HEALTH CARE REFORM SPECIAL ALERT

VOLUME 2

Timothy Stoltzfus Jost
Robert L. Willett Professor
Washington and Lee University School of Law

David J. Edquist
von Briesen, s.c.
Milwaukee

Brian Kopp, Eric Paley, David L. Bacon and David S. Foster
Nixon Peabody
New York, San Francisco, Los Angeles

Brian K. French
Nixon Peabody
Boston

Gerald W. Paulukonis, Esq.

QUESTIONS ABOUT THIS PUBLICATION?

For questions about the **Editorial Content** appearing in these volumes or reprint permission, please call:
Caroline Conway, J.D. at .... 1-800-424-0651 (ext. 4424)
Email: .... Caroline.Conway@lexisnexis.com
For assistance with replacement pages, shipments, billing or other customer service matters, please call:

Customer Services Department at . . . . (800) 833-9844
Outside the United States and Canada, please call . . . . (518) 487-3000
Fax Number . . . . (518) 487-3584
Customer Service Website . . . . http://www.lexisnexis.com/custserv/
For information on other Matthew Bender publications, please call

Your account manager or . . . . (800) 223-1940
Outside the United States and Canada, please call . . . . (518) 487-3000

ISBN: 978-1-4224-7837-0

Cite this publication as:

[Vol. no.] Health Care Reform Special Alert § [sec. no.] (Matthew Bender, Rev. Ed.)

Example:
1 Health Care Reform Special Alert § 1.01 (Matthew Bender, Rev. Ed.)

This publication is designed to provide accurate and authoritative information in regard to the subject matter covered. It is sold with the understanding that the publisher is not engaged in rendering legal, accounting, or other professional services. If legal advice or other expert assistance is required, the services of a competent professional should be sought.

Editorial Offices
121 Chanlon Rd., New Providence, NJ 07974 (908) 464-6800
201 Mission St., San Francisco, CA 94105-1831 (415) 908-3200
www.lexisnexis.com

MATTHEW BENDER

(2010–Pub.1610)

Statement on Fair Use

LexisNexis Matthew Bender recognizes the balance that must be achieved between the operation of the fair use doctrine, whose basis is to avoid the rigid application of the copyright statute, and the protection of the creative rights and economic interests of authors, publishers and other copyright holders.

We are also aware of the countervailing forces that exist between the ever greater technological advances for making both print and electronic copies and the reduction in the value of copyrighted works that must result from a consistent and pervasive reliance on these new copying technologies. It is LexisNexis Matthew Bender's position that if the "progress of science and useful arts" is promoted by granting copyright protection to authors, such progress may well be impeded if copyright protection is diminished in the name of fair use. (See Nimmer on Copyright § 13.05[E][1].) This holds true whether the parameters of the fair use doctrine are considered in either the print or the electronic environment as it is the integrity of the copyright that is at issue, not the media under which the protected work may become available. Therefore, the fair use guidelines we propose apply equally to our print and electronic information, and apply, within §§ 107 and 108 of the Copyright Act, regardless of the professional status of the user.

Our draft guidelines would allow for the copying of limited materials, which would include synopses and tables of contents, primary source and government materials that may have a minimal amount of editorial enhancements, individual forms to aid in the drafting of applications and pleadings, and miscellaneous pages from any of our newsletters, treatises and practice guides. This copying would be permitted provided it is performed for internal use and solely for the purpose of facilitating individual research or for creating documents produced in the course of the user's professional practice, and the original from which the copy is made has been purchased or licensed as part of the user's existing in-house collection.

LexisNexis Matthew Bender fully supports educational awareness programs designed to increase the public's recognition of its fair use rights. We also support the operation of collective licensing organizations with regard to our print and electronic information.

Table of Contents

Table of Contents

CONTRIBUTING AUTHORS

DAVID L. BACON

David Bacon is a partner in Nixon Peabody LLP's Labor & Employment practice group. His practice focuses on ERISA and employee benefits, the federal health care reform legislation (the Patient Protection and Affordable Care Act, or PPACA) enacted in 2010, multiemployer pension plan withdrawal liability, class action defense, labor and employment law, and federal securities law. He has significant experience in ERISA fiduciary liability cases, class action defense, tax shelter litigation, securities litigation, wrongful termination and EEO. Mr. Bacon has represented clients in civil litigation, insurance defense, unfair competition, trademark and copyright law, and products liability defense and specializes in trial and appellate practice, including Supreme Court practice. Mr. Pitts received his J.D. from Harvard Law School and his B.A. from Harvard University, magna cum laude, Phi Beta Kappa.

DAVID J. EDQUIST

David Edquist is a Shareholder in the Milwaukee office of von Briesen & Roper, s.c. Mr. Edquist advises health care clients on Stark, anti-kickback/fraud and abuse, tax exemption and corporate governance. Mr. Edquist obtained a BBA-Finance degree from UW – Madison in 1977 and a law degree from the University of Virginia in 1980. von Briesen & Roper provides comprehensive legal services to the health care industry nationwide, for clients ranging from multi-hospital integrated systems and academic medical centers to rural and critical access hospitals, imaging centers, and physician clinics.

DAVID S. FOSTER

David Foster is a partner in Nixon Peabody LLP's Labor & Employment practice group. Mr. Foster has extensive experience with ERISA and other employee benefits and executive compensation matters. After clerking for Judge Archie O. Dawson in the United States District Court for the Southern District of New York, David Foster was an associate with Debevoise & Plimpton in New York City, gaining broad experience, particularly in the area of taxation, including pension and employee benefits and international taxation. David served in the U.S. Treasury Department in Washington, D.C. from 1972 to 1977 as the chief Treasury Department spokesman for the pension legislation which became the Employee Retirement Income Security Act of 1974 (ERISA). Then, as International Tax Counsel, he was the chief administration spokesman for international tax policy. He received the Exceptional Service Medal from the U.S. Treasury Department in 1977. Mr. Foster received his LL.B., cum laude, from Harvard Law School and his B.A. from Amherst College, magna cum laude (Phi Beta Kappa and Sigma Xi).

BRIAN K. FRENCH

Brian French is a member of Nixon Peabody's Government Investigations and White Collar Defense team. He focuses his practice on representing companies and individuals involved in criminal and other government investigations and related civil litigation, including investigations and litigation under the False Claims Act, the Federal Food, Drug and Cosmetic Act, the Federal Anti-Kickback Statute, and state consumer fraud statutes. Mr. French received his J.D. from Boston College Law School and his B.A. from University of Massachusetts at Amherst, B.A., cum laude, Phi Beta Kappa. Mr. French is a frequent lecturer at pharmaceutical and medical device conferences. In 2005 and 2007, Boston Magazine identified him as a "Rising Star" in its annual "Super Lawyer" survey of Massachusetts attorneys.

TIMOTHY S. JOST

Timothy Stoltzfus Jost, J.D., holds the Robert L. Willett Family Professorship of Law at the Washington and Lee University School of Law. He is a coauthor of a casebook, Health Law, used widely throughout the United States in teaching health law and now in its sixth edition. He is also the author of Health Care at Risk, A Critique of the Consumer-Driven Movement, Health Care Coverage Determinations: An International Comparative Study, Readings in Comparative Health Law and Bioethics, and numerous articles and book chapters on health care regulation and comparative health law and policy. He has written numerous monographs on legal issues in health care reform for national organizations, and in recent months has been interviewed by CNN, ABC News, Fox News, the New York Times, AP and other news media.

BRIAN KOPP

Brian Kopp is a member of Nixon Peabody. Mr. Kopp's practice focuses on the variety of legal issues that impact employee benefit plans and executive compensation. He drafts and counsels employers on all types of traditional benefit plans, including defined benefit pension plans, defined contribution plans, 401(k) plans, multiemployer plans, medical benefit plans, cafeteria plans, disability plans, and other benefit plans. This counseling includes advising clients on the federal and state laws that apply to benefit plans, such as the Employee Retirement Income Security Action ("ERISA") and its fiduciary duty, prohibited transaction, reporting/disclosure, and withdrawal liability rules. Mr. Kopp received his J.D. from Cornell Law School, magna cum laude, an M.S. in Accounting from New York University Graduate School of Business Administration, and a B.A. from Colgate University.

ERIC PALEY

Eric Paley is a member of Nixon Peabody's Employee Benefits and Executive Compensation team within the Labor and Employment Practice Group. Mr. Paley focuses his practice on the law and regulations governing retirement plans (e.g., pension, profit-sharing, 401(k), and 403(b) plan compliance), welfare plans (e.g., group health plan, group insurance plan, cafeteria plan, HIPAA, and COBRA compliance), nonqualified deferred compensation plans and equity compensation plans. A significant portion of Mr. Paley's practice also involves counseling retirement and welfare plan committees on their fiduciary responsibilities under ERISA. Mr. Paley received his J.D. from Syracuse University College of Law, magna cum laude, and his B.A. from Cornell University.

§ 300gg-18. Bringing down the cost of health care coverage [Caution: This section is effective for plan years beginning on after the date that is 6 months after enactment of Act March 23, 2010, P. L. 111-148, as provided by § 1004(a) of such Act, which appears as 42 USCS § 300gg-11 note.]

(a) Clear accounting for costs. A health insurance issuer offering group or individual health insurance coverage (including a grandfathered health plan) shall, with respect to each plan year, submit to the Secretary a report concerning the ratio of the incurred loss (or incurred claims) plus the loss adjustment expense (or change in contract reserves) to earned premiums. Such report shall include the percentage of total premium revenue, after accounting for collections or receipts for risk adjustment and risk corridors and payments of reinsurance, that such coverage expends—

(1) on reimbursement for clinical services provided to enrollees under such coverage;

(2) for activities that improve health care quality; and

(3) on all other non-claims costs, including an explanation of the nature of such costs, and excluding Federal and State taxes and licensing or regulatory fees.The Secretary shall make reports received under this section available to the public on the Internet website of the Department of Health and Human Services.

(b) Ensuring that consumers receive value for their premium payments. (1) Requirement to provide value for premium payments. (A) Requirement. Beginning not later than January 1, 2011, a health insurance issuer offering group or individual health insurance coverage (including a grandfathered health plan) shall, with respect to each plan year, provide an annual rebate to each enrollee under such coverage, on a pro rata basis, if the ratio of the amount of premium revenue expended by the issuer on costs described in paragraphs (1) and (2) of subsection (a) to the total amount of premium revenue (excluding Federal and State taxes and licensing or regulatory fees and after accounting for payments or receipts for risk adjustment, risk corridors, and reinsurance under sections 1341, 1342, and 1343 of the Patient Protection and Affordable Care Act [42 USCS §§ 18061, 18062, and 18063]) for the plan year (except as provided in subparagraph (B)(ii)), is less than—

(i) with respect to a health insurance issuer offering coverage in the large group market, 85 percent, or such higher percentage as a State may by regulation determine; or

(ii) with respect to a health insurance issuer offering coverage in the small group market or in the individual market, 80 percent, or such higher percentage as a State may by regulation determine, except that the Secretary may adjust such percentage with respect to a State if the Secretary determines that the application of such 80 percent may destabilize the individual market in such State.

(B) Rebate amount. (i) Calculation of amount. The total amount of an annual rebate required under this paragraph shall be in an amount equal to the product of—

(I) the amount by which the percentage described in clause (i) or (ii) of subparagraph (A) exceeds the ratio described in such subparagraph; and

(II) the total amount of premium revenue (excluding Federal and State taxes and licensing or regulatory fees and after accounting for payments or receipts for risk adjustment, risk corridors, and reinsurance under sections 1341, 1342, and 1343 of the Patient Protection and Affordable Care Act [42 USCS §§ 18061, 18062, and 18063]) for such plan year.

(ii) Calculation based on average ratio. Beginning on January 1, 2014, the determination made under subparagraph (A) for the year involved shall be based on the averages of the premiums expended on the costs described in such subparagraph and total premium revenue for each of the previous 3 years for the plan.

(2) Consideration in setting percentages. In determining the percentages under paragraph (1), a State shall seek to ensure adequate participation by health insurance issuers, competition in the health insurance market in the State, and value for consumers so that premiums are used for clinical services and quality improvements.

(3) Enforcement. The Secretary shall promulgate regulations for enforcing the provisions of this section and may provide for appropriate penalties.

(c) Definitions. Not later than December 31, 2010, and subject to the certification of the Secretary, the National Association of Insurance Commissioners shall establish uniform definitions of the activities reported under subsection (a) and standardized methodologies for calculating measures of such activities, including definitions of which activities, and in what regard such activities, constitute activities described in subsection (a)(2). Such methodologies shall be designed to take into account the special circumstances of smaller plans, different types of plans, and newer plans.

(d) Adjustments. The Secretary may adjust the rates described in subsection (b) if the Secretary determines appropriate on account of the volatility of the individual market due to the establishment of State Exchanges.

(e) Standard hospital charges. Each hospital operating within the United States shall for each year establish (and update) and make public (in accordance with guidelines developed by the Secretary) a list of the hospital's standard charges for items and services provided by the hospital, including for diagnosis-related groups established under section 1886(d)(4) of the Social Security Act [42 USCS § 1395ww(d)(4)].

(July 1, 1944, ch 373, Title XXVII, Part A, Subpart II, § 2718, as added and amended March 23, 2010, P. L. 111-148, Title I, Subtitle A, § 1001(5), Title X, Subtitle A, § 10101(f), 124 Stat. 136, 885.)

§ 300gg-19. Appeals process [Caution: This section is effective for plan years beginning on after the date that is 6 months after enactment of Act March 23, 2010, P. L. 111-148, as provided by § 1004(a) of such Act, which appears as 42 USCS § 300gg-11 note.]

(a) Internal claims appeals. (1) In general. A group health plan and a health insurance issuer offering group or individual health insurance coverage shall implement an effective appeals process for appeals of coverage determinations and claims, under which the plan or issuer shall, at a minimum—

(A) have in effect an internal claims appeal process;

(B) provide notice to enrollees, in a culturally and linguistically appropriate manner, of available internal and external appeals processes, and the availability of any applicable office of health insurance consumer assistance or ombudsman established under section 2793 [42 USCS § 300gg-93] to assist such enrollees with the appeals processes; and

(C) allow an enrollee to review their file, to present evidence and testimony as part of the appeals process, and to receive continued coverage pending the outcome of the appeals process.

(2) Established processes. To comply with paragraph (1)—

(A) a group health plan and a health insurance issuer offering group health coverage shall provide an internal claims and appeals process that initially incorporates the claims and appeals procedures (including urgent claims) set forth at section 2560.503-1 of title 29, Code of Federal Regulations, as published on November 21, 2000 (65 Fed. Reg. 70256), and shall update such process in accordance with any standards established by the Secretary of Labor for such plans and issuers; and

(B) a health insurance issuer offering individual health coverage, and any other issuer not subject to subparagraph (A), shall provide an internal claims and appeals process that initially incorporates the claims and appeals procedures set forth under applicable law (as in existence on the date of enactment of this section), and shall update such process in accordance with any standards established by the Secretary of Health and Human Services for such issuers.

(b) External review. A group health plan and a health insurance issuer offering group or individual health insurance coverage—

(1) shall comply with the applicable State external review process for such plans and issuers that, at a minimum, includes the consumer protections set forth in the Uniform External Review Model Act promulgated by the National Association of Insurance Commissioners and is binding on such plans; or

(2) shall implement an effective external review process that meets minimum standards established by the Secretary through guidance and that is similar to the process described under paragraph (1)—

(A) if the applicable State has not established an external review process that meets the requirements of paragraph (1); or

(B) if the plan is a self-insured plan that is not subject to State insurance regulation (including a State law that establishes an external review process described in paragraph (1)).

(c) Secretary authority. The Secretary may deem the external review process of a group health plan or health insurance issuer, in operation as of the date of enactment of this section [enacted March 23, 2010], to be in compliance with the applicable process established under subsection (b), as determined appropriate by the Secretary.

(July 1, 1944, ch 373, Title XXVII, Part A, Subpart II, § 2719, as added and amended March 23, 2010, P. L. 111-148, Title I, Subtitle A, § 1001(5), Title X, Subtitle A, § 10101(g), 124 Stat. 137, 887.)

§ 300gg-19a. Patient protections

(a) Choice of health care professional. If a group health plan, or a health insurance issuer offering group or individual health insurance coverage, requires or provides for designation by a participant, beneficiary, or enrollee of a participating primary care provider, then the plan or issuer shall permit each participant, beneficiary, and enrollee to designate any participating primary care provider who is available to accept such individual.

(b) Coverage of emergency services. (1) In general. If a group health plan, or a health insurance issuer offering group or individual health insurance issuer, provides or covers any benefits with respect to services in an emergency department of a hospital, the plan or issuer shall cover emergency services (as defined in paragraph (2)(B))—

(A) without the need for any prior authorization determination;

(B) whether the health care provider furnishing such services is a participating provider with respect to such services;

(C) in a manner so that, if such services are provided to a participant, beneficiary, or enrollee—

(i) by a nonparticipating health care provider with or without prior authorization; or

(ii)(I) such services will be provided without imposing any requirement under the plan for prior authorization of services or any limitation on coverage where the provider of services does not have a contractual relationship with the plan for the providing of services that is more restrictive than the requirements or limitations that apply to emergency department services received from providers who do have such a contractual relationship with the plan; and

(II) if such services are provided out-of-network, the cost-sharing requirement (expressed as a copayment amount or coinsurance rate) is the same requirement that would apply if such services were provided in-network;

(D) without regard to any other term or condition of such coverage (other than exclusion or coordination of benefits, or an affiliation or waiting period, permitted under section 2701 of this Act [42 USCS § 300gg], section 701 of the Employee Retirement Income Security Act of 1974 [29 USCS § 1181], or section 9801 of the Internal Revenue Code of 1986 [26 USCS § 9801], and other than applicable cost-sharing).

(2) Definitions. In this subsection:

(A) Emergency medical condition. The term "emergency medical condition" means a medical condition manifesting itself by acute symptoms of sufficient severity (including severe pain) such that a prudent layperson, who possesses an average knowledge of health and medicine, could reasonably expect the absence of immediate medical attention to result in a condition described in clause (i), (ii), or (iii) of section 1867(e)(1)(A) of the Social Security Act [42 USCS § 1395dd(e)(1)(A)].

(B) Emergency services. The term "emergency services" means, with respect to an emergency medical condition—

(i) a medical screening examination (as required under section 1867 of the Social Security Act [42 USCS § 1395dd]) that is within the capability of the emergency department of a hospital, including ancillary services routinely available to the emergency department to evaluate such emergency medical condition, and

(ii) within the capabilities of the staff and facilities available at the hospital, such further medical examination and treatment as are required under section 1867 of such Act [42 USCS § 1395dd] to stabilize the patient.

(C) Stabilize. The term "to stabilize", with respect to an emergency medical condition (as defined in subparagraph (A)), has the meaning give in section 1867(e)(3) of the Social Security Act (42 U.S.C. 1395dd(e)(3)).

(c) Access to pediatric care. (1) Pediatric care. In the case of a person who has a child who is a participant, beneficiary, or enrollee under a group health plan, or health insurance coverage offered by a health insurance issuer in the group or individual market, if the plan or issuer requires or provides for the designation of a participating primary care provider for the child, the plan or issuer shall permit such person to designate a physician (allopathic or osteopathic) who specializes in pediatrics as the child's primary care provider if such provider participates in the network of the plan or issuer.

(2) Construction. Nothing in paragraph (1) shall be construed to waive any exclusions of coverage under the terms and conditions of the plan or health insurance coverage with respect to coverage of pediatric care.

(d) Patient access to obstetrical and gynecological care. (1) General rights. (A) Direct access. A group health plan, or health insurance issuer offering group or individual health insurance coverage, described in paragraph (2) may not require authorization or referral by the plan, issuer, or any person (including a primary care provider described in paragraph (2)(B)) in the case of a female participant, beneficiary, or enrollee who seeks coverage for obstetrical or gynecological care provided by a participating health care professional who specializes in obstetrics or gynecology. Such professional shall agree to otherwise adhere to such plan's or issuer's policies and procedures, including procedures regarding referrals and obtaining prior authorization and providing services pursuant to a treatment plan (if any) approved by the plan or issuer.

(B) Obstetrical and gynecological care. A group health plan or health insurance issuer described in paragraph (2) shall treat the provision of obstetrical and gynecological care, and the ordering of related obstetrical and gynecological items and services, pursuant to the direct access described under subparagraph (A), by a participating health care professional who specializes in obstetrics or gynecology as the authorization of the primary care provider.

(2) Application of paragraph. A group health plan, or health insurance issuer offering group or individual health insurance coverage, described in this paragraph is a group health plan or coverage that—

(A) provides coverage for obstetric or gynecologic care; and

(B) requires the designation by a participant, beneficiary, or enrollee of a participating primary care provider.

(3) Construction. Nothing in paragraph (1) shall be construed to—

(A) waive any exclusions of coverage under the terms and conditions of the plan or health insurance coverage with respect to coverage of obstetrical or gynecological care; or

(B) preclude the group health plan or health insurance issuer involved from requiring that the obstetrical or gynecological provider notify the primary care health care professional or the plan or issuer of treatment decisions.

(July 1, 1944, ch 373, Title XXVII, Part A, Subpart II, § 2719A, as added March 23, 2010, P. L. 111-148, Title X, Subtitle A, § 10101(h), 124 Stat. 888.)

Exclusion of Plans; Enforcement; Preemption

§ 300gg-21. Exclusion of certain plans

(a) Limitation on application of provisions relating to group health plans. (1) In general. The requirements of subparts 1 and 2 [42 USCS §§ 300gg et seq. and 300gg-11 et seq.] shall apply with respect to group health plans only—

(A) subject to paragraph (2), in the case of a plan that is a nonfederal governmental plan, and

(B) with respect to health insurance coverage offered in connection with a group health plan (including such a plan that is a church plan or a governmental plan).

(2) Treatment of nonfederal governmental plans. (A) Election to be excluded. Except as provided in subparagraph (D) or (E), if the plan sponsor of a nonfederal governmental plan which is a group health plan to which the provisions of subparts 1 and 2 [42 USCS §§ 300gg et seq. and 300gg-11 et seq.] otherwise apply makes an election under this subparagraph (in such form and manner as the Secretary may by regulations prescribe), then the requirements of such subparts insofar as they apply directly to group health plans (and not merely to group health insurance coverage) shall not apply to such governmental plans for such period except as provided in this paragraph.

(B) Period of election. An election under subparagraph (A) shall apply—

(i) for a single specified plan year, or

(ii) in the case of a plan provided pursuant to a collective bargaining agreement, for the term of such agreement.

An election under clause (i) may be extended through subsequent elections under this paragraph.

(C) Notice to enrollees. Under such an election, the plan shall provide for—

(i) notice to enrollees (on an annual basis and at the time of enrollment under the plan) of the fact and consequences of such election, and

(ii) certification and disclosure of creditable coverage under the plan with respect to enrollees in accordance with section 2701(e) [42 USCS § 300gg(e)].

(D) Election not applicable to requirements concerning genetic information. The election described in subparagraph (A) shall not be available with respect to the provisions of subsections (a)(1)(F), (b)(3), (c), and (d) of section 2702 [42 USCS § 300gg-1] and the provisions of sections 2701 and 2702(b) [42 USCS §§ 300gg and 300gg-1(b)] to the extent that such provisions apply to genetic information.

(E) Election not applicable. The election described in subparagraph (A) shall not be available with respect to the provisions of subparts I and II [42 USCS §§ 300gg et seq. and 300gg-11 et seq.].

(b) Exception for certain benefits. The requirements of subparts 1 and 2 [42 USCS §§ 300gg et seq. and 300gg-11 et seq.] shall not apply to any individual coverage or any group health plan (or group health insurance coverage) in relation to its provision of excepted benefits described in section 2791(c)(1).

(c) Exception for certain benefits if certain conditions met. (1) Limited, excepted benefits. The requirements of subparts 1 and 2 [42 USCS §§ 300gg et seq. and 300gg-11 et seq.] shall not apply to any individual coverage or any group health plan (and group health insurance coverage offered in connection with a group health plan) in relation to its provision of excepted benefits described in section 2791(c)(2) [42 USCS § 300gg-91(c)(2)] if the benefits—

(A) are provided under a separate policy, certificate, or contract of insurance; or

(B) are otherwise not an integral part of the plan.

(2) Noncoordinated, excepted benefits. The requirements of subparts 1 and 2 [42 USCS §§ 300gg et seq. and 300gg-11 et seq.] shall not apply to any individual coverage or any group health plan (and group health insurance coverage offered in connection with a group health plan) in relation to its provision of excepted benefits described in section 2791(c)(3) [42 USCS § 300gg-91(c)(3)] if all of the following conditions are met:

(A) The benefits are provided under a separate policy, certificate, or contract of insurance.

(B) There is no coordination between the provision of such benefits and any exclusion of benefits under any group health plan maintained by the same plan sponsor.

(C) Such benefits are paid with respect to an event without regard to whether benefits are provided with respect to such an event under any group health plan maintained by the same plan sponsor or, with respect to individual coverage, under any health insurance coverage maintained by the same health insurance issuer.

(3) Supplemental excepted benefits. The requirements of this part shall not apply to any individual coverage or any group health plan (and group health insurance coverage) in relation to its provision of excepted benefits described in section 27971(c)(4) if the benefits are provided under a separate policy, certificate, or contract of insurance.

(d) Treatment of partnerships. For purposes of this part [42 USCS §§ 300gg-21 et seq.]—

(1) Treatment as a group health plan. Any plan, fund, or program which would not be (but for this subsection) an employee welfare benefit plan and which is established or maintained by a partnership, to the extent that such plan, fund, or program provides medical care (including items and services paid for as medical care) to present or former partners in the partnership or to their dependents (as defined under the terms of the plan, fund, or program), directly or through insurance, reimbursement, or otherwise, shall be treated (subject to paragraph (2)) as an employee welfare benefit plan which is a group health plan.

(2) Employer. In the case of a group health plan, the term 'employer' also includes the partnership in relation to any partner.

(3) Participants of group health plans. In the case of a group health plan, the term "participant" also includes—

(A) in connection with a group health plan maintained by a partnership, an individual who is a partner in relation to the partnership, or

(B) in connection with a group health plan maintained by a self-employed individual (under which one or more employees are participants), the self-employed individual,

if such individual is, or may become, eligible to receive a benefit under the plan or such individual's beneficiaries may be eligible to receive any such benefit.

(July 1, 1944, ch 373, Title XXVII, Part A, Subpart 2 [4] [3], § 2722 [2735] [2721], as added Aug. 21, 1996, P. L. 104-191, Title I, Subtitle A, Part 1, § 102(a), 110 Stat. 1967; Sept. 26, 1996, P. L. 104-204, Title VI, § 604(a)(2), (b)(1), 110 Stat. 2939, 2941; May 21, 2008, P. L. 110-233, Title I, § 102(c), 122 Stat. 895; March 23, 2010, P. L. 111-148, Title I, Subtitle A, § 1001(4), Subtitle G, § 1563(a), (c)(11), (12) [1562(a), (c)(11), (12)], Title X, Subtitle A, § 10107(a), (b)(1), 124 Stat. 130, 264, 268, 911.)

§ 300gg-22. Enforcement

(a) State enforcement. (1) State authority. Subject to section 2723 [42 USCS § 300gg-23], each State may require that health insurance issuers that issue, sell, renew, or offer health insurance coverage in the State in the individual or group market meet the requirements of this part [42 USCS §§ 300gg et seq.] with respect to such issuers.

(2) Failure to implement provisions. In the case of a determination by the Secretary that a State has failed to substantially enforce a provision (or provisions) in this part [42 USCS §§ 300gg et seq.] with respect to health insurance issuers in the State, the Secretary shall enforce such provision (or provisions) under subsection (b) insofar as they relate to the issuance, sale, renewal, and offering of health insurance coverage in connection with group health plans or individual health insurance coverage in such State.

(b) Secretarial enforcement authority. (1) Limitation. The provisions of this subsection shall apply to enforcement of a provision (or provisions) of this part [42 USCS §§ 300gg et seq.] only—

(A) as provided under subsection (a)(2); and

(B) with respect to individual health insurance coverage or group health plans that are non-Federal governmental plans.

(2) Imposition of penalties. In the cases described in paragraph (1)—

(A) In general. Subject to the succeeding provisions of this subsection, any non-Federal governmental plan that is a group health plan and any health insurance issuer that fails to meet a provision of this part applicable to such plan or issuer is subject to a civil money penalty under this subsection.

(B) Liability for penalty. In the case of a failure by—

(i) a health insurance issuer, the issuer is liable for such penalty, or

(ii) a group health plan that is a non-Federal governmental plan which is—

(I) sponsored by 2 or more employers, the plan is liable for such penalty, or

(II) not so sponsored, the employer is liable for such penalty.

(C) Amount of penalty. (i) In general. The maximum amount of penalty imposed under this paragraph is $100 for each day for each individual with respect to which such a failure occurs.

(ii) Considerations in imposition. In determining the amount of any penalty to be assessed under this paragraph, the Secretary shall take into account the previous record of compliance of the entity being assessed with the applicable provisions of this part [42 USCS §§ 300gg et seq.] and the gravity of the violation.

(iii) Limitations. (I) Penalty not to apply where failure not discovered exercising reasonable diligence. No civil money penalty shall be imposed under this paragraph on any failure during any period for which it is established to the satisfaction of the Secretary that none of the entities against whom the penalty would be imposed knew, or exercising reasonable diligence would have known, that such failure existed.

(II) Penalty not to apply to failures corrected within 30 days. No civil money penalty shall be imposed under this paragraph on any failure if such failure was due to reasonable cause and not to willful neglect, and such failure is corrected during the 30-day period beginning on the first day any of the entities against whom the penalty would be imposed knew, or exercising reasonable diligence would have known, that such failure existed.

(D) Administrative review. (i) Opportunity for hearing. The entity assessed shall be afforded an opportunity for hearing by the Secretary upon request made within 30 days after the date of the issuance of a notice of assessment. In such hearing the decision shall be made on the record pursuant to section 554 of title 5, United States Code. If no hearing is requested, the assessment shall constitute a final and unappealable order.

(ii) Hearing procedure. If a hearing is requested, the initial agency decision shall be made by an administrative law judge, and such decision shall become the final order unless the Secretary modifies or vacates the decision. Notice of intent to modify or vacate the decision of the administrative law judge shall be issued to the parties within 30 days after the date of the decision of the judge. A final order which takes effect under this paragraph shall be subject to review only as provided under subparagraph (E).

(E) Judicial review. (i) Filing of action for review. Any entity against whom an order imposing a civil money penalty has been entered after an agency hearing under this paragraph may obtain review by the United States district court for any district in which such entity is located or the United States District Court for the District of Columbia by filing a notice of appeal in such court within 30 days from the date of such order, and simultaneously sending a copy of such notice by registered mail to the Secretary.

(ii) Certification of administrative record. The Secretary shall promptly certify and file in such court the record upon which the penalty was imposed.

(iii) Standard for review. The findings of the Secretary shall be set aside only if found to be unsupported by substantial evidence as provided by section 706(2)(E) of title 5, United States Code.

(iv) Appeal. Any final decision, order, or judgment of the district court concerning such review shall be subject to appeal as provided in chapter 83 of title 28 of such Code [28 USCS §§ 1291 et seq.].

(F) Failure to pay assessment; maintenance of action. (i) Failure to pay assessment. If any entity fails to pay an assessment after it has become a final and unappealable order, or after the court has entered final judgment in favor of the Secretary, the Secretary shall refer the matter to the Attorney General who shall recover the amount assessed by action in the appropriate United States district court.

(ii) Nonreviewability. In such action the validity and appropriateness of the final order imposing the penalty shall not be subject to review.

(G) Payment of penalties. Except as otherwise provided, penalties collected under this paragraph shall be paid to the Secretary (or other officer) imposing the penalty and shall be available without appropriation and until expended for the purpose of enforcing the provisions with respect to which the penalty was imposed.

(3) Enforcement authority relating to genetic discrimination. (A) General rule. In the cases described in paragraph (1), notwithstanding the provisions of paragraph (2)(C), the succeeding subparagraphs of this paragraph shall apply with respect to an action under this subsection by the Secretary with respect to any failure of a health insurance issuer in connection with a group health plan, to meet the requirements of subsection (a)(1)(F), (b)(3), (c), or (d) of section 2702 [42 USCS § 300gg-1] or section 2701 or 2702(b)(1) [42 USCS § 300gg or 300gg-1(b)(1)] with respect to genetic information in connection with the plan.

(B) Amount. (i) In general. The amount of the penalty imposed under this paragraph shall be $100 for each day in the noncompliance period with respect to each participant or beneficiary to whom such failure relates.

(ii) Noncompliance period. For purposes of this paragraph, the term "noncompliance period" means, with respect to any failure, the period—

(I) beginning on the date such failure first occurs; and

(II) ending on the date the failure is corrected.

(C) Minimum penalties where failure discovered. Notwithstanding clauses (i) and (ii) of subparagraph (D):

(i) In general. In the case of 1 or more failures with respect to an individual—

(I) which are not corrected before the date on which the plan receives a notice from the Secretary of such violation; and

(II) which occurred or continued during the period involved;

the amount of penalty imposed by subparagraph (A) by reason of such failures with respect to such individual shall not be less than $2,500.

(ii) Higher minimum penalty where violations are more than de minimis. To the extent violations for which any person is liable under this paragraph for any year are more than de minimis, clause (i) shall be applied by substituting "$15,000" for "$2,500" with respect to such person.

(D) Limitations. (i) Penalty not to apply where failure not discovered exercising reasonable diligence. No penalty shall be imposed by subparagraph (A) on any failure during any period for which it is established to the satisfaction of the Secretary that the person otherwise liable for such penalty did not know, and exercising reasonable diligence would not have known, that such failure existed.

(ii) Penalty not to apply to failures corrected within certain periods. No penalty shall be imposed by subparagraph (A) on any failure if—

(I) such failure was due to reasonable cause and not to willful neglect; and

(II) such failure is corrected during the 30-day period beginning on the first date the person otherwise liable for such penalty knew, or exercising reasonable diligence would have known, that such failure existed.

(iii) Overall limitation for unintentional failures. In the case of failures which are due to reasonable cause and not to willful neglect, the penalty imposed by subparagraph (A) for failures shall not exceed the amount equal to the lesser of—

(I) 10 percent of the aggregate amount paid or incurred by the employer (or predecessor employer) during the preceding taxable year for group health plans; or

(II) $500,000.

(E) Waiver by Secretary. In the case of a failure which is due to reasonable cause and not to willful neglect, the Secretary may waive part or all of the penalty imposed by subparagraph (A) to the extent that the payment of such penalty would be excessive relative to the failure involved.

(July 1, 1944, ch 373, Title XXVII, Part A, Subpart 2 [4] [3], § 2723 [2736] [2722], as added Aug. 21, 1996, P. L. 104-191, Title I, Subtitle A, Part 1, § 102(a), 110 Stat. 1968; Sept. 26, 1996, P. L. 104-204, Title VI, § 604(a)(2), 110 Stat. 2939; May 21, 2008, P. L. 110-233, Title I, § 102(a)(5), 122 Stat. 891; March 23, 2010, P. L. 111-148, Title I, Subtitle A, § 1001(4), Subtitle G, § 1563(c)(13) [1562(c)(13)], Title X, Subtitle A, § 10107(b)(1), 124 Stat. 130, 269, 911.)

§ 300gg-23. Preemption; State flexibility; construction

(a) Continued applicability of State law with respect to health insurance issuers. (1) In general. Subject to paragraph (2) and except as provided in subsection (b), this part [42 USCS §§ 300gg et seq.] and part C [42 USCS §§ 300gg-91 et seq.] insofar as it relates to this part [42 USCS §§ 300gg et seq.] shall not be construed to supersede any provision of State law which establishes, implements, or continues in effect any standard or requirement solely relating to health insurance issuers in connection with individual or group health insurance coverage except to the extent that such standard or requirement prevents the application of a requirement of this part [42 USCS §§ 300gg et seq.].

(2) Continued preemption with respect to group health plans. Nothing in this part [42 USCS §§ 300gg et seq.] shall be construed to affect or modify the provisions of section 514 of the Employee Retirement Income Security Act of 1974 [29 USCS § 1144] with respect to group health plans.

(b) Special rules in case of portability requirements. (1) In general. Subject to paragraph (2), the provisions of this part [42 USCS §§ 300gg et seq.] relating to health insurance coverage offered by a health insurance issuer supersede any provision of State law which establishes, implements, or continues in effect a standard or requirement applicable to imposition of a preexisting condition exclusion specifically governed by section 701 which differs from the standards or requirements specified in such section.

(2) Exceptions. Only in relation to health insurance coverage offered by a health insurance issuer, the provisions of this part [42 USCS §§ 300gg et seq.] do not supersede any provision of State law to the extent that such provision—

(i) substitutes for the reference to "6-month period" in section 2701(a)(1) [42 USCS § 300gg(a)(1)] a reference to any shorter period of time;

(ii) substitutes for the reference to "12 months" and "18 months" in section 2701(a)(2) [42 USCS § 300gg(a)(2)] a reference to any shorter period of time;

(iii) substitutes for the references to "63" days in sections 2701(c)(2)(A) and 2701(d)(4)(A) [42 USCS § 300gg(c)(2)(A), (d)(4)(A)] a reference to any greater number of days;

(iv) substitutes for the reference to "30-day period" in sections 2701(b)(2) and 2701(d)(1) [42 USCS § 300gg(b)(2), (d)(1)] a reference to any greater period;

(v) prohibits the imposition of any preexisting condition exclusion in cases not described in section 2701(d) [42 USCS § 300gg(d)] or expands the exceptions described in such section;

(vi) requires special enrollment periods in addition to those required under section 2701(f) [42 USCS § 300gg(f)]; or

(vii) reduces the maximum period permitted in an affiliation period under section 2701(g)(1)(B) [42 USCS § 300gg(g)(1)(B)].

(c) Rules of construction. Nothing in this part [42 USCS §§ 300gg et seq.] (other than section 2704 [42 USCS § 300gg-4]) shall be construed as requiring a group health plan or health insurance coverage to provide specific benefits under the terms of such plan or coverage.

(d) Definitions. For purposes of this section—

(1) State law. The term "State law" includes all laws, decisions, rules, regulations, or other State action having the effect of law, of any State. A law of the United States applicable only to the District of Columbia shall be treated as a State law rather than a law of the United States.

(2) State. The term "State" includes a State (including the Northern Mariana Islands), any political subdivisions of a State or such Islands, or any agency or instrumentality of either.

(July 1, 1944, ch 373, Title XXVII, Part A, Subpart 2 [4] [3], § 2724 [2737] [2723], as added Aug. 21, 1996, P. L. 104-191, Title I, Subtitle A, Part 1, § 102(a), 110 Stat. 1971; Sept. 26, 1996, P. L. 104-204, Title VI, § 604(a)(2), (b)(2), 110 Stat. 2939, 2941; March 23, 2010, P. L. 111-148, Title I, Subtitle A, § 1002(4), Subtitle G, § 1563(c)(14) [1562(c)(14)], Title X, Subtitle A, § 10107(b)(1), 124 Stat. 130, 269, 911.)

§ 300gg-25. Standards relating to benefits for mothers and newborns

(a) Requirements for minimum hospital stay following birth. (1) In general. A group health plan, and a health insurance issuer offering group or individual health insurance coverage, may not—

(A) except as provided in paragraph (2)—

(i) restrict benefits for any hospital length of stay in connection with childbirth for the mother or newborn child, following a normal vaginal delivery, to less than 48 hours, or

(ii) restrict benefits for any hospital length of stay in connection with childbirth for the mother or newborn child, following a cesarean section, to less than 96 hours, or

(B) require that a provider obtain authorization from the plan or the issuer for prescribing any length of stay required under subparagraph (A) (without regard to paragraph (2)).

(2) Exception. Paragraph (1)(A) shall not apply in connection with any group health plan or health insurance issuer in any case in which the decision to discharge the mother or her newborn child prior to the expiration of the minimum length of stay otherwise required

under paragraph (1)(A) is made by an attending provider in consultation with the mother.

(b) Prohibitions. A group health plan, and a health insurance issuer offering group or individual health insurance coverage, may not—

(1) deny to the mother or her newborn child eligibility, or continued eligibility, to enroll or to renew coverage under the terms of the plan or coverage, solely for the purpose of avoiding the requirements of this section;

(2) provide monetary payments or rebates to mothers to encourage such mothers to accept less than the minimum protections available under this section;

(3) penalize or otherwise reduce or limit the reimbursement of an attending provider because such provider provided care to an individual participant or beneficiary in accordance with this section;

(4) provide incentives (monetary or otherwise) to an attending provider to induce such provider to provide care to an individual participant or beneficiary in a manner inconsistent with this section; or

(5) subject to subsection (c)(3), restrict benefits for any portion of a period within a hospital length of stay required under subsection (a) in a manner which is less favorable than the benefits provided for any preceding portion of such stay.

(c) Rules of construction. (1) Nothing in this section shall be construed to require a mother who is a participant or beneficiary—

(A) to give birth in a hospital; or

(B) to stay in the hospital for a fixed period of time following the birth of her child.

(2) This section shall not apply with respect to any group health plan, or any health insurance issuer offering group or individual health insurance coverage, which does not provide benefits for hospital lengths of stay in connection with childbirth for a mother or her newborn child.

(3) Nothing in this section shall be construed as preventing a group health plan or health insurance issuer from imposing deductibles, coinsurance, or other cost-sharing in relation to benefits for hospital lengths of stay in connection with childbirth for a mother or newborn child under the plan (or under health insurance coverage offered in connection with a group health plan), except that such coinsurance or other cost-sharing for any portion of a period within a hospital length of stay required under subsection (a) may not be greater than such coinsurance or cost-sharing for any preceding portion of such stay.

(d) Notice. A group health plan under this part shall comply with the notice requirement under section 711(d) of the Employee Retirement Income Security Act of 1974 [29 USCS § 1185(d)] with respect to the requirements of this section as if such section applied to such plan.

(e) Level and type of reimbursements. Nothing in this section shall be construed to prevent a group health plan or a health insurance issuer offering group or individual health insurance coverage from negotiating the level and type of reimbursement with a provider for care provided in accordance with this section.

(f) Preemption; exception for health insurance coverage in certain States. (1) In general. The requirements of this section shall not apply with respect to health insurance coverage if there is a State law (as defined in section 2723(d)(1) [42 USCS §§ 300gg-23(d)(1)]) for a State that regulates such coverage that is described in any of the following subparagraphs:

(A) Such State law requires such coverage to provide for at least a 48-hour hospital length of stay following a normal vaginal delivery and at least a 96-hour hospital length of stay following a cesarean section.

(B) Such State law requires such coverage to provide for maternity and pediatric care in accordance with guidelines established by the American College of Obstetricians and Gynecologists, the American Academy of Pediatrics, or other established professional medical associations.

(C) Such State law requires, in connection with such coverage for maternity care, that the hospital length of stay for such care is left to the decision of (or required to be made by) the attending provider in consultation with the mother.

(2) Construction. Section 2723(a)(1) [42 USCS §§ 300gg-23(a)(1)] shall not be construed as superseding a State law described in paragraph (1).

(Act July 1, 1944, ch 373, Title XXVII, Part A, Subpart 2, § 2725 [2704], as added Sept. 26, 1996, P. L. 104-204, Title VI, § 604(a)(3), 110 Stat. 2939; March 23, 2010, P. L. 111-148, Title I, Subtitle A, § 1001(2), Subtitle G, § 1563(c)(3) [1562(c)(3)], Title X, Subtitle A, § 10107(b)(1), 124 Stat. 130, 265, 911.)

HISTORY; ANCILLARY LAWS AND DIRECTIVES

Redesignation:

This section, enacted as § 2704 of Part A of Title XXVII of Act July 1, 1944, ch 373, was redesignated § 2725 of such Part by Act March 23, 2010, P. L.

111-148, Title I, Subtitle A, § 1001(2), 124 Stat. 130.

Section 1562 of Act March 23, 2010, P. L. 111-148, which amended this section, was redesignated § 1563 of such Act by § 10107(b)(1) of the Act.

§ 300gg-26. Parity in mental health and substance use disorder benefits

(a) In general. (1) Aggregate lifetime limits. In the case of a group health plan or a health insurance issuer offering group or individual health insurance coverage that provides both medical and surgical benefits and mental health or substance use disorder benefits—

(A) No lifetime limit. If the plan or coverage does not include an aggregate lifetime limit on substantially all medical and surgical benefits, the plan or coverage may not impose any aggregate lifetime limit on mental health or substance use disorder benefits.

(B) Lifetime limit. If the plan or coverage includes an aggregate lifetime limit on substantially all medical and surgical benefits (in this paragraph referred to as the "applicable lifetime limit"), the plan or coverage shall either—

(i) apply the applicable lifetime limit both to the medical and surgical benefits to which it otherwise would apply and to mental health and substance use disorder benefits and not distinguish in the application of such limit between such medical and surgical benefits and mental health and substance use disorder benefits; or

(ii) not include any aggregate lifetime limit on mental health or substance use disorder benefits that is less than the applicable lifetime limit.

(C) Rule in case of different limits. In the case of a plan or coverage that is not described in subparagraph (A) or (B) and that includes no or different aggregate lifetime limits on different categories of medical and surgical benefits, the Secretary shall establish rules under which subparagraph (B) is applied to such plan or coverage with respect to mental health and substance use disorder benefits by substituting for the applicable lifetime limit an average aggregate lifetime limit that is computed taking into account the weighted average of the aggregate lifetime limits applicable to such categories.

(2) Annual limits. In the case of a group health plan or a health insurance issuer offering group or individual health insurance coverage that provides both medical and surgical benefits and mental health or substance use disorder benefits—

(A) No annual limit. If the plan or coverage does not include an annual limit on substantially all medical and surgical benefits, the plan or coverage may not impose any annual limit on mental health or substance use disorder benefits.

(B) Annual limit. If the plan or coverage includes an annual limit on substantially all medical and surgical benefits (in this paragraph referred to as the "applicable annual limit"), the plan or coverage shall either—

(i) apply the applicable annual limit both to medical and surgical benefits to which it otherwise would apply and to mental health and substance use disorder benefits and not distinguish in the application of such limit between such medical and surgical benefits and mental health and substance use disorder benefits; or

(ii) not include any annual limit on mental health or substance use disorder benefits that is less than the applicable annual limit.

(C) Rule in case of different limits. In the case of a plan or coverage that is not described in subparagraph (A) or (B) and that includes no or different annual limits on different categories of medical and surgical benefits, the Secretary shall establish rules under which subparagraph (B) is applied to such plan or coverage with respect to mental health and substance use disorder benefits by substituting for the applicable annual limit an average annual limit that is computed taking into account the weighted average of the annual limits applicable to such categories.

(3) Financial requirements and treatment limitations. (A) In general. In the case of a group health plan or a health insurance issuer offering group or individual health insurance coverage that provides both medical and surgical benefits and mental health or substance use disorder benefits, such plan or coverage shall ensure that—

(i) the financial requirements applicable to such mental health or substance use disorder benefits are no more restrictive than the predominant financial requirements applied to substantially all medical and surgical benefits covered by the plan (or coverage), and there are no separate cost sharing requirements that are applicable only with respect to mental health or substance use disorder benefits; and

(ii) the treatment limitations applicable to such mental health or substance use disorder benefits are no more restrictive than the predominant treatment limitations applied to substantially all medical and surgical benefits covered by the plan (or coverage) and there are no separate treatment limitations that are applicable only with respect to mental health or substance use disorder benefits.

(B) Definitions. In this paragraph:

(i) Financial requirement. The term "financial requirement" includes deductibles, copayments, coinsurance, and out-of-pocket expenses, but excludes an aggregate lifetime limit and an annual limit subject to paragraphs (1) and (2).

(ii) Predominant. A financial requirement or treatment limit is considered to be predominant if it is the most common or frequent of such type of limit or requirement.

(iii) Treatment limitation. The term "treatment limitation" includes limits on the frequency of treatment, number of visits, days of coverage, or other similar limits on the scope or duration of treatment.

(4) Availability of plan information. The criteria for medical necessity determinations made under the plan with respect to mental health or substance use disorder benefits (or the health insurance coverage offered in connection with the plan with respect to such benefits) shall be made available by the plan administrator (or the health insurance issuer offering such coverage) in accordance with regulations to any current or potential participant, beneficiary, or contracting provider upon request. The reason for any denial under the plan (or coverage) of reimbursement or payment for services with respect to mental health or substance use disorder benefits in the case of any participant or beneficiary shall, on request or as otherwise required, be made available by the plan administrator (or the health insurance issuer offering such coverage) to the participant or beneficiary in accordance with regulations.

(5) Out-of-network providers. In the case of a plan or coverage that provides both medical and surgical benefits and mental health or substance use disorder benefits, if the plan or coverage provides coverage for medical or surgical benefits provided by out-of-network providers, the plan or coverage shall provide coverage for mental health or substance use disorder benefits provided by out-of-network providers in a manner that is consistent with the requirements of this section.

(b) Construction. Nothing in this section shall be construed—

(1) as requiring a group health plan or a health insurance issuer offering group or individual health insurance coverage to provide any mental health or substance use disorder benefits; or

(2) in the case of a group health plan or a health insurance issuer offering group or individual health insurance coverage that provides mental health or substance use disorder benefits, as affecting the terms and conditions of the plan or coverage relating to such benefits under the plan or coverage, except as provided in subsection (a).

(c) Exemptions. (1) Small employer exemption. This section shall not apply to any group health plan and a health insurance issuer offering group or individual health insurance coverage for any plan year of a small employer (as defined in section 2791(e)(4) [42 USCS § 300gg-91(e)(4)], except that for purposes of this paragraph such term shall include employers with 1 employee in the case of an employer residing in a State that permits small groups to include a single individual).

(2) Cost exemption. (A) In general. With respect to a group health plan or a health insurance issuer offering group or individual health insurance coverage, if the application of this section to such plan (or coverage) results in an increase for the plan year involved of the actual total costs of coverage with respect to medical and surgical benefits and mental health and substance use disorder benefits under the plan (as determined and certified under subparagraph (C)) by an amount that exceeds the applicable percentage described in subparagraph (B) of the actual total plan costs, the provisions of this section shall not apply to such plan (or coverage) during the following plan year, and such exemption shall apply to the plan (or coverage) for 1 plan year. An employer may elect to continue to apply mental health and substance use disorder parity pursuant to this section with respect to the group health plan (or coverage) involved regardless of any increase in total costs.

(B) Applicable percentage. With respect to a plan (or coverage), the applicable percentage described in this subparagraph shall be—

(i) 2 percent in the case of the first plan year in which this section is applied; and

(ii) 1 percent in the case of each subsequent plan year.

(C) Determinations by actuaries. Determinations as to increases in actual costs under a plan (or coverage) for purposes of this section shall be made and certified by a qualified and licensed actuary who is a member in good standing of the American Academy of Actuaries. All such determinations shall be in a written report prepared by the actuary. The report, and all underlying documentation relied upon by the actuary, shall be maintained by the group health plan or health insurance issuer for a period of 6 years following the notification made under subparagraph (E).

(D) 6-month determinations. If a group health plan (or a health insurance issuer offering coverage in connection with a group health plan) seeks an exemption under this paragraph, determinations under subparagraph (A) shall be made after such plan (or coverage) has complied with this section for the first 6 months of the plan year involved.

(E) Notification. (i) In general. A group health plan (or a health insurance issuer offering coverage in connection with a group health plan) that, based upon a certification described under subparagraph (C), qualifies for an exemption under this paragraph, and elects to implement the exemption, shall promptly notify the Secretary, the appropriate State agencies, and participants and beneficiaries in the plan of such election.

(ii) Requirement. A notification to the Secretary under clause (i) shall include—

(I) a description of the number of covered lives under the plan (or coverage) involved at the time of the notification, and as applicable, at the time of any prior election of the cost-exemption under this paragraph by such plan (or coverage);

(II) for both the plan year upon which a cost exemption is sought and the year prior, a description of the actual total costs of coverage with respect to medical and surgical benefits and mental health and substance use disorder benefits under the plan; and

(III) for both the plan year upon which a cost exemption is sought and the year prior, the actual total costs of coverage with respect to mental health and substance use disorder benefits under the plan.

(iii) Confidentiality. A notification to the Secretary under clause (i) shall be confidential. The Secretary shall make available, upon request and on not more than an annual basis, an anonymous itemization of such notifications, that includes—

(I) a breakdown of States by the size and type of employers submitting such notification; and

(II) a summary of the data received under clause (ii).

(F) Audits by appropriate agencies. To determine compliance with this paragraph, the Secretary may audit the books and records of a group health plan or health insurance issuer relating to an exemption, including any actuarial reports prepared pursuant to subparagraph (C), during the 6 year period following the notification of such exemption under subparagraph (E). A State agency receiving a notification under subparagraph (E) may also conduct such an audit with respect to an exemption covered by such notification.

(d) Separate application to each option offered. In the case of a group health plan that offers a participant or beneficiary two or more benefit package options under the plan, the requirements of this section shall be applied separately with respect to each such option.

(e) Definitions. For purposes of this section—

(1) Aggregate lifetime limit. The term "aggregate lifetime limit" means, with respect to benefits under a group health plan or health insurance coverage, a dollar limitation on the total amount that may be paid with respect to such benefits under the plan or health insurance coverage with respect to an individual or other coverage unit.

(2) Annual limit. The term "annual limit" means, with respect to benefits under a group health plan or health insurance coverage, a dollar limitation on the total amount of benefits that may be paid with respect to such benefits in a 12-month period under the plan or health insurance coverage with respect to an individual or other coverage unit.

(3) Medical or surgical benefits. The term "medical or surgical benefits" means benefits with respect to medical or surgical services, as defined under the terms of the plan or coverage (as the case may be), but does not include mental health benefits.

(4) Mental health benefits. The term "mental health benefits" means benefits with respect to services for mental health conditions, as defined under the terms of the plan and in accordance with applicable Federal and State law.

(5) Substance use disorder benefits. The term "substance use disorder benefits" means benefits with respect to services for substance use disorders, as defined under the terms of the plan and in accordance with applicable Federal and State law.

(July 1, 1944, ch 373, Title XXVII, Part A, Subpart 2, § 2706 [2705], as added Sept. 26, 1996, P. L. 104-204, Title VII, § 703(a), 110 Stat. 2947; Jan. 10, 2002, P. L. 107-116, Title VII, § 701(b), 115 Stat. 2228; Dec. 2, 2002, P. L. 107-313, § 2(b), 116 Stat. 2457; Dec. 19, 2003, P. L. 108-197, § 2(b), 117 Stat. 2898; Oct. 4, 2004, P. L. 108-311, Title III, § 302(c), 118 Stat. 1179; Dec. 30, 2005, P. L. 109-151, § 1(b), 119 Stat. 2886; Dec. 20, 2006, P. L. 109-432, Div A, Title I, § 115(c), 120 Stat. 2941; June 17, 2008, P. L. 110-245, Title IV, § 401(c), 122 Stat. 1650; Oct. 3, 2008, P. L. 110-343, Div C, Title V, Subtitle B, § 512(b), (g)(2), 122 Stat. 3885,

3892; March 23, 2010, P. L. 111-148, Title I, Subtitle A, § 1001(2), Subtitle G, § 1563(c)(4) [1562(c)(4)], Title X, Subtitle A, § 10107(b)(1), 124 Stat. 130, 265, 911.)

HISTORY; ANCILLARY LAWS AND DIRECTIVES

Redesignation:

This section, enacted as § 2705 of Part A of Title XXVII of Act July 1, 1944, ch 373, was redesignated § 2726 of such Part by Act March 23, 2010, P. L. 111-148, Title I, Subtitle A, § 1001(2), 124 Stat. 130.)

Section 1562 of Act March 23, 2010, P. L. 111-148, which amended this section, was redesignated § 1563 of such Act by § 10107(b)(1) of the Act.

§ 300gg-27. Required coverage for reconstructive surgery following mastectomies

The provisions of section 713 of the Employee Retirement Income Security Act of 1974 [29 USCS § 1185b] shall apply to group health plans, and [and] health insurance issuers offering group or individual health insurance coverage, as if included in this subpart [42 USCS § 300gg-21 et seq.].

(July 1, 1944, ch 373, Title XXVII, Part A, Subpart 2, § 2727 [2706], as added Oct. 21, 1998, P. L. 105-277, Div A, § 101(f) [Title IX, § 903(a)], 112 Stat. 2681-438; March 23, 2010, P. L. 111-148, Title I, Subtitle A, § 1001(2), Subtitle G, § 1563(c)(5) [1562(c)(5)], Title X, Subtitle A, § 10107(b)(1), 124 Stat. 130, 266, 911.)

HISTORY; ANCILLARY LAWS AND DIRECTIVES

Redesignation:

This section, enacted as § 2706 of Part A of Title XXVII of Act July 1, 1944, ch 373, was redesignated § 2727 of such Part by Act March 23, 2010, P. L. 111-148, Title I, Subtitle A, § 1001(2), 124 Stat. 130.

Section 1562 of Act March 23, 2010, P. L. 111-148, which amended this section, was redesignated § 1563 of such Act by § 10107(b)(1) of the Act.

§ 300gg-28. Coverage of dependent students on medically necessary leave of absence

(a) Medically necessary leave of absence. In this section, the term "medically necessary leave of absence" means, with respect to a dependent child described in subsection (b)(2) in connection with a group health plan or individual health insurance coverage, a leave of absence of such child from a postsecondary educational institution (including an institution of higher education as defined in section 102 of the Higher Education Act of 1965 [20 USCS § 1002]), or any other change in enrollment of such child at such an institution, that—

(1) commences while such child is suffering from a serious illness or injury;

(2) is medically necessary; and

(3) causes such child to lose student status for purposes of coverage under the terms of the plan or coverage.

(b) Requirement to continue coverage. (1) In general. In the case of a dependent child described in paragraph (2), a group health plan, or a health insurance issuer that offers group or individual health insurance coverage, shall not terminate coverage of such child under such plan or health insurance coverage due to a medically necessary leave of absence before the date that is the earlier of—

(A) the date that is 1 year after the first day of the medically necessary leave of absence; or

(B) the date on which such coverage would otherwise terminate under the terms of the plan or health insurance coverage.

(2) Dependent child described. A dependent child described in this paragraph is, with respect to a group health plan or individual health insurance coverage, a beneficiary under the plan who—

(A) is a dependent child, under the terms of the plan or coverage, of a participant or beneficiary under the plan or coverage; and

(B) was enrolled in the plan or coverage, on the basis of being a student at a postsecondary educational institution (as described in subsection (a)), immediately before the first day of the medically necessary leave of absence involved.

(3) Certification by physician. Paragraph (1) shall apply to a group health plan or individual health insurance coverage only if the plan or issuer of the coverage has received written certification by a treating physician of the dependent child which states that the child is suffering from a serious illness or injury and that the leave of absence (or other change of enrollment) described in subsection (a) is medically necessary.

(c) Notice. A group health plan, and a health insurance issuer that offers group or individual health insurance coverage, shall include, with any notice regarding a requirement for certification of student status for coverage under the plan or coverage, a description of the terms of this section for continued coverage during medically necessary leaves of absence. Such description shall be in language which is understandable to the typical plan participant.

(d) No change in benefits. A dependent child whose benefits are continued under this section shall be entitled to the same benefits as if (during the medically necessary leave of absence) the child continued to be a covered student at the institution of higher education and was not on a medically necessary leave of absence.

(e) Continued application in case of changed coverage. If—

(1) a dependent child of a participant or beneficiary is in a period of coverage under a group health plan or individual health insurance coverage, pursuant to a medically necessary leave of absence of the child described in subsection (b);

(2) the manner in which the participant or beneficiary is covered under the plan changes, whether through a change in health insurance coverage or health insurance issuer, a change between health insurance coverage and self-insured coverage, or otherwise; and

(3) the coverage as so changed continues to provide coverage of beneficiaries as dependent children,

this section shall apply to coverage of the child under the changed coverage for the remainder of the period of the medically necessary leave of absence of the dependent child under the plan in the same manner as it would have applied if the changed coverage had been the previous coverage.

(July 1, 1944, ch 373, Title XXVII, Part A, Subpart 2, § 2728 [2707], as added Oct. 9, 2008, P. L. 110-381, § 2(b)(1), 122 Stat. 4083; March 23, 2010, P. L. 111-148, Title I, Subtitle A, § 1001(2), Subtitle G, § 1563(c)(6) [1562(c)(6)], Title X, Subtitle A, § 10107(b)(1), 124 Stat. 130, 266, 911.)

HISTORY; ANCILLARY LAWS AND DIRECTIVES

Redesignation:

This section, enacted as § 2707 of Part A of Title XXVII of Act July 1, 1944, ch 373, was redesignated § 2728 of such Part by Act March 23, 2010, P. L. 111-148, Title I, Subtitle A, § 1001(2), 124 Stat. 130.

Section 1562 of Act March 23, 2010, P. L. 111-148, which amended this section, was redesignated § 1563 of such Act by § 10107(b)(1) of the Act.

Individual Market Rules

General Provisions

§ 300gg-62. Preemption and application

(a) In general. Subject to subsection (b), nothing in this part (or part C [42 USCS § 300gg-91 et seq.] insofar as it applies to this part [42 USCS § 300gg-41 et seq.]) shall be construed to prevent a State from establishing, implementing, or continuing in effect standards and requirements unless such standards and requirements prevent the application of a requirement of this part [42 USCS § 300gg-41 et seq.].

(b) Rules of construction. (1) Nothing in this part [42 USCS § 300gg-41 et seq.] (or part C [42 USCS § 300gg-91 et seq.] insofar as it applies to this part [42 USCS § 300gg-41 et seq.]) shall be construed to affect or modify the provisions of section 514 of the Employee Retirement Income Security Act of 1974 (29 U.S.C. 1144).

(2) Nothing in this part [42 USCS §§ 300gg-41 et seq.] (other than section 2751 [42 USCS § 300gg-51]) shall be construed as requiring health insurance coverage offered in the individual market to provide specific benefits under the terms of such coverage.

(c) Application of part A provisions. (1) In general. The provisions of part A [42 USCS §§ 300gg et seq.] shall apply to health insurance issuers providing health insurance coverage in the individual market in a State as provided for in such part.

(2) Clarification. To the extent that any provision of this part [42 USCS § 300gg-41 et seq.] conflicts with a provision of part A [42 USCS §§ 300gg et seq.] with respect to health insurance issuers providing health insurance coverage in the individual market in a State, the provisions of such part A [42 USCS §§ 300gg et seq.] shall apply.

(July 1, 1944, ch 373, Title XXVII, Part B, Subpart 3, § 2762 [2746], as added Aug. 21, 1996, P. L. 104-191, Title I, Subtitle B, § 111(a), 110 Stat. 1987; Sept. 26, 1996, P. L. 104-204, Title VI, § 605(a)(2), (3), (b)(3), 110 Stat. 2941, 2942; March 23, 2010, P. L. 111-148, Title I, Subtitle G, § 1563(c)(15) [1562(c)(15)], Title X, Subtitle A, § 10107(b)(1), 124 Stat. 269, 911.)

Definitions; Miscellaneous Provisions

§ 300gg-91. Definitions

(a) Group health plan. (1) Definition. The term "group health plan" means an employee welfare benefit plan (as defined in section 3(1) of the Employee Retirement Income Security Act of 1974 [29 USCS § 1002(1)]) to the extent that the plan provides medical care (as defined in paragraph (2)) and including items and services paid for as medical care) to employees or their dependents (as defined under the terms of the plan) directly or through insurance, reimbursement, or otherwise.

(2) Medical care. The term "medical care" means amounts paid for—

(A) the diagnosis, cure, mitigation, treatment, or prevention of disease, or amounts paid for the purpose of affecting any structure or function of the body,

(B) amounts paid for transportation primarily for and essential to medical care referred to in subparagraph (A), and

(C) amounts paid for insurance covering medical care referred to in subparagraphs (A) and (B).

(3) Treatment of certain plans as group health plan for notice provision. A program under which creditable coverage described in subparagraph (C), (D), (E), or (F) of section 2701(c)(1) [42 USCS § 300gg(c)(1)] is provided shall be treated as a group health plan for purposes of applying section 2701(e) [42 USCS § 300gg(e)].

(b) Definitions relating to health insurance. (1) Health insurance coverage. The term "health insurance coverage" means benefits consisting of medical care (provided directly, through insurance or reimbursement, or otherwise and including items and services paid for as medical care) under any hospital or medical service policy or certificate, hospital or medical service plan contract, or health maintenance organization contract offered by a health insurance issuer.

(2) Health insurance issuer. The term "health insurance issuer" means an insurance company, insurance service, or insurance organization (including a health maintenance organization, as defined in paragraph (3)) which is licensed to engage in the business of insurance in a State and which is subject to State law which regulates insurance (within the meaning of section 514(b)(2) of the Employee Retirement Income Security Act of 1974 [29 USCS § 1144(b)(2)]). Such term does not include a group health plan.

(3) Health maintenance organization. The term "health maintenance organization" means—

(A) a Federally qualified health maintenance organization (as defined in section 1301(a) [42 USCS § 300e(a)]),

(B) an organization recognized under State law as a health maintenance organization, or

(C) a similar organization regulated under State law for solvency in the same manner and to the same extent as such a health maintenance organization.

(4) Group health insurance coverage. The term "group health insurance coverage" means, in connection with a group health plan, health insurance coverage offered in connection with such plan.

(5) Individual health insurance coverage. The term "individual health insurance coverage" means health insurance coverage offered to individuals in the individual market, but does not include short-term limited duration insurance.

(c) Excepted benefits. For purposes of this title [42 USCS §§ 300gg et seq.], the term "excepted benefits" means benefits under one or more (or any combination thereof) of the following:

(1) Benefits not subject to requirements. (A) Coverage only for accident, or disability income insurance, or any combination thereof.

(B) Coverage issued as a supplement to liability insurance.

(C) Liability insurance, including general liability insurance and automobile liability insurance.

(D) Workers' compensation or similar insurance.

(E) Automobile medical payment insurance.

(F) Credit-only insurance.

(G) Coverage for on-site medical clinics.

(H) Other similar insurance coverage, specified in regulations, under which benefits for medical care are secondary or incidental to other insurance benefits.

(2) Benefits not subject to requirements if offered separately. (A) Limited scope dental or vision benefits.

(B) Benefits for long-term care, nursing home care, home health care, community-based care, or any combination thereof.

(C) Such other similar, limited benefits as are specified in regulations.

(3) Benefits not subject to requirements if offered as independent, noncoordinated benefits. (A) Coverage only for a specified disease or illness.

(B) Hospital indemnity or other fixed indemnity insurance.

(4) Benefits not subject to requirements if offered as separate insurance policy. Medicare supplemental health insurance (as defined under section 1882(g)(1) of the Social Security Act [42 USCS § 1395ss(g)(1)]), coverage supplemental to the coverage provided under chapter 55 of title 10, United States Code [10 USCS §§ 1071 et seq.], and similar supplemental coverage provided to coverage under a group health plan.

(d) Other definitions (1) Applicable State authority. The term "applicable State authority" means, with respect to a health insurance issuer in a State, the State insurance commissioner or official or officials designated by the State to enforce the requirements of this title [42 USCS §§ 300gg et seq.] for the State involved with respect to such issuer.

(2) Beneficiary. The term "beneficiary" has the meaning given such term under section 3(8)

of the Employee Retirement Income Security Act of 1974 [29 USCS § 1002(8)].

(3) Bona fide association. The term "bona fide association" means, with respect to health insurance coverage offered in a State, an association which—

(A) has been actively in existence for at least 5 years;

(B) has been formed and maintained in good faith for purposes other than obtaining insurance;

(C) does not condition membership in the association on any health status-related factor relating to an individual (including an employee of an employer or a dependent of an employee);

(D) makes health insurance coverage offered through the association available to all members regardless of any health status-related factor relating to such members (or individuals eligible for coverage through a member);

(E) does not make health insurance coverage offered through the association available other than in connection with a member of the association; and

(F) meets such additional requirements as may be imposed under State law.

(4) COBRA continuation provision. The term "COBRA continuation provision" means any of the following:

(A) Section 4980B of the Internal Revenue Code of 1986 [26 USCS § 4980B], other than subsection (f)(1) of such section insofar as it relates to pediatric vaccines.

(B) Part 6 of subtitle B of title I of the Employee Retirement Income Security Act of 1974 [29 USCS §§ 1161 et seq.], other than section 609 of such Act [29 USCS § 1169].

(C) Title XXII of this Act [42 USCS §§ 300bb et seq.].

(5) Employee. The term "employee" has the meaning given such term under section 3(6) of the Employee Retirement Income Security Act of 1974 [29 USCS § 1002(6)].

(6) Employer. The term "employer" has the meaning given such term under section 3(5) of the Employee Retirement Income Security Act of 1974 [29 USCS § 1002(5)], except that such term shall include only employers of two or more employees.

(7) Church plan. The term "church plan" has the meaning given such term under section 3(33) of the Employee Retirement Income Security Act of 1974 [29 USCS § 1002(33)].

(8) Governmental plan. (A) The term "governmental plan" has the meaning given such term under section 3(32) of the Employee Retirement Income Security Act of 1974 [29 USCS § 1002(32)] and any Federal governmental plan.

(B) Federal governmental plan. The term "Federal governmental plan" means a governmental plan established or maintained for its employees by the Government of the United States or by any agency or instrumentality of such Government.

(C) Non-Federal governmental plan. The term "non-Federal governmental plan" means a governmental plan that is not a Federal governmental plan.

(9) Health status-related factor. The term "health status-related factor" means any of the factors described in section 2702(a)(1) [42 USCS § 300gg-1(a)(1)].

(10) Network plan. The term "network plan" means health insurance coverage of a health insurance issuer under which the financing and delivery of medical care (including items and services paid for as medical care) are provided, in whole or in part, through a defined set of providers under contract with the issuer.

(11) Participant. The term "participant" has the meaning given such term under section 3(7) of the Employee Retirement Income Security Act of 1974 [29 USCS § 1002(7)].

(12) Placed for adoption defined. The term "placement", or being "placed", for adoption, in connection with any placement for adoption of a child with any person, means the assumption and retention by such person of a legal obligation for total or partial support of such child in anticipation of adoption of such child. The child's placement with such person terminates upon the termination of such legal obligation.

(13) Plan sponsor. The term "plan sponsor" has the meaning given such term under section 3(16)(B) of the Employee Retirement Income Security Act of 1974 [29 USCS § 1002(16)(B)].

(14) State. The term "State" means each of the several States, the District of Columbia, Puerto Rico, the Virgin Islands, Guam, American Samoa, and the Northern Mariana Islands.

(15) Family member. The term "family member" means, with respect to any individual—

(A) a dependent (as such term is used for purposes of section 2701(f)(2) [42 USCS § 300gg(f)(2)]) of such individual; and

(B) any other individual who is a first-degree, second-degree, third-degree, or fourth-degree relative of such individual or of an individual described in subparagraph (A).

(16) Genetic information. (A) In general. The term "genetic information" means, with respect to any individual, information about—

(i) such individual's genetic tests,

(ii) the genetic tests of family members of

such individual, and

(iii) the manifestation of a disease or disorder in family members of such individual.

(B) Inclusion of genetic services and participation in genetic research. Such term includes, with respect to any individual, any request for, or receipt of, genetic services, or participation in clinical research which includes genetic services, by such individual or any family member of such individual.

(C) Exclusions. The term "genetic information" shall not include information about the sex or age of any individual.

(17) Genetic test. (A) In general. The term "genetic test" means an analysis of human DNA, RNA, chromosomes, proteins, or metabolites, that detects genotypes, mutations, or chromosomal changes.

(B) Exceptions. The term "genetic test" does not mean—

(i) an analysis of proteins or metabolites that does not detect genotypes, mutations, or chromosomal changes; or

(ii) an analysis of proteins or metabolites that is directly related to a manifested disease, disorder, or pathological condition that could reasonably be detected by a health care professional with appropriate training and expertise in the field of medicine involved.

(18) Genetic services. The term "genetic services" means—

(A) a genetic test;

(B) genetic counseling (including obtaining, interpreting, or assessing genetic information); or

(C) genetic education.

(19) Underwriting purposes. The term "underwriting purposes" means, with respect to any group health plan, or health insurance coverage offered in connection with a group health plan—

(A) rules for, or determination of, eligibility (including enrollment and continued eligibility) for benefits under the plan or coverage;

(B) the computation of premium or contribution amounts under the plan or coverage;

(C) the application of any pre-existing condition exclusion under the plan or coverage; and

(D) other activities related to the creation, renewal, or replacement of a contract of health insurance or health benefits.

(20) Qualified health plan. The term "qualified health plan" has the meaning given such term in section 1301(a) of the Patient Protection and Affordable Care Act [42 USCS § 18021(a)].

(21) Exchange. The term "Exchange" means an American Health Benefit Exchange established under section 1311 of the Patient Protection and Affordable Care Act [42 USCS § 18031].

(e) Definitions relating to markets and small employers. For purposes of this title [42 USCS §§ 300gg et seq.]:

(1) Individual market. (A) In general. The term "individual market" means the market for health insurance coverage offered to individuals other than in connection with a group health plan.

(B) Treatment of very small groups. (i) In general. Subject to clause (ii), such terms includes coverage offered in connection with a group health plan that has fewer than two participants as current employees on the first day of the plan year.

(ii) State exception. Clause (i) shall not apply in the case of a State that elects to regulate the coverage described in such clause as coverage in the small group market.

(2) Large employer. The term "large employer" means, in connection with a group health plan with respect to a calendar year and a plan year, an employer who employed an average of at least 101 employees on business days during the preceding calendar year and who employs at least 2 employees on the first day of the plan year.

(3) Large group market. The term "large group market" means the health insurance market under which individuals obtain health insurance coverage (directly or through any arrangement) on behalf of themselves (and their dependents) through a group health plan maintained by a large employer.

(4) Small employer. The term "small employer" means, in connection with a group health plan with respect to a calendar year and a plan year, an employer who employed an average of at least 1 but not more than 50 employees on business days during the preceding calendar year and who employs at least 1 employees on the first day of the plan year.

(5) Small group market. The term "small group market" means the health insurance market under which individuals obtain health insurance coverage (directly or through any arrangement) on behalf of themselves (and their dependents) through a group health plan maintained by a small employer.

(6) Application of certain rules in determination of employer size. For purposes of this subsection—

(A) Application of aggregation rule for employers. all [All] persons treated as a single employer under subsection (b), (c), (m), or (o) of section 414 of the Internal Revenue Code of

1986 [26 USCS § 414] shall be treated as 1 employer.

(B) Employers not in existence in preceding year. In the case of an employer which was not in existence throughout the preceding calendar year, the determination of whether such employer is a small or large employer shall be based on the average number of employees that it is reasonably expected such employer will employ on business days in the current calendar year.

(C) Predecessors. Any reference in this subsection to an employer shall include a reference to any predecessor of such employer.

(July 1, 1944, ch 373, Title XXVII, Part C, § 2791, as added Aug. 21, 1996, P. L. 104-191, Title I, Subtitle A, Part 1, § 102(a), 110 Stat. 1972; May 21, 2008, P. L. 110-233, Title I, § 102(a)(4), 122 Stat. 890; March 23, 2010, P. L. 111-148, Title I, Subtitle G, § 1563(b), (c)(16) [1562(b), (c)(16)], Title X, Subtitle A, § 10107(b)(1), 124 Stat. 264, 269, 911.)

§ 300gg-93. Health insurance consumer information

(a) In general. The Secretary shall award grants to States to enable such States (or the Exchanges operating in such States) to establish, expand, or provide support for—

(1) offices of health insurance consumer assistance; or

(2) health insurance ombudsman programs.

(b) Eligibility. (1) In general. To be eligible to receive a grant, a State shall designate an independent office of health insurance consumer assistance, or an ombudsman, that, directly or in coordination with State health insurance regulators and consumer assistance organizations, receives and responds to inquiries and complaints concerning health insurance coverage with respect to Federal health insurance requirements and under State law.

(2) Criteria. A State that receives a grant under this section shall comply with criteria established by the Secretary for carrying out activities under such grant.

(c) Duties. The office of health insurance consumer assistance or health insurance ombudsman shall—

(1) assist with the filing of complaints and appeals, including filing appeals with the internal appeal or grievance process of the group health plan or health insurance issuer involved and providing information about the external appeal process;

(2) collect, track, and quantify problems and inquiries encountered by consumers;

(3) educate consumers on their rights and responsibilities with respect to group health plans and health insurance coverage;

(4) assist consumers with enrollment in a group health plan or health insurance coverage by providing information, referral, and assistance; and

(5) resolve problems with obtaining premium tax credits under section 36B of the Internal Revenue Code of 1986 [26 USCS § 36B].

(d) Data collection. As a condition of receiving a grant under subsection (a), an office of health insurance consumer assistance or ombudsman program shall be required to collect and report data to the Secretary on the types of problems and inquiries encountered by consumers. The Secretary shall utilize such data to identify areas where more enforcement action is necessary and shall share such information with State insurance regulators, the Secretary of Labor, and the Secretary of the Treasury for use in the enforcement activities of such agencies.

(e) Funding. (1) Initial funding. There is hereby appropriated to the Secretary, out of any funds in the Treasury not otherwise appropriated, $30,000,000 for the first fiscal year for which this section applies to carry out this section. Such amount shall remain available without fiscal year limitation.

(2) Authorization for subsequent years. There is authorized to be appropriated to the Secretary for each fiscal year following the fiscal year described in paragraph (1), such sums as may be necessary to carry out this section.

(July 1, 1944, ch 373, Title XXVII, Part C, § 2793, as added March 23, 2010, P. L. 111-148, Title I, Subtitle A, § 1002, 124 Stat. 138.)

§ 300gg-94. Ensuring that consumers get value for their dollars

(a) Initial premium review process. (1) In general. The Secretary, in conjunction with States, shall establish a process for the annual review, beginning with the 2010 plan year and subject to subsection (b)(2)(A), of unreasonable increases in premiums for health insurance coverage.

(2) Justification and disclosure. The process established under paragraph (1) shall require health insurance issuers to submit to the Secretary and the relevant State a justification for an unreasonable premium increase prior to the implementation of the increase. Such issuers shall prominently post such information on their Internet websites. The Secretary shall ensure the public disclosure of information on

such increases and justifications for all health insurance issuers.

(b) Continuing premium review process. (1) Informing Secretary of premium increase patterns. As a condition of receiving a grant under subsection (c)(1), a State, through its Commissioner of Insurance, shall—

(A) provide the Secretary with information about trends in premium increases in health insurance coverage in premium rating areas in the State; and

(B) make recommendations, as appropriate, to the State Exchange about whether particular health insurance issuers should be excluded from participation in the Exchange based on a pattern or practice of excessive or unjustified premium increases.

(2) Monitoring by Secretary of premium increases.

(A) In general. Beginning with plan years beginning in 2014, the Secretary, in conjunction with the States and consistent with the provisions of subsection (a)(2), shall monitor premium increases of health insurance coverage offered through an Exchange and outside of an Exchange.

(B) Consideration in opening exchange. In determining under section 1312(f)(2)(B) of the Patient Protection and Affordable Care Act [42 USCS § 18032(f)(2)(B)] whether to offer qualified health plans in the large group market through an Exchange, the State shall take into account any excess of premium growth outside of the Exchange as compared to the rate of such growth inside the Exchange.

(c) Grants in support of process. (1) Premium review grants during 2010 through 2014. The Secretary shall carry out a program to award grants to States during the 5-year period beginning with fiscal year 2010 to assist such States in carrying out subsection (a), including—

(A) in reviewing and, if appropriate under State law, approving premium increases for health insurance coverage;

(B) in providing information and recommendations to the Secretary under subsection (b)(1); and

(C) in establishing centers (consistent with subsection (d)) at academic or other nonprofit institutions to collect medical reimbursement information from health insurance issuers, to analyze and organize such information, and to make such information available to such issuers, health care providers, health researchers, health care policy makers, and the general public.

(2) Funding. (A) In general. Out of all funds in the Treasury not otherwise appropriated, there are appropriated to the Secretary $250,000,000, to be available for expenditure for grants under paragraph (1) and subparagraph (B).

(B) Further availability for insurance reform and consumer protection. If the amounts appropriated under subparagraph (A) are not fully obligated under grants under paragraph (1) by the end of fiscal year 2014, any remaining funds shall remain available to the Secretary for grants to States for planning and implementing the insurance reforms and consumer protections under part A [42 USCS §§ 300gg et seq.].

(C) Allocation. The Secretary shall establish a formula for determining the amount of any grant to a State under this subsection. Under such formula—

(i) the Secretary shall consider the number of plans of health insurance coverage offered in each State and the population of the State; and

(ii) no State qualifying for a grant under paragraph (1) shall receive less than $1,000,000, or more than $5,000,000 for a grant year.

(d) Medical reimbursement data centers. (1) Functions. A center established under subsection (c)(1)(C) shall—

(A) develop fee schedules and other database tools that fairly and accurately reflect market rates for medical services and the geographic differences in those rates;

(B) use the best available statistical methods and data processing technology to develop such fee schedules and other database tools;

(C) regularly update such fee schedules and other database tools to reflect changes in charges for medical services;

(D) make health care cost information readily available to the public through an Internet website that allows consumers to understand the amounts that health care providers in their area charge for particular medical services; and

(E) regularly publish information concerning the statistical methodologies used by the center to analyze health charge data and make such data available to researchers and policy makers.

(2) Conflicts of interest. A center established under subsection (c)(1)(C) shall adopt by-laws that ensures that the center (and all members of the governing board of the center) is independent and free from all conflicts of interest. Such by-laws shall ensure that the center is not controlled or influenced by, and does not have any corporate relation to, any individual or entity that may make or receive payments for

health care services based on the center's analysis of health care costs.

(3) Rule of construction. Nothing in this subsection shall be construed to permit a center established under subsection (c)(1)(C) to compel health insurance issuers to provide data to the center.

(July 1, 1944, ch 373, Title XXVII, Part C, § 2794, as added and amended March 23, 2010, P. L. 111-148, Title I, Subtitle A, § 1003, Title X, Subtitle A, § 10101(i), 124 Stat. 139, 891.)

§ 300gg-95. Uniform fraud and abuse referral format

The Secretary shall request the National Association of Insurance Commissioners to develop a model uniform report form for private health insurance issuer seeking to refer suspected fraud and abuse to State insurance departments or other responsible State agencies for investigation. The Secretary shall request that the National Association of Insurance Commissioners develop recommendations for uniform reporting standards for such referrals.

(July 1, 1944, ch 373, Title XXVII, Part C, § 2794, as added March 23, 2010, P. L. 111-148, Title VI, Subtitle G, § 6603, 124 Stat. 780.)

NATIONAL ALL-HAZARDS PREPAREDNESS FOR PUBLIC HEALTH EMERGENCIES

STRENGTHENING PUBLIC HEALTH SURVEILLANCE SYSTEMS

§ 300hh-31. Epidemiology-laboratory capacity grants

(a) In general. Subject to the availability of appropriations, the Secretary, acting through the Director of the Centers for Disease Control and Prevention, shall establish an Epidemiology and Laboratory Capacity Grant Program to award grants to State health departments as well as local health departments and tribal jurisdictions that meet such criteria as the Director determines appropriate. Academic centers that assist State and eligible local and tribal health departments may also be eligible for funding under this section as the Director determines appropriate. Grants shall be awarded under this section to assist public health agencies in improving surveillance for, and response to, infectious diseases and other conditions of public health importance by—

(1) strengthening epidemiologic capacity to identify and monitor the occurrence of infectious diseases and other conditions of public health importance;

(2) enhancing laboratory practice as well as systems to report test orders and results electronically;

(3) improving information systems including developing and maintaining an information exchange using national guidelines and complying with capacities and functions determined by an advisory council established and appointed by the Director; and

(4) developing and implementing prevention and control strategies.

(b) Authorization of appropriations. There are authorized to be appropriated to carry out this section $190,000,000 for each of fiscal years 2010 through 2013, of which—

(1) not less than $95,000,000 shall be made available each such fiscal year for activities under paragraphs (1) and (4) of subsection (a);

(2) not less than $60,000,000 shall be made available each such fiscal year for activities under subsection (a)(3); and

(3) not less than $32,000,000 shall be made available each such fiscal year for activities under subsection (a)(2).

(July 1, 1944, ch 373, Title XXVIII, Subtitle C, § 2821, as added March 23, 2010, P. L. 111-148, Title IV, Subtitle C, § 4304, 124 Stat. 584.)

HEALTH INFORMATION TECHNOLOGY AND QUALITY

OTHER PROVISIONS

§ 300jj-51. Health information technology enrollment standards and protocols

(a) In general. (1) Standards and protocols. Not later than 180 days after the date of enactment of this title [enacted March 23, 2010], the Secretary, in consultation with the HIT Policy Committee and the HIT Standards Committee, shall develop interoperable and secure standards and protocols that facilitate enrollment of individuals in Federal and State health and human services programs, as determined by the Secretary.

(2) Methods. The Secretary shall facilitate enrollment in such programs through methods determined appropriate by the Secretary, which shall include providing individuals and third parties authorized by such individuals and their designees notification of eligibility and verification of eligibility required under such programs.

(b) Content. The standards and protocols for electronic enrollment in the Federal and

State programs described in subsection (a) shall allow for the following:

(1) Electronic matching against existing Federal and State data, including vital records, employment history, enrollment systems, tax records, and other data determined appropriate by the Secretary to serve as evidence of eligibility and in lieu of paper-based documentation.

(2) Simplification and submission of electronic documentation, digitization of documents, and systems verification of eligibility.

(3) Reuse of stored eligibility information (including documentation) to assist with retention of eligible individuals.

(4) Capability for individuals to apply, recertify and manage their eligibility information online, including at home, at points of service, and other community-based locations.

(5) Ability to expand the enrollment system to integrate new programs, rules, and functionalities, to operate at increased volume, and to apply streamlined verification and eligibility processes to other Federal and State programs, as appropriate.

(6) Notification of eligibility, recertification, and other needed communication regarding eligibility, which may include communication via email and cellular phones.

(7) Other functionalities necessary to provide eligibles with streamlined enrollment process.

(c) Approval and notification. With respect to any standard or protocol developed under subsection (a) that has been approved by the HIT Policy Committee and the HIT Standards Committee, the Secretary—

(1) shall notify States of such standards or protocols; and

(2) may require, as a condition of receiving Federal funds for the health information technology investments, that States or other entities incorporate such standards and protocols into such investments.

(d) Grants for implementation of appropriate enrollment HIT. (1) In general. The Secretary shall award grant to eligible entities to develop new, and adapt existing, technology systems to implement the HIT enrollment standards and protocols developed under subsection (a) (referred to in this subsection as "appropriate HIT technology").

(2) Eligible entities. To be eligible for a grant under this subsection, an entity shall—

(A) be a State, political subdivision of a State, or a local governmental entity; and

(B) submit to the Secretary an application at such time, in such manner, and containing—

(i) a plan to adopt and implement appropriate enrollment technology that includes—

(I) proposed reduction in maintenance costs of technology systems;

(II) elimination or updating of legacy systems; and

(III) demonstrated collaboration with other entities that may receive a grant under this section that are located in the same State, political subdivision, or locality;

(ii) an assurance that the entity will share such appropriate enrollment technology in accordance with paragraph (4); and

(iii) such other information as the Secretary may require.

(3) Sharing. (A) In general. The Secretary shall ensure that appropriate enrollment HIT adopted under grants under this subsection is made available to other qualified State, qualified political subdivisions of a State, or other appropriate qualified entities (as described in subparagraph (B)) at no cost.

(B) Qualified entities. The Secretary shall determine what entities are qualified to receive enrollment HIT under subparagraph (A), taking into consideration the recommendations of the HIT Policy Committee and the HIT Standards Committee.

(July 1, 1944, ch 373, Title XXX, Subtitle C, § 3021, as added March 23, 2010, P. L. 111-148, Title I, Subtitle G, § 1561, 124 Stat. 262.)

DATA COLLECTION, ANALYSIS, AND QUALITY

§ 300kk. Data collection, analysis, and quality

(a) Data collection. (1) In general. The Secretary shall ensure that, by not later than 2 years after the date of enactment of this title [enacted March 23, 2010], any federally conducted or supported health care or public health program, activity or survey (including Current Population Surveys and American Community Surveys conducted by the Bureau of Labor Statistics and the Bureau of the Census) collects and reports, to the extent practicable—

(A) data on race, ethnicity, sex, primary language, and disability status for applicants, recipients, or participants;

(B) data at the smallest geographic level such as State, local, or institutional levels if such data can be aggregated;

(C) sufficient data to generate statistically reliable estimates by racial, ethnic, sex, primary language, and disability status subgroups for applicants, recipients or participants using, if needed, statistical oversamples of these subpopulations; and

(D) any other demographic data as deemed appropriate by the Secretary regarding health disparities.

(2) Collection standards. In collecting data described in paragraph (1), the Secretary or designee shall—

(A) use Office of Management and Budget standards, at a minimum, for race and ethnicity measures;

(B) develop standards for the measurement of sex, primary language, and disability status;

(C) develop standards for the collection of data described in paragraph (1) that, at a minimum—

(i) collects self-reported data by the applicant, recipient, or participant; and

(ii) collects data from a parent or legal guardian if the applicant, recipient, or participant is a minor or legally incapacitated;

(D) survey health care providers and establish other procedures in order to assess access to care and treatment for individuals with disabilities and to identify—

(i) locations where individuals with disabilities access primary, acute (including intensive), and long-term care;

(ii) the number of providers with accessible facilities and equipment to meet the needs of the individuals with disabilities, including medical diagnostic equipment that meets the minimum technical criteria set forth in section 510 of the Rehabilitation Act of 1973 [29 USCS § 794f]; and

(iii) the number of employees of health care providers trained in disability awareness and patient care of individuals with disabilities; and

(E) require that any reporting requirement imposed for purposes of measuring quality under any ongoing or federally conducted or supported health care or public health program, activity, or survey includes requirements for the collection of data on individuals receiving health care items or services under such programs activities by race, ethnicity, sex, primary language, and disability status.

(3) Data management. In collecting data described in paragraph (1), the Secretary, acting through the National Coordinator for Health Information Technology shall—

(A) develop national standards for the management of data collected; and

(B) develop interoperability and security systems for data management.

(b) Data analysis. (1) In general. For each federally conducted or supported health care or public health program or activity, the Secretary shall analyze data collected under paragraph (a) to detect and monitor trends in health disparities (as defined for purposes of section 485E [42 USCS § 287c-31]) at the Federal and State levels.

(2) [Not enacted]

(c) Data reporting and dissemination. (1) In general. The Secretary shall make the analyses described in (b) available to—

(A) the Office of Minority Health;

(B) the National Center on Minority Health and Health Disparities;

(C) the Agency for Healthcare Research and Quality;

(D) the Centers for Disease Control and Prevention;

(E) the Centers for Medicare & Medicaid Services;

(F) the Indian Health Service and epidemiology centers funded under the Indian Health Care Improvement Act [25 USCS §§ 1601 et seq.];

(G) the Office of Rural health;

(H) other agencies within the Department of Health and Human Services; and

(I) other entities as determined appropriate by the Secretary.

(2) Reporting of data. The Secretary shall report data and analyses described in (a) and (b) through—

(A) public postings on the Internet websites of the Department of Health and Human Services; and

(B) any other reporting or dissemination mechanisms determined appropriate by the Secretary.

(3) Availability of data. The Secretary may make data described in (a) and (b) available for additional research, analyses, and dissemination to other Federal agencies, non-governmental entities, and the public, in accordance with any Federal agency's data user agreements.

(d) Limitations on use of data. Nothing in this section shall be construed to permit the use of information collected under this section in a manner that would adversely affect any individual.

(e) Protection and sharing of data. (1) Privacy and other safeguards. The Secretary shall ensure (through the promulgation of regulations or otherwise) that—

(A) all data collected pursuant to subsection (a) is protected—

(i) under privacy protections that are at least as broad as those that the Secretary applies to other health data under the regulations promulgated under section 264(c) of the

Health Insurance Portability and Accountability Act of 1996 (Public Law 104-191; 110 Stat. 2033) [42 USCS § 1320d-2 note]; and

(ii) from all inappropriate internal use by any entity that collects, stores, or receives the data, including use of such data in determinations of eligibility (or continued eligibility) in health plans, and from other inappropriate uses, as defined by the Secretary; and

(B) all appropriate information security safeguards are used in the collection, analysis, and sharing of data collected pursuant to subsection (a).

(2) Data sharing. The Secretary shall establish procedures for sharing data collected pursuant to subsection (a), measures relating to such data, and analyses of such data, with other relevant Federal and State agencies including the agencies, centers, and entities within the Department of Health and Human Services specified in subsection (c)(1).

(f) Data on rural underserved populations. The Secretary shall ensure that any data collected in accordance with this section regarding racial and ethnic minority groups are also collected regarding underserved rural and frontier populations.

(g) Authorization of appropriations. For the purpose of carrying out this section, there are authorized to be appropriated such sums as may be necessary for each of fiscal years 2010 through 2014.

(h) Requirement for implementation. Notwithstanding any other provision of this section, data may not be collected under this section unless funds are directly appropriated for such purpose in an appropriations Act.

(i) Consultation. The Secretary shall consult with the Director of the Office of Personnel Management, the Secretary of Defense, the Secretary of Veterans Affairs, the Director of the Bureau of the Census, the Commissioner of Social Security, and the head of other appropriate Federal agencies in carrying out this section.

(July 1, 1944, ch 373, Title XXXI, § 3101, as added March 23, 2010, P. L. 111-148, Title IV, Subtitle D, § 4302(a), 124 Stat. 578.)

COMMUNITY LIVING ASSISTANCE SERVICES AND SUPPORTS

§ 300ll. Purpose [Caution: This section takes effect on January 1, 2011, pursuant to § 8002(e) of Act March 23, 2010, P. L. 111-148, which appears as a note to this section.]

The purpose of this title [42 USCS §§ 300ll et seq.] is to establish a national voluntary insurance program for purchasing community living assistance services and supports in order to—

(1) provide individuals with functional limitations with tools that will allow them to maintain their personal and financial independence and live in the community through a new financing strategy for community living assistance services and supports;

(2) establish an infrastructure that will help address the Nation's community living assistance services and supports needs;

(3) alleviate burdens on family caregivers; and

(4) address institutional bias by providing a financing mechanism that supports personal choice and independence to live in the community.

(July 1, 1944, ch 373, Title XXXII, § 3201, as added March 23, 2010, P. L. 111-148, Title VIII, § 8002(a)(1), 124 Stat. 828.)

HISTORY; ANCILLARY LAWS AND DIRECTIVES

Effective date of section:

This section takes effect on January 1, 2011, pursuant to § 8002(e) of Act March 23, 2010, P. L. 111-148, which appears as a note to this section.

Other provisions:

Personal Care Attendants Workforce Advisory Panel. Act March 23, 2010, P. L. 111-148, Title VIII, § 8002(c), 124 Stat. 846, provides:

"(1) Establishment. Not later than 90 days after the date of enactment of this Act, the Secretary of Health and Human Services shall establish a Personal Care Attendants Workforce Advisory Panel for the purpose of examining and advising the Secretary and Congress on workforce issues related to personal care attendant workers, including with respect to the adequacy of the number of such workers, the salaries, wages, and benefits of such workers, and access to the services provided by such workers.

"(2) Membership. In appointing members to the Personal Care Attendants Workforce Advisory Panel, the Secretary shall ensure that such members include the following:

"(A) Individuals with disabilities of all ages.
"(B) Senior individuals.
"(C) Representatives of individuals with disabilities.
"(D) Representatives of senior individuals.
"(E) Representatives of workforce and labor organizations.
"(F) Representatives of home and community-based service providers.
"(G) Representatives of assisted living providers.".

Effective date of March 23, 2010 amendments. Act March 23, 2010, P. L. 111-148, Title VIII, § 8002(e), 124 Stat. 847, provides: "The amendments made by subsections (a), (b), and (d) [adding 42 USCS §§ 300ll et seq, and amending 42 USCS §§ 1396a(a) and 1396p note] take effect on January 1, 2011.".

Rule of construction of March 23, 2010 amendments. Act March 23, 2010, P. L. 111-148, Title VIII, § 8002(f), 124 Stat. 847, provides: "Nothing in this title or the amendments made by this title [adding 42 USCS §§ 300ll et seq. generally; for full classification, consult USCS Tables volumes] are intended to replace or displace public or private disability insurance benefits, including such benefits that are for income replacement.".

§ 300ll-1. Definitions [Caution: This section takes effect on January 1, 2011, pursuant to § 8002(e) of Act March 23, 2010, P. L. 111-148, which appears as 42 USCS § 300ll note.]

In this title [42 USCS §§ 300ll et seq.]:

(1) Active enrollee. The term "active enrollee" means an individual who is enrolled in the CLASS program in accordance with section 3204 [42 USCS § 300ll-3] and who has paid any premiums due to maintain such enrollment.

(2) Actively employed. The term "actively employed" means an individual who—

(A) is reporting for work at the individual's usual place of employment or at another location to which the individual is required to travel because of the individual's employment (or in the case of an individual who is a member of the uniformed services, is on active duty and is physically able to perform the duties of the individual's position); and

(B) is able to perform all the usual and customary duties of the individual's employment on the individual's regular work schedule.

(3) Activities of daily living. The term "activities of daily living" means each of the following activities specified in section 7702B(c)(2)(B) of the Internal Revenue Code of 1986 [26 USCS § 7702B(c)(2)(B)]:

(A) Eating.

(B) Toileting.

(C) Transferring.

(D) Bathing.

(E) Dressing.

(F) Continence.

(4) CLASS program. The term "CLASS program" means the program established under this title [42 USCS §§ 300ll et seq.].

(5) Eligibility assessment system. The term "Eligibility Assessment System" means the entity established by the Secretary under section 3205(a)(2) [42 USCS § 300ll-4(a)(2)] to make functional eligibility determinations for the CLASS program.

(6) Eligible beneficiary. (A) In general. The term "eligible beneficiary" means any individual who is an active enrollee in the CLASS program and, as of the date described in subparagraph (B)—

(i) has paid premiums for enrollment in such program for at least 60 months;

(ii) has earned, with respect to at least 3 calendar years that occur during the first 60 months for which the individual has paid premiums for enrollment in the program, at least an amount equal to the amount of wages and self-employment income which an individual must have in order to be credited with a quarter of coverage under section 213(d) of the Social Security Act for the year [42 USCS § 413(d)]; and

(iii) has paid premiums for enrollment in such program for at least 24 consecutive months, if a lapse in premium payments of more than 3 months has occurred during the period that begins on the date of the individual's enrollment and ends on the date of such determination.

(B) Date described. For purposes of subparagraph (A), the date described in this subparagraph is the date on which the individual is determined to have a functional limitation described in section 3203(a)(1)(C) [42 USCS § 300ll-2(a)(1)(C)] that is expected to last for a continuous period of more than 90 days.

(C) Regulations. The Secretary shall promulgate regulations specifying exceptions to the minimum earnings requirements under subparagraph (A)(ii) for purposes of being considered an eligible beneficiary for certain populations.

(7) Hospital; nursing facility; intermediate care facility for the mentally retarded; institution for mental diseases. The terms "hospital", "nursing facility", "intermediate care facility for the mentally retarded", and "institution for mental diseases" have the meanings given such terms for purposes of Medicaid.

(8) CLASS independence advisory council. The term "CLASS Independence Advisory Council" or "Council" means the Advisory Council established under section 3207 [42 USCS § 300ll-6] to advise the Secretary.

(9) CLASS independence benefit plan. The term "CLASS Independence Benefit Plan" means the benefit plan developed and designated by the Secretary in accordance with section 3203 [42 USCS § 300ll-2].

(10) CLASS Independence Fund. The term "CLASS Independence Fund" or "Fund" means the fund established under section 3206 [42 USCS § 300ll-5].

(11) Medicaid. The term "Medicaid" means the program established under title XIX of the Social Security Act (42 U.S.C. 1396 et seq.).

(12) Poverty line. The term "poverty line" has the meaning given that term in section 2110(c)(5) of the Social Security Act (42 U.S.C.

1397jj(c)(5)).

(13) Protection and Advocacy System. The term "Protection and Advocacy System" means the system for each State established under section 143 of the Developmental Disabilities Assistance and Bill of Rights Act of 2000 (42 U.S.C. 15043).

(July 1, 1944, ch 373, Title XXXII, § 3202, as added March 23, 2010, P. L. 111-148, Title VIII, § 8002(a)(1), 124 Stat. 828.)

§ 300ll-2. CLASS Independence Benefit Plan [Caution: This section takes effect on January 1, 2011, pursuant to § 8002(e) of Act March 23, 2010, P. L. 111-148, which appears as 42 USCS § 300ll note.]

(a) Process for development. (1) In general. The Secretary, in consultation with appropriate actuaries and other experts, shall develop at least 3 actuarially sound benefit plans as alternatives for consideration for designation by the Secretary as the CLASS Independence Benefit Plan under which eligible beneficiaries shall receive benefits under this title [42 USCS §§ 300ll et seq.]. Each of the plan alternatives developed shall be designed to provide eligible beneficiaries with the benefits described in section 3205 [42 USCS § 300ll-4] consistent with the following requirements:

(A) Premiums. (i) In general. Beginning with the first year of the CLASS program, and for each year thereafter, subject to clauses (ii) and (iii), the Secretary shall establish all premiums to be paid by enrollees for the year based on an actuarial analysis of the 75-year costs of the program that ensures solvency throughout such 75-year period.

(ii) Nominal premium for poorest individuals and full-time students. (I) In general. The monthly premium for enrollment in the CLASS program shall not exceed the applicable dollar amount per month determined under subclause (II) for—

(aa) any individual whose income does not exceed the poverty line; and

(bb) any individual who has not attained age 22, and is actively employed during any period in which the individual is a full-time student (as determined by the Secretary).

(II) Applicable dollar amount. The applicable dollar amount described in this subclause is the amount equal to $5, increased by the percentage increase in the consumer price index for all urban consumers (U.S. city average) for each year occurring after 2009 and before such year.

(iii) Class Independence Fund reserves. At such time as the CLASS program has been in operation for 10 years, the Secretary shall establish all premiums to be paid by enrollees for the year based on an actuarial analysis that accumulated reserves in the CLASS Independence Fund would not decrease in that year. At such time as the Secretary determines the CLASS program demonstrates a sustained ability to finance expected yearly expenses with expected yearly premiums and interest credited to the CLASS Independence Fund, the Secretary may decrease the required amount of CLASS Independence Fund reserves.

(B) Vesting period. A 5-year vesting period for eligibility for benefits.

(C) Benefit triggers. A benefit trigger for provision of benefits that requires a determination that an individual has a functional limitation, as certified by a licensed health care practitioner, described in any of the following clauses that is expected to last for a continuous period of more than 90 days:

(i) The individual is determined to be unable to perform at least the minimum number (which may be 2 or 3) of activities of daily living as are required under the plan for the provision of benefits without substantial assistance (as defined by the Secretary) from another individual.

(ii) The individual requires substantial supervision to protect the individual from threats to health and safety due to substantial cognitive impairment.

(iii) The individual has a level of functional limitation similar (as determined under regulations prescribed by the Secretary) to the level of functional limitation described in clause (i) or (ii).

(D) Cash benefit. Payment of a cash benefit that satisfies the following requirements:

(i) Minimum required amount. The benefit amount provides an eligible beneficiary with not less than an average of $50 per day (as determined based on the reasonably expected distribution of beneficiaries receiving benefits at various benefit levels).

(ii) Amount scaled to functional ability. The benefit amount is varied based on a scale of functional ability, with not less than 2, and not more than 6, benefit level amounts.

(iii) Daily or weekly. The benefit is paid on a daily or weekly basis.

(iv) No lifetime or aggregate limit. The benefit is not subject to any lifetime or aggregate limit.

(2) Review and recommendation by the class independence advisory council. The CLASS Independence Advisory Council shall—

(A) evaluate the alternative benefit plans

developed under paragraph (1); and

(B) recommend for designation as the CLASS Independence Benefit Plan for offering to the public the plan that the Council determines best balances price and benefits to meet enrollees' needs in an actuarially sound manner, while optimizing the probability of the long-term sustainability of the CLASS program.

(3) Designation by the Secretary. Not later than October 1, 2012, the Secretary, taking into consideration the recommendation of the CLASS Independence Advisory Council under paragraph (2)(B), shall designate a benefit plan as the CLASS Independence Benefit Plan. The Secretary shall publish such designation, along with details of the plan and the reasons for the selection by the Secretary, in a final rule that allows for a period of public comment.

(b) Additional premium requirements. (1) Adjustment of premiums. (A) In general. Except as provided in subparagraphs (B), (C), (D), and (E), the amount of the monthly premium determined for an individual upon such individual's enrollment in the CLASS program shall remain the same for as long as the individual is an active enrollee in the program.

(B) Recalculated premium if required for program solvency. (i) In general. Subject to clause (ii), if the Secretary determines, based on the most recent report of the Board of Trustees of the CLASS Independence Fund, the advice of the CLASS Independence Advisory Council, and the annual report of the Inspector General of the Department of Health and Human Services, and waste, fraud, and abuse, or such other information as the Secretary determines appropriate, that the monthly premiums and income to the CLASS Independence Fund for a year are projected to be insufficient with respect to the 20-year period that begins with that year, the Secretary shall adjust the monthly premiums for individuals enrolled in the CLASS program as necessary (but maintaining a nominal premium for enrollees whose income is below the poverty line or who are full-time students actively employed).

(ii) Exemption from increase. Any increase in a monthly premium imposed as result of a determination described in clause (i) shall not apply with respect to the monthly premium of any active enrollee who—

(I) has attained age 65;

(II) has paid premiums for enrollment in the program for at least 20 years; and

(III) is not actively employed.

(C) Recalculated premium if reenrollment after more than a 3-month lapse. (i) In general. The reenrollment of an individual after a 90-day period during which the individual failed to pay the monthly premium required to maintain the individual's enrollment in the CLASS program shall be treated as an initial enrollment for purposes of age-adjusting the premium for reenrollment in the program.

(ii) Credit for prior months if reenrolled within 5 years. An individual who reenrolls in the CLASS program after such a 90-day period and before the end of the 5-year period that begins with the first month for which the individual failed to pay the monthly premium required to maintain the individual's enrollment in the program shall be—

(I) credited with any months of paid premiums that accrued prior to the individual's lapse in enrollment; and

(II) notwithstanding the total amount of any such credited months, required to satisfy section 3202(6)(A)(ii) [42 USCS § 300ll-1(6)(A)(ii)] before being eligible to receive benefits.

(D) No longer status as a full-time student. An individual subject to a nominal premium on the basis of being described in subsection (a)(1)(A)(ii)(I)(bb) who ceases to be described in that subsection, beginning with the first month following the month in which the individual ceases to be so described, shall be subject to the same monthly premium as the monthly premium that applies to an individual of the same age who first enrolls in the program under the most similar circumstances as the individual (such as the first year of eligibility for enrollment in the program or in a subsequent year).

(E) Penalty for reenollment after 5-year lapse. In the case of an individual who reenrolls in the CLASS program after the end of the 5-year period described in subparagraph (C)(ii), the monthly premium required for the individual shall be the age-adjusted premium that would be applicable to an initially enrolling individual who is the same age as the reenrolling individual, increased by the greater of—

(i) an amount that the Secretary determines is actuarially sound for each month that occurs during the period that begins with the first month for which the individual failed to pay the monthly premium required to maintain the individual's enrollment in the CLASS program and ends with the month preceding the month in which the reenollment is effective; or

(ii) 1 percent of the applicable age-adjusted premium for each such month occurring in such period.

(2) Administrative expenses. In determining the monthly premiums for the CLASS program the Secretary may factor in costs for adminis-

tering the program, not to exceed for any year in which the program is in effect under this title [42 USCS §§ 300ll et seq.], an amount equal to 3 percent of all premiums paid during the year.

(3) No underwriting requirements. No underwriting (other than on the basis of age in accordance with subparagraphs (D) and (E) of paragraph (1)) shall be used to—

(A) determine the monthly premium for enrollment in the CLASS program; or

(B) prevent an individual from enrolling in the program.

(c) Self-attestation and verification of income. The Secretary shall establish procedures to—

(1) permit an individual who is eligible for the nominal premium required under subsection (a)(1)(A)(ii) to self-attest that their income does not exceed the poverty line or that their status as a full-time student who is actively employed;

(2) verify, using procedures similar to the procedures used by the Commissioner of Social Security under section 1631(e)(1)(B)(ii) of the Social Security Act [42 USCS § 1383(e)(1)(B)(ii)] and consistent with the requirements applicable to the conveyance of data and information under section 1942 of such Act [42 USCS § 300x-52], the validity of such self-attestation; and

(3) require an individual to confirm, on at least an annual basis, that their income does not exceed the poverty line or that they continue to maintain such status.

(July 1, 1944, ch 373, Title XXXII, § 3203, as added and amended March 23, 2010, P. L. 111-148, Title VIII, § 8002(a)(1), Title X, Subtitle G, § 10801(a)(1), 124 Stat. 830, 1015.)

§ 300ll-3. Enrollment and disenrollment requirements [Caution: This section takes effect on January 1, 2011, pursuant to § 8002(e) of Act March 23, 2010, P. L. 111-148, which appears as 42 USCS § 300ll note.]

(a) Automatic enrollment. (1) In general. Subject to paragraph (2), the Secretary, in coordination with the Secretary of the Treasury, shall establish procedures under which each individual described in subsection (c) may be automatically enrolled in the CLASS program by an employer of such individual in the same manner as an employer may elect to automatically enroll employees in a plan under section 401(k), 403(b), or 457 of the Internal Revenue Code of 1986 [26 USCS § 401(k), 403(b), or 457].

(2) Alternative enrollment procedures. The procedures established under paragraph (1) shall provide for an alternative enrollment process for an individual described in subsection (c) in the case of such an individual—

(A) who is self-employed;

(B) who has more than 1 employer; or

(C) whose employer does not elect to participate in the automatic enrollment process established by the Secretary.

(3) Administration. (A) In general. The Secretary and the Secretary of the Treasury shall, by regulation, establish procedures to ensure that an individual is not automatically enrolled in the CLASS program by more than 1 employer.

(B) Form. Enrollment in the CLASS program shall be made in such manner as the Secretary may prescribe in order to ensure ease of administration.

(b) Election to opt-out. An individual described in subsection (c) may elect to waive enrollment in the CLASS program at any time in such form and manner as the Secretary and the Secretary of the Treasury shall prescribe.

(c) Individual described. For purposes of enrolling in the CLASS program, an individual described in this paragraph is an individual—

(1) who has attained age 18;

(2) who—

(A) receives wages or income on which there is imposed a tax under section 3101(a) or 3201(a) of the Internal Revenue Code of 1986 [26 USCS § 3101(a) or 3201(a)]; or

(B) derives self-employment income on which there is imposed a tax under section 1401(a) of the Internal Revenue Code of 1986 [26 USCS § 1401(a)];

(3) who is actively employed; and

(4) who is not—

(A) a patient in a hospital or nursing facility, an intermediate care facility for the mentally retarded, or an institution for mental diseases and receiving medical assistance under Medicaid; or

(B) confined in a jail, prison, other penal institution or correctional facility, or by court order pursuant to conviction of a criminal offense or in connection with a verdict or finding described in section 202(x)(1)(A)(ii) of the Social Security Act (42 U.S.C. 402(x)(1)(A)(ii)).

(d) Rule of construction. Nothing in this title [42 USCS §§ 300ll et seq.] shall be construed as requiring an active enrollee to continue to satisfy subparagraph (A) or (B) of subsection (c)(2) in order to maintain enrollment in the CLASS program.

(e) Payment. (1) Payroll deduction. An

amount equal to the monthly premium for the enrollment in the CLASS program of an individual shall be deducted from the wages or self-employment income of such individual in accordance with such procedures as the Secretary, in coordination with the Secretary of the Treasury, shall establish for employers who elect to deduct and withhold such premiums on behalf of enrolled employees.

(2) Alternative payment mechanism. The Secretary, in coordination with the Secretary of the Treasury, shall establish alternative procedures for the payment of monthly premiums by an individual enrolled in the CLASS program—

(A) who does not have an employer who elects to deduct and withhold premiums in accordance with paragraph (1); or

(B) who does not earn wages or derive self-employment income.

(f) Transfer of premiums collected. (1) In general. During each calendar year the Secretary of the Treasury shall deposit into the CLASS Independence Fund a total amount equal, in the aggregate, to 100 percent of the premiums collected during that year.

(2) Transfers based on estimates. The amount deposited pursuant to paragraph (1) shall be transferred in at least monthly payments to the CLASS Independence Fund on the basis of estimates by the Secretary and certified to the Secretary of the Treasury of the amounts collected in accordance with subparagraphs (A) and (B) of paragraph (5). Proper adjustments shall be made in amounts subsequently transferred to the Fund to the extent prior estimates were in excess of, or were less than, actual amounts collected.

(g) Other enrollment and disenrollment opportunities. The Secretary, in coordination with the Secretary of the Treasury, shall establish procedures under which—

(1) an individual who, in the year of the individual's initial eligibility to enroll in the CLASS program, has not enrolled in the program, is eligible to elect to enroll in the program, in such form and manner as the Secretaries shall establish, only during an open enrollment period established by the Secretaries that is specific to the individual and that may not occur more frequently than biennially after the date on which the individual first elected to waive enrollment in the program; and

(2) an individual shall only be permitted to disenroll from the program (other than for nonpayment of premiums) during an annual disenrollment period established by the Secretaries and in such form and manner as the Secretaries shall establish.

(July 1, 1944, ch 373, Title XXXII, § 3204, as added and amended March 23, 2010, P. L. 111-148, Title VIII, § 8002(a)(1), Title X, Subtitle G, § 10801(a)(2), 124 Stat. 834, 1015.)

§ 300ll-4. Benefits [Caution: This section takes effect on January 1, 2011, pursuant to § 8002(e) of Act March 23, 2010, P. L. 111-148, which appears as 42 USCS § 300ll note.]

(a) Determination of eligibility. (1) Application for receipt of benefits. The Secretary shall establish procedures under which an active enrollee shall apply for receipt of benefits under the CLASS Independence Benefit Plan.

(2) Eligibility assessments. (A) In general. Not later than January 1, 2012, the Secretary shall—

(i) establish an Eligibility Assessment System (other than a service with which the Commissioner of Social Security has entered into an agreement, with respect to any State, to make disability determinations for purposes of title II or XVI of the Social Security Act [42 USCS §§ 401 et seq. or 1381 et seq.]) to provide for eligibility assessments of active enrollees who apply for receipt of benefits;

(ii) enter into an agreement with the Protection and Advocacy System for each State to provide advocacy services in accordance with subsection (d); and

(iii) enter into an agreement with public and private entities to provide advice and assistance counseling in accordance with subsection (e).

(B) Regulations. The Secretary shall promulgate regulations to develop an expedited nationally equitable eligibility determination process, as certified by a licensed health care practitioner, an appeals process, and a redetermination process, as certified by a licensed health care practitioner, including whether an active enrollee is eligible for a cash benefit under the program and if so, the amount of the cash benefit (in accordance the sliding scale established under the plan).

(C) Presumptive eligibility for certain institutionalized enrollees planning to discharge. An active enrollee shall be deemed presumptively eligible if the enrollee—

(i) has applied for, and attests is eligible for, the maximum cash benefit available under the sliding scale established under the CLASS Independence Benefit Plan;

(ii) is a patient in a hospital (but only if the

hospitalization is for long-term care), nursing facility, intermediate care facility for the mentally retarded, or an institution for mental diseases; and

(iii) is in the process of, or about to begin the process of, planning to discharge from the hospital, facility, or institution, or within 60 days from the date of discharge from the hospital, facility, or institution.

(D) Appeals. The Secretary shall establish procedures under which an applicant for benefits under the CLASS Independence Benefit Plan shall be guaranteed the right to appeal an adverse determination.

(b) Benefits. An eligible beneficiary shall receive the following benefits under the CLASS Independence Benefit Plan:

(1) Cash benefit. A cash benefit established by the Secretary in accordance with the requirements of section 3203(a)(1)(D) [42 USCS § 300ll-2(a)(1)(D)] that—

(A) the first year in which beneficiaries receive the benefits under the plan, is not less than the average dollar amount specified in clause (i) of such section; and

(B) for any subsequent year, is not less than the average per day dollar limit applicable under this subparagraph for the preceding year, increased by the percentage increase in the consumer price index for all urban consumers (U.S. city average) over the previous year.

(2) Advocacy services. Advocacy services in accordance with subsection (d).

(3) Advice and assistance counseling. Advice and assistance counseling in accordance with subsection (e).

(4) Administrative expenses. Advocacy services and advise and assistance counseling services under paragraphs (2) and (3) of this subsection shall be included as administrative expenses under section 3203(b)(3) [42 USCS § 300ll-2(b)(3)].

(c) Payment of benefits. (1) Life independence account. (A) In general. The Secretary shall establish procedures for administering the provision of benefits to eligible beneficiaries under the CLASS Independence Benefit Plan, including the payment of the cash benefit for the beneficiary into a Life Independence Account established by the Secretary on behalf of each eligible beneficiary.

(B) Use of cash benefits. Cash benefits paid into a Life Independence Account of an eligible beneficiary shall be used to purchase nonmedical services and supports that the beneficiary needs to maintain his or her independence at home or in another residential setting of their choice in the community, including (but not limited to) home modifications, assistive technology, accessible transportation, homemaker services, respite care, personal assistance services, home care aides, and nursing support. Nothing in the preceding sentence shall prevent an eligible beneficiary from using cash benefits paid into a Life Independence Account for obtaining assistance with decision making concerning medical care, including the right to accept or refuse medical or surgical treatment and the right to formulate advance directives or other written instructions recognized under State law, such as a living will or durable power of attorney for health care, in the case that an injury or illness causes the individual to be unable to make health care decisions.

(C) Electronic management of funds. The Secretary shall establish procedures for—

(i) crediting an account established on behalf of a beneficiary with the beneficiary's cash daily benefit;

(ii) allowing the beneficiary to access such account through debit cards; and

(iii) accounting for withdrawals by the beneficiary from such account.

(D) Primary payor rules for beneficiaries who are enrolled in Medicaid. In the case of an eligible beneficiary who is enrolled in Medicaid, the following payment rules shall apply:

(i) Institutionalized beneficiary. If the beneficiary is a patient in a hospital, nursing facility, intermediate care facility for the mentally retarded, or an institution for mental diseases, the beneficiary shall retain an amount equal to 5 percent of the beneficiary's daily or weekly cash benefit (as applicable) (which shall be in addition to the amount of the beneficiary's personal needs allowance provided under Medicaid), and the remainder of such benefit shall be applied toward the facility's cost of providing the beneficiary's care, and Medicaid shall provide secondary coverage for such care.

(ii) Beneficiaries receiving home and community-based services. (I) 50 percent of benefit retained by beneficiary. Subject to subclause (II), if a beneficiary is receiving medical assistance under Medicaid for home and community based services, the beneficiary shall retain an amount equal to 50 percent of the beneficiary's daily or weekly cash benefit (as applicable), and the remainder of the daily or weekly cash benefit shall be applied toward the cost to the State of providing such assistance (and shall not be used to claim Federal matching funds under Medicaid), and Medicaid shall provide secondary coverage for the remainder of any costs incurred in providing such assistance.

(II) Requirement for state offset. A State

shall be paid the remainder of a beneficiary's daily or weekly cash benefit under subclause (I) only if the State home and community-based waiver under section 1115 of the Social Security Act (42 U.S.C. 1315) or subsection (c) or (d) of section 1915 of such Act (42 U.S.C. 1396n), or the State plan amendment under subsection (i) of such section does not include a waiver of the requirements of section 1902(a)(1) of the Social Security Act (relating to statewideness) or of section 1902(a)(10)(B) of such Act (relating to comparability) and the State offers at a minimum case management services, personal care services, habilitation services, and respite care under such a waiver or State plan amendment.

(III) Definition of home and community-based services. In this clause, the term "home and community-based services" means any services which may be offered under a home and community-based waiver authorized for a State under section 1115 of the Social Security Act (42 U.S.C. 1315) or subsection (c) or (d) of section 1915 of such Act (42 U.S.C. 1396n) or under a State plan amendment under subsection (i) of such section.

(iii) Beneficiaries enrolled in programs of all-inclusive care for the elderly (pace). (I) In general. Subject to subclause (II), if a beneficiary is receiving medical assistance under Medicaid for PACE program services under section 1934 of the Social Security Act (42 U.S.C. 1396u-4), the beneficiary shall retain an amount equal to 50 percent of the beneficiary's daily or weekly cash benefit (as applicable), and the remainder of the daily or weekly cash benefit shall be applied toward the cost to the State of providing such assistance (and shall not be used to claim Federal matching funds under Medicaid), and Medicaid shall provide secondary coverage for the remainder of any costs incurred in providing such assistance.

(II) Institutionalized recipients of pace program services. If a beneficiary receiving assistance under Medicaid for PACE program services is a patient in a hospital, nursing facility, intermediate care facility for the mentally retarded, or an institution for mental diseases, the beneficiary shall be treated as in institutionalized beneficiary under clause (i).

(2) Authorized representatives. (A) In general.The Secretary shall establish procedures to allow access to a beneficiary's cash benefits by an authorized representative of the eligible beneficiary on whose behalf such benefits are paid.

(B) Quality assurance and protection against fraud and abuse. The procedures established under subparagraph (A) shall ensure that authorized representatives of eligible beneficiaries comply with standards of conduct established by the Secretary, including standards requiring that such representatives provide quality services on behalf of such beneficiaries, do not have conflicts of interest, and do not misuse benefits paid on behalf of such beneficiaries or otherwise engage in fraud or abuse.

(3) Commencement of benefits. Benefits shall be paid to, or on behalf of, an eligible beneficiary beginning with the first month in which an application for such benefits is approved.

(4) Rollover option for lump-sum payment. An eligible beneficiary may elect to—

(A) defer payment of their daily or weekly benefit and to rollover any such deferred benefits from month-to-month, but not from year-to-year; and

(B) receive a lump-sum payment of such deferred benefits in an amount that may not exceed the lesser of—

(i) the total amount of the accrued deferred benefits; or

(ii) the applicable annual benefit.

(5) Period for determination of annual benefits. (A) In general. The applicable period for determining with respect to an eligible beneficiary the applicable annual benefit and the amount of any accrued deferred benefits is the 12-month period that commences with the first month in which the beneficiary began to receive such benefits, and each 12-month period thereafter.

(B) Inclusion of increased benefits. The Secretary shall establish procedures under which cash benefits paid to an eligible beneficiary that increase or decrease as a result of a change in the functional status of the beneficiary before the end of a 12-month benefit period shall be included in the determination of the applicable annual benefit paid to the eligible beneficiary.

(C) Recoupment of unpaid, accrued benefits. (i) In general. The Secretary, in coordination with the Secretary of the Treasury, shall recoup any accrued benefits in the event of—

(I) the death of a beneficiary; or

(II) the failure of a beneficiary to elect under paragraph (4)(B) to receive such benefits as a lump-sum payment before the end of the 12-month period in which such benefits accrued.

(ii) Payment into class independence fund. Any benefits recouped in accordance with clause (i) shall be paid into the CLASS Independence Fund and used in accordance with section 3206 [42 USCS § 300ll-5].

(6) Requirement to recertify eligibility for receipt of benefits. An eligible beneficiary shall periodically, as determined by the Secretary—

(A) recertify by submission of medical evidence the beneficiary's continued eligibility for receipt of benefits; and

(B) submit records of expenditures attributable to the aggregate cash benefit received by the beneficiary during the preceding year.

(7) Supplement, not supplant other health care benefits. Subject to the Medicaid payment rules under paragraph (1)(D), benefits received by an eligible beneficiary shall supplement, but not supplant, other health care benefits for which the beneficiary is eligible under Medicaid or any other Federally funded program that provides health care benefits or assistance.

(d) Advocacy services. An agreement entered into under subsection (a)(2)(A)(ii) shall require the Protection and Advocacy System for the State to—

(1) assign, as needed, an advocacy counselor to each eligible beneficiary that is covered by such agreement and who shall provide an eligible beneficiary with—

(A) information regarding how to access the appeals process established for the program;

(B) assistance with respect to the annual recertification and notification required under subsection (c)(6); and

(C) such other assistance with obtaining services as the Secretary, by regulation, shall require; and

(2) ensure that the System and such counselors comply with the requirements of subsection (h).

(e) Advice and assistance counseling. An agreement entered into under subsection (a)(2)(A)(iii) shall require the entity to assign, as requested by an eligible beneficiary that is covered by such agreement, an advice and assistance counselor who shall provide an eligible beneficiary with information regarding—

(1) accessing and coordinating long-term services and supports in the most integrated setting;

(2) possible eligibility for other benefits and services;

(3) development of a service and support plan;

(4) information about programs established under the Assistive Technology Act of 1998 and the services offered under such programs;

(5) available assistance with decision making concerning medical care, including the right to accept or refuse medical or surgical treatment and the right to formulate advance directives or other written instructions recognized under State law, such as a living will or durable power of attorney for health care, in the case that an injury or illness causes the individual to be unable to make health care decisions; and

(6) such other services as the Secretary, by regulation, may require.

(f) No effect on eligibility for other benefits. Benefits paid to an eligible beneficiary under the CLASS program shall be disregarded for purposes of determining or continuing the beneficiary's eligibility for receipt of benefits under any other Federal, State, or locally funded assistance program, including benefits paid under titles II, XVI, XVIII, XIX, or XXI of the Social Security Act (42 U.S.C. 401 et seq., 1381 et seq., 1395 et seq., 1396 et seq., 1397aa et seq.), under the laws administered by the Secretary of Veterans Affairs, under low-income housing assistance programs, or under the supplemental nutrition assistance program established under the Food and Nutrition Act of 2008 (7 U.S.C. 2011 et seq.).

(g) Rule of construction. Nothing in this title [42 USCS §§ 300ll et seq.] shall be construed as prohibiting benefits paid under the CLASS Independence Benefit Plan from being used to compensate a family caregiver for providing community living assistance services and supports to an eligible beneficiary.

(h) Protection against conflict of interests. The Secretary shall establish procedures to ensure that the Eligibility Assessment System, the Protection and Advocacy System for a State, advocacy counselors for eligible beneficiaries, and any other entities that provide services to active enrollees and eligible beneficiaries under the CLASS program comply with the following:

(1) If the entity provides counseling or planning services, such services are provided in a manner that fosters the best interests of the active enrollee or beneficiary.

(2) The entity has established operating procedures that are designed to avoid or minimize conflicts of interest between the entity and an active enrollee or beneficiary.

(3) The entity provides information about all services and options available to the active enrollee or beneficiary, to the best of its knowledge, including services available through other entities or providers.

(4) The entity assists the active enrollee or beneficiary to access desired services, regardless of the provider.

(5) The entity reports the number of active enrollees and beneficiaries provided with assis-

tance by age, disability, and whether such enrollees and beneficiaries received services from the entity or another entity.

(6) If the entity provides counseling or planning services, the entity ensures that an active enrollee or beneficiary is informed of any financial interest that the entity has in a service provider.

(7) The entity provides an active enrollee or beneficiary with a list of available service providers that can meet the needs of the active enrollee or beneficiary.

(July 1, 1944, ch 373, Title XXXII, § 3205, as added March 23, 2010, P. L. 111-148, Title VIII, § 8002(a)(1), 124 Stat. 836.)

§ 300ll-5. CLASS Independence Fund [Caution: This section takes effect on January 1, 2011, pursuant to § 8002(e) of Act March 23, 2010, P. L. 111-148, which appears as 42 USCS § 300ll note.]

(a) Establishment of CLASS Independence Fund. There is established in the Treasury of the United States a trust fund to be known as the "CLASS Independence Fund". The Secretary of the Treasury shall serve as Managing Trustee of such Fund. The Fund shall consist of all amounts derived from payments into the Fund under sections 3204(f) and 3205(c)(5)(C)(ii) [42 USCS § 300ll-3(f) and 300ll-4(c)(5)(C)(ii)], and remaining after investment of such amounts under subsection (b), including additional amounts derived as income from such investments. The amounts held in the Fund are appropriated and shall remain available without fiscal year limitation—

(1) to be held for investment on behalf of individuals enrolled in the CLASS program;

(2) to pay the administrative expenses related to the Fund and to investment under subsection (b); and

(3) to pay cash benefits to eligible beneficiaries under the CLASS Independence Benefit Plan.

(b) Investment of Fund balance. The Secretary of the Treasury shall invest and manage the CLASS Independence Fund in the same manner, and to the same extent, as the Federal Supplementary Medical Insurance Trust Fund may be invested and managed under subsections (c), (d), and (e) of section 1841(d) of the Social Security Act (42 U.S.C. 1395t).

(c) Board of Trustees. (1) In general. With respect to the CLASS Independence Fund, there is hereby created a body to be known as the Board of Trustees of the CLASS Independence Fund (hereinafter in this section referred to as the "Board of Trustees") composed of the Secretary of the Treasury, the Secretary of Labor, and the Secretary of Health and Human Services, all ex officio, and of two members of the public (both of whom may not be from the same political party), who shall be nominated by the President for a term of 4 years and subject to confirmation by the Senate. A member of the Board of Trustees serving as a member of the public and nominated and confirmed to fill a vacancy occurring during a term shall be nominated and confirmed only for the remainder of such term. An individual nominated and confirmed as a member of the public may serve in such position after the expiration of such member's term until the earlier of the time at which the member's successor takes office or the time at which a report of the Board is first issued under paragraph (2) after the expiration of the member's term. The Secretary of the Treasury shall be the Managing Trustee of the Board of Trustees. The Board of Trustees shall meet not less frequently than once each calendar year. A person serving on the Board of Trustees shall not be considered to be a fiduciary and shall not be personally liable for actions taken in such capacity with respect to the Trust Fund.

(2) Duties. (A) In general. It shall be the duty of the Board of Trustees to do the following:

(i) Hold the CLASS Independence Fund.

(ii) Report to the Congress not later than the first day of April of each year on the operation and status of the CLASS Independence Fund during the preceding fiscal year and on its expected operation and status during the current fiscal year and the next 2 fiscal years.

(iii) Report immediately to the Congress whenever the Board is of the opinion that the amount of the CLASS Independence Fund is not actuarially sound in regards to the projection under section 3203(b)(1)(B)(i) [42 USCS § 300ll-2(b)(1)(B)(i)].

(iv) Review the general policies followed in managing the CLASS Independence Fund, and recommend changes in such policies, including necessary changes in the provisions of law which govern the way in which the CLASS Independence Fund is to be managed.

(B) Report. The report provided for in subparagraph (A)(ii) shall—

(i) include—

(I) a statement of the assets of, and the disbursements made from, the CLASS Independence Fund during the preceding fiscal year;

(II) an estimate of the expected income to,

and disbursements to be made from, the CLASS Independence Fund during the current fiscal year and each of the next 2 fiscal years;

(III) a statement of the actuarial status of the CLASS Independence Fund for the current fiscal year, each of the next 2 fiscal years, and as projected over the 75-year period beginning with the current fiscal year; and

(IV) an actuarial opinion by the Chief Actuary of the Centers for Medicare & Medicaid Services certifying that the techniques and methodologies used are generally accepted within the actuarial profession and that the assumptions and cost estimates used are reasonable; and

(ii) be printed as a House document of the session of the Congress to which the report is made.

(C) Recommendations. If the Board of Trustees determines that enrollment trends and expected future benefit claims on the CLASS Independence Fund are not actuarially sound in regards to the projection under section 3203(b)(1)(B)(i) [42 USCS § 300ll-2(b)(1)(B)(i)] and are unlikely to be resolved with reasonable premium increases or through other means, the Board of Trustees shall include in the report provided for in subparagraph (A)(ii) recommendations for such legislative action as the Board of Trustees determine to be appropriate, including whether to adjust monthly premiums or impose a temporary moratorium on new enrollments.

(July 1, 1944, ch 373, Title XXXII, § 3206, as added March 23, 2010, P. L. 111-148, Title VIII, § 8002(a)(1), 124 Stat. 842.)

§ 300ll-6. CLASS Independence Advisory Council [Caution: This section takes effect on January 1, 2011, pursuant to § 8002(e) of Act March 23, 2010, P. L. 111-148, which appears as 42 USCS § 300ll note.]

(a) Establishment. There is hereby created an Advisory Committee to be known as the "CLASS Independence Advisory Council".

(b) Membership. (1) In general. The CLASS Independence Advisory Council shall be composed of not more than 15 individuals, not otherwise in the employ of the United States—

(A) who shall be appointed by the President without regard to the civil service laws and regulations; and

(B) a majority of whom shall be representatives of individuals who participate or are likely to participate in the CLASS program, and shall include representatives of older and younger workers, individuals with disabilities, family caregivers of individuals who require services and supports to maintain their independence at home or in another residential setting of their choice in the community, individuals with expertise in long-term care or disability insurance, actuarial science, economics, and other relevant disciplines, as determined by the Secretary.

(2) Terms. (A) In general. The members of the CLASS Independence Advisory Council shall serve overlapping terms of 3 years (unless appointed to fill a vacancy occurring prior to the expiration of a term, in which case the individual shall serve for the remainder of the term).

(B) Limitation. A member shall not be eligible to serve for more than 2 consecutive terms.

(3) Chair. The President shall, from time to time, appoint one of the members of the CLASS Independence Advisory Council to serve as the Chair.

(c) Duties. The CLASS Independence Advisory Council shall advise the Secretary on matters of general policy in the administration of the CLASS program established under this title [42 USCS §§ 300ll et seq.] and in the formulation of regulations under this title including with respect to—

(1) the development of the CLASS Independence Benefit Plan under section 3203 [42 USCS § 300ll-2];

(2) the determination of monthly premiums under such plan; and

(3) the financial solvency of the program.

(d) Application of FACA. The Federal Advisory Committee Act (5 U.S.C. App.), other than section 14 of that Act [5 USCS Appx], shall apply to the CLASS Independence Advisory Council.

(e) Authorization of Appropriations. (1) In general. There are authorized to be appropriated to the CLASS Independence Advisory Council to carry out its duties under this section, such sums as may be necessary for fiscal year 2011 and for each fiscal year thereafter.

(2) Availability. Any sums appropriated under the authorization contained in this section shall remain available, without fiscal year limitation, until expended.

(July 1, 1944, ch 373, Title XXXII, § 3207, as added March 23, 2010, P. L. 111-148, Title VIII, § 8002(a)(1), 124 Stat. 844.)

§ 300ll-7. Solvency and fiscal independence; regulations; annual report [Caution: This section takes effect on January 1, 2011, pursuant to § 8002(e) of Act

March 23, 2010, P. L. 111-148, which appears as 42 USCS § 300ll note.]

(a) Solvency. The Secretary shall regularly consult with the Board of Trustees of the CLASS Independence Fund and the CLASS Independence Advisory Council, for purposes of ensuring that enrollees premiums are adequate to ensure the financial solvency of the CLASS program, both with respect to fiscal years occurring in the near-term and fiscal years occurring over 20- and 75-year periods, taking into account the projections required for such periods under subsections (a)(1)(A)(i) and (b)(1)(B)(i) of section 3202 [42 USCS § 300ll-1].

(b) No taxpayer funds used to pay benefits. No taxpayer funds shall be used for payment of benefits under a CLASS Independent Benefit Plan. For purposes of this subsection, the term "taxpayer funds" means any Federal funds from a source other than premiums deposited by CLASS program participants in the CLASS Independence Fund and any associated interest earnings.

(c) Regulations. The Secretary shall promulgate such regulations as are necessary to carry out the CLASS program in accordance with this title [42 USCS §§ 300ll et seq.]. Such regulations shall include provisions to prevent fraud and abuse under the program.

(d) Annual report. Beginning January 1, 2014, the Secretary shall submit an annual report to Congress on the CLASS program. Each report shall include the following:

(1) The total number of enrollees in the program.

(2) The total number of eligible beneficiaries during the fiscal year.

(3) The total amount of cash benefits provided during the fiscal year.

(4) A description of instances of fraud or abuse identified during the fiscal year.

(5) Recommendations for such administrative or legislative action as the Secretary determines is necessary to improve the program, ensure the solvency of the program, or to prevent the occurrence of fraud or abuse.

(July 1, 1944, ch 373, Title XXXII, § 3208, as added March 23, 2010, P. L. 111-148, Title VIII, § 8002(a)(1), 124 Stat. 845.)

§ 300ll-8. Inspector General's report [Caution: This section takes effect on January 1, 2011, pursuant to § 8002(e) of Act March 23, 2010, P. L. 111-148, which appears as 42 USCS § 300ll note.]

The Inspector General of the Department of Health and Human Services shall submit an annual report to the Secretary and Congress relating to the overall progress of the CLASS program and of the existence of waste, fraud, and abuse in the CLASS program. Each such report shall include findings in the following areas:

(1) The eligibility determination process.

(2) The provision of cash benefits.

(3) Quality assurance and protection against waste, fraud, and abuse.

(4) Recouping of unpaid and accrued benefits.

(July 1, 1944, ch 373, Title XXXII, § 3209, as added March 23, 2010, P. L. 111-148, Title VIII, § 8002(a)(1), 124 Stat. 845.)

§ 300ll-9. Tax treatment of program [Caution: This section takes effect on January 1, 2011, pursuant to § 8002(e) of Act March 23, 2010, P. L. 111-148, which appears as 42 USCS § 300ll note.]

The CLASS program shall be treated for purposes of the Internal Revenue Code of 1986 [26 USCS §§ 1 et seq.] in the same manner as a qualified long-term care insurance contract for qualified long-term care services.

(July 1, 1944, ch 373, Title XXXII, § 3210, as added March 23, 2010, P. L. 111-148, Title VIII, § 8002(a)(1), 124 Stat. 846.)

CHAPTER 7. SOCIAL SECURITY ACT

TITLE II. FEDERAL OLD-AGE, SURVIVORS, AND DISABILITY INSURANCE BENEFITS

§ 405. Evidence and procedure for establishment of benefits

(a) Rules and regulations; procedures. The Commissioner of Social Security shall have full power and authority to make rules and regulations and to establish procedures, not inconsistent with the provisions of this title [42 USCS §§ 401 et seq.], which are necessary or appropriate to carry out such provisions, and shall adopt reasonable and proper rules and regulations to regulate and provide for the nature and extent of the proofs and evidence and the method of taking and furnishing the same in order to establish the right to benefits hereunder.

(b) Administrative determination of entitlement to benefits; findings of fact; hearings; investigations; evidentiary hearings in reconsiderations of disability benefit terminations. (1) The Commissioner of Social Security is directed to make findings of fact, and decisions as to the rights of any individual applying for a payment under this title [42 USCS §§ 401 et seq.]. Any such decision by the Commissioner of Social Security which involves a determination of disability and which is in whole or in part unfavorable to such individual shall contain a statement of the case, in understandable language, setting forth a discussion of the evidence, and stating the Commissioner's determination and the reason or reasons upon which it is based. Upon request by any such individual or upon request by a wife, divorced wife, surviving divorced mother, surviving divorced father husband, divorced husband, widower, surviving divorced husband, child, or parent who makes a showing in writing that his or her rights may be prejudiced by any decision the Commissioner of Social Security has rendered, the Commissioner shall give such applicant and such other individual reasonable notice and opportunity for a hearing with respect to such decision, and, if a hearing is held, shall, on the basis of evidence adduced at the hearing, affirm, modify, or reverse the Commissioner's findings of fact and such decision. Any such request with respect to such a decision must be filed within sixty days after notice of such decision is received by the individual making such request. The Commissioner of Social Security is further authorized, on the Commissioner's own motion, to hold such hearings and to conduct such investigations and other proceedings as the Commissioner may deem necessary or proper for the administration of this title [42 USCS §§ 401 et seq.]. In the course of any hearing, investigation or other proceeding, the Commissioner may administer oaths and affirmations, examine witnesses and receive evidence. Evidence may be received at any hearing before the Commissioner of Social Security even though inadmissible under rules of evidence applicable to court procedure.

(2) In any case where—

(A) an individual is a recipient of disability insurance benefits, or of child's, widow's, or widower's insurance benefits based on disability,

(B) the physical or mental impairment on the basis of which such benefits are payable is found to have ceased, not to have existed, or to no longer be disabling, and

(C) as a consequence of the finding described in subparagraph (B), such individual is determined by the Commissioner of Social Security not to be entitled to such benefits,

any reconsideration of the finding described in subparagraph (B), in connection with a reconsideration by the Commissioner of Social Security (before any hearing under paragraph (1) on the issue of such entitlement) of the Commissioner's determination described in subparagraph (C), shall be made only after opportunity for an evidentiary hearing, with regard to the finding described in subparagraph (B), which is reasonably accessible to such individual. Any reconsideration of a finding described in subparagraph (B) may be made either by the State agency or the Commissioner of Social Security where the finding was originally made by the State agency, and shall be made by the Commissioner of Social Security where the finding was originally made by the Commissioner of Social Security. In the case of a reconsideration by a State agency of a finding described in subparagraph (B) which was originally made by such State agency, the evidentiary hearing shall be held by an adjudicatory unit of the State agency other than the unit that made the finding described in subparagraph (B). In the case of a reconsideration by the Commissioner of Social Security of a finding described in subparagraph (B) which was originally made by the Commissioner of Social Security, the evidentiary hearing shall be held by a person other than the person or persons who made the finding described in subparagraph (B).

(3)(A) A failure to timely request review of an initial adverse determination with respect to an application for any benefit under this title [42 USCS §§ 401 et seq.] or an adverse determination on reconsideration of such an initial determination shall not serve as a basis for denial of a subsequent application for any benefit under this title [42 USCS §§ 401 et seq.] if the applicant demonstrates that the applicant, or any other individual referred to in paragraph (1), failed to so request such a review acting in good faith reliance upon incorrect, incomplete, or misleading information, relating to the consequences of reapplying for benefits in lieu of seeking review of an adverse determination, provided by any officer or employee of the Social Security Administration or any State agency acting under section 221 [42 USCS § 441].

(B) In any notice of an adverse determination with respect to which a review may be requested under paragraph (1), the Commissioner of Social Security shall describe in clear and specific language the effect on possible entitlement to benefits under this title [42 USCS §§ 401 et seq.] of choosing to reapply in lieu of requesting review of the determination.

(c) Records of wages and self-employ-

ment income. (1) For the purposes of this subsection—

(A) The term "year" means a calendar year when used with respect to wages and a taxable year when used with respect to self-employment income.

(B) The term "time limitation" means a period of three years, three months, and fifteen days.

(C) The term "survivor" means an individual's spouse, surviving divorced wife, surviving divorced husband, surviving divorced mother, surviving divorced father, child, or parent, who survives such individual.

(D) The term "period" when used with respect to self-employment income means a taxable year and when used with respect to wages means—

(i) a quarter if wages were reported or should have been reported on a quarterly basis on tax returns filed with the Secretary of the Treasury or his delegate under section 6011 of the Internal Revenue Code of 1986 [26 USCS § 6011] or regulations thereunder (or on reports filed by a State under section 218(e) [42 USCS § 418(e)] (as in effect prior to December 31, 1986) or regulations thereunder),

(ii) a year if wages were reported or should have been reported on a yearly basis on such tax returns or reports, or

(iii) the half year beginning January 1 or July 1 in the case of wages which were reported or should have been reported for calendar year 1937.

(2)(A) On the basis of information obtained by or submitted to the Commissioner of Social Security, and after such verification thereof as the Commissioner deems necessary, the Commissioner of Social Security shall establish and maintain records of the amounts of wages paid to, and the amounts of self-employment income derived by, each individual and of the periods in which such wages were paid and such income was derived and, upon request, shall inform any individual or his survivor, or the legal representative of such individual or his estate, of the amounts of wages and self-employment income of such individual and the periods during which such wages were paid and such income was derived, as shown by such records at the time of such request.

(B)(i) In carrying out the Commissioner's duties under subparagraph (A) and subparagraph (F), the Commissioner of Social Security shall take affirmative measures to assure that social security account numbers will, to the maximum extent practicable, be assigned to all members of appropriate groups of categories of individuals by assigning such numbers (or ascertaining that such numbers have already been assigned):

(I) to aliens at the time of their lawful admission to the United States either for permanent residence or under other authority of law permitting them to engage in employment in the United States and to other aliens at such time as their status is so changed as to make it lawful for them to engage in such employment;

(II) to any individual who is an applicant for or recipient of benefits under any program financed in whole or in part from Federal funds including any child on whose behalf such benefits are claimed by another person; and

(III) to any other individual when it appears that he could have been but was not assigned an account number under the provisions of subclauses (I) or (II) but only after such investigation as is necessary to establish to the satisfaction of the Commissioner of Social Security, the identity of such individual, the fact that an account number has not already been assigned to such individual, and the fact that such individual is a citizen or a noncitizen who is not, because of his alien status, prohibited from engaging in employment;

and, in carrying out such duties, the Commissioner of Social Security is authorized to take affirmative measures to assure the issuance of social security numbers:

(IV) to or on behalf of children who are below school age at the request of their parents or guardians; and

(V) to children of school age at the time of their first enrollment in school.

(ii) The Commissioner of Social Security shall require of applicants for social security account numbers such evidence as may be necessary to establish the age, citizenship, or alien status, and true identity of such applicants, and to determine which (if any) social security account number has previously been assigned to such individual. With respect to an application for a social security account number for an individual who has not attained the age of 18 before such application, such evidence shall include the information described in subparagraph (C)(ii).

(iii) In carrying out the requirements of this subparagraph, the Commissioner of Social Security shall enter into such agreements as may be necessary with the Attorney General and other officials and with State and local welfare agencies and school authorities (including nonpublic school authorities).

(C)(i) It is the policy of the United States that any State (or political subdivision thereof) may, in the administration of any tax, general public assistance, driver's license, or motor vehicle registration law within its jurisdiction, utilize the social security account numbers issued by the Commissioner of Social Security for the purpose of establishing the identification of individuals affected by such law, and may require any individual who is or appears to be so affected to furnish to such State (or political subdivision thereof) or any agency thereof having administrative responsibility for the law involved, the social security account number (or numbers, if he has more than one such number) issued to him by the Commissioner of Social Security.

(ii) In the administration of any law involving the issuance of a birth certificate, each State shall require each parent to furnish to such State (or political subdivision thereof) or any agency thereof having administrative responsibility for the law involved, the social security account number (or numbers, if the parent has more than one such number) issued to the parent unless the State (in accordance with regulations prescribed by the Commissioner of Social Security) finds good cause for not requiring the furnishing of such number. The State shall make numbers furnished under this subclause available to the Commissioner of Social Security and the agency administering the State's plan under part D of title IV [42 USCS §§ 651 et seq.] in accordance with Federal or State law and regulation. Such numbers shall not be recorded on the birth certificate. A State shall not use any social security account number, obtained with respect to the issuance by the State of a birth certificate, for any purpose other than for the enforcement of child support orders in effect in the State, unless section 7(a) of the Privacy Act of 1974 [5 USCS § 552a note] does not prohibit the State from requiring the disclosure of such number, by reason of the State having adopted, before January 1, 1975, a statute or regulation requiring such disclosure.

(iii)(I) In the administration of section 9 of the Food and Nutrition Act of 2008 (7 U.S.C 2018) involving the determination of the qualifications of applicants under such Act, the Secretary of Agriculture may require each applicant retail store or wholesale food concern to furnish to the Secretary of Agriculture the social security account number of each individual who is an officer of the store or concern and, in the case of a privately owned applicant, furnish the social security account numbers of the owners of such applicant. No officer or employee of the Department of Agriculture shall have access to any such number for any purpose other than the establishment and maintenance of a list of the names and social security account numbers of such individuals for use in determining those applicants who have been previously sanctioned or convicted under section 12 or 15 of such Act (7 U.S.C. 2021 or 2024).

(II) The Secretary of Agriculture may share any information contained in any list referred to in subclause (I) with any other agency or instrumentality of the United States which otherwise has access to social security account numbers in accordance with this subsection or other applicable Federal law, except that the Secretary of Agriculture may share such information only to the extent that such Secretary determines such sharing would assist in verifying and matching such information against information maintained by such other agency or instrumentality. Any such information shared pursuant to this subclause may be used by such other agency or instrumentality only for the purpose of effective administration and enforcement of the Food and Nutrition Act of 2008 or for the purpose of investigation of violations of other Federal laws or enforcement of such laws.

(III) The Secretary of Agriculture, and the head of any other agency or instrumentality referred to in this subclause, shall restrict, to the satisfaction of the Commissioner of Social Security, access to social security account numbers obtained pursuant to this clause only to officers and employees of the United States whose duties or responsibilities require access for the purposes described in subclause (II).

(IV) The Secretary of Agriculture, and the head of any agency or instrumentality with which information is shared pursuant to clause (II), shall provide such other safeguards as the Commissioner of Social Security determines to be necessary or appropriate to protect the confidentiality of the social security account numbers.

(iv) In the administration of section 506 of the Federal Crop Insurance Act [7 USCS § 1506], the Federal Crop Insurance Corporation may require each policyholder and each reinsured company to furnish to the insurer or to the Corporation the social security account number of such policyholder, subject to the requirements of this clause. No officer or employee of the Federal Crop Insurance Corporation shall have access to any such number for any purpose other than the establishment of a system of records necessary for the effective administration of such Act [7 USCS §§ 1501 et seq.]. The Manager of the Corporation may require each policyholder to provide to the Manager, at such times and in such manner as prescribed by the Manager, the social security account number of each individual that holds or acquires a substantial beneficial interest in the policyholder. For purposes of this clause, the term "substantial beneficial interest" means not less than 5 percent of all beneficial interest in the policyholder. The Secretary of Agriculture shall restrict, to the satisfaction of the Commissioner of Social Security, access to social security account numbers obtained pursuant to this clause only to officers and employees of the United States or authorized persons whose duties or responsibilities require access for the administration of the Federal Crop Insurance Act. The Secretary of Agriculture shall provide such other safeguards as the Commissioner of Social Security determines to be necessary or appropriate to protect the confidentiality of such social security account numbers. For purposes of this clause the term "authorized person" means an officer or employee of an insurer whom the Manager of the Corporation designates by rule, subject to appropriate safeguards including a prohibition against the release of such social security account number (other than to the Corporation) by such person.

(v) If and to the extent that any provision of Federal law heretofore enacted is inconsistent with the policy set forth in clause (i), such provision shall, on and after the date of the enactment of this subparagraph [enacted Oct. 4, 1976], be null, void, and of no effect. If and to the extent that any such provision is inconsistent with the requirement set forth in clause (ii), such provision shall, on and after the date of the enactment of such subclause, be null, void, and of no effect.

(vi)(I) For purposes of clause (i) of this subparagraph, an agency of a State (or political subdivision thereof) charged with the administration of any general public assistance, driver's license, or motor vehicle registration law which did not use the social security account number for identification under a law or regulation adopted before January 1, 1975, may require an individual to disclose his or her social security number to such agency solely for the purpose of administering the laws referred to in clause (i) above and for the purpose of responding to requests for information from an agency administering a program funded under part A of title IV [42 USCS §§ 601 et seq.] or an agency operating pursuant to the provisions of part D of such title [42 USCS §§ 651 et seq.].

(II) Any State or political subdivision thereof (and any person acting as an agent of such an agency or instrumentality), in the administration of any driver's license or motor vehicle registration law within its jurisdiction, may not display a social security account number issued by the Commissioner of Social Security (or any derivative of such number) on any driver's license, motor vehicle registration, or personal identification card (as defined in section 7212(a)(2) of the 9/11 Commission Implementation Act of 2004 [49 USCS § 30301 note]), or include, on any such license, registration, or personal identification card, a magnetic strip, bar code, or other means of communication which conveys such number (or derivative thereof).

(vii) For purposes of this subparagraph, the term "State" includes the District of Columbia, the Commonwealth of Puerto Rico, the Virgin Islands, Guam, the Commonwealth of the Northern Marianas, and the Trust Territory of the Pacific Islands.

(viii)(I) Social security account numbers and related records that are obtained or maintained by authorized persons pursuant to any provision of law, enacted on or after October 1, 1990, shall be confidential, and no authorized person shall disclose any such social security account number or related record.

(II) Paragraphs (1), (2), and (3) of section 7213(a) of the Internal Revenue Code of 1986 [26 USCS § 7213(a)] shall apply with respect to the unauthorized willful disclosure to any person of social security account numbers and related records obtained or maintained by an authorized person pursuant to a provision of law enacted on or after October 1, 1990, in the same manner and to the same extent as such paragraphs as such paragraphs apply with respect to unauthorized disclosures of returns and return information described in such paragraphs. Paragraph (4) of such 7213(a) of such Code [26 USCS § 7213(a)(4)] shall apply with respect to the willful offer of any item of material value in exchange for any such social security account number or related record in the same manner and to the same extent as such paragraph applies with respect to offers (in exchange for any return or return information) described in such paragraph.

(III) For purposes of this clause, the term "authorized person" means an officer or employee of the United States, an officer or employee of any State, political subdivision of a State, or agency of a State or political subdivision of a State, and any other person (or officer or employee thereof), who has or had access to social security account numbers or related records pursuant to any provision of law enacted on or after October 1, 1990. For purposes of this subclause, the term "officer or employee" includes a former officer or employee.

(IV) For purposes of this clause, the term "related record" means any record, list, or compilation that indicates, directly or indirectly, the identity of any individual with respect to whom a social security account number or a request for a social security account number is maintained pursuant to this clause.

(ix) In the administration of the provisions of chapter 81 of title 5, United States Code [5 USCS §§ 8101 et seq.], and the Longshore and Harbor Workers' Compensation Act (33 U.S.C. 901 et seq.), the Secretary of Labor may require by regulation that any person filing a notice of injury or a claim for benefits under such provisions provide as part of such notice or claim such person's social security account number, subject to the requirements of this clause. No officer or employee of the Department of Labor shall have access to any such number for any purpose other than the establishment of a system of records necessary for the effective administration of such provisions. The Secretary of Labor shall restrict, to the satisfaction of the Commissioner of Social Security, access to social security account numbers obtained pursuant to this clause to officers and employees of the United States whose duties or responsibilities require access for the administration or enforcement of such provisions. The Secretary of Labor shall provide such other safeguards as the Commissioner of Social Security determines to be necessary or appropriate to protect the confidentiality of the social security account numbers.

(x) The Secretary of Health and Human Services, and the Exchanges established under section 1311 of the Patient Protection and Affordable Care Act [42 USCS § 18031], are authorized to collect and use the names and social security account numbers of individuals as required to administer the provisions of, and the amendments made by, the such Act.

(D)(i) It is the policy of the United States that—

(I) any State (or any political subdivision of a State) and any authorized blood donation facility may utilize the social security account numbers issued by the Commissioner of Social Security for the purpose of identifying blood donors, and

(II) any State (or political subdivision of a State) may require any individual who donates blood within such State (or political subdivision) to furnish to such State (or political subdivision), to any agency thereof having related administrative responsibility, or to any authorized blood donation facility the social security account number (or numbers, if the donor has more than one such number) issued to the donor by the Commissioner of Social Security.

(ii) If and to the extent that any provision of Federal law enacted before the date of the enactment of this subparagraph [enacted Nov. 10, 1988] is inconsistent with the policy set forth in clause (i), such provision shall, on and after such date, be null, void, and of no effect.

(iii) For purposes of this subparagraph—

(I) the term "authorized blood donation facility" means an entity described in section 1141(h)(1)(B) [42 USCS § 1320b-11(h)(1)(B)], and

(II) the term "State" includes the District of Columbia, the Commonwealth of Puerto Rico, the Virgin Islands, Guam, the Commonwealth of the Northern Marianas, and the Trust Territory of the Pacific Islands.

(E)(i) It is the policy of the United States that—

(I) any State (or any political subdivision of a State) may utilize the social security account numbers issued by the Commissioner of Social Security for the additional purposes described in clause (ii) if such numbers have been collected and are otherwise utilized by such State (or political subdivision) in accordance with applicable law, and

(II) any district court of the United States may use, for such additional purposes, any such social security account numbers which have been so collected and are so utilized by any State.

(ii) The additional purposes described in this clause are the following:

(I) Identifying duplicate names of individuals on master lists used for jury selection purposes.

(II) Identifying on such master lists those individuals who are ineligible to serve on a jury by reason of their conviction of a felony.

(iii) To the extent that any provision of Federal law enacted before the date of the enactment of this subparagraph is inconsistent with the policy set forth in clause (i), such provision shall, on and after that date, be null, void, and of no effect.

(iv) For purposes of this subparagraph, the term "State" has the meaning such term has in subparagraph (D).

(F) The Commissioner of Social Security shall require, as a condition for receipt of benefits under this title [42 USCS §§ 401 et seq.], that an individual furnish satisfactory proof of a social security account number assigned to such individual by the Commissioner of Social Security or, in the case of an individual to whom no such number has been assigned, that such individual make proper application for assignment of such a number.

(G) The Commissioner of Social Security shall issue a social security card to each individual at the time of the issuance of a social security account number to such individual. The social security card shall be made of banknote paper, and (to the maximum extent practicable) shall be a card which cannot be counterfeited.

(H) The Commissioner of Social Security shall share with the Secretary of the Treasury the information obtained by the Commissioner pursuant to the second sentence of subparagraph (B)(ii) and to subparagraph (C)(ii) for the purpose of administering those sections of the Internal Revenue Code of 1986 which grant tax benefits based on support or residence of children.

(3) The Commissioner's records shall be evidence for the purpose of proceedings before the Commissioner of Social Security or any court of the amounts of wages paid to, and self-employment income derived by, an individual and of the periods in which such wages were paid and such income was derived. The absence of an entry in such records as to wages alleged to have been paid to, or as to self-employment income alleged to have been derived by, an individual in any period shall be evidence that no such alleged wages were paid to, or that no such alleged income was derived by, such individual during such period.

(4) Prior to the expiration of the time limitation following any year the Commissioner of Social Security may, if it is brought to the Commissioner's attention that any entry of wages or self-employment income in the Commissioner's records for such year is erroneous or that any item of wages or self-employment income for such year has been omitted from such records, correct such entry or include such omitted item in the Commissioner's records, as the case may be. After the expiration of the time limitation following any year—

(A) the Commissioner's records (with changes, if any, made pursuant to paragraph (5)) of the amounts of wages paid to, and self-employment income derived by, an individual during any period in such year shall be conclusive for the purposes of this title [42 USCS §§ 401 et seq.];

(B) the absence of an entry in the Commissioner's records as to the wages alleged to have been paid by an employer to an individual during any period in such year shall be presumptive evidence for the purposes of this title [42 USCS §§ 401 et seq.] that no such alleged wages were paid to such individuals in such period; and

(C) the absence of an entry in the Commissioner's records as to the self-employment income alleged to have been derived by an individual in such year shall be conclusive for the purposes of this title [42 USCS §§ 401 et seq.] that no such alleged self-employment income was derived by such individual in such year unless it is shown that he filed a tax return of his self-employment income for such year before the expiration of the time limitation following such year, in which case the Commissioner of Social Security shall include in the Commissioner's records the self-employment income of such individual for such year.

(5) After the expiration of the time limitation following any year in which wages were paid or alleged to have been paid to, or self-employment income was derived or alleged to have been derived by, an individual, the Commissioner of Social Security may change or delete any entry with respect to wages or self-employment income in the Commissioner's records of such year for such individual or include in the Commissioner's records of such year for such individual any omitted item of wages or self-employment income but only—

(A) if an application for monthly benefits or for a lump-sum death payment was filed within the time limitation following such year; except that no such change, deletion, or inclusion may be made pursuant to this subparagraph after a final decision upon the application for monthly benefits or lump-sum death payment;

(B) if within the time limitation following such year an individual or his survivor makes a request for a change or deletion, or for an inclusion of an omitted item, and alleges in writing that the Commissioner's records of the wages paid to, or the self-employment income derived by, such individual in such year are in one or more respects erroneous; except that no such change, deletion, or inclusion may be made pursuant to this subparagraph after a final decision upon such request. Written notice of the Commissioner's decision on any such request shall be given to the individual who made the request;

(C) to correct errors apparent on the face of such records;

(D) to transfer items to records of the Railroad Retirement Board if such items were credited under this title [42 USCS §§ 401 et seq.] when they should have been credited under the Railroad Retirement Act of 1937 or 1974, or to enter items transferred by the Railroad Retirement Board which have been credited under the Railroad Retirement Act of 1937 or 1974 when they should have been credited under this title [42 USCS §§ 401 et seq.];

(E) to delete or reduce the amount of any entry which is erroneous as a result of fraud;

(F) to conform his records to—

(i) tax returns or portions thereof (including information returns and other written statements) filed with the Commissioner of Internal Revenue under title VIII of the Social Security Act [42 USCS §§ 1001 et seq.], under subchapter E of chapter 1 or subchapter A of chapter 9 of the Internal Revenue Code of 1939, under chapter 2 or 21 of the Internal Revenue Code of 1954 or the Internal Revenue Code of 1986 [26 USCS §§ 1401 et seq., or 3101 et seq.], or under regulations made under authority of such title, subchapter, or chapter;

(ii) wage reports filed by a State pursuant to an agreement under section 218 [42 USCS § 418] or regulations of the Commissioner of Social Security thereunder; or

(iii) assessments of amounts due under an agreement pursuant to section 218 [42 USCS § 418] (as in effect prior to December 31, 1986), if such assessments are made within the period specified in subsection (q) of such section [42 USCS § 418(q)] (as so in effect), or allowances of credits or refunds of overpayments by a State under an agreement pursuant to such section;

except that no amount of self-employment income of an individual for any taxable year (if such return or statement was filed after the expiration of the time limitation following the taxable year) shall be included in the Commissioner's records pursuant to this subparagraph;

(G) to correct errors made in the allocation, to individuals or periods, of wages or self-employment income entered in the records of the Commissioner of Social Security;

(H) to include wages paid during any period in such year to an individual by an employer;

(I) to enter items which constitute remuneration for employment under subsection (o), such entries to be in accordance with certified reports of records made by the Railroad Retirement Board pursuant to section 5(k)(3) of the Railroad Retirement Act of 1937 [45 USCS § 228e(k)(3)] or section 7(b)(7) of the Railroad Retirement Act of 1974 [45 USCS § 231f(b)(7)]; or

(J) to include self-employment income for any taxable year, up to, but not in excess of, the amount of wages deleted by the Commissioner of Social Security as payments erroneously included in such records as wages paid to such individual, if such income (or net earnings from self-employment), not already included in such records as self-employment income, is included in a return or statement (referred to in subparagraph (F)) filed before the expiration of the time limitation following the taxable year in which such deletion of wages is made.

(6) Written notice of any deletion or reduction under paragraph (4) or (5) shall be given to the individual whose record is involved or to his survivor, except that (A) in the case of a deletion or reduction with respect to any entry of wages such notice shall be given to such individual only if he has previously been notified by the Commissioner of Social Security of the amount of his wages for the period involved, and (B) such notice shall be given to such survivor only if he or the individual whose record is involved has previously been notified by the Commissioner of Social Security of the amount of such individual's wages and self-employment income for the period involved.

(7) Upon request in writing (within such period, after any change or refusal of a request for a change of the Commissioner's records pursuant to this subsection, as the Commissioner of Social Security may prescribe), opportunity for hearing with respect to such change or refusal shall be afforded to any individual or his survivor. If a hearing is held pursuant to this paragraph the Commissioner of Social Security shall make findings of fact and a decision based upon the evidence adduced at such hearing and shall include any omitted items, or change or delete any entry, in the Commissioner's records as may be required by such findings and decision.

(8) A translation into English by a third party of a statement made in a foreign language by an applicant for or beneficiary of monthly insurance benefits under this title [42 USCS §§ 401 et seq.] shall not be regarded as reliable for any purpose under this title [42 USCS §§ 401 et seq.] unless the third party, under penalty of perjury—

(A) certifies that the translation is accurate; and

(B) discloses the nature and scope of the relationship between the third party and the applicant or recipient, as the case may be.

(9) Decisions of the Commissioner of Social Security under this subsection shall be reviewable by commencing a civil action in the United States district court as provided in subsection

(g).

(d) Issuance of subpenas in administrative proceedings. For the purpose of any hearing, investigation, or other proceeding authorized or directed under this title [42 USCS §§ 401 et seq.], or relative to any other matter within the the Commissioner's jurisdiction hereunder, the Commissioner of Social Security shall have power to issue subpenas requiring the attendance and testimony of witnesses and the production of any evidence that relates to any matter under investigation or in question before the Commissioner of Social Security. Such attendance of witnesses and production of evidence at the designated place of such hearing, investigation, or other proceeding may be required from any place in the United States or in any Territory or possession thereof. Subpenas of the Commissioner of Social Security shall be served by anyone authorized by the Commissioner (1) by delivering a copy thereof to the individual named therein, or (2) by registered mail or by certified mail addressed to such individual at his last dwelling place or principal place of business. A verified return by the individual so serving the subpena setting forth the manner of service, or, in the case of service by registered mail or by certified mail, the return post-office receipt therefor signed by the individual so served, shall be proof of service. Witnesses so subpenaed shall be paid the same fees and mileage as are paid witnesses in the district courts of the United States.

(e) Judicial enforcement of subpenas; contempt. In case of contumacy by, or refusal to obey a subpena duly served upon, any person, any district court of the United States for the judicial district in which said person charged with contumacy or refusal to obey is found or resides or transacts business, upon application by the Commissioner of Social Security, shall have jurisdiction to issue an order requiring such person to appear and give testimony, or to appear and produce evidence, or both; any failure to obey such order of the court may be punished by said court as contempt thereof.

(f) [Repealed]

(g) Judicial review. Any individual, after any final decision of the Commissioner of Social Security made after a hearing to which he was a party, irrespective of the amount in controversy, may obtain a review of such decision by a civil action commenced within sixty days after the mailing to him of notice of such decision or within such further time as the Commissioner of Social Security may allow. Such action shall be brought in the district court of the United States for the judicial district in which the plaintiff resides, or has his principal place of business, or, if he does not reside or have his principal place of business within any such judicial district, in the District Court of the United States for the District of Columbia [United States District Court for the District of Columbia]. As part of the Commissioner's answer the Commissioner of Social Security shall file a certified copy of the transcript of the record including the evidence upon which the findings and decision complained of are based. The court shall have power to enter, upon the pleadings and transcript of the record, a judgment affirming, modifying, or reversing the decision of the Commissioner of Social Security, with or without remanding the cause for a rehearing. The findings of the Commissioner of Social Security as to any fact, if supported by substantial evidence, shall be conclusive, and where a claim has been denied by the Commissioner of Social Security or a decision is rendered under subsection (b) hereof which is adverse to an individual who was a party to the hearing before the Commissioner of Social Security, because of failure of the claimant or such individual to submit proof in conformity with any regulation prescribed under subsection (a) hereof, the court shall review only the question of conformity with such regulations and the validity of such regulations. The court may, on motion of the Commissioner of Social Security made for good cause shown before the Commissioner files the Commissioner's answer, remand the case to the Commissioner of Social Security for further action by the Commissioner of Social Security, and it may at any time order additional evidence to be taken before the Commissioner of Social Security, but only upon a showing that there is new evidence which is material and that there is good cause for the failure to incorporate such evidence into the record in a prior proceeding; and the Commissioner of Social Security shall, after the case is remanded, and after hearing such additional evidence if so ordered, modify or affirm the Commissioner's findings of fact or the Commissioner's decision, or both, and shall file with the court any such additional and modified findings of fact and decision, and, in any case in which the Commissioner has not made a decision fully favorable to the individual, a transcript of the additional record and testimony upon which the Commissioner's action in modifying or affirming was based. Such additional or modified findings of fact and decision shall be reviewable only to the extent provided for review of the original findings of fact and decision. The judgment of the court shall be final except that it shall be subject to review in the same manner as a judgment in other civil actions. Any action instituted in accordance with this subsection shall survive notwithstanding any change in the person occupying the office of Commissioner of Social Security or any vacancy in such office.

(h) Finality of Commissioner's decision. The findings and decisions of the Commissioner of Social Security after a hearing shall be binding upon all individuals who were parties to such hearing. No findings of fact or decision of the Commissioner of Social Security shall be reviewed by any person, tribunal, or governmental agency except as herein provided. No action against the United States, the Commissioner of Social Security, or any officer or employee thereof shall be brought under section 1331 or 1346 of title 28, United States Code [28 USCS § 1331 or 1346], to recover on any claim arising under this title [42 USCS §§ 401 et seq.].

(i) Certification for payment. Upon final decision of the Commissioner of Social Security, or upon final judgment of any court of competent jurisdiction, that any person is entitled to any payment or payments under this title [42 USCS §§ 401 et seq.], the Commissioner of Social Security shall certify to the Managing Trustee the name and address of the person so entitled to receive such payment or payments, the amount of such payment or payments, and the time at which such payment or payments should be made, and the Managing Trustee, through the Fiscal Service of the Department of the Treasury, and prior to any action thereon by the General Accounting Office [Government Accountability Office], shall make payment in accordance with the certification of the Commissioner of Social Security (except that in the case of (A) an individual who will have completed ten years of service (or five or more years of service, all of which accrues after December 31, 1995) creditable under the Railroad Retirement Act of 1937 or the Railroad Retirement Act of 1974, (B) the wife or husband of such an individual, (C) any survivor of such an individual if such survivor is entitled, or could upon application become entitled, to an annuity under section 2 of the Railroad Retirement Act of 1974 [45 USCS § 231a], and (D) any other person entitled to benefits under section 202 of this Act [42 USCS § 402] on the basis of the wages and self-employment income of such an individual (except a survivor of such an individual where such individual did not have a current connection with the railroad industry, as defined in the Railroad Retirement Act of 1974 [45 USCS §§ 231 et seq.], at the time of his death), such certification shall be made to the Railroad Retirement Board which shall provide for such payment or payments to such person on behalf of the Managing Trustee in accordance with the provisions of the Railroad Retirement Act of 1974): *Provided,* That where a review of the Commissioner's decision is or may be sought under subsection (g) the Commissioner of Social Security may withhold certification of payment pending such review. The Managing Trustee shall not be held personally liable for any payment or payments made in accordance with a certification by the Commissioner of Social Security.

(j) Representative payees. (1)(A) If the Commissioner of Social Security determines that the interest of any individual under this title [42 USCS §§ 401 et seq.] would be served thereby, certification of payment of such individual's benefit under this title [42 USCS §§ 401 et seq.] may be made, regardless of the legal competency or incompetency of the individual, either for direct payment to the individual, or for his or her use and benefit, to another individual, or an organization, with respect to whom the requirements of paragraph (2) have been met (hereinafter in this subsection referred to as the individual's "representative payee"). If the Commissioner of Social Security or a court of competent jurisdiction determines that a representative payee has misused any individual's benefit paid to such representative payee pursuant to this subsection or section 807 or 1631(a)(2) [42 USCS § 1007 or 1383(a)(2)], the Commissioner of Social Security shall promptly revoke certification for payment of benefits to such representative payee pursuant to this subsection and certify payment to an alternative representative payee or, if the interest of the individual under this title [42 USCS §§ 401 et seq.] would be served thereby, to the individual.

(B) In the case of an individual entitled to benefits based on disability, the payment of such benefits shall be made to a representative payee if the Commissioner of Social Security determines that such payment would serve the interest of the individual because the individual also has an alcoholism or drug addiction condition (as determined by the Commissioner) and the individual is incapable of managing such benefits.

(2)(A) Any certification made under paragraph (1) for payment of benefits to an individual's representative payee shall be made on the basis of—

(i) an investigation by the Commissioner of Social Security of the person to serve as representative payee, which shall be conducted in advance of such certification and shall, to the extent practicable, include a face-to-face interview with such person, and

(ii) adequate evidence that such certification is in the interest of such individual (as determined by the Commissioner of Social Security in regulations).

(B)(i) As part of the investigation referred to in subparagraph (A)(i), the Commissioner of Social Security shall—

(I) require the person being investigated to submit documented proof of the identity of such person, unless information establishing such identity has been submitted with an application for benefits under this title, title VIII, or title XVI [42 USCS §§ 401 et seq., 1001 et seq. or 1381 et seq.],

(II) verify such person's social security account number (or employer identification number),

(III) determine whether such person has been convicted of a violation of section 208, 811, or 1632 [42 USCS § 408, 1011, or 1383a],

(IV) obtain information concerning whether such person has been convicted of any other offense under Federal or State law which resulted in imprisonment for more than 1 year,

(V) obtain information concerning whether such person is a person described in section 202(x)(1)(A)(iv) [42 USCS § 402(x)(1)(A)(iv)], and

(VI) determine whether certification of payment of benefits to such person has been revoked pursuant to this subsection, the designation of such person as a representative payee has been revoked pursuant to section 807(a) [42 USCS § 1007(a)], or payment of benefits to such person has been terminated pursuant to section 1631(a)(2)(A)(iii) [42 USCS § 1383(a)(2)(A)(iii)] by reason of misuse of funds paid as benefits under this title, title VIII, or title XVI [42 USCS §§ 401 et seq., 1001 et seq. or 1381 et seq.].

(ii) The Commissioner of Social Security shall establish and maintain a centralized file, which shall be updated periodically and which shall be in a form which renders it readily retrievable by each servicing office of the Social Security Administration. Such file shall consist of—

(I) a list of the names and social security account numbers (or employer identification numbers) of all persons with respect to whom certification of payment of benefits has been revoked on or after January 1, 1991, pursuant to this subsection, whose designation as a representative payee has been revoked pursuant to section 807(a) [42 USCS § 1007(a)], or with respect to whom payment of benefits has been terminated on or after such date pursuant to section 1631(a)(2)(A)(iii) [42 USCS § 1383(a)(2)(A)(iii)], by reason of misuse of funds paid as benefits under this title, title VIII, or title XVI [42 USCS §§ 401 et seq., 1001 et seq., or 1381 et seq.], and

(II) a list of the names and social security account numbers (or employer identification numbers) of all persons who have been convicted of a violation of section 208, 811, or 1632 [42 USCS § 408, 1011 or 1383a].

(iii) Notwithstanding the provisions of section 552a of title 5, United States Code [5 USCS § 552a], or any other provision of Federal or State law (other than section 6103 of the Internal Revenue Code of 1986 [26 USCS § 6103] and section 1106(c) of this Act [42 USCS § 1306(c)]), the Commissioner shall furnish any Federal, State, or local law enforcement officer, upon the written request of the officer, with the current address, social security account number, and photograph (if applicable) of any person investigated under this paragraph, if the officer furnishes the Commissioner with the name of such person and such other identifying information as may reasonably be required by the Commissioner to establish the unique identity of such person, and notifies the Commissioner that—

(I) such person is described in section 202(x)(1)(A)(iv) [42 USCS § 402(x)(1)(A)(iv)],

(II) such person has information that is necessary for the officer to conduct the officer's official duties, and

(III) the location or apprehension of such person is within the officer's official duties.

(C)(i) Benefits of an individual may not be certified for payment to any other person pursuant to this subsection if—

(I) such person has previously been convicted as described in subparagraph (B)(i)(III),

(II) except as provided in clause (ii), certification of payment of benefits to such person under this subsection has previously been revoked as described in subparagraph (B)(i)(VI) the designation of such person as a representative payee has been revoked pursuant to section 807(a) [42 USCS § 1007(a)], or payment of benefits to such person pursuant to section 1631(a)(2)(A)(ii) [42 USCS § 1383(a)(2)(A)(ii)] has previously been terminated as described in section 1631(a)(2)(B)(ii)(VI) [42 USCS

§ 1383(a)(2)(B)(ii)(VI)],

(III) except as provided in clause (iii), such person is a creditor of such individual who provides such individual with goods or services for consideration,

(IV) such person has previously been convicted as described in subparagraph (B)(i)(IV), unless the Commissioner determines that such certification would be appropriate notwithstanding such conviction, or

(V) such person is a person described in section 202(x)(1)(A)(iv) [42 USCS § 402(x)(1)(A)(iv)].

(ii) The Commissioner of Social Security shall prescribe regulations under which the Commissioner of Social Security may grant exemptions to any person from the provisions of clause (i)(II) on a case-by-case basis if such exemption is in the best interest of the individual whose benefits would be paid to such person pursuant to this subsection.

(iii) Clause (i)(III) shall not apply with respect to any person who is a creditor referred to therein if such creditor is—

(I) a relative of such individual if such relative resides in the same household as such individual,

(II) a legal guardian or legal representative of such individual,

(III) a facility that is licensed or certified as a care facility under the law of a State or a political subdivision of a State,

(IV) a person who is an administrator, owner, or employee of a facility referred to in subclause (III) if such individual resides in such facility, and the certification of payment to such facility or such person is made only after good faith efforts have been made by the local servicing office of the Social Security Administration to locate an alternative representative payee to whom such certification of payment would serve the best interests of such individual, or

(V) an individual who is determined by the Commissioner of Social Security, on the basis of written findings and under procedures which the Commissioner of Social Security shall prescribe by regulation, to be acceptable to serve as a representative payee.

(iv) The procedures referred to in clause (iii)(V) shall require the individual who will serve as representative payee to establish, to the satisfaction of the Commissioner of Social Security, that—

(I) such individual poses no risk to the beneficiary,

(II) the financial relationship of such individual to the beneficiary poses no substantial conflict of interest, and

(III) no other more suitable representative payee can be found.

(v) In the case of an individual described in paragraph (1)(B), when selecting such individual's representative payee, preference shall be given to—

(I) a certified community-based nonprofit social service agency (as defined in paragraph (10)),

(II) a Federal, State, or local government agency whose mission is to carry out income maintenance, social service, or health care-related activities,

(III) a State or local government agency with fiduciary responsibilities, or

(IV) a designee of an agency (other than of a Federal agency) referred to in the preceding subclauses of this clause, if the Commissioner of Social Security deems it appropriate,

unless the Commissioner of Social Security determines that selection of a family member would be appropriate.

(D)(i) Subject to clause (ii), if the Commissioner of Social Security makes a determination described in the first sentence of paragraph (1) with respect to any individual's benefit and determines that direct payment of the benefit to the individual would cause substantial harm to the individual, the Commissioner of Social Security may defer (in the case of initial entitlement) or suspend (in the case of existing entitlement) direct payment of such benefit to the individual, until such time as the selection of a representative payee is made pursuant to this subsection.

(ii)(I) Except as provided in subclause (II), any deferral or suspension of direct payment of a benefit pursuant to clause (i) shall be for a period of not more than 1 month.

(II) Subclause (I) shall not apply in any case in which the individual is, as of the date of the Commissioner's determination, legally incompetent, under the age of 15 years, or described in paragraph (1)(B).

(iii) Payment pursuant to this subsection of any benefits which are deferred or suspended pending the selection of a representative payee shall be made to the individual or the representative payee as a single sum or over such period of time as the Commissioner of Social Security determines is in the best interest of the individual entitled to such benefits.

(E)(i) Any individual who is dissatisfied with a determination by the Commissioner of Social Security to certify payment of such individual's benefit to a representative payee under paragraph (1) or with the designation of a particular person to serve as representative payee shall be entitled to a hearing by the Commissioner of Social Security to the same extent as is provided in subsection (b), and to judicial review of the Commissioner's final decision as is provided in subsection (g).

(ii) In advance of the certification of payment of an individual's benefit to a representative payee under paragraph (1), the Commissioner of Social Security shall provide written notice of the Commissioner's initial determination to certify such payment. Such notice shall be provided to such individual, except that, if such individual—

(I) is under the age of 15,

(II) is an unemancipated minor under the age of 18, or

(III) is legally incompetent,

then such notice shall be provided solely to the legal guardian or legal representative of such individual.

(iii) Any notice described in clause (ii) shall be clearly written in language that is easily understandable to the reader, shall identify the person to be designated as such individual's representative payee, and shall explain to the reader the right under clause (i) of such individual or of such individual's legal guardian or legal representative—

(I) to appeal a determination that a representative payee is necessary for such individual,

(II) to appeal the designation of a particular person to serve as the representative payee of such individual, and

(III) to review the evidence upon which such designation is based and submit additional evidence.

(3)(A) In any case where payment under this title [42 USCS §§ 401 et seq.] is made to a person other than the individual entitled to such payment, the Commissioner of Social Security shall establish a system of accountability monitoring whereby such person shall report not less often than annually with respect to the use of such payments. The Commissioner of Social Security shall establish and implement statistically valid procedures for reviewing such reports in order to identify instances in which such persons are not properly using such payments.

(B) Subparagraph (A) shall not apply in any case where the other person to whom such payment is made is a State institution. In such cases, the Commissioner of Social Security shall establish a system of accountability monitoring for institutions in each State.

(C) Subparagraph (A) shall not apply in any case where the individual entitled to such payment is a resident of a Federal institution and the other person to whom such payment is made is the institution.

(D) Notwithstanding subparagraphs (A), (B), and (C), the Commissioner of Social Security may require a report at any time from any person receiving payments on behalf of another, if the Commissioner of Social Security has reason to believe that the person receiving such payments is misusing such payments.

(E) In any case in which the person described in subparagraph (A) or (D) receiving payments on behalf of another fails to submit a report required by the Commissioner of Social Security under subparagraph (A) or (D), the Commissioner may, after furnishing notice to such person and the individual entitled to such payment, require that such person appear in person at a field office of the Social Security Administration serving the area in which the individual resides in order to receive such payments.

(F) The Commissioner of Social Security shall maintain a centralized file, which shall be updated periodically and which shall be in a form which will be readily retrievable by each servicing office of the Social Security Administration, of—

(i) the address and the social security account number (or employer identification number) of each representative payee who is receiving benefit payments pursuant to this subsection, section 807 [42 USCS § 1007], or section 1631(a)(2) [42 USCS § 1383(a)(2)], and

(ii) the address and social security account number of each individual for whom each representative payee is reported to be providing services as representative payee pursuant to this subsection, section 807 [42 USCS § 1007], or section 1631(a)(2) [42 USCS § 1383(a)(2)].

(G) Each servicing office of the Administration shall maintain a list, which shall be updated periodically, of public agencies and certified community-based nonprofit social service agencies (as defined in paragraph (10)) which are qualified to serve as representative payees pursuant to this subsection or section 807 or 1631(a)(2) [42 USCS § 1007 or 1383(a)(2)] and which are located in the area served by such servicing office.

(4)(A)(i) Except as provided in the next sentence, a qualified organization may collect from an individual a monthly fee for expenses (including overhead) incurred by such organization in providing services performed as such individual's representative payee pursuant to this subsection if such fee does not exceed the lesser of—

(I) 10 percent of the monthly benefit involved, or

(II) $25.00 per month ($50.00 per month in any case in which the individual is described in paragraph (1)(B)).

A qualified organization may not collect a fee from an individual for any month with respect to which the Commissioner of Social Security or a court of competent jurisdiction has determined that the organization misused all or part of the individual's benefit, and any amount so collected by the qualified organization for such month shall be treated as a misused part of the individual's benefit for purposes of paragraphs (5) and (6). The Commissioner of Social Security shall adjust annually (after 1995) each dollar amount set forth in subclause (II) under procedures providing for adjustments in the same manner and to the same extent as adjustments are provided for under the procedures used to adjust benefit amounts under section 215(i)(2)(A) [42 USCS § 415(i)(2)(A)], except that any amount so adjusted that is not a multiple of $1.00 shall be rounded to the nearest multiple of $1.00.

(ii) In the case of an individual who is no longer currently entitled to monthly insurance benefits under this title [42 USCS §§ 401 et seq.] but to whom all past-due benefits have not been paid, for purposes of clause (i), any amount of such past-due benefits payable in any month shall be treated as a monthly benefit referred to in clause (i)(I).

Any agreement providing for a fee in excess of the amount permitted under this subparagraph shall be void and shall be treated as misuse by such organization of such individual's benefits.

(B) For purposes of this paragraph, the term "qualified organization" means any State or local government agency whose mission is to carry out income maintenance, social service, or health care-related activities, any State or local government agency with fiduciary responsibilities, or any certified community-based nonprofit social service agency (as defined in paragraph (10)), if such agency, in accordance with any applicable regulations of the Commissioner of Social Security—

(i) regularly provides services as the representative payee, pursuant to this subsection or section 807 or 1631(a)(2) [42 USCS § 1007 or 1383(a)(2)], concurrently to 5 or more individuals, [and]

(ii) demonstrates to the satisfaction of the Commissioner of Social Security that such agency is not otherwise a creditor of any such individual.

The Commissioner of Social Security shall prescribe regulations under which the Commissioner of Social Security may grant an exception from clause (ii) for any individual on a case-by-case basis if such exception is in the best interests of such individual.

(C) Any qualified organization which knowingly charges or collects, directly or indirectly, any fee in excess of the maximum fee prescribed under subparagraph (A) or makes any agreement, directly or indirectly, to charge or collect any fee in excess of such maximum fee, shall be fined in accordance with title 18, United States Code, or imprisoned not more than 6 months, or both.

(5) In cases where the negligent failure of the Commissioner of Social Security to investigate or monitor a representative payee results in misuse of benefits by the representative payee, the Commissioner of Social Security shall certify for payment to the beneficiary or the beneficiary's alternative representative payee an amount equal to such misused benefits. In any case in which a representative payee that—

(A) is not an individual (regardless of whether it is a "qualified organization" within the meaning of paragraph (4)(B)); or

(B) is an individual who, for any month during a period when misuse occurs, serves 15 or more individuals who are beneficiaries under this title [42 USCS §§ 401 et seq.], title VIII [42 USCS §§ 1001 et seq.], title XVI [42 USCS §§ 1381 et seq.], or any combination of such titles;

misuses all or part of an individual's benefit paid to such representative payee, the Commissioner of Social Security shall certify for payment to the beneficiary or the beneficiary's alternative representative payee an amount equal to the amount of such benefit so misused. The provisions of this paragraph are subject to the limitations of paragraph (7)(B). The Commissioner of Social Security shall make a good faith effort to obtain restitution from the terminated representative payee.

(6)(A) In addition to such other reviews of representative payees as the Commissioner of Social Security may otherwise conduct, the Commissioner shall provide for the periodic onsite review of any person or agency located in the United States that receives the benefits payable under this title [42 USCS §§ 401 et seq.] (alone or in combination with benefits payable under title VIII [42 USCS §§ 1001 et seq.] or title XVI [42 USCS §§ 1381 et seq.]) to another individual pursuant to the appointment of such person or agency as a representative payee under this subsection, section 807 [42 USCS § 1007], or section 1631(a)(2) [42 USCS § 1383(a)(2)] in any case in which—

(i) the representative payee is a person who serves in that capacity with respect to 15 or more such individuals;

(ii) the representative payee is a certified community-based nonprofit social service agency (as defined in paragraph (10) of this subsection or section 1631(a)(2)(I) [42 USCS § 1383(a)(2)(I)]); or

(iii) the representative payee is an agency (other than an agency described in clause (ii)) that serves in that capacity with respect to 50 or more such individuals.

(B) Within 120 days after the end of each fiscal year, the Commissioner shall submit to the Committee on Ways and Means of the House of Representatives and the Committee on Finance of the Senate a report on the results of periodic onsite reviews conducted during the fiscal year pursuant to subparagraph (A) and of any other reviews of representative payees conducted during such fiscal year in connection with benefits under this title [42 USCS §§ 401 et seq.]. Each such report shall describe in detail all problems identified in such reviews and any corrective action taken or planned to be taken to correct such problems, and shall include—

(i) the number of such reviews;

(ii) the results of such reviews;

(iii) the number of cases in which the representative payee was changed and why;

(iv) the number of cases involving the exercise of expedited, targeted oversight of the representative payee by the Commissioner conducted upon receipt of an allegation of misuse of funds, failure to pay a vendor, or a similar irregularity;

(v) the number of cases discovered in which there was a misuse of funds;

(vi) how any such cases of misuse of funds were dealt with by the Commissioner;

(vii) the final disposition of such cases of misuse of funds, including any criminal penalties imposed; and

(viii) such other information as the Commissioner deems appropriate.

(7) (A) If the Commissioner of Social Security or a court of competent jurisdiction determines that a representative payee that is not a Federal, State, or local government agency has misused all or part of an individual's benefit that was paid to such representative payee under this subsection, the representative payee shall be liable for the amount misused, and such amount (to the extent not repaid by the representative payee) shall be treated as an overpayment of benefits under this title [42 USCS §§ 401 et seq.] to the representative payee for all purposes of this Act [42 USCS §§ 301 et seq.] and related laws pertaining to the recovery of such overpayments. Subject to subparagraph (B), upon recovering all or any part of such amount, the Commissioner shall certify an amount equal to the recovered amount for payment to such individual or such individual's alternative representative payee.

(B) The total of the amount certified for payment to such individual or such individual's alternative representative payee under subparagraph (A) and the amount certified for payment under paragraph (5) may not exceed the total benefit amount misused by the representative payee with respect to such individual.

(8) For purposes of this subsection, the term "benefit based on disability" of an individual means a disability insurance benefit of such individual under section 223 [42 USCS § 423] or a child's, widow's, or widower's insurance benefit of such individual under section 202 [42 USCS § 402] based on such individual's disability.

(9) For purposes of this subsection, misuse of benefits by a representative payee occurs in any case in which the representative payee receives payment under this title [42 USCS §§ 401 et seq.] for the use and benefit of another person and converts such payment, or any part thereof, to a use other than for the use and benefit of such other person. The Commissioner of Social Security may prescribe by regulation the meaning of the term "use and benefit" for purposes of this paragraph.

(10) For purposes of this subsection, the term "certified community-based nonprofit social service agency" means a community-based nonprofit social service agency which is in compliance with requirements, under regulations which shall be prescribed by the Commissioner, for annual certification to the Commissioner that it is bonded in accordance with requirements specified by the Commissioner and that it is licensed in each State in which it serves as a representative payee (if licensing is available in the State) in accordance with requirements specified by the Commissioner. Any such annual certification shall include a copy of any independent audit on the agency which may have been performed since the previous certification.

(k) Payments to incompetents. Any payment made after December 31, 1939, under conditions set forth in subsection (j) any payment made before January 1, 1940, to, or on behalf of, a legally incompetent individual, and any payment made after December 31, 1939, to a legally incompetent individual without knowledge by the Commissioner of Social Security of incompetency prior to certification of payment, if otherwise valid under this title [42 USCS §§ 401 et seq.], shall be a complete settlement and satisfaction of any claim, right, or interest in and to such payment.

(l) Delegation of powers and duties by Commissioner of Social Security. The Commissioner of Social Security is authorized to delegate to any member, officer, or employee of the Social Security Administration designated by the Commissioner any of the powers conferred upon the Commissioner by this section, and is authorized to be represented by the Commissioner's own attorneys in any court in any case or proceeding arising under the provisions of subsection (e).

(m) [Repealed]

(n) Joint payments. The Commissioner of Social Security may, in the Commissioner's discretion, certify to the Managing Trustee any two or more individuals of the same family for joint payment of the total benefits payable to such individuals for any month, and if one of such individuals dies before a check representing such joint payment is negotiated, payment of the amount of such unnegotiated check to the surviving individual or individuals may be authorized in accordance with regulations of the Secretary of the Treasury; except that appropriate adjustment or recovery shall be made under section 204(a) [42 USCS § 404(a)] with respect to so much of the amount of such check as exceeds the amount to which such surviving individual or individuals are entitled under this title [42 USCS §§ 401 et seq.] for such month.

(o) Crediting of compensation under the Railroad Retirement Act. If there is no person who would be entitled, upon application therefor, to an annuity under section 5 of the Railroad Retirement Act of 1974 [45 USCS § 231a], or to a lump-sum payment under section 6(b) of such Act [45 USCS § 231e(b)], with respect to the death of an employee (as defined in such Act), then, notwithstanding section 210(a)(10) of this Act [42 USCS § 410(a)(10)], compensation (as defined in such Railroad Retirement Act, but excluding compensation attributable as having been paid during any month on account of military service creditable under section 3(i) of such Act [45 USCS § 231b(i)] if wages are deemed to have been paid to such employee during such month under subsection (a) or (e) of section 217 of this Act [42 USCS § 417(a) or (e)]) of such employee shall constitute remuneration for employment for purposes of determining (A) entitlement to and the amount of any lump-sum death payment under this title [42 USCS §§ 401 et seq.] on the basis of such employee's wages and self-employment income and (B) entitlement to and the amount of any monthly benefit under this title [42 USCS §§ 401 et seq.], for the month in which such employee died or for any month thereafter, on the basis of such wages and self-employment income. For such purposes, compensation (as so defined) paid in a calendar year before 1978 shall, in the absence of evidence to the contrary, be presumed to have been paid in equal proportions with respect to all months in the year in which the employee rendered services for such compensation.

(p) Special rules in case of Federal service. (1) With respect to service included as employment under section 210 [42 USCS § 410] which is performed in the employ of the United States or in the employ of any instrumentality which is wholly owned by the United States, including service, performed as a member of a uniformed service, to which the provisions of subsection (l)(1) of such section [42 USCS § 410(l)(1)] are applicable, and including service, performed as a volunteer or volunteer leader within the meaning of the Peace Corps Act, to which the provisions of section 210(o) [42 USCS § 410(o)] are applicable, the Commissioner of Social Security shall not make determinations as to the amounts of remuneration for such service, or the periods in which or for which such remuneration was paid, but shall accept the determinations with respect thereto of the head of the appropriate Federal agency or instrumentality, and of such agents as such head may designate, as evidenced by returns filed in accordance with the provisions of section 3122 of the Internal Revenue Code of 1954 [26 USCS § 3122] and certifications made pursuant to this subsection. Such determinations shall be final and conclusive. Nothing in this paragraph shall be construed to affect the Commissioner's authority to determine under sections 209 and 210 [42 USCS §§ 409, 410] whether any such service constitutes employment, the periods of such employment, and whether remuneration paid for any such service constitutes wages.

(2) The head of any such agency or instrumentality is authorized and directed, upon written request of the Commissioner of Social Security, to make certification to the Commis-

sioner with respect to any matter determinable for the Commissioner of Social Security by such head or his agents under this subsection, which the Commissioner of Social Security finds necessary in administering this title [42 USCS §§ 401 et seq.].

(3) The provisions of paragraphs (1) and (2) shall be applicable in the case of service performed by a civilian employee, not compensated from funds appropriated by the Congress, in the Army and Air Force Exchange Service, Army and Air Force Motion Picture Service, Navy Exchanges, Marine Corps Exchanges, or other activities, conducted by an instrumentality of the United States subject to the jurisdiction of the Secretary of Defense, at installations of the Department of Defense for the comfort, pleasure, contentment, and mental and physical improvement of personnel of such Department; and for purposes of paragraphs (1) and (2) the Secretary of Defense shall be deemed to be the head of such instrumentality. The provisions of paragraphs (1) and (2) shall be applicable also in the case of service performed by a civilian employee, not compensated from funds appropriated by the Congress, in the Coast Guard Exchanges or other activities, conducted by an instrumentality of the United States subject to the jurisdiction of the Secretary of Homeland Security, at installations of the Coast Guard for the comfort, pleasure, contentment, and mental and physical improvement of personnel of the Coast Guard; and for purposes of paragraphs (1) and (2) the Secretary of Homeland Security shall be deemed to be the head of such instrumentality.

(q) Expedited benefit payments. (1) The Commissioner of Social Security shall establish and put into effect procedures under which expedited payment of monthly insurance benefits under this title [42 USCS §§ 401 et seq.] will, subject to paragraph (4) of this subsection, be made as set forth in paragraphs (2) and (3) of this subsection.

(2) In any case in which—

(A) an individual makes an allegation that a monthly benefit under this title [42 USCS §§ 401 et seq.] was due him in a particular month but was not paid to him, and

(B) such individual submits a written request for the payment of such benefit—

(i) in the case of an individual who received a regular monthly benefit in the month preceding the month with respect to which such allegation is made, not less than 30 days after the 15th day of the month with respect to which such allegation is made (and in the event that such request is submitted prior to the expiration of such 30-day period, it shall be deemed to have been submitted upon the expiration of such period), and

(ii) in any other case, not less than 90 days after the later of (I) the date on which such benefit is alleged to have been due, or (II) the date on which such individual furnished the last information requested by the Commissioner of Social Security (and such written request will be deemed to be filed on the day on which it was filed, or the ninetieth day after the first day on which the Commissioner of Social Security has evidence that such allegation is true, whichever is later),

the Commissioner of Social Security shall, if the Commissioner finds that benefits are due, certify such benefits for payment, and payment shall be made within 15 days immediately following the date on which the written request is deemed to have been filed.

(3) In any case in which the Commissioner of Social Security determines that there is evidence, although additional evidence might be required for a final decision, that an allegation described in paragraph (2)(A) is true, the Commissioner may make a preliminary certification of such benefit for payment even though the 30-day or 90-day periods described in paragraph (2)(B)(i) and (B)(ii) have not elapsed.

(4) Any payment made pursuant to a certification under paragraph (3) of this subsection shall not be considered an incorrect payment for purposes of determining the liability of the certifying or disbursing officer.

(5) For purposes of this subsection, benefits payable under section 228 [42 USCS § 428] shall be treated as monthly insurance benefits payable under this title [42 USCS §§ 401 et seq.]. However, this subsection shall not apply with respect to any benefit for which a check has been negotiated, or with respect to any benefit alleged to be due under either section 223 [42 USCS § 423], or section 202 [42 USCS § 402] to a wife, husband, or child of an individual entitled to or applying for benefits under section 223 [42 USCS § 423], or to a child who has attained age 18 and is under a disability, or to a widow or widower on the basis of being under a disability.

(r) Use of death certificates to correct program information. (1) The Commissioner of Social Security shall undertake to establish a program under which—

(A) States (or political subdivisions thereof) voluntarily contract with the Commissioner of Social Security to furnish the Commissioner of Social Security periodically with information (in a form established by the Commissioner of

Social Security in consultation with the States) concerning individuals with respect to whom death certificates (or equivalent documents maintained by the States or subdivisions) have been officially filed with them; and

(B) there will be (i) a comparison of such information on such individuals with information on such individuals in the records being used in the administration of this Act [42 USCS §§ 301 et seq.], (ii) validation of the results of such comparisons, and (iii) corrections in such records to accurately reflect the status of such individuals.

(2) Each State (or political subdivision thereof) which furnishes the Commissioner of Social Security with information on records of deaths in the State or subdivision under this subsection may be paid by the Commissioner of Social Security from amounts available for administration of this Act [42 USCS §§ 301 et seq.] the reasonable costs (established by the Commissioner of Social Security in consultations with the States) for transcribing and transmitting such information to the Commissioner of Social Security.

(3) In the case of individuals with respect to whom federally funded benefits are provided by (or through) a Federal or State agency other than under this Act [42 USCS §§ 301 et seq.], the Commissioner of Social Security shall to the extent feasible provide such information through a cooperative arrangement with such agency, for ensuring proper payment of those benefits with respect to such individuals if—

(A) under such arrangement the agency provides reimbursement to the Commissioner of Social Security for the reasonable cost of carrying out such arrangement, and

(B) such arrangement does not conflict with the duties of the Commissioner of Social Security under paragraph (1).

(4) The Commissioner of Social Security may enter into similar agreements with States to provide information for their use in programs wholly funded by the States if the requirements of subparagraphs (A) and (B) of paragraph (3) are met.

(5) The Commissioner of Social Security may use or provide for the use of such records as may be corrected under this section, subject to such safeguards as the Commissioner of Social Security determines are necessary or appropriate to protect the information from unauthorized use or disclosure, for statistical and research activities conducted by Federal and State agencies.

(6) Information furnished to the Commissioner of Social Security under this subsection may not be used for any purpose other than the purpose described in this subsection and is exempt from disclosure under section 552 of title 5, United States Code, and from the requirements of section 552a of such title.

(7) The Commissioner of Social Security shall include information on the status of the program established under this section and impediments to the effective implementation of the program in the 1984 report required under section 704 of the Act [42 USCS § 904].

(8)(A) The Commissioner of Social Security shall, upon the request of the official responsible for a State driver's license agency pursuant to the Help America Vote Act of 2002—

(i) enter into an agreement with such official for the purpose of verifying applicable information, so long as the requirements of subparagraphs (A) and (B) of paragraph (3) are met; and

(ii) include in such agreement safeguards to assure the maintenance of the confidentiality of any applicable information disclosed and procedures to permit such agency to use the applicable information for the purpose of maintaining its records.

(B) Information provided pursuant to an agreement under this paragraph shall be provided at such time, in such place, and in such manner as the Commissioner determines appropriate.

(C) The Commissioner shall develop methods to verify the accuracy of information provided by the agency with respect to applications for voter registration, for whom the last 4 digits of a social security number are provided instead of a driver's license number.

(D) For purposes of this paragraph—

(i) the term "applicable information" means information regarding whether—

(I) the name (including the first name and any family forename or surname), the date of birth (including the month, day, and year), and social security number of an individual provided to the Commissioner match the information contained in the Commissioner's records, and

(II) such individual is shown on the records of the Commissioner as being deceased; and

(ii) the term "State driver's license agency" means the State agency which issues driver's licenses to individuals within the State and maintains records relating to such licensure.

(E) Nothing in this paragraph may be construed to require the provision of applicable information with regard to a request for a record of an individual if the Commissioner determines there are exceptional circumstances warranting an exception (such as safety of the individual or interference with an investigation).

(F) Applicable information provided by the Commission pursuant to an agreement under this paragraph or by an individual to any agency that has entered into an agreement under this paragraph shall be considered as strictly confidential and shall be used only for the purposes described in this paragraph and for carrying out an agreement under this paragraph. Any officer or employee or former officer or employee of a State, or any officer or employee or former officer or employee of a contractor of a State who, without the written authority of the Commissioner, publishes or communicates any applicable information in such individual's possession by reason of such employment or position as such an officer, shall be guilty of a felony and upon conviction thereof shall be fined or imprisoned, or both, as described in section 208 [42 USCS § 408].

(9)(A) The Commissioner of Social Security shall, upon the request of the Secretary or the Inspector General of the Department of Health and Human Services—

(i) enter into an agreement with the Secretary or such Inspector General for the purpose of matching data in the system of records of the Social Security Administration and the system of records of the Department of Health and Human Services; and

(ii) include in such agreement safeguards to assure the maintenance of the confidentiality of any information disclosed.

(B) For purposes of this paragraph, the term 'system of records' has the meaning given such term in section 552a(a)(5) of title 5, United States Code.

(s) Notice requirements. The Commissioner of Social Security shall take such actions as are necessary to ensure that any notice to one or more individuals issued pursuant to this title [42 USCS §§ 401 et seq.] by the Commissioner of Social Security or by a State agency—

(1) is written in simple and clear language, and

(2) includes the address and telephone number of the local office of the Social Security Administration which serves the recipient.

In the case of any such notice which is not generated by a local servicing office, the requirements of paragraph (2) shall be treated as satisfied if such notice includes the address of the local office of the Social Security Administration which services the recipient of the notice and a telephone number through which such office can be reached.

(t) Same-day personal interviews at field offices in cases where time is of the essence. In any case in which an individual visits a field office of the Social Security Administration and represents during the visit to an officer or employee of the Social Security Administration in the office that the individual's visit is occasioned by—

(1) the receipt of a notice from the Social Security Administration indicating a time limit for response by the individual, or

(2) the theft, loss, or nonreceipt of a benefit payment under this title [42 USCS §§ 401 et seq.],

the Commissioner of Social Security shall ensure that the individual is granted a face-to-face interview at the office with an officer or employee of the Social Security Administration before the close of business on the day of the visit.

(u) Redetermination of entitlement in cases of fraud or similar fault. (1)(A) The Commissioner of Social Security shall immediately redetermine the entitlement of individuals to monthly insurance benefits under this title [42 USCS §§ 401 et seq.] if there is reason to believe that fraud or similar fault was involved in the application of the individual for such benefits, unless a United States attorney, or equivalent State prosecutor, with jurisdiction over potential or actual related criminal cases, certifies, in writing, that there is a substantial risk that such action by the Commissioner of Social Security with regard to beneficiaries in a particular investigation would jeopardize the criminal prosecution of a person involved in a suspected fraud.

(B) When redetermining the entitlement, or making an initial determination of entitlement, of an individual under this title [42 USCS §§ 401 et seq.], the Commissioner of Social Security shall disregard any evidence if there is reason to believe that fraud or similar fault was involved in the providing of such evidence.

(2) For purposes of paragraph (1), similar fault is involved with respect to a determination if—

(A) an incorrect or incomplete statement that is material to the determination is knowingly made; or

(B) information that is material to the determination is knowingly concealed.

(3) If, after redetermining pursuant to this subsection the entitlement of an individual to monthly insurance benefits, the Commissioner of Social Security determines that there is insufficient evidence to support such entitle-

ment, the Commissioner of Social Security may terminate such entitlement and may treat benefits paid on the basis of such insufficient evidence as overpayments.

(Aug. 14, 1935, ch 531, Title II, § 205, 49 Stat. 624; Aug. 10, 1939, ch 666, Title II, § 201, 53 Stat. 1368; Aug. 28, 1950, ch 809, Title I, §§ 101(b)(2), 108(a)–(c), 109(b), 64 Stat. 488, 518, 523; July 18, 1952, ch 945, § 5(b), 66 Stat. 775; Sept. 1, 1954, ch 1206, Title I, § 101(c)(3), 68 Stat. 1054; Aug. 1, 1956, ch 836, Title I, §§ 107(b), 111(a), 117, 70 Stat. 829, 831, 834; Aug. 1, 1956, ch 837, Title IV, § 402(b), 70 Stat. 871; June 11, 1960, P. L. 86-507, § 1(35), 74 Stat. 202; Sept. 13, 1960, P. L. 86-778, Title I, §§ 102(f)(2), 103(j)(2)(E), Title VII, § 702(a), 74 Stat. 933, 938, 993; Sept. 22, 1961, P. L. 87-293, Title II, § 202(b)(3), 75 Stat. 626; July 30, 1965, P. L. 89-97, Title III, §§ 308(d)(9), (10), 330, 79 Stat. 379, 401; Jan. 2, 1968, P. L. 90-248, Title I, Part 4, § 171(a), 81 Stat. 876; Oct. 15, 1970, P. L. 91-452, Title II, § 236, 84 Stat. 930; Oct. 30, 1972, P. L. 92-603, Title I, § 137, 86 Stat. 1364; Oct. 16, 1974, P. L. 93-445, Title III, §§ 302(a), 303, 88 Stat. 1358; Jan. 2, 1976, P. L. 94-202, § 4, 89 Stat. 1136; Oct. 4, 1976, P. L. 94-455, Title XII, § 1211(b), 90 Stat. 1711; Dec. 20, 1977, P. L. 95-216, Title III, Part E, Subpart 1, § 353(f)(2), 91 Stat. 1554; Nov. 6, 1978, P. L. 95-600, Title VII, § 703(j)(14)(B), 92 Stat. 2942; June 9, 1980, P. L. 96-265, Title III, §§ 305(a), 307, 94 Stat. 457, 458; Jan. 12, 1983, P. L. 97-455, § 4(a), 96 Stat. 2499; April 20, 1983, P. L. 98-21, Title III, Part A, §§ 301(d), 309(i), Part C, §§ 336, 345(a), 97 Stat. 111, 117, 130, 137; July 18, 1984, P. L. 98-369, Division B, Title VI, Subtitle D, §§ 2661(h)(1), (2), 2663(a)(4), (j)(4), 98 Stat. 1157, 1162, 1171; Oct. 9, 1984, P. L. 98-460, § 16(a), 98 Stat. 1809; Oct. 21, 1986, P. L. 99-509, Title IX, Subtitle A, § 9002(c)(2)(A)(B), 100 Stat. 1971; Oct. 13, 1988, P. L. 100-485, Title I, Subtitle C, § 125(a), 102 Stat. 2353; Nov. 10, 1988, P. L. 100-647, Title VIII, Subtitle A, §§ 8008(a), 8009(a), 8015(a)(1), 8016(a)(1), 102 Stat. 3783, 3787, 3790, 3792; Dec. 19, 1989, P. L. 101-239, Title X, Subtitle C, §§ 10303(a), 10304, 103 Stat. 2482, 2483; Nov. 5, 1990, P. L. 101-508, Title V, Subtitle B, §§ 5105(a)(1)(A), (2)(A)(i), (B), (3)(A)(i), (b)(1)(A), (c)(1), (d)(1)(A), 5107(a)(1), 5109(a)(1), 104 Stat. 1388-254, 1388-255, 1388-260, 1388-263, 1388-265, 1388-269, 1388-271; Nov. 28, 1990, P. L. 101-624, Title XVII, Subtitle A, § 1735(a), (b), Title XXII, Subtitle A, §§ 2201(b), (c), 104 Stat. 3791, 3792, 3951, 3952; Aug. 15, 1994, P. L. 103-296, Title I, §§ 107(a)(1), (2), (4), Title II, § 201(a)(1)(A), (B), (2)(A)–(C), 206(a)(1), (d)(1), Title III, §§ 304(a), 316(a), 318, 321(a)(7)–(11), (c)(3), (6)(B), (f)(2)(A), 108 Stat. 1477, 1478, 1483, 1490, 1491, 1492, 1509, 1514, 1520, 1531, 1533, 1536, 1538, 1541; March 29, 1996, P. L. 104-121, Title I, § 105(a)(2), 110 Stat. 852; Aug. 22, 1996, P. L. 104-193, Title I, § 108(a)(1), 110 Stat. 2164; Aug. 5, 1997, P. L. 105-34, Title X, Subtitle I, § 1090(b)(1), 111 Stat. 962; Dec. 14, 1999, P. L. 106-169, Title II, Subtitle B, § 251(b)(2), 113 Stat. 1854; Dec. 21, 2001, P. L. 107-90, Title I, § 103(i)(3), 115 Stat. 882; Oct. 29, 2002, P. L. 107-252, Title III, Subtitle A, § 303(a)(5)(C), 116 Stat. 1711; March 2, 2004, P. L. 108-203, Title I, Subtitle A, §§ 101(a), 102(a)(1), (b)(1), 103(a), 104(a), 105(a), 106(a), Title IV, Subtitle B, § 411(a), 118 Stat. 495, 497, 498, 500, 503, 504, 505, 527; Dec. 17, 2004, P. L. 108-458, Title VII, Subtitle B, § 7214(a), 118 Stat. 3832; July 11, 2006, P. L. 109-241, Title IX, § 902(n), 120 Stat. 568; May 22, 2008, P. L. 110-234, Title IV, Subtitle A, Part I, § 4002(b)(1)(B), (2)(V), 122 Stat. 1096, 1097; June 18, 2008, P. L. 110-246, § 4(a), Title IV, Subtitle A, Part I, § 4002(b)(1)(B), (2)(V), 122 Stat. 1664, 1857, 1858; March 23, 2010, P. L. 111-148, Title I, Subtitle E, Part I, Subpart B, § 1414(a)(2), Title VI, Subtitle E, § 6402(b)(3), 124 Stat. 237, 756.)

TITLE IV. GRANTS TO STATES FOR AID AND SERVICES TO NEEDY FAMILIES WITH CHILDREN AND FOR CHILD-WELFARE SERVICES

PART A. BLOCK GRANTS TO STATES FOR TEMPORARY ASSISTANCE FOR NEEDY FAMILIES

§ 602. Eligible States; State plan

(a) In general. As used in this part [42 USCS §§ 601 et seq.], the term "eligible State" means, with respect to a fiscal year, a State that, during the 27-month period ending with the close of the 1st quarter of the fiscal year, has submitted to the Secretary a plan that the Secretary has found includes the following:

(1) Outline of family assistance program. (A) General provisions. A written document that outlines how the State intends to do the following:

(i) Conduct a program, designed to serve all political subdivisions in the State (not necessarily in a uniform manner), that provides assistance to needy families with (or expecting) children and provides parents with job preparation, work, and support services to enable them to leave the program and become self-sufficient.

(ii) Require a parent or caretaker receiving assistance under the program to engage in work (as defined by the State) once the State determines the parent or caretaker is ready to engage in work, or once the parent or caretaker has received assistance under the program for 24 months (whether or not consecutive), whichever is earlier, consistent with section 407(e)(2) [42 USCS § 607(e)(2)].

(iii) Ensure that parents and caretakers receiving assistance under the program engage in work activities in accordance with section 407 [42 USCS § 607].

(iv) Take such reasonable steps as the State deems necessary to restrict the use and disclosure of information about individuals and families receiving assistance under the program attributable to funds provided by the Federal Government.

(v) Establish goals and take action to prevent and reduce the incidence of out-of-wedlock pregnancies, with special emphasis on teenage pregnancies, and establish numerical goals for reducing the illegitimacy ratio of the State (as defined in section 403(a)(2)(C)(iii) [42 USCS § 603(a)(2)(C)(iii)]) for calendar years 1996 through 2005.

(vi) Conduct a program, designed to reach State and local law enforcement officials, the education system, and relevant counseling services, that provides education and training on the problem of statutory rape so that teenage pregnancy prevention programs may be expanded in scope to include men.

(B) Special provisions. (i) The document shall indicate whether the State intends to treat families moving into the State from another State differently than other families under the program, and if so, how the State intends to treat such families under the program.

(ii) The document shall indicate whether the State intends to provide assistance under the program to individuals who are not citizens of the United States, and if so, shall include an overview of such assistance.

(iii) The document shall set forth objective criteria for the delivery of benefits and the determination of eligibility and for fair and equitable treatment, including an explanation of how the State will provide opportunities for recipients who have been adversely affected to be heard in a State administrative or appeal process.

(iv) Not later than 1 year after the date of enactment of this section [enacted Aug. 22, 1996], unless the chief executive officer of the State opts out of this provision by notifying the Secretary, a State shall, consistent with the exception provided in section 407(e)(2) [42 USCS § 607(e)(2)], require a parent or caretaker receiving assistance under the program who, after receiving such assistance for 2 months is not exempt from work requirements and is not engaged in work, as determined under section 407(c) [42 USCS § 607(c)], to participate in community service employment, with minimum hours per week and tasks to be determined by the State.

(v) **[Caution: This clause takes effect on January 1, 2011, as provided by § 6703(a)(2)(B) of Act March 23, 2010, P. L. 111-148, which appears as a note to this section.]** The document shall indicate whether the State intends to assist individuals to train for, seek, and maintain employment—

(I) providing direct care in a long-term care facility (as such terms are defined under section 2011 [42 USCS § 1397j]); or

(II) in other occupations related to elder care determined appropriate by the State for which the State identifies an unmet need for service personnel,

and, if so, shall include an overview of such assistance.

(2) Certification that the State will operate a child support enforcement program. A certification by the chief executive officer of the State that, during the fiscal year, the State will operate a child support enforcement program under the State plan approved under part D [42 USCS §§ 651 et seq.].

(3) Certification that the State will operate a foster care and adoption assistance program. A certification by the chief executive officer of the State that, during the fiscal year, the State will operate a foster care and adoption assistance program under the State plan approved under part E [42 USCS §§ 670 et seq.], and that the State will take such actions as are necessary to ensure that children receiving assistance under such part are eligible for medical assistance under the State plan under title XIX [42 USCS §§ 1396 et seq.].

(4) Certification of the administration of the program. A certification by the chief executive officer of the State specifying which State agency or agencies will administer and supervise the program referred to in paragraph (1) for the fiscal year, which shall include assurances that local governments and private sector organizations—

(A) have been consulted regarding the plan and design of welfare services in the State so that services are provided in a manner appropriate to local populations; and

(B) have had at least 45 days to submit comments on the plan and the design of such services.

(5) Certification that the State will provide Indians with equitable access to assistance. A certification by the chief executive officer of the State that, during the fiscal year, the State will provide each member of an Indian tribe, who is domiciled in the State and is not eligible for assistance under a tribal family assistance plan approved under section 412 [42 USCS § 612], with equitable access to assistance under the State program funded under this part [42 USCS §§ 601 et seq.] attributable to funds provided by the Federal Government.

(6) Certification of standards and procedures to ensure against program fraud and abuse. A certification by the chief executive officer of the State that the State has established and is enforcing standards and procedures to ensure against program fraud and abuse, including standards and procedures concerning nepotism, conflicts of interest among individuals responsible for the administration and supervision of the State program, kickbacks, and the use of political patronage.

(7) Optional certification of standards and procedures to ensure that the State will screen for and identify domestic violence. (A) In general. At the option of the State, a certification by the chief executive officer of the State that the State has established and is enforcing standards and procedures to—

(i) screen and identify individuals receiving assistance under this part [42 USCS §§ 601 et seq.] with a history of domestic violence while maintaining the confidentiality of such individuals;

(ii) refer such individuals to counseling and supportive services; and

(iii) waive, pursuant to a determination of good cause, other program requirements such as time limits (for so long as necessary) for individuals receiving assistance, residency requirements, child support cooperation requirements, and family cap provisions, in cases where compliance with such requirements would make it more difficult for individuals receiving assistance under this part to escape domestic violence or unfairly penalize such individuals who are or have been victimized by such violence, or individuals who are at risk of further domestic violence.

(B) Domestic violence defined. For purposes of this paragraph, the term "domestic violence" has the same meaning as the term "battered or subjected to extreme cruelty", as defined in section 408(a)(7)(C)(iii) [42 USCS § 608(a)(7)(C)(iii)].

(b) Plan amendments. Within 30 days after a State amends a plan submitted pursuant to subsection (a), the State shall notify the Secretary of the amendment.

(c) Public availability of State plan summary. The State shall make available to the public a summary of any plan or plan amendment submitted by the State under this section.

(Aug. 14, 1935, ch 531, Title IV, Part A, § 402, as added Aug. 22, 1996, P. L. 104-193, Title I, § 103(a), 110 Stat. 2113; Aug. 5, 1997, P. L. 105-33, Title V, Subtitle F, Ch 1, §§ 5501, 5514(c). 111 Stat. 606, 620; Dec. 14, 1999, P. L. 106-169, Title IV, § 401(a), 113 Stat. 1858; March 23, 2010, P. L. 111-148, Title VI, Subtitle H, § 6703(a)(2)(A), 124 Stat. 798.)

HISTORY; ANCILLARY LAWS AND DIRECTIVES

Other provisions:

Effective date of March 23, 2010 amendment. Act March 23, 2010, P. L. 111-148, Title VI, Subtitle H, § 6703(a)(2)(B), 124 Stat. 798, provides: "The amendment made by subparagraph (A) [adding subsec. (a)(1)(B)(v) of this section] shall take effect on January 1, 2011.".

§ 604. Use of grants

(a) General rules. Subject to this part [42 USCS §§ 601 et seq.], a State to which a grant is made under section 403 [42 USCS § 603] may use the grant—

(1) in any manner that is reasonably calculated to accomplish the purpose of this part [42 USCS §§ 601 et seq.], including to provide low income households with assistance in meeting home heating and cooling costs; or

(2) in any manner that the State was authorized to use amounts received under part A or F [former 42 USCS §§ 601 et seq. or 681 et seq.], as such parts were in effect on September 30, 1995, or (at the option of the State) August 21, 1996.

(b) Limitation on use of grant for administrative purposes. (1) Limitation. A State to which a grant is made under section 403 [42 USCS § 603] shall not expend more than 15 percent of the grant for administrative purposes.

(2) Exception. Paragraph (1) shall not apply to the use of a grant for information technology and computerization needed for tracking or monitoring required by or under this part [42

USCS §§ 601 et seq.].

(c) Authority to treat interstate immigrants under rules of former State [Caution: In Saenz v Roe (May 17, 1999) 143 L Ed 2d 689, 119 S Ct 1518, 1999 US LEXIS 3174, 67 USLW 4291, the Supreme Court held that it was beyond the power of Congress to authorize, by enactment of this subsection, a durational residency requirement for welfare benefits that violated the Fourteenth Amendment.]. A State operating a program funded under this part [42 USCS §§ 601 et seq.] may apply to a family the rules (including benefit amounts) of the program funded under this part [42 USCS §§ 601 et seq.] of another State if the family has moved to the State from the other State and has resided in the State for less than 12 months.

(d) Authority to use portion of grant for other purposes. (1) In general. Subject to paragraph (2), a State may use not more than 30 percent of the amount of any grant made to the State under section 403(a) [42 USCS § 603(a)] for a fiscal year to carry out a State program pursuant to any or all of the following provisions of law:

(A) [Subtitle] subtitle 1 of Title [title] XX of this Act [42 USCS §§ 1397 et seq.].

(B) The Child Care and Development Block Grant Act of 1990 [42 USCS §§ 9858 et seq.].

(2) Limitation on amount transferable to subtitle 1 of title XX programs. (A) In general. A State may use not more than the applicable percent of the amount of any grant made to the State under section 403(a) [42 USCS § 603(a)] for a fiscal year to carry out State programs pursuant to subtitle 1 of title XX [42 USCS §§ 1397 et seq.].

(B) Applicable percent. For purposes of subparagraph (A), the applicable percent is 4.25 percent in the case of fiscal year 2001 and each succeeding fiscal year.

(3) Applicable rules. (A) In general. Except as provided in subparagraph (B) of this paragraph, any amount paid to a State under this part [42 USCS §§ 601 et seq.] that is used to carry out a State program pursuant to a provision of law specified in paragraph (1) shall not be subject to the requirements of this part [42 USCS §§ 601 et seq.], but shall be subject to the requirements that apply to Federal funds provided directly under the provision of law to carry out the program, and the expenditure of any amount so used shall not be considered to be an expenditure under this part [42 USCS §§ 601 et seq.].

(B) Exception relating to subtitle 1 of title XX programs. All amounts paid to a State under this part [42 USCS §§ 601 et seq.] that are used to carry out State programs pursuant to subtitle 1 of title XX [42 USCS §§ 1397 et seq.] shall be used only for programs and services to children or their families whose income is less than 200 percent of the income official poverty line (as defined by the Office of Management and Budget, and revised annually in accordance with section 673(2) of the Omnibus Budget Reconciliation Act of 1981 [42 USCS § 9902(2)]) applicable to a family of the size involved.

(e) Authority to carry over certain amounts for benefits or services or for future contingencies. A State or tribe may use a grant made to the State or tribe under this part [42 USCS §§ 601 et seq.] for any fiscal year to provide, without fiscal year limitation, any benefit or service that may be provided under the State or tribal program funded under this part [42 USCS §§ 601 et seq.].

(f) Authority to operate employment placement program. A State to which a grant is made under section 403 [42 USCS § 603] may use the grant to make payments (or provide job placement vouchers) to State-approved public and private job placement agencies that provide employment placement services to individuals who receive assistance under the State program funded under this part [42 USCS §§ 601 et seq.].

(g) Implementation of electronic benefit transfer system. A State to which a grant is made under section 403 [42 USCS § 603] is encouraged to implement an electronic benefit transfer system for providing assistance under the State program funded under this part [42 USCS §§ 601 et seq.], and may use the grant for such purpose.

(h) Use of funds for individual development accounts. (1) In general. A State to which a grant is made under section 403 [42 USCS § 603] may use the grant to carry out a program to fund individual development accounts (as defined in paragraph (2)) established by individuals eligible for assistance under the State program funded under this part [42 USCS §§ 601 et seq.].

(2) Individual development accounts. (A) Establishment. Under a State program carried out under paragraph (1), an individual development account may be established by or on behalf of an individual eligible for assistance under the State program operated under this part [42 USCS §§ 601 et seq.] for the purpose of enabling the individual to accumulate funds for a qualified purpose described in subparagraph (B).

(B) Qualified purpose. A qualified purpose described in this subparagraph is 1 or more of the following, as provided by the qualified entity providing assistance to the individual under this subsection:

(i) Postsecondary educational expenses. Postsecondary educational expenses paid from an individual development account directly to an eligible educational institution.

(ii) First home purchase. Qualified acquisition costs with respect to a qualified principal residence for a qualified first-time homebuyer, if paid from an individual development account directly to the persons to whom the amounts are due.

(iii) Business capitalization. Amounts paid from an individual development account directly to a business capitalization account which is established in a federally insured financial institution and is restricted to use solely for qualified business capitalization expenses.

(C) Contributions to be from earned income. An individual may only contribute to an individual development account such amounts as are derived from earned income, as defined in section 911(d)(2) of the Internal Revenue Code of 1986 [26 USCS § 911(d)(2)].

(D) Withdrawal of funds. The Secretary shall establish such regulations as may be necessary to ensure that funds held in an individual development account are not withdrawn except for 1 or more of the qualified purposes described in subparagraph (B).

(3) Requirements. (A) In general. An individual development account established under this subsection shall be a trust created or organized in the United States and funded through periodic contributions by the establishing individual and matched by or through a qualified entity for a qualified purpose (as described in paragraph (2)(B)).

(B) Qualified entity. As used in this subsection, the term "qualified entity" means—

(i) a not-for-profit organization described in section 501(c)(3) of the Internal Revenue Code of 1986 [26 USCS § 501(c)(3)] and exempt from taxation under section 501(a) of such Code [26 USCS § 501(a)]; or

(ii) a State or local government agency acting in cooperation with an organization described in clause (i).

(4) No reduction in benefits. Notwithstanding any other provision of Federal law (other than the Internal Revenue Code of 1986 [26 USCS §§ 1 et seq.]) that requires consideration of 1 or more financial circumstances of an individual, for the purpose of determining eligibility to receive, or the amount of, any assistance or benefit authorized by such law to be provided to or for the benefit of such individual, funds (including interest accruing) in an individual development account under this subsection shall be disregarded for such purpose with respect to any period during which such individual maintains or makes contributions into such an account.

(5) Definitions. As used in this subsection—

(A) Eligible educational institution. The term "eligible educational institution" means the following:

(i) An institution described in section 481(a)(1) or 1201(a) of the Higher Education Act of 1965 (20 U.S.C. 1088(a)(1) or 1141(a)), as such sections are in effect on the date of the enactment of this subsection [enacted Aug. 22, 1996].

(ii) An area vocational education school (as defined in subparagraph (C) or (D) of section 521(4) of the Carl D. Perkins Vocational and Applied Technology Education Act (20 U.S.C. 2471(4))) which is in any State (as defined in section 521(33) of such Act [20 USCS § 521(33)]), as such sections are in effect on the date of the enactment of this subsection [enacted Aug. 22, 1996].

(B) Post-secondary educational expenses. The term "post-secondary educational expenses" means—

(i) tuition and fees required for the enrollment or attendance of a student at an eligible educational institution, and

(ii) fees, books, supplies, and equipment required for courses of instruction at an eligible educational institution.

(C) Qualified acquisition costs. The term "qualified acquisition costs" means the costs of acquiring, constructing, or reconstructing a residence. The term includes any usual or reasonable settlement, financing, or other closing costs.

(D) Qualified business. The term "qualified business" means any business that does not contravene any law or public policy (as determined by the Secretary).

(E) Qualified business capitalization expenses. The term "qualified business capitalization expenses" means qualified expenditures for the capitalization of a qualified business pursuant to a qualified plan.

(F) Qualified expenditures. The term "qualified expenditures" means expenditures included in a qualified plan, including capital, plant, equipment, working capital, and inventory expenses.

(G) Qualified first-time homebuyer. (i) In

general. The term "qualified first-time homebuyer" means a taxpayer (and, if married, the taxpayer's spouse) who has no present ownership interest in a principal residence during the 3-year period ending on the date of acquisition of the principal residence to which this subsection applies.

(ii) Date of acquisition. The term "date of acquisition" means the date on which a binding contract to acquire, construct, or reconstruct the principal residence to which this subparagraph applies is entered into.

(H) Qualified plan. The term "qualified plan" means a business plan which—

(i) is approved by a financial institution, or by a nonprofit loan fund having demonstrated fiduciary integrity,

(ii) includes a description of services or goods to be sold, a marketing plan, and projected financial statements, and

(iii) may require the eligible individual to obtain the assistance of an experienced entrepreneurial advisor.

(I) Qualified principal residence. The term "qualified principal residence" means a principal residence (within the meaning of section 1034 of the Internal Revenue Code of 1986 [26 USCS § 1034]), the qualified acquisition costs of which do not exceed 100 percent of the average area purchase price applicable to such residence (determined in accordance with paragraphs (2) and (3) of section 143(e) of such Code [26 USCS § 143(e)]).

(i) Sanction welfare recipients for failing to ensure that minor dependent children attend school. A State to which a grant is made under section 403 [42 USCS § 603] shall not be prohibited from sanctioning a family that includes an adult who has received assistance under any State program funded under this part [42 USCS §§ 601 et seq.] attributable to funds provided by the Federal Government or under the supplemental nutrition assistance program, as defined in section 3(l) of the Food and Nutrition Act of 2008 [7 USCS § 2012(l)], if such adult fails to ensure that the minor dependent children of such adult attend school as required by the law of the State in which the minor children reside.

(j) Requirement for high school diploma or equivalent. A State to which a grant is made under section 403 [42 USCS § 603] shall not be prohibited from sanctioning a family that includes an adult who is older than age 20 and younger than age 51 and who has received assistance under any State program funded under this part [42 USCS §§ 601 et seq.] attributable to funds provided by the Federal Government or under the supplemental nutrition assistance program, as defined in section 3(l) of the Food and Nutrition Act of 2008 [7 USCS § 2012(l)], if such adult does not have, or is not working toward attaining, a secondary school diploma or its recognized equivalent unless such adult has been determined in the judgment of medical, psychiatric, or other appropriate professionals to lack the requisite capacity to complete successfully a course of study that would lead to a secondary school diploma or its recognized equivalent.

(k) Limitations on use of grant for matching under certain Federal transportation program. (1) Use limitations. A State to which a grant is made under section 403 [42 USCS § 603] may not use any part of the grant to match funds made available under section 3037 of the Transportation Equity Act for the 21st Century [49 USCS § 5309 note], unless—

(A) the grant is used for new or expanded transportation services (and not for construction) that benefit individuals described in subparagraph (C), and not to subsidize current operating costs;

(B) the grant is used to supplement and not supplant other State expenditures on transportation;

(C) the preponderance of the benefits derived from such use of the grant accrues to individuals who are—

(i) recipients of assistance under the State program funded under this part [42 USCS §§ 601 et seq.];

(ii) former recipients of such assistance;

(iii) noncustodial parents who are described in section 403(a)(5)(C)(iii) [42 USCS § 603(a)(5)(C)(iii)]; and

(iv) low-income individuals who are at risk of qualifying for such assistance; and

(D) the services provided through such use of the grant promote the ability of such recipients to engage in work activities (as defined in section 407(d) [42 USCS § 607(d)]).

(2) Amount limitation. From a grant made to a State under section 403(a) [42 USCS § 603(a)], the amount that a State uses to match funds described in paragraph (1) of this subsection shall not exceed the amount (if any) by which 30 percent of the total amount of the grant exceeds the amount (if any) of the grant that is used by the State to carry out any State program described in subsection (d)(1) of this section.

(3) Rule of interpretation. The provision by a State of a transportation benefit under a program conducted under section 3037 of the Transportation Equity Act for the 21st Century

[49 USCS § 5309 note], to an individual who is not otherwise a recipient of assistance under the State program funded under this part [42 USCS §§ 601 et seq.], using funds from a grant made under section 403(a) of this Act [42 USCS § 603(a)], shall not be considered to be the provision of assistance to the individual under the State program funded under this part [42 USCS §§ 601 et seq.].

(Aug. 14, 1935, ch 531, Title IV, Part A, § 404, as added Aug. 22, 1996, P. L. 104-193, Title I, § 103(a), 110 Stat. 2124; Aug. 5, 1997, P. L. 105-33, Title V, Subtitle A, § 5002(a), Subtitle F, Ch 1, §§ 5503, 5514(c), 111 Stat. 593, 609, 620; June 9, 1998, P. L. 105-178, Title VIII, Subtitle D, § 8401(b), 112 Stat. 499; July 16, 1998, P. L. 105-200, Title IV, § 403(a), 112 Stat. 670; Nov. 29, 1999, P. L. 106-113, Div B, § 1000(a)(4), 113 Stat. 1535; Dec. 14, 1999, P. L. 106-169, Title IV, § 401(l), 113 Stat. 1858; May 22, 2008, P. L. 110-234, Title IV, Subtitle A, Part I, § 4002(b)(1)(A), (B), (2)(V), Part III, § 4115(c)(2)(G), 122 Stat. 1096, 1097, 1110; June 18, 2008, P. L. 110-246, § 4(a), Title IV, Subtitle A, Part I, § 4002(b)(1)(A), (B), (2)(V), Part III, § 4115(c)(2)(G), 122 Stat. 1664, 1857, 1858, 1871; Feb. 17, 2009, P. L. 111-5, Div B, Title II, Subtitle B, § 2103, 123 Stat. 449; March 23, 2010, P. L. 111-148, Title VI, Subtitle H, § 6703(d)(2)(A), 124 Stat. 803.)

PART B. CHILD AND FAMILY SERVICES

SUBPART 1. STEPHANIE TUBBS JONES CHILD WELFARE SERVICES PROGRAM

§ 622. State plans for child welfare services

(a) Joint development. In order to be eligible for payment under this subpart [42 USCS §§ 621 et seq.], a State must have a plan for child welfare services which has been developed jointly by the Secretary and the State agency designated pursuant to subsection (b)(1), and which meets the requirements of subsection (b).

(b) Requisite features of State plans. Each plan for child welfare services under this subpart [42 USCS §§ 621 et seq.] shall—

(1) provide that (A) the individual or agency that administers or supervises the administration of the State's services program under subtitle 1 of title XX [42 USCS §§ 1397 et seq.] will administer or supervise the administration of the plan (except as otherwise provided in section 103(d) of the Adoption Assistance and Child Welfare Act of 1980 [note to this section]), and (B) to the extent that child welfare services are furnished by the staff of the State agency or local agency administering the plan, a single organizational unit in such State or local agency, as the case may be, will be responsible for furnishing such child welfare services;

(2) provide for coordination between the services provided for children under the plan and the services and assistance provided under subtitle 1 of title XX [42 USCS §§ 1397 et seq.], under the State program funded under part A [42 USCS §§ 601 et seq.], under the State plan approved under subpart 2 of this part [42 USCS §§ 629 et seq.], under the State plan approved [under the State plan approved] under part E [42 USCS §§ 670 et seq.], and under other State programs having a relationship to the program under this subpart [42 USCS §§ 621 et seq.], with a view to provision of welfare and related services which will best promote the welfare of such children and their families;

(3) include a description of the services and activities which the State will fund under the State program carried out pursuant to this subpart [42 USCS §§ 621 et seq.], and how the services and activities will achieve the purpose of this subpart [42 USCS §§ 621 et seq.];

(4) contain a description of—

(A) the steps the State will take to provide child welfare services statewide and to expand and strengthen the range of existing services and develop and implement services to improve child outcomes; and

(B) the child welfare services staff development and training plans of the State;

(5) provide, in the development of services for children, for utilization of the facilities and experience of voluntary agencies in accordance with State and local programs and arrangements, as authorized by the State;

(6) provide that the agency administering or supervising the administration of the plan will furnish such reports, containing such information, and participate in such evaluations, as the Secretary may require;

(7) provide for the diligent recruitment of potential foster and adoptive families that reflect the ethnic and racial diversity of children in the State for whom foster and adoptive homes are needed;

(8) provide assurances that the State—

(A) is operating, to the satisfaction of the Secretary—

(i) a statewide information system from which can be readily determined the status, demographic characteristics, location, and goals for the placement of every child who is (or, within the immediately preceding 12 months, has been) in foster care;

(ii) a case review system (as defined in section 475(5) [42 USCS § 675(5)]) for each child receiving foster care under the supervision of the State;

(iii) a service program designed to help children—

(I) where safe and appropriate, return to families from which they have been removed; or

(II) be placed for adoption, with a legal guardian, or, if adoption or legal guardianship is determined not to be appropriate for a child, in some other planned, permanent living arrangement, which may include a residential educational program; and

(iv) a preplacement preventive services program designed to help children at risk of foster care placement remain safely with their families; and

(B) has in effect policies and administrative and judicial procedures for children abandoned at or shortly after birth (including policies and procedures providing for legal representation of the children) which enable permanent decisions to be made expeditiously with respect to the placement of the children;

(9) contain a description, developed after consultation with tribal organizations (as defined in section 4 of the Indian Self-Determination and Education Assistance Act [25 USCS § 450b]) in the State, of the specific measures taken by the State to comply with the Indian Child Welfare Act [25 USCS §§ 1901 et seq.];

(10) contain assurances that the State shall make effective use of cross-jurisdictional resources (including through contracts for the purchase of services), and shall eliminate legal barriers, to facilitate timely adoptive or permanent placements for waiting children;

(11) contain a description of the activities that the State has undertaken for children adopted from other countries, including the provision of adoption and post-adoption services;

(12) provide that the State shall collect and report information on children who are adopted from other countries and who enter into State custody as a result of the disruption of a placement for adoption or the dissolution of an adoption, including the number of children, the agencies who handled the placement or adoption, the plans for the child, and the reasons for the disruption or dissolution;

(13) demonstrate substantial, ongoing, and meaningful collaboration with State courts in the development and implementation of the State plan under subpart 1 [42 USCS §§ 621 et seq.], the State plan approved under subpart 2 [42 USCS §§ 629 et seq.], and the State plan approved under part E [42 USCS §§ 670 et seq.], and in the development and implementation of any program improvement plan required under section 1123A [42 USCS § 1320a-2a];

(14) not later than October 1, 2007, include assurances that not more than 10 percent of the expenditures of the State with respect to activities funded from amounts provided under this subpart [42 USCS §§ 621 et seq.] will be for administrative costs;

(15)(A) provides that the State will develop, in coordination and collaboration with the State agency referred to in paragraph (1) and the State agency responsible for administering the State plan approved under title XIX [42 USCS §§ 1396 et seq.], and in consultation with pediatricians, other experts in health care, and experts in and recipients of child welfare services, a plan for the ongoing oversight and coordination of health care services for any child in a foster care placement, which shall ensure a coordinated strategy to identify and respond to the health care needs of children in foster care placements, including mental health and dental health needs, and shall include an outline of—

(i) a schedule for initial and follow-up health screenings that meet reasonable standards of medical practice;

(ii) how health needs identified through screenings will be monitored and treated;

(iii) how medical information for children in care will be updated and appropriately shared, which may include the development and implementation of an electronic health record;

(iv) steps to ensure continuity of health care services, which may include the establishment of a medical home for every child in care;

(v) the oversight of prescription medicines;

(vi) how the State actively consults with and involves physicians or other appropriate medical or non-medical professionals in assessing the health and well-being of children in foster care and in determining appropriate medical treatment for the children; and

(vii) **[Caution: This clause takes effect on October 1, 2010, as provided by**

§ 2955(d) of Act March 23, 2010, P. L. 111-148, which appears as a note to this section.] steps to ensure that the components of the transition plan development process required under section 475(5)(H) [42 USCS § 675(5)(H)] that relate to the health care needs of children aging out of foster care, including the requirements to include options for health insurance, information about a health care power of attorney, health care proxy, or other similar document recognized under State law, and to provide the child with the option to execute such a document, are met; and

(B) subparagraph (A) shall not be construed to reduce or limit the responsibility of the State agency responsible for administering the State plan approved under title XIX [42 USCS §§ 1396 et seq.] to administer and provide care and services for children with respect to whom services are provided under the State plan developed pursuant to this subpart;

(16) provide that, not later than 1 year after the date of the enactment of this paragraph [enacted Sept. 28, 2006], the State shall have in place procedures providing for how the State programs assisted under this subpart, subpart 2 of this part, or part E [42 USCS §§ 621 et seq., 629 et seq., or 670 et seq.] would respond to a disaster, in accordance with criteria established by the Secretary which should include how a State would—

(A) identify, locate, and continue availability of services for children under State care or supervision who are displaced or adversely affected by a disaster;

(B) respond, as appropriate, to new child welfare cases in areas adversely affected by a disaster, and provide services in those cases;

(C) remain in communication with caseworkers and other essential child welfare personnel who are displaced because of a disaster;

(D) preserve essential program records; and

(E) coordinate services and share information with other States; and

(17) not later than October 1, 2007, describe the State standards for the content and frequency of caseworker visits for children who are in foster care under the responsibility of the State, which, at a minimum, ensure that the children are visited on a monthly basis and that the caseworker visits are well-planned and focused on issues pertinent to case planning and service delivery to ensure the safety, permanency, and well-being of the children.

(c) Definitions. In this subpart [42 USCS §§ 621 et seq.]:

(1) Administrative costs. The term "administrative costs" means costs for the following, but only to the extent incurred in administering the State plan developed pursuant to this subpart [42 USCS §§ 621 et seq.]: procurement, payroll management, personnel functions (other than the portion of the salaries of supervisors attributable to time spent directly supervising the provision of services by caseworkers), management, maintenance and operation of space and property, data processing and computer services, accounting, budgeting, auditing, and travel expenses (except those related to the provision of services by caseworkers or the oversight of programs funded under this subpart [42 USCS §§ 621 et seq.]).

(2) Other terms. For definitions of other terms used in this part [42 USCS §§ 621 et seq.], see section 475 [42 USCS § 675].

(Aug. 14, 1935, ch 531, Title IV, Part B, Subpart 1, § 422, as added Jan. 2, 1968, P. L. 90-248, Title II, Part 3, § 240(c), (d), 81 Stat. 912, 915; Jan. 4, 1975, P. L. 93-647, Part A, § 3(a)(6), (7), (h), 88 Stat. 2348, 2349; June 17, 1980, P. L. 96-272, Title I, § 103(a), 94 Stat. 517; Dec. 19, 1989, P. L. 101-239, Title X, Subtitle D, § 10403(b)(1), 103 Stat. 2488; Aug. 10, 1993, P. L. 103-66, Title XIII, Ch 2, Subch C, Part I, § 13711(a)(1), (b)(1), 107 Stat. 649, 655; Oct. 20, 1994, P. L. 103-382, Title V, Part E, Subpart 1, § 554, 108 Stat. 4057; Oct. 31, 1994, P. L. 103-432, Title II, Subtitle A, §§ 202(a), 204(a), 108 Stat. 4453, 4456; Aug. 22, 1996, P. L. 104-193, Title I, § 108(b), 110 Stat. 2165; Aug. 5, 1997, P. L. 105-33, Title V, Subtitle F, Ch 5, § 5592(a)(1)(A), (2), 111 Stat. 644; Nov. 19, 1997, P. L. 105-89, Title I, § 102(1), Title II, § 202(a), 111 Stat. 2117, 2125; July 16, 1998, P. L. 105-200, Title IV, § 410(b), 112 Stat. 673; Oct. 6, 2000, P. L. 106-279, Title II, § 205, 114 Stat. 837; Feb. 8, 2006, P. L. 109-171, Title VII, Subtitle D, § 7401(b), 120 Stat. 150; July 3, 2006, P. L. 109-239, § 13, 120 Stat. 514; Sept. 28, 2006, P. L. 109-288, §§ 6(c), 7(a), 120 Stat. 1244, 1248; Oct. 7, 2008, P. L. 110-351, Title II, § 205, 122 Stat. 3961; March 23, 2010, P. L. 111-148, Title II, Subtitle L, § 2955(c), Title VI, Subtitle H, § 6703(d)(2)(B), 124 Stat. 352, 803.)

HISTORY; ANCILLARY LAWS AND DIRECTIVES

Other provisions:

Effective date of March 23, 2010 amendments. Act March 23, 2010, P. L. 111-148, Title II, Subtitle L, § 2955(d), 124 Stat. 353, provides: "The amendments made by this section [amending 42 USCS §§ 622, 675, and 677] take effect on October 1, 2010.".

PART E. FEDERAL PAYMENTS FOR FOSTER CARE AND ADOPTION ASSISTANCE

§ 671. State plan for foster care and adoption assistance

(a) Requisite features of State plan. In order for a State to be eligible for payments under this part [42 USCS §§ 670 et seq.], it shall have a plan approved by the Secretary which—

(1) provides for foster care maintenance payments in accordance with section 472 [42 USCS § 672] and for adoption assistance in accordance with section 473 [42 USCS § 673];

(2) provides that the State agency responsible for administering the program authorized by subpart 1 of part B of this title [42 USCS §§ 620 et seq.] shall administer, or supervise the administration of, the program authorized by this part [42 USCS §§ 670 et seq.];

(3) provides that the plan shall be in effect in all political subdivisions of the State, and, if administered by them, be mandatory upon them;

(4) provides that the State shall assure that the programs at the local level assisted under this part [42 USCS §§ 670 et seq.] will be coordinated with the programs at the State or local level assisted under parts A and B of this title [42 USCS §§ 601 et seq., 620 et seq.], under subtitle 1 of title XX of this Act [42 USCS §§ 1397 et seq.], and under any other appropriate provision of Federal law;

(5) provides that the State will, in the administration of its programs under this part [42 USCS §§ 670 et seq.], use such methods relating to the establishment and maintenance of personnel standards on a merit basis as are found by the Secretary to be necessary for the proper and efficient operation of the programs, except that the Secretary shall exercise no authority with respect to the selection, tenure of office, or compensation of any individual employed in accordance with such methods;

(6) provides that the State agency referred to in paragraph (2) (hereinafter in this part [42 USCS §§ 670 et seq.] referred to as the "State agency") will make such reports, in such form and containing such information as the Secretary may from time to time require, and comply with such provisions as the Secretary may from time to time find necessary to assure the correctness and verification of such reports;

(7) provides that the State agency will monitor and conduct periodic evaluations of activities carried out under this part [42 USCS §§ 670 et seq.];

(8) subject to subsection (c), provides safeguards which restrict the use of or disclosure of information concerning individuals assisted under the State plan to purposes directly connected with (A) the administration of the plan of the State approved under this part [42 USCS §§ 670 et seq.], the plan or program of the State under part A, B, or D of this title [42 USCS §§ 601 et seq., 620 et seq., 651 et seq.] or under title I, V, X, XIV, XVI [42 USCS §§ 301 et seq., 701 et seq., 1201 et seq., 1351 et seq., 1381 et seq.] (as in effect in Puerto Rico, Guam, and the Virgin Islands), XIX, or XX [42 USCS §§ 1396 et seq., 1397 et seq.], or the supplemental security income program established by title XVI [42 USCS §§ 1381 et seq.], (B) any investigation, prosecution, or criminal or civil proceeding, conducted in connection with the administration of any such plan or program, (C) the administration of any other Federal or federally assisted program which provides assistance, in cash or in kind, or services, directly to individuals on the basis of need, (D) any audit or similar activity conducted in connection with the administration of any such plan or program by any governmental agency which is authorized by law to conduct such audit or activity, and (E) reporting and providing information pursuant to paragraph (9) to appropriate authorities with respect to known or suspected child abuse or neglect; and the safeguards so provided shall prohibit disclosure, to any committee or legislative body (other than an agency referred to in clause (D) with respect to any activity referred to in such clause), of any information which identifies by name or address any such applicant or recipient; except that nothing contained herein shall preclude a State from providing standards which restrict disclosures to purposes more limited than those specified herein, or which, in the case of adoptions, prevent disclosure entirely;

(9) provides that the State agency will—

(A) report to an appropriate agency or official, known or suspected instances of physical or mental injury, sexual abuse or exploitation, or negligent treatment or maltreatment of a child receiving aid under part B or this part [42 USCS §§ 620 et seq. or 671 et seq.] under circumstances which indicate that the child's health or welfare is threatened thereby; and

(B) provide such information with respect to a situation described in subparagraph (A) as the State agency may have;

(10) provides for the establishment or designation of a State authority or authorities which

shall be responsible for establishing and maintaining standards for foster family homes and child care institutions which are reasonably in accord with recommended standards of national organizations concerned with standards for such institutions or homes, including standards related to admission policies, safety, sanitation, and protection of civil rights, provides that the standards so established shall be applied by the State to any foster family home or child care institution receiving funds under this part [42 USCS §§ 670 et seq.] or part B of this title [42 USCS §§ 620 et seq.], and provides that a waiver of any such standard may be made only on a case-by-case basis for nonsafety standards (as determined by the State) in relative foster family homes for specific children in care;

(11) provides for periodic review of the standards referred to in the preceding paragraph and amounts paid as foster care maintenance payments and adoption assistance to assure their continuing appropriateness;

(12) provides for granting an opportunity for a fair hearing before the State agency to any individual whose claim for benefits available pursuant to this part [42 USCS §§ 670 et seq.] is denied or is not acted upon with reasonable promptness;

(13) provides that the State shall arrange for a periodic and independently conducted audit of the programs assisted under this part [42 USCS §§ 670 et seq.] and part B of this title [42 USCS §§ 620 et seq.], which shall be conducted no less frequently than once every three years;

(14) provides (A) specific goals (which shall be established by State law on or before October 1, 1982) for each fiscal year (commencing with the fiscal year which begins on October 1, 1983) as to the maximum number of children (in absolute numbers or as a percentage of all children in foster care with respect to whom assistance under the plan is provided during such year) who, at any time during such year, will remain in foster care after having been in such care for a period in excess of twenty-four months, and (B) a description of the steps which will be taken by the State to achieve such goals;

(15) provides that—

(A) in determining reasonable efforts to be made with respect to a child, as described in this paragraph, and in making such reasonable efforts, the child's health and safety shall be the paramount concern;

(B) except as provided in subparagraph (D), reasonable efforts shall be made to preserve and reunify families—

(i) prior to the placement of a child in foster care, to prevent or eliminate the need for removing the child from the child's home; and

(ii) to make it possible for a child to safely return to the child's home;

(C) if continuation of reasonable efforts of the type described in subparagraph (B) is determined to be inconsistent with the permanency plan for the child, reasonable efforts shall be made to place the child in a timely manner in accordance with the permanency plan (including, if appropriate, through an interstate placement), and to complete whatever steps are necessary to finalize the permanent placement of the child;

(D) reasonable efforts of the type described in subparagraph (B) shall not be required to be made with respect to a parent of a child if a court of competent jurisdiction has determined that—

(i) the parent has subjected the child to aggravated circumstances (as defined in State law, which definition may include but need not be limited to abandonment, torture, chronic abuse, and sexual abuse);

(ii) the parent has—

(I) committed murder (which would have been an offense under section 1111(a) of title 18, United States Code, if the offense had occurred in the special maritime or territorial jurisdiction of the United States) of another child of the parent;

(II) committed voluntary manslaughter (which would have been an offense under section 1112(a) of title 18, United States Code, if the offense had occurred in the special maritime or territorial jurisdiction of the United States) of another child of the parent;

(III) aided or abetted, attempted, conspired, or solicited to commit such a murder or such a voluntary manslaughter; or

(IV) committed a felony assault that results in serious bodily injury to the child or another child of the parent; or

(iii) the parental rights of the parent to a sibling have been terminated involuntarily;

(E) if reasonable efforts of the type described in subparagraph (B) are not made with respect to a child as a result of a determination made by a court of competent jurisdiction in accordance with subparagraph (D)—

(i) a permanency hearing (as described in section 475(5)(C) [42 USCS § 675(5)(C)]), which considers in-State and out-of-State permanent placement options for the child, shall be held for the child within 30 days after the determination; and

(ii) reasonable efforts shall be made to place

the child in a timely manner in accordance with the permanency plan, and to complete whatever steps are necessary to finalize the permanent placement of the child; and

(F) reasonable efforts to place a child for adoption or with a legal guardian, including identifying appropriate in-State and out-of-State placements may be made concurrently with reasonable efforts of the type described in subparagraph (B);

(16) provides for the development of a case plan (as defined in section 475(1) [42 USCS § 675(1)]) for each child receiving foster care maintenance payments under the State plan and provides for a case review system which meets the requirements described in section 475(5)(B) [42 USCS § 675(5)(B)] with respect to each such child;

(17) provides that, where appropriate, all steps will be taken, including cooperative efforts with the State agencies administering the program funded under part A [42 USCS §§ 601 et seq.] and plan approved under part D [42 USCS §§ 651 et seq.], to secure an assignment to the State of any rights to support on behalf of each child receiving foster care maintenance payments under this part [42 USCS §§ 670 et seq.];

(18) not later than January 1, 1997, provides that neither the State nor any other entity in the State that receives funds from the Federal Government and is involved in adoption or foster care placements may—

(A) deny to any person the opportunity to become an adoptive or a foster parent, on the basis of the race, color, or national origin of the person, or of the child, involved; or

(B) delay or deny the placement of a child for adoption or into foster care, on the basis of the race, color, or national origin of the adoptive or foster parent, or the child, involved;

(19) provides that the State shall consider giving preference to an adult relative over a non-related caregiver when determining a placement for a child, provided that the relative caregiver meets all relevant State child protection standards;

(20)(A) provides procedures for criminal records checks, including fingerprint-based checks of national crime information databases (as defined in section 534(e)(3)(A) of title 28, United States Code [28 USCS § 534(e)(3)(A)]), for any prospective foster or adoptive parent before the foster or adoptive parent may be finally approved for placement of a child regardless of whether foster care maintenance payments or adoption assistance payments are to be made on behalf of the child under the State plan under this part [42 USCS §§ 670 et seq.], including procedures requiring that—

(i) in any case involving a child on whose behalf such payments are to be so made in which a record check reveals a felony conviction for child abuse or neglect, for spousal abuse, for a crime against children (including child pornography), or for a crime involving violence, including rape, sexual assault, or homicide, but not including other physical assault or battery, if a State finds that a court of competent jurisdiction has determined that the felony was committed at any time, such final approval shall not be granted; and

(ii) in any case involving a child on whose behalf such payments are to be so made in which a record check reveals a felony conviction for physical assault, battery, or a drug-related offense, if a State finds that a court of competent jurisdiction has determined that the felony was committed within the past 5 years, such final approval shall not be granted; and

(B) provides that the State shall—

(i) check any child abuse and neglect registry maintained by the State for information on any prospective foster or adoptive parent and on any other adult living in the home of such a prospective parent, and request any other State in which any such prospective parent or other adult has resided in the preceding 5 years, to enable the State to check any child abuse and neglect registry maintained by such other State for such information, before the prospective foster or adoptive parent may be finally approved for placement of a child, regardless of whether foster care maintenance payments or adoption assistance payments are to be made on behalf of the child under the State plan under this part [42 USCS §§ 670 et seq.];

(ii) comply with any request described in clause (i) that is received from another State; and

(iii) have in place safeguards to prevent the unauthorized disclosure of information in any child abuse and neglect registry maintained by the State; and to prevent any such information obtained pursuant to this subparagraph from being used for a purpose other than the conducting of background checks in foster or adoptive placement cases; and

(C) provides procedures for criminal records checks, including fingerprint-based checks of national crime information databases (as defined in section 534(e)(3)(A) of title 28, United States Code [28 USCS § 534(e)(3)(A)]), on any relative guardian, and for checks described in subparagraph (B) of this paragraph on any relative guardian and any other adult living in the home of any relative guardian, before the relative guardian may receive kinship guardianship assistance payments on behalf of the child under the State plan under this part [42 USCS §§ 670 et seq.];

(D) [Redesignated]

(21) provides for health insurance coverage (including, at State option, through the program under the State plan approved under title XIX [42 USCS §§ 1396 et seq.]) for any child who has been determined to be a child with special needs, for whom there is in effect an adoption assistance agreement (other than an agreement under this part [42 USCS §§ 670 et seq.]) between the State and an adoptive parent or parents, and who the State has determined cannot be placed with an adoptive parent or parents without medical assistance because such child has special needs for medical, mental health, or rehabilitative care, and that with respect to the provision of such health insurance coverage—

(A) such coverage may be provided through 1 or more State medical assistance programs;

(B) the State, in providing such coverage, shall ensure that the medical benefits, including mental health benefits, provided are of the same type and kind as those that would be provided for children by the State under title XIX [42 USCS §§ 1396 et seq.];

(C) in the event that the State provides such coverage through a State medical assistance program other than the program under title XIX [42 USCS §§ 1396 et seq.], and the State exceeds its funding for services under such other program, any such child shall be deemed to be receiving aid or assistance under the State plan under this part [42 USCS §§ 670 et seq.] for purposes of section 1902(a)(10)(A)(i)(I) [42 USCS § 1396a(a)(10)(A)(i)(I)]; and

(D) in determining cost-sharing requirements, the State shall take into consideration the circumstances of the adopting parent or parents and the needs of the child being adopted consistent, to the extent coverage is provided through a State medical assistance program, with the rules under such program;

(22) provides that, not later than January 1, 1999, the State shall develop and implement standards to ensure that children in foster care placements in public or private agencies are provided quality services that protect the safety and health of the children;

(23) provides that the State shall not—

(A) deny or delay the placement of a child for adoption when an approved family is available outside of the jurisdiction with responsibility for handling the case of the child; or

(B) fail to grant an opportunity for a fair hearing, as described in paragraph (12), to an individual whose allegation of a violation of subparagraph (A) of this paragraph is denied by the State or not acted upon by the State with reasonable promptness;

(24) include [includes] a certification that, before a child in foster care under the responsibility of the State is placed with prospective foster parents, the prospective foster parents will be prepared adequately with the appropriate knowledge and skills to provide for the needs of the child, and that such preparation will be continued, as necessary, after the placement of the child;

(25) provide [provides] that the State shall have in effect procedures for the orderly and timely interstate placement of children; and procedures implemented in accordance with an interstate compact, if incorporating with the procedures prescribed by paragraph (26), shall be considered to satisfy the requirement of this paragraph;

(26) provides that—

(A)(i) within 60 days after the State receives from another State a request to conduct a study of a home environment for purposes of assessing the safety and suitability of placing a child in the home, the State shall, directly or by contract—

(I) conduct and complete the study; and

(II) return to the other State a report on the results of the study, which shall address the extent to which placement in the home would meet the needs of the child; and

(ii) in the case of a home study begun on or before September 30, 2008, if the State fails to comply with clause (i) within the 60-day period as a result of circumstances beyond the control of the State (such as a failure by a Federal agency to provide the results of a background check, or the failure by any entity to provide completed medical forms, requested by the State at least 45 days before the end of the 60-day period), the State shall have 75 days to comply with clause (i) if the State documents the circumstances involved and certifies that completing the home study is in the best interests of the child; except that

(iii) this subparagraph shall not be construed to require the State to have completed, within the applicable period, the parts of the home study involving the education and training of the prospective foster or adoptive parents;

(B) the State shall treat any report described in subparagraph (A) that is received from another State or an Indian tribe (or from a private agency under contract with another State) as meeting any requirements imposed by the State for the completion of a home study before placing a child in the home, unless, within 14 days after receipt of the report, the State determines, based on grounds that are specific to the content of the report, that making a decision in reliance on the report would be contrary to the welfare of the child; and

(C) the State shall not impose any restriction on the ability of a State agency administering, or supervising the administration of, a State program operated under a State plan approved under this part [42 USCS §§ 670 et seq.] to contract with a private agency for the conduct of a home study described in subparagraph (A);

(27) provides that, with respect to any child in foster care under the responsibility of the State under this part or part B [42 USCS §§ 670 et seq. or 621 et seq.] and without regard to whether foster care maintenance payments are made under section 472 [42 USCS § 672] on behalf of the child, the State has in effect procedures for verifying the citizenship or immigration status of the child;

(28) at the option of the State, provides for the State to enter into kinship guardianship assistance agreements to provide kinship guardianship assistance payments on behalf of children to grandparents and other relatives who have assumed legal guardianship of the children for whom they have cared as foster parents and for whom they have committed to care on a permanent basis, as provided in section 473(d) [42 USCS § 673(d)];

(29) provides that, within 30 days after the removal of a child from the custody of the parent or parents of the child, the State shall exercise due diligence to identify and provide notice to all adult grandparents and other adult relatives of the child (including any other adult relatives suggested by the parents), subject to exceptions due to family or domestic violence, that—

(A) specifies that the child has been or is being removed from the custody of the parent or parents of the child;

(B) explains the options the relative has under Federal, State, and local law to participate in the care and placement of the child, including any options that may be lost by failing to respond to the notice;

(C) describes the requirements under paragraph (10) of this subsection to become a foster family home and the additional services and supports that are available for children placed in such a home; and

(D) if the State has elected the option to make kinship guardianship assistance payments under paragraph (28) of this subsection, describes how the relative guardian of the child may subsequently enter into an agreement with the State under section 473(d) [42 USCS § 673(d)] to receive the payments;

(30) provides assurances that each child who has attained the minimum age for compulsory school attendance under State law and with respect to whom there is eligibility for a payment under the State plan is a full-time elementary or secondary school student or has completed secondary school, and for purposes of this paragraph, the term "elementary or secondary school student" means, with respect to a child, that the child is—

(A) enrolled (or in the process of enrolling) in an institution which provides elementary or secondary education, as determined under the law of the State or other jurisdiction in which the institution is located;

(B) instructed in elementary or secondary education at home in accordance with a home school law of the State or other jurisdiction in which the home is located;

(C) in an independent study elementary or secondary education program in accordance with the law of the State or other jurisdiction in which the program is located, which is administered by the local school or school district; or

(D) incapable of attending school on a full-time basis due to the medical condition of the child, which incapability is supported by regularly updated information in the case plan of the child;

(31) provides that reasonable efforts shall be made—

(A) to place siblings removed from their home in the same foster care, kinship guardianship, or adoptive placement, unless the State documents that such a joint placement would be contrary to the safety or well-being of any of the siblings; and

(B) in the case of siblings removed from their home who are not so jointly placed, to provide for frequent visitation or other ongoing interaction between the siblings, unless that State documents that frequent visitation or other ongoing interaction would be contrary to the safety or well-being of any of the siblings;

(32) provides that the State will negotiate in good faith with any Indian tribe, tribal organization or tribal consortium in the State that requests to develop an agreement with the State to administer all or part of the program under this part [42 USCS §§ 670 et seq.] on

behalf of Indian children who are under the authority of the tribe, organization, or consortium, including foster care maintenance payments on behalf of children who are placed in State or tribally licensed foster family homes, adoption assistance payments, and, if the State has elected to provide such payments, kinship guardianship assistance payments under section 473(d) [42 USCS § 673(d)], and tribal access to resources for administration, training, and data collection under this part [42 USCS §§ 670 et seq.]; and

(33) provides that the State will inform any individual who is adopting, or whom the State is made aware is considering adopting, a child who is in foster care under the responsibility of the State of the potential eligibility of the individual for a Federal tax credit under section 23 of the Internal Revenue Code of 1986 [26 USCS § 23].

(b) Approval of plan by Secretary. The Secretary shall approve any plan which complies with the provisions of subsection (a) of this section.

(c) Use of child welfare records in State court proceedings. Subsection (a)(8) shall not be construed to limit the flexibility of a State in determining State policies relating to public access to court proceedings to determine child abuse and neglect or other court hearings held pursuant to part B or this part [42 USCS §§ 620 et seq. or 670 et seq.], except that such policies shall, at a minimum, ensure the safety and well-being of the child, parents, and family.

(Aug. 14, 1935, ch 531, Title IV, Part E, § 471, as added June 17, 1980, P. L. 96-272, Title I, § 101(a)(1), 94 Stat. 501; Aug. 13, 1981, P. L. 97-35, Title XXIII, Subtitle C, § 2353(r), 95 Stat. 874; Sept. 3, 1982, P. L. 97-248, Title I, Subtitle D, § 160(d), 96 Stat. 400; Aug. 16, 1984, P. L. 98-378, § 11(c), 98 Stat. 1318; Oct. 22, 1986, P. L. 99-514, Title XVII, § 1711(c)(2), 100 Stat. 2784; Oct. 13, 1988, P. L. 100-485, Title II, § 202(c)(1), 102 Stat. 2378; Nov. 5, 1990, P. L. 101-508, Title V, Subtitle A, Ch 4, § 5054, 104 Stat. 1388-229; Aug. 10, 1993, P. L. 103-66, Title XIII, Ch 2, Subch C, Part I, § 13711(b)(4), 107 Stat. 655; Oct. 31, 1994, P. L. 103-432, Title II, Subtitle A, § 203(b), 108 Stat. 4456; Aug. 20, 1996, P. L. 104-188, Title I, Subtitle H, § 1808(a), 110 Stat. 1903; Aug. 22, 1996, P. L. 104-193, Title I, § 108(d)(2), Title V, § 505, 110 Stat. 2166, 2278; Aug. 5, 1997, P. L. 105-33, Title V, Subtitle F, Ch 5, § 5591(b), 111 Stat. 643; Nov. 19, 1997, P. L. 105-89, Title I, §§ 101(a), 106, Title III, §§ 306, 308, 111 Stat. 2116, 2120, 2132, 2133; July 16, 1998, P. L. 105-200, Title III, § 301(a), 112 Stat. 658; Dec. 14, 1999, P. L. 106-169, Title I, Subtitle B, § 112(a), Title IV, § 401(o), 113 Stat. 1829, 1859; Feb. 8, 2006, P. L. 109-171, Title VII, Subtitle D, § 7401(c), 120 Stat. 150; July 3, 2006, P. L. 109-239, §§ 3, 4(a)(1), 10, 120 Stat. 508, 513; July 27, 2006, P. L. 109-248, Title I, Subtitle C, § 152(a), (b), 120 Stat. 608; Dec. 20, 2006, P. L. 109-432, Div B, Title IV, § 405(c)(1)(B)(i), 120 Stat. 2999; Oct. 7, 2008, P. L. 110-351, Title I, §§ 101(a), (c)(2), 103, 104(a), Title II, §§ 204(b), 206, Title III, § 301(c)(1)(A), Title IV, § 403, 122 Stat. 3950, 3951, 3956, 3957, 3960, 3962, 3969, 3979; March 23, 2010, P. L. 111-148, Title VI, Subtitle H, § 6703(d)(2)(B), 124 Stat. 803.)

§ 672. Foster care maintenance payments program [Caution: See prospective amendment note below.]

(a) In general. (1) Eligibility. Each State with a plan approved under this part shall make foster care maintenance payments on behalf of each child who has been removed from the home of a relative specified in section 406(a) [42 USCS § 606(a)] (as in effect on July 16, 1996) into foster care if—

(A) the removal and foster care placement met, and the placement continues to meet, the requirements of paragraph (2); and

(B) the child, while in the home, would have met the AFDC eligibility requirement of paragraph (3).

(2) Removal and foster care placement requirements. The removal and foster care placement of a child meet the requirements of this paragraph if—

(A) the removal and foster care placement are in accordance with—

(i) a voluntary placement agreement entered into by a parent or legal guardian of the child who is the relative referred to in paragraph (1); or

(ii) a judicial determination to the effect that continuation in the home from which removed would be contrary to the welfare of the child and that reasonable efforts of the type described in section 471(a)(15) [42 USCS § 671(a)(15)] for a child have been made;

(B) the child's placement and care are the responsibility of—

(i) the State agency administering the State plan approved under section 471 [42 USCS § 671];

(ii) any other public agency with which the State agency administering or supervising the administration of the State plan has made an agreement which is in effect; or

(iii) an Indian tribe or a tribal organization

(as defined in section 479B(a) [42 USCS § 679c(a)]) or a tribal consortium that has a plan approved under section 471 [42 USCS § 671] in accordance with section 479B [42 USCS § 679c]; and

(C) the child has been placed in a foster family home or child-care institution.

(3) AFDC eligibility requirement. (A) In general. A child in the home referred to in paragraph (1) would have met the AFDC eligibility requirement of this paragraph if the child—

(i) would have received aid under the State plan approved under section 402 [42 USCS § 602] (as in effect on July 16, 1996) in the home, in or for the month in which the agreement was entered into or court proceedings leading to the determination referred to in paragraph (2)(A)(ii) of this subsection were initiated; or

(ii)(I) would have received the aid in the home, in or for the month referred to in clause (i), if application had been made therefor; or

(II) had been living in the home within 6 months before the month in which the agreement was entered into or the proceedings were initiated, and would have received the aid in or for such month, if, in such month, the child had been living in the home with the relative referred to in paragraph (1) and application for the aid had been made.

(B) Resources determination. For purposes of subparagraph (A), in determining whether a child would have received aid under a State plan approved under section 402 [42 USCS § 602] (as in effect on July 16, 1996), a child whose resources (determined pursuant to section 402(a)(7)(B) [42 USCS § 602(a)(7)(B)], as so in effect) have a combined value of not more than $10,000 shall be considered a child whose resources have a combined value of not more than $1,000 (or such lower amount as the State may determine for purposes of section 402(a)(7)(B) [42 USCS § 602(a)(7)(B)]).

(4) Eligibility of certain alien children. Subject to title IV of the Personal Responsibility and Work Opportunity Reconciliation Act of 1996, if the child is an alien disqualified under section 245A(h) or 210(f) of the Immigration and Nationality Act [8 USCS § 1255a(h) or 1160(f)] from receiving aid under the State plan approved under section 402 [42 USCS § 602] in or for the month in which the agreement described in paragraph (2)(A)(i) was entered into or court proceedings leading to the determination described in paragraph (2)(A)(ii) were initiated, the child shall be considered to satisfy the requirements of paragraph (3), with respect to the month, if the child would have satisfied the requirements but for the disqualification.

(b) Additional qualifications. Foster care maintenance payments may be made under this part [42 USCS §§ 670 et seq.] only on behalf of a child described in subsection (a) of this section who is—

(1) in the foster family home of an individual, whether the payments therefor are made to such individual or to a public or private child-placement or child-agency, or

(2) in a child-care institution, whether the payments therefor are made to such institution or to a public or private child-placement or child-care agency, which payments shall be limited so as to include in such payments only those items which are included in the term "foster care maintenance payments" (as defined in section 475(4) [42 USCS § 675(4)]).

(c) "Foster family home" and "child-care institution" defined. For the purposes of this part [42 USCS § 670 et seq.], (1) the term "foster family home" means a foster family home for children which is licensed by the State in which it is situated or has been approved, by the agency of such State having responsibility for licensing homes of this type, as meeting the standards established for such licensing; and (2) the term "child-care institution" means a private child-care institution, or a public child-care institution which accommodates no more than twenty-five children, which is licensed by the State in which it is situated or has been approved, by the agency of such State responsible for licensing or approval of institutions of this type, as meeting the standards established for such licensing, but the term shall not include detention facilities, forestry camps, training schools, or any other facility operated primarily for the detention of children who are determined to be delinquent.

(d) Children removed from their homes pursuant to voluntary placement agreements. Notwithstanding any other provision of this title [42 USCS §§ 601 et seq.], Federal payments may be made under this part [42 USCS §§ 671 et seq.] with respect to amounts expended by any State as foster care maintenance payments under this section, in the case of children removed from their homes pursuant to voluntary placement agreements as described in subsection (a), only if (at the time such amounts were expended) the State has fulfilled all of the requirements of section 422(b)(8) [42 USCS § 622(b)(8)].

(e) Placements in best interests of child. No Federal payment may be made under this part [42 USCS §§ 670 et seq.] with respect to amounts expended by any State as foster care maintenance payments under this section, in the case of any child who was removed from his or her home pursuant to a voluntary placement agreement as described in subsection (a) and has remained in voluntary placement for a period in excess of 180 days, unless there has been a judicial determination by a court of competent jurisdiction (within the first 180 days of such placement) to the effect that such placement is in the best interests of the child.

(f) "Voluntary placement" and "voluntary placement agreement" defined. For the purposes of this part [42 USCS §§ 670 et seq.] and part B of this title [42 USCS §§ 620 et seq.], (1) the term "voluntary placement" means an out-of-home placement of a minor, by or with participation of a State agency, after the parents or guardians of the minor have requested the assistance of the agency and signed a voluntary placement agreement; and (2) the term "voluntary placement agreement" means a written agreement, binding on the parties to the agreement, between the State agency, any other agency acting on its behalf, and the parents or guardians of a minor child which specifies, at a minimum, the legal status of the child and the rights and obligations of the parents or guardians, the child, and the agency while the child is in placement.

(g) Revocation of voluntary placement agreement. In any case where—

(1) the placement of a minor child in foster care occurred pursuant to a voluntary placement agreement entered into by the parents or guardians of such child as provided in subsection (a), and

(2) such parents or guardians request (in such manner and form as the Secretary may prescribe) that the child be returned to their home or to the home of a relative,

the voluntary placement agreement shall be deemed to be revoked unless the State agency opposes such request and obtains a judicial determination, by a court of competent jurisdiction, that the return of the child to such home would be contrary to the child's best interests.

(h) Aid for dependent children; assistance for minor children in needy families. (1) For purposes of title XIX [42 USCS §§ 1396 et seq.], any child with respect to whom foster care maintenance payments are made under this section is deemed to be a dependent child as defined in section 406 (as in effect as of July 16, 1996) and deemed to be a recipient of aid to families with dependent children under part A of this title (as so in effect). For purposes of subtitle 1 of title XX [42 USCS §§ 1397 et seq.], any child with respect to whom foster care maintenance payments are made under this section is deemed to be a minor child in a needy family under a State program funded under part A of this title [42 USCS §§ 601 et seq.] and is deemed to be a recipient of assistance under such part.

(2) For purposes of paragraph (1), a child whose costs in a foster family home or child care institution are covered by the foster care maintenance payments being made with respect to the child's minor parent, as provided in section 475(4)(B) [42 USCS § 675(4)(B)], shall be considered a child with respect to whom foster care maintenance payments are made under this section.

(i) Administrative costs associated with otherwise eligible children not in licensed foster care settings. Expenditures by a State that would be considered administrative expenditures for purposes of section 474(a)(3) [42 USCS § 674(a)(3)] if made with respect to a child who was residing in a foster family home or child-care institution shall be so considered with respect to a child not residing in such a home or institution—

(1) in the case of a child who has been removed in accordance with subsection (a) of this section from the home of a relative specified in section 406(a) [42 USCS § 606(a)] (as in effect on July 16, 1996), only for expenditures—

(A) with respect to a period of not more than the lesser of 12 months or the average length of time it takes for the State to license or approve a home as a foster home, in which the child is in the home of a relative and an application is pending for licensing or approval of the home as a foster family home; or

(B) with respect to a period of not more than 1 calendar month when a child moves from a facility not eligible for payments under this part into a foster family home or child care institution licensed or approved by the State; and

(2) in the case of any other child who is potentially eligible for benefits under a State plan approved under this part and at imminent risk of removal from the home, only if—

(A) reasonable efforts are being made in accordance with section 471(a)(15) [42 USCS § 671(a)(15)] to prevent the need for, or if necessary to pursue, removal of the child from the home; and

(B) the State agency has made, not less often than every 6 months, a determination (or redetermination) as to whether the child remains at imminent risk of removal from the home.

(Aug. 14, 1935, ch 531, Title IV, Part E, § 472, as added June 17, 1980, P. L. 96-272, Title I, § 101(a)(1), 94 Stat. 503; June 17, 1980, P. L. 96-272, Title I, § 102(a)(1) in part, (2), 94 Stat. 513, 514; Nov. 6, 1986, P. L. 99-603, Title II, § 201(b)(2)(A), Title III, §§ 302(b)(2), 303(e)(2), 100 Stat. 3403, 3422, 3431; Dec. 22, 1987, P. L. 100-203, Title IX, Subtitle B, Part 2, §§ 9133(b)(2), 9139(a), 101 Stat. 1330-314, 321; Oct. 31, 1994, P. L. 103-432, Title II, Subtitle A, § 202(d)(3), 108 Stat. 4454; Aug. 22, 1996, P. L. 104-193, Title I, § 108(d)(3), (4), Title V, § 501, 110 Stat. 2166, 2277; Aug. 5, 1997, P. L. 105-33, Title V, Subtitle F, Ch 1, § 5513(b)(1), (2), Ch 5, § 5592(b), 111 Stat. 620, 644; Nov. 19, 1997, P. L. 105-89, Title I, § 101(c), 111 Stat. 2117; Dec. 14, 1999, P. L. 106-169, Title I, Subtitle B, § 111, 113 Stat. 1829; Nov. 22, 2005, P. L. 109-113, § 2, 119 Stat. 2371; Feb. 8, 2006, P. L. 109-171, Title VII, Subtitle D, §§ 7403(a), 7404(a), 120 Stat. 151; Sept. 28, 2006, P. L. 109-288, § 6(f)(6), 120 Stat. 1247; Oct. 7, 2008, P. L. 110-351, Title II, § 201(b), Title III, § 301(a)(2), 122 Stat. 3958, 3967; March 23, 2010, P. L. 111-148, Title VI, Subtitle H, § 6703(d)(2)(B), 124 Stat. 803.)

HISTORY; ANCILLARY LAWS AND DIRECTIVES

Prospective amendments:

Amendment of subsec. (c)(2), effective on October 1, 2010. Act Oct. 7, 2008, P. L. 110-351 Title II, § 201(b), 122 Stat. 3958 (effective on 10/1/2010, as provided by § 201(d) of such Act, which appears as a note to this section), provides: "Section 472(c)(2) of such Act (42 U.S.C. 672(c)(2)) is amended by inserting 'except, in the case of a child who has attained 18 years of age, the term shall include a supervised setting in which the individual is living independently, in accordance with such conditions as the Secretary shall establish in regulations,' before 'but'.".

§ 673. Adoption and guardianship assistance program [Caution: See prospective amendment note below.]

(a) Agreements with adoptive parents of children with special needs; State payments; qualifying children; amount of payments; changes in circumstances; placements period prior to adoption; nonrecurring adoption expenses. (1)(A) Each State having a plan approved under this part shall enter into adoption assistance agreements (as defined in section 475(3) [42 USCS § 675(3)]) with the adoptive parents of children with special needs.

(B) Under any adoption assistance agreement entered into by a State with parents who adopt a child with special needs, the State—

(i) shall make payments of nonrecurring adoption expenses incurred by or on behalf of such parents in connection with the adoption of such child, directly through the State agency or through another public or nonprofit private agency, in amounts determined under paragraph (3), and

(ii) in any case where the child meets the requirements of paragraph (2), may make adoption assistance payments to such parents, directly through the State agency or through another public or nonprofit private agency, in amounts so determined.

(2)(A) For purposes of paragraph (1)(B)(ii), a child meets the requirements of this paragraph if—

(i) in the case of a child who is not an applicable child for the fiscal year (as defined in subsection (e)), the child—

(I)(aa) was removed from the home of a relative specified in section 406(a) [42 USCS § 606(a)] (as in effect on July 16, 1996) and placed in foster care in accordance with a voluntary placement agreement with respect to which Federal payments are provided under section 474 [42 USCS § 674] (or section 403 [42 USCS § 603], as such section was in effect on July 16, 1996), or in accordance with a judicial determination to the effect that continuation in the home would be contrary to the welfare of the child; and met the requirements of section 472(a)(3) [42 USCS § 672(a)(3)] with respect to the home referred to in subitem (AA) of this item;

(bb) meets all of the requirements of title XVI [42 USCS §§ 1381 et seq.] with respect to eligibility for supplemental security income benefits; or

(cc) is a child whose costs in a foster family home or child-care institution are covered by the foster care maintenance payments being made with respect to the minor parent of the child as provided in section 475(4)(B) [42 USCS § 675(4)(B)]; and

(II) has been determined by the State, pursuant to subsection (c)(1) of this section, to be a child with special needs; or

(ii) in the case of a child who is an applicable child for the fiscal year (as so defined), the child—

(I)(aa) at the time of initiation of adoption proceedings was in the care of a public or licensed private child placement agency or Indian tribal organization pursuant to— an involuntary removal of the child from the home in accordance with a judicial determination to the effect that continuation in the home would be contrary to the welfare of the child; or a voluntary placement agreement or voluntary relinquishment;

(bb) meets all medical or disability requirements of title XVI [42 USCS § 1381 et seq.] with respect to eligibility for supplemental security income benefits; or

(cc) was residing in a foster family home or child care institution with the child's minor parent, and the child's minor parent was in such foster family home or child care institution pursuant to— an involuntary removal of the child from the home in accordance with a judicial determination to the effect that continuation in the home would be contrary to the welfare of the child; or a voluntary placement agreement or voluntary relinquishment; and

(II) has been determined by the State, pursuant to subsection (c)(2), to be a child with special needs.

(B) Section 472(a)(4) [42 USCS § 672(a)(4)] shall apply for purposes of subparagraph (A) of this paragraph, in any case in which the child is an alien described in such section.

(C) A child shall be treated as meeting the requirements of this paragraph for the purpose of paragraph (1)(B)(ii) if—

(i) in the case of a child who is not an applicable child for the fiscal year (as defined in subsection (e)), the child—

(I) meets the requirements of subparagraph (A)(i)(II);

(II) was determined eligible for adoption assistance payments under this part [42 USCS §§ 670 et seq.] with respect to a prior adoption;

(III) is available for adoption because—

(aa) the prior adoption has been dissolved, and the parental rights of the adoptive parents have been terminated; or

(bb) the child's adoptive parents have died; and

(IV) fails to meet the requirements of subparagraph (A)(i) but would meet such requirements if—

(aa) the child were treated as if the child were in the same financial and other circumstances the child was in the last time the child was determined eligible for adoption assistance payments under this part [42 USCS §§ 670 et seq.]; and

(bb) the prior adoption were treated as never having occurred; or

(ii) in the case of a child who is an applicable child for the fiscal year (as so defined), the child meets the requirements of subparagraph (A)(ii)(II), is determined eligible for adoption assistance payments under this part [42 USCS §§ 670 et seq.] with respect to a prior adoption (or who would have been determined eligible for such payments had the Adoption and Safe Families Act of 1997 been in effect at the time that such determination would have been made), and is available for adoption because the prior adoption has been dissolved and the parental rights of the adoptive parents have been terminated or because the child's adoptive parents have died.

(D) In determining the eligibility for adoption assistance payments of a child in a legal guardianship arrangement described in section 471(a)(28) [42 USCS § 671(a)(28)], the placement of the child with the relative guardian involved and any kinship guardianship assistance payments made on behalf of the child shall be considered never to have been made.

(3) The amount of the payments to be made in any case under clauses (i) and (ii) of paragraph (1)(B) shall be determined through agreement between the adoptive parents and the State or local agency administering the program under this section, which shall take into consideration the circumstances of the adopting parents and the needs of the child being adopted, and may be readjusted periodically, with the concurrence of the adopting parents (which may be specified in the adoption assistance agreement), depending upon changes in such circumstances. However, in no case may the amount of the adoption assistance payment made under clause (ii) of paragraph (1)(B) exceed the foster care maintenance payment which would have been paid during the period if the child with respect to whom the adoption assistance payment is made had been in a foster family home.

(4) Notwithstanding the preceding paragraph, (A) no payment may be made to parents with respect to any child who has attained the age of eighteen (or, where the State determines that the child has a mental or physical handicap which warrants the continuation of assistance, the age of twenty-one), and (B) no payment may be made to parents with respect to any child if the State determines that the parents are no longer legally responsible for the support of the child or if the State determines that the child is no longer receiving any support from such parents. Parents who have been receiving adoption assistance payments under this section shall keep the State or local agency administering the program under this section informed of circumstances which would, pursuant to this subsection, make them ineligible for such assistance payments, or eligible for assistance payments in a different amount.

(5) For purposes of this part [42 USCS §§ 670 et seq.], individuals with whom a child

(who has been determined by the State, pursuant to subsection (c), to be a child with special needs) is placed for adoption in accordance with applicable State and local law shall be eligible for such payments, during the period of the placement, on the same terms and subject to the same conditions as if such individuals had adopted such child.

(6)(A) For purposes of paragraph (1)(B)(i), the term "nonrecurring adoption expenses" means reasonable and necessary adoption fees, court costs, attorney fees, and other expenses which are directly related to the legal adoption of a child with special needs and which are not incurred in violation of State or Federal law.

(B) A State's payment of nonrecurring adoption expenses under an adoption assistance agreement shall be treated as an expenditure made for the proper and efficient administration of the State plan for purposes of section 474(a)(3)(E) [42 USCS § 674(a)(3)(E)].

(7)(A) Notwithstanding any other provision of this subsection, no payment may be made to parents with respect to any applicable child for a fiscal year that—

(i) would be considered a child with special needs under subsection (c)(2);

(ii) is not a citizen or resident of the United States; and

(iii) was adopted outside of the United States or was brought into the United States for the purpose of being adopted.

(B) Subparagraph (A) shall not be construed as prohibiting payments under this part [42 USCS §§ 670 et seq.] for an applicable child described in subparagraph (A) that is placed in foster care subsequent to the failure, as determined by the State, of the initial adoption of the child by the parents described in subparagraph (A).

(8) A State shall spend an amount equal to the amount of savings (if any) in State expenditures under this part [42 USCS §§ 670 et seq.] resulting from the application of paragraph (2)(A)(ii) to all applicable children for a fiscal year to provide to children or families any service (including post-adoption services) that may be provided under this part [42 USCS §§ 670 et seq.] or part B [42 USCS §§ 621 et seq.].

(b) Aid for dependent children; assistance for minor children in needy families. (1) For purposes of title XIX [42 USCS §§ 1396 et seq.], any child who is described in paragraph (3) is deemed to be a dependent child as defined in section 406 [former 42 USCS § 606] (as in effect as of July 16, 1996) and deemed to be a recipient of aid to families with dependent children under part A of this title [former 42 USCS §§ 601 et seq.] (as so in effect) in the State where such child resides.

(2) For purposes of subtitle 1 of title XX [42 USCS §§ 1397 et seq.], any child who is described in paragraph (3) is deemed to be a minor child in a needy family under a State program funded under part A of this title [42 USCS §§ 601 et seq.] and deemed to be a recipient of assistance under such part.

(3) A child described in this paragraph is any child—

(A)(i) who is a child described in subsection (a)(2), and

(ii) with respect to whom an adoption assistance agreement is in effect under this section (whether or not adoption assistance payments are provided under the agreement or are being made under this section), including any such child who has been placed for adoption in accordance with applicable State and local law (whether or not an interlocutory or other judicial decree of adoption has been issued),

(B) with respect to whom foster care maintenance payments are being made under section 472 [42 USCS § 672], or

(C) with respect to whom kinship guardianship assistance payments are being made pursuant to subsection (d).

(4) For purposes of paragraphs (1) and (2), a child whose costs in a foster family home or child-care institution are covered by the foster care maintenance payments being made with respect to the child's minor parent, as provided in section 475(4)(B) [42 USCS § 675(4)(B)], shall be considered a child with respect to whom foster care maintenance payments are being made under section 472 [42 USCS § 672].

(c) Children with special needs. For purposes of this section—

(1) in the case of a child who is not an applicable child for a fiscal year, the child shall not be considered a child with special needs unless—

(A) the State has determined that the child cannot or should not be returned to the home of his parents; and

(B) the State had first determined (A) that there exists with respect to the child a specific factor or condition (such as his ethnic background, age, or membership in a minority or sibling group, or the presence of factors such as medical conditions or physical, mental, or emotional handicaps) because of which it is reasonable to conclude that such child cannot be placed with adoptive parents without providing adoption assistance under this section or medical assistance under title XIX [42 USCS §§ 1396 et seq.], and (B) that, except where it would be against the best interests of the child because of such factors as the existence of significant emotional ties with prospective adoptive parents while in the care of such parents as a foster child, a reasonable, but unsuccessful, effort has been made to place the child with appropriate adoptive parents without providing adoption assistance under this section or medical assistance under title XIX [42 USCS §§ 1396 et seq.]; or

(2) in the case of a child who is an applicable child for a fiscal year, the child shall not be considered a child with special needs unless—

(A) the State has determined, pursuant to a criterion or criteria established by the State, that the child cannot or should not be returned to the home of his parents;

(B)(i) the State has determined that there exists with respect to the child a specific factor or condition (such as ethnic background, age, or membership in a minority or sibling group, or the presence of factors such as medical conditions or physical, mental, or emotional handicaps) because of which it is reasonable to conclude that the child cannot be placed with adoptive parents without providing adoption assistance under this section and medical assistance under title XIX [42 USCS §§ 1396 et seq.]; or

(ii) the child meets all medical or disability requirements of title XVI [42 USCS §§ 1381 et seq.] with respect to eligibility for supplemental security income benefits; and

(C) the State has determined that, except where it would be against the best interests of the child because of such factors as the existence of significant emotional ties with prospective adoptive parents while in the care of the parents as a foster child, a reasonable, but unsuccessful, effort has been made to place the child with appropriate adoptive parents without providing adoption assistance under this section or medical assistance under title XIX [42 USCS §§ 1396 et seq.].

(d) Kinship guardianship assistance payments for children. (1) Kinship guardianship assistance agreement. (A) In general. In order to receive payments under section 474(a)(5) [42 USCS § 674(a)(5)], a State shall—

(i) negotiate and enter into a written, binding kinship guardianship assistance agreement with the prospective relative guardian of a child who meets the requirements of this paragraph; and

(ii) provide the prospective relative guardian with a copy of the agreement.

(B) Minimum requirements. The agreement shall specify, at a minimum—

(i) the amount of, and manner in which, each kinship guardianship assistance payment will be provided under the agreement, and the manner in which the payment may be adjusted periodically, in consultation with the relative guardian, based on the circumstances of the relative guardian and the needs of the child;

(ii) the additional services and assistance that the child and relative guardian will be eligible for under the agreement;

(iii) the procedure by which the relative guardian may apply for additional services as needed; and

(iv) subject to subparagraph (D), that the State will pay the total cost of nonrecurring expenses associated with obtaining legal guardianship of the child, to the extent the total cost does not exceed $2,000.

(C) Interstate applicability. The agreement shall provide that the agreement shall remain in effect without regard to the State residency of the relative guardian.

(D) No effect on Federal reimbursement. Nothing in subparagraph (B)(iv) shall be construed as affecting the ability of the State to obtain reimbursement from the Federal Government for costs described in that subparagraph.

(2) Limitations on amount of kinship guardianship assistance payment. A kinship guardianship assistance payment on behalf of a child shall not exceed the foster care maintenance payment which would have been paid on behalf of the child if the child had remained in a foster family home.

(3) Child's eligibility for a kinship guardianship assistance payment. (A) In general. A child is eligible for a kinship guardianship assistance payment under this subsection if the State agency determines the following:

(i) The child has been—

(I) removed from his or her home pursuant to a voluntary placement agreement or as a result of a judicial determination to the effect that continuation in the home would be contrary to the welfare of the child; and

(II) eligible for foster care maintenance payments under section 472 [42 USCS § 672] while residing for at least 6 consecutive months in the home of the prospective relative guardian.

(ii) Being returned home or adopted are not appropriate permanency options for the child.

(iii) The child demonstrates a strong attachment to the prospective relative guardian and the relative guardian has a strong commitment to caring permanently for the child.

(iv) With respect to a child who has attained 14 years of age, the child has been consulted regarding the kinship guardianship arrangement.

(B) Treatment of siblings. With respect to a child described in subparagraph (A) whose sibling or siblings are not so described—

(i) the child and any sibling of the child may be placed in the same kinship guardianship arrangement, in accordance with section 471(a)(31) [42 USCS § 671(a)(31)], if the State agency and the relative agree on the appropriateness of the arrangement for the siblings; and

(ii) kinship guardianship assistance payments may be paid on behalf of each sibling so placed.

(e) Applicable child defined. (1) On the basis of age. (A) In general. Subject to paragraphs (2) and (3), in this section, the term "applicable child" means a child for whom an adoption assistance agreement is entered into under this section during any fiscal year described in subparagraph (B) if the child attained the applicable age for that fiscal year before the end of that fiscal year.

(B) Applicable age. For purposes of subparagraph (A), the applicable age for a fiscal year is as follows:

In the case of fiscal year:	The applicable age is:
2010	16
2011	14
2012	12
2013	10
2014	8
2015	6
2016	4
2017	2
2018 or thereafter	any age.

(2) Exception for duration in care. Notwithstanding paragraph (1) of this subsection, beginning with fiscal year 2010, such term shall include a child of any age on the date on which an adoption assistance agreement is entered into on behalf of the child under this section if the child—

(A) has been in foster care under the responsibility of the State for at least 60 consecutive months; and

(B) meets the requirements of subsection (a)(2)(A)(ii).

(3) Exception for member of a sibling group. Notwithstanding paragraphs (1) and (2) of this subsection, beginning with fiscal year 2010, such term shall include a child of any age on the date on which an adoption assistance agreement is entered into on behalf of the child under this section without regard to whether the child is described in paragraph (2)(A) of this subsection if the child—

(A) is a sibling of a child who is an applicable child for the fiscal year under paragraph (1) or (2) of this subsection;

(B) is to be placed in the same adoption placement as an applicable child for the fiscal year who is their sibling; and

(C) meets the requirements of subsection (a)(2)(A)(ii).

(Aug. 14, 1935, ch 531, Title IV, Part E, § 473, as added June 17, 1980, P. L. 96-272, Title I, §§ 101(a)(1), 94 Stat. 504; June 17, 1980, P. L. 96-272, Title I, § 102(a)(3), 94 Stat. 514; April 7, 1986, P. L. 99-272, Title XII, Subtitle C, § 12305(a), (b)(1), 100 Stat. 293; Oct. 22, 1986, P. L. 99-514, Title XVII, § 1711(a), (b), (c)(3)–(5), 100 Stat. 2783, 2784, Nov. 6, 1986, P. L. 99-603, Title II, § 201(b)(2)(B), 100 Stat. 3403; Dec. 22, 1987, P. L. 100-203, Title IX, Subtitle B, Part 2, §§ 9133(b), (3), (4), 9139(b), 101 Stat. 1330-314, 1330-321; Oct. 31, 1994, P. L. 103-432, Title II, Subtitle F, §§ 265(b), 266(a), 108 Stat. 4469; Aug. 22, 1996, P. L. 104-193, Title I, § 108(d)(5), (6), 110 Stat. 2167; Aug. 5, 1997, P. L. 105-33, Title V, Subtitle F, Ch 1, § 5513(b)(3), (4), 111 Stat. 620; Nov. 19, 1997, P. L. 105-89, Title III, § 307(a), 111 Stat. 2133; Feb. 8, 2006, P. L. 109-171, Title VII, Subtitle D, § 7404(b), 120 Stat. 153; Oct. 7, 2008, P. L. 110-351, Title I, § 101(b), (c)(1), (5), (f), Title II, § 201(c), Title IV, § 402, 122 Stat. 3950, 3953, 3958, 3975; March 23, 2010, P. L. 111-148, Title VI, Subtitle H, § 6703(d)(2)(B), 124 Stat. 803.)

HISTORY; ANCILLARY LAWS AND DIRECTIVES

Prospective amendments:

Amendment of subsec. (a)(4), effective on October 1, 2010. Act Oct. 7, 2008, P. L. 110-351, Title II, § 201(c), 122 Stat. 3958 (effective on 10/1/2010, as provided by § 201(d) of such Act, which appears as 42 USCS § 672 note), provides:

"Section 473(a)(4) of such Act (42 U.S.C. 673(a)(4)) is amended to read as follows:

" '(4) (A) Notwithstanding any other provision of this section, a payment may not be made pursuant to this section to parents or relative guardians with respect to a child—

" '(i) who has attained—

" '(I) 18 years of age, or such greater age as the State may elect under section 475(8)(B)(iii) [42 USCS § 675(8)(B)(iii)]; or

" '(II) 21 years of age, if the State determines that the child has a mental or physical handicap which warrants the continuation of assistance;

" '(ii) who has not attained 18 years of age, if the State determines that the parents or relative guardians, as the case may be, are no longer legally responsible for the support of the child; or

" '(iii) if the State determines that the child is no longer receiving any support from the parents or relative guardians, as the case may be.

" '(B) Parents or relative guardians who have been receiving adoption assistance payments or kinship guardianship assistance payments under this section shall keep the State or local agency administering the program under this section informed of circumstances which would, pursuant to this subsection, make them ineligible for the payments, or eligible for the payments in a different amount.'.".

§ 675. Definitions [Caution: See prospective amendment note below.]

As used in this part [42 USCS §§ 670 et seq.] or part B of this title [42 USCS §§ 620 et seq.]:

(1) The term "case plan" means a written document which includes at least the following:

(A) A description of the type of home or institution in which a child is to be placed, including a discussion of the safety and appropriateness of the placement and how the agency which is responsible for the child plans to carry out the voluntary placement agreement entered into or judicial determination made with respect to the child in accordance with section 472(a)(1) [42 USCS § 672(a)(1)].

(B) A plan for assuring that the child receives safe and proper care and that services are provided to the parents, child, and foster parents in order to improve the conditions in the parents' home, facilitate return of the child to his own safe home or the permanent placement of the child, and address the needs of the child while in foster care, including a discussion of the appropriateness of the services that have been provided to the child under the plan.

(C) The health and education records of the child, including the most recent information available regarding—

(i) the names and addresses of the child's health and educational providers;

(ii) the child's grade level performance;

(iii) the child's school record;

(iv) a record of the child's immunizations;

(v) the child's known medical problems;

(vi) the child's medications; and

(vii) any other relevant health and education information concerning the child determined to be appropriate by the State agency.

(viii) [Redesignated]

(D) Where appropriate, for a child age 16 or over, a written description of the programs and services which will help such child prepare for the transition from foster care to independent living.

(E) In the case of a child with respect to whom the permanency plan is adoption or placement in another permanent home, documentation of the steps the agency is taking to find an adoptive family or other permanent living arrangement for the child, to place the child with an adoptive family, a fit and willing relative, a legal guardian, or in another planned permanent living arrangement, and to finalize the adoption or legal guardianship. At a minimum, such documentation shall include child specific recruitment efforts such as the use of State, regional, and national adoption exchanges including electronic exchange systems to facilitate orderly and timely in-State and interstate placements.

(F) In the case of a child with respect to whom the permanency plan is placement with a relative and receipt of kinship guardianship assistance payments under section 473(d) [42 USCS § 673(d)], a description of—

(i) the steps that the agency has taken to determine that it is not appropriate for the child to be returned home or adopted;

(ii) the reasons for any separation of siblings during placement;

(iii) the reasons why a permanent placement with a fit and willing relative through a kinship guardianship assistance arrangement is in the child's best interests;

(iv) the ways in which the child meets the eligibility requirements for a kinship guardianship assistance payment;

(v) the efforts the agency has made to discuss adoption by the child's relative foster parent as a more permanent alternative to legal guardianship and, in the case of a relative foster parent who has chosen not to pursue adoption, documentation of the reasons therefor; and

(vi) the efforts made by the State agency to discuss with the child's parent or parents the kinship guardianship assistance arrangement, or the reasons why the efforts were not made.

(G) A plan for ensuring the educational stability of the child while in foster care, including—

(i) assurances that the placement of the child in foster care takes into account the appropriateness of the current educational setting and the proximity to the school in which the child is enrolled at the time of placement; and

(ii)(I) an assurance that the State agency has coordinated with appropriate local educational agencies (as defined under section 9101 of the Elementary and Secondary Education Act of 1965 [20 USCS § 7801]) to ensure that the child remains in the school in which the child is enrolled at the time of placement; or

(II) if remaining in such school is not in the best interests of the child, assurances by the State agency and the local educational agencies to provide immediate and appropriate enrollment in a new school, with all of the educational records of the child provided to the school.

(2) The term "parents" means biological or adoptive parents or legal guardians, as determined by applicable State law.

(3) The term "adoption assistance agreement" means a written agreement, binding on the parties to the agreement, between the State agency, other relevant agencies, and the prospective adoptive parents of a minor child which at a minimum (A) specifies the nature and amount of any payments, services, and assistance to be provided under such agreement, and (B) stipulates that the agreement shall remain in effect regardless of the State of which the adoptive parents are residents at any given time. The agreement shall contain provisions for the protection (under an interstate compact approved by the Secretary or otherwise) of the interests of the child in cases where the adoptive parents and child move to another State while the agreement is effective.

(4)(A) The term "foster care maintenance payments" means payments to cover the cost of (and the cost of providing) food, clothing, shelter, daily supervision, school supplies, a child's personal incidentals, liability insurance with respect to a child, reasonable travel to the child's home for visitation, and reasonable travel for the child to remain in the school in which the child is enrolled at the time of placement. In the case of institutional care, such term shall include the reasonable costs of administration and operation of such institution as are necessarily required to provide the items described in the preceding sentence.

(B) In cases where—

(i) a child placed in a foster family home or child-care institution is the parent of a son or daughter who is in the same home or institution, and

(ii) payments described in subparagraph (A) are being made under this part with respect to such child,

the foster care maintenance payments made with respect to such child as otherwise determined under subparagraph (A) shall also include such amounts as may be necessary to cover the cost of the items described in that subparagraph with respect to such son or daughter.

(5) The term "case review system" means a procedure for assuring that—

(A) each child has a case plan designed to achieve placement in a safe setting that is the least restrictive (most family like) and most appropriate setting available and in close proximity to the parents' home, consistent with the best interest and special needs of the child, which—

(i) if the child has been placed in a foster family home or child-care institution a substantial distance from the home of the parents of the child, or in a State different from the State in which such home is located, sets forth the reasons why such placement is in the best interests of the child, and

(ii) if the child has been placed in foster care outside the State in which the home of the parents of the child is located, requires that, periodically, but not less frequently than every 6 months, a caseworker on the staff of the State agency of the State in which the home of the parents of the child is located, of the State in which the child has been placed, or of a private agency under contract with either such State, visit such child in such home or institution and submit a report on such visit to the State agency of the State in which the home of the parents of the child is located,

(B) the status of each child is reviewed periodically but no less frequently than once every six months by either a court or by administrative review (as defined in paragraph (6)) in order to determine the safety of the child, the continuing necessity for and appropriateness of the placement, the extent of compliance with the case plan, and the extent of progress which has been made toward alleviating or mitigating the causes necessitating placement in foster care, and to project a likely date by which the child may be returned to and safely maintained in the home or placed for adoption or legal guardianship,

(C) with respect to each such child, (i) procedural safeguards will be applied, among other things, to assure each child in foster care under the supervision of the State of a permanency hearing to be held, in a family or juvenile court or another court (including a tribal court) of competent jurisdiction, or by an administrative body appointed or approved by the court, no later than 12 months after the date the child is considered to have entered foster care (as determined under subparagraph (F)) (and not less frequently than every 12 months thereafter during the continuation of foster care), which hearing shall determine the permanency plan for the child that includes whether, and if applicable when, the child will be returned to the parent, placed for adoption and the State will file a petition for termination of parental rights, or referred for legal guardianship, or (in cases where the State agency has documented to the State court a compelling reason for determining that it would not be in the best interests of the child to return home, be referred for termination of parental rights, or be placed for adoption, with a fit and willing relative, or with a legal guardian) placed in another planned permanent living arrangement, in the case of a child who will not be returned to the parent, the hearing shall consider in-State and out-of-State placement options, and, in the case of a child described in subparagraph (A)(ii), the hearing shall determine whether the out-of-State placement continues to be appropriate and in the best interests of the child, and, in the case of a child who has attained age 16, the services needed to assist the child to make the transition from foster care to independent living; (ii) procedural safeguards shall be applied with respect to parental rights pertaining to the removal of the child from the home of his parents, to a change in the child's placement, and to any determination affecting visitation privileges of parents; and (iii) procedural safeguards shall be applied to assure that in any permanency hearing held with respect to the child, including any hearing regarding the transition of the child from foster care to independent living, the court or administrative body conducting the hearing consults, in an age-appropriate manner, with the child regarding the proposed permanency or transition plan for the child; [,]

(D) a child's health and education record (as described in paragraph (1)(A)) is reviewed and updated, and a copy of the record is supplied to the foster parent or foster care provider with whom the child is placed, at the time of each placement of the child in foster care, and is supplied to the child at no cost at the time the child leaves foster care if the child is leaving foster care by reason of having attained the age of majority under State law; [,]

(E) in the case of a child who has been in foster care under the responsibility of the State for 15 of the most recent 22 months, or, if a court of competent jurisdiction has determined a child to be an abandoned infant (as defined under State law) or has made a determination that the parent has committed murder of another child of the parent, committed voluntary manslaughter of another child of the parent, aided or abetted, attempted, conspired, or solicited to commit such a murder or such a voluntary manslaughter, or committed a felony assault that has resulted in serious bodily injury to the child or to another child of the parent, the State shall file a petition to terminate the parental rights of the child's parents (or, if such a petition has been filed by another party, seek to be joined as a party to the petition), and, concurrently, to identify, recruit, process, and approve a qualified family for an adoption, unless—

(i) at the option of the State, the child is being cared for by a relative;

(ii) a State agency has documented in the case plan (which shall be available for court review) a compelling reason for determining that filing such a petition would not be in the best interests of the child; or

(iii) the State has not provided to the family of the child, consistent with the time period in the State case plan, such services as the State deems necessary for the safe return of the child to the child's home, if reasonable efforts of the type described in section 471(a)(15)(B)(ii) [42 USCS § 671(a)(15)(B)(ii)] are required to be made with respect to the child;

(F) a child shall be considered to have entered foster care on the earlier of—

(i) the date of the first judicial finding that the child has been subjected to child abuse or neglect; or

(ii) the date that is 60 days after the date on which the child is removed from the home;

(G) the foster parents (if any) of a child and any preadoptive parent or relative providing care for the child are provided with notice of, and a right to be heard in, any proceeding to be held with respect to the child, except that this subparagraph shall not be construed to require that any foster parent, preadoptive parent, or relative providing care for the child be made a party to such a proceeding solely on the basis of such notice and right to be heard; and

(H) during the 90-day period immediately prior to the date on which the child will attain 18 years of age, or such greater age as the State may elect under paragraph (8)(B)(iii), whether during that period foster care maintenance payments are being made on the child's behalf or the child is receiving benefits or services under section 477 [42 USCS § 677], a caseworker on the staff of the State agency, and, as appropriate, other representatives of the child provide the child with assistance and support in developing a transition plan that is personalized at the direction of the child, includes specific options on housing, health insurance, education, local opportunities for mentors and continuing support services, and work force supports and employment services, and is as detailed as the child may elect.

(6) The term "administrative review" means a review open to the participation of the parents of the child, conducted by a panel of appropriate persons at least one of whom is not responsible for the case management of, or the delivery of services to, either the child or the parents who are the subject of the review.

(7) The term "legal guardianship" means a judicially created relationship between child and caretaker which is intended to be permanent and self-sustaining as evidenced by the transfer to the caretaker of the following parental rights with respect to the child: protection, education, care and control of the person, custody of the person, and decisionmaking. The term "legal guardian" means the caretaker in such a relationship.

(8) **[Caution: This paragraph takes effect on Oct. 1, 2010, pursuant to § 201(d) of Act Oct. 7, 2008, P. L. 110-351, which appears as 42 USCS § 672 note.]** (A) Subject to subparagraph (B), the term "child" means an individual who has not attained 18 years of age.

(B) At the option of a State, the term shall include an individual—

(i)(I) who is in foster care under the responsibility of the State;

(II) with respect to whom an adoption assistance agreement is in effect under section 473 [42 USCS § 673] if the child had attained 16 years of age before the agreement became effective; or

(III) with respect to whom a kinship guardianship assistance agreement is in effect under section 473(d) [42 USCS § 673(d)] if the child had attained 16 years of age before the agreement became effective;

(ii) who has attained 18 years of age;

(iii) who has not attained 19, 20, or 21 years of age, as the State may elect; and

(iv) who is—

(I) completing secondary education or a program leading to an equivalent credential;

(II) enrolled in an institution which provides post-secondary or vocational education;

(III) participating in a program or activity designed to promote, or remove barriers to, employment;

(IV) employed for at least 80 hours per month; or

(V) incapable of doing any of the activities described in subclauses (I) through (IV) due to a medical condition, which incapability is supported by regularly updated information in the case plan of the child.

(Aug. 14, 1935, ch 531, Title IV, Part E, § 475, as added June 17, 1980, P. L. 96-272, Title I, § 101(a)(1), 94 Stat. 510; June 17, 1980, P. L. 96-272, Title I, § 102(a)(4), 94 Stat. 514; Apr. 7, 1986, P. L. 99-272, Title XII, Subtitle C, §§ 12305(b)(2), 12307(b), 100 Stat. 293, 296; Oct. 22, 1986, P. L. 99-514, Title XVII, § 1711(c)(6), 100 Stat. 2784; Dec. 22, 1987, P. L. 100-203, Title IX, Subtitle B, Part 2, § 9133(a), 101 Stat. 1330-314; Nov. 10, 1988, P. L. 100-647, Title VIII, Subtitle B, § 8104(e), 102 Stat. 3797; Dec. 19, 1989, P. L. 101-239, Title VIII, § 8007(a), (b), 103 Stat. 2462; Oct. 31, 1994, P. L. 103-432, Title II, Subtitle A, §§ 206(a), (b), 209(a), (b), Subtitle F, § 265(c), 108 Stat. 4457, 4459, 4469; Nov. 19, 1997, P. L. 105-89, Title I, §§ 101(b), 102(2), 103(a), (b), 104, 107, Title III, § 302, 111 Stat. 2117, 2118, 2120, 2121, 2128; July 3, 2006, P. L. 109-239, §§ 6–8(a), 11, 12, 120 Stat. 512–514; Sept. 28, 2006, P. L. 109-288, § 10, 120 Stat. 1255; Oct. 7, 2008, P. L. 110-351, Title I, § 101(c)(4), Title II, §§ 201(a), 202, 204(a), 122 Stat. 3952, 3957, 3959, 3960; March 23, 2010, P. L. 111-148, Title II, Subtitle L, § 2955(a), 124 Stat. 352.)

HISTORY; ANCILLARY LAWS AND DIRECTIVES

Prospective amendments:

Amendment of para. (5)(H), effective October 1, 2010. Act March 23, 2010, P. L. 111-148, Title II, Subtitle L, § 2955(a), 124 Stat. 352 (effective on 10/1/2010, as provided by § 2955(d) of such Act, which appears as 42 USCS § 622 note), provides: "Section 475(5)(H) of the Social Security Act (42 U.S.C. 675(5)(H)) is amended by inserting 'includes information about the importance of designating another individual to make health care treatment decisions on behalf of the child if the child becomes unable to participate in such decisions and the child does not have, or does not want, a relative who would otherwise be authorized under State law to make such decisions, and provides the child with the option to execute a health care power of attorney, health care proxy, or other similar document recognized under State law,' after 'employment services,'.".

§ 677. John H. Chafee Foster Care Independence Program

(a) Purpose. The purpose of this section is to provide States with flexible funding that will enable programs to be designed and conducted—

(1) to identify children who are likely to remain in foster care until 18 years of age and to help these children make the transition to self-sufficiency by providing services such as assistance in obtaining a high school diploma, career exploration, vocational training, job placement and retention, training in daily living skills, training in budgeting and financial management skills, substance abuse prevention, and preventive health activities (including smoking avoidance, nutrition education,

and pregnancy prevention);

(2) to help children who are likely to remain in foster care until 18 years of age receive the education, training, and services necessary to obtain employment;

(3) to help children who are likely to remain in foster care until 18 years of age prepare for and enter postsecondary training and education institutions;

(4) to provide personal and emotional support to children aging out of foster care, through mentors and the promotion of interactions with dedicated adults;

(5) to provide financial, housing, counseling, employment, education, and other appropriate support and services to former foster care recipients between 18 and 21 years of age to complement their own efforts to achieve self-sufficiency and to assure that program participants recognize and accept their personal responsibility for preparing for and then making the transition from adolescence to adulthood;

(6) to make available vouchers for education and training, including postsecondary training and education, to youths who have aged out of foster care; and

(7) to provide the services referred to in this subsection to children who, after attaining 16 years of age, have left foster care for kinship guardianship or adoption.

(b) Applications. (1) In general. A State may apply for funds from its allotment under subsection (c) for a period of five consecutive fiscal years by submitting to the Secretary, in writing, a plan that meets the requirements of paragraph (2) and the certifications required by paragraph (3) with respect to the plan.

(2) State plan. A plan meets the requirements of this paragraph if the plan specifies which State agency or agencies will administer, supervise, or oversee the programs carried out under the plan, and describes how the State intends to do the following:

(A) Design and deliver programs to achieve the purposes of this section.

(B) Ensure that all political subdivisions in the State are served by the program, though not necessarily in a uniform manner.

(C) Ensure that the programs serve children of various ages and at various stages of achieving independence.

(D) Involve the public and private sectors in helping adolescents in foster care achieve independence.

(E) Use objective criteria for determining eligibility for benefits and services under the programs, and for ensuring fair and equitable treatment of benefit recipients.

(F) Cooperate in national evaluations of the effects of the programs in achieving the purposes of this section.

(3) Certifications. The certifications required by this paragraph with respect to a plan are the following:

(A) A certification by the chief executive officer of the State that the State will provide assistance and services to children who have left foster care because they have attained 18 years of age, and who have not attained 21 years of age.

(B) A certification by the chief executive officer of the State that not more than 30 percent of the amounts paid to the State from its allotment under subsection (c) for a fiscal year will be expended for room or board for children who have left foster care because they have attained 18 years of age, and who have not attained 21 years of age.

(C) A certification by the chief executive officer of the State that none of the amounts paid to the State from its allotment under subsection (c) will be expended for room or board for any child who has not attained 18 years of age.

(D) A certification by the chief executive officer of the State that the State will use training funds provided under the program of Federal payments for foster care and adoption assistance to provide training to help foster parents, adoptive parents, workers in group homes, and case managers understand and address the issues confronting adolescents preparing for independent living, and will, to the extent possible, coordinate such training with the independent living program conducted for adolescents.

(E) A certification by the chief executive officer of the State that the State has consulted widely with public and private organizations in developing the plan and that the State has given all interested members of the public at least 30 days to submit comments on the plan.

(F) A certification by the chief executive officer of the State that the State will make every effort to coordinate the State programs receiving funds provided from an allotment made to the State under subsection (c) with other Federal and State programs for youth (especially transitional living youth projects funded under part B of title III of the Juvenile Justice and Delinquency Prevention Act of 1974 [42 USCS §§ 5714-1 et seq.]), abstinence education programs, local housing programs, programs for disabled youth (especially sheltered workshops), and school-to-work programs offered by high schools or local workforce agencies.

(G) A certification by the chief executive officer of the State that each Indian tribe in the State has been consulted about the programs to be carried out under the plan; that there have been efforts to coordinate the programs with such tribes; that benefits and services under the programs will be made available to Indian children in the State on the same basis as to other children in the State; and that the State will negotiate in good faith with any Indian tribe, tribal organization, or tribal consortium in the State that does not receive an allotment under subsection (j)(4) for a fiscal year and that requests to develop an agreement with the State to administer, supervise, or oversee the programs to be carried out under the plan with respect to the Indian children who are eligible for such programs and who are under the authority of the tribe, organization, or consortium and to receive from the State an appropriate portion of the State allotment under subsection (c) for the cost of such administration, supervision, or oversight.

(H) A certification by the chief executive officer of the State that the State will ensure that adolescents participating in the program under this section participate directly in designing their own program activities that prepare them for independent living and that the adolescents accept personal responsibility for living up to their part of the program.

(I) A certification by the chief executive officer of the State that the State has established and will enforce standards and procedures to prevent fraud and abuse in the programs carried out under the plan.

(J) A certification by the chief executive officer of the State that the State educational and training voucher program under this section is in compliance with the conditions specified in subsection (i), including a statement describing methods the State will use—

(i) to ensure that the total amount of educational assistance to a youth under this section and under other Federal and Federally supported programs does not exceed the limitation specified in subsection (i)(5); and

(ii) to avoid duplication of benefits under this and any other Federal or Federally assisted benefit program.

(K) **[Caution: This subparagraph takes effect on October 1, 2010, as provided by § 2955(d) of Act March 23, 2010, P. L. 111-148, which appears as 42 USCS § 622 note.]** A certification by the chief executive officer of the State that the State will ensure that an adolescent participating in the program under this section are provided with education about the importance of designating another individual to make health care treatment decisions on behalf of the adolescent if the adolescent becomes unable to participate in such decisions and the adolescent does not have, or does not want, a relative who would otherwise be authorized under State law to make such decisions, whether a health care power of attorney, health care proxy, or other similar document is recognized under State law, and how to execute such a document if the adolescent wants to do so.

(4) Approval. The Secretary shall approve an application submitted by a State pursuant to paragraph (1) for a period if—

(A) the application is submitted on or before June 30 of the calendar year in which such period begins; and

(B) the Secretary finds that the application contains the material required by paragraph (1).

(5) Authority to implement certain amendments; notification. A State with an application approved under paragraph (4) may implement any amendment to the plan contained in the application if the application, incorporating the amendment, would be approvable under paragraph (4). Within 30 days after a State implements any such amendment, the State shall notify the Secretary of the amendment.

(6) Availability. The State shall make available to the public any application submitted by the State pursuant to paragraph (1), and a brief summary of the plan contained in the application.

(c) Allotments to States. (1) General program allotment. From the amount specified in subsection (h)(1) that remains after applying subsection (g)(2) for a fiscal year, the Secretary shall allot to each State with an application approved under subsection (b) for the fiscal year the amount which bears the ratio to such remaining amount equal to the State foster care ratio, as adjusted in accordance with paragraph (2).

(2) Hold harmless provision. (A) In general. The Secretary shall allot to each State whose allotment for a fiscal year under paragraph (1) is less than the greater of $500,000 or the amount payable to the State under this section for fiscal year 1998, an additional amount equal to the difference between such allotment and such greater amount.

(B) Ratable reduction of certain allotments. In the case of a State not described in subparagraph (A) of this paragraph for a fiscal year, the Secretary shall reduce the amount allotted to the State for the fiscal year under paragraph (1) by the amount that bears the same ratio to the sum of the differences determined under subparagraph (A) of this paragraph for the fiscal year as the excess of the amount so allotted over the greater of $500,000 or the amount payable to the State under this section for fiscal year 1998 bears to the sum of such excess amounts determined for all such States.

(3) Voucher program allotment. From the amount, if any, appropriated pursuant to subsection (h)(2) for a fiscal year, the Secretary may allot to each State with an application approved under subsection (b) for the fiscal year an amount equal to the State foster care ratio multiplied by the amount so specified.

(4) State foster care ratio. In this subsection, the term "State foster care ratio" means the ratio of the number of children in foster care under a program of the State in the most recent fiscal year for which the information is available to the total number of children in foster care in all States for the most recent fiscal year.

(d) Use of funds. (1) In general. A State to which an amount is paid from its allotment under subsection (c) may use the amount in any manner that is reasonably calculated to accomplish the purposes of this section.

(2) No supplantation of other funds available for same general purposes. The amounts paid to a State from its allotment under subsection (c) shall be used to supplement and not supplant any other funds which are available for the same general purposes in the State.

(3) Two-year availability of funds. Payments made to a State under this section for a fiscal year shall be expended by the State in the fiscal year or in the succeeding fiscal year.

(4) Reallocation of unused funds. If a State does not apply for funds under this section for a fiscal year within such time as may be provided by the Secretary, the funds to which the State would be entitled for the fiscal year shall be reallocated to 1 or more other States on the basis of their relative need for additional payments under this section, as determined by the Secretary.

(e) Penalties. (1) Use of grant in violation of this part. If the Secretary is made aware, by an audit conducted under chapter 75 of title 31, United States Code [31 USCS §§ 7501 et seq.], or by any other means, that a program receiving funds from an allotment made to a State under subsection (c) has been operated in a manner that is inconsistent with, or not disclosed in the State application approved under subsection (b), the Secretary shall assess a penalty against the State in an amount equal to not less than 1 percent and not more than 5 percent of the amount of the allotment.

(2) Failure to comply with data reporting requirement. The Secretary shall assess a penalty against a State that fails during a fiscal year to comply with an information collection plan implemented under subsection (f) in an amount equal to not less than 1 percent and not more than 5 percent of the amount allotted to the State for the fiscal year.

(3) Penalties based on degree of noncompliance. The Secretary shall assess penalties under this subsection based on the degree of noncompliance.

(f) Data collection and performance measurement. (1) In general. The Secretary, in consultation with State and local public officials responsible for administering independent living and other child welfare programs, child welfare advocates, Members of Congress, youth service providers, and researchers, shall—

(A) develop outcome measures (including measures of educational attainment, high school diploma, employment, avoidance of dependency, homelessness, nonmarital childbirth, incarceration, and high-risk behaviors) that can be used to assess the performance of States in operating independent living programs;

(B) identify data elements needed to track—

(i) the number and characteristics of children receiving services under this section;

(ii) the type and quantity of services being provided; and

(iii) State performance on the outcome measures; and

(C) develop and implement a plan to collect the needed information beginning with the second fiscal year beginning after the date of the enactment of this section [enacted Dec. 14, 1999].

(2) Report to the Congress. Within 12 months after the date of the enactment of this section [enacted Dec. 14, 1999], the Secretary shall submit to the Committee on Ways and Means of the House of Representatives and the Committee on Finance of the Senate a report detailing the plans and timetable for collecting from the States the information described in paragraph (1) and a proposal to impose penalties consistent with paragraph (e)(2) on States that do not report data.

(g) Evaluations. (1) In general. The Secretary shall conduct evaluations of such State programs funded under this section as the Secretary deems to be innovative or of potential national significance. The evaluation of any such program shall include information on the effects of the program on education, employment, and personal development. To the maximum extent practicable, the evaluations shall be based on rigorous scientific standards including random assignment to treatment and control groups. The Secretary is encouraged to work directly with State and local governments to design methods for conducting the evaluations, directly or by grant, contract, or cooperative agreement.

(2) Funding of evaluations. The Secretary shall reserve 1.5 percent of the amount specified in subsection (h) for a fiscal year to carry out, during the fiscal year, evaluation, technical assistance, performance measurement, and data collection activities related to this section, directly or through grants, contracts, or cooperative agreements with appropriate entities.

(h) Limitations on authorization of appropriations. To carry out this section and for payments to States under section 474(a)(4) [42 USCS § 674(a)(4)], there are authorized to be appropriated to the Secretary for each fiscal year—

(1) $140,000,000, which shall be available for all purposes under this section; and

(2) an additional $60,000,000, which are authorized to be available for payments to States for education and training vouchers for youths who age out of foster care, to assist the youths to develop skills necessary to lead independent and productive lives.

(i) Educational and training vouchers. The following conditions shall apply to a State educational and training voucher program under this section:

(1) Vouchers under the program may be available to youths otherwise eligible for services under the State program under this section.

(2) For purposes of the voucher program, youths who, after attaining 16 years of age, are adopted from, or enter kinship guardianship from, foster care may be considered to be youths otherwise eligible for services under the State program under this section.

(3) The State may allow youths participating in the voucher program on the date they attain 21 years of age to remain eligible until they attain 23 years of age, as long as they are enrolled in a postsecondary education or training program and are making satisfactory progress toward completion of that program.

(4) The voucher or vouchers provided for an individual under this section—

(A) may be available for the cost of attendance at an institution of higher education, as defined in section 102 of the Higher Education Act of 1965 [20 USCS § 1002]; and

(B) shall not exceed the lesser of $5,000 per year or the total cost of attendance, as defined in section 472 of that Act [20 USCS § 1087ll].

(5) The amount of a voucher under this section may be disregarded for purposes of determining the recipient's eligibility for, or the amount of, any other Federal or Federally supported assistance, except that the total amount of educational assistance to a youth under this section and under other Federal and Federally supported programs shall not exceed the total cost of attendance, as defined in section 472 of the Higher Education Act of 1965 [20 USCS § 1087ll], and except that the State agency shall take appropriate steps to prevent duplication of benefits under this and other Federal or Federally supported programs.

(6) The program is coordinated with other appropriate education and training programs.

(j) Authority for an Indian tribe, tribal organization, or tribal consortium to receive an allotment. (1) In general. An Indian tribe, tribal organization, or tribal consortium with a plan approved under section 479B [42 USCS § 679c], or which is receiving funding to provide foster care under this part pursuant to a cooperative agreement or contract with a State, may apply for an allotment out of any funds authorized by paragraph (1) or (2) (or both) of subsection (h) of this section.

(2) Application. A tribe, organization, or consortium desiring an allotment under paragraph (1) of this subsection shall submit an application to the Secretary to directly receive such allotment that includes a plan which—

(A) satisfies such requirements of paragraphs (2) and (3) of subsection (b) as the Secretary determines are appropriate;

(B) contains a description of the tribe's, organization's, or consortium's consultation process regarding the programs to be carried out under the plan with each State for which a portion of an allotment under subsection (c) would be redirected to the tribe, organization, or consortium; and

(C) contains an explanation of the results of such consultation, particularly with respect to—

(i) determining the eligibility for benefits and services of Indian children to be served under the programs to be carried out under the plan; and

(ii) the process for consulting with the State in order to ensure the continuity of benefits and services for such children who will transition from receiving benefits and services under programs carried out under a State plan under subsection (b)(2) to receiving benefits and services under programs carried out under a plan under this subsection.

(3) Payments. The Secretary shall pay an Indian tribe, tribal organization, or tribal consortium with an application and plan approved under this subsection from the allotment determined for the tribe, organization, or consortium under paragraph (4) of this subsection in the same manner as is provided in section 474(a)(4) [42 USCS § 674(a)(4)] (and, where requested, and if funds are appropriated, section 474(e) [42 USCS § 674(e)]) with respect to a State, or in such other manner as is determined appropriate by the Secretary, except that in no case shall an Indian tribe, a tribal organization, or a tribal consortium receive a lesser proportion of such funds than a State is authorized to receive under those sections.

(4) Allotment. From the amounts allotted to a State under subsection (c) of this section for a fiscal year, the Secretary shall allot to each Indian tribe, tribal organization, or tribal consortium with an application and plan approved under this subsection for that fiscal year an amount equal to the tribal foster care ratio determined under paragraph (5) of this subsection for the tribe, organization, or consortium multiplied by the allotment amount of the State within which the tribe, organization, or consortium is located. The allotment determined under this paragraph is deemed to be a part of the allotment determined under section 477(c) [42 USCS § 677(c)] for the State in which the Indian tribe, tribal organization, or tribal consortium is located.

(5) Tribal foster care ratio. For purposes of paragraph (4), the tribal foster care ratio means, with respect to an Indian tribe, tribal organization, or tribal consortium, the ratio of—

(A) the number of children in foster care under the responsibility of the Indian tribe, tribal organization, or tribal consortium (either directly or under supervision of the State), in the most recent fiscal year for which the information is available; to

(B) the sum of—

(i) the total number of children in foster care under the responsibility of the State within which the Indian tribe, tribal organization, or tribal consortium is located; and

(ii) the total number of children in foster care under the responsibility of all Indian tribes, tribal organizations, or tribal consortia in the State (either directly or under supervision of the State) that have a plan approved under this subsection.

(Aug. 14, 1935, ch 531, Title IV, Part E, § 477, as added Apr. 7, 1986, P. L. 99-272, Title XII, Subtitle C, § 12307(a), 100 Stat. 294; Nov. 10, 1988, P. L. 100-647, Title VIII, Subtitle B, § 8104(a)–(d), (f) 102 Stat. 3796; Dec. 19, 1989, P. L. 101-239, Title VIII, § 8002(a), (b), 103 Stat. 2452; Nov. 5, 1990, P. L. 101-508, Title V, Subtitle A, Ch 5, § 5073(a), 104 Stat. 1388-233; Aug. 10, 1993, P. L. 103-66, Title XIII, Ch 2, Subch C, Part I, § 13714(a), 107 Stat. 657; Nov. 19, 1997, P. L. 105-89, Title III, § 304, 111 Stat. 2130; Dec. 14, 1999, P. L. 106-169, Title I, Subtitle A, § 101(b), 113 Stat. 1824; Jan. 17, 2002, P. L. 107-133, Title II, §§ 201(a)–(e), 202(a), 115 Stat. 2422, 2425; Oct. 7, 2008, P. L. 110-351, Title I, § 101(e), Title III, § 301(b), (c)(1)(B), 122 Stat. 3953, 3967, 3969; March 23, 2010, P. L. 111-148, Title II, Subtitle L, § 2955(b), 124 Stat. 352.)

TITLE V. MATERNAL AND CHILD HEALTH SERVICES BLOCK GRANT

§ 701. Authorization of appropriations; purposes; definitions

(a) To improve the health of all mothers and children consistent with the applicable health status goals and national health objectives established by the Secretary under the Public Health Service Act for the year 2000, there are authorized to be appropriated $850,000,000 for fiscal year 2001 and each fiscal year thereafter—

(1) for the purpose of enabling each State—

(A) to provide and to assure mothers and children (in particular those with low income or with limited availability of health services) access to quality maternal and child health services:

(B) to reduce infant mortality and the incidence of preventable diseases and handicapping conditions among children, to reduce the need for inpatient and long-term care services, to increase the number of children (especially preschool children) appropriately immunized against disease and the number of low income children receiving health assessments and follow-up diagnostic and treatment services, and otherwise to promote the health of mothers and infants by providing prenatal, delivery, and postpartum care for low income, at-risk pregnant women, and to promote the health of children by providing preventive and primary care services for low income children;

(C) to provide rehabilitation services for blind and disabled individuals under the age of 16 receiving benefit under title XVI [42 USCS §§ 1381 et seq.], to the extent medical assistance for such services is not provided under title XIX [42 USCS §§ 1396 et seq.]; and

(D) to provide and to promote family-centered, community-based, coordinated care (including care coordination services, as defined in subsection (b)(3)) for children with special health care needs and to facilitate the development of community-based systems of services for such children and their families;

(2) for the purpose of enabling the Secretary (through grants, contracts, or otherwise) to provide for special projects of regional and national significance, research, and training with respect to maternal and child health and children with special health care needs (including early intervention training and services development), for genetic disease testing, counseling, and information development and dissemination programs, for grants (including funding for comprehensive hemophilia diagnostic treatment centers) relating to hemophilia without regard to age, and for the screening of newborns for sickle cell anemia, and other genetic disorders and follow-up services; and

(3) subject to section 502(b) [42 USCS § 702(b)] for the purpose of enabling the Secretary (through grants, contracts, or otherwise) to provide for developing and expanding the following—

(A) maternal and infant health home visiting programs in which case management services as defined in subparagraphs (A) and (B) of subsection (b)(4), health education services, and related social support services are provided in the home to pregnant women or families with an infant up to the age one by an appropriate health professional or by a qualified nonprofessional acting under the supervision of a health care professional,

(B) projects designed to increase the participation of obstetricians and pediatricians under the program under this title [42 USCS §§ 701 et seq.] and under state plans approved under title XIX [42 USCS §§ 1396 et seq.],

(C) integrated maternal and child health service delivery systems (of the type described in section 1136 [42 USCS § 1320b-6] and using, once developed, the model application form developed under section 6506(a) of the Omnibus Budget Reconciliation Act of 1989) [note to this section],

(D) maternal and child health centers which (i) provide prenatal, delivery, and postpartum care for pregnant women and preventive and primary care services for infants up to age one, and (ii) operate under the direction of a not-for-profit hospital,

(E) maternal and child health projects to serve rural populations, and

(F) outpatient and community based services programs (including day care services) for children with special health care needs whose medical services are provided primarily through inpatient institutional care.

Funds appropriated under this section may only be used in a manner consistent with the Assisted Suicide Funding Restriction Act of 1997.

(b) For purposes of this title [42 USCS §§ 701 et seq.]:

(1) The term "consolidated health programs" means the programs administered under the provisions of—

(A) this title [42 USCS §§ 701 et seq.] (relating to maternal and child health and services for children with special health care needs),

(B) section 1615(c) of this Act [42 USCS § 1382d(c)] (relating to supplemental security income for disabled children),

(C) sections 316 (relating to lead-based paint poisoning prevention programs), 1101 (relating to genetic disease programs), 1121 (relating to sudden infant death syndrome programs) and 1131 (relating to hemophilia treatment centers) of the Public Health Service Act, and

(D) title VI of the Health Services and Centers Amendments of 1978 (Public Law 95-626; relating to adolescent pregnancy grants),

as such provisions were in effect before the date of the enactment of the Maternal and Child Health Services Block Grant Act [enacted Aug. 13, 1981].

(2) The term "low income" means, with respect to an individual or family, such an individual or family with an income determined to be below the income official poverty line defined by the Office of Management and Budget and revised annually in accordance with section 673(2) of the Omnibus Budget Reconciliation Act of 1981 [42 USCS § 9902(2)].

(3) The term "care coordination services" means services to promote the effective and efficient organization and utilization of resources to assure access to necessary comprehensive services for children with special health care needs and their families.

(4) The term "case management services" means—

(A) with respect to pregnant women, services to assure access to quality prenatal, delivery, and postpartum care; and

(B) with respect to infants up to age one, services to assure access to quality preventive and primary care services.

(c)(1)(A) For the purpose of enabling the Secretary (through grants, contracts, or otherwise) to provide for special projects of regional and national significance for the development and support of family-to-family health information centers described in paragraph (2), there is appropriated to the Secretary, out of any money in the Treasury not otherwise appropriated—

(i) $3,000,000 for fiscal year 2007;

(ii) $4,000,000 for fiscal year 2008; and

(iii) $5,000,000 for each of fiscal years 2009 through 2012.

(B) Funds appropriated or authorized to be appropriated under subparagraph (A) shall—

(i) be in addition to amounts appropriated under subsection (a) and retained under section 502(a)(1) [42 USCS § 702(a)(1)] for the purpose of carrying out activities described in subsection (a)(2); and

(ii) remain available until expended.

(2) The family-to-family health information centers described in this paragraph are centers that—

(A) assist families of children with disabilities or special health care needs to make informed choices about health care in order to promote good treatment decisions, cost-effectiveness, and improved health outcomes for such children;

(B) provide information regarding the health care needs of, and resources available for, such children;

(C) identify successful health delivery models for such children;

(D) develop with representatives of health care providers, managed care organizations, health care purchasers, and appropriate State agencies, a model for collaboration between families of such children and health professionals;

(E) provide training and guidance regarding caring for such children;

(F) conduct outreach activities to the families of such children, health professionals, schools, and other appropriate entities and individuals; and

(G) are staffed—

(i) by such families who have expertise in Federal and State public and private health care systems; and

(ii) by health professionals.

(3) The Secretary shall develop family-to-family health information centers described in paragraph (2) in accordance with the following:

(A) With respect to fiscal year 2007, such centers shall be developed in not less than 25 States.

(B) With respect to fiscal year 2008, such centers shall be developed in not less than 40 States.

(C) With respect to fiscal year 2009 and each fiscal year thereafter, such centers shall be developed in all States.

(4) The provisions of this title [42 USCS §§ 701 et seq.] that are applicable to the funds made available to the Secretary under section 502(a)(1) [42 USCS § 702(a)(1)] apply in the same manner to funds made available to the Secretary under paragraph (1)(A).

(5) For purposes of this subsection, the term "State" means each of the 50 States and the District of Columbia.

(Aug. 14, 1935, ch 531, Title V, § 501, as added Aug. 13, 1981, P. L. 97-35, Title XXI, Subtitle D, § 2192(a), 95 Stat. 818; Sept. 3, 1982, P. L. 97-248, Title I, Subtitle B, § 137(b)(1), (2), 96 Stat 376; July 18, 1984, P. L. 98-369, Division B, Title III, Subtitle B, § 2372(a), 98 Stat. 1110; April 7, 1986, P. L. 99-272, Title IX, Subtitle B, § 9527(a)–(c), 100 Stat. 219; Oct. 21, 1986, P. L. 99-509, Title IX, Subtitle E, Part 5, § 9441(a), 100 Stat. 2071; Dec. 22, 1987, P. L. 100-203, Title IV, Subtitle B, Part 2, § 4118(p)(8), 101 Stat. 1330-159; Dec. 19, 1989, P. L. 101-239, Title VI, Subtitle C, § 6501(a), 103 Stat. 2273; Oct. 31, 1994, P. L. 103-432, Title II, § 201, 108 Stat. 4453; April 30, 1997, P. L. 105-12, § 9(d), 111 Stat. 27; Dec. 21, 2000, P. L. 106-554, § 1(a)(6), 114 Stat. 2763; Feb. 8, 2006, P. L. 109-171, Title VI, Subtitle A, Ch. 6, Subch. A, § 6064, 120 Stat. 100; March 23, 2010, P. L. 111-148, Title V, Subtitle F, § 5507(b), 124 Stat. 668.)

§ 710. Separate program for abstinence education

(a) In general. For the purpose described in subsection (b), the Secretary shall, for each of fiscal years 2010 through 2014, allot to each State which has transmitted an application for the fiscal year under section 505(a) [42 USCS § 705(a)] an amount equal to the product of—

(1) the amount appropriated in subsection (d) for the fiscal year; and

(2) the percentage determined for the State under section 502(c)(1)(B)(ii) [42 USCS § 702(c)(1)(B)].

(b) Purpose of allotment. (1) The purpose of an allotment under subsection (a) to a State is to enable the State to provide abstinence education, and at the option of the State, where appropriate, mentoring, counseling, and adult supervision to promote abstinence from sexual activity, with a focus on those groups which are most likely to bear children out-of-wedlock.

(2) For purposes of this section, the term

"abstinence education" means an educational or motivational program which—

(A) has as its exclusive purpose, teaching the social, psychological, and health gains to be realized by abstaining from sexual activity;

(B) teaches abstinence from sexual activity outside marriage as the expected standard for all school age children;

(C) teaches that abstinence from sexual activity is the only certain way to avoid out-of-wedlock pregnancy, sexually transmitted diseases, and other associated health problems;

(D) teaches that a mutually faithful monogamous relationship in context of marriage is the expected standard of human sexual activity;

(E) teaches that sexual activity outside of the context of marriage is likely to have harmful psychological and physical effects;

(F) teaches that bearing children out-of-wedlock is likely to have harmful consequences for the child, the child's parents, and society;

(G) teaches young people how to reject sexual advances and how alcohol and drug use increases vulnerability to sexual advances; and

(H) teaches the importance of attaining self-sufficiency before engaging in sexual activity.

(c) Applicability of 42 USCS §§ 703, 707, and 708. (1) Sections 503, 507, and 508 [42 USCS §§ 703, 707, 708] apply to allotments under subsection (a) to the same extent and in the same manner as such sections apply to allotments under section 502(c) [42 USCS § 702(c)].

(2) Sections 505 and 506 [42 USCS §§ 705, 706] apply to allotments under subsection (a) to the extent determined by the Secretary to be appropriate.

(d) Appropriations. For the purpose of allotments under subsection (a), there is appropriated, out of any money in the Treasury not otherwise appropriated, an additional $50,000,000 for each of the fiscal years 2010 through 2014. The appropriation under the preceding sentence for a fiscal year is made on October 1 of the fiscal year (except that such appropriation shall be made on the date of enactment of the Patient Protection and Affordable Care Act [enacted March 23, 2010] in the case of fiscal year 2010).

(Aug. 14, 1935, ch 531, Title V, § 510, as added Aug. 22, 1996, P. L. 104-193, Title IX, § 912, 110 Stat. 2353; June 30, 2003, P. L. 108-40, § 6, 117 Stat. 837; March 23, 2010, P. L. 111-148, Title II, Subtitle L, § 2954, 124 Stat. 352.)

§ 711. Maternal, infant, and early childhood home visiting programs

(a) Purposes. The purposes of this section are—

(1) to strengthen and improve the programs and activities carried out under this title [42 USCS §§ 701 et seq.];

(2) to improve coordination of services for at risk communities; and

(3) to identify and provide comprehensive services to improve outcomes for families who reside in at risk communities.

(b) Requirement for all States to assess statewide needs and identify at risk communities. (1) In general. Not later than 6 months after the date of enactment of this section, each State shall, as a condition of receiving payments from an allotment for the State under section 502 [42 USCS § 702] for fiscal year 2011, conduct a statewide needs assessment (which shall be separate from the statewide needs assessment required under section 505(a) [42 USCS § 705(a)]) that identifies—

(A) communities with concentrations of—

(i) premature birth, low-birth weight infants, and infant mortality, including infant death due to neglect, or other indicators of at-risk prenatal, maternal, newborn, or child health;

(ii) poverty;

(iii) crime;

(iv) domestic violence;

(v) high rates of high-school drop-outs;

(vi) substance abuse;

(vii) unemployment; or

(viii) child maltreatment;

(B) the quality and capacity of existing programs or initiatives for early childhood home visitation in the State including—

(i) the number and types of individuals and families who are receiving services under such programs or initiatives;

(ii) the gaps in early childhood home visitation in the State; and

(iii) the extent to which such programs or initiatives are meeting the needs of eligible families described in subsection (k)(2); and

(C) the State's capacity for providing substance abuse treatment and counseling services to individuals and families in need of such treatment or services.

(2) Coordination with other assessments. In conducting the statewide needs assessment required under paragraph (1), the State shall coordinate with, and take into account, other appropriate needs assessments conducted by the State, as determined by the Secretary, including the needs assessment required under

section 505(a) [42 USCS § 705(a)] (both the most recently completed assessment and any such assessment in progress), the communitywide strategic planning and needs assessments conducted in accordance with section 640(g)(1)(C) of the Head Start Act [42 USCS § 9835(g)(1)(C)], and the inventory of current unmet needs and current community-based and prevention-focused programs and activities to prevent child abuse and neglect, and other family resource services operating in the State required under section 205(3) of the Child Abuse Prevention and Treatment Act [42 USCS § 5116d(3)].

(3) Submission to the Secretary. Each State shall submit to the Secretary, in such form and manner as the Secretary shall require—

(A) the results of the statewide needs assessment required under paragraph (1); and

(B) a description of how the State intends to address needs identified by the assessment, particularly with respect to communities identified under paragraph (1)(A), which may include applying for a grant to conduct an early childhood home visitation program in accordance with the requirements of this section.

(c) Grants for early childhood home visitation programs. (1) Authority to make grants. In addition to any other payments made under this title [42 USCS §§ 701 et seq.] to a State, the Secretary shall make grants to eligible entities to enable the entities to deliver services under early childhood home visitation programs that satisfy the requirements of subsection (d) to eligible families in order to promote improvements in maternal and prenatal health, infant health, child health and development, parenting related to child development outcomes, school readiness, and the socioeconomic status of such families, and reductions in child abuse, neglect, and injuries.

(2) Authority to use initial grant funds for planning or implementation. An eligible entity that receives a grant under paragraph (1) may use a portion of the funds made available to the entity during the first 6 months of the period for which the grant is made for planning or implementation activities to assist with the establishment of early childhood home visitation programs that satisfy the requirements of subsection (d).

(3) Grant duration. The Secretary shall determine the period of years for which a grant is made to an eligible entity under paragraph (1).

(4) Technical assistance. The Secretary shall provide an eligible entity that receives a grant under paragraph (1) with technical assistance in administering programs or activities conducted in whole or in part with grant funds.

(d) Requirements. The requirements of this subsection for an early childhood home visitation program conducted with a grant made under this section are as follows:

(1) Quantifiable, measurable improvement in benchmark areas. (A) In general. The eligible entity establishes, subject to the approval of the Secretary, quantifiable, measurable 3- and 5-year benchmarks for demonstrating that the program results in improvements for the eligible families participating in the program in each of the following areas:

(i) Improved maternal and newborn health.

(ii) Prevention of child injuries, child abuse, neglect, or maltreatment, and reduction of emergency department visits.

(iii) Improvement in school readiness and achievement.

(iv) Reduction in crime or domestic violence.

(v) Improvements in family economic self-sufficiency.

(vi) Improvements in the coordination and referrals for other community resources and supports.

(B) Demonstration of improvements after 3 years. (i) Report to the Secretary. Not later than 30 days after the end of the 3rd year in which the eligible entity conducts the program, the entity submits to the Secretary a report demonstrating improvement in at least 4 of the areas specified in subparagraph (A).

(ii) Corrective action plan. If the report submitted by the eligible entity under clause (i) fails to demonstrate improvement in at least 4 of the areas specified in subparagraph (A), the entity shall develop and implement a plan to improve outcomes in each of the areas specified in subparagraph (A), subject to approval by the Secretary. The plan shall include provisions for the Secretary to monitor implementation of the plan and conduct continued oversight of the program, including through submission by the entity of regular reports to the Secretary.

(iii) Technical assistance. (I) In general. The Secretary shall provide an eligible entity required to develop and implement an improvement plan under clause (ii) with technical assistance to develop and implement the plan. The Secretary may provide the technical assistance directly or through grants, contracts, or cooperative agreements.

(II) Advisory panel. The Secretary shall establish an advisory panel for purposes of obtaining recommendations regarding the technical assistance provided to entities in accordance with subclause (I).

(iv) No improvement or failure to submit

report. If the Secretary determines after a period of time specified by the Secretary that an eligible entity implementing an improvement plan under clause (ii) has failed to demonstrate any improvement in the areas specified in subparagraph (A), or if the Secretary determines that an eligible entity has failed to submit the report required under clause (i), the Secretary shall terminate the entity's grant and may include any unexpended grant funds in grants made to nonprofit organizations under subsection (h)(2)(B).

(C) Final report. Not later than December 31, 2015, the eligible entity shall submit a report to the Secretary demonstrating improvements (if any) in each of the areas specified in subparagraph (A).

(2) Improvements in outcomes for individual families. (A) In general. The program is designed, with respect to an eligible family participating in the program, to result in the participant outcomes described in subparagraph (B) that the eligible entity identifies on the basis of an individualized assessment of the family, are relevant for that family.

(B) Participant outcomes. The participant outcomes described in this subparagraph are the following:

(i) Improvements in prenatal, maternal, and newborn health, including improved pregnancy outcomes

(ii) Improvements in child health and development, including the prevention of child injuries and maltreatment and improvements in cognitive, language, social-emotional, and physical developmental indicators.

(iii) Improvements in parenting skills.

(iv) Improvements in school readiness and child academic achievement.

(v) Reductions in crime or domestic violence.

(vi) Improvements in family economic self-sufficiency.

(vii) Improvements in the coordination of referrals for, and the provision of, other community resources and supports for eligible families, consistent with State child welfare agency training.

(3) Core components. The program includes the following core components: (A) Service delivery model or models. (i) In general. Subject to clause (ii), the program is conducted using 1 or more of the service delivery models described in item (aa) or (bb) of subclause (I) or in subclause (II) selected by the eligible entity:

(I) The model conforms to a clear consistent home visitation model that has been in existence for at least 3 years and is research-based, grounded in relevant empirically-based knowledge, linked to program determined outcomes, associated with a national organization or institution of higher education that has comprehensive home visitation program standards that ensure high quality service delivery and continuous program quality improvement, and has demonstrated significant, (and in the case of the service delivery model described in item (aa), sustained) positive outcomes, as described in the benchmark areas specified in paragraph (1)(A) and the participant outcomes described in paragraph (2)(B), when evaluated using well-designed and rigorous—

(aa) randomized controlled research designs, and the evaluation results have been published in a peer-reviewed journal; or

(bb) quasi-experimental research designs.

(II) The model conforms to a promising and new approach to achieving the benchmark areas specified in paragraph (1)(A) and the participant outcomes described in paragraph (2)(B), has been developed or identified by a national organization or institution of higher education, and will be evaluated through well-designed and rigorous process.

(ii) Majority of grant funds used for evidence-based models. An eligible entity shall use not more than 25 percent of the amount of the grant paid to the entity for a fiscal year for purposes of conducting a program using the service delivery model described in clause (i)(II).

(iii) Criteria for evidence of effectiveness of models. The Secretary shall establish criteria for evidence of effectiveness of the service delivery models and shall ensure that the process for establishing the criteria is transparent and provides the opportunity for public comment.

(B) Additional requirements. (i) The program adheres to a clear, consistent model that satisfies the requirements of being grounded in empirically-based knowledge related to home visiting and linked to the benchmark areas specified in paragraph (1)(A) and the participant outcomes described in paragraph (2)(B) related to the purposes of the program.

(ii) The program employs well-trained and competent staff, as demonstrated by education or training, such as nurses, social workers, educators, child development specialists, or other well-trained and competent staff, and provides ongoing and specific training on the model being delivered.

(iii) The program maintains high quality supervision to establish home visitor competencies.

(iv) The program demonstrates strong organizational capacity to implement the activities involved.

(v) The program establishes appropriate linkages and referral networks to other community resources and supports for eligible families.

(vi) The program monitors the fidelity of program implementation to ensure that services are delivered pursuant to the specified model.

(4) Priority for serving high-risk populations. The eligible entity gives priority to providing services under the program to the following:

(A) Eligible families who reside in communities in need of such services, as identified in the statewide needs assessment required under subsection (b)(1)(A).

(B) Low-income eligible families.

(C) Eligible families who are pregnant women who have not attained age 21.

(D) Eligible families that have a history of child abuse or neglect or have had interactions with child welfare services.

(E) Eligible families that have a history of substance abuse or need substance abuse treatment.

(F) Eligible families that have users of tobacco products in the home.

(G) Eligible families that are or have children with low student achievement.

(H) Eligible families with children with developmental delays or disabilities.

(I) Eligible families who, or that include individuals who, are serving or formerly served in the Armed Forces, including such families that have members of the Armed Forces who have had multiple deployments outside of the United States.

(e) Application requirements. An eligible entity desiring a grant under this section shall submit an application to the Secretary for approval, in such manner as the Secretary may require, that includes the following:

(1) A description of the populations to be served by the entity, including specific information regarding how the entity will serve high risk populations described in subsection (d)(4).

(2) An assurance that the entity will give priority to serving low-income eligible families and eligible families who reside in at risk communities identified in the statewide needs assessment required under subsection (b)(1)(A).

(3) The service delivery model or models described in subsection (d)(3)(A) that the entity will use under the program and the basis for the selection of the model or models.

(4) A statement identifying how the selection of the populations to be served and the service delivery model or models that the entity will use under the program for such populations is consistent with the results of the statewide needs assessment conducted under subsection (b).

(5) The quantifiable, measurable benchmarks established by the State to demonstrate that the program contributes to improvements in the areas specified in subsection (d)(1)(A).

(6) An assurance that the entity will obtain and submit documentation or other appropriate evidence from the organization or entity that developed the service delivery model or models used under the program to verify that the program is implemented and services are delivered according to the model specifications.

(7) Assurances that the entity will establish procedures to ensure that—

(A) the participation of each eligible family in the program is voluntary; and

(B) services are provided to an eligible family in accordance with the individual assessment for that family.

(8) Assurances that the entity will—

(A) submit annual reports to the Secretary regarding the program and activities carried out under the program that include such information and data as the Secretary shall require; and

(B) participate in, and cooperate with, data and information collection necessary for the evaluation required under subsection (g)(2) and other research and evaluation activities carried out under subsection (h)(3).

(9) A description of other State programs that include home visitation services, including, if applicable to the State, other programs carried out under this title [42 USCS §§ 701 et seq.] with funds made available from allotments under section 502(c) [42 USCS § 702(c)], programs funded under title IV [42 USCS §§ 601 et seq.], title II of the Child Abuse Prevention and Treatment Act [42 USCS §§ 5116 et seq.] (relating to community-based grants for the prevention of child abuse and neglect), and section 645A of the Head Start Act [42 USCS § 9840a] (relating to Early Head Start programs).

(10) Other information as required by the Secretary.

(f) Maintenance of effort. Funds provided to an eligible entity receiving a grant under this section shall supplement, and not supplant, funds from other sources for early childhood home visitation programs or initiatives.

(g) Evaluation. (1) Independent, expert advisory panel. The Secretary, in accordance with subsection (h)(1)(A), shall appoint an independent advisory panel consisting of experts in program evaluation and research, education, and early childhood development—

(A) to review, and make recommendations on, the design and plan for the evaluation required under paragraph (2) within 1 year after the date of enactment of this section;

(B) to maintain and advise the Secretary regarding the progress of the evaluation; and

(C) to comment, if the panel so desires, on the report submitted under paragraph (3).

(2) Authority to conduct evaluation. On the basis of the recommendations of the advisory panel under paragraph (1), the Secretary shall, by grant, contract, or interagency agreement, conduct an evaluation of the statewide needs assessments submitted under subsection (b) and the grants made under subsections (c) and (h)(3)(B). The evaluation shall include—

(A) an analysis, on a State-by-State basis, of the results of such assessments, including indicators of maternal and prenatal health and infant health and mortality, and State actions in response to the assessments; and

(B) an assessment of—

(i) the effect of early childhood home visitation programs on child and parent outcomes, including with respect to each of the benchmark areas specified in subsection (d)(1)(A) and the participant outcomes described in subsection (d)(2)(B);

(ii) the effectiveness of such programs on different populations, including the extent to which the ability of programs to improve participant outcomes varies across programs and populations; and

(iii) the potential for the activities conducted under such programs, if scaled broadly, to improve health care practices, eliminate health disparities, and improve health care system quality, efficiencies, and reduce costs.

(3) Report. Not later than March 31, 2015, the Secretary shall submit a report to Congress on the results of the evaluation conducted under paragraph (2) and shall make the report publicly available.

(h) Other provisions. (1) Intra-agency collaboration. The Secretary shall ensure that the Maternal and Child Health Bureau and the Administration for Children and Families collaborate with respect to carrying out this section, including with respect to—

(A) reviewing and analyzing the statewide needs assessments required under subsection (b), the awarding and oversight of grants awarded under this section, the establishment of the advisory panels required under subsections (d)(1)(B)(iii)(II) and (g)(1), and the evaluation and report required under subsection (g); and

(B) consulting with other Federal agencies with responsibility for administering or evaluating programs that serve eligible families to coordinate and collaborate with respect to research related to such programs and families, including the Office of the Assistant Secretary for Planning and Evaluation of the Department of Health and Human Services, the Centers for Disease Control and Prevention, the National Institute of Child Health and Human Development of the National Institutes of Health, the Office of Juvenile Justice and Delinquency Prevention of the Department of Justice, and the Institute of Education Sciences of the Department of Education.

(2) Grants to eligible entities that are not States. (A) Indian Tribes, Tribal Organizations, or Urban Indian Organizations. The Secretary shall specify requirements for eligible entities that are Indian Tribes (or a consortium of Indian Tribes), Tribal Organizations, or Urban Indian Organizations to apply for and conduct an early childhood home visitation program with a grant under this section. Such requirements shall, to the greatest extent practicable, be consistent with the requirements applicable to eligible entities that are States and shall require an Indian Tribe (or consortium), Tribal Organization, or Urban Indian Organization to—

(i) conduct a needs assessment similar to the assessment required for all States under subsection (b); and

(ii) establish quantifiable, measurable 3- and 5-year benchmarks consistent with subsection (d)(1)(A).

(B) Nonprofit organizations. If, as of the beginning of fiscal year 2012, a State has not applied or been approved for a grant under this section, the Secretary may use amounts appropriated under paragraph (1) of subsection (j) that are available for expenditure under paragraph (3) of that subsection to make a grant to an eligible entity that is a nonprofit organization described in subsection (k)(1)(B) to conduct an early childhood home visitation program in the State. The Secretary shall specify the requirements for such an organization to apply for and conduct the program which shall, to the greatest extent practicable, be consistent with the requirements applicable to eligible entities that are States and shall require the organization to—

(i) carry out the program based on the needs assessment conducted by the State under subsection (b); and

(ii) establish quantifiable, measurable 3- and 5-year benchmarks consistent with subsection (d)(1)(A).

(3) Research and other evaluation activities. (A) In general. The Secretary shall carry out a continuous program of research and evaluation activities in order to increase knowledge about the implementation and effectiveness of home visiting programs, using random assignment designs to the maximum extent feasible. The Secretary may carry out such activities directly, or through grants, cooperative agreements, or contracts.

(B) Requirements. The Secretary shall ensure that—

(i) evaluation of a specific program or project is conducted by persons or individuals not directly involved in the operation of such program or project; and

(ii) the conduct of research and evaluation activities includes consultation with independent researchers, State officials, and developers and providers of home visiting programs on topics including research design and administrative data matching.

(4) Report and recommendation. Not later than December 31, 2015, the Secretary shall submit a report to Congress regarding the programs conducted with grants under this section. The report required under this paragraph shall include—

(A) information regarding the extent to which eligible entities receiving grants under this section demonstrated improvements in each of the areas specified in subsection (d)(1)(A);

(B) information regarding any technical assistance provided under subsection (d)(1)(B)(iii)(I), including the type of any such assistance provided; and

(C) recommendations for such legislative or administrative action as the Secretary determines appropriate.

(i) Application of other provisions of title. (1) In general. Except as provided in paragraph (2), the other provisions of this title [42 USCS §§ 701 et seq.] shall not apply to a grant made under this section.

(2) Exceptions. The following provisions of this title [42 USCS §§ 701 et seq.] shall apply to a grant made under this section to the same extent and in the same manner as such provisions apply to allotments made under section 502(c) [42 USCS § 702(c)]:

(A) Section 504(b)(6) [42 USCS § 704(b)(6)] (relating to prohibition on payments to excluded individuals and entities).

(B) Section 504(c) [42 USCS § 704(c)] (relating to the use of funds for the purchase of technical assistance).

(C) Section 504(d) [42 USCS § 704(d)] (relating to a limitation on administrative expenditures).

(D) Section 506 [42 USCS § 706] (relating to reports and audits), but only to the extent determined by the Secretary to be appropriate for grants made under this section.

(E) Section 507 [42 USCS § 707] (relating to penalties for false statements).

(F) Section 508 [42 USCS § 708] (relating to nondiscrimination).

(G) Section 509(a) [42 USCS § 709(a)] (relating to the administration of the grant program).

(j) Appropriations. (1) In general. Out of any funds in the Treasury not otherwise appropriated, there are appropriated to the Secretary to carry out this section—

(A) $100,000,000 for fiscal year 2010;

(B) $250,000,000 for fiscal year 2011;

(C) $350,000,000 for fiscal year 2012;

(D) $400,000,000 for fiscal year 2013; and

(E) $400,000,000 for fiscal year 2014.

(2) Reservations. Of the amount appropriated under this subsection for a fiscal year, the Secretary shall reserve—

(A) 3 percent of such amount for purposes of making grants to eligible entities that are Indian Tribes (or a consortium of Indian Tribes), Tribal Organizations, or Urban Indian Organizations; and

(B) 3 percent of such amount for purposes of carrying out subsections (d)(1)(B)(iii), (g), and (h)(3).

(3) Availability. Funds made available to an eligible entity under this section for a fiscal year shall remain available for expenditure by the eligible entity through the end of the second succeeding fiscal year after award. Any funds that are not expended by the eligible entity during the period in which the funds are available under the preceding sentence may be used for grants to nonprofit organizations under subsection (h)(2)(B).

(k) Definitions. In this section:

(1) Eligible entity. (A) In general. The term "eligible entity" means a State, an Indian Tribe, Tribal Organization, or Urban Indian Organization, Puerto Rico, Guam, the Virgin Islands, the Northern Mariana Islands, and American Samoa.

(B) Nonprofit organizations. Only for purposes of awarding grants under subsection (h)(2)(B), such term shall include a nonprofit organization with an established record of providing early childhood home visitation programs or initiatives in a State or several States.

(2) Eligible family. The term "eligible family" means—

(A) a woman who is pregnant, and the father of the child if the father is available; or

(B) a parent or primary caregiver of a child, including grandparents or other relatives of the child, and foster parents, who are serving as the child's primary caregiver from birth to kindergarten entry, and including a noncustodial parent who has an ongoing relationship with, and at times provides physical care for, the child.

(3) Indian Tribe; Tribal Organization. The terms "Indian Tribe" and "Tribal Organization", and "Urban Indian Organization" have the meanings given such terms in section 4 of the Indian Health Care Improvement Act [25 USCS § 1603].

(Aug. 14, 1935, ch 531, Title V, § 511, as added March 23, 2010, P. L. 111-148, Title II, Subtitle L, § 2951, 124 Stat. 334.)

§ 712. Services to individuals with a postpartum condition and their families

(a) In general. In addition to any other payments made under this title [42 USCS §§ 701 et seq.] to a State, the Secretary may make grants to eligible entities for projects for the establishment, operation, and coordination of effective and cost-efficient systems for the delivery of essential services to individuals with or at risk for postpartum conditions and their families.

(b) Certain activities. To the extent practicable and appropriate, the Secretary shall ensure that projects funded under subsection (a) provide education and services with respect to the diagnosis and management of postpartum conditions for individuals with or at risk for postpartum conditions and their families. The Secretary may allow such projects to include the following:

(1) Delivering or enhancing outpatient and home-based health and support services, including case management and comprehensive treatment services.

(2) Delivering or enhancing inpatient care management services that ensure the well-being of the mother and family and the future development of the infant.

(3) Improving the quality, availability, and organization of health care and support services (including transportation services, attendant care, homemaker services, day or respite care, and providing counseling on financial assistance and insurance).

(4) Providing education about postpartum conditions to promote earlier diagnosis and treatment. Such education may include—

(A) providing complete information on postpartum conditions, symptoms, methods of coping with the illness, and treatment resources; and

(B) in the case of a grantee that is a State, hospital, or birthing facility—

(i) providing education to new mothers and fathers, and other family members as appropriate, concerning postpartum conditions before new mothers leave the health facility; and

(ii) ensuring that training programs regarding such education are carried out at the health facility.

(c) Integration with other programs. To the extent practicable and appropriate, the Secretary may integrate the grant program under this section with other grant programs carried out by the Secretary, including the program under section 330 of the Public Health Service Act [42 USCS § 254b].

(d) Requirements. The Secretary shall establish requirements for grants made under this section that include a limit on the amount of grants funds that may be used for administration, accounting, reporting, or program oversight functions and a requirement for each eligible entity that receives a grant to submit, for each grant period, a report to the Secretary that describes how grant funds were used during such period.

(e) Technical assistance. The Secretary may provide technical assistance to entities seeking a grant under this section in order to assist such entities in complying with the requirements of this section.

(f) Application of other provisions of title. (1) In general. Except as provided in paragraph (2), the other provisions of this title [42 USCS §§ 701 et seq.] shall not apply to a grant made under this section.

(2) Exceptions. The following provisions of this title [42 USCS §§ 701 et seq.] shall apply to a grant made under this section to the same extent and in the same manner as such provisions apply to allotments made under section 502(c) [42 USCS § 702(c)]:

(A) Section 504(b)(6) [42 USCS § 704(b)(6)] (relating to prohibition on payments to excluded individuals and entities).

(B) Section 504(c) [42 USCS § 704(c)] (relating to the use of funds for the purchase of technical assistance).

(C) Section 504(d) [42 USCS § 704(d)] (relating to a limitation on administrative expenditures).

(D) Section 506 [42 USCS § 706] (relating to reports and audits), but only to the extent determined by the Secretary to be appropriate for grants made under this section.

(E) Section 507 [42 USCS § 707] (relating to penalties for false statements).

(F) Section 508 [42 USCS § 708] (relating to nondiscrimination).

(G) Section 509(a) [42 USCS § 709(a)] (relating to the administration of the grant program).

(g) Definitions. In this section:

(1) The term "eligible entity"—

(A) means a public or nonprofit private entity; and

(B) includes a State or local government, public-private partnership, recipient of a grant under section 330H of the Public Health Service Act [42 USCS § 254c-8] (relating to the Healthy Start Initiative), public or nonprofit private hospital, community-based organization, hospice, ambulatory care facility, community health center, migrant health center, public housing primary care center, or homeless health center.

(2) The term "postpartum condition" means postpartum depression or postpartum psychosis.

(Aug. 14, 1935, ch 531, Title V, § 512, as added March 23, 2010, P. L. 111-148, Title II, Subtitle L, § 2952(b), 124 Stat. 345.)

HISTORY; ANCILLARY LAWS AND DIRECTIVES

Other provisions:

Research on postpartum conditions. Act March 23, 2010, P. L. 111-148, Title II, Subtitle L, § 2952(a), 124 Stat. 344, provides:

"(1) Expansion and intensification of activities. The Secretary of Health and Human Services (in this subsection and subsection (c) referred to as the 'Secretary') is encouraged to continue activities on postpartum depression or postpartum psychosis (in this subsection and subsection (c) referred to as "postpartum conditions"), including research to expand the understanding of the causes of, and treatments for, postpartum conditions. Activities under this paragraph shall include conducting and supporting the following:

"(A) Basic research concerning the etiology and causes of the conditions.

"(B) Epidemiological studies to address the frequency and natural history of the conditions and the differences among racial and ethnic groups with respect to the conditions.

"(C) The development of improved screening and diagnostic techniques.

"(D) Clinical research for the development and evaluation of new treatments.

"(E) Information and education programs for health care professionals and the public, which may include a coordinated national campaign to increase the awareness and knowledge of postpartum conditions. Activities under such a national campaign may—

"(i) include public service announcements through television, radio, and other means; and

"(ii) focus on—

"(I) raising awareness about screening;

"(II) educating new mothers and their families about postpartum conditions to promote earlier diagnosis and treatment; and

"(III) ensuring that such education includes complete information concerning postpartum conditions, including its symptoms, methods of coping with the illness, and treatment resources.

"(2) Sense of Congress regarding longitudinal study of relative mental health consequences for women of resolving a pregnancy. (A) Sense of Congress. It is the sense of Congress that the Director of the National Institute of Mental Health may conduct a nationally representative longitudinal study (during the period of fiscal years 2010 through 2019) of the relative mental health consequences for women of resolving a pregnancy (intended and unintended) in various ways, including carrying the pregnancy to term and parenting the child, carrying the pregnancy to term and placing the child for adoption, miscarriage, and having an abortion. This study may assess the incidence, timing, magnitude, and duration of the immediate and long-term mental health consequences (positive or negative) of these pregnancy outcomes.

"(B) Report. Subject to the completion of the study under subsection (a), beginning not later than 5 years after the date of the enactment of this Act, and periodically thereafter for the duration of the study, such Director may prepare and submit to the Congress reports on the findings of the study.

§ 713. Personal responsibility education

(a) Allotments to States. (1) Amount. (A) In general. For the purpose described in subsection (b), subject to the succeeding provisions of this section, for each of fiscal years 2010 through 2014, the Secretary shall allot to each State an amount equal to the product of—

(i) the amount appropriated under subsection (f) for the fiscal year and available for allotments to States after the application of subsection (c); and

(ii) the State youth population percentage determined under paragraph (2).

(B) Minimum allotment. (i) In general. Each State allotment under this paragraph for a fiscal year shall be at least $250,000.

(ii) Pro rata adjustments. The Secretary shall adjust on a pro rata basis the amount of the State allotments determined under this paragraph for a fiscal year to the extent necessary to comply with clause (i).

(C) Application required to access allotments. (i) In general. A State shall not be paid from its allotment for a fiscal year unless the State submits an application to the Secretary for the fiscal year and the Secretary approves the application (or requires changes to the application that the State satisfies) and meets such additional requirements as the Secretary may specify.

(ii) Requirements. The State application shall contain an assurance that the State has complied with the requirements of this section in preparing and submitting the application and shall include the following as well as such additional information as the Secretary may require:

(I) Based on data from the Centers for Disease Control and Prevention National Center for Health Statistics, the most recent pregnancy rates for the State for youth ages 10 to 14 and youth ages 15 to 19 for which data are available, the most recent birth rates for such youth populations in the State for which data are available, and trends in those rates for the most recently preceding 5-year period for which such data are available.

(II) State-established goals for reducing the pregnancy rates and birth rates for such youth populations.

(III) A description of the State's plan for using the State allotments provided under this section to achieve such goals, especially among youth populations that are the most high-risk or vulnerable for pregnancies or otherwise have special circumstances, including youth in foster care, homeless youth, youth with HIV/AIDS, pregnant youth who are under 21 years of age, mothers who are under 21 years of age, and youth residing in areas with high birth rates for youth.

(2) State youth population percentage. (A) In general. For purposes of paragraph (1)(A)(ii), the State youth population percentage is, with respect to a State, the proportion (expressed as a percentage) of—

(i) the number of individuals who have attained age 10 but not attained age 20 in the State; to

(ii) the number of such individuals in all States.

(B) Determination of number of youth. The number of individuals described in clauses (i) and (ii) of subparagraph (A) in a State shall be determined on the basis of the most recent Bureau of the Census data.

(3) Availability of State allotments. Subject to paragraph (4)(A), amounts allotted to a State pursuant to this subsection for a fiscal year shall remain available for expenditure by the State through the end of the second succeeding fiscal year.

(4) Authority to award grants from State allotments to local organizations and entities in nonparticipating States. (A) Grants from unexpended allotments. If a State does not submit an application under this section for fiscal year 2010 or 2011, the State shall no longer be eligible to submit an application to receive funds from the amounts allotted for the State for each of fiscal years 2010 through 2014 and such amounts shall be used by the Secretary to award grants under this paragraph for each of fiscal years 2012 through 2014. The Secretary also shall use any amounts from the allotments of States that submit applications under this section for a fiscal year that remain unexpended as of the end of the period in which the allotments are available for expenditure under paragraph (3) for awarding grants under this paragraph.

(B) 3-year grants. (i) In general. The Secretary shall solicit applications to award 3-year grants in each of fiscal years 2012, 2013, and 2014 to local organizations and entities to conduct, consistent with subsection (b), programs and activities in States that do not submit an application for an allotment under this section for fiscal year 2010 or 2011.

(ii) Faith-based organizations or consortia. The Secretary may solicit and award grants under this paragraph to faith-based organizations or consortia.

(C) Evaluation. An organization or entity awarded a grant under this paragraph shall agree to participate in a rigorous Federal evaluation.

(5) Maintenance of effort. No payment shall be made to a State from the allotment determined for the State under this subsection or to a local organization or entity awarded a grant under paragraph (4), if the expenditure of non-federal funds by the State, organization, or entity for activities, programs, or initiatives for which amounts from allotments and grants under this subsection may be expended is less than the amount expended by the State, organization, or entity for such programs or initiatives for fiscal year 2009.

(6) Data collection and reporting. A State or local organization or entity receiving funds under this section shall cooperate with such requirements relating to the collection of data and information and reporting on outcomes regarding the programs and activities carried out with such funds, as the Secretary shall specify.

(b) Purpose. (1) In general. The purpose of an allotment under subsection (a)(1) to a State is to enable the State (or, in the case of grants made under subsection (a)(4)(B), to enable a local organization or entity) to carry out personal responsibility education programs consistent with this subsection.

(2) Personal responsibility education pro-

grams. (A) In general. In this section, the term "personal responsibility education program" means a program that is designed to educate adolescents on—

(i) both abstinence and contraception for the prevention of pregnancy and sexually transmitted infections, including HIV/AIDS, consistent with the requirements of subparagraph (B); and

(ii) at least 3 of the adulthood preparation subjects described in subparagraph (C).

(B) Requirements. The requirements of this subparagraph are the following:

(i) The program replicates evidence-based effective programs or substantially incorporates elements of effective programs that have been proven on the basis of rigorous scientific research to change behavior, which means delaying sexual activity, increasing condom or contraceptive use for sexually active youth, or reducing pregnancy among youth.

(ii) The program is medically-accurate and complete.

(iii) The program includes activities to educate youth who are sexually active regarding responsible sexual behavior with respect to both abstinence and the use of contraception.

(iv) The program places substantial emphasis on both abstinence and contraception for the prevention of pregnancy among youth and sexually transmitted infections.

(v) The program provides age-appropriate information and activities.

(vi) The information and activities carried out under the program are provided in the cultural context that is most appropriate for individuals in the particular population group to which they are directed.

(C) Adulthood preparation subjects. The adulthood preparation subjects described in this subparagraph are the following:

(i) Healthy relationships, including marriage and family interactions.

(ii) Adolescent development, such as the development of healthy attitudes and values about adolescent growth and development, body image, racial and ethnic diversity, and other related subjects.

(iii) Financial literacy.

(iv) Parent-child communication.

(v) Educational and career success, such as developing skills for employment preparation, job seeking, independent living, financial self-sufficiency, and workplace productivity.

(vi) Healthy life skills, such as goal-setting, decision making, negotiation, communication and interpersonal skills, and stress management.

(c) Reservations of funds. (1) Grants to implement innovative strategies. From the amount appropriated under subsection (f) for the fiscal year, the Secretary shall reserve $10,000,000 of such amount for purposes of awarding grants to entities to implement innovative youth pregnancy prevention strategies and target services to high-risk, vulnerable, and culturally under-represented youth populations, including youth in foster care, homeless youth, youth with HIV/AIDS, pregnant women who are under 21 years of age and their partners, mothers who are under 21 years of age and their partners, and youth residing in areas with high birth rates for youth. An entity awarded a grant under this paragraph shall agree to participate in a rigorous Federal evaluation of the activities carried out with grant funds.

(2) Other reservations. From the amount appropriated under subsection (f) for the fiscal year that remains after the application of paragraph (1), the Secretary shall reserve the following amounts:

(A) Grants for Indian tribes or tribal organizations. The Secretary shall reserve 5 percent of such remainder for purposes of awarding grants to Indian tribes and tribal organizations in such manner, and subject to such requirements, as the Secretary, in consultation with Indian tribes and tribal organizations, determines appropriate.

(B) Secretarial responsibilities. (i) Reservation of funds. The Secretary shall reserve 10 percent of such remainder for expenditures by the Secretary for the activities described in clauses (ii) and (iii).

(ii) Program support. The Secretary shall provide, directly or through a competitive grant process, research, training and technical assistance, including dissemination of research and information regarding effective and promising practices, providing consultation and resources on a broad array of teen pregnancy prevention strategies, including abstinence and contraception, and developing resources and materials to support the activities of recipients of grants and other State, tribal, and community organizations working to reduce teen pregnancy. In carrying out such functions, the Secretary shall collaborate with a variety of entities that have expertise in the prevention of teen pregnancy, HIV and sexually transmitted infections, healthy relationships, financial literacy, and other topics addressed through the personal responsibility education programs.

(iii) Evaluation. The Secretary shall evaluate the programs and activities carried out with funds made available through allotments or grants under this section.

(d) Administration. (1) In general. The Secretary shall administer this section through the Assistant Secretary for the Administration for Children and Families within the Department of Health and Human Services.

(2) Application of other provisions of title. (A) In general. Except as provided in subparagraph (B), the other provisions of this title [42 USCS §§ 701 et seq.] shall not apply to allotments or grants made under this section.

(B) Exceptions. The following provisions of this title [42 USCS §§ 701 et seq.] shall apply to allotments and grants made under this section to the same extent and in the same manner as such provisions apply to allotments made under section 502(c) [42 USCS § 702(c)]:

(i) Section 504(b)(6) [42 USCS § 704(b)(6)] (relating to prohibition on payments to excluded individuals and entities).

(ii) Section 504(c) [42 USCS § 704(c)] (relating to the use of funds for the purchase of technical assistance).

(iii) Section 504(d) [42 USCS § 704(d)] (relating to a limitation on administrative expenditures).

(iv) Section 506 [42 USCS § 706] (relating to reports and audits), but only to the extent determined by the Secretary to be appropriate for grants made under this section.

(v) Section 507 [42 USCS § 707] (relating to penalties for false statements).

(vi) Section 508 [42 USCS § 708] (relating to nondiscrimination).

(e) Definitions. In this section:

(1) Age-appropriate. The term "age-appropriate", with respect to the information in pregnancy prevention, means topics, messages, and teaching methods suitable to particular ages or age groups of children and adolescents, based on developing cognitive, emotional, and behavioral capacity typical for the age or age group.

(2) Medically accurate and complete. The term "medically accurate and complete" means verified or supported by the weight of research conducted in compliance with accepted scientific methods and—

(A) published in peer-reviewed journals, where applicable; or

(B) comprising information that leading professional organizations and agencies with relevant expertise in the field recognize as accurate, objective, and complete.

(3) Indian tribes; tribal organizations. The terms "Indian tribe" and "Tribal organization" have the meanings given such terms in section 4 of the Indian Health Care Improvement Act (25 U.S.C. 1603)).

(4) Youth. The term "youth" means an individual who has attained age 10 but has not attained age 20.

(f) Appropriation. For the purpose of carrying out this section, there is appropriated, out of any money in the Treasury not otherwise appropriated, $75,000,000 for each of fiscal years 2010 through 2014. Amounts appropriated under this subsection shall remain available until expended.

(Aug. 14, 1935, ch 531, Title V, § 513, as added and amended March 23, 2010, P. L. 111-148, Title II, Subtitle L, § 2953, Title X, Subtitle B, Part I, § 10201(h), 124 Stat. 347, 922.)

TITLE VII. ADMINISTRATION

§ 914. Office of Women's Health

(a) Establishment. The Secretary shall establish within the Office of the Administrator of the Health Resources and Services Administration, an office to be known as the Office of Women's Health. The Office shall be headed by a director who shall be appointed by the Administrator.

(b) Purpose. The Director of the Office shall—

(1) report to the Administrator on the current Administration level of activity regarding women's health across, where appropriate, age, biological, and sociocultural contexts;

(2) establish short-range and long-range goals and objectives within the Health Resources and Services Administration for women's health and, as relevant and appropriate, coordinate with other appropriate offices on activities within the Administration that relate to health care provider training, health service delivery, research, and demonstration projects, for issues of particular concern to women;

(3) identify projects in women's health that should be conducted or supported by the bureaus of the Administration;

(4) consult with health professionals, nongovernmental organizations, consumer organizations, women's health professionals, and other individuals and groups, as appropriate, on Administration policy with regard to women; and

(5) serve as a member of the Department of Health and Human Services Coordinating Committee on Women's Health (established under section 229(b)(4) of the Public Health Service Act [42 USCS § 237a(b)(4)]).

(c) Continued administration of exist-

ing programs. The Director of the Office shall assume the authority for the development, implementation, administration, and evaluation of any projects carried out through the Health Resources and Services Administration relating to women's health on the date of enactment of this section.

(d) Definitions. For purposes of this section:

(1) Administration. The term "Administration" means the Health Resources and Services Administration.

(2) Administrator. The term "Administrator" means the Administrator of the Health Resources and Services Administration.

(3) Office. The term "Office" means the Office of Women's Health established under this section in the Administration.

(e) Authorization of appropriations. For the purpose of carrying out this section, there are authorized to be appropriated such sums as may be necessary for each of the fiscal years 2010 through 2014.

(Aug. 14, 1935, ch 531, Title VII, § 713, as added March 23, 2010, P. L. 111-148, Title III, Subtitle F, § 3509(f), 124 Stat. 535.)

TITLE XI. GENERAL PROVISIONS, PEER REVIEW, AND ADMINISTRATIVE SIMPLIFICATION

PART A. GENERAL PROVISIONS

§ 1305. Short title of chapter

This Act may be cited as the "Social Security Act".

(Aug. 14, 1935, ch 531, Title XI, Part A, § 1105, 49 Stat. 648; Oct. 30, 1972, P. L. 92-603, Title II, § 249F(a), 86 Stat. 1429.)

HISTORY; ANCILLARY LAWS AND DIRECTIVES

Short title:

Act March 23, 2010, P. L. 111-148, Title VI, Subtitle H, § 6701, 124 Stat. 782, provides: "This subtitle [adding 42 USCS §§ 1397j et seq. generally; for full classification, consult USCS Tables volumes] may be cited as the 'Elder Justice Act of 2009'.".

§ 1308. Additional grants to Puerto Rico, the Virgin Islands, Guam, and American Samoa; limitation on total payments [Caution: See prospective amendment note below.]

(a) Limitation on total payments to each territory. (1) In general. Notwithstanding any other provision of this Act [42 USCS §§ 301 et seq.] (except for paragraph (2) of this subsection), the total amount certified by the Secretary of Health and Human Services under titles I, X, XIV, and XVI [42 USCS §§ 301 et seq., 1201 et seq., 1351 et seq., 1381 et seq.], under parts A and E of title IV [42 USCS §§ 601 et seq., 670 et seq.], and under subsection (b) of this section, for payment to any territory for a fiscal year shall not exceed the ceiling amount for the territory for the fiscal year.

(2) Certain payments disregarded. Paragraph (1) of this subsection shall be applied without regard to any payment made under section 403(a)(2), 403(a)(4), 403(a)(5), 403(c)(3), 406, or 413(f) [42 USCS § 603(a)(2), (4), (5), (c)(3), 606, or 613(f)].

(b) Entitlement to matching grant. (1) In general. Each territory shall be entitled to receive from the Secretary for each fiscal year a grant in an amount equal to 75 percent of the amount (if any) by which—

(A) the total expenditures of the territory during the fiscal year under the territory programs funded under parts A and E of title IV [42 USCS §§ 601 et seq. and 670 et seq.], including any amount paid to the State under part A of title IV [42 USCS §§ 601 et seq.] that is transferred in accordance with section 404(d) [42 USCS § 604(d)] and expended under the program to which transferred; exceeds

(B) the sum of—

(i) the amount of the family assistance grant payable to the territory without regard to section 409 [42 USCS § 609]; and

(ii) the total amount expended by the territory during fiscal year 1995 pursuant to parts A and F of title IV [42 USCS §§ 601 et seq. and 681 et seq.] (as so in effect), other than for child care.

(2) Appropriation. Out of any money in the Treasury of the United States not otherwise appropriated, there are appropriated for fiscal years 1997 through 2003, such sums as are necessary for grants under this paragraph.

(c) Definitions. As used in this section:

(1) Territory. The term "territory" means Puerto Rico, the Virgin Islands, Guam, and American Samoa.

(2) Ceiling amount. The term "ceiling amount" means, with respect to a territory and a fiscal year, the mandatory ceiling amount with respect to the territory, reduced for the fiscal year in accordance with subsection (e), and reduced by the amount of any penalty imposed on the territory under any provision of law specified in subsection (a) during the fiscal

year.

(3) Family assistance grant. The term "family assistance grant" has the meaning given such term by section 403(a)(1)(B) [42 USCS § 603(a)(1)(B)].

(4) Mandatory ceiling amount. The term "mandatory ceiling amount" means—

(A) $107,255,000 with respect to Puerto Rico;

(B) $4,686,000 with respect to Guam;

(C) $3,554,000 with respect to the Virgin Islands; and

(D) $1,000,000 with respect to American Samoa.

(5) Total amount expended by the territory. The term "total amount expended by the territory"—

(A) does not include expenditures during the fiscal year from amounts made available by the Federal Government; and

(B) when used with respect to fiscal year 1995, also does not include—

(i) expenditures during fiscal year 1995 under subsection (g) or (i) of section 402 [former 42 USCS § 602(g) or (i)] (as in effect on September 30, 1995); or

(ii) any expenditures during fiscal year 1995 for which the territory (but for section 1108 [42 USCS § 1308], as in effect on September 30, 1995) would have received reimbursement from the Federal Government.

(d) Authority to transfer funds to certain programs. A territory to which an amount is paid under subsection (b) of this section may use the amount in accordance with section 404(d) [42 USCS § 604(d)].

(e) [Deleted]

(f) Total amount certified under 42 USCS §§ 1396 et seq. Subject to subsection (g) and section 1935(e)(1)(B) [42 USCS § 1396u-5(e)(1)(B)], the total amount certified by the Secretary under title XIX [42 USCS §§ 1396 et seq.] with respect to a fiscal year for payment to—

(1) Puerto Rico shall not exceed (A) $116,500,000 for fiscal year 1994 and (B) for each succeeding fiscal year the amount provided in this paragraph for the preceding fiscal year increased by the percentage increase in the medical care component of the consumer price index for all urban consumers (as published by the Bureau of Labor Statistics) for the twelve-month period ending in March preceding the beginning of the fiscal year, rounded to the nearest $100,000;

(2) the Virgin Islands shall not exceed (A) $3,837,500 for fiscal year 1994, and (B) for each succeeding fiscal year the amount provided in this paragraph for the preceding fiscal year increased by the percentage increase referred to in paragraph (1)(B), rounded to the nearest $10,000;

(3) Guam shall not exceed (A) $3,685,000 for fiscal year 1994, and (B) for each succeeding fiscal year the amount provided in this paragraph for the preceding fiscal year increased by the percentage increase referred to in paragraph (1)(B), rounded to the nearest $10,000;

(4) Northern Mariana Islands shall not exceed (A) $1,110,000 for fiscal year 1994, and (B) for each succeeding fiscal year the amount provided in this paragraph for the preceding fiscal year increased by the percentage increase referred to in paragraph (1)(B), rounded to the nearest $10,000; and

(5) American Samoa shall not exceed (A) $2,140,000 for fiscal year 1994, and (B) for each succeeding fiscal year the amount provided in this paragraph for the preceding fiscal year increased by the percentage increase referred to in paragraph (1)(B), rounded to the nearest $10,000.

(g) Medicaid payments to Territories for fiscal year 1998 and thereafter. (1) Fiscal year 1998. With respect to fiscal year 1998, the amounts otherwise determined for Puerto Rico, the Virgin Islands, Guam, the Northern Mariana Islands, and American Samoa under subsection (f) for such fiscal year shall be increased by the following amounts:

(A) For Puerto Rico, $30,000,000.

(B) For the Virgin Islands, $750,000.

(C) For Guam, $750,000.

(D) For the Northern Mariana Islands, $500,000.

(E) For American Samoa, $500,000.

(2) Fiscal year 1999 and thereafter. Notwithstanding subsection (f) and subject to paragraphs (3) and (5) and section 1323(a)(2) of the Patient Protection and Affordable Care Act [42 USCS § 18043(a)(2)], with respect to fiscal year 1999 and any fiscal year thereafter, the total amount certified by the Secretary under title XIX [42 USCS §§ 1396 et seq.] for payment to—

(A) Puerto Rico shall not exceed the sum of the amount provided in this subsection for the preceding fiscal year increased by the percentage increase in the medical care component of the Consumer Price Index for all urban consumers (as published by the Bureau of Labor Statistics) for the 12-month period ending in March preceding the beginning of the fiscal year, rounded to the nearest $100,000;

(B) the Virgin Islands shall not exceed the sum of the amount provided in this subsection for the preceding fiscal year increased by the percentage increase referred to in subparagraph (A), rounded to the nearest $10,000;

(C) Guam shall not exceed the sum of the amount provided in this subsection for the preceding fiscal year increased by the percentage increase referred to in subparagraph (A), rounded to the nearest $10,000;

(D) the Northern Mariana Islands shall not exceed the sum of the amount provided in this subsection for the preceding fiscal year increased by the percentage increase referred to in subparagraph (A), rounded to the nearest $10,000; and

(E) American Samoa shall not exceed the sum of the amount provided in this subsection for the preceding fiscal year increased by the percentage increase referred to in subparagraph (A), rounded to the nearest $10,000.

(3) Fiscal years 2006 and 2007 for certain insular areas. The amounts otherwise determined under this subsection for Puerto Rico, the Virgin Islands, Guam, the Northern Mariana Islands, and American Samoa for fiscal year 2006 and fiscal year 2007 shall be increased by the following amounts:

(A) For Puerto Rico, $12,000,000 for fiscal year 2006 and $12,000,000 for fiscal year 2007.

(B) For the Virgin Islands, $2,500,000 for fiscal year 2006 and $5,000,000 for fiscal year 2007.

(C) For Guam, $2,500,000 for fiscal year 2006 and $5,000,000 for fiscal year 2007.

(D) For the Northern Mariana Islands, $1,000,000 for fiscal year 2006 and $2,000,000 for fiscal year 2007.

(E) For American Samoa, $2,000,000 for fiscal year 2006 and $4,000,000 for fiscal year 2007.

Such amounts shall not be taken into account in applying paragraph (2) for fiscal year 2007 but shall be taken into account in applying such paragraph for fiscal year 2008 and subsequent fiscal years.

(4) Exclusion of certain expenditures from payment limits. With respect to fiscal years beginning with fiscal year 2009, if Puerto Rico, the Virgin Islands, Guam, the Northern Mariana Islands, or American Samoa qualify for a payment under subparagraph (A)(i), (B), or (F) of section 1903(a)(3) [42 USCS § 1396b(a)(3)] for a calendar quarter of such fiscal year, the payment shall not be taken into account in applying subsection (f) (as increased in accordance with paragraphs (1), (2), (3), and (4) [(5)] of this subsection) to such commonwealth or territory for such fiscal year.

(5) Additional increase. The Secretary shall increase the amounts otherwise determined under this subsection for Puerto Rico, the Virgin Islands, Guam, the Northern Mariana Islands, and American Samoa (after the application of subsection (f) and the preceding paragraphs of this subsection) for the period beginning July 1, 2011, and ending on September 30, 2019, by such amounts that the total additional payments under title XIX [42 USCS §§ 1396 et seq.] to such territories equals $6,300,000,000 for such period. The Secretary shall increase such amounts in proportion to the amounts applicable to such territories under this subsection and subsection (f) on the date of enactment of this paragraph [enacted March 30, 2010].

(Aug. 14, 1935, ch 531, Title XI, Part A, § 1108, as added Aug. 28, 1950, ch 809, Title III, Part 6, § 361(g), 64 Stat. 558; Aug. 1, 1956, ch 836, Title III, Part VI, § 351(c), 70 Stat. 855; Aug. 28, 1958, P. L. 85-840, Title V, §§ 507(a), 508, 72 Stat. 1051; Sept. 13, 1960, P. L. 86-778, Title VI, § 602, 74 Stat. 992; May 8, 1961, P. L. 87-31, § 6, 75 Stat. 78; June 30, 1961, P. L. 87-64, Title III, § 303(d), 75 Stat. 143; July 25, 1962, P. L. 87-543, Title I, Part E, § 151, 76 Stat. 206; July 30, 1965, P. L. 89-97, Title II, Part 1, § 208(a)(2), Title IV, § 408(a), 79 Stat. 355, 422; Jan. 2, 1968, P. L. 90-248, Title II, Part 4, § 248(a)(1), 81 Stat. 918; Oct. 30, 1972, P. L. 92-603, Title II, §§ 249F(a), 271(a), (b), 272(b), 86 Stat. 1429, 1451; Jan. 4, 1975, P. L. 93-647, Part A, § 3(i), 88 Stat. 2350; Nov. 6, 1978, P. L. 95-600, Title VIII, § 802(b), 92 Stat. 2945; June 17, 1980, P. L. 96-272, Title II, § 207(c), Title III, § 305(a), (b), 94 Stat. 526, 529, 530; Aug. 13, 1981, P. L. 97-35, Title XXI, Subtitle C, ch 1, § 2162(b)(1), Subtitle D, § 2193(c)(1), Title XXIII, Subtitle C, § 2353(f), 95 Stat. 806, 827, 872; Sept. 3, 1982, P. L. 97-248, Title I, Subtitle B, § 136(b), Subtitle D, § 160(a), 96 Stat. 375, 400; July 18, 1984, P. L. 98-369, Division B, Title III, Subtitle B, § 2365(a), 98 Stat. 1108; Dec. 22, 1987, P. L. 100-203, Title IV, Subtitle B, Part 2, § 4111(a), 101 Stat. 1330-148; Oct. 13, 1988, P. L. 100-485, Title II, § 202(c)(2), (3), Title VI, §§ 601(b), (c)(2), 602(a), 102 Stat. 2378, 2407, 2408; Aug. 10, 1993, P. L. 103-66, Title XIII, Ch 2, Subch B, Part V, § 13641(a), 107 Stat. 646; Aug. 22, 1996, P. L. 104-193, Title I, § 103(a), 110 Stat. 2160; Aug. 5, 1997, P. L. 105-33, Title IV, Subtitle H, Ch 3, § 4726, Title V, Subtitle A, § 5001(b), Subtitle F, Ch 1, § 5512, 111 Stat. 519, 589, 619; June 30, 2003, P. L. 108-40, § 3(b), 117 Stat. 836; Dec. 8, 2003, P. L. 108-173, Title I, § 103(d)(2), 117 Stat. 2159; Feb. 8, 2006, P. L. 109-171, Title VI, Subtitle A, Ch. 5,

§ 6055, 120 Stat. 96; Feb. 4, 2009, P. L. 111-3, Title I, Subtitle A, § 109, 123 Stat. 25; Feb. 17, 2009, P. L. 111-5, Div B, Title II, Subtitle B, § 2101(c), (d)(1), 123 Stat. 449; March 23, 2010, P. L. 111-148, Title II, Subtitle A, § 2005(a), (b), Title X, Subtitle B, Part I, § 10201(d), 124 Stat. 283, 919; March 30, 2010, P. L. 111-152, Title I, Subtitle C, § 1204(b)(1), (2)(A), 124 Stat. 1056.)

HISTORY; ANCILLARY LAWS AND DIRECTIVES

Prospective amendments:

Amendment of subsec. (a)(2), effective October 1, 2010. Act Feb. 17, 2009, P. L. 111-5, Div B, Title II, Subtitle B, § 2101(d)(1), 123 Stat. 449, provides: "Effective October 1, 2010, section 1108(a)(2) of the Social Security Act (42 U.S.C. 1308(a)(2)) is amended by striking '403(c)(3),' (as added by subsection (c)).".

§ 1315. Demonstration projects

(a) Waiver of State plan requirements; costs regarded as State plan expenditures; availability of appropriations. In the case of any experimental, pilot, or demonstration project which, in the judgment of the Secretary, is likely to assist in promoting the objectives of title I, X, XIV, XVI, or XIX, or part A or D of title IV [42 USCS §§ 301 et seq., 601 et seq., 651 et seq., 1201 et seq., 1351 et seq., 1381 et seq., 1396 et seq.] in a State or States—

(1) the Secretary may waive compliance with any of the requirements of section 2, 402, 454, 1002, 1402, 1602, or 1902 [42 USCS §§ 302, 654, 1202, 1352, 1382, 1396a,], as the case may be, to the extent and for the period he finds necessary to enable such State or States to carry out such project, and

(2)(A) costs of such project which would not otherwise be included as expenditures under section 3, 455, 1003, 1403, 1603, or 1903 [42 USCS §§ 603, 655, 1203, 1353, 1383, 1396b,], as the case may be, and which are not included as part of the costs of projects under section 1110 [42 USCS § 1310], shall, to the extent and for the period prescribed by the Secretary, be regarded as expenditures under the State plan or plans approved under such title, or for administration of such State plan or plans, as may be appropriate, and

(B) costs of such project which would not otherwise be a permissible use of funds under part A of title IV [42 USCS §§ 601 et seq.] and which are not included as part of the costs of projects under section 1110 [42 USCS § 1310], shall to the extent and for the period prescribed by the Secretary, be regarded as a permissible use of funds under such part

In addition, not to exceed $4,000,000 of the aggregate amount appropriated for payments to States under such titles for any fiscal year beginning after June 30, 1967, shall be available, under such terms and conditions as the Secretary may establish, for payments to States to cover so much of the cost of such projects as is not covered by payments under such titles and is not included as part of the cost of projects for purposes of section 1110 [42 USCS § 1310].

(b) Child support enforcement program. In the case of any experimental, pilot, or demonstration project undertaken under subsection (a) to assist in promoting the objectives of part D of title IV [42 USCS §§ 651 et seq.] the project—

(1) must be designed to improve the financial well-being of children or otherwise improve the operation of the child support program;

(2) may not permit modifications in the child support program which would have the effect of disadvantaging children in need of support; and

(3) must not result in increased cost to the Federal Government under part A of such title [42 USCS §§ 601 et seq.].

(c) Demonstration projects to test alternative definitions of employment. (1)(A) The Secretary shall enter into agreements with up to 8 States submitting applications under this subsection for the purpose of conducting demonstration projects in such States to test and evaluate the use, with respect to individuals who received aid under part A of title IV [42 USCS §§ 601 et seq.] in the preceding month (on the basis of the unemployment of the parent who is the principal earner), of a number greater than 100 for the number of hours per month that such individuals may work and still be considered to be unemployed for purposes of section 407 [42 USCS § 607]. If any State submits an application under this subsection for the purpose of conducting a demonstration project to test and evaluate the total elimination of the 100-hour rule, the Secretary shall approve at least one such application.

(B) If any State with an agreement under this subsection so requests, the demonstration project conducted pursuant to such agreement may test and evaluate the complete elimination of the 100-hour rule and of any other durational standard that might be applied in defining unemployment for purposes of determining eligibility under section 407 [42 USCS § 607].

(2) Notwithstanding section 402(a)(1) [42 USCS § 602(a)(1)], a demonstration project conducted under this subsection may be con-

ducted in one or more political subdivisions of the State.

(3) An agreement under this subsection shall be entered into between the Secretary and the State agency designated under section 402(a)(3) [42 USCS § 602(a)(3)]. Such agreement shall provide for the payment of aid under the applicable State plan under part A of title IV [42 USCS §§ 601 et seq.] as though section 407 [42 USCS § 607] had been modified to reflect the definition of unemployment used in the demonstration project but shall also provide that such project shall otherwise be carried out in accordance with all of the requirements and conditions of section 407 [42 USCS § 607] (and, except as provided in paragraph (2), any related requirements and conditions under part A of title IV [42 USCS §§ 601 et seq.]).

(4) A demonstration project under this subsection may be commenced any time after September 30, 1990, and shall be conducted for such period of time as the agreement with the Secretary may provide; except that, in no event may a demonstration project under this section be conducted after September 30, 1995.

(5)(A) Any State with an agreement under this subsection shall evaluate the comparative cost and employment effects of the use of the definition of unemployment in its demonstration project under this section by use of experimental and control groups comprised of a random sample of individuals receiving aid under section 407 [42 USCS § 607] and shall furnish the Secretary with such information as the Secretary determines to be necessary to evaluate the results of the project conducted by the State.

(B) The Secretary shall report the results of the demonstration projects conducted under this subsection to the Congress not later than 6 months after all such projects are completed.

(d) Demonstration projects. (1) An application or renewal of any experimental, pilot, or demonstration project undertaken under subsection (a) to promote the objectives of title XIX or XXI [42 USCS §§ 1396 et seq. or 1397aa et seq.] in a State that would result in an impact on eligibility, enrollment, benefits, cost-sharing, or financing with respect to a State program under title XIX or XXI [42 USCS §§ 1396 et seq. or 1397aa et seq.] (in this subsection referred to as a "demonstration project") shall be considered by the Secretary in accordance with the regulations required to be promulgated under paragraph (2).

(2) Not later than 180 days after the date of enactment of this subsection [enacted March 23, 2010], the Secretary shall promulgate regulations relating to applications for, and renewals of, a demonstration project that provide for—

(A) a process for public notice and comment at the State level, including public hearings, sufficient to ensure a meaningful level of public input;

(B) requirements relating to—

(i) the goals of the program to be implemented or renewed under the demonstration project;

(ii) the expected State and Federal costs and coverage projections of the demonstration project; and

(iii) the specific plans of the State to ensure that the demonstration project will be in compliance with title XIX or XXI [42 USCS §§ 1396 et seq. or 1397aa et seq.];

(C) a process for providing public notice and comment after the application is received by the Secretary, that is sufficient to ensure a meaningful level of public input;

(D) a process for the submission to the Secretary of periodic reports by the State concerning the implementation of the demonstration project; and

(E) a process for the periodic evaluation by the Secretary of the demonstration project.

(3) The Secretary shall annually report to Congress concerning actions taken by the Secretary with respect to applications for demonstration projects under this section.

(e) Extension of State-wide comprehensive demonstration projects for which waivers granted. (1) The provisions of this subsection shall apply to the extension of any State-wide comprehensive demonstration project (in this subsection referred to as "waiver project") for which a waiver of compliance with requirements of title XIX [42 USCS §§ 1396 et seq.] is granted under subsection (a).

(2) During the 6-month period ending 1 year before the date the waiver under subsection (a) with respect to a waiver project would otherwise expire, the chief executive officer of the State which is operating the project may submit to the Secretary a written request for an extension, of up to 3 years (5 years, in the case of a waiver described in section 1915(h)(2) [42 USCS § 1396n(h)(2)]), of the project.

(3) If the Secretary fails to respond to the request within 6 months after the date it is submitted, the request is deemed to have been granted.

(4) If such a request is granted, the deadline for submittal of a final report under the waiver

project is deemed to have been extended until the date that is 1 year after the date the waiver project would otherwise have expired.

(5) The Secretary shall release an evaluation of each such project not later than 1 year after the date of receipt of the final report.

(6) Subject to paragraphs (4) and (7), the extension of a waiver project under this subsection shall be on the same terms and conditions (including applicable terms and conditions relating to quality and access of services, budget neutrality, data and reporting requirements, and special population protections) that applied to the project before its extension under this subsection.

(7) If an original condition of approval of a waiver project was that Federal expenditures under the project not exceed the Federal expenditures that would otherwise have been made, the Secretary shall take such steps as may be necessary to ensure that, in the extension of the project under this subsection, such condition continues to be met. In applying the previous sentence, the Secretary shall take into account the Secretary's best estimate of rates of change in expenditures at the time of the extension.

(f) Application for extension of waiver project; submission; approval. An application by the chief executive officer of a State for an extension of a waiver project the State is operating under an extension under subsection (e) (in this subsection referred to as the "waiver project") shall be submitted and approved or disapproved in accordance with the following:

(1) The application for an extension of the waiver project shall be submitted to the Secretary at least 120 days prior to the expiration of the current period of the waiver project.

(2) Not later than 45 days after the date such application is received by the Secretary, the Secretary shall notify the State if the Secretary intends to review the terms and conditions of the waiver project. A failure to provide such notification shall be deemed to be an approval of the application.

(3) Not later than 45 days after the date a notification is made in accordance with paragraph (2), the Secretary shall inform the State of proposed changes in the terms and conditions of the waiver project. A failure to provide such information shall be deemed to be an approval of the application.

(4) During the 30-day period that begins on the date information described in paragraph (3) is provided to a State, the Secretary shall negotiate revised terms and conditions of the waiver project with the State.

(5)(A) Not later than 120 days after the date an application for an extension of the waiver project is submitted to the Secretary (or such later date agreed to by the chief executive officer of the State), the Secretary shall—

(i) approve the application subject to such modifications in the terms and conditions—

(I) as have been agreed to by the Secretary and the State; or

(II) in the absence of such agreement, as are determined by the Secretary to be reasonable, consistent with the overall objectives of the waiver project, and not in violation of applicable law; or

(ii) disapprove the application.

(B) A failure by the Secretary to approve or disapprove an application submitted under this subsection in accordance with the requirements of subparagraph (A) shall be deemed to be an approval of the application subject to such modifications in the terms and conditions as have been agreed to (if any) by the Secretary and the State.

(6) An approval of an application for an extension of a waiver project under this subsection shall be for a period not to exceed 3 years (5 years, in the case of a waiver described in section 1915(h)(2) [42 USCS § 1396n(h)(2)]).

(7) An extension of a waiver project under this subsection shall be subject to the final reporting and evaluation requirements of paragraphs (4) and (5) of subsection (e) (taking into account the extension under this subsection with respect to any timing requirements imposed under those paragraphs).

(Aug. 14, 1935, ch 531, Title XI, Part A, § 1115, as added July 25, 1962, P. L. 87-543, Title I, Part B, § 122, 76 Stat. 192; July 30, 1965, P. L. 89-97, Title I, Part 2, § 121(c)(3), 79 Stat. 352; June 29, 1967, P. L. 90-36, § 2, 81 Stat. 94; Jan. 2, 1968, P. L. 90-248, Title II, Part 3, § 241(c)(4), Part 4, § 247, 81 Stat. 917, 918; Oct. 30, 1972, P. L. 92-603, Title II, § 249F(a), 86 Stat. 1429; Dec. 31, 1973, P. L. 93-223, § 18(z-2)(1)(B), 87 Stat. 973; Jan. 4, 1975, P. L. 93-647, Part A, § 3(c), 88 Stat. 2349; Dec. 20, 1977, P. L. 95-216, Title IV, § 404, 91 Stat. 1562; Aug. 13, 1981, P. L. 97-35, Title XXIII, Subtitle C, § 2353(g), 95 Stat. 872; July 18, 1984, P. L. 98-369, Division B, Title VI, Subtitle D, § 2663(e)(5), 98 Stat. 1168; Aug. 16, 1984, P. L. 98-378, § 10, 98 Stat. 1317; April 7, 1986, P. L. 99-272, Title XIV, § 14001(b)(2), 100 Stat. 328; Oct. 13, 1988, P. L. 100-485, Title V, § 503, 102 Stat. 2402; Aug. 22, 1996, P. L. 104-193, Title I, § 108(g)(2), 110 Stat. 2168; Aug. 5, 1997, P. L. 105-33, Title IV, Subtitle H, Ch 6, § 4757(a), 111 Stat. 527; Dec. 21, 2000, P. L.

106-554, § 1(a)(6), 114 Stat. 2763; March 23, 2010, P. L. 111-148, Title II, Subtitle H, § 2601(b), Title X, Subtitle B, Part I, § 10201(i), 124 Stat. 315, 922.)

§ 1315a. Center for Medicare and Medicaid Innovation

(a) Center for Medicare and Medicaid Innovation established. (1) In general. There is created within the Centers for Medicare & Medicaid Services a Center for Medicare and Medicaid Innovation (in this section referred to as the "CMI") to carry out the duties described in this section. The purpose of the CMI is to test innovative payment and service delivery models to reduce program expenditures under the applicable titles while preserving or enhancing the quality of care furnished to individuals under such titles. In selecting such models, the Secretary shall give preference to models that also improve the coordination, quality, and efficiency of health care services furnished to applicable individuals defined in paragraph (4)(A).

(2) Deadline. The Secretary shall ensure that the CMI is carrying out the duties described in this section by not later than January 1, 2011.

(3) Consultation. In carrying out the duties under this section, the CMI shall consult representatives of relevant Federal agencies, and clinical and analytical experts with expertise in medicine and health care management. The CMI shall use open door forums or other mechanisms to seek input from interested parties.

(4) Definitions. In this section:

(A) Applicable individual. The term "applicable individual" means—

(i) an individual who is entitled to, or enrolled for, benefits under part A of title XVIII [42 USCS §§ 1395c et seq.] or enrolled for benefits under part B of such title [42 USCS §§ 1395j et seq.];

(ii) an individual who is eligible for medical assistance under title XIX [42 USCS §§ 1396 et seq.], under a State plan or waiver; or

(iii) an individual who meets the criteria of both clauses (i) and (ii).

(B) Applicable title. The term "applicable title" means title XVIII [42 USCS §§ 1395 et seq.], title XIX [42 USCS §§ 1396 et seq.], or both.

(5) Testing within certain geographic areas. For purposes of testing payment and service delivery models under this section, the Secretary may elect to limit testing of a model to certain geographic areas.

(b) Testing of models (Phase I). (1) In general. The CMI shall test payment and service delivery models in accordance with selection criteria under paragraph (2) to determine the effect of applying such models under the applicable title (as defined in subsection (a)(4)(B)) on program expenditures under such titles and the quality of care received by individuals receiving benefits under such title.

(2) Selection of models to be tested. (A) In general. The Secretary shall select models to be tested from models where the Secretary determines that there is evidence that the model addresses a defined population for which there are deficits in care leading to poor clinical outcomes or potentially avoidable expenditures. The Secretary shall focus on models expected to reduce program costs under the applicable title while preserving or enhancing the quality of care received by individuals receiving benefits under such title. The models selected under this subparagraph may include, but are not limited to, the models described in subparagraph (B).

(B) Opportunities. The models described in this subparagraph are the following models:

(i) Promoting broad payment and practice reform in primary care, including patient-centered medical home models for high-need applicable individuals, medical homes that address women's unique health care needs, and models that transition primary care practices away from fee-for-service based reimbursement and toward comprehensive payment or salary-based payment.

(ii) Contracting directly with groups of providers of services and suppliers to promote innovative care delivery models, such as through risk-based comprehensive payment or salary-based payment.

(iii) Utilizing geriatric assessments and comprehensive care plans to coordinate the care (including through interdisciplinary teams) of applicable individuals with multiple chronic conditions and at least one of the following:

(I) An inability to perform 2 or more activities of daily living.

(II) Cognitive impairment, including dementia.

(iv) Promote care coordination between providers of services and suppliers that transition health care providers away from fee-for-service based reimbursement and toward salary-based payment.

(v) Supporting care coordination for chronically-ill applicable individuals at high risk of hospitalization through a health information technology-enabled provider network that includes care coordinators, a chronic disease registry, and home tele-health technology.

(vi) Varying payment to physicians who order advanced diagnostic imaging services (as defined in section 1834(e)(1)(B) [42 USCS § 1395m(e)(1)(B)]) according to the physician's adherence to appropriateness criteria for the ordering of such services, as determined in consultation with physician specialty groups and other relevant stakeholders.

(vii) Utilizing medication therapy management services, such as those described in section 935 of the Public Health Service Act [42 USCS § 299b-35].

(viii) Establishing community-based health teams to support small-practice medical homes by assisting the primary care practitioner in chronic care management, including patient self-management, activities.

(ix) Assisting applicable individuals in making informed health care choices by paying providers of services and suppliers for using patient decision-support tools, including tools that meet the standards developed and identified under section 936(c)(2)(A) of the Public Health Service Act [42 USCS § 299b-36(c)(2)(A)], that improve applicable individual and caregiver understanding of medical treatment options.

(x) Allowing States to test and evaluate fully integrating care for dual eligible individuals in the State, including the management and oversight of all funds under the applicable titles with respect to such individuals.

(xi) Allowing States to test and evaluate systems of all-payer payment reform for the medical care of residents of the State, including dual eligible individuals.

(xii) Aligning nationally recognized, evidence-based guidelines of cancer care with payment incentives under title XVIII [42 USCS §§ 1395 et seq.] in the areas of treatment planning and follow-up care planning for applicable individuals described in clause (i) or (iii) of subsection (a)(4)(A) with cancer, including the identification of gaps in applicable quality measures.

(xiii) Improving post-acute care through continuing care hospitals that offer inpatient rehabilitation, long-term care hospitals, and home health or skilled nursing care during an inpatient stay and the 30 days immediately following discharge.

(xiv) Funding home health providers who offer chronic care management services to applicable individuals in cooperation with interdisciplinary teams.

(xv) Promoting improved quality and reduced cost by developing a collaborative of high-quality, low-cost health care institutions that is responsible for—

(I) developing, documenting, and disseminating best practices and proven care methods;

(II) implementing such best practices and proven care methods within such institutions to demonstrate further improvements in quality and efficiency; and

(III) providing assistance to other health care institutions on how best to employ such best practices and proven care methods to improve health care quality and lower costs.

(xvi) Facilitate inpatient care, including intensive care, of hospitalized applicable individuals at their local hospital through the use of electronic monitoring by specialists, including intensivists and critical care specialists, based at integrated health systems.

(xvii) Promoting greater efficiencies and timely access to outpatient services (such as outpatient physical therapy services) through models that do not require a physician or other health professional to refer the service or be involved in establishing the plan of care for the service, when such service is furnished by a health professional who has the authority to furnish the service under existing State law.

(xviii) Establishing comprehensive payments to Healthcare Innovation Zones, consisting of groups of providers that include a teaching hospital, physicians, and other clinical entities, that, through their structure, operations, and joint-activity deliver a full spectrum of integrated and comprehensive health care services to applicable individuals while also incorporating innovative methods for the clinical training of future health care professionals.

(xix) Utilizing, in particular in entities located in medically underserved areas and facilities of the Indian Health Service (whether operated by such Service or by an Indian tribe or tribal organization (as those terms are defined in section 4 of the Indian Health Care Improvement Act [25 USCS § 1603])), telehealth services—

(I) in treating behavioral health issues (such as post-traumatic stress disorder) and stroke; and

(II) to improve the capacity of non-medical providers and non-specialized medical providers to provide health services for patients with chronic complex conditions.

(xx) Utilizing a diverse network of providers of services and suppliers to improve care coordination for applicable individuals described in subsection (a)(4)(A)(i) with 2 or more chronic conditions and a history of prior-year hospitalization through interventions developed under the Medicare Coordinated Care Demonstration Project under section 4016 of the Balanced Budget Act of 1997 (42 U.S.C. 1395b-1 note).

(C) Additional factors for consideration. In selecting models for testing under subparagraph (A), the CMI may consider the following additional factors:

(i) Whether the model includes a regular process for monitoring and updating patient care plans in a manner that is consistent with the needs and preferences of applicable individuals.

(ii) Whether the model places the applicable individual, including family members and other informal caregivers of the applicable individual, at the center of the care team of the applicable individual.

(iii) Whether the model provides for in-person contact with applicable individuals.

(iv) Whether the model utilizes technology, such as electronic health records and patient-based remote monitoring systems, to coordinate care over time and across settings.

(v) Whether the model provides for the maintenance of a close relationship between care coordinators, primary care practitioners, specialist physicians, community-based organizations, and other providers of services and suppliers.

(vi) Whether the model relies on a team-based approach to interventions, such as comprehensive care assessments, care planning, and self-management coaching.

(vii) Whether, under the model, providers of services and suppliers are able to share information with patients, caregivers, and other providers of services and suppliers on a real time basis.

(viii) Whether the model demonstrates effective linkage with other public sector or private sector payers.

(3) Budget neutrality. (A) Initial period. The Secretary shall not require, as a condition for testing a model under paragraph (1), that the design of such model ensure that such model is budget neutral initially with respect to expenditures under the applicable title.

(B) Termination or modification. The Secretary shall terminate or modify the design and implementation of a model unless the Secretary determines (and the Chief Actuary of the Centers for Medicare & Medicaid Services, with respect to program spending under the applicable title, certifies), after testing has begun, that the model is expected to—

(i) improve the quality of care (as determined by the Administrator of the Centers for Medicare & Medicaid Services) without increasing spending under the applicable title;

(ii) reduce spending under the applicable title without reducing the quality of care; or

(iii) improve the quality of care and reduce spending.

Such termination may occur at any time after such testing has begun and before completion of the testing.

(4) Evaluation. (A) In general. The Secretary shall conduct an evaluation of each model tested under this subsection. Such evaluation shall include an analysis of—

(i) the quality of care furnished under the model, including the measurement of patient-level outcomes and patient-centeredness criteria determined appropriate by the Secretary; and

(ii) the changes in spending under the applicable titles by reason of the model.

(B) Information. The Secretary shall make the results of each evaluation under this paragraph available to the public in a timely fashion and may establish requirements for States and other entities participating in the testing of models under this section to collect and report information that the Secretary determines is necessary to monitor and evaluate such models.

(C) Measure selection. To the extent feasible, the Secretary shall select measures under this paragraph that reflect national priorities for quality improvement and patient-centered care consistent with the measures described in 1890(b)(7)(B) [42 USCS § 1395aaa(b)(7)(B)].

(c) Expansion of models (Phase II). Taking into account the evaluation under subsection (b)(4), the Secretary may, through rulemaking, expand (including implementation on a nationwide basis) the duration and the scope of a model that is being tested under subsection (b) or a demonstration project under section 1866C, to the extent determined appropriate by the Secretary, if—

(1) the Secretary determines that such expansion is expected to—

(A) reduce spending under applicable title without reducing the quality of care; or

(B) improve the quality of patient care without increasing spending; and

(2) the Chief Actuary of the Centers for Medicare & Medicaid Services certifies that such expansion would reduce (or would not result in any increase in) net program spending under applicable titles; and

(3) the Secretary determines that such expansion would not deny or limit the coverage or provision of benefits under the applicable title

for applicable individuals.

In determining which models or demonstration projects to expand under the preceding sentence, the Secretary shall focus on models and demonstration projects that improve the quality of patient care and reduce spending.

(d) Implementation. (1) Waiver authority. The Secretary may waive such requirements of titles XI and XVIII [42 USCS §§ 1301 et seq. and 1395 et seq.] and of sections 1902(a)(1), 1902(a)(13), and 1903(m)(2)(A)(iii) [42 USCS § 1395a(a)(1), (a)(13), and (m)(2)(A)(iii)] as may be necessary solely for purposes of carrying out this section with respect to testing models described in subsection (b).

(2) Limitations on review. There shall be no administrative or judicial review under section 1869 [42 USCS § 1395ff], section 1878 [42 USCS § 1395oo], or otherwise of—

(A) the selection of models for testing or expansion under this section;

(B) the selection of organizations, sites, or participants to test those models selected;

(C) the elements, parameters, scope, and duration of such models for testing or dissemination;

(D) determinations regarding budget neutrality under subsection (b)(3);

(E) the termination or modification of the design and implementation of a model under subsection (b)(3)(B); and

(F) determinations about expansion of the duration and scope of a model under subsection (c), including the determination that a model is not expected to meet criteria described in paragraph (1) or (2) of such subsection.

(3) Administration. Chapter 35 of title 44, United States Code [44 USCS §§ 3501 et seq.], shall not apply to the testing and evaluation of models or expansion of such models under this section.

(e) Application to CHIP. The Center may carry out activities under this section with respect to title XXI [42 USCS §§ 1397aa et seq.] in the same manner as provided under this section with respect to the program under the applicable titles.

(f) Funding. (1) In general. There are appropriated, from amounts in the Treasury not otherwise appropriated—

(A) $5,000,000 for the design, implementation, and evaluation of models under subsection (b) for fiscal year 2010;

(B) $10,000,000,000 for the activities initiated under this section for the period of fiscal years 2011 through 2019; and

(C) the amount described in subparagraph (B) for the activities initiated under this section for each subsequent 10-year fiscal period (beginning with the 10-year fiscal period beginning with fiscal year 2020).

Amounts appropriated under the preceding sentence shall remain available until expended.

(2) Use of certain funds. Out of amounts appropriated under subparagraphs (B) and (C) of paragraph (1), not less than $25,000,000 shall be made available each such fiscal year to design, implement, and evaluate models under subsection (b).

(g) Report to Congress. Beginning in 2012, and not less than once every other year thereafter, the Secretary shall submit to Congress a report on activities under this section. Each such report shall describe the models tested under subsection (b), including the number of individuals described in subsection (a)(4)(A)(i) and of individuals described in subsection (a)(4)(A)(ii) participating in such models and payments made under applicable titles for services on behalf of such individuals, any models chosen for expansion under subsection (c), and the results from evaluations under subsection (b)(4). In addition, each such report shall provide such recommendations as the Secretary determines are appropriate for legislative action to facilitate the development and expansion of successful payment models.

(Aug. 14, 1935, ch 531, Title XI, Part A, § 1115A, as added and amended March 23, 2010, P. L. 111-148, Title III, Subtitle A, Part III, § 3021(a), Title X, Subtitle C, § 10306, 124 Stat. 389, 939.)

HISTORY; ANCILLARY LAWS AND DIRECTIVES

Other provisions:

Medicaid Global Payment System Demonstration Project. Act March 23, 2010, P. L. 111-148, Title II, Subtitle I, § 2705, 124 Stat. 324, provides:

"(a) In general. The Secretary of Health and Human Services (referred to in this section as the "Secretary") shall, in coordination with the Center for Medicare and Medicaid Innovation (as established under section 1115A of the Social Security Act [this section], as added by section 3021 of this Act), establish the Medicaid Global Payment System Demonstration Project under which a participating State shall adjust the payments made to an eligible safety net hospital system or network from a fee-for-service payment structure to a global capitated payment model.

"(b) Duration and scope. The demonstration project conducted under this section shall operate during a period of fiscal years 2010 through 2012. The Secretary shall select not more than 5 States to participate in the demonstration project.

"(c) Eligible safety net hospital system or network. For purposes of this section, the term "eligible safety net hospital system or network" means a large, safety net hospital system or network (as defined by the

Secretary) that operates within a State selected by the Secretary under subsection (b).

"(d) Evaluation. (1) Testing. The Innovation Center shall test and evaluate the demonstration project conducted under this section to examine any changes in health care quality outcomes and spending by the eligible safety net hospital systems or networks.

"(2) Budget neutrality. During the testing period under paragraph (1), any budget neutrality requirements under section 1115A(b)(3) of the Social Security Act [subsec. (b)(3) of this section] (as so added) shall not be applicable.

"(3) Modification. During the testing period under paragraph (1), the Secretary may, in the Secretary's discretion, modify or terminate the demonstration project conducted under this section.

"(e) Report. Not later than 12 months after the date of completion of the demonstration project under this section, the Secretary shall submit to Congress a report containing the results of the evaluation and testing conducted under subsection (d), together with recommendations for such legislation and administrative action as the Secretary determines appropriate.

"(f) Authorization of appropriations. There are authorized to be appropriated such sums as are necessary to carry out this section.".

§ 1315b. Providing Federal coverage and payment coordination for dual eligible beneficiaries

(a) Establishment of Federal Coordinated Health Care Office. (1) In general. Not later than March 1, 2010, the Secretary of Health and Human Services (in this section referred to as the "Secretary") shall establish a Federal Coordinated Health Care Office.

(2) Establishment and reporting to CMS Administrator. The Federal Coordinated Health Care Office—

(A) shall be established within the Centers for Medicare & Medicaid Services; and

(B) have as the Office a Director who shall be appointed by, and be in direct line of authority to, the Administrator of the Centers for Medicare & Medicaid Services.

(b) Purpose. The purpose of the Federal Coordinated Health Care Office is to bring together officers and employees of the Medicare and Medicaid programs at the Centers for Medicare & Medicaid Services in order to—

(1) more effectively integrate benefits under the Medicare program under title XVIII of the Social Security Act [42 USCS §§ 1395 et seq.] and the Medicaid program under title XIX of such Act [42 USCS §§ 1396 et seq.]; and

(2) improve the coordination between the Federal Government and States for individuals eligible for benefits under both such programs in order to ensure that such individuals get full access to the items and services to which they are entitled under titles XVIII and XIX of the Social Security Act [42 USCS §§ 1395 et seq. and 1396 et seq.].

(c) Goals. The goals of the Federal Coordinated Health Care Office are as follows:

(1) Providing dual eligible individuals full access to the benefits to which such individuals are entitled under the Medicare and Medicaid programs.

(2) Simplifying the processes for dual eligible individuals to access the items and services they are entitled to under the Medicare and Medicaid programs.

(3) Improving the quality of health care and long-term services for dual eligible individuals.

(4) Increasing dual eligible individuals' understanding of and satisfaction with coverage under the Medicare and Medicaid programs.

(5) Eliminating regulatory conflicts between rules under the Medicare and Medicaid programs.

(6) Improving care continuity and ensuring safe and effective care transitions for dual eligible individuals.

(7) Eliminating cost-shifting between the Medicare and Medicaid program and among related health care providers.

(8) Improving the quality of performance of providers of services and suppliers under the Medicare and Medicaid programs.

(d) Specific responsibilities. The specific responsibilities of the Federal Coordinated Health Care Office are as follows:

(1) Providing States, specialized MA plans for special needs individuals (as defined in section 1859(b)(6) of the Social Security Act (42 U.S.C. 1395w-28(b)(6))), physicians and other relevant entities or individuals with the education and tools necessary for developing programs that align benefits under the Medicare and Medicaid programs for dual eligible individuals.

(2) Supporting State efforts to coordinate and align acute care and long-term care services for dual eligible individuals with other items and services furnished under the Medicare program.

(3) Providing support for coordination of contracting and oversight by States and the Centers for Medicare & Medicaid Services with respect to the integration of the Medicare and Medicaid programs in a manner that is supportive of the goals described in paragraph (3).

(4) To consult and coordinate with the Medicare Payment Advisory Commission established under section 1805 of the Social Security Act (42 U.S.C. 1395b-6) and the Medicaid and CHIP Payment and Access Commission established under section 1900 of such Act (42 U.S.C. 1396) with respect to policies relating to the

enrollment in, and provision of, benefits to dual eligible individuals under the Medicare program under title XVIII of the Social Security Act [42 USCS §§ 1395 et seq.] and the Medicaid program under title XIX of such Act [42 USCS §§ 1396 et seq.].

(5) To study the provision of drug coverage for new full-benefit dual eligible individuals (as defined in section 1935(c)(6) of the Social Security Act (42 U.S.C. 1396u-5(c)(6)), as well as to monitor and report annual total expenditures, health outcomes, and access to benefits for all dual eligible individuals.

(e) Report. The Secretary shall, as part of the budget transmitted under section 1105(a) of title 31, United States Code, submit to Congress an annual report containing recommendations for legislation that would improve care coordination and benefits for dual eligible individuals.

(f) Dual eligible defined. In this section, the term "dual eligible individual" means an individual who is entitled to, or enrolled for, benefits under part A of title XVIII of the Social Security Act [42 USCS §§ 1395c et seq.], or enrolled for benefits under part B of title XVIII of such Act [42 USCS §§ 1395j et seq.], and is eligible for medical assistance under a State plan under title XIX of such Act [42 USCS §§ 1396 et seq.] or under a waiver of such plan.

(March 23, 2010, P. L. 111-148, Title II, Subtitle H, § 2602, 124 Stat. 315.)

§ 1320a-3. Disclosure of ownership and related information; procedure; definitions; scope of requirements

(a)(1) The Secretary shall by regulation or by contract provision provide that each disclosing entity (as defined in paragraph (2)) shall—

(A) as a condition of the disclosing entity's participation in, or certification or recertification under, any of the programs established by titles V, XVIII, and XIX [42 USCS §§ 701 et seq., 1395 et seq., 1396 et seq.], or

(B) as a condition for the approval or renewal of a contract or agreement between the disclosing entity and the Secretary or the appropriate State agency under any of the programs established under titles V, XVIII, and XIX [42 USCS §§ 701 et seq., 1395 et seq., 1396 et seq.],

supply the Secretary or the appropriate State agency with full and complete information as to the identity of each person with an ownership or control interest (as defined in paragraph (3)) in the entity or in any subcontractor (as defined by the Secretary in regulations) in which the entity directly or indirectly has a 5 per centum or more ownership interest and supply the Secretary with [the] both the employer identification number (assigned pursuant to section 6109 of the Internal Revenue Code of 1986 [26 USCS § 6109]) and social security account number (assigned under section 205(c)(2)(B) [42 USCS § 405(c)(2)(B)]) of the disclosing entity, each person with an ownership or control interest (as defined in subsection (a)(3)), and any subcontractor in which the entity directly or indirectly has a 5 percent or more ownership interest.

(2) As used in this section, the term "disclosing entity" means an entity which is—

(A) a provider of services (as defined in section 1861(u) [42 USCS § 1395x(u)], other than a fund), an independent clinical laboratory, a renal disease facility, a managed care entity, as defined in section 1932(a)(1)(B) [42 USCS § 1396u-2(a)(1)(B)], or a health maintenance organization (as defined in section 1301(a) of the Public Health Service Act [42 USCS § 300e(a)]);

(B) an entity (other than an individual practitioner or group of practitioners) that furnishes, or arranges for the furnishing of, items or services with respect to which payment may be claimed by the entity under any plan or program established pursuant to title V [42 USCS §§ 701 et seq.] or under a State plan approved under title XIX [42 USCS §§ 1396 et seq.]; or

(C) a carrier or other agency or organization that is acting as a fiscal intermediary or agent with respect to one or more providers of services (for purposes of part A or part B of title XVIII [42 USCS §§ 1395c et seq., 1395j et seq.], or both, or for purposes of a State plan approved under title XIX [42 USCS §§ 1396 et seq.]) pursuant to (i) an agreement under section 1816 [42 USCS § 1395h], (ii) a contract under section 1842 [42 USCS § 1395u], or (iii) an agreement with a single State agency administering or supervising the administration of a State plan approved under title XIX [42 USCS §§ 1396 et seq.].

(3) As used in this section, the term "person with an ownership or control interest" means, with respect to an entity, a person who—

(A)(i) has directly or indirectly (as determined by the Secretary in regulations) an ownership interest of 5 per centum or more in the entity; or

(ii) is the owner of a whole or part interest in any mortgage, deed of trust, note, or other obligation secured (in whole or in part) by the entity or any of the property or assets thereof, which whole or part interest is equal to or exceeds 5 per centum of the total property and assets of the entity; or

(B) is an officer or director of the entity, if the entity is organized as a corporation; or

(C) is a partner in the entity, if the entity is organized as a partnership.

(b) To the extent determined to be feasible under regulations of the Secretary, a disclosing entity shall also include in the information supplied under subsection (a)(1), with respect to each person with an ownership or control interest in the entity, the name of any other disclosing entity with respect to which the person is a person with an ownership or control interest.

(c) Required disclosure of ownership and additional disclosable parties information. (1) Disclosure. A facility shall have the information described in paragraph (2) available—

(A) during the period beginning on the date of the enactment of this subsection [enacted March 23, 2010] and ending on the date such information is made available to the public under section 6101(b) of the Patient Protection and Affordable Care Act [note to this section] for submission to the Secretary, the Inspector General of the Department of Health and Human Services, the State in which the facility is located, and the State long-term care ombudsman in the case where the Secretary, the Inspector General, the State, or the State long-term care ombudsman requests such information; and

(B) beginning on the effective date of the final regulations promulgated under paragraph (3)(A), for reporting such information in accordance with such final regulations.

Nothing in subparagraph (A) shall be construed as authorizing a facility to dispose of or delete information described in such subparagraph after the effective date of the final regulations promulgated under paragraph (3)(A).

(2) Information described. (A) In general. The following information is described in this paragraph:

(i) The information described in subsections (a) and (b), subject to subparagraph (C).

(ii) The identity of and information on—

(I) each member of the governing body of the facility, including the name, title, and period of service of each such member;

(II) each person or entity who is an officer, director, member, partner, trustee, or managing employee of the facility, including the name, title, and period of service of each such person or entity; and

(III) each person or entity who is an additional disclosable party of the facility.

(iii) The organizational structure of each additional disclosable party of the facility and a description of the relationship of each such additional disclosable party to the facility and to one another.

(B) Special rule where information is already reported or submitted. To the extent that information reported by a facility to the Internal Revenue Service on Form 990, information submitted by a facility to the Securities and Exchange Commission, or information otherwise submitted to the Secretary or any other Federal agency contains the information described in clauses (i), (ii), or (iii) of subparagraph (A), the facility may provide such Form or such information submitted to meet the requirements of paragraph (1).

(C) Special rule. In applying subparagraph (A)(i)—

(i) with respect to subsections (a) and (b), "ownership or control interest" shall include direct or indirect interests, including such interests in intermediate entities; and

(ii) subsection (a)(3)(A)(ii) shall include the owner of a whole or part interest in any mortgage, deed of trust, note, or other obligation secured, in whole or in part, by the entity or any of the property or assets thereof, if the interest is equal to or exceeds 5 percent of the total property or assets of the entirety.

(3) Reporting. (A) In general. Not later than the date that is 2 years after the date of the enactment of this subsection [enacted March 23, 2010], the Secretary shall promulgate final regulations requiring, effective on the date that is 90 days after the date on which such final regulations are published in the Federal Register, a facility to report the information described in paragraph (2) to the Secretary in a standardized format, and such other regulations as are necessary to carry out this subsection. Such final regulations shall ensure that the facility certifies, as a condition of participation and payment under the program under title XVIII or XIX [42 USCS §§ 1395 et seq. or 1396 et seq.], that the information reported by the facility in accordance with such final regulations is, to the best of the facility's knowledge, accurate and current.

(B) Guidance. The Secretary shall provide guidance and technical assistance to States on how to adopt the standardized format under subparagraph (A).

(4) No effect on existing reporting requirements. Nothing in this subsection shall reduce, diminish, or alter any reporting requirement for a facility that is in effect as of the date of the

enactment of this subsection [enacted March 23, 2010].

(5) Definitions. In this subsection:

(A) Additional disclosable party. The term "additional disclosable party" means, with respect to a facility, any person or entity who—

(i) exercises operational, financial, or managerial control over the facility or a part thereof, or provides policies or procedures for any of the operations of the facility, or provides financial or cash management services to the facility;

(ii) leases or subleases real property to the facility, or owns a whole or part interest equal to or exceeding 5 percent of the total value of such real property; or

(iii) provides management or administrative services, management or clinical consulting services, or accounting or financial services to the facility.

(B) Facility. The term "facility" means a disclosing entity which is—

(i) a skilled nursing facility (as defined in section 1819(a) [42 USCS § 1395i-3(a)]); or

(ii) a nursing facility (as defined in section 1919(a) [42 USCS § 1396r(a)]).

(C) Managing employee. The term "managing employee" means, with respect to a facility, an individual (including a general manager, business manager, administrator, director, or consultant) who directly or indirectly manages, advises, or supervises any element of the practices, finances, or operations of the facility.

(D) Organizational structure. The term "organizational structure" means, in the case of—

(i) a corporation, the officers, directors, and shareholders of the corporation who have an ownership interest in the corporation which is equal to or exceeds 5 percent;

(ii) a limited liability company, the members and managers of the limited liability company (including, as applicable, what percentage each member and manager has of the ownership interest in the limited liability company);

(iii) a general partnership, the partners of the general partnership;

(iv) a limited partnership, the general partners and any limited partners of the limited partnership who have an ownership interest in the limited partnership which is equal to or exceeds 10 percent;

(v) a trust, the trustees of the trust;

(vi) an individual, contact information for the individual; and

(vii) any other person or entity, such information as the Secretary determines appropriate.

(Aug. 14, 1935, ch 531, Title XI, Part A, § 1124, as added Oct. 25, 1977, P. L. 95-142, § 3(a)(1), 91 Stat. 1177; Dec. 5, 1980, P. L. 96-499, Title IX, Part A, Subpart II, § 912(a), 94 Stat. 2619; Aug 13, 1981, P. L. 97-35, Title XXIII, Subtitle C, § 2353(i), 95 Stat. 872; Aug. 18, 1987, P. L. 100-93, § 11, 101 Stat. 697; Aug. 5, 1997, P. L. 105-33, Title IV, Subtitle D, Ch 2, § 4313(a), Subtitle H, Ch 1, § 4705(c), 111 Stat. 388, 506; March 23, 2010, P. L. 111-148, Title VI, Subtitle B, Part I, § 6101(a), 124 Stat. 699.)

HISTORY; ANCILLARY LAWS AND DIRECTIVES

Other provisions:

Public availability of information. Act March 23, 2010, P. L. 111-148, Title VI, Subtitle B, Part I, § 6101(b), 124 Stat. 702, provides: "Not later than the date that is 1 year after the date on which the final regulations promulgated under section 1124(c)(3)(A) of the Social Security Act [subsec. (c)(3)(A) of this section], as added by subsection (a), are published in the Federal Register, the Secretary of Health and Human Services shall make the information reported in accordance with such final regulations available to the public in accordance with procedures established by the Secretary.".

§ 1320a-7. Exclusion of certain individuals and entities from participation in Medicare and State health care programs

(a) Mandatory exclusion. The Secretary shall exclude the following individuals and entities from participation in any Federal health care program (as defined in section 1128B(f) [42 USCS § 1320a-7b(f)]):

(1) Conviction of program-related crimes. Any individual or entity that has been convicted of a criminal offense related to the delivery of an item or service under title XVIII [42 USCS §§ 1395 et seq.] or under any State health care program.

(2) Conviction relating to patient abuse. Any individual or entity that has been convicted, under Federal or State law, of a criminal offense relating to neglect or abuse of patients in connection with the delivery of a health care item or service.

(3) Felony conviction relating to health care fraud. Any individual or entity that has been convicted for an offense which occurred after the date of the enactment of the Health Insurance Portability and Accountability Act of 1996 [enacted Aug. 21, 1996], under Federal or State law, in connection with the delivery of a health care item or service or with respect to any act or omission in a health care program (other than those specifically described in paragraph (1)) operated by or financed in whole or in part by any Federal, State, or local government agency,

of a criminal offense consisting of a felony relating to fraud, theft, embezzlement, breach of fiduciary responsibility, or other financial misconduct.

(4) Felony conviction relating to controlled substance. Any individual or entity that has been convicted for an offense which occurred after the date of the enactment of the Health Insurance Portability and Accountability Act of 1996 [enacted Aug. 21, 1996], under Federal or State law, of a criminal offense consisting of a felony relating to the unlawful manufacture, distribution, prescription, or dispensing of a controlled substance.

(b) Permissive exclusion. The Secretary may exclude the following individuals and entities from participation in any Federal health care program (as defined in section 1128B(f) [42 USCS § 1320a-7b(f)]):

(1) Conviction relating to fraud. Any individual or entity that has been convicted for an offense which occurred after the date of the enactment of the Health Insurance Portability and Accountability Act of 1996 [enacted Aug. 21, 1996], under Federal or State law—

(A) of a criminal offense consisting of a misdemeanor relating to fraud, theft, embezzlement, breach of fiduciary responsibility, or other financial misconduct—

(i) in connection with the delivery of a health care item or service, or

(ii) with respect to any act or omission in a health care program (other than those specifically described in subsection (a)(1)) operated by or financed in whole or in part by any Federal, State, or local government agency; or

(B) of a criminal offense relating to fraud, theft, embezzlement, breach of fiduciary responsibility, or other financial misconduct with respect to any act or omission in a program (other than a health care program) operated by or financed in whole or in part by any Federal, State, or local government agency.

(2) Conviction relating to obstruction of an investigation or audit. Any individual or entity that has been convicted, under Federal or State law, in connection with the interference with or obstruction of any investigation or audit related to—

(i) any offense described in paragraph (1) or in subsection (a); or

(ii) the use of funds received, directly or indirectly, from any Federal health care program (as defined in section 1128B(f) [42 USCS § 1320a-7b(f)]).

(3) Misdemeanor conviction relating to controlled substance. Any individual or entity that has been convicted, under Federal or State law, of a criminal offense consisting of a misdemeanor relating to the unlawful manufacture, distribution, prescription, or dispensing of a controlled substance.

(4) License revocation or suspension. Any individual or entity—

(A) whose license to provide health care has been revoked or suspended by any State licensing authority, or who otherwise lost such a license or the right to apply for or renew such a license, for reasons bearing on the individual's or entity's professional competence, professional performance, or financial integrity, or

(B) who surrendered such a license while a formal disciplinary proceeding was pending before such an authority and the proceeding concerned the individual's or entity's professional competence, professional performance, or financial integrity.

(5) Exclusion or suspension under Federal or State health care program. Any individual or entity which has been suspended or excluded from participation, or otherwise sanctioned, under—

(A) any Federal program, including programs of the Department of Defense or the Department of Veterans Affairs, involving the provision of health care, or

(B) a State health care program,

for reasons bearing on the individual's or entity's professional competence, professional performance, or financial integrity.

(6) Claims for excessive charges or unnecessary services and failure of certain organizations to furnish medically necessary services. Any individual or entity that the Secretary determines—

(A) has submitted or caused to be submitted bills or requests for payment (where such bills or requests are based on charges or cost) under title XVIII [42 USCS §§ 1395 et seq.] or a State health care program containing charges (or, in applicable cases, requests for payment of costs) for items or services furnished substantially in excess of such individual's or entity's usual charges (or, in applicable cases, substantially in excess of such individual's or entity's costs) for such items or services, unless the Secretary finds there is good cause for such bills or requests containing such charges or costs;

(B) has furnished or caused to be furnished items or services to patients (whether or not eligible for benefits under title XVIII [42 USCS §§ 1395 et seq.] or under a State health care program) substantially in excess of the needs of such patients or of a quality which fails to meet professionally recognized standards of health care;

(C) is—

(i) a health maintenance organization (as defined in section 1903(m) [42 USCS § 1396b(m)]) providing items and services under a State plan approved under title XIX [42 USCS §§ 1396 et seq.], or

(ii) an entity furnishing services under a waiver approved under section 1915(b)(1) [42 USCS § 1396n(b)(1)],

and has failed substantially to provide medically necessary items and services that are required (under law or the contract with the State under title XIX [42 USCS §§ 1396 et seq.]) to be provided to individuals covered under that plan or waiver, if the failure has adversely affected (or has a substantial likelihood of adversely affecting) these individuals; or

(D) is an entity providing items and services as an eligible organization under a risk-sharing contract under section 1876 [42 USCS § 1395mm] and has failed substantially to provide medically necessary items and services that are required (under law or such contract) to be provided to individuals covered under the risk-sharing contract, if the failure has adversely affected (or has a substantial likelihood of adversely affecting) these individuals.

(7) Fraud, kickbacks, and other prohibited activities. Any individual or entity that the Secretary determines has committed an act which is described in section 1128A, 1128B, or 1129 [42 USCS § 1320a-7a, 1320a-7b, or 1320a-8].

(8) Entities controlled by a sanctioned individual. Any entity with respect to which the Secretary determines that a person—

(A)(i) who has a direct or indirect ownership or control interest of 5 percent or more in the entity or with an ownership or control interest (as defined in section 1124(a)(3) [42 USCS § 1320a-3(a)(3)]) in that entity,

(ii) who is an officer, director, agent, or managing employee (as defined in section 1126(b) [42 USCS § 1320a-5(b)]) of that entity; or

(iii) who was described in clause (i) but is no longer so described because of a transfer of ownership or control interest, in anticipation of (or following) a conviction, assessment, or exclusion described in subparagraph (B) against the person, to an immediate family member (as defined in subsection (j)(1)) or a member of the household of the person (as defined in subsection (j)(2)) who continues to maintain an interest described in such clause—

is a person—

(B)(i) who has been convicted of any offense described in subsection (a) or in paragraph (1), (2), or (3) of this subsection;

(ii) against whom a civil monetary penalty has been assessed under section 1128A or 1129 [42 USCS § 1320a-7a or 1320a-8]; or

(iii) who has been excluded from participation under a program under title XVIII [42 USCS §§ 1395 et seq.] or under a State health care program.

(9) Failure to disclose required information. Any entity that did not fully and accurately make any disclosure required by section 1124, section 1124A, or section 1126 [42 USCS § 1320a-3, 1320a-3a, or 1320a-5].

(10) Failure to supply requested information on subcontractors and suppliers. Any disclosing entity (as defined in section 1124(a)(2) [42 USCS § 1320a-3(a)(2)]) that fails to supply (within such period as may be specified by the Secretary in regulations) upon request specifically addressed to the entity by the Secretary or by the State agency administering or supervising the administration of a State health care program—

(A) full and complete information as to the ownership of a subcontractor (as defined by the Secretary in regulations) with whom the entity has had, during the previous 12 months, business transactions in an aggregate amount in excess of $25,000, or

(B) full and complete information as to any significant business transactions (as defined by the Secretary in regulations), occurring during the five-year period ending on the date of such request, between the entity and any wholly owned supplier or between the entity and any subcontractor.

(11) Failure to supply payment information. Any individual or entity furnishing, ordering, referring for furnishing, or certifying the need for items or services for which payment may be made under title XVIII [42 USCS §§ 1395 et seq.] or a State health care program that fails to provide such information as the Secretary or the appropriate State agency finds necessary to determine whether such payments are or were due and the amounts thereof, or has refused to permit such examination of its records by or on behalf of the Secretary or that agency as may be necessary to verify such information.

(12) Failure to grant immediate access. Any individual or entity that fails to grant immediate access, upon reasonable request (as defined by the Secretary in regulations) to any of the following:

(A) To the Secretary, or to the agency used by the Secretary, for the purpose specified in the first sentence of section 1864(a) [42 USCS § 1395aa(a)] (relating to compliance with conditions of participation or payment).

(B) To the Secretary or the State agency, to perform the reviews and surveys required under State plans under paragraphs (26), (31), and (33) of section 1902(a) and under section 1903(g) [42 USCS §§ 1396a(a)(26), (31), (33), 1396b(g)].

(C) To the Inspector General of the Department of Health and Human Services, for the purpose of reviewing records, documents, and other data necessary to the performance of the statutory functions of the Inspector General.

(D) To a State medicaid fraud control unit (as defined in section 1903(q) [42 USCS § 1396b(q)]), for the purpose of conducting activities described in that section.

(13) Failure to take corrective action. Any hospital that fails to comply substantially with a corrective action required under section 1886(f)(2)(B) [42 USCS § 1395ww(f)(2)(B)].

(14) Default on health education loan or scholarship obligations. Any individual who the Secretary determines is in default on repayments of scholarship obligations or loans in connection with health professions education made or secured, in whole or in part, by the Secretary and with respect to whom the Secretary has taken all reasonable steps available to the Secretary to secure repayment of such obligations or loans, except that (A) the Secretary shall not exclude pursuant to this paragraph a physician who is the sole community physician or sole source of essential specialized services in a community if a State requests that the physician not be excluded, and (B) the Secretary shall take into account, in determining whether to exclude any other physician pursuant to this paragraph, access of beneficiaries to physician services for which payment may be made under title XVIII or XIX [42 USCS §§ 1395 et seq. or 1396 et seq.].

(15) Individuals controlling a sanctioned entity. (A) Any individual—

(i) who has a direct or indirect ownership or control interest in a sanctioned entity and who knows or should know (as defined in section 1128A(i)(6) [1128A(i)(7)] [42 USCS § 1320a-7a(i)(7)]) of the action constituting the basis for the conviction or exclusion described in subparagraph (B); or

(ii) who is an officer or managing employee (as defined in section 1126(b) [42 USCS § 1320a-5(b)]) of such an entity.

(B) For purposes of subparagraph (A), the term "sanctioned entity" means an entity—

(i) that has been convicted of any offense described in subsection (a) or in paragraph (1), (2), or (3) of this subsection; or

(ii) that has been excluded from participation under a program under title XVIII [42 USCS §§ 1395 et seq.] or under a State health care program.

(16) Making false statements or misrepresentation of material facts. Any individual or entity that knowingly makes or causes to be made any false statement, omission, or misrepresentation of a material fact in any application, agreement, bid, or contract to participate or enroll as a provider of services or supplier under a Federal health care program (as defined in section 1128B(f) [42 USCS § 1320a-7b(f)]), including Medicare Advantage organizations under part C of title XVIII [42 USCS §§ 1395w-21 et seq.], prescription drug plan sponsors under part D of title XVIII [42 USCS §§ 1395w-101 et seq.], Medicaid managed care organizations under title XIX [42 USCS § 1396 et seq.], and entities that apply to participate as providers of services or suppliers in such managed care organizations and such plans.

(c) Notice, effective date, and period of exclusion. (1) An exclusion under this section or under section 1128A [42 USCS § 1320a-7a] shall be effective at such time and upon such reasonable notice to the public and to the individual or entity excluded as may be specified in regulations consistent with paragraph (2).

(2)(A) Except as provided in subparagraph (B), such an exclusion shall be effective with respect to services furnished to an individual on or after the effective date of the exclusion.

(B) Unless the Secretary determines that the health and safety of individuals receiving services warrants the exclusion taking effect earlier, an exclusion shall not apply to payments made under title XVIII [42 USCS §§ 1395 et seq.] or under a State health care program for—

(i) inpatient institutional services furnished to an individual who was admitted to such institution before the date of the exclusion, or

(ii) home health services and hospice care furnished to an individual under a plan of care established before the date of the exclusion,

until the passage of 30 days after the effective date of the exclusion.

(3)(A) The Secretary shall specify, in the notice of exclusion under paragraph (1) and the written notice under section 1128A [42 USCS § 1320a-7a], the minimum period (or, in the case of an exclusion of an individual under subsection (b)(12) or in the case described in subparagraph (G), the period) of the exclusion.

(B) Subject to subparagraph (G), in the case of an exclusion under subsection (a), the minimum period of exclusion shall be not less than five years, except that, upon the request of the administrator of a Federal health care program (as defined in section 1128B(f) [42 USCS § 1320a-7b(f)]) who determines that the exclusion would impose a hardship on beneficiaries (as defined in section 1128A(i)(5) [42 USCS § 1320a-7a(i)(5)]) of that program, the Secretary may, after consulting with the Inspector General of the Department of Health and Human Services, waive the exclusion under subsection (a)(1), (a)(3), or (a)(4) with respect to that program in the case of an individual or entity that is the sole community physician or sole source of essential specialized services in a community. The Secretary's decision whether to waive the exclusion shall not be reviewable.

(C) In the case of an exclusion of an individual under subsection (b)(12), the period of the exclusion shall be equal to the sum of—

(i) the length of the period in which the individual failed to grant the immediate access described in that subsection, and

(ii) an additional period, not to exceed 90 days, set by the Secretary.

(D) Subject to subparagraph (G), in the case of an exclusion of an individual or entity under paragraph (1), (2), or (3) of subsection (b), the period of the exclusion shall be 3 years, unless the Secretary determines in accordance with published regulations that a shorter period is appropriate because of mitigating circumstances or that a longer period is appropriate because of aggravating circumstances.

(E) In the case of an exclusion of an individual or entity under subsection (b)(4) or (b)(5), the period of the exclusion shall not be less than the period during which the individual's or entity's license to provide health care is revoked, suspended, or surrendered, or the individual or the entity is excluded or suspended from a Federal or State health care program.

(F) In the case of an exclusion of an individual or entity under subsection (b)(6)(B), the period of the exclusion shall be not less than 1 year.

(G) In the case of an exclusion of an individual under subsection (a) based on a conviction occurring on or after the date of the enactment of this subparagraph [enacted Aug. 5, 1997], if the individual has (before, on, or after such date) been convicted—

(i) on one previous occasion of one or more offenses for which an exclusion may be effected under such subsection, the period of the exclusion shall be not less than 10 years, or

(ii) on 2 or more previous occasions of one or more offenses for which an exclusion may be effected under such subsection, the period of the exclusion shall be permanent.

(d) Notice to State agencies and exclusion under State health care programs. (1) Subject to paragraph (3), the Secretary shall exercise the authority under this section and section 1128A [42 USCS § 1320a-7a] in a manner that results in an individual's or entity's exclusion from all the programs under title XVIII [42 USCS §§ 1395 et seq.] and all the State health care programs in which the individual or entity may otherwise participate.

(2) The Secretary shall promptly notify each appropriate State agency administering or supervising the administration of each State health care program (and, in the case of an exclusion effected pursuant to subsection (a) and to which section 304(a)(5) of the Controlled Substances Act [21 USCS § 824(a)(5)] may apply, the Attorney General)—

(A) of the fact and circumstances of each exclusion effected against an individual or entity under this section or section 1128A [42 USCS § 1320a-7a], and

(B) of the period (described in paragraph (3)) for which the State agency is directed to exclude the individual or entity from participation in the State health care program.

(3)(A) Except as provided in subparagraph (B), the period of the exclusion under a State health care program under paragraph (2) shall be the same as any period of exclusion under title XVIII [42 USCS §§ 1395 et seq.].

(B)(i) The Secretary may waive an individual's or entity's exclusion under a State health care program under paragraph (2) if the Secretary receives and approves a request for the waiver with respect to the individual or entity from the State agency administering or supervising the administration of the program.

(ii) A State health care program may provide for a period of exclusion which is longer than the period of exclusion under title XVIII [42 USCS §§ 1395 et seq.].

(e) Notice to State licensing agencies. The Secretary shall—

(1) promptly notify the appropriate State or local agency or authority having responsibility for the licensing or certification of an individual or entity excluded (or directed to be excluded) from participation under this section or section 1128A [42 USCS § 1320a-7a], of the fact and circumstances of the exclusion,

(2) request that appropriate investigations be made and sanctions invoked in accordance with applicable State law and policy, and

(3) request that the State or local agency or

authority keep the Secretary and the Inspector General of the Department of Health and Human Services fully and currently informed with respect to any actions taken in response to the request.

(f) Notice, hearing, and judicial review. (1) Subject to paragraph (2), any individual or entity that is excluded (or directed to be excluded) from participation under this section is entitled to reasonable notice and opportunity for a hearing thereon by the Secretary to the same extent as is provided in section 205(b) [42 USCS § 405(b)], and to judicial review of the Secretary's final decision after such hearing as is provided in section 205(g) [42 USCS § 405(g)], except that, in so applying such sections and section 205(l) [42 USCS § 405(l)], any reference therein to the Commissioner of Social Security or the Social Security Administration shall be considered a reference to the Secretary or the Department of Health and Human Services, respectively.

(2) Unless the Secretary determines that the health or safety of individuals receiving services warrants the exclusion taking effect earlier, any individual or entity that is the subject of an adverse determination under subsection (b)(7) shall be entitled to a hearing by an administrative law judge (as provided under section 205(b) [42 USCS § 405(b)]) on the determination under subsection (b)(7) before any exclusion based upon the determination takes effect.

(3) The provisions of section 205(h) [42 USCS § 405(h)] shall apply with respect to this section and sections 1128A, 1129, and 1156 [42 USCS §§ 1320a-7a, 1320a-8, 1320c-5] to the same extent as it is applicable with respect to title II [42 USCS §§ 401 et seq.], except that, in so applying such section and section 205(l) [42 USCS § 405(l)], any reference therein to the Commissioner of Social Security shall be considered a reference to the Secretary.

(4) The provisions of subsections (d) and (e) of section 205 [42 USCS § 405] shall apply with respect to this section to the same extent as they are applicable with respect to title II [42 USCS §§ 401 et seq.]. The Secretary may delegate the authority granted by section 205(d) [42 USCS § 405(d)] (as made applicable to this section) to the Inspector General of the Department of Health and Human Services for purposes of any investigation under this section.

(g) Application for termination of exclusion. (1) An individual or entity excluded (or directed to be excluded) from participation under this section or section 1128A [42 USCS § 1320a-7a] may apply to the Secretary, in the manner specified by the Secretary in regulations and at the end of the minimum period of exclusion provided under subsection (c)(3) and at such other times as the Secretary may provide, for termination of the exclusion effected under this section or section 1128A [42 USCS § 1320a-7a].

(2) The Secretary may terminate the exclusion if the Secretary determines, on the basis of the conduct of the applicant which occurred after the date of the notice of exclusion or which was unknown to the Secretary at the time of the exclusion, that—

(A) there is no basis under subsection (a) or (b) or section 1128A(a) [42 USCS § 1320a-7a(a)] for a continuation of the exclusion, and

(B) there are reasonable assurances that the types of actions which formed the basis for the original exclusion have not recurred and will not recur.

(3) The Secretary shall promptly notify each appropriate State agency administering or supervising the administration of each State health care program (and, in the case of an exclusion effected pursuant to subsection (a) and to which section 304(a)(5) of the Controlled Substances Act [21 USCS § 824(a)(5)] may apply, the Attorney General) of the fact and circumstances of each termination of exclusion made under this subsection.

(h) "State health care program" defined. For purposes of this section and sections 1128A and 1128B [42 USCS §§ 1320a-7a, 1320a-7b], the term "State health care program" means—

(1) a State plan approved under title XIX [42 USCS §§ 1396 et seq.],

(2) any program receiving funds under title V [42 USCS §§ 701 et seq.] or from an allotment to a State under such title,

(3) any program receiving funds under subtitle 1 of title XX [42 USCS §§ 1397 et seq.] or from an allotment to a State under such subtitle, or

(4) a State child health plan approved under title XXI [42 USCS §§ 1397aa et seq.].

(i) "Convicted" defined. For purposes of subsections (a) and (b), an individual or entity is considered to have been "convicted" of a criminal offense—

(1) when a judgment of conviction has been entered against the individual or entity by a Federal, State, or local court, regardless of whether there is an appeal pending or whether the judgment of conviction or other record relating to criminal conduct has been expunged;

(2) when there has been a finding of guilt against the individual or entity by a Federal, State, or local court;

(3) when a plea of guilty or nolo contendere by the individual or entity has been accepted by a Federal, State, or local court; or

(4) when the individual or entity has entered into participation in a first offender, deferred adjudication, or other arrangement or program where judgment of conviction has been withheld.

(j) Definition of immediate family member and member of household. For purposes of subsection (b)(8)(A)(iii):

(1) The term "immediate family member" means, with respect to a person—

(A) the husband or wife of the person;

(B) the natural or adoptive parent, child, or sibling of the person;

(C) the stepparent, stepchild, stepbrother, or stepsister of the person;

(D) the father-, mother-, daughter-, son-, brother-, or sister-in-law of the person;

(E) the grandparent or grandchild of the person; and

(F) the spouse of a grandparent or grandchild of the person.

(2) The term "member of the household" means, with respect to any person, any individual sharing a common abode as part of a single family unit with the person, including domestic employees and others who live together as a family unit, but not including a roomer or boarder.

(Aug. 14, 1935, ch 531, Title XI, Part A, § 1128, as added Dec. 5, 1980, P. L. 96-499, Title IX, Part A, Subtitle II, § 913(a), 94 Stat. 2619; Aug. 13, 1981, P. L. 97-35, Title XXI, Subtitle A, Ch 2, § 2105(b) Title XXIII, Subtitle C, § 2353(k), 95 Stat. 791, 873; July 18, 1984, P. L. 98-369, Division B, Title III, Subtitle A, Part II, § 2333(a), (b), 98 Stat. 1089; Oct. 21, 1986, P. L. 99-509, Title IX, Subtitle D, Part 2, § 9317(c), 100 Stat. 2008; Aug. 18, 1987, P. L. 100-93, § 2, 101 Stat. 680; Dec. 22, 1987, P. L. 100-203, Title IV, Subtitle B, Part 2, § 4118(e)(2)–(5), 101 Stat. 1330-155; July 1, 1988, P. L. 100-360, Title IV, Subtitle B, § 411(k)(10)(B)(ii), (C), (D), 102 Stat. 795; Oct. 13, 1988, P. L. 100-485, Title VI, § 608(d)(26)(H), 102 Stat. 2422; Dec. 19, 1989, P. L. 101-239, Title VI, Subtitle B, Part 2, § 6411(d)(1), 103 Stat. 2270; Nov. 5, 1990, P. L. 101-508, Title V, Subtitle A, Part 2, Subpart B, § 4164(b)(3), 104 Stat. 1388-102; June 13, 1991, P. L. 102-54, § 13(q)(3)(A)(ii), 105 Stat. 279; Aug. 15, 1994, P. L. 103-296, Title I, § 108(b)(9), Title II, § 206(b)(2), 108 Stat. 1483, 1513; Aug. 21, 1996, P. L. 104-191, Title II, Subtitle B, §§ 211–213, 110 Stat. 2003; Aug. 5, 1997, P. L. 105-33, Title IV, Subtitle D, Ch 1, §§ 4301, 4303(a), Ch 3, § 4331(c), Subtitle J, Ch 1, § 4901(b)(2), 111 Stat. 382, 396, 570; Dec. 8, 2003, P. L. 108-173, Title IX, Subtitle E, § 949, 117 Stat. 2426; March 23, 2010, P. L. 111-148, Title VI, Subtitle E, §§ 6402(d)(1), (e), (k), 6406(c), 6408(c), Subtitle H, § 6703(d)(3)(A), 124 Stat. 757, 759, 763, 769, 772, 804.)

HISTORY; ANCILLARY LAWS AND DIRECTIVES

Other provisions:

Application of amendments made by § 6406 of Act March 23, 2010. Act March 23, 2010, P. L. 111-148, Title VI, Subtitle E, § 6406(d), 124 Stat. 769, provides: "The amendments made by this section [amending 42 USCS §§ 1320a-7, 1395u, and 1395cc] shall apply to orders, certifications, and referrals made on or after January 1, 2010.".

Appplication of amendments made by § 6408 of Act March 23, 2010. Act March 23, 2010, P. L. 111-148, Title VI, Subtitle E, § 6408(d), 124 Stat. 772, provides:

"(1) In general. Except as provided in paragraph (2), the amendments made by this section [amending 42 USCS §§ 1320a-7, 1320a-7a, 1395w-27] shall apply to acts committed on or after January 1, 2010.

"(2) Exception. The amendments made by subsection (b)(1) [amending 42 USCS § 1395w-27(d)(2)] take effect on the date of enactment of this Act.".

§ 1320a-7a. Civil monetary penalties

(a) Improperly filed claims. Any person (including an organization, agency, or other entity, but excluding a beneficiary, as defined in subsection (i)(5)) that—

(1) knowingly presents or causes to be presented to an officer, employee, or agent of the United States, or of any department or agency thereof, or of any State agency (as defined in subsection (i)(1)), a claim (as defined in subsection (i)(2)) that the Secretary determines—

(A) is for a medical or other item or service that the person knows or should know was not provided as claimed, including any person who engages in a pattern or practice of presenting or causing to be presented a claim for an item or service that is based on a code that the person knows or should know will result in a greater payment to the person than the code the person knows or should know is applicable to the item or service actually provided,

(B) is for a medical or other item or service and the person knows or should know the claim is false or fraudulent,

(C) is presented for a physician's service (or an item or service incident to a physician's service) by a person who knows or should know that the individual who furnished (or supervised the furnishing of) the service—

(i) was not licensed as a physician,

(ii) was licensed as a physician, but such license had been obtained through a misrepresentation of material fact (including cheating on an examination required for licensing), or

(iii) represented to the patient at the time the service was furnished that the physician was certified in a medical specialty by a medical specialty board when the individual was not so certified,

(D) is for a medical or other item or service furnished during a period in which the person was excluded from the Federal health care program (as defined in section 1128B(f) [42 USCS § 1320a-7b(f)]) under which the claim was made pursuant to Federal law. [, or]

(E) is for a pattern of medical or other items or services that a person knows or should know are not medically necessary;

(2) knowingly presents or causes to be presented to any person a request for payment which is in violation of the terms of (A) an assignment under section 1842(b)(3)(B)(ii) [42 USCS § 1395u(b)(3)(B)(ii)], or (B) an agreement with a State agency (or other requirement of a State plan under title XIX [42 USCS §§ 1396 et seq.]) not to charge a person for an item or service in excess of the amount permitted to be charged, or (C) an agreement to be a participating physician or supplier under section 1842(h)(1) [42 USCS § 1395u(h)(1)], or (D) an agreement pursuant to section 1866(a)(1)(G) [42 USCS § 1395cc(a)(1)(G)];

(3) knowingly gives or causes to be given to any person, with respect to coverage under title XVIII [42 USCS §§ 1395 et seq.] of inpatient hospital services subject to the provisions of section 1886 [42 USCS § 1395ww], information that he knows or has reason to know is false or misleading, and that could reasonably be expected to influence the decision when to discharge such person or another individual from the hospital;

(4) in the case of a person who is not an organization, agency, or other entity, is excluded from participating in a program under title XVIII [42 USCS §§ 1395 et seq.] or a State health care program in accordance with this subsection or under section 1128 [42 USCS § 1320a-7] and who, at the time of a violation of this subsection—

(A) retains a direct or indirect ownership or control interest in an entity that is participating in a program under title XVIII [42 USCS §§ 1395 et seq.] or a State health care program, and who knows or should know of the action constituting the basis for the exclusion; or

(B) is an officer or managing employee (as defined in section 1126(b) [42 USCS § 1320a-5(b)]) of such an entity;

(5) offers to or transfers remuneration to any individual eligible for benefits under title XVIII of this Act [42 USCS §§ 1395 et seq.], or under a State health care program (as defined in section 1128(h) [42 USCS § 1320a-7(h)]) that such person knows or should know is likely to influence such individual to order or receive from a particular provider, practitioner, or supplier any item or service for which payment may be made, in whole or in part, under title XVIII [42 USCS §§ 1395 et seq.], or a State health care program (as so defined);

(6) arranges or contracts (by employment or otherwise) with an individual or entity that the person knows or should know is excluded from participation in a Federal health care program (as defined in section 1128B(f) [42 USCS § 1320a-7b(f)]), for the provision of items or services for which payment may be made under such a program;

(7) commits an act described in paragraph (1) or (2) of section 1128B(b) [42 USCS § 1320a-7b(b)];

(8) knowingly makes, uses, or causes to be made or used, a false record or statement material to a false or fraudulent claim for payment for items and services furnished under a Federal health care program; [or]

(9) fails to grant timely access, upon reasonable request (as defined by the Secretary in regulations), to the Inspector General of the Department of Health and Human Services, for the purpose of audits, investigations, evaluations, or other statutory functions of the Inspector General of the Department of Health and Human Services;

[(10)](8) orders or prescribes a medical or other item or service during a period in which the person was excluded from a Federal health care program (as so defined), in the case where the person knows or should know that a claim for such medical or other item or service will be made under such a program;

[(11)](9) knowingly makes or causes to be made any false statement, omission, or misrepresentation of a material fact in any application, bid, or contract to participate or enroll as a provider of services or a supplier under a Federal health care program (as so defined), including Medicare Advantage organizations under part C of title XVIII [42 USCS §§ 1395w-21 et seq.], prescription drug plan sponsors under part D of title XVIII [42 USCS §§ 1395w-101 et seq.], Medicaid managed care organizations under title XIX [42 USCS §§ 1396 et seq.], and entities that apply to participate as providers of services or suppliers in such managed care organizations and such plans;

[(12)](10) knows of an overpayment (as defined in paragraph (4) of section 1128J(d) [42 USCS § 1320a-7k(d)]) and does not report and return the overpayment in accordance with such section;

shall be subject, in addition to any other penalties that may be prescribed by law, to a civil money penalty of not more than $10,000 for each item or service (or, in cases under paragraph (3), $15,000 for each individual with respect to whom false or misleading information was given; in cases under paragraph (4), $10,000 for each day the prohibited relationship occurs; in cases under paragraph (7), $50,000 for each such act, in cases under paragraph (8), $50,000 for each false record or statement, or in cases under paragraph (9), $15,000 for each day of the failure described in such paragraph); or in cases under paragraph (9) [paragraph [(11)](9)], $50,000 for each false statement or misrepresentation of a material fact). In addition, such a person shall be subject to an assessment of not more than 3 times the amount claimed for each such item or service in lieu of damages sustained by the United States or a State agency because of such claim (or, in cases under paragraph (7), damages of not more than 3 times the total amount of remuneration offered, paid, solicited, or received, without regard to whether a portion of such remuneration was offered, paid, solicited, or received for a lawful purpose; or in cases under paragraph (9) [paragraph [(11)](9)], an assessment of not more than 3 times the total amount claimed for each item or service for which payment was made based upon the application containing the false statement or misrepresentation of a material fact). In addition the Secretary may make a determination in the same proceeding to exclude the person from participation in the Federal health care programs (as defined in section 1128B(f)(1) [42 USCS § 1320a-7b(f)(1)]) and to direct the appropriate State agency to exclude the person from participation in any State health care program.

(b) Payments to induce reduction or limitation of services. (1) If a hospital or a critical access hospital knowingly makes a payment, directly or indirectly, to a physician as an inducement to reduce or limit services provided with respect to individuals who—

(A) are entitled to benefits under part A or part B of title XVIII [42 USCS §§ 1395c et seq., 1395j et seq] or to medical assistance under a State plan approved under title XIX [42 USCS §§ 1396 et seq.], and

(B) are under the direct care of the physician, the hospital or a critical access hospital shall be subject, in addition to any other penalties that may be prescribed by law, to a civil money penalty of not more than $2,000 for each such individual with respect to whom the payment is made.

(2) Any physician who knowingly accepts receipt of a payment described in paragraph (1) shall be subject, in addition to any other penalties that may be prescribed by law, to a civil money penalty of not more than $2,000 for each individual described in such paragraph with respect to whom the payment is made.

(3)(A) Any physician who executes a document described in subparagraph (B) with respect to an individual knowing that all of the requirements referred to in such subparagraph are not met with respect to the individual shall be subject to a civil monetary penalty of not more than the greater of—

(i) $5,000, or

(ii) three times the amount of the payments under title XVIII [42 USCS §§ 1395 et seq.] for home health services which are made pursuant to such certification.

(B) A document described in this subparagraph is any document that certifies, for purposes of title XVIII [42 USCS §§ 1395 et seq.], that an individual meets the requirements of section 1814(a)(2)(C) or 1835(a)(2)(A) [42 USCS § 1395f(a)(2)(C) or 1395n(a)(2)(A)] in the case of home health services furnished to the individual.

(c) Initiation of proceeding; authorization by Attorney General, notice, etc., estoppel, failure to comply with order or procedure. (1) The Secretary may initiate a proceeding to determine whether to impose a civil money penalty, assessment, or exclusion under subsection (a) or (b) only as authorized by the Attorney General pursuant to procedures agreed upon by them. The Secretary may not initiate an action under this section with respect to any claim, request for payment, or other occurrence described in this section later than six years after the date the claim was presented, the request for payment was made, or the occurrence took place. The Secretary may initiate an action under this section by serving notice of the action in any manner authorized by Rule 4 of the Federal Rules of Civil Procedure.

(2) The Secretary shall not make a determination adverse to any person under subsection

(a) or (b) until the person has been given written notice and an opportunity for the determination to be made on the record after a hearing at which the person is entitled to be represented by counsel, to present witnesses, and to cross-examine witnesses against the person.

(3) In a proceeding under subsection (a) or (b) which—

(A) is against a person who has been convicted (whether upon a verdict after trial or upon a plea of guilty or nolo contendere) of a Federal crime charging fraud or false statements, and

(B) involves the same transaction as in the criminal action,

the person is estopped from denying the essential elements of the criminal offense.

(4) The official conducting a hearing under this section may sanction a person, including any party or attorney, for failing to comply with an order or procedure, failing to defend an action, or other misconduct as would interfere with the speedy, orderly, or fair conduct of the hearing. Such sanction shall reasonably relate to the severity and nature of the failure or misconduct. Such sanction may include—

(A) in the case of refusal to provide or permit discovery, drawing negative factual inferences or treating such refusal as an admission by deeming the matter, or certain facts, to be established,

(B) prohibiting a party from introducing certain evidence or otherwise supporting a particular claim or defense,

(C) striking pleadings, in whole or in part,

(D) staying the proceedings,

(E) dismissal of the action,

(F) entering a default judgment,

(G) ordering the party or attorney to pay attorneys' fees and other costs caused by the failure or misconduct, and

(H) refusing to consider any motion or other action which is not filed in a timely manner.

(d) Amount or scope of penalty, assessment, or exclusion. In determining the amount or scope of any penalty, assessment, or exclusion imposed pursuant to subsection (a) or (b), the Secretary shall take into account—

(1) the nature of claims and the circumstances under which they were presented,

(2) the degree of culpability, history of prior offenses, and financial condition of the person presenting the claims, and

(3) such other matters as justice may require.

(e) Review by courts of appeals. Any person adversely affected by a determination of the Secretary under this section may obtain a review of such determination in the United States Court of Appeals for the circuit in which the person resides, or in which the claim was presented, by filing in such court (within sixty days following the date the person is notified of the Secretary's determination) a written petition requesting that the determination be modified or set aside. A copy of the petition shall be forthwith transmitted by the clerk of the court to the Secretary, and thereupon the Secretary shall file in the Court [court] the record in the proceeding as provided in section 2112 of title 28, United States Code. Upon such filing, the court shall have jurisdiction of the proceeding and of the question determined therein, and shall have the power to make and enter upon the pleadings, testimony, and proceedings set forth in such record a decree affirming, modifying, remanding for further consideration, or setting aside, in whole or in part, the determination of the Secretary and enforcing the same to the extent that such order is affirmed or modified. No objection that has not been urged before the Secretary shall be considered by the court, unless the failure or neglect to urge such objection shall be excused because of extraordinary circumstances. The findings of the Secretary with respect to questions of fact, if supported by substantial evidence on the record considered as a whole, shall be conclusive. If any party shall apply to the court for leave to adduce additional evidence and shall show to the satisfaction of the court that such additional evidence is material and that there were reasonable grounds for the failure to adduce such evidence in the hearing before the Secretary, the court may order such additional evidence to be taken before the Secretary and to be made a part of the record. The Secretary may modify his findings as to the facts, or make new findings, by reason of additional evidence so taken and filed, and he shall file with the court such modified or new findings, which findings with respect to questions of fact, if supported by substantial evidence on the record considered as a whole, shall be conclusive, and his recommendations, if any, for the modification or setting aside of his original order. Upon the filing of the record with it, the jurisdiction of the court shall be exclusive and its judgment and decree shall be final, expect that the same shall be subject to review by the Supreme Court of the United States, as provided in section 1254 of title 28, United States Code.

(f) Compromise of penalties and assessments; recovery; use of funds recovered. Civil money penalties and assessments imposed under this section may be compromised by the Secretary and may be recovered in a civil action in the name of the United States brought in United States district court for the district where the claim was presented, or where the claimant resides, as determined by the Secretary. Amounts recovered under this section shall be paid to the Secretary and disposed of as follows:

(1)(A) In the case of amounts recovered arising out of a claim under title XIX [42 USCS §§ 1396 et seq.], there shall be paid to the State agency an amount bearing the same proportion to the total amount recovered as the State's share of the amount paid by the State agency for such claim bears to the total amount paid for such claim.

(B) In the case of amounts recovered arising out of a claim under an allotment to a State under title V [42 USCS §§ 701 et seq.], there shall be paid to the State agency an amount equal to three-sevenths of the amount recovered.

(2) Such portion of the amounts recovered as is determined to have been paid out of the trust funds under sections 1817 and 1841 [42 USCS §§ 1395i, 1395t] shall be repaid to such trust funds.

(3) With respect to amounts recovered arising out of a claim under a Federal health care program (as defined in section 1128B(f) [42 USCS § 1320a-7b(f)]), the portion of such amounts as is determined to have been paid by the program shall be repaid to the program, and the portion of such amounts attributable to the amounts recovered under this section by reason of the amendments made by the Health Insurance Portability and Accountability Act of 1996 (as estimated by the Secretary) shall be deposited into the Federal Hospital Insurance Trust Fund pursuant to section 1817(k)(2)(C) [42 USCS § 1395i(k)(2)(C)].

(4) The remainder of the amounts recovered shall be deposited as miscellaneous receipts of the Treasury of the United States.

The amount of such penalty or assessment, when finally determined, or the amount agreed upon in compromise, may be deducted from any sum then or later owing by the United States or a State agency to the person against whom the penalty or assessment has been assessed.

(g) Finality of determination respecting penalty, assessment, or exclusion. A determination by the Secretary to impose a penalty, assessment, or exclusion under subsection (a) or (b) shall be final upon the expiration of the sixty-day period referred to in subsection (e). Matters that were raised or that could have been raised in a hearing before the Secretary or in an appeal pursuant to subsection (e) may not be raised as a defense to a civil action by the United States to collect a penalty or assessment assessed under this section.

(h) Notification of appropriate entities of finality of determination. Whenever the Secretary's determination to impose a penalty, assessment, or exclusion under subsection (a) or (b) becomes final, he shall notify the appropriate State or local medical or professional organization, the appropriate State agency or agencies administering or supervising the administration of State health care programs (as defined in section 1128(h) [42 USCS § 1320a-7(h)]), and the appropriate utilization and quality control peer review organization, and the appropriate State or local licensing agency or organization (including the agency specified in section 1864(a) and 1902(a)(33) [42 USCS §§ 1395aa(a), 1396a(a)(33)]) that such a penalty or assessment has become final and the reasons therefor.

(i) Definitions. For the purposes of this section:

(1) The term "State agency" means the agency established or designated to administer or supervise the administration of the State plan under title XIX of this Act [42 USCS §§ 1396 et seq.] or designated to administer the State's program under title V or subtitle 1 of title XX of this Act [42 USCS §§ 701 et seq. or 1397 et seq.].

(2) The term "claim" means an application for payments for items and services under a Federal health care program (as defined in section 1128B(f) [42 USCS § 1320a-7b(f)]).

(3) The term "item or service" includes (A) any particular item, device, medical supply, or service claimed to have been provided to a patient and listed in an itemized claim for payment, and (B) in the case of a claim based on costs, any entry in the cost report, books of account or other documents supporting such claim.

(4) The term "agency of the United States" includes any contractor acting as a fiscal intermediary, carrier, or fiscal agent or any other claims processing agent for a Federal health care program (as so defined).

(5) The term "beneficiary" means an individual who is eligible to receive items or services for which payment may be made under a Federal health care program (as so defined) but does not include a provider, supplier, or practitioner.

(6) The term "remuneration" includes the waiver of coinsurance and deductible amounts

(or any part thereof), and transfers of items or services for free or for other than fair market value. The term "remuneration" does not include—

(A) the waiver of coinsurance and deductible amounts by a person, if—

(i) the waiver is not offered as part of any advertisement or solicitation;

(ii) the person does not routinely waive coinsurance or deductible amounts; and

(iii) the person—

(I) waives the coinsurance and deductible amounts after determining in good faith that the individual is in financial need; or

(II) fails to collect coinsurance or deductible amounts after making reasonable collection efforts;

(B) subject to subsection (n), any permissible practice described in any subparagraph of section 1128B(b)(3) [42 USCS § 1320a-7b(b)(3)] or in regulations issued by the Secretary;

(C) differentials in coinsurance and deductible amounts as part of a benefit plan design as long as the differentials have been disclosed in writing to all beneficiaries, third party payers, and providers, to whom claims are presented and as long as the differentials meet the standards as defined in regulations promulgated by the Secretary not later than 180 days after the date of the enactment of the Health Insurance Portability and Accountability Act of 1996 [enacted Aug. 21, 1996];

(D) incentives given to individuals to promote the delivery of preventive care as determined by the Secretary in regulations so promulgated;

(E) a reduction in the copayment amount for covered OPD services under section 1833(t)(5)(B); [or]

(F) any other remuneration which promotes access to care and poses a low risk of harm to patients and Federal health care programs (as defined in section 1128B(f) [42 USCS § 1320a-7b(f)] and designated by the Secretary under regulations);

(G) the offer or transfer of items or services for free or less than fair market value by a person, if—

(i) the items or services consist of coupons, rebates, or other rewards from a retailer;

(ii) the items or services are offered or transferred on equal terms available to the general public, regardless of health insurance status; and

(iii) the offer or transfer of the items or services is not tied to the provision of other items or services reimbursed in whole or in part by the program under title XVIII [42 USCS §§ 1395 et seq.] or a State health care program (as defined in section 1128(h) [42 USCS § 1320a-7(h)]);

(H) the offer or transfer of items or services for free or less than fair market value by a person, if—

(i) the items or services are not offered as part of any advertisement or solicitation;

(ii) the items or services are not tied to the provision of other services reimbursed in whole or in part by the program under title XVIII [42 USCS §§ 1395 et seq.] or a State health care program (as so defined);

(iii) there is a reasonable connection between the items or services and the medical care of the individual; and

(iv) the person provides the items or services after determining in good faith that the individual is in financial need; or

(I) effective on a date specified by the Secretary (but not earlier than January 1, 2011), the waiver by a PDP sponsor of a prescription drug plan under part D of title XVIII [42 USCS §§ 1395w-101 et seq.] or an MA organization offering an MA-PD plan under part C of such title [42 USCS §§ 1395w-21 et seq.] of any copayment for the first fill of a covered part D drug (as defined in section 1860D-2(e) [42 USCS § 1395w-102(e)]) that is a generic drug for individuals enrolled in the prescription drug plan or MA-PD plan, respectively.

(7) The term "should know" means that a person, with respect to information—

(A) acts in deliberate ignorance of the truth or falsity of the information; or

(B) acts in reckless disregard of the truth or falsity of the information,

and no proof of specific intent to defraud is required.

(j) Subpoenas. (1) The provisions of subsections (d) and (e) of section 205 [42 USCS § 405(d), (e)] shall apply with respect to this section to the same extent as they are applicable with respect to title II [42 USCS §§ 401 et seq.]. The Secretary may delegate the authority granted by section 205(d) [42 USCS § 405(d)] (as made applicable to this section) to the Inspector General of the Department of Health and Human Services for purposes of any investigation under this section.

(2) The Secretary may delegate authority granted under this section and under section 1128 [42 USCS § 1320a-7] to the Inspector General of the Department of Health and Human Services.

(k) Injunctions. Whenever the Secretary has reason to believe that any person has engaged, is engaging, or is about to engage in any activity which makes the person subject to a civil monetary penalty under this section, the Secretary may bring an action in an appropriate district court of the United States (or, if applicable, a United States court of any territory) to enjoin such activity, or to enjoin the person from concealing, removing, encumbering, or disposing of assets which may be required in order to pay a civil monetary penalty if any such penalty were to be imposed or to seek other appropriate relief.

(l) Liability of principal for acts of agent. A principal is liable for penalties, assessments, and an exclusion under this section for the actions of the principal's agent acting within the scope of the agency.

(m) Claims within jurisdiction of other departments or agencies. (1) For purposes of this section, with respect to a Federal health care program not contained in this Act [42 USCS §§ 301 et seq.], references to the Secretary in this section shall be deemed to be references to the Secretary or Administrator of the department or agency with jurisdiction over such program and references to the Inspector General of the Department of Health and Human Services in this section shall be deemed to be references to the Inspector General of the applicable department or agency.

(2)(A) The Secretary and Administrator of the departments and agencies referred to in paragraph (1) may include in any action pursuant to this section, claims within the jurisdiction of other Federal departments or agencies as long as the following conditions are satisfied:

(i) The case involves primarily claims submitted to the Federal health care programs of the department or agency initiating the action.

(ii) The Secretary or Administrator of the department or agency initiating the action gives notice and an opportunity to participate in the investigation to the Inspector General of the department or agency with primary jurisdiction over the Federal health care programs to which the claims were submitted.

(B) If the conditions specified in subparagraph (A) are fulfilled, the Inspector General of the department or agency initiating the action is authorized to exercise all powers granted under the Inspector General Act of 1978 (5 U.S.C. App.) with respect to the claims submitted to the other departments or agencies to the same manner and extent as provided in that Act with respect to claims submitted to such departments or agencies.

(n) Safe harbor for payment of medigap premiums. (1) Subparagraph (B) of subsection (i)(6) shall not apply to a practice described in paragraph (2) unless—

(A) the Secretary, through the Inspector General of the Department of Health and Human Services, promulgates a rule authorizing such a practice as an exception to remuneration; and

(B) the remuneration is offered or transferred by a person under such rule during the 2-year period beginning on the date the rule is first promulgated.

(2) A practice described in this paragraph [subsection] is a practice under which a health care provider or facility pays, in whole or in part, premiums for medicare supplemental policies for individuals entitled to benefits under part A of title XVIII [42 USCS §§ 1395c et seq.] pursuant to section 226A [42 USCS § 426-1].

(Aug. 14, 1935, ch 531, Title XI, Part A, § 1128A, as added Aug. 13, 1981, P. L. 97-35, Title XXI, Subtitle A, ch 2, § 2105(a), 95 Stat. 789; Sept. 3, 1982, P. L. 97-248, Title I, Subtitle B, § 137(b)(26), 96 Stat. 380; July 18, 1984, P. L. 98-369, Division B, Title III, Subtitle A, Part I, § 2306(f)(1), Part II, § 2354(a)(3), 98 Stat. 1073, 1100; Oct. 21, 1986, P. L. 99-509, Title IX, Subtitle D, Part 2, §§ 9313(c)(1), 9317(a),(b), 100 Stat. 2003, 2008; Aug. 18, 1987, P. L. 100-93, § 3, 101 Stat. 686; Dec. 22, 1987, P. L. 100-203, Title IV, Subtitle A, Part 2, Subpart C, § 4039(h)(1), Subtitle B, Part 2, § 4118(e)(1)(A), (B), (6)–(10), 101 Stat. 1330-81, 155; July 1, 1988, P. L. 100-360, Title II, Subtitle A, § 202(c)(2), Title IV, Subtitle B, § 411(e) (3), (k)(10)(B)(I), (III), (D), 102 Stat. 715, 775, 795; Oct. 13, 1988, P. L. 100-485, Title VI, § 608(d)(26)(H)–(K), 102 Stat. 2422; Dec. 13, 1989, P. L. 101-234, Title II, § 201(a)(1), 103 Stat. 1981; Dec. 19, 1989, P. L. 101-239, Title VI, Subtitle A, Part 1, Subpart A, § 6003(g)(3)(D)(i), 103 Stat. 2153; Nov. 5, 1990, P. L. 101-508, Title IV, Subtitle A, Part 3, §§ 4204(a)(3), 4207(h), Subtitle B, Part 4, Subpart C, § 4731(b)(1), Subpart E, § 4753, 104 Stat. 1388-109, 1388-123, 1388-195, 1388-208; Oct. 31, 1994, P. L. 103-432, Title I, Subtitle C, § 160(d)(4), 108 Stat. 4444; Aug. 21, 1996, P. L. 104-191, Title II, Subtitle D, §§ 231(a)–(e), (h), 232(a), 110 Stat. 2012, 2014, 2015; Aug. 5, 1997, P. L. 105-33, Title IV, Subtitle C, § 4201(c)(1), Subtitle D, § 4304(a), (b), Ch 3, § 4331(e), Subtitle F, Ch 2, § 4523(c), 111 Stat. 373, 383, 396, 449; Oct. 21, 1998, P. L. 105-277, Div J, Title V, Subtitle B, § 5201(a), (b)(1), 112 Stat. 2681-916; March 23, 2010, P. L. 111-148, Title VI, Subtitle E, §§ 6402(d)(2), 6408(a), Subtitle H, § 6703(d)(3)(B), 124 Stat. 757, 770, 804.)

§ 1320a-7b. Criminal penalties for acts involving Federal health care programs

(a) Making or causing to be made false statements or representations. Whoever—

(1) knowingly and willfully makes or causes to be made any false statement or representation of a material fact in any application for any benefit or payment under a Federal health care program (as defined in subsection (f)),

(2) at any time knowingly and willfully makes or causes to be made any false statement or representation of a material fact for use in determining rights to such benefit or payment,

(3) having knowledge of the occurrence of any event affecting (A) his initial or continued right to any such benefit or payment, or (B) the initial or continued right to any such benefit or payment of any other individual in whose behalf he has applied for or is receiving such benefit or payment, conceals or fails to disclose such event with an intent fraudulently to secure such benefit or payment either in a greater amount or quantity than is due or when no such benefit or payment is authorized,

(4) having made application to receive any such benefit or payment for the use and benefit of another and having received it, knowingly and willfully converts such benefit or payment or any part thereof to a use other than for the use and benefit of such other person,

(5) presents or causes to be presented a claim for a physician's service for which payment may be made under a Federal health care program and knows that the individual who furnished the service was not licensed as a physician, or

(6) for a fee knowingly and willfully counsels or assists an individual to dispose of assets (including by any transfer in trust) in order for the individual to become eligible for medical assistance under a State plan under title XIX [42 USCS §§ 1396 et seq.], if disposing of the assets results in the imposition of a period of ineligibility for such assistance under section 1917(c) [42 USCS § 1396p(c)],

shall (i) in the case of such a statement, representation, concealment, failure, or conversion by any other person in connection with the furnishing (by that person) of items or services for which payment is or may be made under the program, be guilty of a felony and upon conviction thereof fined not more than $25,000 or imprisoned for not more than five years or both, or (ii) in the case of such a statement, representation, concealment, failure, conversion, or provision of counsel or assistance by any other person, be guilty of a misdemeanor and upon conviction thereof fined not more than $10,000 or imprisoned for not more than one year, or both. In addition, in any case where an individual who is otherwise eligible for assistance under a Federal health care program is convicted of an offense under the preceding provisions of this subsection, the administrator of such program may at its option (notwithstanding any other provision of such program) limit, restrict, or suspend the eligibility of that individual for such period (not exceeding one year) as it deems appropriate; but the imposition of a limitation, restriction, or suspension with respect to the eligibility of any individual under this sentence shall not affect the eligibility of any other person for assistance under the plan, regardless of the relationship between that individual and such other person.

(b) Illegal remunerations. (1) Whoever knowingly and willfully solicits or receives any remuneration (including any kickback, bribe, or rebate) directly or indirectly, overtly or covertly, in cash or in kind—

(A) in return for referring an individual to a person for the furnishing or arranging for the furnishing of any item or service for which payment may be made in whole or in part under a Federal health care program, or

(B) in return for purchasing, leasing, ordering, or arranging for or recommending purchasing, leasing, or ordering any good, facility, service, or item for which payment may be made in whole or in part under a Federal health care program,

shall be guilty of a felony and upon conviction thereof, shall be fined not more than $25,000 or imprisoned for not more than five years, or both.

(2) Whoever knowingly and willfully offers or pays any remuneration (including any kickback, bribe, or rebate) directly or indirectly, overtly or covertly, in cash or in kind to any person to induce such person—

(A) to refer an individual to a person for the furnishing or arranging for the furnishing of any item or service for which payment may be made in whole or in part under a Federal health care program, or

(B) to purchase, lease, order, or arrange for or recommend purchasing, leasing, or ordering any good, facility, service, or item for which payment may be made in whole or in part under a Federal health care program,

shall be guilty of a felony and upon conviction thereof, shall be fined not more than $25,000 or imprisoned for not more than five years, or both.

(3) Paragraphs (1) and (2) shall not apply

to—

(A) a discount or other reduction in price obtained by a provider of services or other entity under a Federal health care program if the reduction in price is properly disclosed and appropriately reflected in the costs claimed or charges made by the provider or entity under a Federal health care program;

(B) any amount paid by an employer to an employee (who has a bona fide employment relationship with such employer) for employment in the provision of covered items or services;

(C) any amount paid by a vendor of goods or services to a person authorized to act as a purchasing agent for a group of individuals or entities who are furnishing services reimbursed under a Federal health care program if—

(i) the person has a written contract, with each such individual or entity, which specifies the amount to be paid the person, which amount may be a fixed amount or a fixed percentage of the value of the purchases made by each such individual or entity under the contract, and

(ii) in the case of an entity that is a provider of services (as defined in section 1861(u) [42 USCS § 1395x(u)]), the person discloses (in such form and manner as the Secretary requires) to the entity and, upon request, to the Secretary the amount received from each such vendor with respect to purchases made by or on behalf of the entity;

(D) a waiver of any coinsurance under part B of title XVIII [42 USCS §§ 1395j et seq.] by a Federally qualified health care center with respect to an individual who qualifies for subsidized services under a provision of the Public Health Service Act;

(E) any payment practice specified by the Secretary in regulations promulgated pursuant to section 14(a) of the Medicare and Medicaid Patient and Program Protection Act of 1987 [note to this section] or in regulations under section 1860D-3(e)(6) [1860D-4(e)(6)] [42 USCS § 1395w-104(e)(6)];

(F) any remuneration between an organization and an individual or entity providing items or services, or a combination thereof, pursuant to a written agreement between the organization and the individual or entity if the organization is an eligible organization under section 1876 [42 USCS § 1395mm] or if the written agreement, through a risk-sharing arrangement, places the individual or entity at substantial financial risk for the cost or utilization of the items or services, or a combination thereof, which the individual or entity is obligated to provide;

(G) the waiver or reduction by pharmacies (including pharmacies of the Indian Health Service, Indian tribes, tribal organizations, and urban Indian organizations) of any cost-sharing imposed under part D of title XVIII [42 USCS §§ 1395w-101 et seq.], if the conditions described in clauses (i) through (iii) of section 1128A(i)(6)(A) [42 USCS § 1320a-7a(i)(6)(A)] are met with respect to the waiver or reduction (except that, in the case of such a waiver or reduction on behalf of a subsidy eligible individual (as defined in section 1860D-14(a)(3) [42 USCS § 1395w-114(a)(3)]), section 1128A(i)(6)(A) [42 USCS § 1320a-7a(i)(6)(A)] shall be applied without regard to clauses (ii) and (iii) of that section);

(H) any remuneration between a federally qualified health center (or an entity controlled by such a health center) and an MA organization pursuant to a written agreement described in section 1853(a)(4) [42 USCS § 1395w-23(a)(4)];

(I) any remuneration between a health center entity described under clause (i) or (ii) of section 1905(l)(2)(B) [42 USCS § 1396d(l)(2)(B)] and any individual or entity providing goods, items, services, donations, loans, or a combination thereof, to such health center entity pursuant to a contract, lease, grant, loan, or other agreement, if such agreement contributes to the ability of the health center entity to maintain or increase the availability, or enhance the quality, of services provided to a medically underserved population served by the health center entity; and

(J) **[Caution: This subparagraph applies to drugs dispensed on or after July 1, 2010, as provided by § 3301(d)(3) of Act March 23, 2010, P. L. 111-148, which appears as a note to this section.]** a discount in the price of an applicable drug (as defined in paragraph (2) of section 1860D-14A(g) [42 USCS § 1395w-114a(g)]) of a manufacturer that is furnished to an applicable beneficiary (as defined in paragraph (1) of such section) under the Medicare coverage gap discount program under section 1860D-14A [42 USCS § 1395w-114a].

(c) False statements or representations with respect to condition or operation of institutions. Whoever knowingly and willfully makes or causes to be made, or induces or seeks to induce the making of, any false statement or representation of a material fact with respect to the conditions or operation of any institution, facility, or entity in order that such institution, facility, or entity may qualify (either upon initial certification or upon recertification) as a hospital, critical access hospital, skilled nursing facility, nursing facility, intermediate care facility for the mentally retarded, home health agency, or other entity (including an eligible organization under section 1876(b) [42 USCS § 1395mm(b)]) for which certification is required under title XVIII [42 USCS §§ 1395 et seq.] or a State health care program (as defined in section 1128(h) [42 USCS § 1320a-7(h)]), or with respect to information required to be provided under section 1124A [42 USCS § 1320a-3a], shall be guilty of a felony and upon conviction thereof shall be fined not more than $25,000 or imprisoned for not more than five years, or both.

(d) Illegal patient admittance and retention practices. Whoever knowingly and willfully—

(1) charges, for any service provided to a patient under a State plan approved under title XIX [42 USCS §§ 1396 et seq.], money or other consideration at a rate in excess of the rates established by the State (or, in the case of services provided to an individual enrolled with a medicaid managed care organization under title XIX under a contract under section 1903(m) [42 USCS § 1396b(m)] or under a contractual, referral, or other arrangement under such contract, at a rate in excess of the rate permitted under such contract), or

(2) charges, solicits, accepts, or receives, in addition to any amount otherwise required to be paid under a State plan approved under title XIX [42 USCS §§ 1396 et seq.], any gift, money, donation, or other consideration (other than a charitable, religious, or philanthropic contribution from an organization or from a person unrelated to the patient)—

(A) as a precondition of admitting a patient to a hospital, nursing facility, or intermediate care facility for the mentally retarded, or

(B) as a requirement for the patient's continued stay in such a facility,

when the cost of the services provided therein to the patient is paid for (in whole or in part) under the State plan,

shall be guilty of a felony and upon conviction thereof shall be fined not more than $25,000 or imprisoned for not more than five years, or both.

(e) Violation of assignment terms. Whoever accepts assignments described in section 1842(b)(3)(B)(ii) [42 USCS § 1395u(b)(3)(B)(ii)] or agrees to be a participating physician or supplier under section 1842(h)(1) [42 USCS § 1395a(h)(1)] and knowingly, willfully, and repeatedly violates the term of such assignments or agreement, shall be guilty of a misdemeanor and upon conviction thereof shall be fined not more than $2,000 or imprisoned for not more than six months, or both.

(f) "Federal health care program" defined. For purposes of this section, the term "Federal health care program" means—

(1) any plan or program that provides health benefits, whether directly, through insurance, or otherwise, which is funded directly, in whole or in part, by the United States Government (other than the health insurance program under chapter 89 of title 5, United States Code [5 USCS §§ 8901 et seq.]); or

(2) any State health care program, as defined in section 1128(h) [42 USCS § 1320a-7(h)].

(g) Kickbacks. In addition to the penalties provided for in this section or section 1128A [42 USCS § 1320a-7a], a claim that includes items or services resulting from a violation of this section constitutes a false or fraudulent claim for purposes of subchapter III of chapter 37 of title 31, United States Code [31 USCS §§ 3721 et seq.].

(h) Intent. With respect to violations of this section, a person need not have actual knowledge of this section or specific intent to commit a violation of this section.

(Aug. 14, 1935, ch 531, Title XI [XVIII, Part C] [XIX], § 1128B [1877(d)] [1909], as added Oct. 30, 1972, P. L. 92-603, Title II, §§ 242(c), 278(b)(9), 86 Stat. 1419, 1454; Oct. 25, 1977, P. L. 95-142, § 4(a), (b), 91 Stat. 1179, 1181; Dec. 5, 1980, P. L. 96-499, Title IX, Part A, Subpart II, § 917 in part, 94 Stat. 2625; July 18, 1984, P. L. 98-369, Division B, Title III, Subtitle A, Part I, § 2306(f)(2), 98 Stat. 1073; Aug. 18, 1987, P. L. 100-93, §§ 4(a)–(d), 14(b), 101 Stat. 688, 689, 697; Dec. 22, 1987, P. L. 100-203, Title IV, Subtitle A, Part 2, Subpt. C, § 4039(a), Subtitle C, Part 2, § 4211(h)(7), 101 Stat. 1330-81, 1330-206; July 1, 1988, P. L. 100-360, Title IV, Subtitle B, § 411(a)(3)(B), 102 Stat. 768; Dec. 19, 1989, P. L. 101-239, Title VI, Subtitle A, Part 1, Subpart A, § 6003(g)(3)(D)(ii), 103 Stat. 2153; Nov. 5, 1990, P. L. 101-508, Title IV, Subtitle A, Part 2, Subpart B, §§ 4161(a)(4), 4164(b)(2), 104 Stat. 1388-94, 1388-102; Oct. 31, 1994, P. L. 103-432, Title I, Subtitle B, Part II, § 133(a)(2), 108 Stat. 4421; Aug. 21, 1996, P. L. 104-191, Title II, Subtitle A, § 204(a), Subtitle B, § 216(a), 110 Stat. 1999, 2007; Aug. 5, 1997, P. L. 105-33, Title IV, Subtitle C, § 4201(c)(1), Subtitle H, Ch 1, § 4704(b), Ch 4, § 4734, 111 Stat. 373, 498, 522; Dec. 8, 2003, P. L. 108-173, Title I, § 101(e)(2), (8)(A), Title II, Subtitle D, § 237(d), Title IV, Subtitle D,

§ 431(a), 117 Stat. 2150, 2152, 2213, 2287; March 23, 2010, P. L. 111-148, Title III, Subtitle D, § 3301(d)(1), Title VI, Subtitle E, § 6402(f), 124 Stat. 468, 759.)

HISTORY; ANCILLARY LAWS AND DIRECTIVES

Other provisions:

Appplication of amendments made by § 3301(d) of Act March 23, 2010. Act March 23, 2010, P. L. 111-148, Title III, Subtitle D, § 3301(d)(3), 124 Stat. 468, provides: "The amendments made by this subsection [amending 42 USCS §§ 1320a-7b(b)(3) and 1396r-8(c)(1)(C)] shall apply to drugs dispensed on or after July 1, 2010.".

§ 1320a-7c. Fraud and abuse control program [Caution: See prospective amendment note below.]

(a) Establishment of program (1) In general. Not later than January 1, 1997, the Secretary, acting through the Office of the Inspector General of the Department of Health and Human Services, and the Attorney General shall establish a program—

(A) to coordinate Federal, State, and local law enforcement programs to control fraud and abuse with respect to health plans,

(B) to conduct investigations, audits, evaluations, and inspections relating to the delivery of and payment for health care in the United States,

(C) to facilitate the enforcement of the provisions of sections 1128, 1128A, and 1128B [42 USCS §§ 1320a-7, 1320a-7a, 1320a-7b] and other statutes applicable to health care fraud and abuse,

(D) to provide for the modification and establishment of safe harbors and to issue advisory opinions and special fraud alerts pursuant to section 1128D [42 USCS § 1320a-7d], and

(E) to provide for the reporting and disclosure of certain final adverse actions against health care providers, suppliers, or practitioners pursuant to the data collection system established under section 1128E [42 USCS § 1320a-7e].

(2) Coordination with health plans. In carrying out the program established under paragraph (1), the Secretary and the Attorney General shall consult with, and arrange for the sharing of data with representatives of health plans.

(3) Guidelines. (A) In general. The Secretary and the Attorney General shall issue guidelines to carry out the program under paragraph (1). The provisions of sections 553, 556, and 557 of title 5, United States Code, shall not apply in the issuance of such guidelines.

(B) Information guidelines. (i) In general. Such guidelines shall include guidelines relating to the furnishing of information by health plans, providers, and others to enable the Secretary and the Attorney General to carry out the program (including coordination with health plans under paragraph (2)).

(ii) Confidentiality. Such guidelines shall include procedures to assure that such information is provided and utilized in a manner that appropriately protects the confidentiality of the information and the privacy of individuals receiving health care services and items.

(iii) Qualified immunity for providing information. The provisions of section 1157(a) [42 USCS § 1320c-6(a)] (relating to limitation on liability) shall apply to a person providing information to the Secretary or the Attorney General in conjunction with their performance of duties under this section.

(4) Ensuring access to documentation. The Inspector General of the Department of Health and Human Services is authorized to exercise such authority described in paragraphs (3) through (9) of section 6 of the Inspector General Act of 1978 (5 U.S.C. App.) as necessary with respect to the activities under the fraud and abuse control program established under this subsection.

(5) Authority of Inspector General. Nothing in this Act [42 USCS §§ 301 et seq.] shall be construed to diminish the authority of any Inspector General, including such authority as provided in the Inspector General Act of 1978 (5 U.S.C. App.).

(b) Additional use of funds by Inspector General. (1) Reimbursements for investigations. The Inspector General of the Department of Health and Human Services is authorized to receive and retain for current use reimbursement for the costs of conducting investigations and audits and for monitoring compliance plans when such costs are ordered by a court, voluntarily agreed to by the payor, or otherwise.

(2) Crediting. Funds received by the Inspector General under paragraph (1) as reimbursement for costs of conducting investigations shall be deposited to the credit of the appropriation from which initially paid, or to appropriations for similar purposes currently available at the time of deposit, and shall remain available for obligation for 1 year from the date of the deposit of such funds.

(c) "Health plan" defined. For purposes of this section, the term "health plan" means a plan or program that provides health benefits, whether directly, through insurance, or otherwise, and includes—

(1) a policy of health insurance;

(2) a contract of a service benefit organization; and

(3) a membership agreement with a health maintenance organization or other prepaid health plan.

(Aug. 14, 1935, ch 531, Title XI, Part A, § 1128C, as added Aug. 21, 1996, P. L. 104-191, Title II, Subtitle A, § 201(a), 110 Stat. 1992; March 23, 2010, P. L. 111-148, Title VI, Subtitle E, § 6403(c), 124 Stat. 766.)

HISTORY; ANCILLARY LAWS AND DIRECTIVES

Prospective amendments:

Amendment of subsec. (a)(1), effective on later of March 23, 2011, or effective date of regulations. Act March 23, 2010, P. L. 111-148, Title VI, Subtitle E, § 6403(c), 124 Stat. 766 (effective as provided by § 6403(d)(6) of such Act, which appears as 42 USCS § 1320a-7e note), provides:

"Section 1128C(a)(1) of the Social Security Act (42 U.S.C. 1320a-7c(a)(1)) is amended—

"(1) in subparagraph (C), by adding 'and' after the comma at the end;

"(2) in subparagraph (D), by striking ', and' and inserting a period; and

"(3) by striking subparagraph (E).".

§ 1320a-7e. Health care fraud and abuse data collection program [Caution: See prospective amendment note below.]

(a) General purpose. Not later than January 1, 1997, the Secretary shall establish a national health care fraud and abuse data collection program for the reporting of final adverse actions (not including settlements in which no findings of liability have been made) against health care providers, suppliers, or practitioners as required by subsection (b), with access as set forth in subsection (c), and shall maintain a database of the information collected under this section.

(b) Reporting of information. (1) In general. Each Government agency and health plan shall report any final adverse action (not including settlements in which no findings of liability have been made) taken against a health care provider, supplier, or practitioner.

(2) Information to be reported. The information to be reported under paragraph (1) includes:

(A) The name and TIN (as defined in section 7701(a)(41) of the Internal Revenue Code of 1986 [26 USCS § 7701(a)(41)]) of any health care provider, supplier, or practitioner who is the subject of a final adverse action.

(B) The name (if known) of any health care entity with which a health care provider, supplier, or practitioner, who is the subject of a final adverse action, is affiliated or associated.

(C) The nature of the final adverse action and whether such action is on appeal.

(D) A description of the acts or omissions and injuries upon which the final adverse action was based, and such other information as the Secretary determines by regulation is required for appropriate interpretation of information reported under this section.

(3) Confidentiality. In determining what information is required, the Secretary shall include procedures to assure that the privacy of individuals receiving health care services is appropriately protected.

(4) Timing and form of reporting. The information required to be reported under this subsection shall be reported regularly (but not less often than monthly) and in such form and manner as the Secretary prescribes. Such information shall first be required to be reported on a date specified by the Secretary.

(5) To whom reported. The information required to be reported under this subsection shall be reported to the Secretary.

(6) Sanctions for failure to report. (A) Health plans. Any health plan that fails to report information on an adverse action required to be reported under this subsection shall be subject to a civil money penalty of not more than $25,000 for each such adverse action not reported. Such penalty shall be imposed and collected in the same manner as civil money penalties under subsection (a) of section 1128A [42 USCS § 1320a-7a] are imposed and collected under that section.

(B) Governmental agencies. The Secretary shall provide for a publication of a public report that identifies those Government agencies that have failed to report information on adverse actions as required to be reported under this subsection.

(c) Disclosure and correction of information. (1) Disclosure. With respect to the information about final adverse actions (not including settlements in which no findings of liability have been made) reported to the Secretary under this section with respect to a health care provider, supplier, or practitioner, the Secretary shall, by regulation, provide for—

(A) disclosure of the information, upon request, to the health care provider, supplier, or licensed practitioner, and

(B) procedures in the case of disputed accuracy of the information.

(2) Corrections. Each Government agency and health plan shall report corrections of information already reported about any final

adverse action taken against a health care provider, supplier, or practitioner, in such form and manner that the Secretary prescribes by regulation.

(d) Access to reported information. (1) Availability. The information in the database maintained under this section shall be available to Federal and State government agencies and health plans pursuant to procedures that the Secretary shall provide by regulation.

(2) Fees for disclosure. The Secretary may establish or approve reasonable fees for the disclosure of information in such database (other than with respect to requests by Federal agencies). The amount of such a fee shall be sufficient to recover the full costs of operating the database. Such fees shall be available to the Secretary or, in the Secretary's discretion to the agency designated under this section to cover such costs.

(e) Protection from liability for reporting. No person or entity, including the agency designated by the Secretary in subsection (b)(5) shall be held liable in any civil action with respect to any report made as required by this section, without knowledge of the falsity of the information contained in the report.

(f) Coordination with National Practitioner Data Bank. The Secretary shall implement this section in such a manner as to avoid duplication with the reporting requirements established for the National Practitioner Data Bank under the Health Care Quality Improvement Act of 1986 (42 U.S.C. 11101 et seq.).

(g) Definitions and special rules. For purposes of this section:

(1) Final adverse action. (A) In general. The term "final adverse action" includes:

(i) Civil judgments against a health care provider, supplier, or practitioner in Federal or State court related to the delivery of a health care item or service.

(ii) Federal or State criminal convictions related to the delivery of a health care item or service.

(iii) Actions by Federal or State agencies responsible for the licensing and certification of health care providers, suppliers, and licensed health care practitioners, including—

(I) formal or official actions, such as revocation or suspension of a license (and the length of any such suspension), reprimand, censure or probation,

(II) any other loss of license or the right to apply for, or renew, a license of the provider, supplier, or practitioner, whether by operation of law, voluntary surrender, non-renewability, or otherwise, or

(III) any other negative action or finding by such Federal or State agency that is publicly available information.

(iv) Exclusion from participation in Federal or State health care programs (as defined in sections 1128B(f) and 1128(h) [42 USCS §§ 1320a-7b(f), 1320a-7(h)], respectively).

(v) Any other adjudicated actions or decisions that the Secretary shall establish by regulation.

(B) Exception. The term does not include any action with respect to a malpractice claim.

(2) Practitioner. The terms "licensed health care practitioner", "licensed practitioner", and "practitioner" mean, with respect to a State, an individual who is licensed or otherwise authorized by the State to provide health care services (or any individual who, without authority holds himself or herself out to be so licensed or authorized).

(3) Government agency. The term "Government agency" shall include:

(A) The Department of Justice.

(B) The Department of Health and Human Services.

(C) Any other Federal agency that either administers or provides payment for the delivery of health care services, including, but not limited to the Department of Defense and the Department of Veterans Affairs.

(D) State law enforcement agencies.

(E) State medicaid fraud control units.

(F) Federal or State agencies responsible for the licensing and certification of health care providers and licensed health care practitioners.

(4) Health plan. The term "health plan" has the meaning given such term by section 1128C(c) [42 USCS § 1320a-7c(c)].

(5) Determination of conviction. For purposes of paragraph (1), the existence of a conviction shall be determined under paragraphs (1) through (4) of section 1128(i) [42 USCS § 1320a-7(i)(1)–(4)].

(Aug. 14, 1935, ch 531, Title XI, Part A, § 1128E, as added Aug. 21, 1996, P. L. 104-191, Title II, Subtitle C, § 221(a), 110 Stat. 2009; Aug. 5, 1997, P. L. 105-33, Title IV, Subtitle D, Ch 3, § 4331(a)(2), (b), (d), 111 Stat. 395, 396; March 23, 2010, P. L. 111-148, Title VI, Subtitle E, § 6403(a), 124 Stat. 763.)

HISTORY; ANCILLARY LAWS AND DIRECTIVES

Prospective amendments:

Amendment of section, effective on later of March 23, 2011, or effective date of regulations. Act March 23, 2010, P. L. 111-148, Title VI, Subtitle E, § 6403(a), 124 Stat. 763 (effective as provided by § 6403(d)(6) of such Act, which appears as a note to this section), provides:

"Section 1128E of the Social Security Act (42 U.S.C. 1320a-7e) is amended—

"(1) by striking subsection (a) and inserting the following:

" '(a) In general. The Secretary shall maintain a national health care fraud and abuse data collection program under this section for the reporting of certain final adverse actions (not including settlements in which no findings of liability have been made) against health care providers, suppliers, or practitioners as required by subsection (b), with access as set forth in subsection (d), and shall furnish the information collected under this section to the National Practitioner Data Bank established pursuant to the Health Care Quality Improvement Act of 1986 (42 U.S.C. 11101 et seq.).';

"(2) by striking subsection (d) and inserting the following:

" '(d) Access to reported information. (1) Availability. The information collected under this section shall be available from the National Practitioner Data Bank to the agencies, authorities, and officials which are provided under section 1921(b) [42 USCS § 1396r-2(b)] information reported under section 1921(a) [42 USCS § 1396r-2(a)].

" '(2) Fees for disclosure. The Secretary may establish or approve reasonable fees for the disclosure of information under this section. The amount of such a fee may not exceed the costs of processing the requests for disclosure and of providing such information. Such fees shall be available to the Secretary to cover such costs.';

"(3) by striking subsection (f) and inserting the following:

" '(f) Appropriate coordination. In implementing this section, the Secretary shall provide for the maximum appropriate coordination with part B of the Health Care Quality Improvement Act of 1986 (42 U.S.C. 11131 et seq.) and section 1921 [42 USCS § 1396r-2].'; and

"(4) in subsection (g)—

"(A) in paragraph (1)(A)—

"(i) in clause (iii)—

"(I) by striking 'or State' each place it appears;

"(II) by redesignating subclauses (II) and (III) as subclauses (III) and (IV), respectively; and

"(III) by inserting after subclause (I) the following new subclause:

" '(II) any dismissal or closure of the proceedings by reason of the provider, supplier, or practitioner surrendering their license or leaving the State or jurisdiction'; and

"(ii) by striking clause (iv) and inserting the following:

" '(iv) Exclusion from participation in a Federal health care program (as defined in section 1128B(f) [42 USCS § 1320a-7b(f)]).';

"(B) in paragraph (3)—

"(i) by striking subparagraphs (D) and (E); and

"(ii) by redesignating subparagraph (F) as subparagraph (D); and

"(C) in subparagraph (D) (as so redesignated), by striking 'or State'.".

Other provisions:

Transition process; effective date of March 23, 2010 amendments. Act March 23, 2010, P. L. 111-148, Title VI, Subtitle E, § 6403(d), 124 Stat. 766, provides:

"(1) In general. Effective on the date of enactment of this Act, the Secretary of Health and Human Services (in this section referred to as the "Secretary") shall implement a transition process under which, by not later than the end of the transition period described in paragraph (5), the Secretary shall cease operating the Healthcare Integrity and Protection Data Bank established under section 1128E of the Social Security Act [42 USCS § 1320a-7e] (as in effect before the effective date specified in paragraph (6)) and shall transfer all data collected in the Healthcare Integrity and Protection Data Bank to the National Practitioner Data Bank established pursuant to the Health Care Quality Improvement Act of 1986 (42 U.S.C. 11101 et seq.). During such transition process, the Secretary shall have in effect appropriate procedures to ensure that data collection and access to the Healthcare Integrity and Protection Data Bank and the National Practitioner Data Bank are not disrupted.

"(2) Regulations. The Secretary shall promulgate regulations to carry out the amendments made by subsections (a) and (b) [amending 42 USCS §§ 1320a-7e and 1396r-2].

"(3) Funding. (A) Availability of fees. Fees collected pursuant to section 1128E(d)(2) of the Social Security Act [42 USCS § 1320a-7e(d)(2)] prior to the effective date specified in paragraph (6) for the disclosure of information in the Healthcare Integrity and Protection Data Bank shall be available to the Secretary, without fiscal year limitation, for payment of costs related to the transition process described in paragraph (1). Any such fees remaining after the transition period is complete shall be available to the Secretary, without fiscal year limitation, for payment of the costs of operating the National Practitioner Data Bank.

"(B) Availability of additional funds. In addition to the fees described in subparagraph (A), any funds available to the Secretary or to the Inspector General of the Department of Health and Human Services for a purpose related to combating health care fraud, waste, or abuse shall be available to the extent necessary for operating the Healthcare Integrity and Protection Data Bank during the transition period, including systems testing and other activities necessary to ensure that information formerly reported to the Healthcare Integrity and Protection Data Bank will be accessible through the National Practitioner Data Bank after the end of such transition period.

"(4) Special provision for access to the National Practitioner Data Bank by the Department of Veterans Affairs. (A) In general. Notwithstanding any other provision of law, during the 1-year period that begins on the effective date specified in paragraph (6), the information described in subparagraph (B) shall be available from the National Practitioner Data Bank to the Secretary of Veterans Affairs without charge.

"(B) Information described. For purposes of subparagraph (A), the information described in this subparagraph is the information that would, but for the amendments made by this section, have been available to the Secretary of Veterans Affairs from the Healthcare Integrity and Protection Data Bank.

"(5) Transition period defined. For purposes of this subsection, the term "transition period" means the period that begins on the date of enactment of this Act and ends on the later of—

"(A) the date that is 1 year after such date of enactment; or

"(B) the effective date of the regulations promulgated under paragraph (2).

"(6) Effective date. The amendments made by

subsections (a), (b), and (c) [amending 42 USCS §§ 1320a-7e, 1395r-2, and 1320a-7c] shall take effect on the first day after the final day of the transition period.".

§ 1320a-7h. Transparency reports and reporting of physician ownership or investment interests

(a) Transparency reports. (1) Payments or other transfers of value. (A) In general. On March 31, 2013, and on the 90th day of each calendar year beginning thereafter, any applicable manufacturer that provides a payment or other transfer of value to a covered recipient (or to an entity or individual at the request of or designated on behalf of a covered recipient), shall submit to the Secretary, in such electronic form as the Secretary shall require, the following information with respect to the preceding calendar year:

(i) The name of the covered recipient.

(ii) The business address of the covered recipient and, in the case of a covered recipient who is a physician, the specialty and National Provider Identifier of the covered recipient.

(iii) The amount of the payment or other transfer of value.

(iv) The dates on which the payment or other transfer of value was provided to the covered recipient.

(v) A description of the form of the payment or other transfer of value, indicated (as appropriate for all that apply) as—

(I) cash or a cash equivalent;

(II) in-kind items or services;

(III) stock, a stock option, or any other ownership interest, dividend, profit, or other return on investment; or

(IV) any other form of payment or other transfer of value (as defined by the Secretary).

(vi) A description of the nature of the payment or other transfer of value, indicated (as appropriate for all that apply) as—

(I) consulting fees;

(II) compensation for services other than consulting;

(III) honoraria;

(IV) gift;

(V) entertainment;

(VI) food;

(VII) travel (including the specified destinations);

(VIII) education;

(IX) research;

(X) charitable contribution;

(XI) royalty or license;

(XII) current or prospective ownership or investment interest;

(XIII) direct compensation for serving as faculty or as a speaker for a medical education program;

(XIV) grant; or

(XV) any other nature of the payment or other transfer of value (as defined by the Secretary).

(vii) If the payment or other transfer of value is related to marketing, education, or research specific to a covered drug, device, biological, or medical supply, the name of that covered drug, device, biological, or medical supply.

(viii) Any other categories of information regarding the payment or other transfer of value the Secretary determines appropriate.

(B) Special rule for certain payments or other transfers of value. In the case where an applicable manufacturer provides a payment or other transfer of value to an entity or individual at the request of or designated on behalf of a covered recipient, the applicable manufacturer shall disclose that payment or other transfer of value under the name of the covered recipient.

(2) Physician ownership. In addition to the requirement under paragraph (1)(A), on March 31, 2013, and on the 90th day of each calendar year beginning thereafter, any applicable manufacturer or applicable group purchasing organization shall submit to the Secretary, in such electronic form as the Secretary shall require, the following information regarding any ownership or investment interest (other than an ownership or investment interest in a publicly traded security and mutual fund, as described in section 1877(c) [42 USCS § 1395nn]) held by a physician (or an immediate family member of such physician (as defined for purposes of section 1877(a) [42 USCS § 1395nn(a)])) in the applicable manufacturer or applicable group purchasing organization during the preceding year:

(A) The dollar amount invested by each physician holding such an ownership or investment interest.

(B) The value and terms of each such ownership or investment interest.

(C) Any payment or other transfer of value provided to a physician holding such an ownership or investment interest (or to an entity or individual at the request of or designated on behalf of a physician holding such an ownership or investment interest), including the information described in clauses (i) through (viii) of paragraph (1)(A), except that in applying such clauses, "physician" shall be substituted for "covered recipient" each place it appears.

(D) Any other information regarding the

ownership or investment interest the Secretary determines appropriate.

(b) Penalties for noncompliance. (1) Failure to report. (A) In general. Subject to subparagraph (B) except as provided in paragraph (2), any applicable manufacturer or applicable group purchasing organization that fails to submit information required under subsection (a) in a timely manner in accordance with rules or regulations promulgated to carry out such subsection, shall be subject to a civil money penalty of not less than $1,000, but not more than $10,000, for each payment or other transfer of value or ownership or investment interest not reported as required under such subsection. Such penalty shall be imposed and collected in the same manner as civil money penalties under subsection (a) of section 1128A [42 USCS § 1320a-7a] are imposed and collected under that section.

(B) Limitation. The total amount of civil money penalties imposed under subparagraph (A) with respect to each annual submission of information under subsection (a) by an applicable manufacturer or applicable group purchasing organization shall not exceed $150,000.

(2) Knowing failure to report. (A) In general. Subject to subparagraph (B), any applicable manufacturer or applicable group purchasing organization that knowingly fails to submit information required under subsection (a) in a timely manner in accordance with rules or regulations promulgated to carry out such subsection, shall be subject to a civil money penalty of not less than $10,000, but not more than $100,000, for each payment or other transfer of value or ownership or investment interest not reported as required under such subsection. Such penalty shall be imposed and collected in the same manner as civil money penalties under subsection (a) of section 1128A [42 USCS § 1320a-7a] are imposed and collected under that section.

(B) Limitation. The total amount of civil money penalties imposed under subparagraph (A) with respect to each annual submission of information under subsection (a) by an applicable manufacturer or applicable group purchasing organization shall not exceed $1,000,000.

(3) Use of funds. Funds collected by the Secretary as a result of the imposition of a civil money penalty under this subsection shall be used to carry out this section.

(c) Procedures for submission of information and public availability. (1) In general. (A) Establishment. Not later than October 1, 2011, the Secretary shall establish procedures—

(i) for applicable manufacturers and applicable group purchasing organizations to submit information to the Secretary under subsection (a); and

(ii) for the Secretary to make such information submitted available to the public.

(B) Definition of terms. The procedures established under subparagraph (A) shall provide for the definition of terms (other than those terms defined in subsection (e)), as appropriate, for purposes of this section.

(C) Public availability. Except as provided in subparagraph (E), the procedures established under subparagraph (A)(ii) shall ensure that, not later than September 30, 2013, and on June 30 of each calendar year beginning thereafter, the information submitted under subsection (a) with respect to the preceding calendar year is made available through an Internet website that—

(i) is searchable and is in a format that is clear and understandable;

(ii) contains information that is presented by the name of the applicable manufacturer or applicable group purchasing organization, the name of the covered recipient, the business address of the covered recipient, the specialty of the covered recipient, the value of the payment or other transfer of value, the date on which the payment or other transfer of value was provided to the covered recipient, the form of the payment or other transfer of value, indicated (as appropriate) under subsection (a)(1)(A)(v), the nature of the payment or other transfer of value, indicated (as appropriate) under subsection (a)(1)(A)(vi), and the name of the covered drug, device, biological, or medical supply, as applicable;

(iii) contains information that is able to be easily aggregated and downloaded;

(iv) contains a description of any enforcement actions taken to carry out this section, including any penalties imposed under subsection (b), during the preceding year;

(v) contains background information on industry-physician relationships;

(vi) in the case of information submitted with respect to a payment or other transfer of value described in subparagraph (E)(i), lists such information separately from the other information submitted under subsection (a) and designates such separately listed information as funding for clinical research;

(vii) contains any other information the Secretary determines would be helpful to the average consumer;

(viii) does not contain the National Provider Identifier of the covered recipient, and

(ix) subject to subparagraph (D), provides the applicable manufacturer, applicable group purchasing organization, or covered recipient an opportunity to review and submit corrections to the information submitted with respect to the applicable manufacturer, applicable group purchasing organization, or covered recipient, respectively, for a period of not less than 45 days prior to such information being made available to the public.

(D) Clarification of time period for review and corrections. In no case may the 45-day period for review and submission of corrections to information under subparagraph (C)(ix) prevent such information from being made available to the public in accordance with the dates described in the matter preceding clause (i) in subparagraph (C).

(E) Delayed publication for payments made pursuant to product research or development agreements and clinical investigations. (i) In general. In the case of information submitted under subsection (a) with respect to a payment or other transfer of value made to a covered recipient by an applicable manufacturer pursuant to a product research or development agreement for services furnished in connection with research on a potential new medical technology or a new application of an existing medical technology or the development of a new drug, device, biological, or medical supply, or by an applicable manufacturer in connection with a clinical investigation regarding a new drug, device, biological, or medical supply, the procedures established under subparagraph (A)(ii) shall provide that such information is made available to the public on the first date described in the matter preceding clause (i) in subparagraph (C) after the earlier of the following:

(I) The date of the approval or clearance of the covered drug, device, biological, or medical supply by the Food and Drug Administration.

(II) Four calendar years after the date such payment or other transfer of value was made.

(ii) Confidentiality of information prior to publication. Information described in clause (i) shall be considered confidential and shall not be subject to disclosure under section 552 of title 5, United States Code, or any other similar Federal, State, or local law, until on or after the date on which the information is made available to the public under such clause.

(2) Consultation. In establishing the procedures under paragraph (1), the Secretary shall consult with the Inspector General of the Department of Health and Human Services, affected industry, consumers, consumer advocates, and other interested parties in order to ensure that the information made available to the public under such paragraph is presented in the appropriate overall context.

(d) Annual reports and relation to State laws. (1) Annual report to Congress. Not later than April 1 of each year beginning with 2013, the Secretary shall submit to Congress a report that includes the following:

(A) The information submitted under subsection (a) during the preceding year, aggregated for each applicable manufacturer and applicable group purchasing organization that submitted such information during such year (except, in the case of information submitted with respect to a payment or other transfer of value described in subsection (c)(1)(E)(i), such information shall be included in the first report submitted to Congress after the date on which such information is made available to the public under such subsection).

(B) A description of any enforcement actions taken to carry out this section, including any penalties imposed under subsection (b), during the preceding year.

(2) Annual reports to States. Not later than September 30, 2013 and on June 30 of each calendar year thereafter, the Secretary shall submit to States a report that includes a summary of the information submitted under subsection (a) during the preceding year with respect to covered recipients in the State (except, in the case of information submitted with respect to a payment or other transfer of value described in subsection (c)(1)(E)(i), such information shall be included in the first report submitted to States after the date on which such information is made available to the public under such subsection).

(3) Relation to State laws. (A) In general. In the case of a payment or other transfer of value provided by an applicable manufacturer that is received by a covered recipient (as defined in subsection (e)) on or after January 1, 2012, subject to subparagraph (B), the provisions of this section shall preempt any statute or regulation of a State or of a political subdivision of a State that requires an applicable manufacturer (as so defined) to disclose or report, in any format, the type of information (as described in subsection (a)) regarding such payment or other transfer of value.

(B) No preemption of additional requirements. Subparagraph (A) shall not preempt any statute or regulation of a State or of a political subdivision of a State that requires the disclosure or reporting of information—

(i) not of the type required to be disclosed or reported under this section;

(ii) described in subsection (e)(10)(B), except in the case of information described in clause (i) of such subsection;

(iii) by any person or entity other than an applicable manufacturer (as so defined) or a covered recipient (as defined in subsection (e)); or

(iv) to a Federal, State, or local governmental agency for public health surveillance, investigation, or other public health purposes or health oversight purposes.

(C) Nothing in subparagraph (A) shall be construed to limit the discovery or admissibility of information described in such subparagraph in a criminal, civil, or administrative proceeding.

(4) Consultation. The Secretary shall consult with the Inspector General of the Department of Health and Human Services on the implementation of this section.

(e) Definitions. In this section:

(1) Applicable group purchasing organization. The term "applicable group purchasing organization" means a group purchasing organization (as defined by the Secretary) that purchases, arranges for, or negotiates the purchase of a covered drug, device, biological, or medical supply which is operating in the United States, or in a territory, possession, or commonwealth of the United States.

(2) Applicable manufacturer. The term "applicable manufacturer" means a manufacturer of a covered drug, device, biological, or medical supply which is operating in the United States, or in a territory, possession, or commonwealth of the United States.

(3) Clinical investigation. The term "clinical investigation" means any experiment involving 1 or more human subjects, or materials derived from human subjects, in which a drug or device is administered, dispensed, or used.

(4) Covered device. The term "covered device" means any device for which payment is available under title XVIII [42 USCS §§ 1395 et seq.] or a State plan under title XIX or XXI [42 USCS §§ 1396 et seq. or 1397aa et seq.] (or a waiver of such a plan).

(5) Covered drug, device, biological, or medical supply. The term "covered drug, device, biological, or medical supply" means any drug, biological product, device, or medical supply for which payment is available under title XVIII or a State plan under title XIX or XXI [42 USCS §§ 1396 et seq. or 1397aa et seq.] (or a waiver of such a plan).

(6) Covered recipient. (A) In general. Except as provided in subparagraph (B), the term "covered recipient" means the following:

(i) A physician.

(ii) A teaching hospital.

(B) Exclusion. Such term does not include a physician who is an employee of the applicable manufacturer that is required to submit information under subsection (a).

(7) Employee. The term "employee" has the meaning given such term in section 1877(h)(2) [42 USCS § 1395nn(h)(2)].

(8) Knowingly. The term "knowingly" has the meaning given such term in section 3729(b) of title 31, United States Code.

(9) Manufacturer of a covered drug, device, biological, or medical supply. The term "manufacturer of a covered drug, device, biological, or medical supply" means any entity which is engaged in the production, preparation, propagation, compounding, or conversion of a covered drug, device, biological, or medical supply (or any entity under common ownership with such entity which provides assistance or support to such entity with respect to the production, preparation, propagation, compounding, conversion, marketing, promotion, sale, or distribution of a covered drug, device, biological, or medical supply).

(10) Payment or other transfer of value. (A) In general. The term "payment or other transfer of value" means a transfer of anything of value. Such term does not include a transfer of anything of value that is made indirectly to a covered recipient through a third party in connection with an activity or service in the case where the applicable manufacturer is unaware of the identity of the covered recipient.

(B) Exclusions. An applicable manufacturer shall not be required to submit information under subsection (a) with respect to the following:

(i) A transfer of anything the value of which is less than $10, unless the aggregate amount transferred to, requested by, or designated on behalf of the covered recipient by the applicable manufacturer during the calendar year exceeds $100. For calendar years after 2012, the dollar amounts specified in the preceding sentence shall be increased by the same percentage as the percentage increase in the consumer price index for all urban consumers (all items; U.S. city average) for the 12-month period ending with June of the previous year.

(ii) Product samples that are not intended to be sold and are intended for patient use.

(iii) Educational materials that directly benefit patients or are intended for patient use.

(iv) The loan of a covered device for a short-term trial period, not to exceed 90 days, to permit evaluation of the covered device by the covered recipient.

(v) Items or services provided under a contractual warranty, including the replacement of a covered device, where the terms of the warranty are set forth in the purchase or lease agreement for the covered device.

(vi) A transfer of anything of value to a covered recipient when the covered recipient is a patient and not acting in the professional capacity of a covered recipient.

(vii) Discounts (including rebates).

(viii) In-kind items used for the provision of charity care.

(ix) A dividend or other profit distribution from, or ownership or investment interest in, a publicly traded security and mutual fund (as described in section 1877(c) [42 USCS § 1395nn(c)]).

(x) In the case of an applicable manufacturer who offers a self-insured plan, payments for the provision of health care to employees under the plan.

(xi) In the case of a covered recipient who is a licensed non-medical professional, a transfer of anything of value to the covered recipient if the transfer is payment solely for the non-medical professional services of such licensed non-medical professional.

(xii) In the case of a covered recipient who is a physician, a transfer of anything of value to the covered recipient if the transfer is payment solely for the services of the covered recipient with respect to a civil or criminal action or an administrative proceeding.

(11) Physician. The term "physician" has the meaning given that term in section 1861(r) [42 USCS § 1395x(r)].

(Aug. 14, 1935, ch 531, Title XI, Part A, § 1128G, as added March 23, 2010, P. L. 111-148, Title VI, Subtitle A, § 6002, 124 Stat. 689.)

§ 1320a-7i. Reporting of information relating to drug samples

(a) In general. Not later than April 1 of each year (beginning with 2012), each manufacturer and authorized distributor of record of an applicable drug shall submit to the Secretary (in a form and manner specified by the Secretary) the following information with respect to the preceding year:

(1) In the case of a manufacturer or authorized distributor of record which makes distributions by mail or common carrier under subsection (d)(2) of section 503 of the Federal Food, Drug, and Cosmetic Act (21 U.S.C. 353), the identity and quantity of drug samples requested and the identity and quantity of drug samples distributed under such subsection during that year, aggregated by—

(A) the name, address, professional designation, and signature of the practitioner making the request under subparagraph (A)(i) of such subsection, or of any individual who makes or signs for the request on behalf of the practitioner; and

(B) any other category of information determined appropriate by the Secretary.

(2) In the case of a manufacturer or authorized distributor of record which makes distributions by means other than mail or common carrier under subsection (d)(3) of such section 503 [21 USCS § 353], the identity and quantity of drug samples requested and the identity and quantity of drug samples distributed under such subsection during that year, aggregated by—

(A) the name, address, professional designation, and signature of the practitioner making the request under subparagraph (A)(i) of such subsection, or of any individual who makes or signs for the request on behalf of the practitioner; and

(B) any other category of information determined appropriate by the Secretary.

(b) Definitions. In this section:

(1) Applicable drug. The term "applicable drug" means a drug—

(A) which is subject to subsection (b) of such section 503 [21 USCS § 353]; and

(B) for which payment is available under title XVIII [42 USCS §§ 1395 et seq.] or a State plan under title XIX or XXI [42 USCS §§ 1396 et seq. or 1397aa et seq.] (or a waiver of such a plan).

(2) Authorized distributor of record. The term "authorized distributor of record" has the meaning given that term in subsection (e)(3)(A) of such section.

(3) Manufacturer. The term "manufacturer" has the meaning given that term for purposes of subsection (d) of such section.

(Aug. 14, 1935, ch 531, Title XI, Part A, § 1128H, as added March 23, 2010, P. L. 111-148, Title VI, Subtitle A, § 6004, 124 Stat. 697.)

§ 1320a-7j. Accountability requirements for facilities

(a) Definition of facility. In this section, the term "facility" means—

(1) a skilled nursing facility (as defined in section 1819(a) [42 USCS § 1395i-3(a)]); or

(2) a nursing facility (as defined in section 1919(a) [42 USCS § 1396r(a)]).

(b) Effective compliance and ethics programs. (1) Requirement. On or after the date that is 36 months after the date of the enactment of this section [enacted March 23, 2010], a facility shall, with respect to the entity that operates the facility (in this subparagraph referred to as the "operating organization" or "organization"), have in operation a compliance and ethics program that is effective in preventing and detecting criminal, civil, and administrative violations under this Act [42 USCS §§ 301 et seq.] and in promoting quality of care consistent with regulations developed under paragraph (2).

(2) Development of regulations. (A) In general. Not later than the date that is 2 years after such date of the enactment [enacted March 23, 2010], the Secretary, working jointly with the Inspector General of the Department of Health and Human Services, shall promulgate regulations for an effective compliance and ethics program for operating organizations, which may include a model compliance program.

(B) Design of regulations. Such regulations with respect to specific elements or formality of a program shall, in the case of an organization that operates 5 or more facilities, vary with the size of the organization, such that larger organizations should have a more formal program and include established written policies defining the standards and procedures to be followed by its employees. Such requirements may specifically apply to the corporate level management of multi unit nursing home chains.

(C) Evaluation. Not later than 3 years after the date of the promulgation of regulations under this paragraph, the Secretary shall complete an evaluation of the compliance and ethics programs required to be established under this subsection. Such evaluation shall determine if such programs led to changes in deficiency citations, changes in quality performance, or changes in other metrics of patient quality of care. The Secretary shall submit to Congress a report on such evaluation and shall include in such report such recommendations regarding changes in the requirements for such programs as the Secretary determines appropriate.

(3) Requirements for compliance and ethics programs. In this subsection, the term "compliance and ethics program" means, with respect to a facility, a program of the operating organization that—

(A) has been reasonably designed, implemented, and enforced so that it generally will be effective in preventing and detecting criminal, civil, and administrative violations under this Act [42 USCS §§ 301 et seq.] and in promoting quality of care; and

(B) includes at least the required components specified in paragraph (4).

(4) Required components of program. The required components of a compliance and ethics program of an operating organization are the following:

(A) The organization must have established compliance standards and procedures to be followed by its employees and other agents that are reasonably capable of reducing the prospect of criminal, civil, and administrative violations under this Act [42 USCS §§ 301 et seq.].

(B) Specific individuals within high-level personnel of the organization must have been assigned overall responsibility to oversee compliance with such standards and procedures and have sufficient resources and authority to assure such compliance.

(C) The organization must have used due care not to delegate substantial discretionary authority to individuals whom the organization knew, or should have known through the exercise of due diligence, had a propensity to engage in criminal, civil, and administrative violations under this Act [42 USCS §§ 301 et seq.].

(D) The organization must have taken steps to communicate effectively its standards and procedures to all employees and other agents, such as by requiring participation in training programs or by disseminating publications that explain in a practical manner what is required.

(E) The organization must have taken reasonable steps to achieve compliance with its standards, such as by utilizing monitoring and auditing systems reasonably designed to detect criminal, civil, and administrative violations under this Act [42 USCS §§ 301 et seq.] by its employees and other agents and by having in place and publicizing a reporting system whereby employees and other agents could report violations by others within the organization without fear of retribution.

(F) The standards must have been consistently enforced through appropriate disciplinary mechanisms, including, as appropriate, discipline of individuals responsible for the failure to detect an offense.

(G) After an offense has been detected, the organization must have taken all reasonable steps to respond appropriately to the offense and to prevent further similar offenses, including any necessary modification to its program to prevent and detect criminal, civil, and administrative violations under this Act [42 USCS §§ 301 et seq.].

(H) The organization must periodically undertake reassessment of its compliance program to identify changes necessary to reflect changes within the organization and its facilities.

(c) Quality assurance and performance improvement program. (1) In general. Not later than December 31, 2011, the Secretary shall establish and implement a quality assurance and performance improvement program (in this subparagraph referred to as the "QAPI program") for facilities, including multi unit chains of facilities. Under the QAPI program, the Secretary shall establish standards relating to quality assurance and performance improvement with respect to facilities and provide technical assistance to facilities on the development of best practices in order to meet such standards. Not later than 1 year after the date on which the regulations are promulgated under paragraph (2), a facility must submit to the Secretary a plan for the facility to meet such standards and implement such best practices, including how to coordinate the implementation of such plan with quality assessment and assurance activities conducted under sections 1819(b)(1)(B) [42 USCS § 1395i-3(b)(1)(B)] and 1919(b)(1)(B) [42 USCS § 1396r(b)(1)(B)], as applicable.

(2) Regulations. The Secretary shall promulgate regulations to carry out this subsection.

(f) Standardized complaint form [Caution: This subsection takes effect March 23, 2011, pursuant to § 6105(b) of Act March 23, 2010, PL. 111-148, which appears as a note to this section.]. (1) Development by the Secretary. The Secretary shall develop a standardized complaint form for use by a resident (or a person acting on the resident's behalf) in filing a complaint with a State survey and certification agency and a State long-term care ombudsman program with respect to a facility.

(2) Complaint forms and resolution processes. (A) Complaint forms. The State must make the standardized complaint form developed under paragraph (1) available upon request to—

(i) a resident of a facility; and

(ii) any person acting on the resident's behalf.

(B) Complaint resolution process. The State must establish a complaint resolution process in order to ensure that the legal representative of a resident of a facility or other responsible party is not denied access to such resident or otherwise retaliated against if they have complained about the quality of care provided by the facility or other issues relating to the facility. Such complaint resolution process shall include—

(i) procedures to assure accurate tracking of complaints received, including notification to the complainant that a complaint has been received;

(ii) procedures to determine the likely severity of a complaint and for the investigation of the complaint; and

(iii) deadlines for responding to a complaint and for notifying the complainant of the outcome of the investigation.

(3) Rule of construction. Nothing in this subsection shall be construed as preventing a resident of a facility (or a person acting on the resident's behalf) from submitting a complaint in a manner or format other than by using the standardized complaint form developed under paragraph (1) (including submitting a complaint orally).

(g) Submission of staffing information based on payroll data in a uniform format. Beginning not later than 2 years after the date of the enactment of this subsection [enacted March 23, 2010], and after consulting with State long-term care ombudsman programs, consumer advocacy groups, provider stakeholder groups, employees and their representatives, and other parties the Secretary deems appropriate, the Secretary shall require a facility to electronically submit to the Secretary direct care staffing information (including information with respect to agency and contract staff) based on payroll and other verifiable and auditable data in a uniform format (according to specifications established by the Secretary in consultation with such programs, groups, and parties). Such specifications shall require that the information submitted under the preceding sentence—

(1) specify the category of work a certified employee performs (such as whether the employee is a registered nurse, licensed practical nurse, licensed vocational nurse, certified nursing assistant, therapist, or other medical personnel);

(2) include resident census data and information on resident case mix;

(3) include a regular reporting schedule; and

(4) include information on employee turnover and tenure and on the hours of care provided by each category of certified employees referenced in paragraph (1) per resident per day.

Nothing in this subsection shall be construed

as preventing the Secretary from requiring submission of such information with respect to specific categories, such as nursing staff, before other categories of certified employees. Information under this subsection with respect to agency and contract staff shall be kept separate from information on employee staffing.

(h) Notification of facility closure [Caution: This subsection takes effect March 23, 2011, pursuant to § 6113(c) of Act March 23, 2010, PL. 111-148, which appears as a note to this section.]. (1) In general. Any individual who is the administrator of a facility must—

(A) submit to the Secretary, the State long-term care ombudsman, residents of the facility, and the legal representatives of such residents or other responsible parties, written notification of an impending closure—

(i) subject to clause (ii), not later than the date that is 60 days prior to the date of such closure; and

(ii) in the case of a facility where the Secretary terminates the facility's participation under this title [42 USCS §§ 1301 et seq.], not later than the date that the Secretary determines appropriate;

(B) ensure that the facility does not admit any new residents on or after the date on which such written notification is submitted; and

(C) include in the notice a plan for the transfer and adequate relocation of the residents of the facility by a specified date prior to closure that has been approved by the State, including assurances that the residents will be transferred to the most appropriate facility or other setting in terms of quality, services, and location, taking into consideration the needs, choice, and best interests of each resident.

(2) Relocation. (A) In general. The State shall ensure that, before a facility closes, all residents of the facility have been successfully relocated to another facility or an alternative home and community-based setting.

(B) Continuation of payments until residents relocated. The Secretary may, as the Secretary determines appropriate, continue to make payments under this title with respect to residents of a facility that has submitted a notification under paragraph (1) during the period beginning on the date such notification is submitted and ending on the date on which the resident is successfully relocated.

(3) Sanctions. Any individual who is the administrator of a facility that fails to comply with the requirements of paragraph (1)—

(A) shall be subject to a civil monetary penalty of up to $100,000;

(B) may be subject to exclusion from participation in any Federal health care program (as defined in section 1128B(f) [42 USCS § 1320a-7b(f)]); and

(C) shall be subject to any other penalties that may be prescribed by law.

(4) Procedure. The provisions of section 1128A [42 USCS § 1320a-7a] (other than subsections (a) and (b) and the second sentence of subsection (f)) shall apply to a civil money penalty or exclusion under paragraph (3) in the same manner as such provisions apply to a penalty or proceeding under section 1128A(a) [42 USCS § 1320a-7a(a)].

(Aug. 14, 1935, ch 531, Title XI, Part A, § 1128I, as added and amended March 23, 2010, P. L. 111-148, Title VI, Subtitle B, Part I, §§ 6102, 6105(a), 6106, Part II, § 6113(a), 124 Stat. 702, 711, 712, 718.)

HISTORY; ANCILLARY LAWS AND DIRECTIVES

Other provisions:

Effective date of amendment made by § 6105 of Act March 23, 2010. Act March 23, 2010, P. L. 111-148, Title VI, Subtitle B, Part I, § 6105(b), 124 Stat. 712, provides: "The amendment made by this section [adding subsec. (f) of this section] shall take effect 1 year after the date of the enactment of this Act.".

National independent monitor demonstration project. Act March 23, 2010, P. L. 111-148, Title VI, Subtitle B, Part II, § 6112, 124 Stat. 716, provides:

"(a) Establishment. (1) In general. The Secretary, in consultation with the Inspector General of the Department of Health and Human Services, shall conduct a demonstration project to develop, test, and implement an independent monitor program to oversee interstate and large intrastate chains of skilled nursing facilities and nursing facilities.

"(2) Selection. The Secretary shall select chains of skilled nursing facilities and nursing facilities described in paragraph (1) to participate in the demonstration project under this section from among those chains that submit an application to the Secretary at such time, in such manner, and containing such information as the Secretary may require.

"(3) Duration. The Secretary shall conduct the demonstration project under this section for a 2-year period.

"(4) Implementation. The Secretary shall implement the demonstration project under this section not later than 1 year after the date of the enactment of this Act.

"(b) Requirements. The Secretary shall evaluate chains selected to participate in the demonstration project under this section based on criteria selected by the Secretary, including where evidence suggests that a number of the facilities of the chain are experiencing serious safety and quality of care problems. Such criteria may include the evaluation of a chain that includes a number of facilities participating in the "Special Focus Facility" program (or a successor program) or multiple facilities with a record of repeated serious safety and quality of care deficiencies.

"(c) Responsibilities. An independent monitor that enters into a contract with the Secretary to participate in the conduct of the demonstration project under this section shall—

"(1) conduct periodic reviews and prepare root-cause quality and deficiency analyses of a chain to assess if facilities of the chain are in compliance with State and Federal laws and regulations applicable to the facilities;

"(2) conduct sustained oversight of the efforts of the chain, whether publicly or privately held, to achieve compliance by facilities of the chain with State and Federal laws and regulations applicable to the facilities;

"(3) analyze the management structure, distribution of expenditures, and nurse staffing levels of facilities of the chain in relation to resident census, staff turnover rates, and tenure;

"(4) report findings and recommendations with respect to such reviews, analyses, and oversight to the chain and facilities of the chain, to the Secretary, and to relevant States; and

"(5) publish the results of such reviews, analyses, and oversight.

"(d) Implementation of recommendations. (1) Receipt of finding by chain. Not later than 10 days after receipt of a finding of an independent monitor under subsection (c)(4), a chain participating in the demonstration project shall submit to the independent monitor a report—

"(A) outlining corrective actions the chain will take to implement the recommendations in such report; or

"(B) indicating that the chain will not implement such recommendations, and why it will not do so.

"(2) Receipt of report by independent monitor. Not later than 10 days after receipt of a report submitted by a chain under paragraph (1), an independent monitor shall finalize its recommendations and submit a report to the chain and facilities of the chain, the Secretary, and the State or States, as appropriate, containing such final recommendations.

"(e) Cost of appointment. A chain shall be responsible for a portion of the costs associated with the appointment of independent monitors under the demonstration project under this section. The chain shall pay such portion to the Secretary (in an amount and in accordance with procedures established by the Secretary).

"(f) Waiver authority. The Secretary may waive such requirements of titles XVIII and XIX of the Social Security Act (42 U.S.C. 1395 et seq.; 1396 et seq.) as may be necessary for the purpose of carrying out the demonstration project under this section.

"(g) Authorization of appropriations. There are authorized to be appropriated such sums as may be necessary to carry out this section.

"(h) Definitions. In this section:

"(1) Additional disclosable party. The term 'additional disclosable party' has the meaning given such term in section 1124(c)(5)(A) of the Social Security Act [42 USCS § 1320a-3(c)(5)(A)], as added by section 4201(a).

"(2) Facility. The term 'facility' means a skilled nursing facility or a nursing facility.

"(3) Nursing facility. The term 'nursing facility' has the meaning given such term in section 1919(a) of the Social Security Act (42 U.S.C. 1396r(a)).

"(4) Secretary. The term 'Secretary' means the Secretary of Health and Human Services, acting through the Assistant Secretary for Planning and Evaluation.

"(5) Skilled nursing facility. The term 'skilled nursing facility' has the meaning given such term in section 1819(a) of the Social Security Act (42 U.S.C. 1395(a)).

"(i) Evaluation and report. (1) Evaluation. The Secretary, in consultation with the Inspector General of the Department of Health and Human Services, shall evaluate the demonstration project conducted under this section.

"(2) Report. Not later than 180 days after the completion of the demonstration project under this section, the Secretary shall submit to Congress a report containing the results of the evaluation conducted under paragraph (1), together with recommendations—

"(A) as to whether the independent monitor program should be established on a permanent basis;

"(B) if the Secretary recommends that such program be so established, on appropriate procedures and mechanisms for such establishment; and

"(C) for such legislation and administrative action as the Secretary determines appropriate.".

Effective date of amendments made by § 6113 of Act March 23, 2010. Act March 23, 2010, P. L. 111-148, Title VI, Subtitle B, Part II, § 6113(c), 124 Stat. 720, provides: "The amendments made by this section [adding 42 USCS § 1320a-7j(h) and amending 42 USCS § 1395i-3(h)(4)] shall take effect 1 year after the date of the enactment of this Act.".

§ 1320a-7k. Medicare and Medicaid program integrity provisions

(a) Data matching. (1) Integrated data repository. (A) Inclusion of certain data. (i) In general. The Integrated Data Repository of the Centers for Medicare & Medicaid Services shall include, at a minimum, claims and payment data from the following:

(I) The programs under titles XVIII and XIX [42 USCS §§ 1395 et seq. and 1396 et seq.] (including parts A, B, C, and D of title XVIII [42 USCS §§ 1395c et seq., 1395j et seq., 1395w-21 et seq., and 1395w-101 et seq.]).

(II) The program under title XXI [42 USCS §§ 1397aa et seq.].

(III) Health-related programs administered by the Secretary of Veterans Affairs.

(IV) Health-related programs administered by the Secretary of Defense.

(V) The program of old-age, survivors, and disability insurance benefits established under title II [42 USCS §§ 401 et seq.].

(VI) The Indian Health Service and the Contract Health Service program.

(ii) Priority for inclusion of certain data. Inclusion of the data described in subclause (I) of such clause in the Integrated Data Repository shall be a priority. Data described in subclauses (II) through (VI) of such clause shall be included in the Integrated Data Repository as appropriate.

(B) Data sharing and matching. (i) In general. The Secretary shall enter into agreements with the individuals described in clause (ii) under which such individuals share and match data in the system of records of the respective agencies of such individuals with data in the system of records of the Department of Health and Human Services for the purpose of identifying potential fraud, waste, and abuse under the programs under titles XVIII and XIX [42 USCS §§ 1395 et seq. and 1396 et seq.].

(ii) Individuals described. The following individuals are described in this clause:

(I) The Commissioner of Social Security.

(II) The Secretary of Veterans Affairs.

(III) The Secretary of Defense.

(IV) The Director of the Indian Health Service.

(iii) Definition of system of records. For purposes of this paragraph, the term "system of records" has the meaning given such term in section 552a(a)(5) of title 5, United States Code.

(2) Access to claims and payment databases. For purposes of conducting law enforcement and oversight activities and to the extent consistent with applicable information, privacy, security, and disclosure laws, including the regulations promulgated under the Health Insurance Portability and Accountability Act of 1996 and section 552a of title 5, United States Code, and subject to any information systems security requirements under such laws or otherwise required by the Secretary, the Inspector General of the Department of Health and Human Services and the Attorney General shall have access to claims and payment data of the Department of Health and Human Services and its contractors related to titles XVIII, XIX, and XXI [42 USCS §§ 1395 et seq., 1396 et seq., and 1397aa et seq.].

(b) OIG authority to obtain information. (1) In general. Notwithstanding and in addition to any other provision of law, the Inspector General of the Department of Health and Human Services may, for purposes of protecting the integrity of the programs under titles XVIII and XIX [42 USCS §§ 1395 et seq. and 1396 et seq.], obtain information from any individual (including a beneficiary provided all applicable privacy protections are followed) or entity that—

(A) is a provider of medical or other items or services, supplier, grant recipient, contractor, or subcontractor; or

(B) directly or indirectly provides, orders, manufactures, distributes, arranges for, prescribes, supplies, or receives medical or other items or services payable by any Federal health care program (as defined in section 1128B(f) [42 USCS § 1320a-7b(f)]) regardless of how the item or service is paid for, or to whom such payment is made.

(2) Inclusion of certain information. Information which the Inspector General may obtain under paragraph (1) includes any supporting documentation necessary to validate claims for payment or payments under title XVIII or XIX [42 USCS §§ 1395 et seq. or 1396 et seq.], including a prescribing physician's medical records for an individual who is prescribed an item or service which is covered under part B of title XVIII [42 USCS §§ 1395j et seq.], a covered part D drug (as defined in section 1860D-2(e) [42 USCS § 1395w-102(e)]) for which payment is made under an MA-PD plan under part C of such title [42 USCS §§ 1395w-21 et seq.], or a prescription drug plan under part D of such title [42 USCS §§ 1395w-101 et seq.], and any records necessary for evaluation of the economy, efficiency, and effectiveness of the programs under titles XVIII and XIX [42 USCS §§ 1395 et seq. and 1396 et seq.].

(c) Administrative remedy for knowing participation by beneficiary in health care fraud scheme. (1) In general. In addition to any other applicable remedies, if an applicable individual has knowingly participated in a Federal health care fraud offense or a conspiracy to commit a Federal health care fraud offense, the Secretary shall impose an appropriate administrative penalty commensurate with the offense or conspiracy.

(2) Applicable individual. For purposes of paragraph (1), the term "applicable individual" means an individual—

(A) entitled to, or enrolled for, benefits under part A of title XVIII [42 USCS §§ 1395c et seq.] or enrolled under part B of such title [42 USCS §§ 1395j et seq.];

(B) eligible for medical assistance under a State plan under title XIX [42 USCS §§ 1396 et seq.] or under a waiver of such plan; or

(C) eligible for child health assistance under a child health plan under title XXI [42 USCS §§ 1397aa et seq.].

(d) Reporting and returning of overpayments. (1) In general. If a person has received an overpayment, the person shall—

(A) report and return the overpayment to the Secretary, the State, an intermediary, a carrier, or a contractor, as appropriate, at the correct address; and

(B) notify the Secretary, State, intermediary, carrier, or contractor to whom the overpayment was returned in writing of the reason for the overpayment.

(2) Deadline for reporting and returning overpayments. An overpayment must be reported and returned under paragraph (1) by the later of—

(A) the date which is 60 days after the date on which the overpayment was identified; or

(B) the date any corresponding cost report is due, if applicable.

(3) Enforcement. Any overpayment retained by a person after the deadline for reporting and returning the overpayment under paragraph (2) is an obligation (as defined in section 3729(b)(3) of title 31, United States Code) for purposes of section 3729 of such title [31 USCS § 3729].

(4) Definitions. In this subsection:

(A) Knowing and knowingly. The terms "knowing" and "knowingly" have the meaning given those terms in section 3729(b) of title 31, United States Code.

(B) Overpayment. The term "overpayment" means any funds that a person receives or retains under title XVIII or XIX [42 USCS §§ 1395 et seq. or 1396 et seq.] to which the person, after applicable reconciliation, is not entitled under such title.

(C) Person. (i) In general. The term "person" means a provider of services, supplier, Medicaid managed care organization (as defined in section 1903(m)(1)(A) [42 USCS § 1396b(m)(1)(A)]), Medicare Advantage organization (as defined in section 1859(a)(1) [42 USCS § 1395w-28(a)(1)]), or PDP sponsor (as defined in section 1860D-41(a)(13) [42 USCS § 1395w-151(a)(13)]).

(ii) Exclusion. Such term does not include a beneficiary.

(e) Inclusion of national provider identifier on all applications and claims. The Secretary shall promulgate a regulation that requires, not later than January 1, 2011, all providers of medical or other items or services and suppliers under the programs under titles XVIII and XIX [42 USCS §§ 1395 et seq. and 1396 et seq.] that qualify for a national provider identifier to include their national provider identifier on all applications to enroll in such programs and on all claims for payment submitted under such programs.

(Aug. 14, 1935, ch 531, Title XI, Part A, § 1128J, as added March 23, 2010, P. L. 111-148, Title VI, Subtitle E, § 6402(a), 124 Stat. 753.)

§ 1320a-7l. Nationwide program for national and State background checks on direct patient access employees of long-term care facilities and providers

(a) In general. The Secretary of Health and Human Services (in this section referred to as the "Secretary"), shall establish a program to identify efficient, effective, and economical procedures for long term care facilities or providers to conduct background checks on prospective direct patient access employees on a nationwide basis (in this subsection, such program shall be referred to as the "nationwide program"). Except for the following modifications, the Secretary shall carry out the nationwide program under similar terms and conditions as the pilot program under section 307 of the Medicare Prescription Drug, Improvement, and Modernization Act of 2003 [note to this section] (Public Law 108-173; 117 Stat. 2257), including the prohibition on hiring abusive workers and the authorization of the imposition of penalties by a participating State under subsection (b)(3)(A) and (b)(6), respectively, of such section 307 [note to this section]:

(1) Agreements. (A) Newly participating States. The Secretary shall enter into agreements with each State—

(i) that the Secretary has not entered into an agreement with under subsection (c)(1) of such section 307 [note to this section];

(ii) that agrees to conduct background checks under the nationwide program on a Statewide basis; and

(iii) that submits an application to the Secretary containing such information and at such time as the Secretary may specify.

(B) Certain previously participating states. The Secretary shall enter into agreements with each State—

(i) that the Secretary has entered into an agreement with under such subsection (c)(1), but only in the case where such agreement did not require the State to conduct background checks under the program established under subsection (a) of such section 307 [note to this section] on a Statewide basis;

(ii) that agrees to conduct background checks under the nationwide program on a Statewide basis; and

(iii) that submits an application to the Secretary containing such information and at such time as the Secretary may specify.

(2) Nonapplication of selection criteria. The selection criteria required under subsection (c)(3)(B) of such section 307 [note to this section] shall not apply.

(3) Required fingerprint check as part of criminal history background check. The procedures established under subsection (b)(1) of such section 307 [note to this section] shall—

(A) require that the long-term care facility or provider (or the designated agent of the long-term care facility or provider) obtain State and national criminal history background checks on the prospective employee through such means as the Secretary determines appropriate, efficient, and effective that utilize a search of State-based abuse and neglect registries and databases, including the abuse and neglect registries of another State in the case where a prospective employee previously resided in that State, State criminal history records, the records of any proceedings in the State that may contain disqualifying information about prospective employees (such as proceedings conducted by State professional licensing and disciplinary boards and State Medicaid Fraud Control Units), and Federal criminal history records, including a fingerprint check using the Integrated Automated Fingerprint Identification System of the Federal Bureau of Investigation;

(B) require States to describe and test methods that reduce duplicative fingerprinting, including providing for the development of "rap back" capability by the State such that, if a direct patient access employee of a long-term care facility or provider is convicted of a crime following the initial criminal history background check conducted with respect to such employee, and the employee's fingerprints match the prints on file with the State law enforcement department, the department will immediately inform the State and the State will immediately inform the long-term care facility or provider which employs the direct patient access employee of such conviction; and

(C) require that criminal history background checks conducted under the nationwide program remain valid for a period of time specified by the Secretary.

(4) State requirements. An agreement entered into under paragraph (1) shall require that a participating State—

(A) be responsible for monitoring compliance with the requirements of the nationwide program;

(B) have procedures in place to—

(i) conduct screening and criminal history background checks under the nationwide program in accordance with the requirements of this section;

(ii) monitor compliance by long-term care facilities and providers with the procedures and requirements of the nationwide program;

(iii) as appropriate, provide for a provisional period of employment by a long-term care facility or provider of a direct patient access employee, not to exceed 60 days, pending completion of the required criminal history background check and, in the case where the employee has appealed the results of such background check, pending completion of the appeals process, during which the employee shall be subject to direct on-site supervision (in accordance with procedures established by the State to ensure that a long-term care facility or provider furnishes such direct on-site supervision);

(iv) provide an independent process by which a provisional employee or an employee may appeal or dispute the accuracy of the information obtained in a background check performed under the nationwide program, including the specification of criteria for appeals for direct patient access employees found to have disqualifying information which shall include consideration of the passage of time, extenuating circumstances, demonstration of rehabilitation, and relevancy of the particular disqualifying information with respect to the current employment of the individual;

(v) provide for the designation of a single State agency as responsible for—

(I) overseeing the coordination of any State and national criminal history background checks requested by a long-term care facility or provider (or the designated agent of the long-term care facility or provider) utilizing a search of State and Federal criminal history records, including a fingerprint check of such records;

(II) overseeing the design of appropriate privacy and security safeguards for use in the review of the results of any State or national criminal history background checks conducted regarding a prospective direct patient access employee to determine whether the employee has any conviction for a relevant crime;

(III) immediately reporting to the long-term care facility or provider that requested the criminal history background check the results of such review; and

(IV) in the case of an employee with a conviction for a relevant crime that is subject to reporting under section 1128E of the Social Security Act (42 U.S.C. 1320a-7e), reporting the existence of such conviction to the database established under that section;

(vi) determine which individuals are direct patient access employees (as defined in paragraph (6)(B)) for purposes of the nationwide program;

(vii) as appropriate, specify offenses, including convictions for violent crimes, for purposes of the nationwide program; and

(viii) describe and test methods that reduce duplicative fingerprinting, including providing for the development of "rap back" capability such that, if a direct patient access employee of a long-term care facility or provider is convicted of a crime following the initial criminal history background check conducted with respect to such employee, and the employee's fingerprints match the prints on file with the State law enforcement department—

(I) the department will immediately inform the State agency designated under clause (v) and such agency will immediately inform the facility or provider which employs the direct patient access employee of such conviction; and

(II) the State will provide, or will require the facility to provide, to the employee a copy of the results of the criminal history background check conducted with respect to the employee at no charge in the case where the individual requests such a copy.

(5) Payments. (A) Newly participating States. (i) In general. As part of the application submitted by a State under paragraph (1)(A)(iii), the State shall guarantee, with respect to the costs to be incurred by the State in carrying out the nationwide program, that the State will make available (directly or through donations from public or private entities) a particular amount of non-Federal contributions, as a condition of receiving the Federal match under clause (ii).

(ii) Federal match. The payment amount to each State that the Secretary enters into an agreement with under paragraph (1)(A) shall be 3 times the amount that the State guarantees to make available under clause (i), except that in no case may the payment amount exceed $3,000,000.

(B) Previously participating States. (i) In general. As part of the application submitted by a State under paragraph (1)(B)(iii), the State shall guarantee, with respect to the costs to be incurred by the State in carrying out the nationwide program, that the State will make available (directly or through donations from public or private entities) a particular amount of non-Federal contributions, as a condition of receiving the Federal match under clause (ii).

(ii) Federal match. The payment amount to each State that the Secretary enters into an agreement with under paragraph (1)(B) shall be 3 times the amount that the State guarantees to make available under clause (i), except that in no case may the payment amount exceed $1,500,000.

(6) Definitions. Under the nationwide program:

(A) Conviction for a relevant crime. The term "conviction for a relevant crime" means any Federal or State criminal conviction for—

(i) any offense described in section 1128(a) of the Social Security Act (42 U.S.C. 1320a-7); or

(ii) such other types of offenses as a participating State may specify for purposes of conducting the program in such State.

(B) Disqualifying information. The term "disqualifying information" means a conviction for a relevant crime or a finding of patient or resident abuse.

(C) Finding of patient or resident abuse. The term "finding of patient or resident abuse" means any substantiated finding by a State agency under section 1819(g)(1)(C) or 1919(g)(1)(C) of the Social Security Act (42 U.S.C. 1395i-3(g)(1)(C), 1396r(g)(1)(C)) or a Federal agency that a direct patient access employee has committed—

(i) an act of patient or resident abuse or neglect or a misappropriation of patient or resident property; or

(ii) such other types of acts as a participating State may specify for purposes of conducting the program in such State.

(D) Direct patient access employee. The term "direct patient access employee" means any individual who has access to a patient or resident of a long-term care facility or provider through employment or through a contract with such facility or provider and has duties that involve (or may involve) one-on-one contact with a patient or resident of the facility or provider, as determined by the State for purposes of the nationwide program. Such term does not include a volunteer unless the volunteer has duties that are equivalent to the duties of a direct patient access employee and those duties involve (or may involve) one-on-one contact with a patient or resident of the long-term care facility or provider.

(E) Long-term care facility or provider. The term "long-term care facility or provider" means the following facilities or providers which receive payment for services under title XVIII or XIX of the Social Security Act [42 USCS §§ 1395 et seq. or 1396 et seq.]:

(i) A skilled nursing facility (as defined in section 1819(a) of the Social Security Act (42 U.S.C. 1395i-3(a))).

(ii) A nursing facility (as defined in section 1919(a) of such Act (42 U.S.C. 1396r(a))).

(iii) A home health agency.

(iv) A provider of hospice care (as defined in section 1861(dd)(1) of such Act (42 U.S.C. 1395x(dd)(1))).

(v) A long-term care hospital (as described in section 1886(d)(1)(B)(iv) of such Act (42 U.S.C. 1395ww(d)(1)(B)(iv))).

(vi) A provider of personal care services.

(vii) A provider of adult day care.

(viii) A residential care provider that arranges for, or directly provides, long-term care services, including an assisted living facility that provides a level of care established by the Secretary.

(ix) An intermediate care facility for the mentally retarded (as defined in section 1905(d) of such Act (42 U.S.C. 1396d(d))).

(x) Any other facility or provider of long-term care services under such titles as the participating State determines appropriate.

(7) Evaluation and report. (A) Evaluation. (i) In general. The Inspector General of the Department of Health and Human Services shall conduct an evaluation of the nationwide program.

(ii) Inclusion of specific topics. The evaluation conducted under clause (i) shall include the following:

(I) A review of the various procedures implemented by participating States for long-term care facilities or providers, including staffing agencies, to conduct background checks of direct patient access employees under the nationwide program and identification of the most appropriate, efficient, and effective procedures for conducting such background checks.

(II) An assessment of the costs of conducting such background checks (including start up and administrative costs).

(III) A determination of the extent to which conducting such background checks leads to any unintended consequences, including a reduction in the available workforce for long-term care facilities or providers.

(IV) An assessment of the impact of the nationwide program on reducing the number of incidents of neglect, abuse, and misappropriation of resident property to the extent practicable.

(V) An evaluation of other aspects of the nationwide program, as determined appropriate by the Secretary.

(B) Report. Not later than 180 days after the completion of the nationwide program, the Inspector General of the Department of Health and Human Services shall submit a report to Congress containing the results of the evaluation conducted under subparagraph (A).

(b) Funding. (1) Notification. The Secretary of Health and Human Services shall notify the Secretary of the Treasury of the amount necessary to carry out the nationwide program under this section for the period of fiscal years 2010 through 2012, except that in no case shall such amount exceed $160,000,000.

(2) Transfer of funds. (A) In general. Out of any funds in the Treasury not otherwise appropriated, the Secretary of the Treasury shall provide for the transfer to the Secretary of Health and Human Services of the amount specified as necessary to carry out the nationwide program under paragraph (1). Such amount shall remain available until expended.

(B) Reservation of funds for conduct of evaluation. The Secretary may reserve not more than $3,000,000 of the amount transferred under subparagraph (A) to provide for the conduct of the evaluation under subsection (a)(7)(A).

(March 23, 2010, P. L. 111-148, Title VI, Subtitle C, § 6201, 124 Stat. 721.)

HISTORY; ANCILLARY LAWS AND DIRECTIVES

Other provisions:

Pilot program for national and State background checks on direct patient access employees of long-term care facilities or providers. Act Dec. 8, 2003, P. L. 108-173, Title III, § 307, 117 Stat. 2257, provides:

"(a) Authority to conduct program. The Secretary, in consultation with the Attorney General, shall establish a pilot program to identify efficient, effective, and economical procedures for long term care facilities or providers to conduct background checks on prospective direct patient access employees.

"(b) Requirements. (1) In general. Under the pilot program, a long-term care facility or provider in a participating State, prior to employing a direct patient access employee that is first hired on or after the commencement date of the pilot program in the State, shall conduct a background check on the employee in accordance with such procedures as the participating State shall establish.

"(2) Procedures. (A) In general. The procedures established by a participating State under paragraph (1) should be designed to—

"(i) give a prospective direct access patient employee notice that the long-term care facility or provider is required to perform background checks with respect to new employees;

"(ii) require, as a condition of employment, that the employee—

"(I) provide a written statement disclosing any disqualifying information;

"(II) provide a statement signed by the employee authorizing the facility to request national and State criminal history background checks;

"(III) provide the facility with a rolled set of the employee's fingerprints; and

"(IV) provide any other identification information the participating State may require;

"(iii) require the facility or provider to check any available registries that would be likely to contain disqualifying information about a prospective employee of a long-term care facility or provider; and

"(iv) permit the facility or provider to obtain State and national criminal history background checks on the prospective employee through a 10-fingerprint check that utilizes State criminal records and the Integrated Automated Fingerprint Identification System of the Federal Bureau of Investigation.

"(B) Elimination of unnecessary checks. The procedures established by a participating State under paragraph (1) shall permit a long-term care facility or provider to terminate the background check at any stage at which the facility or provider obtains disqualifying information regarding a prospective direct patient access employee.

"(3) Prohibition on hiring of abusive workers. (A) In general. A long-term care facility or provider may not knowingly employ any direct patient access employee who has any disqualifying information.

"(B) Provisional employment. (i) In general. Under the pilot program, a participating State may permit a long-term care facility or provider to provide for a provisional period of employment for a direct patient access employee pending completion of a background check, subject to such supervision during the employee's provisional period of employment as the participating State determines appropriate.

"(ii) Special consideration for certain facilities and providers. In determining what constitutes appropriate supervision of a provisional employee, a participating State shall take into account cost or other burdens that would be imposed on small rural long-term care facilities or providers, as well as the nature of care delivered by such facilities or providers that are home health agencies or providers of hospice care.

"(4) Use of information; immunity from liability. (A) Use of information. A participating State shall ensure that a long-term care facility or provider that obtains information about a direct patient access employee pursuant to a background check uses such information only for the purpose of determining the suitability of the employee for employment.

"(B) Immunity from liability. A participating State shall ensure that a long-term care facility or provider that, in denying employment for an individual selected for hire as a direct patient access employee (including during any period of provisional employment), reasonably relies upon information obtained through a background check of the individual, shall not be liable in any action brought by the individual based on the employment determination resulting from the information.

"(5) Agreements with employment agencies. A participating State may establish procedures for facilitating the conduct of background checks on prospective direct patient access employees that are hired by a long-term care facility or provider through an employment agency (including a temporary employment agency).

"(6) Penalties. A participating State may impose such penalties as the State determines appropriate to enforce the requirements of the pilot program conducted in that State.

"(c) Participating States. (1) In general. The Secretary shall enter into agreements with not more than 10 States to conduct the pilot program under this section in such States.

"(2) Requirements for States. An agreement entered into under paragraph (1) shall require that a participating State—

"(A) be responsible for monitoring compliance with the requirements of the pilot program;

"(B) have procedures by which a provisional employee or an employee may appeal or dispute the accuracy of the information obtained in a background check performed under the pilot program; and

"(C) agree to—

"(i) review the results of any State or national criminal history background checks conducted regarding a prospective direct patient access employee to determine whether the employee has any conviction for a relevant crime;

"(ii) immediately report to the entity that requested the criminal history background checks the results of such review; and

"(iii) in the case of an employee with a conviction for a relevant crime that is subject to reporting under section 1128E of the Social Security Act (42 U.S.C. 1320a-7e), report the existence of such conviction to the database established under that section.

"(3) Application and selection criteria. (A) Application. A State seeking to participate in the pilot program established under this section, shall submit an application to the Secretary containing such information and at such time as the Secretary may specify.

"(B) Selection criteria. (i) In general. In selecting States to participate in the pilot program, the Secretary shall establish criteria to ensure—

"(I) geographic diversity;

"(II) the inclusion of a variety of long-term care facilities or providers;

"(III) the evaluation of a variety of payment mechanisms for covering the costs of conducting the background checks required under the pilot program; and

"(IV) the evaluation of a variety of penalties (monetary and otherwise) used by participating States to enforce the requirements of the pilot program in such States.

"(ii) Additional criteria. The Secretary shall, to the greatest extent practicable, select States to participate in the pilot program in accordance with the following:

"(I) At least one participating State should permit long-term care facilities or providers to provide for a provisional period of employment pending completion of a background check and at least one such State should not permit such a period of employment.

"(II) At least one participating State should establish procedures under which employment agencies (including temporary employment agencies) may contact the State directly to conduct background checks on prospective direct patient access employees.

"(III) At least one participating State should include patient abuse prevention training (including behavior training and interventions) for managers and employees of long-term care facilities and providers as part of the pilot program conducted in that State.

"(iii) Inclusion of States with existing programs. Nothing in this section shall be construed as prohibiting any State which, as of the date of the enactment of this Act, has procedures for conducting background checks on behalf of any entity described in subsection (g)(5) from being selected to participate in the pilot program conducted under this section.

"(d) Payments. Of the amounts made available under subsection (f) to conduct the pilot program under this section, the Secretary shall—

"(1) make payments to participating States for the costs of conducting the pilot program in such States; and

"(2) reserve up to 4 percent of such amounts to conduct the evaluation required under subsection (e).

"(e) Evaluation. The Secretary, in consultation with the Attorney General, shall conduct by grant, contract, or interagency agreement an evaluation of the pilot program conducted under this section. Such evaluation shall—

"(1) review the various procedures implemented by participating States for long-term care facilities or providers to conduct background checks of direct patient access employees and identify the most efficient, effective, and economical procedures for conducting such background checks;

"(2) assess the costs of conducting such background checks (including start-up and administrative costs);

"(3) consider the benefits and problems associated with requiring employees or facilities or providers to pay the costs of conducting such background checks;

"(4) consider whether the costs of conducting such

background checks should be allocated between the medicare and medicaid programs and if so, identify an equitable methodology for doing so;
"(5) determine the extent to which conducting such background checks leads to any unintended consequences, including a reduction in the available workforce for such facilities or providers;
"(6) review forms used by participating States in order to develop, in consultation with the Attorney General, a model form for such background checks;
"(7) determine the effectiveness of background checks conducted by employment agencies; and
"(8) recommend appropriate procedures and payment mechanisms for implementing a national criminal background check program for such facilities and providers.

"(f) Funding. Out of any funds in the Treasury not otherwise appropriated, there are appropriated to the Secretary to carry out the pilot program under this section for the period of fiscal years 2004 through 2007, $25,000,000.

"(g) Definitions. In this section:
"(1) Conviction for a relevant crime. The term 'conviction for a relevant crime' means any Federal or State criminal conviction for—

"(A) any offense described in section 1128(a) of the Social Security Act (42 U.S.C. 1320a-7); and

"(B) such other types of offenses as a participating State may specify for purposes of conducting the pilot program in such State.
"(2) Disqualifying information. The term 'disqualifying information' means a conviction for a relevant crime or a finding of patient or resident abuse.
"(3) Finding of patient or resident abuse. The term 'finding of patient or resident abuse' means any substantiated finding by a State agency under section 1819(g)(1)(C) or 1919(g)(1)(C) of the Social Security Act (42 U.S.C. 1395i-3(g)(1)(C), 1396r(g)(1)(C)) or a Federal agency that a direct patient access employee has committed—

"(A) an act of patient or resident abuse or neglect or a misappropriation of patient or resident property; or

"(B) such other types of acts as a participating State may specify for purposes of conducting the pilot program in such State.
"(4) Direct patient access employee. The term 'direct patient access employee' means any individual (other than a volunteer) that has access to a patient or resident of a long-term care facility or provider through employment or through a contract with such facility or provider, as determined by a participating State for purposes of conducting the pilot program in such State.
"(5) Long-term care facility or provider. (A) In general. The term 'long-term care facility or provider' means the following facilities or providers which receive payment for services under title XVIII or XIX of the Social Security Act [42 USCS §§ 1395 et seq. or 1396 et seq.]:

"(i) A skilled nursing facility (as defined in section 1819(a) of the Social Security Act) (42 U.S.C. 1395i-3(a)).

"(ii) A nursing facility (as defined in section 1919(a) in such Act) (42 U.S.C. 1396r(a)).

"(iii) A home health agency.

"(iv) A provider of hospice care (as defined in section 1861(dd)(1) of such Act) (42 U.S.C. 1395x(dd)(1)).

"(v) A long-term care hospital (as described in section 1886(d)(1)(B)(iv) of such Act) (42 U.S.C. 1395ww(d)(1)(B)(iv)).

"(vi) A provider of personal care services.

"(vii) A residential care provider that arranges for, or directly provides, long-term care services.

"(viii) An intermediate care facility for the mentally retarded (as defined in section 1905(d) of such Act) 42 U.S.C. 1396d(d)).

"(B) Additional facilities or providers. During the first year in which a pilot program under this section is conducted in a participating State, the State may expand the list of facilities or providers under subparagraph (A) (on a phased-in basis or otherwise) to include such other facilities or providers of long-term care services under such titles as the participating State determines appropriate. "(C) Exceptions. Such term does not include—

"(i) any facility or entity that provides, or is a provider of, services described in subparagraph (A) that are exclusively provided to an individual pursuant to a self-directed arrangement that meets such requirements as the participating State may establish in accordance with guidance from the Secretary; or

"(ii) any such arrangement that is obtained by a patient or resident functioning as an employer.
"(6) Participating State. The term 'participating State' means a State with an agreement under subsection (c)(1).".

§ 1320b-9. Improved access to, and delivery of, health care for Indians under titles XIX and XXI

(a) Agreements with States for Medicaid and CHIP outreach on or near reservations to increase the enrollment of Indians in those programs. (1) In general. In order to improve the access of Indians residing on or near a reservation to obtain benefits under the Medicaid and State children's health insurance programs established under titles XIX and XXI [42 USCS §§ 1396 et seq. and 1397aa et seq.], the Secretary shall encourage the State to take steps to provide for enrollment on or near the reservation. Such steps may include outreach efforts such as the outstationing of eligibility workers, entering into agreements with the Indian Health Service, Indian Tribes, Tribal Organizations, and Urban Indian Organizations to provide outreach, education regarding eligibility and benefits, enrollment, and translation services when such services are appropriate.

(2) Construction. Nothing in paragraph (1) shall be construed as affecting arrangements entered into between States and the Indian Health Service, Indian Tribes, Tribal Organizations, or Urban Indian Organizations for such Service, Tribes, or Organizations to conduct administrative activities under such titles.

(b) Requirement to facilitate cooperation. The Secretary, acting through the Centers for Medicare & Medicaid Services, shall take such steps as are necessary to facilitate cooperation with, and agreements between,

States and the Indian Health Service, Indian Tribes, Tribal Organizations, or Urban Indian Organizations with respect to the provision of health care items and services to Indians under the programs established under title XIX or XXI [42 USCS §§ 1396 et seq. or 1397aa et seq.].

(c) Definition of Indian; Indian Tribe; Indian Health Program; Tribal Organization; Urban Indian Organization. For purposes of this section, title XIX [42 USCS §§ 1396 et seq.], and title XXI [42 USCS §§ 1397aa et seq.], the terms "Indian", "Indian Tribe", "Indian Health Program", "Tribal Organization", and "Urban Indian Organization" have the meanings given those terms in section 4 of the Indian Health Care Improvement Act [25 USCS § 1603].

(Aug. 14, 1935, ch 531, Title XI, Part A, § 1139, as added Dec. 22, 1987, P. L. 100-203, Title IX, Subtitle B, Part 2, § 9136, 101 Stat. 1330-316; Nov. 10, 1988, P. L. 100-647, Title VIII, Subtitle C, § 8201, 102 Stat. 3798; June 30, 1989, P. L. 101-45, Title IV, § 409, 103 Stat. 130; Dec. 19, 1989, P. L. 101-239, Title VI, Subtitle A, Part 3, Subpart B, § 6221, 103 Stat. 2255; Nov. 5, 1990, P. L. 101-508, Title IV, Subtitle A, Part 3, § 4207(k)(6), Title V, Subtitle A, Ch 4, § 5057, 104 Stat. 1388-125, 1388-230; Oct. 31, 1994, P. L. 103-432, Title I, Subtitle C, § 160(d)(4), Title II, Subtitle F, § 264(d), 108 Stat. 4444, 4468; Feb. 4, 2009, P. L. 111-3, Title II, Subtitle A, § 202(a), 123 Stat. 39; March 23, 2010, P. L. 111-148, Title II, Subtitle K, § 2901(d), 124 Stat. 333.)

§ 1320b-9a. Child health quality measures

(a) Development of an initial core set of health care quality measures for children enrolled in Medicaid or CHIP. (1) In general. Not later than January 1, 2010, the Secretary shall identify and publish for general comment an initial, recommended core set of child health quality measures for use by State programs administered under titles XIX and XXI [42 USCS §§ 1396 et seq. and 1397aa et seq.], health insurance issuers and managed care entities that enter into contracts with such programs, and providers of items and services under such programs.

(2) Identification of initial core measures. In consultation with the individuals and entities described in subsection (b)(3), the Secretary shall identify existing quality of care measures for children that are in use under public and privately sponsored health care coverage arrangements, or that are part of reporting systems that measure both the presence and duration of health insurance coverage over time.

(3) Recommendations and dissemination. Based on such existing and identified measures, the Secretary shall publish an initial core set of child health quality measures that includes (but is not limited to) the following:

(A) The duration of children's health insurance coverage over a 12-month time period.

(B) The availability and effectiveness of a full range of—

(i) preventive services, treatments, and services for acute conditions, including services to promote healthy birth, prevent and treat premature birth, and detect the presence or risk of physical or mental conditions that could adversely affect growth and development; and

(ii) treatments to correct or ameliorate the effects of physical and mental conditions, including chronic conditions and, with respect to dental care, conditions requiring the restoration of teeth, relief of pain and infection, and maintenance of dental health, in infants, young children, school-age children, and adolescents.

(C) The availability of care in a range of ambulatory and inpatient health care settings in which such care is furnished.

(D) The types of measures that, taken together, can be used to estimate the overall national quality of health care for children, including children with special needs, and to perform comparative analyses of pediatric health care quality and racial, ethnic, and socioeconomic disparities in child health and health care for children.

(4) Encourage voluntary and standardized reporting. Not later than 2 years after the date of enactment of the Children's Health Insurance Program Reauthorization Act of 2009 [enacted Feb. 4, 2009], the Secretary, in consultation with States, shall develop a standardized format for reporting information and procedures and approaches that encourage States to use the initial core measurement set to voluntarily report information regarding the quality of pediatric health care under titles XIX and XXI [42 USCS §§ 1396 et seq. and 1397aa et seq.].

(5) Adoption of best practices in implementing quality programs. The Secretary shall disseminate information to States regarding best practices among States with respect to measuring and reporting on the quality of health care for children, and shall facilitate the adoption of such best practices. In developing best practices approaches, the Secretary shall give particular attention to State measurement techniques that ensure the timeliness and accuracy

of provider reporting, encourage provider reporting compliance, encourage successful quality improvement strategies, and improve efficiency in data collection using health information technology.

(6) Reports to Congress. Not later than January 1, 2011, and every 3 years thereafter, the Secretary shall report to Congress on—

(A) the status of the Secretary's efforts to improve—

(i) quality related to the duration and stability of health insurance coverage for children under titles XIX and XXI [42 USCS §§ 1396 et seq. and 1397aa et seq.];

(ii) the quality of children's health care under such titles, including preventive health services, dental care, health care for acute conditions, chronic health care, and health services to ameliorate the effects of physical and mental conditions and to aid in growth and development of infants, young children, school-age children, and adolescents with special health care needs; and

(iii) the quality of children's health care under such titles across the domains of quality, including clinical quality, health care safety, family experience with health care, health care in the most integrated setting, and elimination of racial, ethnic, and socioeconomic disparities in health and health care;

(B) the status of voluntary reporting by States under titles XIX and XXI [42 USCS §§ 1396 et seq. and 1397aa et seq.], utilizing the initial core quality measurement set; and

(C) any recommendations for legislative changes needed to improve the quality of care provided to children under titles XIX and XXI [42 USCS §§ 1396 et seq. and 1397aa et seq.], including recommendations for quality reporting by States.

(7) Technical assistance. The Secretary shall provide technical assistance to States to assist them in adopting and utilizing core child health quality measures in administering the State plans under titles XIX and XXI [42 USCS §§ 1396 et seq. and 1397aa et seq.].

(8) Definition of core set. In this section, the term "core set" means a group of valid, reliable, and evidence-based quality measures that, taken together—

(A) provide information regarding the quality of health coverage and health care for children;

(B) address the needs of children throughout the developmental age span; and

(C) allow purchasers, families, and health care providers to understand the quality of care in relation to the preventive needs of children, treatments aimed at managing and resolving acute conditions, and diagnostic and treatment services whose purpose is to correct or ameliorate physical, mental, or developmental conditions that could, if untreated or poorly treated, become chronic.

(b) Advancing and improving pediatric quality measures. (1) Establishment of pediatric quality measures program. Not later than January 1, 2011, the Secretary shall establish a pediatric quality measures program to—

(A) improve and strengthen the initial core child health care quality measures established by the Secretary under subsection (a);

(B) expand on existing pediatric quality measures used by public and private health care purchasers and advance the development of such new and emerging quality measures; and

(C) increase the portfolio of evidence-based, consensus pediatric quality measures available to public and private purchasers of children's health care services, providers, and consumers.

(2) Evidence-based measures. The measures developed under the pediatric quality measures program shall, at a minimum, be—

(A) evidence-based and, where appropriate, risk adjusted;

(B) designed to identify and eliminate racial and ethnic disparities in child health and the provision of health care;

(C) designed to ensure that the data required for such measures is collected and reported in a standard format that permits comparison of quality and data at a State, plan, and provider level;

(D) periodically updated; and

(E) responsive to the child health needs, services, and domains of health care quality described in clauses (i), (ii), and (iii) of subsection (a)(6)(A).

(3) Process for pediatric quality measures program. In identifying gaps in existing pediatric quality measures and establishing priorities for development and advancement of such measures, the Secretary shall consult with—

(A) States;

(B) pediatricians, children's hospitals, and other primary and specialized pediatric health care professionals (including members of the allied health professions) who specialize in the care and treatment of children, particularly children with special physical, mental, and developmental health care needs;

(C) dental professionals, including pediatric dental professionals;

(D) health care providers that furnish primary health care to children and families who live in urban and rural medically underserved communities or who are members of distinct population sub-groups at heightened risk for poor health outcomes;

(E) national organizations representing children, including children with disabilities and children with chronic conditions;

(F) national organizations representing consumers and purchasers of children's health care;

(G) national organizations and individuals with expertise in pediatric health quality measurement; and

(H) voluntary consensus standards setting organizations and other organizations involved in the advancement of evidence-based measures of health care.

(4) Developing, validating, and testing a portfolio of pediatric quality measures. As part of the program to advance pediatric quality measures, the Secretary shall—

(A) award grants and contracts for the development, testing, and validation of new, emerging, and innovative evidence-based measures for children's health care services across the domains of quality described in clauses (i), (ii), and (iii) of subsection (a)(6)(A); and

(B) award grants and contracts for—

(i) the development of consensus on evidence-based measures for children's health care services;

(ii) the dissemination of such measures to public and private purchasers of health care for children; and

(iii) the updating of such measures as necessary.

(5) Revising, strengthening, and improving initial core measures. Beginning no later than January 1, 2013, and annually thereafter, the Secretary shall publish recommended changes to the core measures described in subsection (a) that shall reflect the testing, validation, and consensus process for the development of pediatric quality measures described in subsection paragraphs (1) through (4).

(6) Definition of pediatric quality measure. In this subsection, the term "pediatric quality measure" means a measurement of clinical care that is capable of being examined through the collection and analysis of relevant information, that is developed in order to assess 1 or more aspects of pediatric health care quality in various institutional and ambulatory health care settings, including the structure of the clinical care system, the process of care, the outcome of care, or patient experiences in care.

(7) Construction. Nothing in this section shall be construed as supporting the restriction of coverage, under title XIX or XXI [42 USCS §§ 1396 et seq. and 1397aa et seq.] or otherwise, to only those services that are evidence-based.

(c) Annual State reports regarding State-specific quality of care measures applied under Medicaid or CHIP. (1) Annual State reports. Each State with a State plan approved under title XIX [42 USCS §§ 1396 et seq.] or a State child health plan approved under title XXI [42 USCS §§ 1397aa et seq.] shall annually report to the Secretary on the—

(A) State-specific child health quality measures applied by the States under such plans, including measures described in subparagraphs (A) and (B) of subsection (a)(6); and

(B) State-specific information on the quality of health care furnished to children under such plans, including information collected through external quality reviews of managed care organizations under section 1932 of the Social Security Act (42 U.S.C. 1396u-4) and benchmark plans under sections 1937 and 2103 of such Act (42 U.S.C. 1396u-7, 1397cc).

(2) Publication. Not later than September 30, 2010, and annually thereafter, the Secretary shall collect, analyze, and make publicly available the information reported by States under paragraph (1).

(d) Demonstration projects for improving the quality of children's health care and the use of health information technology. (1) In general. During the period of fiscal years 2009 through 2013, the Secretary shall award not more than 10 grants to States and child health providers to conduct demonstration projects to evaluate promising ideas for improving the quality of children's health care provided under title XIX or XXI [42 USCS §§ 1396 et seq. and 1397aa et seq.], including projects to—

(A) experiment with, and evaluate the use of, new measures of the quality of children's health care under such titles (including testing the validity and suitability for reporting of such measures);

(B) promote the use of health information technology in care delivery for children under such titles;

(C) evaluate provider-based models which improve the delivery of children's health care services under such titles, including care management for children with chronic conditions and the use of evidence-based approaches to improve the effectiveness, safety, and efficiency of health care services for children; or

(D) demonstrate the impact of the model electronic health record format for children developed and disseminated under subsection (f) on improving pediatric health, including the effects of chronic childhood health conditions, and pediatric health care quality as well as reducing health care costs.

(2) Requirements. In awarding grants under this subsection, the Secretary shall ensure that—

(A) only 1 demonstration project funded under a grant awarded under this subsection shall be conducted in a State; and

(B) demonstration projects funded under grants awarded under this subsection shall be conducted evenly between States with large urban areas and States with large rural areas.

(3) Authority for multistate projects. A demonstration project conducted with a grant awarded under this subsection may be conducted on a multistate basis, as needed.

(4) Funding. $20,000,000 of the amount appropriated under subsection (i) for a fiscal year shall be used to carry out this subsection.

(e) Childhood obesity demonstration project. (1) Authority to conduct demonstration. The Secretary, in consultation with the Administrator of the Centers for Medicare & Medicaid Services, shall conduct a demonstration project to develop a comprehensive and systematic model for reducing childhood obesity by awarding grants to eligible entities to carry out such project. Such model shall—

(A) identify, through self-assessment, behavioral risk factors for obesity among children;

(B) identify, through self-assessment, needed clinical preventive and screening benefits among those children identified as target individuals on the basis of such risk factors;

(C) provide ongoing support to such target individuals and their families to reduce risk factors and promote the appropriate use of preventive and screening benefits; and

(D) be designed to improve health outcomes, satisfaction, quality of life, and appropriate use of items and services for which medical assistance is available under title XIX [42 USCS §§ 1396 et seq.] or child health assistance is available under title XXI [42 USCS §§ 1397aa et seq.] among such target individuals.

(2) Eligibility entities. For purposes of this subsection, an eligible entity is any of the following:

(A) A city, county, or Indian tribe.

(B) A local or tribal educational agency.

(C) An accredited university, college, or community college.

(D) A Federally-qualified health center.

(E) A local health department.

(F) A health care provider.

(G) A community-based organization.

(H) Any other entity determined appropriate by the Secretary, including a consortia or partnership of entities described in any of subparagraphs (A) through (G).

(3) Use of funds. An eligible entity awarded a grant under this subsection shall use the funds made available under the grant to—

(A) carry out community-based activities related to reducing childhood obesity, including by—

(i) forming partnerships with entities, including schools and other facilities providing recreational services, to establish programs for after school and weekend community activities that are designed to reduce childhood obesity;

(ii) forming partnerships with daycare facilities to establish programs that promote healthy eating behaviors and physical activity; and

(iii) developing and evaluating community educational activities targeting good nutrition and promoting healthy eating behaviors;

(B) carry out age-appropriate school-based activities that are designed to reduce childhood obesity, including by—

(i) developing and testing educational curricula and intervention programs designed to promote healthy eating behaviors and habits in youth, which may include—

(I) after hours physical activity programs; and

(II) science-based interventions with multiple components to prevent eating disorders including nutritional content, understanding and responding to hunger and satiety, positive body image development, positive self-esteem development, and learning life skills (such as stress management, communication skills, problemsolving and decisionmaking skills), as well as consideration of cultural and developmental issues, and the role of family, school, and community;

(ii) providing education and training to educational professionals regarding how to promote a healthy lifestyle and a healthy school environment for children;

(iii) planning and implementing a healthy lifestyle curriculum or program with an emphasis on healthy eating behaviors and physical activity; and

(iv) planning and implementing healthy lifestyle classes or programs for parents or guardians, with an emphasis on healthy eating behaviors and physical activity for children;

(C) carry out educational, counseling, promotional, and training activities through the local health care delivery systems including by—

(i) promoting healthy eating behaviors and physical activity services to treat or prevent eating disorders, being overweight, and obesity;

(ii) providing patient education and counseling to increase physical activity and promote healthy eating behaviors;

(iii) training health professionals on how to identify and treat obese and overweight individuals which may include nutrition and physical activity counseling; and

(iv) providing community education by a health professional on good nutrition and physical activity to develop a better understanding of the relationship between diet, physical activity, and eating disorders, obesity, or being overweight; and

(D) provide, through qualified health professionals, training and supervision for community health workers to—

(i) educate families regarding the relationship between nutrition, eating habits, physical activity, and obesity;

(ii) educate families about effective strategies to improve nutrition, establish healthy eating patterns, and establish appropriate levels of physical activity; and

(iii) educate and guide parents regarding the ability to model and communicate positive health behaviors.

(4) Priority. In awarding grants under paragraph (1), the Secretary shall give priority to awarding grants to eligible entities—

(A) that demonstrate that they have previously applied successfully for funds to carry out activities that seek to promote individual and community health and to prevent the incidence of chronic disease and that can cite published and peer-reviewed research demonstrating that the activities that the entities propose to carry out with funds made available under the grant are effective;

(B) that will carry out programs or activities that seek to accomplish a goal or goals set by the State in the Healthy People 2010 plan of the State;

(C) that provide non-Federal contributions, either in cash or in-kind, to the costs of funding activities under the grants;

(D) that develop comprehensive plans that include a strategy for extending program activities developed under grants in the years following the fiscal years for which they receive grants under this subsection;

(E) located in communities that are medically underserved, as determined by the Secretary;

(F) located in areas in which the average poverty rate is at least 150 percent or higher of the average poverty rate in the State involved, as determined by the Secretary; and

(G) that submit plans that exhibit multisectoral, cooperative conduct that includes the involvement of a broad range of stakeholders, including—

(i) community-based organizations;

(ii) local governments;

(iii) local educational agencies;

(iv) the private sector;

(v) State or local departments of health;

(vi) accredited colleges, universities, and community colleges;

(vii) health care providers;

(viii) State and local departments of transportation and city planning; and

(ix) other entities determined appropriate by the Secretary.

(5) Program design. (A) Initial design. Not later than 1 year after the date of enactment of the Children's Health Insurance Program Reauthorization Act of 2009 [enacted Feb. 4, 2009], the Secretary shall design the demonstration project. The demonstration should draw upon promising, innovative models and incentives to reduce behavioral risk factors. The Administrator of the Centers for Medicare & Medicaid Services shall consult with the Director of the Centers for Disease Control and Prevention, the Director of the Office of Minority Health, the heads of other agencies in the Department of Health and Human Services, and such professional organizations, as the Secretary determines to be appropriate, on the design, conduct, and evaluation of the demonstration.

(B) Number and project areas. Not later than 2 years after the date of enactment of the Children's Health Insurance Program Reauthorization Act of 2009 [enacted Feb. 4, 2009], the Secretary shall award 1 grant that is specifically designed to determine whether programs similar to programs to be conducted by other grantees under this subsection should be implemented with respect to the general population of children who are eligible for child health assistance under State child health plans under title XXI [42 USCS §§ 1397aa et seq.] in order to reduce the incidence of childhood obesity among such population.

(6) Report to Congress. Not later than 3 years after the date the Secretary implements the demonstration project under this subsection, the Secretary shall submit to Congress a report that describes the project, evaluates the effectiveness and cost effectiveness of the

project, evaluates the beneficiary satisfaction under the project, and includes any such other information as the Secretary determines to be appropriate.

(7) Definitions. In this subsection:

(A) Federally-qualified health center. The term "Federally-qualified health center" has the meaning given that term in section 1905(l)(2)(B) [42 USCS § 1396d(l)(2)(B)].

(B) Indian tribe. The term "Indian tribe" has the meaning given that term in section 4 of the Indian Health Care Improvement Act (25 U.S.C. 1603).

(C) Self-assessment. The term "self-assessment" means a form that—

(i) includes questions regarding—

(I) behavioral risk factors;

(II) needed preventive and screening services; and

(III) target individuals' preferences for receiving follow-up information;

(ii) is assessed using such computer generated assessment programs; and

(iii) allows for the provision of such ongoing support to the individual as the Secretary determines appropriate.

(D) Ongoing support. The term "ongoing support" means—

(i) to provide any target individual with information, feedback, health coaching, and recommendations regarding—

(I) the results of a self-assessment given to the individual;

(II) behavior modification based on the self-assessment; and

(III) any need for clinical preventive and screening services or treatment including medical nutrition therapy;

(ii) to provide any target individual with referrals to community resources and programs available to assist the target individual in reducing health risks; and

(iii) to provide the information described in clause (i) to a health care provider, if designated by the target individual to receive such information.

(8) Appropriation. Out of any funds in the Treasury not otherwise appropriated, there is appropriated to carry out this subsection, $25,000,000 for the period of fiscal years 2010 through 2014.

(f) Development of model electronic health record format for children enrolled in Medicaid or CHIP. (1) In general. Not later than January 1, 2010, the Secretary shall establish a program to encourage the development and dissemination of a model electronic health record format for children enrolled in the State plan under title XIX [42 USCS §§ 1396 et seq.] or the State child health plan under title XXI [42 USCS §§ 1397aa et seq.] that is—

(A) subject to State laws, accessible to parents, caregivers, and other consumers for the sole purpose of demonstrating compliance with school or leisure activity requirements, such as appropriate immunizations or physicals;

(B) designed to allow interoperable exchanges that conform with Federal and State privacy and security requirements;

(C) structured in a manner that permits parents and caregivers to view and understand the extent to which the care their children receive is clinically appropriate and of high quality; and

(D) capable of being incorporated into, and otherwise compatible with, other standards developed for electronic health records.

(2) Funding. $5,000,000 of the amount appropriated under subsection (i) for a fiscal year shall be used to carry out this subsection.

(g) Study of pediatric health and health care quality measures. (1) In general. Not later than July 1, 2010, the Institute of Medicine shall study and report to Congress on the extent and quality of efforts to measure child health status and the quality of health care for children across the age span and in relation to preventive care, treatments for acute conditions, and treatments aimed at ameliorating or correcting physical, mental, and developmental conditions in children. In conducting such study and preparing such report, the Institute of Medicine shall—

(A) consider all of the major national population-based reporting systems sponsored by the Federal Government that are currently in place, including reporting requirements under Federal grant programs and national population surveys and estimates conducted directly by the Federal Government;

(B) identify the information regarding child health and health care quality that each system is designed to capture and generate, the study and reporting periods covered by each system, and the extent to which the information so generated is made widely available through publication;

(C) identify gaps in knowledge related to children's health status, health disparities among subgroups of children, the effects of social conditions on children's health status and use and effectiveness of health care, and the relationship between child health status and family income, family stability and preservation, and children's school readiness and educational achievement and attainment; and

(D) make recommendations regarding improving and strengthening the timeliness, quality, and public transparency and accessibility of information about child health and health care quality.

(2) Funding. Up to $1,000,000 of the amount appropriated under subsection (i) for a fiscal year shall be used to carry out this subsection.

(h) Rule of construction. Notwithstanding any other provision in this section, no evidence based quality measure developed, published, or used as a basis of measurement or reporting under this section may be used to establish an irrebuttable presumption regarding either the medical necessity of care or the maximum permissible coverage for any individual child who is eligible for and receiving medical assistance under title XIX [42 USCS §§ 1396 et seq.] or child health assistance under title XXI [42 USCS §§ 1397aa et seq.].

(i) Appropriation. Out of any funds in the Treasury not otherwise appropriated, there is appropriated for each of fiscal years 2009 through 2013, $45,000,000 for the purpose of carrying out this section (other than subsection (e)). Funds appropriated under this subsection shall remain available until expended.

(Aug. 14, 1935, ch 531, Title XI, Part A, § 1139A, as added and amended Feb. 4, 2009, P. L. 111-3, Title IV, § 401(a), Title V, § 501(g), 123 Stat. 72, 88; March 23, 2010, P. L. 111-148, Title IV, Subtitle D, § 4306, 124 Stat. 587.)

§ 1320b-9b. Adult health quality measures

(a) Development of core set of health care quality measures for adults eligible for benefits under Medicaid. The Secretary shall identify and publish a recommended core set of adult health quality measures for Medicaid eligible adults in the same manner as the Secretary identifies and publishes a core set of child health quality measures under section 1139A [42 USCS § 1320b-9a], including with respect to identifying and publishing existing adult health quality measures that are in use under public and privately sponsored health care coverage arrangements, or that are part of reporting systems that measure both the presence and duration of health insurance coverage over time, that may be applicable to Medicaid eligible adults.

(b) Deadlines. (1) Recommended measures. Not later than January 1, 2011, the Secretary shall identify and publish for comment a recommended core set of adult health quality measures for Medicaid eligible adults.

(2) Dissemination. Not later than January 1, 2012, the Secretary shall publish an initial core set of adult health quality measures that are applicable to Medicaid eligible adults.

(3) Standardized reporting. Not later than January 1, 2013, the Secretary, in consultation with States, shall develop a standardized format for reporting information based on the initial core set of adult health quality measures and create procedures to encourage States to use such measures to voluntarily report information regarding the quality of health care for Medicaid eligible adults.

(4) Reports to Congress. Not later than January 1, 2014, and every 3 years thereafter, the Secretary shall include in the report to Congress required under section 1139A(a)(6) [42 USCS § 1320b-9a(a)(6)] information similar to the information required under that section with respect to the measures established under this section.

(5) Establishment of Medicaid quality measurement program. (A) In general. Not later than 12 months after the release of the recommended core set of adult health quality measures under paragraph (1)), the Secretary shall establish a Medicaid Quality Measurement Program in the same manner as the Secretary establishes the pediatric quality measures program under section 1139A(b) [42 USCS § 1320b-9a(b)]. The aggregate amount awarded by the Secretary for grants and contracts for the development, testing, and validation of emerging and innovative evidence-based measures under such program shall equal the aggregate amount awarded by the Secretary for grants under section 1139A(b)(4)(A) [42 USCS § 1320b-9a(b)(4)(A)] [.]

(B) Revising, strengthening, and improving initial core measures. Beginning not later than 24 months after the establishment of the Medicaid Quality Measurement Program, and annually thereafter, the Secretary shall publish recommended changes to the initial core set of adult health quality measures that shall reflect the results of the testing, validation, and consensus process for the development of adult health quality measures.

(c) Construction. Nothing in this section shall be construed as supporting the restriction of coverage, under title XIX or XXI [42 USCS §§ 1396 et seq. or 1397aa et seq.] or otherwise, to only those services that are evidence-based, or in anyway limiting available services.

(d) Annual State reports regarding State-specific quality of care measures applied under Medicaid. (1) Annual State reports. Each State with a State plan or waiver approved under title XIX [42 USCS §§ 1396 et seq.] shall annually report (separately or as part of the annual report required under section 1139A(c) [42 USCS § 1320b-9a(c)]), to the Secretary on the—

(A) State-specific adult health quality measures applied by the State under the such plan, including measures described in subsection (a)(5); and

(B) State-specific information on the quality of health care furnished to Medicaid eligible adults under such plan, including information collected through external quality reviews of managed care organizations under section 1932 [42 USCS § 1396u-2] and benchmark plans under section 1937 [42 USCS § 1396u-7].

(2) Publication. Not later than September 30, 2014, and annually thereafter, the Secretary shall collect, analyze, and make publicly available the information reported by States under paragraph (1).

(e) Appropriation. Out of any funds in the Treasury not otherwise appropriated, there is appropriated for each of fiscal years 2010 through 2014, $60,000,000 for the purpose of carrying out this section. Funds appropriated under this subsection shall remain available until expended.

(Aug. 14, 1935, ch 531, Title XI, Part A, § 1139, as added March 23, 2010, P. L. 111-148, Title II, Subtitle I, § 2701, 124 Stat. 317.)

§ 1320b-23. Pharmacy benefit managers transparency requirements

(a) Provision of information. A health benefits plan or any entity that provides pharmacy benefits management services on behalf of a health benefits plan (in this section referred to as a "PBM") that manages prescription drug coverage under a contract with—

(1) a PDP sponsor of a prescription drug plan or an MA organization offering an MA-PD plan under part D of title XVIII [42 USCS §§ 1395w-101 et seq.]; or

(2) a qualified health benefits plan offered through an exchange established by a State under section 1311 of the Patient Protection and Affordable Care Act [USCS § note],

shall provide the information described in subsection (b) to the Secretary and, in the case of a PBM, to the plan with which the PBM is under contract with, at such times, and in such form and manner, as the Secretary shall specify.

(b) Information described. The information described in this subsection is the following with respect to services provided by a health benefits plan or PBM for a contract year:

(1) The percentage of all prescriptions that were provided through retail pharmacies compared to mail order pharmacies, and the percentage of prescriptions for which a generic drug was available and dispensed (generic dispensing rate), by pharmacy type (which includes an independent pharmacy, chain pharmacy, supermarket pharmacy, or mass merchandiser pharmacy that is licensed as a pharmacy by the State and that dispenses medication to the general public), that is paid by the health benefits plan or PBM under the contract.

(2) The aggregate amount, and the type of rebates, discounts, or price concessions (excluding bona fide service fees, which include but are not limited to distribution service fees, inventory management fees, product stocking allowances, and fees associated with administrative services agreements and patient care programs (such as medication compliance programs and patient education programs)) that the PBM negotiates that are attributable to patient utilization under the plan, and the aggregate amount of the rebates, discounts, or price concessions that are passed through to the plan sponsor, and the total number of prescriptions that were dispensed.

(3) The aggregate amount of the difference between the amount the health benefits plan pays the PBM and the amount that the PBM pays retail pharmacies, and mail order pharmacies, and the total number of prescriptions that were dispensed.

(c) Confidentiality. Information disclosed by a health benefits plan or PBM under this section is confidential and shall not be disclosed by the Secretary or by a plan receiving the information, except that the Secretary may disclose the information in a form which does not disclose the identity of a specific PBM, plan, or prices charged for drugs, for the following purposes:

(1) As the Secretary determines to be necessary to carry out this section or part D of title XVIII [42 USCS § 1395w-101].

(2) To permit the Comptroller General to review the information provided.

(3) To permit the Director of the Congressional Budget Office to review the information provided.

(4) To States to carry out section 1311 of the Patient Protection and Affordable Care Act [42 USCS § 18031].

(d) Penalties. The provisions of subsection (b)(3)(C) of section 1927 [42 USCS § 1396r-8] shall apply to a health benefits plan or PBM that fails to provide information required under subsection (a) on a timely basis or that knowingly provides false information in the same manner as such provisions apply to a manufacturer with an agreement under that section.

(Aug 14, 1935, ch 531, Title XI, Part A, § 1150A, as added March 23, 2010, P. L. 111-148, Title VI, Subtitle A, § 6005, 124 Stat. 698.)

§ 1320b-25. Reporting to law enforcement of crimes occurring in Federally funded long-term care facilities

(a) Determination and notification. (1) Determination. The owner or operator of each long-term care facility that receives Federal funds under this Act shall annually determine whether the facility received at least $10,000 in such Federal funds during the preceding year.

(2) Notification. If the owner or operator determines under paragraph (1) that the facility received at least $10,000 in such Federal funds during the preceding year, such owner or operator shall annually notify each covered individual (as defined in paragraph (3)) of that individual's obligation to comply with the reporting requirements described in subsection (b).

(3) Covered individual defined. In this section, the term "covered individual" means each individual who is an owner, operator, employee, manager, agent, or contractor of a long-term care facility that is the subject of a determination described in paragraph (1).

(b) Reporting requirements. (1) In general. Each covered individual shall report to the Secretary and 1 or more law enforcement entities for the political subdivision in which the facility is located any reasonable suspicion of a crime (as defined by the law of the applicable political subdivision) against any individual who is a resident of, or is receiving care from, the facility.

(2) Timing. If the events that cause the suspicion—

(A) result in serious bodily injury, the individual shall report the suspicion immediately, but not later than 2 hours after forming the suspicion; and

(B) do not result in serious bodily injury, the individual shall report the suspicion not later than 24 hours after forming the suspicion.

(c) Penalties. (1) In general. If a covered individual violates subsection (b)—

(A) the covered individual shall be subject to a civil money penalty of not more than $200,000; and

(B) the Secretary may make a determination in the same proceeding to exclude the covered individual from participation in any Federal health care program (as defined in section 1128B(f) [42 USCS § 1320a-7b(f)]).

(2) Increased harm. If a covered individual violates subsection (b) and the violation exacerbates the harm to the victim of the crime or results in harm to another individual—

(A) the covered individual shall be subject to a civil money penalty of not more than $300,000; and

(B) the Secretary may make a determination in the same proceeding to exclude the covered individual from participation in any Federal health care program (as defined in section 1128B(f) [42 USCS § 1320a-7b(f)]).

(3) Excluded individual. During any period for which a covered individual is classified as an excluded individual under paragraph (1)(B) or (2)(B), a long-term care facility that employs such individual shall be ineligible to receive Federal funds under this Act [42 USCS §§ 301 et seq.].

(4) Extenuating circumstances. (A) In general. The Secretary may take into account the financial burden on providers with underserved populations in determining any penalty to be imposed under this subsection.

(B) Underserved population defined. In this paragraph, the term "underserved population" means the population of an area designated by the Secretary as an area with a shortage of elder justice programs or a population group designated by the Secretary as having a shortage of such programs. Such areas or groups designated by the Secretary may include—

(i) areas or groups that are geographically isolated (such as isolated in a rural area);

(ii) racial and ethnic minority populations; and

(iii) populations underserved because of special needs (such as language barriers, disabilities, alien status, or age).

(d) Additional penalties for retaliation. (1) In general. A long-term care facility may not—

(A) discharge, demote, suspend, threaten, harass, or deny a promotion or other employment-related benefit to an employee, or in any other manner discriminate against an employee in the terms and conditions of employment because of lawful acts done by the employee; or

(B) file a complaint or a report against a nurse or other employee with the appropriate State professional disciplinary agency because of lawful acts done by the nurse or employee,

for making a report, causing a report to be made, or for taking steps in furtherance of making a report pursuant to subsection (b)(1).

(2) Penalties for retaliation. If a long-term care facility violates subparagraph (A) or (B) of paragraph (1) the facility shall be subject to a civil money penalty of not more than $200,000 or the Secretary may classify the entity as an excluded entity for a period of 2 years pursuant to section 1128(b) [42 USCS § 1320a-7(b)], or both.

(3) Requirement to post notice. Each long-term care facility shall post conspicuously in an appropriate location a sign (in a form specified by the Secretary) specifying the rights of employees under this section. Such sign shall include a statement that an employee may file a complaint with the Secretary against a long-term care facility that violates the provisions of this subsection and information with respect to the manner of filing such a complaint.

(e) Procedure. The provisions of section 1128A [42 USCS § 1320a-7a] (other than subsections (a) and (b) and the second sentence of subsection (f)) shall apply to a civil money penalty or exclusion under this section in the same manner as such provisions apply to a penalty or proceeding under section 1128A(a) [42 USCS § 1320a-7a].

(f) Definitions. In this section, the terms "elder justice", "long-term care facility", and "law enforcement" have the meanings given those terms in section 2011 [42 USCS § 1397j].

(Aug. 14, 1935, ch 531, Title XI, Part A, § 1150B, as added March 23, 2010, P. L. 111-148, Title VI, Subtitle H, § 6703(b)(3), 124 Stat. 800.)

PART C. ADMINISTRATIVE SIMPLIFICATION

§ 1320d. Definitions

For purposes of this part [42 USCS §§ 1320d et seq.]:

(1) Code set. The term "code set" means any set of codes used for encoding data elements, such as tables of terms, medical concepts, medical diagnostic codes, or medical procedure codes.

(2) Health care clearinghouse. The term "health care clearinghouse" means a public or private entity that processes or facilitates the processing of nonstandard data elements of health information into standard data elements.

(3) Health care provider. The term "health care provider" includes a provider of services (as defined in section 1861(u) [42 USCS § 1395x(u)]), a provider of medical or other health services (as defined in section 1861(s) [42 USCS § 1395x(s)]), and any other person furnishing health care services or supplies.

(4) Health information. The term "health information" means any information, whether oral or recorded in any form or medium, that—

(A) is created or received by a health care provider, health plan, public health authority, employer, life insurer, school or university, or health care clearinghouse; and

(B) relates to the past, present, or future physical or mental health or condition of an individual, the provision of health care to an individual, or the past, present, or future payment for the provision of health care to an individual.

(5) Health plan. The term "health plan" means an individual or group plan that provides, or pays the cost of, medical care (as such term is defined in section 2791 of the Public Health Service Act [42 USCS § 300gg-91]). Such term includes the following, and any combination thereof:

(A) A group health plan (as defined in section 2791(a) of the Public Health Service Act [42 USCS § 300gg-91(a)]), but only if the plan—

(i) has 50 or more participants (as defined in section 3(7) of the Employee Retirement Income Security Act of 1974 [29 USCS § 1002(7)]); or

(ii) is administered by an entity other than the employer who established and maintains the plan.

(B) A health insurance issuer (as defined in section 2791(b) of the Public Health Service Act [42 USCS § 300gg-91(b)]).

(C) A health maintenance organization (as defined in section 2791(b) of the Public Health Service Act [42 USCS § 300gg-91(b)]).

(D) Parts [Part] A, B, C, or D of the Medicare program under title XVIII [42 USCS §§ 1395c et seq., 1395j et seq., 1395w-21 et seq., or 1395w-101 et seq.].

(E) The medicaid program under title XIX [42 USCS §§ 1396 et seq.].

(F) A Medicare supplemental policy (as defined in section 1882(g)(1) [42 USCS § 1395ss(g)(1)]).

(G) A long-term care policy, including a nursing home fixed indemnity policy (unless the Secretary determines that such a policy does not provide sufficiently comprehensive coverage of a benefit so that the policy should be treated as a health plan).

(H) An employee welfare benefit plan or any

other arrangement which is established or maintained for the purpose of offering or providing health benefits to the employees of 2 or more employers.

(I) The health care program for active military personnel under title 10, United States Code.

(J) The veterans health care program under chapter 17 of title 38, United States Code [38 USCS §§ 1701 et seq.].

(K) The Civilian Health and Medical Program of the Uniformed Services (CHAMPUS), as defined in section 1072(4) of title 10, United States Code.

(L) The Indian health service program under the Indian Health Care Improvement Act (25 U.S.C. 1601 et seq.).

(M) The Federal Employees Health Benefit Plan under chapter 89 of title 5, United States Code [5 USCS §§ 8901 et seq.].

(6) Individually identifiable health information. The term "individually identifiable health information" means any information, including demographic information collected from an individual, that—

(A) is created or received by a health care provider, health plan, employer, or health care clearinghouse; and

(B) relates to the past, present, or future physical or mental health or condition of an individual, the provision of health care to an individual, or the past, present, or future payment for the provision of health care to an individual, and—

(i) identifies the individual; or

(ii) with respect to which there is a reasonable basis to believe that the information can be used to identify the individual.

(7) Standard. The term "standard", when used with reference to a data element of health information or a transaction referred to in section 1173(a)(1) [42 USCS § 1320d-2(a)(1)], means any such data element or transaction that meets each of the standards and implementation specifications adopted or established by the Secretary with respect to the data element or transaction under sections 1172 through 1174 [42 USCS §§ 1320d-1 through 1320d-3].

(8) Standard setting organization. The term "standard setting organization" means a standard setting organization accredited by the American National Standards Institute, including the National Council for Prescription Drug Programs, that develops standards for information transactions, data elements, or any other standard that is necessary to, or will facilitate, the implementation of this part [42 USCS §§ 1320d et seq.].

(9) Operating rules. The term "operating rules" means the necessary business rules and guidelines for the electronic exchange of information that are not defined by a standard or its implementation specifications as adopted for purposes of this part [42 USCS §§ 1320d et seq.].

(Aug. 14, 1935, ch 531, Title XI, Part C, § 1171, as added Aug. 21, 1996, P. L. 104-191, Title II, Subtitle F, § 262(a), 110 Stat. 2021; Dec. 27, 2001, P. L. 107-105, § 4, 115 Stat. 1007; Feb. 17, 2009, P. L. 111-5, Div A, Title XIII, Subtitle A, Part 1, § 13102, 123 Stat. 242; March 23, 2010, P. L. 111-148, Title I, Subtitle B, § 1104(b)(1), 124 Stat. 147.)

HISTORY; ANCILLARY LAWS AND DIRECTIVES

Other provisions:

Purpose of Subtitle F of Title II of Act Aug. 21, 1996. Act Aug. 21, 1996, P. L. 104-191, Title II, Subtitle F, § 261, 110 Stat. 2021; March 23, 2010, P. L. 111-148, Title I, Subtitle B, § 1104(a), 124 Stat. 146 (effective on enactment as provided by § 1105 of such Act, which appears as a note to this section), provides: "It is the purpose of this subtitle [enacting 42 USCS §§ 1320d et seq., among other things; for full classification, consult USCS Tables volumes] to improve the Medicare program under title XVIII of the Social Security Act [42 USCS §§ 1395 et seq.], the medicaid program under title XIX of such Act [42 USCS §§ 1396 et seq.], and the efficiency and effectiveness of the health care system, by encouraging the development of a health information system through the establishment of uniform standards and requirements for the electronic transmission of certain health information and to reduce the clerical burden on patients, health care providers, and health plans.".

Effective date of Subtitle B of Title I of Act March 23, 2010. Act March 23, 2010, P. L. 111-148, Title I, Subtitle B, § 1005, 124 Stat. 154, provides: "This subtitle [for full classification, consult USCS Tables volumes] shall take effect on the date of enactment of this Act.".

§ 1320d-2. Standards for information transactions and data elements

(a) Standards to enable electronic exchange. (1) In general. The Secretary shall adopt standards for transactions, and data elements for such transactions, to enable health information to be exchanged electronically, that are appropriate for—

(A) the financial and administrative transactions described in paragraph (2); and

(B) other financial and administrative transactions determined appropriate by the Secretary, consistent with the goals of improving the operation of the health care system and reducing administrative costs, and subject to the requirements under paragraph (5).

(2) Transactions. The transactions referred to in paragraph (1)(A) are transactions with respect to the following:

(A) Health claims or equivalent encounter information.

(B) Health claims attachments.

(C) Enrollment and disenrollment in a health plan.

(D) Eligibility for a health plan.

(E) Health care payment and remittance advice.

(F) Health plan premium payments.

(G) First report of injury.

(H) Health claim status.

(I) Referral certification and authorization.

(J) Electronic funds transfers.

(3) Accommodation of specific providers. The standards adopted by the Secretary under paragraph (1) shall accommodate the needs of different types of health care providers.

(4) Requirements for financial and administrative transactions. (A) In general. The standards and associated operating rules adopted by the Secretary shall—

(i) to the extent feasible and appropriate, enable determination of an individual's eligibility and financial responsibility for specific services prior to or at the point of care;

(ii) be comprehensive, requiring minimal augmentation by paper or other communications;

(iii) provide for timely acknowledgment, response, and status reporting that supports a transparent claims and denial management process (including adjudication and appeals); and

(iv) describe all data elements (including reason and remark codes) in unambiguous terms, require that such data elements be required or conditioned upon set values in other fields, and prohibit additional conditions (except where necessary to implement State or Federal law, or to protect against fraud and abuse).

(B) Reduction of clerical burden. In adopting standards and operating rules for the transactions referred to under paragraph (1), the Secretary shall seek to reduce the number and complexity of forms (including paper and electronic forms) and data entry required by patients and providers.

(5) Consideration of standardization of activities and items. (A) In general. For purposes of carrying out paragraph (1)(B), the Secretary shall solicit, not later than January 1, 2012, and not less than every 3 years thereafter, input from entities described in subparagraph (B) on—

(i) whether there could be greater uniformity in financial and administrative activities and items, as determined appropriate by the Secretary; and

(ii) whether such activities should be considered financial and administrative transactions (as described in paragraph (1)(B)) for which the adoption of standards and operating rules would improve the operation of the health care system and reduce administrative costs.

(B) Solicitation of input. For purposes of subparagraph (A), the Secretary shall seek input from—

(i) the National Committee on Vital and Health Statistics, the Health Information Technology Policy Committee, and the Health Information Technology Standards Committee; and

(ii) standard setting organizations and stakeholders, as determined appropriate by the Secretary.

(b) Unique health identifiers. (1) In general. The Secretary shall adopt standards providing for a standard unique health identifier for each individual, employer, health plan, and health care provider for use in the health care system. In carrying out the preceding sentence for each health plan and health care provider, the Secretary shall take into account multiple uses for identifiers and multiple locations and specialty classifications for health care providers.

(2) Use of identifiers. The standards adopted under paragraph (1) shall specify the purposes for which a unique health identifier may be used.

(c) Code sets. (1) In general. The Secretary shall adopt standards that—

(A) select code sets for appropriate data elements for the transactions referred to in subsection (a)(1) from among the code sets that have been developed by private and public entities; or

(B) establish code sets for such data elements if no code sets for the data elements have been developed.

(2) Distribution. The Secretary shall establish efficient and low-cost procedures for distribution (including electronic distribution) of code sets and modifications made to such code sets under section 1174(b) [42 USCS § 1320d-3(b)].

(d) Security standards for health information. (1) Security standards. The Secretary shall adopt security standards that—

(A) take into account—

(i) the technical capabilities of record systems used to maintain health information;

(ii) the costs of security measures;

(iii) the need for training persons who have access to health information;

(iv) the value of audit trails in computerized record systems; and

(v) the needs and capabilities of small health care providers and rural health care providers (as such providers are defined by the Secretary); and

(B) ensure that a health care clearinghouse, if it is part of a larger organization, has policies and security procedures which isolate the activities of the health care clearinghouse with respect to processing information in a manner that prevents unauthorized access to such information by such larger organization.

(2) Safeguards. Each person described in section 1172(a) [42 USCS § 1320d-1] who maintains or transmits health information shall maintain reasonable and appropriate administrative, technical, and physical safeguards—

(A) to ensure the integrity and confidentiality of the information;

(B) to protect against any reasonably anticipated—

(i) threats or hazards to the security or integrity of the information; and

(ii) unauthorized uses or disclosures of the information; and

(C) otherwise to ensure compliance with this part [42 USCS §§ 1320d et seq.] by the officers and employees of such person.

(e) Electronic signature. (1) Standards. The Secretary, in coordination with the Secretary of Commerce, shall adopt standards specifying procedures for the electronic transmission and authentication of signatures with respect to the transactions referred to in subsection (a)(1).

(2) Effect of compliance. Compliance with the standards adopted under paragraph (1) shall be deemed to satisfy Federal and State statutory requirements for written signatures with respect to the transactions referred to in subsection (a)(1).

(f) Transfer of information among health plans. The Secretary shall adopt standards for transferring among health plans appropriate standard data elements needed for the coordination of benefits, the sequential processing of claims, and other data elements for individuals who have more than one health plan.

(g) Operating rules. (1) In general. The Secretary shall adopt a single set of operating rules for each transaction referred to under subsection (a)(1) with the goal of creating as much uniformity in the implementation of the electronic standards as possible. Such operating rules shall be consensus-based and reflect the necessary business rules affecting health plans and health care providers and the manner in which they operate pursuant to standards issued under Health Insurance Portability and Accountability Act of 1996.

(2) Operating rules development. In adopting operating rules under this subsection, the Secretary shall consider recommendations for operating rules developed by a qualified nonprofit entity that meets the following requirements:

(A) The entity focuses its mission on administrative simplification.

(B) The entity demonstrates a multi-stakeholder and consensus-based process for development of operating rules, including representation by or participation from health plans, health care providers, vendors, relevant Federal agencies, and other standard development organizations.

(C) The entity has a public set of guiding principles that ensure the operating rules and process are open and transparent, and supports nondiscrimination and conflict of interest policies that demonstrate a commitment to open, fair, and nondiscriminatory practices.

(D) The entity builds on the transaction standards issued under Health Insurance Portability and Accountability Act of 1996.

(E) The entity allows for public review and updates of the operating rules.

(3) Review and recommendations. The National Committee on Vital and Health Statistics shall—

(A) advise the Secretary as to whether a nonprofit entity meets the requirements under paragraph (2);

(B) review the operating rules developed and recommended by such nonprofit entity;

(C) determine whether such operating rules represent a consensus view of the health care stakeholders and are consistent with and do not conflict with other existing standards;

(D) evaluate whether such operating rules are consistent with electronic standards adopted for health information technology; and

(E) submit to the Secretary a recommendation as to whether the Secretary should adopt such operating rules.

(4) Implementation. (A) In general. The Secretary shall adopt operating rules under this subsection, by regulation in accordance with subparagraph (C), following consideration of the operating rules developed by the nonprofit entity described in paragraph (2) and the recommendation submitted by the National

Committee on Vital and Health Statistics under paragraph (3)(E) and having ensured consultation with providers.

(B) Adoption requirements; effective dates. (i) Eligibility for a health plan and health claim status. The set of operating rules for eligibility for a health plan and health claim status transactions shall be adopted not later than July 1, 2011, in a manner ensuring that such operating rules are effective not later than January 1, 2013, and may allow for the use of a machine readable identification card.

(ii) Electronic funds transfers and health care payment and remittance advice. The set of operating rules for electronic funds transfers and health care payment and remittance advice transactions shall—

(I) allow for automated reconciliation of the electronic payment with the remittance advice; and

(II) be adopted not later than July 1, 2012, in a manner ensuring that such operating rules are effective not later than January 1, 2014.

(iii) Health claims or equivalent encounter information, enrollment and disenrollment in a health plan, health plan premium payments, referral certification and authorization. The set of operating rules for health claims or equivalent encounter information, enrollment and disenrollment in a health plan, health plan premium payments, and referral certification and authorization transactions shall be adopted not later than July 1, 2014, in a manner ensuring that such operating rules are effective not later than January 1, 2016.

(C) Expedited rulemaking. The Secretary shall promulgate an interim final rule applying any standard or operating rule recommended by the National Committee on Vital and Health Statistics pursuant to paragraph (3). The Secretary shall accept and consider public comments on any interim final rule published under this subparagraph for 60 days after the date of such publication.

(h) Compliance. (1) Health plan certification. (A) Eligibility for a health plan, health claim status, electronic funds transfers, health care payment and remittance advice. Not later than December 31, 2013, a health plan shall file a statement with the Secretary, in such form as the Secretary may require, certifying that the data and information systems for such plan are in compliance with any applicable standards (as described under paragraph (7) of section 1171 [42 USCS § 1320d]) and associated operating rules (as described under paragraph (9) of such section) for electronic funds transfers, eligibility for a health plan, health claim status, and health care payment and remittance advice, respectively.

(B) Health claims or equivalent encounter information, enrollment and disenrollment in a health plan, health plan premium payments, health claims attachments, referral certification and authorization. Not later than December 31, 2015, a health plan shall file a statement with the Secretary, in such form as the Secretary may require, certifying that the data and information systems for such plan are in compliance with any applicable standards and associated operating rules for health claims or equivalent encounter information, enrollment and disenrollment in a health plan, health plan premium payments, health claims attachments, and referral certification and authorization, respectively. A health plan shall provide the same level of documentation to certify compliance with such transactions as is required to certify compliance with the transactions specified in subparagraph (A).

(2) Documentation of compliance. A health plan shall provide the Secretary, in such form as the Secretary may require, with adequate documentation of compliance with the standards and operating rules described under paragraph (1). A health plan shall not be considered to have provided adequate documentation and shall not be certified as being in compliance with such standards, unless the health plan—

(A) demonstrates to the Secretary that the plan conducts the electronic transactions specified in paragraph (1) in a manner that fully complies with the regulations of the Secretary; and

(B) provides documentation showing that the plan has completed end-to-end testing for such transactions with their partners, such as hospitals and physicians.

(3) Service contracts. A health plan shall be required to ensure that any entities that provide services pursuant to a contract with such health plan shall comply with any applicable certification and compliance requirements (and provide the Secretary with adequate documentation of such compliance) under this subsection.

(4) Certification by outside entity. The Secretary may designate independent, outside entities to certify that a health plan has complied with the requirements under this subsection, provided that the certification standards employed by such entities are in accordance with any standards or operating rules issued by the Secretary.

(5) Compliance with revised standards and

operating rules. (A) In general. A health plan (including entities described under paragraph (3)) shall file a statement with the Secretary, in such form as the Secretary may require, certifying that the data and information systems for such plan are in compliance with any applicable revised standards and associated operating rules under this subsection for any interim final rule promulgated by the Secretary under subsection (i) that—

(i) amends any standard or operating rule described under paragraph (1) of this subsection; or

(ii) establishes a standard (as described under subsection (a)(1)(B)) or associated operating rules (as described under subsection (i)(5)) for any other financial and administrative transactions.

(B) Date of compliance. A health plan shall comply with such requirements not later than the effective date of the applicable standard or operating rule.

(6) Audits of health plans. The Secretary shall conduct periodic audits to ensure that health plans (including entities described under paragraph (3)) are in compliance with any standards and operating rules that are described under paragraph (1) or subsection (i)(5).

(i) Review and amendment of standards and operating rules. (1) Establishment. Not later than January 1, 2014, the Secretary shall establish a review committee (as described under paragraph (4)).

(2) Evaluations and reports. (A) Hearings. Not later than April 1, 2014, and not less than biennially thereafter, the Secretary, acting through the review committee, shall conduct hearings to evaluate and review the adopted standards and operating rules established under this section.

(B) Report. Not later than July 1, 2014, and not less than biennially thereafter, the review committee shall provide recommendations for updating and improving such standards and operating rules. The review committee shall recommend a single set of operating rules per transaction standard and maintain the goal of creating as much uniformity as possible in the implementation of the electronic standards.

(3) Interim final rulemaking. (A) In general. Any recommendations to amend adopted standards and operating rules that have been approved by the review committee and reported to the Secretary under paragraph (2)(B) shall be adopted by the Secretary through promulgation of an interim final rule not later than 90 days after receipt of the committee's report.

(B) Public comment. (i) Public comment period. The Secretary shall accept and consider public comments on any interim final rule published under this paragraph for 60 days after the date of such publication.

(ii) Effective date. The effective date of any amendment to existing standards or operating rules that is adopted through an interim final rule published under this paragraph shall be 25 months following the close of such public comment period.

(4) Review committee. (A) Definition. For the purposes of this subsection, the term "review committee" means a committee chartered by or within the Department of Health and Human services that has been designated by the Secretary to carry out this subsection, including—

(i) the National Committee on Vital and Health Statistics; or

(ii) any appropriate committee as determined by the Secretary.

(B) Coordination of HIT standards. In developing recommendations under this subsection, the review committee shall ensure coordination, as appropriate, with the standards that support the certified electronic health record technology approved by the Office of the National Coordinator for Health Information Technology.

(5) Operating rules for other standards adopted by the Secretary. The Secretary shall adopt a single set of operating rules (pursuant to the process described under subsection (g)) for any transaction for which a standard had been adopted pursuant to subsection (a)(1)(B).

(j) Penalties. (1) Penalty fee. (A) In general. Not later than April 1, 2014, and annually thereafter, the Secretary shall assess a penalty fee (as determined under subparagraph (B)) against a health plan that has failed to meet the requirements under subsection (h) with respect to certification and documentation of compliance with—

(i) the standards and associated operating rules described under paragraph (1) of such subsection; and

(ii) a standard (as described under subsection (a)(1)(B)) and associated operating rules (as described under subsection (i)(5)) for any other financial and administrative transactions.

(B) Fee amount. Subject to subparagraphs (C), (D), and (E), the Secretary shall assess a penalty fee against a health plan in the amount of $1 per covered life until certification is complete. The penalty shall be assessed per person covered by the plan for which its data systems for major medical policies are not in compliance and shall be imposed against the health plan for each day that the plan is not in compliance with the requirements under subsection (h).

(C) Additional penalty for misrepresentation. A health plan that knowingly provides inaccurate or incomplete information in a statement of certification or documentation of compliance under subsection (h) shall be subject to a penalty fee that is double the amount that would otherwise be imposed under this subsection.

(D) Annual fee increase. The amount of the penalty fee imposed under this subsection shall be increased on an annual basis by the annual percentage increase in total national health care expenditures, as determined by the Secretary.

(E) Penalty limit. A penalty fee assessed against a health plan under this subsection shall not exceed, on an annual basis—

(i) an amount equal to $20 per covered life under such plan; or

(ii) an amount equal to $40 per covered life under the plan if such plan has knowingly provided inaccurate or incomplete information (as described under subparagraph (C)).

(F) Determination of covered individuals. The Secretary shall determine the number of covered lives under a health plan based upon the most recent statements and filings that have been submitted by such plan to the Securities and Exchange Commission.

(2) Notice and dispute procedure. The Secretary shall establish a procedure for assessment of penalty fees under this subsection that provides a health plan with reasonable notice and a dispute resolution procedure prior to provision of a notice of assessment by the Secretary of the Treasury (as described under paragraph (4)(B)).

(3) Penalty fee report. Not later than May 1, 2014, and annually thereafter, the Secretary shall provide the Secretary of the Treasury with a report identifying those health plans that have been assessed a penalty fee under this subsection.

(4) Collection of penalty fee. (A) In general. The Secretary of the Treasury, acting through the Financial Management Service, shall administer the collection of penalty fees from health plans that have been identified by the Secretary in the penalty fee report provided under paragraph (3).

(B) Notice. Not later than August 1, 2014, and annually thereafter, the Secretary of the Treasury shall provide notice to each health plan that has been assessed a penalty fee by the Secretary under this subsection. Such notice shall include the amount of the penalty fee assessed by the Secretary and the due date for payment of such fee to the Secretary of the Treasury (as described in subparagraph (C)).

(C) Payment due date. Payment by a health plan for a penalty fee assessed under this subsection shall be made to the Secretary of the Treasury not later than November 1, 2014, and annually thereafter.

(D) Unpaid penalty fees. Any amount of a penalty fee assessed against a health plan under this subsection for which payment has not been made by the due date provided under subparagraph (C) shall be—

(i) increased by the interest accrued on such amount, as determined pursuant to the underpayment rate established under section 6621 of the Internal Revenue Code of 1986 [26 USCS § 6621]; and

(ii) treated as a past-due, legally enforceable debt owed to a Federal agency for purposes of section 6402(d) of the Internal Revenue Code of 1986 [26 USCS § 6402(d)].

(E) Administrative fees. Any fee charged or allocated for collection activities conducted by the Financial Management Service will be passed on to a health plan on a pro-rata basis and added to any penalty fee collected from the plan.

(Aug. 14, 1935, ch 531, Title XI, Part C, § 1173, as added Aug. 21, 1996, P. L. 104-191, Title II, Subtitle F, § 262(a), 110 Stat. 2024; March 23, 2010, P. L. 111-148, Title I, Subtitle B, § 1104(b)(2), Title X, Subtitle A, § 10109(a), 124 Stat. 147, 915.)

HISTORY; ANCILLARY LAWS AND DIRECTIVES

Other provisions:

Promulgation of rules. Act March 23, 2010, P. L. 111-148, Title I, Subtitle B, § 1104(c), 124 Stat. 153 (effective on enactment, as provided by § 1105 of such Act, which appears as 42 USCS § 1320d note), provides:

"(1) Unique health plan identifier. The Secretary shall promulgate a final rule to establish a unique health plan identifier (as described in section 1173(b) of the Social Security Act (42 U.S.C. 1320d-2(b))) based on the input of the National Committee on Vital and Health Statistics. The Secretary may do so on an interim final basis and such rule shall be effective not later than October 1, 2012.

"(2) Electronic funds transfer. The Secretary shall promulgate a final rule to establish a standard for electronic funds transfers (as described in section 1173(a)(2)(J) of the Social Security Act, as added by subsection (b)(2)(A)) [subsec. (a)(2)(J) of this section]. The Secretary may do so on an interim final basis and shall adopt such standard not later than January 1, 2012, in a manner ensuring that such standard is effective not later than January 1, 2014.

"(3) Health claims attachments. The Secretary

shall promulgate a final rule to establish a transaction standard and a single set of associated operating rules for health claims attachments (as described in section 1173(a)(2)(B) of the Social Security Act (42 U.S.C. 1320d-2(a)(2)(B))) that is consistent with the X12 Version 5010 transaction standards. The Secretary may do so on an interim final basis and shall adopt a transaction standard and a single set of associated operating rules not later than January 1, 2014, in a manner ensuring that such standard is effective not later than January 1, 2016.".

Activities and items for initial consideration; ICD coding crosswalks. Act March 23, 2010, P. L. 111-148, Title X, Subtitle A, § 10109(b), (c), 124 Stat. 916, provides:

"(b) Activities and items for initial consideration. For purposes of section 1173(a)(5) of the Social Security Act [subsec. (a)(5) of this section], as added by subsection (a), the Secretary of Health and Human Services (in this section referred to as the 'Secretary') shall, not later than January 1, 2012, seek input on activities and items relating to the following areas:

"(1) Whether the application process, including the use of a uniform application form, for enrollment of health care providers by health plans could be made electronic and standardized.

"(2) Whether standards and operating rules described in section 1173 of the Social Security Act [this section] should apply to the health care transactions of automobile insurance, worker's compensation, and other programs or persons not described in section 1172(a) of such Act (42 U.S.C. 1320d-1(a)).

"(3) Whether standardized forms could apply to financial audits required by health plans, Federal and State agencies (including State auditors, the Office of the Inspector General of the Department of Health and Human Services, and the Centers for Medicare & Medicaid Services), and other relevant entities as determined appropriate by the Secretary.

"(4) Whether there could be greater transparency and consistency of methodologies and processes used to establish claim edits used by health plans (as described in section 1171(5) of the Social Security Act (42 U.S.C. 1320d(5))).

"(5) Whether health plans should be required to publish their timeliness of payment rules.

"(c) ICD coding crosswalks. (1) ICD-9 to ICD-10 crosswalk. The Secretary shall task the ICD-9-CM Coordination and Maintenance Committee to convene a meeting, not later than January 1, 2011, to receive input from appropriate stakeholders (including health plans, health care providers, and clinicians) regarding the crosswalk between the Ninth and Tenth Revisions of the International Classification of Diseases (ICD-9 and ICD-10, respectively) that is posted on the website of the Centers for Medicare & Medicaid Services, and make recommendations about appropriate revisions to such crosswalk.

"(2) Revision of crosswalk. For purposes of the crosswalk described in paragraph (1), the Secretary shall make appropriate revisions and post any such revised crosswalk on the website of the Centers for Medicare & Medicaid Services.

"(3) Use of revised crosswalk. For purposes of paragraph (2), any revised crosswalk shall be treated as a code set for which a standard has been adopted by the Secretary for purposes of section 1173(c)(1)(B) of the Social Security Act (42 U.S.C. 1320d-2(c)(1)(B)).

"(4) Subsequent crosswalks. For subsequent revisions of the International Classification of Diseases that are adopted by the Secretary as a standard code set under section 1173(c) of the Social Security Act (42 U.S.C. 1320d-2(c)), the Secretary shall, after consultation with the appropriate stakeholders, post on the website of the Centers for Medicare & Medicaid Services a crosswalk between the previous and subsequent version of the International Classification of Diseases not later than the date of implementation of such subsequent revision.".

PART D. Comparative Clinical Effectiveness Research

§ 1320e. Comparative clinical effectiveness research

(a) Definitions. In this section:

(1) Board. The term "Board" means the Board of Governors established under subsection (f).

(2) Comparative clinical effectiveness research; research. (A) In general. The terms "comparative clinical effectiveness research" and "research" mean research evaluating and comparing health outcomes and the clinical effectiveness, risks, and benefits of 2 or more medical treatments, services, and items described in subparagraph (B).

(B) Medical treatments, services, and items described. The medical treatments, services, and items described in this subparagraph are health care interventions, protocols for treatment, care management, and delivery, procedures, medical devices, diagnostic tools, pharmaceuticals (including drugs and biologicals), integrative health practices, and any other strategies or items being used in the treatment, management, and diagnosis of, or prevention of illness or injury in, individuals.

(3) Conflict of interest. The term "conflict of interest" means an association, including a financial or personal association, that have the potential to bias or have the appearance of biasing an individual's decisions in matters related to the Institute or the conduct of activities under this section.

(4) Real conflict of interest. The term "real conflict of interest" means any instance where a member of the Board, the methodology committee established under subsection (d)(6), or an advisory panel appointed under subsection (d)(4), or a close relative of such member, has received or could receive either of the following:

(A) A direct financial benefit of any amount deriving from the result or findings of a study conducted under this section.

(B) A financial benefit from individuals or companies that own or manufacture medical treatments, services, or items to be studied under this section that in the aggregate exceeds $10,000 per year. For purposes of the preceding sentence, a financial benefit includes honoraria, fees, stock, or other financial benefit and the current value of the member or close relative's already existing stock holdings, in addition to any direct financial benefit deriving from the results or findings of a study conducted under this section.

(b) Patient-Centered Outcomes Research Institute. (1) Establishment. There is authorized to be established a nonprofit corporation, to be known as the "Patient-Centered Outcomes Research Institute" (referred to in this section as the "Institute") which is neither an agency nor establishment of the United States Government.

(2) Application of provisions. The Institute shall be subject to the provisions of this section, and, to the extent consistent with this section, to the District of Columbia Nonprofit Corporation Act.

(3) Funding of comparative clinical effectiveness research. For fiscal year 2010 and each subsequent fiscal year, amounts in the Patient-Centered Outcomes Research Trust Fund (referred to in this section as the "PCORTF") under section 9511 of the Internal Revenue Code of 1986 [26 USCS § 9511] shall be available, without further appropriation, to the Institute to carry out this section.

(c) Purpose. The purpose of the Institute is to assist patients, clinicians, purchasers, and policy-makers in making informed health decisions by advancing the quality and relevance of evidence concerning the manner in which diseases, disorders, and other health conditions can effectively and appropriately be prevented, diagnosed, treated, monitored, and managed through research and evidence synthesis that considers variations in patient subpopulations, and the dissemination of research findings with respect to the relative health outcomes, clinical effectiveness, and appropriateness of the medical treatments, services, and items described in subsection (a)(2)(B).

(d) Duties. (1) Identifying research priorities and establishing research project agenda. (A) Identifying research priorities. The Institute shall identify national priorities for research, taking into account factors of disease incidence, prevalence, and burden in the United States (with emphasis on chronic conditions), gaps in evidence in terms of clinical outcomes, practice variations and health disparities in terms of delivery and outcomes of care, the potential for new evidence to improve patient health, well-being, and the quality of care, the effect on national expenditures associated with a health care treatment, strategy, or health conditions, as well as patient needs, outcomes, and preferences, the relevance to patients and clinicians in making informed health decisions, and priorities in the National Strategy for quality care established under section 399H of the Public Health Service Act [42 USCS § 280F] that are consistent with this section.

(B) Establishing research project agenda. The Institute shall establish and update a research project agenda for research to address the priorities identified under subparagraph (A), taking into consideration the types of research that might address each priority and the relative value (determined based on the cost of conducting research compared to the potential usefulness of the information produced by research) associated with the different types of research, and such other factors as the Institute determines appropriate.

(2) Carrying out research project agenda. (A) Research. The Institute shall carry out the research project agenda established under paragraph (1)(B) in accordance with the methodological standards adopted under paragraph (9) using methods, including the following:

(i) Systematic reviews and assessments of existing and future research and evidence including original research conducted subsequent to the date of the enactment of this section [enacted March 23, 2010].

(ii) Primary research, such as randomized clinical trials, molecularly informed trials, and observational studies.

(iii) Any other methodologies recommended by the methodology committee established under paragraph (6) that are adopted by the Board under paragraph (9).

(B) Contracts for the management of funding and conduct of research. (i) Contracts. (I) In general. In accordance with the research project agenda established under paragraph (1)(B), the Institute shall enter into contracts for the management of funding and conduct of research in accordance with the following:

(aa) Appropriate agencies and instrumentalities of the Federal Government.

(bb) Appropriate academic research, private sector research, or study-conducting entities.

(II) Preference. In entering into contracts under subclause (I), the Institute shall give preference to the Agency for Healthcare Research and Quality and the National Institutes of Health, but only if the research to be conducted or managed under such contract is authorized by the governing statutes of such Agency or Institutes.

(ii) Conditions for contracts. A contract entered into under this subparagraph shall require that the agency, instrumentality, or other entity—

(I) abide by the transparency and conflicts of interest requirements under subsection (h) that apply to the Institute with respect to the research managed or conducted under such contract;

(II) comply with the methodological standards adopted under paragraph (9) with respect to such research;

(III) consult with the expert advisory panels for clinical trials and rare disease appointed under clauses (ii) and (iii), respectively, of paragraph (4)(A);

(IV) subject to clause (iv), permit a researcher who conducts original research, as described in subparagraph (A)(ii), under the contract for the agency, instrumentality, or other entity to have such research published in a peer-reviewed journal or other publication, as long as the researcher enters into a data use agreement with the Institute for use of the data from the original research, as appropriate;

(V) have appropriate processes in place to manage data privacy and meet ethical standards for the research;

(VI) comply with the requirements of the Institute for making the information available to the public under paragraph (8); and

(VII) comply with other terms and conditions determined necessary by the Institute to carry out the research agenda adopted under paragraph (2).

(iii) Coverage of copayments or coinsurance. A contract entered into under this subparagraph may allow for the coverage of copayments or coinsurance, or allow for other appropriate measures, to the extent that such coverage or other measures are necessary to preserve the validity of a research project, such as in the case where the research project must be blinded.

(iv) Subsequent use of the data. The Institute shall not allow the subsequent use of data from original research in work-for-hire contracts with individuals, entities, or instrumentalities that have a financial interest in the results, unless approved under a data use agreement with the Institute.

(C) Review and update of evidence. The Institute shall review and update evidence on a periodic basis as appropriate.

(D) Taking into account potential differences. Research shall be designed, as appropriate, to take into account the potential for differences in the effectiveness of health care treatments, services, and items as used with various subpopulations, such as racial and ethnic minorities, women, age, and groups of individuals with different comorbidities, genetic and molecular sub-types, or quality of life preferences and include members of such subpopulations as subjects in the research as feasible and appropriate.

(E) Differences in treatment modalities. Research shall be designed, as appropriate, to take into account different characteristics of treatment modalities that may affect research outcomes, such as the phase of the treatment modality in the innovation cycle and the impact of the skill of the operator of the treatment modality.

(3) Data collection. (A) In general. The Secretary shall, with appropriate safeguards for privacy, make available to the Institute such data collected by the Centers for Medicare & Medicaid Services under the programs under titles XVIII, XIX, and XXI [42 USCS §§ 1395 et seq., 1396 et seq., and 1397aa et seq.], as well as provide access to the data networks developed under section 937(f) of the Public Health Service Act [42 USCS § 299b-37(f)], as the Institute and its contractors may require to carry out this section. The Institute may also request and obtain data from Federal, State, or private entities, including data from clinical databases and registries.

(B) Use of data. The Institute shall only use data provided to the Institute under subparagraph (A) in accordance with laws and regulations governing the release and use of such data, including applicable confidentiality and privacy standards.

(4) Appointing expert advisory panels. (A) Appointment. (i) In general. The Institute may appoint permanent or ad hoc expert advisory panels as determined appropriate to assist in identifying research priorities and establishing the research project agenda under paragraph (1) and for other purposes.

(ii) Expert advisory panels for clinical trials. The Institute shall appoint expert advisory panels in carrying out randomized clinical trials under the research project agenda under paragraph (2)(A)(ii). Such expert advisory panels shall advise the Institute and the agency, instrumentality, or entity conducting the research on the research question involved and the research design or protocol, including important patient subgroups and other parameters of the research. Such panels shall be available as a resource for technical questions that may arise during the conduct of such research.

(iii) Expert advisory panel for rare disease. In the case of a research study for rare disease, the Institute shall appoint an expert advisory panel for purposes of assisting in the design of the research study and determining the relative value and feasibility of conducting the research study.

(B) Composition. An expert advisory panel appointed under subparagraph (A) shall include representatives of practicing and research clinicians, patients, and experts in scientific and health services research, health services delivery, and evidence-based medicine who have experience in the relevant topic, and as appropriate, experts in integrative health and primary prevention strategies. The Institute may include a technical expert of each manufacturer or each medical technology that is included under the relevant topic, project, or category for which the panel is established.

(5) Supporting patient and consumer representatives. The Institute shall provide support and resources to help patient and consumer representatives effectively participate on the Board and expert advisory panels appointed by the Institute under paragraph (4).

(6) Establishing methodology committee. (A) In general. The Institute shall establish a standing methodology committee to carry out the functions described in subparagraph (C).

(B) Appointment and composition. The methodology committee established under subparagraph (A) shall be composed of not more than 15 members appointed by the Comptroller General of the United States. Members appointed to the methodology committee shall be experts in their scientific field, such as health services research, clinical research, comparative clinical effectiveness research, biostatistics, genomics, and research methodologies. Stakeholders with such expertise may be appointed to the methodology committee. In addition to the members appointed under the first sentence, the Directors of the National Institutes of Health and the Agency for Healthcare Research and Quality (or their designees) shall each be included as members of the methodology committee.

(C) Functions. Subject to subparagraph (D), the methodology committee shall work to develop and improve the science and methods of comparative clinical effectiveness research by, not later than 18 months after the establishment of the Institute, directly or through subcontract, developing and periodically updating the following:

(i) Methodological standards for research. Such methodological standards shall provide specific criteria for internal validity, generalizability, feasibility, and timeliness of research and for health outcomes measures, risk adjustment, and other relevant aspects of research and assessment with respect to the design of research. Any methodological standards developed and updated under this subclause shall be scientifically based and include methods by which new information, data, or advances in technology are considered and incorporated into ongoing research projects by the Institute, as appropriate. The process for developing and updating such standards shall include input from relevant experts, stakeholders, and decisionmakers, and shall provide opportunities for public comment. Such standards shall also include methods by which patient subpopulations can be accounted for and evaluated in different types of research. As appropriate, such standards shall build on existing work on methodological standards for defined categories of health interventions and for each of the major categories of comparative clinical effectiveness research methods (determined as of the date of enactment of the Patient Protection and Affordable Care Act [enacted March 23, 2010]).

(ii) A translation table that is designed to provide guidance and act as a reference for the Board to determine research methods that are most likely to address each specific research question.

(D) Consultation and conduct of examinations. The methodology committee may consult and contract with the Institute of Medicine of the National Academies and academic, nonprofit, or other private and governmental entities with relevant expertise to carry out activities described in subparagraph (C) and may consult with relevant stakeholders to carry out such activities.

(E) Reports. The methodology committee shall submit reports to the Board on the committee's performance of the functions described in subparagraph (C). Reports shall contain recommendations for the Institute to adopt methodological standards developed and updated by the methodology committee as well as other actions deemed necessary to comply with such methodological standards.

(7) Providing for a peer-review process for primary research. (A) In general. The Institute shall ensure that there is a process for peer review of primary research described in subparagraph (A)(ii) of paragraph (2) that is conducted under such paragraph. Under such process—

(i) evidence from such primary research shall be reviewed to assess scientific integrity and adherence to methodological standards adopted under paragraph (9); and

(ii) a list of the names of individuals contributing to any peer-review process during the preceding year or years shall be made public and included in annual reports in accordance with paragraph (10)(D).

(B) Composition. Such peer-review process shall be designed in a manner so as to avoid bias and conflicts of interest on the part of the reviewers and shall be composed of experts in the scientific field relevant to the research under review.

(C) Use of existing processes. (i) Processes of another entity. In the case where the Institute enters into a contract or other agreement with another entity for the conduct or management of research under this section, the Institute may utilize the peer-review process of such entity if such process meets the requirements under subparagraphs (A) and (B).

(ii) Processes of appropriate medical journals. The Institute may utilize the peer-review process of appropriate medical journals if such process meets the requirements under subparagraphs (A) and (B).

(8) Release of research findings. (A) In general. The Institute shall, not later than 90 days after the conduct or receipt of research findings under this part, make such research findings available to clinicians, patients, and the general public. The Institute shall ensure that the research findings—

(i) convey the findings of research in a manner that is comprehensible and useful to patients and providers in making health care decisions;

(ii) fully convey findings and discuss considerations specific to certain subpopulations, risk factors, and comorbidities, as appropriate;

(iii) include limitations of the research and what further research may be needed as appropriate;

(iv) do not include practice guidelines, coverage recommendations, payment, or policy recommendations; and

(v) not include any data which would violate the privacy of research participants or any confidentiality agreements made with respect to the use of data under this section.

(B) Definition of research findings. In this paragraph, the term "research findings" means the results of a study or assessment.

(9) Adoption. Subject to subsection (h)(1), the Institute shall adopt the national priorities identified under paragraph (1)(A), the research project agenda established under paragraph (1)(B), the methodological standards developed and updated by the methodology committee under paragraph (6)(C)(i), and any peer-review process provided under paragraph (7) by majority vote. In the case where the Institute does not adopt such processes in accordance with the preceding sentence, the processes shall be referred to the appropriate staff or entity within the Institute (or, in the case of the methodological standards, the methodology committee) for further review.

(10) Annual reports. The Institute shall submit an annual report to Congress and the President, and shall make the annual report available to the public. Such report shall contain—

(A) a description of the activities conducted under this section, research priorities identified under paragraph (1)(A) and methodological standards developed and updated by the methodology committee under paragraph (6)(C)(i) that are adopted under paragraph (9) during the preceding year;

(B) the research project agenda and budget of the Institute for the following year;

(C) any administrative activities conducted by the Institute during the preceding year;

(D) the names of individuals contributing to any peer-review process under paragraph (7), without identifying them with a particular research project; and

(E) any other relevant information (including information on the membership of the Board, expert advisory panels, methodology committee, and the executive staff of the Institute, any conflicts of interest with respect to these individuals, and any bylaws adopted by the Board during the preceding year).

(e) Administration. (1) In general. Subject to paragraph (2), the Board shall carry out the duties of the Institute.

(2) Nondelegable duties. The activities described in subsections (d)(1) and (d)(9) are nondelegable.

(f) Board of Governors. (1) In general. The Institute shall have a Board of Governors, which shall consist of the following members:

(A) The Director of Agency for Healthcare Research and Quality (or the Director's designee).

(B) The Director of the National Institutes of Health (or the Director's designee).

(C) Seventeen members appointed, not later than 6 months after the date of enactment of this section [enacted March 23, 2010], by the Comptroller General of the United States as follows:

(i) 3 members representing patients and health care consumers.

(ii) 7 members representing physicians and

providers, including 4 members representing physicians (at least 1 of whom is a surgeon), 1 nurse, 1 State-licensed integrative health care practitioner, and 1 representative of a hospital.

(iii) 3 members representing private payers, of whom at least 1 member shall represent health insurance issuers and at least 1 member shall represent employers who self-insure employee benefits.

(iv) 3 members representing pharmaceutical, device, and diagnostic manufacturers or developers.

(v) 1 member representing quality improvement or independent health service researchers.

(vi) 2 members representing the Federal Government or the States, including at least 1 member representing a Federal health program or agency.

(2) Qualifications. The Board shall represent a broad range of perspectives and collectively have scientific expertise in clinical health sciences research, including epidemiology, decisions sciences, health economics, and statistics. In appointing the Board, the Comptroller General of the United States shall consider and disclose any conflicts of interest in accordance with subsection (h)(4)(B). Members of the Board shall be recused from relevant Institute activities in the case where the member (or an immediate family member of such member) has a real conflict of interest directly related to the research project or the matter that could affect or be affected by such participation.

(3) Terms; vacancies. A member of the Board shall be appointed for a term of 6 years, except with respect to the members first appointed, whose terms of appointment shall be staggered evenly over 2-year increments. No individual shall be appointed to the Board for more than 2 terms. Vacancies shall be filled in the same manner as the original appointment was made.

(4) Chairperson and Vice-Chairperson. The Comptroller General of the United States shall designate a Chairperson and Vice Chairperson of the Board from among the members of the Board. Such members shall serve as Chairperson or Vice Chairperson for a period of 3 years.

(5) Compensation. Each member of the Board who is not an officer or employee of the Federal Government shall be entitled to compensation (equivalent to the rate provided for level IV of the Executive Schedule under section 5315 of title 5, United States Code) and expenses incurred while performing the duties of the Board. An officer or employee of the Federal government who is a member of the Board shall be exempt from compensation.

(6) Director and staff; experts and consultants. The Board may employ and fix the compensation of an Executive Director and such other personnel as may be necessary to carry out the duties of the Institute and may seek such assistance and support of, or contract with, experts and consultants that may be necessary for the performance of the duties of the Institute.

(7) Meetings and hearings. The Board shall meet and hold hearings at the call of the Chairperson or a majority of its members. Meetings not solely concerning matters of personnel shall be advertised at least 7 days in advance and open to the public. A majority of the Board members shall constitute a quorum, but a lesser number of members may meet and hold hearings.

(g) Financial and governmental oversight. (1) Contract for audit. The Institute shall provide for the conduct of financial audits of the Institute on an annual basis by a private entity with expertise in conducting financial audits.

(2) Review and annual reports. (A) Review. The Comptroller General of the United States shall review the following:

(i) Not less frequently than on an annual basis, the financial audits conducted under paragraph (1).

(ii) Not less frequently than every 5 years, the processes established by the Institute, including the research priorities and the conduct of research projects, in order to determine whether information produced by such research projects is objective and credible, is produced in a manner consistent with the requirements under this section, and is developed through a transparent process.

(iii) Not less frequently than every 5 years, the dissemination and training activities and data networks established under section 937 of the Public Health Service Act [42 USCS § 299b-37], including the methods and products used to disseminate research, the types of training conducted and supported, and the types and functions of the data networks established, in order to determine whether the activities and data are produced in a manner consistent with the requirements under such section.

(iv) Not less frequently than every 5 years, the overall effectiveness of activities conducted under this section and the dissemination, training, and capacity building activities conducted under section 937 of the Public Health Service Act [42 USCS § 299b-37]. Such review shall include an analysis of the extent to which research findings are used by health care decision-makers, the effect of the dissemination of such findings on reducing practice variation and disparities in health care, and the effect of the research conducted and disseminated on innovation and the health care economy of the United States.

(v) Not later than 8 years after the date of enactment of this section [enacted March 23, 2010], the adequacy and use of the funding for the Institute and the activities conducted under section 937 of the Public Health Service Act [42 USCS § 299b-37], including a determination as to whether, based on the utilization of research findings by public and private payers, funding sources for the Patient-Centered Outcomes Research Trust Fund under section 9511 of the Internal Revenue Code of 1986 [26 USCS § 9511] are appropriate and whether such sources of funding should be continued or adjusted.

(B) Annual reports. Not later than April 1 of each year, the Comptroller General of the United States shall submit to Congress a report containing the results of the review conducted under subparagraph (A) with respect to the preceding year (or years, if applicable), together with recommendations for such legislation and administrative action as the Comptroller General determines appropriate.

(h) Ensuring transparency, credibility, and access. The Institute shall establish procedures to ensure that the following requirements for ensuring transparency, credibility, and access are met:

(1) Public comment periods. The Institute shall provide for a public comment period of not less than 45 days and not more than 60 days prior to the adoption under subsection (d)(9) of the national priorities identified under subsection (d)(1)(A), the research project agenda established under subsection (d)(1)(B), the methodological standards developed and updated by the methodology committee under subsection (d)(6)(C)(i), and the peer-review process provided under paragraph (7), and after the release of draft findings with respect to systematic reviews of existing research and evidence.

(2) Additional forums. The Institute shall support forums to increase public awareness and obtain and incorporate public input and feedback through media (such as an Internet website) on research priorities, research findings, and other duties, activities, or processes the Institute determines appropriate.

(3) Public availability. The Institute shall make available to the public and disclose through the official public Internet website of the Institute the following:

(A) Information contained in research findings as specified in subsection (d)(9).

(B) The process and methods for the conduct of research, including the identity of the entity and the investigators conducing such research and any conflicts of interests of such parties, any direct or indirect links the entity has to industry, and research protocols, including measures taken, methods of research and analysis, research results, and such other information the Institute determines appropriate) concurrent with the release of research findings.

(C) Notice of public comment periods under paragraph (1), including deadlines for public comments.

(D) Subsequent comments received during each of the public comment periods.

(E) In accordance with applicable laws and processes and as the Institute determines appropriate, proceedings of the Institute.

(4) Disclosure of conflicts of interest. (A) In general. A conflict of interest shall be disclosed in the following manner:

(i) By the Institute in appointing members to an expert advisory panel under subsection (d)(4), in selecting individuals to contribute to any peer-review process under subsection (d)(7), and for employment as executive staff of the Institute.

(ii) By the Comptroller General in appointing members of the methodology committee under subsection (d)(6);

(iii) By the Institute in the annual report under subsection (d)(10), except that, in the case of individuals contributing to any such peer review process, such description shall be in a manner such that those individuals cannot be identified with a particular research project.

(B) Manner of disclosure. Conflicts of interest shall be disclosed as described in subparagraph (A) as soon as practicable on the Internet web site of the Institute and of the Government Accountability Office. The information disclosed under the preceding sentence shall include the type, nature, and magnitude of the interests of the individual involved, except to the extent that the individual recuses himself or herself from participating in the consideration of or any other activity with respect to the study as to which the potential conflict exists.

(i) Rules. The Institute, its Board or staff, shall be prohibited from accepting gifts, bequeaths, or donations of services or property. In addition, the Institute shall be prohibited from establishing a corporation or generating revenues from activities other than as provided under this section.

(j) Rules of construction. (1) Coverage. Nothing in this section shall be construed—

(A) to permit the Institute to mandate coverage, reimbursement, or other policies for any public or private payer; or

(B) as preventing the Secretary from covering the routine costs of clinical care received by an individual entitled to, or enrolled for, benefits under title XVIII, XIX, or XXI [42 USCS §§ 1395 et seq., 1396 et seq., or 1397aa et seq.] in the case where such individual is participating in a clinical trial and such costs would otherwise be covered under such title with respect to the beneficiary.

(Aug. 14, 1935, ch 531, Title XI, Part D, § 1181, as added and amended March 23, 2010, P. L. 111-148, Title VI, Subtitle D, § 6301(a), Title X, Subtitle F, § 10602, 124 Stat. 727, 1005.)

§ 1320e-1. Limitations on certain uses of comparative clinical effectiveness research

(a) The Secretary may only use evidence and findings from research conducted under section 1181 [42 USCS § 1320e] to make a determination regarding coverage under title XVIII [42 USCS §§ 1395 et seq.] if such use is through an iterative and transparent process which includes public comment and considers the effect on subpopulations.

(b) Nothing in section 1181 [42 USCS § 1320e] shall be construed as—

(1) superceding or modifying the coverage of items or services under title XVIII [42 USCS §§ 1395 et seq.] that the Secretary determines are reasonable and necessary under section 1862(l)(1) [42 USCS § 1395y(l)(1)]; or

(2) authorizing the Secretary to deny coverage of items or services under such title solely on the basis of comparative clinical effectiveness research.

(c)(1) The Secretary shall not use evidence or findings from comparative clinical effectiveness research conducted under section 1181 [42 USCS § 1320e] in determining coverage, reimbursement, or incentive programs under title XVIII [42 USCS §§ 1395 et seq.] in a manner that treats extending the life of an elderly, disabled, or terminally ill individual as of lower value than extending the life of an individual who is younger, nondisabled, or not terminally ill.

(2) Paragraph (1) shall not be construed as preventing the Secretary from using evidence or findings from such comparative clinical effectiveness research in determining coverage, reimbursement, or incentive programs under title XVIII [42 USCS §§ 1395 et seq.] based upon a comparison of the difference in the effectiveness of alternative treatments in extending an individual's life due to the individual's age, disability, or terminal illness.

(d)(1) The Secretary shall not use evidence or findings from comparative clinical effectiveness research conducted under section 1181 [42 USCS § 1320e] in determining coverage, reimbursement, or incentive programs under title XVIII [42 USCS §§ 1395 et seq.] in a manner that precludes, or with the intent to discourage, an individual from choosing a health care treatment based on how the individual values the tradeoff between extending the length of their life and the risk of disability.

(2)(A) Paragraph (1) shall not be construed to—

(i) limit the application of differential copayments under title XVIII [42 USCS §§ 1395 et seq.] based on factors such as cost or type of service; or

(ii) prevent the Secretary from using evidence or findings from such comparative clinical effectiveness research in determining coverage, reimbursement, or incentive programs under such title based upon a comparison of the difference in the effectiveness of alternative health care treatments in extending an individual's life due to that individual's age, disability, or terminal illness.

(3) Nothing in the provisions of, or amendments made by the Patient Protection and Affordable Care Act, shall be construed to limit comparative clinical effectiveness research or any other research, evaluation, or dissemination of information concerning the likelihood that a health care treatment will result in disability.

(e) The Patient-Centered Outcomes Research Institute established under section 1181(b)(1) [42 USCS § 1320e(b)(1)] shall not develop or employ a dollars-per-quality adjusted life year (or similar measure that discounts the value of a life because of an individual's disability) as a threshold to establish what type of health care is cost effective or recommended. The Secretary shall not utilize such an adjusted life year (or such a similar measure) as a threshold to determine coverage, reimbursement, or incentive programs under title XVIII [42 USCS §§ 1395 et seq.].

(Aug. 14, 1935, ch 531, Title XI, Part D, § 1182, as added March 23, 2010, P. L. 111-148, Title VI, Subtitle D, § 6301(c), 124 Stat. 740.)

§ 1320e-2. Trust Fund transfers to Patient-Centered Outcomes Research Trust

Fund

(a) In general. The Secretary shall provide for the transfer, from the Federal Hospital Insurance Trust Fund under section 1817 [42 USCS § 1395i] and the Federal Supplementary Medical Insurance Trust Fund under section 1841 [42 USCS § 1395t], in proportion (as estimated by the Secretary) to the total expenditures during such fiscal year that are made under title XVIII [42 USCS §§ 1395 et seq.] from the respective trust fund, to the Patient-Centered Outcomes Research Trust Fund (referred to in this section as the "PCORTF") under section 9511 of the Internal Revenue Code of 1986 [26 USCS § 9511], of the following:

(1) For fiscal year 2013, an amount equal to $1 multiplied by the average number of individuals entitled to benefits under part A [42 USCS §§ 1395c et seq.], or enrolled under part B [42 USCS §§ 1395j et seq.], of title XVIII during such fiscal year.

(2) For each of fiscal years 2014, 2015, 2016, 2017, 2018, and 2019, an amount equal to $2 multiplied by the average number of individuals entitled to benefits under part A [42 USCS §§ 1395c et seq.], or enrolled under part B [42 USCS §§ 1395j et seq.], of title XVIII during such fiscal year.

(b) Adjustments for increases in health care spending. In the case of any fiscal year beginning after September 30, 2014, the dollar amount in effect under subsection (a)(2) for such fiscal year shall be equal to the sum of such dollar amount for the previous fiscal year (determined after the application of this subsection), plus an amount equal to the product of—

(1) such dollar amount for the previous fiscal year, multiplied by

(2) the percentage increase in the projected per capita amount of National Health Expenditures, as most recently published by the Secretary before the beginning of the fiscal year.

(Aug. 14, 1935, ch 531, Title XI, Part D, § 1183, as added March 23, 2010, P. L. 111-148, Title VI, Subtitle D, § 6301(d), 124 Stat. 741.)

TITLE XVIII. HEALTH INSURANCE FOR THE AGED AND DISABLED

§ 1395. Prohibition against any Federal interference

Nothing in this title [42 USCS §§ 1395 et seq.] shall be construed to authorize any Federal officer or employee to exercise any supervision or control over the practice of medicine or the manner in which medical services are provided, or over the selection, tenure, or compensation of any officer or employee of any institution, agency, or person providing health services; or to exercise any supervision or control over the administration or operation of any such institution, agency, or person.

(Aug. 14, 1935, ch 531, Title XVIII, § 1801, as added July 30, 1965, P. L. 89-97, Title I, Part 1, § 102(a), 79 Stat. 291.)

HISTORY; ANCILLARY LAWS AND DIRECTIVES

Other provisions:

Protecting and improving guaranteed Medicare benefits. Act March 23, 2010, P. L. 111-148, Title III, Subtitle G, § 3601, 124 Stat. 538, provides:

"(a) Protecting guaranteed Medicare benefits. Nothing in the provisions of, or amendments made by, this Act [for full classification, consult USCS Tables volumes] shall result in a reduction of guaranteed benefits under title XVIII of the Social Security Act [42 USCS §§ 1395 et seq.].

"(b) Ensuring that Medicare savings benefit the Medicare program and Medicare beneficiaries. Savings generated for the Medicare program under title XVIII of the Social Security Act [42 USCS §§ 1395 et seq.] under the provisions of, and amendments made by, this Act [for full classification, consult USCS Tables volumes shall extend the solvency of the Medicare trust funds, reduce Medicare premiums and other cost-sharing for beneficiaries, and improve or expand guaranteed Medicare benefits and protect access to Medicare providers.".

§ 1395b-1. Incentives for economy while maintaining or improving quality in the provision of health services

(a) Grants and contracts to develop and engage in experiments and demonstration projects. (1) The Secretary of Health, Education, and Welfare [Secretary of Health and Human Services] is authorized, either directly or through grants to public or private agencies, institutions, and organizations or contracts with public or private agencies, institutions, and organizations, to develop and engage in experiments and demonstration projects for the following purposes:

(A) to determine whether, and if so which, changes in methods of payment or reimbursement (other than those dealt with in section 222(a) of the Social Security Amendments of 1972 [note to this section]) for health care and services under health programs established by the Social Security Act, including a change to methods based on negotiated rates, would have the effect of increasing the efficiency and economy of health services under such programs through the creation of additional incentives to these ends without adversely affecting the quality of such services;

(B) to determine whether payments for services other than those for which payment may be made under such programs (and which are incidental to services for which payment may be made under such programs) would, in the judgment of the Secretary, result in more economical provision and more effective utilization of services for which payment may be made under such program, where such services are furnished by organizations and institutions which have the capability of providing—

(i) comprehensive health care services,

(ii) mental health care services (as defined by section 401(c) of the Mental Retardation Facilities and Community Health Centers Construction Act of 1963),

(iii) ambulatory health care services (including surgical services provided on an outpatient basis), or

(iv) institutional services which may substitute, at lower cost, for hospital care;

(C) to determine whether the rates of payment or reimbursement for health care services, approved by a State for purposes of the administration of one or more of its laws, when utilized to determine the amount to be paid for services furnished in such State under the health programs established by the Social Security Act, would have the effect of reducing the costs of such programs without adversely affecting the quality of such services;

(D) to determine whether payments under such programs based on a single combined rate of reimbursement or charge for the teaching activities and patient care which residents, interns, and supervising physicians render in connection with a graduate medical education program in a patient facility would result in more equitable and economical patient care arrangements without adversely affecting the quality of such care;

(E) to determine whether coverage of intermediate care facility services and homemaker services would provide suitable alternatives to posthospital benefits presently provided under title XVIII of the Social Security Act [42 USCS §§ 1395 et seq.]; such experiment and demonstration projects may include:

(i) counting each day of care in an intermediate care facility as one day of care in a skilled nursing facility, if such care was for a condition for which the individual was hospitalized,

(ii) covering the services of homemakers for a maximum of 21 days, if institutional services are not medically appropriate,

(iii) determining whether such coverage would reduce long-range costs by reducing the lengths of stay in hospitals and skilled nursing facilities, and

(iv) establishing alternative eligibility requirements and determining the probable cost of applying each alternative, if the project suggests that such extension of coverage would be desirable;

(F) to determine whether, and if so which type of, fixed price or performance incentive contract would have the effect of inducing to the greatest degree effective, efficient, and economical performance of agencies and organizations making payment under agreements or contracts with the Secretary for health care and services under health programs established by the Social Security Act;

(G) to determine under what circumstances payment for services would be appropriate and the most appropriate, equitable, and noninflationary methods and amounts of reimbursement under health care programs established by the Social Security Act for services, which are performed independently by an assistant to a physician, including a nurse practitioner (whether or not performed in the office of or at a place at which such physician is physically present), and—

(i) which such assistant is legally authorized to perform by the State or political subdivision wherein such services are performed, and

(ii) for which such physician assumes full legal and ethical responsibility as to the necessity, propriety, and quality thereof;

(H) to establish an experimental program to provide day-care services, which consist of such personal care, supervision, and services as the Secretary shall by regulation prescribe, for individuals eligible to enroll in the supplemental medical insurance program established under part B of title XVIII and title XIX of the Social Security Act [42 USCS §§ 1395j et seq. and 1397 et seq.], in day-care centers which meet such standards as the Secretary shall by regulation establish;

(I) to determine whether the services of clinical psychologists may be made more generally available to persons eligible for services under titles XVIII and XIX of this Act [42 USCS §§ 1395 et seq. and 1397 et seq.] in a manner consistent with quality of care and equitable and efficient administration;

(J) to develop or demonstrate improved methods for the investigation and prosecution of fraud in the provision of care or services under the health programs established by the Social Security Act; and

(K) to determine whether the use of competitive bidding in the awarding of contracts, or the use of other methods of reimbursement, under part B of title XI [42 USCS §§ 1320c et seq.] would be efficient and effective methods of furthering the purposes of that part [42 USCS §§ 1320c et seq.]

For purposes of this subsection, "health programs established by the Social Security Act" means the program established by title XVIII of such Act [42 USCS §§ 1395 et seq.] and a program established by a plan of a State approved under title XIX of such Act [42 USCS §§ 1396 et seq.].

(2) Grants, payments under contracts, and other expenditures made for experiments and demonstration projects under paragraph (1) shall be made in appropriate part from the Federal Hospital Insurance Trust Fund (established by section 1817 of the Social Security Act [42 USCS § 1395i]) and the Federal Supplementary Medical Insurance Trust Fund (established by section 1841 of the Social Security Act [42 USCS § 1395t]) and from funds appropriated under title XIX of such Act [42 USCS §§ 1396 et seq.]. Grants and payments under contracts may be made either in advance or by way of reimbursement, as may be determined by the Secretary, and shall be made in such installments and on such conditions as the Secretary finds necessary to carry out the purpose of this section. With respect to any such grant, payment, or other expenditure, the amount to be paid from each of such trust funds (and from funds appropriated under such title XIX [42 USCS §§ 1396 et seq.]) shall be determined by the Secretary, giving due regard to the purposes of the experiment or project involved.

(b) Waiver of certain payment or reimbursement requirements; advice and recommendations of specialists preceding experiments and demonstration projects. In the case of any experiment or demonstration project under subsection (a), the Secretary may waive compliance with the requirements of titles XVIII and XIX of the Social Security Act [42 USCS §§ 1395 et seq. and 1396 et seq.] insofar as such requirements relate to reimbursement or payment on the basis of reasonable cost, or (in the case of physicians) on the basis of reasonable charge, or to reimbursement or payment only for such services or items as may be specified in the experiment [or demonstration project]; and costs incurred in such experiment or demonstration project in excess of the costs which would otherwise be reimbursed or paid under such titles may be reimbursed or paid to the extent that such waiver applies to them (with such excess being borne by the Secretary). No experiment or demonstration project shall be engaged in or developed under subsection (a) until the Secretary obtains the advice and recommendations of specialists who are competent to evaluate the proposed experiment or demonstration project as to the soundness of its objectives, the possibilities of securing productive results, the adequacy of resources to conduct the proposed experiment or demonstration project, and its relationship to other similar experiments and projects already completed or in process.

(Jan. 2, 1968, P. L. 90-248, Title IV, § 402(a), (b), 81 Stat. 930, 931; Oct. 30, 1972, P. L. 92-603, Title II, §§ 222(b), 278(b)(2), 86 Stat. 1391, 1453; Oct. 25, 1977, P. L. 95-142, § 17(d), 91 Stat. 1202; Aug. 13, 1981, P. L. 97-35, Title XXI, Subtitle D, § 2193(d), 95 Stat. 828; Sept. 3, 1982, P. L. 97-248, Title I, Subtitle C, § 147, 96 Stat. 394; July 18, 1984, P. L. 98-369, Division B, Title III, Subtitle A, Part II, § 2331(b), 98 Stat. 1088.)

HISTORY; ANCILLARY LAWS AND DIRECTIVES

Other provisions:

Community-Based Care Transitions Program. Act March 23, 2010, P. L. 111-148, Title III, Subtitle A, Part III, § 3026, 124 Stat. 413, provides:

"(a) In general. The Secretary shall establish a Community-Based Care Transitions Program under which the Secretary provides funding to eligible entities that furnish improved care transition services to high-risk Medicare beneficiaries.

"(b) Definitions. In this section:

"(1) Eligible entity. The term 'eligible entity' means the following:

"(A) A subsection (d) hospital (as defined in section 1886(d)(1)(B) of the Social Security Act (42 U.S.C. 1395ww(d)(1)(B))) identified by the Secretary as having a high readmission rate, such as under section 1886(q) of the Social Security Act [42 USCS § 1395ww(q)], as added by section 3025.

"(B) An appropriate community-based organization that provides care transition services under this section across a continuum of care through arrangements with subsection (d) hospitals (as so defined) to furnish the services described in subsection (c)(2)(B)(i) and whose governing body includes sufficient representation of multiple health care stakeholders (including consumers).

"(2) High-risk Medicare beneficiary. The term 'high-risk Medicare beneficiary' means a Medicare beneficiary who has attained a minimum hierarchical condition category score, as determined by the Secretary, based on a diagnosis of multiple chronic conditions or other risk factors associated with a hospital readmission or substandard transition into post-hospitalization care, which may include 1 or more of the following:

"(A) Cognitive impairment.

"(B) Depression.

"(C) A history of multiple readmissions.

"(D) Any other chronic disease or risk factor as determined by the Secretary.

"(3) Medicare beneficiary. The term 'Medicare beneficiary' means an individual who is entitled to benefits under part A of title XVIII of the Social Security Act (42 U.S.C. 1395 et seq.) [42 USCS §§ 1395c et seq.] and enrolled under part B of such title [42 USCS §§ 1395j et seq.], but not enrolled under part C of such title [42 USCS §§ 1395w-21 et seq.].

"(4) Program. The term 'program' means the program conducted under this section.

"(5) Readmission. The term 'readmission' has the meaning given such term in section 1886(q)(5)(E) of the Social Security Act [42 USCS § 1395ww(q)(5)(E)], as added by section 3025.

"(6) Secretary. The term 'Secretary' means the Secretary of Health and Human Services.

"(c) Requirements. (1) Duration. (A) In general. The program shall be conducted for a 5-year period, beginning January 1, 2011.

"(B) Expansion. The Secretary may expand the duration and the scope of the program, to the extent determined appropriate by the Secretary, if the Secretary determines (and the Chief Actuary of the Centers for Medicare & Medicaid Services, with respect to spending under this title, certifies) that such expansion would reduce spending under this title without reducing quality.

"(2) Application; participation. (A) In general. (i) Application. An eligible entity seeking to participate in the program shall submit an application to the Secretary at such time, in such manner, and containing such information as the Secretary may require.

"(ii) Partnership. If an eligible entity is a hospital, such hospital shall enter into a partnership with a community-based organization to participate in the program.

"(B) Intervention proposal. Subject to subparagraph (C), an application submitted under subparagraph (A)(i) shall include a detailed proposal for at least 1 care transition intervention, which may include the following:

"(i) Initiating care transition services for a high-risk Medicare beneficiary not later than 24 hours prior to the discharge of the beneficiary from the eligible entity.

"(ii) Arranging timely post-discharge follow-up services to the high-risk Medicare beneficiary to provide the beneficiary (and, as appropriate, the primary caregiver of the beneficiary) with information regarding responding to symptoms that may indicate additional health problems or a deteriorating condition.

"(iii) Providing the high-risk Medicare beneficiary (and, as appropriate, the primary caregiver of the beneficiary) with assistance to ensure productive and timely interactions between patients and post-acute and outpatient providers.

"(iv) Assessing and actively engaging with a high-risk Medicare beneficiary (and, as appropriate, the primary caregiver of the beneficiary) through the provision of self-management support and relevant information that is specific to the beneficiary's condition.

"(v) Conducting comprehensive medication review and management (including, if appropriate, counseling and self-management support).

"(C) Limitation. A care transition intervention proposed under subparagraph (B) may not include payment for services required under the discharge planning process described in section 1861(ee) of the Social Security Act (42 U.S.C. 1395x(ee)).

"(3) Selection. In selecting eligible entities to participate in the program, the Secretary shall give priority to eligible entities that—

"(A) participate in a program administered by the Administration on Aging to provide concurrent care transitions interventions with multiple hospitals and practitioners; or

"(B) provide services to medically underserved populations, small communities, and rural areas.

"(d) Implementation. Notwithstanding any other provision of law, the Secretary may implement the provisions of this section by program instruction or otherwise.

"(e) Waiver authority. The Secretary may waive such requirements of titles XI and XVIII of the Social Security Act [42 USCS §§ 1301 et seq. and 1395 et seq.] as may be necessary to carry out the program.

"(f) Funding. For purposes of carrying out this section, the Secretary of Health and Human Services shall provide for the transfer, from the Federal Hospital Insurance Trust Fund under section 1817 of the Social Security Act (42 U.S.C. 1395i) and the Federal Supplementary Medical Insurance Trust Fund under section 1841 of such Act (42 U.S.C. 1395t), in such proportion as the Secretary determines appropriate, of $500,000,000, to the Centers for Medicare & Medicaid Services Program Management Account for the period of fiscal years 2011 through 2015. Amounts transferred under the preceding sentence shall remain available until expended.".

Pilot testing pay-for-performance programs for certain Medicare providers. Act March 23, 2010, P. L. 111-148, Title X, Subtitle C, § 10326, 124 Stat. 961, provides:

"(a) In general. Not later than January 1, 2016, the Secretary of Health and Human Services (in this section referred to as the 'Secretary') shall, for each provider described in subsection (b), conduct a separate pilot program under title XVIII of the Social Security Act [42 USCS §§ 1395 et seq.] to test the implementation of a value-based purchasing program for payments under such title for the provider.

"(b) Providers described. The providers described in this paragraph are the following:

"(1) Psychiatric hospitals (as described in clause (i) of section 1886(d)(1)(B) of such Act (42 U.S.C. 1395ww(d)(1)(B))) and psychiatric units (as described in the matter following clause (v) of such section).

"(2) Long-term care hospitals (as described in clause (iv) of such section).

"(3) Rehabilitation hospitals (as described in clause (ii) of such section).

"(4) PPS-exempt cancer hospitals (as described in clause (v) of such section).

"(5) Hospice programs (as defined in section 1861(dd)(2) of such Act (42 U.S.C. 1395x(dd)(2))).

"(c) Waiver authority. The Secretary may waive such requirements of titles XI and XVIII of the Social Security Act [42 USCS §§ 1301 et seq. and 1395 et seq.] as may be necessary solely for purposes of carrying out the pilot programs under this section.

"(d) No additional program expenditures. Payments under this section under the separate pilot program for value based purchasing (as described in subsection (a)) for each provider type described in paragraphs (1) through (5) of subsection (b) for applicable items and services under title XVIII of the Social Security Act [42 USCS §§ 1395 et seq.] for a year shall be established in a manner that does not result in spending more under each such value based purchasing program for such year than would otherwise be expended for such provider type for such year if the pilot program were not implemented, as estimated by the Secretary.

"(e) Expansion of pilot program. The Secretary

may, at any point after January 1, 2018, expand the duration and scope of a pilot program conducted under this subsection, to the extent determined appropriate by the Secretary, if—

"(1) the Secretary determines that such expansion is expected to—

"(A) reduce spending under title XVIII of the Social Security Act [42 USCS §§ 1395 et seq.] without reducing the quality of care; or

"(B) improve the quality of care and reduce spending;

"(2) the Chief Actuary of the Centers for Medicare & Medicaid Services certifies that such expansion would reduce program spending under such title XVIII [42 USCS §§ 1395 et seq.]; and

"(3) the Secretary determines that such expansion would not deny or limit the coverage or provision of benefits under such title XIII [42 USCS §§ 1301 et seq.] for Medicare beneficiaries.".

§ 1395b-3. Health insurance advisory service for medicare beneficiaries

(a) In general. The Secretary of Health and Human Services shall establish a health insurance advisory service program (in this section referred to as the "beneficiary assistance program") to assist medicare-eligible individuals with the receipt of services under the medicare and medicaid programs and other health insurance programs.

(b) Outreach elements. The beneficiary assistance program shall provide assistance—

(1) through operation using local Federal offices that provide information on the medicare program,

(2) using community outreach programs, and

(3) using a toll-free telephone information service.

(c) Assistance provided. The beneficiary assistance program shall provide for information, counseling, and assistance for medicare-eligible individuals with respect to at least the following:

(1) With respect to the medicare program—

(A) eligibility,

(B) benefits (both covered and not covered),

(C) the process of payment for services,

(D) rights and process for appeals of determinations,

(E) other medicare-related entities (such as peer review organizations, fiscal intermediaries, and carriers), and

(F) recent legislative and administrative changes in the medicare program.

(2) With respect to the medicaid program—

(A) eligibility, benefits, and the application process,

(B) linkages between the medicaid and medicare programs, and

(C) referral to appropriate State and local agencies involved in the medicaid program.

(3) With respect to medicare supplemental policies—

(A) the program under section 1882 of the Social Security Act [42 USCS § 1395ss] and standards required under such program,

(B) how to make informed decisions on whether to purchase such policies and on what criteria to use in evaluating different policies,

(C) appropriate Federal, State, and private agencies that provide information and assistance in obtaining benefits under such policies, and

(D) other issues deemed appropriate by the Secretary.

The beneficiary assistance program also shall provide such other services as the Secretary deems appropriate to increase beneficiary understanding of, and confidence in, the medicare program and to improve the relationship between beneficiaries and the program.

(d) Educational material. The Secretary, through the Administrator of the Centers for Medicare & Medicaid Services, shall develop appropriate educational materials and other appropriate techniques to assist employees in carrying out this section.

(e) Notice to beneficiaries. The Secretary shall take such steps as are necessary to assure that medicare-eligible beneficiaries and the general public are made aware of the beneficiary assistance program.

(f) Report. The Secretary shall include, in an annual report transmitted to the Congress, a report on the beneficiary assistance program and on other health insurance informational and counseling services made available to medicare-eligible individuals. The Secretary shall include in the report recommendations for such changes as may be desirable to improve the relationship between the medicare program and medicare-eligible individuals.

(Nov. 5, 1990, P. L. 101-508, Title IV, Subtitle A, Part 4, § 4359, 104 Stat. 1388-137; Dec. 8, 2003, P. L. 108-173, Title IX, § 900(e)(6)(G), 117 Stat. 2374.)

HISTORY; ANCILLARY LAWS AND DIRECTIVES

Other provisions:

Medicare enrollment assistance. Act July 15, 2008, P. L. 110-275, Title I, Subtitle A, Part II, § 119, 122 Stat. 2508; March 23, 2010, P. L. 111-148, Title III, Subtitle D, § 3306, 124 Stat. 470, provides:

"(a) Additional funding for State health insurance assistance programs. (1) Grants. (A) In general. The Secretary of Health and Human Services (in this section referred to as the 'Secretary') shall use amounts made available under subparagraph (B) to make grants to States for State health insurance assistance programs receiving assistance under section 4360 of the Omnibus Budget Reconciliation Act of 1990 [42 USCS § 1395b-4].

"(B) Funding. For purposes of making grants under this subsection, the Secretary shall provide for the transfer, from the Federal Hospital Insurance Trust Fund under section 1817 of the Social Security Act (42 U.S.C. 1395i) and the Federal Supplementary Medical Insurance Trust Fund under section 1841 of such Act (42 U.S.C. 1395t), in the same proportion as the Secretary determines under section 1853(f) of such Act (42 U.S.C. 1395w-23(f)), to the Centers for Medicare & Medicaid Services Program Management Account—

"(i) for fiscal year 2009, of $7,500,000; and

"(ii) for the period of fiscal years 2010 through 2012, of $15,000,000.

"Amounts appropriated under this subparagraph shall remain available until expended.

"(2) Amount of grants. The amount of a grant to a State under this subsection from the total amount made available under paragraph (1) shall be equal to the sum of the amount allocated to the State under paragraph (3)(A) and the amount allocated to the State under subparagraph (3)(B).

"(3) Allocation to States. (A) Allocation based on percentage of low-income beneficiaries. The amount allocated to a State under this subparagraph from ⅔ of the total amount made available under paragraph (1) shall be based on the number of individuals who meet the requirement under subsection (a)(3)(A)(ii) of section 1860D-14 of the Social Security Act (42 U.S.C. 1395w-114) but who have not enrolled to receive a subsidy under such section 1860D-14 [42 USCS § 1395w-114] relative to the total number of individuals who meet the requirement under such subsection (a)(3)(A)(ii) in each State, as estimated by the Secretary.

"(B) Allocation based on percentage of rural beneficiaries. The amount allocated to a State under this subparagraph from ⅓ of the total amount made available under paragraph (1) shall be based on the number of part D eligible individuals (as defined in section 1860D-1(a)(3)(A) of such Act (42 U.S.C. 1395w-101(a)(3)(A))) residing in a rural area relative to the total number of such individuals in each State, as estimated by the Secretary.

"(4) Portion of grant based on percentage of low-income beneficiaries to be used to provide outreach to individuals who may be subsidy eligible individuals or eligible for the Medicare Savings Program. Each grant awarded under this subsection with respect to amounts allocated under paragraph (3)(A) shall be used to provide outreach to individuals who may be subsidy eligible individuals (as defined in section 1860D-14(a)(3)(A) of the Social Security Act (42 U.S.C. 1395w-114(a)(3)(A)) or eligible for the Medicare Savings Program (as defined in subsection (f)).

"(b) Additional funding for area agencies on aging. (1) Grants. (A) In general. The Secretary, acting through the Assistant Secretary for Aging, shall make grants to States for area agencies on aging (as defined in section 102 of the Older Americans Act of 1965 (42 U.S.C. 3002)) and Native American programs carried out under the Older Americans Act of 1965 (42 U.S.C. 3001 et seq.).

"(B) Funding. For purposes of making grants under this subsection, the Secretary shall provide for the transfer, from the Federal Hospital Insurance Trust Fund under section 1817 of the Social Security Act (42 U.S.C. 1395i) and the Federal Supplementary Medical Insurance Trust Fund under section 1841 of such Act (42 U.S.C. 1395t), in the same proportion as the Secretary determines under section 1853(f) of such Act (42 U.S.C. 1395w-23(f)), to the Administration on Aging—

"(i) for fiscal year 2009, of $7,500,000; and

"(ii) for the period of fiscal years 2010 through 2012, of $15,000,000.

"Amounts appropriated under this subparagraph shall remain available until expended.

"(2) Amount of grant and allocation to States based on percentage of low-income and rural beneficiaries. The amount of a grant to a State under this subsection from the total amount made available under paragraph (1) shall be determined in the same manner as the amount of a grant to a State under subsection (a), from the total amount made available under paragraph (1) of such subsection, is determined under paragraph (2) and subparagraphs (A) and (B) of paragraph (3) of such subsection.

"(3) Required use of funds. (A) All funds. Subject to subparagraph (B), each grant awarded under this subsection shall be used to provide outreach to eligible Medicare beneficiaries regarding the benefits available under title XVIII of the Social Security Act [42 USCS §§ 1395 et seq.].

"(B) Outreach to individuals who may be subsidy eligible individuals or eligible for the Medicare Savings Program. Subsection (a)(4) shall apply to each grant awarded under this subsection in the same manner as it applies to a grant under subsection (a).

"(c) Additional funding for Aging and Disability Resource Centers. (1) Grants. (A) In general. The Secretary shall make grants to Aging and Disability Resource Centers under the Aging and Disability Resource Center grant program that are established centers under such program on the date of the enactment of this Act.

"(B) Funding. For purposes of making grants under this subsection, the Secretary shall provide for the transfer, from the Federal Hospital Insurance Trust Fund under section 1817 of the Social Security Act (42 U.S.C. 1395i) and the Federal Supplementary Medical Insurance Trust Fund under section 1841 of such Act (42 U.S.C. 1395t), in the same proportion as the Secretary determines under section 1853(f) of such Act (42 U.S.C. 1395w-23(f)), to the Administration on Aging—

"(i) for fiscal year 2009, of $5,000,000; and

"(ii) for the period of fiscal years 2010 through 2012, of $10,000,000.

"Amounts appropriated under this subparagraph shall remain available until expended.

"(2) Required use of funds. Each grant awarded under this subsection shall be used to provide outreach to individuals regarding the benefits available under the Medicare prescription drug benefit under part D of title XVIII of the Social Security Act [42 USCS §§ 1395w-101 et seq.] and under the Medicare Savings Program.

"(d) Coordination of efforts to inform older Americans about benefits available under Federal and State programs. (1) In general. The Secretary, acting through the Assistant Secretary for Aging, in cooperation with related Federal agency partners, shall make a grant to, or enter into a contract with, a qualified, experienced entity under which the entity shall—

"(A) maintain and update web-based decision support tools, and integrated, person-centered systems, designed to inform older individuals (as defined in section 102 of the Older Americans Act of 1965 (42 U.S.C. 3002)) about the full range of benefits for which the individuals may be eligible under Federal and State programs;

"(B) utilize cost-effective strategies to find older individuals with the greatest economic need (as defined in such section 102) and inform the individuals of the programs;

"(C) develop and maintain an information clearinghouse on best practices and the most cost-effective methods for finding older individuals with greatest economic need and informing the individuals of the programs; and

"(D) provide, in collaboration with related Federal agency partners administering the Federal programs, training and technical assistance on the most effective outreach, screening, and follow-up strategies for the Federal and State programs.

"(2) Funding. For purposes of making a grant or entering into a contract under paragraph (1), the Secretary shall provide for the transfer, from the Federal Hospital Insurance Trust Fund under section 1817 of the Social Security Act (42 U.S.C. 1395i) and the Federal Supplementary Medical Insurance Trust Fund under section 1841 of such Act (42 U.S.C. 1395t), in the same proportion as the Secretary determines under section 1853(f) of such Act (42 U.S.C. 1395w-23(f)), to the Administration on Aging—

"(i) for fiscal year 2009, of $5,000,000; and

"(ii) for the period of fiscal years 2010 through 2012, of $5,000,000.

"Amounts appropriated under this subparagraph shall remain available until expended.

"(e) Reprogramming funds from Medicare, Medicaid, and SCHIP Extension Act of 2007. The Secretary shall only use the $5,000,000 in funds allocated to make grants to States for Area Agencies on Aging and Aging Disability and Resource Centers for the period of fiscal years 2008 through 2009 under section 118 of the Medicare, Medicaid, and SCHIP Extension Act of 2007 (Public Law 110-173) [unclassified] for the sole purpose of providing outreach to individuals regarding the benefits available under the Medicare prescription drug benefit under part D of title XVIII of the Social Security Act [42 USCS §§ 1395w-101 et seq.]. The Secretary shall republish the request for proposals issued on April 17, 2008, in order to comply with the preceding sentence.

"(f) Medicare Savings Program defined. For purposes of this section, the term 'Medicare Savings Program' means the program of medical assistance for payment of the cost of medicare cost-sharing under the Medicaid program pursuant to sections 1902(a)(10)(E) and 1933 of the Social Security Act (42 U.S.C. 1396a(a)(10)(E), 1396u-3).

"(g) Secretarial authority to enlist support in conducting certain outreach activities. The Secretary may request that an entity awarded a grant under this section support the conduct of outreach activities aimed at preventing disease and promoting wellness. Notwithstanding any other provision of this section, an entity may use a grant awarded under this subsection to support the conduct of activities described in the preceding sentence.".

§ 1395b-6. Medicare Payment Advisory Commission

(a) Establishment. There is hereby established as an agency of Congress the Medicare Payment Advisory Commission (in this section referred to as the "Commission").

(b) Duties. (1) Review of payment policies and annual reports. The Commission shall—

(A) review payment policies under this title [42 USCS §§ 1395 et seq.], including the topics described in paragraph (2);

(B) make recommendations to Congress concerning such payment policies;

(C) by not later than March 15 [of each year], submit a report to Congress containing the results of such reviews and its recommendations concerning such policies; and

(D) by not later than June 15 of each year, submit a report to Congress containing an examination of issues affecting the medicare program, including the implications of changes in health care delivery in the United States and in the market for health care services on the medicare program and including a review of the estimate of the conversion factor submitted under section 1848(d)(1)(E)(ii) [42 USCS § 1395w-4(d)(1)(E)(ii)], and (beginning with 2012) containing an examination of the topics described in paragraph (9), to the extent feasible.

(2) Specific topics to be reviewed. (A) Medicare+Choice program. Specifically, the Commission shall review, with respect to the Medicare+Choice program under part C [42 USCS §§ 1395w-21 et seq.], the following:

(i) The methodology for making payment to plans under such program, including the making of differential payments and the distribution of differential updates among different payment areas.

(ii) The mechanisms used to adjust payments for risk and the need to adjust such mechanisms to take into account health status of beneficiaries.

(iii) The implications of risk selection both among Medicare+Choice organizations and between the Medicare+Choice option and the original medicare fee-for-service option.

(iv) The development and implementation of mechanisms to assure the quality of care for those enrolled with Medicare+Choice organizations.

(v) The impact of the Medicare+Choice program on access to care for medicare beneficiaries.

(vi) Other major issues in implementation and further development of the Medicare+Choice program.

(B) Original medicare fee-for-service system. Specifically, the Commission shall review payment policies under parts A and B [42 USCS §§ 1395c et seq. and 1395j et seq.], including—

(i) the factors affecting expenditures for the efficient provision of services in different sectors, including the process for updating hospital, skilled nursing facility, physician, and other fees,

(ii) payment methodologies, and

(iii) their relationship to access and quality of care for medicare beneficiaries.

(C) Interaction of medicare payment policies with health care delivery generally. Specifically, the Commission shall review the effect of payment policies under this title [42 USCS §§ 1395 et seq.] on the delivery of health care services other than under this title [42 USCS §§ 1395 et seq.] and assess the implications of changes in health care delivery in the United States and in the general market for health care services on the medicare program.

(3) Comments on certain secretarial reports. If the Secretary submits to Congress (or a committee of Congress) a report that is required by law and that relates to payment policies under this title [42 USCS §§ 1395 et seq.], the Secretary shall transmit a copy of the report to the Commission. The Commission shall review the report and, not later than 6 months after the date of submittal of the Secretary's report to Congress, shall submit to the appropriate committees of Congress written comments on such report. Such comments may include such recommendations as the Commission deems appropriate.

(4) Review and comment on the Independent Medicare Advisory Board [Independent Payment Advisory Board] or secretarial proposal. If the Independent Medicare Advisory Board [Independent Payment Advisory Board] (as established under subsection (a) of section 1899A [42 USCS § 1395kkk]) or the Secretary submits a proposal to the Commission under such section in a year, the Commission shall review the proposal and, not later than March 1 of that year, submit to the Committee on Ways and Means and the Committee on Energy and Commerce of the House of Representatives and the Committee on Finance of the Senate written comments on such proposal. Such comments may include such recommendations as the Commission deems appropriate.

(5) Agenda and additional reviews. The Commission shall consult periodically with the chairmen and ranking minority members of the appropriate committees of Congress regarding the Commission's agenda and progress towards achieving the agenda. The Commission may conduct additional reviews, and submit additional reports to the appropriate committees of Congress, from time to time on such topics relating to the program under this title [42 USCS §§ 1395 et seq.] as may be requested by such chairmen and members and as the Commission deems appropriate.

(6) Availability of reports. The Commission shall transmit to the Secretary a copy of each report submitted under this subsection and shall make such reports available to the public.

(7) Appropriate committees of Congress. For purposes of this section, the term "appropriate committees of Congress" means the Committees on Ways and Means and Commerce of the House of Representatives and the Committee on Finance of the Senate.

(8) Voting and reporting requirements. With respect to each recommendation contained in a report submitted under paragraph (1), each member of the Commission shall vote on the recommendation, and the Commission shall include, by member, the results of that vote in the report containing the recommendation.

(9) Examination of budget consequences. Before making any recommendations, the Commission shall examine the budget consequences of such recommendations, directly or through consultation with appropriate expert entities.

[(10)](9) Review and annual report on Medicaid and commercial trends. The Commission shall review and report on aggregate trends in spending, utilization, and financial performance under the Medicaid program under title XIX and the private market for health care services with respect to providers for which, on an aggregate national basis, a significant portion of revenue or services is associated with the Medicaid program. Where appropriate, the Commission shall conduct such review in consultation with the Medicaid and CHIP Payment and Access Commission established under section 1900 [42 USCS § 1396] (in this section referred to as "MACPAC").

[(11)](10) Coordinate and consult with the Federal Coordinated Health Care Office. The Commission shall coordinate and consult with the Federal Coordinated Health Care Office established under section 2081 [2602] of the Patient Protection and Affordable Care Act [42 USCS § 1315b] before making any recommendations regarding dual eligible individuals.

[(12)](11) Interaction of Medicaid and Medicare. The Commission shall consult with MACPAC in carrying out its duties under this section, as appropriate. Responsibility for analysis of and recommendations to change Medicare policy regarding Medicare beneficiaries, including Medicare beneficiaries who are dually eligible for Medicare and Medicaid, shall rest with the Commission. Responsibility for analysis of and recommendations to change

Medicaid policy regarding Medicaid beneficiaries, including Medicaid beneficiaries who are dually eligible for Medicare and Medicaid, shall rest with MACPAC.

(c) Membership. (1) Number and appointment. The Commission shall be composed of 17 members appointed by the Comptroller General.

(2) Qualifications. (A) In general. The membership of the Commission shall include individuals with national recognition for their expertise in health finance and economics, actuarial science, health facility management, health plans and integrated delivery systems, reimbursement of health facilities, allopathic and osteopathic physicians, and other providers of health services, and other related fields, who provide a mix of different professionals, broad geographic representation, and a balance between urban and rural representatives.

(B) Inclusion. The membership of the Commission shall include (but not be limited to) physicians and other health professionals, experts in the area of pharmaco-economics or prescription drug benefit programs, employers, third-party payers, individuals skilled in the conduct and interpretation of biomedical, health services, and health economics research and expertise in outcomes and effectiveness research and technology assessment. Such membership shall also include representatives of consumers and the elderly.

(C) Majority nonproviders. Individuals who are directly involved in the provision, or management of the delivery, of items and services covered under this title [42 USCS §§ 1395 et seq.] shall not constitute a majority of the membership of the Commission.

(D) Ethical disclosure. The Comptroller General shall establish a system for public disclosure by members of the Commission of financial and other potential conflicts of interest relating to such members. Members of the Commission shall be treated as employees of Congress for purposes of applying title I of the Ethics in Government Act of 1978 (Public Law 95-521) [5 USCS Appx].

(3) Terms. (A) In general. The terms of members of the Commission shall be for 3 years except that the Comptroller General shall designate staggered terms for the members first appointed.

(B) Vacancies. Any member appointed to fill a vacancy occurring before the expiration of the term for which the member's predecessor was appointed shall be appointed only for the remainder of that term. A member may serve after the expiration of that member's term until a successor has taken office. A vacancy in the Commission shall be filled in the manner in which the original appointment was made.

(4) Compensation. While serving on the business of the Commission (including traveltime), a member of the Commission shall be entitled to compensation at the per diem equivalent of the rate provided for level IV of the Executive Schedule under section 5315 of title 5, United States Code; and while so serving away from home and the member's regular place of business, a member may be allowed travel expenses, as authorized by the Chairman of the Commission. Physicians serving as personnel of the Commission may be provided a physician comparability allowance by the Commission in the same manner as Government physicians may be provided such an allowance by an agency under section 5948 of title 5, United States Code, and for such purpose subsection (i) of such section shall apply to the Commission in the same manner as it applies to the Tennessee Valley Authority. For purposes of pay (other than pay of members of the Commission) and employment benefits, rights, and privileges, all personnel of the Commission shall be treated as if they were employees of the United States Senate.

(5) Chairman; Vice Chairman. The Comptroller General shall designate a member of the Commission, at the time of appointment of the member as Chairman and a member as Vice Chairman for that term of appointment, except that in the case of vacancy of the Chairmanship or Vice Chairmanship, the Comptroller General may designate another member for the remainder of that member's term.

(6) Meetings. The Commission shall meet at the call of the Chairman.

(d) Director and staff; experts and consultants. Subject to such review as the Comptroller General deems necessary to assure the efficient administration of the Commission, the Commission may—

(1) employ and fix the compensation of an Executive Director (subject to the approval of the Comptroller General) and such other personnel as may be necessary to carry out its duties (without regard to the provisions of title 5, United States Code, governing appointments in the competitive service);

(2) seek such assistance and support as may be required in the performance of its duties from appropriate Federal departments and agencies;

(3) enter into contracts or make other arrangements, as may be necessary for the conduct of the work of the Commission (without

regard to section 3709 of the Revised Statutes (41 U.S.C. 5));

(4) make advance, progress, and other payments which relate to the work of the Commission;

(5) provide transportation and subsistence for persons serving without compensation; and

(6) prescribe such rules and regulations as it deems necessary with respect to the internal organization and operation of the Commission.

(e) Powers. (1) Obtaining official data. The Commission may secure directly from any department or agency of the United States information necessary to enable it to carry out this section. Upon request of the Chairman, the head of that department or agency shall furnish that information to the Commission on an agreed upon schedule.

(2) Data collection. In order to carry out its functions, the Commission shall—

(A) utilize existing information, both published and unpublished, where possible, collected and assessed either by its own staff or under other arrangements made in accordance with this section,

(B) carry out, or award grants or contracts for, original research and experimentation, where existing information is inadequate, and

(C) adopt procedures allowing any interested party to submit information for the Commission's use in making reports and recommendations.

(3) Access of GAO to information. The Comptroller General shall have unrestricted access to all deliberations, records, and nonproprietary data of the Commission, immediately upon request.

(4) Periodic audit. The Commission shall be subject to periodic audit by the Comptroller General.

(f) Authorization of appropriations. (1) Request for appropriations. The Commission shall submit requests for appropriations in the same manner as the Comptroller General submits requests for appropriations, but amounts appropriated for the Commission shall be separate from amounts appropriated for the Comptroller General.

(2) Authorization. There are authorized to be appropriated such sums as may be necessary to carry out the provisions of this section. Sixty percent of such appropriation shall be payable from the Federal Hospital Insurance Trust Fund, and 40 percent of such appropriation shall be payable from the Federal Supplementary Medical Insurance Trust Fund.

(Aug. 14, 1935, ch 531, Title XVIII, § 1805, as added Aug. 5, 1997, P. L. 105-33, Title IV, Subtitle A, Ch 3, § 4022(a), 111 Stat. 350; Oct. 21, 1998, P. L. 105-277, Div J, Title V, Subtitle B, § 5202(a), 112 Stat. 2681-917; Nov. 29, 1999, P. L. 106-113, Div B, § 1000(a)(6), 113 Stat. 1536; Dec. 21, 2000, P. L. 106-554, § 1(a)(6), 114 Stat. 2763; Dec. 8, 2003, P. L. 108-173, Title VII, Subtitle D, § 735(a), (b), (c)(1), (e)(1), 117 Stat. 2353, 2354; Dec. 29, 2007, P. L. 110-173, Title III, § 301, 121 Stat. 2514; March 23, 2010, P. L. 111-148, Title II, Subtitle J, § 2801(b), Title III, Subtitle E, § 3403(c), 124 Stat. 332, 507.)

PART A. HOSPITAL INSURANCE BENEFITS FOR THE AGED AND DISABLED

§ 1395d. Scope of benefits

(a) Entitlement to payment for inpatient hospital services, post-hospital extended care services, home health services, and hospice care. The benefits provided to an individual by the insurance program under this part [42 USCS §§ 1395c et seq.] shall consist of entitlement to have payment made on his behalf or, in the case of payments referred to in section 1814(d)(2) [42 USCS § 1395f(d)(2)] to him (subject to the provisions of this part [42 USCS §§ 1395c et seq.]) for—

(1) inpatient hospital services or inpatient critical access hospital services for up to 150 days during any spell of illness minus 1 day for each day of such services in excess of 90 received during any preceding spell of illness (if such individual was entitled to have payment for such services made under this part [42 USCS §§ 1395c et seq.] unless he specifies in accordance with regulations of the Secretary that he does not desire to have such payment made);

(2) (A) post-hospital extended care services for up to 100 days during any spell of illness, and (B) to the extent provided in subsection (f), extended care services that are not post-hospital extended care services;

(3) in the case of individuals not enrolled in part B [42 USCS §§ 1395j et seq.], home health services, and in the case of individuals so enrolled, post-institutional home health services furnished during a home health spell of illness for up to 100 visits during such spell of illness;

(4) in lieu of certain other benefits, hospice care with respect to the individual during up to

two periods of 90 days each and an unlimited number of subsequent periods of 60 days each with respect to which the individual makes an election under subsection (d)(1); and

(5) **[Caution: This paragraph applies to services provided by a hospice program on or after January 1, 2005, pursuant to § 512(d) of Act Dec. 8, 2003, P. L. 108-173, which appears as a note to this section.]** for individuals who are terminally ill, have not made an election under subsection (d)(1), and have not previously received services under this paragraph, services that are furnished by a physician (as defined in section 1861(r)(1) [42 USCS § 1395x(r)(1)]) who is either the medical director or an employee of a hospice program and that—

(A) consist of—

(i) an evaluation of the individual's need for pain and symptom management, including the individual's need for hospice care; and

(ii) counseling the individual with respect to hospice care and other care options; and

(B) may include advising the individual regarding advanced care planning.

(b) Services not covered. Payment under this part [42 USCS §§ 1395c et seq.] for services furnished an individual during a spell of illness may not (subject to subsection (c)) be made for—

(1) inpatient hospital services furnished to him during such spell after such services have been furnished to him for 150 days during such spell minus 1 day for each day of inpatient hospital services in excess of 90 received during any preceding spell of illness (if such individual was entitled to have payment for such services made under this part [42 USCS §§ 1395c et seq.] unless he specifies in accordance with regulations of the Secretary that he does not desire to have such payment made);

(2) post-hospital extended care services furnished to him during such spell after such services have been furnished to him for 100 days during such spell; or

(3) inpatient psychiatric hospital services furnished to him after such services have been furnished to him for a total of 190 days during his lifetime.

Payment under this part [42 USCS §§ 1395c et seq.] for post-institutional home health services furnished an individual during a home health spell of illness may not be made for such services beginning after such services have been furnished for a total of 100 visits during such spell.

(c) Inpatients of psychiatric hospitals. If an individual is an inpatient of a psychiatric hospital on the first day of the first month for which he is entitled to benefits under this part [42 USCS §§ 1395c et seq.], the days on which he was an inpatient of such a hospital in the 150-day period immediately before such first day shall be included in determining the number of days limit under subsection (b)(1) insofar as such limit applies to (1) inpatient psychiatric hospital services, or (2) inpatient hospital services for an individual who is an inpatient primarily for the diagnosis or treatment of mental illness (but shall not be included in determining such number of days limit insofar as it applies to other inpatient hospital services or in determining the 190-day limit under subsection (b)(3)).

(d) Hospice care; election; waiver of rights; revocation; change of election. (1) Payment under this part [42 USCS §§ 1395c et seq.] may be made for hospice care provided with respect to an individual only during two periods of 90 days each, a subsequent period of 30 days and an unlimited number of subsequent periods of 60 days each, if the individual makes an election under this paragraph to receive hospice care under this part [42 USCS §§ 1395c et seq.] provided by, or under arrangements made by, a particular hospice program instead of certain other benefits under this title [42 USCS §§ 1395 et seq.].

(2)(A) Except as provided in subparagraphs (B) and (C) and except in such exceptional and unusual circumstances as the Secretary may provide, if an individual makes such an election for a period with respect to a particular hospice program, the individual shall be deemed to have waived all rights to have payment made under this title [42 USCS §§ 1395 et seq.] with respect to—

(i) hospice care provided by another hospice program (other than under arrangements made by the particular hospice program) during the period, and

(ii) services furnished during the period that are determined (in accordance with guidelines of the Secretary) to be—

(I) related to the treatment of the individual's condition with respect to which a diagnosis of terminal illness has been made or

(II) equivalent to (or duplicative of) hospice care;

except that clause (ii) shall not apply to physicians' services furnished by the individual's attending physician (if not an employee of the hospice program) or to services provided by (or under arrangements made by) the hospice program.

(B) After an individual makes such an election with respect to a 90-day period or a subsequent 60-day period, the individual may revoke the election during the period, in which case—

(i) the revocation shall act as a waiver of the right to have payment made under this part [42 USCS §§ 1395c et seq.] for any hospice care benefits for the remaining time in such period and (for purposes of subsection (a)(4) and subparagraph (A)) the individual shall be deemed to have been provided such benefits during such entire period, and

(ii) the individual may at any time after the revocation execute a new election for a subsequent period, if the individual otherwise is entitled to hospice care benefits with respect to such a period.

(C) An individual may, once in each such period, change the hospice program with respect to which the election is made and such change shall not be considered a revocation of an election under subparagraph (B).

(D) For purposes of this title [42 USCS §§ 1395 et seq.], an individual's election with respect to a hospice program shall no longer be considered to be in effect with respect to that hospice program after the date the individual's revocation or change of election with respect to that election takes effect.

(e) Services taken into account. For purposes of subsections (b) and (c), inpatient hospital services, inpatient psychiatric hospital services, and post-hospital extended care services shall be taken into account only if payment is or would be, except for this section or the failure to comply with the request and certification requirements of or under section 1814(a) [42 USCS § 1395f(a)], made with respect to such services under this part [42 USCS §§ 1395c et seq.].

(f) Coverage of extended care services without regard to three-day prior hospitalization requirement. (1) The Secretary shall provide for coverage, under clause (B) of subsection (a)(2), of extended care services which are not post-hospital extended care services at such time and for so long as the Secretary determines, and under such terms and conditions (described in paragraph (2)) as the Secretary finds appropriate, that the inclusion of such services will not result in any increase in the total of payments made under this title [42 USCS §§ 1395 et seq.] and will not alter the acute care nature of the benefit described in subsection (a)(2).

(2) The Secretary may provide—

(A) for such limitations on the scope and extent of services described in subsection (a)(2)(B) and on the categories of individuals who may be eligible to receive such services, and

(B) notwithstanding sections 1814, 1861(v), and 1866 [42 USCS §§ 1395f, 1395x(v), and 1395ww], for such restrictions and alternatives on the amounts and methods of payment for services described in such subsection,

as may be necessary to carry out paragraph (1).

(g) "Spell of illness" defined. For definition of "spell of illness", and for definitions of other terms used in this part [42 USCS §§ 1395c et seq.], see section 1861 [42 USCS § 1395x].

(Aug. 14, 1935, ch 531, Title XVIII, Part A, § 1812, as added July 30, 1965, P. L. 89-97, Title I, Part 1, § 102(a), 79 Stat. 291; Jan. 2, 1968, P. L. 90-248, Title I, Part 3, §§ 129(c)(2), 137(a), 138(a), 143(b), 146(a), 81 Stat. 847, 853, 854, 857, 859; Dec. 5, 1980, P. L. 96-499, Title IX, Part B, Subpart I, §§ 930(b)–(d), 931(a), 94 Stat. 2631, 2633; Aug. 13, 1981, P. L. 97-35, Title XXI, Subtitle B, ch 1, § 2121(a), 95 Stat. 796; Sept. 3, 1982, P. L. 97-248, Title I, Subtitle A, Part II, §§ 122(b), 123, 96 Stat. 356, 364; Jan. 12, 1983, P. L. 97-448, Title III, § 309(b)(5), 96 Stat. 2409; July 1, 1988, P. L. 100-360, Title I, Subtitle A, § 101, 102 Stat. 684; Dec. 13, 1989, P. L. 101-234, Title I, § 101(a)(1), 103 Stat. 1979; Dec. 19, 1989, P. L. 101-239, Title VI, Subtitle A, Part 1, Subpart A, § 6003(g)(3)(B)(i), 103 Stat. 2152; Nov. 5, 1990, P. L. 101-508, Title IV, Subtitle A, Part 1, § 4006(a), 104 Stat. 1388-43; Oct. 31, 1994, P. L. 103-432, Title I, Subtitle A, § 102(g)(1), 108 Stat. 4404; Aug. 5, 1997, P. L. 105-33, Title IV, Subtitle C, § 4201(c)(1), Subtitle E, Ch 4, § 4443(a), (b)(1), Subtitle G, Ch 1, Subch B, § 4611(a), 111 Stat. 373, 423, 472; Nov. 29, 1999, P. L. 106-113, Div B, § 1000(a)(6), 113 Stat. 1536; Dec. 8, 2003, P. L. 108-173, Title V, Subtitle B, § 512(a), Title VII, Subtitle D, § 736(c)(1), 117 Stat. 2299, 2356.)

HISTORY; ANCILLARY LAWS AND DIRECTIVES

Other provisions:

Medicare hospice concurrent care demonstration program. Act March 23, 2010, P. L. 111-148, Title III, Subtitle B, Part III, § 3140, 124 Stat. 440, provides:

"(a) Establishment. (1) In general. The Secretary of Health and Human Services (in this section referred to as the 'Secretary') shall establish a Medicare Hospice Concurrent Care demonstration program at participating hospice programs under which Medicare beneficiaries are furnished, during the same period, hospice care and any other items or services covered under title XVIII of the Social Security Act (42 U.S.C. 1395 et seq.) from funds otherwise paid under such title to such hospice programs.

"(2) Duration. The demonstration program under this section shall be conducted for a 3-year period.

"(3) Sites. The Secretary shall select not more than 15 hospice programs at which the demonstration program under this section shall be conducted. Such hospice programs shall be located in urban and rural areas.

"(b) Independent evaluation and reports. (1) Independent evaluation. The Secretary shall provide for the conduct of an independent evaluation of the demonstration program under this section. Such independent evaluation shall determine whether the demonstration program has improved patient care, quality of life, and cost-effectiveness for Medicare beneficiaries participating in the demonstration program.

"(2) Reports. The Secretary shall submit to Congress a report containing the results of the evaluation conducted under paragraph (1), together with such recommendations as the Secretary determines appropriate.

"(c) Budget neutrality. With respect to the 3-year period of the demonstration program under this section, the Secretary shall ensure that the aggregate expenditures under title XVIII [42 USCS §§ 1395 et seq.] for such period shall not exceed the aggregate expenditures that would have been expended under such title if the demonstration program under this section had not been implemented.".

Protecting home health benefits. Act March 23, 2010, P. L. 111-148, Title III, Subtitle B, Part III, § 3143, 124 Stat. 442, provides: "Nothing in the provisions of, or amendments made by, this Act [for full classification, consult USCS Tables volumes] shall result in the reduction of guaranteed home health benefits under title XVIII of the Social Security Act [42 USCS §§ 1395 et seq.].".

§ 1395f. Conditions of and limitations on payment for services

(a) Requirement of requests and certifications. Except as provided in subsections (d) and (g) and in section 1876 [42 USCS § 1395mm], payment for services furnished an individual may be made only to providers of services which are eligible therefor under section 1866 [42 USCS § 1395cc] and only if—

(1) written request, signed by such individual, except in cases in which the Secretary finds it impracticable for the individual to do so, is filed for such payment in such form, in such manner, and by such person or persons as the Secretary may be regulation prescribe, no later than the close of the period ending 1 calendar year after the date of service;

(2) **[Caution: For provisions applicable to written orders and certifications made before July 1, 2010, and to items and services furnished before January 1, 2011, see 2010 amendment notes below.]** a physician, or, in the case of services described in subparagraph (B), a physician, or a nurse practitioner or clinical nurse specialist who does not have a direct or indirect employment relationship with the facility but is working in collaboration with a physician, or, in the case of services described in subparagraph (C), a physician enrolled under section 1866(j) [42 USCS § 1395cc(j)], certifies (and recertifies, where such services are furnished over a period of time, in such cases, with such frequency, and accompanied by such supporting material, appropriate to the case involved, as may be provided by regulations, except that the first of such recertifications shall be required in each case of inpatient hospital services not later than the 20th day of such period) that—

(A) in the case of inpatient psychiatric hospital services, such services are or were required to be given on an inpatient basis, by or under the supervision of a physician, for the psychiatric treatment of an individual; and (i) such treatment can or could reasonably be expected to improve the condition for which such treatment is or was necessary or (ii) inpatient diagnostic study is or was medically required and such services are or were necessary for such purposes;

(B) in the case of post-hospital extended care services, such services are or were required to be given because the individual needs or needed on a daily basis skilled nursing care (provided directly by or requiring the supervision of skilled nursing personnel) or other skilled rehabilitation services, which as a practical matter can only be provided in a skilled nursing facility on an inpatient basis, for any of the conditions with respect to which he was receiving inpatient hospital services (or services which would constitute inpatient hospital services if the institution met the requirements of paragraphs (6) and (9) of section 1861(e) [42 USCS § 1395x(e)(6) and (9)] prior to transfer to the skilled nursing facility or for a condition requiring such extended care services which arose after such transfer and while he was still in the facility for treatment of the condition or conditions for which he was receiving such inpatient hospital services;

(C) in the case of home health services, such services are or were required because the individual is or was confined to his home (except when receiving items and services referred to in section 1861(m)(7) [42 USCS § 1395x(m)(7)]) and needs or needed skilled nursing care (other than solely venipuncture for the purpose of obtaining a blood sample) on an intermittent basis or physical or speech therapy or, in the case of an individual who has been furnished home health services based on such a need and who no longer has such a need for such care or therapy, continues or continued to need occupational therapy; a plan for furnishing such services to such individual has been established and is periodically reviewed by a physician; such services are or were furnished while the individual was under the care of a physician, and, in the case of a certification made by a physician after January 1, 2010, prior to making such certification the physician must document that the physician himself or herself, or a nurse practitioner or clinical nurse specialist (as those terms are defined in section 1861(aa)(5) [42 USCS § 1395x(aa)(5)]) who is working in collaboration with the physician in accordance with State law, or a certified nurse-midwife (as defined in section 1861(gg) [42 USCS § 1395x(gg)]) as authorized by State law, or a physician assistant (as defined in section 1861(aa)(5) [42 USCS § 1395x(aa)(5)]) under the supervision of the physician, has had a face-to-face encounter (including through use of telehealth, subject to the requirements in section 1834(m) [42 USCS § 1395m(m)], and other than with respect to encounters that are incident to services involved) with the individual within a reasonable timeframe as determined by the Secretary; or

(D) in the case of inpatient hospital services in connection with the care, treatment, filling, removal, or replacement of teeth or structures directly supporting teeth, the individual, because of his underlying medical condition and clinical status or because of the severity of the dental procedure, requires hospitalization in connection with the provision of such services;

(3) with respect to inpatient hospital services (other than inpatient psychiatric hospital services) which are furnished over a period of time, a physician certifies that such services are required to be given on an inpatient basis for such individual's medical treatment, or that inpatient diagnostic study is medically required and such services are necessary for such purpose, except that (A) such certification shall be furnished only in such cases, with such frequency, and accompanied by such supporting material, appropriate to the cases involved, as may be provided by regulations, and (B) the first such certification required in accordance with clause (A) shall be furnished no later than the 20th day of such period;

(4) in the case of inpatient psychiatric hospital services, the services are those which the records of the hospital indicate were furnished to the individual during periods when he was receiving (A) intensive treatment services, (B) admission and related services necessary for a diagnostic study, or (C) equivalent services;

(5) with respect to inpatient hospital services furnished such individual after the 20th day of a continuous period of such services, there was not in effect, at the time of admission of such individual to the hospital, a decision under section 1866(d) [42 USCS § 1395cc(d)] (based on a finding that utilization review of long-stay cases is not being made in such hospital);

(6) with respect to inpatient hospital services or post-hospital extended care services furnished such individual during a continuous period, a finding has not been made (by the physician members of the committee or group, as described in section 1861(k)(4) [42 USCS § 1395x(k)(4)], including any finding made in the course of a sample or other review of admissions to the institution) pursuant to the system of utilization review that further inpatient hospital services or further post-hospital extended care services, as the case may be, are not medically necessary; except that, if such a finding has been made, payment may be made for such services furnished before the 4th day after the date on which the hospital or skilled nursing facility, as the case may be, received notice of such finding;

(7) in the case of hospice care provided an individual—

(A)(i) in the first 90-day period—

(I) the individual's attending physician (as defined in section 1861(dd)(3)(B) [42 USCS § 1395x(dd)(3)(B)]) (which for purposes of this subparagraph does not include a nurse practitioner), and

(II) the medical director (or physician member of the interdisciplinary group described in section 1861(dd)(2)(B) [42 USCS § 1395x(dd)(2)(B)]) of the hospice program providing (or arranging for) the care,

each certify in writing at the beginning of the period, that the individual is terminally ill (as defined in section 1861(dd)(3)(A) [42 USCS § 1395x(dd)(3)(A)]) based on the physician's or medical director's clinical judgment regarding the normal course of the individual's illness, and

(ii) in a subsequent 90- or 60-day period, the medical director or physician described in clause (i)(II) recertifies at the beginning of the period that the individual is terminally ill based on such clinical judgment;

(B) a written plan for providing hospice care with respect to such individual has been established (before such care is provided by, or under arrangements made by, that hospice program) and is periodically reviewed by the individual's attending physician and by the medical director (and the interdisciplinary group described in section 1861(dd)(2)(B) [42 USCS

§ 1395x(dd)(2)(B)]) of the hospice program;

(C) such care is being or was provided pursuant to such plan of care; and

(D) on and after January 1, 2011—

(i) a hospice physician or nurse practitioner has a face-to-face encounter with the individual to determine continued eligibility of the individual for hospice care prior to the 180th-day recertification and each subsequent recertification under subparagraph (A)(ii) and attests that such visit took place (in accordance with procedures established by the Secretary); and

(ii) in the case of hospice care provided an individual for more than 180 days by a hospice program for which the number of such cases for such program comprises more than a percent (specified by the Secretary) of the total number of such cases for all programs under this title [42 USCS §§ 1395 et seq.], the hospice care provided to such individual is medically reviewed (in accordance with procedures established by the Secretary); and

(8) in the case of inpatient critical access hospital services, a physician certifies that the individual may reasonably be expected to be discharged or transferred to a hospital within 96 hours after admission to the critical access hospital.

[Caution: For provisions applicable to items and services furnished before January 1, 2011, see 2010 amendment note below.] To the extent provided by regulations, the certification and recertification requirements of paragraph (2) shall be deemed satisfied where, at a later date, a physician, nurse practitioner, clinical nurse specialist, or physician assistant (as the case may be) makes certification of the kind provided in subparagraph (A), (B), (C), or (D) of paragraph (2) (whichever would have applied), but only where such certification is accompanied by such medical and other evidence as may be required by such regulations. With respect to the physician certification required by paragraph (2) for home health services furnished to any individual by a home health agency (other than an agency which is a governmental entity) and with respect to the establishment and review of a plan for such services, the Secretary shall prescribe regulations which shall become effective no later than July 1, 1981, and which prohibit a physician who has a significant ownership interest in, or a significant financial or contractual relationship with, such home health agency from performing such certification and from establishing or reviewing such plan, except that such prohibition shall not apply with respect to a home health agency which is a sole community home health agency (as determined by the Secretary). For purposes of the preceding sentence, service by a physician as an uncompensated officer or director of a home health agency shall not constitute having a significant ownership interest in, or a significant financial or contractual relationship with, such agency. For purposes of paragraph (2)(C), an individual shall be considered to be "confined to his home" if the individual has a condition, due to an illness or injury, that restricts the ability of the individual to leave his or her home except with the assistance of another individual or the aid of a supportive device (such as crutches, a cane, a wheelchair, or a walker), or if the individual has a condition such that leaving his or her home is medically contraindicated. While an individual does not have to be bedridden to be considered "confined to his home", the condition of the individual should be such that there exists a normal inability to leave home and that leaving home requires a considerable and taxing effort by the individual. Any absence of an individual from the home attributable to the need to receive health care treatment, including regular absences for the purpose of participating in therapeutic, psychosocial, or medical treatment in an adult day-care program that is licensed or certified by a State, or accredited, to furnish adult day-care services in the State shall not disqualify an individual from being considered to be "confined to his home". Any other absence of an individual from the home shall not so disqualify an individual if the absence is of infrequent or of relatively short duration. For purposes of the preceding sentence, any absence for the purpose of attending a religious service shall be deemed to be an absence of infrequent or short duration. In applying paragraph (1), the Secretary may specify exceptions to the 1 calendar year period specified in such paragraph.

(b) Amount paid to provider of services. The amount paid to any provider of services (other than a hospice program providing hospice care, other than a critical access hospital providing inpatient critical access hospital services, and other than a home health agency with respect to durable medical equipment) with respect to services for which payment may be made under this part [42 USCS §§ 1395c et seq.] shall, subject to the provisions of sections 1813, 1886, and 1895 [42 USCS §§ 1395e, 1395ww, and 1395fff], be—

(1) except as provided in paragraph (3), the lesser of (A) the reasonable cost of such services, as determined under section 1861(v) [42

USCS § 1395x(v)] and as further limited by section 1881(b)(2)(B) [42 USCS § 1395rr(b)(2)(B)], or (B) the customary charges with respect to such services;

(2) if such services are furnished by a public provider of services, or by another provider which demonstrates to the satisfaction of the Secretary that a significant portion of its patients are low-income (and requests that payment be made under this paragraph), free of charge or at nominal charges to the public, the amount determined on the basis of those items (specified in regulations prescribed by the Secretary) included in the determination of such reasonable cost which the Secretary finds will provide fair compensation to such provider for such services; or

(3) if some or all of the hospitals in a State have been reimbursed for services (for which payment may be made under this part [42 USCS §§ 1395c et seq.]) pursuant to a reimbursement system approved as a demonstration project under section 402 of the Social Security Amendments of 1967 [42 USCS §§ 1395b-1 and 1395ll] or section 222 of the Social Security Amendments of 1972 [42 USCS §§ 1395b-1 and note and 1395ll], if the rate of increase in such hospitals in their costs per hospital inpatient admission of individuals entitled to benefits under this part [42 USCS §§ 1395c et seq.] over the duration of such project was equal to or less than such rate of increase for admissions of such individuals with respect to all hospitals in the United States during such period, and if either the State has legislative authority to operate such system and the State elects to have reimbursement to such hospitals made in accordance with this paragraph or the system is operated through a voluntary agreement of hospitals and such hospitals elect to have reimbursement to those hospitals made in accordance with this paragraph, then, subject to section 1886(d)(3)(B)(ix)(III) [42 USCS § 1395ww(d)(3)(B)(ix)(III)], the Secretary may provide for continuation of reimbursement to such hospitals under such system until the Secretary determines that—

(A) a third-party payor reimburses such a hospital on a basis other than under such system, or

(B) the aggregate rate of increase from January 1, 1981, to the most recent date for which annual data are available in such hospitals in costs per hospital inpatient admission of individuals entitled to benefits under this part [42 USCS §§ 1395c et seq.] is greater than such rate of increase for admissions of such individuals with respect to all hospitals in the United States for such period.

In the case of any State which has had such a demonstration project reimbursement system in continuous operation since July 1, 1977, the Secretary shall provide under paragraph (3) for continuation of reimbursement to hospitals in the State under such system until the first day of the 37th month beginning after the date the Secretary determines and notifies the Governor of the State that either of the conditions described in subparagraph (A) or (B) of such paragraph has occurred. If, by the end of such 36-month period, the Secretary determines, based on evidence submitted by the Governor of the State, that neither of the conditions described in subparagraph (A) or (B) of paragraph (3) continues to apply, the Secretary shall continue without interruption payment to hospitals in the State under the State's system. If, by the end of such 36-month period, the Secretary determines, based on such evidence, that either of the conditions described in subparagraph (A) or (B) of such paragraph continues to apply, the Secretary shall (i) collect any net excess reimbursement to hospitals in the State during such 36-month period (basing such net excess reimbursement on the net difference, if any, in the rate of increase in costs per hospital inpatient admission under the State system compared to the rate of increase in such costs with respect to all hospitals in the United States over the 36-month period, as measured by including the cumulative savings under the State system based on the difference in the rate of increase in costs per hospital inpatient admission under the State system as compared to the rate of increase in such costs with respect to all hospitals in the United States between January 1, 1981, and the date of the Secretary's initial notice), and (ii) provide a reasonable period, not to exceed 2 years, for transition from the State system to the national payment system. For purposes of applying paragraph (3), there shall be taken into account incentive payments, and payment adjustments under subsection (b)(3)(B)(ix) or (n) of section 1886 [42 USCS § 1395ww].

(c) No payments to Federal providers of services. Subject to section 1880 [42 USCS § 1395qq], no payment may be made under this part [42 USCS §§ 1395c et seq.] (except under subsection (d) or subsection (h)) to any Federal provider of services, except a provider of services which the Secretary determines is providing services to the public generally as a community institution or agency; and no such payment may be made to any provider of services for any item or service which such provider is obligated by a law of, or a contract with, the United States to render at public expense.

(d) Payments for emergency hospital services. (1) Payments shall also be made to any hospital for inpatient hospital services furnished in a calendar year, by the hospital or under arrangements (as defined in section 1861(w) [42 USCS § 1395x(w)]) with it, to an individual entitled to hospital insurance benefits under section 226 [42 USCS § 426] even though such hospital does not have an agreement in effect under this title [42 USCS §§ 1395 et seq.] if (A) such services were emergency services, (B) the Secretary would be required to make such payment if the hospital had such an agreement in effect and otherwise met the conditions of payment hereunder, and (C) such hospital has elected to claim payments for all such inpatient emergency services and for the emergency outpatient services referred to in section 1835(b) [42 USCS § 1395n(b)] furnished during such year. Such payments shall be made only in the amounts provided under subsection (b) and then only if such hospital agrees to comply, with respect to the emergency services provided, with the provisions of section 1866(a) [42 USCS § 1395cc(a)].

(2) Payment may be made on the basis of an itemized bill to an individual entitled to hospital insurance benefits under section 226 [42 USCS § 426] for services described in paragraph (1) which are emergency services if (A) payment cannot be made under paragraph (1) solely because the hospital does not elect to claim such payment, and (B) such individual files application (submitted within such time and in such form and manner and by such person, and containing and supported by such information as the Secretary shall by regulations prescribe) for reimbursement.

(3) The amounts payable under the preceding paragraph with respect to services described therein shall, subject to the provisions of section 1813 [42 USCS § 1395e], be equal to 60 percent of the hospital's reasonable charges for routine services furnished in the accommodations occupied by the individual or in semiprivate accommodations (as defined in section 1861(v)(4) [42 USCS § 1395x(v)(4)]), whichever is less, plus 80 percent of the hospital's reasonable charges for ancillary services. If separate charges for routine and ancillary services are not made by the hospital, reimbursement may be based on two-thirds of the hospital's reasonable charges for the services received but not to exceed the charges which would have been made if the patient had occupied semiprivate accommodations. For purposes of the preceding provisions of this paragraph, the term "routine services" shall mean the regular room, dietary, and nursing services, minor medical and surgical supplies and the use of equipment and facilities for which a separate charge is not customarily made; the term "ancillary services" shall mean those special services for which charges are customarily made in addition to routine services.

(e) Payment for inpatient hospital services prior to notification of noneligibility. Notwithstanding that an individual is not entitled to have payment made under this part [42 USCS §§ 1395c et seq.] for inpatient hospital services furnished by any hospital, payment shall be made to such hospital (unless it elects not to receive such payment or, if payment has already been made by or on behalf of such individual, fails to refund such payment within the time specified by the Secretary) for such services which are furnished to the individual prior to notification to such hospital from the Secretary of his lack of entitlement, if such payments are precluded only by reason of section 1812 [42 USCS § 1395d] and if such hospital complies with the requirements of and regulations under this title [42 USCS §§ 1395 et seq.] with respect to such payments, has acted in good faith and without knowledge of such lack of entitlement, and has acted reasonably in assuming entitlement existed. Payment under the preceding sentence may not be made for services furnished an individual pursuant to any admission after the 6th elapsed day (not including as an elapsed day Saturday, Sunday, or a legal holiday) after the day on which such admission occurred.

(f) Payment for certain inpatient hospital services furnished outside the United States. (1) Payment shall be made for inpatient hospital services furnished to an individual entitled to hospital insurance benefits under section 226 [42 USCS § 426] by a hospital located outside the United States, or under arrangements (as defined in section 1861(w) [42 USCS § 1395x(w)]) with it, if—

(A) such individual is a resident of the United States, and

(B) such hospital was closer to, or substantially more accessible from, the residence of such individual than the nearest hospital within the United States which was adequately equipped to deal with, and was available for the treatment of, such individual's illness or injury.

(2) Payment may also be made for emergency inpatient hospital services furnished to

an individual entitled to hospital insurance benefits under section 226 [42 USCS § 426] by a hospital located outside the United States if—

(A) such individual was physically present—

(i) in a place within the United States; or

(ii) at a place within Canada while traveling without unreasonable delay by the most direct route (as determined by the Secretary) between Alaska and another State;

at the time the emergency which necessitated such inpatient hospital services occurred, and

(B) such hospital was closer to, or substantially more accessible from, such place than the nearest hospital within the United States which was adequately equipped to deal with, and was available for the treatment of, such individual's illness or injury.

(3) Payment shall be made in the amount provided under subsection (b) to any hospital for the inpatient hospital services described in paragraph (1) or (2) furnished to an individual by the hospital or under arrangements (as defined in section 1861(w) [42 USCS § 1395x(w)]) with it if (A) the Secretary would be required to make such payment if the hospital had an agreement in effect under this title [42 USCS §§ 1395 et seq.] and otherwise met the conditions of payment hereunder, (B) such hospital elects to claim such payment, and (C) such hospital agrees to comply, with respect to such services, with the provisions of section 1866(a) [42 USCS § 1395cc(a)].

(4) Payment for the inpatient hospital services described in paragraph (1) or (2) furnished to an individual entitled to hospital insurance benefits under section 226 [42 USCS § 426] may be made on the basis of an itemized bill to such individual if (A) payment for such services cannot be made under paragraph (3) solely because the hospital does not elect to claim such payment, and (B) such individual files application (submitted within such time and in such form and manner and by such person, and continuing and supported by such information as the Secretary shall by regulations prescribe) for reimbursement. The amount payable with respect to such services shall, subject to the provisions of section 1813 [42 USCS § 1395e], be equal to the amount which would be payable under subsection (d)(3).

(g) Payment to physicians for services rendered in teaching hospital. For purposes of services for which the reasonable cost thereof is determined under section 1861(v)(1)(D) [42 USCS § 1395x(v)(1)(D)] (or would be if section 1886 [42 USCS § 1395ww] did not apply), payment under this part [42 USCS §§ 1395c et seq.] shall be made to such fund as may be designated by the organized medical staff of the hospital in which such services were furnished or, if such services were furnished in such hospital by the faculty of a medical school, to such fund as may be designated by such faculty, but only if—

(1) such hospital has an agreement with the Secretary under section 1866 [42 USCS § 1395cc], and

(2) the Secretary has received written assurances that (A) such payment will be used by such fund solely for the improvement of care of hospital patients or for educational or charitable purposes and (B) the individuals who were furnished such services or any other persons will not be charged for such services (or if charged, provision will be made for return of any moneys incorrectly collected).

(h) Payment for specified hospital services provided in Department of Veterans Affairs hospitals; amount of payment. (1) Payments shall also be made to any hospital operated by the Department of Veterans Affairs for inpatient hospital services furnished in a calendar year by the hospital, or under arrangements (as defined in section 1861(w) [42 USCS § 1395x(w)]) with it, to an individual entitled to hospital benefits under section 226 [42 USCS § 426] even though the hospital is a Federal provider of services if (A) the individual was not entitled to have the services furnished to him free of charge by the hospital, (B) the individual was admitted to the hospital in the reasonable belief on the part of the admitting authorities that the individual was a person who was entitled to have the services furnished to him free of charge, (C) the authorities of the hospital, in admitting the individual, and the individual, acted in good faith, and (D) the services were furnished during a period ending with the close of the day on which the authorities operating the hospital first became aware of the fact that the individual was not entitled to have the services furnished to him by the hospital free of charge, or (if later) ending with the first day on which it was medically feasible to remove the individual from the hospital by discharging him therefrom or transferring him to a hospital which has in effect an agreement under this title [42 USCS §§ 1395 et seq.].

(2) Payment for services described in paragraph (1) shall be in an amount equal to the charge imposed by the Secretary of Veterans Affairs for such services, or (if less) the amount

that would be payable for such services under subsection (b) and section 1886 [42 USCS § 1395ww] (as estimated by the Secretary). Any such payment shall be made to the entity to which payment for the services involved would have been payable, if payment for such services had been made by the individual receiving the services involved (or by another private person acting on behalf of such individual).

(i) Payment for hospice care. (1)(A) Subject to the limitation under paragraph (2) and the provisions of section 1813(a)(4) [42 USCS § 1395e(a)(4)] and except as otherwise provided in this paragraph the amount paid to a hospice program with respect to hospice care for which payment may be made under this part [42 USCS §§ 1395c et seq.] shall be an amount equal to the costs which are reasonable and related to the cost of providing hospice care or which are based on such other tests of reasonableness as the Secretary may prescribe in regulations (including those authorized under section 1861(v)(1)(A) [42 USCS § 1395x(v)(1)(A)]), except that no payment may be made for bereavement counseling and no reimbursement may be made for other counseling services (including nutritional and dietary counseling) as separate services.

(B) Notwithstanding subparagraph (A), for hospice care furnished on or after April 1, 1986, the daily rate of payment per day for routine home care shall be $63.17 and the daily rate of payment for other services included in hospice care shall be the daily rate of payment recognized under subparagraph (A) as of July 1, 1985, increased by $10.

(C)(i) With respect to routine home care and other services included in hospice care furnished on or after January 1, 1990, and on or before September 30, 1990, the payment rates for such care and services shall be 120 percent of such rates in effect as of September 30, 1989.

(ii) With respect to routine home care and other services included in hospice care furnished during a subsequent fiscal year (before the first fiscal year in which the payment revisions described in paragraph (6)(D) are implemented), the payment rates for such care and services shall be the payment rates in effect under this subparagraph during the previous fiscal year increased by—

(I) for a fiscal year ending on or before September 30, 1993, the market basket percentage increase (as defined in section 1886(b)(3)(B)(iii) [42 USCS § 1395ww(b)(3)(B)(iii)]) for the fiscal year;

(II) for fiscal year 1994, the market basket percentage increase for the fiscal year minus 2.0 percentage points;

(III) for fiscal year 1995, the market basket percentage increase for the fiscal year minus 1.5 percentage points;

(IV) for fiscal year 1996, the market basket percentage increase for the fiscal year minus 1.5 percentage points;

(V) for fiscal year 1997, the market basket percentage increase for the fiscal year minus 0.5 percentage point;

(VI) for each of fiscal years 1998 through 2002, the market basket percentage increase for the fiscal year involved minus 1.0 percentage points, plus, in the case of fiscal year 2001, 5.0 percentage points; and

(VII) for a subsequent fiscal year (before the first fiscal year in which the payment revisions described in paragraph (6)(D) are implemented), subject to clause (iv),[,] the market basket percentage increase for the fiscal year.

(iii) With respect to routine home care and other services included in hospice care furnished during fiscal years subsequent to the first fiscal year in which payment revisions described in paragraph (6)(D) are implemented, the payment rates for such care and services shall be the payment rates in effect under this clause during the preceding fiscal year increased by, subject to clause (iv), the market basket percentage increase (as defined in section 1886(b)(3)(B)(iii) [42 USCS § 1395ww(b)(3)(B)(iii)]) for the fiscal year.

(iv) After determining the market basket percentage increase under clause (ii)(VII) or (iii), as applicable, with respect to fiscal year 2013 and each subsequent fiscal year, the Secretary shall reduce such percentage—

(I) for 2013 and each subsequent fiscal year, by the productivity adjustment described in section 1886(b)(3)(B)(xi)(II) [42 USCS § 1395ww(b)(3)(B)(xi)(II)]; and

(II) subject to clause (v), for each of fiscal years 2013 through 2019, by 0.3 percentage point.

The application of this clause may result in the market basket percentage increase under clause (ii)(VII) or (iii), as applicable, being less than 0.0 for a fiscal year, and may result in payment rates under this subsection for a fiscal year being less than such payment rates for the preceding fiscal year.

(v) Clause (iv)(II) shall be applied with respect to any of fiscal years 2014 through 2019 by substituting "0.0 percentage points" for "0.3 percentage point", if for such fiscal year—

(I) the excess (if any) of—

(aa) the total percentage of the non-elderly

insured population for the preceding fiscal year (based on the most recent estimates available from the Director of the Congressional Budget Office before a vote in either House on the Patient Protection and Affordable Care Act that, if determined in the affirmative, would clear such Act for enrollment); over

(bb) the total percentage of the non-elderly insured population for such preceding fiscal year (as estimated by the Secretary); exceeds

(II) 5 percentage points.

(2)(A) The amount of payment made under this part [42 USCS §§ 1395c et seq.] for hospice care provided by (or under arrangements made by) a hospice program for an accounting year may not exceed the "cap amount" for the year (computed under subparagraph (B)) multiplied by the number of medicare beneficiaries in the hospice program in that year (determined under subparagraph (C)).

(B) For purposes of subparagraph (A), the "cap amount" for a year is $6,500, increased or decreased, for accounting years that end after October 1, 1984, by the same percentage as the percentage increase or decrease, respectively, in the medical care expenditure category of the Consumer Price Index for All Urban Consumers (United States city average), published by the Bureau of Labor Statistics, from March 1984 to the fifth month of the accounting year.

(C) For purposes of subparagraph (A), the "number of medicare beneficiaries" in a hospice program in an accounting year is equal to the number of individuals who have made an election under subsection (d) with respect to the hospice program and have been provided hospice care by (or under arrangements made by) the hospice program under this part [42 USCS §§ 1395c et seq.] in the accounting year, such number reduced to reflect the proportion of hospice care that each such individual was provided in a previous or subsequent accounting year or under a plan of care established by another hospice program.

(D) A hospice program shall submit claims for payment for hospice care furnished in an individual's home under this title [42 USCS §§ 1395 et seq.] only on the basis of the geographic location at which the service is furnished, as determined by the Secretary.

(3) Hospice programs providing hospice care for which payment is made under this subsection shall submit to the Secretary such data with respect to the costs for providing such care for each fiscal year, beginning with fiscal year 1999, as the Secretary determines necessary.

(4) The amount paid to a hospice program with respect to the services under section 1812(a)(5) [42 USCS § 1395d(a)(5)] for which payment may be made under this part shall be equal to an amount established for an office or other outpatient visit for evaluation and management associated with presenting problems of moderate severity and requiring medical decisionmaking of low complexity under the fee schedule established under section 1848(b) [42 USCS § 1395w-4(b)], other than the portion of such amount attributable to the practice expense component.

(5) Quality reporting. (A) Reduction in update for failure to report. (i) In general. For purposes of fiscal year 2014 and each subsequent fiscal year, in the case of a hospice program that does not submit data to the Secretary in accordance with subparagraph (C) with respect to such a fiscal year, after determining the market basket percentage increase under paragraph (1)(C)(ii)(VII) or paragraph (1)(C)(iii), as applicable, and after application of paragraph (1)(C)(iv), with respect to the fiscal year, the Secretary shall reduce such market basket percentage increase by 2 percentage points.

(ii) Special rule. The application of this subparagraph may result in the market basket percentage increase under paragraph (1)(C)(ii)(VII) or paragraph (1)(C)(iii), as applicable, being less than 0.0 for a fiscal year, and may result in payment rates under this subsection for a fiscal year being less than such payment rates for the preceding fiscal year.

(B) Noncumulative application. Any reduction under subparagraph (A) shall apply only with respect to the fiscal year involved and the Secretary shall not take into account such reduction in computing the payment amount under this subsection for a subsequent fiscal year.

(C) Submission of quality data. For fiscal year 2014 and each subsequent fiscal year, each hospice program shall submit to the Secretary data on quality measures specified under subparagraph (D). Such data shall be submitted in a form and manner, and at a time, specified by the Secretary for purposes of this subparagraph.

(D) Quality measures. (i) In general. Subject to clause (ii), any measure specified by the Secretary under this subparagraph must have been endorsed by the entity with a contract under section 1890(a) [42 USCS § 1395aaa(a)].

(ii) Exception. In the case of a specified area or medical topic determined appropriate by the Secretary for which a feasible and practical measure has not been endorsed by the entity with a contract under section 1890(a) [42 USCS

§ 1395aaa(a)], the Secretary may specify a measure that is not so endorsed as long as due consideration is given to measures that have been endorsed or adopted by a consensus organization identified by the Secretary.

(iii) Time frame. Not later than October 1, 2012, the Secretary shall publish the measures selected under this subparagraph that will be applicable with respect to fiscal year 2014.

(E) Public availability of data submitted. The Secretary shall establish procedures for making data submitted under subparagraph (C) available to the public. Such procedures shall ensure that a hospice program has the opportunity to review the data that is to be made public with respect to the hospice program prior to such data being made public. The Secretary shall report quality measures that relate to hospice care provided by hospice programs on the Internet website of the Centers for Medicare & Medicaid Services.

(6)(A) The Secretary shall collect additional data and information as the Secretary determines appropriate to revise payments for hospice care under this subsection pursuant to subparagraph (D) and for other purposes as determined appropriate by the Secretary. The Secretary shall begin to collect such data by not later than January 1, 2011.

(B) The additional data and information to be collected under subparagraph (A) may include data and information on—

(i) charges and payments;

(ii) the number of days of hospice care which are attributable to individuals who are entitled to, or enrolled for, benefits under part A [42 USCS §§ 1395c et seq.]; and

(iii) with respect to each type of service included in hospice care—

(I) the number of days of hospice care attributable to the type of service;

(II) the cost of the type of service; and

(III) the amount of payment for the type of service;

(iv) charitable contributions and other revenue of the hospice program;

(v) the number of hospice visits;

(vi) the type of practitioner providing the visit; and

(vii) the length of the visit and other basic information with respect to the visit.

(C) The Secretary may collect the additional data and information under subparagraph (A) on cost reports, claims, or other mechanisms as the Secretary determines to be appropriate.

(D)(i) Notwithstanding the preceding paragraphs of this subsection, not earlier than October 1, 2013, the Secretary shall, by regulation, implement revisions to the methodology for determining the payment rates for routine home care and other services included in hospice care under this part, as the Secretary determines to be appropriate. Such revisions may be based on an analysis of data and information collected under subparagraph (A). Such revisions may include adjustments to per diem payments that reflect changes in resource intensity in providing such care and services during the course of the entire episode of hospice care.

(ii) Revisions in payment implemented pursuant to clause (i) shall result in the same estimated amount of aggregate expenditures under this title for hospice care furnished in the fiscal year in which such revisions in payment are implemented as would have been made under this title for such care in such fiscal year if such revisions had not been implemented.

(E) The Secretary shall consult with hospice programs and the Medicare Payment Advisory Commission regarding the additional data and information to be collected under subparagraph (A) and the payment revisions under subparagraph (D).

(7) In the case of hospice care provided by a hospice program under arrangements under section 1861(dd)(5)(D) [42 USCS § 1395x(dd)(5)(D)] made by another hospice program, the hospice program that made the arrangements shall bill and be paid for the hospice care.

(j) Elimination of lesser-of-cost-or-charges provision. (1) The lesser-of-cost-or-charges provisions (described in paragraph (2)) will not apply in the case of services provided by a class of provider of services if the Secretary determines and certifies to Congress that the failure of such provisions to apply to the services provided by that class of providers will not result in any increase in the amount of payments made for those services under this title [42 USCS §§ 1395 et seq.]. Such change will take effect with respect to services furnished, or cost reporting periods of providers, on or after such date as the Secretary shall provide in the certification. Such change for a class of provider shall be discontinued if the Secretary determines and notifies Congress that such change has resulted in an increase in the amount of payments made under this title [42 USCS §§ 1395 et seq.] for services provided by that class of provider.

(2) The lesser-of-cost-or-charges provisions referred to in paragraph (1) are as follows:

(A) Clause (B) of paragraph (1) and paragraph (2) of subsection (b).

(B) Section 1834(a)(1)(B) [42 USCS § 1395m(a)(1)(B)].

(C) So much of subparagraph (A) of section 1833(a)(2) [42 USCS § 1395l(a)(2)(A)] as provides for payment other than of the reasonable cost of such services, as determined under section 1861(v) [42 USCS § 1395x(v)].

(D) Subclause (II) of clause (i) and clause (ii) of section 1833(a)(2)(B) [42 USCS § 1395 l(a)(2)(B)(i)(II) and (ii)].

(k) Payments to home health agencies for durable medical equipment. The amount paid to any home health agency with respect to durable medical equipment for which payment may be made under this part [42 USCS §§ 1395c et seq.] shall be the amount described in section 1834(a)(1) [42 USCS § 1395m(a)(1)].

(l) Payment for inpatient critical access hospital services. (1) Except as provided in the subsequent paragraphs of this subsection, the amount of payment under this part [42 USCS §§ 1395c et seq.] for inpatient critical access hospital services is equal to 101 percent of the reasonable costs of the critical access hospital in providing such services.

(2) In the case of a distinct part psychiatric or rehabilitation unit of a critical access hospital described in section 1820(c)(2)(E) [42 USCS § 1395i-4(c)(2)(E)], the amount of payment for inpatient critical access hospital services of such unit shall be equal to the amount of the payment that would otherwise be made if such services were inpatient hospital services of a distinct part psychiatric or rehabilitation unit, respectively, described in the matter following clause (v) of section 1886(d)(1)(B) [42 USCS § 1395ww(d)(1)(B)].

(3)(A) The following rules shall apply in determining payment and reasonable costs under paragraph (1) for costs described in subparagraph (C) for a critical access hospital that would be a meaningful EHR user (as would be determined under paragraph (3) of section 1886(n) [42 USCS § 1395ww(n)]) for an EHR reporting period for a cost reporting period beginning during a payment year if such critical access hospital was treated as an eligible hospital under such section:

(i) The Secretary shall compute reasonable costs by expensing such costs in a single payment year and not depreciating such costs over a period of years (and shall include as costs with respect to cost reporting periods beginning during a payment year costs from previous cost reporting periods to the extent they have not been fully depreciated as of the period involved).

(ii) There shall be substituted for the Medicare share that would otherwise be applied under paragraph (1) a percent (not to exceed 100 percent) equal to the sum of—

(I) the Medicare share (as would be specified under paragraph (2)(D) of section 1886(n) [42 USCS § 1395ww(n)]) for such critical access hospital if such critical access hospital was treated as an eligible hospital under such section; and

(II) 20 percentage points.

(B) The payment under this paragraph with respect to a critical access hospital shall be paid through a prompt interim payment (subject to reconciliation) after submission and review of such information (as specified by the Secretary) necessary to make such payment, including information necessary to apply this paragraph. In no case may payment under this paragraph be made with respect to a cost reporting period beginning during a payment year after 2015 and in no case may a critical access hospital receive payment under this paragraph with respect to more than 4 consecutive payment years.

(C) The costs described in this subparagraph are costs for the purchase of certified EHR technology to which purchase depreciation (excluding interest) would apply if payment was made under paragraph (1) and not under this paragraph.

(D) For purposes of this paragraph, paragraph (4), and paragraph (5), the terms "certified EHR technology", "eligible hospital", "EHR reporting period", and "payment year" have the meanings given such terms in sections 1886(n) [42 USCS § 1395ww(n)].

(4)(A) Subject to subparagraph (C), for cost reporting periods beginning in fiscal year 2015 or a subsequent fiscal year, in the case of a critical access hospital that is not a meaningful EHR user (as would be determined under paragraph (3) of section 1886(n) [42 USCS § 1395ww(n)] if such critical access hospital was treated as an eligible hospital under such section) for an EHR reporting period with respect to such fiscal year, paragraph (1) shall be applied by substituting the applicable percent under subparagraph (B) for the percent described in such paragraph (1).

(B) The percent described in this subparagraph is—

(i) for fiscal year 2015, 100.66 percent;

(ii) for fiscal year 2016, 100.33 percent; and

(iii) for fiscal year 2017 and each subsequent fiscal year, 100 percent.

(C) The provisions of subclause (II) of section

1886(b)(3)(B)(ix) [42 USCS § 1395ww(b)(3)(B)(ix)] shall apply with respect to subparagraph (A) for a critical access hospital with respect to a cost reporting period beginning in a fiscal year in the same manner as such subclause applies with respect to subclause (I) of such section for a subsection (d) hospital with respect to such fiscal year.

(5) There shall be no administrative or judicial review under section 1869 [42 USCS § 1395ff], section 1878 [42 USCS § 1395oo], or otherwise, of—

(A) the methodology and standards for determining the amount of payment and reasonable cost under paragraph (3) and payment adjustments under paragraph (4), including selection of periods under section 1886(n)(2) [42 USCS § 1395ww(n)(2)] for determining, and making estimates or using proxies of, inpatient-bed-days, hospital charges, charity charges, and Medicare share under subparagraph (D) of section 1886(n)(2) [42 USCS § 1395ww(n)(2)];

(B) the methodology and standards for determining a meaningful EHR user under section 1886(n)(3) as would apply if the hospital was treated as an eligible hospital under section 1886(n) [42 USCS § 1395ww(n)], and the hardship exception under paragraph (4)(C);

(C) the specification of EHR reporting periods under section 1886(n)(6)(B) [42 USCS § 1395ww(n)(6)(B)] as applied under paragraphs (3) and (4); and

(D) the identification of costs for purposes of paragraph (3)(C).

(Aug. 14, 1935, ch 531, Title XVIII, Part A, § 1814, as added July 30, 1965, P. L. 89-97, Title I, Part 1, § 102(a), 79 Stat. 294; Jan. 2, 1968, P. L. 90-248, Title I, Part 3, §§ 126(a), 129(c)(5), (6)(A), 143(c), 81 Stat. 846, 848, 857; Oct. 30, 1972, P. L. 92-603, Title II, §§ 211(a), 226(c)(1), 227(b), 228(a), 233(a), 234(g)(1), 238(a), 247(a), 256(a), 278(a)(1)–(3), (b)(4), (17), 281(e), 86 Stat. 1382, 1404, 1405, 1407, 1411, 1413, 1416, 1425, 1447, 1453, 1454, 1456; Dec. 31, 1973, P. L. 93-233, § 18(k)(1), (2), 87 Stat. 970; Sept. 30, 1976, P. L. 94-437, Title IV, § 401(a), 90 Stat. 1408; Oct. 25, 1977, P. L. 95-142, § 23(a), (b), 91 Stat. 1208; June 13, 1978, P. L. 95-292, § 4 (f), 92 Stat. 315; Dec. 5, 1980, P. L. 96-499, Title IX, Part A, Subpart I, §§ 903(a), 930(e), (f), 931(b), 936(b), Subpart II, § 941(a), (b), 94 Stat. 2614, 2631, 2633, 2640, 2641; Aug. 13, 1981, P. L. 97-35, Title XXI, Subtitle B, Ch 1, §§ 2121(b), 2122(a)(1), 95 Stat. 796; Sept. 3, 1982, P. L. 97-248, Title I, Subtitle A, Part I, Subpart A, § 101(c)(1), Part II, § 122(c)(1), (2), 96 Stat. 335, 357; Jan. 12, 1983, P. L. 97-448, Title III, § 309(b)(7), 96 Stat. 2409; April 20, 1983, P. L. 98-21, Title VI, §§ 601(d), 602(b) in part, (c), 97 Stat. 152, 163; Aug. 29, 1983, P. L. 98-90, § 1, 97 Stat. 606; July 18, 1984, P. L. 98-369, Division B, Title III, Subtitle A, Part I, §§ 2308(b)(2)(A), 2321(a), (f), Part II, §§ 2335(a), 2336(a), (b), 2354(b)(1), 98 Stat. 1074, 1084, 1085, 1090, 1091, 1100; Nov. 8, 1984, P. L. 98-617, §§ 1, 3(a)(3), (b)(1), 98 Stat. 3294, 3296; April 7, 1986, P. L. 99-272, Title IX, Subtitle A, Part 1, Subpart B, § 9123(b), 100 Stat. 168; Dec. 22, 1987, P. L. 100-203, Title IV, Subtitle A, Part 1, § 4008(b)(1), Part 2, Subpart B, § 4024(a), Part 3, Subpart B, § 4062(d)(1), 101 Stat. 1330-55, 1330-73, 1330-108; July 1, 1988, P. L. 100-360, Title I, Subtitle A, § 104(d)(2), 102 Stat. 688; Dec. 13, 1989, P. L. 101-234, Title I, § 101(a)(1), 103 Stat. 1979; Dec. 19, 1989, P. L. 101-239, Title VI, Subtitle A, Part 1, Subpart A, § 6003(g)(3)(B)(ii), (iii), 6005(a),(b), Subpart B, § 6028, 103 Stat. 2152, 2160, 2168; Nov. 5, 1990, P. L. 101-508, Title IV, Subtitle A, Part 1, §§ 4006(b), 4008(i)(3), (m)(3)(A), 104 Stat. 1388-43, 1388a-51; June 13, 1991, P. L. 102-54, § 13(q)(3)(A)(iii), (iv), (B)(iv), 105 Stat. 279; Aug. 10, 1993, P. L. 103-66, Title XIII, Ch 2, Subch A, Part I, § 13504, 107 Stat. 579; Oct. 31, 1994, P. L. 103-432, Title I, Subtitle A, §§ 102(a)(3), (d), 106(b)(1)(A), 110(d)(1), 108 Stat. 4402, 4403, 4405, 4408; Aug. 5, 1997, P. L. 105-33, Title IV, Subtitle C, § 4201(c)(1), (3), Subtitle E, Ch 4, §§ 4441, 4442(a), 4443(b)(2), 4448, Subtitle G, Ch 1, Subch A, § 4603(c)(1), Subch B, § 4615(a), 111 Stat. 373, 422, 423, 424, 470, 475; Dec. 21, 2000, P. L. 106-554, § 1(a)(6), 114 Stat. 2763; Dec. 8, 2003, P. L. 108-173, Title IV, Subtitle A, §§ 405(a)(1), (g)(2), 408(b), Title V, Subtitle B, § 512(b), Title VII, Subtitle D, § 736(a)(1), (2), (c)(2)(A), Title IX, Subtitle E, § 946(b), 117 Stat. 2266, 2269, 2270, 2299, 2354, 2356, 2425; Feb. 17, 2009, P. L. 111-5, Div B, Title IV, Subtitle A, § 4102(a)(2), (b)(2), (d)(1), 123 Stat. 481, 483, 486; March 23, 2010, P. L. 111-148, Title III, Subtitle A, Part I, § 3004(c), Subtitle B, Part I, § 3108(a), Part III, § 3132, Subtitle E, § 3401(g), Title VI, Subtitle E, §§ 6404(a)(1), 6405(b)(1), 6407(a)(1), Title X, Subtitle C, § 10319(f), Subtitle F, §§ 10604(1), 10605(a), 124 Stat. 370, 418, 430, 484, 767, 768, 769, 949, 1006.)

HISTORY; ANCILLARY LAWS AND DIRECTIVES

References in text:

The "Patient Protection and Affordable Care Act", referred to in subsec. (i)(1)(C), is Act March 23, 2010, P. L. 111-148. For full classification of such Act, consult USCS Tables volumes.

Amendments:

2010. Act March 23, 2010, in subsec. (a), in para. (2)(C), deleted "and" following "reviewed by a physician;", and inserted ", and, in the case of a certification made by a physician after January 1, 2010, prior to making such certification the physician must document that the physician himself or herself, or a nurse practitioner or clinical nurse specialist (as those terms are defined in section 1861(aa)(5)) who is working in collaboration with the physician in accordance with State law, or a certified nurse-midwife (as defined in section 1861(gg)) as authorized by State law, or a physician assistant (as defined in section 1861(aa)(5)) under the supervision of the physician, has had a face-to-face encounter (including through use of telehealth, subject to the requirements in section 1834(m), and other than with respect to encounters that are incident to services involved) with the individual within a reasonable timeframe as determined by the Secretary", and in para. (7), in subpara. (B), deleted "and" following the concluding semicolon, and added subpara. (D); and in subsec. (i), in para. (1)(C), in cl. (ii), in the introductory matter, inserted "(before the first fiscal year in which the payment revisions described in paragraph (6)(D) are implemented)", and in subcl. (VII), inserted "(before the first fiscal year in which the payment revisions described in paragraph (6)(D) are implemented), subject to clause (iv),", and added cls. (iii)–(v), redesignated para. (5) as para. (7), and inserted new paras. (5) and (6).

Section 10319(f) of such Act further, in subsec. (i)(1)(C), in cls. (iv)(II) and (v), substituted "0.3" for "0.5".

Such Act further (applicable to items and services furnished on or after 1/1/2011, as provided by § 3108(b) of such Act, which appears as a note to this section), in subsec. (a), in para. (2), substituted ", a clinical nurse specialist, or a physician assistant (as those terms are defined in section 1861(aa)(5))" for "or clinical nurse specialist", and in the concluding matter, substituted "clinical nurse specialist, or physician assistant" for "or clinical nurse specialist".

Such Act further (applicable to services furnished on or after 1/1/2010, as provided by § 6404(b)(1) of such Act, which appears as a note to this section), in subsec. (a), in para. (1), substituted "period ending 1 calendar year after the date of service;" for "period of 3 calendar years following the year in which such services are furnished (deeming any services furnished in the last 3 calendar months of any calendar year to have been furnished in the succeeding calendar year) except that where the Secretary deems that efficient administration so requires, such period may be reduced to not less than 1 calendar year;", and in the concluding matter, added the sentence beginning "In applying paragraph (1), . . .".

Such Act further (applicable to written orders and certifications made on or after 7/1/2010, as provided by § 6405(d) of such Act, which appears as a note to this section), in subsec. (a)(2), in the introductory matter, inserted "or, in the case of services described in subparagraph (C), a physician enrolled under section 1866(j),".

Other provisions:

Application of amendments made by § 3108 of Act March 23, 2010. Act March 23, 2010, P. L. 111-148, Title III, Subtitle B, Part I, § 3108(b), 124 Stat. 418, provides: "The amendments made by this section [amending subsec. (a) of this section] shall apply to items and services furnished on or after January 1, 2011.".

Application of amendments made by § 6404 of Act March 23, 2010. Act March 23, 2010, P. L. 111-148, Title VI, Subtitle E, § 6404(b), 124 Stat. 768, provides:

"(1) In general. The amendments made by subsection (a) [amending 42 USCS §§ 1395f, 1395n, and 1395u] shall apply to services furnished on or after January 1, 2010.

"(2) Services furnished before 2010. In the case of services furnished before January 1, 2010, a bill or request for payment under section 1814(a)(1), 1842(b)(3)(B), or 1835(a) [42 USCS § 1395f(a)(1), 1395u(b)(3)(B), or 1395n(a)] shall be filed not later that December 31, 2010.".

Application to other items or services. Act March 23, 2010, P. L. 111-148, Title VI, Subtitle E, § 6405(c), 124 Stat. 768, provides: "The Secretary may extend the requirement applied by the amendments made by subsections (a) and (b) [amending 42 USCS §§ 1395f, 1395m, and 1395n] to durable medical equipment and home health services (relating to requiring certifications and written orders to be made by enrolled physicians and health professions) to all other categories of items or services under title XVIII of the Social Security Act (42 U.S.C. 1395 et seq.), including covered part D drugs as defined in section 1860D-2(e) of such Act (42 U.S.C. 1395w-102), that are ordered, prescribed, or referred by a physician enrolled under section 1866(j) of such Act (42 U.S.C. 1395cc(j)) or an eligible professional under section 1848(k)(3)(B) of such Act (42 U.S.C. 1395w-4(k)(3)(B)).".

Application of amendments made by § 6405 of Act March 23, 2010. Act March 23, 2010, P. L. 111-148, Title VI, Subtitle E, § 6405(d), 124 Stat. 769, provides: "The amendments made by this section [amending 42 USCS §§ 1395f, 1395m, and 1395n] shall apply to written orders and certifications made on or after July 1, 2010.".

Application to other areas under Medicare. Act March 23, 2010, P. L. 111-148, Title VI, Subtitle E, § 6407(c), 124 Stat. 770, provides: "The Secretary may apply the face-to-face encounter requirement described in the amendments made by subsections (a) and (b) [amending 42 USCS §§ 1395f, 1395m, and 1395n] to other items and services for which payment is provided under title XVIII of the Social Security Act [42 USCS §§ 1395 et seq.] based upon a finding that such an decision would reduce the risk of waste, fraud, or abuse.".

Application to Medicaid. Act March 23, 2010, P. L. 111-148, Title VI, Subtitle E, § 6407(d), 124 Stat. 770, provides: "The requirements pursuant to the amendments made by subsections (a) and (b) [amending 42 USCS §§ 1395f, 1395m, and 1395n] shall apply in the case of physicians making certifications for home health services under title XIX of the Social Security Act [42 USCS §§ 1396 et seq.] in the same manner and to the same extent as such requirements apply in the case of physicians making such certifications under title XVIII of such Act [42 USCS §§ 1395 et seq.].".

§ 1395i. Federal Hospital Insurance Trust Fund

(a) Creation; deposits; transfers from Treasury. There is hereby created on the books of the Treasury of the United States a trust fund to be known as the "Federal Hospital Insurance Trust Fund" (hereinafter in this section referred to as the "Trust Fund"). The Trust Fund shall consist of such gifts and bequests as may be made as provided in section 201(i)(1) [42 USCS § 401(i)(1)], and such amounts as may be deposited in, or appropriated to, such fund as provided in this part [42 USCS §§ 1395c et seq.]. There are hereby appropriated to the Trust Fund for the fiscal year ending June 30, 1966, and for each fiscal year thereafter, out of any moneys in the Treasury not otherwise appropriated, amounts equivalent to 100 per centum of—

(1) the taxes imposed by sections 3101(b) and 3111(b) of the Internal Revenue Code of 1954 [1986] [26 USCS §§ 3101(b) and 3111(b)] with respect to wages reported to the Secretary of the Treasury or his delegate pursuant to subtitle F of such Code [26 USCS §§ 6001 et seq.] after December 31, 1965, as determined by the Secretary of the Treasury by applying the applicable rates of tax under such sections to such wages, which wages shall be certified by the Commissioner of Social Security on the basis of records of wages established and maintained by the Commissioner of Social Security in accordance with such reports; and

(2) the taxes imposed by section 1401(b) of the Internal Revenue Code of 1954 [1986] [26 USCS § 1401(b)] with respect to self-employment income reported to the Secretary of the Treasury or his delegate on tax returns under subtitle F of such Code [26 USCS §§ 6001 et seq.], as determined by the Secretary of the Treasury by applying the applicable rate of tax under such section to such self-employment income, which self-employment income shall be certified by the Commissioner of Social Security on the basis of records of self-employment established and maintained by the Commissioner of Social Security in accordance with such returns.

The amounts appropriated by the preceding sentence shall be transferred from time to time from the general fund in the Treasury to the Trust Fund, such amounts to be determined on the basis of estimates by the Secretary of the Treasury of the taxes, specified in the preceding sentence, paid to or deposited into the Treasury; and proper adjustments shall be made in amounts subsequently transferred to the extent prior estimates were in excess of or were less than the taxes specified in such sentence.

(b) Board of Trustees; composition; meetings; duties. With respect to the Trust Fund, there is hereby created a body to be known as the Board of Trustees of the Trust Fund (hereinafter in this section referred to as the "Board of Trustees") composed of the Commissioner of Social Security, the Secretary of the Treasury, the Secretary of Labor, and the Secretary of Health and Human Services, all ex officio, and of two members of the public (both of whom may not be from the same political party), who shall be nominated by the President for a term of four years and subject to confirmation by the Senate. A member of the Board of Trustees serving as a member of the public and nominated and confirmed to fill a vacancy occurring during a term shall be nominated and confirmed only for the remainder of such term. An individual nominated and confirmed as a member of the public may serve in such position after the expiration of such member's term until the earlier of the time at which the member's successor takes office or the time at which a report of the Board is first issued under paragraph (2) after the expiration of the member's term. The Secretary of the Treasury shall be the Managing Trustee of the Board of Trustees (hereinafter in this section referred to as the "Managing Trustee"). The Administrator of the Centers for Medicare & Medicaid Services shall serve as the Secretary of the Board of Trustees. The Board of Trustees shall meet not less frequently than once each calendar year. It shall be the duty of the Board of Trustees to—

(1) Hold the Trust Fund;

(2) Report to the Congress not later than the first day of April of each year on the operation and status of the Trust Fund during the preceding fiscal year and on its expected operation and status during the current fiscal year and the next 2 fiscal years;

(3) Report immediately to the Congress whenever the Board is of the opinion that the amount of the Trust Fund is unduly small; and

(4) Review the general policies followed in managing the Trust Fund, and recommend changes in such policies, including necessary changes in the provisions of law which govern the way in which the Trust Fund is to be managed.

The report provided for in paragraph (2) shall include a statement of the assets of, and the disbursements made from, the Trust Fund during the preceding fiscal year, an estimate of the expected income to, and disbursements to be made from, the Trust Fund during the current fiscal year and each of the next 2 fiscal years, and a statement of the actuarial status of the Trust Fund. Such report shall also include an actuarial opinion by the Chief Actuary of the Centers for Medicare & Medicaid Services certifying that the techniques and methodologies used are generally accepted within the actuarial profession and that the assumptions and cost estimates used are reasonable. Such report shall be printed as a House document of the session of the Congress to which the report is made. A person serving on the Board of Trustees shall not be considered to be a fiduciary and shall not be personally liable for actions taken in such capacity with respect to the Trust Fund. Each report provided under paragraph (2) beginning with the report in 2005 shall include the information specified in section 801(a) of the Medicare Prescription Drug, Improvement, and Modernization Act of 2003 [note to this section].

(c) Investment of Trust Fund by Managing Trustee. It shall be the duty of the Managing Trustee to invest such portion of the Trust Fund as is not, in his judgment, required to meet current withdrawals. Such investments may be made only in interest-bearing obligations of the United States or in obligations guaranteed as to both principal and interest by the United States. For such purpose such obligations may be acquired (1) on original issue at the issue price, or (2) by purchase of outstanding obligations at the market price. The purposes for which obligations of the United States may be issued under chapter 31 of title 31, United States Code [31 USCS §§ 3101 et seq.], are hereby extended to authorize the issuance at par of public-debt obligations for purchase by the Trust Fund. Such obligations issued for purchase by the Trust Fund shall have maturities fixed with due regard for the needs of the Trust Fund and shall bear interest at a rate equal to the average market yield (computed by the Managing Trustee on the basis of market quotations as of the end of the calendar month next preceding the date of such issue) on all marketable interest-bearing obligations of the United States then forming a part of the public debt which are not due or callable until after the expiration of 4 years from the end of such calendar month; except that where such average market yield is not a multiple of one-eighth of 1 per centum, the rate of interest on such obligations shall be the multiple of one-eighth of 1 per centum nearest such market yield. The Managing Trustee may purchase other interest-bearing obligations of the United States or obligations guaranteed as to both principal and interest by the United States, on original issue or at the market price, only where he determines that the purchase of such other obligations is in the public interest.

(d) Authority of Managing Trustee to sell obligations. Any obligations acquired by the Trust Fund (except public-debt obligations issued exclusively to the Trust Fund) may be sold by the Managing Trustee at the market price, and such public-debt obligations may be redeemed at par plus accrued interest.

(e) Interest on and proceeds from sale or redemption of obligations. The interest on, and the proceeds from the sale or redemption of, any obligations held in the Trust Fund shall be credited to and form a part of the Trust Fund.

(f) Payment of estimated taxes. (1) The Managing Trustee is directed to pay from time to time from the Trust Fund into the Treasury the amount estimated by him as taxes imposed under section 3101(b) [26 USCS § 3101(b)] which are subject to refund under section 6413(c) of the Internal Revenue Code of 1954 [1986] [26 USCS § 6413(c)] with respect to wages paid after December 31, 1965. Such taxes shall be determined on the basis of the records of wages established and maintained by the Commissioner of Social Security in accordance with the wages reported to the Secretary of the Treasury or his delegate pursuant to subtitle F of the Internal Revenue Code of 1954 [1986] [26 USCS §§ 6001 et seq.], and the Commissioner of Social Security shall furnish the Managing Trustee such information as may be required by the Managing Trustee for such purpose. The payments by the Managing Trustee shall be covered into the Treasury as repayments to the account for refunding internal revenue collections.

(2) Repayments made under paragraph (1) shall not be available for expenditures but shall be carried to the surplus fund of the Treasury. If it subsequently appears that the estimates under such paragraph in any particular period were too high or too low, appropriate adjustments shall be made by the Managing Trustee in future payments.

(g) Transfers from other Funds. There shall be transferred periodically (but not less often than once each fiscal year) to the Trust Fund from the Federal Old-Age and Survivors Insurance Trust Fund and from the Federal Disability Insurance Trust Fund amounts equivalent to the amounts not previously so transferred which the Secretary of Health and Human Services shall have certified as overpayments (other than amounts so certified to the Railroad Retirement Board) pursuant to section 1870(b) of this Act [42 USCS § 1395gg(b)]. There shall be transferred periodically (but not less often than once each fiscal year) to the Trust Fund from the Railroad Retirement Account amounts equivalent to the amounts not previously so transferred which the Secretary of Health and Human Services shall have certified as overpayments to the Railroad Retirement Board pursuant to section 1870(b) of this Act [42 USCS § 1395gg(b)].

(h) Payments from Trust Fund amounts certified by Secretary. The Managing Trustee shall also pay from time to time from the Trust Fund such amounts as the Secretary of Health and Human Services certifies are necessary to make the payments provided for by this part [42 USCS §§ 1395c et seq.], and the payments with respect to administrative expenses in accordance with section 201(g)(1) [42 USCS § 401(g)(1)].

(i) Payment of travel expenses for travel within United States; reconsideration interviews and proceedings before administrative law judges. There are authorized to be made available for expenditure out of the Trust Fund such amounts as are required to pay travel expenses, either on an actual cost or commuted basis, to parties, their representatives, and all reasonably necessary witnesses for travel within the United States (as defined in section 210(i) [42 USCS § 410(i)]) to attend reconsideration interviews and proceedings before administrative law judges with respect to any determination under this title [42 USCS §§ 1395 et seq.]. The amount available under the preceding sentence for payment for air travel by any person shall not exceed the coach fare for air travel between the points involved unless the use of first-class accommodations is required (as determined under regulations of the Secretary) because of such person's health condition or the unavailability of alternative accommodations; and the amount available for payment for other travel by any person shall not exceed the cost of travel (between the points involved) by the most economical and expeditious means of transportation appropriate to such person's health condition, as specified in such regulations. The amount available for payment under this subsection for travel by a representative to attend an administrative proceeding before an administrative law judge or other adjudicator shall not exceed the maximum amount allowable under this subsection for such travel originating within the geographic area of the office having jurisdiction over such proceeding.

(j) Loans from other Funds; interest; repayment; report to Congress. (1) If at any time prior to January 1988 the Managing Trustee determines that borrowing authorized under this subsection is appropriate in order to best meet the need for financing the benefit payments from the Federal Hospital Insurance Trust Fund, the Managing Trustee may, subject to paragraph (5), borrow such amounts as he determines to be appropriate from either the Federal Old-Age and Survivors Insurance Trust Fund or the Federal Disability Insurance Trust Fund for transfer to and deposit in the Federal Hospital Insurance Trust Fund.

(2) In any case where a loan has been made to the Federal Hospital Insurance Trust Fund under paragraph (1), there shall be transferred on the last day of each month after such loan is made, from such Trust Fund to the lending Trust Fund, the total interest accrued to such day with respect to the unrepaid balance of such loan at a rate equal to the rate which the lending Trust Fund would earn on the amount involved if the loan were an investment under subsection (c) (even if such an investment would earn interest at a rate different than the rate earned by investments redeemed by the lending fund in order to make the loan).

(3)(A) If in any month after a loan has been made to the Federal Hospital Insurance Trust Fund under paragraph (1), the Managing Trustee determines that the assets of such Trust Fund are sufficient to permit repayment of all or part of any loans made to such Fund under paragraph (1), he shall make such repayments as he determines to be appropriate.

(B)(i) If on the last day of any year after a loan has been made under paragraph (1) by the Federal Old-Age and Survivors Insurance Trust Fund or the Federal Disability Insurance Trust Fund to the Federal Hospital Insurance Trust Fund, the Managing Trustee determines that the Hospital Insurance Trust Fund ratio exceeds 15 percent, he shall transfer from such Trust Fund to the lending trust fund an amount that—

(I) together with any amounts transferred to another lending trust fund under this paragraph for such year, will reduce the Hospital Insurance Trust Fund ratio to 15 percent; and

(II) does not exceed the outstanding balance of such loan.

(ii) Amounts required to be transferred under clause (i) shall be transferred on the last day of the first month of the year succeeding the year in which the determination described in clause (i) is made.

(iii) For purposes of this subparagraph, the term "Hospital Insurance Trust Fund ratio" means, with respect to any calendar year, the ratio of—

(I) the balance in the Federal Hospital Insurance Trust Fund, as of the last day of such calendar year; to

(II) the amount estimated by the Secretary to be the total amount to be paid from the Federal Hospital Insurance Trust Fund during the calendar year following such calendar year (other than payments of interest on, and repayments of, loans from the Federal Old-Age and Survivors Insurance Trust Fund and the Federal Disability Insurance Trust Fund under paragraph (1)), and reducing the amount of any transfer to the Railroad Retirement Account by the amount of any transfers into such Trust Fund from the Railroad Retirement Account.

(C)(i) The full amount of all loans made under paragraph (1) (whether made before or after January 1, 1983) shall be repaid at the earliest feasible date and in any event no later than December 31, 1989.

(ii) For the period after December 31, 1987 and before January 1, 1990, the Managing Trustee shall transfer each month from the Federal Hospital Insurance Trust Fund to any Trust Fund that is owed any amount by the Federal Hospital Insurance Trust Fund on a loan made under paragraph (1), an amount not less than an amount equal to (I) the amount owed to such Trust Fund by the Federal Hospital Insurance Trust Fund at the beginning of such month (plus the interest accrued on the outstanding balance of such loan during such month), divided by (II) the number of months elapsing after the preceding month and before January 1990. The Managing Trustee may, during this period, transfer larger amounts than prescribed by the preceding sentence.

(4) The Board of Trustees shall make a timely report to the Congress of any amounts transferred (including interest payments) under this subsection.

(5)(A) No amounts may be loaned by the Federal Old-Age and Survivors Insurance Trust Fund or the Federal Disability Insurance Trust Fund under paragraph (1) during any month if the OASDI trust fund ratio for such month is less than 10 percent.

(B) For purposes of this paragraph, the term "OASDI trust fund ratio" means, with respect to any month, the ratio of—

(i) the combined balance in the Federal Old-Age and Survivors Insurance Trust Fund and the Federal Disability Insurance Trust Fund, reduced by the outstanding amount of any loan (including interest thereon) theretofore made to either such Trust Fund from the Federal Hospital Insurance Trust Fund under section 201(l) [42 USCS § 401(l)], as of the last day of the second month preceding such month, to

(ii) the amount obtained by multiplying by twelve the total amount which (as estimated by the Secretary) will be paid from the Federal Old-Age and Survivors Insurance Trust Fund and the Federal Disability Insurance Trust Fund during the month for which such ratio is to be determined for all purposes authorized by section 201 [42 USCS § 401] (other than payments of interest on, or repayments of, loans from the Federal Hospital Insurance Trust Fund under section 201(l) [42 USCS § 401(l)], but excluding any transfer payments between such trust funds and reducing the amount of any transfers to the Railroad Retirement Account by the amount of any transfers into either such trust fund from that Account.

(k) Health Care Fraud and Abuse Control Account. (1) Establishment. There is hereby established in the Trust Fund an expenditure account to be known as the "Health Care Fraud and Abuse Control Account" (in this subsection referred to as the "Account").

(2) Appropriated amounts to Trust Fund. (A) In general. There are hereby appropriated to the Trust Fund—

(i) such gifts and bequests as may be made as provided in subparagraph (B);

(ii) such amounts as may be deposited in the Trust Fund as provided in sections 242(b) and 249(c) of the Health Insurance Portability and Accountability Act of 1996 [notes to this section], and title XI [42 USCS §§ 1301 et seq.]; and

(iii) such amounts as are transferred to the Trust Fund under subparagraph (C).

(B) Authorization to accept gifts. The Trust Fund is authorized to accept on behalf of the United States money gifts and bequests made unconditionally to the Trust Fund, for the benefit of the Account or any activity financed through the Account.

(C) Transfer of amounts. The Managing Trustee shall transfer to the Trust Fund, under rules similar to the rules in section 9601 of the Internal Revenue Code of 1986 [26 USCS § 9601], an amount equal to the sum of the following:

(i) Criminal fines recovered in cases involving a Federal health care offense (as defined in section 24(a) of title 18, United States Code).

(ii) Civil monetary penalties and assessments imposed in health care cases, including amounts recovered under titles XI, XVIII, and XIX [42 USCS §§ 1301 et seq., 1395 et seq., 1396 et seq.], and chapter 38 of title 31, United States Code [31 USCS §§ 3801 et seq.] (except as otherwise provided by law).

(iii) Amounts resulting from the forfeiture of

property by reason of a Federal health care offense.

(iv) Penalties and damages obtained and otherwise creditable to miscellaneous receipts of the general fund of the Treasury obtained under sections 3729 through 3733 of title 31, United States Code (known as the False Claims Act), in cases involving claims related to the provision of health care items and services (other than funds awarded to a relator, for restitution or otherwise authorized by law).

(D) Application. Nothing in subparagraph (C)(iii) shall be construed to limit the availability of recoveries and forfeitures obtained under title I of the Employee Retirement Income Security Act of 1974 for the purpose of providing equitable or remedial relief for employee welfare benefit plans, and for participants and beneficiaries under such plans, as authorized under such title.

(3) Appropriated amounts to account for fraud and abuse control program, etc. (A) Departments of Health and Human Services and Justice. (i) In general. There are hereby appropriated to the Account from the Trust Fund such sums as the Secretary and the Attorney General certify are necessary to carry out the purposes described in subparagraph (C), to be available without further appropriation until expended, in an amount not to exceed—

(I) for fiscal year 1997, $104,000,000;

(II) for each of the fiscal years 1998 through 2003, the limit for the preceding fiscal year, increased by 15 percent;

(III) for each of fiscal years 2004, 2005, and 2006, the limit for fiscal year 2003; and

(IV) for each fiscal year after fiscal year 2006, the limit under this clause for the preceding fiscal year, increased by the percentage increase in the consumer price index for all urban consumers (all items; United States city average) over the previous year.

(ii) Medicare and medicaid activities. For each fiscal year, of the amount appropriated in clause (i), the following amounts shall be available only for the purposes of the activities of the Office of the Inspector General of the Department of Health and Human Services with respect to the programs under this title and title XIX [42 USCS §§ 1395 et seq. and 1396 et seq.]—

(I) for fiscal year 1997, not less than $60,000,000 and not more than $70,000,000;

(II) for fiscal year 1998, not less than $80,000,000 and not more than $90,000,000;

(III) for fiscal year 1999, not less than $90,000,000 and not more than $100,000,000;

(IV) for fiscal year 2000, not less than $110,000,000 and not more than $120,000,000;

(V) for fiscal year 2001, not less than $120,000,000 and not more than $130,000,000;

(VI) for fiscal year 2002, not less than $140,000,000 and not more than $150,000,000;

(VII) for each of fiscal years 2003, 2004, 2005, and 2006, not less than $150,000,000 and not more than $160,000,000;

(VIII) for fiscal year 2007, not less than $160,000,000, increased by the percentage increase in the consumer price index for all urban consumers (all items; United States city average) over the previous year; and

(IX) for each fiscal year after fiscal year 2007, not less than the amount required under this clause for the preceding fiscal year, increased by the percentage increase in the consumer price index for all urban consumers (all items; United States city average) over the previous year.

(B) Federal Bureau of Investigation. There are hereby appropriated from the general fund of the United States Treasury and hereby appropriated to the Account for transfer to the Federal Bureau of Investigation to carry out the purposes described in subparagraph (C), to be available without further appropriation until expended—

(i) for fiscal year 1997, $47,000,000;

(ii) for fiscal year 1998, $56,000,000;

(iii) for fiscal year 1999, $66,000,000;

(iv) for fiscal year 2000, $76,000,000;

(v) for fiscal year 2001, $88,000,000;

(vi) for fiscal year 2002, $101,000,000;

(vii) for each of fiscal years 2003, 2004, 2005, and 2006, $114,000,000; and

(viii) for each fiscal year after fiscal year 2006, the amount to be appropriated under this subparagraph for the preceding fiscal year, increased by the percentage increase in the consumer price index for all urban consumers (all items; United States city average) over the previous year.

(C) Use of funds. The purposes described in this subparagraph are to cover the costs (including equipment, salaries and benefits, and travel and training) of the administration and operation of the health care fraud and abuse control program established under section 1128C(a) [42 USCS § 1320a-7c(a)], including the costs of—

(i) prosecuting health care matters (through criminal, civil, and administrative proceedings);

(ii) investigations;

(iii) financial and performance audits of health care programs and operations;

(iv) inspections and other evaluations; and

(v) provider and consumer education regarding compliance with the provisions of title XI [42 USCS §§ 1301 et seq.].

(4) Appropriated amounts to account for Medicare Integrity Program. (A) In general. There are hereby appropriated to the Account from the Trust Fund for each fiscal year such amounts as are necessary for activities described in paragraph (3)(C) and to carry out the Medicare Integrity Program under section 1893 [42 USCS § 1395ddd], subject to subparagraphs (B), (C), and (D) and to be available without further appropriation until expended.

(B) Amounts specified. Subject to subparagraph (C), the amount appropriated under subparagraph (A) for a fiscal year is as follows:

(i) For fiscal year 1997, such amount shall be not less than $430,000,000 and not more than $440,000,000.

(ii) For fiscal year 1998, such amount shall be not less than $490,000,000 and not more than $500,000,000.

(iii) For fiscal year 1999, such amount shall be not less than $550,000,000 and not more than $560,000,000.

(iv) For fiscal year 2000, such amount shall be not less than $620,000,000 and not more than $630,000,000.

(v) For fiscal year 2001, such amount shall be not less than $670,000,000 and not more than $680,000,000.

(vi) For fiscal year 2002, such amount shall be not less than $690,000,000 and not more than $700,000,000.

(vii) For each fiscal year after fiscal year 2002, such amount shall be not less than $710,000,000 and not more than $720,000,000.

(C) Adjustments. The amount appropriated under subparagraph (A) for a fiscal year is increased as follows:

(i) For fiscal year 2006, $100,000,000.

(ii) For each fiscal year after 2010, by the percentage increase in the consumer price index for all urban consumers (all items; United States city average) over the previous year.

(D) Expansion of the Medicare-Medicaid Data Match Program. The amount appropriated under subparagraph (A) for a fiscal year is further increased as follows for purposes of carrying out section 1893(b)(6) [42 USCS § 1395ddd(b)(6)] for the respective fiscal year:

(i) $12,000,000 for fiscal year 2006.

(ii) $24,000,000 for fiscal year 2007.

(iii) $36,000,000 for fiscal year 2008.

(iv) $48,000,000 for fiscal year 2009.

(v) $60,000,000 for fiscal year 2010 and each fiscal year thereafter.

(5) Annual report. Not later than January 1, the Secretary and the Attorney General shall submit jointly a report to Congress which identifies—

(A) the amounts appropriated to the Trust Fund for the previous fiscal year under paragraph (2)(A) and the source of such amounts; and

(B) the amounts appropriated from the Trust Fund for such year under paragraph (3) and the justification for the expenditure of such amounts.

(6) GAO report. Not later than June 1, 1998, and January 1 of 2000, 2002, and 2004, the Comptroller General of the United States shall submit a report to Congress which—

(A) identifies—

(i) the amounts appropriated to the Trust Fund for the previous two fiscal years under paragraph (2)(A) and the source of such amounts; and

(ii) the amounts appropriated from the Trust Fund for such fiscal years under paragraph (3) and the justification for the expenditure of such amounts;

(B) identifies any expenditures from the Trust Fund with respect to activities not involving the program under this title [42 USCS §§ 1395 et seq.];

(C) identifies any savings to the Trust Fund, and any other savings, resulting from expenditures from the Trust Fund; and

(D) analyzes such other aspects of the operation of the Trust Fund as the Comptroller General of the United States considers appropriate.

(7) Additional funding. In addition to the funds otherwise appropriated to the Account from the Trust Fund under paragraphs (3) and (4) and for purposes described in paragraphs (3)(C) and (4)(A), there are hereby appropriated an additional $10,000,000 to such Account from such Trust Fund for each of fiscal years 2011 through 2020. The funds appropriated under this paragraph shall be allocated in the same proportion as the total funding appropriated with respect to paragraphs (3)(A) and (4)(A) was allocated with respect to fiscal year 2010, and shall be available without further appropriation until expended.

(8) Additional funding. (A) In general. In addition to the funds otherwise appropriated to the Account from the Trust Fund under paragraphs (3)(C) and (4)(A) and for purposes described in paragraphs (3)(C) and (4)(A), there are hereby appropriated to such Account from such Trust Fund the following additional amounts:

(i) For fiscal year 2011, $95,000,000.

(ii) For fiscal year 2012, $55,000,000.

(iii) For each of fiscal years 2013 and 2014, $30,000,000.

(iv) For each of fiscal years 2015 and 2016, $20,000,000.

(B) Allocation. The funds appropriated under this paragraph shall be allocated in the same proportion as the total funding appropriated with respect to paragraphs (3)(A) and (4)(A) was allocated with respect to fiscal year 2010, and shall be available without further appropriation until expended.

(Aug. 14, 1935, ch 531, Title XVIII, Part A, § 1817, as added July 30, 1965, P. L. 89-97, Title I, Part 1, § 102(a), 79 Stat. 299; Jan. 2, 1968, P. L. 90-248, Title I, Part 4, § 169(a), 81 Stat. 875; Oct. 30, 1972, P. L. 92-603, Title I, § 132(d), 86 Stat. 1361; June 13, 1978, P. L. 95-292, § 5, 92 Stat. 315; June 9, 1980, P. L. 96-265, Title III, § 310(c), 94 Stat. 460; Dec. 29, 1981, P. L. 97-123, Title II, § 1(b), 95 Stat. 1659; April 20, 1983, P. L. 98-21, Title I, Part E, §§ 141(b), 142(b)(1), (2)(A), (3), (4), Part F, § 154(b), Title III, Part C, § 341(b), 97 Stat. 98, 100, 101, 107, 135; July 18, 1984, P. L. 98-369, Division B, Title III, Subtitle A, Part II, §§ 2337(a), 2354(b)(2), Title VI, Subtitle D, § 2663(j)(2)(F)(i), 98 Stat. 1091, 1100, 1160; April 7, 1986, P. L. 99-272, Title IX, Subtitle A, Part 2, Subpart B, § 9213(b) in part, 100 Stat. 180; July 1, 1988, P. L. 100-360, Title II, Subtitle B, § 212(c)(3), 102 Stat. 741; Nov. 10, 1988, P. L. 100-647, Title VIII, Subtitle A, § 8005(a), 102 Stat. 3781; Dec. 13, 1989, P. L. 101-234, Title II, § 202(a), 103 Stat. 1981; Nov. 5, 1990, P. L. 101-508, Title V, Subtitle B, § 5106(c), 104 Stat. 1388-268; Aug. 15, 1994, P. L. 103-296, Title I, § 108(c)(1), 108 Stat. 1485; Aug. 21, 1996, P. L. 104-191, Title II, Subtitle A, § 201(b), 110 Stat. 1993; Aug. 5, 1997, P. L. 105-33, Title IV, Subtitle D, Ch 2, § 4318, 111 Stat. 392; Nov. 29, 1999, P. L. 106-113, Div B, § 1000(a)(6), 113 Stat. 1536; Dec. 8, 2003, P. L. 108-173, Title VII, Subtitle D, § 736(a)(5), (6), Title VIII, Subtitle A, § 801(d)(1), Title IX, § 900(e)(1)(D), 117 Stat. 2355, 2359, 2371; Feb. 8, 2006, P. L. 109-171, Title V, Subtitle C, § 5204, Title VI, Subtitle A, Ch. 3, § 6034(d)(2), 120 Stat. 48, 78; Dec. 20, 2006, P. L. 109-432, Div B, Title III, § 303, 120 Stat. 2992; March 23, 2010, P. L. 111-148, Title VI, Subtitle E, § 6402(i), 124 Stat. 760; March 30, 2010, P. L. 111-152, Title I, Subtitle D, § 1303(a), 124 Stat. 1057.)

§ 1395i-3. Requirements for, and assuring quality of care in, skilled nursing facilities [Caution: See prospective amendment notes below.]

(a) "Skilled nursing facility" defined. In this title [42 USCS §§ 1395 et seq.], the term "skilled nursing facility" means an institution (or a distinct part of an institution) which—

(1) is primarily engaged in providing to residents—

(A) skilled nursing care and related services for residents who require medical or nursing care, or

(B) rehabilitation services for the rehabilitation of injured, disabled, or sick persons,

and is not primarily for the care and treatment of mental diseases;

(2) has in effect a transfer agreement (meeting the requirements of section 1861(l) [42 USCS § 1395x(l)]) with one or more hospitals having agreements in effect under section 1866 [42 USCS § 1395cc]; and

(3) meets the requirements for a skilled nursing facility described in subsections (b), (c), and (d) of this section.

(b) Requirements relating to provision of services. (1) Quality of life. (A) In general. A skilled nursing facility must care for its residents in such a manner and in such an environment as will promote maintenance or enhancement of the quality of life of each resident.

(B) Quality assessment and assurance. A skilled nursing facility must maintain a quality assessment and assurance committee, consisting of the director of nursing services, a physician designated by the facility, and at least 3 other members of the facility's staff, which (i) meets at least quarterly to identify issues with respect to which quality assessment and assurance activities are necessary and (ii) develops and implements appropriate plans of action to correct identified quality deficiencies. A State or the Secretary may not require disclosure of the records of such committee except insofar as such disclosure is related to the compliance of such committee with the requirements of this subparagraph.

(2) Scope of services and activities under plan of care. A skilled nursing facility must provide services to attain or maintain the highest practicable physical, mental, and psychosocial well-being of each resident, in accordance with a written plan of care which—

(A) describes the medical, nursing, and psychosocial needs of the resident and how such needs will be met;

(B) is initially prepared, with the participation to the extent practicable of the resident or the resident's family or legal representative, by a team which includes the resident's attending physician and a registered professional nurse with responsibility for the resident; and

(C) is periodically reviewed and revised by such team after each assessment under paragraph (3).

(3) Residents' assessment. (A) Requirement. A skilled nursing facility must conduct a comprehensive, accurate, standardized, reproducible assessment of each resident's functional capacity, which assessment—

(i) describes the resident's capability to perform daily life functions and significant impairments in functional capacity;

(ii) is based on a uniform minimum data set specified by the Secretary under subsection (f)(6)(A);

(iii) uses an instrument which is specified by the State under subsection (e)(5); and

(iv) includes the identification of medical problems.

(B) Certification. (i) In general. Each such assessment must be conducted or coordinated (with the appropriate participation of health professionals) by a registered professional nurse who signs and certifies the completion of the assessment. Each individual who completes a portion of such an assessment shall sign and certify as to the accuracy of that portion of the assessment.

(ii) Penalty for falsification. (I) An individual who willfully and knowingly certifies under clause (i) a material and false statement in a resident assessment is subject to a civil money penalty of not more than $1,000 with respect to each assessment.

(II) An individual who willfully and knowingly causes another individual to certify under clause (i) a material and false statement in a resident assessment is subject to a civil money penalty of not more than $5,000 with respect to each assessment.

(III) The provisions of section 1128A [42 USCS § 1320a-7a] (other than subsections (a) and (b)) shall apply to a civil money penalty under this clause in the same manner as such provisions apply to a penalty or proceeding under section 1128A(a) [42 USCS § 1320a-7a(a)].

(iii) Use of independent assessors. If a State determines, under a survey under subsection (g) or otherwise, that there has been a knowing and willful certification of false assessments under this paragraph, the State may require (for a period specified by the State) that resident assessments under this paragraph be conducted and certified by individuals who are independent of the facility and who are approved by the State.

(C) Frequency. (i) In general. Subject to timeframes prescribed by the Secretary under section 1888(e)(6) [42 USCS § 1395yy(e)(6)], such an assessment must be conducted—

(I) promptly upon (but no later than 14 days after the date of) admission for each individual admitted on or after October 1, 1990, and by not later than January 1, 1991, for each resident of the facility on that date;

(II) promptly after a significant change in the resident's physical or mental condition; and

(III) in no case less often than once every 12 months.

(ii) Resident review. The skilled nursing facility must examine each resident no less frequently than once every 3 months and, as appropriate, revise the resident's assessment to assure the continuing accuracy of the assessment.

(D) Use. The results of such an assessment shall be used in developing, reviewing, and revising the resident's plan of care under paragraph (2).

(E) Coordination. Such assessments shall be coordinated with any State-required preadmission screening program to the maximum extent practicable in order to avoid duplicative testing and effort.

(4) Provision of services and activities. (A) In general. To the extent needed to fulfill all plans of care described in paragraph (2), a skilled nursing facility must provide, directly or under arrangements (or, with respect to dental services, under agreements) with others for the provision of—

(i) nursing services and specialized rehabilitative services to attain or maintain the highest practicable physical, mental, and psychosocial well-being of each resident;

(ii) medically-related social services to attain or maintain the highest practicable physical, mental, and psychosocial well-being of each resident;

(iii) pharmaceutical services (including procedures that assure the accurate acquiring, receiving, dispensing, and administering of all drugs and biologicals) to meet the needs of each resident;

(iv) dietary services that assure that the meals meet the daily nutritional and special dietary needs of each resident;

(v) an on-going program, directed by a qualified professional, of activities designed to meet the interests and the physical, mental, and psychosocial well-being of each resident;

(vi) routine and emergency dental services to meet the needs of each resident; and

(vii) treatment and services required by mentally ill and mentally retarded residents not otherwise provided or arranged for (or required to be provided or arranged for) by the State.

The services provided or arranged by the facility must meet professional standards of quality. Nothing in clause (vi) shall be construed as requiring a facility to provide or arrange for dental services described in that clause without additional charge.

(B) Qualified persons providing services. Services described in clauses (i), (ii), (iii), (iv), and (vi) of subparagraph (A) must be provided by qualified persons in accordance with each resident's written plan of care.

(C) Required nursing care. (i) In general. Except as provided in clause (ii), a skilled nursing facility must provide 24-hour licensed nursing service which is sufficient to meet nursing needs of its residents and must use the services of a registered professional nurse at least 8 consecutive hours a day, 7 days a week.

(ii) Exception. To the extent that clause (i) may be deemed to require that a skilled nursing facility engage the services of a registered professional nurse for more than 40 hours a week, the Secretary is authorized to waive such requirement if the Secretary finds that—

(I) the facility is located in a rural area and the supply of skilled nursing facility services in such area is not sufficient to meet the needs of individuals residing therein,

(II) the facility has one full-time registered professional nurse who is regularly on duty at such facility 40 hours a week,

(III) the facility either has only patients whose physicians have indicated (through physicians' orders or admission notes) that each such patient does not require the services of a registered nurse or a physician for a 48-hour period, or has made arrangements for a registered professional nurse or a physician to spend such time at such facility as may be indicated as necessary by the physician to provide necessary skilled nursing services on days when the regular full-time registered professional nurse is not on duty,

(IV) the Secretary provides notice of the waiver to the State long-term care ombudsman (established under section 307(a)(12) of the Older Americans Act of 1965 [42 USCS § 3027(a)(12)]) and the protection and advocacy system in the State for the mentally ill and the mentally retarded, and

(V) the facility that is granted such a waiver notifies residents of the facility (or, where appropriate, the guardians or legal representatives of such residents) and members of their immediate families of the waiver.

A waiver under this subparagraph shall be subject to annual renewal.

(5) Required training of nurse aides. (A) In general. (i) Except as provided in clause (ii), a skilled nursing facility must not use on a full-time basis any individual as a nurse aide in the facility on or after October 1, 1990 for more than 4 months unless the individual—

(I) has completed a training and competency evaluation program, or a competency evaluation program, approved by the State under subsection (e)(1)(A), and

(II) is competent to provide nursing or nursing-related services.

(ii) A skilled nursing facility must not use on a temporary, per diem, leased, or on any basis other than as a permanent employee any individual as a nurse aide in the facility on or after January 1, 1991, unless the individual meets the requirements described in clause (i).

(B) Offering competency evaluation programs for current employees. A skilled nursing facility must provide, for individuals used as a nurse aide [nurse aides] by the facility as of January 1, 1990, for a competency evaluation program approved by the State under subsection (e)(1) and such preparation as may be necessary for the individual to complete such a program by October 1, 1990.

(C) Competency. The skilled nursing facility must not permit an individual, other than in a training and competency evaluation program approved by the State, to serve as a nurse aide or provide services of a type for which the individual has not demonstrated competency and must not use such an individual as a nurse aide unless the facility has inquired of any State registry established under subsection (e)(2)(A) that the facility believes will include information concerning the individual.

(D) Re-training required. For purposes of subparagraph (A), if, since an individual's most recent completion of a training and competency evaluation program, there has been a continuous period of 24 consecutive months during none of which the individual performed nursing or nursing-related services for monetary compensation, such individual shall complete a new training and competency evaluation program or a new competency evaluation program.

(E) Regular in-service education. The skilled nursing facility must provide such regular performance review and regular in-service education as assures that individuals used as nurse aides are competent to perform services as nurse aides, including training for individuals providing nursing and nursing-related services to residents with cognitive impairments.

(F) Nurse aide defined. In this paragraph, the term "nurse aide" means any individual providing nursing or nursing-related services to residents in a skilled nursing facility, but does not include an individual—

(i) who is a licensed health professional (as defined in subparagraph (G)) or a registered dietician, or

(ii) who volunteers to provide such services without monetary compensation.

(G) Licensed health professional defined. In this paragraph, the term "licensed health professional" means a physician, physician assistant, nurse practitioner, physical, speech, or occupational therapist, physical or occupational therapy assistant, registered professional nurse, licensed practical nurse, licensed or certified social worker, registered respiratory therapist, or certified respiratory therapy technician.

(6) Physician supervision and clinical records. A skilled nursing facility must—

(A) require that the medical care of every resident be provided under the supervision of a physician;

(B) provide for having a physician available to furnish necessary medical care in case of emergency; and

(C) maintain clinical records on all residents, which records include the plans of care (described in paragraph (2)) and the residents' assessments (described in paragraph (3)).

(7) Required social services. In the case of a skilled nursing facility with more than 120 beds, the facility must have at least one social worker (with at least a bachelor's degree in social work or similar professional qualifications) employed full-time to provide or assure the provision of social services.

(8) Information on nurse staffing. (A) In general. A skilled nursing facility shall post daily for each shift the current number of licensed and unlicensed nursing staff directly responsible for resident care in the facility. The information shall be displayed in a uniform manner (as specified by the Secretary) and in a clearly visible place.

(B) Publication of data. A skilled nursing facility shall, upon request, make available to the public the nursing staff data described in subparagraph (A).

(c) Requirements relating to residents' rights. (1) General rights. (A) Specified rights. A skilled nursing facility must protect and promote the rights of each resident, including each of the following rights:

(i) Free choice. The right to choose a personal attending physician, to be fully informed in advance about care and treatment, to be fully informed in advance of any changes in care or treatment that may affect the resident's well-being, and (except with respect to a resident adjudged incompetent) to participate in planning care and treatment or changes in care and treatment.

(ii) Free from restraints. The right to be free from physical or mental abuse, corporal punishment, involuntary seclusion, and any physical or chemical restraints imposed for purposes of discipline or convenience and not required to treat the resident's medical symptoms. Restraints may only be imposed—

(I) to ensure the physical safety of the resident or other residents, and

(II) only upon the written order of a physician that specifies the duration and circumstances under which the restraints are to be used (except in emergency circumstances specified by the Secretary until such an order could reasonably be obtained).

(iii) Privacy. The right to privacy with regard to accommodations, medical treatment, written and telephonic communications, visits, and meetings of family and of resident groups.

(iv) Confidentiality. The right to confidentiality of personal and clinical records and to access to current clinical records of the resident upon request by the resident or the resident's legal representative, within 24 hours (excluding hours occurring during a weekend or holiday) after making such a request.

(v) Accommodation of needs. The right—

(I) to reside and receive services with reasonable accommodation of individual needs and preferences, except where the health or safety of the individual or other residents would be endangered, and

(II) to receive notice before the room or roommate of the resident in the facility is changed.

(vi) Grievances. The right to voice grievances with respect to treatment or care that is (or fails to be) furnished, without discrimination or reprisal for voicing the grievances and the right to prompt efforts by the facility to resolve grievances the resident may have, including those with respect to the behavior of other residents.

(vii) Participation in resident and family groups. The right of the resident to organize and participate in resident groups in the facility and the right of the resident's family to meet in the facility with the families of other residents in the facility.

(viii) Participation in other activities. The right of the resident to participate in social, religious, and community activities that do not interfere with the rights of other residents in the facility.

(ix) Examination of survey results. The right to examine, upon reasonable request, the results of the most recent survey of the facility conducted by the Secretary or a State with respect to the facility and any plan of correction in effect with respect to the facility.

(x) Refusal of certain transfers. The right to refuse a transfer to another room within the facility, if a purpose of the transfer is to relocate the resident from a portion of the facility that is a skilled nursing facility (for purposes of this title [42 USCS §§ 1395 et seq.]) to a portion of the facility that is not such a skilled nursing facility.

(xi) Other rights. Any other right established by the Secretary.

Clause (iii) shall not be construed as requiring the provision of a private room. A resident's exercise of a right to refuse transfer under clause (x) shall not affect the resident's eligibility or entitlement to benefits under this title [42 USCS §§ 1395 et seq.] or to medical assistance under title XIX of this Act [42 USCS §§ 1396 et seq.].

(B) Notice of rights and services. A skilled nursing facility must—

(i) inform each resident, orally and in writing at the time of admission to the facility, of the resident's legal rights during the stay at the facility;

(ii) make available to each resident, upon reasonable request, a written statement of such rights (which statement is updated upon changes in such rights) including the notice (if any) of the State developed under section 1919(e)(6) [42 USCS § 1396r(e)(6)]; and

(iii) inform each other resident, in writing before or at the time of admission and periodically during the resident's stay, of services available in the facility and of related charges for such services, including any charges for services not covered under this title [42 USCS §§ 1395 et seq.] or by the facility's basic per diem charge.

The written description of legal rights under this subparagraph shall include a description of the protection of personal funds under paragraph (6) and a statement that a resident may file a complaint with a State survey and certification agency respecting resident abuse and neglect and misappropriation of resident property in the facility.

(C) Rights of incompetent residents. In the case of a resident adjudged incompetent under the laws of a State, the rights of the resident under this title [42 USCS §§ 1395 et seq.] shall devolve upon, and, to the extent judged necessary by a court of competent jurisdiction, be exercised by, the person appointed under State law to act on the resident's behalf.

(D) Use of psychopharmacologic drugs. Psychopharmacologic drugs may be administered only on the orders of a physician and only as part of a plan (included in the written plan of care described in paragraph (2)) designed to eliminate or modify the symptoms for which the drugs are prescribed and only if, at least annually, an independent, external consultant reviews the appropriateness of the drug plan of each resident receiving such drugs. In determining whether such a consultant is qualified to conduct reviews under the preceding sentence, the Secretary shall take into account the needs of nursing facilities under this title to have access to the services of such a consultant on a timely basis.

(E) Information respecting advance directives. A skilled nursing facility must comply with the requirement of section 1866(f) [42 USCS § 1395cc(f)] (relating to maintaining written policies and procedures respecting advance directives).

(2) Transfer and discharge rights. (A) In general. A skilled nursing facility must permit each resident to remain in the facility and must not transfer or discharge the resident from the facility unless—

(i) the transfer or discharge is necessary to meet the resident's welfare and the resident's welfare cannot be met in the facility;

(ii) the transfer or discharge is appropriate because the resident's health has improved sufficiently so the resident no longer needs the services provided by the facility;

(iii) the safety of individuals in the facility is endangered;

(iv) the health of individuals in the facility would otherwise be endangered;

(v) the resident has failed, after reasonable and appropriate notice, to pay (or to have paid under this title or title XIX [42 USCS §§ 1395 et seq. or 1396 et seq.] on the resident's behalf) for a stay at the facility; or

(vi) the facility ceases to operate.

In each of the cases described in clauses (i) through (v), the basis for the transfer or discharge must be documented in the resident's clinical record. In the cases described in clauses (i) and (ii), the documentation must be made by the resident's physician, and in the cases described in clauses (iii) and (iv) the documentation must be made by a physician.

(B) Pre-transfer and pre-discharge notice. (i) In general. Before effecting a transfer or discharge of a resident, a skilled nursing facility must—

(I) notify the resident (and, if known, a family member of the resident or legal representative) of the transfer or discharge and the reasons therefor,

(II) record the reasons in the resident's clinical record (including any documentation required under subparagraph (A)), and

(III) include in the notice the items described in clause (iii).

(ii) Timing of notice. The notice under clause (i)(I) must be made at least 30 days in advance of the resident's transfer or discharge except—

(I) in a case described in clause (iii) or (iv) of subparagraph (A);

(II) in a case described in clause (ii) of subparagraph (A), where the resident's health improves sufficiently to allow a more immediate transfer or discharge;

(III) in a case described in clause (i) of subparagraph (A), where a more immediate transfer or discharge is necessitated by the resident's urgent medical needs; or

(IV) in a case where a resident has not resided in the facility for 30 days.

In the case of such exceptions, notice must be given as many days before the date of the transfer or discharge as is practicable.

(iii) Items included in notice. Each notice under clause (i) must include—

(I) for transfers or discharges effected on or after October 1, 1990, notice of the resident's right to appeal the transfer or discharge under the State process established under subsection (e)(3); and

(II) the name, mailing address, and telephone number of the State long-term care ombudsman (established under title III or VII of the Older Americans Act of 1965 [42 USCS §§ 3021 et seq. or 3058 et seq.] in accordance with section 712 of the Act [42 USCS § 3058g]).

(C) Orientation. A skilled nursing facility must provide sufficient preparation and orientation to residents to ensure safe and orderly transfer or discharge from the facility.

(3) Access and visitation rights. A skilled nursing facility must—

(A) permit immediate access to any resident by any representative of the Secretary, by any representative of the State, by an ombudsman described in paragraph (2)(B)(iii)(II), or by the resident's individual physician;

(B) permit immediate access to a resident, subject to the resident's right to deny or withdraw consent at any time, by immediate family or other relatives of the resident;

(C) permit immediate access to a resident, subject to reasonable restrictions and the resident's right to deny or withdraw consent at any time, by others who are visiting with the consent of the resident;

(D) permit reasonable access to a resident by any entity or individual that provides health, social, legal, or other services to the resident, subject to the resident's right to deny or withdraw consent at any time; and

(E) permit representatives of the State ombudsman (described in paragraph (2)(B)(iii)(II)), with the permission of the resident (or the resident's legal representative) and consistent with State law, to examine a resident's clinical records.

(4) Equal access to quality care. A skilled nursing facility must establish and maintain identical policies and practices regarding transfer, discharge, and covered services under this title for all individuals regardless of source of payment.

(5) Admissions policy. (A) Admissions. With respect to admissions practices, a skilled nursing facility must—

(i)(I) not require individuals applying to reside or residing in the facility to waive their rights to benefits under this title [42 USCS §§ 1395 et seq.] or under a State plan under title XIX [42 USCS §§ 1396 et seq.], (II) not require oral or written assurance that such individuals are not eligible for, or will not apply for, benefits under this title [42 USCS §§ 1395 et seq.] or such a State plan, and (III) prominently display in the facility and provide to such individuals written information about how to apply for and use such benefits and how to receive refunds for previous payments covered by such benefits; and

(ii) not require a third party guarantee of payment to the facility as a condition of admission (or expedited admission) to, or continued stay in, the facility.

(B) Construction. (i) No preemption of stricter standards. Subparagraph (A) shall not be construed as preventing States or political subdivisions therein from prohibiting, under State or local law, the discrimination against individuals who are entitled to medical assistance under this title [42 USCS §§ 1395 et seq.] with respect to admissions practices of skilled nursing facilities.

(ii) Contracts with legal representatives. Subparagraph (A)(ii) shall not be construed as preventing a facility from requiring an individual, who has legal access to a resident's income or resources available to pay for care in the facility, to sign a contract (without incurring personal financial liability) to provide payment from the resident's income or resources for such care.

(6) Protection of resident funds. (A) In general. The skilled nursing facility—

(i) may not require residents to deposit their personal funds with the facility, and

(ii) upon the written authorization of the resident, must hold, safeguard, and account for such personal funds under a system established and maintained by the facility in accordance with this paragraph.

(B) Management of personal funds. Upon written authorization of a resident under subparagraph (A)(ii), the facility must manage and account for the personal funds of the resident deposited with the facility as follows:

(i) Deposit. The facility must deposit any amount of personal funds in excess of $100 with respect to a resident in an interest bearing account (or accounts) that is separate from any of the facility's operating accounts and credits [credit] all interest earned on such separate account to such account. With respect to any other personal funds, the facility must maintain such funds in a non-interest bearing account or petty cash fund.

(ii) Accounting and records. The facility must assure a full and complete separate accounting of each such resident's personal funds, maintain a written record of all financial transactions involving the personal funds of a resident deposited with the facility, and afford the resident (or a legal representative of the resident) reasonable access to such record.

(iii) Conveyance upon death. Upon the death of a resident with such an account, the facility must convey promptly the resident's personal funds (and a final accounting of such funds) to the individual administering the resident's estate.

(C) Assurance of financial security. The facility must purchase a surety bond, or otherwise provide assurance satisfactory to the Secretary, to assure the security of all personal funds of residents deposited with the facility.

(D) Limitation on charges to personal funds. The facility may not impose a charge against the personal funds of a resident for any item or service for which payment is made under this title or title XIX [42 USCS §§ 1395 et seq. or 1396 et seq.].

(d) Requirements relating to administration and other matters. (1) Administration. (A) In general. A skilled nursing facility must be administered in a manner that enables it to use its resources effectively and efficiently to attain or maintain the highest practicable physical, mental, and psychosocial well-being of each resident (consistent with requirements established under subsection (f)(5)).

(B) Required notices. If a change occurs in—

(i) the persons with an ownership or control interest (as defined in section 1124(a)(3) [42 USCS § 1320a-3(a)(3)]) in the facility,

(ii) the persons who are officers, directors, agents, or managing employees (as defined in section 1126(b) [42 USCS § 1320a-5(b)]) of the facility,

(iii) the corporation, association, or other company responsible for the management of the facility, or

(iv) the individual who is the administrator or director of nursing of the facility,

the skilled nursing facility must provide notice to the State agency responsible for the licensing of the facility, at the time of the change, of the change and of the identity of each new person, company, or individual described in the respective clause.

(C) Skilled nursing facility administrator. The administrator of a skilled nursing facility must meet standards established by the Secretary under subsection (f)(4).

(2) Licensing and Life Safety Code. (A) Licensing. A skilled nursing facility must be licensed under applicable State and local law.

(B) Life Safety Code. A skilled nursing facility must meet such provisions of such edition (as specified by the Secretary in regulation) of the Life Safety Code of the National Fire Protection Association as are applicable to nursing homes; except that—

(i) the Secretary may waive, for such periods as he deems appropriate, specific provisions of such Code which if rigidly applied would result in unreasonable hardship upon a facility, but only if such waiver would not adversely affect the health and safety of residents or personnel, and

(ii) the provisions of such Code shall not apply in any State if the Secretary finds that in such State there is in effect a fire and safety code, imposed by State law, which adequately protects residents of and personnel in skilled nursing facilities.

(3) Sanitary and infection control and physical environment. A skilled nursing facility must—

(A) establish and maintain an infection control program designed to provide a safe, sanitary, and comfortable environment in which residents reside and to help prevent the development and transmission of disease and infection, and

(B) be designed, constructed, equipped, and maintained in a manner to protect the health and safety of residents, personnel, and the general public.

(4) Miscellaneous. (A) Compliance with Federal, State, and local laws and professional standards. A skilled nursing facility must operate and provide services in compliance with all applicable Federal, State, and local laws and regulations (including the requirements of section 1124 [42 USCS § 1320a-3]) and with accepted professional standards and principles which apply to professionals providing services in such a facility.

(B) Other. A skilled nursing facility must meet such other requirements relating to the health, safety, and well-being of residents or relating to the physical facilities thereof as the Secretary may find necessary.

(e) State requirements relating to skilled nursing facility requirements. The requirements, referred to in section 1864(d) [42 USCS § 1395aa(d)], with respect to a State are as follows:

(1) Specification and review of nurse aide training and competency evaluation programs and of nurse aide competency evaluation programs. The State must—

(A) by not later than January 1, 1989, specify those training and competency evaluation programs, and those competency evaluation programs, that the State approves for purposes of subsection (b)(5) and that meet the requirements established under subsection (f)(2), and

(B) by not later than January 1, 1990, provide for the review and reapproval of such programs, at a frequency and using a methodology consistent with the requirements established under subsection (f)(2)(A)(iii).

The failure of the Secretary to establish requirements under subsection (f)(2) shall not relieve any State of its responsibility under this paragraph.

(2) Nurse aide registry. (A) In general. By not later than January 1, 1989, the State shall establish and maintain a registry of all individuals who have satisfactorily completed a nurse aide training and competency evaluation program, or a nurse aide competency evaluation program, approved under paragraph (1) in the State, or any individual described in subsection (f)(2)(B)(ii) or in subparagraph (B), (C), or (D) of section 6901(b)(4) of the Omnibus Budget Reconciliation Act of 1989 [note to this section].

(B) Information in registry. The registry under subparagraph (A) shall provide (in accordance with regulations of the Secretary) for the inclusion of specific documented findings by a State under subsection (g)(1)(C) of resident neglect or abuse or misappropriation of resident property involving an individual listed in the registry, as well as any brief statement of the individual disputing the findings, but shall not include any allegations of resident abuse or neglect or misappropriation of resident property that are not specifically documented by the State under such subsection. The State shall make available to the public information in the registry. In the case of inquiries to the registry concerning an individual listed in the registry, any information disclosed concerning such a finding shall also include disclosure of any such statement in the registry relating to the finding or a clear and accurate summary of such a statement.

(C) Prohibition against charges. A State may not impose any charges on a nurse aide relating to the registry established and maintained under subparagraph (A).

(3) State appeals process for transfers and discharges. The State, for transfers and discharges from skilled nursing facilities effected on or after October 1, 1989, must provide for a fair mechanism for hearing appeals on transfers of residents of such facilities. Such mechanism must meet the guidelines established by the Secretary under subsection (f)(3); but the failure of the Secretary to establish such guidelines shall not relieve any State of its responsibility to provide for such a fair mechanism.

(4) Skilled nursing facility administrator standards. By not later than January 1, 1990, the State must have implemented and enforced the skilled nursing facility administrator standards developed under subsection (f)(4) respecting the qualification of administrators of skilled nursing facilities.

(5) Specification of resident assessment instrument. Effective July 1, 1990, the State shall specify the instrument to be used by nursing facilities in the State in complying with the requirement of subsection (b)(3)(A)(iii). Such instrument shall be—

(A) one of the instruments designated under subsection (f)(6)(B), or

(B) an instrument which the Secretary has approved as being consistent with the minimum data set of core elements, common definitions, and utilization guidelines specified by the Secretary under subsection (f)(6)(A).

(f) Responsibilities of Secretary relating to skilled nursing facility requirements. (1) General responsibility. It is the duty and responsibility of the Secretary to assure that requirements which govern the provision of care in skilled nursing facilities under this title [42 USCS §§ 1395 et seq.], and the enforcement of such requirements, are adequate to protect the health, safety, welfare, and rights of residents and to promote the effective and efficient use of public moneys.

(2) Requirements for nurse aide training and competency evaluation programs and for nurse aide competency evaluation of programs. (A) In general. For purposes of subsections (b)(5) and (e)(1)(A), the Secretary shall establish, by not later than September 1, 1988—

(i) requirements for the approval of nurse aide training and competency evaluation programs, including requirements relating to (I) the areas to be covered in such a program (including at least basic nursing skills, personal care skills, recognition of mental health and social service needs, care of cognitively impaired residents, basic restorative services, and residents' rights) and content of the curriculum, (II) minimum hours of initial and ongoing training and retraining (including not less than 75 hours in the case of initial training), (III) qualifications of instructors, and (IV) procedures for determination of competency;

(ii) requirements for the approval of nurse aide competency evaluation programs, including requirement relating to the areas to be covered in such a program, including at least basic nursing skills, personal care skills, recognition of mental health and social service needs, care of cognitively impaired residents, basic restorative services, residents' rights, and procedures for determination of competency;

(iii) requirements respecting the minimum frequency and methodology to be used by a State in reviewing such programs compliance with the requirements for such programs; and

(iv) requirements, under both such programs, that—

(I) provide procedures for determining competency that permit a nurse aide, at the nurse aide's option, to establish competency through procedures or methods other than the passing of a written examination and to have the competency evaluation conducted at the nursing facility at which the aide is (or will be) employed (unless the facility is described in subparagraph (B)(iii)(I)),

(II) prohibit the imposition on a nurse aide who is employed by (or who has received an offer of employment from) a facility on the date on which the aide begins either such program of any charges (including any charges for textbooks and other required course materials and any charges for the competency evaluation) for either such program, and

(III) in the case of a nurse aide not described in subclause (II) who is employed by (or who has received an offer of employment from) a facility not later than 12 months after completing either such program, the State shall provide for the reimbursement of costs incurred in completing such program on a prorata [pro rata] basis during the period in which the nurse aide is so employed.

(B) Approval of certain programs. Such requirements—

(i) may permit approval of programs offered by or in facilities (subject to clause (iii)), as well as outside facilities (including employee organizations), and of programs in effect on the date of the enactment of this section [enacted Dec. 22, 1987];

(ii) shall permit a State to find that an individual who has completed (before July 1, 1989) a nurse aide training and competency evaluation program shall be deemed to have completed such a program approved under subsection (b)(5) if the State determines that, at the time the program was offered, the program met the requirements for approval under such paragraph; and

(iii) subject to subparagraphs (C) and (D), shall prohibit approval of such a program—

(I) offered by or in a skilled nursing facility which, within the previous 2 years—

(a) has operated under a waiver under subsection (b)(4)(C)(ii)(II);

(b) has been subject to an extended (or partial extended) survey under subsection (g)(2)(B)(i) or section 1919(g)(2)(B)(i) [42 USCS § 1396r(g)(2)(B)(i)], unless the survey shows that the facility is in compliance with the requirements of subsections (b), (c), and (d) of this section; or

(c) has been assessed a civil money penalty described in subsection (h)(2)(B)(ii) or section 1919(h)(2)(A)(ii) [42 USCS § 1396r(h)(2)(A)(ii)] of not less than $5,000, or has been subject to a remedy described in clause (i) or (iii) of subsection (h)(2)(B), subsection (h)(4), section 1919(h)(1)(B)(i) [42 USCS § 1396r(h)(1)(B)(i)], or in clause (i), (iii), or (iv) of section 1919(h)(2)(A) [42 USCS § 1396r(h)(2)(A)(i), (iii), or (iv)], or

(II) offered by or in a skilled nursing facility unless the State makes the determination, upon an individual's completion of the program, that the individual is competent to provide nursing and nursing-related services in skilled nursing facilities.

A State may not delegate (through subcontract or otherwise) its responsibility under clause (iii)(II) to the skilled nursing facility.

(C) Waiver authorized. Clause (iii)(I) of subparagraph (B) shall not apply to a program offered in (but not by) a nursing facility (or skilled nursing facility for purposes of title XVIII [42 USCS §§ 1395 et seq.]) in a State if the State—

(i) determines that there is no other such program offered within a reasonable distance of the facility,

(ii) assures, through an oversight effort, that an adequate environment exists for operating the program in the facility, and

(iii) provides notice of such determination and assurances to the State long-term care ombudsman.

(D) Waiver of disapproval of nurse-aide training programs. Upon application of a nursing facility, the Secretary may waive the application of subparagraph (B)(iii)(I)(c) if the imposition of the civil monetary penalty was not related to the quality of care provided to residents of the facility. Nothing in this subparagraph shall be construed as eliminating any requirement upon a facility to pay a civil monetary penalty described in the preceding sentence.

(3) Federal guidelines for State appeals process for transfers and discharges. For purposes of subsections (c)(2)(B)(iii)(I) and (e)(3), by not later than October 1, 1988, the Secretary shall establish guidelines for minimum standards which State appeals processes under subsection (e)(3) must meet to provide a fair mechanism for hearing appeals on transfers and discharges of residents from skilled nursing facilities.

(4) Secretarial standards for qualification of administrators. For purposes of subsections (d)(1)(C) and (e)(4), the Secretary shall develop, by not later than March 1, 1989, standards to be applied in assuring the qualifications of administrators of skilled nursing facilities.

(5) Criteria for administration. The Secretary shall establish criteria for assessing a skilled nursing facility's compliance with the requirement of subsection (d)(1) with respect to—

(A) its governing body and management,

(B) agreements with hospitals regarding transfers of residents to and from the hospitals and to and from other skilled nursing facilities,

(C) disaster preparedness,

(D) direction of medical care by a physician,

(E) laboratory and radiological services,

(F) clinical records, and

(G) resident and advocate participation.

(6) Specification of resident assessment data set and instruments. The Secretary shall—

(A) not later than January 1, 1989, specify a minimum data set of core elements and common definitions for use by nursing facilities in conducting the assessments required under subsection (b)(3), and establish guidelines for utilization of the data set; and

(B) by not later than April 1, 1990, designate one or more instruments which are consistent with the specification made under subparagraph (A) and which a State may specify under subsection (e)(5)(A) for use by nursing facilities in complying with the requirements of subsection (b)(3)(A)(iii).

(7) List of items and services furnished in skilled nursing facilities not chargeable to the personal funds of a resident. (A) Regulations required. Pursuant to the requirement of section 21(b) of the Medicare-Medicaid Anti-Fraud and Abuse Amendments of 1977 [42 USCS § 1395x note], the Secretary shall issue regulations, on or before the first day of the seventh month to begin after the date of enactment of this section [enacted Dec. 22, 1987], that define those costs which may be charged to the personal funds of residents in skilled nursing facilities who are individuals receiving benefits under this part [42 USCS §§ 1395c et seq.] and those costs which are to be included in the reasonable cost (or other payment amount) under this title [42 USCS §§ 1395 et seq.] for extended care services.

(B) Rule if failure to publish regulations. If the Secretary does not issue the regulations under subparagraph (A) on or before the date required in such subparagraph, in the case of a resident of a skilled nursing facility who is eligible to receive benefits under this part [42 USCS §§ 1395c et seq.], the costs which may not be charged to the personal funds of such resident (and for which payment is considered to be made under this title [42 USCS §§ 1395 et seq.]) shall include, at a minimum, the costs for routine personal hygiene items and services furnished by the facility.

(8) Special focus facility program. (A) In general. The Secretary shall conduct a special focus facility program for enforcement of requirements for skilled nursing facilities that the Secretary has identified as having substantially failed to meet applicable requirement of this Act.

(B) Periodic surveys. Under such program the Secretary shall conduct surveys of each facility in the program not less than once every 6 months.

(g) Survey and certification process. (1) State and Federal responsibility. (A) In general. Pursuant to an agreement under section 1864 [42 USCS § 1395aa], each State shall be responsible for certifying, in accordance with surveys conducted under paragraph (2), the compliance of skilled nursing facilities (other than facilities of the State) with the requirements of subsections (b), (c), and (d). The Secretary shall be responsible for certifying, in accordance with surveys conducted under paragraph (2), the compliance of State skilled nursing facilities with the requirements of such subsections.

(B) Educational program. Each State shall conduct periodic educational programs for the staff and residents (and their representatives) of skilled nursing facilities in order to present current regulations, procedures, and policies under this section.

(C) Investigation of allegations of resident neglect and abuse and misappropriation of resident property. The State shall provide, through the agency responsible for surveys and certification of nursing facilities under this subsection, for a process for the receipt and timely review and investigation of allegations of neglect and abuse and misappropriation of resident property by a nurse aide of a resident in a nursing facility of by another individual used by the facility in providing services to such a resident. The State shall, after providing the individual involved with a written notice of the allegations (including a statement of the availability of a hearing for the individual to rebut the allegations) and the opportunity for a hearing on the record, make a written finding as to the accuracy of the allegations. If the State finds that a nurse aide has neglected or abused a resident or misappropriated resident property in a facility, the State shall notify the nurse aide and the registry of such finding. If the State finds that any other individual used by the facility has neglected or abused a resident or misappropriated resident property in a facility, the State shall notify the appropriate licensure authority. A State shall not make a finding that an individual has neglected a resident if the individual demonstrates that such neglect was caused by factors beyond the control of the individual.

(D) Removal of name from nurse aide registry. (i) In general. In the case of a finding of neglect under subparagraph (C), the State shall establish a procedure to permit a nurse aide to petition the State to have his or her name removed from the registry upon a determination by the State that—

(I) the employment and personal history of the nurse aide does not reflect a pattern of abusive behavior or neglect; and

(II) the neglect involved in the original finding was a singular occurrence.

(ii) Timing of determination. In no case shall a determination on a petition submitted under clause (i) be made prior to the expiration of the 1-year period beginning on the date on which the name of the petitioner was added to the registry under subparagraph (C).

(E) Construction. The failure of the Secretary to issue regulations to carry out this subsection shall not relieve a State of its responsibility under this subsection.

(2) Surveys. (A) Standard survey. (i) In general. Each skilled nursing facility shall be subject to a standard survey, to be conducted without any prior notice to the facility. Any individual who notifies (or causes to be notified) a skilled nursing facility of the time or date on which such a survey is scheduled to be conducted is subject to a civil money penalty of not to exceed $2,000. The provisions of section 1128A [42 USCS § 1320a-7a] (other than subsections (a) and (b)) shall apply to a civil money penalty under the previous sentence in the same manner as such provisions apply to a penalty or proceeding under section 1128A(a) [42 USCS § 1320a-7a(a)]. The Secretary shall review each State's procedures for the scheduling and conduct of standard surveys to assure that the State has taken all reasonable steps to avoid giving notice of such a survey through the scheduling procedures and the conduct of the surveys themselves.

(ii) Contents. Each standard survey shall include, for a case-mix stratified sample of residents—

(I) a survey of the quality of care furnished, as measured by indicators of medical, nursing, and rehabilitative care, dietary and nutrition services, activities and social participation, and sanitation, infection control, and the physical environment,

(II) written plans of care provided under subsection (b)(2) and an audit of the residents' assessments under subsection (b)(3) to determine the accuracy of such assessments and the adequacy of such plans of care, and

(III) a review of compliance with residents' rights under subsection (c).

(iii) Frequency. (I) In general. Each skilled nursing facility shall be subject to a standard survey not later than 15 months after the date of the previous standard survey conducted under this subparagraph. The Statewide average interval between standard surveys of skilled nursing facilities under this subsection shall not exceed 12 months.

(II) Special surveys. If not otherwise conducted under subclause (I), a standard survey (or an abbreviated standard survey) may be conducted within 2 months of any change of ownership, administration, management of a skilled nursing facility, or the director of nursing in order to determine whether the change has resulted in any decline in the quality of care furnished in the facility.

(B) Extended surveys. (i) In general. Each skilled nursing facility which is found, under a standard survey, to have provided substandard quality of care shall be subject to an extended survey. Any other facility may, at the Secretary's or State's discretion, be subject to such an extended survey (or a partial extended survey).

(ii) Timing. The extended survey shall be conducted immediately after the standard survey (or, if not practicable, not later than 2 weeks after the date of completion of the standard survey).

(iii) Contents. In such an extended survey, the survey team shall review and identify the policies and procedures which produced such substandard quality of care and shall determine whether the facility has complied with all the requirements described in subsections (b), (c), and (d). Such review shall include an expansion of the size of the sample of residents' assessments reviewed and a review of the staffing, of in-service training, and, if appropriate, of contracts with consultants.

(iv) Construction. Nothing in this paragraph shall be construed as requiring an extended or partial extended survey as a prerequisite to imposing a sanction against a facility under subsection (h) on the basis of findings in a standard survey.

(C) Survey protocol. Standard and extended surveys shall be conducted—

(i) based upon a protocol which the Secretary has developed, tested, and validated by not later than January 1, 1990, and

(ii) by individuals, of a survey team, who meet such minimum qualifications as the Secretary establishes by not later than such date.

The failure of the Secretary to develop, test, or validate such protocols or to establish such minimum qualifications shall not relieve any State of its responsibility (or the Secretary of the Secretary's responsibility) to conduct surveys under this subsection.

(D) Consistency of surveys. Each State and the Secretary shall implement programs to measure and reduce inconsistency in the application of survey results among surveyors.

(E) Survey teams. (i) In general. Surveys under this subsection shall be conducted by a multidisciplinary team of professionals (including a registered professional nurse).

(ii) Prohibition of conflicts of interest. A State may not use as a member of a survey team under this subsection an individual who is serving (or has served within the previous 2 years) as a member of the staff of, or as a consultant to, the facility surveyed respecting compliance with the requirements of subsections (b), (c), and (d), or who has a personal or familial financial interest in the facility being surveyed.

(iii) Training. The Secretary shall provide for the comprehensive training of State and Federal surveyors in the conduct of standard and extended surveys under this subsection, including the auditing of resident assessments and plans of care. No individual shall serve as a member of a survey team unless the individual has successfully completed a training and testing program in survey and certification techniques that has been approved by the Secretary.

(3) Validation surveys. (A) In general. The Secretary shall conduct onsite surveys of a representative sample of skilled nursing facilities in each State, within 2 months of the date of surveys conducted under paragraph (2) by the State, in a sufficient number to allow inferences about the adequacies of each State's surveys conducted under paragraph (2). In conducting such surveys, the Secretary shall use the same survey protocols as the State is required to use under paragraph (2). If the State has determined that an individual skilled nursing facility meets the requirements of subsections (b), (c), and (d), but the Secretary determines that the facility does not meet such requirements, the Secretary's determination as to the facility's noncompliance with such requirements is binding and supersedes that of the State survey.

(B) Scope. With respect to each State, the Secretary shall conduct surveys under subparagraph (A) each year with respect to at least 5 percent of the number of skilled nursing facilities surveyed by the State in the year, but in no case less than 5 skilled nursing facilities in the State.

(C) Remedies for substandard performance. If the Secretary finds, on the basis of such surveys, that a State has failed to perform surveys as required under paragraph (2) or that a State's survey and certification performance otherwise is not adequate, the Secretary shall provide for an appropriate remedy, which may include the training of survey teams in the

State.

(D) Special surveys of compliance. Where the Secretary has reason to question the compliance of a skilled nursing facility with any of the requirements of subsections (b), (c), and (d), the Secretary may conduct a survey of the facility and, on the basis of that survey, make independent and binding determinations concerning the extent to which the skilled nursing facility meets such requirements.

(4) Investigation of complaints and monitoring compliance. Each State shall maintain procedures and adequate staff to—

(A) investigate complaints of violations of requirements by skilled nursing facilities, and

(B) monitor, on-site, on a regular, as needed basis, a skilled nursing facility's compliance with the requirements of subsections (b), (c), and (d), if—

(i) the facility has been found not to be in compliance with such requirements and is in the process of correcting deficiencies to achieve such compliance;

(ii) the facility was previously found not to be in compliance with such requirements, has corrected deficiencies to achieve such compliance, and verification of continued compliance is indicated; or

(iii) the State has reason to question the compliance of the facility with such requirements.

A State may maintain and utilize a specialized team (including an attorney, an auditor, and appropriate health care professionals) for the purpose of identifying, surveying, gathering and preserving evidence, and carrying out appropriate enforcement actions against substandard skilled nursing facilities.

(5) Disclosure of results of inspections and activities. (A) Public information. Each State, and the Secretary, shall make available to the public—

(i) information respecting all surveys and certifications made respecting skilled nursing facilities, including statements of deficiencies, within 14 calendar days after such information is made available to those facilities, and approved plans of correction,

(ii) copies of cost reports of such facilities filed under this title [42 USCS §§ 1395 et seq.] or title XIX [42 USCS §§ 1396 et seq.],

(iii) copies of statements of ownership under section 1124 [42 USCS § 1320a-3], and

(iv) information disclosed under section 1126 [42 USCS § 1320a-5].

(B) Notice to ombudsman. Each State shall notify the State long-term care ombudsman (established under title III or VII of the Older Americans Act of 1965 [42 USCS §§ 3021 et seq. or 3058 et seq.] in accordance with section 712 of the Act [42 USCS § 3058g]) of the State's findings of noncompliance with any of the requirements of subsections (b), (c), and (d), or of any adverse action taken against a skilled nursing facility under paragraph (1), (2), or (4) of subsection (h), with respect to a skilled nursing facility in the State.

(C) Notice to physicians and skilled nursing facility administrator licensing board. If a State finds that a skilled nursing facility has provided substandard quality of care, the State shall notify—

(i) the attending physician of each resident with respect to which such finding is made, and

(ii) the State board responsible for the licensing of the skilled nursing facility administrator at the facility.

(D) Access to fraud control units. Each State shall provide its State medicaid fraud and abuse control unit (established under section 1903(q) [42 USCS § 1396b(q)]) with access to all information of the State agency responsible for surveys and certifications under this subsection.

(E) **[Caution: This subparagraph takes effect 1 year after enactment of Act March 23, 2010, P. L. 111-148, as provided by § 6103(a)(2)(B) of such Act, which appears as a note to this section.]** Submission of survey and certification information to the Secretary. In order to improve the timeliness of information made available to the public under subparagraph (A) and provided on the Nursing Home Compare Medicare website under subsection (i), each State shall submit information respecting any survey or certification made respecting a skilled nursing facility (including any enforcement actions taken by the State) to the Secretary not later than the date on which the State sends such information to the facility. The Secretary shall use the information submitted under the preceding sentence to update the information provided on the Nursing Home Compare Medicare website as expeditiously as practicable but not less frequently than quarterly.

(h) Enforcement process. (1) In general. If a State finds, on the basis of a standard, extended, or partial extended survey under subsection (g)(2) or otherwise, that a skilled nursing facility no longer meets a requirement of subsection (b), (c), or (d), and further finds that the facility's deficiencies—

(A) immediately jeopardize the health or safety of its residents, the State shall recommend to the Secretary that the Secretary take such action as described in paragraph (2)(A)(i); or

(B) do not immediately jeopardize the health or safety of its residents, the State may recommend to the Secretary that the Secretary take such action as described in paragraph (2)(A)(ii).

If a State finds that a skilled nursing facility meets the requirements of subsections (b), (c), and (d), but, as of a previous period, did not meet such requirements, the State may recommend a civil money penalty under paragraph (2)(B)(ii) for the days in which it finds that the facility was not in compliance with such requirements.

(2) Secretarial authority. (A) In general. With respect to any skilled nursing facility in a State, if the Secretary finds, or pursuant to a recommendation of the State under paragraph (1) finds, that a skilled nursing facility no longer meets a requirement of subsection (b), (c), (d), or (e), and further finds that the facility's deficiencies—

(i) immediately jeopardize the health or safety of its residents, the Secretary shall take immediate action to remove the jeopardy and correct the deficiencies through the remedy specified in subparagraph (B)(iii), or terminate the facility's participation under this title [42 USCS §§ 1395 et seq.] and may provide, in addition, for one or more of the other remedies described in subparagraph (B); or

(ii) do not immediately jeopardize the health or safety of its residents, the Secretary may impose any of the remedies described in subparagraph (B).

Nothing in this subparagraph shall be construed as restricting the remedies available to the Secretary to remedy a skilled nursing facility's deficiencies. If the Secretary finds, or pursuant to the recommendation of the State under paragraph (1) finds, that a skilled nursing facility meets such requirements but, as of a previous period, did not meet such requirements, the Secretary may provide for a civil money penalty under subparagraph (B)(ii) for the days on which he finds that the facility was not in compliance with such requirements.

(B) Specified remedies. The Secretary may take the following actions with respect to a finding that a facility has not met an applicable requirement:

(i) Denial of payment. The Secretary may deny any further payments under this title [42 USCS §§ 1395 et seq.] with respect to all individuals entitled to benefits under this title [42 USCS §§ 1395 et seq.] in the facility or with respect to such individuals admitted to the facility after the effective date of the finding.

(ii) Authority with respect to civil money penalties. (I) In general. Subject to subclause (II), the Secretary may impose a civil money penalty in an amount not to exceed $10,000 for each day of noncompliance. The provisions of section 1128A [42 USCS § 1320a-7a] (other than subsections (a) and (b)) shall apply to a civil money penalty under the previous sentence in the same manner as such provisions apply to a penalty or proceeding under section 1128A(a) [42 USCS § 1320a-7a(a)].

(II) **[Caution: This subclause takes effect 1 year after enactment of Act March 23, 2011, P. L. 111-148, as provided by § 6111(c) of such Act, which appears as a note to this section.]** Reduction of civil money penalties in certain circumstances. Subject to subclause (III), in the case where a facility self-reports and promptly corrects a deficiency for which a penalty was imposed under this clause not later than 10 calendar days after the date of such imposition, the Secretary may reduce the amount of the penalty imposed by not more than 50 percent.

(III) **[Caution: This subclause takes effect 1 year after enactment of Act March 23, 2011, P. L. 111-148, as provided by § 6111(c) of such Act, which appears as a note to this section.]** Prohibitions on reduction for certain deficiencies. (aa) Repeat deficiencies. The Secretary may not reduce the amount of a penalty under subclause (II) if the Secretary had reduced a penalty imposed on the facility in the preceding year under such subclause with respect to a repeat deficiency.

(bb) Certain other deficiencies. The Secretary may not reduce the amount of a penalty under subclause (II) if the penalty is imposed on the facility for a deficiency that is found to result in a pattern of harm or widespread harm, immediately jeopardizes the health or safety of a resident or residents of the facility, or results in the death of a resident of the facility.

(IV) **[Caution: This subclause takes effect 1 year after enactment of Act March 23, 2011, P. L. 111-148, as provided by § 6111(c) of such Act, which appears as a note to this section.]** Collection of civil money penalties. In the case of a civil money penalty imposed under this clause, the Secretary shall issue regulations that—

(aa) subject to item (cc), not later than 30 days after the imposition of the penalty, provide for the facility to have the opportunity to participate in an independent informal dispute resolution process which generates a written record prior to the collection of such penalty;

(bb) in the case where the penalty is imposed for each day of noncompliance, provide that a penalty may not be imposed for any day during the period beginning on the initial day of the imposition of the penalty and ending on the day on which the informal dispute resolution process under item (aa) is completed;

(cc) may provide for the collection of such civil money penalty and the placement of such amounts collected in an escrow account under the direction of the Secretary on the earlier of the date on which the informal dispute resolution process under item (aa) is completed or the date that is 90 days after the date of the imposition of the penalty;

(dd) may provide that such amounts collected are kept in such account pending the resolution of any subsequent appeals;

(ee) in the case where the facility successfully appeals the penalty, may provide for the return of such amounts collected (plus interest) to the facility; and

(ff) in the case where all such appeals are unsuccessful, may provide that some portion of such amounts collected may be used to support activities that benefit residents, including assistance to support and protect residents of a facility that closes (voluntarily or involuntarily) or is decertified (including offsetting costs of relocating residents to home and community-based settings or another facility), projects that support resident and family councils and other consumer involvement in assuring quality care in facilities, and facility improvement initiatives approved by the Secretary (including joint training of facility staff and surveyors, technical assistance for facilities implementing quality assurance programs, the appointment of temporary management firms, and other activities approved by the Secretary).

(iii) Appointment of temporary management. In consultation with the State, the Secretary may appoint temporary management to oversee the operation of the facility and to assure the health and safety of the facility's residents, where there is a need for temporary management while—

(I) there is an orderly closure of the facility, or

(II) improvements are made in order to bring the facility into compliance with all the requirements of subsections (b), (c), and (d).

The temporary management under this clause shall not be terminated under subclause (II) until the Secretary has determined that the facility has the management capability to ensure continued compliance with all the requirements of subsections (b), (c), and (d).

The Secretary shall specify criteria, as to when and how each of such remedies is to be applied, the amounts of any fines, and the severity of each of these remedies, to be used in the imposition of such remedies. Such criteria shall be designed so as to minimize the time between the identification of violations and final imposition of the remedies and shall provide for the imposition of incrementally more severe fines for repeated or uncorrected deficiencies. In addition, the Secretary may provide for other specified remedies, such as directed plans of correction.

(C) Continuation of payments pending remediation. The Secretary may continue payments, over a period of not longer than 6 months after the effective date of the findings, under this title [42 USCS §§ 1395 et seq.] with respect to a skilled nursing facility not in compliance with a requirement of subsection (b), (c), or (d), if—

(i) the State survey agency finds that it is more appropriate to take alternative action to assure compliance of the facility with the requirements than to terminate the certification of the facility,

(ii) the State has submitted a plan and timetable for corrective action to the Secretary for approval and the Secretary approves the plan of corrective action, and

(iii) the facility agrees to repay to the Federal Government payments received under this subparagraph if the corrective action is not taken in accordance with the approved plan and timetable.

The Secretary shall establish guidelines for approval of corrective actions requested by States under this subparagraph.

(D) Assuring prompt compliance. If a skilled nursing facility has not complied with any of the requirements of subsections (b), (c), and (d), within 3 months after the date the facility is found to be out of compliance with such requirements, the Secretary shall impose the remedy described in subparagraph (B)(i) for all individuals who are admitted to the facility after such date.

(E) Repeated noncompliance. In the case of a skilled nursing facility which, on 3 consecutive standard surveys conducted under subsection (g)(2), has been found to have provided substandard quality of care, the Secretary shall (regardless of what other remedies are provided)—

(i) impose the remedy described in subparagraph (B)(i), and

(ii) monitor the facility under subsection

(g)(4)(B),

until the facility has demonstrated, to the satisfaction of the Secretary, that it is in compliance with the requirements of subsections (b), (c), and (d), and that it will remain in compliance with such requirements.

(3) Effective period of denial of payment. A finding to deny payment under this subsection shall terminate when the Secretary finds that the facility is in substantial compliance with all the requirements of subsections (b), (c), and (d).

(4) Immediate termination of participation for facility where Secretary finds noncompliance and immediate jeopardy. If the Secretary finds that a skilled nursing facility has not met a requirement of subsection (b), (c), or (d), and finds that the failure immediately jeopardizes the health or safety of its residents, the Secretary shall take immediate action to remove the jeopardy and correct the deficiencies through the remedy specified in paragraph (2)(B)(iii), or the Secretary, subject to section 1128I(h) [42 USCS § 1320a-7j(h)], shall terminate the facility's participation under this title [42 USCS §§ 1395 et seq.]. If the facility's participation under this title [42 USCS §§ 1395 et seq.] is terminated, the State shall provide for the safe and orderly transfer of the residents eligible under this title [42 USCS §§ 1395 et seq.] consistent with the requirements of subsection (c)(2) and section 1128I(h) [42 USCS § 1320a-7j(h)].

(5) Construction. The remedies provided under this subsection are in addition to those otherwise available under State or Federal law and shall not be construed as limiting such other remedies, including any remedy available to an individual at common law. The remedies described in clauses (i), (ii)(IV), and (iii) of paragraph (2)(B) may be imposed during the pendency of any hearing.

(6) Sharing of information. Notwithstanding any other provision of law, all information concerning skilled nursing facilities required by this section to be filed with the Secretary or a State agency shall be made available by such facilities to Federal or State employees for purposes consistent with the effective administration of programs established under this title and title XIX [42 USCS §§ 1395 et seq. and 1396 et seq.], including investigations by State medicaid fraud control units.

(i) Nursing Home Compare website. (1) Inclusion of additional information. (A) In general. The Secretary shall ensure that the Department of Health and Human Services includes, as part of the information provided for comparison of nursing homes on the official Internet website of the Federal Government for Medicare beneficiaries (commonly referred to as the "Nursing Home Compare" Medicare website) (or a successor website), the following information in a manner that is prominent, updated on a timely basis, easily accessible, readily understandable to consumers of long-term care services, and searchable:

(i) Staffing data for each facility (including resident census data and data on the hours of care provided per resident per day) based on data submitted under section 1128I(g) [42 USCS § 1320a-7j(g)], including information on staffing turnover and tenure, in a format that is clearly understandable to consumers of long-term care services and allows such consumers to compare differences in staffing between facilities and State and national averages for the facilities. Such format shall include—

(I) concise explanations of how to interpret the data (such as a plain English explanation of data reflecting "nursing home staff hours per resident day");

(II) differences in types of staff (such as training associated with different categories of staff);

(III) the relationship between nurse staffing levels and quality of care; and

(IV) an explanation that appropriate staffing levels vary based on patient case mix.

(ii) Links to State Internet websites with information regarding State survey and certification programs, links to Form 2567 State inspection reports (or a successor form) on such websites, information to guide consumers in how to interpret and understand such reports, and the facility plan of correction or other response to such report. Any such links shall be posted on a timely basis.

(iii) The standardized complaint form developed under section 1128I(f) [42 USCS § 1320a-7j(f)], including explanatory material on what complaint forms are, how they are used, and how to file a complaint with the State survey and certification program and the State long-term care ombudsman program.

(iv) Summary information on the number, type, severity, and outcome of substantiated complaints.

(v) The number of adjudicated instances of criminal violations by a facility or the employees of a facility—

(I) that were committed inside the facility;

(II) with respect to such instances of violations or crimes committed inside of the facility that were the violations or crimes of abuse, neglect, and exploitation, criminal sexual abuse, or other violations or crimes that resulted in serious bodily injury; and

(III) the number of civil monetary penalties levied against the facility, employees, contractors, and other agents.

(B) Deadline for provision of information. (i) In general. Except as provided in clause (ii), the Secretary shall ensure that the information described in subparagraph (A) is included on such website (or a successor website) not later than 1 year after the date of the enactment of this subsection [enacted March 23, 2010].

(ii) Exception. The Secretary shall ensure that the information described in subparagraph (A)(i) is included on such website (or a successor website) not later than the date on which the requirements under section 1128I(g) [42 USCS § 1320a-7j(g)] are implemented.

(2) Review and modification of website. (A) In general. The Secretary shall establish a process—

(i) to review the accuracy, clarity of presentation, timeliness, and comprehensiveness of information reported on such website as of the day before the date of the enactment of this subsection; and

(ii) not later than 1 year after the date of the enactment of this subsection [enacted March 23, 2010], to modify or revamp such website in accordance with the review conducted under clause (i).

(B) Consultation. In conducting the review under subparagraph (A)(i), the Secretary shall consult with—

(i) State long-term care ombudsman programs;

(ii) consumer advocacy groups;

(iii) provider stakeholder groups; and

(iv) any other representatives of programs or groups the Secretary determines appropriate.

(j) Construction. Where requirements or obligations under this section are identical to those provided under section 1919 of this Act [42 USCS § 1396r], the fulfillment of those requirements or obligations under section 1919 [42 USCS § 1396r] shall be considered to be the fulfillment of the corresponding requirements or obligations under this section.

(Aug. 14, 1935, ch 531, Title XVIII, Part A, § 1819, as added and amended Dec. 22, 1987, P. L. 100-203, Title IV, Subtitle C, Part 1, §§ 4201(a)(3), 4202(a)(2), 4203(a)(2), 4206, 101 Stat. 1330-160, 1330-175, 1330-179, 1330-182; July 1, 1988, P. L. 100-360, Title IV, Subtitle B, § 411(l)(1)(A), (2)(A)–(D), (F)–(K), (L)(i), (4), (5), (7), 102 Stat. 800-805; Oct. 13, 1988, P. L. 100-485, Title VI, § 608(d)(27)(A), (C), (I), (L), 102 Stat. 2422, 2423; Dec. 19, 1989, P. L. 101-239, Title VI, Subtitle F, § 6901(b)(1), (3), (d)(4), 103 Stat. 2298, 2301; Nov. 5, 1990, P. L. 101-508, Title IV, Subtitle A, Part 1, § 4008(h)(1)(B)–(F)(i), (G), (2)(B)–(N), (m)(3)(F), Part 3, § 4206(d)(1), 104 Stat. 1388-46, 1388-116; Sept. 30, 1992, P. L. 102-375, Title VII, § 708(a)(1)(A), 106 Stat. 1292; Oct. 31, 1994, P. L. 103-432, Title I, Subtitle A, § 106(c)(1)(A), (2)(A), (3)(A), (4)(A), (B), (d)(1)–(5), 110(b), 108 Stat. 4405–4407, 4408; May 15, 1997, P. L. 105-15, § 1, 111 Stat. 34; Aug. 5, 1997, P. L. 105-33, Title IV, Subtitle E, Ch 3, § 4432(b)(5)(A), Subtitle H, Ch 6, § 4755(a), 111 Stat. 421, 526; Dec. 21, 2000, P. L. 106-554, § 1(a)(6), 114 Stat. 2763; Dec. 8, 2003, P. L. 108-173, Title VII, Subtitle D, § 736(a)(8), Title IX, Subtitle D, § 932(c)(2), 117 Stat. 2355, 2401; March 23, 2010, P. L. 111-148, Title VI, Subtitle B, Part I, §§ 6101(c)(1), 6103(a)(1), (2)(A), (3), (c)(1), Part II, § 6111(a), 6113(b), Part III, § 6121(a), 124 Stat. 702, 704, 706, 709, 713, 719, 720.)

HISTORY; ANCILLARY LAWS AND DIRECTIVES

Prospective amendments:

Amendment of subsec. (d)(1), effective on the date on which the Secretary makes public the information reported in accordance with final regulations promulgated. Act March 23, 2010, P. L. 111-148, Title VI, Subtitle B, Part I, § 6101(c)(1)(A), 124 Stat. 702 (effective on the date on which the Secretary makes public the information reported in accordance with final regulations promulgated, as provided by § 6101(c)(2) of such Act, which appears as 42 USCS § 1395i-3 note), provides: "Section 1919(d)(1) of the Social Security Act (42 U.S.C. 1396r(d)(1)) is amended by striking subparagraph (B) and redesignating subparagraph (C) as subparagraph (B).".

Amendment of subsec. (d)(1), effective March 23, 2011. Act March 23, 2010, P. L. 111-148, Title VI, Subtitle B, Part I, § 6103(c)(1), 124 Stat. 710 (effective 1 year after enactment, as provided by § 6013(c)(3) of such Act, which appears as a note to this section), provides:

"Section 1819(d)(1) of the Social Security Act (42 U.S.C. 1395i-3(d)(1)), as amended by section 6101, is amended by adding at the end the following new subparagraph:

" '(C) Availability of survey, certification, and complaint investigation reports. A skilled nursing facility must—

" '(i) have reports with respect to any surveys, certifications, and complaint investigations made respecting the facility during the 3 preceding years available for any individual to review upon request; and

" '(ii) post notice of the availability of such reports in areas of the facility that are prominent and accessible to the public.

"The facility shall not make available under clause (i) identifying information about complainants or residents.'.".

Amendment of subsecs. (b)(5)(F) and (f)(2)(A), effective March 23, 2011. Act March 23, 2010, P. L. 111-148, Title VI, Subtitle B, Part III, § 6121(a), 124

Stat. 720 (effective 1 year after enactment, as provided by § 6121(c) of such Act, which appears as a note to this section), provides:

"(1) In general. Section 1819(f)(2)(A)(i)(I) of the Social Security Act (42 U.S.C. 1395i-3(f)(2)(A)(i)(I)) is amended by inserting '(including, in the case of initial training and, if the Secretary determines appropriate, in the case of ongoing training, dementia management training, and patient abuse prevention training' before ', (II)'.

"(2) Clarification of definition of nurse aide. Section 1819(b)(5)(F) of the Social Security Act (42 U.S.C. 1395i-3(b)(5)(F)) is amended by adding at the end the following flush sentence:

" 'Such term includes an individual who provides such services through an agency or under a contract with the facility.'.".

Other provisions:

Effective date of amendments made by § 6101(c) of Act March 23, 2010. Act March 23, 2010, P. L. 111-148, Title VI, Subtitle B, Part I, § 6101(c)(2), 124 Stat. 702, provides: "The amendments made by paragraph (1) [amending 42 USCS §§ 1395i-3(d)(1) and 1396r(d)(1)] shall take effect on the date on which the Secretary makes the information described in subsection (b)(1) available to the public under such subsection.".

Effective date of amendment made by § 6103(a)(2) of Act March 23, 2010. Act March 23, 2010, P. L. 111-148, Title VI, Subtitle B, Part I, § 6103(a)(2)(B), 124 Stat. 706, provides: "The amendment made by this paragraph [adding subsec. (g)(5)(E) of this section] shall take effect 1 year after the date of the enactment of this Act.".

Effective date of amendments made by § 6103(c) of Act March 23, 2010. Act March 23, 2010, P. L. 111-148, Title VI, Subtitle B, Part I, § 6103(c)(3), 124 Stat. 710, provides: "The amendments made by this subsection [amending 42 USCS §§ 1395i-3(d)(1) and 1396r(d)(1)] shall take effect 1 year after the date of the enactment of this Act.".

Guidance to States on Form 2567 State inspection reports and complaint investigation reports. Act March 23, 2010, P. L. 111-148, Title VI, Subtitle B, Part I, § 6103(d)(1), (3), 124 Stat. 710, provides:

"(1) Guidance. The Secretary of Health and Human Services (in this subtitle referred to as the 'Secretary') shall provide guidance to States on how States can establish electronic links to Form 2567 State inspection reports (or a successor form), complaint investigation reports, and a facility's plan of correction or other response to such Form 2567 State inspection reports (or a successor form) on the Internet website of the State that provides information on skilled nursing facilities and nursing facilities and the Secretary shall, if possible, include such information on Nursing Home Compare.".

"* * * * *

"(3) Definitions. In this subsection [this note and amending 42 USCS § 1396(a)(9)]:

"(A) Nursing facility. The term 'nursing facility' has the meaning given such term in section 1919(a) of the Social Security Act (42 U.S.C. 1396r(a)).

"(B) Secretary. The term 'Secretary' means the Secretary of Health and Human Services.

"(C) Skilled nursing facility. The term 'skilled nursing facility' has the meaning given such term in section 1819(a) of the Social Security Act (42 U.S.C. 1395i-3(a)).".

Development of consumer rights information page on Nursing Home Compare website. Act March 23, 2010, P. L. 111-148, Title VI, Subtitle B, Part I, § 6103(e), 124 Stat. 710, provides:

"Not later than 1 year after the date of enactment of this Act, the Secretary shall ensure that the Department of Health and Human Services, as part of the information provided for comparison of nursing facilities on the Nursing Home Compare Medicare website develops and includes a consumer rights information page that contains links to descriptions of, and information with respect to, the following:

"(1) The documentation on nursing facilities that is available to the public.

"(2) General information and tips on choosing a nursing facility that meets the needs of the individual.

"(3) General information on consumer rights with respect to nursing facilities.

"(4) The nursing facility survey process (on a national and State-specific basis).

"(5) On a State-specific basis, the services available through the State long-term care ombudsman for such State.".

Effective date of amendments made by § 6111 of Act March 23, 2010. Act March 23, 2010, P. L. 111-148, Title VI, Subtitle B, Part II, § 6111(c), 124 Stat. 716, provides: "The amendments made by this section [amending 42 USCS §§ 1395i-3(h) and 1396r(h)] shall take effect 1 year after the date of the enactment of this Act.".

National demonstration projects on culture change and use of information technology in nursing homes. Act March 23, 2010, P. L. 111-148, Title VI, Subtitle B, Part II, § 6114, 124 Stat. 720, provides:

"(a) In general. The Secretary shall conduct 2 demonstration projects, 1 for the development of best practices in skilled nursing facilities and nursing facilities that are involved in the culture change movement (including the development of resources for facilities to find and access funding in order to undertake culture change) and 1 for the development of best practices in skilled nursing facilities and nursing facilities for the use of information technology to improve resident care.

"(b) Conduct of demonstration projects. (1) Grant award. Under each demonstration project conducted under this section, the Secretary shall award 1 or more grants to facility-based settings for the development of best practices described in subsection (a) with respect to the demonstration project involved. Such award shall be made on a competitive basis and may be allocated in 1 lump-sum payment.

"(2) Consideration of special needs of residents. Each demonstration project conducted under this section shall take into consideration the special needs of residents of skilled nursing facilities and nursing facilities who have cognitive impairment, including dementia.

"(c) Duration and implementation. (1) Duration. The demonstration projects shall each be conducted for a period not to exceed 3 years.

"(2) Implementation. The demonstration projects shall each be implemented not later than 1 year after the date of the enactment of this Act.

"(d) Definitions. In this section:

"(1) Nursing facility. The term "nursing facility" has the meaning given such term in section 1919(a) of the Social Security Act (42 U.S.C. 1396r(a)).

"(2) Secretary. The term "Secretary" means the Secretary of Health and Human Services.

"(3) Skilled nursing facility. The term "skilled nursing

facility" has the meaning given such term in section 1819(a) of the Social Security Act (42 U.S.C. 1395(a)).

"(e) Authorization of appropriations. There are authorized to be appropriated such sums as may be necessary to carry out this section.

"(f) Report. Not later than 9 months after the completion of the demonstration project, the Secretary shall submit to Congress a report on such project, together with recommendations for such legislation and administrative action as the Secretary determines appropriate.".

Effective date of amendments made by § 6121 of Act March 23, 2010. Act March 23, 2010, P. L. 111-148, Title VI, Subtitle B, Part III, § 6121(c), 124 Stat. 721, provides: "The amendments made by this section [amending 42 USCS §§ 1395i-3 and 1396r] shall take effect 1 year after the date of the enactment of this Act.".

§ 1395i-3a. Protecting residents of long-term care facilities

(1) National Training Institute for surveyors.

(A) In general. The Secretary of Health and Human Services shall enter into a contract with an entity for the purpose of establishing and operating a National Training Institute for Federal and State surveyors. Such Institute shall provide and improve the training of surveyors with respect to investigating allegations of abuse, neglect, and misappropriation of property in programs and long-term care facilities that receive payments under title XVIII or XIX of the Social Security Act [42 USCS §§ 1395 et seq. or 1396 et seq.].

(B) Activities carried out by the Institute. The contract entered into under subparagraph (A) shall require the Institute established and operated under such contract to carry out the following activities:

(i) Assess the extent to which State agencies use specialized surveyors for the investigation of reported allegations of abuse, neglect, and misappropriation of property in such programs and long-term care facilities.

(ii) Evaluate how the competencies of surveyors may be improved to more effectively investigate reported allegations of such abuse, neglect, and misappropriation of property, and provide feedback to Federal and State agencies on the evaluations conducted.

(iii) Provide a national program of training, tools, and technical assistance to Federal and State surveyors on investigating reports of such abuse, neglect, and misappropriation of property.

(iv) Develop and disseminate information on best practices for the investigation of such abuse, neglect, and misappropriation of property.

(v) Assess the performance of State complaint intake systems, in order to ensure that the intake of complaints occurs 24 hours per day, 7 days a week (including holidays).

(vi) To the extent approved by the Secretary of Health and Human Services, provide a national 24 hours per day, 7 days a week (including holidays), back-up system to State complaint intake systems in order to ensure optimum national responsiveness to complaints of such abuse, neglect, and misappropriation of property.

(vii) Analyze and report annually on the following:

(I) The total number and sources of complaints of such abuse, neglect, and misappropriation of property.

(II) The extent to which such complaints are referred to law enforcement agencies.

(III) General results of Federal and State investigations of such complaints.

(viii) Conduct a national study of the cost to State agencies of conducting complaint investigations of skilled nursing facilities and nursing facilities under sections 1819 and 1919, respectively, of the Social Security Act (42 U.S.C. 1395i-3; 1396r), and making recommendations to the Secretary of Health and Human Services with respect to options to increase the efficiency and cost-effectiveness of such investigations.

(C) Authorization. There are authorized to be appropriated to carry out this paragraph, for the period of fiscal years 2011 through 2014, $12,000,000.

(2) Grants to State survey agencies.

(A) In general. The Secretary of Health and Human Services shall make grants to State agencies that perform surveys of skilled nursing facilities or nursing facilities under sections 1819 or 1919, respectively, of the Social Security Act (42 U.S.C. 1395i-3; 1395r).

(B) Use of funds. A grant awarded under subparagraph (A) shall be used for the purpose of designing and implementing complaint investigations systems that—

(i) promptly prioritize complaints in order to ensure a rapid response to the most serious and urgent complaints;

(ii) respond to complaints with optimum effectiveness and timeliness; and

(iii) optimize the collaboration between local authorities, consumers, and providers, including—

(I) such State agency;

(II) the State Long-Term Care Ombudsman;

(III) local law enforcement agencies;

(IV) advocacy and consumer organizations;

(V) State aging units;

(VI) Area Agencies on Aging; and

(VII) other appropriate entities.

(C) Authorization. There are authorized to be appropriated to carry out this paragraph, for each of fiscal years 2011 through 2014, $5,000,000.

(March 23, 2010, P. L. 111-148, Title VI, Subtitle H, § 6703(b)(1), (2), 124 Stat. 798.)

HISTORY; ANCILLARY LAWS AND DIRECTIVES

Explanatory notes:

This section was enacted as part of Act March 23, 2010, P. L. 111-148, and not as part of the Social Security Act, Act Aug. 14, 1935, ch 531, which generally comprises this chapter.

Other provisions:

Definitions. Act March 23, 2010, P. L. 111-148, Title VI, Subtitle H, § 6702, 124 Stat. 782, provides: "Except as otherwise specifically provided, any term that is defined in section 2011 of the Social Security Act [42 USCS § 1397j] (as added by section 6703(a)) and is used in this subtitle [for full classification, consult USCS Tables volumes] has the meaning given such term by such section.".

§ 1395i-4. Medicare rural hospital flexibility program

(a) Establishment. Any State that submits an application in accordance with subsection (b) may establish a medicare rural hospital flexibility program described in subsection (c).

(b) Application. A State may establish a medicare rural hospital flexibility program described in subsection (c) if the State submits to the Secretary at such time and in such form as the Secretary may require an application containing—

(1) assurances that the State—

(A) has developed, or is in the process of developing, a State rural health care plan that—

(i) provides for the creation of 1 or more rural health networks (as defined in subsection (d)) in the State;

(ii) promotes regionalization of rural health services in the State; and

(iii) improves access to hospital and other health services for rural residents of the State; and

(B) has developed the rural health care plan described in subparagraph (A) in consultation with the hospital association of the State, rural hospitals located in the State, and the State Office of Rural Health (or, in the case of a State in the process of developing such plan, that assures the Secretary that the State will consult with its State hospital association, rural hospitals located in the State, and the State Office of Rural Health in developing such plan);

(2) assurances that the State has designated (consistent with the rural health care plan described in paragraph (1)(A)), or is in the process of so designating, rural nonprofit or public hospitals or facilities located in the State as critical access hospitals; and

(3) such other information and assurances as the Secretary may require.

(c) Medicare rural hospital flexibility program described. (1) In general. A State that has submitted an application in accordance with subsection (b), may establish a medicare rural hospital flexibility program that provides that—

(A) the State shall develop at least 1 rural health network (as defined in subsection (d)) in the State; and

(B) at least 1 facility in the State shall be designated as a critical access hospital in accordance with paragraph (2).

(2) State designation of facilities. (A) In general. A State may designate 1 or more facilities as a critical access hospital in accordance with subparagraphs (B), (C), and (D).

(B) Criteria for designation as critical access hospital. A State may designate a facility as a critical access hospital if the facility—

(i) is a hospital that is located in a county (or equivalent unit of local government) in a rural area (as defined in section 1886(d)(2)(D) [42 USCS § 1395ww(d)(2)(D)]) or is treated as being located in a rural area pursuant to section 1886(d)(8)(E) [42 USCS § 1395ww(d)(8)(E)], and that—

(I) is located more than a 35-mile drive (or, in the case of mountainous terrain or in areas with only secondary roads available, a 15-mile drive) from a hospital, or another facility described in this subsection; or

(II) is certified before January 1, 2006, by the State as being a necessary provider of health care services to residents in the area;

(ii) makes available 24-hour emergency care services that a State determines are necessary for ensuring access to emergency care services in each area served by a critical access hospital;

(iii) provides not more than 25 acute care inpatient beds (meeting such standards as the Secretary may establish) for providing inpatient care for a period that does not exceed, as determined on an annual, average basis, 96 hours per patient;

(iv) meets such staffing requirements as would apply under section 1861(e) [42 USCS § 1395x(e)] to a hospital located in a rural area, except that—

(I) the facility need not meet hospital standards relating to the number of hours during a day, or days during a week, in which the facility must be open and fully staffed, except insofar as the facility is required to make available emergency care services as determined under clause (ii) and must have nursing services available on a 24-hour basis, but need not otherwise staff the facility except when an inpatient is present;

(II) the facility may provide any services otherwise required to be provided by a full-time, on site dietitian, pharmacist, laboratory technician, medical technologist, and radiological technologist on a part-time, off site basis under arrangements as defined in section 1861(w)(1) [42 USCS § 1395x(w)(1)]; and

(III) the inpatient care described in clause (iii) may be provided by a physician assistant, nurse practitioner, or clinical nurse specialist subject to the oversight of a physician who need not be present in the facility; and

(v) meets the requirements of section 1861(aa)(2)(I) [42 USCS § 1395x(aa)(2)(I)].

(C) Recently closed facilities. A State may designate a facility as a critical access hospital if the facility—

(i) was a hospital that ceased operations on or after the date that is 10 years before the date of the enactment of this subparagraph [enacted Nov. 29, 1999]; and

(ii) as of the effective date of such designation, meets the criteria for designation under subparagraph (B).

(D) Downsized facilities. A State may designate a health clinic or a health center (as defined by the State) as a critical access hospital if such clinic or center—

(i) is licensed by the State as a health clinic or a health center;

(ii) was a hospital that was downsized to a health clinic or health center; and

(iii) as of the effective date of such designation, meets the criteria for designation under subparagraph (B).

(E) Authority to establish psychiatric and rehabilitation distinct part units. (i) In general. Subject to the succeeding provisions of this subparagraph, a critical access hospital may establish—

(I) a psychiatric unit of the hospital that is a distinct part of the hospital; and

(II) a rehabilitation unit of the hospital that is a distinct part of the hospital,

if the distinct part meets the requirements (including conditions of participation) that would otherwise apply to the distinct part if the distinct part were established by a subsection (d) hospital in accordance with the matter following clause (v) of section 1886(d)(1)(B) [42 USCS § 1395ww(d)(1)(B)], including any regulations adopted by the Secretary under such section.

(ii) Limitation on number of beds. The total number of beds that may be established under clause (i) for a distinct part unit may not exceed 10.

(iii) Exclusion of beds from bed count. In determining the number of beds of a critical access hospital for purposes of applying the bed limitations referred to in subparagraph (B)(iii) and subsection (f), the Secretary shall not take into account any bed established under clause (i).

(iv) Effect of failure to meet requirements. If a psychiatric or rehabilitation unit established under clause (i) does not meet the requirements described in such clause with respect to a cost reporting period, no payment may be made under this title to the hospital for services furnished in such unit during such period. Payment to the hospital for services furnished in the unit may resume only after the hospital has demonstrated to the Secretary that the unit meets such requirements.

(d) "Rural health network" defined. (1) In general. In this section, the term "rural health network" means, with respect to a State, an organization consisting of—

(A) at least 1 facility that the State has designated or plans to designate as a critical access hospital; and

(B) at least 1 hospital that furnishes acute care services.

(2) Agreements. (A) In general. Each critical access hospital that is a member of a rural health network shall have an agreement with respect to each item described in subparagraph (B) with at least 1 hospital that is a member of the network.

(B) Items described. The items described in this subparagraph are the following:

(i) Patient referral and transfer.

(ii) The development and use of communications systems including (where feasible)—

(I) telemetry systems; and

(II) systems for electronic sharing of patient data.

(iii) The provision of emergency and non-emergency transportation among the facility and the hospital.

(C) Credentialing and quality assurance. Each critical access hospital that is a member of a rural health network shall have an agreement with respect to credentialing and quality assurance with at least—

(i) 1 hospital that is a member of the network;

(ii) 1 peer review organization or equivalent

entity; or

(iii) 1 other appropriate and qualified entity identified in the State rural health care plan.

(e) Certification by the Secretary. The Secretary shall certify a facility as a critical access hospital if the facility—

(1) is located in a State that has established a medicare rural hospital flexibility program in accordance with subsection (c);

(2) is designated as a critical access hospital by the State in which it is located; and

(3) meets such other criteria as the Secretary may require.

(f) Permitting maintenance of swing beds. Nothing in this section shall be construed to prohibit a State from designating or the Secretary from certifying a facility as a critical access hospital solely because, at the time the facility applies to the State for designation as a critical access hospital, there is in effect an agreement between the facility and the Secretary under section 1883 [42 USCS § 1395tt] under which the facility's inpatient hospital facilities are used for the provision of extended care services, so long as the total number of beds that may be used at any time for the furnishing of either such services or acute care inpatient services does not exceed 25 beds. For purposes of the previous sentence, any bed of a unit of the facility that is licensed as a distinct-part skilled nursing facility at the time the facility applies to the State for designation as a critical access hospital shall not be counted.

(g) Grants. (1) Medicare rural hospital flexibility program. The Secretary may award grants to States that have submitted applications in accordance with subsection (b) for—

(A) engaging in activities relating to planning and implementing a rural health care plan;

(B) engaging in activities relating to planning and implementing rural health networks;

(C) designating facilities as critical access hospitals; and

(D) providing support for critical access hospitals for quality improvement, quality reporting, performance improvements, and benchmarking.

(2) Rural emergency medical services. (A) In general. The Secretary may award grants to States that have submitted applications in accordance with subparagraph (B) for the establishment or expansion of a program for the provision of rural emergency medical services.

(B) Application. An application is in accordance with this subparagraph if the State submits to the Secretary at such time and in such form as the Secretary may require an application containing the assurances described in subparagraphs (A)(ii), (A)(iii), and (B) of subsection (b)(1) and paragraph (3) of that subsection.

(3) Upgrading data systems. (A) Grants to hospitals. The Secretary may award grants to hospitals that have submitted applications in accordance with subparagraph (C) to assist eligible small rural hospitals in meeting the costs of implementing data systems required to meet requirements established under the medicare program pursuant to amendments made by the Balanced Budget Act of 1997 and to assist such hospitals in participating in delivery system reforms under the provisions of and amendments made by the Patient Protection and Affordable Care Act, such as value-based purchasing programs, accountable care organizations under section 1899 [42 USCS § 1395jjj], the National pilot program on payment bundling under section 1866D [42 USCS § 1395cc-4], and other delivery system reform programs determined appropriate by the Secretary.

(B) Eligible small rural hospital defined. For purposes of this paragraph, the term "eligible small rural hospital" means a non-Federal, short-term general acute care hospital that—

(i) is located in a rural area (as defined for purposes of section 1886(d) [42 USCS § 1395ww(d)]); and

(ii) has less than 50 beds.

(C) Application. A hospital seeking a grant under this paragraph shall submit an application to the Secretary on or before such date and in such form and manner as the Secretary specifies.

(D) Amount of grant. A grant to a hospital under this paragraph may not exceed $50,000.

(E) Use of funds. A hospital receiving a grant under this paragraph may use the funds for the purchase of computer software and hardware, the education and training of hospital staff on computer information systems, to offset costs related to the implementation of prospective payment systems and to participate in delivery system reforms under the provisions of and amendments made by the Patient Protection and Affordable Care Act, such as value-based purchasing programs, accountable care organizations under section 1899 [42 USCS § 1395jjj], the National pilot program on payment bundling under section 1866D [42 USCS § 1395c-4], and other delivery system reform programs determined appropriate by the Secretary.

(F) Reports. (i) Information. A hospital receiving a grant under this section shall furnish the Secretary with such information as the Secretary may require to evaluate the project for which the grant is made and to ensure that the grant is expended for the purposes for which it is made.

(ii) Timing of submission. (I) Interim reports. The Secretary shall report to the Committee on Ways and Means of the House of Representatives and the Committee on Finance of the Senate at least annually on the grant program established under this section, including in such report information on the number of grants made, the nature of the projects involved, the geographic distribution of grant recipients, and such other matters as the Secretary deems appropriate.

(II) Final report. The Secretary shall submit a final report to such committees not later than 180 days after the completion of all of the projects for which a grant is made under this section.

(4) Additional requirements with respect to flex grants. With respect to grants awarded under paragraph (1) or (2) from funds appropriated for fiscal year 2005 and subsequent fiscal years—

(A) Consultation with the state hospital association and rural hospitals on the most appropriate ways to use grants. A State shall consult with the hospital association of such State and rural hospitals located in such State on the most appropriate ways to use the funds under such grant.

(B) Limitation on use of grant funds for administrative expenses. A State may not expend more than the lesser of—

(i) 15 percent of the amount of the grant for administrative expenses; or

(ii) the State's federally negotiated indirect rate for administering the grant.

(5) Use of funds for Federal administrative expenses. Of the total amount appropriated for grants under paragraphs (1) and (2) for a fiscal year (for each of fiscal years 2005 through 2008) and, of the total amount appropriated for grants under paragraphs (1), (2), and (6) for a fiscal year (beginning with fiscal year 2009), up to 5 percent of such amount shall be available to the Health Resources and Services Administration for purposes of administering such grants.

(6) Providing mental health services and other health services to veterans and other residents of rural areas. (A) Grants to States. The Secretary may award grants to States that have submitted applications in accordance with subparagraph (B) for increasing the delivery of mental health services or other health care services deemed necessary to meet the needs of veterans of Operation Iraqi Freedom and Operation Enduring Freedom living in rural areas (as defined for purposes of section 1886(d) [42 USCS § 1395ww(d)] and including areas that are rural census tracks, as defined by the Administrator of the Health Resources and Services Administration), including for the provision of crisis intervention services and the detection of post-traumatic stress disorder, traumatic brain injury, and other signature injuries of veterans of Operation Iraqi Freedom and Operation Enduring Freedom, and for referral of such veterans to medical facilities operated by the Department of Veterans Affairs, and for the delivery of such services to other residents of such rural areas.

(B) Application. (i) In general. An application is in accordance with this subparagraph if the State submits to the Secretary at such time and in such form as the Secretary may require an application containing the assurances described in subparagraphs (A)(ii) and (A)(iii) of subsection (b)(1).

(ii) Consideration of regional approaches, networks, or technology. The Secretary may, as appropriate in awarding grants to States under subparagraph (A), consider whether the application submitted by a State under this subparagraph includes 1 or more proposals that utilize regional approaches, networks, health information technology, telehealth, or telemedicine to deliver services described in subparagraph (A) to individuals described in that subparagraph. For purposes of this clause, a network may, as the Secretary determines appropriate, include Federally qualified health centers (as defined in section 1861(aa)(4) [42 USCS § 1395x(aa)(4)]), rural health clinics (as defined in section 1861(aa)(2) [42 USCS § 1395x(aa)(2)]), home health agencies (as defined in section 1861(o) [42 USCS § 1395x(o)]), community mental health centers (as defined in section 1861(ff)(3)(B) [42 USCS § 1395x(ff)(3)(B)]) and other providers of mental health services, pharmacists, local government, and other providers deemed necessary to meet the needs of veterans.

(iii) Coordination at local level. The Secretary shall require, as appropriate, a State to demonstrate consultation with the hospital association of such State, rural hospitals located in such State, providers of mental health services, or other appropriate stakeholders for the provision of services under a grant awarded under this paragraph.

(iv) Special consideration of certain applications. In awarding grants to States under subparagraph (A), the Secretary shall give special consideration to applications submitted by States in which veterans make up a high percentage (as determined by the Secretary) of the total population of the State. Such consideration shall be given without regard to the number of veterans of Operation Iraqi Freedom and Operation Enduring Freedom living in the areas in which mental health services and other health care services would be delivered under the application.

(C) Coordination with VA. The Secretary shall, as appropriate, consult with the Director of the Office of Rural Health of the Department of Veterans Affairs in awarding and administering grants to States under subparagraph (A).

(D) Use of funds. A State awarded a grant under this paragraph may, as appropriate, use the funds to reimburse providers of services described in subparagraph (A) to individuals described in that subparagraph.

(E) Limitation on use of grant funds for administrative expenses. A State awarded a grant under this paragraph may not expend more than 15 percent of the amount of the grant for administrative expenses.

(F) Independent evaluation and final report. The Secretary shall provide for an independent evaluation of the grants awarded under subparagraph (A). Not later than 1 year after the date on which the last grant is awarded to a State under such subparagraph, the Secretary shall submit a report to Congress on such evaluation. Such report shall include an assessment of the impact of such grants on increasing the delivery of mental health services and other health services to veterans of the United States Armed Forces living in rural areas (as so defined and including such areas that are rural census tracks), with particular emphasis on the impact of such grants on the delivery of such services to veterans of Operation Enduring Freedom and Operation Iraqi Freedom, and to other individuals living in such rural areas.

(7) Critical access hospitals transitioning to skilled nursing facilities and assisted living facilities. (A) Grants. The Secretary may award grants to eligible critical access hospitals that have submitted applications in accordance with subparagraph (B) for assisting such hospitals in the transition to skilled nursing facilities and assisted living facilities.

(B) Application. An applicable critical access hospital seeking a grant under this paragraph shall submit an application to the Secretary on or before such date and in such form and manner as the Secretary specifies.

(C) Additional requirements. The Secretary may not award a grant under this paragraph to an eligible critical access hospital unless—

(i) local organizations or the State in which the hospital is located provides matching funds; and

(ii) the hospital provides assurances that it will surrender critical access hospital status under this title within 180 days of receiving the grant.

(D) Amount of grant. A grant to an eligible critical access hospital under this paragraph may not exceed $1,000,000.

(E) Funding. There are appropriated from the Federal Hospital Insurance Trust Fund under section 1817 [42 USCS § 1395i] for making grants under this paragraph, $5,000,000 for fiscal year 2008.

(F) Eligible critical access hospital defined. For purposes of this paragraph, the term "eligible critical access hospital" means a critical access hospital that has an average daily acute census of less than 0.5 and an average daily swing bed census of greater than 10.0.

(h) Grandfathering provisions. (1) In general. Any medical assistance facility operating in Montana and any rural primary care hospital designated by the Secretary under this section prior to the date of the enactment of the Balanced Budget Act of 1997 [enacted Aug. 5, 1997] shall be deemed to have been certified by the Secretary under subsection (e) as a critical access hospital if such facility or hospital is otherwise eligible to be designated by the State as a critical access hospital under subsection (c).

(2) Continuation of medical assistance facility and rural primary care hospital terms. Notwithstanding any other provision of this title [42 USCS §§ 1395 et seq.], with respect to any medical assistance facility or rural primary care hospital described in paragraph (1), any reference in this title [42 USCS §§ 1395 et seq.] to a "critical access hospital" shall be deemed to be a reference to a "medical assistance facility" or "rural primary care hospital".

(3) State authority to waive 35-mile rule. In the case of a facility that was designated as a critical access hospital before January 1, 2006, and was certified by the State as being a necessary provider of health care services to residents in the area under subsection (c)(2)(B)(i)(II), as in effect before such date, the authority under such subsection with respect to any redesignation of such facility shall continue to apply notwithstanding the amendment made by section 405(h)(1) of the Medicare Pre-

scription Drug, Improvement, and Modernization Act of 2003.

(i) Waiver of conflicting part A provisions. The Secretary is authorized to waive such provisions of this part [42 USCS §§ 1395c et seq.] and part D [part E] [42 USCS §§ 1395x et seq.] as are necessary to conduct the program established under this section.

(j) Authorization of appropriations. There are authorized to be appropriated from the Federal Hospital Insurance Trust Fund for making grants to all States under subsection (g), $25,000,000 in each of the fiscal years 1998 through 2002, for making grants to all States under paragraphs (1) and (2) of subsection (g), $35,000,000 in each of fiscal years 2005 through 2008, for making grants to all States under paragraphs (1) and (2) of subsection (g), $55,000,000 in each of fiscal years 2009 and 2010, for making grants to all States under paragraph (6) of subsection (g), $50,000,000 in each of fiscal years 2009 and 2010, to remain available until expended and for making grants to all States under subsection (g), such sums as may be necessary in each of fiscal years 2011 and 2012, to remain available until expended.

(Aug. 14, 1935, ch 531, Title XVIII, Part A, § 1820, as added Dec. 19, 1989, P. L. 101-239, Title VI, Subtitle A, Part 1, Subpart A, § 6003(g)(1)(A), 103 Stat. 2145; Nov. 5, 1990, P. L. 101-508, Title IV, Subtitle A, Part 1, § 4008(d), (m)(2)(B), 104 Stat. 1388-44, 1388-53; Oct. 31, 1994, P. L. 103-432, Title I, Subtitle A, § 102(a)(1), (2), (b)(1)(A), (2), (c), (f), (h), 108 Stat. 4401–4404; Aug. 5, 1997, P. L. 105-33, Title IV, Subtitle C, § 4201(a), 111 Stat. 329, 369; Nov. 29, 1999, P. L. 106-113, Div B, § 1000(a)(6), 113 Stat. 1536; Dec. 8, 2003, P. L. 108-173, Title IV, Subtitle A, § 405(e)(1), (2), (f), (g)(1), (h), 117 Stat. 2267, 2269; July 15, 2008, P. L. 110-275, Title I, Subtitle B, § 121, 122 Stat. 2511; March 23, 2010, P. L. 111-148, Title III, Subtitle B, Part II, § 3129(a), (b), 124 Stat. 426.)

HISTORY; ANCILLARY LAWS AND DIRECTIVES

Other provisions:

Demonstration project on community health integration models in certain rural counties. Act July 15, 2008, P. L. 110-275, Title I, Subtitle B, § 123, 122 Stat. 2514; March 23, 2010, P. L. 111-148, Title III, Subtitle B, Part II, § 3126, 124 Stat. 425, provides:

"(a) In general. The Secretary shall establish a demonstration project to allow eligible entities to develop and test new models for the delivery of health care services in eligible counties for the purpose of improving access to, and better integrating the delivery of, acute care, extended care, and other essential health care services to Medicare beneficiaries.

"(b) Purpose. The purpose of the demonstration project under this section is to—

"(1) explore ways to increase access to, and improve the adequacy of, payments for acute care, extended care, and other essential health care services provided under the Medicare and Medicaid programs in eligible counties; and

"(2) evaluate regulatory challenges facing such providers and the communities they serve.

"(c) Requirements. The following requirements shall apply under the demonstration project:

"(1) Health care providers in eligible counties selected to participate in the demonstration project under subsection (d)(3) shall (when determined appropriate by the Secretary), instead of the payment rates otherwise applicable under the Medicare program, be reimbursed at a rate that covers at least the reasonable costs of the provider in furnishing acute care, extended care, and other essential health care services to Medicare beneficiaries.

"(2) Methods to coordinate the survey and certification process under the Medicare program and the Medicaid program across all health service categories included in the demonstration project shall be tested with the goal of assuring quality and safety while reducing administrative burdens, as appropriate, related to completing such survey and certification process.

"(3) Health care providers in eligible counties selected to participate in the demonstration project under subsection (d)(3) and the Secretary shall work with the State to explore ways to revise reimbursement policies under the Medicaid program to improve access to the range of health care services available in such eligible counties.

"(4) The Secretary shall identify regulatory requirements that may be revised appropriately to improve access to care in eligible counties.

"(5) Other essential health care services necessary to ensure access to the range of health care services in eligible counties selected to participate in the demonstration project under subsection (d)(3) shall be identified. Ways to ensure adequate funding for such services shall also be explored.

"(d) Application process. (1) Eligibility. (A) In general. Eligibility to participate in the demonstration project under this section shall be limited to eligible entities.

"(B) Eligible entity defined. In this section, the term 'eligible entity' means an entity that—

"(i) is a Rural Hospital Flexibility Program grantee under section 1820(g) of the Social Security Act (42 U.S.C. 1395i-4(g)); and

"(ii) is located in a State in which at least 65 percent of the counties in the State are counties that have 6 or less residents per square mile.

"(2) Application. (A) In general. An eligible entity seeking to participate in the demonstration project under this section shall submit an application to the Secretary at such time, in such manner, and containing such information as the Secretary may require.

"(B) Limitation. The Secretary shall select eligible entities located in not more than 4 States to participate in the demonstration project under this section.

"(3) Selection of eligible counties. An eligible entity selected by the Secretary to participate in the demonstration project under this section shall select eligible counties in the State in which the entity is located in which to conduct the demonstration project.

"(4) Eligible county defined. In this section, the term 'eligible county' means a county that meets the following requirements:

"(A) The county has 6 or less residents per square mile.

"(B) As of the date of the enactment of this Act, a facility designated as a critical access hospital which meets the following requirements was located in the county:

"(i) As of the date of the enactment of this Act, the critical access hospital furnished 1 or more of the following:

"(I) Home health services.

"(II) Hospice care.

"(ii) As of the date of the enactment of this Act, the critical access hospital has an average daily inpatient census of 5 or less.

"(C) As of the date of the enactment of this Act, skilled nursing facility services were available in the county in—

"(i) a critical access hospital using swing beds; or

"(ii) a local nursing home.

"(e) Administration. (1) In general. The demonstration project under this section shall be administered jointly by the Administrator of the Office of Rural Health Policy of the Health Resources and Services Administration and the Administrator of the Centers for Medicare & Medicaid Services, in accordance with paragraphs (2) and (3).

"(2) HRSA duties. In administering the demonstration project under this section, the Administrator of the Office of Rural Health Policy of the Health Resources and Services Administration shall—

"(A) award grants to the eligible entities selected to participate in the demonstration project; and

"(B) work with such entities to provide technical assistance related to the requirements under the project.

"(3) CMS duties. In administering the demonstration project under this section, the Administrator of the Centers for Medicare & Medicaid Services shall determine which provisions of titles XVIII and XIX of the Social Security Act (42 U.S.C. 1395 et seq.; 1396 et seq.) the Secretary should waive under the waiver authority under subsection (i) that are relevant to the development of alternative reimbursement methodologies, which may include, as appropriate, covering at least the reasonable costs of the provider in furnishing acute care, extended care, and other essential health care services to Medicare beneficiaries and coordinating the survey and certification process under the Medicare and Medicaid programs, as appropriate, across all service categories included in the demonstration project.

"(f) Duration. (1) In general. The demonstration project under this section shall be conducted for a 3-year period beginning on October 1, 2009.

"(2) Beginning date of demonstration project. The demonstration project under this section shall be considered to have begun in a State on the date on which the eligible counties selected to participate in the demonstration project under subsection (d)(3) begin operations in accordance with the requirements under the demonstration project.

"(g) Funding. (1) CMS. (A) In general. The Secretary shall provide for the transfer, in appropriate part from the Federal Hospital Insurance Trust Fund established under section 1817 of the Social Security Act (42 U.S.C. 1395i) and the Federal Supplementary Medical Insurance Trust Fund established under section 1841 of such Act (42 U.S.C. 1395t), of such sums as are necessary for the costs to the Centers for Medicare & Medicaid Services of carrying out its duties under the demonstration project under this section.

"(B) Budget neutrality. In conducting the demonstration project under this section, the Secretary shall ensure that the aggregate payments made by the Secretary do not exceed the amount which the Secretary estimates would have been paid if the demonstration project under this section was not implemented.

"(2) HRSA. There are authorized to be appropriated to the Office of Rural Health Policy of the Health Resources and Services Administration $800,000 for each of fiscal years 2010, 2011, and 2012 for the purpose of carrying out the duties of such Office under the demonstration project under this section, to remain available for the duration of the demonstration project.

"(h) Report. (1) Interim report. Not later than the date that is 2 years after the date on which the demonstration project under this section is implemented, the Administrator of the Office of Rural Health Policy of the Health Resources and Services Administration, in coordination with the Administrator of the Centers for Medicare & Medicaid Services, shall submit a report to Congress on the status of the demonstration project that includes initial recommendations on ways to improve access to, and the availability of, health care services in eligible counties based on the findings of the demonstration project.

"(2) Final report. Not later than 1 year after the completion of the demonstration project, the Administrator of the Office of Rural Health Policy of the Health Resources and Services Administration, in coordination with the Administrator of the Centers for Medicare & Medicaid Services, shall submit a report to Congress on such project, together with recommendations for such legislation and administrative action as the Secretary determines appropriate.

"(i) Waiver authority. The Secretary may waive such requirements of titles XVIII and XIX of the Social Security Act (42 U.S.C. 1395 et seq.; 1396 et seq.) as may be necessary and appropriate for the purpose of carrying out the demonstration project under this section.

"(j) Definitions. In this section:

"(1) Extended care services. The term 'extended care services' means the following:

"(A) Home health services.

"(B) Covered skilled nursing facility services.

"(C) Hospice care.

"(2) Covered skilled nursing facility services. The term 'covered skilled nursing facility services' has the meaning given such term in section 1888(e)(2)(A) of the Social Security Act (42 U.S.C. 1395yy(e)(2)(A)).

"(3) Critical access hospital. The term 'critical access hospital' means a facility designated as a critical access hospital under section 1820(c) of such Act (42 U.S.C. 1395i-4(c)).

"(4) Home health services. The term 'home health services' has the meaning given such term in section 1861(m) of such Act (42 U.S.C. 1395x(m)).

"(5) Hospice care. The term 'hospice care' has the meaning given such term in section 1861(dd) of such Act (42 U.S.C. 1395x(dd)).

"(6) Medicaid program. The term 'Medicaid program' means the program under title XIX of such Act (42 U.S.C. 1396 et seq.).

"(7) Medicare program. The term 'Medicare program' means the program under title XVIII of such Act (42 U.S.C. 1395 et seq.).

"(8) Other essential health care services. The term

'other essential health care services' means the following:

"(A) Ambulance services (as described in section 1861(s)(7) of the Social Security Act (42 U.S.C. 1395x(s)(7))).

"(B) Physicians' services (as defined in section 1861(q) of the Social Security Act (42 U.S.C. 1395x(q)).

"(C) Public health services (as defined by the Secretary).

"(D) Other health care services determined appropriate by the Secretary.

"(9) Secretary. The term 'Secretary' means the Secretary of Health and Human Services.".

Application of amendments made by § 3129 of Act March 23, 2010. Act March 23, 2010, P. L. 111-148, Title III, Subtitle B, Part II, § 3129(c), 124 Stat. 427, provides: "The amendments made by this section [amending subsecs. (g)(3) and (j) of this section] shall apply to grants made on or after January 1, 2010.".

PART B. SUPPLEMENTARY MEDICAL INSURANCE BENEFITS FOR THE AGED AND DISABLED

§ 1395l. Payment of benefits

(a) Amounts. Except as provided in section 1876 [42 USCS § 1395mm], and subject to the succeeding provisions of this section, there shall be paid from the Federal Supplementary Medical Insurance Trust Fund, in the case of each individual who is covered under the insurance program established by this part [42 USCS §§ 1395j et seq.] and incurs expenses for services with respect to which benefits are payable under this part [42 USCS §§ 1395j et seq.], amounts equal to—

(1) **[Caution: For provisions applicable to items and services furnished before January 1, 2011, see 2010 amendment notes below.]** in the case of services described in section 1832(a)(1) [42 USCS § 1395k(a)(1)]—80 percent of the reasonable charges for the services; except that (A) an organization which provides medical and other health services (or arranges for their availability) on a prepayment basis (and either is sponsored by a union or employer, or does not provide, or arrange for the provision of, any inpatient hospital services) may elect to be paid 80 percent of the reasonable cost of services for which payment may be made under this part [42 USCS §§ 1395j et seq.] on behalf of individuals enrolled in such organization in lieu of 80 percent of the reasonable charges for such services if the organization undertakes to charge such individuals no more than 20 percent of such reasonable cost plus any amounts payable by them as a result of subsection (b), (B) with respect to items and services described in section 1861(s)(10)(A) [42 USCS § 1395x(s)(10)(A)], the amounts paid shall be 100 percent of the reasonable charges for such items and services, (C) with respect to expenses incurred for those physicians' services for which payment may be made under this part [42 USCS §§ 1395j et seq.] that are described in section 1862(a)(4) [42 USCS § 1395y(a)(4)], the amounts paid shall be subject to such limitations as may be prescribed by regulations, (D) with respect to clinical diagnostic laboratory tests for which payment is made under this part [42 USCS §§ 1395j et seq.] (i) on the basis of a fee schedule under subsection (h)(1) or section 1834(d)(1) [42 USCS § 1395m(d)(1)], the amount paid shall be equal to 80 percent (or 100 percent, in the case of such tests for which payment is made on an assignment-related basis) of the lesser of the amount determined under such fee schedule, the limitation amount for that test determined under subsection (h)(4)(B), or the amount of the charges billed for the tests, or (ii) on the basis of a negotiated rate established under subsection (h)(6), the amount paid shall be equal to 100 percent of such negotiated rate, [,] (E) with respect to services furnished to individuals who have been determined to have end stage renal disease, the amounts paid shall be determined subject to the provisions of section 1881 [42 USCS § 1395rr], (F) with respect to clinical social worker services under section 1861(s)(2)(N) [42 USCS § 1395x(s)(2)(N)], the amounts paid shall be 80 percent of the lesser of (i) the actual charge for the services or (ii) 75 percent of the amount determined for payment of a psychologist under clause (L), (G) with respect to facility services furnished in connection with a surgical procedure specified pursuant to subsection (i)(1)(A) and furnished to an individual in an ambulatory surgical center described in such subsection, for services furnished beginning with the implementation date of a revised payment system for such services in such facilities specified in subsection (i)(2)(D), the amounts paid shall be 80 percent of the lesser of the actual charge for the services or the amount determined by the Secretary under such revised payment system, (H) with respect to services of a certified registered nurse anesthetist under section 1861(s)(11) [42 USCS § 1395x(s)(11)], the amounts paid shall be 80 percent of the least of the actual charge, the prevailing charge that would be recognized (or, for services furnished on or after January 1, 1992, the fee schedule amount provided under section 1848 [42 USCS § 1395w-4]) if the services had been performed by an anesthesiolo-

gist, or the fee schedule for such services established by the Secretary in accordance with subsection (1), (I) with respect to covered items (described in section 1834(a)(13) [42 USCS § 1395m(a)(13)]), the amounts paid shall be the amounts described in section 1834(a)(1) [42 USCS § 1395m(a)(1)], [and] (J) with respect to expenses incurred for radiologist services (as defined in section 1834(b)(6) [42 USCS § 1395m(b)(6)]), subject to section 1848 [42 USCS § 1395w-4], the amounts paid shall be 80 percent of the lesser of the actual charge for the services or the amount provided under the fee schedule established under section 1834(b) [42 USCS § 1395m(b)], (K) with respect to certified nurse-midwife services under section 1861(s)(2)(L) [42 USCS § 1395x(s)(2)(L)], the amounts paid shall be 80 percent of the lesser of the actual charge for the services or the amount determined by a fee schedule established by the Secretary for the purposes of this subparagraph (but in no event shall such fee schedule exceed 65 percent of the prevailing charge that would be allowed for the same service performed by a physician, or, for services furnished on or after January 1, 1992, 65 percent (or 100 percent for services furnished on or after January 1, 2011) of the fee schedule amount provided under section 1848 [42 USCS § 1395w-4] for the same service performed by a physician), (L) with respect to qualified psychologist services under section 1861(s)(2)(M) [42 USCS § 1395x(s)(2)(M)], the amounts paid shall be 80 percent of the lesser of the actual charge for the services or the amount determined by a fee schedule established by the Secretary for the purposes of this subparagraph, (M) with respect to prosthetic devices and orthotics and prosthetics (as defined in section 1834(h)(4) [42 USCS § 1395m(h)(4)]), the amounts paid shall be the amounts described in section 1834(h)(1) [42 USCS § 1395m(h)(1)], (N) with respect to expenses incurred for physicians' services (as defined in section 1848(j)(3) [42 USCS § 1395w-4(j)(3)]) other than personalized prevention plan services (as defined in section 1861(hhh)(1) [42 USCS § 1395x(hhh)(1)]), the amounts paid shall be 80 percent of the payment basis determined under section 1848(a)(1) [42 USCS § 1395w-4(a)(1)], (O) with respect to services described in 1861(s)(2)(K) [42 USCS § 1395x(s)(2)(K)] (relating to services furnished by physician assistants, nurse practitioners, or clinic nurse specialists), the amounts paid shall be equal to 80 percent of (i) the lesser of the actual charge or 85 percent of the fee schedule amount provided under section 1848 [42 USCS § 1395w-4], or (ii) in the case of services as an assistant at surgery, the lesser of the actual charge or 85 percent of the amount that would otherwise be recognized if performed by a physician who is serving as an assistant at surgery, (P) with respect to surgical dressings, the amounts paid shall be the amounts determined under section 1834(i) [42 USCS § 1395m(i)], (Q) with respect to items or services for which fee schedules are established pursuant to section 1842(s) [42 USCS § 1395u(s)], the amounts paid shall be 80 percent of the lesser of the actual charge or the fee schedule established in such section, (R) with respect to ambulance services, (i) the amounts paid shall be 80 percent of the lesser of the actual charge for the services or the amount determined by a fee schedule established by the Secretary under section 1834(l) [42 USCS § 1395m(l)] and (ii) with respect to ambulance services described in section 1834(l)(8) [42 USCS § 1395m(l)(8)], the amounts paid shall be the amounts determined under section 1834(g) [42 USCS § 1395m(g)] for outpatient critical access hospital services, (S) with respect to drugs and biologicals (including intravenous immune globulin (as defined in section 1861(zz) [42 USCS § 1395x(zz)])) not paid on a cost or prospective payment basis as otherwise provided in this part [42 USCS §§ 1395j et seq.] (other than items and services described in subparagraph (B)), the amounts paid shall be 80 percent of the lesser of the actual charge or the payment amount established in section 1842(o) [42 USCS § 1395u(o)] (or, if applicable, under section 1847, 1847A, or 1847B [42 USCS § 1395w-3, 1395w-3a, or 1395w-3b]), (T) with respect to medical nutrition therapy services (as defined in section 1861(vv) [42 USCS § 1395x(vv)]), the amount paid shall be 80 percent (or 100 percent if such services are recommended with a grade of A or B by the United States Preventive Services Task Force for any indication or population and are appropriate for the individual) of the lesser of the actual charge for the services or 85 percent of the amount determined under the fee schedule established under section 1848(b) [42 USCS § 1395w-4(b)] for the same services if furnished by a physician, (U) with respect to facility fees described in section 1834(m)(2)(B) [42 USCS § 1395m(m)(2)(B)], the amounts paid shall be 80 percent of the lesser of the actual charge or the amounts specified in such section, (V) notwithstanding subparagraphs (I) (relating to durable medical equipment), (M) (relating to prosthetic devices and orthotics and prosthetics), and (Q) (relating to 1842(s) items), with respect to competitively priced items and services (described in section 1847(a)(2) [42 USCS § 1395w-3(a)(2)]) that are furnished in a competitive area, the amounts paid shall be the amounts described in section 1847(b)(5) [42 USCS § 1395w-3(b)(5)], (W) with respect to additional preventive services (as defined in section 1861(ddd)(1) [42 USCS § 1395x(ddd)(1)]), the amount paid shall be (i) in the case of such services which are clinical diagnostic laboratory tests, the amount determined under subparagraph (D) (if such subparagraph were applied, by substituting "100 percent" for "80 percent"), and (ii) in the case of all other such services, 100 percent of the lesser of the actual charge for the service or the amount determined under a fee schedule established by the Secretary for purposes of this subparagraph, (X) with respect to personalized prevention plan services (as defined in section 1861(hhh)(1) [42 USCS § 1395x(hhh)(1)]), the amount paid shall be 100 percent of the lesser of the actual charge for the services or the amount determined under the payment basis determined under section 1848 [42 USCS § 1395w-4], (Y) with respect to preventive services described in subparagraphs (A) and (B) of section 1861(ddd)(3) [42 USCS § 1395x(ddd)(3)] that are appropriate for the individual and, in the case of such services described in subparagraph (A), are recommended with a grade of A or B by the United States Preventive Services Task Force for any indication or population, the amount paid shall be 100 percent of (i) except as provided in clause (ii), the lesser of the actual charge for the services or the amount determined under the fee schedule that applies to such services under this part [42 USCS §§ 1395j et seq.], and (ii) in the case of such services that are covered OPD services (as defined in subsection (t)(1)(B)), the amount determined under subsection (t), and (Z) with respect to Federally qualified health center services for which payment is made under section 1834(o) [42 USCS § 1395m(o)], the amounts paid shall be 80 percent of the lesser of the actual charge or the amount determined under such section;

(2) in the case of services described in section 1832(a)(2) [42 USCS § 1395k(a)(2)] (except those services described in subparagraphs (C), (D), (E), (F), (G), (H), and (I) of such section and unless otherwise specified in section 1881 [42 USCS § 1395rr])—

(A) with respect to home health services (other than a covered osteoporosis drug) (as defined in section 1861(kk) [42 USCS § 1395x(kk)]), the amount determined under the prospective payment system under section 1895 [42 USCS § 1395fff];

(B) with respect to other items and services (except those described in subparagraph (C), (D), or (E) of this paragraph and except as may be provided in section 1886 or section 1888(e)(9) [42 USCS § 1395ww or 1395yy(e)(9)])—

(i) furnished before January 1, 1999, the lessor of—

(I) the reasonable cost of such services, as determined under section 1861(v) [42 USCS § 1395x(v)], or

(II) the customary charges with respect to such services,

less the amount a provider may charge as described in clause (ii) of section 1866(a)(2)(A) [42 USCS § 1395cc(a)(2)(A)(ii)], but in no case may the payment for such other services exceed 80 percent of such reasonable cost, or

(ii) if such services are furnished before January 1, 1999, by a public provider of services, or by another provider which demonstrates to the satisfaction of the Secretary that a significant portion of its patients are low-income (and requests that payment be made under this clause), free of charge or at nominal charges to the public, 80 percent of the amount determined in accordance with section 1814(b)(2) [42 USCS § 1395f(b)(2)], or

(iii) if such services are furnished on or after January 1, 1999, the amount determined under subsection (t), or

(iv) if (and for so long as) the conditions described in section 1814(b)(3) [42 USCS § 1395f(b)(3)] are met, the amounts determined under the reimbursement system described in such section;

(C) with respect to services described in the second sentence of section 1861(p) [42 USCS § 1395x(p)], 80 percent of the reasonable charges for such services;

(D) with respect to clinical diagnostic laboratory tests for which payment is made under this part [42 USCS §§ 1395j et seq.] (i) on the basis of a fee schedule determined under subsection (h)(1) or section 1834(d)(1) [42 USCS § 1395m(d)(1)], the amount paid shall be equal to 80 percent (or 100 percent, in the case of such tests for which payment is made on an assignment-related basis or to a provider having an agreement under section 1866 [42 USCS § 1395cc]) of the lesser of the amount determined under such fee schedule or the amount of the charges billed for the tests, or (ii) on the basis of a negotiated rate established under subsection (h)(6), the amount paid shall be equal to 100 percent of such negotiated rate for such tests;

(E) with respect to—

(i) outpatient hospital radiology services (including diagnostic and therapeutic radiology, nuclear medicine and CAT scan procedures, magnetic resonance imaging, and ultrasound and other imaging services, but excluding screening mammography and, for services furnished on or after January 1, 2005, diagnostic mammography), and

(ii) effective for procedures performed on or after October 1, 1989, diagnostic procedures (as defined by the Secretary) described in section 1861(s)(3) [42 USCS § 1395x(s)(3)] (other than diagnostic x-ray tests and diagnostic laboratory tests),

the amount determined under subsection (n) or, for services or procedures performed on or after January 1, 1999, subsection (t);

(F) with respect to a covered osteoporosis drug (as defined in section 1861(kk) [42 USCS § 1395x(kk)]) furnished by a home health agency, 80 percent of the reasonable cost of such service, as determined under section 1861(v) [42 USCS § 1395x(v)];

(G) with respect to items and services described in section 1861(s)(10)(A) [42 USCS § 1395x(s)(10)(A)], the lesser of—

(i) the reasonable cost of such services, as determined under section 1861(v) [42 USCS § 1395x(v)], or

(ii) the customary charges with respect to such services;

(H) **[Caution: This subparagraph applies to services furnished on or after January 1, 2011, as provided by § 4103(e) of Act March 23, 2010, P. L. 111-148, which appears as a note to this section.]** with respect to personalized prevention plan services (as defined in section 1861(hhh)(1) [42 USCS § 1395x(hhh)(1)]) furnished by an outpatient department of a hospital, the amount determined under paragraph (1)(X); and

(I) **[Caution: This subparagraph applies to services furnished on or after January 1, 2011, as provided by § 4104(d) of Act March 23, 2010, P. L. 111-148, which appears as a note to this section.]** with respect to preventive services described in subparagraphs (A) and (B) of section 1861(ddd)(3) [42 USCS § 1395x(ddd)(3)] that are appropriate for the individual and are furnished by an outpatient department of a hospital and, in the case of such services described in subparagraph (A), are recommended with a grade of A or B by the United States Preventive Services Task Force for any indication or population, the amount determined under paragraph (1)(W) or (1)(Y),

or, if such services are furnished by a public provider of services, or by another provider which demonstrates to the satisfaction of the Secretary that a significant portion of its patients are low-income (and requests that payment be made under this provision), free of charge or at nominal charges to the public, the amount determined in accordance with section 1814(b)(2) [42 USCS § 1395f(b)(2)];

(3) in the case of services described in section 1832(a)(2)(D) [42 USCS § 1395k(a)(2)(D)]—

(A) except as provided in subparagraph (B), the costs which are reasonable and related to the cost of furnishing such services or which are based on such other tests of reasonableness as the Secretary may prescribe in regulations, including those authorized under section 1861(v)(1)(A) [42 USCS § 1395x(v)(1)(A)], less the amount a provider may charge as described in clause (ii) of section 1866(a)(2)(A) [42 USCS § 1395cc(a)(2)(A)], but in no case may the payment for such services (other than for items and services described in section 1861(s)(10)(A) [42 USCS § 1395x(s)(10)(A)]) exceed 80 percent of such costs; or

(B) with respect to the services described in clause (ii) of section 1832(a)(2)(D) [42 USCS § 1395k(a)(2)(D)] that are furnished to an individual enrolled with a MA plan under part C [42 USCS §§ 1395w-21 et seq.] pursuant to a written agreement described in section 1853(a)(4) [42 USCS § 1395w-23(a)(4)], the amount (if any) by which—

(i) the amount of payment that would have otherwise been provided (I) under subparagraph (A) (calculated as if "100 percent" were substituted for "80 percent" in such subparagraph) for such services if the individual had not been so enrolled, or (II) in the case of such services furnished on or after the implementation date of the prospective payment system under section 1834(o) [42 USCS § 1395m(o)], under such section (calculated as if "100 percent" were substituted for "80 percent" in such section) for such services if the individual had not been so enrolled; exceeds

(ii) the amount of the payments received under such written agreement for such services (not including any financial incentives provided for in such agreement such as risk pool payments, bonuses, or withholds),

less the amount the federally qualified health center may charge as described in section 1857(e)(3)(B) [42 USCS § 1395w-27(e)(3)(B)];

(4) in the case of facility services described

in section 1832(a)(2)(F) [42 USCS § 1395k(a)(2)(F)], and outpatient hospital facility services furnished in connection with surgical procedures specified by the Secretary pursuant to section 1833(i)(1)(A) [subsec. (i)(1)(A) of this section], the applicable amount as determined under paragraph (2) or (3) of subsection (i) or subsection (t);

(5) in the case of covered items (described in section 1834(a)(13) [42 USCS § 1395m(a)(13)]) the amounts described in section 1834(a)(1) [42 USCS § 1395m(a)(1)];

(6) in the case of outpatient critical access hospital services, the amounts described in section 1834(g) [42 USCS § 1395m(g)];

(7) in the case of prosthetic devices and orthotics and prosthetics (as described in section 1834(h)(4) [42 USCS § 1395m(h)(4)]), the amounts described in section 1834(h) [42 USCS § 1395m(h)];

(8) in the case of—

(A) outpatient physical therapy services, outpatient speech-language pathology services, and outpatient occupational therapy services furnished—

(i) by a rehabilitation agency, public health agency, clinic, comprehensive outpatient rehabilitation facility, or skilled nursing facility,

(ii) by a home health agency to an individual who is not homebound, or

(iii) by another entity under an arrangement with an entity described in clause (i) or (ii); and

(B) outpatient physical therapy services, outpatient speech-language pathology services, and outpatient occupational therapy services furnished—

(i) by a hospital to an outpatient or to a hospital inpatient who is entitled to benefits under part A [42 USCS §§ 1395c et seq.] but has exhausted benefits for inpatient hospital services during a spell of illness or is not so entitled to benefits under part A [42 USCS §§ 1395c et seq.], or

(ii) by another entity under an arrangement with a hospital described in clause (i),

the amounts described in section 1834(k) [42 USCS § 1395m(k)]; and

(9) in the case of services described in section 1832(a)(2)(E) [42 USCS § 1395k(a)(2)(E)] that are not described in paragraph (8), the amounts described in section 1834(k) [42 USCS § 1395m(k)].

Paragraph (3)(A) shall not apply to Federally qualified health center services furnished on or after the implementation date of the prospective payment system under section 1834(o) [42 USCS § 1395m(o)].

(b) Deductible provision [Caution: For provisions applicable to items and services furnished on or before Jan. 1, 2011, see 2010 amendment notes below.]. Before applying subsection (a) with respect to expenses incurred by an individual during any calendar year, the total amount of the expenses incurred by such individual during such year (which would, except for this subsection, constitute incurred expenses from which benefits payable under subsection (a) are determinable) shall be reduced by a deductible of $75 for calendar years before 1991, $100 for 1991 through 2004, $110 for 2005, and for a subsequent year the amount of such deductible for the previous year increased by the annual percentage increase in the monthly actuarial rate under section 1839(a)(1) [42 USCS § 1395r(a)(1)] ending with such subsequent year (rounded to the nearest $1); except that (1) such total amount shall not include expenses incurred for preventive services described in subparagraph (A) of section 1861(ddd)(3) that are recommended with a grade of A or B by the United States Preventive Services Task Force for any indication or population and are appropriate for the individual [.], (2) such deductible shall not apply with respect to home health services (other than a covered osteoporosis drug (as defined in section 1861(kk) [42 USCS § 1395x(kk)])), (3) such deductible shall not apply with respect to clinical diagnostic laboratory tests for which payment is made under this part [42 USCS §§ 1395j et seq.] (A) under subsection (a)(1)(D)(i) or (a)(2)(D)(i) on an assignment-related basis, or to a provider having an agreement under section 1866 [42 USCS § 1395cc], or (B) on the basis of a negotiated rate determined under subsection (h)(6), (4) such deductible shall not apply to Federally qualified health center services, (5) such deductible shall not apply with respect to screening mammography (as described in section 1861(jj) [42 USCS § 1395x(jj)]), (6) such deductible shall not apply with respect to screening pap smear and screening pelvic exam (as described in section 1861(nn) [42 USCS § 1395x(nn)]), (7) such deductible shall not apply with respect to ultrasound screening for abdominal aortic aneurysm (as defined in section 1861(bbb) [42 USCS § 1395x(bbb)]), (8) such deductible shall not apply with respect to colorectal cancer screening tests (as described in section 1861(pp)(1) [42 USCS § 1395x(pp)(1)]), (9) such deductible shall not apply with respect to an initial preventive physical examination (as defined in section 1861(ww) [42 USCS § 1395x(ww)]), and (10) such deductible shall not apply with respect to personalized prevention plan services (as defined in section 1861(hhh)(1) [42 USCS § 1395x(hhh)(1)]). The total amount of the expenses incurred by an individual as determined under the preceding sentence shall, after the reduction specified in such sentence, be further reduced by an amount equal to the expenses incurred for the first three pints of whole blood (or equivalent quantities of packed red blood cells, as defined under regulations) furnished to the individual during the calendar year, except that such deductible for such blood shall in accordance with regulations be appropriately reduced to the extent that there has been a replacement of such blood (or equivalent quantities of packed red blood cells, as so defined); and for such purposes blood (or equivalent quantities of packed red blood cells, as so defined) furnished such individual shall be deemed replaced when the institution or other person furnishing such blood (or such equivalent quantities of packed red blood cells, as so defined) is given one pint of blood for each pint of blood (or equivalent quantities of packed red blood cells, as so defined) furnished such individual with respect to which a deduction is made under this sentence. The deductible under the previous sentence for blood or blood cells furnished an individual in a year shall be reduced to the extent that a deductible has been imposed under section 1813(a)(2) [42 USCS § 1395e(a)(2)] to blood or blood cells furnished the individual in the year. Paragraph (1) of the first sentence of this subsection shall apply with respect to a colorectal cancer screening test regardless of the code that is billed for the establishment of a diagnosis as a result of the test, or for the removal of tissue or other matter or other procedure that is furnished in connection with, as a result of, and in the same clinical encounter as the screening test.

(c) Copayment rates for Medicare outpatient psychiatric services. (1) Notwithstanding any other provision of this part, with respect to expenses incurred in a calendar year in connection with the treatment of mental, psychoneurotic, and personality disorders of an individual who is not an inpatient of a hospital at the time such expenses are incurred, there shall be considered as incurred expenses for purposes of subsections (a) and (b)—

(A) for expenses incurred in years prior to 2010, only 62½ percent of such expenses;

(B) for expenses incurred in 2010 or 2011, only 68¾ percent of such expenses;

(C) for expenses incurred in 2012, only 75 percent of such expenses;

(D) for expenses incurred in 2013, only 81¼ percent of such expenses; and

(E) for expenses incurred in 2014 or any subsequent calendar year, 100 percent of such expenses.

(2) For purposes of subparagraphs (A) through (D) of paragraph (1), the term "treatment" does not include brief office visits (as defined by the Secretary) for the sole purpose of monitoring or changing drug prescriptions used in the treatment of such disorders or partial hospitalization services that are not directly provided by a physician.

(d) Nonduplication of payments. No payment may be made under this part [42 USCS §§ 1395j et seq.] with respect to any services furnished an individual to the extent that such individual is entitled (or would be entitled except for section 1813 [42 USCS § 1395e]) to have payment made with respect to such services under part A [42 USCS §§ 1395c et seq.].

(e) Information for determination of amounts due. No payment shall be made to any provider of services or other person under this part [42 USCS §§ 1395j et seq.] unless there has been furnished such information as may be necessary in order to determine the amounts due such provider or other person under this part [42 USCS §§ 1395j et seq.] for the period with respect to which the amounts are being paid or for any prior period.

(f) Updating maximum rate of payment per visit for independent rural health clinics. In establishing limits under subsection (a) on payment for rural health clinic services provided by rural health clinics (other than such clinics in hospitals with less than 50 beds), the Secretary shall establish such limit, for services provided—

(1) in 1988, after March 31, at $46 per visit, and

(2) in a subsequent year, at the limit established under this subsection for the previous year increased by the percentage increase in the MEI (as defined in section 1842(i)(3) [42 USCS § 1395u(i)(3)]) applicable to primary care services (as defined in section 1842(i)(4) [42 USCS § 1395u(i)(4)]) furnished as of the first day of that year.

(g) Physical therapy services. (1) Subject to paragraphs (4) and (5), in the case of physical therapy services of the type described in section 1861(p) [42 USCS § 1395x(p)] and speech-language pathology services of the type described in such section through the application of section 1861(ll)(2) [42 USCS § 1395x(ll)(2)], but not described in section 1833(a)(8)(B) [subsec. (a)(8)(B) of this section], and physical therapy services and speech-language pathology services of such type which are furnished by a physician or as incident to physicians' services, with respect to expenses incurred in any calendar year, no more than the amount specified in paragraph (2) for the year shall be considered as incurred expenses for purposes of subsections (a) and (b).

(2) The amount specified in this paragraph—

(A) for 1999, 2000, and 2001, is $1,500, and

(B) for a subsequent year is the amount specified in this paragraph for the preceding year increased by the percentage increase in the MEI (as defined in section 1842(i)(3) [42 USCS § 1395u(i)(3)]) for such subsequent year; except that if an increase under subparagraph (B) for a year is not a multiple of $10, it shall be rounded to the nearest multiple of $10.

(3) Subject to paragraphs (4) and (5), in the case of occupational therapy services (of the type that are described in section 1861(p) [42 USCS § 1395x(p)] (but not described in section 1833(a)(8)(B) [subsec. (a)(8)(B) of this section]) through the operation of section 1861(g) [42 USCS § 1395x(g)] and of such type which are furnished by a physician or as incident to physicians' services), with respect to expenses incurred in any calendar year, no more than the amount specified in paragraph (2) for the year shall be considered as incurred expenses for purposes of subsections (a) and (b).

(4) This subsection shall not apply to expenses incurred with respect to services furnished during 2000, 2001, 2002, 2004, and 2005.

(5) With respect to expenses incurred during the period beginning on January 1, 2006, and ending on December 31, 2010, for services, the Secretary shall implement a process under which an individual enrolled under this part may, upon request of the individual or a person on behalf of the individual, obtain an exception from the uniform dollar limitation specified in paragraph (2), for services described in paragraphs (1) and (3) if the provision of such services is determined to be medically necessary. Under such process, if the Secretary does not make a decision on such a request for an exception within 10 business days of the date of the Secretary's receipt of the request, the Secretary shall be deemed to have found the services to be medically necessary.

(h) Fee schedules for clinical diagnostic laboratory tests; percentage of prevailing charge level; nominal fee for samples; adjustments; recipients of payments; negotiated payment rate. (1)(A) Subject to section 1834(d)(1) [42 USCS § 1395m(d)(1)], the Secretary shall establish fee schedules for clinical diagnostic laboratory tests (including prostate cancer screening tests under section 1861(oo) [42 USCS § 1395x(oo)] consisting of prostate-specific antigen blood tests) for which payment is made under this part [42 USCS §§ 1395j et seq.], other than such tests performed by a provider of services for an inpatient of such provider.

(B) In the case of clinical diagnostic laboratory tests performed by a physician or by a laboratory (other than tests performed by a qualified hospital laboratory (as defined in subparagraph (D)) for outpatients of such hospital), the fee schedules established under subparagraph (A) shall be established on a regional, statewide, or carrier service area basis (as the Secretary may determine to be appropriate) for tests furnished on or after July 1, 1984.

(C) In the case of clinical diagnostic laboratory tests performed by a qualified hospital laboratory (as defined in subparagraph (D)) for outpatients of such hospital, the fee schedules established under subparagraph (A) shall be established on a regional, statewide, or carrier service area basis (as the Secretary may determine to be appropriate) for tests furnished on or after July 1, 1984.

(D) In this subsection, the term "qualified hospital laboratory" means a hospital laboratory, in a sole community hospital (as defined in section 1886(d)(5)(D)(iii) [42 USCS § 1395ww(d)(5)(D)(iii)]) which provides some clinical diagnostic laboratory tests 24 hours a day in order to serve a hospital emergency room which is available to provide services 24 hours a day and 7 days a week.

(2)(A)(i) Except as provided in paragraph (4), the Secretary shall set the fee schedules at 60 percent (or, in the case of a test performed by a qualified hospital laboratory in a sole community hospital (as defined in paragraph (1)(D)) for outpatients of such hospital, 62 percent) of the prevailing charge level determined pursuant to the third and fourth sentences of section 1842(b)(3) [42 USCS § 1395u(b)(3)] for similar clinical diagnostic laboratory tests for the applicable region, State, or area for the 12-month period beginning July 1, 1984, adjusted annually (to become effective on January 1 of each year) by, subject to clause (iv), a percentage increase or decrease equal to the percentage increase or decrease in the Consumer Price Index for All Urban Consumers (United States city average) minus, for each of the years 2009 and 2010, 0.5 percentage points, and subject to such other adjustments as the Secretary determines are justified by technological changes.

(ii) Notwithstanding clause (i)—

(I) any change in the fee schedules which would have become effective under this subsection for tests furnished on or after January 1, 1988, shall not be effective for tests furnished during the 3-month period beginning on January 1, 1988,

(II) the Secretary shall not adjust the fee schedules under clause (i) to take into account any increase in the consumer price index for 1988,

(III) the annual adjustment in the fee schedules determined under clause (i) for each of the years 1991, 1992, and 1993 shall be 2 percent, and

(IV) the annual adjustment in the fee schedules determined under clause (i) for each of the years 1994 and 1995, 1998 through 2002, and 2004 through 2008 shall be 0 percent.

(iii) In establishing fee schedules under clause (i) with respect to automated tests and tests (other than cytopathology tests) which before July 1, 1984, the Secretary made subject to a limit based on lowest charge levels under the sixth sentence of section 1842(b)(3) [42 USCS § 1395u(b)(3)] performed after March 31, 1988, the Secretary shall reduce by 8.3 percent the fee schedules otherwise established for 1988, and such reduced fee schedules shall serve as the base for 1989 and subsequent years.

(iv) After determining the adjustment to the fee schedules under clause (i), the Secretary shall reduce such adjustment—

(I) for 2011 and each subsequent year, by the productivity adjustment described in section 1886(b)(3)(B)(xi)(II); and

(II) for each of 2011 through 2015, by 1.75 percentage points.

Subclause (I) shall not apply in a year where the adjustment to the fee schedules determined under clause (i) is 0.0 or a percentage decrease for a year. The application of the productivity adjustment under subclause (I) shall not result in an adjustment to the fee schedules under clause (i) being less than 0.0 for a year. The application of subclause (II) may result in an adjustment to the fee schedules under clause (i) being less than 0.0 for a year, and may result in payment rates for a year being less than such payment rates for the preceding year.

(B) The Secretary may make further adjustments or exceptions to the fee schedules to assure adequate reimbursement of (i) emergency laboratory tests needed for the provision of bona fide emergency services, and (ii) certain low volume high-cost tests where highly sophisticated equipment or extremely skilled personnel are necessary to assure quality.

(3) In addition to the amounts provided under the fee schedules, the Secretary shall provide for and establish (A) a nominal fee to cover the appropriate costs in collecting the sample on which a clinical diagnostic laboratory test was performed and for which payment is made under this part [42 USCS §§ 1395j et seq.], except that not more than one such fee may be provided under this paragraph with respect to samples collected in the same encounter, and (B) a fee to cover the transportation and personnel expenses for trained personnel to travel to the location of an individual to collect the sample, except that such a fee may be provided only with respect to an individual who is homebound or an inpatient in an inpatient facility (other than a hospital). In establishing a fee to cover the transportation and personnel expenses for trained personnel to travel to the location of an individual to collect a sample, the Secretary shall provide a method for computing the fee based on the number of miles traveled and the personnel costs associated with the collection of each individual sample, but the Secretary shall only be required to apply such method in the case of tests furnished during the period beginning on April 1, 1989, and ending on December 31, 1990, by a laboratory that establishes to the satisfaction of the Secretary (based on data for the 12-month period ending June 30, 1988) that (i) the laboratory is dependent upon payments under this title [42 USCS §§ 1395 et seq.] for at least 80 percent of its collected revenues for clinical diagnostic laboratory tests, (ii) at least 85 percent of its gross revenues for such tests are attributable to tests performed with respect to individuals who are homebound or who are residents in a nursing facility, and (iii) the laboratory provided such tests for residents in nursing facilities representing at least 20 percent of the number of such facilities in the State in which the laboratory is located.

(4)(A) In establishing any fee schedule under this subsection, the Secretary may provide for an adjustment to take into account, with respect to the portion of the expenses of clinical diagnostic laboratory tests attributable to wages, the relative difference between a region's or local area's wage rates and the wage rate presumed in the data on which the schedule is based.

(B) For purposes of subsections (a)(1)(D)(i)

and (a)(2)(D)(i), the limitation amount for a clinical diagnostic laboratory test performed—

(i) on or after July 1, 1986, and before April 1, 1988, is equal to 115 percent of the median of all the fee schedules established for that test for that laboratory setting under paragraph (1),

(ii) after March 31, 1988, and before January 1, 1990, is equal to the median of all the fee schedules established for that test for that laboratory setting under paragraph (1),

(iii) after December 31, 1989, and before January 1, 1991, is equal to 93 percent of the median of all the fee schedules established for that test for that laboratory setting under paragraph (1),

(iv) after December 31, 1990, and before January 1, 1994, is equal to 88 percent of such median,

(v) after December 31, 1993, and before January 1, 1995, is equal to 84 percent of such median,

(vi) after December 31, 1994, and before January 1, 1996, is equal to 80 percent of such median,

(vii) after December 31, 1995, and before January 1, 1998, is equal to 76 percent of such median, and

(viii) after December 31, 1997, is equal to 74 percent of such median (or 100 percent of such median in the case of a clinical diagnostic laboratory test performed on or after January 1, 2001, that the Secretary determines is a new test for which no limitation amount has previously been established under this subparagraph).

(5)(A) In the case of a bill or request for payment for a clinical diagnostic laboratory test for which payment may otherwise be made under this part [42 USCS §§ 1395j et seq.] on an assignment-related basis or under a provider agreement under section 1866 [42 USCS § 1395cc], payment may be made only to the person or entity which performed or supervised the performance of such test; except that—

(i) if a physician performed or supervised the performance of such test, payment may be made to another physician with whom he shares his practice.

(ii) in the case of a test performed at the request of a laboratory by another laboratory, payment may be made to the referring laboratory but only if—

(I) the referring laboratory is located in, or is part of, a rural hospital,

(II) the referring laboratory is wholly owned by the entity performing such test, the referring laboratory wholly owns the entity performing such test, or both the referring laboratory and the entity performing such test are wholly-owned by a third entity, or

(III) not more than 30 percent of the clinical diagnostic laboratory tests for which such referring laboratory (but not including a laboratory described in subclause (II)) [,] receives requests for testing during the year in which the test is performed [,] are performed by another laboratory, and

(iii) in the case of a clinical diagnostic laboratory test provided under an arrangement (as defined in section 1861(w)(1) [42 USCS § 1395x(w)(1)]) made by a hospital, critical access hospital, or skilled nursing facility, payment shall be made to the hospital or skilled nursing facility.

(B) In the case of such a bill or request for payment for a clinical diagnostic laboratory test for which payment may otherwise be made under this part [42 USCS §§ 1395j et seq.], and which is not described in subparagraph (A), payment may be made to the beneficiary only on the basis of the itemized bill of the person or entity which performed or supervised the performance of the test.

(C) Payment for a clinical diagnostic laboratory test, including a test performed in a physician's office but excluding a test performed by a rural health clinic may only be made on an assignment-related basis or to a provider of services with an agreement in effect under section 1866 [42 USCS § 1395cc].

(D) A person may not bill for a clinical diagnostic laboratory test, including a test performed in a physician's office but excluding a test performed by a rural health clinic, other than on an assignment-related basis. If a person knowingly and willfully and on a repeated basis bills for a clinical diagnostic laboratory test in violation of the previous sentence, the Secretary may apply sanctions against the person in the same manner as the Secretary may apply sanctions against a physician in accordance with paragraph (2) of section 1842(j) [42 USCS § 1395u(j)(2)] in the same manner such paragraphs apply with respect to a physician. Paragraph (4) of such section shall apply in this subparagraph in the same manner as such paragraph applies to such section.

(6) In the case of any diagnostic laboratory test payment for which is not made on the basis of a fee schedule under paragraph (1), the Secretary may establish a payment rate which is acceptable to the person or entity performing the test and which would be considered the full charge for such tests. Such negotiated rate shall be limited to an amount not in excess of the total payment that would have been made

for the services in the absence of such rate.

(7) Notwithstanding paragraphs (1) and (4), the Secretary shall establish a national minimum payment amount under this subsection for a diagnostic or screening pap smear laboratory test (including all cervical cancer screening technologies that have been approved by the Food and Drug Administration as a primary screening method for detection of cervical cancer) equal to $14.60 for tests furnished in 2000. For such tests furnished in subsequent years, such national minimum payment amount shall be adjusted annually as provided in paragraph (2).

(8)(A) The Secretary shall establish by regulation procedures for determining the basis for, and amount of, payment under this subsection for any clinical diagnostic laboratory test with respect to which a new or substantially revised HCPCS code is assigned on or after January 1, 2005 (in this paragraph referred to as "new tests").

(B) Determinations under subparagraph (A) shall be made only after the Secretary—

(i) makes available to the public (through an Internet website and other appropriate mechanisms) a list that includes any such test for which establishment of a payment amount under this subsection is being considered for a year;

(ii) on the same day such list is made available, causes to have published in the Federal Register notice of a meeting to receive comments and recommendations (and data on which recommendations are based) from the public on the appropriate basis under this subsection for establishing payment amounts for the tests on such list;

(iii) not less than 30 days after publication of such notice convenes a meeting, that includes representatives of officials of the Centers for Medicare & Medicaid Services involved in determining payment amounts, to receive such comments and recommendations (and data on which the recommendations are based);

(iv) taking into account the comments and recommendations (and accompanying data) received at such meeting, develops and makes available to the public (through an Internet website and other appropriate mechanisms) a list of proposed determinations with respect to the appropriate basis for establishing a payment amount under this subsection for each such code, together with an explanation of the reasons for each such determination, the data on which the determinations are based, and a request for public written comments on the proposed determination; and

(v) taking into account the comments received during the public comment period, develops and makes available to the public (through an Internet website and other appropriate mechanisms) a list of final determinations of the payment amounts for such tests under this subsection, together with the rationale for each such determination, the data on which the determinations are based, and responses to comments and suggestions received from the public.

(C) Under the procedures established pursuant to subparagraph (A), the Secretary shall—

(i) set forth the criteria for making determinations under subparagraph (A); and

(ii) make available to the public the data (other than proprietary data) considered in making such determinations.

(D) The Secretary may convene such further public meetings to receive public comments on payment amounts for new tests under this subsection as the Secretary deems appropriate.

(E) For purposes of this paragraph:

(i) The term "HCPCS" refers to the Health Care Procedure Coding System.

(ii) A code shall be considered to be "substantially revised" if there is a substantive change to the definition of the test or procedure to which the code applies (such as a new analyte or a new methodology for measuring an existing analyte-specific test).

(9) Notwithstanding any other provision in this part [42 USCS §§ 1395j et seq.], in the case of any diagnostic laboratory test for HbA1c that is labeled by the Food and Drug Administration for home use and is furnished on or after April 1, 2008, the payment rate for such test shall be the payment rate established under this part for a glycated hemoglobin test (identified as of October 1, 2007, by HCPCS code 83036 (and any succeeding codes)).

(i) Outpatient surgery. (1) The Secretary shall, in consultation with appropriate medical organizations—

(A) specify those surgical procedures which are appropriately (when considered in terms of the proper utilization of hospital inpatient facilities) performed on an inpatient basis in a hospital but which also can be performed safely on an ambulatory basis in an ambulatory surgical center (meeting the standards specified under section 1832(a)(2)(F)(i) [42 USCS § 1395k(a)(2)(F)(i)]), critical access hospital, or hospital outpatient department, and

(B) specify those surgical procedures which are appropriately (when considered in terms of the proper utilization of hospital inpatient facilities) performed on an inpatient basis in a hospital but which also can be performed safely on an ambulatory basis in a physician's office.

The lists of procedures established under subparagraphs (A) and (B) shall be reviewed and updated not less often than every 2 years, in consultation with appropriate trade and professional organizations.

(2)(A) For services furnished prior to the implementation of the system described in subparagraph (D), subject to subparagraph (E), the amount of payment to be made for facility services furnished in connection with a surgical procedure specified pursuant to paragraph (1)(A) and furnished to an individual in an ambulatory surgical center described in such paragraph shall be equal to 80 percent of a standard overhead amount established by the Secretary (with respect to each such procedure) on the basis of the Secretary's estimate of a fair fee which—

(i) takes into account the costs incurred by such centers, or classes of centers, generally in providing services furnished in connection with the performance of such procedure, as determined in accordance with a survey (based upon a representative sample of procedures and facilities) of the actual audited costs incurred by such centers in providing such services,

(ii) takes such costs into account in such a manner as will assure that the performance of the procedure in such a center will result in substantially less amounts paid under this title [42 USCS §§ 1395 et seq.] than would have been paid if the procedure had been performed on an inpatient basis in a hospital, and

(iii) in the case of insertion of an intraocular lens during or subsequent to cataract surgery includes payment which is reasonable and related to the cost of acquiring the class of lens involved.

Each amount so established shall be reviewed and updated not later than July 1, 1987, and annually thereafter to take account of varying conditions in different areas.

(B) The amount of payment to be made under this part [42 USCS §§ 1395j et seq.] for facility services furnished, in connection with a surgical procedure specified pursuant to paragraph (1)(B), in a physician's office shall be equal to 80 percent of a standard overhead amount established by the Secretary (with respect to each such procedure) on the basis of the Secretary's estimate of a fair fee which—

(i) takes into account additional costs, not usually included in the professional fee, incurred by physicians in securing, maintaining, and staffing the facilities and ancillary services appropriate for the performance of such procedure in the physician's office, and

(ii) takes such items into account in such a manner which will assure that the performance of such procedure in the physician's office will result in substantially less amounts paid under this title [42 USCS §§ 1395 et seq.] than would have been paid if the services had been furnished on an inpatient basis in a hospital.

Each amount so established shall be reviewed and updated not later than July 1, 1987, and annually thereafter and may be adjusted by the Secretary, when appropriate, to take account of varying conditions in different areas.

(C)(i) Notwithstanding the second sentence of each of subparagraphs (A) and (B), except as otherwise specified in clauses (ii), (iii), and (iv), if the Secretary has not updated amounts established under such subparagraphs or under subparagraph (D), with respect to facility services furnished during a fiscal year (beginning with fiscal year 1986 or a calendar year (beginning with 2006)), such amounts shall be increased by the percentage increase in the Consumer Price Index for all urban consumers (U.S. city average) as estimated by the Secretary for the 12-month period ending with the midpoint of the year involved.

(ii) In each of the fiscal years 1998 through 2002, the increase under this subparagraph shall be reduced (but not below zero) by 2.0 percentage points.

(iii) In fiscal year 2004, beginning with April 1, 2004, the increase under this subparagraph shall be the Consumer Price Index for all urban consumers (U.S. city average) as estimated by the Secretary for the 12-month period ending with March 31, 2003, minus 3.0 percentage points.

(iv) In fiscal year 2005, the last quarter of calendar year 2005, and each of calendar years 2006 through 2009, the increase under this subparagraph shall be 0 percent.

(D)(i) Taking into account the recommendations in the report under section 626(d) of Medicare Prescription Drug, Improvement, and Modernization Act of 2003 [note to this section], the Secretary shall implement a revised payment system for payment of surgical services furnished in ambulatory surgical centers.

(ii) In the year the system described in clause (i) is implemented, such system shall be designed to result in the same aggregate amount of expenditures for such services as would be made if this subparagraph did not apply, as estimated by the Secretary and taking into account reduced expenditures that would apply if subparagraph (E) were to continue to apply, as estimated by the Secretary.

(iii) The Secretary shall implement the system described in clause (i) for periods in a manner so that it is first effective beginning on or after January 1, 2006, and not later than January 1, 2008.

(iv) The Secretary may implement such system in a manner so as to provide for a reduction in any annual update for failure to report on quality measures in accordance with paragraph (7).

(v) In implementing the system described in clause (i) for 2011 and each subsequent year, any annual update under such system for the year, after application of clause (iv), shall be reduced by the productivity adjustment described in section 1886(b)(3)(B)(xi)(II) [42 USCS § 1395ww(b)(3)(B)(xi)(II)]. The application of the preceding sentence may result in such update being less than 0.0 for a year, and may result in payment rates under the system described in clause (i) for a year being less than such payment rates for the preceding year.

(vi) There shall be no administrative or judicial review under section 1869 [42 USCS § 1395ff], 1878 [42 USCS § 1395oo], or otherwise, of the classification system, the relative weights, payment amounts, and the geographic adjustment factor, if any, under this subparagraph.

(E) With respect to surgical procedures furnished on or after January 1, 2007, and before the effective date of the implementation of a revised payment system under subparagraph (D), if—

(i) the standard overhead amount under subparagraph (A) for a facility service for such procedure, without the application of any geographic adjustment, exceeds

(ii) the Medicare OPD fee schedule amount established under the prospective payment system for hospital outpatient department services under paragraph (3)(D) of section 1833(t) [42 USCS § 1395l(t)] for such service for such year, determined without regard to geographic adjustment under paragraph (2)(D) of such section,

the Secretary shall substitute under subparagraph (A) the amount described in clause (ii) for the standard overhead amount for such service referred to in clause (i).

(3)(A) The aggregate amount of the payments to be made under this part [42 USCS §§ 1395j et seq.] for outpatient hospital facility services or critical access hospital services furnished before January 1, 1999, in connection with surgical procedures specified under paragraph (1)(A) shall be equal to the lesser of—

(i) the amount determined with respect to such services under subsection (a)(2)(B); or

(ii) the blend amount (described in subparagraph (B)).

(B)(i) The blend amount for a cost reporting period is the sum of—

(I) the cost proportion (as defined in clause (ii)(I)) of the amount described in subparagraph (A)(i), and

(II) the ASC proportion (as defined in clause (ii)(II)) of the standard overhead amount payable with respect to the same surgical procedure as if it were provided in an ambulatory surgical center in the same area, as determined under paragraph (2)(A), less the amount a provider may charge as described in clause (ii) of section 1866(a)(2)(A) [42 USCS § 1395cc(a)(2)(A)].

(ii) Subject to paragraph (4), in this paragraph:

(I) The term "cost proportion" means 75 percent for cost reporting periods beginning in fiscal year 1988, 50 percent for portions of cost reporting periods beginning on or after October 1, 1988, and ending on or before December 31, 1990, and 42 percent for portions of cost reporting periods beginning on or after January 1, 1991.

(II) The term "ASC proportion" means 25 percent for cost reporting periods beginning in fiscal year 1988, 50 percent for portions of cost reporting periods beginning on or after October 1, 1988, and ending on or before December 31, 1990, and 58 percent for portions of cost reporting periods beginning on or after January 1, 1991.

(4)(A) In the case of a hospital that—

(i) makes application to the Secretary and demonstrates that it specializes in eye services or eye and ear services (as determined by the Secretary),

(ii) receives more than 30 percent of its total revenues from outpatient services, and

(iii) on October 1, 1987—

(I) was an eye specialty hospital or an eye and ear specialty hospital, or

(II) was operated as an eye or eye and ear unit (as defined in subparagraph (B)) of a general acute care hospital which, on the date of the application described in clause (i), operates less than 20 percent of the beds that the hospital operated on October 1, 1987, and has sold or otherwise disposed of a substantial portion of the hospital's other acute care operations,the cost proportion and ASC proportion in effect under subclauses (I) and (II) of paragraph (3)(B)(ii) for cost reporting periods beginning in fiscal year 1988 shall remain in effect for cost reporting periods beginning on or after October 1, 1988, and before January 1, 1995.

(B) For purposes of [this] subparagraph (A)(iii)(II), the term "eye or eye and ear unit" means a physically separate or distinct unit containing separate surgical suites devoted solely to eye or eye and ear services.

(5)(A) The Secretary is authorized to provide by regulations that in the case of a surgical procedure, specified by the Secretary pursuant to paragraph (1)(A), performed in an ambulatory surgical center described in such paragraph, there shall be paid (in lieu of any amounts otherwise payable under this part [42 USCS §§ 1395j et seq.]) with respect to the facility services furnished by such center and with respect to all related services furnished by such center and with respect to all related services (including physicians' services, laboratory, X-ray, and diagnostic services) a single all-inclusive fee established pursuant to subparagraph (B), if all parties furnishing all such services agree to accept such fee (to be divided among the parties involved in such manner as they shall have previously agreed upon) as full payment for the services furnished.

(B) In implementing this paragraph, the Secretary shall establish with respect to each surgical procedure specified pursuant to paragraph (1)(A) the amount of the all-inclusive fee for such procedure, taking into account such factors as may be appropriate. The amount so established with respect to any surgical procedure shall be reviewed periodically and may be adjusted by the Secretary, when appropriate, to take account of varying conditions in different areas.

(6) Any person, including a facility having an agreement under section 1832(a)(2)(F)(i) [42 USCS § 1395k(a)(2)(F)(i), who knowingly and willfully presents, or causes to be presented, a bill or request for payment, for an intraocular lens inserted during or subsequent to cataract surgery for which payment may be made under paragraph (2)(A)(iii), is subject to a civil money penalty of not to exceed $2,000. The provisions of section 1128A [42 USCS § 1320a-7a] (other than subsections (a) and (b)) shall apply to a civil money penalty under the previous sentence in the same manner as such provisions apply to a penalty or proceeding under section 1128A(a) [42 USCS § 1320a-7a(a)].

(7)(A) For purposes of paragraph (2)(D)(iv), the Secretary may provide, in the case of an ambulatory surgical center that does not submit, to the Secretary in accordance with this paragraph, data required to be submitted on measures selected under this paragraph with respect to a year, any annual increase provided under the system established under paragraph (2)(D) for such year shall be reduced by 2.0 percentage points. A reduction under this subparagraph shall apply only with respect to the year involved and the Secretary shall not take into account such reduction in computing any annual increase factor for a subsequent year.

(B) Except as the Secretary may otherwise provide, the provisions of subparagraphs (B), (C), (D), and (E) of paragraph (17) of section 1833(t) [subsec. (t) of this section] shall apply with respect to services of ambulatory surgical centers under this paragraph in a similar manner to the manner in which they apply under such paragraph and, for purposes of this subparagraph, any reference to a hospital, outpatient setting, or outpatient hospital services is deemed a reference to an ambulatory surgical center, the setting of such a center, or services of such a center, respectively.

(j) Accrual of interest on balance of excess or deficit not paid. Whenever a final determination is made that the amount of payment made under this part [42 USCS §§ 1395j et seq.] either to a provider of services or to another person pursuant to an assignment under section 1842(b)(3)(B)(ii) [42 USCS § 1395u(b)(3)(B)(ii)] was in excess of or less than the amount of payment that is due, and payment of such excess or deficit is not made (or effected by offset) within 30 days of the date of the determination, interest shall accrue on the balance of such excess or deficit not paid or offset (to the extent that the balance is owed by or owing to the provider) at a rate determined in accordance with the regulations of the Secretary of the Treasury applicable to charges for late payments.

(k) Hepatitis B vaccine. With respect to services described in section 1861(s)(10)(B) [42 USCS § 1395x(s)(10)(B)], the Secretary may provide, instead of the amount of payment otherwise provided under this part [42 USCS §§ 1395j et seq.], for payment of such an amount or amounts as reasonably reflects the general cost of efficiently providing such services.

(l) Fee schedule for services of certified registered nurse anesthetists. (1)(A) The Secretary shall establish a fee schedule for services of certified registered nurse anesthetists under section 1861(s)(11) [42 USCS § 1395x(s)(11)].

(B) In establishing the fee schedule under

this paragraph the Secretary may utilize a system of time units, a system of base and time units, or any appropriate methodology.

(C) The provisions of this subsection shall not apply to certain services furnished in certain hospitals in rural areas under the provisions of section 9320(k) of the Omnibus Budget Reconciliation Act of 1986, as amended by section 6132 of the Omnibus Budget Reconciliation Act of 1989 [42 USCS § 1395k note].

(2) Except as provided in paragraph (3), the fee schedule established under paragraph (1) shall be initially based on audited data from cost reporting periods ending in fiscal year 1985 and such other data as the Secretary determines necessary.

(3)(A) In establishing the initial fee schedule for those services, the Secretary shall adjust the fee schedule to the extent necessary to ensure that the estimated total amount which will be paid under this title for those services plus applicable coinsurance in 1989 will equal the estimated total amount which would be paid under this title for those services in 1989 if the services were included as inpatient hospital services and payment for such services was made under part A [42 USCS §§ 1395c et seq.] in the same manner as payment was made in fiscal year 1987, adjusted to take into account changes in prices and technology relating to the administration of anesthesia.

(B) The Secretary shall also reduce the prevailing charge of physicians for medical direction of a certified registered nurse anesthetist, or the fee schedule for services of certified registered nurse anesthetists, or both, to the extent necessary to ensure that the estimated total amount which will be paid under this title plus applicable coinsurance for such medical direction and such services in 1989 and 1990 will not exceed the estimated total amount which would have been paid plus applicable coinsurance but for the enactment of the amendments made by section 9320 of the Omnibus Budget Reconciliation Act of 1986. A reduced prevailing charge under this subparagraph shall become the prevailing charge but for subsequent years for purposes of applying the economic index under the fourth sentence of section 1842(b)(3) [42 USCS § 1395u(b)(3)].

(4)(A) Except as provided in subparagraphs (C) and (D), in determining the amount paid under the fee schedule under this subsection for services furnished on or after January 1, 1991, by a certified registered nurse anesthetist who is not medically directed—

(i) the conversion factor shall be—

(I) for services furnished in 1991, $15.50,

(II) for services furnished in 1992, $15.75,

(III) for services furnished in 1993, $16.00,

(IV) for services furnished in 1994, $16.25,

(V) for services furnished in 1995, $16.50,

(VI) for services furnished in 1996, $16.75, and

(VII) for services furnished in calendar years after 1996, the previous year's conversion factor increased by the update determined under section 1848(d) [42 USCS § 1395w-4(d)] for physician anesthesia services for that year;

(ii) the payment areas to be used shall be the fee schedule areas used under section 1848 [42 USCS § 1395w-4] (or, in the case of services furnished during 1991, the localities used under section 1842(b) [42 USCS § 1395u(b)]) for purposes of computing payments for physicians' services that are anesthesia services;

(iii) the geographic adjustment factors to be applied to the conversion factor under clause (i) for services in a fee schedule area or locality is [are]—

(I) in the case of services furnished in 1991, the geographic work index value and the geographic practice cost index value specified in section 1842(q)(1)(B) [42 USCS § 1395u(q)(1)(B)] for physicians' services that are anesthesia services furnished in the area or locality, and

(II) in the case of services furnished after 1991, the geographic work index value, the geographic practice cost index value, and the geographic malpractice index value used for determining payments for physicians' services that are anesthesia services under section 1848 [42 USCS § 1395w-4],

with 70 percent of the conversion factor treated as attributable to work and 30 percent as attributable to overhead for services furnished in 1991 (and the portions attributable to work, practice expenses, and malpractice expenses in 1992 and thereafter being the same as is applied under section 1848 [42 USCS § 1395w-4]).

(B)(i) Except as provided in clause (ii) and subparagraph (D), in determining the amount paid under the fee schedule under this subsection for services furnished on or after January 1, 1991, and before January 1, 1994, by a certified registered nurse anesthetist who is medically directed, the Secretary shall apply the same methodology specified in subparagraph (A).

(ii) The conversion factor used under clause (i) shall be—

(I) for services furnished in 1991, $10.50,

(II) for services furnished in 1992, $10.75, and

(III) for services furnished in 1993, $11.00.

(iii) In the case of services of a certified registered nurse anesthetist who is medically directed or medically supervised by a physician which are furnished on or after January 1, 1994, the fee schedule amount shall be one-half of the amount described in section 1848(a)(5)[(4)](B) [42 USCS § 1395w-4(a)(4)(B)] with respect to the physician.

(C) Notwithstanding subclauses (I) through (V) of subparagraph (A)(i)—

(i) in the case of a 1990 conversion factor that is greater than $16.50, the conversion factor for a calendar year after 1990 and before 1996 shall be the 1990 conversion factor reduced by the product of the last digit of the calendar year and one-fifth of the amount by which the 1990 conversion factor exceeds $16.50; and

(ii) in the case of a 1990 conversion factor that is greater than $15.49 but less than $16.51, the conversion factor for a calendar year after 1990 and before 1996 shall be the greater of—

(I) the 1990 conversion factor, or

(II) the conversion factor specified in subparagraph (A)(i) for the year involved.

(D) Notwithstanding subparagraph (C), in no case may the conversion factor used to determine payment for services in a fee schedule area or locality under this subsection, as adjusted by the adjustment factors specified in subparagraphs [subparagraph] (A)(iii), exceed the conversion factor used to determine the amount paid for physicians' services that are anesthesia services in the area or locality.

(5)(A) Payment for the services of a certified registered nurse anesthetist (for which payment may otherwise be made under this part [42 USCS §§ 1395j et seq.]) may be made on the basis of a claim or request for payment presented by the certified registered nurse anesthetist furnishing such services, or by a hospital, critical access hospital, physician, group practice, or ambulatory surgical center with which the certified registered nurse anesthetist furnishing such services has an employment or contractual relationship that provides for payment to be made under this part [42 USCS §§ 1395j et seq.] for such services to such hospital, critical access hospital, physician, group practice, or ambulatory surgical center.

(B) No hospital or critical access hospital that presents a claim or request for payment for services of a certified nurse anesthetist under this part [42 USCS §§ 1395j et seq.] may treat any uncollected coinsurance amount imposed under this part [42 USCS §§ 1395j et seq.] with respect to such services as a bad debt of such hospital or critical access hospital for purposes of this title [42 USCS §§ 1395 et seq.].

(6) If an adjustment under paragraph (3)(B) results in a reduction in the reasonable charge for a physicians' service and a nonparticipating physician furnishes the service to an individual entitled to benefits under this part [42 USCS §§ 1395j et seq.] after the effective date of the reduction, the physician's actual charge is subject to a limit under section 1842(j)(1)(D) [42 USCS § 1395u(j)(1)(D)].

(m) Incentive payments for physicians' services furnished in underserved areas. (1) In the case of physicians' services furnished in a year to an individual, who is covered under the insurance program established by this part [42 USCS §§ 1395j et seq.] and who incurs expenses for such services, in an area that is designated (under section 332(a)(1)(A) of the Public Health Service Act [42 USCS § 256(a)(1)(A)]) as a health professional shortage area as identified by the Secretary prior to the beginning of such year, in addition to the amount otherwise paid under this part [42 USCS §§ 1395j et seq.], there also shall be paid to the physician (or to an employer or facility in the cases described in clause (A) of section 1842(b)(6) [42 USCS § 1395u(b)(6)(A)]) (on a monthly or quarterly basis) from the Federal Supplementary Medical Insurance Trust Fund an amount equal to 10 percent of the payment amount for the service under this part [42 USCS §§ 1395j et seq.].

(2) For each health professional shortage area identified in paragraph (1) that consists of an entire county, the Secretary shall provide for the additional payment under paragraph (1) without any requirement on the physician to identify the health professional shortage area involved. The Secretary may implement the previous sentence using the method specified in subsection (u)(4)(C).

(3) The Secretary shall post on the Internet website of the Centers for Medicare & Medicaid Services a list of the health professional shortage areas identified in paragraph (1) that consist of a partial county to facilitate the additional payment under paragraph (1) in such areas.

(4) There shall be no administrative or judicial review under section 1869 [42 USCS § 1395ff], section 1878 [42 USCS § 1395oo], or otherwise, respecting—

(A) the identification of a county or area;

(B) the assignment of a specialty of any

physician under this paragraph;

(C) the assignment of a physician to a county under this subsection; or

(D) the assignment of a postal ZIP Code to a county or other area under this subsection.

(n) Payments to hospital outpatient departments for radiology; amount; definition. [(1)](A) The aggregate amount of the payments to be made for all or part of a cost reporting period for services described in subsection (a)(2)(E)(i) furnished under this part [42 USCS §§ 1395j et seq.] on or after October 1, 1988, and before January 1, 1999, and for services described in subsection (a)(2)(E)(ii) furnished under this part [42 USCS §§ 1395j et seq.] on or after October 1, 1989, and before January 1, 1999, shall be equal to the lesser of—

(i) the amount determined with respect to such services under subsection (a)(2)(B), or

(ii) the blend amount for radiology services and diagnostic procedures determined in accordance with subparagraph (B).

(B)(i) The blend amount for radiology services and diagnostic procedures for a cost reporting period is the sum of—

(I) the cost proportion (as defined in clause (ii)) of the amount described in subparagraph (A)(i); and

(II) the charge proportion (as defined in clause (ii)(II)) of 62 percent (for services described in subsection (a)(2)(E)(i)), or (for procedures described in subsection (a)(2)(E)(ii)), 42 percent or such other percent established by the Secretary (or carriers acting pursuant to guidelines issued by the Secretary) based on prevailing charges established with actual charge data, of the prevailing charge or (for services described in subsection (a)(2)(E)(i) furnished on or after April 1, 1989 and for services described in subsection (a)(2)(E)(ii) furnished on or after January 1, 1992) the fee schedule amount established for participating physicians for the same services as if they were furnished in a physician's office in the same locality as determined under section 1842(b) [42 USCS § 1395u(b)] (or, in the case of services furnished on or after January 1, 1992, under section 1848 [42 USCS § 1395w-4]), less the amount a provider may charge as described in clause (ii) of section 1866(a)(2)(A) [42 USCS § 1395cc(a)(2)(A)].

(ii) In this subparagraph:

(I) The term "cost proportion" means 50 percent, except that such term means 65 percent in the case of outpatient radiology services for portions of cost reporting periods which occur in fiscal year 1989 and in the case of diagnostic procedures described in subsection (a)(2)(E)(ii) for portions of cost reporting periods which occur in fiscal year 1990, and such term means 42 percent in the case of outpatient radiology services for portions of cost reporting periods beginning on or after January 1, 1991.

(II) The term "charge proportion" means 100 percent minus the cost proportion.

(o) Limitation on benefit for payment for therapeutic shoes for individuals with server diabetic foot disease. (1) In the case of shoes described in section 1861(s)(12) [42 USCS § 1395x(s)(12)]—

(A) no payment may be made under this part [42 USCS §§ 1395j et seq.], with respect to any individual for any year, for the furnishing of—

(i) more than one pair of custom molded shoes (including inserts provided with such shoes) and 2 additional pairs of inserts for such shoes, or

(ii) more than one pair of extra-depth shoes (not including inserts provided with such shoes) and 3 pairs of inserts for such shoes, and

(B) with respect to expenses incurred in any calendar year, no more than the amount of payment applicable under paragraph (2) shall be considered as incurred expenses for purposes of subsections (a) and (b).

Payment for shoes (or inserts) under this part [42 USCS §§ 1395j et seq.] shall be considered to include payment for any expenses for the fitting of such shoes (or inserts).

(2)(A) Except as provided by the Secretary under subparagraphs (B) and (C), the amount of payment under this paragraph for custom molded shoes, extra-depth shoes, and inserts shall be the amount determined for such items by the Secretary under section 1834(h) [42 USCS § 1395m(h)].

(B) The Secretary may establish payment amounts for shoes and inserts that are lower than the amount established under section 1834(h) [42 USCS § 1395m(h)] if the Secretary finds that shoes and inserts of an appropriate quality are readily available at or below the amount established under such section.

(C) In accordance with procedures established by the Secretary, an individual entitled to benefits with respect to shoes described in section 1861(s)(12) [42 USCS § 1395x(s)(12)] may substitute modification of such shoes instead of obtaining one (or more, as specified by the Secretary) pair of inserts (other than the original pair of inserts with respect to such shoes). In such case, the Secretary shall substitute, for the payment amount established under section 1834(h) [42 USCS § 1395m(h)], a payment amount that the Secretary estimates will assure that there is no net increase in expenditures under this subsection as a result of this subparagraph.

(3) In this title [42 USCS §§ 1395 et seq.], the term "shoes" includes, except for purposes of subparagraphs (A)(ii) and (B) of paragraph (2), inserts for extra-depth shoes.

(p) [Deleted]

(q) Requests for payment to include information on referring physician (1) Each request for payment, or bill submitted, for an item or service furnished by an entity for which payment may be made under this part [42 USCS §§ 1395j et seq.] and for which the entity knows or has reason to believe there has been a referral by a referring physician (within the meaning of section 1877 [42 USCS § 1395nn]) shall include the name and unique physician identification number for the referring physician.

(2)(A) In the case of a request for payment for an item or service furnished by an entity under this part [42 USCS §§ 1395j et seq.] on an assignment-related basis and for which information is required to be provided under paragraph (1) but not included, payment may be denied under this part [42 USCS §§ 1395j et seq.].

(B) In the case of a request for payment for an item or service furnished by an entity under this part [42 USCS §§ 1395j et seq.] not submitted on an assignment-related basis and for which information is required to be provided under paragraph (1) but not included—

(i) if the entity knowingly and willfully fails to provide such information promptly upon request of the Secretary or a carrier, the entity may be subject to a civil money penalty in an amount not to exceed $2,000, and

(ii) if the entity knowingly, willfully, and in repeated cases fails, after being notified by the Secretary of the obligations and requirements of this subsection to provide the information required under paragraph (1), the entity may be subject to exclusion from participation in the programs under this Act for a period not to exceed 5 years, in accordance with the procedures of subsections (c), (f), and (g) of section 1128 [42 USCS § 1320a-7(c), (f), and (g)].

The provisions of section 1128A [42 USCS § 1320a-7a] (other than subsections (a) and (b)) shall apply to civil money penalties under clause (i) in the same manner as they apply to a penalty or proceeding under section 1128A(a) [42 USCS § 1320a-7a(a)].

(r) Cap on prevailing charge; billing only on assignment-related basis. (1) With respect to services described in section 1861(s)(2)(K)(ii) [42 USCS § 1395x(s)(2)(K)(ii)] (relating to nurse practitioner or clinical nurse specialist services), payment may be made on the basis of a claim or request for payment presented by the nurse practitioner or clinical nurse specialist furnishing such services, or by a hospital, critical access hospital, skilled nursing facility or nursing facility (as defined in section 1919(a) [42 USCS § 1396r(a)]), physician, group practice, or ambulatory surgical center with which the nurse practitioner or clinical nurse specialist has an employment or contractual relationship that provides for payment to be made under this part [42 USCS §§ 1395j et seq.] for such services to such hospital, physician, group practice, or ambulatory surgical center.

(2) No hospital or critical access hospital that presents a claim or request for payment under this part [42 USCS §§ 1395j et seq.] for services described in section 1861(s)(2)(K)(ii) [42 USCS § 1395x(s)(2)(K)(ii)] may treat any uncollected coinsurance amount imposed under this part [42 USCS §§ 1395j et seq.] with respect to such services as a bad debt of such hospital for purposes of this title [42 USCS §§ 1395 et seq.].

(s) Other prepaid organizations. The Secretary may not provide for payment under subsection (a)(1)(A) with respect to an organization unless the organization provides assurances satisfactory to the Secretary that the organization meets the requirement of section 1866(f) [42 USCS § 1395cc(f)] (relating to maintaining written policies and procedures respecting advance directives).

(t) Prospective payment system for hospital outpatient department services. (1) Amount of payment. (A) In general. With respect to covered OPD services (as defined in subparagraph (B)) furnished during a year beginning with 1999, the amount of payment under this part [42 USCS §§ 1395j et seq.] shall be determined under a prospective payment system established by the Secretary in accordance with this subsection.

(B) Definition of covered OPD services. For purposes of this subsection, the term "covered OPD services"—

(i) means hospital outpatient services designated by the Secretary;

(ii) subject to clause (iv), includes inpatient hospital services designated by the Secretary that are covered under this part [42 USCS §§ 1395j et seq.] and furnished to a hospital inpatient who (I) is entitled to benefits under part A [42 USCS §§ 1395c et seq.] but has exhausted benefits for inpatient hospital services during a spell of illness, or (II) is not so entitled;

(iii) includes implantable items described in paragraph (3), (6), or (8) of section 1861(s); but

(iv) **[Caution: For provisions applicable to services furnished before January 1, 2011, see 2010 amendment notes below.]** does not include any therapy services described in subsection (a)(8) or ambulance services, for which payment is made under a fee schedule described in section 1834(k) or section 1834(l) [42 USCS § 1395m(k) or (l)] and does not include screening mammography (as defined in section 1861(jj) [42 USCS § 1395x(jj)]), diagnostic mammography, personalized prevention plan services (as defined in section 1861(hhh)(1) [42 USCS § 1395x(hhh)(1)]), or preventive services described in subparagraphs (A) and (B) of section 1861(ddd)(3) [42 USCS § 1395x(ddd)(3)] that are appropriate for the individual and, in the case of such services described in subparagraph (A), are recommended with a grade of A or B by the United States Preventive Services Task Force for any indication or population.

(2) System requirements. Under the payment system—

(A) the Secretary shall develop a classification system for covered OPD services;

(B) the Secretary may establish groups of covered OPD services, within the classification system described in subparagraph (A), so that services classified within each group are comparable clinically and with respect to the use of resources and so that an implantable item is classified to the group that includes the service to which the item relates;

(C) the Secretary shall, using data on claims from 1996 and using data from the most recent available cost reports, establish relative payment weights for covered OPD services (and any groups of such services described in subparagraph (B)) based on median (or, at the election of the Secretary, mean) hospital costs and shall determine projections of the frequency of utilization of each such service (or group of services) in 1999;

(D) subject to paragraph (19), the Secretary shall determine a wage adjustment factor to adjust the portion of payment and coinsurance attributable to labor-related costs for relative differences in labor and labor-related costs across geographic regions in a budget neutral manner;

(E) the Secretary shall establish, in a budget neutral manner, outlier adjustments under paragraph (5) and transitional pass-through payments under paragraph (6) and other adjustments as determined to be necessary to ensure equitable payments, such as adjustments for certain classes of hospitals;

(F) the Secretary shall develop a method for controlling unnecessary increases in the volume of covered OPD services;

(G) the Secretary shall create additional groups of covered OPD services that classify separately those procedures that utilize contrast agents from those that do not; and

(H) with respect to devices of brachytherapy consisting of a seed or seeds (or radioactive source), the Secretary shall create additional groups of covered OPD services that classify such devices separately from the other services (or group of services) paid for under this subsection in a manner reflecting the number, isotope, and radioactive intensity of such devices furnished, including separate groups for palladium-103 and iodine-125 devices and for stranded and non-stranded devices furnished on or after July 1, 2007.

For purposes of subparagraph (B), items and services within a group shall not be treated as "comparable with respect to the use of resources" if the highest median cost (or mean cost, if elected by the Secretary under subparagraph (C)) for an item or service within the group is more than 2 times greater than the lowest median cost (or mean cost, if so elected) for an item or service within the group; except that the Secretary may make exceptions in unusual cases, such as low volume items and services, but may not make such an exception in the case of a drug or biological that has been designated as an orphan drug under section 526 of the Federal Food, Drug and Cosmetic Act [21 USCS § 360bb].

(3) Calculation of base amounts. (A) Aggregate amounts that would be payable if deductibles were disregarded. The Secretary shall estimate the sum of—

(i) the total amounts that would be payable from the Trust Fund under this part [42 USCS §§ 1395j et seq.] for covered OPD services in 1999, determined without regard to this subsection, as though the deductible under section 1833(b) [subsec. (b) of this section] did not apply, and

(ii) the total amounts of copayments estimated to be paid under this subsection by beneficiaries to hospitals for covered OPD services in 1999, as though the deductible under section 1833(b) [subsec. (b) of this section] did not apply.

(B) Unadjusted copayment amount. (i) In general. For purposes of this subsection, subject to clause (ii), the "unadjusted copayment amount" applicable to a covered OPD service (or group of such services) is 20 percent of the national median of the charges for the service (or services within the group) furnished during 1996, updated to 1999 using the Secretary's estimate of charge growth during the period.

(ii) Adjusted to be 20 percent when fully phased in. If the pre-deductible payment percentage for a covered OPD service (or group of such services) furnished in a year would be equal to or exceed 80 percent, then the unadjusted copayment amount shall be 20 percent of amount determined under subparagraph (D).

(iii) Rules for new services. The Secretary shall establish rules for establishment of an unadjusted copayment amount for a covered OPD service not furnished during 1996, based upon its classification within a group of such services.

(C) Calculation of conversion factors. (i) For 1999. (I) In general. The Secretary shall establish a 1999 conversion factor for determining the medicare OPD fee schedule amounts for each covered OPD service (or group of such services) furnished in 1999. Such conversion factor shall be established on the basis of the weights and frequencies described in paragraph (2)(C) and in such a manner that the sum for all services and groups of the products (described in subclause (II) for each such service or group) equals the total projected amount described in subparagraph (A).

(II) Product described. The Secretary shall determine for each service or group the product of the medicare OPD fee schedule amounts (taking into account appropriate adjustments described in paragraphs (2)(D) and (2)(E)) and the estimated frequencies for such service or group.

(ii) Subsequent years. Subject to paragraph (8)(B), the Secretary shall establish a conversion factor for covered OPD services furnished in subsequent years in an amount equal to the conversion factor established under this subparagraph and applicable to such services furnished in the previous year increased by the OPD fee schedule increase factor specified under clause (iv) for the year involved.

(iii) Adjustment for service mix changes. Insofar as the Secretary determines that the adjustments for service mix under paragraph (2) for a previous year (or estimates that such adjustments for a future year) did (or are likely to) result in a change in aggregate payments under this subsection during the year that are a result of changes in the coding or classification of covered OPD services that do not reflect real changes in service mix, the Secretary may adjust the conversion factor computed under this subparagraph for subsequent years so as to eliminate the effect of such coding or classification changes.

(iv) OPD fee schedule increase factor. For purposes of this subparagraph, subject to paragraph (17) and subparagraph (F) of this paragraph, the "OPD fee schedule increase factor" for services furnished in a year is equal to the market basket percentage increase applicable under section 1886(b)(3)(B)(iii) [42 USCS § 1395ww(b)(3)(B)(iii)] to hospital discharges occurring during the fiscal year ending in such year, reduced by 1 percentage point for such factor for services furnished in each of 2000 and 2002. In applying the previous sentence for years beginning with 2000, the Secretary may substitute for the market basket percentage increase an annual percentage increase that is computed and applied with respect to covered OPD services furnished in a year in the same manner as the market basket percentage increase is determined and applied to inpatient hospital services for discharges occurring in a fiscal year.

(D) Calculation of medicare OPD fee schedule amounts. The Secretary shall compute a medicare OPD fee schedule amount for each covered OPD service (or group of such services) furnished in a year, in an amount equal to the product of—

(i) the conversion factor computed under subparagraph (C) for the year, and

(ii) the relative payment weight (determined under paragraph (2)(C)) for the service or group.

(E) Pre-deductible payment percentage. The pre-deductible payment percentage for a covered OPD service (or group of such services) furnished in a year is equal to the ratio of—

(i) the medicare OPD fee schedule amount established under subparagraph (D) for the year, minus the unadjusted copayment amount determined under subparagraph (B) for the service or group, to

(ii) the medicare OPD fee schedule amount determined under subparagraph (D) for the year for such service or group.

(F) Productivity and other adjustment. After determining the OPD fee schedule increase factor under subparagraph (C)(iv), the Secretary shall reduce such increase factor—

(i) for 2012 and subsequent years, by the productivity adjustment described in section 1886(b)(3)(B)(xi)(II) [42 USCS § 1395ww(b)(3)(B)(xi)(II)]; and

(ii) for each of 2010 through 2019, by the

adjustment described in subparagraph (G).

The application of this subparagraph may result in the increase factor under subparagraph (C)(iv) being less than 0.0 for a year, and may result in payment rates under the payment system under this subsection for a year being less than such payment rates for the preceding year.

(G) Other adjustment. For purposes of subparagraph (F)(ii), the adjustment described in this subparagraph is—

(i) for each of 2010 and 2011, 0.25 percentage point;

(ii) for each of 2012 and 2013, 0.1 percentage point;

(iii) for 2014, 0.3 percentage point;

(iv) for each of 2015 and 2016, 0.2 percentage point; and

(v) for each of 2017, 2018, and 2019, 0.75 percentage point.

(4) Medicare payment amount. The amount of payment made from the Trust Fund under this part [42 USCS §§ 1395j et seq.] for a covered OPD service (and such services classified within a group) furnished in a year is determined, subject to paragraph (7), as follows:

(A) Fee schedule adjustments. The medicare OPD fee schedule amount (computed under paragraph (3)(D)) for the service or group and year is adjusted for relative differences in the cost of labor and other factors determined by the Secretary, as computed under paragraphs (2)(D) and (2)(E).

(B) Subtract applicable deductible. Reduce the adjusted amount determined under subparagraph (A) by the amount of the deductible under section 1833(b) [subsec. (b) of this section], to the extent applicable.

(C) Apply payment proportion to remainder. The amount of payment is the amount so determined under subparagraph (B) multiplied by the pre-deductible payment percentage (as determined under paragraph (3)(E)) for the service or group and year involved, plus the amount of any reduction in the copayment amount attributable to paragraph (8)(C).

(5) Outlier adjustment. (A) In general. Subject to subparagraph (D), the Secretary shall provide for an additional payment for each covered OPD service (or group of services) for which a hospital's charges, adjusted to cost, exceed—

(i) a fixed multiple of the sum of—

(I) the applicable medicare OPD fee schedule amount determined under paragraph (3)(D), as adjusted under paragraph (4)(A) (other than for adjustments under this paragraph or paragraph (6)); and

(II) any transitional pass-through payment under paragraph (6); and

(ii) at the option of the Secretary, such fixed dollar amount as the Secretary may establish.

(B) Amount of adjustment. The amount of the additional payment under subparagraph (A) shall be determined by the Secretary and shall approximate the marginal cost of care beyond the applicable cutoff point under such subparagraph.

(C) Limit on aggregate outlier adjustments. (i) In general. The total of the additional payments made under this paragraph for covered OPD services furnished in a year (as estimated by the Secretary before the beginning of the year) may not exceed the applicable percentage (specified in clause (ii)) of the total program payments estimated to be made under this subsection for all covered OPD services furnished in that year. If this paragraph is first applied to less than a full year, the previous sentence shall apply only to the portion of such year.

(ii) Applicable percentage. For purposes of clause (i), the term "applicable percentage" means a percentage specified by the Secretary up to (but not to exceed)—

(I) for a year (or portion of a year) before 2004, 2.5 percent; and

(II) for 2004 and thereafter, 3.0 percent.

(D) Transitional authority. In applying subparagraph (A) for covered OPD services furnished before January 1, 2002, the Secretary may—

(i) apply such subparagraph to a bill for such services related to an outpatient encounter (rather than for a specific service or group of services) using OPD fee schedule amounts and transitional pass-through payments covered under the bill; and

(ii) use an appropriate cost-to-charge ratio for the hospital involved (as determined by the Secretary), rather than for specific departments within the hospital.

(E) Exclusion of separate drug and biological APCs from outlier payments. No additional payment shall be made under subparagraph (A) in the case of ambulatory payment classification groups established separately for drugs or biologicals.

(6) Transitional pass-through for additional costs of innovative medical devices, drugs, and biologicals. (A) In general. The Secretary shall provide for an additional payment under this paragraph for any of the following that are provided as part of a covered OPD service (or group of services):

(i) Current orphan drugs. A drug or biological that is used for a rare disease or condition with respect to which the drug or biological has been designated as an orphan drug under section 526 of the Federal Food, Drug and Cosmetic Act [21 USCS § 360bb] if payment for the drug or biological as an outpatient hospital service under this part [42 USCS §§ 1395j et seq.] was being made on the first date that the system under this subsection is implemented.

(ii) Current cancer therapy drugs and biologicals and brachytherapy. A drug or biological that is used in cancer therapy, including (but not limited to) a chemotherapeutic agent, an antiemetic, a hematopoietic growth factor, a colony stimulating factor, a biological response modifier, a bisphosphonate, and a device of brachytherapy or temperature monitored cryoablation, if payment for such drug, biological, or device as an outpatient hospital service under this part was being made on such first date.

(iii) Current radiopharmaceutical drugs and biological products. A radiopharmaceutical drug or biological product used in diagnostic, monitoring, and therapeutic nuclear medicine procedures if payment for the drug or biological as an outpatient hospital service under this part [42 USCS §§ 1395j et seq.] was being made on such first date.

(iv) New medical devices, drugs, and biologicals. A medical device, drug, or biological not described in clause (i), (ii), or (iii) if—

(I) payment for the device, drug, or biological as an outpatient hospital service under this part [42 USCS §§ 1395j et seq.] was not being made as of December 31, 1996; and

(II) the cost of the drug or biological or the average cost of the category of devices is not insignificant in relation to the OPD fee schedule amount (as calculated under paragraph (3)(D)) payable for the service (or group of services) involved.

(B) Use of categories in determining eligibility of a device for pass-through payments. The following provisions apply for purposes of determining whether a medical device qualifies for additional payments under clause (ii) or (iv) of subparagraph (A):

(i) Establishment of initial categories. (I) In general. The Secretary shall initially establish under this clause categories of medical devices based on type of device by April 1, 2001. Such categories shall be established in a manner such that each medical device that meets the requirements of clause (ii) or (iv) of subparagraph (A) as of January 1, 2001, is included in such a category and no such device is included in more than one category. For purposes of the preceding sentence, whether a medical device meets such requirements as of such date shall be determined on the basis of the program memoranda issued before such date.

(II) Authorization of implementation other than through regulations. The categories may be established under this clause by program memorandum or otherwise, after consultation with groups representing hospitals, manufacturers of medical devices, and other affected parties.

(ii) Establishing criteria for additional categories. (I) In general. The Secretary shall establish criteria that will be used for creation of additional categories (other than those established under clause (i)) through rulemaking (which may include use of an interim final rule with comment period).

(II) Standard. Such categories shall be established under this clause in a manner such that no medical device is described by more than one category. Such criteria shall include a test of whether the average cost of devices that would be included in a category and are in use at the time the category is established is not insignificant, as described in subparagraph (A)(iv)(II).

(III) Deadline. Criteria shall first be established under this clause by July 1, 2001. The Secretary may establish in compelling circumstances categories under this clause before the date such criteria are established.

(IV) Adding categories. The Secretary shall promptly establish a new category of medical devices under this clause for any medical device that meets the requirements of subparagraph (A)(iv) and for which none of the categories in effect (or that were previously in effect) is appropriate.

(iii) Period for which category is in effect. A category of medical devices established under clause (i) or (ii) shall be in effect for a period of at least 2 years, but not more than 3 years, that begins—

(I) in the case of a category established under clause (i), on the first date on which payment was made under this paragraph for any device described by such category (including payments made during the period before April 1, 2001); and

(II) in the case of any other category, on the first date on which payment is made under this paragraph for any medical device that is described by such category.

(iv) Requirements treated as met. A medical device shall be treated as meeting the requirements of subparagraph (A)(iv), regardless of whether the device meets the requirement of subclause (I) of such subparagraph, if—

(I) the device is described by a category established and in effect under clause (i); or

(II) the device is described by a category established and in effect under clause (ii) and an application under section 515 of the Federal Food, Drug, and Cosmetic Act [21 USCS § 360e] has been approved with respect to the device, or the device has been cleared for market under section 510(k) of such Act [21 USCS § 360(k)], or the device is exempt from the requirements of section 510(k) of such Act [21 USCS § 360(k)] pursuant to subsection (l) or (m) of section 510 of such Act [21 USCS § 360] or section 520(g) of such Act [21 USCS § 360j(g)].

Nothing in this clause shall be construed as requiring an application or prior approval (other than that described in subclause (II)) in order for a covered device described by a category to qualify for payment under this paragraph.

(C) Limited period of payment. (i) Drugs and biologicals. The payment under this paragraph with respect to a drug or biological shall only apply during a period of at least 2 years, but not more than 3 years, that begins—

(I) on the first date this subsection is implemented in the case of a drug or biological described in clause (i), (ii), or (iii) of subparagraph (A) and in the case of a drug or biological described in subparagraph (A)(iv) and for which payment under this part is made as an outpatient hospital service before such first date; or

(II) in the case of a drug or biological described in subparagraph (A)(iv) not described in subclause (I), on the first date on which payment is made under this part for the drug or biological as an outpatient hospital service.

(ii) Medical devices. Payment shall be made under this paragraph with respect to a medical device only if such device-

(I) is described by a category of medical devices established and in effect under subparagraph (B); and

(II) is provided as part of a service (or group of services) paid for under this subsection and provided during the period for which such category is in effect under such subparagraph.

(D) Amount of additional payment. Subject to subparagraph (E)(iii), the amount of the payment under this paragraph with respect to a device, drug, or biological provided as part of a covered OPD service is—

(i) in the case of a drug or biological, the amount by which the amount determined under section 1842(o) [42 USCS § 1395u] (or if the drug or biological is covered under a competitive acquisition contract under section 1847B [42 USCS § 1395w-3b], an amount determined by the Secretary equal to the average price for the drug or biological for all competitive acquisition areas and year established under such section as calculated and adjusted by the Secretary for purposes of this paragraph) for the drug or biological exceeds the portion of the otherwise applicable medicare OPD fee schedule that the Secretary determines is associated with the drug or biological; or

(ii) in the case of a medical device, the amount by which the hospital's charges for the device, adjusted to cost, exceeds the portion of the otherwise applicable medicare OPD fee schedule that the Secretary determines is associated with the device.

(E) Limit on aggregate annual adjustment. (i) In general. The total of the additional payments made under this paragraph for covered OPD services furnished in a year (as estimated by the Secretary before the beginning of the year) may not exceed the applicable percentage (specified in clause (ii)) of the total program payments estimated to be made under this subsection for all covered OPD services furnished in that year. If this paragraph is first applied to less than a full year, the previous sentence shall apply only to the portion of such year.

(ii) Applicable percentage. For purposes of clause (i), the term "applicable percentage" means—

(I) for a year (or portion of a year) before 2004, 2.5 percent; and

(II) for 2004 and thereafter, a percentage specified by the Secretary up to (but not to exceed) 2.0 percent.

(iii) Uniform prospective reduction if aggregate limit projected to be exceeded. If the Secretary estimates before the beginning of a year that the amount of the additional payments under this paragraph for the year (or portion thereof) as determined under clause (i) without regard to this clause will exceed the limit established under such clause, the Secretary shall reduce pro rata the amount of each of the additional payments under this paragraph for that year (or portion thereof) in order to ensure that the aggregate additional payments under this paragraph (as so estimated) do not exceed such limit.

(F) Limitation of application of functional equivalence standard. (i) In general. The Secretary may not publish regulations that apply a functional equivalence standard to a drug or biological under this paragraph.

(ii) Application. Clause (i) shall apply to the application of a functional equivalence standard to a drug or biological on or after the date of enactment of the Medicare Prescription Drug, Improvement, and Modernization Act of 2003 [enacted Dec. 8, 2003] unless—

(I) such application was being made to such drug or biological prior to such date of enactment; and

(II) the Secretary applies such standard to such drug or biological only for the purpose of determining eligibility of such drug or biological for additional payments under this paragraph and not for the purpose of any other payments under this title [42 USCS §§ 1395 et seq.].

(iii) Rule of construction. Nothing in this subparagraph shall be construed to effect the Secretary's authority to deem a particular drug to be identical to another drug if the 2 products are pharmaceutically equivalent and bioequivalent, as determined by the Commissioner of Food and Drugs.

(7) Transitional adjustment to limit decline in payment. (A) Before 2002. Subject to subparagraph (D), for covered OPD services furnished before January 1, 2002, for which the PPS amount (as defined in subparagraph (E)) is—

(i) at least 90 percent, but less than 100 percent, of the pre-BBA amount (as defined in subparagraph (F)), the amount of payment under this subsection shall be increased by 80 percent of the amount of such difference;

(ii) at least 80 percent, but less than 90 percent, of the pre-BBA amount, the amount of payment under this subsection shall be increased by the amount by which (I) the product of 0.71 and the pre-BBA amount, exceeds (II) the product of 0.70 and the PPS amount;

(iii) at least 70 percent, but less than 80 percent, of the pre-BBA amount, the amount of payment under this subsection shall be increased by the amount by which (I) the product of 0.63 and the pre-BBA amount, exceeds (II) the product of 0.60 and the PPS amount; or

(iv) less than 70 percent of the pre-BBA amount, the amount of payment under this subsection shall be increased by 21 percent of the pre-BBA amount.

(B) 2002. Subject to subparagraph (D), for covered OPD services furnished during 2002, for which the PPS amount is—

(i) at least 90 percent, but less than 100 percent, of the pre-BBA amount, the amount of payment under this subsection shall be increased by 70 percent of the amount of such difference;

(ii) at least 80 percent, but less than 90 percent, of the pre-BBA amount, the amount of payment under this subsection shall be increased by the amount by which (I) the product of 0.61 and the pre-BBA amount, exceeds (II) the product of 0.60 and the PPS amount; or

(iii) less than 80 percent of the pre-BBA amount, the amount of payment under this subsection shall be increased by 13 percent of the pre-BBA amount.

(C) 2003. Subject to subparagraph (D), for covered OPD services furnished during 2003, for which the PPS amount is—

(i) at least 90 percent, but less than 100 percent, of the pre-BBA amount, the amount of payment under this subsection shall be increased by 60 percent of the amount of such difference; or

(ii) less than 90 percent of the pre-BBA amount, the amount of payment under this subsection shall be increased by 6 percent of the pre-BBA amount.

(D) Hold harmless provisions. (i) Temporary treatment for certain rural hospitals. (I) In the case of a hospital located in a rural area and that has not more than 100 beds or a sole community hospital (as defined in section 1886(d)(5)(D)(iii) [42 USCS § 1395ww(d)(5)(D)(iii)]) located in a rural area, for covered OPD services furnished before January 1, 2006, for which the PPS amount is less than the pre-BBA amount, the amount of payment under this subsection shall be increased by the amount of such difference.

(II) In the case of a hospital located in a rural area and that has not more than 100 beds and that is not a sole community hospital (as defined in section 1886(d)(5)(D)(iii) [42 USCS § 1395ww(d)(5)(D)(iii)]), for covered OPD services furnished on or after January 1, 2006, and before January 1, 2011, for which the PPS amount is less than the pre-BBA amount, the amount of payment under this subsection shall be increased by the applicable percentage of the amount of such difference. For purposes of the preceding sentence, the applicable percentage shall be 95 percent with respect to covered OPD services furnished in 2006, 90 percent with respect to such services furnished in 2007, and 85 percent with respect to such services furnished in 2008, 2009, or 2010.

(III) In the case of a sole community hospital (as defined in section 1886(d)(5)(D)(iii) [42 USCS § 1395ww(d)(5)(D)(iii)]) that has not more than 100 beds, for covered OPD services furnished on or after January 1, 2009, and before January 1, 2011, for which the PPS amount is less than the pre-BBA amount, the amount of payment under this subsection shall be increased by 85 percent of the amount of such difference. In the case of covered OPD services furnished on or after January 1, 2010, and before January 1, 2011, the preceding sentence shall be applied without regard to the 100-bed limitation.

(ii) Permanent treatment for cancer hospitals and children's hospitals. In the case of a hospital described in clause (iii) or (v) of section 1886(d)(1)(B) [42 USCS § 1395ww(d)(1)(B)], for covered OPD services for which the PPS amount is less than the pre-BBA amount, the amount of payment under this subsection shall be increased by the amount of such difference.

(E) PPS amount defined. In this paragraph, the term "PPS amount" means, with respect to covered OPD services, the amount payable under this title for such services (determined without regard to this paragraph), including amounts payable as copayment under paragraph (8), coinsurance under section 1866(a)(2)(A)(ii) [42 USCS § 1395cc(a)(2)(A)(ii)], and the deductible under section 1833(b) [subsec. (b) of this section].

(F) Pre-BBA amount defined. (i) In general. In this paragraph, the "pre-BBA amount" means, with respect to covered OPD services furnished by a hospital in a year, an amount equal to the product of the reasonable cost of the hospital for such services for the portions of the hospital's cost reporting period (or periods) occurring in the year and the base OPD payment-to-cost ratio for the hospital (as defined in clause (ii)).

(ii) Base payment-to-cost-ratio defined. For purposes of this subparagraph, the "base payment-to-cost ratio" for a hospital means the ratio of—

(I) the hospital's reimbursement under this part for covered OPD services furnished during the cost reporting period ending in 1996 (or in the case of a hospital that did not submit a cost report for such period, during the first subsequent cost reporting period ending before 2001 for which the hospital submitted a cost report), including any reimbursement for such services through cost-sharing described in subparagraph (E), to

(II) the reasonable cost of such services for such period.

The Secretary shall determine such ratios as if the amendments made by section 4521 of the Balanced Budget Act of 1997 were in effect in 1996.

(G) Interim payments. The Secretary shall make payments under this paragraph to hospitals on an interim basis, subject to retrospective adjustments based on settled cost reports.

(H) No effect on copayments. Nothing in this paragraph shall be construed to affect the unadjusted copayment amount described in paragraph (3)(B) or the copayment amount under paragraph (8).

(I) Application without regard to budget neutrality. The additional payments made under this paragraph—

(i) shall not be considered an adjustment under paragraph (2)(E); and

(ii) shall not be implemented in a budget neutral manner.

(8) Copayment amount. (A) In general. Except as provided in subparagraphs (B) and (C), the copayment amount under this subsection is the amount by which the amount described in paragraph (4)(B) exceeds the amount of payment determined under paragraph (4)(C).

(B) Election to offer reduced copayment amount. The Secretary shall establish a procedure under which a hospital, before the beginning of a year (beginning with 1999), may elect to reduce the copayment amount otherwise established under subparagraph (A) for some or all covered OPD services to an amount that is not less than 20 percent of the medicare OPD fee schedule amount (computed under paragraph (3)(D)) for the service involved. Under such procedures, such reduced copayment amount may not be further reduced or increased during the year involved and the hospital may disseminate information on the reduction of copayment amount effected under this subparagraph.

(C) Limitation on copayment amount. (i) To inpatient hospital deductible amount. In no case shall the copayment amount for a procedure performed in a year exceed the amount of the inpatient hospital deductible established under section 1813(b) [42 USCS § 1395e(b)] for that year.

(ii) To specified percentage. The Secretary shall reduce the national unadjusted copayment amount for a covered OPD service (or group of such services) furnished in a year in a manner so that the effective copayment rate (determined on a national unadjusted basis) for that service in the year does not exceed the following percentage:

(I) For procedures performed in 2001, on or after April 1, 2001, 57 percent.

(II) For procedures performed in 2002 or 2003, 55 percent.

(III) For procedures performed in 2004, 50 percent.

(IV) For procedures performed in 2005, 45 percent.

(V) For procedures performed in 2006 and thereafter, 40 percent.

(D) No impact on deductibles. Nothing in this paragraph shall be construed as affecting a hospital's authority to waive the charging of a deductible under section 1833(b) [subsec. (b) of this section].

(E) Computation ignoring outlier and pass-through adjustments. The copayment amount shall be computed under subparagraph (A) as if the adjustments under paragraphs (5) and (6) (and any adjustment made under paragraph (2)(E) in relation to such adjustments) had not occurred.

(9) Periodic review and adjustments components of prospective payment system. (A) Periodic review. The Secretary shall review not less often than annually and revise the groups, the relative payment weights, and the wage and other adjustments described in paragraph (2) to take into account changes in medical practice, changes in technology, the addition of new services, new cost data, and other relevant information and factors. The Secretary shall consult with an expert outside advisory panel composed of an appropriate selection of representatives of providers to review (and advise the Secretary concerning) the clinical integrity of the groups and weights. Such panel may use data collected or developed by entities and organizations (other than the Department of Health and Human Services) in conducting such review.

(B) Budget neutrality adjustment. If the Secretary makes adjustments under subparagraph (A), then the adjustments for a year may not cause the estimated amount of expenditures under this part [42 USCS §§ 1395j et seq.] for the year to increase or decrease from the estimated amount of expenditures under this part [42 USCS §§ 1395j et seq.] that would have been made if the adjustments had not been made. In determining adjustments under the preceding sentence for 2004 and 2005, the Secretary shall not take into account under this subparagraph or paragraph (2)(E) any expenditures that would not have been made but for the application of paragraph (14).

(C) Update factor. If the Secretary determines under methodologies described in paragraph (2)(F) that the volume of services paid for under this subsection increased beyond amounts established through those methodologies, the Secretary may appropriately adjust the update to the conversion factor otherwise applicable in a subsequent year.

(10) Special rule for ambulance services. The Secretary shall pay for hospital outpatient services that are ambulance services on the basis described in section 1861(v)(1)(U) [42 USCS § 1395x(v)(1)(U)], or, if applicable, the fee schedule established under section 1834(l) [42 USCS § 1395m(l)].

(11) Special rules for certain hospitals. In the case of hospitals described in clause (iii) or (v) of section 1886(d)(1)(B) [42 USCS § 1395ww(d)(1)(B)]—

(A) the system under this subsection shall not apply to covered OPD services furnished before January 1, 2000; and

(B) the Secretary may establish a separate conversion factor for such services in a manner that specifically takes into account the unique costs incurred by such hospitals by virtue of their patient population and service intensity.

(12) Limitation on review. There shall be no administrative or judicial review under section 1869 [42 USCS § 1395ff], 1878 [42 USCS § 1395oo], or otherwise of—

(A) the development of the classification system under paragraph (2), including the establishment of groups and relative payment weights for covered OPD services, of wage adjustment factors, other adjustments, and methods described in paragraph (2)(F);

(B) the calculation of base amounts under paragraph (3);

(C) periodic adjustments made under paragraph (6);

(D) the establishment of a separate conversion factor under paragraph (8)(B); and

(E) the determination of the fixed multiple, or a fixed dollar cutoff amount, the marginal cost of care, or applicable percentage under paragraph (5) or the determination of insignificance of cost, the duration of the additional payments, the determination and deletion of initial and new categories (consistent with subparagraphs (B) and (C) of paragraph (6)), the portion of the medicare OPD fee schedule amount associated with particular devices, drugs, or biologicals, and the application of any pro rata reduction under paragraph (6).

(13) Authorization of adjustment for rural hospitals. (A) Study. The Secretary shall conduct a study to determine if, under the system under this subsection, costs incurred by hospitals located in rural areas by ambulatory payment classification groups (APCs) exceed those costs incurred by hospitals located in urban areas.

(B) Authorization of adjustment. Insofar as the Secretary determines under subparagraph (A) that costs incurred by hospitals located in rural areas exceed those costs incurred by hospitals located in urban areas, the Secretary shall provide for an appropriate adjustment under paragraph (2)(E) to reflect those higher costs by January 1, 2006.

(14) Drug APC payment rates. (A) In general. The amount of payment under this subsection for a specified covered outpatient drug (defined in subparagraph (B)) that is furnished as part of a covered OPD service (or group of services)—

(i) in 2004, in the case of—

(I) a sole source drug shall in no case be less than 88 percent, or exceed 95 percent, of the reference average wholesale price for the drug;

(II) an innovator multiple source drug shall in no case exceed 68 percent of the reference average wholesale price for the drug; or

(III) a noninnovator multiple source drug shall in no case exceed 46 percent of the reference average wholesale price for the drug;

(ii) in 2005, in the case of—

(I) a sole source drug shall in no case be less than 83 percent, or exceed 95 percent, of the reference average wholesale price for the drug;

(II) an innovator multiple source drug shall in no case exceed 68 percent of the reference average wholesale price for the drug; or

(III) a noninnovator multiple source drug shall in no case exceed 46 percent of the reference average wholesale price for the drug; or

(iii) in a subsequent year, shall be equal, subject to subparagraph (E)—

(I) to the average acquisition cost for the drug for that year (which, at the option of the Secretary, may vary by hospital group (as defined by the Secretary based on volume of covered OPD services or other relevant characteristics)), as determined by the Secretary taking into account the hospital acquisition cost survey data under subparagraph (D); or

(II) if hospital acquisition cost data are not available, the average price for the drug in the year established under section 1842(o), section 1847A, or section 1847B [42 USCS § 1395(u), 1395w-3a, or 1395w-3b], as the case may be, as calculated and adjusted by the Secretary as necessary for purposes of this paragraph.

(B) Specified covered outpatient drug defined. (i) In general. In this paragraph, the term "specified covered outpatient drug" means, subject to clause (ii), a covered outpatient drug (as defined in section 1927(k)(2) [42 USCS § 1396r-8(k)(2)]) for which a separate ambulatory payment classification group (APC) has been established and that is—

(I) a radiopharmaceutical; or

(II) a drug or biological for which payment was made under paragraph (6) (relating to pass-through payments) on or before December 31, 2002.

(ii) Exception. Such term does not include—

(I) a drug or biological for which payment is first made on or after January 1, 2003, under paragraph (6);

(II) a drug or biological for which a temporary HCPCS code has not been assigned; or

(III) during 2004 and 2005, an orphan drug (as designated by the Secretary).

(C) Payment for designated orphan drugs during 2004 and 2005. The amount of payment under this subsection for an orphan drug designated by the Secretary under subparagraph (B)(ii)(III) that is furnished as part of a covered OPD service (or group of services) during 2004 and 2005 shall equal such amount as the Secretary may specify.

(D) Acquisition cost survey for hospital outpatient drugs. (i) Annual GAO surveys in 2004 and 2005. (I) In general. The Comptroller General of the United States shall conduct a survey in each of 2004 and 2005 to determine the hospital acquisition cost for each specified covered outpatient drug. Not later than April 1, 2005, the Comptroller General shall furnish data from such surveys to the Secretary for use in setting the payment rates under subparagraph (A) for 2006.

(II) Recommendations. Upon the completion of such surveys, the Comptroller General shall recommend to the Secretary the frequency and methodology of subsequent surveys to be conducted by the Secretary under clause (ii).

(ii) Subsequent secretarial surveys. The Secretary, taking into account such recommendations, shall conduct periodic subsequent surveys to determine the hospital acquisition cost for each specified covered outpatient drug for use in setting the payment rates under subparagraph (A).

(iii) Survey requirements. The surveys conducted under clauses (i) and (ii) shall have a large sample of hospitals that is sufficient to generate a statistically significant estimate of the average hospital acquisition cost for each specified covered outpatient drug. With respect to the surveys conducted under clause (i), the Comptroller General shall report to Congress on the justification for the size of the sample used in order to assure the validity of such estimates.

(iv) Differentiation in cost. In conducting surveys under clause (i), the Comptroller General shall determine and report to Congress if there is (and the extent of any) variation in hospital acquisition costs for drugs among hospitals based on the volume of covered OPD services performed by such hospitals or other relevant characteristics of such hospitals (as defined by the Comptroller General).

(v) Comment on proposed rates. Not later than 30 days after the date the Secretary promulgated proposed rules setting forth the payment rates under subparagraph (A) for 2006, the Comptroller General shall evaluate such proposed rates and submit to Congress a report regarding the appropriateness of such rates based on the surveys the Comptroller General has conducted under clause (i).

(E) Adjustment in payment rates for overhead costs. (i) MedPAC report on drug APC design. The Medicare Payment Advisory Commission shall submit to the Secretary, not later than July 1, 2005, a report on adjustment of payment for ambulatory payment classifications for specified covered outpatient drugs to take into account overhead and related expenses, such as pharmacy services and handling costs. Such report shall include—

(I) a description and analysis of the data available with regard to such expenses;

(II) a recommendation as to whether such a payment adjustment should be made; and

(III) if such adjustment should be made, a recommendation regarding the methodology for making such an adjustment.

(ii) Adjustment authorized. The Secretary may adjust the weights for ambulatory payment classifications for specified covered outpatient drugs to take into account the recommendations contained in the report submitted under clause (i).

(F) Classes of drugs. For purposes of this paragraph:

(i) Sole source drugs. The term "sole source drug" means—

(I) a biological product (as defined under section 1861(t)(1) [42 USCS § 1395x(t)(1)]); or

(II) a single source drug (as defined in section 1927(k)(7)(A)(iv) [42 USCS § 1396r-8(k)(7)(A)(iv)]).

(ii) Innovator multiple source drugs. The term "innovator multiple source drug" has the meaning given such term in section 1927(k)(7)(A)(ii) [42 USCS § 1396r-8(k)(7)(A)(ii)].

(iii) Noninnovator multiple source drugs. The term "noninnovator multiple source drug" has the meaning given such term in section 1927(k)(7)(A)(iii) [42 USCS § 1396r-8(k)(7)(A)(iii)].

(G) Reference average wholesale price. The term "reference average wholesale price" means, with respect to a specified covered outpatient drug, the average wholesale price for the drug as determined under section 1842(o) [42 USCS § 1395u(o)] as of May 1, 2003.

(H) Inapplicability of expenditures in determining conversion, weighting, and other adjustment factors. Additional expenditures resulting from this paragraph shall not be taken into account in establishing the conversion, weighting, and other adjustment factors for 2004 and 2005 under paragraph (9), but shall be taken into account for subsequent years.

(15) Payment for new drugs and biologicals until HCPCS code assigned. With respect to payment under this part for an outpatient drug or biological that is covered under this part and is furnished as part of covered OPD services for which a HCPCS code has not been assigned, the amount provided for payment for such drug or biological under this part shall be equal to 95 percent of the average wholesale price for the drug or biological.

(16) Miscellaneous provisions. (A) Application of reclassification of certain hospitals. If a hospital is being treated as being located in a rural area under section 1886(d)(8)(E) [42 USCS § 1395ww(d)(8)(E)], that hospital shall be treated under this subsection as being located in that rural area.

(B) Threshold for establishment of separate APCs for drugs. The Secretary shall reduce the threshold for the establishment of separate ambulatory payment classification groups (APCs) with respect to drugs or biologicals to $50 per administration for drugs and biologicals furnished in 2005 and 2006.

(C) Payment for devices of brachytherapy and therapeutic radiopharmaceuticals at charges adjusted to cost. Notwithstanding the preceding provisions of this subsection, for a device of brachytherapy consisting of a seed or seeds (or radioactive source) furnished on or after January 1, 2004, and before January 1, 2010, and for therapeutic radiopharmaceuticals furnished on or after January 1, 2008, and before January 1, 2010, the payment basis for the device or therapeutic radiopharmaceutical under this subsection shall be equal to the hospital's charges for each device or therapeutic radiopharmaceutical furnished, adjusted to cost. Charges for such devices or therapeutic radiopharmaceuticals shall not be included in determining any outlier payment under this subsection.

(17) Quality reporting. (A) Reduction in update for failure to report. (i) In general. For purposes of paragraph (3)(C)(iv) for 2009 and each subsequent year, in the case of a subsection (d) hospital (as defined in section

1886(d)(1)(B) [42 USCS § 1395ww(d)(1)(B)]) that does not submit, to the Secretary in accordance with this paragraph, data required to be submitted on measures selected under this paragraph with respect to such a year, the OPD fee schedule increase factor under paragraph (3)(C)(iv) for such year shall be reduced by 2.0 percentage points.

(ii) Non-cumulative application. A reduction under this subparagraph shall apply only with respect to the year involved and the Secretary shall not take into account such reduction in computing the OPD fee schedule increase factor for a subsequent year.

(B) Form and manner of submission. Each subsection (d) hospital shall submit data on measures selected under this paragraph to the Secretary in a form and manner, and at a time, specified by the Secretary for purposes of this paragraph.

(C) Development of outpatient measures. (i) In general. The Secretary shall develop measures that the Secretary determines to be appropriate for the measurement of the quality of care (including medication errors) furnished by hospitals in outpatient settings and that reflect consensus among affected parties and, to the extent feasible and practicable, shall include measures set forth by one or more national consensus building entities.

(ii) Construction. Nothing in this paragraph shall be construed as preventing the Secretary from selecting measures that are the same as (or a subset of) the measures for which data are required to be submitted under section 1886(b)(3)(B)(viii) [42 USCS § 1395ww(b)(3)(B)(viii)].

(D) Replacement of measures. For purposes of this paragraph, the Secretary may replace any measures or indicators in appropriate cases, such as where all hospitals are effectively in compliance or the measures or indicators have been subsequently shown not to represent the best clinical practice.

(E) Availability of data. The Secretary shall establish procedures for making data submitted under this paragraph available to the public. Such procedures shall ensure that a hospital has the opportunity to review the data that are to be made public with respect to the hospital prior to such data being made public. The Secretary shall report quality measures of process, structure, outcome, patients' perspectives on care, efficiency, and costs of care that relate to services furnished in outpatient settings in hospitals on the Internet website of the Centers for Medicare & Medicaid Services.

(18) Authorization of adjustment for cancer hospitals. (A) Study. The Secretary shall conduct a study to determine if, under the system under this subsection, costs incurred by hospitals described in section 1886(d)(1)(B)(v) [42 USCS § 1395ww(d)(1)(B)(v)] with respect to ambulatory payment classification groups exceed those costs incurred by other hospitals furnishing services under this subsection (as determined appropriate by the Secretary). In conducting the study under this subparagraph, the Secretary shall take into consideration the cost of drugs and biologicals incurred by such hospitals.

(B) Authorization of adjustment. Insofar as the Secretary determines under subparagraph (A) that costs incurred by hospitals described in section 1886(d)(1)(B)(v) [42 USCS § 1395ww(d)(1)(B)(v)] exceed those costs incurred by other hospitals furnishing services under this subsection, the Secretary shall provide for an appropriate adjustment under paragraph (2)(E) to reflect those higher costs effective for services furnished on or after January 1, 2011.

(19) Floor on area wage adjustment factor for hospital outpatient department services in frontier States. (A) In general. Subject to subparagraph (B), with respect to covered OPD services furnished on or after January 1, 2011, the area wage adjustment factor applicable under the payment system established under this subsection to any hospital outpatient department which is located in a frontier State (as defined in section 1886(d)(3)(E)(iii)(II) [42 USCS § 1395ww(d)(3)(E)(iii)(II)]) may not be less than 1.00. The preceding sentence shall not be applied in a budget neutral manner.

(B) Limitation. This paragraph shall not apply to any hospital outpatient department located in a State that receives a non-labor related share adjustment under section 1886(d)(5)(H) [42 USCS § 1395ww(d)(5)(H)].

(u) Incentive payments for physician scarcity areas. (1) In general. In the case of physicians' services furnished on or after January 1, 2005, and before July 1, 2008—

(A) by a primary care physician in a primary care scarcity county (identified under paragraph (4)); or

(B) by a physician who is not a primary care physician in a specialist care scarcity county (as so identified),

in addition to the amount of payment that would otherwise be made for such services under this part [42 USCS §§ 1395j et seq.], there also shall be paid an amount equal to 5 percent of the payment amount for the service under this part [42 USCS §§ 1395j et seq.].

(2) Determination of ratios of physicians to medicare beneficiaries in area. Based upon available data, the Secretary shall establish for each county or equivalent area in the United States, the following:

(A) Number of physicians practicing in the area. The number of physicians who furnish physicians' services in the active practice of medicine or osteopathy in that county or area, other than physicians whose practice is exclusively for the Federal Government, physicians who are retired, or physicians who only provide administrative services. Of such number, the number of such physicians who are—

(i) primary care physicians; or

(ii) physicians who are not primary care physicians.

(B) Number of medicare beneficiaries residing in the area. The number of individuals who are residing in the county and are entitled to benefits under part A [42 USCS §§ 1395c et seq.] or enrolled under this part [42 USCS §§ 1395j et seq.], or both (in this subsection referred to as "individuals").

(C) Determination of ratios. (i) Primary care ratio. The ratio (in this paragraph referred to as the "primary care ratio") of the number of primary care physicians (determined under subparagraph (A)(i)), to the number of individuals determined under subparagraph (B).

(ii) Specialist care ratio. The ratio (in this paragraph referred to as the "specialist care ratio") of the number of other physicians (determined under subparagraph (A)(ii)), to the number of individuals determined under subparagraph (B).

(3) Ranking of counties. The Secretary shall rank each such county or area based separately on its primary care ratio and its specialist care ratio.

(4) Identification of counties. (A) In general. The Secretary shall identify—

(i) those counties and areas (in this paragraph referred to as "primary care scarcity counties") with the lowest primary care ratios that represent, if each such county or area were weighted by the number of individuals determined under paragraph (2)(B), an aggregate total of 20 percent of the total of the individuals determined under such paragraph; and

(ii) those counties and areas (in this subsection referred to as "specialist care scarcity counties") with the lowest specialist care ratios that represent, if each such county or area were weighted by the number of individuals determined under paragraph (2)(B), an aggregate total of 20 percent of the total of the individuals determined under such paragraph.

(B) Periodic revisions. The Secretary shall periodically revise the counties or areas identified in subparagraph (A) (but not less often than once every three years) unless the Secretary determines that there is no new data available on the number of physicians practicing in the county or area or the number of individuals residing in the county or area, as identified in paragraph (2).

(C) Identification of counties where service is furnished. For purposes of paying the additional amount specified in paragraph (1), if the Secretary uses the 5-digit postal ZIP Code where the service is furnished, the dominant county of the postal ZIP Code (as determined by the United States Postal Service, or otherwise) shall be used to determine whether the postal ZIP Code is in a scarcity county identified in subparagraph (A) or revised in subparagraph (B).

(D) Special rule. With respect to physicians' services furnished on or after January 1, 2008, and before July 1, 2008, for purposes of this subsection, the Secretary shall use the primary care scarcity counties and the specialty care scarcity counties (as identified under the preceding provisions of this paragraph) that the Secretary was using under this subsection with respect to physicians' services furnished on December 31, 2007.

(E) Judicial review. There shall be no administrative or judicial review under section 1869 [42 USCS § 1395ff], 1878 [42 USCS § 1395oo], or otherwise, respecting—

(i) the identification of a county or area;

(ii) the assignment of a specialty of any physician under this paragraph;

(iii) the assignment of a physician to a county under paragraph (2); or

(iv) the assignment of a postal ZIP Code to a county or other area under this subsection.

(5) Rural census tracts. To the extent feasible, the Secretary shall treat a rural census tract of a metropolitan statistical area (as determined under the most recent modification of the Goldsmith Modification, originally published in the Federal Register on February 27, 1992 (57 Fed. Reg. 6725)), as an equivalent area for purposes of qualifying as a primary care scarcity county or specialist care scarcity county under this subsection.

(6) Physician defined. For purposes of this paragraph, the term "physician" means a physician described in section 1861(r)(1) [42 USCS § 1395x(r)(1)] and the term "primary care physician" means a physician who is identified in the available data as a general practitioner, family practice practitioner, general internist,

or obstetrician or gynecologist.

(7) Publication of list of counties; posting on website. With respect to a year for which a county or area is identified or revised under paragraph (4), the Secretary shall identify such counties or areas as part of the proposed and final rule to implement the physician fee schedule under section 1848 [42 USCS § 1395w-4] for the applicable year. The Secretary shall post the list of counties identified or revised under paragraph (4) on the Internet website of the Centers for Medicare & Medicaid Services.

(v) Increase of FQHC payment limits. In the case of services furnished by Federally qualified health centers (as defined in section 1861(aa)(4) [42 USCS § 1395x(aa)(4)]), the Secretary shall establish payment limits with respect to such services under this part [42 USCS §§ 1395j et seq.] for services furnished—

(1) in 2010, at the limits otherwise established under this part for such year increased by $5; and

(2) in a subsequent year, at the limits established under this subsection for the previous year increased by the percentage increase in the MEI (as defined in section 1842(i)(3) [42 USCS § 1395u(i)(3)]) for such subsequent year.

(w) Methods of payment. The Secretary may develop alternative methods of payment for items and services provided under clinical trials and comparative effectiveness studies sponsored or supported by an agency of the Department of Health and Human Services, as determined by the Secretary, to those that would otherwise apply under this section, to the extent such alternative methods are necessary to preserve the scientific validity of such trials or studies, such as in the case where masking the identity of interventions from patients and investigators is necessary to comply with the particular trial or study design.

(x) Incentive payments for primary care services. (1) In general. In the case of primary care services furnished on or after January 1, 2011, and before January 1, 2016, by a primary care practitioner, in addition to the amount of payment that would otherwise be made for such services under this part [42 USCS §§ 1395j et seq.], there also shall be paid (on a monthly or quarterly basis) an amount equal to 10 percent of the payment amount for the service under this part [42 USCS §§ 1395j et seq.].

(2) Definitions. In this subsection:

(A) Primary care practitioner. The term "primary care practitioner" means an individual—

(i) who—

(I) is a physician (as described in section 1861(r)(1) [42 USCS § 1395x(r)(1)]) who has a primary specialty designation of family medicine, internal medicine, geriatric medicine, or pediatric medicine; or

(II) is a nurse practitioner, clinical nurse specialist, or physician assistant (as those terms are defined in section 1861(aa)(5) [42 USCS § 1395x(aa)(5)]); and

(ii) for whom primary care services accounted for at least 60 percent of the allowed charges under this part [42 USCS §§ 1395j et seq.] for such physician or practitioner in a prior period as determined appropriate by the Secretary.

(B) Primary care services. The term "primary care services" means services identified, as of January 1, 2009, by the following HCPCS codes (and as subsequently modified by the Secretary):

(i) 99201 through 99215.

(ii) 99304 through 99340.

(iii) 99341 through 99350.

(3) Coordination with other payments. The amount of the additional payment for a service under this subsection and subsection (m) shall be determined without regard to any additional payment for the service under subsection (m) and this subsection, respectively.

(4) Limitation on review. There shall be no administrative or judicial review under section 1869 [42 USCS § 1395ff], 1878 [42 USCS § 1395oo], or otherwise, respecting the identification of primary care practitioners under this subsection.

(y) Incentive payments for major surgical procedures furnished in health professional shortage areas. (1) In general. In the case of major surgical procedures furnished on or after January 1, 2011, and before January 1, 2016, by a general surgeon in an area that is designated (under section 332(a)(1)(A) of the Public Health Service Act [42 USCS § 256(a)(1)(A)]) as a health professional shortage area as identified by the Secretary prior to the beginning of the year involved, in addition to the amount of payment that would otherwise be made for such services under this part [42 USCS §§ 1395j et seq.], there also shall be paid (on a monthly or quarterly basis) an amount equal to 10 percent of the payment amount for the service under this part [42 USCS §§ 1395j et seq.].

(2) Definitions. In this subsection:

(A) General surgeon. In this subsection, the term "general surgeon" means a physician (as described in section 1861(r)(1) [42 USCS § 1395x(r)(1)]) who has designated CMS specialty code 02-General Surgery as their primary specialty code in the physician's enrollment under section 1866(j) [42 USCS § 1395cc(j)].

(B) Major surgical procedures. The term "major surgical procedures" means physicians' services which are surgical procedures for which a 10-day or 90-day global period is used for payment under the fee schedule under section 1848(b) [42 USCS § 1395w-4(b)].

(3) Coordination with other payments. The amount of the additional payment for a service under this subsection and subsection (m) shall be determined without regard to any additional payment for the service under subsection (m) and this subsection, respectively.

(4) Application. The provisions of paragraph (2) and (4) of subsection (m) shall apply to the determination of additional payments under this subsection in the same manner as such provisions apply to the determination of additional payments under subsection (m).

(Aug. 14, 1935, ch 531, Title XVIII, Part B, § 1833, as added July 30, 1965, P. L. 89-97, Title I, Part 1, § 102(a), 79 Stat. 302; Jan. 2, 1968, P. L. 90-248, Title I, Part 3, §§ 129(c)(7), (8), 131(a), (b), 132(b), 135(c), 81 Stat. 848–850, 853; Oct. 30, 1972, P. L. 92-603, Title II, §§ 204(a), 211(c)(4), 226(c)(2), 233(b), 245(d), 251(a)(2), (3), 279, 299K(a), 86 Stat. 1377, 1384, 1404, 1411, 1424, 1445, 1454, 1464; Oct. 25, 1977, P. L. 95-142, § 16(a), 91 Stat. 1200; Dec. 13, 1977, P. L. 95-210, § 1(b), 91 Stat. 1485; June 13, 1978, P. L. 95-292, § 4(b), (c), 92 Stat. 315; Oct. 19, 1980, P. L. 96-473, § 6(j), 94 Stat. 2266; Dec. 5, 1980, P. L. 96-499, Title IX, Part A, Subpart III, § 918(a)(4), Part B, Subpart I, §§ 930(h), 932(a)(1), 934(b), (d)(1), (3), 935(a), Subpart II, §§ 942, 943(a), 94 Stat. 2626, 2631, 2634, 2637, 2639, 2641; Dec. 28, 1980, P. L. 96-611, § 1(b)(1), (2), 94 Stat. 3566; Aug. 13, 1981, P. L. 97-35, Title XXI, Subtitle A, Ch 2, § 2106(a) Subtitle B, Ch 2, §§ 2133(a), 2134(a), 95 Stat. 792, 797; Sept. 3, 1982, P. L. 97-248, Title I, Subtitle A, Part I, Subpart A, § 101(c)(2), Subpart B, § 112(a), (b), Subpart C, § 117(a)(2), Subtitle C, § 148(d), 96 Stat. 336, 340, 355, 394; July 18, 1984, P. L. 98-369, Division B, Title III, Subtitle A, Part I, §§ 2303(a)–(d), 2305(a)–(d), 2308(b)(2)(B), 2321(b), (d)(1)–(3), (4)(A), 2323(b)(1), (2), (4), Part II, § 2354(b)(5), (7), 98 Stat. 1064, 1069, 1074, 1084-1086, 1100; Nov. 8, 1984, P. L. 98-617, § 3(b)(3), 98 Stat. 3295; April 7, 1986, P. L. 99-272, Title IX, Subtitle A, Part 3, Subpart A, § 9303(a)(1), (b)(1)–(3), Part 4, § 9401(b)(1), (2)(A)–(E), 100 Stat. 188, 189, 198, 199; Oct. 21, 1986, P. L. 99-509, Title IX, Subtitle D, Part 2, § 9320(e)(1), (2), Part 3, §§ 9337(b), 9339(e)(1), (b)(1), (2), (c)(1), 9343(a), (b), (e)(2), 100 Stat. 2014, 2032, 2035, 2038-2040; Dec. 22, 1987, P. L. 100-203, Title IV, Subtitle A, Part 3, Subpart A, §§ 4043(a), 4045(c)(2)(A), 4049(a) 4055 [4054], Subpart B, §§ 4062(d)(3), 4063(b), (e), 4064(a)(b), (c), 4066(a)(b), 4067(a), 4068(a), Subpart C, §§ 4070(a), (b)(4), 4072(b), 4073(b)(2)(t), 4077(b)(3), (4), 4073(b), 4077(b)(2), Subpart D, §§ 4084(a), 4085(b)(1), (i)(1)–(3), (21)(D)(i), (22)(B), (23), 101 Stat. 1330-85, 1330-86, 1330-87, 1330-88, 1330-90, 1330-98, 1330-108–1330-113, 1330-117, 1330-118, 1330-129–1330-133; July 1, 1988, P. L. 100-360, Title I, Subtitle A, § 104(d)(7), Title II, Subtitle A, §§ 201(a), 202(b)(1)–(3), 203(c)(1)(A)–(E), 204(d)(1), 205(c), Subtitle B, § 212(c)(2), Title IV, Subtitle B, § 411(f)(2)(D), (8)(B)(i), (C), (12)(A), (14), (g)(1)(E), (2)(D), (E), (3)(A)–(F), (4)(C), (5), (h)(1)(A), (3)(B), (4)(B)–(C), (7)(C), (D), (i)(3), (4)(B), (C)(ii), (iv), (vi), 102 Stat. 689, 699, 704, 722, 729, 730, 741, 777, 779-789; Oct. 13, 1988, P. L. 100-485, Title VI, § 608(d)(4), (22)(B), (23)(A) 102 Stat. 2414, 2420, 2421; Nov. 10, 1988, P. L. 100-647, Title VIII, Subtitle E, Part III, §§ 8421(a), 8422(a), 102 Stat. 3802; Dec. 13, 1989, P. L. 101-234, Title II, §§ 201(a)(1), 202(a), 103 Stat. 1981; Dec. 19, 1989, P. L. 101-239, Title VI, Subtitle A, Part 1, Subpart A, § 6003(e)(2)(A), (g)(3)(D)(vii), Part 2, Subpart A, §§ 6102(c)(1), (e)(1), (5), (6)(A), (7), (f)(2), 6111(a), (b)(1), 6113(b)(3)(B), (d), 6116(b)(1), Subpart B, §§ 6131(a)(1), (b), 6133(a), Part 3, Subpart A, § 6204(b), 103 Stat. 2143, 2153, 2184, 2187, 2188, 2189, 2213, 2217, 2219, 2221, 2222, 2241; Nov. 5, 1990, P. L. 101-508, Title IV, Subtitle A, Part 1, § 4008(m)(2)(C), Part 2, Subpart A, §§ 4104(b)(1), 4118(f)(2)(D), Subpart B, §§ 4151(c)(1), (2), 4153(a)(2)(B), (C), 4154(a), (b)(1), (c)(1), (e)(1), 4155(b)(2), (3), 4160, 4161(a)(3)(B), 4163(d)(1), Part 2, § 4206(b)(2), Part 3, § 4302, 104 Stat. 1388-53, 1388-59, 1388-70, 1388-73, 1388-83, 1388-84, 1388-85, 1388-86, 1388-87, 1388-91, 1388-93, 1388-100, 1388-116, 1388-125; Nov. 16, 1990, P. L. 101-597, Title IV, § 401(c)(2), 104 Stat. 3035.; Aug. 10, 1993, P. L. 103-66, Title XIII, Ch 2, Subch A, Part II, Subpart A, § 13516(b), Subpart C, § 13532(a), Subpart D, § 13544(b)(2), Subpart E, §§ 13551, 13555(a), 107 Stat. 584, 586, 590, 592; Oct. 31, 1994, P. L. 103-432, Title I, Subtitle B, Part I, § 123(b)(2)(A), (e), Part III, § 141(a), (c)(1), 147(a), (d), (e)(2), (3), (f)(6)(C)–(E), Subtitle C, § 156(a)(2)(B), 160(d)(1), 108 Stat. 4411, 4412, 4424, 4425, 4429, 4430, 4432, 4440, 4443; Aug. 5, 1997, P. L. 105-33, Title IV, Subtitle A, Ch 1, Subch A, § 4002(j)(1)(A), Subtitle B,

§§ 4101(b), 4102(b), 4103(b), 4104(c)(1), (2), Subtitle (C), §§ 4201(c)(1), 4205(a)(1)(A), (2), Subtitle D, Ch 2, § 4315(b), Subtitle E, Ch 3, § 4432(b)(5)(C), Subtitle F, Ch 1, Subch B, §§ 4511(b), 4512(b)(1), Ch 2, §§ 4521(a), (b), 4523(a), (d)(1)(A)(i), (B), (2), (3), Ch 3, § 4531(b)(1), Ch 4, § 4541(a)(1), (c), (d)(1), Ch 5, §§ 4553(a), (b), 4555, 4556(b), Subtitle G, Ch 1, Subch A, § 4603(c)(2)(A), 111 Stat. 330, 360–362, 365, 373, 376, 390, 421, 442–445, 449–451, 454, 456, 460, 462, 463, 471; Nov. 29, 1999, P. L. 106-113, Div B, § 1000(a)(6), 113 Stat. 1536; Dec. 21, 2000, P. L. 106-554, § 1(a)(6), 114 Stat. 2763; Dec. 8, 2003, P. L. 108-173, Title II, Subtitle D, § 237(a), Title III, §§ 302(b)(2), 303(i)(3)(A), Title IV, Subtitle B, §§ 411(a)(1), (b), 413(a), (b)(1), Title VI, Subtitle B, § 614(a), (b), Subtitle C, §§ 621(a)(1)–(5), (b)(1), (2), 622, 624(a)(1), 626(a)–(c), 627(a), 628, 629, Subtitle D, § 642(b), Title VII, Subtitle D, § 736(b)(1), (2), Title IX, Subtitle E, § 942(b), 117 Stat. 2212, 2229, 2254, 2274, 2275, 2306, 2307, 2310, 2311, 2318, 2320, 2321, 2322, 2355, 2421; Feb. 8, 2006, P. L. 109-171, Title V, Subtitle B, Ch. 1, §§ 5103, 5105, 5107(a)(1), Ch. 2, §§ 5112(e), 5113(a), 120 Stat. 40, 41, 42, 44; Dec. 20, 2006, P. L. 109-432, Div B, Title I, §§ 107(a), (b)(1), 109(a)(1), (b), Title II, § 201, 120 Stat. 2983, 2984, 2985, 2986; Dec. 29, 2007, P. L. 110-173, Title I, §§ 102, 105, 106, 113, 121 Stat. 2495, 2496, 2501; July 15, 2008, P. L. 110-275, Title I, Subtitle A, Part I, §§ 101(a)(2), (b)(2), 102, Subtitle C, Part II, §§ 141, 142, 143(b)(2), (3), 145(a)(2), (b), 147, 151(a), Subtitle F, § 184, 122 Stat. 2497, 2498, 2542, 2547, 2548, 2550, 2587; March 2, 2010, P. L. 111-144, § 6, 124 Stat. 46; March 23, 2010, P. L. 111-148, Title III, Subtitle B, Part I, §§ 3103, 3114, Part II, § 3121, Part III, § 3138, Subtitle E, § 3401(i), (k), (l), Title IV, Subtitle B, §§ 4103(c)(1), (3), (4), 4104(b), (c), Title V, Subtitle F, § 5501(a)(1), (b)(1), Title X, Subtitle B, Part III, § 10221(a), (b)(4), Subtitle C, §§ 10319(g), 10324(b), Subtitle D, § 10406, Subtitle E, § 10501(i)(3)(B), (C), 124 Stat. 417, 423, 439, 485, 486, 556, 557, 652, 653, 935, 936, 949, 960, 975, 998; March 30, 2010, P. L. 111-152, Title I, Subtitle B, § 1105(e), 124 Stat. 1049.)

HISTORY; ANCILLARY LAWS AND DIRECTIVES

Amendments:

2010. Act March 2, 2010, in subsec. (g)(5), substituted "March 31, 2010" for "December 31, 2009".

Act March 23, 2010, purported to amend subsec. (g)(5) by substituting "December 31, 2010" for "December 31, 2009"; however, because of prior amendments, the amendment has been executed by substituting "December 31, 2010" for "March 31, 2010" in order to effectuate the probable intent of Congress.

Such Act further, in subsec. (a), in para. (1)(K), inserted "(or 100 percent for services furnished on or after January 1, 2011), and in para. (3)(B)(i), inserted the subclause "(I)" designation, inserted ", or" and subcl. (II), and added the concluding matter beginning "Paragraph (3)(A) . . ."; in subsec. (h)(2)(A), in cl. (i), inserted ", subject to clause (iv)," and substituted "and 2010" for "through 2013", and added cl. (iv); in subsec. (i)(2)(D), redesignated cl. (v) as cl. (vi), and inserted new cl. (v); in subsec. (t), in para. (2)(D), inserted "subject to paragraph (19),", in para. (3), in subpara. (C)(iv), inserted "and subparagraph (F) of this paragraph", and added subparas. (F) and (G), in para. (7)(D)(i), in subcl. (II), substituted "2011" for "2010" and ", 2009, or 2010" for "or 2009", and in subcl. (III), substituted "January 1, 2011" for "January 1, 2010", and added the sentence beginning "In the case of covered OPD services . . .", and added paras. (18) and (19); and added subsecs. (x) and (y).

Such Act further (applicable to services furnished on or after 1/1/2011, as provided by § 4103(e) of such Act, which appears as a note to this section), in subsec. (a), in para. (1), in subpara. (N), inserted "other than personalized prevention plan services (as defined in section 1861(hhh)(1))", deleted "and" before "(W)", and inserted ", and (X) with respect to personalized prevention plan services (as defined in section 1861(hhh)(1)), the amount paid shall be 100 percent of the lesser of the actual charge for the services or the amount determined under the payment basis determined under section 1848", and in para. (2), in subpara. (F), deleted "and" at the end, in subpara. (G)(ii), substituted "; and" for a concluding comma, and added subpara. (H); in subsec. (b), deleted "and" before "(9)", and inserted ", and (10) such deductible shall not apply with respect to personalized prevention plan services (as defined in section 1861(hhh)(1))"; and in subsec. (t)(1)(B)(iv), substituted ", diagnostic mammography, or personalized prevention plan services (as defined in section 1861(hhh)(1))" for "and diagnostic mammography".

Such Act further (as amended by § 10406 of such Act, and applicable to items and services furnished on or after 1/1/2011, as provided by § 4104(d) of such Act, which appears as a note to this section), in subsec. (a), in para. (1), in subpara. (T), inserted "(or 100 percent if such services are recommended with a grade of A or B by the United States Preventive Services Task Force for any indication or population and are appropriate for the individual)", in subpara. (W), in cl. (i), inserted "(if such subparagraph were applied, by substituting '100 percent' for '80 percent')", and in cl. (ii), substituted "100 percent" for "80 percent", deleted "and" before "(X)", and inserted ", and (Y) with respect to preventive services described in subparagraphs (A) and (B) of section 1861(ddd)(3) that are appropriate for the individual and, in the case of such services described in subparagraph (A), are recommended with a grade of A or B by the United States Preventive Services Task Force for any indication or population, the amount paid shall be 100 percent of (i) except as provided in clause (ii), the lesser of the actual charge for the services or the amount determined under the fee schedule that applies to such services under this part, and (ii) in the case of such services that are covered OPD services (as defined in subsection (t)(1)(B)), the amount determined under subsection (t)", and, in para. (2), in subpara. (G)(ii), deleted "and" following the concluding semicolon, in subpara. (H), substituted "; and" for a concluding comma, and added subpara. (I); in subsec. (b), substituted "preventive services described in subparagraph (A) of section 1861(ddd)(3) that are recommended with a grade of A or B by the United States Preventive Services Task Force for any indication or population and are appropriate for the individual." for "items and services described in section 1861(s)(10)(A)", and added the sentence beginning "Paragraph (1) of the first sentence. . . "; and, in subsec. (t)(1)(B)(iv), deleted "or" preceding "personalized prevention services" and inserted ", or preventive services described in subparagraphs (A) and (B) of section 1861(ddd)(3) that are appropriate for the individual and, in the case of such services described in subparagraph (A), are recommended with a grade of A or B by the United States Preventive Services Task Force for any indication or population".

Section 10221(a) of such Act further, in subsec. (a)(1)(B), inserted "or 1880(e) after "section 1861(s)(10)(A); however, this amendment was repealed by § 10221(b)(4) of such Act.

Section 10319(g) of such Act further, in subsec. (t)(3)(G)(i), in subcl. (I), deleted "and" following the concluding semicolon, redesignated subcl. (II) as subcl. (III), inserted new subcl. (II), and, in subcl. (III), as redesignated, substituted "2014" for "2012".

Section 10501(i)(3)(B) of such Act further, in subsec. (a), in para. (1), deleted "and" preceding "(Y)", and inserted ", and (Z) with respect to Federally qualified health center services for which payment is made under section 1834(o), the amounts paid shall be 80 percent of the lesser of the actual charge or the amount determined under such section", and in para. (3)(B)(i), inserted "(I)" and ", or (II) in the case of such services furnished on or after the implementation date of the prospective payment system under section 1834(o), under such section (calculated as if '100 percent' were substituted for '80 percent' in such section) for such services if the individual had not been so enrolled", and added the concluding matter.

Act March 30, 2010, in subsec. (t)(3)(G), in cl. (i), in subcl. (II), deleted "and" following the concluding semicolon, substituted subcls. (III)–(V) for former subcl. (III), which read: "(III) subject to clause (ii), for each of 2014 through 2019, 0.2 percentage point.", deleted cl. (ii), which read:

"(ii) Reduction of other adjustment. Clause (i)(II) shall be applied with respect to any of 2014 through 2019 by substituting '0.0 percentage points' for '0.2 percentage point', if for such year—

"(I) the excess (if any) of—

"(aa) the total percentage of the non-elderly insured population for the preceding year (based on the most recent estimates available from the Director of the Congressional Budget Office before a vote in either House on the Patient Protection and Affordable Care Act that, if determined in the affirmative, would clear such Act for enrollment); over

"(bb) the total percentage of the non-elderly insured population for such preceding year (as estimated by the Secretary); exceeds

"(II) 5 percentage points.",

substituted "(G) Other adjustment. For purposes" for "(G) Other adjustment. (i) In general. For purposes", and redesignated subcls. (I)–(V) as cls. (i)–(v), respectively.

Other provisions:

Treatment of certain complex diagnostic laboratory tests. Act March 23, 2010, P. L. 111-148, Title III, Subtitle B, Part I, § 3113, 124 Stat. 422, provides:

"(a) Demonstration project. (1) In general. The Secretary of Health and Human Services (in this section referred to as the 'Secretary') shall conduct a demonstration project under part B title XVIII of the Social Security Act [42 USCS §§ 1395j et seq.] under which separate payments are made under such part for complex diagnostic laboratory tests provided to individuals under such part. Under the demonstration project, the Secretary shall establish appropriate payment rates for such tests.

"(2) Covered complex diagnostic laboratory test defined. In this section, the term 'complex diagnostic laboratory test' means a diagnostic laboratory test—

"(A) that is an analysis of gene protein expression, topographic genotyping, or a cancer chemotherapy sensitivity assay;

"(B) that is determined by the Secretary to be a laboratory test for which there is not an alternative test having equivalent performance characteristics;

"(C) which is billed using a Health Care Procedure Coding System (HCPCS) code other than a not otherwise classified code under such Coding System;

"(D) which is approved or cleared by the Food and Drug Administration or is covered under title XVIII of the Social Security Act [42 USCS §§ 1395 et seq.]; and

"(E) is described in section 1861(s)(3) of the Social Security Act (42 U.S.C. 1395x(s)(3)).

"(3) Separate payment defined. In this section, the term 'separate payment' means direct payment to a laboratory (including a hospital-based or independent laboratory) that performs a complex diagnostic laboratory test with respect to a specimen collected from an individual during a period in which the individual is a patient of a hospital if the test is performed after such period of hospitalization and if separate payment would not otherwise be made under title XVIII of the Social Security Act [42 USCS §§ 1395 et seq.] by reason of sections 1862(a)(14) and 1866(a)(1)(H)(i) of the such Act (42 U.S.C. 1395y(a)(14); 42 U.S.C. 1395cc(a)(1)(H)(i)).

"(b) Duration. Subject to subsection (c)(2), the Secretary shall conduct the demonstration project under this section for the 2-year period beginning on July 1, 2011.

"(c) Payments and limitation. Payments under the demonstration project under this section shall—

"(1) be made from the Federal Supplemental Medical Insurance Trust Fund under section 1841 of the Social Security Act (42 U.S.C. 1395t); and

"(2) may not exceed $100,000,000.

"(d) Report. Not later than 2 years after the completion of the demonstration project under this section, the Secretary shall submit to Congress a report on the project. Such report shall include—

"(1) an assessment of the impact of the demonstration project on access to care, quality of care, health outcomes, and expenditures under title XVIII of the Social Security Act [42 USCS §§ 1395 et seq.] (including any savings under such title); and

"(2) such recommendations as the Secretary determines appropriate.

"(e) Implementation funding. For purposes of administering this section (including preparing and submitting the report under subsection (d)), the Secretary shall provide for the transfer, from the Federal Supplemental Medical Insurance Trust Fund under section 1841 of the Social Security Act (42 U.S.C. 1395t), to the Centers for Medicare & Medicaid Services Program Management Account, of $5,000,000. Amounts transferred under the preceding sentence shall remain available until expended.".

Application of amendments made by § 4103

of Act March 23, 2010. Act March 23, 2010, P. L. 111-148, Title IV, Subtitle B, § 4103(e), 124 Stat. 557, provides: "The amendments made by this section [amending 42 USCS §§ 1395l, 1395w-4, 1395x, and 1395y] shall apply to services furnished on or after January 1, 2011.".

Application of amendments made by § 4104 of Act March 23, 2010. Act March 23, 2010, P. L. 111-148, Title IV, Subtitle B, § 4104(d), 124 Stat. 558, provides: "The amendments made by this section [amending 42 USCS §§ 1395l and 1395x] shall apply to items and services furnished on or after January 1, 2011.".

§ 1395m. Special payment rules for particular items and services

(a) Payment for durable medical equipment. (1) General rule for payment. (A) In general. With respect to a covered item (as defined in paragraph (13)) for which payment is determined under this subsection, payment shall be made in the frequency specified in paragraphs (2) through (7) and in an amount equal to 80 percent of the payment basis described in subparagraph (B).

(B) Payment basis. Subject to subparagraph (F)(i), the payment basis described in this subparagraph is the lesser of—

(i) the actual charge for the item, or

(ii) the payment amount recognized under paragraphs (2) through (7) of this subsection for the item;

except that clause (i) shall not apply if the covered item is furnished by a public home health agency (or by another home health agency which demonstrates to the satisfaction of the Secretary that a significant portion of its patients are low income) free of charge or at nominal charges to the public.

(C) Exclusive payment rule. Subject to subparagraph (F)(ii), this subsection shall constitute the exclusive provision of this title [42 USCS §§ 1395 et seq.] for payment for covered items under this part [42 USCS §§ 1395j et seq.] or under part A [42 USCS §§ 1395c et seq.] to a home health agency.

(D) Reduction in fee schedules for certain items. With respect to a seat-lift chair or transcutaneous electrical nerve stimulator furnished on or after April 1, 1990, the Secretary shall reduce the payment amount applied under subparagraph (B)(ii) for such an item by 15 percent, and, in the case of a transcutaneous electrical nerve stimulator furnished on or after January 1, 1991, the Secretary shall further reduce such payment amount (as previously reduced) by 45 percent.

(E) Clinical conditions for coverage. (i) In general. The Secretary shall establish standards for clinical conditions for payment for covered items under this subsection.

(ii) Requirements. The standards established under clause (i) shall include the specification of types or classes of covered items that require, as a condition of payment under this subsection, a face-to-face examination of the individual by a physician (as defined in section 1861(r) [42 USCS § 1395x(r)]), a physician assistant, nurse practitioner, or a clinical nurse specialist (as those terms are defined in section 1861(aa)(5) [42 USCS § 1395x(aa)(5)]) and a prescription for the item.

(iii) Priority of establishment of standards. In establishing the standards under this subparagraph, the Secretary shall first establish standards for those covered items for which the Secretary determines there has been a proliferation of use, consistent findings of charges for covered items that are not delivered, or consistent findings of falsification of documentation to provide for payment of such covered items under this part [42 USCS §§ 1395j et seq.].

(iv) Standards for power wheelchairs. Effective on the date of the enactment of this subparagraph, in the case of a covered item consisting of a motorized or power wheelchair for an individual, payment may not be made for such covered item unless a physician (as defined in section 1861(r)(1) [42 USCS § 1395x(r)(1)]), a physician assistant, nurse practitioner, or a clinical nurse specialist (as those terms are defined in section 1861(aa)(5) [42 USCS § 1395x(aa)(5)]) has conducted a face-to-face examination of the individual and written a prescription for the item.

(v) Limitation on payment for covered items. Payment may not be made for a covered item under this subsection unless the item meets any standards established under this subparagraph for clinical condition of coverage.

(F) Application of competitive acquisition; limitation of inherent reasonableness authority. In the case of covered items furnished on or after January 1, 2011, subject to subparagraph (G), that are included in a competitive acquisition program in a competitive acquisition area under section 1847(a) [42 USCS § 1395w-3(a)]—

(i) the payment basis under this subsection for such items and services furnished in such area shall be the payment basis determined under such competitive acquisition program;

(ii) the Secretary may (and, in the case of covered items furnished on or after January 1, 2016, subject to clause (iii), shall) use information on the payment determined under such competitive acquisition programs to adjust the payment amount otherwise recognized under subparagraph (B)(ii) for an area that is not a competitive acquisition area under section 1847 [42 USCS § 1395w-3] and in the case of such adjustment, paragraph (10)(B) shall not be applied.

(iii) in the case of covered items furnished on or after January 1, 2016, the Secretary shall continue to make such adjustments described in clause (ii) as, under such competitive acquisition programs, additional covered items are phased in or information is updated as contracts under section 1847 [42 USCS § 1395w-3] are recompeted in accordance with section 1847(b)(3)(B) [42 USCS § 1395w-3(b)(3)(B)].

(G) Use of information on competitive bid rates. The Secretary shall specify by regulation the methodology to be used in applying the provisions of subparagraph (F)(ii) and subsection (h)(1)(H)(ii). In promulgating such regulation, the Secretary shall consider the costs of items and services in areas in which such provisions would be applied compared to the payment rates for such items and services in competitive acquisition areas.

(2) Payment for inexpensive and other routinely purchased durable medical equipment. (A) In general. Payment for an item of durable medical equipment (as defined in paragraph (13))—

(i) the purchase price of which does not exceed $150,

(ii) which the Secretary determines is acquired at least 75 percent of the time by purchase, or

(iii) which is an accessory used in conjunction with a nebulizer, aspirator, or a ventilator excluded under paragraph (3)(A),

shall be made on a rental basis or in a lump-sum amount for the purchase of the item. The payment amount recognized for purchase or rental of such equipment is the amount specified in subparagraph (B) for purchase or rental, except that the total amount of payments with respect to an item may not exceed the payment amount specified in subparagraph (B) with respect to the purchase of the item.

(B) Payment amount. For purposes of subparagraph (A), the amount specified in this subparagraph, with respect to the purchase or rental of an item furnished in a carrier service area—

(i) in 1989 and in 1990 is the average reasonable charge in the area for the purchase or rental, respectively, of the item for the 12-month period ending on June 30, 1987, increased by the percentage increase in the consumer price index for all urban consumers (U.S. city average) for the 6-month period ending with December 1987;

(ii) in 1991 is the sum of (I) 67 percent of the local payment amount for the item or device computed under subparagraph (C)(i)(I) for 1991, and (II) 33 percent of the national limited payment amount for the item or device computed under subparagraph (C)(ii) for 1991;

(iii) in 1992 is the sum of (I) 33 percent of the local payment amount for the item or device computed under subparagraph (C)(i)(II) for 1992, and (II) 67 percent of the national limited payment amount for the item or device computed under subparagraph (C)(ii) for 1992; and

(iv) in 1993 and each subsequent year is the national limited payment amount for the item or device computed under subparagraph (C)(ii) for that year (reduced by 10 percent, in the case of a blood glucose testing strip furnished after 1997 for an individual with diabetes).

(C) Computation of local payment amount and national limited payment amount. For purposes of subparagraph (B)—

(i) the local payment amount for an item or device for a year is equal to—

(I) for 1991, the amount specified in subparagraph (B)(i) for 1990 increased by the covered item update for 1991, and

(II) for 1992, 1993, and 1994, the amount determined under this clause for the preceding year increased by the covered item update for the year; and

(ii) the national limited payment amount for an item or device for a year is equal to—

(I) for 1991, the local payment amount determined under clause (i) for such item or device for that year, except that the national limited payment amount may not exceed 100 percent of the weighted average of all local payment amounts determined under such clause for such item for that year and may not be less than 85 percent of the weighted average of all local payment amounts determined under such clause for such item,

(II) for 1992 and 1993, the amount determined under this clause for the preceding year increased by the covered item update for such subsequent year,

(III) for 1994, the local payment amount determined under clause (i) for such item or device for that year, except that the national limited payment amount may not exceed 100 percent of the median of all local payment amounts determined under such clause for such item for that year and may not be less than 85 percent of the median of all local payment amounts determined under such clause for such item or device for that year, and

(IV) for each subsequent year, the amount determined under this clause for the preceding year increased by the covered item update for such subsequent year.

(3) Payment for items requiring frequent and substantial servicing. (A) In general. Payment for a covered item (such as IPPB machines and ventilators, excluding ventilators that are either continuous airway pressure devices or intermittent assist devices with continuous airway pressure devices) for which there must be frequent and substantial servicing in order to avoid risk to the patient's health shall be made on a monthly basis for the rental of the item and the amount recognized is the amount specified in subparagraph (B).

(B) Payment amount. For purposes of subparagraph (A), the amount specified in this subparagraph, with respect to an item or device furnished in a carrier service area—

(i) in 1989 and in 1990 is the average reasonable charge in the area for the rental of the item or device for the 12-month period ending with June 1987, increased by the percentage increase in the consumer price index for all urban consumers (U.S. city average) for the 6-month period ending with December 1987;

(ii) in 1991 is the sum of (I) 67 percent of the local payment amount for the item or device computed under subparagraph (C)(i)(I) for 1991, and (II) 33 percent of the national limited payment amount for the item or device computed under subparagraph (C)(ii) for 1991;

(iii) in 1992 is the sum of (I) 33 percent of the local payment amount for the item or device computed under subparagraph (C)(i)(II) for 1992, and (II) 67 percent of the national limited payment amount for the item or device computed under subparagraph (C)(ii) for 1992; and

(iv) in 1993 and each subsequent year is the national limited payment amount for the item or device computed under subparagraph (C)(ii) for that year.

(C) Computation of local payment amount and national limited payment amount. For purposes of subparagraph (B)—

(i) the local payment amount for an item or device for a year is equal to—

(I) for 1991, the amount specified in subparagraph (B)(i) for 1990 increased by the covered item update for 1991, and

(II) for 1992, 1993, and 1994, the amount determined under this clause for the preceding year increased by the covered item update for the year; and

(ii) the national limited payment amount for an item or device for a year is equal to—

(I) for 1991, the local payment amount determined under clause (i) for such item or device for that year, except that the national limited payment amount may not exceed 100 percent of the weighted average of all local payment amounts determined under such clause for such item for that year and may not be less than 85 percent of the weighted average of all local payment amounts determined under such clause for such item,

(II) for 1992 and 1993, the amount determined under this clause for the preceding year increased by the covered item update for such subsequent year,

(III) for 1994, the local payment amount determined under clause (i) for such item or device for that year, except that the national limited payment amount may not exceed 100 percent of the median of all local payment amounts determined under such clause for such item for that year and may not be less than 85 percent of the median of all local payment amounts determined under such clause for such item or device for that year, and

(IV) for each subsequent year, the amount determined under this clause for the preceding year increased by the covered item update for such subsequent year.

(4) Payment for certain customized items. Payment with respect to a covered item that is uniquely constructed or substantially modified to meet the specific needs of an individual patient, and for the reason cannot be grouped with similar items for purposes of payment under this title [42 USCS §§ 1395 et seq.], shall be made in a lump-sum amount (A) for the purchase of the item in a payment amount based upon the carrier's individual consideration for that item, and (B) for the reasonable and necessary maintenance and servicing for parts and labor not covered by the supplier's or manufacturer's warranty, when necessary during the period of medical need, and the amount recognized for such maintenance and servicing shall be paid on a lump-sum, as needed basis upon the carrier's individual consideration for that item.

(5) Payment for oxygen and oxygen equipment. (A) In general. Payment for oxygen and oxygen equipment shall be made on a monthly basis in the monthly payment amount recognized under paragraph (9) for oxygen and oxygen equipment (other than portable oxygen equipment), subject to subparagraphs (B), (C), (E), and (F).

(B) Add-on for portable oxygen equipment. When portable oxygen equipment is used, but subject to subparagraph (D), the payment amount recognized under subparagraph (A) shall be increased by the monthly payment amount recognized under paragraph (9) for portable oxygen equipment.

(C) Volume adjustment. When the attending physician prescribes an oxygen flow rate—

(i) exceeding 4 liters per minute, the payment amount recognized under subparagraph (A), subject to subparagraph (D), shall be increased by 50 percent, or

(ii) of less than 1 liter per minute, the payment amount recognized under subparagraph (A) shall be decreased by 50 percent.

(D) Limit on adjustment. When portable oxygen equipment is used and the attending physician prescribes an oxygen flow rate exceeding 4 liters per minute, there shall only be an increase under either subparagraph (B) or (C), whichever increase is larger, and not under both such subparagraphs.

(E) Recertification for patients receiving home oxygen therapy. In the case of a patient receiving home oxygen therapy services who, at the time such services are initiated, has an initial arterial blood gas value at or above a partial pressure of 56 or an arterial oxygen saturation at or above 89 percent (or such other values, pressures, or criteria as the Secretary may specify) no payment may be made under this part [42 USCS §§ 1395j et seq.] for such services after the expiration of the 90-day period that begins on the date the patient first receives such services unless the patient's attending physician certifies that, on the basis of a follow-up test of the patient's arterial blood gas value or arterial oxygen saturation conducted during the final 30 days of such 90-day period, there is a medical need for the patient to continue to receive such services.

(F) Rental cap. (i) In general. Payment for oxygen equipment (including portable oxygen equipment) under this paragraph may not extend over a period of continuous use (as determined by the Secretary) of longer than 36 months.

(ii) Payments and rules after rental cap. After the 36th continuous month during which payment is made for the equipment under this paragraph—

(I) the supplier furnishing such equipment under this subsection shall continue to furnish the equipment during any period of medical need for the remainder of the reasonable useful lifetime of the equipment, as determined by the Secretary;

(II) payments for oxygen shall continue to be made in the amount recognized for oxygen under paragraph (9) for the period of medical need; and

(III) maintenance and servicing payments shall, if the Secretary determines such payments are reasonable and necessary, be made (for parts and labor not covered by the supplier's or manufacturer's warranty, as determined by the Secretary to be appropriate for the equipment), and such payments shall be in an amount determined to be appropriate by the Secretary.

(6) Payment for other covered items (other than durable medical equipment). Payment for other covered items (other than durable medical equipment and other covered items described in paragraph (3), (4), or (5)) shall be made in a lump-sum amount for the purchase of the item in the amount of the purchase price recognized under paragraph (8).

(7) Payment for other items of durable medical equipment. (A) Payment. In the case of an item of durable medical equipment not described in paragraphs (2) through (6), the following rules shall apply:

(i) Rental. (I) In general. Except as provided in clause (iii), payment for the item shall be made on a monthly basis for the rental of the item during the period of medical need (but payments under this clause may not extend over a period of continuous use (as determined by the Secretary) of longer than 13 months).

(II) Payment amount. Subject to subclause (III) and subparagraph (B), the amount recognized for the item, for each of the first 3 months of such period, is 10 percent of the purchase price recognized under paragraph (8) with respect to the item, and, for each of the remaining months of such period, is 7.5 percent of such purchase price.

(III) Special rule for power-driven wheelchairs **[Caution: This subclause takes effect on January 1, 2011, and applies to power-driven wheelchairs furnished on or after such date, as provided by § 3136(c) of Act March 23, 2010, P. L. 111-148, which appears as a note to this section.]**. For purposes of payment for power-driven wheelchairs, subclause (II) shall be applied by substituting "15 percent" and "6 percent" for "10 percent" and "7.5 percent", respectively.

(ii) Ownership after rental. On the first day that begins after the 13th continuous month during which payment is made for the rental of an item under clause (i), the supplier of the item shall transfer title to the item to the individual.

(iii) Purchase agreement option for complex, rehabilitative power-driven wheelchairs. In the case of a complex, rehabilitative power-driven wheelchair, at the time the supplier furnishes the item, the supplier shall offer the individual the option to purchase the item, and payment for such item shall be made on a lump-sum basis if the individual exercises such option.

(iv) Maintenance and servicing. After the supplier transfers title to the item under clause (ii) or in the case of a power-driven wheelchair for which a purchase agreement has been entered into under clause (iii), maintenance and servicing payments shall, if the Secretary determines such payments are reasonable and necessary, be made (for parts and labor not covered by the supplier's or manufacturer's warranty, as determined by the Secretary to be appropriate for the particular type of durable medical equipment), and such payments shall be in an amount determined to be appropriate by the Secretary.

(B) Range for rental amounts. (i) For 1989. For items furnished during 1989, the payment amount recognized under subparagraph (A)(i) shall not be more than 115 percent, and shall not be less than 85 percent, of the prevailing charge established for rental of the item in January 1987, increased by the percentage increase in the consumer price index for all urban consumers (U.S. city average) for the 6-month period ending with December 1987.

(ii) For 1990. For items furnished during 1990, clause (i) shall apply in the same manner as it applies to items furnished during 1989.

(C) Replacement of items. (i) Establishment of reasonable useful lifetime. In accordance with clause (iii), the Secretary shall determine and establish a reasonable useful lifetime for items of durable medical equipment for which payment may be made under this paragraph.

(ii) Payment for replacement items. If the reasonable lifetime of such an item, as so established, has been reached during a continuous period of medical need, or the carrier determines that the item is lost or irreparably damaged, the patient may elect to have payment for an item serving as a replacement for such item made—

(I) on a monthly basis for the rental of the replacement item in accordance with subparagraph (A); or

(II) in the case of an item for which a purchase agreement has been entered into under subparagraph (A)(iii), in a lump-sum amount for the purchase of the item.

(iii) Length of reasonable useful lifetime. The reasonable useful lifetime of an item of durable medical equipment under this subparagraph shall be equal to 5 years, except that, if the Secretary determines that, on the basis of prior experience in making payments for such an item under this title [42 USCS §§ 1395 et seq.], a reasonable useful lifetime of 5 years is not appropriate with respect to a particular item, the Secretary shall establish an alternative reasonable lifetime for such item.

(8) Purchase price recognized for miscellaneous devices and items. For purposes of paragraphs (6) and (7), the amount that is recognized under this paragraph as the purchase price for a covered item is the amount described in subparagraph (C) of this paragraph, determined as follows:

(A) Computation of local purchase price. Each carrier under section 1842 [42 USCS § 1395u] shall compute a base local purchase price for the item as follows:

(i) The carrier shall compute a base local purchase price, for each item described—

(I) in paragraph (6) equal to the average reasonable charge in the locality for the purchase of the item for the 12-month period ending with June 1987, or

(II) in paragraph (7) equal to the average of the purchase prices on the claims submitted on an assignment-related basis for the unused item supplied during the 6-month period ending with December 1986.

(ii) The carrier shall compute a local purchase price, with respect to the furnishing of each particular item—

(I) in 1989 and 1990, equal to the base local purchase price computed under clause (i) increased by the percentage increase in the consumer price index for all urban consumers (U.S. city average) for the 6-month period ending with December 1987,

(II) in 1991, equal to the local purchase price computed under this clause for the previous year, increased by the covered item update for 1991, and decreased by the percentage by which the average of the reasonable charges for claims paid for all items described in paragraph (7) is lower than the average of the purchase prices submitted for such items during the final 9 months of 1988; [,] or

(III) in 1992, 1993, and 1994, equal to the local purchase price computed under this clause for the previous year increased by the covered item update for the year.

(B) Computation of national limited purchase price. With respect to the furnishing of a particular item in a year, the Secretary shall compute a national limited purchase price—

(i) for 1991, equal to the local purchase price computed under subparagraph (A)(ii) for the item for the year, except that such national limited purchase price may not exceed 100 percent of the weighted average of all local purchase prices for the item computed under such subparagraph for the year, and may not be less than 85 percent of the weighted average of all local purchase prices for the item computed under such subparagraph for the year;

(ii) for 1992 and 1993, the amount determined under this subparagraph for the preceding year increased by the covered item update for such subsequent year;

(iii) for 1994, the local purchase price computed under subparagraph (A)(ii) for the item for the year, except that such national limited purchase price may not exceed 100 percent of the median of all local purchase prices computed for the item under such subparagraph for the year and may not be less than 85 percent of the median of all local purchase prices computed under such subparagraph for the item for the year; and

(iv) for each subsequent year, equal to the amount determined under this subparagraph for the preceding year increased by the covered item update for such subsequent year.

(C) Purchase price recognized. For purposes of paragraphs (6) and (7), the amount that is recognized under this paragraph as the purchase price for each item furnished—

(i) in 1989 or 1990, is 100 percent of the local purchase price computed under subparagraph (A)(ii)(I);

(ii) in 1991, is the sum of (I) 67 percent of the local purchase price computed under subparagraph (A)(ii)(II) for 1991, and (II) 33 percent of the national limited purchase price computed under subparagraph (B) for 1991;

(iii) in 1992, is the sum of (I) 33 percent of the local purchase price computed under subparagraph (A)(ii)(III) for 1992, and (II) 67 percent of the national limited purchase price computed under subparagraph (B) for 1992; and

(iv) in 1993 or a subsequent year, is the national limited purchase price computed under subparagraph (B) for that year.

(9) Monthly payment amount recognized with respect to oxygen and oxygen equipment. For purposes of paragraph (5), the amount that is recognized under this paragraph for payment for oxygen and oxygen equipment is the monthly payment amount described in subparagraph (C) of this paragraph. Such amount shall be computed separately (i) for all items of oxygen and oxygen equipment (other than portable oxygen equipment) and (ii) for portable oxygen equipment (each such group referred to in this paragraph as an "item").

(A) Computation of local monthly payment rate. Each carrier under this section shall compute a base local payment rate for each item as follows:

(i) The carrier shall compute a base local average monthly payment rate per beneficiary as an amount equal to (I) the total reasonable charges for the item during the 12-month period ending with December 1986, divided by (II) the total number of months for all beneficiaries receiving the item in the area during the 12-month period for which the carrier made payment for the item under this title [42 USCS §§ 1395 et seq.].

(ii) The carrier shall compute a local average monthly payment rate for the item applicable—

(I) to 1989 and 1990, equal to 95 percent of the base local average monthly payment rate computed under clause (i) for the item increased by the percentage increase in the consumer price index for all urban consumers (U.S. city average) for the 6-month period ending with December 1987, or

(II) to 1991, 1992, 1993, and 1994, equal to the local average monthly payment rate computed under this clause for the item for the previous year increased by the covered item increase for the year.

(B) Computation of national limited monthly payment rate. With respect to the furnishing of an item in a year, the Secretary shall compute a national limited monthly payment rate equal to—

(i) for 1991, the local monthly payment rate computed under subparagraph (A)(ii)(II) for the item for the year, except that such national limited monthly payment rate may not exceed 100 percent of the weighted average of all local monthly payment rates computed for the item under such subparagraph for the year, and may not be less than 85 percent of the weighted average of all local monthly payment rates computed for the item under such subparagraph for the year;

(ii) for 1992 and 1993, the amount determined under this subparagraph for the preceding year increased by the covered item update for such subsequent year;

(iii) for 1994, the local monthly payment rate computed under subparagraph (A)(ii) for the item for the year, except that such national limited monthly payment rate may not exceed 100 percent of the median of all local monthly payment rates computed for the item under such subparagraph for the year and may not be less than 85 percent of the median of all local monthly payment rates computed for the item under such subparagraph for the year;

(iv) for 1995, 1996, and 1997, equal to the amount determined under this subparagraph for the preceding year increased by the covered item update for such subsequent year;

(v) for 1998, 75 percent of the amount determined under this subparagraph for 1997; and

(vi) for 1999 and each subsequent year, 70 percent of the amount determined under this subparagraph for 1997.

(C) Monthly payment amount recognized. For purposes of paragraph (5), the amount that is recognized under this paragraph as the base monthly payment amount for each item furnished—

(i) in 1989 and in 1990, is 100 percent of the local average monthly payment rate computed under subparagraph (A)(ii) for the item;

(ii) in 1991, is the sum of (I) 67 percent of the local average monthly payment rate computed under subparagraph (A)(ii)(II) for the item for 1991, and (II) 33 percent of the national limited monthly payment rate computed under subparagraph (B)(i) for the item for 1991;

(iii) in 1992, is the sum of (I) 33 percent of the local average monthly payment rate computed under subparagraph (A)(ii)(II) for the item for 1992, and (II) 67 percent of the national limited monthly payment rate computed under subparagraph (B)(ii) for the item for 1992; and

(iv) in a subsequent year, is the regional monthly payment rate computed under subparagraph (B) for the item for that year.

(D) Authority to create classes. (i) In general. Subject to clause (ii), the Secretary may establish separate classes for any item of oxygen and oxygen equipment and separate national limited monthly payment rates for each of such classes.

(ii) Budget neutrality. The Secretary may take actions under clause (i) only to the extent such actions do not result in expenditures for any year to be more or less than the expenditures which would have been made if such actions had not been taken.

(10) Exceptions and adjustments. (A) Areas outside continental United States. Exceptions to the amounts recognized under the previous provisions of this subsection shall be made to take into account the unique circumstances of covered items furnished in Alaska, Hawaii, or Puerto Rico.

(B) Adjustment for inherent reasonableness. The Secretary is authorized to apply the provisions of paragraphs (8) and (9) of section 1842(b) [42 USCS § 1395u(b)] to covered items and suppliers of such items and payments under this subsection in an area and with respect to covered items and services for which the Secretary does not make a payment amount adjustment under paragraph (1)(F).

(C) Transcutaneous electrical nerve stimulator (TENS). In order to permit an attending physician time to determine whether the purchase of a transcutaneous electrical nerve stimulator is medically appropriate for a particular patient, the Secretary may determine an appropriate payment amount for the initial rental of such item for a period of not more than 2 months. If such item is subsequently purchased, the payment amount with respect to such purchase is the payment amount determined under paragraph (2).

(11) Improper billing and requirement of physician order. (A) Improper billing for certain rental items. Notwithstanding any other provision of this title [42 USCS §§ 1395 et seq.], a supplier of a covered item for which payment is made under this subsection and which is furnished on a rental basis shall continue to supply the item without charge (other than a charge provided under this subsection for the maintenance and servicing of the item) after rental payments may no longer be made under this subsection. If a supplier knowingly and willfully violates the previous sentence, the Secretary may apply sanctions against the supplier under section 1842(j)(2) [42 USCS § 1395u(j)(2)] in the same manner such sanctions may apply with respect to a physician.

(B) Requirement of physician order. (i) **[Caution: For provisions applicable to written orders and certifications made before July 1, 2010, see 2010 amendment note below.]** In general. The Secretary is authorized to require, for specified covered items, that payment may be made under this subsection with respect to the item only if a physician enrolled under section 1866(j) [42 USCS § 1395cc(j)] or an eligible professional under section 1848(k)(3)(B) [42 USCS § 1395w-4(k)(3)(B)] that is enrolled under section 1866(j) [42 USCS § 1395cc(j)] has communicated to the supplier, before delivery of the item, a written order for the item.

(ii) Requirement for face to face encounter. The Secretary shall require that such an order be written pursuant to the physician documenting that a physician, a physician assistant, a nurse practitioner, or a clinical nurse specialist (as those terms are defined in section 1861(aa)(5) [42 USCS § 1395x(aa)(5)]) has had a face-to-face encounter (including through use of telehealth under subsection (m) and other than with respect to encounters that are incident to services involved) with the individual involved during the 6-month period preceding such written order, or other reasonable timeframe as determined by the Secretary.

(12) Regional carriers. The Secretary may designate, by regulation under section 1842 [42 USCS § 1395u], one carrier for one or more entire regions to process all claims within the region for covered items under this section.

(13) "Covered item" defined. In this subsection, the term "covered item" means durable medical equipment (as defined in section 1861(n) [42 USCS § 1395x(n)]), including such equipment described in section 1861(m)(5) [42 USCS § 1395x(m)(5)], but not including implantable items for which payment may be made under section 1833(t) [42 USCS § 1395l(t)][)].

(14) Covered item update. In this subsection, the term "covered item update" means, with respect to a year—

(A) for 1991 and 1992, the percentage increase in the consumer price index for all urban consumers (U.S. city average) for the 12-month period ending with June of the previous year reduced by 1 percentage point;

(B) for 1993, 1994, 1995, 1996, and 1997, the percentage increase in the consumer price index for all urban consumers (U.S. city average) for the 12-month period ending with June of the previous year;

(C) for each of the years 1998 through 2000, 0 percentage points;

(D) for 2001, the percentage increase in the consumer price index for all urban consumers (U.S. city average) for the 12-month period ending with June 2000;

(E) for 2002, 0 percentage points;

(F) for 2003, the percentage increase in the consumer price index for all urban consumers (U.S. urban average) for the 12-month period ending with June of the 2002;

(G) for 2004 through 2006—

(i) subject to clause (ii), in the case of class III medical devices described in section 513(a)(1)(C) of the Federal Food, Drug, and Cosmetic Act (21 U.S.C. 360(c)(1)(C) [21 USCS § 360c(c)(1)(C)]), the percentage increase described in subparagraph (B) for the year involved; and

(ii) in the case of covered items not described in clause (i), 0 percentage points;

(H) for 2007—

(i) subject to clause (ii), in the case of class III medical devices described in section 513(a)(1)(C) of the Federal Food, Drug, and Cosmetic Act (21 U.S.C. 360(c)(1)(C) [21 USCS § 360c(c)(1)(C)]), the percentage change determined by the Secretary to be appropriate taking into account recommendations contained in the report of the Comptroller General of the United States under section 302(c)(1)(B) of the Medicare Prescription Drug, Improvement, and Modernization Act of 2003 [note to this section]; and

(ii) in the case of covered items not described in clause (i), 0 percentage points;

(I) for 2008—

(i) subject to clause (ii), in the case of class III medical devices described in section 513(a)(1)(C) of the Federal Food, Drug, and Cosmetic Act (21 U.S.C. 360(c)(1)(C) [21 USCS § 360c(c)(1)(C)]), the percentage increase described in subparagraph (B) (as applied to the payment amount for 2007 determined after the application of the percentage change under subparagraph (H)(i)); and

(ii) in the case of covered items not described in clause (i), 0 percentage points;

(J) for 2009—

(i) in the case of items and services furnished in any geographic area, if such items or services were selected for competitive acquisition in any area under the competitive acquisition program under section 1847(a)(1)(B)(i)(I) [42 USCS § 1395w-3(a)(1)(B)(i)(I)] before July 1, 2008, including related accessories but only if furnished with such items and services selected for such competition and diabetic supplies but only if furnished through mail order, -9.5 percent; or

(ii) in the case of other items and services, the percentage increase in the consumer price index for all urban consumers (U.S. urban average) for the 12-month period ending with June 2008;

(K) for 2010, the percentage increase in the consumer price index for all urban consumers (U.S. urban average) for the 12-month period ending with June of the previous year;

(L) for 2011 and each subsequent year—

(i) the percentage increase in the consumer price index for all urban consumers (United States city average) for the 12-month period ending with June of the previous year, reduced by—

(ii) the productivity adjustment described in section 1886(b)(3)(B)(xi)(II) [42 USCS § 1395ww(b)(3)(B)(xi)(II)].

The application of subparagraph (L)(ii) may result in the covered item update under this paragraph being less than 0.0 for a year, and may result in payment rates under this subsection for a year being less than such payment rates for the preceding year.

(15) Advance determinations of coverage for certain items. (A) Development of lists of items by Secretary. The Secretary may develop and periodically update a list of items for which payment may be made under this subsection that the Secretary determines, on the basis of prior payment experience, are frequently subject to unnecessary utilization throughout a carrier's entire service area or a portion of such area.

(B) Development of lists of suppliers by Secretary. The Secretary may develop and periodically update a list of suppliers of items for which payment may be made under this subsection with respect to whom—

(i) the Secretary has found that a substantial number of claims for payment under this part for items furnished by the supplier have been denied on the basis of the application of section 1862(a)(1) [42 USCS § 1395y(a)(1)]; or

(ii) the Secretary has identified a pattern of overutilization resulting from the business practice of the supplier.

(C) Determinations of coverage in advance. A carrier shall determine in advance of delivery of an item whether payment for the item may not be made because the item is not covered or because of the application of section 1862(a)(1) [42 USCS § 1395y(a)(1)] if—

(i) the item is included on the list developed by the Secretary under subparagraph (A);

(ii) the item is furnished by a supplier included on the list developed by the Secretary under subparagraph (B); or

(iii) the item is a customized item (other than inexpensive items specified by the Secretary) and the patient to whom the item is to be furnished or the supplier requests that such advance determination be made.

(16) Disclosure of information and surety bond. The Secretary shall not provide for the issuance (or renewal) of a provider number for a supplier of durable medical equipment, for purposes of payment under this part [42 USCS §§ 1395j et seq.] for durable medical equipment furnished by the supplier, unless the supplier provides the Secretary on a continuing basis—

(A) with—

(i) full and complete information as to the identity of each person with an ownership or control interest (as defined in section 1124(a)(3) [42 USCS § 1320a-3(a)(3)]) in the supplier or in any subcontractor (as defined by the Secretary in regulations) in which the supplier directly or indirectly has a 5 percent or more ownership interest; and

(ii) to the extent determined to be feasible under regulations of the Secretary, the name of any disclosing entity (as defined in section 1124(a)(2) [42 USCS § 1320a-3(a)(2)]) with respect to which a person with such an ownership or control interest in the supplier is a person with such an ownership or control interest in the disclosing entity; and

(B) with a surety bond in a form specified by the Secretary and in an amount that is not less than $50,000 that the Secretary determines is commensurate with the volume of the billing of the supplier.

The Secretary may waive the requirement of a bond under subparagraph (B) in the case of a supplier that provides a comparable surety bond under State law. The Secretary, at the Secretary's discretion, may impose the requirements of the first sentence with respect to some or all providers of items or services under part A [42 USCS §§ 1395c et seq.] or some or all suppliers or other persons (other than physicians or other practitioners, as defined in section 1842(b)(18)(C) [42 USCS § 1395u(b)(18)(C)]) who furnish items or services under this part [42 USCS §§ 1395j et seq.].

(17) Prohibition against unsolicited telephone contacts by suppliers. (A) In general. A supplier of a covered item under this subsection may not contact an individual enrolled under this part by telephone regarding the furnishing of a covered item to the individual unless 1 of the following applies:

(i) The individual has given written permission to the supplier to make contact by telephone regarding the furnishing of a covered item.

(ii) The supplier has furnished a covered item to the individual and the supplier is contacting the individual only regarding the furnishing of such covered item.

(iii) If the contact is regarding the furnishing of a covered item other than a covered item already furnished to the individual, the supplier has furnished at least 1 covered item to the individual during the 15-month period preceding the date on which the supplier makes such contact.

(B) Prohibiting payment for items furnished subsequent to unsolicited contacts. If a supplier knowingly contacts an individual in violation of subparagraph (A), no payment may be made under this part for any item subsequently furnished to the individual by the supplier.

(C) Exclusion from program for suppliers engaging in pattern of unsolicited contacts. If a supplier knowingly contacts individuals in violation of subparagraph (A) to such an extent that the supplier's conduct establishes a pattern of contacts in violation of such subparagraph, the Secretary shall exclude the supplier from participation in the programs under this Act, in accordance with the procedures set forth in subsections (c), (f), and (g) of section 1128 [42 USCS § 1320a-7].

(18) Refund of amounts collected for certain disallowed items. (A) In general. If a nonparticipating supplier furnishes to an individual enrolled under this part [42 USCS §§ 1395j et seq.] a covered item for which no payment may be made under this part by reason of paragraph (17)(B), the supplier shall refund on a timely basis to the patient (and shall be liable to the patient for) any amounts collected from the patient for the item, unless—

(i) the supplier establishes that the supplier did not know and could not reasonably have been expected to know that payment may not be made for the item by reason of paragraph (17)(B), or

(ii) before the item was furnished, the patient was informed that payment under this part may not be made for that item and the patient has agreed to pay for that item.

(B) Sanctions. If a supplier knowingly and willfully fails to make refunds in violation of subparagraph (A), the Secretary may apply sanctions against the supplier in accordance with section 1842(j)(2) [42 USCS § 1395u(j)(2)].

(C) Notice. Each carrier with a contract in effect under this part [42 USCS §§ 1395j et seq.] with respect to suppliers of covered items shall send any notice of denial of payment for covered items by reason of paragraph (17)(B) and for which payment is not requested on an assignment-related basis to the supplier and the patient involved.

(D) Timely basis defined. A refund under subparagraph (A) is considered to be on a timely basis only if—

(i) in the case of a supplier who does not request reconsideration or seek appeal on a timely basis, the refund is made within 30 days after the date the supplier receives a denial notice under subparagraph (C), or

(ii) in the case in which such a reconsideration or appeal is taken, the refund is made within 15 days after the date the supplier receives notice of an adverse determination on reconsideration or appeal.

(19) Certain upgraded items. (A) Individual's right to choose upgraded item. Notwithstanding any other provision of this title [42 USCS §§ 1395 et seq.], the Secretary may issue regulations under which an individual may purchase or rent from a supplier an item of upgraded durable medical equipment for which payment would be made under this subsection if the item were a standard item.

(B) Payments to supplier. In the case of the purchase or rental of an upgraded item under subparagraph (A)—

(i) the supplier shall receive payment under this subsection with respect to such item as if such item were a standard item; and

(ii) the individual purchasing or renting the item shall pay the supplier an amount equal to the difference between the supplier's charge and the amount under clause (i).

In no event may the supplier's charge for an upgraded item exceed the applicable fee schedule amount (if any) for such item.

(C) Consumer protection safeguards. Any regulations under subparagraph (A) shall provide for consumer protection standards with respect to the furnishing of upgraded equipment under subparagraph (A). Such regulations shall provide for—

(i) determination of fair market prices with respect to an upgraded item;

(ii) full disclosure of the availability and price of standard items and proof of receipt of such disclosure information by the beneficiary before the furnishing of the upgraded item;

(iii) conditions of participation for suppliers in the billing arrangement;

(iv) sanctions of suppliers who are determined to engage in coercive or abusive practices, including exclusion; and

(v) such other safeguards as the Secretary determines are necessary.

(20) Identification of quality standards. (A) In general. Subject to subparagraph (C), the Secretary shall establish and implement quality standards for suppliers of items and services described in subparagraph (D) to be applied by recognized independent accreditation organizations (as designated under subparagraph (B)) and with which such suppliers shall be required to comply in order to—

(i) furnish any such item or service for which payment is made under this part [42 USCS §§ 1395j et seq.]; and

(ii) receive or retain a provider or supplier number used to submit claims for reimbursement for any such item or service for which payment may be made under this title [42 USCS §§ 1395 et seq.].

(B) Designation of independent accreditation organizations **[Caution: For provisions applicable to accreditations of hospitals granted before July 15, 2010, see 2008 amendment note below.]**. Not later than the date that is 1 year after the date on which the Secretary implements the quality standards under subparagraph (A), notwithstanding section 1865(a) [42 USCS § 1395bb(a)], the Secretary shall designate and approve one or more independent accreditation organizations for purposes of such subparagraph.

(C) Quality standards. The quality standards described in subparagraph (A) may not be less stringent than the quality standards that would otherwise apply if this paragraph did not apply and shall include consumer services standards.

(D) Items and services described. The items and services described in this subparagraph are the following items and services, as the Secretary determines appropriate:

(i) Covered items (as defined in paragraph (13)) for which payment may otherwise be made under this subsection.

(ii) Prosthetic devices and orthotics and prosthetics described in section 1834(h)(4) [subsec. (h)(4) of this section].

(iii) Items and services described in section 1842(s)(2) [42 USCS § 1395u(s)(2)].

(E) Implementation. The Secretary may establish by program instruction or otherwise the quality standards under this paragraph, including subparagraph (F), after consultation with representatives of relevant parties. Such standards shall be applied prospectively and shall be published on the Internet website of the Centers for Medicare & Medicaid Services.

(F) Application of accreditation requirement. In implementing quality standards under this paragraph—

(i) subject to clause (ii) and subparagraph (G), the Secretary shall require suppliers furnishing items and services described in subparagraph (D) on or after October 1, 2009, directly or as a subcontractor for another entity, to have submitted to the Secretary evidence of accreditation by an accreditation organization designated under subparagraph (B) as meeting applicable quality standards, except that the Secretary shall not require under this clause pharmacies to obtain such accreditation before January 1, 2010, except that the Secretary shall not require a pharmacy to have submitted to the Secretary such evidence of accreditation prior to January 1, 2011; and

(ii) in applying such standards and the accreditation requirement of clause (i) with respect to eligible professionals (as defined in section 1848(k)(3)(B) [42 USCS § 1395w-4(k)(3)(B)]), and including such other persons, such as orthotists and prosthetists, as specified by the Secretary, furnishing such items and services—

(I) such standards and accreditation requirement shall not apply to such professionals and persons unless the Secretary determines that the standards being applied are designed specifically to be applied to such professionals and persons; and

(II) the Secretary may exempt such professionals and persons from such standards and requirement if the Secretary determines that licensing, accreditation, or other mandatory quality requirements apply to such professionals and persons with respect to the furnishing of such items and services.

(G) Application of accreditation requirement to certain pharmacies. (i) In general. With respect to items and services furnished on or after January 1, 2011, in implementing quality standards under this paragraph—

(I) subject to subclause (II), in applying such standards and the accreditation requirement of subparagraph (F)(i) with respect to pharmacies described in clause (ii) furnishing such items and services, such standards and accreditation requirement shall not apply to such pharmacies; and

(II) the Secretary may apply to such pharmacies an alternative accreditation requirement established by the Secretary if the Secretary determines such alternative accreditation requirement is more appropriate for such pharmacies.

(ii) Pharmacies described. A pharmacy described in this clause is a pharmacy that meets each of the following criteria:

(I) The total billings by the pharmacy for such items and services under this title are less than 5 percent of total pharmacy sales, as determined based on the average total pharmacy sales for the previous 3 calendar years, 3 fiscal years, or other yearly period specified by the Secretary.

(II) The pharmacy has been enrolled under section 1866(j) [42 USCS § 1395cc(j)] as a supplier of durable medical equipment, prosthetics, orthotics, and supplies, has been issued (which may include the renewal of) a provider number for at least 5 years, and for which a final adverse action (as defined in section 424.57(a) of title 42, Code of Federal Regulations) has not been imposed in the past 5 years.

(III) The pharmacy submits to the Secretary an attestation, in a form and manner, and at a time, specified by the Secretary, that the pharmacy meets the criteria described in subclauses (I) and (II). Such attestation shall be subject to section 1001 of title 18, United States Code.

(IV) The pharmacy agrees to submit materials as requested by the Secretary, or during the course of an audit conducted on a random sample of pharmacies selected annually, to verify that the pharmacy meets the criteria described in subclauses (I) and (II). Materials submitted under the preceding sentence shall include a certification by an accountant on behalf of the pharmacy or the submission of tax returns filed by the pharmacy during the relevant periods, as requested by the Secretary.

(21) Special payment rule for specified items and supplies. (A) In general. Notwithstanding the preceding provisions of this subsection, for specified items and supplies (described in subparagraph (B)) furnished during 2005, the payment amount otherwise determined under this subsection for such specified items and supplies shall be reduced by the percentage difference between—

(i) the amount of payment otherwise determined for the specified item or supply under this subsection for 2002, and

(ii) the amount of payment for the specified item or supply under chapter 89 of title 5, United States Code [5 USCS §§ 8901 et seq.], as identified in the column entitled "Median FEHP Price" in the table entitled "SUMMARY OF MEDICARE PRICES COMPARED TO VA, MEDICAID, RETAIL, AND FEHP PRICES FOR 16 ITEMS" included in the Testimony of the Inspector General before the Senate Committee on Appropriations, June 12, 2002, or any subsequent report by the Inspector General.

(B) Specified item or supply described. For purposes of subparagraph (A), a specified item or supply means oxygen and oxygen equipment, standard wheelchairs (including standard power wheelchairs), nebulizers, diabetic supplies consisting of lancets and testing strips, hospital beds, and air mattresses, but only if the HCPCS code for the item or supply is identified in a table referred to in subparagraph (A)(ii).

(C) Application of update to special payment amount. The covered item update under paragraph (14) for specified items and supplies for 2006 and each subsequent year shall be applied to the payment amount under subparagraph (A) unless payment is made for such items and supplies under section 1847 [42 USCS § 1395w-3].

(b) Fee schedules for radiologist services. (1) Development. The Secretary shall develop—

(A) a relative value scale to serve as the basis for the payment for radiologist services under this part [42 USCS §§ 1395j et seq.], and

(B) using such scale and appropriate conversion factors and subject to subsection (c)(1)(A), fee schedules (on a regional, statewide, locality, or carrier service area basis) for payment for radiologist services under this part [42 USCS §§ 1395j et seq.], to be implemented for such services furnished during 1989.

(2) Consultation. In carrying out paragraph (1), the Secretary shall regularly consult closely with the Physician Payment Review Commission [Medicare Payment Advisory Commission], the American College of Radiology, and other organizations representing physicians or suppliers who furnish radiologist services and shall share with them the data and data analysis being used to make the determinations under paragraph (1), including data on variations in current medicare payments by geographic area, and by service and physician specialty.

(3) Considerations. In developing the relative value scale and fee schedules under paragraph (1), the Secretary—

(A) shall take into consideration variations in the cost of furnishing such services among geographic areas and among different sites where services are furnished, and

(B) may also take into consideration such other factors respecting the manner in which physicians in different specialties furnish such services as may be appropriate to assure that payment amounts are equitable and designed to promote effective and efficient provision of radiologist services by physicians in the different specialties.

(4) Savings. (A) Budget neutral fee schedules. The Secretary shall develop preliminary fee schedules for 1989, which are designed to result in the same amount of aggregate payments (net of any coinsurance and deductibles under sections 1833(a)(1)(J) and 1833(b) [42 USCS § 1395l(a)(1)(J) and (b)]) for radiologist services furnished in 1989 as would have been made if this subsection had not been enacted.

(B) Initial savings. The fee schedules established for payment purposes under this subsection for services furnished in 1989 shall be 97 percent of the amounts permitted under the preliminary fee schedules developed under subparagraph (A).

(C) 1990 Fee schedules. For radiologist services (other than portable X-ray services) furnished under this part [42 USCS §§ 1395j et seq.] during 1990, after March 31 of such year, the conversion factors used under this subsection shall be 96 percent of the conversion factors that applied under this subsection as of December 31, 1989.

(D) 1991 fee schedules. For radiologist services (other than portable X-ray services) furnished under this part [42 USCS §§ 1395j et seq.] during 1991, the conversion factors used in a locality under this subsection shall, subject to clause (vii), be reduced to the adjusted conversion factor for the locality determined as follows:

(i) National weighted average conversion factor. The Secretary shall estimate the national weighted average of the conversion factors used under this subsection for services furnished during 1990 beginning on April 1, using the best available data.

(ii) Reduced national weighted average. The national weighted average estimated under clause (i) shall be reduced by 13 percent.

(iii) Computation of 1990 locality index relative to national average. The Secretary shall establish an index which reflects, for each locality, the ratio of the conversion factor used in the locality under this subsection to the national weighted average estimated under clause (i).

(iv) Adjusted conversion factor. The adjusted conversion factor for the professional or technical component of a service in a locality is the sum of ½ of the locally-adjusted amount determined under clause (v) and ½ of the GPCI-adjusted amount determined under clause (vi).

(v) Locally-adjusted amount. For purposes of clause (iv), the locally adjusted amount determined under this clause is the product of (I) the national weighted average conversion factor computed under clause (ii), and (II) the index value established under clause (iii) for the locality.

(vi) GPCI-adjusted amount. For purposes of clause (iv), the GPCI-adjusted amount determined under this clause is the sum of—

(I) the product of (a) the portion of the reduced national weighted average conversion factor computed under clause (ii) which is attributable to physician work and (b) the geographic work index value for the locality (specified in Addendum C to the Model Fee Schedule for Physician Services (published on September 4, 1990, 55 Federal Register pp. 36238–36243)); and

(II) the product of (a) the remaining portion of the reduced national weighted average conversion factor computed under clause (ii), and (b) the geographic practice cost index value specified in section 1842(b)(14)(C)(iv) [42 USCS § 1395u(b)(14)(C)(iv)] for the locality.

In applying this clause with respect to the professional component of a service, 80 percent of the conversion factor shall be considered to be attributable to physician work and with respect to the technical component of the service, 0 percent shall be considered to be attributable to physician work.

(vii) Limits on conversion factor. The conversion factor to be applied to a locality to the professional or technical component of a service shall not be reduced under this subparagraph by more than 9.5 percent below the conversion factor applied in the locality under subparagraph (C) to such component, but in no case shall the conversion factor be less than 60 percent of the national weighted average of the conversion factors (computed under clause (i)).

(E) Rule for certain scanning services. In the case of the technical components of magnetic resonance imaging (MRI) services and computer assisted tomography (CAT) services furnished after December 31, 1990, the amount otherwise payable shall be reduced by 10 percent.

(F) Subsequent updating. For radiologist services furnished in subsequent years, the fee schedules shall be the schedules for the previous year updated by the percentage increase in the MEI(as defined in section 1842(i)(3) [42 USCS § 1395u(i)(3)]) for the year.

(G) Nonparticipating physicians and suppliers. Each fee schedule so established shall provide that the payment rate recognized for nonparticipating physicians and suppliers is equal to the appropriate percent (as defined in section 1842(b)(4)(A)(iv) [42 USCS § 1395u(b)(4)(A)(iv)]) of the payment rate recognized for participating physicians and suppliers.

(5) Limiting charges of nonparticipating physicians and suppliers. (A) In general. In the case of radiologist services furnished after January 1, 1989, for which payment is made under a fee schedule under this subsection, if a nonparticipating physician or supplier furnishes the service to an individual entitled to benefits under this part [42 USCS §§ 1395j et seq.], the physician or supplier may not charge the individual more than the limiting charge (as defined in subparagraph (B)).

(B) Limiting charge defined. In subparagraph (A), the term "limiting charge" means, with respect to a service furnished—

(i) in 1989, 125 percent of the amount specified for the service in the appropriate fee schedule established under paragraph (1),

(ii) in 1990, 120 percent of the amount specified for the service in the appropriate fee schedule established under paragraph (1), and

(iii) after 1990, 115 percent of the amount specified for the service in the appropriate fee schedule established under paragraph (1).

(C) Enforcement. If a physician or supplier knowingly and willfully bills in violation of subparagraph (A), the Secretary may apply sanctions against such physician or supplier in accordance with section 1842(j)(2) [42 USCS § 1395u(j)(2)] in the same manner as such sanctions may apply to a physician.

(6) Radiologist services defined. For the purposes of this subsection and section 1833(a)(1)(J) [42 USCS § 1395l(a)(1)(J)], the term "radiologist services" only includes radiology services performed by, or under the direction or supervision of, a physician—

(A) who is certified, or eligible to be certified, by the American Board of Radiology, or

(B) for whom radiology services account for at least 50 percent of the total amount of charges made under this part [42 USCS §§ 1395j et seq.].

(c) Payment and standards for screening mammography. (1) In general. With respect to expenses incurred for screening mammography (as defined in section 1861(jj) [42 USCS § 1395x(jj)]), payment may be made only—

(A) for screening mammography conducted consistent with the frequency permitted under paragraph (2); and

(B) if the screening mammography is conducted by a facility that has a certificate (or provisional certificate) issued under section 354 of the Public Health Service Act [42 USCS § 263b].

(2) Frequency covered. (A) In general. Subject to revision by the Secretary under subparagraph (B)—

(i) no payment may be made under this part for screening mammography performed on a woman under 35 years of age;

(ii) payment may be made under this part for only one screening mammography performed on a woman over 34 years of age, but under 40 years of age; and

(iii) in the case of a woman over 39 years of age, payment may not be made under this part for screening mammography performed within 11 months following the month in which a previous screening mammography was performed.

(B) Revision of frequency. (i) Review. The Secretary, in consultation with the Director of the National Cancer Institute, shall review periodically the appropriate frequency for performing screening mammography, based on age and such other factors as the Secretary believes to be pertinent.

(ii) Revision of frequency. The Secretary, taking into consideration the review made under clause (i), may revise from time to time the frequency with which screening mammography may be paid for under this subsection.

(d) Frequency limits and payment for colorectal cancer screening tests. (1) Screening fecal-occult blood tests. (A) Payment amount. The payment amount for colorectal cancer screening tests consisting of screening fecal-occult blood tests is equal to the payment amount established for diagnostic fecal-occult blood tests under section 1833(h) [42 USCS § 1395l(h)].

(B) Frequency limit. No payment may be made under this part [42 USCS §§ 1395j et seq.] for a colorectal cancer screening test consisting of a screening fecal-occult blood test—

(i) if the individual is under 50 years of age; or

(ii) if the test is performed within the 11 months after a previous screening fecal-occult blood test.

(2) Screening flexible sigmoidoscopies. (A) Fee schedule. With respect to colorectal cancer screening tests consisting of screening flexible sigmoidoscopies, payment under section 1848 [42 USCS § 1395w-4] shall be consistent with payment under such section for similar or related services.

(B) Payment limit. In the case of screening flexible sigmoidoscopy services, payment under this part [42 USCS §§ 1395j et seq.] shall not exceed such amount as the Secretary specifies, based upon the rates recognized for diagnostic flexible sigmoidoscopy services.

(C) Facility payment limit. (i) In general. Notwithstanding subsections (i)(2)(A) and (t) of section 1833 [42 USCS § 1395l(i)(2)(A) and (t)], in the case of screening flexible sigmoidoscopy services furnished on or after January 1, 1999, that—

(I) in accordance with regulations, may be performed in an ambulatory surgical center and for which the Secretary permits ambulatory surgical center payments under this part [42 USCS §§ 1395j et seq.], and

(II) are performed in an ambulatory surgical center or hospital outpatient department,

payment under this part [42 USCS §§ 1395j et seq.] shall be based on the lesser of the amount under the fee schedule that would apply to such services if they were performed in a hospital outpatient department in an area or the amount under the fee schedule that would apply to such services if they were performed in an ambulatory surgical center in the same area.

(ii) Limitation on coinsurance. Notwithstanding any other provision of this title [42

USCS §§ 1395 et seq.], in the case of a beneficiary who receives the services described in clause (i)—

(I) in computing the amount of any applicable copayment, the computation of such coinsurance shall be based upon the fee schedule under which payment is made for the services, and

(II) the amount of such coinsurance is equal to 25 percent of the payment amount under the fee schedule described in subclause (I).

(D) Special rule for detected lesions. If during the course of such screening flexible sigmoidoscopy, a lesion or growth is detected which results in a biopsy or removal of the lesion or growth, payment under this part [42 USCS §§ 1395j et seq.] shall not be made for the screening flexible sigmoidoscopy but shall be made for the procedure classified as a flexible sigmoidoscopy with such biopsy or removal.

(E) Frequency limit. No payment may be made under this part [42 USCS §§ 1395j et seq.] for a colorectal cancer screening test consisting of a screening flexible sigmoidoscopy—

(i) if the individual is under 50 years of age; or

(ii) if the procedure is performed within the 47 months after a previous screening flexible sigmoidoscopy or, in the case of an individual who is not at high risk for colorectal cancer, if the procedure is performed within the 119 months after a previous screening colonoscopy.

(3) Screening colonoscopy. (A) Fee schedule. With respect to colorectal cancer screening test consisting of a screening colonoscopy, payment under section 1848 shall be consistent with payment amounts under such section for similar or related services.

(B) Payment limit. In the case of screening colonoscopy services, payment under this part [42 USCS §§ 1395j et seq.] shall not exceed such amount as the Secretary specifies, based upon the rates recognized for diagnostic colonoscopy services.

(C) Facility payment limit. (i) In general. Notwithstanding subsections (i)(2)(A) and (t) of section 1833 [42 USCS § 1395l(i)(2)(A) and (t)], in the case of screening colonoscopy services furnished on or after January 1, 1999, that are performed in an ambulatory surgical center or a hospital outpatient department, payment under this part [42 USCS §§ 1395j et seq.] shall be based on the lesser of the amount under the fee schedule that would apply to such services if they were performed in a hospital outpatient department in an area or the amount under the fee schedule that would apply to such services if they were performed in an ambulatory surgical center in the same area.

(ii) Limitation on coinsurance. Notwithstanding any other provision of this title [42 USCS §§ 1395 et seq.], in the case of a beneficiary who receives the services described in clause (i)—

(I) in computing the amount of any applicable coinsurance, the computation of such coinsurance shall be based upon the fee schedule under which payment is made for the services, and

(II) the amount of such coinsurance is equal to 25 percent of the payment amount under the fee schedule described in subclause (I).

(D) Special rule for detected lesions. If during the course of such screening colonoscopy, a lesion or growth is detected which results in a biopsy or removal of the lesion or growth, payment under this part [42 USCS §§ 1395j et seq.] shall not be made for the screening colonoscopy but shall be made for the procedure classified as a colonoscopy with such biopsy or removal.

(E) Frequency limit. No payment may be made under this part [42 USCS §§ 1395j et seq.] for a colorectal cancer screening test consisting of a screening colonoscopy for individuals at high risk for colorectal cancer if the procedure is performed within the 23 months after a previous screening colonoscopy or for other individuals if the procedure is performed within the 119 months after a previous screening colonoscopy or within 47 months after a previous screening flexible sigmoidoscopy.

(e) Accreditation requirement for advanced diagnostic imaging services. (1) In general. (A) In general. Beginning with January 1, 2012, with respect to the technical component of advanced diagnostic imaging services for which payment is made under the fee schedule established under section 1848(b) [42 USCS § 1395w-4] and that are furnished by a supplier, payment may only be made if such supplier is accredited by an accreditation organization designated by the Secretary under paragraph (2)(B)(i).

(B) Advanced diagnostic imaging services defined. In this subsection, the term "advanced diagnostic imaging services" includes—

(i) diagnostic magnetic resonance imaging, computed tomography, and nuclear medicine (including positron emission tomography); and

(ii) such other diagnostic imaging services, including services described in section 1848(b)(4)(B) [42 USCS § 1395w-4(b)(4)(B)] (excluding X-ray, ultrasound, and fluoroscopy), as specified by the Secretary in consultation with physician specialty organizations and other stakeholders.

(C) Supplier defined. In this subsection, the term "supplier" has the meaning given such term in section 1861(d) [42 USCS § 1395x(d)].

(2) Accreditation organizations. (A) Factors for designation of accreditation organizations. The Secretary shall consider the following factors in designating accreditation organizations under subparagraph (B)(i) and in reviewing and modifying the list of accreditation organizations designated pursuant to subparagraph (C):

(i) The ability of the organization to conduct timely reviews of accreditation applications.

(ii) Whether the organization has established a process for the timely integration of new advanced diagnostic imaging services into the organization's accreditation program.

(iii) Whether the organization uses random site visits, site audits, or other strategies for ensuring accredited suppliers maintain adherence to the criteria described in paragraph (3).

(iv) The ability of the organization to take into account the capacities of suppliers located in a rural area (as defined in section 1886(d)(2)(D) [42 USCS § 1395ww(d)(2)(D)]).

(v) Whether the organization has established reasonable fees to be charged to suppliers applying for accreditation.

(vi) Such other factors as the Secretary determines appropriate.

(B) Designation. Not later than January 1, 2010, the Secretary shall designate organizations to accredit suppliers furnishing the technical component of advanced diagnostic imaging services. The list of accreditation organizations so designated may be modified pursuant to subparagraph (C).

(C) Review and modification of list of accreditation organizations. (i) In general. The Secretary shall review the list of accreditation organizations designated under subparagraph (B) taking into account the factors under subparagraph (A). Taking into account the results of such review, the Secretary may, by regulation, modify the list of accreditation organizations designated under subparagraph (B).

(ii) Special rule for accreditations done prior to removal from list of designated accreditation organizations. In the case where the Secretary removes an organization from the list of accreditation organizations designated under subparagraph (B), any supplier that is accredited by the organization during the period beginning on the date on which the organization is designated as an accreditation organization under subparagraph (B) and ending on the date on which the organization is removed from such list shall be considered to have been accredited by an organization designated by the Secretary under subparagraph (B) for the remaining period such accreditation is in effect.

(3) Criteria for accreditation. The Secretary shall establish procedures to ensure that the criteria used by an accreditation organization designated under paragraph (2)(B) to evaluate a supplier that furnishes the technical component of advanced diagnostic imaging services for the purpose of accreditation of such supplier is specific to each imaging modality. Such criteria shall include—

(A) standards for qualifications of medical personnel who are not physicians and who furnish the technical component of advanced diagnostic imaging services;

(B) standards for qualifications and responsibilities of medical directors and supervising physicians, including standards that recognize the considerations described in paragraph (4);

(C) procedures to ensure that equipment used in furnishing the technical component of advanced diagnostic imaging services meets performance specifications;

(D) standards that require the supplier have procedures in place to ensure the safety of persons who furnish the technical component of advanced diagnostic imaging services and individuals to whom such services are furnished;

(E) standards that require the establishment and maintenance of a quality assurance and quality control program by the supplier that is adequate and appropriate to ensure the reliability, clarity, and accuracy of the technical quality of diagnostic images produced by such supplier; and

(F) any other standards or procedures the Secretary determines appropriate.

(4) Recognition in standards for the evaluation of medical directors and supervising physicians. The standards described in paragraph (3)(B) shall recognize whether a medical director or supervising physician—

(A) in a particular specialty receives training in advanced diagnostic imaging services in a residency program;

(B) has attained, through experience, the necessary expertise to be a medical director or a supervising physician;

(C) has completed any continuing medical education courses relating to such services; or

(D) has met such other standards as the Secretary determines appropriate.

(5) Rule for accreditations made prior to designation. In the case of a supplier that is accredited before January 1, 2010, by an ac-

creditation organization designated by the Secretary under paragraph (2)(B) as of January 1, 2010, such supplier shall be considered to have been accredited by an organization designated by the Secretary under such paragraph as of January 1, 2012, for the remaining period such accreditation is in effect.

(f) Reduction in payments for physician pathology services during 1991. (1) In general. For physician pathology services furnished under this part [42 USCS §§ 1395j et seq.] during 1991, the prevailing charges used in a locality under this part [42 USCS §§ 1395j et seq.] shall be 7 percent below the prevailing charges used in the locality under this part [42 USCS §§ 1395j et seq.] in 1990 after March 31.

(2) Limitation. The prevailing charge for the technical and professional components of an [a] physician pathology service furnished by a physician through an independent laboratory shall not be reduced pursuant to paragraph (1) to the extent that such reduction would reduce such prevailing charge below 115 percent of the prevailing charge for the professional component of such service when furnished by a hospital-based physician in the same locality. For purposes of the preceding sentence, an independent laboratory is a laboratory that is independent of a hospital and separate from the attending or consulting physicians' office.

(g) Payment for outpatient critical access hospital services. (1) In general. The amount of payment for outpatient critical access hospital services of a critical access hospital is equal to 101 percent of the reasonable costs of the hospital in providing such services, unless the hospital makes the election under paragraph (2).

(2) Election of cost-based hospital outpatient service payment plus fee schedule for professional services. A critical access hospital may elect to be paid for outpatient critical access hospital services amounts equal to the sum of the following, less the amount that such hospital may charge as described in section 1866(a)(2)(A) [42 USCS § 1395cc(a)(2)(A)]:

(A) Facility fee. With respect to facility services, not including any services for which payment may be made under subparagraph (B), 101 percent of the reasonable costs of the critical access hospital in providing such services.

(B) Fee schedule for professional services. With respect to professional services otherwise included within outpatient critical access hospital services, 115 percent of such amounts as would otherwise be paid under this part if such services were not included in outpatient critical access hospital services. Subsections (x) and (y) of section 1833 [42 USCS § 1395l] shall not be taken into account in determining the amounts that would otherwise be paid pursuant to the preceding sentence.

The Secretary may not require, as a condition for applying subparagraph (B) with respect to a critical access hospital, that each physician or other practitioner providing professional services in the hospital must assign billing rights with respect to such services, except that such subparagraph shall not apply to those physicians and practitioners who have not assigned such billing rights.

(3) Disregarding charges. The payment amounts under this subsection shall be determined without regard to the amount of the customary or other charge.

(4) Treatment of clinical diagnostic laboratory services. No coinsurance, deductible, copayment, or other cost-sharing otherwise applicable under this part [42 USCS §§ 1395j et seq.] shall apply with respect to clinical diagnostic laboratory services furnished as an outpatient critical access hospital service. Nothing in this title [42 USCS §§ 1395 et seq.] shall be construed as providing for payment for clinical diagnostic laboratory services furnished as part of outpatient critical access hospital services, other than on the basis described in this subsection. For purposes of the preceding sentence and section 1861(mm)(3) [42 USCS § 1395x(mm)(3)], clinical diagnostic laboratory services furnished by a critical access hospital shall be treated as being furnished as part of outpatient critical access services without regard to whether the individual with respect to whom such services are furnished is physically present in the critical access hospital, or in a skilled nursing facility or a clinic (including a rural health clinic) that is operated by a critical access hospital, at the time the specimen is collected.

(5) Coverage of costs for certain emergency room on-call providers. In determining the reasonable costs of outpatient critical access hospital services under paragraphs (1) and (2)(A), the Secretary shall recognize as allowable costs, amounts (as defined by the Secretary) for reasonable compensation and related costs for physicians, physician assistants, nurse practitioners, and clinical nurse specialists who are on-call (as defined by the Secretary) to provide emergency services but who are not present on the premises of the critical access hospital involved, and are not otherwise furnishing services covered under this title [42 USCS §§ 1395 et seq.] and are not on-call at any

other provider or facility.

(h) Payment for prosthetic devices and orthotics and prosthetics. (1) General rule for payment. (A) In general. Payment under this subsection for prosthetic devices and orthotics and prosthetics shall be made in a lump-sum amount for the purchase of the item in an amount equal to 80 percent of the payment basis described in subparagraph (B).

(B) Payment basis. Except as provided in subparagraphs (C), (E), and (H)(i), the payment basis described in this subparagraph is the lesser of—

(i) the actual charge for the item; or

(ii) the amount recognized under paragraph (2) as the purchase price for the item.

(C) Exception for certain public home health agencies. Subparagraph (B)(i) shall not apply to an item furnished by a public home health agency (or by another home health agency which demonstrates to the satisfaction of the Secretary that a significant portion of its patients are low income) free of charge or at nominal charges to the public.

(D) Exclusive payment rule. Subject to subparagraph (H)(ii), this subsection shall constitute the exclusive provision of this title [42 USCS §§ 1395 et seq.] for payment for prosthetic devices, orthotics, and prosthetics under this part [42 USCS §§ 1395j et seq.] or under part A [42 USCS §§ 1395c et seq.] to a home health agency.

(E) Exception for certain items. Payment for ostomy supplies, tracheostomy supplies, and urologicals shall be made in accordance with subparagraphs (B) and (C) of section 1834(a)(2) [subsec. (a)(2)(B), (C) of this section].

(F) Special payment rules for certain prosthetics and custom-fabricated orthotics. (i) In general. No payment shall be made under this subsection for an item of custom-fabricated orthotics described in clause (ii) or for an item of prosthetics unless such item is—

(I) furnished by a qualified practitioner; and

(II) fabricated by a qualified practitioner or a qualified supplier at a facility that meets such criteria as the Secretary determines appropriate.

(ii) Description of custom-fabricated item. (I) In general. An item described in this clause is an item of custom-fabricated orthotics that requires education, training, and experience to custom-fabricate and that is included in a list established by the Secretary in subclause (II). Such an item does not include shoes and shoe inserts.

(II) List of items. The Secretary, in consultation with appropriate experts in orthotics (including national organizations representing manufacturers of orthotics), shall establish and update as appropriate a list of items to which this subparagraph applies. No item may be included in such list unless the item is individually fabricated for the patient over a positive model of the patient.

(iii) Qualified practitioner defined. In this subparagraph, the term "qualified practitioner" means a physician or other individual who—

(I) is a qualified physical therapist or a qualified occupational therapist;

(II) in the case of a State that provides for the licensing of orthotics and prosthetics, is licensed in orthotics or prosthetics by the State in which the item is supplied; or

(III) in the case of a State that does not provide for the licensing of orthotics and prosthetics, is specifically trained and educated to provide or manage the provision of prosthetics and custom-designed or -fabricated orthotics, and is certified by the American Board for Certification in Orthotics and Prosthetics, Inc. or by the Board for Orthotist/Prosthetist Certification, or is credentialed and approved by a program that the Secretary determines, in consultation with appropriate experts in orthotics and prosthetics, has training and education standards that are necessary to provide such prosthetics and orthotics.

(iv) Qualified supplier defined. In this subparagraph, the term "qualified supplier" means any entity that is accredited by the American Board for Certification in Orthotics and Prosthetics, Inc. or by the Board for Orthotist/Prosthetist Certification, or accredited and approved by a program that the Secretary determines has accreditation and approval standards that are essentially equivalent to those of such Board.

(G) Replacement of prosthetic devices and parts. (i) In general. Payment shall be made for the replacement of prosthetic devices which are artificial limbs, or for the replacement of any part of such devices, without regard to continuous use or useful lifetime restrictions if an ordering physician determines that the provision of a replacement device, or a replacement part of such a device, is necessary because of any of the following:

(I) A change in the physiological condition of the patient.

(II) An irreparable change in the condition of the device, or in a part of the device.

(III) The condition of the device, or the part of the device, requires repairs and the cost of such repairs would be more than 60 percent of the cost of a replacement device, or, as the case may be, of the part being replaced.

(ii) Confirmation may be required if device or part being replaced is less than 3 years old. If a physician determines that a replacement device, or a replacement part, is necessary pursuant to clause (i)—

(I) such determination shall be controlling; and

(II) such replacement device or part shall be deemed to be reasonable and necessary for purposes of section 1862(a)(1)(A) [42 USCS § 1395y(a)(1)(A)];

except that if the device, or part, being replaced is less than 3 years old (calculated from the date on which the beneficiary began to use the device or part), the Secretary may also require confirmation of necessity of the replacement device or replacement part, as the case may be.

(H) Application of competitive acquisition to orthotics; limitation of inherent reasonableness authority. In the case of orthotics described in paragraph (2)(C) of section 1847(a) [42 USCS § 1395w-3(a)] furnished on or after January 1, 2011, subject to subsection (a)(1)(G), that are included in a competitive acquisition program in a competitive acquisition area under such section—

(i) the payment basis under this subsection for such orthotics furnished in such area shall be the payment basis determined under such competitive acquisition program; and

(ii) the Secretary may use information on the payment determined under such competitive acquisition programs to adjust the payment amount otherwise recognized under subparagraph (B)(ii) for an area that is not a competitive acquisition area under section 1847 [42 USCS § 1395w-3], and in the case of such adjustment, paragraphs (8) and (9) of section 1842(b) [42 USCS § 1395u(b)] shall not be applied.

(2) Purchase price recognized. For purposes of paragraph (1), the amount that is recognized under this paragraph as the purchase price for prosthetic devices, orthotics, and prosthetics is the amount described in subparagraph (C) of this paragraph, determined as follows:

(A) Computation of local purchase price. Each carrier under section 1842 [42 USCS § 1395u] shall compute a base local purchase price for the item as follows:

(i) The carrier shall compute a base local purchase price for each item equal to the average reasonable charge in the locality for the purchase of the item for the 12-month period ending with June 1987.

(ii) The carrier shall compute a local purchase price, with respect to the furnishing of each particular item—

(I) in 1989 and 1990, equal to the base local purchase price computed under clause (i) increased by the percentage increase in the consumer price index for all urban consumers (United States city average) for the 6-month period ending with December 1987, or

(II) in 1991, 1992 or 1993, equal to the local purchase price computed under this clause for the previous year increased by the applicable percentage increase for the year.

(B) Computation of regional purchase price. With respect to the furnishing of a particular item in each region (as defined by the Secretary), the Secretary shall compute a regional purchase price—

(i) for 1992, equal to the average (weighted by relative volume of all claims among carriers) of the local purchase prices for the carriers in the region computed under subparagraph (A)(ii)(II) for the year, and

(ii) for each subsequent year, equal to the regional purchase price computed under this subparagraph for the previous year increased by the applicable percentage increase for the year.

(C) Purchase price recognized. For purposes of paragraph (1) and subject to subparagraph (D), the amount that is recognized under this paragraph as the purchase price for each item furnished—

(i) in 1989, 1990, or 1991, is 100 percent of the local purchase price computed under subparagraph (A)(ii);

(ii) in 1992, is the sum of (I) 75 percent of the local purchase price computed under subparagraph (A)(ii)(II) for 1992, and (II) 25 percent of the regional purchase price computed under subparagraph (B) for 1992;

(iii) in 1993, is the sum of (I) 50 percent of the local purchase price computed under subparagraph (A)(ii)(II) for 1993, and (II) 50 percent of the regional purchase price computed under subparagraph (B) for 1993; and

(iv) in 1994 or a subsequent year, is the regional purchase price computed under subparagraph (B) for that year.

(D) Range on amount recognized. The amount that is recognized under subparagraph (C) as the purchase price for an item furnished—

(i) in 1992, may not exceed 125 percent, and may not be lower than 85 percent, of the average of the purchase prices recognized under such subparagraph for all the carrier service areas in the United States in that year; and

(ii) in a subsequent year, may not exceed 120 percent, and may not be lower than 90 percent, of the average of the purchase prices recognized under such subparagraph for all the carrier service areas in the United States in that year.

(3) Applicability of certain provisions relating to durable medical equipment. Paragraphs (12), (15), and (17) and subparagraphs (A) and (B) of paragraph (10) and paragraph (11) of subsection (a) shall apply to prosthetic devices, orthotics, and prosthetics in the same manner as such provisions apply to covered items under such subsection.

(4) Definitions. In this subsection—

(A) the term "applicable percentage increase" means—

(i) for 1991, 0 percent;

(ii) for 1992 and 1993, the percentage increase in the consumer price index for all urban consumers (United States city average) for the 12-month period ending with June of the previous year; [,]

(iii) for 1994 and 1995, 0 percent;

(iv) for 1996 and 1997, the percentage increase in the consumer price index for all urban consumers (United States city average) for the 12-month period ending with June of the previous year; [,]

(v) for each of the years 1998 through 2000, 1 percent;

(vi) for 2001, the percentage increase in the consumer price index for all urban consumers (U.S. city average) for the 12-month period ending with June 2000;

(vii) for 2002, 1 percent;

(viii) for 2003, the percentage increase in the consumer price index for all urban consumers (United States city average) for the 12-month period ending with June of the previous year;

(ix) for 2004, 2005, and 2006, 0 percent;

(x) for each of 2007 through 2010, the percentage increase in the consumer price index for all urban consumers (United States city average) for the 12-month period ending with June of the previous year; and

(xi) for 2011 and each subsequent year—

(I) the percentage increase in the consumer price index for all urban consumers (United States city average) for the 12-month period ending with June of the previous year, reduced by—

(II) the productivity adjustment described in section 1886(b)(3)(B)(xi)(II) [42 USCS § 1395ww(b)(3)(B)(xi)(II)].

The application of subparagraph (A)(xi)(II) may result in the applicable percentage increase under subparagraph (A) being less than 0.0 for a year, and may result in payment rates under this subsection for a year being less than such payment rates for the preceding year.

(B) the term "prosthetic devices" has the meaning given such term in section 1861(s)(8) [42 USCS § 1395x(s)(8)], except that such term does not include parenteral and enteral nutrition nutrients, supplies, and equipment and does not include an implantable item for which payment may be made under section 1833(t) [42 USCS § 1395l(t)]; and

(C) the term "orthotics and prosthetics" has the meaning given such term in section 1861(s)(9) [42 USCS § 1395x(s)(9)] (and includes shoes described in section 1861(s)(12) [42 USCS § 1395x(s)(12)]), but does not include intraocular lenses or medical supplies (including catheters, catheter supplies, ostomy bags, and supplies related to ostomy care) furnished by a home health agency under section 1861(m)(5) [42 USCS § 1395x(m)(5)].

(i) Payment for surgical dressings. (1) In general. Payment under this subsection for surgical dressings (described in section 1861(s)(5) [42 USCS § 1395x(s)(5)]) shall be made in a lump sum amount for the purchase of the item in an amount equal to 80 percent of the lesser of—

(A) the actual charge for the item; or

(B) a payment amount determined in accordance with the methodology described in subparagraphs (B) and (C) of subsection (a)(2) (except that in applying such methodology, the national limited payment amount referred to in such subparagraphs shall be initially computed based on local payment amounts using average reasonable charges for the 12-month period ending December 31, 1992, increased by the covered item updates described in such subsection for 1993 and 1994).

(2) Exceptions. Paragraph (1) shall not apply to surgical dressings that are—

(A) furnished as an incident to a physician's professional service; or

(B) furnished by a home health agency.

(j) Requirements for suppliers of medical equipment and supplies. (1) Issuance and renewal of supplier number. (A) Payment. Except as provided in subparagraph (C), no payment may be made under this part after the date of the enactment of the Social Security Act Amendments of 1994 [enacted Oct. 31, 1994] for items furnished by a supplier of medical equipment and supplies unless such supplier obtains (and renews at such intervals as the Secretary may require) a supplier number.

(B) Standards for possessing a supplier number. A supplier may not obtain a supplier number unless—

(i) for medical equipment and supplies furnished on or after the date of the enactment of the Social Security Act Amendments of 1994 [enacted Oct. 31, 1994] and before January 1, 1996, the supplier meets standards prescribed by the Secretary in regulations issued on June 18, 1992; and

(ii) for medical equipment and supplies furnished on or after January 1, 1996, the supplier meets revised standards prescribed by the Secretary (in consultation with representatives of suppliers of medical equipment and supplies, carriers, and consumers) that shall include requirements that the supplier—

(I) comply with all applicable State and Federal licensure and regulatory requirements;

(II) maintain a physical facility on an appropriate site;

(III) have proof of appropriate liability insurance; and

(IV) meet such other requirements as the Secretary may specify.

(C) Exception for items furnished as incident to a physician's service. Subparagraph (A) shall not apply with respect to medical equipment and supplies furnished incident to a physician's service.

(D) Prohibition against multiple supplier numbers. The Secretary may not issue more than one supplier number to any supplier of medical equipment and supplies unless the issuance of more than one number is appropriate to identify subsidiary or regional entities under the supplier's ownership or control.

(E) Prohibition against delegation of supplier determinations. The Secretary may not delegate (other than by contract under section 1842 [42 USCS § 1395u]) the responsibility to determine whether suppliers meet the standards necessary to obtain a supplier number.

(2) Certificates of medical necessity. (A) Limitation on information provided by suppliers on certificates of medical necessity. (i) In general. Effective 60 days after the date of the enactment of the Social Security Act Amendments of 1994 [enacted Oct. 31, 1994], a supplier of medical equipment and supplies may distribute to physicians, or to individuals entitled to benefits under this part [42 USCS §§ 1395j et seq.], a certificate of medical necessity for commercial purposes which contains no more than the following information completed by the supplier:

(I) An identification of the supplier and the beneficiary to whom such medical equipment and supplies are furnished.

(II) A description of such medical equipment and supplies.

(III) Any product code identifying such medical equipment and supplies.

(IV) Any other administrative information (other than information relating to the beneficiary's medical condition) identified by the Secretary.

(ii) Information on payment amount and charges. If a supplier distributes a certificate of medical necessity containing any of the information permitted to be supplied under clause (i), the supplier shall also list on the certificate of medical necessity the fee schedule amount and the supplier's charge for the medical equipment or supplies being furnished prior to distribution of such certificate to the physician.

(iii) Penalty. Any supplier of medical equipment and supplies who knowingly and willfully distributes a certificate of medical necessity in violation of clause (i) or fails to provide the information required under clause (ii) is subject to a civil money penalty in an amount not to exceed $1,000 for each such certificate of medical necessity so distributed. The provisions of section 1128A [42 USCS § 1320a-7a] (other than subsections (a) and (b)) shall apply to civil money penalties under this subparagraph in the same manner as they apply to a penalty or proceeding under section 1128A(a) [42 USCS § 1320a-7a(a)].

(B) Definition. For purposes of this paragraph, the term "certificate of medical necessity" means a form or other document containing information required by the carrier to be submitted to show that an item is reasonable and necessary for the diagnosis or treatment of illness or injury or to improve the functioning of a malformed body member.

(3) Coverage and review criteria. The Secretary shall annually review the coverage and utilization of items of medical equipment and supplies to determine whether such items should be made subject to coverage and utilization review criteria, and if appropriate, shall develop and apply such criteria to such items.

(4) Limitation on patient liability. If a supplier of medical equipment and supplies (as defined in paragraph (5))—

(A) furnishes an item or service to a beneficiary for which no payment may be made by reason of paragraph (1);

(B) furnishes an item or service to a beneficiary for which payment is denied in advance under subsection (a)(15); or

(C) furnishes an item or service to a beneficiary for which payment is denied under section 1862(a)(1) [42 USCS § 1395y(a)(1)];

any expenses incurred for items and services furnished to an individual by such a supplier not on an assigned basis shall be the responsibility of such supplier. The individual shall have no financial responsibility for such expenses and the supplier shall refund on a timely basis to the individual (and shall be liable to the individual for) any amounts collected from the individual for such items or services. The provisions of subsection (a)(18) shall apply to refunds required under the previous sentence in the same manner as such provisions apply to refunds under such subsection.

(5) Definition. The term "medical equipment and supplies" means—

(A) durable medical equipment (as defined in section 1861(n) [42 USCS § 1395x(n)]);

(B) prosthetic devices (as described in section 1861(s)(8) [42 USCS § 1395x(s)(8)]);

(C) orthotics and prosthetics (as described in section 1861(s)(9) [42 USCS § 1395x(s)(9)]);

(D) surgical dressings (as described in section 1861(s)(5) [42 USCS § 1395x(s)(5)]);

(E) such other items as the Secretary may determine; and

(F) for purposes of paragraphs (1) and (3)—

(i) home dialysis supplies and equipment (as described in section 1861(s)(2)(F) [42 USCS § 1395x(s)(2)(F)]),

(ii) immunosuppressive drugs (as described in section 1861(s)(2)(J) [42 USCS § 1395x(s)(2)(J)]),

(iii) therapeutic shoes for diabetics (as described in section 1861(s)(12) [42 USCS § 1395x(s)(12)]),

(iv) oral drugs prescribed for use as an anticancer therapeutic agent (as described in section 1861(s)(2)(Q) [42 USCS § 1395x(s)(2)(Q)]), and

(v) self-administered erythropoetin (as described in section 1861(s)(2)(P) [42 USCS § 1395x(s)(2)(P)]).

(k) Payment for outpatient therapy services and comprehensive outpatient rehabilitation services. (1) In general. With respect to services described in section 1833(a)(8) or 1833(a)(9) [42 USCS § 1395l(a)(8) or (9)] for which payment is determined under this subsection, the payment basis shall be—

(A) for services furnished during 1998, the amount determined under paragraph (2); or

(B) for services furnished during a subsequent year, 80 percent of the lesser of—

(i) the actual charge for the services, or

(ii) the applicable fee schedule amount (as defined in paragraph (3)) for the services.

(2) Payment in 1998 based upon adjusted reasonable costs. The amount under this paragraph for services is the lesser of—

(A) the charges imposed for the services, or

(B) the adjusted reasonable costs (as defined in paragraph (4)) for the services,

less 20 percent of the amount of the charges imposed for such services.

(3) Applicable fee schedule amount. In this subsection, the term "applicable fee schedule amount" means, with respect to services furnished in a year, the amount determined under the fee schedule established under section 1848 [42 USCS § 1395w-4] for such services furnished during the year or, if there is no such fee schedule established for such services, the amount determined under the fee schedule established for such comparable services as the Secretary specifies.

(4) Adjusted reasonable costs. In paragraph (2), the term "adjusted reasonable costs" means, with respect to any services, reasonable costs determined for such services, reduced by 10 percent. The 10-percent reduction shall not apply to services described in section 1833(a)(8)(B) [42 USCS § 1395l(a)(8)(B)] (relating to services provided by hospitals).

(5) Uniform coding. For claims for services submitted on or after April 1, 1998, for which the amount of payment is determined under this subsection, the claim shall include a code (or codes) under a uniform coding system specified by the Secretary that identifies the services furnished.

(6) Restraint on billing. The provisions of subparagraphs (A) and (B) of section 1842(b)(18) [42 USCS § 1395u(b)(18)] shall apply to therapy services for which payment is made under this subsection in the same manner as they apply to services provided by a practitioner described in section 1842(b)(18)(C) [42 USCS § 1395u(b)(18)(C)].

(l) Establishment of fee schedule for ambulance services. (1) In general. The Secretary shall establish a fee schedule for payment for ambulance services whether provided directly by a supplier or provider or under arrangement with a provider under this part [42 USCS §§ 1395j et seq.] through a negotiated rulemaking process described in title 5, United States Code, and in accordance with the requirements of this subsection.

(2) Considerations. In establishing such fee schedule, the Secretary shall—

(A) establish mechanisms to control increases in expenditures for ambulance services under this part [42 USCS §§ 1395j et seq.];

(B) establish definitions for ambulance services which link payments to the type of services provided;

(C) consider appropriate regional and operational differences;

(D) consider adjustments to payment rates to account for inflation and other relevant factors; and

(E) phase in the application of the payment rates under the fee schedule in an efficient and fair manner consistent with paragraph (11), except that such phase-in shall provide for full payment of any national mileage rate for ambulance services provided by suppliers that are paid by carriers in any of the 50 States where payment by a carrier for such services for all such suppliers in such State did not, prior to the implementation of the fee schedule, include a separate amount for all mileage within the county from which the beneficiary is transported.

(3) Savings. In establishing such fee schedule, the Secretary shall—

(A) ensure that the aggregate amount of payments made for ambulance services under this part [42 USCS §§ 1395j et seq.] during 2000 does not exceed the aggregate amount of payments which would have been made for such services under this part [42 USCS §§ 1395j et seq.] during such year if the amendments made by section 4531(a) of the Balanced Budget Act of 1997 continued in effect, except that in making such determination the Secretary shall assume an update in such payments for 2002 equal to percentage increase in the consumer price index for all urban consumers (U.S. city average) for the 12-month period ending with June of the previous year reduced in the case of 2002 by 1.0 percentage points;

(B) set the payment amounts provided under the fee schedule for services furnished in 2001 and each subsequent year at amounts equal to the payment amounts under the fee schedule for services furnished during the previous year, increased, subject to subparagraph (C) and the succeeding sentence of this paragraph, by the percentage increase in the consumer price index for all urban consumers (U.S. city average) for the 12-month period ending with June of the previous year reduced in the case of 2002 by 1.0 percentage points.

(C) for 2011 and each subsequent year, after determining the percentage increase under subparagraph (B) for the year, reduce such percentage increase by the productivity adjustment described in section 1886(b)(3)(B)(xi)(II) [42 USCS § 1395ww(b)(3)(B)(xi)(II)].

The application of subparagraph (C) may result in the percentage increase under subparagraph (B) being less than 0.0 for a year, and may result in payment rates under the fee schedule under this subsection for a year being less than such payment rates for the preceding year.

(4) Consultation. In establishing the fee schedule for ambulance services under this subsection, the Secretary shall consult with various national organizations representing individuals and entities who furnish and regulate ambulance services and share with such organizations relevant data in establishing such schedule.

(5) Limitation on review. There shall be no administrative or judicial review under section 1869 [42 USCS § 1395ff] or otherwise of the amounts established under the fee schedule for ambulance services under this subsection, including matters described in paragraph (2).

(6) Restraint on billing. The provisions of subparagraphs (A) and (B) of section 1842(b)(18) [42 USCS § 1395u(b)(18)] shall apply to ambulance services for which payment is made under this subsection in the same manner as they apply to services provided by a practitioner described in section 1842(b)(18)(C) [42 USCS § 1395u(b)(18)(C)].

(7) Coding system. The Secretary may require the claim for any services for which the amount of payment is determined under this subsection to include a code (or codes) under a uniform coding system specified by the Secretary that identifies the services furnished.

(8) Services furnished by critical access hospitals. Notwithstanding any other provision of this subsection, the Secretary shall pay 101 percent of the reasonable costs incurred in furnishing ambulance services if such services are furnished—

(A) by a critical access hospital (as defined in section 1861(mm)(1) [42 USCS § 1395x(mm)(1)]), or

(B) by an entity that is owned and operated by a critical access hospital,

but only if the critical access hospital or entity is the only provider or supplier of ambulance services that is located within a 35-mile drive of such critical access hospital.

(9) Transitional assistance for rural providers. In the case of ground ambulance services furnished on or after July 1, 2001, and before January 1, 2004, for which the transportation originates in a rural area (as defined in section 1886(d)(2)(D) [42 USCS § 1395ww(d)(2)(D)]) or in a rural census tract of a metropolitan statistical area (as determined under the most recent modification of the Goldsmith Modification, originally published in the Federal Register on February 27, 1992 (57 Fed. Reg. 6725)), the fee

schedule established under this subsection shall provide that, with respect to the payment rate for mileage for a trip above 17 miles, and up to 50 miles, the rate otherwise established shall be increased by not less than ½ of the additional payment per mile established for the first 17 miles of such a trip originating in a rural area.

(10) Phase-in providing floor using blend of fee schedule and regional fee schedules. In carrying out the phase-in under paragraph (2)(E) for each level of ground service furnished in a year, the portion of the payment amount that is based on the fee schedule shall be the greater of the amount determined under such fee schedule (without regard to this paragraph) or the following blended rate of the fee schedule under paragraph (1) and of a regional fee schedule for the region involved:

(A) For 2004 (for services furnished on or after July 1, 2004), the blended rate shall be based 20 percent on the fee schedule under paragraph (1) and 80 percent on the regional fee schedule.

(B) For 2005, the blended rate shall be based 40 percent on the fee schedule under paragraph (1) and 60 percent on the regional fee schedule.

(C) For 2006, the blended rate shall be based 60 percent on the fee schedule under paragraph (1) and 40 percent on the regional fee schedule.

(D) For 2007, 2008, and 2009, the blended rate shall be based 80 percent on the fee schedule under paragraph (1) and 20 percent on the regional fee schedule.

(E) For 2010 and each succeeding year, the blended rate shall be based 100 percent on the fee schedule under paragraph (1).

For purposes of this paragraph, the Secretary shall establish a regional fee schedule for each of the nine census divisions (referred to in section 1886(d)(2) [42 USCS § 1395ww(d)(2)]) using the methodology (used in establishing the fee schedule under paragraph (1)) to calculate a regional conversion factor and a regional mileage payment rate and using the same payment adjustments and the same relative value units as used in the fee schedule under such paragraph.

(11) Adjustment in payment for certain long trips. In the case of ground ambulance services furnished on or after July 1, 2004, and before January 1, 2009, regardless of where the transportation originates, the fee schedule established under this subsection shall provide that, with respect to the payment rate for mileage for a trip above 50 miles the per mile rate otherwise established shall be increased by ¼ of the payment per mile otherwise applicable to miles in excess of 50 miles in such trip.

(12) Assistance for rural providers furnishing services in low population density areas. (A) In general. In the case of ground ambulance services furnished on or after July 1, 2004, and before January 1, 2011, for which the transportation originates in a qualified rural area (identified under subparagraph (B)(iii)), the Secretary shall provide for a percent increase in the base rate of the fee schedule for a trip established under this subsection. In establishing such percent increase, the Secretary shall estimate the average cost per trip for such services (not taking into account mileage) in the lowest quartile as compared to the average cost per trip for such services (not taking into account mileage) in the highest quartile of all rural county populations.

(B) Identification of qualified rural areas. (i) Determination of population density in area. Based upon data from the United States decennial census for the year 2000, the Secretary shall determine, for each rural area, the population density for that area.

(ii) Ranking of areas. The Secretary shall rank each such area based on such population density.

(iii) Identification of qualified rural areas. The Secretary shall identify those areas (in subparagraph (A) referred to as "qualified rural areas") with the lowest population densities that represent, if each such area were weighted by the population of such area (as used in computing such population densities), an aggregate total of 25 percent of the total of the population of all such areas.

(iv) Rural area. For purposes of this paragraph, the term "rural area" has the meaning given such term in section 1886(d)(2)(D) [42 USCS § 1395ww(d)(2)(D)]. If feasible, the Secretary shall treat a rural census tract of a metropolitan statistical area (as determined under the most recent modification of the Goldsmith Modification, originally published in the Federal Register on February 27, 1992 (57 Fed. Reg. 6725) as a rural area for purposes of this paragraph.

(v) Judicial review. There shall be no administrative or judicial review under section 1869 [42 USCS § 1395ff], 1878 [42 USCS § 1395oo], or otherwise, respecting the identification of an area under this subparagraph.

(13) Temporary increase for ground ambulance services. (A) In general. After computing the rates with respect to ground ambulance services under the other applicable provisions of this subsection, in the case of such services furnished on or after July 1, 2004, and before

January 1, 2007, and for such services furnished on or after July 1, 2008, and before January 1, 2011, for which the transportation originates in—

(i) a rural area described in paragraph (9) or in a rural census tract described in such paragraph, the fee schedule established under this section shall provide that the rate for the service otherwise established, after the application of any increase under paragraphs (11) and (12), shall be increased by 2 percent (or 3 percent if such service is furnished on or after July 1, 2008, and before January 1, 2011); and

(ii) an area not described in clause (i), the fee schedule established under this subsection shall provide that the rate for the service otherwise established, after the application of any increase under paragraph (11), shall be increased by 1 percent (or 2 percent if such service is furnished on or after July 1, 2008, and before January 1, 2011).

(B) Application of increased payments after applicable period. The increased payments under subparagraph (A) shall not be taken into account in calculating payments for services furnished after the applicable period specified in such subparagraph.

(14) Providing appropriate coverage of rural air ambulance services. (A) In general. The regulations described in section 1861(s)(7) [42 USCS § 1395x(s)(7)] shall provide, to the extent that any ambulance services (whether ground or air) may be covered under such section, that a rural air ambulance service (as defined in subparagraph (C)) is reimbursed under this subsection at the air ambulance rate if the air ambulance service—

(i) is reasonable and necessary based on the health condition of the individual being transported at or immediately prior to the time of the transport; and

(ii) complies with equipment and crew requirements established by the Secretary.

(B) Satisfaction of requirement of medically necessary. The requirement of subparagraph (A)(i) is deemed to be met for a rural air ambulance service if—

(i) subject to subparagraph (D), such service is requested by a physician or other qualified medical personnel (as specified by the Secretary) who certifies or reasonably determines that the individual's condition is such that the time needed to transport the individual by land or the instability of transportation by land poses a threat to the individual's survival or seriously endangers the individual's health; or

(ii) such service is furnished pursuant to a protocol that is established by a State or regional emergency medical service (EMS) agency and recognized or approved by the Secretary under which the use of an air ambulance is recommended, if such agency does not have an ownership interest in the entity furnishing such service.

(C) Rural air ambulance service defined. For purposes of this paragraph, the term "rural air ambulance service" means fixed wing and rotary wing air ambulance service in which the point of pick up of the individual occurs in a rural area (as defined in section 1886(d)(2)(D) [42 USCS § 1395ww(d)(2)(D)]) or in a rural census tract of a metropolitan statistical area (as determined under the most recent modification of the Goldsmith Modification, originally published in the Federal Register on February 27, 1992 (57 Fed. Reg. 6725)).

(D) Limitation. (i) In general. Subparagraph (B)(i) shall not apply if there is a financial or employment relationship between the person requesting the rural air ambulance service and the entity furnishing the ambulance service, or an entity under common ownership with the entity furnishing the air ambulance service, or a financial relationship between an immediate family member of such requester and such an entity.

(ii) Exception. Where a hospital and the entity furnishing rural air ambulance services are under common ownership, clause (i) shall not apply to remuneration (through employment or other relationship) by the hospital of the requester or immediate family member if the remuneration is for provider-based physician services furnished in a hospital (as described in section 1887 [42 USCS § 1395xx]) which are reimbursed under part A [42 USCS §§ 1395c et seq.] and the amount of the remuneration is unrelated directly or indirectly to the provision of rural air ambulance services.

(m) Payment for telehealth services. (1) In general. The Secretary shall pay for telehealth services that are furnished via a telecommunications system by a physician (as defined in section 1861(r) [42 USCS § 1395x(r)]) or a practitioner (described in section 1842(b)(18)(C) [42 USCS § 1395u(b)(18)(C)]) to an eligible telehealth individual enrolled under this part notwithstanding that the individual physician or practitioner providing the telehealth service is not at the same location as the beneficiary. For purposes of the preceding sentence, in the case of any Federal telemedicine demonstration program conducted in Alaska or Hawaii, the term "telecommunications system" includes store-and-forward technologies that provide for the asynchronous transmission of health care information in single or multimedia formats.

(2) Payment amount. (A) Distant site. The Secretary shall pay to a physician or practitioner located at a distant site that furnishes a telehealth service to an eligible telehealth individual an amount equal to the amount that such physician or practitioner would have been paid under this title [42 USCS §§ 1395 et seq.] had such service been furnished without the use of a telecommunications system.

(B) Facility fee for originating site. With respect to a telehealth service, subject to section 1833(a)(1)(U) [42 USCS § 1395l(a)(1)(U)], there shall be paid to the originating site a facility fee equal to—

(i) for the period beginning on October 1, 2001, and ending on December 31, 2001, and for 2002, $20; and

(ii) for a subsequent year, the facility fee specified in clause (i) or this clause for the preceding year increased by the percentage increase in the MEI (as defined in section 1842(i)(3) [42 USCS § 1395u(i)(3)]) for such subsequent year.

(C) Telepresenter not required. Nothing in this subsection shall be construed as requiring an eligible telehealth individual to be presented by a physician or practitioner at the originating site for the furnishing of a service via a telecommunications system, unless it is medically necessary (as determined by the physician or practitioner at the distant site).

(3) Limitation on beneficiary charges. (A) Physician and practitioner. The provisions of section 1848(g) [42 USCS § 1395w-4(g)] and subparagraphs (A) and (B) of section 1842(b)(18) [42 USCS § 1395u(b)(18)] shall apply to a physician or practitioner receiving payment under this subsection in the same manner as they apply to physicians or practitioners under such sections.

(B) Originating site. The provisions of section 1842(b)(18) [42 USCS § 1395u(b)(18)] shall apply to originating sites receiving a facility fee in the same manner as they apply to practitioners under such section.

(4) Definitions. For purposes of this subsection:

(A) Distant site. The term "distant site" means the site at which the physician or practitioner is located at the time the service is provided via a telecommunications system.

(B) Eligible telehealth individual. The term "eligible telehealth individual" means an individual enrolled under this part who receives a telehealth service furnished at an originating site.

(C) Originating site. (i) In general. The term "originating site" means only those sites described in clause (ii) at which the eligible telehealth individual is located at the time the service is furnished via a telecommunications system and only if such site is located—

(I) in an area that is designated as a rural health professional shortage area under section 332(a)(1)(A) of the Public Health Service Act (42 U.S.C. 254e(a)(1)(A));

(II) in a county that is not included in a Metropolitan Statistical Area; or

(III) from an entity that participates in a Federal telemedicine demonstration project that has been approved by (or receives funding from) the Secretary of Health and Human Services as of December 31, 2000.

(ii) Sites described. The sites referred to in clause (i) are the following sites:

(I) The office of a physician or practitioner.

(II) A critical access hospital (as defined in section 1861(mm)(1) [42 USCS § 1395x(mm)(1)]).

(III) A rural health clinic (as defined in section 1861(aa)(2) [42 USCS § 1395x(aa)(2)]).

(IV) A federally qualified health center (as defined in section 1861(aa)(4) [42 USCS § 1395x(aa)(4)]).

(V) A hospital (as defined in section 1861(e) [42 USCS § 1395x(e)]).

(VI) A hospital-based or critical access hospital-based renal dialysis center (including satellites).

(VII) A skilled nursing facility (as defined in section 1819(a) [42 USCS § 1395i-3(a)]).

(VIII) A community mental health center (as defined in section 1861(ff)(3)(B) [42 USCS § 1395x(ff)(3)(B)]).

(D) Physician. The term "physician" has the meaning given that term in section 1861(r) [42 USCS § 1395x(r)].

(E) Practitioner. The term "practitioner" has the meaning given that term in section 1842(b)(18)(C) [42 USCS § 1395u(b)(18)(C)].

(F) Telehealth service. (i) In general. The term "telehealth service" means professional consultations, office visits, and office psychiatry services (identified as of July 1, 2000, by HCPCS codes 99241–99275, 99201–99215, 90804–90809, and 90862 (and as subsequently modified by the Secretary)), and any additional service specified by the Secretary.

(ii) Yearly update. The Secretary shall establish a process that provides, on an annual basis, for the addition or deletion of services (and HCPCS codes), as appropriate, to those specified in clause (i) for authorized payment under paragraph (1).

(n) Authority to modify or eliminate coverage of certain preventive services. Notwithstanding any other provision of this title, effective beginning on January 1, 2010, if the Secretary determines appropriate, the Secretary may—

(1) modify—

(A) the coverage of any preventive service described in subparagraph (A) of section 1861(ddd)(3) [42 USCS § 1395x(ddd)(3)] to the extent that such modification is consistent with the recommendations of the United States Preventive Services Task Force; and

(B) the services included in the initial preventive physical examination described in subparagraph (B) of such section; and

(2) provide that no payment shall be made under this title for a preventive service described in subparagraph (A) of such section that has not received a grade of A, B, C, or I by such Task Force.

(o) Development and implementation of prospective payment system. (1) Development. (A) In general. The Secretary shall develop a prospective payment system for payment for Federally qualified health center services furnished by Federally qualified health centers under this title [42 USCS §§ 1395 et seq.]. Such system shall include a process for appropriately describing the services furnished by Federally qualified health centers and shall establish payment rates for specific payment codes based on such appropriate descriptions of services. Such system shall be established to take into account the type, intensity, and duration of services furnished by Federally qualified health centers. Such system may include adjustments, including geographic adjustments, determined appropriate by the Secretary.

(B) Collection of data and evaluation. By not later than January 1, 2011, the Secretary shall require Federally qualified health centers to submit to the Secretary such information as the Secretary may require in order to develop and implement the prospective payment system under this subsection, including the reporting of services using HCPCS codes.

(2) Implementation. (A) In general. Notwithstanding section 1833(a)(3)(A) [42 USCS § 1395l(a)(3)(A)], the Secretary shall provide, for cost reporting periods beginning on or after October 1, 2014, for payments of prospective payment rates for Federally qualified health center services furnished by Federally qualified health centers under this title [42 USCS §§ 1395 et seq.] in accordance with the prospective payment system developed by the Secretary under paragraph (1).

(B) Payments. (i) Initial payments. The Secretary shall implement such prospective payment system so that the estimated aggregate amount of prospective payment rates (determined prior to the application of section 1833(a)(1)(Z) [42 USCS § 1395l(a)(1)(Z)]) under this title [42 USCS §§ 1395 et seq.] for Federally qualified health center services in the first year that such system is implemented is equal to 100 percent of the estimated amount of reasonable costs (determined without the application of a per visit payment limit or productivity screen and prior to the application of section 1866(a)(2)(A)(ii) [42 USCS § 1395ww(a)(2)(A)(ii)]) that would have occurred for such services under this title [42 USCS §§ 1395 et seq.] in such year if the system had not been implemented.

(ii) Payments in subsequent years. Payment rates in years after the year of implementation of such system shall be the payment rates in the previous year increased—

(I) in the first year after implementation of such system, by the percentage increase in the MEI (as defined in section 1842(i)(3) [42 USCS § 1395u(i)(3)]) for the year involved; and

(II) in subsequent years, by the percentage increase in a market basket of Federally qualified health center goods and services as promulgated through regulations, or if such an index is not available, by the percentage increase in the MEI (as defined in section 1842(i)(3) [42 USCS § 1395u(i)(3)]) for the year involved.

(C) Preparation for PPS implementation. Notwithstanding any other provision of law, the Secretary may establish and implement by program instruction or otherwise the payment codes to be used under the prospective payment system under this section.

(Aug. 14, 1935, ch 531, Title XVIII, Part B, § 1834 as added and amended Dec. 22, 1987, P. L. 100-203, Title IV, Subtitle A, Part 3, Subpart A, § 4049(a)(2), Subpart B, § 4062(b) 101 Stat. 1330-91, 1330-100; July 1, 1988, P. L. 100-360, Title II, Subtitle A, §§ 202(b)(4), 203(c)(1)(F), 204(b), Title IV, Subtitle B, § 411(2)(3)(C)(ii), (f)(8)(A), (B)(ii), (D)(g)(1)(A), (B), 102 Stat. 704, 722, 726, 768, 779–782; Oct. 13, 1988, P. L. 100-485, Title VI, § 608(d)(21)(C)(22)(A), 102 Stat. 2420; Dec. 13, 1989, P. L. 101-234, Title II, §§ 201(a)(1), 301(b)(1), (c)(1), 103 Stat. 1981, 1985; Dec. 19, 1989, P. L. 101-239, Title VI, Subtitle A, Part 2, Subpart A, §§ 6102(f)(1), 6105(a), 6112(a), (c), (d)(1), (e)(2), 6116(b)(2), Subpart B, § 6140, 103 Stat. 2188, 2210, 2214, 2215, 2216, 2220, 2224; Nov. 5, 1990, P. L.

101-508, Title IV, Subtitle A, Part 2, Subpart A, §§ 4102(a), (d), (f), 4104(a), Subpart B, §§ 4152(a)(1), (b), (c)(1)–(4)(B)(i), (e), (f)(1), (g)(1), 4153(a)(1), (2)(D), 4163(b), 104 Stat. 1388-58, 1388-59, 1388-74, 1388-79, 1388-81, 1388-97; Aug. 10, 1993, P. L. 103-66, Title XIII, Ch 2, Subch A, Part II, Subpart D, §§ 13542(a), 13543(a), (b), 13544(a)(1), (2), (b)(1), 13545(a), 13546, 107 Stat. 587–590; Oct. 31, 1994, P. L. 103-432, Title I, Subtitle A, § 102(e), Subtitle B, Part I, § 126(b)(1)–(5), (g)(1), (10)(B), Part II, §§ 131(a), 132(a), (b), 133(a)(1), 134(a)(1), 135(a)(1), (b)(1), (3), (d), (e)(2)–(5), Part III, § 145(a), Subtitle C, § 156(a)(2)(C), 108 Stat. 4403, 4414–4416, 4421–4424, 4427, 4440; Aug. 5, 1997, P. L. 105-33, Title IV, Subtitle B, §§ 4101(a), (c), 4104(b), 4105(b)(2), Subtitle C, § 4201(c)(5), Subtitle D, Ch 2, §§ 4312(a), (c), 4316(b), Subtitle F, Ch 3, § 4531(b)(2), Ch 4, § 4541(a)(2), Ch 5, §§ 4551(a), (c)(1), 4552(a), (b), 111 Stat. 360, 363, 367, 374, 386, 387, 392, 451, 455, 457–459; Nov. 29, 1999, P. L. 106-113, Div B, § 1000(a)(6), 113 Stat. 1536; Dec. 21, 2000, P. L. 106-554, § 1(a)(6), 114 Stat. 2763; Dec. 8, 2003, P. L. 108-173, Title III, § 302(a), (c)(1)(A), (2), (3), (d)(1), (2), Title IV, Subtitle A, § 405(a)(1), (b)(1), (d)(1), Subtitle B, §§ 414(a)–(c)(1), (d), 415(a), Title VI, Subtitle C, § 627(b)(1), Title VII, Subtitle D, § 736(b)(4), (5), 117 Stat. 2223, 2230, 2231, 2266, 2267, 2278, 2280, 2281, 2321, 2356; Feb. 8, 2006, P. L. 109-171, Title V, Subtitle B, Ch. 1, § 5101(a)(1), (b)(1), Ch. 2, § 5113(b), 120 Stat. 37, 38, 44; July 15, 2008, P. L. 110-275, Title I, Subtitle B, § 125(b)(5), Subtitle C, Part I, § 135(a)(1), Part II, §§ 144(b)(1), 146(a), (b)(2)(A), 148(a), 149(a), 154(a)(2)(A), (3), (4), (b)(1)(A), (d)(2), 122 Stat. 2519, 2532, 2547, 2548, 2549, 2563, 2564, 2567; Oct. 13, 2009, P. L. 111-72, § 1(a), 123 Stat. 2059; March 23, 2010, P. L. 111-148, Title III, Subtitle B, Part I, §§ 3105(a), (c), 3109(a), Part II, § 3128(a), Part III, § 3136(a), (b), Subtitle E, § 3401(j), (m), (n), Title IV, Subtitle B, § 4105(a), Title V, Subtitle F, § 5501(a)(2), (b)(2), 5502(b), Title VI, Subtitle E, §§ 6402(g)(1), 6405(a), 6407(b), 6410(b), Title X, Subtitle C, § 10311(a), (c), Subtitle E, § 10501(i)(1), (3)(A), 124 Stat. 417, 418, 426, 437, 486, 487, 558, 653, 654, 759, 768, 770, 773, 942, 943, 997.)

HISTORY; ANCILLARY LAWS AND DIRECTIVES

Amendments:

2008. Act July 15, 2008 (applicable to accreditations of hospitals granted on or after 7/15/2010, as provided by § 125(d) of such Act, which appears as 42 USCS § 1395bb note), in subsec. (a)(20)(B), substituted "section 1865(a)" for "section 1865(b)".

Such Act further added subsec. (e); and in subsec. (l)(13), in subpara. (A), in the introductory matter, inserted "and for such services furnished on or after July 1, 2008, and before January 1, 2010", in cl. (i), inserted "(or 3 percent if such service is furnished on or after July 1, 2008, and before January 1, 2010)", and in cl. (ii), inserted "(or 2 percent if such service is furnished on or after July 1, 2008, and before January 1, 2010)", and, in subpara. (B), in the heading, substituted "applicable period" for "2006", and in the text, inserted "applicable".

Such Act further (effective 1/1/2009, as provided by § 144(b)(2) of such Act, which appears as a note to this section), in subsec. (a)(5)(F), substituted the subparagraph heading for one which read "Ownership of equipment", and substituted cl. (ii) for one which read:

"(ii) Ownership. (I) Transfer of title. On the first day that begins after the 36th continuous month during which payment is made for the equipment under this paragraph, the supplier of the equipment shall transfer title to the equipment to the individual.

"(II) Payments for oxygen and maintenance and servicing. After the supplier transfers title to the equipment under subclause (I)—

"(aa) payments for oxygen shall continue to be made in the amount recognized for oxygen under paragraph (9) for the period of medical need; and

"(bb) maintenance and servicing payments shall, if the Secretary determines such payments are reasonable and necessary, be made (for parts and labor not covered by the supplier's or manufacturer's warranty, as determined by the Secretary to be appropriate for the equipment), and such payments shall be in an amount determined to be appropriate by the Secretary.".

Such Act further (applicable to services furnished on or after enactment, as provided by § 146(b)(2)(B) of such Act, which appears as a note to this section), in subsec. (l)(14)(B)(i), substituted "certifies or reasonably determines" for "reasonably determines or certifies".

Such Act further (applicable to services furnished on or after 7/1/2009, as provided by § 148(a) of such Act, which appears as a note to this section), in subsec. (g)(4), in the heading, substituted "Treatment of" for "No beneficiary cost-sharing for", and added the sentence beginning "For purposes of the preceding sentence . . .".

Such Act further (applicable to services furnished on or after 1/1/2009, as provided by § 149(c) of such Act, which appears as a note to this section), in subsec. (m)(4)(C)(ii), added subcls. (VI)–(VIII).

Such Act further (effective as of 6/30/2008, as provided by § 154(e) of such Act, which appears as a note to this section), in subsec. (a), in para. (1), in subpara. (E)(ii), substituted "1861(r)" for "1861(r)(1)", in subpara. (F), in the introductory matter, substituted "January 1, 2011" for "January 1, 2009" and inserted "subject to subparagraph (G),", and added subpara. (G), in para. (14), in subparas. (H) and (I), deleted "and" following the concluding semicolon, redesignated subpara. (J) as subpara. (M), and inserted new subparas. (J)–(L), and in para. (20), in subpara. (E), inserted "including subparagraph (F)," and added subpara. (F); and, in subsec. (h)(1)(H), in the introductory matter, substituted "January 1, 2011" for "January 1, 2009" and inserted "subject to subsection (a)(1)(G),".

2010. Act March 23, 2010, in subsec. (a), in para. (1)(F), in cl. (i), deleted "and" following the concluding semicolon, in cl. (ii), inserted "(and, in the case of covered items furnished on or after January 1, 2016, subject to clause (iii), shall)", and added cl. (iii), in para. (7)(C)(ii)(II), deleted "(A)(ii) or" before "(A)(iii)", in para. (11)(B), designated the existing provisions as cl. (i), inserted the clause heading, and added cl. (ii), in para. (14), in subpara. (K), deleted "2011, 2012, and 2013, following "2010,", and added "and" at the end, substituted subpara. (L) for subparas. (L) and (M), which read:

"(L) for 2014—

"(i) in the case of items and services described in subparagraph (J)(i) for which a payment adjustment has not been made under subsection (a)(1)(F)(ii) in any previous year, the percentage increase in the consumer price index for all urban consumers (U.S. urban average) for the 12-month period ending with June 2013, plus 2.0 percentage points; or

"(ii) in the case of other items and services, the percentage increase in the consumer price index for all urban consumers (U.S. urban average) for the 12-month period ending with June 2013; and

"(M) for a subsequent year, the percentage increase in the consumer price index for all urban consumers (U.S. urban average) for the 12-month period ending with June of the previous year.",

and added the concluding matter, in para. (16)(B), inserted "that the Secretary determines is commensurate with the volume of the billing of the supplier", and in para. (20), in subpara. (F)(i), inserted "and subparagraph (G)" and ", except that the Secretary shall not require a pharmacy to have submitted to the Secretary such evidence of accreditation prior to January 1, 2011", and added subpara. (G); in subsec. (g)(2)(B), added the sentence beginning "Section 1833(x) . . .", and substituted "Subsections (x) and (y) of section 1833" for "Section 1833(x)"; in subsec. (h)(4), in subpara. (A), in cl. (ix), deleted "and" following the concluding semicolon, in cl. (x), substituted "for each of 2007 through 2010" for "a subsequent year" and added "and" at the end, added cl. (xi) and the concluding matter; in subsec. (l), in para. (3), in subpara. (A), deleted "and" following the concluding semicolon, in subpara. (B), inserted ", subject to subparagraph (C) and the succeeding sentence of this paragraph," and substituted "; and" for a concluding period, and added subpara. (C) and the concluding matter, in para. (12)(A), substituted "2010, and on or after April 1, 2010, and before January 1, 2011" for "2010", and in para. (13)(A), in the introductory matter, substituted "2007, for" for "2007, and for" and "2010, and for such services furnished on or after April 1, 2010, and before January 1, 2011,", and, in cls. (i) and (ii), inserted ", and on or after April 1, 2010, and before January 1, 2011"; and added subsecs. (n) and (o).

Such Act further (repealed by § 10501(i)(1) of such Act), added subsec. (n), which read:

"(n) Development and implementation of prospective payment system. (1) Development. (A) In general The Secretary shall develop a prospective payment system for payment for Federally qualified health services furnished by Federally qualified health centers under this title. Such system shall include a process for appropriately describing the services furnished by Federally qualified health centers.

"(B) Collection of data and evaluation. The Secretary shall require Federally qualified health centers to submit to the Secretary such information as the Secretary may require in order to develop and implement the prospective payment system under this paragraph and paragraph (2), respectively, including the reporting of services using HCPCS codes.

"(2) Implementation. (A) In general. Notwithstanding section 1833(a)(3)(B), the Secretary shall provide, for cost reporting periods beginning on or after October 1, 2014, for payments for Federally qualified health services furnished by Federally qualified health centers under this title in accordance with the prospective payment system developed by the Secretary under paragraph (1).

"(B) Payments. (i) Initial payments. The Secretary shall implement such prospective payment system so that the estimated amount of expenditures under this title for Federally qualified health services in the first year that the prospective payment system is implemented is equal to 103 percent of the estimated amount of expenditures under this title that would have occurred for such services in such year if the system had not been implemented.

"(ii) Payments in subsequent years. In the year after the first year of implementation of such system, and in each subsequent year, the payment rate for Federally qualified health services furnished in the year shall be equal to the payment rate established for such services furnished in the preceding year under this subparagraph increased by the percentage increase in the MEI (as defined in 1842(i)(3)) for the year involved.".

Section 10311(a) of such Act further, in subsec. (l)(13)(A), in the introductory matter, substituted "2007, and for" for "2007, for", and "2011" for "2010, and for such services furnished on or after April 1, 2010, and before January 1, 2011", in cls. (i) and (ii), deleted ", and on or after April 1, 2010, and before January 1, 2011" following "January 1, 2010", and substituted "January 1, 2011" for "January 1, 2010".

Section 10311(c) of such Act further, in subsec. (l)(12)(A), substituted "2011" for "2010, and on or after April 1, 2010, and before January 1, 2011".

Such Act further (effective as if included in the enactment of § 405(a) of Act Dec. 8, 2003, as provided by § 3128(b) of the 2010 Act, which appears as a note to this section), in subsecs. (g)(2)(A) and (l)(8), inserted "101 percent of".

Such Act further (effective on 1/1/2011 and applicable to power-driven wheelchairs furnished on or after such date, as provided by § 3136(c) of such Act, which appears as a note to this section), in subsec. (a)(7)(A), in cl. (i), in subcl. (II), inserted "subclause (III) and", and added subcl. (III), and in cl. (iii), in the heading and text, inserted "complex, rehabilitative".

Such Act further (applicable to written orders and certifications made on or after 7/1/2010, as provided by § 6405(d) of such Act, which appears as 42 USCS § 1395f note), in subsec. (a)(11)(B), inserted "enrolled under section 1866(j) or an eligible professional under section 1848(k)(3)(B) that is enrolled under section 1866(j)".

Other provisions:

Construction of subsec. (a)(20)(F)(i). Act Oct. 13, 2009, P. L. 111-72, § 1(b), 123 Stat. 2059, provides: "Nothing in subsection (a) [amending subsec. (a)(20)(F)(i) of this section] shall be construed as affecting the application of an accreditation requirement for pharmacies to qualify for bidding in a competitive acquisition area under section 1847 of the Social Security Act (42 U.S.C. 1395w-3).".

Administration. Act March 23, 2010, P. L. 111-148, Title III, Subtitle B, Part I, § 3109(b), 124 Stat. 419, provides: "Notwithstanding any other provision of law, the Secretary may implement the amendments made by subsection (a) [amending subsec. (a)(20) of this section] by program instruction or otherwise.".

Rule of construction. Act March 23, 2010, P. L. 111-148, Title III, Subtitle B, Part I, § 3109(c), 124 Stat. 420, provides: "Nothing in the provisions of or amendments made by this section [amending subsec. (a)(20) of this section and appearing in part as a note to this section] shall be construed as affecting the application of an accreditation requirement for pharmacies to qualify for bidding in a competitive acquisition area under section 1847 of the Social Security Act (42 U.S.C. 1395w-3).".

Effective date of amendments made by § 3128 of Act March 23, 2010. Act March 23, 2010, P. L. 111-148, Title III, Subtitle B, Part II, § 3128(b), 124 Stat. 426, provides: "The amendments made by subsection (a) [amending subsecs. (g)(2)(A) and (l)(8) of this section] shall take effect as if included in the enactment of section 405(a) of the Medicare Prescription Drug, Improvement, and Modernization Act of 2003 (Public Law 108-173; 117 Stat. 2266).".

Effective date and applicability of amendments made by § 3136(a) of Act March 23, 2010. Act March 23, 2010, P. L. 111-148, Title III, Subtitle B, Part III, § 3136(c), 124 Stat. 438, provides:

"(1) In general. Subject to paragraph (2), the amendments made by subsection (a) [amending subsec. (a)(7)(A) of this section] shall take effect on January 1, 2011, and shall apply to power-driven wheelchairs furnished on or after such date.

"(2) Application to competitive bidding. The amendments made by subsection (a) shall not apply to payment made for items and services furnished pursuant to contracts entered into under section 1847 of the Social Security Act (42 U.S.C. 1395w-3) prior to January 1, 2011, pursuant to the implementation of subsection (a)(1)(B)(i)(I) of such section 1847.".

Construction of subsec. (n). Act March 23, 2010, P. L. 111-148, Title IV, Subtitle B, § 4105(b), 124 Stat. 559, provides: "Nothing in the amendment made by paragraph (1) [adding subsec. (n) of this section] shall be construed to affect the coverage of diagnostic or treatment services under title XVIII of the Social Security Act [42 USCS §§ 1395 et seq.].".

§ 1395n. Procedure for payment of claims of providers of services

(a) Conditions for payment for services described in 42 USCS § 1395k(a)(2). Except as provided in subsections (b), (c), and (e), payment for services described in section 1832(a)(2) [42 USCS § 1395k(a)(2)] furnished an individual may be made only to providers of services which are eligible therefor under section 1866(a) [42 USCS § 1395cc(a)], and only if—

(1) written request, signed by such individual, except in cases in which the Secretary finds it impracticable for the individual to do so, is filed for such payment in such form, in such manner and by such person or persons as the Secretary may by regulation prescribe, no later than the close of the period ending 1 calendar year after the date of service; and

(2) **[Caution: For provisions applicable to written orders and certifications made before July 1, 2010, see 2010 amendment note below.]** a physician, or, in the case of services described in subparagraph (A), a physician enrolled under section 1866(j) [42 USCS § 1395cc(j)], certifies (and recertifies, where such services are furnished over a period of time, in such cases, with such frequency, and accompanied by such supporting material, appropriate to the case involved, as may be provided by regulations) that—

(A) in the case of home health services (i) such services are or were required because the individual is or was confined to his home (except when receiving items and services referred to in section 1861(m)(7) [42 USCS § 1395x(m)(7)]) and needs or needed skilled nursing care (other than solely venipuncture for the purpose of obtaining a blood sample) on an intermittent basis or physical or speech therapy or, in the case of an individual who has been furnished home health services based on such a need and who no longer has such a need for such care or therapy, continues or continued to need occupational therapy, (ii) a plan for furnishing such services to such individual has been established and is periodically reviewed by a physician, (iii) such services are or were furnished while the individual is or was under the care of a physician, and (iv) in the case of a certification after January 1, 2010, prior to making such certification the physician must document that the physician, or a nurse practitioner or clinical nurse specialist (as those terms are defined in section 1861(aa)(5) [42 USCS § 1395x(aa)(5)]) who is working in collaboration with the physician in accordance with State law, or a certified nurse-midwife (as defined in section 1861(gg) [42 USCS § 1395x(gg)]) as authorized by State law, or a physician assistant (as defined in section 1861(aa)(5) [42 USCS § 1395x(aa)(5)]) under the supervision of the physician, has had a face-to-face encounter (including through use of telehealth and other than with respect to encounters that are incident to services involved) with the individual during the 6-month period preceding such certification, or other reasonable timeframe as determined by the Secretary;

(B) in the case of medical and other health services, except services described in subparagraphs (B), (C), and (D) of section 1861(s)(2) [42 USCS § 1395x(s)(2)(B)–(D)], such services are or were medically required;

(C) in the case of outpatient physical therapy services or outpatient occupational therapy services, (i) such services are or were required because the individual needed physical therapy services or outpatient occupational therapy services, respectively, (ii) a plan for furnishing such services has been established by a physician or by the qualified physical therapist or qualified occupational therapist, respectively, providing such services and is periodically reviewed by a physician, and (iii) such services are or were furnished while the individual is or was under the care of a physician;

(D) in the case of outpatient speech pathology services, (i) such services are or were required because the individual needed speech pathology services, (ii) a plan for furnishing such services has been established by a physician or by the speech pathologist providing such services and is periodically reviewed by a physician, and (iii) such services are or were furnished while the individual is or was under the care of a physician;

(E) in the case of comprehensive outpatient rehabilitation facility services, (i) such services are or were required because the individual needed skilled rehabilitation services, (ii) a plan for furnishing such services has been established and is periodically reviewed by a physician, and (iii) such services are or were furnished while the individual is or was under the care of a physician; and

(F) in the case of partial hospitalization services, (i) the individual would require inpatient psychiatric care in the absence of such services, (ii) an individualized, written plan for furnishing such services has been established by a physician and is reviewed periodically by a physician, and (iii) such services are or were furnished while the individual is or was under the care of a physician.

For purposes of this section, the term "provider of services" shall include a clinic, rehabilitation agency, or public health agency if, in the case of a clinic or rehabilitation agency, such clinic or agency meets the requirements of section 1861(p)(4)(A) [42 USCS § 1395x(p)(4)(A)] (or meets the requirements of such section through the operation of subsection (g) or (ll)(2) of section 1861 [42 USCS § 1395x]), or if, in the case of a public health agency, such agency meets the requirements of section 1861(p)(4)(B) [42 USCS § 1395x(p)(4)(B)], (or meets the requirements of such section through the operation of subsection (g) or (ll)(2) of section 1861 [42 USCS § 1395x]), but only with respect to the furnishing of outpatient physical therapy services (as therein defined) or (through the operation of subsection (g) or (ll)(2) of section 1861 [42 USCS § 1395x]) with respect to the furnishing of outpatient occupational therapy services or outpatient speech-language pathology services, respectively.

To the extent provided by regulations, the certification and recertification requirements of paragraph (2) shall be deemed satisfied where, at a later date, a physician makes a certification of the kind provided in subparagraph (A) or (B) of paragraph (2) (whichever would have applied), but only where such certification is accompanied by such medical and other evidence as may be required by such regulations. With respect to the physician certification required by paragraph (2) for home health services furnished to any individual by a home health agency (other than an agency which is a governmental entity) and with respect to the establishment and review of a plan for such services, the Secretary shall prescribe regulations which shall become effective no later than July 1, 1981, and which prohibit a physician who has a significant ownership interest in, or a significant financial or contractual relationship with, such home health agency from performing such certification and from establishing or reviewing such plan, except that such prohibition shall not apply with respect to a home health agency which is a sole community home health agency (as determined by the Secretary). For purposes of the preceding sentence, service by a physician as an uncompensated officer or director of a home health agency shall not constitute having a significant ownership interest in, or a significant financial or contractual relationship with, such agency. For purposes of paragraph (2)(A), an individual shall be considered to be "confined to his home" if the individual has a condition, due to an illness or injury, that restricts the ability of the individual to leave his or her home except with the assistance of another individual or the aid of a supportive device (such as crutches, a cane, a wheelchair, or a walker), or if the individual has a condition such that leaving his or her home is medically contraindicated. While an individual does not have to be bedridden to be considered "confined to his home", the condition of the individual should be such that there exists a normal inability to leave home and that leaving home requires a considerable and taxing effort by the individual. Any absence of an individual from the home attributable to the need to receive health care treatment, including regular absences for the purpose of participating in therapeutic, psychosocial, or medical treatment in an adult day-care program that is licensed or certified by a State, or accredited, to furnish adult day-care services in the State shall not disqualify an individual from being considered to be "confined to his home". Any other absence of an individual from the home shall not so disqualify an individual if the absence is of infrequent or of relatively short duration. For purposes of the preceding sentence, any absence for the purpose of attending a religious service shall be deemed to be an absence of infrequent or short duration. In applying paragraph (1), the Secretary may specify exceptions to the 1 calendar year period specified in such paragraph.

(b) Conditions for payment for services described in 42 USCS § 1395x(s). (1) Payment may also be made to any hospital for services described in section 1861(s) [42 USCS § 1395x(s)] furnished as an outpatient service by a hospital or by others under arrangements made by it to an individual entitled to benefits under this part [42 USCS §§ 1395j et seq.] even though such hospital does not have an agreement in effect under this title [42 USCS §§ 1395 et seq.] if (A) such services were emergency services, (B) the Secretary would be required to make such payment if the hospital had such an agreement in effect and otherwise met the conditions of payment hereunder, and (C) such hospital has made an election pursuant to section 1814(d)(1)(C) [42 USCS § 1395f(d)(1)(C)] with respect to the calendar year in which such emergency services are provided. Such payments shall be made only in the amounts provided under section 1833(a)(2) [42 USCS § 1395l(a)(2)] and then only if such hospital agrees to comply, with respect to the emergency services provided, with the provisions of section 1866(a) [42 USCS § 1395cc(a)].

(2) Payment may also be made on the basis of an itemized bill to an individual for services described in paragraph (1) of this subsection if (A) payment cannot be made under such paragraph (1) solely because the hospital does not elect, in accordance with section 1814(d)(1)(C) [42 USCS § 1395f(d)(1)(C)], to claim such payments and (B) such individual files application (submitted within such time and in such form and manner, and containing and supported by such information as the Secretary shall by regulations prescribe) for reimbursement. The amounts payable under this paragraph shall, subject to the provisions of section 1833 [42 USCS § 1395l], be equal to 80 percent of the hospital's reasonable charges for such services.

(c) Collection of charges from individuals for services specified in 42 USCS § 1395x(s). Notwithstanding the provisions of this section and sections 1832, 1833, and 1866(a)(1)(A) [42 USCS §§ 1395k, 1395l and 1395cc(a)(1)(A)], a hospital or a critical access hospital may, subject to such limitations as may be prescribed by regulations, collect from an individual the customary charges for services specified in section 1861(s) [42 USCS § 1395x(s)] and furnished to him by such hospital as an outpatient, but only if such charges for such services do not exceed the applicable supplementary medical insurance deductible, and such customary charges shall be regarded as expenses incurred by such individual with respect to which benefits are payable in accordance with section 1833(a)(1) [42 USCS § 1395l(a)(1)]. Payments under this title [42 USCS §§ 1395 et seq.] to hospitals which have elected to make collections from individuals in accordance with the preceding sentence shall be adjusted periodically to place the hospital in the same position it would have been had it instead been reimbursed in accordance with section 1833(a)(2) [42 USCS § 1395l(a)(2)] (or, in the case of a critical access hospital, in accordance with section 1833(a)(6) [42 USCS § 1395l(a)(6)]). A critical access hospital shall be considered a hospital for purposes of this subsection.

(d) Payment to Federal provider of services or other Federal agencies prohibited. Subject to section 1880 [42 USCS § 1395qq], no payment may be made under this part [42 USCS §§ 1395j et seq.] to any Federal provider of services or other Federal agency, except a provider of services which the Secretary determines is providing services to the public generally as a community institution or agency; and no such payment may be made to any provider of services or other person for any item or service which such provider or person is obligated by a law of, or a contract with, the United States to render at public expense.

(e) Payment to fund designated by medical staff or faculty of medical school. For purposes of services (1) which are inpatient hospital services by reason of paragraph (7) of section 1861(b) [42 USCS § 1395x(b)(7)] or for which entitlement exists by reason of clause (II) of section 1832(a)(2)(B)(i) [42 USCS § 1395k(a)(2)(B)(i)(II)], and (2) for which the reasonable cost thereof is determined under section 1861(v)(1)(D) [42 USCS § 1395x(v)(1)(D)] (or would be if section 1886 [42 USCS § 1395ww] did not apply), payment under this part [42 USCS §§ 1395j et seq.] shall be made to such fund as may be designated by the organized medical staff of the hospital in which such services were furnished or, if such services were furnished in such hospital by the faculty of a medical school, to such fund as may be designated by such faculty, but only if—

(A) such hospital has an agreement with the Secretary under section 1866 [42 USCS § 1395cc], and

(B) the Secretary has received written assurances (i) that such payment will be used by such fund solely for the improvement of care to patients in such hospital or for educational or charitable purposes and (ii) the individuals who were furnished such services or any other persons will not be charged for such services (or if charged provision will be made for return of any moneys incorrectly collected).

(Aug. 14, 1935, ch 531, Title XVIII, Part B, § 1835, as added July 30, 1965, P. L. 89-97, Title I, Part 1, § 102(a), 79 Stat. 303; Jan. 2, 1968, P. L. 90-248, Title I, Part 3, §§ 126(b), 129(c)(9)(A), (B), 130(a), (b), 133(e), 81 Stat. 846, 848, 849, 851; Oct. 30, 1972, P. L. 92-603, Title II, §§ 204(b), 227(e)(2), 251(b)(2), 281(f), 283(b), 86 Stat. 1377, 1406, 1445, 1456; Sept. 30, 1976, P. L. 94-437, Title IV, § 401(a) in part, 90 Stat. 1408; Dec. 5, 1980, P. L. 96-499, Title IX, Part B, Subpart I, §§ 930(e), (j), 933(b), Subpart II, § 944(a), 94 Stat. 2631, 2632, 2635, 2642; Aug. 13, 1981, P. L. 97-35, Title XXI, Subtitle A, ch 2, § 2106(b)(1), Subtitle B, ch 1, § 2122(a)(1), 95 Stat. 792, 796; April 20, 1983, P. L. 98-21, Title VI, § 602(b) in part, 97 Stat. 163; July 18, 1984, P. L. 98-369, Division B, Title III, Subtitle A, Part II, §§ 2336(a) in part, (b) in part, 2342(b), 2354(b)(1), (8), (9), 98 Stat. 1091, 1094, 1100; Nov. 8, 1984, P. L. 98-617, § 3(a)(3), 98 Stat. 3295; Oct. 21, 1986, P. L. 99-509, Title IX, Subtitle D, Part 3, § 9337(c)(1), (2) in part, 100 Stat. 2033; Dec. 22, 1987, P. L. 100-203, Title IV, Subtitle A, Part 2, Subpart B, § 4024(b), Part 3, Subpart C, § 4070(b)(3), Subpart D, § 4085(i)(4), 101 Stat. 1330-115, 1330-132; July 1, 1988, P. L. 100-360, Title II, Subtitle A, §§ 203(d)(1), 205(d), 102 Stat. 724, 731; Dec. 13, 1989, P. L. 101-234, Title II, § 201(a)(1), 103 Stat. 1981; Dec. 19, 1989, P. L. 101-239, Title VI, Subtitle A, Part 1, Subpart A, § 6003(g)(3)(D)(viii), 103 Stat. 2153; Nov. 5, 1990, P. L. 101-508, Title IV, Subtitle A, Part 1, § 4008(m)(2)(D), 104 Stat. 1388-53; Aug. 5, 1997, P. L. 105-33, Title IV, Subtitle C, § 4201(c)(1), Subtitle G, Ch 1, Subch B, § 4615(a), 111 Stat. 373, 475; Dec. 21, 2000, P. L. 106-554, § 1(a)(6), 114 Stat. 2763; Dec. 8, 2003, P. L. 108-173, Title VII, Subtitle D, § 736(c)(2)(B), 117 Stat. 2356; July 15, 2008, P. L. 110-275, Title I, Subtitle C, Part II, § 143(b)(4), 122 Stat. 2543; March 23, 2010, P. L. 111-148, Title VI, Subtitle E, §§ 6404(a)(2)(B), 6405(b)(2), 6407(a)(2), Title X, Subtitle F, §§ 10604(2), 10605(b), 124 Stat. 768, 770, 1006.)

HISTORY; ANCILLARY LAWS AND DIRECTIVES

Amendments: 2010. Act March 23, 2010 (applicable to services furnished on or after 1/1/2010, as provided by § 6404(b)(1) of such Act, which appears as 42 USCS § 1395f note), in subsec. (a), in para. (1), substituted "period ending 1 calendar year after the date of service;" for "period of 3 calendar years following the year in which such services are furnished (deeming any services furnished in the last 3 calendar months of any calendar year to have been furnished in the succeeding calendar year) except that, where the Secretary deems that efficient administration so requires, such period may be reduced to not less than 1 calendar year;", and in the concluding matter, added the sentence beginning "In applying paragraph (1), . . .".

Such Act further (as amended by § 10604(b) of such Act and applicable to written orders and certifications made on or after 7/1/2010, as provided by § 6405(d) of such Act, which appears as 42 USCS § 1395f note), in subsec. (a)(2), in the introductory matter, inserted ", or, in the case of services described in subparagraph (A), a physician enrolled under section 1866(j),".

Such Act further, in subsec. (a)(2)(A), deleted "and" before "(iii)", and inserted ", and (iv) in the case of a certification after January 1, 2010, prior to making such certification the physician must document that the physician, or a nurse practitioner or clinical nurse specialist (as those terms are defined in section 1861(aa)(5)) who is working in collaboration with the physician in accordance with State law, or a certified nurse-midwife (as defined in section 1861(gg)) as authorized by State law, or a physician assistant (as defined in section 1861(aa)(5)) under the supervision of the physician, has had a face-to-face encounter (including through use of telehealth and other than with respect to encounters that are incident to services involved) with the individual during the 6-month period preceding such certification, or other reasonable timeframe as determined by the Secretary".

§ 1395p. Enrollment periods

(a) Generally; regulations. An individual may enroll in the insurance program established by this part [42 USCS §§ 1395j et seq.] only in such manner and form as may be prescribed by regulations, and only during an enrollment period prescribed in or under this section.

(b) [Repealed]

(c) Initial general enrollment period; eligible individuals before March 1, 1966. In the case of individuals who first satisfy paragraph (1) or (2) of section 1836 [42 USCS § 1395o(1) or (2)] before March 1, 1966, the initial general enrollment period shall begin on the first day of the second month which begins after the date of enactment of this title [enacted July 30, 1965] and shall end on May 31, 1966. For purposes of this subsection and subsection (d), an individual who has attained age 65 and who satisfies paragraph (1) of section 1836 [42 USCS § 1395o(1)] but not paragraph (2) of such section [42 USCS § 1395o(2)] shall be treated as satisfying such paragraph (1) on the first day on which he is (or on filing application would have been) entitled to hospital insurance benefits under part A [42 USCS §§ 1395c et seq.].

(d) Eligible individuals on or after March 1, 1966. In the case of an individual who first satisfies paragraph (1) or (2) of section 1836 [42 USCS § 1395(1) or (2)] on or after March 1, 1966, his initial enrollment period shall begin on the first day of the third month before the month in which he first satisfies such paragraphs and shall end seven months later. Where the Secretary finds that an individual who has attained age 65 failed to enroll under this part [42 USCS §§ 1395j et seq.] during his initial enrollment period (based on a determination by the Secretary of the month in which such individual attained age 65), because such individual (relying on documentary evidence) was mistaken as to his correct date of birth, the Secretary shall establish for such individual an initial enrollment period based on his attaining age 65 at the time shown in such documentary evidence (with a coverage period determined under section 1838 [42 USCS § 1395q] as though he had attained such age at that time).

(e) General enrollment period. There shall be a general enrollment period during the period beginning on January 1 and ending on March 31 of each year.

(f) Individuals deemed enrolled in the medical insurance program. Any individual—

(1) who is eligible under section 1836 [42 USCS § 1395o] to enroll in the medical insurance program by reason of entitlement to hospital insurance benefits as described in paragraph (1) of such section, and

(2) whose initial enrollment period under subsection (d) begins after March 31, 1973, and

(3) who is residing in the United States, exclusive of Puerto Rico,

shall be deemed to have enrolled in the medical insurance program established by this part [42 USCS §§ 1395j et seq.].

(g) Commencement of enrollment period. All of the provisions of this section shall apply to individuals satisfying subsection (f), except that—

(1) in the case of an individual who satisfies subsection (f) by reason of entitlement to disability insurance benefits described in section 226(b) [42 USCS § 426(b)], his initial enrollment period shall begin on the first day of the later of (A) April 1973 or (B) the third month before the 25th month of such entitlement, and shall reoccur with each continuous period of eligibility (as defined in section 1839(d) [42 USCS § 1395r(d)]) and upon attainment of age 65;

(2)(A) in the case of an individual who is entitled to monthly benefits under section 202 or 223 [42 USCS §§ 402 or 423] on the first day of his initial enrollment period or becomes entitled to monthly benefits under section 202 [42 USCS § 402] during the first 3 months of such period, his enrollment shall be deemed to have occurred in the third month of his initial enrollment period, and

(B) in the case of an individual who is not entitled to benefits under section 202 [42 USCS § 402] on the first day of his initial enrollment period and does not become so entitled during the first 3 months of such period, his enrollment shall be deemed to have occurred in the month in which he files the application establishing his entitlement to hospital insurance benefits provided such filing occurs during the last 4 months of his initial enrollment period; and

(3) in the case of an individual who would otherwise satisfy subsection (f) but does not establish his entitlement to hospital insurance benefits until after the last day of his initial enrollment period (as defined in subsection (d) of this section), his enrollment shall be deemed to have occurred on the first day of the earlier of the then current or immediately succeeding general enrollment period (as defined in subsection (e) of this section).

(h) Waiver of enrollment period requirements where individual's rights were prejudiced by administrative error or inaction. In any case where the Secretary finds that an individual's enrollment or nonenrollment in the insurance program established by this part [42 USCS §§ 1395j et seq.] or part A [42 USCS §§ 1395c et seq.] pursuant to section 1818 [42 USCS § 1395i-2] is unintentional, inadvertent, or erroneous and is the result of the error, misrepresentation, or inaction of an officer, employee, or agent of the Federal Government, or its instrumentalities, the Secretary may take such action (including the designation for such individual of a special initial or subsequent enrollment period, with a coverage period determined on the basis thereof and with appropriate adjustments of premiums) as may be necessary to correct or eliminate the effects of such error, misrepresentation, or inaction.

(i) Special enrollment periods. (1) In the case of an individual who—

(A) at the time the individual first satisfies paragraph (1) or (2) of section 1836 [42 USCS § 1395o(1) or (2)] is enrolled in a group health plan described in section 1862(b)(1)(A)(v) [42 USCS § 1395y(b)(1)(A)(v)] by reason of the individual's (or the individual's spouse's) current employment status, and

(B) has elected not to enroll (or to be deemed enrolled) under this section during the individual's initial enrollment period,

there shall be a special enrollment period described in paragraph (3). In the case of an individual not described in the previous sentence who has not attained the age of 65, at the time the individual first satisfies paragraph (1) of section 1836 [42 USCS § 1395o(1)], is enrolled in a large group health plan (as that term is defined in section 1862(b)(1)(B)(iii) [42 USCS § 1395y(b)(1)(B)(iii)]) by reason of the individual's current employment status (or the current employment status of a family member of the individual), and has elected not to enroll (or to be deemed enrolled) under this section during the individual's initial enrollment period, there shall be a special enrollment period described in paragraph (3)(B).

(2) In the case of an individual who—

(A) (i) has enrolled (or has been deemed to have enrolled) in the medical insurance program established under this part [42 USCS §§ 1395j et seq.] during the individual's initial enrollment period, or (ii) is an individual described in paragraph (1)(A);

(B) has enrolled in such program during any subsequent special enrollment period under this subsection during which the individual was not enrolled in a group health plan described in section 1862(b)(1)(A)(v) [42 USCS § 1395y(b)(1)(A)(v)] by reason of the individual's (or individual's spouse's) current employment status; and

(C) has not terminated enrollment under this section at any time at which the individual is not enrolled in such a group health plan by reason of the individual's (or individual's spouse's) current employment status,

there shall be a special enrollment period described in paragraph (3). In the case of an individual not described in the previous sentence who has not attained the age of 65, has enrolled (or has been deemed to have enrolled) in the medical insurance program established under this part [42 USCS §§ 1395j et seq.] during the individual's initial enrollment period, or is an individual described in the second sentence of paragraph (1), has enrolled in such program during any subsequent special enrollment period under this subsection during which the individual was not enrolled in a large group health plan (as that term is defined in section 1862(b)(1)(B)(iii) [42 USCS § 1395y(b)(1)(B)(iii)]) by reason of the individual's current employment status (or the current employment status of a family member of the individual), and has not terminated enrollment under this section at any time at which the individual is not enrolled in such a large group health plan by reason of the individual's current employment status (or the current employment status of a family member of the individual), there shall be a special enrollment period described in paragraph (3)(B).

(3)(A) The special enrollment period referred to in the first sentences of paragraphs (1) and (2) is the period including each month during any part of which the individual is enrolled in a group health plan described in section 1862(b)(1)(A)(v) [42 USCS § 1395y(b)(1)(A)(v)] by reason of current employment status ending with the last day of the eighth consecutive month in which the individual is at no time so enrolled.

(B) The special enrollment period referred to in the second sentences of paragraphs (1) and (2) is the period including each month during any part of which the individual is enrolled in a large group health plan (as that term is defined in section 1862(b)(1)(B)(iii) [42 USCS § 1395y(b)(1)(B)(iii)]) by reason of the individual's current employment status (or the current employment status of a family member of the individual) and ending with the last day of the eighth consecutive month in which the individual is at no time so enrolled.

(4)(A) In the case of an individual who is entitled to benefits under part A [42 USCS §§ 1395c et seq.] pursuant to section 226(b) [42 USCS § 426(b)] and—

(i) who at the time the individual first satisfies paragraph (1) of section 1836 [42 USCS § 1395o(1)]—

(I) is enrolled in a group health plan described in section 1862(b)(1)(A)(v) [42 USCS § 1395y(b)(1)(A)(v)] by reason of the individual's current or former employment or by reason of the current or former employment status of a member of the individual's family, and

(II) has elected not to enroll (or to be deemed enrolled) under this section during the individual's initial enrollment period; and

(ii) whose continuous enrollment under such group health plan is involuntarily terminated at a time when the enrollment under the plan is not by reason of the individual's current employment or by reason of the current employment of a member of the individual's family,

there shall be a special enrollment period described in subparagraph (B).

(B) The special enrollment period referred to in subparagraph (A) is the 6-month period beginning on the first day of the month which includes the date of the enrollment termination described in subparagraph (A)(ii).

(j) Persons who have ALS. In applying this section in the case of an individual who is entitled to benefits under part A [42 USCS §§ 1395c et seq.] pursuant to the operation of section 226(h) [42 USCS § 426(h)], the following special rules apply:

(1) The initial enrollment period under subsection (d) shall begin on the first day of the first month in which the individual satisfies the requirement of section 1836(1) [42 USCS § 1395o(1)].

(2) In applying subsection (g)(1), the initial enrollment period shall begin on the first day of the first month of entitlement to disability insurance benefits referred to in such subsection.

(k) Special enrollment period. (1) In the case of an individual who—

(A) at the time the individual first satisfies paragraph (1) or (2) of section 1836 [42 USCS § 1395o], is described in paragraph (3), and has elected not to enroll (or to be deemed enrolled) under this section during the individual's initial enrollment period; or

(B) has terminated enrollment under this section during a month in which the individual is described in paragraph (3),

there shall be a special enrollment period described in paragraph (2).

(2) The special enrollment period described in this paragraph is the 6-month period beginning on the first day of the month which includes the date that the individual is no longer described in paragraph (3).

(3) For purposes of paragraph (1), an individual described in this paragraph is an individual who—

(A) is serving as a volunteer outside of the United States through a program—

(i) that covers at least a 12-month period; and

(ii) that is sponsored by an organization described in section 501(c)(3) of the Internal Revenue Code of 1986 [26 USCS § 501(c)(3)] and exempt from taxation under section 501(a) of such Code [26 USCS § 501(a)]; and

(B) demonstrates health insurance coverage while serving in the program.

(l) Part B special enrollment period for disabled TRICARE beneficiaries. (1) In the case of any individual who is a covered beneficiary (as defined in section 1072(5) of title 10, United States Code) at the time the individual is entitled to part A [42 USCS §§ 1395c et seq.] under section 226(b) [42 USCS § 426(b)] or section 226A [42 USCS § 426-1] and who is eligible to enroll but who has elected not to enroll (or to be deemed enrolled) during the individual's initial enrollment period, there shall be a special enrollment period described in paragraph (2).

(2) The special enrollment period described in this paragraph, with respect to an individual, is the 12-month period beginning on the day after the last day of the initial enrollment period of the individual or, if later, the 12-month period beginning with the month the individual is notified of enrollment under this section.

(3) In the case of an individual who enrolls during the special enrollment period provided under paragraph (1), the coverage period under this part shall begin on the first day of the month in which the individual enrolls, or, at the option of the individual, the first month after the end of the individual's initial enrollment period.

(4) An individual may only enroll during the special enrollment period provided under paragraph (1) one time during the individual's lifetime.

(5) The Secretary shall ensure that the materials relating to coverage under this part that are provided to an individual described in paragraph (1) prior to the individual's initial enrollment period contain information concerning the impact of not enrolling under this part, including the impact on health care benefits under the TRICARE program under chapter 55 of title 10, United States Code [42 USCS §§ 1071 et seq.].

(6) The Secretary of Defense shall collaborate with the Secretary of Health and Human Services and the Commissioner of Social Security to provide for the accurate identification of individuals described in paragraph (1). The Secretary of Defense shall provide such individuals with notification with respect to this subsection. The Secretary of Defense shall collaborate with the Secretary of Health and Human Services and the Commissioner of Social Security to ensure appropriate follow up pursuant to any notification provided under the preceding sentence.

(Aug. 14, 1935, ch 531, Title XVIII, Part B, § 1837, as added July 30, 1965, P. L. 89-97,

Title I, Part 1, § 102(a), 79 Stat. 304; April 8, 1966, P. L. 89-384, § 3(a), (b), 80 Stat. 105; Jan. 2, 1968, P. L. 90-248, Title I, Part 3, §§ 136(a), 145(a), (b), 81 Stat. 853, 859; Oct. 30, 1972, P. L. 92-603, Title II, §§ 201(c)(2), 206(a), 259(a), 260, 86 Stat. 1372, 1378, 1448; June 9, 1980, P. L. 96-265, Title I, § 103(a)(3), 94 Stat. 444; Dec. 5, 1980, P. L. 96-499, Title IX, Part B, Subpart II, § 945(a), (b), 94 Stat. 2642; Aug. 13, 1981, P. L. 97-35, Title XXI, Subtitle B, Ch 4, § 2151(a)(1), (2), 95 Stat. 801; July 18, 1984, P. L. 98-369, Division B, Title III, Subtitle A, Part II, §§ 2338(b), 2354(b)(10), 98 Stat. 1092, 1101; April 7, 1986, P. L. 99-272, Title IX, Subtitle A, Part 2, Subtitle A, § 9201(c)(1), Subpart B, § 9219(a)(2), 100 Stat. 171, 182; Oct. 21, 1986, P. L. 99-509, Title IX, Subtitle D, Part 2, § 9319(c)(1)–(3), 100 Stat. 2011; Oct. 22, 1986, P. L. 99-514, Title XVIII, Subtitle C, Ch 1, § 1895(b)(12), 100 Stat. 2934; Dec. 19, 1989, P. L. 101-239, Title VI, Subtitle A, Part 3, Subpart A, § 6202(b)(4)(C), (c)(1), 103 Stat. 2233, 2234; Oct. 31, 1994, P. L. 103-432, Title I, Subtitle B, Part III, § 147(f)(1)(A), Subtitle C, § 151(c)(2), 108 Stat. 4430, 4435; Aug. 5, 1997, P. L. 105-33, Title IV, Subtitle F, Ch 6, Subch B, § 4581(b)(1), Subtitle G, Ch 3, § 4631(a)(2), 111 Stat. 465, 486; Dec. 21, 2000, P. L. 106-554, § 1(a)(6), 114 Stat. 2763; Feb. 8, 2006, P. L. 109-171, Title V, Subtitle B, Ch. 2, § 5115(a)(2)(A), 120 Stat. 45; March 23, 2010, P. L. 111-148, Title III, Subtitle B, Part I, § 3110(a)(1), 124 Stat. 420.)

HISTORY; ANCILLARY LAWS AND DIRECTIVES

Other provisions:

Applicability of March 23, 2010 amendment. Act March 23, 2010, P. L. 111-148, Title III, Subtitle B, Part I, § 3110(a)(2), 124 Stat. 420, provides: "The amendment made by paragraph (1) [adding subsec. (l) of this section] shall apply to elections made with respect to initial enrollment periods that end after the date of the enactment of this Act.".

§ 1395r. Amount of premiums for individuals enrolled under 42 USCS §§ 1395j et seq.

(a) Determination of monthly actuarial rates and premiums. (1) The Secretary shall, during September of 1983 and of each year thereafter, determine the monthly actuarial rate for enrollees age 65 and over which shall be applicable for the succeeding calendar year. Such actuarial rate shall be the amount the Secretary estimates to be necessary so that the aggregate amount for such calendar year with respect to those enrollees age 65 and older will equal one-half of the total of the benefits and administrative costs which he estimates will be payable from the Federal Supplementary Medical Insurance Trust Fund for services performed and related administrative costs incurred in such calendar year with respect to such enrollees. In calculating the monthly actuarial rate, the Secretary shall include an appropriate amount for a contingency margin. In applying this paragraph there shall not be taken into account additional payments under section 1848(o) [42 USCS § 1395w-4(o)] and section 1853(l)(3) [42 USCS § 1395w-23(l)(3)] and the Government contribution under section 1844(a)(3) [42 USCS § 1395w(a)(3)].

(2) The monthly premium of each individual enrolled under this part [42 USCS §§ 1395j et seq.] for each month after December 1983 shall be the amount determined under paragraph (3), adjusted as required in accordance with subsections (b), (c), (f), and (i), and to reflect any credit provided under section 1854(b)(1)(C)(ii)(III) [42 USCS § 1395w-24(b)(1)(C)(ii)(III)].

(3) The Secretary, during September of each year, shall determine and promulgate a monthly premium rate for the succeeding calendar year that (except as provided in subsection (g)) is equal to 50 percent of the monthly actuarial rate for enrollees age 65 and over, determined according to paragraph (1), for that succeeding calendar year. Whenever the Secretary promulgates the dollar amount which shall be applicable as the monthly premium rate for any period, he shall, at the time such promulgation is announced, issue a public statement setting forth the actuarial assumptions and bases employed by him in arriving at the amount of an adequate actuarial rate for enrollees age 65 and older as provided in paragraph (1).

(4) The Secretary shall also, during September of 1983 and of each year thereafter, determine the monthly actuarial rate for disabled enrollees under age 65 which shall be applicable for the succeeding calendar year. Such actuarial rate shall be the amount the Secretary estimates to be necessary so that the aggregate amount for such calendar year with respect to disabled enrollees under age 65 will equal one-half of the total of the benefits and administrative costs which he estimates will be payable from the Federal Supplementary Medical Insurance Trust Fund for services performed and related administrative costs incurred in such calendar year with respect to such enrollees. In calculating the monthly actuarial rate under this paragraph, the Secretary shall include an appropriate amount for a

contingency margin.

(b) Increase in monthly premiums. In the case of an individual whose coverage period began pursuant to an enrollment after his initial enrollment period (determined pursuant to subsection (c) or (d) of section 1837 [42 USCS § 1395p(c) or (d)]) and not pursuant to a special enrollment period under subsection (i)(4) or (l) of section 1837 [42 USCS § 1395p], the monthly premium determined under subsection (a) (without regard to any adjustment under subsection (i)) shall be increased by 10 percent of the monthly premium so determined for each full 12 months (in the same continuous period of eligibility) in which he could have been but was not enrolled. For purposes of the preceding sentence, there shall be taken into account (1) the months which elapsed between the close of his initial enrollment period and the close of the enrollment period in which he enrolled, plus (in the case of an individual who reenrolls) (2) the months which elapsed between the date of termination of a previous coverage period and the close of the enrollment period in which he reenrolled, but there shall not be taken into account months for which the individual can demonstrate that the individual was enrolled in a group health plan described in section 1862(b)(1)(A)(v) [42 USCS § 1395y(b)(1)(A)(v)] by reason of the individual's (or the individual's spouse's) current employment status or months during which the individual has not attained the age of 65 and for which the individual can demonstrate that the individual was enrolled in a large group health plan (as that term is defined in section 1862(b)(1)(B)(iii) [42 USCS § 1395y(b)(1)(B)(iii)]) by reason of the individual's current employment status (or the current employment status of a family member of the individual) or months for which the individual can demonstrate that the individual was an individual described in section 1837(k)(3) [42 USCS § 1395p(k)(3)]. Any increase in an individual's monthly premium under the first sentence of this subsection with respect to a particular continuous period of eligibility shall not be applicable with respect to any other continuous period of eligibility which such individual may have. No increase in the premium shall be effected for a month in the case of an individual who enrolls under this part during 2001, 2002, 2003, or 2004 and who demonstrates to the Secretary before December 31, 2004, that the individual is a covered beneficiary (as defined in section 1072(5) of title 10, United States Code). The Secretary of Health and Human Services shall consult with the Secretary of Defense in identifying individuals described in the previous sentence.

(c) Premiums rounded to nearest multiple of 10 cents. If any monthly premium determined under the foregoing provisions of this section is not a multiple of 10 cents, such premium shall be rounded to the nearest multiple of 10 cents.

(d) "Continuous period of eligibility" defined. For purposes of subsection (b) (and section 1837(g)(1) [42 USCS § 1395p(g)(1)]), an individual's "continuous period of eligibility" is the period beginning with the first day on which he is eligible to enroll under section 1836 [42 USCS § 1395o] and ending with his death; except that any period during all of which an individual satisfied paragraph (1) of section 1836 [42 USCS § 1395o(1)] and which terminated in or before the month preceding the month in which he attained age 65 shall be a separate "continuous period of eligibility" with respect to such individual (and each such period which terminates shall be deemed not to have existed for purposes of subsequently applying this section).

(e) State payment of Part B late enrollment premium increases. (1) Upon the request of a State (or any appropriate State or local governmental entity specified by the Secretary), the Secretary may enter into an agreement with the State (or such entity) under which the State (or such entity) agrees to pay on a quarterly or other periodic basis to the Secretary (to be deposited in the Treasury to the credit of the Federal Supplementary Medical Insurance Trust Fund) an amount equal to the amount of the part B late enrollment premium increases with respect to the premiums for eligible individuals (as defined in paragraph (3)(A)).

(2) No part B late enrollment premium increase shall apply to an eligible individual for premiums for months for which the amount of such an increase is payable under an agreement under paragraph (1).

(3) In this subsection:

(A) The term "eligible individual" means an individual who is enrolled under this part B [42 USCS §§ 1395j et seq.] and who is within a class of individuals specified in the agreement under paragraph (1).

(B) The term "part B late enrollment premium increase" means any increase in a premium as a result of the application of subsection (b).

(f) Limitation on increase in monthly premium. For any calendar year after 1988, if an individual is entitled to monthly benefits under section 202 or 223 [42 USCS § 402 or 423] or to a monthly annuity under section 3(a), 4(a), or 4(f) of the Railroad Retirement Act of 1974 [45 USCS §§ 231b(a), 231c(a) or (f)] for November and December of the preceding year, if the monthly premium of the individual under this section for December and for January is deducted from those benefits under section 1840(a)(1) or section 1840(b)(1) [42 USCS § 1395s(a)(1) or (b)(1)], and if the amount of the individual's premium is not adjusted for such January under subsection (i), the monthly premium otherwise determined under this section for an individual for that year shall not be increased, pursuant to this subsection, to the extent that such increase would reduce the amount of benefits payable to that individual for that December below the amount of benefits payable to that individual for that November (after the deduction of the premium under this section). For purposes of this subsection, retroactive adjustments or payments and deductions on account of work shall not be taken into account in determining the monthly benefits to which an individual is entitled under section 202 or 223 [42 USCS § 402 or 423] or under the Railroad Retirement Act of 1974.

(g) Exclusions from estimate of benefits and administrative costs. In estimating the benefits and administrative costs which will be payable from the Federal Supplementary Medical Insurance Trust Fund for a year for purposes of determining the monthly premium rate under subsection (a)(3), the Secretary shall exclude an estimate of any benefits and administrative costs attributable to—

(1) the application of section 1861(v)(1)(L)(viii) [42 USCS § 1395x(v)(1)(L)(viii)] or to the establishment under section 1861(v)(1)(L)(i)(V) [42 USCS § 1395x(v)(1)(L)(i)(V)] of a per visit limit at 106 percent of the median (instead of 105 percent of the median), but only to the extent payment for home health services under this title [42 USCS §§ 1395 et seq.] is not being made under section 1895 [42 USCS § 1395fff] (relating to prospective payment for home health services); and

(2) the medicare prescription drug discount card and transitional assistance program under section 1860D-31 [42 USCS § 1395w-141].

(h) Potential application of comparative cost adjustment in CCA areas. (1) In general. Certain individuals who are residing in a CCA area under section 1860C-1 [42 USCS § 1395w-29] who are not enrolled in an MA plan under part C [42 USCS §§ 1395w-21 et seq.] may be subject to a premium adjustment under subsection (f) of such section for months in which the CCA program under such section is in effect in such area.

(2) No effect on late enrollment penalty or income-related adjustment in subsidies. Nothing in this subsection or section 1860C-1(f) [42 USCS § 1395w-29(f)] shall be construed as affecting the amount of any premium adjustment under subsection (b) or (i). Subsection (f) shall be applied without regard to any premium adjustment referred to in paragraph (1).

(3) Implementation. In order to carry out a premium adjustment under this subsection and section 1860C-1(f) [42 USCS § 1395w-29(f)] (insofar as it is effected through the manner of collection of premiums under section 1840(a) [42 USCS § 1395s(a)]), the Secretary shall transmit to the Commissioner of Social Security—

(A) at the beginning of each year, the name, social security account number, and the amount of the premium adjustment (if any) for each individual enrolled under this part for each month during the year; and

(B) periodically throughout the year, information to update the information previously transmitted under this paragraph for the year.

(i) Reduction in premium subsidy based on income. (1) In general. In the case of an individual whose modified adjusted gross income exceeds the threshold amount under paragraph (2), the monthly amount of the premium subsidy applicable to the premium under this section for a month after December 2006 shall be reduced (and the monthly premium shall be increased) by the monthly adjustment amount specified in paragraph (3).

(2) Threshold amount. For purposes of this subsection, subject to paragraph (6), the threshold amount is—

(A) except as provided in subparagraph (B), $80,000, and

(B) in the case of a joint return, twice the amount applicable under subparagraph (A) for the calendar year.

(3) Monthly adjustment amount. (A) In general. Subject to subparagraph (B), the monthly adjustment amount specified in this paragraph for an individual for a month in a year is equal to the product of the following:

(i) Sliding scale percentage. Subject to paragraph (6), the applicable percentage specified in the table in subparagraph (C) for the individual minus 25 percentage points.

(ii) Unsubsidized part B premium amount. 200 percent of the monthly actuarial rate for enrollees age 65 and over (as determined under subsection (a)(1) for the year).

(B) 3-year phase in. The monthly adjustment amount specified in this paragraph for an individual for a month in a year before 2009 is equal to the following percentage of the monthly adjustment amount specified in subparagraph (A):

(i) For 2007, 33 percent.

(ii) For 2008, 67 percent.

(iii), (iv) [Deleted]

(C) Applicable percentage. (i) In general.

If the modified adjusted gross income is:	The applicable percentage is:
More than $80,000 but not more than $100,000	35 percent
More than $100,000 but not more than $150,000	50 percent
More than $150,000 but not more than $200,000	65 percent
More than $200,000	80 percent.

(ii) Joint returns. In the case of a joint return, clause (i) shall be applied by substituting dollar amounts which are twice the dollar amounts otherwise applicable under clause (i) for the calendar year.

(iii) Married individuals filing separate returns. In the case of an individual who—

(I) is married as of the close of the taxable year (within the meaning of section 7703 of the Internal Revenue Code of 1986 [26 USCS § 7703]) but does not file a joint return for such year, and

(II) does not live apart from such individual's spouse at all times during the taxable year,

clause (i) shall be applied by reducing each of the dollar amounts otherwise applicable under such clause for the calendar year by the threshold amount for such year applicable to an unmarried individual.

(4) Modified adjusted gross income. (A) In general. For purposes of this subsection, the term "modified adjusted gross income" means adjusted gross income (as defined in section 62 of the Internal Revenue Code of 1986 [26 USCS § 62])—

(i) determined without regard to sections 135, 911, 931, and 933 of such Code [26 USCS §§ 135, 911, 931, and 933]; and

(ii) increased by the amount of interest received or accrued during the taxable year which is exempt from tax under such Code.

In the case of an individual filing a joint return, any reference in this subsection to the modified adjusted gross income of such individual shall be to such return's modified adjusted gross income.

(B) Taxable year to be used in determining modified adjusted gross income. (i) In general. In applying this subsection for an individual's premiums in a month in a year, subject to clause (ii) and subparagraph (C), the individual's modified adjusted gross income shall be such income determined for the individual's last taxable year beginning in the second calendar year preceding the year involved.

(ii) Temporary use of other data. If, as of October 15 before a calendar year, the Secretary of the Treasury does not have adequate data for an individual in appropriate electronic form for the taxable year referred to in clause (i), the individual's modified adjusted gross income shall be determined using the data in such form from the previous taxable year. Except as provided in regulations prescribed by the Commissioner of Social Security in consultation with the Secretary, the preceding sentence shall cease to apply when adequate data in appropriate electronic form are available for the individual for the taxable year referred to in clause (i), and proper adjustments shall be made to the extent that the premium adjustments determined under the preceding sentence were inconsistent with those determined using such taxable year.

(iii) Non-filers. In the case of individuals with respect to whom the Secretary of the Treasury does not have adequate data in appropriate electronic form for either taxable year referred to in clause (i) or clause (ii), the Commissioner of Social Security, in consultation with the Secretary, shall prescribe regulations which provide for the treatment of the premium adjustment with respect to such individual under this subsection, including regulations which provide for—

(I) the application of the highest applicable percentage under paragraph (3)(C) to such individual if the Commissioner has information which indicates that such individual's modified adjusted gross income might exceed the threshold amount for the taxable year referred to in clause (i), and

(II) proper adjustments in the case of the application of an applicable percentage under subclause (I) to such individual which is inconsistent with such individual's modified adjusted gross income for such taxable year.

(C) Use of more recent taxable year. (i) In general. The Commissioner of Social Security in consultation with the Secretary of the Treasury shall establish a procedures under which an individual's modified adjusted gross income shall, at the request of such individual, be determined under this subsection—

(I) for a more recent taxable year than the taxable year otherwise used under subparagraph (B), or

(II) by such methodology as the Commissioner, in consultation with such Secretary, determines to be appropriate, which may include a methodology for aggregating or disaggregating information from tax returns in the case of marriage or divorce.

(ii) Standard for granting requests. A request under clause (i)(I) to use a more recent taxable year may be granted only if—

(I) the individual furnishes to such Commissioner with respect to such year such documentation, such as a copy of a filed Federal income tax return or an equivalent document, as the Commissioner specifies for purposes of determining the premium adjustment (if any) under this subsection; and

(II) the individual's modified adjusted gross income for such year is significantly less than such income for the taxable year determined under subparagraph (B) by reason of the death of such individual's spouse, the marriage or divorce of such individual, or other major life changing events specified in regulations prescribed by the Commissioner in consultation with the Secretary.

(5) Inflation adjustment. (A) In general. In the case of any calendar year beginning after 2007, each dollar amount in paragraph (2) or (3) shall be increased by an amount equal to—

(i) such dollar amount, multiplied by

(ii) the percentage (if any) by which the average of the Consumer Price Index for all urban consumers (United States city average) for the 12-month period ending with August of the preceding calendar year exceeds such average for the 12-month period ending with August 2006.

(B) Rounding. If any dollar amount after being increased under subparagraph (A) is not a multiple of $1,000, such dollar amount shall be rounded to the nearest multiple of $1,000.

(6) Temporary adjustment to income thresholds. Notwithstanding any other provision of this subsection, during the period beginning on January 1, 2011, and ending on December 31, 2019—

(A) the threshold amount otherwise applicable under paragraph (2) shall be equal to such amount for 2010; and

(B) the dollar amounts otherwise applicable under paragraph (3)(C)(i) shall be equal to such dollar amounts for 2010.

(7) Joint return defined. For purposes of this subsection, the term "joint return" has the meaning given to such term by section 7701(a)(38) of the Internal Revenue Code of 1986 [26 USCS § 7701(a)(38)].

(Aug. 14, 1935, ch 531, Title XVIII, Part B, § 1839, as added July 30, 1965, P. L. 89-97, Title I, Part 1, § 102(a), 79 Stat. 305; Jan. 2, 1968, P. L. 90-248, Title I, Part 3, § 145(d), 81 Stat. 859; Oct. 30, 1972, P. L. 92-603, Title II, §§ 201(c)(4), (5), 203(a)–(d), 86 Stat. 1373, 1376, 1377; Dec. 31, 1975, P. L. 94-182, Title I, § 104(a), 89 Stat. 1052; Dec. 20, 1977, P. L. 95-216, § 205(e), 91 Stat. 1529; Dec. 5, 1980, P. L. 96-499, Title IX, Part B, Subpart II, § 945(c)(2), 94 Stat. 2642; Aug. 13, 1981, P. L. 97-35, Title XXI, Subtitle B, ch 4, § 2151(a)(4), 95 Stat. 802; Sept. 3, 1982, P. L. 97-248, Title I, Subtitle A, Part II, § 124(a), (b), 96 Stat. 364; Jan. 12, 1983, P. L. 97-448, Title III, § 309(b)(8), 96 Stat. 2409; April 20, 1983, P. L. 98-21, Title VI, § 606(a)(1), (2), (3)(A)–(C), 97 Stat. 169, 170; July 18, 1984, P. L. 98-369, Division B, Title III, Subtitle A, Part II, § 2338(a), 98 Stat. 1091; July 18, 1984, P. L. 98-369, Division B, Title III, Subtitle A, Part I, § 2302(a), (b), 98 Stat. 1063; Nov. 8, 1984, P. L. 98-617, § 3(b)(4), 98 Stat. 3295; April 7, 1986, P. L. 99-272, Title IX, Subtitle A, Part 2, Subpart B, § 9219(a)(1), Part 3, Subpart B, § 9313, 100 Stat. 182, 194; Oct. 21, 1986, P. L. 99-509, Title IX, Subtitle A, § 9001(c), Subtitle D, Part 2, § 9319(c)(4), 100 Stat. 1970, 2012; Dec. 22, 1987, P. L. 100-203, Title IV, Subtitle A, Part 3, Subpart C, § 4080, 101 Stat. 1330-126; July 1, 1988, P. L. 100-360, Title II, Subtitle B, § 211(a)–(c)(1), 102 Stat. 733, 738; Oct. 13, 1988, P. L. 100-485, Title VI, § 608(d)(9), 102 Stat. 2415; Dec. 13, 1989, P. L. 101-234, Title II, § 202(a), 103 Stat. 1981; Dec. 19, 1989, P. L. 101-239, Title VI, Subtitle A, Part 3, Subpart A, § 6202(b)(4)(C), (c)(2), Part 4, § 6301, 103 Stat. 2233, 2234, 2258, Nov. 5, 1990, P. L. 101-508, Title IV, Subtitle A, Part 4, § 4301, 104 Stat. 1388-125; Aug. 10, 1993, P. L. 103-66, Title XIII, Ch 2, Subch A, Part IV, § 13571, 107 Stat. 609; Oct. 31, 1994, P. L. 103-432, Title I, Subtitle B, Part III, § 144, Subtitle C, § 151(c)(3), 108 Stat. 4427, 4435; Aug. 5, 1997, P. L. 105-33, Title IV, Subtitle F, Ch 6, Subch A, § 4571(a), (b)(1), Subch B, §§ 4581(a), 4582, Subtitle G,

Ch 3, § 4631(a)(2), 111 Stat. 464, 465, 486; Oct. 21, 1998, P. L. 105-277, Div J, Title V, Subtitle A, § 5101(e), 112 Stat. 2681-915; Dec. 21, 2000, P. L. 106-554, § 1(a)(6), 114 Stat. 2763; Dec. 8, 2003, P. L. 108-173, Title I, § 105(a), Title II, Subtitle C, § 222(l)(2)(A), Subtitle E, § 241(b)(2)(A), Title VI, Subtitle C, § 625(a)(1), Title VII, Subtitle D, § 736(b)(7), Title VIII, Subtitle B, § 811(a), (b)(1), 117 Stat. 2166, 2206, 2220, 2317, 2356, 2364; Feb. 8, 2006, P. L. 109-171, Title V, Subtitle B, Ch. 2, §§ 5111, 5115(a)(1), 120 Stat. 43, 45; Feb. 17, 2009, P. L. 111-5, Div B, Title IV, Subtitle A, § 4103(a)(1), 123 Stat. 487; March 23, 2010, P. L. 111-148, Title III, Subtitle B, Part I, § 3110(b), Subtitle E, § 3402, 124 Stat. 420, 488.)

§ 1395t. Federal Supplementary Medical Insurance Fund

(a) Creation; deposits; fund transfers. There is hereby created on the books of the Treasury of the United States a trust fund to be known as the "Federal Supplementary Medical Insurance Trust Fund" (hereinafter in this section referred to as the "Trust Fund"). The Trust Fund shall consist of such gifts and bequests as may be made as provided in section 201(i)(1) [42 USCS § 401(i)(1)], such amounts as may be deposited in, or appropriated to, such fund as provided in this part [42 USCS §§ 1395j et seq.] or section 9008(c) of the Patient Protection and Affordable Care Act of 2009 [26 USCS prec § 4001 note], and such amounts as may be deposited in, or appropriated to, the Medicare Prescription Drug Account established by section 1860D-16 [42 USCS § 1395w-116] or the Transitional Assistance Account established by section 1860D-31(k)(1) [42 USCS § 1395w-141(k)(1)].

(b) Board of Trustees; composition; meetings; duties. With respect to the Trust Fund, there is hereby created a body to be known as the Board of Trustees of the Trust Fund (hereinafter in this section referred to as the "Board of Trustees") composed of the Commissioner of Social Security, the Secretary of the Treasury, the Secretary of Labor, and the Secretary of Health and Human Services, all ex officio, and of two members of the public (both of whom may not be from the same political party), who shall be nominated by the President for a term of four years and subject to confirmation by the Senate. A member of the Board of Trustees serving as a member of the public and nominated and confirmed to fill a vacancy occurring during a term shall be nominated and confirmed only for the remainder of such term. An individual nominated and confirmed as a member of the public may serve in such position after the expiration of such member's term until the earlier of the time at which the member's successor takes office or the time at which a report of the Board is first issued under paragraph (2) after the expiration of the member's term. The Secretary of the Treasury shall be the Managing Trustee of the Board of Trustees (hereinafter in this section referred to as the "Managing Trustee"). The Administrator of the Centers for Medicare & Medicaid Services shall serve as the Secretary of the Board of Trustees. The Board of Trustees shall meet not less frequently than once each calendar year. It shall be the duty of the Board of Trustees to—

(1) Hold the Trust Fund;

(2) Report to the Congress not later than the first day of April of each year on the operation and status of the Trust Fund during the preceding fiscal year and on its expected operation and status during the current fiscal year and the next 2 fiscal years;

(3) Report immediately to the Congress whenever the Board is of the opinion that the amount of the Trust Fund is unduly small; and

(4) Review the general policies followed in managing the Trust Fund, and recommend changes in such policies, including necessary changes in the provisions of law which govern the way in which the Trust Fund is to be managed.

The report provided for in paragraph (2) shall include a statement of the assets of, and the disbursements made from, the Trust Fund during the preceding fiscal year, an estimate of the expected income to, and disbursements to be made from, the Trust Fund during the current fiscal year and each of the next 2 fiscal years, and a statement of the actuarial status of the Trust Fund. Such report shall also include an actuarial opinion by the Chief Actuary of the Centers for Medicare & Medicaid Services certifying that the techniques and methodologies used are generally accepted within the actuarial profession and that the assumptions and cost estimates used are reasonable. Such report shall be printed as a House document of the session of the Congress to which the report is made. A person serving on the Board of Trustees shall not be considered to be a fiduciary and shall not be personally liable for actions taken in such capacity with respect to the Trust Fund. Each report provided under paragraph (2) beginning with the report in 2005 shall include the information specified in section 801(a) of the Medicare Prescription Drug, Improvement, and Modernization Act of

2003 [42 USCS § 1395i note].

(c) Investment of Trust Fund by Managing Trustee. It shall be the duty of the Managing Trustee to invest such portion of the Trust Fund as is not, in his judgment, required to meet current withdrawals. Such investments may be made only in interest-bearing obligations of the United States or in obligations guaranteed as to both principal and interest by the United States. For such purpose such obligations may be acquired (1) on original issue at the issue price, or (2) by purchase of outstanding obligations at the market price. The purposes for which obligations of the United States may be issued under chapter 31 of title 31, United States Code [31 USCS §§ 3101 et seq.], are hereby extended to authorize the issuance at par of public-debt obligations for purchase by the Trust Fund. Such obligations issued for purchase by the Trust Fund shall have maturities fixed with due regard for the needs of the Trust Fund and shall bear interest at a rate equal to the average market yield (computed by the Managing Trustee on the basis of market quotations as of the end of the calendar month next preceding the date of such issue) on all marketable interest-bearing obligations of the United States then forming a part of the public debt which are not due or callable until after the expiration of 4 years from the end of such calendar month; except that where such average market yield is not a multiple of one-eighth of 1 per centum, the rate of interest on such obligations shall be the multiple of one-eighth of 1 per centum nearest such market yield. The Managing Trustee may purchase other interest-bearing obligations of the United States or obligations guaranteed as to both principal and interest by the United States, on original issue or at the market price, only where he determines that the purchase of such other obligations is in the public interest.

(d) Authority of Managing Trustee to sell obligations. Any obligations acquired by the Trust Fund (except public-debt obligations issued exclusively to the Trust Fund) may be sold by the Managing Trustee at the market price, and such public-debt obligations may be redeemed at par plus accrued interest.

(e) Interest on or proceeds from sale or redemption of obligations. The interest on, and the proceeds from the sale or redemption of, any obligations held in the Trust Fund shall be credited to and form a part of the Trust Fund.

(f) Transfers to other Funds. There shall be transferred periodically (but not less often than once each fiscal year) to the Trust Fund from the Federal Old-Age and Survivors Insurance Trust Fund and from the Federal Disability Insurance Trust Fund amounts equivalent to the amounts not previously so transferred which the Secretary of Health and Human Services shall have certified as overpayments (other than amounts so certified to the Railroad Retirement Board) pursuant to section 1870(b) of this Act [42 USCS § 1395gg(b)]. There shall be transferred periodically (but not less often than once each fiscal year) to the Trust Fund from the Railroad Retirement Account amounts equivalent to the amounts not previously so transferred which the Secretary of Health and Human Services shall have certified as overpayments to the Railroad Retirement Board pursuant to section 1870(b) of this Act [42 USCS § 1395gg(b)].

(g) Payments from Trust Fund of amounts provided for by 42 USCS §§ 1395j et seq. or with respect to administrative expenses. The Managing Trustee shall pay from time to time from the Trust Fund such amounts as the Secretary of Health and Human Services certifies are necessary to make the payments provided for by this part [42 USCS §§ 1395j et seq.], and the payments with respect to administrative expenses in accordance with section 201(g)(1) [42 USCS § 401(g)(1)]. The payments provided for under part D [42 USCS §§ 1395w-101 et seq.], other than under section 1860D-31(k)(2) [42 USCS § 1395w-141(k)(2)], shall be made from the Medicare Prescription Drug Account in the Trust Fund. The payments provided for under section 1860D-31(k)(2) [42 USCS § 1395w-141(k)(2)] shall be made from the Transitional Assistance Account in the Trust Fund.

(h) Payments from Trust Fund of costs incurred by Director of the Office of Personnel Management. The Managing Trustee shall pay from time to time from the Trust Fund such amounts as the Secretary of Health and Human Services certifies are necessary to pay the costs incurred by the Director of the Office of Personnel Management in making deductions pursuant to section 1840(d) [42 USCS § 1395s(d)] or pursuant to section 1860D-13(c)(1) or 1854(d)(2)(A) [42 USCS § 1395w-113(c)(1) or 1395w-24(d)(2)(A)] (in which case payments shall be made in appropriate part from the Medicare Prescription Drug Account in the Trust Fund). During each fiscal year, or after the close of such fiscal year, the Director of the Office of Personnel Management shall certify to the Secretary the amount of the costs the Director incurred in making such deductions, and such certified amount shall be the basis for the amount of such costs certified by the Secretary to the Managing Trustee.

(i) Payments from Trust Fund of costs incurred by Railroad Retirement Board. The Managing Trustee shall pay from time to time from the Trust Fund such amounts as the Secretary of Health and Human Services certifies are necessary to pay the costs incurred by the Railroad Retirement Board for services performed pursuant to section 1840(b)(1) and section 1842(g) [42 USCS §§ 1395s(b)(1) and 1395u(g)] and pursuant to sections 1860D-13(c)(1) and 1854(d)(2)(A) [42 USCS §§ 1395w-113(c)(1) and 1395w-24(d)(2)(A)] (in which case payments shall be made in appropriate part from the Medicare Prescription Drug Account in the Trust Fund). During each fiscal year or after the close of such fiscal year, the Railroad Retirement Board shall certify to the Secretary the amount of the costs it incurred in performing such services and such certified amount shall be the basis for the amount of such costs certified by the Secretary to the Managing Trustee.

(Aug. 14, 1935, ch 531, Title XVIII, Part B, § 1841, as added July 30, 1965, P. L. 89-97, Title I, Part 1, § 102(a), 79 Stat. 308; Jan. 2, 1968, P. L. 90-248, Title I, Part 4, § 169(a), 81 Stat. 875; Oct. 30, 1972, P. L. 92-603, Title I, § 132(e), Title II, § 263(d)(4), (e), 86 Stat. 1361, 1449; June 13, 1978, P. L. 95-292, § 5, 92 Stat. 315; April 20, 1983, P. L. 98-21, Title I, Part F, § 154(c), Title III, Part C, § 341(c), 97 Stat. 107, 135; July 18, 1984, P. L. 98-369, Division B, Title III, Subtitle A, Part II, §§ 2354(b)(2), (11), (12), 2663(j)(2)(F)(iii), 98 Stat. 1100, 1101, 1170; April 7, 1986, P. L. 99-272, Title IX, Subtitle A, Part 2, Subpart B, § 9213(b) in part, 100 Stat. 180; July 1, 1988, P. L. 100-360, Title II, Subtitle B, § 212(b)(2), (c)(4), 102 Stat. 740, 741; Nov. 10, 1988, P. L. 100-647, Title VIII, Subtitle A, § 8005(a), 102 Stat. 3781; Dec. 13, 1989, P. L. 101-234, Title II, § 202(a), 103 Stat. 1981; Aug. 15, 1994, P. L. 103-296, Title I, § 108(c)(3), 108 Stat. 1485; Dec. 8, 2003, P. L. 108-173, Title I, §§ 101(e)(3)(C), 105(d), Title VIII, Subtitle A, § 801(d)(2), Title IX, § 900(e)(1)(E), 117 Stat. 2151, 2166, 2359, 2371; March 23, 2010, P. L. 111-148, Title IX, Subtitle A, § 9008(k), 124 Stat. 862.)

§ 1395u. Provisions relating to the administration of part B

(a) The administration of this part [42 USCS §§ 1395j et seq.] shall be conducted through contracts with medicare administrative contractors under section 1874A [42 USCS § 1395kk-1].

(b) Applicability of competitive bidding provisions; findings as to financial responsibility, etc., of carrier; contractual duties imposed by contract. (1) [Deleted]

(2)

(A), (B) [Deleted]

(C) In the case of residents of nursing facilities who receive services described in clause (i) or (ii) of section 1861(s)(2)(K) [42 USCS § 1395x(s)(2)(K)] performed by a member of a team, the Secretary shall instruct medicare administrative contractors to develop mechanisms which permit routine payment under this part for up to 1.5 visits per month per resident. In the previous sentence, the term "team" refers to a physician and includes a physician assistant acting under the supervision of the physician or a nurse practitioner working in collaboration with that physician, or both.

(D), (E) [Deleted]

(3) The Secretary—

(A) shall take such action as may be necessary to assure that, where payment under this part [42 USCS §§ 1395j et seq.] for a service is on a cost basis, the cost is reasonable cost (as determined under section 1861(v) [42 USCS § 1395x(v)]);

(B) shall take such action as may be necessary to assure that, where payment under this part [42 USCS §§ 1395j et seq.] for a service is on a charge basis, such charge will be reasonable and not higher than the charge applicable, for a comparable service and under comparable circumstances, to the policyholders and subscribers of the medicare administrative contractor, and such payment will (except as otherwise provided in section 1870(f) [42 USCS § 1395gg(f)]) be made—

(i) on the basis of an itemized bill; or

(ii) on the basis of an assignment under the terms of which (I) the reasonable charge is the full charge for the service, (II) the physician or other person furnishing such service agrees not to charge (and to refund amounts already collected) for services for which payment under this title [42 USCS §§ 1395 et seq.] is denied under section 1154(a)(2) [42 USCS § 1320c-3(a)(2)] by reason of a determination under section 1154(a)(1)(B) [42 USCS § 1320c-3(a)(1)(B)], and (III) the physician or other person furnishing such service agrees not to charge (and to refund amounts already collected) for such service if payment may not be made therefor by reason of the provisions of paragraph (1) of section 1862(a) [42 USCS § 1395y(a)(1)], and if the individual to whom such service was furnished was without fault in incurring the expenses of such service, and if the Secretary's determination that payment (pursuant to such assignment) was incorrect and was made subsequent to the third year following the year in which notice of such payment was sent to such individual; except that the Secretary may reduce such three-year period to not less than one year if he finds such reduction is consistent with the objectives of this title [42 USCS §§ 1395 et seq.] (except in the case of physicians' services and ambulance service furnished as described in section 1862(a)(4) [42 USCS § 1395y(a)(4)], other than for purposes of section 1870(f) [42 USCS § 1395gg(f)]);

but (in the case of bills submitted, or requests for payment made, after March 1968) only if the bill is submitted, or a written request for payment is made in such other form as may be permitted under regulations, no later than the period ending 1 calendar year after the date of service;

(C)–(E) [Deleted]

(F) shall take such action as may be necessary to assure that where payment under this part [42 USCS §§ 1395j et seq.] for a service rendered is on a charge basis, such payment shall be determined on the basis of the charge that is determined in accordance with this section on the basis of customary and prevailing charge levels in effect at the time the service was rendered or, in the case of services rendered more than 12 months before the year in which the bill is submitted or request for payment is made, on the basis of such levels in effect for the 12-month period preceding such year;

(G) shall, for a service that is furnished with respect to an individual enrolled under this part, that is not paid on an assignment-related basis, and that is subject to a limiting charge under section 1848(g) [42 USCS § 1395w-4(g)]—

(i) determine, prior to making payment, whether the amount billed for such service exceeds the limiting charge applicable under section 1848(g)(2) [42 USCS § 1395w-4(g)];

(ii) notify the physician, supplier, or other person periodically (but not less often than once every 30 days) of determinations that amounts billed exceeded such applicable limiting charges; and

(iii) provide for prompt response to inquiries of physicians, suppliers, and other persons concerning the accuracy of such limiting charges for their services;

(H) shall implement—

(i) programs to recruit and retain physicians as participating physicians in the area served by the medicare administrative contractor, including educational and outreach activities and the use of professional relations personnel to handle billing and other problems relating to payment of claims of participating physicians; and

(ii) programs to familiarize beneficiaries with the participating physician program and to assist such beneficiaries in locating participating physicians;

(I) [Deleted]

(J), (K) [Repealed]

(L) shall monitor and profile physicians' billing patterns within each area or locality and provide comparative data to physicians whose utilization patterns vary significantly from other physicians in the same payment area or locality.

In determining the reasonable charge for services for purposes of this paragraph, there shall be taken into consideration the customary charges for similar services generally made by the physician or other person furnishing such services, as well as the prevailing charges in the locality for similar services. No charge may be determined to be reasonable in the case of bills submitted or requests for payment made under this part [42 USCS §§ 1395j et seq.] after December 31, 1970, if it exceeds the higher of (i) the prevailing charge recognized by the carrier and found acceptable by the Secretary for similar services in the same locality in administering this part [42 USCS §§ 1395j et seq.] on December 31, 1970, or (ii) the prevailing charge level that, on the basis of statistical data and methodology acceptable to the Secretary, would cover 75 percent of the customary charges made for similar services in the same locality during the 12-month period ending on the March 31 last preceding the start of the twelve-month period (beginning October 1 of each year) in which the service is rendered. In the case of physicians' services the prevailing charge level determined for purposes of clause (ii) of the preceding sentence for any twelve-month period (beginning after June 30, 1973) specified in clause (ii) of such sentence may not exceed (in the aggregate) the level determined under such clause for the fiscal year ending June 30, 1973, or (with respect to physicians' services furnished in a year after 1987) the level determined under this sentence (or under any other provision of law affecting the prevailing charge level) for the previous year except to the extent that the Secretary finds, on the basis of appropriate economic index data, that such higher level is justified by year-to-year economic changes. With respect to power-operated wheelchairs for which payment may be made in accordance with section 1861(s)(6) [42 USCS § 1395x(s)(6)], charges determined to be reasonable may not exceed the lowest charge at which power-operated wheelchairs are available in the locality. In the case of medical services, supplies, and equipment (including equipment servicing) that, in the judgment of the Secretary, do not generally vary significantly in quality from one supplier to another, the charges incurred after December 31, 1972, determined to be reasonable may not exceed the lowest charge levels at which such services, supplies, and equipment are widely and consistently available in a locality except to the extent and under the circumstances specified by the Secretary. The requirement in subparagraph (B) that a bill be submitted or request for payment be made by the close of the following calendar year shall not apply if (I) failure to submit the bill or request the payment by the close of such year is due to the error or misrepresentation of an officer, employee, fiscal intermediary, carrier, medicare administrative contractor, or agent of the Department of Health and Human Services performing functions under this title [42 USCS §§ 1395 et seq.] and acting within the scope of his or its authority, and (II) the bill is submitted or the payment is requested promptly after such error or misrepresentation is eliminated or corrected. The amount of any charges for outpatient services which shall be considered reasonable shall be subject to the limitations established by regulations issued by the Secretary pursuant to section 1861(v)(1)(K) [42 USCS § 1395x(v)(1)(K)], and in determining the reasonable charge for such services, the Secretary may limit such reasonable charge to a percentage of the amount of the prevailing charge for similar services furnished in a physician's office, taking into account the extent to which overhead costs associated with such outpatient services have been included in the reasonable cost or charge of the facility. In applying subparagraph (B), the Secretary may specify exceptions to the 1 calendar year period specified in such subparagraph.

(4)(A)(i) In determining the prevailing charge levels under the third and fourth sentences of paragraph (3) for physicians' services furnished during the 15-month period beginning July 1, 1984, the Secretary shall not set any level higher than the same level as was set for the 12-month period beginning July 1, 1983.

(ii)(I) In determining the prevailing charge levels under the third and fourth sentences of paragraph (3) for physicians' services furnished during the 8-month period beginning May 1, 1986, by a physician who is not a participating physician (as defined in subsection (h)(1)) at the time of furnishing the services, the Secretary shall not set any level higher than the same level as was set for the 12-month period beginning July 1, 1983.

(II) In determining the prevailing charge levels under the fourth sentence of paragraph (3) for physicians' services furnished during the 8-month period beginning May 1, 1986, by a physician who is a participating physician (as defined in subsection (h)(1)) at the time of furnishing the services, the Secretary shall permit an additional one percentage point increase in the increase otherwise permitted under that sentence.

(iii) In determining the maximum allowable prevailing charges which may be recognized consistent with the index described in the fourth sentence of paragraph (3) for physicians' services furnished on or after January 1, 1987, by participating physicians, the Secretary shall treat the maximum allowable prevailing charges recognized as of December 31, 1986, under such sentence with respect to participating physicians as having been justified by economic changes.

(iv) The reasonable charge for physicians' services furnished on or after January 1, 1987, and before January 1, 1992, by a nonparticipating physician shall be no greater than the applicable percent of the prevailing charge levels established under the third and fourth sentences of paragraph (3) (or under any other applicable provision of law affecting the prevailing charge level). In the previous sentence, the term "applicable percent" means for services furnished (I) on or after January 1, 1987, and before April 1, 1988, 96 percent, (II) on or after April 1, 1988, and before January 1, 1989, 95.5 percent, and (III) on or after January 1, 1989, 95 percent.

(v) In determining the prevailing charge levels under the third and fourth sentences of paragraph (3) for physicians' services furnished during the 3-month period beginning January 1, 1988, the Secretary shall not set any level higher than the same level as was set for the 12-month period beginning January 1, 1987.

(vi) Before each year (beginning with 1989), the Secretary shall establish a prevailing charge floor for primary care services (as defined in subsection (i)(4) equal to 60 percent of the estimated average prevailing charge levels based on the best available data (determined, for participating physicians under the third and fourth sentences of paragraph (3) and under paragraph (4), without regard to this clause and without regard to physician specialty) for such service for all localities in the United States (weighted by the relative frequency of the service in each locality) for the year.

(vii) Beginning with 1987, the percentage increase in the MEI (as defined in subsection (i)(3)) for each year shall be the same for nonparticipating physicians as for participating physicians.

(B)(i) In determining the reasonable charge under paragraph (3) for physicians' services furnished during the 15-month period beginning July 1, 1984, the customary charges shall be the same customary charges as were recognized under this section for the 12-month period beginning July 1, 1983.

(ii) In determining the reasonable charge under paragraph (3) for physicians' services furnished during the 8-month period beginning May 1, 1986, by a physician who is not a participating physician (as defined in subsection (h)(1)) at the time of furnishing the services—

(I) if the physician was not a participating physician at any time during the 12-month period beginning on October 1, 1984, the customary charges shall be the same customary charges as were recognized under this section for the 12-month period beginning July 1, 1983, and

(II) if the physician was a participating physician at any time during the 12-month period beginning on October 1, 1984, the physician's customary charges shall be determined based upon the physician's actual charges billed during the 12-month period ending on March 31, 1985.

(iii) In determining the reasonable charge under paragraph (3) for physicians' services furnished during the 3-month period beginning January 1, 1988, the customary charges shall be the same customary charges as were recognized under this section for the 12-month period beginning January 1, 1987.

(iv) In determining the reasonable charge under paragraph (3) for physicians' services (other than primary care services, as defined in subsection (i)(4)) furnished during 1991, the customary charges shall be the same customary charges as were recognized under this section for the 9-month period beginning April 1, 1990. In a case in which subparagraph (F) applies (relating to new physicians) so as to limit the customary charges of a physician during 1990 to a percent of prevailing charges, the previous sentence shall not prevent such limit on customary charges under such subparagraph from increasing in 1991 to a higher percent of such prevailing charges.

(C) In determining the prevailing charge levels under the third and fourth sentences of paragraph (3) for physicians' services furnished during periods beginning after September 30, 1985, the Secretary shall treat the level as set under subparagraph (A)(i) as having fully provided for the economic changes which would have been taken into account but for the limitations contained in subparagraph (A)(i).

(D)(i) In determining the customary charges for physicians' services furnished during the 8-month period beginning May 1, 1986, or the 12-month period beginning January 1, 1987, by a physician who was not a participating physician (as defined in subsection (h)(1)) on September 30, 1985, the Secretary shall not recognize increases in actual charges for services furnished during the 15-month period beginning on July 1, 1984, above the level of the physician's actual charges billed in the 3-month period ending on June 30, 1984.

(ii) In determining the customary charges for physicians' services furnished during the 12-month period beginning January 1, 1987, by a physician who is not a participating physician (as defined in subsection (h)(1)) on April 30, 1986, the Secretary shall not recognize increases in actual charges for services furnished during the 7-month period beginning on October 1, 1985, above the level of the physician's actual charges billed during the 3-month period ending on June 30, 1984.

(iii) In determining the customary charges for physicians' services furnished during the 12-month period beginning January 1, 1987, or January 1, 1988, by a physician who is not a participating physician (as defined in subsection (h)(1)) on December 31, 1986, the Secretary shall not recognize increases in actual charges for services furnished during the 8-month period beginning on May 1, 1986, above the level of the physician's actual charges billed during the 3-month period ending on June 30, 1984.

(iv) In determining the customary charges for a physicians' service furnished on or after January 1, 1988, if a physician was a nonparticipating physician in a previous year (beginning with 1987), the Secretary shall not recognize any amount of such actual charges (for that service furnished during such previous year) that exceeds the maximum allowable actual charge for such service established under subsection (j)(1)(C).

(E)(i) For purposes of this part [42 USCS §§ 1395j et seq.] for physicians' services furnished in 1987, the percentage increase in the MEI is 3.2 percent.

(ii) For purposes of this part [42 USCS §§ 1395j et seq.] for physicians' services furnished in 1988, on or after April 1, the percentage increase in the MEI is—

(I) 3.6 percent for primary care services (as defined in subsection (i)(4)), and

(II) 1 percent for other physicians' services.

(iii) For purposes of this part [42 USCS §§ 1395j et seq.] for physicians' services furnished in 1989, the percentage increase in the MEI is—

(I) 3.0 percent for primary care services, and

(II) 1 percent for other physicians' services.

(iv) For purposes of this part [42 USCS §§ 1395j et seq.] for items and services furnished in 1990, after March 31, 1990, the percentage increase in the MEI is—

(I) 0 percent for radiology services, for anesthesia services, and for other services specified in the list referred to in paragraph (14)(C)(i),

(II) 2 percent for other services (other than primary care services), and

(III) such percentage increase in the MEI (as defined in subsection (i)(3)) as would be otherwise determined for primary care services (as defined in subsection (i)(4)).

(v) For purposes of this part [42 USCS §§ 1395j et seq.] for items and services furnished in 1991, the percentage increase in the MEI is—

(I) 0 percent for services (other than primary care services), and

(II) 2 percent for primary care services (as defined in subsection (i)(4)).

(5) [Deleted]

(6) No payment under this part [42 USCS §§ 1395j et seq.] for a service provided to any individual shall (except as provided in section 1870 [42 USCS § 1395gg]) be made to anyone other than such individual or (pursuant to an assignment described in subparagraph (B)(ii) of paragraph (3)) the physician or other person who provided the service, except that (A) payment may be made (i) to the employer of such physician or other person if such physician or other person is required as a condition of his employment to turn over his fee for such service to his employer, or (ii) where the service was provided under a contractual arrangement between such physician or other person and an entity, to the entity if, under the contractual arrangement, the entity submits the bill for the service and the contractual arrangement meets such program integrity and other safeguards as the Secretary may determine to be appropriate, (B) payment may be made to an entity (i) which provides coverage of the services under a health benefits plan, but only to the extent that payment is not made under this part [42 USCS §§ 1395j et seq.], (ii) which has paid the person who provided the service an amount (including the amount payable under this part [42 USCS §§ 1395j et seq.]) which that person has accepted as payment in full for the service, and (iii) to which the individual has agreed in writing that payment may be made under this part [42 USCS §§ 1395j et seq.], (C) in the case of services described in clause (i) of section 1861(s)(2)(K) [42 USCS § 1395x(s)(2)(K)], payment shall be made to either (i) the employer of the physician assistant involved, or (ii) with respect to a physician assistant who was the owner of a rural health clinic (as described in section 1861(aa)(2) [42 USCS § 1395x(aa)(2)]) for a continuous period beginning prior to the date of the enactment of the Balanced Budget Act of 1997 [enacted on Aug. 5, 1997] and ending on the date that the Secretary determines such rural health clinic no longer meets the requirements of section 1861(aa)(2) [42 USCS § 1395x(aa)(2)], payment may be made directly to the physician assistant, (D) payment may be made to a physician for physicians' services (and services furnished incident to such services) furnished by a second physician to patients of the first physician if (i) the first physician is unavailable to provide the services; (ii) the services are furnished pursuant to an arrangement between the two physicians that (I) is informal and reciprocal, or (II) involves per diem or other fee-for-time compensation for such services; (iii) the services are not provided by the second physician over a continuous period of more than 60 days or are provided over a longer continuous period during all of which the first physician has been called or ordered to active duty as a member of a reserve component of the Armed Forces; and (iv) the claim form submitted to the medicare administrative contractor for such services includes the second physician's unique identifier (provided under the system established under subsection (r)) and indicates that the claim meets the requirements of this subparagraph for payment to the first physician, (E) in the case of an item or service (other than services described in section 1888(e)(2)(A)(ii) [42 USCS § 1395rr(e)(2)(A)(ii)]) furnished by, or under arrangements made by, a skilled nursing facil-

ity to an individual who (at the time the item or service is furnished) is a resident of a skilled nursing facility, payment shall be made to the facility, (F) in the case of home health services (including medical supplies described in section 1861(m)(5) [42 USCS § 1395x(m)(5)], but excluding durable medical equipment to the extent provided for in such section) furnished to an individual who (at the time the item or service is furnished) is under a plan of care of a home health agency, payment shall be made to the agency (without regard to whether or not the item or service was furnished by the agency, by others under arrangement with them made by the agency, or when any other contracting or consulting arrangement, or otherwise), (G) in the case of services in a hospital or clinic to which section 1880(e) [42 USCS § 1395qq(e)] applies, payment shall be made to such hospital or clinic, and (H) in the case of services described in section 1861(aa)(3) [42 USCS § 1395x(aa)(3)] that are furnished by a health care professional under contract with a Federally qualified health center, payment shall be made to the center. No payment which under the preceding sentence may be made directly to the physician or other person providing the service involved (pursuant to an assignment described in subparagraph (B)(ii) of paragraph (3)) shall be made to anyone else under a reassignment or power of attorney (except to an employer or entity as described in subparagraph (A) of such sentence); but nothing in this subsection shall be construed (i) to prevent the making of such a payment in accordance with an assignment from the individual to whom the service was provided or a reassignment from the physician or other person providing such service if such assignment or reassignment is made to a governmental agency or entity or is established by or pursuant to the order of a court of competent jurisdiction, or (ii) to preclude an agent of the physician or other person providing the service from receiving any such payment if (but only if) such agent does so pursuant to an agency agreement under which the compensation to be paid to the agent for his services for or in connection with the billing or collection of payments due such physician or other person under this title [42 USCS §§ 1395 et seq.] is unrelated (directly or indirectly) to the amount of such payments or the billings therefor, and is not dependent upon the actual collection of any such payment. For purposes of subparagraph (C) of the first sentence of this paragraph, an employment relationship may include any independent contractor arrangement, and employer status shall be determined in accordance with the law of the State in which the services described in such clause are performed.

(7)(A) In the case of physicians' services furnished to a patient in a hospital with a teaching program approved as specified in section 1861(b)(6) [42 USCS § 1395x(b)(6)] but which does not meet the conditions described in section 1861(b)(7) [42 USCS § 1395x(b)(7)], the Secretary shall not provide (except on the basis described in subparagraph (C)) for payment for such services under this part [42 USCS §§ 1395j et seq.]—

(i) unless—

(I) the physician renders sufficient personal and identifiable physicians' services to the patient to exercise full, personal control over the management of the portion of the case for which the payment is sought,

(II) the services are of the same character as the services the physician furnishes to patients not entitled to benefits under this title [42 USCS §§ 1395 et seq.], and

(III) at least 25 percent of the hospital's patients (during a representative past period, as determined by the Secretary) who were not entitled to benefits under this title [42 USCS §§ 1395 et seq.] and who were furnished services described in subclauses (I) and (II) paid all or a substantial part of charges (other than nominal charges) imposed for such services; and

(ii) to the extent that the payment is based upon a reasonable charge for the services in excess of the customary charge as determined in accordance with subparagraph (B).

(B) The customary charge for such services in a hospital shall be determined in accordance with regulations issued by the Secretary and taking into account the following factors:

(i) In the case of a physician who is not a teaching physician (as defined by the Secretary), the Secretary shall take into account the amounts the physician charges for similar services in the physician's practice outside the teaching setting.

(ii) In the case of a teaching physician, if the hospital, its physicians, or other appropriate billing entity has established one or more schedules of charges which are collected for medical and surgical services, the Secretary shall base payment under this title [42 USCS §§ 1395 et seq.] on the greatest of—

(I) the charges (other than nominal charges) which are most frequently collected in full or substantial part with respect to patients who were not entitled to benefits under this title [42 USCS §§ 1395 et seq.] and who were furnished services described in subclauses (I) and (II) of subparagraph (A)(i),

(II) the mean of the charges (other than nominal charges) which were collected in full or substantial part with respect to such patients, or

(III) 85 percent of the prevailing charges paid for similar services in the same locality.

(iii) If all the teaching physicians in a hospital agree to have payment made for all of their physicians' services under this part [42 USCS §§ 1395j et seq.] furnished to patients in such hospital on an assignment-related basis, the customary charge for such services shall be equal to 90 percent of the prevailing charges paid for similar services in the same locality.

(C) In the case of physicians' services furnished to a patient in a hospital with a teaching program approved as specified in section 1861(b)(6) [42 USCS § 1395x(b)(6)] but which does not meet the conditions described in section 1861(b)(7) [42 USCS § 1395x(b)(7)], if the conditions described in subclauses (I) and (II) of subparagraph (A)(i) are met and if the physician elects payment to be determined under this subparagraph, the Secretary shall provide for payment for such services under this part [42 USCS §§ 1395j et seq.] on the basis of regulations of the Secretary governing reimbursement for the services of hospital-based physicians (and not on any other basis).

(D)(i) In the case of physicians' services furnished to a patient in a hospital with a teaching program approved as specified in section 1861(b)(6) [42 USCS § 1395x(b)(6)] but which does not meet the conditions described in section 1861(b)(7) [42 USCS § 1395x(b)(7)], no payment shall be made under this part [42 USCS §§ 1395j et seq.] for services of assistants at surgery with respect to a surgical procedure if such hospital has a training program relating to the medical specialty required for such surgical procedure and a qualified individual on the staff of the hospital is available to provide such services; except that payment may be made under this part [42 USCS §§ 1395j et seq.] for such services, to the extent that such payment is otherwise allowed under this paragraph, if such services, as determined under regulations of the Secretary—

(I) are required due to exceptional medical circumstances,

(II) are performed by team physicians needed to perform complex medical procedures, or

(III) constitute concurrent medical care relating to a medical condition which requires the presence of, and active care by, a physician of another specialty during surgery,

and under such other circumstances as the Secretary determines by regulation to be appropriate.

(ii) For purposes of this subparagraph, the term "assistant at surgery" means a physician who actively assists the physician in charge of a case in performing a surgical procedure.

(iii) The Secretary shall determine appropriate methods of reimbursement of assistants at surgery where such services are reimbursable under this part [42 USCS §§ 1395j et seq.].

(8)(A) (i) The Secretary shall by regulation—

(I) describe the factors to be used in determining the cases (of particular items or services) in which the application of this title [42 USCS §§ 1395 et seq.] to payment under this part [42 USCS §§ 1395j et seq.](other than to physicians' services paid under section 1848 [42 USCS § 1395w-4]) results in the determination of an amount that, because of its being grossly excessive or grossly deficient, is not inherently reasonable, and

(II) provide in those cases for the factors to be considered in determining an amount that is realistic and equitable.

(ii) Notwithstanding the determination made in clause (i), the Secretary may not apply factors that would increase or decrease the payment under this part [42 USCS §§ 1395j et seq.] during any year for any particular item or service by more than 15 percent from such payment during the preceding year except as provided in subparagraph (B).

(B) The Secretary may make a determination under this subparagraph that would result in an increase or decrease under subparagraph (A) of more than 15 percent of the payment amount for a year, but only if—

(i) the Secretary's determination takes into account the factors described in subparagraph (C) and any additional factors the Secretary determines appropriate,

(ii) the Secretary's determination takes into account the potential impacts described in subparagraph (D), and

(iii) the Secretary complies with the procedural requirements of paragraph (9).

(C) The factors described in this subparagraph are as follows:

(i) The programs established under this title [42 USCS §§ 1395 et seq.] and title XIX [42 USCS §§ 1396 et seq.] are the sole or primary sources of payment for an item or service.

(ii) The payment amount does not reflect changing technology, increased facility with that technology, or reductions in acquisition or production costs.

(iii) The payment amount for an item or service under this part [42 USCS §§ 1395j et seq.] is substantially higher or lower than the payment made for the item or service by other purchasers.

(D) The potential impacts of a determination under subparagraph (B) on quality, access, and beneficiary liability, including the likely effects on assignment rates and participation rates.

(9)(A) The Secretary shall consult with representatives of suppliers or other individuals who furnish an item or service before making a determination under paragraph (8)(B) with regard to that item or service.

(B) The Secretary shall publish notice of a proposed determination under paragraph (8)(B) in the Federal Register—

(i) specifying the payment amount proposed to be established with respect to an item or service,

(ii) explaining the factors and data that the Secretary took into account in determining the payment amount so specified, and

(iii) explaining the potential impacts described in paragraph (8)(D).

(C) After publication of the notice required by subparagraph (B), the Secretary shall allow not less than 60 days for public comment on the proposed determination.

(D)(i) Taking into consideration the comments made by the public, the Secretary shall publish in the Federal Register a final determination under paragraph (8)(B) with respect to the payment amount to be established with respect to the item or service.

(ii) A final determination published pursuant to clause (i) shall explain the factors and data that the Secretary took into consideration in making the final determination.

(10)(A)(i) In determining the reasonable charge for procedures described in subparagraph (B) and performed during the 9-month period beginning on April 1, 1988, the prevailing charge for such procedure shall be the prevailing charge otherwise recognized for such procedure for 1987—

(I) subject to clause (iii), reduced by 2.0 percent, and

(II) further reduced by the applicable percentage specified in clause (ii).

(ii) For purposes of clause (i), the applicable percentage specified in this clause is—

(I) 15 percent, in the case of a prevailing charge otherwise recognized (without regard to this paragraph and determined without regard to physician specialty) that is at least 150 percent of the weighted national average (as determined by the Secretary) of such prevailing charges for such procedure for all localities in the United States for 1987;

(II) 0 percent, in the case of a prevailing charge that does not exceed 85 percent of such weighted national average; and

(III) in the case of any other prevailing charge, a percent determined on the basis of a straight-line sliding scale, equal to 3/13 of a percentage point for each percent by which the prevailing charge exceeds 85 percent of such weighted national average.

(iii) In no case shall the reduction under clause (i) for a procedure result in a prevailing charge in a locality for 1988 which is less than 85 percent of the Secretary's estimate of the weighted national average of such prevailing charges for such procedure for all localities in the United States for 1987 (based upon the best available data and determined without regard to physician specialty) after making the reduction described in clause (i)(I).

(B) The procedures described in this subparagraph are as follows: bronchoscopy, carpal tunnel repair, cataract surgery (including subsequent inspection of an intra-ocular lens), coronary artery bypass surgery, diagnostic and/or therapeutic dilation and curettage, knee arthroscopy, knee arthroplasty, pacemaker implantation surgery, total hip replacement, suprapubic prostatectomy, transurethral resection of the prostate, and upper gastrointestinal endoscopy.

(C) In the case of a reduction in the reasonable charge for a physicians' service under subparagraph (A), if a nonparticipating physician furnishes the service to an individual entitled to benefits under this part [42 USCS §§ 1395j et seq.], after the effective date of such reduction, the physician's actual charge is subject to a limit under subsection (j)(1)(D).

(D) There shall be no administrative or judicial review under section 1869 [42 USCS § 1395ff] or otherwise of any determination under subparagraph (A) or under paragraph (11)(B)(ii).

(11)(A) In providing payment for cataract eyeglasses and cataract contact lenses, and professional services relating to them, under this part [42 USCS §§ 1395j et seq.], each carrier shall—

(i) provide for separate determinations of the payment amount for the eyeglasses and lenses and of the payment amount for the professional services of a physician (as defined in section 1861(r) [42 USCS § 1395x(r)]), and

(ii) not recognize as reasonable for such eyeglasses and lenses more than such amount as the Secretary establishes in guidelines relating to the inherent reasonableness of charges for such eyeglasses and lenses.

(B)(i) In determining the reasonable charge under paragraph (3) for a cataract surgical procedure, subject to clause (ii), the prevailing charge for such procedure otherwise recognized for participating and nonparticipating physicians shall be reduced by 10 percent with respect to procedures performed in 1987.

(ii) In no case shall the reduction under clause (i) for a surgical procedure result in a prevailing charge in a locality for a year which is less than 75 percent of the weighted national average of such prevailing charges for such procedure for all the localities in the United States for 1986.

(C)(i) The prevailing charge level determined with respect to A-mode ophthalmic ultrasound procedures may not exceed 5 percent of the prevailing charge level established with respect to extra-capsular cataract removal with lens insertion.

(ii) The reasonable charge for an intraocular lens inserted during or subsequent to cataract surgery in a physician's office may not exceed the actual acquisition cost for the lens (taking into account any discount) plus a handling fee (not to exceed 5 percent of such actual acquisition cost).

(D) In the case of a reduction in the reasonable charge for a physicians' service or item under subparagraph (B) or (C), if a nonparticipating physician furnishes the service or item to an individual entitled to benefits under this part [42 USCS §§ 1395j et seq.] after the effective date of such reduction, the physician's actual charge is subject to a limit under subsection (j)(1)(D).

(12) [Repealed]

(13)(A) In determining payments under section 1833(l) and section 1848 [42 USCS §§ 1395l(l), 1395w-4] for anesthesia services furnished on or after January 1, 1994, the methodology for determining the base and time units used shall be the same for services furnished by physicians, for medical direction by physicians of two, three, or four certified registered nurse anesthetists, or for services furnished by a certified registered nurse anesthetist (whether or not medically directed) and shall be based on the methodology in effect, for anesthesia services furnished by physicians, as of the date of the enactment of the Omnibus Budget Reconciliation Act of 1993 [enacted Aug. 10, 1993].

(B) The Secretary shall require claims for physicians' services for medical direction of nurse anesthetists during the periods in which the provisions of subparagraph (A) apply to indicate the number of such anesthetists being medically directed concurrently at any time during the procedure, the name of each nurse anesthetist being directed, and the type of procedure for which the services are provided.

(14)(A)(i) In determining the reasonable charge for a physicians' service specified in subparagraph (C)(i) and furnished during the 9-month period beginning on April 1, 1990, the prevailing charge for such service shall be the prevailing charge otherwise recognized for such service for 1989 reduced by 15 percent or, if less, ⅓ of the percent (if any) by which the prevailing charge otherwise applied in the locality in 1989 exceeds the locally-adjusted reduced prevailing amount (as determined under subparagraph (B)(i)) for the service.

(ii) In determining the reasonable charge for a physicians' service specified in subparagraph (C)(i) and furnished during 1991, the prevailing charge for such service shall be the prevailing charge otherwise recognized for such service for the period during 1990 beginning on April 1, reduced by the same amount as the amount of the reduction effected under this paragraph (as amended by the Omnibus Budget Reconciliation Act of 1990) for such service during such period.

(B) For purposes of this paragraph:

(i) The "locally-adjusted reduced prevailing amount" for a locality for a physicians' service is equal to the product of—

(I) the reduced national weighted average prevailing charge for the service (specified under clause (ii)), and

(II) the adjustment factor (specified under clause (iii)) for the locality.

(ii) The "reduced national weighted average prevailing charge" for a physicians' service is equal to the national weighted average prevailing charge for the service (specified in subparagraph (C)(ii)) reduced by the percentage change (specified in subparagraph (C)(iii)) for the service.

(iii) The "adjustment factor", for a physicians' service for a locality, is the sum of—

(I) the practice expense component (percent), divided by 100, specified in appendix A (pages 187 through 194) of the Report of the Medicare and Medicaid Health Budget Reconciliation Amendments of 1989, prepared by the Subcommittee on Health and the Environment of the Committee on Energy and Commerce, House of Representatives, (Committee Print 101-M, 101st Congress, 1st Session) for the service, multiplied by the geographic practice cost index value (specified in subparagraph (C)(iv)) for the locality, and

(II) 1 minus the practice expense component (percent), divided by 100.

(C) For purposes of this paragraph:

(i) The procedures specified (by code and description) in the Overvalued Procedures List for Finance Committee, Revised September 20, 1989, prepared by the Physician Payment Review Commission [Medicare Payment Advisory Commission] which specification is of physicians' services that have been identified as overvalued by at least 10 percent based on a comparison of payments for such services under a resource-based relative value scale and of the national average prevailing charges under this part [42 USCS §§ 1395j et seq.].

(ii) The "national weighted average prevailing charge" specified in this clause, for a physicians' service specified in clause (i), is the national weighted average prevailing charge for the service in 1989 as determined by the Secretary using the best data available.

(iii) The "percentage change" specified in this clause, for a physicians' service specified in clause (i), is the percent difference (but expressed as a positive number) specified for the service in the list referred to in clause (i).

(iv) The geographic practice cost index value specified in this clause for a locality is the Geographic Overhead Costs Index specified for the locality in table 1 of the September 1989 Supplement to the Geographic Medicare Economic Index: Alternative Approaches (prepared by the Urban Institute and the Center for Health Economics Research).

(D) In the case of a reduction in the prevailing charge for a physicians' service under subparagraph (A), if a nonparticipating physician furnishes the service to an individual entitled to benefits under this part [42 USCS §§ 1395j et seq.], after the effective date of such reduction, the physician's actual charge is subject to a limit under subsection (j)(1)(D).

(15)(A) In determining the reasonable charge for surgery, radiology, and diagnostic physicians' services which the Secretary shall designate (based on their high volume of expenditures under this part [42 USCS §§ 1395j et seq.]) and for which the prevailing charge (but for this paragraph) differs by physician specialty, the prevailing charge for such a service may not exceed the prevailing charge or fee schedule amount for that specialty of physicians that furnish the service most frequently nationally.

(B) In the case of a reduction in the prevailing charge for a physician's service under subparagraph (A), if a nonparticipating physician furnishes the service to an individual entitled to benefits under this part [42 USCS §§ 1395j et seq.], after the effective date of the reduction, the physician's actual charge is subject to a limit under subsection (j)(1)(D).

(16)(A) In determining the reasonable charge for all physicians' services other than physicians' services specified in subparagraph (B) furnished during 1991, the prevailing charge for a locality shall be 6.5 percent below the prevailing charges used in the locality under this part [42 USCS §§ 1395j et seq.] in 1990 after March 31.

(B) For purposes of subparagraph (A), the physicians' services specified in this subparagraph are as follows:

(i) Radiology, anesthesia and physician pathology services, the technical components of diagnostic tests specified in paragraph (17) and physicians' services specified in paragraph (14)(C)(i).

(ii) Primary care services specified in subsection (i)(4), hospital inpatient medical services, consultations, other visits, preventive medicine visits, psychiatric services, emergency care facility services, and critical care services.

(iii) Partial mastectomy; tendon sheath injections; and small joint arthrocentesis; femoral fracture and trochanteric fracture treatments; endotracheal intubation; thoracentesis; thoracostomy; aneurysm repair; cystourethroscopy; transurethral fulguration and resection; tympanoplasty with mastoidectomy; and ophthalmoscopy.

(17) With respect to payment under this part [42 USCS §§ 1395j et seq.] for the technical (as distinct from professional) component of diagnostic tests (other than clinical diagnostic laboratory tests, tests specified in paragraph (14)(C)(i), and radiology services, including portable x-ray services) which the Secretary shall designate (based on their high volume of expenditures under this part [42 USCS §§ 1395j et seq.]), the reasonable charge for such technical component (including the applicable portion of a global service) may not exceed the national median of such charges for all localities, as estimated by the Secretary using the best available data.

(18)(A) Payment for any service furnished by a practitioner described in subparagraph (C) and for which payment may be made under this part [42 USCS §§ 1395j et seq.] on a reasonable charge or fee schedule basis may only be made under this part [42 USCS §§ 1395j et seq.] on an assignment-related basis.

(B) A practitioner described in subparagraph (C) or other person may not bill (or collect any amount from) the individual or another person for any service described in subparagraph (A), except for deductible and coinsurance amounts applicable under this part [42 USCS §§ 1395j et seq.]. No person is liable for payment of any amounts billed for such a service in violation of the previous sentence. If a practitioner or other person knowingly and willfully bills (or collects an amount) for such a service in violation of such sentence, the Secretary may apply sanctions against the practitioner or other person in the same manner as the Secretary may apply sanctions against a physician in accordance with subsection (j)(2) in the same manner as such section applies with respect to a physician. Paragraph (4) of subsection (j) shall apply in this subparagraph in the same manner as such paragraph applies to such section.

(C) A practitioner described in this subparagraph is any of the following:

(i) A physician assistant, nurse practitioner, or clinical nurse specialist (as defined in section 1861(aa)(5) [42 USCS § 1395x(aa)(5)]).

(ii) A certified registered nurse anesthetist (as defined in section 1861(bb)(2) [42 USCS § 1395x(bb)(2)]).

(iii) A certified nurse-midwife (as defined in section 1861(gg)(2) [42 USCS § 1395x(gg)(2)]).

(iv) A clinical social worker (as defined in section 1861(hh)(1) [42 USCS § 1395x(hh)(1)]).

(v) A clinical psychologist (as defined by the Secretary for purposes of section 1861(ii) [42 USCS § 1395x(ii)]).

(vi) A registered dietitian or nutrition professional.

(D) For purposes of this paragraph, a service furnished by a practitioner described in subparagraph (C) includes any services and supplies furnished as incident to the service as would otherwise be covered under this part if furnished by a physician or as incident to a physician's service.

(19) For purposes of section 1833(a)(1) [42 USCS § 1395m(a)(1)], the reasonable charge for ambulance services (as described in section 1861(s)(7) [42 USCS § 1395x(s)(7)]) provided during calendar year 1998 and calendar year 1999 may not exceed the reasonable charge for such services provided during the previous calendar year (after application of this paragraph), increased by the percentage increase in the consumer price index for all urban consumers (U.S. city average) as estimated by the Secretary for the 12-month period ending with the midpoint of the year involved reduced by 1.0 percentage point.

(c) Advances of funds to carrier; prompt payment of claim. (1) [Deleted]

(2)(A) Each contract under section 1874A [42 USCS § 1395kk-1] that provides for making payments under this part [42 USCS §§ 1395j et seq.] shall provide that payment shall be issued, mailed, or otherwise transmitted with respect to not less than 95 percent of all claims submitted under this part [42 USCS §§ 1395j et seq.]—

(i) which are clean claims, and

(ii) for which payment is not made on a periodic interim payment basis,

within the applicable number of calendar days after the date on which the claim is received.

(B) In this paragraph:

(i) The term "clean claim" means a claim that has no defect or impropriety (including any lack of any required substantiating documentation) or particular circumstance requiring special treatment that prevents timely payment from being made on the claim under this part [42 USCS §§ 1395j et seq.].

(ii) The term "applicable number of calendar days" means—

(I) with respect to claims received in the 12-month period beginning October 1, 1986, 30 calendar days,

(II) with respect to claims received in the 12-month period beginning October 1, 1987, 26 calendar days (or 19 calendar days with respect to claims submitted by participating physicians),

(III) with respect to claims received in the 12-month period beginning October 1, 1988, 25 calendar days (or 18 calendar days with respect to claims submitted by participating physicians),

(IV) with respect to claims received in the 12-month period beginning October 1, 1989, and claims received in any succeeding 12-month period ending on or before September 30, 1993, 24 calendar days (or 17 calendar days with respect to claims submitted by participating physicians), and

(V) with respect to claims received in the 12-month period beginning October 1, 1993, and claims received in any succeeding 12-month period, 30 calendar days.

(C) If payment is not issued, mailed, or otherwise transmitted within the applicable number of calendar days (as defined in clause (ii) of subparagraph (B)) after a clean claim (as defined in clause (i) of such subparagraph) is received, interest shall be paid at the rate used for purposes of section 3902(a) of title 31,

United States Code (relating to interest penalties for failure to make prompt payments) for the period beginning on the day after the required payment date and ending on the date on which payment is made.

(3)(A) Each contract under this section which provides for the disbursement of funds, as described in section 1874A(a)(3)(B) [42 USCS § 1395kk-1(a)(3)(B)], shall provide that no payment shall be issued, mailed, or otherwise transmitted with respect to any claim submitted under this title [42 USCS §§ 1395 et seq.] within the applicable number of calendar days after the date on which the claim is received.

(B) In this paragraph, the term "applicable number of calendar days" means—

(i) with respect to claims submitted electronically as prescribed by the Secretary, 13 days, and

(ii) with respect to claims submitted otherwise, 28 days.

(4) Neither a medicare administrative contractor nor the Secretary may impose a fee under this title [42 USCS §§ 1395 et seq.]—

(A) for the filing of claims related to physicians' services,

(B) for an error in filing a claim relating to physicians' services or for such a claim which is denied,

(C) for any appeal under this title with respect to physicians' services,

(D) for applying for (or obtaining) a unique identifier under subsection (r), or

(E) for responding to inquiries respecting physicians' services or for providing information with respect to medical review of such services.

(5), (6) [Deleted]

(d)–(f) [Repealed]

(g) Authority of Railroad Retirement Board to enter into contracts with carriers. The Railroad Retirement Board shall, in accordance with such regulations as the Secretary may prescribe, contract with a medicare administrative contractor or contractors to perform the functions set out in this section with respect to individuals entitled to benefits as qualified railroad retirement beneficiaries pursuant to section 226(a) of this Act [42 USCS § 426(a)] and section 7(d) of the Railroad Retirement Act of 1974 [45 USCS § 231f(d)].

(h) Participating physician or supplier; agreements with Secretary; publication of directories; availability; inclusion of program in explanation of benefits; payment of claims on assignment-related basis. (1) Any physician or supplier may voluntarily enter into an agreement with the Secretary to become a participating physician or supplier. For purposes of this section, the term "participating physician or supplier" means a physician or supplier (excluding any provider of services) who, before the beginning of any year beginning with 1984, enters into an agreement with the Secretary which provides that such physician or supplier will accept payment under this part [42 USCS §§ 1395j et seq.] on an assignment-related basis for all items and services furnished to individuals enrolled under this part [42 USCS §§ 1395j et seq.] during such year. In the case of a newly licensed physician or a physician who begins a practice in a new area, or in the case of a new supplier who begins a new business, or in such similar cases as the Secretary may specify, such physician or supplier may enter into such an agreement after the beginning of a year, for items and services furnished during the remainder of the year.

(2) The Secretary shall maintain a toll-free telephone number or numbers at which individuals enrolled under this part [42 USCS §§ 1395j et seq.] may obtain the names, addresses, specialty, and telephone numbers of participating physicians and suppliers, and may request a copy of an appropriate directory published under paragraph (4). The Secretary shall, without charge, mail a copy of such directory upon such a request.

(3)(A) In any case in which [a] medicare administrative contractor having a contract under section 1874A [42 USCS § 1395kk-1] that provides for making payments under this part [42 USCS §§ 1395j et seq.] is able to develop a system for the electronic transmission to such contractor of bills for services, such contractor shall establish direct lines for the electronic receipt of claims from participating physicians and suppliers.

(B) The Secretary shall establish a procedure whereby an individual enrolled under this part may assign, in an appropriate manner on the form claiming a benefit under this part [42 USCS §§ 1395j et seq.] for an item or service furnished by a participating physician or supplier, the individual's rights of payment under a medicare supplemental policy (described in section 1882(g)(1) [42 USCS § 1395ss(g)(1)]) in which the individual is enrolled. In the case such an assignment is properly executed and a payment determination is made by a medicare administrative contractor with a contract under this section, the contractor shall transmit to the private entity issuing the medicare supplemental policy notice of such fact and shall include an explanation of benefits and any additional information that the Secretary may determine to be appropriate in order to enable the entity to decide whether (and the amount of) any payment is due under the policy. The Secretary may enter into agreements for the transmittal of such information to entities electronically. The Secretary shall impose user fees for the transmittal of information under this subparagraph by a medicare administrative contractor, whether electronically or otherwise, and such user fees shall be collected and retained by the contractor.

(4) At the beginning of each year the Secretary shall publish directories (for appropriate local geographic areas) containing the name, address, and specialty of all participating physicians and suppliers (as defined in paragraph (1)) for that area for that year. Each directory shall be organized to make the most useful presentation of the information (as determined by the Secretary) for individuals enrolled under this part [42 USCS §§ 1395j et seq.]. Each participating physician directory for an area shall provide an alphabetical listing of all participating physicians practicing in the area and an alphabetical listing by locality and specialty of such physicians.

(5)(A) The Secretary shall promptly notify individuals enrolled under this part [42 USCS §§ 1395j et seq.] through an annual mailing of the participation program under this subsection and the publication and availability of the directories and shall make appropriate area directory or directories available in each district and branch office of the Social Security Administration, in the offices of medicare administrative contractors, and to senior citizen organizations.

(B) The annual notice provided under subparagraph (A) shall include—

(i) a description of the participation program,

(ii) an explanation of the advantages to beneficiaries of obtaining covered services through a participating physician or supplier,

(iii) an explanation of the assistance offered by medicare administrative contractors in obtaining the names of participating physicians and suppliers, and

(iv) the toll-free telephone number under paragraph (2)(A) for inquiries concerning the program and for requests for free copies of appropriate directories.

(6) The Secretary shall provide that the directories shall be available for purchase by the public. The Secretary shall provide that each appropriate area directory is sent to each participating physician located in that area and that an appropriate number of copies of each such directory is sent to hospitals located in the area. Such copies shall be sent free of charge.

(7) The Secretary shall provide that each explanation of benefits provided under this part [42 USCS §§ 1395j et seq.] for services furnished in the United States, in conjunction with the payment of claims under section 1833(a)(1) [42 USCS § 1395l(a)(1)] (made other than on an assignment-related basis, shall include—

(A) a prominent reminder of the participating physician and supplier program established under this subsection (including the limitation on charges that may be imposed by such physicians and suppliers) and a clear statement of any amounts charged for the particular items or services on the claim involved above the amount recognized under this part [42 USCS §§ 1395j et seq.]),

(B) the toll-free telephone number or numbers, maintained under paragraph (2), at which an individual enrolled under this part [42 USCS §§ 1395j et seq.] may obtain information on participating physicians and suppliers,

(C) (i) an offer of assistance to such an individual in obtaining the names of participating physicians of appropriate specialty and (ii) an offer to provide a free copy of the appropriate participating physician directory, and

(D) in the case of services for which the billed amount exceeds the limiting charge imposed under section 1848(g) [42 USCS § 1395w-4(g)], information regarding such applicable limiting charge (including information concerning the right to a refund under section 1848(g)(1)(A)(iv) [42 USCS § 1395w-4(g)(1)(A)(iv)]).

(8) The Secretary may refuse to enter into an agreement with a physician or supplier under this subsection, or may terminate or refuse to renew such agreement, in the event that such physician or supplier has been convicted of a felony under Federal or State law for an offense which the Secretary determines is detrimental to the best interests of the program or program beneficiaries.

(9) The Secretary may revoke enrollment, for a period of not more than one year for each act, for a physician or supplier under section 1866(j) [42 USCS § 1395cc(j)] if such physician or supplier fails to maintain and, upon request of the Secretary, provide access to documentation relating to written orders or requests for payment for durable medical equipment, certifications for home health services, or referrals for other items or services written or ordered by

such physician or supplier under this title, as specified by the Secretary.

(i) Definitions. For purposes of this title [42 USCS §§ 1395 et seq.]:

(1) A claim is considered to be paid on an "assignment-related basis" if the claim is paid on the basis of an assignment described in subsection (b)(3)(B)(ii), in accordance with subsection (b)(6)(B), or under the procedure described in section 1870(f)(1) [42 USCS § 1395gg(f)(1)].

(2) The term "participating physician" refers, with respect to the furnishing of services, to a physician who at the time of furnishing the services is a participating physician (under subsection (h)(1)); the term "nonparticipating physician" refers, with respect to the furnishing of services, to a physician who at the time of furnishing the services is not a participating physician; and the term "nonparticipating supplier or other person" means a supplier or other person (excluding a provider of services) that is not a participating physician or supplier (as defined in subsection (h)(1)).

(3) The term "percentage increase in the MEI" means, with respect to physicians' services furnished in a year, the percentage increase in the medicare economic index (referred to in the fourth sentence of subsection (b)(3)) applicable to such services furnished as of the first day of that year.

(4) The term "primary care services" means physicians' services which constitute office medical services, emergency department services, home medical services, skilled nursing, intermediate care, and long-term care medical services, or nursing home, boarding home, domiciliary, or custodial care medical services.

(j) Monitoring of charges by nonparticipating physicians; sanctions and penalties for excess charges. (1)(A) In the case of a physician who is not a participating physician for items and services furnished during a portion of the 30-month period beginning July 1, 1984, the Secretary shall monitor the physician's actual charges to individuals enrolled under this part for physicians' services during that portion of that period. If such physician knowingly and willfully bills individuals enrolled under this part [42 USCS §§ 1395j et seq.] for actual charges in excess of such physician's actual charges for the calendar quarter beginning on April 1, 1984, the Secretary may apply sanctions against such physician in accordance with paragraph (2).

(B)(i) During any period (on or after January 1, 1987, and before the date specified in clause (ii)), during which a physician is a nonparticipating physician, the Secretary shall monitor the actual charges of each such physician for physicians' services furnished to individuals enrolled under this part [42 USCS §§ 1395j et seq.]. If such physician knowingly and willfully bills on a repeated basis for such a service an actual charge in excess of the maximum allowable actual charge determined under subparagraph (C) for that service, the Secretary may apply sanctions against such physician in accordance with paragraph (2).

(ii) Clause (i) shall not apply to services furnished after December 31, 1990.

(C)(i) For a particular physicians' service furnished by a nonparticipating physician to individuals enrolled under this part during a year, for purposes of subparagraph (B), the maximum allowable actual charge is determined as follows: If the physician's maximum allowable actual charge for that service in the previous year was—

(I) less than 115 percent of the applicable percent (as defined in subsection (b)(4)(A)(iv)) of the prevailing charge for the year and service involved, the maximum allowable actual charge for the year involved is the greater of the maximum allowable actual charge described in subclause (II) or the charge described in clause (ii), or

(II) equal to, or greater than, 115 percent of the applicable percent (as defined in subsection (b)(4)(A)(iv)) of the prevailing charge for the year and service involved, the maximum allowable actual charge is 101 percent of the physician's maximum allowable actual charge for the service for the previous year.

(ii) For purposes of clause (i)(I), the charge described in this clause for a particular physicians' service furnished in a year is the maximum allowable actual charge for the service of the physician for the previous year plus the product of (I) the applicable fraction (as defined in clause (iii)) and (II) the amount by which 115 percent of the prevailing charge for the year involved for such service furnished by nonparticipating physicians, exceeds the physician's maximum allowable actual charge for the service for the previous year.

(iii) In clause (ii), the "applicable fraction" is—

(I) for 1987, ¼,

(II) for 1988, ⅓,

(III) for 1989, ½, and

(IV) for any subsequent year, 1.

(iv) For purposes of determining the maximum allowable actual charge under clauses (i) and (ii) for 1987, in the case of a physicians' service for which the physician has actual charges for the calendar quarter beginning on April 1, 1984, the "maximum allowable actual charge" for 1986 is the physician's actual charge for such service furnished during such quarter.

(v) For purposes of determining the maximum allowable actual charge under clauses (i) and (ii) for a year after 1986, in the case of a physicians' service for which the physician has no actual charges for the calendar quarter beginning on April 1, 1984, and for which a maximum allowable actual charge has not been previously established under this clause, the "maximum allowable actual charge" for the previous year shall be the 50th percentile of the customary charges for the service (weighted by frequency of the service) performed by nonparticipating physicians in the locality during the 12-month period ending June 30 of that previous year.

(vi) For purposes of this subparagraph, a "physician's actual charge" for a physicians' service furnished in a year or other period is the weighted average (or, at the option of the Secretary for a service furnished in the calendar quarter beginning April 1, 1984, the median) of the physician's charges for such service furnished in the year or other period.

(vii) In the case of a nonparticipating physician who was a participating physician during a previous period, for the purpose of computing the physician's maximum allowable actual charge during the physician's period of nonparticipation, the physician shall be deemed to have had a maximum allowable actual charge during the period of participation, and such deemed maximum allowable actual charge shall be determined according to clauses (i) through (vi).

(viii) Notwithstanding any other provision of this subparagraph, the maximum allowable actual charge for a particular physician's service furnished by a nonparticipating physician to individuals enrolled under this part [42 USCS §§ 1395j et seq.] during the 3-month period beginning on January 1, 1988, shall be the amount determined under this subparagraph for 1987. The maximum allowable actual charge for any such service otherwise determined under this subparagraph for 1988 shall take effect on April 1, 1988.

(ix) If there is a reduction under subsection (b)(13) in the reasonable charge for medical direction furnished by a nonparticipating physician, the maximum allowable actual charge otherwise permitted under this subsection for such services shall be reduced in the same manner and in the same percentage as the reduction in such reasonable charge.

(D)(i) If an action described in clause (ii) results in a reduction in a reasonable charge for a physicians' service or item and a nonparticipating physician furnishes the service or item to an individual entitled to benefits under this part [42 USCS §§ 1395j et seq.] after the effective date of such action, the physician may not charge the individual more than 125 percent of the reduced payment allowance (as defined in clause (iii)) plus (for services or items furnished during the 12-month period (or 9-month period in the case of an action described in clause (ii)(II)) beginning on the effective date of the action) ½ of the amount by which the physician's maximum allowable actual charge for the service or item for the previous 12-month period exceeds such 125 percent level.

(ii) The first sentence of clause (i) shall apply to—

(I) an adjustment under subsection (b)(8)(B) (relating to inherent reasonableness),

(II) a reduction under subsection (b)(10)(A) or (b)(14)(A) (relating to certain overpriced procedures),

(III) a reduction under subsection (b)(11)(B) (relating to certain cataract procedures),

(IV) a prevailing charge limit established under subsection (b)(11)(C)(i) or (b)(15)(A),

(V) a reasonable charge limit established under subsection (b)(11)(C)(ii), and

(VI) an adjustment under section 1833(l)(3)(B) [42 USCS § 1395l(l)(3)(B)] (relating to physician supervision of certified registered nurse anesthetists).

(iii) In clause (i), the term "reduced payment allowance" means, with respect to an action—

(I) under subsection (b)(8)(B), the inherently reasonable charge established under subsection (b)(8);

(II) under subsection (b)(10)(A), (b)(11)(B), (b)(11)(C)(i), (b)(14)(A), or (b)(15)(A) or under section 1833(l)(3)(B) [42 USCS § 13951(1)(3)(B)], the prevailing charge for the service after the action; or

(III) under subsection (b)(11)(C)(ii), the payment allowance established under such subsection.

(iv) If a physician knowingly and willfully bills in violation of clause (i) (whether or not such charge violates subparagraph (B)), the Secretary may apply sanctions against such physician in accordance with paragraph (2).

(v) Clause (i) shall not apply to items and services furnished after December 31, 1990.

(2) Subject to paragraph (3), the sanctions which the Secretary may apply under this

paragraph are—

(A) excluding a physician from participation in the programs under this Act [42 USCS §§ 301 et seq.] for a period not to exceed 5 years, in accordance with the procedures of subsections (c), (f), and (g) of section 1128 [42 USCS § 1320a-7(c), (f), and (g)], or

(B) civil monetary penalties and assessments, in the same manner as such penalties and assessments are authorized under section 1128A(a) [42 USCS § 1320a-7a(a)],

or both. The provisions of section 1128A [42 USCS § 1320a-7a] (other than the first 2 sentences of subsection (a) and other than subsection (b)) shall apply to a civil money penalty and assessment under subparagraph (B) in the same manner as such provisions apply to a penalty, assessment, or proceeding under section 1128A(a) [42 USCS § 1320a-7a(a)], except to the extent such provisions are inconsistent with subparagraph (A) or paragraph (3).

(3)(A) The Secretary may not exclude a physician pursuant to paragraph (2)(A) if such physician is a sole community physician or sole source of essential specialized services in a community.

(B) The Secretary shall take into account access of beneficiaries to physicians' services for which payment may be made under this part [42 USCS §§ 1395j et seq.] in determining whether to bar a physician from participation under paragraph (2)(A).

(4) The Secretary may, out of any civil monetary penalty or assessment collected from a physician pursuant to this subsection, make a payment to a beneficiary enrolled under this part [42 USCS §§ 1395j et seq.] in the nature of restitution for amounts paid by such beneficiary to such physician which was determined to be an excess charge under paragraph (1).

(k) Sanctions for billing services of assistant at cataract operations. (1) If a physician knowingly and willfully presents or causes to be presented a claim or bills an individual enrolled under this part [42 USCS §§ 1395j et seq.] for charges for services as an assistant at surgery for which payment may not be made by reason of section 1862(a)(15) [42 USCS § 1395y(a)(15)], the Secretary may apply sanctions against such physician in accordance with subsection (j)(2) in the case of surgery performed on or after March 1, 1987.

(2) If a physician knowingly and willfully presents or causes to be presented a claim or bills an individual enrolled under this part [42 USCS §§ 1395j et seq.] for charges that includes a charge for an assistant at surgery for which payment may not be made by reason of section 1862(a)(15) [42 USCS § 1395y(a)(15)], the Secretary may apply sanctions against such physician in accordance with subsection (j)(2) in the case of surgery performed on or after March 1, 1987.

(l) Prohibition of unassigned billing of services determined to be medically unnecessary by carrier. (1)(A) Subject to subparagraph (C), if—

(i) a nonparticipating physician furnishes services to an individual enrolled for benefits under this part [42 USCS §§ 1395j et seq.],

(ii) payment for such services is not accepted on an assignment-related basis,

(iii) (I) a medicare administrative contractor determines under this part [42 USCS §§ 1395j et seq.] or a peer review organization determines under part B of title XI [42 USCS §§ 1320c et seq.] that payment may not be made by reason of section 1862(a)(1) [42 USCS § 1395y(a)(1)] because a service otherwise covered under this title is not reasonable and necessary under the standards described in that section or (II) payment under this title for such services is denied under section 1154(a)(2) [42 USCS § 1320c-3(a)(2)] by reason of a determination under section 1154(a)(1)(B) [42 USCS § 1320c-3(a)(1)(B)], and

(iv) the physician has collected any amounts for such services,

the physician shall refund on a timely basis to the individual (and shall be liable to the individual for) any amounts so collected.

(B) A refund under subparagraph (A) is considered to be on a timely basis only if—

(i) in the case of a physician who does not request reconsideration or seek appeal on a timely basis, the refund is made within 30 days after the date the physician receives a denial notice under paragraph (2), or

(ii) in the case in which such a reconsideration or appeal is taken, the refund is made within 15 days after the date the physician receives notice of an adverse determination on reconsideration or appeal.

(C) Subparagraph (A) shall not apply to the furnishing of a service by a physician to an individual in the case described in subparagraph (A)(ii)(I) if—

(i) the physician establishes that the physician did not know and could not reasonably have been expected to know that payment may not be made for the service by reason of section 1862(a)(1) [42 USCS § 1395y(a)(1)], or

(ii) before the service was provided, the individual was informed that payment under this part [42 USCS §§ 1395j et seq.] may not be made for the specific service and the individual has agreed to pay for that service.

(2) Each medicare administrative contractor with a contract in effect under this section with respect to physicians and each peer review organization with a contract under part B of title XI [42 USCS §§ 1320c et seq.] shall send any notice of denial of payment for physicians' services based on section 1862(a)(1) and for which payment is not requested on an assignment-related basis to the physician and the individual involved.

(3) If a physician knowingly and willfully fails to make refunds in violation of paragraph (1)(A), the Secretary may apply sanctions against such physician in accordance with subsection (j)(2).

(m) Disclosure of information of unassigned claims for certain physicians' services. (1) In the case of a nonparticipating physician who—

(A) performs an elective surgical procedure for an individual enrolled for benefits under this part [42 USCS §§ 1395j et seq.] and for which the physician's actual charge is at least $500, and

(B) does not accept payment for such procedure on an assignment-related basis,

the physician must disclose to the individual, in writing and in a form approved by the Secretary, the physician's estimated actual charge for the procedure, the estimated approved charge under this part [42 USCS §§ 1395j et seq.] for the procedure, the excess of the physician's actual charge over the approved charge, and the coinsurance amount applicable to the procedure. The written estimate may not be used as the basis for, or evidence in, a civil suit.

(2) A physician who fails to make a disclosure required under paragraph (1) with respect to a procedure shall refund on a timely basis to the individual (and shall be liable to the individual for) any amounts collected for the procedure in excess of the charges recognized and approved under this part [42 USCS §§ 1395j et seq.].

(3) If a physician knowingly and willfully fails to comply with paragraph (2), the Secretary may apply sanctions against such physician in accordance with subsection (j)(2).

(4) The Secretary shall provide for such monitoring of requests for payment for physicians' services to which paragraph (1) applies as is necessary to assure compliance with paragraph (2).

(n) Elimination of markup for certain purchased services. (1) If a physician's bill or a request for payment for services billed by a physician includes a charge for a diagnostic test described in section 1861(s)(3) [42 USCS § 1395x(s)(3)] (other than a clinical diagnostic laboratory test) for which the bill or request for payment does not indicate that the billing physician personally performed or supervised the performance of the test or that another physician with whom the physician who shares a practice personally performed or supervised the performance of the test, the amount payable with respect to the test shall be determined as follows:

(A) If the bill or request for payment indicates that the test was performed by a supplier, identifies the supplier, and indicates the amount the supplier charged the billing physician, payment for the test (less the applicable deductible and coinsurance amounts) shall be the actual acquisition costs (net of any discounts) or, if lower, the supplier's reasonable charge (or other applicable limit) for the test.

(B) If the bill or request for payment (i) does not indicate who performed the test, or (ii) indicates that the test was performed by a supplier but does not identify the supplier or include the amount charged by the supplier, no payment shall be made under this part [42 USCS §§ 1395j et seq.].

(2) A physician may not bill an individual enrolled under this part [42 USCS §§ 1395j et seq.]—

(A) any amount other than the payment amount specified in paragraph (1)(A) and any applicable deductible and coinsurance for a diagnostic test for which payment is made pursuant to paragraph (1)(A), or

(B) any amount for a diagnostic test for which payment may not be made pursuant to paragraph (1)(B).

(3) If a physician knowingly and willfully in repeated cases bills one or more individuals in violation of paragraph (2), the Secretary may apply sanctions against such physician in accordance with section 1842(j)(2) [subsec. (j)(2) of this section].

(o) Reimbursement for drugs and biologicals. (1) If a physician's, supplier's, or any other person's bill or request for payment for services includes a charge for a drug or biological for which payment may be made under this part [42 USCS §§ 1395j et seq.] and the drug or biological is not paid on a cost or prospective payment basis as otherwise provided in this part [42 USCS §§ 1395j et seq.], the amount payable for the drug or biological is equal to the following:

(A) In the case of any of the following drugs or biologicals, 95 percent of the average wholesale price:

(i) A drug or biological furnished before January 1, 2004.

(ii) Blood clotting factors furnished during 2004.

(iii) A drug or biological furnished during 2004 that was not available for payment under this part [42 USCS §§ 1395j et seq.] as of April 1, 2003.

(iv) A vaccine described in subparagraph (A) or (B) of section 1861(s)(10) [42 USCS § 1395x(s)(10)] furnished on or after January 1, 2004.

(v) A drug or biological furnished during 2004 in connection with the furnishing of renal dialysis services if separately billed by renal dialysis facilities.

(B) In the case of a drug or biological furnished during 2004 that is not described in—

(i) clause (ii), (iii), (iv), or (v) of subparagraph (A),

(ii) subparagraph (D)(i), or

(iii) subparagraph (F),

the amount determined under paragraph (4).

(C) In the case of a drug or biological that is not described in subparagraph (A)(iv), (D)(i), or (F) furnished on or after January 1, 2005, the amount provided under section 1847, section 1847A, section 1847B, or section 1881(b)(13) [42 USCS § 1395w-3, 1395w-3a, 1395w-3b, or 1395rr(b)(13)], as the case may be for the drug or biological.

(D)(i) Except as provided in clause (ii), in the case of infusion drugs furnished through an item of durable medical equipment covered under section 1861(n) [42 USCS § 1395x(n)] on or after January 1, 2004, 95 percent of the average wholesale price for such drug in effect on October 1, 2003.

(ii) In the case of such infusion drugs furnished in a competitive acquisition area under section 1847 [42 USCS § 1395w-3] on or after January 1, 2007, the amount provided under section 1847 [42 USCS § 1395w-3].

(E) In the case of a drug or biological, consisting of intravenous immune globulin, furnished—

(i) in 2004, the amount of payment provided under paragraph (4); and

(ii) in 2005 and subsequent years, the amount of payment provided under section 1847A [42 USCS § 1395w-3a].

(F) In the case of blood and blood products (other than blood clotting factors), the amount of payment shall be determined in the same manner as such amount of payment was determined on October 1, 2003.

(G) In the case of inhalation drugs or biologicals furnished through durable medical equipment covered under section 1861(n) [42 USCS § 1395x(n)] that are furnished—

(i) in 2004, the amount provided under paragraph (4) for the drug or biological; and

(ii) in 2005 and subsequent years, the amount provided under section 1847A [42 USCS § 1395w-3a] for the drug or biological.

(2) If payment for a drug or biological is made to a licensed pharmacy approved to dispense drugs or biologicals under this part [42 USCS §§ 1395j et seq.], the Secretary may pay a dispensing fee (less the applicable deductible and coinsurance amounts) to the pharmacy. This paragraph shall not apply in the case of payment under paragraph (1)(C).

(3)(A) Payment for a charge for any drug or biological for which payment may be made under this part may be made only on an assignment-related basis.

(B) The provisions of subsection (b)(18)(B) shall apply to charges for such drugs or biologicals in the same manner as they apply to services furnished by a practitioner described in subsection (b)(18)(C).

(4)(A) Subject to the succeeding provisions of this paragraph, the amount of payment for a drug or biological under this paragraph furnished in 2004 is equal to 85 percent of the average wholesale price (determined as of April 1, 2003) for the drug or biological.

(B) The Secretary shall substitute for the percentage under subparagraph (A) for a drug or biological the percentage that would apply to the drug or biological under the column entitled "Average of GAO and OIG data (percent)" in the table entitled "Table 3. Medicare Part B Drugs in the Most Recent GAO and OIG Studies" published on August 20, 2003, in the Federal Register (68 Fed. Reg. 50445).

(C)(i) The Secretary may substitute for the percentage under subparagraph (A) a percentage that is based on data and information submitted by the manufacturer of the drug or biological by October 15, 2003.

(ii) The Secretary may substitute for the percentage under subparagraph (A) with respect to drugs and biologicals furnished during 2004 on or after April 1, 2004, a percentage that is based on data and information submitted by the manufacturer of the drug or biological after October 15, 2003, and before January 1, 2004.

(D) In no case may the percentage substituted under subparagraph (B) or (C) be less than 80 percent.

(5)(A) Subject to subparagraph (B), in the

case of clotting factors furnished on or after January 1, 2005, the Secretary shall, after reviewing the January 2003 report to Congress by the Comptroller General of the United States entitled "Payment for Blood Clotting Factor Exceeds Providers Acquisition Cost", provide for a separate payment, to the entity which furnishes to the patient blood clotting factors, for items and services related to the furnishing of such factors in an amount that the Secretary determines to be appropriate. Such payment amount may take into account any or all of the following:

(i) The mixing (if appropriate) and delivery of factors to an individual, including special inventory management and storage requirements.

(ii) Ancillary supplies and patient training necessary for the self-administration of such factors.

(B) In determining the separate payment amount under subparagraph (A) for blood clotting factors furnished in 2005, the Secretary shall ensure that the total amount of payments under this part [42 USCS §§ 1395j et seq.] (as estimated by the Secretary) for such factors under paragraph (1)(C) and such separate payments for such factors does not exceed the total amount of payments that would have been made for such factors under this part [42 USCS §§ 1395j et seq.] (as estimated by the Secretary) if the amendments made by section 303 of the Medicare Prescription Drug, Improvement, and Modernization Act of 2003 had not been enacted.

(C) The separate payment amount under this subparagraph for blood clotting factors furnished in 2006 or a subsequent year shall be equal to the separate payment amount determined under this paragraph for the previous year increased by the percentage increase in the consumer price index for medical care for the 12-month period ending with June of the previous year.

(6) In the case of an immunosuppressive drug described in subparagraph (J) of section 1861(s)(2) [42 USCS § 1395x(s)(2)] and an oral drug described in subparagraph (Q) or (T) of such section, the Secretary shall pay to the pharmacy a supplying fee for such a drug determined appropriate by the Secretary (less the applicable deductible and coinsurance amounts).

(7) There shall be no administrative or judicial review under section 1869 [42 USCS § 1395ff], section 1878 [42 USCS § 1395oo], or otherwise, of determinations of payment amounts, methods, or adjustments under paragraphs (4) through (6).

(p) Requiring submission of diagnostic information. (1) Each request for payment, or bill submitted, for an item or service furnished by a physician or practitioner specified in subsection (b)(18)(C) for which payment may be made under this part [42 USCS §§ 1395j et seq.] shall include the appropriate diagnosis code (or codes) as established by the Secretary for such item or service.

(2) In the case of a request for payment for an item or service furnished by a physician or practitioner specified in subsection (b)(18)(C) on an assignment-related basis which does not include the code (or codes) required under paragraph (1), payment may be denied under this part [42 USCS §§ 1395j et seq.].

(3) In the case of a request for payment for an item or service furnished by a physician not submitted on an assignment-related basis and which does not include the code (or codes) required under paragraph (1)—

(A) if the physician knowingly and willfully fails to provide the code (or codes) promptly upon request of the Secretary or a medicare administrative contractor, the physician may be subject to a civil money penalty in an amount not to exceed $2,000, and

(B) if the physician knowingly, willfully, and in repeated cases fails, after being notified by the Secretary of the obligations and requirements of this subsection, to include the code (or codes) required under paragraph (1), the physician may be subject to the sanction described in section 1842(j)(2)(A) [subsec. (j)(2)(A) of this section].

The provisions of section 1128A [42 USCS § 1320a-7a] (other than subsections (a) and (b)) shall apply to civil money penalties under subparagraph (A) in the same manner as they apply to a penalty or proceeding under section 1128A(a) [42 USCS § 1320a-7a(a)].

(4) In the case of an item or service defined in paragraph (3), (6), (8), or (9) of subsection 1861(s) [42 USCS § 1395x(s)] ordered by a physician or a practitioner specified in subsection (b)(18)(C), but furnished by another entity, if the Secretary (or fiscal agent of the Secretary) requires the entity furnishing the item or service to provide diagnostic or other medical information in order for payment to be made to the entity, the physician or practitioner shall provide that information to the entity at the time that the item or service is ordered by the physician or practitioner.

(q) Anesthesia services; counting actual time units. (1)(A) The Secretary, in consultation with groups representing physicians who furnish anesthesia services, shall establish by regulation a relative value guide for use in all localities in making payment for physician anesthesia services furnished under this part [42 USCS §§ 1395j et seq.]. Such guide shall be designed so as to result in expenditures under this title [42 USCS §§ 1395 et seq.] for such services in an amount that would not exceed the amount of such expenditures which would otherwise occur.

(B) For physician anesthesia services furnished under this part [42 USCS §§ 1395j et seq.] during 1991, the prevailing charge conversion factor used in a locality under this subsection shall, subject to clause (iv), be reduced to the adjusted prevailing charge conversion factor for the locality determined as follows:

(i) The Secretary shall estimate the national weighted average of the prevailing charge conversion factors used under this subsection for services furnished during 1990 after March 31, using the best available data.

(ii) The national weighted average estimated under clause (i) shall be reduced by 7 percent.

(iii) The adjusted prevailing charge conversion factor for a locality is the sum of—

(I) the product of (a) the portion of the reduced national weighted average prevailing charge conversion factor computed under clause (ii) which is attributable to physician work and (b) the geographic work index value for the locality (specified in Addendum C to the Model Fee Schedule for Physician Services (published on September 4, 1990, 55 Federal Register pp. 36238–36243)); and

(II) the product of (a) the remaining portion of the reduced national weighted average prevailing charge conversion factor computed under clause (ii) and (b) the geographic practice cost index value specified in section 1842(b)(14)(C)(iv) [subsec. (b)(14)(C)(iv) of this section] for the locality.

In applying this clause, 70 percent of the prevailing charge conversion factor shall be considered to be attributable to physician work.

(iv) The prevailing charge conversion factor to be applied to a locality under this subparagraph shall not be reduced by more than 15 percent below the prevailing charge conversion factor applied in the locality for the period during 1990 after March 31, but in no case shall the prevailing charge conversion factor be less than 60 percent of the national weighted average of the prevailing charge conversion factors (computed under clause (i)).

(2) For purposes of payment for anesthesia services (whether furnished by physicians or by certified registered nurse anesthetists) under this part [42 USCS §§ 1395j et seq.], the time units shall be counted based on actual time rather than rounded to full time units.

(r) Establishment of physician identification system. The Secretary shall establish a system which provides for a unique identifier for each physician who furnishes services for which payment may be made under this title [42 USCS §§ 1395 et seq.]. Under such system, the Secretary may impose appropriate fees on such physicians to cover the costs of investigation and recertification activities with respect to the issuance of the identifiers.

(s) Establishment of fee schedule. (1)(A) Subject to paragraph (3), the Secretary may implement a statewide or other areawide fee schedule to be used for payment of any item or service described in paragraph (2) which is paid on a reasonable charge basis.

(B) Any fee schedule established under this paragraph for such item or service shall be updated—

(i) for years before 2011—

(I) subject to subclause (II), by the percentage increase in the consumer price index for all urban consumers (United States city average) for the 12-month period ending with June of the preceding year; and

(II) for items and services described in paragraph (2)(D) for 2009, section 1834(a)(14)(J) [42 USCS § 1395m(a)(14)(J)] shall apply under this paragraph instead of the percentage increase otherwise applicable; and

(ii) for 2011 and subsequent years—

(I) the percentage increase in the consumer price index for all urban consumers (United States city average) for the 12-month period ending with June of the previous year, reduced by—

(II) the productivity adjustment described in section 1886(b)(3)(B)(xi)(II) [42 USCS § 1395ww(b)(3)(B)(xi)(II)].

The application of subparagraph (B)(ii)(II) may result in the update under this paragraph being less than 0.0 for a year, and may result in payment rates under any fee schedule established under this paragraph for a year being less than such payment rates for the preceding year.

(2) The items and services described in this paragraph are as follows:

(A) Medical supplies.

(B) Home dialysis supplies and equipment (as defined in section 1881(b)(8) [42 USCS § 1395rr(b)(8)]).

(C) [Deleted]

(D) Parenteral and enteral nutrients, equipment, and supplies.

(E) Electromyogram devices.

(F) Salivation devices.

(G) Blood products.

(H) Transfusion medicine.

(3) In the case of items and services described in paragraph (2)(D) that are included in a competitive acquisition program in a competitive acquisition area under section 1847(a) [42 USCS § 1395w-3(a)]—

(A) the payment basis under this subsection for such items and services furnished in such area shall be the payment basis determined under such competitive acquisition program; and

(B) the Secretary may use information on the payment determined under such competitive acquisition programs to adjust the payment amount otherwise applicable under paragraph (1) for an area that is not a competitive acquisition area under section 1847 [42 USCS § 1395w-3], and in the case of such adjustment, paragraphs (8) and (9) of section 1842(b) [42 USCS § 1395u(b)] shall not be applied.

(t) Facility provider number required on claims submitted by physicians. Each request for payment, or bill submitted, for an item or service furnished to an individual who is a resident of a skilled nursing facility, for which payment may be made under this part [42 USCS §§ 1395j et seq.] shall include the facility's medicare provider number.

(u) Each request for payment, or bill submitted, for a drug furnished to an individual for the treatment of anemia in connection with the treatment of cancer shall include (in a form and manner specified by the Secretary) information on the hemoglobin or hematocrit levels for the individual.

(Aug. 14, 1935, ch 531, Title XVIII, Part B, § 1842, as added July 30, 1965, P. L. 89-97, Title I, Part 1, § 102(a), 79 Stat. 309; Jan. 2, 1968, P. L. 90-248, Title I, Part 3, § 125(a), Part 4, § 154(d), 81 Stat. 845, 863; Oct. 30, 1972, P. L. 92-603, Title II, §§ 211(c)(3), 224(a), 227(e)(3), 236(a), 258(a), 262(a), 263(d)(5), 281(d), 86 Stat. 1384, 1395, 1407, 1414, 1447–1449, 1455; Oct. 16, 1974, P. L. 93-445, Title III, § 307, 88 Stat. 1358; Dec. 31, 1975, P. L. 94-182, Title I, § 101(a), 89 Stat. 1051; July 16, 1976, P. L. 94-368, §§ 2, 3(a), (b), 90 Stat. 997; Oct. 25, 1977, P. L. 95-142, § 2(a)(1), 91 Stat. 1175; Dec. 20, 1977, P. L. 95-216, Title V, § 501(b), 91 Stat. 1565; Dec. 5, 1980, P. L. 96-499, Title IX, Part A, Subpart II, § 918(a)(1), Part B, Subpart II, §§ 946(a), (b), 948(b), 94 Stat. 2625, 2642, 2643; Aug. 13, 1981, P. L. 97-35, Title XXI, Subtitle B, ch 3, § 2142(b), 95 Stat. 798; Sept. 3, 1982, P. L. 97-248, Title I, Subtitle A, Part I, Subpart A, § 104(a), Subpart B, § 113(a), Part III, § 128(d)(1), 96 Stat. 336, 340, 367; July 18, 1984, P. L. 98-369, Division B, Title III, Subtitle A, Part I, §§ 2303(e), 2306(a), (b)(1), (c), 2307(a)(1), (2), 2326(c)(2), (d)(2), Part II, §§ 2339, 2354(b)(13), (14), Title IV, Subtitle D, § 2663(j)(2)(F)(iv), 98 Stat. 1066, 1070, 1071, 1073, 1087, 1088, 1093, 1101, 1170; Nov. 8, 1984, P. L. 98-617, § 3(a)(1), (b)(5), (6), 98 Stat. 3295, 3296; April 7, 1986, P. L. 99-272, Title IX, Subtitle A, Part 2, Subpart B, § 9219(b)(1)(A), (2)(A), Part 3, Subpart A, §§ 9301(b)(1), (2), (c)(2)–(4), (d)(1)–(3), 9304(a), 9306(a), 9307(c), 100 Stat. 182–188, 190, 193, 194; Oct. 21, 1986, P. L. 99-509, Title IX, Subtitle D, Part 2, § 9311(c), Part 3, §§ 9331(a)(1)–(3), (b)(1)–(3), 9332(b)(1), (2), 9333(a), (b), 9334(a), 9338, 9341(a)(2), 100 Stat. 1998, 2017, 2018, 2022, 2024, 2025, 2027, 2034, 2037; Oct. 22, 1986, P. L. 99-514, Title XVIII, Subtitle C, Ch 1, § 1895(b)(14), 100 Stat. 2934, as amended Oct. 21, 1986, P. L. 99-509, Title IX, Subtitle D, Part 1, § 9307(c)(2)(A) 99 Stat. 1995; Oct. 22, 1986, P. L. 99-514, Title XVIII, Subtitle C, Ch 1, § 1895(b)(15), (16)(A), 100 Stat. 2934; Oct. 21, 1986, P. L. 99-509, Title IX, Subtitle D, Part 2, § 9320(e)(3), Part 3, §§ 9331(c)(3)(A), 9332(a)(1), (c)(1), (d)(1), 100 Stat. 2015, 2020–2023; Aug. 18, 1987, P. L. 100-93, § 8(c)(2), 101 Stat. 692; Dec. 22, 1987, P. L. 100-203, Title IV, Subtitle A, Part 2, Subpart C, §§ 4031(a)(2), 4035(a)(2), Part 3, Subpart A, §§ 4041(a)(1), (3)(A), 4042, 4044(a), 4045(a), (c)(1), (2)(B), (D), 4046(a), 4047(a), 4048(a), (e), 4051(a), 4052(a), 4053(a), Subpart B, § 4063(a), Subpart D, §§ 4081(a), 4082(c), 4085(g)(1), (i)(5)–(7), (22)(C), (24)–(27), Part 4, § 4096(a)(1), 101 Stat. 1330-76, 1330-78, 1330-83, 1330-85, 1330-86, 1330-88, 1330-89, 1330-93, 1330-95, 1330-97, 1330-109, 1330-126, 1330-128, 1330-131, 1330-132, 1330-139; July 1, 1988, P. L. 100-360, Title II, Subtitle A, §§ 201(c), 202(c), (e)(1)–(5), (g), Subtitle C, § 223(b), (c), Title IV, Subtitle B, § 411(a)(3)(C)(i), (f)(1)(A), (B), (2)–(4)(C), (5), (6)(B), (7), (9), (11)(A), (14), (g)(2)(A)–(C), (i)(1)(A), (2), (3), (4)(C)(vi), (j)(4)(A), 102 Stat. 702, 713, 716, 717 747, 768, 776–783, 787–791; Oct. 13, 1988, P. L. 100-485, Title VI, § 608(d)(5)(A)–(D), (F), (G), (17), (21)(A), (B), (D), (24)(B), 102 Stat. 2414, 2418, 2420, 2421; Dec. 13, 1989, P. L. 101-234, Title II, §§ 201(a), 301(b)(2), (6), (c)(2), (d)(3), 103 Stat. 1981, 1985, 1986; Dec. 19, 1989, P. L. 101-239, Title VI, Subtitle A, Part 1, Subpart A,

§ 6003(g)(3)(D)(ix), Part 2, Subpart A, §§ 6102(b), (e)(2)–(4), (9), 6104, 6106(a), 6107(b), 6108(a)(1), (b)(1), (2), 6114(b), (c), Part 3, Subpart A, § 6202(d)(2), 103 Stat. 2153, 2184, 2187, 2188, 2208, 2210, 2212, 2213, 2218, 2235; Nov. 5, 1990, P. L. 101-508, Title IV, Subtitle A, Part 2, Subpart A, § 4101(a), (b)(1), 4103, 4105(a)(1), (2), (b)(1), 4106(a)(1), (b)(2), 4108(a), 4110(a), 4118(a)(1), (2), (f)(2)(B), (C), (i)(1), (j)(2), Subpart B, § 4155(c), 104 Stat. 1388-54, 1388-58, 1388-59, 1388-61, 1388-63, 1388-66; Nov. 16, 1990, P. L. 101-597, Title IV, § 401(c)(2), 104 Stat. 3035; Aug. 10, 1993, P. L. 103-66, Title XIII, Ch 2, Subch A, Part II, Subpart A, §§ 13515(a)(2), 13516(a)(2), 13517(b), Part III, § 13568(a), (b), 107 Stat. 583–585, 608; Oct. 31, 1994, P. L. 103-432, Title I, Subtitle B, Part I, §§ 123(b)(1), (2)(B), (c), 125(a), (b)(1), 126(a)(1), (c), (e), (g)(9), (h)(2), Part II, § 135(b)(2), Subtitle C, § 151(b)(1)(B), (2)(B), 108 Stat. 4411–4416, 4423, 4434; Aug. 21, 1996, P. L. 104-191, Title II, Subtitle A, § 202(b)(2), Subtitle C, § 221(b), 110 Stat. 1998, 2011; Aug. 5, 1997, P. L. 105-33, Title IV, Subtitle C, §§ 4201(c)(1), 4205(d)(3)(B), Subtitle D, Ch 1, § 4302(b), Ch 2, §§ 4315(a), 4316(a), 4317(a), (b), Ch 3, § 4432(b)(2), (4), Subtitle F, Ch 1, Subch B, § 4512(b)(2), (c), Ch 3, § 4531(a)(2), Ch 5, 4556(a), Subtitle G, Ch 1, Subch A, § 4603(c)(2)(B)(i), Subch B, § 4611(d), 111 Stat. 373, 377, 382, 390, 392, 421, 444, 450, 462, 471, 473; Nov. 29, 1999, P. L. 106-113, Div B, § 1000(a)(6), 113 Stat. 1536; Dec. 21, 2000, P. L. 106-554, § 1(a)(6), 114 Stat. 2763; Dec. 8, 2003, P. L. 108-173, Title III, §§ 302(d)(3), 303(b), (e), (g)(1), (i)(1), 305(a), Title VI, Subtitle C, § 627(b)(2), Title VII, Subtitle D, § 736(b)(8), (9), Title IX, Subtitle B, § 911(c), Subtitle E, § 952(a), (b), 117 Stat. 2233, 2238, 2252, 2253, 2254, 2255, 2321, 2356, 2383, 2427; Feb. 8, 2006, P. L. 109-171, Title V, Subtitle B, Ch. 2, §§ 5114(a)(2), 5202(a)(2), 120 Stat. 45, 47; Dec. 20, 2006, P. L. 109-432, Div B, Title I, § 110(a), Title II, § 205(b)(2), Title IV, § 405(c)(2)(A)(i), 120 Stat. 2985, 2989, 2999; Aug. 3, 2007, P. L. 110-54, § 1(a), 121 Stat. 551; Dec. 29, 2007, P. L. 110-173, Title I, § 116, 121 Stat. 2507; July 15, 2008, P. L. 110-275, Title I, Subtitle C, Part I, § 137, Part II, § 154(a)(2)(B), 122 Stat. 2540, 2563; March 23, 2010, P. L. 111-148, Title III, Subtitle E, § 3401(o), Title VI, Subtitle E, §§ 6404(a)(2)(A), 6406(a), 124 Stat. 488, 768, 769.)

§ 1395w-3. Competitive acquisition of certain items and services

(a) Establishment of competitive acquisition programs. (1) Implementation of programs. (A) In general. The Secretary shall establish and implement programs under which competitive acquisition areas are established throughout the United States for contract award purposes for the furnishing under this part [42 USCS §§ 1395j et seq.] of competitively priced items and services (described in paragraph (2)) for which payment is made under this part [42 USCS §§ 1395j et seq.]. Such areas may differ for different items and services.

(B) Phased-in implementation. The programs—

(i) shall be phased in among competitive acquisition areas in a manner consistent with subparagraph (D) so that the competition under the programs occurs in—

(I) 10 of the largest metropolitan statistical areas in 2007;

(II) an additional 91 of the largest metropolitan statistical areas in 2011; and

(III) additional areas after 2011 (or, in the case of national mail order for items and services, after 2010); and

(ii) may be phased in first among the highest cost and highest volume items and services or those items and services that the Secretary determines have the largest savings potential.

(C) Waiver of certain provisions. In carrying out the programs, the Secretary may waive such provisions of the Federal Acquisition Regulation as are necessary for the efficient implementation of this section, other than provisions relating to confidentiality of information and such other provisions as the Secretary determines appropriate.

(D) Changes in competitive acquisition programs. (i) Round 1 of competitive acquisition program. Notwithstanding subparagraph (B)(i)(I) and in implementing the first round of the competitive acquisition programs under this section—

(I) the contracts awarded under this section before the date of the enactment of this subparagraph are terminated, no payment shall be made under this title on or after the date of the enactment of this subparagraph based on such a contract, and, to the extent that any damages may be applicable as a result of the termination of such contracts, such damages shall be payable from the Federal Supplementary Medical Insurance Trust Fund under section 1841;

(II) the Secretary shall conduct the competition for such round in a manner so that it occurs in 2009 with respect to the same items and services and the same areas, except as provided in subclauses (III) and (IV);

(III) the Secretary shall exclude Puerto Rico so that such round of competition covers 9, instead of 10, of the largest metropolitan statistical areas; and

(IV) there shall be excluded negative pressure wound therapy items and services.

Nothing in subclause (I) shall be construed to provide an independent cause of action or right to administrative or judicial review with regard to the termination provided under such subclause.

(ii) Round 2 of competitive acquisition program. In implementing the second round of the competitive acquisition programs under this section described in subparagraph (B)(i)(II)—

(I) the metropolitan statistical areas to be included shall be those metropolitan statistical areas selected by the Secretary for such round as of June 1, 2008;

(II) the Secretary shall include the next 21 largest metropolitan statistical areas by total population (after those selected under subclause (I)) for such round; and

(III) the Secretary may subdivide metropolitan statistical areas with populations (based upon the most recent data from the Census Bureau) of at least 8,000,000 into separate areas for competitive acquisition purposes.

(iii) Exclusion of certain areas in subsequent rounds of competitive acquisition programs. In implementing subsequent rounds of the competitive acquisition programs under this section, including under subparagraph (B)(i)(III), for competitions occurring before 2015, the Secretary shall exempt from the competitive acquisition program (other than national mail order) the following:

(I) Rural areas.

(II) Metropolitan statistical areas not selected under round 1 or round 2 with a population of less than 250,000.

(III) Areas with a low population density within a metropolitan statistical area that is otherwise selected, as determined for purposes of paragraph (3)(A).

(E) Verification by OIG. The Inspector General of the Department of Health and Human Services shall, through post-award audit, survey, or otherwise, assess the process used by the Centers for Medicare & Medicaid Services to conduct competitive bidding and subsequent pricing determinations under this section that are the basis for pivotal bid amounts and single payment amounts for items and services in competitive bidding areas under rounds 1 and 2 of the competitive acquisition programs under this section and may continue to verify such calculations for subsequent rounds of such programs.

(F) Supplier feedback on missing financial documentation. (i) In general. In the case of a bid where one or more covered documents in connection with such bid have been submitted not later than the covered document review date specified in clause (ii), the Secretary—

(I) shall provide, by not later than 45 days (in the case of the first round of the competitive acquisition programs as described in subparagraph (B)(i)(I)) or 90 days (in the case of a subsequent round of such programs) after the covered document review date, for notice to the bidder of all such documents that are missing as of the covered document review date; and

(II) may not reject the bid on the basis that any covered document is missing or has not been submitted on a timely basis, if all such missing documents identified in the notice provided to the bidder under subclause (I) are submitted to the Secretary not later than 10 business days after the date of such notice.

(ii) Covered document review date. The covered document review date specified in this clause with respect to a competitive acquisition program is the later of—

(I) the date that is 30 days before the final date specified by the Secretary for submission of bids under such program; or

(II) the date that is 30 days after the first date specified by the Secretary for submission of bids under such program.

(iii) Limitations of process. The process provided under this subparagraph—

(I) applies only to the timely submission of covered documents;

(II) does not apply to any determination as to the accuracy or completeness of covered documents submitted or whether such documents meet applicable requirements;

(III) shall not prevent the Secretary from rejecting a bid based on any basis not described in clause (i)(II); and

(IV) shall not be construed as permitting a bidder to change bidding amounts or to make other changes in a bid submission.

(iv) Covered document defined. In this subparagraph, the term "covered document" means a financial, tax, or other document required to be submitted by a bidder as part of an original bid submission under a competitive acquisition program in order to meet required financial standards. Such term does not include other documents, such as the bid itself or accreditation documentation.

(2) Items and services described. The items and services referred to in paragraph (1) are the following:

(A) Durable medical equipment and medical supplies. Covered items (as defined in section 1834(a)(13) [42 USCS § 1395m(a)(13)]) for which payment would otherwise be made under section 1834(a) [42 USCS § 1395m(a)], including items used in infusion and drugs (other than inhalation drugs) and supplies used in conjunction with durable medical equipment, but excluding class III devices under the Federal Food, Drug, and Cosmetic Act and excluding certain complex rehabilitative power wheelchairs recognized by the Secretary as classified within group 3 or higher (and related accessories when furnished in connection with such wheelchairs).

(B) Other equipment and supplies. Items and services described in section 1842(s)(2)(D) [42 USCS § 1395u(s)(2)(D)], other than parenteral nutrients, equipment, and supplies.

(C) Off-the-shelf orthotics. Orthotics described in section 1861(s)(9) [42 USCS § 1395x(s)(9)] for which payment would otherwise be made under section 1834(h) [42 USCS § 1395m(h)] which require minimal self-adjustment for appropriate use and do not require expertise in trimming, bending, molding, assembling, or customizing to fit to the individual.

(3) Exception authority. In carrying out the programs under this section, the Secretary may exempt—

(A) rural areas and areas with low population density within urban areas that are not competitive, unless there is a significant national market through mail order for a particular item or service; and

(B) items and services for which the application of competitive acquisition is not likely to result in significant savings.

(4) Special rule for certain rented items of durable medical equipment and oxygen. In the case of a covered item for which payment is made on a rental basis under section 1834(a) [42 USCS § 1395m(a)] and in the case of payment for oxygen under section 1834(a)(5) [42 USCS § 1395m(a)(5)], the Secretary shall establish a process by which rental agreements for the covered items and supply arrangements with oxygen suppliers entered into before the application of the competitive acquisition program under this section for the item may be continued notwithstanding this section. In the case of any such continuation, the supplier involved shall provide for appropriate servicing and replacement, as required under section 1834(a) [42 USCS § 1395m(a)].

(5) Physician authorization. (A) In general. With respect to items or services included within a particular HCPCS code, the Secretary may establish a process for certain items and services under which a physician may prescribe a particular brand or mode of delivery of an item or service within such code if the physician determines that use of the particular item or service would avoid an adverse medical outcome on the individual, as determined by the Secretary.

(B) No effect on payment amount. A prescription under subparagraph (A) shall not affect the amount of payment otherwise applicable for the item or service under the code involved.

(6) Application. For each competitive acquisition area in which the program is implemented under this subsection with respect to items and services, the payment basis determined under the competition conducted under subsection (b) shall be substituted for the payment basis otherwise applied under section 1834(a), section 1834(h), or section 1842(s) [42 USCS § 1395m(a), 1395m(h), or 1395u(s)], as appropriate.

(7) Exemption from competitive acquisition. The programs under this section shall not apply to the following:

(A) Certain off-the-shelf orthotics. Items and services described in paragraph (2)(C) if furnished—

(i) by a physician or other practitioner (as defined by the Secretary) to the physician's or practitioner's own patients as part of the physician's or practitioner's professional service; or

(ii) by a hospital to the hospital's own patients during an admission or on the date of discharge.

(B) Certain durable medical equipment. Those items and services described in paragraph (2)(A)—

(i) that are furnished by a hospital to the hospital's own patients during an admission or on the date of discharge; and

(ii) to which such programs would not apply, as specified by the Secretary, if furnished by a physician to the physician's own patients as part of the physician's professional service.

(b) Program requirements. (1) In general. The Secretary shall conduct a competition among entities supplying items and services described in subsection (a)(2) for each competitive acquisition area in which the program is implemented under subsection (a) with respect to such items and services.

(2) Conditions for awarding contract. (A) In general. The Secretary may not award a contract to any entity under the competition conducted in an competitive acquisition area pur-

suant to paragraph (1) to furnish such items or services unless the Secretary finds all of the following:

(i) The entity meets applicable quality standards specified by the Secretary under section 1834(a)(20) [42 USCS § 1395m(a)(20)].

(ii) The entity meets applicable financial standards specified by the Secretary, taking into account the needs of small providers.

(iii) The total amounts to be paid to contractors in a competitive acquisition area are expected to be less than the total amounts that would otherwise be paid.

(iv) Access of individuals to a choice of multiple suppliers in the area is maintained.

(B) Timely implementation of program. Any delay in the implementation of quality standards under section 1834(a)(20) [42 USCS § 1395m(a)(20)] or delay in the receipt of advice from the program oversight committee established under subsection (c) shall not delay the implementation of the competitive acquisition program under this section.

(3) Contents of contract. (A) In general. A contract entered into with an entity under the competition conducted pursuant to paragraph (1) is subject to terms and conditions that the Secretary may specify.

(B) Term of contracts. The Secretary shall recompete contracts under this section not less often than once every 3 years.

(C) Disclosure of subcontractors. (i) Initial disclosure. Not later than 10 days after the date a supplier enters into a contract with the Secretary under this section, such supplier shall disclose to the Secretary, in a form and manner specified by the Secretary, the information on—

(I) each subcontracting relationship that such supplier has in furnishing items and services under the contract; and

(II) whether each such subcontractor meets the requirement of section 1834(a)(20)(F)(i) [42 USCS § 1395m(a)(20)(F)(i)], if applicable to such subcontractor.

(ii) Subsequent disclosure. Not later than 10 days after such a supplier subsequently enters into a subcontracting relationship described in clause (i)(II), such supplier shall disclose to the Secretary, in such form and manner, the information described in subclauses (I) and (II) of clause (i).

(4) Limit on number of contractors. (A) In general. The Secretary may limit the number of contractors in a competitive acquisition area to the number needed to meet projected demand for items and services covered under the contracts. In awarding contracts, the Secretary shall take into account the ability of bidding entities to furnish items or services in sufficient quantities to meet the anticipated needs of individuals for such items or services in the geographic area covered under the contract on a timely basis.

(B) Multiple winners. The Secretary shall award contracts to multiple entities submitting bids in each area for an item or service.

(5) Payment. (A) In general. Payment under this part [42 USCS §§ 1395j et seq.] for competitively priced items and services described in subsection (a)(2) shall be based on bids submitted and accepted under this section for such items and services. Based on such bids the Secretary shall determine a single payment amount for each item or service in each competitive acquisition area.

(B) Reduced beneficiary cost-sharing. (i) Application of coinsurance. Payment under this section for items and services shall be in an amount equal to 80 percent of the payment basis described in subparagraph (A).

(ii) Application of deductible. Before applying clause (i), the individual shall be required to meet the deductible described in section 1833(b) [42 USCS § 1395l(b)].

(C) Payment on assignment-related basis. Payment for any item or service furnished by the entity may only be made under this section on an assignment-related basis.

(D) Construction. Nothing in this section shall be construed as precluding the use of an advanced beneficiary notice with respect to a competitively priced item and service.

(6) Participating contractors. (A) In general. Except as provided in subsection (a)(4), payment shall not be made for items and services described in subsection (a)(2) furnished by a contractor and for which competition is conducted under this section unless—

(i) the contractor has submitted a bid for such items and services under this section; and

(ii) the Secretary has awarded a contract to the contractor for such items and services under this section.

(B) Bid defined. In this section, the term 'bid' means an offer to furnish an item or service for a particular price and time period that includes, where appropriate, any services that are attendant to the furnishing of the item or service.

(C) Rules for mergers and acquisitions. In applying subparagraph (A) to a contractor, the contractor shall include a successor entity in the case of a merger or acquisition, if the successor entity assumes such contract along with any liabilities that may have occurred thereunder.

(D) Protection of small suppliers. In developing procedures relating to bids and the awarding of contracts under this section, the Secretary shall take appropriate steps to ensure that small suppliers of items and services have an opportunity to be considered for participation in the program under this section.

(7) Consideration in determining categories for bids. The Secretary may consider the clinical efficiency and value of specific items within codes, including whether some items have a greater therapeutic advantage to individuals.

(8) Authority to contract for education, monitoring, outreach, and complaint services. The Secretary may enter into contracts with appropriate entities to address complaints from individuals who receive items and services from an entity with a contract under this section and to conduct appropriate education of and outreach to such individuals and monitoring quality of services with respect to the program.

(9) Authority to contract for implementation. The Secretary may contract with appropriate entities to implement the competitive bidding program under this section.

(10) Special rule in case of competition for diabetic testing strips. (A) In general. With respect to the competitive acquisition program for diabetic testing strips conducted after the first round of the competitive acquisition programs, if an entity does not demonstrate to the Secretary that its bid covers types of diabetic testing strip products that, in the aggregate and taking into account volume for the different products, cover 50 percent (or such higher percentage as the Secretary may specify) of all such types of products, the Secretary shall reject such bid. The volume for such types of products may be determined in accordance with such data (which may be market based data) as the Secretary recognizes.

(B) Study of types of testing strip products. Before 2011, the Inspector General of the Department of Health and Human Services shall conduct a study to determine the types of diabetic testing strip products by volume that could be used to make determinations pursuant to subparagraph (A) for the first competition under the competitive acquisition program described in such subparagraph and submit to the Secretary a report on the results of the study. The Inspector General shall also conduct such a study and submit such a report before the Secretary conducts a subsequent competitive acquistion [acquisition] program described in subparagraph (A).

(11) No administrative or judicial review. There shall be no administrative or judicial review under section 1869 [42 USCS § 1395ff], section 1878 [42 USCS § 1395oo], or otherwise, of—

(A) the establishment of payment amounts under paragraph (5);

(B) the awarding of contracts under this section;

(C) the designation of competitive acquisition areas under subsection (a)(1)(A) and the identification of areas under subsection (a)(1)(D)(iii);

(D) the phased-in implementation under subsection (a)(1)(B) and implementation of subsection (a)(1)(D);

(E) the selection of items and services for competitive acquisition under subsection (a)(2);

(F) the bidding structure and number of contractors selected under this section; or

(G) the implementation of the special rule described in paragraph (10).

(c) Program Advisory and Oversight Committee. (1) Establishment. The Secretary shall establish a Program Advisory and Oversight Committee (hereinafter in this section referred to as the "Committee").

(2) Membership; terms. The Committee shall consist of such members as the Secretary may appoint who shall serve for such term as the Secretary may specify.

(3) Duties. (A) Advice. The Committee shall provide advice to the Secretary with respect to the following functions:

(i) The implementation of the program under this section.

(ii) The establishment of financial standards for purposes of subsection (b)(2)(A)(ii).

(iii) The establishment of requirements for collection of data for the efficient management of the program.

(iv) The development of proposals for efficient interaction among manufacturers, providers of services, suppliers (as defined in section 1861(d) [42 USCS § 1395x(d)]), and individuals.

(v) The establishment of quality standards under section 1834(a)(20) [42 USCS § 1395m(a)(20)].

(B) Additional duties. The Committee shall perform such additional functions to assist the Secretary in carrying out this section as the Secretary may specify.

(4) Inapplicability of FACA. The provisions of the Federal Advisory Committee Act (5 U.S.C. App.) shall not apply.

(5) Termination. The Committee shall terminate on December 31, 2011.

(d) Report. Not later than July 1, 2011, the

Secretary shall submit to Congress a report on the programs under this section. The report shall include information on savings, reductions in cost-sharing, access to and quality of items and services, and satisfaction of individuals.

(e) [Deleted]

(f) Competitive acquisition ombudsman. The Secretary shall provide for a competitive acquisition ombudsman within the Centers for Medicare & Medicaid Services in order to respond to complaints and inquiries made by suppliers and individuals relating to the application of the competitive acquisition program under this section. The ombudsman may be within the office of the Medicare Beneficiary Ombudsman appointed under section 1808(c) [42 USCS § 1395b-9(c)]. The ombudsman shall submit to Congress an annual report on the activities under this subsection, which report shall be coordinated with the report provided under section 1808(c)(2)(C) [42 USCS § 1395b-9(c)(2)(C)].

(Act Aug. 14, 1935, ch 531, Title XVIII, Part B, § 1847, as added Aug. 5, 1997, P. L. 105-33, Title IV, Subtitle D, Ch 2, § 4319(a), 111 Stat. 392; Nov. 29, 1999, P. L. 106-113, Div B, § 1000(a)(6), 113 Stat. 1536; Dec. 8, 2003, P. L. 108-173, Title III, § 302(b)(1), 117 Stat. 2224; July 15, 2008, P. L. 110-275, Title I, Subtitle C, Part II, §§ 145(a)(1), 154(a)(1), (b)(2), (3), (c)(2)(A), (B), (d)(1), (3), (4), 122 Stat. 2547, 2560, 2565, 2566, 2567; March 23, 2010, P. L. 111-148, Title VI, Subtitle E, § 6410(a), 124 Stat. 773.)

§ 1395w-3a. Use of average sales price payment methodology

(a) Application. (1) In general. Except as provided in paragraph (2), this section shall apply to payment for drugs and biologicals that are described in section 1842(o)(1)(C) [42 USCS § 1395u(o)(1)(C)] and that are furnished on or after January 1, 2005.

(2) Election. This section shall not apply in the case of a physician who elects under subsection (a)(1)(A)(ii) of section 1847B [42 USCS § 1395w-3b] for that section to apply instead of this section for the payment for drugs and biologicals.

(b) Payment amount. (1) In general. Subject to paragraph (7) and subsections (d)(3)(C) and (e), the amount of payment determined under this section for the billing and payment code for a drug or biological (based on a minimum dosage unit) is, subject to applicable deductible and coinsurance—

(A) in the case of a multiple source drug (as defined in subsection (c)(6)(C)), 106 percent of the amount determined under paragraph (3) for a multiple source drug furnished before April 1, 2008, or 106 percent of the amount determined under paragraph (6) for a multiple source drug furnished on or after April 1, 2008;

(B) in the case of a single source drug or biological (as defined in subsection (c)(6)(D)), 106 percent of the amount determined under paragraph (4); and

(C) **[Caution: This subparagraph is applicable as provided by § 3139(b) of Act March 23, 2010, P. L. 111-148, which appears as a note to this section.]** in the case of a biosimilar biological product (as defined in subsection (c)(6)(H)), the amount determined under paragraph (8).

(2) Specification of unit. (A) Specification by manufacturer. The manufacturer of a drug or biological shall specify the unit associated with each National Drug Code (including package size) as part of the submission of data under section 1927(b)(3)(A)(iii) [42 USCS § 1396r-8(b)(3)(A)(iii)].

(B) Unit defined. In this section, the term "unit" means, with respect to each National Drug Code (including package size) associated with a drug or biological, the lowest identifiable quantity (such as a capsule or tablet, milligram of molecules, or grams) of the drug or biological that is dispensed, exclusive of any diluent without reference to volume measures pertaining to liquids. For years after 2004, the Secretary may establish the unit for a manufacturer to report and methods for counting units as the Secretary determines appropriate to implement this section.

(3) Multiple source drug. For all drug products included within the same multiple source drug billing and payment code, the amount specified in this paragraph is the volume-weighted average of the average sales prices reported under section 1927(b)(3)(A)(iii) [42 USCS § 1396r-8(b)(3)(A)(iii)] determined by—

(A) computing the sum of the products (for each National Drug Code assigned to such drug products) of—

(i) the manufacturer's average sales price (as defined in subsection (c)); and

(ii) the total number of units specified under paragraph (2) sold; and

(B) dividing the sum determined under subparagraph (A) by the sum of the total number of units under subparagraph (A)(ii) for all National Drug Codes assigned to such drug products.

(4) Single source drug or biological. The amount specified in this paragraph for a single

source drug or biological is the lesser of the following:

(A) Average sales price. The average sales price as determined using the methodology applied under paragraph (3) for single source drugs and biologicals furnished before April 1, 2008, and using the methodology applied under paragraph (6) for single source drugs and biologicals furnished on or after April 1, 2008, for all National Drug Codes assigned to such drug or biological product.

(B) Wholesale acquisition cost (WAC). The wholesale acquisition cost (as defined in subsection (c)(6)(B)) using the methodology applied under paragraph (3) for single source drugs and biologicals furnished before April 1, 2008, and using the methodology applied under paragraph (6) for single source drugs and biologicals furnished on or after April 1, 2008, for all National Drug Codes assigned to such drug or biological product.

(5) Basis for payment amount. The payment amount shall be determined under this subsection based on information reported under subsection (f) and without regard to any special packaging, labeling, or identifiers on the dosage form or product or package.

(6) Use of volume-weighted average sales prices in calculation of average sales price. (A) In general. For all drug products included within the same multiple source drug billing and payment code, the amount specified in this paragraph is the volume-weighted average of the average sales prices reported under section 1927(b)(3)(A)(iii) [42 USCS § 1396r-8(b)(3)(A)(iii)] determined by—

(i) computing the sum of the products (for each National Drug Code assigned to such drug products) of—

(I) the manufacturer's average sales price (as defined in subsection (c)), determined by the Secretary without dividing such price by the total number of billing units for the National Drug Code for the billing and payment code; and

(II) the total number of units specified under paragraph (2) sold; and

(ii) dividing the sum determined under clause (i) by the sum of the products (for each National Drug Code assigned to such drug products) of—

(I) the total number of units specified under paragraph (2) sold; and

(II) the total number of billing units for the National Drug Code for the billing and payment code.

(B) Billing unit defined. For purposes of this subsection, the term "billing unit" means the identifiable quantity associated with a billing and payment code, as established by the Secretary.

(7) Special rule. Beginning with April 1, 2008, the payment amount for—

(A) each single source drug or biological described in section 1842(o)(1)(G) [42 USCS § 1395u(o)(1)(G)] that is treated as a multiple source drug because of the application of subsection (c)(6)(C)(ii) is the lower of—

(i) the payment amount that would be determined for such drug or biological applying such subsection; or

(ii) the payment amount that would have been determined for such drug or biological if such subsection were not applied; and

(B) a multiple source drug described in section 1842(o)(1)(G) [42 USCS § 1395u(o)(1)(G)] (excluding a drug or biological that is treated as a multiple source drug because of the application of such subsection) is the lower of—

(i) the payment amount that would be determined for such drug or biological taking into account the application of such subsection; or

(ii) the payment amount that would have been determined for such drug or biological if such subsection were not applied.

(8) Biosimilar biological product **[Caution: This paragraph is applicable as provided by § 3139(b) of Act March 23, 2010, P. L. 111-148, which appears as a note to this section.]**. The amount specified in this paragraph for a biosimilar biological product described in paragraph (1)(C) is the sum of—

(A) the average sales price as determined using the methodology described under paragraph (6) applied to a biosimilar biological product for all National Drug Codes assigned to such product in the same manner as such paragraph is applied to drugs described in such paragraph; and

(B) 6 percent of the amount determined under paragraph (4) for the reference biological product (as defined in subsection (c)(6)(I)).

(c) Manufacturer's average sales price. (1) In general. For purposes of this section, subject to paragraphs (2) and (3), the manufacturer's "average sales price" means, of a drug or biological for a National Drug Code for a calendar quarter for a manufacturer for a unit—

(A) the manufacturer's sales to all purchasers (excluding sales exempted in paragraph (2)) in the United States for such drug or biological in the calendar quarter; divided by

(B) the total number of such units of such drug or biological sold by the manufacturer in such quarter.

(2) Certain sales exempted from computa-

tion. In calculating the manufacturer's average sales price under this subsection, the following sales shall be excluded:

(A) Sales exempt from best price. Sales exempt from the inclusion in the determination of "best price" under section 1927(c)(1)(C)(i) [42 USCS § 1396r-8(c)(1)(C)(i)].

(B) Sales at nominal charge. Such other sales as the Secretary identifies as sales to an entity that are merely nominal in amount (as applied for purposes of section 1927(c)(1)(C)(ii)(III) [42 USCS § 1396r-8(c)(1)(C)(ii)(III)], except as the Secretary may otherwise provide).

(3) Sale price net of discounts. In calculating the manufacturer's average sales price under this subsection, such price shall include volume discounts, prompt pay discounts, cash discounts, free goods that are contingent on any purchase requirement, chargebacks, and rebates (other than rebates under section 1927 [42 USCS § 1396r-8]). For years after 2004, the Secretary may include in such price other price concessions, which may be based on recommendations of the Inspector General, that would result in a reduction of the cost to the purchaser.

(4) Payment methodology in cases where average sales price during first quarter of sales is unavailable. In the case of a drug or biological during an initial period (not to exceed a full calendar quarter) in which data on the prices for sales for the drug or biological is not sufficiently available from the manufacturer to compute an average sales price for the drug or biological, the Secretary may determine the amount payable under this section for the drug or biological based on—

(A) the wholesale acquisition cost; or

(B) the methodologies in effect under this part [42 USCS §§ 1395j et seq.] on November 1, 2003, to determine payment amounts for drugs or biologicals.

(5) Frequency of determinations. (A) In general on a quarterly basis. The manufacturer's average sales price, for a drug or biological of a manufacturer, shall be calculated by such manufacturer under this subsection on a quarterly basis. In making such calculation insofar as there is a lag in the reporting of the information on rebates and chargebacks under paragraph (3) so that adequate data are not available on a timely basis, the manufacturer shall apply a methodology based on a 12-month rolling average for the manufacturer to estimate costs attributable to rebates and chargebacks. For years after 2004, the Secretary may establish a uniform methodology under this subparagraph to estimate and apply such costs.

(B) Updates in payment amounts. The payment amounts under subsection (b) shall be updated by the Secretary on a quarterly basis and shall be applied based upon the manufacturer's average sales price calculated for the most recent calendar quarter for which data is available.

(C) Use of contractors; implementation. The Secretary may contract with appropriate entities to calculate the payment amount under subsection (b). Notwithstanding any other provision of law, the Secretary may implement, by program instruction or otherwise, any of the provisions of this section.

(6) Definitions and other rules. In this section:

(A) Manufacturer. The term "manufacturer" means, with respect to a drug or biological, the manufacturer (as defined in section 1927(k)(5) [42 USCS § 1396r-8(k)(5)]).

(B) Wholesale acquisition cost. The term "wholesale acquisition cost" means, with respect to a drug or biological, the manufacturer's list price for the drug or biological to wholesalers or direct purchasers in the United States, not including prompt pay or other discounts, rebates or reductions in price, for the most recent month for which the information is available, as reported in wholesale price guides or other publications of drug or biological pricing data.

(C) Multiple source drug. (i) In general. The term "multiple source drug" means, for a calendar quarter, a drug for which there are 2 or more drug products which—

(I) are rated as therapeutically equivalent (under the Food and Drug Administration's most recent publication of "Approved Drug Products with Therapeutic Equivalence Evaluations"),

(II) except as provided in subparagraph (E), are pharmaceutically equivalent and bioequivalent, as determined under subparagraph (F) and as determined by the Food and Drug Administration, and

(III) are sold or marketed in the United States during the quarter.

(ii) Exception. With respect to single source drugs or biologicals that are within the same billing and payment code as of October 1, 2003, the Secretary shall treat such single source drugs or biologicals as if the single source drugs or biologicals were multiple source drugs.

(D) Single source drug or biological. The term "single source drug or biological" means—

(i) a biological; or

(ii) a drug which is not a multiple source drug and which is produced or distributed under a new drug application approved by the Food and Drug Administration, including a drug product marketed by any cross-licensed producers or distributors operating under the new drug application.

(E) Exception from pharmaceutical equivalence and bioequivalence requirement. Subparagraph (C)(ii) shall not apply if the Food and Drug Administration changes by regulation the requirement that, for purposes of the publication described in subparagraph (C)(i), in order for drug products to be rated as therapeutically equivalent, they must be pharmaceutically equivalent and bioequivalent, as defined in subparagraph (F).

(F) Determination of pharmaceutical equivalence and bioequivalence. For purposes of this paragraph—

(i) drug products are pharmaceutically equivalent if the products contain identical amounts of the same active drug ingredient in the same dosage form and meet compendial or other applicable standards of strength, quality, purity, and identity; and

(ii) drugs are bioequivalent if they do not present a known or potential bioequivalence problem, or, if they do present such a problem, they are shown to meet an appropriate standard of bioequivalence.

(G) Inclusion of vaccines. In applying provisions of section 1927 [42 USCS § 1396r-8] under this section, "other than a vaccine" is deemed deleted from section 1927(k)(2)(B) [42 USCS § 1396r-8(k)(2)(B)].

(H) Biosimilar biological product **[Caution: This subparagraph is applicable as provided by § 3139(b) of Act March 23, 2010, P. L. 111-148, which appears as a note to this section.]**. The term "biosimilar biological product" means a biological product approved under an abbreviated application for a license of a biological product that relies in part on data or information in an application for another biological product licensed under section 351 of the Public Health Service Act [42 USCS § 262].

(I) Reference biological product **[Caution: This subparagraph is applicable as provided by § 3139(b) of Act March 23, 2010, P. L. 111-148, which appears as a note to this section.]**. The term "reference biological product" means the biological product licensed under such section 351 [42 USCS § 262] that is referred to in the application described in subparagraph (H) of the biosimilar biological product.

(d) Monitoring of market prices. (1) In general. The Inspector General of the Department of Health and Human Services shall conduct studies, which may include surveys, to determine the widely available market prices of drugs and biologicals to which this section applies, as the Inspector General, in consultation with the Secretary, determines to be appropriate.

(2) Comparison of prices. Based upon such studies and other data for drugs and biologicals, the Inspector General shall compare the average sales price under this section for drugs and biologicals with—

(A) the widely available market price for such drugs and biologicals (if any); and

(B) the average manufacturer price (as determined under section 1927(k)(1) [42 USCS § 1396r-8(k)(1)]) for such drugs and biologicals.

(3) Limitation on average sales price. (A) In general. The Secretary may disregard the average sales price for a drug or biological that exceeds the widely available market price or the average manufacturer price for such drug or biological by the applicable threshold percentage (as defined in subparagraph (B)).

(B) Applicable threshold percentage defined. In this paragraph, the term "applicable threshold percentage" means—

(i) in 2005, in the case of an average sales price for a drug or biological that exceeds widely available market price or the average manufacturer price, 5 percent; and

(ii) in 2006 and subsequent years, the percentage applied under this subparagraph subject to such adjustment as the Secretary may specify for the widely available market price or the average manufacturer price, or both.

(C) Authority to adjust average sales price. If the Inspector General finds that the average sales price for a drug or biological exceeds such widely available market price or average manufacturer price for such drug or biological by the applicable threshold percentage, the Inspector General shall inform the Secretary (at such times as the Secretary may specify to carry out this subparagraph) and the Secretary shall, effective as of the next quarter, substitute for the amount of payment otherwise determined under this section for such drug or biological the lesser of—

(i) the widely available market price for the drug or biological (if any); or

(ii) 103 percent of the average manufacturer price (as determined under section 1927(k)(1) [42 USCS § 1396r-8(k)(1)]) for the drug or biological.

(4) Civil money penalty. (A) In general. If

the Secretary determines that a manufacturer has made a misrepresentation in the reporting of the manufacturer's average sales price for a drug or biological, the Secretary may apply a civil money penalty in an amount of up to $10,000 for each such price misrepresentation and for each day in which such price misrepresentation was applied.

(B) Procedures. The provisions of section 1128A [42 USCS § 1320a-7a] (other than subsections (a) and (b)) shall apply to civil money penalties under subparagraph (B) in the same manner as they apply to a penalty or proceeding under section 1128A(a) [42 USCS § 1320a-7a(a)].

(5) Widely available market price. (A) In general. In this subsection, the term "widely available market price" means the price that a prudent physician or supplier would pay for the drug or biological. In determining such price, the Inspector General shall take into account the discounts, rebates, and other price concessions routinely made available to such prudent physicians or suppliers for such drugs or biologicals.

(B) Considerations. In determining the price under subparagraph (A), the Inspector General shall consider information from one or more of the following sources:

(i) Manufacturers.

(ii) Wholesalers.

(iii) Distributors.

(iv) Physician supply houses.

(v) Specialty pharmacies.

(vi) Group purchasing arrangements.

(vii) Surveys of physicians.

(viii) Surveys of suppliers.

(ix) Information on such market prices from insurers.

(x) Information on such market prices from private health plans.

(e) Authority to use alternative payment in response to public health emergency. In the case of a public health emergency under section 319 of the Public Health Service Act [42 USCS § 247d] in which there is a documented inability to access drugs and biologicals, and a concomitant increase in the price, of a drug or biological which is not reflected in the manufacturer's average sales price for one or more quarters, the Secretary may use the wholesale acquisition cost (or other reasonable measure of drug or biological price) instead of the manufacturer's average sales price for such quarters and for subsequent quarters until the price and availability of the drug or biological has stabilized and is substantially reflected in the applicable manufacturer's average sales price.

(f) Quarterly report on average sales price. For requirements for reporting the manufacturer's average sales price (and, if required to make payment, the manufacturer's wholesale acquisition cost) for the drug or biological under this section, see section 1927(b)(3) [42 USCS § 1396r-8(b)(3)].

(g) Judicial review. There shall be no administrative or judicial review under section 1869 [42 USCS § 1395ff], section 1878 [42 USCS § 1395oo], or otherwise, of—

(1) determinations of payment amounts under this section, including the assignment of National Drug Codes to billing and payment codes;

(2) the identification of units (and package size) under subsection (b)(2);

(3) the method to allocate rebates, chargebacks, and other price concessions to a quarter if specified by the Secretary;

(4) the manufacturer's average sales price when it is used for the determination of a payment amount under this section; and

(5) the disclosure of the average manufacturer price by reason of an adjustment under subsection (d)(3)(C) or (e).

(Aug. 14, 1935, ch 531, Title XVIII, Part B, § 1847A, as added Dec. 8, 2003, P. L. 108-173, Title III, § 303(c)(1), 117 Stat. 2239; Dec. 29, 2007, P. L. 110-173, Title I, § 112, 121 Stat. 2500; March 23, 2010, P. L. 111-148, Title III, Subtitle B, Part III, § 3139(a), 124 Stat. 439.)

HISTORY; ANCILLARY LAWS AND DIRECTIVES

Other provisions:

Application of March 23, 2010 amendments. Act March 23, 2010, P. L. 111-148, Title III, Subtitle B, Part III, § 3139(b), 124 Stat. 440, provides: "The amendments made by subsection (a) [amending subsecs. (b) and (c)(6) of this section] shall apply to payments for biosimilar biological products beginning with the first day of the second calendar quarter after enactment of legislation providing for a biosimilar pathway (as determined by the Secretary).".

§ 1395w-4. Payment for physicians' services

(a) Payment based on fee schedule. (1) In general. Effective for all physicians' services (as defined in subsection (j)(3)) furnished under this part during a year (beginning with 1992) for which payment is otherwise made on the basis of a reasonable charge or on the basis of a fee schedule under section 1834(b) [42 USCS § 1395m(b)], payment under this part [42 USCS §§ 1395j et seq.] shall instead be based on the lesser of—

(A) the actual charge for the service, or

(B) subject to the succeeding provisions of this subsection, the amount determined under the fee schedule established under subsection (b) for services furnished during that year (in this subsection referred to as the "fee schedule amount").

(2) Transition to full fee schedule. (A) Limiting reductions and increases to 15 percent in 1992. (i) Limit on increase. In the case of a service in a fee schedule area (as defined in subsection (j)(2)) for which the adjusted historical payment basis (as defined in subparagraph (D)) is less than 85 percent of the fee schedule amount for services furnished in 1992, there shall be substituted for the fee schedule amount an amount equal to the adjusted historical payment basis plus 15 percent of the fee schedule amount otherwise established (without regard to this paragraph).

(ii) Limit in reduction. In the case of a service in a fee schedule area for which the adjusted historical payment basis exceeds 115 percent of the fee schedule amount for services furnished in 1992, there shall be substituted for the fee schedule amount an amount equal to the adjusted historical payment basis minus 15 percent of the fee schedule amount otherwise established (without regard to this paragraph).

(B) Special rule for 1993, 1994, and 1995. If a physicians' service in a fee schedule area is subject to the provisions of subparagraph (A) in 1992, for physicians' services furnished in the area—

(i) during 1993, there shall be substituted for the fee schedule amount an amount equal to the sum of—

(I) 75 percent of the fee schedule amount determined under subparagraph (A), adjusted by the update established under subsection (d)(3) for 1993, and

(II) 25 percent of the fee schedule amount determined under paragraph (1) for 1993 without regard to this paragraph;

(ii) during 1994, there shall be substituted for the fee schedule amount an amount equal to the sum of—

(I) 67 percent of the fee schedule amount determined under clause (i), adjusted by the update established under subsection (d)(3) for 1994 and as adjusted under subsection (c)(2)(F)(ii) and under section 13515(b) of the Omnibus Budget Reconciliation Act of 1993 [42 USCS § 1395u note], and

(II) 33 percent of the fee schedule amount determined under paragraph (1) for 1994 without regard to this paragraph; and

(iii) during 1995, there shall be substituted for the fee schedule amount an amount equal to the sum of—

(I) 50 percent of the fee schedule amount determined under clause (ii) adjusted by the update established under subsection (d)(3) for 1995, and

(II) 50 percent of the fee schedule amount determined under paragraph (1) for 1995 without regard to this paragraph.

(C) Special rule for anesthesia and radiology services. With respect to physicians' services which are anesthesia services, the Secretary shall provide for a transition in the same manner as a transition is provided for other services under subparagraph (B). With respect to radiology services, "109 percent" and "9 percent" shall be substituted for "115 percent" and "15 percent", respectively, in subparagraph (A)(ii).

(D) "Adjusted historical payment basis" defined. (i) In general. In this paragraph, the term "adjusted historical payment basis" means, with respect to a physicians' service furnished in a fee schedule area, the weighted average prevailing charge applied in the area for the service in 1991 (as determined by the Secretary without regard to physician specialty and as adjusted to reflect payments for services with customary charges below the prevailing charge or other payment limitations imposed by law or regulation) adjusted by the update established under subsection (d)(3) for 1992.

(ii) Application to radiology services. In applying clause (i) in the case of physicians' services which are radiology services (including radiologist services, as defined in section 1834(b)(6) [42 USCS § 1395m(b)(6)]), but excluding nuclear medicine services that are subject to section 6105(b) of the Omnibus Budget Reconciliation Act of 1989 [42 USCS § 1395m note], there shall be substituted for the weighted average prevailing charge the amount provided under the fee schedule established for the service for the fee schedule area under section 1834(b) [42 USCS § 1395m(b)].

(iii) Nuclear medicine services. In applying clause (i) in the case of physicians' services which are nuclear medicine services, there shall be substituted for the weighted average prevailing charge the amount provided under section 6105(b) of the Omnibus Budget Reconciliation Act of 1989 [42 USCS § 1395m note].

(3) Incentives for participating physicians and suppliers. In applying paragraph (1)(B) in the case of a nonparticipating physician or a nonparticipating supplier or other person, the fee schedule amount shall be 95 percent of such amount otherwise applied under this subsection (without regard to this paragraph). In the

case of physicians' services (including services which the Secretary excludes pursuant to subsection (j)(3)) of a nonparticipating physician, supplier, or other person for which payment is made under this part [42 USCS §§ 1395j et seq.] on a basis other than the fee schedule amount, the payment shall be based on 95 percent of the payment basis for such services furnished by a participating physician, supplier, or other person.

(4) Special rule for medical direction. (A) In general. With respect to physicians' services furnished on or after January 1, 1994, and consisting of medical direction of two, three, or four concurrent anesthesia cases, except as provided in paragraph (5), the fee schedule amount to be applied shall be equal to one-half of the amount described in subparagraph (B).

(B) Amount. The amount described in this subparagraph, for a physician's medical direction of the performance of anesthesia services, is the following percentage of the fee schedule amount otherwise applicable under this section if the anesthesia services were personally performed by the physician alone:

(i) For services furnished during 1994, 120 percent.

(ii) For services furnished during 1995, 115 percent.

(iii) For services furnished during 1996, 110 percent.

(iv) For services furnished during 1997, 105 percent.

(v) For services furnished after 1997, 100 percent.

(5) Incentives for electronic prescribing.

(A) Adjustment. (i) In general. Subject to subparagraph (B) and subsection (m)(2)(B), with respect to covered professional services furnished by an eligible professional during 2012, 2013 or 2014, if the eligible professional is not a successful electronic prescriber for the reporting period for the year (as determined under subsection (m)(3)(B)), the fee schedule amount for such services furnished by such professional during the year (including the fee schedule amount for purposes of determining a payment based on such amount) shall be equal to the applicable percent of the fee schedule amount that would otherwise apply to such services under this subsection (determined after application of paragraph (3) but without regard to this paragraph).

(ii) Applicable percent. For purposes of clause (i), the term "applicable percent" means—

(I) for 2012, 99 percent;

(II) for 2013, 98.5 percent; and

(III) for 2014, 98 percent.

(B) Significant hardship exception. The Secretary may, on a case-by-case basis, exempt an eligible professional from the application of the payment adjustment under subparagraph (A) if the Secretary determines, subject to annual renewal, that compliance with the requirement for being a successful electronic prescriber would result in a significant hardship, such as in the case of an eligible professional who practices in a rural area without sufficient Internet access.

(C) Application. (i) Physician reporting system rules. Paragraphs (5), (6), and (8) of subsection (k) shall apply for purposes of this paragraph in the same manner as they apply for purposes of such subsection.

(ii) Incentive payment validation rules. Clauses (ii) and (iii) of subsection (m)(5)(D) shall apply for purposes of this paragraph in a similar manner as they apply for purposes of such subsection.

(D) Definitions. For purposes of this paragraph:

(i) Eligible professional; covered professional services. The terms "eligible professional" and "covered professional services" have the meanings given such terms in subsection (k)(3).

(ii) Physician reporting system. The term "physician reporting system" means the system established under subsection (k).

(iii) Reporting period. The term "reporting period" means, with respect to a year, a period specified by the Secretary.

(6) Special rule for teaching anesthesiologists. With respect to physicians' services furnished on or after January 1, 2010, in the case of teaching anesthesiologists involved in the training of physician residents in a single anesthesia case or two concurrent anesthesia cases, the fee schedule amount to be applied shall be 100 percent of the fee schedule amount otherwise applicable under this section if the anesthesia services were personally performed by the teaching anesthesiologist alone and paragraph (4) shall not apply if—

(A) the teaching anesthesiologist is present during all critical or key portions of the anesthesia service or procedure involved; and

(B) the teaching anesthesiologist (or another anesthesiologist with whom the teaching anesthesiologist has entered into an arrangement) is immediately available to furnish anesthesia services during the entire procedure.

(7) Incentives for meaningful use of certified EHR technology. (A) Adjustment. (i) In general. Subject to subparagraphs (B) and (D),

with respect to covered professional services furnished by an eligible professional during 2015 or any subsequent payment year, if the eligible professional is not a meaningful EHR user (as determined under subsection (o)(2)) for an EHR reporting period for the year, the fee schedule amount for such services furnished by such professional during the year (including the fee schedule amount for purposes of determining a payment based on such amount) shall be equal to the applicable percent of the fee schedule amount that would otherwise apply to such services under this subsection (determined after application of paragraph (3) but without regard to this paragraph).

(ii) Applicable percent. Subject to clause (iii), for purposes of clause (i), the term "applicable percent" means—

(I) for 2015, 99 percent (or, in the case of an eligible professional who was subject to the application of the payment adjustment under section 1848(a)(5) for 2014, 98 percent);

(II) for 2016, 98 percent; and

(III) for 2017 and each subsequent year, 97 percent.

(iii) Authority to decrease applicable percentage for 2018 and subsequent years. For 2018 and each subsequent year, if the Secretary finds that the proportion of eligible professionals who are meaningful EHR users (as determined under subsection (o)(2)) is less than 75 percent, the applicable percent shall be decreased by 1 percentage point from the applicable percent in the preceding year, but in no case shall the applicable percent be less than 95 percent.

(B) Significant hardship exception. The Secretary may, on a case-by-case basis, exempt an eligible professional from the application of the payment adjustment under subparagraph (A) if the Secretary determines, subject to annual renewal, that compliance with the requirement for being a meaningful EHR user would result in a significant hardship, such as in the case of an eligible professional who practices in a rural area without sufficient Internet access. In no case may an eligible professional be granted an exemption under this subparagraph for more than 5 years.

(C) Application of physician reporting system rules. Paragraphs (5), (6), and (8) of subsection (k) shall apply for purposes of this paragraph in the same manner as they apply for purposes of such subsection.

(D) Non-application to hospital-based eligible professionals. No payment adjustment may be made under subparagraph (A) in the case of hospital-based eligible professionals (as defined in subsection (o)(1)(C)(ii)).

(E) Definitions. For purposes of this paragraph:

(i) Covered professional services. The term "covered professional services" has the meaning given such term in subsection (k)(3).

(ii) EHR reporting period. The term "EHR reporting period" means, with respect to a year, a period (or periods) specified by the Secretary.

(iii) Eligible professional. The term "eligible professional" means a physician, as defined in section 1861(r) [42 USCS § 1395x(r)].

(8) Incentives for quality reporting. (A) Adjustment. (i) In general. With respect to covered professional services furnished by an eligible professional during 2015 or any subsequent year, if the eligible professional does not satisfactorily submit data on quality measures for covered professional services for the quality reporting period for the year (as determined under subsection (m)(3)(A)), the fee schedule amount for such services furnished by such professional during the year (including the fee schedule amount for purposes of determining a payment based on such amount) shall be equal to the applicable percent of the fee schedule amount that would otherwise apply to such services under this subsection (determined after application of paragraphs (3), (5), and (7), but without regard to this paragraph).

(ii) Applicable percent. For purposes of clause (i), the term "applicable percent" means—

(I) for 2015, 98.5 percent; and

(II) for 2016 and each subsequent year, 98 percent.

(B) Application. (i) Physician reporting system rules. Paragraphs (5), (6), and (8) of subsection (k) shall apply for purposes of this paragraph in the same manner as they apply for purposes of such subsection.

(ii) Incentive payment validation rules. Clauses (ii) and (iii) of subsection (m)(5)(D) shall apply for purposes of this paragraph in a similar manner as they apply for purposes of such subsection.

(C) Definitions. For purposes of this paragraph:

(i) Eligible professional; covered professional services. The terms "eligible professional" and "covered professional services" have the meanings given such terms in subsection (k)(3).

(ii) Physician reporting system. The term "physician reporting system" means the system established under subsection (k).

(iii) Quality reporting period. The term "quality reporting period" means, with respect to a year, a period specified by the Secretary.

(b) Establishment of fee schedules. (1) In general. Before November 1 of the preceding year, for each year beginning with 1998, subject to subsection (p), the Secretary shall establish, by regulation, fee schedules that establish payment amounts for all physicians' services furnished in all fee schedule areas (as defined in subsection (j)(2)) for the year. Except as provided in paragraph (2), each such payment amount for a service shall be equal to the product of—

(A) the relative value for the service (as determined in subsection (c)(2)),

(B) the conversion factor (established under subsection (d)) for the year, and

(C) the geographic adjustment factor (established under subsection (e)(2)) for the service for the fee schedule area.

(2) Treatment of radiology services and anesthesia services. (A) Radiology services. With respect to radiology services (including radiologist services, as defined in section 1834(b)(6) [42 USCS § 1395m(b)(6)]), the Secretary shall base the relative values on the relative value scale developed under section 1834(b)(1)(A) [42 USCS § 1395m(b)(1)(A)], with appropriate modifications of the relative values to assure that the relative values established for radiology services which are similar or related to other physicians' services are consistent with the relative values established for those similar or related services.

(B) Anesthesia services. In establishing the fee schedule for anesthesia services for which a relative value guide has been established under section 4048(b) of the Omnibus Budget Reconciliation Act of 1987 [42 USCS § 1395u note], the Secretary shall use, to the extent practicable, such relative value guide, with appropriate adjustment of the conversion factor, in a manner to assure that the fee schedule amounts for anesthesia services are consistent with the fee schedule amounts for other services determined by the Secretary to be of comparable value. In applying the previous sentence, the Secretary shall adjust the conversion factor by geographic adjustment factors in the same manner as such adjustment is made under paragraph (1)(C).

(C) Consultation. The Secretary shall consult with the Physician Payment Review Commission [Medicare Payment Advisory Commission] and organizations representing physicians or suppliers who furnish radiology services and anesthesia services in applying subparagraphs (A) and (B).

(3) Treatment of interpretation of electrocardiograms. The Secretary—

(A) shall make separate payment under this section for the interpretation of electrocardiograms performed or ordered to be performed as part of or in conjunction with a visit to or a consultation with a physician, and

(B) shall adjust the relative values established for visits and consultations under subsection (c) so as not to include relative value units for interpretations of electrocardiograms in the relative value for visits and consultations.

(4) Special rule for imaging services. (A) In general. In the case of imaging services described in subparagraph (B) furnished on or after January 1, 2007, if—

(i) the technical component (including the technical component portion of a global fee) of the service established for a year under the fee schedule described in paragraph (1) without application of the geographic adjustment factor described in paragraph (1)(C), exceeds

(ii) the Medicare OPD fee schedule amount established under the prospective payment system for hospital outpatient department services under paragraph (3)(D) of section 1833(t) [42 USCS § 1395l(t)] for such service for such year, determined without regard to geographic adjustment under paragraph (2)(D) of such section,

the Secretary shall substitute the amount described in clause (ii), adjusted by the geographic adjustment factor described in paragraph (1)(C), for the fee schedule amount for such technical component for such year.

(B) Imaging services described. For purposes of subparagraph (A), imaging services described in this subparagraph are imaging and computer-assisted imaging services, including X-ray, ultrasound (including echocardiography), nuclear medicine (including positron emission tomography), magnetic resonance imaging, computed tomography, and fluoroscopy, but excluding diagnostic and screening mammography, and for 2010 and 2011, dual-energy x-ray absorptiometry services (as described in paragraph (6)).

(C) Adjustment in imaging utilization rate. With respect to fee schedules established for 2011 and subsequent years, in the methodology for determining practice expense relative value units for expensive diagnostic imaging equipment under the final rule published by the Secretary in the Federal Register on November 25, 2009 (42 CFR 410 et al.), the Secretary shall use a 75 percent assumption instead of the utilization rates otherwise established in such final rule.

(D) Adjustment in technical component discount on single-session imaging involving consecutive body parts. For services furnished on or after July 1, 2010, the Secretary shall increase the reduction in payments attributable to the multiple procedure payment reduction applicable to the technical component for imaging under the final rule published by the Secretary in the Federal Register on November 21, 2005 (part 405 of title 42, Code of Federal Regulations) from 25 percent to 50 percent.

(5) Treatment of intensive cardiac rehabilitation program. (A) In general. In the case of an intensive cardiac rehabilitation program described in section 1861(eee)(4) [42 USCS § 1395x(eee)(4)], the Secretary shall substitute the Medicare OPD fee schedule amount established under the prospective payment system for hospital outpatient department service under paragraph (3)(D) of section 1833(t) [42 USCS § 1395l(t)] for cardiac rehabilitation (under HCPCS codes 93797 and 93798 for calendar year 2007, or any succeeding HCPCS codes for cardiac rehabilitation).

(B) Definition of session. Each of the services described in subparagraphs (A) through (E) of section 1861(eee)(3) [42 USCS § 1395x(eee)(3)], when furnished for one hour, is a separate session of intensive cardiac rehabilitation.

(C) Multiple sessions per day. Payment may be made for up to 6 sessions per day of the series of 72 one-hour sessions of intensive cardiac rehabilitation services described in section 1861(eee)(4)(B) [42 USCS § 1395x(eee)(4)(B)].

(6) Treatment of bone mass scans. For dual-energy x-ray absorptiometry services (identified in 2006 by HCPCS codes 76075 and 76077 (and any succeeding codes)) furnished during 2010 and 2011, instead of the payment amount that would otherwise be determined under this section for such years, the payment amount shall be equal to 70 percent of the product of—

(A) the relative value for the service (as determined in subsection (c)(2)) for 2006;

(B) the conversion factor (established under subsection (d)) for 2006; and

(C) the geographic adjustment factor (established under subsection (e)(2)) for the service for the fee schedule area for 2010 and 2011, respectively.

(c) Determination of relative values for physicians' services. (1) Division of physicians' services into components. In this section, with respect to a physicians' service:

(A) Work component defined. The term "work component" means the portion of the resources used in furnishing the service that reflects physician time and intensity in furnishing the service. Such portion shall—

(i) include activities before and after direct patient contact, and

(ii) be defined, with respect to surgical procedures, to reflect a global definition including pre-operative and post-operative physicians' services.

(B) Practice expense component defined. The term "practice expense component" means the portion of the resources used in furnishing the service that reflects the general categories of expenses (such as office rent and wages of personnel, but excluding malpractice expenses) comprising practice expenses.

(C) Malpractice component defined. The term "malpractice component" means the portion of the resources used in furnishing the service that reflects malpractice expenses in furnishing the service.

(2) Determination of relative values. (A) In general. (i) Combination of units for components. The Secretary shall develop a methodology for combining the work, practice expense, and malpractice relative value units, determined under subparagraph (C), for each service in a manner to produce a single relative value for that service. Such relative values are subject to adjustment under subparagraph (F)(i) and section 13515(b) of the Omnibus Budget Reconciliation Act of 1993 [42 USCS § 1395u note].

(ii) Extrapolation. The Secretary may use extrapolation and other techniques to determine the number of relative value units for physicians' services for which specific data are not available and shall take into account recommendations of the Physician Payment Review Commission [Medicare Payment Advisory Commission] and the results of consultations with organizations representing physicians who provide such services.

(B) Periodic review and adjustments in relative values. (i) Periodic review. The Secretary, not less often than every 5 years, shall review the relative values established under this paragraph for all physicians' services.

(ii) Adjustments. (I) In general. The Secretary shall, to the extent the Secretary determines to be necessary and subject to subclause (II), adjust the number of such units to take into account changes in medical practice, coding changes, new data on relative value components, or the addition of new procedures. The Secretary shall publish an explanation of the basis for such adjustments.

(II) Limitation on annual adjustments. Subject to clauses (iv) and (v), the adjustments under subclause (I) for a year may not cause the amount of expenditures under this part [42 USCS §§ 1395j et seq.] for the year to differ by more than $20,000,000 from the amount of expenditures under this part [42 USCS §§ 1395j et seq.] that would have been made if such adjustments had not been made.

(iii) Consultation. The Secretary, in making adjustments under clause (ii), shall consult with the Medicare Payment Advisory Commission and organizations representing physicians.

(iv) Exemption of certain additional expenditures from budget neutrality. The additional expenditures attributable to—

(I) subparagraph (H) shall not be taken into account in applying clause (ii)(II) for 2004;

(II) subparagraph (I) insofar as it relates to a physician fee schedule for 2005 or 2006 shall not be taken into account in applying clause (ii)(II) for drug administration services under the fee schedule for such year for a specialty described in subparagraph (I)(ii)(II);

(III) subparagraph (J) insofar as it relates to a physician fee schedule for 2005 or 2006 shall not be taken into account in applying clause (ii)(II) for drug administration services under the fee schedule for such year; and

(IV) subsection (b)(6) shall not be taken into account in applying clause (ii)(II) for 2010 or 2011.

(v) Exemption of certain reduced expenditures from budget-neutrality calculation. The following reduced expenditures, as estimated by the Secretary, shall not be taken into account in applying clause (ii)(II):

(I) Reduced payment for multiple imaging procedures. Effective for fee schedules established beginning with 2007, reduced expenditures attributable to the multiple procedure payment reduction for imaging under the final rule published by the Secretary in the Federal Register on November 21, 2005 (42 CFR 405, et al.) insofar as it relates to the physician fee schedules for 2006 and 2007.

(II) OPD payment cap for imaging services. Effective for fee schedules established beginning with 2007, reduced expenditures attributable to subsection (b)(4).

(III) Change in utilization rate for certain imaging services. Effective for fee schedules established beginning with 2011, reduced expenditures attributable to the change in the utilization rate applicable to 2011, as described in subsection (b)(4)(C).

(IV), (V) [Deleted]

(VI) Additional reduced payment for multiple imaging procedures. Effective for fee schedules established beginning with 2010 (but not applied for services furnished prior to July 1, 2010), reduced expenditures attributable to the increase in the multiple procedure payment reduction from 25 to 50 percent (as described in subsection (b)(4)(D)).

(vi) Alternative application of budget-neutrality adjustment. Notwithstanding subsection (d)(9)(A), effective for fee schedules established beginning with 2009, with respect to the 5-year review of work relative value units used in fee schedules for 2007 and 2008, in lieu of continuing to apply budget-neutrality adjustments required under clause (ii) for 2007 and 2008 to work relative value units, the Secretary shall apply such budget-neutrality adjustments to the conversion factor otherwise determined for years beginning with 2009.

(vii) Adjustment for certain physician incentive payments. Fifty percent of the additional expenditures under this part attributable to subsections (x) and (y) of section 1833 [42 USCS § 1395l(x), (y)] for a year (as estimated by the Secretary) shall be taken into account in applying clause (ii)(II) for 2011 and subsequent years. In lieu of applying the budget-neutrality adjustments required under clause (ii)(II) to relative value units to account for such costs for the year, the Secretary shall apply such budget-neutrality adjustments to the conversion factor otherwise determined for the year. For 2011 and subsequent years, the Secretary shall increase the incentive payment otherwise applicable under section 1833(m) [42 USCS § 1395l(m)] by a percent estimated to be equal to the additional expenditures estimated under the first sentence of this clause for such year that is applicable to physicians who primarily furnish services in areas designated (under section 332(a)(1)(A) of the Public Health Service Act [42 USCS § 254e]) as health professional shortage areas.

(C) Computation of relative value units for components. For purposes of this section for each physicians' service—

(i) Work relative value units. The Secretary shall determine a number of work relative value units for the service based on the relative resources incorporating physician time and intensity required in furnishing the service.

(ii) Practice expense relative value units. The Secretary shall determine a number of practice expense relative value units for the service for years before 1999 equal to the product of—

(I) the base allowed charges (as defined in subparagraph (D)) for the service, and

(II) the practice expense percentage for the

service (as determined under paragraph (3)(C)(ii)),

and for years beginning with 1999 based on the relative practice expense resources involved in furnishing the service. For 1999, such number of units shall be determined based 75 percent on such product and based 25 percent on the relative practice expense resources involved in furnishing the service. For 2000, such number of units shall be determined based 50 percent on such product and based 50 percent on such relative practice expense resources. For 2001, such number of units shall be determined based 25 percent on such product and based 75 percent on such relative practice expense resources. For a subsequent year, such number of units shall be determined based entirely on such relative practice expense resources.

(iii) Malpractice relative value units. The Secretary shall determine a number of malpractice relative value units for the service for years before 2000 equal to the product of—

(I) the base allowed charges (as defined in subparagraph (D)) for the service, and

(II) the malpractice percentage for the service (as determined under paragraph (3)(C)(iii)),

and for years beginning with 2000 based on the malpractice expense resources involved in furnishing the service.

(D) Base allowed charges defined. In this paragraph, the term "base allowed charges" means, with respect to a physician's service, the national average allowed charges for the service under this part [42 USCS §§ 1395j et seq.] for services furnished during 1991, as estimated by the Secretary using the most recent data available.

(E) Reduction in practice expense relative value units for certain services. (i) In general. Subject to clause (ii), the Secretary shall reduce the practice expense relative value units applied to services described in clause (iii) furnished in—

(I) 1994, by 25 percent of the number by which the number of practice expense relative value units (determined for 1994 without regard to this subparagraph) exceeds the number of work relative value units determined for 1994,

(II) 1995, by an additional 25 percent of such excess, and

(III) 1996, by an additional 25 percent of such excess.

(ii) Floor on reductions. The practice expense relative value units for a physician's service shall not be reduced under this subparagraph to a number less than 128 percent of the number of work relative value units.

(iii) Services covered. For purposes of clause (i), the services described in this clause are physicians' services that are not described in clause (iv) and for which—

(I) there are work relative value units, and

(II) the number of practice expense relative value units (determined for 1994) exceeds 128 percent of the number of work relative value units (determined for such year).

(iv) Excluded services. For purposes of clause (iii), the services described in this clause are services which the Secretary determines at least 75 percent of which are provided under this title in an office setting.

(F) Budget neutrality adjustments. The Secretary—

(i) shall reduce the relative values for all services (other than anesthesia services) established under this paragraph (and, in the case of anesthesia services, the conversion factor established by the Secretary for such services) by such percentage as the Secretary determines to be necessary so that, beginning in 1996, the amendment made by section 13514(a) of the Omnibus Budget Reconciliation Act of 1993 would not result in expenditures under this section that exceed the amount of such expenditures that would have been made if such amendment had not been made, and

(ii) shall reduce the amounts determined under subsection (a)(2)(B)(ii)(I) by such percentage as the Secretary determines to be required to assure that, taking into account the reductions made under clause (i), the amendment made by section 13514(a) of the Omnibus Budget Reconciliation Act of 1993 would not result in expenditures under this section in 1994 that exceed the amount of such expenditures that would have been made if such amendment had not been made.

(G) Adjustments in relative value units for 1998. (i) In general. The Secretary shall—

(I) subject to clauses (iv) and (v), reduce the practice expense relative value units applied to any services described in clause (ii) furnished in 1998 to a number equal to 110 percent of the number of work relative value units, and

(II) increase the practice expense relative value units for office visit procedure codes during 1998 by a uniform percentage which the Secretary estimates will result in an aggregate increase in payments for such services equal to the aggregate decrease in payments by reason of subclause (I).

(ii) Services covered. For purposes of clause (i), the services described in this clause are physicians' services that are not described in clause (iii) and for which—

(I) there are work relative value units, and

(II) the number of practice expense relative value units (determined for 1998) exceeds 110 percent of the number of work relative value units (determined for such year).

(iii) Excluded services. For purposes of clause (ii), the services described in this clause are services which the Secretary determines at least 75 percent of which are provided under this title in an office setting.

(iv) Limitation on aggregate reallocation. If the application of clause (i)(I) would result in an aggregate amount of reductions under such clause in excess of $390,000,000, such clause shall be applied by substituting for 110 percent such greater percentage as the Secretary estimates will result in the aggregate amount of such reductions equaling $390,000,000.

(v) No reduction for certain services. Practice expense relative value units for a procedure performed in an office or in a setting out of an office shall not be reduced under clause (i) if the in-office or out-of-office practice expense relative value, respectively, for the procedure would increase under the proposed rule on resource-based practice expenses issued by the Secretary on June 18, 1997 (62 Federal Register 33158 et seq.).

(H) Adjustments in practice expense relative value units for certain drug administration services beginning in 2004. (i) Use of survey data. In establishing the physician fee schedule under subsection (b) with respect to payments for services furnished on or after January 1, 2004, the Secretary shall, in determining practice expense relative value units under this subsection, utilize a survey submitted to the Secretary as of January 1, 2003, by a physician specialty organization pursuant to section 212 of the Medicare, Medicaid, and SCHIP Balanced Budget Refinement Act of 1999 [note to this section] if the survey—

(I) covers practice expenses for oncology drug administration services; and

(II) meets criteria established by the Secretary for acceptance of such surveys.

(ii) Pricing of clinical oncology nurses in practice expense methodology. If the survey described in clause (i) includes data on wages, salaries, and compensation of clinical oncology nurses, the Secretary shall utilize such data in the methodology for determining practice expense relative value units under subsection (c).

(iii) Work relative value units for certain drug administration services. In establishing the relative value units under this paragraph for drug administration services described in clause (iv) furnished on or after January 1, 2004, the Secretary shall establish work relative value units equal to the work relative value units for a level 1 office medical visit for an established patient.

(iv) Drug administration services described. The drug administration services described in this clause are physicians' services—

(I) which are classified as of October 1, 2003, within any of the following groups of procedures: therapeutic or diagnostic infusions (excluding chemotherapy); chemotherapy administration services; and therapeutic, prophylactic, or diagnostic injections;

(II) for which there are no work relative value units assigned under this subsection as of such date; and

(III) for which national relative value units have been assigned under this subsection as of such date.

(I) Adjustments in practice expense relative value units for certain drug administration services beginning with 2005. (i) In general. In establishing the physician fee schedule under subsection (b) with respect to payments for services furnished on or after January 1, 2005 or 2006, the Secretary shall adjust the practice expense relative value units for such year consistent with clause (ii).

(ii) Use of supplemental survey data. (I) In general. Subject to subclause (II), if a specialty submits to the Secretary by not later than March 1, 2004, for 2005, or March 1, 2005, for 2006, data that includes expenses for the administration of drugs and biologicals for which the payment amount is determined pursuant to section 1842(o), the Secretary shall use such supplemental survey data in carrying out this subparagraph for the years involved insofar as they are collected and provided by entities and organizations consistent with the criteria established by the Secretary pursuant to section 212(a) of the Medicare, Medicaid, and SCHIP Balanced Budget Refinement Act of 1999 [note to this section].

(II) Limitation on specialty. Subclause (I) shall apply to a specialty only insofar as not less than 40 percent of payments for the specialty under this title in 2002 are attributable to the administration of drugs and biologicals, as determined by the Secretary.

(III) Application. This clause shall not apply with respect to a survey to which subparagraph (H)(i) applies.

(J) Provisions for appropriate reporting and billing for physicians' services associated with the administration of covered outpatient drugs and biologicals. (i) Evaluation of codes. The Secretary shall promptly evaluate existing drug administration codes for physicians' services to ensure accurate reporting and billing for such services, taking into account levels of complexity of the administration and resource consumption.

(ii) Use of existing processes. In carrying out clause (i), the Secretary shall use existing processes for the consideration of coding changes and, to the extent coding changes are made, shall use such processes in establishing relative values for such services.

(iii) Implementation. In carrying out clause (i), the Secretary shall consult with representatives of physician specialties affected by the implementation of section 1847A or section 1847B [42 USCS § 1395w-3a or 1395w-3b], and shall take such steps within the Secretary's authority to expedite such considerations under clause (ii).

(iv) Subsequent, budget neutral adjustments permitted. Nothing in subparagraph (H) or (I) or this subparagraph shall be construed as preventing the Secretary from providing for adjustments in practice expense relative value units under (and consistent with) subparagraph (B) for years after 2004, 2005, or 2006, respectively.

(K) Potentially misvalued codes. (i) In general. The Secretary shall—

(I) periodically identify services as being potentially misvalued using criteria specified in clause (ii); and

(II) review and make appropriate adjustments to the relative values established under this paragraph for services identified as being potentially misvalued under subclause (I).

(ii) Identification of potentially misvalued codes. For purposes of identifying potentially misvalued services pursuant to clause (i)(I), the Secretary shall examine (as the Secretary determines to be appropriate) codes (and families of codes as appropriate) for which there has been the fastest growth; codes (and families of codes as appropriate) that have experienced substantial changes in practice expenses; codes for new technologies or services within an appropriate period (such as 3 years) after the relative values are initially established for such codes; multiple codes that are frequently billed in conjunction with furnishing a single service; codes with low relative values, particularly those that are often billed multiple times for a single treatment; codes which have not been subject to review since the implementation of the RBRVS (the so-called "Harvard-valued codes"); and such other codes determined to be appropriate by the Secretary.

(iii) Review and adjustments. (I) The Secretary may use existing processes to receive recommendations on the review and appropriate adjustment of potentially misvalued services described in clause (i)(II).

(II) The Secretary may conduct surveys, other data collection activities, studies, or other analyses as the Secretary determines to be appropriate to facilitate the review and appropriate adjustment described in clause (i)(II).

(III) The Secretary may use analytic contractors to identify and analyze services identified under clause (i)(I), conduct surveys or collect data, and make recommendations on the review and appropriate adjustment of services described in clause (i)(II).

(IV) The Secretary may coordinate the review and appropriate adjustment described in clause (i)(II) with the periodic review described in subparagraph (B).

(V) As part of the review and adjustment described in clause (i)(II), including with respect to codes with low relative values described in clause (ii), the Secretary may make appropriate coding revisions (including using existing processes for consideration of coding changes) which may include consolidation of individual services into bundled codes for payment under the fee schedule under subsection (b).

(VI) The provisions of subparagraph (B)(ii)(II) shall apply to adjustments to relative value units made pursuant to this subparagraph in the same manner as such provisions apply to adjustments under subparagraph (B)(ii)(II).

(L) Validating relative value units. (i) In general. The Secretary shall establish a process to validate relative value units under the fee schedule under subsection (b).

(ii) Components and elements of work. The process described in clause (i) may include validation of work elements (such as time, mental effort and professional judgment, technical skill and physical effort, and stress due to risk) involved with furnishing a service and may include validation of the pre-, post-, and intra-service components of work.

(iii) Scope of codes. The validation of work relative value units shall include a sampling of codes for services that is the same as the codes listed under subparagraph (K)(ii).

(iv) Methods. The Secretary may conduct the validation under this subparagraph using methods described in subclauses (I) through (V) of subparagraph (K)(iii) as the Secretary determines to be appropriate.

(v) Adjustments. The Secretary shall make appropriate adjustments to the work relative value units under the fee schedule under subsection (b). The provisions of subparagraph (B)(ii)(II) shall apply to adjustments to relative value units made pursuant to this subparagraph in the same manner as such provisions apply to adjustments under subparagraph (B)(ii)(II).

(3) Component percentages. For purposes of paragraph (2), the Secretary shall determine a work percentage, a practice expense percentage, and a malpractice percentage for each physician's service as follows:

(A) Division of services by specialty. For each physician's service or class of physicians' services, the Secretary shall determine the average percentage of each such service or class of services that is performed, nationwide, under this part [42 USCS §§ 1395j et seq.] by physicians in each of the different physician specialties (as identified by the Secretary).

(B) Division of specialty by component. The Secretary shall determine the average percentage division of resources, among the work component, the practice expense component, and the malpractice component, used by physicians in each of such specialties in furnishing physicians' services. Such percentages shall be based on national data that describe the elements of physician practice costs and revenues, by physician specialty. The Secretary may use extrapolation and other techniques to determine practice costs and revenues for specialties for which adequate data are not available.

(C) Determination of component percentages. (i) Work percentage. The work percentage for a service (or class of services) is equal to the sum (for all physician specialties) of—

(I) the average percentage division for the work component for each physician specialty (determined under subparagraph (B)), multiplied by

(II) the proportion (determined under subparagraph (A)) of such service (or services) performed by physicians in that specialty.

(ii) Practice expense percentage. For years before 2002, the practice expense percentage for a service (or class of services) is equal to the sum (for all physician specialties) of—

(I) the average percentage division for the practice expense component for each physician specialty (determined under subparagraph (B)), multiplied by

(II) the proportion (determined under subparagraph (A)) of such service (or services) performed by physicians in that specialty.

(iii) Malpractice percentage. For years before 1999, the malpractice percentage for a service (or class of services) is equal to the sum (for all physician specialties) of—

(I) the average percentage division for the malpractice component for each physician specialty (determined under subparagraph (B)), multiplied by

(II) the proportion (determined under subparagraph (A)) of such service (or services) performed by physicians in that specialty.

(D) Periodic recomputation. The Secretary may, from time to time, provide for the recomputation of work percentages, practice expense percentages, and malpractice percentages determined under this paragraph.

(4) Ancillary policies. The Secretary may establish ancillary policies (with respect to the use of modifiers, local codes, and other matters) as may be necessary to implement this section.

(5) Coding. The Secretary shall establish a uniform procedure coding system for the coding of all physicians' services. The Secretary shall provide for an appropriate coding structure for visits and consultations. The Secretary may incorporate the use of time in the coding for visits and consultations. The Secretary, in establishing such coding system, shall consult with the Physician Payment Review Commission [Medicare Payment Advisory Commission] and other organizations representing physicians.

(6) No variation for specialists. The Secretary may not vary the conversion factor or the number of relative value units for a physicians' service based on whether the physician furnishing the service is a specialist or based on the type of specialty of the physician.

(d) Conversion factors. (1) Establishment. (A) In general. The conversion factor for each year shall be the conversion factor established under this subsection for the previous year (or, in the case of 1992, specified in subparagraph (B)) adjusted by the update (established under paragraph (3)) for the year involved (for years before 2001) and, for years beginning with 2001, multiplied by the update (established under paragraph (4)) for the year involved.

(B) Special provision for 1992. For purposes of subparagraph (A), the conversion factor specified in this subparagraph is a conversion factor (determined by the Secretary) which, if this section were to apply during 1991 using such conversion factor, would result in the same aggregate amount of payments under this part [42 USCS §§ 1395j et seq.] for physicians' services as the estimated aggregate amount of the payments under this part for such services in 1991.

(C) Special rules for 1998. Except as provided in subparagraph (D), the single conversion factor for 1998 under this subsection shall be the conversion factor for primary care services for 1997, increased by the Secretary's estimate of the weighted average of the three separate updates that would otherwise occur were it not for the enactment of chapter 1 of subtitle F of title IV of the Balanced Budget Act of 1997.

(D) Special rules for anesthesia services. The separate conversion factor for anesthesia services for a year shall be equal to 46 percent of the single conversion factor established for other physicians' services, except as adjusted for changes in work, practice expense, or malpractice relative value units.

(E) Publication and dissemination of information. The Secretary shall—

(i) cause to have published in the Federal Register not later than November 1 of each year (beginning with 2000) the conversion factor which will apply to physicians' services for the succeeding year, the update determined under paragraph (4) for such succeeding year, and the allowed expenditures under such paragraph for such succeeding year; and

(ii) make available to the Medicare Payment Advisory Commission and the public by March 1 of each year (beginning with 2000) an estimate of the sustainable growth rate and of the conversion factor which will apply to physicians' services for the succeeding year and data used in making such estimate.

(2) [Deleted]

(3) Update for 1999 and 2000. (A) In general. Unless otherwise provided by law, subject to subparagraph (D) and the budget-neutrality factor determined by the Secretary under subsection (c)(2)(B)(ii), the update to the single conversion factor established in paragraph (1)(C) for 1999 and 2000 is equal to the product of—

(i) 1 plus the Secretary's estimate of the percentage increase in the MEI (as defined in section 1842(i)(3) [42 USCS § 1395u(i)(3)]) for the year (divided by 100), and

(ii) 1 plus the Secretary's estimate of the update adjustment factor for the year (divided by 100),

minus 1 and multiplied by 100.

(B) Update adjustment factor. For purposes of subparagraph (A)(ii), the "update adjustment factor" for a year is equal (as estimated by the Secretary) to—

(i) the difference between (I) the sum of the allowed expenditures for physicians' services (as determined under subparagraph (C)) for the period beginning April 1, 1997, and ending on March 31 of the year involved, and (II) the amount of actual expenditures for physicians' services furnished during the period beginning April 1, 1997, and ending on March 31 of the preceding year; divided by

(ii) the actual expenditures for physicians' services for the 12-month period ending on March 31 of the preceding year, increased by the sustainable growth rate under subsection (f) for the fiscal year which begins during such 12-month period.

(C) Determination of allowed expenditures. For purposes of this paragraph and paragraph (4), the allowed expenditures for physicians' services for the 12-month period ending with March 31 of—

(i) 1997 is equal to the actual expenditures for physicians' services furnished during such 12-month period, as estimated by the Secretary; or

(ii) a subsequent year is equal to the allowed expenditures for physicians' services for the previous year, increased by the sustainable growth rate under subsection (f) for the fiscal year which begins during such 12-month period.

(D) Restriction on variation from medicare economic index. Notwithstanding the amount of the update adjustment factor determined under subparagraph (B) for a year, the update in the conversion factor under this paragraph for the year may not be—

(i) greater than 100 times the following amount: (1.03 + (MEI percentage/100)) − 1; or

(ii) less than 100 times the following amount: (0.93 + (MEI percentage/100)) − 1,

where "MEI percentage" means the Secretary's estimate of the percentage increase in the MEI (as defined in section 1842(i)(3) [42 USCS § 1395u(i)(3)]) for the year involved.

(4) Update for years beginning with 2001. (A) In general. Unless otherwise provided by law, subject to the budget-neutrality factor determined by the Secretary under subsection (c)(2)(B)(ii) and subject to adjustment under subparagraph (F), the update to the single conversion factor established in paragraph (1)(C) for a year beginning with 2001 is equal to the product of—

(i) 1 plus the Secretary's estimate of the percentage increase in the MEI (as defined in section 1842(i)(3) [42 USCS § 1395u(i)(3)]) for the year (divided by 100); and

(ii) 1 plus the Secretary's estimate of the update adjustment factor under subparagraph (B) for the year.

(B) Update adjustment factor. For purposes of subparagraph (A)(ii), subject to subparagraph (D) and the succeeding paragraphs of this subsection, the "update adjustment factor" for a year is equal (as estimated by the Secretary) to the sum of the following:

(i) Prior year adjustment component. An amount determined by—

(I) computing the difference (which may be positive or negative) between the amount of the allowed expenditures for physicians' services for the prior year (as determined under subparagraph (C)) and the amount of the actual expenditures for such services for that year;

(II) dividing that difference by the amount of the actual expenditures for such services for that year; and

(III) multiplying that quotient by 0.75.

(ii) Cumulative adjustment component. An amount determined by—

(I) computing the difference (which may be positive or negative) between the amount of the allowed expenditures for physicians' services (as determined under subparagraph (C)) from April 1, 1996, through the end of the prior year and the amount of the actual expenditures for such services during that period;

(II) dividing that difference by actual expenditures for such services for the prior year as increased by the sustainable growth rate under subsection (f) for the year for which the update adjustment factor is to be determined; and

(III) multiplying that quotient by 0.33.

(C) Determination of allowed expenditures. For purposes of this paragraph:

(i) Period up to April 1, 1999. The allowed expenditures for physicians' services for a period before April 1, 1999, shall be the amount of the allowed expenditures for such period as determined under paragraph (3)(C).

(ii) Transition to calendar year allowed expenditures. Subject to subparagraph (E), the allowed expenditures for—

(I) the 9-month period beginning April 1, 1999, shall be the Secretary's estimate of the amount of the allowed expenditures that would be permitted under paragraph (3)(C) for such period; and

(II) the year of 1999, shall be the Secretary's estimate of the amount of the allowed expenditures that would be permitted under paragraph (3)(C) for such year.

(iii) Years beginning with 2000. The allowed expenditures for a year (beginning with 2000) is equal to the allowed expenditures for physicians' services for the previous year, increased by the sustainable growth rate under subsection (f) for the year involved.

(D) Restriction on update adjustment factor. The update adjustment factor determined under subparagraph (B) for a year may not be less than −0.07 or greater than 0.03.

(E) Recalculation of allowed expenditures for updates beginning with 2001. For purposes of determining the update adjustment factor for a year beginning with 2001, the Secretary shall recompute the allowed expenditures for previous periods beginning on or after April 1, 1999, consistent with subsection (f)(3).

(F) Transitional adjustment designed to provide for budget neutrality. Under this subparagraph the Secretary shall provide for an adjustment to the update under subparagraph (A)—

(i) for each of 2001, 2002, 2003, and 2004, of −0.2 percent; and

(ii) for 2005 of +0.8 percent.

(5) Update for 2004 and 2005. The update to the single conversion factor established in paragraph (1)(C) for each of 2004 and 2005 shall be not less than 1.5 percent.

(6) Update for 2006. The update to the single conversion factor established in paragraph (1)(C) for 2006 shall be 0 percent.

(7) Conversion factor for 2007. (A) In general. The conversion factor that would otherwise be applicable under this subsection for 2007 shall be the amount of such conversion factor divided by the product of—

(i) 1 plus the Secretary's estimate of the percentage increase in the MEI (as defined in section 1842(i)(3) [42 USCS § 1395u(i)(3)]) for 2007 (divided by 100); and

(ii) 1 plus the Secretary's estimate of the update adjustment factor under paragraph (4)(B) for 2007.

(B) No effect on computation of conversion factor for 2008. The conversion factor under this subsection shall be computed under paragraph (1)(A) for 2008 as if subparagraph (A) had never applied.

(8) Update for 2008. (A) In general. Subject to paragraph (7)(B), in lieu of the update to the single conversion factor established in paragraph (1)(C) that would otherwise apply for 2008, the update to the single conversion factor shall be 0.5 percent.

(B) No effect on computation of conversion factor for 2009. The conversion factor under this subsection shall be computed under paragraph (1)(A) for 2009 and subsequent years as if subparagraph (A) had never applied.

(9) Update for 2009. (A) In general. Subject to paragraphs (7)(B) and (8)(B), in lieu of the update to the single conversion factor established in paragraph (1)(C) that would otherwise apply for 2009, the update to the single

conversion factor shall be 1.1 percent.

(B) No effect on computation of conversion factor for 2010 and subsequent years. The conversion factor under this subsection shall be computed under paragraph (1)(A) for 2010 and subsequent years as if subparagraph (A) had never applied.

(10) Update for portion of 2010. (A) In general. Subject to paragraphs (7)(B), (8)(B), and (9)(B), in lieu of the update to the single conversion factor established in paragraph (1)(C) that would otherwise apply for 2010 for the period beginning on January 1, 2010, and ending on May 31, 2010, the update to the single conversion factor shall be 0 percent for 2010.

(B) No effect on computation of conversion factor for remaining portion of 2010 and subsequent years. The conversion factor under this subsection shall be computed under paragraph (1)(A) for the period beginning on June 1, 2010, and ending on December 31, 2010, and for 2011 and subsequent years as if subparagraph (A) had never applied.

(e) Geographic adjustment factors. (1) Establishment of geographic indices. (A) In general. Subject to subparagraphs (B), (C), (E), (G), (H), and (I), the Secretary shall establish—

(i) an index which reflects the relative costs of the mix of goods and services comprising practice expenses (other than malpractice expenses) in the different fee schedule areas compared to the national average of such costs,

(ii) an index which reflects the relative costs of malpractice expenses in the different fee schedule areas compared to the national average of such costs, and

(iii) an index which reflects ¼ of the difference between the relative value of physicians' work effort in each of the different fee schedule areas and the national average of such work effort.

(B) Class-specific geographic cost-of-practice indices. The Secretary may establish more than one index under subparagraph (A)(i) in the case of classes of physicians' services, if, because of differences in the mix of goods and services comprising practice expenses for the different classes of services, the application of a single index under such clause to different classes of such services would be substantially inequitable.

(C) Periodic review and adjustments in geographic adjustment factors. The Secretary, not less often than every 3 years, shall, in consultation with appropriate representatives of physicians, review the indices established under subparagraph (A) and the geographic index values applied under this subsection for all fee schedule areas. Based on such review, the Secretary may revise such index and adjust such index values, except that, if more than 1 year has elasped [elapsed] since the date of the last previous adjustment, the adjustment to be applied in the first year of the next adjustment shall be ½ of the adjustment that otherwise would be made.

(D) Use of recent data. In establishing indices and index values under this paragraph, the Secretary shall use the most recent data available relating to practice expenses, malpractice expenses, and physician work effort in different fee schedule areas.

(E) Floor at 1.0 on work geographic index. After calculating the work geographic index in subparagraph (A)(iii), for purposes of payment for services furnished on or after January 1, 2004, and before January 1, 2011, the Secretary shall increase the work geographic index to 1.00 for any locality for which such work geographic index is less than 1.00.

(F) [Not enacted]

(G) Floor for practice expense, malpractice, and work geographic indices for services furnished in Alaska. For purposes of payment for services furnished in Alaska on or after January 1, 2004, and before January 1, 2006, after calculating the practice expense, malpractice, and work geographic indices in clauses (i), (ii), and (iii) of subparagraph (A) and in subparagraph (B), the Secretary shall increase any such index to 1.67 if such index would otherwise be less than 1.67. For purposes of payment for services furnished in the State described in the preceding sentence on or after January 1, 2009, after calculating the work geographic index in subparagraph (A)(iii), the Secretary shall increase the work geographic index to 1.5 if such index would otherwise be less than 1.5[.]

(H) Practice expense geographic adjustment for 2010 and subsequent years. (i) For 2010. Subject to clause (iii), for services furnished during 2010, the employee wage and rent portions of the practice expense geographic index described in subparagraph (A)(i) shall reflect ½ of the difference between the relative costs of employee wages and rents in each of the different fee schedule areas and the national average of such employee wages and rents.

(ii) For 2011. Subject to clause (iii), for services furnished during 2011, the employee wage and rent portions of the practice expense geographic index described in subparagraph (A)(i) shall reflect ½ of the difference between the relative costs of employee wages and rents in each of the different fee schedule areas and the national average of such employee wages and rents.

(iii) Hold harmless. The practice expense portion of the geographic adjustment factor applied in a fee schedule area for services furnished in 2010 or 2011 shall not, as a result of the application of clause (i) or (ii), be reduced below the practice expense portion of the geographic adjustment factor under subparagraph (A)(i) (as calculated prior to the application of such clause (i) or (ii), respectively) for such area for such year.

(iv) Analysis. The Secretary shall analyze current methods of establishing practice expense geographic adjustments under subparagraph (A)(i) and evaluate data that fairly and reliably establishes distinctions in the costs of operating a medical practice in the different fee schedule areas. Such analysis shall include an evaluation of the following:

(I) The feasibility of using actual data or reliable survey data developed by medical organizations on the costs of operating a medical practice, including office rents and non-physician staff wages, in different fee schedule areas.

(II) The office expense portion of the practice expense geographic adjustment described in subparagraph (A)(i), including the extent to which types of office expenses are determined in local markets instead of national markets.

(III) The weights assigned to each of the categories within the practice expense geographic adjustment described in subparagraph (A)(i).

(v) Revision for 2012 and subsequent years. As a result of the analysis described in clause (iv), the Secretary shall, not later than January 1, 2012, make appropriate adjustments to the practice expense geographic adjustment described in subparagraph (A)(i) to ensure accurate geographic adjustments across fee schedule areas, including—

(I) basing the office rents component and its weight on office expenses that vary among fee schedule areas; and

(II) considering a representative range of professional and non-professional personnel employed in a medical office based on the use of the American Community Survey data or other reliable data for wage adjustments.

Such adjustments shall be made without regard to adjustments made pursuant to clauses (i) and (ii) and shall be made in a budget neutral manner.

(I) Floor for practice expense index for services furnished in frontier States. (i) In general. Subject to clause (ii), for purposes of payment for services furnished in a frontier State (as defined in section 1886(d)(3)(E)(iii)(II) [42 USCS § 1395ww(d)(3)(E)(iii)(II)]) on or after January 1, 2011, after calculating the practice expense index in subparagraph (A)(i), the Secretary shall increase any such index to 1.00 if such index would otherwise be less that 1.00. The preceding sentence shall not be applied in a budget neutral manner.

(ii) Limitation. This subparagraph shall not apply to services furnished in a State that receives a non-labor related share adjustment under section 1886(d)(5)(H) [42 USCS § 1395ww(d)(5)(H)].

(2) Computation of geographic adjustment factor. For purposes of subsection (b)(1)(C), for all physicians' services for each fee schedule area the Secretary shall establish a geographic adjustment factor equal to the sum of the geographic cost-of-practice adjustment factor (specified in paragraph (3)), the geographic malpractice adjustment factor (specified in paragraph (4)), and the geographic physician work adjustment factor (specified in paragraph (5)) for the service and the area.

(3) Geographic cost-of-practice adjustment factor. For purposes of paragraph (2), the "geographic cost-of-practice adjustment factor", for a service for a fee schedule area, is the product of—

(A) the proportion of the total relative value for the service that reflects the relative value units for the practice expense component, and

(B) the geographic cost-of-practice index value for the area for the service, based on the index established under paragraph (1)(A)(i) or (1)(B) (as the case may be).

(4) Geographic malpractice adjustment factor. For purposes of paragraph (2), the "geographic malpractice adjustment factor", for a service for a fee schedule area, is the product of—

(A) the proportion of the total relative value for the service that reflects the relative value units for the malpractice component, and

(B) the geographic malpractice index value for the area, based on the index established under paragraph (1)(A)(ii).

(5) Geographic physician work adjustment factor. For purposes of paragraph (2), the "geographic physician work adjustment factor", for a service for a fee schedule area, is the product of—

(A) the proportion of the total relative value for the service that reflects the relative value units for the work component, and

(B) the geographic physician work index value for the area, based on the index established under paragraph (1)(A)(iii).

(f) Sustainable growth rate. (1) Publication. The Secretary shall cause to have published in the Federal Register not later than—

(A) November 1, 2000, the sustainable growth rate for 2000 and 2001; and

(B) November 1 of each succeeding year the sustainable growth rate for such succeeding year and each of the preceding 2 years.

(2) Specification of growth rate. The sustainable growth rate for all physicians' services for a fiscal year (beginning with fiscal year 1998 and ending with fiscal year 2000) and a year beginning with 2000 shall be equal to the product of—

(A) 1 plus the Secretary's estimate of the weighted average percentage increase (divided by 100) in the fees for all physicians' services in the applicable period involved,

(B) 1 plus the Secretary's estimate of the percentage change (divided by 100) in the average number of individuals enrolled under this part [42 USCS §§ 1395j et seq.] (other than Medicare+Choice plan enrollees) from the previous applicable period to the applicable period involved,

(C) 1 plus the Secretary's estimate of the annual average percentage growth in real gross domestic product per capita (divided by 100) during the 10-year period ending with the applicable period involved, and

(D) 1 plus the Secretary's estimate of the percentage change (divided by 100) in expenditures for all physicians' services in the applicable period (compared with the previous applicable period) which will result from changes in law and regulations, determined without taking into account estimated changes in expenditures resulting from the update adjustment factor determined under subsection (d)(3)(B) or (d)(4)(B), as the case may be,

minus 1 and multiplied by 100.

(3) Data to be used. For purposes of determining the update adjustment factor under subsection (d)(4)(B) for a year beginning with 2001, the sustainable growth rates taken into consideration in the determination under paragraph (2) shall be determined as follows.

(A) For 2001. For purposes of such calculations for 2001, the sustainable growth rates for fiscal year 2000 and the years 2000 and 2001 shall be determined on the basis of the best data available to the Secretary as of September 1, 2000.

(B) For 2002. For purposes of such calculations for 2002, the sustainable growth rates for fiscal year 2000 and for years 2000, 2001, and 2002 shall be determined on the basis of the best data available to the Secretary as of September 1, 2001.

(C) For 2003 and succeeding years. For purposes of such calculations for a year after 2002—

(i) the sustainable growth rates for that year and the preceding 2 years shall be determined on the basis of the best data available to the Secretary as of September 1 of the year preceding the year for which the calculation is made; and

(ii) the sustainable growth rate for any year before a year described in clause (i) shall be the rate as most recently determined for that year under this subsection.

Nothing in this paragraph shall be construed as affecting the sustainable growth rates established for fiscal year 1998 or fiscal year 1999.

(4) Definitions. In this subsection:

(A) Services included in physicians' services. The term "physicians' services" includes other items and services (such as clinical diagnostic laboratory tests and radiology services), specified by the Secretary, that are commonly performed or furnished by a physician or in a physician's office, but does not include services furnished to a Medicare+Choice plan enrollee.

(B) Medicare+choice plan enrollee. The term "Medicare+Choice plan enrollee" means, with respect to a fiscal year, an individual enrolled under this part [42 USCS §§ 1395j et seq.] who has elected to receive benefits under this title [42 USCS §§ 1395 et seq.] for the fiscal year through a Medicare+Choice plan offered under part C [42 USCS §§ 1395w-21 et seq.], and also includes an individual who is receiving benefits under this part [42 USCS §§ 1395j et seq.] through enrollment with an eligible organization with a risk-sharing contract under section 1876 [42 USCS § 1395mm].

(C) Applicable period. The term "applicable period" means—

(i) a fiscal year, in the case of fiscal year 1998, fiscal year 1999, and fiscal year 2000; or

(ii) a calendar year with respect to a year beginning with 2000; as the case may be.

(g) Limitation on beneficiary liability. (1) Limitation on actual charges. (A) In general. In the case of a nonparticipating physician or nonparticipating supplier or other person (as defined in section 1842(i)(2) [42 USCS § 1395u(i)(2)]) who does not accept payment on an assignment-related basis for a physician's service furnished with respect to an individual enrolled under this part [42 USCS §§ 1395j et seq.], the following rules apply:

(i) Application of limiting charge. No person

may bill or collect an actual charge for the service in excess of the limiting charge described in paragraph (2) for such service.

(ii) No liability for excess charges. No person is liable for payment of any amounts billed for the service in excess of such limiting charge.

(iii) Correction of excess charges. If such a physician, supplier, or other person bills, but does not collect, an actual charge for a service in violation of clause (i), the physician, supplier, or other person shall reduce on a timely basis the actual charge billed for the service to an amount not to exceed the limiting charge for the service.

(iv) Refund of excess collections. If such a physician, supplier, or other person collects an actual charge for a service in violation of clause (i), the physician, supplier, or other person shall provide on a timely basis a refund to the individual charged in the amount by which the amount collected exceeded the limiting charge for the service. The amount of such a refund shall be reduced to the extent the individual has an outstanding balance owed by the individual to the physician.

(B) Sanctions. If a physician, supplier, or other person—

(i) knowingly and willfully bills or collects for services in violation of subparagraph (A)(i) on a repeated basis, or

(ii) fails to comply with clause (iii) or (iv) of subparagraph (A) on a timely basis,

the Secretary may apply sanctions against the physician, supplier, or other person in accordance with paragraph (2) of section 1842(j) [42 USCS § 1395u(j)]. In applying this subparagraph, paragraph (4) of such section applies in the same manner as such paragraph applies to such section and any reference in such section to a physician is deemed also to include a reference to a supplier or other person under this subparagraph.

(C) Timely basis. For purposes of this paragraph, a correction of a bill for an excess charge or refund of an amount with respect to a violation of subparagraph (A)(i) in the case of a service is considered to be provided "on a timely basis", if the reduction or refund is made not later than 30 days after the date the physician, supplier, or other person is notified by the carrier under this part [42 USCS §§ 1395j et seq.] of such violation and of the requirements of subparagraph (A).

(2) "Limiting charge" defined. (A) For 1991. For physicians' services of a physician furnished during 1991, other than radiologist services subject to section 1834(b) [42 USCS § 1395m(b)], the "limiting charge" shall be the same percentage (or, if less, 25 percent) above the recognized payment amount under this part [42 USCS §§ 1395j et seq.] with respect to the physician (as a nonparticipating physician) as the percentage by which—

(i) the maximum allowable actual charge (as determined under section 1842(j)(1)(C) [42 USCS § 1395u(j)(1)(C)] as of December 31, 1990, or, if less, the maximum actual charge otherwise permitted for the service under this part [42 USCS §§ 1395j et seq.] as of such date) for the service of the physician, exceeds

(ii) the recognized payment amount for the service of the physician (as a nonparticipating physician) as of such date.

In the case of evaluation and management services (as specified in section 1842(b)(16)(B)(ii) [42 USCS § 1395u(b)(16)(B)(ii)]), the preceding sentence shall be applied by substituting "40 percent" for "25 percent".

(B) For 1992. For physicians' services furnished during 1992, other than radiologist services subject to section 1834(b) [42 USCS § 1395m(b)], the "limiting charge" shall be the same percentage (or, if less, 20 percent) above the recognized payment amount under this part [42 USCS §§ 1395j et seq.] for nonparticipating physicians as the percentage by which—

(i) the limiting charge (as determined under subparagraph (A) as of December 31, 1991) for the service, exceeds

(ii) the recognized payment amount for the service for nonparticipating physicians as of such date.

(C) After 1992. For physicians' services furnished in a year after 1992, the "limiting charge" shall be 115 percent of the recognized payment amount under this part [42 USCS §§ 1395j et seq.] for nonparticipating physicians or for nonparticipating suppliers or other persons.

(D) Recognized payment amount. In this section, the term "recognized payment amount" means, for services furnished on or after January 1, 1992, the fee schedule amount determined under subsection (a) (or, if payment under this part [42 USCS §§ 1395j et seq.] is made on a basis other than the fee schedule under this section, 95 percent of the other payment basis), and, for services furnished during 1991, the applicable percentage (as defined in section 1842(b)(4)(A)(iv) [42 USCS § 1395u(b)(4)(A)(iv)]) of the prevailing charge (or fee schedule amount) for nonparticipating physicians for that year.

(3) Limitation on charges for medicare ben-

eficiaries eligible for medicaid benefits. (A) In general. Payment for physicians' services furnished on or after April 1, 1990, to an individual who is enrolled under this part [42 USCS §§ 1395j et seq.] and eligible for any medical assistance (including as a qualified medicare beneficiary, as defined in section 1905(p)(1) [42 USCS § 1396d(p)(1)]) with respect to such services under a State plan approved under title XIX [42 USCS §§ 1396 et seq.] may only be made on an assignment-related basis and the provisions of section 1902(n)(3)(A) [42 USCS § 1396a(n)(3)(A)] apply to further limit permissible charges under this section.

(B) Penalty. A person may not bill for physicians' services subject to subparagraph (A) other than on an assignment-related basis. No person is liable for payment of any amounts billed for such a service in violation of the previous sentence. If a person knowingly and willfully bills for physicians' services in violation of the first sentence, the Secretary may apply sanctions against the person in accordance with section 1842(j)(2) [42 USCS § 1395u(j)(2)].

(4) Physician submission of claims. (A) In general. For services furnished on or after September 1, 1990, within 1 year after the date of providing a service for which payment is made under this part [42 USCS §§ 1395j et seq.] on a reasonable charge or fee schedule basis, a physician, supplier, or other person (or an employer or facility in the cases described in section 1842(b)(6)(A) [42 USCS § 1395u(b)(6)(A)])—

(i) shall complete and submit a claim for such service on a standard claim form specified by the Secretary to the carrier on behalf of a beneficiary, and

(ii) may not impose any charge relating to completing and submitting such a form.

(B) Penalty. (i) With respect to an assigned claim wherever a physician, provider, supplier or other person (or an employer or facility in the cases described in section 1842(b)(6)(A) [42 USCS § 1395u(b)(6)(A)]) fails to submit such a claim as required in subparagraph (A), the Secretary shall reduce by 10 percent the amount that would otherwise be paid for such claim under this part [42 USCS §§ 1395j et seq.].

(ii) If a physician, supplier, or other person (or an employer or facility in the cases described in section 1842(b)(6)(A) [42 USCS § 1395u(b)(6)(A)]) fails to submit a claim required to be submitted under subparagraph (A) or imposes a charge in violation of such subparagraph, the Secretary shall apply the sanction with respect to such a violation in the same manner as a sanction may be imposed under section 1842(p)(3) [42 USCS § 1395u(p)(3)] for a violation of section 1842(p)(1) [42 USCS § 1395u(p)(1)].

(5) Electronic billing; direct deposit. The Secretary shall encourage and develop a system providing for expedited payment for claims submitted electronically. The Secretary shall also encourage and provide incentives allowing for direct deposit as payments for services furnished by participating physicians. The Secretary shall provide physicians with such technical information as necessary to enable such physicians to submit claims electronically. The Secretary shall submit a plan to Congress on this paragraph by May 1, 1990.

(6) Monitoring of charges. (A) In general. The Secretary shall monitor—

(i) the actual charges of nonparticipating physicians for physicians' services furnished on or after January 1, 1991, to individuals enrolled under this part [42 USCS §§ 1395j et seq.], and

(ii) changes (by specialty, type of service, and geographic area) in (I) the proportion of expenditures for physicians' services provided under this part [42 USCS §§ 1395j et seq.] by participating physicians, (II) the proportion of expenditures for such services for which payment is made under this part on an assignment-related basis, and (III) the amounts charged above the recognized payment amounts under this part [42 USCS §§ 1395j et seq.].

(B) Report. The Secretary shall, by not later than April 15 of each year (beginning in 1992), report to the Congress information on the extent to which actual charges exceed limiting charges, the number and types of services involved, and the average amount of excess charges and information regarding the changes described in subparagraph (A)(ii).

(C) Plan. If the Secretary finds that there has been a significant decrease in the proportions described in subclauses (I) and (II) of subparagraph (A)(ii) or an increase in the amounts described in subclause (III) of that subparagraph, the Secretary shall develop a plan to address such a problem and transmit to Congress recommendations regarding the plan. The Medicare Payment Advisory Commission shall review the Secretary's plan and recommendations and transmit to Congress its comments regarding such plan and recommendations.

(7) Monitoring of utilization and access. (A) In general. The Secretary shall monitor—

(i) changes in the utilization of and access to

services furnished under this part [42 USCS §§ 1395j et seq.] within geographic, population, and service related categories,

(ii) possible sources of inappropriate utilization of services furnished under this part [42 USCS §§ 1395j et seq.] which contribute to the overall level of expenditures under this part [42 USCS §§ 1395j et seq.], and

(iii) factors underlying these changes and their interrelationships.

(B) Report. The Secretary shall by not later than April 15[,] of each year (beginning with 1991) report to the Congress on the changes described in subparagraph (A)(i) and shall include in the report an examination of the factors (including factors relating to different services and specific categories and groups of services and geographic and demographic variations in utilization) which may contribute to such changes.

(C) Recommendations. The Secretary shall include in each annual report under subparagraph (B) recommendations—

(i) addressing any identified patterns of inappropriate utilization,

(ii) on utilization review,

(iii) on physician education or patient education,

(iv) addressing any problems of beneficiary access to care made evident by the monitoring process, and

(v) on such other matters as the Secretary deems appropriate.

The Medicare Payment Advisory Commission shall comment on the Secretary's recommendations and in developing its comments, the Commission shall convene and consult a panel of physician experts to evaluate the implications of medical utilization patterns for the quality of and access to patient care.

(h) Sending information to physicians. Before the beginning of each year (beginning with 1992), the Secretary shall send to each physician or nonparticipating supplier or other person furnishing physicians' services (as defined in section 1848(j)(3) [subsec. (j)(3) of this section]) furnishing physicians' services under this part [42 USCS §§ 1395j et seq.], for services commonly performed by the physician, supplier, or other person, information on fee schedule amounts that apply for the year in the fee schedule area for participating and nonparticipating physicians, and the maximum amount that may be charged consistent with subsection (g)(2). Such information shall be transmitted in conjunction with notices to physicians, suppliers, and other persons under section 1842(h) [42 USCS § 1395u(h)] (relating to the participating physician program) for a year.

(i) Miscellaneous provisions. (1) Restriction on administrative and judicial review. There shall be no administrative or judicial review under section 1869 [42 USCS § 1395ff] or otherwise of—

(A) the determination of the adjusted historical payment basis (as defined in subsection (a)(2)(D)(i)),

(B) the determination of relative values and relative value units under subsection (c), including adjustments under subsections (c)(2)(F), (c)(2)(H), and (c)(2)(I) and section 13515(b) of the Omnibus Budget Reconciliation Act of 1993 [42 USCS § 1395u note],

(C) the determination of conversion factors under subsection (d), including without limitation a prospective redetermination of the sustainable growth rates for any or all previous fiscal years,

(D) the establishment of geographic adjustment factors under subsection (e), and

(E) the establishment of the system for the coding of physicians' services under this section.

(2) Assistants-at-surgery. (A) In general. Subject to subparagraph (B), in the case of a surgical service furnished by a physician, if payment is made separately under this part [42 USCS §§ 1395j et seq.] for the services of a physician serving as an assistant-at-surgery, the fee schedule amount shall not exceed 16 percent of the fee schedule amount otherwise determined under this section for the global surgical service involved.

(B) Denial of payment in certain cases. If the Secretary determines, based on the most recent data available, that for a surgical procedure (or class of surgical procedures) the national average percentage of such procedure performed under this part [42 USCS §§ 1395j et seq.] which involve the use of a physician as an assistant at surgery is less than 5 percent, no payment may be made under this part [42 USCS §§ 1395j et seq.] for services of an assistant at surgery involved in the procedure.

(3) No comparability adjustment. For physicians' services for which payment under this part [42 USCS §§ 1395j et seq.] is determined under this section—

(A) a carrier may not make any adjustment in the payment amount under section 1842(b)(3)(B) [42 USCS § 1395u(b)(3)(B)] on the basis that the payment amount is higher than the charge applicable, for comparable services and under comparable circumstances, to the policyholders and subscribers of the carrier,

(B) no payment adjustment may be made under section 1842(b)(8) [42 USCS § 1395u(b)(8)], and

(C) section 1842(b)(9) [42 USCS § 1395u(b)(9)] shall not apply.

(j) Definitions. In this section:

(1) Category. For services furnished before January 1, 1998, the term "category" means, with respect to physicians' services, surgical services, and all physicians' services other than surgical services (as defined by the Secretary and including anesthesia services), primary care services (as defined in section 1842(i)(4) [42 USCS § 1395u(i)(4)]), and all other physicians' services. The Secretary shall define surgical services and publish such definition in the Federal Register no later than May 1, 1990, after consultation with organizations representing physicians.

(2) Fee schedule area. The term "fee schedule area" means a locality used under section 1842(b) [42 USCS § 1395u(b)] for purposes of computing payment amounts for physicians' services.

(3) Physicians' services. The term "physicians" services' includes items and services described in paragraphs (1), (2)(A), (2)(D), (2)(G), (2)(P) (with respect to services described in subparagraphs (A) and (C) of section 1861(oo)(2) [42 USCS § 1395x(oo)(2)]), (2)(R) (with respect to services described in subparagraphs (B), (C), and (D) of section 1861(pp)(1) [42 USCS § 1395x(pp)(1)]), (2)(S), (2)(W), (2)(AA), (2)(DD), (2)(EE), (2)(FF) (including administration of the health risk assessment), (3), (4), (13), (14) (with respect to services described in section 1861(nn)(2) [42 USCS § 1395x(nn)(2)]), and (15) of section 1861(s) [42 USCS § 1395x(s)] (other than clinical diagnostic laboratory tests and, except for purposes of subsections (a)(3), (g), and (h)[,] such other items and services as the Secretary may specify).

(4) Practice expenses. The term "practice expenses" includes all expenses for furnishing physicians' services, excluding malpractice expenses, physician compensation, and other physician fringe benefits.

(k) Quality reporting system. (1) In general. The Secretary shall implement a system for the reporting by eligible professionals of data on quality measures specified under paragraph (2). Such data shall be submitted in a form and manner specified by the Secretary (by program instruction or otherwise), which may include submission of such data on claims under this part [42 USCS §§ 1395j et seq.].

(2) Use of consensus-based quality measures. (A) For 2007. (i) In general. For purposes of applying this subsection for the reporting of data on quality measures for covered professional services furnished during the period beginning July 1, 2007, and ending December 31, 2007, the quality measures specified under this paragraph are the measures identified as 2007 physician quality measures under the Physician Voluntary Reporting Program as published on the public website of the Centers for Medicare & Medicaid Services as of the date of the enactment of this subsection [enacted Dec. 20, 2006], except as may be changed by the Secretary based on the results of a consensus-based process in January of 2007, if such change is published on such website by not later than April 1, 2007.

(ii) Subsequent refinements in application permitted. The Secretary may, from time to time (but not later than July 1, 2007), publish on such website (without notice or opportunity for public comment) modifications or refinements (such as code additions, corrections, or revisions) for the application of quality measures previously published under clause (i), but may not, under this clause, change the quality measures under the reporting system.

(iii) Implementation. Notwithstanding any other provision of law, the Secretary may implement by program instruction or otherwise this subsection for 2007.

(B) For 2008 and 2009. (i) In general. For purposes of reporting data on quality measures for covered professional services furnished during 2008 and 2009, the quality measures specified under this paragraph for covered professional services shall be measures that have been adopted or endorsed by a consensus organization (such as the National Quality Forum or AQA), that include measures that have been submitted by a physician specialty, and that the Secretary identifies as having used a consensus-based process for developing such measures. Such measures shall include structural measures, such as the use of electronic health records and electronic prescribing technology.

(ii) Proposed set of measures. Not later than August 15 of each of 2007 and 2008, the Secretary shall publish in the Federal Register a proposed set of quality measures that the Secretary determines are described in clause (i) and would be appropriate for eligible professionals to use to submit data to the Secretary in 2008 or 2009, as applicable. The Secretary shall provide for a period of public comment on such set of measures.

(iii) Final set of measures. Not later than

November 15 of each of 2007 and 2008, the Secretary shall publish in the Federal Register a final set of quality measures that the Secretary determines are described in clause (i) and would be appropriate for eligible professionals to use to submit data to the Secretary in 2008 or 2009, as applicable.

(C) For 2010 and subsequent years. (i) In general. Subject to clause (ii), for purposes of reporting data on quality measures for covered professional services furnished during 2010 and each subsequent year, subject to subsection (m)(3)(C), the quality measures (including electronic prescribing quality measures) specified under this paragraph shall be such measures selected by the Secretary from measures that have been endorsed by the entity with a contract with the Secretary under section 1890(a) [42 USCS § 1395aaa(a)].

(ii) Exception. In the case of a specified area or medical topic determined appropriate by the Secretary for which a feasible and practical measure has not been endorsed by the entity with a contract under section 1890(a) [42 USCS § 1395aaa(a)], the Secretary may specify a measure that is not so endorsed as long as due consideration is given to measures that have been endorsed or adopted by a consensus organization identified by the Secretary, such as the AQA alliance.

(D) Opportunity to provide input on measures for 2009 and subsequent years. For each quality measure (including an electronic prescribing quality measure) adopted by the Secretary under subparagraph (B) (with respect to 2009) or subparagraph (C), the Secretary shall ensure that eligible professionals have the opportunity to provide input during the development, endorsement, or selection of measures applicable to services they furnish.

(3) Covered professional services and eligible professionals defined. For purposes of this subsection:

(A) Covered professional services. The term "covered professional services" means services for which payment is made under, or is based on, the fee schedule established under this section and which are furnished by an eligible professional.

(B) Eligible professional. The term "eligible professional" means any of the following:

(i) A physician.

(ii) A practitioner described in section 1842(b)(18)(C) [42 USCS § 1395u(b)(18)(C)].

(iii) A physical or occupational therapist or a qualified speech-language pathologist.

(iv) Beginning with 2009, a qualified audiologist (as defined in section 1861(ll)(3)(B) [42 USCS § 1395x(ll)(3)(B)]).

(4) Use of registry-based reporting. As part of the publication of proposed and final quality measures for 2008 under clauses (ii) and (iii) of paragraph (2)(B), the Secretary shall address a mechanism whereby an eligible professional may provide data on quality measures through an appropriate medical registry (such as the Society of Thoracic Surgeons National Database) or through a Maintenance of Certification program operated by a specialty body of the American Board of Medical Specialties that meets the criteria for such a registry, as identified by the Secretary.

(5) Identification units. For purposes of applying this subsection, the Secretary may identify eligible professionals through billing units, which may include the use of the Provider Identification Number, the unique physician identification number (described in section 1833(q)(1) [42 USCS § 1395l(q)(1)]), the taxpayer identification number, or the National Provider Identifier. For purposes of applying this subsection for 2007, the Secretary shall use the taxpayer identification number as the billing unit.

(6) Education and outreach. The Secretary shall provide for education and outreach to eligible professionals on the operation of this subsection.

(7) Limitations on review. There shall be no administrative or judicial review under section 1869 [42 USCS § 1395ff], section 1878 [42 USCS § 1395oo], or otherwise, of the development and implementation of the reporting system under paragraph (1), including identification of quality measures under paragraph (2) and the application of paragraphs (4) and (5).

(8) Implementation. The Secretary shall carry out this subsection acting through the Administrator of the Centers for Medicare & Medicaid Services.

(l) Physician Assistance and Quality Initiative Fund. (1) Establishment. The Secretary shall establish under this subsection a Physician Assistance and Quality Initiative Fund (in this subsection referred to as the "Fund") which shall be available to the Secretary for physician payment and quality improvement initiatives, which may include application of an adjustment to the update of the conversion factor under subsection (d).

(2) Funding. (A) Amount available. (i) In general. Subject to clause (ii), there shall be available to the Fund the following amounts:

(I) For expenditures during 2008, an amount equal to $150,500,000.

(II) For expenditures during 2009, an

amount equal to $24,500,000.

(III), (IV) [Deleted]

(ii) Limitations on expenditures. (I) 2008. The amount available for expenditures during 2008 shall be reduced as provided by subparagraph (A) of section 225(c)(1) [unclassified] and section 524 of the Departments of Labor, Health and Human Services, and Education, and Related Agencies Appropriations Act, 2008 (division G of the Consolidated Appropriations Act, 2008).

(II) 2009. The amount available for expenditures during 2009 shall be reduced as provided by subparagraph (B) of such section 225(c)(1) [unclassified].

(III), (IV) [Deleted]

(B) Timely obligation of all available funds for services. The Secretary shall provide for expenditures from the Fund in a manner designed to provide (to the maximum extent feasible) for the obligation of the entire amount available for expenditures, after application of subparagraph (A)(ii), during—

(i) for payment with respect to physicians' services furnished during 2008; and

(ii) 2009 for payment with respect to physicians' services furnished during 2009.

(iii), (iv) [Deleted]

(C) Payment from Trust Fund. The amount specified in subparagraph (A) shall be available to the Fund, as expenditures are made from the Fund, from the Federal Supplementary Medical Insurance Trust Fund under section 1841 [42 USCS § 1395t].

(D) Funding limitation. Amounts in the Fund shall be available in advance of appropriations in accordance with subparagraph (B) but only if the total amount obligated from the Fund does not exceed the amount available to the Fund under subparagraph (A). The Secretary may obligate funds from the Fund only if the Secretary determines (and the Chief Actuary of the Centers for Medicare & Medicaid Services and the appropriate budget officer certify) that there are available in the Fund sufficient amounts to cover all such obligations incurred consistent with the previous sentence.

(E) Construction. In the case that expenditures from the Fund are applied to, or otherwise affect, a conversion factor under subsection (d) for a year, the conversion factor under such subsection shall be computed for a subsequent year as if such application or effect had never occurred.

(m) Incentive payments for quality reporting. (1) Incentive payments. (A) In general. For 2007 through 2014, with respect to covered professional services furnished during a reporting period by an eligible professional, if—

(i) there are any quality measures that have been established under the physician reporting system that are applicable to any such services furnished by such professional for such reporting period; and

(ii) the eligible professional satisfactorily submits (as determined under this subsection) to the Secretary data on such quality measures in accordance with such reporting system for such reporting period,

in addition to the amount otherwise paid under this part, there also shall be paid to the eligible professional (or to an employer or facility in the cases described in clause (A) of section 1842(b)(6) [42 USCS § 1395u(b)(6)]) or, in the case of a group practice under paragraph (3)(C), to the group practice, from the Federal Supplementary Medical Insurance Trust Fund established under section 1841 [42 USCS § 1395t] an amount equal to the applicable quality percent of the Secretary's estimate (based on claims submitted not later than 2 months after the end of the reporting period) of the allowed charges under this part for all such covered professional services furnished by the eligible professional (or, in the case of a group practice under paragraph (3)(C), by the group practice) during the reporting period.

(B) Applicable quality percent. For purposes of subparagraph (A), the term "applicable quality percent" means—

(i) for 2007 and 2008, 1.5 percent;

(ii) for 2009 and 2010, 2.0 percent;

(iii) for 2011, 1.0 percent; and

(iv) for 2012, 2013, and 2014, 0.5 percent.

(2) Incentive payments for electronic prescribing. (A) In general. Subject to subparagraph (D), for 2009 through 2013, with respect to covered professional services furnished during a reporting period by an eligible professional, if the eligible professional is a successful electronic prescriber for such reporting period, in addition to the amount otherwise paid under this part, there also shall be paid to the eligible professional (or to an employer or facility in the cases described in clause (A) of section 1842(b)(6) [42 USCS § 1395u(b)(6)]) or, in the case of a group practice under paragraph (3)(C), to the group practice, from the Federal Supplementary Medical Insurance Trust Fund established under section 1841 [42 USCS § 1395t] an amount equal to the applicable electronic prescribing percent of the Secretary's estimate (based on claims submitted not later than 2 months after the end of the reporting period) of the allowed charges under this part

for all such covered professional services furnished by the eligible professional (or, in the case of a group practice under paragraph (3)(C), by the group practice) during the reporting period.

(B) Limitation with respect to electronic prescribing quality measures. The provisions of this paragraph and subsection (a)(5) shall not apply to an eligible professional (or, in the case of a group practice under paragraph (3)(C), to the group practice) if, for the reporting period (or, for purposes of subsection (a)(5), for the reporting period for a year)—

(i) the allowed charges under this part for all covered professional services furnished by the eligible professional (or group, as applicable) for the codes to which the electronic prescribing quality measure applies (as identified by the Secretary and published on the Internet website of the Centers for Medicare & Medicaid Services as of January 1, 2008, and as subsequently modified by the Secretary) are less than 10 percent of the total of the allowed charges under this part for all such covered professional services furnished by the eligible professional (or the group, as applicable); or

(ii) if determined appropriate by the Secretary, the eligible professional does not submit (including both electronically and nonelectronically) a sufficient number (as determined by the Secretary) of prescriptions under part D [42 USCS §§ 1395w-101 et seq.].

If the Secretary makes the determination to apply clause (ii) for a period, then clause (i) shall not apply for such period.

(C) Applicable electronic prescribing percent. For purposes of subparagraph (A), the term "applicable electronic prescribing percent" means—

(i) for 2009 and 2010, 2.0 percent;

(ii) for 2011 and 2012, 1.0 percent; and

(iii) for 2013, 0.5 percent.

(D) Limitation with respect to EHR incentive payments. The provisions of this paragraph shall not apply to an eligible professional (or, in the case of a group practice under paragraph (3)(C), to the group practice) if, for the EHR reporting period the eligible professional (or group practice) receives an incentive payment under subsection (o)(1)(A) with respect to a certified EHR technology (as defined in subsection (o)(4)) that has the capability of electronic prescribing.

(3) Satisfactory reporting and successful electronic prescriber described. (A) In general. For purposes of paragraph (1), an eligible professional shall be treated as satisfactorily submitting data on quality measures for covered professional services for a reporting period (or, for purposes of subsection (a)(8), for the quality reporting period for the year) if quality measures have been reported as follows:

(i) Three or fewer quality measures applicable. If there are no more than 3 quality measures that are provided under the physician reporting system and that are applicable to such services of such professional furnished during the period, each such quality measure has been reported under such system in at least 80 percent of the cases in which such measure is reportable under the system.

(ii) Four or more quality measures applicable. If there are 4 or more quality measures that are provided under the physician reporting system and that are applicable to such services of such professional furnished during the period, at least 3 such quality measures have been reported under such system in at least 80 percent of the cases in which the respective measure is reportable under the system.

For years after 2008, quality measures for purposes of this subparagraph shall not include electronic prescribing quality measures.

(B) Successful electronic prescriber. (i) In general. For purposes of paragraph (2) and subsection (a)(5), an eligible professional shall be treated as a successful electronic prescriber for a reporting period (or, for purposes of subsection (a)(5), for the reporting period for a year) if the eligible professional meets the requirement described in clause (ii), or, if the Secretary determines appropriate, the requirement described in clause (iii). If the Secretary makes the determination under the preceding sentence to apply the requirement described in clause (iii) for a period, then the requirement described in clause (ii) shall not apply for such period.

(ii) Requirement for submitting data on electronic prescribing quality measures. The requirement described in this clause is that, with respect to covered professional services furnished by an eligible professional during a reporting period (or, for purposes of subsection (a)(5), for the reporting period for a year), if there are any electronic prescribing quality measures that have been established under the physician reporting system and are applicable to any such services furnished by such professional for the period, such professional reported each such measure under such system in at least 50 percent of the cases in which such measure is reportable by such professional under such system.

(iii) Requirement for electronically prescribing under part D. The requirement described in this clause is that the eligible professional electronically submitted a sufficient number (as determined by the Secretary) of prescriptions under part D [42 USCS §§ 1395w-101 et seq.] during the reporting period (or, for purposes of subsection (a)(5), for the reporting period for a year).

(iv) Use of part D data. Notwithstanding sections 1860D-15(d)(2)(B) and 1860D-15(f)(2) [42 USCS § 1395w-115(d)(2)(B) and (f)(2)], the Secretary may use data regarding drug claims submitted for purposes of section 1860D-15 [42 USCS § 1395w-115] that are necessary for purposes of clause (iii), paragraph (2)(B)(ii), and paragraph (5)(G).

(v) Standards for electronic prescribing. To the extent practicable, in determining whether eligible professionals meet the requirements under clauses (ii) and (iii) for purposes of clause (i), the Secretary shall ensure that eligible professionals utilize electronic prescribing systems in compliance with standards established for such systems pursuant to the Part D Electronic Prescribing Program under section 1860D-4(e) [42 USCS § 1395w-104(e)].

(C) Satisfactory reporting measures for group practices. (i) In general. By January 1, 2010, the Secretary shall establish and have in place a process under which eligible professionals in a group practice (as defined by the Secretary) shall be treated as satisfactorily submitting data on quality measures under subparagraph (A) and as meeting the requirement described in subparagraph (B)(ii) for covered professional services for a reporting period (or, for purposes of subsection (a)(5), for a reporting period for a year, or, for purposes of subsection (a)(8), for a quality reporting period for the year) if, in lieu of reporting measures under subsection (k)(2)(C), the group practice reports measures determined appropriate by the Secretary, such as measures that target high-cost chronic conditions and preventive care, in a form and manner, and at a time, specified by the Secretary.

(ii) Statistical sampling model. The process under clause (i) shall provide for the use of a statistical sampling model to submit data on measures, such as the model used under the Physician Group Practice demonstration project under section 1866A [42 USCS § 1395cc-1].

(iii) No double payments. Payments to a group practice under this subsection by reason of the process under clause (i) shall be in lieu of the payments that would otherwise be made under this subsection to eligible professionals in the group practice for satisfactorily submitting data on quality measures.

(D) Authority to revise satisfactorily reporting data. For years after 2009, the Secretary, in consultation with stakeholders and experts, may revise the criteria under this subsection for satisfactorily submitting data on quality measures under subparagraph (A) and the criteria for submitting data on electronic prescribing quality measures under subparagraph (B)(ii).

(4) Form of payment. The payment under this subsection shall be in the form of a single consolidated payment.

(5) Application. (A) Physician reporting system rules. Paragraphs (5), (6), and (8) of subsection (k) shall apply for purposes of this subsection in the same manner as they apply for purposes of such subsection.

(B) Coordination with other bonus payments. The provisions of this subsection shall not be taken into account in applying subsections (m) and (u) of section 1833 and any payment under such subsections shall not be taken into account in computing allowable charges under this subsection.

(C) Implementation. Notwithstanding any other provision of law, for 2007, 2008, and 2009, the Secretary may implement by program instruction or otherwise this subsection.

(D) Validation. (i) In general. Subject to the succeeding provisions of this subparagraph, for purposes of determining whether a measure is applicable to the covered professional services of an eligible professional under this subsection for 2007 and 2008, the Secretary shall presume that if an eligible professional submits data for a measure, such measure is applicable to such professional.

(ii) Method. The Secretary may establish procedures to validate (by sampling or other means as the Secretary determines to be appropriate) whether measures applicable to covered professional services of an eligible professional have been reported.

(iii) Denial of payment authority. If the Secretary determines that an eligible professional (or, in the case of a group practice under paragraph (3)(C), the group practice) has not reported measures applicable to covered professional services of such professional, the Secretary shall not pay the incentive payment under this subsection. If such payments for such period have already been made, the Secretary shall recoup such payments from the eligible professional (or the group practice).

(E) Limitations on review. Except as provided in subparagraph (I), there shall be no administrative or judicial review under section 1869 [42 USCS § 1395ff], section 1878 [42 USCS § 1395oo], or otherwise of—

(i) the determination of measures applicable to services furnished by eligible professionals under this subsection;

(ii) the determination of satisfactory reporting under this subsection;

(iii) the determination of a successful electronic prescriber under paragraph (3), the limitation under paragraph (2)(B), and the exception under subsection (a)(5)(B); and

(iv) the determination of any incentive payment under this subsection and the payment adjustment under paragraphs (5)(A) and (8)(A) of subsection (a).

(F) Extension. For 2008 and subsequent years, the Secretary shall establish alternative criteria for satisfactorily reporting under this subsection and alternative reporting periods under paragraph (6)(C) for reporting groups of measures under subsection (k)(2)(B) and for reporting using the method specified in subsection (k)(4).

(G) Posting on website. The Secretary shall post on the Internet website of the Centers for Medicare & Medicaid Services, in an easily understandable format, a list of the names of the following:

(i) The eligible professionals (or, in the case of reporting under paragraph (3)(C), the group practices) who satisfactorily submitted data on quality measures under this subsection.

(ii) The eligible professionals (or, in the case of reporting under paragraph (3)(C), the group practices) who are successful electronic prescribers.

(H) Feedback. The Secretary shall provide timely feedback to eligible professionals on the performance of the eligible professional with respect to satisfactorily submitting data on quality measures under this subsection.

(I) Informal appeals process. The Secretary shall, by not later than January 1, 2011, establish and have in place an informal process for eligible professionals to seek a review of the determination that an eligible professional did not satisfactorily submit data on quality measures under this subsection.

(6) Definitions. For purposes of this subsection:

(A) Eligible professional; covered professional services. The terms "eligible professional" and "covered professional services" have the meanings given such terms in subsection (k)(3).

(B) Physician reporting system. The term "physician reporting system" means the system established under subsection (k).

(C) Reporting period. (i) In general. Subject to clauses (ii) and (iii), the term "reporting period" means—

(I) for 2007, the period beginning on July 1, 2007, and ending on December 31, 2007; and

(II) for 2008 and subsequent years, the entire year.

(ii) Authority to revise reporting period. For years after 2009, the Secretary may revise the reporting period under clause (i) if the Secretary determines such revision is appropriate, produces valid results on measures reported, and is consistent with the goals of maximizing scientific validity and reducing administrative burden. If the Secretary revises such period pursuant to the preceding sentence, the term "reporting period" shall mean such revised period.

(iii) Reference. Any reference in this subsection to a reporting period with respect to the application of subsection (a)(5) [or] (a)(8) shall be deemed a reference to the reporting period under subsection (a)(5)(D)(iii) or the quality reporting period under subsection (a)(8)(D)(iii), respectively.

(7) Integration of physician quality reporting and EHR reporting. Not later than January 1, 2012, the Secretary shall develop a plan to integrate reporting on quality measures under this subsection with reporting requirements under subsection (o) relating to the meaningful use of electronic health records. Such integration shall consist of the following:

(A) The selection of measures, the reporting of which would both demonstrate—

(i) meaningful use of an electronic health record for purposes of subsection (o); and

(ii) quality of care furnished to an individual.

(B) Such other activities as specified by the Secretary.

[(8)](7) Additional incentive payment. (A) In general. For 2011 through 2014, if an eligible professional meets the requirements described in subparagraph (B), the applicable quality percent for such year, as described in clauses (iii) and (iv) of paragraph (1)(B), shall be increased by 0.5 percentage points.

(B) Requirements described. In order to qualify for the additional incentive payment described in subparagraph (A), an eligible professional shall meet the following requirements:

(i) The eligible professional shall—

(I) satisfactorily submit data on quality measures for purposes of paragraph (1) for a year; and

(II) have such data submitted on their behalf through a Maintenance of Certification Program (as defined in subparagraph (C)(i)) that meets—

(aa) the criteria for a registry (as described in subsection (k)(4)); or

(bb) an alternative form and manner determined appropriate by the Secretary.

(ii) The eligible professional, more frequently than is required to qualify for or maintain board certification status—

(I) participates in such a Maintenance of Certification program for a year; and

(II) successfully completes a qualified Maintenance of Certification Program practice assessment (as defined in subparagraph (C)(ii)) for such year.

(iii) A Maintenance of Certification program submits to the Secretary, on behalf of the eligible professional, information—

(I) in a form and manner specified by the Secretary, that the eligible professional has successfully met the requirements of clause (ii) (which may be in the form of a structural measure);

(II) if requested by the Secretary, on the survey of patient experience with care (as described in subparagraph (C)(ii)(II)); and

(III) as the Secretary may require, on the methods, measures, and data used under the Maintenance of Certification Program and the qualified Maintenance of Certification Program practice assessment.

(C) Definitions. For purposes of this paragraph:

(i) The term "Maintenance of Certification Program" means a continuous assessment program, such as qualified American Board of Medical Specialties Maintenance of Certification program or an equivalent program (as determined by the Secretary), that advances quality and the lifelong learning and self-assessment of board certified specialty physicians by focusing on the competencies of patient care, medical knowledge, practice-based learning, interpersonal and communication skills and professionalism. Such a program shall include the following:

(I) The program requires the physician to maintain a valid, unrestricted medical license in the United States.

(II) The program requires a physician to participate in educational and self-assessment programs that require an assessment of what was learned.

(III) The program requires a physician to demonstrate, through a formalized, secure examination, that the physician has the fundamental diagnostic skills, medical knowledge, and clinical judgment to provide quality care in their respective specialty.

(IV) The program requires successful completion of a qualified Maintenance of Certification Program practice assessment as described in clause (ii).

(ii) The term "qualified Maintenance of Certification Program practice assessment" means an assessment of a physician's practice that—

(I) includes an initial assessment of an eligible professional's practice that is designed to demonstrate the physician's use of evidence-based medicine;

(II) includes a survey of patient experience with care; and

(III) requires a physician to implement a quality improvement intervention to address a practice weakness identified in the initial assessment under subclause (I) and then to remeasure to assess performance improvement after such intervention.

(n) Physician Feedback Program. (1) Establishment. (A) In general. (i) Establishment. The Secretary shall establish a Physician Feedback Program (in this subsection referred to as the "Program").

(ii) Reports on resources. The Secretary shall use claims data under this title [42 USCS §§ 1395 et seq.] (and may use other data) to provide confidential reports to physicians (and, as determined appropriate by the Secretary, to groups of physicians) that measure the resources involved in furnishing care to individuals under this title [42 USCS §§ 1395 et seq.].

(iii) Inclusion of certain information. If determined appropriate by the Secretary, the Secretary may include information on the quality of care furnished to individuals under this title [42 USCS §§ 1395 et seq.] by the physician (or group of physicians) in such reports.

(B) Resource use. The resources described in subparagraph (A)(ii) may be measured—

(i) on an episode basis;

(ii) on a per capita basis; or

(iii) on both an episode and a per capita basis.

(2) Implementation. The Secretary shall implement the Program by not later than January 1, 2009.

(3) Data for reports. To the extent practicable, reports under the Program shall be based on the most recent data available.

(4) Authority to focus initial application. The Secretary may focus the initial application of the Program as appropriate, such as focusing the Program on—

(A) physician specialties that account for a

certain percentage of all spending for physicians' services under this title [42 USCS §§ 1395 et seq.];

(B) physicians who treat conditions that have a high cost or a high volume, or both, under this title [42 USCS §§ 1395 et seq.];

(C) physicians who use a high amount of resources compared to other physicians;

(D) physicians practicing in certain geographic areas; or

(E) physicians who treat a minimum number of individuals under this title [42 USCS §§ 1395 et seq.].

(5) Authority to exclude certain information if insufficient information. The Secretary may exclude certain information regarding a service from a report under the Program with respect to a physician (or group of physicians) if the Secretary determines that there is insufficient information relating to that service to provide a valid report on that service.

(6) Adjustment of data. To the extent practicable, the Secretary shall make appropriate adjustments to the data used in preparing reports under the Program, such as adjustments to take into account variations in health status and other patient characteristics. For adjustments for reports on utilization under paragraph (9), see subparagraph (D) of such paragraph.

(7) Education and outreach. The Secretary shall provide for education and outreach activities to physicians on the operation of, and methodologies employed under, the Program.

(8) Disclosure exemption. Reports under the Program shall be exempt from disclosure under section 552 of title 5, United States Code.

(9) Reports on utilization. (A) Development of episode grouper. (i) In general. The Secretary shall develop an episode grouper that combines separate but clinically related items and services into an episode of care for an individual, as appropriate.

(ii) Timeline for development. The episode grouper described in subparagraph (A) shall be developed by not later than January 1, 2012.

(iii) Public availability. The Secretary shall make the details of the episode grouper described in subparagraph (A) available to the public.

(iv) Endorsement. The Secretary shall seek endorsement of the episode grouper described in subparagraph (A) by the entity with a contract under section 1890(a) [42 USCS § 1385aaa(a)].

(B) Reports on utilization. Effective beginning with 2012, the Secretary shall provide reports to physicians that compare, as determined appropriate by the Secretary, patterns of resource use of the individual physician to such patterns of other physicians.

(C) Analysis of data. The Secretary shall, for purposes of preparing reports under this paragraph, establish methodologies as appropriate, such as to—

(i) attribute episodes of care, in whole or in part, to physicians;

(ii) identify appropriate physicians for purposes of comparison under subparagraph (B); and

(iii) aggregate episodes of care attributed to a physician under clause (i) into a composite measure per individual.

(D) Data adjustment. In preparing reports under this paragraph, the Secretary shall make appropriate adjustments, including adjustments—

(i) to account for differences in socioeconomic and demographic characteristics, ethnicity, and health status of individuals (such as to recognize that less healthy individuals may require more intensive interventions); and

(ii) to eliminate the effect of geographic adjustments in payment rates (as described in subsection (e)).

(E) Public availability of methodology. The Secretary shall make available to the public—

(i) the methodologies established under subparagraph (C);

(ii) information regarding any adjustments made to data under subparagraph (D); and

(iii) aggregate reports with respect to physicians.

(F) Definition of physician. In this paragraph:

(i) In general. The term "physician" has the meaning given that term in section 1861(r)(1) [42 USCS § 1395x(r)(1)].

(ii) Treatment of groups. Such term includes, as the Secretary determines appropriate, a group of physicians.

(G) Limitations on review. There shall be no administrative or judicial review under section 1869 [42 USCS § 1395ff], section 1878 [42 USCS § 1395oo], or otherwise of the establishment of the methodology under subparagraph (C), including the determination of an episode of care under such methodology.

(10) Coordination with other value-based purchasing reforms. The Secretary shall coordinate the Program with the value-based payment modifier established under subsection (p) and, as the Secretary determines appropriate, other similar provisions of this title [42 USCS §§ 1395 et seq.].

(o) Incentives for adoption and mean-

ingful use of certified EHR technology. (1) Incentive payments. (A) In general. (i) In general. Subject to the succeeding subparagraphs of this paragraph, with respect to covered professional services furnished by an eligible professional during a payment year (as defined in subparagraph (E)), if the eligible professional is a meaningful EHR user (as determined under paragraph (2)) for the EHR reporting period with respect to such year, in addition to the amount otherwise paid under this part, there also shall be paid to the eligible professional (or to an employer or facility in the cases described in clause (A) of section 1842(b)(6) [42 USCS § 1395u(b)(6)]), from the Federal Supplementary Medical Insurance Trust Fund established under section 1841 [42 USCS § 1395t] an amount equal to 75 percent of the Secretary's estimate (based on claims submitted not later than 2 months after the end of the payment year) of the allowed charges under this part for all such covered professional services furnished by the eligible professional during such year.

(ii) No incentive payments with respect to years after 2016. No incentive payments may be made under this subsection with respect to a year after 2016.

(B) Limitations on amounts of incentive payments. (i) In general. In no case shall the amount of the incentive payment provided under this paragraph for an eligible professional for a payment year exceed the applicable amount specified under this subparagraph with respect to such eligible professional and such year.

(ii) Amount. Subject to clauses (iii) through (v), the applicable amount specified in this subparagraph for an eligible professional is as follows:

(I) For the first payment year for such professional, $15,000 (or, if the first payment year for such eligible professional is 2011 or 2012, $18,000).

(II) For the second payment year for such professional, $12,000.

(III) For the third payment year for such professional, $8,000.

(IV) For the fourth payment year for such professional, $4,000.

(V) For the fifth payment year for such professional, $2,000.

(VI) For any succeeding payment year for such professional, $0.

(iii) Phase down for eligible professionals first adopting EHR after 2013. If the first payment year for an eligible professional is after 2013, then the amount specified in this subparagraph for a payment year for such professional is the same as the amount specified in clause (ii) for such payment year for an eligible professional whose first payment year is 2013.

(iv) Increase for certain eligible professionals. In the case of an eligible professional who predominantly furnishes services under this part in an area that is designated by the Secretary (under section 332(a)(1)(A) of the Public Health Service Act [42 USCS § 254e(a)(1)(A)]) as a health professional shortage area, the amount that would otherwise apply for a payment year for such professional under subclauses (I) through (V) of clause (ii) shall be increased by 10 percent. In implementing the preceding sentence, the Secretary may, as determined appropriate, apply provisions of subsections (m) and (u) of section 1833 [42 USCS § 1395l] in a similar manner as such provisions apply under such subsection.

(v) No incentive payment if first adopting after 2014. If the first payment year for an eligible professional is after 2014 then the applicable amount specified in this subparagraph for such professional for such year and any subsequent year shall be $0.

(C) Non-application to hospital-based eligible professionals. (i) In general. No incentive payment may be made under this paragraph in the case of a hospital-based eligible professional.

(ii) Hospital-based eligible professional. For purposes of clause (i), the term "hospital-based eligible professional" means, with respect to covered professional services furnished by an eligible professional during the EHR reporting period for a payment year, an eligible professional, such as a pathologist, anesthesiologist, or emergency physician, who furnishes substantially all of such services in a hospital inpatient or emergency room setting and through the use of the facilities and equipment, including qualified electronic health records, of the hospital. The determination of whether an eligible professional is a hospital-based eligible professional shall be made on the basis of the site of service (as defined by the Secretary) and without regard to any employment or billing arrangement between the eligible professional and any other provider.

(D) Payment. (i) Form of payment. The payment under this paragraph may be in the form of a single consolidated payment or in the form of such periodic installments as the Secretary may specify.

(ii) Coordination of application of limitation for professionals in different practices. In the case of an eligible professional furnishing covered professional services in more than one practice (as specified by the Secretary), the Secretary shall establish rules to coordinate the incentive payments, including the application of the limitation on amounts of such incentive payments under this paragraph, among such practices.

(iii) Coordination with medicaid. The Secretary shall seek, to the maximum extent practicable, to avoid duplicative requirements from Federal and State governments to demonstrate meaningful use of certified EHR technology under this title and title XIX [42 USCS §§ 1395 et seq. and 1396 et seq.]. The Secretary may also adjust the reporting periods under such title and such subsections in order to carry out this clause.

(E) Payment year defined. (i) In general. For purposes of this subsection, the term "payment year" means a year beginning with 2011.

(ii) First, second, etc. payment year. The term "first payment year" means, with respect to covered professional services furnished by an eligible professional, the first year for which an incentive payment is made for such services under this subsection. The terms "second payment year", "third payment year", "fourth payment year", and "fifth payment year" mean, with respect to covered professional services furnished by such eligible professional, each successive year immediately following the first payment year for such professional.

(2) Meaningful EHR user. (A) In general. For purposes of paragraph (1), an eligible professional shall be treated as a meaningful EHR user for an EHR reporting period for a payment year (or, for purposes of subsection (a)(7), for an EHR reporting period under such subsection for a year) if each of the following requirements is met:

(i) Meaningful use of certified EHR technology. The eligible professional demonstrates to the satisfaction of the Secretary, in accordance with subparagraph (C)(i), that during such period the professional is using certified EHR technology in a meaningful manner, which shall include the use of electronic prescribing as determined to be appropriate by the Secretary.

(ii) Information exchange. The eligible professional demonstrates to the satisfaction of the Secretary, in accordance with subparagraph (C)(i), that during such period such certified EHR technology is connected in a manner that provides, in accordance with law and standards applicable to the exchange of information, for the electronic exchange of health information to improve the quality of health care, such as promoting care coordination.

(iii) Reporting on measures using EHR. Subject to subparagraph (B)(ii) and using such certified EHR technology, the eligible professional submits information for such period, in a form and manner specified by the Secretary, on such clinical quality measures and such other measures as selected by the Secretary under subparagraph (B)(i).

The Secretary may provide for the use of alternative means for meeting the requirements of clauses (i), (ii), and (iii) in the case of an eligible professional furnishing covered professional services in a group practice (as defined by the Secretary). The Secretary shall seek to improve the use of electronic health records and health care quality over time by requiring more stringent measures of meaningful use selected under this paragraph.

(B) Reporting on measures. (i) Selection. The Secretary shall select measures for purposes of subparagraph (A)(iii) but only consistent with the following:

(I) The Secretary shall provide preference to clinical quality measures that have been endorsed by the entity with a contract with the Secretary under section 1890(a) [42 USCS § 1395aaa(a)].

(II) Prior to any measure being selected under this subparagraph, the Secretary shall publish in the Federal Register such measure and provide for a period of public comment on such measure.

(ii) Limitation. The Secretary may not require the electronic reporting of information on clinical quality measures under subparagraph (A)(iii) unless the Secretary has the capacity to accept the information electronically, which may be on a pilot basis.

(iii) Coordination of reporting of information. In selecting such measures, and in establishing the form and manner for reporting measures under subparagraph (A)(iii), the Secretary shall seek to avoid redundant or duplicative reporting otherwise required, including reporting under subsection (k)(2)(C).

(C) Demonstration of meaningful use of certified EHR technology and information exchange. (i) In general. A professional may satisfy the demonstration requirement of clauses (i) and (ii) of subparagraph (A) through means specified by the Secretary, which may include—

(I) an attestation;

(II) the submission of claims with appropriate coding (such as a code indicating that a patient encounter was documented using certified EHR technology);

(III) a survey response;

(IV) reporting under subparagraph (A)(iii); and

(V) other means specified by the Secretary.

(ii) Use of part D data. Notwithstanding sections 1860D-15(d)(2)(B) and 1860D-15(f)(2) [42 USCS § 1395w-115(d)(2)(B), (f)(2)], the Secretary may use data regarding drug claims submitted for purposes of section 1860D-15 [42 USCS § 1395w-115] that are necessary for purposes of subparagraph (A).

(3) Application. (A) Physician reporting system rules. Paragraphs (5), (6), and (8) of subsection (k) shall apply for purposes of this subsection in the same manner as they apply for purposes of such subsection.

(B) Coordination with other payments. The provisions of this subsection shall not be taken into account in applying the provisions of subsection (m) of this section and of section 1833(m) [42 USCS § 1395l(m)] and any payment under such provisions shall not be taken into account in computing allowable charges under this subsection.

(C) Limitations on review. There shall be no administrative or judicial review under section 1869 [42 USCS § 1395ff], section 1878 [42 USCS § 1395oo], or otherwise, of—

(i) the methodology and standards for determining payment amounts under this subsection and payment adjustments under subsection (a)(7)(A), including the limitation under paragraph (1)(B) and coordination under clauses (ii) and (iii) of paragraph (1)(D);

(ii) the methodology and standards for determining a meaningful EHR user under paragraph (2), including selection of measures under paragraph (2)(B), specification of the means of demonstrating meaningful EHR use under paragraph (2)(C), and the hardship exception under subsection (a)(7)(B);

(iii) the methodology and standards for determining a hospital-based eligible professional under paragraph (1)(C); and

(iv) the specification of reporting periods under paragraph (5) and the selection of the form of payment under paragraph (1)(D)(i).

(D) Posting on website. The Secretary shall post on the Internet website of the Centers for Medicare & Medicaid Services, in an easily understandable format, a list of the names, business addresses, and business phone numbers of the eligible professionals who are meaningful EHR users and, as determined appropriate by the Secretary, of group practices receiving incentive payments under paragraph (1).

(4) Certified EHR technology defined. For purposes of this section, the term "certified EHR technology" means a qualified electronic health record (as defined in section 3000(13) of the Public Health Service Act [42 USCS § 300jj(13)]) that is certified pursuant to section 3001(c)(5) of such Act [42 USCS § 300jj-11(c)(5)] as meeting standards adopted under section 3004 of such Act [42 USCS § 300jj-14] that are applicable to the type of record involved (as determined by the Secretary, such as an ambulatory electronic health record for office-based physicians or an inpatient hospital electronic health record for hospitals).

(5) Definitions. For purposes of this subsection:

(A) Covered professional services. The term "covered professional services" has the meaning given such term in subsection (k)(3).

(B) EHR reporting period. The term "EHR reporting period" means, with respect to a payment year, any period (or periods) as specified by the Secretary.

(C) Eligible professional. The term "eligible professional" means a physician, as defined in section 1861(r) [42 USCS § 1395x(r)].

(p) Establishment of value-based payment modifier. (1) In general. The Secretary shall establish a payment modifier that provides for differential payment to a physician or a group of physicians under the fee schedule established under subsection (b) based upon the quality of care furnished compared to cost (as determined under paragraphs (2) and (3), respectively) during a performance period. Such payment modifier shall be separate from the geographic adjustment factors established under subsection (e).

(2) Quality. (A) In general. For purposes of paragraph (1), quality of care shall be evaluated, to the extent practicable, based on a composite of measures of the quality of care furnished (as established by the Secretary under subparagraph (B)).

(B) Measures. (i) The Secretary shall establish appropriate measures of the quality of care furnished by a physician or group of physicians to individuals enrolled under this part, such as measures that reflect health outcomes. Such measures shall be risk adjusted as determined appropriate by the Secretary.

(ii) The Secretary shall seek endorsement of the measures established under this subparagraph by the entity with a contract under section 1890(a) [42 USCS § 1395aaa(a)].

(3) Costs. For purposes of paragraph (1), costs shall be evaluated, to the extent practicable, based on a composite of appropriate measures of costs established by the Secretary

(such as the composite measure under the methodology established under subsection (n)(9)(C)(iii)) that eliminate the effect of geographic adjustments in payment rates (as described in subsection (e)), and take into account risk factors (such as socioeconomic and demographic characteristics, ethnicity, and health status of individuals (such as to recognize that less healthy individuals may require more intensive interventions) and other factors determined appropriate by the Secretary.

(4) Implementation. (A) Publication of measures, dates of implementation, performance period.—Not later than January 1, 2012, the Secretary shall publish the following:

(i) The measures of quality of care and costs established under paragraphs (2) and (3), respectively.

(ii) The dates for implementation of the payment modifier (as determined under subparagraph (B)).

(iii) The initial performance period (as specified under subparagraph (B)(ii)).

(B) Deadlines for implementation. (i) Initial implementation. Subject to the preceding provisions of this subparagraph, the Secretary shall begin implementing the payment modifier established under this subsection through the rulemaking process during 2013 for the physician fee schedule established under subsection (b).

(ii) Initial performance period. (I) In general. The Secretary shall specify an initial performance period for application of the payment modifier established under this subsection with respect to 2015.

(II) Provision of information during initial performance period.—During the initial performance period, the Secretary shall, to the extent practicable, provide information to physicians and groups of physicians about the quality of care furnished by the physician or group of physicians to individuals enrolled under this part compared to cost (as determined under paragraphs (2) and (3), respectively) with respect to the performance period.

(iii) Application. The Secretary shall apply the payment modifier established under this subsection for items and services furnished—

(I) beginning on January 1, 2015, with respect to specific physicians and groups of physicians the Secretary determines appropriate; and

(II) beginning not later than January 1, 2017, with respect to all physicians and groups of physicians.

(C) Budget neutrality. The payment modifier established under this subsection shall be implemented in a budget neutral manner.

(5) Systems-based care. The Secretary shall, as appropriate, apply the payment modifier established under this subsection in a manner that promotes systems-based care.

(6) Consideration of special circumstances of certain providers. In applying the payment modifier under this subsection, the Secretary shall, as appropriate, take into account the special circumstances of physicians or groups of physicians in rural areas and other underserved communities.

(7) Application. For purposes of the initial application of the payment modifier established under this subsection during the period beginning on January 1, 2015, and ending on December 31, 2016, the term "physician" has the meaning given such term in section 1861(r) [42 USCS § 1395x(r)]. On or after January 1, 2017, the Secretary may apply this subsection to eligible professionals (as defined in subsection (k)(3)(B)) as the Secretary determines appropriate.

(8) Definitions. For purposes of this subsection:

(A) Costs. The term "costs" means expenditures per individual as determined appropriate by the Secretary. In making the determination under the preceding sentence, the Secretary may take into account the amount of growth in expenditures per individual for a physician compared to the amount of such growth for other physicians.

(B) Performance period. The term "performance period" means a period specified by the Secretary.

(9) Coordination with other value-based purchasing reforms. The Secretary shall coordinate the value-based payment modifier established under this subsection with the Physician Feedback Program under subsection (n) and, as the Secretary determines appropriate, other similar provisions of this title.

(10) Limitations on review. There shall be no administrative or judicial review under section 1869 [42 USCS § 1395ff], section 1878 [42 USCS § 1395oo], or otherwise of—

(A) the establishment of the value-based payment modifier under this subsection;

(B) the evaluation of quality of care under paragraph (2), including the establishment of appropriate measures of the quality of care under paragraph (2)(B);

(C) the evaluation of costs under paragraph (3), including the establishment of appropriate measures of costs under such paragraph;

(D) the dates for implementation of the value-based payment modifier;

(E) the specification of the initial performance period and any other performance period under paragraphs (4)(B)(ii) and (8)(B), respectively;

(F) the application of the value-based payment modifier under paragraph (7); and

(G) the determination of costs under paragraph (8)(A).

(Aug. 14, 1935, ch 531, Title XVIII, Part B, § 1848, as added Dec. 19, 1989, P. L. 101-239, Title VI, Subtitle A, Part 2, Subpart A, § 6102(a), 103 Stat. 2169; Nov. 5, 1990, P. L. 101-508, Title IV, Subtitle A, Part 2, Subpart A, §§ 4102(b), (g)(2), 4104(b)(2), 4105(a)(3), (c), 4106(b)(1), 4107(a)(1), 4109(a), 4116, 4118(b)–(f)(1), (k), 104 Stat. 1388-56, 1388-57–1388-60, 1388-61–1388-63, 1388-65, 1388-67, 1388-68, 1388-71; Aug. 10, 1993, P. L. 103-66, Title XIII, Ch 2, Subch A, Part II, Subpart A, §§ 13511(a), 13512–13514(a), (b), 13515(a)(1), (c), 13516(a)(2), 13517(a), 13518(a), 107 Stat. 580–586; Oct. 31, 1994, P. L. 103-432, Title I, Subtitle B, Part I, §§ 121(b)(1), (2), 122(a), (b), 123(a), (d), 126(b)(6), (g)(2)(B), (5)–(7), (10)(A), 108 Stat. 4409, 4410, 4412, 4415, 4416; Aug. 5, 1997, P. L. 105-33, Title IV, Subtitle A, Ch 3, § 4022(b)(2)(B), (C), Subtitle B, §§ 4102(d), 4103(d), 4104(d), 4105(a)(2), 4106(b), Subtitle F, Ch 1, Subch A, §§ 4501, 4502(a)(1), (b), 4503, Subtitle F, Ch 1, Subch A, §§ 4504(a), 4505(a), (b), (e), (f)(1), Subtitle G, Ch 3, § 4644(d), Subtitle H, Ch 2, § 4714(b)(2), 111 Stat. 354, 361, 362, 365, 366, 368, 432–437, 488, 510; Nov. 29, 1999, P. L. 106-113, Div B, § 1000(a)(6), 113 Stat. 1536; Dec. 21, 2000, P. L. 106-554, § 1(a)(6), 114 Stat. 2763; Feb. 20, 2003, P. L. 108-7, Div N, Title IV, § 402(a), 117 Stat. 548; Dec. 8, 2003, P. L. 108-173, Title III, § 303(a)(1), (g)(2), Title IV, Subtitle B, § 412, Title VI, Subtitle A, §§ 601(a)(1), (2), (b)(1), 602, Subtitle B, § 611(c), Title VII, Subtitle D, § 736(b)(10), 117 Stat. 2233, 2253, 2274, 2300, 2301, 2304, 2356; Feb. 8, 2006, P. L. 109-171, Title V, Subtitle B, Ch. 1, §§ 5102, 5104(a), Ch. 2, § 5112(c), 120 Stat. 37, 39, 40, 44; Dec. 20, 2006, P. L. 109-432, Div B, Title I, §§ 101(a), (b), (d), 102, 120 Stat. 2975, 2980, 2981; Sept. 29, 2007, P. L. 110-90, § 6, 121 Stat. 985; Dec. 26, 2007, P. L. 110-161, Div G, Title II, § 225(c)(2), Title V, § 524, 121 Stat. 2190, 2212; Dec. 29, 2007, P. L. 110-173, Title I, §§ 101(a)(1), (2)(A), (b)(1), 103, 121 Stat. 2493, 2494, 2495; June 30, 2008, P. L. 110-252, Title VII, § 7002(c), 122 Stat. 2395; July 15, 2008, P. L. 110-275, Title I, Subtitle C, Part I, §§ 131(a)–(b)(4)(A), (5), (c)(1), 132(a), (b), 133(b), 134, 139(a), Part II, §§ 144(a)(2), 152(b)(1)(C), 122 Stat. 2520, 2525, 2526, 2528, 2532, 2541, 2546, 2552; Feb. 17, 2009, P. L. 111-5, Div B, Title IV, Subtitle A, § 4101(a), (b), (f), 123 Stat. 467, 476; Dec. 19, 2009, P. L. 111-119, Div B, § 1011(a), 123 Stat. 3473; March 2, 2010, P. L. 111-144, § 5, 124 Stat. 46; March 23, 2010, P. L. 111-148, Title III, Subtitle A, Part I, §§ 3002(a)–(c)(1), (d)–(f), 3003(a), 3007, Subtitle B, Part I, §§ 3101, 3102, 3111(a)(1), Part III, §§ 3134(a), 3135(a), (b), Title IV, Subtitle B, § 4103(c)(2), Title V, Subtitle F, § 5501(c), Title X, Subtitle C, §§ 10310, 10324(c), 10327(a), Subtitle E, § 10501(h), 124 Stat. 363, 365, 373, 415, 421, 434, 436, 556, 654, 942, 960, 962, 997; March 30, 2010, P. L. 111-152, Title I, Subtitle B, § 1107, 1108, 124 Stat. 1050; April 15, 2010, P. L. 111-157, §§ 4, 5(a)(1), 124 Stat. 1117.)

HISTORY; ANCILLARY LAWS AND DIRECTIVES

Other provisions:

Adjustment for medicare mental health services. Act July 15, 2008, P. L. 110-275, Title I, Subtitle C, Part I, § 138, 122 Stat. 2541; March 23, 2010, P. L. 111-148, Title III, Subtitle B, Part I, § 3107, 124 Stat. 418, provides:

"(a) Payment adjustment. (1) In general. For purposes of payment for services furnished under the physician fee schedule under section 1848 of the Social Security Act (42 U.S.C. 1395w-4) during the period beginning on July 1, 2008, and ending on December 31, 2010, the Secretary of Health and Human Services shall increase the fee schedule otherwise applicable for specified services by 5 percent.

"(2) Nonapplication of budget-neutrality. The budget-neutrality provision of section 1848(c)(2)(B)(ii) of the Social Security Act (42 U.S.C. 1395w-4(c)(2)(B)(ii)) shall not apply to the adjustments described in paragraph (1).

"(b) Definition of specified services. In this section, the term 'specified services' means procedure codes for services in the categories of the Health Care Common Procedure Coding System, established by the Secretary of Health and Human Services under section 1848(c)(5) of the Social Security Act (42 U.S.C. 1395w-4(c)(5)), as of July 1, 2007, and as subsequently modified by the Secretary, consisting of psychiatric therapeutic procedures furnished in office or other outpatient facility settings or in inpatient hospital, partial hospital, or residential care facility settings, but only with respect to such services in such categories that are in the subcategories of services which are—

"(1) insight oriented, behavior modifying, or supportive psychotherapy; or

"(2) interactive psychotherapy.

"(c) Implementation. Notwithstanding any other provision of law, the Secretary may implement this section by program instruction or otherwise.".

Applicability of amendments made by § 144(a) of Act July 15, 2008. Act July 15, 2008, P. L. 110-275, Title I, Subtitle C, Part II, § 144(a)(3), 122 Stat. 2547, provides: "The amendments made by this subsection [amending 42 USCS §§ 1395w-4 and 1395x] shall apply to items and services furnished on or after January 1, 2010.".

Applicability of amendments made by § 152(b) of Act July 15, 2008. Act July 15, 2008, P. L. 110-275, Title I, Subtitle C, Part II, § 152(b)(2), 122 Stat. 2553, provides: "The amendments made by this subsection [amending 42 USCS §§ 1395w-4, 1395x, and 1395y] shall apply to services furnished on or after January 1, 2010.".

Applicability of amendment made by § 3002(c) of Act March 23, 2010. Act March 23, 2010, P. L. 111-148, Title III, Subtitle A, Part I, § 3002(c)(2), 124 Stat. 365, provides: "The amendment made by paragraph (1) [amending subsec. (k)(4) of this section] shall apply for years after 2010.".

Authority. Act March 23, 2010, P. L. 111-148, Title III, Subtitle A, Part I, § 3002(c)(3), as added Title X, Subtitle C, § 10327(b), 124 Stat. 963, provides: "For years after 2014, if the Secretary of Health and Human Services determines it to be appropriate, the Secretary may incorporate participation in a Maintenance of Certification Program and successful completion of a qualified Maintenance of Certification Program practice assessment into the composite of measures of quality of care furnished pursuant to the physician fee schedule payment modifier, as described in section 1848(p)(2) of the Social Security Act (42 U.S.C. 1395w-4(p)(2)).".

Implementation of amendments made by § 3111(a) of Act March 23, 2010. Act March 23, 2010, P. L. 111-148, Title III, Subtitle B, Part I, § 3111(a)(2), 124 Stat. 421, provides: "Notwithstanding any other provision of law, the Secretary may implement the amendments made by paragraph (1) [amending subsecs. (b)(4)(B), (b)(6), and (c)(2)(B) of this section] by program instruction or otherwise.".

Implementation of subsec. (c)(2)(K), (L). Act March 23, 2010, P. L. 111-148, Title III, Subtitle B, Part III, § 3134(b)(1), provides:

"(A) Chapter 35 of title 44, United States Code [42 USCS §§ 3501 et seq.] and the provisions of the Federal Advisory Committee Act (5 U.S.C. App.) shall not apply to this section or the amendment made by this section [adding 42 USCS § 1395w-4(c)(2)(K), (L)].

"(B) Notwithstanding any other provision of law, the Secretary may implement subparagraphs (K) and (L) of 1848(c)(2) of the Social Security Act, as added by subsection (a), by program instruction or otherwise.

"(C) Section 4505(d) of the Balanced Budget Act of 1997 [note to this section] is repealed.

"(D) Except for provisions related to confidentiality of information, the provisions of the Federal Acquisition Regulation shall not apply to this section or the amendment made by this section.".

§ 1395w-5. Public reporting of performance information

(a) In general. (1) Development. Not later than January 1, 2011, the Secretary shall develop a Physician Compare Internet website with information on physicians enrolled in the Medicare program under section 1866(j) of the Social Security Act (42 U.S.C. 1395cc(j)) and other eligible professionals who participate in the Physician Quality Reporting Initiative under section 1848 of such Act (42 U.S.C. 1395w-4).

(2) Plan. Not later than January 1, 2013, and with respect to reporting periods that begin no earlier than January 1, 2012, the Secretary shall also implement a plan for making publicly available through Physician Compare, consistent with subsection (c), information on physician performance that provides comparable information for the public on quality and patient experience measures with respect to physicians enrolled in the Medicare program under such section 1866(j) [42 USCS § 1395cc(j)]. To the extent scientifically sound measures that are developed consistent with the requirements of this section are available, such information, to the extent practicable, shall include—

(A) measures collected under the Physician Quality Reporting Initiative;

(B) an assessment of patient health outcomes and the functional status of patients;

(C) an assessment of the continuity and coordination of care and care transitions, including episodes of care and risk-adjusted resource use;

(D) an assessment of efficiency;

(E) an assessment of patient experience and patient, caregiver, and family engagement;

(F) an assessment of the safety, effectiveness, and timeliness of care; and

(G) other information as determined appropriate by the Secretary.

(b) Other required considerations. In developing and implementing the plan described in subsection (a)(2), the Secretary shall, to the extent practicable, include—

(1) processes to assure that data made public, either by the Centers for Medicare & Medicaid Services or by other entities, is statistically valid and reliable, including risk adjustment mechanisms used by the Secretary;

(2) processes by which a physician or other eligible professional whose performance on measures is being publicly reported has a reasonable opportunity, as determined by the Secretary, to review his or her individual results before they are made public;

(3) processes by the Secretary to assure that the implementation of the plan and the data made available on Physician Compare provide a robust and accurate portrayal of a physician's performance;

(4) data that reflects the care provided to all patients seen by physicians, under both the Medicare program and, to the extent practicable, other payers, to the extent such information would provide a more accurate portrayal of physician performance;

(5) processes to ensure appropriate attribution of care when multiple physicians and other providers are involved in the care of a patient;

(6) processes to ensure timely statistical performance feedback is provided to physicians concerning the data reported under any program subject to public reporting under this section; and

(7) implementation of computer and data systems of the Centers for Medicare & Medicaid Services that support valid, reliable, and accurate public reporting activities authorized under this section.

(c) Ensuring patient privacy. The Secretary shall ensure that information on physician performance and patient experience is not disclosed under this section in a manner that violates sections 552 or 552a of title 5, United States Code, with regard to the privacy of individually identifiable health information.

(d) Feedback from multi-stakeholder groups. The Secretary shall take into consideration input provided by multi-stakeholder groups, consistent with sections 1890(b)(7) and 1890A of the Social Security Act [42 USCS § 1395aaa(b)(7) and 1395aaa-1], as added by section 3014 of this Act, in selecting quality measures for use under this section.

(e) Consideration of transition to value-based purchasing. In developing the plan under this subsection (a)(2), the Secretary shall, as the Secretary determines appropriate, consider the plan to transition to a value-based purchasing program for physicians and other practitioners developed under section 131 of the Medicare Improvements for Patients and Providers Act of 2008 (Public Law 110-275).

(f) Report to Congress. Not later than January 1, 2015, the Secretary shall submit to Congress a report on the Physician Compare Internet website developed under subsection (a)(1). Such report shall include information on the efforts of and plans made by the Secretary to collect and publish data on physician quality and efficiency and on patient experience of care in support of value-based purchasing and consumer choice, together with recommendations for such legislation and administrative action as the Secretary determines appropriate.

(g) Expansion. At any time before the date on which the report is submitted under subsection (f), the Secretary may expand (including expansion to other providers of services and suppliers under title XVIII of the Social Security Act [42 USCS §§ 1395 et seq.]) the information made available on such website.

(h) Financial incentives to encourage consumers to choose high quality providers. The Secretary may establish a demonstration program, not later than January 1, 2019, to provide financial incentives to Medicare beneficiaries who are furnished services by high quality physicians, as determined by the Secretary based on factors in subparagraphs (A) through (G) of subsection (a)(2). In no case may Medicare beneficiaries be required to pay increased premiums or cost sharing or be subject to a reduction in benefits under title XVIII of the Social Security Act [42 USCS §§ 1395 et seq.] as a result of such demonstration program. The Secretary shall ensure that any such demonstration program does not disadvantage those beneficiaries without reasonable access to high performing physicians or create financial inequities under such title.

(i) Definitions. In this section:

(1) Eligible professional. The term "eligible professional" has the meaning given that term for purposes of the Physician Quality Reporting Initiative under section 1848 of the Social Security Act (42 U.S.C. 1395w-4).

(2) Physician. The term "physician" has the meaning given that term in section 1861(r) of such Act (42 U.S.C. 1395x(r)).

(3) Physician compare. The term "Physician Compare" means the Internet website developed under subsection (a)(1).

(4) Secretary. The term "Secretary" means the Secretary of Health and Human Services.

(March 23, 2010, P. L. 111-148, Title X, Subtitle C, § 10331, 124 Stat. 966.)

PART C. MEDICARE+CHOICE PROGRAM

§ 1395w-21. Eligibility, election, and enrollment

(a) Choice of medicare benefits through Medicare+Choice plans. (1) In general. Subject to the provisions of this section, each Medicare+Choice eligible individual (as defined in paragraph (3)) is entitled to elect to receive benefits (other than qualified prescription drug benefits) under this title [42 USCS §§ 1395 et seq.]—

(A) through the original medicare fee-for-service program under parts A and B [42 USCS §§ 1395c et seq. and 1395j et seq.], or

(B) through enrollment in a Medicare+Choice plan under this part [42 USCS §§ 1395w-21 et seq.],

and may elect qualified prescription drug coverage in accordance with section 1860D-1 [42 USCS § 1395w-101].

(2) Types of Medicare+Choice plans that may be available. A Medicare+Choice plan may

be any of the following types of plans of health insurance:

(A) Coordinated care plans (including regional plans). (i) In general. Coordinated care plans which provide health care services, including but not limited to health maintenance organization plans (with or without point of service options), plans offered by provider-sponsored organizations (as defined in section 1855(d) [42 USCS § 1395w-25(d)]), and regional or local preferred provider organization plans (including MA regional plans).

(ii) Specialized MA plans for special needs individuals. Specialized MA plans for special needs individuals (as defined in section 1859(b)(6) [42 USCS § 1395w-28(b)(6)]) may be any type of coordinated care plan.

(B) Combination of MSA plan and contributions to Medicare+Choice MSA. An MSA plan, as defined in section 1859(b)(3) [42 USCS § 1395w-28(b)(3)], and a contribution into a Medicare+Choice medical savings account (MSA).

(C) Private fee-for-service plans. A Medicare+Choice private fee-for-service plan, as defined in section 1859(b)(2) [42 USCS § 1395w-28(b)(2)].

(3) Medicare+choice eligible individual. (A) In general. In this title [42 USCS §§ 1395 et seq.], subject to subparagraph (B), the term "Medicare+Choice eligible individual" means an individual who is entitled to benefits under part A [42 USCS §§ 1395c et seq.]and enrolled under part B [42 USCS §§ 1395j et seq.].

(B) Special rule for end-stage renal disease. Such term shall not include an individual medically determined to have end-stage renal disease, except that—

(i) an individual who develops end-stage renal disease while enrolled in a Medicare+Choice plan may continue to be enrolled in that plan; and

(ii) in the case of such an individual who is enrolled in a Medicare+Choice plan under clause (i) (or subsequently under this clause), if the enrollment is discontinued under circumstances described in subsection (e)(4)(A), then the individual will be treated as a "Medicare+Choice eligible individual" for purposes of electing to continue enrollment in another Medicare+Choice plan.

(b) Special rules. (1) Residence requirement. (A) In general. Except as the Secretary may otherwise provide and except as provided in subparagraph (C), an individual is eligible to elect a Medicare+Choice plan offered by a Medicare+Choice organization only if the plan serves the geographic area in which the individual resides.

(B) Continuation of enrollment permitted. Pursuant to rules specified by the Secretary, the Secretary shall provide that an MA local plan may offer to all individuals residing in a geographic area the option to continue enrollment in the plan, notwithstanding that the individual no longer resides in the service area of the plan, so long as the plan provides that individuals exercising this option have, as part of the benefits under the original medicare fee-for-service program option, reasonable access within that geographic area to the full range of basic benefits, subject to reasonable cost sharing liability in obtaining such benefits.

(C) Continuation of enrollment permitted where service changed. Notwithstanding subparagraph (A) and in addition to subparagraph (B), if a Medicare+Choice organization eliminates from its service area a Medicare+Choice payment area that was previously within its service area, the organization may elect to offer individuals residing in all or portions of the affected area who would otherwise be ineligible to continue enrollment the option to continue enrollment in an MA local plan it offers so long as—

(i) the enrollee agrees to receive the full range of basic benefits (excluding emergency and urgently needed care) exclusively at facilities designated by the organization within the plan service area; and

(ii) there is no other Medicare+Choice plan offered in the area in which the enrollee resides at the time of the organization's election.

(2) Special rule for certain individuals covered under FEHBP or eligible for veterans or military health benefits, veterans. (A) FEHBP. An individual who is enrolled in a health benefit plan under chapter 89 of title 5 [5 USCS §§ 8901 et seq.], United States Code, is not eligible to enroll in an MSA plan until such time as the Director of the Office of Management and Budget certifies to the Secretary that the Office of Personnel Management has adopted policies which will ensure that the enrollment of such individuals in such plans will not result in increased expenditures for the Federal Government for health benefit plans under such chapter.

(B) VA and DOD. The Secretary may apply rules similar to the rules described in subparagraph (A) in the case of individuals who are eligible for health care benefits under chapter 55 of title 10, United States Code [10 USCS §§ 1071 et seq.], or under chapter 17 of title 38 of such Code [38 USCS §§ 1701 et seq.].

(3) Limitation on eligibility of qualified

medicare beneficiaries and other medicaid beneficiaries to enroll in an MSA plan. An individual who is a qualified medicare beneficiary (as defined in section 1905(p)(1) [42 USCS § 1396d(p)(1)]), a qualified disabled and working individual (described in section 1905(s) [42 USCS § 1396d(s)]), an individual described in section 1902(a)(10)(E)(iii) [42 USCS § 1396a(a)(10)(E)(iii)], or otherwise entitled to medicare cost-sharing under a State plan under title XIX [42 USCS §§ 1396 et seq.] is not eligible to enroll in an MSA plan.

(4) Coverage under MSA plans. (A) In general. Under rules established by the Secretary, an individual is not eligible to enroll (or continue enrollment) in an MSA plan for a year unless the individual provides assurances satisfactory to the Secretary that the individual will reside in the United States for at least 183 days during the year.

(B) Evaluation. The Secretary shall regularly evaluate the impact of permitting enrollment in MSA plans under this part [42 USCS §§ 1395w-21 et seq.] on selection (including adverse selection), use of preventive care, access to care, and the financial status of the Trust Funds under this title [42 USCS §§ 1395 et seq.].

(C) Reports. The Secretary shall submit to Congress periodic reports on the numbers of individuals enrolled in such plans and on the evaluation being conducted under subparagraph (B).

(c) Process for exercising choice. (1) In general. The Secretary shall establish a process through which elections described in subsection (a) are made and changed, including the form and manner in which such elections are made and changed. Such elections shall be made or changed only during coverage election periods specified under subsection (e) and shall become effective as provided in subsection (f).

(2) Coordination through Medicare+Choice organizations. (A) Enrollment. Such process shall permit an individual who wishes to elect a Medicare+Choice plan offered by a Medicare+Choice organization to make such election through the filing of an appropriate election form with the organization.

(B) Disenrollment. Such process shall permit an individual, who has elected a Medicare+Choice plan offered by a Medicare+Choice organization and who wishes to terminate such election, to terminate such election through the filing of an appropriate election form with the organization.

(3) Default. (A) Initial election. (i) In general. Subject to clause (ii), an individual who fails to make an election during an initial election period under subsection (e)(1) is deemed to have chosen the original medicare fee-for-service program option.

(ii) Seamless continuation of coverage. The Secretary may establish procedures under which an individual who is enrolled in a health plan (other than Medicare+Choice plan) offered by a Medicare+Choice organization at the time of the initial election period and who fails to elect to receive coverage other than through the organization is deemed to have elected the Medicare+Choice plan offered by the organization (or, if the organization offers more than one such plan, such plan or plans as the Secretary identifies under such procedures).

(B) Continuing periods. An individual who has made (or is deemed to have made) an election under this section is considered to have continued to make such election until such time as—

(i) the individual changes the election under this section, or

(ii) the Medicare+Choice plan with respect to which such election is in effect is discontinued or, subject to subsection (b)(1)(B), no longer serves the area in which the individual resides.

(d) Providing information to promote informed choice. (1) In general. The Secretary shall provide for activities under this subsection to broadly disseminate information to medicare beneficiaries (and prospective medicare beneficiaries) on the coverage options provided under this section in order to promote an active, informed selection among such options.

(2) Provision of notice. (A) Open season notification. At least 15 days before the beginning of each annual, coordinated election period (as defined in subsection (e)(3)(B)), the Secretary shall mail to each Medicare+Choice eligible individual residing in an area the following:

(i) General information. The general information described in paragraph (3).

(ii) List of plans and comparison of plan options. A list identifying the Medicare+Choice plans that are (or will be) available to residents of the area and information described in paragraph (4) concerning such plans. Such information shall be presented in a comparative form.

(iii) Additional information. Any other information that the Secretary determines will assist the individual in making the election under this section.

The mailing of such information shall be coordinated, to the extent practicable, with the mailing of any annual notice under section 1804 [42 USCS § 1395b-2].

(B) Notification to newly eligible

Medicare+Choice eligible individuals. To the extent practicable, the Secretary shall, not later than 30 days before the beginning of the initial Medicare+Choice enrollment period for an individual described in subsection (e)(1), mail to the individual the information described in subparagraph (A).

(C) Form. The information disseminated under this paragraph shall be written and formatted using language that is easily understandable by medicare beneficiaries.

(D) Periodic updating. The information described in subparagraph (A) shall be updated on at least an annual basis to reflect changes in the availability of Medicare+Choice plans and the benefits and Medicare+Choice monthly basic and supplemental beneficiary premiums for such plans.

(3) General information. General information under this paragraph, with respect to coverage under this part [42 USCS §§ 1395w-21 et seq.] during a year, shall include the following:

(A) Benefits under original medicare fee-for-service program option. A general description of the benefits covered under the original medicare fee-for-service program under parts A and B [42 USCS §§ 1395c et seq. and 1395j et seq.], including—

(i) covered items and services,

(ii) beneficiary cost sharing, such as deductibles, coinsurance, and copayment amounts, and

(iii) any beneficiary liability for balance billing.

(B) Election procedures. Information and instructions on how to exercise election options under this section.

(C) Rights. A general description of procedural rights (including grievance and appeals procedures) of beneficiaries under the original medicare fee-for-service program and the Medicare+Choice program and the right to be protected against discrimination based on health status-related factors under section 1852(b) [42 USCS § 1395w-22(b)].

(D) Information on medigap and medicare select. A general description of the benefits, enrollment rights, and other requirements applicable to medicare supplemental policies under section 1882 [42 USCS § 1395ss] and provisions relating to medicare select policies described in section 1882(t) [42 USCS § 1395ss(t)].

(E) Potential for contract termination. The fact that a Medicare+Choice organization may terminate its contract, refuse to renew its contract, or reduce the service area included in its contract, under this part [42 USCS §§ 1395w-21 et seq.], and the effect of such a termination, nonrenewal, or service area reduction may have on individuals enrolled with the Medicare+Choice plan under this part [42 USCS §§ 1395w-21 et seq.].

(F) Catastrophic coverage and single deductible. In the case of an MA regional plan, a description of the catastrophic coverage and single deductible applicable under the plan.

(4) Information comparing plan options. Information under this paragraph, with respect to a Medicare+Choice plan for a year, shall include the following:

(A) Benefits. The benefits covered under the plan, including the following:

(i) Covered items and services beyond those provided under the original medicare fee-for-service program.

(ii) Any beneficiary cost sharing, including information on the single deductible (if applicable) under section 1858(b)(1) [42 USCS § 1395w-27a(b)(1)].

(iii) Any maximum limitations on out-of-pocket expenses.

(iv) In the case of an MSA plan, differences in cost sharing, premiums, and balance billing under such a plan compared to under other Medicare+Choice plans.

(v) In the case of a Medicare+Choice private fee-for-service plan, differences in cost sharing, premiums, and balance billing under such a plan compared to under other Medicare+Choice plans.

(vi) The extent to which an enrollee may obtain benefits through out-of-network health care providers.

(vii) The extent to which an enrollee may select among in-network providers and the types of providers participating in the plan's network.

(viii) The organization's coverage of emergency and urgently needed care.

(B) Premiums. (i) In general. The monthly amount of the premium charged to an individual.

(ii) Reductions. The reduction in part B [42 USCS §§ 1395j et seq.] premiums, if any.

(C) Service area. The service area of the plan.

(D) Quality and performance. To the extent available, plan quality and performance indicators for the benefits under the plan (and how they compare to such indicators under the original medicare fee-for-service program under parts A and B [42 USCS §§ 1395c et seq. and 1395j et seq.] in the area involved), including—

(i) disenrollment rates for medicare enrollees electing to receive benefits through the plan for the previous 2 years (excluding disenrollment due to death or moving outside the plan's service area),

(ii) information on medicare enrollee satisfaction,

(iii) information on health outcomes, and

(iv) the recent record regarding compliance of the plan with requirements of this part [42 USCS §§ 1395w-21 et seq.] (as determined by the Secretary).

(E) Supplemental benefits. Supplemental health care benefits, including any reductions in cost-sharing under section 1852(a)(3) [42 USCS § 1395w-22(a)(3)] and the terms and conditions (including premiums) for such benefits.

(5) Maintaining a toll-free number and internet site. The Secretary shall maintain a toll-free number for inquiries regarding Medicare+Choice options and the operation of this part [42 USCS §§ 1395w-21 et seq.] in all areas in which Medicare+Choice plans are offered and an Internet site through which individuals may electronically obtain information on such options and Medicare+Choice plans.

(6) Use of non-Federal entities. The Secretary may enter into contracts with non-Federal entities to carry out activities under this subsection.

(7) Provision of information. A Medicare+Choice organization shall provide the Secretary with such information on the organization and each Medicare+Choice plan it offers as may be required for the preparation of the information referred to in paragraph (2)(A).

(e) Coverage election periods. (1) Initial choice upon eligibility to make election if Medicare+Choice plans available to individual. If, at the time an individual first becomes entitled to benefits under part A [42 USCS §§ 1395c et seq.] and enrolled under part B [42 USCS §§ 1395j et seq.], there is one or more Medicare+Choice plans offered in the area in which the individual resides, the individual shall make the election under this section during a period specified by the Secretary such that if the individual elects a Medicare+Choice plan during the period, coverage under the plan becomes effective as of the first date on which the individual may receive such coverage. If any portion of an individual's initial enrollment period under part B [42 USCS §§ 1395j et seq.] occurs after the end of the annual, coordinated election period described in paragraph (3)(B)(iii), the initial enrollment period under this part [42 USCS §§ 1395w-21 et seq.] shall further extend through the end of the individual's initial enrollment period under part B [42 USCS §§ 1395j et seq.].

(2) Open enrollment and disenrollment opportunities. Subject to paragraph (5)—

(A) Continuous open enrollment and disenrollment through 2005. At any time during the period beginning January 1, 1998, and ending on December 31, 2005, a Medicare+Choice eligible individual may change the election under subsection (a)(1).

(B) Continuous open enrollment and disenrollment for first 6 months during 2006. (i) In general. Subject to clause (ii), subparagraph (C)(iii), and subparagraph (D), at any time during the first 6 months of 2006, or, if the individual first becomes a Medicare+Choice eligible individual during 2006, during the first 6 months during 2006 in which the individual is a Medicare+Choice eligible individual, a Medicare+Choice eligible individual may change the election under subsection (a)(1).

(ii) Limitation of one change. An individual may exercise the right under clause (i) only once. The limitation under this clause shall not apply to changes in elections effected during an annual, coordinated election period under paragraph (3) or during a special enrollment period under the first sentence of paragraph (4).

(C) **[Caution: For provisions applicable before 2011, see 2010 amendment note below.]** Annual 45-day period for disenrollment from MA plans to elect to receive benefits under the original Medicare fee-for-service program. Subject to subparagraph (D), at any time during the first 45 days of a year (beginning with 2011), an individual who is enrolled in a Medicare Advantage plan may change the election under subsection (a)(1), but only with respect to coverage under the original Medicare fee-for-service program under parts A and B [42 USCS §§ 1395c et seq. and 1395j et seq.], and may elect qualified prescription drug coverage in accordance with section 1860D-1 [42 USCS § 1395w-101].

(D) Continuous open enrollment for institutionalized individuals. At any time after 2005 in the case of a Medicare+Choice eligible individual who is institutionalized (as defined by the Secretary), the individual may elect under subsection (a)(1)—

(i) to enroll in a Medicare+Choice plan; or

(ii) to change the Medicare+Choice plan in which the individual is enrolled.

(E) Limited continuous open enrollment of original fee-for-service enrollees in medicare advantage non-prescription drug plans. (i) In general. On any date during the period beginning on January 1, 2007, and ending on July 31, 2007, on which a Medicare Advantage eligible individual is an unenrolled fee-for-service individual (as defined in clause (ii)), the individual may elect under subsection (a)(1) to enroll in a Medicare Advantage plan that is not an MA-PD plan.

(ii) Unenrolled fee-for-service individual defined. In this subparagraph, the term "unenrolled fee-for-service individual" means, with respect to a date, a Medicare Advantage eligible individual who—

(I) is receiving benefits under this title through enrollment in the original medicare fee-for-service program under parts A and B [42 USCS §§ 1395c et seq. and 1395j et seq.];

(II) is not enrolled in an MA plan on such date; and

(III) as of such date is not otherwise eligible to elect to enroll in an MA plan.

(iii) Limitation of one change during the applicable period. An individual may exercise the right under clause (i) only once during the period described in such clause.

(iv) No effect on coverage under a prescription drug plan. Nothing in this subparagraph shall be construed as permitting an individual exercising the right under clause (i)—

(I) who is enrolled in a prescription drug plan under part D [42 USCS §§ 1395w-101 et seq.], to disenroll from such plan or to enroll in a different prescription drug plan; or

(II) who is not enrolled in a prescription drug plan, to enroll in such a plan.

(3) Annual, coordinated election period. (A) In general. Subject to paragraph (5), each individual who is eligible to make an election under this section may change such election during an annual, coordinated election period.

(B) Annual, coordinated election period. For purposes of this section, the term "annual, coordinated election period" means—

(i) with respect to a year before 2002, the month of November before such year;

(ii) with respect to 2002, 2003, 2004, and 2005, the period beginning on November 15 and ending on December 31 of the year before such year;

(iii) with respect to 2006, the period beginning on November 15, 2005, and ending on May 15, 2006;

(iv) with respect to 2007, 2008, 2009, and 2010, the period beginning on November 15 and ending on December 31 of the year before such year; and

(v) with respect to 2012 and succeeding years, the period beginning on October 15 and ending on December 7 of the year before such year.

(C) Medicare+Choice health information fairs. During the fall season of each year (beginning with 1999) and during the period described in subparagraph (B)(iii), in conjunction with the annual coordinated election period defined in subparagraph (B), the Secretary shall provide for a nationally coordinated educational and publicity campaign to inform Medicare+Choice eligible individuals about Medicare+Choice plans and the election process provided under this section.

(D) Special information campaigns. During November 1998 the Secretary shall provide for an educational and publicity campaign to inform Medicare+Choice eligible individuals about the availability of Medicare+Choice plans, and eligible organizations with risk-sharing contracts under section 1876 [42 USCS § 1395mm], offered in different areas and the election process provided under this section. During the period described in subparagraph (B)(iii), the Secretary shall provide for an educational and publicity campaign to inform MA eligible individuals about the availability of MA plans (including MA-PD plans) offered in different areas and the election process provided under this section.

(4) Special election periods. Effective as of January 1, 2006, an individual may discontinue an election of a Medicare+Choice plan offered by a Medicare+Choice organization other than during an annual, coordinated election period and make a new election under this section if—

(A) (i) the certification of the organization or plan under this part [42 USCS §§ 1395w-21 et seq.] has been terminated, or the organization or plan has notified the individual of an impending termination of such certification; or

(ii) the organization has terminated or otherwise discontinued providing the plan in the area in which the individual resides, or has notified the individual of an impending termination or discontinuation of such plan;

(B) the individual is no longer eligible to elect the plan because of a change in the individual's place of residence or other change in circumstances (specified by the Secretary, but not including termination of the individual's enrollment on the basis described in clause (i) or (ii) of subsection (g)(3)(B));

(C) the individual demonstrates (in accordance with guidelines established by the Secretary) that—

(i) the organization offering the plan substantially violated a material provision of the organization's contract under this part [42 USCS §§ 1395w-21 et seq.] in relation to the individual (including the failure to provide an enrollee on a timely basis medically necessary care for which benefits are available under the plan or the failure to provide such covered care in accordance with applicable quality standards); or

(ii) the organization (or an agent or other entity acting on the organization's behalf) materially misrepresented the plan's provisions in marketing the plan to the individual; or

(D) the individual meets such other exceptional conditions as the Secretary may provide.

Effective as of January 1, 2006, an individual who, upon first becoming eligible for benefits under part A [42 USCS §§ 1395c et seq.] at age 65, enrolls in a Medicare+Choice plan under this part [42 USCS §§ 1395w-21 et seq.], the individual may discontinue the election of such plan, and elect coverage under the original fee-for-service plan, at any time during the 12-month period beginning on the effective date of such enrollment.

(5) Special rules for MSA plans. Notwithstanding the preceding provisions of this subsection, an individual—

(A) may elect an MSA plan only during—

(i) an initial open enrollment period described in paragraph (1), or

(ii) an annual, coordinated election period described in paragraph (3)(B);

(B) subject to subparagraph (C), may not discontinue an election of an MSA plan except during the periods described in clause (ii) or (iii) of subparagraph (A) and under the first sentence of paragraph (4); and

(C) who elects an MSA plan during an annual, coordinated election period, and who never previously had elected such a plan, may revoke such election, in a manner determined by the Secretary, by not later than December 15 following the date of the election.

(6) Open enrollment periods. Subject to paragraph (5), a Medicare+Choice organization—

(A) shall accept elections or changes to elections during the initial enrollment periods described in paragraph (1), during the month of November 1998 and during the annual, coordinated election period under paragraph (3) for each subsequent year, and during special election periods described in the first sentence of paragraph (4); and

(B) may accept other changes to elections at such other times as the organization provides.

(f) Effectiveness of elections and changes of elections. (1) During initial coverage election period. An election of coverage made during the initial coverage election period under subsection (e)(1) shall take effect upon the date the individual becomes entitled to benefits under part A [42 USCS §§ 1395c et seq.] and enrolled under part B [42 USCS §§ 1395j et seq.], except as the Secretary may provide (consistent with section 1838 [42 USCS § 1395q]) in order to prevent retroactive coverage.

(2) During continuous open enrollment periods. An election or change of coverage made under subsection (e)(2) shall take effect with the first day of the first calendar month following the date on which the election or change is made.

(3) Annual, coordinated election period. An election or change of coverage made during an annual, coordinated election period (as defined in subsection (e)(3)(B), other than the period described in clause (iii) of such subsection) in a year shall take effect as of the first day of the following year.

(4) Other periods. An election or change of coverage made during any other period under subsection (e)(4) shall take effect in such manner as the Secretary provides in a manner consistent (to the extent practicable) with protecting continuity of health benefit coverage.

(g) Guaranteed issue and renewal. (1) In general. Except as provided in this subsection, a Medicare+Choice organization shall provide that at any time during which elections are accepted under this section with respect to a Medicare+Choice plan offered by the organization, the organization will accept without restrictions individuals who are eligible to make such election.

(2) Priority. If the Secretary determines that a Medicare+Choice organization, in relation to a Medicare+Choice plan it offers, has a capacity limit and the number of Medicare+Choice eligible individuals who elect the plan under this section exceeds the capacity limit, the organization may limit the election of individuals of the plan under this section but only if priority in election is provided—

(A) first to such individuals as have elected the plan at the time of the determination, and

(B) then to other such individuals in such a manner that does not discriminate, on a basis described in section 1852(b) [42 USCS § 1395w-22(b)], among the individuals (who seek to elect the plan).

The preceding sentence shall not apply if it would result in the enrollment of enrollees substantially nonrepresentative, as determined in accordance with regulations of the

Secretary, of the medicare population in the service area of the plan.

(3) Limitation on termination of election. (A) In general. Subject to subparagraph (B), a Medicare+Choice organization may not for any reason terminate the election of any individual under this section for a Medicare+Choice plan it offers.

(B) Basis for termination of election. A Medicare+Choice organization may terminate an individual's election under this section with respect to a Medicare+Choice plan it offers if—

(i) any Medicare+Choice monthly basic and supplemental beneficiary premiums required with respect to such plan are not paid on a timely basis (consistent with standards under section 1856 [42 USCS § 1395w-26] that provide for a grace period for late payment of such premiums),

(ii) the individual has engaged in disruptive behavior (as specified in such standards), or

(iii) the plan is terminated with respect to all individuals under this part [42 USCS §§ 1395w-21 et seq.] in the area in which the individual resides.

(C) Consequence of termination. (i) Terminations for cause. Any individual whose election is terminated under clause (i) or (ii) of subparagraph (B) is deemed to have elected the original medicare fee-for-service program option described in subsection (a)(1)(A).

(ii) Termination based on plan termination or service area reduction. Any individual whose election is terminated under subparagraph (B)(iii) shall have a special election period under subsection (e)(4)(A) in which to change coverage to coverage under another Medicare+Choice plan. Such an individual who fails to make an election during such period is deemed to have chosen to change coverage to the original medicare fee-for-service program option described in subsection (a)(1)(A).

(D) Organization obligation with respect to election forms. Pursuant to a contract under section 1857 [42 USCS § 1395w-27], each Medicare+Choice organization receiving an election form under subsection (c)(2) shall transmit to the Secretary (at such time and in such manner as the Secretary may specify) a copy of such form or such other information respecting the election as the Secretary may specify.

(h) Approval of marketing material and application forms. (1) Submission. No marketing material or application form may be distributed by a Medicare+Choice organization to (or for the use of) Medicare+Choice eligible individuals unless—

(A) at least 45 days (or 10 days in the case described in paragraph (5)) before the date of distribution the organization has submitted the material or form to the Secretary for review, and

(B) the Secretary has not disapproved the distribution of such material or form.

(2) Review. The standards established under section 1856 [42 USCS § 1395w-26] shall include guidelines for the review of any material or form submitted and under such guidelines the Secretary shall disapprove (or later require the correction of) such material or form if the material or form is materially inaccurate or misleading or otherwise makes a material misrepresentation.

(3) Deemed approval (1-stop shopping). In the case of material or form that is submitted under paragraph (1)(A) to the Secretary or a regional office of the Department of Health and Human Services and the Secretary or the office has not disapproved the distribution of marketing material or form under paragraph (1)(B) with respect to a Medicare+Choice plan in an area, the Secretary is deemed not to have disapproved such distribution in all other areas covered by the plan and organization except with regard to that portion of such material or form that is specific only to an area involved.

(4) Prohibition of certain marketing practices. Each Medicare+Choice organization shall conform to fair marketing standards, in relation to Medicare+Choice plans offered under this part [42 USCS §§ 1395w-21 et seq.], included in the standards established under section 1856 [42 USCS § 1395w-26]. Such standards—

(A) shall not permit a Medicare+Choice organization to provide for, subject to subsection (j)(2)(C), cash, gifts, prizes, or other monetary rebates as an inducement for enrollment or otherwise;

(B) may include a prohibition against a Medicare+Choice organization (or agent of such an organization) completing any portion of any election form used to carry out elections under this section on behalf of any individual;

(C) shall not permit a Medicare Advantage organization (or the agents, brokers, and other third parties representing such organization) to conduct the prohibited activities described in subsection (j)(1); and

(D) shall only permit a Medicare Advantage organization (and the agents, brokers, and other third parties representing such organization) to conduct the activities described in subsection (j)(2) in accordance with the limitations established under such subsection.

(5) Special treatment of marketing material following model marketing language. In the case of marketing material of an organization that uses, without modification, proposed model language specified by the Secretary, the period specified in paragraph (1)(A) shall be reduced from 45 days to 10 days.

(6) Required inclusion of plan type in plan name. For plan years beginning on or after January 1, 2010, a Medicare Advantage organization must ensure that the name of each Medicare Advantage plan offered by the Medicare Advantage organization includes the plan type of the plan (using standard terminology developed by the Secretary).

(7) Strengthening the ability of States to act in collaboration with the Secretary to address fraudulent or inappropriate marketing practices. (A) Appointment of agents and brokers. Each Medicare Advantage organization shall—

(i) only use agents and brokers who have been licensed under State law to sell Medicare Advantage plans offered by the Medicare Advantage organization;

(ii) in the case where a State has a State appointment law, abide by such law; and

(iii) report to the applicable State the termination of any such agent or broker, including the reasons for such termination (as required under applicable State law).

(B) Compliance with State information requests. Each Medicare Advantage organization shall comply in a timely manner with any request by a State for information regarding the performance of a licensed agent, broker, or other third party representing the Medicare Advantage organization as part of an investigation by the State into the conduct of the agent, broker, or other third party.

(i) Effect of election of Medicare+Choice plan option. (1) Payments to organizations. Subject to sections 1852(a)(5), 1853(a)(4), 1853(g), 1853(h), 1886(d)(11), 1886(h)(3)(D), and 1853(m) [42 USCS §§ 1395w-22(a)(5), 1395w-23(a)(4), 1395w-23(g), 1395w-23(h), 1395ww(d)(11), 1395ww(h)(3)(D), and 1395w-23(m)], payments under a contract with a Medicare+Choice organization under section 1853(a) [42 USCS § 1395w-23(a)] with respect to an individual electing a Medicare+Choice plan offered by the organization shall be instead of the amounts which (in the absence of the contract) would otherwise be payable under parts A and B [42 USCS §§ 1395c et seq. and 1395j et seq.] for items and services furnished to the individual.

(2) Only organization entitled to payment. Subject to sections 1853(a)(4), 1853(e), 1853(g), 1853(h), 1857(f)(2), 1858(h), 1886(d)(11), and 1886(h)(3)(D) [42 USCS §§ 1395w-23(a)(4), 1395w-23(e), 1395w-23(g), 1395w-23(h), 1395w-27(f)(2), 1395w-27a(h), 1395ww(d)(11), and 1395ww(h)(3)(D)], only the Medicare+Choice organization shall be entitled to receive payments from the Secretary under this title [42 USCS §§ 1395 et seq.] for services furnished to the individual.

(j) Prohibited activities described and limitations on the conduct of certain other activities. (1) Prohibited activities described. The following prohibited activities are described in this paragraph:

(A) Unsolicited means of direct contact. Any unsolicited means of direct contact of prospective enrollees, including soliciting door-to-door or any outbound telemarketing without the prospective enrollee initiating contact.

(B) Cross-selling. The sale of other non-health related products (such as annuities and life insurance) during any sales or marketing activity or presentation conducted with respect to a Medicare Advantage plan.

(C) Meals. The provision of meals of any sort, regardless of value, to prospective enrollees at promotional and sales activities.

(D) Sales and marketing in health care settings and at educational events. Sales and marketing activities for the enrollment of individuals in Medicare Advantage plans that are conducted—

(i) in health care settings in areas where health care is delivered to individuals (such as physician offices and pharmacies), except in the case where such activities are conducted in common areas in health care settings; and

(ii) at educational events.

(2) Limitations. The Secretary shall establish limitations with respect to at least the following:

(A) Scope of marketing appointments. The scope of any appointment with respect to the marketing of a Medicare Advantage plan. Such limitation shall require advance agreement with a prospective enrollee on the scope of the marketing appointment and documentation of such agreement by the Medicare Advantage organization. In the case where the marketing appointment is in person, such documentation shall be in writing.

(B) Co-branding. The use of the name or logo of a co-branded network provider on Medicare Advantage plan membership and marketing materials.

(C) Limitation of gifts to nominal dollar value. The offering of gifts and other promotional items other than those that are of nominal value (as determined by the Secretary) to prospective enrollees at promotional activities.

(D) Compensation. The use of compensation other than as provided under guidelines established by the Secretary. Such guidelines shall ensure that the use of compensation creates incentives for agents and brokers to enroll individuals in the Medicare Advantage plan that is intended to best meet their health care needs.

(E) Required training, annual retraining, and testing of agents, brokers, and other third parties. The use by a Medicare Advantage organization of any individual as an agent, broker, or other third party representing the organization that has not completed an initial training and testing program and does not complete an annual retraining and testing program.

(Aug. 14, 1935, ch 531, Title XVIII, Part C, § 1851, as added Aug. 5, 1997, P. L. 105-33, Title IV, Subtitle A, Ch 1, Subch A, § 4001, 111 Stat. 276; Nov. 29, 1999, P. L. 106-113, Div B, § 1000(a)(6), 113 Stat. 1536; Dec. 21, 2000, P. L. 106-554, § 1(a)(6), 114 Stat. 2763; June 12, 2002, P. L. 107-188, Title V, Subtitle C, § 532(a), (c)(1), 116 Stat. 696; Dec. 8, 2003, P. L. 108-173, Title I, § 102(a), (c)(1), Title II, Subtitle C, §§ 221(a)(1), (d)(5), 222(l)(3)(A), (B), (D), (E), Subtitle D, §§ 231(a), 233(b), (d), 237(b)(2)(A), 117 Stat. 2152, 2154, 2180, 2193, 2206, 2207, 2209, 2213; Dec. 20, 2006, P. L. 109-432, Div B, Title II, § 206(a), 120 Stat. 2990; July 18, 2007, P. L. 110-48, § 2, 121 Stat. 244; July 15, 2008, P. L. 110-275, Title I, Subtitle A, Part I, § 103(a)(1), (b)(1), (c)(1), (d)(1), 122 Stat. 2498, 2499, 2500, 2501; Feb. 17, 2009, P. L. 111-5, Div B, Title IV, Subtitle A, § 4102(d)(2), 123 Stat. 486; March 23, 2010, P. L. 111-148, Title III, Subtitle C, §§ 3201(e)(2)(A)(i), 3204(a)(1), (b), 124 Stat. 446, 456; March 30, 2010, P. L. 111-152, Title I, Subtitle B, § 1102(a), 124 Stat. 1040.)

HISTORY; ANCILLARY LAWS AND DIRECTIVES

Amendments:

2010. Act March 23, 2010 (effective on 1/1/2012, as provided by § 3201(e)(2)(B) of such Act, which appears as a note to this section, and repealed by § 1102(a) of Act March 30, 2010, effective as if included in the enactment of Act March 23, 2010), in subsec. (b)(1), deleted subpara. (C).

Such Act further (applicable to 2011 and succeeding years, as provided by § 3204(a)(2) of such Act), in subsec. (e)(2), substituted subpara. (C) for one which read:

"(C) Continuous open enrollment and disenrollment for first 3 months in subsequent years. (i) In general. Subject to clauses (ii) and (iii) and subparagraph (D), at any time during the first 3 months of a year after 2006, or, if the individual first becomes a Medicare+Choice eligible individual during a year after 2006, during the first 3 months of such year in which the individual is a Medicare+Choice eligible individual, a Medicare+Choice eligible individual may change the election under subsection (a)(1).

"(ii) Limitation of one change during open enrollment period each year. An individual may exercise the right under clause (i) only once during the applicable 3-month period described in such clause in each year. The limitation under this clause shall not apply to changes in elections effected during an annual, coordinated election period under paragraph (3) or during a special enrollment period under paragraph (4).

"(iii) Limitation on exercise of right with respect to prescription drug coverage. Effective for plan years beginning on or after January 1, 2006, in applying clause (i) (and clause (i) of subparagraph (B)) in the case of an individual who—

"(I) is enrolled in an MA plan that does provide qualified prescription drug coverage, the individual may exercise the right under such clause only with respect to coverage under the original fee-for-service plan or coverage under another MA plan that does not provide such coverage and may not exercise such right to obtain coverage under an MA-PD plan or under a prescription drug plan under part D; or

"(II) is enrolled in an MA-PD plan, the individual may exercise the right under such clause only with respect to coverage under another MA-PD plan (and not an MA plan that does not provide qualified prescription drug coverage) or under the original fee-for-service plan and coverage under a prescription drug plan under part D.".

Such Act further, in subsec. (e)(3)(B), in cl. (iii), deleted "and" following the concluding semicolon, in cl. (iv), substituted ", 2008, 2009, and 2010" for "and succeeding years, and substituted the "; and" for a concluding period, and added cl. (v).

Other provisions:

Repeal of provisions relating to effective date of amendments made by § 3201(e)(2) of Act March 23, 2010. Act March 23, 2010, P. L. 111-148, Title III, Subtitle C, § 3201(e)(2)(B), 124 Stat. 447, which formerly appeared as a note to this section, was repealed by Act March 30, 2010, P. L. 111-152, Title I, Subtitle B, § 1102(a), effective as if included in the enactment of Act March 23, 2010. Such note provided that the amendments made by § 3201(e)(2) of the Act to 42 USCS §§ 1395w-21, 1395w-23, and 1395w-24 should take effect on January 1, 2012.

No cuts in guaranteed benefits. Act March 23, 2010, P. L. 111-148, Title III, Subtitle G, § 3602, 124 Stat. 538, provides: "Nothing in this Act [for full classification, consult USCS Tables volumes] shall result in the reduction or elimination of any benefits guaranteed by law to participants in Medicare Advantage plans.".

§ 1395w-22. Benefits and beneficiary protections

(a) Basic benefits. (1) Requirement. (A) In general. Except as provided in section 1859(b)(3) [42 USCS § 1395w-28(b)(3)] for MSA plans and except as provided in paragraph (6) for MA regional plans, each Medicare+Choice plan shall provide to members enrolled under this part [42 USCS

§§ 1395w-21 et seq.], through providers and other persons that meet the applicable requirements of this title [42 USCS §§ 1395 et seq.] and part A of title XI [42 USCS §§ 1301 et seq.], benefits under the original medicare fee-for-service program option (and, for plan years before 2006, additional benefits required under section 1854(f)(1)(A) [42 USCS § 1395w-24(f)(1)(A)]).

(B) Benefits under the original medicare fee-for-service program option defined. (i) In general. For purposes of this part [42 USCS §§ 1395w-21 et seq.], the term "benefits under the original medicare fee-for-service program option" means those items and services (other than hospice care) for which benefits are available under parts A and B [42 USCS §§ 1395c et seq. and 1395j et seq.] to individuals entitled to benefits under part A [42 USCS §§ 1395c et seq.] and enrolled under part B [42 USCS §§ 1395j et seq.], with cost-sharing for those services as required under parts A and B [42 USCS §§ 1395c et seq. and 1395j et seq.] or, subject to clause (iii), an actuarially equivalent level of cost-sharing as determined in this part [42 USCS §§ 1395w-21 et seq.],.

(ii) Special rule for regional plans. In the case of an MA regional plan in determining an actuarially equivalent level of cost-sharing with respect to benefits under the original medicare fee-for-service program option, there shall only be taken into account, with respect to the application of section 1858(b)(2) [42 USCS § 1395w-27a(b)(2)], such expenses only with respect to subparagraph (A) of such section.

(iii) Limitation on variation of cost sharing for certain benefits **[Caution: This clause applies to plan years beginning on or after Jan. 1, 2011, pursuant to § 3202(a)(2) of Act March 23, 2010, P. L. 111-148, which appears as a note to this section.]**. Subject to clause (v), cost-sharing for services described in clause (iv) shall not exceed the cost-sharing required for those services under parts A and B [42 USCS §§ 1395c et seq. and 1395j et seq.].

(iv) Services described **[Caution: This clause applies to plan years beginning on or after Jan. 1, 2011, pursuant to § 3202(a)(2) of Act March 23, 2010, P. L. 111-148, which appears as a note to this section.]**. The following services are described in this clause:

(I) Chemotherapy administration services.

(II) Renal dialysis services (as defined in section 1881(b)(14)(B) [42 USCS § 1395rr(b)(14)(B)]).

(III) Skilled nursing care.

(IV) Such other services that the Secretary determines appropriate (including services that the Secretary determines require a high level of predictability and transparency for beneficiaries).

(v) Exception **[Caution: This clause applies to plan years beginning on or after Jan. 1, 2011, pursuant to § 3202(a)(2) of Act March 23, 2010, P. L. 111-148, which appears as a note to this section.]**. In the case of services described in clause (iv) for which there is no cost-sharing required under parts A and B [42 USCS §§ 1395c et seq. and 1395j et seq.], cost-sharing may be required for those services in accordance with clause (i).

(2) Satisfaction of requirement. (A) In general. A Medicare+Choice plan (other than an MSA plan) offered by a Medicare+Choice organization satisfies paragraph (1)(A), with respect to benefits for items and services furnished other than through a provider or other person that has a contract with the organization offering the plan, if the plan provides payment in an amount so that—

(i) the sum of such payment amount and any cost sharing provided for under the plan, is equal to at least

(ii) the total dollar amount of payment for such items and services as would otherwise be authorized under parts A and B [42 USCS §§ 1395c et seq. and 1395j et seq.] (including any balance billing permitted under such parts).

(B) Reference to related provisions. For provision relating to—

(i) limitations on balance billing against Medicare+Choice organizations for non-contract providers, see sections 1852(k) and 1866(a)(1)(O) [42 USCS §§ 1395w-22(k) and 1395cc(a)(1)(O)], and

(ii) limiting actuarial value of enrollee liability for covered benefits, see section 1854(e) [42 USCS § 1395w-24(e)].

(C) Election of uniform coverage determination. In the case of a Medicare+Choice organization that offers a Medicare+Choice plan in an area in which more than one local coverage determination is applied with respect to different parts of the area, the organization may elect to have the local coverage determination for the part of the area that is most beneficial to Medicare+Choice enrollees (as identified by the Secretary) apply with respect to all Medicare+Choice enrollees enrolled in the plan.

(3) Supplemental benefits. (A) Benefits included subject to Secretary's approval. Each Medicare+Choice organization may provide to individuals enrolled under this part [42 USCS

§§ 1395w-21 et seq.], other than under an MSA plan (without affording those individuals an option to decline the coverage), supplemental health care benefits that the Secretary may approve. The Secretary shall approve any such supplemental benefits unless the Secretary determines that including such supplemental benefits would substantially discourage enrollment by Medicare+Choice eligible individuals with the organization.

(B) At enrollees' option. (i) In general. Subject to clause (ii), a Medicare+Choice organization may provide to individuals enrolled under this part [42 USCS §§ 1395w-21 et seq.] supplemental health care benefits that the individuals may elect, at their option, to have covered.

(ii) Special rule for MSA plans. A Medicare+Choice organization may not provide, under an MSA plan, supplemental health care benefits that cover the deductible described in section 1859(b)(2)(B) [42 USCS § 1395w-28(b)(2)(B)]. In applying the previous sentence, health benefits described in section 1882(u)(2)(B) [42 USCS § 1395ss(u)(2)(B)] shall not be treated as covering such deductible.

(C) Application to Medicare+Choice private fee-for-service plans. Nothing in this paragraph shall be construed as preventing a Medicare+Choice private fee-for-service plan from offering supplemental benefits that include payment for some or all of the balance billing amounts permitted consistent with section 1852(k) [42 USCS § 1395w-22(k)] and coverage of additional services that the plan finds to be medically necessary.

Such benefits may include reductions in cost-sharing below the actuarial value specified in section 1854(e)(4)(B) [42 USCS § 1395w-24(e)(4)(B)].

(4) Organization as secondary payer. Notwithstanding any other provision of law, a Medicare+Choice organization may (in the case of the provision of items and services to an individual under a Medicare+Choice plan under circumstances in which payment under this title [42 USCS §§ 1395 et seq.] is made secondary pursuant to section 1862(b)(2) [42 USCS § 1395y(b)(2)]) charge or authorize the provider of such services to charge, in accordance with the charges allowed under a law, plan, or policy described in such section—

(A) the insurance carrier, employer, or other entity which under such law, plan, or policy is to pay for the provision of such services, or

(B) such individual to the extent that the individual has been paid under such law, plan, or policy for such services.

(5) National coverage determinations and legislative changes in benefits. If there is a national coverage determination or legislative change in benefits required to be provided under this part [42 USCS §§ 1395w-21 et seq.] made in the period beginning on the date of an announcement under section 1853(b) [42 USCS § 1395w-23(b)] and ending on the date of the next announcement under such section and the Secretary projects that the determination will result in a significant change in the costs to a Medicare+Choice organization of providing the benefits that are the subject of such national coverage determination and that such change in costs was not incorporated in the determination of the annual Medicare+Choice capitation rate under section 1853 [42 USCS § 1395w-23] included in the announcement made at the beginning of such period, then, unless otherwise required by law—

(A) such determination or legislative change in benefits shall not apply to contracts under this part [42 USCS §§ 1395w-21 et seq.] until the first contract year that begins after the end of such period, and

(B) if such coverage determination or legislative change provides for coverage of additional benefits or coverage under additional circumstances, section 1851(i)(1) [42 USCS § 1395w-21(i)(1)] shall not apply to payment for such additional benefits or benefits provided under such additional circumstances until the first contract year that begins after the end of such period.

The projection under the previous sentence shall be based on an analysis by the Chief Actuary of the Centers for Medicare & Medicaid Services of the actuarial costs associated with the coverage determination or legislative change in benefits.

(6) Special benefit rules for regional plans. In the case of an MA plan that is an MA regional plan, benefits under the plan shall include the benefits described in paragraphs (1) and (2) of section 1858(b) [42 USCS § 1395w-27a(b)].

(7) Limitation on cost-sharing for dual eligibles and qualified medicare beneficiaries. In the case of an individual who is a full-benefit dual eligible individual (as defined in section 1935(c)(6) [42 USCS § 1396u-5(c)(6)]) or a qualified medicare beneficiary (as defined in section 1905(p)(1) [42 USCS § 1396d(p)(1)]) and who is enrolled in a specialized Medicare Advantage plan for special needs individuals described in section 1859(b)(6)(B)(ii) [42 USCS § 1395w-28(b)(6)(B)(ii)], the plan may not impose cost-sharing that exceeds the amount of

cost-sharing that would be permitted with respect to the individual under title XIX [42 USCS §§ 1396 et seq.] if the individual were not enrolled in such plan.

(b) Antidiscrimination. (1) Beneficiaries. (A) In general. A Medicare+Choice organization may not deny, limit, or condition the coverage or provision of benefits under this part [42 USCS §§ 1395w-21 et seq.], for individuals permitted to be enrolled with the organization under this part [42 USCS §§ 1395w-21 et seq.], based on any health status-related factor described in section 2702(a)(1) of the Public Health Service Act [42 USCS § 300gg-1(a)(1)]. The Secretary shall not approve a plan of an organization if the Secretary determines that the design of the plan and its benefits are likely to substantially discourage enrollment by certain MA eligible individuals with the organization.

(B) Construction. Subparagraph (A) shall not be construed as requiring a Medicare+Choice organization to enroll individuals who are determined to have end-stage renal disease, except as provided under section 1851(a)(3)(B) [42 USCS § 1395w-21(a)(3)(B)].

(2) Providers. A Medicare+Choice organization shall not discriminate with respect to participation, reimbursement, or indemnification as to any provider who is acting within the scope of the provider's license or certification under applicable State law, solely on the basis of such license or certification. This paragraph shall not be construed to prohibit a plan from including providers only to the extent necessary to meet the needs of the plan's enrollees or from establishing any measure designed to maintain quality and control costs consistent with the responsibilities of the plan.

(c) Disclosure requirements. (1) Detailed description of plan provisions. A Medicare+Choice organization shall disclose, in clear, accurate, and standardized form to each enrollee with a Medicare+Choice plan offered by the organization under this part [42 USCS §§ 1395w-21 et seq.] at the time of enrollment and at least annually thereafter, the following information regarding such plan:

(A) Service area. The plan's service area.

(B) Benefits. Benefits offered under the plan, including information described in section 1851(d)(3)(A) [42 USCS § 1395w-21(d)(3)(A)] and exclusions from coverage and, if it is an MSA plan, a comparison of benefits under such a plan with benefits under other Medicare+Choice plans.

(C) Access. The number, mix, and distribution of plan providers, out-of-network coverage (if any) provided by the plan, and any point-of-service option (including the supplemental premium for such option).

(D) Out-of-area coverage. Out-of-area coverage provided by the plan.

(E) Emergency coverage. Coverage of emergency services, including—

(i) the appropriate use of emergency services, including use of the 911 telephone system or its local equivalent in emergency situations and an explanation of what constitutes an emergency situation;

(ii) the process and procedures of the plan for obtaining emergency services; and

(iii) the locations of (I) emergency departments, and (II) other settings, in which plan physicians and hospitals provide emergency services and post-stabilization care.

(F) Supplemental benefits. Supplemental benefits available from the organization offering the plan, including—

(i) whether the supplemental benefits are optional,

(ii) the supplemental benefits covered, and

(iii) the Medicare+Choice monthly supplemental beneficiary premium for the supplemental benefits.

(G) Prior authorization rules. Rules regarding prior authorization or other review requirements that could result in nonpayment.

(H) Plan grievance and appeals procedures. All plan appeal or grievance rights and procedures.

(I) Quality improvement program. A description of the organization's quality improvement program under subsection (e).

(2) Disclosure upon request. Upon request of a Medicare+Choice eligible individual, a Medicare+Choice organization must provide the following information to such individual:

(A) The general coverage information and general comparative plan information made available under clauses (i) and (ii) of section 1851(d)(2)(A) [42 USCS § 1395w-21(d)(2)(A)].

(B) Information on procedures used by the organization to control utilization of services and expenditures.

(C) Information on the number of grievances, redeterminations, and appeals and on the disposition in the aggregate of such matters.

(D) An overall summary description as to the method of compensation of participating physicians.

(d) Access to services. (1) In general. A Medicare+Choice organization offering a Medicare+Choice plan may select the providers from whom the benefits under the plan are provided so long as—

(A) the organization makes such benefits available and accessible to each individual electing the plan within the plan service area with reasonable promptness and in a manner which assures continuity in the provision of benefits;

(B) when medically necessary the organization makes such benefits available and accessible 24 hours a day and 7 days a week;

(C) the plan provides for reimbursement with respect to services which are covered under subparagraphs (A) and (B) and which are provided to such an individual other than through the organization, if—

(i) the services were not emergency services (as defined in paragraph (3)), but (I) the services were medically necessary and immediately required because of an unforeseen illness, injury, or condition, and (II) it was not reasonable given the circumstances to obtain the services through the organization,

(ii) the services were renal dialysis services and were provided other than through the organization because the individual was temporarily out of the plan's service area, or

(iii) the services are maintenance care or post-stabilization care covered under the guidelines established under paragraph (2);

(D) the organization provides access to appropriate providers, including credentialed specialists, for medically necessary treatment and services; and

(E) coverage is provided for emergency services (as defined in paragraph (3)) without regard to prior authorization or the emergency care provider's contractual relationship with the organization.

(2) Guidelines respecting coordination of post-stabilization care. A Medicare+Choice plan shall comply with such guidelines as the Secretary may prescribe relating to promoting efficient and timely coordination of appropriate maintenance and post-stabilization care of an enrollee after the enrollee has been determined to be stable under section 1867 [42 USCS § 1395dd].

(3) Definition of emergency services. In this subsection—

(A) In general. The term "emergency services" means, with respect to an individual enrolled with an organization, covered inpatient and outpatient services that—

(i) are furnished by a provider that is qualified to furnish such services under this title [42 USCS §§ 1395 et seq.], and

(ii) are needed to evaluate or stabilize an emergency medical condition (as defined in subparagraph (B)).

(B) Emergency medical condition based on prudent layperson. The term "emergency medical condition" means a medical condition manifesting itself by acute symptoms of sufficient severity (including severe pain) such that a prudent layperson, who possesses an average knowledge of health and medicine, could reasonably expect the absence of immediate medical attention to result in—

(i) placing the health of the individual (or, with respect to a pregnant woman, the health of the woman or her unborn child) in serious jeopardy,

(ii) serious impairment to bodily functions, or

(iii) serious dysfunction of any bodily organ or part.

(4) Assuring access to services in Medicare+Choice private fee-for-service plans. In addition to any other requirements under this part [42 USCS §§ 1395w-21 et seq.], in the case of a Medicare+Choice private fee-for-service plan, the organization offering the plan must demonstrate to the Secretary that the organization has sufficient number and range of health care professionals and providers willing to provide services under the terms of the plan. Subject to paragraphs (5) and (6), the Secretary shall find that an organization has met such requirement with respect to any category of health care professional or provider if, with respect to that category of provider—

(A) the plan has established payment rates for covered services furnished by that category of provider that are not less than the payment rates provided for under part A [42 USCS §§ 1395c et seq.], part B [42 USCS §§ 1395j et seq.], or both, for such services, or

(B) the plan has contracts or agreements (other than deemed contracts or agreements under subsection (j)(6)) with a sufficient number and range of providers within such category to meet the access standards in subparagraphs (A) through (E) of paragraph (1),

or a combination of both. The previous sentence shall not be construed as restricting the persons from whom enrollees under such a plan may obtain covered benefits, except that, if a plan entirely meets such requirement with respect to a category of health care professional or provider on the basis of subparagraph (B), it may provide for a higher beneficiary copayment in the case of health care professionals and providers of that category who do not have contracts or agreements (other than deemed contracts or agreements under subsection (j)(6)) to provide covered services under the terms of the plan.

(5) Requirement of certain nonemployer medicare advantage private fee-for-service plans to use contracts with providers. (A) In general. For plan year 2011 and subsequent plan years, in the case of a Medicare Advantage private fee-for-service plan not described in paragraph (1) or (2) of section 1857(i) [42 USCS § 1395w-27(i)] operating in a network area (as defined in subparagraph (B)), the plan shall meet the access standards under paragraph (4) in that area only through entering into written contracts as provided for under subparagraph (B) of such paragraph and not, in whole or in part, through the establishment of payment rates meeting the requirements under subparagraph (A) of such paragraph.

(B) Network area defined. For purposes of subparagraph (A), the term "network area" means, for a plan year, an area which the Secretary identifies (in the Secretary's announcement of the proposed payment rates for the previous plan year under section 1853(b)(1)(B) [42 USCS § 1395w-23(b)(1)(B)]) as having at least 2 network-based plans (as defined in subparagraph (C)) with enrollment under this part as of the first day of the year in which such announcement is made.

(C) Network-based plan defined. (i) In general. For purposes of subparagraph (B), the term "network-based plan" means—

(I) except as provided in clause (ii), a Medicare Advantage plan that is a coordinated care plan described in section 1851(a)(2)(A)(i) [USCS § 1395w-21(a)(2)(A)(i)];

(II) a network-based MSA plan; and

(III) a reasonable cost reimbursement plan under section 1876 [42 USCS § 1395mm].

(ii) Exclusion of non-network regional PPOs. The term "network-based plan" shall not include an MA regional plan that, with respect to the area, meets access adequacy standards under this part [42 USCS §§ 1395w-21 et seq.] substantially through the authority of section 422.112(a)(1)(ii) of title 42, Code of Federal Regulations, rather than through written contracts.

(6) Requirement of all employer Medicare Advantage private fee-for-service plans to use contracts with providers. For plan year 2011 and subsequent plan years, in the case of a Medicare Advantage private fee-for-service plan that is described in paragraph (1) or (2) of section 1857(i) [42 USCS § 1395w-27(i)], the plan shall meet the access standards under paragraph (4) only through entering into written contracts as provided for under subparagraph (B) of such paragraph and not, in whole or in part, through the establishment of payment rates meeting the requirements under subparagraph (A) of such paragraph.

(e) Quality improvement program. (1) In general. Each MA organization shall have an ongoing quality improvement program for the purpose of improving the quality of care provided to enrollees in each MA plan offered by such organization.

(2) Chronic care improvement programs. As part of the quality improvement program under paragraph (1), each MA organization shall have a chronic care improvement program. Each chronic care improvement program shall have a method for monitoring and identifying enrollees with multiple or sufficiently severe chronic conditions that meet criteria established by the organization for participation under the program.

(3) Data. (A) Collection, analysis, and reporting. (i) In general. Except as provided in clauses (ii) and (iii) with respect to plans described in such clauses and subject to subparagraph (B), as part of the quality improvement program under paragraph (1), each MA organization shall provide for the collection, analysis, and reporting of data that permits the measurement of health outcomes and other indices of quality. With respect to MA private fee-for-service plans and MSA plans, the requirements under the preceding sentence may not exceed the requirements under this subparagraph with respect to MA local plans that are preferred provider organization plans, except that, for plan year 2010, the limitation under clause (iii) shall not apply and such requirements shall apply only with respect to administrative claims data.

(ii) Special requirements for specialized MA plans for special needs individuals. In addition to the data required to be collected, analyzed, and reported under clause (i) and notwithstanding the limitations under subparagraph (B), as part of the quality improvement program under paragraph (1), each MA organization offering a specialized Medicare Advantage plan for special needs individuals shall provide for the collection, analysis, and reporting of data that permits the measurement of health outcomes and other indices of quality with respect to the requirements described in paragraphs (2) through (5) of subsection (f). Such data may be based on claims data and shall be at the plan level.

(iii) Application to local preferred provider organizations and MA regional plans. Clause (i) shall apply to MA organizations with respect to MA local plans that are preferred provider organization plans and to MA regional plans only insofar as services are furnished by providers or services, physicians, and other health care practitioners and suppliers that have contracts with such organization to furnish services under such plans.

(iv) Definition of preferred provider organization plan. In this subparagraph, the term "preferred provider organization plan" means an MA plan that—

(I) has a network of providers that have agreed to a contractually specified reimbursement for covered benefits with the organization offering the plan;

(II) provides for reimbursement for all covered benefits regardless of whether such benefits are provided within such network of providers; and

(III) is offered by an organization that is not licensed or organized under State law as a health maintenance organization.

(B) Limitations. (i) Types of data. The Secretary shall not collect under subparagraph (A) data on quality, outcomes, and beneficiary satisfaction to facilitate consumer choice and program administration other than the types of data that were collected by the Secretary as of November 1, 2003.

(ii) Changes in types of data. Subject to subclause (iii), the Secretary may only change the types of data that are required to be submitted under subparagraph (A) after submitting to Congress a report on the reasons for such changes that was prepared in consultation with MA organizations and private accrediting bodies.

(iii) Construction. Nothing in the subsection shall be construed as restricting the ability of the Secretary to carry out the duties under section 1851(d)(4)(D) [42 USCS § 1395w-21(d)(4)(D)].

(4) Treatment of accreditation. (A) In general The Secretary shall provide that a Medicare+Choice organization is deemed to meet all the requirements described in any specific clause of subparagraph (B) if the organization is accredited (and periodically reaccredited) by a private accrediting organization under a process that the Secretary has determined assures that the accrediting organization applies and enforces standards that meet or exceed the standards established under section 1856 [42 USCS § 1395w-26] to carry out the requirements in such clause.

(B) Requirements described. The provisions described in this subparagraph are the following:

(i) Paragraphs (1) through (3) of this subsection (relating to quality improvement programs).

(ii) Subsection (b) (relating to antidiscrimination).

(iii) Subsection (d) (relating to access to services).

(iv) Subsection (h) (relating to confidentiality and accuracy of enrollee records).

(v) Subsection (i) (relating to information on advance directives).

(vi) Subsection (j) (relating to provider participation rules).

(vii) The requirements described in section 1860D-4(j) [42 USCS § 1395w-104(j)], to the extent such requirements apply under section 1860D-21(c) [42 USCS § 1395w-131(c)].

(C) Timely action on applications **[Caution: For provisions applicable to accreditations of hospitals granted before July 15, 2010, see 2008 amendment note below.]**. The Secretary shall determine, within 210 days after the date the Secretary receives an application by a private accrediting organization and using the criteria specified in section 1865(a)(2) [42 USCS § 1395bb(a)(2)], whether the process of the private accrediting organization meets the requirements with respect to any specific clause in subparagraph (B) with respect to which the application is made. The Secretary may not deny such an application on the basis that it seeks to meet the requirements with respect to only one, or more than one, such specific clause.

(D) Construction. Nothing in this paragraph shall be construed as limiting the authority of the Secretary under section 1857 [42 USCS § 1395w-27], including the authority to terminate contracts with Medicare+Choice organizations under subsection (c)(2) of such section.

(f) Grievance mechanism. Each Medicare+Choice organization must provide meaningful procedures for hearing and resolving grievances between the organization (including any entity or individual through which the organization provides health care services) and enrollees with Medicare+Choice plans of the organization under this part [42 USCS §§ 1395w-21 et seq.].

(g) Coverage determinations, reconsiderations, and appeals. (1) Determinations by organization. (A) In general. A Medicare+Choice organization shall have a procedure for making determinations regarding whether an individual enrolled with the plan of the organization under this part [42 USCS §§ 1395w-21 et seq.] is entitled to receive a health service under this section and the amount (if any) that the individual is required to pay with respect to such service. Subject to paragraph (3), such procedures shall provide for such determination to be made on a timely basis.

(B) Explanation of determination. Such a determination that denies coverage, in whole or in part, shall be in writing and shall include a statement in understandable language of the reasons for the denial and a description of the reconsideration and appeals processes.

(2) Reconsiderations. (A) In general. The organization shall provide for reconsideration of a determination described in paragraph (1)(B) upon request by the enrollee involved. The reconsideration shall be within a time period specified by the Secretary, but shall be made, subject to paragraph (3), not later than 60 days after the date of the receipt of the request for reconsideration.

(B) Physician decision on certain reconsiderations. A reconsideration relating to a determination to deny coverage based on a lack of medical necessity shall be made only by a physician with appropriate expertise in the field of medicine which necessitates treatment who is other than a physician involved in the initial determination.

(3) Expedited determinations and reconsiderations. (A) Receipt of requests. (i) Enrollee requests. An enrollee in a Medicare+Choice plan may request, either in writing or orally, an expedited determination under paragraph (1) or an expedited reconsideration under paragraph (2) by the Medicare+Choice organization.

(ii) Physician requests. A physician, regardless whether the physician is affiliated with the organization or not, may request, either in writing or orally, such an expedited determination or reconsideration.

(B) Organization procedures. (i) In general. The Medicare+Choice organization shall maintain procedures for expediting organization determinations and reconsiderations when, upon request of an enrollee, the organization determines that the application of the normal time frame for making a determination (or a reconsideration involving a determination) could seriously jeopardize the life or health of the enrollee or the enrollee's ability to regain maximum function.

(ii) Expedition required for physician requests. In the case of a request for an expedited determination or reconsideration made under subparagraph (A)(ii), the organization shall expedite the determination or reconsideration if the request indicates that the application of the normal time frame for making a determination (or a reconsideration involving a determination) could seriously jeopardize the life or health of the enrollee or the enrollee's ability to regain maximum function.

(iii) Timely response. In cases described in clauses (i) and (ii), the organization shall notify the enrollee (and the physician involved, as appropriate) of the determination or reconsideration under time limitations established by the Secretary, but not later than 72 hours of the time of receipt of the request for the determination or reconsideration (or receipt of the information necessary to make the determination or reconsideration), or such longer period as the Secretary may permit in specified cases.

(4) Independent review of certain coverage denials. The Secretary shall contract with an independent, outside entity to review and resolve in a timely manner reconsiderations that affirm denial of coverage, in whole or in part. The provisions of section 1869(c)(5) [42 USCS § 1395ff(c)(5)] shall apply to independent outside entities under contract with the Secretary under this paragraph.

(5) An enrollee with a Medicare+Choice plan of a Medicare+Choice organization under this part [42 USCS §§ 1395w-21 et seq.] who is dissatisfied by reason of the enrollee's failure to receive any health service to which the enrollee believes the enrollee is entitled and at no greater charge than the enrollee believes the enrollee is required to pay is entitled, if the amount in controversy is $100 or more, to a hearing before the Secretary to the same extent as is provided in section 205(b) [42 USCS § 405(b)], and in any such hearing the Secretary shall make the organization a party. If the amount in controversy is $1,000 or more, the individual or organization shall, upon notifying the other party, be entitled to judicial review of the Secretary's final decision as provided in section 205(g) [42 USCS § 405(g)], and both the individual and the organization shall be entitled to be parties to that judicial review. In applying subsections (b) and (g) of section 205 [42 USCS § 405(b) and (g)] as provided in this paragraph, and in applying section 205(l) [42 USCS § 405(l)] thereto, any reference therein to the Commissioner of Social Security or the Social Security Administration shall be considered a reference to the Secretary or the Department of Health and Human Services, respectively. The provisions of section 1869(b)(1)(E)(iii) [42 USCS § 1395ff(b)(1)(E)(iii)] shall apply with respect to dollar amounts specified in the first 2 sentences of this paragraph in the same manner as they apply to the dollar amounts specified in

section 1869(b)(1)(E)(i) [42 USCS § 1395ff(b)(1)(E)(i)].

(h) Confidentiality and accuracy of enrollee records. Insofar as a Medicare+Choice organization maintains medical records or other health information regarding enrollees under this part [42 USCS §§ 1395w-21 et seq.], the Medicare+Choice organization shall establish procedures—

(1) to safeguard the privacy of any individually identifiable enrollee information;

(2) to maintain such records and information in a manner that is accurate and timely; and

(3) to assure timely access of enrollees to such records and information.

(i) Information on advance directives. Each Medicare+Choice organization shall meet the requirement of section 1866(f) [42 USCS § 1395cc(f)] (relating to maintaining written policies and procedures respecting advance directives).

(j) Rules regarding provider participation. (1) Procedures. Insofar as a Medicare+Choice organization offers benefits under a Medicare+Choice plan through agreements with physicians, the organization shall establish reasonable procedures relating to the participation (under an agreement between a physician and the organization) of physicians under such a plan. Such procedures shall include—

(A) providing notice of the rules regarding participation,

(B) providing written notice of participation decisions that are adverse to physicians, and

(C) providing a process within the organization for appealing such adverse decisions, including the presentation of information and views of the physician regarding such decision.

(2) Consultation in medical policies. A Medicare+Choice organization shall consult with physicians who have entered into participation agreements with the organization regarding the organization's medical policy, quality, and medical management procedures.

(3) Prohibiting interference with provider advice to enrollees. (A) In general. Subject to subparagraphs (B) and (C), a Medicare+Choice organization (in relation to an individual enrolled under a Medicare+Choice plan offered by the organization under this part [42 USCS §§ 1395w-21 et seq.]) shall not prohibit or otherwise restrict a covered health care professional (as defined in subparagraph (D)) from advising such an individual who is a patient of the professional about the health status of the individual or medical care or treatment for the individual's condition or disease, regardless of whether benefits for such care or treatment are provided under the plan, if the professional is acting within the lawful scope of practice.

(B) Conscience protection. Subparagraph (A) shall not be construed as requiring a Medicare+Choice plan to provide, reimburse for, or provide coverage of a counseling or referral service if the Medicare+Choice organization offering the plan—

(i) objects to the provision of such service on moral or religious grounds; and

(ii) in the manner and through the written instrumentalities such Medicare+Choice organization deems appropriate, makes available information on its policies regarding such service to prospective enrollees before or during enrollment and to enrollees within 90 days after the date that the organization or plan adopts a change in policy regarding such a counseling or referral service.

(C) Construction. Nothing in subparagraph (B) shall be construed to affect disclosure requirements under State law or under the Employee Retirement Income Security Act of 1974.

(D) Health care professional defined. For purposes of this paragraph, the term "health care professional" means a physician (as defined in section 1861(r) [42 USCS § 1395x(r)]) or other health care professional if coverage for the professional's services is provided under the Medicare+Choice plan for the services of the professional. Such term includes a podiatrist, optometrist, chiropractor, psychologist, dentist, physician assistant, physical or occupational therapist and therapy assistant, speech-language pathologist, audiologist, registered or licensed practical nurse (including nurse practitioner, clinical nurse specialist, certified registered nurse anesthetist, and certified nurse-midwife), licensed certified social worker, registered respiratory therapist, and certified respiratory therapy technician.

(4) Limitations on physician incentive plans. (A) In general. No Medicare+Choice organization may operate any physician incentive plan (as defined in subparagraph (B)) unless the organization provides assurances satisfactory to the Secretary that the following requirements are met:

(i) No specific payment is made directly or indirectly under the plan to a physician or physician group as an inducement to reduce or limit medically necessary services provided with respect to a specific individual enrolled with the organization.

(ii) If the plan places a physician or physician group at substantial financial risk (as determined by the Secretary) for services not provided by the physician or physician group, the organization provides stop-loss protection for the physician or group that is adequate and appropriate, based on standards developed by the Secretary that take into account the number of physicians placed at such substantial financial risk in the group or under the plan and the number of individuals enrolled with the organization who receive services from the physician or group.

(B) Physician incentive plan defined. In this paragraph, the term "physician incentive plan" means any compensation arrangement between a Medicare+Choice organization and a physician or physician group that may directly or indirectly have the effect of reducing or limiting services provided with respect to individuals enrolled with the organization under this part [42 USCS §§ 1395w-21 et seq.].

(5) Limitation on provider indemnification. A Medicare+Choice organization may not provide (directly or indirectly) for a health care professional, provider of services, or other entity providing health care services (or group of such professionals, providers, or entities) to indemnify the organization against any liability resulting from a civil action brought for any damage caused to an enrollee with a Medicare+Choice plan of the organization under this part [42 USCS §§ 1395w-21 et seq.] by the organization's denial of medically necessary care.

(6) Special rules for Medicare+Choice private fee-for-service plans. For purposes of applying this part [42 USCS §§ 1395w-21 et seq.] (including subsection (k)(1)) and section 1866(a)(1)(O) [42 USCS § 1395cc(a)(1)(O)], a hospital (or other provider of services), a physician or other health care professional, or other entity furnishing health care services is treated as having an agreement or contract in effect with a Medicare+Choice organization (with respect to an individual enrolled in a Medicare+Choice private fee-for-service plan it offers), if—

(A) the provider, professional, or other entity furnishes services that are covered under the plan to such an enrollee; and

(B) before providing such services, the provider, professional, or other entity—

(i) has been informed of the individual's enrollment under the plan, and

(ii) either—

(I) has been informed of the terms and conditions of payment for such services under the plan, or

(II) is given a reasonable opportunity to obtain information concerning such terms and conditions,

in a manner reasonably designed to effect informed agreement by a provider.

The previous sentence shall only apply in the absence of an explicit agreement between such a provider, professional, or other entity and the Medicare+Choice organization.

(7) Promotion of e-prescribing by MA plans. (A) In general. An MA-PD plan may provide for a separate payment or otherwise provide for a differential payment for a participating physician that prescribes covered part D drugs in accordance with an electronic prescription drug program that meets standards established under section 1860D-4(e) [42 USCS § 1395w-104(e)].

(B) Considerations. Such payment may take into consideration the costs of the physician in implementing such a program and may also be increased for those participating physicians who significantly increase—

(i) formulary compliance;

(ii) lower cost, therapeutically equivalent alternatives;

(iii) reductions in adverse drug interactions; and

(iv) efficiencies in filing prescriptions through reduced administrative costs.

(C) Structure. Additional or increased payments under this subsection may be structured in the same manner as medication therapy management fees are structured under section 1860D-4(c)(2)(E) [42 USCS § 1395w-104(c)(2)(E)].

(k) Treatment of services furnished by certain providers. (1) In general. Except as provided in paragraph (2), a physician or other entity (other than a provider of services) that does not have a contract establishing payment amounts for services furnished to an individual enrolled under this part [42 USCS §§ 1395w-21 et seq.] with a Medicare+Choice organization described in section 1851(a)(2)(A) [42 USCS § 1395w-21(a)(2)(A)] or with an organization offering an MSA plan shall accept as payment in full for covered services under this title [42 USCS §§ 1395 et seq.] that are furnished to such an individual the amounts that the physician or other entity could collect if the individual were not so enrolled. Any penalty or other provision of law that applies to such a payment with respect to an individual entitled to benefits under this title [42 USCS §§ 1395 et seq.] (but not enrolled with a Medicare+Choice organization under this part [42 USCS §§ 1395w-21 et seq.]) also applies with respect to an individual so enrolled.

(2) Application to Medicare+Choice private fee-for-service plans. (A) Balance billing limits under Medicare+Choice private fee-for-service plans in case of contract providers. (i) In general. In the case of an individual enrolled in a Medicare+Choice private fee-for-service plan under this part [42 USCS §§ 1395w-21 et seq.], a physician, provider of services, or other entity that has a contract (including through the operation of subsection (j)(6)) establishing a payment rate for services furnished to the enrollee shall accept as payment in full for covered services under this title [42 USCS §§ 1395 et seq.] that are furnished to such an individual an amount not to exceed (including any deductibles, coinsurance, copayments, or balance billing otherwise permitted under the plan) an amount equal to 115 percent of such payment rate.

(ii) Procedures to enforce limits. The Medicare+Choice organization that offers such a plan shall establish procedures, similar to the procedures described in section 1848(g)(1)(A) [42 USCS § 1395w-4(g)(1)(A)], in order to carry out the previous sentence.

(iii) Assuring enforcement. If the Medicare+Choice organization fails to establish and enforce procedures required under clause (ii), the organization is subject to intermediate sanctions under section 1857(g) [42 USCS § 1395w-27(g)].

(B) Enrollee liability for noncontract providers. For provision—

(i) establishing minimum payment rate in the case of noncontract providers under a Medicare+Choice private fee-for-service plan, see section 1852(a)(2) [42 USCS § 1395w-22(a)(2)]; or

(ii) limiting enrollee liability in the case of covered services furnished by such providers, see paragraph (1) and section 1866(a)(1)(O) [42 USCS § 1395cc(a)(1)(O)].

(C) Information on beneficiary liability. (i) In general. Each Medicare+Choice organization that offers a Medicare+Choice private fee-for-service plan shall provide that enrollees under the plan who are furnished services for which payment is sought under the plan are provided an appropriate explanation of benefits (consistent with that provided under parts A and B [42 USCS §§ 1395c et seq. and 1395j et seq.] and, if applicable, under medicare supplemental policies) that includes a clear statement of the amount of the enrollee's liability (including any liability for balance billing consistent with this subsection) with respect to payments for such services.

(ii) Advance notice before receipt of inpatient hospital services and certain other services. In addition, such organization shall, in its terms and conditions of payments to hospitals for inpatient hospital services and for other services identified by the Secretary for which the amount of the balance billing under subparagraph (A) could be substantial, require the hospital to provide to the enrollee, before furnishing such services and if the hospital imposes balance billing under subparagraph (A)—

(I) notice of the fact that balance billing is permitted under such subparagraph for such services, and

(II) a good faith estimate of the likely amount of such balance billing (if any), with respect to such services, based upon the presenting condition of the enrollee.

(l) Return to home skilled nursing facilities for covered post-hospital extended care services. (1) Ensuring return to home SNF. (A) In general. In providing coverage of post-hospital extended care services, a Medicare+Choice plan shall provide for such coverage through a home skilled nursing facility if the following conditions are met:

(i) Enrollee election. The enrollee elects to receive such coverage through such facility.

(ii) SNF agreement. The facility has a contract with the Medicare+Choice organization for the provision of such services, or the facility agrees to accept substantially similar payment under the same terms and conditions that apply to similarly situated skilled nursing facilities that are under contract with the Medicare+Choice organization for the provision of such services and through which the enrollee would otherwise receive such services.

(B) Manner of payment to home SNF. The organization shall provide payment to the home skilled nursing facility consistent with the contract or the agreement described in subparagraph (A)(ii), as the case may be.

(2) No less favorable coverage. The coverage provided under paragraph (1) (including scope of services, cost-sharing, and other criteria of coverage) shall be no less favorable to the enrollee than the coverage that would be provided to the enrollee with respect to a skilled nursing facility the post-hospital extended care services of which are otherwise covered under the Medicare+Choice plan.

(3) Rule of construction. Nothing in this subsection shall be construed to do the following:

(A) To require coverage through a skilled nursing facility that is not otherwise qualified to provide benefits under part A [1395c et seq.] for medicare beneficiaries not enrolled in a

Medicare+Choice plan.

(B) To prevent a skilled nursing facility from refusing to accept, or imposing conditions upon the acceptance of, an enrollee for the receipt of post-hospital extended care services.

(4) Definitions. In this subsection:

(A) Home skilled nursing facility. The term "home skilled nursing facility" means, with respect to an enrollee who is entitled to receive post-hospital extended care services under a Medicare+Choice plan, any of the following skilled nursing facilities:

(i) SNF residence at time of admission. The skilled nursing facility in which the enrollee resided at the time of admission to the hospital preceding the receipt of such post-hospital extended care services.

(ii) SNF in continuing care retirement community. A skilled nursing facility that is providing such services through a continuing care retirement community (as defined in subparagraph (B)) which provided residence to the enrollee at the time of such admission.

(iii) SNF residence of spouse at time of discharge. The skilled nursing facility in which the spouse of the enrollee is residing at the time of discharge from such hospital.

(B) Continuing care retirement community. The term "continuing care retirement community" means, with respect to an enrollee in a Medicare+Choice plan, an arrangement under which housing and health-related services are provided (or arranged) through an organization for the enrollee under an agreement that is effective for the life of the enrollee or for a specified period.

(Aug. 14, 1935, ch 531, Title XVIII, Part C, § 1852, as added Aug. 5, 1997, P. L. 105-33, Title IV, Subtitle A, Ch 1, Subch A, § 4001, 111 Stat. 286; Nov. 29, 1999, P. L. 106-113, Div B, § 1000(a)(6), 113 Stat. 1536; Dec. 21, 2000, P. L. 106-554, § 1(a)(6), 114 Stat. 2763; Dec. 8, 2003, P. L. 108-173, Title I, § 102(b), Title II, Subtitle B, § 211(j), Subtitle C, §§ 221(d)(3), 222(a)(2), (3), (h), (l)(1), Subtitle D, § 233(a)(1), (2), (c), Title VII, Subtitle C, § 722(a), (b), Title IX, § 900(e)(1)(F), Subtitle D, § 940(b)(2)(A), Title E, § 948(b)(2), 117 Stat. 2153, 2180, 2193, 2195, 2204, 2206, 2209, 2347, 2371, 2417, 2426; July 15, 2008, P. L. 110-275, Title I, Subtitle B, § 125(b)(6), Subtitle D, §§ 162(a)(1)–(3)(A), 163(a), (b), 164(f)(1), 165(a), 122 Stat. 2519, 2569, 2571, 2574, 2575; March 23, 2010, P. L. 111-148, Title III, Subtitle C, § 3202(a)(1), 124 Stat. 454.)

HISTORY; ANCILLARY LAWS AND DIRECTIVES

Amendments:

2010. Act March 23, 2010 (applicable to plan years beginning on or after 1/1/2011, as provided by § 3202(a)(2) of such Act, which appears as a note to this section), in subsec. (a)(1)(B), in cl. (i), inserted ", subject to clause (iii),", and added cls. (iii)–(v).

Other provisions:

Applicability of amendments made by § 3202(a) of Act March 23, 2010. Act March 23, 2010, P. L. 111-148, Title III, Subtitle C, § 3202(a)(2), 124 Stat. 454, provides: "The amendments made by this subsection [amending subsec. (a)(1)(B) of this section] shall apply to plan years beginning on or after January 1, 2011.".

§ 1395w-23. Payments to Medicare+Choice organizations

(a) Payments to organizations. (1) Monthly payments. (A) In general. Under a contract under section 1857 [42 USCS § 1395w-27] and subject to subsections (e), (g), (i), and (l) and section 1859(e)(4) [42 USCS § 1395w-28(e)(4)], the Secretary shall make monthly payments under this section in advance to each Medicare+Choice organization, with respect to coverage of an individual under this part [42 USCS §§ 1395w-21 et seq.] in a Medicare+Choice payment area for a month, in an amount determined as follows:

(i) Payment before 2006. For years before 2006, the payment amount shall be equal to 1/12 of the annual MA capitation rate (as calculated under subsection (c)(1)) with respect to that individual for that area, adjusted under subparagraph (C) and reduced by the amount of any reduction elected under section 1854(f)(1)(E) [42 USCS § 1395w-24(f)(1)(E)].

(ii) Payment for original fee-for-service benefits beginning with 2006. For years beginning with 2006, the amount specified in subparagraph (B).

(B) Payment amount for original fee-for-service benefits beginning with 2006. (i) Payment of bid for plans with bids below benchmark. In the case of a plan for which there are average per capita monthly savings described in section 1854(b)(3)(C) or 1854(b)(4)(C) [42 USCS § 1395w-24(b)(3)(C) or (4)(C)], as the case may be, the amount specified in this subparagraph is equal to the unadjusted MA statutory non-drug monthly bid amount, adjusted under subparagraph (C) and (if applicable) under subparagraphs (F) and (G), plus the amount (if any) of any rebate under subparagraph (E).

(ii) Payment of benchmark for plans with bids at or above benchmark. In the case of a plan for which there are no average per capita monthly savings described in section 1854(b)(3)(C) or 1854(b)(4)(C) [42 USCS § 1395w-24(b)(3)(C) or (4)(C)], as the case may be, the amount specified in this subparagraph is equal to the MA area-specific non-drug monthly benchmark amount, adjusted under subparagraph (C) and (if applicable) under subparagraphs (F) and (G).

(iii) Payment of benchmark for MSA plans. Notwithstanding clauses (i) and (ii), in the case of an MSA plan, the amount specified in this subparagraph is equal to the MA area-specific non-drug monthly benchmark amount, adjusted under subparagraph (C).

(iv) Authority to apply frailty adjustment under pace payment rules for certain specialized MA plans for special needs individuals. (I) In general. Notwithstanding the preceding provisions of this paragraph, for plan year 2011 and subsequent plan years, in the case of a plan described in subclause (II), the Secretary may apply the payment rules under section 1894(d) [42 USCS § 1395eee(d)] (other than paragraph (3) of such section) rather than the payment rules that would otherwise apply under this part, but only to the extent necessary to reflect the costs of treating high concentrations of frail individuals.

(II) Plan described. A plan described in this subclause is a specialized MA plan for special needs individuals described in section 1859(b)(6)(B)(ii) [42 USCS § 1395w-28(b)(6)(B)(ii)] that is fully integrated with capitated contracts with States for Medicaid benefits, including long-term care, and that have similar average levels of frailty (as determined by the Secretary) as the PACE program.

(C) Demographic adjustment, including adjustment for health status. (i) In general. The Secretary shall adjust the payment amount under subparagraph (A)(i) and the amount specified under subparagraph (B)(i), (B)(ii), and (B)(iii) for such risk factors as age, disability status, gender, institutional status, and such other factors as the Secretary determines to be appropriate, including adjustment for health status under paragraph (3), so as to ensure actuarial equivalence. The Secretary may add to, modify, or substitute for such adjustment factors if such changes will improve the determination of actuarial equivalence.

(ii) Application of coding adjustment. For 2006 and each subsequent year:

(I) In applying the adjustment under clause (i) for health status to payment amounts, the Secretary shall ensure that such adjustment reflects changes in treatment and coding practices in the fee-for-service sector and reflects differences in coding patterns between Medicare Advantage plans and providers under part A and B [42 USCS §§ 1395c et seq. and 1395j et seq.] to the extent that the Secretary has identified such differences.

(II) In order to ensure payment accuracy, the Secretary shall annually conduct an analysis of the differences described in subclause (I). The Secretary shall complete such analysis by a date necessary to ensure that the results of such analysis are incorporated on a timely basis into the risk scores for 2008 and subsequent years. In conducting such analysis, the Secretary shall use data submitted with respect to 2004 and subsequent years, as available and updated as appropriate.

(III) In calculating each year's adjustment, the adjustment factor shall be for 2014, not less than the adjustment factor applied for 2010, plus 1.3 percentage points; for each of years 2015 through 2018, not less than the adjustment factor applied for the previous year, plus 0.25 percentage point; and for 2019 and each subsequent year, not less than 5.7 percent.

(IV) Such adjustment shall be applied to risk scores until the Secretary implements risk adjustment using Medicare Advantage diagnostic, cost, and use data.

(iii) Improvements to risk adjustment for special needs individuals with chronic health conditions. (I) In general. For 2011 and subsequent years, for purposes of the adjustment under clause (i) with respect to individuals described in subclause (II), the Secretary shall use a risk score that reflects the known underlying risk profile and chronic health status of similar individuals. Such risk score shall be used instead of the default risk score for new enrollees in Medicare Advantage plans that are not specialized MA plans for special needs individuals (as defined in section 1859(b)(6) [42 USCS § 1395w-28(b)(6)]).

(II) Individuals described. An individual described in this subclause is a special needs individual described in subsection (b)(6)(B)(iii) who enrolls in a specialized MA plan for special needs individuals on or after January 1, 2011.

(III) Evaluation. For 2011 and periodically thereafter, the Secretary shall evaluate and revise the risk adjustment system under this subparagraph in order to, as accurately as possible, account for higher medical and care coordination costs associated with frailty, individuals with multiple, comorbid chronic conditions, and individuals with a diagnosis of mental illness, and also to account for costs that may be associated with higher concentrations of beneficiaries with those conditions.

(IV) Publication of evaluation and revisions. The Secretary shall publish, as part of an announcement under subsection (b), a description of any evaluation conducted under subclause (III) during the preceding year and any revisions made under such subclause as a result of such evaluation.

(D) Separate payment for Federal drug subsidies. In the case of an enrollee in an MA-PD plan, the MA organization offering such plan also receives—

(i) subsidies under section 1860D-15 [42 USCS § 1395w-115] (other than under subsection (g)); and

(ii) reimbursement for premium and cost-sharing reductions for low-income individuals under section 1860D-14(c)(1)(C) [42 USCS § 1395w-114(c)(1)(C)].

(E) Payment of rebate for plans with bids below benchmark. In the case of a plan for which there are average per capita monthly savings described in section 1854(b)(3)(C) or 1854(b)(4)(C) [42 USCS § 1395w-24(b)(3)(C) or (4)(C)], as the case may be, the amount specified in this subparagraph is the amount of the monthly rebate computed under section 1854(b)(1)(C)(i) [42 USCS § 1395w-24(b)(1)(C)(i)] for that plan and year (as reduced by the amount of any credit provided under section 1854(b)(1)(C)(iv) [42 USCS § 1395w-24(b)(1)(C)(iv)]).

(F) Adjustment for intra-area variations. (i) Intra-regional variations. In the case of payment with respect to an MA regional plan for an MA region, the Secretary shall also adjust the amounts specified under subparagraphs (B)(i) and (B)(ii) in a manner to take into account variations in MA local payment rates under this part among the different MA local areas included in such region.

(ii) Intra-service area variations. In the case of payment with respect to an MA local plan for a service area that covers more than one MA local area, the Secretary shall also adjust the amounts specified under subparagraphs (B)(i) and (B)(ii) in a manner to take into account variations in MA local payment rates under this part among the different MA local areas included in such service area.

(G) Adjustment relating to risk adjustment. The Secretary shall adjust payments with respect to MA plans as necessary to ensure that—

(i) the sum of—

(I) the monthly payment made under subparagraph (A)(ii); and

(II) the MA monthly basic beneficiary premium under section 1854(b)(2)(A) [42 USCS § 1395w-24(b)(2)(A)]; equals

(ii) the unadjusted MA statutory non-drug monthly bid amount, adjusted in the manner described in subparagraph (C) and, for an MA regional plan, subparagraph (F).

(H) Special rule for end-stage renal disease. The Secretary shall establish separate rates of payment to a Medicare+Choice organization with respect to classes of individuals determined to have end-stage renal disease and enrolled in a Medicare+Choice plan of the organization. Such rates of payment shall be actuarially equivalent to rates that would have been paid with respect to other enrollees in the MA payment area (or such other area as specified by the Secretary) under the provisions of this section as in effect before the date of the enactment of the Medicare Prescription Drug, Improvement, and Modernization Act of 2003 [enacted Dec. 8, 2003]. In accordance with regulations, the Secretary shall provide for the application of the seventh sentence of section 1881(b)(7) [42 USCS § 1395rr(b)(7)] to payments under this section covering the provision of renal dialysis treatment in the same manner as such sentence applies to composite rate payments described in such sentence. In establishing such rates, the Secretary shall provide for appropriate adjustments to increase each rate to reflect the demonstration rate (including the risk adjustment methodology associated with such rate) of the social health maintenance organization end-stage renal disease capitation demonstrations (established by section 2355 of the Deficit Reduction Act of 1984 [unclassified], as amended by section 13567(b) of the Omnibus Budget Reconciliation Act of 1993), and shall compute such rates by taking into account such factors as renal treatment modality, age, and the underlying cause of the end-stage renal disease. The Secretary may apply the competitive bidding methodology provided for in this section, with appropriate adjustments to account for the risk adjustment methodology applied to end stage renal disease payments.

(2) Adjustment to reflect number of enrollees. (A) In general. The amount of payment under this subsection may be retroactively adjusted to take into account any difference between the actual number of individuals enrolled with an organization under this part [42 USCS §§ 1395w-21 et seq.] and the number of such individuals estimated to be so enrolled in determining the amount of the advance payment.

(B) Special rule for certain enrollees. (i) In general. Subject to clause (ii), the Secretary may make retroactive adjustments under subparagraph (A) to take into account individuals enrolled during the period beginning on the date on which the individual enrolls with a

Medicare+Choice organization under a plan operated, sponsored, or contributed to by the individual's employer or former employer (or the employer or former employer of the individual's spouse) and ending on the date on which the individual is enrolled in the organization under this part [42 USCS §§ 1395w-21 et seq.], except that for purposes of making such retroactive adjustments under this subparagraph, such period may not exceed 90 days.

(ii) Exception. No adjustment may be made under clause (i) with respect to any individual who does not certify that the organization provided the individual with the disclosure statement described in section 1852(c) [42 USCS § 1395w-22(c)] at the time the individual enrolled with the organization.

(3) Establishment of risk adjustment factors. (A) Report. The Secretary shall develop, and submit to Congress by not later than March 1, 1999, a report on the method of risk adjustment of payment rates under this section, to be implemented under subparagraph (C), that accounts for variations in per capita costs based on health status. Such report shall include an evaluation of such method by an outside, independent actuary of the actuarial soundness of the proposal. (B) Data collection. In order to carry out this paragraph, the Secretary shall require Medicare+Choice organizations (and eligible organizations with risk-sharing contracts under section 1876 [42 USCS § 1395mm]) to submit data regarding inpatient hospital services for periods beginning on or after July 1, 1997, and data regarding other services and other information as the Secretary deems necessary for periods beginning on or after July 1, 1998. The Secretary may not require an organization to submit such data before January 1, 1998.

(C) Initial implementation. (i) In general. The Secretary shall first provide for implementation of a risk adjustment methodology that accounts for variations in per capita costs based on health status and other demographic factors for payments by no later than January 1, 2000.

(ii) Phase-in. Except as provided in clause (iv), such risk adjustment methodology shall be implemented in a phased-in manner so that the methodology insofar as it makes adjustments to capitation rates for health status applies to—

(I) 10 percent of 1/12 of the annual Medicare+Choice capitation rate in 2000 and each succeeding year through 2003;

(II) 30 percent of such capitation rate in 2004;

(III) 50 percent of such capitation rate in 2005;

(IV) 75 percent of such capitation rate in 2006; and

(V) 100 percent of such capitation rate in 2007 and succeeding years.

(iii) Data for risk adjustment methodology. Such risk adjustment methodology for 2004 and each succeeding year, shall be based on data from inpatient hospital and ambulatory settings.

(iv) Full implementation of risk adjustment for congestive heart failure enrollees for 2001. (I) Exemption from phase-in. Subject to subclause (II), the Secretary shall fully implement the risk adjustment methodology described in clause (i) with respect to each individual who has had a qualifying congestive heart failure inpatient diagnosis (as determined by the Secretary under such risk adjustment methodology) during the period beginning on July 1, 1999, and ending on June 30, 2000, and who is enrolled in a coordinated care plan that is the only coordinated care plan offered on January 1, 2001, in the service area of the individual.

(II) Period of application. Subclause (I) shall only apply during the 1-year period beginning on January 1, 2001.

(D) Uniform application to all types of plans. Subject to section 1859(e)(4) [42 USCS § 1395w-28(e)(4)], the methodology shall be applied uniformly without regard to the type of plan.

(4) Payment rule for federally qualified health center services. If an individual who is enrolled with an MA plan under this part receives a service from a federally qualified health center that has a written agreement with the MA organization that offers such plan for providing such a service (including any agreement required under section 1857(e)(3) [42 USCS § 1395w-27(e)(3)])—

(A) the Secretary shall pay the amount determined under section 1833(a)(3)(B) [42 USCS § 1395l(a)(3)(B)] directly to the federally qualified health center not less frequently than quarterly; and

(B) the Secretary shall not reduce the amount of the monthly payments under this subsection as a result of the application of subparagraph (A).

(b) Annual announcement of payment rates. (1) Annual announcements. (A) For 2005. The Secretary shall determine, and shall announce (in a manner intended to provide notice to interested parties), not later than the second Monday in May of 2004, with respect to each MA payment area, the following:

(i) MA capitation rates. The annual MA capitation rate for each MA payment area for 2005.

(ii) Adjustment factors. The risk and other factors to be used in adjusting such rates under subsection (a)(1)(C) for payments for months in 2005.

(B) For 2006 and subsequent years. For a year after 2005—

(i) Initial announcement. The Secretary shall determine, and shall announce (in a manner intended to provide notice to interested parties), not later than the first Monday in April before the calendar year concerned, with respect to each MA payment area, the following:

(I) MA capitation rates; ma local area benchmark. The annual MA capitation rate for each MA payment area for the year.

(II) Adjustment factors. The risk and other factors to be used in adjusting such rates under subsection (a)(1)(C) for payments for months in such year.

(ii) Regional benchmark announcement. The Secretary shall determine, and shall announce (in a manner intended to provide notice to interested parties), on a timely basis before the calendar year concerned, with respect to each MA region and each MA regional plan for which a bid was submitted under section 1854 [42 USCS § 1395w-24], the MA region-specific non-drug monthly benchmark amount for that region for the year involved.

(iii) Benchmark announcement for CCA local areas. The Secretary shall determine, and shall announce (in a manner intended to provide notice to interested parties), on a timely basis before the calendar year concerned, with respect to each CCA area (as defined in section 1860C-1(b)(1)(A) [42 USCS § 1395w-29(b)(1)(A)]), the CCA non-drug monthly benchmark amount under section 1860C-1(e)(1) [42 USCS § 1395w-29(e)(1)] for that area for the year involved.

(2) Advance notice of methodological changes. At least 45 days before making the announcement under paragraph (1) for a year, the Secretary shall provide for notice to Medicare+Choice organizations of proposed changes to be made in the methodology from the methodology and assumptions used in the previous announcement and shall provide such organizations an opportunity to comment on such proposed changes.

(3) Explanation of assumptions. In each announcement made under paragraph (1), the Secretary shall include an explanation of the assumptions and changes in methodology used in such announcement. (4) Continued computation and publication of county-specific per capita fee-for-service expenditure information. The Secretary, through the Chief Actuary of the Centers for Medicare & Medicaid Services, shall provide for the computation and publication, on an annual basis beginning with 2001 at the time of publication of the annual Medicare+Choice capitation rates under paragraph (1), of the following information for the original medicare fee-for-service program under parts A and B [42 USCS §§ 1395c et seq. and 1395j et seq.] (exclusive of individuals eligible for coverage under section 226A [42 USCS § 426-1]) for each Medicare+Choice payment area for the second calendar year ending before the date of publication:

(A) Total expenditures per capita per month, computed separately for part A [42 USCS §§ 1395c et seq.] and for part B [42 USCS §§ 1395j et seq.].

(B) The expenditures described in subparagraph (A) reduced by the best estimate of the expenditures (such as graduate medical education and disproportionate share hospital payments) not related to the payment of claims.

(C) The average risk factor for the covered population based on diagnoses reported for medicare inpatient services, using the same methodology as is expected to be applied in making payments under subsection (a).

(D) Such average risk factor based on diagnoses for inpatient and other sites of service, using the same methodology as is expected to be applied in making payments under subsection (a).

(c) Calculation of annual Medicare+Choice capitation rates. (1) In general. For purposes of this part [42 USCS §§ 1395w-21 et seq.], subject to paragraphs (6)(C) and (7), each annual Medicare+Choice capitation rate, for a Medicare+Choice payment area that is an MA local area for a contract year consisting of a calendar year, is equal to the largest of the amounts specified in the following subparagraph (A), (B), (C), or (D):

(A) Blended capitation rate. For a year before 2005, the sum of—

(i) the area-specific percentage (as specified under paragraph (2) for the year) of the annual area-specific Medicare+Choice capitation rate for the Medicare+Choice payment area, as determined under paragraph (3) for the year, and

(ii) the national percentage (as specified under paragraph (2) for the year) of the input-price-adjusted annual national Medicare+Choice capitation rate, as determined under paragraph (4) for the year,

multiplied (for a year other than 2004) by

the budget neutrality adjustment factor determined under paragraph (5).

(B) Minimum amount. 12 multiplied by the following amount:

(i) For 1998, $367 (but not to exceed, in the case of an area outside the 50 States and the District of Columbia, 150 percent of the annual per capita rate of payment for 1997 determined under section 1876(a)(1)(C) [42 USCS § 1395mm(a)(1)(C)] for the area).

(ii) For 1999 and 2000, the minimum amount determined under clause (i) or this clause, respectively, for the preceding year, increased by the national per capita Medicare+Choice growth percentage described in paragraph (6)(A) applicable to 1999 or 2000, respectively.

(iii)(I) Subject to subclause (II), for 2001, for any area in a Metropolitan Statistical Area with a population of more than 250,000, $525, and for any other area $475.

(II) In the case of an area outside the 50 States and the District of Columbia, the amount specified in this clause shall not exceed 120 percent of the amount determined under clause (ii) for such area for 2000.

(iv) For 2002, 2003, and 2004, the minimum amount specified in this clause (or clause (iii)) for the preceding year increased by the national per capita Medicare+Choice growth percentage, described in paragraph (6)(A) for that succeeding year.

(C) Minimum percentage increase. (i) For 1998, 102 percent of the annual per capita rate of payment for 1997 determined under section 1876(a)(1)(C) [42 USCS § 1395mm(a)(1)(C)] for the Medicare+Choice payment area.

(ii) For 1999 and 2000, 102 percent of the annual Medicare+Choice capitation rate under this paragraph for the area for the previous year.

(iii) For 2001, 103 percent of the annual Medicare+Choice capitation rate under this paragraph for the area for 2000.

(iv) For 2002 and 2003, 102 percent of the annual Medicare+Choice capitation rate under this paragraph for the area for the previous year.

(v) For 2004 and each succeeding year, the greater of—

(I) 102 percent of the annual MA capitation rate under this paragraph for the area for the previous year; or

(II) the annual MA capitation rate under this paragraph for the area for the previous year increased by the national per capita MA growth percentage, described in paragraph (6) for that succeeding year, but not taking into account any adjustment under paragraph (6)(C) for a year before 2004.

(D) 100 percent of fee-for-service costs. (i) In general. For each year specified in clause (ii), the adjusted average per capita cost for the year involved, determined under section 1876(a)(4) [42 USCS § 1395mm(a)(4)] and adjusted as appropriate for the purpose of risk adjustment, for the MA payment area for individuals who are not enrolled in an MA plan under this part for the year, but adjusted to exclude costs attributable to payments under sections[,] 1848(o), [and] 1886(n) and 1886(h) [42 USCS §§ 1395w-4(o), 1395ww(h), (n)].

(ii) Periodic rebasing. The provisions of clause (i) shall apply for 2004 and for subsequent years as the Secretary shall specify (but not less than once every 3 years).

(iii) Inclusion of costs of VA and DOD military facility services to medicare-eligible beneficiaries. In determining the adjusted average per capita cost under clause (i) for a year, such cost shall be adjusted to include the Secretary's estimate, on a per capita basis, of the amount of additional payments that would have been made in the area involved under this title if individuals entitled to benefits under this title had not received services from facilities of the Department of Defense or the Department of Veterans Affairs.

(2) Area-specific and national percentages. For purposes of paragraph (1)(A)—

(A) for 1998, the "area-specific percentage" is 90 percent and the "national percentage" is 10 percent,

(B) for 1999, the "area-specific percentage" is 82 percent and the "national percentage" is 18 percent,

(C) for 2000, the "area-specific percentage" is 74 percent and the "national percentage" is 26 percent,

(D) for 2001, the "area-specific percentage" is 66 percent and the "national percentage" is 34 percent,

(E) for 2002, the "area-specific percentage" is 58 percent and the "national percentage" is 42 percent, and

(F) for a year after 2002, the "area-specific percentage" is 50 percent and the "national percentage" is 50 percent.

(3) Annual area-specific Medicare+Choice capitation rate. (A) In general. For purposes of paragraph (1)(A), subject to subparagraphs (B) and (E), the annual area-specific Medicare+Choice capitation rate for a Medicare+Choice payment area—

(i) for 1998 is, subject to subparagraph (D), the annual per capita rate of payment for 1997 determined under section 1876(a)(1)(C) [42 USCS § 1395mm(a)(1)(C)] for the area, increased by the national per capita Medicare+Choice growth percentage for 1998 (described in paragraph (6)(A)); or

(ii) for a subsequent year is the annual area-specific Medicare+Choice capitation rate for the previous year determined under this paragraph for the area, increased by the national per capita Medicare+Choice growth percentage for such subsequent year.

(B) Removal of medical education from calculation of adjusted average per capita cost. (i) In general. In determining the area-specific Medicare+Choice capitation rate under subparagraph (A) for a year (beginning with 1998), the annual per capita rate of payment for 1997 determined under section 1876(a)(1)(C) [42 USCS § 1395mm(a)(1)(C)] shall be adjusted to exclude from the rate the applicable percent (specified in clause (ii)) of the payment adjustments described in subparagraph (C).

(ii) Applicable percent. For purposes of clause (i), the applicable percent for—

(I) 1998 is 20 percent,

(II) 1999 is 40 percent,

(III) 2000 is 60 percent,

(IV) 2001 is 80 percent, and

(V) a succeeding year is 100 percent.

(C) Payment adjustment. (i) In general. Subject to clause (ii), the payment adjustments described in this subparagraph are payment adjustments which the Secretary estimates were payable during 1997—

(I) for the indirect costs of medical education under section 1886(d)(5)(B) [42 USCS § 1395ww(d)(5)(B)], and

(II) for direct graduate medical education costs under section 1886(h) [42 USCS § 1395ww(h)].

(ii) Treatment of payments covered under state hospital reimbursement system. To the extent that the Secretary estimates that an annual per capita rate of payment for 1997 described in clause (i) reflects payments to hospitals reimbursed under section 1814(b)(3) [42 USCS § 1395f(b)(3)], the Secretary shall estimate a payment adjustment that is comparable to the payment adjustment that would have been made under clause (i) if the hospitals had not been reimbursed under such section.

(D) Treatment of areas with highly variable payment rates. In the case of a Medicare+Choice payment area for which the annual per capita rate of payment determined under section 1876(a)(1)(C) [42 USCS § 1395mm(a)(1)(C)] for 1997 varies by more than 20 percent from such rate for 1996, for purposes of this subsection the Secretary may substitute for such rate for 1997 a rate that is more representative of the costs of the enrollees in the area.

(E) Inclusion of costs of DOD and VA military facility services to medicare-eligible beneficiaries. In determining the area-specific MA capitation rate under subparagraph (A) for a year (beginning with 2004), the annual per capita rate of payment for 1997 determined under section 1876(a)(1)(C) [42 USCS § 1395mm(a)(1)(C)] shall be adjusted to include in the rate the Secretary's estimate, on a per capita basis, of the amount of additional payments that would have been made in the area involved under this title if individuals entitled to benefits under this title had not received services from facilities of the Department of Defense or the Department of Veterans Affairs.

(4) Input-price-adjusted annual national Medicare+Choice capitation rate. (A) In general. For purposes of paragraph (1)(A), the input-price-adjusted annual national Medicare+Choice capitation rate for a Medicare+Choice payment area for a year is equal to the sum, for all the types of medicare services (as classified by the Secretary), of the product (for each such type of service) of—

(i) the national standardized annual Medicare+Choice capitation rate (determined under subparagraph (B)) for the year,

(ii) the proportion of such rate for the year which is attributable to such type of services, and

(iii) an index that reflects (for that year and that type of services) the relative input price of such services in the area compared to the national average input price of such services.

In applying clause (iii), the Secretary may, subject to subparagraph (C), apply those indices under this title [42 USCS §§ 1395 et seq.]that are used in applying (or updating) national payment rates for specific areas and localities.

(B) National standardized annual Medicare+Choice capitation rate. In subparagraph (A)(i), the "national standardized annual Medicare+Choice capitation rate" for a year is equal to—

(i) the sum (for all Medicare+Choice payment areas) of the product of—

(I) the annual area-specific Medicare+Choice capitation rate for that year for the area under paragraph (3), and

(II) the average number of medicare beneficiaries residing in that area in the year, multiplied by the average of the risk factor weights used to adjust payments under subsection (a)(1)(A) for such beneficiaries in such area; divided by

(ii) the sum of the products described in clause (i)(II) for all areas for that year.

(C) Special rules for 1998. In applying this paragraph for 1998—

(i) medicare services shall be divided into 2 types of services: part A [42 USCS §§ 1395c et seq.] services and part B [42 USCS §§ 1395j et seq.] services;

(ii) the proportions described in subparagraph (A)(ii)—

(I) for part A [42 USCS §§ 1395c et seq.] services shall be the ratio (expressed as a percentage) of the national average annual per capita rate of payment for part A [42 USCS §§ 1395c et seq.] for 1997 to the total national average annual per capita rate of payment for parts A and B [42 USCS §§ 1395c et seq. and 1395j et seq.] for 1997, and

(II) for part B [42 USCS §§ 1395j et seq.] services shall be 100 percent minus the ratio described in subclause (I);

(iii) for part A [42 USCS §§ 1395c et seq.] services, 70 percent of payments attributable to such services shall be adjusted by the index used under section 1886(d)(3)(E) [42 USCS § 1395ww(d)(3)(E)] to adjust payment rates for relative hospital wage levels for hospitals located in the payment area involved;

(iv) for part B [42 USCS §§ 1395j et seq.] services—

(I) 66 percent of payments attributable to such services shall be adjusted by the index of the geographic area factors under section 1848(e) [42 USCS § 1395w-4(e)] used to adjust payment rates for physicians' services furnished in the payment area, and

(II) of the remaining 34 percent of the amount of such payments, 40 percent shall be adjusted by the index described in clause (iii); and

(v) the index values shall be computed based only on the beneficiary population who are 65 years of age or older and who are not determined to have end stage renal disease.

The Secretary may continue to apply the rules described in this subparagraph (or similar rules) for 1999.

(5) Payment adjustment budget neutrality factor. For purposes of paragraph (1)(A), for each year (other than 2004), the Secretary shall determine a budget neutrality adjustment factor so that the aggregate of the payments under this part [42 USCS §§ 1395w-21 et seq.] (other than those attributable to subsections (a)(c)(3)(iv), (a)(4), and (i)) shall equal the aggregate payments that would have been made under this part [42 USCS §§ 1395w-21 et seq.] if payment were based entirely on area-specific capitation rates.

(6) National per capita Medicare+Choice growth percentage defined. (A) In general. In this part [42 USCS §§ 1395w-21 et seq.], the "national per capita Medicare+Choice growth percentage" for a year is the percentage determined by the Secretary, by March 1st before the beginning of the year involved, to reflect the Secretary's estimate of the projected per capita rate of growth in expenditures under this title [42 USCS §§ 1395 et seq.] for an individual entitled to benefits under part A [42 USCS §§ 1395c et seq.] and enrolled under part B [42 USCS §§ 1395j et seq.], excluding expenditures attributable to subsections (a)(7) and (o) of section 1848 [42 USCS § 1395w-4] and subsections (b)(3)(B)(ix) and (n) of section 1886 [42 USCS § 1395ww], reduced by the number of percentage points specified in subparagraph (B) for the year. Separate determinations may be made for aged enrollees, disabled enrollees, and enrollees with end-stage renal disease.

(B) Adjustment. The number of percentage points specified in this subparagraph is—

(i) for 1998, 0.8 percentage points,

(ii) for 1999, 0.5 percentage points,

(iii) for 2000, 0.5 percentage points,

(iv) for 2001, 0.5 percentage points,

(v) for 2002, 0.3 percentage points, and

(vi) for a year after 2002, 0 percentage points.

(C) Adjustment for over or under projection of national per capita Medicare+Choice growth percentage. Beginning with rates calculated for 1999, before computing rates for a year as described in paragraph (1), the Secretary shall adjust all area-specific and national Medicare+Choice capitation rates (and beginning in 2000, the minimum amount) for the previous year for the differences between the projections of the national per capita Medicare+Choice growth percentage for that year and previous years and the current estimate of such percentage for such years, except that for purposes of paragraph (1)(C)(v)(II), no such adjustment shall be made for a year before 2004.

(7) Adjustment for national coverage determinations and legislative changes in benefits. If the Secretary makes a determination with respect to coverage under this title or there is a change in benefits required to be provided under this part that the Secretary projects will result in a significant increase in the costs to Medicare+Choice of providing benefits under

contracts under this part (for periods after any period described in section 1852(a)(5) [42 USCS § 1395w-22(a)(5)]), the Secretary shall adjust appropriately the payments to such organizations under this part. Such projection and adjustment shall be based on an analysis by the Chief Actuary of the Centers for Medicare & Medicaid Services of the actuarial costs associated with the new benefits.

(d) MA payment area; MA local area; MA region defined. (1) MA payment area. In this part [42 USCS §§ 1395w-21 et seq.], except as provided in this subsection, the term "MA payment area" means—

(A) with respect to an MA local plan, an MA local area (as defined in paragraph (2)); and

(B) with respect to an MA regional plan, an MA region (as established under section 1858(a)(2) [42 USCS § 1395w-27a(a)(2)]).

(2) MA local area. The term "MA local area" means a county or equivalent area specified by the Secretary.

(3) Rule for ESRD beneficiaries. In the case of individuals who are determined to have end stage renal disease, the Medicare+Choice payment area shall be a State or such other payment area as the Secretary specifies.

(4) Geographic adjustment. (A) In general. Upon written request of the chief executive officer of a State for a contract year (beginning after 1998) made by not later than February 1 of the previous year, the Secretary shall make a geographic adjustment to a Medicare+Choice payment area in the State otherwise determined under paragraph (1) for local MA plans—

(i) to a single statewide Medicare+Choice payment area,

(ii) to the metropolitan based system described in subparagraph (C), or

(iii) to consolidating into a single Medicare+Choice payment area noncontiguous counties (or equivalent areas described in paragraph (1)(A)) within a State.

Such adjustment shall be effective for payments for months beginning with January of the year following the year in which the request is received.

(B) Budget neutrality adjustment. In the case of a State requesting an adjustment under this paragraph, the Secretary shall initially (and annually thereafter) adjust the payment rates otherwise established under this section with respect to MA local plans for Medicare+Choice payment areas in the State in a manner so that the aggregate of the payments under this section for such plans in the State shall not exceed the aggregate payments that would have been made under this section for such plans for Medicare+Choice payment areas in the State in the absence of the adjustment under this paragraph.

(C) Metropolitan based system. The metropolitan based system described in this subparagraph is one in which—

(i) all the portions of each metropolitan statistical area in the State or in the case of a consolidated metropolitan statistical area, all of the portions of each primary metropolitan statistical area within the consolidated area within the State, are treated as a single Medicare+Choice payment area, and

(ii) all areas in the State that do not fall within a metropolitan statistical area are treated as a single Medicare+Choice payment area.

(D) Areas. In subparagraph (C), the terms "metropolitan statistical area", "consolidated metropolitan statistical area", and "primary metropolitan statistical area" mean any area designated as such by the Secretary of Commerce.

(e) Special rules for individuals electing MSA plans. (1) In general. If the amount of the Medicare+Choice monthly MSA premium (as defined in section 1854(b)(2)(C) [42 USCS § 1395w-24(b)(2)(C)]) for an MSA plan for a year is less than 1/12 of the annual Medicare+Choice capitation rate applied under this section for the area and year involved, the Secretary shall deposit an amount equal to 100 percent of such difference in a Medicare+Choice MSA established (and, if applicable, designated) by the individual under paragraph (2).

(2) Establishment and designation of Medicare+Choice medical savings account as requirement for payment of contribution. In the case of an individual who has elected coverage under an MSA plan, no payment shall be made under paragraph (1) on behalf of an individual for a month unless the individual—

(A) has established before the beginning of the month (or by such other deadline as the Secretary may specify) a Medicare+Choice MSA (as defined in section 138(b)(2) of the Internal Revenue Code of 1986 [26 USCS § 138(b)(2)]), and

(B) if the individual has established more than one such Medicare+Choice MSA, has designated one of such accounts as the individual's Medicare+Choice MSA for purposes of this part [42 USCS §§ 1395w-21 et seq.].

Under rules under this section, such an individual may change the designation of such account under subparagraph (B) for purposes of this part [42 USCS §§ 1395w-21 et seq.].

(3) Lump-sum deposit of medical savings account contribution. In the case of an individual electing an MSA plan effective beginning with a month in a year, the amount of the contribution to the Medicare+Choice MSA on behalf of the individual for that month and all successive months in the year shall be deposited during that first month. In the case of a termination of such an election as of a month before the end of a year, the Secretary shall provide for a procedure for the recovery of deposits attributable to the remaining months in the year.

(f) Payments from trust funds. The payment to a Medicare+Choice organization under this section for individuals enrolled under this part [42 USCS §§ 1395w-21 et seq.] with the organization and for payments under subsection (l) and subsection (m) and payments to a Medicare+Choice MSA under subsection (e)(1) shall be made from the Federal Hospital Insurance Trust Fund and the Federal Supplementary Medical Insurance Trust Fund in such proportion as the Secretary determines reflects the relative weight that benefits under part A [42 USCS §§ 1395c et seq.] and under part B [42 USCS §§ 1395j et seq.] represents of the actuarial value of the total benefits under this title [42 USCS §§ 1395 et seq.]. Payments to MA organizations for statutory drug benefits provided under this title [42 USCS §§ 1395 et seq.] are made from the Medicare Prescription Drug Account in the Federal Supplementary Medical Insurance Trust Fund. Monthly payments otherwise payable under this section for October 2000 shall be paid on the first business day of such month. Monthly payments otherwise payable under this section for October 2001 shall be paid on the last business day of September 2001. Monthly payments otherwise payable under this section for October 2006 shall be paid on the first business day of October 2006.

(g) Special rule for certain inpatient hospital stays. In the case of an individual who is receiving inpatient hospital services from a subsection (d) hospital (as defined in section 1886(d)(1)(B) [42 USCS § 1395ww(d)(1)(B)]), a rehabilitation hospital described in section 1886(d)(1)(B)(ii) [42 USCS § 1395ww(d)(1)(B)(ii)] or a distinct part rehabilitation unit described in the matter following clause (v) of section 1886(d)(1)(B) [42 USCS § 1395ww(d)(1)(B)], or a long-term care hospital (described in section 1886(d)(1)(B)(iv) [42 USCS § 1395ww(d)(1)(B)(iv)]) as of the effective date of the individual's—

(1) election under this part [42 USCS §§ 1395w-21 et seq.] of a Medicare+Choice plan offered by a Medicare+Choice organization—

(A) payment for such services until the date of the individual's discharge shall be made under this title [42 USCS §§ 1395 et seq.] through the Medicare+Choice plan or the original medicare fee-for-service program option described in section 1851(a)(1)(A) [42 USCS § 1395w-21(a)(1)(A)] (as the case may be) elected before the election with such organization,

(B) the elected organization shall not be financially responsible for payment for such services until the date after the date of the individual's discharge, and

(C) the organization shall nonetheless be paid the full amount otherwise payable to the organization under this part [42 USCS §§ 1395w-21 et seq.]; or

(2) termination of election with respect to a Medicare+Choice organization under this part [42 USCS §§ 1395w-21 et seq.]—

(A) the organization shall be financially responsible for payment for such services after such date and until the date of the individual's discharge,

(B) payment for such services during the stay shall not be made under section 1886(d) [42 USCS § 1395ww(d)] or other payment provision under this title for inpatient services for the type of facility, hospital, or unit involved, described in the matter preceding paragraph (1), as the case may be, or by any succeeding Medicare+Choice organization, and

(C) the terminated organization shall not receive any payment with respect to the individual under this part [42 USCS §§ 1395w-21 et seq.] during the period the individual is not enrolled.

(h) Special rule for hospice care. (1) Information. A contract under this part [42 USCS §§ 1395w-21 et seq.] shall require the Medicare+Choice organization to inform each individual enrolled under this part [42 USCS §§ 1395w-21 et seq.] with a Medicare+Choice plan offered by the organization about the availability of hospice care if—

(A) a hospice program participating under this title [42 USCS §§ 1395 et seq.] is located within the organization's service area; or

(B) it is common practice to refer patients to hospice programs outside such service area.

(2) Payment. If an individual who is enrolled with a Medicare+Choice organization under this part [42 USCS §§ 1395w-21 et seq.] makes an election under section 1812(d)(1) [42 USCS

§ 1395d(d)(1)] to receive hospice care from a particular hospice program—

(A) payment for the hospice care furnished to the individual shall be made to the hospice program elected by the individual by the Secretary;

(B) payment for other services for which the individual is eligible notwithstanding the individual's election of hospice care under section 1812(d)(1) [42 USCS § 1395d(d)(1)], including services not related to the individual's terminal illness, shall be made by the Secretary to the Medicare+Choice organization or the provider or supplier of the service instead of payments calculated under subsection (a); and

(C) the Secretary shall continue to make monthly payments to the Medicare+Choice organization in an amount equal to the value of the additional benefits required under section 1854(f)(1)(A) [42 USCS § 1395w-24(f)(1)(A)].

(i) New entry bonus. (1) In general. Subject to paragraphs (2) and (3), in the case of Medicare+Choice payment area in which a Medicare+Choice plan has not been offered since 1997 (or in which all organizations that offered a plan since such date have filed notice with the Secretary, as of October 13, 1999, that they will not be offering such a plan as of January 1, 2000, or filed notice with the Secretary as of October 3, 2000, that they will not be offering such a plan as of January 1, 2001), the amount of the monthly payment otherwise made under this section shall be increased—

(A) only for the first 12 months in which any Medicare+Choice plan is offered in the area, by 5 percent of the total monthly payment otherwise computed for such payment area; and

(B) only for the subsequent 12 months, by 3 percent of the total monthly payment otherwise computed for such payment area.

(2) Period of application. Paragraph (1) shall only apply to payment for Medicare+Choice plans which are first offered in a Medicare+Choice payment area during the 2-year period beginning on January 1, 2000.

(3) Limitation to organization offering first plan in an area. Paragraph (1) shall only apply to payment to the first Medicare+Choice organization that offers a Medicare+Choice plan in each Medicare+Choice payment area, except that if more than one such organization first offers such a plan in an area on the same date, paragraph (1) shall apply to payment for such organizations.

(4) Construction. Nothing in paragraph (1) shall be construed as affecting the calculation of the annual Medicare+Choice capitation rate under subsection (c) for any payment area or as applying to payment for any period not described in such paragraph and paragraph (2).

(5) Offered defined. In this subsection, the term "offered" means, with respect to a Medicare+Choice plan as of a date, that a Medicare+Choice eligible individual may enroll with the plan on that date, regardless of when the enrollment takes effect or when the individual obtains benefits under the plan.

(j) Computation of benchmark amounts. For purposes of this part [42 USCS §§ 1395w-21 et seq.], subject to subsection (o), the term "MA area-specific non-drug monthly benchmark amount" means for a month in a year—

(1) with respect to—

(A) a service area that is entirely within an MA local area, subject to section 1860C-1(d)(2)(A) [42 USCS § 1395w-29(d)(2)(A)], an amount equal to 1/12 of the annual MA capitation rate under section 1853(c)(1) [42 USCS § 1395w-23(c)(1)] for the area for the year (or, for 2007, 2008, 2009, and 2010, 1/12 of the applicable amount determined under subsection (k)(1) for the area for the year; for 2011, 1/12 of the applicable amount determined under subsection (k)(1) for the area for 2010; and, beginning with 2012, 1/12 of the blended benchmark amount determined under subsection (n)(1) for the area for the year), adjusted as appropriate (for years before 2007) for the purpose of risk adjustment; or

(B) a service area that includes more than one MA local area, an amount equal to the average of the amounts described in subparagraph (A) for each such local MA area, weighted by the projected number of enrollees in the plan residing in the respective local MA areas (as used by the plan for purposes of the bid and disclosed to the Secretary under section 1854(a)(6)(A)(iii) [42 USCS § 1395w-24(a)(6)(A)(iii)]), adjusted as appropriate (for years before 2007) for the purpose of risk adjustment; or

(2) with respect to an MA region for a month in a year, the MA region-specific non-drug monthly benchmark amount, as defined in section 1858(f) [42 USCS § 1395w-27a] for the region for the year.

(k) Determination of applicable amount for purposes of calculating the benchmark amounts. (1) Applicable amount defined. For purposes of subsection (j), subject to paragraphs (2) and (4), the term "applicable amount" means for an area—

(A) for 2007—

(i) if such year is not specified under subsection (c)(1)(D)(ii), an amount equal to the amount specified in subsection (c)(1)(C) for the area for 2006—

(I) first adjusted by the rescaling factor for 2006 for the area (as made available by the Secretary in the announcement of the rates on April 4, 2005, under subsection (b)(1), but excluding any national adjustment factors for coding intensity and risk adjustment budget neutrality that were included in such factor); and

(II) then increased by the national per capita MA growth percentage, described in subsection (c)(6) for 2007, but not taking into account any adjustment under subparagraph (C) of such subsection for a year before 2004;

(ii) if such year is specified under subsection (c)(1)(D)(ii), an amount equal to the greater of—

(I) the amount determined under clause (i) for the area for the year; or

(II) the amount specified in subsection (c)(1)(D) for the area for the year; and

(B) for a subsequent year—

(i) if such year is not specified under subsection (c)(1)(D)(ii), an amount equal to the amount determined under this paragraph for the area for the previous year (determined without regard to paragraphs (2) and (4)), increased by the national per capita MA growth percentage, described in subsection (c)(6) for that succeeding year, but not taking into account any adjustment under subparagraph (C) of such subsection for a year before 2004; and

(ii) if such year is specified under subsection (c)(1)(D)(ii), an amount equal to the greater of—

(I) the amount determined under clause (i) for the area for the year; or

(II) the amount specified in subsection (c)(1)(D) for the area for the year.

(2) Phase-out of budget neutrality factor. (A) In general. Except as provided in subparagraph (D), in the case of 2007 through 2010, the applicable amount determined under paragraph (1) shall be multiplied by a factor equal to 1 plus the product of—

(i) the percent determined under subparagraph (B) for the year; and

(ii) the applicable phase-out factor for the year under subparagraph (C).

(B) Percent determined. (i) In general. For purposes of subparagraph (A)(i), subject to clause (iv), the percent determined under this subparagraph for a year is a percent equal to a fraction the numerator of which is described in clause (ii) and the denominator of which is described in clause (iii).

(ii) Numerator based on difference between demographic rate and risk rate. (I) In general. The numerator described in this clause is an amount equal to the amount by which the demographic rate described in subclause (II) exceeds the risk rate described in subclause (III).

(II) Demographic rate. The demographic rate described in this subclause is the Secretary's estimate of the total payments that would have been made under this part in the year if all the monthly payment amounts for all MA plans were equal to 1/12 of the annual MA capitation rate under subsection (c)(1) for the area and year, adjusted pursuant to subsection (a)(1)(C).

(III) Risk rate. The risk rate described in this subclause is the Secretary's estimate of the total payments that would have been made under this part in the year if all the monthly payment amounts for all MA plans were equal to the amount described in subsection (j)(1)(A) (determined as if this paragraph had not applied) under subsection (j) for the area and year, adjusted pursuant to subsection (a)(1)(C).

(iii) Denominator based on risk rate. The denominator described in this clause is equal to the total amount estimated for the year under clause (ii)(III).

(iv) Requirements. In estimating the amounts under the previous clauses, the Secretary shall—

(I) use a complete set of the most recent and representative Medicare Advantage risk scores under subsection (a)(3) that are available from the risk adjustment model announced for the year;

(II) adjust the risk scores to reflect changes in treatment and coding practices in the fee-for-service sector;

(III) adjust the risk scores for differences in coding patterns between Medicare Advantage plans and providers under the original Medicare fee-for-service program under parts A and B to the extent that the Secretary has identified such differences, as required in subsection (a)(1)(C);

(IV) as necessary, adjust the risk scores for late data submitted by Medicare Advantage organizations;

(V) as necessary, adjust the risk scores for lagged cohorts; and

(VI) as necessary, adjust the risk scores for changes in enrollment in Medicare Advantage plans during the year.

(v) Authority. In computing such amounts the Secretary may take into account the estimated health risk of enrollees in preferred provider organization plans (including MA regional plans) for the year.

(C) Applicable phase-out factor. For purposes of subparagraph (A)(ii), the term "applicable phase-out factor" means—

(i) for 2007, 0.55;

(ii) for 2008, 0.40;

(iii) for 2009, 0.25; and

(iv) for 2010, 0.05.

(D) Termination of application. Subparagraph (A) shall not apply in a year if the amount estimated under subparagraph (B)(ii)(III) for the year is equal to or greater than the amount estimated under subparagraph (B)(ii)(II) for the year.

(3) No revision in percent. (A) In general. The Secretary may not make any adjustment to the percent determined under paragraph (2)(B) for any year.

(B) Rule of construction. Nothing in this subsection shall be construed to limit the authority of the Secretary to make adjustments to the applicable amounts determined under paragraph (1) as appropriate for purposes of updating data or for purposes of adopting an improved risk adjustment methodology.

(4) Phase-out of the indirect costs of medical education from capitation rates. (A) In general. After determining the applicable amount for an area for a year under paragraph (1) (beginning with 2010), the Secretary shall adjust such applicable amount to exclude from such applicable amount the phase-in percentage (as defined in subparagraph (B)(i)) for the year of the Secretary's estimate of the standardized costs for payments under section 1886(d)(5)(B) [42 USCS § 1395ww(d)(5)(B)] in the area for the year. Any adjustment under the preceding sentence shall be made prior to the application of paragraph (2).

(B) Percentages defined. For purposes of this paragraph:

(i) Phase-in percentage. The term "phase-in percentage" means, for an area for a year, the ratio (expressed as a percentage, but in no case greater than 100 percent) of—

(I) the maximum cumulative adjustment percentage for the year (as defined in clause (ii)); to

(II) the standardized IME cost percentage (as defined in clause (iii)) for the area and year.

(ii) Maximum cumulative adjustment percentage. The term "maximum cumulative adjustment percentage" means, for—

(I) 2010, 0.60 percent; and

(II) a subsequent year, the maximum cumulative adjustment percentage for the previous year increased by 0.60 percentage points.

(iii) Standardized IME cost percentage. The term "standardized IME cost percentage" means, for an area for a year, the per capita costs for payments under section 1886(d)(5)(B) [42 USCS § 1395ww(d)(5)(B)] (expressed as a percentage of the fee-for-service amount specified in subparagraph (C)) for the area and the year.

(C) Fee-for-service amount. The fee-for-service amount specified in this subparagraph for an area for a year is the amount specified under subsection (c)(1)(D) for the area and the year.

(l) Application of eligible professional incentives for certain MA organizations for adoption and meaningful use of certified EHR technology. (1) In general. Subject to paragraphs (3) and (4), in the case of a qualifying MA organization, the provisions of sections 1848(o) and 1848(a)(7) [42 USCS § 1395w-4(a)(7), (o)] shall apply with respect to eligible professionals described in paragraph (2) of the organization who the organization attests under paragraph (6) to be meaningful EHR users in a similar manner as they apply to eligible professionals under such sections. Incentive payments under paragraph (3) shall be made to and payment adjustments under paragraph (4) shall apply to such qualifying organizations.

(2) Eligible professional described. With respect to a qualifying MA organization, an eligible professional described in this paragraph is an eligible professional (as defined for purposes of section 1848(o) [42 USCS § 1395w-4(o)]) who—

(A)(i) is employed by the organization; or

(ii)(I) is employed by, or is a partner of, an entity that through contract with the organization furnishes at least 80 percent of the entity's Medicare patient care services to enrollees of such organization; and

(II) furnishes at least 80 percent of the professional services of the eligible professional covered under this title to enrollees of the organization; and

(B) furnishes, on average, at least 20 hours per week of patient care services.

(3) Eligible professional incentive payments. (A) In general. In applying section 1848(o) [42 USCS § 1395w-4(o)] under paragraph (1), instead of the additional payment amount under section 1848(o)(1)(A) [42 USCS § 1395w-4(o)(1)(A)] and subject to subparagraph (B), the Secretary may substitute an amount determined by the Secretary to the extent feasible and practical to be similar to the estimated amount in the aggregate that would be payable if payment for services furnished by such professionals was payable under part B [42 USCS

§§ 1395j et seq.] instead of this part [42 USCS §§ 1395w-21 et seq.].

(B) Avoiding duplication of payments. (i) In general. In the case of an eligible professional described in paragraph (2)—

(I) that is eligible for the maximum incentive payment under section 1848(o)(1)(A) [42 USCS § 1395w-4(o)(1)(A)] for the same payment period, the payment incentive shall be made only under such section and not under this subsection; and

(II) that is eligible for less than such maximum incentive payment for the same payment period, the payment incentive shall be made only under this subsection and not under section 1848(o)(1)(A) [42 USCS § 1395w-4(o)(1)(A)].

(ii) Methods. In the case of an eligible professional described in paragraph (2) who is eligible for an incentive payment under section 1848(o)(1)(A) [42 USCS § 1395w-4(o)(1)(A)] but is not described in clause (i) for the same payment period, the Secretary shall develop a process—

(I) to ensure that duplicate payments are not made with respect to an eligible professional both under this subsection and under section 1848(o)(1)(A) [42 USCS § 1395w-4(o)(1)(A)]; and

(II) to collect data from Medicare Advantage organizations to ensure against such duplicate payments.

(C) Fixed schedule for application of limitation on incentive payments for all eligible professionals. In applying section 1848(o)(1)(B)(ii) [42 USCS § 1395w-4(o)(1)(B)(ii)] under subparagraph (A), in accordance with rules specified by the Secretary, a qualifying MA organization shall specify a year (not earlier than 2011) that shall be treated as the first payment year for all eligible professionals with respect to such organization.

(4) Payment adjustment. (A) In general. In applying section 1848(a)(7) [42 USCS § 1395w-4(a)(7)] under paragraph (1), instead of the payment adjustment being an applicable percent of the fee schedule amount for a year under such section, subject to subparagraph (D), the payment adjustment under paragraph (1) shall be equal to the percent specified in subparagraph (B) for such year of the payment amount otherwise provided under this section for such year.

(B) Specified percent. The percent specified under this subparagraph for a year is 100 percent minus a number of percentage points equal to the product of—

(i) the number of percentage points by which the applicable percent (under section 1848(a)(7)(A)(ii) [42 USCS § 1395w-4(a)(7)(A)(ii)]) for the year is less than 100 percent; and

(ii) the Medicare physician expenditure proportion specified in subparagraph (C) for the year.

(C) Medicare physician expenditure proportion. The Medicare physician expenditure proportion under this subparagraph for a year is the Secretary's estimate of the proportion, of the expenditures under parts A and B [42 USCS §§ 1395c et seq. and 1395j et seq.] that are not attributable to this part [42 USCS §§ 1395w-21 et seq.], that are attributable to expenditures for physicians' services.

(D) Application of payment adjustment. In the case that a qualifying MA organization attests that not all eligible professionals of the organization are meaningful EHR users with respect to a year, the Secretary shall apply the payment adjustment under this paragraph based on the proportion of all such eligible professionals of the organization that are not meaningful EHR users for such year.

(5) Qualifying MA organization defined. In this subsection and subsection (m), the term "qualifying MA organization" means a Medicare Advantage organization that is organized as a health maintenance organization (as defined in section 2791(b)(3) of the Public Health Service Act [42 USCS § 300gg-91(b)(3)]).

(6) Meaningful EHR user attestation. For purposes of this subsection and subsection (m), a qualifying MA organization shall submit an attestation, in a form and manner specified by the Secretary which may include the submission of such attestation as part of submission of the initial bid under section 1854(a)(1)(A)(iv) [42 USCS § 1395w-24(a)(1)(A)(iv)], identifying—

(A) whether each eligible professional described in paragraph (2), with respect to such organization is a meaningful EHR user (as defined in section 1848(o)(2) [42 USCS § 1395w-4(o)(2)]) for a year specified by the Secretary; and

(B) whether each eligible hospital described in subsection (m)(1), with respect to such organization, is a meaningful EHR user (as defined in section 1886(n)(3) [42 USCS § 1395ww]) for an applicable period specified by the Secretary.

(7) Posting on website. The Secretary shall post on the Internet website of the Centers for Medicare & Medicaid Services, in an easily understandable format, a list of the names, business addresses, and business phone numbers of—

(A) each qualifying MA organization receiving an incentive payment under this subsection for eligible professionals of the organization; and

(B) the eligible professionals of such organization for which such incentive payment is based.

(8) Limitation on review. There shall be no administrative or judicial review under section 1869 [42 USCS § 1395ff], section 1878 [42 USCS § 1395oo], or otherwise, of—

(A) the methodology and standards for determining payment amounts and payment adjustments under this subsection, including avoiding duplication of payments under paragraph (3)(B) and the specification of rules for the fixed schedule for application of limitation on incentive payments for all eligible professionals under paragraph (3)(C);

(B) the methodology and standards for determining eligible professionals under paragraph (2); and

(C) the methodology and standards for determining a meaningful EHR user under section 1848(o)(2) [42 USCS § 1395w-4(o)(2)], including specification of the means of demonstrating meaningful EHR use under section 1848(o)(3)(C) [42 USCS § 1395w-4(o)(3)(C)] and selection of measures under section 1848(o)(3)(B) [42 USCS § 1395w-4(o)(3)(B)].

(m) Application of eligible hospital incentives for certain MA organizations for adoption and meaningful use of certified EHR technology. (1) Application. Subject to paragraphs (3) and (4), in the case of a qualifying MA organization, the provisions of sections 1886(n) and 1886(b)(3)(B)(ix) [42 USCS § 1395ww(b)(3)(B)(ix), (n)] shall apply with respect to eligible hospitals described in paragraph (2) of the organization which the organization attests under subsection (l)(6) to be meaningful EHR users in a similar manner as they apply to eligible hospitals under such sections. Incentive payments under paragraph (3) shall be made to and payment adjustments under paragraph (4) shall apply to such qualifying organizations.

(2) Eligible hospital described. With respect to a qualifying MA organization, an eligible hospital described in this paragraph is an eligible hospital (as defined in section 1886(n)(6)(A) [42 USCS § 1395ww(n)(6)(A)]) that is under common corporate governance with such organization and serves individuals enrolled under an MA plan offered by such organization.

(3) Eligible hospital incentive payments. (A) In general. In applying section 1886(n)(2) [42 USCS § 1395ww(n)(2)] under paragraph (1), instead of the additional payment amount under section 1886(n)(2), there shall be substituted an amount determined by the Secretary to be similar to the estimated amount in the aggregate that would be payable if payment for services furnished by such hospitals was payable under part A instead of this part. In implementing the previous sentence, the Secretary—

(i) shall, insofar as data to determine the discharge related amount under section 1886(n)(2)(C) [42 USCS § 1395ww(n)(2)(C)] for an eligible hospital are not available to the Secretary, use such alternative data and methodology to estimate such discharge related amount as the Secretary determines appropriate; and

(ii) shall, insofar as data to determine the medicare share described in section 1886(n)(2)(D) [42 USCS § 1395ww(n)(2)(D)] for an eligible hospital are not available to the Secretary, use such alternative data and methodology to estimate such share, which data and methodology may include use of the inpatient-bed-days (or discharges) with respect to an eligible hospital during the appropriate period which are attributable to both individuals for whom payment may be made under part A or individuals enrolled in an MA plan under a Medicare Advantage organization under this part as a proportion of the estimated total number of patient-bed-days (or discharges) with respect to such hospital during such period.

(B) Avoiding duplication of payments. (i) In general. In the case of a hospital that for a payment year is an eligible hospital described in paragraph (2) and for which at least one-third of their discharges (or bed-days) of Medicare patients for the year are covered under part A, payment for the payment year shall be made only under section 1886(n) [42 USCS § 1395ww(n)] and not under this subsection.

(ii) Methods. In the case of a hospital that is an eligible hospital described in paragraph (2) and also is eligible for an incentive payment under section 1886(n) but is not described in clause (i) for the same payment period, the Secretary shall develop a process—

(I) to ensure that duplicate payments are not made with respect to an eligible hospital both under this subsection and under section 1886(n) [42 USCS § 1395ww(n)]; and

(II) to collect data from Medicare Advantage organizations to ensure against such duplicate payments.

(4) Payment adjustment. (A) Subject to paragraph (3), in the case of a qualifying MA organization (as defined in section 1853(l)(5) [42 USCS § 1395w-23(l)(5)]), if, according to the attestation of the organization submitted under subsection (l)(6) for an applicable period, one or more eligible hospitals (as defined in section 1886(n)(6)(A) [42 USCS § 1395ww(n)(6)(A)]) that are under common corporate governance with such organization and that serve individuals enrolled under a plan offered by such organization are not meaningful EHR users (as defined in section 1886(n)(3) [42 USCS § 1395ww(n)(3)]) with respect to a period, the payment amount payable under this section for such organization for such period shall be the percent specified in subparagraph (B) for such period of the payment amount otherwise provided under this section for such period.

(B) Specified percent. The percent specified under this subparagraph for a year is 100 percent minus a number of percentage points equal to the product of—

(i) the number of the percentage point reduction effected under section 1886(b)(3)(B)(ix)(I) [42 USCS § 1395ww(b)(3)(B)(ix)(I)] for the period; and

(ii) the Medicare hospital expenditure proportion specified in subparagraph (C) for the year.

(C) Medicare hospital expenditure proportion. The Medicare hospital expenditure proportion under this subparagraph for a year is the Secretary's estimate of the proportion, of the expenditures under parts A and B [42 USCS §§ 1395c et seq. and 1395j et seq.] that are not attributable to this part [42 USCS §§ 1395w-21 et seq.], that are attributable to expenditures for inpatient hospital services.

(D) Application of payment adjustment. In the case that a qualifying MA organization attests that not all eligible hospitals are meaningful EHR users with respect to an applicable period, the Secretary shall apply the payment adjustment under this paragraph based on a methodology specified by the Secretary, taking into account the proportion of such eligible hospitals, or discharges from such hospitals, that are not meaningful EHR users for such period.

(5) Posting on website. The Secretary shall post on the Internet website of the Centers for Medicare & Medicaid Services, in an easily understandable format—

(A) a list of the names, business addresses, and business phone numbers of each qualifying MA organization receiving an incentive payment under this subsection for eligible hospitals described in paragraph (2); and

(B) a list of the names of the eligible hospitals for which such incentive payment is based.

(6) Limitations on review. There shall be no administrative or judicial review under section 1869 [42 USCS § 1395ff], section 1878 [42 USCS § 1395oo], or otherwise, of—

(A) the methodology and standards for determining payment amounts and payment adjustments under this subsection, including avoiding duplication of payments under paragraph (3)(B);

(B) the methodology and standards for determining eligible hospitals under paragraph (2); and

(C) the methodology and standards for determining a meaningful EHR user under section 1886(n)(3) [42 USCS § 1395ww(n)(3)], including specification of the means of demonstrating meaningful EHR use under subparagraph (C) of such section and selection of measures under subparagraph (B) of such section.

(n) Determination of blended benchmark amount. (1) In general. For purposes of subsection (j), subject to paragraphs (3), (4), and (5), the term "blended benchmark amount" means for an area—

(A) for 2012 the sum of—

(i) ½ of the applicable amount for the area and year; and

(ii) ½ of the amount specified in paragraph (2)(A) for the area and year; and

(B) for a subsequent year the amount specified in paragraph (2)(A) for the area and year.

(2) Specified amount. (A) In general. The amount specified in this subparagraph for an area and year is the product of—

(i) the base payment amount specified in subparagraph (E) for the area and year adjusted to take into account the phase-out in the indirect costs of medical education from capitation rates described in subsection (k)(4); and

(ii) the applicable percentage for the area for the year specified under subparagraph (B).

(B) Applicable percentage. Subject to subparagraph (D), the applicable percentage specified in this subparagraph for an area for a year in the case of an area that is ranked—

(i) in the highest quartile under subparagraph (C) for the previous year is 95 percent;

(ii) in the second highest quartile under such subparagraph for the previous year is 100 percent;

(iii) in the third highest quartile under such subparagraph for the previous year is 107.5 percent; or

(iv) in the lowest quartile under such subparagraph for the previous year is 115 percent.

(C) Periodic ranking. For purposes of this paragraph in the case of an area located—

(i) in 1 of the 50 States or the District of Columbia, the Secretary shall rank such area in each year specified under subsection (c)(1)(D)(ii) based upon the level of the amount specified in subparagraph (A)(i) for such areas; or

(ii) in a territory, the Secretary shall rank such areas in each such year based upon the level of the amount specified in subparagraph (A)(i) for such area relative to quartile rankings computed under clause (i).

(D) 1-year transition for changes in applicable percentage. If, for a year after 2012, there is a change in the quartile in which an area is ranked compared to the previous year, the applicable percentage for the area in the year shall be the average of—

(i) the applicable percentage for the area for the previous year; and

(ii) the applicable percentage that would otherwise apply for the area for the year.

(E) Base payment amount. Subject to subparagraph (F), the base payment amount specified in this subparagraph—

(i) for 2012 is the amount specified in subsection (c)(1)(D) for the area for the year; or

(ii) for a subsequent year that—

(I) is not specified under subsection (c)(1)(D)(ii), is the base amount specified in this subparagraph for the area for the previous year, increased by the national per capita MA growth percentage, described in subsection (c)(6) for that succeeding year, but not taking into account any adjustment under subparagraph (C) of such subsection for a year before 2004; and

(II) is specified under subsection (c)(1)(D)(ii), is the amount specified in subsection (c)(1)(D) for the area for the year.

(F) Application of indirect medical education phase-out. The base payment amount specified in subparagraph (E) for a year shall be adjusted in the same manner under paragraph (4) of subsection (k) as the applicable amount is adjusted under such subsection.

(3) Alternative phase-ins. (A) 4-year phase-in for certain areas. If the difference between the applicable amount (as defined in subsection (k)) for an area for 2010 and the projected 2010 benchmark amount (as defined in subparagraph (C)) for the area is at least $30 but less than $50, the blended benchmark amount for the area is—

(i) for 2012 the sum of—

(I) ¾ of the applicable amount for the area and year; and

(II) ¼ of the amount specified in paragraph (2)(A) for the area and year;

(ii) for 2013 the sum of—

(I) ½ of the applicable amount for the area and year; and

(II) ½ of the amount specified in paragraph (2)(A) for the area and year;

(iii) for 2014 the sum of—

(I) ¼ of the applicable amount for the area and year; and

(II) ¾ of the amount specified in paragraph (2)(A) for the area and year; and

(iv) for a subsequent year the amount specified in paragraph (2)(A) for the area and year.

(B) 6-year phase-in for certain areas. If the difference between the applicable amount (as defined in subsection (k)) for an area for 2010 and the projected 2010 benchmark amount (as defined in subparagraph (C)) for the area is at least $50, the blended benchmark amount for the area is—

(i) for 2012 the sum of—

(I) ⅚ of the applicable amount for the area and year; and

(II) ⅙ of the amount specified in paragraph (2)(A) for the area and year;

(ii) for 2013 the sum of—

(I) ⅔ of the applicable amount for the area and year; and

(II) ⅓ of the amount specified in paragraph (2)(A) for the area and year;

(iii) for 2014 the sum of—

(I) ½ of the applicable amount for the area and year; and

(II) ½ of the amount specified in paragraph (2)(A) for the area and year;

(iv) for 2015 the sum of—

(I) ⅓ of the applicable amount for the area and year; and

(II) ⅔ of the amount specified in paragraph (2)(A) for the area and year; and

(v) for 2016 the sum of—

(I) ⅙ of the applicable amount for the area and year; and

(II) ⅚ of the amount specified in paragraph (2)(A) for the area and year; and

(vi) for a subsequent year the amount specified in paragraph (2)(A) for the area and year.

(C) Projected 2010 benchmark amount. The projected 2010 benchmark amount described in this subparagraph for an area is equal to the sum of—

(i) ½ of the applicable amount (as defined in subsection (k)) for the area for 2010; and

(ii) ½ of the amount specified in paragraph (2)(A) for the area for 2010 but determined as if there were substituted for the applicable percentage specified in clause (ii) of such paragraph the sum of—

(I) the applicable percent that would be specified under subparagraph (B) of paragraph (2) (determined without regard to subparagraph (D) of such paragraph) for the area for 2010 if any reference in such paragraph to "the previous year" were deemed a reference to 2010; and

(II) the applicable percentage increase that would apply to a qualifying plan in the area under subsection (o) as if any reference in such subsection to 2012 were deemed a reference to 2010 and as if the determination of a qualifying county under paragraph (3)(B) of such subsection were made for 2010.

(4) Cap on benchmark amount. In no case shall the blended benchmark amount for an area for a year (determined taking into account subsection (o)) be greater than the applicable amount that would (but for the application of this subsection) be determined under subsection (k)(1) for the area for the year.

(5) Non-application to PACE plans. This subsection shall not apply to payments to a PACE program under section 1894 [42 USCS § 1395eee].

(6) Application of performance bonuses. For plan years beginning on or after January 1, 2014, any performance bonus paid to an MA plan under this subsection shall be used for the purposes, and in the priority order, described in subclauses (I) through (III) of section 1854(b)(1)(C)(iii) [42 USCS § 1395w-24(b)(1)(C)(iii)].

(o) Applicable percentage quality increases. (1) In general. Subject to the succeeding paragraphs, in the case of a qualifying plan with respect to a year beginning with 2012, the applicable percentage under subsection (n)(2)(B) shall be increased on a plan or contract level, as determined by the Secretary—

(A) for 2012, by 1.5 percentage points;

(B) for 2013, by 3.0 percentage points; and

(C) for 2014 or a subsequent year, by 5.0 percentage points.

(2) Increase for qualifying plans in qualifying counties. The increase applied under paragraph (1) for a qualifying plan located in a qualifying county for a year shall be doubled.

(3) Qualifying plans and qualifying county defined; application of increases to low enrollment and new plans. For purposes of this subsection:

(A) Qualifying plan. (i) In general. The term "qualifying plan" means, for a year and subject to paragraph (4), a plan that had a quality rating under paragraph (4) of 4 stars or higher based on the most recent data available for such year.

(ii) Application of increases to low enrollment plans. (I) 2012. For 2012, the term "qualifying plan" includes an MA plan that the Secretary determines is not able to have a quality rating under paragraph (4) because of low enrollment.

(II) 2013 and subsequent years. For 2013 and subsequent years, for purposes of determining whether an MA plan with low enrollment (as defined by the Secretary) is included as a qualifying plan, the Secretary shall establish a method to apply to MA plans with low enrollment (as defined by the Secretary) the computation of quality rating and the rating system under paragraph (4).

(iii) Application of increases to new plans. (I) In general. A new MA plan that meets criteria specified by the Secretary shall be treated as a qualifying plan, except that in applying paragraph (1), the applicable percentage under subsection (n)(2)(B) shall be increased—

(aa) for 2012, by 1.5 percentage points;

(bb) for 2013, by 2.5 percentage points; and

(cc) for 2014 or a subsequent year, by 3.5 percentage points.

(II) New MA plan defined. The term "new MA plan" means, with respect to a year, a plan offered by an organization or sponsor that has not had a contract as a Medicare Advantage organization in the preceding 3-year period.

(B) Qualifying county. The term "qualifying county" means, for a year, a county—

(i) that has an MA capitation rate that, in 2004, was based on the amount specified in subsection (c)(1)(B) for a Metropolitan Statistical Area with a population of more than 250,000;

(ii) for which, as of December 2009, of the Medicare Advantage eligible individuals residing in the county at least 25 percent of such individuals were enrolled in Medicare Advantage plans; and

(iii) that has per capita fee-for-service spending that is lower than the national monthly per capita cost for expenditures for individuals enrolled under the original medicare fee-for-service program for the year.

(4) Quality determinations for application of increase. (A) Quality determination. The quality rating for a plan shall be determined according to a 5-star rating system (based on the data collected under section 1852(e)).

(B) Plans that failed to report. An MA plan which does not report data that enables the Secretary to rate the plan for purposes of this paragraph shall be counted as having a rating of fewer than 3.5 stars.

(5) Exception for PACE plans. This subsection shall not apply to payments to a PACE program under section 1894 [42 USCS § 1395eee].

(Aug. 14, 1935, ch 531, Title XVIII, Part C, § 1853, as added Aug. 5, 1997, P. L. 105-33, Title IV, Subtitle A, Ch 1, Subch A, § 4001, 111 Stat. 299; Nov. 29, 1999, P. L. 106-113, Div B, § 1000(a)(6), 113 Stat. 1536; Dec. 21, 2000, P. L. 106-554, § 1(a)(6), 114 Stat. 2763; June 12, 2002, P. L. 107-188, Title V, Subtitle C, § 532(d)(1), 116 Stat. 696; Dec. 8, 2003, P. L. 108-173, Title I, § 101(e)(3)(D), Title II, Subtitle B, § 211(a)–(e)(1), Subtitle C, §§ 221(d)(1), (4), 222(d)–(f), (i), Subtitle D, § 237(b)(1), (2)(B), Subtitle E, § 241(b)(1), Title VII, Subtitle D, § 736(d)(1), Title IX, § 900(e)(1)(G), 117 Stat. 2151, 2176, 2192, 2193, 2200, 2204, 2212, 2213, 2220, 2357, 2371; Feb. 8, 2006, P. L. 109-171, Title V, Subtitle D, § 5301, 120 Stat. 48; July 15, 2008, P. L. 110-275, Title I, Subtitle D, § 161(a), (b), 122 Stat. 2568; Feb. 17, 2009, P. L. 111-5, Div B, Title IV, Subtitle A, §§ 4101(c), (e), 4102(c), (d)(3), 123 Stat. 473, 476, 484, 486; March 23, 2010, P. L. 111-148, Title III, Subtitle C, § 3201(a)(1), (2)(A), (b), (e)(2)(A)(ii)–(iv), (f)(1), (g), (h), (i)(2), 3202(b)(2), 3203, 3205(b), (f), Title X, Subtitle III, § 10318, 124 Stat. 442, 444, 445, 446, 447, 450, 455, 456, 457, 458, 948; March 30, 2010, P. L. 111-152, Title I, Subtitle B, § 1102(a)–(c)(3), (e), 124 Stat. 1040, 1046.)

§ 1395w-24. Premiums and bid amounts

(a) Submission of proposed premiums, bid amounts, and related information. (1) In general. (A) Initial submission. Not later than the second Monday in September of 2002, 2003, and 2004 (or the first Monday in June of each subsequent year), each MA organization shall submit to the Secretary, in a form and manner specified by the Secretary and for each MA plan for the service area (or segment of such an area if permitted under subsection (h)) in which it intends to be offered in the following year the following:

(i) The information described in paragraph (2), (3), (4), or (6)(A) for the type of plan and year involved.

(ii) The plan type for each plan.

(iii) The enrollment capacity (if any) in relation to the plan and area.

(B) Beneficiary rebate information. In the case of a plan required to provide a monthly rebate under subsection (b)(1)(C) for a year, the MA organization offering the plan shall submit to the Secretary, in such form and manner and at such time as the Secretary specifies, information on—

(i) the manner in which such rebate will be provided under clause (ii) of such subsection; and

(ii) the MA monthly prescription drug beneficiary premium (if any) and the MA monthly supplemental beneficiary premium (if any).

(C) Paperwork reduction for offering of MA regional plans nationally or in multi-region areas. The Secretary shall establish requirements for information submission under this subsection in a manner that promotes the offering of MA regional plans in more than one region (including all regions) through the filing of consolidated information.

(2) Information required for coordinated care plans before 2006. For a Medicare+Choice plan described in section 1851(a)(2)(A) [42 USCS § 1395w-21(a)(2)(A)] for a year before 2006, the information described in this paragraph is as follows:

(A) Basic (and additional) benefits. For benefits described in section 1852(a)(1)(A) [42 USCS § 1395w-22(a)(1)(A)]—

(i) the adjusted community rate (as defined in subsection (f)(3));

(ii) the Medicare+Choice monthly basic beneficiary premium (as defined in subsection (b)(2)(A));

(iii) a description of deductibles, coinsurance, and copayments applicable under the plan and the actuarial value of such deductibles, coinsurance, and copayments, described in subsection (e)(1)(A); and

(iv) if required under subsection (f)(1), a description of the additional benefits to be provided pursuant to such subsection and the value determined for such proposed benefits under such subsection.

(B) Supplemental benefits. For benefits described in section 1852(a)(3) [42 USCS § 1395w-22(a)(3)]—

(i) the adjusted community rate (as defined in subsection (f)(3));

(ii) the Medicare+Choice monthly supplemental beneficiary premium (as defined in subsection (b)(2)(B)); and

(iii) a description of deductibles, coinsurance, and copayments applicable under the plan and the actuarial value of such deductibles, coinsurance, and copayments, described in subsection (e)(2).

(3) Requirements for MSA plans. For an MSA plan for any year, the information described in this paragraph is as follows:

(A) Basic (and additional) benefits. For benefits described in section 1852(a)(1)(A) [42 USCS § 1395w-22(a)(1)(A)], the amount of the Medicare+Choice monthly MSA premium.

(B) Supplemental benefits. For benefits described in section 1852(a)(3) [42 USCS § 1395w-22(a)(3)], the amount of the Medicare+Choice monthly supplementary beneficiary premium.

(4) Requirements for private fee-for-service plans before 2006. For a Medicare+Choice plan described in section 1851(a)(2)(C) [42 USCS § 1395w-21(a)(2)(C)] for benefits described in section 1852(a)(1)(A) [42 USCS § 1395w-22(a)(1)(A)] for a year before 2006, the information described in this paragraph is as follows:

(A) Basic (and additional) benefits. For benefits described in section 1852(a)(1)(A) [42 USCS § 1395w-22(a)(1)(A)]—

(i) the adjusted community rate (as defined in subsection (f)(3));

(ii) the amount of the Medicare+Choice monthly basic beneficiary premium;

(iii) a description of the deductibles, coinsurance, and copayments applicable under the plan, and the actuarial value of such deductibles, coinsurance, and copayments, as described in subsection (e)(4)(A); and

(iv) if required under subsection (f)(1), a description of the additional benefits to be provided pursuant to such subsection and the value determined for such proposed benefits under such subsection.

(B) Supplemental benefits. For benefits described in section 1852(a)(3) [42 USCS § 1395w-22(a)(3)], the amount of the Medicare+Choice monthly supplemental beneficiary premium (as defined in subsection (b)(2)(B)).

(5) Review. (A) In general. Subject to subparagraph (B), the Secretary shall review the adjusted community rates, the amounts of the basic and supplemental premiums, and values filed under paragraphs (2) and (4) of this subsection and shall approve or disapprove such rates, amounts, and values so submitted. The Chief Actuary of the Centers for Medicare & Medicaid Services shall review the actuarial assumptions and data used by the Medicare+Choice organization with respect to such rates, amounts, and values so submitted to determine the appropriateness of such assumptions and data.

(B) Exception. The Secretary shall not review, approve, or disapprove the amounts submitted under paragraph (3) or, in the case of an MA private fee-for-service plan, subparagraphs (A)(ii) and (B) of paragraph (4).

(C) Rejection of bids **[Caution: This subparagraph applies to bids submitted for contract years beginning on or after January 1, 2011, as provided by § 3209(c) of Act March 23, 2010, P. L. 111-148, which appears as a note to this section.]**. (i) In general. Nothing in this section shall be construed as requiring the Secretary to accept any or every bid submitted by an MA organization under this subsection.

(ii) Authority to deny bids that propose significant increases in cost sharing or decreases in benefits. The Secretary may deny a bid submitted by an MA organization for an MA plan if it proposes significant increases in cost sharing or decreases in benefits offered under the plan.

(6) Submission of bid amounts by MA organizations beginning in 2006. (A) Information to be submitted. For an MA plan (other than an MSA plan) for a plan year beginning on or after January 1, 2006, the information described in this subparagraph is as follows:

(i) The monthly aggregate bid amount for the provision of all items and services under the plan, which amount shall be based on average revenue requirements (as used for purposes of section 1302(8) of the Public Health Service Act [42 USCS § 300e-1(8)]) in the payment area for an enrollee with a national average risk profile for the factors described in section 1853(a)(1)(C) [42 USCS § 1395w-23(a)(1)(C)] (as specified by the Secretary).

(ii) The proportions of such bid amount that are attributable to—

(I) the provision of benefits under the original medicare fee-for-service program option (as defined in section 1852(a)(1)(B) [42 USCS § 1395w-22(a)(1)(B)]);

(II) the provision of basic prescription drug coverage; and

(III) the provision of supplemental health care benefits.

(iii) The actuarial basis for determining the amount under clause (i) and the proportions described in clause (ii) and such additional information as the Secretary may require to verify such actuarial bases and the projected number of enrollees in each MA local area.

(iv) A description of deductibles, coinsurance, and copayments applicable under the plan and the actuarial value of such deductibles, coinsurance, and copayments, described in subsection (e)(4)(A).

(v) With respect to qualified prescription drug coverage, the information required under section 1860D-4 [42 USCS § 1395w-104], as incorporated under section 1860D-11(b)(2) [42 USCS § 1395w-111(b)(2)], with respect to such coverage.

In the case of a specialized MA plan for special needs individuals, the information described in this subparagraph is such information as the Secretary shall specify.

(B) Acceptance and negotiation of bid amounts. (i) Authority. Subject to clauses (iii) and (iv), the Secretary has the authority to negotiate regarding monthly bid amounts submitted under subparagraph (A) (and the proportions described in subparagraph (A)(ii)), including supplemental benefits provided under subsection (b)(1)(C)(ii)(I) and in exercising such authority the Secretary shall have authority similar to the authority of the Director of the Office of Personnel Management with respect to health benefits plans under chapter 89 of title 5, United States Code [5 USCS §§ 8901 et seq.].

(ii) Application of FEHBP standard. Subject to clause (iv), the Secretary may only accept such a bid amount or proportion if the Secretary determines that such amount and proportions are supported by the actuarial bases provided under subparagraph (A) and reasonably and equitably reflects the revenue requirements (as used for purposes of section 1302(8) of the Public Health Service Act [42 USCS § 300e-1(8)]) of benefits provided under that plan.

(iii) Noninterference. In order to promote competition under this part and part D and in carrying out such parts, the Secretary may not require any MA organization to contract with a particular hospital, physician, or other entity or individual to furnish items and services under this title or require a particular price structure for payment under such a contract to the extent consistent with the Secretary's authority under this part.

(iv) Exception. In the case of a plan described in section 1851(a)(2)(C) [42 USCS § 1395w-21(a)(2)(C)], the provisions of clauses (i) and (ii) shall not apply and the provisions of paragraph (5)(B), prohibiting the review, approval, or disapproval of amounts described in such paragraph, shall apply to the negotiation and rejection of the monthly bid amounts and the proportions referred to in subparagraph (A).

(b) Monthly premium charged. (1) In general. (A) Rule for other than MSA plans. Subject to the rebate under subparagraph (C), the monthly amount (if any) of the premium charged to an individual enrolled in a Medicare+Choice plan (other than an MSA plan) offered by a Medicare+Choice organization shall be equal to the sum of the Medicare+Choice monthly basic beneficiary premium, the Medicare+Choice monthly supplementary beneficiary premium (if any), and, if the plan provides qualified prescription drug coverage, the MA monthly prescription drug beneficiary premium.

(B) MSA plans. The monthly amount of the premium charged to an individual enrolled in an MSA plan offered by a Medicare+Choice organization shall be equal to the Medicare+Choice monthly supplemental beneficiary premium (if any).

(C) Beneficiary rebate rule. (i) Requirement. The MA plan shall provide to the enrollee a monthly rebate equal to 75 percent (or the applicable rebate percentage specified in clause (iii) in the case of plan years beginning on or after January 1, 2012) of the average per capita savings (if any) described in paragraph (3)(C) or (4)(C), as applicable to the plan and year involved.

(ii) Form of rebate for plan years before 2012. For plan years before 2012, a rebate required under this subparagraph shall be provided through the application of the amount of the rebate toward one or more of the following:

(I) Provision of supplemental health care benefits and payment for premium for supplemental benefits. The provision of supplemental health care benefits described in section 1852(a)(3) [42 USCS § 1395w-22(a)(3)] in a manner specified under the plan, which may include the reduction of cost-sharing otherwise applicable as well as additional health care benefits which are not benefits under the original medicare fee-for-service program option, or crediting toward an MA monthly supplemental beneficiary premium (if any).

(II) Payment for premium for prescription drug coverage. Crediting toward the MA monthly prescription drug beneficiary premium.

(III) Payment toward part B premium. Crediting toward the premium imposed under part B [42 USCS §§ 1395j et seq.] (determined without regard to the application of subsections (b), (h), and (i) of section 1839 [42 USCS § 1395r]).

(iii) Applicable rebate percentage. The applicable rebate percentage specified in this clause for a plan for a year, based on the system under section 1853(o)(4)(A) [42 USCS § 1395w-23(o)(4)(A)], is the sum of—

(I) the product of the old phase-in proportion for the year under clause (iv) and 75 percent; and

(II) the product of the new phase-in proportion for the year under clause (iv) and the final applicable rebate percentage under clause (v).

(iv) Old and new phase-in proportions. For purposes of clause (iv)—

(I) for 2012, the old phase-in proportion is ⅔ and the new phase-in proportion is ⅓;

(II) for 2013, the old phase-in proportion is ⅓ and the new phase-in proportion is ⅔; and

(III) for 2014 and any subsequent year, the old phase-in proportion is 0 and the new phase-in proportion is 1.

(v) Final applicable rebate percentage. Subject to clause (vi), the final applicable rebate percentage under this clause is—

(I) in the case of a plan with a quality rating under such system of at least 4.5 stars, 70 percent;

(II) in the case of a plan with a quality rating under such system of at least 3.5 stars and less than 4.5 stars, 65 percent; and

(III) in the case of a plan with a quality rating under such system of less than 3.5 stars, 50 percent.

(vi) Treatment of low enrollment and new plans. For purposes of clause (v)—

(I) for 2012, in the case of a plan described in subclause (I) of subsection (o)(3)(A)(ii), the plan shall be treated as having a rating of 4.5 stars; and

(II) for 2012 or a subsequent year, in the case of a new MA plan (as defined under subclause (III) of subsection (o)(3)(A)(iii)) that is treated as a qualifying plan pursuant to subclause (I) of such subsection, the plan shall be treated as having a rating of 3.5 stars.

(vii) Disclosure relating to rebates. The plan shall disclose to the Secretary information on the form and amount of the rebate provided under this subparagraph or the actuarial value in the case of supplemental health care benefits.

(viii) Application of part B premium reduction. Insofar as an MA organization elects to provide a rebate under this subparagraph under a plan as a credit toward the part B premium under clause (ii)(III), the Secretary shall apply such credit to reduce the premium under section 1839 [42 USCS § 1395r] of each enrollee in such plan as provided in section 1840(i) [42 USCS § 1395s(i)].

(2) Premium and bid terminology defined. For purposes of this part [42 USCS §§ 1395w-21 et seq.]:

(A) MA monthly basic beneficiary premium. The term "MA monthly basic beneficiary premium" means, with respect to an MA plan—

(i) described in section 1853(a)(1)(B)(i) [42 USCS § 1395w-23(a)(1)(B)(i)] (relating to plans providing rebates), zero; or

(ii) described in section 1853(a)(1)(B)(ii) [42 USCS § 1395w-23(a)(1)(B)(ii)], the amount (if any) by which the unadjusted MA statutory non-drug monthly bid amount (as defined in subparagraph (E)) exceeds the applicable unadjusted MA area-specific non-drug monthly benchmark amount (as defined in section 1853(j) [42 USCS § 1395w-23(j)]).

(B) MA monthly prescription drug beneficiary premium. The term "MA monthly prescription drug beneficiary premium" means, with respect to an MA plan, the base beneficiary premium (as determined under section 1860D-13(a)(2) [42 USCS § 1395w-113(a)(2)] and as adjusted under section 1860D-13(a)(1)(B) [42 USCS § 1395w-113(a)(1)(B)]), less the amount of rebate credited toward such amount under section 1854(b)(1)(C)(ii)(II) [42 USCS § 1395w-24(b)(1)(C)(ii)(II)].

(C) MA monthly supplemental beneficiary premium. (i) In general. The term "MA monthly supplemental beneficiary premium" means, with respect to an MA plan, the portion of the aggregate monthly bid amount submitted under clause (i) of subsection (a)(6)(A) for the year that is attributable under clause (ii)(III) of such subsection to the provision of supplemental health care benefits, less the amount of rebate credited toward such portion under section 1854(b)(1)(C)(ii)(I) [42 USCS § 1395w-24(b)(1)(C)(ii)(I)].

(ii) Application of MA monthly supplementary beneficiary premium. For plan years beginning on or after January 1, 2012, any MA monthly supplementary beneficiary premium charged to an individual enrolled in an MA plan shall be used for the purposes, and in the priority order, described in subclauses (I) through (III) of paragraph (1)(C)(iii).

(D) Medicare+Choice monthly MSA premium. The term "Medicare+Choice monthly MSA premium" means, with respect to a Medicare+Choice plan, the amount of such premium filed under subsection (a)(3)(A) for the plan.

(E) Unadjusted MA statutory non-drug monthly bid amount. The term "unadjusted MA statutory non-drug monthly bid amount" means the portion of the bid amount submitted under clause (i) of subsection (a)(6)(A) for the year that is attributable under clause (ii)(I) of such subsection to the provision of benefits under the original medicare fee-for-service program option (as defined in section 1852(a)(1)(B) [42 USCS § 1395w-22(a)(1)(B)]).

(3) Computation of average per capita monthly savings for local plans. For purposes of paragraph (1)(C)(i), the average per capita

monthly savings referred to in such paragraph for an MA local plan and year is computed as follows:

(A) Determination of statewide average risk adjustment for local plans. (i) In general. Subject to clause (iii), the Secretary shall determine, at the same time rates are promulgated under section 1853(b)(1) [42 USCS § 1395w-23(b)(1)] (beginning with 2006) for each State, the average of the risk adjustment factors to be applied under section 1853(a)(1)(C) [42 USCS § 1395w-23(a)(1)(C)] to payment for enrollees in that State for MA local plans.

(ii) Treatment of States for first year in which local plan offered. In the case of a State in which no MA local plan was offered in the previous year, the Secretary shall estimate such average. In making such estimate, the Secretary may use average risk adjustment factors applied to comparable States or applied on a national basis.

(iii) Authority to determine risk adjustment for areas other than States. The Secretary may provide for the determination and application of risk adjustment factors under this subparagraph on the basis of areas other than States or on a plan-specific basis.

(B) Determination of risk adjusted benchmark and risk-adjusted bid for local plans. For each MA plan offered in a local area in a State, the Secretary shall—

(i) adjust the applicable MA area-specific non-drug monthly benchmark amount (as defined in section 1853(j)(1) [42 USCS § 1395w-23(j)(1)]) for the area by the average risk adjustment factor computed under subparagraph (A); and

(ii) adjust the unadjusted MA statutory non-drug monthly bid amount by such applicable average risk adjustment factor.

(C) Determination of average per capita monthly savings. The average per capita monthly savings described in this subparagraph for an MA local plan is equal to the amount (if any) by which—

(i) the risk-adjusted benchmark amount computed under subparagraph (B)(i); exceeds

(ii) the risk-adjusted bid computed under subparagraph (B)(ii).

(4) Computation of average per capita monthly savings for regional plans. For purposes of paragraph (1)(C)(i), the average per capita monthly savings referred to in such paragraph for an MA regional plan and year is computed as follows:

(A) Determination of regionwide average risk adjustment for regional plans. (i) In general. The Secretary shall determine, at the same time rates are promulgated under section 1853(b)(1) [42 USCS § 1395w-23(b)(1)] (beginning with 2006) for each MA region the average of the risk adjustment factors to be applied under section 1853(a)(1)(C) [42 USCS § 1395w-23(a)(1)(C)] to payment for enrollees in that region for MA regional plans.

(ii) Treatment of regions for first year in which regional plan offered. In the case of an MA region in which no MA regional plan was offered in the previous year, the Secretary shall estimate such average. In making such estimate, the Secretary may use average risk adjustment factors applied to comparable regions or applied on a national basis.

(iii) Authority to determine risk adjustment for areas other than regions. The Secretary may provide for the determination and application of risk adjustment factors under this subparagraph on the basis of areas other than MA regions or on a plan-specific basis.

(B) Determination of risk-adjusted benchmark and risk-adjusted bid for regional plans. For each MA regional plan offered in a region, the Secretary shall—

(i) adjust the applicable MA area-specific non-drug monthly benchmark amount (as defined in section 1853(j)(2) [42 USCS § 1395w-23(j)(2)]) for the region by the average risk adjustment factor computed under subparagraph (A); and

(ii) adjust the unadjusted MA statutory non-drug monthly bid amount by such applicable average risk adjustment factor.

(C) Determination of average per capita monthly savings. The average per capita monthly savings described in this subparagraph for an MA regional plan is equal to the amount (if any) by which—

(i) the risk-adjusted benchmark amount computed under subparagraph (B)(i); exceeds

(ii) the risk-adjusted bid computed under subparagraph (B)(ii).

(c) Uniform premium and bid amounts. Except as permitted under section 1857(i) [42 USCS § 1395w-27(i)], the MA monthly bid amount submitted under subsection (a)(6), the amounts of the MA monthly basic, prescription drug, and supplemental beneficiary premiums, and the MA monthly MSA premium charged under subsection (b) of an MA organization under this part may not vary among individuals enrolled in the plan.

(d) Terms and conditions of imposing premiums. (1) In general. Each Medicare+Choice organization shall permit the payment of Medicare+Choice monthly basic, prescription drug, and supplemental beneficiary premiums on a monthly basis, may terminate election of individuals for a Medicare+Choice plan for failure to make premium payments only in accordance with section 1851(g)(3)(B)(i) [42 USCS § 1395w-21(g)(3)(B)(i)], and may not provide for cash or other monetary rebates as an inducement for enrollment or otherwise.

(2) Beneficiary's option of payment through withholding from social security payment or use of electronic funds transfer mechanism. In accordance with regulations, an MA organization shall permit each enrollee, at the enrollee's option, to make payment of premiums (if any) under this part to the organization through—

(A) withholding from benefit payments in the manner provided under section 1840 [42 USCS § 1395s] with respect to monthly premiums under section 1839 [42 USCS § 1395r];

(B) an electronic funds transfer mechanism (such as automatic charges of an account at a financial institution or a credit or debit card account); or

(C) such other means as the Secretary may specify, including payment by an employer or under employment-based retiree health coverage (as defined in section 1860D-22(c)(1) [42 USCS § 1395w-132(c)(1)]) on behalf of an employee or former employee (or dependent).

All premium payments that are withheld under subparagraph (A) shall be credited to the appropriate Trust Fund (or Account thereof), as specified by the Secretary, under this title and shall be paid to the MA organization involved. No charge may be imposed under an MA plan with respect to the election of the payment option described in subparagraph (A). The Secretary shall consult with the Commissioner of Social Security and the Secretary of the Treasury regarding methods for allocating premiums withheld under subparagraph (A) among the appropriate Trust Funds and Account.

(3) Information necessary for collection. In order to carry out paragraph (2)(A) with respect to an enrollee who has elected such paragraph to apply, the Secretary shall transmit to the Commissioner of Social Security—

(A) by the beginning of each year, the name, social security account number, consolidated monthly beneficiary premium described in paragraph (4) owed by such enrollee for each month during the year, and other information determined appropriate by the Secretary, in consultation with the Commissioner of Social Security; and

(B) periodically throughout the year, information to update the information previously transmitted under this paragraph for the year.

(4) Consolidated monthly beneficiary premium. In the case of an enrollee in an MA plan, the Secretary shall provide a mechanism for the consolidation of—

(A) the MA monthly basic beneficiary premium (if any);

(B) the MA monthly supplemental beneficiary premium (if any); and

(C) the MA monthly prescription drug beneficiary premium (if any).

(e) Limitation on enrollee liability. (1) For basic and additional benefits before 2006. For periods before 2006, in no event may—

(A) the Medicare+Choice monthly basic beneficiary premium (multiplied by 12) and the actuarial value of the deductibles, coinsurance, and copayments applicable on average to individuals enrolled under this part [42 USCS §§ 1395w-21 et seq.] with a Medicare+Choice plan described in section 1851(a)(2)(A) [42 USCS § 1395w-21(a)(2)(A)] of an organization with respect to required benefits described in section 1852(a)(1)(A) [42 USCS § 1395w-22(a)(1)(A)] and additional benefits (if any) required under subsection (f)(1)(A) for a year, exceed

(B) the actuarial value of the deductibles, coinsurance, and copayments that would be applicable on average to individuals entitled to benefits under part A [42 USCS §§ 1395c et seq.] and enrolled under part B [42 USCS §§ 1395j et seq.] if they were not members of a Medicare+Choice organization for the year.

(2) For supplemental benefits before 2006. For periods before 2006, if the Medicare+Choice organization provides to its members enrolled under this part [42 USCS §§ 1395w-21 et seq.] in a Medicare+Choice plan described in section 1851(a)(2)(A) [42 USCS § 1395w-21(a)(2)(A)] with respect to supplemental benefits described in section 1852(a)(3) [42 USCS § 1395w-22(a)(3)], the sum of the Medicare+Choice monthly supplemental beneficiary premium (multiplied by 12) charged and the actuarial value of its deductibles, coinsurance, and copayments charged with respect to such benefits may not exceed the adjusted community rate for such benefits (as defined in subsection (f)(3)).

(3) Determination on other basis. If the Secretary determines that adequate data are not available to determine the actuarial value under paragraph (1)(A), (2), or (4), the Secretary may determine such amount with respect to all individuals in same geographic area, the State, or in the United States, eligible to enroll in the Medicare+Choice plan involved under this part [42 USCS §§ 1395w-21 et seq.] or on the basis

of other appropriate data.

(4) Special rule for private fee-for-service plans and for basic benefits beginning in 2006. With respect to a Medicare+Choice private fee-for-service plan (other than a plan that is an MSA plan) and for periods beginning with 2006, with respect to an MA plan described in section 1851(a)(2)(A) [42 USCS § 13952-21(a)(2)(A)], in no event may—

(A) the actuarial value of the deductibles, coinsurance, and copayments applicable on average to individuals enrolled under this part [42 USCS §§ 1395w-21 et seq.] with such a plan of an organization with respect to benefits under the original medicare fee-for-service program option, exceed

(B) the actuarial value of the deductibles, coinsurance, and copayments that would be applicable with respect to such benefits on average to individuals entitled to benefits under part A [42 USCS §§ 1395c et seq.] and enrolled under part B [42 USCS §§ 1395j et seq.] if they were not members of a Medicare+Choice organization for the year.

(f) Requirement for additional benefits before 2006. (1) Requirement. (A) In general. For years before 2006, each Medicare+Choice organization (in relation to a Medicare+Choice plan, other than an MSA plan, it offers) shall provide that if there is an excess amount (as defined in subparagraph (B)) for the plan for a contract year, subject to the succeeding provisions of this subsection, the organization shall provide to individuals such additional benefits (as the organization may specify) in a value which the Secretary determines is at least equal to the adjusted excess amount (as defined in subparagraph (C)).

(B) Excess amount. For purposes of this paragraph, the "excess amount", for an organization for a plan, is the amount (if any) by which—

(i) the average of the capitation payments made to the organization under section 1853 [42 USCS § 1395w-23] for the plan at the beginning of contract year, exceeds

(ii) the actuarial value of the required benefits described in section 1852(a)(1)(A) [42 USCS § 1395w-22(a)(1)(A)] under the plan for individuals under this part [42 USCS §§ 1395w-21 et seq.], as determined based upon an adjusted community rate described in paragraph (3) (as reduced for the actuarial value of the coinsurance, copayments, and deductibles under parts A and B [42 USCS §§ 1395c et seq. and 1395j et seq.]).

(C) Adjusted excess amount. For purposes of this paragraph, the "adjusted excess amount", for an organization for a plan, is the excess amount reduced to reflect any amount withheld and reserved for the organization for the year under paragraph (2).

(D) Uniform application. This paragraph shall be applied uniformly for all enrollees for a plan.

(E) Premium reductions. (i) In general. Subject to clause (ii), as part of providing any additional benefits required under subparagraph (A), a Medicare+Choice organization may elect a reduction in its payments under section 1853(a)(1)(A) [42 USCS § 1395w-23(a)(1)(A)] with respect to a Medicare+Choice plan and the Secretary shall apply such reduction to reduce the premium under section 1839 [42 USCS § 1395r] of each enrollee in such plan as provided in section 1840(i) [42 USCS § 1395s(i)].

(ii) Amount of reduction. The amount of the reduction under clause (i) with respect to any enrollee in a Medicare+Choice plan—

(I) may not exceed 125 percent of the premium described under section 1839(a)(3) [42 USCS § 1395r(a)(3)]; and

(II) shall apply uniformly to each enrollee of the Medicare+Choice plan to which such reduction applies.

(F) Construction. Nothing in this subsection shall be construed as preventing a Medicare+Choice organization from providing supplemental benefits (described in section 1852(a)(3) [42 USCS § 1395w-22(a)(3)]) that are in addition to the health care benefits otherwise required to be provided under this paragraph and from imposing a premium for such supplemental benefits.

(2) Stabilization fund. A Medicare+Choice organization may provide that a part of the value of an excess amount described in paragraph (1) be withheld and reserved in the Federal Hospital Insurance Trust Fund and in the Federal Supplementary Medical Insurance Trust Fund (in such proportions as the Secretary determines to be appropriate) by the Secretary for subsequent annual contract periods, to the extent required to stabilize and prevent undue fluctuations in the additional benefits offered in those subsequent periods by the organization in accordance with such paragraph. Any of such value of the amount reserved which is not provided as additional benefits described in paragraph (1)(A) to individuals electing the Medicare+Choice plan of the organization in accordance with such paragraph prior to the end of such periods, shall revert for the use of such trust funds.

(3) Adjusted community rate. For purposes

of this subsection, subject to paragraph (4), the term "adjusted community rate" for a service or services means, at the election of a Medicare+Choice organization, either—

(A) the rate of payment for that service or services which the Secretary annually determines would apply to an individual electing a Medicare+Choice plan under this part [42 USCS §§ 1395w-21 et seq.] if the rate of payment were determined under a "community rating system" (as defined in section 1302(8) of the Public Health Service Act [42 USCS § 300e-1(8)], other than subparagraph (C)), or

(B) such portion of the weighted aggregate premium, which the Secretary annually estimates would apply to such an individual, as the Secretary annually estimates is attributable to that service or services,

but adjusted for differences between the utilization characteristics of the individuals electing coverage under this part [42 USCS §§ 1395w-21 et seq.] and the utilization characteristics of the other enrollees with the plan (or, if the Secretary finds that adequate data are not available to adjust for those differences, the differences between the utilization characteristics of individuals selecting other Medicare+Choice coverage, or Medicare+Choice eligible individuals in the area, in the State, or in the United States, eligible to elect Medicare+Choice coverage under this part [42 USCS §§ 1395w-21 et seq.] and the utilization characteristics of the rest of the population in the area, in the State, or in the United States, respectively).

(4) Determination based on insufficient data. For purposes of this subsection, if the Secretary finds that there is insufficient enrollment experience to determine an average of the capitation payments to be made under this part [42 USCS §§ 1395w-21 et seq.] at the beginning of a contract period or to determine (in the case of a newly operated provider-sponsored organization or other new organization) the adjusted community rate for the organization, the Secretary may determine such an average based on the enrollment experience of other contracts entered into under this part [42 USCS §§ 1395w-21 et seq.] and may determine such a rate using data in the general commercial marketplace.

(g) Prohibition of State imposition of premium taxes. No State may impose a premium tax or similar tax with respect to payments to Medicare+Choice organizations under section 1853 [42 USCS § 1395w-23] or premiums paid to such organizations under this part [42 USCS §§ 1395w-21 et seq.].

(h) Permitting use of segments of service areas. The Secretary shall permit a Medicare+Choice organization to elect to apply the provisions of this section uniformly to separate segments of a service area (rather than uniformly to an entire service area) as long as such segments are composed of one or more Medicare+Choice payment areas.

(Aug. 14, 1935, ch 531, Title XVIII, Part C, § 1854, as added Aug. 5, 1997, P. L. 105-33, Title IV, Subtitle A, Ch 1, Subch A, § 4001, 111 Stat. 308; Nov. 29, 1999, P. L. 106-113, Div B, § 1000(a)(6), 113 Stat. 1536; Dec. 21, 2000, P. L. 106-554, § 1(a)(6), 114 Stat. 2763; June 12, 2002, P. L. 107-188, Title V, Subtitle C, § 532(b)(1), 116 Stat. 696; Dec. 8, 2003, P. L. 108-173, Title II, Subtitle C, § 222(a)(1), (b), (c), (g), Subtitle D, § 232(b), Title IX, § 900(e)(1)(H), 117 Stat. 2193, 2196, 2203, 2208, 2371; March 23, 2010, P. L. 111-148, Title III, Subtitle C, §§ 3201(a)(2)(B), (c)–(d)(2), (e)(2)(A)(v), 3202(b)(1), (3), 3209(a), 124 Stat. 444, 447, 454, 455, 460; March 30, 2010, P. L. 111-152, Title I, Subtitle B, § 1102(a), (d), 124 Stat. 1040, 1045.)

HISTORY; ANCILLARY LAWS AND DIRECTIVES

Other provisions:

Repeal of provisions relating to application of amendments made by § 3201(d) of Act March 23, 2010. Act March 23, 2010, P. L. 111-148, Title III, Subtitle C, § 3201(d)(3), 124 Stat. 445, which formerly appeared as a note to this section, was repealed by Act March 30, 2010, P. L. 111-152, Title I, Subtitle B, § 1102(a), effective as if include in the enactment of Act March 23, 2010. Such note provided that the amendments to subsec. (a)(6) of this section should apply to bid amounts submitted on or after January 1, 2012.

Application of amendments made by § 3209 of Act March 23, 2010. Act March 23, 2010, P. L. 111-148, Title III, Subtitle C, § 3209(c), 124 Stat. 460, provides: "The amendments made by this section [adding 42 USCS §§ 1395w-24(a)(5)(C) and 1395w-111(d)(3)] shall apply to bids submitted for contract years beginning on or after January 1, 2011.".

§ 1395w-27. Contracts with Medicare+Choice organizations

(a) In general. The Secretary shall not permit the election under section 1851 [42 USCS § 1395w-21] of a Medicare+Choice plan offered by a Medicare+Choice organization under this part [42 USCS §§ 1395w-21 et seq.], and no payment shall be made under section 1853 [42 USCS § 1395w-23] to an organization, unless the Secretary has entered into a contract under this section with the organization with respect to the offering of such plan. Such a contract with an organization may cover more than 1

Medicare+Choice plan. Such contract shall provide that the organization agrees to comply with the applicable requirements and standards of this part [42 USCS §§ 1395w-21 et seq.] and the terms and conditions of payment as provided for in this part [42 USCS §§ 1395w-21 et seq.].

(b) Minimum enrollment requirements. (1) In general. Subject to paragraph (2), the Secretary may not enter into a contract under this section with a Medicare+Choice organization unless the organization has—

(A) at least 5,000 individuals (or 1,500 individuals in the case of an organization that is a provider-sponsored organization) who are receiving health benefits through the organization, or

(B) at least 1,500 individuals (or 500 individuals in the case of an organization that is a provider-sponsored organization) who are receiving health benefits through the organization if the organization primarily serves individuals residing outside of urbanized areas.

(2) Application to MSA plans. In applying paragraph (1) in the case of a Medicare+Choice organization that is offering an MSA plan, paragraph (1) shall be applied by substituting covered lives for individuals.

(3) Allowing transition. The Secretary may waive the requirement of paragraph (1) during the first 3 contract years with respect to an organization.

(c) Contract period and effectiveness. (1) Period. Each contract under this section shall be for a term of at least 1 year, as determined by the Secretary, and may be made automatically renewable from term to term in the absence of notice by either party of intention to terminate at the end of the current term.

(2) Termination authority. In accordance with procedures established under subsection (h), the Secretary may at any time terminate any such contract if the Secretary determines that the organization—

(A) has failed substantially to carry out the contract;

(B) is carrying out the contract in a manner inconsistent with the efficient and effective administration of this part [42 USCS §§ 1395w-21 et seq.]; or

(C) no longer substantially meets the applicable conditions of this part [42 USCS §§ 1395w-21 et seq.].

(3) Effective date of contracts. The effective date of any contract executed pursuant to this section shall be specified in the contract, except that in no case shall a contract under this section which provides for coverage under an MSA plan be effective before January 1999 with respect to such coverage.

(4) Previous terminations. (A) In general. The Secretary may not enter into a contract with a Medicare+Choice organization if a previous contract with that organization under this section was terminated at the request of the organization within the preceding 2-year period, except as provided in subparagraph (B) and except in such other circumstances which warrant special consideration, as determined by the Secretary.

(B) Earlier re-entry permitted where change in payment policy. Subparagraph (A) shall not apply with respect to the offering by a Medicare+Choice organization of a Medicare+Choice plan in a Medicare+Choice payment area if during the 6-month period beginning on the date the organization notified the Secretary of the intention to terminate the most recent previous contract, there was a legislative change enacted (or a regulatory change adopted) that has the effect of increasing payment amounts under section 1853 [42 USCS § 1395w-23] for that Medicare+Choice payment area.

(5) Contracting authority. The authority vested in the Secretary by this part [42 USCS §§ 1395w-21 et seq.] may be performed without regard to such provisions of law or regulations relating to the making, performance, amendment, or modification of contracts of the United States as the Secretary may determine to be inconsistent with the furtherance of the purpose of this title [42 USCS §§ 1395 et seq.].

(d) Protections against fraud and beneficiary protections. (1) Periodic auditing. The Secretary shall provide for the annual auditing of the financial records (including data relating to medicare utilization and costs, including allowable costs under section 1858(c) [42 USCS § 1395w-27a(c)]) of at least one-third of the Medicare+Choice organizations offering Medicare+Choice plans under this part [42 USCS §§ 1395w-21 et seq.]. The Comptroller General shall monitor auditing activities conducted under this subsection.

(2) Inspection and audit. Each contract under this section shall provide that the Secretary, or any person or organization designated by the Secretary—

(A) shall have the right to timely inspect or otherwise evaluate (i) the quality, appropriateness, and timeliness of services performed under the contract, and (ii) the facilities of the organization when there is reasonable evidence of some need for such inspection, and

(B) shall have the right to timely audit and inspect any books and records of the Medicare+Choice organization that pertain (i) to the ability of the organization to bear the risk of potential financial losses, or (ii) to services performed or determinations of amounts payable under the contract.

(3) Enrollee notice at time of termination. Each contract under this section shall require the organization to provide (and pay for) written notice in advance of the contract's termination, as well as a description of alternatives for obtaining benefits under this title [42 USCS §§ 1395 et seq.], to each individual enrolled with the organization under this part [42 USCS §§ 1395w-21 et seq.].

(4) Disclosure. (A) In general. Each Medicare+Choice organization shall, in accordance with regulations of the Secretary, report to the Secretary financial information which shall include the following:

(i) Such information as the Secretary may require demonstrating that the organization has a fiscally sound operation.

(ii) A copy of the report, if any, filed with the Secretary containing the information required to be reported under section 1124 [42 USCS § 1320a-3] by disclosing entities.

(iii) A description of transactions, as specified by the Secretary, between the organization and a party in interest. Such transactions shall include—

(I) any sale or exchange, or leasing of any property between the organization and a party in interest;

(II) any furnishing for consideration of goods, services (including management services), or facilities between the organization and a party in interest, but not including salaries paid to employees for services provided in the normal course of their employment and health services provided to members by hospitals and other providers and by staff, medical group (or groups), individual practice association (or associations), or any combination thereof; and

(III) any lending of money or other extension of credit between an organization and a party in interest.

The Secretary may require that information reported respecting an organization which controls, is controlled by, or is under common control with, another entity be in the form of a consolidated financial statement for the organization and such entity.

(B) Party in interest defined. For the purposes of this paragraph, the term "party in interest" means—

(i) any director, officer, partner, or employee responsible for management or administration of a Medicare+Choice organization, any person who is directly or indirectly the beneficial owner of more than 5 percent of the equity of the organization, any person who is the beneficial owner of a mortgage, deed of trust, note, or other interest secured by, and valuing more than 5 percent of the organization, and, in the case of a Medicare+Choice organization organized as a nonprofit corporation, an incorporator or member of such corporation under applicable State corporation law;

(ii) any entity in which a person described in clause (i)—

(I) is an officer or director;

(II) is a partner (if such entity is organized as a partnership);

(III) has directly or indirectly a beneficial interest of more than 5 percent of the equity; or

(IV) has a mortgage, deed of trust, note, or other interest valuing more than 5 percent of the assets of such entity;

(iii) any person directly or indirectly controlling, controlled by, or under common control with an organization; and

(iv) any spouse, child, or parent of an individual described in clause (i).

(C) Access to information. Each Medicare+Choice organization shall make the information reported pursuant to subparagraph (A) available to its enrollees upon reasonable request.

(5) Loan information. The contract shall require the organization to notify the Secretary of loans and other special financial arrangements which are made between the organization and subcontractors, affiliates, and related parties.

(6) Review to ensure compliance with care management requirements for specialized Medicare Advantage plans for special needs individuals. In conjunction with the periodic audit of a specialized Medicare Advantage plan for special needs individuals under paragraph (1), the Secretary shall conduct a review to ensure that such organization offering the plan meets the requirements described in section 1859(f)(5) [42 USCS § 1395w-28(f)(5)].

(e) Additional contract terms. (1) In general. The contract shall contain such other terms and conditions not inconsistent with this part [42 USCS §§ 1395w-21 et seq.] (including requiring the organization to provide the Secretary with such information) as the Secretary may find necessary and appropriate.

(2) Cost-sharing in enrollment-related costs. (A) In general. A Medicare+Choice organization and a PDP sponsor under part D [42 USCS

§§ 1395w-101 et seq.] shall pay the fee established by the Secretary under subparagraph (B).

(B) Authorization. The Secretary is authorized to charge a fee to each Medicare+Choice organization with a contract under this part [42 USCS §§ 1395w-21 et seq.] and each PDP sponsor with a contract under part D [42 USCS §§ 1395w-101 et seq.] that is equal to the organization's or sponsor's pro rata share (as determined by the Secretary) of the aggregate amount of fees which the Secretary is directed to collect in a fiscal year. Any amounts collected shall be available without further appropriation to the Secretary for the purpose of carrying out section 1851 [42 USCS § 1395w-21] (relating to enrollment and dissemination of information), section 1860D-1(c) [42 USCS § 1395w-101(c)], and section 4360 of the Omnibus Budget Reconciliation Act of 1990 [42 USCS § 1395b-4] (relating to the health insurance counseling and assistance program).

(C) Authorization of appropriations. There are authorized to be appropriated for the purposes described in subparagraph (B) for each fiscal year beginning with fiscal year 2001 and ending with fiscal year 2005 an amount equal to $100,000,000, and for each fiscal year beginning with fiscal year 2006 an amount equal to $200,000,000, reduced by the amount of fees authorized to be collected under this paragraph and section 1860D-12(b)(3)(D) [42 USCS § 1395w-112(b)(3)(D)] for the fiscal year.

(D) Limitation. In any fiscal year the fees collected by the Secretary under subparagraph (B) shall not exceed the lesser of—

(i) the estimated costs to be incurred by the Secretary in the fiscal year in carrying out the activities described in section 1851 [42 USCS § 1395w-21] and section 1860D-1(c) [42 USCS § 1395w-101(c)] and section 4360 of the Omnibus Budget Reconciliation Act of 1990 [42 USCS § 1395b-4]; or

(ii)(I) $200,000,000 in fiscal year 1998;

(II) $150,000,000 in fiscal year 1999;

(III) $100,000,000 in fiscal year 2000;

(IV) the Medicare+Choice portion (as defined in subparagraph (E)) of $100,000,000 in fiscal year 2001 and each succeeding fiscal year before fiscal year 2006; and

(V) the applicable portion (as defined in subparagraph (F)) of $200,000,000 in fiscal year 2006 and each succeeding fiscal year.

(E) Medicare+Choice portion defined. In this paragraph, the term "Medicare+Choice portion" means, for a fiscal year, the ratio, as estimated by the Secretary, of—

(i) the average number of individuals enrolled in Medicare+Choice plans during the fiscal year, to

(ii) the average number of individuals entitled to benefits under part A [42 USCS §§ 1395c et seq.], and enrolled under part B [42 USCS §§ 1395j et seq.], during the fiscal year.

(F) Applicable portion defined. In this paragraph, the term "applicable portion" means, for a fiscal year—

(i) with respect to MA organizations, the Secretary's estimate of the total proportion of expenditures under this title that are attributable to expenditures made under this part (including payments under part D [42 USCS §§ 1395w-101 et seq.] that are made to such organizations); or

(ii) with respect to PDP sponsors, the Secretary's estimate of the total proportion of expenditures under this title that are attributable to expenditures made to such sponsors under part D [42 USCS §§ 1395w-101 et seq.].

(3) Agreements with federally qualified health centers. (A) Payment levels and amounts. A contract under this section with an MA organization shall require the organization to provide, in any written agreement described in section 1853(a)(4) [42 USCS § 1395w-23(a)(4)] between the organization and a federally qualified health center, for a level and amount of payment to the federally qualified health center for services provided by such health center that is not less than the level and amount of payment that the plan would make for such services if the services had been furnished by a entity providing similar services that was not a federally qualified health center.

(B) Cost-sharing. Under the written agreement referred to in subparagraph (A), a federally qualified health center must accept the payment amount referred to in such subparagraph plus the Federal payment provided for in section 1833(a)(3)(B) [42 USCS § 1395l(a)(3)(B)] as payment in full for services covered by the agreement, except that such a health center may collect any amount of cost-sharing permitted under the contract under this section, so long as the amounts of any deductible, coinsurance, or copayment comply with the requirements under section 1854(e) [42 USCS § 1395w-24(e)].

(4) Requirement for minimum medical loss ratio. If the Secretary determines for a contract year (beginning with 2014) that an MA plan has failed to have a medical loss ratio of at least .85—

(A) the MA plan shall remit to the Secretary an amount equal to the product of—

(i) the total revenue of the MA plan under

this part for the contract year; and

(ii) the difference between .85 and the medical loss ratio;

(B) for 3 consecutive contract years, the Secretary shall not permit the enrollment of new enrollees under the plan for coverage during the second succeeding contract year; and

(C) the Secretary shall terminate the plan contract if the plan fails to have such a medical loss ratio for 5 consecutive contract years.

(f) Prompt payment by Medicare+Choice organization. (1) Requirement. A contract under this part [42 USCS §§ 1395w-21 et seq.] shall require a Medicare+Choice organization to provide prompt payment (consistent with the provisions of sections 1816(c)(2) and 1842(c)(2) [42 USCS §§ 1395h(c)(2) and 1395u(c)(2)]) of claims submitted for services and supplies furnished to enrollees pursuant to the contract, if the services or supplies are not furnished under a contract between the organization and the provider or supplier (or in the case of a Medicare+Choice private fee-for-service plan, if a claim is submitted to such organization by an enrollee).

(2) Secretary's option to bypass noncomplying organization. In the case of a Medicare+Choice eligible organization which the Secretary determines, after notice and opportunity for a hearing, has failed to make payments of amounts in compliance with paragraph (1), the Secretary may provide for direct payment of the amounts owed to providers and suppliers (or, in the case of a Medicare+Choice private fee-for-service plan, amounts owed to the enrollees) for covered services and supplies furnished to individuals enrolled under this part [42 USCS §§ 1395w-21 et seq.] under the contract. If the Secretary provides for the direct payments, the Secretary shall provide for an appropriate reduction in the amount of payments otherwise made to the organization under this part [42 USCS §§ 1395w-21 et seq.] to reflect the amount of the Secretary's payments (and the Secretary's costs in making the payments).

(3) Incorporation of certain prescription drug plan contract requirements. The following provisions shall apply to contracts with a Medicare Advantage organization offering an MA-PD plan in the same manner as they apply to contracts with a PDP sponsor offering a prescription drug plan under part D [42 USCS §§ 1395w-101 et seq.]:

(A) Prompt payment. Section 1860D-12(b)(4) [42 USCS § 1395w-112(b)(4)].

(B) Submission of claims by pharmacies located in or contracting with long-term care facilities. Section 1860D-12(b)(5) [42 USCS § 1395w-112(b)(5)].

(C) Regular update of prescription drug pricing standard. Section 1860D-12(b)(6) [42 USCS § 1395w-112(b)(6)].

(g) Intermediate sanctions. (1) In general. If the Secretary determines that a Medicare+Choice organization with a contract under this section—

(A) fails substantially to provide medically necessary items and services that are required (under law or under the contract) to be provided to an individual covered under the contract, if the failure has adversely affected (or has substantial likelihood of adversely affecting) the individual;

(B) imposes premiums on individuals enrolled under this part [42 USCS §§ 1395w-21 et seq.] in excess of the amount of the Medicare+Choice monthly basic and supplemental beneficiary premiums permitted under section 1854 [42 USCS § 1395w-24];

(C) acts to expel or to refuse to re-enroll an individual in violation of the provisions of this part [42 USCS §§ 1395w-21 et seq.];

(D) engages in any practice that would reasonably be expected to have the effect of denying or discouraging enrollment (except as permitted by this part [42 USCS §§ 1395w-21 et seq.]) by eligible individuals with the organization whose medical condition or history indicates a need for substantial future medical services;

(E) misrepresents or falsifies information that is furnished—

(i) to the Secretary under this part [42 USCS §§ 1395w-21 et seq.], or

(ii) to an individual or to any other entity under this part [42 USCS §§ 1395w-21 et seq.];

(F) fails to comply with the applicable requirements of section 1852(j)(3) or 1852(k)(2)(A)(ii) [42 USCS § 1395w-22(j)(3) or (k)(2)(A)(ii)];

(G) employs or contracts with any individual or entity that is excluded from participation under this title [42 USCS §§ 1395 et seq.] under section 1128 or 1128A [42 USCS § 1320a-7 or 1320a-7a] for the provision of health care, utilization review, medical social work, or administrative services or employs or contracts with any entity for the provision (directly or indirectly) through such an excluded individual or entity of such services;

(H) except as provided under subparagraph (C) or (D) of section 1860D-1(b)(1) [42 USCS § 1395w-101(b)(1)], enrolls an individual in any plan under this part without the prior consent of the individual or the designee of the individual;

(I) transfers an individual enrolled under this part from one plan to another without the prior consent of the individual or the designee of the individual or solely for the purpose of earning a commission;

(J) fails to comply with marketing restrictions described in subsections (h) and (j) of section 1851 [42 USCS § 1395w-21] or applicable implementing regulations or guidance; or

(K) employs or contracts with any individual or entity who engages in the conduct described in subparagraphs (A) through (J) of this paragraph;

the Secretary may provide, in addition to any other remedies authorized by law, for any of the remedies described in paragraph (2). The Secretary may provide, in addition to any other remedies authorized by law, for any of the remedies described in paragraph (2), if the Secretary determines that any employee or agent of such organization, or any provider or supplier who contracts with such organization, has engaged in any conduct described in subparagraphs (A) through (K) of this paragraph.

(2) Remedies. The remedies described in this paragraph are—

(A) civil money penalties of not more than $25,000 for each determination under paragraph (1) or, with respect to a determination under subparagraph (D) or (E)(i) of such paragraph, of not more than $100,000 for each such determination, except with respect to a determination under subparagraph (E), an assessment of not more than the amount claimed by such plan or plan sponsor based upon the misrepresentation or falsified information involved, plus, with respect to a determination under paragraph (1)(B), double the excess amount charged in violation of such paragraph (and the excess amount charged shall be deducted from the penalty and returned to the individual concerned), and plus, with respect to a determination under paragraph (1)(D), $15,000 for each individual not enrolled as a result of the practice involved,

(B) suspension of enrollment of individuals under this part [42 USCS §§ 1395w-21 et seq.] after the date the Secretary notifies the organization of a determination under paragraph (1) and until the Secretary is satisfied that the basis for such determination has been corrected and is not likely to recur, or

(C) suspension of payment to the organization under this part [42 USCS §§ 1395w-21 et seq.] for individuals enrolled after the date the Secretary notifies the organization of a determination under paragraph (1) and until the Secretary is satisfied that the basis for such determination has been corrected and is not likely to recur.

(3) Other intermediate sanctions. In the case of a Medicare+Choice organization for which the Secretary makes a determination under subsection (c)(2) the basis of which is not described in paragraph (1), the Secretary may apply the following intermediate sanctions:

(A) Civil money penalties of not more than $25,000 for each determination under subsection (c)(2) if the deficiency that is the basis of the determination has directly adversely affected (or has the substantial likelihood of adversely affecting) an individual covered under the organization's contract.

(B) Civil money penalties of not more than $10,000 for each week beginning after the initiation of civil money penalty procedures by the Secretary during which the deficiency that is the basis of a determination under subsection (c)(2) exists.

(C) Suspension of enrollment of individuals under this part [42 USCS §§ 1395w-21 et seq.] after the date the Secretary notifies the organization of a determination under subsection (c)(2) and until the Secretary is satisfied that the deficiency that is the basis for the determination has been corrected and is not likely to recur.

(D) Civil monetary penalties of not more than $100,000, or such higher amount as the Secretary may establish by regulation, where the finding under subsection (c)(2)(A) is based on the organization's termination of its contract under this section other than at a time and in a manner provided for under subsection (a).

(4) Civil money penalties. The provisions of section 1128A [42 USCS § 1320a-7a] (other than subsections (a) and (b)) shall apply to a civil money penalty under paragraph (2) or (3) in the same manner as they apply to a civil money penalty or proceeding under section 1128A(a) [42 USCS § 1320a-7a(a)].

(h) Procedures for termination. (1) In general. The Secretary may terminate a contract with a Medicare+Choice organization under this section in accordance with formal investigation and compliance procedures established by the Secretary under which—

(A) the Secretary provides the organization with the reasonable opportunity to develop and implement a corrective action plan to correct the deficiencies that were the basis of the Secretary's determination under subsection (c)(2); and

(B) the Secretary provides the organization with reasonable notice and opportunity for hearing (including the right to appeal an initial decision) before terminating the contract.

(2) Exception for imminent and serious risk to health. Paragraph (1) shall not apply if the Secretary determines that a delay in termination, resulting from compliance with the procedures specified in such paragraph prior to termination, would pose an imminent and serious risk to the health of individuals enrolled under this part [42 USCS §§ 1395w-21 et seq.] with the organization.

(i) Medicare+Choice program compatibility with employer or union group health plans. (1) Contracts with MA organizations. To facilitate the offering of Medicare+Choice plans under contracts between Medicare+Choice organizations and employers, labor organizations, or the trustees of a fund established by 1 or more employers or labor organizations (or combination thereof) to furnish benefits to the entity's employees, former employees (or combination thereof) or members or former members (or combination thereof) of the labor organizations, the Secretary may waive or modify requirements that hinder the design of, the offering of, or the enrollment in such Medicare+Choice plans.

(2) Employer sponsored MA plans. To facilitate the offering of MA plans by employers, labor organizations, or the trustees of a fund established by one or more employers or labor organizations (or combination thereof) to furnish benefits to the entity's employees, former employees (or combination thereof) or members or former members (or combination thereof) of the labor organizations, the Secretary may waive or modify requirements that hinder the design of, the offering of, or the enrollment in such MA plans. Notwithstanding section 1851(g) [42 USCS § 1395w-21(g)], an MA plan described in the previous sentence may restrict the enrollment of individuals under this part to individuals who are beneficiaries and participants in such plan.

(Aug. 14, 1935, ch 531, Title XVIII, Part C, § 1857, as added Aug. 5, 1997, P. L. 105-33, Title IV, Subtitle A, Ch 1, Subch A, § 4001, 111 Stat. 319; Nov. 29, 1999, P. L. 106-113, Div B, § 1000(a)(6), 113 Stat. 1536; Dec. 21, 2000, P. L. 106-554, § 1(a)(6), 114 Stat. 2763; Dec. 8, 2003, P. L. 108-173, Title II, Subtitle C, § 222(j), (k), (l)(3)(C), Subtitle D, § 237(c), Title IX, § 900(e)(1)(I), 117 Stat. 2205, 2207, 2213, 2372; July 15, 2008, P. L. 110-275, Title I, Subtitle D, § 164(d)(2), Subtitle E, Part I, §§ 171(b), 172(a)(2), 173(b), 122 Stat. 2574, 2580, 2581; March 23, 2010, P. L. 111-148, Title VI, Subtitle E, § 6408(b), 124 Stat. 771; March 30, 2010, P. L. 111-152, Title I, Subtitle B, § 1103, 124 Stat. 1047.)

HISTORY; ANCILLARY LAWS AND DIRECTIVES

Other provisions:

Technical correction to MA private fee-for-service plans. Act March 23, 2010, P. L. 111-148, Title III, Subtitle C, § 3207, 124 Stat. 459, provides: "For plan year 2011 and subsequent plan years, to the extent that the Secretary of Health and Human Services is applying the 2008 service area extension waiver policy (as modified in the April 11, 2008, Centers for Medicare & Medicaid Services' memorandum with the subject '2009 Employer Group Waiver-Modification of the 2008 Service Area Extension Waiver Granted to Certain MA Local Coordinated Care Plans') to Medicare Advantage coordinated care plans, the Secretary shall extend the application of such waiver policy to employers who contract directly with the Secretary as a Medicare Advantage private fee-for-service plan under section 1857(i)(2) of the Social Security Act (42 U.S.C. 1395w-27(i)(2)) and that had enrollment as of October 1, 2009.".

§ 1395w-27a. Special rules for MA regional plans

(a) Regional service area; establishment of MA regions. (1) Coverage of entire MA region. The service area for an MA regional plan shall consist of an entire MA region established under paragraph (2) and the provisions of section 1854(h) [42 USCS § 1395w-24(h)] shall not apply to such a plan.

(2) Establishment of MA regions. (A) MA region. For purposes of this title [42 USCS §§ 1395 et seq.], the term "MA region" means such a region within the 50 States and the District of Columbia as established by the Secretary under this paragraph.

(B) Establishment. (i) Initial establishment. Not later than January 1, 2005, the Secretary shall first establish and publish MA regions.

(ii) Periodic review and revision of service areas. The Secretary may periodically review MA regions under this paragraph and, based on such review, may revise such regions if the Secretary determines such revision to be appropriate.

(C) Requirements for MA regions. The Secretary shall establish, and may revise, MA regions under this paragraph in a manner consistent with the following:

(i) Number of regions. There shall be no fewer than 10 regions, and no more than 50 regions.

(ii) Maximizing availability of plans. The regions shall maximize the availability of MA regional plans to all MA eligible individuals without regard to health status, especially those residing in rural areas.

(D) Market survey and analysis. Before establishing MA regions, the Secretary shall conduct a market survey and analysis, including an examination of current insurance markets, to determine how the regions should be established.

(3) National plan. Nothing in this subsection shall be construed as preventing an MA regional plan from being offered in more than one MA region (including all regions).

(b) Application of single deductible and catastrophic limit on out-of-pocket expenses. An MA regional plan shall include the following:

(1) Single deductible. Any deductible for benefits under the original medicare fee-for-service program option shall be a single deductible (instead of a separate inpatient hospital deductible and a part B deductible) and may be applied differentially for in-network services and may be waived for preventive or other items and services.

(2) Catastrophic limit. (A) In-network. A catastrophic limit on out-of-pocket expenditures for in-network benefits under the original medicare fee-for-service program option.

(B) Total. A catastrophic limit on out-of-pocket expenditures for all benefits under the original medicare fee-for-service program option.

(c) Portion of total payments to an organization subject to risk for 2006 and 2007. (1) Application of risk corridors. (A) In general. This subsection shall only apply to MA regional plans offered during 2006 or 2007.

(B) Notification of allowable costs under the plan. In the case of an MA organization that offers an MA regional plan in an MA region in 2006 or 2007, the organization shall notify the Secretary, before such date in the succeeding year as the Secretary specifies, of—

(i) its total amount of costs that the organization incurred in providing benefits covered under the original medicare fee-for-service program option for all enrollees under the plan in the region in the year and the portion of such costs that is attributable to administrative expenses described in subparagraph (C); and

(ii) its total amount of costs that the organization incurred in providing rebatable integrated benefits (as defined in subparagraph (D)) and with respect to such benefits the portion of such costs that is attributable to administrative expenses described in subparagraph (C) and not described in clause (i) of this subparagraph.

(C) Allowable costs defined. For purposes of this subsection, the term "allowable costs" means, with respect to an MA regional plan for a year, the total amount of costs described in subparagraph (B) for the plan and year, reduced by the portion of such costs attributable to administrative expenses incurred in providing the benefits described in such subparagraph.

(D) Rebatable integrated benefits. For purposes of this subsection, the term "rebatable integrated benefits" means such non-drug supplemental benefits under subclause (I) of section 1854(b)(1)(C)(ii) [42 USCS § 1395w-24(b)(1)(C)(ii)] pursuant to a rebate under such section that the Secretary determines are integrated with the benefits described in subparagraph (B)(i).

(2) Adjustment of payment. (A) No adjustment if allowable costs within 3 percent of target amount. If the allowable costs for the plan for the year are at least 97 percent, but do not exceed 103 percent, of the target amount for the plan and year, there shall be no payment adjustment under this subsection for the plan and year.

(B) Increase in payment if allowable costs above 103 percent of target amount. (i) Costs between 103 and 108 percent of target amount. If the allowable costs for the plan for the year are greater than 103 percent, but not greater than 108 percent, of the target amount for the plan and year, the Secretary shall increase the total of the monthly payments made to the organization offering the plan for the year under section 1853(a) [42 USCS § 1395w-23(a)] by an amount equal to 50 percent of the difference between such allowable costs and 103 percent of such target amount.

(ii) Costs above 108 percent of target amount. If the allowable costs for the plan for the year are greater than 108 percent of the target amount for the plan and year, the Secretary shall increase the total of the monthly payments made to the organization offering the plan for the year under section 1853(a) [42 USCS § 1395w-23(a)] by an amount equal to the sum of—

(I) 2.5 percent of such target amount; and

(II) 80 percent of the difference between such allowable costs and 108 percent of such target amount.

(C) Reduction in payment if allowable costs below 97 percent of target amount. (i) Costs between 92 and 97 percent of target amount. If the allowable costs for the plan for the year are less than 97 percent, but greater than or equal to 92 percent, of the target amount for the plan and year, the Secretary shall reduce the total of the monthly payments made to the organization offering the plan for the year under section 1853(a) [42 USCS § 1395w-23(a)] by an amount (or otherwise recover from the plan an amount) equal to 50 percent of the difference between 97 percent of the target amount and such allowable costs.

(ii) Costs below 92 percent of target amount. If the allowable costs for the plan for the year are less than 92 percent of the target amount for the plan and year, the Secretary shall reduce the total of the monthly payments made to the organization offering the plan for the year under section 1853(a) [42 USCS § 1395w-23(a)] by an amount (or otherwise recover from the plan an amount) equal to the sum of—

(I) 2.5 percent of such target amount; and

(II) 80 percent of the difference between 92 percent of such target amount and such allowable costs.

(D) Target amount described. For purposes of this paragraph, the term "target amount" means, with respect to an MA regional plan offered by an organization in a year, an amount equal to—

(i) the sum of—

(I) the total monthly payments made to the organization for enrollees in the plan for the year that are attributable to benefits under the original medicare fee-for-service program option (as defined in section 1852(a)(1)(B) [42 USCS § 1395w-22(a)(1)(B)]);

(II) the total of the MA monthly basic beneficiary premium collectable for such enrollees for the year; and

(III) the total amount of the rebates under section 1854(b)(1)(C)(ii) [42 USCS § 1395w-24(b)(1)(C)(ii)] that are attributable to rebatable integrated benefits; reduced by

(ii) the amount of administrative expenses assumed in the bid insofar as the bid is attributable to benefits described in clause (i)(I) or (i)(III).

(3) Disclosure of information. (A) In general. Each contract under this part [42 USCS §§ 1395w-21 et seq.] shall provide—

(i) that an MA organization offering an MA regional plan shall provide the Secretary with such information as the Secretary determines is necessary to carry out this subsection; and

(ii) that, pursuant to section 1857(d)(2)(B) [42 USCS § 1395w-27(d)(2)(B)], the Secretary has the right to inspect and audit any books and records of the organization that pertain to the information regarding costs provided to the Secretary under paragraph (1)(B).

(B) Restriction on use of information. Information disclosed or obtained pursuant to the provisions of this subsection may be used by officers, employees, and contractors of the Department of Health and Human Services only for the purposes of, and to the extent necessary in, carrying out this subsection.

(d) Organizational and financial requirements. (1) In general. In the case of an MA organization that is offering an MA regional plan in an MA region and—

(A) meets the requirements of section 1855(a)(1) [42 USCS § 1395w-25(a)(1)] with respect to at least one such State in such region; and

(B) with respect to each other State in such region in which it does not meet requirements, it demonstrates to the satisfaction of the Secretary that it has filed the necessary application to meet such requirements,

the Secretary may waive such requirement with respect to each State described in subparagraph (B) for such period of time as the Secretary determines appropriate for the timely processing of such an application by the State (and, if such application is denied, through the end of such plan year as the Secretary determines appropriate to provide for a transition).

(2) Selection of appropriate State. In applying paragraph (1) in the case of an MA organization that meets the requirements of section 1855(a)(1) [42 USCS § 1395w-25(a)(1)] with respect to more than one State in a region, the organization shall select, in a manner specified by the Secretary among such States, one State the rules of which shall apply in the case of the States described in paragraph (1)(B).

(e) [Deleted]

(f) Computation of applicable MA region-specific non-drug monthly benchmark amounts. (1) Computation for regions. For purposes of section 1853(j)(2) [42 USCS § 1395w-23(j)(2)] and this section, subject to subsection (e), the term "MA region-specific non-drug monthly benchmark amount" means, with respect to an MA region for a month in a year, the sum of the 2 components described in paragraph (2) for the region and year. The Secretary shall compute such benchmark amount for each MA region before the beginning of each annual, coordinated election period under section 1851(e)(3)(B) [42 USCS § 1395w-21(e)(3)(B)] for each year (beginning with 2006).

(2) 2 components. For purposes of paragraph (1), the 2 components described in this paragraph for an MA region and a year are the

following:

(A) Statutory component. The product of the following:

(i) Statutory region-specific non-drug amount. The statutory region-specific non-drug amount (as defined in paragraph (3)) for the region and year.

(ii) Statutory national market share. The statutory national market share percentage, determined under paragraph (4) for the year.

(B) Plan-bid component. The product of the following:

(i) Weighted average of MA plan bids in region. The weighted average of the plan bids for the region and year (as determined under paragraph (5)(A)).

(ii) Non-statutory market share. 1 minus the statutory national market share percentage, determined under paragraph (4) for the year.

(3) Statutory region-specific non-drug amount. For purposes of paragraph (2)(A)(i), the term "statutory region-specific non-drug amount" means, for an MA region and year, an amount equal the sum (for each MA local area within the region) of the product of—

(A) MA area-specific non-drug monthly benchmark amount under section 1853(j)(1)(A) [42 USCS § 1395w-23(j)(1)(A)] for that area and year; and

(B) the number of MA eligible individuals residing in the local area, divided by the total number of MA eligible individuals residing in the region.

(4) Computation of statutory market share percentage. (A) In general. The Secretary shall determine for each year a statutory national market share percentage that is equal to the proportion of MA eligible individuals nationally who were not enrolled in an MA plan during the reference month.

(B) Reference month defined. For purposes of this part [42 USCS §§ 1395w-21 et seq.], the term "reference month" means, with respect to a year, the most recent month during the previous year for which the Secretary determines that data are available to compute the percentage specified in subparagraph (A) and other relevant percentages under this part [42 USCS §§ 1395w-21 et seq.].

(5) Determination of weighted average MA bids for a region. (A) In general. For purposes of paragraph (2)(B)(i), the weighted average of plan bids for an MA region and a year is the sum, for MA regional plans described in subparagraph (D) in the region and year, of the products (for each such plan) of the following:

(i) Monthly MA statutory non-drug bid amount. The unadjusted MA statutory non-drug monthly bid amount for the plan.

(ii) Plan's share of MA enrollment in region. The factor described in subparagraph (B) for the plan.

(B) Plan's share of MA enrollment in region. (i) In general. Subject to the succeeding provisions of this subparagraph, the factor described in this subparagraph for a plan is equal to the number of individuals described in subparagraph (C) for such plan, divided by the total number of such individuals for all MA regional plans described in subparagraph (D) for that region and year.

(ii) Single plan rule. In the case of an MA region in which only a single MA regional plan is being offered, the factor described in this subparagraph shall be equal to 1.

(iii) Equal division among multiple plans in year in which plans are first available. In the case of an MA region in the first year in which any MA regional plan is offered, if more than one MA regional plan is offered in such year, the factor described in this subparagraph for a plan shall (as specified by the Secretary) be equal to—

(I) 1 divided by the number of such plans offered in such year; or

(II) a factor for such plan that is based upon the organization's estimate of projected enrollment, as reviewed and adjusted by the Secretary to ensure reasonableness and as is certified by the Chief Actuary of the Centers for Medicare & Medicaid Services.

(C) Counting of individuals. For purposes of subparagraph (B)(i), the Secretary shall count for each MA regional plan described in subparagraph (D) for an MA region and year, the number of individuals who reside in the region and who were enrolled under such plan under this part [42 USCS §§ 1395w-21 et seq.] during the reference month.

(D) Plans covered. For an MA region and year, an MA regional plan described in this subparagraph is an MA regional plan that is offered in the region and year and was offered in the region in the reference month.

(g) Election of uniform coverage determination. Instead of applying section 1852(a)(2)(C) [42 USCS § 1395w-22(a)(2)(C)] with respect to an MA regional plan, the organization offering the plan may elect to have a local coverage determination for the entire MA region be the local coverage determination applied for any part of such region (as selected by the organization).

(h) Assuring network adequacy. (1) In general. For purposes of enabling MA organizations that offer MA regional plans to meet applicable provider access requirements under section 1852 [42 USCS § 1395w-22] with respect to such plans, the Secretary may provide for payment under this section to an essential hospital that provides inpatient hospital services to enrollees in such a plan where the MA organization offering the plan certifies to the Secretary that the organization was unable to reach an agreement between the hospital and the organization regarding provision of such services under the plan. Such payment shall be available only if—

(A) the organization provides assurances satisfactory to the Secretary that the organization will make payment to the hospital for inpatient hospital services of an amount that is not less than the amount that would be payable to the hospital under section 1886 [42 USCS § 1395ww] with respect to such services; and

(B) with respect to specific inpatient hospital services provided to an enrollee, the hospital demonstrates to the satisfaction of the Secretary that the hospital's costs of such services exceed the payment amount described in subparagraph (A).

(2) Payment amounts. The payment amount under this subsection for inpatient hospital services provided by a subsection (d) hospital to an enrollee in an MA regional plan shall be, subject to the limitation of funds under paragraph (3), the amount (if any) by which—

(A) the amount of payment that would have been paid for such services under this title [42 USCS §§ 1395 et seq.] if the enrollees were covered under the original medicare fee-for-service program option and the hospital were a critical access hospital; exceeds

(B) the amount of payment made for such services under paragraph (1)(A).

(3) Available amounts. There shall be available for payments under this subsection—

(A) in 2006, $25,000,000; and

(B) in each succeeding year the amount specified in this paragraph for the preceding year increased by the market basket percentage increase (as defined in section 1886(b)(3)(B)(iii) [42 USCS § 1395ww(b)(3)(B)(iii)]) for the fiscal year ending in such succeeding year.

Payments under this subsection shall be made from the Federal Hospital Insurance Trust Fund.

(4) Essential hospital. In this subsection, the term "essential hospital" means, with respect to an MA regional plan offered by an MA organization, a subsection (d) hospital (as defined in section 1886(d) [42 USCS § 1395ww(d)]) that the Secretary determines, based upon an application filed by the organization with the Secretary, is necessary to meet the requirements referred to in paragraph (1) for such plan.

(Aug. 14, 1935, ch 531, Title XVIII, Part C, § 1858, as added Dec. 8, 2003, P. L. 108-173, Title II, Subtitle C, § 221(c), 117 Stat. 2181; Dec. 20, 2006, P. L. 109-432, Div B, Title III, § 301, 120 Stat. 2990; July 18, 2007, P. L. 110-48, § 3, 121 Stat. 244; Dec. 29, 2007, P. L. 110-173, Title I, § 110, 121 Stat. 2497; July 15, 2008, P. L. 110-275, Title I, Subtitle D, § 166, 122 Stat. 2575; March 11, 2009, P. L. 111-8, Div G, Title I, § 1301(f), 123 Stat. 829; March 23, 2010, P. L. 111-148, Title III, Subtitle C, § 3201(a)(2)(C), (f)(2), Title X, Subtitle C, § 10327(c)(1), 124 Stat. 444, 450, 964; March 30, 2010, P. L. 111-152, Title I, Subtitle B, § 1102(a), 124 Stat. 1040.)

HISTORY; ANCILLARY LAWS AND DIRECTIVES

Other provisions:

Transition. Act March 23, 2010, P. L. 111-148, Title X, Subtitle C, § 10327(c)(2), 124 Stat. 964, provides: "Any amount contained in the MA Regional Plan Stabilization Fund as of the date of the enactment of this Act shall be transferred to the Federal Supplementary Medical Insurance Trust Fund.".

§ 1395w-28. Definitions; miscellaneous provisions

(a) Definitions relating to Medicare+Choice organizations. In this part [42 USCS §§ 1395w-21 et seq.]—

(1) Medicare+Choice organization. The term "Medicare+Choice organization" means a public or private entity that is certified under section 1856 [42 USCS § 1395w-26] as meeting the requirements and standards of this part [42 USCS §§ 1395w-21 et seq.] for such an organization.

(2) Provider-sponsored organization. The term "provider-sponsored organization" is defined in section 1855(d)(1) [42 USCS § 1395w-25(d)(1)].

(b) Definitions relating to Medicare+Choice plans. (1) Medicare+choice plan. The term "Medicare+Choice plan" means health benefits coverage offered under a policy, contract, or plan by a Medicare+Choice organization pursuant to and in accordance with a contract under section 1857 [42 USCS § 1395w-27].

(2) Medicare+Choice private fee-for-service plan. The term "Medicare+Choice private fee-for-service plan" means a Medicare+Choice plan that—

(A) reimburses hospitals, physicians, and

other providers at a rate determined by the plan on a fee-for-service basis without placing the provider at financial risk;

(B) does not vary such rates for such a provider based on utilization relating to such provider; and

(C) does not restrict the selection of providers among those who are lawfully authorized to provide the covered services and agree to accept the terms and conditions of payment established by the plan.

Nothing in subparagraph (B) shall be construed to preclude a plan from varying rates for such a provider based on the specialty of the provider, the location of the provider, or other factors related to such provider that are not related to utilization, or to preclude a plan from increasing rates for such a provider based on increased utilization of specified preventive or screening services.

(3) MSA plan. (A) In general. The term "MSA plan" means a Medicare+Choice plan that—

(i) provides reimbursement for at least the items and services described in section 1852(a)(1) [42 USCS § 1395w-22(a)(1)] in a year but only after the enrollee incurs countable expenses (as specified under the plan) equal to the amount of an annual deductible (described in subparagraph (B));

(ii) counts as such expenses (for purposes of such deductible) at least all amounts that would have been payable under parts A and B [42 USCS §§ 1395c et seq. and 1395j et seq.], and that would have been payable by the enrollee as deductibles, coinsurance, or copayments, if the enrollee had elected to receive benefits through the provisions of such parts; and

(iii) provides, after such deductible is met for a year and for all subsequent expenses for items and services referred to in clause (i) in the year, for a level of reimbursement that is not less than—

(I) 100 percent of such expenses, or

(II) 100 percent of the amounts that would have been paid (without regard to any deductibles or coinsurance) under parts A and B [42 USCS §§ 1395c et seq. and 1395j et seq.] with respect to such expenses,

whichever is less.

(B) Deductible. The amount of annual deductible under an MSA plan—

(i) for contract year 1999 shall be not more than $6,000; and

(ii) for a subsequent contract year shall be not more than the maximum amount of such deductible for the previous contract year under this subparagraph increased by the national per capita Medicare+Choice growth percentage under section 1853(c)(6) [42 USCS § 1395w-23(c)(6)] for the year.

If the amount of the deductible under clause (ii) is not a multiple of $50, the amount shall be rounded to the nearest multiple of $50.

(4) MA regional plan. The term "MA regional plan" means an MA plan described in section 1851(a)(2)(A)(i) [42 USCS § 1395w-21(a)(2)(A)(i)]—

(A) that has a network of providers that have agreed to a contractually specified reimbursement for covered benefits with the organization offering the plan;

(B) that provides for reimbursement for all covered benefits regardless of whether such benefits are provided within such network of providers; and

(C) the service area of which is one or more entire MA regions.

(5) MA local plan. The term "MA local plan" means an MA plan that is not an MA regional plan.

(6) Specialized MA plans for special needs individuals. (A) In general. The term "specialized MA plan for special needs individuals" means an MA plan that exclusively serves special needs individuals (as defined in subparagraph (B)) and that, as of January 1, 2010, meets the applicable requirements of paragraph (2), (3), or (4) of subsection (f), as the case may be.

(B) Special needs individual. The term "special needs individual" means an MA eligible individual who—

(i) is institutionalized (as defined by the Secretary);

(ii) is entitled to medical assistance under a State plan under title XIX [42 USCS §§ 1396 et seq.]; or

(iii) meets such requirements as the Secretary may determine would benefit from enrollment in such a specialized MA plan described in subparagraph (A) for individuals with severe or disabling chronic conditions who have one or more comorbid and medically complex chronic conditions that are substantially disabling or life threatening, have a high risk of hospitalization or other significant adverse health outcomes, and require specialized delivery systems across domains of care.

The Secretary may waive application of section 1851(a)(3)(B) [42 USCS § 1395w-21(a)(3)(B)] in the case of an individual described in clause (i), (ii), or (iii) of this subparagraph and may apply rules similar to the rules of section 1894(c)(4) [42 USCS § 1395eee(c)(4)] for continued eligibility of special needs individuals.

(c) Other references to other terms. (1) Medicare+choice eligible individual. The term "Medicare+Choice eligible individual" is defined in section 1851(a)(3) [42 USCS § 1395w-21(a)(3)].

(2) Medicare+choice payment area. The term "Medicare+Choice payment area" is defined in section 1853(d) [42 USCS § 1395w-23(d)].

(3) National per capita Medicare+Choice growth percentage. The "national per capita Medicare+Choice growth percentage" is defined in section 1853(c)(6) [42 USCS § 1395w-23(c)(6)].

(4) Medicare+choice monthly basic beneficiary premium; Medicare+Choice monthly supplemental beneficiary premium. The terms "Medicare+Choice monthly basic beneficiary premium" and "Medicare+Choice monthly supplemental beneficiary premium" are defined in section 1854(a)(2) [42 USCS § 1395w-24(a)(2)].

(5) MA local area. The term "MA local area" is defined in section 1853(d)(2) [42 USCS § 1395w-23(d)(2)].

(d) Coordinated acute and long-term care benefits under a Medicare+Choice plan. Nothing in this part [42 USCS §§ 1395w-21 et seq.] shall be construed as preventing a State from coordinating benefits under a medicaid plan under title XIX with those provided under a Medicare+Choice plan in a manner that assures continuity of a full-range of acute care and long-term care services to poor elderly or disabled individuals eligible for benefits under this title [42 USCS §§ 1395 et seq.] and under such plan.

(e) Restriction on enrollment for certain Medicare+Choice plans. (1) In general. In the case of a Medicare+Choice religious fraternal benefit society plan described in paragraph (2), notwithstanding any other provision of this part [42 USCS §§ 1395w-21 et seq.] to the contrary and in accordance with regulations of the Secretary, the society offering the plan may restrict the enrollment of individuals under this part [42 USCS §§ 1395w-21 et seq.] to individuals who are members of the church, convention, or group described in paragraph (3)(B) with which the society is affiliated.

(2) Medicare+choice religious fraternal benefit society plan described. For purposes of this subsection, a Medicare+Choice religious fraternal benefit society plan described in this paragraph is a Medicare+Choice plan described in section 1851(a)(2) [42 USCS § 1395w-21(a)(2)] that—

(A) is offered by a religious fraternal benefit society described in paragraph (3) only to members of the church, convention, or group described in paragraph (3)(B); and

(B) permits all such members to enroll under the plan without regard to health status-related factors.

Nothing in this subsection shall be construed as waiving any plan requirements relating to financial solvency.

(3) Religious fraternal benefit society defined. For purposes of paragraph (2)(A), a "religious fraternal benefit society" described in this section is an organization that—

(A) is described in section 501(c)(8) of the Internal Revenue Code of 1986 [26 USCS § 501(c)(8)] and is exempt from taxation under section 501(a) of such Act [26 USCS § 501(a)];

(B) is affiliated with, carries out the tenets of, and shares a religious bond with, a church or convention or association of churches or an affiliated group of churches;

(C) offers, in addition to a Medicare+Choice religious fraternal benefit society plan, health coverage to individuals not entitled to benefits under this title [42 USCS §§ 1395 et seq.] who are members of such church, convention, or group; and

(D) does not impose any limitation on membership in the society based on any health status-related factor.

(4) Payment adjustment. Under regulations of the Secretary, in the case of individuals enrolled under this part [42 USCS §§ 1395w-21 et seq.] under a Medicare+Choice religious fraternal benefit society plan described in paragraph (2), the Secretary shall provide for such adjustment to the payment amounts otherwise established under section 1854 [42 USCS § 1395w-24] as may be appropriate to assure an appropriate payment level, taking into account the actuarial characteristics and experience of such individuals.

(f) Requirements regarding enrollment in specialized MA plans for special needs individuals. (1) Requirements for enrollment. In the case of a specialized MA plan for special needs individuals (as defined in subsection (b)(6)), notwithstanding any other provision of this part and in accordance with regulations of the Secretary and for periods before January 1, 2014, the plan may restrict the enrollment of individuals under the plan to individuals who are within one or more classes of special needs individuals.

(2) Additional requirements for institutional SNPs. In the case of a specialized MA plan for special needs individuals described in subsec-

tion (b)(6)(B)(i), the applicable requirements described in this paragraph are as follows:

(A) Each individual that enrolls in the plan on or after January 1, 2010, is a special needs individuals described in subsection (b)(6)(B)(i). In the case of an individual who is living in the community but requires an institutional level of care, such individual shall not be considered a special needs individual described in subsection (b)(6)(B)(i) unless the determination that the individual requires an institutional level of care was made—

(i) using a State assessment tool of the State in which the individual resides; and

(ii) by an entity other than the organization offering the plan.

(B) The plan meets the requirements described in paragraph (5).

(C) If applicable, the plan meets the requirement described in paragraph (7).

(3) Additional requirements for dual SNPs. In the case of a specialized MA plan for special needs individuals described in subsection (b)(6)(B)(ii), the applicable requirements described in this paragraph are as follows:

(A) Each individual that enrolls in the plan on or after January 1, 2010, is a special needs individuals described in subsection (b)(6)(B)(ii).

(B) The plan meets the requirements described in paragraph (5).

(C) The plan provides each prospective enrollee, prior to enrollment, with a comprehensive written statement (using standardized content and format established by the Secretary) that describes—

(i) the benefits and cost-sharing protections that the individual is entitled to under the State Medicaid program under title XIX [42 USCS §§ 1396 et seq.]; and

(ii) which of such benefits and cost-sharing protections are covered under the plan.

Such statement shall be included with any description of benefits offered by the plan.

(D) The plan has a contract with the State Medicaid agency to provide benefits, or arrange for benefits to be provided, for which such individual is entitled to receive as medical assistance under title XIX [42 USCS §§ 1396 et seq.]. Such benefits may include long-term care services consistent with State policy.

(E) If applicable, the plan meets the requirement described in paragraph (7).

(4) Additional requirements for severe or disabling chronic condition SNPs. In the case of a specialized MA plan for special needs individuals described in subsection (b)(6)(B)(iii), the applicable requirements described in this paragraph are as follows:

(A) Each individual that enrolls in the plan on or after January 1, 2010, is a special needs individual described in subsection (b)(6)(B)(iii).

(B) The plan meets the requirements described in paragraph (5).

(C) If applicable, the plan meets the requirement described in paragraph (7).

(5) Care management requirements for all SNPs. The requirements described in this paragraph are that the organization offering a specialized MA plan for special needs individuals—

(A) have in place an evidenced-based model of care with appropriate networks of providers and specialists; and

(B) with respect to each individual enrolled in the plan—

(i) conduct an initial assessment and an annual reassessment of the individual's physical, psychosocial, and functional needs;

(ii) develop a plan, in consultation with the individual as feasible, that identifies goals and objectives, including measurable outcomes as well as specific services and benefits to be provided; and

(iii) use an interdisciplinary team in the management of care.

(6) Transition and exception regarding restriction on enrollment. (A) In general. Subject to subparagraph (C), the Secretary shall establish procedures for the transition of applicable individuals to—

(i) a Medicare Advantage plan that is not a specialized MA plan for special needs individuals (as defined in subsection (b)(6)); or

(ii) the original Medicare fee-for-service program under parts A and B [42 USCS §§ 1395c et seq. and 1395j et seq.].

(B) Applicable individuals. For purposes of clause (i), the term "applicable individual" means an individual who—

(i) is enrolled under a specialized MA plan for special needs individuals (as defined in subsection (b)(6)); and

(ii) is not within the 1 or more of the classes of special needs individuals to which enrollment under the plan is restricted to.

(C) Exception. The Secretary shall provide for an exception to the transition described in subparagraph (A) for a limited period of time for individuals enrolled under a specialized MA plan for special needs individuals described in subsection (b)(6)(B)(ii) who are no longer eligible for medical assistance under title XIX [42 USCS §§ 1396 et seq.].

(D) Timeline for initial transition. The Secretary shall ensure that applicable individuals enrolled in a specialized MA plan for special needs individuals (as defined in subsection (b)(6)) prior to January 1, 2010, are transitioned to a plan or the program described in subparagraph (A) by not later than January 1, 2013.

(7) Authority to require special needs plans be NCQA approved. For 2012 and subsequent years, the Secretary shall require that a Medicare Advantage organization offering a specialized MA plan for special needs individuals be approved by the National Committee for Quality Assurance (based on standards established by the Secretary).

(g) Special rules for senior housing facility plans. (1) In general. In the case of a Medicare Advantage senior housing facility plan described in paragraph (2), notwithstanding any other provision of this part to the contrary and in accordance with regulations of the Secretary, the service area of such plan may be limited to a senior housing facility in a geographic area.

(2) Medicare Advantage senior housing facility plan described. For purposes of this subsection, a Medicare Advantage senior housing facility plan is a Medicare Advantage plan that—

(A) restricts enrollment of individuals under this part to individuals who reside in a continuing care retirement community (as defined in section 1852(l)(4)(B) [42 USCS § 1395w-22(l)(4)(B)]);

(B) provides primary care services onsite and has a ratio of accessible physicians to beneficiaries that the Secretary determines is adequate;

(C) provides transportation services for beneficiaries to specialty providers outside of the facility; and

(D) has participated (as of December 31, 2009) in a demonstration project established by the Secretary under which such a plan was offered for not less than 1 year.

(Aug. 14, 1935, ch 531, Title XVIII, Part C, § 1859, as added Aug. 5, 1997, P. L. 105-33, Title IV, Subtitle A, Ch 1, Subch A, § 4001, 111 Stat. 325; Nov. 29, 1999, P. L. 106-113, Div B, § 1000(a)(6), 113 Stat. 1536; Dec. 8, 2003, P. L. 108-173, Title II, Subtitle C, § 221(b)(1), (d)(2), Subtitle D, § 231(b), (c), 117 Stat. 2181, 2193, 2207; Dec. 29, 2007, P. L. 110-173, Title I, § 108(a), 121 Stat. 2496; July 15, 2008, P. L. 110-275, Title I, Subtitle D, §§ 162(b), 164(a), (c)(1), (d)(1), (e)(1), 122 Stat. 2571, 2572, 2573, 2574; March 23, 2010, P. L. 111-148, Title III, Subtitle C, §§ 3205(a), (c), (e), (g), 3208(a), 124 Stat. 457, 458, 459.)

HISTORY; ANCILLARY LAWS AND DIRECTIVES

Other provisions:

Specialized Medicare Advantage plans for special needs individuals. Act July 15, 2008, P. L. 110-275, Title I, Subtitle D, § 164(c)(2)–(4), 122 Stat. 2573; March 23, 2010, P. L. 111-148, Title III, Subtitle C, § 3205(d), 124 Stat. 458, provides:

"(2) Authority to operate but no service area expansion for dual SNPs that do not meet certain requirements. Notwithstanding subsection (f) of section 1859 of the Social Security Act (42 U.S.C. 1395w-28), during the period beginning on January 1, 2010, and ending on December 31, 2012, in the case of a specialized Medicare Advantage plan for special needs individuals described in subsection (b)(6)(B)(ii) of such section, as amended by this section, that does not meet the requirement described in subsection (f)(3)(D) of such section, the Secretary of Health and Human Services—

"(A) shall permit such plan to be offered under part C of title XVIII of such Act [42 USCS §§ 1395w-21 et seq.]; and

"(B) shall not permit an expansion of the service area of the plan under such part C.

(3) Resources for State medicaid agencies. The Secretary of Health and Human Services shall provide for the designation of appropriate staff and resources that can address State inquiries with respect to the coordination of State and Federal policies for specialized MA plans for special needs individuals described in section 1859(b)(6)(B)(ii) of the Social Security Act (42 U.S.C. 1395w-28(b)(6)(B)(ii)), as amended by this section.

"(4) No requirement for contract. Nothing in the provisions of, or amendments made by, this subsection shall require a State to enter into a contract with a Medicare Advantage organization with respect to a specialized MA plan for special needs individuals described in section 1859(b)(6)(B)(ii) of the Social Security Act (42 U.S.C. 1395w-28(b)(6)(B)(ii)), as amended by this section.".

Effective date and applicability of subsec. (g). Act March 23, 2010, P. L. 111-148, Title III, Subtitle C, § 3208(b), 124 Stat. 460, provides: "The amendment made by this section [adding subsec. (g) of this section] shall take effect on January 1, 2010, and shall apply to plan years beginning on or after such date.".

§ 1395w-29. [Repealed]

HISTORY; ANCILLARY LAWS AND DIRECTIVES

This section (Act Aug. 14, 1935, ch 531, Title XVIII, Part C, § 1860C-1, as added Dec. 8, 2003, P. L. 108-173, Title II, Subtitle E, § 241(a), 117 Stat. 2214; March 23, 2010, P. L. 111-148, Title III, Subtitle C, § 3201(a)(2)(D), 124 Stat. 444; March 30, 2010, P. L. 111-152, Title I, Subtitle B, § 1102(a), 124 Stat. 1040) was repealed by Act March 30, 2010, P. L. 111-152, Title I, Subtitle B, § 1102(f), 124 Stat. 1046. It established the comparative cost adjustment (CCA) program.

PART D. VOLUNTARY PRESCRIPTION DRUG BENEFIT PROGRAM

SUBPART 1. Part D Eligible Individuals and Prescription Drug Benefits

§ 1395w-101. Eligibility, enrollment, and information

(a) Provision of qualified prescription drug coverage through enrollment in plans. (1) In general. Subject to the succeeding provisions of this part [42 USCS §§ 1395w-101 et seq.], each part D eligible individual (as defined in paragraph (3)(A)) is entitled to obtain qualified prescription drug coverage (described in section 1860D-2(a) [42 USCS § 1395w-102(a)]) as follows:

(A) Fee-for-service enrollees may receive coverage through a prescription drug plan. A part D eligible individual who is not enrolled in an MA plan may obtain qualified prescription drug coverage through enrollment in a prescription drug plan (as defined in section 1860D-41(a)(14) [42 USCS § 1395w-151(a)(14)]).

(B) Medicare Advantage enrollees. (i) Enrollees in a plan providing qualified prescription drug coverage receive coverage through the plan. A part D eligible individual who is enrolled in an MA-PD plan obtains such coverage through such plan.

(ii) Limitation on enrollment of MA plan enrollees in prescription drug plans. Except as provided in clauses (iii) and (iv), a part D eligible individual who is enrolled in an MA plan may not enroll in a prescription drug plan under this part [42 USCS §§ 1395w-101 et seq.].

(iii) Private fee-for-service enrollees in ma plans not providing qualified prescription drug coverage permitted to enroll in a prescription drug plan. A part D eligible individual who is enrolled in an MA private fee-for-service plan (as defined in section 1859(b)(2) [42 USCS § 1395w-28(b)(2)]) that does not provide qualified prescription drug coverage may obtain qualified prescription drug coverage through enrollment in a prescription drug plan.

(iv) Enrollees in MSA plans permitted to enroll in a prescription drug plan. A part D eligible individual who is enrolled in an MSA plan (as defined in section 1859(b)(3) [42 USCS § 1395w-28(b)(3)]) may obtain qualified prescription drug coverage through enrollment in a prescription drug plan.

(2) Coverage first effective January 1, 2006. Coverage under prescription drug plans and MA-PD plans shall first be effective on January 1, 2006.

(3) Definitions. For purposes of this part [42 USCS §§ 1395w-101 et seq.]:

(A) Part D eligible individual. The term "part D eligible individual" means an individual who is entitled to benefits under part A [42 USCS §§ 1395c et seq.] or enrolled under part B [42 USCS §§ 1395j et seq.].

(B) MA plan. The term "MA plan" has the meaning given such term in section 1859(b)(1) [42 USCS § 1395w-28(b)(1)].

(C) MA-PD plan. The term "MA-PD plan" means an MA plan that provides qualified prescription drug coverage.

(b) Enrollment process for prescription drug plans. (1) Establishment of process. (A) In general. The Secretary shall establish a process for the enrollment, disenrollment, termination, and change of enrollment of part D eligible individuals in prescription drug plans consistent with this subsection.

(B) Application of MA rules. In establishing such process, the Secretary shall use rules similar to (and coordinated with) the rules for enrollment, disenrollment, termination, and change of enrollment with an MA-PD plan under the following provisions of section 1851 [42 USCS § 1395w-21]:

(i) Residence requirements. Section 1851(b)(1)(A) [42 USCS § 1395w-21(b)(1)(A)], relating to residence requirements.

(ii) Exercise of choice. Section 1851(c) [42 USCS § 1395w-21(c)] (other than paragraph (3)(A) of such section), relating to exercise of choice.

(iii) Coverage election periods. Subject to paragraphs (2) and (3) of this subsection, section 1851(e) [42 USCS § 1395w-21(e)] (other than subparagraphs (B), (C), and (E) of paragraph (2) and the second sentence of paragraph (4) of such section), relating to coverage election periods, including initial periods, annual coordinated election periods, special election periods, and election periods for exceptional circumstances.

(iv) Coverage periods. Section 1851(f) [42 USCS § 1395w-21(f)], relating to effectiveness of elections and changes of elections.

(v) Guaranteed issue and renewal. Section 1851(g) [42 USCS § 1395w-21(g)] (other than paragraph (2) of such section and clause (i) and the second sentence of clause (ii) of paragraph (3)(C) of such section), relating to guaranteed issue and renewal.

(vi) Marketing material and application forms. Section 1851(h) [42 USCS § 1395w-21(h)], relating to approval of marketing material and application forms.

In applying clauses (ii), (iv), and (v) of this subparagraph, any reference to section 1851(e) [42 USCS § 1395w-21(e)] shall be treated as a reference to such section as applied pursuant to clause (iii) of this subparagraph.

(C) Special rule. The process established under subparagraph (A) shall include, except as provided in subparagraph (D), in the case of a part D eligible individual who is a full-benefit dual eligible individual (as defined in section 1935(c)(6) [42 USCS § 1396u-5(c)(6)]) who has failed to enroll in a prescription drug plan or an MA-PD plan, for the enrollment in a prescription drug plan that has a monthly beneficiary premium that does not exceed the premium assistance available under section 1860D-14(a)(1)(A) [42 USCS § 1395w-114(a)(1)(A)]). If there is more than one such plan available, the Secretary shall enroll such an individual on a random basis among all such plans in the PDP region. Nothing in the previous sentence shall prevent such an individual from declining or changing such enrollment.

(D) Special rule for plans that waive de minimis premiums **[Caution: This subparagraph applies to premiums for months, and enrollments for plan years, beginning after January 1, 2011, as provided by § 3303(c) of Act March 23, 2010, P. L. 111-148, which appears as a note to this section.]**. The process established under subparagraph (A) may include, in the case of a part D eligible individual who is a subsidy eligible individual (as defined in section 1860D-14(a)(3) [42 USCS § 1395w-114(a)(3)]) who has failed to enroll in a prescription drug plan or an MA-PD plan, for the enrollment in a prescription drug plan or MA-PD plan that has waived the monthly beneficiary premium for such subsidy eligible individual under section 1860D-14(a)(5) [42 USCS § 1395w-114(a)(5)]. If there is more than one such plan available, the Secretary shall enroll such an individual under the preceding sentence on a random basis among all such plans in the PDP region. Nothing in the previous sentence shall prevent such an individual from declining or changing such enrollment.

(2) Initial enrollment period. (A) Program initiation. In the case of an individual who is a part D eligible individual as of November 15, 2005, there shall be an initial enrollment period that shall be the same as the annual, coordinated open election period described in section 1851(e)(3)(B)(iii) [42 USCS § 1395w-21(e)(3)(B)(iii)], as applied under paragraph (1)(B)(iii).

(B) Continuing periods. In the case of an individual who becomes a part D eligible individual after November 15, 2005, there shall be an initial enrollment period which is the period under section 1851(e)(1) [42 USCS § 1395w-21(e)(1)], as applied under paragraph (1)(B)(iii) of this section, as if "entitled to benefits under part A [42 USCS §§ 1395c et seq.] or enrolled under part B [42 USCS §§ 1395j et seq.]" were substituted for "entitled to benefits under part A [42 USCS §§ 1395c et seq.] and enrolled under part B [42 USCS §§ 1395j et seq.]", but in no case shall such period end before the period described in subparagraph (A).

(3) Additional special enrollment periods. The Secretary shall establish special enrollment periods, including the following:

(A) Involuntary loss of creditable prescription drug coverage. (i) In general. In the case of a part D eligible individual who involuntarily loses creditable prescription drug coverage (as defined in section 1860D-13(b)(4) [42 USCS § 1395w-113(b)(4)]).

(ii) Notice. In establishing special enrollment periods under clause (i), the Secretary shall take into account when the part D eligible individuals are provided notice of the loss of creditable prescription drug coverage.

(iii) Failure to pay premium. For purposes of clause (i), a loss of coverage shall be treated as voluntary if the coverage is terminated because of failure to pay a required beneficiary premium.

(iv) Reduction in coverage. For purposes of clause (i), a reduction in coverage so that the coverage no longer meets the requirements under section 1860D-13(b)(5) [42 USCS § 1395w-113(b)(5)] (relating to actuarial equivalence) shall be treated as an involuntary loss of coverage.

(B) Errors in enrollment. In the case described in section 1837(h) [42 USCS § 1395p(h)] (relating to errors in enrollment), in the same manner as such section applies to part B [42 USCS §§ 1395j et seq.].

(C) Exceptional circumstances. In the case of part D eligible individuals who meet such exceptional conditions (in addition to those conditions applied under paragraph (1)(B)(iii)) as the Secretary may provide.

(D) Medicaid coverage. In the case of an individual (as determined by the Secretary) who is a full-benefit dual eligible individual (as defined in section 1935(c)(6) [42 USCS § 1396u-5(c)(6)]).

(E) Discontinuance of MA-PD election during first year of eligibility. In the case of a part D eligible individual who discontinues enrollment in an MA-PD plan under the second sentence of section 1851(e)(4) [42 USCS § 1395w-21(e)(4)] at the time of the election of coverage under such sentence under the original medicare fee-for-service program.

(4) Information to facilitate enrollment. (A) In general. Notwithstanding any other provi-

sion of law but subject to subparagraph (B), the Secretary may provide to each PDP sponsor and MA organization such identifying information about part D eligible individuals as the Secretary determines to be necessary to facilitate efficient marketing of prescription drug plans and MA-PD plans to such individuals and enrollment of such individuals in such plans.

(B) Limitation. (i) Provision of information. The Secretary may provide the information under subparagraph (A) only to the extent necessary to carry out such subparagraph.

(ii) Use of information. Such information provided by the Secretary to a PDP sponsor or an MA organization may be used by such sponsor or organization only to facilitate marketing of, and enrollment of part D eligible individuals in, prescription drug plans and MA-PD plans.

(5) Reference to enrollment procedures for MA-PD plans. For rules applicable to enrollment, disenrollment, termination, and change of enrollment of part D eligible individuals in MA-PD plans, see section 1851 [42 USCS § 1395w-21].

(6) Reference to penalties for late enrollment. Section 1860D-13(b) [42 USCS § 1395w-113(b)] imposes a late enrollment penalty for part D eligible individuals who—

(A) enroll in a prescription drug plan or an MA-PD plan after the initial enrollment period described in paragraph (2); and

(B) fail to maintain continuous creditable prescription drug coverage during the period of non-enrollment.

(c) Providing information to beneficiaries. (1) Activities. The Secretary shall conduct activities that are designed to broadly disseminate information to part D eligible individuals (and prospective part D eligible individuals) regarding the coverage provided under this part [42 USCS §§ 1395w-101 et seq.]. Such activities shall ensure that such information is first made available at least 30 days prior to the initial enrollment period described in subsection (b)(2)(A).

(2) Requirements. The activities described in paragraph (1) shall—

(A) be similar to the activities performed by the Secretary under section 1851(d) [42 USCS § 1395w-21(d)], including dissemination (including through the toll-free telephone number 1-800-MEDICARE) of comparative information for prescription drug plans and MA-PD plans; and

(B) be coordinated with the activities performed by the Secretary under such section and under section 1804 [42 USCS § 1395b-2].

(3) Comparative information. (A) In general. Subject to subparagraph (B), the comparative information referred to in paragraph (2)(A) shall include a comparison of the following with respect to qualified prescription drug coverage:

(i) Benefits. The benefits provided under the plan.

(ii) Monthly beneficiary premium. The monthly beneficiary premium under the plan.

(iii) Quality and performance. The quality and performance under the plan.

(iv) Beneficiary cost-sharing. The cost-sharing required of part D eligible individuals under the plan.

(v) Consumer satisfaction surveys. The results of consumer satisfaction surveys regarding the plan conducted pursuant to section 1860D-4(d) [42 USCS § 1395w-104(d)].

(B) Exception for unavailability of information. The Secretary is not required to provide comparative information under clauses (iii) and (v) of subparagraph (A) with respect to a plan—

(i) for the first plan year in which it is offered; and

(ii) for the next plan year if it is impracticable or the information is otherwise unavailable.

(4) Information on late enrollment penalty. The information disseminated under paragraph (1) shall include information concerning the methodology for determining the late enrollment penalty under section 1860D-13(b) [42 USCS § 1395w-113(b)].

(Aug. 4, 1935, ch 531, Title XVIII, Part D, Subpart 1, § 1860D-1, as added Dec. 8, 2003, P. L. 108-173, Title I, § 101(a)(2), 117 Stat. 2071; Dec. 20, 2006, P. L. 109-432, Div B, Title II, § 206(b), 120 Stat. 2990; March 23, 2010, P. L. 111-148, Title III, Subtitle D, § 3303(b), 124 Stat. 469.)

HISTORY; ANCILLARY LAWS AND DIRECTIVES

Other provisions:

Application of amendments made by § 3303 of Act March 23, 2010. Act March 23, 2010, P. L. 111-148, Title III, Subtitle D, § 3303(c), 124 Stat. 469, provides: "The amendments made by this subsection [amending 42 USCS §§ 1395w-101(b)(1) and 1395w-114(a)] shall apply to premiums for months, and enrollments for plan years, beginning on or after January 1, 2011.".

Office of the Inspector General studies and reports. Act March 23, 2010, P. L. 111-148, Title III, Subtitle D, § 3313, 124 Stat. 477, provides:

"(a) Study and annual report on part D formularies' inclusion of drugs commonly used by dual eligibles. (1) Study. The Inspector General of the Department of Health and Human Services shall conduct a study of the extent to which formularies used by prescription drug plans and MA-PD plans under part D include drugs commonly used by full-benefit dual eligible individuals (as defined in section 1935(c)(6) of the Social Security Act (42 U.S.C. 1396u-5(c)(6))).

"(2) Annual reports. Not later than July 1 of each year (beginning with 2011), the Inspector General shall submit to Congress a report on the study conducted under paragraph (1), together with such recommendations as the Inspector General determines appropriate.

"(b) Study and report on prescription drug prices under Medicare part D and Medicaid. (1) Study. (A) In general. The Inspector General of the Department of Health and Human Services shall conduct a study on prices for covered part D drugs under the Medicare prescription drug program under part D of title XVIII of the Social Security Act [42 USCS §§ 1395w-101 et seq.] and for covered outpatient drugs under title XIX [42 USCS §§ 1396 et seq.]. Such study shall include the following:

"(i) A comparison, with respect to the 200 most frequently dispensed covered part D drugs under such program and covered outpatient drugs under such title (as determined by the Inspector General based on volume and expenditures), of—

"(I) the prices paid for covered part D drugs by PDP sponsors of prescription drug plans and Medicare Advantage organizations offering MA-PD plans; and

"(II) the prices paid for covered outpatient drugs by a State plan under title XIX [42 USCS §§ 1396 et seq.].

"(ii) An assessment of—

"(I) the financial impact of any discrepancies in such prices on the Federal Government; and

"(II) the financial impact of any such discrepancies on enrollees under part D or individuals eligible for medical assistance under a State plan under title XIX [42 USCS §§ 1396 et seq.].

"(B) Price. For purposes of subparagraph (A), the price of a covered part D drug or a covered outpatient drug shall include any rebate or discount under such program or such title, respectively, including any negotiated price concession described in section 1860D-2(d)(1)(B) of the Social Security Act (42 U.S.C. 1395w-102(d)(1)(B)) or rebate under an agreement under section 1927 of the Social Security Act (42 U.S.C. 1396r-8).

"(C) Authority to collect any necessary information. Notwithstanding any other provision of law, the Inspector General of the Department of Health and Human Services shall be able to collect any information related to the prices of covered part D drugs under such program and covered outpatient drugs under such title XIX [42 USCS §§ 1396 et seq.] necessary to carry out the comparison under subparagraph (A).

"(2) Report. (A) In general. Not later than October 1, 2011, subject to subparagraph (B), the Inspector General shall submit to Congress a report containing the results of the study conducted under paragraph (1), together with recommendations for such legislation and administrative action as the Inspector General determines appropriate.

"(B) Limitation on information contained in report. The report submitted under subparagraph (A) shall not include any information that the Inspector General determines is proprietary or is likely to negatively impact the ability of a PDP sponsor or a State plan under title XIX [42 USCS §§ 1396 et seq.] to negotiate prices for covered part D drugs or covered outpatient drugs, respectively.

"(3) Definitions. In this section:

"(A) Covered part D drug. The term 'covered part D drug' has the meaning given such term in section 1860D-2(e) of the Social Security Act (42 U.S.C. 1395w-102(e)).

"(B) Covered outpatient drug. The term 'covered outpatient drug' has the meaning given such term in section 1927(k) of such Act (42 U.S.C. 1396r(k)).

"(C) MA-PD plan. The term 'MA-PD plan' has the meaning given such term in section 1860D-41(a)(9) of such Act (42 U.S.C. 1395w-151(a)(9)).

"(D) Medicare Advantage organization. The term 'Medicare Advantage organization' has the meaning given such term in section 1859(a)(1) of such Act (42 U.S.C. 1395w-28)(a)(1)).

"(E) PDP sponsor. The term 'PDP sponsor' has the meaning given such term in section 1860D-41(a)(13) of such Act (42 U.S.C. 1395w-151(a)(13)).

"(F) Prescription drug plan. The term 'prescription drug plan' has the meaning given such term in section 1860D-41(a)(14) of such Act (42 U.S.C. 1395w-151(a)(14)).".

§ 1395w-102. Prescription drug benefits

(a) Requirements. (1) In general. For purposes of this part and part C [42 USCS §§ 1395w-101 et seq. and 1395w-21 et seq.], the term "qualified prescription drug coverage" means either of the following:

(A) Standard prescription drug coverage with access to negotiated prices. Standard prescription drug coverage (as defined in subsection (b)) and access to negotiated prices under subsection (d).

(B) Alternative prescription drug coverage with at least actuarially equivalent benefits and access to negotiated prices. Coverage of covered part D drugs which meets the alternative prescription drug coverage requirements of subsection (c) and access to negotiated prices under subsection (d), but only if the benefit design of such coverage is approved by the Secretary, as provided under subsection (c).

(2) Permitting supplemental prescription drug coverage. (A) In general. Subject to subparagraph (B), qualified prescription drug coverage may include supplemental prescription drug coverage consisting of either or both of the following:

(i) Certain reductions in cost-sharing. (I) In general. A reduction in the annual deductible, a reduction in the coinsurance percentage, or an increase in the initial coverage limit with respect to covered part D drugs, or any combination thereof, insofar as such a reduction or increase increases the actuarial value of benefits above the actuarial value of basic prescription drug coverage.

(II) Construction. Nothing in this paragraph shall be construed as affecting the application of subsection (c)(3).

(ii) Optional drugs. Coverage of any product that would be a covered part D drug but for the application of subsection (e)(2)(A).

(B) Requirement. A PDP sponsor may not offer a prescription drug plan that provides supplemental prescription drug coverage pursuant to subparagraph (A) in an area unless the sponsor also offers a prescription drug plan in the area that only provides basic prescription drug coverage.

(3) Basic prescription drug coverage. For purposes of this part and part C [42 USCS §§ 1395w-101 et seq. and 1395w-21 et seq.], the term "basic prescription drug coverage" means either of the following:

(A) Coverage that meets the requirements of paragraph (1)(A).

(B) Coverage that meets the requirements of paragraph (1)(B) but does not have any supplemental prescription drug coverage described in paragraph (2)(A).

(4) Application of secondary payor provisions. The provisions of section 1852(a)(4) [42 USCS § 1395w-22(a)(4)] shall apply under this part [42 USCS §§ 1395w-101 et seq.] in the same manner as they apply under part C [42 USCS §§ 1395w-21 et seq.].

(5) Construction. Nothing in this subsection shall be construed as changing the computation of incurred costs under subsection (b)(4).

(b) Standard prescription drug coverage. For purposes of this part and part C [42 USCS §§ 1395w-101 et seq. and 1395w-21 et seq.], the term "standard prescription drug coverage" means coverage of covered part D drugs that meets the following requirements:

(1) Deductible. (A) In general. The coverage has an annual deductible—

(i) for 2006, that is equal to $250; or

(ii) for a subsequent year, that is equal to the amount specified under this paragraph for the previous year increased by the percentage specified in paragraph (6) for the year involved.

(B) Rounding. Any amount determined under subparagraph (A)(ii) that is not a multiple of $5 shall be rounded to the nearest multiple of $5.

(2) Benefit structure. (A) 25 percent coinsurance. Subject to subparagraphs (C) and (D), the coverage has coinsurance (for costs above the annual deductible specified in paragraph (1) and up to the initial coverage limit under paragraph (3)) that is—

(i) equal to 25 percent; or

(ii) actuarially equivalent (using processes and methods established under section 1860D-11(c) [42 USCS § 1395w-111(c)]) to an average expected payment of 25 percent of such costs.

(B) Use of tiers. Nothing in this part [42 USCS §§ 1395w-101 et seq.] shall be construed as preventing a PDP sponsor or an MA organization from applying tiered copayments under a plan, so long as such tiered copayments are consistent with subparagraphs (A)(ii), (C), and (D).

(C) Coverage for generic drugs in coverage gap. (i) In general. Except as provided in paragraph (4), the coverage for an applicable beneficiary (as defined in section 1860D-14A(g)(1) [42 USCS § 1395w-114a(g)(1)]) has coinsurance (for costs above the initial coverage limit under paragraph (3) and below the out-of-pocket threshold) for covered part D drugs that are not applicable drugs under section 1860D-14A(g)(2) [42 USCS § 1395w-114a(g)(2)] that is—

(I) equal to the generic-gap coinsurance percentage (specified in clause (ii)) for the year; or

(II) actuarially equivalent (using processes and methods established under section 1860D-11(c) [42 USCS § 1395w-111(c)]) to an average expected payment of such percentage of such costs for covered part D drugs that are not applicable drugs under section 1860D-14A(g)(2) [42 USCS § 1395w-114a(g)(2)].

(ii) Generic-gap coinsurance percentage. The generic-gap coinsurance percentage specified in this clause for—

(I) 2011 is 93 percent;

(II) 2012 and each succeeding year before 2020 is the generic-gap coinsurance percentage under this clause for the previous year decreased by 7 percentage points; and

(III) 2020 and each subsequent year is 25 percent.

(D) Coverage for applicable drugs in coverage gap. (i) In general. Except as provided in paragraph (4), the coverage for an applicable beneficiary (as defined in section 1860D-14A(g)(1) [42 USCS § 1395w-114a(g)(1)]) has coinsurance (for costs above the initial coverage limit under paragraph (3) and below the out-of-pocket threshold) for the negotiated price (as defined in section 1860D-14A(g)(6) [42 USCS § 1395w-114a(g)(6)]) of covered part D drugs that are applicable drugs under section 1860D-14A(g)(2) [42 USCS § 1395w-114a(g)(2)] that is—

(I) equal to the difference between the applicable gap percentage (specified in clause (ii) for the year) and the discount percentage specified in section 1860D-14A(g)(4)(A) [42 USCS § 1395w-114a(g)(4)(A)] for such applicable drugs; or

(II) actuarially equivalent (using processes and methods established under section 1860D-11(c) [42 USCS § 1395w-111(c)]) to an average expected payment of such percentage of such costs, for covered part D drugs that are applicable drugs under section 1860D-14A(g)(2) [42 USCS § 1395w-114a(g)(2)].

(ii) Applicable gap percentage. The applicable gap percentage specified in this clause for—

(I) 2013 and 2014 is 97.5 percent;

(II) 2015 and 2016 is 95 percent;

(III) 2017 is 90 percent;

(IV) 2018 is 85 percent;

(V) 2019 is 80 percent; and

(VI) 2020 and each subsequent year is 75 percent.

(3) Initial coverage limit. (A) In general. Except as provided in paragraphs (2)(C), (2)(D), and (4), the coverage has an initial coverage limit on the maximum costs that may be recognized for payment purposes (including the annual deductible)—

(i) for 2006, that is equal to $2,250; or

(ii) for a subsequent year, that is equal to the amount specified in this paragraph for the previous year, increased by the annual percentage increase described in paragraph (6) for the year involved.

(B) Rounding. Any amount determined under subparagraph (A)(ii) that is not a multiple of $10 shall be rounded to the nearest multiple of $10.

(4) Protection against high out-of-pocket expenditures. (A) In general. (i) In general. The coverage provides benefits, after the part D eligible individual has incurred costs (as described in subparagraph (C)) for covered part D drugs in a year equal to the annual out-of-pocket threshold specified in subparagraph (B), with cost-sharing that is equal to the greater of—

(I) a copayment of $2 for a generic drug or a preferred drug that is a multiple source drug (as defined in section 1927(k)(7)(A)(i) [42 USCS § 1396r-8(k)(7)(A)(i)]) and $5 for any other drug; or

(II) coinsurance that is equal to 5 percent.

(ii) Adjustment of amount. For a year after 2006, the dollar amounts specified in clause (i)(I) shall be equal to the dollar amounts specified in this subparagraph for the previous year, increased by the annual percentage increase described in paragraph (6) for the year involved. Any amount established under this clause that is not a multiple of a 5 cents shall be rounded to the nearest multiple of 5 cents.

(B) Annual out-of-pocket threshold. (i) In general. For purposes of this part [42 USCS §§ 1395w-101 et seq.], the "annual out-of-pocket threshold" specified in this subparagraph—

(I) for 2006, is equal to $3,600;

(II) for each of years 2007 through 2013, is equal to the amount specified in this subparagraph for the previous year, increased by the annual percentage increase described in paragraph (6) for the year involved;

(III) for 2014 and 2015, is equal to the amount specified in this subparagraph for the previous year, increased by the annual percentage increase described in paragraph (6) for the year involved, minus 0.25 percentage point;

(IV) for each of years 2016 through 2019, is equal to the amount specified in this subparagraph for the previous year, increased by the lesser of—

(aa) the annual percentage increase described in paragraph (7) for the year involved, plus 2 percentage points; or

(bb) the annual percentage increase described in paragraph (6) for the year;

(V) for 2020, is equal to the amount that would have been applied under this subparagraph for 2020 if the amendments made by section 1101(d)(1) of the Health Care and Education Reconciliation Act of 2010 had not been enacted; or

(VI) for a subsequent year, is equal to the amount specified in this subparagraph for the previous year, increased by the annual percentage increase described in paragraph (6) for the year involved.

(ii) Rounding. Any amount determined under clause (i)(II) that is not a multiple of $50 shall be rounded to the nearest multiple of $50.

(C) Application. Except as provided in subparagraph (E), in applying subparagraph (A)—

(i) incurred costs shall only include costs incurred with respect to covered part D drugs for the annual deductible described in paragraph (1), for cost-sharing described in paragraph (2), and for amounts for which benefits are not provided because of the application of the initial coverage limit described in paragraph (3), but does not include any costs incurred for covered part D drugs which are not included (or treated as being included) in the plan's formulary;

(ii) **[Caution: For provisions applicable to costs incurred before January 1, 2011, see 2010 amendment note below.]** subject to clause (iii), such costs shall be treated as incurred only if they are paid by the part D eligible individual (or by another person, such as a family member, on behalf of the individual) and the part D eligible individual (or other person) is not reimbursed through insurance or otherwise, a group health plan, or other third-party payment arrangement (other than under such section or such a Program) for such costs; and

(iii) **[Caution: This clause applies to costs incurred on or after January 1, 2011, as provided by § 3314(b) of Act March 23, 2010, P. L. 111-148, which appears as a note to this section.]** such costs shall be treated as incurred and shall not be considered to be reimbursed under clause (ii) if such costs are borne or paid—

(I) under section 1860D-14 [42 USCS § 1395w-114];

(II) under a State Pharmaceutical Assistance Program;

(III) by the Indian Health Service, an Indian tribe or tribal organization, or an urban Indian organization (as defined in section 4 of the Indian Health Care Improvement Act [25 USCS § 1603]); or

(IV) under an AIDS Drug Assistance Program under part B of title XXVI of the Public Health Service Act [42 USCS §§ 300ff-21 et seq.].

(D) Information regarding third-party reimbursement. (i) Procedures for exchanging information. In order to accurately apply the requirements of subparagraph (C)(ii), the Secretary is authorized to establish procedures, in coordination with the Secretary of the Treasury and the Secretary of Labor—

(I) for determining whether costs for part D eligible individuals are being reimbursed through insurance or otherwise, a group health plan, or other third-party payment arrangement; and

(II) for alerting the PDP sponsors and MA organizations that offer the prescription drug plans and MA-PD plans in which such individuals are enrolled about such reimbursement arrangements.

(ii) Authority to request information from enrollees. A PDP sponsor or an MA organization may periodically ask part D eligible individuals enrolled in a prescription drug plan or an MA-PD plan offered by the sponsor or organization whether such individuals have or expect to receive such third-party reimbursement. A material misrepresentation of the information described in the preceding sentence by an individual (as defined in standards set by the Secretary and determined through a process established by the Secretary) shall constitute grounds for termination of enrollment in any plan under section 1851(g)(3)(B) [42 USCS § 1395w-21(g)(3)(B)] (and as applied under this part [42 USCS §§ 1395w-101 et seq.] under section 1860D-1(b)(1)(B)(v) [42 USCS § 1395w-101(b)(1)(B)(v)]) for a period specified by the Secretary.

(E) **[Caution: This subparagraph applies to costs incurred on or after July 1, 2010, as provided by § 3301(c)(2) of Act March 23, 2010, P. L. 111-148, which appears as a note to this section.]** Inclusion of costs of applicable drugs under Medicare coverage gap discount program. In applying subparagraph (A), incurred costs shall include the negotiated price (as defined in paragraph (6) of section 1860D-14A(g) [42 USCS § 1395w-114a(g)]) of an applicable drug (as defined in paragraph (2) of such section) of a manufacturer that is furnished to an applicable beneficiary (as defined in paragraph (1) of such section) under the Medicare coverage gap discount program under section 1860D-14A [42 USCS § 1395w-114a], regardless of whether part of such costs were paid by a manufacturer under such program, except that incurred costs shall not include the portion of the negotiated price that represents the reduction in coinsurance resulting from the application of paragraph (2)(D).

(5) Construction. Nothing in this part [42 USCS §§ 1395w-101 et seq.] shall be construed as preventing a PDP sponsor or an MA organization offering an MA-PD plan from reducing to zero the cost-sharing otherwise applicable to preferred or generic drugs.

(6) Annual percentage increase. The annual percentage increase specified in this paragraph for a year is equal to the annual percentage increase in average per capita aggregate expenditures for covered part D drugs in the United States for part D eligible individuals, as determined by the Secretary for the 12-month period ending in July of the previous year using such methods as the Secretary shall specify.

(7) Additional annual percentage increase. The annual percentage increase specified in this paragraph for a year is equal to the annual percentage increase in the consumer price index for all urban consumers (United States city average) for the 12-month period ending in July of the previous year.

(c) Alternative prescription drug coverage requirements. A prescription drug plan or an MA-PD plan may provide a different prescription drug benefit design from standard prescription drug coverage so long as the Secretary determines (consistent with section 1860D-11(c) [42 USCS § 1395w-111(c)]) that the following requirements are met and the plan applies for, and receives, the approval of the Secretary for such benefit design:

(1) Assuring at least actuarially equivalent coverage. (A) Assuring equivalent value of total coverage. The actuarial value of the total coverage is at least equal to the actuarial value

of standard prescription drug coverage.

(B) Assuring equivalent unsubsidized value of coverage. The unsubsidized value of the coverage is at least equal to the unsubsidized value of standard prescription drug coverage. For purposes of this subparagraph, the unsubsidized value of coverage is the amount by which the actuarial value of the coverage exceeds the actuarial value of the subsidy payments under section 1860D-15 [42 USCS § 1395w-115] with respect to such coverage.

(C) Assuring standard payment for costs at initial coverage limit. The coverage is designed, based upon an actuarially representative pattern of utilization, to provide for the payment, with respect to costs incurred that are equal to the initial coverage limit under subsection (b)(3) for the year, of an amount equal to at least the product of—

(i) the amount by which the initial coverage limit described in subsection (b)(3) for the year exceeds the deductible described in subsection (b)(1) for the year; and

(ii) 100 percent minus the coinsurance percentage specified in subsection (b)(2)(A)(i).

(2) Maximum required deductible. The deductible under the coverage shall not exceed the deductible amount specified under subsection (b)(1) for the year.

(3) Same protection against high out-of-pocket expenditures. The coverage provides the coverage required under subsection (b)(4).

(d) Access to negotiated prices. (1) Access. (A) In general. Under qualified prescription drug coverage offered by a PDP sponsor offering a prescription drug plan or an MA organization offering an MA-PD plan, the sponsor or organization shall provide enrollees with access to negotiated prices used for payment for covered part D drugs, regardless of the fact that no benefits may be payable under the coverage with respect to such drugs because of the application of a deductible or other cost-sharing or an initial coverage limit (described in subsection (b)(3)).

(B) Negotiated prices. For purposes of this part [42 USCS §§ 1395w-101 et seq.], negotiated prices shall take into account negotiated price concessions, such as discounts, direct or indirect subsidies, rebates, and direct or indirect remunerations, for covered part D drugs, and include any dispensing fees for such drugs.

(C) Medicaid-related provisions. The prices negotiated by a prescription drug plan, by an MA-PD plan with respect to covered part D drugs, or by a qualified retiree prescription drug plan (as defined in section 1860D-22(a)(2) [42 USCS § 1395w-132(a)(2)]) with respect to such drugs on behalf of part D eligible individuals, shall (notwithstanding any other provision of law) not be taken into account for the purposes of establishing the best price under section 1927(c)(1)(C) [42 USCS § 1396r-8(c)(1)(C)].

(2) Disclosure. A PDP sponsor offering a prescription drug plan or an MA organization offering an MA-PD plan shall disclose to the Secretary (in a manner specified by the Secretary) the aggregate negotiated price concessions described in paragraph (1)(B) made available to the sponsor or organization by a manufacturer which are passed through in the form of lower subsidies, lower monthly beneficiary prescription drug premiums, and lower prices through pharmacies and other dispensers. The provisions of section 1927(b)(3)(D) [42 USCS § 1396r-8(b)(3)(D)] apply to information disclosed to the Secretary under this paragraph.

(3) Audits. To protect against fraud and abuse and to ensure proper disclosures and accounting under this part [42 USCS §§ 1395w-101 et seq.] and in accordance with section 1857(d)(2)(B) [42 USCS § 1395w-27(d)(2)(B)] (as applied under section 1860D-12(b)(3)(C) [42 USCS § 1395w-112(b)(3)(C)]), the Secretary may conduct periodic audits, directly or through contracts, of the financial statements and records of PDP sponsors with respect to prescription drug plans and MA organizations with respect to MA-PD plans.

(e) Covered part D drug defined. (1) In general. Except as provided in this subsection, for purposes of this part [42 USCS §§ 1395w-101 et seq.], the term "covered part D drug" means—

(A) a drug that may be dispensed only upon a prescription and that is described in subparagraph (A)(i), (A)(ii), or (A)(iii) of section 1927(k)(2) [42 USCS § 1396r-8(k)(2)]; or

(B) a biological product described in clauses (i) through (iii) of subparagraph (B) of such section or insulin described in subparagraph (C) of such section and medical supplies associated with the injection of insulin (as defined in regulations of the Secretary),

and such term includes a vaccine licensed under section 351 of the Public Health Service Act [42 USCS § 262] (and, for vaccines administered on or after January 1, 2008, its administration) and any use of a covered part D drug for a medically accepted indication (as defined in paragraph (4)).

(2) Exclusions. (A) In general **[Caution: For provisions applicable to prescriptions dispensed before January 1, 2013, see 2008**

amendment note below.]. Such term does not include drugs or classes of drugs, or their medical uses, which may be excluded from coverage or otherwise restricted under section 1927(d)(2) [42 USCS § 1396r-8(d)(2)], other than subparagraph (E) of such section (relating to smoking cessation agents), other than subparagraph (I) of such section (relating to barbiturates) if the barbiturate is used in the treatment of epilepsy, cancer, or a chronic mental health disorder, and other than subparagraph (J) of such section (relating to benzodiazepines), or under section 1927(d)(3) [42 USCS § 1396r-8(d)(3)], as such sections were in effect on the date of the enactment of this part [enacted Dec. 8, 2003]. Such term also does not include a drug when used for the treatment of sexual or erectile dysfunction, unless such drug were used to treat a condition, other than sexual or erectile dysfunction, for which the drug has been approved by the Food and Drug Administration.

(B) Medicare covered drugs. A drug prescribed for a part D eligible individual that would otherwise be a covered part D drug under this part [42 USCS §§ 1395w-101 et seq.] shall not be so considered if payment for such drug as so prescribed and dispensed or administered with respect to that individual is available (or would be available but for the application of a deductible) under part A or B [42 USCS §§ 1395c et seq. or 1395j et seq.] for that individual.

(3) Application of general exclusion provisions. A prescription drug plan or an MA-PD plan may exclude from qualified prescription drug coverage any covered part D drug—

(A) for which payment would not be made if section 1862(a) [42 USCS § 1395y(a)] applied to this part [42 USCS §§ 1395w-101 et seq.]; or

(B) which is not prescribed in accordance with the plan or this part [42 USCS §§ 1395w-101 et seq.].

Such exclusions are determinations subject to reconsideration and appeal pursuant to subsections (g) and (h), respectively, of section 1860D-4 [42 USCS § 1395w-104].

(4) Medically accepted indication defined. (A) In general. For purposes of paragraph (1), the term "medically accepted indication"' has the meaning given that term—

(i) in the case of a covered part D drug used in an anticancer chemotherapeutic regimen, in section 1861(t)(2)(B) [42 USCS § 1395x(t)(2)(B)], except that in applying such section—

(I) "prescription drug plan or MA-PD plan" shall be substituted for "carrier" each place it appears; and

(II) subject to subparagraph (B), the compendia described in section 1927(g)(1)(B)(i)(III) [42 USCS § 1396r-8(g)(1)(B)(i)(III)] shall be included in the list of compendia described in clause (ii)(I) section 1861(t)(2)(B) [42 USCS § 1395x(t)(2)(B)]; and

(ii) in the case of any other covered part D drug, in section 1927(k)(6) [42 USCS § 1396r-8(k)(6)].

(B) Conflict of interest. On and after January 1, 2010, subparagraph (A)(i)(II) shall not apply unless the compendia described in section 1927(g)(1)(B)(i)(III) [42 USCS § 1396r-8(g)(1)(B)(i)(III)] meets the requirement in the third sentence of section 1861(t)(2)(B) [42 USCS § 1395x(t)(2)(B)].

(C) Update. For purposes of applying subparagraph (A)(ii), the Secretary shall revise the list of compendia described in section 1927(g)(1)(B)(i) [42 USCS § 1396r-8(g)(1)(B)(i)] as is appropriate for identifying medically accepted indications for drugs. Any such revision shall be done in a manner consistent with the process for revising compendia under section 1861(t)(2)(B) [42 USCS § 1395x(t)(2)(B)].

(Aug. 4, 1935, ch 531, Title XVIII, Part D, Subpart 1, § 1860D-2, as added Dec. 8, 2003, P. L. 108-173, Title I, § 101(a)(2), 117 Stat. 2075; Oct. 20, 2005, P. L. 109-91, Title I, § 103(a), 119 Stat. 2092; Dec. 20, 2006, P. L. 109-432, Div B, Title II, § 202(b), 120 Stat. 2986; July 15, 2008, P. L. 110-275, Title I, Subtitle E, Part II, § 175(a), Subtitle F, § 182(a)(1), 122 Stat. 2581, 2583; March 23, 2010, P. L. 111-148, Title III, Subtitle D, §§ 3301(c)(1), 3314(a), 3315, 124 Stat. 467, 478, 479; March 30, 2010, P. L. 111-152, Title I, Subtitle B, § 1101(a)(2), (b)(3), (d), 124 Stat. 1037, 1038, 1039.)

HISTORY; ANCILLARY LAWS AND DIRECTIVES

Amendments:

2008. Act July 15, 2008 (applicable to prescriptions dispensed on or after 1/1/2013, as provided by § 175(b) of such Act, which appears as a note to this section), in subsec. (e)(2)(A), inserted "other than subparagraph (I) of such section (relating to barbiturates) if the barbiturate is used in the treatment of epilepsy, cancer, or a chronic mental health disorder, and other than subparagraph (J) of such section (relating to benzodiazepines),".

Such Act further (applicable to plan years beginning on or after 1/1/2009, as provided by § 182(a)(2) of such Act, which appears as a note to this section), in subsec. (e), in para. (1), in the concluding matter, substituted "(as defined in paragraph (4))" for "(as defined in section 1927(k)(6))", and added para. (4).

2010. Act March 23, 2010 (applicable to costs incurred on of after 7/1/2010, as provided by § 3301(c)(2) of such Act, which appears as a note to this section), in subsec. (b)(4), in subpara. (C), in the introductory matter, substituted "Except as provided in subparagraph (E), in applying" for "In applying", and added subpara. (E).

Such Act further (applicable to costs incurred on or after 1/1/2011, as provided by § 3314(b) of such Act, which appears as a note to this section), in subsec. (b)(4)(C), in cl. (i), deleted "and" following the concluding semicolon, in cl. (ii), inserted "subject to clause (iii),", deleted ", under section 1860D-14, or under a State Pharmaceutical Assistance Program" before "and the part D", and substituted "; and" for a concluding period, and added cl. (iii).

Section 3315 of such Act further (repealed by § 1101(a)(2) of Act March 30, 2010, which appears as a note to this section), in subsec. (b), in para. (3)(A), substituted "paragraphs (4) and (7)" for "paragraph (4)", and added para. (7), which read:

"(7) Increase in initial coverage limit in 2010. (A) In general. For the plan year beginning on January 1, 2010, the initial coverage limit described in paragraph (3)(B) otherwise applicable shall be increased by $500.

"(B) Application. In applying subparagraph (A)—

"(i) except as otherwise provided in this subparagraph, there shall be no change in the premiums, bids, or any other parameters under this part or part C;

"(ii) costs that would be treated as incurred costs for purposes of applying paragraph (4) but for the application of subparagraph (A) shall continue to be treated as incurred costs;

"(iii) the Secretary shall establish procedures, which may include a reconciliation process, to fully reimburse PDP sponsors with respect to prescription drug plans and MA organizations with respect to MA-PD plans for the reduction in beneficiary cost sharing associated with the application of subparagraph (A);

"(iv) the Secretary shall develop an estimate of the additional increased costs attributable to the application of this paragraph for increased drug utilization and financing and administrative costs and shall use such estimate to adjust payments to PDP sponsors with respect to prescription drug plans under this part and MA organizations with respect to MA-PD plans under part C; and

"(v) the Secretary shall establish procedures for retroactive reimbursement of part D eligible individuals who are covered under such a plan for costs which are incurred before the date of initial implementation of subparagraph (A) and which would be reimbursed under such a plan if such implementation occurred as of January 1, 2010.

"(C) No effect on subsequent years. The increase under subparagraph (A) shall only apply with respect to the plan year beginning on January 1, 2010, and the initial coverage limit for plan years beginning on or after January 1, 2011, shall be determined as if subparagraph (A) had never applied.".

Act March 30, 2010, in subsec. (b), in para. (2), in subpara. (A), substituted "Subject to subparagraphs (C) and (D), the coverage" for "The covergae", and in subpara. (B), substituted "subparagraphs (A)(ii), (C), and (D)" for "subparagraph (A)(ii)", and added subparas. (C) and (D), in para. (3)(A), substituted "paragraphs (2)(C), (2)(D), and (4)" for "paragraph (4)", in para. (4), in subpara. (B)(i), in subcl. (I), deleted "or" following the concluding semicolon, redesignated subcl. (II) as subcl. (VI), and inserted new subcls. (II)–(V), and in subpara. (E), inserted ", except that incurred costs shall not include the portion of the negotiated price that represents the reduction in coinsurance resulting from the application of paragraph (2)(D)", and added para. (7).

Other provisions:

Application of amendments made by § 3301(c) of Act March 23, 2010. Act March 23, 2010, P. L. 111-148, Title III, Subtitle D, § 3301(c)(2), 124 Stat. 468, provides: "The amendments made by this subsection [amending subsec. (b)(4) of this section] shall apply to costs incurred on or after July 1, 2010.".

Application of amendments made by § 3314 of Act March 23, 2010. Act March 23, 2010, P. L. 111-148, Title III, Subtitle D, § 3314, 124 Stat. 479, provides: "The amendments made by subsection (a) [amending subsec. (b)(4)(C) of this section] shall apply to costs incurred on or after January 1, 2011.".

Repeal of amendments made by § 3315 of Act March 23, 2010. Act March 30, 2010, P. L. 111-152, Title I, Subtitle B, § 1101(a)(2), 124 Stat. 1037, provides: "Section 3315 of the Patient Protection and Affordable Care Act (including the amendments made by such section) [amending subsec. (b)(3)(A) and adding subsec. (b)(7) of this section] is repealed, and any provision of law amended or repealed by such sections is hereby restored or revived as if such section had not been enacted into law.".

§ 1395w-104. Beneficiary protections for qualified prescription drug coverage

(a) Dissemination of information. (1) General information. (A) Application of MA information. A PDP sponsor shall disclose, in a clear, accurate, and standardized form to each enrollee with a prescription drug plan offered by the sponsor under this part [42 USCS §§ 1395w-101 et seq.] at the time of enrollment and at least annually thereafter, the information described in section 1852(c)(1) [42 USCS § 1395w-22(c)(1)] relating to such plan, insofar as the Secretary determines appropriate with respect to benefits provided under this part [42 USCS §§ 1395w-101 et seq.], and including the information described in subparagraph (B).

(B) Drug specific information. The information described in this subparagraph is information concerning the following:

(i) Access to specific covered part D drugs, including access through pharmacy networks.

(ii) How any formulary (including any tiered formulary structure) used by the sponsor functions, including a description of how a part D eligible individual may obtain information on the formulary consistent with paragraph (3).

(iii) Beneficiary cost-sharing requirements and how a part D eligible individual may obtain information on such requirements, including tiered or other copayment level applicable to each drug (or class of drugs), consistent with paragraph (3).

(iv) The medication therapy management program required under subsection (c).

(2) Disclosure upon request of general coverage, utilization, and grievance information.

Upon request of a part D eligible individual who is eligible to enroll in a prescription drug plan, the PDP sponsor offering such plan shall provide information similar (as determined by the Secretary) to the information described in subparagraphs (A), (B), and (C) of section 1852(c)(2) [42 USCS § 1395w-22(c)(2)] to such individual.

(3) Provision of specific information. (A) Response to beneficiary questions. Each PDP sponsor offering a prescription drug plan shall have a mechanism for providing specific information on a timely basis to enrollees upon request. Such mechanism shall include access to information through the use of a toll-free telephone number and, upon request, the provision of such information in writing.

(B) Availability of information on changes in formulary through the internet. A PDP sponsor offering a prescription drug plan shall make available on a timely basis through an Internet website information on specific changes in the formulary under the plan (including changes to tiered or preferred status of covered part D drugs).

(4) Claims information. A PDP sponsor offering a prescription drug plan must furnish to each enrollee in a form easily understandable to such enrollees—

(A) an explanation of benefits (in accordance with section 1806(a) [42 USCS § 1395b-7(a)] or in a comparable manner); and

(B) when prescription drug benefits are provided under this part [42 USCS §§ 1395w-101 et seq.], a notice of the benefits in relation to—

(i) the initial coverage limit for the current year; and

(ii) the annual out-of-pocket threshold for the current year.

Notices under subparagraph (B) need not be provided more often than as specified by the Secretary and notices under subparagraph (B)(ii) shall take into account the application of section 1860D-2(b)(4)(C) [42 USCS § 1395w-102(b)(4)(C)] to the extent practicable, as specified by the Secretary.

(b) Access to covered part D drugs. (1) Assuring pharmacy access. (A) Participation of any willing pharmacy. A prescription drug plan shall permit the participation of any pharmacy that meets the terms and conditions under the plan.

(B) Discounts allowed for network pharmacies. For covered part D drugs dispensed through in-network pharmacies, a prescription drug plan may, notwithstanding subparagraph (A), reduce coinsurance or copayments for part D eligible individuals enrolled in the plan below the level otherwise required. In no case shall such a reduction result in an increase in payments made by the Secretary under section 1860D-15 [42 USCS § 1395w-115] to a plan.

(C) Convenient access for network pharmacies. (i) In general. The PDP sponsor of the prescription drug plan shall secure the participation in its network of a sufficient number of pharmacies that dispense (other than by mail order) drugs directly to patients to ensure convenient access (consistent with rules established by the Secretary).

(ii) Application of TRICARE standards. The Secretary shall establish rules for convenient access to in-network pharmacies under this subparagraph that are no less favorable to enrollees than the rules for convenient access to pharmacies included in the statement of work of solicitation (#MDA906-03-R-0002) of the Department of Defense under the TRICARE Retail Pharmacy (TRRx) as of March 13, 2003.

(iii) Adequate emergency access. Such rules shall include adequate emergency access for enrollees.

(iv) Convenient access in long-term care facilities. Such rules may include standards with respect to access for enrollees who are residing in long-term care facilities and for pharmacies operated by the Indian Health Service, Indian tribes and tribal organizations, and urban Indian organizations (as defined in section 4 of the Indian Health Care Improvement Act [25 USCS § 1603]).

(D) Level playing field. Such a sponsor shall permit enrollees to receive benefits (which may include a 90-day supply of drugs or biologicals) through a pharmacy (other than a mail order pharmacy), with any differential in charge paid by such enrollees.

(E) Not required to accept insurance risk. The terms and conditions under subparagraph (A) may not require participating pharmacies to accept insurance risk as a condition of participation.

(2) Use of standardized technology. (A) In general. The PDP sponsor of a prescription drug plan shall issue (and reissue, as appropriate) such a card (or other technology) that may be used by an enrollee to assure access to negotiated prices under section 1860D-2(d) [42 USCS § 1395w-102(d)].

(B) Standards. (i) In general. The Secretary shall provide for the development, adoption, or recognition of standards relating to a standardized format for the card or other technology required under subparagraph (A). Such standards shall be compatible with part C of title XI

[42 USCS §§ 1320d et seq.] and may be based on standards developed by an appropriate standard setting organization.

(ii) Consultation. In developing the standards under clause (i), the Secretary shall consult with the National Council for Prescription Drug Programs and other standard setting organizations determined appropriate by the Secretary.

(iii) Implementation. The Secretary shall develop, adopt, or recognize the standards under clause (i) by such date as the Secretary determines shall be sufficient to ensure that PDP sponsors utilize such standards beginning January 1, 2006.

(3) Requirements on development and application of formularies. If a PDP sponsor of a prescription drug plan uses a formulary (including the use of tiered cost-sharing), the following requirements must be met:

(A) Development and revision by a pharmacy and therapeutic (P&T) committee. (i) In general. The formulary must be developed and reviewed by a pharmacy and therapeutic committee. A majority of the members of such committee shall consist of individuals who are practicing physicians or practicing pharmacists (or both).

(ii) Inclusion of independent experts. Such committee shall include at least one practicing physician and at least one practicing pharmacist, each of whom—

(I) is independent and free of conflict with respect to the sponsor and plan; and

(II) has expertise in the care of elderly or disabled persons.

(B) Formulary development. In developing and reviewing the formulary, the committee shall—

(i) base clinical decisions on the strength of scientific evidence and standards of practice, including assessing peer-reviewed medical literature, such as randomized clinical trials, pharmacoeconomic studies, outcomes research data, and on such other information as the committee determines to be appropriate; and

(ii) take into account whether including in the formulary (or in a tier in such formulary) particular covered part D drugs has therapeutic advantages in terms of safety and efficacy.

(C) Inclusion of drugs in all therapeutic categories and classes. (i) In general. Subject to subparagraph (G), the formulary must include drugs within each therapeutic category and class of covered part D drugs, although not necessarily all drugs within such categories and classes.

(ii) Model guidelines. The Secretary shall request the United States Pharmacopeia to develop, in consultation with pharmaceutical benefit managers and other interested parties, a list of categories and classes that may be used by prescription drug plans under this paragraph and to revise such classification from time to time to reflect changes in therapeutic uses of covered part D drugs and the additions of new covered part D drugs.

(iii) Limitation on changes in therapeutic classification. The PDP sponsor of a prescription drug plan may not change the therapeutic categories and classes in a formulary other than at the beginning of each plan year except as the Secretary may permit to take into account new therapeutic uses and newly approved covered part D drugs.

(D) Provider and patient education. The PDP sponsor shall establish policies and procedures to educate and inform health care providers and enrollees concerning the formulary.

(E) Notice before removing drug from formulary or changing preferred or tier status of drug. Any removal of a covered part D drug from a formulary and any change in the preferred or tiered cost-sharing status of such a drug shall take effect only after appropriate notice is made available (such as under subsection (a)(3)) to the Secretary, affected enrollees, physicians, pharmacies, and pharmacists.

(F) Periodic evaluation of protocols. In connection with the formulary, the sponsor of a prescription drug plan shall provide for the periodic evaluation and analysis of treatment protocols and procedures.

(G) Required inclusion of drugs in certain categories and classes **[Caution: For provisions applicable to plan years before 2011, see 2010 amendment note below.]**. (i) Formulary requirements. (I) In general. Subject to subclause (II), a PDP sponsor offering a prescription drug plan shall be required to include all covered part D drugs in the categories and classes identified by the Secretary under clause (ii)(I).

(II) Exceptions. The Secretary may establish exceptions that permit a PDP sponsor offering a prescription drug plan to exclude from its formulary a particular covered part D drug in a category or class that is otherwise required to be included in the formulary under subclause (I) (or to otherwise limit access to such a drug, including through prior authorization or utilization management).

(ii) Identification of drugs in certain categories and classes. (I) In general. Subject to clause (iv), the Secretary shall identify, as appropriate, categories and classes of drugs for which the Secretary determines are of clinical concern.

(II) Criteria. The Secretary shall use criteria established by the Secretary in making any determination under subclause (I).

(iii) Implementation. The Secretary shall establish the criteria under clause (ii)(II) and any exceptions under clause (i)(II) through the promulgation of a regulation which includes a public notice and comment period.

(iv) Requirement for certain categories and classes until criteria established. Until such time as the Secretary establishes the criteria under clause (ii)(II) the following categories and classes of drugs shall be identified under clause (ii)(I):

(I) Anticonvulsants.

(II) Antidepressants.

(III) Antineoplastics.

(IV) Antipsychotics.

(V) Antiretrovirals.

(VI) Immunosuppressants for the treatment of transplant rejection.

(H) Use of single, uniform exceptions and appeals process **Caution: This paragraph applies to exceptions and appeals on or after January 1, 2012, as provided by § 3312(b) of Act March 23, 2010, P. L. 111-148, which appears as a note to this section.]**. Notwithstanding any other provision of this part [42 USCS §§ 1395w-101 et seq.], each PDP sponsor of a prescription drug plan shall—

(i) use a single, uniform exceptions and appeals process (including, to the extent the Secretary determines feasible, a single, uniform model form for use under such process) with respect to the determination of prescription drug coverage for an enrollee under the plan; and

(ii) provide instant access to such process by enrollees through a toll-free telephone number and an Internet website.

The requirements of this paragraph may be met by a PDP sponsor directly or through arrangements with another entity.

(c) Cost and utilization management; quality assurance; medication therapy management program. (1) In general. The PDP sponsor shall have in place, directly or through appropriate arrangements, with respect to covered part D drugs, the following:

(A) A cost-effective drug utilization management program, including incentives to reduce costs when medically appropriate, such as through the use of multiple source drugs (as defined in section 1927(k)(7)(A)(i) [42 USCS § 1396r-8(k)(7)(A)(i)]).

(B) Quality assurance measures and systems to reduce medication errors and adverse drug interactions and improve medication use.

(C) A medication therapy management program described in paragraph (2).

(D) A program to control fraud, abuse, and waste.

Nothing in this section shall be construed as impairing a PDP sponsor from utilizing cost management tools (including differential payments) under all methods of operation.

(2) Medication therapy management program. (A) Description. (i) In general. A medication therapy management program described in this paragraph is a program of drug therapy management that may be furnished by a pharmacist and that is designed to assure, with respect to targeted beneficiaries described in clause (ii), that covered part D drugs under the prescription drug plan are appropriately used to optimize therapeutic outcomes through improved medication use, and to reduce the risk of adverse events, including adverse drug interactions. Such a program may distinguish between services in ambulatory and institutional settings.

(ii) Targeted beneficiaries described. Targeted beneficiaries described in this clause are part D eligible individuals who—

(I) have multiple chronic diseases (such as diabetes, asthma, hypertension, hyperlipidemia, and congestive heart failure);

(II) are taking multiple covered part D drugs; and

(III) are identified as likely to incur annual costs for covered part D drugs that exceed a level specified by the Secretary.

(B) Elements. Such program may include elements that promote—

(i) enhanced enrollee understanding to promote the appropriate use of medications by enrollees and to reduce the risk of potential adverse events associated with medications, through beneficiary education, counseling, and other appropriate means;

(ii) increased enrollee adherence with prescription medication regimens through medication refill reminders, special packaging, and other compliance programs and other appropriate means; and

(iii) detection of adverse drug events and patterns of overuse and underuse of prescription drugs.

(C) Required interventions. For plan years beginning on or after the date that is 2 years after the date of the enactment of the Patient Protection and Affordable Care Act [enacted March 23, 2010], prescription drug plan sponsors shall offer medication therapy management services to targeted beneficiaries described in subparagraph (A)(ii) that include, at a minimum, the following to increase adherence to prescription medications or other goals deemed necessary by the Secretary:

(i) An annual comprehensive medication review furnished person-to-person or using telehealth technologies (as defined by the Secretary) by a licensed pharmacist or other qualified provider. The comprehensive medication review—

(I) shall include a review of the individual's medications and may result in the creation of a recommended medication action plan or other actions in consultation with the individual and with input from the prescriber to the extent necessary and practicable; and

(II) shall include providing the individual with a written or printed summary of the results of the review. The Secretary, in consultation with relevant stakeholders, shall develop a standardized format for the action plan under subclause (I) and the summary under subclause (II).

(ii) Follow-up interventions as warranted based on the findings of the annual medication review or the targeted medication enrollment and which may be provided person-to-person or using telehealth technologies (as defined by the Secretary).

(D) Assessment. The prescription drug plan sponsor shall have in place a process to assess, at least on a quarterly basis, the medication use of individuals who are at risk but not enrolled in the medication therapy management program, including individuals who have experienced a transition in care, if the prescription drug plan sponsor has access to that information.

(E) Automatic enrollment with ability to opt-out. The prescription drug plan sponsor shall have in place a process to—

(i) subject to clause (ii), automatically enroll targeted beneficiaries described in subparagraph (A)(ii), including beneficiaries identified under subparagraph (D), in the medication therapy management program required under this subsection; and

(ii) permit such beneficiaries to opt-out of enrollment in such program.

[(F)](E) Development of program in cooperation with licensed pharmacists. Such program shall be developed in cooperation with licensed and practicing pharmacists and physicians.

[(G)](F) Coordination with care management plans. The Secretary shall establish guidelines for the coordination of any medication therapy management program under this paragraph with respect to a targeted beneficiary with any care management plan established with respect to such beneficiary under a chronic care improvement program under section 1807 [42 USCS § 1395b-8].

[(H)](G) Considerations in pharmacy fees. The PDP sponsor of a prescription drug plan shall take into account, in establishing fees for pharmacists and others providing services under such plan, the resources used, and time required to, implement the medication therapy management program under this paragraph. Each such sponsor shall disclose to the Secretary upon request the amount of any such management or dispensing fees. The provisions of section 1927(b)(3)(D) [42 USCS § 1396r-8(b)(3)(D)] apply to information disclosed under this subparagraph.

(3) Reducing wasteful dispensing of outpatient prescription drugs in long-term care facilities **[Caution: This paragraph applies to plan years beginning on or after January 1, 2012, as provided by § 3310(b) of Act March 23, 2010, P. L. 111-148, which appears as a note to this section.]**. The Secretary shall require PDP sponsors of prescription drug plans to utilize specific, uniform dispensing techniques, as determined by the Secretary, in consultation with relevant stakeholders (including representatives of nursing facilities, residents of nursing facilities, pharmacists, the pharmacy industry (including retail and long-term care pharmacy), prescription drug plans, MA-PD plans, and any other stakeholders the Secretary determines appropriate), such as weekly, daily, or automated dose dispensing, when dispensing covered part D drugs to enrollees who reside in a long-term care facility in order to reduce waste associated with 30-day fills.

(d) Consumer satisfaction surveys. In order to provide for comparative information under section 1860D-1(c)(3)(A)(v) [42 USCS § 1395w-101(c)(3)(A)(v)], the Secretary shall conduct consumer satisfaction surveys with respect to PDP sponsors and prescription drug plans in a manner similar to the manner such surveys are conducted for MA organizations and MA plans under part C [42 USCS §§ 1395w-21 et seq.].

(e) Electronic prescription program. (1) Application of standards. As of such date as the Secretary may specify, but not later than 1 year after the date of promulgation of final standards under paragraph (4)(D), prescriptions and other information described in paragraph (2)(A) for covered part D drugs prescribed for part D eligible individuals that are transmitted electronically shall be transmitted only in accordance with such standards under an electronic prescription drug program that meets the requirements of paragraph (2).

(2) Program requirements. Consistent with uniform standards established under paragraph (3)—

(A) Provision of information to prescribing health care professional and dispensing pharmacies and pharmacists. An electronic prescription drug program shall provide for the electronic transmittal to the prescribing health care professional and to the dispensing pharmacy and pharmacist of the prescription and information on eligibility and benefits (including the drugs included in the applicable formulary, any tiered formulary structure, and any requirements for prior authorization) and of the following information with respect to the prescribing and dispensing of a covered part D drug:

(i) Information on the drug being prescribed or dispensed and other drugs listed on the medication history, including information on drug-drug interactions, warnings or cautions, and, when indicated, dosage adjustments.

(ii) Information on the availability of lower cost, therapeutically appropriate alternatives (if any) for the drug prescribed.

(B) Application to medical history information. Effective on and after such date as the Secretary specifies and after the establishment of appropriate standards to carry out this subparagraph, the program shall provide for the electronic transmittal in a manner similar to the manner under subparagraph (A) of information that relates to the medical history concerning the individual and related to a covered part D drug being prescribed or dispensed, upon request of the professional or pharmacist involved.

(C) Limitations. Information shall only be disclosed under subparagraph (A) or (B) if the disclosure of such information is permitted under the Federal regulations (concerning the privacy of individually identifiable health information) promulgated under section 264(c) of the Health Insurance Portability and Accountability Act of 1996 [42 USCS § 1320d-2 note].

(D) Timing. To the extent feasible, the information exchanged under this paragraph shall be on an interactive, real-time basis.

(3) Standards. (A) In general. The Secretary shall provide consistent with this subsection for the promulgation of uniform standards relating to the requirements for electronic prescription drug programs under paragraph (2).

(B) Objectives. Such standards shall be consistent with the objectives of improving—

(i) patient safety;

(ii) the quality of care provided to patients; and

(iii) efficiencies, including cost savings, in the delivery of care.

(C) Design criteria. Such standards shall—

(i) be designed so that, to the extent practicable, the standards do not impose an undue administrative burden on prescribing health care professionals and dispensing pharmacies and pharmacists;

(ii) be compatible with standards established under part C of title XI [42 USCS §§ 1320d et seq.], standards established under subsection (b)(2)(B)(i), and with general health information technology standards; and

(iii) be designed so that they permit electronic exchange of drug labeling and drug listing information maintained by the Food and Drug Administration and the National Library of Medicine.

(D) Permitting use of appropriate messaging. Such standards shall allow for the messaging of information only if it relates to the appropriate prescribing of drugs, including quality assurance measures and systems referred to in subsection (c)(1)(B).

(E) Permitting patient designation of dispensing pharmacy. (i) In general. Consistent with clause (ii), such standards shall permit a part D eligible individual to designate a particular pharmacy to dispense a prescribed drug.

(ii) No change in benefits. Clause (i) shall not be construed as affecting—

(I) the access required to be provided to pharmacies by a prescription drug plan; or

(II) the application of any differences in benefits or payments under such a plan based on the pharmacy dispensing a covered part D drug.

(4) Development, promulgation, and modification of standards. (A) Initial standards. Not later than September 1, 2005, the Secretary shall develop, adopt, recognize, or modify initial uniform standards relating to the requirements for electronic prescription drug programs described in paragraph (2) taking into consideration the recommendations (if any) from the National Committee on Vital and Health Statistics (as established under section 306(k) of the Public Health Service Act (42 U.S.C. 242k(k))) under subparagraph (B).

(B) Role of NCVHS. The National Committee on Vital and Health Statistics shall develop recommendations for uniform standards relating to such requirements in consultation with the following:

(i) Standard setting organizations (as defined in section 1171(8) [42 USCS § 1320d(8)])[.]

(ii) Practicing physicians.

(iii) Hospitals.

(iv) Pharmacies.

(v) Practicing pharmacists.

(vi) Pharmacy benefit managers.

(vii) State boards of pharmacy.

(viii) State boards of medicine.

(ix) Experts on electronic prescribing.

(x) Other appropriate Federal agencies.

(C) Pilot project to test initial standards. (i) In general. During the 1-year period that begins on January 1, 2006, the Secretary shall conduct a pilot project to test the initial standards developed under subparagraph (A) prior to the promulgation of the final uniform standards under subparagraph (D) in order to provide for the efficient implementation of the requirements described in paragraph (2).

(ii) Exception. Pilot testing of standards is not required under clause (i) where there already is adequate industry experience with such standards, as determined by the Secretary after consultation with effected standard setting organizations and industry users.

(iii) Voluntary participation of physicians and pharmacies. In order to conduct the pilot project under clause (i), the Secretary shall enter into agreements with physicians, physician groups, pharmacies, hospitals, PDP sponsors, MA organizations, and other appropriate entities under which health care professionals electronically transmit prescriptions to dispensing pharmacies and pharmacists in accordance with such standards.

(iv) Evaluation and report. (I) Evaluation. The Secretary shall conduct an evaluation of the pilot project conducted under clause (i).

(II) Report to Congress. Not later than April 1, 2007, the Secretary shall submit to Congress a report on the evaluation conducted under subclause (I).

(D) Final standards. Based upon the evaluation of the pilot project under subparagraph (C)(iv)(I) and not later than April 1, 2008, the Secretary shall promulgate uniform standards relating to the requirements described in paragraph (2).

(5) Relation to State laws. The standards promulgated under this subsection shall supersede any State law or regulation that—

(A) is contrary to the standards or restricts the ability to carry out this part [42 USCS §§ 1395w-101 et seq.]; and

(B) pertains to the electronic transmission of medication history and of information on eligibility, benefits, and prescriptions with respect to covered part D drugs under this part [42 USCS §§ 1395w-101 et seq.].

(6) Establishment of safe harbor. The Secretary, in consultation with the Attorney General, shall promulgate regulations that provide for a safe harbor from sanctions under paragraphs (1) and (2) of section 1128B(b) [42 USCS § 1320a-7b(b)] and an exception to the prohibition under subsection (a)(1) of section 1877 [42 USCS § 1395nn] with respect to the provision of nonmonetary remuneration (in the form of hardware, software, or information technology and training services) necessary and used solely to receive and transmit electronic prescription information in accordance with the standards promulgated under this subsection—

(A) in the case of a hospital, by the hospital to members of its medical staff;

(B) in the case of a group practice (as defined in section 1877(h)(4) [42 USCS § 1395nn(h)(4)]), by the practice to prescribing health care professionals who are members of such practice; and

(C) in the case of a PDP sponsor or MA organization, by the sponsor or organization to pharmacists and pharmacies participating in the network of such sponsor or organization, and to prescribing health care professionals.

(f) Grievance mechanism. Each PDP sponsor shall provide meaningful procedures for hearing and resolving grievances between the sponsor (including any entity or individual through which the sponsor provides covered benefits) and enrollees with prescription drug plans of the sponsor under this part [42 USCS §§ 1395w-101 et seq.] in accordance with section 1852(f) [42 USCS § 1395w-22(f)].

(g) Coverage determinations and reconsiderations. (1) Application of coverage determination and reconsideration provisions. A PDP sponsor shall meet the requirements of paragraphs (1) through (3) of section 1852(g) [42 USCS § 1395w-22(g)] with respect to covered benefits under the prescription drug plan it offers under this part [42 USCS §§ 1395w-101 et seq.] in the same manner as such requirements apply to an MA organization with respect to benefits it offers under an MA plan under part C [42 USCS §§ 1395w-21 et seq.].

(2) Request for a determination for the treatment of tiered formulary drug. In the case of a prescription drug plan offered by a PDP sponsor that provides for tiered cost-sharing for drugs included within a formulary and provides lower cost-sharing for preferred drugs included within the formulary, a part D eligible

individual who is enrolled in the plan may request an exception to the tiered cost-sharing structure. Under such an exception, a nonpreferred drug could be covered under the terms applicable for preferred drugs if the prescribing physician determines that the preferred drug for treatment of the same condition either would not be as effective for the individual or would have adverse effects for the individual or both. A PDP sponsor shall have an exceptions process under this paragraph consistent with guidelines established by the Secretary for making a determination with respect to such a request. Denial of such an exception shall be treated as a coverage denial for purposes of applying subsection (h).

(h) Appeals. (1) In general. Subject to paragraph (2), a PDP sponsor shall meet the requirements of paragraphs (4) and (5) of section 1852(g) [42 USCS § 1395w-22(g)] with respect to benefits (including a determination related to the application of tiered cost-sharing described in subsection (g)(2)) in a manner similar (as determined by the Secretary) to the manner such requirements apply to an MA organization with respect to benefits under the original medicare fee-for-service program option it offers under an MA plan under part C [42 USCS §§ 1395w-21 et seq.]. In applying this paragraph only the part D eligible individual shall be entitled to bring such an appeal.

(2) Limitation in cases on nonformulary determinations. A part D eligible individual who is enrolled in a prescription drug plan offered by a PDP sponsor may appeal under paragraph (1) a determination not to provide for coverage of a covered part D drug that is not on the formulary under the plan only if the prescribing physician determines that all covered part D drugs on any tier of the formulary for treatment of the same condition would not be as effective for the individual as the nonformulary drug, would have adverse effects for the individual, or both.

(3) Treatment of nonformulary determinations. If a PDP sponsor determines that a plan provides coverage for a covered part D drug that is not on the formulary of the plan, the drug shall be treated as being included on the formulary for purposes of section 1860D-2(b)(4)(C)(i) [42 USCS § 1395w-102(b)(4)(C)(i)].

(i) Privacy, confidentiality, and accuracy of enrollee records. The provisions of section 1852(h) [42 USCS § 1395w-22(h)] shall apply to a PDP sponsor and prescription drug plan in the same manner as it applies to an MA organization and an MA plan.

(j) Treatment of accreditation. Subparagraph (A) of section 1852(e)(4) [42 USCS § 1395w-22(e)(4)] (relating to treatment of accreditation) shall apply to a PDP sponsor under this part [42 USCS §§ 1395w-101 et seq.] with respect to the following requirements, in the same manner as it applies to an MA organization with respect to the requirements in subparagraph (B) (other than clause (vii) thereof) of such section:

(1) Subsection (b) of this section (relating to access to covered part D drugs).

(2) Subsection (c) of this section (including quality assurance and medication therapy management).

(3) Subsection (i) of this section (relating to confidentiality and accuracy of enrollee records).

(k) Public disclosure of pharmaceutical prices for equivalent drugs. (1) In general. A PDP sponsor offering a prescription drug plan shall provide that each pharmacy that dispenses a covered part D drug shall inform an enrollee of any differential between the price of the drug to the enrollee and the price of the lowest priced generic covered part D drug under the plan that is therapeutically equivalent and bioequivalent and available at such pharmacy.

(2) Timing of notice. (A) In general. Subject to subparagraph (B), the information under paragraph (1) shall be provided at the time of purchase of the drug involved, or, in the case of dispensing by mail order, at the time of delivery of such drug.

(B) Waiver. The Secretary may waive subparagraph (A) in such circumstances as the Secretary may specify.

(l) Requirements with respect to sales and marketing activities. The following provisions shall apply to a PDP sponsor (and the agents, brokers, and other third parties representing such sponsor) in the same manner as such provisions apply to a Medicare Advantage organization (and the agents, brokers, and other third parties representing such organization):

(1) The prohibition under section 1851(h)(4)(C) [42 USCS § 1395w-21(h)(4)(C)] on conducting activities described in section 1851(j)(1) [42 USCS § 1395w-21(j)(1)].

(2) The requirement under section 1851(h)(4)(D) [42 USCS § 1395w-21(h)(4)(D)] to conduct activities described in section 1851(j)(2) [42 USCS § 1395w-21(j)(2)] in accordance with the limitations established under such subsection.

(3) The inclusion of the plan type in the plan

name under section 1851(h)(6) [42 USCS § 1395w-21(h)(6)].

(4) The requirements regarding the appointment of agents and brokers and compliance with State information requests under subparagraphs (A) and (B), respectively, of section 1851(h)(7) [42 USCS § 1395w-21(h)(7)].

(Aug. 4, 1935, ch 531, Title XVIII, Part D, Subpart 1, § 1860D-4, as added Dec. 8, 2003, P. L. 108-173, Title I, § 101(a)(2), 117 Stat. 2082; July 15, 2008, P. L. 110-275, Title I, Subtitle A, Part I, § 103(a)(2), (b)(2), (c)(2), (d)(2), Subtitle E, Part II, § 176, 122 Stat. 2499, 2500, 2501, 2581; March 23, 2010, P. L. 111-148, Title III, Subtitle D, §§ 3307(a), 3310(a), 3312(a), Title X, Subtitle C, § 10328(a), 124 Stat. 471, 475, 476, 964.)

HISTORY; ANCILLARY LAWS AND DIRECTIVES

Amendments:

2010. Act March 23, 2010 (applicable to plan year 2011 and subsequent plan years, as provided by § 3307(b) of such Act, which appears as a note to this section), in subsec. (b)(3), substituted subpara. (G) for one which read:

"(G) Required inclusion of drugs in certain categories and classes. (i) Identification of drugs in certain categories and classes. Beginning with plan year 2010, the Secretary shall identify, as appropriate, categories and classes of drugs for which both of the following criteria are met:

"(I) Restricted access to drugs in the category or class would have major or life threatening clinical consequences for individuals who have a disease or disorder treated by the drugs in such category or class.

"(II) There is significant clinical need for such individuals to have access to multiple drugs within a category or class due to unique chemical actions and pharmacological effects of the drugs within the category or class, such as drugs used in the treatment of cancer.

"(ii) Formulary requirements. Subject to clause (iii), PDP sponsors offering prescription drug plans shall be required to include all covered part D drugs in the categories and classes identified by the Secretary under clause (i).

"(iii) Exceptions. The Secretary may establish exceptions that permits a PDP sponsor of a prescription drug plan to exclude from its formulary a particular covered part D drug in a category or class that is otherwise required to be included in the formulary under clause (ii) (or to otherwise limit access to such a drug, including through prior authorization or utilization management). Any exceptions established under the preceding sentence shall be provided under a process that—

"(I) ensures that any exception to such requirement is based upon scientific evidence and medical standards of practice (and, in the case of antiretroviral medications, is consistent with the Department of Health and Human Services Guidelines for the Use of Antiretroviral Agents in HIV-1-Infected Adults and Adolescents); and

"(II) includes a public notice and comment period.".

Such Act further (applicable to plan years beginning on or after 1/1/2012, as provided by § 3310(b) of such Act, which appears as a note to this section), added subsec. (c)(3).

Such Act further (applicable to exceptions and appears on or after 1/1/2010, as provided by § 3312(b) of such Act, which appears as a note to this section), added subsec. (b)(3)(H).

Such Act further, in subsec. (c)(2), redesignated subparas. (C), (D), and (E) as subparas. [(F)](E), [(G)](F), and [(H)](G), respectively, and inserted new subparas. (C)–(E).

Other provisions:

Application of amendment made by § 3307 of Act March 23, 2010. Act March 23, 2010, P. L. 111-148, Title III, Subtitle D, § 3307(b), 124 Stat. 472, provides: "The amendments made by this section [amending subsec. (b)(3)(G) of this section] shall apply to plan year 2011 and subsequent plan years.".

Application of amendment made by § 3310 of Act March 23, 2010. Act March 23, 2010, P. L. 111-148, Title III, Subtitle D, § 3310(b), 124 Stat. 475, provides: "The amendment made by subsection (a) [adding subsec. (c)(3) of this section] shall apply to plan years beginning on or after January 1, 2012.".

Application of amendment made by § 3312 of Act March 23, 2010. Act March 23, 2010, P. L. 111-148, Title III, Subtitle D, § 3312(b), 124 Stat. 476, provides: "The amendment made by subsection (a) [adding subsec. (b)(3)(H) of this section] shall apply to exceptions and appeals on or after January 1, 2012.".

Rule of construction. Act March 23, 2010, P. L. 111-148, Title X, Subtitle C, § 10328(b), 124 Stat. 965, provides: "Nothing in this section [adding subsec. (c)(2)(C)–(E) of this section] shall limit the authority of the Secretary of Health and Human Services to modify or broaden requirements for a medication therapy management program under part D of title XVIII of the Social Security Act [42 USCS §§ 1395w-101 et seq.] or to study new models for medication therapy management through the Center for Medicare and Medicaid Innovation under section 1115A of such Act [42 USCS § 1315a], as added by section 3021.".

SUBPART 2. Presciption Drug Plans; PDP Sponsors; Financing

§ 1395w-111. PDP regions; submission of bids; plan approval

(a) Establishment of PDP regions; service areas. (1) Coverage of entire PDP region. The service area for a prescription drug plan shall consist of an entire PDP region established under paragraph (2).

(2) Establishment of PDP regions. (A) In general. The Secretary shall establish, and may revise, PDP regions in a manner that is consistent with the requirements for the establishment and revision of MA regions under subparagraphs (B) and (C) of section 1858(a)(2) [42 USCS § 1395w-27a(a)(2)].

(B) Relation to MA regions. To the extent practicable, PDP regions shall be the same as MA regions under section 1858(a)(2) [42 USCS § 1395w-27a(a)(2)]. The Secretary may establish PDP regions which are not the same as MA regions if the Secretary determines that the establishment of different regions under this part [42 USCS §§ 1395w-101 et seq.] would improve access to benefits under this part [42 USCS §§ 1395w-101 et seq.].

(C) Authority for territories. The Secretary shall establish, and may revise, PDP regions for areas in States that are not within the 50 States or the District of Columbia.

(3) National plan. Nothing in this subsection shall be construed as preventing a prescription drug plan from being offered in more than one PDP region (including all PDP regions).

(b) Submission of bids, premiums, and related information. (1) In general. A PDP sponsor shall submit to the Secretary information described in paragraph (2) with respect to each prescription drug plan it offers. Such information shall be submitted at the same time and in a similar manner to the manner in which information described in paragraph (6) of section 1854(a) [42 USCS § 1395w-24(a)] is submitted by an MA organization under paragraph (1) of such section.

(2) Information described. The information described in this paragraph is information on the following:

(A) Coverage provided. The prescription drug coverage provided under the plan, including the deductible and other cost-sharing.

(B) Actuarial value. The actuarial value of the qualified prescription drug coverage in the region for a part D eligible individual with a national average risk profile for the factors described in section 1860D-15(c)(1)(A) [42 USCS § 1395w-115(c)(1)(A)] (as specified by the Secretary).

(C) Bid. Information on the bid, including an actuarial certification of—

(i) the basis for the actuarial value described in subparagraph (B) assumed in such bid;

(ii) the portion of such bid attributable to basic prescription drug coverage and, if applicable, the portion of such bid attributable to supplemental benefits;

(iii) assumptions regarding the reinsurance subsidy payments provided under section 1860D-15(b) [42 USCS § 1395w-115(b)] subtracted from the actuarial value to produce such bid; and

(iv) administrative expenses assumed in the bid.

(D) Service area. The service area for the plan.

(E) Level of risk assumed. (i) In general. Whether the PDP sponsor requires a modification of risk level under clause (ii) and, if so, the extent of such modification. Any such modification shall apply with respect to all prescription drug plans offered by a PDP sponsor in a PDP region. This subparagraph shall not apply to an MA-PD plan.

(ii) Risk levels described. A modification of risk level under this clause may consist of one or more of the following:

(I) Increase in Federal percentage assumed in initial risk corridor. An equal percentage point increase in the percents applied under subparagraphs (B)(i), (B)(ii)(I), (C)(i), and (C)(ii)(I) of section 1860D-15(e)(2) [42 USCS § 1395w-115(e)(2)]. In no case shall the application of previous sentence prevent the application of a higher percentage under section 1869D-15(e)(2)(B)(iii) [1860D-15(e)(2)(B)(iii)] [42 USCS § 1395w-115(e)(2)(B)(iii)].

(II) Increase in Federal percentage assumed in second risk corridor. An equal percentage point increase in the percents applied under subparagraphs (B)(ii)(II) and (C)(ii)(II) of section 1860D-15(e)(2) [42 USCS § 1395w-115(e)(2)].

(III) Decrease in size of risk corridors. A decrease in the threshold risk percentages specified in section 1860D-15(e)(3)(C) [42 USCS § 1395w-115(e)(3)(C)].

(F) Additional information. Such other information as the Secretary may require to carry out this part [42 USCS §§ 1395w-101 et seq.].

(3) Paperwork reduction for offering of prescription drug plans nationally or in multiregion areas. The Secretary shall establish requirements for information submission under this subsection in a manner that promotes the offering of such plans in more than one PDP region (including all regions) through the filing of consolidated information.

(c) Actuarial valuation. (1) Processes. For purposes of this part [42 USCS §§ 1395w-101 et seq.], the Secretary shall establish processes and methods for determining the actuarial valuation of prescription drug coverage, including—

(A) an actuarial valuation of standard prescription drug coverage under section 1860D-2(b) [42 USCS § 1395w-102(b)];

(B) actuarial valuations relating to alternative prescription drug coverage under section 1860D-2(c)(1) [42 USCS § 1395w-102(c)(1)];

(C) an actuarial valuation of the reinsurance subsidy payments under section 1860D-15(b) [42 USCS § 1395w-115(b)];

(D) the use of generally accepted actuarial principles and methodologies; and

(E) applying the same methodology for determinations of actuarial valuations under subparagraphs (A) and (B).

(2) Accounting for drug utilization. Such processes and methods for determining actuarial valuation shall take into account the effect that providing alternative prescription drug coverage (rather than standard prescription drug coverage) has on drug utilization.

(3) Responsibilities. (A) Plan responsibilities. PDP sponsors and MA organizations are responsible for the preparation and submission of actuarial valuations required under this part [42 USCS §§ 1395w-101 et seq.] for prescription drug plans and MA-PD plans they offer.

(B) Use of outside actuaries. Under the processes and methods established under paragraph (1), PDP sponsors offering prescription drug plans and MA organizations offering MA-PD plans may use actuarial opinions certified by independent, qualified actuaries to establish actuarial values.

(d) Review of information and negotiation. (1) Review of information. The Secretary shall review the information filed under subsection (b) for the purpose of conducting negotiations under paragraph (2).

(2) Negotiation regarding terms and conditions. Subject to subsection (i), in exercising the authority under paragraph (1), the Secretary—

(A) has the authority to negotiate the terms and conditions of the proposed bid submitted and other terms and conditions of a proposed plan; and

(B) has authority similar to the authority of the Director of the Office of Personnel Management with respect to health benefits plans under chapter 89 of title 5, United States Code [5 USCS §§ 8901 et seq.].

(3) Rejection of bids **[Caution: This subparagraph applies to bids submitted for contract years beginning on or after January 1, 2011, as provided by § 3209(c) of Act March 23, 2010, P. L. 111-148, which appears as 42 USCS § 1395w-24 note.]**. Paragraph (5)(C) of section 1854(a) [42 USCS § 1395w-24(a)] shall apply with respect to bids submitted by a PDP sponsor under subsection (b) in the same manner as such paragraph applies to bids submitted by an MA organization under such section 1854(a) [42 USCS § 1395w-24(a)].

(e) Approval of proposed plans. (1) In general. After review and negotiation under subsection (d), the Secretary shall approve or disapprove the prescription drug plan.

(2) Requirements for approval. The Secretary may approve a prescription drug plan only if the following requirements are met:

(A) Compliance with requirements. The plan and the PDP sponsor offering the plan comply with the requirements under this part [42 USCS §§ 1395w-101 et seq.], including the provision of qualified prescription drug coverage.

(B) Actuarial determinations. The Secretary determines that the plan and PDP sponsor meet the requirements under this part [42 USCS §§ 1395w-101 et seq.] relating to actuarial determinations, including such requirements under section 1860D-2(c) [42 USCS § 1395w-102(c)].

(C) Application of FEHBP standard. (i) In general. The Secretary determines that the portion of the bid submitted under subsection (b) that is attributable to basic prescription drug coverage is supported by the actuarial bases provided under such subsection and reasonably and equitably reflects the revenue requirements (as used for purposes of section 1302(8)(C) of the Public Health Service Act [42 USCS § 300e-1(8)(C)]) for benefits provided under that plan, less the sum (determined on a monthly per capita basis) of the actuarial value of the reinsurance payments under section 1860D-15(b) [42 USCS § 1395w-115(b)].

(ii) Supplemental coverage. The Secretary determines that the portion of the bid submitted under subsection (b) that is attributable to supplemental prescription drug coverage pursuant to section 1860D-2(a)(2) [42 USCS § 1395w-102(a)(2)] is supported by the actuarial bases provided under such subsection and reasonably and equitably reflects the revenue requirements (as used for purposes of section 1302(8)(C) of the Public Health Service Act [42 USCS § 300e-1(8)(C)]) for such coverage under the plan.

(D) Plan design. (i) In general. The Secretary does not find that the design of the plan and its benefits (including any formulary and tiered formulary structure) are likely to substantially discourage enrollment by certain part D eligible individuals under the plan.

(ii) Use of categories and classes in formularies. The Secretary may not find that the design of categories and classes within a formulary violates clause (i) if such categories and classes are consistent with guidelines (if any) for such categories and classes established by the United States Pharmacopeia.

(f) Application of limited risk plans. (1) Conditions for approval of limited risk plans. The Secretary may only approve a limited risk plan (as defined in paragraph (4)(A)) for a PDP region if the access requirements under section 1860D-3(a) [42 USCS § 1395w-103(a)] would not be met for the region but for the approval of such a plan (or a fallback prescription drug plan under subsection (g)).

(2) Rules. The following rules shall apply with respect to the approval of a limited risk plan in a PDP region:

(A) Limited exercise of authority. Only the minimum number of such plans may be approved in order to meet the access requirements under section 1860D-3(a) [42 USCS § 1395w-103(a)].

(B) Maximizing assumption of risk. The Secretary shall provide priority in approval for those plans bearing the highest level of risk (as computed by the Secretary), but the Secretary may take into account the level of the bids submitted by such plans.

(C) No full underwriting for limited risk plans. In no case may the Secretary approve a limited risk plan under which the modification of risk level provides for no (or a de minimis) level of financial risk.

(3) Acceptance of all full risk contracts. There shall be no limit on the number of full risk plans that are approved under subsection (e).

(4) Risk-plans defined. For purposes of this subsection:

(A) Limited risk plan. The term "limited risk plan" means a prescription drug plan that provides basic prescription drug coverage and for which the PDP sponsor includes a modification of risk level described in subparagraph (E) of subsection (b)(2) in its bid submitted for the plan under such subsection. Such term does not include a fallback prescription drug plan.

(B) Full risk plan. The term "full risk plan" means a prescription drug plan that is not a limited risk plan or a fallback prescription drug plan.

(g) Guaranteeing access to coverage. (1) Solicitation of bids. (A) In general. Separate from the bidding process under subsection (b), the Secretary shall provide for a process for the solicitation of bids from eligible fallback entities (as defined in paragraph (2)) for the offering in all fallback service areas (as defined in paragraph (3)) in one or more PDP regions of a fallback prescription drug plan (as defined in paragraph (4)) during the contract period specified in paragraph (5).

(B) Acceptance of bids. (i) In general. Except as provided in this subparagraph, the provisions of subsection (e) shall apply with respect to the approval or disapproval of fallback prescription drug plans. The Secretary shall enter into contracts under this subsection with eligible fallback entities for the offering of fallback prescription drug plans so approved in fallback service areas.

(ii) Limitation of 1 plan for all fallback service areas in a PDP region. With respect to all fallback service areas in any PDP region for a contract period, the Secretary shall approve the offering of only 1 fallback prescription drug plan.

(iii) Competitive procedures. Competitive procedures (as defined in section 4(5) of the Office of Federal Procurement Policy Act (41 U.S.C. 403(5))) shall be used to enter into a contract under this subsection. The provisions of subsection (d) of section 1874A [42 USCS § 1395kk-1] shall apply to a contract under this section in the same manner as they apply to a contract under such section.

(iv) Timing. The Secretary shall approve a fallback prescription drug plan for a PDP region in a manner so that, if there are any fallback service areas in the region for a year, the fallback prescription drug plan is offered at the same time as prescription drug plans would otherwise be offered.

(v) No national fallback plan. The Secretary shall not enter into a contract with a single fallback entity for the offering of fallback plans throughout the United States.

(2) Eligible fallback entity. For purposes of this section, the term "eligible fallback entity" means, with respect to all fallback service areas in a PDP region for a contract period, an entity that—

(A) meets the requirements to be a PDP sponsor (or would meet such requirements but for the fact that the entity is not a risk-bearing entity); and

(B) does not submit a bid under section 1860D-11(b) [42 USCS § 1395w-111(b)] for any prescription drug plan for any PDP region for the first year of such contract period.

For purposes of subparagraph (B), an entity shall be treated as submitting a bid with respect to a prescription drug plan if the entity is acting as a subcontractor of a PDP sponsor that is offering such a plan. The previous sentence shall not apply to entities that are subcontractors of an MA organization except insofar as such organization is acting as a PDP sponsor with respect to a prescription drug plan.

(3) Fallback service area. For purposes of this subsection, the term "fallback service area" means, for a PDP region with respect to a year, any area within such region for which the Secretary determines before the beginning of the year that the access requirements of the first sentence of section 1860D-3(a) [42 USCS § 1395w-103(a)] will not be met for part D eligible individuals residing in the area for the

year.

(4) Fallback prescription drug plan. For purposes of this part [42 USCS §§ 1395w-101 et seq.], the term "fallback prescription drug plan" means a prescription drug plan that—

(A) only offers the standard prescription drug coverage and access to negotiated prices described in section 1860D-2(a)(1)(A) [42 USCS § 1395w-102(a)(1)(A)] and does not include any supplemental prescription drug coverage; and

(B) meets such other requirements as the Secretary may specify.

(5) Payments under the contract. (A) In general. A contract entered into under this subsection shall provide for—

(i) payment for the actual costs (taking into account negotiated price concessions described in section 1860D-2(d)(1)(B) [42 USCS § 1395w-102(d)(1)(B)]) of covered part D drugs provided to part D eligible individuals enrolled in a fallback prescription drug plan offered by the entity; and

(ii) payment of management fees that are tied to performance measures established by the Secretary for the management, administration, and delivery of the benefits under the contract.

(B) Performance measures. The performance measures established by the Secretary pursuant to subparagraph (A)(ii) shall include at least measures for each of the following:

(i) Costs. The entity contains costs to the Medicare Prescription Drug Account and to part D eligible individuals enrolled in a fallback prescription drug plan offered by the entity through mechanisms such as generic substitution and price discounts.

(ii) Quality programs. The entity provides such enrollees with quality programs that avoid adverse drug reactions and overutilization and reduce medical errors.

(iii) Customer service. The entity provides timely and accurate delivery of services and pharmacy and beneficiary support services.

(iv) Benefit administration and claims adjudication. The entity provides efficient and effective benefit administration and claims adjudication.

(6) Monthly beneficiary premium. Except as provided in section 1860D-13(b) [42 USCS § 1395w-113(b)] (relating to late enrollment penalty) and subject to section 1860D-14 [42 USCS § 1395w-114] (relating to low-income assistance), the monthly beneficiary premium to be charged under a fallback prescription drug plan offered in all fallback service areas in a PDP region shall be uniform and shall be equal to 25.5 percent of an amount equal to the Secretary's estimate of the average monthly per capita actuarial cost, including administrative expenses, under the fallback prescription drug plan of providing coverage in the region, as calculated by the Chief Actuary of the Centers for Medicare & Medicaid Services. In calculating such administrative expenses, the Chief Actuary shall use a factor that is based on similar expenses of prescription drug plans that are not fallback prescription drug plans.

(7) General contract terms and conditions. (A) In general. Except as may be appropriate to carry out this section, the terms and conditions of contracts with eligible fallback entities offering fallback prescription drug plans under this subsection shall be the same as the terms and conditions of contracts under this part [42 USCS §§ 1395w-101 et seq.] for prescription drug plans.

(B) Period of contract. (i) In general. Subject to clause (ii), a contract approved for a fallback prescription drug plan for fallback service areas for a PDP region under this section shall be for a period of 3 years (except as may be renewed after a subsequent bidding process).

(ii) Limitation. A fallback prescription drug plan may be offered under a contract in an area for a year only if that area is a fallback service area for that year.

(C) Entity not permitted to market or brand fallback prescription drug plans. An eligible fallback entity with a contract under this subsection may not engage in any marketing or branding of a fallback prescription drug plan.

(h) Annual report on use of limited risk plans and fallback plans. The Secretary shall submit to Congress an annual report that describes instances in which limited risk plans and fallback prescription drug plans were offered under subsections (f) and (g). The Secretary shall include in such report such recommendations as may be appropriate to limit the need for the provision of such plans and to maximize the assumption of financial risk under section subsection (f).

(i) Noninterference. In order to promote competition under this part [42 USCS §§ 1395w-101 et seq.] and in carrying out this part [42 USCS §§ 1395w-101 et seq.], the Secretary—

(1) may not interfere with the negotiations between drug manufacturers and pharmacies and PDP sponsors; and

(2) may not require a particular formulary or institute a price structure for the reimbursement of covered part D drugs.

(j) Coordination of benefits. A PDP sponsor offering a prescription drug plan shall permit State Pharmaceutical Assistance Programs and Rx plans under sections 1860D-23 and 1860D-24 [42 USCS §§ 1395w-133 and 1395w-134] to coordinate benefits with the plan and, in connection with such coordination with such a Program, not to impose fees that are unrelated to the cost of coordination.

(Aug. 4, 1935, ch 531, Title XVIII, Part D, Subpart 2, § 1860D-11, as added Dec. 8, 2003, P. L. 108-173, Title I, § 101(a)(2), 117 Stat. 2092; March 23, 2010, P. L. 111-148, Title III, Subtitle C, § 3209(b), 124 Stat. 460.)

§ 1395w-113. Premiums; late enrollment penalty

(a) Monthly beneficiary premium. (1) Computation. (A) In general. The monthly beneficiary premium for a prescription drug plan is the base beneficiary premium computed under paragraph (2) as adjusted under this paragraph.

(B) Adjustment to reflect difference between bid and national average bid. (i) Above average bid. If for a month the amount of the standardized bid amount (as defined in paragraph (5)) exceeds the amount of the adjusted national average monthly bid amount (as defined in clause (iii)), the base beneficiary premium for the month shall be increased by the amount of such excess.

(ii) Below average bid. If for a month the amount of the adjusted national average monthly bid amount for the month exceeds the standardized bid amount, the base beneficiary premium for the month shall be decreased by the amount of such excess.

(iii) Adjusted national average monthly bid amount defined. For purposes of this subparagraph, the term "adjusted national average monthly bid amount" means the national average monthly bid amount computed under paragraph (4), as adjusted under section 1860D-15(c)(2) [42 USCS § 1395w-115(c)(2)].

(C) Increase for supplemental prescription drug benefits. The base beneficiary premium shall be increased by the portion of the PDP approved bid that is attributable to supplemental prescription drug benefits.

(D) Increase for late enrollment penalty. The base beneficiary premium shall be increased by the amount of any late enrollment penalty under subsection (b).

(E) Decrease for low-income assistance. The monthly beneficiary premium is subject to decrease in the case of a subsidy eligible individual under section 1860D-14 [42 USCS § 1395w-114].

(F) Increase based on income. The monthly beneficiary premium shall be increased pursuant to paragraph (7).

(G) Uniform premium. Except as provided in subparagraphs (D), (E), and (F), the monthly beneficiary premium for a prescription drug plan in a PDP region is the same for all part D eligible individuals enrolled in the plan.

(2) Base beneficiary premium. The base beneficiary premium under this paragraph for a prescription drug plan for a month is equal to the product—

(A) the beneficiary premium percentage (as specified in paragraph (3)); and

(B) the national average monthly bid amount (computed under paragraph (4)) for the month.

(3) Beneficiary premium percentage. For purposes of this subsection, the beneficiary premium percentage for any year is the percentage equal to a fraction

(A) the numerator of which is 25.5 percent; and

(B) the denominator of which is 100 percent minus a percentage equal to—

(i) the total reinsurance payments which the Secretary estimates are payable under section 1860D-15(b) [42 USCS § 1395w-115(b)] with respect to the coverage year; divided by

(ii) the sum of—

(I) the amount estimated under clause (i) for the year; and

(II) the total payments which the Secretary estimates will be paid to prescription drug plans and MA-PD plans that are attributable to the standardized bid amount during the year, taking into account amounts paid by the Secretary and enrollees.

(4) Computation of national average monthly bid amount. (A) In general. For each year (beginning with 2006) the Secretary shall compute a national average monthly bid amount equal to the average of the standardized bid amounts (as defined in paragraph (5)) for each prescription drug plan and for each MA-PD plan described in section 1851(a)(2)(A)(i) [42 USCS § 1395w-21(a)(2)(A)(i)]. Such average does not take into account the bids submitted for MSA plans, MA private fee-for-service plan, and specialized MA plans for special needs individuals, PACE programs under section 1894 [42 USCS § 1395eee] (pursuant to section 1860D-21(f) [42 USCS § 1395w-131(f)]), and under reasonable cost reimbursement contracts under section 1876(h) [42 USCS § 1395mm(h)] (pursuant to section 1860D-21(e) [42 USCS § 1395w-131(e)]).

(B) Weighted average. (i) In general. The

monthly national average monthly bid amount computed under subparagraph (A) for a year shall be a weighted average, with the weight for each plan being equal to the average number of part D eligible individuals enrolled in such plan in the reference month (as defined in section 1858(f)(4) [42 USCS § 1395w-27a(f)(4)]).

(ii) Special rule for 2006. For purposes of applying this paragraph for 2006, the Secretary shall establish procedures for determining the weighted average under clause (i) for 2005.

(5) Standardized bid amount defined. For purposes of this subsection, the term "standardized bid amount" means the following:

(A) Prescription drug plans. (i) Basic coverage. In the case of a prescription drug plan that provides basic prescription drug coverage, the PDP approved bid (as defined in paragraph (6)).

(ii) Supplemental coverage. In the case of a prescription drug plan that provides supplemental prescription drug coverage, the portion of the PDP approved bid that is attributable to basic prescription drug coverage.

(B) MA-PD plans. In the case of an MA-PD plan, the portion of the accepted bid amount that is attributable to basic prescription drug coverage.

(6) PDP approved bid defined. For purposes of this part [42 USCS §§ 1395w-101 et seq.], the term "PDP approved bid" means, with respect to a prescription drug plan, the bid amount approved for the plan under this part [42 USCS §§ 1395w-101 et seq.].

(7) Increase in base beneficiary premium based on income. (A) In general. In the case of an individual whose modified adjusted gross income exceeds the threshold amount applicable under paragraph (2) of section 1839(i) [42 USCS § 1395r(i)] (including application of paragraph (5) of such section) for the calendar year, the monthly amount of the beneficiary premium applicable under this section for a month after December 2010 shall be increased by the monthly adjustment amount specified in subparagraph (B).

(B) Monthly adjustment amount. The monthly adjustment amount specified in this subparagraph for an individual for a month in a year is equal to the product of—

(i) the quotient obtained by dividing—

(I) the applicable percentage determined under paragraph (3)(C) of section 1839(i) [42 USCS § 1395r(i)] (including application of paragraph (5) of such section) for the individual for the calendar year reduced by 25.5 percent; by

(II) 25.5 percent; and

(ii) the base beneficiary premium (as computed under paragraph (2)).

(C) Modified adjusted gross income. For purposes of this paragraph, the term "modified adjusted gross income" has the meaning given such term in subparagraph (A) of section 1839(i)(4) [42 USCS § 1395r(i)(4)], determined for the taxable year applicable under subparagraphs (B) and (C) of such section.

(D) Determination by Commissioner of Social Security. The Commissioner of Social Security shall make any determination necessary to carry out the income-related increase in the base beneficiary premium under this paragraph.

(E) Procedures to assure correct income-related increase in base beneficiary premium. (i) Disclosure of base beneficiary premium. Not later than September 15 of each year beginning with 2010, the Secretary shall disclose to the Commissioner of Social Security the amount of the base beneficiary premium (as computed under paragraph (2)) for the purpose of carrying out the income-related increase in the base beneficiary premium under this paragraph with respect to the following year.

(ii) Additional disclosure. Not later than October 15 of each year beginning with 2010, the Secretary shall disclose to the Commissioner of Social Security the following information for the purpose of carrying out the income-related increase in the base beneficiary premium under this paragraph with respect to the following year:

(I) The modified adjusted gross income threshold applicable under paragraph (2) of section 1839(i) [42 USCS § 1395r(i)] (including application of paragraph (5) of such section).

(II) The applicable percentage determined under paragraph (3)(C) of section 1839(i) [42 USCS § 1395r(i)] (including application of paragraph (5) of such section).

(III) The monthly adjustment amount specified in subparagraph (B).

(IV) Any other information the Commissioner of Social Security determines necessary to carry out the income-related increase in the base beneficiary premium under this paragraph.

(F) Rule of construction. The formula used to determine the monthly adjustment amount specified under subparagraph (B) shall only be used for the purpose of determining such monthly adjustment amount under such subparagraph.

(b) Late enrollment penalty. (1) In general. Subject to the succeeding provisions of this subsection, in the case of a part D eligible individual described in paragraph (2) with respect to a continuous period of eligibility, there shall be an increase in the monthly beneficiary premium established under subsection (a) in an amount determined under paragraph (3).

(2) Individuals subject to penalty. A part D eligible individual described in this paragraph is, with respect to a continuous period of eligibility, an individual for whom there is a continuous period of 63 days or longer (all of which in such continuous period of eligibility) beginning on the day after the last date of the individual's initial enrollment period under section 1860D-1(b)(2) [42 USCS § 1395w-101(b)(2)] and ending on the date of enrollment under a prescription drug plan or MA-PD plan during all of which the individual was not covered under any creditable prescription drug coverage.

(3) Amount of penalty. (A) In general. The amount determined under this paragraph for a part D eligible individual for a continuous period of eligibility is the greater of—

(i) an amount that the Secretary determines is actuarially sound for each uncovered month (as defined in subparagraph (B)) in the same continuous period of eligibility; or

(ii) 1 percent of the base beneficiary premium (computed under subsection (a)(2)) for each such uncovered month in such period.

(B) Uncovered month defined. For purposes of this subsection, the term "uncovered month" means, with respect to a part D eligible individual, any month beginning after the end of the initial enrollment period under section 1860D-1(b)(2) [42 USCS § 1395w-101(b)(2)] unless the individual can demonstrate that the individual had creditable prescription drug coverage (as defined in paragraph (4)) for any portion of such month.

(4) Creditable prescription drug coverage defined. For purposes of this part [42 USCS §§ 1395w-101 et seq.], the term "creditable prescription drug coverage" means any of the following coverage, but only if the coverage meets the requirement of paragraph (5):

(A) Coverage under prescription drug plan or MA-PD plan. Coverage under a prescription drug plan or under an MA-PD plan.

(B) Medicaid. Coverage under a medicaid plan under title XIX [42 USCS §§ 1396 et seq.] or under a waiver under section 1115 [42 USCS § 1315].

(C) Group health plan. Coverage under a group health plan, including a health benefits plan under chapter 89 of title 5, United States Code [5 USCS §§ 8901 et seq.] (commonly known as the Federal employees health benefits program), and a qualified retiree prescription drug plan (as defined in section 1860D-22(a)(2) [42 USCS § 1395w-132(a)(2)]).

(D) State pharmaceutical assistance program. Coverage under a State pharmaceutical assistance program described in section 1860D-23(b)(1) [42 USCS § 1395w-133(b)(1)].

(E) Veterans' coverage of prescription drugs. Coverage for veterans, and survivors and dependents of veterans, under chapter 17 of title 38, United States Code [38 USCS §§ 1701 et seq.].

(F) Prescription drug coverage under Medigap policies. Coverage under a medicare supplemental policy under section 1882 [42 USCS § 1395ss] that provides benefits for prescription drugs (whether or not such coverage conforms to the standards for packages of benefits under section 1882(p)(1) [42 USCS § 1395ss(p)(1)]).

(G) Military coverage (including TRICARE). Coverage under chapter 55 of title 10, United States Code [10 USCS §§ 1071 et seq.].

(H) Other coverage. Such other coverage as the Secretary determines appropriate.

(5) Actuarial equivalence requirement. Coverage meets the requirement of this paragraph only if the coverage is determined (in a manner specified by the Secretary) to provide coverage of the cost of prescription drugs the actuarial value of which (as defined by the Secretary) to the individual equals or exceeds the actuarial value of standard prescription drug coverage (as determined under section 1860D-11(c) [42 USCS § 1395w-111(c)]).

(6) Procedures to document creditable prescription drug coverage. (A) In general. The Secretary shall establish procedures (including the form, manner, and time) for the documentation of creditable prescription drug coverage, including procedures to assist in determining whether coverage meets the requirement of paragraph (5).

(B) Disclosure by entities offering creditable prescription drug coverage. (i) In general. Each entity that offers prescription drug coverage of the type described in subparagraphs (B) through (H) of paragraph (4) shall provide for disclosure, in a form, manner, and time consistent with standards established by the Secretary, to the Secretary and part D eligible individuals of whether the coverage meets the requirement of paragraph (5) or whether such coverage is changed so it no longer meets such requirement.

(ii) Disclosure of non-creditable coverage. In the case of such coverage that does not meet such requirement, the disclosure to part D eligible individuals under this subparagraph shall include information regarding the fact that because such coverage does not meet such requirement there are limitations on the periods in a year in which the individuals may enroll under a prescription drug plan or an MA-PD plan and that any such enrollment is subject to a late enrollment penalty under this subsection.

(C) Waiver of requirement. In the case of a part D eligible individual who was enrolled in prescription drug coverage of the type described in subparagraphs (B) through (H) of paragraph (4) which is not creditable prescription drug coverage because it does not meet the requirement of paragraph (5), the individual may apply to the Secretary to have such coverage treated as creditable prescription drug coverage if the individual establishes that the individual was not adequately informed that such coverage did not meet such requirement.

(7) Continuous period of eligibility. (A) In general. Subject to subparagraph (B), for purposes of this subsection, the term "continuous period of eligibility" means, with respect to a part D eligible individual, the period that begins with the first day on which the individual is eligible to enroll in a prescription drug plan under this part [42 USCS §§ 1395w-101 et seq.] and ends with the individual's death.

(B) Separate period. Any period during all of which a part D eligible individual is entitled to hospital insurance benefits under part A [42 USCS §§ 1395c et seq.] and—

(i) which terminated in or before the month preceding the month in which the individual attained age 65; or

(ii) for which the basis for eligibility for such entitlement changed between section 226(b) [42 USCS § 426(b)] and section 226(a) [42 USCS § 426(a)], between 226(b) [42 USCS § 426(b)] and section 226A [42 USCS § 426-1], or between section 226A [42 USCS § 426-1] and section 226(a) [42 USCS § 426(a)],

shall be a separate continuous period of eligibility with respect to the individual (and each such period which terminates shall be deemed not to have existed for purposes of subsequently applying this paragraph).

(8) Waiver of penalty for subsidy-eligible individuals. In no case shall a part D eligible individual who is determined to be a subsidy eligible individual (as defined in section 1860D-14(a)(3) [42 USCS § 1395w-114(a)(3)]) be subject to an increase in the monthly beneficiary premium established under subsection (a).

(c) Collection of monthly beneficiary premiums. (1) In general. Subject to paragraphs (2), (3), and (4), the provisions of section 1854(d) [42 USCS § 1395w-24(d)] shall apply to PDP sponsors and premiums (and any late enrollment penalty) under this part [42 USCS §§ 1395w-101 et seq.] in the same manner as they apply to MA organizations and beneficiary premiums under part C [42 USCS §§ 1395w-21 et seq.], except that any reference to a Trust Fund is deemed for this purpose a reference to the Medicare Prescription Drug Account.

(2) Crediting of late enrollment penalty. (A) Portion attributable to increased actuarial costs. With respect to late enrollment penalties imposed under subsection (b), the Secretary shall specify the portion of such a penalty that the Secretary estimates is attributable to increased actuarial costs assumed by the PDP sponsor or MA organization (and not taken into account through risk adjustment provided under section 1860D-15(c)(1) [42 USCS § 1395w-115(c)(1)] or through reinsurance payments under section 1860D-15(b) [42 USCS § 1395w-115(b)]) as a result of such late enrollment.

(B) Collection through withholding. In the case of a late enrollment penalty that is collected from a part D eligible individual in the manner described in section 1854(d)(2)(A) [42 USCS § 1395w-24(d)(2)(A)], the Secretary shall provide that only the portion of such penalty estimated under subparagraph (A) shall be paid to the PDP sponsor or MA organization offering the part D plan in which the individual is enrolled.

(C) Collection by plan. In the case of a late enrollment penalty that is collected from a part D eligible individual in a manner other than the manner described in section 1854(d)(2)(A) [42 USCS § 1395w-24(d)(2)(A)], the Secretary shall establish procedures for reducing payments otherwise made to the PDP sponsor or MA organization by an amount equal to the amount of such penalty less the portion of such penalty estimated under subparagraph (A).

(3) Fallback plans. In applying this subsection in the case of a fallback prescription drug plan, paragraph (2) shall not apply and the monthly beneficiary premium shall be collected in the manner specified in section 1854(d)(2)(A) [42 USCS § 1395w-24(d)(2)(A)] (or such other manner as may be provided under section 1840 [42 USCS § 1395s] in the case of monthly premiums under section 1839 [42 USCS § 1395r]).

(4) Collection of monthly adjustment amount. (A) In general. Notwithstanding any provision of this subsection or section 1854(d)(2) [42 USCS § 1395w-24(d)(2)], subject to subparagraph (B), the amount of the income-related increase in the base beneficiary pre-

mium for an individual for a month (as determined under subsection (a)(7)) shall be paid through withholding from benefit payments in the manner provided under section 1840 [42 USCS § 1395s].

(B) Agreements. In the case where the monthly benefit payments of an individual that are withheld under subparagraph (A) are insufficient to pay the amount described in such subparagraph, the Commissioner of Social Security shall enter into agreements with the Secretary, the Director of the Office of Personnel Management, and the Railroad Retirement Board as necessary in order to allow other agencies to collect the amount described in subparagraph (A) that was not withheld under such subparagraph.

(Aug. 4, 1935, ch 531, Title XVIII, Part D, Subpart 2, § 1860D-13, as added Dec. 8, 2003, P. L. 108-173, Title I, § 101(a)(2), 117 Stat. 2102; July 15, 2008, P. L. 110-275, Title I, Subtitle A, Part II, § 114(a)(1), 122 Stat. 2506; March 23, 2010, P. L. 111-148, Title III, Subtitle D, § 3308(a), (b)(1), 124 Stat. 472.)

§ 1395w-114. Premium and cost-sharing subsidies for low-income individuals

(a) Income-related subsidies for individuals with income up to 150 percent of poverty line. (1) Individuals with income below 135 percent of poverty line. In the case of a subsidy eligible individual (as defined in paragraph (3)) who is determined to have income that is below 135 percent of the poverty line applicable to a family of the size involved and who meets the resources requirement described in paragraph (3)(D) or who is covered under this paragraph under paragraph (3)(B)(i), the individual is entitled under this section to the following:

(A) Full premium subsidy. An income-related premium subsidy equal to 100 percent of the amount described in subsection (b)(1), but not to exceed the premium amount specified in subsection (b)(2)(B).

(B) Elimination of deductible. A reduction in the annual deductible applicable under section 1860D-2(b)(1) [42 USCS § 1395w-102(b)(1)] to $0.

(C) Continuation of coverage above the initial coverage limit. The continuation of coverage from the initial coverage limit (under paragraph (3) of section 1860D-2(b) [42 USCS § 1395w-102(b)]) for expenditures incurred through the total amount of expenditures at which benefits are available under paragraph (4) of such section, subject to the reduced cost-sharing described in subparagraph (D).

(D) Reduction in cost-sharing below out-of-pocket threshold. (i) Institutionalized individuals. In the case of an individual who is a full-benefit dual eligible individual and who is an institutionalized individual or couple (as defined in section 1902(q)(1)(B) [42 USCS § 1396a(q)(1)(B)]) or, effective on a date specified by the Secretary (but in no case earlier than January 1, 2012), who would be such an institutionalized individual or couple, if the full-benefit dual eligible individual were not receiving services under a home and community-based waiver authorized for a State under section 1115 [42 USCS § 1315] or subsection (c) or (d) of section 1915 [42 USCS § 1396n] or under a State plan amendment under subsection (i) of such section or services provided through enrollment in a Medicaid managed care organization with a contract under section 1903(m) [42 USCS § 1396b(m)] or under section 1932 [42 USCS § 1396u-2], the elimination of any beneficiary coinsurance described in section 1860D-2(b)(2) [42 USCS § 1395w-102(b)(2)] (for all amounts through the total amount of expenditures at which benefits are available under section 1860D-2(b)(4) [42 USCS § 1395w-102(b)(4)]).

(ii) Lowest income dual eligible individuals. In the case of an individual not described in clause (i) who is a full-benefit dual eligible individual and whose income does not exceed 100 percent of the poverty line applicable to a family of the size involved, the substitution for the beneficiary coinsurance described in section 1860D-2(b)(2) [42 USCS § 1395w-102(b)(2)] (for all amounts through the total amount of expenditures at which benefits are available under section 1860D-2(b)(4) [42 USCS § 1395w-102(b)(4)]) of a copayment amount that does not exceed $1 for a generic drug or a preferred drug that is a multiple source drug (as defined in section 1927(k)(7)(A)(i) [42 USCS § 1396r-8(k)(7)(A)(i)]) and $3 for any other drug, or, if less, the copayment amount applicable to an individual under clause (iii).

(iii) Other individuals. In the case of an individual not described in clause (i) or (ii), the substitution for the beneficiary coinsurance described in section 1860D-2(b)(2) [42 USCS § 1395w-102(b)(2)] (for all amounts through the total amount of expenditures at which benefits are available under section 1860D-2(b)(4) [42 USCS § 1395w-102(b)(4)]) of a copayment amount that does not exceed the copayment amount specified under section 1860D-2(b)(4)(A)(i)(I) [42 USCS § 1395w-102(b)(4)(A)(i)(I)] for the drug and year involved.

(E) Elimination of cost-sharing above annual out-of-pocket threshold. The elimination of any cost-sharing imposed under section 1860D-2(b)(4)(A) [42 USCS § 1395w-102(b)(4)(A)].

(2) Other individuals with income below 150 percent of poverty line. In the case of a subsidy eligible individual who is not described in paragraph (1), the individual is entitled under this section to the following:

(A) Sliding scale premium subsidy. An income-related premium subsidy determined on a linear sliding scale ranging from 100 percent of the amount described in paragraph (1)(A) for individuals with incomes at or below 135 percent of such level to 0 percent of such amount for individuals with incomes at 150 percent of such level.

(B) Reduction of deductible. A reduction in the annual deductible applicable under section 1860D-2(b)(1) [42 USCS § 1395w-102(b)(1)] to $50.

(C) Continuation of coverage above the initial coverage limit. The continuation of coverage from the initial coverage limit (under paragraph (3) of section 1860D-2(b) [42 USCS § 1395w-102(b)]) for expenditures incurred through the total amount of expenditures at which benefits are available under paragraph (4) of such section, subject to the reduced coinsurance described in subparagraph (D).

(D) Reduction in cost-sharing below out-of-pocket threshold. The substitution for the beneficiary coinsurance described in section 1860D-2(b)(2) [42 USCS § 1395w-102(b)(2)] (for all amounts above the deductible under subparagraph (B) through the total amount of expenditures at which benefits are available under section 1860D-2(b)(4) [42 USCS § 1395w-102(b)(4)]) of coinsurance of "15 percent" instead of coinsurance of "25 percent" in section 1860D-2(b)(2) [42 USCS § 1395w-102(b)(2)].

(E) Reduction of cost-sharing above annual out-of-pocket threshold. Subject to subsection (c), the substitution for the cost-sharing imposed under section 1860D-2(b)(4)(A) [42 USCS § 1395w-102(b)(4)(A)] of a copayment or coinsurance not to exceed the copayment or coinsurance amount specified under section 1860D-2(b)(4)(A)(i)(I) [42 USCS § 1395w-102(b)(4)(A)(i)(I)] for the drug and year involved.

(3) Determination of eligibility. (A) Subsidy eligible individual defined. For purposes of this part [42 USCS §§ 1395w-101 et seq.], subject to subparagraph (F), the term "subsidy eligible individual" means a part D eligible individual who—

(i) is enrolled in a prescription drug plan or MA-PD plan;

(ii) has income below 150 percent of the poverty line applicable to a family of the size involved; and

(iii) meets the resources requirement described in subparagraph (D) or (E).

(B) Determinations. (i) In general. The determination of whether a part D eligible individual residing in a State is a subsidy eligible individual and whether the individual is described in paragraph (1) shall be determined under the State plan under title XIX [42 USCS §§ 1396 et seq.] for the State under section 1935(a) [42 USCS § 1396u-5(a)] or by the Commissioner of Social Security. There are authorized to be appropriated to the Social Security Administration such sums as may be necessary for the determination of eligibility under this subparagraph.

(ii) Effective period. Determinations under this subparagraph shall be effective beginning with the month in which the individual applies for a determination that the individual is a subsidy eligible individual and shall remain in effect for a period specified by the Secretary, but not to exceed 1 year.

(iii) Redeterminations and appeals through medicaid. Redeterminations and appeals, with respect to eligibility determinations under clause (i) made under a State plan under title XIX [42 USCS §§ 1396 et seq.], shall be made in accordance with the frequency of, and manner in which, redeterminations and appeals of eligibility are made under such plan for purposes of medical assistance under such title.

(iv) Redeterminations and appeals through Commissioner. With respect to eligibility determinations under clause (i) made by the Commissioner of Social Security—

(I) redeterminations shall be made at such time or times as may be provided by the Commissioner;

(II) the Commissioner shall establish procedures for appeals of such determinations that are similar to the procedures described in the third sentence of section 1631(c)(1)(A) [42 USCS § 1383(c)(1)(A)]; and

(III) judicial review of the final decision of the Commissioner made after a hearing shall be available to the same extent, and with the same limitations, as provided in subsections (g) and (h) of section 205 [42 USCS § 405].

(v) Treatment of medicaid beneficiaries. Subject to subparagraph (F), the Secretary—

(I) shall provide that part D eligible individuals who are full-benefit dual eligible individuals (as defined in section 1935(c)(6) [42 USCS § 1396u-5(c)(6)]) or who are recipients of supplemental security income benefits under title XVI [42 USCS §§ 1381 et seq.] shall be treated as subsidy eligible individuals described in paragraph (1); and

(II) may provide that part D eligible individuals not described in subclause (I) who are determined for purposes of the State plan under title XIX [42 USCS §§ 1396 et seq.] to be eligible for medical assistance under clause (i), (iii), or (iv) of section 1902(a)(10)(E) [42 USCS § 1396a(a)(10)(E)] are treated as being determined to be subsidy eligible individuals described in paragraph (1). Insofar as the Secretary determines that the eligibility requirements under the State plan for medical assistance referred to in subclause (II) are substantially the same as the requirements for being treated as a subsidy eligible individual described in paragraph (1), the Secretary shall provide for the treatment described in such subclause.

(vi) Special rule for widows and widowers **[Caution: This clause takes effect on January 1, 2011, as provided by § 3304(b) of Act March 23, 2010, P. L. 111-148, which appears as a note to this section.]**. Notwithstanding the preceding provisions of this subparagraph, in the case of an individual whose spouse dies during the effective period for a determination or redetermination that has been made under this subparagraph, such effective period shall be extended through the date that is 1 year after the date on which the determination or redetermination would (but for the application of this clause) otherwise cease to be effective.

(C) Income determinations. For purposes of applying this section—

(i) in the case of a part D eligible individual who is not treated as a subsidy eligible individual under subparagraph (B)(v), income shall be determined in the manner described in section 1905(p)(1)(B) [42 USCS § 1396d(p)(1)(B)], without regard to the application of section 1902(r)(2) [42 USCS § 1396a(r)(2)] and except that support and maintenance furnished in kind shall not be counted as income; and

(ii) the term "poverty line" has the meaning given such term in section 673(2) of the Community Services Block Grant Act (42 U.S.C. 9902(2)), including any revision required by such section.

Nothing in clause (i) shall be construed to affect the application of section 1902(r)(2) [42 USCS § 1396a(r)(2)] for the determination of eligibility for medical assistance under title XIX [42 USCS §§ 1396 et seq.].

(D) Resource standard applied to full low-income subsidy to be based on three times SSI resource standard. The resources requirement of this subparagraph is that an individual's resources (as determined under section 1613 [42 USCS § 1382b] for purposes of the supplemental security income program subject to the life insurance policy exclusion provided under subparagraph (G)) do not exceed—

(i) for 2006 three times the maximum amount of resources that an individual may have and obtain benefits under that program; and

(ii) for a subsequent year the resource limitation established under this clause for the previous year increased by the annual percentage increase in the consumer price index (all items; U.S. city average) as of September of such previous year.

Any resource limitation established under clause (ii) that is not a multiple of $10 shall be rounded to the nearest multiple of $10.

(E) Alternative resource standard. (i) In general. The resources requirement of this subparagraph is that an individual's resources (as determined under section 1613 [42 USCS § 1382b] for purposes of the supplemental security income program subject to the life insurance policy exclusion provided under subparagraph (G)) do not exceed—

(I) for 2006, $10,000 (or $20,000 in the case of the combined value of the individual's assets or resources and the assets or resources of the individual's spouse); and

(II) for a subsequent year the dollar amounts specified in this subclause (or subclause (I)) for the previous year increased by the annual percentage increase in the consumer price index (all items; U.S. city average) as of September of such previous year.

Any dollar amount established under subclause (II) that is not a multiple of $10 shall be rounded to the nearest multiple of $10.

(ii) Use of simplified application form and process. The Secretary, jointly with the Commissioner of Social Security, shall—

(I) develop a model, simplified application form and process consistent with clause (iii) for the determination and verification of a part D eligible individual's assets or resources under this subparagraph; and

(II) provide such form to States.

(iii) Documentation and safeguards. Under such process—

(I) the application form shall consist of an attestation under penalty of perjury regarding the level of assets or resources (or combined assets and resources in the case of a married part D eligible individual) and valuations of general classes of assets or resources;

(II) such form shall be accompanied by copies of recent statements (if any) from financial institutions in support of the application; and

(III) matters attested to in the application shall be subject to appropriate methods of verification.

(iv) Methodology flexibility. The Secretary may permit a State in making eligibility determinations for premium and cost-sharing subsidies under this section to use the same asset or resource methodologies that are used with respect to eligibility for medical assistance for medicare cost-sharing described in section 1905(p) [42 USCS § 1396d(p)] so long as the Secretary determines that the use of such methodologies will not result in any significant differences in the number of individuals determined to be subsidy eligible individuals.

(F) Treatment of territorial residents. In the case of a part D eligible individual who is not a resident of the 50 States or the District of Columbia, the individual is not eligible to be a subsidy eligible individual under this section but may be eligible for financial assistance with prescription drug expenses under section 1935(e) [42 USCS § 1396u-5(e)].

(G) Life insurance policy exclusion. In determining the resources of an individual (and the eligible spouse of the individual, if any) under section 1613 [42 USCS § 1382b] for purposes of subparagraphs (D) and (E) no part of the value of any life insurance policy shall be taken into account.

(4) Indexing dollar amounts. (A) Copayment for lowest income dual eligible individuals. The dollar amounts applied under paragraph (1)(D)(ii)—

(i) for 2007 shall be the dollar amounts specified in such paragraph increased by the annual percentage increase in the consumer price index (all items; U.S. city average) as of September of such previous year; or

(ii) for a subsequent year shall be the dollar amounts specified in this clause (or clause (i)) for the previous year increased by the annual percentage increase in the consumer price index (all items; U.S. city average) as of September of such previous year.

Any amount established under clause (i) or (ii), that is based on an increase of $1 or $3, that is not a multiple of 5 cents or 10 cents, respectively, shall be rounded to the nearest multiple of 5 cents or 10 cents, respectively.

(B) Reduced deductible. The dollar amount applied under paragraph (2)(B)—

(i) for 2007 shall be the dollar amount specified in such paragraph increased by the annual percentage increase described in section 1860D-2(b)(6) [42 USCS § 1395w-102(b)(6)] for 2007; or

(ii) for a subsequent year shall be the dollar amount specified in this clause (or clause (i)) for the previous year increased by the annual percentage increase described in section 1860D-2(b)(6) [42 USCS § 1395w-102(b)(6)] for the year involved.

Any amount established under clause (i) or (ii) that is not a multiple of $1 shall be rounded to the nearest multiple of $1.

(5) Waiver of de minimis premiums **[Caution: This paragraph applies to premiums for months beginning after January 1, 2011, as provided by § 3303(c) of Act March 23, 2010, P. L. 111-148, which appears as 42 USCS § 1395w-101 note.]**. The Secretary shall, under procedures established by the Secretary, permit a prescription drug plan or an MA-PD plan to waive the monthly beneficiary premium for a subsidy eligible individual if the amount of such premium is de minimis. If such premium is waived under the plan, the Secretary shall not reassign subsidy eligible individuals enrolled in the plan to other plans based on the fact that the monthly beneficiary premium under the plan was greater than the low-income benchmark premium amount.

(b) Premium subsidy amount. (1) In general. The premium subsidy amount described in this subsection for a subsidy eligible individual residing in a PDP region and enrolled in a prescription drug plan or MA-PD plan is the low-income benchmark premium amount (as defined in paragraph (2)) for the PDP region in which the individual resides or, if greater, the amount specified in paragraph (3).

(2) Low-income benchmark premium amount defined. (A) In general. For purposes of this subsection, the term "low-income benchmark premium amount" means, with respect to a PDP region in which—

(i) all prescription drug plans are offered by the same PDP sponsor, the weighted average of the amounts described in subparagraph (B)(i) for such plans; or

(ii) there are prescription drug plans offered by more than one PDP sponsor, the weighted average of amounts described in subparagraph (B) for prescription drug plans and MA-PD plans described in section 1851(a)(2)(A)(i) [42 USCS § 1395w-21(a)(2)(A)(i)] offered in such region.

(B) Premium amounts described. The premium amounts described in this subparagraph are, in the case of—

(i) a prescription drug plan that is a basic prescription drug plan, the monthly beneficiary premium for such plan;

(ii) a prescription drug plan that provides alternative prescription drug coverage the actuarial value of which is greater than that of standard prescription drug coverage, the portion of the monthly beneficiary premium that is attributable to basic prescription drug coverage; and

(iii) **[Caution: For provisions applicable to premiums for months beginning before January 1, 2011, see 2010 amendment note below.]** an MA-PD plan, the portion of the MA monthly prescription drug beneficiary premium that is attributable to basic prescription drug benefits (described in section 1852(a)(6)(B)(ii) [42 USCS § 1395w-22(a)(6)(B)(ii)]) and determined before the application of the monthly rebate computed under section 1854(b)(1)(C)(i) [42 USCS § 1395w-24(b)(1)(C)(i)] for that plan and year involved and, in the case of a qualifying plan, before the application of the increase under section 1853(o) [42 USCS § 1395w-23(o)] for that plan and year involved.

The premium amounts described in this subparagraph do not include any amounts attributable to late enrollment penalties under section 1860D-13(b) [42 USCS § 1395w-113(b)].

(3) Access to 0 premium plan. In no case shall the premium subsidy amount under this subsection for a PDP region be less than the lowest monthly beneficiary premium for a prescription drug plan that offers basic prescription drug coverage in the region.

(c) Administration of subsidy program. (1) In general. The Secretary shall provide a process whereby, in the case of a part D eligible individual who is determined to be a subsidy eligible individual and who is enrolled in a prescription drug plan or is enrolled in an MA-PD plan—

(A) the Secretary provides for a notification of the PDP sponsor or the MA organization offering the plan involved that the individual is eligible for a subsidy and the amount of the subsidy under subsection (a);

(B) the sponsor or organization involved reduces the premiums or cost-sharing otherwise imposed by the amount of the applicable subsidy and submits to the Secretary information on the amount of such reduction;

(C) the Secretary periodically and on a timely basis reimburses the sponsor or organization for the amount of such reductions; and

(D) the Secretary ensures the confidentiality of individually identifiable information.

In applying subparagraph (C), the Secretary shall compute reductions based upon imposition under subsections (a)(1)(D) and (a)(2)(E) of unreduced copayment amounts applied under such subsections.

(2) Use of capitated form of payment. The reimbursement under this section with respect to cost-sharing subsidies may be computed on a capitated basis, taking into account the actuarial value of the subsidies and with appropriate adjustments to reflect differences in the risks actually involved.

(d) Facilitation of reassignments. Beginning not later than January 1, 2011, the Secretary shall, in the case of a subsidy eligible individual who is enrolled in one prescription drug plan and is subsequently reassigned by the Secretary to a new prescription drug plan, provide the individual, within 30 days of such reassignment, with—

(1) information on formulary differences between the individual's former plan and the plan to which the individual is reassigned with respect to the individual's drug regimens; and

(2) a description of the individual's right to request a coverage determination, exception, or reconsideration under section 1860D-4(g) [42 USCS § 1395w-104(g)], bring an appeal under section 1860D-4(h) [42 USCS § 1395w-104(h)], or resolve a grievance under section 1860D-4(f) [42 USCS § 1395w-104(f)].

(e) Relation to medicaid program. For special provisions under the medicaid program relating to medicare prescription drug benefits, see section 1935 [42 USCS § 1396u-5].

(Aug. 4, 1935, ch 531, Title XVIII, Part D, Subpart 2, § 1860D-14, as added Dec. 8, 2003, P. L. 108-173, Title I, § 101(a)(2), 117 Stat. 2107; July 15, 2008, P. L. 110-275, Title I, Subtitle A, Part II, §§ 114(a)(2), 116(a), 117(a), 122 Stat. 2506, 2507; March 23, 2010, P. L. 111-148, Title III, Subtitle D, §§ 3302(a), 3303(a), 3304(a), 3305, 3309, 124 Stat. 468, 469, 470, 475; March 30, 2010, P. L. 111-152, Title I, Subtitle B, § 1102(c)(4), 124 Stat. 1045.)

HISTORY; ANCILLARY LAWS AND DIRECTIVES

Amendments:

2010. Act March 23, 2010 (applicable to premiums for months beginning on or after 1/1/2011, as provided by § 3302(b) of such Act, which appears as a note to this section), in subsec. (b)(2)(B)(iii), inserted ", determined without regard to any reduction in such premium as a result of any beneficiary rebate under section 1854(b)(1)(C) or bonus payment under section

1853(n)".

Such Act further (applicable to premiums for months, and enrollments for plan years, beginning on or after 1/1/2011, as provided by § 3303(c) of such Act, which appears as 42 USCS § 1395w-101 note), added subsec. (a)(5).

Such Act further (effective on 1/1/2011, as provided by § 3304(b) of such Act, which appears as a note to this section), added subsec. (a)(3)(B)(vi).

Such Act further, in subsec. (a)(1)(D)(i), inserted "or, effective on a date specified by the Secretary (but in no case earlier than January 1, 2012), who would be such an institutionalized individual or couple, if the full-benefit dual eligible individual were not receiving services under a home and community-based waiver authorized for a State under section 1115 or subsection (c) or (d) of section 1915 or under a State plan amendment under subsection (i) of such section or services provided through enrollment in a Medicaid managed care organization with a contract under section 1903(m) or under section 1932"; redesignated subsec. (d) as subsec. (e); and inserted new subsec. (d).

Act March 30, 2010, in subsec. (b)(2)(B)(iii), substituted "and determined before the application of the monthly rebate computed under section 1854(b)(1)(C)(i) for that plan and year involved and, in the case of a qualifying plan, before the application of the increase under section 1853(o) for that plan and year involved" for ", determined without regard to any reduction in such premium as a result of any beneficiary rebate under section 1854(b)(1)(C) or bonus payment under section 1853(n)".

Other provisions:

Application of amendment made by § 3302 of Act March 23, 2010. Act March 23, 2010, P. L. 111-148, Title III, Subtitle D, § 3302(b), 124 Stat. 468, provides: "The amendment made by subsection (a) [amending subsec. (b)(2)(B)(ii) of this section] shall apply to premiums for months beginning on or after January 1, 2011.".

Application of amendment made by § 3304 of Act March 23, 2010. Act March 23, 2010, P. L. 111-148, Title III, Subtitle D, § 3304(b), 124 Stat. 470, provides: "The amendment made by subsection (a) [adding subsec. (a)(3)(B)(vi) of this section] shall take effect on January 1, 2011.".

§ 1395w-114a. Medicare coverage gap discount program

(a) Establishment. The Secretary shall establish a Medicare coverage gap discount program (in this section referred to as the "program") by not later than January 1, 2011. Under the program, the Secretary shall enter into agreements described in subsection (b) with manufacturers and provide for the performance of the duties described in subsection (c)(1). The Secretary shall establish a model agreement for use under the program by not later than 180 days after the date of the enactment of this section [enacted March 23, 2010], in consultation with manufacturers, and allow for comment on such model agreement.

(b) Terms of agreement. (1) In general. (A) Agreement. An agreement under this section shall require the manufacturer to provide applicable beneficiaries access to discounted prices for applicable drugs of the manufacturer.

(B) Provision of discounted prices at the point-of-sale. Except as provided in subsection (c)(1)(A)(iii), such discounted prices shall be provided to the applicable beneficiary at the pharmacy or by the mail order service at the point-of-sale of an applicable drug.

(C) Timing of agreement. (i) Special rule for 2011. In order for an agreement with a manufacturer to be in effect under this section with respect to the period beginning on January 1, 2011, and ending on December 31, 2011, the manufacturer shall enter into such agreement [not later than] not later than 30 days after the date of the establishment of a model agreement under subsection (a).

(ii) 2012 and subsequent years. In order for an agreement with a manufacturer to be in effect under this section with respect to plan year 2012 or a subsequent plan year, the manufacturer shall enter into such agreement (or such agreement shall be renewed under paragraph (4)(A)) not later than January 30 of the preceding year.

(2) Provision of appropriate data. Each manufacturer with an agreement in effect under this section shall collect and have available appropriate data, as determined by the Secretary, to ensure that it can demonstrate to the Secretary compliance with the requirements under the program.

(3) Compliance with requirements for administration of program. Each manufacturer with an agreement in effect under this section shall comply with requirements imposed by the Secretary or a third party with a contract under subsection (d)(3), as applicable, for purposes of administering the program, including any determination under clause (i) of subsection (c)(1)(A) or procedures established under such subsection (c)(1)(A).

(4) Length of agreement. (A) In general. An agreement under this section shall be effective for an initial period of not less than 18 months and shall be automatically renewed for a period of not less than 1 year unless terminated under subparagraph (B).

(B) Termination. (i) By the Secretary. The Secretary may provide for termination of an agreement under this section for a knowing and willful violation of the requirements of the agreement or other good cause shown. Such termination shall not be effective earlier than 30 days after the date of notice to the manufacturer of such termination. The Secretary shall provide, upon request, a manufacturer with a hearing concerning such a termination, and such hearing shall take place prior to the effective date of the termination with sufficient time for such effective date to be repealed if the Secretary determines appropriate.

(ii) By a manufacturer. A manufacturer may terminate an agreement under this section for any reason. Any such termination shall be effective, with respect to a plan year—

(I) if the termination occurs before January 30 of a plan year, as of the day after the end of the plan year; and

(II) if the termination occurs on or after January 30 of a plan year, as of the day after the end of the succeeding plan year.

(iii) Effectiveness of termination. Any termination under this subparagraph shall not affect discounts for applicable drugs of the manufacturer that are due under the agreement before the effective date of its termination.

(iv) Notice to third party. The Secretary shall provide notice of such termination to a third party with a contract under subsection (d)(3) within not less than 30 days before the effective date of such termination.

(c) Duties described and special rule for supplemental benefits. (1) Duties described. The duties described in this subsection are the following:

(A) Administration of program. Administering the program, including—

(i) the determination of the amount of the discounted price of an applicable drug of a manufacturer;

(ii) except as provided in clause (iii), the establishment of procedures under which discounted prices are provided to applicable beneficiaries at pharmacies or by mail order service at the point-of-sale of an applicable drug;

(iii) in the case where, during the period beginning on January 1, 2011, and ending on December 31, 2011, it is not practicable to provide such discounted prices at the point-of-sale (as described in clause (ii)), the establishment of procedures to provide such discounted prices as soon as practicable after the point-of-sale;

(iv) the establishment of procedures to ensure that, not later than the applicable number of calendar days after the dispensing of an applicable drug by a pharmacy or mail order service, the pharmacy or mail order service is reimbursed for an amount equal to the difference between—

(I) the negotiated price of the applicable drug; and

(II) the discounted price of the applicable drug;

(v) the establishment of procedures to ensure that the discounted price for an applicable drug under this section is applied before any coverage or financial assistance under other health benefit plans or programs that provide coverage or financial assistance for the purchase or provision of prescription drug coverage on behalf of applicable beneficiaries as the Secretary may specify;

(vi) the establishment of procedures to implement the special rule for supplemental benefits under paragraph (2); and

(vii) providing a reasonable dispute resolution mechanism to resolve disagreements between manufacturers, applicable beneficiaries, and the third party with a contract under subsection (d)(3).

(B) Monitoring compliance. (i) In general. The Secretary shall monitor compliance by a manufacturer with the terms of an agreement under this section.

(ii) Notification. If a third party with a contract under subsection (d)(3) determines that the manufacturer is not in compliance with such agreement, the third party shall notify the Secretary of such noncompliance for appropriate enforcement under subsection (e).

(C) Collection of data from prescription drug plans and MA-PD plans. The Secretary may collect appropriate data from prescription drug plans and MA-PD plans in a timeframe that allows for discounted prices to be provided for applicable drugs under this section.

(2) Special rule for supplemental benefits. For plan year 2011 and each subsequent plan year, in the case where an applicable beneficiary has supplemental benefits with respect to applicable drugs under the prescription drug plan or MA-PD plan that the applicable beneficiary is enrolled in, the applicable beneficiary shall not be provided a discounted price for an applicable drug under this section until after such supplemental benefits have been applied with respect to the applicable drug.

(d) Administration. (1) In general. Subject to paragraph (2), the Secretary shall provide for the implementation of this section, including the performance of the duties described in subsection (c)(1).

(2) Limitation. (A) In general. Subject to subparagraph (B), in providing for such implementation, the Secretary shall not receive or distribute any funds of a manufacturer under the program.

(B) Exception. The limitation under subparagraph (A) shall not apply to the Secretary with respect to drugs dispensed during the period beginning on January 1, 2011, and ending on December 31, 2011, but only if the Secretary determines that the exception to such limitation under this subparagraph is necessary in order for the Secretary to begin implementation of this section and provide applicable beneficiaries timely access to discounted prices during such period.

(3) Contract with third parties. The Secretary shall enter into a contract with 1 or more third parties to administer the requirements established by the Secretary in order to carry out this section. At a minimum, the contract with a third party under the preceding sentence shall require that the third party—

(A) receive and transmit information between the Secretary, manufacturers, and other individuals or entities the Secretary determines appropriate;

(B) receive, distribute, or facilitate the distribution of funds of manufacturers to appropriate individuals or entities in order to meet the obligations of manufacturers under agreements under this section;

(C) provide adequate and timely information to manufacturers, consistent with the agreement with the manufacturer under this section, as necessary for the manufacturer to fulfill its obligations under this section; and

(D) permit manufacturers to conduct periodic audits, directly or through contracts, of the data and information used by the third party to determine discounts for applicable drugs of the manufacturer under the program.

(4) Performance requirements. The Secretary shall establish performance requirements for a third party with a contract under paragraph (3) and safeguards to protect the independence and integrity of the activities carried out by the third party under the program under this section.

(5) Implementation. The Secretary may implement the program under this section by program instruction or otherwise.

(6) Administration. Chapter 35 of title 44, United States Code [42 USCS §§ 3501 et seq.], shall not apply to the program under this section.

(e) Enforcement. (1) Audits. Each manufacturer with an agreement in effect under this section shall be subject to periodic audit by the Secretary.

(2) Civil money penalty. (A) In general. The Secretary shall impose a civil money penalty on a manufacturer that fails to provide applicable beneficiaries discounts for applicable drugs of the manufacturer in accordance with such agreement for each such failure in an amount the Secretary determines is commensurate with the sum of—

(i) the amount that the manufacturer would have paid with respect to such discounts under the agreement, which will then be used to pay the discounts which the manufacturer had failed to provide; and

(ii) 25 percent of such amount.

(B) Application. The provisions of section 1128A [42 USCS § 1320a-7a] (other than subsections (a) and (b)) shall apply to a civil money penalty under this paragraph in the same manner as such provisions apply to a penalty or proceeding under section 1128A(a) [42 USCS § 1320a-7a].

(f) Clarification regarding availability of other covered part D drugs. Nothing in this section shall prevent an applicable beneficiary from purchasing a covered part D drug that is not an applicable drug (including a generic drug or a drug that is not on the formulary of the prescription drug plan or MA-PD plan that the applicable beneficiary is enrolled in).

(g) Definitions. In this section:

(1) Applicable beneficiary. The term "applicable beneficiary" means an individual who, on the date of dispensing a covered part D drug—

(A) is enrolled in a prescription drug plan or an MA-PD plan;

(B) is not enrolled in a qualified retiree prescription drug plan;

(C) is not entitled to an income-related subsidy under section 1860D-14(a) [42 USCS § 1395w-114(a)]; and

(D) who—

(i) has reached or exceeded the initial coverage limit under section 1860D-2(b)(3) [42 USCS § 1395w-102(b)(3)] during the year; and

(ii) has not incurred costs for covered part D drugs in the year equal to the annual out-of-pocket threshold specified in section 1860D-2(b)(4)(B) [42 USCS § 1395w-102(b)(4)(B)].

(2) Applicable drug. The term "applicable drug" means, with respect to an applicable beneficiary, a covered part D drug—

(A) approved under a new drug application under section 505(b) of the Federal Food, Drug, and Cosmetic Act [21 USCS § 355] or, in the case of a biologic product, licensed under section 351 of the Public Health Service Act [42 USCS § 262] (other than a product licensed under subsection (k) of such section 351 [42 USCS § 262]); and

(B)(i) if the PDP sponsor of the prescription drug plan or the MA organization offering the MA-PD plan uses a formulary, which is on the formulary of the prescription drug plan or MA-PD plan that the applicable beneficiary is enrolled in;

(ii) if the PDP sponsor of the prescription drug plan or the MA organization offering the MA-PD plan does not use a formulary, for which benefits are available under the prescription drug plan or MA-PD plan that the applicable beneficiary is enrolled in; or

(iii) is provided through an exception or appeal.

(3) Applicable number of calendar days. The term "applicable number of calendar days" means—

(A) with respect to claims for reimbursement submitted electronically, 14 days; and

(B) with respect to claims for reimbursement submitted otherwise, 30 days.

(4) Discounted price. (A) In general. The term "discounted price" means 50 percent of the negotiated price of the applicable drug of a manufacturer.

(B) Clarification. Nothing in this section shall be construed as affecting the responsibility of an applicable beneficiary for payment of a dispensing fee for an applicable drug.

(C) Special case for certain claims. In the case where the entire amount of the negotiated price of an individual claim for an applicable drug with respect to an applicable beneficiary does not fall at or above the initial coverage limit under section 1860D-2(b)(3) [42 USCS § 1395w-102(b)(3)] and below the annual out-of-pocket threshold specified in section 1860D-2(b)(4)(B) [42 USCS § 1395w-102(b)(4)(B)] for the year, the manufacturer of the applicable drug shall provide the discounted price under this section on only the portion of the negotiated price of the applicable drug that falls at or above such initial coverage limit and below such annual out-of-pocket threshold.

(5) Manufacturer. The term "manufacturer" means any entity which is engaged in the production, preparation, propagation, compounding, conversion, or processing of prescription drug products, either directly or indirectly by extraction from substances of natural origin, or independently by means of chemical synthesis, or by a combination of extraction and chemical synthesis. Such term does not include a wholesale distributor of drugs or a retail pharmacy licensed under State law.

(6) Negotiated price. The term "negotiated price" has the meaning given such term in section 423.100 of title 42, Code of Federal Regulations (as in effect on the date of enactment of this section), except that such negotiated price shall not include any dispensing fee for the applicable drug.

(7) Qualified retiree prescription drug plan. The term "qualified retiree prescription drug plan" has the meaning given such term in section 1860D-22(a)(2) [42 USCS § 1395w-132(a)(2)].

(Aug. 4, 1935, ch 531, Title XVIII, Part D, Subpart 2, § 1860D-14A, as added March 23, 2010, P. L. 111-148, Title III, Subtitle D, § 3301(b), 124 Stat. 462; March 30, 2010, P. L. 111-152, Title I, Subtitle B, § 1101(b)(2), 124 Stat. 1037.)

§ 1395w-115. Subsidies for part D eligible individuals for qualified prescription drug coverage

(a) Subsidy payment. In order to reduce premium levels applicable to qualified prescription drug coverage for part D eligible individuals consistent with an overall subsidy level of 74.5 percent for basic prescription drug coverage, to reduce adverse selection among prescription drug plans and MA-PD plans, and to promote the participation of PDP sponsors under this part [42 USCS §§ 1395w-101 et seq.] and MA organizations under part C [42 USCS §§ 1395w-21 et seq.], the Secretary shall provide for payment to a PDP sponsor that offers a prescription drug plan and an MA organization that offers an MA-PD plan of the following subsidies in accordance with this section:

(1) Direct subsidy. A direct subsidy for each part D eligible individual enrolled in a prescription drug plan or MA-PD plan for a month equal to—

(A) the amount of the plan's standardized bid amount (as defined in section 1860D-13(a)(5) [42 USCS § 1395w-113(a)(5)]), adjusted under subsection (c)(1), reduced by

(B) the base beneficiary premium (as computed under paragraph (2) of section 1860D-13(a) [42 USCS § 1395w-113(a)] and as adjusted under paragraph (1)(B) of such section).

(2) Subsidy through reinsurance. The reinsurance payment amount (as defined in subsection (b)).

This section constitutes budget authority in advance of appropriations Acts and represents the obligation of the Secretary to provide for the payment of amounts provided under this section.

(b) Reinsurance payment amount. (1) In general. The reinsurance payment amount under this subsection for a part D eligible individual enrolled in a prescription drug plan or MA-PD plan for a coverage year is an amount equal to 80 percent of the allowable reinsurance costs (as specified in paragraph (2)) attributable to that portion of gross covered prescription drug costs as specified in paragraph (3) incurred in the coverage year after such individual has incurred costs that exceed the annual out-of-pocket threshold specified in section 1860D-2(b)(4)(B) [42 USCS § 1395w-102(b)(4)(B)].

(2) Allowable reinsurance costs. For purposes of this section, the term "allowable reinsurance costs" means, with respect to gross covered prescription drug costs under a prescription drug plan offered by a PDP sponsor or an MA-PD plan offered by an MA organization, the part of such costs that are actually paid (net of discounts, chargebacks, and average percentage rebates) by the sponsor or organization or by (or on behalf of) an enrollee under the plan, but in no case more than the part of such costs that would have been paid under the plan if the prescription drug coverage under the plan were basic prescription drug coverage, or, in the case of a plan providing supplemental prescription drug coverage, if such coverage were standard prescription drug coverage.

(3) Gross covered prescription drug costs. For purposes of this section, the term "gross covered prescription drug costs" means, with respect to a part D eligible individual enrolled in a prescription drug plan or MA-PD plan during a coverage year, the costs incurred under the plan, not including administrative costs, but including costs directly related to the dispensing of covered part D drugs during the year and costs relating to the deductible. Such costs shall be determined whether they are paid by the individual or under the plan, regardless of whether the coverage under the plan exceeds basic prescription drug coverage.

(4) Coverage year defined. For purposes of this section, the term "coverage year" means a calendar year in which covered part D drugs are dispensed if the claim for such drugs (and payment on such claim) is made not later than such period after the end of such year as the Secretary specifies.

(c) Adjustments relating to bids. (1) Health status risk adjustment. (A) Establishment of risk adjustors. The Secretary shall establish an appropriate methodology for adjusting the standardized bid amount under subsection (a)(1)(A) to take into account variation in costs for basic prescription drug coverage among prescription drug plans and MA-PD plans based on the differences in actuarial risk of different enrollees being served. Any such risk adjustment shall be designed in a manner so as not to result in a change in the aggregate amounts payable to such plans under subsection (a)(1) and through that portion of the monthly beneficiary prescription drug premiums described in subsection (a)(1)(B) and MA monthly prescription drug beneficiary premiums.

(B) Considerations. In establishing the methodology under subparagraph (A), the Secretary may take into account the similar methodologies used under section 1853(a)(3) [42 USCS § 1395w-23(a)(3)] to adjust payments to MA organizations for benefits under the original medicare fee-for-service program option.

(C) Data collection. In order to carry out this paragraph, the Secretary shall require—

(i) PDP sponsors to submit data regarding drug claims that can be linked at the individual level to part A and part B [42 USCS §§ 1395c et seq. and 1395j et seq.] data and such other information as the Secretary determines necessary; and

(ii) MA organizations that offer MA-PD plans to submit data regarding drug claims that can be linked at the individual level to other data that such organizations are required to submit to the Secretary and such other information as the Secretary determines necessary.

(D) Publication. At the time of publication of risk adjustment factors under section 1853(b)(1)(B)(i)(II) [42 USCS § 1395w-23(b)(1)(B)(i)(II)], the Secretary shall publish the risk adjusters established under this paragraph for the succeeding year.

(2) Geographic adjustment. (A) In general. Subject to subparagraph (B), for purposes of section 1860D-13(a)(1)(B)(iii) [42 USCS § 1395w-113(a)(1)(B)(iii)], the Secretary shall establish an appropriate methodology for adjusting the national average monthly bid amount (computed under section 1860D-13(a)(4) [42 USCS § 1395w-113(a)(4)]) to take into account differences in prices for covered part D drugs among PDP regions.

(B) De minimis rule. If the Secretary determines that the price variations described in subparagraph (A) among PDP regions are de minimis, the Secretary shall not provide for adjustment under this paragraph.

(C) Budget neutral adjustment. Any adjustment under this paragraph shall be applied in a manner so as to not result in a change in the aggregate payments made under this part [42 USCS §§ 1395w-101 et seq.] that would have been made if the Secretary had not applied such adjustment.

(d) Payment methods. (1) In general. Payments under this section shall be based on such a method as the Secretary determines. The Secretary may establish a payment method by which interim payments of amounts under this section are made during a year based on the Secretary's best estimate of amounts that will be payable after obtaining all of the information.

(2) Requirement for provision of information. (A) Requirement. Payments under this section to a PDP sponsor or MA organization are conditioned upon the furnishing to the Secretary, in a form and manner specified by the Secretary, of such information as may be required to carry out this section.

(B) Restriction on use of information. Information disclosed or obtained pursuant to subparagraph (A) may be used by officers, employees, and contractors of the Department of Health and Human Services only for the purposes of, and to the extent necessary in, carrying out this section.

(3) Source of payments. Payments under this section shall be made from the Medicare Prescription Drug Account.

(4) Application of enrollee adjustment. The provisions of section 1853(a)(2) [42 USCS § 1395w-23(a)(2)] shall apply to payments to PDP sponsors under this section in the same manner as they apply to payments to MA organizations under section 1853(a) [42 USCS § 1395w-23(a)].

(e) Portion of total payments to a sponsor or organization subject to risk (application of risk corridors). (1) Computation of adjusted allowable risk corridor costs. (A) In general. For purposes of this subsection, the term "adjusted allowable risk corridor costs" means, for a plan for a coverage year (as defined in subsection (b)(4))—

(i) the allowable risk corridor costs (as defined in subparagraph (B)) for the plan for the year, reduced by

(ii) the sum of (I) the total reinsurance payments made under subsection (b) to the sponsor of the plan for the year, and (II) the total subsidy payments made under section 1860D-14 [42 USCS § 1395w-114] to the sponsor of the plan for the year.

(B) Allowable risk corridor costs. For purposes of this subsection, the term "allowable risk corridor costs" means, with respect to a prescription drug plan offered by a PDP sponsor or an MA-PD plan offered by an MA organization, the part of costs (not including administrative costs, but including costs directly related to the dispensing of covered part D drugs during the year) incurred by the sponsor or organization under the plan that are actually paid (net of discounts, chargebacks, and average percentage rebates) by the sponsor or organization under the plan, but in no case more than the part of such costs that would have been paid under the plan if the prescription drug coverage under the plan were basic prescription drug coverage, or, in the case of a plan providing supplemental prescription drug coverage, if such coverage were basic prescription drug coverage taking into account the adjustment under section 1860D-11(c)(2) [42 USCS § 1395w-111(c)(2)]. In computing allowable costs under this paragraph, the Secretary shall compute such costs based upon imposition under paragraphs (1)(D) and (2)(E) of section 1860D-14(a) [42 USCS § 1395w-114(a)] of the maximum amount of copayments permitted under such paragraphs.

(2) Adjustment of payment. (A) No adjustment if adjusted allowable risk corridor costs within risk corridor. If the adjusted allowable risk corridor costs (as defined in paragraph (1)) for the plan for the year are at least equal to the first threshold lower limit of the risk corridor (specified in paragraph (3)(A)(i)), but not greater than the first threshold upper limit of the risk corridor (specified in paragraph (3)(A)(iii)) for the plan for the year, then no payment adjustment shall be made under this subsection.

(B) Increase in payment if adjusted allowable risk corridor costs above upper limit of risk corridor. (i) Costs between first and second threshold upper limits. If the adjusted allowable risk corridor costs for the plan for the year are greater than the first threshold upper limit, but not greater than the second threshold upper limit, of the risk corridor for the plan for the year, the Secretary shall increase the total of the payments made to the sponsor or organization offering the plan for the year under this section by an amount equal to 50 percent (or, for 2006 and 2007, 75 percent or 90 percent if the conditions described in clause (iii) are met for the year) of the difference between such adjusted allowable risk corridor costs and the first threshold upper limit of the risk corridor.

(ii) Costs above second threshold upper limits. If the adjusted allowable risk corridor costs for the plan for the year are greater than the second threshold upper limit of the risk corridor for the plan for the year, the Secretary shall increase the total of the payments made to the sponsor or organization offering the plan for the year under this section by an amount equal to the sum of—

(I) 50 percent (or, for 2006 and 2007, 75 percent or 90 percent if the conditions described in clause (iii) are met for the year) of the difference between the second threshold upper limit and the first threshold upper limit;

and

(II) 80 percent of the difference between such adjusted allowable risk corridor costs and the second threshold upper limit of the risk corridor.

(iii) Conditions for application of higher percentage for 2006 and 2007. The conditions described in this clause are met for 2006 or 2007 if the Secretary determines with respect to such year that—

(I) at least 60 percent of prescription drug plans and MA-PD plans to which this subsection applies have adjusted allowable risk corridor costs for the plan for the year that are more than the first threshold upper limit of the risk corridor for the plan for the year; and

(II) such plans represent at least 60 percent of part D eligible individuals enrolled in any prescription drug plan or MA-PD plan.

(C) Reduction in payment if adjusted allowable risk corridor costs below lower limit of risk corridor. (i) Costs between first and second threshold lower limits. If the adjusted allowable risk corridor costs for the plan for the year are less than the first threshold lower limit, but not less than the second threshold lower limit, of the risk corridor for the plan for the year, the Secretary shall reduce the total of the payments made to the sponsor or organization offering the plan for the year under this section by an amount (or otherwise recover from the sponsor or organization an amount) equal to 50 percent (or, for 2006 and 2007, 75 percent) of the difference between the first threshold lower limit of the risk corridor and such adjusted allowable risk corridor costs.

(ii) Costs below second threshold lower limit. If the adjusted allowable risk corridor costs for the plan for the year are less the second threshold lower limit of the risk corridor for the plan for the year, the Secretary shall reduce the total of the payments made to the sponsor or organization offering the plan for the year under this section by an amount (or otherwise recover from the sponsor or organization an amount) equal to the sum of—

(I) 50 percent (or, for 2006 and 2007, 75 percent) of the difference between the first threshold lower limit and the second threshold lower limit; and

(II) 80 percent of the difference between the second threshold upper limit of the risk corridor and such adjusted allowable risk corridor costs.

(3) Establishment of risk corridors. (A) In general. For each plan year the Secretary shall establish a risk corridor for each prescription drug plan and each MA-PD plan. The risk corridor for a plan for a year shall be equal to a range as follows:

(i) First threshold lower limit. The first threshold lower limit of such corridor shall be equal to—

(I) the target amount described in subparagraph (B) for the plan; minus

(II) an amount equal to the first threshold risk percentage for the plan (as determined under subparagraph (C)(i)) of such target amount.

(ii) Second threshold lower limit. The second threshold lower limit of such corridor shall be equal to—

(I) the target amount described in subparagraph (B) for the plan; minus

(II) an amount equal to the second threshold risk percentage for the plan (as determined under subparagraph (C)(ii)) of such target amount.

(iii) First threshold upper limit. The first threshold upper limit of such corridor shall be equal to the sum of—

(I) such target amount; and

(II) the amount described in clause (i)(II).

(iv) Second threshold upper limit. The second threshold upper limit of such corridor shall be equal to the sum of—

(I) such target amount; and

(II) the amount described in clause (ii)(II).

(B) Target amount described. The target amount described in this paragraph is, with respect to a prescription drug plan or an MA-PD plan in a year, the total amount of payments paid to the PDP sponsor or MA-PD organization for the plan for the year, taking into account amounts paid by the Secretary and enrollees, based upon the standardized bid amount (as defined in section 1860D-13(a)(5) [42 USCS § 1395w-113(a)(5)] and as risk adjusted under subsection (c)(1)), reduced by the total amount of administrative expenses for the year assumed in such standardized bid.

(C) First and second threshold risk percentage defined. (i) First threshold risk percentage. Subject to clause (iii), for purposes of this section, the first threshold risk percentage is—

(I) for 2006 and 2007, and 2.5 percent;

(II) for 2008 through 2011, 5 percent; and

(III) for 2012 and subsequent years, a percentage established by the Secretary, but in no case less than 5 percent.

(ii) Second threshold risk percentage. Subject to clause (iii), for purposes of this section, the second threshold risk percentage is—

(I) for 2006 and 2007, 5 percent;

(II) for 2008 through 2011, 10 percent; and

(III) for 2012 and subsequent years, a percentage established by the Secretary that is greater than the percent established for the year under clause (i)(III), but in no case less than 10 percent.

(iii) Reduction of risk percentage to ensure 2 plans in an area. Pursuant to section 1860D-11(b)(2)(E)(ii) [42 USCS § 1395w-111(b)(2)(E)(ii)], a PDP sponsor may submit a bid that requests a decrease in the applicable first or second threshold risk percentages or an increase in the percents applied under paragraph (2).

(4) Plans at risk for entire amount of supplemental prescription drug coverage. A PDP sponsor and MA organization that offers a plan that provides supplemental prescription drug benefits shall be at full financial risk for the provision of such supplemental benefits.

(5) No effect on monthly premium. No adjustment in payments made by reason of this subsection shall affect the monthly beneficiary premium or the MA monthly prescription drug beneficiary premium.

(f) Disclosure of information. (1) In general. Each contract under this part [42 USCS §§ 1395w-101 et seq.] and under part C [42 USCS §§ 1395w-21 et seq.] shall provide that—

(A) the PDP sponsor offering a prescription drug plan or an MA organization offering an MA-PD plan shall provide the Secretary with such information as the Secretary determines is necessary to carry out this section; and

(B) the Secretary shall have the right in accordance with section 1857(d)(2)(B) [42 USCS § 1395w-27(d)(2)(B)] (as applied under section 1860D-12(b)(3)(C) [42 USCS § 1395w-112(b)(3)(C)]) to inspect and audit any books and records of a PDP sponsor or MA organization that pertain to the information regarding costs provided to the Secretary under subparagraph (A).

(2) Restriction on use of information. Information disclosed or obtained pursuant to the provisions of this section may be used—

(A) by officers, employees, and contractors of the Department of Health and Human Services for the purposes of, and to the extent necessary in—

(i) carrying out this section; and

(ii) conducting oversight, evaluation, and enforcement under this title [42 USCS §§ 1395 et seq.]; and

(B) by the Attorney General and the Comptroller General of the United States for the purposes of, and to the extent necessary in, carrying out health oversight activities.

(g) Payment for fallback prescription drug plans. In lieu of the amounts otherwise payable under this section to a PDP sponsor offering a fallback prescription drug plan (as defined in section 1860D-3(c)(4) [42 USCS § 1395w-103(c)(4)]), the amount payable shall be the amounts determined under the contract for such plan pursuant to section 1860D-11(g)(5) [42 USCS § 1395w-111(g)(5)].

(Aug. 4, 1935, ch 531, Title XVIII, Part D, Subpart 2, § 1860D-15, as added Dec. 8, 2003, P. L. 108-173, Title I, § 101(a)(2), 117 Stat. 2113; March 23, 2010, P. L. 111-148, Title VI, Subtitle E, § 6402(b)(1), 124 Stat. 756.)

SUBPART 5. DEFINITIONS AND MISCELLANEOUS PROVISIONS

§ 1395w-153. Condition for coverage of drugs under this part

(a) In general. In order for coverage to be available under this part [42 USCS §§ 1395w-101 et seq.] for covered part D drugs (as defined in section 1860D-2(e) [42 USCS § 1395w-102(e)]) of a manufacturer, the manufacturer must—

(1) participate in the Medicare coverage gap discount program under section 1860D-14A [42 USCS § 1395w-114a];

(2) have entered into and have in effect an agreement described in subsection (b) of such section with the Secretary; and

(3) have entered into and have in effect, under terms and conditions specified by the Secretary, a contract with a third party that the Secretary has entered into a contract with under subsection (d)(3) of such section.

(b) Effective date. Subsection (a) shall apply to covered part D drugs dispensed under this part on or after January 1, 2011.

(c) Authorizing coverage for drugs not covered under agreements. Subsection (a) shall not apply to the dispensing of a covered part D drug if—

(1) the Secretary has made a determination that the availability of the drug is essential to the health of beneficiaries under this part; or

(2) the Secretary determines that in the period beginning on January 1, 2011, [and ending on] December 31, 2011, there were extenuating circumstances.

(d) Definition of manufacturer. In this section, the term "manufacturer" has the meaning given such term in section 1860D-14A(g)(5) [42 USCS § 1395w-114a(g)(5)].

(Aug. 4, 1935, ch 531, Title XVIII, Part D, Subpart 5, § 1860D-43, as added March 23, 2010, P. L. 111-148, Title III, Subtitle D, § 3301(a), 124 Stat. 461; March 30, 2010, P. L. 111-152, Title I, Subtitle B, § 1101(b)(1), 124 Stat. 1037.)

§ 1395w-154. Improved Medicare prescription drug plan and MA-PD plan complaint system

(a) In general. The Secretary shall develop and maintain a complaint system, that is widely known and easy to use, to collect and maintain information on MA-PD plan and prescription drug plan complaints that are received (including by telephone, letter, e-mail, or any other means) by the Secretary (including by a regional office of the Department of Health and Human Services, the Medicare Beneficiary Ombudsman, a subcontractor, a carrier, a fiscal intermediary, and a Medicare administrative contractor under section 1874A of the Social Security Act (42 U.S.C. 1395kk)) through the date on which the complaint is resolved. The system shall be able to report and initiate appropriate interventions and monitoring based on substantial complaints and to guide quality improvement.

(b) Model electronic complaint form. The Secretary shall develop a model electronic complaint form to be used for reporting plan complaints under the system. Such form shall be prominently displayed on the front page of the Medicare.gov Internet website and on the Internet website of the Medicare Beneficiary Ombudsman.

(c) Annual reports by the Secretary. The Secretary shall submit to Congress annual reports on the system. Such reports shall include an analysis of the number and types of complaints reported in the system, geographic variations in such complaints, the timeliness of agency or plan responses to such complaints, and the resolution of such complaints.

(d) Definitions. In this section:

(1) MA-PD plan. The term "MA-PD plan" has the meaning given such term in section 1860D-41(a)(9) of such Act (42 U.S.C. 1395w-151(a)(9)).

(2) Prescription drug plan. The term "prescription drug plan" has the meaning given such term in section 1860D-41(a)(14) of such Act (42 U.S.C. 1395w-151(a)(14)).

(3) Secretary. The term "Secretary" means the Secretary of Health and Human Services.

(4) System. The term "system" means the plan complaint system developed and maintained under subsection (a).

(March 23, 2010, P. L. 111-148, Title III, Subtitle D, § 3311, 124 Stat. 475.)

PART E. MISCELLANEOUS PROVISIONS

§ 1395x. Definitions

For purpose of this title [42 USCS §§ 1395 et seq.]—

(a) Spell of illness. The term "spell of illness" with respect to any individual means a period of consecutive days—

(1) beginning with the first day (not included in a previous spell of illness) (A) on which such individual is furnished inpatient hospital services, inpatient critical access hospital services or extended care services, and (B) which occurs in a month for which he is entitled to benefits under part A [42 USCS §§ 1395c et seq.], and

(2) ending with the close of the first period of 60 consecutive days thereafter on each of which he is neither an inpatient of a hospital or critical access hospital nor an inpatient of a facility described in section 1819(a)(2) [42 USCS § 1395i-3 (a)(2)] or subsection (y)(1).

(b) Inpatient hospital services. The term "inpatient hospital services" means the following items and services furnished to an inpatient of a hospital and (except as provided in paragraph (3)) by the hospital—

(1) bed and board;

(2) such nursing services and other related services, such use of hospital facilities, and such medical social services as are ordinarily furnished by the hospital for the care and treatment of inpatients, and such drugs, biologicals, supplies, appliances, and equipment, for use in the hospital, as are ordinarily furnished by such hospital for the care and treatment of inpatients; and

(3) such other diagnostic or therapeutic items or services, furnished by the hospital or by others under arrangements with them made by the hospital, as are ordinarily furnished to inpatients either by such hospital or by others under such arrangements;

excluding, however—

(4) medical or surgical services provided by a physician, resident, or, services described by subsection (s)(2)(K), certified nurse-midwife services, qualified psychologist services, and services of a certified registered nurse anesthetist; and

(5) the services of a private-duty nurse or other private-duty attendant.

Paragraph (4) shall not apply to services provided in a hospital by—

(6) an intern or a resident-in-training under a teaching program approved by the Council on Medical Education of the American Medical Association or, in the case of an osteopathic hospital, approved by the Committee on Hospitals of the Bureau of Professional Education of the American Osteopathic Association, or, in the case of services in a hospital or osteopathic hospital by an intern or resident-in-training in the field of dentistry, approved by the Council on Dental Education of the American Dental Association, or in the case of services in a hospital or osteopathic hospital by an intern or resident-in-training in the field of podiatry, approved by the Council on Podiatric Medical Education of the American Podiatric Medical Association; or

(7) a physician where the hospital has a teaching program approved as specified in paragraph (6), if (A) the hospital elects to receive any payment due under this title [42 USCS §§ 1395 et seq.] for reasonable costs of such services, and (B) all physicians in such hospital agree not to bill charges for professional services rendered in such hospital to individuals covered under the insurance program established by this title [42 USCS §§ 1395 et seq.].

(c) Inpatient psychiatric hospital services. The term "inpatient psychiatric hospital services" means inpatient hospital services furnished to an inpatient of a psychiatric hospital.

(d) Supplier. The term "supplier" means, unless the context otherwise requires, a physician or other practitioner, a facility, or other entity (other than a provider of services) that furnishes items or services under this title [42 USCS §§ 1395 et seq.].

(e) Hospital [Caution: For provisions applicable to accreditions of hospitals granted before July 15, 2010, see 2008 amendment note below.]. The term "hospital" (except for purposes of sections 1814(d), 1814(f), and 1835(b) [42 USCS §§ 1395f(d), (f), and 1395n(b)], subsection (a)(2) of this section, paragraph (7) of this subsection, and subsection (i) of this section) means an institution which—

(1) is primarily engaged in providing, by or under the supervision of physicians, to inpatients (A) diagnostic services and therapeutic services for medical diagnosis, treatment, and care of injured, disabled, or sick persons, or (B) rehabilitation services for the rehabilitation of injured, disabled, or sick persons;

(2) maintains clinical records on all patients;

(3) has bylaws in effect with respect to its staff of physicians;

(4) has a requirement that every patient with respect to whom payment may be made under this title [42 USCS §§ 1395 et seq.] must be under the care of a physician, except that a patient receiving qualified psychologist services (as defined in subsection (ii)) may be under the care of a clinical psychologist with respect to such services to the extent permitted under State law;

(5) provides 24-hour nursing service rendered or supervised by a registered professional nurse, and has a licensed practical nurse or registered professional nurse on duty at all times; except that until January 1, 1979, the Secretary is authorized to waive the requirement of this paragraph for any one-year period with respect to any institution, insofar as such requirement relates to the provision of twenty-four-hour nursing service rendered or supervised by a registered professional nurse (except that in any event a registered professional nurse must be present on the premises to render or supervise the nursing service provided, during at least the regular daytime shift), where immediately preceding such one-year period he finds that—

(A) such institution is located in a rural area and the supply of hospital services in such area is not sufficient to meet the needs of individuals residing therein,

(B) the failure of such institution to qualify as a hospital would seriously reduce the availability of such services to such individuals, and

(C) such institution has made and continues to make a good faith effort to comply with this paragraph, but such compliance is impeded by the lack of qualified nursing personnel in such area;

(6)(A) has in effect a hospital utilization review plan which meets the requirements of subsection (k) and (B) has in place a discharge planning process that meets the requirements of subsection (ee);

(7) in the case of an institution in any State in which State or applicable local law provides for the licensing of hospitals, (A) is licensed pursuant to such law or (B) is approved, by the agency of such State or locality responsible for licensing hospitals, as meeting the standards established for such licensing;

(8) has in effect an overall plan and budget that meets the requirements of subsection (z); and

(9) meets such other requirements as the Secretary finds necessary in the interest of the health and safety of individuals who are fur-

nished services in the institution.

For purposes of subsection (a)(2), such term includes any institution which meets the requirements of paragraph (1) of this subsection. For purposes of sections 1814(d) [42 USCS § 1395f(d)] and 1835(b) [42 USCS § 1395n(b)] (including determination of whether an individual received inpatient hospital services or diagnostic services for purposes of such sections), section 1814(f)(2) [42 USCS § 1395f(f)(2)], and subsection (i) of this section, such term includes any institution which (i) meets the requirements of paragraphs (5) and (7) of this subsection, (ii) is not primarily engaged in providing the services described in section 1861(j)(1)(A) [subsec. (j)(1)(A) of this section] and (iii) is primarily engaged in providing, by or under the supervision of individuals referred to in paragraph (1) of section 1861(r) [subsec. (r)(1) of this section], to inpatients diagnostic services and therapeutic services for medical diagnosis, treatment, and care of injured, disabled, or sick persons, or rehabilitation services for the rehabilitation of injured, disabled, or sick persons. For purposes of section 1814(f)(1) [42 USCS § 1395f(f)(1)], such term includes an institution which (i) is a hospital for purposes of sections 1814(d), 1814(f)(2), and 1835(b) [42 USCS §§ 1395f(d), (f)(2), and 1395n(b)] and (ii) is accredited by a national accreditation body recognized by the Secretary under section 1865(a), or is accredited by or approved by a program of the country in which such institution is located if the Secretary finds the accreditation or comparable approval standards of such program to be essentially equivalent to those of such a national accreditation body.[.] Notwithstanding the preceding provisions of this subsection, such term shall not, except for purposes of subsection (a)(2) include any institution which is primarily for the care and treatment of mental diseases unless it is a psychiatric hospital (as defined in subsection (f)). The term "hospital" also includes a religious nonmedical health care institution (as defined in subsection (ss)(1)), but only with respect to items and services ordinarily furnished by such institution to inpatients, and payment may be made with respect to services provided by or in such an institution only to such extent and under such conditions, limitations, and requirements (in addition to or in lieu of the conditions, limitations, and requirements otherwise applicable) as may be provided in regulations consistent with section 1821 [42 USCS § 1395i-5]. For provisions deeming certain requirements of this subsection to be met in the case of accredited institutions, see section 1865 [42 USCS § 1395bb]. The term "hospital" also includes a facility of fifty beds or less which is located in an area determined by the Secretary to meet the definition relating to a rural area described in subparagraph (A) of paragraph (5) of this subsection and which meets the other requirements of this subsection, except that—

(A) with respect to the requirements for nursing services applicable after December 31, 1978, such requirements shall provide for temporary waiver of the requirements, for such period as the Secretary deems appropriate, where (i) the facility's failure to fully comply with the requirements is attributable to a temporary shortage of qualified nursing personnel in the area in which the facility is located, (ii) a registered professional nurse is present on the premises to render or supervise the nursing service provided during at least the regular daytime shift, and (iii) the Secretary determines that the employment of such nursing personnel as are available to the facility during such temporary period will not adversely affect the health and safety of patients;

(B) with respect to the health and safety requirements promulgated under paragraph (9), such requirements shall be applied by the Secretary to a facility herein defined in such manner as to assure that personnel requirements take into account the availability of technical personnel and the educational opportunities for technical personnel in the area in which such facility is located, and the scope of services rendered by such facility; and the Secretary, by regulations, shall provide for the continued participation of such a facility where such personnel requirements are not fully met, for such period as the Secretary determines that (i) the facility is making good faith efforts to fully comply with the personnel requirements, (ii) the employment by the facility of such personnel as are available to the facility will not adversely affect the health and safety of patients, and (iii) if the Secretary has determined that because of the facility's waiver under this subparagraph the facility should limit its scope of services in order not to adversely affect the health and safety of the facility's patients, the facility is so limiting the scope of services it provides; and

(C) with respect to the fire and safety requirements promulgated under paragraph (9), the Secretary (i) may, waive, for such period as he deems appropriate, specific provisions of such requirements which if rigidly applied would result in unreasonable hardship for such a facility and which, if not applied, would not jeopardize the health and safety of patients, and (ii) may accept a facility's compliance with all applicable State codes relating to fire and safety in lieu of compliance with the fire and safety requirements promulgated under paragraph (9), if he determines that such State has in effect fire and safety codes, imposed by State law, which adequately protect patients.

The term "hospital" does not include, unless the context otherwise requires, a critical access hospital (as defined in section 1861(mm)(1) [subsec. (mm)(1) of this section]).

(f) Psychiatric hospital. The term "psychiatric hospital" means an institution which—

(1) is primarily engaged in providing, by or under the supervision of a physician, psychiatric services for the diagnosis and treatment of mentally ill persons;

(2) satisfies the requirements of paragraphs (3) through (9) of subsection (e);

(3) maintains clinical records on all patients and maintains such records as the Secretary finds to be necessary to determine the degree and intensity of the treatment provided to individuals entitled to hospital insurance benefits under part A [42 USCS §§ 1395c et seq.] and

(4) meets such staffing requirements as the Secretary finds necessary for the institution to carry out an active program of treatment for individuals who are furnished services in the institution.

In the case of an institution which satisfies paragraphs (1) and (2) of the preceding sentence and which contains a distinct part which also satisfies paragraphs (3) and (4) of such sentence, such distinct part shall be considered to be a "psychiatric hospital".

(g) Outpatient occupational therapy services. The term "outpatient occupational therapy services" has the meaning given the term "outpatient physical therapy services" in subsection (p), except that "occupational" shall be substituted for "physical" each place it appears therein.

(h) Extended care services. The term "extended care services" means the following items and services furnished to an inpatient of a skilled nursing facility and (except as provided in paragraphs (3), (6), and (7)) by such skilled nursing facility—

(1) nursing care provided by or under the supervision of a registered professional nurse;

(2) bed and board in connection with the furnishing of such nursing care;

(3) physical or occupational therapy or speech-language pathology services furnished by the skilled nursing facility or by others under arrangements with them made by the facility;

(4) medical social services;

(5) such drugs, biologicals, supplies, appliances, and equipment, furnished for use in the skilled nursing facility, as are ordinarily furnished by such facility for the care and treatment of inpatients;

(6) medical services provided by an intern or resident-in-training of a hospital with which the facility has in effect a transfer agreement (meeting the requirements of subsection (l)), under a teaching program of such hospital approved as provided in the last sentence of subsection (b), and other diagnostic or therapeutic services provided by a hospital with which the facility has such an agreement in effect; and

(7) such other services necessary to the health of the patients as are generally provided by skilled nursing facilities, or by others under arrangements with them made by the facility;

excluding, however, any item or service if it would not be included under subsection (b) if furnished to an inpatient of a hospital.

(i) Post-hospital extended care services. The term "post-hospital extended care services" means extended care services furnished an individual after transfer from a hospital in which he was an inpatient for not less than 3 consecutive days before his discharge from the hospital in connection with such transfer. For purposes of the preceding sentence, items and services shall be deemed to have been furnished to an individual after transfer from a hospital, and he shall be deemed to have been an inpatient in the hospital immediately before transfer therefrom, if he is admitted to the skilled nursing facility (A) within 30 days after discharge from such hospital, or (B) within such time as it would be medically appropriate to begin an active course of treatment, in the case of an individual whose condition is such that skilled nursing facility care would not be medically appropriate within 30 days after discharge from a hospital; and an individual shall be deemed not to have been discharged from a skilled nursing facility if, within 30 days after discharge therefrom, he is admitted to such facility or any other skilled nursing facility.

(j) Skilled nursing facility. The term "skilled nursing facility" has the meaning given such term in section 1819(a) [42 USCS § 1395i-3(a)].

(k) Utilization review. A utilization review plan of a hospital or skilled nursing facility shall be considered sufficient if it is applicable to services furnished by the institution to individuals entitled to insurance benefits under this title [42 USCS §§ 1395 et seq.] and if it provides—

(1) for the review, on a sample or other basis, of admissions to the institution, the duration of stays therein, and the professional services (including drugs and biologicals) furnished, (A) with respect to the medical necessity of the services, and (B) for the purpose of promoting the most efficient use of available health facilities and services;

(2) for such review to be made by either (A) a staff committee of the institution composed of two or more physicians (of which at least two must be physicians described in subsection (r)(1) of this section), with or without participation of other professional personnel, or (B) a group outside the institution which is similarly composed and (i) which is established by the local medical society and some or all of the hospitals and skilled nursing facilities in the locality, or (ii) if (and for as long as) there has not been established such a group which serves such institution, which is established in such other manner as may be approved by the Secretary;

(3) for such review, in each case of inpatient hospital services or extended care services furnished to such an individual during a continuous period of extended duration, as of such days of such period (which may differ for different classes of cases) as may be specified in regulations, with such review to be made as promptly as possible, after each day so specified, and in no event later than one week following such day; and

(4) for prompt notification to the institution, the individual, and his attending physician of any finding (made after opportunity for consultation to such attending physician) by the physician members of such committee or group that any further stay in the institution is not medically necessary.

The review committee must be composed as provided in clause (B) of paragraph (2) rather than as provided in clause (A) of such paragraph in the case of any hospital or skilled nursing facility where, because of the small size of the institution, or (in the case of a skilled nursing facility) because of lack of an organized medical staff, or for such other reason or reasons as may be included in regulations, it is impracticable for the institution to have a properly functioning staff committee for the purposes of this subsection. If the Secretary determines that the utilization review procedures established pursuant to title XIX [42 USCS §§ 1396 et seq.] are superior in their effectiveness to the procedures required under this section, he may, to the extent that he deems it appropriate, require for purposes of this title [42 USCS §§ 1395 et seq.] that the procedures established pursuant to title XIX [42 USCS §§ 1396 et seq.] be utilized instead of the procedures required by this section.

(l) Agreements for transfer between skilled nursing facilities and hospitals. A hospital and a skilled nursing facility shall be considered to have a transfer agreement in effect if, by reason of a written agreement between them or (in case the two institutions are under common control) by reason of a written undertaking by the person or body which controls them, there is reasonable assurance that—

(1) transfer of patients will be effected between the hospital and the skilled nursing facility whenever such transfer is medically appropriate as determined by the attending physician; and

(2) there will be interchange of medical and other information necessary or useful in the care and treatment of individuals transferred between the institutions, or in determining whether such individuals can be adequately cared for otherwise than in either of such institutions.

Any skilled nursing facility which does not have such an agreement in effect, but which is found by a State agency (of the State in which such facility is situated) with which an agreement under section 1864 [42 USCS § 1395aa] is in effect (or, in the case of a State in which no such agency has an agreement under section 1864 [42 USCS § 1395aa], by the Secretary) to have attempted in good faith to enter into such an agreement with a hospital sufficiently close to the facility to make feasible the transfer between them of patients and the information referred to in paragraph (2), shall be considered to have such an agreement in effect if and for so long as such agency (or the Secretary, as the case may be) finds that to do so is in the public interest and essential to assuring extended care services for persons in the community who are eligible for payments with respect to such services under this title [42 USCS §§ 1395 et seq.].

(m) Home health services. The term "home health services" means the following items and services furnished to an individual, who is under the care of a physician, by a home health agency or by others under arrangements with them made by such agency, under a plan (for furnishing such items and services to such individual) established and periodically reviewed by a physician, which items and services are, except as provided in paragraph (7), provided on a visiting basis in a place of residence used as such individual's home—

(1) part-time or intermittent nursing care provided by or under the supervision of a registered professional nurse;

(2) physical or occupational therapy or speech-language pathology services;

(3) medical social services under the direction of a physician;

(4) to the extent permitted in regulations, part-time or intermittent services of a home health aide who has successfully completed a training program approved by the Secretary;

(5) medical supplies (including catheters, catheter supplies, ostomy bags, and supplies related to ostomy care, and a covered osteoporosis drug (as defined in subsection (kk)), but excluding other drugs and biologicals) and durable medical equipment while under such a plan;

(6) in the case of a home health agency which is affiliated or under common control with a hospital, medical services provided by an intern or resident-in-training of such hospital, under a teaching program of such hospital approved as provided in the last sentence of subsection (b); and

(7) any of the foregoing items and services which are provided on an out-patient basis, under arrangements made by the home health agency, at a hospital or skilled nursing facility, or at a rehabilitation center which meets such standards as may be prescribed in regulations, and—

(A) the furnishing of which involves the use of equipment of such a nature that the items and services cannot readily be made available to the individual in such place of residence, or

(B) which are furnished at such facility while he is there to receive any such item or service described in clause (A),

but not including transportation of the individual in connection with any such item or service;

excluding, however, any item or service if it would not be included under subsection (b) if furnished to an inpatient of a hospital. For purposes of paragraphs (1) and (4), the term "part-time or intermittent services" means skilled nursing and home health aide services furnished any number of days per week as long as they are furnished (combined) less than 8 hours each day and 28 or fewer hours each week (or, subject to review on a case-by-case basis as to the need for care, less than 8 hours each day and 35 or fewer hours per week). For purposes of sections 1814(a)(2)(C) and 1835(a)(2)(A) [42 USCS §§ 1395f(a)(2)(C) and 1395n(a)(2)(A)], "intermittent" means skilled nursing care that is either provided or needed on fewer than 7 days each week, or less than 8 hours of each day for periods of 21 days or less (with extensions in exceptional circumstances when the need for additional care is finite and predictable).

(n) Durable medical equipment. The term "durable medical equipment" includes iron lungs, oxygen tents, hospital beds, and wheelchairs (which may include a power-operated vehicle that may be appropriately used as a wheelchair, but only where the use of such a vehicle is determined to be necessary on the basis of the individual's medical and physical condition and the vehicle meets such safety requirements as the Secretary may prescribe) used in the patient's home (including an institution used as his home other than an institution that meets the requirements of subsection (e)(1) of this section or of section 1819(a)(1) [42 USCS § 1395i-3(a)(1)]), whether furnished on a rental basis or purchased, and includes blood-testing strips and blood glucose monitors for individuals with diabetes without regard to whether the individual has Type I or Type II diabetes or to the individual's use of insulin (as determined under standards established by the Secretary in consultation with the appropriate organizations); except that such term does not include such equipment furnished by a supplier who has used, for the demonstration and use of specific equipment, an individual who has not met such minimum training standards as the Secretary may establish with respect to the demonstration and use of such specific equipment. With respect to a seat-lift chair, such term includes only the seat-lift mechanism and does not include the chair.

(o) Home health agency. The term "home health agency" means a public agency or private organization, or a subdivision of such an agency or organization, which—

(1) is primarily engaged in providing skilled nursing services and other therapeutic services;

(2) has policies, established by a group of professional personnel (associated with the agency or organization), including one or more physicians and one or more registered professional nurses, to govern the services (referred to in paragraph (1)) which it provides, and provides for supervision of such services by a physician or registered professional nurse;

(3) maintains clinical records on all patients;

(4) in the case of an agency or organization in any State in which State or applicable local law provides for the licensing of agencies or organizations of this nature, (A) is licensed pursuant to such law, or (B) is approved, by the agency of such State or locality responsible for licensing agencies or organizations of this nature, as meeting the standards established for such licensing;

(5) has in effect an overall plan and budget that meets the requirements of subsection (z);

(6) meets the conditions of participation specified in section 1891(a) [42 USCS §§ 1395bbb(a)] such other conditions of participation as the Secretary may find necessary in the interest of the health and safety of individuals who are furnished services by such agency or organization;

(7) provides the Secretary with a surety bond—

(A) effective for a period of 4 years (as specified by the Secretary) or in the case of a change in the ownership or control of the agency (as determined by the Secretary) during or after such 4-year period, an additional period of time that the Secretary determines appropriate, such additional period not to exceed 4 years from the date of such change in ownership or control;

(B) in a form specified by the Secretary; and

(C) for a year in the period described in subparagraph (A) in an amount that is equal to the lesser of $50,000 or 10 percent of the aggregate amount of payments to the agency under this title and title XIX [42 USCS §§ 1395 et seq. and 1396 et seq.] for that year, as estimated by the Secretary that the Secretary determines is commensurate with the volume of the billing of the home health agency; and

(8) meets such additional requirements (including conditions relating to bonding or establishing of escrow accounts as the Secretary finds necessary for the financial security of the program) as the Secretary finds necessary for the effective and efficient operation of the program;

except that for purposes of part A [42 USCS §§ 1395c et seq.] such term shall not include any agency or organization which is primarily for the care and treatment of mental diseases. The Secretary may waive the requirement of a surety bond under paragraph (7) in the case of an agency or organization that provides a comparable surety bond under State law.

(p) Outpatient physical therapy services. The term "outpatient physical therapy services" means physical therapy services furnished by a provider of services, a clinic, rehabilitation agency, or a public health agency, or by others under an arrangement with, and under the supervision of, such provider, clinic, rehabilitation agency, or public health agency to an individual as an outpatient—

(1) who is under the care of a physician (as defined in paragraph (1), (3), or (4) of section 1861(r) [subsec. (r) of this section]), and

(2) with respect to whom a plan prescribing the type, amount, and duration of physical therapy services that are to be furnished such individual has been established by a physician (as so defined) or by a qualified physical therapist and is periodically reviewed by a physician (as so defined);

excluding, however—

(3) any item or service if it would not be included under subsection (b) if furnished to an inpatient of a hospital; and

(4) any such service—

(A) if furnished by a clinic or rehabilitation agency, or by others under arrangements with such clinic or agency, unless such clinic or rehabilitation agency—

(i) provides an adequate program of physical therapy services for outpatients and has the facilities and personnel required for such program or required for the supervision of such a program, in accordance with such requirements as the Secretary may specify,

(ii) has policies, established by a group of professional personnel, including one or more physicians (associated with the clinic or rehabilitation agency) and one or more qualified physical therapists, to govern the services (referred to in clause (i)) it provides,

(iii) maintains clinical records on all patients,

(iv) if such clinic or agency is situated in a State in which State or applicable local law provides for the licensing of institutions of this nature, (I) is licensed pursuant to such law, or (II) is approved by the agency of such State or locality responsible for licensing institutions of this nature, as meeting the standards established for such licensing; and

(v) meets such other conditions relating to the health and safety of individuals who are furnished services by such clinic or agency on an outpatient basis, as the Secretary may find necessary, and provides the Secretary on a continuing basis with a surety bond in a form specified by the Secretary and in an amount that is not less than $50,000,or

(B) if furnished by a public health agency, unless such agency meets such other conditions relating to health and safety of individuals who are furnished services by such agency on an outpatient basis, as the Secretary may find necessary.

The term "outpatient physical therapy services" also includes physical therapy services furnished an individual by a physical therapist (in his office or in such individual's home) who meets licensing and other standards prescribed by the Secretary in regulations, otherwise than under an arrangement with and under the supervision of a provider of services, clinic, rehabilitation agency, or public health agency, if the furnishing of such services meets such conditions relating to health and safety as the Secretary may find necessary. In addition, such term includes physical therapy services which meet the requirements of the first sentence of this subsection except that they are furnished to an individual as an inpatient of a hospital or extended care facility. Nothing in this subsection shall be construed as requiring, with respect to outpatients who are not entitled to benefits under this title [42 USCS §§ 1395 et seq.], a physical therapist to provide outpatient physical therapy services only to outpatients who are under the care of a physician or pursuant to a plan of care established by a physician. The Secretary may waive the requirement of a surety bond under paragraph (4)(A)(v) in the case of a clinic or agency that provides a comparable surety bond under State law.

(q) Physicians' services. The term "physicians' services" means professional services performed by physicians, including surgery, consultation, and home, office, and institutional calls (but not including services described in subsection (b)(6)).

(r) Physician. The term "physician", when used in connection with the performance of any function or action, means (1) a doctor of medicine or osteopathy legally authorized to practice medicine and surgery by the State in which he performs such function or action (including a physician within the meaning of section 1101(a)(7) [42 USCS § 1301(a)(7)]), (2) a doctor of dental surgery or of dental medicine who is legally authorized to practice dentistry by the State in which he performs such function and who is acting within the scope of his license when he performs such functions, (3) a doctor of podiatric medicine for the purposes of subsections (k), (m), (p)(1), and (s) of this section and sections 1814(a), 1832(a)(2)(F)(ii), and 1835 [42 USCS §§ 1395f(a), 1395k(a)(2)(F)(ii), and 1395n] but only with respect to functions which he is legally authorized to perform as such by the State in which he performs them, (4) a doctor of optometry, but only for purposes of subsection (p)(1) and with respect to the provision of items or services described in subsection (s) which he is legally authorized to perform as a doctor of optometry by the State in which he performs them, or (5) a chiropractor who is licensed as such by the State (or in a State which does not license chiropractors as such, is legally authorized to perform the services of a chiropractor in the jurisdiction in which he performs such services), and who meets uniform minimum standards promulgated by the Secretary, but only for the purpose of sections 1861(s)(1) and 1861(s)(2)(A) [subsecs. (s)(1) and (s)(2)(A) of this section] and only with respect to treatment by means of manual manipulation of the spine (to correct a subluxation which he is legally authorized to perform by the State or jurisdiction in which such treatment is provided. For the purposes of section 1862(a)(4) [42 USCS § 1395y(a)(4)] and subject to the limitations and conditions provided in the previous sentence, such term includes a doctor of one of the arts, specified in such previous sentence, legally authorized to practice such art in the country in which the inpatient hospital services (referred to in such section 1862(a)(4) [42 USCS § 1395y(a)(4)] are furnished.

(s) Medical and other health services. The term "medical and other health services" means any of the following items or services:

(1) physicians' services;

(2)(A) services and supplies (including drugs and biologicals which are not usually self-administered by the patient) furnished as an incident to a physician's professional service, or kinds which are commonly furnished in physicians' offices and are commonly either rendered without charge or included in the physicians' bills (or would have been so included but for the application of section 1847B [42 USCS § 1395w-3b]);

(B) hospital services (including drugs and biologicals which are not usually self-administered by the patient) incident to physicians' services rendered to outpatients and partial hospitalization services incident to such services;

(C) diagnostic services which are—

(i) furnished to an individual as an outpatient by a hospital or by others under arrangements with them made by a hospital, and

(ii) ordinarily furnished by such hospital (or by others under such arrangements) to its outpatients for the purpose of diagnostic study;

(D) outpatient physical therapy services, outpatient speech-language pathology services, and outpatient occupational therapy services;

(E) rural health clinic services and Federally

qualified health center services;

(F) home dialysis supplies and equipment, self-care home dialysis support services, and institutional dialysis services and supplies, and, for items and services furnished on or after January 1, 2011, renal dialysis services (as defined in section 1881(b)(14)(B) [42 USCS § 1395rr(b)(14)(B)]);

(G) antigens (subject to quantity limitations prescribed in regulations by the Secretary) prepared by a physician, as defined in section 1861(r)(1) [subsec. (r)(1) of this section], for a particular patient, including antigens so prepared which are forwarded to another qualified person (including a rural health clinic) for administration to such patient, from time to time, by or under the supervision of another such physician;

(H)(i) services furnished pursuant to a contract under section 1876 [42 USCS § 1395mm] to a member of an eligible organization by a physician assistant or by a nurse practitioner (as defined in subsection (aa)(5)) and such services and supplies furnished as an incident to his service to such a member as would otherwise be covered under this part [42 USCS §§ 1395x et seq.] if furnished by a physician or as an incident to a physician's service; and

(ii) services furnished pursuant to a risk-sharing contract under section 1876(g) [42 USCS § 1395mm(g)] to a member of an eligible organization by a clinical psychologist (as defined by the Secretary) or by a clinical social worker (as defined in subsection (hh)(2)), and such services and supplies furnished as an incident to such clinical psychologist's services or clinical social worker's services to such a member as would otherwise be covered under this part [42 USCS §§ 1395x et seq.] if furnished by a physician or as an incident to a physician's service;

(I) blood clotting factors, for hemophilia patients competent to use such factors to control bleeding without medical or other supervision, and items related to the administration of such factors, subject to utilization controls deemed necessary by the Secretary for the efficient use of such factors;

(J) prescription drugs used in immunosuppressive therapy furnished, to an individual who receives an organ transplant for which payment is made under this title [42 USCS §§ 1395 et seq.];

(K)(i) services which would be physicians' services and services described in subsections (ww)(1) and (hhh) if furnished by a physician (as defined in subsection (r)(1)) and which are performed by a physician assistant (as defined in subsection (aa)(5)) under the supervision of a physician (as so defined) and which the physician assistant is legally authorized to perform by the State in which the services are performed, and such services and supplies furnished as incident to such services as would be covered under subparagraph (A) if furnished incident to a physician's professional service, but only if no facility or other provider charges or is paid any amounts with respect to the furnishing of such services, [and]

(ii) services which would be physicians' services and services described in subsections (ww)(1) and (hhh) if furnished by a physician (as defined in subsection (r)(1)) and which are performed by a nurse practitioner or clinical nurse specialist (as defined in subsection (aa)(5)) working in collaboration (as defined in subsection (aa)(6)) with a physician (as defined in subsection (r)(1)) which the nurse practitioner or clinical nurse specialist is legally authorized to perform by the State in which the services are performed, and such services and supplies furnished as an incident to such services as would be covered under subparagraph (A) if furnished incident to a physician's professional service, but only if no facility or other provider charges or is paid any amounts with respect to the furnishing of such services;

(L) certified nurse-midwife services;

(M) qualified psychologist services;

(N) clinical social worker services (as defined in subsection (hh)(2));

(O) erythropoietin for dialysis patients competent to use such drug without medical or other supervision with respect to the administration of such drug, subject to methods and standards established by the Secretary by regulation for the safe and effective use of such drug, and items related to the administration of such drug;

(P) prostate cancer screening tests (as defined in subsection (oo));

(Q) an oral drug (which is approved by the Federal Food and Drug Administration) prescribed for use as an anticancer chemotherapeutic agent for a given indication, and containing an active ingredient (or ingredients), which is the same indication and active ingredient (or ingredients) as a drug which the carrier determines would be covered pursuant to subparagraph (A) or (B) if the drug could not be self-administered;

(R) colorectal cancer screening tests (as defined in subsection (pp));

(S) diabetes outpatient self-management training services (as defined in subsection (qq));

(T) an oral drug (which is approved by the

Federal Food and Drug Administration) prescribed for use as an acute anti-emetic used as part of an anticancer chemotherapeutic regimen if the drug is administered by a physician (or as prescribed by a physician)—

(i) for use immediately before, at, or within 48 hours after the time of the administration of the anticancer chemotherapeutic agent; and

(ii) as a full replacement for the anti-emetic therapy which would otherwise be administered intravenously;

(U) screening for glaucoma (as defined in subsection (uu)) for individuals determined to be at high risk for glaucoma, individuals with a family history of glaucoma and individuals with diabetes;

(V) medical nutrition therapy services (as defined in subsection (vv)(1)) in the case of a beneficiary with diabetes or a renal disease who—

(i) has not received diabetes outpatient self-management training services within a time period determined by the Secretary;

(ii) is not receiving maintenance dialysis for which payment is made under section 1881 [42 USCS § 1395rr]; and

(iii) meets such other criteria determined by the Secretary after consideration of protocols established by dietitian or nutrition professional organizations;

(W) an initial preventive physical examination (as defined in subsection (ww));

(X) cardiovascular screening blood tests (as defined in subsection (xx)(1));

(Y) diabetes screening tests (as defined in subsection (yy));

(Z) intravenous immune globulin for the treatment of primary immune deficiency diseases in the home (as defined in subsection (zz));

(AA) ultrasound screening for abdominal aortic aneurysm (as defined in subsection (bbb)) for an individual—

(i) who receives a referral for such an ultrasound screening as a result of an initial preventive physical examination (as defined in section 1861(ww)(1) [subsec. (ww)(1) of this section]);

(ii) who has not been previously furnished such an ultrasound screening under this title [42 USCS §§ 1395 et seq.]; and

(iii) who—

(I) has a family history of abdominal aortic aneurysm; or

(II) manifests risk factors included in a beneficiary category recommended for screening by the United States Preventive Services Task Force regarding abdominal aortic aneurysms;

(BB) additional preventive services (described in subsection (ddd)(1));

(CC) items and services furnished under a cardiac rehabilitation program (as defined in subsection (eee)(1)) or under a pulmonary rehabilitation program (as defined in subsection (fff)(1));

(DD) items and services furnished under an intensive cardiac rehabilitation program (as defined in subsection (eee)(4));

(EE) kidney disease education services (as defined in subsection (ggg)); and

(FF) **[Caution: This subparagraph applies to services furnished on or after January 1, 2011, as provided by § 4103(e) of Act March 23, 2010, P. L. 111-148, which appears as 42 USCS § 1395l note.]** personalized prevention plan services (as defined in subsection (hhh));

(3) diagnostic X-ray tests (including tests under the supervision of a physician, furnished in a place of residence used as the patient's home, if the performance of such tests meets such conditions relating to health and safety as the Secretary may find necessary and including diagnostic mammography if conducted by a facility that has a certificate (or provisional certificate) issued under section 354 of the Public Health Service Act [42 USCS § 263b], diagnostic laboratory tests, and other diagnostic tests;

(4) X-ray, radium, and radioactive isotope therapy, including materials and services of technicians;

(5) surgical dressings, and splints, casts, and other devices used for reduction of fractures and dislocations;

(6) durable medical equipment;

(7) ambulance service where the use of other methods of transportation is contraindicated by the individual's condition, but, subject to section 1834(l)(14) [42 USCS § 1395m(l)(14)], only to the extent provided in regulations;

(8) prosthetic devices (other than dental) which replace all or part of an internal body organ (including colostomy bags and supplies directly related to colostomy care), including replacement of such devices, and including one pair of conventional eyeglasses or contact lenses furnished subsequent to each cataract surgery with insertion of an intraocular lens

(9) leg, arm, back, and neck braces, and artificial legs, arms, and eyes, including replacements if required because of a change in the patient's physical condition;

(10)(A) pneumococcal vaccine and its administration and subject to section 4071(b) of the Omnibus Budget Reconciliation Act of 1987 [note to this section], influenza vaccine and its administration; and

(B) hepatitis B vaccine and its administration, furnished to an individual who is at high or intermediate risk of contracting hepatitis B (as determined by the Secretary under regulations); and

(11) services of a certified registered nurse anesthetist (as defined in subsection (bb));

(12) subject to section 4072(e) of the Omnibus Budget Reconciliation Act of 1987 [note to this section], extra-depth shoes with inserts or custom molded shoes with inserts for an individual with diabetes, if—

(A) the physician who is managing the individual's diabetic condition (i) documents that the individual has peripheral neuropathy with evidence of callus formation, a history of preulcerative calluses, a history of previous ulceration, foot deformity, or previous amputation, or poor circulation, and (ii) certifies that the individual needs such shoes under a comprehensive plan of care related to the individual's diabetic condition;

(B) the particular type of shoes are prescribed by a podiatrist or other qualified physician (as established by the Secretary); and

(C) the shoes are fitted and furnished by a podiatrist or other qualified individual (such as a pedorthist or orthotist, as established by the Secretary) who is not the physician described in subparagraph (A) (unless the Secretary finds that the physician is the only such qualified individual in the area);

(13) screening mammography (as defined in subsection (jj);

(14) screening pap smear and screening pelvic exam; and

(15) bone mass measurement (as defined in subsection (rr)).

No diagnostic tests performed in any laboratory, including a laboratory that is part of a rural health clinic, or a hospital (which, for purposes of this sentence, means an institution considered a hospital for purposes of section 1814(d) [42 USCS § 1395f(d)]) shall be included within paragraph (3) unless such laboratory—

(16) if situated in any State in which State or applicable local law provides for licensing of establishments of this nature, (A) is licensed pursuant to such law, or (B) is approved, by the agency of such State or locality responsible for licensing establishments of this nature, as meeting the standards established for such licensing; and

(17)(A) meets the certification requirements under section 353 of the Public Health Service Act [42 USCS § 263a]; and

(B) meets such other conditions relating to the health and safety of individuals with respect to whom such tests are performed as the Secretary may find necessary.

There shall be excluded from the diagnostic services specified in paragraph (2)(C) any item or service (except services referred to in paragraph (1)) which would not be included under subsection (b) if it were furnished to an inpatient of a hospital. None of the items and services referred to in the preceding paragraphs (other than paragraphs (1) and (2)(A)) of this subsection which are furnished to a patient of an institution which meets the definition of a hospital for purposes of section 1814(d) [42 USCS § 1395f(d)] shall be included unless such other conditions are met as the Secretary may find necessary relating to health and safety of individuals with respect to whom such items and services are furnished.

(t) Drugs and biologicals. (1) The term "drugs" and the term "biologicals", except for purposes of subsection (m)(5) and paragraph (2) of this section, include only such drugs (including contrast agents) and biologicals, respectively, as are included (or approved for inclusion) in the United States Pharmacopoeia, the National Formulary, or the United States Homeopathic Pharmacopoeia, or in New Drugs or Accepted Dental Remedies (except for any drugs and biologicals unfavorably evaluated therein), or as are approved by the pharmacy and drug therapeutics committee (or equivalent committee) of the medical staff of the hospital furnishing such drugs and biologicals for use in such hospital.

(2)(A) For purposes of paragraph (1), the term "drugs" also includes any drugs or biologicals used in an anticancer chemotherapeutic regimen for a medically accepted indication (as described in subparagraph (B)).

(B) In subparagraph (A), the term "medically accepted indication", with respect to the use of a drug, includes any use which has been approved by the Food and Drug Administration for the drug, and includes another use of the drug if—

(i) the drug has been approved by the Food and Drug Administration; and

(ii)(I) such use is supported by one or more citations which are included (or approved for inclusion) in one or more of the following compendia: the American Hospital Formulary Service-Drug Information, the American Medical Association Drug Evaluations, the United States Pharmacopoeia-Drug Information (or its successor publications), and other authoritative compendia as identified by the Secretary, unless the Secretary has determined that the use is not medically appropriate or the use is identified as not indicated in one or more such compendia, or

(II) the carrier involved determines, based upon guidance provided by the Secretary to carriers for determining accepted uses of drugs, that such use is medically accepted based on supportive clinical evidence in peer reviewed medical literature appearing in publications which have been identified for purposes of this subclause by the Secretary.

The Secretary may revise the list of compendia in clause (ii)(I) as is appropriate for identifying medically accepted indications for drugs. On and after January 1, 2010, no compendia may be included on the list of compendia under this subparagraph unless the compendia has a publicly transparent process for evaluating therapies and for identifying potential conflicts of interests.

(u) Provider of services. The term "provider of services" means a hospital, critical access hospital, skilled nursing facility, comprehensive outpatient rehabilitation facility, home health agency, hospice program, or, for purposes of section 1814(g) [42 USCS § 1395f(g)] and section 1835(e) [42 USCS § 1395n(e)], a fund.

(v) Reasonable costs. (1)(A) The reasonable cost of any services shall be the cost actually incurred, excluding therefrom any part of incurred cost found to be unnecessary in the efficient delivery of needed health services, and shall be determined in accordance with regulations establishing the method or methods to be used, and the items to be included, in determining such costs for various types or classes of institutions, agencies, and services; except that in any case to which paragraph (2) or (3) applies, the amount of the payment determined under such paragraph with respect to the services involved shall be considered the reasonable cost of such services. In prescribing the regulations referred to in the preceding sentence, the Secretary shall consider, among other things, the principles generally applied by national organizations or established prepayment organizations (which have developed such principles) in computing the amount of payment, to be made by persons other than the recipients of services, to providers of services on account of services furnished to such recipients by such providers. Such regulations may provide for determination of the costs of services on a per diem, per unit, per capita, or other basis, may provide for using different methods in different circumstances, may provide for the use of estimates of costs of particular items or services[,] may provide for the establishment of limits on the direct or indirect overall incurred costs or incurred costs of specific items or services or groups of items or services to be recognized as reasonable based on estimates of the costs necessary in the efficient delivery of needed health services to individuals covered by the insurance programs established under this title [42 USCS §§ 1395 et seq.], and may provide for the use of charges or a percentage of charges where this method reasonably reflects the costs. Such regulations shall (i) take into account both direct and indirect costs of providers of services (excluding therefrom any such costs, including standby costs, which are determined in accordance with regulations to be unnecessary in the efficient delivery of services covered by the insurance programs established under this title [42 USCS §§ 1395 et seq.]) in order that, under the methods of determining costs, the necessary costs of efficiently delivering covered services to individuals covered by the insurance programs established by this title [42 USCS §§ 1395 et seq.] will not be borne by individuals not so covered, and the costs with respect to individuals not so covered will not be borne by such insurance programs, and (ii) provide for the making of suitable retroactive corrective adjustments where, for a provider of services for any fiscal period, the aggregate reimbursement produced by the methods of determining costs proves to be either inadequate or excessive.

(B) In the case of extended care services, the regulations under subparagraph (A) shall not include provision for specific recognition of a return on equity capital.

(C) Where a hospital has an arrangement with a medical school under which the faculty of such school provides services at such hospital, an amount not in excess of the reasonable cost of such services to the medical school shall be included in determining the reasonable cost to the hospital of furnishing services—

(i) for which payment may be made under part A [42 USCS §§ 1395c et seq.], but only if—

(I) payment for such services as furnished under such arrangement would be made under part A [42 USCS §§ 1395c et seq.] to the hospital had such services been furnished by the hospital, and

(II) such hospital pays to the medical school at least the reasonable cost of such services to the medical school, or

(ii) for which payment may be made under part B, [42 USCS §§ 1395j et seq.] but only if such hospital pays to the medical school at least the reasonable cost of such services to the medical school.

(D) Where (i) physicians furnish services which are either inpatient hospital services (including services in conjunction with the teaching programs of such hospital) by reason of paragraph (7) of subsection (b) or for which entitlement exists by reason of clause (II) of section 1832(a)(2)(B)(i) [42 USCS § 1395k(a)(2)(B)(i)(II)], and (ii) such hospital (or medical school under arrangement with such hospital) incurs no actual cost in the furnishing of such services, the reasonable cost of such services shall (under regulations of the Secretary) be deemed to be the cost such hospital or medical school would have incurred had it paid a salary to such physicians rendering such services approximately equivalent to the average salary paid to all physicians employed by such hospital (or if such employment does not exist, or is minimal in such hospital, by similar hospitals in a geographic area of sufficient size to assure reasonable inclusion of sufficient physicians in development of such average salary).

(E) Such regulations may, in the case of skilled nursing facilities in any State, provide for the use of rates, developed by the State in which such facilities are located, for the payment of the cost of skilled nursing facility services furnished under the State's plan approved under title XIX [42 USCS §§ 1396 et seq.] (and such rates may be increased by the Secretary on a class or size of institution or on a geographical basis by a percentage factor not in excess of 10 percent to take into account determinable items or services or other requirements under this title [42 USCS §§ 1395 et seq.] not otherwise included in the computation of such State rates), if the Secretary finds that such rates are reasonably related to (but not necessarily limited to) analyses undertaken by such State of costs of care in comparable facilities in such State. Notwithstanding the previous sentence, such regulations with respect to skilled nursing facilities shall take into account (in a manner consistent with subparagraph (A) and based on patient-days of services furnished) the costs (including the costs of services required to attain or maintain the highest practicable physical, mental, and psychosocial well-being of each resident eligible for benefits under this title [42 USCS §§ 1395 et seq.]) of such facilities complying with the requirements of subsections (b), (c), and (d) of section 1819 [42 USCS § 1395i-3(b), (c), and (d)] (including the costs of conducting nurse aide training and competency evaluation programs and competency evaluation programs).

(F) Such regulations shall require each provider of services (other than a fund) to make reports to the Secretary of information described in section 1121(a) [42 USCS § 1320a(a)] in accordance with the uniform reporting system (established under such section) for that type of provider.

(G)(i) In any case in which a hospital provides inpatient services to an individual that would constitute post-hospital extended care services if provided by a skilled nursing facility and a quality control and peer review organization (or, in the absence of such a qualified organization, the Secretary or such agent as the Secretary may designate) determines that inpatient hospital services for the individual are not medically necessary but post-hospital extended care services for the individual are medically necessary and such post-hospital extended care services are not otherwise available to the individual (as determined in accordance with criteria established by the Secretary) at the time of such determination, payment for such services provided to the individual shall continue to be made under this title [42 USCS §§ 1395 et seq.] at the payment rate described in clause (ii) during the period in which—

(I) such post-hospital extended care services for the individual are medically necessary and not otherwise available to the individual (as so determined),

(II) inpatient hospital services for the individual are not medically necessary, and

(III) the individual is entitled to have payment made for post-hospital extended care services under this title [42 USCS §§ 1395 et seq.],

except that if the Secretary determines that there is not an excess of hospital beds in such hospital and (subject to clause (iv), there is not an excess of hospital beds in the area of such hospital, such payment shall be made (during such period) on the basis of the amount otherwise payable under part A [42 USCS §§ 1395c et seq.] with respect to inpatient hospital services.

(ii)(I) Except as provided in subclause (II), the payment rate referred to in clause (i) is a rate equal to the estimated adjusted Statewide average rate per patient-day paid for services provided in skilled nursing facilities under the State plan approved under title XIX [42 USCS §§ 1396 et seq.] for the State in which such hospital is located, or, if the State in which the hospital is located does not have a State plan approved under title XIX [42 USCS §§ 1396 et seq.], the estimated adjusted State-wide average allowable costs per patient-day for extended care services under this title [42 USCS §§ 1395 et seq.] in that State.

(II) If a hospital has a unit which is a skilled nursing facility, the payment rate referred to in clause (i) for the hospital is a rate equal to the lesser of the rate described in subclause (I) or the allowable costs in effect under this title [42 USCS §§ 1395 et seq.] for extended care services provided to patients of such unit.

(iii) Any day on which an individual receives inpatient services for which payment is made under this subparagraph shall, for purposes of this Act (other than this subparagraph), be deemed to be a day on which the individual received inpatient hospital services.

(iv) In determining under clause (i), in the case of a public hospital, whether or not there is an excess of hospital beds in the area of such hospital, such determination shall be made on the basis of only the public hospitals (including the hospital) which are in the area of the hospital and which are under common ownership with that hospital.

(H) In determining such reasonable cost with respect to home health agencies, the Secretary may not include—

(i) any costs incurred in connection with bonding or establishing an escrow account by any such agency as a result of the surety bond requirement described in subsection (o)(7) and the financial security requirement described in subsection (o)(8);

(ii) in the case of home health agencies to which the surety bond requirement described in subsection (o)(7) and the financial security requirement described in subsection (o)(8) apply, any costs attributed to interest charged such an agency in connection with amounts borrowed by the agency to repay overpayments made under this title [42 USCS §§ 1395 et seq.] to the agency, except that such costs may be included in reasonable cost if the Secretary determines that the agency was acting in good faith in borrowing the amounts;

(iii) in the case of contracts entered into by a home health agency after the date of the enactment of this subparagraph [enacted Dec. 5, 1980] for the purpose of having services furnished for or on behalf of such agency, any cost incurred by such agency pursuant to any such contract which is entered into for a period exceeding five years; and

(iv) in the case of contracts entered into by a home health agency before the date of the enactment of this subparagraph [enacted Dec. 5, 1980] for the purpose of having services furnished for or on behalf of such agency, any cost incurred by such agency pursuant to any such contract, which determines the amount payable by the home health agency on the basis of a percentage of the agency's reimbursement or claim for reimbursement for services furnished by the agency, to the extent that such cost exceeds the reasonable value of the services furnished on behalf of such agency.

(I) In determining such reasonable cost, the Secretary may not include any costs incurred by a provider with respect to any services furnished in connection with matters for which payment may be made under this title [42 USCS §§ 1395 et seq.] and furnished pursuant to a contract between the provider and any of its subcontractors which is entered into after the date of the enactment of this subparagraph [enacted Dec. 5, 1980] and the value or cost of which is $10,000 or more over a twelve-month period unless the contract contains a clause to the effect that—

(i) until the expiration of four years after the furnishing of such services pursuant to such contract, the subcontractor shall make available, upon written request by the Secretary, or upon request by the Comptroller General, or any of their duly authorized representatives, the contract, and books, documents and records of such subcontractor that are necessary to certify the nature and extent of such costs, and

(ii) if the subcontractor carries out any of the duties of the contract through a subcontract, with a value or cost of $10,000 or more over a twelve-month period, with a related organization, such subcontract shall contain a clause to the effect that until the expiration of four years after the furnishing of such services pursuant to such subcontract, the related organization shall make available, upon written request by the Secretary, or upon request by the Comptroller General, or any of their duly authorized representatives, the subcontract, and books, documents and records of such organization that are necessary to verify the nature and extent of such costs.

The Secretary shall prescribe in regulation [regulations] criteria and procedures which the Secretary shall use in obtaining access to books, documents, and records under clauses required in contracts and subcontracts under this subparagraph.

(J) Such regulations may not provide for any inpatient routine salary cost differential as a reimbursable cost for hospitals and skilled nursing facilities.

(K)(i) The Secretary shall issue regulations that provide, to the extent feasible, for the establishment of limitations on the amount of any costs or charges that shall be considered reasonable with respect to services provided on an outpatient basis by hospitals (other than bona fide emergency services as defined in clause (ii), or clinics (other than rural health clinics), which are reimbursed on a cost basis or on the basis of cost related charges, and by physicians utilizing such outpatient facilities. Such limitations shall be reasonably related to the charges in the same area for similar services provided in physicians' offices. Such regulations shall provide for exceptions to such limitations in cases where similar services are not generally available in physicians' offices in the area to individuals entitled to benefits under this title [42 USCS §§ 1395 et seq.].

(ii) For purposes of clause (i), the term "bona fide emergency services" means services provided in a hospital emergency room after the sudden onset of a medical condition manifesting itself by acute symptoms of sufficient severity (including severe pain) such that the absence of immediate medical attention could reasonably be expected to result in—

(I) placing the patient's health in serious jeopardy;

(II) serious impairment to bodily functions; or

(III) serious dysfunction of any bodily organ or part.

(L)(i) The Secretary, in determining the amount of the payments that may be made under this title [42 USCS §§ 1395 et seq.] with respect to services furnished by home health agencies, may not recognize as reasonable (in the efficient delivery of such services) costs for the provision of such services by an agency to the extent these costs exceed (on the aggregate for the agency) for cost reporting periods beginning on or after—

(I) July 1, 1985, and before July 1, 1986, 120 percent of the mean of the labor-related and nonlabor per visit costs for freestanding home health agencies,

(II) July 1, 1986, and before July 1, 1987, 115 percent of such mean,

(III) July 1, 1987, and before October 1, 1997, 112 percent of such mean,

(IV) October 1, 1997, and before October 1, 1998, 105 percent of the median of the labor-related and nonlabor per visit costs for freestanding home health agencies, or

(V) October 1, 1998, 106 percent of such median.

(ii) Effective for cost reporting periods beginning on or after July 1, 1986, such limitations shall be applied on an aggregate basis for the agency, rather than on a discipline specific basis. The Secretary may provide for such exemptions and exceptions to such limitation as he deems appropriate.

(iii) Not later than July 1, 1991, and annually thereafter (but not for cost reporting periods beginning on or after July 1, 1994, and before July 1, 1996, or on or after July 1, 1997, and before October 1, 1997), the Secretary shall establish limits under this subparagraph for cost reporting periods beginning on or after such date by utilizing the area wage index applicable under section 1886(d)(3)(E) [42 USCS § 1395ww(d)(3)(E)] and determined using the survey of the most recent available wages and wage-related costs of hospitals located in the geographic area in which the home health service is furnished (determined without regard to whether such hospitals have been reclassified to a new geographic area pursuant to section 1886(d)(8)(B) [42 USCS § 1395ww(d)(8)(B)], a decision of the Medicare Geographic Classification Review Board under section 1886(d)(10) [42 USCS § 1395ww(d)(10)], or a decision of the Secretary).

(iv) In establishing limits under this subparagraph for cost reporting periods beginning after September 30, 1997, the Secretary shall not take into account any changes in the home health market basket, as determined by the Secretary, with respect to cost reporting periods which began on or after July 1, 1994, and before July 1, 1996.

(v) For services furnished by home health agencies for cost reporting periods beginning on or after October 1, 1997, subject to clause (viii)(I), the Secretary shall provide for an interim system of limits. Payment shall not exceed the costs determined under the preceding provisions of this subparagraph or, if lower, the product of—

(I) an agency-specific per beneficiary annual limitation calculated based 75 percent on 98 percent of the reasonable costs (including nonroutine medical supplies) for the agency's 12-month cost reporting period ending during fiscal year 1994, and based 25 percent on 98 percent of the standardized regional average of such costs for the agency's census division, as applied to such agency, for cost reporting periods ending during fiscal year 1994, such costs updated by the home health market basket index; and

(II) the agency's unduplicated census count of patients (entitled to benefits under this title [42 USCS §§ 1395 et seq.]) for the cost reporting period subject to the limitation.

(vi) For services furnished by home health agencies for cost reporting periods beginning on or after October 1, 1997, the following rules apply:

(I) For new providers and those providers without a 12-month cost reporting period ending in fiscal year 1994 subject to clauses (viii)(II) and (viii)(III), the per beneficiary limitation shall be equal to the median of these limits (or the Secretary's best estimates thereof) applied to other home health agencies as determined by the Secretary. A home health agency that has altered its corporate structure or name shall not be considered a new provider for this purpose.

(II) For beneficiaries who use services furnished by more than one home health agency, the per beneficiary limitations shall be prorated among the agencies.

(vii)(I) Not later than January 1, 1998, the Secretary shall establish per visit limits applicable for fiscal year 1998, and not later than April 1, 1998, the Secretary shall establish per beneficiary limits under clause (v)(I) for fiscal year 1998.

(II) Not later than August 1 of each year (beginning in 1998) the Secretary shall establish the limits applicable under this subparagraph for services furnished during the fiscal year beginning October 1 of the year.

(viii)(I) In the case of a provider with a 12-month cost reporting period ending in fiscal year 1994, if the limit imposed under clause (v) (determined without regard to this subclause) for a cost reporting period beginning during or after fiscal year 1999 is less than the median described in clause (vi)(I) (but determined as if any reference in clause (v) to "98 percent" were a reference to "100 percent"), the limit otherwise imposed under clause (v) for such provider and period shall be increased by ⅓ of such difference.

(II) Subject to subclause (IV), for new providers and those providers without a 12-month cost reporting period ending in fiscal year 1994, but for which the first cost reporting period begins before fiscal year 1999, for cost reporting periods beginning during or after fiscal year 1999, the per beneficiary limitation described in clause (vi)(I) shall be equal to the median described in such clause (determined as if any reference in clause (v) to "98 percent" were a reference to "100 percent").

(III) Subject to subclause (IV), in the case of a new provider for which the first cost reporting period begins during or after fiscal year 1999, the limitation applied under clause (vi)(I) (but only with respect to such provider) shall be equal to 75 percent of the median described in clause (vi)(I).

(IV) In the case of a new provider or a provider without a 12-month cost reporting period ending in fiscal year 1994, subclause (II) shall apply, instead of subclause (III), to a home health agency which filed an application for home health agency provider status under this title [42 USCS §§ 1395 et seq.] before September 15, 1998, or which was approved as a branch of its parent agency before such date and becomes a subunit of the parent agency or a separate agency on or after such date.

(V) Each of the amounts specified in subclauses (I) through (III) are such amounts as adjusted under clause (iii) to reflect variations in wages among different areas.

(ix) Notwithstanding the per beneficiary limit under clause (viii), if the limit imposed under clause (v) (determined without regard to this clause) for a cost reporting period beginning during or after fiscal year 2000 is less than the median described in clause (vi)(I) (but determined as if any reference in clause (v) to "98 percent" were a reference to "100 percent"), the limit otherwise imposed under clause (v) for such provider and period shall be increased by 2 percent.

(x) Notwithstanding any other provision of this subparagraph, in updating any limit under this subparagraph by a home health market basket index for cost reporting periods beginning during each of fiscal years 2000, 2002, and 2003, the update otherwise provided shall be reduced by 1.1 percentage points. With respect to cost reporting periods beginning during fiscal year 2001, the update to any limit under this subparagraph shall be the home health market basket index.

(M) Such regulations shall provide that costs respecting care provided by a provider of services, pursuant to an assurance under title VI or XVI of the Public Health Service Act [42 USCS §§ 291 et seq. or 300q et seq.] that the provider will make available a reasonable volume of services to persons unable to pay therefor, shall not be allowable as reasonable costs.

(N) In determining such reasonable costs, costs incurred for activities directly related to influencing employees respecting unionization may not be included.

(O)(i) In establishing an appropriate allowance for depreciation and for interest on capital indebtedness with respect to an asset of a provider of services which has undergone a change of ownership, such regulations shall provide, except as provided in clause (iii), that the valuation of the asset after such change of ownership shall be the historical cost of the asset, as recognized under this title [42 USCS §§ 1395 et seq.], less depreciation allowed, to the owner of record as of the date of enactment of the Balanced Budget Act of 1997 [enacted August 5, 1997] (or, in the case of an asset not in existence as of that date, the first owner of record of the asset after that date).

(ii) Such regulations shall not recognize, as reasonable in the provision of health care services, costs (including legal fees, accounting and administrative costs, travel costs, and the costs of feasibility studies) attributable to the negotiation or settlement of the sale or purchase of any capital asset (by acquisition or merger) for which any payment has previously been made under this title [42 USCS §§ 1395 et seq.].

(iii) In the case of the transfer of a hospital from ownership by a State to ownership by a nonprofit corporation without monetary consideration, the basis for capital allowances to the new owner shall be the book value of the hospital to the State at the time of the transfer.

(P) If such regulations provide for the payment for a return on equity capital (other than with respect to costs of inpatient hospital services), the rate of return to be recognized, for determining the reasonable cost of services furnished in a cost reporting period, shall be equal to the average of the rates of interest, for each of the months any part of which is included in the period, on obligations issued for purchase by the Federal Hospital Insurance Trust Fund.

(Q) Except as otherwise explicitly authorized, the Secretary is not authorized to limit the rate of increase on allowable costs of approved medical educational activities.

(R) In determining such reasonable cost, costs incurred by a provider of services representing a beneficiary in an unsuccessful appeal of a determination described in section 1869(b) [42 USCS § 1395ff(b)] shall not be allowable as reasonable costs.

(S)(i) Such regulations shall not include provision for specific recognition of any return on equity capital with respect to hospital outpatient departments.

(ii)(I) Such regulations shall provide that, in determining the amount of the payments that may be made under this title [42 USCS §§ 1395 et seq.] with respect to all the capital-related costs of outpatient hospital services, the Secretary shall reduce the amounts of such payments otherwise established under this title [42 USCS §§ 1395 et seq.] by 15 percent for payments attributable to portions of cost reporting periods occurring during fiscal year 1990, by 15 percent for payments attributable to portions of cost reporting periods occurring during fiscal year 1991, and by 10 percent for payments attributable to portions of cost reporting periods occurring during fiscal years 1992 through 1999 and until the first date that the prospective payment system under section 1833(t) [42 USCS § 1395l(t)] is implemented.

(II) The Secretary shall reduce the reasonable cost of outpatient hospital services (other than the capital-related costs of such services) otherwise determined pursuant to section 1833(a)(2)(B)(i)(I) [42 USCS § 1395l(a)(2)(B)(i)(I)] by 5.8 percent for payments attributable to portions of cost reporting periods occurring during fiscal years 1991 through 1999 and until the first date that the prospective payment system under section 1833(t) [42 USCS § 1395l(t)] is implemented.

(III) Subclauses (I) and (II) shall not apply to payments with respect to the costs of hospital out-patient services provided by any hospital that is a sole community hospital (as defined in section 1886(d)(5)(D)(iii) [42 USCS § 1395ww(d)(5)(D)(iii)]) or a critical access hospital (as defined in section 1861(mm)(1) [subsec. (mm)(1) of this section]).

(IV) In applying subclauses (I) and (II) to services for which payment is made on the basis of a blend amount under section 1833(i)(3)(A)(ii) or 1833(n)(1)(A)(ii) [42 USCS § 1395l(i)(3)(A)(ii) or (n)(1)(A)(ii)], the costs reflected in the amounts described in sections 1833(i)(3)(B)(i)(I) and 1833(n)(1)(B)(i)(I) [42 USCS § 1395l(i)(3)(B)(i)(I) and (n)(1)(B)(i)(I)], respectively, shall be reduced in accordance with such subclause [subclauses].

(T) In determining such reasonable costs for hospitals, no reduction in copayments under section 1833(t)(8)(B) [42 USCS § 1395l(t)(8)(B)] shall be treated as a bad debt and the amount of bad debts otherwise treated as allowable costs which are attributable to the deductibles and coinsurance amounts under this title [42 USCS §§ 1395 et seq.] shall be reduced—

(i) for cost reporting periods beginning during fiscal year 1998, by 25 percent of such amount otherwise allowable,

(ii) for cost reporting periods beginning during fiscal year 1999, by 40 percent of such amount otherwise allowable,

(iii) for cost reporting periods beginning during fiscal year 2000, by 45 percent of such amount otherwise allowable, and

(iv) for cost reporting periods beginning during a subsequent fiscal year, by 30 percent of such amount otherwise allowable.

(U) In determining the reasonable cost of ambulance services (as described in subsection (s)(7)) provided during fiscal year 1998, during fiscal year 1999, and during so much of fiscal year 2000 as precedes January 1, 2000, the Secretary shall not recognize the costs per trip in excess of costs recognized as reasonable for ambulance services provided on a per trip basis during the previous fiscal year (after application of this subparagraph), increased by the percentage increase in the consumer price index for all urban consumers (U.S. city average) as estimated by the Secretary for the 12-month period ending with the midpoint of the fiscal year involved reduced by 1.0 percentage point. For ambulance services provided after June 30, 1998, the Secretary may provide that claims for such services must include a code (or codes) under a uniform coding system specified by the Secretary that identifies the services furnished.

(V) In determining such reasonable costs for skilled nursing facilities with respect to cost reporting periods beginning on or after October 1, 2005, the amount of bad debts otherwise treated as allowed costs which are attributable to the coinsurance amounts under this title [42 USCS §§ 1395 et seq.] for individuals who are entitled to benefits under part A [42 USCS §§ 1395c et seq.] and—

(i) are not described in section 1935(c)(6)(A)(ii) [42 USCS § 1396u-5(c)(6)(A)(ii)] shall be reduced by 30 percent of such amount otherwise allowable; and

(ii) are described in such section shall not be reduced.

(2)(A) If the bed and board furnished as part of inpatient hospital services (including inpatient tuberculosis hospital services and inpatient psychiatric hospital services) or post-hospital extended care services is in accomodations [accommodations] more expensive than semi-private accomodations [accommodations], the amount taken into account for purposes of payment under this title [42 USCS §§ 1395 et seq.] with respect to such services may not exceed the amount that would be taken into account with respect to such services if furnished in such semi-private accommodations unless the more expensive accomodations [accommodations] were required for medical reasons.

(B) Where a provider of services which has an agreement in effect under this title [42 USCS §§ 1395 et seq.] furnishes to an individual items or services which are in excess of or more expensive than the items or services with respect to which payment may be made under part A or part B [42 USCS §§ 1395c et seq. or 1395j et seq.], as the case may be, the Secretary shall take into account for purposes of payment to such provider of services only the items or services with respect to which such payment may be made.

(3) If the bed and board furnished as part of inpatient hospital services (including inpatient tuberculosis hospital services and inpatient psychiatric hospital services) or post-hospital extended care services is in accommodations other than, but not more expensive than, semi-private accommodations and the use of such other accommodations rather than semi-private accommodations was neither at the request of the patient nor for a reason which the Secretary determines is consistent with the purposes of this title [42 USCS §§ 1395 et seq.], the amount of the payment with respect to such bed and board under part A [42 USCS §§ 1395c et seq.] shall be the amount otherwise payable under this title [42 USCS §§ 1395 et seq.] for such bed and board furnished in semi-private accommodations minus the difference between the charge customarily made by the hospital or skilled nursing facility for bed and board in semi-private accommodations and the charge customarily made by it for bed and board in the accommodations furnished.

(4) If a provider of services furnishes items or services to an individual which are in excess of or more expensive than the items or services determined to be necessary in the efficient delivery of needed health services and charges are imposed for such more expensive items or services under the authority granted in section 1866(a)(2)(B)(ii), the amount of payment with respect to such items or services otherwise due such provider in any fiscal period shall be reduced to the extent that such payment plus such charges exceed the cost actually incurred for such items or services in the fiscal period in which such charges are imposed.

(5)(A) Where physical therapy services, occupational therapy services, speech therapy services, or other therapy services or services of other health-related personnel (other than physicians) are furnished under an arrangement with a provider of services or other organization, specified in the first sentence of subsection (p) (including through the operation of subsection (g)) the amount included in any payment to such provider or other organization under this title [42 USCS §§ 1395 et seq.] as the reasonable cost of such services (as furnished under such arrangements) shall not exceed an amount equal to the salary which would reasonably have been paid for such services (together with any additional costs that would have been incurred by the provider or other organization) to the person performing them if they had been performed in an employment relationship with such provider or other organization (rather than under such arrangement) plus the cost of such other expenses (including a reasonable allowance for traveltime and other reasonable types of expense related to any differences in acceptable methods of organization for the provision of such therapy) incurred by such person, as the Secretary may in regulations determine to be appropriate.

(B) Notwithstanding the provisions of subparagraph (A), if a provider of services or other organization specified in the first sentence of section 1861(p) [subsec. (p) of this section] requires the services of a therapist on a limited part-time basis, or only to perform intermittent services, the Secretary may make payment on the basis of a reasonable rate per unit of service, even though such rate is greater per unit of time than salary related amounts, where he finds that such greater payment is, in the aggregate, less than the amount that would have been paid if such organization had employed a therapist on a full- or part-time salary basis.

(6) For purposes of this subsection, the term "semi-private accommodations" means two-bed, three-bed, or four-bed accommodations.

(7)(A) For limitation on Federal participation for capital expenditures which are out of conformity with a comprehensive plan of a State or areawide planning agency, see section 1122 [42 USCS § 1320a-1].

(B) For further limitations on reasonable cost and determination of payment amounts for operating costs of inpatient hospital services and waivers for certain States, see section 1886 [42 USCS § 1395ww].

(C) For provisions restricting payment for provider-based physicians' services and for payments under certain percentage arrangements, see section 1887 [42 USCS § 1395xx].

(D) For further limitations on reasonable cost and determination of payment amounts for routine service costs of skilled nursing facilities, see subsections (a) through (c) of section 1888 [42 USCS §§ 1395yy(a)–(c)].

(8) Items unrelated to patient care. Reasonable costs do not include costs for the following—

(i) entertainment, including tickets to sporting and other entertainment events;

(ii) gifts or donations;

(iii) personal use of motor vehicles;

(iv) costs for fines and penalties resulting from violations of Federal, State, or local laws; and

(v) education expenses for spouses or other dependents of providers of services, their employees or contractors.

(w) Arrangements for certain services; payments pursuant to arrangements for utilization review activities. (1) The term "arrangements" is limited to arrangements under which receipt of payment by the hospital, critical access hospital, skilled nursing facility, home health agency, or hospice program (whether in its own right or as agent), with respect to services for which an individual is entitled to have payment made under this title [42 USCS §§ 1395 et seq.], discharges the liability of such individual or any other person to pay for the services.

(2) Utilization review activities conducted, in accordance with the requirements of the program established under part B of title XI of the Social Security Act [42 USCS §§ 1320c et seq.] with respect to services furnished by a hospital or critical access hospital to patients insured under part A of this title [42 USCS §§ 1395c et seq.] or entitled to have payment made for such services under part B of this title [42 USCS § 1395j et seq.] or under a State plan approved under title XIX [42 USCS §§ 1396 et seq.] by a quality control and peer review organization designated for the area in which such hospital or critical access hospital is located shall be deemed to have been conducted pursuant to arrangements between such hospital or critical access hospital and such organization under which such hospital or critical access hospital is obligated to pay to such organization, as a condition of receiving payment for hospital or critical access hospital services so furnished under this part [42 USCS §§ 1395x et seq.] or under such a State plan, such amount as is reasonably incurred and requested (as determined under regulations of the Secretary) by such organization in conducting such review activities with respect to services furnished by such hospital or critical access hospital to such patients.

(x) State and United States. The terms "State" and "United States" have the meaning given to them by subsections (h) and (i), respectively, of section 210 [42 USCS § 410(h) and (i)].

(y) Extended care in religious nonmedical health care institutions. (1) The term "skilled nursing facility" also includes a religious nonmedical health care institution (as defined in subsection (ss)(1)), but only (except for purposes of subsection (a)(2)) with respect to items and services ordinarily furnished by such an institution to inpatients, and payment may be made with respect to services provided by or in such an institution only to such extent and under such conditions, limitations, and requirements (in addition to or in lieu of the conditions, limitations, and requirements otherwise applicable) as may be provided in regulations consistent with section 1821 [42 USCS § 1395i-5].

(2) Notwithstanding any other provision of this title [42 USCS §§ 1395 et seq.], payment under part A [42 USCS §§ 1395c et seq.] may not be made for services furnished an individual in a skilled nursing facility to which paragraph (1) applies unless such individual elects, in accordance with regulations, for a spell of illness to have such services treated as post-hospital extended care services for purposes of such part [42 USCS §§ 1395c et seq.]; and payment under part A [42 USCS §§ 1395c et seq.] may not be made for extended care services—

(A) furnished an individual during such spell of illness in a skilled nursing facility to which paragraph (1) applies after—

(i) such services have been furnished to him in such a facility for 30 days during such spell, or

(ii) such services have been furnished to him during such spell in a skilled nursing facility to which such paragraph does not apply; or

(B) furnished an individual during such spell of illness in a skilled nursing facility to which paragraph (1) does not apply after such services have been furnished to him during such spell in a skilled nursing facility to which such paragraph applies.

(3) The amount payable under part A [42 USCS §§ 1395c et seq.] for post-hospital extended care services furnished an individual during any spell of illness in a skilled nursing facility to which paragraph (1) applies shall be reduced by a coinsurance amount equal to one-eighth of the inpatient hospital deductible for each day before the 31st day on which he is furnished such services in such a facility during such spell (and the reduction under this paragraph shall be in lieu of any reduction under section 1813(a)(3) [42 USCS § 1395e(a)(3)]).

(4) For purposes of subsection (i), the determination of whether services furnished by or in an institution described in paragraph (1) constitute post-hospital extended care services shall be made in accordance with and subject to such conditions, limitations, and requirements as may be provided in regulations.

(z) Institutional planning. An overall plan and budget of a hospital, skilled nursing facility, comprehensive outpatient rehabilitation facility, or home health agency shall be considered sufficient if it—

(1) provides for an annual operating budget which includes all anticipated income and expenses related to items which would, under generally accepted accounting principles, be considered income and expense items (except that nothing in this paragraph shall require that there be prepared, in connection with any budget, an item-by-item identification of the components of each type of anticipated expenditure or income);

(2)(A) provides for a capital expenditures plan for at least a 3-year period (including the year to which the operating budget described in paragraph (1) is applicable) which includes and identifies in detail the anticipated sources of financing for, and the objectives of, each anticipated expenditures in excess of $600,000 (or such lesser amount as may be established by the State under section 1122(g)(1) [42 USCS § 1320a-1(g)(1)] in which the hospital is located) related to the acquisition of land, the improvement of land, buildings, and equipment, and the replacement, modernization, and expansion of the buildings and equipment which would, under generally accepted accounting principles, be considered capital items;

(B) provides that such plan is submitted to the agency designated under section 1122(b) [42 USCS § 1320a-1(b)], or if no such agency is designated, to the appropriate health planning agency in the State (but this subparagraph shall not apply in the case of a facility exempt from review under section 1122 [42 USCS § 1320a-1] by reason of section 1122(j) [42 USCS § 1320a-1(j)]);

(3) provides for review and updating at least annually; and

(4) is prepared, under the direction of the governing body of the institution or agency, by a committee consisting of representatives of the governing body, the administrative staff, and the medical staff (if any) of the institution or agency.

(aa) Rural health clinic services and Federally qualified health center services. (1) The term "rural health clinic services" means—

(A) physicians' services and such services and supplies as are covered under section 1861(s)(2)(A) [subsec. (s)(2)(A) of this section] if furnished as an incident to a physician's professional service and items and services described in section 1861(s)(10) [subsec. (s)(10) of this section],

(B) such services furnished by a physician assistant or a nurse practitioner (as defined in paragraph (5)), by a clinical psychologist (as defined by the Secretary) or by a clinical social worker (as defined in subsection (hh)(1)), and such services and supplies furnished as an incident to his service as would otherwise be covered if furnished by a physician or as an incident to a physician's service, and

(C) in the case of a rural health clinic located in an area in which there exists a shortage of home health agencies, part-time or intermittent nursing care and related medical supplies (other than drugs and biologicals) furnished by a registered professional nurse or licensed practical nurse to a homebound individual under a written plan of treatment (i) established and periodically reviewed by a physician described in paragraph (2)(B), or (ii) established by a nurse practitioner or physician assistant and periodically reviewed and approved by a physician described in paragraph (2)(B),

when furnished to an individual as an outpatient of a rural health clinic.

(2) The term "rural health clinic" means a facility which—

(A) is primarily engaged in furnishing to outpatients services described in subparagraphs (A) and (B) of paragraph (1);

(B) in the case of a facility which is not a physician-directed clinic, has an arrangement (consistent with the provisions of State and local law relative to the practice, performance, and delivery of health services) with one or more physicians (as defined in subsection (r)(1)) under which provision is made for the periodic review by such physicians of covered services furnished by physician assistants and nurse practitioners, the supervision and guidance by such physicians of physician assistants and nurse practitioners, the preparation by such physicians of such medical orders for care and treatment of clinic patients as may be necessary, and the availability of such physicians for such referral of and consultation for patients as is necessary and for advice and assistance in the management of medical emergencies; and, in the case of a physician-directed clinic, has one or more of its staff physicians perform the activities accomplished through such an arrangement;

(C) maintains clinical records on all patients;

(D) has arrangements with one or more hospitals, having agreements in effect under section 1866 [42 USCS § 1395cc], for the referral and admission of patients requiring inpatient services or such diagnostic or other specialized services as are not available at the clinic;

(E) has written policies, which are developed with the advice of (and with provision for review of such policies from time to time by) a group of professional personnel, including one or more physicians and one or more physician assistants or nurse practitioners, to govern those services described in paragraph (1) which it furnishes;

(F) has a physician, physician assistant, or nurse practitioner responsible for the execution of policies described in subparagraph (E) and relating to the provision of the clinic's services;

(G) directly provides routine diagnostic services, including clinical laboratory services, as prescribed in regulations by the Secretary, and has prompt access to additional diagnostic services from facilities meeting requirements under this title [42 USCS §§ 1395 et seq.];

(H) in compliance with State and Federal law, has available for administering to patients of the clinic at least such drugs and biologicals as are determined by the Secretary to be necessary for the treatment of emergency cases (as defined in regulations) and has appropriate procedures or arrangements for storing, administering, and dispensing any drugs and biologicals;

(I) has a quality assessment and performance improvement program, and appropriate procedures for review of utilization of clinic services, as the Secretary may specify;

(J) has a nurse practitioner, a physician assistant, or a certified nurse-midwife (as defined in subsection (gg)) available to furnish patient care services not less than 50 percent of the time the clinic operates; and

(K) meets such other requirements as the Secretary may find necessary in the interest of the health and safety of the individuals who are furnished services by the clinic.

For the purposes of this title [42 USCS §§ 1395 et seq.], such term includes only a facility which (i) is located in an area that is not an urbanized area (as defined by the Bureau of the Census) and in which there are insufficient numbers of needed health care practitioners (as determined by the Secretary), and that, within the previous 4-year period, has been designated by the chief executive officer of the State and certified by the Secretary as an area with a shortage of personal health services or designated by the Secretary either (I) as an area with a shortage of personal health services under section 330(b)(3) or 1302(7) of the Public Health Service Act, (II) as a health professional shortage area described in section

332(a)(1)(A) of that Act [42 USCS § 254e(a)(1)(A)] because of its shortage of primary medical care manpower, (III) as a high impact area described in section 329(a)(5) of that Act [42 USCS § 254b(a)(5)], or (IV) as an area which includes a population group which the Secretary determines has a health manpower shortage under section 332(a)(1)(B) of that Act [42 USCS § 256(a)(1)(B)], (ii) has filed an agreement with the Secretary by which it agrees not to charge any individual or other person for items or services for which such individual is entitled to have payment made under this title [42 USCS §§ 1395 et seq.], except for the amount of any deductible or coinsurance amount imposed with respect to such items or services (not in excess of the amount customarily charged for such items and services by such clinic), pursuant to subsections (a) and (b) of section 1833 [42 USCS § 1395l(a) and (b)], (iii) employs a physician assistant or nurse practitioner, and (iv) is not a rehabilitation agency or a facility which is primarily for the care and treatment of mental diseases. A facility that is in operation and qualifies as a rural health clinic under this title or title XIX [42 USCS §§ 1395 et seq. or 1396 et seq.] and that subsequently fails to satisfy the requirement of clause (i) shall be considered, for purposes of this title and title XIX [42 USCS §§ 1395 et seq. or 1396 et seq.], as still satisfying the requirement of such clause if it is determined, in accordance with criteria established by the Secretary in regulations, to be essential to the delivery of primary care services that would otherwise be unavailable in the geographic area served by the clinic. If a State agency has determined under section 1864(a) [42 USCS § 1395laa(a)] that a facility is a rural health clinic and the facility has applied to the Secretary for approval as such a clinic, the Secretary shall notify the facility of the Secretary's approval or disapproval not later than 60 days after the date of the State agency determination or the application (whichever is later).

(3) The term "Federally qualified health center services" means—

(A) services of the type described in subparagraphs (A) through (C) of paragraph (1) and services described in subsections (qq) and (vv); and

(B) preventive primary health services that a center is required to provide under section 330 of the Public Health Service Act [42 USCS § 254b],

when furnished to an individual as an outpatient of a Federally qualified health center by the center or by a health care professional under contract with the center and, for this purpose, any reference to a rural health clinic or a physician described in paragraph (2)(B) is deemed a reference to a Federally qualified health center or a physician at the center, respectively.

(4) The term "Federally qualified health center" means an entity which—

(A)(i) is receiving a grant under section 330 of the Public Health Service Act [42 USCS § 254b], or

(ii) (I) is receiving funding from such a grant under a contract with the recipient of such a grant, and (II) meets the requirements to receive a grant under section 330 of such Act [42 USCS § 254b];

(B) based on the recommendation of the Health Resources and Services Administration within the Public Health Service, is determined by the Secretary to meet the requirements for receiving such a grant;

(C) was treated by the Secretary, for purposes of part B [42 USCS §§ 1395j et seq.], as a comprehensive Federally funded health center as of January 1, 1990; or

(D) is an outpatient health program or facility operated by a tribe or tribal organization under the Indian Self-Determination Act or by an urban Indian organization receiving funds under title V of the Indian Health Care Improvement Act [25 USCS §§ 1651 et seq.].

(5)(A) The term "physician assistant" and the term "nurse practitioner" mean, for purposes of this title [42 USCS §§ 1395 et seq.], a physician assistant or nurse practitioner who performs such services as such individual is legally authorized to perform (in the State in which the individual performs such services) in accordance with State law (or the State regulatory mechanism provided by State law), and who meets such training, education, and experience requirements (or any combination thereof) as the Secretary may prescribe in regulations.

(B) The term "clinical nurse specialist" means, for purposes of this title, an individual who—

(i) is a registered nurse and is licensed to practice nursing in the State in which the clinical nurse specialist services are performed; and

(ii) holds a master's degree in a defined clinical area of nursing from an accredited educational institution.

(6) The term "collaboration" means a process in which a nurse practitioner works with a physician to deliver health care services within

the scope of the practitioner's professional expertise, with medical direction and appropriate supervision as provided for in jointly developed guidelines or other mechanisms as defined by the law of the State in which the services are performed.

(7)(A) The Secretary shall waive for a 1-year period the requirements of paragraph (2) that a rural health clinic employ a physician assistant, nurse practitioner or certified nurse midwife or that such clinic require such providers to furnish services at least 50 percent of the time that the clinic operates for any facility that requests such waiver if the facility demonstrates that the facility has been unable, despite reasonable efforts, to hire a physician assistant, nurse practitioner, or certified nurse-midwife in the previous 90-day period. (B) The Secretary may not grant such a waiver under subparagraph (A) to a facility if the request for the waiver is made less than 6 months after the date of the expiration of any previous such waiver for the facility, or if the facility has not yet been determined to meet the requirements (including subparagraph (J) of the first sentence of paragraph (2)) of a rural health clinic. (C) A waiver which is requested under this paragraph shall be deemed granted unless such request is denied by the Secretary within 60 days after the date such request is received.

(bb) Services of a certified registered nurse anesthetist. (1) The term "services of a certified registered nurse anesthetist" means anesthesia services and related care furnished by a certified registered nurse anesthetist (as defined in paragraph (2)) which the nurse anesthetist is legally authorized to perform as such by the State in which the services are furnished.

(2) The term "certified registered nurse anesthetist" means a certified registered nurse anesthetist licensed by the State who meets such education, training, and other requirements relating to anesthesia services and related care as the Secretary may prescribe. In prescribing such requirements the Secretary may use the same requirements as those established by a national organization for the certification of nurse anesthetists. Such term also includes, as prescribed by the Secretary, an anesthesiologist assistant.

(cc) Comprehensive outpatient rehabilitation facility services. (1) The term "comprehensive outpatient rehabilitation facility services" means the following items and services furnished by a physician or other qualified professional personnel (as defined in regulations by the Secretary) to an individual who is an outpatient of a comprehensive outpatient rehabilitation facility under a plan (for furnishing such items and services to such individual) established and periodically reviewed by a physician—

(A) physicians' services;

(B) physical therapy, occupational therapy, speech-language pathology services, and respiratory therapy;

(C) prosthetic and orthotic devices, including testing, fitting, or training in the use of prosthetic and orthotic devices;

(D) social and psychological services;

(E) nursing care provided by or under the supervision of a registered professional nurse;

(F) drugs and biologicals which cannot, as determined in accordance with regulations, be self-administered;

(G) supplies and durable medical equipment; and

(H) such other items and services as are medically necessary for the rehabilitation of the patient and are ordinarily furnished by comprehensive inpatient rehabilitation facilities,

excluding, however, any item or service if it would not be included under subsection (b) if furnished to an outpatient of a hospital. In the case of physical therapy, occupational therapy, and speech pathology services, there shall be no requirement that the item or service be furnished at any single fixed location if the item or service is furnished pursuant to such plan and payments are not otherwise made for the item or service under this title [42 USCS §§ 1395 et seq.].

(2) The term "comprehensive outpatient rehabilitation facility" means a facility which—

(A) is primarily engaged in providing (by or under the supervision of physicians) diagnostic, therapeutic, and restorative services to outpatients for the rehabilitation of injured, disabled, or sick persons;

(B) provides at least the following comprehensive outpatient rehabilitation services: (i) physicians' services (rendered by physicians, as defined in section 1861(r)(1) [subsec. (r)(1) of this section], who are available at the facility on a full- or part-time basis); (ii) physical therapy; and (iii) social or psychological services;

(C) maintains clinical records on all patients;

(D) has policies established by a group of professional personnel (associated with the facility), including one or more physicians defined in subsection (r)(1) to govern the comprehensive outpatient rehabilitation services it furnishes, and provides for the carrying out of such policies by a full- or part-time physician referred to in subparagraph (B)(i);

(E) has a requirement that every patient must be under the care of a physician;

(F) in the case of a facility in any State in which State or applicable local law provides for the licensing of facilities of this nature (i) is licensed pursuant to such law, or (ii) is approved by the agency of such State or locality, responsible for licensing facilities of this nature, as meeting the standards established for such licensing;

(G) has in effect a utilization review plan in accordance with regulations prescribed by the Secretary;

(H) has in effect an overall plan and budget that meets the requirements of subsection (z);

(I) provides the Secretary on a continuing basis with a surety bond in a form specified by the Secretary and in an amount that is not less than $50,000; and

(J) meets such other conditions of participation as the Secretary may find necessary in the interest of the health and safety of individuals who are furnished services by such facility, including conditions concerning qualifications of personnel in these facilities.

The Secretary may waive the requirement of a surety bond under subparagraph (I) in the case of a facility that provides a comparable surety bond under State law.

(dd) Hospice care; hospice program; definitions; certification; waiver by Secretary. (1) The term "hospice care" means the following items and services provided to a terminally ill individual by, or by others under arrangements made by, a hospice program under a written plan (for providing such care to such individual) established and periodically reviewed by the individual's attending physician and by the medical director (and by the interdisciplinary group described in paragraph (2)(B)) of the program—

(A) nursing care provided by or under the supervision of a registered professional nurse,

(B) physical or occupational therapy, or speech-language pathology services,

(C) medical social services under the direction of a physician,

(D) (i) services of a home health aide who has successfully completed a training program approved by the Secretary and (ii) homemaker services,

(E) medical supplies (including drugs and biologicals) and the use of medical appliances, while under such a plan,

(F) physicians' services,

(G) short-term inpatient care (including both respite care and procedures necessary for pain control and acute and chronic symptom management) in an inpatient facility meeting such conditions as the Secretary determines to be appropriate to provide such care, but such respite care may be provided only on an intermittent, nonroutine, and occasional basis and may not be provided consecutively over longer than five days,

(H) counseling (including dietary counseling) with respect to care of the terminally ill individual and adjustment to his death, and

(I) any other item or service which is specified in the plan and for which payment may otherwise be made under this title [42 USCS §§ 1395 et seq.].

The care and services described in subparagraphs (A) and (D) may be provided on a 24-hour, continuous basis only during periods of crisis (meeting criteria established by the Secretary) and only as necessary to maintain the terminally ill individual at home.

(2) The term "hospice program" means a public agency or private organization (or a subdivision thereof) which—

(A)(i) is primarily engaged in providing the care and services described in paragraph (1) and makes such services available (as needed) on a 24-hour basis and which also provides bereavement counseling for the immediate family of terminally ill individuals and services described in section 1812(a)(5) [42 USCS § 1395d(a)(5)],

(ii) provides for such care and services in individuals' homes, on an outpatient basis, and on a short-term inpatient basis, directly or under arrangements made by the agency or organization, except that—

(I) the agency or organization must routinely provide directly substantially all of each of the services described in subparagraphs (A), (C), and (H) of paragraph (1), except as otherwise provided in paragraph (5), and

(II) in the case of other services described in paragraph (1) which are not provided directly by the agency or organization, the agency or organization must maintain professional management responsibility for all such services furnished to an individual, regardless of the location or facility in which such services are furnished; and

(iii) provides assurances satisfactory to the Secretary that the aggregate number of days of inpatient care described in paragraph (1)(G) provided in any 12-month period to individuals who have an election in effect under section 1812(d) [42 USCS § 1395d(d)] with respect to that agency or organization does not exceed 20 percent of the aggregate number of days during that period on which such elections for such individuals are in effect;

(B) has an interdisciplinary group of personnel which—

(i) includes at least—

(I) one physician (as defined in subsection (r)(1)),

(II) one registered professional nurse, and

(III) one social worker,

employed by or, in the case of a physician described in subclause (I), under contract with the agency or organization, and also includes at least one pastoral or other counselor,

(ii) provides (or supervises the provision of) the care and services described in paragraph (1), and

(iii) establishes the policies governing the provision of such care and services;

(C) maintains central clinical records on all patients;

(D) does not discontinue the hospice care it provides with respect to a patient because of the inability of the patient to pay for such care;

(E) (i) utilizes volunteers in its provision of care and services in accordance with standards set by the Secretary, which standards shall ensure a continuing level of effort to utilize such volunteers, and (ii) maintains records on the use of these volunteers and the cost savings and expansion of care and services achieved through the use of these volunteers;

(F) in the case of an agency or organization in any State in which State or applicable local law provides for the licensing of agencies or organizations of this nature, is licensed pursuant to such law; and

(G) meets such other requirements as the Secretary may find necessary in the interest of the health and safety of the individuals who are provided care and services by such agency or organization.

(3)(A) An individual is considered to be "terminally ill" if the individual has a medical prognosis that the individual's life expectancy is 6 months or less.

(B) The term "attending physician" means, with respect to an individual, the physician (as defined in subsection (r)(1)) or nurse practitioner (as defined in subsection (aa)(5)), who may be employed by a hospice program, whom the individual identifies as having the most significant role in the determination and delivery of medical care to the individual at the time the individual makes an election to receive hospice care.

(4)(A) An entity which is certified as a provider of services other than a hospice program shall be considered, for purposes of certification as a hospice program, to have met any requirements under paragraph (2) which are also the same requirements for certification as such other type of provider. The Secretary shall coordinate surveys for determining certification under this title [42 USCS §§ 1395 et seq.] so as to provide, to the extent feasible, for simultaneous surveys of an entity which seeks to be certified as a hospice program and as a provider of services of another type.

(B) Any entity which is certified as a hospice program and as a provider of another type shall have separate provider agreements under section 1866 [42 USCS § 1395cc] and shall file separate cost reports with respect to costs incurred in providing hospice care and in providing other services and items under this title [42 USCS §§ 1395 et seq.].

(5)(A) The Secretary may waive the requirements of paragraph (2)(A)(ii)(I) for an agency or organization with respect to all or part of the nursing care described in paragraph (1)(A) if such agency or organization—

(i) is located in an area which is not an urbanized area (as defined by the Bureau of the Census);

(ii) was in operation on or before January 1, 1983; and

(iii) has demonstrated a good faith effort (as determined by the Secretary) to hire a sufficient number of nurses to provide such nursing care directly.

(B) Any waiver, which is in such form and containing such information as the Secretary may require and which is requested by an agency or organization under subparagraph (A) or (C), shall be deemed to be granted unless such request is denied by the Secretary within 60 days after the date such request is received by the Secretary. The granting of a waiver under subparagraph (A) or (C) shall not preclude the granting of any subsequent waiver request should such a waiver again become necessary.

(C) The Secretary may waive the requirements of paragraph (2)(A)(i) and (2)(A)(ii) for an agency or organization with respect to the services described in paragraph (1)(B) and, with respect to dietary counseling, paragraph (1)(H), if such agency or organization—

(i) is located in an area which is not an urbanized area (as defined by the Bureau of Census), and

(ii) demonstrates to the satisfaction of the Secretary that the agency or organization has been unable, despite diligent efforts, to recruit appropriate personnel.

(D) In extraordinary, exigent, or other non-routine circumstances, such as unanticipated periods of high patient loads, staffing shortages due to illness or other events, or temporary travel of a patient outside a hospice program's service area, a hospice program may enter into arrangements with another hospice program for the provision by that other program of services described in paragraph (2)(A)(ii)(I). The provisions of paragraph (2)(A)(ii)(II) shall apply with respect to the services provided under such arrangements.

(E) A hospice program may provide services described in paragraph (1)(A) other than directly by the program if the services are highly specialized services of a registered professional nurse and are provided non-routinely and so infrequently so that the provision of such services directly would be impracticable and prohibitively expensive.

(ee) Discharge planning process. (1) A discharge planning process of a hospital shall be considered sufficient if it is applicable to services furnished by the hospital to individuals entitled to benefits under this title [42 USCS §§ 1395 et seq.] and if it meets the guidelines and standards established by the Secretary under paragraph (2).

(2) The Secretary shall develop guidelines and standards for the discharge planning process in order to ensure a timely and smooth transition to the most appropriate type of and setting for post-hospital or rehabilitative care. The guidelines and standards shall include the following:

(A) The hospital must identify, at an early stage of hospitalization, those patients who are likely to suffer adverse health consequences upon discharge in the absence of adequate discharge planning.

(B) Hospitals must provide a discharge planning evaluation for patients identified under subparagraph (A) and for other patients upon the request of the patient, patient's representative, or patient's physician.

(C) Any discharge planning evaluation must be made on a timely basis to ensure that appropriate arrangements for post-hospital care will be made before discharge and to avoid unnecessary delays in discharge.

(D) A discharge planning evaluation must include an evaluation of a patient's likely need for appropriate post-hospital services, including hospice care and post-hospital extended services, and the availability of those services, including the availability of home health services through individuals and entities that participate in the program under this title [42 USCS § 1395 et seq.] and that serve the area in which the patient resides and that request to be listed by the hospital as available and, in the case of individuals who are likely to need post-hospital extended care services, the availability of such services through facilities that participate in the program under this title [42 USCS § 1395 et seq.] and that serve the area in which the patient resides.

(E) The discharge planning evaluation must be included in the patient's medical record for use in establishing an appropriate discharge plan and the results of the evaluation must be discussed with the patient (or the patient's representative).

(F) Upon the request of a patient's physician, the hospital must arrange for the development and initial implementation of a discharge plan for the patient.

(G) Any discharge planning evaluation or discharge plan required under this paragraph must be developed by, or under the supervision of, a registered professional nurse, social worker, or other appropriately qualified personnel.

(H) Consistent with section 1802 [42 USCS § 1395a], the discharge plan shall—

(i) not specify or otherwise limit the qualified provider which may provide post-hospital home health services, and

(ii) identify (in a form and manner specified by the Secretary) any entity to whom the individual is referred in which the hospital has a disclosable financial interest (as specified by the Secretary consistent with section 1866(a)(1)(S) [42 USCS § 1395cc(a)(1)(S)]) or which has such an interest in the hospital.

(3) With respect to a discharge plan for an individual who is enrolled with a Medicare+Choice organization under a Medicare+Choice plan and is furnished inpatient hospital services by a hospital under a contract with the organization—

(A) the discharge planning evaluation under paragraph (2)(D) is not required to include information on the availability of home health services through individuals and entities which do not have a contract with the organization; and

(B) notwithstanding subparagraph (H)(i) [(2)(H)(i)], the plan may specify or limit the provider (or providers) of post-hospital home health services or other post-hospital services under the plan.

(ff) Partial hospitalization services. (1) The term "partial hospitalization services" means the items and services described in paragraph (2) prescribed by a physician and provided under a program described in paragraph (3) under the supervision of a physician pursuant to an individualized, written plan of treatment established and periodically reviewed by a physician (in consultation with appropriate staff participating in such program), which plan sets forth the physician's diagnosis, the type, amount, frequency, and duration of the items and services provided under the plan, and the goals for treatment under the plan.

(2) The items and services described in this paragraph are—

(A) individual and group therapy with physicians or psychologists (or other mental health professionals to the extent authorized under State law),

(B) occupational therapy requiring the skills of a qualified occupational therapist,

(C) services of social workers, trained psychiatric nurses, and other staff trained to work with psychiatric patients,

(D) drugs and biologicals furnished for therapeutic purposes (which cannot, as determined in accordance with regulations, be self-administered),

(E) individualized activity therapies that are not primarily recreational or diversionary,

(F) family counseling (the primary purpose of which is treatment of the individual's condition),

(G) patient training and education (to the extent that training and educational activities are closely and clearly related to individual's care and treatment),

(H) diagnostic services, and

(I) such other items and services as the Secretary may provide (but in no event to include meals and transportation);

that are reasonable and necessary for the diagnosis or active treatment of the individual's condition, reasonably expected to improve or maintain the individual's condition and functional level and to prevent relapse or hospitalization, and furnished pursuant to such guidelines relating to frequency and duration of services as the Secretary shall by regulation establish (taking into account accepted norms of medical practice and the reasonable expectation of patient improvement).

(3) **[Caution: For provisions applicable to items and services furnished before April 1, 2011, see March 30, 2010 amendment note below.]** (A) A program described in this paragraph is a program which is furnished by a hospital to its outpatients or by a community mental health center (as defined in subparagraph (B)), and which is a distinct and organized intensive ambulatory treatment service offering less than 24-hour-daily care other than in an individual's home or in an inpatient or residential setting.

(B) For purposes of subparagraph (A), the term "community mental health center" means an entity that—

(i)(I) provides the mental health services described in section 1913(c)(1) of the Public Health Service Act [42 USCS § 300x-2(c)(1)]; or

(II) in the case of an entity operating in a State that by law precludes the entity from providing itself the service described in subparagraph (E) of such section, provides for such service by contract with an approved organization or entity (as determined by the Secretary);

(ii) meets applicable licensing or certification requirements for community mental health centers in the State in which it is located;

(iii) provides at least 40 percent of its services to individuals who are not eligible for benefits under this title [42 USCS §§ 1395 et seq.]; and

(iv) meets such additional conditions as the Secretary shall specify to ensure (I) the health and safety of individuals being furnished such services, (II) the effective and efficient furnishing of such services, and (III) the compliance of such entity with the criteria described in section 1931(c)(1) of the Public Health Service Act [42 USCS § 300x-31(c)(1)].

(gg) Certified nurse-midwife services. (1) The term "certified nurse-midwife services" means such services furnished by a certified nurse-midwife (as defined in paragraph (2)) and such services and supplies furnished as an incident to the nurse-midwife's service which the certified nurse-midwife is legally authorized to perform under State law (or the State regulatory mechanism provided by State law) as would otherwise be covered if furnished by a physician or as an incident to a physicians' service.

(2) The term "certified nurse-midwife" means a registered nurse who has successfully completed a program of study and clinical experience meeting guidelines prescribed by the Secretary, or has been certified by an organization recognized by the Secretary.

(hh) Clinical social worker; clinical social worker services. (1) The term "clinical social worker" means an individual who—

(A) possesses a master's or doctor's degree in social work;

(B) after obtaining such degree has performed at least 2 years of supervised clinical social work; and

(C)(i) is licensed or certified as a clinical social worker by the State in which the services are performed, or

(ii) in the case of an individual in a State which does not provide for licensure or certification—

(I) has completed at least 2 years or 3,000 hours of postmaster's degree supervised clinical social work practice under the supervision of a master's level social worker in an appropriate setting (as determined by the Secretary), and

(II) meets such other criteria as the Secretary establishes.

(2) The term "clinical social worker services" means services performed by a clinical social worker (as defined in paragraph (1)) for the diagnosis and treatment of mental illnesses (other than services furnished to an inpatient of a hospital and other than services furnished to an inpatient of a skilled nursing facility which the facility is required to provide as a requirement for participation) which the clinical social worker is legally authorized to perform under State law (or the State regulatory mechanism provided by State law) of the State in which such services are performed as would otherwise be covered if furnished by a physician or as an incident to a physician's professional service.

(ii) Qualified psychologist services. The term "qualified psychologist services" means such services and such services and supplies furnished as an incident to his service furnished by a clinical psychologist (as defined by the Secretary) which the psychologist is legally authorized to perform under State law (or the State regulatory mechanism provided by State law) as would otherwise be covered if furnished by a physician or as an incident to a physician's service.

(jj) Screening mammography. The term "screening mammography" means a radiologic procedure provided to a woman for the purpose of early detection of breast cancer and includes a physician's interpretation of the results of the procedure.

(kk) Covered osteoporosis drug. The term "covered osteoporosis drug" means an injectable drug approved for the treatment of post-menopausal osteoporosis provided to an individual by a home health agency if, in accordance with regulations promulgated by the Secretary—

(1) the individual's attending physician certifies that the individual has suffered a bone fracture related to post-menopausal osteoporosis and that the individual is unable to learn the skills needed to self-administer such drug or is otherwise physically or mentally incapable of self-administering such drug; and

(2) the individual is confined to the individual's home (except when receiving items and services referred to in subsection (m)(7)).

(ll) Speech-language pathology services; audiology services. (1) The term "speech-language pathology services" means such speech, language, and related function assessment and rehabilitation services furnished by a qualified speech-language pathologist as the speech-language pathologist is legally authorized to perform under State law (or the State regulatory mechanism provided by State law) as would otherwise be covered if furnished by a physician.

(2) The term "outpatient speech-language pathology services" has the meaning given the term "outpatient physical therapy services" in subsection (p), except that in applying such subsection—

(A) "speech-language pathology" shall be substituted for "physical therapy" each place it appears; and

(B) "speech-language pathologist" shall be substituted for "physical therapist" each place it appears.

(3) The term "audiology services" means such hearing and balance assessment services furnished by a qualified audiologist as the audiologist is legally authorized to perform under State law (or the State regulatory mechanism provided by State law), as would otherwise be covered if furnished by a physician.

(4) In this subsection:

(A) The term "qualified speech-language pathologist" means an individual with a master's or doctoral degree in speech-language pathology who—

(i) is licensed as a speech-language pathologist by the State in which the individual furnishes such services, or

(ii) in the case of an individual who furnishes services in a State which does not license speech-language pathologists, has successfully completed 350 clock hours of supervised clinical practicum (or is in the process of accumulating such supervised clinical experience), performed not less than 9 months of supervised full-time speech-language pathology services after obtaining a master's or doctoral degree in speech-language pathology or a related field, and successfully completed a national examination in speech-language pathology approved by the Secretary.

(B) The term "qualified audiologist" means an individual with a master's or doctoral degree in audiology who—

(i) is licensed as an audiologist by the State in which the individual furnishes such services, or

(ii) in the case of an individual who furnishes services in a State which does not license audiologists, has successfully completed 350 clock hours of supervised clinical practicum (or is in the process of accumulating such supervised clinical experience), performed not less than 9 months of supervised full-time audiology services after obtaining a master's or doctoral degree in audiology or a related field, and successfully completed a national examination in audiology approved by the Secretary.

(mm) Critical access hospital; critical access hospital services. (1) The term "critical access hospital" means a facility certified by the Secretary as a critical access hospital under section 1820(e) [42 USCS § 1395i-4(e)].

(2) The term "inpatient critical access hospital services" means items and services, furnished to an inpatient of a critical access hospital by such facility, that would be inpatient hospital services if furnished to an inpatient of a hospital by a hospital.

(3) The term "outpatient critical access hospital services" means medical and other health services furnished by a critical access hospital on an outpatient basis.

(nn) Screening pap smear; screening pelvic exam. (1) The term "screening pap smear" means a diagnostic laboratory test consisting of a routine exfoliative cytology test (Papanicolaou test) provided to a woman for the purpose of early detection of cervical or vaginal cancer and includes a physician's interpretation of the results of the test, if the individual involved has not had such a test during the preceding 2 years, or during the preceding year in the case of a woman described in paragraph (3).

(2) The term "screening pelvic exam" means a pelvic examination provided to a woman if the woman involved has not had such an examination during the preceding 2 years, or during the preceding year in the case of a woman described in paragraph (3), and includes a clinical breast examination.

(3) A woman described in this paragraph is a woman who—

(A) is of childbearing age and has had a test described in this subsection during any of the preceding 3 years that indicated the presence of cervical or vaginal cancer or other abnormality; or

(B) is at high risk of developing cervical or vaginal cancer (as determined pursuant to factors identified by the Secretary).

(oo) Prostate cancer screening tests. (1) The term "prostate cancer screening test" means a test that consists of any (or all) of the procedures described in paragraph (2) provided for the purpose of early detection of prostate cancer to a man over 50 years of age who has not had such a test during the preceding year.

(2) The procedures described in this paragraph are as follows:

(A) A digital rectal examination.

(B) A prostate-specific antigen blood test.

(C) For years beginning after 2002, such other procedures as the Secretary finds appropriate for the purpose of early detection of prostate cancer, taking into account changes in technology and standards of medical practice, availability, effectiveness, costs, and such other factors as the Secretary considers appropriate.

(pp) Colorectal cancer screening tests. (1) The term "colorectal cancer screening test" means any of the following procedures furnished to an individual for the purpose of early detection of colorectal cancer:

(A) Screening fecal-occult blood test.

(B) Screening flexible sigmoidoscopy.

(C) Screening colonoscopy.

(D) Such other tests or procedures, and modifications to tests and procedures under this subsection, with such frequency and payment limits, as the Secretary determines appropriate, in consultation with appropriate organizations.

(2) An "individual at high risk for colorectal cancer" is an individual who, because of family history, prior experience of cancer or precursor neoplastic polyps, a history of chronic digestive disease condition (including inflammatory bowel disease, Crohn's Disease, or ulcerative colitis), the presence of any appropriate recognized gene markers for colorectal cancer, or other predisposing factors, faces a high risk for colorectal cancer.

(qq) Diabetes outpatient self-management training services. (1) The term "diabetes outpatient self-management training services" means educational and training services furnished (at such times as the Secretary determines appropriate) to an individual with diabetes by a certified provider (as described in paragraph (2)(A)) in an outpatient setting by an individual or entity who meets the quality standards described in paragraph (2)(B), but only if the physician who is managing the individual's diabetic condition certifies that such services are needed under a comprehensive plan of care related to the individual's diabetic condition to ensure therapy compliance or to provide the individual with necessary skills and knowledge (including skills related to the self-administration of injectable drugs) to participate in the management of the individual's condition.

(2) In paragraph (1)—

(A) a "certified provider" is a physician, or other individual or entity designated by the Secretary, that, in addition to providing diabetes outpatient self-management training services, provides other items or services for which payment may be made under this title [42 USCS §§ 1395 et seq.]; and

(B) a physician, or such other individual or entity, meets the quality standards described in this paragraph if the physician, or individual or entity, meets quality standards established by the Secretary, except that the physician or other individual or entity shall be deemed to have met such standards if the physician or other individual or entity meets applicable standards originally established by the National Diabetes Advisory Board and subsequently revised by organizations who participated in the establishment of standards by such Board, or is recognized by an organization that represents individuals (including individuals under this title [42 USCS §§ 1395 et seq.]) with diabetes as meeting standards for furnishing the services.

(rr) Bone mass measurement. (1) The term "bone mass measurement" means a radiologic or radioisotopic procedure or other procedure approved by the Food and Drug Administration performed on a qualified individual (as defined in paragraph (2)) for the purpose of identifying bone mass or detecting bone loss or determining bone quality, and includes a physician's interpretation of the results of the procedure.

(2) For purposes of this subsection, the term "qualified individual" means an individual who is (in accordance with regulations prescribed by the Secretary)—

(A) an estrogen-deficient woman at clinical risk for osteoporosis;

(B) an individual with vertebral abnormalities;

(C) an individual receiving long-term glucocorticoid steroid therapy;

(D) an individual with primary hyperparathyroidism; or

(E) an individual being monitored to assess the response to or efficacy of an approved osteoporosis drug therapy.

(3) The Secretary shall establish such standards regarding the frequency with which a qualified individual shall be eligible to be provided benefits for bone mass measurement under this title [42 USCS §§ 1395 et seq.]. Religious Nonmedical Health Care Institution

(ss) Religious nonmedical health care institution. (1) The term "religious nonmedical health care institution" means an institution that—

(A) is described in subsection (c)(3) of section 501 of the Internal Revenue Code of 1986 [26 USCS § 501(c)(3)] and is exempt from taxes under subsection (a) of such section;

(B) is lawfully operated under all applicable Federal, State, and local laws and regulations;

(C) provides only nonmedical nursing items and services exclusively to patients who choose to rely solely upon a religious method of healing and for whom the acceptance of medical health services would be inconsistent with their religious beliefs;

(D) provides such nonmedical items and services exclusively through nonmedical nursing personnel who are experienced in caring for the physical needs of such patients;

(E) provides such nonmedical items and services to inpatients on a 24-hour basis;

(F) on the basis of its religious beliefs, does not provide through its personnel or otherwise medical items and services (including any medical screening, examination, diagnosis, prognosis, treatment, or the administration of drugs) for its patients;

(G)(i) is not owned by, under common ownership with, or has an ownership interest in, a provider of medical treatment or services;

(ii) is not affiliated with—

(I) a provider of medical treatment or services, or

(II) an individual who has an ownership interest in a provider of medical treatment or services;

(H) has in effect a utilization review plan which—

(i) provides for the review of admissions to the institution, of the duration of stays therein, of cases of continuous extended duration, and of the items and services furnished by the institution,

(ii) requires that such reviews be made by an appropriate committee of the institution that includes the individuals responsible for overall administration and for supervision of nursing personnel at the institution,

(iii) provides that records be maintained of the meetings, decisions, and actions of such committee, and

(iv) meets such other requirements as the Secretary finds necessary to establish an effective utilization review plan;

(I) provides the Secretary with such information as the Secretary may require to implement section 1821 [42 USCS § 1395i-5], including information relating to quality of care and coverage determinations; and

(J) meets such other requirements as the Secretary finds necessary in the interest of the health and safety of individuals who are furnished services in the institution.

(2) To the extent that the Secretary finds that the accreditation of an institution by a State, regional, or national agency or association provides reasonable assurances that any or all of the requirements of paragraph (1) are met or exceeded, the Secretary may treat such institution as meeting the condition or conditions with respect to which the Secretary made such finding.

(3)(A) (i) In administering this subsection and section 1821 [42 USCS § 1395i-5], the Secretary shall not require any patient of a religious nonmedical health care institution to undergo medical screening, examination, diagnosis, prognosis, or treatment or to accept any other medical health care service, if such patient (or legal representative of the patient) objects thereto on religious grounds.

(ii) Clause (i) shall not be construed as preventing the Secretary from requiring under section 1821(a)(2) [42 USCS § 1395i-5(a)(2)] the provision of sufficient information regarding an individual's condition as a condition for receipt of benefits under part A [42 USCS §§ 1395c et seq.] for services provided in such an institution.

(B)(i) In administering this subsection and section 1821 [42 USCS § 1395i-5], the Secretary shall not subject a religious nonmedical health care institution or its personnel to any medical supervision, regulation, or control, insofar as such supervision, regulation, or control would be contrary to the religious beliefs observed by the institution or such personnel.

(ii) Clause (i) shall not be construed as preventing the Secretary from reviewing items and services billed by the institution to the extent the Secretary determines such review to be necessary to determine whether such items and services were not covered under part A [42 USCS §§ 1395c et seq.], are excessive, or are fraudulent.

(4)(A) For purposes of paragraph (1)(G)(i), an ownership interest of less than 5 percent shall not be taken into account.

(B) For purposes of paragraph (1)(G)(ii), none of the following shall be considered to create an affiliation:

(i) An individual serving as an uncompensated director, trustee, officer, or other member of the governing body of a religious nonmedical health care institution.

(ii) An individual who is a director, trustee, officer, employee, or staff member of a religious nonmedical health care institution having a family relationship with an individual who is affiliated with (or has an ownership interest in) a provider of medical treatment or services.

(iii) An individual or entity furnishing goods or services as a vendor to both providers of medical treatment or services and religious nonmedical health care institutions.

(tt) Post-institutional home health services; home health spell of illness. (1) The term "post-institutional home health services" means home health services furnished to an individual—

(A) after discharge from a hospital or critical access hospital in which the individual was an inpatient for not less than 3 consecutive days before such discharge if such home health services were initiated within 14 days after the date of such discharge; or

(B) after discharge from a skilled nursing facility in which the individual was provided post-hospital extended care services if such home health services were initiated within 14 days after the date of such discharge.

(2) The term "home health spell of illness" with respect to any individual means a period of consecutive days—

(A) beginning with the first day (not included in a previous home health spell of illness) (i) on which such individual is furnished post-institutional home health services, and (ii) which occurs in a month for which the individual is entitled to benefits under part A [42 USCS §§ 1395c et seq.], and

(B) ending with the close of the first period of 60 consecutive days thereafter on each of which the individual is neither an inpatient of a hospital or critical access hospital nor an inpatient of a facility described in section 1819(a)(1) [42 USCS § 1395i-3(a)(1)] or subsection (y)(1) nor provided home health services.

(uu) Screening for glaucoma. The term "screening for glaucoma" means a dilated eye examination with an intraocular pressure measurement, and a direct ophthalmoscopy or a slit-lamp biomicroscopic examination for the early detection of glaucoma which is furnished by or under the direct supervision of an optometrist or ophthalmologist who is legally authorized to furnish such services under State law (or the State regulatory mechanism provided by State law) of the State in which the services are furnished, as would otherwise be covered if furnished by a physician or as an incident to a physician's professional service, if the individual involved has not had such an examination in the preceding year.

(vv) Medical nutrition therapy services; registered dietitian or nutrition professional. (1) The term "medical nutrition therapy services" means nutritional diagnostic, therapy, and counseling services for the purpose of disease management which are furnished by a registered dietitian or nutrition professional (as defined in paragraph (2)) pursuant to a referral by a physician (as defined in subsection (r)(1)).

(2) Subject to paragraph (3), the term "registered dietitian or nutrition professional" means an individual who—

(A) holds a baccalaureate or higher degree granted by a regionally accredited college or university in the United States (or an equivalent foreign degree) with completion of the academic requirements of a program in nutrition or dietetics, as accredited by an appropriate national accreditation organization recognized by the Secretary for this purpose;

(B) has completed at least 900 hours of supervised dietetics practice under the supervision of a registered dietitian or nutrition professional; and

(C)(i) is licensed or certified as a dietitian or nutrition professional by the State in which the services are performed; or

(ii) in the case of an individual in a State that does not provide for such licensure or certification, meets such other criteria as the Secretary establishes.

(3) Subparagraphs (A) and (B) of paragraph (2) shall not apply in the case of an individual who, as of the date of the enactment of this subsection [enacted Dec. 21, 2000], is licensed or certified as a dietitian or nutrition professional by the State in which medical nutrition therapy services are performed.

(ww) Initial preventive physical examination. (1) The term "initial preventive physical examination" means physicians' services consisting of a physical examination (including measurement of height, weight[,] body mass index,[,] and blood pressure) with the goal of health promotion and disease detection and includes education, counseling, and referral with respect to screening and other preventive services described in paragraph (2) and end-of-life planning (as defined in paragraph (3)) upon the agreement with the individual, but does not include clinical laboratory tests.

(2) The screening and other preventive services described in this paragraph include the following:

(A) Pneumococcal, influenza, and hepatitis B vaccine and administration under subsection (s)(10).

(B) Screening mammography as defined in subsection (jj).

(C) Screening pap smear and screening pelvic exam as defined in subsection (nn).

(D) Prostate cancer screening tests as defined in subsection (oo).

(E) Colorectal cancer screening tests as defined in subsection (pp).

(F) Diabetes outpatient self-management training services as defined in subsection (qq)(1).

(G) Bone mass measurement as defined in subsection (rr).

(H) Screening for glaucoma as defined in subsection (uu).

(I) Medical nutrition therapy services as defined in subsection (vv).

(J) Cardiovascular screening blood tests as defined in subsection (xx)(1).

(K) Diabetes screening tests as defined in subsection (yy).

(L) Ultrasound screening for abdominal aortic aneurysm as defined in section 1861(bbb) [subsec. (bbb) of this section].

(M) An electrocardiogram.

(N) Additional preventive services (as defined in subsection (ddd)(1)).

(3) For purposes of paragraph (1), the term "end-of-life planning" means verbal or written information regarding—

(A) an individual's ability to prepare an advance directive in the case that an injury or illness causes the individual to be unable to make health care decisions; and

(B) whether or not the physician is willing to follow the individual's wishes as expressed in an advance directive.

(xx) Cardiovascular screening blood test. (1) The term "cardiovascular screening blood test" means a blood test for the early detection of cardiovascular disease (or abnormalities associated with an elevated risk of cardiovascular disease) that tests for the following:

(A) Cholesterol levels and other lipid or triglyceride levels.

(B) Such other indications associated with the presence of, or an elevated risk for, cardiovascular disease as the Secretary may approve for all individuals (or for some individuals determined by the Secretary to be at risk for cardiovascular disease), including indications measured by noninvasive testing.

The Secretary may not approve an indication under subparagraph (B) for any individual unless a blood test for such is recommended by the United States Preventive Services Task Force.

(2) The Secretary shall establish standards, in consultation with appropriate organizations, regarding the frequency for each type of cardiovascular screening blood tests, except that such frequency may not be more often than once every 2 years.

(yy) Diabetes screening tests. (1) The term "diabetes screening tests" means testing furnished to an individual at risk for diabetes (as defined in paragraph (2)) for the purpose of early detection of diabetes, including—

(A) a fasting plasma glucose test; and

(B) such other tests, and modifications to tests, as the Secretary determines appropriate, in consultation with appropriate organizations.

(2) For purposes of paragraph (1), the term "individual at risk for diabetes" means an individual who has any of the following risk factors for diabetes:

(A) Hypertension.

(B) Dyslipidemia.

(C) Obesity, defined as a body mass index greater than or equal to 30 kg/m^2.

(D) Previous identification of an elevated impaired fasting glucose.

(E) Previous identification of impaired glucose tolerance.

(F) A risk factor consisting of at least 2 of the following characteristics:

(i) Overweight, defined as a body mass index greater than 25, but less than 30, kg/m^2.

(ii) A family history of diabetes.

(iii) A history of gestational diabetes mellitus or delivery of a baby weighing greater than 9 pounds.

(iv) 65 years of age or older.

(3) The Secretary shall establish standards, in consultation with appropriate organizations, regarding the frequency of diabetes screening tests, except that such frequency may not be more often than twice within the 12-month period following the date of the most recent diabetes screening test of that individual.

(zz) Intravenous immune globulin. The term "intravenous immune globulin" means an approved pooled plasma derivative for the treatment in the patient's home of a patient with a diagnosed primary immune deficiency disease, but not including items or services related to the administration of the derivative, if a physician determines administration of the derivative in the patient's home is medically appropriate.

(aaa) Extended care in religious nonmedical health care institutions. (1) The term "home health agency" also includes a religious nonmedical health care institution (as defined in subsection (ss)(1)), but only with respect to items and services ordinarily furnished by such an institution to individuals in their homes, and that are comparable to items and services furnished to individuals by a home health agency that is not religious nonmedical health care institution.

(2)(A) Subject to subparagraphs (B), payment may be made with respect to services provided by such an institution only to such extent and under such conditions, limitations, and requirements (in addition to or in lieu of the conditions, limitations, and requirements otherwise applicable) as may be provided in regulations consistent with section 1821 [42 USCS § 1395i-5].

(B) Notwithstanding any other provision of this title [42 USCS §§ 1395 et seq.], payment may not be made under subparagraph (A)—

(i) in a year insofar as such payments exceed $700,000; and

(ii) after December 31, 2006.

(bbb) Ultrasound screening for abdominal aortic aneurysm. The term "ultrasound screening for abdominal aortic aneurysm" means—

(1) a procedure using sound waves (or such other procedures using alternative technologies, of commensurate accuracy and cost, that the Secretary may specify) provided for the early detection of abdominal aortic aneurysm; and

(2) includes a physician's interpretation of the results of the procedure.

(ccc) Long-term care hospital. The term "long-term care hospital" means a hospital which—

(1) is primarily engaged in providing inpatient services, by or under the supervision of a physician, to Medicare beneficiaries whose medically complex conditions require a long hospital stay and programs of care provided by a long-term care hospital;

(2) has an average inpatient length of stay (as determined by the Secretary) of greater than 25 days, or meets the requirements of clause (II) of section 1886(d)(1)(B)(iv) [42 USCS § 1395ww(d)(1)(B)(iv)];

(3) satisfies the requirements of subsection (e); and

(4) meets the following facility criteria:

(A) the institution has a patient review process, documented in the patient medical record, that screens patients prior to admission for appropriateness of admission to a long-term care hospital, validates within 48 hours of admission that patients meet admission criteria for long-term care hospitals, regularly evaluates patients throughout their stay for continuation of care in a long-term care hospital, and assesses the available discharge options when patients no longer meet such continued stay criteria;

(B) the institution has active physician involvement with patients during their treatment through an organized medical staff, physician-directed treatment with physician onsite availability on a daily basis to review patient progress, and consulting physicians on call and capable of being at the patient's side within a moderate period of time, as determined by the Secretary; and

(C) the institution has interdisciplinary team treatment for patients, requiring interdisciplinary teams of health care professionals, including physicians, to prepare and carry out an individualized treatment plan for each patient.

(ddd) Additional preventive services; preventive services [Caution: For provisions applicable to items and services furnished before January 1, 2011, see 2010 amendment note below.]. (1) The term "additional preventive services" means services not described in subparagraph (A) or (C) of paragraph (3) that identify medical conditions or risk factors and that the Secretary determines are—

(A) reasonable and necessary for the prevention or early detection of an illness or disability;

(B) recommended with a grade of A or B by the United States Preventive Services Task Force; and

(C) appropriate for individuals entitled to benefits under part A [42 USCS §§ 1395c et seq.] or enrolled under part B [42 USCS §§ 1395j et seq.].

(2) In making determinations under paragraph (1) regarding the coverage of a new service, the Secretary shall use the process for making national coverage determinations (as defined in section 1869(f)(1)(B) [42 USCS § 1395ff(f)(1)(B)]) under this title [42 USCS §§ 1395 et seq.]. As part of the use of such process, the Secretary may conduct an assessment of the relation between predicted outcomes and the expenditures for such service and may take into account the results of such assessment in making such determination.

(3) The term "preventive services" means the following:

(A) The screening and preventive services described in subsection (ww)(2) (other than the service described in subparagraph (M) of such subsection).

(B) An initial preventive physical examination (as defined in subsection (ww)).

(C) Personalized prevention plan services (as defined in subsection (hhh)(1)).

(eee) Cardiac rehabilitation program; intensive cardiac rehabilitation program. (1) The term "cardiac rehabilitation program" means a physician-supervised program (as described in paragraph (2)) that furnishes the items and services described in paragraph (3).

(2) A program described in this paragraph is a program under which—

(A) items and services under the program are delivered—

(i) in a physician's office;

(ii) in a hospital on an outpatient basis; or

(iii) in other settings determined appropriate by the Secretary.

(B) a physician is immediately available and accessible for medical consultation and medical emergencies at all times items and services are being furnished under the program, except that, in the case of items and services furnished under such a program in a hospital, such availability shall be presumed; and

(C) individualized treatment is furnished under a written plan established, reviewed, and signed by a physician every 30 days that describes—

(i) the individual's diagnosis;

(ii) the type, amount, frequency, and duration of the items and services furnished under the plan; and

(iii) the goals set for the individual under the plan.

(3) The items and services described in this paragraph are—

(A) physician-prescribed exercise;

(B) cardiac risk factor modification, including education, counseling, and behavioral intervention (to the extent such education, counseling, and behavioral intervention is closely related to the individual's care and treatment and is tailored to the individual's needs);

(C) psychosocial assessment;

(d) outcomes assessment; and

(E) such other items and services as the Secretary may determine, but only if such items and services are—

(i) reasonable and necessary for the diagnosis or active treatment of the individual's condition;

(ii) reasonably expected to improve or maintain the individual's condition and functional level; and

(iii) furnished under such guidelines relating to the frequency and duration of such items and services as the Secretary shall establish, taking into account accepted norms of medical practice and the reasonable expectation of improvement of the individual.

(4) (A) The term "intensive cardiac rehabilitation program" means a physician-supervised program (as described in paragraph (2)) that furnishes the items and services described in paragraph (3) and has shown, in peer-reviewed published research, that it accomplished—

(i) one or more of the following:

(I) positively affected the progression of coronary heart disease; or

(II) reduced the need for coronary bypass surgery; or

(III) reduced the need for percutaneous coronary interventions; and

(ii) a statistically significant reduction in 5 or more of the following measures from their level before receipt of cardiac rehabilitation services to their level after receipt of such services:

(I) low density lipoprotein;

(II) triglycerides;

(III) body mass index;

(IV) systolic blood pressure;

(V) diastolic blood pressure; or

(VI) the need for cholesterol, blood pressure, and diabetes medications.

(B) To be eligible for an intensive cardiac rehabilitation program, an individual must have—

(i) had an acute myocardial infarction within the preceding 12 months;

(ii) had coronary bypass surgery;

(iii) stable angina pectoris;

(iv) had heart valve repair or replacement;

(v) had percutaneous transluminal coronary angioplasty (PTCA) or coronary stenting; or

(vi) had a heart or heart-lung transplant.

(C) An intensive cardiac rehabilitation program may be provided in a series of 72 one-hour sessions (as defined in section 1848(b)(5) [42 USCS § 1395w-4(b)(5)]), up to 6 sessions per day, over a period of up to 18 weeks.

(5) The Secretary shall establish standards to ensure that a physician with expertise in the management of individuals with cardiac pathophysiology who is licensed to practice medicine in the State in which a cardiac rehabilitation program (or the intensive cardiac rehabilitation program, as the case may be) is offered—

(A) is responsible for such program; and

(B) in consultation with appropriate staff, is involved substantially in directing the progress of individual in the program.

(fff) Pulmonary rehabilitation program. (1) The term "pulmonary rehabilitation program" means a physician-supervised program (as described in subsection (eee)(2) with respect to a program under this subsection) that furnishes the items and services described in paragraph (2).

(2) The items and services described in this paragraph are—

(A) physician-prescribed exercise;

(B) education or training (to the extent the education or training is closely and clearly related to the individual's care and treatment and is tailored to such individual's needs);

(C) psychosocial assessment;

(D) outcomes assessment; and

(E) such other items and services as the Secretary may determine, but only if such items and services are—

(i) reasonable and necessary for the diagnosis or active treatment of the individual's condition;

(ii) reasonably expected to improve or maintain the individual's condition and functional level; and

(iii) furnished under such guidelines relating to the frequency and duration of such items and services as the Secretary shall establish, taking into account accepted norms of medical practice and the reasonable expectation of improvement of the individual.

(3) The Secretary shall establish standards to ensure that a physician with expertise in the management of individuals with respiratory pathophysiology who is licensed to practice medicine in the State in which a pulmonary rehabilitation program is offered—

(A) is responsible for such program; and

(B) in consultation with appropriate staff, is involved substantially in directing the progress of individual in the program.

(ggg) Kidney disease education services.

(1) The term "kidney disease education services" means educational services that are—

(A) furnished to an individual with stage IV chronic kidney disease who, according to accepted clinical guidelines identified by the Secretary, will require dialysis or a kidney transplant;

(B) furnished, upon the referral of the physician managing the individual's kidney condition, by a qualified person (as defined in paragraph (2)); and

(C) designed—

(i) to provide comprehensive information (consistent with the standards set under paragraph (3)) regarding—

(I) the management of comorbidities, including for purposes of delaying the need for dialysis;

(II) the prevention of uremic complications; and

(III) each option for renal replacement therapy (including hemodialysis and peritoneal dialysis at home and in-center as well as vascular access options and transplantation);

(ii) to ensure that the individual has the opportunity to actively participate in the choice of therapy; and

(iii) to be tailored to meet the needs of the individual involved.

(2) (A) The term "qualified person" means—

(i) a physician (as defined in section 1861(r)(1) [subsec. (r)(1) of this section]) or a physician assistant, nurse practitioner, or clinical nurse specialist (as defined in section 1861(aa)(5) [subsec. (aa)(5) of this section]), who furnishes services for which payment may be made under the fee schedule established under section 1848 [42 USCS § 1395w-4]; and

(ii) a provider of services located in a rural area (as defined in section 1886(d)(2)(D) [42 USCS § 1395ww(d)(2)(D)]).

(B) Such term does not include a provider of services (other than a provider of services described in subparagraph (A)(ii)) or a renal dialysis facility.

(3) The Secretary shall set standards for the content of such information to be provided under paragraph (1)(C)(i) after consulting with physicians, other health professionals, health educators, professional organizations, accrediting organizations, kidney patient organizations, dialysis facilities, transplant centers, network organizations described in section 1881(c)(2) [42 USCS § 1395rr(c)(2)], and other knowledgeable persons. To the extent possible the Secretary shall consult with persons or entities described in the previous sentence, other than a dialysis facility, that has not received industry funding from a drug or biological manufacturer or dialysis facility.

(4) No individual shall be furnished more than 6 sessions of kidney disease education services under this title [42 USCS §§ 1395 et seq.].

(hhh) Annual wellness visit [Caution: This subsection applies to services furnished on or after January 1, 2011, as provided by § 4103(e) of Act March 23, 2010, P. L. 111-148, which appears as 42 USCS § 1395l note.]. (1) The term "personalized prevention plan services" means the creation of a plan for an individual—

(A) that includes a health risk assessment (that meets the guidelines established by the Secretary under paragraph (4)(A)) of the individual that is completed prior to or as part of the same visit with a health professional described in paragraph (3); and

(B) that—

(i) takes into account the results of the health risk assessment; and

(ii) may contain the elements described in paragraph (2).

(2) Subject to paragraph (4)(H), the elements described in this paragraph are the following:

(A) The establishment of, or an update to, the individual's medical and family history.

(B) A list of current providers and suppliers that are regularly involved in providing medical care to the individual (including a list of all prescribed medications).

(C) A measurement of height, weight, body mass index (or waist circumference, if appropriate), blood pressure, and other routine measurements.

(D) Detection of any cognitive impairment.

(E) The establishment of, or an update to, the following:

(i) A screening schedule for the next 5 to 10 years, as appropriate, based on recommendations of the United States Preventive Services Task Force and the Advisory Committee on Immunization Practices, and the individual's health status, screening history, and age-appropriate preventive services covered under this title.

(ii) A list of risk factors and conditions for which primary, secondary, or tertiary prevention interventions are recommended or are underway, including any mental health conditions or any such risk factors or conditions that have been identified through an initial preventive physical examination (as described under subsection (ww)(1)), and a list of treatment options and their associated risks and benefits.

(F) The furnishing of personalized health advice and a referral, as appropriate, to health education or preventive counseling services or programs aimed at reducing identified risk factors and improving self-management, or community-based lifestyle interventions to reduce health risks and promote self-management and wellness, including weight loss, physical activity, smoking cessation, fall prevention, and nutrition.

(G) Any other element determined appropriate by the Secretary.

(3) A health professional described in this paragraph is—

(A) a physician;

(B) a practitioner described in clause (i) of section 1842(b)(18)(C) [42 USCS § 1395u(b)(18)(C)]; or

(C) a medical professional (including a health educator, registered dietitian, or nutrition professional) or a team of medical professionals, as determined appropriate by the Secretary, under the supervision of a physician.

(4)(A) For purposes of paragraph (1)(A), the Secretary, not later than 1 year after the date of enactment of this subsection [enacted March 23, 2010], shall establish publicly available guidelines for health risk assessments. Such guidelines shall be developed in consultation with relevant groups and entities and shall provide that a health risk assessment—

(i) identify chronic diseases, injury risks, modifiable risk factors, and urgent health needs of the individual; and

(ii) may be furnished—

(I) through an interactive telephonic or web-based program that meets the standards established under subparagraph (B);

(II) during an encounter with a health care professional;

(III) through community-based prevention programs; or

(IV) through any other means the Secretary determines appropriate to maximize accessibility and ease of use by beneficiaries, while ensuring the privacy of such beneficiaries.

(B) Not later than 1 year after the date of enactment of this subsection [enacted March 23, 2010], the Secretary shall establish standards for interactive telephonic or web-based programs used to furnish health risk assessments under subparagraph (A)(ii)(I). The Secretary may utilize any health risk assessment developed under section 4004(f) of the Patient Protection and Affordable Care Act [42 USCS § 300u-12] as part of the requirement to develop a personalized prevention plan to comply with this subparagraph.

(C)(i) Not later than 18 months after the date of enactment of this subsection [enacted March 23, 2010], the Secretary shall develop and make available to the public a health risk assessment model. Such model shall meet the guidelines under subparagraph (A) and may be used to meet the requirement under paragraph (1)(A).

(ii) Any health risk assessment that meets the guidelines under subparagraph (A) and is approved by the Secretary may be used to meet the requirement under paragraph (1)(A).

(D) The Secretary may coordinate with community-based entities (including State Health Insurance Programs, Area Agencies on Aging, Aging and Disability Resource Centers, and the Administration on Aging) to—

(i) ensure that health risk assessments are accessible to beneficiaries; and

(ii) provide appropriate support for the completion of health risk assessments by beneficiaries.

(E) The Secretary shall establish procedures to make beneficiaries and providers aware of the requirement that a beneficiary complete a health risk assessment prior to or at the same time as receiving personalized prevention plan services.

(F) To the extent practicable, the Secretary shall encourage the use of, integration with, and coordination of health information technology (including use of technology that is compatible with electronic medical records and personal health records) and may experiment with the use of personalized technology to aid in the development of self-management skills and management of and adherence to provider recommendations in order to improve the health status of beneficiaries.

(G) A beneficiary shall be eligible to receive only an initial preventive physical examination (as defined under subsection (ww)(1)) during the 12-month period after the date that the beneficiary's coverage begins under part B [42 USCS §§ 1395j et seq.] and shall be eligible to receive personalized prevention plan services under this subsection each year thereafter provided that the beneficiary has not received either an initial preventive physical examination or personalized prevention plan services within the preceding 12-month period.

(H) The Secretary shall issue guidance that—

(i) identifies elements under paragraph (2) that are required to be provided to a beneficiary as part of their first visit for personalized prevention plan services; and

(ii) establishes a yearly schedule for appropriate provision of such elements thereafter.

(Aug. 14, 1935, ch 531, Title XVIII, Part E [D] [C], § 1861, as added July 30, 1965, P. L. 89-97, Title I, Part 1, § 102(a), 79 Stat. 313; Nov. 2, 1966, P. L. 89-713, § 7, 80 Stat. 1111; Jan. 2, 1968, P. L. 90-248, Title I, Part 3, §§ 127(a), 129(a), (b), (c)(9)(C)–(11), 132(a), 133(a), (b), 134(a), 143(a), 144(a)–(d), 81 Stat. 846–850, 852, 857, 858; Jan. 12, 1971, P. L. 91-690, 84 Stat. 2074; Oct. 30, 1972, P. L. 92-603, Title II, §§ 211(b), (c)(2), 221(c)(4), 223(a)–(d), (f), 227(a), (c), (d)(1), (f), 234(a)–(f), 237(c), 244(c), 246(b), 248, 249(b), 251(a)(1), (b)(1), (c), 252(a), 256(b), 264(a), 265, 267, 273(a), 276(a), 278(a)(4)–(15), (b)(6), (10), (11), (13), 283(a), 86

Stat. 1383, 1384, 1389, 1393, 1394, 1404–1407, 1412, 1413, 1416, 1423–1426, 1445–1447, 1449–1454, 1456; Dec. 31, 1975, P. L. 94-182, Title I, §§ 102, 106(a), 112(a)(1), 89 Stat. 1051, 1052, 1055; Oct. 25, 1977, P. L. 95-142, §§ 3(a)(2), 5(m), 19(b)(1), 21(a), 91 Stat. 1178, 1191, 1204, 1207; Dec. 13, 1977, P. L. 95-210, § 1(d), (g), (h), 91 Stat. 1485, 1487, 1488; Dec. 20, 1977, P. L. 95-216, Title V, § 501(a), 91 Stat. 1564; June 13, 1978, P. L. 95-292, § 4(d), 92 Stat. 315; Dec. 5, 1980, P. L. 96-499, Title IX, Part A, Subpart I, § 902(a)(1), Subpart II, § 915(a), Part B, Subpart I, §§ 930(k)–(n), (p), 931(c), (d), 933(c)–(e), 936(a), 937(a), 938(a), Subpart II, § 948(a)(1), 949, 950, 951(a), (b), 952(a) [952], 94 Stat. 2612, 2623, 2632, 2633, 2635, 2639, 2640, 2643, 2645, 2646; Dec. 28, 1980, P. L. 96-611, § 1(a)(1), (b)(3), 94 Stat. 3566; Aug. 13, 1981, P. L. 97-35, Title XXI, Subtitle A, Ch 1, § 2102(a), Ch 3, § 2114, Subtitle B, Ch 1, § 2121(c), (d), Ch 3, §§ 2141(a), 2142(a), 2144(a), Subtitle D, § 2193(c)(9), 95 Stat. 787, 796–799, 828; Sept. 3, 1982, P. L. 97-248, Title I, Subtitle A, Part I, Subpart A, §§ 101(a)(2), (d), 102(a), 103(a), 105(a), 106(a), 107(a), 108(a)(2), 109(b), Subpart B, § 114(b), Part II, § 122(d), Part III, §§ 127(l), 128(a)(1), (d)(2), Subtitle C, § 148(b), 96 Stat. 335–339, 350, 359, 366, 367, 394; Jan. 12, 1983, P. L. 97-448, Title III, § 309(a)(4), 96 Stat. 2408; April 20, 1983, P. L. 98-21, Title VI, §§ 602(d), 607(b)(2), (d), 97 Stat. 163, 171, 172; July 18, 1984, P. L. 98-369, Division B, Title III, Subtitle A, Part I, §§ 2314(a), 2318(a), (b), 2319(a), 2321(e), 2322(a), 2323(a), 2324(a), Part II, §§ 2335(b), 2340(a), 2341(a), (c), 2342(a), 2343(a), (b), 2354(b)(18)–(29), 98 Stat. 1079, 1081, 1082, 1085, 1086, 1090, 1093, 1094, 1101; Nov. 8, 1984, P. L. 98-617, § 3(a)(4), (b)(7), 98 Stat. 3295, 3296; April 7, 1986, P. L. 99-272, Title IX, Subtitle A, Part 1, Subpart A, §§ 9107(b), 9110(a), Part 2, Subpart A, § 9202(i)(1), Subpart B, § 9219(b)(1)(B), (3)(A), 100 Stat. 160, 162, 177, 182, 183; Oct. 21, 1986, P. L. 99-509, Title IX, Subtitle D, Part 1, § 9305(c)(1), (2), Part 2, §§ 9313(a)(2), 9315(a), 9320(b), (c), (f), Part 3, §§ 9335(c)(1), 9336(a), 9337(d), (g), 9338(a), 100 Stat. 1989, 2002, 2005, 2013, 2015, 2029, 2032, 2033, 2034; Dec. 22, 1987, P. L. 100-203, Title IV, Subtitle A, Part 1, § 4009(e)(1), (f), Part 2, Subpart B, § 4021(a), 4026(a)(1), Part 2, Subpart C, § 4039(b), Part 3, Subpart B, §§ 4064(e)(1), 4065(a), Part 3, Subpart C, §§ 4070(b)(1), (2), 4071(a), 4072(a), 4073(a), (c), 4074(a), (b), 4075(a), 4076(a), 4077(a)(1), (b)(1), (4) [(5)], 4078, Subpart D, § 4084(c)(1), 4085(i), (9)–(14), Subtitle C, Part 1, § 4201(a)(1), (b), (d), 100 Stat. 1330-58, 1330-67, 1330-74, 1330-81, 1330-111, 1330-112, 1330-114, 1330-116, 1330-118, 1330-119, 1330-120, 1330-121, 1330-132, 1330-160, 1330-174; July 1, 1988, P. L. 100-360, Title I, Subtitle A, § 104(d)(4), Title II, §§ 202(a)(1), (2), 203(e)(1), 204(a)(1), 206(a), Title IV, Subtitle B, § 411(d)(1)(B)(i), (h)(1)(B), (2), (3)(A), (4)(D), (5)–(7)(A), (E), (F), (i)(3), (l)(1)(B), 102 Stat. 689, 702, 725, 731, 773, 785–788, 801; Oct. 13, 1988, P. L. 100-485, Title VI, § 608(d)(6)(A), (23)(B), (27)(B) 102 Stat. 2412, 2421, 2422; Nov. 10, 1988, P. L. 100-647, Title VIII, Subtitle E, Part III, §§ 8423(a), 8424(a), 102 Stat. 3803; Dec. 13, 1989, P. L. 101-234, Title I, §§ 101(a)(1), 201(a)(1), 103 Stat. 1979, 1981; Dec. 19, 1989, P. L. 101-239, Title VI, Subtitle A, Part 1, Subpart A, § 6003(g)(3)(A), (C)(i), (D)(x), Part 2, Subpart A, §§ 6110, 6112(e)(1), 6113(a)–(b)(2), 6114(a), (d), 6115(a), 6116(a)(1), Part 2, Subpart B, §§ 6131(a)(2), 6141(a), Part 3, Subpart B, § 6213(a)–(c), 103 Stat. 2151–2153, 2213, 2215–2217, 2218, 2219, 2221, 2225, 2250; Nov. 5, 1990, P. L. 101-508, Title IV, Subtitle A, Part 1, § 4008(h)(2)(A)(i), Part 2, Subpart B, §§ 4151(a), (b)(1), 4153(b)(2)(A), 4155(a), (d), 4156(a), 4157(a), 4161(a)(1), (2), (5), 4162(a), 4163(a), Part 3, §§ 4201(d)(1), 4207(d)(1), 104 Stat. 1388-48, 1388-71, 1388-72, 1388-74, 1388-84, 1388-87, 1388-88, 1388-93, 1388-94, 1388-96, 1388-104, 1388-120; Nov. 16, 1990, P. L. 101-597, Title IV, § 401(c)(2), 104 Stat. 3035; Nov. 5, 1990, P. L. 101-508, Title IV, Subtitle A, Part 1, § 4008(h)(2)(A)(i), Part 2, Subpart B, §§ 4151(a), (b)(1), 4153(b)(2)(A), 4155(a), (d), 4156(a), 4157(a), 4161(a)(1), (2), (5), 4162(a), 4163(a), Part 3, §§ 4201(d)(1), 4207(d)(1), 104 Stat. 1388-48, 1388-71, 1388-72, 1388-74, 1388-84, 1388-87, 1388-88, 1388-93, 1388-94, 1388-96, 1388-104, 1388-120; Nov. 16, 1990, P. L. 101-597, Title IV, § 401(c)(2), 104 Stat. 3035; Aug. 10, 1993, P. L. 103-66, Title XIII, Ch 2, Subch A, Part I, § 13503(c)(1), Part II, Subpart B, § 13521, Subpart E, §§ 13553(a), (b), 13554(a), 13556(a), Part III, §§ 13564(a)(2), (b)(1), 13565, 13566(b), 107 Stat. 579, 586, 591, 592, 607; Oct. 31, 1994, P. L. 103-432, Title I, Subtitle A, §§ 102(g)(4), 104, 107(a), Subtitle B, Part III, § 145(b), 146(a), (b), 147(e)(1), (4), (5), (f)(3), (4), (6)(A), (B), (E), Subtitle C, §§ 158(a)(1), 160(d)(4), 108 Stat. 4404, 4405, 4407, 4427, 4428, 4430–4432, 4442, 4444; Oct. 11, 1996, P. L. 104-299, § 4(b)(1), 110 Stat. 3645; Aug. 5, 1997, P. L. 105-33, Title IV, Subtitle A, Ch 1, Subch A, § 4001, Subtitle B, §§ 4102(a), (c), 4103(a), 4104(a)(1), 4105(a)(1), (b)(1), 4106(a), Subtitle C, § 4201(c), 4205(b)(1), (c)(1), (d)(1), (2), (3)(A), Subtitle D,

Ch 2, §§ 4312(b)(1), (2), (d), (e), 4320, 4321(a), Subtitle E, Ch 1, § 4404(a), Ch 3, § 4432(b)(5)(D), (E), Ch 4, 4444(a), 4445, 4446, Ch 5, 4451, 4454(a)(1), Subtitle F, Ch 1, Subch B, 4511(a)(1)–(2)(B), (d), 4512(a), 4513(a), Ch 2, § 4522, Ch 3, § 4531(a)(1), Ch 5, § 4557(a), Subtitle G, Ch 1, Subch A, §§ 4601(a), 4602(a)–(c), 4604(b), Subch B, §§ 4611(b), 4612(a), 111 Stat. 275, 360, 361, 362, 366, 367, 373, 376, 386, 394, 400, 421, 423–426, 442–444, 450, 463, 466, 472, 474; Oct. 21, 1998, P. L. 105-277, Div J, Title V, Subtitle A, § 5101(a), (b), (d)(1), 112 Stat. 2681-913, 2681-914; Nov. 29, 1999, P. L. 106-113, Div B, § 1000(a)(6), 113 Stat. 1536; Dec. 21, 2000, P. L. 106-554, § 1(a)(6), 114 Stat. 2763; Dec. 8, 2003, P. L. 108-173, Title I, § 101(a)(1), Title III, § 303(i)(2), Title IV, Subtitle A, § 408(a), Subtitle B, §§ 414(f)(2) [414(g)(2)], 415(b), Title V, Subtitle B, § 512(c), Title VI, Subtitle B, §§ 611(a), (b), (d)(2), 612(a), (b), 613(a), (b), Subtitle D, § 642(a), Title VII, Subtitle A, § 706(b), Subtitle D, § 736(a)(10), (11), (b)(3), (11), (12), (c)(4), Title IX, Subtitle A, § 901(b), Subtitle C, § 926(b)(1), Subtitle E, § 946(a), 117 Stat. 2071, 2254, 2270, 2281, 2282, 2299, 2303, 2304, 2305, 2322, 2339, 2355, 2356, 2374, 2396, 2424; Feb. 8, 2006, P. L. 109-171, Title V, Subtitle A, § 5004, Ch. 2, §§ 5112(a), (b), 5114(a)(1), (b), Title VI, Subtitle A, Ch. 1, § 6001(f)(1), 120 Stat. 32, 43, 45, 58; Dec. 29, 2007, P. L. 110-173, Title I, § 114(a), 121 Stat. 2501; July 15, 2008, P. L. 110-275, Title I, Subtitle A, Part I, § 101(a)(1), (b)(1), Subtitle B, § 125(b)(2), Subtitle C, Part II, §§ 143(a), (b)(5), (6), 144(a)(1), 152(b)(1)(A), (B), 153(b)(3)(B), Subtitle F, § 182(b), 122 Stat. 2496, 2497, 2519, 2542, 2543, 2544, 2551, 2556, 2583; Oct. 8, 2008, P. L. 110-355, § 7(a), 122 Stat. 3995; Oct. 1, 2009, P. L. 111-68, Div A, Title I, § 1501(e)(2), 123 Stat. 2041; March 23, 2010, P. L. 111-148, Title IV, Subtitle B, §§ 4103(a), (b), 4104(a), Title V, Subtitle F, § 5502(a)(1), Title VI, Subtitle E, § 6402(g)(2), Title X, Subtitle D, § 10402(b), Subtitle E, § 10501(i)(2)(A), 124 Stat. 553, 557, 654, 759, 975, 997; March 30, 2010, P. L. 111-152, Title I, Subtitle D, § 1301(a), (b), 124 Stat. 1057.)

HISTORY; ANCILLARY LAWS AND DIRECTIVES

Prospective amendments:

Amendment of subsec. (aa)(3)(A), applicable to services furnished on or after Jan. 1, 2011. Act March 23, 2010, P. L. 111-148, Title X, Subtitle E, § 10501(i)(2)(A), 124 Stat. 997 (applicable to services furnished on or after 1/1/2011, 2011, as provided by § 10501(i)(2)(B) of such Act, which appears as a note to this section), provides: "Section 1861(aa)(3)(A) of the Social Security Act (42 U.S.C. 1395w(aa)(3)(A)) is amended to read as follows:

" '(A) services of the type described in subparagraphs (A) through (C) of paragraph (1) and preventive services (as defined in section 1861(ddd)(3)); and'.".

Amendments:

2008. Act July 15, 2008 (applicable to services furnished on or after 1/1/2009, as provided by § 101(c) of such Act, which appears as 42 USCS § 1395l note), in subsec. (s)(2), in subpara. (Z), deleted "and" following the concluding semicolon, in subpara. (AA)(iii)(II), added "and" at the end, and added subpara. (BB); in subsec. (ww), in para. (1), inserted "body mass index," deleted ", and an electrocardiogram" following "blood pressure", and inserted "and end-of-life planning (as defined in paragraph (3)) upon the agreement with the individual", in para. (2), added subparas. (M) and (N), and added para. (3); and added subsec. (ddd).

Such Act further (applicable to accreditations of hospitals granted on or after 7/15/2010, as provided by § 125(d) of such Act, which appears as 42 USCS § 1395bb note), in subsec. (e), in the concluding matter, substituted "and (ii) is accredited by a national accreditation body recognized by the Secretary under section 1865(a), or is accredited by or approved by a program of the country in which such institution is located if the Secretary finds the accreditation or comparable approval standards of such program to be essentially equivalent to those of such a national accreditation body." for "and (ii) is accredited by the Joint Commission on Accreditation of Hospitals, or is accredited by or approved by a program of the country in which such institution is located if the Secretary finds the accreditation or comparable approval standards of such program to be essentially equivalent to those of the Joint Commission on Accreditation of Hospitals".

Such Act further (applicable to services furnished on or after 7/1/2009, as provided by § 143(c) of such Act, which appears as 42 USCS § 1395k note), in subsec. (p), in the concluding matter, deleted "The term 'outpatient physical therapy services' also includes speech-language pathology services furnished by a provider of services, a clinic, rehabilitation agency, or by a public health agency, or by others under an arrangement with, and under the supervision of, such provider, clinic, rehabilitation agency, or public health agency to an individual as an outpatient, subject to the conditions prescribed in this subsection." following "extended care facility."; in subsec. (s)(2)(D), inserted ", outpatient speech-language pathology services,"; and in subsec. (ll), redesignated paras. (2) and (3) as paras. (3) and (4), respectively, and inserted new para. (2).

Such Act further (applicable to items and services furnished on or after 1/1/2010, as provided by § 144(a)(3) of such Act, which appears as 42 USCS § 1395w-4 note), in subsec. (s)(2), in subpara. (AA)(iii)(II), deleted "and" following the concluding semicolon, and added subparas. (CC) and (DD); and added subsecs. (eee) and (fff).

Such Act further (applicable to services furnished on or after 1/1/2010, as provided by § 152(b)(2) of such Act, which appears as 42 USCS § 1395w-4 note), in subsec. (s)(2), in subpara. (CC), deleted "and" following the concluding semicolon, in subpara. (DD), added "and" following the semicolon, and added subpara. (EE); and added subsec. (ggg).

Such Act further, in subsec. (s)(2)(F), inserted ", and, for items and services furnished on or after January 1, 2011, renal dialysis services (as defined in section 1881(b)(14)(B))"; and in subsec. (t)(2)(B), in the concluding matter, added the sentence beginning "On and after January 1, 2010, . . .".

Act Oct. 8, 2008 (effective on enactment, as provided by § 7(b) of such Act, which appears as a note to this section), in subsec. (aa)(2), in the concluding matter, substituted "4-year period" for "3-year period".

2010. Act March 23, 2010 (applicable to services furnished on or after 1/1/2011, as provided by § 4103(e) of such Act, which appears as 42 USCS § 1395l note), in subsec. (s)(2), in subpara. (K), in cls. (i) and (ii), substituted "subsections (ww)(1) and (hhh)" for "subsection (ww)(1), in subpara. (DD), deleted "and" following the concluding semicolon, in subpara. (EE), added "and" following the semicolon, and added subpara. (FF); and added subsec. (hhh).

Such Act further (applicable to items and services furnished on or after 1/1/2011, as provided by § 4104(d) of such Act, which appears as 42 USCS § 1395l note), in subsec. (ddd), in the heading, inserted "; preventive services", in para. (1), substituted "not described in subparagraph (A) or (C) of paragraph (3)" for "not otherwise described in this title", and added para. (3).

Such Act further, in subsec. (o)(7)(C), inserted "that the Secretary determines is commensurate with the volume of the billing of the home health agency".

Such Act further (applicable to services furnished on or after 1/1/2011, as provided by § 5502(a)(2), and repealed by § 10501(i)(1) of such Act), amended subsec. (aa)(3)(A) to read: "(A) services of the type described subparagraphs (A) through (C) of paragraph (1) and preventive services (as defined in section 1861(ddd)(3)); and".

Section 10402(b) of such Act further, in subsec. (hhh)(4), substituted subpara. (G) for one which read: "(G) (i) A beneficiary shall only be eligible to receive an initial preventive physical examination (as defined under subsection (ww)(1)) at any time during the 12-month period after the date that the beneficiary's coverage begins under part B and shall be eligible to receive personalized prevention plan services under this subsection provided that the beneficiary has not received such services within the preceding 12-month period.

"(ii) The Secretary shall establish procedures to make beneficiaries aware of the option to select an initial preventive physical examination or personalized prevention plan services during the period of 12 months after the date that a beneficiary's coverage begins under part B, which shall include information regarding any relevant differences between such services.".

Act March 30, 2010 (applicable to items and services furnished on or after 4/1/2011, pursuant to § 1301(c) of such Act, which appears as a note to this section), in subsec. (ff)(3), in subpara. (A), inserted "other than in an individual's home or in an inpatient or residential setting", and in subpara. (B), in cl. (ii), deleted "and" following the concluding semicolon, redesignated cl. (iii) as cl. (iv), and inserted new cl. (iii).

Other provisions:

Repeal of provisions relating to effective date of amendments made by § 5502(a)(1) of Act March 23, 2010. Act March 23, 2010, P. L. 111-148, Title V, Subtitle F, § 5502(a)(2) 124 Stat. 654 which provided that the amendment made by paragraph (1) [amending subsec. (aa)(3)(A) of this section] shall apply to services furnished on or after January 1, 2011, was repealed by § 10501(i)(1) of such Act.

Applicability of amendments made by § 10501(i)(2)(B) of Act March 23, 2010. Act March 23, 2010, P. L. 111-148, Title X, Subtitle E, § 10501(i)(2)(B), 124 Stat. 997, provides: "The amendment made by subparagraph (A) [amending subsec. (aa)(3)(A) of this section] shall apply to services furnished on or after January 1, 2011.".

Application of amendments made by § 1301 of Act March 30, 2010. Act March 30, 2010, P. L. 111-152, Title I, Subtitle D, § 1301(c), 124 Stat. 1057, provides: "The amendments made by this section [amending subsec. (ff) of this section] shall apply to items and services furnished on or after the first day of the first calendar quarter that begins at least 12 months after the date of the enactment of this Act.".

§ 1395y. Exclusions from coverage and medicare as secondary payer

(a) Items or services specifically excluded. Notwithstanding any other provision of this title [42 USCS §§ 1395 et seq.], no payment may be made under part A or part B [42 USCS §§ 1395c et seq. or 1395j et seq.] for any expenses incurred for items or services—

(1)(A) which, except for items and services described in a succeeding subparagraph or additional preventive services (as described in section 1861(ddd)(1) [42 USCS § 1395x(ddd)(1)]), are not reasonable and necessary for the diagnosis or treatment of illness or injury or to improve the functioning of a malformed body member,

(B) in the case of items and services described in section 1861(s)(10) [42 USCS § 1395x(s)(10)], which are not reasonable and necessary for the prevention of illness,

(C) in the case of hospice care, which are not reasonable and necessary for the palliation or management of terminal illness,

(D) in the case of clinical care items and services provided with the concurrence of the Secretary and with respect to research and experimentation conducted by, or under contract with, the Medicare Payment Advisory Commission or the Secretary, which are not reasonable and necessary to carry out the purposes of section 1886(e)(6),

(E) in the case of research conducted pursuant to section 1142 [42 USCS § 1320b-12], which is not reasonable and necessary to carry out the purposes of that section,

(F) in the case of screening mammography, which is performed more frequently than is covered under section 1834(c)(2) [42 USCS § 1395m(c)(2)] or which is not conducted by a facility described in section 1834(c)(1)(B) [42 USCS § 1395m(c)(1)(B)], in the case of screening pap smear and screening pelvic exam, which is performed more frequently than is provided under section 1861(nn) [42 USCS § 1395x(nn)], and, in the case of screening for glaucoma, which is performed more frequently than is provided under section 1861(uu) [42 USCS § 1395x(uu)],

(G) in the case of prostate cancer screening tests (as defined in section 1861(oo)), which are performed more frequently than is covered under such section,

(H) in the case of colorectal cancer screening tests, which are performed more frequently than is covered under section 1834(d) [42 USCS § 1395m(d)],

(I) the frequency and duration of home health services which are in excess of normative guidelines that the Secretary shall establish by regulation,

(J) in the case of a drug or biological specified in section 1847A(c)(6)(C) [42 USCS § 1395w-3a(c)(6)(C)] for which payment is made under part B [42 USCS §§ 1395j et seq.] that is furnished in a competitive area under section 1847B [42 USCS § 1395w-3b], that is not furnished by an entity under a contract under such section,

(K) in the case of an initial preventive physical examination, which is performed more than 1 year after the date the individual's first coverage period begins under part B [42 USCS §§ 1395j et seq.],

(L) in the case of cardiovascular screening blood tests (as defined in section 1861(xx)(1) [42 USCS § 1395x(xx)(1)]), which are performed more frequently than is covered under section 1861(xx)(2) [42 USCS § 1395x(xx)(2)],

(M) in the case of a diabetes screening test (as defined in section 1861(yy)(1) [42 USCS § 1395x(yy)(1)]), which is performed more frequently than is covered under section 1861(yy)(3) [42 USCS § 1395x(yy)(3)],

(N) in the case of ultrasound screening for abdominal aortic aneurysm which is performed more frequently than is provided for under section 1861(s)(2)(AA) [42 USCS § 1395x(s)(2)(AA)],

(O) in the case of kidney disease education services (as defined in paragraph (1) of section 1861(ggg) [42 USCS § 1395x(ggg)]), which are furnished in excess of the number of sessions covered under paragraph (4) of such section, and

(P) **[Caution: This subparagraph applies to services furnished on or after January 1, 2011, as provided by § 4103(e) of Act March 23, 2010, P. L. 111-148, which appears as 42 USCS § 1395l note.]** in the case of personalized prevention plan services (as defined in section 1861(hhh)(1) [42 USCS § 1395x(hhh)(1)]), which are performed more frequently than is covered under such section;

(2) for which the individual furnished such items or services has no legal obligation to pay, and which no other person (by reason of such individual's membership in a prepayment plan or otherwise) has a legal obligation to provide or pay for, except in the case of Federally qualified health center services;

(3) which are paid for directly or indirectly by a governmental entity (other than under this Act and other than under a health benefits or insurance plan established for employees of such an entity), except in the case of rural health clinic services, as defined in section 1861(aa)(1) [42 USCS § 1395x(aa)(1)], in the case of Federally qualified health center services, as defined in section 1861(aa)(3) [42 USCS § 1395x(aa)(3)], in the case of services for which payment may be made under section 1880(e) [42 USCS § 1395qq(e)], and in such other cases as the Secretary may specify;

(4) which are not provided within the United States (except for inpatient hospital services furnished outside the United States under the conditions described in section 1814(f) [42 USCS § 1395(f)] and, subject to such conditions, limitations, and requirements as are provided under or pursuant to this title [42 USCS §§ 1395 et seq.], physicians' services and ambulance services furnished an individual in conjunction with such inpatient hospital services but only for the period during which such inpatient hospital services were furnished);

(5) which are required as a result of war, or of an act of war, occurring after the effective date of such individual's current coverage under such part [42 USCS §§ 1395c et seq. or 1395j et seq.];

(6) which constitute personal comfort items (except, in the case of hospice care, as is otherwise permitted under paragraph (1)(C));

(7) where such expenses are for routine physical checkups, eyeglasses (other than eyewear described in section 1861(s)(8) [42 USCS § 1395x(s)(8)]) or eye examinations for the purpose of prescribing, fitting, or changing eyeglasses, procedures performed (during the course of any eye examination) to determine the refractive state of the eyes, hearing aids or examinations therefor, or immunizations (except as otherwise allowed under section 1861(s)(10) [42 USCS § 1395x(s)(10)] and subparagraph (B), (F), (G), (H), (K), or (P) of paragraph (1));

(8) where such expenses are for orthopedic shoes or other supportive devices for the feet, other than shoes furnished pursuant to section

1861(s)(12) [42 USCS § 1395x(s)(12)];

(9) where such expenses are for custodial care (except, in the case of hospice care, as is otherwise permitted under paragraph (1)(C));

(10) where such expenses are for cosmetic surgery or are incurred in connection therewith, except as required for the prompt repair of accidental injury or for improvement of the functioning of a malformed body member;

(11) where such expenses constitute charges imposed by immediate relatives of such individual or members of his household;

(12) where such expenses are for services in connection with the care, treatment, filling, removal, or replacement of teeth or structures directly supporting teeth, except that payment may be made under part A [42 USCS §§ 1395c et seq.] in the case of inpatient hospital services in connection with the provision of such dental services if the individual, because of his underlying medical condition and clinical status or because of the severity of the dental procedure, requires hospitalization in connection with the provision of such services;

(13) where such expenses are for—

(A) the treatment of flat foot conditions and the prescription of supportive devices therefor,

(B) the treatment of subluxations of the foot, or

(C) routine foot care (including the cutting or removal of corns or calluses, the trimming of nails, and other routine hygienic care);

(14) which are other than physicians' services (as defined in regulations promulgated specifically for purposes of this paragraph), services described by section 1861(s)(2)(K) [42 USCS § 1395x(s)(2)(K)], certified nurse-midwife services, qualified psychologist services, and services of a certified registered nurse anesthetist, and which are furnished to an individual who is a patient of a hospital or critical access hospital by an entity other than the hospital or critical access hospital, unless the services are furnished under arrangements (as defined in section 1861(w)(1) [42 USCS § 1395x(w)(1)]) with the entity made by the hospital or critical access hospital;

(15)(A) which are for services of an assistant at surgery in a cataract operation (including subsequent insertion of an intraocular lens) unless, before the surgery is performed, the appropriate utilization and quality control peer review organization (under part B of title XI [42 USCS §§ 1320c et seq.]) or a carrier under section 1842 [42 USCS § 1395u] has approved of the use of such an assistant in the surgical procedure based on the existence of a complicating medical condition, or

(B) which are for services of an assistant at surgery to which section 1848(i)(2)(B) [42 USCS § 1395w-4(i)(2)(B)] applies;

(16) in the case in which funds may not be used for such items and services under the Assisted Suicide Funding Restriction Act of 1997;

(17) where the expenses are for an item or service furnished in a competitive acquisition area (as established by the Secretary under section 1847(a) [42 USCS § 1395w-3(a)]) by an entity other than an entity with which the Secretary has entered into a contract under section 1847(b) [42 USCS § 1395w-3(b)] for the furnishing of such an item or service in that area, unless the Secretary finds that the expenses were incurred in a case of urgent need, or in other circumstances specified by the Secretary;

(18) which are covered skilled nursing facility services described in section 1888(e)(2)(A)(i) [42 USCS § 1395yy(e)(2)(A)(i)] and which are furnished to an individual who is a resident of a skilled nursing facility during a period in which the resident is provided covered post-hospital extended care services (or, for services described in section 1861(s)(2)(D) [42 USCS § 1395x(s)(2)(D)], which are furnished to such an individual without regard to such period), by an entity other than the skilled nursing facility, unless the services are furnished under arrangements (as defined in section 1861(w)(1) [42 USCS § 1395x(w)(1)]) with the entity made by the skilled nursing facility;

(19) which are for items or services which are furnished pursuant to a private contract described in section 1802(b) [42 USCS § 1395a(b)];

(20) in the case of outpatient physical therapy services, outpatient speech-language pathology services, or outpatient occupational therapy services furnished as an incident to a physician's professional services (as described in section 1861(s)(2)(A) [42 USCS § 1395x(s)(2)(A)]), that do not meet the standards and conditions (other than any licensing requirement specified by the Secretary) under the second sentence of section 1861(p) [42 USCS § 1395x(p)] (or under such sentence through the operation of subsection (g) or (ll)(2) of section 1861 [42 USCS § 1395x]) as such standards and conditions would apply to such therapy services if furnished by a therapist;

(21) where such expenses are for home health services (including medical supplies described in section 1861(m)(5) [42 USCS § 1395x(m)(5)], but excluding durable medical equipment to the extent provided for in such

section) furnished to an individual who is under a plan of care of the home health agency if the claim for payment for such services is not submitted by the agency;

(22) subject to subsection (h), for which a claim is submitted other than in an electronic form specified by the Secretary;

(23) **[Caution: This paragraph applies to advanced diagnostic imaging services furnished on or after January 1, 2012, as provided by § 135(a)(2)(B) of Act July 15, 2008, P. L. 110-275, which appears as a note to this section.]** which are the technical component of advanced diagnostic imaging services described in section 1834(e)(1)(B) [42 USCS § 1395m(e)(1)(B)] for which payment is made under the fee schedule established under section 1848(b) [42 USCS § 1395w-4(b)] and that are furnished by a supplier (as defined in section 1861(d) [42 USCS § 1395x(d)]), if such supplier is not accredited by an accreditation organization designated by the Secretary under section 1834(e)(2)(B) [42 USCS § 1395m(e)(2)(B)];

(24) where such expenses are for renal dialysis services (as defined in subparagraph (B) of section 1881(b)(14) [42 USCS § 1395rr(b)(14)]) for which payment is made under such section unless such payment is made under such section to a provider of services or a renal dialysis facility for such services; or

(25) not later than January 1, 2014, for which the payment is other than by electronic funds transfer (EFT) or an electronic remittance in a form as specified in ASC X12 835 Health Care Payment and Remittance Advice or subsequent standard.

Paragraph (7) shall not apply to Federally qualified health center services described in section 1861(aa)(3)(B) [42 USCS § 1395x(aa)(3)(B)]. In making a national coverage determination (as defined in paragraph (1)(B) of section 1869(f) [42 USCS § 1395ff(f)]) the Secretary shall ensure consistent with subsection (l) that the public is afforded notice and opportunity to comment prior to implementation by the Secretary of the determination; meetings of advisory committees with respect to the determination are made on the record; in making the determination, the Secretary has considered applicable information (including clinical experience and medical, technical, and scientific evidence) with respect to the subject matter of the determination; and in the determination, provide a clear statement of the basis for the determination (including responses to comments received from the public), the assumptions underlying that basis, and make available to the public the data (other than proprietary data) considered in making the determination.

(b) Medicare as secondary payer. (1) Requirements of group health plans. (A) Working aged under group health plans. (i) In general. A group health plan—

(I) may not take into account that an individual (or the individual's spouse) who is covered under the plan by virtue of the individual's current employment status with an employer is entitled to benefits under this title under section 226(a) [42 USCS § 426(a)], and

(II) shall provide that any individual age 65 or older (and the spouse age 65 or older of any individual) who has current employment status with an employer shall be entitled to the same benefits under the plan under the same conditions as any such individual (or spouse) under age 65.

(ii) Exclusion of group health plan of a small employer. Clause (i) shall not apply to a group health plan unless the plan is a plan of, or contributed to by, an employer that has 20 or more employees for each working day in each of 20 or more calendar weeks in the current calendar year or the preceding calendar year.

(iii) Exception for small employers in multiemployer or multiple employer group health plans. Clause (i) also shall not apply with respect to individuals enrolled in a multiemployer or multiple employer group health plan if the coverage of the individuals under the plan is by virtue of current employment status with an employer that does not have 20 or more individuals in current employment status for each working day in each of 20 or more calendar weeks in the current calendar year and the preceding calendar year; except that the exception provided in this clause shall only apply if the plan elects treatment under this clause.

(iv) Exception for individuals with end stage renal disease. Subparagraph (C) shall apply instead of clause (i) to an item or service furnished in a month to an individual if for the month the individual is, or (without regard to entitlement under section 226 [42 USCS § 426]) would upon application be, entitled to benefits under section 226A [42 USCS § 426-1].

(v) "Group health plan" defined. In this subparagraph, and subparagraph (C), the term "group health plan" has the meaning given such term in section 5000(b)(1) of the Internal Revenue Code of 1986 [26 USCS § 5000(b)(1)], without regard to section 5000(d) of such Code [26 USCS § 5000(d)].

(B) Disabled individuals in large group

health plans. (i) In general. A large group health plan (as defined in clause (iii)) may not take into account that an individual (or a member of the individual's family) who is covered under the plan by virtue of the individual's current employment status with an employer is entitled to benefits under this title [42 USCS §§ 1395 et seq.] under section 226(b) [42 USCS § 426(b)].

(ii) Exception for individuals with end stage renal disease. Subparagraph (C) shall apply instead of clause (i) to an item or service furnished in a month to an individual if for the month the individual is, or (without regard to entitlement under section 226 [42 USCS § 426]) would upon application be, entitled to benefits under section 226A [42 USCS § 426-1].

(iii) Large group health plan defined. In this subparagraph, the term "large group health plan" has the meaning given such term in section 5000(b)(2) of the Internal Revenue Code of 1986 [26 USCS § 5000(b)(2)], without regard to section 5000(d) of such Code [26 USCS § 5000(d)].

(C) Individuals with end stage renal disease. A group health plan (as defined in subparagraph (A)(v))—

(i) may not take into account that an individual is entitled to or eligible for benefits under this title [42 USCS §§ 1395 et seq.] under section 226A [42 USCS § 426-1] during the 12-month period which begins with the first month in which the individual becomes entitled to benefits under part A [42 USCS §§ 1395c et seq.] under the provisions of section 226A [42 USCS § 426-1], or, if earlier, the first month in which the individual would have been entitled to benefits under such part under the provisions of section 226A [42 USCS § 426-1] if the individual had filed an application for such benefits; and

(ii) may not differentiate in the benefits it provides between individuals having end stage renal disease and other individuals covered by such plan on the basis of the existence of end stage renal disease, the need for renal dialysis, or in any other manner;

except that clause (ii) shall not prohibit a plan from paying benefits secondary to this title [42 USCS §§ 1395 et seq.] when an individual is entitled to or eligible for benefits under this title [42 USCS §§ 1395 et seq.] under section 226A [42 USCS § 426-1] after the end of the 12-month period described in clause (i). Effective for items and services furnished on or after February 1, 1991, and before the date of enactment of the Balanced Budget Act of 1997 [enacted Aug. 5, 1997], (with respect to periods beginning on or after February 1, 1990), this subparagraph shall be applied by substituting "18-month" for "12-month" each place it appears. Effective for items and services furnished on or after the date of enactment of the Balanced Budget Act of 1997 [enacted Aug. 5, 1997] [,] (with respect to periods beginning on or after the date that is 18 months prior to such date), clauses (i) and (ii) shall be applied by substituting "30-month" for "12-month" each place it appears.

(D) Treatment of certain members of religious orders. In this subsection, an individual shall not be considered to be employed, or an employee, with respect to the performance of services as a member of a religious order which are considered employment only by virtue of an election made by the religious order under section 3121(r) of the Internal Revenue Code of 1986 [26 USCS § 3121(r)].

(E) General provisions. For purposes of this subsection: (i) Aggregation rules. (I) All employers treated as a single employer under subsection (a) or (b) of section 52 of the Internal Revenue Code of 1986 [26 USCS § 52(a) or (b)] shall be treated as a single employer.

(II) All employees of the members of an affiliated service group (as defined in section 414(m) of such Code [26 USCS § 414(m)]) shall be treated as employed by a single employer.

(III) Leased employees (as defined in section 414(n)(2) of such Code [26 USCS § 414(n)(2)]) shall be treated as employees of the person for whom they perform services to the extent they are so treated under section 414(n) of such Code [26 USCS § 414(n)].

In applying sections of the Internal Revenue Code of 1986 [26 USCS §§ 1 et seq.] under this clause, the Secretary shall rely upon regulations and decisions of the Secretary of the Treasury respecting such sections.

(ii) Current employment status defined. An individual has "current employment status" with an employer if the individual is an employee, is the employer, or is associated with the employer in a business relationship.

(iii) Treatment of self-employed persons as employers. The term "employer" includes a self-employed person.

(F) Limitation on beneficiary liability. An individual who is entitled to benefits under this title [42 USCS §§ 1395 et seq.] and is furnished an item or service for which such benefits are incorrectly paid is not liable for repayment of such benefits under this paragraph unless payment of such benefits was made to the individual.

(2) Medicare secondary payer. (A) In general. Payment under this title [42 USCS §§ 1395 et seq.] may not be made, except as provided in subparagraph (B), with respect to any item or service to the extent that—

(i) payment has been made, or can reasonably be expected to be made, with respect to the item or service as required under paragraph (1), or

(ii) payment has been made or can reasonably be expected to be made under a workmen's compensation law or plan of the United States or a State or under an automobile or liability insurance policy or plan (including a self-insured plan) or under no fault insurance.

In this subsection, the term "primary plan" means a group health plan or large group health plan, to the extent that clause (i) applies, and a workmen's compensation law or plan, an automobile or liability insurance policy or plan (including a self-insured plan) or no fault insurance, to the extent that clause (ii) applies. An entity that engages in a business, trade, or profession shall be deemed to have a self-insured plan if it carries its own risk (whether by a failure to obtain insurance, or otherwise) in whole or in part.

(B) Conditional payment. (i) Authority to make conditional payment. The Secretary may make payment under this title with respect to an item or service if a primary plan described in subparagraph (A)(ii) has not made or cannot reasonably be expected to make payment with respect to such item or service promptly (as determined in accordance with regulations). Any such payment by the Secretary shall be conditioned on reimbursement to the appropriate Trust Fund in accordance with the succeeding provisions of this subsection. (ii) Repayment required. A primary plan, and an entity that receives payment from a primary plan, shall reimburse the appropriate Trust Fund for any payment made by the Secretary under this title [42 USCS §§ 1395 et seq.] with respect to an item or service if it is demonstrated that such primary plan has or had a responsibility to make payment with respect to such item or service. A primary plan's responsibility for such payment may be demonstrated by a judgment, a payment conditioned upon the recipient's compromise, waiver, or release (whether or not there is a determination or admission of liability) of payment for items or services included in a claim against the primary plan or the primary plan's insured, or by other means. If reimbursement is not made to the appropriate Trust Fund before the expiration of the 60-day period that begins on the date notice of, or information related to, a primary plan's responsibility for such payment or other information is received, the Secretary may charge interest (beginning with the date on which the notice or other information is received) on the amount of the reimbursement until reimbursement is made (at a rate determined by the Secretary in accordance with regulations of the Secretary of the Treasury applicable to charges for late payments).

(iii) Action by United States. In order to recover payment made under this title [42 USCS §§ 1395 et seq.] for an item or service, the United States may bring an action against any or all entities that are or were required or responsible (directly, as an insurer or self-insurer, as a third-party administrator, as an employer that sponsors or contributes to a group health plan, or large group health plan, or otherwise) to make payment with respect to the same item or service (or any portion thereof) under a primary plan. The United States may, in accordance with paragraph (3)(A) collect double damages against any such entity. In addition, the United States may recover under this clause from any entity that has received payment from a primary plan or from the proceeds of a primary plan's payment to any entity. The United States may not recover from a third-party administrator under this clause in cases where the third-party administrator would not be able to recover the amount at issue from the employer or group health plan and is not employed by or under contract with the employer or group health plan at the time the action for recovery is initiated by the United States or for whom it provides administrative services due to the insolvency or bankruptcy of the employer or plan.

(iv) Subrogation rights. The United States shall be subrogated (to the extent of payment made under this title [42 USCS §§ 1395 et seq.] for such an item or service) to any right under this subsection of an individual or any other entity to payment with respect to such item or service under a primary plan.

(v) Waiver of rights. The Secretary may waive (in whole or in part) the provisions of this subparagraph in the case of an individual claim if the Secretary determines that the waiver is in the best interests of the program established under this title [42 USCS §§ 1395 et seq.].

(vi) Claims-filing period. Notwithstanding any other time limits that may exist for filing a claim under an employer group health plan, the United States may seek to recover conditional payments in accordance with this subparagraph where the request for payment is submitted to the entity required or responsible under this subsection to pay with respect to the item or service (or any portion thereof) under a primary plan within the 3-year period beginning on the date on which the item or service was furnished.

(C) Treatment of questionnaires. The Secretary may not fail to make payment under subparagraph (A) solely on the ground that an individual failed to complete a questionnaire concerning the existence of a primary plan.

(3) Enforcement. (A) Private cause of action. There is established a private cause of action for damages (which shall be in an amount double the amount otherwise provided) in the case of a primary plan which fails to provide for primary payment (or appropriate reimbursement) in accordance with paragraphs (1) and (2)(A).

(B) Reference to excise tax with respect to nonconforming group health plans. For provision imposing an excise tax with respect to nonconforming group health plans, see section 5000 of the Internal Revenue Code of 1986 [26 USCS § 5000].

(C) Prohibition of financial incentives not to enroll in a group health plan or a large group health plan. It is unlawful for an employer or other entity to offer any financial or other incentive for an individual entitled to benefits under this title [42 USCS §§ 1395 et seq.] not to enroll (or to terminate enrollment) under a group health plan or a large group health plan which would (in the case of such enrollment) be a primary plan (as defined in paragraph (2)(A)). Any entity that violates the previous sentence is subject to a civil money penalty of not to exceed $5,000 for each such violation. The provisions of section 1128A [42 USCS § 1320a-7a] (other than subsections (a) and (b)) shall apply to a civil money penalty under the previous sentence in the same manner as such provisions apply to a penalty or proceeding under section 1128A(a) [42 USCS § 1320a-7a(a)].

(4) Coordination of benefits. Where payment for an item or service by a primary plan is less than the amount of the charge for such item or service and is not payment in full, payment may be made under this title [42 USCS §§ 1395 et seq.] (without regard to deductibles and coinsurance under this title [42 USCS §§ 1395 et seq.]) for the remainder of such charge, but—

(A) payment under this title [42 USCS §§ 1395 et seq.] may not exceed an amount which would be payable under this title [42 USCS §§ 1395 et seq.] for such item or service if paragraph (2)(A) did not apply; and

(B) payment under this title [42 USCS §§ 1395 et seq.], when combined with the amount payable under the primary plan, may not exceed—

(i) in the case of an item or service payment for which is determined under this title [42 USCS §§ 1395 et seq.] on the basis of reasonable cost (or other cost-related basis) or under section 1886 [42 USCS § 1395ww], the amount which would be payable under this title [42 USCS §§ 1395 et seq.] on such basis, and

(ii) in the case of an item or service for which payment is authorized under this title [42 USCS §§ 1395 et seq.] on another basis—

(I) the amount which would be payable under the primary plan (without regard to deductibles and coinsurance under such plan), or

(II) the reasonable charge or other amount which would be payable under this title [42 USCS §§ 1395 et seq.] (without regard to deductibles and coinsurance under this title [42 USCS §§ 1395 et seq.]),

whichever is greater.

(5) Identification of secondary payer situations. (A) Requesting matching information. (i) Commissioner of Social Security. The Commissioner of Social Security shall, not less often than annually, transmit to the Secretary of the Treasury a list of the names and TINs of medicare beneficiaries (as defined in section 6103(1)(12) of the Internal Revenue Code of 1986 [26 USCS § 6103(l)(12)]) and request that the Secretary disclose to the Commissioner the information described in subparagraph (A) of such section.

(ii) Administrator. The Administrator of the Centers for Medicare & Medicaid Services shall request, not less often than annually, the Commissioner of the Social Security Administration to disclose to the Administrator the information described in subparagraph (B) of section 6103(l)(12) of the Internal Revenue Code of 1986 [26 USCS § 6103(l)(12)(B)].

(B) Disclosure to fiscal intermediaries and carriers. In addition to any other information provided under this title [42 USCS §§ 1395 et seq.] to fiscal intermediaries and carriers, the Administrator shall disclose to such intermediaries and carriers (or to such a single intermediary or carrier as the Secretary may designate) the information received under subparagraph (A) for purposes of carrying out this subsection.

(C) Contacting employers. (i) In general. With respect to each individual (in this subparagraph referred to as an "employee") who was furnished a written statement under section 6051 of the Internal Revenue Code of 1986 [26 USCS § 6051] by a qualified employer (as defined in section 6103(l)(12)(E)(iii) of such Code [26 USCS § 6103(l)(12)(E)(iii)]), as disclosed under subparagraph (B), the appropriate fiscal intermediary or carrier shall contact the employer in order to determine during what period the employee or employee's spouse may be (or have been) covered under a group health plan of the employer and the nature of the coverage that is or was provided under the plan (including the name, address, and identifying number of the plan).

(ii) Employer response. Within 30 days of the date of receipt of the inquiry, the employer shall notify the intermediary or carrier making the inquiry as to the determinations described in clause (i). An employer (other than a Federal or other governmental entity) who willfully or repeatedly fails to provide timely and accurate notice in accordance with the previous sentence shall be subject to a civil money penalty of not to exceed $1,000 for each individual with respect to which such an inquiry is made. The provisions of section 1128A [42 USCS § 1320a-7a] (other than subsections (a) and (b)) shall apply to a civil money penalty under the previous sentence in the same manner as such provisions apply to a penalty or proceeding under section 1128A(a) [42 USCS § 1320a-7a(a)].

(D) Obtaining information from beneficiaries. Before an individual applies for benefits under part A [42 USCS §§ 1395c et seq.] or enrolls under part B [42 USCS §§ 1395j et seq.], the Administrator shall mail the individual a questionnaire to obtain information on whether the individual is covered under a primary plan and the nature of the coverage provided under the plan, including the name, address, and identifying number of the plan.

(6) Screening requirements for providers and suppliers. (A) In general. Notwithstanding any other provision of this title [42 USCS §§ 1395 et seq.], no payment may be made for any item or service furnished under part B [42 USCS §§ 1395j et seq.] unless the entity furnishing such item or service completes (to the best of its knowledge and on the basis of information obtained from the individual to whom the item or service is furnished) the portion of the claim form relating to the availability of other health benefit plans.

(B) Penalties. An entity that knowingly, willfully, and repeatedly fails to complete a claim form in accordance with subparagraph (A) or provides inaccurate information relating to the availability of other health benefit plans on a claim form under such subparagraph shall be subject to a civil money penalty of not to exceed $2,000 for each such incident. The provisions of section 1128A [42 USCS § 1320a-7a] (other than subsections (a) and (b)) shall apply to a civil money penalty under the previous sentence in the same manner as such provisions apply to a penalty or proceeding under section 1128A(a) [42 USCS § 1320a-7a(a)].

(7) Required submission of information by group health plans. (A) Requirement. On and after the first day of the first calendar quarter beginning after the date that is 1 year after the date of the enactment of this paragraph [enacted Dec. 29, 2007], an entity serving as an insurer or third party administrator for a group health plan, as defined in paragraph (1)(A)(v), and, in the case of a group health plan that is self-insured and self-administered, a plan administrator or fiduciary, shall—

(i) secure from the plan sponsor and plan participants such information as the Secretary shall specify for the purpose of identifying situations where the group health plan is or has been a primary plan to the program under this title [42 USCS §§ 1395 et seq.]; and

(ii) submit such information to the Secretary in a form and manner (including frequency) specified by the Secretary.

(B) Enforcement. (i) In general. An entity, a plan administrator, or a fiduciary described in subparagraph (A) that fails to comply with the requirements under such subparagraph shall be subject to a civil money penalty of $1,000 for each day of noncompliance for each individual for which the information under such subparagraph should have been submitted. The provisions of subsections (e) and (k) of section 1128A [42 USCS § 1320a-7a] shall apply to a civil money penalty under the previous sentence in the same manner as such provisions apply to a penalty or proceeding under section 1128A(a) [42 USCS § 1320a-7a(a)]. A civil money penalty under this clause shall be in addition to any other penalties prescribed by law and in addition to any Medicare secondary payer claim under this title with respect to an individual.

(ii) Deposit of amounts collected. Any amounts collected pursuant to clause (i) shall be deposited in the Federal Hospital Insurance Trust Fund under section 1817 [42 USCS § 1395i].

(C) Sharing of information. Notwithstanding any other provision of law, under terms and conditions established by the Secretary, the

Secretary—

(i) shall share information on entitlement under Part A [42 USCS §§ 1395c et seq.] and enrollment under Part B under this title [42 USCS §§ 1395j et seq.] with entities, plan administrators, and fiduciaries described in subparagraph (A);

(ii) may share the entitlement and enrollment information described in clause (i) with entities and persons not described in such clause; and

(iii) may share information collected under this paragraph as necessary for purposes of the proper coordination of benefits.

(D) Implementation. Notwithstanding any other provision of law, the Secretary may implement this paragraph by program instruction or otherwise.

(8) Required submission of information by or on behalf of liability insurance (including self-insurance), no fault insurance, and workers' compensation laws and plans. (A) Requirement. On and after the first day of the first calendar quarter beginning after the date that is 18 months after the date of the enactment of this paragraph [enacted Dec. 29, 2007], an applicable plan shall—

(i) determine whether a claimant (including an individual whose claim is unresolved) is entitled to benefits under the program under this title [42 USCS §§ 1395 et seq.] on any basis; and

(ii) if the claimant is determined to be so entitled, submit the information described in subparagraph (B) with respect to the claimant to the Secretary in a form and manner (including frequency) specified by the Secretary.

(B) Required information. The information described in this subparagraph is—

(i) the identity of the claimant for which the determination under subparagraph (A) was made; and

(ii) such other information as the Secretary shall specify in order to enable the Secretary to make an appropriate determination concerning coordination of benefits, including any applicable recovery claim.

(C) Timing. Information shall be submitted under subparagraph (A)(ii) within a time specified by the Secretary after the claim is resolved through a settlement, judgment, award, or other payment (regardless of whether or not there is a determination or admission of liability).

(D) Claimant. For purposes of subparagraph (A), the term "claimant" includes—

(i) an individual filing a claim directly against the applicable plan; and

(ii) an individual filing a claim against an individual or entity insured or covered by the applicable plan.

(E) Enforcement. (i) In general. An applicable plan that fails to comply with the requirements under subparagraph (A) with respect to any claimant shall be subject to a civil money penalty of $1,000 for each day of noncompliance with respect to each claimant. The provisions of subsections (e) and (k) of section 1128A [42 USCS § 1320a-7a] shall apply to a civil money penalty under the previous sentence in the same manner as such provisions apply to a penalty or proceeding under section 1128A(a) [42 USCS § 1320a-7a(a)]. A civil money penalty under this clause shall be in addition to any other penalties prescribed by law and in addition to any Medicare secondary payer claim under this title [42 USCS §§ 1395 et seq.] with respect to an individual.

(ii) Deposit of amounts collected. Any amounts collected pursuant to clause (i) shall be deposited in the Federal Hospital Insurance Trust Fund.

(F) Applicable plan. In this paragraph, the term "applicable plan" means the following laws, plans, or other arrangements, including the fiduciary or administrator for such law, plan, or arrangement:

(i) Liability insurance (including self-insurance).

(ii) No fault insurance.

(iii) Workers' compensation laws or plans.

(G) Sharing of information. The Secretary may share information collected under this paragraph as necessary for purposes of the proper coordination of benefits.

(H) Implementation. Notwithstanding any other provision of law, the Secretary may implement this paragraph by program instruction or otherwise.

(c) Drug products. No payment may be made under part B [42 USCS §§ 1395j et seq.] for any expenses incurred for—

(1) a drug product—

(A) which is described in section 107(c)(3) of the Drug Amendments of 1962 [21 USCS § 321 note],

(B) which may be dispensed only upon prescription,

(C) for which the Secretary has issued a notice of an opportunity for a hearing under subsection (e) of section 505 of the Federal Food, Drug, and Cosmetic Act [21 USCS § 355(e)] on a proposed order of the Secretary to withdraw approval of an application for such drug product under such section because the Secretary has determined that the drug is less than effective for all conditions of use prescribed, recommended, or suggested in its labeling, and

(D) for which the Secretary has not determined there is a compelling justification for its medical need; and

(2) any other drug product—

(A) which is identical, related, or similar (as determined in accordance with section 310.6 of title 21 of the Code of Federal Regulations) to a drug product described in paragraph (1), and

(B) for which the Secretary has not determined there is a compelling justification for its medical need,

until such time as the Secretary withdraws such proposed order.

(d) Payment for EMTALA-mandated screening and stabilization services. For purposes of subsection (a)(1)(A), in the case of any item or service that is required to be provided pursuant to section 1867 [42 USCS § 1395dd] to an individual who is entitled to benefits under this title [42 USCS §§ 1395 et seq.], determinations as to whether the item or service is reasonable and necessary shall be made on the basis of the information available to the treating physician or practitioner (including the patient's presenting symptoms or complaint) at the time the item or service was ordered or furnished by the physician or practitioner (and not on the patient's principal diagnosis). When making such determinations with respect to such an item or service, the Secretary shall not consider the frequency with which the item or service was provided to the patient before or after the time of the admission or visit.

(e) Item or service by excluded individual or entity or at direction of excluded physician; limitation of liability of beneficiaries with respect to services furnished by excluded individuals and entities. (1) No payment may be made under this title [42 USCS §§ 1395 et seq.] with respect to any item or service (other than an emergency item or service, not including items or services furnished in an emergency room of a hospital) furnished—

(A) by an individual or entity during the period when such individual or entity is excluded pursuant to section 1128, 1128A, 1156 or 1842(j)(2) [42 USCS § 1320a-7, 1320a-7a, 1320c-5, or 1395u(j)(2)] from participation in the program under this title [42 USCS §§ 1395 et seq.]; or

(B) at the medical direction or on the prescription of a physician during the period when he is excluded pursuant to section 1128, 1128A, 1156 or 1842(j)(2) [42 USCS § 1320a-7, 1320a-7a, 1320c-5, or 1395u(j)(2)] from participation in the program under this title [42 USCS §§ 1395 et seq.] and when the person furnishing such item or service knew or had reason to know of the exclusion (after a reasonable time period after reasonable notice has been furnished to the person).

(2) Where an individual eligible for benefits under this title [42 USCS §§ 1395 et seq.] submits a claim for payment for items or services furnished by an individual or entity excluded from participation in the programs under this title [42 USCS §§ 1395 et seq.], pursuant to section 1128, 1128A, 1156, 1160 [42 USCS § 1320a-7, 1320a-7a, 1320c-5, 1320c-9] (as in effect on September 2, 1982), 1842(j)(2), 1862(d) [42 USCS § 1395u(j)(2), 1395y(d)] (as in effect on the date of the enactment of the Medicare and Medicaid Patient and Program Protection Act of 1987 [enacted Aug. 18, 1987]), or 1866 [42 USCS § 1395cc], and such beneficiary did not know or have reason to know that such individual or entity was so excluded, then, to the extent permitted by this title [42 USCS §§ 1395 et seq.], and notwithstanding such exclusion, payment shall be made for such items or services. In each such case the Secretary shall notify the beneficiary of the exclusion of the individual or entity furnishing the items or services. Payment shall not be made for items or services furnished by an excluded individual or entity to a beneficiary after a reasonable time (as determined by the Secretary in regulations) after the Secretary has notified the beneficiary of the exclusion of that individual or entity.

(f) Utilization guidelines for provision of home health services. The Secretary shall establish utilization guidelines for the determination of whether or not payment may be made, consistent with paragraph (1)(A) of subsection (a), under part A or part B [42 USCS §§ 1395c et seq. or 1395j et seq.] for expenses incurred with respect to the provision of home health services, and shall provide for the implementation of such guidelines through a process of selective postpayment coverage review by intermediaries or otherwise.

(g) Contracts with utilization and quality control peer review organizations. The Secretary shall, in making the determinations under paragraphs (1) and (9) of subsection (a), and for the purposes of promoting the effective, efficient, and economical delivery of health care services, and of promoting the quality of services of the type for which payment may be made under this title [42 USCS §§ 1395 et seq.], enter into contracts with utilization and quality control peer review organizations pursuant to part B of title XI of this Act [42 USCS §§ 1320c et seq.].

(h) Waiver of electronic submission of claims. (1) The Secretary—

(A) shall waive the application of subsection (a)(22) in cases in which—

(i) there is no method available for the submission of claims in an electronic form; or

(ii) the entity submitting the claim is a small provider of services or supplier; and

(B) may waive the application of such subsection in such unusual cases as the Secretary finds appropriate.

(2) For purposes of this subsection, the term "small provider of services or supplier" means—

(A) a provider of services with fewer than 25 full-time equivalent employees; or

(B) a physician, practitioner, facility, or supplier (other than provider of services) with fewer than 10 full-time equivalent employees.

(i) Awards and contracts for original research and experimentation of new and existing medical procedures; conditions. In order to supplement the activities of the Medicare Payment Advisory Commission under section 1886(e) [42 USCS § 1395ww(e)] in assessing the safety, efficacy, and cost-effectiveness of new and existing medical procedures, the Secretary may carry out, or award grants or contracts for, original research and experimentation of the type described in clause (ii) of section 1886(e)(6)(E) [42 USCS § 1395ww(e)(6)(E)(ii)] with respect to such a procedure if the Secretary finds that—

(1) such procedure is not of sufficient commercial value to justify research and experimentation by a commercial organization;

(2) research and experimentation with respect to such procedure is not of a type that may appropriately be carried out by an institute, division, or bureau of the National Institutes of Health; and

(3) such procedure has the potential to be more cost-effective in the treatment of a condition than procedures currently in use with respect to such condition.

(j) Advisory committees with respect to exclusions from medicare coverage. (1) Any advisory committee appointed to advise the Secretary on matters relating to the interpretation, application, or implementation of subsection (a)(1) shall assure the full participation of a nonvoting member in the deliberations of the advisory committee, and shall provide such nonvoting member access to all information and data made available to voting members of the advisory committee, other than information that—

(A) is exempt from disclosure pursuant to subsection (a) of section 552 of title 5, United States Code, by reason of subsection (b)(4) of such section (relating to trade secrets); or

(B) the Secretary determines would present a conflict of interest relating to such nonvoting member.

(2) If an advisory committee described in paragraph (1) organizes into panels of experts according to types of items or services considered by the advisory committee, any such panel of experts may report any recommendation with respect to such items or services directly to the Secretary without the prior approval of the advisory committee or an executive committee thereof.

(k) Treatment of certain dental claims. (1) Subject to paragraph (2), a group health plan (as defined in subsection (a)(1)(A)(v)) providing supplemental or secondary coverage to individuals also entitled to services under this title shall not require a medicare claims determination under this title for dental benefits specifically excluded under subsection (a)(12) as a condition of making a claims determination for such benefits under the group health plan.

(2) A group health plan may require a claims determination under this title in cases involving or appearing to involve inpatient dental hospital services or dental services expressly covered under this title pursuant to actions taken by the Secretary.

(l) National and local coverage determination process. (1) Factors and evidence used in making national coverage determinations. The Secretary shall make available to the public the factors considered in making national coverage determinations of whether an item or service is reasonable and necessary. The Secretary shall develop guidance documents to carry out this paragraph in a manner similar to the development of guidance documents under section 701(h) of the Federal Food, Drug, and Cosmetic Act (21 U.S.C. 371(h)).

(2) Timeframe for decisions on requests for national coverage determinations. In the case of a request for a national coverage determination that—

(A) does not require a technology assessment from an outside entity or deliberation from the Medicare Coverage Advisory Committee, the decision on the request shall be made not later than 6 months after the date of the request; or

(B) requires such an assessment or deliberation and in which a clinical trial is not requested, the decision on the request shall be made not later than 9 months after the date of the request.

(3) Process for public comment in national coverage determinations. (A) Period for proposed decision. Not later than the end of the 6-month period (or 9-month period for requests described in paragraph (2)(B)) that begins on the date a request for a national coverage determination is made, the Secretary shall make a draft of proposed decision on the request available to the public through the Internet website of the Centers for Medicare & Medicaid Services or other appropriate means.

(B) 30-day period for public comment. Beginning on the date the Secretary makes a draft of the proposed decision available under subparagraph (A), the Secretary shall provide a 30-day period for public comment on such draft.

(C) 60-day period for final decision. Not later than 60 days after the conclusion of the 30-day period referred to under subparagraph (B), the Secretary shall—

(i) make a final decision on the request;

(ii) include in such final decision summaries of the public comments received and responses to such comments;

(iii) make available to the public the clinical evidence and other data used in making such a decision when the decision differs from the recommendations of the Medicare Coverage Advisory Committee; and

(iv) in the case of a final decision under clause (i) to grant the request for the national coverage determination, the Secretary shall assign a temporary or permanent code (whether existing or unclassified) and implement the coding change.

(4) Consultation with outside experts in certain national coverage determinations. With respect to a request for a national coverage determination for which there is not a review by the Medicare Coverage Advisory Committee, the Secretary shall consult with appropriate outside clinical experts.

(5) Local coverage determination process. (A) Plan to promote consistency of coverage determinations. The Secretary shall develop a plan to evaluate new local coverage determinations to determine which determinations should be adopted nationally and to what extent greater consistency can be achieved among local coverage determinations.

(B) Consultation. The Secretary shall require the fiscal intermediaries or carriers providing services within the same area to consult on all new local coverage determinations within the area.

(C) Dissemination of information. The Secretary should serve as a center to disseminate information on local coverage determinations among fiscal intermediaries and carriers to reduce duplication of effort.

(6) National and local coverage determination defined. For purposes of this subsection—

(A) National coverage determination. The term "national coverage determination" means a determination by the Secretary with respect to whether or not a particular item or service is covered nationally under this title.

(B) Local coverage determination. The term "local coverage determination" has the meaning given that in section 1869(f)(2)(B) [42 USCS § 1395ff(f)(2)(B)].

(m) Coverage of routine costs associated with certain clinical trials of category A devices. (1) In general. In the case of an individual entitled to benefits under part A [42 USCS §§ 1395c et seq.], or enrolled under part B [42 USCS §§ 1395j et seq.], or both who participates in a category A clinical trial, the Secretary shall not exclude under subsection (a)(1) payment for coverage of routine costs of care (as defined by the Secretary) furnished to such individual in the trial.

(2) Category A clinical trial. For purposes of paragraph (1), a "category A clinical trial" means a trial of a medical device if—

(A) the trial is of an experimental/investigational (category A) medical device (as defined in regulations under section 405.201(b) of title 42, Code of Federal Regulations (as in effect as of September 1, 2003));

(B) the trial meets criteria established by the Secretary to ensure that the trial conforms to appropriate scientific and ethical standards; and

(C) in the case of a trial initiated before January 1, 2010, the device involved in the trial has been determined by the Secretary to be intended for use in the diagnosis, monitoring, or treatment of an immediately life-threatening disease or condition.

(n) Requirement of a surety bond for certain providers of services and suppliers. (1) In general. The Secretary may require a provider of services or supplier described in paragraph (2) to provide the Secretary on a continuing basis with a surety bond in a form specified by the Secretary in an amount (not less than $50,000) that the Secretary determines is commensurate with the volume of the billing of the provider of services or supplier.

The Secretary may waive the requirement of a bond under the preceding sentence in the case of a provider of services or supplier that provides a comparable surety bond under State law.

(2) Provider of services or supplier described. A provider of services or supplier described in this paragraph is a provider of services or supplier the Secretary determines appropriate based on the level of risk involved with respect to the provider of services or supplier, and consistent with the surety bond requirements under sections 1834(a)(16)(B) and 1861(o)(7)(C) [42 USCS §§ 1395m(a)(16)(B) and 1395x(o)(7)(C)].

(o) Suspension of payments pending investigation of credible allegations of fraud. (1) In general. The Secretary may suspend payments to a provider of services or supplier under this title pending an investigation of a credible allegation of fraud against the provider of services or supplier, unless the Secretary determines there is good cause not to suspend such payments.

(2) Consultation. The Secretary shall consult with the Inspector General of the Department of Health and Human Services in determining whether there is a credible allegation of fraud against a provider of services or supplier.

(3) Promulgation of regulations. The Secretary shall promulgate regulations to carry out this subsection and section 1903(i)(2)(C) [42 USCS § 1396b(i)(2)(C)].

(Aug. 14, 1935, ch 531, Title XVIII, Part E [D] [C], § 1862, as added July 30, 1965, P.L. 89-97 Title I, Part 1, § 102(a), 79 Stat. 325; Jan. 2, 1968, P. L. 90-248, Title I, Part 3, §§ 127(b), 128, 81 Stat. 846, 847; Oct. 30, 1972, P. L. 92-603, Title II, §§ 210, 211(c)(1), 229(a), 256(c), 86 Stat. 1382, 1384, 1408, 1447; Dec. 31, 1973, P. L. 93-233, § 18(k)(3), 87 Stat. 970; Oct. 26, 1974, P. L. 93-480, § 4(a), 88 Stat. 1454; Dec. 31, 1975, P. L. 94-182, Title I, § 103, 89 Stat. 1051; Oct. 25, 1977, P. L. 95-142, §§ 7(a), 13(a), (b)(1), (2), 91 Stat. 1192, 1197, 1198; Dec. 13, 1977, P. L. 95-210, § 1(f), 91 Stat. 1487; June 17, 1980, P. L. 96-272, Title III, § 308(a), 94 Stat. 531; Dec. 5, 1980, P. L. 96-499, Title IX, Part A, Subpart II, § 913(b), Part B, Subpart I, §§ 936(c), 939(a), Subpart II, § 953, 94 Stat. 2620, 2640, 2647; Dec. 28, 1980, P. L. 96-611, § 1(a)(3), 94 Stat. 3566; Aug. 13, 1981, P. L. 97-35, Title XXI, Subtitle A, Ch 1, § 2103(a)(1) Subtitle B, Ch 3, § 2146(a), Ch 4, 2152(a), 95 Stat. 787, 800, 802; Sept. 3, 1982, P. L. 97-248, Title I, Subtitle A, Part I, Subpart C, § 116(b), Part II, § 122(f), (g)(1), Part III, § 128(a)(2)–(4), Subtitle C, §§ 142, 148(a), 96 Stat. 353, 362, 366, 381, 394; Jan. 12, 1983, P. L. 97-448, Title III, § 309(b)(10), 96 Stat. 2409; April 20, 1983, P. L. 98-21, Title VI, §§ 601(f), 602(e), 97 Stat. 162; July 18, 1984, P. L. 98-369, Division B, Title III, Subtitle A, Part I, §§ 2301(a), 2304(c), 2313(c), Part II, §§ 2344(a)–(c), 2354(b)(30), (31), 98 Stat. 1063, 1068, 1078, 1095, 1101; April 7, 1986, P. L. 99-272, Title IX, Subtitle A, Part 2, Subpart A, § 9201(a), Part 3, Subpart A, § 9307(a), Part 4, § 9401(c), 100 Stat. 170, 193, 199; Oct. 21, 1986, P. L. 99-509, Title IX, Subtitle D, Part 2, §§ 9316(b), 9319(a), (b), 9320(h)(1), Part 3, 9343(c)(1), 100 Stat. 2007, 2010, 2015, 2039; Aug. 18, 1987, P. L. 100-93, § 8(c)(1), (3), 101 Stat. 692, 693; Dec. 22, 1987, P. L. 100-203, Title IV, Subtitle A, Part 1, § 4009(j)(6)(C), Part 2, Subpart C, §§ 4034(a), 4036(a)(1), 4039(c)(1), Part 3, Subpart D, §§ 4072(c), 4085(i)(15), (16), 101 Stat. 1330-77, 1330-79, 1330-82, 1330-117, 1330-133; July 1, 1988, P. L. 100-360, Title II, Subtitle A, §§ 202(d), 204(d)(2), 205(e)(1), Title IV, Subtitle B, § 411(f)(4)(D)(i), (ii)(iv)(i)(4)(D), 102 Stat. 715, 729, 731, 778, 790; Oct. 13, 1988, P. L. 100-485, Title VI, § 608(d)(24)(C)(i), (ii)(III), 102 Stat. 2421; Dec. 13, 1989, P. L. 101-234, Title II, § 201(a)(1), 103 Stat. 1981; Dec. 19, 1989, P. L. 101-239, Title VI, Subtitle A, Part 1, Subpart A, § 6003(g)(3)(D)(xi), Part 2, Subpart A, §§ 6103(b)(3)(B), 6115(b), Part 3, Subpart A, § 6202(a)(2)(A), (b)(1), (e)(1), Subtitle B, Part 2, § 6411(d)(2), 103 Stat 2154, 2199, 2219, 2228, 2229, 2234, 2271; Nov. 5, 1990, P. L. 101-508, Title IV, Subtitle A, Part 2, Subpart A, § 4107(b), Subpart B, §§ 4153(b)(2)(B), 4157(c)(1), 4161(a)(3)(C), 4163(d)(2), 4203(a)(1), (b), (c), 4204(g)(1), 104 Stat. 1388-62, 1388-84, 1388-89, 1388-94, 1388-100, 1388-107, 1388-112; Aug. 10, 1993, P. L. 103-66, Title XIII, Ch 2, Subch A, Part III, §§ 13561(a)(1), (b), (c), (d)(1), (e)(1), Part V, 13581(b), 107 Stat. 593-595, 611; Oct. 31, 1994, P. L. 103-432, Title I, Subtitle B, Part III, §§ 145(c)(1), 147(e)(6), Subtitle C, §§ 151(a)(1)(A), (C), (2)(A), (b)(3)(A), (B), (c)(1), (4)–(6), (9), 156(a)(2)(D), 157(b)(7), 108 Stat. 4427, 4430, 4432–4436, 4441, 4442; Oct. 2, 1996, P. L. 104-224, § 1, 110 Stat. 3031; Oct. 2, 1996, P. L. 104-226, § 1(b)(1), 110 Stat. 3033; April 30, 1997, P. L. 105-12, § 9(a)(1), 111 Stat. 26; Aug. 5, 1997, P. L. 105-33, Title IV, Subtitle A, Ch 1, Subch A, § 4001, Ch 3, § 4022(b)(1)(B), Subtitle B, §§ 4102(c), 4103(c), 4104(c)(3), Subtitle C, § 4201(c)(1), Subtitle D, Ch 2, § 4319(b), Subtitle E, Ch 3, § 4432(b)(1), Subtitle F, Ch 1, Subch A, § 4507(a)(2)(B), Subch B, § 4511(a)(2)(C), Ch 4, § 4541(b), Subtitle G,

Ch 1, Subch A, § 4603(c)(2)(C), Subch B, § 4614(a), Ch 3, §§ 4631(a)(1), (b), (c)(1), 4632(a), 4633(a), (b), 111 Stat. 275, 354, 361, 362, 365, 373, 394, 420, 440, 442, 456, 471, 474, 486, 487; Nov. 29, 1999, P. L. 106-113, Div B, § 1000(a)(6), 113 Stat. 1536; Dec. 21, 2000, P. L. 106-554, § 1(a)(6), 114 Stat. 2763; Dec. 27, 2001, P. L. 107-105, § 3(a), 115 Stat. 1006; Dec. 8, 2003, P. L. 108-173, Title I, § 101(a)(1), Title III, §§ 301(a)–(c), 303(i)(3)(B), Title VI, Subtitle B, §§ 611(d)(1), 612(c), 613(c), Title VII, Subtitle D, § 731(a)(1), (b)(1), Title IX, § 900(e)(1)(J), Subtitle E, §§ 944(a)(1), 948(a), 950(a), 117 Stat. 2071, 2221, 2254, 2304, 2305, 2306, 2349, 2351, 2372, 2422, 2425, 2426; Feb. 8, 2006, P. L. 109-171, Title V, Subtitle B, Ch. 2, § 5112(d), 120 Stat. 44; Dec. 29, 2007, P. L. 110-173, Title I, § 111(a), 121 Stat. 2497; July 15, 2008, P. L. 110-275, Title I, Subtitle A, Part I, § 101(a)(3), (b)(3), (4), Subtitle C, Part I, § 135(a)(2)(A), Part II, §§ 143(b)(7), 152(b)(1)(D), 153(b)(2), 122 Stat. 2497, 2498, 2535, 2543, 2552, 2555; March 23, 2010, P. L. 111-148, Title I, Subtitle B, § 1104(d), Title IV, Subtitle B, § 4103(d), Title VI, Subtitle E, § 6402(g)(3), (h)(1), 124 Stat. 153, 556, 759.)

§ 1395aa. Agreements with States

(a) Use of State agencies to determine compliance by providers of services with conditions of participation. The Secretary shall make an agreement with any State which is able and willing to do so under which the services of the State health agency or other appropriate State agency (or the appropriate local agencies) will be utilized by him for the purpose of determining whether an institution therein is a hospital or skilled nursing facility, or whether an agency therein is a home health agency, or whether an agency is a hospice program or whether a facility therein is a rural health clinic as defined in section 1861(aa)(2) [42 USCS § 1395x(aa)(2)], a critical access hospital, as defined in section 1861(mm)(1) [42 USCS § 1395x(mm)(1)], or a comprehensive outpatient rehabilitation facility as defined in section 1861(cc)(2) [42 USCS § 1395x(cc)(2)], or whether a laboratory meets the requirements of paragraphs (16) and (17) of section 1861(s) [42 USCS § 1395x(s)(16) and (17)], or whether a clinic, rehabilitation agency or public health agency meets the requirements of subparagraph (A) or (B), as the case may be, of section 1861(p)(4) [42 USCS § 1395x(p)(4)(A) or (B)], or whether an ambulatory surgical center meets the standards specified under section 1832(a)(2)(F)(i) [42 USCS § 1395k(a)(2)(F)(i)]. To the extent that the Secretary finds it appropriate, an institution or agency which such a State (or local) agency certifies is a hospital, skilled nursing facility, rural health clinic, comprehensive outpatient rehabilitation facility, home health agency, or hospice program (as those terms are defined in section 1861 [42 USCS § 1395x]) may be treated as such by the Secretary. Any State agency which has such an agreement may (subject to approval of the Secretary) furnish to a skilled nursing facility, after proper request by such facility, such specialized consultative services (which such agency is able and willing to furnish in a manner satisfactory to the Secretary) as such facility may need to meet one or more of the conditions specified in section 1819(a) [42 USCS § 1395i-3(a)]. Any such services furnished by a State agency shall be deemed to have been furnished pursuant to such agreement. Within 90 days following the completion of each survey of any health care facility, ambulatory surgical center, rural health clinic, comprehensive outpatient rehabilitation facility, laboratory, clinic, agency, or organization by the appropriate State or local agency described in the first sentence of this subsection, the Secretary shall make public in readily available form and place, and require (in the case of skilled nursing facilities) the posting in a place readily accessible to patients (and patients' representatives), the pertinent findings of each such survey relating to the compliance of each such health care facility, ambulatory surgical center, rural health clinic, comprehensive outpatient rehabilitation facility, laboratory, clinic, agency, or organization with (1) the statutory conditions of participation imposed under this title [42 USCS §§ 1395 et seq.] and (2) the major additional conditions which the Secretary finds necessary in the interest of health and safety of individuals who are furnished care or services by any such health care facility, laboratory, clinic, agency, or organization. Any agreement under this subsection shall provide for the appropriate State or local agency to maintain a toll-free hotline (1) to collect, maintain, and continually update information on home health agencies located in the State or locality that are certified to participate in the program established under this title [42 USCS §§ 1395 et seq.] (which information shall include any significant deficiencies found with respect to patient care in the most recent certification survey conducted by a State agency or accreditation survey conducted by a private accreditation agency under section 1865 [42 USCS § 1395bb] with respect to the home health agency, when that survey was completed, whether corrective actions have been taken or are planned, and the sanctions, if any, imposed under this title [42 USCS §§ 1395 et seq.] with respect to the agency) and (2) to receive complaints (and answer questions) with respect to home health agencies in the State or locality. Any such agreement shall provide for such State or local agency to maintain a unit for investigating such complaints that possesses enforcement authority and has access to survey and certification reports, information gathered by any private accreditation agency utilized by the Secretary under section 1865 [42 USCS § 1395bb], and consumer medical records (but only with the consent of the consumer or his or her legal representative).

(b) Payment in advance or by way of reimbursement to State for performance of functions of subsection (a). The Secretary shall pay any such State, in advance or by way of reimbursement, as may be provided in the agreement with it (and may make adjustments in such payments on account of overpayments or underpayments previously made), for the reasonable cost of performing the functions specified in subsection (a), and for the Federal Hospital Insurance Trust Fund's fair share of the costs attributable to the planning and other efforts directed toward coordination of activities in carrying out its agreement and other activities related to the provision of services similar to those for which payment may be made under part A [42 USCS §§ 1395c et seq.], or related to the facilities and personnel required for the provision of such services, or related to improving the quality of such services.

(c) Use of State or local agencies to survey hospitals [Caution: For provisions applicable to accreditations of hospitals granted before July 15, 2010, see 2008 amendment note below.]. The Secretary is authorized to enter into an agreement with any State under which the appropriate State or local agency which performs the certification function described in subsection (a) will survey, on a selective sample basis (or where the Secretary finds that a survey is appropriate because of substantial allegations of the existence of a significant deficiency or deficiencies which would, if found to be present, adversely affect health and safety of patients), provider entities that, pursuant to section 1865(a)(1) [42 USCS § 1395bb(a)(1)], are treated as meeting the conditions or requirements of this title [42 USCS §§ 1395 et seq.]. The Secretary shall pay for such services in the manner prescribed in subsection (b).

(d) Fulfillment of requirements by State. The Secretary may not enter an agreement under this section with a State with respect to determining whether an institution therein is a skilled nursing facility unless the State meets the requirements specified in section 1819(e) and section 1819(g) [42 USCS § 1395i-3(e) and (g)] and the establishment of remedies under sections 1819(h)(2)(B) and 1819(h)(2)(C) [42 USCS § 1395i-3(h)(2)(B) and (h)(2)(C)] (relating to establishment and application of remedies).

(e) Prohibition of user fees for survey and certification. Notwithstanding any other provision of law, the Secretary may not impose, or require a State to impose, any fee on any facility or entity subject to a determination under subsection (a), or any renal dialysis facility subject to the requirements of section 1881(b)(1) [42 USCS § 1395rr(b)(1)], for any such determination or any survey relating to determining the compliance of such facility or entity with any requirement of this title [42 USCS §§ 1395 et seq.] (other than any fee relating to section 353 of the Public Health Service Act [42 USCS § 263a]).

(Aug. 14, 1935, ch 531, Title XVIII, Part E [D] [C], § 1864, as added July 30, 1965, P. L. 89-97, Title I, Part 1, § 102(a), 79 Stat. 326; Jan. 2, 1968, P. L. 90-248, Title I, Part 3, § 133(f), Title II, Part 2, § 228(b), 81 Stat. 852, 904; Oct. 30, 1972, P. L. 92-603, Title II, §§ 244(a), 277, 278(a)(16), (b)(15), 299D(a), 86 Stat. 1422, 1452–1454, 1461; Dec. 13, 1977, P. L. 95-210, § 1(i), 91 Stat. 1488; Dec. 5, 1980, P. L. 96-499, Title IX, Part B, Subpart I, §§ 933(g), 934(c)(2), 94 Stat. 2637, 2639; Dec. 28, 1980, P. L. 96-611, § 1(a)(2), 94 Stat. 3566; Sept. 3, 1982, P. L. 97-248, Title I, Subtitle A, Part II, § 122(g)(3), 96 Stat. 362; July 18, 1984, P. L. 98-369, Division B, Title III, Subtitle A, Part II, § 2354(b)(17), 98 Stat. 1101; Oct. 21, 1986, P. L. 99-509, Title IX, Subtitle D, Part 2, § 9320(h)(3), 100 Stat. 2105; Dec. 22, 1987, P. L. 100-203, Title IV, Subtitle A, Part 2, Subpart B, § 4025(a), Subtitle C, Part 1, §§ 4201(a)(2), (d)(4), 4202(a)(1), (c)(1), 4203(a)(1), 4212(b), 101 Stat. 1330-160, 1330-74, 1330-179, 1330-212; July 1, 1988, P. L. 100-360, Title II, Subtitle A, §§ 203(e)(3) 204(c)(2), (d)(3), Title IV, Subtitle B, § 411(d)(4)(A), (l)(1)(C), 102 Stat. 725, 728, 729, 774; Oct. 13, 1988, P. L. 100-485, Title VI, § 608(d)(20)(B), (C), (27)(B), 102 Stat. 2419, 2422; Dec. 13, 1989, P. L. 101-234, Title II, § 201(a)(1), 103 Stat. 1981; Dec. 19, 1989, P. L. 101-239, Title VI, Subtitle A, Part 1, Subpart A, § 6003(g)(3)(C)(iii), Part 2, Subpart A, § 6115(c), 103 Stat. 2152, 2219; Nov. 5, 1990, P.

L. 101-508, Title IV, Subtitle A, Part 2, Subpart B, §§ 4154(d)(1), 4163(c)(2), 4207(g), 104 Stat. 1388-85, 1388-100, 1388-123; Nov. 5, 1990, P. L. 101-508, Title IV, Subtitle A, Part 2, Subpart B, §§ 4154(d)(1), 4163(c)(2), 4207(g), 104 Stat. 1388-85, 1388-100, 1388-123; Oct. 31, 1994, P. L. 103-432, Title I, Subtitle B, Part III, § 145(c)(3), Subtitle C, § 160(a)(1), (d)(4), 108 Stat. 4427, 4443, 4444; April 26, 1996, P. L. 104-134, Title I [Title V, § 516(c)(1)], 110 Stat. 1321-247; May 2, 1996, P. L. 104-140, § 1(a), 110 Stat. 1327; Aug. 5, 1997, P. L. 105-33, Title IV, Subtitle A, Chapter 1, Subchapter A, § 4001, Subtitle B, § 4106(c), Subtitle C, § 4201(c)(1), 111 Stat. 275, 368, 373; Dec. 8, 2003, P. L. 108-173, Title I, § 101(a)(1), 117 Stat. 2071; July 15, 2008, P. L. 110-275, Title I, Subtitle B, § 125(b)(3), 122 Stat. 2519.)

HISTORY; ANCILLARY LAWS AND DIRECTIVES

Amendments:

2008. Act July 15, 2008 (applicable to accreditations of hospitals granted on or after 7/15/2010, as provided by § 125(d) of such Act, which appears as 42 USCS § 1395bb note), in subsec. (c), substituted "pursuant to section 1865(a)(1)" for "pursuant to subsection (a) or (b)(1) of section 1865".

Other provisions:

Transfer of provisions relating to pilot program for national and State background checks on direct patient access employees of long-term care facilities or providers. Act Dec. 8, 2003, P. L. 108-173, Title III, § 307, 117 Stat. 2257, which formerly appeared as a note to this section, was transferred by the compilers of the official United States Code and now appears as 42 USCS § 1320a-7l note.

§ 1395cc. Agreements with providers of services; enrollment processes

(a) Filing of agreements; eligibility for payment; charges with respect to items and services. (1) Any provider of services (except a fund designated for purposes of section 1814(g) and section 1835(e) [42 USCS §§ 1395f(g) and 1395n(e)]) shall be qualified to participate under this title [42 USCS §§ 1395 et seq.] and shall be eligible for payments under this title [42 USCS §§ 1395 et seq.] if it files with the Secretary an agreement—

(A) (i) not to charge, except as provided in paragraph (2), any individual or any other person for items or services for which such individual is entitled to have payment made under this title [42 USCS §§ 1395 et seq.] (or for which he would be so entitled if such provider of services had complied with the procedural and other requirements under or pursuant to this title [42 USCS §§ 1395 et seq.] or for which such provider is paid pursuant to the provisions of section 1814(e) [42 USCS § 1395f(e)]), and (ii) not to impose any charge that is prohibited under section 1902(n)(3) [42 USCS § 1396a(n)(3)],

(B) not to charge any individual or any other person for items or services for which such individual is not entitled to have payment made under this title [42 USCS §§ 1395 et seq.] because payment for expenses incurred for such items or services may not be made by reason of the provisions of paragraph (1) or (9) of section 1862(a) [42 USCS § 1395y(a)(1) or (9)] but only if (i) such individual was without fault in incurring such expenses and (ii) the Secretary's determination that such payment may not be made for such items and services was made after the third year following the year in which notice of such payment was sent to such individual; except that the Secretary may reduce such three-year period to not less than one year if he finds such reduction is consistent with the objectives of this title [42 USCS §§ 1395 et seq.],

(C) to make adequate provision for return (or other disposition, in accordance with regulations) of any moneys incorrectly collected from such individual or other person,

(D) to promptly notify the Secretary of its employment of an individual who, at any time during the year preceding such employment, was employed in a managerial, accounting, auditing, or similar capacity (as determined by the Secretary by regulation) by an agency or organization which serves as a fiscal intermediary or carrier (for purposes of part A or part B, or both, of this title [42 USCS §§ 1395c et seq. or 1395j et seq.]) with respect to the provider,

(E) to release data with respect to patients of such provider upon request to an organization having a contract with the Secretary under part B of title XI [42 USCS §§ 1320c et seq.] as may be necessary (i) to allow such organization to carry out its functions under such contract, or (ii) to allow such organization to carry out similar review functions under any contract the organization may have with a private or public agency paying for health care in the same area with respect to patients who authorize release of such data for such purposes,

(F)(i) in the case of hospitals which provide hospital services for which payment may be made under subsection (b), (c), or (d) of section 1886 [42 USCS § 1395ww(b), (c), or (d)], to maintain an agreement with a professional standards review organization (if there is such an organization in existence in the area in which the hospital is located) or with a utilization and quality control peer review organization which has a contract with the Secretary under part B of title XI [42 USCS §§ 1320c et seq.] for the area in which the hospital is located, under which the organization will perform functions under that part [42 USCS §§ 1320c et seq.] with respect to the review of the validity of diagnostic information provided by such hospital, the completeness, adequacy, and quality of care provided, the appropriateness of admissions and discharges, and the appropriateness of care provided for which additional payments are sought under section 1886(d)(5) [42 USCS § 1395ww(d)(5)], with respect to inpatient hospital services for which payment may be made under part A of this title [42 USCS §§ 1395c et seq.] (and for purposes of payment under this title [42 USCS §§ 1395 et seq.], the cost of such agreement to the hospital shall be considered a cost incurred by such hospital in providing inpatient services under part A [42 USCS §§ 1395c et seq.], and (I) shall be paid directly by the Secretary to such organization on behalf of such hospital in accordance with a rate per review established by the Secretary, (II) shall be transferred from the Federal Hospital Insurance Trust Fund, without regard to amounts appropriated in advance in appropriation Acts, in the same manner as transfers are made for payment for services provided directly to beneficiaries, and (III) shall not be less in the aggregate for a fiscal year than the aggregate amount expended in fiscal year 1988 for direct and administrative costs (adjusted for inflation and for any direct or administrative costs incurred as a result of review functions added with respect to a subsequent fiscal year) of such reviews),

(ii) in the case of hospitals, critical access hospitals, skilled nursing facilities, and home health agencies, to maintain an agreement with a utilization and quality control peer review organization (which has a contract with the Secretary under part B of title XI [42 USCS §§ 1320c et seq.] for the area in which the hospital, facility, or agency is located) to perform the functions described in paragraph (3)(A),

(G) in the case of hospitals which provide inpatient hospital services for which payment may be made under subsection (b) or (d) of section 1886 [42 USCS § 1395ww(b) or (d)], not to charge any individual or any other person for inpatient hospital services for which such individual would be entitled to have payment made under part A [42 USCS §§ 1395c et seq.] but for a denial or reduction of payments under section 1886(f)(2) [42 USCS § 1395ww(f)(2)],

(H)(i) in the case of hospitals which provide services for which payment may be made under this title [42 USCS §§ 1395 et seq.] and in the case of critical access hospitals which provide critical access hospital services, to have all items and services (other than physicians' services as defined in regulations for purposes of section 1862(a)(14) [42 USCS § 1395y(a)(14)], and other than services described by section 1861(s)(2)(K) [42 USCS § 1395x(s)(2)(K)], certified nurse-midwife services, qualified psychologist services, and services of a certified registered nurse anesthetist) (I) that are furnished to an individual who is a patient of the hospital, and (II) for which the individual is entitled to have payment made under this title [42 USCS §§ 1395 et seq.], furnished by the hospital or otherwise under arrangements (as defined in section 1861(w)(1) [42 USCS § 1395x(w)(1)]) made by the hospital,

(ii) in the case of skilled nursing facilities which provide covered skilled nursing facility services—

(I) that are furnished to an individual who is a resident of the skilled nursing facility during a period in which the resident is provided covered post-hospital extended care services (or, for services described in section 1861(s)(2)(D) [42 USCS § 1395x(s)(2)(D)], that are furnished to such an individual without regard to such period), and

(II) for which the individual is entitled to have payment made under this title [42 USCS §§ 1395 et seq.],

to have items and services (other than services described in section 1888(e)(2)(A)(ii) [42 USCS § 1395yy(e)(2)(A)(ii)]) furnished by the skilled nursing facility or otherwise under arrangements (as defined in section 1861(w)(1) [42 USCS § 1395x(w)(1)]) made by the skilled nursing facility,

(I) in the case of a hospital or critical access hospital—

(i) to adopt and enforce a policy to ensure compliance with the requirements of section 1867 [42 USCS § 1395dd] and to meet the requirements of such section,

(ii) to maintain medical and other records related to individuals transferred to or from the hospital for a period of five years from the date of the transfer, and

(iii) to maintain a list of physicians who are on call for duty after the initial examination to provide treatment necessary to stabilize an individual with an emergency medical condition,

(J) in the case of hospitals which provide inpatient hospital services for which payment may be made under this title [42 USCS §§ 1395 et seq.], to be a participating provider of medical care under any health plan contracted for under section 1079 or 1086 of title 10, or under section 613 [1713] of title 38, United States Code, in accordance with admission practices, payment methodology, and amounts as prescribed under joint regulations issued by the Secretary and by the Secretaries of Defense and Transportation, in implementation of sections 1079 and 1086 of title 10, United States Code,

(K) not to charge any individual or any other person for items or services for which payment under this title [42 USCS §§ 1395 et seq.] is denied under section 1154(a)(2) [42 USCS § 1320c-3(a)(2)] by reason of a determination under section 1154(a)(1)(B) [42 USCS § 1320c-3(a)(1)(B)],

(L) in the case of hospitals which provide inpatient hospital services for which payment may be made under this title [42 USCS §§ 1395 et seq.], to be a participating provider of medical care under section 603 [1703] of title 38, United States Code, in accordance with such admission practices, and such payment methodology and amounts, as are prescribed under joint regulations issued by the Secretary and by the Secretary of Veterans Affairs in implementation of such section,

(M) in the case of hospitals, to provide to each individual who is entitled to benefits under part A [42 USCS §§ 1395c et seq.] (or to a person acting on the individual's behalf), at or about the time of the individual's admission as an inpatient to the hospital, a written statement (containing such language as the Secretary prescribes consistent with this paragraph) which explains—

(i) the individual's rights to benefits for inpatient hospital services and for post-hospital services under this title [42 USCS §§ 1395 et seq.],

(ii) the circumstances under which such an individual will and will not be liable for charges for continued stay in the hospital,

(iii) the individual's right to appeal denials of benefits for continued inpatient hospital services, including the practical steps to initiate such an appeal, and

(iv) the individual's liability for payment for services if such a denial of benefits is upheld on appeal,

and which provides such additional information as the Secretary may specify,

(N) in the case of hospitals and critical access hospitals—

(i) to make available to its patients the directory or directories of participating physicians (published under section 1842(h)(4) [42 USCS § 1395u(h)(4)]) for the area served by the hospital or critical access hospital,

(ii) if hospital personnel (including staff of any emergency or outpatient department) refer a patient to a nonparticipating physician for further medical care on an outpatient basis, the personnel must inform the patient that the physician is a nonparticipating physician and, whenever practicable, must identify at least one qualified participating physician who is listed in such a directory and from whom the patient may receive the necessary services,

(iii) to post conspicuously in any emergency department a sign (in a form specified by the Secretary) specifying rights of individuals under section 1867 [42 USCS § 1395dd] with respect to examination and treatment for emergency medical conditions and women in labor, and

(iv) to post conspicuously (in a form specified by the Secretary) information indicating whether or not the hospital participates in the medicaid program under a State plan approved under title XIX [42 USCS §§ 1396 et seq.],

(O) to accept as payment in full for services that are covered under this title [42 USCS §§ 1395 et seq.] and are furnished to any individual enrolled with a Medicare+Choice organization under part C [42 USCS §§ 1395w-21 et seq.], with a PACE provider under section 1894 or 1934 [42 USCS § 1395eee or 1396u-4], or with an eligible organization with a risk-sharing contract under section 1876 [42 USCS § 1395mm], under section 1876(i)(2)(A) [42 USCS § 1395mm(i)(2)(A)] (as in effect before February 1, 1985), under section 402(a) of the Social Security Amendments of 1967 [42 USCS § 1395b-1], or under section 222(a) of the Social Security Amendments of 1972, which does not have a contract (or, in the case of a PACE provider, contract or other agreement) establishing payment amounts for services furnished to members of the organization or PACE program eligible individuals enrolled with the PACE provider, the amounts that would be made as a payment in full under this title [42 USCS §§ 1395 et seq.] (less any payments under sections 1886(d)(11) and 1886(h)(3)(D) [42 USCS §§ 1395ww(d)(11) and (h)(3)(D)]) if the individuals were not so enrolled,

(P) in the case of home health agencies which provide home health services to individuals entitled to benefits under this title [42 USCS §§ 1395 et seq.] who require catheters, catheter supplies, ostomy bags, and supplies related to ostomy care (described in section 1861(m)(5) [42 USCS § 1395x(m)(5)]), to offer to furnish such supplies to such an individual as part of their furnishing of home health services,

(Q) in the case of hospitals, skilled nursing facilities, home health agencies, and hospice programs, to comply with the requirement of subsection (f) (relating to maintaining written policies and procedures respecting advance directives),

(R) to contract only with a health care clearinghouse (as defined in section 1171 [42 USCS § 1320d]) that meets each standard and implementation specification adopted or established under part C of title XI [42 USCS §§ 1320d et seq.] on or after the date on which the health care clearinghouse is required to comply with the standard or specification,

(S) **[Caution: This subparagraph takes effect on such date, on or after issuance of implementing regulations, as the Secretary specifies in such regulations, as provided by § 4321(d)(2) of Act Aug. 5, 1997, P. L. 105-33, which appears as a note to 42 USCS § 1320b-16.]** in the case of a hospital that has a financial interest (as specified by the Secretary in regulations) in an entity to which individuals are referred as described in section 1861(ee)(2)(H)(ii) [42 USCS § 1395x(ee)(2)], or in which such an entity has such a financial interest, or in which another entity has such a financial interest (directly or indirectly) with such hospital and such an entity, to maintain and disclose to the Secretary (in a form and manner specified by the Secretary) information on—

(i) the nature of such financial interest,

(ii) the number of individuals who were discharged from the hospital and who were identified as requiring home health services, and

(iii) the percentage of such individuals who received such services from such provider (or another such provider),

(T) in the case of hospitals and critical access hospitals, to furnish to the Secretary such data as the Secretary determines appropriate pursuant to subparagraph (E) of section 1886(d)(12) [42 USCS § 1395ww(d)(12)] to carry out such section,

(U) in the case of hospitals which furnish inpatient hospital services for which payment may be made under this title [42 USCS §§ 1395 et seq.], to be a participating provider of medical care both—

(i) under the contract health services program funded by the Indian Health Service and operated by the Indian Health Service, an Indian tribe, or tribal organization (as those terms are defined in section 4 of the Indian Health Care Improvement Act [25 USCS § 1603]), with respect to items and services that are covered under such program and furnished to an individual eligible for such items and services under such program; and

(ii) under any program funded by the Indian Health Service and operated by an urban Indian organization with respect to the purchase of items and services for an eligible urban Indian (as those terms are defined in such section 4),

in accordance with regulations promulgated by the Secretary regarding admission practices, payment methodology, and rates of payment (including the acceptance of no more than such payment rate as payment in full for such items and services,

(V) in the case of hospitals that are not otherwise subject to the Occupational Safety and Health Act of 1970 (or a State occupational safety and health plan that is approved under 18(b) of such Act [29 USCS § 667(b)]), to comply with the Bloodborne Pathogens standard under section 1910.1030 of title 29 of the Code of Federal Regulations (or as subsequently redesignated), [and]

(W) in the case of a hospital described in section 1886(d)(1)(B)(v) [42 USCS § 1395ww(d)(1)(B)(v)], to report quality data to the Secretary in accordance with subsection (k). [, and]

[(X)](W) maintain and, upon request of the Secretary, provide access to documentation relating to written orders or requests for payment for durable medical equipment, certifications for home health services, or referrals for other items or services written or ordered by the provider under this title, as specified by the Secretary.

In the case of a hospital which has an agreement in effect with an organization described in subparagraph (F), which organization's contract with the Secretary under part B of title XI [42 USCS §§ 1320c et seq.] is terminated on or after October 1, 1984, the hospital shall not be determined to be out of compliance with the requirement of such subparagraph during the six month period beginning on the date of the termination of that contract.

(2)(A) A provider of services may charge such individual or other person (i) the amount of any deduction or coinsurance amount imposed pursuant to section 1813(a)(1), (a)(3), or (a)(4), section 1833(b), or section 1861(y)(3) [42 USCS §§ 1395e(a)(1), (3), or (4), 1395l(b), or 1395x(y)(3)] with respect to such items and services (not in excess of the amount customarily charged for such items and services by such provider), and (ii) an amount equal to 20 per centum of the reasonable charges for such items and services (not in excess of 20 per centum of the amount customarily charged for such items and services by such provider) for which payment is made under part B [42 USCS §§ 1395j et seq.] or which are durable medical equipment furnished as home health services (but in the case of items and services furnished to individuals with end-stage renal disease, an amount equal to 20 percent of the estimated amounts for such items and services calculated on the basis established by the Secretary). In the case of items and services described in section 1833(c) [42 USCS § 1395l(c)], clause (ii) of the preceding sentence shall be applied by substituting for 20 percent the proportion which is appropriate under such section [42 USCS § 1395l]. A provider of services may not impose a charge under clause (ii) of the first sentence of this subparagraph with respect to items and services described in section 1861(s)(10)(A) [42 USCS § 1395x(s)(10)(A)] and with respect to clinical diagnostic laboratory tests for which payment is made under part B [42 USCS §§ 1395j et seq.]. Notwithstanding the first sentence of this subparagraph, a home health agency may charge such an individual or person, with respect to covered items subject to payment under section 1834(a) [42 USCS § 1395m(a)], the amount of any deduction imposed under section 1833(b) [42 USCS § 1395l(b)] and 20 percent of the payment basis described in section 1834(a)(1)(B) [42 USCS § 1395m(a)(1)(B)]. In the case of items and services for which payment is made under part B [42 USCS §§ 1395j et seq.] under the prospective payment system established under section 1833(t) [42 USCS § 1395l(t)], clause (ii) of the first sentence shall be applied by substituting for 20 percent of the reasonable charge, the applicable copayment amount established under section 1833(t)(5) [42 USCS § 1395l(t)(5)]. In the case of services described in section 1833(a)(8) or section 1833(a)(9) [42 USCS § 1395l(a)(8) or (9)] for which payment is made under part B [42 USCS §§ 1395j et seq.] under section 1834(k) [42 USCS § 1395m(k)], clause (ii) of the first sentence shall be applied by substituting for 20 percent of the reasonable charge for such services 20 percent of the lesser of the actual charge or the applicable fee schedule amount (as defined in such section) for such services.

(B) Where a provider of services has furnished, at the request of such individual, items or services which are in excess of or more expensive than the items or services with respect to which payment may be made under this title [42 USCS §§ 1395 et seq.], such provider of services may also charge such individual or other person for such more expensive items or services to the extent that the amount customarily charged by it for the items or services furnished at such request exceeds the amount customarily charged by it for the items or services with respect to which payment may be made under this title [42 USCS §§ 1395 et seq.].

(C) A provider of services may in accordance with its customary practice also appropriately charge any such individual for any whole blood (or equivalent quantities of packed red blood cells, as defined under regulations) furnished him with respect to which a deductible is imposed under section 1813(a)(2) [42 USCS § 1395e(a)(2)], except that (i) any excess of such charge over the cost to such provider for the blood (or equivalent quantities of packed red blood cells, as so defined) shall be deducted from any payment to such provider under this title [42 USCS §§ 1395 et seq.], (ii) no such charge may be imposed for the cost of administration of such blood (or equivalent quantities of packed red blood cells, as so defined), and (iii) such charge may not be made to the extent such blood (or equivalent quantities of packed red blood cells, as so defined) has been replaced on behalf of such individual or arrangements have been made for its replacement on his behalf. For purposes of subparagraph (C), whole blood (or equivalent quantities of packed red blood cells, as so defined) furnished an individual shall be deemed replaced when the provider of services is given one pint of blood for each pint of blood (or equivalent quantities of packed red blood cells, as so defined) furnished such individual with respect to which a deduction is imposed under section 1813(a)(2) [42 USCS § 1395e(a)(2)].

(D) Where a provider of services customarily furnishes items or services which are in excess of or more expensive than the items or services with respect to which payment may be made under this title [42 USCS §§ 1395 et seq.], such provider, notwithstanding the preceding provisions of this paragraph, may not, under the authority of section 1866(a)(2)(B)(ii) [subsec. (a)(2)(B)(ii) of this section], charge any individual or other person any amount for such items or services in excess of the amount of the payment which may otherwise be made for such items or services under this title [42 USCS §§ 1395 et seq.] if the admitting physician has a direct or indirect financial interest in such provider.

(3)(A) Under the agreement required under paragraph (1)(F)(ii), the peer review organization must perform functions (other than those covered under an agreement under paragraph (1)(F)(i)) under the third sentence of section 1154(a)(4)(A) [42 USCS § 1320c-3(a)(4)(A)] and under section 1154(a)(14) [42 USCS § 1320c-3(a)(14)] with respect to services, furnished by the hospital, critical access hospital, facility, or agency involved, for which payment may be made under this title [42 USCS §§ 1395 et seq.].

(B) For purposes of payment under this title [42 USCS §§ 1395 et seq.], the cost of such an agreement to the hospital, critical access hospital, facility, or agency shall be considered a cost incurred by such hospital, critical access hospital, facility, or agency in providing covered services under this title [42 USCS §§ 1395 et seq.] and shall be paid directly by the Secretary to the peer review organization on behalf of such hospital, facility, or agency in accordance with a schedule established by the Secretary.

(C) Such payments—

(i) shall be transferred in appropriate proportions from the Federal Hospital Insurance Trust Fund and from the Federal Supplementary Medical Insurance Trust Fund, without regard to amounts appropriated in advance in appropriation Acts, in the same manner as transfers are made for payment for services provided directly to beneficiaries, and

(ii) shall not be less in the aggregate for a fiscal year—

(I) in the case of hospitals, than the amount specified in paragraph (1)(F)(i)(III), and

(II) in the case of facilities, critical access hospitals, and agencies, than the amounts the Secretary determines to be sufficient to cover the costs of such organizations' conducting the activities described in subparagraph (A) with respect to such facilities, critical access hospitals, or agencies under part B of title XI [42 USCS § 1320c et seq.].

(b) Termination or nonrenewal of agreements. (1) A provider of services may terminate an agreement with the Secretary under this section at such time and upon such notice to the Secretary and the public as may be provided in regulations, except that notice of more than six months shall not be required.

(2) The Secretary may refuse to enter into an agreement under this section or, upon such reasonable notice to the provider and the public as may be specified in regulations, may refuse to renew or may terminate such an agreement after the Secretary—

(A) has determined that the provider fails to comply substantially with the provisions of the agreement, with the provisions of this title [42 USCS §§ 1395 et seq.] and regulations thereunder, or with a corrective action required under section 1886(f)(2)(B) [42 USCS § 1395ww(f)(2)(B)],

(B) has determined that the provider fails substantially to meet the applicable provisions of section 1861 [42 USCS § 1395x],

(C) has excluded the provider from participation in a program under this title [42 USCS §§ 1395 et seq.] pursuant to section 1128 or section 1128A [42 USCS § 1320a-7 or 1320a-7a], or

(D) has ascertained that the provider has been convicted of a felony under Federal or State law for an offense which the Secretary determines is detrimental to the best interests of the program or program beneficiaries.

(3) A termination of an agreement or a refusal to renew an agreement under this subsection shall become effective on the same date and in the same manner as an exclusion from participation under the programs under this title [42 USCS §§ 1395 et seq.] becomes effective under section 1128(c) [42 USCS § 1320a-7(c)].

(4)(A) A hospital that fails to comply with the requirement of subsection (a)(1)(V) (relating to the Bloodborne Pathogens standard) is subject to a civil money penalty in an amount described in subparagraph (B), but is not subject to termination of an agreement under this section.

(B) The amount referred to in subparagraph (A) is an amount that is similar to the amount of civil penalties that may be imposed under section 17 of the Occupational Safety and Health Act of 1970 [29 USCS § 666] for a violation of the Bloodborne Pathogens standard referred to in subsection (a)(1)(U) by a hospital that is subject to the provisions of such Act.

(C) A civil money penalty under this paragraph shall be imposed and collected in the same manner as civil money penalties under subsection (a) of section 1128A [42 USCS § 1320a-7a] are imposed and collected under that section.

(c) Refiling after termination or nonrenewal; agreements with skilled nursing facilities. (1) Where the Secretary has terminated or has refused to renew an agreement under this title [42 USCS §§ 1395 et seq.] with a provider of services, such provider may not file another agreement under this title [42

USCS §§ 1395 et seq.] unless the Secretary finds that the reason for the termination or nonrenewal has been removed and that there is reasonable assurance that it will not recur.

(2) Where an agreement filed under this title [42 USCS §§ 1395 et seq.] by a provider of services has been terminated by the Secretary, the Secretary shall promptly notify each State agency which administers or supervises the administration of a State plan approved under title XIX [42 USCS §§ 1396 et seq.] of such termination.

(d) Decision to withhold payment for failure to review long-stay cases. If the Secretary finds that there is a substantial failure to make timely review in accordance with section 1861(k) [42 USCS § 1395x(k)] of long-stay cases in a hospital, he may, in lieu of terminating his agreement with such hospital, decide that, with respect to any individual admitted to such hospital after a subsequent date specified by him, no payment shall be made under this title [42 USCS §§ 1395 et seq.] for inpatient hospital services (including inpatient psychiatric hospital services) after the 20th day of a continuous period of such services. Such decision may be made effective only after such notice to the hospital and to the public, as may be prescribed by regulations, and its effectiveness shall terminate when the Secretary finds that the reason therefor has been removed and that there is reasonable assurance that it will not recur. The Secretary shall not make any such decision except after reasonable notice and opportunity for hearing to the institution or agency affected thereby.

(e) "Provider of services" defined. For purposes of this section, the term "provider of services" shall include—

(1) a clinic, rehabilitation agency, or public health agency if, in the case of a clinic or rehabilitation agency, such clinic or agency meets the requirements of section 1861(p)(4)(A) [42 USCS § 1395x(p)(4)(A)] (or meets the requirements of such section through the operation of subsection (g) or (ll)(2) of section 1861 [42 USCS § 1395x]), or if, in the case of a public health agency, such agency meets the requirements of section 1861(p)(4)(B) [42 USCS § 1395x(p)(4)(B)] (or meets the requirements of such section through the operation of subsection (g) or (ll)(2) of section 1861 [42 USCS § 1395x]), but only with respect to the furnishing of outpatient physical therapy services (as therein defined), (through the operation of section 1861(g) [42 USCS § 1395x(g)]) with respect to the furnishing of outpatient occupational therapy services, or (through the operation of section 1861(ll)(2) [42 USCS § 1395x(ll)(2)]) with respect to the furnishing of outpatient speech-language pathology; and

(2) a community mental health center (as defined in section 1861(ff)(3)(B) [42 USCS § 1395x(ff)(3)(B)]), but only with respect to the furnishing of partial hospitalization services (as described in section 1861(ff)(1) [42 USCS § 1395x(ff)(1)]).

(f) Maintenance of written policies and procedures. (1) For purposes of subsection (a)(1)(Q) and sections 1819(c)(2)(E), 1833(s), 1855(i), 1876(c)(8), and 1891(a)(6) [42 USCS §§ 1395i-3(c)(2)(E), 1395l(s), 1395w-25(i), 1395mm(c)(8), and 1395bbb(a)(6)], the requirement of this subsection is that a provider of services, Medicare+Choice organization, or prepaid or eligible organization (as the case may be) maintain written policies and procedures with respect to all adult individuals receiving medical care by or through the provider or organization—

(A) to provide written information to each such individual concerning—

(i) an individual's rights under State law (whether statutory or as recognized by the courts of the State) to make decisions concerning such medical care, including the right to accept or refuse medical or surgical treatment and the right to formulate advance directives (as defined in paragraph (3)), and

(ii) the written policies of the provider or organization respecting the implementation of such rights;

(B) to document in a prominent part of the individual's current medical record whether or not the individual has executed an advance directive;

(C) not to condition the provision of care or otherwise discriminate against an individual based on whether or not the individual has executed an advance directive;

(D) to ensure compliance with requirements of State law (whether statutory or as recognized by the courts of the State) respecting advance directives at facilities of the provider or organization; and

(E) to provide (individually or with others) for education for staff and the community on issues concerning advance directives.

Subparagraph (C) shall not be construed as requiring the provision of care which conflicts with an advance directive.

(2) The written information described in paragraph (1)(A) shall be provided to an adult individual—

(A) in the case of a hospital, at the time of

the individual's admission as an inpatient,

(B) in the case of a skilled nursing facility, at the time of the individual's admission as a resident,

(C) in the case of a home health agency, in advance of the individual coming under the care of the agency,

(D) in the case of a hospice program, at the time of initial receipt of hospice care by the individual from the program, and

(E) in the case of an eligible organization (as defined in section 1876(b) [42 USCS § 1395mm(b)]) or an organization provided payments under section 1833(a)(1)(A) [42 USCS § 1395l(a)(1)(A)] or a Medicare+Choice organization, at the time of enrollment of the individual with the organization.

(3) In this subsection, the term "advance directive" means a written instruction, such as a living will or durable power of attorney for health care, recognized under State law (whether statutory or as recognized by the courts of the State) and relating to the provision of such care when the individual is incapacitated.

(4) For construction relating to this subsection, see section 7 of the Assisted Suicide Funding Restriction Act of 1997 [42 USCS § 14406] (relating to clarification respecting assisted suicide, euthanasia, and mercy killing).

(g) Penalties for improper billing. Except as permitted under subsection (a)(2), any person who knowingly and willfully presents, or causes to be presented, a bill or request for payment inconsistent with an arrangement under subsection (a)(1)(H) or in violation of the requirement for such an arrangement, is subject to a civil money penalty of not to exceed $2,000. The provisions of section 1128A [42 USCS § 1320a-7a] (other than subsections (a) and (b)) shall apply to a civil money penalty under the previous sentence in the same manner as such provisions apply to a penalty or proceeding under section 1128A(a) [42 USCS § 1320a-7a(a)].

(h) Dissatisfaction with determination of Secretary; appeal by institutions or agencies; single notice and hearing. (1)(A) Except as provided in paragraph (2), an institution or agency dissatisfied with a determination by the Secretary that it is not a provider of services or with a determination described in subsection (b)(2) shall be entitled to a hearing thereon by the Secretary (after reasonable notice) to the same extent as is provided in section 205(b) [42 USCS § 405(b)], and to judicial review of the Secretary's final decision after such hearing as is provided in section 205(g) [42 USCS § 405(g)], except that, in so applying such sections and in applying section 205(l) [42 USCS § 405(l)] thereto, any reference therein to the Commissioner of Social Security or the Social Security Administration shall be considered a reference to the Secretary or the Department of Health and Human Services, respectively.

(B) An institution or agency described in subparagraph (A) that has filed for a hearing under subparagraph (A) shall have expedited access to judicial review under this subparagraph in the same manner as providers of services, suppliers, and individuals entitled to benefits under part A [42 USCS §§ 1395c et seq.] or enrolled under part B [42 USCS §§ 1395j et seq.], or both, may obtain expedited access to judicial review under the process established under section 1869(b)(2) [42 USCS § 1395r(b)(2)]. Nothing in this subparagraph shall be construed to affect the application of any remedy imposed under section 1819 [42 USCS § 1395i-3] during the pendency of an appeal under this subparagraph.

(C)(i) The Secretary shall develop and implement a process to expedite proceedings under this subsection in which—

(I) the remedy of termination of participation has been imposed;

(II) a remedy described in clause (i) or (iii) of section 1819(h)(2)(B) [42 USCS § 1395i-3(h)(2)(B)] has been imposed, but only if such remedy has been imposed on an immediate basis; or

(III) a determination has been made as to a finding of substandard quality of care that results in the loss of approval of a skilled nursing facility's nurse aide training program.

(ii) Under such process under clause (i), priority shall be provided in cases of termination described in clause (i)(I).

(iii) Nothing in this subparagraph shall be construed to affect the application of any remedy imposed under section 1819 [42 USCS § 1395i-3] during the pendency of an appeal under this subparagraph.

(2) An institution or agency is not entitled to separate notice and opportunity for a hearing under both section 1128 [42 USCS § 1320a-7] and this section with respect to a determination or determinations based on the same underlying facts and issues.

(i) Intermediate sanctions for psychiatric hospitals. (1) If the Secretary determines that a psychiatric hospital which has an agreement in effect under this section no longer meets the requirements for a psychiatric hospital under this title [42 USCS §§ 1395 et seq.]

and further finds that the hospital's deficiencies—

(A) immediately jeopardize the health and safety of its patients, the Secretary shall terminate such agreement; or

(B) do not immediately jeopardize the health and safety of its patients, the Secretary may terminate such agreement, or provide that no payment will be made under this title [42 USCS §§ 1395 et seq.] with respect to any individual admitted to such hospital after the effective date of the finding, or both.

(2) If a psychiatric hospital, found to have deficiencies described in paragraph (1)(B), has not complied with the requirements of this title—

(A) within 3 months after the date the hospital is found to be out of compliance with such requirements, the Secretary shall provide that no payment will be made under this title [42 USCS §§ 1395 et seq.] with respect to any individual admitted to such hospital after the end of such 3-month period, or

(B) within 6 months after the date the hospital is found to be out of compliance with such requirements, no payment may be made under this title with respect to any individual in the hospital until the Secretary finds that the hospital is in compliance with the requirements of this title [42 USCS §§ 1395 et seq.].

(j) Enrollment process for providers of services and suppliers. (1) Enrollment process. (A) In general. The Secretary shall establish by regulation a process for the enrollment of providers of services and suppliers under this title [42 USCS §§ 1395 et seq.]. Such process shall include screening of providers and suppliers in accordance with paragraph (2), a provisional period of enhanced oversight in accordance with paragraph (3), disclosure requirements in accordance with paragraph (4), the imposition of temporary enrollment moratoria in accordance with paragraph (5), and the establishment of compliance programs in accordance with paragraph (6).

(B) Deadlines. The Secretary shall establish by regulation procedures under which there are deadlines for actions on applications for enrollment (and, if applicable, renewal of enrollment). The Secretary shall monitor the performance of medicare administrative contractors in meeting the deadlines established under this subparagraph.

(C) Consultation before changing provider enrollment forms. The Secretary shall consult with providers of services and suppliers before making changes in the provider enrollment forms required of such providers and suppliers to be eligible to submit claims for which payment may be made under this title [42 USCS §§ 1395 et seq.].

(2) Provider screening. (A) Procedures. Not later than 180 days after the date of enactment of this paragraph [enacted March 23, 2010], the Secretary, in consultation with the Inspector General of the Department of Health and Human Services, shall establish procedures under which screening is conducted with respect to providers of medical or other items or services and suppliers under the program under this title [42 USCS §§ 1395 et seq.], the Medicaid program under title XIX [42 USCS §§ 1396 et seq.], and the CHIP program under title XXI [42 USCS §§ 1397aa et seq.].

(B) Level of screening. The Secretary shall determine the level of screening conducted under this paragraph according to the risk of fraud, waste, and abuse, as determined by the Secretary, with respect to the category of provider of medical or other items or services or supplier. Such screening—

(i) shall include a licensure check, which may include such checks across States; and

(ii) may, as the Secretary determines appropriate based on the risk of fraud, waste, and abuse described in the preceding sentence, include—

(I) a criminal background check;

(II) fingerprinting;

(III) unscheduled and unannounced site visits, including preenrollment site visits;

(IV) database checks (including such checks across States); and

(V) such other screening as the Secretary determines appropriate.

(C) Application fees.

(i) Institutional providers. Except as provided in clause (ii), the Secretary shall impose a fee on each institutional provider of medical or other items or services or supplier (such as a hospital or skilled nursing facility) with respect to which screening is conducted under this paragraph in an amount equal to—

(I) for 2010, $500; and

(II) for 2011 and each subsequent year, the amount determined under this clause for the preceding year, adjusted by the percentage change in the consumer price index for all urban consumers (all items; United States city average) for the 12-month period ending with June of the previous year.

(ii) Hardship exception; waiver for certain Medicaid providers. The Secretary may, on a case-by-case basis, exempt a provider of medical or other items or services or supplier from the imposition of an application fee under this subparagraph if the Secretary determines that the imposition of the application fee would result in a hardship. The Secretary may waive the application fee under this subparagraph for providers enrolled in a State Medicaid program for whom the State demonstrates that imposition of the fee would impede beneficiary access to care.

(iii) Use of funds. Amounts collected as a result of the imposition of a fee under this subparagraph shall be used by the Secretary for program integrity efforts, including to cover the costs of conducting screening under this paragraph and to carry out this subsection and section 1128J [42 USCS § 1320a-7k].

(D) Application and enforcement. (i) New providers of services and suppliers. The screening under this paragraph shall apply, in the case of a provider of medical or other items or services or supplier who is not enrolled in the program under this title, title XIX, or title XXI [42 USCS §§ 1395 et seq., 1396 et seq., or 1397aa et seq.] as of the date of enactment of this paragraph [enacted March 23, 2010], on or after the date that is 1 year after such date of enactment.

(ii) Current providers of services and suppliers. The screening under this paragraph shall apply, in the case of a provider of medical or other items or services or supplier who is enrolled in the program under this title, title XIX, or title XXI [42 USCS §§ 1395 et seq., 1396 et seq., or 1397aa et seq.] as of such date of enactment [March 23, 2010], on or after the date that is 2 years after such date of enactment.

(iii) Revalidation of enrollment. Effective beginning on the date that is 180 days after such date of enactment [March 23, 2010], the screening under this paragraph shall apply with respect to the revalidation of enrollment of a provider of medical or other items or services or supplier in the program under this title, title XIX, or title XXI [42 USCS §§ 1395 et seq., 1396 et seq., or 1397aa et seq.].

(iv) Limitation on enrollment and revalidation of enrollment. In no case may a provider of medical or other items or services or supplier who has not been screened under this paragraph be initially enrolled or reenrolled in the program under this title, title XIX, or title XXI [42 USCS §§ 1395 et seq., 1396 et seq., or 1397aa et seq.] on or after the date that is 3 years after such date of enactment [enacted March 23, 2010].

(E) Expedited rulemaking. The Secretary may promulgate an interim final rule to carry out this paragraph.

(3) Provisional period of enhanced oversight for new providers of services and suppliers. (A) In general. The Secretary shall establish procedures to provide for a provisional period of not less than 30 days and not more than 1 year during which new providers of medical or other items or services and suppliers, as the Secretary determines appropriate, including categories of providers or suppliers, would be subject to enhanced oversight, such as prepayment review and payment caps, under the program under this title [42 USCS §§ 1395 et seq.], the Medicaid program under title XIX [42 USCS §§ 1396 et seq.]. and the CHIP program under title XXI [42 USCS §§ 1397aa et seq.].

(B) Implementation. The Secretary may establish by program instruction or otherwise the procedures under this paragraph.

(4) 90-day period of enhanced oversight for initial claims of DME suppliers. For periods beginning after January 1, 2011, if the Secretary determines that there is a significant risk of fraudulent activity among suppliers of durable medical equipment, in the case of a supplier of durable medical equipment who is within a category or geographic area under title XVIII [42 USCS §§ 1395 et seq.] identified pursuant to such determination and who is initially enrolling under such title, the Secretary shall, notwithstanding sections 1816(c), 1842(c), and 1869(a)(2) [42 USCS § 1395h(c), 1395u(c), and 1395ff(a)(2)], withhold payment under such title with respect to durable medical equipment furnished by such supplier during the 90-day period beginning on the date of the first submission of a claim under such title for durable medical equipment furnished by such supplier.

(5) Increased disclosure requirements. (A) Disclosure. A provider of medical or other items or services or supplier who submits an application for enrollment or revalidation of enrollment in the program under this title, title XIX, or title XXI [42 USCS §§ 1395 et seq., 1396 et seq., or 1397aa et seq.] on or after the date that is 1 year after the date of enactment of this paragraph [enacted March 23, 2010] shall disclose (in a form and manner and at such time as determined by the Secretary) any current or previous affiliation (directly or indirectly) with a provider of medical or other items or services or supplier that has uncollected debt, has been or is subject to a payment suspension under a Federal health care program (as defined in section 1128B(f)), has been excluded from participation under the program under this title [42 USCS §§ 1395 et seq.], the Medicaid program under title XIX [42 USCS §§ 1396 et seq.], or the CHIP program under

title XXI [42 USCS §§ 1397aa et seq.], or has had its billing privileges denied or revoked.

(B) Authority to deny enrollment. If the Secretary determines that such previous affiliation poses an undue risk of fraud, waste, or abuse, the Secretary may deny such application. Such a denial shall be subject to appeal in accordance with paragraph (7).

(6) Authority to adjust payments of providers of services and suppliers with the same tax identification number for past-due obligations. (A) In general. Notwithstanding any other provision of this title [42 USCS §§ 1395 et seq.], in the case of an applicable provider of services or supplier, the Secretary may make any necessary adjustments to payments to the applicable provider of services or supplier under the program under this title [42 USCS §§ 1395 et seq.] in order to satisfy any past-due obligations described in subparagraph (B)(ii) of an obligated provider of services or supplier.

(B) Definitions. In this paragraph:

(i) In general. The term "applicable provider of services or supplier" means a provider of services or supplier that has the same taxpayer identification number assigned under section 6109 of the Internal Revenue Code of 1986 [26 USCS § 6109] as is assigned to the obligated provider of services or supplier under such section, regardless of whether the applicable provider of services or supplier is assigned a different billing number or national provider identification number under the program under this title than is assigned to the obligated provider of services or supplier.

(ii) Obligated provider of services or supplier. The term "obligated provider of services or supplier" means a provider of services or supplier that owes a past-due obligation under the program under this title [42 USCS §§ 1395 et seq.] (as determined by the Secretary).

(7) Temporary moratorium on enrollment of new providers. (A) In general. The Secretary may impose a temporary moratorium on the enrollment of new providers of services and suppliers, including categories of providers of services and suppliers, in the program under this title [42 USCS §§ 1395 et seq.], under the Medicaid program under title XIX [42 USCS §§ 1396 et seq.], or under the CHIP program under title XXI [42 USCS §§ 1397aa et seq.] if the Secretary determines such moratorium is necessary to prevent or combat fraud, waste, or abuse under either such program.

(B) Limitation on review. There shall be no judicial review under section 1869 [42 USCS § 1395ff], section 1878 [42 USCS § 1395oo], or otherwise, of a temporary moratorium imposed under subparagraph (A).

(8) Compliance programs. (A) In general. On or after the date of implementation determined by the Secretary under subparagraph (C), a provider of medical or other items or services or supplier within a particular industry sector or category shall, as a condition of enrollment in the program under this title, title XIX, or title XXI [42 USCS §§ 1395 et seq., 1396 et seq., or 1397aa et seq.], establish a compliance program that contains the core elements established under subparagraph (B) with respect to that provider or supplier and industry or category.

(B) Establishment of core elements. The Secretary, in consultation with the Inspector General of the Department of Health and Human Services, shall establish core elements for a compliance program under subparagraph (A) for providers or suppliers within a particular industry or category.

(C) Timeline for implementation. The Secretary shall determine the timeline for the establishment of the core elements under subparagraph (B) and the date of the implementation of subparagraph (A) for providers or suppliers within a particular industry or category. The Secretary shall, in determining such date of implementation, consider the extent to which the adoption of compliance programs by a provider of medical or other items or services or supplier is widespread in a particular industry sector or with respect to a particular provider or supplier category.

(8) Hearing rights in cases of denial or nonrenewal. A provider of services or supplier whose application to enroll (or, if applicable, to renew enrollment) under this title is denied may have a hearing and judicial review of such denial under the procedures that apply under subsection (h)(1)(A) to a provider of services that is dissatisfied with a determination by the Secretary.

(k) Quality reporting by cancer hospitals. (1) In general. For purposes of fiscal year 2014 and each subsequent fiscal year, a hospital described in section 1886(d)(1)(B)(v) [42 USCS § 1395ww(d)(1)(B)(v)] shall submit data to the Secretary in accordance with paragraph (2) with respect to such a fiscal year.

(2) Submission of quality data. For fiscal year 2014 and each subsequent fiscal year, each hospital described in such section shall submit to the Secretary data on quality measures specified under paragraph (3). Such data shall be submitted in a form and manner, and at a time, specified by the Secretary for purposes of this subparagraph.

(3) Quality measures. (A) In general. Subject to subparagraph (B), any measure specified by the Secretary under this paragraph must have been endorsed by the entity with a contract under section 1890(a) [42 USCS § 1395aaa(a)].

(B) Exception. In the case of a specified area or medical topic determined appropriate by the Secretary for which a feasible and practical measure has not been endorsed by the entity with a contract under section 1890(a) [42 USCS § 1395aaa(a)], the Secretary may specify a measure that is not so endorsed as long as due consideration is given to measures that have been endorsed or adopted by a consensus organization identified by the Secretary.

(C) Time frame. Not later than October 1, 2012, the Secretary shall publish the measures selected under this paragraph that will be applicable with respect to fiscal year 2014.

(4) Public availability of data submitted. The Secretary shall establish procedures for making data submitted under paragraph (4) available to the public. Such procedures shall ensure that a hospital described in section 1886(d)(1)(B)(v) [42 USCS § 1395ww(d)(1)(B)(v)] has the opportunity to review the data that is to be made public with respect to the hospital prior to such data being made public. The Secretary shall report quality measures of process, structure, outcome, patients' perspective on care, efficiency, and costs of care that relate to services furnished in such hospitals on the Internet website of the Centers for Medicare & Medicaid Services.

(Aug. 14, 1935, ch 531, Title XVIII, Part E [D] [C], § 1866, as added July 30, 1965, P. L. 89-97, Title I, Part 1, § 102(a), 79 Stat. 327; Jan. 2, 1968, P. L. 90-248, Title I, Part 3, §§ 129(c)(12), 133(c), 135(b), 81 Stat. 849, 851, 852; Oct. 30, 1972, P. L. 92-603, Title II, §§ 223(e), (g), 227(d)(2), 229(b), 249A(b)–(d), 278(a)(17), (b)(18), 281(c), 86 Stat. 1394, 1406, 1409, 1427, 1453–1455; Oct. 25, 1977, P. L. 95-142, §§ 3(b), 8(b), 13(b)(3), 15(a), 91 Stat. 1178, 1194, 1198, 1200; Dec. 13, 1977, P. L. 95-210, § 2(e), 91 Stat. 1489; June 13, 1978, P. L. 95-292, § 4(e), 92 Stat. 315; June 17, 1980, P. L. 96-272, Title III, § 308(b), 94 Stat. 531; Dec. 5, 1980, P. L. 96-499, Title IX, Part A, Subpart II, § 916(a), 94 Stat. 2623; Dec. 28, 1980, P. L. 96-611, § 1(b)(4), 94 Stat. 3566; Aug. 13, 1981, P. L. 97-35, Title XXI, Subtitle B, Ch 4, § 2153, 95 Stat. 802; Sept. 3, 1982, P. L. 97-248, Title I, Subtitle A, Part II, § 122(g)(5), (6), Part II, § 128(a)(5), (d)(4), Subtitle C, § 144, 96 Stat. 362, 366, 367, 393; Jan. 12, 1983, P. L. 97-448, Title III, § 309(a)(5), (b)(11), 96 Stat. 2408, 2409; April 20, 1983, P. L. 98-21, Title VI, § 602(f), (l)(2), 97 Stat. 163, 166; July 18, 1984, P. L. 98-369, Division B, Title III, Subtitle A, Part I, §§ 2303(f), 2315(d), 2321(c), 2323(b)(3), Part II, §§ 2335(d), 2347(a), 2348(a), 2354(b)(33), (34), 98 Stat. 1066, 1080, 1084, 1086, 1090, 1096, 1097, 1102; April 7, 1986, P. L. 99-272, Title IX, Subtitle A, Part 1, Subpart B, §§ 9121(a), 9122(a), Part 4, §§ 9401(b)(2)(F), 9402(a), 9403(b), 100 Stat. 164, 167, 199, 200; Oct. 21, 1986, P. L. 99-509, Title IX, Subtitle D, Part 1, § 9305(b)(1), Part 2, § 9320(h)(2), Part 3, §§ 9332(e)(1), 9337(c)(2) in part, 9343(c)(2), (3), Part 4, § 9353(e)(1), 100 Stat. 1989, 2015, 2024, 2033, 2039, 2046; Oct. 22, 1986, P. L. 99-514, Title XVIII, Subtitle C, Ch 1, § 1855(b)(5), 100 Stat. 2933; Oct. 28, 1986, P. L. 99-576, Title II, Part D, § 233(a), 100 Stat. 3265; Aug. 18, 1987, P. L. 100-93, § 8(d), 101 Stat. 693; Dec. 22, 1987, P. L. 100-203, Title IV, Subtitle A, Part 2, Subpart A, § 4012(a), Part 3, Subpart B, § 4062(d)(4), Subpart D, § 4085(i)(17), Part 4, § 4097(a), (b), Title IV, Subtitle C, Part 2, § 4212(e)(4), 101 Stat. 1330-60, 1330-109, 1330-133, 1330-140, 1330-213; July 1 1988, P. L. 100-360, Title I, Subtitle A, § 104(d)(5), Title II, §§ 201(b), 202(h)(1), Title IV, Subtitle B, § 411(c)(2)(A)(i), (C), (g)(1)(D), (i)(4)(C)(vi), (j)(5), 102 Stat. 689, 702, 718, 772, 782, 790, 791; Oct. 13, 1988, P. L. 100-485, Title VI, § 608(d)(3)(F), (19)(A), (f)(1), 102 Stat. 2414, 2419, 2424; Dec. 13, 1989, P. L. 101-234, Title I, § 101(a)(1), Title II, § 201(a)(1), Title III, § 301(b)(4), (1), 103 Stat. 1979, 1981, 1985, 1986; Dec. 19, 1989, P. L. 101-239, Title VI, Subtitle A, Part 1, Subpart A, § 6003(g)(3)(D)(xii), (xiii), Subpart B, §§ 6017, 6018(a), 6020, Part 2, Subpart A, § 6112(e)(3), 103 Stat. 2154, 2165, 2166, 2216; Nov. 5, 1990, P. L. 101-508, Title IV, Subtitle A, Part 1, § 4008(b)(3)(B), (m)(3) [(F)](G), Part 2, Subpart B, §§ 4153(d)(1), 4157(c)(2), 4162(b)(2), Part 3, § 4206(a), 104 Stat. 1388-44, 1388-54, 1388-84, 1388-89, 1388-96, 1388-115; June 13, 1991, P. L. 102-54, § 13(q)(3)(F), 105 Stat. 280; Aug. 15, 1994, P. L. 103-296, Title I, § 108(c)(5), 108 Stat. 1485; Oct. 31, 1994, P. L. 103-432, Title I, Subtitle A, § 106(b)(1)(B), Subtitle B, § 147(e)(7), Subtitle C, § 156(a)(2)(E), 160(d)(2), 108 Stat. 4406, 4430, 4441, 4443; Aug. 21, 1996, P. L. 104-191, Title II, Subtitle F, § 262(b)(1), 110 Stat. 2031; April 30, 1997, P. L. 105-12, § 9(a)(2), 111 Stat. 26; Aug. 5, 1997, P. L. 105-33, Title IV, Subtitle A, Ch 1, Subch A, §§ 4001, 4002(d), (e), Subtitle C, § 4201(c)(1), Subtitle D, Ch 1, § 4302(a), Ch 2, § 4321(b), Subtitle E, Ch 3, § 4432(b)(5)(F), Ch 4, § 4541(a)(3), Subtitle F, Ch 1, Subch B,

§ 4511(a)(2)(D), Ch 2, § 4523(b), Subtitle G, Ch 4, § 4641(a), Subtitle H, Ch 2, § 4714(b)(1), 111 Stat. 275, 329, 373, 382, 395, 422, 442, 449, 456, 487, 510; Nov. 29, 1999, P. L. 106-113, Div B, § 1000(a)(6), 113 Stat. 1536; Dec. 21, 2000, P. L. 106-554, § 1(a)(6), 114 Stat. 2763; Dec. 8, 2003, P. L. 108-173, Title I, § 101(a)(1), Title II, Subtitle D, § 236(a)(1), Title V, Subtitle A, § 505(b), 506(a), Title VII, Subtitle D, § 736(a)(13), Title IX, Subtitle D, §§ 932(b), (c)(1), 936(a), 947(a), 117 Stat. 2071, 2210, 2294, 2355, 2400, 2411, 2425; July 15, 2008, P. L. 110-275, Title I, Subtitle C, Part II, § 143(b)(8), 122 Stat. 2543; March 23, 2010, P. L. 111-148, Title III, Subtitle A, Part I, § 3005, Title VI, Subtitle E, §§ 6401(a), 6406(b), Title X, Subtitle F, § 10603, 124 Stat. 371, 747, 769, 1006; March 30, 2010, P. L. 111-152, Title I, Subtitle D, § 1304, 124 Stat. 1058.)

HISTORY; ANCILLARY LAWS AND DIRECTIVES

Other provisions:

Disclosure of Medicare terminated providers and suppliers to States. Act March 23, 2010, P. L. 111-148, Title VI, Subtitle E, § 6401(b)(2), 124 Stat. 752, provides: "The Administrator of the Centers for Medicare & Medicaid Services shall establish a process for making available to the each State agency with responsibility for administering a State Medicaid plan (or a waiver of such plan) under title XIX of the Social Security Act [42 USCS §§ 1395 et seq.] or a child health plan under title XXI [42 USCS §§ 1397aa et seq.] the name, national provider identifier, and other identifying information for any provider of medical or other items or services or supplier under the Medicare program under title XVIII [42 USCS §§ 1395 et seq.] or under the CHIP program under title XXI [42 USCS §§ 1397aa et seq.] that is terminated from participation under that program within 30 days of the termination (and, with respect to all such providers or suppliers who are terminated from the Medicare program on the date of enactment of this Act, within 90 days of such date).".

§ 1395cc-3. Health care quality demonstration program

(a) Definitions. In this section:

(1) Beneficiary. The term "beneficiary" means an individual who is entitled to benefits under part A [42 USCS §§ 1395c et seq.] and enrolled under part B [42 USCS §§ 1395j et seq.], including any individual who is enrolled in a Medicare Advantage plan under part C [42 USCS §§ 1395w-21 et seq.].

(2) Health care group. (A) In general. The term "health care group" means—

(i) a group of physicians that is organized at least in part for the purpose of providing physician's services under this title [42 USCS §§ 1395 et seq.];

(ii) an integrated health care delivery system that delivers care through coordinated hospitals, clinics, home health agencies, ambulatory surgery centers, skilled nursing facilities, rehabilitation facilities and clinics, and employed, independent, or contracted physicians; or

(iii) an organization representing regional coalitions of groups or systems described in clause (i) or (ii).

(B) Inclusion. As the Secretary determines appropriate, a health care group may include a hospital or any other individual or entity furnishing items or services for which payment may be made under this title [42 USCS §§ 1395 et seq.] that is affiliated with the health care group under an arrangement structured so that such hospital, individual, or entity participates in a demonstration project under this section.

(3) Physician. Except as otherwise provided for by the Secretary, the term "physician" means any individual who furnishes services that may be paid for as physicians' services under this title [42 USCS §§ 1395 et seq.].

(b) Demonstration projects. The Secretary shall establish a demonstration program under which the Secretary shall approve demonstration projects that examine health delivery factors that encourage the delivery of improved quality in patient care, including—

(1) the provision of incentives to improve the safety of care provided to beneficiaries;

(2) the appropriate use of best practice guidelines by providers and services by beneficiaries;

(3) reduced scientific uncertainty in the delivery of care through the examination of variations in the utilization and allocation of services, and outcomes measurement and research;

(4) encourage shared decision making between providers and patients;

(5) the provision of incentives for improving the quality and safety of care and achieving the efficient allocation of resources;

(6) the appropriate use of culturally and ethnically sensitive health care delivery; and

(7) the financial effects on the health care marketplace of altering the incentives for care delivery and changing the allocation of resources.

(c) Administration by contract. (1) In general. Except as otherwise provided in this section, the Secretary may administer the demonstration program established under this section in a manner that is similar to the manner in which the demonstration program established under section 1866A [42 USCS

§ 1395cc-1] is administered in accordance with section 1866B [42 USCS § 1395cc-2].

(2) Alternative payment systems. A health care group that receives assistance under this section may, with respect to the demonstration project to be carried out with such assistance, include proposals for the use of alternative payment systems for items and services provided to beneficiaries by the group that are designed to—

(A) encourage the delivery of high quality care while accomplishing the objectives described in subsection (b); and

(B) streamline documentation and reporting requirements otherwise required under this title [42 USCS §§ 1395 et seq.].

(3) Benefits. A health care group that receives assistance under this section may, with respect to the demonstration project to be carried out with such assistance, include modifications to the package of benefits available under the original medicare fee-for-service program under parts A and B [42 USCS §§ 1395c et seq. and 1395j et seq.] or the package of benefits available through a Medicare Advantage plan under part C [42 USCS §§ 1395w-21 et seq.]. The criteria employed under the demonstration program under this section to evaluate outcomes and determine best practice guidelines and incentives shall not be used as a basis for the denial of medicare benefits under the demonstration program to patients against their wishes (or if the patient is incompetent, against the wishes of the patient's surrogate) on the basis of the patient's age or expected length of life or of the patient's present or predicted disability, degree of medical dependency, or quality of life.

(d) Eligibility criteria. To be eligible to receive assistance under this section, an entity shall—

(1) be a health care group;

(2) meet quality standards established by the Secretary, including—

(A) the implementation of continuous quality improvement mechanisms that are aimed at integrating community-based support services, primary care, and referral care;

(B) the implementation of activities to increase the delivery of effective care to beneficiaries;

(C) encouraging patient participation in preference-based decisions;

(D) the implementation of activities to encourage the coordination and integration of medical service delivery; and

(E) the implementation of activities to measure and document the financial impact on the health care marketplace of altering the incentives of health care delivery and changing the allocation of resources; and

(3) meet such other requirements as the Secretary may establish.

(e) Waiver authority. The Secretary may waive such requirements of titles XI and XVIII [42 USCS §§ 1301 et seq. and 1395 et seq.] as may be necessary to carry out the purposes of the demonstration program established under this section.

(f) Budget neutrality. With respect to the period of the demonstration program under subsection (b), the aggregate expenditures under this title [42 USCS §§ 1395 et seq.] for such period shall not exceed the aggregate expenditures that would have been expended under this title [42 USCS §§ 1395 et seq.] if the program established under this section had not been implemented.

(g) Notice requirements. In the case of an individual that receives health care items or services under a demonstration program carried out under this section, the Secretary shall ensure that such individual is notified of any waivers of coverage or payment rules that are applicable to such individual under this title [42 USCS §§ 1395 et seq.] as a result of the participation of the individual in such program.

(h) Participation and support by Federal agencies. In carrying out the demonstration program under this section, the Secretary may direct—

(1) the Director of the National Institutes of Health to expand the efforts of the Institutes to evaluate current medical technologies and improve the foundation for evidence-based practice;

(2) the Administrator of the Agency for Healthcare Research and Quality to, where possible and appropriate, use the program under this section as a laboratory for the study of quality improvement strategies and to evaluate, monitor, and disseminate information relevant to such program; and

(3) the Administrator of the Centers for Medicare & Medicaid Services and the Administrator of the Center for Medicare Choices to support linkages of relevant medicare data to registry information from participating health care groups for the beneficiary populations served by the participating groups, for analysis supporting the purposes of the demonstration program, consistent with the applicable provisions of the Health Insurance Portability and Accountability Act of 1996.

(Aug. 14, 1935, ch 531, Title XVIII, Part E, § 1866C, as added Dec. 8, 2003, P. L. 108-173,

Title VI, Subtitle D, § 646, 117 Stat. 2324; March 23, 2010, P. L. 111-148, Title III, Subtitle A, Part III, § 3021(c), 124 Stat. 395.)

§ 1395cc-4. National pilot program on payment bundling

(a) Implementation. (1) In general. The Secretary shall establish a pilot program for integrated care during an episode of care provided to an applicable beneficiary around a hospitalization in order to improve the coordination, quality, and efficiency of health care services under this title [42 USCS §§ 1395 et seq.].

(2) Definitions. In this section:

(A) Applicable beneficiary. The term "applicable beneficiary" means an individual who—

(i) is entitled to, or enrolled for, benefits under part A [42 USCS §§ 1395c et seq.] and enrolled for benefits under part B of such title [42 USCS §§ 1395j et seq.], but not enrolled under part C [42 USCS §§ 1395w-21 et seq.] or a PACE program under section 1894 [42 USCS § 1395eee]; and

(ii) is admitted to a hospital for an applicable condition.

(B) Applicable condition. The term "applicable condition" means 1 or more of 10 conditions selected by the Secretary. In selecting conditions under the preceding sentence, the Secretary shall take into consideration the following factors:

(i) Whether the conditions selected include a mix of chronic and acute conditions.

(ii) Whether the conditions selected include a mix of surgical and medical conditions.

(iii) Whether a condition is one for which there is evidence of an opportunity for providers of services and suppliers to improve the quality of care furnished while reducing total expenditures under this title [42 USCS §§ 1395 et seq.].

(iv) Whether a condition has significant variation in—

(I) the number of readmissions; and

(II) the amount of expenditures for post-acute care spending under this title [42 USCS §§ 1395 et seq.].

(v) Whether a condition is high-volume and has high post-acute care expenditures under this title [42 USCS §§ 1395 et seq.].

(vi) Which conditions the Secretary determines are most amenable to bundling across the spectrum of care given practice patterns under this title [42 USCS §§ 1395 et seq.].

(C) Applicable services. The term "applicable services" means the following:

(i) Acute care inpatient services.

(ii) Physicians' services delivered in and outside of an acute care hospital setting.

(iii) Outpatient hospital services, including emergency department services.

(iv) Post-acute care services, including home health services, skilled nursing services, inpatient rehabilitation services, and inpatient hospital services furnished by a long-term care hospital.

(v) Other services the Secretary determines appropriate.

(D) Episode of care. (i) In general. Subject to clause (ii), the term "episode of care" means, with respect to an applicable condition and an applicable beneficiary, the period that includes—

(I) the 3 days prior to the admission of the applicable beneficiary to a hospital for the applicable condition;

(II) the length of stay of the applicable beneficiary in such hospital; and

(III) the 30 days following the discharge of the applicable beneficiary from such hospital.

(ii) Establishment of period by the secretary. The Secretary, as appropriate, may establish a period (other than the period described in clause (i)) for an episode of care under the pilot program.

(E) Physicians' services. The term "physicians' services" has the meaning given such term in section 1861(q) [42 USCS § 1395x(q)].

(F) Pilot program. The term "pilot program" means the pilot program under this section.

(G) Provider of services. The term "provider of services" has the meaning given such term in section 1861(u) [42 USCS § 1395x(u)].

(H) Readmission. The term "readmission" has the meaning given such term in section 1886(q)(5)(E) [42 USCS § 1395ww(q)(5)(E)].

(I) Supplier. The term "supplier" has the meaning given such term in section 1861(d) [42 USCS § 1395x(d)].

(3) Deadline for implementation. The Secretary shall establish the pilot program not later than January 1, 2013.

(b) Developmental phase. (1) Determination of patient assessment instrument. The Secretary shall determine which patient assessment instrument (such as the Continuity Assessment Record and Evaluation (CARE) tool) shall be used under the pilot program to evaluate the applicable condition of an applicable beneficiary for purposes of determining the most clinically appropriate site for the provision of post-acute care to the applicable beneficiary.

(2) Development of quality measures for an episode of care and for post-acute care. (A) In

general. The Secretary, in consultation with the Agency for Healthcare Research and Quality and the entity with a contract under section 1890(a) of the Social Security Act [42 USCS § 1395aaa(a)], shall develop quality measures for use in the pilot program—

(i) for episodes of care; and

(ii) for post-acute care.

(B) Site-neutral post-acute care quality measures. Any quality measures developed under subparagraph (A)(ii) shall be site-neutral.

(C) Coordination with quality measure development and endorsement procedures. The Secretary shall ensure that the development of quality measures under subparagraph (A) is done in a manner that is consistent with the measures developed and endorsed under section 1890 and 1890A [42 USCS §§ 1395aaa and 1395aaa-1] that are applicable to all post-acute care settings.

(c) Details. (1) Duration. (A) In general. Subject to subparagraph (B), the pilot program shall be conducted for a period of 5 years.

(B) Expansion. The Secretary may, at any point after January 1, 2016, expand the duration and scope of the pilot program, to the extent determined appropriate by the Secretary, if—

(i) the Secretary determines that such expansion is expected to—

(I) reduce spending under title XVIII of the Social Security Act [42 USCS §§ 1395 et seq.] without reducing the quality of care; or

(II) improve the quality of care and reduce spending;

(ii) the Chief Actuary of the Centers for Medicare & Medicaid Services certifies that such expansion would reduce program spending under such title XVIII [42 USCS §§ 1395 et seq.]; and

(iii) the Secretary determines that such expansion would not deny or limit the coverage or provision of benefits under this title [42 USCS §§ 1395 et seq.] for individuals.

(2) Participating providers of services and suppliers. (A) In general. An entity comprised of providers of services and suppliers, including a hospital, a physician group, a skilled nursing facility, and a home health agency, who are otherwise participating under this title [42 USCS §§ 1395 et seq.], may submit an application to the Secretary to provide applicable services to applicable individuals under this section.

(B) Requirements. The Secretary shall develop requirements for entities to participate in the pilot program under this section. Such requirements shall ensure that applicable beneficiaries have an adequate choice of providers of services and suppliers under the pilot program.

(3) Payment methodology. (A) In general. (i) Establishment of payment methods. The Secretary shall develop payment methods for the pilot program for entities participating in the pilot program. Such payment methods may include bundled payments and bids from entities for episodes of care. The Secretary shall make payments to the entity for services covered under this section.

(ii) No additional program expenditures. Payments under this section for applicable items and services under this title [42 USCS §§ 1395 et seq.] (including payment for services described in subparagraph (B)) for applicable beneficiaries for a year shall be established in a manner that does not result in spending more for such entity for such beneficiaries than would otherwise be expended for such entity for such beneficiaries for such year if the pilot program were not implemented, as estimated by the Secretary.

(B) Inclusion of certain services. A payment methodology tested under the pilot program shall include payment for the furnishing of applicable services and other appropriate services, such as care coordination, medication reconciliation, discharge planning, transitional care services, and other patient-centered activities as determined appropriate by the Secretary.

(C) Bundled payments. (i) In general. A bundled payment under the pilot program shall—

(I) be comprehensive, covering the costs of applicable services and other appropriate services furnished to an individual during an episode of care (as determined by the Secretary); and

(II) be made to the entity which is participating in the pilot program.

(ii) Requirement for provision of applicable services and other appropriate services. Applicable services and other appropriate services for which payment is made under this subparagraph shall be furnished or directed by the entity which is participating in the pilot program.

(D) Payment for post-acute care services after the episode of care. The Secretary shall establish procedures, in the case where an applicable beneficiary requires continued post-acute care services after the last day of the episode of care, under which payment for such services shall be made.

(4) Quality measures. (A) In general. The

Secretary shall establish quality measures (including quality measures of process, outcome, and structure) related to care provided by entities participating in the pilot program. Quality measures established under the preceding sentence shall include measures of the following:

(i) Functional status improvement.

(ii) Reducing rates of avoidable hospital readmissions.

(iii) Rates of discharge to the community.

(iv) Rates of admission to an emergency room after a hospitalization.

(v) Incidence of health care acquired infections.

(vi) Efficiency measures.

(vii) Measures of patient-centeredness of care.

(viii) Measures of patient perception of care.

(ix) Other measures, including measures of patient outcomes, determined appropriate by the Secretary.

(B) Reporting on quality measures. (i) In general. A entity shall submit data to the Secretary on quality measures established under subparagraph (A) during each year of the pilot program (in a form and manner, subject to clause (iii), specified by the Secretary).

(ii) Submission of data through electronic health record. To the extent practicable, the Secretary shall specify that data on measures be submitted under clause (i) through the use of an qualified electronic health record (as defined in section 3000(13) of the Public Health Service Act (42 U.S.C. 300jj-11(13)) in a manner specified by the Secretary.

(d) Waiver. The Secretary may waive such provisions of this title and title XI [42 USCS §§ 1395 et seq. and 1301 et seq.] as may be necessary to carry out the pilot program.

(e) Independent evaluation and reports on pilot program. (1) Independent evaluation. The Secretary shall conduct an independent evaluation of the pilot program, including the extent to which the pilot program has—

(A) improved quality measures established under subsection (c)(4)(A);

(B) improved health outcomes;

(C) improved applicable beneficiary access to care; and

(D) reduced spending under this title [42 USCS §§ 1395 et seq.].

(2) Reports. (A) Interim report. Not later than 2 years after the implementation of the pilot program, the Secretary shall submit to Congress a report on the initial results of the independent evaluation conducted under paragraph (1).

(B) Final report. Not later than 3 years after the implementation of the pilot program, the Secretary shall submit to Congress a report on the final results of the independent evaluation conducted under paragraph (1).

(f) Consultation. The Secretary shall consult with representatives of small rural hospitals, including critical access hospitals (as defined in section 1861(mm)(1) [42 USCS § 1395x(mm)(1)]), regarding their participation in the pilot program. Such consultation shall include consideration of innovative methods of implementing bundled payments in hospitals described in the preceding sentence, taking into consideration any difficulties in doing so as a result of the low volume of services provided by such hospitals.

(g) Application of pilot program to continuing care hospitals. (1) In general. In conducting the pilot program, the Secretary shall apply the provisions of the program so as to separately pilot test the continuing care hospital model.

(2) Special rules. In pilot testing the continuing care hospital model under paragraph (1), the following rules shall apply:

(A) Such model shall be tested without the limitation to the conditions selected under subsection (a)(2)(B).

(B) Notwithstanding subsection (a)(2)(D), an episode of care shall be defined as the full period that a patient stays in the continuing care hospital plus the first 30 days following discharge from such hospital.

(3) Continuing care hospital defined. In this subsection, the term "continuing care hospital" means an entity that has demonstrated the ability to meet patient care and patient safety standards and that provides under common management the medical and rehabilitation services provided in inpatient rehabilitation hospitals and units (as defined in section 1886(d)(1)(B)(ii) [42 USCS § 1395ww(d)(1)(B)(ii)]), long term care hospitals (as defined in section 1886(d)(1)(B)(iv)(I) [42 USCS § 1395ww(d)(1)(B)(iv)(I)]), and skilled nursing facilities (as defined in section 1819(a) [42 USCS § 1395i-3(a)]) that are located in a hospital described in section 1886(d) [42 USCS § 1395ww(d)].

(h) Administration. Chapter 35 of title 44, United States Code [44 USCS §§ 3501 et seq.], shall not apply to the selection, testing, and evaluation of models or the expansion of such models under this section.

(Aug. 14, 1935, ch 531, Title XVIII, Part E, § 1866D, as added and amended March 23, 2010, P. L. 111-148, Title III, Subtitle A, Part

III, § 3023, Title X, Subtitle C, § 10308, 124 Stat. 399, 941.)

§ 1395cc-5. Independence at home medical practice demonstration program

(a) Establishment. (1) In general. The Secretary shall conduct a demonstration program (in this section referred to as the "demonstration program") to test a payment incentive and service delivery model that utilizes physician and nurse practitioner directed home-based primary care teams designed to reduce expenditures and improve health outcomes in the provision of items and services under this title [42 USCS §§ 1395 et seq.] to applicable beneficiaries (as defined in subsection (d)).

(2) Requirement. The demonstration program shall test whether a model described in paragraph (1), which is accountable for providing comprehensive, coordinated, continuous, and accessible care to high-need populations at home and coordinating health care across all treatment settings, results in—

(A) reducing preventable hospitalizations;

(B) preventing hospital readmissions;

(C) reducing emergency room visits;

(D) improving health outcomes commensurate with the beneficiaries' stage of chronic illness;

(E) improving the efficiency of care, such as by reducing duplicative diagnostic and laboratory tests;

(F) reducing the cost of health care services covered under this title [42 USCS §§ 1395 et seq.]; and

(G) achieving beneficiary and family caregiver satisfaction.

(b) Independence at home medical practice. (1) Independence at home medical practice defined. In this section:

(A) In general. The term "independence at home medical practice" means a legal entity that—

(i) is comprised of an individual physician or nurse practitioner or group of physicians and nurse practitioners that provides care as part of a team that includes physicians, nurses, physician assistants, pharmacists, and other health and social services staff as appropriate who have experience providing home-based primary care to applicable beneficiaries, make in-home visits, and are available 24 hours per day, 7 days per week to carry out plans of care that are tailored to the individual beneficiary's chronic conditions and designed to achieve the results in subsection (a);

(ii) is organized at least in part for the purpose of providing physicians' services;

(iii) has documented experience in providing home-based primary care services to high-cost chronically ill beneficiaries, as determined appropriate by the Secretary;

(iv) furnishes services to at least 200 applicable beneficiaries (as defined in subsection (d)) during each year of the demonstration program;

(v) has entered into an agreement with the Secretary;

(vi) uses electronic health information systems, remote monitoring, and mobile diagnostic technology; and

(vii) meets such other criteria as the Secretary determines to be appropriate to participate in the demonstration program.

The entity shall report on quality measures (in such form, manner, and frequency as specified by the Secretary, which may be for the group, for providers of services and suppliers, or both) and report to the Secretary (in a form, manner, and frequency as specified by the Secretary) such data as the Secretary determines appropriate to monitor and evaluate the demonstration program.

(B) Physician. The term "physician" includes, except as the Secretary may otherwise provide, any individual who furnishes services for which payment may be made as physicians' services and has the medical training or experience to fulfill the physician's role described in subparagraph (A)(i).

(2) Participation of nurse practitioners and physician assistants. Nothing in this section shall be construed to prevent a nurse practitioner or physician assistant from participating in, or leading, a home-based primary care team as part of an independence at home medical practice if—

(A) all the requirements of this section are met;

(B) the nurse practitioner or physician assistant, as the case may be, is acting consistent with State law; and

(C) the nurse practitioner or physician assistant has the medical training or experience to fulfill the nurse practitioner or physician assistant role described in paragraph (1)(A)(i).

(3) Inclusion of providers and practitioners. Nothing in this subsection shall be construed as preventing an independence at home medical practice from including a provider of services or a participating practitioner described in section 1842(b)(18)(C) [42 USCS § 1395u(b)(18)(C)] that is affiliated with the practice under an arrangement structured so that such provider of services or practitioner

participates in the demonstration program and shares in any savings under the demonstration program.

(4) Quality and performance standards. The Secretary shall develop quality performance standards for independence at home medical practices participating in the demonstration program.

(c) Payment methodology. (1) Establishment of target spending level. The Secretary shall establish an estimated annual spending target, for the amount the Secretary estimates would have been spent in the absence of the demonstration, for items and services covered under parts A and B [42 USCS §§ 1395c et seq. and 1395j et seq.] furnished to applicable beneficiaries for each qualifying independence at home medical practice under this section. Such spending targets shall be determined on a per capita basis. Such spending targets shall include a risk corridor that takes into account normal variation in expenditures for items and services covered under parts A and B [42 USCS §§ 1395c et seq. and 1395j et seq.] furnished to such beneficiaries with the size of the corridor being related to the number of applicable beneficiaries furnished services by each independence at home medical practice. The spending targets may also be adjusted for other factors as the Secretary determines appropriate.

(2) Incentive payments. Subject to performance on quality measures, a qualifying independence at home medical practice is eligible to receive an incentive payment under this section if actual expenditures for a year for the applicable beneficiaries it enrolls are less than the estimated spending target established under paragraph (1) for such year. An incentive payment for such year shall be equal to a portion (as determined by the Secretary) of the amount by which actual expenditures (including incentive payments under this paragraph) for applicable beneficiaries under parts A and B [42 USCS §§ 1395c et seq. and 1395j et seq.] for such year are estimated to be less than 5 percent less than the estimated spending target for such year, as determined under paragraph (1).

(d) Applicable beneficiaries. (1) Definition. In this section, the term "applicable beneficiary" means, with respect to a qualifying independence at home medical practice, an individual who the practice has determined—

(A) is entitled to benefits under part A [42 USCS §§ 1395c et seq.] and enrolled for benefits under part B [42 USCS §§ 1395j et seq.];

(B) is not enrolled in a Medicare Advantage plan under part C [42 USCS §§ 1395w-21 et seq.] or a PACE program under section 1894 [42 USCS § 1395eee];

(C) has 2 or more chronic illnesses, such as congestive heart failure, diabetes, other dementias designated by the Secretary, chronic obstructive pulmonary disease, ischemic heart disease, stroke, Alzheimer's Disease and neurodegenerative diseases, and other diseases and conditions designated by the Secretary which result in high costs under this title [42 USCS §§ 1395 et seq.];

(D) within the past 12 months has had a nonelective hospital admission;

(E) within the past 12 months has received acute or subacute rehabilitation services;

(F) has 2 or more functional dependencies requiring the assistance of another person (such as bathing, dressing, toileting, walking, or feeding); and

(G) meets such other criteria as the Secretary determines appropriate.

(2) Patient election to participate. The Secretary shall determine an appropriate method of ensuring that applicable beneficiaries have agreed to enroll in an independence at home medical practice under the demonstration program. Enrollment in the demonstration program shall be voluntary.

(3) Beneficiary access to services. Nothing in this section shall be construed as encouraging physicians or nurse practitioners to limit applicable beneficiary access to services covered under this title [42 USCS §§ 1395 et seq.] and applicable beneficiaries shall not be required to relinquish access to any benefit under this title [42 USCS §§ 1395 et seq.] as a condition of receiving services from an independence at home medical practice.

(e) Implementation. (1) Starting date. The demonstration program shall begin no later than January 1, 2012. An agreement with an independence at home medical practice under the demonstration program may cover not more than a 3-year period.

(2) No physician duplication in demonstration participation. The Secretary shall not pay an independence at home medical practice under this section that participates in section 1899 [42 USCS § 1395jjj].

(3) No beneficiary duplication in demonstration participation. The Secretary shall ensure that no applicable beneficiary enrolled in an independence at home medical practice under this section is participating in the programs under section 1899 [42 USCS § 1395jjj].

(4) Preference. In approving an indepen-

dence at home medical practice, the Secretary shall give preference to practices that are—

(A) located in high-cost areas of the country;

(B) have experience in furnishing health care services to applicable beneficiaries in the home; and

(C) use electronic medical records, health information technology, and individualized plans of care.

(5) Limitation on number of practices. In selecting qualified independence at home medical practices to participate under the demonstration program, the Secretary shall limit the number of such practices so that the number of applicable beneficiaries that may participate in the demonstration program does not exceed 10,000.

(6) Waiver. The Secretary may waive such provisions of this title and title XI [42 USCS §§ 1395 et seq. and 1301 et seq.] as the Secretary determines necessary in order to implement the demonstration program.

(7) Administration. Chapter 35 of title 44, United States Code [44 USCS §§ 3501 et seq.], shall not apply to this section.

(f) Evaluation and monitoring. (1) In general. The Secretary shall evaluate each independence at home medical practice under the demonstration program to assess whether the practice achieved the results described in subsection (a).

(2) Monitoring applicable beneficiaries. The Secretary may monitor data on expenditures and quality of services under this title [42 USCS §§ 1395 et seq.] after an applicable beneficiary discontinues receiving services under this title [42 USCS §§ 1395 et seq.] through a qualifying independence at home medical practice.

(g) Reports to Congress. The Secretary shall conduct an independent evaluation of the demonstration program and submit to Congress a final report, including best practices under the demonstration program. Such report shall include an analysis of the demonstration program on coordination of care, expenditures under this title [42 USCS §§ 1395 et seq.], applicable beneficiary access to services, and the quality of health care services provided to applicable beneficiaries.

(h) Funding. For purposes of administering and carrying out the demonstration program, other than for payments for items and services furnished under this title [42 USCS §§ 1395 et seq.] and incentive payments under subsection (c), in addition to funds otherwise appropriated, there shall be transferred to the Secretary for the Center for Medicare & Medicaid Services Program Management Account from the Federal Hospital Insurance Trust Fund under section 1817 [42 USCS § 1395i] and the Federal Supplementary Medical Insurance Trust Fund under section 1841 [42 USCS § 1395t] (in proportions determined appropriate by the Secretary) $5,000,000 for each of fiscal years 2010 through 2015. Amounts transferred under this subsection for a fiscal year shall be available until expended.

(i) Termination. (1) Mandatory termination. The Secretary shall terminate an agreement with an independence at home medical practice if—

(A) the Secretary estimates or determines that such practice will not receive an incentive payment for the second of 2 consecutive years under the demonstration program; or

(B) such practice fails to meet quality standards during any year of the demonstration program.

(2) Permissive termination. The Secretary may terminate an agreement with an independence at home medical practice for such other reasons determined appropriate by the Secretary.

(Aug. 14, 1935, ch 531, Title XVIII, Part E, § 1866E [1866D], as added and amended March 23, 2010, P. L. 111-148, Title III, Subtitle A, Part III, § 3024, Title X, Subtitle C, § 10308(b)(2), 124 Stat. 404, 942.)

§ 1395ee. Council for Technology and Innovation

(a) [Repealed]

(b) Council for Technology and Innovation. (1) Establishment. The Secretary shall establish a Council for Technology and Innovation within the Centers for Medicare & Medicaid Services (in this section referred to as "CMS").

(2) Composition. The Council shall be composed of senior CMS staff and clinicians and shall be chaired by the Executive Coordinator for Technology and Innovation (appointed or designated under paragraph (4)).

(3) Duties. The Council shall coordinate the activities of coverage, coding, and payment processes under this title [42 USCS §§ 1395 et seq.] with respect to new technologies and procedures, including new drug therapies, and shall coordinate the exchange of information on new technologies between CMS and other entities that make similar decisions.

(4) Executive Coordinator for Technology and Innovation. The Secretary shall appoint (or designate) a noncareer appointee (as defined in section 3132(a)(7) of title 5, United States

Code) who shall serve as the Executive Coordinator for Technology and Innovation. Such executive coordinator shall report to the Administrator of CMS, shall chair the Council, shall oversee the execution of its duties, and shall serve as a single point of contact for outside groups and entities regarding the coverage, coding, and payment processes under this title [42 USCS §§ 1395 et seq.].

(Aug. 14, 1935, ch 531, Title XVIII, Part E [D] [C], § 1868, as added Nov. 5, 1990, P. L. 101-508, Title IV, Subtitle A, Part 2, Subpart A, § 4112, 104 Stat. 1388-64; Aug. 5, 1997, P. L. 105-33, Title IV, Subtitle A, Chapter 1, Subchapter A, § 4001, 111 Stat. 275; Dec. 8, 2003, P. L. 108-173, Title I, § 101(a)(1), Title IX, Subtitle E, § 942(a), 117 Stat. 2071, 2420; March 23, 2010, P. L. 111-148, Title III, Subtitle B, Part III, § 3134(b)(2), 124 Stat. 435.)

§ 1395kk. Administration of insurance programs

(a) Functions of Secretary; performance directly or by contract. Except as otherwise provided in this title [42 USCS §§ 1395 et seq.] and in the Railroad Retirement Act of 1974, the insurance programs established by this title [42 USCS §§ 1395 et seq.] shall be administered by the Secretary. The Secretary may perform any of his functions under this title [42 USCS §§ 1395 et seq.] directly, or by contract providing for payment in advance or by way of reimbursement, and in such installments, as the Secretary may deem necessary.

(b) Contracts to secure special data, actuarial information, etc. The Secretary may contract with any person, agency, or institution to secure on a reimbursable basis such special data, actuarial information, and other information as may be necessary in the carrying out of his functions under this title [42 USCS §§ 1395 et seq.].

(c) Oaths and affirmations. In the course of any hearing, investigation, or other proceeding, that he is authorized to conduct under this title [42 USCS §§ 1395 et seq.], the Secretary may administer oaths and affirmations.

(d) Inclusion of medicare provider and supplier payments in Federal Payment Levy Program. (1) In general. The Centers for Medicare & Medicaid Services shall take all necessary steps to participate in the Federal Payment Levy Program under section 6331(h) of the Internal Revenue Code of 1986 [26 USCS § 6331(h)] as soon as possible and shall ensure that—

(A) at least 50 percent of all payments under parts A and B [42 USCS §§ 1395c et seq. and 1395j et seq.] are processed through such program beginning within 1 year after the date of the enactment of this section;

(B) at least 75 percent of all payments under parts A and B [42 USCS §§ 1395c et seq. and 1395j et seq.] are processed through such program beginning within 2 years after such date; and

(C) all payments under parts A and B [42 USCS §§ 1395c et seq. and 1395j et seq.] are processed through such program beginning not later than September 30, 2011.

(2) Assistance. The Financial Management Service and the Internal Revenue Service shall provide assistance to the Centers for Medicare & Medicaid Services to ensure that all payments described in paragraph (1) are included in the Federal Payment Levy Program by the deadlines specified in that subsection.

(e) Availability of Medicare data [Caution: This subsection takes effect on January 1, 2012, as provided by § 10332(b) of Act March 23, 2010, P. L. 111-148, which appears as a note to this section]. (1) In general. Subject to paragraph (4), the Secretary shall make available to qualified entities (as defined in paragraph (2)) data described in paragraph (3) for the evaluation of the performance of providers of services and suppliers.

(2) Qualified entities. For purposes of this subsection, the term "qualified entity" means a public or private entity that—

(A) is qualified (as determined by the Secretary) to use claims data to evaluate the performance of providers of services and suppliers on measures of quality, efficiency, effectiveness, and resource use; and

(B) agrees to meet the requirements described in paragraph (4) and meets such other requirements as the Secretary may specify, such as ensuring security of data.

(3) Data described. The data described in this paragraph are standardized extracts (as determined by the Secretary) of claims data under parts A, B, and D [42 USCS §§ 1395c et seq., 1395j et seq., and 1395w-101 et seq.] for items and services furnished under such parts for one or more specified geographic areas and time periods requested by a qualified entity. The Secretary shall take such actions as the Secretary deems necessary to protect the identity of individuals entitled to or enrolled for benefits under such parts.

(4) Requirements. (A) Fee. Data described in paragraph (3) shall be made available to a qualified entity under this subsection at a fee equal to the cost of making such data available.

Any fee collected pursuant to the preceding sentence shall be deposited into the Federal Supplementary Medical Insurance Trust Fund under section 1841 [42 USCS § 1395t].

(B) Specification of uses and methodologies. A qualified entity requesting data under this subsection shall—

(i) submit to the Secretary a description of the methodologies that such qualified entity will use to evaluate the performance of providers of services and suppliers using such data;

(ii)(I) except as provided in subclause (II), if available, use standard measures, such as measures endorsed by the entity with a contract under section 1890(a) [42 USCS § 1395aaa(a)] and measures developed pursuant to section 931 of the Public Health Service Act [42 USCS § 299b-31]; or

(II) use alternative measures if the Secretary, in consultation with appropriate stakeholders, determines that use of such alternative measures would be more valid, reliable, responsive to consumer preferences, cost-effective, or relevant to dimensions of quality and resource use not addressed by such standard measures;

(iii) include data made available under this subsection with claims data from sources other than claims data under this title in the evaluation of performance of providers of services and suppliers;

(iv) only include information on the evaluation of performance of providers and suppliers in reports described in subparagraph (C);

(v) make available to providers of services and suppliers, upon their request, data made available under this subsection; and

(vi) prior to their release, submit to the Secretary the format of reports under subparagraph (C).

(C) Reports. Any report by a qualified entity evaluating the performance of providers of services and suppliers using data made available under this subsection shall—

(i) include an understandable description of the measures, which shall include quality measures and the rationale for use of other measures described in subparagraph (B)(ii)(II), risk adjustment methods, physician attribution methods, other applicable methods, data specifications and limitations, and the sponsors, so that consumers, providers of services and suppliers, health plans, researchers, and other stakeholders can assess such reports;

(ii) be made available confidentially, to any provider of services or supplier to be identified in such report, prior to the public release of such report, and provide an opportunity to appeal and correct errors;

(iii) only include information on a provider of services or supplier in an aggregate form as determined appropriate by the Secretary; and

(iv) except as described in clause (ii), be made available to the public.

(D) Approval and limitation of uses. The Secretary shall not make data described in paragraph (3) available to a qualified entity unless the qualified entity agrees to release the information on the evaluation of performance of providers of services and suppliers. Such entity shall only use such data, and information derived from such evaluation, for the reports under subparagraph (C). Data released to a qualified entity under this subsection shall not be subject to discovery or admission as evidence in judicial or administrative proceedings without consent of the applicable provider of services or supplier.

(Aug. 14, 1935, ch 531, Title XVIII, Part E [D] [C], § 1874, as added July 30, 1965, P. L. 89-97, Title I, Part 1, §§ 102(a), 111(a), 79 Stat. 332, 340; Oct. 30, 1972, P. L. 92-603, Title II, § 289, 86 Stat. 1457; Oct. 16, 1974, P. L. 93-445, Title III, § 310, 88 Stat. 1359; Aug. 5, 1997, P. L. 105-33, Title IV, Subtitle A, Ch 1, Subch A, § 4001, 111 Stat. 275; Dec. 8, 2003, P. L. 108-173, Title I, § 101(a)(1), 117 Stat. 2071; July 15, 2008, P. L. 110-275, Title I, Subtitle F, § 189(a), 122 Stat. 2590; March 23, 2010, P. L. 111-148, Title X, Subtitle C, § 10332, 124 Stat. 968.)

HISTORY; ANCILLARY LAWS AND DIRECTIVES

Other provisions:

Effective date of March 23, 2010 amendment. Act March 23, 2010, P. L. 111-148, Title X, § 10332(b), 124 Stat. 970, provides: "The amendment made by subsection (a) [adding subsec. (e) of this section] shall take effect on January 1, 2012.".

§ 1395mm. Payments to health maintenance organizations and competitive medical plans

(a) Rates and adjustments. (1)(A) The Secretary shall annually determine, and shall announce (in a manner intended to provide notice to interested parties) not later than September 7 before the calendar year concerned—

(i) a per capita rate of payment for each class of individuals who are enrolled under this section with an eligible organization which has entered into a risk-sharing contract and who are entitled to benefits under part A [42 USCS §§ 1395c et seq.] and enrolled under part B [42 USCS §§ 1395j et seq.], and

(ii) a per capita rate of payment for each class of individuals who are so enrolled with such an organization and who are enrolled under part B [42 USCS §§ 1395j et seq.] only.

For purposes of this section, the term "risk-sharing contract" means a contract entered into under subsection (g) and the term "reasonable cost reimbursement contract" means a contract entered into under subsection (h).

(B) The Secretary shall define appropriate classes of members, based on age, disability status, and such other factors as the Secretary determines to be appropriate, so as to ensure actuarial equivalence. The Secretary may add to, modify, or substitute for such classes, if such changes will improve the determination of actuarial equivalence.

(C) The annual per capita rate of payment for each such class shall be equal to 95 percent of the adjusted average per capita cost (as defined in paragraph (4)) for that class.

(D) In the case of an eligible organization with a risk-sharing contract, the Secretary shall make monthly payments in advance and in accordance with the rate determined under subparagraph (C) and except as provided in subsection (g)(2), to the organization for each individual enrolled with the organization under this section.

(E)(i) The amount of payment under this paragraph may be retroactively adjusted to take into account any difference between the actual number of individuals enrolled in the plan under this section and the number of such individuals estimated to be so enrolled in determining the amount of the advance payment.

(ii)(I) Subject to subclause (II), the Secretary may make retroactive adjustments under clause (i) to take into account individuals enrolled during the period beginning on the date on which the individual enrolls with an eligible organization (which has a risk-sharing contract under this section) under a health benefit plan operated, sponsored, or contributed to by the individual's employer or former employer (or the employer or former employer of the individual's spouse) and ending on the date on which the individual is enrolled in the plan under this section, except that for purposes of making such retroactive adjustments under this clause, such period may not exceed 90 days.

(II) No adjustment may be made under subclause (I) with respect to any individual who does not certify that the organization provided the individual with the explanation described in subsection (c)(3)(E) at the time the individual enrolled with the organization.

(F)(i) At least 45 days before making the announcement under subparagraph (A) for a year (beginning with the announcement for 1991), the Secretary shall provide for notice to eligible organizations of proposed changes to be made in the methodology or benefit coverage assumptions from the methodology and assumptions used in the previous announcement and shall provide such organizations an opportunity to comment on such proposed changes.

(ii) In each announcement made under subparagraph (A) for a year (beginning with the announcement for 1991), the Secretary shall include an explanation of the assumptions (including any benefit coverage assumptions) and changes in methodology used in the announcement in sufficient detail so that eligible organizations can compute per capita rates of payment for classes of individuals located in each county (or equivalent area) which is in whole or in part within the service area of such an organization.

(2) With respect to any eligible organization which has entered into a reasonable cost reimbursement contract, payments shall be made to such plan in accordance with subsection (h)(2) rather than paragraph (1).

(3) Subject to subsection (c)(2)(B)(ii) and (c)(7), payments under a contract to an eligible organization under paragraph (1) or (2) shall be instead of the amounts which (in the absence of the contract) would be otherwise payable, pursuant to sections 1814(b) and 1833(a) [42 USCS §§ 1395f(b) and 1395l(a)], for services furnished by or through the organization to individuals enrolled with the organization under this section.

(4) For purposes of this section, the term "adjusted average per capita cost" means the average per capita amount that the Secretary estimates in advance (on the basis of actual experience, or retrospective actuarial equivalent based upon an adequate sample and other information and data, in a geographic area served by an eligible organization or in a similar area, with appropriate adjustments to assure actuarial equivalence) would be payable in any contract year for services covered under parts A and B [42 USCS §§ 1395c et seq. and 1395j et seq.], or part B [42 USCS §§ 1395j et seq.] only, and types of expenses otherwise reimbursable under parts A and B [42 USCS §§ 1395c et seq. and 1395j et seq.], or part B [42 USCS §§ 1395j et seq.] only (including administrative costs incurred by organizations described in sections 1816 and 1842 [42 USCS §§ 1395h and 1395u]), if the services were to be furnished by other than an eligible organization or, in the case of services covered only

under section 1861(s)(2)(H) [42 USCS § 1395x(s)(2)(H)], if the services were to be furnished by a physician or as an incident to a physician's service.

(5) The payment to an eligible organization under this section for individuals enrolled under this section with the organization and entitled to benefits under part A [42 USCS §§ 1395c et seq.] and enrolled under part B [42 USCS §§ 1395j et seq.] shall be made from the Federal Hospital Insurance Trust Fund and the Federal Supplementary Medical Insurance Trust Fund. The portion of that payment to the organization for a month to be paid by each trust fund shall be determined as follows:

(A) In regard to expenditures by eligible organizations having risk-sharing contracts, the allocation shall be determined each year by the Secretary based on the relative weight that benefits from each fund contribute to the adjusted average per capita cost.

(B) In regard to expenditures by eligible organizations operating under a reasonable cost reimbursement contract, the initial allocation shall be based on the plan's most recent budget, such allocation to be adjusted, as needed, after cost settlement to reflect the distribution of actual expenditures.

The remainder of that payment shall be paid by the former trust fund.

(6) Subject to subsections (c)(2)(B)(ii) and (c)(7), if an individual is enrolled under this section with an eligible organization having a risk-sharing contract, only the eligible organization shall be entitled to receive payments from the Secretary under this title [42 USCS §§ 1395 et seq.] for services furnished to the individual.

(b) Definitions; requirements. For purposes of this section, the term "eligible organization" means a public or private entity (which may be a health maintenance organization or a competitive medical plan), organized under the laws of any State, which—

(1) is a qualified health maintenance organization (as defined in section 1310(d) of the Public Health Service Act [42 USCS § 300e-9(d)]), or

(2) meets the following requirements:

(A) The entity provides to enrolled members at least the following health care services:

(i) Physicians' services performed by physicians (as defined in section 1861(r)(1) [42 USCS § 1395x(r)(1)]).

(ii) Inpatient hospital services.

(iii) Laboratory, X-ray, emergency, and preventive services.

(iv) Out-of-area coverage.

(B) The entity is compensated (except for deductibles, coinsurance, and copayments) for the provision of health care services to enrolled members by a payment which is paid on a periodic basis without regard to the date the health care services are provided and which is fixed without regard to the frequency, extent, or kind of health care service actually provided to a member.

(C) The entity provides physicians' services primarily (i) directly through physicians who are either employees or partners of such organization, or (ii) through contracts with individual physicians or one or more groups of physicians (organized on a group practice or individual practice basis).

(D) The entity assumes full financial risk on a prospective basis for the provision of the health care services listed in subparagraph (A), except that such entity may—

(i) obtain insurance or make other arrangements for the cost of providing to any enrolled member health care services listed in subparagraph (A) the aggregate value of which exceeds $5,000 in any year,

(ii) obtain insurance or make other arrangements for the cost of health care service listed in subparagraph (A) provided to its enrolled members other than through the entity because medical necessity required their provision before they could be secured through the entity,

(iii) obtain insurance or make other arrangements for not more than 90 percent of the amount by which its costs for any of its fiscal years exceed 115 percent of its income for such fiscal year, and

(iv) make arrangements with physicians or other health professionals, health care institutions, or any combination of such individuals or institutions to assume all or part of the financial risk on a prospective basis for the provision of basic health services by the physicians or other health professionals or through the institutions.

(E) The entity has made adequate provision against the risk of insolvency, which provision is satisfactory to the Secretary.

Paragraph (2)(A)(ii) shall not apply to an entity which had contracted with a single State agency administering a State plan approved under title XIX [42 USCS §§ 1396 et seq.] for the provision of services (other than inpatient hospital services) to individuals eligible for such services under such State plan on a prepaid risk basis prior to 1970.

(c) Enrollment in plan; duties of organization to enrollees. (1) The Secretary may not enter into a contract under this section with an eligible organization unless it meets the requirements of this subsection and subsection (e) with respect to members enrolled under this section.

(2)(A) The organization must provide to members enrolled under this section, through providers and other persons that meet the applicable requirements of this title [42 USCS §§ 1395 et seq.] and part A of title XI [42 USCS §§ 1301 et seq.]—

(i) only those services covered under parts A and B of this title [42 USCS §§ 1395c et seq. and 1395j et seq.], for those members entitled to benefits under part A [42 USCS §§ 1395c et seq.] and enrolled under part B [42 USCS §§ 1395j et seq.], or

(ii) only those services covered under part B [42 USCS §§ 1395j et seq.], for those members enrolled only under such part,

which are available to individuals residing in the geographic area served by the organization, except that (I) the organization may provide such members with such additional health care services as the members may elect, at their option, to have covered, and (II) in the case of an organization with a risk-sharing contract, the organization may provide such members with such additional health care services as the Secretary may approve. The Secretary shall approve any such additional health care services which the organization proposes to offer to such members, unless the Secretary determines that including such additional services will substantially discourage enrollment by covered individuals with the organization.

(B) If there is a national coverage determination made in the period beginning on the date of an announcement under subsection (a)(1)(A) and ending on the date of the next announcement under such subsection that the Secretary projects will result in a significant change in the costs to the organization of providing the benefits that are the subject of such national coverage determination and that was not incorporated in the determination of the per capita rate of payment included in the announcement made at the beginning of such period—

(i) such determination shall not apply to risk-sharing contracts under this section until the first contract year that begins after the end of such period; and

(ii) if such coverage determination provides for coverage of additional benefits or under additional circumstances, subsection (a)(3) shall not apply to payment for such additional benefits or benefits provided under such additional circumstances until the first contract year that begins after the end of such period,

unless otherwise required by law.

(3)(A)(i) Each eligible organization must have an open enrollment period, for the enrollment of individuals under this section, of at least 30 days duration every year and including the period or periods specified under clause (ii), and must provide that at any time during which enrollments are accepted, the organization will accept up to the limits of its capacity (as determined by the Secretary) and without restrictions, except as may be authorized in regulations, individuals who are eligible to enroll under subsection (d) in the order in which they apply for enrollment, unless to do so would result in failure to meet the requirements of subsection (f) or would result in the enrollment of enrollees substantially nonrepresentative, as determined in accordance with regulations of the Secretary, of the population in the geographic area served by the organization.

(ii)(I) If a risk-sharing contract under this section is not renewed or is otherwise terminated, eligible organizations with risk-sharing contracts under this section and serving a part of the same service area as under the terminated contract are required to have an open enrollment period for individuals who were enrolled under the terminated contract as of the date of notice of such termination. If a risk-sharing contract under this section is renewed in a manner that discontinues coverage for individuals residing in part of the service area, eligible organizations with risk-sharing contracts under this section and enrolling individuals residing in that part of the service area are required to have an open enrollment period for individuals residing in the part of the service area who were enrolled under the contract as of the date of notice of such discontinued coverage.

(II) The open enrollment periods required under subclause (I) shall be for 30 days and shall begin 30 days after the date that the Secretary provides notice of such requirement.

(III) Enrollment under this clause shall be effective 30 days after the end of the open enrollment period, or, if the Secretary determines that such date is not feasible, such other date as the Secretary specifies.

(B) An individual may enroll under this section with an eligible organization in such manner as may be prescribed in regulations and may terminate his enrollment with the eligible organization as of the beginning of the first calendar month following the date on which the request is made for such termination (or, in the case of financial insolvency of the organization, as may be prescribed by regulations) or, in the case of such an organization with a reasonable cost reimbursement contract, as may be prescribed by regulations. In the case of an individual's termination of enrollment, the organization shall provide the individual with a copy of the written request for termination of enrollment and a written explanation of the period (ending on the effective date of the termination) during which the individual continues to be enrolled with the organization and may not receive benefits under this title other than through the organization.

(C) The Secretary may prescribe the procedures and conditions under which an eligible organization that has entered into a contract with the Secretary under this subsection may inform individuals eligible to enroll under this section with the organization about the organization, or may enroll such individuals with the organization. No brochures, application forms, or other promotional or informational material may be distributed by an organization to (or for the use of) individuals eligible to enroll with the organization under this section unless (i) at least 45 days before its distribution, the organization has submitted the material to the Secretary for review and (ii) the Secretary has not disapproved the distribution of the material. The Secretary shall review all such material submitted and shall disapprove such material if the Secretary determines, in the Secretary's discretion, that the material is materially inaccurate or misleading or otherwise makes a material misrepresentation.

(D) The organization must provide assurances to the Secretary that it will not expel or refuse to re-enroll any such individual because of the individual's health status or requirements for health care services, and that it will notify each such individual of such fact at the time of the individual's enrollment.

(E) Each eligible organization shall provide each enrollee, at the time of enrollment and not less frequently than annually thereafter, an explanation of the enrollee's rights under this section, including an explanation of—

(i) the enrollee's rights to benefits from the organization,

(ii) the restrictions on payments under this title [42 USCS §§ 1395 et seq.] for services furnished other than by or through the organization,

(iii) out-of-area coverage provided by the organization,

(iv) the organization's coverage of emergency services and urgently needed care, and

(v) appeal rights of enrollees.

(F) Each eligible organization that provides items and services pursuant to a contract under this section shall provide assurances to the Secretary that in the event the organization ceases to provide such items and services, the organization shall provide or arrange for supplemental coverage of benefits under this title [42 USCS §§ 1395 et seq.] related to a pre-existing condition with respect to any exclusion period, to all individuals enrolled with the entity who receive benefits under this title [42 USCS §§ 1395 et seq.], for the lesser of six months or the duration of such period.

(G)(i) Each eligible organization having a risk-sharing contract under this section shall notify individuals eligible to enroll with the organization under this section and individuals enrolled with the organization under this section that—

(I) the organization is authorized by law to terminate or refuse to renew the contract, and

(II) termination or nonrenewal of the contract may result in termination of the enrollments of individuals enrolled with the organization under this section.

(ii) The notice required by clause (i) shall be included in—

(I) any marketing materials described in subparagraph (C) that are distributed by an eligible organization to individuals eligible to enroll under this section with the organization, and

(II) any explanation provided to enrollees by the organization pursuant to subparagraph (E).

(4) The organization must—

(A) make the services described in paragraph (2) (and such other health care services as such individuals have contracted for) (i) available and accessible to each such individual, within the area served by the organization, with reasonable promptness and in a manner which assures continuity, and (ii) when medically necessary, available and accessible twenty-four hours a day and seven days a week, and

(B) provide for reimbursement with respect to services which are described in subparagraph (A) and which are provided to such an individual other than through the organization, if (i) the services were medically necessary and immediately required because of an unforeseen illness, injury, or condition and (ii) it was not reasonable given the circumstances to obtain the services through the organization.

(5)(A) The organization must provide meaningful procedures for hearing and resolving grievances between the organization (including any entity or individual through which the organization provides health care services) and members enrolled with the organization under this section.

(B) A member enrolled with an eligible organization under this section who is dissatisfied by reason of his failure to receive any health service to which he believes he is entitled and at no greater charge than he believes he is required to pay is entitled, if the amount in controversy is $100 or more, to a hearing before the Secretary to the same extent as is provided in section 205(b) [42 USCS § 405(b)], and in any such hearing the Secretary shall make the eligible organization a party. If the amount in controversy is $1,000 or more, the individual or eligible organization shall, upon notifying the other party, be entitled to judicial review of the Secretary's final decision as provided in section 205(g) [42 USCS § 405(g)], and both the individual and the eligible organization shall be entitled to be parties to that judicial review. In applying sections 205(b) and 205(g) [42 USCS § 405(b) and (g)] as provided in this subparagraph, and in applying section 205(l) [42 USCS § 405(l)] thereto, any reference therein to the Commissioner of Social Security or the Social Security Administration shall be considered a reference to the Secretary or the Department of Health and Human Services, respectively. The provisions of section 1869(b)(1)(E)(iii) [42 USCS § 1395ff(b)(1)(E)(iii)] shall apply with respect to dollar amounts specified in the first 2 sentences of this subparagraph in the same manner as they apply to the dollar amounts specified in section 1869(b)(1)(E)(i) [42 USCS § 1395ff(b)(1)(E)(i)].

(6) The organization must have arrangements, established in accordance with regulations of the Secretary, for an ongoing quality assurance program for health care services it provides to such individuals, which program (A) stresses health outcomes and (B) provides review by physicians and other health care professionals of the process followed in the provision of such health care services.

(7) A risk-sharing contract under this section shall provide that in the case of an individual who is receiving inpatient hospital services from a subsection (d) hospital (as defined in section 1886(d)(1)(B) [42 USCS § 1395ww(d)(1)(B)]) as of the effective date of the individual's—

(A) enrollment with an eligible organization under this section—

(i) payment for such services until the date of the individual's discharge shall be made under this title [42 USCS §§ 1395 et seq.] as if the individual were not enrolled with the organization,

(ii) the organization shall not be financially responsible for payment for such services until the date after the date of the individual's discharge, and

(iii) the organization shall nonetheless be paid the full amount otherwise payable to the organization under this section; or

(B) termination of enrollment with an eligible organization under this section—

(i) the organization shall be financially responsible for payment for such services after such date and until the date of the individual's discharge,

(ii) payment for such services during the stay shall not be made under section 1886(d) [42 USCS § 1395ww(d)], and

(iii) the organization shall not receive any payment with respect to the individual under this section during the period the individual is not enrolled.

(8) A contract under this section shall provide that the eligible organization shall meet the requirement of section 1866(f) [42 USCS § 1395cc(f)] (relating to maintaining written policies and procedures respecting advance directives).

(d) Right to enroll with contracting organization in geographic area. Subject to the provisions of subsection (c)(3), every individual entitled to benefits under part A [42 USCS §§ 1395c et seq.] and enrolled under part B [42 USCS §§ 1395j et seq.] or enrolled under part B [42 USCS §§ 1395j et seq.] only (other than an individual medically determined to have end-stage renal disease) shall be eligible to enroll under this section with any eligible organization with which the Secretary has entered into a contract under this section and which serves the geographic area in which the individual resides.

(e) Limitation on charges; election of coverage; "adjusted community rate" defined; workmen's compensation and insurance benefits. (1) In no case may—

(A) the portion of an eligible organization's premium rate and the actuarial value of its deductibles, coinsurance, and copayments charged (with respect to services covered under parts A and B [42 USCS §§ 1395c et seq. and 1395j et seq.]) to individuals who are enrolled under this section with the organization and who are entitled to benefits under part A [42 USCS §§ 1395c et seq.] and enrolled under part B [42 USCS §§ 1395j et seq.], or

(B) the portion of its premium rate and the actuarial value of its deductibles, coinsurance, and copayments charged (with respect to services covered under part B [42 USCS §§ 1395j et seq.]) to individuals who are enrolled under this section with the organization and enrolled under part B [42 USCS §§ 1395j et seq.] only

exceed the actuarial value of the coinsurance and deductibles that would be applicable on the average to individuals enrolled under this section with the organization (or, if the Secretary finds that adequate data are not available to determine that actuarial value, the actuarial value of the coinsurance and deductibles applicable on the average to individuals in the area, in the State, or in the United States, eligible to enroll under this section with the organization, or other appropriate data) and entitled to benefits under part A [42 USCS §§ 1395c et seq.] and enrolled under part B [42 USCS §§ 1395j et seq.], or enrolled under part B [42 USCS §§ 1395j et seq.] only, respectively, if they were not members of an eligible organization.

(2) If the eligible organization provides to its members enrolled under this section services in addition to services covered under parts A and B of this title [42 USCS §§ 1395c et seq. and 1395j et seq.], election of coverage for such additional services (unless such services have been approved by the Secretary under subsection (c)(2)) shall be optional for such members and such organization shall furnish such members with information on the portion of its premium rate or other charges applicable to such additional services. In no case may the sum of—

(A) the portion of such organization's premium rate charged, with respect to such additional services, to members enrolled under this section, and

(B) the actuarial value of its deductibles, coinsurance, and copayments charged, with respect to such services to such members

exceed the adjusted community rate for such services.

(3) For purposes of this section, the term "adjusted community rate" for a service or services means, at the election of an eligible organization, either—

(A) the rate of payment for that service or services which the Secretary annually determines would apply to a member enrolled under this section with an eligible organization if the rate of payment were determined under a "community rating system" (as defined in section 1302(8) of the Public Health Service Act [42 USCS § 300e-1(8)], other than subparagraph (C)), or

(B) such portion of the weighted aggregate premium, which the Secretary annually estimates would apply to a member enrolled under this section with the eligible organization, as the Secretary annually estimates is attributable to that service or services,

but adjusted for differences between the utilization characteristics of the members enrolled with the eligible organization under this section and the utilization characteristics of the other members of the organization (or, if the Secretary finds that adequate data are not available to adjust for those differences, the differences between the utilization characteristics of members in other eligible organizations, or individuals in the area, in the State, or in the United States, eligible to enroll under this section with an eligible organization and the utilization characteristics of the rest of the population in the area, in the State, or in the United States, respectively).

(4) Notwithstanding any other provision of law, the eligible organization may (in the case of the provision of services to a member enrolled under this section for an illness or injury for which the member is entitled to benefits under a workmen's compensation law or plan of the United States or a State, under an automobile or liability insurance policy or plan, including a self-insured plan, or under no fault insurance) charge or authorize the provider of such services to charge, in accordance with the charges allowed under such law or policy—

(A) the insurance carrier, employer, or other entity which under such law, plan, or policy is to pay for the provision of such services, or

(B) such member to the extent that the member has been paid under such law, plan, or policy for such services.

(f) Membership requirements. (1) For contract periods beginning before January 1, 1999, each eligible organization with which the Secretary enters into a contract under this section shall have, for the duration of such contract, an enrolled membership at least one-half of which consists of individuals who are not entitled to benefits under this title [42 USCS §§ 1395 et seq.].

(2) Subject to paragraph (4), the Secretary may modify or waive the requirement imposed by paragraph (1)—

(A) to the extent that more than 50 percent of the population of the area served by the organization consists of individuals who are entitled to benefits under this title [42 USCS §§ 1395 et seq.] or under a State plan approved under title XIX [42 USCS §§ 1396 et seq.], or

(B) in the case of an eligible organization that is owned and operated by a governmental entity, only with respect to a period of three years beginning on the date the organization first enters into a contract under this section, and only if the organization has taken and is making reasonable efforts to enroll individuals who are not entitled to benefits under this title [42 USCS §§ 1395 et seq.] or under a State plan approved under title XIX [42 USCS §§ 1396 et seq.].

(3) If the Secretary determines that an eligible organization has failed to comply with the requirements of this subsection, the Secretary may provide for the suspension of enrollment of individuals under this section or of payment to the organization under this section for individuals newly enrolled with the organization, after the date the Secretary notifies the organization of such noncompliance.

(4) Effective for contract periods beginning after December 31, 1996, the Secretary may waive or modify the requirement imposed by paragraph (1) to the extent the Secretary finds that it is in the public interest.

(g) Risk-sharing contract. (1) The Secretary may enter a risk-sharing contract with any eligible organization, as defined in subsection (b), which has at least 5,000 members, except that the Secretary may enter into such a contract with an eligible organization that has fewer members if the organization primarily serves members residing outside of urbanized areas.

(2) Each risk-sharing contract shall provide that—

(A) if the adjusted community rate, as defined in subsection (e)(3), for services under parts A and B [42 USCS §§ 1395c et seq. and 1395j et seq.] (as reduced for the actuarial value of the coinsurance and deductibles under those parts) for members enrolled under this section with the organization and entitled to benefits under part A [42 USCS §§ 1395c et seq.] and enrolled in part B [42 USCS §§ 1395j et seq.], or

(B) if the adjusted community rate for services under part B [42 USCS §§ 1395j et seq.] (as reduced for the actuarial value of the coinsurance and deductibles under that part) for members enrolled under this section with the organization and entitled to benefits under part B [42 USCS §§ 1395j et seq.] only

is less than the average of the per capita rates of payment to be made under subsection (a)(1) at the beginning of an annual contract period for members enrolled under this section with the organization and entitled to benefits under part A [42 USCS §§ 1395c et seq.] and enrolled in part B [42 USCS §§ 1395j et seq.], or enrolled in part B [42 USCS §§ 1395j et seq.] only, respectively, the eligible organization shall provide to members enrolled under a risk-sharing contract under this section with the organization and entitled to benefits under part A [42 USCS §§ 1395c et seq.] and enrolled in part B [42 USCS §§ 1395j et seq.], or enrolled in part B [42 USCS §§ 1395j et seq.] only, respectively, the additional benefits described in paragraph (3) which are selected by the eligible organization and which the Secretary finds are at least equal in value to the difference between that average per capita payment and the adjusted community rate (as so reduced); except that this paragraph shall not apply with respect to any organization which elects to receive a lesser payment to the extent that there is no longer a difference between the average per capita payment and adjusted community rate (as so reduced). and except that an organization (with the approval of the Secretary) may provide that a part of the value of such additional benefits be withheld and reserved by the Secretary as provided in paragraph (5). If the Secretary finds that there is insufficient enrollment experience to determine an average of the per capita rates of payment to be made under subsection (a)(1) at the beginning of a contract period, the Secretary may determine such an average based on the enrollment experience of other contracts entered into under this section.

(3) The additional benefits referred to in paragraph (2) are—

(A) the reduction of the premium rate or other charges made with respect to services furnished by the organization to members enrolled under this section, or

(B) the provision of additional health benefits,

or both.

(4) [Repealed]

(5) An organization having a risk-sharing contract under this section may (with the approval of the Secretary) provide that a part of the value of additional benefits otherwise required to be provided by reason of paragraph (2) be withheld and reserved in the Federal Hospital Insurance Trust Fund and in the Federal Supplementary Medical Insurance Trust Fund (in such proportions as the Secretary determines to be appropriate) by the Secretary for subsequent annual contract periods, to the extent required to stabilize and prevent undue fluctuations in the additional benefits offered in those subsequent periods by the organization in accordance with paragraph (3). Any of such value of additional benefits which

is not provided to members of the organization in accordance with paragraph (3) prior to the end of such period, shall revert for the use of such trust funds.

(6) (A) A risk-sharing contract under this section shall require the eligible organization to provide prompt payment (consistent with the provisions of sections 1816(c)(2) and 1842(c)(2) [42 USCS §§ 1395h(c)(2) and 1395u(c)(2)]) of claims submitted for services and supplies furnished to individuals pursuant to such contract, if the services or supplies are not furnished under a contract between the organization and the provider or supplier.

(B) In the case of an eligible organization which the Secretary determines, after notice and opportunity for a hearing, has failed to make payments of amounts in compliance with subparagraph (A), the Secretary may provide for direct payment of the amounts owed to providers and suppliers for such covered services furnished to individuals enrolled under this section under the contract. If the Secretary provides for such direct payments, the Secretary shall provide for an appropriate reduction in the amount of payments otherwise made to the organization under this section to reflect the amount of the Secretary's payments (and costs incurred by the Secretary in making such payments).

(h) Reasonable cost reimbursement contract; requirements. (1) If—

(A) the Secretary is not satisfied that an eligible organization has the capacity to bear the risk of potential losses under a risk-sharing contract under this section, or

(B) the eligible organization so elects or has an insufficient number of members to be eligible to enter into a risk-sharing contract under subsection (g)(1),

the Secretary may, if he is otherwise satisfied that the eligible organization is able to perform its contractual obligations effectively and efficiently, enter into a contract with such organization pursuant to which such organization is reimbursed on the basis of its reasonable cost (as defined in section 1861(v) [42 USCS § 1395x(v)]) in the manner prescribed in paragraph (3).

(2) A reasonable cost reimbursement contract under this subsection may, at the option of such organization, provide that the Secretary—

(A) will reimburse hospitals and skilled nursing facilities either for the reasonable cost (as determined under section 1861(v) [42 USCS § 1395x(v)]) or for payment amounts determined in accordance with section 1886 [42 USCS § 1395ww], as applicable, of services furnished to individuals enrolled with such organization pursuant to subsection (d), and

(B) will deduct the amount of such reimbursement from payment which would otherwise be made to such organization.

If such an eligible organization pays a hospital or skilled nursing facility directly, the amount paid shall not exceed the reasonable cost of the services (as determined under section 1861(v) [42 USCS § 1395x(v)]) or the amount determined under section 1886 [42 USCS § 1395ww], as applicable, unless such organization demonstrates to the satisfaction of the Secretary that such excess payments are justified on the basis of advantages gained by the organization.

(3) Payments made to an organization with a reasonable cost reimbursement contract shall be subject to appropriate retroactive corrective adjustment at the end of each contract year so as to assure that such organization is paid for the reasonable cost actually incurred (excluding any part of incurred cost found to be unnecessary in the efficient delivery of health services) or the amounts otherwise determined under section 1886 [42 USCS § 1395ww] for the types of expenses otherwise reimbursable under this title [42 USCS §§ 1395 et seq.] for providing services covered under this title [42 USCS §§ 1395 et seq.] to individuals described in subsection (a)(1).

(4) Any reasonable cost reimbursement contract with an eligible organization under this subsection shall provide that the Secretary shall require, at such time following the expiration of each accounting period of the eligible organization (and in such form and in such detail) as he may prescribe—

(A) that the organization report to him in an independently certified financial statement its per capita incurred cost based on the types of components of expenses otherwise reimbursable under this title [42 USCS §§ 1395 et seq.] for providing services described in subsection (a)(1), including therein, in accordance with accounting procedures prescribed by the Secretary, its methods of allocating costs between individuals enrolled under this section and other individuals enrolled with such organization;

(B) that failure to report such information as may be required may be deemed to constitute evidence of likely overpayment on the basis of which appropriate collection action may be taken;

(C) that in any case in which an eligible organization is related to another organization by common ownership or control, a consolidated financial statement shall be filed and that the allowable costs for such organization may not include costs for the types of expense otherwise reimbursable under this title [42 USCS §§ 1395 et seq.], in excess of those which would be determined to be reasonable in accordance with regulations (providing for limiting reimbursement to costs rather than charges to the eligible organization by related organizations and owners) issued by the Secretary; and

(D) that in any case in which compensation is paid by an eligible organization substantially in excess of what is normally paid for similar services by similar practitioners (regardless of method of compensation), such compensation may as appropriate be considered to constitute a distribution of profits.

(5)(A) After the date of the enactment of this paragraph [enacted Aug. 5, 1997], the Secretary may not enter into a reasonable cost reimbursement contract under this subsection (if the contract is not in effect as of such date), except for a contract with an eligible organization which, immediately previous to entering into such contract, had an agreement in effect under section 1833(a)(1)(A) [42 USCS § 1395l(a)(1)(A)].

(B) Subject to subparagraph (C), the Secretary shall approve an application for a modification to a reasonable cost contract under this section in order to expand the service area of such contract if—

(i) such application is submitted to the Secretary on or before September 1, 2003; and

(ii) the Secretary determines that the organization with the contract continues to meet the requirements applicable to such organizations and contracts under this section.

(C)(i) Subject to clause (ii), a reasonable cost reimbursement contract under this subsection may be extended or renewed indefinitely.

(ii) For any period beginning on or after January 1, 2013, a reasonable cost reimbursement contract under this subsection may not be extended or renewed for a service area insofar as such area during the entire previous year was within the service area of—

(I) 2 or more MA regional plans described in clause (iii), provided that all such plans are not offered by the same Medicare Advantage organization; or

(II) 2 or more MA local plans described in clause (iii), provided that all such plans are not offered by the same Medicare Advantage organization.

(iii) A plan described in this clause for a year for a service area is a plan described in section 1851(a)(2)(A)(i) [42 USCS § 1395w-21(a)(2)(A)(i)] if the service area for the year meets the following minimum enrollment requirements:

(I) With respect to any portion of the area involved that is within a Metropolitan Statistical Area with a population of more than 250,000 and counties contiguous to such Metropolitan Statistical Area that are not in another Metropolitan Statistical Area with a population of more than 250,000, 5,000 individuals. If the service area includes a portion in more than 1 Metropolitan Statistical Area with a population of more than 250,000, the minimum enrollment determination under the preceding sentence shall be made with respect to each such Metropolitan Statistical Area (and such applicable contiguous counties to such Metropolitan Statistical Area).

(II) With respect to any other portion of such area, 1,500 individuals.

(i) Duration; termination, effective date, and terms of contract; powers and duties of Secretary. (1) Each contract under this section shall be for a term of at least one year, as determined by the Secretary, and may be made automatically renewable from term to term in the absence of notice by either party of intention to terminate at the end of the current term; except that in accordance with procedures established under paragraph (9), the Secretary may at any time terminate any such contract or may impose the intermediate sanctions described in paragraph (6)(B) or (6)(C) (whichever is applicable) on the eligible organization if the Secretary determines that the organization—

(A) has failed substantially to carry out the contract;

(B) is carrying out the contract in a manner substantially inconsistent with the efficient and effective administration of this section; or

(C) no longer substantially meets the applicable conditions of subsections (b), (c), (e), and (f).

(2) The effective date of any contract executed pursuant to this section shall be specified in the contract.

(3) Each contract under this section—

(A) shall provide that the Secretary, or any person or organization designated by him—

(i) shall have the right to inspect or otherwise evaluate (I) the quality, appropriateness, and timeliness of services performed under the contract and (II) the facilities of the organization when there is reasonable evidence of some need for such inspection, and

(ii) shall have the right to audit and inspect any books and records of the eligible organization that pertain (I) to the ability of the organization to bear the risk of potential financial losses, or (II) to services performed or determinations of amounts payable under the contract;

(B) shall require the organization with a risk-sharing contract to provide (and pay for) written notice in advance of the contract's termination, as well as a description of alternatives for obtaining benefits under this title [42 USCS §§ 1395 et seq.], to each individual enrolled under this section with the organization; and

(C)(i) shall require the organization to comply with subsections (a) and (c) of section 1318 of the Public Health Service Act [42 USCS § 300e-17(a) and (c)] (relating to disclosure of certain financial information) and with the requirement of section 1301(c)(8) of such Act (relating to liability arrangements to protect members);

(ii) shall require the organization to provide and supply information (described in section 1866(b)(2)(C)(ii) [42 USCS § 1395cc(b)(2)(C)(ii)]) in the manner such information is required to be provided or supplied under that section;

(iii) shall require the organization to notify the Secretary of loans and other special financial arrangements which are made between the organization and subcontractors, affiliates, and related parties; and

(D) shall contain such other terms and conditions not inconsistent with this section (including requiring the organization to provide the Secretary with such information) as the Secretary may find necessary and appropriate.

(4) The Secretary may not enter into a risk-sharing contract with an eligible organization if a previous risk-sharing contract with that organization under this section was terminated at the request of the organization within the preceding five-year period, except in circumstances which warrant special consideration, as determined by the Secretary.

(5) The authority vested in the Secretary by this section may be performed without regard to such provisions of law or regulations relating to the making, performance, amendment, or modification of contracts of the United States as the Secretary may determine to be inconsistent with the furtherance of the purpose of this title [42 USCS §§ 1395 et seq.].

(6)(A) If the Secretary determines that an eligible organization with a contract under this section—

(i) fails substantially to provide medically necessary items and services that are required (under law or under the contract) to be provided to an individual covered under the contract, if the failure has adversely affected (or has substantial likelihood of adversely affecting) the individual;

(ii) imposes premiums on individuals enrolled under this section in excess of the premiums permitted;

(iii) acts to expel or to refuse to re-enroll an individual in violation of the provisions of this section;

(iv) engages in any practice that would reasonably be expected to have the effect of denying or discouraging enrollment (except as permitted by this section) by eligible individuals with the organization whose medical condition or history indicates a need for substantial future medical services;

(v) misrepresents or falsifies information that is furnished—

(I) to the Secretary under this section, or

(II) to an individual or to any other entity under this section;

(vi) fails to comply with the requirements of subsection (g)(6)(A) or paragraph (8); or

(vii) in the case of a risk-sharing contract, employs or contracts with any individual or entity that is excluded from participation under this title [42 USCS §§ 1395 et seq.] under section 1128 or 1128A [42 USCS § 1320a-7 or 1320a-7a] for the provision of health care, utilization review, medical social work, or administrative services or employs or contracts with any entity for the provision (directly or indirectly) through such an excluded individual or entity of such services;

the Secretary may provide, in addition to any other remedies authorized by law, for any of the remedies described in subparagraph (B).

(B) The remedies described in this subparagraph are—

(i) civil money penalties of not more than $25,000 for each determination under subparagraph (A) or, with respect to a determination under clause (iv) or (v)(I) of such subparagraph, of not more than $100,000 for each such determination, plus, with respect to a determination under subparagraph (A)(ii), double the excess amount charged in violation of such subparagraph (and the excess amount charged shall be deducted from the penalty and returned to the individual concerned), and plus, with respect to a determination under subparagraph (A)(iv), $15,000 for each individual not enrolled as a result of the practice involved,

(ii) suspension of enrollment of individuals under this section after the date the Secretary notifies the organization of a determination under subparagraph (A) and until the Secretary is satisfied that the basis for such determination has been corrected and is not likely to recur, or

(iii) suspension of payment to the organization under this section for individuals enrolled after the date the Secretary notifies the organization of a determination under subparagraph (A) and until the Secretary is satisfied that the basis for such determination has been corrected and is not likely to recur.

(C) In the case of an eligible organization for which the Secretary makes a determination under paragraph (1), the basis of which is not described in subparagraph (A), the Secretary may apply the following intermediate sanctions:

(i) Civil money penalties of not more than $25,000 for each determination under paragraph (1) if the deficiency that is the basis of the determination has directly adversely affected (or has the substantial likelihood of adversely affecting) an individual covered under the organization's contract.

(ii) Civil money penalties of not more than $10,000 for each week beginning after the initiation of procedures by the Secretary under paragraph (9) during which the deficiency that is the basis of a determination under paragraph (1) exists.

(iii) Suspension of enrollment of individuals under this section after the date the Secretary notifies the organization of a determination under paragraph (1) and until the Secretary is satisfied that the deficiency that is the basis for the determination has been corrected and is not likely to recur.

(D) The provisions of section 1128A [42 USCS § 1320a-7a] (other than subsections (a) and (b)) shall apply to a civil money penalty under subparagraph (B)(i) or (C)(i) in the same manner as such provisions apply to a civil money penalty or proceeding under section 1128A(a) [42 USCS § 1320a-7a(a)].

(7)(A) Each risk-sharing contract with an eligible organization under this section shall provide that the organization will maintain a written agreement with a utilization and quality control peer review organization (which has a contract with the Secretary under part B of title XI [42 USCS §§ 1320c et seq.] for the area in which the eligible organization is located) or with an entity selected by the Secretary under section 1154(a)(4)(C) [42 USCS § 1320c-3(a)(4)(C)] under which the review organization will perform functions under section 1154(a)(4)(B) [42 USCS § 1320c-3(a)(4)(B)] and section 1154(a)(14) [42 USCS § 1320c-3(a)(14)] (other than those performed under contracts described in section 1866(a)(1)(F) [42 USCS 1395cc(a)(1)(F)]) with respect to services, furnished by the eligible organization, for which payment may be made under this title [42 USCS §§ 1395 et seq.].

(B) For purposes of payment under this title [42 USCS §§ 1395 et seq.], the cost of such agreement to the eligible organization shall be considered a cost incurred by a provider of services in providing covered services under this title [42 USCS §§ 1395 et seq.] and shall be paid directly by the Secretary to the review organization on behalf of such eligible organization in accordance with a schedule established by the Secretary.

(C) Such payments—

(i) shall be transferred in appropriate proportions from the Federal Hospital Insurance Trust Fund and from the Supplementary Medical Insurance Trust Fund, without regard to amounts appropriated in advance in appropriation Acts, in the same manner as transfers are made for payment for services provided directly to beneficiaries, and

(ii) shall not be less in the aggregate for such organizations for a fiscal year than the amounts the Secretary determines to be sufficient to cover the costs of such organizations' conducting activities described in subparagraph (A) with respect to such eligible organizations under part B of title XI [42 USCS §§ 1320c et seq.].

(8)(A) Each contract with an eligible organization under this section shall provide that the organization may not operate any physician incentive plan (as defined in subparagraph (B)) unless the following requirements are met:

(i) No specific payment is made directly or indirectly under the plan to a physician or physician group as an inducement to reduce or limit medically necessary services provided with respect to a specific individual enrolled with the organization.

(ii) If the plan places a physician or physician group at substantial financial risk (as determined by the Secretary) for services not provided by the physician or physician group, the organization—

(I) provides stop-loss protection for the physician or group that is adequate and appropriate, based on standards developed by the Secretary that take into account the number of physicians placed at such substantial financial risk in the group or under the plan and the number of individuals enrolled with the organization who receive services from the physician or the physician group, and

(II) conducts periodic surveys of both individuals enrolled and individuals previously enrolled with the organization to determine the degree of access of such individuals to services provided by the organization and satisfaction with the quality of such services.

(iii) The organization provides the Secretary with descriptive information regarding the plan, sufficient to permit the Secretary to determine whether the plan is in compliance with the requirements of this subparagraph.

(B) In this paragraph, the term "physician incentive plan" means any compensation arrangement between an eligible organization and a physician or physician group that may directly or indirectly have the effect of reducing or limiting services provided with respect to individuals enrolled with the organization.

(9) The Secretary may terminate a contract with an eligible organization under this section or may impose the intermediate sanctions described in paragraph (6) on the organization in accordance with formal investigation and compliance procedures established by the Secretary under which—

(A) the Secretary first provides the organization with the reasonable opportunity to develop and implement a corrective action plan to correct the deficiencies that were the basis of the Secretary's determination under paragraph (1) and the organization fails to develop or implement such a plan;

(B) in deciding whether to impose sanctions, the Secretary considers aggravating factors such as whether an organization has a history of deficiencies or has not taken action to correct deficiencies the Secretary has brought to the organization's attention;

(C) there are no unreasonable or unnecessary delays between the finding of a deficiency and the imposition of sanctions; and

(D) the Secretary provides the organization with reasonable notice and opportunity for hearing (including the right to appeal an initial decision) before imposing any sanction or terminating the contract.

(j) Payment in full and limitation on actual charges; physicians, providers of services, or renal dialysis facilities not under contract with organization. (1)(A) In the case of physicians' services or renal dialysis services described in paragraph (2) which are furnished by a participating physician to an individual enrolled with an eligible organization under this section and enrolled under part B [42 USCS §§ 1395j et seq.], the applicable participation agreement is deemed to provide that the physician or provider of services or renal dialysis facility will accept as payment in full from the eligible organization the amount that would be payable to the physician or provider of services or renal dialysis facility under part B [42 USCS §§ 1395j et seq.] and from the individual under such part, if the individual were not enrolled with an eligible organization under this section.

(B) In the case of physicians' services described in paragraph (2) which are furnished by a nonparticipating physician, the limitations on actual charges for such services otherwise applicable under part B [42 USCS §§ 1395j et seq.] (to services furnished by individuals not enrolled with an eligible organization under this section) shall apply in the same manner as such limitations apply to services furnished to individuals not enrolled with such an organization.

(2) The physicians' services described in this paragraph are physicians' services which are furnished to an enrollee of an eligible organization under this section by a physician, provider of services, or renal dialysis facility who is not under a contract with the organization.

(k) Risk-sharing contracts. (1) Except as provided in paragraph (2)—

(A) on or after the date standards for Medicare+Choice organizations and plans are first established under section 1856(b)(1) [42 USCS § 1395w-26(b)(1)], the Secretary shall not enter into any risk-sharing contract under this section with an eligible organization; and

(B) for any contract year beginning on or after January 1, 1999, the Secretary shall not renew any such contract.

(2) An individual who is enrolled in part B [42 USCS §§ 1395j et seq.] only and is enrolled in an eligible organization with a risk-sharing contract under this section on December 31, 1998, may continue enrollment in such organization in accordance with regulations described in section 1856(b)(1) [42 USCS § 1395w-26(b)(1)].

(3) Notwithstanding subsection (a), the Secretary shall provide that payment amounts under risk-sharing contracts under this section for months in a year (beginning with January 1998) shall be computed—

(A) with respect to individuals entitled to benefits under both parts A and B, by substituting payment rates under section 1853(a) [42 USCS § 1395w-23(a)] for the payment rates otherwise established under section 1876(a) [42 USCS § 1395mm(a)], and

(B) with respect to individuals only entitled to benefits under part B [42 USCS §§ 1395j et seq.], by substituting an appropriate proportion of such rates (reflecting the relative proportion of payments under this title attributable to such part) for the payment rates otherwise established under subsection (a).

(4) The following requirements shall apply to eligible organizations with risk-sharing contracts under this section in the same manner as they apply to Medicare+Choice organizations under part C [42 USCS §§ 1395w-21 et seq.]:

(A) Data collection requirements under section 1853(a)(3)(B) [42 USCS § 1395w-23(a)(3)(B)].

(B) Restrictions on imposition of premium taxes under section 1854(g) [42 USCS § 1395w-24(g)] in relating to payments to such organizations under this section.

(C) The requirement to accept enrollment of new enrollees during November 1998 under section 1851(e)(6) [42 USCS § 1395w-21(e)(6)].

(D) Payments under section 1857(e)(2) [42 USCS § 1395w-27(e)(2)].

(Aug. 14, 1935, ch 531, Title XVIII, Part E [D] [C], § 1876, as added Oct. 30, 1972, P. L. 92-603, Title II, §§ 226(a), 278(b)(3), 86 Stat. 1396, 1453; Dec. 31, 1973, P. L. 93-233, § 18(m), (n), 87 Stat. 970, 971; Oct. 8, 1976, P. L. 94-460, Title II, § 201(a)–(d), 90 Stat. 1956; June 13, 1978, P. L. 95-292, § 5, 92 Stat. 315; Sept. 3, 1982, P. L. 97-248, Title I, Subtitle A, Part I, Subpart B, § 114(a), 96 Stat. 341; Jan. 12, 1983, P. L. 97-448, Title III, § 309(b)(12), 96 Stat. 2409; April 20, 1983, P. L. 98-21, Title VI, §§ 602(g), 606(a)(2)(H), 97 Stat. 164, 171; July 18, 1984, P. L. 98-369, Division B, Title III, Subtitle A, Part II, §§ 2350(a)(1), (b)(1), (2), (c), 2354(b)(37), (38), 98 Stat. 1097, 1098, 1102; April 7, 1986, P. L. 99-272, Title IX, Subtitle A, Part 2, Subpart B, § 9211(a)–(d), 100 Stat. 178; Oct. 21, 1986, P. L. 99-509, Title IX, Subtitle D, Part 2, § 9312(b)(1), (c)(1), (2), (d)(1), (e)(1), (f), Part 4, § 9353(e)(2), 100 Stat. 1999-2001, 2047; Oct. 22, 1986, P. L. 99-514, Title XVIII, Subtitle C, Ch 1, § 1895(b)(11)(A), 100 Stat. 2934; Dec. 22, 1987, P. L. 100-203, Title IV, Subtitle A, Part 2, Subpt. A, §§ 4011(a)(1), (b)(1), 4012(b), 4014, 4018(a), 4039(h)(8), 101 Stat. 1330-60, 1330-61, 1330-65; July 1, 1988, P. L. 100-360, Title II, Subtitle A, § 202(f), Subtitle B, § 211(c)(3), Subtitle C, § 224, Title IV, Subtitle B, § 411(c)(1), (3), (4), (6), (e)(3), 102 Stat. 717, 738, 748, 773, 776; Oct. 13, 1988, P. L. 100-485, Title VI, § 608(d)(19)(B), 102 Stat. 2419; Nov. 10, 1988, P. L. 100-647, Title VIII, Subtitle E, Part II, § 8412(a), 102 Stat. 3801; Dec. 13, 1989, P. L. 101-234, Title II, §§ 201(a)(1), 202(a), 103 Stat. 1981; Dec. 19, 1989, P. L. 101-239, Title VI, Subtitle A, Part 3, Subpart A, § 6206(a)(1), (b)(1), Subpart B, § 6212(b)(1), (c)(2), Subtitle B, Part 2, § 6411(d)(3)(A), 103 Stat. 2244, 2250, 2271; Nov. 5, 1990, P. L. 101-508, Title IV, Subtitle A, Part 3, §§ 4204(a)(1), (2), (c)(1), (2), (d)(1), (e)(1), 4206(b)(1), 104 Stat. 1388-108, 1388-116; Aug. 15, 1994, P. L. 103-296, Title I, § 108(c)(6), 108 Stat. 1486; Oct. 31, 1994, P. L. 103-432, Title I, Subtitle C, § 157(b)(1), (4), 108 Stat. 4442; Aug. 21, 1996, P. L. 104-191, Title II, Subtitle B, § 215(a), (b), Subtitle D, § 231(g), 110 Stat. 2005, 2014; Aug. 5, 1997, P. L. 105-33, Title IV, Subtitle A, Ch 1, Subch A, §§ 4001, 4002(a), (b)(1), (2)(A), 111 Stat. 275, 328; Nov. 29, 1999, P. L. 106-113, Div B, § 1000(a)(6), 113 Stat. 1536; Dec. 21, 2000, P. L. 106-554, § 1(a)(6), 114 Stat. 2763; Dec. 8, 2003, P. L. 108-173, Title I, § 101(a)(1), Title II, Subtitle D, § 234, Title VII, Subtitle D, § 736(d)(2), Title IX, Subtitle D, § 940(b)(2)(B), 117 Stat. 2071, 2209, 2357, 2417; Dec. 29, 2007, P. L. 110-173, Title I, § 109, 121 Stat. 2497; July 15, 2008, P. L. 110-275, Title I, Subtitle D, § 167(a)–(c), 122 Stat. 2575; March 23, 2010, P. L. 111-148, Title III, Subtitle C, § 3206, 124 Stat. 459.)

§ 1395nn. Limitation on certain physician referrals

(a) Prohibition of certain referrals. (1) In general. Except as provided in subsection (b), if a physician (or an immediate family member of such physician) has a financial relationship with an entity specified in paragraph (2), then—

(A) the physician may not make a referral to the entity for the furnishing of designated health services for which payment otherwise may be made under this title [42 USCS §§ 1395 et seq.], and

(B) the entity may not present or cause to be presented a claim under this title [42 USCS §§ 1395 et seq.] or bill to any individual, third party payor, or other entity for designated health services furnished pursuant to a referral prohibited under subparagraph (A).

(2) Financial relationship specified. For purposes of this section, a financial relationship of a physician (or an immediate family member of such physician) with an entity specified in this paragraph is—

(A) except as provided in subsections (c) and (d), an ownership or investment interest in the entity, or

(B) except as provided in subsection (e), a compensation arrangement (as defined in subsection (h)(1)) between the physician (or an immediate family member of such physician) and the entity.

An ownership or investment interest described in subparagraph (A) may be through equity, debt, or other means and includes an interest in an entity that holds an ownership or investment interest in any entity providing the designated health service.

(b) General exceptions to both ownership and compensation arrangement prohibitions. Subsection (a)(1) shall not apply in the following cases:

(1) Physicians' services. In the case of physicians' services (as defined in section 1861(q) [42 USCS § 1395x(q)]) provided personally by (or under the personal supervision of) another physician in the same group practice (as defined in subsection (h)(4)) as the referring physician.

(2) In-office ancillary services. In the case of services (other than durable medical equipment (excluding infusion pumps) and parenteral and enteral nutrients, equipment, and supplies)—

(A) that are furnished—

(i) personally by the referring physician, personally by a physician who is a member of the same group practice as the referring physician, or personally by individuals who are directly supervised by the physician or by another physician in the group practice, and

(ii)(I) in a building in which the referring physician (or another physician who is a member of the same group practice) furnishes physicians' services unrelated to the furnishing of designated health services, or

(II) in the case of a referring physician who is a member of a group practice, in another building which is used by the group practice—

(aa) for the provision of some or all of the group's clinical laboratory services, or

(bb) for the centralized provision of the group's designated health services (other than clinical laboratory services),

unless the Secretary determines other terms and conditions under which the provision of such services does not present a risk of program or patient abuse, and

(B) that are billed by the physician performing or supervising the services, by a group practice of which such physician is a member under a billing number assigned to the group practice, or by an entity that is wholly owned by such physician or such group practice,

if the ownership or investment interest in such services meets such other requirements as the Secretary may impose by regulation as needed to protect against program or patient abuse. Such requirements shall, with respect to magnetic resonance imaging, computed tomography, positron emission tomography, and any other designated health services specified under subsection (h)(6)(D) that the Secretary determines appropriate, include a requirement that the referring physician inform the individual in writing at the time of the referral that the individual may obtain the services for which the individual is being referred from a person other than a person described in subparagraph (A)(i) and provide such individual with a written list of suppliers (as defined in section 1861(d) [42 USCS § 1395x(d)]) who furnish such services in the area in which such individual resides.

(3) Prepaid plans. In the case of services furnished by an organization—

(A) with a contract under section 1876 [42 USCS § 1395mm] to an individual enrolled with the organization,

(B) described in section 1833(a)(1)(A) [42 USCS § 1395l(a)(1)(A)] to an individual enrolled with the organization,

(C) receiving payments on a prepaid basis, under a demonstration project under section 402(a) of the Social Security Amendments of 1967 [42 USCS § 1395b-1(a)] or under section 222(a) of the Social Security Amendments of 1972 [42 USCS § 1395b-1 note], to an individual enrolled with the organization,

(D) that is a qualified health maintenance organization (within the meaning of section 1310(d) of the Public Health Service Act [42 USCS § 300e-9(d)]) to an individual enrolled with the organization, or

(E) that is a Medicare+Choice organization under part C [42 USCS §§ 1395w-21 et seq.] that is offering a coordinated care plan described in section 1851(a)(2)(A) [42 USCS § 1395w-21(a)(2)(A)] to an individual enrolled with the organization.

(4) Other permissible exceptions. In the case of any other financial relationship which the Secretary determines, and specifies in regulations, does not pose a risk of program or patient abuse.

(5) Electronic prescribing. An exception established by regulation under section 1860D-3(e)(6) [1860D-4(e)(6)] [42 USCS § 1395w-104(e)(6)].

(c) General exception related only to ownership or investment prohibition for ownership in publicly traded securities and mutual funds. Ownership of the following shall not be considered to be an ownership or investment interest described in subsection (a)(2)(A):

(1) Ownership of investment securities (including shares or bonds, debentures, notes, or other debt instruments) which may be purchased on terms generally available to the

public and which are—

(A)(i) securities listed on the New York Stock Exchange, the American Stock Exchange, or any regional exchange in which quotations are published on a daily basis, or foreign securities listed on a recognized foreign, national, or regional exchange in which quotations are published on a daily basis, or

(ii) traded under an automated interdealer quotation system operated by the National Association of Securities Dealers, and

(B) in a corporation that had, at the end of the corporation's most recent fiscal year, or on average during the previous 3 fiscal years, stockholder equity exceeding $75,000,000.

(2) Ownership of shares in a regulated investment company as defined in section 851(a) of the Internal Revenue Code of 1986 [26 USCS § 851(a)], if such company had, at the end of the company's most recent fiscal year, or on average during the previous 3 fiscal years, total assets exceeding $75,000,000.

(d) Additional exceptions related only to ownership or investment prohibition. The following, if not otherwise excepted under subsection (b), shall not be considered to be an ownership or investment interest described in subsection (a)(2)(A):

(1) Hospitals in Puerto Rico. In the case of designated health services provided by a hospital located in Puerto Rico.

(2) Rural providers. In the case of designated health services furnished in a rural area (as defined in section 1886(d)(2)(D) [42 USCS § 1395ww(d)(2)(D)]) by an entity, if—

(A) substantially all of the designated health services furnished by the entity are furnished to individuals residing in such a rural area;

(B) effective for the 18-month period beginning on the date of the enactment of the Medicare Prescription Drug, Improvement, and Modernization Act of 2003 [enacted Dec. 8, 2003], the entity is not a specialty hospital (as defined in subsection (h)(7)); and

(C) in the case where the entity is a hospital, the hospital meets the requirements of paragraph (3)(D).

(3) Hospital ownership. In the case of designated health services provided by a hospital (other than a hospital described in paragraph (1)) if—

(A) the referring physician is authorized to perform services at the hospital;

(B) effective for the 18-month period beginning on the date of the enactment of the Medicare Prescription Drug, Improvement, and Modernization Act of 2003 [enacted Dec. 8, 2003], the hospital is not a specialty hospital (as defined in subsection (h)(7));

(C) the ownership or investment interest is in the hospital itself (and not merely in a subdivision of the hospital); and

(D) the hospital meets the requirements described in subsection (i)(1) not later than 18 months after the date of the enactment of this subparagraph.

(e) Exceptions relating to other compensation arrangements. The following shall not be considered to be a compensation arrangement described in subsection (a)(2)(B):

(1) Rental of office space; rental of equipment. (A) Office space. Payments made by a lessee to a lessor for the use of premises if—

(i) the lease is set out in writing, signed by the parties, and specifies the premises covered by the lease,

(ii) the space rented or leased does not exceed that which is reasonable and necessary for the legitimate business purposes of the lease or rental and is used exclusively by the lessee when being used by the lessee, except that the lessee may make payments for the use of space consisting of common areas if such payments do not exceed the lessee's pro rata share of expenses for such space based upon the ratio of the space used exclusively by the lessee to the total amount of space (other than common areas) occupied by all persons using such common areas,

(iii) the lease provides for a term of rental or lease for at least 1 year,

(iv) the rental charges over the term of the lease are set in advance, are consistent with fair market value, and are not determined in a manner that takes into account the volume or value of any referrals or other business generated between the parties,

(v) the lease would be commercially reasonable even if no referrals were made between the parties, and

(vi) the lease meets such other requirements as the Secretary may impose by regulation as needed to protect against program or patient abuse.

(B) Equipment. Payments made by a lessee of equipment to the lessor of the equipment for the use of the equipment if—

(i) the lease is set out in writing, signed by the parties, and specifies the equipment covered by the lease,

(ii) the equipment rented or leased does not exceed that which is reasonable and necessary for the legitimate business purposes of the lease or rental and is used exclusively by the lessee when being used by the lessee,

(iii) the lease provides for a term of rental or

lease of at least 1 year,

(iv) the rental charges over the term of the lease are set in advance, are consistent with fair market value, and are not determined in a manner that takes into account the volume or value of any referrals or other business generated between the parties,

(v) the lease would be commercially reasonable even if no referrals were made between the parties, and

(vi) the lease meets such other requirements as the Secretary may impose by regulation as needed to protect against program or patient abuse.

(2) Bona fide employment relationships. Any amount paid by an employer to a physician (or an immediate family member of such physician) who has a bona fide employment relationship with the employer for the provision of services if—

(A) the employment is for identifiable services,

(B) the amount of the remuneration under the employment—

(i) is consistent with the fair market value of the services, and

(ii) is not determined in a manner that takes into account (directly or indirectly) the volume or value of any referrals by the referring physician,

(C) the remuneration is provided pursuant to an agreement which would be commercially reasonable even if no referrals were made to the employer, and

(D) the employment meets such other requirements as the Secretary may impose by regulation as needed to protect against program or patient abuse.

Subparagraph (B)(ii) shall not prohibit the payment of remuneration in the form of a productivity bonus based on services performed personally by the physician (or an immediate family member of such physician).

(3) Personal service arrangements. (A) In general. Remuneration from an entity under an arrangement (including remuneration for specific physicians' services furnished to a nonprofit blood center) if—

(i) the arrangement is set out in writing, signed by the parties, and specifies the services covered by the arrangement,

(ii) the arrangement covers all of the services to be provided by the physician (or an immediate family member of such physician) to the entity,

(iii) the aggregate services contracted for do not exceed those that are reasonable and necessary for the legitimate business purposes of the arrangement,

(iv) the term of the arrangement is for at least 1 year,

(v) the compensation to be paid over the term of the arrangement is set in advance, does not exceed fair market value, and except in the case of a physician incentive plan described in subparagraph (B), is not determined in a manner that takes into account the volume or value of any referrals or other business generated between the parties,

(vi) the services to be performed under the arrangement do not involve the counseling or promotion or a business arrangement or other activity that violates any State or Federal law, and

(vii) the arrangement meets such other requirements as the Secretary may impose by regulation as needed to protect against program or patient abuse.

(B) Physician incentive plan exception. (i) In general. In the case of a physician incentive plan (as defined in clause (ii)) between a physician and an entity, the compensation may be determined in a manner (through a withhold, capitation, bonus, or otherwise) that takes into account directly or indirectly the volume or value of any referrals or other business generated between the parties, if the plan meets the following requirements:

(I) No specific payment is made directly or indirectly under the plan to a physician or a physician group as an inducement to reduce or limit medically necessary services provided with respect to a specific individual enrolled with the entity.

(II) In the case of a plan that places a physician or a physician group at substantial financial risk as determined by the Secretary pursuant to section 1876(i)(8)(A)(ii) [42 USCS § 1395mm(i)(8)(A)(ii)], the plan complies with any requirements the Secretary may impose pursuant to such section.

(III) Upon request by the Secretary, the entity provides the Secretary with access to descriptive information regarding the plan, in order to permit the Secretary to determine whether the plan is in compliance with the requirements of this clause.

(ii) Physician incentive plan defined. For purposes of this subparagraph, the term "physician incentive plan" means any compensation arrangement between an entity and a physician or physician group that may directly or indirectly have the effect of reducing or limiting services provided with respect to individuals enrolled with the entity.

(4) Remuneration unrelated to the provision

of designated health services. In the case of remuneration which is provided by a hospital to a physician if such remuneration does not relate to the provision of designated health services.

(5) Physician recruitment. In the case of remuneration which is provided by a hospital to a physician to induce the physician to relocate to the geographic area served by the hospital in order to be a member of the medical staff of the hospital, if—

(A) the physician is not required to refer patients to the hospital,

(B) the amount of the remuneration under the arrangement is not determined in a manner that takes into account (directly or indirectly) the volume or value of any referrals by the referring physician, and

(C) the arrangement meets such other requirements as the Secretary may impose by regulation as needed to protect against program or patient abuse.

(6) Isolated transactions. In the case of an isolated financial transaction, such as a one-time sale of property or practice, if—

(A) the requirements described in subparagraphs (B) and (C) of paragraph (2) are met with respect to the entity in the same manner as they apply to an employer, and

(B) the transaction meets such other requirements as the Secretary may impose by regulation as needed to protect against program or patient abuse.

(7) Certain group practice arrangements with a hospital. [(A)] In general. An arrangement between a hospital and a group under which designated health services are provided by the group but are billed by the hospital if—

(i) with respect to services provided to an inpatient of the hospital, the arrangement is pursuant to the provision of inpatient hospital services under section 1861(b)(3) [42 USCS § 1395x(b)(3)],

(ii) the arrangement began before December 19, 1989, and has continued in effect without interruption since such date,

(iii) with respect to the designated health services covered under the arrangement, substantially all of such services furnished to patients of the hospital are furnished by the group under the arrangement,

(iv) the arrangement is pursuant to an agreement that is set out in writing and that specifies the services to be provided by the parties and the compensation for services provided under the agreement,

(v) the compensation paid over the term of the agreement is consistent with fair market value and the compensation per unit of services is fixed in advance and is not determined in a manner that takes into account the volume or value of any referrals or other business generated between the parties,

(vi) the compensation is provided pursuant to an agreement which would be commercially reasonable even if no referrals were made to the entity, and

(vii) the arrangement between the parties meets such other requirements as the Secretary may impose by regulation as needed to protect against program or patient abuse.

(8) Payments by a physician for items and services. Payments made by a physician—

(A) to a laboratory in exchange for the provision of clinical laboratory services, or

(B) to an entity as compensation for other items or services if the items or services are furnished at a price that is consistent with fair market value.

(f) Reporting requirements. Each entity providing covered items or services for which payment may be made under this title [42 USCS §§ 1395 et seq.] shall provide the Secretary with the information concerning the entity's ownership, investment, and compensation arrangements, including—

(1) the covered items and services provided by the entity, and

(2) the names and unique physician identification numbers of all physicians with an ownership or investment interest (as described in subsection (a)(2)(A)), or with a compensation arrangement (as described in subsection (a)(2)(B)), in the entity, or whose immediate relatives have such an ownership or investment interest or who have such a compensation relationship with the entity.

Such information shall be provided in such form, manner, and at such times as the Secretary shall specify. The requirement of this subsection shall not apply to designated health services provided outside the United States or to entities which the Secretary determines provides [provide] services for which payment may be made under this title [42 USCS §§ 1395 et seq.] very infrequently.

(g) Sanctions. (1) Denial of payment. No payment may be made under this title [42 USCS §§ 1395 et seq.] for a designated health service which is provided in violation of subsection (a)(1).

(2) Requiring refunds for certain claims. If a person collects any amounts that were billed in violation of subsection (a)(1), the person shall be liable to the individual for, and shall refund on a timely basis to the individual, any

amounts so collected.

(3) Civil money penalty and exclusion for improper claims. Any person that presents or causes to be presented a bill or a claim for a service that such person knows or should know is for a service for which payment may not be made under paragraph (1) or for which a refund has not been made under paragraph (2) shall be subject to a civil money penalty of not more than $15,000 for each such service. The provisions of section 1128A [42 USCS § 1320a-7a] (other than the first sentence of subsection (a) and other than subsection (b)) shall apply to a civil money penalty under the previous sentence in the same manner as such provisions apply to a penalty or proceeding under section 1128A(a) [42 USCS § 1320a-7a(a)].

(4) Civil money penalty and exclusion for circumvention schemes. Any physician or other entity that enters into an arrangement or scheme (such as a cross-referral arrangement) which the physician or entity knows or should know has a principal purpose of assuring referrals by the physician to a particular entity which, if the physician directly made referrals to such entity, would be in violation of this section, shall be subject to a civil money penalty of not more than $100,000 for each such arrangement or scheme. The provisions of section 1128A [42 USCS § 1320a-7a] (other than the first sentence of subsection (a) and other than subsection (b)) shall apply to a civil money penalty under the previous sentence in the same manner as such provisions apply to a penalty or proceeding under section 1128A(a) [42 USCS § 1320a-7a(a)].

(5) Failure to report information. Any person who is required, but fails, to meet a reporting requirement of subsection (f) is subject to a civil money penalty of not more than $10,000 for each day for which reporting is required to have been made. The provisions of section 1128A [42 USCS § 1320a-7a] (other than the first sentence of subsection (a) and other than subsection (b)) shall apply to a civil money penalty under the previous sentence in the same manner as such provisions apply to a penalty or proceeding under section 1128A(a) [42 USCS § 1320a-7a(a)].

(6) Advisory opinions. (A) In general. The Secretary shall issue written advisory opinions concerning whether a referral relating to designated health services (other than clinical laboratory services) is prohibited under this section. Each advisory opinion issued by the Secretary shall be binding as to the Secretary and the party or parties requesting the opinion.

(B) Application of certain rules. The Secretary shall, to the extent practicable, apply the rules under subsections (b)(3) and (b)(4) and take into account the regulations promulgated under subsection (b)(5) of section 1128D [42 USCS § 1320a-7d(b)(5)] in the issuance of advisory opinions under this paragraph.

(C) Regulations. In order to implement this paragraph in a timely manner, the Secretary may promulgate regulations that take effect on an interim basis, after notice and pending opportunity for public comment.

(D) Applicability. This paragraph shall apply to requests for advisory opinions made after the date which is 90 days after the date of the enactment of this paragraph [enacted Aug. 5, 1997] and before the close of the period described in section 1128D(b)(6) [42 USCS § 1320a-7d(b)(6)].

(h) Definitions and special rules. For purposes of this section:

(1) Compensation arrangement; remuneration. (A) The term "compensation arrangement" means any arrangement involving any remuneration between a physician (or an immediate family member of such physician) and an entity other than an arrangement involving only remuneration described in subparagraph (C).

(B) The term "remuneration" includes any remuneration, directly or indirectly, overtly or covertly, in cash or in kind.

(C) Remuneration described in this subparagraph is any remuneration consisting of any of the following:

(i) The forgiveness of amounts owed for inaccurate tests or procedures, mistakenly performed tests or procedures, or the correction of minor billing errors.

(ii) The provision of items, devices, or supplies that are used solely to—

(I) collect, transport, process, or store specimens for the entity providing the item, device, or supply, or

(II) order or communicate the results of tests or procedures for such entity.

(iii) A payment made by an insurer or a self-insured plan to a physician to satisfy a claim, submitted on a fee for service basis, for the furnishing of health services by that physician to an individual who is covered by a policy with the insurer or by the self-insured plan, if—

(I) the health services are not furnished, and the payment is not made, pursuant to a contract or other arrangement between the insurer or the plan and the physician,

(II) the payment is made to the physician on

behalf of the covered individual and would otherwise be made directly to such individual,

(III) the amount of the payment is set in advance, does not exceed fair market value, and is not determined in a manner that takes into account directly or indirectly the volume or value of any referrals, and

(IV) the payment meets such other requirements as the Secretary may impose by regulation as needed to protect against program or patient abuse.

(2) Employee. An individual is considered to be "employed by" or an "employee" of an entity if the individual would be considered to be an employee of the entity under the usual common law rules applicable in determining the employer-employee relationship (as applied for purposes of section 3121(d)(2) of the Internal Revenue Code of 1986 [26 USCS § 3121(d)(2)]).

(3) Fair market value. The term "fair market value" means the value in arms length transactions, consistent with the general market value, and, with respect to rentals or leases, the value of rental property for general commercial purposes (not taking into account its intended use) and, in the case of a lease of space, not adjusted to reflect the additional value the prospective lessee or lessor would attribute to the proximity or convenience to the lessor where the lessor is a potential source of patient referrals to the lessee.

(4) Group practice. (A) Definition of group practice. The term "group practice" means a group of 2 or more physicians legally organized as a partnership, professional corporation, foundation, not-for-profit corporation, faculty practice plan, or similar association—

(i) in which each physician who is a member of the group provides substantially the full range of services which the physician routinely provides, including medical care, consultation, diagnosis, or treatment, through the joint use of shared office space, facilities, equipment and personnel,

(ii) for which substantially all of the services of the physicians who are members of the group are provided through the group and are billed under a billing number assigned to the group and amounts so received are treated as receipts of the group,

(iii) in which the overhead expenses of and the income from the practice are distributed in accordance with methods previously determined,

(iv) except as provided in subparagraph (B)(i), in which no physician who is a member of the group directly or indirectly receives compensation based on the volume or value of referrals by the physician,

(v) in which members of the group personally conduct no less than 75 percent of the physician-patient encounters of the group practice, and

(vi) which meets such other standards as the Secretary may impose by regulation.

(B) Special rules. (i) Profits and productivity bonuses. A physician in a group practice may be paid a share of overall profits of the group, or a productivity bonus based on services personally performed or services incident to such personally performed services, so long as the share or bonus is not determined in any manner which is directly related to the volume or value of referrals by such physician.

(ii) Faculty practice plans. In the case of a faculty practice plan associated with a hospital, institution of higher education, or medical school with an approved medical residency training program in which physician members may provide a variety of different specialty services and provide professional services both within and outside the group, as well as perform other tasks such as research, subparagraph (A) shall be applied only with respect to the services provided within the faculty practice plan.

(5) Referral; referring physician. (A) Physicians' services. Except as provided in subparagraph (C), in the case of an item or service for which payment may be made under part B, the request by a physician for the item or service, including the request by a physician for a consultation with another physician (and any test or procedure ordered by, or to be performed by (or under the supervision of) that other physician), constitutes a "referral" by a "referring physician".

(B) Other items. Except as provided in subparagraph (C), the request or establishment of a plan of care by a physician which includes the provision of the designated health service constitutes a "referral" by a "referring physician".

(C) Clarification respecting certain services integral to a consultation by certain specialists. A request by a pathologist for clinical diagnostic laboratory tests and pathological examination services, a request by a radiologist for diagnostic radiology services, and a request by a radiation oncologist for radiation therapy, if such services are furnished by (or under the supervision of) such pathologist, radiologist, or radiation oncologist pursuant to a consultation requested by another physician does not constitute a "referral" by a "referring physician".

(6) Designated health services. The term "designated health services" means any of the

following items or services:

(A) Clinical laboratory services.

(B) Physical therapy services.

(C) Occupational therapy services.

(D) Radiology services, including magnetic resonance imaging, computerized axial tomography scans, and ultrasound services.

(E) Radiation therapy services and supplies.

(F) Durable medical equipment and supplies.

(G) Parenteral and enteral nutrients, equipment, and supplies.

(H) Prosthetics, orthotics, and prosthetic devices and supplies.

(I) Home health services.

(J) Outpatient prescription drugs.

(K) Inpatient and outpatient hospital services.

(L) Outpatient speech-language pathology services.

(7) Specialty hospital. (A) In general. For purposes of this section, except as provided in subparagraph (B), the term "specialty hospital" means a subsection (d) hospital (as defined in section 1886(d)(1)(B) [42 USCS § 1395ww(d)(1)(B)]) that is primarily or exclusively engaged in the care and treatment of one of the following categories:

(i) Patients with a cardiac condition.

(ii) Patients with an orthopedic condition.

(iii) Patients receiving a surgical procedure.

(iv) Any other specialized category of services that the Secretary designates as inconsistent with the purpose of permitting physician ownership and investment interests in a hospital under this section.

(B) Exception. For purposes of this section, the term "specialty hospital" does not include any hospital—

(i) determined by the Secretary—

(I) to be in operation before November 18, 2003; or

(II) under development as of such date;

(ii) for which the number of physician investors at any time on or after such date is no greater than the number of such investors as of such date;

(iii) for which the type of categories described in subparagraph (A) at any time on or after such date is no different than the type of such categories as of such date;

(iv) for which any increase in the number of beds occurs only in the facilities on the main campus of the hospital and does not exceed 50 percent of the number of beds in the hospital as of November 18, 2003, or 5 beds, whichever is greater; and

(v) that meets such other requirements as the Secretary may specify.

(i) Requirements for hospitals to qualify for rural provider and hospital exception to ownership or investment prohibition. (1) Requirements described. For purposes of subsection (d)(3)(D), the requirements described in this paragraph for a hospital are as follows:

(A) Provider agreement. The hospital had—

(i) physician ownership or investment on December 31, 2010; and

(ii) a provider agreement under section 1866 [42 USCS § 1395cc] in effect on such date.

(B) Limitation on expansion of facility capacity. Except as provided in paragraph (3), the number of operating rooms, procedure rooms, and beds for which the hospital is licensed at any time on or after the date of the enactment of this subsection is no greater than the number of operating rooms, procedure rooms, and beds for which the hospital is licensed as of such date.

(C) Preventing conflicts of interest. (i) The hospital submits to the Secretary an annual report containing a detailed description of—

(I) the identity of each physician owner or investor and any other owners or investors of the hospital; and

(II) the nature and extent of all ownership and investment interests in the hospital.

(ii) The hospital has procedures in place to require that any referring physician owner or investor discloses to the patient being referred, by a time that permits the patient to make a meaningful decision regarding the receipt of care, as determined by the Secretary—

(I) the ownership or investment interest, as applicable, of such referring physician in the hospital; and

(II) if applicable, any such ownership or investment interest of the treating physician.

(iii) The hospital does not condition any physician ownership or investment interests either directly or indirectly on the physician owner or investor making or influencing referrals to the hospital or otherwise generating business for the hospital.

(iv) The hospital discloses the fact that the hospital is partially owned or invested in by physicians—

(I) on any public website for the hospital; and

(II) in any public advertising for the hospital.

(D) Ensuring bona fide investment. (i) The percentage of the total value of the ownership or investment interests held in the hospital, or in an entity whose assets include the hospital, by physician owners or investors in the aggregate does not exceed such percentage as of the date of enactment of this subsection [enacted March 23, 2010].

(ii) Any ownership or investment interests that the hospital offers to a physician owner or investor are not offered on more favorable terms than the terms offered to a person who is not a physician owner or investor.

(iii) The hospital (or any owner or investor in the hospital) does not directly or indirectly provide loans or financing for any investment in the hospital by a physician owner or investor.

(iv) The hospital (or any owner or investor in the hospital) does not directly or indirectly guarantee a loan, make a payment toward a loan, or otherwise subsidize a loan, for any individual physician owner or investor or group of physician owners or investors that is related to acquiring any ownership or investment interest in the hospital.

(v) Ownership or investment returns are distributed to each owner or investor in the hospital in an amount that is directly proportional to the ownership or investment interest of such owner or investor in the hospital.

(vi) Physician owners and investors do not receive, directly or indirectly, any guaranteed receipt of or right to purchase other business interests related to the hospital, including the purchase or lease of any property under the control of other owners or investors in the hospital or located near the premises of the hospital.

(vii) The hospital does not offer a physician owner or investor the opportunity to purchase or lease any property under the control of the hospital or any other owner or investor in the hospital on more favorable terms than the terms offered to an individual who is not a physician owner or investor.

(E) Patient safety. (i) Insofar as the hospital admits a patient and does not have any physician available on the premises to provide services during all hours in which the hospital is providing services to such patient, before admitting the patient—

(I) the hospital discloses such fact to a patient; and

(II) following such disclosure, the hospital receives from the patient a signed acknowledgment that the patient understands such fact.

(ii) The hospital has the capacity to—

(I) provide assessment and initial treatment for patients; and

(II) refer and transfer patients to hospitals with the capability to treat the needs of the patient involved.

(F) Limitation on application to certain converted facilities. The hospital was not converted from an ambulatory surgical center to a hospital on or after the date of enactment of this subsection [enacted March 23, 2010].

(2) Publication of information reported. The Secretary shall publish, and update on an annual basis, the information submitted by hospitals under paragraph (1)(C)(i) on the public Internet website of the Centers for Medicare & Medicaid Services.

(3) Exception to prohibition on expansion of facility capacity. (A) Process. (i) Establishment. The Secretary shall establish and implement a process under which a hospital that is an applicable hospital (as defined in subparagraph (E)) or is a high Medicaid facility described in subparagraph (F) may apply for an exception from the requirement under paragraph (1)(B).

(ii) Opportunity for community input. The process under clause (i) shall provide individuals and entities in the community in which the applicable hospital applying for an exception is located with the opportunity to provide input with respect to the application.

(iii) Timing for implementation. The Secretary shall implement the process under clause (i) on February 1, 2012.

(iv) Regulations. Not later than January 1, 2012, the Secretary shall promulgate regulations to carry out the process under clause (i).

(B) Frequency. The process described in subparagraph (A) shall permit an applicable hospital to apply for an exception up to once every 2 years.

(C) Permitted increase. (i) In general. Subject to clause (ii) and subparagraph (D), an applicable hospital granted an exception under the process described in subparagraph (A) may increase the number of operating rooms, procedure rooms, and beds for which the applicable hospital is licensed above the baseline number of operating rooms, procedure rooms, and beds of the applicable hospital (or, if the applicable hospital has been granted a previous exception under this paragraph, above the number of operating rooms, procedure rooms, and beds for which the hospital is licensed after the application of the most recent increase under such an exception).

(ii) 100 percent increase limitation. The Secretary shall not permit an increase in the number of operating rooms, procedure rooms, and beds for which an applicable hospital is licensed under clause (i) to the extent such increase would result in the number of operating rooms, procedure rooms, and beds for which the applicable hospital is licensed exceeding 200 percent of the baseline number of operating rooms, procedure rooms, and beds of the applicable hospital.

(iii) Baseline number of operating rooms, procedure rooms, and beds. In this paragraph, the term "baseline number of operating rooms, procedure rooms, and beds" means the number of operating rooms, procedure rooms, and beds for which the applicable hospital is licensed as of the date of enactment of this subsection [enacted March 23, 2010] (or, in the case of a hospital that did not have a provider agreement in effect as of such date but does have such an agreement in effect on December 31, 2010, the effective date of such provider agreement).

(D) Increase limited to facilities on the main campus of the hospital. Any increase in the number of operating rooms, procedure rooms, and beds for which an applicable hospital is licensed pursuant to this paragraph may only occur in facilities on the main campus of the applicable hospital.

(E) Applicable hospital. In this paragraph, the term "applicable hospital" means a hospital—

(i) that is located in a county in which the percentage increase in the population during the most recent 5-year period (as of the date of the application under subparagraph (A)) is at least 150 percent of the percentage increase in the population growth of the State in which the hospital is located during that period, as estimated by Bureau of the Census;

(ii) whose annual percent of total inpatient admissions that represent inpatient admissions under the program under title XIX [42 USCS §§ 1396 et seq.] is equal to or greater than the average percent with respect to such admissions for all hospitals located in the county in which the hospital is located;

(iii) that does not discriminate against beneficiaries of Federal health care programs and does not permit physicians practicing at the hospital to discriminate against such beneficiaries;

(iv) that is located in a State in which the average bed capacity in the State is less than the national average bed capacity; and

(v) that has an average bed occupancy rate that is greater than the average bed occupancy rate in the State in which the hospital is located.

(F) High Medicaid facility described. A high Medicaid facility described in this subparagraph is a hospital that—

(i) is not the sole hospital in a county;

(ii) with respect to each of the 3 most recent years for which data are available, has an annual percent of total inpatient admissions that represent inpatient admissions under title XIX [42 USCS §§ 1396 et seq.] that is estimated to be greater than such percent with respect to such admissions for any other hospital located in the county in which the hospital is located; and

(iii) meets the conditions described in subparagraph (E)(iii).

(G) Procedure rooms. In this subsection, the term "procedure rooms" includes rooms in which catheterizations, angiographies, angiograms, and endoscopies are performed, except such term shall not include emergency rooms or departments (exclusive of rooms in which catheterizations, angiographies, angiograms, and endoscopies are performed).

(H) Publication of final decisions. Not later than 60 days after receiving a complete application under this paragraph, the Secretary shall publish in the Federal Register the final decision with respect to such application.

(I) Limitation on review. There shall be no administrative or judicial review under section 1869 [42 USCS § 1395ff], section 1878 [42 USCS § 1395oo], or otherwise of the process under this paragraph (including the establishment of such process).

(4) Collection of ownership and investment information. For purposes of subparagraphs (A)(i) and (D)(i) of paragraph (1), the Secretary shall collect physician ownership and investment information for each hospital.

(5) Physician owner or investor defined. For purposes of this subsection, the term "physician owner or investor" means a physician (or an immediate family member of such physician) with a direct or an indirect ownership or investment interest in the hospital.

(6) Clarification. Nothing in this subsection shall be construed as preventing the Secretary from revoking a hospital's provider agreement if not in compliance with regulations implementing section 1866 [42 USCS § 1395cc].

(Aug. 14, 1935, ch 531, Title XVIII, Part E [D] [C], § 1877, as added Dec. 19, 1989, P. L. 101-239, Title VI, Subtitle A, Part 3, Subpart A, § 6204(a), 103 Stat. 2236; Nov. 5, 1990, P. L. 101-508, Title IV, Subtitle A, Part 3, § 4207(e)(1)–(3), (k)(2), 104 Stat. 1388-122, 1388-124; Aug. 10, 1993, P. L. 103-66, Title XIII, Ch 2, Subch A, Part III, § 13562(a), 107 Stat. 596; Oct. 31, 1994, P. L. 103-432, Title I, Subtitle C, §§ 152(a), (b), 160(d)(4), 108 Stat. 4436, 4444; Aug. 5, 1997, P. L. 105-33, Title IV,

Subtitle A, Chapter 1, Subchapter A, § 4001, Subtitle D, Ch 2, § 4314, 111 Stat. 275, 389; Nov. 29, 1999, P. L. 106-113, Div B, § 1000(a)(6), 113 Stat. 1536; Dec. 8, 2003, P. L. 108-173, Title I, § 101(a)(1), (e)(8)(B), Title V, Subtitle A, § 507(a), 117 Stat. 2071, 2152, 2295; July 15, 2008, P. L. 110-275, Title I, Subtitle C, Part II, § 143(b)(9), 122 Stat. 2543; March 23, 2010, P. L. 111-148, Title VI, Subtitle A, §§ 6001(a), 6003(a), Title X, Subtitle F, § 10601(a), 124 Stat. 684, 697, 1005; March 30, 2010, P. L. 111-152, Title I, Subtitle B, § 1106, 124 Stat. 1049.)

HISTORY; ANCILLARY LAWS AND DIRECTIVES

Other provisions:

Enforcement. Act March 23, 2010, P. L. 111-148, Title VI, Subtitle A, § 6001(b), 124 Stat. 689; amended Title X, Subtitle F, § 10601(b), 124 Stat 1005, provides:

"(1) Ensuring compliance. The Secretary of Health and Human Services shall establish policies and procedures to ensure compliance with the requirements described in subsection (i)(1) of section 1877 of the Social Security Act [subsec. (i)(1) of this section], as added by subsection (a)(3), beginning on the date such requirements first apply. Such policies and procedures may include unannounced site reviews of hospitals.

"(2) Audits. Beginning not later than May 1, 2012, the Secretary of Health and Human Services shall conduct audits to determine if hospitals violate the requirements referred to in paragraph (1).".

Application of amendment made by § 6003 of Act March 23, 2010. Act March 23, 2010, P. L. 111-148, Title VI, Subtitle A, § 6003(b), 124 Stat. 697, provides: "The amendment made by this section [amending subsec. (b)(2) of this section] shall apply to services furnished on or after January 1, 2010.".

Medicare self-referral disclosure protocol. Act March 23, 2010, P. L. 111-148, Title VI, Subtitle E, § 6409, 124 Stat. 772, provides:

"(a) Development of self-referral disclosure protocol. (1) In general. The Secretary of Health and Human Services, in cooperation with the Inspector General of the Department of Health and Human Services, shall establish, not later than 6 months after the date of the enactment of this Act, a protocol to enable health care providers of services and suppliers to disclose an actual or potential violation of section 1877 of the Social Security Act (42 U.S.C. 1395nn) pursuant to a self-referral disclosure protocol (in this section referred to as an 'SRDP'). The SRDP shall include direction to health care providers of services and suppliers on—

"(A) a specific person, official, or office to whom such disclosures shall be made; and

"(B) instruction on the implication of the SRDP on corporate integrity agreements and corporate compliance agreements.

"(2) Publication on Internet website of SRDP information. The Secretary of Health and Human Services shall post information on the public Internet website of the Centers for Medicare & Medicaid Services to inform relevant stakeholders of how to disclose actual or potential violations pursuant to an SRDP.

"(3) Relation to advisory opinions. The SRDP shall be separate from the advisory opinion process set forth in regulations implementing section 1877(g) of the Social Security Act [subsec. (g) of this section].

"(b) Reduction in amounts owed. The Secretary of Health and Human Services is authorized to reduce the amount due and owing for all violations under section 1877 of the Social Security Act [this section] to an amount less than that specified in subsection (g) of such section. In establishing such amount for a violation, the Secretary may consider the following factors:

"(1) The nature and extent of the improper or illegal practice.

"(2) The timeliness of such self-disclosure.

"(3) The cooperation in providing additional information related to the disclosure.

"(4) Such other factors as the Secretary considers appropriate.

"(c) Report. Not later than 18 months after the date on which the SRDP protocol is established under subsection (a)(1), the Secretary shall submit to Congress a report on the implementation of this section. Such report shall include—

"(1) the number of health care providers of services and suppliers making disclosures pursuant to the SRDP;

"(2) the amounts collected pursuant to the SRDP;

"(3) the types of violations reported under the SRDP; and

"(4) such other information as may be necessary to evaluate the impact of this section.".

§ 1395qq. Indian Health Service facilities

(a) Eligibility for payments; conditions and requirements. A hospital or skilled nursing facility of the Indian Health Service, whether operated by such Service or by an Indian tribe or tribal organization (as those terms are defined in section 4 of the Indian Health Care Improvement Act [25 USCS § 1603]), shall be eligible for payments under this title [42 USCS §§ 1395 et seq.], notwithstanding sections 1814(c) [42 USCS § 1395f(c)] and 1835(d) [42 USCS § 1395n(d)], if and for so long as it meets all of the conditions and requirements for such payments which are applicable generally to hospitals or skilled nursing facilities (as the case may be) under this title [42 USCS §§ 1395 et seq.].

(b) Eligibility based on submission of plan to achieve compliance with conditions and requirements; twelve-month period. Notwithstanding subsection (a), a hospital or skilled nursing facility of the Indian Health Service which does not meet all of the conditions and requirements of this title [42 USCS §§ 1395 et seq.] which are applicable generally to hospitals or skilled nursing facilities (as the case may be), but which submits to the Secretary within six months after the date of the enactment of this section [enacted Sept. 30, 1976] an acceptable plan for achieving compliance with such conditions and requirements, shall be deemed to meet such conditions and requirements (and to be eligible for payments under this title [42 USCS §§ 1395 et seq.]), without regard to the extent of its actual compliance with such conditions and requirements, during the first 12 months after the month in which such plan is submitted.

(c) Payments into special fund for improvements to achieve compliance with conditions and requirements; certification of compliance by Secretary. Notwithstanding any other provision of this title [42 USCS §§ 1395 et seq.], payments to which any hospital or skilled nursing facility of the Indian Health Service is entitled by reason of this section shall be placed in a special fund to be held by the Secretary and used by him (to such extent or in such amounts as are provided in appropriation Acts) exclusively for the purpose of making any improvements in the hospitals and skilled nursing facilities of such Service which may be necessary to achieve compliance with the applicable conditions and requirements of this title [42 USCS §§ 1395 et seq.]. The preceding sentence shall cease to apply when the Secretary determines and certifies that substantially all of the hospitals and skilled nursing facilities of such Service in the United States are in compliance with such conditions and requirements.

(d) Report by Secretary; status of facilities in complying with conditions and requirements. The annual report of the Secretary which is required by section 701 [801] of the Indian Health Care Improvement Act [25 USCS § 1671] shall include (along with the matters specified in section 403 of such Act [25 USCS § 1671 note]) a detailed statement of the status of the hospitals and skilled nursing facilities of the Service in terms of their compliance with the applicable conditions and requirements of this title [42 USCS §§ 1395 et seq.] and of the progress being made by such hospitals and facilities (under plans submitted under subsection (b) and otherwise) toward the achievement of such compliance.

(e) Payment of physician and nonphysician services in certain Indian providers. (1)(A) Notwithstanding section 1835(d) [42 USCS § 1395n(d)], subject to subparagraph (B), the Secretary shall make payment under part B [42 USCS §§ 1395j et seq.] to a hospital or an ambulatory care clinic (whether provider-based or freestanding) that is operated by the Indian Health Service or by an Indian tribe or tribal organization (as defined for purposes of subsection (a)) for services described in paragraph (2) (and for items and services furnished on or after January 1, 2005, all items and services for which payment may be made under part B [42 USCS §§ 1395j et seq.]) furnished in or at the direction of the hospital or clinic under the same situations, terms, and conditions as would apply if the services were furnished in or at the direction of such a hospital or clinic that was not operated by such Service, tribe, or organization.

(B) Payment shall not be made for services under subparagraph (A) to the extent that payment is otherwise made for such services under this title [42 USCS §§ 1395 et seq.].

(2) The services described in this paragraph are the following:

(A) Services for which payment is made under section 1848 [42 USCS § 1395w-4].

(B) Services furnished by a practitioner described in section 1842(b)(18)(C) [42 USCS § 1395u(b)(18)(C)] for which payment under part B [42 USCS §§ 1395j et seq.] is made under a fee schedule.

(C) Services furnished by a physical therapist or occupational therapist as described in section 1861(p) [42 USCS § 1395x(p)] for which payment under part B [42 USCS §§ 1395j et seq.] is made under a fee schedule.

(3) Subsection (c) shall not apply to payments made under this subsection.

(f) Direct billing by Alaska Native and American Indian organizations. For provisions relating to the authority of certain Indian tribes, tribal organizations, and Alaska Native health organizations to elect to directly bill for, and receive payment for, health care services provided by a hospital or clinic of such tribes or organizations and for which payment may be made under this title [42 USCS §§ 1395 et seq.], see section 405 of the Indian Health Care Improvement Act (25 U.S.C. 1645).

(Aug. 14, 1935, ch 531, Title XVIII, Part E [D] [C], § 1880, as added Sept. 30, 1976, P. L. 94-437, Title IV, § 401(b), 90 Stat. 1408; Aug. 5, 1997, P. L. 105-33, Title IV, Subtitle A, Ch 1, Subch A, § 4001, 111 Stat. 275; Nov. 1, 2000, P. L. 106-417, § 3(b)(1), 114 Stat. 1815; Dec. 21, 2000, P. L. 106-554, § 1(a)(6), 114 Stat. 2763; Dec. 8, 2003, P. L. 108-173, Title I, § 101(a)(1), Title VI, Subtitle C, § 630, 117 Stat. 2071, 2321; March 23, 2010, P. L. 111-148, Title II, Subtitle K, § 2902(a), Title X, Subtitle B, Part III, § 10221(a), (b)(4), 124 Stat. 333, 935, 936.)

HISTORY; ANCILLARY LAWS AND DIRECTIVES

Other provisions:

Application of March 23, 2010 amendment. Act March 23, 2010, P. L. 111-148, Title II, Subtitle K, § 2902(b), 124 Stat. 333, provides: "The amendments made by this section [amending subsec. (e)(1)(A) of this section] shall apply to items or services furnished on or after January 1, 2010.".

§ 1395rr. End stage renal disease program

(a) Type, duration, and scope of benefits. The benefits provided by parts A and B of this title [42 USCS §§ 1395c et seq. and 1395j et seq.] shall include benefits for individuals who have been determined to have end stage renal disease as provided in section 226A [42 USCS § 426-1], and benefits for kidney donors as provided in subsection (d) of this section. Notwithstanding any other provision of this title [42 USCS §§ 1395 et seq.], the type, duration, and scope of the benefit provided by parts A and B [42 USCS §§ 1395c et seq. and 1395j et seq.] with respect to individuals who have been determined to have end stage renal disease and who are entitled to such benefits without regard to section 226A [42 USCS § 426-1] shall in no case be less than the type, duration, and scope of the benefits so provided for individuals entitled to such benefits solely by reason of that section.

(b) Payments with respect to services; dialysis; regulations; physicians' services; target reimbursement rates; home dialysis supplies and equipment; self-care home dialysis support services; self-care dialysis units; hepatitis B vaccine. (1) Payments under this title [42 USCS §§ 1395 et seq.] with respect to services, in addition to services for which payment would otherwise be made under this title [42 USCS §§ 1395 et seq.], furnished to individuals who have been determined to have end stage renal disease shall include (A) payments on behalf of such individuals to providers of services and renal dialysis facilities which meet such requirements as the Secretary shall by regulation prescribe for institutional dialysis services and supplies (including self-dialysis services in a self-care dialysis unit maintained by the provider or facility), transplantation services, self-care home dialysis support services which are furnished by the provider or facility, and routine professional services performed by a physician during a maintenance dialysis episode if payments for his other professional services furnished to an individual who has end stage renal disease are made on the basis specified in paragraph (3)(A) of this subsection, (B) payments to or on behalf of such individuals for home dialysis supplies and equipment, and (C) payments to a supplier of home dialysis supplies and equipment that is not a provider of services, a renal dialysis facility, or a physician for self-administered erythropoietin as described in section 1861(s)(2)(P) if the Secretary finds that the patient receiving such drug from such a supplier can safely and effectively administer the drug (in accordance with the applicable methods and standards established by the Secretary pursuant to such section). The requirements prescribed by the Secretary under subparagraph (A) shall include requirements for a minimum utilization rate for transplantations.

(2)(A) With respect to payments for dialysis services furnished by providers of services and renal dialysis facilities to individuals determined to have end stage renal disease for which payments may be made under part B of this title [42 USCS §§ 1395j et seq.], such payments (unless otherwise provided in this section) shall be equal to 80 percent of the amounts determined in accordance with subparagraph (B); and with respect to payments for services for which payments may be made under part A of this title [42 USCS §§ 1395c et seq.], the amounts of such payments (which amounts shall not exceed, in respect to costs in procuring organs attributable to payments made to an organ procurement agency or histocompatibility laboratory, the costs incurred by that agency or laboratory) shall be determined in accordance with section 1861(v) [42 USCS § 1395x(v)] or section 1886 [42 USCS § 1395ww] (if applicable). Payments shall be made to a renal dialysis facility only if it agrees to accept such payments as payment in full for covered services, except for payment by the individual of 20 percent of the estimated amounts for such services calculated on the basis established by the Secretary under subparagraph (B) and the deductible amount imposed by section 1833(b) [42 USCS § 1395l(b)].

(B) The Secretary shall prescribe in regulations any methods and procedures to (i) determine the costs incurred by providers of services and renal dialysis facilities in furnishing covered services to individuals determined to have end stage renal disease, and (ii) determine, on a cost-related basis or other economical and equitable basis (including any basis authorized under section 1861(v) [42 USCS § 1395x(v)]) and consistent with any regulations promulgated under paragraph (7), the amounts of payments to be made for part B [42 USCS §§ 1395j et seq.] services furnished by such providers and facilities to such individuals.

(C) Such regulations, in the case of services furnished by proprietary providers and facilities (other than hospital outpatient departments) may include, if the Secretary finds it feasible and appropriate, provision for recognition of a reasonable rate of return on equity capital, providing such rate of return does not exceed the rate of return stipulated in section 1861(v)(1)(B) [42 USCS § 1395x(v)(1)(B)].

(D) For purposes of section 1878 [42 USCS § 1395oo], a renal dialysis facility shall be treated as a provider of services.

(3) With respect to payments for physicians' services furnished to individuals determined to have end stage renal disease, the Secretary shall pay 80 percent of the amounts calculated for such services—

(A) on a reasonable charge basis (but may, in such case, make payment on the basis of the prevailing charges of other physicians for comparable services or, for services furnished on or after January 1, 1992, on the basis described in section 1848 [42 USCS § 1395w-4]) except that payment may not be made under this subparagraph for routine services furnished during a maintenance dialysis episode, or

(B) on a comprehensive monthly fee or other basis (which effectively encourages the efficient delivery of dialysis services and provides incentives for the increased use of home dialysis) for an aggregate of services provided over a period of time (as defined in regulations).

(4)(A) Pursuant to agreements with approved providers of services and renal dialysis facilities, the Secretary may make payments to such providers and facilities for the cost of home dialysis supplies and equipment and self-care home dialysis support services furnished to patients whose self-care home dialysis is under the direct supervision of such provider or facility, on the basis of a target reimbursement rate (as defined in paragraph (6)) or on the basis of a method established under paragraph (7).

(B) The Secretary shall make payments to a supplier of home dialysis supplies and equipment furnished to a patient whose self-care home dialysis is not under the direct supervision of an approved provider of services or renal dialysis facility only in accordance with a written agreement under which—

(i) the patient certifies that the supplier is the sole provider of such supplies and equipment to the patient,

(ii) the supplier agrees to receive payment for the cost of such supplies and equipment only on an assignment-related basis, and

(iii) the supplier certifies that it has entered into a written agreement with an approved provider of services or renal dialysis facility under which such provider or facility agrees to furnish to such patient all self-care home dialysis support services and all other necessary dialysis services and supplies, including institutional dialysis services and supplies and emergency services.

(5) An agreement under paragraph (4) shall require, in accordance with regulations prescribed by the Secretary, that the provider or facility will—

(A) assume full responsibility for directly obtaining or arranging for the provision of—

(i) such medically necessary dialysis equipment as is prescribed by the attending physician;

(ii) dialysis equipment maintenance and repair services;

(iii) the purchase and delivery of all necessary medical supplies; and

(iv) where necessary, the services of trained home dialysis aides;

(B) perform all such administrative functions and maintain such information and records as the Secretary may require to verify the transactions and arrangements described in subparagraph (A);

(C) submit such cost reports, data, and information as the Secretary may require with respect to the costs incurred for equipment, supplies, and services furnished to the facility's home dialysis patient population; and

(D) provide for full access for the Secretary to all such records, data, and information as he may require to perform his functions under this section.

(6) The Secretary shall establish, for each calendar year, commencing with January 1, 1979, a target reimbursement rate for home dialysis which shall be adjusted for regional variations in the cost of providing home dialysis. In establishing such a rate, the Secretary shall include—

(A) the Secretary's estimate of the cost of providing medically necessary home dialysis supplies and equipment;

(B) an allowance, in an amount determined by the Secretary, to cover the cost of providing personnel to aid in home dialysis; and

(C) an allowance, in an amount determined by the Secretary, to cover administrative costs and to provide an incentive for the efficient delivery of home dialysis;

but in no event (except as may be provided in regulations under paragraph (7)) shall such target rate exceed 75 percent of the national average payment, adjusted for regional variations, for maintenance dialysis services furnished in approved providers and facilities during the preceding fiscal year. Any such target rate so established shall be utilized, without renegotiation of the rate, throughout the calendar year for which it is established. During the last quarter of each calendar year, the Secretary shall establish a home dialysis target reimbursement rate for the next calendar year based on the most recent data available to the Secretary at the time. In establishing any rate under this paragraph, the Secretary may utilize a competitive-bid procedure, a prenegotiated rate procedure, or any other procedure (including methods established under paragraph (7)) which the Secretary determines is appropriate and feasible in order to carry out this paragraph in an effective and efficient manner.

(7) Subject to paragraph (12), the Secretary shall provide by regulation for a method (or methods) for determining prospectively the amounts of payments to be made for dialysis services furnished by providers of services and renal dialysis facilities to individuals in a facility and to such individuals at home. Such method (or methods) shall provide for the prospective determination of a rate (or rates) for each mode of care based on a single composite weighted formula (which takes into account the mix of patients who receive dialysis services at a facility or at home and the relative costs of providing such services in such settings) for hospital-based facilities and such a single composite weighted formula for other renal dialysis facilities, or based on such other method or combination of methods which differentiate between hospital-based facilities and other renal dialysis facilities and which the Secretary determines, after detailed analysis, will more effectively encourage the more efficient delivery of dialysis services and will provide greater incentives for increased use of home dialysis than through the single composite weighted formulas. The amount of a payment made under any method other than a method based on a single composite weighted formula may not exceed the amount (or, in the case of continuous cycling peritoneal dialysis, 130 percent of the amount) of the median payment that would have been made under the formula for hospital-based facilities. Subject to section 422(a)(2) of the Medicare, Medicaid, and SCHIP Benefits Improvement and Protection Act of 2000 [note to this section], the Secretary shall provide for such exceptions to such methods as may be warranted by unusual circumstances (including the special circumstances of sole facilities located in isolated, rural areas and of pediatric facilities). Each application for such an exception shall be deemed to be approved unless the Secretary disapproves it by not later than 60 working days after the date the application is filed. The Secretary may provide that such method will serve in lieu of any target reimbursement rate that would otherwise be established under paragraph (6). The Secretary shall reduce the amount of each composite rate payment under this paragraph for each treatment by 50 cents (subject to such adjustments as may be required to reflect modes of dialysis other than hemodialysis) and provide for payment of such amount to the organizations (designated under subsection (c)(1)(A)) for such organizations' necessary and proper administrative costs incurred in carrying out the responsibilities described in subsection (c)(2). The Secretary shall provide that amounts paid under the previous sentence shall be distributed to the organizations described in subsection (c)(1)(A) to ensure equitable treatment of all such network organizations. The Secretary in distributing any such payments to network organizations shall take into account—

(A) the geographic size of the network area;

(B) the number of providers of end stage renal disease services in the network area;

(C) the number of individuals who are entitled to end stage renal disease services in the network area; and

(D) the proportion of the aggregate administrative funds collected in the network area.

The Secretary shall increase the amount of each composite rate payment for dialysis services furnished during 2000 by 1.2 percent above such composite rate payment amounts for such services furnished on December 31, 1999, for such services furnished on or after January 1, 2001, and before January 1, 2005, by 2.4 percent above such composite rate payment amounts for such services furnished on December 31, 2000, and for such services furnished on or after January 1, 2005, by 1.6 percent above such composite rate payment amounts for such services furnished on December 31, 2004.

(8) For purposes of this title [42 USCS §§ 1395 et seq.], the term "home dialysis supplies and equipment" means medically necessary supplies and equipment (including supportive equipment) required by an individual suffering from end stage renal disease in connection with renal dialysis carried out in his home (as defined in regulations), including obtaining, installing, and maintaining such equipment.

(9) For purposes of this title [42 USCS §§ 1395 et seq.], the term "self-care home dial-

ysis support services", to the extent permitted in regulation, means—

(A) periodic monitoring of the patient's home adaptation, including visits by qualified provider or facility personnel (as defined in regulations), so long as this is done in accordance with a plan prepared and periodically reviewed by a professional team (as defined in regulations) including the individual's physician;

(B) installation and maintenance of dialysis equipment;

(C) testing and appropriate treatment of the water; and

(D) such additional supportive services as the Secretary finds appropriate and desirable.

(10) For purposes of this title [42 USCS §§ 1395 et seq.], the term "self-care dialysis unit" means a renal dialysis facility or a distinct part of such facility or of a provider of services, which has been approved by the Secretary to make self-dialysis services, as defined by the Secretary in regulations, available to individuals who have been trained for self-dialysis. A self-care dialysis unit must, at a minimum, furnish the services, equipment and supplies needed for self-care dialysis, have patient-staff ratios which are appropriate to self-dialysis (allowing for such appropriate lesser degree of ongoing medical supervision and assistance of ancillary personnel than is required for full care maintenance dialysis), and meet such other requirements as the Secretary may prescribe with respect to the quality and cost-effectiveness of services.

(11)(A) Hepatitis B vaccine and its administration, when provided to a patient determined to have end stage renal disease, shall not be included as dialysis services for purposes of payment under any prospective payment amount or comprehensive fee established under this section. Payment for such vaccine and its administration shall be made separately in accordance with section 1833 [42 USCS § 1395l].

(B) Erythropoietin, when provided to a patient determined to have end stage renal disease, shall not be included as a dialysis service for purposes of payment under any prospective payment amount or comprehensive fee established under this section, and subject to paragraphs (12) and (13) payment for such item shall be made separately—

(i) in the case of erythropoietin provided by a physician, in accordance with section 1833 [42 USCS § 1395l]; and

(ii) in the case of erythropoietin provided by a provider of services, renal dialysis facility, or other supplier of home dialysis supplies and equipment—

(I) for erythropoietin provided during 1994, in an amount equal to $10 per thousand units (rounded to the nearest 100 units), and

(II) for erythropoietin provided during a subsequent year, in an amount determined to be appropriate by the Secretary, except that such amount may not exceed the amount determined under this clause for the previous year increased by the percentage increase (if any) in the implicit price deflator for gross national product (as published by the Department of Commerce) for the second quarter of the preceding year over the implicit price deflator for the second quarter of the second preceding year.

(C) The amount payable to a supplier of home dialysis supplies and equipment that is not a provider of services, a renal dialysis facility, or a physician for erythropoietin shall be determined in the same manner as the amount payable to a renal dialysis facility for such item.

(12)(A) Subject to paragraph (14), in lieu of payment under paragraph (7) beginning with services furnished on January 1, 2005, the Secretary shall establish a basic case-mix adjusted prospective payment system for dialysis services furnished by providers of services and renal dialysis facilities in a year to individuals in a facility and to such individuals at home. The case-mix under such system shall be for a limited number of patient characteristics. Under such system, the payment rate for dialysis services furnished on or after January 1, 2009, by providers of services shall be the same as the payment rate (computed without regard to this sentence) for such services furnished by renal dialysis facilities, and in applying the geographic index under subparagraph (D) to providers of services, the labor share shall be based on the labor share otherwise applied for renal dialysis facilities.

(B) The system described in subparagraph (A) shall include—

(i) the services comprising the composite rate established under paragraph (7); and

(ii) the difference between payment amounts under this title [42 USCS §§ 1395 et seq.] for separately billed drugs and biologicals (including erythropoietin) and acquisition costs of such drugs and biologicals, as determined by the Inspector General reports to the Secretary as required by section 623(c) of the Medicare Prescription Drug, Improvement, and Modernization Act of 2003 [note to this section]—

(I) beginning with 2005, for such drugs and biologicals for which a billing code exists prior to January 1, 2004; and

(II) beginning with 2007, for such drugs and biologicals for which a billing code does not exist prior to January 1, 2004,

adjusted to 2005, or 2007, respectively, as determined to be appropriate by the Secretary.

(C)(i) In applying subparagraph (B)(ii) for 2005, such payment amounts under this title [42 USCS §§ 1395 et seq.] shall be determined using the methodology specified in paragraph (13)(A)(i).

(ii) For 2006, the Secretary shall provide for an adjustment to the payments under clause (i) to reflect the difference between the payment amounts using the methodology under paragraph (13)(A)(i) and the payment amount determined using the methodology applied by the Secretary under paragraph (13)(A)(iii) of such paragraph, as estimated by the Secretary.

(D) The Secretary shall adjust the payment rates under such system by a geographic index as the Secretary determines to be appropriate. If the Secretary applies a geographic index under this paragraph that differs from the index applied under paragraph (7) the Secretary shall phase-in the application of the index under this paragraph over a multiyear period.

(E)(i) Such system shall be designed to result in the same aggregate amount of expenditures for such services, as estimated by the Secretary, as would have been made for 2005 if this paragraph did not apply.

(ii) The adjustment made under subparagraph (B)(ii)(II) shall be done in a manner to result in the same aggregate amount of expenditures after such adjustment as would otherwise have been made for such services for 2006 or 2007, respectively, as estimated by the Secretary, if this paragraph did not apply.

(F) Beginning with 2006, the Secretary shall annually increase the basic case-mix adjusted payment amounts established under this paragraph, by an amount determined by—

(i) applying the estimated growth in expenditures for drugs and biologicals (including erythropoietin) that are separately billable to the component of the basic case-mix adjusted system described in subparagraph (B)(ii); and

(ii) converting the amount determined in clause (i) to an increase applicable to the basic case-mix adjusted payment amounts established under subparagraph (B).

Except as provided in subparagraph (G), nothing in this paragraph or paragraph (14) shall be construed as providing for an update to the composite rate component of the basic case-mix adjusted system under subparagraph (B) or under the system under paragraph (14).

(G) The Secretary shall increase the amount of the composite rate component of the basic case-mix adjusted system under subparagraph (B) for dialysis services—

(i) furnished on or after January 1, 2006, and before April 1, 2007, by 1.6 percent above the amount of such composite rate component for such services furnished on December 31, 2005;

(ii) furnished on or after April 1, 2007, and before January 1, 2009, by 1.6 percent above the amount of such composite rate component for such services furnished on March 31, 2007;

(iii) furnished on or after January 1, 2009, and before January 1, 2010, by 1.0 percent above the amount of such composite rate component for such services furnished on December 31, 2008; and

(iv) furnished on or after January 1, 2010, by 1.0 percent above the amount of such composite rate component for such services furnished on December 31, 2009.

(H) There shall be no administrative or judicial review under section 1869 [42 USCS § 1395ff], section 1878 [42 USCS § 1395oo], or otherwise, of the case-mix system, relative weights, payment amounts, the geographic adjustment factor, or the update for the system established under this paragraph, or the determination of the difference between medicare payment amounts and acquisition costs for separately billed drugs and biologicals (including erythropoietin) under this paragraph and paragraph (13).

(13)(A) Subject to paragraph (14), the payment amounts under this title [42 USCS §§ 1395 et seq.] for separately billed drugs and biologicals furnished in a year, beginning with 2004, are as follows:

(i) For such drugs and biologicals (other than erythropoietin) furnished in 2004, the amount determined under section 1842(o)(1)(A)(v) [USCS § 1395u(o)(1)(A)(v)] for the drug or biological.

(ii) For such drugs and biologicals (including erythropoietin) furnished in 2005, the acquisition cost of the drug or biological, as determined by the Inspector General reports to the Secretary as required by section 623(c) of the Medicare Prescription Drug, Improvement, and Modernization Act of 2003 [note to this section]. Insofar as the Inspector General has not determined the acquisition cost with respect to a drug or biological, the Secretary shall determine the payment amount for such drug or biological.

(iii) For such drugs and biologicals (including erythropoietin) furnished in 2006 and subsequent years, such acquisition cost or the amount determined under section 1847A [42 USCS § 1395w-3a] for the drug or biological, as the Secretary may specify.

(B) Drugs and biologicals (including erythropoietin) which were separately billed under this subsection on the day before the date of the enactment of the Medicare Prescription Drug, Improvement, and Modernization Act of 2003 [enacted Dec. 8, 2003] shall continue to be separately billed on and after such date, subject to paragraph (14).

(14)(A)(i) Subject to subparagraph (E), for services furnished on or after January 1, 2011, the Secretary shall implement a payment system under which a single payment is made under this title to a provider of services or a renal dialysis facility for renal dialysis services (as defined in subparagraph (B)) in lieu of any other payment (including a payment adjustment under paragraph (12)(B)(ii)) and for such services and items furnished pursuant to paragraph (4).

(ii) In implementing the system under this paragraph the Secretary shall ensure that the estimated total amount of payments under this title for 2011 for renal dialysis services shall equal 98 percent of the estimated total amount of payments for renal dialysis services, including payments under paragraph (12)(B)(ii), that would have been made under this title with respect to services furnished in 2011 if such system had not been implemented. In making the estimation under subclause (I), the Secretary shall use per patient utilization data from 2007, 2008, or 2009, whichever has the lowest per patient utilization.

(B) For purposes of this paragraph, the term "renal dialysis services" includes—

(i) items and services included in the composite rate for renal dialysis services as of December 31, 2010;

(ii) erythropoiesis stimulating agents and any oral form of such agents that are furnished to individuals for the treatment of end stage renal disease;

(iii) other drugs and biologicals that are furnished to individuals for the treatment of end stage renal disease and for which payment was (before the application of this paragraph) made separately under this title, and any oral equivalent form of such drug or biological; and

(iv) diagnostic laboratory tests and other items and services not described in clause (i) that are furnished to individuals for the treatment of end stage renal disease.

Such term does not include vaccines.

(C) The system under this paragraph may provide for payment on the basis of services furnished during a week or month or such other appropriate unit of payment as the Secretary specifies.

(D) Such system—

(i) shall include a payment adjustment based on case mix that may take into account patient weight, body mass index, comorbidities, length of time on dialysis, age, race, ethnicity, and other appropriate factors;

(ii) shall include a payment adjustment for high cost outliers due to unusual variations in the type or amount of medically necessary care, including variations in the amount of erythropoiesis stimulating agents necessary for anemia management;

(iii) shall include a payment adjustment that reflects the extent to which costs incurred by low-volume facilities (as defined by the Secretary) in furnishing renal dialysis services exceed the costs incurred by other facilities in furnishing such services, and for payment for renal dialysis services furnished on or after January 1, 2011, and before January 1, 2014, such payment adjustment shall not be less than 10 percent; and

(iv) may include such other payment adjustments as the Secretary determines appropriate, such as a payment adjustment—

(I) for pediatric providers of services and renal dialysis facilities;

(II) by a geographic index, such as the index referred to in paragraph (12)(D), as the Secretary determines to be appropriate; and

(III) for providers of services or renal dialysis facilities located in rural areas.

The Secretary shall take into consideration the unique treatment needs of children and young adults in establishing such system.

(E)(i) The Secretary shall provide for a four-year phase-in (in equal increments) of the payment amount under the payment system under this paragraph, with such payment amount being fully implemented for renal dialysis services furnished on or after January 1, 2014.

(ii) A provider of services or renal dialysis facility may make a one-time election to be excluded from the phase-in under clause (i) and be paid entirely based on the payment amount under the payment system under this paragraph. Such an election shall be made prior to January 1, 2011, in a form and manner specified by the Secretary, and is final and may not be rescinded.

(iii) The Secretary shall make an adjustment to the payments under this paragraph for years during which the phase-in under clause (i) is applicable so that the estimated total amount of payments under this paragraph, including payments under this subparagraph, shall equal the estimated total amount of payments that would otherwise occur under this paragraph without such phase-in.

(F)(i)(I) Subject to subclause (II) and clause (ii), beginning in 2012, the Secretary shall annually increase payment amounts established under this paragraph by an ESRD market basket percentage increase factor for a bundled payment system for renal dialysis services that reflects changes over time in the prices of an appropriate mix of goods and services included in renal dialysis services.

(II) For 2012 and each subsequent year, after determining the increase factor described in subclause (I), the Secretary shall reduce such increase factor by the productivity adjustment described in section 1886(b)(3)(B)(xi)(II) [42 USCS § 1395ww(b)(3)(B)(xi)(II)]. The application of the preceding sentence may result in such increase factor being less than 0.0 for a year, and may result in payment rates under the payment system under this paragraph for a year being less than such payment rates for the preceding year.

(ii) For years during which a phase-in of the payment system pursuant to subparagraph (E) is applicable, the following rules shall apply to the portion of the payment under the system that is based on the payment of the composite rate that would otherwise apply if the system under this paragraph had not been enacted:

(I) The update under clause (i) shall not apply.

(II) Subject to clause (i)(II), the Secretary shall annually increase such composite rate by the ESRD market basket percentage increase factor described in clause (i)(I).

(G) There shall be no administrative or judicial review under section 1869 [42 USCS § 1395ff], section 1878 [42 USCS § 1395oo], or otherwise of the determination of payment amounts under subparagraph (A), the establishment of an appropriate unit of payment under subparagraph (C), the identification of renal dialysis services included in the bundled payment, the adjustments under subparagraph (D), the application of the phase-in under subparagraph (E), and the establishment of the market basket percentage increase factors under subparagraph (F).

(H) Erythropoiesis stimulating agents and other drugs and biologicals shall be treated as prescribed and dispensed or administered and available only under part B [42 USCS §§ 1395j et seq.] if they are—

(i) furnished to an individual for the treatment of end stage renal disease; and

(ii) included in subparagraph (B) for purposes of payment under this paragraph.

(c) Renal disease network areas; coordinating councils, executive committees, and medical review boards; national end stage renal disease medical information system; functions of network organizations. (1)(A)(i) For the purpose of assuring effective and efficient administration of the benefits provided under this section, the Secretary shall, in accordance with such criteria as he finds necessary to assure the performance of the responsibilities and functions specified in paragraph (2)—

(I) establish at least 17 end stage renal disease network areas, and

(II) for each such area, designate a network administrative organization which, in accordance with regulations of the Secretary, shall establish (aa) a network council of renal dialysis and transplant facilities located in the area and (bb) a medical review board, which has a membership including at least one patient representative and physicians, nurses, and social workers engaged in treatment relating to end stage renal disease. The Secretary shall publish in the Federal Register a description of the geographic area that he determines, after consultation with appropriate professional and patient organizations, constitutes each network area and the criteria on the basis of which such determination is made.

(ii)(I) In order to determine whether the Secretary should enter into, continue, or terminate an agreement with a network administrative organization designated for an area established under clause (i), the Secretary shall develop and publish in the Federal Register standards, criteria, and procedures to evaluate an applicant organization's capabilities to perform (and, in the case of an organization with which such an agreement is in effect, actual performance of) the responsibilities described in paragraph (2). The Secretary shall evaluate each applicant based on quality and scope of services and may not accord more than 20 percent of the weight of the evaluation to the element of price.

(II) An agreement with a network administrative organization may be terminated by the Secretary only if he finds, after applying such standards and criteria, that the organization has failed to perform its prescribed responsibilities effectively and efficiently. If such an agreement is to be terminated, the Secretary shall select a successor to the agreement on the basis of competitive bidding and in a manner that provides an orderly transition.

(B) At least one patient representative shall serve as a member of each network council and each medical review board.

(C) The Secretary shall, in regulations, prescribe requirements with respect to membership in network organizations by individuals (and the relatives of such individuals) (i) who have an ownership or control interest in a facility or provider which furnishes services referred to in section 1861(s)(2)(F) [42 USCS § 1395x(s)(2)(F)], or (ii) who have received remuneration from any such facility or provider in excess of such amounts as constitute reasonable compensation for services (including time and effort relative to the provision of professional medical services) or goods supplied to such facility or provider; and such requirements shall provide for the definition, disclosure, and, to the maximum extent consistent with effective administration, prevention of potential or actual financial or professional conflicts of interest with respect to decisions concerning the appropriateness, nature, or site of patient care.

(2) The network organizations of each network shall be responsible, in addition to such other duties and functions as may be prescribed by the Secretary, for—

(A) encouraging, consistent with sound medical practice, the use of those treatment settings most compatible with the successful rehabilitation of the patient and the participation of patients, providers of services, and renal disease facilities in vocational rehabilitation programs;

(B) developing criteria and standards relating to the quality and appropriateness of patient care and with respect to working with patients, facilities, and providers in encouraging participation in vocational rehabilitation programs; and network goals with respect to the placement of patients in self-care settings and undergoing or preparing for transplantation;

(C) evaluating the procedure by which facilities and providers in the network assess the appropriateness of patients for proposed treatment modalities;

(D) implementing a procedure for evaluating and resolving patient grievances;

(E) conducting on-site reviews of facilities and providers as necessary (as determined by a medical review board or the Secretary), utilizing standards of care established by the network organization to assure proper medical care;

(F) collecting, validating, and analyzing such data as are necessary to prepare the reports required by subparagraph (H) and to assure the maintenance of the registry established under paragraph (7);

(G) identifying facilities and providers that are not cooperating toward meeting network goals and assisting such facilities and providers in developing appropriate plans for correction and reporting to the Secretary on facilities and providers that are not providing appropriate medical care; and

(H) submitting an annual report to the Secretary on July 1 of each year which shall include a full statement of the network's goals, data on the network's performance in meeting its goals (including data on the comparative performance of facilities and providers with respect to the identification and placement of suitable candidates in self-care settings and transplantation and encouraging participation in vocational rehabilitation programs), identification of those facilities that have consistently failed to cooperate with network goals, and recommendations with respect to the need for additional or alternative services or facilities in the network in order to meet the network goals, including self-dialysis training, transplantation, and organ procurement facilities.

(3) Where the Secretary determines, on the basis of the data contained in the network's annual report and such other relevant data as may be available to him, that a facility or provider has consistently failed to cooperate with network plans and goals or to follow the recommendations of the medical review board, he may terminate or withhold certification of such facility or provider (for purposes of payment for services furnished to individuals with end stage renal disease) until he determines that such provider or facility is making reasonable and appropriate efforts to cooperate with the network's plans and goals. If the Secretary determines that the facility's or provider's failure to cooperate with network plans and goals does not jeopardize patient health or safety or justify termination of certification, he may instead, after reasonable notice to the provider or facility and to the public, impose such other sanctions as he determines to be appropriate, which sanctions may include denial of reimbursement with respect to some or all patients admitted to the facility after the date of notice to the facility or provider, and graduated reduction in reimbursement for all patients.

(4) The Secretary shall, in determining whether to certify additional facilities or expansion of existing facilities within a network, take into account the network's goals and per-

formance as reflected in the network's annual report.

(5) The Secretary, after consultation with appropriate professional and planning organizations, shall provide such guidelines with respect to the planning and delivery of renal disease services as are necessary to assist network organizations in their development of their respective networks' goals to promote the optimum use of self-dialysis and transplantation by suitable candidates for such modalities.

(6) It is the intent of the Congress that the maximum practical number of patients who are medically, socially, and psychologically suitable candidates for home dialysis or transplantation should be so treated and that the maximum practical number of patients who are suitable candidates for vocational rehabilitation services be given access to such services and encouraged to return to gainful employment. The Secretary shall consult with appropriate professional and network organizations and consider available evidence relating to developments in research, treatment methods, and technology for home dialysis and transplantation.

(7) The Secretary shall establish a national end stage renal disease registry the purpose of which shall be to assemble and analyze the data reported by network organizations, transplant centers, and other sources on all end stage renal disease patients in a manner that will permit—

(A) the preparation of the annual report to the Congress required under subsection (g);

(B) an identification of the economic impact, cost-effectiveness, and medical efficacy of alternative modalities of treatment;

(C) an evaluation with respect to the most appropriate allocation of resources for the treatment and research into the cause of end stage renal disease;

(D) the determination of patient mortality and morbidity rates, and trends in such rates, and other indices of quality of care; and

(E) such other analyses relating to the treatment and management of end stage renal disease as will assist the Congress in evaluating the end stage renal disease program under this section.

The Secretary shall provide for such coordination of data collection activities, and such consolidation of existing end stage renal disease data systems, as is necessary to achieve the purpose of such registry, shall determine the appropriate location of the registry, and shall provide for the appointment of a professional advisory group to assist the Secretary in the formulation of policies and procedures relevant to the management of such registry.

(8) The provisions of sections 1157 and 1160 [42 USCS §§ 1320c-6 and 1320c-9] shall apply with respect to network administrative organizations (including such organizations as medical review boards) with which the Secretary has entered into agreements under this subsection.

(d) Donors of kidney for transplant surgery. Notwithstanding any provision to the contrary in section 226 [42 USCS § 426] any individual who donates a kidney for transplant surgery shall be entitled to benefits under parts A and B of this title [42 USCS §§ 1395c et seq. and 1395j et seq.] with respect to such donation. Reimbursement for the reasonable expenses incurred by such an individual with respect to a kidney donation shall be made (without regard to the deductible, premium, and coinsurance provisions of this title [42 USCS §§ 1395 et seq.]), in such manner as may be prescribed by the Secretary in regulations, for all reasonable preparatory, operation, and postoperation recovery expenses associated with such donation, including but not limited to the expenses for which payment could be made if he were an eligible individual for purposes of parts A and B of this title [42 USCS §§ 1395c et seq. and 1395j et seq.] without regard to this subsection. Payments for postoperation recovery expenses shall be limited to the actual period of recovery.

(e) Reimbursement of providers, facilities, and nonprofit entities for costs of artificial kidney and automated dialysis peritoneal machines for home dialysis. (1) Notwithstanding any other provision of this title [42 USCS §§ 1395 et seq.], the Secretary may, pursuant to agreements with approved providers of services, renal dialysis facilities, and nonprofit entities which the Secretary finds can furnish equipment economically and efficiently, reimburse such providers, facilities, and nonprofit entities (without regard to the deductible and coinsurance provisions of this title [42 USCS §§ 1395 et seq.]) for the reasonable cost of the purchase, installation, maintenance and reconditioning for subsequent use of artificial kidney and automated dialysis peritoneal machines (including supportive equipment) which are to be used exclusively by entitled individuals dialyzing at home.

(2) An agreement under this subsection shall require that the provider, facility, or entity will—

(A) make the equipment available for use only by entitled individuals dialyzing at home;

(B) recondition the equipment, as needed, for reuse by such individuals throughout the useful life of the equipment, including modification of the equipment consistent with advances in research and technology;

(C) provide for full access for the Secretary to all records and information relating to the purchase, maintenance, and use of the equipment; and

(D) submit such reports, data, and information as the Secretary may require with respect to the cost, management, and use of the equipment.

(3) For purposes of this section, the term "supportive equipment" includes blood pumps, heparin pumps, bubble detectors, other alarm systems, and such other items as the Secretary may determine are medically necessary.

(f) Experiments, studies, and pilot projects. (1) The Secretary shall initiate and carry out, at selected locations in the United States, pilot projects under which financial assistance in the purchase of new or used durable medical equipment for renal dialysis is provided to individuals suffering from end stage renal disease at the time home dialysis is begun, with provision for a trial period to assure successful adaptation to home dialysis before the actual purchase of such equipment.

(2) The Secretary shall conduct experiments to evaluate methods for reducing the costs of the end stage renal disease program. Such experiments shall include (without being limited to) reimbursement for nurses and dialysis technicians to assist with home dialysis, and reimbursement to family members assisting with home dialysis.

(3) The Secretary shall conduct experiments to evaluate methods of dietary control for reducing the costs of the end stage renal disease program, including (without being limited to) the use of protein-controlled products to delay the necessity for, or reduce the frequency of, dialysis in the treatment of end stage renal disease.

(4) The Secretary shall conduct a comprehensive study of methods for increasing public participation in kidney donation and other organ donation programs.

(5) The Secretary shall conduct a full and complete study of the reimbursement of physicians for services furnished to patients with end stage renal disease under this title [42 USCS §§ 1395 et seq.], giving particular attention to the range of payments to physicians for such services, the average amounts of such payments, and the number of hours devoted to furnishing such services to patients at home, in renal disease facilities, in hospitals, and elsewhere.

(6) The Secretary shall conduct a study of the number of patients with end stage renal disease who are not eligible for benefits with respect to such disease under this title [42 USCS §§ 1395 et seq.] (by reason of this section or otherwise), and of the economic impact of such noneligibility of such individuals. Such study shall include consideration of mechanisms whereby governmental and other health plans might be instituted or modified to permit the purchase of actuarially sound coverage for the costs of end stage renal disease.

(7)(A) The Secretary shall establish protocols on standards and conditions for the reuse of dialyzer filters for those facilities and providers which voluntarily elect to reuse such filters.

(B) With respect to dialysis services furnished on or after January 1, 1988 (or July 1, 1988, with respect to protocols that relate to the reuse of bloodlines), no dialysis facility may reuse dialysis supplies (other than dialyzer filters) unless the Secretary has established a protocol with respect to the reuse of such supplies and the facility follows the protocol so established.

(C) The Secretary shall incorporate protocols established under this paragraph, and the requirement of subparagraph (B), into the requirements for facilities prescribed under subsection (b)(1)(A) and failure to follow such a protocol or requirement subjects such a facility to denial of participation in the program established under this section and to denial of payment for dialysis treatment not furnished in compliance with such a protocol or in violation of such requirement.

(8) The Secretary shall submit to the Congress no later than October 1, 1979, a full report on the experiments conducted under paragraphs (1), (2), (3), and (7), and the studies under paragraphs (4), (5), (6), and (7). Such report shall include any recommendations for legislative changes which the Secretary finds necessary or desirable as a result of such experiments and studies.

(g) Conditional approval of dialysis facilities; restriction-of-payments; notice to public and facility; notice and hearing; judicial review. (1) In any case where the Secretary—

(A) finds that a renal dialysis facility is not in substantial compliance with requirements for such facilities prescribed under subsection (b)(1)(A),

(B) finds that the facility's deficiencies do not immediately jeopardize the health and safety of patients, and

(C) has given the facility a reasonable opportunity to correct its deficiencies,

the Secretary may, in lieu of terminating approval of the facility, determine that pay+ment under this title [42 USCS §§ 1395 et seq.] shall be made to the facility only for services furnished to individuals who were patients of the facility before the effective date of the notice.

(2) The Secretary's decision to restrict payments under this subsection shall be made effective only after such notice to the public and to the facility as may be prescribed in regulations, and shall remain in effect until (A) the Secretary finds that the facility is in substantial compliance with the requirements under subsection (b)(1)(A), or (B) the Secretary terminates the agreement under this title [42 USCS §§ 1395 et seq.] with the facility.

(3) A facility dissatisfied with a determination by the Secretary under paragraph (1) shall be entitled to a hearing thereon by the Secretary (after reasonable notice) to the same extent as is provided in section 205(b) [42 USCS § 405(b)], and to judicial review of the Secretary's final decision after such hearing as is provided in section 205(g) [42 USCS § 405(g)], except that, in so applying such sections and in applying section 205(l) [42 USCS § 405(l)] thereto, any reference therein to the Commissioner of Social Security or the Social Security Administration shall be considered a reference to the Secretary or the Department of Health and Human Services, respectively.

(h) Quality incentives in the end-stage renal disease program. (1) Quality incentives. (A) In general. With respect to renal dialysis services (as defined in subsection (b)(14)(B)) furnished on or after January 1, 2012, in the case of a provider of services or a renal dialysis facility that does not meet the requirement described in subparagraph (B) with respect to the year, payments otherwise made to such provider or facility under the system under subsection (b)(14) for such services shall be reduced by up to 2.0 percent, as determined appropriate by the Secretary.

(B) Requirement. The requirement described in this subparagraph is that the provider or facility meets (or exceeds) the total performance score under paragraph (3) with respect to performance standards established by the Secretary with respect to measures specified in paragraph (2).

(C) No effect in subsequent years. The reduction under subparagraph (A) shall apply only with respect to the year involved, and the Secretary shall not take into account such reduction in computing the single payment amount under the system under paragraph (14) in a subsequent year.

(2) Measures. (A) In general. The measures specified under this paragraph with respect to the year involved shall include—

(i) measures on anemia management that reflect the labeling approved by the Food and Drug Administration for such management and measures on dialysis adequacy;

(ii) to the extent feasible, such measure (or measures) of patient satisfaction as the Secretary shall specify; and

(iii) such other measures as the Secretary specifies, including, to the extent feasible, measures on—

(I) iron management;

(II) bone mineral metabolism; and

(III) vascular access, including for maximizing the placement of arterial venous fistula.

(B) Use of endorsed measures. (i) In general. Subject to clause (ii), any measure specified by the Secretary under subparagraph (A)(iii) must have been endorsed by the entity with a contract under section 1890(a) [42 USCS § 1395aaa(a)].

(ii) Exception. In the case of a specified area or medical topic determined appropriate by the Secretary for which a feasible and practical measure has not been endorsed by the entity with a contract under section 1890(a) [42 USCS § 1395aaa(a)], the Secretary may specify a measure that is not so endorsed as long as due consideration is given to measures that have been endorsed or adopted by a consensus organization identified by the Secretary.

(C) Updating measures. The Secretary shall establish a process for updating the measures specified under subparagraph (A) in consultation with interested parties.

(D) Consideration. In specifying measures under subparagraph (A), the Secretary shall consider the availability of measures that address the unique treatment needs of children and young adults with kidney failure.

(3) Performance scores. (A) Total performance score. (i) In general. Subject to clause (ii), the Secretary shall develop a methodology for assessing the total performance of each provider of services and renal dialysis facility based on performance standards with respect to the measures selected under paragraph (2) for a performance period established under paragraph (4)(D) (in this subsection referred to as the "total performance score").

(ii) Application. For providers of services and renal dialysis facilities that do not meet (or exceed) the total performance score established by the Secretary, the Secretary shall ensure that the application of the methodology developed under clause (i) results in an appropriate distribution of reductions in payment under paragraph (1) among providers and facilities achieving different levels of total performance scores, with providers and facilities achieving the lowest total performance scores receiving the largest reduction in payment under paragraph (1)(A).

(iii) Weighting of measures. In calculating the total performance score, the Secretary shall weight the scores with respect to individual measures calculated under subparagraph (B) to reflect priorities for quality improvement, such as weighting scores to ensure that providers of services and renal dialysis facilities have strong incentives to meet or exceed anemia management and dialysis adequacy performance standards, as determined appropriate by the Secretary.

(B) Performance score with respect to individual measures. The Secretary shall also calculate separate performance scores for each measure, including for dialysis adequacy and anemia management.

(4) Performance standards. (A) Establishment. Subject to subparagraph (E), the Secretary shall establish performance standards with respect to measures selected under paragraph (2) for a performance period with respect to a year (as established under subparagraph (D)).

(B) Achievement and improvement. The performance standards established under subparagraph (A) shall include levels of achievement and improvement, as determined appropriate by the Secretary.

(C) Timing. The Secretary shall establish the performance standards under subparagraph (A) prior to the beginning of the performance period for the year involved.

(D) Performance period. The Secretary shall establish the performance period with respect to a year. Such performance period shall occur prior to the beginning of such year.

(E) Special rule. The Secretary shall initially use as the performance standard for the measures specified under paragraph (2)(A)(i) for a provider of services or a renal dialysis facility the lesser of—

(i) the performance of such provider or facility for such measures in the year selected by the Secretary under the second sentence of subsection (b)(14)(A)(ii); or

(ii) a performance standard based on the national performance rates for such measures in a period determined by the Secretary.

(5) Limitation on review. There shall be no administrative or judicial review under section 1869 [42 USCS § 1395ff], section 1878 [42 USCS § 1395oo], or otherwise of the following:

(A) The determination of the amount of the payment reduction under paragraph (1).

(B) The establishment of the performance standards and the performance period under paragraph (4).

(C) The specification of measures under paragraph (2).

(D) The methodology developed under paragraph (3) that is used to calculate total performance scores and performance scores for individual measures.

(6) Public reporting. (A) In general. The Secretary shall establish procedures for making information regarding performance under this subsection available to the public, including—

(i) the total performance score achieved by the provider of services or renal dialysis facility under paragraph (3) and appropriate comparisons of providers of services and renal dialysis facilities to the national average with respect to such scores; and

(ii) the performance score achieved by the provider or facility with respect to individual measures.

(B) Opportunity to review. The procedures established under subparagraph (A) shall ensure that a provider of services and a renal dialysis facility has the opportunity to review the information that is to be made public with respect to the provider or facility prior to such data being made public.

(C) Certificates. (i) In general. The Secretary shall provide certificates to providers of services and renal dialysis facilities who furnish renal dialysis services under this section to display in patient areas. The certificate shall indicate the total performance score achieved by the provider or facility under paragraph (3).

(ii) Display. Each facility or provider receiving a certificate under clause (i) shall prominently display the certificate at the provider or facility.

(D) Web-based list. The Secretary shall establish a list of providers of services and renal dialysis facilities who furnish renal dialysis services under this section that indicates the total performance score and the performance score for individual measures achieved by the provider and facility under paragraph (3). Such information shall be posted on the Internet website of the Centers for Medicare & Medicaid Services in an easily understandable format.

(Aug. 14, 1935, ch 531, Title XVIII, Part E [D] [C], § 1881, as added June 13, 1978, P. L. 95-292, § 2, 92 Stat. 308; Dec. 5, 1980, P. L. 96-499, Title IX, Part B, Subpart II, § 957, 94 Stat. 2648; Aug. 13, 1981, P. L. 97-35, Title XXI, Subtitle B, Ch 3, § 2145(a), 95 Stat. 799; April 20, 1983, P. L. 98-21, Title VI, § 602(i), 97 Stat. 165; July 18, 1984, P. L. 98-369, Division B, Title III, Subtitle A, Part I, § 2323(c), Part II, §§ 2352(a), 2354(b)(41), 98 Stat. 1086, 1099, 1100; Nov. 8, 1984, P. L. 98-617, § 3(b)(8), 98 Stat. 3296; Oct. 21, 1986, P. L. 99-509, Title IX, Subtitle D, Part 3, § 9335(a)(2), (d)(1), (e)–(i)(1), (j)(1), (k)(1), 100 Stat. 2028-2032; Aug. 18, 1987, P. L. 100-93, § 12, 101 Stat. 697; Dec. 22, 1987, P. L. 100-203, Title IV, Subtitle A, Part 2, Subpt. C, § 4036(b), (c)(2), (d)(5), Part 3, Subpt. B, § 4065(b), 101 Stat. 1330-79, 1330-80, 1330-112; Dec. 19, 1989, P. L. 101-239, Title VI, Subtitle A, Part 2, Subpart A, § 6102(e)(8), Part 3, Subpart A, § 6203(b)(1), (2), Subpart B, § 6219(a), (b), 103 Stat. 2188, 2235, 2254; Nov. 5, 1990, P. L. 101-508, Title IV, Subtitle A, Part 2, § 4201(c)(1), (d)(2), 104 Stat. 1388-103; Aug. 10, 1993, P. L. 103-66, Title XIII, Ch 2, Subch A, Part III, § 13566(a), 107 Stat. 607; Aug. 15, 1994, P. L. 103-296, Title I, § 108(c)(5), 108 Stat. 1495; Oct. 31, 1994, P. L. 103-432, Title I, Subtitle C, § 160(d)(3), 108 Stat. 4444; Aug. 5, 1997, P. L. 105-33, Title IV, Subtitle A, Ch 1, Subch A, § 4001, 111 Stat. 275; Nov. 29, 1999, P. L. 106-113, Div B, § 1000(a)(6), 113 Stat. 1536; Dec. 21, 2000, P. L. 106-554, § 1(a)(6), 114 Stat. 2763; Dec. 8, 2003, P. L. 108-173, Title I, § 101(a)(1), Title VI, Subtitle C, § 623(a), (b)(2), (d), 117 Stat. 2071, 2312, 2313; Feb. 8, 2006, P. L. 109-171, Title V, Subtitle B, Ch. 1, § 5106, 120 Stat. 42; Dec. 20, 2006, P. L. 109-432, Div B, Title I, § 103(a), 120 Stat. 2981; July 15, 2008, P. L. 110-275, Title I, Subtitle C, Part II, § 153(a), (b)(1), (3)(A), (c), 122 Stat. 2553, 2556; March 23, 2010, P. L. 111-148, Title III, Subtitle E, § 3401(h), 124 Stat. 485.)

§ 1395rr-1. Medicare coverage for individuals exposed to environmental health hazards

(a) Deeming of individuals as eligible for Medicare benefits. (1) In general. For purposes of eligibility for benefits under this title [42 USCS §§ 1395 et seq.], an individual determined under subsection (c) to be an environmental exposure affected individual described in subsection (e)(2) shall be deemed to meet the conditions specified in section 226(a) [42 USCS § 426(a)].

(2) Discretionary deeming. For purposes of eligibility for benefits under this title [42 USCS §§ 1395 et seq.], the Secretary may deem an individual determined under subsection (c) to be an environmental exposure affected individual described in subsection (e)(3) to meet the conditions specified in section 226(a) [42 USCS § 426(a)].

(3) Effective date of coverage. An Individual who is deemed eligible for benefits under this title [42 USCS §§ 1395 et seq.] under paragraph (1) or (2) shall be—

(A) entitled to benefits under the program under Part A [42 USCS §§ 1395c et seq.] as of the date of such deeming; and

(B) eligible to enroll in the program under Part B [42 USCS §§ 1395j et seq.] beginning with the month in which such deeming occurs.

(b) Pilot program for care of certain individuals residing in emergency declaration areas. (1) Program; purpose. (A) Primary pilot program. The Secretary shall establish a pilot program in accordance with this subsection to provide innovative approaches to furnishing comprehensive, coordinated, and cost-effective care under this title [42 USCS §§ 1395 et seq.] to individuals described in paragraph (2)(A).

(B) Optional pilot programs. The Secretary may establish a separate pilot program, in accordance with this subsection, with respect to each geographic area subject to an emergency declaration (other than the declaration of June 17, 2009), in order to furnish such comprehensive, coordinated and cost-effective care to individuals described in subparagraph (2)(B) who reside in each such area.

(2) Individual described. For purposes of paragraph (1), an individual described in this paragraph is an individual who enrolls in part B [42 USCS §§ 1395j et seq.], submits to the Secretary an application to participate in the applicable pilot program under this subsection, and—

(A) is an environmental exposure affected individual described in subsection (e)(2) who resides in or around the geographic area subject to an emergency declaration made as of June 17, 2009; or

(B) is an environmental exposure affected individual described in subsection (e)(3) who—

(i) is deemed under subsection (a)(2); and

(ii) meets such other criteria or conditions for participation in a pilot program under paragraph (1)(B) as the Secretary specifies.

(3) Flexible benefits and services. A pilot program under this subsection may provide for the furnishing of benefits, items, or services not otherwise covered or authorized under this title

[42 USCS §§ 1395 et seq.], if the Secretary determines that furnishing such benefits, items, or services will further the purposes of such pilot program (as described in paragraph (1)).

(4) Innovative reimbursement methodologies. For purposes of the pilot program under this subsection, the Secretary—

(A) shall develop and implement appropriate methodologies to reimburse providers for furnishing benefits, items, or services for which payment is not otherwise covered or authorized under this title [42 USCS §§ 1395 et seq.], if such benefits, items, or services are furnished pursuant to paragraph (3); and

(B) may develop and implement innovative approaches to reimbursing providers for any benefits, items, or services furnished under this subsection.

(5) Limitation. Consistent with section 1862(b) [42 USCS § 1395y(b)], no payment shall be made under the pilot program under this subsection with respect to benefits, items, or services furnished to an environmental exposure affected individual (as defined in subsection (e)) to the extent that such individual is eligible to receive such benefits, items, or services through any other public or private benefits plan or legal agreement.

(6) Waiver authority. The Secretary may waive such provisions of this title and title XI [42 USCS §§ 1395 et seq. and 1301 et seq.] as are necessary to carry out pilot programs under this subsection.

(7) Funding. For purposes of carrying out pilot programs under this subsection, the Secretary shall provide for the transfer, from the Federal Hospital Insurance Trust Fund under section 1817 [42 USCS § 1395i] and the Federal Supplementary Medical Insurance Trust Fund under section 1841 [42 USCS § 1395t], in such proportion as the Secretary determines appropriate, of such sums as the Secretary determines necessary, to the Centers for Medicare & Medicaid Services Program Management Account.

(8) Waiver of budget neutrality. The Secretary shall not require that pilot programs under this subsection be budget neutral with respect to expenditures under this title [42 USCS §§ 1395 et seq.].

(c) Determinations. (1) By the Commissioner of Social Security. For purposes of this section, the Commissioner of Social Security, in consultation with the Secretary, and using the cost allocation method prescribed in section 201(g) [42 USCS § 401(g)], shall determine whether individuals are environmental exposure affected individuals.

(2) By the Secretary. The Secretary shall determine eligibility for pilot programs under subsection (b).

(d) Emergency declaration defined. For purposes of this section, the term "emergency declaration" means a declaration of a public health emergency under section 104(a) of the Comprehensive Environmental Response, Compensation, and Liability Act of 1980 [42 USCS § 9604(a)].

(e) Environmental exposure affected individual defined. (1) In general. For purposes of this section, the term "environmental exposure affected individual" means—

(A) an individual described in paragraph (2); and

(B) an individual described in paragraph (3).

(2) Individual described. (A) In general. An individual described in this paragraph is any individual who—

(i) is diagnosed with 1 or more conditions described in subparagraph (B);

(ii) as demonstrated in such manner as the Secretary determines appropriate, has been present for an aggregate total of 6 months in the geographic area subject to an emergency declaration specified in subsection (b)(2)(A), during a period ending—

(I) not less than 10 years prior to such diagnosis; and

(II) prior to the implementation of all the remedial and removal actions specified in the Record of Decision for Operating Unit 4 and the Record of Decision for Operating Unit 7;

(iii) files an application for benefits under this title [42 USCS §§ 1395 et seq.] (or has an application filed on behalf of the individual), including pursuant to this section; and

(iv) is determined under this section to meet the criteria in this subparagraph.

(B) Conditions described. For purposes of subparagraph (A), the following conditions are described in this subparagraph:

(i) Asbestosis, pleural thickening, or pleural plaques as established by—

(I) interpretation by a "B Reader" qualified physician of a plain chest x-ray or interpretation of a computed tomographic radiograph of the chest by a qualified physician, as determined by the Secretary; or

(II) such other diagnostic standards as the Secretary specifies, except that this clause shall not apply to pleural thickening or pleural plaques unless there are symptoms or conditions requiring medical treatment as a result of these diagnoses.

(ii) Mesothelioma, or malignancies of the

lung, colon, rectum, larynx, stomach, esophagus, pharynx, or ovary, as established by—

(I) pathologic examination of biopsy tissue;

(II) cytology from bronchioalveolar lavage; or

(III) such other diagnostic standards as the Secretary specifies.

(iii) Any other diagnosis which the Secretary, in consultation with the Commissioner of Social Security, determines is an asbestos-related medical condition, as established by such diagnostic standards as the Secretary specifies.

(3) Other individual described. An individual described in this paragraph is any individual who—

(A) is not an individual described in paragraph (2);

(B) is diagnosed with a medical condition caused by the exposure of the individual to a public health hazard to which an emergency declaration applies, based on such medical conditions, diagnostic standards, and other criteria as the Secretary specifies;

(C) as demonstrated in such manner as the Secretary determines appropriate, has been present for an aggregate total of 6 months in the geographic area subject to the emergency declaration involved, during a period determined appropriate by the Secretary;

(D) files an application for benefits under this title [42 USCS §§ 1395 et seq.] (or has an application filed on behalf of the individual), including pursuant to this section; and

(E) is determined under this section to meet the criteria in this paragraph.

(Aug. 14, 1935, ch 531, Title XVIII, Part E, § 1881A, as added March 23, 2010, P. L. 111-148, Title X, Subtitle C, § 10323(a), 124 Stat. 954.)

§ 1395ss. Certification of Medicare supplemental health insurance policies

(a) Submission of policy by insurer. (1) The Secretary shall establish a procedure whereby medicare supplemental policies (as defined in subsection (g)(1)) may be certified by the Secretary as meeting minimum standards and requirements set forth in subsection (c). Such procedure shall provide an opportunity for any insurer to submit any such policy, and such additional data as the Secretary finds necessary, to the Secretary for his examination and for his certification thereof as meeting the standards and requirements set forth in subsection (c). Subject to subsections (k)(3), (m), and (n), such certification shall remain in effect if the insurer files a notarized statement with the Secretary no later than June 30 of each year stating that the policy continues to meet such standards and requirements and if the insurer submits such additional data as the Secretary finds necessary to independently verify the accuracy of such notarized statement. Where the Secretary determines such a policy meets (or continues to meet) such standards and requirements, he shall authorize the insurer to have printed on such policy (but only in accordance with such requirements and conditions as the Secretary may prescribe) an emblem which the Secretary shall cause to be designed for use as an indication that a policy has received the Secretary's certification. The Secretary shall provide each State commissioner or superintendent of insurance with a list of all the policies which have received his certification.

(2) No medicare supplemental policy may be issued in a State on or after the date specified in subsection (p)(1)(c) unless—

(A) the State's regulatory program under subsection (b)(1) provides for the application and enforcement of the standards and requirements set forth in such subsection (including the 1991 NAIC Model Regulation or 1991 Federal Regulation (as the case may be)) by the date specified in subsection (p)(1)(c); or

(B) if the State's program does not provide for the application and enforcement of such standards and requirements, the policy has been certified by the Secretary under paragraph (1) as meeting the standards and requirements set forth in subsection (c) (including such applicable standards) by such date.

Any person who issues a medicare supplemental policy, on and after the effective date specified in subsection (p)(1)(C), in violation of this paragraph is subject to a civil money penalty of not to exceed $25,000 for each such violation. The provisions of section 1128A [42 USCS § 1320a-7a] (other than the first sentence of subsection (a) and other than subsection (b)) shall apply to a civil money penalty under the previous sentence in the same manner as such provisions apply to a penalty or proceeding under section 1128A(a) [42 USCS § 132a-7a(a)].

(b) Standards and requirements; periodic review by Secretary. (1) **[Caution: For application and termination of Nov. 5, 1990 amendment of this section, see § 4358(c) of Act Nov. 5, 1990, P. L. 101-508, which appears as a note to this section.]** Any medicare supplemental policy issued in any State which the Secretary determines has established under State law a regulatory program that—

(A) **[Caution: For application and termination of 1990 amendment, see § 4358(c) of Act Nov. 4, 1990, P. L. 101-508, which appears as a note to this section.]** provides for the application and enforcement of standards with respect to such policies equal to or more stringent than the NAIC Model Standards (as defined in subsection (g)(2)(A)), except as otherwise provided by subparagraph (H);

(B) includes requirements equal to or more stringent than the requirements described in paragraphs (2) through (5) of subsection (c);

(C) provides that—

(i) information with respect to the actual ratio of benefits provided to premiums collected under such policies will be reported to the State on forms conforming to those developed by the National Association of Insurance Commissioners for such purpose, or

(ii) such ratios will be monitored under the program in an alternative manner approved by the Secretary, and that a copy of each such policy, the most recent premium for each such policy, and a listing of the ratio of benefits provided to premiums collected for the most recent 3-year period for each such policy issued or sold in the State is maintained and made available to interested persons;

(D) provides for application and enforcement of the standards and requirements described in subparagraphs (A), (B), and (C) to all medicare supplemental policies (as defined in subsection (g)(1)) issued in such State,

(E) provides the Secretary periodically (but at least annually) with a list containing the name and address of the issuer of each such policy and the name and number of each such policy (including an indication of policies that have been previously approved, newly approved, or withdrawn from approval since the previous list was provided),

(F) reports to the Secretary on the implementation and enforcement of standards and requirements of this paragraph at intervals established by the Secretary,

(G) provides for a process for approving or disapproving proposed premium increases with respect to such policies, and establishes a policy for the holding of public hearings prior to approval of a premium increase, and

(H) **[Caution: For application and termination of this subparagraph, see § 4358(c) of Act Nov. 4, 1990, P. L. 101-508, which appears as a note to this section.]** in the case of a policy that meets the standards under subparagraph (A) except that benefits under the policy are limited to items and services furnished by certain entities (or reduced benefits are provided when items or services are furnished by other entities), provides for the application of requirements equal to or more stringent than the requirements under subsection (t),

shall be deemed (subject to subsections (k)(3), (m), and (n), for so long as the Secretary finds that such State regulatory program continues to meet the standards and requirements of this paragraph) to meet the standards and requirements set forth in subsection (c). Each report required under subparagraph (F) shall include information on loss ratios of policies sold in the State, frequency and types of instances in which policies approved by the State fail to meet the standards and requirements of this paragraph, actions taken by the State to bring such policies into compliance, information regarding State programs implementing consumer protection provisions, and such further information as the Secretary in consultation with the National Association of Insurance Commissioners may specify.

(2) The Secretary periodically shall review State regulatory programs to determine if they continue to meet the standards and requirements specified in paragraph (1). If the Secretary finds that a State regulatory program no longer meets the standards and requirements, before making a final determination, the Secretary shall provide the State an opportunity to adopt such a plan of correction as would permit the State regulatory program to continue to meet such standards and requirements. If the Secretary makes a final determination that the State regulatory program, after such an opportunity, fails to meet such standards and requirements, the program shall no longer be considered to have in operation a program meeting such standards and requirements.

(3) Notwithstanding paragraph (1), a medicare supplemental policy offered in a State shall not be deemed to meet the standards and requirements set forth in subsection (c), with respect to an advertisement (whether through written, radio, or television medium) used (or, at a State's option, to be used) for the policy in the State, unless the entity issuing the policy provides a copy of each advertisement to the Commissioner of Insurance (or comparable officer identified by the Secretary) of that State for review or approval to the extent it may be required under State law.

(c) Requisite findings. The Secretary shall certify under this section any medicare supplemental policy, or continue certification of such a policy, only if he finds that such policy (or, with respect to paragraph (3) or the requirement described in subsection (s), the issuer of the policy)—

(1) **[Caution: For application and termination of Nov. 5, 1990 amendment of this section, see § 4358(c) of Act Nov. 5, 1990, P. L. 101-508, which appears as a note to this section.]** meets or exceeds (either in a single policy or, in the case of nonprofit hospital and medical service associations, in one or more policies issued in conjunction with one another) the NAIC Model Standards (except as otherwise provided by subsection (t));

(2) meets the requirements of subsection (r);

(3)(A) accepts a notice under section 1842(h)(3)(B) [42 USCS § 1395u(h)(3)(B)] as a claim form for benefits under such policy in lieu of any claim form otherwise required and agrees to make a payment determination on the basis of the information contained in such notice;

(B) where such a notice is received—

(i) provides notice to such physician or supplier and the beneficiary of the payment determination under the policy, and

(ii) provides any payment covered by such policy directly to the participating physician or supplier involved;

(C) provides each enrollee at the time of enrollment a card listing the policy name and number and a single mailing address to which notices under section 1842(h)(3)(B) [42 USCS § 1395u(h)(3)(B)] respecting the policy are to be sent;

(D) agrees to pay any user fees established under section 1842(h)(3)(B) [42 USCS § 1395u(h)(3)(B)] with respect to information transmitted to the issuer of the policy; and

(E) provides to the Secretary at least annually, for transmittal to carriers, a single mailing address to which notices under section 1842(h)(3)(B) [42 USCS § 1395u(h)(3)(B)] respecting the policy are to be sent;

(4) may, during a period of not less than 30 days after the policy is issued, be returned for a full refund of any premiums paid (without regard to the manner in which the purchase of the policy was solicited); and

(5) meets the applicable requirements of subsections (o) through (t).

(d) Criminal penalties; civil penalties for certain violations. (1) Whoever knowingly and willfully makes or causes to be made or induces or seeks to induce the making of any false statement or representation of a material fact with respect to the compliance of any policy with the standards and requirements set forth in subsection (c) or in regulations promulgated pursuant to such subsection, or with respect to the use of the emblem designed by the Secretary under subsection (a), shall be fined under title 18, United States Code, or imprisoned not more than 5 years, or both, and, in addition to or in lieu of such a criminal penalty, is subject to a civil money penalty of not to exceed $5,000 for each such prohibited act.

(2) Whoever falsely assumes or pretends to be acting, or misrepresents in any way that he is acting, under the authority of or in association with, the program of health insurance established by this title [42 USCS §§ 1395 et seq.], or any Federal agency, for the purpose of selling or attempting to sell insurance, or in such pretended character demands, or obtains money, paper, documents, or anything of value, shall be fined under title 18, United States Code, or imprisoned not more than 5 years, or both, and, in addition to or in lieu of such a criminal penalty, is subject to a civil money penalty of not to exceed $5,000 for each such prohibited act.

(3)(A)(i) It is unlawful for a person to sell or issue to an individual entitled to benefits under part A [42 USCS §§ 1395c et seq.] or enrolled under part B of this title [42 USCS §§ 1395j et seq.] (including an individual electing a Medicare+Choice plan under section 1851)—

(I) a health insurance policy with knowledge that the policy duplicates health benefits to which the individual is otherwise entitled under this title or title XIX [42 USCS §§ 1395 et seq. or 1396 et seq.],

(II) in the case of an individual not electing a Medicare+Choice plan, a medicare supplemental policy with knowledge that the individual is entitled to benefits under another medicare supplemental policy or in the case of an individual electing a Medicare+Choice plan, a medicare supplemental policy with knowledge that the policy duplicates health benefits to which the individual is otherwise entitled under the Medicare+Choice plan or under another medicare supplemental policy, or

(III) a health insurance policy (other than a medicare supplemental policy) with knowledge that the policy duplicates health benefits to which the individual is otherwise entitled, other than benefits to which the individual is entitled under a requirement of State or Federal law.

(ii) Whoever violates clause (i) shall be fined under title 18, United States Code, or imprisoned not more than 5 years, or both, and, in addition to or in lieu of such a criminal penalty, is subject to a civil money penalty of not to exceed $25,000 (or $15,000 in the case of a person other than the issuer of the policy) for each such prohibited act.

(iii) A seller (who is not the issuer of a health insurance policy) shall not be considered to violate clause (i)(II) with respect to the sale of a medicare supplemental policy if the policy is sold in compliance with subparagraph (B).

(iv) For purposes of this subparagraph, a health insurance policy (other than a Medicare supplemental policy) providing for benefits which are payable to or on behalf of an individual without regard to other health benefit coverage of such individual is not considered to "duplicate" any health benefits under this title [42 USCS §§ 1395 et seq.], under title XIX [42 USCS §§ 1396 et seq.], or under a health insurance policy, and subclauses (I) and (III) of clause (i) do not apply to such a policy.

(v) For purposes of this subparagraph, a health insurance policy (or a rider to an insurance contract which is not a health insurance policy) is not considered to "duplicate" health benefits under this title or under another health insurance policy if it—

(I) provides health care benefits only for long-term care, nursing home care, home health care, or community-based care, or any combination thereof,

(II) coordinates against or excludes items and services available or paid for under this title or under another health insurance policy, and

(III) for policies sold or issued on or after the end of the 90-day period beginning on the date of enactment of the Health Insurance Portability and Accountability Act of 1996 [enacted Aug. 21, 1996] discloses such coordination or exclusion in the policy's outline of coverage.

For purposes of this clause, the terms "coordinates" and "coordination" mean, with respect to a policy in relation to health benefits under this title or under another health insurance policy, that the policy under its terms is secondary to, or excludes from payment, items and services to the extent available or paid for under this title [42 USCS §§ 1395 et seq.] or under another health insurance policy.

(vi)(I) An individual entitled to benefits under part A [42 USCS §§ 1395c et seq.] or enrolled under part B of this title [42 USCS §§ 1395j et seq.] who is applying for a health insurance policy (other than a policy described in subclause (III)) shall be furnished a disclosure statement described in clause (vii) for the type of policy being applied for. Such statement shall be furnished as a part of (or together with) the application for such policy.

(II) Whoever issues or sells a health insurance policy (other than a policy described in subclause (III)) to an individual described in subclause (I) and fails to furnish the appropriate disclosure statement as required under such subclause shall be fined under title 18, United States Code, or imprisoned not more than 5 years, or both, and, in addition to or in lieu of such a criminal penalty, is subject to a civil money penalty of not to exceed $25,000 (or $15,000 in the case of a person other than the issuer of the policy) for each such violation.

(III) A policy described in this subclause (to which subclauses (I) and (II) do not apply) is a Medicare supplemental policy, a policy described in clause (v), or a health insurance policy identified under 60 Federal Register 30880 (June 12, 1995) as a policy not required to have a disclosure statement.

(IV) Any reference in this section to the revised NAIC model regulation (referred to in subsection (m)(1)(A)) is deemed a reference to such regulation as revised by section 171(m)(2) of the Social Security Act Amendments of 1994 (Public Law 103-432) and as modified by substituting, for the disclosure required under section 16D(2), disclosure under subclause (I) of an appropriate disclosure statement under clause (vii).

(vii) The disclosure statement described in this clause for a type of policy is the statement specified under subparagraph (D) of this paragraph (as in effect before the date of the enactment of the Health Insurance Portability and Accountability Act of 1996 [enacted Aug. 21, 1996]) for that type of policy, as revised as follows:

(I) In each statement, amend the second line to read as follows:

"THIS IS NOT MEDICARE SUPPLEMENT INSURANCE".

(II) In each statement, strike the third line and insert the following: **"Some health care services paid for by Medicare may also trigger the payment of benefits under this policy."**.

(III) In each statement not described in subclause (V), strike the boldface matter that begins **"This insurance"** and all that follows up to the next paragraph that begins **"Medicare"**.

(IV) In each statement not described in subclause (V), insert before the boxed matter (that states **"Before You Buy This Insurance"**) the following: **"This policy must pay benefits without regard to other health benefit coverage to which you may be entitled under Medicare or other insurance."**.

(V) In a statement relating to policies providing both nursing home and non-institutional coverage, to policies providing nursing home benefits only, or policies providing home care benefits only, amend the sentence that begins "Federal law" to read as follows: "Federal law requires us to inform you that in certain situations this insurance may pay for some care also covered by Medicare.".

(viii)(I) Subject to subclause (II), nothing in this subparagraph shall restrict or preclude a State's ability to regulate health insurance policies, including any health insurance policy that is described in clause (iv), (v), or (vi)(III).

(II) A State may not declare or specify, in statute, regulation, or otherwise, that a health insurance policy (other than a Medicare supplemental policy) or rider to an insurance contract which is not a health insurance policy, that is described in clause (iv), (v), or (vi)(III) and that is sold, issued, or renewed to an individual entitled to benefits under part A [42 USCS §§ 1395c et seq.] or enrolled under part B [42 USCS §§ 1395j et seq.] "duplicates" health benefits under this title [42 USCS §§ 1395 et seq.] or under a Medicare supplemental policy.

(B)(i) It is unlawful for a person to issue or sell a medicare supplemental policy to an individual entitled to benefits under part A [42 USCS §§ 1395c et seq.] or enrolled under part B [42 USCS §§ 1395j et seq.], whether directly, through the mail, or otherwise, unless—

(I) the person obtains from the individual, as part of the application for the issuance or purchase and on a form described in clause ii, a written statement signed by the individual stating, to the best of the individual's knowledge, what health insurance policies (including any Medicare+Choice plan) the individual has, from what source, and whether the individual is entitled to any medical assistance under title XIX [42 USCS §§ 1396 et seq.], whether as a qualified medicare beneficiary or otherwise, and

(II) the written statement is accompanied by a written acknowledgment, signed by the seller of the policy, of the request for and receipt of such statement.

(ii) The statement required by clause (i) shall be made on a form that—

(I) states in substance that a medicare-eligible individual does not need more than one medicare supplemental policy,

(II) states in substance that individuals may be eligible for benefits under the State medicaid program under title XIX [42 USCS §§ 1396 et seq.] and that such individuals who are entitled to benefits under that program usually do not need a medicare supplemental policy and that benefits and premiums under any such policy shall be suspended upon request of the policyholder during the period (of not longer than 24 months) of entitlement to benefits under such title [42 USCS §§ 1396 et seq.] and may be reinstituted upon loss of such entitlement, and

(III) states that counseling services may be available in the State to provide advice concerning the purchase of medicare supplemental policies and enrollment under the medicaid program and may provide the telephone number for such services.

(iii)(I) Except as provided in subclauses (II) and (III), if the statement required by clause (i) is not obtained or indicates that the individual has a medicare supplemental policy or indicates that the individual is entitled to any medical assistance under title XIX [42 USCS §§ 1396 et seq.], the sale of a medicare supplemental policy shall be considered to be a violation of subparagraph (A).

(II) Subclause (I) shall not apply in the case of an individual who has a medicare supplemental policy, if the individual indicates in writing, as part of the application for purchase, that the policy being purchased replaces such other policy and indicates an intent to terminate the policy being replaced when the new policy becomes effective and the issuer or seller certifies in writing that such policy will not, to the best of the issuer's or seller's knowledge, duplicate coverage (taking into account any such replacement).

(III) If the statement required by clause (i) is obtained and indicates that the individual is entitled to any medical assistance under title XIX [42 USCS §§ 1396 et seq.], the sale of the policy is not in violation of clause (i) (insofar as such clause relates to such medical assistance), if (aa) a State medicaid plan under such title pays the premiums for the policy, (bb) in the case of a qualified medicare beneficiary described in section 1905(p)(1) [42 USCS § 1396d(p)(1)], the policy provides for coverage of outpatient prescription drugs, or (cc) the only medical assistance to which the individual is entitled under the State plan is medicare cost sharing described in section 1905(p)(3)(A)(ii) [42 USCS § 1396d(p)(3)(A)].

(iv) Whoever issues or sells a medicare supplemental policy in violation of this subparagraph shall be fined under title 18, United States Code, or imprisoned not more than 5 years, or both, and, in addition to or in lieu of such a criminal penalty, is subject to a civil money penalty of not to exceed $25,000 (or $15,000 in the case of a seller who is not the issuer of a policy) for each such violation.

(C) Subparagraph (A) shall not apply with respect to the sale or issuance of a group policy or plan of one or more employers or labor organizations, or of the trustees of a fund established by one or more employers or labor organizations (or combination thereof), for employees or former employees (or combination thereof) or for members or former members (or combination thereof) of the labor organizations.

(4)(A) Whoever knowingly, directly or through his agent, mails or causes to be mailed any matter for a prohibited purpose (as determined under subparagraph (B)) shall be fined under title 18, United States Code, or imprisoned not more than 5 years, or both, and, in addition to or in lieu of such a criminal penalty, is subject to a civil money penalty of not to exceed $5,000 for each such prohibited act.

(B) For purposes of subparagraph (A), a prohibited purpose means the advertising, solicitation, or offer for sale of a medicare supplemental policy, or the delivery of such a policy, in or into any State in which such policy has not been approved by the State commissioner or superintendent of insurance.

(C) Subparagraph (A) shall not apply in the case of a person who mails or causes to be mailed a medicare supplemental policy into a State if such person has ascertained that the party insured under such policy to whom (or on whose behalf) such policy is mailed is located in such State on a temporary basis.

(D) Subparagraph (A) shall not apply in the case of a person who mails or causes to be mailed a duplicate copy of a medicare supplemental policy previously issued to the party to whom (or on whose behalf) such duplicate copy is mailed.

(E) Subparagraph (A) shall not apply in the case of an issuer who mails or causes to be mailed a policy, certificate, or other matter solely to comply with the requirements of subsection (q).

(5) The provisions of section 1128A [42 USCS § 1320a-7a] (other than subsections (a) and (b)) shall apply to civil money penalties under paragraphs (1), (2), (3)(A), and (4)(A) in the same manner as such provisions apply to penalties and proceedings under section 1128A(a) [42 USCS § 1320a-7a(a)].

(e) Dissemination of information. (1) The Secretary shall provide to all individuals entitled to benefits under this title [42 USCS §§ 1395 et seq.] (and, to the extent feasible, to individuals about to become so entitled) such information as will permit such individuals to evaluate the value of medicare supplemental policies to them and the relationship of any such policies to benefits provided under this title [42 USCS §§ 1395 et seq.].

(2) The Secretary shall—

(A) inform all individuals entitled to benefits under this title [42 USCS §§ 1395 et seq.] (and, to the extent feasible, individuals about to become so entitled) of—

(i) the actions and practices that are subject to sanctions under subsection (d), and

(ii) the manner in which they may report any such action or practice to an appropriate official of the Department of Health and Human Services (or to an appropriate State official), and

(B) publish the toll-free telephone number for individuals to report suspected violations of the provisions of such subsection.

(3) The Secretary shall provide individuals entitled to benefits under this title [42 USCS §§ 1395 et seq.] and, to the extent feasible, individuals about to become so entitled) with a listing of the addresses and telephone numbers of State and Federal agencies and offices that provide information and assistance to individuals with respect to the selection of medicare supplemental policies.

(f) Study and evaluation of comparative effectiveness of various State approaches to regulating medicare supplemental policies; report to Congress no later than January 1, 1982; periodic evaluations. (1)(A) The Secretary shall, in consultation with Federal and State regulatory agencies, the National Association of Insurance Commissioners, private insurers, and organizations representing consumers and the aged, conduct a comprehensive study and evaluation of the comparative effectiveness of various State approaches to the regulation of medicare supplemental policies in (i) limiting marketing and agent abuse, (ii) assuring the dissemination of such information to individuals entitled to benefits under this title [42 USCS §§ 1395 et seq.] (and to other consumers) as is necessary to permit informed choice, (iii) promoting policies which provide reasonable economic benefits for such individuals, (iv) reducing the purchase of unnecessary duplicative coverage, (v) improving price competition, and (vi) establishing effective approved State regulatory programs described in subsection (b).

(B) Such study shall also address the need for standards or certification of health insurance policies, other than medicare supplemental policies, sold to individuals eligible for benefits under this title [42 USCS §§ 1395 et seq.].

(C) The Secretary shall, no later than January 1, 1982, submit a report to the Congress on the results of such study and evaluation, accompanied by such recommendations as the Secretary finds warranted by such results with respect to the need for legislative or administrative changes to accomplish the objectives set forth in subparagraphs (A) and (B), including the need for a mandatory Federal regulatory program to assure the marketing of appropriate types of medicare supplemental policies, and such other means as he finds may be appropriate to enhance effective State regulation of such policies.

(2) The Secretary shall submit to the Congress no later than July 1, 1982, and periodically as may be appropriate thereafter (but not less often than once every 2 years), a report evaluating the effectiveness of the certification procedure and the criminal penalties established under this section, and shall include in such reports an analysis of—

(A) the impact of such procedure and penalties on the types, market share, value, and cost to individuals entitled to benefits under this title [42 USCS §§ 1395 et seq.] of medicare supplemental policies which have been certified by the Secretary;

(B) the need for any change in the certification procedure to improve its administration or effectiveness; and

(C) whether the certification program and criminal penalties should be continued.

(3) The Secretary shall provide information via a toll-free telephone number on medicare supplemental policies (including the relationship of State programs under title XIX [42 USCS §§ 1396 et seq.] to such policies).

(g) Definitions. (1) For purposes of this section, a medicare supplemental policy is a health insurance policy or other health benefit plan offered by a private entity to individuals who are entitled to have payment made under this title [42 USCS §§ 1395 et seq.], which provides reimbursement for expenses incurred for services and items for which payment may be made under this title [42 USCS §§ 1395 et seq.] but which are not reimbursable by reason of the applicability of deductibles, coinsurance amounts, or other limitations imposed pursuant to this title [42 USCS §§ 1395 et seq.]; but does not include a prescription drug plan under part D [42 USCS §§ 1395w-101 et seq.] or a Medicare+Choice plan or any such policy or plan of one or more employers or labor organizations, or of the trustees of a fund established by one or more employers or labor organizations (or combination thereof), for employees or former employees (or combination thereof) or for members or former members (or combination thereof) of the labor organizations and does not include a policy or plan of an eligible organization (as defined in section 1876(b) [42 USCS § 1395mm(b)]) if the policy or plan provides benefits pursuant to a contract under section 1876 [42 USCS § 1395mm] or an approved demonstration project described in section 603(c) of the Social Security Amendments of 1983 [unclassified], section 2355 of the Deficit Reduction Act of 1984 [unclassified], or section 9412(b) of the Omnibus Budget Reconciliation Act of 1986 [unclassified], or a policy or plan of an organization if the policy or plan provides benefits pursuant to an agreement under section 1833(a)(1)(A) [42 USCS § 1395l(a)(1)(A)]. For purposes of this section, the term "policy" includes a certificate issued under such policy.

(2) For purposes of this section:

(A) The term "NAIC Model Standards" means the "NAIC Model Regulation to Implement the Individual Accident and Sickness Insurance Minimum Standards Act", adopted by the National Association of Insurance Commissioners on June 6, 1979, as it applies to medicare supplemental policies.

(B) The term "State with an approved regulatory program" means a State for which the Secretary has made a determination under subsection (b)(1).

(C) The State in which a policy is issued means—

(i) in the case of an individual policy, the State in which the policyholder resides; and

(ii) in the case of a group policy, the State in which the holder of the master policy resides.

(h) Rules and regulations. The Secretary shall prescribe such regulations as may be necessary for the effective, efficient, and equitable administration of the certification procedure established under this section. The Secretary shall first issue final regulations to implement the certification procedure established under subsection (a) not later than March 1, 1981.

(i) Commencement of certification program. (1) No medicare supplemental policy shall be certified and no such policy may be issued bearing the emblem authorized by the Secretary under subsection (a) until July 1, 1982. On and after such date policies certified by the Secretary may bear such emblem, including policies which were issued prior to such date and were subsequently certified, and insurers may notify holders of such certified policies issued prior to such date using such emblem in the notification.

(2)(A) The Secretary shall not implement the certification program established under subsection (a) with respect to policies issued in a State unless the Panel makes a finding that such State cannot be expected to have established, by July 1, 1982, an approved State regulatory program meeting the standards and requirements of subsection (b)(1). If the Panel makes such a finding, the Secretary shall implement such program under subsection (a) with respect to medicare supplemental policies issued in such State, until such time as the Panel determines that such State has a program that meets the standards and requirements of subsection (b)(1).

(B) Any finding by the Panel under subparagraph (A) shall be transmitted in writing, not later than January 1, 1982, to the Committee on Finance of the Senate and to the Committee on Interstate and Foreign Commerce [Committee on Energy and Commerce] and the Committee on Ways and Means of the House of Representatives and shall not become effective until 60 days after the date of its transmittal to the Committees of the Congress under this subparagraph. In counting such days, days on which either House is not in session because of an adjournment sine die or an adjournment of more than three days to a day certain are excluded in the computation.

(j) State regulation of policies issued in other States. Nothing in this section shall be construed so as to affect the right of any State to regulate medicare supplemental policies which, under the provisions of this section, are considered to be issued in another State.

(k) Amended NAIC Model Regulation or Federal model standards applicable; effective date; medicare supplemental policy and State regulatory program meeting applicable standards. (1)(A) If, within the 90-day period beginning on the date of the enactment of this subsection [enacted July 1, 1988] the National Association of Insurance Commissioners (in this subsection referred to as the "Association") amends the NAIC Model Regulation adopted on June 6, 1979 (as it relates to medicare supplemental policies), with respect to matters such as minimum benefit standards, loss ratios, disclosure requirements, and replacement requirements and provisions otherwise necessary to reflect the changes in law made by the Medicare Catastrophic Coverage Act of 1988, except as provided in subsection (m), subsection (g)(2)(A) shall be applied in a State, effective on and after the date specified in subparagraph (B), as if the reference to the Model Regulation adopted on June 6, 1979, were a reference to the Model Regulation as amended by the Association in accordance with this paragraph (in this subsection and subsection (l) referred to as the "amended NAIC Model Regulation").

(B) The date specified in this subparagraph for a State is the earlier of the date the State adopts standards equal to or more stringent than the amended NAIC Model Regulation or 1 year after the date the Association first adopts such amended Regulation.

(2)(A) If the Association does not amend the NAIC Model Regulation within the 90-day period specified in paragraph (1)(A), the Secretary shall promulgate, not later than 60 days after the end of such period, Federal model standards (in this subsection and subsection (l) referred to as "Federal model standards") for medicare supplemental policies to reflect the changes in law made by the Medicare Catastrophic Coverage Act of 1988, and subsection (g)(2)(A) shall be applied in a State, effective on and after the date specified in subparagraph (B), as if the reference to the Model Regulation adopted on June 6, 1979, were a reference to Federal model standards.

(B) The date specified in this subparagraph for a State is the earlier of the date the State adopts standards equal to or more stringent than the Federal model standards or 1 year after the date the Secretary first promulgates such standards.

(3) Notwithstanding any other provision of this section (except as provided in subsections (l), (m), and (n))—

(A) no medicare supplemental policy may be certified by the Secretary pursuant to subsection (a),

(B) no certification made pursuant to subsection (a) shall remain in effect, and

(C) no State regulatory program shall be found to meet (or to continue to meet) the requirements of subsection (b)(1)(A),

unless such policy meets (or such program provides for the application of standards equal to or more stringent than) the standards set forth in the amended NAIC Model Regulation or the Federal model standards (as the case may be) by the date specified in paragraph (1)(B) or (2)(B) (as the case may be).

(l) Transitional compliance with NAIC Model Transition Regulation; "qualifying medicare supplement policy" and "NAIC Model Transition Regulation" defined; report to Congress respecting State action in adopting equal or more stringent stan-

dards. (1) Until the date specified in paragraph (3), in the case of a qualifying medicare supplemental policy described in paragraph (2) issued—

(A) before January 1, 1989, the policy is deemed to remain in compliance with this section if the insurer issuing the policy complies with the NAIC Model Transition Regulation (including giving notices to subscribers and filing for premium adjustments with the State as described in section 5.B. of such Regulation) by January 1, 1989; or

(B) on or after January 1, 1989, the policy is deemed to be in compliance with this section if the insurer issuing the policy complies with the NAIC Model Transition Regulation before the date of the sale of the policy.

(2) In paragraph (1), the term "qualifying medicare supplemental policy" means a medicare supplemental policy—

(A) issued in a State which—

(i) has not adopted standards equal to or more stringent than the NAIC Model Transition Regulation by January 1, 1989, and

(ii) has not adopted standards equal to or more stringent than the amended NAIC Model Regulation (or Federal model standards) by January 1, 1989; and

(B) which has been issued in compliance with this section (as in effect on June 1, 1988).

(3)(A) The date specified in this paragraph is the earlier of—

(i) the first date a State adopts, after January 1, 1989, standards equal to or more stringent than the NAIC Model Transition Regulation or equal to or more stringent than the amended NAIC Model Regulation (or Federal model standards), as the case may be, or

(ii) the later of (I) the date specified in subsection (k)(1)(B) or (k)(2)(B) (as the case may be), or (II) the date specified in subparagraph (B).

(B) In the case of a State which the Secretary identifies as—

(i) requiring State legislation (other than legislation appropriating funds) in order for medicare supplemental policies to meet standards described in subparagraph (A)(i), but

(ii) having a legislature which is not scheduled to meet in 1989 in a legislative session in which such legislation may be considered,

the date specified in this subparagraph is the first day of the first calendar quarter beginning after the close of the first legislative session of the State legislature that begins on or after January 1, 1989, and in which legislation described in clause (i) may be considered. For purposes of the previous sentence, in the case of a State that has a 2-year legislative session, each year of such session shall be deemed to be a separate regular session of the State legislature.

(4) In the case of a medicare supplemental policy in effect on January 1, 1989, and offered in a State which, as of such date—

(A) has adopted standards equal to or more stringent than the amended NAIC Model Regulation (or Federal model standards), but

(B) does not have in effect standards equal to or more stringent than the NAIC Model Transition Regulation (or otherwise requiring notice substantially the same as the notice required in section 5.B. of such Regulation),

the policy shall not be deemed to meet the standards in subsection (c) unless each individual who is entitled to benefits under this title [42 USCS §§ 1395 et seq.] and is a policyholder under such policy on January 1, 1989, is sent such a notice in any appropriate form by not later than January 31, 1989, that explains—

(A) the improved benefits under this title [42 USCS §§ 1395 et seq.] contained in the Medicare Catastrophic Coverage Act of 1988, and

(B) how these improvements affect the benefits contained in the policies and the premium for the policy.

(5) In this subsection, the term "NAIC Model Transition Regulation" refers to the standards contained in the "Model Regulation to Implement Transitional Requirements for the Conversion of Medicare Supplement Insurance Benefits and Premiums to Conform to Medicare Program Revisions" (as adopted by the National Association of Insurance Commissioners in September 1987).

(m) Revision of amended NAIC Model Regulation and amended Federal model standards; effective dates; medicare supplemental policy and State regulatory program meeting applicable standards. (1)(A) If, within the 90-day period beginning on the date of the enactment of this subsection [enacted Dec. 13, 1989], the National Association of Insurance Commissioners (in this subsection and subsection (n) referred to as the "Association") revises the amended NAIC Model Regulation (referred to in subsection (k)(1)(A) and adopted on September 20, 1988) to improve such regulation and otherwise to reflect the changes in law made by the Medicare Catastrophic Coverage Repeal Act of 1989, subsection (g)(2)(A) shall be applied in a State, effective on and after the date specified in subparagraph (B), as if the reference to the Model Regulation adopted on June 6, 1979, were a reference to the amended NAIC Model

Regulation (referred to in subsection (k)(1)(A)) as revised by the Association in accordance with this paragraph (in this subsection and subsection (n) referred to as the "revised NAIC Model Regulation").

(B) The date specified in this subparagraph for a State is the earlier of the date the State adopts standards equal to or more stringent than the revised NAIC Model Regulation or 1 year after the date the Association first adopts such revised Regulation.

(2)(A) If the Association does not revise the amended NAIC Model Regulation, within the 90-day period specified in paragraph (1)(A), the Secretary shall promulgate, not later than 60 days after the end of such period, revised Federal model standards (in this subsection and subsection (n) referred to as "revised Federal model standards") for medicare supplemental policies to improve such standards and otherwise to reflect the changes in law made by the Medicare Catastrophic Coverage Repeal Act of 1989, subsection (g)(2)(A) shall be applied in a State, effective on and after the date specified in subparagraph (B), as if the reference to the Model Regulation adopted on June 6, 1979, were a reference to the revised Federal model standards.

(B) The date specified in this subparagraph for a State is the earlier of the date the State adopts standards equal to or more stringent than the revised Federal model standards or 1 year after the date the Secretary first promulgates such standards.

(3) Notwithstanding any other provision of this section (except as provided in subsection (n))—

(A) no medicare supplemental policy may be certified by the Secretary pursuant to subsection (a),

(B) no certification made pursuant to subsection (a) shall remain in effect, and

(C) no State regulatory program shall be found to meet (or to continue to meet) the requirements of subsection (b)(1)(A),

unless such policy meets (or such program provides for the application of standards equal to or more stringent than) the standards set forth in the revised NAIC Model Regulation or the revised Federal model standards (as the case may be) by the date specified in paragraph (1)(B) or (2)(B) (as the case may be).

(n) Transition compliance with revision of NAIC Model Regulation and Federal model standards. (1) Until the date specified in paragraph (4), in the case of a qualifying medicare supplemental policy described in paragraph (3) issued in a State—

(A) before the transition deadline, the policy is deemed to remain in compliance with the standards described in subsection (b)(1)(A) only if the insurer issuing the policy complies with the transition provision described in paragraph (2), or

(B) on or after the transition deadline, the policy is deemed to be in compliance with the standards described in subsection (b)(1)(A) only if the insurer issuing the policy complies with the revised NAIC Model Regulation or the revised Federal model standards (as the case may be) before the date of the sale of the policy.

In this paragraph, the term "transition deadline" means 1 year after the date the Association adopts the revised NAIC Model Regulation or 1 year after the date the Secretary promulgates revised Federal model standards (as the case may be).

(2) The transition provision described in this paragraph is—

(A) such transition provision as the Association provides, by not later than December 15, 1989, so as to provide for an appropriate transition (i) to restore benefit provisions which are no longer duplicative as a result of the changes in benefits under this title [42 USCS §§ 1395 et seq.] made by the Medicare Catastrophic Coverage Repeal Act of 1989 and (ii) to eliminate the requirement of payment for the first 8 days of coinsurance for extended care services, or

(B) if the Association does not provide for a transition provision by the date described in subparagraph (A), such transition provision as the Secretary shall provide, by January 1, 1990, so as to provide for an appropriate transition described in subparagraph (A).

(3) In paragraph (1), the term "qualifying medicare supplemental policy" means a medicare supplemental policy which has been issued in compliance with this section as in effect on the date before the date of the enactment of this subsection [enacted Dec. 13, 1989].

(4)(A) The date specified in this paragraph for a policy issued in a State is—

(i) the first date a State adopts, after the date of the enactment of this subsection, standards equal to or more stringent than the revised NAIC Model Regulation (or revised Federal model standards), as the case may be, or

(ii) the date specified in subparagraph (B), whichever is earlier.

(B) In the case of a State which the Secretary identifies, in consultation with the Association, as—

(i) requiring State legislation (other than legislation appropriating funds) in order for medicare supplemental policies to meet standards described in subparagraph (A)(i), but

(ii) having a legislature which is not scheduled to meet in 1990 in a legislative session in which such legislation may be considered,

the date specified in this subparagraph is the first day of the first calendar quarter beginning after the close of the first legislative session of the State legislature that begins on or after January 1, 1990. For purposes of the previous sentence, in the case of a State that has a 2-year legislative session, each year of such session shall be deemed to be a separate regular session of the State legislature.

(5) In the case of a medicare supplemental policy in effect on January 1, 1990, the policy shall not be deemed to meet the standards in subsection (c) unless each individual who is entitled to benefits under this title [42 USCS §§ 1395 et seq.] and is a policyholder or certificate holder under such policy on such date is sent a notice in an appropriate form by not later than January 31, 1990, that explains—

(A) the changes in benefits under this title [42 USCS §§ 1395 et seq.] effected by the Medicare Catastrophic Coverage Repeal Act of 1989, and

(B) how these changes may affect the benefits contained in such policy and the premium for the policy.

(6)(A) Except as provided in subparagraph (B), in the case of an individual who had in effect, as of December 31, 1988, a medicare supplemental policy with an insurer (as a policyholder or, in the case of a group policy, as a certificate holder) and the individual terminated coverage under such policy before the date of the enactment of this subsection [enacted Dec. 13, 1989], no medicare supplemental policy of the insurer shall be deemed to meet the standards in subsection (c) unless the insurer—

(i) provides written notice, no earlier than December 15, 1989, and no later than January 30, 1990, to the policyholder or certificate holder (at the most recent available address) of the offer described in clause (ii), and

(ii) offers the individual, during a period of at least 60 days beginning not later than February 1, 1990, reinstitution of coverage (with coverage effective as of January 1, 1990), under the terms which (I) do not provide for any waiting period with respect to treatment of pre-existing conditions, (II) provides for coverage which is substantially equivalent to coverage in effect before the date of such termination, and (III) provides for classification of premiums on which terms are at least as favorable to the policyholder or certificate holder as the premium classification terms that would have applied to the policyholder or certificate holder had the coverage never terminated.

(B) An insurer is not required to make the offer under subparagraph (A)(ii) in the case of an individual who is a policyholder or certificate holder in another medicare supplemental policy as of the date of the enactment of this subsection, if (as of January 1, 1990) the individual is not subject to a waiting period with respect to treatment of a pre-existing condition under such other policy.

(o) Requirements of group benefits; core group benefits; uniform outline of coverage. The requirements of this subsection are as follows:

(1) Each medicare supplemental policy shall provide for coverage of a group of benefits consistent with subsections (p), (v)[,] (w), and (y).

(2) If the medicare supplemental policy provides for coverage of a group of benefits other than the core group of basic benefits described in subsection (p)(2)(B), the issuer of the policy must make available to the individual a medicare supplemental policy with only such core group of basic benefits.

(3) The issuer of the policy has provided, before the sale of the policy, an outline of coverage that uses uniform language and format (including layout and print size) that facilitates comparison among medicare supplemental policies and comparison with medicare benefits.

(4) The issuer of the medicare supplemental policy complies with subsection (s)(2)(E) and subsection (x).

(5) In addition to the requirement under paragraph (2), the issuer of the policy must make available to the individual at least Medicare supplemental policies with benefit packages classified as "C" or "F".

(p) Standards for group benefits. (1)(A) If, within 9 months after the date of the enactment of this subsection [enacted Nov. 5, 1990], the National Association of Insurance Commissioners (in this subsection referred to as the "Association") changes the revised NAIC Model Regulation (described in subsection (m)) to incorporate—

(i) limitations on the groups or packages of benefits that may be offered under a medicare supplemental policy consistent with paragraphs (2) and (3) of this subsection,

(ii) uniform language and definitions to be used with respect to such benefits,

(iii) uniform format to be used in the policy

with respect to such benefits, and

(iv) other standards to meet the additional requirements imposed by the amendments made by the Omnibus Budget Reconciliation Act of 1990,

subsection (g)(2)(A) shall be applied in each State, effective for policies issued to policyholders on and after the date specified in subparagraph (C), as if the reference to the Model Regulation adopted on June 6, 1979, were a reference to the revised NAIC Model Regulation as changed under this subparagraph (such changed regulation referred to in this section as the "1991 NAIC Model Regulation").

(B) If the Association does not make the changes in the revised NAIC Model Regulation within the 9-month period specified in subparagraph (A), the Secretary shall promulgate, not later than 9 months after the end of such period, a regulation and subsection (g)(2)(A) shall be applied in each State, effective for policies issued to policyholders on and after the date specified in subparagraph (C), as if the reference to the Model Regulation adopted on June 6, 1979, were a reference to the revised NAIC Model Regulation as changed by the Secretary under this subparagraph (such changed regulation referred to in this section as the "1991 Federal Regulation").

(C)(i) Subject to clause (ii), the date specified in this subparagraph for a State is the date the State adopts the 1991 NAIC Model Regulation or 1991 Federal Regulation or 1 year after the date the Association or the Secretary first adopts such standards, whichever is earlier.

(ii) In the case of a State which the Secretary identifies, in consultation with the Association, as—

(I) requiring State legislation (other than legislation appropriating funds) in order for medicare supplemental policies to meet the 1991 NAIC Model Regulation or 1991 Federal Regulation, but

(II) having a legislature which is not scheduled to meet in 1992 in a legislative session in which such legislation may be considered,

the date specified in this subparagraph is the first day of the first calendar quarter beginning after the close of the first legislative session of the State legislature that begins on or after January 1, 1992. For purposes of the previous sentence, in the case of a State that has a 2-year legislative session, each year of such session shall be deemed to be a separate regular session of the State legislature.

(D) In promulgating standards under this paragraph, the Association or Secretary shall consult with a working group composed of representatives of issuers of medicare supplemental policies, consumer groups, medicare beneficiaries, and other qualified individuals. Such representatives shall be selected in a manner so as to assure balanced representation among the interested groups.

(E) If benefits (including deductibles and coinsurance) under this title [42 USCS §§ 1395 et seq.] are changed and the Secretary determines, in consultation with the Association, that changes in the 1991 NAIC Model Regulation or 1991 Federal Regulation are needed to reflect such changes, the preceding provisions of this paragraph shall apply to the modification of standards previously established in the same manner as they applied to the original establishment of such standards.

(2) The benefits under the 1991 NAIC Model Regulation or 1991 Federal Regulation shall provide—

(A) for such groups or packages of benefits as may be appropriate taking into account the considerations specified in paragraph (3) and the requirements of the succeeding subparagraphs;

(B) for identification of a core group of basic benefits common to all policies; and

(C) that, subject to paragraph (4)(B), the total number of different benefit packages (counting the core group of basic benefits described in subparagraph (B) and each other combination of benefits that may be offered as a separate benefit package) that may be established in all the States and by all issuers shall not exceed 10 plus the 2 plans described in paragraph (11)(A).

(3) The benefits under paragraph (2) shall, to the extent possible—

(A) provide for benefits that offer consumers the ability to purchase the benefits that are available in the market as of the date of the enactment of this subsection; and

(B) balance the objectives of (i) simplifying the market to facilitate comparisons among policies, (ii) avoiding adverse selection, (iii) providing consumer choice, (iv) providing market stability, and (v) promoting competition.

(4)(A)(i) Except as provided in subparagraph (B) or paragraph (6), no State with a regulatory program approved under subsection (b)(1) may provide for or permit the grouping of benefits (or language or format with respect to such benefits) under a medicare supplemental policy unless such grouping meets the applicable 1991 NAIC Model Regulation or 1991 Federal Regulation.

(ii) Except as provided in subparagraph (B), the Secretary may not provide for or permit the grouping of benefits (or language or format with respect to such benefits) under a medicare supplemental policy seeking approval by the Secretary unless such grouping meets the applicable 1991 NAIC Model Regulation or 1991 Federal Regulation.

(B) With the approval of the State (in the case of a policy issued in a State with an approved regulatory program) or the Secretary (in the case of any other policy), the issuer of a medicare supplemental policy may offer new or innovative benefits in addition to the benefits provided in a policy that otherwise complies with the applicable 1991 NAIC Model Regulation or 1991 Federal Regulation. Any such new or innovative benefits may include benefits that are not otherwise available and are cost-effective and shall be offered in a manner which is consistent with the goal of simplification of medicare supplemental policies.

(5)(A) Except as provided in subparagraph (B), this subsection shall not be construed as preventing a State from restricting the groups of benefits that may be offered in medicare supplemental policies in the State.

(B) A State with a regulatory program approved under subsection (b)(1) may not restrict under subparagraph (A) the offering of a medicare supplemental policy consisting only of the core group of benefits described in paragraph (2)(B).

(6) The Secretary may waive the application of standards described in clauses (i) through (iii) of paragraph (1)(A) in those States that on the date of enactment of this subsection had in place an alternative simplification program.

(7) This subsection shall not be construed as preventing an issuer of a medicare supplemental policy who otherwise meets the requirements of this section from providing, through an arrangement with a vendor, for discounts from that vendor to policyholders or certificateholders for the purchase of items or services not covered under its medicare supplemental policies.

(8) Any person who sells or issues a medicare supplemental policy, on and after the effective date specified in paragraph (1)(C) (but subject to paragraph (10)), in violation of the applicable 1991 NAIC Model Regulation or 1991 Federal Regulation insofar as such regulation relates to the requirements of subsection (o) or (q) or clause (i), (ii), or (iii) of paragraph (1)(A) is subject to a civil money penalty of not to exceed $25,000 (or $15,000 in the case of a seller who is not an issuer of a policy) for each such violation. The provisions of section 1128A [42 USCS § 1320a-7a] (other than the first sentence of subsection (a) and other than subsection (b)) shall apply to a civil money penalty under the previous sentence in the same manner as such provisions apply to a penalty or proceeding under section 1128A(a) [42 USCS § 1320a-7a(a)].

(9)(A) Anyone who sells a medicare supplemental policy to an individual shall make available for sale to the individual a medicare supplemental policy with only the core group of basic benefits (described in paragraph (2)(B)).

(B) Anyone who sells a medicare supplemental policy to an individual shall provide the individual, before the sale of the policy, an outline of coverage which describes the benefits under the policy. Such outline shall be on a standard form approved by the State regulatory program or the Secretary (as the case may be) consistent with the 1991 NAIC Model Regulation or 1991 Federal Regulation under this subsection.

(C) Whoever sells a medicare supplemental policy in violation of this paragraph is subject to a civil money penalty of not to exceed $25,000 (or $15,000 in the case of a seller who is not the issuer of the policy) for each such violation. The provisions of section 1128A [42 USCS § 1320a-7a] (other than the first sentence of subsection (a) and other than subsection (b)) shall apply to a civil money penalty under the previous sentence in the same manner as such provisions apply to a penalty or proceeding under section 1128A(a) [42 USCS § 1320a-7a(a)].

(D) Subject to paragraph (10), this paragraph shall apply to sales of policies occurring on or after the effective date specified in paragraph (1)(C).

(10) No penalty may be imposed under paragraph (8) or (9) in the case of a seller who is not the issuer of a policy until the Secretary has published a list of the groups of benefit packages that may be sold or issued consistent with paragraph (1)(A)(i).

(11)(A) For purposes of paragraph (2), the benefit packages described in this subparagraph are as follows:

(i) The benefit package classified as "F" under the standards established by such paragraph, except that it has a high deductible feature.

(ii) The benefit package classified as "J" under the standards established by such paragraph, except that it has a high deductible feature.

(B) For purposes of subparagraph (A), a high deductible feature is one which—

(i) requires the beneficiary of the policy to

pay annual out-of-pocket expenses (other than premiums) in the amount specified in subparagraph (C) before the policy begins payment of benefits, and

(ii) covers 100 percent of covered out-of-pocket expenses once such deductible has been satisfied in a year.

(C) The amount specified in this subparagraph—

(i) for 1998 and 1999 is $1,500, and

(ii) for a subsequent year, is the amount specified in this subparagraph for the previous year increased by the percentage increase in the Consumer Price Index for all urban consumers (all items; U.S. city average) for the 12-month period ending with August of the preceding year. If any amount determined under clause (ii) is not a multiple of $10, it shall be rounded to the nearest multiple of $10.

(q) Requirements. The requirements of this subsection are as follows:

(1) Each medicare supplemental policy shall be guaranteed renewable and—

(A) the issuer may not cancel or nonrenew the policy solely on the ground of health status of the individual; and

(B) the issuer shall not cancel or nonrenew the policy for any reason other than nonpayment of premium or material misrepresentation.

(2) If the medicare supplemental policy is terminated by the group policyholder and is not replaced as provided under paragraph (4), the issuer shall offer certificateholders an individual medicare supplemental policy which (at the option of the certificateholder)—

(A) provides for continuation of the benefits contained in the group policy, or

(B) provides for such benefits as otherwise meets [meet] the requirements of this section.

(3) If an individual is a certificateholder in a group medicare supplemental policy and the individual terminates membership in the group, the issuer shall—

(A) offer the certificateholder the conversion opportunity described in paragraph (2), or

(B) at the option of the group policyholder, offer the certificateholder continuation of coverage under the group policy.

(4) If a group medicare supplemental policy is replaced by another group medicare supplemental policy purchased by the same policyholder, [the] issuer of the replacement policy shall offer coverage to all persons covered under the old group policy on its date of termination. Coverage under the new group policy shall not result in any exclusion for preexisting conditions that would have been covered under the group policy being replaced.

(5)(A) Each medicare supplemental policy shall provide that benefits and premiums under the policy shall be suspended at the request of the policyholder for the period (not to exceed 24 months) in which the policyholder has applied for and is determined to be entitled to medical assistance under title XIX [42 USCS §§ 1396 et seq.], but only if the policyholder notifies the issuer of such policy within 90 days after the date the individual becomes entitled to such assistance. If such suspension occurs and if the policyholder or certificate holder loses entitlement to such medical assistance, such policy shall be automatically reinstituted (effective as of the date of termination of such entitlement) under terms described in subsection (n)(6)(A)(ii) as of the termination of such entitlement if the policyholder provides notice of loss of such entitlement within 90 days after the date of such loss.

(B) Nothing in this section shall be construed as affecting the authority of a State, under title XIX [42 USCS §§ 1396 et seq.], to purchase a medicare supplemental policy for an individual otherwise entitled to assistance under such title.

(C) Any person who issues a medicare supplemental policy and fails to comply with the requirements of this paragraph or paragraph (6) is subject to a civil money penalty of not to exceed $25,000 for each such violation. The provisions of section 1128A [42 USCS § 1320a-7a] (other than the first sentence of subsection (a) and other than subsection (b)) shall apply to a civil money penalty under the previous sentence in the same manner as such provisions apply to a penalty or proceeding under section 1128A(a) [42 USCS § 1320a-7a(a)].

(6) Each medicare supplemental policy shall provide that benefits and premiums under the policy shall be suspended at the request of the policyholder if the policyholder is entitled to benefits under section 226(b) [42 USCS § 426(b)] and is covered under a group health plan (as defined in section 1862(b)(1)(A)(v) [42 USCS § 1395y(b)(1)(A)(v)]). If such suspension occurs and if the policyholder or certificate holder loses coverage under the group health plan, such policy shall be automatically reinstituted (effective as of the date of such loss of coverage) under terms described in subsection (n)(6)(A)(ii) as of the loss of such coverage if the policyholder provides notice of loss of such coverage within 90 days after the date of such loss.

(r) Loss ratio of aggregate benefits to

aggregate premiums. (1) A medicare supplemental policy may not be issued or renewed (or otherwise provide coverage after the date described in subsection (p)(1)(C)) in any State unless—

(A) the policy can be expected for periods after the effective date of these provisions (as estimated for the entire period for which rates are computed to provide coverage, on the basis of incurred claims experience and earned premiums for such periods and in accordance with a uniform methodology, including uniform reporting standards, developed by the National Association of Insurance Commissioners) to return to policyholders in the form of aggregate benefits provided under the policy, at least 75 percent of the aggregate amount of premiums collected in the case of group policies and at least 65 percent in the case of individual policies; and

(B) the issuer of the policy provides for the issuance of a proportional refund, or a credit against future premiums of a proportional amount, based on the premium paid and in accordance with paragraph (2), of the amount of premiums received necessary to assure that the ratio of aggregate benefits provided to the aggregate premiums collected (net of such refunds or credits) complies with the expectation required under subparagraph (A), treating policies of the same type as a single policy for each standard package.

For purposes of applying subparagraph (A) only, policies issued as a result of solicitations of individuals through the mails or by mass media advertising (including both print and broadcast advertising) shall be deemed to be individual policies. For the purpose of calculating the refund or credit required under paragraph (1)(B) for a policy issued before the date specified in subsection (p)(1)(C), the refund or credit calculation shall be based on the aggregate benefits provided and premiums collected under all such policies issued by an insurer in a State (separated as to individual and group policies) and shall be based only on aggregate benefits provided and premiums collected under such policies after the date specified in section 171(m)(4) of the Social Security Act Amendments of 1994 [note to this section].

(2)(A) Paragraph (1)(B) shall be applied with respect to each type of policy by standard package. Paragraph (1)(B) shall not apply to a policy until 12 months following issue. The Comptroller General, in consultation with the National Association of Insurance Commissioners, shall submit to Congress a report containing recommendations on adjustments in the percentages under paragraph (1)(A) that may be appropriate. In the case of a policy issued before the date specified in subsection (p)(1)(C), paragraph (1)(B) shall not apply until 1 year after the date specified in section 171(m)(4) of the Social Security Act Amendments of 1994 [note to this section].

(B) A refund or credit required under paragraph (1)(B) shall be made to each policyholder insured under the applicable policy as of the last day of the year involved.

(C) Such a refund or credit shall include interest from the end of the calendar year involved until the date of the refund or credit at a rate as specified by the Secretary for this purpose from time to time which is not less than the average rate of interest for 13-week Treasury notes.

(D) For purposes of this paragraph and paragraph (1)(B), refunds or credits against premiums due shall be made, with respect to a calendar year, not later than the third quarter of the succeeding calendar year.

(3) The provisions of this subsection do not preempt a State from requiring a higher percentage than that specified in paragraph (1)(A).

(4) The Secretary shall submit in October of each year (beginning with 1993) a report to the Committees on Energy and Commerce and Ways and Means of the House of Representatives and the Committee on Finance of the Senate on loss ratios under medicare supplemental policies and the use of sanctions, such as a required rebate or credit or the disallowance of premium increases, for policies that fail to meet the requirements of this subsection (relating to loss ratios). Such report shall include a list of the policies that failed to comply with such loss ratio requirements or other requirements of this section.

(5) The Secretary may perform audits with respect to the compliance of medicare supplemental policies with the loss ratio requirements of this subsection and shall report the results of such audits to the State involved and to the Secretary.

(6)(A) A person who fails to provide refunds or credits as required in paragraph (1)(B) is subject to a civil money penalty of not to exceed $25,000 for each policy issued for which such failure occurred. The provisions of section 1128A [42 USCS § 1320a-7a] (other than the first sentence of subsection (a) and other than subsection (b)) shall apply to a civil money penalty under the previous sentence in the same manner as such provisions apply to a penalty or proceeding under section 1128A(a) [42 USCS § 1320a-7a(a)].

(B) Each issuer of a policy subject to the requirements of paragraph (1)(B) shall be liable to the policyholder or, in the case of a group policy, to the certificate holder for credits required under such paragraph.

(s) Coverage for pre-existing conditions. (1) If a medicare supplemental policy replaces another medicare supplemental policy, the issuer of the replacing policy shall waive any time periods applicable to preexisting conditions, waiting period, elimination periods and probationary periods in the new medicare supplemental policy for similar benefits to the extent such time was spent under the original policy.

(2)(A) The issuer of a medicare supplemental policy may not deny or condition the issuance or effectiveness of a medicare supplemental policy, or discriminate in, the pricing of the policy, because of health status, claims experience, receipt of health care, or medical condition in the case of an individual for whom an application is submitted prior to or during the 6 month period beginning with the first month as of the first day on which the individual is 65 years of age or older and is enrolled for benefits under part B [42 USCS §§ 1395j et seq.].

(B) Subject to subparagraphs (C) and (D), subparagraph (A) shall not be construed as preventing the exclusion of benefits under a policy, during its first 6 months, based on a pre-existing condition for which the policyholder received treatment or was otherwise diagnosed during the 6 months before the policy became effective.

(C) If a medicare supplemental policy or certificate replaces another such policy or certificate which has been in effect for 6 months or longer, the replacing policy may not provide any time period applicable to pre-existing conditions, waiting periods, elimination periods, and probationary periods in the new policy or certificate for similar benefits.

(D) In the case of a policy issued during the 6-month period described in subparagraph (A) to an individual who is 65 years of age or older as of the date of issuance and who as of the date of the application for enrollment has a continuous period of creditable coverage (as defined in section 2701(c) of the Public Health Service Act [42 USCS § 300gg]) of—

(i) at least 6 months, the policy may not exclude benefits based on a pre-existing condition; or

(ii) less than 6 months, if the policy excludes benefits based on a preexisting condition, the policy shall reduce the period of any preexisting condition exclusion by the aggregate of the periods of creditable coverage (if any, as so defined) applicable to the individual as of the enrollment date.

The Secretary shall specify the manner of the reduction under clause (ii), based upon the rules used by the Secretary in carrying out section 2701(a)(3) of such Act [42 USCS § 300gg(a)(3)].

(E) An issuer of a medicare supplemental policy shall not deny or condition the issuance or effectiveness of the policy (including the imposition of any exclusion of benefits under the policy based on a pre-existing condition) and shall not discriminate in the pricing of the policy (including the adjustment of premium rates) of an individual on the basis of the genetic information with respect to such individual.

(F) Rule of construction. Nothing in subparagraph (E) or in subparagraphs (A) or (B) of subsection (x)(2) shall be construed to limit the ability of an issuer of a medicare supplemental policy from, to the extent otherwise permitted under this title

(i) denying or conditioning the issuance or effectiveness of the policy or increasing the premium for an employer based on the manifestation of a disease or disorder of an individual who is covered under the policy; or

(ii) increasing the premium for any policy issued to an individual based on the manifestation of a disease or disorder of an individual who is covered under the policy (in such case, the manifestation of a disease or disorder in one individual cannot also be used as genetic information about other group members and to further increase the premium for the employer).

(3)(A) The issuer of a medicare supplemental policy—

(i) may not deny or condition the issuance or effectiveness of a medicare supplemental policy described in subparagraph (C) that is offered and is available for issuance to new enrollees by such issuer;

(ii) may not discriminate in the pricing of such policy, because of health status, claims experience, receipt of health care, or medical condition; and

(iii) may not impose an exclusion of benefits based on a preexisting condition under such policy,

in the case of an individual described in subparagraph (B) who seeks to enroll under the policy during the period specified in subparagraph (E) and who submits evidence of the date of termination or disenrollment along with the application for such medicare supplemental policy.

(B) An individual described in this subparagraph is an individual described in any of the following clauses:

(i) The individual is enrolled under an employee welfare benefit plan that provides health benefits that supplement the benefits under this title [42 USCS §§ 1395 et seq.] and the plan terminates or ceases to provide all such supplemental health benefits to the individual.

(ii) The individual is enrolled with a Medicare+Choice organization under a Medicare+Choice plan under part C [42 USCS §§ 1395w-21 et seq.], and there are circumstances permitting discontinuance of the individual's election of the plan under the first sentence of section 1851(e)(4) [42 USCS § 1395w-21(e)(4)] or the individual is 65 years of age or older and is enrolled with a PACE provider under section 1894 [42 USCS § 1395eee], and there are circumstances that would permit the discontinuance of the individual's enrollment with such provider under circumstances that are similar to the circumstances that would permit discontinuance of the individual's election under the first sentence of such section if such individual were enrolled in a Medicare+Choice plan.

(iii) The individual is enrolled with an eligible organization under a contract under section 1876 [42 USCS § 1395mm], a similar organization operating under demonstration project authority, effective for periods before April 1, 1999, with an organization under an agreement under section 1833(a)(1)(A) [42 USCS § 1395l(a)(1)(A)], or with an organization under a policy described in subsection (t), and such enrollment ceases under the same circumstances that would permit discontinuance of an individual's election of coverage under the first sentence of section 1851(e)(4) [42 USCS § 1395w-21(e)(4)] and, in the case of a policy described in subsection (t), there is no provision under applicable State law for the continuation or conversion of coverage under such policy.

(iv) The individual is enrolled under a medicare supplemental policy under this section and such enrollment ceases because—

(I) of the bankruptcy or insolvency of the issuer or because of other involuntary termination of coverage or enrollment under such policy and there is no provision under applicable State law for the continuation or conversion of such coverage;

(II) the issuer of the policy substantially violated a material provision of the policy; or

(III) the issuer (or an agent or other entity acting on the issuer's behalf) materially misrepresented the policy's provisions in marketing the policy to the individual.

(v) The individual—

(I) was enrolled under a medicare supplemental policy under this section,

(II) subsequently terminates such enrollment and enrolls, for the first time, with any Medicare+Choice organization under a Medicare+Choice plan under part C [42 USCS §§ 1395w-21 et seq.], any eligible organization under a contract under section 1876 [42 USCS § 1395mm], any similar organization operating under demonstration project authority, any PACE provider under section 1894 [42 USCS § 1395eee], or any policy described in subsection (t), and

(III) the subsequent enrollment under subclause (II) is terminated by the enrollee during any period within the first 12 months of such enrollment (during which the enrollee is permitted to terminate such subsequent enrollment under section 1851(e) [42 USCS § 1395w-21(e)]).

(vi) The individual, upon first becoming eligible for benefits under part A [42 USCS §§ 1395c et seq.] at age 65, enrolls in a Medicare+Choice plan under part C [42 USCS §§ 1395w-21 et seq.] or in a PACE program under section 1894 [42 USCS § 1395eee], and disenrolls from such plan or such program by not later than 12 months after the effective date of such enrollment.

(C) (i) Subject to clauses (ii) and (iii), a medicare supplemental policy described in this subparagraph is a medicare supplemental policy which has a benefit package classified as "A", "B", "C", or "F" under the standards established under subsection (p)(2).

(ii)(I) Subject to subclause (II), only for purposes of an individual described in subparagraph (B)(v), a medicare supplemental policy described in this subparagraph is the same medicare supplemental policy referred to in such subparagraph in which the individual was most recently previously enrolled, if available from the same issuer, or, if not so available, a policy described in clause (i).

(II) If the medicare supplemental policy referred to in subparagraph (B)(v) was a medigap Rx policy (as defined in subsection (v)(6)(A)), a medicare supplemental policy described in this subparagraph is such policy in which the individual was most recently enrolled as modified under subsection (v)(2)(C)(i) or, at the election of the individual, a policy referred to in subsection (v)(3)(A)(i).

(iii) Only for purposes of an individual described in subparagraph (B)(vi) and subject to subsection (v)(1), a medicare supplemental policy described in this subparagraph shall include any medicare supplemental policy.

(iv) For purposes of applying this paragraph in the case of a State that provides for offering of benefit packages other than under the classification referred to in clause (i), the references to benefit packages in such clause are deemed references to comparable benefit packages offered in such State.

(D) At the time of an event described in subparagraph (B) because of which an individual ceases enrollment or loses coverage or benefits under a contract or agreement, policy, or plan, the organization that offers the contract or agreement, the insurer offering the policy, or the administrator of the plan, respectively, shall notify the individual of the rights of the individual under this paragraph, and obligations of issuers of medicare supplemental policies, under subparagraph (A).

(E) For purposes of subparagraph (A), the time period specified in this subparagraph is—

(i) in the case of an individual described in subparagraph (B)(i), the period beginning on the date the individual receives a notice of termination or cessation of all supplemental health benefits (or, if no such notice is received, notice that a claim has been denied because of such a termination or cessation) and ending on the date that is 63 days after the applicable notice;

(ii) in the case of an individual described in clause (ii), (iii), (v), or (vi) of subparagraph (B) whose enrollment is terminated involuntarily, the period beginning on the date that the individual receives a notice of termination and ending on the date that is 63 days after the date the applicable coverage is terminated;

(iii) in the case of an individual described in subparagraph (B)(iv)(I), the period beginning on the earlier of (I) the date that the individual receives a notice of termination, a notice of the issuer's bankruptcy or insolvency, or other such similar notice, if any, and (II) the date that the applicable coverage is terminated, and ending on the date that is 63 days after the date the coverage is terminated;

(iv) in the case of an individual described in clause (ii), (iii), (iv)(II), (iv)(III), (v), or (vi) of subparagraph (B) who disenrolls voluntarily, the period beginning on the date that is 60 days before the effective date of the disenrollment and ending on the date that is 63 days after such effective date; and

(v) in the case of an individual described in subparagraph (B) but not described in the preceding provisions of this subparagraph, the period beginning on the effective date of the disenrollment and ending on the date that is 63 days after such effective date.

(F)(i) Subject to clause (ii), for purposes of this paragraph—

(I) in the case of an individual described in subparagraph (B)(v) (or deemed to be so described, pursuant to this subparagraph) whose enrollment with an organization or provider described in subclause (II) of such subparagraph is involuntarily terminated within the first 12 months of such enrollment, and who, without an intervening enrollment, enrolls with another such organization or provider, such subsequent enrollment shall be deemed to be an initial enrollment described in such subparagraph; and

(II) in the case of an individual described in clause (vi) of subparagraph (B) (or deemed to be so described, pursuant to this subparagraph) whose enrollment with a plan or in a program described in such clause is involuntarily terminated within the first 12 months of such enrollment, and who, without an intervening enrollment, enrolls in another such plan or program, such subsequent enrollment shall be deemed to be an initial enrollment described in such clause.

(ii) For purposes of clauses (v) and (vi) of subparagraph (B), no enrollment of an individual with an organization or provider described in clause (v)(II), or with a plan or in a program described in clause (vi), may be deemed to be an initial enrollment under this clause after the 2-year period beginning on the date on which the individual first enrolled with such an organization, provider, plan, or program.

(4) Any issuer of a medicare supplemental policy that fails to meet the requirements of this subsection is subject to a civil money penalty of not to exceed $5,000 for each such failure. The provisions of section 1128A [42 USCS § 1320a-7a] (other than the first sentence of subsection (a) and other than subsection (b)) shall apply to a civil money penalty under the previous sentence in the same manner as such provisions apply to a penalty or proceeding under section 1128A(a) [42 USCS § 1320a-7a(a)].

(t) Medicare select policies [Caution: For application and termination of this subsection, see § 4358(c) of Act Nov. 5, 1990, P. L. 101-508, which appears as a note to this section.]. (1) If a medicare supplemental policy meets the 1991 NAIC Model Regulation or 1991 Federal Regulation and otherwise complies with the requirements of this section except that benefits under the policy are restricted to items and services furnished by certain entities (or reduced benefits are provided when items or services are furnished by other entities), the policy shall nevertheless be treated as meeting those standards if—

(A) full benefits are provided for items and services furnished through a network of entities which have entered into contracts or agreements with the issuer of the policy;

(B) full benefits are provided for items and services furnished by other entities if the services are medically necessary and immediately required because of an unforeseen illness, injury, or condition and it is not reasonable given the circumstances to obtain the services through the network;

(C) the network offers sufficient access;

(D) the issuer of the policy has arrangements for an ongoing quality assurance program for items and services furnished through the network;

(E)(i) the issuer of the policy provides to each enrollee at the time of enrollment an explanation of (I) the restrictions on payment under the policy for services furnished other than by or through the network, (II) out of area coverage under the policy, (III) the policy's coverage of emergency services and urgently needed care, and (IV) the availability of a policy through the entity that meets the standards in the 1991 NAIC Model Regulation or 1991 Federal Regulation without reference to this subsection and the premium charged for such policy, and

(ii) each enrollee prior to enrollment acknowledges receipt of the explanation provided under clause (i); and

(F) the issuer of the policy makes available to individuals, in addition to the policy described in this subsection, any policy (otherwise offered by the issuer to individuals in the State) that meets the standards in the 1991 NAIC Model Regulation or 1991 Federal Regulation and other requirements of this section without reference to this subsection.

(2) If the Secretary determines that an issuer of a policy approved under paragraph (1)—

(A) fails substantially to provide medically necessary items and services to enrollees seeking such items and services through the issuer's network, if the failure has adversely affected (or has substantial likelihood of adversely affecting) the individual,

(B) imposes premiums on enrollees in excess of the premiums approved by the State,

(C) acts to expel an enrollee for reasons other than nonpayment of premiums, or

(D) does not provide the explanation required under paragraph (1)(E)(i) or does not obtain the acknowledgment required under paragraph (1)(E)(ii),

the issuer is subject to a civil money penalty in an amount not to exceed $25,000 for each such violation. The provisions of section 1128A [42 USCS § 1320a-7a] (other than the first sentence of subsection (a) and other than subsection (b)) shall apply to a civil money penalty under the previous sentence in the same manner as such provisions apply to a penalty or proceeding under section 1128A(a) [42 USCS § 1320a-7a(a)].

(3) The Secretary may enter into a contract with an entity whose policy has been certified under paragraph (1) or has been approved by a State under subsection (b)(1)(H) to determine whether items and services (furnished to individuals entitled to benefits under this title [42 USCS §§ 1395 et seq.] and under that policy) are not allowable under section 1862(a)(1) [42 USCS § 1395y(a)(1)]. Payments to the entity shall be in such amounts as the Secretary may determine, taking into account estimated savings under contracts with carriers and fiscal intermediaries and other factors that the Secretary finds appropriate. Paragraph (1), the first sentence of paragraph (2)(A), paragraph (2)(B), paragraph (3)(C), paragraph (3)(D), and paragraph (3)(E) of section 1842(b) [42 USCS § 1395u(b)] shall apply to the entity.

(u) Additional rules relating to MSA plans and private fee-for-service plans. (1) It is unlawful for a person to sell or issue a policy described in paragraph (2) to an individual with knowledge that the individual has in effect under section 1851 [42 USCS § 1395w-21] an election of an MSA plan or a Medicare+Choice private fee-for-service plan.

(2)(A) A policy described in this subparagraph is a health insurance policy (other than a policy described in subparagraph (B)) that provides for coverage of expenses that are otherwise required to be counted toward meeting the annual deductible amount provided under the MSA plan.

(B) A policy described in this subparagraph is any of the following:

(i) A policy that provides coverage (whether through insurance or otherwise) for accidents, disability, dental care, vision care, or long-term care.

(ii) A policy of insurance to which substantially all of the coverage relates to—

(I) liabilities incurred under workers' compensation laws,

(II) tort liabilities,

(III) liabilities relating to ownership or use of property, or

(IV) such other similar liabilities as the Secretary may specify by regulations.

(iii) A policy of insurance that provides coverage for a specified disease or illness.

(iv) A policy of insurance that pays a fixed amount per day (or other period) of hospitalization.

(v) Rules relating to medigap policies that provide prescription drug coverage. (1) Prohibition on sale, issuance, and renewal of new policies that provide prescription drug coverage. (A) In general. Notwithstanding any other provision of law, on or after January 1, 2006, a medigap Rx policy (as defined in paragraph (6)(A)) may not be sold, issued, or renewed under this section—

(i) to an individual who is a part D enrollee (as defined in paragraph (6)(B)); or

(ii) except as provided in subparagraph (B), to an individual who is not a part D enrollee.

(B) Continuation permitted for non-part D enrollees. Subparagraph (A)(ii) shall not apply to the renewal of a medigap Rx policy that was issued before January 1, 2006.

(C) Construction. Nothing in this subsection shall be construed as preventing the offering on and after January 1, 2006, of "H", "I", and "J" policies described in paragraph (2)(D)(i) if the benefit packages are modified in accordance with paragraph (2)(C).

(2) Elimination of duplicative coverage upon part D enrollment. (A) In general. In the case of an individual who is covered under a medigap Rx policy and enrolls under a part D plan—

(i) before the end of the initial part D enrollment period, the individual may—

(I) enroll in a medicare supplemental policy without prescription drug coverage under paragraph (3); or

(II) continue the policy in effect subject to the modification described in subparagraph (C)(i); or

(ii) after the end of such period, the individual may continue the policy in effect subject to such modification.

(B) Notice required to be provided to current policyholders with medigap Rx policy. No medicare supplemental policy of an issuer shall be deemed to meet the standards in subsection (c) unless the issuer provides written notice (in accordance with standards of the Secretary established in consultation with the National Association of Insurance Commissioners) during the 60-day period immediately preceding the initial part D enrollment period, to each individual who is a policyholder or certificate holder of a medigap Rx policy (at the most recent available address of that individual) of the following:

(i) If the individual enrolls in a plan under part D [42 USCS §§ 1395w-101 et seq.] during the initial enrollment period under section 1860D-1(b)(2)(A) [42 USCS § 1395w-101(b)(2)(A)], the individual has the option of—

(I) continuing enrollment in the individual's current plan, but the plan's coverage of prescription drugs will be modified under subparagraph (C)(i); or

(II) enrolling in another medicare supplemental policy pursuant to paragraph (3).

(ii) If the individual does not enroll in a plan under part D [42 USCS §§ 1395w-101 et seq.] during such period, the individual may continue enrollment in the individual's current plan without change, but—

(I) the individual will not be guaranteed the option of enrollment in another medicare supplemental policy pursuant to paragraph (3); and

(II) if the current plan does not provide creditable prescription drug coverage (as defined in section 1860D-13(b)(4) [42 USCS § 1395w-113(b)(4)]), notice of such fact and that there are limitations on the periods in a year in which the individual may enroll under a part D plan and any such enrollment is subject to a late enrollment penalty.

(iii) Such other information as the Secretary may specify (in consultation with the National Association of Insurance Commissioners), including the potential impact of such election on premiums for medicare supplemental policies.

(C) Modification. (i) In general. The policy modification described in this subparagraph is the elimination of prescription coverage for expenses of prescription drugs incurred after the effective date of the individual's coverage under a part D plan and the appropriate adjustment of premiums to reflect such elimination of coverage.

(ii) Continuation of renewability and application of modification. No medicare supplemental policy of an issuer shall be deemed to meet the standards in subsection (c) unless the issuer—

(I) continues renewability of medigap Rx policies that it has issued, subject to subclause (II); and

(II) applies the policy modification described in clause (i) in the cases described in clauses (i)(II) and (ii) of subparagraph (A).

(D) References to Rx policies. (i) H, I, and J

policies. Any reference to a benefit package classified as "H", "I", or "J" (including the benefit package classified as "J" with a high deductible feature, as described in subsection (p)(11)) under the standards established under subsection (p)(2) shall be construed as including a reference to such a package as modified under subparagraph (C) and such packages as modified shall not be counted as a separate benefit package under such subsection.

(ii) Application in waivered States. Except for the modification provided under subparagraph (C), the waivers previously in effect under subsection (p)(2) shall continue in effect.

(3) Availability of substitute policies with guaranteed issue. (A) In general. The issuer of a medicare supplemental policy—

(i) may not deny or condition the issuance or effectiveness of a medicare supplemental policy that has a benefit package classified as "A", "B", "C", or "F" (including the benefit package classified as "F" with a high deductible feature, as described in subsection (p)(11)), under the standards established under subsection (p)(2), or a benefit package described in subparagraph (A) or (B) of subsection (w)(2) and that is offered and is available for issuance to new enrollees by such issuer;

(ii) may not discriminate in the pricing of such policy, because of health status, claims experience, receipt of health care, or medical condition; and

(iii) may not impose an exclusion of benefits based on a pre-existing condition under such policy,

in the case of an individual described in subparagraph (B) who seeks to enroll under the policy not later than 63 days after the effective date of the individual's coverage under a part D plan.

(B) Individual covered. An individual described in this subparagraph with respect to the issuer of a medicare supplemental policy is an individual who—

(i) enrolls in a part D plan during the initial part D enrollment period;

(ii) at the time of such enrollment was enrolled in a medigap Rx policy issued by such issuer; and

(iii) terminates enrollment in such policy and submits evidence of such termination along with the application for the policy under subparagraph (A).

(C) Special rule for waivered States. For purposes of applying this paragraph in the case of a State that provides for offering of benefit packages other than under the classification referred to in subparagraph (A)(i), the references to benefit packages in such subparagraph are deemed references to comparable benefit packages offered in such State.

(4) Enforcement. (A) Penalties for duplication. The penalties described in subsection (d)(3)(A)(ii) shall apply with respect to a violation of paragraph (1)(A).

(B) Guaranteed issue. The provisions of paragraph (4) of subsection (s) shall apply with respect to the requirements of paragraph (3) in the same manner as they apply to the requirements of such subsection.

(5) Construction. Any provision in this section or in a medicare supplemental policy relating to guaranteed renewability of coverage shall be deemed to have been met with respect to a part D enrollee through the continuation of the policy subject to modification under paragraph (2)(C) or the offering of a substitute policy under paragraph (3). The previous sentence shall not be construed to affect the guaranteed renewability of such a modified or substitute policy.

(6) Definitions. For purposes of this subsection:

(A) Medigap Rx policy. The term "medigap Rx policy" means a medicare supplemental policy—

(i) which has a benefit package classified as "H", "I", or "J" (including the benefit package classified as "J" with a high deductible feature, as described in subsection (p)(11)) under the standards established under subsection (p)(2), without regard to this subsection; and

(ii) to which such standards do not apply (or to which such standards have been waived under subsection (p)(6)) but which provides benefits for prescription drugs.

Such term does not include a policy with a benefit package as classified under clause (i) which has been modified under paragraph (2)(C)(i).

(B) Part D enrollee. The term "part D enrollee" means an individual who is enrolled in a part D plan.

(C) Part D plan. The term "part D plan" means a prescription drug plan or an MA-PD plan (as defined for purposes of part D [42 USCS §§ 1395w-101 et seq.]).

(D) Initial part D enrollment period. The term "initial part D enrollment period" means the initial enrollment period described in section 1860D-1(b)(2)(A) [42 USCS § 1395w-101(b)(2)(A)].

(w) Development of new standards for medicare supplemental policies. (1) In general. The Secretary shall request the National Association of Insurance Commissioners to review and revise the standards for benefit packages under subsection (p)(1), taking into account the changes in benefits resulting from enactment of the Medicare Prescription Drug, Improvement, and Modernization Act of 2003 and to otherwise update standards to reflect other changes in law included in such Act. Such revision shall incorporate the inclusion of the 2 benefit packages described in paragraph (2). Such revisions shall be made consistent with the rules applicable under subsection (p)(1)(E) with the reference to the "1991 NAIC Model Regulation" deemed a reference to the NAIC Model Regulation as published in the Federal Register on December 4, 1998, and as subsequently updated by the National Association of Insurance Commissioners to reflect previous changes in law (and subsection (v)) and the reference to "date of enactment of this subsection" deemed a reference to the date of enactment of the Medicare Prescription Drug, Improvement, and Modernization Act of 2003 [enacted Dec. 8, 2003]. To the extent practicable, such revision shall provide for the implementation of revised standards for benefit packages as of January 1, 2006.

(2) New benefit packages. The benefit packages described in this paragraph are the following (notwithstanding any other provision of this section relating to a core benefit package):

(A) First new benefit package. A benefit package consisting of the following:

(i) Subject to clause (ii), coverage of 50 percent of the cost-sharing otherwise applicable under parts A and B, except there shall be no coverage of the part B deductible and coverage of 100 percent of any cost-sharing otherwise applicable for preventive benefits.

(ii) Coverage for all hospital inpatient coinsurance and 365 extra lifetime days of coverage of inpatient hospital services (as in the current core benefit package).

(iii) A limitation on annual out-of-pocket expenditures under parts A and B to $4,000 in 2006 (or, in a subsequent year, to such limitation for the previous year increased by an appropriate inflation adjustment specified by the Secretary).

(B) Second new benefit package. A benefit package consisting of the benefit package described in subparagraph (A), except as follows:

(i) Substitute "75 percent" for "50 percent" in clause (i) of such subparagraph.

(ii) Substitute "$2,000" for "$4,000" in clause (iii) of such subparagraph.

(x) Limitations on genetic testing and information. (1) Genetic testing. (A) Limitation on requesting or requiring genetic testing. An issuer of a medicare supplemental policy shall not request or require an individual or a family member of such individual to undergo a genetic test.

(B) Rule of construction. Subparagraph (A) shall not be construed to limit the authority of a health care professional who is providing health care services to an individual to request that such individual undergo a genetic test.

(C) Rule of construction regarding payment. (i) In general. Nothing in subparagraph (A) shall be construed to preclude an issuer of a medicare supplemental policy from obtaining and using the results of a genetic test in making a determination regarding payment (as such term is defined for the purposes of applying the regulations promulgated by the Secretary under part C of title XI [42 USCS §§ 1320d et seq.] and section 264 of the Health Insurance Portability and Accountability Act of 1996 [42 USCS § 1320d-2 note], as may be revised from time to time) consistent with subsection (s)(2)(E).

(ii) Limitation. For purposes of clause (i), an issuer of a medicare supplemental policy may request only the minimum amount of information necessary to accomplish the intended purpose.

(D) Research exception. Notwithstanding subparagraph (A), an issuer of a medicare supplemental policy may request, but not require, that an individual or a family member of such individual undergo a genetic test if each of the following conditions is met:

(i) The request is made pursuant to research that complies with part 46 of title 45, Code of Federal Regulations, or equivalent Federal regulations, and any applicable State or local law or regulations for the protection of human subjects in research.

(ii) The issuer clearly indicates to each individual, or in the case of a minor child, to the legal guardian of such child, to whom the request is made that—

(I) compliance with the request is voluntary; and

(II) non-compliance will have no effect on enrollment status or premium or contribution amounts.

(iii) No genetic information collected or acquired under this subparagraph shall be used for underwriting, determination of eligibility to enroll or maintain enrollment status, premium rating, or the creation, renewal, or replacement of a plan, contract, or coverage for health insurance or health benefits.

(iv) The issuer notifies the Secretary in writing that the issuer is conducting activities pursuant to the exception provided for under this subparagraph, including a description of the activities conducted.

(v) The issuer complies with such other conditions as the Secretary may by regulation require for activities conducted under this subparagraph.

(2) Prohibition on collection of genetic information. (A) In general. An issuer of a medicare supplemental policy shall not request, require, or purchase genetic information for underwriting purposes (as defined in paragraph (3)).

(B) Prohibition on collection of genetic information prior to enrollment. An issuer of a medicare supplemental policy shall not request, require, or purchase genetic information with respect to any individual prior to such individual's enrollment under the policy in connection with such enrollment.

(C) Incidental collection. If an issuer of a medicare supplemental policy obtains genetic information incidental to the requesting, requiring, or purchasing of other information concerning any individual, such request, requirement, or purchase shall not be considered a violation of subparagraph (B) if such request, requirement, or purchase is not in violation of subparagraph (A).

(3) Definitions. In this subsection:

(A) Family member. The term "family member" means with respect to an individual, any other individual who is a first-degree, second-degree, third-degree, or fourth-degree relative of such individual.

(B) Genetic information. (i) In general. The term "genetic information" means, with respect to any individual, information about—

(I) such individual's genetic tests,

(II) the genetic tests of family members of such individual, and

(III) subject to clause (iv), the manifestation of a disease or disorder in family members of such individual.

(ii) Inclusion of genetic services and participation in genetic research. Such term includes, with respect to any individual, any request for, or receipt of, genetic services, or participation in clinical research which includes genetic services, by such individual or any family member of such individual.

(iii) Exclusions. The term "genetic information" shall not include information about the sex or age of any individual.

(C) Genetic test. (i) In general. The term "genetic test" means an analysis of human DNA, RNA, chromosomes, proteins, or metabolites, that detects genotypes, mutations, or chromosomal changes.

(ii) Exceptions. The term "genetic test" does not mean—

(I) an analysis of proteins or metabolites that does not detect genotypes, mutations, or chromosomal changes; or

(II) an analysis of proteins or metabolites that is directly related to a manifested disease, disorder, or pathological condition that could reasonably be detected by a health care professional with appropriate training and expertise in the field of medicine involved.

(D) Genetic services. The term "genetic services" means—

(i) a genetic test;

(ii) genetic counseling (including obtaining, interpreting, or assessing genetic information); or

(iii) genetic education.

(E) Underwriting purposes. The term "underwriting purposes" means, with respect to a medicare supplemental policy—

(i) rules for, or determination of, eligibility (including enrollment and continued eligibility) for benefits under the policy;

(ii) the computation of premium or contribution amounts under the policy;

(iii) the application of any pre-existing condition exclusion under the policy; and

(iv) other activities related to the creation, renewal, or replacement of a contract of health insurance or health benefits.

(F) Issuer of a medicare supplemental policy. The term "issuer of a medicare supplemental policy" includes a third-party administrator or other person acting for or on behalf of such issuer.

(4) Genetic information of a fetus or embryo. Any reference in this section to genetic information concerning an individual or family member of an individual shall—

(A) with respect to such an individual or family member of an individual who is a pregnant woman, include genetic information of any fetus carried by such pregnant woman; and

(B) with respect to an individual or family member utilizing an assisted reproductive technology, include genetic information of any embryo legally held by the individual or family member.

(y) Development of new standards for certain medicare supplemental policies. (1) In general. The Secretary shall request the National Association of Insurance Commissioners to review and revise the standards for benefit packages described in paragraph (2) under subsection (p)(1), to otherwise update standards to include requirements for nominal cost sharing to encourage the use of appropriate physicians' services under part B [42 USCS §§ 1395j et seq.]. Such revisions shall be based on evidence published in peer-reviewed journals or current examples used by integrated delivery systems and made consistent with the rules applicable under subsection (p)(1)(E) with the reference to the "1991 NAIC Model Regulation" deemed a reference to the NAIC Model Regulation as published in the Federal Register on December 4, 1998, and as subsequently updated by the National Association of Insurance Commissioners to reflect previous changes in law and the reference to "date of enactment of this subsection" deemed a reference to the date of enactment of the Patient Protection and Affordable Care Act [enacted March 23, 2010]. To the extent practicable, such revision shall provide for the implementation of revised standards for benefit packages as of January 1, 2015.

(2) Benefit packages described. The benefit packages described in this paragraph are benefit packages classified as "C" and "F".

(Aug. 14, 1935, ch 531, Title XVIII, Part E [D] [C], § 1882, as added June 9, 1980, P. L. 96-265, Title V, § 507(a), 94 Stat. 476; Aug. 18, 1987, P. L. 100-93, § 13, 101 Stat. 697; Dec. 22, 1987, P. L. 100-203, Title IV, Subtitle A, Part 3, Subpt. D, § 4081(b), 101 Stat. 1330-126; July 1, 1988, P. L. 100-360, Title II, Subtitle C, § 221(a)–(f) Title IV, Subtitle B, § 411(i)(1)(B), (C), Subtitle C, § 428(b), 102 Stat. 742, 788, 817; Dec. 13, 1989, P. L. 101-234, Title II, § 203(a), 103 Stat. 1981; Nov. 5, 1990, P. L. 101-508, Title IV, Subtitle B, Part 4, § 4207(k)(1), Part 5, §§ 4351–4353(d)(1), 4354(a), (b), 4355(a)–(c), 4356(a), 4357(a), 4358(a), (b)(1), (2), 104 Stat. 1388-124, 1388-125–1388-137; Oct. 31, 1994, P. L. 103-432, Title I, Subtitle C, § 160(d)(4), Subtitle D, § 171(a)–(d)(3)(B), (4), (e)(1), (2), (f)(1), (g), (h)(1), (j)(2), (k), 108 Stat. 4444, 4448, 4449, 4451; Aug. 21, 1996, P. L. 104-191, Title II, Subtitle G, § 271(a), (b), 110 Stat. 2034; Aug. 5, 1997, P. L. 105-33, Title IV, Subtitle A, Ch 1, Subch A, §§ 4001, 4002(j)(2), 4003, Ch 4, §§ 4031(a)–(c), 4032(a), 111 Stat. 275, 330, 355, 359; Nov. 10, 1998, P. L. 105-362, Title VI, § 601(b)(6), 112 Stat. 3286; Nov. 29, 1999, P. L. 106-113, Div B, § 1000(a)(6), 113 Stat. 1536; Dec. 17, 1999, P. L. 106-170, Title II, § 205(a), 113 Stat. 1899; Dec. 21, 2000, P. L. 106-554, § 1(a)(6), 114 Stat. 2763; Dec. 8, 2003, P. L. 108-173, Title I, §§ 101(a)(1), 104(a), (b), Title VII, Subtitle D, § 736(e), 117 Stat. 2071, 2161, 2357; Dec. 26, 2007, P. L. 110-161, Div H, Title I, § 1502(f), 121 Stat. 2250; May 21, 2008, P. L. 110-233, Title I, § 104(a), (b), 122 Stat. 899; July 15, 2008, P. L. 110-275, Title I, Subtitle A, Part I, § 104(b), 122 Stat. 2502; March 23, 2010, P. L. 111-148, Title III, Subtitle C, § 3210, 124 Stat. 460.)

HISTORY; ANCILLARY LAWS AND DIRECTIVES

Other provisions:

Applicability of amendments made by § 4358 of Act Nov. 5, 1990; study. Act Nov. 5, 1990, P. L. 101-508, Title IV, Subtitle A, Part 4, § 4358(c), 104 Stat. 1388-137; Oct. 31, 1994, P. L. 103-432, Title I, Subtitle D, § 172(a), 108 Stat. 4452 (effective as if included in the enactment of Act Nov. 5, 1990, as provided by § 172(b) of the 1994 Act); July 7, 1995, P. L. 104-18, § 1, 109 Stat. 192, provides:

"(1) The amendments made by this section [amending subsecs. (b)(1) and (c)(1) of this section, adding subsec. (t) of this section, and amending 42 USCS § 1320c-3] shall only apply—

"(A) in 15 States (as determined by the Secretary of Health and Human Services) and such other States as elect such amendments to apply to them, and

"(B) subject to paragraph (2), during the 6½-year period beginning with 1992.

For purposes of this paragraph, the term 'State' has the meaning given such term by section 210(h) of the Social Security Act (42 U.S.C. 410(h)).

"(2) (A) The Secretary of Health and Human Services shall conduct a study that compares the health care costs, quality of care, and access to services under medicare select policies with that under other medicare supplemental policies. The study shall be based on surveys of appropriate age-adjusted sample populations. The study shall be completed by June 30, 1997.

"(B) Not later than December 31, 1997, the Secretary shall determine, based on the results of the study under subparagraph (A), if any of the following findings are true:

"(i) The amendments made by this section [amending subsecs. (b)(1) and (c)(1) of this section, adding subsec. (t) of this section, and amending 42 USCS § 1320c-3] have not resulted in savings of premium costs to those enrolled in medicare select policies (in comparison to their enrollment in medicare supplemental policies that are not medicare select policies and that provide comparable coverage).

"(ii) There have been significant additional expenditures under the medicare program as a result of such amendments.

"(iii) Access to and quality of care has been significantly diminished as a result of such amendments.

"(C) The amendments made by this section [amending subsecs. (b)(1) and (c)(1) of this section, adding subsec. (t) of this section, and amending 42 USCS § 1320c-3] shall remain in effect beyond the 6½-year period described in paragraph (1)(B) unless the Secretary determines that any of the findings described in clause (i), (ii), or (iii) of subparagraph (B) are true.

"(3) The Comptroller General shall conduct a study to determine the extent to which individuals who are continuously covered under a medicare supplemental policy are subject to medical underwriting if they change the policy under which they are covered, and to identify options, if necessary, for modifying the medicare supplemental insurance market to make sure that continuously insured beneficiaries are able to switch plans without medical underwriting. By not later than June 30, 1996, the Comptroller General shall submit to the Congress a report on the study. The report shall include a description of the potential impact on the cost and availability of medicare supplemental policies of each option identified in the study.".

Applicability of amendments made by § 4358 of Act Nov. 5, 1990. Act Nov. 5, 1990, P. L. 101-508, Title IV, Subtitle A, Part 5, § 4357(b), 104 Stat. 1388-134, provides: "The amendments made by this section [for full classification, consult USCS Tables volumes] shall only apply in 15 states (as determined by the Secretary of Health and Human Services) and only during the 3-year period beginning in 1992.

Evaluation of 1990 amendments; report to Congress. Act Nov. 5, 1990, P. L. 101-508, Title IV, Subtitle A, Part 5, § 4358(c), 104 Stat. 1388-137, provides: "The Secretary of Health and Human Services shall conduct an evaluation of the amendments made by this section [amending this section and 42 USCS § 1320c-3] and shall report to Congress on such evaluation by not later than January 1, 1995.".

§ 1395ww. Payments to hospitals for inpatient hospital services

(a) Determination of costs for inpatient hospital services; limitations; exemptions; "operating costs of inpatient hospital services" defined. (1)(A)(i) The Secretary, in determining the amount of the payments that may be made under this title [42 USCS §§ 1395 et seq.] with respect to operating costs of inpatient hospital services (as defined in paragraph (4)) shall not recognize as reasonable (in the efficient delivery of health services) costs for the provision of such services by a hospital for a cost reporting period to the extent such costs exceed the applicable percentage (as determined under clause (ii)) of the average of such costs for all hospitals in the same grouping as such hospital for comparable time periods.

(ii) For purposes of clause (i), the applicable percentage for hospital cost reporting periods beginning—

(I) on or after October 1, 1982, and before October 1, 1983, is 120 percent;

(II) on or after October 1, 1983, and before October 1, 1984, is 115 percent; and

(III) on or after October 1, 1984, is 110 percent.

(B)(i) For purposes of subparagraph (A) the Secretary shall establish case mix indexes for all short-term hospitals, and shall set limits for each hospital based upon the general mix of types of medical cases with respect to which such hospital provides services for which payment may be made under this title [42 USCS §§ 1395 et seq.].

(ii) The Secretary shall set such limits for a cost reporting period of a hospital—

(I) by updating available data for a previous period to the immediate preceding cost reporting period by the estimated average rate of change of hospital costs industry-wide, and

(II) by projecting for the cost reporting period by the applicable percentage increase (as defined in subsection (b)(3)(B)).

(C) The limitation established under subparagraph (A) for any hospital shall in no event be lower than the allowable operating costs of inpatient hospital services (as defined in paragraph (4)) recognized under this title [42 USCS §§ 1395 et seq.] for such hospital for such hospital's last cost reporting period prior to the hospital's first cost reporting period for which this section is in effect.

(D) Subparagraph (A) shall not apply to cost reporting periods beginning on or after October 1, 1983.

(2) The Secretary shall provide for such exemptions from, and exceptions and adjustments to, the limitation established under paragraph (1)(A) as he deems appropriate, including those which he deems necessary to take into account—

(A) the special needs of sole community hospitals, of new hospitals, of risk based health maintenance organizations, and of hospitals which provide atypical services or essential community services, and to take into account extraordinary circumstances beyond the hospital's control, medical and paramedical education costs, significantly fluctuating population in the service area of the hospital, and unusual labor costs,

(B) the special needs of psychiatric hospitals and of public or other hospitals that serve a significantly disproportionate number of patients who have low income or are entitled to benefits under part A of this title [42 USCS §§ 1395c et seq.], and

(C) a decrease in the inpatient hospital services that a hospital provides and that are customarily provided directly by similar hospitals which results in a significant distortion in the operating costs of inpatient hospital services.

(3) The limitation established under paragraph (1)(A) shall not apply with respect to any hospital which—

(A) is located outside of a standard metropolitan statistical area, and

(B)(i) has less than 50 beds, and

(ii) was in operation and had less than 50 beds on the date of the enactment of this section [enacted Sept. 3, 1982].

(4) For purposes of this section, the term "operating costs of inpatient hospital services" includes all routine operating costs, ancillary service operating costs, and special care unit

operating costs with respect to inpatient hospital services as such costs are determined on an average per admission or per discharge basis (as determined by the Secretary), and includes the costs of all services for which payment may be made under this title [42 USCS §§ 1395 et seq.] that are provided by the hospital (or by an entity wholly owned or operated by the hospital) to the patient during the 3 days (or, in the case of a hospital that is not a subsection (d) hospital, during the 1 day) immediately preceding the date of the patient's admission if such services are diagnostic services (including clinical diagnostic laboratory tests) or are other services related to the admission (as defined by the Secretary). Such term does not include costs of approved educational activities, a return on equity capital, other capital-related costs (as defined by the Secretary for periods before October 1, 1987), or costs with respect to administering blood clotting factors to individuals with hemophilia.

(b) Computation of payment; definition; exemptions; adjustments. (1) Notwithstanding section 1814(b) [42 USCS § 1395f(b)] but subject to the provisions of section 1813 [42 USCS § 1395e], if the operating costs of inpatient hospital services (as defined in subsection (a)(4)) of a hospital (other than a subsection (d) hospital, as defined in subsection (d)(1)(B) and other than a rehabilitation facility described in subsection (j)(1)) for a cost reporting period subject to this paragraph—

(A) are less than or equal to the target amount (as defined in paragraph (3)) for that hospital for that period, the amount of the payment with respect to such operating costs payable under part A [42 USCS §§ 1395c et seq.] on a per discharge or per admission basis (as the case may be) shall be equal to the amount of such operating costs, plus—

(i) 15 percent of the amount by which the target amount exceeds the amount of the operating costs, or

(ii) 2 percent of the target amount,

whichever is less;

(B) are greater than the target amount but do not exceed 110 percent of the target amount, the amount of the payment with respect to those operating costs payable under part A [42 USCS §§ 1395c et seq.] on a per discharge basis shall equal the target amount; or

(C) are greater than 110 percent of the target amount, the amount of the payment with respect to such operating costs payable under part A [42 USCS §§ 1395c et seq.] on a per discharge or per admission basis (as the case may be) shall be equal to (i) the target amount, plus (ii) in the case of cost reporting periods beginning on or after October 1, 1991, an additional amount equal to 50 percent of the amount by which the operating costs exceed 110 percent of the target amount (except that such additional amount may not exceed 10 percent of the target amount) after any exceptions or adjustments are made to such target amount for the cost reporting period;

plus the amount, if any, provided under paragraph (2), except that in no case may the amount payable under this title [42 USCS §§ 1395 et seq.] (other than on the basis of a DRG prospective payment rate determined under subsection (d)) with respect to operating costs of inpatient hospital services exceed the maximum amount payable with respect to such costs pursuant to subsection (a).

(2)(A) Except as provided in subparagraph (E), in addition to the payment computed under paragraph (1), in the case of an eligible hospital (described in subparagraph (B)) for a cost reporting period beginning on or after October 1, 1997, the amount of payment on a per discharge basis under paragraph (1) shall be increased by the lesser of—

(i) 50 percent of the amount by which the operating costs are less than the expected costs (as defined in subparagraph (D)) for the period; or

(ii) 1 percent of the target amount for the period.

(B) For purposes of this paragraph, an "eligible hospital" means with respect to a cost reporting period, a hospital—

(i) that has received payments under this subsection for at least 3 full cost reporting periods before that cost reporting period, and

(ii) whose operating costs for the period are less than the least of its target amount, its trended costs (as defined in subparagraph (C)), or its expected costs (as defined in subparagraph (D)) for the period.

(C) For purposes of subparagraph (B)(ii), the term "trended costs" means for a hospital cost reporting period ending in a fiscal year—

(i) in the case of a hospital for which its cost reporting period ending in fiscal year 1996 was its third or subsequent full cost reporting period for which it receives payments under this subsection, the lesser of the operating costs or target amount for that hospital for its cost reporting period ending in fiscal year 1996, or

(ii) in the case of any other hospital, the operating costs for that hospital for its third full cost reporting period for which it receives payments under this subsection, increased (in a compounded manner) for each succeeding fiscal year (through the fiscal year involved) by the market basket percentage increase for the fiscal year.

(D) For purposes of this paragraph, the term "expected costs", with respect to the cost reporting period ending in a fiscal year, means the lesser of the operating costs of inpatient hospital services or target amount per discharge for the previous cost reporting period updated by the market basket percentage increase (as defined in paragraph (3)(B)(iii)) for the fiscal year.

(E) (i) In the case of an eligible hospital that is a hospital or unit that is within a class of hospital described in clause (ii) with a 12-month cost reporting period beginning before the enactment of this subparagraph [enacted Nov. 29, 1999], in determining the amount of the increase under subparagraph (A), the Secretary shall substitute for the percentage of the target amount applicable under subparagraph (A)(ii)—

(I) for a cost reporting period beginning on or after October 1, 2000, and before September 30, 2001, 1.5 percent; and

(II) for a cost reporting period beginning on or after October 1, 2001, and before September 30, 2002, 2 percent.

(ii) For purposes of clause (i), each of the following shall be treated as a separate class of hospital:

(I) Hospitals described in clause (i) of subsection (d)(1)(B) and psychiatric units described in the matter following clause (v) of such subsection.

(II) Hospitals described in clause (iv) of such subsection.

(3)(A) Except as provided in subparagraph (C) and succeeding subparagraphs, and in paragraph (7)(A)(ii), for purposes of this subsection, the term "target amount" means, with respect to a hospital for a particular 12-month cost reporting period—

(i) in the case of the first such reporting period for which this subsection is in effect, the allowable operating costs of inpatient hospital services (as defined in subsection (a)(4)) recognized under this title [42 USCS §§ 1395 et seq.] for such hospital for the preceding 12-month cost reporting period, and

(ii) in the case of a later reporting period, the target amount for the preceding 12-month cost reporting period,

increased by the applicable percentage increase under subparagraph (B) for that particular cost reporting period.

(B)(i) For purposes of subsection (d) and subsection (j) for discharges occurring during a fiscal year, the "applicable percentage increase" shall be—

(I) for fiscal year 1986, ½ percent,

(II) for fiscal year 1987, 1.15 percent, and

(III) for fiscal year 1988, 3.0 percent for hospitals located in a rural area, 1.5 percent for hospitals located in a large urban area (as defined in subsection (d)(2)(D)), and 1.0 percent for hospitals located in other urban areas.

(IV) for fiscal year 1989, the market basket percentage increase minus 1.5 percentage points for hospitals located in a rural area, the market basket percentage increase minus 2.0 percentage points for hospitals located in a large urban area, and the market basket percentage increase minus 2.5 percentage points for hospitals located in other urban areas,

(V) for fiscal year 1990, the market basket percentage increase plus 4.22 percentage points for hospitals located in a rural area, the market basket percentage increase plus 0.12 percentage points for hospitals located in a large urban area, and the market basket percentage increase minus 0.53 percentage points for hospitals located in other urban areas,

(VI) for fiscal year 1991, the market basket percentage increase minus 2.0 percentage points for hospitals in a large urban or other urban area, and the market basket percentage increase minus 0.7 percentage point for hospitals located in a rural area,

(VII) for fiscal year 1992, the market basket percentage increase minus 1.6 percentage points for hospitals in a large urban or other urban area, and the market basket percentage increase minus 0.6 percentage point for hospitals located in a rural area,

(VIII) for fiscal year 1993, the market basket percentage increase minus 1.55 percentage point for hospitals in a large urban or other urban area, and the market basket percentage increase minus 0.55 [percentage point] for hospitals located in a rural area,

(IX) for fiscal year 1994, the market basket percentage increase minus 2.5 percentage points for hospitals located in a large urban or other urban area, and the market basket percentage increase minus 1.0 percentage point for hospitals located in a rural area,

(X) for fiscal year 1995, the market basket percentage increase minus 2.5 percentage points for hospitals located in a large urban or other urban area, and such percentage increase for hospitals located in a rural area as will provide for the average standardized amount determined under subsection (d)(3)(A) for hospitals located in a rural area being equal to such average standardized amount for hospitals located in an urban area (other than a large urban area),

(XI) for fiscal year 1996, the market basket percentage increase minus 2.0 percentage points for hospitals in all areas,

(XII) for fiscal year 1997, the market basket percentage increase minus 0.5 percentage point for hospitals in all areas,

(XIII) for fiscal year 1998, 0 percent,

(XIV) for fiscal year 1999, the market basket percentage increase minus 1.9 percentage points for hospitals in all areas,

(XV) for fiscal year 2000, the market basket percentage increase minus 1.8 percentage points for hospitals in all areas,

(XVI) for fiscal year 2001, the market basket percentage increase for hospitals in all areas,

(XVII) for fiscal year 2002, the market basket percentage increase minus 0.55 percentage points for hospitals in all areas,

(XVIII) for fiscal year 2003, the market basket percentage increase minus 0.55 percentage points for hospitals in all areas,

(XIX) for each of fiscal years 2004 through 2006, subject to clause (vii), the market basket percentage increase for hospitals in all areas;[,] and

(XX) for each subsequent fiscal year, subject to clauses (viii), (ix), (xi), and (xii), the market basket percentage increase for hospitals in all areas.

(ii) For purposes of subparagraphs (A) and (E), the "applicable percentage increase" for 12-month cost reporting periods beginning during—

(I) fiscal year 1986, is 0.5 percent,

(II) fiscal year 1987, is 1.15 percent,

(III) fiscal year 1988, is the market basket percentage increase minus 2.0 percentage points,

(IV) a subsequent fiscal year ending on or before September 30, 1993, is the market basket percentage increase,

(V) fiscal years 1994 through 1997, is the market basket percentage increase minus the applicable reduction (as defined in clause (v)(II)), or in the case of a hospital for a fiscal year for which the hospital's update adjustment percentage (as defined in clause (v)(I)) is at least 10 percent, the market basket percentage increase,

(VI) [for] fiscal year 1998, is 0 percent,

(VII) [for] fiscal years 1999 through 2002, is the applicable update factor specified under clause (vi) for the fiscal year, and

(VIII) subsequent fiscal years is the market basket percentage increase.

(iii) For purposes of this subparagraph, the term "market basket percentage increase" means, with respect to cost reporting periods and discharges occurring in a fiscal year, the percentage, estimated by the Secretary before the beginning of the period or fiscal year, by which the cost of the mix of goods and services (including personnel costs but excluding nonoperating costs) comprising routine, ancillary, and special care unit inpatient hospital services, based on an index of appropriately weighted indicators of changes in wages and prices which are representative of the mix of goods and services included in such inpatient hospital services, for the period or fiscal year will exceed the cost of such mix of goods and services for the preceding 12-month cost reporting period or fiscal year.

(iv) For purposes of subparagraphs (C) and (D), the "applicable percentage increase" is—

(I) for 12-month cost reporting periods beginning during fiscal years 1986 through 1993, the applicable percentage increase specified in clause (ii),

(II) for fiscal year 1994, the market basket percentage increase minus 2.3 percentage points (adjusted to exclude any portion of a cost reporting period beginning during fiscal year 1993 for which the applicable percentage increase is determined under subparagraph (I)),

(III) for fiscal year 1995, the market basket percentage increase minus 2.2 percentage points, and

(IV) for fiscal year 1996 and each subsequent fiscal year, the applicable percentage increase under clause (i).

(v) For purposes of clause (ii)(V)—

(I) a hospital's "update adjustment percentage" for a fiscal year is the percentage by which the hospital's allowable operating costs of inpatient hospital services recognized under this title [42 USCS §§ 1395 et seq.] for the cost reporting period beginning in fiscal year 1990 exceeds the hospital's target amount (as determined under subparagraph (A)) for such cost reporting period, increased for each fiscal year (beginning with fiscal year 1994) by the sum of any of the hospital's applicable reductions under subclause (V) for previous fiscal years; and

(II) the "applicable reduction" with respect to a hospital for a fiscal year is the lesser of 1 percentage point or the percentage point difference between 10 percent and the hospital's update adjustment percentage for the fiscal year.

(vi) For purposes of clause (ii)(VII) for a fiscal year, if a hospital's allowable operating costs of inpatient hospital services recognized under this title [42 USCS §§ 1395 et seq.] for the most recent cost reporting period for which information is available—

(I) is equal to, or exceeds, 110 percent of the hospital's target amount (as determined under subparagraph (A)) for such cost reporting period, the applicable update factor specified under this clause is the market basket percentage;

(II) exceeds 100 percent, but is less than 110 percent, of such target amount for the hospital, the applicable update factor specified under this clause is 0 percent or, if greater, the market basket percentage minus 0.25 percentage points for each percentage point by which such allowable operating costs (expressed as a percentage of such target amount) is less than 110 percent of such target amount;

(III) is equal to, or less than 100 percent, but exceeds ⅔ of such target amount for the hospital, the applicable update factor specified under this clause is 0 percent or, if greater, the market basket percentage minus 2.5 percentage points; or

(IV) does not exceed ⅔ of such target amount for the hospital, the applicable update factor specified under this clause is 0 percent.

(vii)(I) For purposes of clause (i)(XIX) for fiscal years 2005 and 2006, in a case of a subsection (d) hospital that does not submit data to the Secretary in accordance with subclause (II) with respect to such a fiscal year, the applicable percentage increase under such clause for such fiscal year shall be reduced by 0.4 percentage points. Such reduction shall apply only with respect to the fiscal year involved, and the Secretary shall not take into account such reduction in computing the applicable percentage increase under clause (i)(XIX) for a subsequent fiscal year.

(II) For fiscal years 2005 and 2006, each subsection (d) hospital shall submit to the Secretary quality data (for a set of 10 indicators established by the Secretary as of November 1, 2003) that relate to the quality of care furnished by the hospital in inpatient settings in a form and manner, and at a time, specified by the Secretary for purposes of this clause, but with respect to fiscal year 2005, the Secretary shall provide for a 30-day grace period for the submission of data by a hospital.

(viii)(I) For purposes of clause (i) for fiscal year 2007 and each subsequent fiscal year, in the case of a subsection (d) hospital that does not submit, to the Secretary in accordance with this clause, data required to be submitted on measures selected under this clause with respect to such a fiscal year, the applicable percentage increase under clause (i) for such fiscal year shall be reduced by 2.0 percentage points (or, beginning with fiscal year 2015, by one-quarter of such applicable percentage increase (determined without regard to clause (ix), (xi), or (xii))). Such reduction shall apply only with respect to the fiscal year involved and the Secretary shall not take into account such reduction in computing the applicable percentage increase under clause (i) for a subsequent fiscal year, and the Secretary and the Medicare Payment Advisory Commission shall carry out the requirements under section 5001(b) of the Deficit Reduction Act of 2005 [note to this section].

(II) Each subsection (d) hospital shall submit data on measures selected under this clause to the Secretary in a form and manner, and at a time, specified by the Secretary for purposes of this clause. The Secretary may require hospitals to submit data on measures that are not used for the determination of value-based incentive payments under subsection (o).

(III) The Secretary shall expand, beyond the measures specified under clause (vii)(II) and consistent with the succeeding subclauses, the set of measures that the Secretary determines to be appropriate for the measurement of the quality of care (including medication errors) furnished by hospitals in inpatient settings.

(IV) Effective for payments beginning with fiscal year 2007, in expanding the number of measures under subclause (III), the Secretary shall begin to adopt the baseline set of performance measures as set forth in the November 2005 report by the Institute of Medicine of the National Academy of Sciences under section 238(b) of the Medicare Prescription Drug, Improvement, and Modernization Act of 2003 [42 USCS § 1395ll note].

(V) Effective for payments for fiscal years 2008 through 2012, the Secretary shall add other measures that reflect consensus among affected parties and, to the extent feasible and practicable, shall include measures set forth by one or more national consensus building entities.

(VI) For purposes of this clause and clause (vii), the Secretary may replace any measures or indicators in appropriate cases, such as where all hospitals are effectively in compliance or the measures or indicators have been subsequently shown not to represent the best clinical practice.

(VII) The Secretary shall establish procedures for making information regarding measures submitted under this clause available to the public. Such procedures shall ensure that a hospital has the opportunity to review the data that are to be made public with respect to the hospital prior to such data being made public. The Secretary shall report quality measures of process, structure, outcome, patients' perspectives on care, efficiency, and costs of care that relate to services furnished in inpatient settings in hospitals on the Internet website of the Centers for Medicare & Medicaid Services.

(VIII) Effective for payments beginning with fiscal year 2013, with respect to quality measures for outcomes of care, the Secretary shall provide for such risk adjustment as the Secretary determines to be appropriate to maintain incentives for hospitals to treat patients with severe illnesses or conditions.

(IX)

(aa) Subject to item (bb), effective for payments beginning with fiscal year 2013, each measure specified by the Secretary under this clause shall be endorsed by the entity with a contract under section 1890(a) [42 USCS § 1395aaa(a)].

(bb) In the case of a specified area or medical topic determined appropriate by the Secretary for which a feasible and practical measure has not been endorsed by the entity with a contract under section 1890(a) [42 USCS § 1395aaa(a)], the Secretary may specify a measure that is not so endorsed as long as due consideration is given to measures that have been endorsed or adopted by a consensus organization identified by the Secretary.

(X) To the extent practicable, the Secretary shall, with input from consensus organizations and other stakeholders, take steps to ensure that the measures specified by the Secretary under this clause are coordinated and aligned with quality measures applicable to—

(aa) physicians under section 1848(k) [42 USCS § 1395w-4(k)]; and

(bb) other providers of services and suppliers under this title [42 USCS §§ 1395 et seq.].

(XI) The Secretary shall establish a process to validate measures specified under this clause as appropriate. Such process shall include the auditing of a number of randomly selected hospitals sufficient to ensure validity of the reporting program under this clause as a whole and shall provide a hospital with an opportunity to appeal the validation of measures reported by such hospital.

(ix)(I) For purposes of clause (i) for fiscal year 2015 and each subsequent fiscal year, in the case of an eligible hospital (as defined in subsection (n)(6)(A)) that is not a meaningful EHR user (as defined in subsection (n)(3)) for an EHR reporting period for such fiscal year, three-quarters of the applicable percentage increase otherwise applicable under clause (i) (determined without regard to clause (viii), (xi), or (xii)) for such fiscal year shall be reduced by 33⅓ percent for fiscal year 2015, 66⅔ percent for fiscal year 2016, and 100 percent for fiscal year 2017 and each subsequent fiscal year. Such reduction shall apply only with respect to the fiscal year involved and the Secretary shall not take into account such reduction in computing the applicable percentage increase under clause (i) for a subsequent fiscal year.

(II) The Secretary may, on a case-by-case basis, exempt a subsection (d) hospital from the application of subclause (I) with respect to a fiscal year if the Secretary determines, subject to annual renewal, that requiring such hospital to be a meaningful EHR user during such fiscal year would result in a significant hardship, such as in the case of a hospital in a rural area without sufficient Internet access. In no case may a hospital be granted an exemption under this subclause for more than 5 years.

(III) For fiscal year 2015 and each subsequent fiscal year, a State in which hospitals are paid for services under section 1814(b)(3) [42 USCS § 1395f(b)(3)] shall adjust the payments to each subsection (d) hospital in the State that is not a meaningful EHR user (as defined in subsection (n)(3)) in a manner that is designed to result in an aggregate reduction in payments to hospitals in the State that is equivalent to the aggregate reduction that would have occurred if payments had been reduced to each subsection (d) hospital in the State in a manner comparable to the reduction under the previous provisions of this clause. The State shall report to the Secretary the methodology it will use to make the payment adjustment under the previous sentence.

(IV) For purposes of this clause, the term "EHR reporting period" means, with respect to a fiscal year, any period (or periods) as specified by the Secretary.

(x)(I) The Secretary shall develop standard Internet website reports tailored to meet the needs of various stakeholders such as hospitals, patients, researchers, and policymakers. The Secretary shall seek input from such stakeholders in determining the type of information that is useful and the formats that best facilitate the use of the information.

(II) The Secretary shall modify the Hospital Compare Internet website to make the use and navigation of that website readily available to individuals accessing it.

(xi)(I) For 2012 and each subsequent fiscal year, after determining the applicable percentage increase described in clause (i) and after application of clauses (viii) and (ix), such percentage increase shall be reduced by the productivity adjustment described in subclause (II).

(II) The productivity adjustment described in this subclause, with respect to a percentage, factor, or update for a fiscal year, year, cost reporting period, or other annual period, is a productivity adjustment equal to the 10-year moving average of changes in annual economy-wide private nonfarm business multi-factor productivity (as projected by the Secretary for the 10-year period ending with the applicable fiscal year, year, cost reporting period, or other annual period).

(III) The application of subclause (I) may result in the applicable percentage increase described in clause (i) being less than 0.0 for a fiscal year, and may result in payment rates under this section for a fiscal year being less than such payment rates for the preceding fiscal year.

(xii) After determining the applicable percentage increase described in clause (i), and after application of clauses (viii), (ix), and (xi), the Secretary shall reduce such applicable percentage increase—

(I) for each of fiscal years 2010 and 2011, by 0.25 percentage point;

(II) for each of fiscal years 2012 and 2013, by 0.1 percentage point;

(III) for fiscal year 2014, 0.3 percentage point;

(IV) for each of fiscal years 2015 and 2016, 0.2 percentage point; and

(V) for each of fiscal years 2017, 2018, and 2019, 0.75 percentage point.

(C) In the case of a hospital that is a sole community hospital (as defined in subsection (d)(5)(D)(iii)), subject to subparagraphs (I) and (L), the term "target amount" means—

(i) with respect to the first 12-month cost reporting period in which this subparagraph is applied to the hospital—

(I) the allowable operating costs of inpatient hospital services (as defined in subsection (a)(4)) recognized under this title [42 USCS §§ 1395 et seq.] for the hospital for the 12-month cost reporting period (in this subparagraph referred to as the "base cost reporting period") preceding the first cost reporting period for which this subsection was in effect with respect to such hospital, increased (in a compounded manner) by—

(II) the applicable percentage increases applied to such hospital under this paragraph for cost reporting periods after the base cost reporting period and up to and including such first 12-month cost reporting period,

(ii) with respect to a later cost reporting period beginning before fiscal year 1994, the target amount for the preceding 12-month cost reporting period, increased by the applicable percentage increase under subparagraph (B)(iv) for discharges occurring in the fiscal year in which that later cost reporting period begins,

(iii) with respect to discharges occurring in fiscal year 1994, the target amount for the cost reporting period beginning in fiscal year 1993 increased by the applicable percentage increase under subparagraph (B)(iv), or

(iv) with respect to discharges occurring in fiscal year 1995 and each subsequent fiscal year, the target amount for the preceding year increased by the applicable percentage increase under subparagraph (B)(iv).

There shall be substituted for the base cost reporting period described in clause (i) a hospital's cost reporting period (if any) beginning during fiscal year 1987 if such substitution results in an increase in the target amount for the hospital.

(D) For cost reporting periods ending on or before September 30, 1994, and for discharges occurring on or after October 1, 1997, and before October 1, 2012, in the case of a hospital that is a medicare-dependent, small rural hospital (as defined in subsection (d)(5)(G)), subject to subparagraph (K), the term "target amount" means—

(i) with respect to the first 12-month cost reporting period in which this subparagraph is applied to the hospital—

(I) the allowable operating costs of inpatient hospital services (as defined in subsection (a)(4)) recognized under this title [42 USCS §§ 1395 et seq.] for the hospital for the 12-month cost reporting period (in this subparagraph referred to as the "base cost reporting period") preceding the first cost reporting period for which this subsection was in effect with respect to such hospital, increased (in a compounded manner) by—

(II) the applicable percentage increases applied to such hospital under this paragraph for cost reporting periods after the base cost reporting period and up to and including such first 12-month cost reporting period, or

(ii) with respect to a later cost reporting period beginning before fiscal year 1994, the target amount for the preceding 12-month cost reporting period, increased by the applicable percentage increase under subparagraph (B)(iv) for discharges occurring in the fiscal year in which that later cost reporting period begins,

(iii) with respect to discharges occurring in fiscal year 1994, the target amount for the cost reporting period beginning in fiscal year 1993 increased by the applicable percentage increase under subparagraph (B)(iv), and

(iv) with respect to discharges occurring during fiscal year 1998 through fiscal year 2012, the target amount for the preceding year increased by the applicable percentage increase under subparagraph (B)(iv).

There shall be substituted for the base cost reporting period described in clause (i) a hospital's cost reporting period (if any) beginning during fiscal year 1987 if such substitution results in an increase in the target amount for the hospital.

(E) In the case of a hospital described in clause (v) of subsection (d)(1)(B), the term "target amount" means—

(i) with respect to the first 12-month cost reporting period in which this subparagraph is applied to the hospital—

(I) the allowable operating costs of inpatient hospital services (as defined in subsection (a)(4)) recognized under this title [42 USCS §§ 1395 et seq.] for the hospital for the 12-month cost reporting period (in this subparagraph referred to as the "base cost reporting period") preceding the first cost reporting period for which this subsection was in effect with respect to such hospital, increased (in a compounded manner) by—

(II) the sum of the applicable percentage increases applied to such hospital under this paragraph for cost reporting periods after the base cost reporting period and up to and including such first 12-month cost reporting period, or

(ii) with respect to a later cost reporting period, the target amount for the preceding 12-month cost reporting period, increased by the applicable percentage increase under subparagraph (B)(ii) for that later cost reporting period.

There shall be substituted for the base cost reporting period described in clause (i) a hospital's cost reporting period (if any) beginning during fiscal year 1987 if such substitution results in an increase in the target amount for the hospital.

(F)(i) In the case of a hospital (or unit described in the matter following clause (v) of subsection (d)(1)(B)) that received payment under this subsection for inpatient hospital services furnished during cost reporting periods beginning before October 1, 1990, that is within a class of hospital described in clause (iii), and that elects (in a form and manner determined by the Secretary) this subparagraph to apply to the hospital, the target amount for the hospital's 12-month cost reporting period beginning during fiscal year 1998 is equal to the average described in clause (ii).

(ii) The average described in this clause for a hospital or unit shall be determined by the Secretary as follows:

(I) The Secretary shall determine the allowable operating costs for inpatient hospital services for the hospital or unit for each of the 5 cost reporting periods for which the Secretary has the most recent settled cost reports as of the date of the enactment of this subparagraph [enacted Aug. 5, 1997].

(II) The Secretary shall increase the amount determined under subclause (I) for each cost reporting period by the applicable percentage increase under subparagraph (B)(ii) for each subsequent cost reporting period up to the cost reporting period described in clause (i).

(III) The Secretary shall identify among such 5 cost reporting periods the cost reporting periods for which the amount determined under subclause (II) is the highest, and the lowest.

(IV) The Secretary shall compute the averages of the amounts determined under subclause (II) for the 3 cost reporting periods not identified under subclause (III).

(iii) For purposes of this subparagraph, each of the following shall be treated as a separate class of hospital:

(I) Hospitals described in clause (i) of subsection (d)(1)(B) and psychiatric units described in the matter following clause (v) of such subsection.

(II) Hospitals described in clause (ii) of such subsection and rehabilitation units described in the matter following clause (v) of such subsection.

(III) Hospitals described in clause (iii) of such subsection.

(IV) Hospitals described in clause (iv) of such subsection.

(V) Hospitals described in clause (v) of such subsection.

(G)(i) In the case of a qualified long-term care hospital (as defined in clause (ii)) that elects (in a form and manner determined by the Secretary) this subparagraph to apply to the hospital, the target amount for the hospital's 12-month cost reporting period beginning during fiscal year 1998 is equal to the allowable operating costs of inpatient hospital services (as defined in subsection (a)(4)) recognized under this title [42 USCS §§ 1395 et seq.] for the hospital for the 12-month cost reporting period beginning during fiscal year 1996, increased by the applicable percentage increase for the cost reporting period beginning during fiscal year 1997.

(ii) In clause (i), a "qualified long-term care hospital" means, with respect to a cost reporting period, a hospital described in clause (iv) of subsection (d)(1)(B) during each of the 2 cost reporting periods for which the Secretary has the most recent settled cost reports as of the date of the enactment of this subparagraph [enacted Aug. 5, 1997] for each of which—

(I) the hospital's allowable operating costs of inpatient hospital services recognized under this title [42 USCS §§ 1395 et seq.] exceeded 115 percent of the hospital's target amount, and

(II) the hospital would have a disproportionate patient percentage of at least 70 percent (as determined by the Secretary under subsection (d)(5)(F)(vi)) if the hospital were a subsection (d) hospital.

(H)(i) In the case of a hospital or unit that is within a class of hospital described in clause (iv), for a cost reporting period beginning during fiscal years 1998 through 2002, the target amount for such a hospital or unit may not exceed the amount as updated up to or for such cost reporting period under clause (ii).

(ii)(I) In the case of a hospital or unit that is within a class of hospital described in clause (iv), the Secretary shall estimate the 75th percentile of the target amounts for such hospitals within such class for cost reporting periods ending during fiscal year 1996, as adjusted under clause (iii).

(II) The Secretary shall update the amount determined under subclause (I), for each cost reporting period after the cost reporting period described in such subclause and up to the first cost reporting period beginning on or after October 1, 1997, by a factor equal to the market basket percentage increase.

(III) For cost reporting periods beginning during each of fiscal years 1999 through 2002, subject to subparagraph (J), the Secretary shall update such amount by a factor equal to the market basket percentage increase.

(iii) In applying clause (ii)(I) in the case of a hospital or unit, the Secretary shall provide for an appropriate adjustment to the labor-related portion of the amount determined under such subparagraph to take into account differences between average wage-related costs in the area of the hospital and the national average of such costs within the same class of hospital.

(iv) For purposes of this subparagraph, each of the following shall be treated as a separate class of hospital:

(I) Hospitals described in clause (i) of subsection (d)(1)(B) and psychiatric units described in the matter following clause (v) of such subsection.

(II) Hospitals described in clause (ii) of such subsection and rehabilitation units described in the matter following clause (v) of such subsection.

(III) Hospitals described in clause (iv) of such subsection.

(I)(i) Subject to subparagraph (L), for cost reporting periods beginning on or after October 1, 2000, in the case of a sole community hospital there shall be substituted for the amount otherwise determined under subsection (d)(5)(D)(i), if such substitution results in a greater amount of payment under this section for the hospital—

(I) with respect to discharges occurring in fiscal year 2001, 75 percent of the amount otherwise applicable to the hospital under subsection (d)(5)(D)(i) (referred to in this clause as the "subsection (d)(5)(D)(i) amount") and 25 percent of the rebased target amount (as defined in clause (ii));

(II) with respect to discharges occurring in fiscal year 2002, 50 percent of the subsection (d)(5)(D)(i) amount and 50 percent of the rebased target amount;

(III) with respect to discharges occurring in fiscal year 2003, 25 percent of the subsection (d)(5)(D)(i) amount and 75 percent of the rebased target amount; and

(IV) with respect to discharges occurring after fiscal year 2003, 100 percent of the rebased target amount.

(ii) For purposes of this subparagraph, the "rebased target amount" has the meaning given the term "target amount" in subparagraph (C) except that—

(I) there shall be substituted for the base cost reporting period the 12-month cost reporting period beginning during fiscal year 1996;

(II) any reference in subparagraph (C)(i) to the "first cost reporting period" described in such subparagraph is deemed a reference to the first cost reporting period beginning on or after October 1, 2000; and

(III) applicable increase percentage shall only be applied under subparagraph (C)(iv) for discharges occurring in fiscal years beginning with fiscal year 2002.

(iii) In no case shall a hospital be denied treatment as a sole community hospital or payment (on the basis of a target rate as such as a hospital) because data are unavailable for any cost reporting period due to changes in ownership, changes in fiscal intermediaries, or other extraordinary circumstances, so long as data for at least one applicable base cost reporting period is available.

(J) For cost reporting periods beginning during fiscal year 2001, for a hospital described in subsection (d)(1)(B)(iv)—

(i) the limiting or cap amount otherwise determined under subparagraph (H) shall be increased by 2 percent; and

(ii) the target amount otherwise determined under subparagraph (A) shall be increased by 25 percent (subject to the limiting or cap amount determined under subparagraph (H), as increased by clause (i)).

(K)(i) With respect to discharges occurring on or after October 1, 2006, in the case of a medicare-dependent, small rural hospital, for purposes of applying subparagraph (D)—

(I) there shall be substituted for the base cost reporting period described in subparagraph (D)(i) the 12-month cost reporting period beginning during fiscal year 2002; and

(II) any reference in such subparagraph to the "first cost reporting period" described in such subparagraph is deemed a reference to the first cost reporting period beginning on or after October 1, 2006.

(ii) This subparagraph shall only apply to a hospital if the substitution described in clause (i)(I) results in an increase in the target amount under subparagraph (D) for the hospital.

(L)(i) For cost reporting periods beginning on or after January 1, 2009, in the case of a sole community hospital there shall be substituted for the amount otherwise determined under subsection (d)(5)(D)(i) of this section, if such substitution results in a greater amount of payment under this section for the hospital, the subparagraph (L) rebased target amount.

(ii) For purposes of this subparagraph, the term "subparagraph (L) rebased target amount" has the meaning given the term "target amount" in subparagraph (C), except that—

(I) there shall be substituted for the base cost reporting period the 12-month cost reporting period beginning during fiscal year 2006;

(II) any reference in subparagraph (C)(i) to the "first cost reporting period" described in such subparagraph is deemed a reference to the first cost reporting period beginning on or after January 1, 2009; and

(III) the applicable percentage increase shall only be applied under subparagraph (C)(iv) for discharges occurring on or after January 1, 2009.

(4)(A)(i) The Secretary shall provide for an exception and adjustment to (and in the case of a hospital described in subsection (d)(1)(B)(iii), may provide an exemption from) the method under this subsection for determining the amount of payment to a hospital where events beyond the hospital's control or extraordinary circumstances, including changes in the case mix of such hospital, create a distortion in the increase in costs for a cost reporting period (including any distortion in the costs for the base period against which such increase is measured). The Secretary may provide for such other exemptions from, and exceptions and adjustments to, such method as the Secretary deems appropriate, including the assignment of a new base period which is more representative, as determined by the Secretary, of the reasonable and necessary cost of inpatient services and including those which he deems necessary to take into account a decrease in the inpatient hospital services that a hospital provides and that are customarily provided directly by similar hospitals which results in a significant distortion in the operating costs of inpatient hospital services. The Secretary shall announce a decision on any request for an exemption, exception, or adjustment under this paragraph not later than 180 days after receiving a completed application from the intermediary for such exemption, exception, or adjustment, and shall include in such decision a detailed explanation of the grounds on which such request was approved or denied.

(ii) The payment reductions under paragraph (3)(B)(ii)(V) shall not be considered by the Secretary in making adjustments pursuant to clause (i). In making such reductions, the Secretary shall treat the applicable update factor described in paragraph (3)(B)(vi) for a fiscal year as being equal to the market basket percentage for that year.

(B) In determining under subparagraph (A) whether to assign a new base period which is more representative of the reasonable and necessary cost to a hospital of providing inpatient services, the Secretary shall take into consideration—

(i) changes in applicable technologies and medical practices, or differences in the severity of illness among patients, that increase the hospital's costs;

(ii) whether increases in wages and wage-related costs for hospitals located in the geographic area in which the hospital is located exceed the average of the increases in such costs paid by hospitals in the United States;

and

(iii) such other factors as the Secretary considers appropriate in determining increases in the hospital's costs of providing inpatient services.

(C) Paragraph (1) shall not apply to payment of hospitals which is otherwise determined under paragraph (3) of section 1814(b) [42 USCS § 1395f(b)(3)].

(5) In the case of any hospital having any cost reporting period of other than a 12-month period, the Secretary shall determine the 12-month period which shall be used for purposes of this section.

(6) In the case of any hospital which becomes subject to the taxes under section 3111 of the Internal Revenue Code of 1954 [1986] [26 USCS § 3111], with respect to any or all of its employees, for part or all of a cost reporting period, and was not subject to such taxes with respect to any or all of its employees for all or part of the 12-month base cost reporting period referred to in subsection (b)(3)(A)(i), the Secretary shall provide for an adjustment by increasing the base period amount described in such subsection for such hospital by an amount equal to the amount of such taxes which would have been paid or accrued by such hospital for such base period if such hospital had been subject to such taxes for all of such base period with respect to all its employees, minus the amount of any such taxes actually paid or accrued for such base period.

(7)(A) Notwithstanding paragraph (1), in the case of a hospital or unit that is within a class of hospital described in subparagraph (B) which first receives payments under this section on or after October 1, 1997—

(i) for each of the first 2 cost reporting periods for which the hospital has a settled cost report, the amount of the payment with respect to operating costs described in paragraph (1) under part A on a per discharge or per admission basis (as the case may be) is equal to the lesser of—

(I) the amount of operating costs for such respective period, or

(II) 110 percent of the national median (as estimated by the Secretary) of the target amount for hospitals in the same class as the hospital for cost reporting periods ending during fiscal year 1996, updated by the hospital market basket increase percentage to the fiscal year in which the hospital first received payments under this section, as adjusted under subparagraph (C); and

(ii) for purposes of computing the target amount for the subsequent cost reporting period, the target amount for the preceding cost reporting period is equal to the amount determined under clause (i) for such preceding period.

(B) For purposes of this paragraph, each of the following shall be treated as a separate class of hospital:

(i) Hospitals described in clause (i) of subsection (d)(1)(B) and psychiatric units described in the matter following clause (v) of such subsection.

(ii) Hospitals described in clause (ii) of such subsection and rehabilitation units described in the matter following clause (v) of such subsection.

(iii) Hospitals described in clause (iv) of such subsection.

(C) In applying subparagraph (A)(i)(II) in the case of a hospital or unit, the Secretary shall provide for an appropriate adjustment to the labor-related portion of the amount determined under such subparagraph to take into account differences between average wage-related costs in the area of the hospital and the national average of such costs within the same class of hospital.

(c) Payment in accordance with State hospital reimbursement control system; amount of payment; discontinuance of payments. (1) The Secretary may provide, in his discretion, that payment with respect to services provided by a hospital in a State may be made in accordance with a hospital reimbursement control system in a State, rather than in accordance with the other provisions of this title [42 USCS §§ 1395 et seq.], if the chief executive officer of the State requests such treatment and if—

(A) the Secretary determines that the system, if approved under this subsection, will apply (i) to substantially all non-Federal acute care hospitals (as defined by the Secretary) in the State and (ii) to the review of at least 75 percent of all revenues or expenses in the State for inpatient hospital services and of revenues or expenses for inpatient hospital services provided under the State's plan approved under title XIX [42 USCS §§ 1396 et seq.];

(B) the Secretary has been provided satisfactory assurances as to the equitable treatment under the system of all entities (including Federal and State programs) that pay hospitals for inpatient hospital services, of hospital employees, and of hospital patients;

(C) the Secretary has been provided satisfactory assurances that under the system, over 36-month periods (the first such period beginning with the first month in which this subsection applies to that system in the State), the amount of payments made under this title [42 USCS §§ 1395 et seq.] under such system will not exceed the amount of payments which would otherwise have been made under this title not using such system;

(D) the Secretary determines that the system will not preclude an eligible organization (as defined in section 1876(b) [42 USCS § 1395mm(b)]) from negotiating directly with hospitals with respect to the organization's rate of payment for inpatient hospital services; and

(E) the Secretary determines that the system requires hospitals to meet the requirement of section 1866(a)(1)(G) [42 USCS § 1395cc(a)(1)(G)] and the system provides for the exclusion of certain costs in accordance with section 1862(a)(14) [42 USCS § 1395y(a)(14)] (except for such waivers thereof as the Secretary provides by regulation).

The Secretary cannot deny the application of a State under this subsection on the ground that the State's hospital reimbursement control system is based on a payment methodology other than on the basis of a diagnosis-related group or on the ground that the amount of payments made under this title [42 USCS §§ 1395 et seq.] under such system must be less than the amount of payments which would otherwise have been made under this title [42 USCS §§ 1395 et seq.] not using such system. If the Secretary determines that the conditions described in subparagraph (C) are based on maintaining payment amounts at no more than a specified percentage increase above the payment amounts in a base period, the State has the option of applying such test (for inpatient hospital services under part A [42 USCS §§ 1395c et seq.]) on an aggregate payment basis or on the basis of the amount of payment per inpatient discharge or admission. If the Secretary determines that the conditions described in subparagraph (C) are based on maintaining aggregate payment amounts below a national average percentage increase in total payments under part A [42 USCS §§ 1395c et seq.] for inpatient hospital services, the Secretary cannot deny the application of a State under this subsection on the ground that the State's rate of increase in such payments for such services must be less than such national average rate of increase.

(2) In determining under paragraph (1)(C) the amount of payment which would otherwise have been made under this title [42 USCS §§ 1395 et seq.] for a State, the Secretary may provide for appropriate adjustment of such amount to take into account previous reductions effected in the amount of payments made under this title [42 USCS §§ 1395 et seq.] in the State due to the operation of the hospital reimbursement control system in the State if the system has resulted in an aggregate rate of increase in operating costs of inpatient hospital services (as defined in subsection (a)(4)) under this title [42 USCS §§ 1395 et seq.] for hospitals in the State which is less than the aggregate rate of increase in such costs under this title [42 USCS §§ 1395 et seq.] for hospitals in the United States.

(3) The Secretary shall discontinue payments under a system described in paragraph (1) if the Secretary—

(A) determines that the system no longer meets the requirements of subparagraphs (A), (D), and (E) of paragraph (1) and, if applicable, the requirements of paragraph (5), or

(B) has reason to believe that the assurances described in subparagraph (B) or (C) of paragraph (1) (or, if applicable, in paragraph (5)) are not being (or will not be) met.

(4) The Secretary shall approve the request of a State under paragraph (1) with respect to a hospital reimbursement control system if—

(A) the requirements of subparagraphs (A), (B), (C), (D), and (E) of paragraph (1) have been met with respect to the system, and

(B) with respect to that system a waiver of certain requirements of title XVIII of the Social Security Act [42 USCS §§ 1395 et seq.] has been approved on or before (and which is in effect as of) the date of the enactment of the Social Security Amendments of 1983 [enacted April 20, 1983], pursuant to section 402(a) of the Social Security Amendments of 1967 [42 USCS § 1395b-1(a)] or section 222(a) of the Social Security Amendments of 1972 [42 USCS § 1395b-1 note].

With respect to a State system described in this paragraph, the Secretary shall judge the effectiveness of such system on the basis of its rate of increase or inflation in inpatient hospital payments for individuals under this title [42 USCS §§ 1395 et seq.], as compared to the national rate of increase or inflation for such payments, with the State retaining the option to have the test applied on the basis of the aggregate payments under the State system as compared to aggregate payments which would have been made under the national system since October 1, 1984, to the most recent date for which annual data are available.

(5) The Secretary shall approve the request of a State under paragraph (1) with respect to a hospital reimbursement control system if—

(A) the requirements of subparagraphs (A), (B), (C), (D), and (E) of paragraph (1) have been met with respect to the system;

(B) the Secretary determines that the system—

(i) is operated directly by the State or by an entity designated pursuant to State law,

(ii) provides for payment of hospitals covered under the system under a methodology (which sets forth exceptions and adjustments, as well as any method for changes in the methodology) by which rates or amounts to be paid for hospital services during a specified period are established under the system prior to the defined rate period, and

(iii) hospitals covered under the system will make such reports (in lieu of cost and other reports, identified by the Secretary, otherwise required under this title [42 USCS §§ 1395 et seq.]) as the Secretary may require in order to properly monitor assurances provided under this subsection;

(C) the State has provided the Secretary with satisfactory assurances that operation of the system will not result in any change in hospital admission practices which result in—

(i) a significant reduction in the proportion of patients (receiving hospital services covered under the system) who have no third-party coverage and who are unable to pay for hospital services,

(ii) a significant reduction in the proportion of individuals admitted to hospitals for inpatient hospital services for which payment is (or is likely to be) less than the anticipated charges for or costs of such services,

(iii) the refusal to admit patients who would be expected to require unusually costly or prolonged treatment for reasons other than those related to the appropriateness of the care available at the hospital, or

(iv) the refusal to provide emergency services to any person who is in need of emergency services if the hospital provides such services;

(D) any change by the State in the system which has the effect of materially reducing payments to hospitals can only take effect upon 60 days notice to the Secretary and to the hospitals the payment to which is likely to be materially affected by the change; and

(E) the State has provided the Secretary with satisfactory assurances that in the development of the system the State has consulted with local governmental officials concerning the impact of the system on public hospitals.

The Secretary shall respond to requests of States under this paragraph within 60 days of the date the request is submitted to the Secretary.

(6) If the Secretary determines that the assurances described in paragraph (1)(C) have not been met with respect to any 36-month period, the Secretary may reduce payments under this title [42 USCS §§ 1395 et seq.] to hospitals under the system in an amount equal to the amount by which the payment under this title [42 USCS §§ 1395 et seq.] under such system for such period exceeded the amount of payments which would otherwise have been made under this title [42 USCS §§ 1395 et seq.] not using such system.

(7) In the case of a State which made a request under paragraph (5) before December 31, 1984, for the approval of a State hospital reimbursement control system and which request was approved—

(A) in applying paragraphs (1)(C) and (6), a reference to a "36-month period" is deemed a reference to a "48-month period", and

(B) in order to allow the State the opportunity to provide the assurances described in paragraph (1)(C) for a 48-month period, the Secretary may not discontinue payments under the system, under the authority of paragraph (3)(A) because the Secretary has reason to believe that such assurances are not being (or will not be) met, before July 1, 1986.

(d) Inpatient hospital service payments on basis of prospective rates; Medicare Geographical Classification Review Board. (1)(A) Notwithstanding section 1814(b) [42 USCS § 1395f(b)] but subject to the provisions of section 1813 [42 USCS § 1395e], the amount of the payment with respect to the operating costs of inpatient hospital services (as defined in subsection (a)(4)) of a subsection (d) hospital (as defined in subparagraph (B)) for inpatient hospital discharges in a cost reporting period or in a fiscal year—

(i) beginning on or after October 1, 1983, and before October 1, 1984, is equal to the sum of—

(I) the target percentage (as defined in subparagraph (C)) of the hospital's target amount for the cost reporting period (as defined in subsection (b)(3)(A), but determined without the application of subsection (a)), and

(II) the DRG percentage (as defined in subparagraph (C)) of the regional adjusted DRG prospective payment rate determined under paragraph (2) for such discharges;

(ii) beginning on or after October 1, 1984, and before October 1, 1987, is equal to the sum of—

(I) the target percentage (as defined in subparagraph (C)) of the hospital's target amount for the cost reporting period (as defined in subsection (b)(3)(A), but determined without the application of subsection (a)), and

(II) the DRG percentage (as defined in subparagraph (C)) of the applicable combined adjusted DRG prospective payment rate determined under subparagraph (D) for such discharges; or

(iii) beginning on or after April 1, 1988, is equal to—

(I) the national adjusted DRG prospective payment rate determined under paragraph (3) for such discharges, or

(II) for discharges occurring during a fiscal year ending on or before September 30, 1996, the sum of 85 percent of the national adjusted DRG prospective payment rate determined under paragraph (3) for such discharges and 15 percent of the regional adjusted DRG prospective payment rate determined under such paragraph, but only if the average standardized amount (described in clause (i)(I) or clause (ii)(I) of paragraph (3)(D)) for hospitals within the region of, and in the same large urban or other area (or, for discharges occurring during a fiscal year ending on or before September 30, 1994, the same large urban or other area) as, the hospital is greater than the average standardized amount (described in the respective clause) for hospitals within the United States in that type of area for discharges occurring during such fiscal year.

(B) As used in this section, the term "subsection (d) hospital" means a hospital located in one of the fifty States or the District of Columbia other than—

(i) a psychiatric hospital (as defined in section 1861(f)) [42 USCS § 1395x(f)],

(ii) a rehabilitation hospital (as defined by the Secretary),

(iii) a hospital whose inpatients are predominantly individuals under 18 years of age,

(iv)(I) a hospital which has an average inpatient length of stay (as determined by the Secretary) of greater than 25 days, or

(II) a hospital that first received payment under this subsection in 1986 which has an average inpatient length of stay (as determined by the Secretary) of greater than 20 days and that has 80 percent or more of its annual medicare inpatient discharges with a principal diagnosis that reflects a finding of neoplastic disease in the 12-month cost reporting period ending in fiscal year 1997, or

(v)(I) a hospital that the Secretary has classified, at any time on or before December 31, 1990[,] (or, in the case of a hospital that, as of the date of the enactment of this clause, is located in a State operating a demonstration project under section 1814(b) [42 USCS § 1395f(b)], on or before December 31, 1991) for purposes of applying exceptions and adjustments to payment amounts under this subsection, as a hospital involved extensively in treatment for or research on cancer,

(II) a hospital that was recognized as a comprehensive cancer center or clinical cancer research center by the National Cancer Institute of the National Institutes of Health as of April 20, 1983, that is located in a State which, as of December 19, 1989, was not operating a demonstration project under section 1814(b), that applied and was denied, on or before December 31, 1990, for classification as a hospital involved extensively in treatment for or research on cancer under this clause (as in effect on the day before the date of the enactment of this subclause), that as of the date of the enactment of this subclause, is licensed for less than 50 acute care beds, and that demonstrates for the 4-year period ending on December 31, 1996, that at least 50 percent of its total discharges have a principal finding of neoplastic disease, as defined in subparagraph (E), or

(III) a hospital that was recognized as a clinical cancer research center by the National Cancer Institute of the National Institutes of Health as of February 18, 1998, that has never been reimbursed for inpatient hospital services pursuant to a reimbursement system under a demonstration project under section 1814(b) [42 USCS § 1395f(b)], that is a freestanding facility organized primarily for treatment of and research on cancer and is not a unit of another hospital, that as of the date of the enactment of this subclause, is licensed for 162 acute care beds, and that demonstrates for the 4-year period ending on June 30, 1999, that at least 50 percent of its total discharges have a principal finding of neoplastic disease, as defined in subparagraph (E);

and, in accordance with regulations of the Secretary, does not include a psychiatric or rehabilitation unit of the hospital which is a distinct part of the hospital (as defined by the Secretary). A hospital that was classified by the Secretary on or before September 30, 1995, as a hospital described in clause (iv) shall continue to be so classified notwithstanding that it is located in the same building as, or on the same campus as, another hospital.

(C) For purposes of this subsection, for cost reporting periods beginning—

(i) on or after October 1, 1983, and before October 1, 1984, the "target percentage" is 75 percent and the "DRG percentage" is 25 percent;

(ii) on or after October 1, 1984, and before October 1, 1985, the "target percentage" is 50 percent and the "DRG percentage" is 50 percent;

(iii) on or after October 1, 1985, and before October 1, 1986, the "target percentage" is 45 percent and the "DRG percentage" is 55 percent; and

(iv) on or after October 1, 1986, and before October 1, 1987, the "target percentage" is 25 percent and the "DRG percentage" is 75 percent.

(D) For purposes of subparagraph (A)(ii)(II), the "applicable combined adjusted DRG prospective payment rate" for discharges occurring—

(i) on or after October 1, 1984, and before October 1, 1986, is a combined rate consisting of 25 percent of the national adjusted DRG prospective payment rate, and 75 percent of the regional adjusted DRG prospective payment rate, determined under paragraph (3) for such discharges; and

(ii) on or after October 1, 1986, and before October 1, 1987, is a combined rate consisting of 50 percent of the national adjusted DRG prospective payment rate, and 50 percent of the regional adjusted DRG prospective payment rate, determined under paragraph (3) for such discharges.

(E) For purposes of subclauses (II) and (III) of subparagraph (B)(v) only, the term "principal finding of neoplastic disease" means the condition established after study to be chiefly responsible for occasioning the admission of a patient to a hospital, except that only discharges with ICD-9-CM principal diagnosis codes of 140 through 239, V58.0, V58.1, V66.1, V66.2, or 990 will be considered to reflect such a principal diagnosis.

(2) The Secretary shall determine a national adjusted DRG prospective payment rate, for each inpatient hospital discharge in fiscal year 1984 involving inpatient hospital services of a subsection (d) hospital in the United States, and shall determine a regional adjusted DRG prospective payment rate for such discharges in each region, for which payment may be made under part A of this title [42 USCS §§ 1395c et seq.]. Each such rate shall be determined for hospitals located in urban or rural areas within the United States or within each such region, respectively, as follows:

(A) The Secretary shall determine the allowable operating costs per discharge of inpatient hospital services for the hospital for the most recent cost reporting period for which data are available.

(B) The Secretary shall update each amount determined under subparagraph (A) for fiscal year 1984 by—

(i) updating for fiscal year 1983 by the estimated average rate of change of hospital costs industry-wide between the cost reporting period used under such subparagraph and fiscal year 1983 and the most recent case-mix data available, and

(ii) projecting for fiscal year 1984 by the applicable percentage increase (as defined in subsection (b)(3)(B)) for fiscal year 1984.

(C) The Secretary shall standardize the amount updated under subparagraph (B) for each hospital by—

(i) excluding an estimate of indirect medical education costs (taking into account, for discharges occurring after September 30, 1986, the amendments made by section 9104(a) of the Medicare and Medicaid Budget Reconciliation Amendments of 1985), except that the Secretary shall not take into account any reduction in the amount of additional payments under paragraph (5)(B)(ii) resulting from the amendment made by section 4621(a)(1) of the Balanced Budget Act of 1997 or any additional payments under such paragraph resulting from the application of section 111 of the Medicare, Medicaid, and SCHIP Balanced Budget Refinement Act of 1999, of section 302 of the Medicare, Medicaid, and SCHIP Benefits Improvement and Protection Act of 2000, or the Medicare Prescription Drug, Improvement, and Modernization Act of 2003,

(ii) adjusting for variations among hospitals by area in the average hospital wage level,

(iii) adjusting for variations in case mix among hospitals, and

(iv) for discharges occurring on or after October 1, 1986, excluding an estimate of the additional payments to certain hospitals to be made under paragraph (5)(F), except that the Secretary shall not exclude additional payments under such paragraph made as a result of the enactment of section 6003(c) of the Omnibus Budget Reconciliation Act of 1989 or the enactment of section 4002(b) of the Omnibus Budget Reconciliation Act of 1990, the enactment of section 303 of the Medicare, Medicaid, and SCHIP Benefits Improvement and Protection Act of 2000, or the enactment of section 402(a)(1) of the Medicare Prescription Drug, Improvement, and Modernization Act of 2003.

(D) The Secretary shall compute an average of the standardized amounts determined under subparagraph (C) for the United States and for each region—

(i) for all subsection (d) hospitals located in

an urban area within the United States or that region, respectively, and

(ii) for all subsection (d) hospitals located in a rural area within the United States or that region, respectively.

For purposes of this subsection, the term "region" means one of the nine census divisions, comprising the fifty States and the District of Columbia, established by the Bureau of the Census for statistical and reporting purposes; the term "urban area" means an area within a Metropolitan Statistical Area (as defined by the Office of Management and Budget) or within such similar area as the Secretary has recognized under subsection (a) by regulation; the term "large urban area" means, with respect to a fiscal year, such an urban area which the Secretary determines (in the publications described in subsection (e)(5) before the fiscal year) has a population of more than 1,000,000 (as determined by the Secretary based on the most recent available population data published by the Bureau of the Census); and the term "rural area" means any area outside such an area or similar area. A hospital located in a Metropolitan Statistical Area shall be deemed to be located in the region in which the largest number of the hospitals in the same Metropolitan Statistical Area are located, or, at the option of the Secretary, the region in which the majority of the inpatient discharges (with respect to which payments are made under this title [42 USCS §§ 1395 et seq.]) from hospitals in the same Metropolitan Statistical Area are made.

(E) The Secretary shall reduce each of the average standardized amounts determined under subparagraph (D) by a proportion equal to the proportion (estimated by the Secretary) of the amount of payments under this subsection based on DRG prospective payment rates which are additional payments described in paragraph (5)(A) (relating to outlier payments).

(F) The Secretary shall adjust each of such average standardized amounts as may be required under subsection (e)(1)(B) for that fiscal year.

(G) For each discharge classified within a diagnosis-related group, the Secretary shall establish a national DRG prospective payment rate and shall establish a regional DRG prospective payment rate for each region, each of which is equal—

(i) for hospitals located in an urban area in the United States or that region (respectively), to the product of—

(I) the average standardized amount (computed under subparagraph (D), reduced under subparagraph (E), and adjusted under subparagraph (F)) for hospitals located in an urban area in the United States or that region, and

(II) the weighting factor (determined under paragraph (4)(B)) for that diagnosis-related group; and

(ii) for hospitals located in a rural area in the United States or that region (respectively), to the product of—

(I) the average standardized amount (computed under subparagraph (D), reduced under subparagraph (E), and adjusted under subparagraph (F)) for hospitals located in a rural area in the United States or that region, and

(II) the weighting factor (determined under paragraph (4)(B)) for that diagnosis-related group.

(H) The Secretary shall adjust the proportion, (as estimated by the Secretary from time to time) of hospitals' costs which are attributable to wages and wage-related costs, of the national and regional DRG prospective payment rates computed under subparagraph (G) for area differences in hospital wage levels by a factor (established by the Secretary) reflecting the relative hospital wage level in the geographic area of the hospital compared to the national average hospital wage level.

(3) The Secretary shall determine a national adjusted DRG prospective payment rate, for each inpatient hospital discharge in a fiscal year after fiscal year 1984 involving inpatient hospital services of a subsection (d) hospital in the United States, and shall determine, for fiscal years before fiscal year 1997, a regional adjusted DRG prospective payment rate for such discharges in each region for which payment may be made under part A of this title [42 USCS §§ 1395c et seq.]. Each such rate shall be determined for hospitals located in large urban, other urban, or rural areas within the United States and within each such region, respectively, as follows:

(A) Updating previous standardized amounts. (i) For discharges occurring in a fiscal year beginning before October 1, 1987, the Secretary shall compute an average standardized amount for hospitals located in an urban area and for hospitals located in a rural area within the United States and for hospitals located in an urban area and for hospitals located in a rural area within each region, equal to the respective average standardized amount computed for the previous fiscal year under paragraph (2)(D) or under this subparagraph, increased for the fiscal year involved by the applicable percentage increase under subsection (b)(3)(B). With respect to discharges occurring on or after October 1, 1987, the Secretary shall compute urban and rural averages on the basis of discharge weighting rather than hospital weighting, making appropriate adjustments to ensure that computation on such basis does not result in total payments under this section that are greater or less than the total payments that would have been made under this section but for this sentence, and making appropriate changes in the manner of determining the reductions under subparagraph (C)(ii).

(ii) For discharges occurring in a fiscal year beginning on or after October 1, 1987, and ending on or before September 30, 1994, the Secretary shall compute an average standardized amount for hospitals located in a large urban area, for hospitals located in a rural area, and for hospitals located in other urban areas, within the United States and within each region, equal to the respective average standardized amount computed for the previous fiscal year under this subparagraph increased by the applicable percentage increase under subsection (b)(3)(B)(i) with respect to hospitals located in the respective areas for the fiscal year involved.

(iii) For discharges occurring in the fiscal year beginning on October 1, 1994, the average standardized amount for hospitals located in a rural area shall be equal to the average standardized amount for hospitals located in an urban area. For discharges occurring on or after October 1, 1994, the Secretary shall adjust the ratio of the labor portion to non-labor portion of each average standardized amount to equal such ratio for the national average of all standardized amounts.

(iv)(I) Subject to subclause (II), for discharges occurring in a fiscal year beginning on or after October 1, 1995, the Secretary shall compute an average standardized amount for hospitals located in a large urban area and for hospitals located in other areas within the United States and within each region equal to the respective average standardized amount computed for the previous fiscal year under this subparagraph increased by the applicable percentage increase under subsection (b)(3)(B)(i) with respect to hospitals located in the respective areas for the fiscal year involved.

(II) For discharges occurring in a fiscal year (beginning with fiscal year 2004), the Secretary shall compute a standardized amount for hospitals located in any area within the United States and within each region equal to the standardized amount computed for the previous fiscal year under this subparagraph for hospitals located in a large urban area (or, beginning with fiscal year 2005, for all hospitals in the previous fiscal year) increased by the applicable percentage increase under subsection (b)(3)(B)(i) for the fiscal year involved.

(v) Average standardized amounts computed under this paragraph shall be adjusted to reflect the most recent case-mix data available.

(vi) Insofar as the Secretary determines that the adjustments under paragraph (4)(C)(i) for a previous fiscal year (or estimates that such adjustments for a future fiscal year) did (or are likely to) result in a change in aggregate payments under this subsection during the fiscal year that are a result of changes in the coding or classification of discharges that do not reflect real changes in case mix, the Secretary may adjust the average standardized amounts computed under this paragraph for subsequent fiscal years so as to eliminate the effect of such coding or classification changes.

(B) The Secretary shall reduce each of the average standardized amounts determined under subparagraph (A) by a factor equal to the proportion of payments under this subsection (as estimated by the Secretary) based on DRG prospective payment amounts which are additional payments described in paragraph (5)(A) (relating to outlier payments).

(C)(i) For discharges occurring in fiscal year 1985, the Secretary shall adjust each of such average standardized amounts as may be required under subsection (e)(1)(B) for that fiscal year.

(ii) For discharges occurring after September 30, 1986, the Secretary shall further reduce each of the average standardized amounts (in a proportion which takes into account the differing effects of the standardization effected under paragraph (2)(C)(i)) so as to provide for a reduction in the total of the payments (attributable to this paragraph) made for discharges occurring on or after October 1, 1986, of an amount equal to the estimated reduction in the payment amounts under paragraph (5)(B) that would have resulted from the enactment of the amendments made by section 9104 of the Medicare and Medicaid Budget Reconciliation Amendments of 1985 and by section 4003(a)(1) of the Omnibus Budget Reconciliation Act of 1987 if the factor described in clause (ii)(II) of paragraph (5)(B) (determined without regard to amendments made by the Omnibus Budget Reconciliation Act of 1990) were applied for discharges occurring on or after such date instead of the factor described in clause (ii) of that paragraph.

(D) For each discharge classified within a diagnosis-related group, the Secretary shall establish for the fiscal year a national DRG prospective payment rate and shall establish, for fiscal years before fiscal year 1997, a regional DRG prospective payment rate for each region which is equal—

(i) for fiscal years before fiscal year 2004, for hospitals located in a large urban area in the United States or that region (respectively), to the product of—

(I) the average standardized amount (computed under subparagraph (A), reduced under subparagraph (B), and adjusted or reduced under subparagraph (C)) for the fiscal year for hospitals located in such a large urban area in the United States or that region, and

(II) the weighting factor (determined under paragraph (4)(B)) for that diagnosis-related group;

(ii) for fiscal years before fiscal year 2004, for hospitals located in other areas in the United States or that region (respectively), to the product of—

(I) the average standardized amount (computed under subparagraph (A), reduced under subparagraph (B), and adjusted or reduced under subparagraph (C)) for the fiscal year for hospitals located in other areas in the United States or that region, and

(II) the weighting factor (determined under paragraph (4)(B)) for that diagnosis-related group; and

(iii) for a fiscal year beginning after fiscal year 2003, for hospitals located in all areas, to the product of—

(I) the applicable standardized amount (computed under subparagraph (A)), reduced under subparagraph (B), and adjusted or reduced under subparagraph (C) for the fiscal year; and

(II) the weighting factor (determined under paragraph (4)(B)) for that diagnosis-related group.

(E) Wage levels. (i) In general. Except as provided in clause (ii) or (iii), the Secretary shall adjust the proportion, (as estimated by the Secretary from time to time) of hospitals' costs which are attributable to wages and wage-related costs, of the DRG prospective payment rates computed under subparagraph (D) for area differences in hospital wage levels by a factor (established by the Secretary) reflecting the relative hospital wage level in the geographic area of the hospital compared to the national average hospital wage level. Not later than October 1, 1990, and October 1, 1993 (and at least every 12 months thereafter), the Secretary shall update the factor under the preceding sentence on the basis of a survey conducted by the Secretary (and updated as appropriate) of the wages and wage-related costs of subsection (d) hospitals in the United States. Not less often than once every 3 years the Secretary (through such survey or otherwise) shall measure the earnings and paid hours of employment by occupational category and shall exclude data with respect to the wages and wage-related costs incurred in furnishing skilled nursing facility services. Any adjustments or updates made under this subparagraph for a fiscal year (beginning with fiscal year 1991) shall be made in a manner that assures that the aggregate payments under this subsection in the fiscal year are not greater or less than those that would have been made in the year without such adjustment. The Secretary shall apply the previous sentence for any period as if the amendments made by section 403(a)(1) of the Medicare Prescription Drug, Improvement, and Modernization Act of 2003 and the amendments made by section 10324(a)(1) of the Patient Protection and Affordable Care Act had not been enacted.

(ii) Alternative proportion to be adjusted beginning in fiscal year 2005. For discharges occurring on or after October 1, 2004, the Secretary shall substitute "62 percent" for the proportion described in the first sentence of clause (i), unless the application of this clause would result in lower payments to a hospital than would otherwise be made.

(iii) Floor on area wage index for hospitals in frontier States. (I) In general. Subject to subclause (IV), for discharges occurring on or after October 1, 2010, the area wage index applicable under this subparagraph to any hospital which is located in a frontier State (as defined in subclause (II)) may not be less than 1.00.

(II) Frontier State defined. In this clause, the term "frontier State" means a State in which at least 50 percent of the counties in the State are frontier counties.

(III) Frontier county defined. In this clause, the term "frontier county" means a county in which the population per square mile is less than 6.

(IV) Limitation. This clause shall not apply to any hospital located in a State that receives a non-labor related share adjustment under paragraph (5)(H).

(4)(A) The Secretary shall establish a classification of inpatient hospital discharges by diagnosis-related groups and a methodology for classifying specific hospital discharges within these groups.

(B) For each such diagnosis-related group the Secretary shall assign an appropriate weighting factor which reflects the relative hospital resources used with respect to discharges classified within that group compared to discharges classified within other groups.

(C)(i) The Secretary shall adjust the classifications and weighting factors established under subparagraphs (A) and (B), for discharges in fiscal year 1988 and at least annually, to reflect changes in treatment patterns, technology (including a new medical service or technology under paragraph (5)(K)), and other factors which may change the relative use of hospital resources.

(ii) For discharges in fiscal year 1990, the Secretary shall reduce the weighting factor for each diagnosis-related group by 1.22 percent.

(iii) Any such adjustment under clause (i) for discharges in a fiscal year (beginning with fiscal year 1991) shall be made in a manner that assures that the aggregate payments under this subsection for discharges in the fiscal year are not greater or less than those that would have been made for discharges in the year without such adjustment.

(iv) [Deleted]

(D)(i) For discharges occurring on or after October 1, 2008, the diagnosis-related group to be assigned under this paragraph for a discharge described in clause (ii) shall be a diagnosis-related group that does not result in higher payment based on the presence of a secondary diagnosis code described in clause (iv).

(ii) A discharge described in this clause is a discharge which meets the following requirements:

(I) The discharge includes a condition identified by a diagnosis code selected under clause (iv) as a secondary diagnosis.

(II) But for clause (i), the discharge would have been classified to a diagnosis-related group that results in a higher payment based on the presence of a secondary diagnosis code selected under clause (iv).

(III) At the time of admission, no code selected under clause (iv) was present.

(iii) As part of the information required to be reported by a hospital with respect to a discharge of an individual in order for payment to be made under this subsection, for discharges occurring on or after October 1, 2007, the information shall include the secondary diagnosis of the individual at admission.

(iv) By not later than October 1, 2007, the Secretary shall select diagnosis codes associated with at least two conditions, each of which codes meets all of the following requirements (as determined by the Secretary):

(I) Cases described by such code have a high cost or high volume, or both, under this title.

(II) The code results in the assignment of a case to a diagnosis-related group that has a higher payment when the code is present as a secondary diagnosis.

(III) The code describes such conditions that could reasonably have been prevented through the application of evidence-based guidelines.

The Secretary may from time to time revise (through addition or deletion of codes) the diagnosis codes selected under this clause so long as there are diagnosis codes associated with at least two conditions selected for discharges occurring during any fiscal year.

(v) In selecting and revising diagnosis codes under clause (iv), the Secretary shall consult with the Centers for Disease Control and Prevention and other appropriate entities.

(vi) Any change resulting from the application of this subparagraph shall not be taken into account in adjusting the weighting factors under subparagraph (C)(i) or in applying budget neutrality under subparagraph (C)(iii).

(5)(A)(i) For discharges occurring during fiscal years ending on or before September 30, 1997, the Secretary shall provide for an additional payment for a subsection (d) hospital for any discharge in a diagnosis-related group, the length of stay of which exceeds the mean length of stay for discharges within that group by a fixed number of days, or exceeds such mean length of stay by some fixed number of standard deviations, whichever is the fewer number of days.

(ii) For cases which are not included in clause (i), a subsection (d) hospital may request additional payments in any case where charges, adjusted to cost, exceed a fixed multiple of the applicable DRG prospective payment rate, or exceed such other fixed dollar amount, whichever is greater, or, for discharges in fiscal years beginning on or after October 1, 1994, exceed the sum of the applicable DRG prospective payment rate plus any amounts payable under subparagraphs (B) and (F) plus a fixed dollar amount determined by the Secretary.

(iii) The amount of such additional payment under clauses (i) and (ii) shall be determined by the Secretary and shall (except as payments under clause (i) are required to be reduced to take into account the requirements of clause (v)) approximate the marginal cost of care beyond the cutoff point applicable under clause (i) or (ii).

(iv) The total amount of the additional payments made under this subparagraph for discharges in a fiscal year may not be less than 5 percent nor more than 6 percent of the total payments projected or estimated to be made based on DRG prospective payment rates for discharges in that year.

(v) The Secretary shall provide that—

(I) the day outlier percentage for fiscal year 1995 shall be 75 percent of the day outlier percentage for fiscal year 1994;

(II) the day outlier percentage for fiscal year 1996 shall be 50 percent of the day outlier percentage for fiscal year 1994; and

(III) the day outlier percentage for fiscal year 1997 shall be 25 percent of the day outlier percentage for fiscal year 1994.

(vi) For purposes of this subparagraph, the term "day outlier percentage" means, for a fiscal year, the percentage of the total additional payments made by the Secretary under this subparagraph for discharges in that fiscal year which are additional payments under clause (i).

(B) The Secretary shall provide for an additional payment amount for subsection (d) hospitals with indirect costs of medical education, in an amount computed in the same manner as the adjustment for such costs under regulations (in effect as of January 1, 1983) under subsection (a)(2), except as follows:

(i) The amount of such additional payment shall be determined by multiplying (I) the sum of the amount determined under paragraph (1)(A)(ii)(II) (or, if applicable, the amount determined under paragraph (1)(A)(iii)) and, for cases qualifying for additional payment under subparagraph (A)(i), the amount paid to the hospital under subparagraph (A), by (II) the indirect teaching adjustment factor described in clause (ii).

(ii) For purposes of clause (i)(II), the indirect teaching adjustment factor is equal to c × A (((1+r) to the nth power) − 1), where "r" is the ratio of the hospital's full-time equivalent interns and residents to beds and "n" equals .405. Subject to clause (ix), for discharges occurring—

(I) on or after October 1, 1988, and before October 1, 1997, "c" is equal to 1.89;

(II) during fiscal year 1998, "c" is equal to 1.72;

(III) during fiscal year 1999, "c" is equal to 1.6;

(IV) during fiscal year 2000, "c" is equal to 1.47;

(V) during fiscal year 2001, "c" is equal to 1.54;

(VI) during fiscal year 2002, "c" is equal to 1.6;

(VII) on or after October 1, 2002, and before April 1, 2004, "c" is equal to 1.35;

(VIII) on or after April 1, 2004, and before October 1, 2004, "c" is equal to 1.47;

(IX) during fiscal year 2005, "c" is equal to 1.42;

(X) during fiscal year 2006, "c" is equal to 1.37;

(XI) during fiscal year 2007, "c" is equal to 1.32; and

(XII) on or after October 1, 2007, "c" is equal to 1.35.

(iii) In determining such adjustment the Secretary shall not distinguish between those interns and residents who are employees of a hospital and those interns and residents who furnish services to a hospital but are not employees of such hospital.

(iv)(I) Effective for discharges occurring on or after October 1, 1997, and before July 1, 2010, all the time spent by an intern or resident in patient care activities under an approved medical residency training program at an entity in a nonhospital setting shall be counted towards the determination of full-time equivalency if the hospital incurs all, or substantially all, of the costs for the training program in that setting.

(II) Effective for discharges occurring on or after July 1, 2010, all the time spent by an intern or resident in patient care activities in a nonprovider setting shall be counted towards the determination of full-time equivalency if a hospital incurs the costs of the stipends and fringe benefits of the intern or resident during the time the intern or resident spends in that setting. If more than one hospital incurs these costs, either directly or through a third party, such hospitals shall count a proportional share of the time, as determined by written agreement between the hospitals, that a resident spends training in that setting.

(v) In determining the adjustment with respect to a hospital for discharges occurring on or after October 1, 1997, the total number of full-time equivalent interns and residents in the fields of allopathic and osteopathic medicine in either a hospital or nonhospital setting may not exceed the number (or, 130 percent of such number in the case of a hospital located in a rural area) of such full-time equivalent interns and residents in the hospital with respect to the hospital's most recent cost reporting period ending on or before December 31, 1996. Rules similar to the rules of subsection (h)(4)(F)(ii) shall apply for purposes of this clause. The provisions of subsections (h)(4)(H)(vi), (h)(7), and (h)(8) shall apply with respect to the first sentence of this clause in the same manner as they apply with respect to subsection (h)(4)(F)(i).

(vi) For purposes of clause (ii)—

(I) "r" may not exceed the ratio of the number of interns and residents, subject to the limit under clause (v), with respect to the hospital for its most recent cost reporting period to the hospital's available beds (as defined by the Secretary) during that cost reporting period, and

(II) for the hospital's cost reporting periods beginning on or after October 1, 1997, subject to the limits described in clauses (iv) and (v), the total number of full-time equivalent residents for payment purposes shall equal the average of the actual full-time equivalent resident count for the cost reporting period and the preceding two cost reporting periods.

In the case of the first cost reporting period beginning on or after October 1, 1997, subclause (II) shall be applied by using the average for such period and the preceding cost reporting period.

(vii) If any cost reporting period beginning on or after October 1, 1997, is not equal to twelve months, the Secretary shall make appropriate modifications to ensure that the average full-time equivalent residency count pursuant to subclause (II) of clause (vi) is based on the equivalent of full twelve-month cost reporting periods.

(viii) Rules similar to the rules of subsection (h)(4)(H) shall apply for purposes of clauses (v) and (vi).

(ix) For discharges occurring on or after July 1, 2005, insofar as an additional payment amount under this subparagraph is attributable to resident positions redistributed to a hospital under subsection (h)(7)(B), in computing the indirect teaching adjustment factor under clause (ii) the adjustment shall be computed in a manner as if "c" were equal to 0.66 with respect to such resident positions.

(x) For discharges occurring on or after July 1, 2011, insofar as an additional payment amount under this subparagraph is attributable to resident positions distributed to a hospital under subsection (h)(8)(B), the indirect teaching adjustment factor shall be computed in the same manner as provided under clause (ii) with respect to such resident positions.

[(xi)](x)(I) The provisions of subparagraph (K) of subsection (h)(4) shall apply under this subparagraph in the same manner as they apply under such subsection.

(II) In determining the hospital's number of full-time equivalent residents for purposes of this subparagraph, all the time spent by an intern or resident in an approved medical residency training program in non-patient care activities, such as didactic conferences and seminars, as such time and activities are defined by the Secretary, that occurs in the hospital shall be counted toward the determination of full-time equivalency if the hospital—

(aa) is recognized as a subsection (d) hospital;

(bb) is recognized as a subsection (d) Puerto Rico hospital;

(cc) is reimbursed under a reimbursement system authorized under section 1814(b)(3) [42 USCS § 1395f(b)(3)]; or

(dd) is a provider-based hospital outpatient department.

(III) In determining the hospital's number of full-time equivalent residents for purposes of this subparagraph, all the time spent by an intern or resident in an approved medical residency training program in research activities that are not associated with the treatment or diagnosis of a particular patient, as such time and activities are defined by the Secretary, shall not be counted toward the determination of full-time equivalency.

(C)(i) The Secretary shall provide for such exceptions and adjustments to the payment amounts established under this subsection (other than under paragraph (9)) as the Secretary deems appropriate to take into account the special needs of regional and national referral centers (including those hospitals of 275 or more beds located in rural areas). A hospital which is classified as a rural hospital may appeal to the Secretary to be classified as a rural referral center under this clause on the basis of criteria (established by the Secretary) which shall allow the hospital to demonstrate that it should be so reclassified by reason of certain of its operating characteristics being similar to those of a typical urban hospital located in the same census region and which shall not require a rural osteopathic hospital to have more than 3,000 discharges in a year in order to be classified as a rural referral center. Such characteristics may include wages, scope of services, service area, and the mix of medical specialties. The Secretary shall publish the criteria not later than August 17, 1984, for implementation by October 1, 1984. An appeal allowed under this clause must be submitted to the Secretary (in such form and manner as the Secretary may prescribe) during the quarter before the first quarter of the hospital's cost reporting period (or, in the case of a cost reporting period beginning during October 1984, during the first quarter of that period), and the Secretary must make a final determination with respect to such appeal within 60 days after the date the appeal was submitted. Any payment adjustments necessitated by a reclassification based upon the appeal shall be effective at the beginning of such cost reporting period.

(ii) The Secretary shall provide, under clause (i), for the classification of a rural hospital as a regional referral center if the hospital has a case mix index equal to or greater than the median case mix index for hospitals (other than hospitals with approved teaching programs) located in an urban area in the same region (as defined in paragraph (2)(D)), has at least 5,000 discharges a year or, if less, the median number of discharges in urban hospitals in the region in which the hospital is located (or, in the case of a rural osteopathic hospital, meets the criterion established by the Secretary under clause (i) with respect to the annual number of discharges for such hospitals), and meets any other criteria established by the Secretary under clause (i).

(D)(i) For any cost reporting period beginning on or after April 1, 1990, with respect to a subsection (d) hospital which is a sole community hospital, payment under paragraph (1)(A) shall be—

(I) an amount based on 100 percent of the hospital's target amount for the cost reporting period, as defined in subsection (b)(3)(C), or

(II) the amount determined under paragraph (1)(A)(iii),

whichever results in greater payment to the hospital.

(ii) In the case of a sole community hospital that experiences, in a cost reporting period compared to the previous cost reporting period, a decrease of more than 5 percent in its total number of inpatient cases due to circumstances beyond its control, the Secretary shall provide for such adjustment to the payment amounts under this subsection (other than under paragraph (9)) as may be necessary to fully compensate the hospital for the fixed costs it incurs in the period in providing inpatient hospital services, including the reasonable cost of maintaining necessary core staff and services.

(iii) For purposes of this title [42 USCS §§ 1395 et seq.], the term "sole community hospital" means any hospital—

(I) that the Secretary determines is located more than 35 road miles from another hospital,

(II) that, by reason of factors such as the time required for an individual to travel to the nearest alternative source of appropriate inpatient care (in accordance with standards promulgated by the Secretary), location, weather conditions, travel conditions, or absence of other like hospitals (as determined by the Secretary), is the sole source of inpatient hospital services reasonably available to individuals in a geographic area who are entitled to benefits under part A [42 USCS §§ 1395c et seq.], or

(III) that is located in a rural area and designated by the Secretary as an essential access community hospital under section 1820(i)(1) [42 USCS § 1395i-4(i)(1)] as in effect on September 30, 1997.

(iv) The Secretary shall promulgate a standard for determining whether a hospital meets the criteria for classification as a sole community hospital under clause (iii)(II) because of the time required for an individual to travel to the nearest alternative source of appropriate inpatient care.

(v) If the Secretary determines that, in the case of a hospital located in a rural area and designated by the Secretary as an essential access community hospital under section 1820(i)(1) [42 USCS § 1395i-4(i)(1)] as in effect on September 30, 1997, the hospital has incurred increases in reasonable costs during a cost reporting period as a result of becoming a member of a rural health network (as defined in section 1820(d) [42 USCS § 1395i-4(d)]) in the State in which it is located, and in incurring such increases, the hospital will increase its costs for subsequent cost reporting periods, the Secretary shall increase the hospital's target amount under subsection (b)(3)(C) to account for such incurred increases.

(E)(i) The Secretary shall estimate the amount of reimbursement made for services described in section 1862(a)(14) [42 USCS § 1395y(a)(14)] with respect to which payment was made under part B [42 USCS §§ 1395j et seq.] in the base reporting periods referred to in paragraph (2)(A) and with respect to which payment is no longer being made.

(ii) The Secretary shall provide for an adjustment to the payment for subsection (d) hospitals in each fiscal year so as appropriately to reflect the net amount described in clause (i).

(F)(i) Subject to subsection (r), for discharges occurring on or after May 1, 1986, the Secretary shall provide, in accordance with this subparagraph, for an additional payment amount for each subsection (d) hospital which—

(I) serves a significantly disproportionate number of low-income patients (as defined in clause (v)), or

(II) is located in an urban area, has 100 or more beds, and can demonstrate that its net inpatient care revenues (excluding any of such revenues attributable to this title or State plans approved under title XIX [42 USCS §§ 1396 et seq.]), during the cost reporting period in which the discharges occur, for indigent care from State and local government sources exceed 30 percent of its total of such net inpatient care revenues during the period.

(ii) Subject to clause (ix), the amount of such payment for each discharge shall be determined by multiplying (I) the sum of the amount determined under paragraph (1)(A)(ii)(II) (or, if applicable, the amount determined under paragraph (1)(A)(iii)) and, for cases qualifying for additional payment under subparagraph (A)(i), the amount paid to the hospital under subparagraph (A) for that discharge, by (II) the disproportionate share adjustment percentage established under clause (iii) or (iv) for the cost reporting period in which the discharge occurs.

(iii) The disproportionate share adjustment percentage for a cost reporting period for a hospital described in clause (i)(II) is equal to 35 percent.

(iv) The disproportionate share adjustment percentage for a cost reporting period for a hospital that is not described in clause (i)(II) and that—

(I) is located in an urban area and has 100 or more beds or is described in the second sentence of clause (v), is equal to the percent determined in accordance with the applicable formula described in clause (vii);

(II) is located in an urban area and has less than 100 beds, is equal to 5 percent or, subject to clause (xiv) and for discharges occurring on or after April 1, 2001, is equal to the percent determined in accordance with clause (xiii);

(III) is located in a rural area and is not described in subclause (IV) or (V) or in the second sentence of clause (v), is equal to 4 percent or, subject to clause (xiv) and for discharges occurring on or after April 1, 2001, is equal to the percent determined in accordance with clause (xii);

(IV) is located in a rural area, is classified as a rural referral center under subparagraph (C), and is classified as a sole community hospital under subparagraph (D), is equal to 10 percent or, if greater, the percent determined in accordance with the applicable formula described in clause (viii) or, subject to clause (xiv) and for discharges occurring on or after April 1, 2001, the greater of the percentages determined under clause (x) or (xi);

(V) is located in a rural area, is classified as a rural referral center under subparagraph (C), and is not classified as a sole community hospital under subparagraph (D), is equal to the percent determined in accordance with the applicable formula described in clause (viii) or, subject to clause (xiv) and for discharges occurring on or after April 1, 2001, is equal to the percent determined in accordance with clause (xi); or

(VI) is located in a rural area, is classified as a sole community hospital under subparagraph (D), and is not classified as a rural referral center under subparagraph (C), is 10 percent or, subject to clause (xiv) and for discharges occurring on or after April 1, 2001, is equal to the percent determined in accordance with clause (x).

(v) In this subparagraph, a hospital "serves a significantly disproportionate number of low income patients" for a cost reporting period if the hospital has a disproportionate patient percentage (as defined in clause (vi)) for that period which equals, or exceeds—

(I) 15 percent, if the hospital is located in an urban area and has 100 or more beds,

(II) 30 percent (or 15 percent, for discharges occurring on or after April 1, 2001), if the hospital is located in a rural area and has more than 100 beds, or is located in a rural area and is classified as a sole community hospital under subparagraph (D),

(III) 40 percent (or 15 percent, for discharges occurring on or after April 1, 2001), if the hospital is located in an urban area and has less than 100 beds, or

(IV) 45 percent (or 15 percent, for discharges occurring on or after April 1, 2001), if the hospital is located in a rural area and is not described in subclause (II).

A hospital located in a rural area and with 500 or more beds also "serves a significantly disproportionate number of low income patients" for a cost reporting period if the hospital has a disproportionate patient percentage (as defined in clause (vi)) for that period which equals or exceeds a percentage specified by the Secretary.

(vi) In this subparagraph, the term "disproportionate patient percentage" means, with respect to a cost reporting period of a hospital, the sum of—

(I) the fraction (expressed as a percentage), the numerator of which is the number of such hospital's patient days for such period which were made up of patients who (for such days) were entitled to benefits under part A of this title [42 USCS §§ 1395c et seq.] and were entitled to supplemental security income benefits (excluding any State supplementation) under title XVI of this Act [42 USCS §§ 1381 et seq.], and the denominator of which is the number of such hospital's patient days for such period which were made up of patients who (for such days) were entitled to benefits under part A of this title [42 USCS §§ 1395c et seq.], and

(II) the fraction (expressed as a percentage), the numerator of which is the number of the hospital's patient days for such period which consist of patients who (for such days) were eligible for medical assistance under a State plan approved under title XIX [42 USCS §§ 1396 et seq.], but who were not entitled to benefits under part A of this title [42 USCS §§ 1395c et seq.], and the denominator of which is the total number of the hospital's patient days for such period.

In determining under subclause (II) the number of the hospital's patient days for such period which consist of patients who (for such days) were eligible for medical assistance under a State plan approved under title XIX [42 USCS §§ 1396 et seq.], the Secretary may, to the extent and for the period the Secretary determines appropriate, include patient days of patients not so eligible but who are regarded as such because they receive benefits under a demonstration project approved under title XI [42 USCS §§ 1301 et seq.].

(vii) The formula used to determine the disproportionate share adjustment percentage for a cost reporting period for a hospital described in clause (iv)(I) is—

(I) in the case of such a hospital with a disproportionate patient percentage (as defined in clause (vi)) greater than 20.2—

(a) for discharges occurring on or after April 1, 1990, and on or before December 31, 1990, (P−20.2)(.65) + 5.62,

(b) for discharges occurring on or after January 1, 1991, and on or before September 30, 1993, (P−20.2)(.7) + 5.62,

(c) for discharges occurring on or after October 1, 1993, and on or before September 30, 1994, (P−20.2)(.8) + 5.88, and

(d) for discharges occurring on or after October 1, 1994, (P−20.2)(.825) + 5.88; or

(II) in the case of any other such hospital—

(a) for discharges occurring on or after April 1, 1990, and on or before December 31, 1990, (P−15)(.6) + 2.5,

(b) for discharges occurring on or after January 1, 1991, and on or before September 30, 1993, (P−15)(.6) + 2.5, [and]

(c) for discharges occurring on or after October 1, 1993, (P−15)(.65) + 2.5,

where "P" is the hospital's disproportionate patient percentage (as defined in clause (vi)).

(viii) Subject to clause (xiv), the formula used to determine the disproportionate share adjustment percentage for a cost reporting period for a hospital described in clause (iv)(IV) or (iv)(V) is the percentage determined in accordance with the following formula: (P−30)(.6) &plus1; 4.0, where "P" is the hospital's disproportionate patient percentage (as defined in clause (vi)).

(ix) In the case of discharges occurring—

(I) during fiscal year 1998, the additional payment amount otherwise determined under clause (ii) shall be reduced by 1 percent;

(II) during fiscal year 1999, such additional payment amount shall be reduced by 2 percent;

(III) during fiscal years 2000 and 2001, such additional payment amount shall be reduced by 3 percent and 2 percent, respectively;

(IV) during fiscal year 2002, such additional payment amount shall be reduced by 3 percent; and

(V) during fiscal year 2003 and each subsequent fiscal year, such additional payment amount shall be reduced by 0 percent.

(x) Subject to clause (xiv), for purposes of clause (iv)(VI) (relating to sole community hospitals), in the case of a hospital for a cost reporting period with a disproportionate patient percentage (as defined in clause (vi)) that—

(I) is less than 19.3, the disproportionate share adjustment percentage is determined in accordance with the following formula: (P−15)(.65) + 2.5;

(II) is equal to or exceeds 19.3, but is less than 30.0, such adjustment percentage is equal to 5.25 percent; or

(III) is equal to or exceeds 30, such adjustment percentage is equal to 10 percent,

where "P" is the hospital's disproportionate patient percentage (as defined in clause (vi)).

(xi) Subject to clause (xiv), for purposes of clause (iv)(V) (relating to rural referral centers), in the case of a hospital for a cost reporting period with a disproportionate patient percentage (as defined in clause (vi)) that—

(I) is less than 19.3, the disproportionate share adjustment percentage is determined in accordance with the following formula: (P−15)(.65) + 2.5;

(II) is equal to or exceeds 19.3, but is less than 30.0, such adjustment percentage is equal to 5.25 percent; or

(III) is equal to or exceeds 30, such adjustment percentage is determined in accordance with the following formula: (P−30)(.6) + 5.25,

where "P" is the hospital's disproportionate

patient percentage (as defined in clause (vi)).

(xii) Subject to clause (xiv), for purposes of clause (iv)(III) (relating to small rural hospitals generally), in the case of a hospital for a cost reporting period with a disproportionate patient percentage (as defined in clause (vi)) that—

(I) is less than 19.3, the disproportionate share adjustment percentage is determined in accordance with the following formula: (P−15)(.65) + 2.5; or

(II) is equal to or exceeds 19.3, such adjustment percentage is equal to 5.25 percent,

where "P" is the hospital's disproportionate patient percentage (as defined in clause (vi)).

(xiii) Subject to clause (xiv), for purposes of clause (iv)(II) (relating to urban hospitals with less than 100 beds), in the case of a hospital for a cost reporting period with a disproportionate patient percentage (as defined in clause (vi)) that—

(I) is less than 19.3, the disproportionate share adjustment percentage is determined in accordance with the following formula: (P−15)(.65) + 2.5; or

(II) is equal to or exceeds 19.3, such adjustment percentage is equal to 5.25 percent,

where "P" is the hospital's disproportionate patient percentage (as defined in clause (vi)).

(xiv)(I) In the case of discharges occurring on or after April 1, 2004, subject to subclause (II), there shall be substituted for the disproportionate share adjustment percentage otherwise determined under clause (iv) (other than subclause (I)) or under clause (viii), (x), (xi), (xii), or (xiii), the disproportionate share adjustment percentage determined under clause (vii) (relating to large, urban hospitals).

(II) Under subclause (I), the disproportionate share adjustment percentage shall not exceed 12 percent for a hospital that is not classified as a rural referral center under subparagraph (C) or, in the case of discharges occurring on or after October 1, 2006, as a medicare-dependent, small rural hospital under subparagraph (G)(iv).

(G)(i) For any cost reporting period beginning on or after April 1, 1990, and before October 1, 1994, or discharges occurring on or after October 1, 1997, and before October 1, 2012, in the case of a subsection (d) hospital which is a medicare-dependent, small rural hospital, payment under paragraph (1)(A) shall be equal to the sum of the amount determined under clause (ii) and the amount determined under paragraph (1)(A)(iii).

(ii) The amount determined under this clause is—

(I) for discharges occurring during the 36-month period beginning with the first day of the cost reporting period that begins on or after April 1, 1990, the amount by which the hospital's target amount for the cost reporting period (as defined in subsection (b)(3)(D)) exceeds the amount determined under paragraph (1)(A)(iii); and

(II) for discharges occurring during any subsequent cost reporting period (or portion thereof) and before October 1, 1994, or discharges occurring on or after October 1, 1997, and before October 1, 2012, 50 percent (or 75 percent in the case of discharges occurring on or after October 1, 2006) of the amount by which the hospital's target amount for the cost reporting period or for discharges in the fiscal year (as defined in subsection (b)(3)(D)) exceeds the amount determined under paragraph (1)(A)(iii).

(iii) In the case of a medicare dependent, small rural hospital that experiences, in a cost reporting period compared to the previous cost reporting period, a decrease of more than 5 percent in its total number of inpatient cases due to circumstances beyond its control, the Secretary shall provide for such adjustment to the payment amounts under this subsection (other than under paragraph (9)) as may be necessary to fully compensate the hospital for the fixed costs it incurs in the period in providing inpatient hospital services, including the reasonable cost of maintaining necessary core staff and services.

(iv) The term "medicare-dependent, small rural hospital" means, with respect to any cost reporting period to which clause (i) applies, any hospital—

(I) located in a rural area,

(II) that has not more than 100 beds,

(III) that is not classified as a sole community hospital under subparagraph (D), and

(IV) for which not less than 60 percent of its inpatient days or discharges during the cost reporting period beginning in fiscal year 1987, or two of the three most recently audited cost reporting periods for which the Secretary has a settled cost report, were attributable to inpatients entitled to benefits under part A [42 USCS §§ 1395c et seq.].

(H) The Secretary may provide for such adjustments to the payment amounts under this subsection as the Secretary deems appropriate to take into account the unique circumstances of hospitals located in Alaska and Hawaii.

(I)(i) The Secretary shall provide by regulation for such other exceptions and adjustments to such payment amounts under this subsection as the Secretary deems appropriate.

(ii) In making adjustments under clause (i) for transfer cases (as defined by the Secretary) in a fiscal year, not taking in account the effect of subparagraph (J), the Secretary may make adjustments to each of the average standardized amounts determined under paragraph (3) to assure that the aggregate payments made under this subsection for such fiscal year are not greater or lesser than those that would have otherwise been made in such fiscal year.

(J)(i) The Secretary shall treat the term "transfer case" (as defined in subparagraph (I)(ii)) as including the case of a qualified discharge (as defined in clause (ii)), which is classified within a diagnosis-related group described in clause (iii), and which occurs on or after October 1, 1998. In the case of a qualified discharge for which a substantial portion of the costs of care are incurred in the early days of the inpatient stay (as defined by the Secretary), in no case may the payment amount otherwise provided under this subsection exceed an amount equal to the sum of—

(I) 50 percent of the amount of payment under this subsection for transfer cases (as established under subparagraph (I)(i)), and

(II) 50 percent of the amount of payment which would have been made under this subsection with respect to the qualified discharge if no transfer were involved.

(ii) For purposes of clause (i), subject to clause (iii), the term "qualified discharge" means a discharge classified with a diagnosis-related group (described in clause (iii)) of an individual from a subsection (d) hospital, if upon such discharge the individual—

(I) is admitted as an inpatient to a hospital or hospital unit that is not a subsection (d) hospital for the provision of inpatient hospital services;

(II) is admitted to a skilled nursing facility;

(III) is provided home health services from a home health agency, if such services relate to the condition or diagnosis for which such individual received inpatient hospital services from the subsection (d) hospital, and if such services are provided within an appropriate period (as determined by the Secretary); or

(IV) for discharges occurring on or after October 1, 2000, the individual receives post discharge services described in clause (iv)(I).

(iii) Subject to clause (iv), a diagnosis-related group described in this clause is—

(I) 1 of 10 diagnosis-related groups selected by the Secretary based upon a high volume of discharges classified within such groups and a disproportionate use of post discharge services described in clause (ii); and

(II) a diagnosis-related group specified by the Secretary under clause (iv)(II).

(iv) The Secretary shall include in the proposed rule published under subsection (e)(5)(A) for fiscal year 2001, a description of the effect of this subparagraph. The Secretary may include in the proposed rule (and in the final rule published under paragraph (6)) for fiscal year 2001 or a subsequent fiscal year, a description of—

(I) post-discharge services not described in subclauses (I), (II), and (III) of clause (ii), the receipt of which results in a qualified discharge; and

(II) diagnosis-related groups described in clause (iii)(I) in addition to the 10 selected under such clause.

(K)(i) Effective for discharges beginning on or after October 1, 2001, the Secretary shall establish a mechanism to recognize the costs of new medical services and technologies under the payment system established under this subsection. Such mechanism shall be established after notice and opportunity for public comment (in the publications required by subsection (e)(5) for a fiscal year or otherwise). Such mechanism shall be modified to meet the requirements of clause (viii).

(ii) The mechanism established pursuant to clause (i) shall—

(I) apply to a new medical service or technology if, based on the estimated costs incurred with respect to discharges involving such service or technology, the DRG prospective payment rate otherwise applicable to such discharges under this subsection is inadequate (applying a threshold specified by the Secretary that is the lesser of 75 percent of the standardized amount (increased to reflect the difference between cost and charges) or 75 percent of one standard deviation for the diagnosis-related group involved);

(II) provide for the collection of data with respect to the costs of a new medical service or technology described in subclause (I) for a period of not less than two years and not more than three years beginning on the date on which an inpatient hospital code is issued with respect to the service or technology;

(III) provide for additional payment to be made under this subsection with respect to discharges involving a new medical service or technology described in subclause (I) that occur during the period described in subclause (II) in an amount that adequately reflects the estimated average cost of such service or technology; and

(IV) provide that discharges involving such a service or technology that occur after the close of the period described in subclause (II) will be classified within a new or existing diagnosis-related group with a weighting factor under paragraph (4)(B) that is derived from cost data collected with respect to discharges occurring during such period.

(iii) For purposes of clause (ii)(II), the term "inpatient hospital code" means any code that is used with respect to inpatient hospital services for which payment may be made under this subsection and includes an alphanumeric code issued under the International Classification of Diseases, 9th Revision, Clinical Modification ("ICD-9-CM") and its subsequent revisions.

(iv) For purposes of clause (ii)(III), the term "additional payment" means, with respect to a discharge for a new medical service or technology described in clause (ii)(I), an amount that exceeds the prospective payment rate otherwise applicable under this subsection to discharges involving such service or technology that would be made but for this subparagraph.

(v) The requirement under clause (ii)(III) for an additional payment may be satisfied by means of a new-technology group (described in subparagraph (L)), an add-on payment, a payment adjustment, or any other similar mechanism for increasing the amount otherwise payable with respect to a discharge under this subsection. The Secretary may not establish a separate fee schedule for such additional payment for such services and technologies, by utilizing a methodology established under subsection (a) or (h) of section 1834 [42 USCS § 1395m] to determine the amount of such additional payment, or by other similar mechanisms or methodologies.

(vi) For purposes of this subparagraph and subparagraph (L), a medical service or technology will be considered a "new medical service or technology" if the service or technology meets criteria established by the Secretary after notice and an opportunity for public comment.

(vii) Under the mechanism under this subparagraph, the Secretary shall provide for the addition of new diagnosis and procedure codes in April 1 of each year, but the addition of such codes shall not require the Secretary to adjust the payment (or diagnosis-related group classification) under this subsection until the fiscal year that begins after such date.

(viii) The mechanism established pursuant to clause (i) shall be adjusted to provide, before publication of a proposed rule, for public input regarding whether a new service or technology represents an advance in medical technology that substantially improves the diagnosis or treatment of individuals entitled to benefits under part A [42 USCS §§ 1395c et seq.] as follows:

(I) The Secretary shall make public and periodically update a list of all the services and technologies for which an application for additional payment under this subparagraph is pending.

(II) The Secretary shall accept comments, recommendations, and data from the public regarding whether the service or technology represents a substantial improvement.

(III) The Secretary shall provide for a meeting at which organizations representing hospitals, physicians, such individuals, manufacturers, and any other interested party may present comments, recommendations, and data to the clinical staff of the Centers for Medicare & Medicaid Services before publication of a notice of proposed rulemaking regarding whether service or technology represents a substantial improvement.

(ix) Before establishing any add-on payment under this subparagraph with respect to a new technology, the Secretary shall seek to identify one or more diagnosis-related groups associated with such technology, based on similar clinical or anatomical characteristics and the cost of the technology. Within such groups the Secretary shall assign an eligible new technology into a diagnosis-related group where the average costs of care most closely approximate the costs of care of using the new technology. No add-on payment under this subparagraph shall be made with respect to such new technology and this clause shall not affect the application of paragraph (4)(C)(iii).

(L)(i) In establishing the mechanism under subparagraph (K), the Secretary may establish new-technology groups into which a new medical service or technology will be classified if, based on the estimated average costs incurred with respect to discharges involving such service or technology, the DRG prospective payment rate otherwise applicable to such discharges under this subsection is inadequate.

(ii) Such groups—

(I) shall not be based on the costs associated with a specific new medical service or technology; but

(II) shall, in combination with the applicable standardized amounts and the weighting factors assigned to such groups under paragraph (4)(B), reflect such cost cohorts as the Secretary determines are appropriate for all new medical services and technologies that are likely to be provided as inpatient hospital services in a fiscal year.

(iii) The methodology for classifying specific hospital discharges within a diagnosis-related group under paragraph (4)(A) or a new-technology group shall provide that a specific hospital discharge may not be classified within both a diagnosis-related group and a new-technology group.

(6) The Secretary shall provide for publication in the Federal Register, on or before the August 1 before each fiscal year (beginning with fiscal year 1984), of a description of the methodology and data used in computing the adjusted DRG prospective payment rates under this subsection, including any adjustments required under subsection (e)(1)(B).

(7) There shall be no administrative or judicial review under section 1878 [42 USCS § 1395oo] or otherwise of—

(A) the determination of the requirement, or the proportional amount, of any adjustment effected pursuant to subsection (e)(1) or the determination of the applicable percentage increase under paragraph (12)(A)(ii), and

(B) the establishment of diagnosis-related groups, of the methodology for the classification of discharges within such groups, and of the appropriate weighting factors thereof under paragraph (4), including the selection and revision of codes under paragraph (4)(D).

(8)(A) In the case of any hospital which is located in an area which is, at any time after April 20, 1983, reclassified from an urban to a rural area, payments to such hospital for the first two cost reporting periods for which such reclassification is effective shall be made as follows:

(i) For the first such cost reporting period, payment shall be equal to the amount payable to such hospital for such reporting period on the basis of the rural classification, plus an amount equal to two-thirds of the amount (if any) by which—

(I) the amount which would have been payable to such hospital for such reporting period on the basis of an urban classification, exceeds

(II) the amount payable to such hospital for such reporting period on the basis of the rural classification.

(ii) For the second such cost reporting period, payment shall be equal to the amount payable to such hospital for such reporting period on the basis of the rural classification, plus an amount equal to one-third of the amount (if any) by which—

(I) the amount which would have been payable to such hospital for such reporting period on the basis of an urban classification, exceeds

(II) the amount payable to such hospital for such reporting period on the basis of the rural classification.

(B)(i) For purposes of this subsection, the Secretary shall treat a hospital located in a rural county adjacent to one or more urban areas as being located in the urban metropolitan statistical area to which the greatest number of workers in the county commute, if the rural county would otherwise be considered part of an urban area, under the standards for designating Metropolitan Statistical Areas (and for designating New England County Metropolitan Areas) described in clause (ii), if the commuting rates used in determining outlying counties (or, for New England, similar recognized areas) were determined on the basis of the aggregate number of resident workers who commute to (and, if applicable under the standards, from) the central county or counties of all contiguous Metropolitan Statistical Areas (or New England County Metropolitan Areas).

(ii) The standards described in this clause for cost reporting periods beginning in a fiscal year—

(I) before fiscal year 2003, are the standards published in the Federal Register on January 3, 1980, or, at the election of the hospital with respect to fiscal years 2001 and 2002, standards so published on March 30, 1990; and

(II) after fiscal year 2002, are the standards published in the Federal Register by the Director of the Office of Management and Budget based on the most recent available decennial population data.

Subparagraphs (C) and (D) shall not apply with respect to the application of subclause (I).

(C)(i) If the application of subparagraph (B) or a decision of the Medicare Geographic Classification Review Board or the Secretary under paragraph (10), by treating hospitals located in a rural county or counties as being located in an urban area, or by treating hospitals located in one urban area as being located in another urban area—

(I) reduces the wage index for that urban area (as applied under this subsection) by 1 percentage point or less, the Secretary, in calculating such wage index under this subsection, shall exclude those hospitals so treated, or

(II) reduces the wage index for that urban area by more than 1 percentage point (as applied under this subsection), the Secretary shall calculate and apply such wage index under this subsection separately to hospitals located in such urban area (excluding all the hospitals so treated) and to the hospitals so treated (as if such hospitals were located in such urban area).

(ii) If the application of subparagraph (B) or a decision of the Medicare Geographic Classification Review Board or the Secretary under paragraph (10), by treating hospitals located in a rural county or counties as not being located in the rural area in a State, reduces the wage index for that rural area (as applied under this subsection), the Secretary shall calculate and apply such wage index under this subsection as if the hospitals so treated had not been excluded from calculation of the wage index for that rural area.

(iii) The application of subparagraph (B) or a decision of the Medicare Geographic Classification Review Board or the Secretary under paragraph (10) may not result in the reduction of any county's wage index to a level below the wage index for rural areas in the State in which the county is located.

(iv) The application of subparagraph (B) or a decision of the Medicare Geographic Classification Review Board or of the Secretary under paragraph (10) may not result in a reduction in an urban area's wage index if—

(I) the urban area has a wage index below the wage index for rural areas in the State in which it is located; or

(II) the urban area is located in a State that is composed of a single urban area.

(v) This subparagraph shall apply with respect to discharges occurring in a fiscal year only if the Secretary uses a method for making adjustments to the DRG prospective payment rate for area differences in hospital wage levels under paragraph (3)(E) for the fiscal year that is based on the use of Metropolitan Statistical Area classifications.

(D) The Secretary shall make a proportional adjustment in the standardized amounts determined under paragraph (3) to assure that the provisions of subparagraphs (B) and (C) or a decision of the Medicare Geographic Classification Review Board or the Secretary under paragraph (10) do not result in aggregate payments under this section that are greater or less than those that would otherwise be made.

(E)(i) For purposes of this subsection, not later than 60 days after the receipt of an application (in a form and manner determined by the Secretary) from a subsection (d) hospital described in clause (ii), the Secretary shall treat the hospital as being located in the rural area (as defined in paragraph (2)(D)) of the State in which the hospital is located.

(ii) For purposes of clause (i), a subsection (d) hospital described in this clause is a subsection (d) hospital that is located in an urban area (as defined in paragraph (2)(D)) and satisfies any of the following criteria:

(I) The hospital is located in a rural census tract of a metropolitan statistical area (as determined under the most recent modification of the Goldsmith Modification, originally published in the Federal Register on February 27, 1992 (57 Fed. Reg. 6725)).

(II) The hospital is located in an area designated by any law or regulation of such State as a rural area (or is designated by such State as a rural hospital).

(III) The hospital would qualify as a rural, regional, or national referral center under paragraph (5)(C) or as a sole community hospital under paragraph (5)(D) if the hospital were located in a rural area.

(IV) The hospital meets such other criteria as the Secretary may specify.

(9)(A) Notwithstanding section 1814(b) [42 USCS § 1395f(b)] but subject to the provisions of section 1813 [42 USCS § 1395e], the amount of the payment with respect to the operating costs of inpatient hospital services of a subsection (d) Puerto Rico hospital for inpatient hospital discharges is equal to the sum of—

(i) the applicable Puerto Rico percentage (specified in subparagraph (E)) of the Puerto Rico adjusted DRG prospective payment rate (determined under subparagraph (B) or (C)) for such discharges,

(ii) the applicable Federal percentage (specified in subparagraph (E)) of—

(I) for discharges beginning in a fiscal year beginning on or after October 1, 1997, and before October 1, 2003, the discharge-weighted average of—

(aa) the national adjusted DRG prospective payment rate (determined under paragraph (3)(D)) for hospitals located in a large urban area,

(bb) such rate for hospitals located in other urban areas, and

(cc) such rate for hospitals located in a rural area,

for such discharges, adjusted in the manner provided in paragraph (3)(E) for different area wage levels; and

(II) for discharges in a fiscal year beginning on or after October 1, 2003, the national DRG prospective payment rate determined under paragraph (3)(D)(iii) for hospitals located in any area for such discharges, adjusted in the manner provided in paragraph (3)(E) for different area wage levels.

As used in this section, the term "subsection (d) Puerto Rico hospital" means a hospital that is located in Puerto Rico and that would be a subsection (d) hospital (as defined in paragraph (1)(B)) if it were located in one of the 50 States.

(B) The Secretary shall determine a Puerto Rico adjusted DRG prospective payment rate, for each inpatient hospital discharge in fiscal year 1988 involving inpatient hospital services of a subsection (d) Puerto Rico hospital for which payment may be made under part A of this title [42 USCS §§ 1395c et seq.]. Such rate shall be determined for such hospitals located in urban or rural areas within Puerto Rico, as follows:

(i) The Secretary shall determine the target amount (as defined in subsection (b)(3)(A)) for the hospital for the cost reporting period beginning in fiscal year 1987 and increase such amount by prorating the applicable percentage increase (as defined in subsection (b)(3)(B)) to update the amount to the midpoint in fiscal year 1988.

(ii) The Secretary shall standardize the amount determined under clause (i) for each hospital by—

(I) excluding an estimate of indirect medical education costs,

(II) adjusting for variations among hospitals by area in the average hospital wage level,

(III) adjusting for variations in case mix among hospitals, and

(IV) excluding an estimate of the additional payments to certain subsection (d) Puerto Rico hospitals to be made under subparagraph (D)(iii) (relating to disproportionate share payments).

(iii) The Secretary shall compute a discharge weighted average of the standardized amounts determined under clause (ii) for all hospitals located in an urban area and for all hospitals located in a rural area (as such terms are defined in paragraph (2)(D)).

(iv) The Secretary shall reduce the average standardized amount by a proportion equal to the proportion (estimated by the Secretary) of the amount of payments under this paragraph which are additional payments described in subparagraph (D)(i) (relating to outlier payments).

(v) For each discharge classified within a diagnosis-related group for hospitals located in an urban or rural area, respectively, the Secretary shall establish a Puerto Rico DRG prospective payment rate equal to the product of—

(I) the average standardized amount (computed under clause (iii) and reduced under clause (iv)) for hospitals located in an urban or rural area, respectively, and

(II) the weighting factor (determined under paragraph (4)(B)) for that diagnosis-related group.

(vi) The Secretary shall adjust the proportion (as estimated by the Secretary from time to time) of hospitals' costs which are attributable to wages and wage-related costs, of the Puerto Rico DRG prospective payment rate computed under clause (v) for area differences in hospital wage levels by a factor (established by the Secretary) reflecting the relative hospital wage level in the geographic area of the hospital compared to the Puerto Rican average hospital wage level.

(C) The Secretary shall determine a Puerto Rico adjusted DRG prospective payment rate, for each inpatient hospital discharge after fiscal year 1988 involving inpatient hospital services of a subsection (d) Puerto Rico hospital for which payment may be made under part A of this title [42 USCS §§ 1395c et seq.]. Such rate shall be determined for hospitals located in urban or rural areas within Puerto Rico as follows:

(i)(I) For discharges in a fiscal year after fiscal year 1988 and before fiscal year 2004, the Secretary shall compute an average standardized amount for hospitals located in an urban area and for hospitals located in a rural area equal to the respective average standardized amount computed for the previous fiscal year under subparagraph (B)(iii) or under this clause, increased for fiscal year 1989 by the applicable percentage increase under subsection (b)(3)(B), and adjusted for subsequent fiscal years in accordance with the final determination of the Secretary under subsection (e)(4), and adjusted to reflect the most recent case-mix data available.

(II) For discharges occurring in a fiscal year (beginning with fiscal year 2004), the Secretary shall compute an average standardized amount for hospitals located in any area of Puerto Rico that is equal to the average standardized amount computed under subclause (I) for fiscal year 2003 for hospitals in a large urban area (or, beginning with fiscal year 2005, for all hospitals in the previous fiscal year) increased by the applicable percentage increase under subsection (b)(3)(B) for the fiscal year involved.

(ii) The Secretary shall reduce each of the average standardized amounts (or for fiscal year 2004 and thereafter, the average standardized amount) by a proportion equal to the proportion (estimated by the Secretary) of the amount of payments under this paragraph which are additional payments described in subparagraph (D)(i) (relating to outlier payments).

(iii) For each discharge classified within a diagnosis-related group for hospitals located in an urban or rural area, respectively, the Secretary shall establish a Puerto Rico DRG prospective payment rate equal to the product of—

(I) the average standardized amount (computed under clause (i) and reduced under clause (ii)), and

(II) the weighting factor (determined under paragraph (4)(B)) for that diagnosis-related group.

(iv)(I) The Secretary shall adjust the proportion (as estimated by the Secretary from time to time) of hospitals' costs which are attributable to wages and wage-related costs, of the Puerto Rico DRG prospective payment rate computed under clause (iii) for area differences in hospital wage levels by a factor (established by the Secretary) reflecting the relative hospital wage level in the geographic area of the hospital compared to the Puerto Rico average hospital wage level. The second and third sentences of paragraph (3)(E)(i) shall apply to subsection (d) Puerto Rico hospitals under this clause in the same manner as they apply to subsection (d) hospitals under such paragraph and, for purposes of this clause, any reference in such paragraph to a subsection (d) hospital is deemed a reference to a subsection (d) Puerto Rico hospital.

(II) For discharges occurring on or after October 1, 2004, the Secretary shall substitute "62 percent" for the proportion described in the first sentence of clause (i), unless the application of this subclause would result in lower payments to a hospital than would otherwise be made.

(D) The following provisions of paragraph (5) shall apply to subsection (d) Puerto Rico hospitals receiving payment under this paragraph in the same manner and to the extent as they apply to subsection (d) hospitals receiving payment under this subsection:

(i) Subparagraph (A) (relating to outlier payments).

(ii) Subparagraph (B) (relating to payments for indirect medical education costs), except that for this purpose the sum of the amount determined under subparagraph (A) of this paragraph and the amount paid to the hospital under clause (i) of this subparagraph shall be substituted for the sum referred to in paragraph (5)(B)(i)(I).

(iii) Subparagraph (F) (relating to disproportionate share payments), except that for this purpose the sum described in clause (ii) of this subparagraph shall be substituted for the sum referred to in paragraph (5)(F)(ii)(I).

(iv) Subparagraph (H) (relating to exceptions and adjustments).

(E) For purposes of subparagraph (A), for discharges occurring—

(i) on or after October 1, 1987, and before October 1, 1997, the applicable Puerto Rico percentage is 75 percent and the applicable Federal percentage is 25 percent;

(ii) on or after October 1, 1997, and before April 1, 2004, the applicable Puerto Rico percentage is 50 percent and the applicable Federal percentage is 50 percent;

(iii) on or after April 1, 2004, and before October 1, 2004, the applicable Puerto Rico percentage is 37.5 percent and the applicable Federal percentage is 62.5 percent; and

(iv) on or after October 1, 2004, the applicable Puerto Rico percentage is 25 percent and the applicable Federal percentage is 75 percent.

(10)(A) There is hereby established the Medicare Geographic Classification Review Board (hereinafter in this paragraph referred to as the "Board").

(B)(i) The Board shall be composed of 5 members appointed by the Secretary without regard to the provisions of title 5, United States Code, governing appointments in the competitive service. Two of such members shall be representative of subsection (d) hospitals located in a rural area under paragraph (2)(D). At least 1 member shall be knowledgeable in the field of analyzing costs with respect to the provision of inpatient hospital services.

(ii) The Secretary shall make initial appointments to the Board as provided in this paragraph within 180 days after the date of the enactment of this paragraph.

(C)(i) The Board shall consider the application of any subsection (d) hospital requesting that the Secretary change the hospital's geographic classification for purposes of determining for a fiscal year—

(I) the hospital's average standardized amount under paragraph (2)(D), or

(II) the factor used to adjust the DRG prospective payment rate for area differences in hospital wage levels that applies to such hospital under paragraph (3)(E).

(ii) A hospital requesting a change in geographic classification under clause (i) for a fiscal year shall submit its application to the Board not later than the first day of the 13-month period ending on September 30 of the preceding fiscal year.

(iii)(I) The Board shall render a decision on an application submitted under clause (i) not later than 180 days after the deadline referred to in clause (ii).

(II) Appeal of decisions of the Board shall be subject to the provisions of section 557b [557(b)] of title 5, United States Code. The Secretary shall issue a decision on such an appeal not later than 90 days after the date on which the appeal is filed. The decision of the Secretary shall be final and shall not be subject to judicial review.

(D)(i) The Secretary shall publish guidelines to be utilized by the Board in rendering decisions on applications submitted under this paragraph, and shall include in such guidelines the following:

(I) Guidelines for comparing wages, taking into account (to the extent the Secretary determines appropriate) occupational mix, in the area in which the hospital is classified and the area in which the hospital is applying to be classified.

(II) Guidelines for determining whether the county in which the hospital is located should be treated as being a part of a particular Metropolitan Statistical Area.

(III) Guidelines for considering information provided by an applicant with respect to the effects of the hospital's geographic classification on access to inpatient hospital services by medicare beneficiaries.

(IV) Guidelines for considering the appropriateness of the criteria used to define New England County Metropolitan Areas.

(ii) Notwithstanding clause (i), if the Secretary uses a method for making adjustments to the DRG prospective payment rate for area differences in hospital wage levels under paragraph (3)(E) that is not based on the use of Metropolitan Statistical Area classifications, the Secretary may revise the guidelines published under clause (i) to the extent such guidelines are used to determine the appropriateness of the geographic area in which the hospital is determined to be located for purposes of making such adjustments.

(iii) Under the guidelines published by the Secretary under clause (i), in the case of a hospital which has ever been classified by the Secretary as a rural referral center under paragraph (5)(C), the Board may not reject the application of the hospital under this paragraph on the basis of any comparison between the average hourly wage of the hospital and the average hourly wage of hospitals in the area in which it is located.

(iv) The Secretary shall publish the guidelines described in clause (i) by July 1, 1990.

(v) Any decision of the Board to reclassify a subsection (d) hospital for purposes of the adjustment factor described in subparagraph (C)(i)(II) for fiscal year 2001 or any fiscal year thereafter shall be effective for a period of 3 fiscal years, except that the Secretary shall establish procedures under which a subsection (d) hospital may elect to terminate such reclassification before the end of such period.

(vi) Such guidelines shall provide that, in making decisions on applications for reclassification for the purposes described in clause (v) for fiscal year 2003 and any succeeding fiscal year, the Board shall base any comparison of the average hourly wage for the hospital with the average hourly wage for hospitals in an area on—

(I) an average of the average hourly wage amount for the hospital from the most recently published hospital wage survey data of the Secretary (as of the date on which the hospital applies for reclassification) and such amount from each of the two immediately preceding surveys; and

(II) an average of the average hourly wage amount for hospitals in such area from the most recently published hospital wage survey data of the Secretary (as of the date on which the hospital applies for reclassification) and such amount from each of the two immediately preceding surveys.

(E)(i) The Board shall have full power and authority to make rules and establish procedures, not inconsistent with the provisions of this title [42 USCS §§ 1395 et seq.] or regulations of the Secretary, which are necessary or appropriate to carry out the provisions of this paragraph. In the course of any hearing the Board may administer oaths and affirmations. The provisions of subsections (d) and (e) of section 205 [42 USCS § 405] with respect to subpenas shall apply to the Board to the same extent as such provisions apply to the Secretary with respect to title II [42 USCS §§ 401 et seq.].

(ii) The Board is authorized to engage such technical assistance and to receive such information as may be required to carry out its functions, and the Secretary shall, in addition, make available to the Board such secretarial, clerical, and other assistance as the Board may require to carry out its functions.

(F)(i) Each member of the Board who is not an officer or employee of the Federal Government shall be compensated at a rate equal to the daily equivalent of the annual rate of basic pay prescribed for grade GS-18 of the General Schedule under section 5332 of title 5, United States Code, for each day (including travel time) during which such member is engaged in the performance of the duties of the Board. Each member of the Board who is an officer or employee of the United States shall serve without compensation in addition to that received for service as an officer or employee of the United States.

(ii) Members of the Board shall be allowed travel expenses, including per diem in lieu of subsistence, at rates authorized for employees of agencies under subchapter I of chapter 57 of title 5, United States Code [5 USCS §§ 5701 et seq.], while away from their homes or regular places of business in the performance of services for the Board.

(11) Additional payments for managed care enrollees. (A) In general. For portions of cost reporting periods occurring on or after January 1, 1998, the Secretary shall provide for an additional payment amount for each applicable discharge of any subsection (d) hospital that has an approved medical residency training program.

(B) Applicable discharge. For purposes of this paragraph, the term "applicable discharge" means the discharge of any individual who is enrolled under a risk-sharing contract with an eligible organization under section 1876 [42 USCS § 1395mm] and who is entitled to benefits under part A [42 USCS §§ 1395c et seq.] or any individual who is enrolled with a Medicare+Choice organization under part C [42 USCS §§ 1395w-21 et seq.].

(C) Determination of amount. The amount of the payment under this paragraph with respect to any applicable discharge shall be equal to the applicable percentage (as defined in subsection (h)(3)(D)(ii)) of the estimated average per discharge amount that would otherwise have been paid under paragraph (5)(B) if the individuals had not been enrolled as described in subparagraph (B).

(D) Special rule for hospitals under reimbursement system. The Secretary shall establish rules for the application of this paragraph to a hospital reimbursed under a reimbursement system authorized under section 1814(b)(3) [42 USCS § 1395f(b)(3)] in the same manner as it would apply to the hospital if it were not reimbursed under such section.

(12) Payment adjustment for low-volume hospitals. (A) In general. In addition to any payments calculated under this section for a subsection (d) hospital, for discharges occurring during a fiscal year (beginning with fiscal year 2005), the Secretary shall provide for an additional payment amount to each low-volume hospital (as defined in subparagraph (C)(i)) for discharges occurring during that fiscal year that is equal to the applicable percentage increase (determined under subparagraph (B) or (D) for the hospital involved) in the amount paid to such hospital under this section for such discharges (determined without regard to this paragraph).

(B) Applicable percentage increase. For discharges occurring in fiscal years 2005 through 2010 and for discharges occurring in fiscal year 2013 and subsequent fiscal years, the Secretary shall determine an applicable percentage increase for purposes of subparagraph (A) as follows:

(i) The Secretary shall determine the empirical relationship for subsection (d) hospitals between the standardized cost-per-case for such hospitals and the total number of discharges of such hospitals and the amount of the additional incremental costs (if any) that are associated with such number of discharges.

(ii) The applicable percentage increase shall be determined based upon such relationship in a manner that reflects, based upon the number of such discharges for a subsection (d) hospital, such additional incremental costs.

(iii) In no case shall the applicable percentage increase exceed 25 percent.

(C) Definitions. (i) Low-volume hospital. For purposes of this paragraph, the term "low-volume hospital" means, for a fiscal year, a subsection (d) hospital (as defined in paragraph (1)(B)) that the Secretary determines is located more than 25 road miles (or, with respect to fiscal years 2011 and 2012, 15 road miles) from another subsection (d) hospital and has less than 800 discharges (or, with respect to fiscal years 2011 and 2012, 1,600 discharges of individuals entitled to, or enrolled for, benefits under part A [42 USCS §§ 1395c et seq.]) during the fiscal year.

(ii) Discharge. For purposes of subparagraph (B) and clause (i), the term "discharge" means an inpatient acute care discharge of an individual regardless of whether the individual is entitled to benefits under part A [42 USCS §§ 1395c et seq.].

(D) Temporary applicable percentage increase. For discharges occurring in fiscal years 2011 and 2012, the Secretary shall determine an applicable percentage increase for purposes of subparagraph (A) using a continuous linear sliding scale ranging from 25 percent for low-volume hospitals with 200 or fewer discharges of individuals entitled to, or enrolled for, benefits under part A [42 USCS §§ 1395c et seq.] in the fiscal year to 0 percent for low-volume hospitals with greater than 1,600 discharges of such individuals in the fiscal year.

(13)(A) In order to recognize commuting patterns among geographic areas, the Secretary shall establish a process through application or otherwise for an increase of the wage index applied under paragraph (3)(E) for subsection (d) hospitals located in a qualifying county described in subparagraph (B) in the amount computed under subparagraph (D) based on out-migration of hospital employees who reside in that county to any higher wage index area.

(B) The Secretary shall establish criteria for a qualifying county under this subparagraph based on the out-migration referred to in subparagraph (A) and differences in the area wage indices. Under such criteria the Secretary shall, utilizing such data as the Secretary determines to be appropriate, establish—

(i) a threshold percentage, established by the Secretary, of the weighted average of the area wage index or indices for the higher wage index areas involved;

(ii) a threshold (of not less than 10 percent) for minimum out-migration to a higher wage index area or areas; and

(iii) a requirement that the average hourly wage of the hospitals in the qualifying county equals or exceeds the average hourly wage of all the hospitals in the area in which the qualifying county is located.

(C) For purposes of this paragraph, the term "higher wage index area" means, with respect to a county, an area with a wage index that exceeds that of the county.

(D) The increase in the wage index under subparagraph (A) for a qualifying county shall be equal to the percentage of the hospital employees residing in the qualifying county who are employed in any higher wage index area multiplied by the sum of the products, for each higher wage index area of—

(i) the difference between—

(I) the wage index for such higher wage index area, and

(II) the wage index of the qualifying county; and

(ii) the number of hospital employees residing in the qualifying county who are employed in such higher wage index area divided by the total number of hospital employees residing in the qualifying county who are employed in any higher wage index area.

(E) The process under this paragraph may be based upon the process used by the Medicare Geographic Classification Review Board under paragraph (10). As the Secretary determines to be appropriate to carry out such process, the Secretary may require hospitals (including subsection (d) hospitals and other hospitals) and critical access hospitals, as required under section 1866(a)(1)(T) [42 USCS § 1395cc(a)(1)(T)], to submit data regarding the location of residence, or the Secretary may use data from other sources.

(F) A wage index increase under this paragraph shall be effective for a period of 3 fiscal years, except that the Secretary shall establish procedures under which a subsection (d) hospital may elect to waive the application of such wage index increase.

(G) A hospital in a county that has a wage index increase under this paragraph for a period and that has not waived the application of such an increase under subparagraph (F) is not eligible for reclassification under paragraph (8) or (10) during that period.

(H) Any increase in a wage index under this paragraph for a county shall not be taken into account for purposes of—

(i) computing the wage index for portions of the wage index area (not including the county) in which the county is located; or

(ii) applying any budget neutrality adjustment with respect to such index under paragraph (8)(D).

(I) The thresholds described in subparagraph (B), data on hospital employees used under this paragraph, and any determination of the Secretary under the process described in subparagraph (E) shall be final and shall not be subject to judicial review.

(e) Proportional adjustments in applicable percentage increases; Prospective Payment Assessment Commission [Medicare Payment Advisory Commission]. (1)(A) For cost reporting periods of hospitals beginning in fiscal year 1984 or fiscal year 1985, the Secretary shall provide for such proportional adjustment in the applicable percentage increase (otherwise applicable to the periods under subsection (b)(3)(B)) as may be necessary to assure that—

(i) the aggregate payment amounts otherwise provided under subsection (d)(1)(A)(i)(I) for that fiscal year for operating costs of inpatient hospital services of hospitals (excluding payments made under section 1866(a)(1)(F)) [42 USCS § 1395cc(a)(1)(F)], are not greater or less than—

(ii) the target percentage (as defined in subsection (d)(1)(C)) of the payment amounts which would have been payable for such services for those same hospitals for that fiscal year under this section under the law as in effect before the date of the enactment of the Social Security Amendments of 1983 [enacted April 20, 1983] (excluding payments made under section 1866(a)(1)(F) [42 USCS § 1395cc(a)(1)(F)];

except that the adjustment made under this subparagraph shall apply only to subsection (d) hospitals and shall not apply for purposes of making computations under subsection (d)(2)(B)(ii) or subsection (d)(3)(A).

(B) For discharges occurring in fiscal year 1984 or fiscal year 1985, the Secretary shall provide under subsections (d)(2)(F) and (d)(3)(C) for such equal proportional adjustment in each of the average standardized amounts otherwise computed for that fiscal year as may be necessary to assure that—

(i) the aggregate payment amounts otherwise provided under subsection (d)(1)(A)(i)(II) and (d)(5) for that fiscal year for operating costs of inpatient hospital services of hospitals (excluding payments made under section 1866(a)(1)(F) [42 USCS § 1395cc(a)(1)(F)]), are not greater or less than—

(ii) the DRG percentage (as defined in subsection (d)(1)(C)) of the payment amounts which would have been payable for such services for those same hospitals for that fiscal year under this section under the law as in effect before the date of the enactment of the Social Security Amendments of 1983 [enacted April 20, 1983] (excluding payments made under section 1866(a)(1)(F) [42 USCS § 1395cc(a)(1)(F)]).

(C) For discharges occurring in fiscal year 1988, the Secretary shall provide for such equal proportional adjustment in each of the average standardized amounts otherwise computed under subsection (d)(3) for that fiscal year as may be necessary to assure that—

(i) the aggregate payment amounts otherwise provided under subsections (d)(1)(A)(iii), (d)(5), and (d)(9) for that fiscal year for operating costs of inpatient hospital services of subsection (d) hospitals and subsection (d) Puerto Rico hospitals, are not greater or less than—

(ii) the payment amounts that would have been payable for such services for those same hospitals for that fiscal year but for the enactment of the amendments made by section 9304 of the Omnibus Budget Reconciliation Act of 1986 [enacted Oct. 21, 1986].

(2) [Deleted]

(3) [Deleted]

(4)(A) Taking into consideration the recommendations of the Commission, the Secretary shall recommend for each fiscal year (beginning with fiscal year 1988) an appropriate change factor for inpatient hospital services for discharges in that fiscal year which will take into account amounts necessary for the efficient and effective delivery of medically appropriate and necessary care of high quality. The appropriate change factor may be different for all large urban subsection (d) hospitals, other urban subsection (d) hospitals, urban subsection (d) Puerto Rico hospitals, rural subsection (d) hospitals, and rural subsection (d) Puerto Rico hospitals, and all other hospitals and units not paid under subsection (d), and may vary among such other hospitals and units.

(B) In addition to the recommendation made under subparagraph (A), the Secretary shall, taking into consideration the recommendations of the Commission under paragraph (2)(B), recommend for each fiscal year (beginning with fiscal year 1992) other appropriate changes in each existing reimbursement policy under this title [42 USCS §§ 1395 et seq.] under which payments to an institution are based upon prospectively determined rates.

(5) The Secretary shall cause to have published in the Federal Register, not later than—

(A) the April 1 before each fiscal year (beginning with fiscal year 1986), the Secretary's proposed recommendation under paragraph (4) for that fiscal year for public comment, and

(B) the August 1 before such fiscal year after such consideration of public comment on the proposal as is feasible in the time available, the Secretary's final recommendation under such paragraph for that year.

The Secretary shall include in the publication referred to in subparagraph (A) for a fiscal year the report of the Commission's recommendations submitted under paragraph (3) for that fiscal year. To the extent that the Secretary's recommendations under paragraph (4) differ from the Commission's recommendations for that fiscal year, the Secretary shall include in the publication referred to in subparagraph (A) an explanation of the Secretary's grounds for not following the Commission's recommendations.

(f) Reporting of costs of hospitals receiving payments on basis of prospective rates. (1)(A) The Secretary shall maintain a system for the reporting of costs of hospitals receiving payments computed under subsection (d).

(B)(i) Subject to clause (ii), the Secretary shall place into effect a standardized electronic cost reporting format for hospitals under this title [42 USCS §§ 1395 et seq.].

(ii) The Secretary may delay or waive the implementation of such format in particular instances where such implementation would result in financial hardship (in particular with respect to hospitals with a small percentage of inpatients entitled to benefits under this title [42 USCS §§ 1395 et seq.]).

(2) If the Secretary determines, based upon information supplied by a utilization and quality control peer review organization under part B of title XI [42 USCS §§ 1320c et seq.], that a hospital, in order to circumvent the payment method established under subsection (b) or (d) of this section, has taken an action that results in the admission of individuals entitled to benefits under part A [42 USCS §§ 1395c et seq.] unnecessarily, unnecessary multiple admissions of the same such individuals, or other inappropriate medical or other practices with respect to such individuals, the Secretary may—

(A) deny payment (in whole or in part) under part A [42 USCS §§ 1395c et seq.] with respect to inpatient hospital services provided with respect to such an unnecessary admission (or subsequent admission of the same individual), or

(B) require the hospital to take other corrective action necessary to prevent or correct the inappropriate practice.

(3) The provisions of subsections (c) through (g) of section 1128 [42 USCS § 1320a-7(c)–(g)] shall apply to determinations made under paragraph (2) in the same manner as they apply to exclusions effected under section 1128(b)(13) [42 USCS § 1320a-7(b)(13)].

(g) Prospective payment of capital-related costs; return on equity capital for hospital. (1)(A) Notwithstanding section 1861(v) [42 USCS § 1395x(v)], instead of any amounts that are otherwise payable under this title [42 USCS §§ 1395 et seq.] with respect to the reasonable costs of subsection (d) hospitals and subsection (d) Puerto Rico hospitals for capital-related costs of inpatient hospital services, the Secretary shall, for hospital cost reporting periods beginning on or after October 1, 1991, provide for payments for such costs in accordance with a prospective payment system established by the Secretary. Aggregate payments made under subsection (d) and this subsection during fiscal years 1992 through 1995 shall be reduced in a manner that results in a reduction (as estimated by the Secretary) in the amount of such payments equal to a 10 percent reduction in the amount of payments attributable to capital-related costs that would otherwise have been made during such fiscal year had the amount of such payments been based on reasonable costs (as defined in section 1861(v) [42 USCS § 1395x(v)]). For discharges occurring after September 30, 1993, the Secretary shall reduce by 7.4 percent the unadjusted standard Federal capital payment rate (as described in 42 CFR 412.308(c), as in effect on the date of the enactment of the Omnibus Budget Reconciliation Act of 1993 [enacted Aug. 10, 1993]) and shall (for hospital cost reporting periods beginning on or after October 1, 1993) redetermine which payment methodology is applied to the hospital under such system to take into account such reduction. In addition to the reduction described in the preceding sentence, for discharges occurring on or after October 1, 1997, the Secretary shall apply the budget neutrality adjustment factor used to determine the Federal capital payment rate in effect on September 30, 1995 (as described in section 412.352 of title 42 of the Code of Federal Regulations), to (i) the unadjusted standard Federal capital payment rate (as described in section 412.308(c) of that title, as in effect on September 30, 1997), and (ii) the unadjusted hospital-specific rate (as described in section 412.328(e)(1) of that title, as in effect on September 30, 1997), and, for discharges occurring on or after October 1, 1997, and before October 1, 2002, reduce the rates described in clauses (i) and (ii) by 2.1 percent.

(B) Such system—

(i) shall provide for (I) a payment on a per discharge basis, and (II) an appropriate weighting of such payment amount as relates to the classification of the discharge;

(ii) may provide for an adjustment to take into account variations in the relative costs of capital and construction for the different types of facilities or areas in which they are located;

(iii) may provide for such exceptions (including appropriate exceptions to reflect capital obligations) as the Secretary determines to be appropriate, and

(iv) may provide for suitable adjustment to reflect hospital occupancy rate.

(C) In this paragraph, the term "capital-related costs" has the meaning given such term by the Secretary under subsection (a)(4) as of September 30, 1987, and does not include a return on equity capital.

(2)(A) The Secretary shall provide that the amount which is allowable, with respect to reasonable costs of inpatient hospital services for which payment may be made under this title [42 USCS §§ 1395 et seq.], for a return on equity capital for hospitals shall, for cost reporting periods beginning on or after the date of the enactment of this subsection [enacted April 20, 1983], be equal to amounts otherwise allowable under regulations in effect on March 1, 1983, except that the rate of return to be recognized shall be equal to the applicable percentage (described in subparagraph (B)) of the average of the rates of interest, for each of the months any part of which is included in the reporting period, on obligations issued for purchase by the Federal Hospital Insurance Trust Fund.

(B) In this paragraph, the "applicable percentage" is—

(i) 75 percent, for cost reporting periods beginning during fiscal year 1987,

(ii) 50 percent, for cost reporting periods beginning during fiscal year 1988,

(iii) 25 percent, for cost reporting periods beginning during fiscal year 1989, and

(iv) 0 percent, for cost reporting periods beginning on or after October 1, 1989.

(3)(A) Except as provided in subparagraph (B), in determining the amount of the payments that may be made under this title with respect to all the capital-related costs of inpatient hospital services of a subsection (d) hospital and a subsection (d) Puerto Rico hospital, the Secretary shall reduce the amounts of such payments otherwise established under this title [42 USCS §§ 1395 et seq.] by—

(i) 3.5 percent for payments attributable to portions of cost reporting periods occurring during fiscal year 1987,

(ii) 7 percent for payments attributable to portions of cost reporting periods or discharges (as the case may be) occurring during fiscal year 1988 on or after October 1, 1987, and before January 1, 1988,

(iii) 12 percent for payments attributable to portions of cost reporting periods or discharges (as the case may be) in fiscal year 1988, occurring on or after January 1, 1988,

(iv) 15 percent for payments attributable to portions of cost reporting periods or discharges (as the case may be) occurring during fiscal year 1989, and

(v) 15 percent for payments attributable to portions of cost reporting periods or discharges (as the case may be) occurring during the period beginning January 1, 1990, and ending September 30, 1991.

(B) Subparagraph (A) shall not apply to payments with respect to the capital-related costs of any hospital that is a sole community hospital (as defined in subsection (d)(5)(D)(iii)) or a critical access hospital (as defined in section 1861(mm)(1) [42 USCS § 1395x(mm)(1)]).

(4) In determining the amount of the payments that are attributable to portions of cost reporting periods occurring during fiscal years 1998 through 2002 and that may be made under this title [42 USCS §§ 1395 et seq.] with respect to capital-related costs of inpatient hospital services of a hospital which is described in clause (i), (ii), or (iv) of subsection (d)(1)(B) or a unit described in the matter after clause (v) of such subsection, the Secretary shall reduce the amounts of such payments otherwise determined under this title [42 USCS §§ 1395 et seq.] by 15 percent.

(h) Payments for direct graduate medical education costs. (1) Substitution of special payment rules. Notwithstanding section 1861(v) [42 USCS §§ 1395x(v)], instead of any amounts that are otherwise payable under this title [42 USCS §§ 1395 et seq.] with respect to the reasonable costs of hospitals for direct graduate medical education costs, the Secretary shall provide for payments for such costs in accordance with paragraph (3) of this subsection. In providing for such payments, the Secretary shall provide for an allocation of such payments between part A and part B [42 USCS §§ 1395c et seq. and 1395j et seq.] (and the trust funds established under the respective parts) as reasonably reflects the proportion of direct graduate medical education costs of hospitals associated with the provision of services under each respective part.

(2) Determination of hospital-specific approved FTE resident amounts. The Secretary shall determine, for each hospital with an approved medical residency training program, an approved FTE resident amount for each cost reporting period beginning on or after July 1, 1985, as follows:

(A) Determining allowable average cost per FTE resident in a hospital's base period. The Secretary shall determine, for the hospital's cost reporting period that began during fiscal year 1984, the average amount recognized as reasonable under this title for direct graduate medical education costs of the hospital for each full-time-equivalent resident.

(B) Updating to the first cost reporting period. (i) In general. The Secretary shall update each average amount determined under subparagraph (A) by the percentage increase in the consumer price index during the 12-month cost reporting period described in such subparagraph.

(ii) Exception. The Secretary shall not perform an update under clause (i) in the case of a hospital if the hospital's reporting period, described in subparagraph (A), began on or after July 1, 1984, and before October 1, 1984.

(C) Amount for first cost reporting period. For the first cost reporting period of the hospital beginning on or after July 1, 1985, the approved FTE resident amount for the hospital is equal to the amount determined under subparagraph (B) increased by 1 percent.

(D) Amount for subsequent cost reporting periods. (i) In general. Except as provided in a subsequent clause, for each subsequent cost reporting period, the approved FTE resident amount for the hospital is equal to the approved FTE resident amount determined under this paragraph for the previous cost reporting period updated, through the midpoint of the period, by projecting the estimated percentage change in the consumer price index during the 12-month period ending at that midpoint, with appropriate adjustments to reflect previous under- or over-estimations under this subparagraph in the projected percentage change in the consumer price index.

(ii) Freeze in update for fiscal years 1994 and 1995. For cost reporting periods beginning during fiscal year 1994 or fiscal year 1995, the approved FTE resident amount for a hospital shall not be updated under clause (i) for a resident who is not a primary care resident (as defined in paragraph (5)(H)) or a resident enrolled in an approved medical residency training program in obstetrics and gynecology.

(iii) Floor for locality adjusted national average per resident amount. The approved FTE resident amount for a hospital for the cost reporting period beginning during fiscal year 2001 shall not be less than 70 percent, and for the cost reporting period beginning during fiscal year 2002 shall not be less than 85 percent, of the locality adjusted national average per resident amount computed under subparagraph (E) for the hospital and period.

(iv) Adjustment in rate of increase for hospitals with FTE approved amount above 140 percent of locality adjusted national average per resident amount. (I) Freeze for fiscal years 2001 and 2002 and 2004 through 2013. For a cost reporting period beginning during fiscal year 2001 or fiscal year 2002 or during the period beginning with fiscal year 2004 and ending with fiscal year 2013, if the approved FTE resident amount for a hospital for the preceding cost reporting period exceeds 140 percent of the locality adjusted national average per resident amount computed under subparagraph (E) for that hospital and period, subject to subclause (III), the approved FTE resident amount for the period involved shall be the same as the approved FTE resident amount for the hospital for such preceding cost reporting period.

(II) 2 percent decrease in update for fiscal years 2003, 2004, and 2005 [fiscal year 2003]. For the cost reporting period beginning during fiscal year 2003, if the approved FTE resident amount for a hospital for the preceding cost reporting period exceeds 140 percent of the locality adjusted national average per resident amount computed under subparagraph (E) for that hospital and preceding period, the approved FTE resident amount for the period involved shall be updated in the manner described in subparagraph (D)(i) except that, subject to subclause (III), the consumer price index applied for a 12-month period shall be reduced (but not below zero) by 2 percentage points.

(III) No adjustment below 140 percent. In no case shall subclause (I) or (II) reduce an approved FTE resident amount for a hospital for a cost reporting period below 140 percent of the locality adjusted national average per resident amount computed under subparagraph (E) for such hospital and period.

(E) Determination of locality adjusted national average per resident amount. The Secretary shall determine a locality adjusted national average per resident amount with respect to a cost reporting period of a hospital beginning during a fiscal year as follows:

(i) Determining hospital single per resident amount. The Secretary shall compute for each hospital operating an approved graduate medical education program a single per resident amount equal to the average (weighted by number of full-time equivalent residents, as determined under paragraph (4)) of the primary care per resident amount and the non-primary care per resident amount computed under paragraph (2) for cost reporting periods ending during fiscal year 1997.

(ii) Standardizing per resident amounts. The Secretary shall compute a standardized per resident amount for each such hospital by dividing the single per resident amount computed under clause (i) by an average of the 3 geographic index values (weighted by the national average weight for each of the work, practice expense, and malpractice components) as applied under section 1848(e) for 1999 for the fee schedule area in which the hospital is located.

(iii) Computing of weighted average. The Secretary shall compute the average of the standardized per resident amounts computed under clause (ii) for such hospitals, with the amount for each hospital weighted by the average number of full-time equivalent residents at such hospital (as determined under paragraph (4)).

(iv) Computing national average per resident amount. The Secretary shall compute the national average per resident amount, for a hospital's cost reporting period that begins during fiscal year 2001, equal to the weighted average computed under clause (iii) increased by the estimated percentage increase in the consumer price index for all urban consumers during the period beginning with the month that represents the midpoint of the cost reporting periods described in clause (i) and ending with the midpoint of the hospital's cost reporting period that begins during fiscal year 2001.

(v) Adjusting for locality. The Secretary shall compute the product of—

(I) the national average per resident amount computed under clause (iv) for the hospital, and

(II) the geographic index value average (described and applied under clause (ii)) for the fee schedule area in which the hospital is located.

(vi) Computing locality adjusted amount. The locality adjusted national per resident amount for a hospital for—

(I) the cost reporting period beginning during fiscal year 2001 is the product computed under clause (v); or

(II) each subsequent cost reporting period is equal to the locality adjusted national per resident amount for the hospital for the previous cost reporting period (as determined under this clause) updated, through the midpoint of the period, by projecting the estimated percentage change in the consumer price index for all urban consumers during the 12-month period ending at that midpoint.

(F) Treatment of certain hospitals. In the case of a hospital that did not have an approved medical residency training program or was not participating in the program under this title [42 USCS §§ 1395 et seq.] for a cost reporting period beginning during fiscal year 1984, the Secretary shall, for the first such period for which it has such a residency training program and is participating under this title [42 USCS §§ 1395 et seq.], provide for such approved FTE resident amount as the Secretary determines to be appropriate, based on approved FTE resident amounts for comparable programs.

(3) Hospital payment amount per resident. (A) In general. The payment amount, for a hospital cost reporting period beginning on or after July 1, 1985, is equal to the product of—

(i) the aggregate approved amount (as defined in subparagraph (B)) for that period, and

(ii) the hospital's medicare patient load (as defined in subparagraph (C)) for that period.

(B) Aggregate approved amount. As used in subparagraph (A), the term "aggregate approved amount" means, for a hospital cost reporting period, the product of—

(i) the hospital's approved FTE resident amount (determined under paragraph (2)) for that period, and

(ii) the weighted average number of full-time-equivalent residents (as determined under paragraph (4)) in the hospital's approved medical residency training programs in that period.

The Secretary shall reduce the aggregate approved amount to the extent payment is made under subsection (k) for residents included in the hospital's count of full-time equivalent residents.

(C) Medicare patient load. As used in subparagraph (A), the term "medicare patient load" means, with respect to a hospital's cost reporting period, the fraction of the total number of inpatient-bed-days (as established by the Secretary) during the period which are attributable to patients with respect to whom payment may be made under part A [42 USCS §§ 1395c et seq.].

(D) Payment for managed care enrollees. (i) In general. For portions of cost reporting periods occurring on or after January 1, 1998, the Secretary shall provide for an additional payment amount under this subsection for services furnished to individuals who are enrolled under a risk-sharing contract with an eligible organization under section 1876 [42 USCS § 1395mm] and who are entitled to part A [42 USCS §§ 1395c et seq.] or with a Medicare+Choice organization under part C [42 USCS §§ 1395w-21 et seq.]. The amount of such a payment shall equal, subject to clause (iii), the applicable percentage of the product of—

(I) the aggregate approved amount (as defined in subparagraph (B)) for that period; and

(II) the fraction of the total number of inpatient-bed days (as established by the Secretary) during the period which are attributable to such enrolled individuals.

(ii) Applicable percentage. For purposes of clause (i), the applicable percentage is—

(I) 20 percent in 1998,

(II) 40 percent in 1999,

(III) 60 percent in 2000,

(IV) 80 percent in 2001, and

(V) 100 percent in 2002 and subsequent years.

(iii) Proportional reduction for nursing and allied health education. The Secretary shall estimate a proportional adjustment in payments to all hospitals determined under clauses (i) and (ii) for portions of cost reporting periods beginning in a year (beginning with 2000) such that the proportional adjustment reduces payments in an amount for such year equal to the total additional payment amounts for nursing and allied health education determined under subsection (l) for portions of cost reporting periods occurring in that year.

(iv) Special rule for hospitals under reimbursement system. The Secretary shall establish rules for the application of this subparagraph to a hospital reimbursed under a reimbursement system authorized under section 1814(b)(3) [42 USCS § 1395f(b)(3)] in the same manner as it would apply to the hospital if it were not reimbursed under such section.

(4) Determination of full-time-equivalent residents. (A) Rules. The Secretary shall establish rules consistent with this paragraph for the computation of the number of full-time-equivalent residents in an approved medical residency training program.

(B) Adjustment for part-year or part-time residents. Such rules shall take into account individuals who serve as residents for only a portion of a period with a hospital or simultaneously with more than one hospital.

(C) Weighting factors for certain residents. Subject to subparagraph (D), such rules shall provide, in calculating the number of full-time-equivalent residents in an approved residency program—

(i) before July 1, 1986, for each resident the weighting factor is 1.00,

(ii) on or after July 1, 1986, for a resident who is in the resident's initial residency period (as defined in paragraph (5)(F)), the weighting factor is 1.00,

(iii) on or after July 1, 1986, and before July 1, 1987, for a resident who is not in the resident's initial residency period (as defined in paragraph (5)(F)), the weighting factor is .75, and

(iv) on or after July 1, 1987, for a resident who is not in the resident's initial residency period (as defined in paragraph (5)(F)), the weighting factor is .50.

(D) Foreign medical graduates required to pass FMGEMS examination. (i) In general. Except as provided in clause (ii), such rules shall provide that, in the case of an individual who is a foreign medical graduate (as defined in paragraph (5)(D)), the individual shall not be counted as a resident on or after July 1, 1986, unless—

(I) the individual has passed the FMGEMS examination (as defined in paragraph (5)(E)), or

(II) the individual has previously received certification from, or has previously passed the examination of, the Educational Commission for Foreign Medical Graduates.

(ii) Transition for current FMGS. On or after July 1, 1986, but before July 1, 1987, in the case of a foreign medical graduate who—

(I) has served as a resident before July 1, 1986, and is serving as a resident after that date, but

(II) has not passed the FMGEMS examination or a previous examination of the Educational Commission for Foreign Medical Graduates before July 1, 1986,

the individual shall be counted as a resident at a rate equal to one-half of the rate at which the individual would otherwise be counted.

(E) Counting time spent in outpatient settings. Subject to subparagraphs (J) and (K), such rules shall provide that only time spent in activities relating to patient care shall be counted and that—

(i) effective for cost reporting periods beginning before July 1, 2010, all the time; so spent by a resident under an approved medical residency training program shall be counted towards the determination of full-time equivalency, without regard to the setting in which the activities are performed, if the hospital incurs all, or substantially all, of the costs for the training program in that setting; and

(ii) effective for cost reporting periods beginning on or after July 1, 2010, all the time so spent by a resident shall be counted towards the determination of full-time equivalency, without regard to the setting in which the activities are performed, if a hospital incurs the costs of the stipends and fringe benefits of the resident during the time the resident spends in that setting. If more than one hospital incurs these costs, either directly or through a third party, such hospitals shall count a proportional share of the time, as determined by written agreement between the hospitals, that a resident spends training in that setting.

Any hospital claiming under this subparagraph for time spent in a nonprovider setting shall maintain and make available to the Secretary records regarding the amount of such time and such amount in comparison with amounts of such time in such base year as the Secretary shall specify.

(F) Limitation on number of residents in allopathic and osteopathic medicine. (i) In general. Such rules shall provide that for purposes of a cost reporting period beginning on or after October 1, 1997, subject to paragraphs (7) and (8), the total number of full-time equivalent residents before application of weighting factors (as determined under this paragraph) with respect to a hospital's approved medical residency training program in the fields of allopathic medicine and osteopathic medicine may not exceed the number (or, 130 percent of such number in the case of a hospital located in a rural area) of such full-time equivalent residents for the hospital's most recent cost reporting period ending on or before December 31, 1996.

(ii) Counting primary care residents on certain approved leaves of absence in base year FTE count. (I) In general. In determining the number of such full-time equivalent residents for a hospital's most recent cost reporting period ending on or before December 31, 1996, for purposes of clause (i), the Secretary shall count an individual to the extent that the individual would have been counted as a primary care resident for such period but for the fact that the individual, as determined by the Secretary, was on maternity or disability leave or a similar approved leave of absence.

(II) Limitation to 3 FTE residents for any hospital. The total number of individuals counted under subclause (I) for a hospital may not exceed 3 full-time equivalent residents.

(G) Counting interns and residents for FY 1998 and subsequent years. (i) In general. For cost reporting periods beginning during fiscal years beginning on or after October 1, 1997, subject to the limit described in subparagraph (F), the total number of full-time equivalent residents for determining a hospital's graduate medical education payment shall equal the average of the actual full-time equivalent resident counts for the cost reporting period and the preceding two cost reporting periods.

(ii) Adjustment for short periods. If any cost reporting period beginning on or after October 1, 1997, is not equal to twelve months, the Secretary shall make appropriate modifications to ensure that the average full-time equivalent resident counts pursuant to clause (i) are based on the equivalent of full twelve-month cost reporting periods.

(iii) Transition rule for 1998. In the case of a hospital's first cost reporting period beginning on or after October 1, 1997, clause (i) shall be applied by using the average for such period and the preceding cost reporting period.

(H) Special rules for application of subparagraphs (f) and (g). (i) New facilities. The Secretary shall, consistent with the principles of subparagraphs (F) and (G) and subject to paragraphs (7) and (8), prescribe rules for the application of such subparagraphs in the case of medical residency training programs established on or after January 1, 1995. In promulgating such rules for purposes of subparagraph (F), the Secretary shall give special consideration to facilities that meet the needs of underserved rural areas.

(ii) Aggregation. The Secretary may prescribe rules which allow institutions which are members of the same affiliated group (as defined by the Secretary) to elect to apply the limitation of subparagraph (F) on an aggregate basis.

(iii) Data collection. The Secretary may require any entity that operates a medical residency training program and to which subparagraphs (F) and (G) apply to submit to the Secretary such additional information as the Secretary considers necessary to carry out such subparagraphs.

(iv) Nonrural hospitals operating training programs in rural areas. In the case of a hospital that is not located in a rural area but establishes separately accredited approved medical residency training programs (or rural tracks) in an rural area or has an accredited training program with an integrated rural track, the Secretary shall adjust the limitation under subparagraph (F) in an appropriate manner insofar as it applies to such programs in such rural areas in order to encourage the training of physicians in rural areas.

(v) Special provider agreement. If an entity enters into a provider agreement pursuant to section 1866(a) [42 USCS § 1395cc(a)] to provide hospital services on the same physical site previously used by Medicare Provider No. 05-0578—

(I) the limitation on the number of total full time equivalent residents under subparagraph (F) and clauses (v) and (vi)(I) of subsection (d)(5)(B) applicable to such provider shall be equal to the limitation applicable under such provisions to Provider No. 05-0578 for its cost reporting period ending on June 30, 2006; and

(II) the provisions of subparagraph (G) and subsection (d)(5)(B)(vi)(II) shall not be applicable to such provider for the first three cost reporting years in which such provider trains residents under any approved medical residency training program.

(vi) Redistribution of residency slots after a hospital closes. (I) In general. Subject to the succeeding provisions of this clause, the Secretary shall, by regulation, establish a process under which, in the case where a hospital (other than a hospital described in clause (v)) with an approved medical residency program closes on or after a date that is 2 years before the date of enactment of this clause, the Secretary shall increase the otherwise applicable resident limit under this paragraph for other hospitals in accordance with this clause.

(II) Priority for hospitals in certain areas. Subject to the succeeding provisions of this clause, in determining for which hospitals the increase in the otherwise applicable resident limit is provided under such process, the Secretary shall distribute the increase to hospitals in the following priority order (with preference given within each category to hospitals that are members of the same affiliated group (as defined by the Secretary under clause (ii)) as the closed hospital):

(aa) First, to hospitals located in the same core-based statistical area as, or a core-based statistical area contiguous to, the hospital that closed.

(bb) Second, to hospitals located in the same State as the hospital that closed.

(cc) Third, to hospitals located in the same region of the country as the hospital that closed.

(dd) Fourth, only if the Secretary is not able to distribute the increase to hospitals described in item (cc), to qualifying hospitals in accordance with the provisions of paragraph (8).

(III) Requirement hospital likely to fill position within certain time period. The Secretary may only increase the otherwise applicable resident limit of a hospital under such process if the Secretary determines the hospital has demonstrated a likelihood of filling the positions made available under this clause within 3 years.

(IV) Limitation. The aggregate number of increases in the otherwise applicable resident limits for hospitals under this clause shall be equal to the number of resident positions in the approved medical residency programs that closed on or after the date described in subclause (I).

(V) Administration. Chapter 35 of title 44, United States Code [44 USCS §§ 3501 et seq.], shall not apply to the implementation of this clause.

(I) [Not enacted]

(J) Treatment of certain nonprovider and didactic activities. Such rules shall provide that all time spent by an intern or resident in an approved medical residency training program in a nonprovider setting that is primarily engaged in furnishing patient care (as defined in paragraph (5)(K)) in non-patient care activities, such as didactic conferences and seminars, but not including research not associated with the treatment or diagnosis of a particular patient, as such time and activities are defined by the Secretary, shall be counted toward the determination of full-time equivalency.

(K) Treatment of certain other activities. In determining the hospital's number of full-time equivalent residents for purposes of this subsection, all the time that is spent by an intern or resident in an approved medical residency training program on vacation, sick leave, or other approved leave, as such time is defined by the Secretary, and that does not prolong the total time the resident is participating in the approved program beyond the normal duration of the program shall be counted toward the determination of full-time equivalency.

(5) Definitions and special rules. As used in this subsection:

(A) Approved medical residency training program. The term "approved medical residency training program" means a residency or other postgraduate medical training program participation in which may be counted toward certification in a specialty or subspecialty and includes formal postgraduate training programs in geriatric medicine approved by the Secretary.

(B) Consumer price index. The term "consumer price index" refers to the Consumer Price Index for All Urban Consumers (United States city average), as published by the Secretary of Commerce.

(C) Direct graduate medical education costs. The term "direct graduate medical education costs" means direct costs of approved educational activities for approved medical residency training programs.

(D) Foreign medical graduate. The term "foreign medical graduate" means a resident who is not a graduate of—

(i) a school of medicine accredited by the Liaison Committee on Medical Education of the American Medical Association and the Association of American Medical Colleges (or approved by such Committee as meeting the standards necessary for such accreditation),

(ii) a school of osteopathy accredited by the American Osteopathic Association, or approved by such Association as meeting the standards necessary for such accreditation, or

(iii) a school of dentistry or podiatry which is accredited (or meets the standards for accreditation) by an organization recognized by the Secretary for such purpose.

(E) FMGEMS examination. The term "FMGEMS examination" means parts I and II of the Foreign Medical Graduate Examination in the Medical Sciences or any successor examination recognized by the Secretary for this purpose.

(F) Initial residency period. The term "initial residency period" means the period of board eligibility, except that—

(i) except as provided in clause (ii), in no case shall the initial period of residency exceed an aggregate period of formal training of more than five years for any individual, and

(ii) a period, of not more than two years, during which an individual is in a geriatric residency or fellowship program or a preventive medicine residency or fellowship program which meets such criteria as the Secretary may establish, shall be treated as part of the initial residency period, but shall not be counted against any limitation on the initial residency period.

Subject to subparagraph (G)(v), the initial residency period shall be determined, with respect to a resident, as of the time the resident enters the residency training program.

(G) Period of board eligibility. (i) General rule. Subject to clauses (ii), (iii), (iv), and (v), the term "period of board eligibility" means, for a resident, the minimum number of years of formal training necessary to satisfy the requirements for initial board eligibility in the particular specialty for which the resident is training.

(ii) Application of 1985-1986 directory. Except as provided in clause (iii), the period of board eligibility shall be such period specified in the 1985-1986 Directory of Residency Training Programs published by the Accreditation Council on Graduate-Medical Education.

(iii) Changes in period of board eligibility. On or after July 1, 1989, if the Accreditation Council on Graduate Medical Education, in its Directory of Residency Training Programs—

(I) increases the minimum number of years of formal training necessary to satisfy the requirements for a specialty, above the period specified in its 1985-1986 Directory, the Secretary may increase the period of board eligibility for that specialty, but not to exceed the period of board eligibility specified in that later Directory, or

(II) decreases the minimum number of years of formal training necessary to satisfy the requirements for a specialty, below the period specified in its 1985-1986 Directory, the Secretary may decrease the period of board eligibility for that specialty, but not below the period of board eligibility specified in that later Directory.

(iv) Special rule for certain primary care combined residency programs. (I) In the case of a resident enrolled in a combined medical residency training program in which all of the individual programs (that are combined) are for training a primary care resident (as defined in subparagraph (H)), the period of board eligibility shall be the minimum number of years of formal training required to satisfy the requirements for initial board eligibility in the longest of the individual programs plus one additional year.

(II) A resident enrolled in a combined medical residency training program that includes an obstetrics and gynecology program shall qualify for the period of board eligibility under subclause (I) if the other programs such resident combines with such obstetrics and gynecology program are for training a primary care resident.

(v) Child neurology training programs. In the case of a resident enrolled in a child neurology residency training program, the period of board eligibility and the initial residency period shall be the period of board eligibility for pediatrics plus 2 years.

(H) Primary care resident. The term "primary care resident" means a resident enrolled in an approved medical residency training program in family medicine, general internal medicine, general pediatrics, preventive medicine, geriatric medicine, or osteopathic general practice.

(I) Resident. The term "resident" includes an intern or other participant in an approved medical residency training program.

(J) Adjustments for certain family practice residency programs. (i) In general. In the case of an approved medical residency training program (meeting the requirements of clause (ii)) of a hospital which received funds from the United States, a State, or a political subdivision of a State or an instrumentality of such a State or political subdivision (other than payments under this title or a State plan under title XIX [42 USCS §§ 1396 et seq.]) for the program during the cost reporting period that began during fiscal year 1984, the Secretary shall—

(I) provide for an average amount under paragraph (2)(A) that takes into account the Secretary's estimate of the amount that would have been recognized as reasonable under this title if the hospital had not received such funds, and

(II) reduce the payment amount otherwise provided under this subsection in an amount equal to the proportion of such program funds received during the cost reporting period involved that is allocable to this title [42 USCS §§ 1395 et seq.].

(ii) Additional requirements. A hospital's approved medical residency program meets the requirements of this clause if—

(I) the program is limited to training for family and community medicine;

(II) the program is the only approved medical residency program of the hospital; and

(III) the average amount determined under paragraph (2)(A) for the hospital (as determined without regard to the increase in such amount described in clause (i)(I)) does not exceed $10,000.

(K) Nonprovider setting that is primarily engaged in furnishing patient care. The term "nonprovider setting that is primarily engaged in furnishing patient care" means a nonprovider setting in which the primary activity is the care and treatment of patients, as defined by the Secretary.

(6) Incentive payment under plans for voluntary reduction in number of residents. (A) In general. In the case of a voluntary residency reduction plan for which an application is approved under subparagraph (B), subject to subparagraph (F), each hospital which is part of the qualifying entity submitting the plan shall be paid an applicable hold harmless percentage (as specified in subparagraph (E)) of the sum of—

(i) the amount (if any) by which—

(I) the amount of payment which would have been made under this subsection if there had been a 5-percent reduction in the number of full-time equivalent residents in the approved medical education training programs of the hospital as of June 30, 1997, exceeds

(II) the amount of payment which is made under this subsection, taking into account the reduction in such number effected under the reduction plan; and

(ii) the amount of the reduction in payment under subsection (d)(5)(B) for the hospital that is attributable to the reduction in number of residents effected under the plan below 95 percent of the number of full-time equivalent residents in such programs of the hospital as of June 30, 1997.

The determination of the amounts under clauses (i) and (ii) for any year shall be made on the basis of the provisions of this title [42 USCS §§ 1395 et seq.] in effect on the application deadline date for the first calendar year to which the reduction plan applies.

(B) Approval of plan applications. The Secretary may not approve the application of an qualifying entity unless—

(i) the application is submitted in a form and manner specified by the Secretary and by not later than November 1, 1999, [;]

(ii) the application provides for the operation of a plan for the reduction in the number of full-time equivalent residents in the approved medical residency training programs of the entity consistent with the requirements of subparagraph (D);

(iii) the entity elects in the application the period of residency training years (not greater than 5) over which the reduction will occur;

(iv) the entity will not reduce the proportion of its residents in primary care (to the total number of residents) below such proportion as in effect as of the applicable time described in subparagraph (D)(v); and

(v) the Secretary determines that the application and the entity and such plan meet such other requirements as the Secretary specifies in regulations.

(C) Qualifying entity. For purposes of this paragraph, any of the following may be a qualifying entity:

(i) Individual hospitals operating one or more approved medical residency training programs.

(ii) Two or more hospitals that operate such programs and apply for treatment under this paragraph as a single qualifying entity.

(iii) A qualifying consortium (as described in section 4628 of the Balanced Budget Act of 1997 [note to this section]).

(D) Residency reduction requirements. (i) Individual hospital applicants. In the case of a qualifying entity described in subparagraph (C)(i), the number of full-time equivalent residents in all the approved medical residency training programs operated by or through the entity shall be reduced as follows:

(I) If the base number of residents exceeds 750 residents, by a number equal to at least 20 percent of such base number.

(II) Subject to subclause (IV), if the base number of residents exceeds 600 but is less than 750 residents, by 150 residents.

(III) Subject to subclause (IV), if the base number of residents does not exceed 600 residents, by a number equal to at least 25 percent of such base number.

(IV) In the case of a qualifying entity which is described in clause (v) and which elects treatment under this subclause, by a number equal to at least 20 percent of the base number.

(ii) Joint applicants. In the case of a qualifying entity described in subparagraph (C)(ii), the number of full-time equivalent residents in the aggregate for all the approved medical residency training programs operated by or through the entity shall be reduced as follows:

(I) Subject to subclause (II), by a number equal to at least 25 percent of the base number.

(II) In the case of such a qualifying entity

which is described in clause (v) and which elects treatment under this subclause, by a number equal to at least 20 percent of the base number.

(iii) Consortia. In the case of a qualifying entity described in subparagraph (C)(iii), the number of full-time equivalent residents in the aggregate for all the approved medical residency training programs operated by or through the entity shall be reduced by a number equal to at least 20 percent of the base number.

(iv) Manner of reduction. The reductions specified under the preceding provisions of this subparagraph for a qualifying entity shall be below the base number of residents for that entity and shall be fully effective not later than the 5th residency training year in which the application under subparagraph (B) is effective.

(v) Entities providing assurance of increase in primary care residents. An entity is described in this clause if—

(I) the base number of residents for the entity is less than 750 or the entity is described in subparagraph (C)(ii); and

(II) the entity represents in its application under subparagraph (B) that it will increase the number of full-time equivalent residents in primary care by at least 20 percent (from such number included in the base number of residents) by not later than the 5th residency training year in which the application under subparagraph (B) is effective.

If a qualifying entity fails to comply with the representation described in subclause (II) by the end of such 5th residency training year, the entity shall be subject to repayment of all amounts paid under this paragraph, in accordance with procedures established to carry out subparagraph (F).

(vi) Base number of residents defined. For purposes of this paragraph, the term "base number of residents" means, with respect to a qualifying entity (or its participating hospitals) operating approved medical residency training programs, the number of full-time equivalent residents in such programs (before application of weighting factors) of the entity as of the most recent residency training year ending before June 30, 1997, or, if less, for any subsequent residency training year that ends before the date the entity makes application under this paragraph.

(E) Applicable hold harmless percentage. For purposes of subparagraph (A), the "applicable hold harmless percentage" for the—

(i) first and second residency training years in which the reduction plan is in effect, 100 percent,

(ii) third such year, 75 percent,

(iii) fourth such year, 50 percent, and

(iv) fifth such year, 25 percent.

(F) Penalty for noncompliance. (i) In general. No payment may be made under this paragraph to a hospital for a residency training year if the hospital has failed to reduce the number of full-time equivalent residents (in the manner required under subparagraph (D)) to the number agreed to by the Secretary and the qualifying entity in approving the application under this paragraph with respect to such year.

(ii) Increase in number of residents in subsequent years. If payments are made under this paragraph to a hospital, and if the hospital increases the number of full-time equivalent residents above the number of such residents permitted under the reduction plan as of the completion of the plan, then, as specified by the Secretary, the entity is liable for repayment to the Secretary of the total amounts paid under this paragraph to the entity.

(G) Treatment of rotating residents. In applying this paragraph, the Secretary shall establish rules regarding the counting of residents who are assigned to institutions the medical residency training programs in which are not covered under approved applications under this paragraph.

(7) Redistribution of unused resident positions. (A) Reduction in limit based on unused positions. (i) Programs subject to reduction. (I) In general. Except as provided in subclause (II), if a hospital's reference resident level (specified in clause (ii)) is less than the otherwise applicable resident limit (as defined in subparagraph (C)(ii)), effective for portions of cost reporting periods occurring on or after July 1, 2005, the otherwise applicable resident limit shall be reduced by 75 percent of the difference between such otherwise applicable resident limit and such reference resident level.

(II) Exception for small rural hospitals. This subparagraph shall not apply to a hospital located in a rural area (as defined in subsection (d)(2)(D)(ii)) with fewer than 250 acute care inpatient beds.

(ii) Reference resident level. (I) In general. Except as otherwise provided in subclauses (II) and (III), the reference resident level specified in this clause for a hospital is the resident level for the most recent cost reporting period of the hospital ending on or before September 30, 2002, for which a cost report has been settled (or, if not, submitted (subject to audit)), as determined by the Secretary.

(II) Use of most recent accounting period to recognize expansion of existing programs. If a hospital submits a timely request to increase its resident level due to an expansion of an existing residency training program that is not reflected on the most recent settled cost report, after audit and subject to the discretion of the Secretary, the reference resident level for such hospital is the resident level for the cost reporting period that includes July 1, 2003, as determined by the Secretary.

(III) Expansions under newly approved programs. Upon the timely request of a hospital, the Secretary shall adjust the reference resident level specified under subclause (I) or (II) to include the number of medical residents that were approved in an application for a medical residency training program that was approved by an appropriate accrediting organization (as determined by the Secretary) before January 1, 2002, but which was not in operation during the cost reporting period used under subclause (I) or (II), as the case may be, as determined by the Secretary.

(iii) Affiliation. The provisions of clause (i) shall be applied to hospitals which are members of the same affiliated group (as defined by the Secretary under paragraph (4)(H)(ii)) as of July 1, 2003.

(B) Redistribution. (i) In general. The Secretary is authorized to increase the otherwise applicable resident limit for each qualifying hospital that submits a timely application under this subparagraph by such number as the Secretary may approve for portions of cost reporting periods occurring on or after July 1, 2005. The aggregate number of increases in the otherwise applicable resident limits under this subparagraph may not exceed the Secretary's estimate of the aggregate reduction in such limits attributable to subparagraph (A).

(ii) Considerations in redistribution. In determining for which hospitals the increase in the otherwise applicable resident limit is provided under clause (i), the Secretary shall take into account the demonstrated likelihood of the hospital filling the positions within the first 3 cost reporting periods beginning on or after July 1, 2005, made available under this subparagraph, as determined by the Secretary.

(iii) Priority for rural and small urban areas. In determining for which hospitals and residency training programs an increase in the otherwise applicable resident limit is provided under clause (i), the Secretary shall distribute the increase to programs of hospitals located in the following priority order:

(I) First, to hospitals located in rural areas (as defined in subsection (d)(2)(D)(ii)).

(II) Second, to hospitals located in urban areas that are not large urban areas (as defined for purposes of subsection (d)).

(III) Third, to other hospitals in a State if the residency training program involved is in a specialty for which there are not other residency training programs in the State.

Increases of residency limits within the same priority category under this clause shall be determined by the Secretary.

(iv) Limitation. In no case shall more than 25 full-time equivalent additional residency positions be made available under this subparagraph with respect to any hospital.

(v) Application of locality adjusted national average per resident amount. With respect to additional residency positions in a hospital attributable to the increase provided under this subparagraph, notwithstanding any other provision of this subsection, the approved FTE resident amount is deemed to be equal to the locality adjusted national average per resident amount computed under paragraph (4)(E) for that hospital.

(vi) Construction. Nothing in this subparagraph shall be construed as permitting the redistribution of reductions in residency positions attributable to voluntary reduction programs under paragraph (6), under a demonstration project approved as of October 31, 2003, under the authority of section 402 of Public Law 90-248, or as affecting the ability of a hospital to establish new medical residency training programs under paragraph (4)(H).

(C) Resident level and limit defined. In this paragraph:

(i) Resident level. The term "resident level" means, with respect to a hospital, the total number of full-time equivalent residents, before the application of weighting factors (as determined under paragraph (4)), in the fields of allopathic and osteopathic medicine for the hospital.

(ii) Otherwise applicable resident limit. The term "otherwise applicable resident limit" means, with respect to a hospital, the limit otherwise applicable under subparagraphs (F)(i) and (H) of paragraph (4) on the resident level for the hospital determined without regard to this paragraph.

(D) Adjustment based on settled cost report. In the case of a hospital with a dual accredited osteopathic and allopathic family practice program for which—

(i) the otherwise applicable resident limit was reduced under subparagraph (A)(i)(I); and

(ii) such reduction was based on a reference

resident level that was determined using a cost report and where a revised or corrected notice of program reimbursement was issued for such cost report between September 1, 2006 and September 15, 2006, whether as a result of an appeal or otherwise, and the reference resident level under such settled cost report is higher than the level used for the reduction under subparagraph (A)(i)(I);

the Secretary shall apply subparagraph (A)(i)(I) using the higher resident reference level and make any necessary adjustments to such reduction. Any such necessary adjustments shall be effective for portions of cost reporting periods occurring on or after July 1, 2005.

(E) Judicial review. There shall be no administrative or judicial review under section 1869 [42 USCS § 1395ff], 1878 [42 USCS § 1395oo], or otherwise, with respect to determinations made under this [this] paragraph, paragraph (8), or paragraph (4)(H)(vi).

(8) Distribution of additional residency positions. (A) Reductions in limit based on unused positions. (i) In general. Except as provided in clause (ii), if a hospital's reference resident level (as defined in subparagraph (H)(i)) is less than the otherwise applicable resident limit (as defined in subparagraph (H)(iii)), effective for portions of cost reporting periods occurring on or after July 1, 2011, the otherwise applicable resident limit shall be reduced by 65 percent of the difference between such otherwise applicable resident limit and such reference resident level.

(ii) Exceptions. This subparagraph shall not apply to—

(I) a hospital located in a rural area (as defined in subsection (d)(2)(D)(ii)) with fewer than 250 acute care inpatient beds;

(II) a hospital that was part of a qualifying entity which had a voluntary residency reduction plan approved under paragraph (6)(B) or under the authority of section 402 of Public Law 90-248, if the hospital demonstrates to the Secretary that it has a specified plan in place for filling the unused positions by not later than 2 years after the date of enactment of this paragraph; or

(III) a hospital described in paragraph (4)(H)(v).

(B) Distribution. (i) In general. The Secretary shall increase the otherwise applicable resident limit for each qualifying hospital that submits an application under this subparagraph by such number as the Secretary may approve for portions of cost reporting periods occurring on or after July 1, 2011. The aggregate number of increases in the otherwise applicable resident limit under this subparagraph shall be equal to the aggregate reduction in such limits attributable to subparagraph (A) (as estimated by the Secretary).

(ii) Requirements. Subject to clause (iii), a hospital that receives an increase in the otherwise applicable resident limit under this subparagraph shall ensure, during the 5-year period beginning on the date of such increase, that—

(I) the number of full-time equivalent primary care residents, as defined in paragraph (5)(H) (as determined by the Secretary), excluding any additional positions under subclause (II), is not less than the average number of full-time equivalent primary care residents (as so determined) during the 3 most recent cost reporting periods ending prior to the date of enactment of this paragraph; and

(II) not less than 75 percent of the positions attributable to such increase are in a primary care or general surgery residency (as determined by the Secretary). The Secretary may determine whether a hospital has met the requirements under this clause during such 5-year period in such manner and at such time as the Secretary determines appropriate, including at the end of such 5-year period.

(iii) Redistribution of positions if hospital no longer meets certain requirements. In the case where the Secretary determines that a hospital described in clause (ii) does not meet either of the requirements under subclause (I) or (II) of such clause, the Secretary shall—

(I) reduce the otherwise applicable resident limit of the hospital by the amount by which such limit was increased under this paragraph; and

(II) provide for the distribution of positions attributable to such reduction in accordance with the requirements of this paragraph.

(C) Considerations in redistribution. In determining for which hospitals the increase in the otherwise applicable resident limit is provided under subparagraph (B), the Secretary shall take into account—

(i) the demonstration likelihood of the hospital filling the positions made available under this paragraph within the first 3 cost reporting periods beginning on or after July 1, 2011, as determined by the Secretary; and

(ii) whether the hospital has an accredited rural training track (as described in paragraph (4)(H)(iv)).

(D) Priority for certain areas. In determining for which hospitals the increase in the otherwise applicable resident limit is provided under subparagraph (B), subject to subparagraph (E), the Secretary shall distribute the increase to hospitals based on the following factors:

(i) Whether the hospital is located in a State with a resident-to-population ratio in the lowest quartile (as determined by the Secretary).

(ii) Whether the hospital is located in a State, a territory of the United States, or the District of Columbia that is among the top 10 States, territories, or Districts in terms of the ratio of—

(I) the total population of the State, territory, or District living in an area designated (under such section 332(a)(1)(A)) as a health professional shortage area (as of the date of enactment of this paragraph [enacted March 23, 2010]); to

(II) the total population of the State, territory, or District (as determined by the Secretary based on the most recent available population data published by the Bureau of the Census).

(iii) Whether the hospital is located in a rural area (as defined in subsection (d)(2)(D)(ii)).

(E) Reservation of positions for certain hospitals. (i) In general. Subject to clause (ii), the Secretary shall reserve the positions available for distribution under this paragraph as follows:

(I) 70 percent of such positions for distribution to hospitals described in clause (i) of subparagraph (D).

(II) 30 percent of such positions for distribution to hospitals described in clause (ii) and (iii) of such subparagraph.

(ii) Exception if positions not redistributed by July 1, 2011. In the case where the Secretary does not distribute positions to hospitals in accordance with clause (i) by July 1, 2011, the Secretary shall distribute such positions to other hospitals in accordance with the considerations described in subparagraph (C) and the priority described in subparagraph (D).

(F) Limitation. A hospital may not receive more than 75 full-time equivalent additional residency positions under this paragraph.

(G) Application of per resident amounts for primary care and nonprimary care. With respect to additional residency positions in a hospital attributable to the increase provided under this paragraph, the approved FTE per resident amounts are deemed to be equal to the hospital per resident amounts for primary care and nonprimary care computed under paragraph (2)(D) for that hospital.

(H) Definitions. In this paragraph:

(i) Reference resident level. The term "reference resident level" means, with respect to a hospital, the highest resident level for any of the 3 most recent cost reporting periods (ending before the date of the enactment of this paragraph) of the hospital for which a cost report has been settled (or, if not, submitted (subject to audit)), as determined by the Secretary.

(ii) Resident level. The term "resident level" has the meaning given such term in paragraph (7)(C)(i).

(iii) Otherwise applicable resident limit. The term "otherwise applicable resident limit" means, with respect to a hospital, the limit otherwise applicable under subparagraphs (F)(i) and (H) of paragraph (4) on the resident level for the hospital determined without regard to this paragraph but taking into account paragraph (7)(A).

(i) Avoiding duplicative payments to hospitals participating in rural demonstration programs. The Secretary shall reduce any payment amounts otherwise determined under this section to the extent necessary to avoid duplication of any payment made under section 4005(e) of the Omnibus Budget Reconciliation Act of 1987 [note to this section].

(j) Prospective payment for inpatient rehabilitation services. (1) Payment during transition period. (A) In general. Notwithstanding section 1814(b) [42 USCS § 1395f(b)], but subject to the provisions of section 1813 [42 USCS § 1395e], the amount of the payment with respect to the operating and capital costs of inpatient hospital services of a rehabilitation hospital or a rehabilitation unit (in this subsection referred to as a "rehabilitation facility"), other than a facility making an election under subparagraph (F) in a cost reporting period beginning on or after October 1, 2000, and before October 1, 2002, is equal to the sum of—

(i) the TEFRA percentage (as defined in subparagraph (C)) of the amount that would have been paid under part A with respect to such costs if this subsection did not apply, and

(ii) the prospective payment percentage (as defined in subparagraph (C)) of the product of (I) the per unit payment rate established under this subsection for the fiscal year in which the payment unit of service occurs, and (II) the number of such payment units occurring in the cost reporting period.

(B) Fully implemented system. Notwithstanding section 1814(b) [42 USCS § 1395f(b)], but subject to the provisions of section 1813 [42 USCS § 1395e], the amount of the payment with respect to the operating and capital costs of inpatient hospital services of a rehabilitation facility for a payment unit in a cost reporting period beginning on or after October 1, 2002, or, in the case of a facility making an election under subparagraph (F), for any cost reporting period described in such subparagraph, is equal to the per unit payment rate established under this subsection for the fiscal year in which the payment unit of service occurs.

(C) TEFRA and prospective payment percentages specified. For purposes of subparagraph (A), for a cost reporting period beginning—

(i) on or after October 1, 2000, and before October 1, 2001, the "TEFRA percentage" is 66⅔ percent and the "prospective payment percentage" is 33⅓ percent; and

(ii) on or after October 1, 2001, and before October 1, 2002, the "TEFRA percentage" is 33⅓ percent and the "prospective payment percentage" is 66⅔ percent.

(D) Payment unit. For purposes of this subsection, the term "payment unit" means a discharge.

(E) Construction relating to transfer authority. Nothing in this subsection shall be construed as preventing the Secretary from providing for an adjustment to payments to take into account the early transfer of a patient from a rehabilitation facility to another site of care.

(F) Election to apply full prospective payment system. A rehabilitation facility may elect, not later than 30 days before its first cost reporting period for which the payment methodology under this subsection applies to the facility, to have payment made to the facility under this subsection under the provisions of subparagraph (B) (rather than subparagraph (A)) for each cost reporting period to which such payment methodology applies.

(2) Patient case mix groups. (A) Establishment. The Secretary shall establish—

(i) classes of patient discharges of rehabilitation facilities by functional-related groups (each in this subsection referred to as a "case mix group"), based on impairment, age, comorbidities, and functional capability of the patient and such other factors as the Secretary deems appropriate to improve the explanatory power of functional independence measure-function related groups; and

(ii) a method of classifying specific patients in rehabilitation facilities within these groups.

(B) Weighting factors. For each case mix group the Secretary shall assign an appropriate weighting which reflects the relative facility resources used with respect to patients classified within that group compared to patients classified within other groups.

(C) Adjustments for case mix. (i) In general. The Secretary shall from time to time adjust the classifications and weighting factors established under this paragraph as appropriate to reflect changes in treatment patterns, technology, case mix, number of payment units for which payment is made under this title [42 USCS §§ 1395 et seq.], and other factors which may affect the relative use of resources. Such adjustments shall be made in a manner so that changes in aggregate payments under the classification system are a result of real changes and are not a result of changes in coding that are unrelated to real changes in case mix.

(ii) Adjustment. Insofar as the Secretary determines that such adjustments for a previous fiscal year (or estimates that such adjustments for a future fiscal year) did (or are likely to) result in a change in aggregate payments under the classification system during the fiscal year that are a result of changes in the coding or classification of patients that do not reflect real changes in case mix, the Secretary shall adjust the per payment unit payment rate for subsequent years so as to eliminate the effect of such coding or classification changes.

(D) Data collection. The Secretary is authorized to require rehabilitation facilities that provide inpatient hospital services to submit such data as the Secretary deems necessary to establish and administer the prospective payment system under this subsection.

(3) Payment rate. (A) In general. The Secretary shall determine a prospective payment rate for each payment unit for which such rehabilitation facility is entitled to receive payment under this title [42 USCS §§ 1395 et seq.]. Subject to subparagraph (B), such rate for payment units occurring during a fiscal year shall be based on the average payment per payment unit under this title [42 USCS §§ 1395 et seq.] for inpatient operating and capital costs of rehabilitation facilities using the most recent data available (as estimated by the Secretary as of the date of establishment of the system) adjusted—

(i) by updating such per-payment-unit amount to the fiscal year involved by the weighted average of the applicable percentage increases provided under subsection (b)(3)(B)(ii) (for cost reporting periods beginning during the fiscal year) covering the period from the midpoint of the period for such data through the midpoint of fiscal year 2000 and by an increase factor (described in subparagraph

(C)) specified by the Secretary for subsequent fiscal years up to the fiscal year involved;

(ii) by reducing such rates by a factor equal to the proportion of payments under this subsection (as estimated by the Secretary) based on prospective payment amounts which are additional payments described in paragraph (4) (relating to outlier and related payments);

(iii) for variations among rehabilitation facilities by area under paragraph (6);

(iv) by the weighting factors established under paragraph (2)(B); and

(v) by such other factors as the Secretary determines are necessary to properly reflect variations in necessary costs of treatment among rehabilitation facilities.

(B) Budget neutral rates. The Secretary shall establish the prospective payment amounts under this subsection for payment units during fiscal years 2001 and 2002 at levels such that, in the Secretary's estimation, the amount of total payments under this subsection for such fiscal years (including any payment adjustments pursuant to paragraphs (4) and (6) but not taking into account any payment adjustment resulting from an election permitted under paragraph (1)(F)) shall be equal to 98 percent for fiscal year 2001 and 100 percent for fiscal year 2002 of the amount of payments that would have been made under this title [42 USCS §§ 1395 et seq.] during the fiscal years for operating and capital costs of rehabilitation facilities had this subsection not been enacted. In establishing such payment amounts, the Secretary shall consider the effects of the prospective payment system established under this subsection on the total number of payment units from rehabilitation facilities and other factors described in subparagraph (A).

(C) Increase factor. (i) In general. For purposes of this subsection for payment units in each fiscal year (beginning with fiscal year 2001), the Secretary shall establish an increase factor subject to clause (ii). Such factor shall be based on an appropriate percentage increase in a market basket of goods and services comprising services for which payment is made under this subsection, which may be the market basket percentage increase described in subsection (b)(3)(B)(iii). The increase factor to be applied under this subparagraph for each of fiscal years 2008 and 2009 shall be 0 percent.

(ii) Productivity and other adjustment. After establishing the increase factor described in clause (i) for a fiscal year, the Secretary shall reduce such increase factor—

(I) for fiscal year 2012 and each subsequent fiscal year, by the productivity adjustment described in section 1886(b)(3)(B)(xi)(II) [subsec. (b)(3)(B)(xi)(II) of this section]; and

(II) for each of fiscal years 2010 through 2019, by the other adjustment described in subparagraph (D).

The application of this clause may result in the increase factor under this subparagraph being less than 0.0 for a fiscal year, and may result in payment rates under this subsection for a fiscal year being less than such payment rates for the preceding fiscal year.

(D) Other adjustment. For purposes of subparagraph (C)(ii)(II), the other adjustment described in this subparagraph is—

(i) for each of fiscal years 2010 and 2011, 0.25 percentage point;

(ii) for each of fiscal years 2012 and 2013, 0.1 percentage point;

(iii) for fiscal year 2014, 0.3 percentage point;

(iv) for each of fiscal years 2015 and 2016, 0.2 percentage point; and

(v) for each of fiscal years 2017, 2018, and 2019, 0.75 percentage point.

(4) Outlier and special payments. (A) Outliers. (i) In general. The Secretary may provide for an additional payment to a rehabilitation facility for patients in a case mix group, based upon the patient being classified as an outlier based on an unusual length of stay, costs, or other factors specified by the Secretary.

(ii) Payment based on marginal cost of care. The amount of such additional payment under clause (i) shall be determined by the Secretary and shall approximate the marginal cost of care beyond the cutoff point applicable under clause (i).

(iii) Total payments. The total amount of the additional payments made under this subparagraph for payment units in a fiscal year may not exceed 5 percent of the total payments projected or estimated to be made based on prospective payment rates for payment units in that year.

(B) Adjustment. The Secretary may provide for such adjustments to the payment amounts under this subsection as the Secretary deems appropriate to take into account the unique circumstances of rehabilitation facilities located in Alaska and Hawaii.

(5) Publication. The Secretary shall provide for publication in the Federal Register, on or before August 1 before each fiscal year (beginning with fiscal year 2001), of the classification and weighting factors for case mix groups under paragraph (2) for such fiscal year and a

description of the methodology and data used in computing the prospective payment rates under this subsection for that fiscal year.

(6) Area wage adjustment. The Secretary shall adjust the proportion (as estimated by the Secretary from time to time) of rehabilitation facilities' costs which are attributable to wages and wage-related costs, of the prospective payment rates computed under paragraph (3) for area differences in wage levels by a factor (established by the Secretary) reflecting the relative hospital wage level in the geographic area of the rehabilitation facility compared to the national average wage level for such facilities. Not later than October 1, 2001 (and at least every 36 months thereafter), the Secretary shall update the factor under the preceding sentence on the basis of information available to the Secretary (and updated as appropriate) of the wages and wage-related costs incurred in furnishing rehabilitation services. Any adjustments or updates made under this paragraph for a fiscal year shall be made in a manner that assures that the aggregated payments under this subsection in the fiscal year are not greater or less than those that would have been made in the year without such adjustment.

(7) Quality reporting. (A) Reduction in update for failure to report. (i) In general. For purposes of fiscal year 2014 and each subsequent fiscal year, in the case of a rehabilitation facility that does not submit data to the Secretary in accordance with subparagraph (C) with respect to such a fiscal year, after determining the increase factor described in paragraph (3)(C), and after application of paragraph (3)(D), the Secretary shall reduce such increase factor for payments for discharges occurring during such fiscal year by 2 percentage points.

(ii) Special rule. The application of this subparagraph may result in the increase factor described in paragraph (3)(C) being less than 0.0 for a fiscal year, and may result in payment rates under this subsection for a fiscal year being less than such payment rates for the preceding fiscal year.

(B) Noncumulative application. Any reduction under subparagraph (A) shall apply only with respect to the fiscal year involved and the Secretary shall not take into account such reduction in computing the payment amount under this subsection for a subsequent fiscal year.

(C) Submission of quality data. For fiscal year 2014 and each subsequent rate year, each rehabilitation facility shall submit to the Secretary data on quality measures specified under subparagraph (D). Such data shall be submitted in a form and manner, and at a time, specified by the Secretary for purposes of this subparagraph.

(D) Quality measures. (i) In general. Subject to clause (ii), any measure specified by the Secretary under this subparagraph must have been endorsed by the entity with a contract under section 1890(a) [42 USCS § 1395aaa(a)].

(ii) Exception. In the case of a specified area or medical topic determined appropriate by the Secretary for which a feasible and practical measure has not been endorsed by the entity with a contract under section 1890(a) [42 USCS § 1395aaa(a)], the Secretary may specify a measure that is not so endorsed as long as due consideration is given to measures that have been endorsed or adopted by a consensus organization identified by the Secretary.

(iii) Time frame. Not later than October 1, 2012, the Secretary shall publish the measures selected under this subparagraph that will be applicable with respect to fiscal year 2014.

(E) Public availability of data submitted. The Secretary shall establish procedures for making data submitted under subparagraph (C) available to the public. Such procedures shall ensure that a rehabilitation facility has the opportunity to review the data that is to be made public with respect to the facility prior to such data being made public. The Secretary shall report quality measures that relate to services furnished in inpatient settings in rehabilitation facilities on the Internet website of the Centers for Medicare & Medicaid Services.

(8) Limitation on review. There shall be no administrative or judicial review under section 1869, 1878 [42 USCS §§ 1395ff, 1395oo], or otherwise of the establishment of—

(A) case mix groups, of the methodology for the classification of patients within such groups, and of the appropriate weighting factors thereof under paragraph (2),

(B) the prospective payment rates under paragraph (3),

(C) outlier and special payments under paragraph (4), and

(D) area wage adjustments under paragraph (6).

(k) Payment to nonhospital providers. (1) In general. For cost reporting periods beginning on or after October 1, 1997, the Secretary may establish rules for payment to qualified nonhospital providers for their direct costs of medical education, if those costs are incurred in the operation of an approved medical residency training program described in subsection (h). Such rules shall specify the amounts, form, and manner in which such payments will be made and the portion of such payments that will be made from each of the trust funds under this title [42 USCS §§ 1395 et seq.].

(2) Qualified nonhospital providers. For purposes of this subsection, the term "qualified nonhospital providers" means—

(A) a Federally qualified health center, as defined in section 1861(aa)(4) [42 USCS § 1395x(aa)(4)];

(B) a rural health clinic, as defined in section 1861(aa)(2) [42 USCS § 1395x(aa)(2)];

(C) Medicare+Choice organizations; and

(D) such other providers (other than hospitals) as the Secretary determines to be appropriate.

(l) Payment for nursing and allied health education for managed care enrollees. (1) In general. For portions of cost reporting periods occurring in a year (beginning with 2000), the Secretary shall provide for an additional payment amount for any hospital that receives payments for the costs of approved educational activities for nurse and allied health professional training under section 1861(v)(1) [42 USCS § 1395x(v)(1)].

(2) Payment amount. The additional payment amount under this subsection for each hospital for portions of cost reporting periods occurring in a year shall be an amount specified by the Secretary in a manner consistent with the following:

(A) Determination of managed care enrollee payment ratio for graduate medical education payments. The Secretary shall estimate the ratio of payments for all hospitals for portions of cost reporting periods occurring in the year under subsection (h)(3)(D) to total direct graduate medical education payments estimated for such portions of periods under subsection (h)(3).

(B) Application to fee-for-service nursing and allied health education payments. Such ratio shall be applied to the Secretary's estimate of total payments for nursing and allied health education determined under section 1861(v) [42 USCS § 1395x(v)] for portions of cost reporting periods occurring in the year to determine a total amount of additional payments for nursing and allied health education to be distributed to hospitals under this subsection for portions of cost reporting periods occurring in the year; except that in no case shall such total amount exceed $60,000,000 in any year.

(C) Application to hospital. The amount of payment under this subsection to a hospital for portions of cost reporting periods occurring in a year is equal to the total amount of payments determined under subparagraph (B) for the year multiplied by the Secretary's estimate of the ratio of—

(i) the product of (I) the Secretary's estimate of the ratio of the amount of payments made under section 1861(v) [42 USCS § 1395x(v)] to the hospital for nursing and allied health education activities for the hospital's cost reporting period ending in the second preceding fiscal year, to the hospital's total inpatient days for such period, and (II) the total number of inpatient days (as established by the Secretary) for such period which are attributable to services furnished to individuals who are enrolled under a risk sharing contract with an eligible organization under section 1876 [42 USCS § 1395mm] and who are entitled to benefits under part A [42 USCS §§ 1395c et seq.] or who are enrolled with a Medicare+Choice organization under part C [42 USCS § 1395w-21 et seq.]; to

(ii) the sum of the products determined under clause (i) for such cost reporting periods.

(m) Prospective payment for long-term care hospitals. (1) Reference to establishment and implementation of system. For provisions related to the establishment and implementation of a prospective payment system for payments under this title [42 USCS §§ 1395 et seq.] for inpatient hospital services furnished by a long-term care hospital described in subsection (d)(1)(B)(iv), see section 123 of the Medicare, Medicaid, and SCHIP Balanced Budget Refinement Act of 1999 [note to this section] and section 307(b) of the Medicare, Medicaid, and SCHIP Benefits Improvement and Protection Act of 2000 [note to this section].

(2) Update for rate year 2008. In implementing the system described in paragraph (1) for discharges occurring during the rate year ending in 2008 for a hospital, the base rate for such discharges for the hospital shall be the same as the base rate for discharges for the hospital occurring during the rate year ending in 2007.

(3) Implementation for rate year 2010 and subsequent years. (A) In general. In implementing the system described in paragraph (1) for rate year 2010 and each subsequent rate year, any annual update to a standard Federal rate for discharges for the hospital during the rate year, shall be reduced—

(i) for rate year 2012 and each subsequent rate year, by the productivity adjustment described in section 1886(b)(3)(B)(xi)(II) [subsec. (b)(3)(B)(xi)(II) of this section]; and

(ii) for each of rate years 2010 through 2019, by the other adjustment described in paragraph (4).

(B) Special rule. The application of this paragraph may result in such annual update being less than 0.0 for a rate year, and may result in payment rates under the system described in paragraph (1) for a rate year being less than such payment rates for the preceding rate year.

(4) Other adjustment. For purposes of paragraph (3)(A)(ii), the other adjustment described in this paragraph is—

(A) for rate year 2010, 0.25 percentage point;

(B) for rate year 2011, 0.50 percentage point;

(C) for each of the rate years beginning in 2012 and 2013, 0.1 percentage point;

(D) for rate year 2014, 0.3 percentage point;

(E) for each of rate years 2015 and 2016, 0.2 percentage point; and

(F) for each of rate years 2017, 2018, and 2019, 0.75 percentage point.

(5) Quality reporting. (A) Reduction in update for failure to report. (i) In general. Under the system described in paragraph (1), for rate year 2014 and each subsequent rate year, in the case of a long-term care hospital that does not submit data to the Secretary in accordance with subparagraph (C) with respect to such a rate year, any annual update to a standard Federal rate for discharges for the hospital during the rate year, and after application of paragraph (3), shall be reduced by 2 percentage points.

(ii) Special rule. The application of this subparagraph may result in such annual update being less than 0.0 for a rate year, and may result in payment rates under the system described in paragraph (1) for a rate year being less than such payment rates for the preceding rate year.

(B) Noncumulative application. Any reduction under subparagraph (A) shall apply only with respect to the rate year involved and the Secretary shall not take into account such reduction in computing the payment amount under the system described in paragraph (1) for a subsequent rate year.

(C) Submission of quality data. For rate year 2014 and each subsequent rate year, each long-term care hospital shall submit to the Secretary data on quality measures specified under subparagraph (D). Such data shall be submitted in a form and manner, and at a time, specified by the Secretary for purposes of this subparagraph.

(D) Quality measures. (i) In general. Subject to clause (ii), any measure specified by the Secretary under this subparagraph must have been endorsed by the entity with a contract under section 1890(a) [42 USCS § 1395aaa(a)].

(ii) Exception. In the case of a specified area or medical topic determined appropriate by the Secretary for which a feasible and practical measure has not been endorsed by the entity with a contract under section 1890(a) [42 USCS § 1395aaa(a)], the Secretary may specify a measure that is not so endorsed as long as due consideration is given to measures that have been endorsed or adopted by a consensus organization identified by the Secretary.

(iii) Time frame. Not later than October 1, 2012, the Secretary shall publish the measures selected under this subparagraph that will be applicable with respect to rate year 2014.

(E) Public availability of data submitted. The Secretary shall establish procedures for making data submitted under subparagraph (C) available to the public. Such procedures shall ensure that a long-term care hospital has the opportunity to review the data that is to be made public with respect to the hospital prior to such data being made public. The Secretary shall report quality measures that relate to services furnished in inpatient settings in long-term care hospitals on the Internet website of the Centers for Medicare & Medicaid Services.

(n) Incentives for adoption and meaningful use of certified EHR technology. (1) In general. Subject to the succeeding provisions of this subsection, with respect to inpatient hospital services furnished by an eligible hospital during a payment year (as defined in paragraph (2)(G)), if the eligible hospital is a meaningful EHR user (as determined under paragraph (3)) for the EHR reporting period with respect to such year, in addition to the amount otherwise paid under this section, there also shall be paid to the eligible hospital, from the Federal Hospital Insurance Trust Fund established under section 1817 [42 USCS § 1395i], an amount equal to the applicable amount specified in paragraph (2)(A) for the hospital for such payment year.

(2) Payment amount. (A) In general. Subject to the succeeding subparagraphs of this paragraph, the applicable amount specified in this subparagraph for an eligible hospital for a payment year is equal to the product of the following:

(i) Initial amount. The sum of—

(I) the base amount specified in subparagraph (B); plus

(II) the discharge related amount specified in subparagraph (C) for a 12-month period selected by the Secretary with respect to such payment year.

(ii) Medicare share. The Medicare share as

specified in subparagraph (D) for the eligible hospital for a period selected by the Secretary with respect to such payment year.

(iii) Transition factor. The transition factor specified in subparagraph (E) for the eligible hospital for the payment year.

(B) Base amount. The base amount specified in this subparagraph is $2,000,000.

(C) Discharge related amount. The discharge related amount specified in this subparagraph for a 12-month period selected by the Secretary shall be determined as the sum of the amount, estimated based upon total discharges for the eligible hospital (regardless of any source of payment) for the period, for each discharge up to the 23,000th discharge as follows:

(i) For the first through 1,149th discharge, $0.

(ii) For the 1,150th through the 23,000th discharge, $200.

(iii) For any discharge greater than the 23,000th, $0.

(D) Medicare share. The Medicare share specified under this subparagraph for an eligible hospital for a period selected by the Secretary for a payment year is equal to the fraction—

(i) the numerator of which is the sum (for such period and with respect to the eligible hospital) of—

(I) the estimated number of inpatient-bed-days (as established by the Secretary) which are attributable to individuals with respect to whom payment may be made under part A [42 USCS §§ 1395c et seq.]; and

(II) the estimated number of inpatient-bed-days (as so established) which are attributable to individuals who are enrolled with a Medicare Advantage organization under part C [42 USCS §§ 1395w-21 et seq.]; and

(ii) the denominator of which is the product of—

(I) the estimated total number of inpatient-bed-days with respect to the eligible hospital during such period; and

(II) the estimated total amount of the eligible hospital's charges during such period, not including any charges that are attributable to charity care (as such term is used for purposes of hospital cost reporting under this title), divided by the estimated total amount of the hospital's charges during such period.

Insofar as the Secretary determines that data are not available on charity care necessary to calculate the portion of the formula specified in clause (ii)(II), the Secretary shall use data on uncompensated care and may adjust such data so as to be an appropriate proxy for charity care including a downward adjustment to eliminate bad debt data from uncompensated care data. In the absence of the data necessary, with respect to a hospital, for the Secretary to compute the amount described in clause (ii)(II), the amount under such clause shall be deemed to be 1. In the absence of data, with respect to a hospital, necessary to compute the amount described in clause (i)(II), the amount under such clause shall be deemed to be 0.

(E) Transition factor specified. (i) In general. Subject to clause (ii), the transition factor specified in this subparagraph for an eligible hospital for a payment year is as follows:

(I) For the first payment year for such hospital, 1.

(II) For the second payment year for such hospital, ¾.

(III) For the third payment year for such hospital, ½.

(IV) For the fourth payment year for such hospital, ¼.

(V) For any succeeding payment year for such hospital, 0.

(ii) Phase down for eligible hospitals first adopting ehr after 2013. If the first payment year for an eligible hospital is after 2013, then the transition factor specified in this subparagraph for a payment year for such hospital is the same as the amount specified in clause (i) for such payment year for an eligible hospital for which the first payment year is 2013. If the first payment year for an eligible hospital is after 2015 then the transition factor specified in this subparagraph for such hospital and for such year and any subsequent year shall be 0.

(F) Form of payment. The payment under this subsection for a payment year may be in the form of a single consolidated payment or in the form of such periodic installments as the Secretary may specify.

(G) Payment year defined. (i) In general. For purposes of this subsection, the term "payment year" means a fiscal year beginning with fiscal year 2011.

(ii) First, second, etc. payment year. The term "first payment year" means, with respect to inpatient hospital services furnished by an eligible hospital, the first fiscal year for which an incentive payment is made for such services under this subsection. The terms "second payment year", "third payment year", and "fourth payment year" mean, with respect to an eligible hospital, each successive year immediately following the first payment year for that hospital.

(3) Meaningful EHR user. (A) In general.

For purposes of paragraph (1), an eligible hospital shall be treated as a meaningful EHR user for an EHR reporting period for a payment year (or, for purposes of subsection (b)(3)(B)(ix), for an EHR reporting period under such subsection for a fiscal year) if each of the following requirements are met:

(i) Meaningful use of certified EHR technology. The eligible hospital demonstrates to the satisfaction of the Secretary, in accordance with subparagraph (C)(i), that during such period the hospital is using certified EHR technology in a meaningful manner.

(ii) Information exchange. The eligible hospital demonstrates to the satisfaction of the Secretary, in accordance with subparagraph (C)(i), that during such period such certified EHR technology is connected in a manner that provides, in accordance with law and standards applicable to the exchange of information, for the electronic exchange of health information to improve the quality of health care, such as promoting care coordination.

(iii) Reporting on measures using EHR. Subject to subparagraph (B)(ii) and using such certified EHR technology, the eligible hospital submits information for such period, in a form and manner specified by the Secretary, on such clinical quality measures and such other measures as selected by the Secretary under subparagraph (B)(i).

The Secretary shall seek to improve the use of electronic health records and health care quality over time by requiring more stringent measures of meaningful use selected under this paragraph.

(B) Reporting on measures. (i) Selection. The Secretary shall select measures for purposes of subparagraph (A)(iii) but only consistent with the following:

(I) The Secretary shall provide preference to clinical quality measures that have been selected for purposes of applying subsection (b)(3)(B)(viii) or that have been endorsed by the entity with a contract with the Secretary under section 1890(a) [42 USCS § 1395aaa(a)].

(II) Prior to any measure (other than a clinical quality measure that has been selected for purposes of applying subsection (b)(3)(B)(viii)) being selected under this subparagraph, the Secretary shall publish in the Federal Register such measure and provide for a period of public comment on such measure.

(ii) Limitations. The Secretary may not require the electronic reporting of information on clinical quality measures under subparagraph (A)(iii) unless the Secretary has the capacity to accept the information electronically, which may be on a pilot basis.

(iii) Coordination of reporting of information. In selecting such measures, and in establishing the form and manner for reporting measures under subparagraph (A)(iii), the Secretary shall seek to avoid redundant or duplicative reporting with reporting otherwise required, including reporting under subsection (b)(3)(B)(viii).

(C) Demonstration of meaningful use of certified EHR technology and information exchange. (i) In general. An eligible hospital may satisfy the demonstration requirement of clauses (i) and (ii) of subparagraph (A) through means specified by the Secretary, which may include—

(I) an attestation;

(II) the submission of claims with appropriate coding (such as a code indicating that inpatient care was documented using certified EHR technology);

(III) a survey response;

(IV) reporting under subparagraph (A)(iii); and

(V) other means specified by the Secretary.

(ii) Use of part D data. Notwithstanding sections 1860D-15(d)(2)(B) and 1860D-15(f)(2) [42 USCS § 1395w-115(d)(2)(B), (f)(2)], the Secretary may use data regarding drug claims submitted for purposes of section 1860D-15 [42 USCS § 1395w-115] that are necessary for purposes of subparagraph (A).

(4) Application. (A) Limitations on review. There shall be no administrative or judicial review under section 1869 [42 USCS § 1395ff], section 1878 [42 USCS § 1395oo], or otherwise, of—

(i) the methodology and standards for determining payment amounts under this subsection and payment adjustments under subsection (b)(3)(B)(ix), including selection of periods under paragraph (2) for determining, and making estimates or using proxies of, discharges under paragraph (2)(C) and inpatient-bed-days, hospital charges, charity charges, and Medicare share under paragraph (2)(D);

(ii) the methodology and standards for determining a meaningful EHR user under paragraph (3), including selection of measures under paragraph (3)(B), specification of the means of demonstrating meaningful EHR use under paragraph (3)(C), and the hardship exception under subsection (b)(3)(B)(ix)(II); and

(iii) the specification of EHR reporting periods under paragraph (6)(B) and the selection of the form of payment under paragraph (2)(F).

(B) Posting on website. The Secretary shall post on the Internet website of the Centers for

Medicare & Medicaid Services, in an easily understandable format, a list of the names of the eligible hospitals that are meaningful EHR users under this subsection or subsection (b)(3)(B)(ix) (and a list of the names of critical access hospitals to which paragraph (3) or (4) of section 1814(l) [42 USCS § 1395f(l)] applies), and other relevant data as determined appropriate by the Secretary. The Secretary shall ensure that an eligible hospital (or critical access hospital) has the opportunity to review the other relevant data that are to be made public with respect to the hospital (or critical access hospital) prior to such data being made public.

(5) Certified EHR technology defined. The term "certified EHR technology" has the meaning given such term in section 1848(o)(4) [42 USCS § 1395w-4(o)(4)].

(6) Definitions. For purposes of this subsection:

(A) EHR reporting period. The term "EHR reporting period" means, with respect to a payment year, any period (or periods) as specified by the Secretary.

(B) Eligible hospital. The term "eligible hospital" means a subsection (d) hospital.

(o) Hospital value-based purchasing program. (1) Establishment. (A) In general. Subject to the succeeding provisions of this subsection, the Secretary shall establish a hospital value-based purchasing program (in this subsection referred to as the 'Program') under which value-based incentive payments are made in a fiscal year to hospitals that meet the performance standards under paragraph (3) for the performance period for such fiscal year (as established under paragraph (4)).

(B) Program to begin in fiscal year 2013. The Program shall apply to payments for discharges occurring on or after October 1, 2012.

(C) Applicability of program to hospitals. (i) In general. For purposes of this subsection, subject to clause (ii), the term "hospital" means a subsection (d) hospital (as defined in subsection (d)(1)(B)).

(ii) Exclusions. The term "hospital" shall not include, with respect to a fiscal year, a hospital—

(I) that is subject to the payment reduction under subsection (b)(3)(B)(viii)(I) for such fiscal year;

(II) for which, during the performance period for such fiscal year, the Secretary has cited deficiencies that pose immediate jeopardy to the health or safety of patients;

(III) for which there are not a minimum number (as determined by the Secretary) of measures that apply to the hospital for the performance period for such fiscal year; or

(IV) for which there are not a minimum number (as determined by the Secretary) of cases for the measures that apply to the hospital for the performance period for such fiscal year.

(iii) Independent analysis. For purposes of determining the minimum numbers under subclauses (III) and (IV) of clause (ii), the Secretary shall have conducted an independent analysis of what numbers are appropriate.

(iv) Exemption. In the case of a hospital that is paid under section 1814(b)(3) [42 USCS § 1395f(b)(3)], the Secretary may exempt such hospital from the application of this subsection if the State which is paid under such section submits an annual report to the Secretary describing how a similar program in the State for a participating hospital or hospitals achieves or surpasses the measured results in terms of patient health outcomes and cost savings established under this subsection.

(2) Measures. (A) In general. The Secretary shall select measures, other than measures of readmissions, for purposes of the Program. Such measures shall be selected from the measures specified under subsection (b)(3)(B)(viii).

(B) Requirements. (i) For fiscal year 2013. For value-based incentive payments made with respect to discharges occurring during fiscal year 2013, the Secretary shall ensure the following:

(I) Conditions or procedures. Measures are selected under subparagraph (A) that cover at least the following 5 specific conditions or procedures:

(aa) Acute myocardial infarction (AMI).

(bb) Heart failure.

(cc) Pneumonia.

(dd) Surgeries, as measured by the Surgical Care Improvement Project (formerly referred to as "Surgical Infection Prevention" for discharges occurring before July 2006).

(ee) Healthcare-associated infections, as measured by the prevention metrics and targets established in the HHS Action Plan to Prevent Healthcare-Associated Infections (or any successor plan) of the Department of Health and Human Services.

(II) HCAHPS. Measures selected under subparagraph (A) shall be related to the Hospital Consumer Assessment of Healthcare Providers and Systems survey (HCAHPS).

(ii) Inclusion of efficiency measures. For value-based incentive payments made with respect to discharges occurring during fiscal year 2014 or a subsequent fiscal year, the Secretary shall ensure that measures selected under subparagraph (A) include efficiency measures, including measures of "Medicare spending per beneficiary". Such measures shall be adjusted for factors such as age, sex, race, severity of illness, and other factors that the Secretary determines appropriate.

(C) Limitations. (i) Time requirement for prior reporting and notice. The Secretary may not select a measure under subparagraph (A) for use under the Program with respect to a performance period for a fiscal year (as established under paragraph (4)) unless such measure has been specified under subsection (b)(3)(B)(viii) and included on the Hospital Compare Internet website for at least 1 year prior to the beginning of such performance period.

(ii) Measure not applicable unless hospital furnishes services appropriate to the measure. A measure selected under subparagraph (A) shall not apply to a hospital if such hospital does not furnish services appropriate to such measure.

(D) Replacing measures. Subclause (VI) of subsection (b)(3)(B)(viii) shall apply to measures selected under subparagraph (A) in the same manner as such subclause applies to measures selected under such subsection.

(3) Performance standards. (A) Establishment. The Secretary shall establish performance standards with respect to measures selected under paragraph (2) for a performance period for a fiscal year (as established under paragraph (4)).

(B) Achievement and improvement. The performance standards established under subparagraph (A) shall include levels of achievement and improvement.

(C) Timing. The Secretary shall establish and announce the performance standards under subparagraph (A) not later than 60 days prior to the beginning of the performance period for the fiscal year involved.

(D) Considerations in establishing standards. In establishing performance standards with respect to measures under this paragraph, the Secretary shall take into account appropriate factors, such as—

(i) practical experience with the measures involved, including whether a significant proportion of hospitals failed to meet the performance standard during previous performance periods;

(ii) historical performance standards;

(iii) improvement rates; and

(iv) the opportunity for continued improvement.

(4) Performance period. For purposes of the Program, the Secretary shall establish the performance period for a fiscal year. Such performance period shall begin and end prior to the beginning of such fiscal year.

(5) Hospital performance score. (A) In general. Subject to subparagraph (B), the Secretary shall develop a methodology for assessing the total performance of each hospital based on performance standards with respect to the measures selected under paragraph (2) for a performance period (as established under paragraph (4)). Using such methodology, the Secretary shall provide for an assessment (in this subsection referred to as the "hospital performance score") for each hospital for each performance period.

(B) Application. (i) Appropriate distribution. The Secretary shall ensure that the application of the methodology developed under subparagraph (A) results in an appropriate distribution of value-based incentive payments under paragraph (6) among hospitals achieving different levels of hospital performance scores, with hospitals achieving the highest hospital performance scores receiving the largest value-based incentive payments.

(ii) Higher of achievement or improvement. The methodology developed under subparagraph (A) shall provide that the hospital performance score is determined using the higher of its achievement or improvement score for each measure.

(iii) Weights. The methodology developed under subparagraph (A) shall provide for the assignment of weights for categories of measures as the Secretary determines appropriate.

(iv) No minimum performance standard. The Secretary shall not set a minimum performance standard in determining the hospital performance score for any hospital.

(v) Reflection of measures applicable to the hospital. The hospital performance score for a hospital shall reflect the measures that apply to the hospital.

(6) Calculation of value-based incentive payments. (A) In general. In the case of a hospital that the Secretary determines meets (or exceeds) the performance standards under paragraph (3) for the performance period for a fiscal year (as established under paragraph (4)), the Secretary shall increase the base operating DRG payment amount (as defined in paragraph (7)(D)), as determined after application of paragraph (7)(B)(i), for a hospital for each discharge occurring in such fiscal year by the value-based incentive payment amount.

(B) Value-based incentive payment amount.

The value-based incentive payment amount for each discharge of a hospital in a fiscal year shall be equal to the product of—

(i) the base operating DRG payment amount (as defined in paragraph (7)(D)) for the discharge for the hospital for such fiscal year; and

(ii) the value-based incentive payment percentage specified under subparagraph (C) for the hospital for such fiscal year.

(C) Value-based incentive payment percentage. (i) In general. The Secretary shall specify a value-based incentive payment percentage for a hospital for a fiscal year.

(ii) Requirements. In specifying the value-based incentive payment percentage for each hospital for a fiscal year under clause (i), the Secretary shall ensure that—

(I) such percentage is based on the hospital performance score of the hospital under paragraph (5); and

(II) the total amount of value-based incentive payments under this paragraph to all hospitals in such fiscal year is equal to the total amount available for value-based incentive payments for such fiscal year under paragraph (7)(A), as estimated by the Secretary.

(7) Funding for value-based incentive payments. (A) Amount. The total amount available for value-based incentive payments under paragraph (6) for all hospitals for a fiscal year shall be equal to the total amount of reduced payments for all hospitals under subparagraph (B) for such fiscal year, as estimated by the Secretary.

(B) Adjustment to payments. (i) In general. The Secretary shall reduce the base operating DRG payment amount (as defined in subparagraph (D)) for a hospital for each discharge in a fiscal year (beginning with fiscal year 2013) by an amount equal to the applicable percent (as defined in subparagraph (C)) of the base operating DRG payment amount for the discharge for the hospital for such fiscal year. The Secretary shall make such reductions for all hospitals in the fiscal year involved, regardless of whether or not the hospital has been determined by the Secretary to have earned a value-based incentive payment under paragraph (6) for such fiscal year.

(ii) No effect on other payments. Payments described in items (aa) and (bb) of subparagraph (D)(i)(II) for a hospital shall be determined as if this subsection had not been enacted.

(C) Applicable percent defined. For purposes of subparagraph (B), the term "applicable percent" means—

(i) with respect to fiscal year 2013, 1.0 percent;

(ii) with respect to fiscal year 2014, 1.25 percent;

(iii) with respect to fiscal year 2015, 1.5 percent;

(iv) with respect to fiscal year 2016, 1.75 percent; and

(v) with respect to fiscal year 2017 and succeeding fiscal years, 2 percent.

(D) Base operating DRG payment amount defined. (i) In general. Except as provided in clause (ii), in this subsection, the term "base operating DRG payment amount" means, with respect to a hospital for a fiscal year—

(I) the payment amount that would otherwise be made under subsection (d) (determined without regard to subsection (q)) for a discharge if this subsection did not apply; reduced by

(II) any portion of such payment amount that is attributable to—

(aa) payments under paragraphs (5)(A), (5)(B), (5)(F), and (12) of subsection (d); and

(bb) such other payments under subsection (d) determined appropriate by the Secretary.

(ii) Special rules for certain hospitals. (I) Sole community hospitals and Medicare-dependent, small rural hospitals. In the case of a Medicare-dependent, small rural hospital (with respect to discharges occurring during fiscal year 2012 and 2013) or a sole community hospital, in applying subparagraph (A)(i), the payment amount that would otherwise be made under subsection (d) shall be determined without regard to subparagraphs (I) and (L) of subsection (b)(3) and subparagraphs (D) and (G) of subsection (d)(5).

(II) Hospitals paid under section 1814. In the case of a hospital that is paid under section 1814(b)(3) [42 USCS § 1395f(b)(3)], the term "base operating DRG payment amount" means the payment amount under such section.

(8) Announcement of net result of adjustments. Under the Program, the Secretary shall, not later than 60 days prior to the fiscal year involved, inform each hospital of the adjustments to payments to the hospital for discharges occurring in such fiscal year under paragraphs (6) and (7)(B)(i).

(9) No effect in subsequent fiscal years. The value-based incentive payment under paragraph (6) and the payment reduction under paragraph (7)(B)(i) shall each apply only with respect to the fiscal year involved, and the Secretary shall not take into account such value-based incentive payment or payment reduction in making payments to a hospital under this section in a subsequent fiscal year.

(10) Public reporting. (A) Hospital specific information. (i) In general. The Secretary shall make information available to the public regarding the performance of individual hospitals under the Program, including—

(I) the performance of the hospital with respect to each measure that applies to the hospital;

(II) the performance of the hospital with respect to each condition or procedure; and

(III) the hospital performance score assessing the total performance of the hospital.

(ii) Opportunity to review and submit corrections. The Secretary shall ensure that a hospital has the opportunity to review, and submit corrections for, the information to be made public with respect to the hospital under clause (i) prior to such information being made public.

(iii) Website. Such information shall be posted on the Hospital Compare Internet website in an easily understandable format.

(B) Aggregate information. The Secretary shall periodically post on the Hospital Compare Internet website aggregate information on the Program, including—

(i) the number of hospitals receiving value-based incentive payments under paragraph (6) and the range and total amount of such value-based incentive payments; and

(ii) the number of hospitals receiving less than the maximum value-based incentive payment available to the hospital for the fiscal year involved and the range and amount of such payments.

(11) Implementation. (A) Appeals. The Secretary shall establish a process by which hospitals may appeal the calculation of a hospital's performance assessment with respect to the performance standards established under paragraph (3)(A) and the hospital performance score under paragraph (5). The Secretary shall ensure that such process provides for resolution of such appeals in a timely manner.

(B) Limitation on review. Except as provided in subparagraph (A), there shall be no administrative or judicial review under section 1869 [42 USCS § 1395ff], section 1878 [42 USCS § 1395oo], or otherwise of the following:

(i) The methodology used to determine the amount of the value-based incentive payment under paragraph (6) and the determination of such amount.

(ii) The determination of the amount of funding available for such value-based incentive payments under paragraph (7)(A) and the payment reduction under paragraph (7)(B)(i).

(iii) The establishment of the performance standards under paragraph (3) and the performance period under paragraph (4).

(iv) The measures specified under subsection (b)(3)(B)(viii) and the measures selected under paragraph (2).

(v) The methodology developed under paragraph (5) that is used to calculate hospital performance scores and the calculation of such scores.

(vi) The validation methodology specified in subsection (b)(3)(B)(viii)(XI).

(C) Consultation with small hospitals. The Secretary shall consult with small rural and urban hospitals on the application of the Program to such hospitals.

(12) Promulgation of regulations. The Secretary shall promulgate regulations to carry out the Program, including the selection of measures under paragraph (2), the methodology developed under paragraph (5) that is used to calculate hospital performance scores, and the methodology used to determine the amount of value-based incentive payments under paragraph (6).

(p) Adjustment to hospital payments for hospital acquired conditions. (1) In general. In order to provide an incentive for applicable hospitals to reduce hospital acquired conditions under this title, with respect to discharges from an applicable hospital occurring during fiscal year 2015 or a subsequent fiscal year, the amount of payment under this section or section 1814(b)(3) [42 USCS § 1395f(b)(3)], as applicable, for such discharges during the fiscal year shall be equal to 99 percent of the amount of payment that would otherwise apply to such discharges under this section or section 1814(b)(3) [42 USCS § 1395f(b)(3)] (determined after the application of subsections (o) and (q) and section 1814(l)(4) [42 USCS § 1395f(l)(4)] but without regard to this subsection).

(2) Applicable hospitals. (A) In general. For purposes of this subsection, the term "applicable hospital" means a subsection (d) hospital that meets the criteria described in subparagraph (B).

(B) Criteria described. (i) In general. The criteria described in this subparagraph, with respect to a subsection (d) hospital, is that the subsection (d) hospital is in the top quartile of all subsection (d) hospitals, relative to the national average, of hospital acquired conditions during the applicable period, as determined by the Secretary.

(ii) Risk adjustment. In carrying out clause (i), the Secretary shall establish and apply an appropriate risk adjustment methodology.

(C) Exemption. In the case of a hospital that is paid under section 1814(b)(3) [42 USCS § 1395f(b)(3)], the Secretary may exempt such hospital from the application of this subsection if the State which is paid under such section submits an annual report to the Secretary describing how a similar program in the State for a participating hospital or hospitals achieves or surpasses the measured results in terms of patient health outcomes and cost savings established under this subsection.

(3) Hospital acquired conditions. For purposes of this subsection, the term "hospital acquired condition" means a condition identified for purposes of subsection (d)(4)(D)(iv) and any other condition determined appropriate by the Secretary that an individual acquires during a stay in an applicable hospital, as determined by the Secretary.

(4) Applicable period. In this subsection, the term "applicable period" means, with respect to a fiscal year, a period specified by the Secretary.

(5) Reporting to hospitals. Prior to fiscal year 2015 and each subsequent fiscal year, the Secretary shall provide confidential reports to applicable hospitals with respect to hospital acquired conditions of the applicable hospital during the applicable period.

(6) Reporting hospital specific information. (A) In general. The Secretary shall make information available to the public regarding hospital acquired conditions of each applicable hospital.

(B) Opportunity to review and submit corrections. The Secretary shall ensure that an applicable hospital has the opportunity to review, and submit corrections for, the information to be made public with respect to the hospital under subparagraph (A) prior to such information being made public.

(C) Website. Such information shall be posted on the Hospital Compare Internet website in an easily understandable format.

(7) Limitations on review. There shall be no administrative or judicial review under section 1869 [42 USCS § 1395ff], section 1878 [42 USCS § 1395oo], or otherwise of the following:

(A) The criteria described in paragraph (2)(A).

(B) The specification of hospital acquired conditions under paragraph (3).

(C) The specification of the applicable period under paragraph (4).

(D) The provision of reports to applicable hospitals under paragraph (5) and the information made available to the public under paragraph (6).

(q) Hospital readmissions reduction program. (1) In general. With respect to payment for discharges from an applicable hospital (as defined in paragraph (5)(C)) occurring during a fiscal year beginning on or after October 1, 2012, in order to account for excess readmissions in the hospital, the Secretary shall make payments (in addition to the payments described in paragraph (2)(A)(ii)) for such a discharge to such hospital under subsection (d) (or section 1814(b)(3) [42 USCS § 1395f(b)(3)], as the case may be) in an amount equal to the product of—

(A) the base operating DRG payment amount (as defined in paragraph (2)) for the discharge; and

(B) the adjustment factor (described in paragraph (3)(A)) for the hospital for the fiscal year.

(2) Base operating DRG payment amount defined. (A) In general. Except as provided in subparagraph (B), in this subsection, the term "base operating DRG payment amount" means, with respect to a hospital for a fiscal year—

(i) the payment amount that would otherwise be made under subsection (d) (determined without regard to subsection (o)) for a discharge if this subsection did not apply; reduced by

(ii) any portion of such payment amount that is attributable to payments under paragraphs (5)(A), (5)(B), (5)(F), and (12) of subsection (d).

(B) Special rules for certain hospitals. (i) Sole community hospitals and Medicare-dependent, small rural hospitals. In the case of a Medicare-dependent, small rural hospital (with respect to discharges occurring during fiscal years 2012 and 2013) or a sole community hospital, in applying subparagraph (A)(i), the payment amount that would otherwise be made under subsection (d) shall be determined without regard to subparagraphs (I) and (L) of subsection (b)(3) and subparagraphs (D) and (G) of subsection (d)(5).

(ii) Hospitals paid under section 1814. In the case of a hospital that is paid under section 1814(b)(3) [42 USCS § 1395f(b)(3)], the Secretary may exempt such hospitals provided that States paid under such section submit an annual report to the Secretary describing how a similar program in the State for a participating hospital or hospitals achieves or surpasses the measured results in terms of patient health outcomes and cost savings established herein with respect to this section.

(3) Adjustment factor. (A) In general. For purposes of paragraph (1), the adjustment factor under this paragraph for an applicable hospital for a fiscal year is equal to the greater

of—

(i) the ratio described in subparagraph (B) for the hospital for the applicable period (as defined in paragraph (5)(D)) for such fiscal year; or

(ii) the floor adjustment factor specified in subparagraph (C).

(B) Ratio. The ratio described in this subparagraph for a hospital for an applicable period is equal to 1 minus the ratio of—

(i) the aggregate payments for excess readmissions (as defined in paragraph (4)(A)) with respect to an applicable hospital for the applicable period; and

(ii) the aggregate payments for all discharges (as defined in paragraph (4)(B)) with respect to such applicable hospital for such applicable period.

(C) Floor adjustment factor. For purposes of subparagraph (A), the floor adjustment factor specified in this subparagraph for—

(i) fiscal year 2013 is 0.99;

(ii) fiscal year 2014 is 0.98; or

(iii) fiscal year 2015 and subsequent fiscal years is 0.97.

(4) Aggregate payments, excess readmission ratio defined. For purposes of this subsection:

(A) Aggregate payments for excess readmissions. The term "aggregate payments for excess readmissions" means, for a hospital for an applicable period, the sum, for applicable conditions (as defined in paragraph (5)(A)), of the product, for each applicable condition, of—

(i) the base operating DRG payment amount for such hospital for such applicable period for such condition;

(ii) the number of admissions for such condition for such hospital for such applicable period; and

(iii) the excess readmissions ratio (as defined in subparagraph (C)) for such hospital for such applicable period minus 1.

(B) Aggregate payments for all discharges. The term "aggregate payments for all discharges" means, for a hospital for an applicable period, the sum of the base operating DRG payment amounts for all discharges for all conditions from such hospital for such applicable period.

(C) Excess readmission ratio. (i) In general. Subject to clause (ii), the term "excess readmissions ratio" means, with respect to an applicable condition for a hospital for an applicable period, the ratio (but not less than 1.0) of—

(I) the risk adjusted readmissions based on actual readmissions, as determined consistent with a readmission measure methodology that has been endorsed under paragraph (5)(A)(ii)(I), for an applicable hospital for such condition with respect to such applicable period; to

(II) the risk adjusted expected readmissions (as determined consistent with such a methodology) for such hospital for such condition with respect to such applicable period.

(ii) Exclusion of certain readmissions. For purposes of clause (i), with respect to a hospital, excess readmissions shall not include readmissions for an applicable condition for which there are fewer than a minimum number (as determined by the Secretary) of discharges for such applicable condition for the applicable period and such hospital.

(5) Definitions. For purposes of this subsection:

(A) Applicable condition. The term "applicable condition" means, subject to subparagraph (B), a condition or procedure selected by the Secretary among conditions and procedures for which—

(i) readmissions (as defined in subparagraph (E)) that represent conditions or procedures that are high volume or high expenditures under this title (or other criteria specified by the Secretary); and

(ii) measures of such readmissions—

(I) have been endorsed by the entity with a contract under section 1890(a) [42 USCS § 1395aaa(a)]; and

(II) such endorsed measures have exclusions for readmissions that are unrelated to the prior discharge (such as a planned readmission or transfer to another applicable hospital).

(B) Expansion of applicable conditions. Beginning with fiscal year 2015, the Secretary shall, to the extent practicable, expand the applicable conditions beyond the 3 conditions for which measures have been endorsed as described in subparagraph (A)(ii)(I) as of the date of the enactment of this subsection to the additional 4 conditions that have been identified by the Medicare Payment Advisory Commission in its report to Congress in June 2007 and to other conditions and procedures as determined appropriate by the Secretary. In expanding such applicable conditions, the Secretary shall seek the endorsement described in subparagraph (A)(ii)(I) but may apply such measures without such an endorsement in the case of a specified area or medical topic determined appropriate by the Secretary for which a feasible and practical measure has not been endorsed by the entity with a contract under section 1890(a) [42 USCS § 1395aaa(a)] as long as due consideration is given to measures that have been endorsed or adopted by a consensus organization identified by the Secretary.

(C) Applicable hospital. The term "applicable hospital" means a subsection (d) hospital or a hospital that is paid under section 1814(b)(3) [42 USCS § 1395f(b)(3)], as the case may be.

(D) Applicable period. The term "applicable period" means, with respect to a fiscal year, such period as the Secretary shall specify.

(E) Readmission. The term "readmission" means, in the case of an individual who is discharged from an applicable hospital, the admission of the individual to the same or another applicable hospital within a time period specified by the Secretary from the date of such discharge. Insofar as the discharge relates to an applicable condition for which there is an endorsed measure described in subparagraph (A)(ii)(I), such time period (such as 30 days) shall be consistent with the time period specified for such measure.

(6) Reporting hospital specific information. (A) In general. The Secretary shall make information available to the public regarding readmission rates of each subsection (d) hospital under the program.

(B) Opportunity to review and submit corrections. The Secretary shall ensure that a subsection (d) hospital has the opportunity to review, and submit corrections for, the information to be made public with respect to the hospital under subparagraph (A) prior to such information being made public.

(C) Website. Such information shall be posted on the Hospital Compare Internet website in an easily understandable format.

(7) Limitations on review. There shall be no administrative or judicial review under section 1869 [42 USCS § 1395ff], section 1878 [42 USCS § 1395oo], or otherwise of the following:

(A) The determination of base operating DRG payment amounts.

(B) The methodology for determining the adjustment factor under paragraph (3), including excess readmissions ratio under paragraph (4)(C), aggregate payments for excess readmissions under paragraph (4)(A), and aggregate payments for all discharges under paragraph (4)(B), and applicable periods and applicable conditions under paragraph (5).

(C) The measures of readmissions as described in paragraph (5)(A)(ii).

(8) Readmission rates for all patients. (A) Calculation of readmission. The Secretary shall calculate readmission rates for all patients (as defined in subparagraph (D)) for a specified hospital (as defined in subparagraph (D)(ii)) for an applicable condition (as defined in paragraph (5)(B)) and other conditions deemed appropriate by the Secretary for an applicable period (as defined in paragraph (5)(D)) in the same manner as used to calculate such readmission rates for hospitals with respect to this title and posted on the CMS Hospital Compare website.

(B) Posting of hospital specific all patient readmission rates. The Secretary shall make information on all patient readmission rates calculated under subparagraph (A) available on the CMS Hospital Compare website in a form and manner determined appropriate by the Secretary. The Secretary may also make other information determined appropriate by the Secretary available on such website.

(C) Hospital submission of all patient data. (i) Except as provided for in clause (ii), each specified hospital (as defined in subparagraph (D)(ii)) shall submit to the Secretary, in a form, manner and time specified by the Secretary, data and information determined necessary by the Secretary for the Secretary to calculate the all patient readmission rates described in subparagraph (A).

(ii) Instead of a specified hospital submitting to the Secretary the data and information described in clause (i), such data and information may be submitted to the Secretary, on behalf of such a specified hospital, by a state or an entity determined appropriate by the Secretary.

(D) Definitions. For purposes of this paragraph:

(i) The term "all patients" means patients who are treated on an inpatient basis and discharged from a specified hospital (as defined in clause (ii)).

(ii) The term "specified hospital" means a subsection (d) hospital, hospitals described in clauses (i) through (v) of subsection (d)(1)(B) and, as determined feasible and appropriate by the Secretary, other hospitals not otherwise described in this subparagraph.

(r) Adjustments to Medicare DSH payments. (1) Empirically justified DSH payments. For fiscal year 2014 and each subsequent fiscal year, instead of the amount of disproportionate share hospital payment that would otherwise be made under subsection (d)(5)(F) to a subsection (d) hospital for the fiscal year, the Secretary shall pay to the subsection (d) hospital 25 percent of such amount (which represents the empirically justified amount for such payment, as determined by the Medicare Payment Advisory Commission in its March 2007 Report to the Congress).

(2) Additional payment. In addition to the payment made to a subsection (d) hospital under paragraph (1), for fiscal year 2014 and

each subsequent fiscal year, the Secretary shall pay to such subsection (d) hospitals an additional amount equal to the product of the following factors:

(A) Factor one. A factor equal to the difference between—

(i) the aggregate amount of payments that would be made to subsection (d) hospitals under subsection (d)(5)(F) if this subsection did not apply for such fiscal year (as estimated by the Secretary); and

(ii) the aggregate amount of payments that are made to subsection (d) hospitals under paragraph (1) for such fiscal year (as so estimated).

(B) Factor two. (i) Fiscal years 2014, 2015, 2016, and 2017. For each of fiscal years 2014, 2015, 2016, and 2017, a factor equal to 1 minus the percent change in the percent of individuals under the age of 65 who are uninsured, as determined by comparing the percent of such individuals—

(I) who are uninsured in 2013, the last year before coverage expansion under the Patient Protection and Affordable Care Act (as calculated by the Secretary based on the most recent estimates available from the Director of the Congressional Budget Office before a vote in either House on the Health Care and Education Reconciliation Act of 2010 that, if determined in the affirmative, would clear such Act for enrollment); and

(II) who are uninsured in the most recent period for which data is available (as so calculated),

minus 0.1 percentage points for fiscal year 2014 and minus 0.2 percentage points for each of fiscal years 2015, 2016, and 2017.

(ii) 2018 and subsequent years. For fiscal year 2018 and each subsequent fiscal year, a factor equal to 1 minus the percent change in the percent of individuals who are uninsured, as determined by comparing the percent of individuals—

(I) who are uninsured in 2013 (as estimated by the Secretary, based on data from the Census Bureau or other sources the Secretary determines appropriate, and certified by the Chief Actuary of the Centers for Medicare & Medicaid Services); and

(II) who are uninsured in the most recent period for which data is available (as so estimated and certified),

minus 0.2 percentage points for each of fiscal years 2018 and 2019.

(C) Factor three. A factor equal to the percent, for each subsection (d) hospital, that represents the quotient of—

(i) the amount of uncompensated care for such hospital for a period selected by the Secretary (as estimated by the Secretary, based on appropriate data (including, in the case where the Secretary determines that alternative data is available which is a better proxy for the costs of subsection (d) hospitals for treating the uninsured, the use of such alternative data)); and

(ii) the aggregate amount of uncompensated care for all subsection (d) hospitals that receive a payment under this subsection for such period (as so estimated, based on such data).

(3) Limitations on review. There shall be no administrative or judicial review under section 1869 [42 USCS § 1395ff], section 1878 [42 USCS § 1395oo], or otherwise of the following:

(A) Any estimate of the Secretary for purposes of determining the factors described in paragraph (2).

(B) Any period selected by the Secretary for such purposes.

(s) Prospective payment for psychiatric hospitals. (1) Reference to establishment and implementation of system. For provisions related to the establishment and implementation of a prospective payment system for payments under this title [42 USCS §§ 1395 et seq.] for inpatient hospital services furnished by psychiatric hospitals (as described in clause (i) of subsection (d)(1)(B)) and psychiatric units (as described in the matter following clause (v) of such subsection), see section 124 of the Medicare, Medicaid, and SCHIP Balanced Budget Refinement Act of 1999 [note to this section].

(2) Implementation for rate year beginning in 2010 and subsequent rate years. (A) In general. In implementing the system described in paragraph (1) for the rate year beginning in 2010 and any subsequent rate year, any update to a base rate for days during the rate year for a psychiatric hospital or unit, respectively, shall be reduced—

(i) for the rate year beginning in 2012 and each subsequent rate year, by the productivity adjustment described in section 1886(b)(3)(B)(xi)(II) [subsec. (b)(3)(B)(xi)(II) of this section]; and

(ii) for each of the rate years beginning in 2010 through 2019, by the other adjustment described in paragraph (3).

(B) Special rule. The application of this paragraph may result in such update being less than 0.0 for a rate year, and may result in payment rates under the system described in paragraph (1) for a rate year being less than such payment rates for the preceding rate year.

(3) Other adjustment. For purposes of paragraph (2)(A)(ii), the other adjustment described

in this paragraph is—

(A) for each of the rate years beginning in 2010 and 2011, 0.25 percentage point;

(B) for each of the rate years beginning in 2012 and 2013, 0.1 percentage point;

(C) for the rate year beginning in 2014, 0.3 percentage point;

(D) for each of the rate years beginning in 2015 and 2016, 0.2 percentage point; and

(E) for each of the rate years beginning in 2017, 2018, and 2019, 0.75 percentage point.

(4) Quality reporting. (A) Reduction in update for failure to report. (i) In general. Under the system described in paragraph (1), for rate year 2014 and each subsequent rate year, in the case of a psychiatric hospital or psychiatric unit that does not submit data to the Secretary in accordance with subparagraph (C) with respect to such a rate year, any annual update to a standard Federal rate for discharges for the hospital during the rate year, and after application of paragraph (2), shall be reduced by 2 percentage points.

(ii) Special rule. The application of this subparagraph may result in such annual update being less than 0.0 for a rate year, and may result in payment rates under the system described in paragraph (1) for a rate year being less than such payment rates for the preceding rate year.

(B) Noncumulative application. Any reduction under subparagraph (A) shall apply only with respect to the rate year involved and the Secretary shall not take into account such reduction in computing the payment amount under the system described in paragraph (1) for a subsequent rate year.

(C) Submission of quality data. For rate year 2014 and each subsequent rate year, each psychiatric hospital and psychiatric unit shall submit to the Secretary data on quality measures specified under subparagraph (D). Such data shall be submitted in a form and manner, and at a time, specified by the Secretary for purposes of this subparagraph.

(D) Quality measures. (i) In general. Subject to clause (ii), any measure specified by the Secretary under this subparagraph must have been endorsed by the entity with a contract under section 1890(a) [42 USCS § 1395aaa(a)].

(ii) Exception. In the case of a specified area or medical topic determined appropriate by the Secretary for which a feasible and practical measure has not been endorsed by the entity with a contract under section 1890(a) [42 USCS § 1395aaa(a)], the Secretary may specify a measure that is not so endorsed as long as due consideration is given to measures that have been endorsed or adopted by a consensus organization identified by the Secretary.

(iii) Time frame. Not later than October 1, 2012, the Secretary shall publish the measures selected under this subparagraph that will be applicable with respect to rate year 2014.

(E) Public availability of data submitted. The Secretary shall establish procedures for making data submitted under subparagraph (C) available to the public. Such procedures shall ensure that a psychiatric hospital and a psychiatric unit has the opportunity to review the data that is to be made public with respect to the hospital or unit prior to such data being made public. The Secretary shall report quality measures that relate to services furnished in inpatient settings in psychiatric hospitals and psychiatric units on the Internet website of the Centers for Medicare & Medicaid Services.

(Aug. 14, 1935, ch 531, Title XVIII, Part E [D] [C], 1886, as added Sept. 3, 1982, P. L. 97-248, Title I, Subtitle A, Part I, Subpart A, § 101(a)(1), 96 Stat. 331; Sept. 3, 1982, P. L. 97-248, Title I, Subtitle A, Part I, Subpart A, § 110, 96 Stat. 339; Jan. 12, 1983, P. L. 97-448, Title III, § 309(b)(13)–(15), 96 Stat. 2409; April 20, 1983, P. L. 98-21, Title VI, 601(a)(1), (2), (b)(1)–(8), (9) in part, (c)–(e), 97 Stat. 149–162; July 18, 1984, P. L. 98-369, Division B, Title III, Subtitle A, Part I, §§ 2307(b)(1), 2310(a), 2311(a)–(c), 2312(a), (b), 2313(a), (b), (d), 2315(a)–(c), Part II, § 2354(b)(42)–(44), 98 Stat. 1073, 1075–1080, 1102; Nov. 8, 1984, P. L. 98-617, § 3(b)(9), 98 Stat. 3296; April 7, 1986, P. L. 99-272, Title IX, Subtitle A, Part 1, Subpart A, §§ 9101(b), (c), 9102(a)–(c), 9104(a), (b), 9105(a)–(c), 9106(a), 9107(a), 9109(a), 9111(a), Subpart B 9127(a), Part 2, Subpart A, § 9202(a), 100 Stat. 153–155, 157–162, 170, 171; July 2, 1986, P. L. 99-349, Title II, § 206, 100 Stat. 749; Oct. 21, 1986, P. L. 99-509, Title IX, Subtitle D, Part 1, §§ 9302(a)(1), (2), (b)(1), (c), (d)(1)(A), (e), 9303(a)–(c), § 9306(a)–(c), Part 2, §§ 9314(a), 9320(g), 9321(e)(2), 100 Stat. 1982, 1985, 1995, 2005, 2015, 2017; Oct. 22, 1986, P. L. 99-514, Title XVIII, Subtitle C, Ch 1, § 1895(a), (b)(2)(A) [(C)] 100 Stat. 2932 as amended Oct. 21, 1986, P. L. 99-509, Title IX, Subtitle D, Part 1, §§ 9304(a)–(c), 9307(c)(1), 100 Stat. 1985, 1995 and Dec. 22, 1987, P. L. 100-203, Title IV, Subtitle A, Part 1, § 4009(j)(6)(A)–(C), 101 Stat. 1330-59; Oct. 22, 1986, P. L. 99-514, Title XVIII, Subtitle C, Ch 1, § 1895(b)(3), (9), 100 Stat. 2932, 2933; Aug. 18, 1987, P. L. 100-93, § 8(c)(4), 101 Stat. 693; Dec. 22, 1987, P. L. 100-203, Title IV, Subtitle A, Part 1, §§ 4002(a), (c)(2), (f)(1), 4003(a)–(c), 4004(a), 4005(a)(1), (c)(1), (d)(1)(A), 4006(a), (b)(1), 4007(b)(1), 4009(d)(1), (j)(4), Part 3, Subpart D, § 4083(b)(1), 101 Stat. 1330-42, 1330-46, 1330-47, 1330-49, 1330-52, 1330-53, 1330-57, 1330-129; July 1, 1988, P. L. 100-360, Title IV, Subtitle B, § 411(b)(1)(A)–(H)(i), (3), (4)(A), (B), (5)(A), (B), (8)(B), 102 Stat. 768-772; Oct. 13, 1988, P. L. 100-485, Title VI, § 608(d)(18)(A), (B), 102 Stat. 2418; Nov. 10, 1988, P. L. 100-647, Title VIII, Subtitle E, Part I, §§ 8401, 8403(a) 102 Stat. 3798; Dec. 13, 1989, P. L. 101-234, Title III, § 301(b)(3), (c)(3), 103 Stat. 1985; Dec. 19, 1989, P. L. 101-239, Title VI, Subtitle A, Part 1, Subpart A, §§ 6002, 6003(a)(1), (b), (c)(1)–(3), (e)(1), (2)(B), (f), (g)(2), (4), (h)(1)–(4), (6), 6004(a)(1), (2), (b)(1), Subpart B, §§ 6011(a), 6015(a), 6022, 103 Stat. 2140–2144, 2151, 2154, 2158–2161, 2164, 2167; Oct. 1, 1990, P. L. 101-403, Title I, § 115(b)(1), 104 Stat. 870; Nov. 5, 1990, P. L. 101-508, Title IV, Subtitle A, Part 1, §§ 4001, 4002(a)(1), (b), (c)(1), (2)(A), (B), (e)(1), (g)(1), (2), (h)(1)(A), (2)(B), 4003(a), 4005(a)(1), (c)(1)(B), (2), 4008(f)(1), (m)(2)(A), 104 Stat. 1388-31, 1388-34, 1388-38, 1388-40, 1388-45; Aug. 10, 1993, P. L. 103-66, Title XIII, Ch 2, Subch A, Part I, §§ 13501(a), (b)(1), (c), (e)(1), (f), 13502, 13505, 13506, Part III, § 13563(a), (b)(1), (c)(1), 107 Stat. 572–574, 576, 577, 578, 579, 605, 606; Oct. 31, 1994, P. L. 103-432, Title I, Subtitle A, §§ 101(a)(1), (b), (c), 102(b)(1)(B), 105, 108, 109, 110(a), (c), Subtitle C, § 153(a), 108 Stat. 4400, 4402, 4405, 4407, 4408, 4437; Aug. 5, 1997, P. L. 105-33, Title IV, Subtitle A, Ch 1, Subch A, § 4001, Ch 3, § 4022(b)(1)(A), Subtitle C, §§ 4201(c)(1), (4), 4202(a), 4204(a)(1), (2), Subtitle E, Ch 1, §§ 4401(a), 4402, 4403(a), 4405(a)–(c), 4406, 4407, Ch 2, Subch A, §§ 4411–4414, 4415(a)–(c), 4416, 4417(a)(1), (b)(1), 4418(a), 4419(a)(1), Subch B, § 4421(a), (b), Subtitle G, Ch 2, Subch A, §§ 4621, 4622, Subch B, §§ 4623–4625, 4626(a), 4627(a), Ch 3, § 4644(a)(1), (b)(1), (c)(1), 111 Stat. 275, 354, 373, 374, 375, 397, 398, 400, 403, 406, 407, 408, 409, 410, 475, 483, 488; Nov. 29, 1999, P. L. 106-113, Div B, § 1000(a)(6), 113 Stat. 1536; Dec. 21, 2000, P. L. 106-554, § 1(a)(4), (6), 114 Stat. 2763; Dec. 8, 2003, P. L. 108-173, Title I, § 101(a)(1), Title IV, Subtitle A, §§ 401(a)–(c), 402, 403, 406, 407(a), Subtitle C, § 422(a), (b)(1), Title V, Subtitle A, §§ 501(a), (b), 502(a), (b), 503(a)–(d)(1), 504, 505(a), Title VII, Subtitle B, § 711, Subtitle D, § 736(a)(9), (15), (c)(6), 117 Stat. 2071, 2262, 2264, 2269, 2284, 2289, 2290, 2291, 2292, 2340, 2355, 2356; Feb. 8, 2006, P. L. 109-171, Title V, Subtitle A, §§ 5001(a), (c), 5002(a), 5003(a)(1), (2)(A), (b)–(d), 120 Stat. 28, 30, 32; Dec. 20, 2006, P. L. 109-432, Div B, Title I, §§ 106(c), 109(a)(2), Title II, § 205(b)(1), 120 Stat. 2983, 2985, 2989; Dec. 26, 2007, P. L. 110-161, Div G, Title II, § 225(a), (b)(1), 121 Stat. 2189; Dec. 29, 2007, P. L. 110-173, Title I, §§ 114(e)(1), 115(a)(1), 121 Stat. 2504, 2506; July 15, 2008, P. L. 110-275, Title I, Subtitle B, § 122, 122 Stat. 2514; Feb. 17, 2009, P. L. 111-5, Div B, Title IV, Subtitle A, § 4102(a)(1), (b)(1), 123 Stat. 477, 482; March 23, 2010, P. L. 111-148, Title III, Subtitle A, Part I, §§ 3001(a)(1)–(3), 3004(a), (b), 3008(a), Part III, § 3025(a), Subtitle B, Part II, §§ 3124(a), (b)(1), 3125, Part III, § 3133, Subtitle E, § 3401(a), (c), (d), (f), Title V, Subtitle F, §§ 5503(a), (b), 5504(a), (b), 5505(a), (b), 5506(a), (b), (e), Title X, Subtitle C, §§ 10309, 10314, 10316, 10319(a)–(c), (e), 10322(a), 10324(a), 10335, 124 Stat. 353, 368, 376, 408, 424, 425, 432, 480, 481, 483, 655, 659, 660, 661, 663, 942, 944, 946, 948, 949, 952, 959, 974; March 30, 2010, P. L. 111-152, Title I, Subtitle B, §§ 1104, 1105(a)–(d), 124 Stat. 1047.)

HISTORY; ANCILLARY LAWS AND DIRECTIVES

Other provisions:

Rural community hospital demonstration program. Act Dec. 8, 2003, P. L. 108-173, Title IV, Subtitle A, § 410A, 117 Stat. 2272; March 23, 2010, P. L. 111-148, Title III, Subtitle B, Part II, § 3123, Title X, Subtitle C, § 10313, 124 Stat. 423, 943, provides:

"(a) Establishment of rural community hospital (RCH) demonstration program. (1) In general. The Secretary shall establish a demonstration program to test the feasibility and advisability of the establishment of rural community hospitals (as defined in subsection (f)(1)) to furnish covered inpatient hospital services (as defined in subsection (f)(2)) to medicare beneficiaries.

"(2) Demonstration areas. The program shall be conducted in rural areas selected by the Secretary in States with low population densities, as determined by the Secretary.

"(3) Application. Each rural community hospital that is located in a demonstration area selected under paragraph (2) that desires to participate in the demonstration program under this section shall submit an application to the Secretary at such time, in such manner, and containing such information as the Secretary may require.

"(4) Selection of hospitals. The Secretary shall select from among rural community hospitals submitting applications under paragraph (3) not more than 15 of such hospitals to participate in the demonstration program under this section.

"(5) Duration. The Secretary shall conduct the demonstration program under this section for a 5-year period (in this section referred to as the 'initial 5-year period') and, as provided in subsection (g), for the 5-year extension period.

"(6) Implementation. The Secretary shall implement the demonstration program not later than January 1, 2005, but may not implement the program before October 1, 2004.

"(b) Payment. (1) In general. The amount of payment under the demonstration program for covered inpatient hospital services furnished in a rural community hospital, other than such services furnished in a psychiatric or rehabilitation unit of the hospital which is a distinct part, is—

"(A) for discharges occurring in the first cost reporting period beginning on or after the implementation of the demonstration program, the reasonable costs of providing such services; and

"(B) for discharges occurring in a subsequent cost reporting period under the demonstration program, the lesser of—

"(i) the reasonable costs of providing such services in the cost reporting period involved; or

"(ii) the target amount (as defined in paragraph (2)), applicable to the cost reporting period involved.

"(2) Target amount. For purposes of paragraph (1)(B)(ii), the term 'target amount' means, with respect to a rural community hospital for a particular 12-month cost reporting period—

"(A) in the case of the second such cost reporting period for which this subsection is in effect, the reasonable costs of providing such covered inpatient hospital services as determined under paragraph (1)(A), and

"(B) in the case of a later cost reporting period, the target amount for the preceding 12-month cost reporting period,

increased by the applicable percentage increase (under clause (i) of section 1886(b)(3)(B) of the Social Security Act (42 U.S.C. 1395ww(b)(3)(B))) in the market basket percentage increase (as defined in clause (iii) of such section) for that particular cost reporting period.

"(c) Funding. (1) In general. The Secretary shall provide for the transfer from the Federal Hospital Insurance Trust Fund under section 1817 of the Social Security Act (42 U.S.C. 1395i) of such funds as are necessary for the costs of carrying out the demonstration program under this section.

"(2) Budget neutrality. In conducting the demonstration program under this section, the Secretary shall ensure that the aggregate payments made by the Secretary do not exceed the amount which the Secretary would have paid if the demonstration program under this section was not implemented.

"(d) Waiver authority. The Secretary may waive such requirements of title XVIII of the Social Security Act (42 U.S.C. 1395 et seq.) as may be necessary for the purpose of carrying out the demonstration program under this section.

"(e) Report. Not later than 6 months after the completion of the demonstration program under this section, the Secretary shall submit to Congress a report on such program, together with recommendations for such legislation and administrative action as the Secretary determines to be appropriate.

"(f) Definitions. In this section:

"(1) Rural community hospital defined. (A) In general. The term 'rural community hospital' means a hospital (as defined in section 1861(e) of the Social Security Act (42 U.S.C. 1395x(e))) that—

"(i) is located in a rural area (as defined in section 1886(d)(2)(D) of such Act (42 U.S.C. 1395ww(d)(2)(D))) or treated as being so located pursuant to section 1886(d)(8)(E) of such Act (42 U.S.C. 1395ww(d)(8)(E));

"(ii) subject to subparagraph (B), has fewer than 51 acute care inpatient beds, as reported in its most recent cost report;

"(iii) makes available 24-hour emergency care services; and

"(iv) is not eligible for designation, or has not been designated, as a critical access hospital under section 1820 [42 USCS § 1395i-4].

"(B) Treatment of psychiatric and rehabilitation units. For purposes of subparagraph (A)(ii), beds in a psychiatric or rehabilitation unit of the hospital which is a distinct part of the hospital shall not be counted.

"(2) Covered inpatient hospital services. The term 'covered inpatient hospital services' means inpatient hospital services, and includes extended care services furnished under an agreement under section 1883 of the Social Security Act (42 U.S.C. 1395tt).

"(g) Five-year extension of demonstration program. (1) In general. Subject to the succeeding provisions of this subsection, the Secretary shall conduct the demonstration program under this section for an additional 5-year period (in this section referred to as the '5-year extension period') that begins on the date immediately following the last day of the initial 5-year period under subsection (a)(5).

"(2) Expansion of demonstration States. Notwithstanding subsection (a)(2), during the 5-year extension period, the Secretary shall expand the number of States with low population densities determined by the Secretary under such subsection to 20. In determining which States to include in such expansion, the Secretary shall use the same criteria and data that the Secretary used to determine the States under such subsection for purposes of the initial 5-year period.

"(3) Increase in maximum number of hospitals participating in the demonstration program. Notwithstanding subsection (a)(4), during the 5-year extension period, not more than 30 rural community hospitals may participate in the demonstration program under this section.

"(4) Hospitals in demonstration program on date of enactment. In the case of a rural community hospital that is participating in the demonstration program under this section as of the last day of the initial 5-year period, the Secretary—

"(A) shall provide for the continued participation of such rural community hospital in the demonstration program during the 5-year extension period unless the rural community hospital makes an election, in such form and manner as the Secretary may specify, to discontinue such participation; and

"(B) in calculating the amount of payment under subsection (b) to the rural community hospital for covered inpatient hospital services furnished by the hospital during such 5-year extension period, shall substitute, under paragraph (1)(A) of such subsection—

"(i) the reasonable costs of providing such services for discharges occurring in the first cost reporting period beginning on or after the first day of the 5-year extension period, for

"(ii) the reasonable costs of providing such services for discharges occurring in the first cost reporting period beginning on or after the implementation of the demonstration program.".

Paperwork Reduction Act not applicable to subsec. (h)(7). Act Dec. 8, 2003, P. L. 108-173, Title IV, Subtitle C, § 422(b)(2), 117 Stat. 2286; March 23, 2010, P. L. 111-148, Title V, Subtitle F, § 5503(c), 124 Stat. 659, provides: "Chapter 35 of title 44, United States Code [44 USCS §§ 3501 et seq.], shall not apply with respect to applications under paragraphs (7) and (8) of subsection (h) of section 1886 of the Social Security Act [this section]".

Medicare demonstration projects to permit gainsharing arrangements. Act Feb. 8, 2006, P. L.

109-171, Title V, Subtitle A, § 5007, 120 Stat. 34; March 23, 2010, P. L. 111-148, Title III, Subtitle A, Part III, § 3027, 124 Stat. 415, provides:

"(a) Establishment. The Secretary shall establish under this section a qualified gainsharing demonstration program under which the Secretary shall approve demonstration projects by not later than November 1, 2006, to test and evaluate methodologies and arrangements between hospitals and physicians designed to govern the utilization of inpatient hospital resources and physician work to improve the quality and efficiency of care provided to Medicare beneficiaries and to develop improved operational and financial hospital performance with sharing of remuneration as specified in the project. Such projects shall be operational by not later than January 1, 2007.

"(b) Requirements described. A demonstration project under this section shall meet the following requirements for purposes of maintaining or improving quality while achieving cost savings:

"(1) Arrangement for remuneration as share of savings. The demonstration project shall involve an arrangement between a hospital and a physician under which the hospital provides remuneration to the physician that represents solely a share of the savings incurred directly as a result of collaborative efforts between the hospital and the physician.

"(2) Written plan agreement. The demonstration project shall be conducted pursuant to a written agreement that—

"(A) is submitted to the Secretary prior to implementation of the project; and

"(B) includes a plan outlining how the project will achieve improvements in quality and efficiency.

"(3) Patient notification. The demonstration project shall include a notification process to inform patients who are treated in a hospital participating in the project of the participation of the hospital in such project.

"(4) Monitoring quality and efficiency of care. The demonstration project shall provide measures to ensure that the quality and efficiency of care provided to patients who are treated in a hospital participating in the demonstration project is continuously monitored to ensure that such quality and efficiency is maintained or improved.

"(5) Independent review. The demonstration project shall certify, prior to implementation, that the elements of the demonstration project are reviewed by an organization that is not affiliated with the hospital or the physician participating in the project.

"(6) Referral limitations. The demonstration project shall not be structured in such a manner as to reward any physician participating in the project on the basis of the volume or value of referrals to the hospital by the physician.

"(c) Waiver of certain restrictions. (1) In general. An incentive payment made by a hospital to a physician under and in accordance with a demonstration project shall not constitute—

"(A) remuneration for purposes of section 1128B of the Social Security Act (42 U.S.C. 1320a-7b);

"(B) a payment intended to induce a physician to reduce or limit services to a patient entitled to benefits under Medicare or a State plan approved under title XIX of such Act [42 USCS §§ 1396 et seq.] in violation of section 1128A of such Act (42 U.S.C. 1320a-7a); or

"(C) a financial relationship for purposes of section 1877 of such Act (42 U.S.C. 1395nn).

"(2) Protection for existing arrangements. In no case shall the failure to comply with the requirements described in paragraph (1) affect a finding made by the Inspector General of the Department of Health and Human Services prior to the date of the enactment of this Act that an arrangement between a hospital and a physician does not violate paragraph (1) or (2) of section 1128A(a) of the Social Security Act (42 U.S.C. 1320a-7(a)).

"(d) Program administration. (1) Solicitation of applications. By not later than 90 days after the date of the enactment of this Act, the Secretary shall solicit applications for approval of a demonstration project, in such form and manner, and at such time specified by the Secretary.

"(2) Number of projects approved. The Secretary shall approve not more than 6 demonstration projects, at least 2 of which shall be located in a rural area.

"(3) Duration. The qualified gainsharing demonstration program under this section shall be conducted for the period beginning on January 1, 2007, and ending on December 31, 2009 (or September 30, 2011, in the case of a demonstration project in operation as of October 1, 2008).

"(e) Reports. (1) Initial report. By not later than December 1, 2006, the Secretary shall submit to Congress a report on the number of demonstration projects that will be conducted under this section.

"(2) Project update. By not later than December 1, 2007, the Secretary shall submit to Congress a report on the details of such projects (including the project improvements towards quality and efficiency described in subsection (b)(2)(B)).

"(3) Quality improvement and savings. By not later than March 31, 2011, the Secretary shall submit to Congress a report on quality improvement and savings achieved as a result of the qualified gainsharing demonstration program established under subsection (a).

"(4) Final report. By not later than March 31, 2013, the Secretary shall submit to Congress a final report on the information described in paragraph (3).

"(f) Funding. (1) In general. Out of any funds in the Treasury not otherwise appropriated, there are appropriated to the Secretary for fiscal year 2006 $6,000,000, and for fiscal year 2010, $1,600,000, to carry out this section.

"(2) Availability. Funds appropriated under paragraph (1) shall remain available for expenditure through fiscal year 2014 or until expended.

"(g) Definitions. For purposes of this section:

"(1) Demonstration project. The term 'demonstration project' means a project implemented under the qualified gainsharing demonstration program established under subsection (a).

"(2) Hospital. The term 'hospital' means a hospital that receives payment under section 1886(d) of the Social Security Act (42 U.S.C. 1395ww(d)), and does not include a critical access hospital (as defined in section 1861(mm) of such Act (42 U.S.C. 1395x(mm))).

"(3) Medicare. The term 'Medicare' means the programs under title XVIII of the Social Security Act [42 USCS §§ 1395 et seq.].

"(4) Physician. The term 'physician' means, with respect to a demonstration project, a physician described in paragraph (1) or (3) of section 1861(r) of the Social Security Act (42 U.S.C. 1395x(r)) who is licensed as such a physician in the area in which the project is located and meets requirements to provide services for which benefits are provided under Medicare. Such term shall be deemed to include a practitioner described in section 1842(e)(18)(C) of such Act

(42 U.S.C. 1395u(e)(18)(C)).
"(5) Secretary. The term 'Secretary' means the Secretary of Health and Human Services.".

Correction of mid-year reclassification expiration. Act Dec. 20, 2006, P. L. 109-432, Div B, Title I, § 106(a), 120 Stat. 2982; Dec. 29, 2007, P. L. 110-173, Title I, § 117(a)(1), 121 Stat. 2507; July 15, 2008, P. L. 110-275, Title I, Subtitle B, § 124(a), 122 Stat. 2518; March 23, 2010, P. L. 111-148, Title III, Subtitle B, Part III, § 3137(a)(1), Title X, Subtitle C, § 10317, 124 Stat. 438, 947, provides: "Notwithstanding any other provision of law, in the case of a subsection (d) hospital (as defined for purposes of section 1886 of the Social Security Act (42 U.S.C. 1395ww)) with respect to which a reclassification of its wage index for purposes of such section would (but for this subsection) expire on March 31, 2007, such reclassification of such hospital shall be extended through September 30, 2010. The previous sentence shall not be effected in a budget-neutral manner.".

[*Special rule and adjustment for certain hospitals in fiscal year 2010.* Act March 23, 2010, P. L. 111-148, Title III, Subtitle B, Part III, § 3137(a)(2), (3), as amended Title X, Subtitle C, § 10317, 124 Stat. 947, provides:

"(2) Special rule for fiscal year 2010. (A) In general. Subject to subparagraph (B), for purposes of implementation of the amendment made by paragraph (1) [note above], including (notwithstanding paragraph (3) of section 117(a) of the Medicare, Medicaid and SCHIP Extension Act of 2007 (Public Law 110-173), as amended by section 124(b) of the Medicare Improvements for Patients and Providers Act of 2008 (Public Law 110-275)) for purposes of the implementation of paragraph (2) of such section 117(a), during fiscal year 2010, the Secretary of Health and Human Services (in this subsection referred to as the 'Secretary') shall use the hospital wage index that was promulgated by the Secretary in the Federal Register on August 27, 2009 (74 Fed. Reg. 43754), and any subsequent corrections.
"(B) Exception. Beginning on April 1, 2010, in determining the wage index applicable to hospitals that qualify for wage index reclassification, the Secretary shall include the average hourly wage data of hospitals whose reclassification was extended pursuant to the amendment made by paragraph (1) [note above], only if including such data results in a higher applicable reclassified wage index.

"(3) Adjustment for certain hospitals in fiscal year 2010. (A) In general. In the case of a subsection (d) hospital (as defined in subsection (d)(1)(B) of section 1886 of the Social Security Act (42 U.S.C. 1395ww)) with respect to which—

"(i) a reclassification of its wage index for purposes of such section was extended pursuant to the amendment made by paragraph (1) [note above],; and

"(ii) the wage index applicable for such hospital for the period beginning on October 1, 2009, and ending on March 31, 2010, was lower than for the period beginning on April 1, 2010, and ending on September 30, 2010, by reason of the application of paragraph (2)(B);
the Secretary shall pay such hospital an additional payment that reflects the difference between the wage index for such periods.
"(B) Timeframe for payments. The Secretary shall make payments required under subparagraph [(A)] by not later than December 31, 2010.".]

Effective date of amendments made by § 225(b) of Div G of Act Dec. 26, 2007. Act Dec. 26, 2007, P. L. 110-161, Div G, Title II, § 225(b)(2), 121 Stat. 2189, provides: "Subject to paragraph (3), the amendments made by paragraph (1) [amending subsec. (h)(7) of this section] shall take effect as if included in the enactment of section 422 of the Medicare Prescription Drug, Improvement, and Modernization Act of 2003 (Public Law 108-173).".

Payment for long-term care hospital services. Act Dec. 29, 2007, P. L. 110-173, Title I, § 114(c), 121 Stat. 2502; Feb. 17, 2009, P. L. 111-5, Div B, Title IV, Subtitle B, § 4302(a), 123 Stat. 495 (effective as if included in the enactment of Act Dec. 29, 2007, as provided by § 4302(c) of such Act); March 23, 2010, P. L. 111-148, Title III, Subtitle B, Part I, § 3106(a), Title X, Subtitle C, § 10312(a), 124 Stat. 418, 943, provides:

"(1) Delay in application of 25 percent patient threshold payment adjustment. The Secretary shall not apply, for cost reporting periods beginning on or after July 1, 2007 a 5-year period—
"(A) section 412.536 of title 42, Code of Federal Regulations, or any similar provision, to freestanding long-term care hospitals or to a long-term care hospital, or satellite facility, that as of December 29, 2007, was co-located with an entity that is a provider-based, off-campus location of a subsection (d) hospital which did not provide services payable under section 1886(d) of the Social Security Act [subsec. (d) of this section] at the off-campus location; and
"(B) such section or section 412.534 of title 42, Code of Federal Regulations, or any similar provisions, to a long-term care hospital identified by the amendment made by section 4417(a) of the Balanced Budget Act of 1997 [amending subsec. (d)(1)(B) of this section] (Public Law 105-33).

"(2) Payment for hospitals-within-hospitals. (A) In general. Payment to an applicable long-term care hospital or satellite facility which is located in a rural area or which is co-located with an urban single or MSA dominant hospital under paragraphs (d)(1), (e)(1), and (e)(4) of section 412.534 of title 42, Code of Federal Regulations, shall not be subject to any payment adjustment under such section if no more than 75 percent of the hospital's Medicare discharges (other than discharges described in paragraph (d)(2) or (e)(3) of such section) are admitted from a co-located hospital.
"(B) Co-located long-term care hospitals and satellite facilities. (i) In general. Payment to an applicable long-term care hospital or satellite facility which is co-located with another hospital shall not be subject to any payment adjustment under section 412.534 of title 42, Code of Federal Regulations, if no more than 50 percent of the hospital's Medicare discharges (other than discharges described in paragraph (c)(3) of such section) are admitted from a co-located hospital.

"(ii) Applicable long-term care hospital or satellite facility defined. In this paragraph, the term 'applicable long-term care hospital or satellite facility' means a hospital or satellite facility that is subject to the transition rules under section 412.534(g) of title 42, Code of Federal Regulations or that is described in section 412.22(h)(3)(i) of such title.
"(C) Effective date. Subparagraphs (A) and (B) shall apply to cost reporting periods beginning on or after October 1, 2007 (or July 1, 2007, in the case of a satellite facility described in section 412.22(h)(3)(i) of title 42, Code of Federal Regulations) for a 3-year period.

"(3) No application of very short-stay outlier policy. The Secretary shall not apply, for the 5-year period beginning on the date of the enactment of this Act, the amendments finalized on May 11, 2007 (72 Federal Register 26904, 26992) made to the short-stay outlier payment provision for long-term care hospitals contained in section 412.529(c)(3)(i) of title 42, Code of Federal Regulations, or any similar provision.

"(4) No application of one-time adjustment to standard amount. The Secretary shall not, for the 5-year period beginning on the date of the enactment of this Act, make the one-time prospective adjustment to long-term care hospital prospective payment rates provided for in section 412.523(d)(3) of title 42, Code of Federal Regulations, or any similar provision.".

Moratorium on the establishment of long-term care hospitals, long-term care satellite facilities and on the increase of long-term care hospital beds in existing long-term care hospitals or satellite facilities. Act Act Dec. 29, 2007, P. L. 110-173, Title I, § 114(d), 121 Stat. 2503; Feb. 17, 2009, P. L. 111-5, Div B, Title IV, Subtitle B, § 4302(b), 123 Stat. 496 (effective as if included in the enactment of Act Dec. 29, 2007, as provided by § 4302(c) of such Act); March 23, 2010, P. L. 111-148, Title III, Subtitle B, Part I, § 3106(b), Title X, Subtitle C, § 10312(b), 124 Stat. 418, 943, provides:

"(1) In general. During the 5-year period beginning on the date of the enactment of this Act, the Secretary shall impose a moratorium for purposes of the Medicare program under title XVIII of the Social Security Act [42 USCS §§ 1395 et seq.]—

"(A) subject to paragraph (2), on the establishment and classification of a long-term care hospital or satellite facility, other than an existing long-term care hospital or facility; and

"(B) subject to paragraph (3), on an increase of long-term care hospital beds in existing long-term care hospitals or satellite facilities.

"(2) Exception for certain long-term care hospitals. The moratorium under paragraph (1)(A) shall not apply to a long-term care hospital that as of the date of the enactment of this Act—

"(A) began its qualifying period for payment as a long-term care hospital under section 412.23(e) of title 42, Code of Federal Regulations, on or before the date of the enactment of this Act;

"(B) has a binding written agreement with an outside, unrelated party for the actual construction, renovation, lease, or demolition for a long-term care hospital, and has expended, before the date of the enactment of this Act, at least 10 percent of the estimated cost of the project (or, if less, $2,500,000); or

"(C) has obtained an approved certificate of need in a State where one is required on or before the date of the enactment of this Act.

"(3) Exception for bed increases during moratorium. (A) In general. Subject to subparagraph (B), the moratorium under paragraph (1)(B) shall not apply to an increase in beds in an existing hospital or satellite facility if the hospital or facility obtained a certificate of need for an increase in beds that is in a State for which such certificate of need is required and that was issued on or after April 1, 2005, and before December 29, 2007, or if the hospital or facility—

"(i) is located in a State where there is only one other long-term care hospital; and

"(ii) requests an increase in beds following the closure or the decrease in the number of beds of another long-term care hospital in the State.

"(B) No effect on certain limitation. The exception under subparagraph (A) shall not effect the limitation on increasing beds under sections 412.22(h)(3) and 412.22(f) of title 42, Code of Federal Regulations.

"(4) Existing hospital or satellite facility defined. For purposes of this subsection, the term 'existing' means, with respect to a hospital or satellite facility, a hospital or satellite facility that received payment under the provisions of subpart O of part 412 of title 42, Code of Federal Regulations, as of the date of the enactment of this Act.

"(5) Judicial review. There shall be no administrative or judicial review under section 1869 of the Social Security Act (42 U.S.C. 1395ff), section 1878 of such Act (42 U.S.C. 1395oo), or otherwise, of the application of this subsection by the Secretary.".

Value-based purchasing demonstration programs. Act March 23, 2010, P. L. 111-148, Title III, Subtitle A, Part I, § 3001(b), 124 Stat. 362, provides:

"(1) Value-based purchasing demonstration program for inpatient critical access hospitals. (A) Establishment. (i) In general. Not later than 2 years after the date of enactment of this Act, the Secretary of Health and Human Services (in this subsection referred to as the 'Secretary') shall establish a demonstration program under which the Secretary establishes a value-based purchasing program under the Medicare program under title XVIII of the Social Security Act [42 USCS §§ 1395 et seq.] for critical access hospitals (as defined in paragraph (1) of section 1861(mm) of such Act (42 U.S.C. 1395x(mm))) with respect to inpatient critical access hospital services (as defined in paragraph (2) of such section) in order to test innovative methods of measuring and rewarding quality and efficient health care furnished by such hospitals.

"(ii) Duration. The demonstration program under this paragraph shall be conducted for a 3-year period.

"(iii) Sites. The Secretary shall conduct the demonstration program under this paragraph at an appropriate number (as determined by the Secretary) of critical access hospitals. The Secretary shall ensure that such hospitals are representative of the spectrum of such hospitals that participate in the Medicare program.

"(B) Waiver authority. The Secretary may waive such requirements of titles XI and XVIII of the Social Security Act [42 USCS §§ 1301 et seq. and 1395 et seq.] as may be necessary to carry out the demonstration program under this paragraph.

"(C) Budget neutrality requirement. In conducting the demonstration program under this section, the Secretary shall ensure that the aggregate payments made by the Secretary do not exceed the amount which the Secretary would have paid if the demonstration program under this section was not implemented.

"(D) Report. Not later than 18 months after the completion of the demonstration program under this paragraph, the Secretary shall submit to Congress a report on the demonstration program together with—

"(i) recommendations on the establishment of a permanent value-based purchasing program under the Medicare program for critical access hospitals with respect to inpatient critical access hospital services; and

"(ii) recommendations for such other legislation and administrative action as the Secretary determines appropriate.

"(2) Value-based purchasing demonstration program for hospitals excluded from hospital value-based purchasing program as a result of insufficient numbers of measures and cases. (A) Establishment.

(i) In general. Not later than 2 years after the date of enactment of this Act, the Secretary shall establish a demonstration program under which the Secretary establishes a value-based purchasing program under the Medicare program under title XVIII of the Social Security Act [42 USCS §§ 1395 et seq.] for applicable hospitals (as defined in clause (ii)) with respect to inpatient hospital services (as defined in section 1861(b) of the Social Security Act (42 U.S.C. 1395x(b))) in order to test innovative methods of measuring and rewarding quality and efficient health care furnished by such hospitals.

"(ii) Applicable hospital defined. For purposes of this paragraph, the term 'applicable hospital' means a hospital described in subclause (III) or (IV) of section 1886(o)(1)(C)(ii) of the Social Security Act [subsec. (o)(1)(C)(ii) of this section], as added by subsection (a)(1).

"(iii) Duration. The demonstration program under this paragraph shall be conducted for a 3-year period.

"(iv) Sites. The Secretary shall conduct the demonstration program under this paragraph at an appropriate number (as determined by the Secretary) of applicable hospitals. The Secretary shall ensure that such hospitals are representative of the spectrum of such hospitals that participate in the Medicare program.

"(B) Waiver authority. The Secretary may waive such requirements of titles XI and XVIII of the Social Security Act [42 USCS §§ 1301 et seq. and 1395 et seq.] as may be necessary to carry out the demonstration program under this paragraph.

"(C) Budget neutrality requirement. In conducting the demonstration program under this section, the Secretary shall ensure that the aggregate payments made by the Secretary do not exceed the amount which the Secretary would have paid if the demonstration program under this section was not implemented.

"(D) Report. Not later than 18 months after the completion of the demonstration program under this paragraph, the Secretary shall submit to Congress a report on the demonstration program together with—

"(i) recommendations on the establishment of a permanent value-based purchasing program under the Medicare program for applicable hospitals with respect to inpatient hospital services; and

"(ii) recommendations for such other legislation and administrative action as the Secretary determines appropriate.".

Hospital wage index improvement. Act March 23, 2010, P. L. 111-148, Title III, Subtitle B, Part III, § 3137(b), 124 Stat. 438, provides:

"(b) Plan for reforming the Medicare hospital wage index system. (1) In general. Not later than December 31, 2011, the Secretary of Health and Human Services (in this section referred to as the 'Secretary') shall submit to Congress a report that includes a plan to reform the hospital wage index system under section 1886 of the Social Security Act [this section].

"(2) Details. In developing the plan under paragraph (1), the Secretary shall take into account the goals for reforming such system set forth in the Medicare Payment Advisory Commission June 2007 report entitled 'Report to Congress: Promoting Greater Efficiency in Medicare', including establishing a new hospital compensation index system that—

"(A) uses Bureau of Labor Statistics data, or other data or methodologies, to calculate relative wages for each geographic area involved;

"(B) minimizes wage index adjustments between and within metropolitan statistical areas and statewide rural areas;

"(C) includes methods to minimize the volatility of wage index adjustments that result from implementation of policy, while maintaining budget neutrality in applying such adjustments;

"(D) takes into account the effect that implementation of the system would have on health care providers and on each region of the country;

"(E) addresses issues related to occupational mix, such as staffing practices and ratios, and any evidence on the effect on quality of care or patient safety as a result of the implementation of the system; and

"(F) provides for a transition.

"(3) Consultation. In developing the plan under paragraph (1), the Secretary shall consult with relevant affected parties.

"(c) Use of particular criteria for determining reclassifications. Notwithstanding any other provision of law, in making decisions on applications for reclassification of a subsection (d) hospital (as defined in paragraph (1)(B) of section 1886(d) of the Social Security Act (42 U.S.C. 1395ww(d)) for the purposes described in paragraph (10)(D)(v) of such section for fiscal year 2011 and each subsequent fiscal year (until the first fiscal year beginning on or after the date that is 1 year after the Secretary of Health and Human Services submits the report to Congress under subsection (b)), the Geographic Classification Review Board established under paragraph (10) of such section shall use the average hourly wage comparison criteria used in making such decisions as of September 30, 2008. The preceding sentence shall be effected in a budget neutral manner.".

Application of budget neutrality on a national basis in the calculation of the Medicare hospital wage index floor. Act March 23, 2010, P. L. 111-148, Title III, Subtitle B, Part III, § 3141, 124 Stat. 441, provides: "In the case of discharges occurring on or after October 1, 2010, for purposes of applying section 4410 of the Balanced Budget Act of 1997 (42 U.S.C. 1395ww note) and paragraph (h)(4) of section 412.64 of title 42, Code of Federal Regulations, the Secretary of Health and Human Services shall administer subsection (b) of such section 4410 and paragraph (e) of such section 412.64 in the same manner as the Secretary administered such subsection (b) and paragraph (e) for discharges occurring during fiscal year 2008 (through a uniform, national adjustment to the area wage index).".

No application prior to April 1, 2010. Act March 23, 2010, P. L. 111-148, Title III, Subtitle E, § 3401(p), 124 Stat. 488, provides: "Notwithstanding the preceding provisions of this section, the amendments made by subsections (a), (c), and (d) [amending subsecs. (b)(3)(B), (j)(3), and (m) of this section] shall not apply to discharges occurring before April 1, 2010.".

Application of amendments made by § 5504 of Act March 23, 2010. Act March 23, 2010, P. L. 111-148, Title V, Subtitle E, § 5504(c), 124 Stat. 660, provides: "The amendments made by this section [amending subsec. (h)(4)(E) of this section] shall not be applied in a manner that requires reopening of any settled hospital cost reports as to which there is not a jurisdictionally proper appeal pending as of the date of the enactment of this Act on the issue of payment for indirect costs of medical education under section 1886(d)(5)(B) of the Social Security Act (42 U.S.C. 1395ww(d)(5)(B)) or for direct graduate medical education costs under section 1886(h) of such Act (42 U.S.C. 1395ww(h)).".

Application of amendments made by § 5505

of Act March 23, 2010. Act March 23, 2010, P. L. 111-148, Title V, Subtitle F, § 5505(d), as added March 23, 2010, P. L. 111-148, Title X, Subtitle E, § 10501(j), 124 Stat. 999, provides:

"(1) In general. Except as otherwise provided, the Secretary of Health and Human Services shall implement the amendments made by this section [amending subsec. (d)(4) and (h)(5) of this section] in a manner so as to apply to cost reporting periods beginning on or after January 1, 1983.

"(2) GME. Section 1886(h)(4)(J) of the Social Security Act [subsec. (h)(4)(J) of this section], as added by subsection (a)(1)(B), shall apply to cost reporting periods beginning on or after July 1, 2009.

"(3) IME. Section 1886(d)(5)(B)(x)(III) of the Social Security Act [subsec. (d)(5)(B)(x)(III) of this section], as added by subsection (b), shall apply to cost reporting periods beginning on or after October 1, 2001. Such section, as so added, shall not give rise to any inference as to how the law in effect prior to such date should be interpreted.".

Application of amendments made by § 5505 of Act March 23, 2010. Act March 23, 2010, P. L. 111-148, Title V, Subtitle F, § 5505(d), 124 Stat. 661, provides: "The amendments made by this section [amending subsec. (d)(4) and (h)(5) of this section] shall not be applied in a manner that requires reopening of any settled cost reports as to which there is not a jurisdictionally proper appeal pending as of the date of the enactment of this Act on the issue of payment for indirect costs of medical education under section 1886(d)(5)(B) of the Social Security Act (42 U.S.C. 1395ww(d)(5)(B)) or for direct graduate medical education costs under section 1886(h) of such Act (42 U.S.C. 1395ww(h)).".

Application of amendments made by § 5506 of Act March 23, 2010. Act March 23, 2010, P. L. 111-148, Title V, Subtitle F, § 5506(c), 124 Stat. 662, provides: "The amendments made by this section [amending subsec. (d)(5) and (h)(5) of this section] shall not be applied in a manner that requires reopening of any settled hospital cost reports as to which there is not a jurisdictionally proper appeal pending as of the date of the enactment of this Act on the issue of payment for indirect costs of medical education under section 1886(d)(5)(B) of the Social Security Act (42 U.S.C. 1395ww(d)(5)(B)) or for direct graduate medical education costs under section 1886(h) of such Act (42 U.S.C. Section 1395ww(h)).".

Effect on temporary FTE cap adjustments. Act March 23, 2010, P. L. 111-148, Title V, Subtitle F, § 5506(d), 124 Stat. 662, provides: "The Secretary of Health and Human Services shall give consideration to the effect of the amendments made by this section [amending subsec. (d)(5) and (h)(5) of this section] on any temporary adjustment to a hospital's FTE cap under section 413.79(h) of title 42, Code of Federal Regulations (as in effect on the date of enactment of this Act) in order to ensure that there is no duplication of FTE slots. Such amendments shall not affect the application of section 1886(h)(4)(H)(v) of the Social Security Act (42 U.S.C. 1395ww(h)(4)(H)(v)).".

Graduate nurse education demonstration. Act March 23, 2010, P. L. 111-148, Title V, Subtitle F, § 5509, 124 Stat. 674, provides:

"(a) In general. (1) Establishment. (A) In general. The Secretary shall establish a graduate nurse education demonstration under title XVIII of the Social Security Act (42 U.S.C. 1395 et seq.) under which an eligible hospital may receive payment for the hospital's reasonable costs (described in paragraph (2)) for the provision of qualified clinical training to advance practice nurses.

"(B) Number. The demonstration shall include up to 5 eligible hospitals.

"(C) Written agreements. Eligible hospitals selected to participate in the demonstration shall enter into written agreements pursuant to subsection (b) in order to reimburse the eligible partners of the hospital the share of the costs attributable to each partner.

"(2) Costs described. (A) In general. Subject to subparagraph (B) and subsection (d), the costs described in this paragraph are the reasonable costs (as described in section 1861(v) of the Social Security Act (42 U.S.C. 1395x(v))) of each eligible hospital for the clinical training costs (as determined by the Secretary) that are attributable to providing advanced practice registered nurses with qualified training.

"(B) Limitation. With respect to a year, the amount reimbursed under subparagraph (A) may not exceed the amount of costs described in subparagraph (A) that are attributable to an increase in the number of advanced practice registered nurses enrolled in a program that provides qualified training during the year and for which the hospital is being reimbursed under the demonstration, as compared to the average number of advanced practice registered nurses who graduated in each year during the period beginning on January 1, 2006, and ending on December 31, 2010 (as determined by the Secretary) from the graduate nursing education program operated by the applicable school of nursing that is an eligible partner of the hospital for purposes of the demonstration.

"(3) Waiver authority. The Secretary may waive such requirements of titles XI and XVIII of the Social Security Act [42 USCS §§ 1301 et seq. and 1395 et seq.] as may be necessary to carry out the demonstration.

"(4) Administration. Chapter 35 of title 44, United States Code [44 USCS §§ 3501 et seq.], shall not apply to the implementation of this section.

"(b) Written agreements with eligible partners. No payment shall be made under this section to an eligible hospital unless such hospital has in effect a written agreement with the eligible partners of the hospital. Such written agreement shall describe, at a minimum—

"(1) the obligations of the eligible partners with respect to the provision of qualified training; and

"(2) the obligation of the eligible hospital to reimburse such eligible partners applicable (in a timely manner) for the costs of such qualified training attributable to partner.

"(c) Evaluation. Not later than October 17, 2017, the Secretary shall submit to Congress a report on the demonstration. Such report shall include an analysis of the following:

"(1) The growth in the number of advanced practice registered nurses with respect to a specific base year as a result of the demonstration.

"(2) The growth for each of the specialties described in subparagraphs (A) through (D) of subsection (e)(1).

"(3) The costs to the Medicare program under title XVIII of the Social Security Act as a result of the demonstration.

"(4) Other items the Secretary determines appropriate and relevant.

"(d) Funding. (1) In general. There is hereby appropriated to the Secretary, out of any funds in the Treasury not otherwise appropriated, $50,000,000 for each of fiscal years 2012 through 2015 to carry out this section, including the design, implementation, monitoring, and evaluation of the demonstration.

"(2) Proration. If the aggregate payments to eligible

hospitals under the demonstration exceed $50,000,000 for a fiscal year described in paragraph (1), the Secretary shall prorate the payment amounts to each eligible hospital in order to ensure that the aggregate payments do not exceed such amount.
"(3) Without fiscal year limitation. Amounts appropriated under this subsection shall remain available without fiscal year limitation.

"(e) Definitions. In this section: (1) Advanced practice registered nurse. The term "advanced practice registered nurse" includes the following:

"(A) A clinical nurse specialist (as defined in subsection (aa)(5) of section 1861 of the Social Security Act (42 U.S.C. 1395x)).

"(B) A nurse practitioner (as defined in such subsection).

"(C) A certified registered nurse anesthetist (as defined in subsection (bb)(2) of such section).

"(D) A certified nurse-midwife (as defined in subsection (gg)(2) of such section).
"(2) Applicable non-hospital community-based care setting. The term 'applicable non-hospital community-based care setting' means a non-hospital community-based care setting which has entered into a written agreement (as described in subsection (b)) with the eligible hospital participating in the demonstration. Such settings include Federally qualified health centers, rural health clinics, and other non-hospital settings as determined appropriate by the Secretary.
"(3) Applicable school of nursing. The term 'applicable school of nursing' means an accredited school of nursing (as defined in section 801 of the Public Health Service Act [42 USCS § 256]) which has entered into a written agreement (as described in subsection (b)) with the eligible hospital participating in the demonstration.
"(4) Demonstration. The term 'demonstration' means the graduate nurse education demonstration established under subsection (a).
"(5) Eligible hospital. The term 'eligible hospital' means a hospital (as defined in subsection (e) of section 1861 of the Social Security Act (42 U.S.C. 1395x)) or a critical access hospital (as defined in subsection (mm)(1) of such section) that has a written agreement in place with—

"(A) 1 or more applicable schools of nursing; and

"(B) 2 or more applicable non-hospital community-based care settings.
"(6) Eligible partners. The term 'eligible partners' includes the following:

"(A) An applicable non-hospital community-based care setting.

"(B) An applicable school of nursing.
"(7) Qualified training. (A) In general. The term 'qualified training' means training—

"(i) that provides an advanced practice registered nurse with the clinical skills necessary to provide primary care, preventive care, transitional care, chronic care management, and other services appropriate for individuals entitled to, or enrolled for, benefits under part A of title XVIII of the Social Security Act [42 USCS §§ 1395c et seq.], or enrolled under part B of such title [42 USCS §§ 1395j et seq.]; and

"(ii) subject to subparagraph (B), at least half of which is provided in a non-hospital community-based care setting.

"(B) Waiver of requirement half of training be provided in non-hospital community-based care setting in certain areas. The Secretary may waive the requirement under subparagraph (A)(ii) with respect to eligible hospitals located in rural or medically underserved areas.
"(8) Secretary. The term 'Secretary' means the Secretary of Health and Human Services.".

Payment for qualifying hospitals. Act March 30, 2010, P. L. 111-152, Title I, Subtitle B, § 1109, 124 Stat. 1051, provides:

"(a) In general. From the amount available under subsection (b), the Secretary of Health and Human Services shall provide for a payment to qualifying hospitals (as defined in subsection (d)) for fiscal years 2011 and 2012 of the amount determined under subsection (c).

"(b) Amounts available. There shall be available from the Federal Hospital Insurance Trust Fund $400,000,000 for payments under this section for fiscal years 2011 and 2012.

"(c) Payment amount. The amount of payment under this section for a qualifying hospital shall be determined, in a manner consistent with the amount available under subsection (b), in proportion to the portion of the amount of the aggregate payments under section 1886(d) of the Social Security Act [subsec. (d) of this section] to the hospital for fiscal year 2009 bears to the sum of all such payments to all qualifying hospitals for such fiscal year.

"(d) Qualifying hospital defined. In this section, the term 'qualifying hospital' means a subsection (d) hospital (as defined for purposes of section 1886(d) of the Social Security Act [subsec. (d) of this section]) that is located in a county that ranks, based upon its ranking in age, sex, and race adjusted spending for benefits under parts A and B under title XVIII of such Act [42 USCS §§ 1395c et seq. and 1395j et seq.] per enrollee, within the lowest quartile of such counties in the United States.".

§ 1395yy. Payment to skilled nursing facilities for routine service costs

(a) Per diem limitations. The Secretary, in determining the amount of the payments which may be made under this title [42 USCS §§ 1395 et seq.] with respect to routine service costs of extended care services shall not recognize as reasonable (in the efficient delivery of health services) per diem costs of such services to the extent that such per diem costs exceed the following per diem limits, except as otherwise provided in this section:

(1) With respect to freestanding skilled nursing facilities located in urban areas, the limit shall be equal to 112 percent of the mean per diem routine service costs for freestanding skilled nursing facilities located in urban areas.

(2) With respect to freestanding skilled nursing facilities located in rural areas, the limit shall be equal to 112 percent of the mean per diem routine service costs for freestanding skilled nursing facilities located in rural areas.

(3) With respect to hospital-based skilled nursing facilities located in urban areas, the limit shall be equal to the sum of the limit for freestanding skilled nursing facilities located in urban areas, plus 50 percent of the amount

by which 112 percent of the mean per diem routine service costs for hospital-based skilled nursing facilities located in urban areas exceeds the limit for freestanding skilled nursing facilities located in urban areas.

(4) With respect to hospital-based skilled nursing facilities located in rural areas, the limit shall be equal to the sum of the limit for freestanding skilled nursing facilities located in rural areas, plus 50 percent of the amount by which 112 percent of the mean per diem routine service costs for hospital-based skilled nursing facilities located in rural areas exceeds the limit for freestanding skilled nursing facilities located in rural areas.

In applying this subsection the Secretary shall make appropriate adjustments to the labor related portion of the costs based upon an appropriate wage index, and shall, for cost reporting periods beginning on or after October 1, 1992, on or after October 1, 1995, and every 2 years thereafter, provide for an update to the per diem cost limits described in this subsection, except that the limits effective for cost reporting periods beginning on or after October 1, 1997, shall be based on the limits effective for cost reporting periods beginning on or after October 1, 1996.

(b) Exception to limitations for hospital-based skilled nursing facility. With respect to a hospital-based skilled nursing facility, the Secretary may not recognize as reasonable the portion of the cost differences between hospital-based and freestanding skilled nursing facilities attributable to excess overhead allocations.

(c) Adjustments in limitations; publication of data. The Secretary may make adjustments in the limits set forth in subsection (a) with respect to any skilled nursing facility to the extent the Secretary deems appropriate, based upon case mix or circumstances beyond the control of the facility. The Secretary shall publish the data and criteria to be used for purposes of this subsection on an annual basis.

(d) Access to skilled nursing facilities. (1) Subject to subsection (e), any skilled nursing facility may choose to be paid under this subsection on the basis of a prospective payment for all routine service costs (including the costs of services required to attain or maintain the highest practicable physical, mental, and psychosocial well-being of each resident eligible for benefits under this title [42 USCS §§ 1395 et seq.]) and capital-related costs of extended care services provided in a cost reporting period if such facility had, in the preceding cost reporting period, fewer than 1,500 patient days with respect to which payments were made under this title [42 USCS §§ 1395 et seq.]. Such prospective payment shall be in lieu of payments which would otherwise be made for routine service costs pursuant to section 1861(v) [42 USCS § 1395x(v)] and subsections (a) through (c) of this section and capital-related costs pursuant to section 1861(v) [42 USCS § 1395x(v)]. This subsection shall not apply to a facility for any cost reporting period immediately following a fiscal year in which such facility had 1,500 or more patient days with respect to which payments were made under this title [42 USCS §§ 1395 et seq.], without regard to whether payments were made under this subsection during such preceding cost reporting period.

(2)(A) The amount of the payment under this section shall be determined on a per diem basis.

(B) Subject to the limitations of subparagraph (C), for skilled nursing facilities located—

(i) in an urban area, the amount shall be equal to 105 percent of the mean of the per diem reasonable routine service and capital-related costs of extended care services for skilled nursing facilities in urban areas within the same region, determined without regard to the limitations of subsection (a) and adjusted for different area wage levels, and

(ii) in a rural area the amount shall be equal to 105 percent of the mean of the per diem reasonable routine service and capital-related costs of extended care services for skilled nursing facilities in rural areas within the same region, determined without regard to the limitations of subsection (a) and adjusted for different area wage levels.

(C) The per diem amounts determined under subparagraph (B) shall not exceed the limit on routine service costs determined under subsection (a) with respect to the facility, adjusted to take into account average capital-related costs with respect to the type and location of the facility.

(3) For purposes of this subsection, urban and rural areas shall be determined in the same manner as for purposes of subsection (a), and the term "region" shall have the same meaning as under section 1886(d)(2)(D) [42 USCS § 1395ww(d)(2)(D)].

(4) The Secretary shall establish the prospective payment amounts for cost reporting period beginning in a fiscal year at least 90 days prior to the beginning of such fiscal year, on the basis of the most recent data available for a 12-month period. A skilled nursing facility

must notify the Secretary of its intention to be paid pursuant to this subsection for a cost reporting period no later than 30 days before the beginning of that period.

(5) The Secretary shall provide for a simplified cost report to be filed by facilities being paid pursuant to this subsection, which shall require only the cost information necessary for determining prospective payment amounts pursuant to paragraph (2) and reasonable costs of ancillary services.

(6) In lieu of payment on a cost basis for ancillary services provided by a facility which is being paid pursuant to this subsection, the Secretary may pay for such ancillary services on a reasonable charge basis if the Secretary determines that such payment basis will provide an equitable level of reimbursement and will ease the reporting burden of the facility.

(7) In computing the rates of payment to be made under this subsection, there shall be taken into account the costs described in the last sentence of section 1861(v)(1)(E) [42 USCS § 1395x(v)(1)(E)] (relating to compliance with nursing facility requirements and of conducting nurse aide training and competency evaluation programs and competency evaluation programs).

(e) Prospective payment. (1) Payment provision. Notwithstanding any other provision of this title [42 USCS §§ 1395 et seq.], subject to paragraphs (7), (11), and (12), the amount of the payment for all costs (as defined in paragraph (2)(B)) of covered skilled nursing facility services (as defined in paragraph (2)(A)) for each day of such services furnished—

(A) in a cost reporting period during the transition period (as defined in paragraph (2)(E)), is equal to the sum of—

(i) the non-Federal percentage of the facility-specific per diem rate (computed under paragraph (3)), and

(ii) the Federal percentage of the adjusted Federal per diem rate (determined under paragraph (4)) applicable to the facility; and

(B) after the transition period is equal to the adjusted Federal per diem rate applicable to the facility.

(2) Definitions. For purposes of this subsection:

(A) Covered skilled nursing facility services. (i) In general. The term "covered skilled nursing facility services"—

(I) means post-hospital extended care services as defined in section 1861(i) [42 USCS § 1395x(i)] for which benefits are provided under part A [42 USCS §§ 1395c et seq.]; and

(II) includes all items and services (other than items and services described in clauses (ii), (iii), and (iv)) for which payment may be made under part B [42 USCS §§ 1395j et seq.] and which are furnished to an individual who is a resident of a skilled nursing facility during the period in which the individual is provided covered post-hospital extended care services.

(ii) Services excluded. Services described in this clause are physicians' services, services described by clauses (i) and (ii) of section 1861(s)(2)(K) [42 USCS § 1395x(s)(2)(K)], certified nurse-midwife services, qualified psychologist services, services of a certified registered nurse anesthetist, items and services described in subparagraphs (F) and (O) of section 1861(s)(2) [42 USCS § 1395x(s)(2)], telehealth services furnished under section 1834(m)(4)(C)(ii)(VII) [42 USCS § 1395m(m)(4)(C)(ii)(VII)], and, only with respect to services furnished during 1998, the transportation costs of electrocardiogram equipment for electrocardiogram test services (HCPCS Code R0076). Services described in this clause do not include any physical, occupational, or speech-language therapy services regardless of whether or not the services are furnished by, or under the supervision of, a physician or other health care professional.

(iii) Exclusion of certain additional items and services. Items and services described in this clause are the following:

(I) Ambulance services furnished to an individual in conjunction with renal dialysis services described in section 1861(s)(2)(F) [42 USCS § 1395x(s)(2)(F)].

(II) Chemotherapy items (identified as of July 1, 1999, by HCPCS codes J9000–J9020; J9040–J9151; J9170–J9185; J9200–J9201; J9206–J9208; J9211; J9230–J9245; and J9265–J9600 (and as subsequently modified by the Secretary)) and any additional chemotherapy items identified by the Secretary.

(III) Chemotherapy administration services (identified as of July 1, 1999, by HCPCS codes 36260–36262; 36489; 36530–36535; 36640; 36823; and 96405–96542 (and as subsequently modified by the Secretary)) and any additional chemotherapy administration services identified by the Secretary.

(IV) Radioisotope services (identified as of July 1, 1999, by HCPCS codes 79030–79440 (and as subsequently modified by the Secretary)) and any additional radioisotope services identified by the Secretary.

(V) Customized prosthetic devices (commonly known as artificial limbs or components of artificial limbs) under the following HCPCS codes (as of July 1, 1999 (and as subsequently modified by the Secretary)), and any additional customized prosthetic devices identified by the Secretary, if delivered to an inpatient for use during the stay in the skilled nursing facility and intended to be used by the individual after discharge from the facility: L5050–L5340; L5500–L5611; L5613–L5986; L5988; L6050–L6370; L6400–L6880; L6920–L7274; and L7362–7366.

(iv) Exclusion of certain rural health clinic and federally qualified health center services. Services described in this clause are—

(I) rural health clinic services (as defined in paragraph (1) of section 1861(aa) [42 USCS § 1395x(aa)]); and

(II) federally qualified health center services (as defined in paragraph (3) of such section);

that would be described in clause (ii) if such services were furnished by an individual not affiliated with a rural health clinic or a federally qualified health center.

(B) All costs. The term "all costs" means routine service costs, ancillary costs, and capital-related costs of covered skilled nursing facility services, but does not include costs associated with approved educational activities.

(C) Non-Federal percentage; Federal percentage. For—

(i) the first cost reporting period (as defined in subparagraph (D)) of a facility, the "non-Federal percentage" is 75 percent and the "Federal percentage" is 25 percent;

(ii) the next cost reporting period of such facility, the "non-Federal percentage" is 50 percent and the "Federal percentage" is 50 percent; and

(iii) the subsequent cost reporting period of such facility, the "non-Federal percentage" is 25 percent and the "Federal percentage" is 75 percent.

(D) First cost reporting period. The term "first cost reporting period" means, with respect to a skilled nursing facility, the first cost reporting period of the facility beginning on or after July 1, 1998.

(E) Transition period. (i) In general. The term "transition period" means, with respect to a skilled nursing facility, the 3 cost reporting periods of the facility beginning with the first cost reporting period.

(ii) Treatment of new skilled nursing facilities. In the case of a skilled nursing facility that first received payment for services under this title [42 USCS §§ 1395 et seq.] on or after October 1, 1995, payment for such services shall be made under this subsection as if all services were furnished after the transition period.

(3) Determination of facility specific per diem rates. The Secretary shall determine a facility-specific per diem rate for each skilled nursing facility not described in paragraph (2)(E)(ii) for a cost reporting period as follows:

(A) Determining base payments. The Secretary shall determine, on a per diem basis, the total of—

(i) the allowable costs of extended care services for the facility for cost reporting periods beginning in fiscal year 1995, including costs associated with facilities described in subsection (d), with appropriate adjustments (as determined by the Secretary) to non-settled cost reports or, in the case of a facility participating in the Nursing Home Case-Mix and Quality Demonstration (RUGS-III), the RUGS-III rate received by the facility during the cost reporting period beginning in 1997, and

(ii) an estimate of the amounts that would be payable under part B (disregarding any applicable deductibles, coinsurance, and copayments) for covered skilled nursing facility services described in paragraph (2)(A)(i)(II) furnished during the applicable cost reporting period described in clause (i) to an individual who is a resident of the facility, regardless of whether or not the payment was made to the facility or to another entity.

In making appropriate adjustments under clause (i), the Secretary shall take into account exceptions and shall take into account exemptions but, with respect to exemptions, only to the extent that routine costs do not exceed 150 percent of the routine cost limits otherwise applicable but for the exemption.

(B) Update to first cost reporting period. The Secretary shall update the amount determined under subparagraph (A), for each cost reporting period after the applicable cost reporting period described in subparagraph (A)(i) and up to the first cost reporting period by a factor equal to the skilled nursing facility market basket percentage increase minus 1.0 percentage point.

(C) Updating to applicable cost reporting period. The Secretary shall update the amount determined under subparagraph (B) for each cost reporting period beginning with the first cost reporting period and up to and including the cost reporting period involved by a factor equal to the facility-specific update factor.

(D) Facility-specific update factor. For purposes of this paragraph, the "facility-specific update factor" for cost reporting periods beginning during—

(i) during each of fiscal years 1998 and 1999, is equal to the skilled nursing facility market basket percentage increase for such fiscal year minus 1 percentage point, and

(ii) during each subsequent fiscal year is equal to the skilled nursing facility market basket percentage increase for such fiscal year.

(4) Federal per diem rate. (A) Determination of historical per diem for facilities. For each skilled nursing facility that received payments for post-hospital extended care services during a cost reporting period beginning in fiscal year 1995 and that was subject to (and not exempted from) the per diem limits referred to in paragraph (1) or (2) of subsection (a) (and facilities described in subsection (d)), the Secretary shall estimate, on a per diem basis for such cost reporting period, the total of—

(i) the allowable costs of extended care services (excluding exceptions payments) for the facility for cost reporting periods beginning in 1995 with appropriate adjustments (as determined by the Secretary) to non-settled cost reports, and

(ii) an estimate of the amounts that would be payable under part B [42 USCS §§ 1395j et seq.] (disregarding any applicable deductibles, coinsurance, and copayments) for covered skilled nursing facility services described in paragraph (2)(A)(i)(II) furnished during such period to an individual who is a resident of the facility, regardless of whether or not the payment was made to the facility or to another entity.

(B) Update to first fiscal year. The Secretary shall update the amount determined under subparagraph (A), for each cost reporting period after the cost reporting period described in subparagraph (A)(i) and up to the first cost reporting period by a factor equal to the skilled nursing facility market basket percentage increase reduced (on an annualized basis) by 1 percentage point.

(C) Computation of standardized per diem rate. The Secretary shall standardize the amount updated under subparagraph (B) for each facility by—

(i) adjusting for variations among facilities by area in the average facility wage level per diem, and

(ii) adjusting for variations in case mix per diem among facilities.

(D) Computation of weighted average per diem rates. (i) All facilities. The Secretary shall compute a weighted average per diem rate for all facilities by computing an average of the standardized amounts computed under subparagraph (C), weighted for each facility by the number of days of extended care services furnished during the cost reporting period referred to in subparagraph (A).

(ii) Freestanding facilities. The Secretary shall compute a weighted average per diem rate for freestanding facilities by computing an average of the standardized amounts computed under subparagraph (C) only for such facilities, weighted for each facility by the number of days of extended care services furnished during the cost reporting period referred to in subparagraph (A).

(iii) Separate computation. The Secretary may compute and apply such averages separately for facilities located in urban and rural areas (as defined in section 1886(d)(2)(D) [42 USCS § 1395ww(d)(2)(D)]).

(E) Updating. (i) Initial period. For the initial period beginning on July 1, 1998, and ending on September 30, 1999, the Secretary shall compute for skilled nursing facilities an unadjusted Federal per diem rate equal to the average of the weighted average per diem rates computed under clauses (i) and (ii) of subparagraph (D), increased by skilled nursing facility market basket percentage change for such period minus 1 percentage point.

(ii) Subsequent fiscal years. The Secretary shall compute an unadjusted Federal per diem rate equal to the Federal per diem rate computed under this subparagraph—

(I) for fiscal year 2000, the rate computed for the initial period described in clause (i), increased by the skilled nursing facility market basket percentage change for the initial period minus 1 percentage point;

(II) for fiscal year 2001, the rate computed for the previous fiscal year increased by the skilled nursing facility market basket percentage change for the fiscal year;

(III) for each of fiscal years 2002 and 2003, the rate computed for the previous fiscal year increased by the skilled nursing facility market basket percentage change for the fiscal year involved minus 0.5 percentage points; and

(IV) for each subsequent fiscal year, the rate computed for the previous fiscal year increased by the skilled nursing facility market basket percentage change for the fiscal year involved.

(F) Adjustment for case mix creep. Insofar as the Secretary determines that the adjustments under subparagraph (G)(i) for a previous fiscal year (or estimates that such adjustments for a future fiscal year) did (or are likely to) result in a change in aggregate payments under this subsection during the fiscal year that are a result of changes in the coding or classification of residents that do not reflect real changes in case mix, the Secretary may adjust unadjusted Federal per diem rates for subsequent fiscal years so as to eliminate the effect of such coding or classification changes.

(G) Determination of Federal rate. The Secretary shall compute for each skilled nursing facility for each fiscal year (beginning with the initial period described in subparagraph (E)(i)) an adjusted Federal per diem rate equal to the unadjusted Federal per diem rate determined under subparagraph (E), as adjusted under subparagraph (F), and as further adjusted as follows:

(i) Adjustment for case mix. The Secretary shall provide for an appropriate adjustment to account for case mix. Such adjustment shall be based on a resident classification system, established by the Secretary, that accounts for the relative resource utilization of different patient types. The case mix adjustment shall be based on resident assessment data and other data that the Secretary considers appropriate.

(ii) Adjustment for geographic variations in labor costs. The Secretary shall adjust the portion of such per diem rate attributable to wages and wage-related costs for the area in which the facility is located compared to the national average of such costs using an appropriate wage index as determined by the Secretary. Such adjustment shall be done in a manner that does not result in aggregate payments under this subsection that are greater or less than those that would otherwise be made if such adjustment had not been made.

(iii) Adjustment for exclusion of certain additional items and services. The Secretary shall provide for an appropriate proportional reduction in payments so that beginning with fiscal year 2001, the aggregate amount of such reductions is equal to the aggregate increase in payments attributable to the exclusion effected under clause (iii) of paragraph (2)(A).

(H) Publication of information on per diem rates. The Secretary shall provide for publication in the Federal Register, before May 1, 1998 (with respect to fiscal period described in subparagraph (E)(i)) and before the August 1 preceding each succeeding fiscal year (with respect to that succeeding fiscal year), of—

(i) the unadjusted Federal per diem rates to be applied to days of covered skilled nursing facility services furnished during the fiscal year,

(ii) the case mix classification system to be applied under subparagraph (G)(i) with respect to such services during the fiscal year, and

(iii) the factors to be applied in making the area wage adjustment under subparagraph (G)(ii) with respect to such services.

(5) Skilled nursing facility market basket index and percentage. For purposes of this subsection:

(A) Skilled nursing facility market basket index. The Secretary shall establish a skilled nursing facility market basket index that reflects changes over time in the prices of an appropriate mix of goods and services included in covered skilled nursing facility services.

(B) Skilled nursing facility market basket percentage. (i) In general. Subject to clause (ii), the term "skilled nursing facility market basket percentage" means, for a fiscal year or other annual period and as calculated by the Secretary, the percentage change in the skilled nursing facility market basket index (established under subparagraph (A)) from the midpoint of the prior fiscal year (or period) to the midpoint of the fiscal year (or other period) involved.

(ii) Adjustment. For fiscal year 2012 and each subsequent fiscal year, after determining the percentage described in clause (i), the Secretary shall reduce such percentage by the productivity adjustment described in section 1886(b)(3)(B)(xi)(II) [42 USCS § 1395ww(b)(3)(B)(xi)(II)]. The application of the preceding sentence may result in such percentage being less than 0.0 for a fiscal year, and may result in payment rates under this subsection for a fiscal year being less than such payment rates for the preceding fiscal year.

(6) Submission of resident assessment data. A skilled nursing facility, or a facility described in paragraph (7)(B), shall provide the Secretary, in a manner and within the timeframes prescribed by the Secretary, the resident assessment data necessary to develop and implement the rates under this subsection. For purposes of meeting such requirement, a skilled nursing facility, or a facility described in paragraph (7), may submit the resident assessment data required under section 1819(b)(3) [42 USCS § 1395i-3(b)(3)], using the standard instrument designated by the State under section 1819(e)(5) [42 USCS § 1395i-3(e)(5)].

(7) Treatment of medicare swing bed hospitals. (A) Transition. Subject to subparagraph (C), the Secretary shall determine an appropriate manner in which to apply this subsection to the facilities described in subparagraph (B) (other than critical access hospitals), taking into account the purposes of this subsection, and shall provide that at the end of the transition period (as defined in paragraph (2)(E)) such facilities shall be paid only under this subsection. Payment shall not be made under

this subsection to such facilities for cost reporting periods beginning before such date (not earlier than July 1, 1999) as the Secretary specifies.

(B) Facilities described. The facilities described in this subparagraph are facilities that have in effect an agreement described in section 1883 [42 USCS § 1395tt].

(C) Exemption from PPS of swing-bed services furnished in critical access hospitals. The prospective payment system established under this subsection shall not apply to services furnished by a critical access hospital pursuant to an agreement under section 1883 [42 USCS § 1395tt].

(8) Limitation on review. There shall be no administrative or judicial review under section 1869, 1878 [42 USCS §§ 1395ff, 1395oo], or otherwise of—

(A) the establishment of Federal per diem rates under paragraph (4), including the computation of the standardized per diem rates under paragraph (4)(C), adjustments and corrections for case mix under paragraphs (4)(F) and (4)(G)(i), adjustments for variations in labor-related costs under paragraph (4)(G)(ii), and adjustments under paragraph (4)(G)(iii);

(B) the establishment of facility specific rates before July 1, 1999 (except any determination of costs paid under part A of this title [42 USCS §§ 1395c et seq.]); and

(C) the establishment of transitional amounts under paragraph (7).

(9) Payment for certain services. In the case of an item or service furnished to a resident of a skilled nursing facility or a part of a facility that includes a skilled nursing facility (as determined under regulations) for which payment would (but for this paragraph) be made under part B [42 USCS §§ 1395j et seq.] in an amount determined in accordance with section 1833(a)(2)(B) [42 USCS § 1395l(a)(2)(B)], the amount of the payment under such part shall be the amount provided under the fee schedule for such item or service. In the case of an item or service described in clause (iii) of paragraph (2)(A) that would be payable under part A [42 USCS §§ 1395c et seq.] but for the exclusion of such item or service under such clause, payment shall be made for the item or service, in an amount otherwise determined under part B of this title [42 USCS §§ 1395j et seq.] for such item or service, from the Federal Hospital Insurance Trust Fund under section 1817 [42 USCS § 1395i] (rather than from the Federal Supplementary Medical Insurance Trust Fund under section 1841 [42 USCS § 1395t]).

(10) Required coding. No payment may be made under part B [42 USCS §§ 1395j et seq.] for items and services (other than services described in paragraph (2)(A)(ii)) furnished to an individual who is a resident of a skilled nursing facility or of a part of a facility that includes a skilled nursing facility (as determined under regulations), unless the claim for such payment includes a code (or codes) under a uniform coding system specified by the Secretary that identifies the items or services furnished.

(11) Permitting facilities to waive 3-year transition. Notwithstanding paragraph (1)(A), a facility may elect to have the amount of the payment for all costs of covered skilled nursing facility services for each day of such services furnished in cost reporting periods beginning no earlier than 30 days before the date of such election determined pursuant to paragraph (1)(B).

(12) Adjustment for residents with AIDS. (A) In general. Subject to subparagraph (B), in the case of a resident of a skilled nursing facility who is afflicted with acquired immune deficiency syndrome (AIDS), the per diem amount of payment otherwise applicable (determined without regard to any increase under section 101 of the Medicare, Medicaid, and SCHIP Balanced Budget Refinement Act of 1999 [unclassified], or under section 314(a) of Medicare, Medicaid, and SCHIP Benefits Improvement and Protection Act of 2000 [unclassified]), shall be increased by 128 percent to reflect increased costs associated with such residents.

(B) Sunset. Subparagraph (A) shall not apply on and after such date as the Secretary certifies that there is an appropriate adjustment in the case mix under paragraph (4)(G)(i) to compensate for the increased costs associated with residents described in such subparagraph.

(f) Reporting of direct care expenditures. (1) In general. For cost reports submitted under this title for cost reporting periods beginning on or after the date that is 2 years after the date of the enactment of this subsection [enacted March 23, 2010], skilled nursing facilities shall separately report expenditures for wages and benefits for direct care staff (breaking out (at a minimum) registered nurses, licensed professional nurses, certified nurse assistants, and other medical and therapy staff).

(2) Modification of form. The Secretary, in consultation with private sector accountants experienced with Medicare and Medicaid nursing facility home cost reports, shall redesign

such reports to meet the requirement of paragraph (1) not later than 1 year after the date of the enactment of this subsection [enacted March 23, 2010].

(3) Categorization by functional accounts. Not later than 30 months after the date of the enactment of this subsection [enacted March 23, 2010], the Secretary, working in consultation with the Medicare Payment Advisory Commission, the Medicaid and CHIP Payment and Access Commission, the Inspector General of the Department of Health and Human Services, and other expert parties the Secretary determines appropriate, shall take the expenditures listed on cost reports, as modified under paragraph (1), submitted by skilled nursing facilities and categorize such expenditures, regardless of any source of payment for such expenditures, for each skilled nursing facility into the following functional accounts on an annual basis:

(A) Spending on direct care services (including nursing, therapy, and medical services).

(B) Spending on indirect care (including housekeeping and dietary services).

(C) Capital assets (including building and land costs).

(D) Administrative services costs.

(4) Availability of information submitted. The Secretary shall establish procedures to make information on expenditures submitted under this subsection readily available to interested parties upon request, subject to such requirements as the Secretary may specify under the procedures established under this paragraph.

(Aug. 14, 1935, ch 531, Title XVIII, Part E [D] [C], § 1888, as added July 18, 1984, P. L. 98-369, Division B, Title III, Subtitle A, Part I, § 2319(b), 98 Stat. 1082; April 7, 1986, P. L. 99-272, Title IX, Subtitle A, Part 1, Subpart B, § 9126(a), (b), Part 2, Subpart B, § 9219(b)(1)(C), 100 Stat. 168, 170, 182; Oct. 22, 1986, P. L. 99-514, Title XVIII, Subtitle C, Ch 1, § 1395(b)(7)(A), (B), 100 Stat. 2933; Dec. 22, 1987, P. L. 100-203, Title IV, Subtitle C, Part 1, § 4201(b)(2), 101 Stat. 1330-174; Nov. 5, 1990, P. L. 101-508, Title IV, Subtitle A, Part 1, § 4008(e)(2), (h)(2)(A)(ii), 104 Stat. 1388-45; Aug. 10, 1993, P. L. 103-66, Title XIII, Ch 2, Subch A, Part I, § 13503(a)(2), (3)(A), 107 Stat. 578; Aug. 5, 1997, P. L. 105-33, Title IV, Subtitle A, Ch 1, Subch A, § 4001, Subtitle E, Ch 3, §§ 4431, 4432(a), (b)(3), (5)(H), Subtitle F, Ch 1, Subch B, § 4511(a)(2)(E), 111 Stat. 275, 414, 421, 422, 442; Nov. 29, 1999, P. L. 106-113, Div B, § 1000(a)(6), 113 Stat. 1536; Dec. 21, 2000, P. L. 106-554, § 1(a)(6), 114 Stat. 2763; Dec. 8, 2003, P. L. 108-173, Title I, § 101(a)(1), Title IV, Subtitle A, § 410(a), Title V, Subtitle B, § 511(a), 117 Stat. 2071, 2271, 2298; July 15, 2008, P. L. 110-275, Title I, Subtitle C, Part II, § 149(b), 122 Stat. 2549; March 23, 2010, P. L. 111-148, Title III, Subtitle E, § 3401(b), Title VI, Subtitle B, Part I, § 6104, 124 Stat. 481, 711.)

§ 1395aaa. Contract with a consensus-based entity regarding performance measurement

(a) Contract. (1) In general. For purposes of activities conducted under this Act [42 USCS §§ 301 et seq.], the Secretary shall identify and have in effect a contract with a consensus-based entity, such as the National Quality Forum, that meets the requirements described in subsection (c). Such contract shall provide that the entity will perform the duties described in subsection (b).

(2) Timing for first contract. As soon as practicable after the date of the enactment of this subsection [enacted July 15, 2008], the Secretary shall enter into the first contract under paragraph (1).

(3) Period of contract. A contract under paragraph (1) shall be for a period of 4 years (except as may be renewed after a subsequent bidding process).

(4) Competitive procedures. Competitive procedures (as defined in section 4(5) of the Office of Federal Procurement Policy Act (41 U.S.C. 403(5))) shall be used to enter into a contract under paragraph (1).

(b) Duties. The duties described in this subsection are the following:

(1) Priority setting process. The entity shall synthesize evidence and convene key stakeholders to make recommendations, with respect to activities conducted under this Act [42 USCS §§ 301 et seq.], on an integrated national strategy and priorities for health care performance measurement in all applicable settings. In making such recommendations, the entity shall—

(A) ensure that priority is given to measures—

(i) that address the health care provided to patients with prevalent, high-cost chronic diseases;

(ii) with the greatest potential for improving the quality, efficiency, and patient-centeredness of health care; and

(iii) that may be implemented rapidly due to existing evidence, standards of care, or other reasons; and

(B) take into account measures that—

(i) may assist consumers and patients in making informed health care decisions;

(ii) address health disparities across groups and areas; and

(iii) address the continuum of care a patient receives, including services furnished by multiple health care providers or practitioners and across multiple settings.

(2) Endorsement of measures. The entity shall provide for the endorsement of standardized health care performance measures. The endorsement process under the preceding sentence shall consider whether a measure—

(A) is evidence-based, reliable, valid, verifiable, relevant to enhanced health outcomes, actionable at the caregiver level, feasible to collect and report, and responsive to variations in patient characteristics, such as health status, language capabilities, race or ethnicity, and income level; and

(B) is consistent across types of health care providers, including hospitals and physicians.

(3) Maintenance of measures. The entity shall establish and implement a process to ensure that measures endorsed under paragraph (2) are updated (or retired if obsolete) as new evidence is developed.

(4) Promotion of the development of electronic health records. The entity shall promote the development and use of electronic health records that contain the functionality for automated collection, aggregation, and transmission of performance measurement information.

(5) Annual report to Congress and the Secretary; secretarial publication and comment. (A) Annual report. By not later than March 1 of each year (beginning with 2009), the entity shall submit to Congress and the Secretary a report containing a description of—

(i) the implementation of quality measurement initiatives under this Act [42 USCS §§ 301 et seq.] and the coordination of such initiatives with quality initiatives implemented by other payers;

(ii) the recommendations made under paragraph (1);

(iii) the performance by the entity of the duties required under the contract entered into with the Secretary under subsection (a);

(iv) gaps in endorsed quality measures, which shall include measures that are within priority areas identified by the Secretary under the national strategy established under section 399HH of the Public Health Service Act [42 USCS § 280j], and where quality measures are unavailable or inadequate to identify or address such gaps;

(v) areas in which evidence is insufficient to support endorsement of quality measures in priority areas identified by the Secretary under the national strategy established under section 399HH of the Public Health Service Act [42 USCS § 280j] and where targeted research may address such gaps; and

(vi) the matters described in clauses (i) and (ii) of paragraph (7)(A).

(B) Secretarial review and publication of annual report. Not later than 6 months after receiving a report under subparagraph (A) for a year, the Secretary shall—

(i) review such report; and

(ii) publish such report in the Federal Register, together with any comments of the Secretary on such report.

(6) Review and endorsement of episode grouper under the physician feedback program. The entity shall provide for the review and, as appropriate, the endorsement of the episode grouper developed by the Secretary under section 1848(n)(9)(A) [42 USCS § 1395w-4(n)(9)(A)]. Such review shall be conducted on an expedited basis.

(7) Convening multi-stakeholder groups. (A) In general. The entity shall convene multi-stakeholder groups to provide input on—

(i) the selection of quality and efficiency measures described in subparagraph (B), from among—

(I) such measures that have been endorsed by the entity; and

(II) such measures that have not been considered for endorsement by such entity but are used or proposed to be used by the Secretary for the collection or reporting of quality and efficiency measures; and

(ii) national priorities (as identified under section 399HH of the Public Health Service Act [42 USCS § 280j]) for improvement in population health and in the delivery of health care services for consideration under the national strategy established under section 399HH of the Public Health Service Act [42 USCS § 280j].

(B) Quality and efficiency measures. (i) In general. Subject to clause (ii), the quality and efficiency measures described in this subparagraph are quality and efficiency measures—

(I) for use pursuant to sections 1814(i)(5)(D), 1833(i)(7), 1833(t)(17), 1848(k)(2)(C), 1866(k)(3), 1881(h)(2)(A)(iii), 1886(b)(3)(B)(viii), 1886(j)(7)(D), 1886(m)(5)(D), 1886(o)(2), 1886(s)(4)(D), and 1895(b)(3)(B)(v) [42 USCS §§ 1395(i)(5)(D), 1395l(i)(7), (t)(17), 1395w-4(k)(2)(C), 1395cc(k)(3), 1395rr(h)(2)(A)(iii), 1395ww(b)(3)(B)(viii), (j)(7)(D), (m)(5)(D), (o)(2), (s)(4)(D), and 1395fff(b)(3)(B)(v)];

(II) for use in reporting performance information to the public; and

(III) for use in health care programs other than for use under this Act [42 USCS §§ 301 et seq.].

(ii) Exclusion. Data sets (such as the outcome and assessment information set for home health services and the minimum data set for skilled nursing facility services) that are used for purposes of classification systems used in establishing payment rates under this title shall not be quality and efficiency measures described in this subparagraph.

(C) Requirement for transparency in process. (i) In general. In convening multi-stakeholder groups under subparagraph (A) with respect to the selection of quality and efficiency measures, the entity shall provide for an open and transparent process for the activities conducted pursuant to such convening.

(ii) Selection of organizations participating in multi-stakeholder groups. The process described in clause (i) shall ensure that the selection of representatives comprising such groups provides for public nominations for, and the opportunity for public comment on, such selection.

(D) Multi-stakeholder group defined. In this paragraph, the term "multi-stakeholder group" means, with respect to a quality and efficiency measure, a voluntary collaborative of organizations representing a broad group of stakeholders interested in or affected by the use of such quality and efficiency measure.

(8) Transmission of multi-stakeholder input. Not later than February 1 of each year (beginning with 2012), the entity shall transmit to the Secretary the input of multi-stakeholder groups provided under paragraph (7).

(c) Requirements described. The requirements described in this subsection are the following:

(1) Private nonprofit. The entity is a private nonprofit entity governed by a board.

(2) Board membership. The members of the board of the entity include—

(A) representatives of health plans and health care providers and practitioners or representatives of groups representing such health plans and health care providers and practitioners;

(B) health care consumers or representatives of groups representing health care consumers; and

(C) representatives of purchasers and employers or representatives of groups representing purchasers or employers.

(3) Entity membership. The membership of the entity includes persons who have experience with—

(A) urban health care issues;

(B) safety net health care issues;

(C) rural and frontier health care issues; and

(D) health care quality and safety issues.

(4) Open and transparent. With respect to matters related to the contract with the Secretary under subsection (a), the entity conducts its business in an open and transparent manner and provides the opportunity for public comment on its activities.

(5) Voluntary consensus standards setting organization. The entity operates as a voluntary consensus standards setting organization as defined for purposes of section 12(d) of the National Technology Transfer and Advancement Act of 1995 (Public Law 104-113) [15 USCS § 272 note] and Office of Management and Budget Revised Circular A-119 (published in the Federal Register on February 10, 1998).

(6) Experience. The entity has at least 4 years of experience in establishing national consensus standards.

(7) Membership fees. If the entity requires a membership fee for participation in the functions of the entity, such fees shall be reasonable and adjusted based on the capacity of the potential member to pay the fee. In no case shall membership fees pose a barrier to the participation of individuals or groups with low or nominal resources to participate in the functions of the entity.

(d) Funding. For purposes of carrying out this section, the Secretary shall provide for the transfer, from the Federal Hospital Insurance Trust Fund under section 1817 [42 USCS § 1395i] and the Federal Supplementary Medical Insurance Trust Fund under section 1841 [42 USCS § 1395t] (in such proportion as the Secretary determines appropriate), of $10,000,000 to the Centers for Medicare & Medicaid Services Program Management Account for each of fiscal years 2009 through 2012.

(Aug. 14, 1935, ch 531, Title XVIII, Part E, § 1890, as added July 15, 2008, P. L. 110-275, Title I, Subtitle F, § 183(a)(1), 122 Stat. 2584; March 23, 2010, P. L. 111-148, Title III, Subtitle A, Part I, § 3003(b), Part II, § 3014(a), Title X, Subtitle C, §§ 10304, 10322(b), 124 Stat. 367, 384, 938, 954.)

§ 1395aaa-1. Quality and efficiency measurement

(a) Multi-stakeholder group input into selection of quality and efficiency mea-

sures. The Secretary shall establish a pre-rulemaking process under which the following steps occur with respect to the selection of quality and efficiency measures described in section 1890(b)(7)(B) [42 USCS § 1395aaa(b)(7)(B)]:

(1) Input. Pursuant to section 1890(b)(7) [42 USCS § 1395aaa(b)(7)], the entity with a contract under section 1890 [42 USCS § 1395aaa] shall convene multi-stakeholder groups to provide input to the Secretary on the selection of quality and efficiency measures described in subparagraph (B) of such paragraph.

(2) Public availability of measures considered for selection. Not later than December 1 of each year (beginning with 2011), the Secretary shall make available to the public a list of quality and efficiency measures described in section 1890(b)(7)(B) [42 USCS § 1395aaa(b)(7)(B)] that the Secretary is considering under this title.

(3) Transmission of multi-stakeholder input. Pursuant to section 1890(b)(8) [42 USCS § 1395aaa(b)(8)], not later than February 1 of each year (beginning with 2012), the entity shall transmit to the Secretary the input of multi-stakeholder groups described in paragraph (1).

(4) Consideration of multi-stakeholder input. The Secretary shall take into consideration the input from multi-stakeholder groups described in paragraph (1) in selecting quality and efficiency measures described in section 1890(b)(7)(B) [42 USCS § 1395aaa(b)(7)(B)] that have been endorsed by the entity with a contract under section 1890 [42 USCS § 1395aaa] and measures that have not been endorsed by such entity.

(5) Rationale for use of quality and efficiency measures. The Secretary shall publish in the Federal Register the rationale for the use of any quality and efficiency measure described in section 1890(b)(7)(B) [42 USCS § 1395aaa(b)(7)(B)] that has not been endorsed by the entity with a contract under section 1890 [42 USCS § 1395aaa].

(6) Assessment of impact. Not later than March 1, 2012, and at least once every three years thereafter, the Secretary shall—

(A) conduct an assessment of the quality and efficiency impact of the use of endorsed measures described in section 1890(b)(7)(B) [42 USCS § 1395aaa(b)(7)(B)]; and

(B) make such assessment available to the public.

(b) Process for dissemination of measures used by the Secretary. (1) In general. The Secretary shall establish a process for disseminating quality and efficiency measures used by the Secretary. Such process shall include the following:

(A) The incorporation of such measures, where applicable, in workforce programs, training curricula, and any other means of dissemination determined appropriate by the Secretary.

(B) The dissemination of such quality and efficiency measures through the national strategy developed under section 399HH of the Public Health Service Act [42 USCS § 280j].

(2) Existing methods. To the extent practicable, the Secretary shall utilize and expand existing dissemination methods in disseminating quality and efficiency measures under the process established under paragraph (1).

(c) Review of quality and efficiency measures used by the Secretary. (1) In general. The Secretary shall—

(A) periodically (but in no case less often than once every 3 years) review quality and efficiency measures described in section 1890(b)(7)(B) [42 USCS § 1395aaa(b)(7)(B)]; and

(B) with respect to each such measure, determine whether to—

(i) maintain the use of such measure; or

(ii) phase out such measure.

(2) Considerations. In conducting the review under paragraph (1), the Secretary shall take steps to—

(A) seek to avoid duplication of measures used; and

(B) take into consideration current innovative methodologies and strategies for quality and efficiency improvement practices in the delivery of health care services that represent best practices for such quality and efficiency improvement and measures endorsed by the entity with a contract under section 1890 [42 USCS § 1395aaa] since the previous review by the Secretary.

(d) Rule of construction. Nothing in this section shall preclude a State from using the quality and efficiency measures identified under sections 1139A and 1139B [42 USCS §§ 1320b-9a and 1320b-9b].

(e) Development of quality and efficiency measures. The Administrator of the Center for Medicare & Medicaid Services shall through contracts develop quality and efficiency measures (as determined appropriate by the Administrator) for use under this Act [42 USCS §§ 301 et seq.]. In developing such measures, the Administrator shall consult with the Director of the Agency for Healthcare Research and Quality.

(f) Hospital acquired conditions. The Secretary shall, to the extent practicable, publicly report on measures for hospital acquired conditions that are currently utilized by the Centers for Medicare & Medicaid Services for the adjustment of the amount of payment to hospitals based on rates of hospital-acquired infections.

(Aug. 14, 1935, ch 531, Title XVIII, Part E, § 1890A, as added and amended March 23, 2010, P. L. 111-148, Title III, Subtitle A, Part II, §§ 3013(b), 3014(b), Title X, Subtitle C, §§ 10303(b), 10304, 124 Stat. 383, 385, 938.)

§ 1395ddd. Medicare Integrity Program

(a) Establishment of Program. There is hereby established the Medicare Integrity Program (in this section referred to as the "Program") under which the Secretary shall promote the integrity of the medicare program by entering into contracts in accordance with this section with eligible entities, or otherwise, to carry out the activities described in subsection (b).

(b) Activities described. The activities described in this subsection are as follows:

(1) Review of activities of providers of services or other individuals and entities furnishing items and services for which payment may be made under this title [42 USCS §§ 1395 et seq.] (including skilled nursing facilities and home health agencies), including medical and utilization review and fraud review (employing similar standards, processes, and technologies used by private health plans, including equipment and software technologies which surpass the capability of the equipment and technologies used in the review of claims under this title [42 USCS §§ 1395 et seq.] as of the date of the enactment of this section).

(2) Audit of cost reports.

(3) Determinations as to whether payment should not be, or should not have been, made under this title [42 USCS §§ 1395 et seq.] by reason of section 1862(b) [42 USCS § 1395y(b)], and recovery of payments that should not have been made.

(4) Education of providers of services, beneficiaries, and other persons with respect to payment integrity and benefit quality assurance issues.

(5) Developing (and periodically updating) a list of items of durable medical equipment in accordance with section 1834(a)(15) [42 USCS § 1395m(a)(15)] which are subject to prior authorization under such section.

(6) The Medicare-Medicaid Data Match Program in accordance with subsection (g).

(c) Eligibility of entities. An entity is eligible to enter into a contract under the Program to carry out any of the activities described in subsection (b) if—

(1) the entity has demonstrated capability to carry out such activities;

(2) in carrying out such activities, the entity agrees to cooperate with the Inspector General of the Department of Health and Human Services, the Attorney General, and other law enforcement agencies, as appropriate, in the investigation and deterrence of fraud and abuse in relation to this title [42 USCS §§ 1395 et seq.] and in other cases arising out of such activities;

(3) the entity complies with such conflict of interest standards as are generally applicable to Federal acquisition and procurement;

(4) the entity agrees to provide the Secretary and the Inspector General of the Department of Health and Human Services with such performance statistics (including the number and amount of overpayments recovered, the number of fraud referrals, and the return on investment of such activities by the entity) as the Secretary or the Inspector General may request; and

(5) the entity meets such other requirements as the Secretary may impose.

In the case of the activity described in subsection (b)(5), an entity shall be deemed to be eligible to enter into a contract under the Program to carry out the activity if the entity is a carrier with a contract in effect under section 1842 [42 USCS § 1395u].

(d) Process for entering into contracts. The Secretary shall enter into contracts under the Program in accordance with such procedures as the Secretary shall by regulation establish, except that such procedures shall include the following:

(1) Procedures for identifying, evaluating, and resolving organizational conflicts of interest that are generally applicable to Federal acquisition and procurement.

(2) Competitive procedures to be used—

(A) when entering into new contracts under this section;

(B) when entering into contracts that may result in the elimination of responsibilities of an individual fiscal intermediary or carrier under section 202(b) of the Health Insurance Portability and Accountability Act of 1996; and

(C) at any other time considered appropriate by the Secretary,

except that the Secretary may continue to contract with entities that are carrying out the activities described in this section pursuant to agreements under section 1816 [42 USCS § 1395h] or contracts under section 1842 [42 USCS § 1395u] in effect on the date of the enactment of this section [enacted Aug. 21, 1996].

(3) Procedures under which a contract under this section may be renewed without regard to any provision of law requiring competition if the contractor has met or exceeded the performance requirements established in the current contract.The Secretary may enter into such contracts without regard to final rules having been promulgated.

(e) Limitation on contractor liability. The Secretary shall by regulation provide for the limitation of a contractor's liability for actions taken to carry out a contract under the Program, and such regulation shall, to the extent the Secretary finds appropriate, employ the same or comparable standards and other substantive and procedural provisions as are contained in section 1157 [42 USCS § 1320c-6].

(f) Recovery of overpayments. (1) Use of repayment plans. (A) In general. If the repayment, within 30 days by a provider of services or supplier, of an overpayment under this title [42 USCS §§ 1395 et seq.] would constitute a hardship (as described in subparagraph (B)), subject to subparagraph (C), upon request of the provider of services or supplier the Secretary shall enter into a plan with the provider of services or supplier for the repayment (through offset or otherwise) of such overpayment over a period of at least 6 months but not longer than 3 years (or not longer than 5 years in the case of extreme hardship, as determined by the Secretary). Interest shall accrue on the balance through the period of repayment. Such plan shall meet terms and conditions determined to be appropriate by the Secretary.

(B) Hardship. (i) In general. For purposes of subparagraph (A), the repayment of an overpayment (or overpayments) within 30 days is deemed to constitute a hardship if—

(I) in the case of a provider of services that files cost reports, the aggregate amount of the overpayments exceeds 10 percent of the amount paid under this title [42 USCS §§ 1395 et seq.] to the provider of services for the cost reporting period covered by the most recently submitted cost report; or

(II) in the case of another provider of services or supplier, the aggregate amount of the overpayments exceeds 10 percent of the amount paid under this title [42 USCS §§ 1395 et seq.] to the provider of services or supplier for the previous calendar year.

(ii) Rule of application. The Secretary shall establish rules for the application of this subparagraph in the case of a provider of services or supplier that was not paid under this title [42 USCS §§ 1395 et seq.] during the previous year or was paid under this title [42 USCS §§ 1395 et seq.] only during a portion of that year.

(iii) Treatment of previous overpayments. If a provider of services or supplier has entered into a repayment plan under subparagraph (A) with respect to a specific overpayment amount, such payment amount under the repayment plan shall not be taken into account under clause (i) with respect to subsequent overpayment amounts.

(C) Exceptions. Subparagraph (A) shall not apply if—

(i) the Secretary has reason to suspect that the provider of services or supplier may file for bankruptcy or otherwise cease to do business or discontinue participation in the program under this title [42 USCS §§ 1395 et seq.]; or

(ii) there is an indication of fraud or abuse committed against the program.

(D) Immediate collection if violation of repayment plan. If a provider of services or supplier fails to make a payment in accordance with a repayment plan under this paragraph, the Secretary may immediately seek to offset or otherwise recover the total balance outstanding (including applicable interest) under the repayment plan.

(E) Relation to no fault provision. Nothing in this paragraph shall be construed as affecting the application of section 1870(c) [42 USCS § 1395gg(c)] (relating to no adjustment in the cases of certain overpayments).

(2) Limitation on recoupment. (A) In general. In the case of a provider of services or supplier that is determined to have received an overpayment under this title [42 USCS §§ 1395 et seq.] and that seeks a reconsideration by a qualified independent contractor on such determination under section 1869(b)(1) [42 USCS § 1395ff(b)(1)], the Secretary may not take any action (or authorize any other person, including any medicare contractor, as defined in subparagraph (C)) to recoup the overpayment until the date the decision on the reconsideration has been rendered. If the provisions of section 1869(b)(1) [42 USCS § 1395ff(b)(1)] (providing for such a reconsideration by a qualified independent contractor) are not in effect, in applying the previous sentence any reference to such a reconsideration shall be treated as a reference to a redetermination by the fiscal intermediary or carrier involved.

(B) Collection with interest. Insofar as the determination on such appeal is against the provider of services or supplier, interest on the overpayment shall accrue on and after the date of the original notice of overpayment. Insofar as such determination against the provider of services or supplier is later reversed, the Secretary shall provide for repayment of the amount recouped plus interest at the same rate as would apply under the previous sentence for the period in which the amount was recouped.

(C) Medicare contractor defined. For purposes of this subsection, the term "medicare contractor" has the meaning given such term in section 1889(g) [42 USCS § 1395zz(g)].

(3) Limitation on use of extrapolation. A medicare contractor may not use extrapolation to determine overpayment amounts to be recovered by recoupment, offset, or otherwise unless the Secretary determines that—

(A) there is a sustained or high level of payment error; or

(B) documented educational intervention has failed to correct the payment error.

There shall be no administrative or judicial review under section 1869 [42 USCS § 1395ff], section 1878 [42 USCS § 1395oo], or otherwise, of determinations by the Secretary of sustained or high levels of payment errors under this paragraph.

(4) Provision of supporting documentation. In the case of a provider of services or supplier with respect to which amounts were previously overpaid, a medicare contractor may request the periodic production of records or supporting documentation for a limited sample of submitted claims to ensure that the previous practice is not continuing.

(5) Consent settlement reforms. (A) In general. The Secretary may use a consent settlement (as defined in subparagraph (D)) to settle a projected overpayment.

(B) Opportunity to submit additional information before consent settlement offer. Before offering a provider of services or supplier a consent settlement, the Secretary shall—

(i) communicate to the provider of services or supplier—

(I) that, based on a review of the medical records requested by the Secretary, a preliminary evaluation of those records indicates that there would be an overpayment;

(II) the nature of the problems identified in such evaluation; and

(III) the steps that the provider of services or supplier should take to address the problems; and

(ii) provide for a 45-day period during which the provider of services or supplier may furnish additional information concerning the medical records for the claims that had been reviewed.

(C) Consent settlement offer. The Secretary shall review any additional information furnished by the provider of services or supplier under subparagraph (B)(ii). Taking into consideration such information, the Secretary shall determine if there still appears to be an overpayment. If so, the Secretary—

(i) shall provide notice of such determination to the provider of services or supplier, including an explanation of the reason for such determination; and

(ii) in order to resolve the overpayment, may offer the provider of services or supplier—

(I) the opportunity for a statistically valid random sample; or

(II) a consent settlement.

The opportunity provided under clause (ii)(I) does not waive any appeal rights with respect to the alleged overpayment involved.

(D) Consent settlement defined. For purposes of this paragraph, the term "consent settlement" means an agreement between the Secretary and a provider of services or supplier whereby both parties agree to settle a projected overpayment based on less than a statistically valid sample of claims and the provider of services or supplier agrees not to appeal the claims involved.

(6) Notice of over-utilization of codes. The Secretary shall establish, in consultation with organizations representing the classes of providers of services and suppliers, a process under which the Secretary provides for notice to classes of providers of services and suppliers served by the contractor in cases in which the contractor has identified that particular billing codes may be overutilized by that class of providers of services or suppliers under the programs under this title [42 USCS §§ 1395 et seq.] (or provisions of title XI [42 USCS §§ 1301 et seq.] insofar as they relate to such programs).

(7) Payment audits. (A) Written notice for post-payment audits. Subject to subparagraph (C), if a medicare contractor decides to conduct a post-payment audit of a provider of services or supplier under this title [42 USCS §§ 1395 et seq.], the contractor shall provide the provider of services or supplier with written notice (which may be in electronic form) of the intent to conduct such an audit.

(B) Explanation of findings for all audits. Subject to subparagraph (C), if a medicare contractor audits a provider of services or supplier under this title [42 USCS §§ 1395 et seq.], the contractor shall—

(i) give the provider of services or supplier a full review and explanation of the findings of the audit in a manner that is understandable to the provider of services or supplier and permits the development of an appropriate corrective action plan;

(ii) inform the provider of services or supplier of the appeal rights under this title [42 USCS §§ 1395 et seq.] as well as consent settlement options (which are at the discretion of the Secretary);

(iii) give the provider of services or supplier an opportunity to provide additional information to the contractor; and

(iv) take into account information provided, on a timely basis, by the provider of services or supplier under clause (iii).

(C) Exception. Subparagraphs (A) and (B) shall not apply if the provision of notice or findings would compromise pending law enforcement activities, whether civil or criminal, or reveal findings of law enforcement-related audits.

(8) Standard methodology for probe sampling. The Secretary shall establish a standard methodology for medicare contractors to use in selecting a sample of claims for review in the case of an abnormal billing pattern.

(g) Medicare-Medicaid Data Match Program. (1) Expansion of program. (A) In general. The Secretary shall enter into contracts with eligible entities for the purpose of ensuring that, beginning with 2006, the Medicare-Medicaid Data Match Program (commonly referred to as the "Medi-Medi Program") is conducted with respect to the program established under this title [42 USCS §§ 1395 et seq.] and State Medicaid programs under title XIX [42 USCS §§ 1396 et seq.] for the purpose of—

(i) identifying program vulnerabilities in the program established under this title [42 USCS §§ 1395 et seq.] and the Medicaid program established under title XIX [42 USCS §§ 1396 et seq.] through the use of computer algorithms to look for payment anomalies (including billing or billing patterns identified with respect to service, time, or patient that appear to be suspect or otherwise implausible);

(ii) working with States, the Attorney General, and the Inspector General of the Department of Health and Human Services to coordinate appropriate actions to protect the Federal and State share of expenditures under the Medicaid program under title XIX [42 USCS §§ 1396 et seq.], as well as the program established under this title [42 USCS §§ 1395 et seq.]; and

(iii) increasing the effectiveness and efficiency of both such programs through cost avoidance, savings, and recoupments of fraudulent, wasteful, or abusive expenditures.

(B) Reporting requirements. The Secretary shall make available in a timely manner any data and statistical information collected by the Medi-Medi Program to the Attorney General, the Director of the Federal Bureau of Investigation, the Inspector General of the Department of Health and Human Services, and the States (including a Medicaid fraud and abuse control unit described in section 1903(q) [42 USCS § 1396b(q)]). Such information shall be disseminated no less frequently than quarterly.

(2) Limited waiver authority. The Secretary shall waive only such requirements of this section and of titles XI and XIX [42 USCS §§ 1301 et seq. and §§ 1396 et seq.] as are necessary to carry out paragraph (1).

(h) Use of recovery audit contractors. (1) In general. Under the Program, the Secretary shall enter into contracts with recovery audit contractors in accordance with this subsection for the purpose of identifying underpayments and overpayments and recouping overpayments under this title [42 USCS §§ 1395 et seq.] with respect to all services for which payment is made under this title [42 USCS §§ 1395 et seq.]. Under the contracts—

(A) payment shall be made to such a contractor only from amounts recovered;

(B) from such amounts recovered, payment—

(i) shall be made on a contingent basis for collecting overpayments; and

(ii) may be made in such amounts as the Secretary may specify for identifying underpayments; and

(C) the Secretary shall retain a portion of the amounts recovered which shall be available to the program management account of the Centers for Medicare & Medicaid Services for purposes of activities conducted under the recovery audit program under this subsection.

(2) Disposition of remaining recoveries. The amounts recovered under such contracts that are not paid to the contractor under paragraph (1) or retained by the Secretary under paragraph (1)(C) shall be applied to reduce expenditures under this title [42 USCS §§ 1395 et seq.].

(3) Nationwide coverage. The Secretary shall enter into contracts under paragraph (1) in a manner so as to provide for activities in all States under such a contract by not later than

January 1, 2010 (not later than December 31, 2010, in the case of contracts relating to payments made under part C or D [42 USCS §§ 1395w-21 et seq. or 1395w-101 et seq.]).

(4) Audit and recovery periods. Each such contract shall provide that audit and recovery activities may be conducted during a fiscal year with respect to payments made under this title [42 USCS §§ 1395 et seq.]—

(A) during such fiscal year; and

(B) retrospectively (for a period of not more than 4 fiscal years prior to such fiscal year).

(5) Waiver. The Secretary shall waive such provisions of this title [42 USCS §§ 1395 et seq.] as may be necessary to provide for payment of recovery audit contractors under this subsection in accordance with paragraph (1).

(6) Qualifications of contractors. (A) In general. The Secretary may not enter into a contract under paragraph (1) with a recovery audit contractor unless the contractor has staff that has the appropriate clinical knowledge of, and experience with, the payment rules and regulations under this title [42 USCS §§ 1395 et seq.] or the contractor has, or will contract with, another entity that has such knowledgeable and experienced staff.

(B) Ineligibility of certain contractors. The Secretary may not enter into a contract under paragraph (1) with a recovery audit contractor to the extent the contractor is a fiscal intermediary under section 1816 [42 USCS § 1395h], a carrier under section 1842 [42 USCS § 1395u], or a medicare administrative contractor under section 1874A [42 USCS § 1395kk-1].

(C) Preference for entities with demonstrated proficiency. In awarding contracts to recovery audit contractors under paragraph (1), the Secretary shall give preference to those risk entities that the Secretary determines have demonstrated more than 3 years direct management experience and a proficiency for cost control or recovery audits with private insurers, health care providers, health plans, under the Medicaid program under title XIX [42 USCS §§ 1396 et seq.], or under this title [42 USCS §§ 1395 et seq.].

(7) Construction relating to conduct of investigation of fraud. A recovery of an overpayment to a individual or entity by a recovery audit contractor under this subsection shall not be construed to prohibit the Secretary or the Attorney General from investigating and prosecuting, if appropriate, allegations of fraud or abuse arising from such overpayment.

(8) Annual report. The Secretary shall annually submit to Congress a report on the use of recovery audit contractors under this subsection. Each such report shall include information on the performance of such contractors in identifying underpayments and overpayments and recouping overpayments, including an evaluation of the comparative performance of such contractors and savings to the program under this title [42 USCS §§ 1395 et seq.].

(9) Special rules relating to parts C and D [42 USCS §§ 1395w-21 et seq., 1395w-101 et seq.]. The Secretary shall enter into contracts under paragraph (1) to require recovery audit contractors to—

(A) ensure that each MA plan under part C [42 USCS §§ 1395w-21 et seq.] has an anti-fraud plan in effect and to review the effectiveness of each such anti-fraud plan;

(B) ensure that each prescription drug plan under part D [42 USCS §§ 1395w-101 et seq.] has an anti-fraud plan in effect and to review the effectiveness of each such anti-fraud plan;

(C) examine claims for reinsurance payments under section 1860D-15(b) [42 USCS § 1395w-115(b)] to determine whether prescription drug plans submitting such claims incurred costs in excess of the allowable reinsurance costs permitted under paragraph (2) of that section; and

(D) review estimates submitted by prescription drug plans by private plans with respect to the enrollment of high cost beneficiaries (as defined by the Secretary) and to compare such estimates with the numbers of such beneficiaries actually enrolled by such plans.

(i) Evaluations and annual report. (1) Evaluations. The Secretary shall conduct evaluations of eligible entities which the Secretary contracts with under the Program not less frequently than every 3 years.

(2) Annual report. Not later than 180 days after the end of each fiscal year (beginning with fiscal year 2011), the Secretary shall submit a report to Congress which identifies—

(A) the use of funds, including funds transferred from the Federal Hospital Insurance Trust Fund under section 1817 [42 USCS § 1395i] and the Federal Supplementary Insurance Trust Fund under section 1841 [42 USCS § 1395t], to carry out this section; and

(B) the effectiveness of the use of such funds.

(July 1, 1944, ch 373, Title XVIII, Part E [D] [C], § 1893, as added Aug. 21, 1996, P. L. 104-191, Title II, Subtitle A, § 202(a), 110 Stat. 1996; Aug. 5, 1997, P. L. 105-33, Title IV, Subtitle A, Ch 1, Subch A, § 4001, 111 Stat. 275; Dec. 8, 2003, P. L. 108-173, Title I, § 101(a)(1), Title VII, Subtitle D, § 736(c)(7), Title IX, Subtitle D, § 935(a), 117 Stat. 2071, 2356, 2407; Feb. 8, 2006, P. L. 109-171, Title VI,

Subtitle A, Ch. 3, § 6034(d)(1), 120 Stat. 77; Dec. 20, 2006, P. L. 109-432, Div B, Title III, § 302(a), 120 Stat. 2991; March 23, 2010, P. L. 111-148, Title VI, Subtitle E, §§ 6402(j)(1), 6411(b), 124 Stat. 762, 775.)

§ 1395eee. Payments to, and coverage of benefits under, programs of all-inclusive care for the elderly (PACE)

(a) Receipt of benefits through enrollment in PACE program; definitions for PACE program related terms. (1) Benefits through enrollment in a PACE program. In accordance with this section, in the case of an individual who is entitled to benefits under part A or enrolled under part B and who is a PACE program eligible individual (as defined in paragraph (5)) with respect to a PACE program offered by a PACE provider under a PACE program agreement—

(A) the individual may enroll in the program under this section; and

(B) so long as the individual is so enrolled and in accordance with regulations—

(i) the individual shall receive benefits under this title [42 USCS §§ 1395 et seq.] solely through such program; and

(ii) the PACE provider is entitled to payment under and in accordance with this section and such agreement for provision of such benefits.

(2) PACE program defined. For purposes of this section, the term "PACE program" means a program of all-inclusive care for the elderly that meets the following requirements:

(A) Operation. The entity operating the program is a PACE provider (as defined in paragraph (3)).

(B) Comprehensive benefits. The program provides comprehensive health care services to PACE program eligible individuals in accordance with the PACE program agreement and regulations under this section.

(C) Transition. In the case of an individual who is enrolled under the program under this section and whose enrollment ceases for any reason (including that the individual no longer qualifies as a PACE program eligible individual, the termination of a PACE program agreement, or otherwise), the program provides assistance to the individual in obtaining necessary transitional care through appropriate referrals and making the individual's medical records available to new providers.

(3) PACE provider defined. (A) In general. For purposes of this section, the term "PACE provider" means an entity that—

(i) subject to subparagraph (B), is (or is a distinct part of) a public entity or a private, nonprofit entity organized for charitable purposes under section 501(c)(3) of the Internal Revenue Code of 1986 [26 USCS § 501(c)(3)]; and

(ii) has entered into a PACE program agreement with respect to its operation of a PACE program.

(B) Treatment of private, for-profit providers. Clause (i) of subparagraph (A) shall not apply—

(i) to entities subject to a demonstration project waiver under subsection (h); and

(ii) after the date the report under section 4804(b) of the Balanced Budget Act of 1997 [note to this section] is submitted, unless the Secretary determines that any of the findings described in subparagraph (A), (B), (C), or (D) of paragraph (2) of such section are true.

(4) PACE program agreement defined. For purposes of this section, the term "PACE program agreement" means, with respect to a PACE provider, an agreement, consistent with this section, section 1934 [42 USCS § 1396u-4] (if applicable), and regulations promulgated to carry out such sections, between the PACE provider and the Secretary, or an agreement between the PACE provider and a State administering agency for the operation of a PACE program by the provider under such sections.

(5) PACE program eligible individual defined. For purposes of this section, the term "PACE program eligible individual" means, with respect to a PACE program, an individual who—

(A) is 55 years of age or older;

(B) subject to subsection (c)(4), is determined under subsection (c) to require the level of care required under the State medicaid plan for coverage of nursing facility services;

(C) resides in the service area of the PACE program; and

(D) meets such other eligibility conditions as may be imposed under the PACE program agreement for the program under subsection (e)(2)(A)(ii).

(6) PACE protocol. For purposes of this section, the term "PACE protocol" means the Protocol for the Program of All-inclusive Care for the Elderly (PACE), as published by On Lok, Inc., as of April 14, 1995, or any successor protocol that may be agreed upon between the Secretary and On Lok, Inc.

(7) PACE demonstration waiver program defined. For purposes of this section, the term "PACE demonstration waiver program" means a demonstration program under either of the following sections (as in effect before the date of their repeal):

(A) Section 603(c) of the Social Security Amendments of 1983 (Public Law 98-21)) [unclassified], as extended by section 9220 of the Consolidated Omnibus Budget Reconciliation Act of 1985 (Public Law 99-272).

(B) Section 9412(b) of the Omnibus Budget Reconciliation Act of 1986 (Public Law 99-509) [unclassified].

(8) State administering agency defined. For purposes of this section, the term "State administering agency" means, with respect to the operation of a PACE program in a State, the agency of that State (which may be the single agency responsible for administration of the State plan under title XIX [42 USCS §§ 1396 et seq.] in the State) responsible for administering PACE program agreements under this section and section 1934 [42 USCS § 1396u-4] in the State.

(9) Trial period defined. (A) In general. For purposes of this section, the term "trial period" means, with respect to a PACE program operated by a PACE provider under a PACE program agreement, the first 3 contract years under such agreement with respect to such program.

(B) Treatment of entities previously operating PACE demonstration waiver programs. Each contract year (including a year occurring before the effective date of this section) during which an entity has operated a PACE demonstration waiver program shall be counted under subparagraph (A) as a contract year during which the entity operated a PACE program as a PACE provider under a PACE program agreement.

(10) Regulations. For purposes of this section, the term "regulations" refers to interim final or final regulations promulgated under subsection (f) to carry out this section and section 1934 [42 USCS § 1396u-4].

(b) Scope of benefits; beneficiary safeguards. (1) In general. Under a PACE program agreement, a PACE provider shall—

(A) provide to PACE program eligible individuals enrolled with the provider, regardless of source of payment and directly or under contracts with other entities, at a minimum—

(i) all items and services covered under this title [42 USCS §§ 1395 et seq.] (for individuals enrolled under this section) and all items and services covered under title XIX [42 USCS §§ 1396 et seq.], but without any limitation or condition as to amount, duration, or scope and without application of deductibles, copayments, coinsurance, or other cost-sharing that would otherwise apply under this title or such title, respectively; and

(ii) all additional items and services specified in regulations, based upon those required under the PACE protocol;

(B) provide such enrollees access to necessary covered items and services 24 hours per day, every day of the year;

(C) provide services to such enrollees through a comprehensive, multidisciplinary health and social services delivery system which integrates acute and long-term care services pursuant to regulations; and

(D) specify the covered items and services that will not be provided directly by the entity, and to arrange for delivery of those items and services through contracts meeting the requirements of regulations.

(2) Quality assurance; patient safeguards. The PACE program agreement shall require the PACE provider to have in effect at a minimum—

(A) a written plan of quality assurance and improvement, and procedures implementing such plan, in accordance with regulations; and

(B) written safeguards of the rights of enrolled participants (including a patient bill of rights and procedures for grievances and appeals) in accordance with regulations and with other requirements of this title [42 USCS §§ 1395 et seq.] and Federal and State law that are designed for the protection of patients.

(3) Treatment of medicare services furnished by noncontract physicians and other entities. (A) Application of medicare advantage requirement with respect to medicare services furnished by noncontract physicians and other entities. Section 1852(k)(1) [42 USCS § 1395w-22(k)(1)] (relating to limitations on balance billing against MA organizations for noncontract physicians and other entities with respect to services covered under this title [42 USCS §§ 1395 et seq.]) shall apply to PACE providers, PACE program eligible individuals enrolled with such PACE providers, and physicians and other entities that do not have a contract or other agreement establishing payment amounts for services furnished to such an individual in the same manner as such section applies to MA organizations, individuals enrolled with such organizations, and physicians and other entities referred to in such section.

(B) Reference to related provision for noncontract providers of services. For the provision relating to limitations on balance billing against PACE providers for services covered under this title [42 USCS §§ 1395 et seq.] furnished by noncontract providers of services, see section 1866(a)(1)(O) [42 USCS § 1395cc(a)(1)(O)].

(4) Reference to related provision for services covered under title XIX but not under this title. For provisions relating to limitations on payments to providers participating under the State plan under title XIX [42 USCS §§ 1396 et seq.] that do not have a contract or other agreement with a PACE provider establishing payment amounts for services covered under such plan (but not under this title [42 USCS §§ 1395 et seq.]) when such services are furnished to enrollees of that PACE provider, see section 1902(a)(66) [42 USCS § 1396a(a)(66)].

(c) Eligibility determinations. (1) In general. The determination of whether an individual is a PACE program eligible individual—

(A) shall be made under and in accordance with the PACE program agreement; and

(B) who is entitled to medical assistance under title XIX [42 USCS §§ 1396 et seq.], shall be made (or who is not so entitled, may be made) by the State administering agency.

(2) Condition. An individual is not a PACE program eligible individual (with respect to payment under this section) unless the individual's health status has been determined by the Secretary or the State administering agency, in accordance with regulations, to be comparable to the health status of individuals who have participated in the PACE demonstration waiver programs. Such determination shall be based upon information on health status and related indicators (such as medical diagnoses and measures of activities of daily living, instrumental activities of daily living, and cognitive impairment) that are part of a uniform minimum data set collected by PACE providers on potential PACE program eligible individuals.

(3) Annual eligibility recertifications. (A) In general. Subject to subparagraph (B), the determination described in subsection (a)(5)(B) for an individual shall be reevaluated at least annually.

(B) Exception. The requirement of annual reevaluation under subparagraph (A) may be waived during a period in accordance with regulations in those cases where the State administering agency determines that there is no reasonable expectation of improvement or significant change in an individual's condition during the period because of the severity of chronic condition, or degree of impairment of functional capacity of the individual involved.

(4) Continuation of eligibility. An individual who is a PACE program eligible individual may be deemed to continue to be such an individual notwithstanding a determination that the individual no longer meets the requirement of subsection (a)(5)(B) if, in accordance with regulations, in the absence of continued coverage under a PACE program the individual reasonably would be expected to meet such requirement within the succeeding 6-month period.

(5) Enrollment; disenrollment. (A) Voluntary disenrollment at any time. The enrollment and disenrollment of PACE program eligible individuals in a PACE program shall be pursuant to regulations and the PACE program agreement and shall permit enrollees to voluntarily disenroll without cause at any time.

(B) Limitations on disenrollment. (i) In general. Regulations promulgated by the Secretary under this section and section 1934 [42 USCS § 1396u-4], and the PACE program agreement, shall provide that the PACE program may not disenroll a PACE program eligible individual except—

(I) for nonpayment of premiums (if applicable) on a timely basis; or

(II) for engaging in disruptive or threatening behavior, as defined in such regulations (developed in close consultation with State administering agencies).

(ii) No disenrollment for noncompliant behavior. Except as allowed under regulations promulgated to carry out clause (i)(II), a PACE program may not disenroll a PACE program eligible individual on the ground that the individual has engaged in noncompliant behavior if such behavior is related to a mental or physical condition of the individual. For purposes of the preceding sentence, the term "noncompliant behavior" includes repeated noncompliance with medical advice and repeated failure to appear for appointments.

(iii) Timely review of proposed nonvoluntary disenrollment. A proposed disenrollment, other than a voluntary disenrollment, shall be subject to timely review and final determination by the Secretary or by the State administering agency (as applicable), prior to the proposed disenrollment becoming effective.

(d) Payments to PACE providers on a capitated basis. (1) In general. In the case of a PACE provider with a PACE program agreement under this section, except as provided in this subsection or by regulations, the Secretary shall make prospective monthly payments of a capitation amount for each PACE program eligible individual enrolled under the agreement under this section in the same manner and from the same sources as payments are made to a Medicare+Choice organization under section 1853 [42 USCS § 1395w-23] (or, for periods beginning before January 1, 1999, to an eligible organization under a risk-sharing contract under section 1876 [42 USCS § 1395mm]). Such payments shall be subject to adjustment in the manner described in section 1853(a)(2) or section 1876(a)(1)(E) [42 USCS § 1395w-23(a)(2) or 1395mm(a)(1)(E)], as the case may be.

(2) Capitation amount. The capitation amount to be applied under this subsection for a provider for a contract year shall be an amount specified in the PACE program agreement for the year. Such amount shall be based upon payment rates established for purposes of payment under section 1853 [42 USCS § 1396w-23] (or, for periods before January 1, 1999, for purposes of risk-sharing contracts under section 1876 [42 USCS § 1395mm]) and shall be adjusted to take into account the comparative frailty of PACE enrollees and such other factors as the Secretary determines to be appropriate. Such amount under such an agreement shall be computed in a manner so that the total payment level for all PACE program eligible individuals enrolled under a program is less than the projected payment under this title [42 USCS §§ 1395 et seq.] for a comparable population not enrolled under a PACE program.

(3) Capitation rates determined without regard to the phase-out of the indirect costs of medical education from the annual Medicare Advantage capitation rate. Capitation amounts under this subsection shall be determined without regard to the application of section 1853(k)(4) [42 USCS § 1395w-23(k)(4)].

(e) PACE program agreement. (1) Requirement. (A) In general. The Secretary, in close cooperation with the State administering agency, shall establish procedures for entering into, extending, and terminating PACE program agreements for the operation of PACE programs by entities that meet the requirements for a PACE provider under this section, section 1934 [42 USCS § 1396u-4], and regulations.

(B) Numerical limitation. (i) In general. The Secretary shall not permit the number of PACE providers with which agreements are in effect under this section or under section 9412(b) of the Omnibus Budget Reconciliation Act of 1986 [unclassified] to exceed—

(I) 40 as of the date of the enactment of this section [enacted Aug. 5, 1997]; or

(II) as of each succeeding anniversary of such date, the numerical limitation under this subparagraph for the preceding year plus 20.

Subclause (II) shall apply without regard to the actual number of agreements in effect as of a previous anniversary date.

(ii) Treatment of certain private, for-profit providers. The numerical limitation in clause (i) shall not apply to a PACE provider that—

(I) is operating under a demonstration project waiver under subsection (h); or

(II) was operating under such a waiver and subsequently qualifies for PACE provider status pursuant to subsection (a)(3)(B)(ii).

(2) Service area and eligibility. (A) In general. A PACE program agreement for a PACE program—

(i) shall designate the service area of the program;

(ii) may provide additional requirements for individuals to qualify as PACE program eligible individuals with respect to the program;

(iii) shall be effective for a contract year, but may be extended for additional contract years in the absence of a notice by a party to terminate and is subject to termination by the Secretary and the State administering agency at any time for cause (as provided under the agreement);

(iv) shall require a PACE provider to meet all applicable State and local laws and requirements; and

(v) shall contain such additional terms and conditions as the parties may agree to, so long as such terms and conditions are consistent with this section and regulations.

(B) Service area overlap. In designating a service area under a PACE program agreement under subparagraph (A)(i), the Secretary (in consultation with the State administering agency) may exclude from designation an area that is already covered under another PACE program agreement, in order to avoid unnecessary duplication of services and avoid impairing the financial and service viability of an existing program.

(3) Data collection; development of outcome measures. (A) Data collection. (i) In general. Under a PACE program agreement, the PACE provider shall—

(I) collect data;

(II) maintain, and afford the Secretary and the State administering agency access to, the records relating to the program, including pertinent financial, medical, and personnel records; and

(III) make available to the Secretary and the State administering agency reports that the Secretary finds (in consultation with State administering agencies) necessary to monitor the operation, cost, and effectiveness of the PACE program under this section and section 1934 [42 USCS § 1396u-4].

(ii) Requirements during trial period. During the first 3 years of operation of a PACE program (either under this section or under a PACE demonstration waiver program), the PACE provider shall provide such additional data as the Secretary specifies in regulations in order to perform the oversight required under paragraph (4)(A).

(B) Development of outcome measures. Under a PACE program agreement, the PACE provider, the Secretary, and the State administering agency shall jointly cooperate in the development and implementation of health status and quality of life outcome measures with respect to PACE program eligible individuals.

(4) Oversight. (A) Annual, close oversight during trial period. During the trial period (as defined in subsection (a)(9)) with respect to a PACE program operated by a PACE provider, the Secretary (in cooperation with the State administering agency) shall conduct a comprehensive annual review of the operation of the PACE program by the provider in order to assure compliance with the requirements of this section and regulations. Such a review shall include—

(i) an on-site visit to the program site;

(ii) comprehensive assessment of a provider's fiscal soundness;

(iii) comprehensive assessment of the provider's capacity to provide all PACE services to all enrolled participants;

(iv) detailed analysis of the entity's substantial compliance with all significant requirements of this section and regulations; and

(v) any other elements the Secretary or State administering agency considers necessary or appropriate.

(B) Continuing oversight. After the trial period, the Secretary (in cooperation with the State administering agency) shall continue to conduct such review of the operation of PACE providers and PACE programs as may be appropriate, taking into account the performance level of a provider and compliance of a provider with all significant requirements of this section and regulations.

(C) Disclosure. The results of reviews under this paragraph shall be reported promptly to the PACE provider, along with any recommendations for changes to the provider's program, and shall be made available to the public upon request.

(5) Termination of PACE provider agreements. (A) In general. Under regulations—

(i) the Secretary or a State administering agency may terminate a PACE program agreement for cause; and

(ii) a PACE provider may terminate an agreement after appropriate notice to the Secretary, the State agency, and enrollees.

(B) Causes for termination. In accordance with regulations establishing procedures for termination of PACE program agreements, the Secretary or a State administering agency may terminate a PACE program agreement with a PACE provider for, among other reasons, the fact that—

(i) the Secretary or State administering agency determines that—

(I) there are significant deficiencies in the quality of care provided to enrolled participants; or

(II) the provider has failed to comply substantially with conditions for a program or provider under this section or section 1934 [42 USCS § 1396u-4]; and

(ii) the entity has failed to develop and successfully initiate, within 30 days of the date of the receipt of written notice of such a determination, a plan to correct the deficiencies, or has failed to continue implementation of such a plan.

(C) Termination and transition procedures. An entity whose PACE provider agreement is terminated under this paragraph shall implement the transition procedures required under subsection (a)(2)(C).

(6) Secretary's oversight; enforcement authority. (A) In general. Under regulations, if the Secretary determines (after consultation with the State administering agency) that a PACE provider is failing substantially to comply with the requirements of this section and regulations, the Secretary (and the State administering agency) may take any or all of the following actions:

(i) Condition the continuation of the PACE program agreement upon timely execution of a corrective action plan.

(ii) Withhold some or all further payments under the PACE program agreement under this section or section 1934 [42 USCS § 1396u-4] with respect to PACE program services furnished by such provider until the deficiencies have been corrected.

(iii) Terminate such agreement.

(B) Application of intermediate sanctions. Under regulations, the Secretary may provide for the application against a PACE provider of remedies described in section 1857(g)(2) [42 USCS § 1395w-27(g)(2)] (or, for periods before January 1, 1999, section 1876(i)(6)(B) [42 USCS § 1395mm(i)(6)(B)]) or 1903(m)(5)(B) [42 USCS § 1396b(m)(5)(B)] in the case of violations by the provider of the type described in section 1857(g)(1) [42 USCS § 1395w-27(g)(1)] (or section 1876(i)(6)(A) [42 USCS § 1395mm(i)(6)(A)] for such periods) or 1903(m)(5)(A) [42 USCS § 1396b(m)(5)(A)], respectively (in relation to agreements, enrollees, and requirements under this section or section 1934 [42 USCS § 1396u-4], respectively).

(7) Procedures for termination or imposition of sanctions. Under regulations, the provisions of section 1857(h) [42 USCS § 1395w-27(h)] (or for periods before January 1, 1999, section 1876(i)(9) [42 USCS § 1395mm(i)(9)]) shall apply to termination and sanctions respecting a PACE program agreement and PACE provider under this subsection in the same manner as they apply to a termination and sanctions with respect to a contract and a Medicare+Choice organization under part C [42 USCS §§ 1395w-21 et seq.] (or for such periods an eligible organization under section 1876 [42 USCS § 1395mm]).

(8) Timely consideration of applications for PACE program provider status. In considering an application for PACE provider program status, the application shall be deemed approved unless the Secretary, within 90 days after the date of the submission of the application to the Secretary, either denies such request in writing or informs the applicant in writing with respect to any additional information that is needed in order to make a final determination with respect to the application. After the date the Secretary receives such additional information, the application shall be deemed approved unless the Secretary, within 90 days of such date, denies such request.

(f) Regulations. (1) In general. The Secretary shall issue interim final or final regulations to carry out this section and section 1934 [42 USCS § 1396u-4].

(2) Use of PACE protocol. (A) In general. In issuing such regulations, the Secretary shall, to the extent consistent with the provisions of this section, incorporate the requirements applied to PACE demonstration waiver programs under the PACE protocol.

(B) Flexibility. In order to provide for reasonable flexibility in adapting the PACE service delivery model to the needs of particular organizations (such as those in rural areas or those that may determine it appropriate to use nonstaff physicians according to State licensing law requirements) under this section and section 1934 [42 USCS § 1396u-4], the Secretary (in close consultation with State administering agencies) may modify or waive provisions of the PACE protocol so long as any such modification or waiver is not inconsistent with and would not impair the essential elements, objectives, and requirements of this section, but may not modify or waive any of the following provisions:

(i) The focus on frail elderly qualifying individuals who require the level of care provided in a nursing facility.

(ii) The delivery of comprehensive, integrated acute and long-term care services.

(iii) The interdisciplinary team approach to care management and service delivery.

(iv) Capitated, integrated financing that allows the provider to pool payments received from public and private programs and individuals.

(v) The assumption by the provider of full financial risk.

(C) Continuation of modifications or waivers of operational requirements under demonstration status. If a PACE program operating under demonstration authority has contractual or other operating arrangements which are not otherwise recognized in regulation and which were in effect on July 1, 2000, the Secretary (in close consultation with, and with the concurrence of, the State administering agency) shall permit any such program to continue such arrangements so long as such arrangements are found by the Secretary and the State to be reasonably consistent with the objectives of the PACE program.

(3) Application of certain additional beneficiary and program protections. (A) In general. In issuing such regulations and subject to subparagraph (B), the Secretary may apply with respect to PACE programs, providers, and agreements such requirements of part C [42 USCS §§ 1395w-21 et seq.] (or, for periods before January 1, 1999, section 1876 [42 USCS § 1395mm]) and sections 1903(m) and 1932 [42 USCS §§ 1396b(m), 1396u-2] relating to protection of beneficiaries and program integrity as would apply to Medicare+Choice organizations under part C [42 USCS §§ 1395w-21 et seq.] (or for such periods eligible organizations under risk-sharing contracts under section 1876 [42 USCS § 1395mm]) and to medicaid managed care organizations under prepaid capitation agreements under section 1903(m) [42 USCS §§ 1396b(m)].

(B) Considerations. In issuing such regulations, the Secretary shall—

(i) take into account the differences between populations served and benefits provided under this section and under part C [42 USCS §§ 1395w-21 et seq.] (or, for periods before January 1, 1999, section 1876 [42 USCS § 1395mm]) and section 1903(m) [42 USCS §§ 1396b(m)];

(ii) not include any requirement that conflicts with carrying out PACE programs under this section; and

(iii) not include any requirement restricting the proportion of enrollees who are eligible for benefits under this title or title XIX [42 USCS §§ 1395 et seq. or 1396 et seq.].

(4) Construction. Nothing in this subsection shall be construed as preventing the Secretary from including in regulations provisions to ensure the health and safety of individuals enrolled in a PACE program under this section that are in addition to those otherwise provided under paragraphs (2) and (3).

(g) Waivers of requirements. With respect to carrying out a PACE program under this section, the following requirements of this title [42 USCS §§ 1395 et seq.] (and regulations relating to such requirements) are waived and shall not apply:

(1) Section 1812 [42 USCS § 1395d], insofar as it limits coverage of institutional services.

(2) Sections 1813, 1814, 1833, and 1886 [42 USCS §§ 1395e, 1395f, 1395l, 1395ww], insofar as such sections relate to rules for payment for benefits.

(3) Sections 1814(a)(2)(B), 1814(a)(2)(C), and 1835(a)(2)(A) [42 USCS §§ 1395f(a)(2)(B), (C), 1395n(a)(2)(A)], insofar as they limit coverage of extended care services or home health services.

(4) Section 1861(i) [42 USCS § 1395x(i)], insofar as it imposes a 3-day prior hospitalization requirement for coverage of extended care services.

(5) Paragraphs (1) and (9) of section 1862(a) [42 USCS § 1395y(a)], insofar as they may prevent payment for PACE program services to individuals enrolled under PACE programs.

(h) Demonstration project for for-profit entities. (1) In general. In order to demonstrate the operation of a PACE program by a private, for-profit entity, the Secretary (in close consultation with State administering agencies) shall grant waivers from the requirement under subsection (a)(3) that a PACE provider may not be a for-profit, private entity.

(2) Similar terms and conditions. (A) In general. Except as provided under subparagraph (B), and paragraph (1), the terms and conditions for operation of a PACE program by a provider under this subsection shall be the same as those for PACE providers that are nonprofit, private organizations.

(B) Numerical limitation. The number of programs for which waivers are granted under this subsection shall not exceed 10. Programs with waivers granted under this subsection shall not be counted against the numerical limitation specified in subsection (e)(1)(B).

(i) Miscellaneous provisions. Nothing in this section or section 1934 [42 USCS § 1396u-4] shall be construed as preventing a PACE provider from entering into contracts with other governmental or nongovernmental payers for the care of PACE program eligible individuals who are not eligible for benefits under part A [42 USCS §§ 1395c et seq.], or enrolled under part B [42 USCS §§ 1395j et seq.], or eligible for medical assistance under title XIX [42 USCS §§ 1396 et seq.].

(Aug. 14, 1935, Ch 531, Title XVIII, Part E [D], § 1894, as added Aug. 5, 1997, P. L. 105-33, Title IV, Subtitle I, § 4801, 111 Stat. 528; Dec. 21, 2000, P. L. 106-554, § 1(a)(6), 114 Stat. 2763; Dec. 8, 2003, P. L. 108-173, Title I, § 101(a)(1), Title II, Subtitle D, § 236(a)(2), 117 Stat. 2071, 2210; July 15, 2008, P. L. 110-275, Title I, Subtitle D, § 161(c), 122 Stat. 2569; March 23, 2010, P. L. 111-148, Title III, Subtitle C, § 3201(i), 124 Stat. 453; March 30, 2010, P. L. 111-152, Title I, Subtitle B, § 1102(a), 124 Stat. 1040.)

§ 1395fff. Prospective payment for home health services

(a) In general. Notwithstanding section 1861(v) [42 USCS § 1395x(v)], the Secretary shall provide, for portions of cost reporting periods occurring on or after October 1, 2000, for payments for home health services in accordance with a prospective payment system established by the Secretary under this section.

(b) System of prospective payment for home health services. (1) In general. The Secretary shall establish under this subsection a prospective payment system for payment for all costs of home health services. Under the system under this subsection all services covered and paid on a reasonable cost basis under the medicare home health benefit as of the date of the enactment of this section [enacted Aug. 5, 1997], including medical supplies, shall be paid for on the basis of a prospective payment amount determined under this subsection and applicable to the services involved. In implementing the system, the Secretary may provide for a transition (of not longer than 4 years) during which a portion of such payment is based on agency-specific costs, but only if such transition does not result in aggregate payments under this title [42 USCS §§ 1395 et seq.] that exceed the aggregate payments that would be made if such a transition did not occur.

(2) Unit of payment. In defining a prospec-

tive payment amount under the system under this subsection, the Secretary shall consider an appropriate unit of service and the number, type, and duration of visits provided within that unit, potential changes in the mix of services provided within that unit and their cost, and a general system design that provides for continued access to quality services.

(3) Payment basis. (A) Initial basis. (i) In general. Under such system the Secretary shall provide for computation of a standard prospective payment amount (or amounts) as follows:

(I) Such amount (or amounts) shall initially be based on the most current audited cost report data available to the Secretary and shall be computed in a manner so that the total amounts payable under the system for the 12-month period beginning on the date the Secretary implements the system shall be equal to the total amount that would have been made if the system had not been in effect and if section 1861(v)(1)(L)(ix) [42 USCS § 1395x(v)(1)(L)(ix)] had not been enacted.

(II) For the 12-month period beginning after the period described in subclause (I), such amount (or amounts) shall be equal to the amount (or amounts) determined under subclause (I), updated under subparagraph (B).

(III) Subject to clause (iii), for periods beginning after the period described in subclause (II), such amount (or amounts) shall be equal to the amount (or amounts) that would have been determined under subclause (I) that would have been made for fiscal year 2001 if the system had not been in effect and if section 1861(v)(1)(L)(ix) [42 USCS § 1395x(v)(1)(L)(ix)] had not been enacted but if the reduction in limits described in clause (ii) had been in effect, updated under subparagraph (B).

Each such amount shall be standardized in a manner that eliminates the effect of variations in relative case mix and area wage adjustments among different home health agencies in a budget neutral manner consistent with the case mix and wage level adjustments provided under paragraph (4)(A). Under the system, the Secretary may recognize regional differences or differences based upon whether or not the services or agency are in an urbanized area.

(ii) Reduction. The reduction described in this clause is a reduction by 15 percent in the cost limits and per beneficiary limits described in section 1861(v)(1)(L) [42 USCS § 1395x(v)(1)(L)], as those limits are in effect on September 30, 2000.

(iii) Adjustment for 2014 and subsequent years. (I) In general. Subject to subclause (II), for 2014 and subsequent years, the amount (or amounts) that would otherwise be applicable under clause (i)(III) shall be adjusted by a percentage determined appropriate by the Secretary to reflect such factors as changes in the number of visits in an episode, the mix of services in an episode, the level of intensity of services in an episode, the average cost of providing care per episode, and other factors that the Secretary considers to be relevant. In conducting the analysis under the preceding sentence, the Secretary may consider differences between hospital-based and freestanding agencies, between for-profit and nonprofit agencies, and between the resource costs of urban and rural agencies. Such adjustment shall be made before the update under subparagraph (B) is applied for the year.

(II) Transition. The Secretary shall provide for a 4-year phase-in (in equal increments) of the adjustment under subclause (I), with such adjustment being fully implemented for 2017. During each year of such phase-in, the amount of any adjustment under subclause (I) for the year may not exceed 3.5 percent of the amount (or amounts) applicable under clause (i)(III) as of the date of enactment of the Patient Protection and Affordable Care Act [enacted March 23, 2010].

(B) Annual update. (i) In general. The standard prospective payment amount (or amounts) shall be adjusted for fiscal year 2002 and for fiscal year 2003 and for each subsequent year (beginning with 2004) in a prospective manner specified by the Secretary by the home health applicable increase percentage (as defined in clause (ii)) applicable to the fiscal year or year involved.

(ii) Home health applicable increase percentage. For purposes of this subparagraph, the term "home health applicable increase percentage" means, with respect to—

(I) each of fiscal years 2002 and 2003, the home health market basket percentage increase (as defined in clause (iii)) minus 1.1 percentage points;

(II) for the last calendar quarter of 2003 and the first calendar quarter of 2004, the home health market basket percentage increase;

(III) the last 3 calendar quarters of 2004, and all of 2005 the home health market basket percentage increase minus 0.8 percentage points;

(IV) 2006, 0 percent; and

(V) any subsequent year, subject to clauses (v) and (vi), the home health market basket percentage increase.

(iii) Home health market basket percentage

increase. For purposes of this subsection, the term "home health market basket percentage increase" means, with respect to a fiscal year or year, a percentage (estimated by the Secretary before the beginning of the fiscal year or year) determined and applied with respect to the mix of goods and services included in home health services in the same manner as the market basket percentage increase under section 1886(b)(3)(B)(iii) [42 USCS § 1395ww(b)(3)(iii)] is determined and applied to the mix of goods and services comprising inpatient hospital services for the fiscal year or year.

(iv) Adjustment for case mix changes. Insofar as the Secretary determines that the adjustments under paragraph (4)(A)(i) for a previous fiscal year or year (or estimates that such adjustments for a future fiscal year or year) did (or are likely to) result in a change in aggregate payments under this subsection during the fiscal year or year that are a result of changes in the coding or classification of different units of services that do not reflect real changes in case mix, the Secretary may adjust the standard prospective payment amount (or amounts) under paragraph (3) for subsequent fiscal years or years so as to eliminate the effect of such coding or classification changes.

(v) Adjustment if quality data not submitted. (I) Adjustment. For purposes of clause (ii)(V), for 2007 and each subsequent year, in the case of a home health agency that does not submit data to the Secretary in accordance with subclause (II) with respect to such a year, the home health market basket percentage increase applicable under such clause for such year shall be reduced by 2 percentage points. Such reduction shall apply only with respect to the year involved, and the Secretary shall not take into account such reduction in computing the prospective payment amount under this section for a subsequent year, and the Medicare Payment Advisory Commission shall carry out the requirements under section 5201(d) of the Deficit Reduction Act of 2005 [unclassified].

(II) Submission of quality data. For 2007 and each subsequent year, each home health agency shall submit to the Secretary such data that the Secretary determines are appropriate for the measurement of health care quality. Such data shall be submitted in a form and manner, and at a time, specified by the Secretary for purposes of this clause.

(III) Public availability of data submitted. The Secretary shall establish procedures for making data submitted under subclause (II) available to the public. Such procedures shall ensure that a home health agency has the opportunity to review the data that is to be made public with respect to the agency prior to such data being made public.

(vi) Adjustments. After determining the home health market basket percentage increase under clause (iii), and after application of clause (v), the Secretary shall reduce such percentage—

(I) for 2015 and each subsequent year, by the productivity adjustment described in section 1886(b)(3)(B)(xi)(II) [42 USCS § 1395ww(b)(3)(B)(xi)(II)]; and

(II) for each of 2011, 2012, and 2013, by 1 percentage point. The application of this clause may result in the home health market basket percentage increase under clause (iii) being less than 0.0 for a year, and may result in payment rates under the system under this subsection for a year being less than such payment rates for the preceding year.

(C) Adjustment for outliers. The Secretary shall reduce the standard prospective payment amount (or amounts) under this paragraph applicable to home health services furnished during a period by such proportion as will result in an aggregate reduction in payments for the period equal to 5 percent of the total payments estimated to be made based on the prospective payment system under this subsection for the period.

(4) Payment computation. (A) In general. The payment amount for a unit of home health services shall be the applicable standard prospective payment amount adjusted as follows:

(i) Case mix adjustment. The amount shall be adjusted by an appropriate case mix adjustment factor (established under subparagraph (B)).

(ii) Area wage adjustment. The portion of such amount that the Secretary estimates to be attributable to wages and wage-related costs shall be adjusted for geographic differences in such costs by an area wage adjustment factor (established under subparagraph (C)) for the area in which the services are furnished or such other area as the Secretary may specify.

(B) Establishment of case mix adjustment factors. The Secretary shall establish appropriate case mix adjustment factors for home health services in a manner that explains a significant amount of the variation in cost among different units of services.

(C) Establishment of area wage adjustment factors. The Secretary shall establish area wage adjustment factors that reflect the relative level of wages and wage-related costs applicable to the furnishing of home health services in a geographic area compared to the national average applicable level. Such factors may be the factors used by the Secretary for purposes of section 1886(d)(3)(E) [42 USCS § 1395ww(d)(3)(E)].

(5) Outliers. (A) In general. Subject to subparagraph (B), the Secretary may provide for an addition or adjustment to the payment amount otherwise made in the case of outliers because of unusual variations in the type or amount of medically necessary care. The total amount of the additional payments or payment adjustments made under this paragraph with respect to a fiscal year or year may not exceed 2.5 percent of the total payments projected or estimated to be made based on the prospective payment system under this subsection in that year.

(B) Program specific outlier cap. The estimated total amount of additional payments or payment adjustments made under subparagraph (A) with respect to a home health agency for a year (beginning with 2011) may not exceed an amount equal to 10 percent of the estimated total amount of payments made under this section (without regard to this paragraph) with respect to the home health agency for the year.

(6) Proration of prospective payment amounts. If a beneficiary elects to transfer to, or receive services from, another home health agency within the period covered by the prospective payment amount, the payment shall be prorated between the home health agencies involved.

(c) Requirements for payment information. With respect to home health services furnished on or after October 1, 1998, no claim for such a service may be paid under this title [42 USCS §§ 1395 et seq.] unless—

(1) the claim has the unique identifier (provided under section 1842(r) [42 USCS § 1395u(r)]) for the physician who prescribed the services or made the certification described in section 1814(a)(2) or 1835(a)(2)(A) [42 USCS § 1395f(a)(2) or 1395n(a)(2)]; and

(2) in the case of a service visit described in paragraph (1), (2), (3), or (4) of section 1861(m) [42 USCS § 1395x(m)], the claim contains a code (or codes) specified by the Secretary that identifies the length of time of the service visit, as measured in 15 minute increments.

(d) Study and report on the development of home health payment revisions in order to ensure access to care and payment for severity of illness. (1) In general. The Secretary of Health and Human Services (in this section referred to as the "Secretary") shall conduct a study on home health agency costs involved with providing ongoing access to care to low-income Medicare beneficiaries or beneficiaries in medically underserved areas, and in treating beneficiaries with varying levels of severity of illness. In conducting the study, the Secretary may analyze items such as the following:

(A) Methods to potentially revise the home health prospective payment system under section 1895 of the Social Security Act (42 U.S.C. 1395fff) to account for costs related to patient severity of illness or to improving beneficiary access to care, such as—

(i) payment adjustments for services that may involve additional or fewer resources;

(ii) changes to reflect resources involved with providing home health services to low-income Medicare beneficiaries or Medicare beneficiaries residing in medically underserved areas;

(iii) ways outlier payments might be revised to reflect costs of treating Medicare beneficiaries with high levels of severity of illness; and

(iv) other issues determined appropriate by the Secretary.

(B) Operational issues involved with potential implementation of potential revisions to the home health payment system, including impacts for both home health agencies and administrative and systems issues for the Centers for Medicare & Medicaid Services, and any possible payment vulnerabilities associated with implementing potential revisions.

(C) Whether additional research might be needed.

(D) Other items determined appropriate by the Secretary.

(2) Considerations. In conducting the study under paragraph (1), the Secretary may consider whether patient severity of illness and access to care could be measured by factors, such as—

(A) population density and relative patient access to care;

(B) variations in service costs for providing care to individuals who are dually eligible under the Medicare and Medicaid programs;

(C) the presence of severe or chronic diseases, which might be measured by multiple, discontinuous home health episodes;

(D) poverty status, such as evidenced by the receipt of Supplemental Security Income under title XVI of the Social Security Act [42 USCS § 1381 et seq.]; and

(E) other factors determined appropriate by the Secretary.

(3) Report. Not later than March 1, 2014, the

Secretary shall submit to Congress a report on the study conducted under paragraph (1), together with recommendations for such legislation and administrative action as the Secretary determines appropriate.

(4) Consultations. In conducting the study under paragraph (1), the Secretary shall consult with appropriate stakeholders, such as groups representing home health agencies and groups representing Medicare beneficiaries.

(5) Medicare demonstration project based on the results of the study. (A) In general. Subject to subparagraph (D), taking into account the results of the study conducted under paragraph (1), the Secretary may, as determined appropriate, provide for a demonstration project to test whether making payment adjustments for home health services under the Medicare program would substantially improve access to care for patients with high severity levels of illness or for low-income or underserved Medicare beneficiaries.

(B) Waiving budget neutrality. The Secretary shall not reduce the standard prospective payment amount (or amounts) under section 1895 of the Social Security Act (42 U.S.C. 1395fff) applicable to home health services furnished during a period to offset any increase in payments during such period resulting from the application of the payment adjustments under subparagraph (A).

(C) No effect on subsequent periods. A payment adjustment resulting from the application of subparagraph (A) for a period—

(i) shall not apply to payments for home health services under title XVIII after such period [42 USCS §§ 1395 et seq.]; and

(ii) shall not be taken into account in calculating the payment amounts applicable for such services after such period.

(D) Duration. If the Secretary determines it appropriate to conduct the demonstration project under this subsection, the Secretary shall conduct the project for a four year period beginning not later than January 1, 2015.

(E) Funding. The Secretary shall provide for the transfer from the Federal Hospital Insurance Trust Fund under section 1817 of the Social Security Act (42 U.S.C. 1395i) and the Federal Supplementary Medical Insurance Trust Fund established under section 1841 of such Act (42 U.S.C. 1395t), in such proportion as the Secretary determines appropriate, of $500,000,000 for the period of fiscal years 2015 through 2018. Such funds shall be made available for the study described in paragraph (1) and the design, implementation and evaluation of the demonstration described in this paragraph. Amounts available under this subparagraph shall be available until expended.

(F) Evaluation and report. If the Secretary determines it appropriate to conduct the demonstration project under this subsection, the Secretary shall—

(i) provide for an evaluation of the project; and

(ii) submit to Congress, by a date specified by the Secretary, a report on the project.

(G) Administration. Chapter 35 of title 44, United States Code [44 USCS §§ 3501 et seq.], shall not apply with respect to this subsection.

(e) Construction related to home health services. (1) Telecommunications. Nothing in this section shall be construed as preventing a home health agency furnishing a home health unit of service for which payment is made under the prospective payment system established by this section for such units of service from furnishing services via a telecommunication system if such services—

(A) do not substitute for in-person home health services ordered as part of a plan of care certified by a physician pursuant to section 1814(a)(2)(C) or 1835(a)(2)(A) [42 USCS § 1395f(a)(2)(C) or 1395n(a)(2)(A)]; and

(B) are not considered a home health visit for purposes of eligibility or payment under this title [42 USCS §§ 1395 et seq.].

(2) Physician certification. Nothing in this section shall be construed as waiving the requirement for a physician certification under section 1814(a)(2)(C) or 1835(a)(2)(A) of such Act (42 U.S.C. 1395f(a)(2)(C), 1395n(a)(2)(A)) for the payment for home health services, whether or not furnished via a telecommunications system.

(Aug. 14, 1935, ch 531, Title XVIII, Part E [D], § 1895, as added Aug. 5, 1997, P. L. 105-33, Title IV, Subtitle G, Ch 1, Subch A, § 4603(a), 111 Stat. 467; Oct. 21, 1998, P. L. 105-277, Div J, Title V, Subtitle A, § 5101(c)(1), (d)(2), 112 Stat. 2681-914; Nov. 29, 1999, P. L. 106-113, Div B, § 1000(a)(6), 113 Stat. 1536; Dec. 21, 2000, P. L. 106-554, § 1(a)(6), 114 Stat. 2763; Dec. 8, 2003, P. L. 108-173, Title I, § 101(a)(1), Title VII, Subtitle A, § 701, 117 Stat. 2071, 2334; Feb. 8, 2006, P. L. 109-171, Title V, Subtitle C, § 5201(a), (c), 120 Stat. 46; March 23, 2010, P. L. 111-148, Title III, Subtitle B, Part III, § 3131(a)(1), (b), Subtitle E, § 3401(e), Title X, Subtitle C, § 10315(a), 10319(d), 124 Stat. 427, 428, 483, 944, 949.)

HISTORY; ANCILLARY LAWS AND DIRECTIVES

Other provisions:

One-year increase for home health services furnished in a rural area. Act Dec. 8, 2003, P. L. 108-173, Title IV, Subtitle C, § 421, 117 Stat. 2283; Feb. 8, 2006, P. L. 109-171, Title V, Subtitle C, § 5201(b), 120 Stat. 46; March 23, 2010, P. L. 111-148, Title III, Subtitle B, Part III, § 3131(c), 124 Stat. 428, provides:

"(a) In general. With respect to episodes and visits ending on or after April 1, 2004, and before April 1, 2005, episodes and visits beginning on or after January 1, 2006, and before January 1, 2007, and episodes and visits ending on or after April 1, 2010, and before January 1, 2016, in the case of home health services furnished in a rural area (as defined in section 1886(d)(2)(D) of the Social Security Act (42 U.S.C. 1395ww(d)(2)(D))), the Secretary shall increase the payment amount otherwise made under section 1895 of such Act (42 U.S.C. 1395fff) for such services by 5 percent (or, in the case of episodes and visits ending on or after April 1, 2010, and before January 1, 2016, 3 percent).

"(b) Waiving budget neutrality. The Secretary shall not reduce the standard prospective payment amount (or amounts) under section 1895 of the Social Security Act (42 U.S.C. 1395fff) applicable to home health services furnished during a period to offset the increase in payments resulting from the application of subsection (a).

"(c) No effect on subsequent periods. The payment increase provided under subsection (a) for a period under such subsection—

"(1) shall not apply to episodes and visits ending after such period; and

"(2) shall not be taken into account in calculating the payment amounts applicable for episodes and visits occurring after such period.".

Study and report on the development of home health payment revisions in order to ensure access to care and payment for severity of illness. Act March 23, 2010, P. L. 111-148, Title III, Subtitle B, Part III, § 3131(d), Title X, Subtitle C, § 10315(b), 124 Stat. 429, 944, provides:

"(1) In general. The Secretary of Health and Human Services (in this section referred to as the 'Secretary') shall conduct a study on home health agency costs involved with providing ongoing access to care to low-income Medicare beneficiaries or beneficiaries in medically underserved areas, and in treating beneficiaries with varying levels of severity of illness. In conducting the study, the Secretary may analyze items such as the following:

"(A) Methods to potentially revise the home health prospective payment system under section 1895 of the Social Security Act (42 U.S.C. 1395fff) to account for costs related to patient severity of illness or to improving beneficiary access to care, such as—

"(i) payment adjustments for services that may involve additional or fewer resources;

"(ii) changes to reflect resources involved with providing home health services to low-income Medicare beneficiaries or Medicare beneficiaries residing in medically underserved areas;

"(iii) ways outlier payments might be revised to reflect costs of treating Medicare beneficiaries with high levels of severity of illness; and

"(iv) other issues determined appropriate by the Secretary.

"(B) Operational issues involved with potential implementation of potential revisions to the home health payment system, including impacts for both home health agencies and administrative and systems issues for the Centers for Medicare & Medicaid Services, and any possible payment vulnerabilities associated with implementing potential revisions.

"(C) Whether additional research might be needed.

"(D) Other items determined appropriate by the Secretary.

"(2) Considerations. In conducting the study under paragraph (1), the Secretary may consider whether patient severity of illness and access to care could be measured by factors, such as—

"(A) population density and relative patient access to care;

"(B) variations in service costs for providing care to individuals who are dually eligible under the Medicare and Medicaid programs;

"(C) the presence of severe or chronic diseases, which might be measured by multiple, discontinuous home health episodes;

"(D) poverty status, such as evidenced by the receipt of Supplemental Security Income under title XVI of the Social Security Act [42 USCS §§ 1381 et seq.]; and

"(E) other factors determined appropriate by the Secretary.

"(3) Report. Not later than March 1, 2014, the Secretary shall submit to Congress a report on the study conducted under paragraph (1), together with recommendations for such legislation and administrative action as the Secretary determines appropriate.

"(4) Consultations. In conducting the study under paragraph (1), the Secretary shall consult with appropriate stakeholders, such as groups representing home health agencies and groups representing Medicare beneficiaries.

"(5) Medicare demonstration project based on the results of the study. (A) In general. Subject to subparagraph (D), taking into account the results of the study conducted under paragraph (1), the Secretary may, as determined appropriate, provide for a demonstration project to test whether making payment adjustments for home health services under the Medicare program would substantially improve access to care for patients with high severity levels of illness or for low-income or underserved Medicare beneficiaries.

"(B) Waiving budget neutrality. The Secretary shall not reduce the standard prospective payment amount (or amounts) under section 1895 of the Social Security Act (42 U.S.C. 1395fff) applicable to home health services furnished during a period to offset any increase in payments during such period resulting from the application of the payment adjustments under subparagraph (A).

"(C) No effect on subsequent periods. A payment adjustment resulting from the application of subparagraph (A) for a period—

"(i) shall not apply to payments for home health services under title XVIII [42 USCS §§ 1395 et seq.] after such period; and

"(ii) shall not be taken into account in calculating the payment amounts applicable for such services after such period.

"(D) Duration. If the Secretary determines it appropriate to conduct the demonstration project under this subsection, the Secretary shall conduct the project for a four year period beginning not later than January 1, 2015.

"(E) Funding. The Secretary shall provide for the transfer from the Federal Hospital Insurance Trust Fund under section 1817 of the Social Security Act (42 U.S.C. 1395i) and the Federal Supplementary Medical Insurance Trust Fund established under section 1841 of such Act (42 U.S.C. 1395t), in such proportion as the Secretary determines appropriate, of $500,000,000 for the period of fiscal years 2015 through 2018. Such funds shall be made available for the study described in paragraph (1) and the design, implementation and evaluation of the demonstration described in this paragraph. Amounts available under this subparagraph shall be available until expended.

"(F) Evaluation and report. If the Secretary determines it appropriate to conduct the demonstration project under this subsection, the Secretary shall—

"(i) provide for an evaluation of the project; and

"(ii) submit to Congress, by a date specified by the Secretary, a report on the project.

"(G) Administration. Chapter 35 of title 44, United States Code [44 USCS §§ 3501 et seq.], shall not apply with respect to this subsection.".

§ 1395iii. Medicare Improvement Fund

(a) Establishment. The Secretary shall establish under this title [42 USCS §§ 1395 et seq.] a Medicare Improvement Fund (in this section referred to as the "Fund") which shall be available to the Secretary to make improvements under the original medicare fee-for-service program under parts A and B [42 USCS §§ 1395c et seq. and 1395j et seq.] for individuals entitled to, or enrolled for, benefits under part A [42 USCS §§ 1395c et seq.] or enrolled under part B [42 USCS §§ 1395j et seq.] including, but not limited to, an increase in the conversion factor under section 1848(d) [42 USCS § 1395w-4] to address, in whole or in part, any projected shortfall in the conversion factor for 2014 relative to the conversion factor for 2008 and adjustments to payments for items and services furnished by providers of services and suppliers under such original medicare fee-for-service program.

(b) Funding. (1) In general. There shall be available to the Fund, for expenditures from the Fund for services furnished during—

(A) fiscal year 2014, $0;

(B) fiscal year 2015, $550,000,000; and

(C) fiscal year 2020 and each subsequent fiscal year, the Secretary's estimate, as of July 1 of the fiscal year, of the aggregate reduction in expenditures under this title during the preceding fiscal year directly resulting from the reduction in payment amounts under sections 1848(a)(7), 1853(l)(4), 1853(m)(4), and 1886(b)(3)(B)(ix) [42 USCS §§ 1395w-4(a)(7), 1395w-23(l)(4), 1395w-23(m)(4), 1395ww(b)(3)(B)(ix)].

(2) Payment from trust funds. The amount specified under paragraph (1) shall be available to the Fund, as expenditures are made from the Fund, from the Federal Hospital Insurance Trust Fund and the Federal Supplementary Medical Insurance Trust Fund in such proportion as the Secretary determines appropriate.

(3) Funding limitation. Amounts in the Fund shall be available in advance of appropriations but only if the total amount obligated from the Fund does not exceed the amount available to the Fund under paragraph (1). The Secretary may obligate funds from the Fund only if the Secretary determines (and the Chief Actuary of the Centers for Medicare & Medicaid Services and the appropriate budget officer certify) that there are available in the Fund sufficient amounts to cover all such obligations incurred consistent with the previous sentence.

(4) No effect on payments in subsequent years. In the case that expenditures from the Fund are applied to, or otherwise affect, a payment rate for an item or service under this title [42 USCS §§ 1395 et seq.] for a year, the payment rate for such item or service shall be computed for a subsequent year as if such application or effect had never occurred.

(Aug. 14, 1935, ch 531, Title XVIII, Subtitle E, § 1898, as added June 30, 2008, P. L. 110-252, Title VII, § 7002(a), 122 Stat. 2394; July 15, 2008, P. L. 110-275, Title I, Subtitle F, § 188(a)(2)(B), 122 Stat. 2589; Oct. 8, 2008, P. L. 110-379, § 6, 122 Stat. 4079; Feb. 17, 2009, P. L. 111-5, Div B, Title IV, Subtitle A, § 4103(b), 123 Stat. 487; Dec. 19, 2009, P. L. 111-119, Div B, § 1011(b), 123 Stat. 3474; March 23, 2010, P. L. 111-148, Title III, Subtitle B, Part I, § 3112, 124 Stat. 421.)

§ 1395jjj. Shared savings program

(a) Establishment. (1) In general. Not later than January 1, 2012, the Secretary shall establish a shared savings program (in this section referred to as the "program") that promotes accountability for a patient population and coordinates items and services under parts A and B [42 USCS §§ 1395c et seq. and 1395j et seq.], and encourages investment in infrastructure and redesigned care processes for high quality and efficient service delivery. Under such program—

(A) groups of providers of services and suppliers meeting criteria specified by the Secretary may work together to manage and coordinate care for Medicare fee-for-service beneficiaries through an accountable care organization (referred to in this section as an "ACO"); and

(B) ACOs that meet quality performance standards established by the Secretary are eligible to receive payments for shared savings under subsection (d)(2).

(2) [Not enacted]

(b) Eligible ACOs. (1) In general. Subject

to the succeeding provisions of this subsection, as determined appropriate by the Secretary, the following groups of providers of services and suppliers which have established a mechanism for shared governance are eligible to participate as ACOs under the program under this section:

(A) ACO professionals in group practice arrangements.

(B) Networks of individual practices of ACO professionals.

(C) Partnerships or joint venture arrangements between hospitals and ACO professionals.

(D) Hospitals employing ACO professionals.

(E) Such other groups of providers of services and suppliers as the Secretary determines appropriate.

(2) Requirements. An ACO shall meet the following requirements:

(A) The ACO shall be willing to become accountable for the quality, cost, and overall care of the Medicare fee-for-service beneficiaries assigned to it.

(B) The ACO shall enter into an agreement with the Secretary to participate in the program for not less than a 3-year period (referred to in this section as the "agreement period").

(C) The ACO shall have a formal legal structure that would allow the organization to receive and distribute payments for shared savings under subsection (d)(2) to participating providers of services and suppliers.

(D) The ACO shall include primary care ACO professionals that are sufficient for the number of Medicare fee-for-service beneficiaries assigned to the ACO under subsection (c). At a minimum, the ACO shall have at least 5,000 such beneficiaries assigned to it under subsection (c) in order to be eligible to participate in the ACO program.

(E) The ACO shall provide the Secretary with such information regarding ACO professionals participating in the ACO as the Secretary determines necessary to support the assignment of Medicare fee-for-service beneficiaries to an ACO, the implementation of quality and other reporting requirements under paragraph (3), and the determination of payments for shared savings under subsection (d)(2).

(F) The ACO shall have in place a leadership and management structure that includes clinical and administrative systems.

(G) The ACO shall define processes to promote evidence-based medicine and patient engagement, report on quality and cost measures, and coordinate care, such as through the use of telehealth, remote patient monitoring, and other such enabling technologies.

(H) The ACO shall demonstrate to the Secretary that it meets patient-centeredness criteria specified by the Secretary, such as the use of patient and caregiver assessments or the use of individualized care plans.

(3) Quality and other reporting requirements. (A) In general. The Secretary shall determine appropriate measures to assess the quality of care furnished by the ACO, such as measures of—

(i) clinical processes and outcomes;

(ii) patient and, where practicable, caregiver experience of care; and

(iii) utilization (such as rates of hospital admissions for ambulatory care sensitive conditions).

(B) Reporting requirements. An ACO shall submit data in a form and manner specified by the Secretary on measures the Secretary determines necessary for the ACO to report in order to evaluate the quality of care furnished by the ACO. Such data may include care transitions across health care settings, including hospital discharge planning and post-hospital discharge follow-up by ACO professionals, as the Secretary determines appropriate.

(C) Quality performance standards. The Secretary shall establish quality performance standards to assess the quality of care furnished by ACOs. The Secretary shall seek to improve the quality of care furnished by ACOs over time by specifying higher standards, new measures, or both for purposes of assessing such quality of care.

(D) Other reporting requirements. The Secretary may, as the Secretary determines appropriate, incorporate reporting requirements and incentive payments related to the physician quality reporting initiative (PQRI) under section 1848 [42 USCS § 1395w-4], including such requirements and such payments related to electronic prescribing, electronic health records, and other similar initiatives under section 1848 [42 USCS § 1395w-4], and may use alternative criteria than would otherwise apply under such section for determining whether to make such payments. The incentive payments described in the preceding sentence shall not be taken into consideration when calculating any payments otherwise made under subsection (d).

(4) No duplication in participation in shared savings programs. A provider of services or supplier that participates in any of the following shall not be eligible to participate in an ACO under this section:

(A) A model tested or expanded under section 1115A [42 USCS § 1315a] that involves shared savings under this title [42 USCS §§ 1395 et seq.], or any other program or demonstration project that involves such shared savings.

(B) The independence at home medical practice pilot program under section 1866E [42 USCS § 1395cc-5].

(c) Assignment of Medicare fee-for-service beneficiaries to ACOs. The Secretary shall determine an appropriate method to assign Medicare fee-for-service beneficiaries to an ACO based on their utilization of primary care services provided under this title by an ACO professional described in subsection (h)(1)(A).

(d) Payments and treatment of savings. (1) Payments. (A) In general. Under the program, subject to paragraph (3), payments shall continue to be made to providers of services and suppliers participating in an ACO under the original Medicare fee-for-service program under parts A and B in the same manner as they would otherwise be made except that a participating ACO is eligible to receive payment for shared savings under paragraph (2) if—

(i) the ACO meets quality performance standards established by the Secretary under subsection (b)(3); and

(ii) the ACO meets the requirement under subparagraph (B)(i).

(B) Savings requirement and benchmark. (i) Determining savings. In each year of the agreement period, an ACO shall be eligible to receive payment for shared savings under paragraph (2) only if the estimated average per capita Medicare expenditures under the ACO for Medicare fee-for-service beneficiaries for parts A and B services, adjusted for beneficiary characteristics, is at least the percent specified by the Secretary below the applicable benchmark under clause (ii). The Secretary shall determine the appropriate percent described in the preceding sentence to account for normal variation in expenditures under this title, based upon the number of Medicare fee-for-service beneficiaries assigned to an ACO.

(ii) Establish and update benchmark. The Secretary shall estimate a benchmark for each agreement period for each ACO using the most recent available 3 years of per-beneficiary expenditures for parts A and B services for Medicare fee-for-service beneficiaries assigned to the ACO. Such benchmark shall be adjusted for beneficiary characteristics and such other factors as the Secretary determines appropriate and updated by the projected absolute amount of growth in national per capita expenditures for parts A and B services under the original Medicare fee-for-service program, as estimated by the Secretary. Such benchmark shall be reset at the start of each agreement period.

(2) Payments for shared savings. Subject to performance with respect to the quality performance standards established by the Secretary under subsection (b)(3), if an ACO meets the requirements under paragraph (1), a percent (as determined appropriate by the Secretary) of the difference between such estimated average per capita Medicare expenditures in a year, adjusted for beneficiary characteristics, under the ACO and such benchmark for the ACO may be paid to the ACO as shared savings and the remainder of such difference shall be retained by the program under this title. The Secretary shall establish limits on the total amount of shared savings that may be paid to an ACO under this paragraph.

(3) Monitoring avoidance of at-risk patients. If the Secretary determines that an ACO has taken steps to avoid patients at risk in order to reduce the likelihood of increasing costs to the ACO the Secretary may impose an appropriate sanction on the ACO, including termination from the program.

(4) Termination. The Secretary may terminate an agreement with an ACO if it does not meet the quality performance standards established by the Secretary under subsection (b)(3).

(e) Administration. Chapter 35 of title 44, United States Code [44 USCS §§ 3501 et seq.], shall not apply to the program.

(f) Waiver authority. The Secretary may waive such requirements of sections 1128A and 1128B [42 USCS §§ 1320a-7a and 1320a-7b] and title XVIII of this Act [42 USCS §§ 1395 et seq.] as may be necessary to carry out the provisions of this section.

(g) Limitations on review. There shall be no administrative or judicial review under section 1869 [42 USCS § 1395ff], section 1878 [42 USCS § 1395oo], or otherwise of—

(1) the specification of criteria under subsection (a)(1)(B);

(2) the assessment of the quality of care furnished by an ACO and the establishment of performance standards under subsection (b)(3);

(3) the assignment of Medicare fee-for-service beneficiaries to an ACO under subsection (c);

(4) the determination of whether an ACO is eligible for shared savings under subsection (d)(2) and the amount of such shared savings, including the determination of the estimated average per capita Medicare expenditures un-

der the ACO for Medicare fee-for-service beneficiaries assigned to the ACO and the average benchmark for the ACO under subsection (d)(1)(B);

(5) the percent of shared savings specified by the Secretary under subsection (d)(2) and any limit on the total amount of shared savings established by the Secretary under such subsection; and

(6) the termination of an ACO under subsection (d)(4).

(h) Definitions. In this section:

(1) ACO professional. The term "ACO professional" means—

(A) a physician (as defined in section 1861(r)(1) [42 USCS § 1395x(r)(1)]); and

(B) a practitioner described in section 1842(b)(18)(C)(i) [42 USCS § 1395u(b)(18)(C)(i)].

(2) Hospital. The term "hospital" means a subsection (d) hospital (as defined in section 1886(d)(1)(B) [42 USCS § 1395ww(d)(1)(B)]).

(3) Medicare fee-for-service beneficiary. The term "Medicare fee-for-service beneficiary" means an individual who is enrolled in the original Medicare fee-for-service program under parts A and B [42 USCS §§ 1395c et seq. and 1395j et seq.] and is not enrolled in an MA plan under part C [42 USCS §§ 1395w-21 et seq.], an eligible organization under section 1876 [42 USCS § 1395mm], or a PACE program under section 1894 [42 USCS § 1395eee].

(i) Option to use other payment models. (1) In general. If the Secretary determines appropriate, the Secretary may use any of the payment models described in paragraph (2) or (3) for making payments under the program rather than the payment model described in subsection (d).

(2) Partial capitation model. (A) In general. Subject to subparagraph (B), a model described in this paragraph is a partial capitation model in which an ACO is at financial risk for some, but not all, of the items and services covered under parts A and B, such as at risk for some or all physicians' services or all items and services under part B [42 USCS §§ 1395j et seq.]. The Secretary may limit a partial capitation model to ACOs that are highly integrated systems of care and to ACOs capable of bearing risk, as determined to be appropriate by the Secretary.

(B) No additional program expenditures. Payments to an ACO for items and services under this title for beneficiaries for a year under the partial capitation model shall be established in a manner that does not result in spending more for such ACO for such beneficiaries than would otherwise be expended for such ACO for such beneficiaries for such year if the model were not implemented, as estimated by the Secretary.

(3) Other payment models. (A) In general. Subject to subparagraph (B), a model described in this paragraph is any payment model that the Secretary determines will improve the quality and efficiency of items and services furnished under this title.

(B) No additional program expenditures. Subparagraph (B) of paragraph (2) shall apply to a payment model under subparagraph (A) in a similar manner as such subparagraph (B) applies to the payment model under paragraph (2).

(j) Involvement in private payer and other third party arrangements. The Secretary may give preference to ACOs who are participating in similar arrangements with other payers.

(k) Treatment of physician group practice demonstration. During the period beginning on the date of the enactment of this section and ending on the date the program is established, the Secretary may enter into an agreement with an ACO under the demonstration under section 1866A [42 USCS § 1395cc-1], subject to rebasing and other modifications deemed appropriate by the Secretary.

(Aug. 14, 1935, ch 531, Title XVIII, Subtitle E, § 1899, as added and amended March 23, 2010, P. L. 111-148, Title III, Subtitle A, Part III, § 3022, Title X, Subtitle C, § 10307, 124 Stat. 395, 940.)

§ 1395kkk. Independent Medicare Advisory Board [Independent Payment Advisory Board]

(a) Establishment. There is established an independent board to be known as the "Independent Medicare Advisory Board [Independent Payment Advisory Board]".

(b) Purpose. It is the purpose of this section to, in accordance with the following provisions of this section, reduce the per capita rate of growth in Medicare spending—

(1) by requiring the Chief Actuary of the Centers for Medicare & Medicaid Services to determine in each year to which this section applies (in this section referred to as "a determination year") the projected per capita growth rate under Medicare for the second year following the determination year (in this section referred to as "an implementation year");

(2) if the projection for the implementation year exceeds the target growth rate for that year, by requiring the Board to develop and submit during the first year following the de-

termination year (in this section referred to as "a proposal year") a proposal containing recommendations to reduce the Medicare per capita growth rate to the extent required by this section; and

(3) by requiring the Secretary to implement such proposals unless Congress enacts legislation pursuant to this section.

(c) Board proposals. (1) Development. (A) In general. The Board shall develop detailed and specific proposals related to the Medicare program in accordance with the succeeding provisions of this section.

(B) Advisory reports. Beginning January 15, 2014, the Board may develop and submit to Congress advisory reports on matters related to the Medicare program, regardless of whether or not the Board submitted a proposal for such year. Such a report may, for years prior to 2020, include recommendations regarding improvements to payment systems for providers of services and suppliers who are not otherwise subject to the scope of the Board's recommendations in a proposal under this section. Any advisory report submitted under this subparagraph shall not be subject to the rules for congressional consideration under subsection (d). In any year (beginning with 2014) that the Board is not required to submit a proposal under this section, the Board shall submit to Congress an advisory report on matters related to the Medicare program.

(2) Proposals. (A) Requirements. Each proposal submitted under this section in a proposal year shall meet each of the following requirements:

(i) If the Chief Actuary of the Centers for Medicare & Medicaid Services has made a determination under paragraph (7)(A) in the determination year, the proposal shall include recommendations so that the proposal as a whole (after taking into account recommendations under clause (v)) will result in a net reduction in total Medicare program spending in the implementation year that is at least equal to the applicable savings target established under paragraph (7)(B) for such implementation year. In determining whether a proposal meets the requirement of the preceding sentence, reductions in Medicare program spending during the 3-month period immediately preceding the implementation year shall be counted to the extent that such reductions are a result of the implementation of recommendations contained in the proposal for a change in the payment rate for an item or service that was effective during such period pursuant to subsection (e)(2)(A).

(ii) The proposal shall not include any recommendation to ration health care, raise revenues or Medicare beneficiary premiums under section 1818, 1818A, or 1839 [42 USCS § 1395i-2, 1395i-2a, or 1395r], increase Medicare beneficiary cost-sharing (including deductibles, coinsurance, and copayments), or otherwise restrict benefits or modify eligibility criteria.

(iii) In the case of proposals submitted prior to December 31, 2018, the proposal shall not include any recommendation that would reduce payment rates for items and services furnished, prior to December 31, 2019, by providers of services (as defined in section 1861(u) [42 USCS § 1395x(u)]) and suppliers (as defined in section 1861(d) [42 USCS § 1395x(d)]) scheduled, pursuant to the amendments made by section 3401 of the Patient Protection and Affordable Care Act, to receive a reduction to the inflationary payment updates of such providers of services and suppliers in excess of a reduction due to productivity in a year in which such recommendations would take effect.

(iv) As appropriate, the proposal shall include recommendations to reduce Medicare payments under parts C and D [42 USCS §§ 1395w-21 et seq. and 1395w-101 et seq.], such as reductions in direct subsidy payments to Medicare Advantage and prescription drug plans specified under paragraph (1) and (2) of section 1860D-15(a) [42 USCS § 1395w-115(a)] that are related to administrative expenses (including profits) for basic coverage, denying high bids or removing high bids for prescription drug coverage from the calculation of the national average monthly bid amount under section 1860D-13(a)(4) [42 USCS § 1395w-113(a)(4)], and reductions in payments to Medicare Advantage plans under clauses (i) and (ii) of section 1853(a)(1)(B) [42 USCS § 1395w-23(a)(1)(B)] that are related to administrative expenses (including profits) and performance bonuses for Medicare Advantage plans under section 1853(n) [42 USCS § 1395w-23(n)]. Any such recommendation shall not affect the base beneficiary premium percentage specified under 1860D-13(a) [42 USCS § 1395w-113(a)] or the full premium subsidy under section 1860D-14(a) [42 USCS § 1395w-114(a)].

(v) The proposal shall include recommendations with respect to administrative funding for the Secretary to carry out the recommendations contained in the proposal.

(vi) The proposal shall only include recommendations related to the Medicare program.

(vii) If the Chief Actuary of the Centers for

Medicare & Medicaid Services has made a determination described in subsection (e)(3)(B)(i)(II) in the determination year, the proposal shall be designed to help reduce the growth rate described in paragraph (8) while maintaining or enhancing beneficiary access to quality care under this title [42 USCS §§ 1395 et seq.].

(B) Additional considerations. In developing and submitting each proposal under this section in a proposal year, the Board shall, to the extent feasible—

(i) give priority to recommendations that extend Medicare solvency;

(ii) include recommendations that—

(I) improve the health care delivery system and health outcomes, including by promoting integrated care, care coordination, prevention and wellness, and quality and efficiency improvement; and

(II) protect and improve Medicare beneficiaries' access to necessary and evidence-based items and services, including in rural and frontier areas;

(iii) include recommendations that target reductions in Medicare program spending to sources of excess cost growth;

(iv) consider the effects on Medicare beneficiaries of changes in payments to providers of services (as defined in section 1861(u) [42 USCS § 1395x(u)]) and suppliers (as defined in section 1861(d) [42 USCS § 1395x(d)]);

(v) consider the effects of the recommendations on providers of services and suppliers with actual or projected negative cost margins or payment updates;

(vi) consider the unique needs of Medicare beneficiaries who are dually eligible for Medicare and the Medicaid program under title XIX [42 USCS §§ 1396 et seq.]; and

(vii) take into account the data and findings contained in the annual reports under subsection (n) in order to develop proposals that can most effectively promote the delivery of efficient, high quality care to Medicare beneficiaries.

(C) No increase in total Medicare program spending. Each proposal submitted under this section shall be designed in such a manner that implementation of the recommendations contained in the proposal would not be expected to result, over the 10-year period starting with the implementation year, in any increase in the total amount of net Medicare program spending relative to the total amount of net Medicare program spending that would have occurred absent such implementation.

(D) Consultation with MedPAC. The Board shall submit a draft copy of each proposal to be submitted under this section to the Medicare Payment Advisory Commission established under section 1805 for its review. The Board shall submit such draft copy by not later than September 1 of the determination year.

(E) Review and comment by the Secretary. The Board shall submit a draft copy of each proposal to be submitted to Congress under this section to the Secretary for the Secretary's review and comment. The Board shall submit such draft copy by not later than September 1 of the determination year. Not later than March 1 of the submission year, the Secretary shall submit a report to Congress on the results of such review, unless the Secretary submits a proposal under paragraph (5)(A) in that year.

(F) Consultations. In carrying out its duties under this section, the Board shall engage in regular consultations with the Medicaid and CHIP Payment and Access Commission under section 1900 [42 USCS § 1396].

(3) Submission of board proposal to Congress and the President. (A) In general. (i) In general. Except as provided in clause (ii) and subsection (f)(3)(B), the Board shall submit a proposal under this section to Congress and the President on January 15 of each year (beginning with 2014).

(ii) Exception. The Board shall not submit a proposal under clause (i) in a proposal year if the year is—

(I) a year for which the Chief Actuary of the Centers for Medicare & Medicaid Services makes a determination in the determination year under paragraph (6)(A) that the growth rate described in clause (i) of such paragraph does not exceed the growth rate described in clause (ii) of such paragraph; or

(II) a year in which the Chief Actuary of the Centers for Medicare & Medicaid Services makes a determination in the determination year that the projected percentage increase (if any) for the medical care expenditure category of the Consumer Price Index for All Urban Consumers (United States city average) for the implementation year is less than the projected percentage increase (if any) in the Consumer Price Index for All Urban Consumers (all items; United States city average) for such implementation year.

(iii) Start-up period. The Board may not submit a proposal under clause (i) prior to January 15, 2014.

(B) Required information. Each proposal submitted by the Board under subparagraph (A)(i) shall include—

(i) the recommendations described in paragraph (2)(A)(i);

(ii) an explanation of each recommendation contained in the proposal and the reasons for including such recommendation;

(iii) an actuarial opinion by the Chief Actuary of the Centers for Medicare & Medicaid Services certifying that the proposal meets the requirements of subparagraphs (A)(i) and (C) of paragraph (2);

(iv) a legislative proposal that implements the recommendations; and

(v) other information determined appropriate by the Board.

(4) Presidential submission to Congress. Upon receiving a proposal from the Secretary under paragraph (5), the President shall within 2 days submit such proposal to Congress.

(5) Contingent secretarial development of proposal. If, with respect to a proposal year, the Board is required, but fails, to submit a proposal to Congress and the President by the deadline applicable under paragraph (3)(A)(i), the Secretary shall develop a detailed and specific proposal that satisfies the requirements of subparagraphs (A) and (C) (and, to the extent feasible, subparagraph (B)) of paragraph (2) and contains the information required paragraph (3)(B)). By not later than January 25 of the year, the Secretary shall transmit—

(A) such proposal to the President; and

(B) a copy of such proposal to the Medicare Payment Advisory Commission for its review.

(6) Per capita growth rate projections by Chief Actuary. (A) In general. Subject to subsection (f)(3)(A), not later than April 30, 2013, and annually thereafter, the Chief Actuary of the Centers for Medicare & Medicaid Services shall determine in each such year whether—

(i) the projected Medicare per capita growth rate for the implementation year (as determined under subparagraph (B)); exceeds

(ii) the projected Medicare per capita target growth rate for the implementation year (as determined under subparagraph (C)).

(B) Medicare per capita growth rate. (i) In general. For purposes of this section, the Medicare per capita growth rate for an implementation year shall be calculated as the projected 5-year average (ending with such year) of the growth in Medicare program spending (calculated as the sum of per capita spending under each of parts A, B, and D [42 USCS §§ 1395c et seq., 1395j et seq., and 1395w-101 et seq.]).

(ii) Requirement. The projection under clause (i) shall—

(I) to the extent that there is projected to be a negative update to the single conversion factor applicable to payments for physicians' services under section 1848(d) [42 USCS § 1395w-4(d)] furnished in the proposal year or the implementation year, assume that such update for such services is 0 percent rather than the negative percent that would otherwise apply; and

(II) take into account any delivery system reforms or other payment changes that have been enacted or published in final rules but not yet implemented as of the making of such calculation.

(C) Medicare per capita target growth rate. For purposes of this section, the Medicare per capita target growth rate for an implementation year shall be calculated as the projected 5-year average (ending with such year) percentage increase in—

(i) with respect to a determination year that is prior to 2018, the average of the projected percentage increase (if any) in—

(I) the Consumer Price Index for All Urban Consumers (all items; United States city average); and

(II) the medical care expenditure category of the Consumer Price Index for All Urban Consumers (United States city average); and

(ii) with respect to a determination year that is after 2017, the nominal gross domestic product per capita plus 1.0 percentage point.

(7) Savings requirement. (A) In general. If, with respect to a determination year, the Chief Actuary of the Centers for Medicare & Medicaid Services makes a determination under paragraph (6)(A) that the growth rate described in clause (i) of such paragraph exceeds the growth rate described in clause (ii) of such paragraph, the Chief Actuary shall establish an applicable savings target for the implementation year.

(B) Applicable savings target. For purposes of this section, the applicable savings target for an implementation year shall be an amount equal to the product of—

(i) the total amount of projected Medicare program spending for the proposal year; and

(ii) the applicable percent for the implementation year.

(C) Applicable percent. For purposes of subparagraph (B), the applicable percent for an implementation year is the lesser of—

(i) in the case of—

(I) implementation year 2015, 0.5 percent;

(II) implementation year 2016, 1.0 percent;

(III) implementation year 2017, 1.25 percent; and

(IV) implementation year 2018 or any subsequent implementation year, 1.5 percent; and

(ii) the projected excess for the implementation year (expressed as a percent) determined under subparagraph (A).

(8) Per capita rate of growth in national health expenditures. In each determination year (beginning in 2018), the Chief Actuary of the Centers for Medicare & Medicaid Services shall project the per capita rate of growth in national health expenditures for the implementation year. Such rate of growth for an implementation year shall be calculated as the projected 5-year average (ending with such year) percentage increase in national health care expenditures.

(d) Congressional consideration. (1) Introduction. (A) In general. On the day on which a proposal is submitted by the Board or the President to the House of Representatives and the Senate under subsection (c)(3)(A)(i) or subsection (c)(4), the legislative proposal (described in subsection (c)(3)(B)(iv)) contained in the proposal shall be introduced (by request) in the Senate by the majority leader of the Senate or by Members of the Senate designated by the majority leader of the Senate and shall be introduced (by request) in the House by the majority leader of the House or by Members of the House designated by the majority leader of the House.

(B) Not in session. If either House is not in session on the day on which such legislative proposal is submitted, the legislative proposal shall be introduced in that House, as provided in subparagraph (A), on the first day thereafter on which that House is in session.

(C) Any member. If the legislative proposal is not introduced in either House within 5 days on which that House is in session after the day on which the legislative proposal is submitted, then any Member of that House may introduce the legislative proposal.

(D) Referral. The legislation introduced under this paragraph shall be referred by the Presiding Officers of the respective Houses to the Committee on Finance in the Senate and to the Committee on Energy and Commerce and the Committee on Ways and Means in the House of Representatives.

(2) Committee consideration of proposal. (A) Reporting bill. Not later than April 1 of any proposal year in which a proposal is submitted by the Board or the President to Congress under this section, the Committee on Ways and Means and the Committee on Energy and Commerce of the House of Representatives and the Committee on Finance of the Senate may report the bill referred to the Committee under paragraph (1)(D) with committee amendments related to the Medicare program.

(B) Calculations. In determining whether a committee amendment meets the requirement of subparagraph (A), the reductions in Medicare program spending during the 3-month period immediately preceding the implementation year shall be counted to the extent that such reductions are a result of the implementation provisions in the committee amendment for a change in the payment rate for an item or service that was effective during such period pursuant to such amendment.

(C) Committee jurisdiction. Notwithstanding rule XV of the Standing Rules of the Senate, a committee amendment described in subparagraph (A) may include matter not within the jurisdiction of the Committee on Finance if that matter is relevant to a proposal contained in the bill submitted under subsection (c)(3).

(D) Discharge. If, with respect to the House involved, the committee has not reported the bill by the date required by subparagraph (A), the committee shall be discharged from further consideration of the proposal.

(3) Limitation on changes to the board recommendations. (A) In general. It shall not be in order in the Senate or the House of Representatives to consider any bill, resolution, or amendment, pursuant to this subsection or conference report thereon, that fails to satisfy the requirements of subparagraphs (A)(i) and (C) of subsection (c)(2).

(B) Limitation on changes to the board recommendations in other legislation. It shall not be in order in the Senate or the House of Representatives to consider any bill, resolution, amendment, or conference report (other than pursuant to this section) that would repeal or otherwise change the recommendations of the Board if that change would fail to satisfy the requirements of subparagraphs (A)(i) and (C) of subsection (c)(2).

(C) Limitation on changes to this subsection. It shall not be in order in the Senate or the House of Representatives to consider any bill, resolution, amendment, or conference report that would repeal or otherwise change this subsection.

(D) Waiver. This paragraph may be waived or suspended in the Senate only by the affirmative vote of three-fifths of the Members, duly chosen and sworn.

(E) Appeals. An affirmative vote of three-fifths of the Members of the Senate, duly chosen and sworn, shall be required in the Senate to sustain an appeal of the ruling of the Chair on a point of order raised under this paragraph.

(4) Expedited procedure. (A) Consideration.

A motion to proceed to the consideration of the bill in the Senate is not debatable.

(B) Amendment. (i) Time limitation. Debate in the Senate on any amendment to a bill under this section shall be limited to 1 hour, to be equally divided between, and controlled by, the mover and the manager of the bill, and debate on any amendment to an amendment, debatable motion, or appeal shall be limited to 30 minutes, to be equally divided between, and controlled by, the mover and the manager of the bill, except that in the event the manager of the bill is in favor of any such amendment, motion, or appeal, the time in opposition thereto shall be controlled by the minority leader or such leader's designee.

(ii) Germane. No amendment that is not germane to the provisions of such bill shall be received.

(iii) Additional time. The leaders, or either of them, may, from the time under their control on the passage of the bill, allot additional time to any Senator during the consideration of any amendment, debatable motion, or appeal.

(iv) Amendment not in order. It shall not be in order to consider an amendment that would cause the bill to result in a net reduction in total Medicare program spending in the implementation year that is less than the applicable savings target established under subsection (c)(7)(B) for such implementation year.

(v) Waiver and appeals. This paragraph may be waived or suspended in the Senate only by the affirmative vote of three-fifths of the Members, duly chosen and sworn. An affirmative vote of three-fifths of the Members of the Senate, duly chosen and sworn, shall be required in the Senate to sustain an appeal of the ruling of the Chair on a point of order raised under this section.

(C) Consideration by the other House. (i) In general. The expedited procedures provided in this subsection for the consideration of a bill introduced pursuant to paragraph (1) shall not apply to such a bill that is received by one House from the other House if such a bill was not introduced in the receiving House.

(ii) Before passage. If a bill that is introduced pursuant to paragraph (1) is received by one House from the other House, after introduction but before disposition of such a bill in the receiving House, then the following shall apply:

(I) The receiving House shall consider the bill introduced in that House through all stages of consideration up to, but not including, passage.

(II) The question on passage shall be put on the bill of the other House as amended by the language of the receiving House.

(iii) After passage. If a bill introduced pursuant to paragraph (1) is received by one House from the other House, after such a bill is passed by the receiving House, then the vote on passage of the bill that originates in the receiving House shall be considered to be the vote on passage of the bill received from the other House as amended by the language of the receiving House.

(iv) Disposition. Upon disposition of a bill introduced pursuant to paragraph (1) that is received by one House from the other House, it shall no longer be in order to consider the bill that originates in the receiving House.

(v) Limitation. Clauses (ii), (iii), and (iv) shall apply only to a bill received by one House from the other House if the bill—

(I) is related only to the program under this title; and

(II) satisfies the requirements of subparagraphs (A)(i) and (C) of subsection (c)(2).

(D) Senate limits on debate. (i) In general. In the Senate, consideration of the bill and on all debatable motions and appeals in connection therewith shall not exceed a total of 30 hours, which shall be divided equally between the majority and minority leaders or their designees.

(ii) Motion to further limit debate. A motion to further limit debate on the bill is in order and is not debatable.

(iii) Motion or appeal. Any debatable motion or appeal is debatable for not to exceed 1 hour, to be divided equally between those favoring and those opposing the motion or appeal.

(iv) Final disposition. After 30 hours of consideration, the Senate shall proceed, without any further debate on any question, to vote on the final disposition thereof to the exclusion of all amendments not then pending before the Senate at that time and to the exclusion of all motions, except a motion to table, or to reconsider and one quorum call on demand to establish the presence of a quorum (and motions required to establish a quorum) immediately before the final vote begins.

(E) Consideration in conference. (i) In general. Consideration in the Senate and the House of Representatives on the conference report or any messages between Houses shall be limited to 10 hours, equally divided and controlled by the majority and minority leaders of the Senate or their designees and the Speaker of the House of Representatives and the minority leader of the House of Representatives or their designees.

(ii) Time limitation. Debate in the Senate on any amendment under this subparagraph shall be limited to 1 hour, to be equally divided between, and controlled by, the mover and the manager of the bill, and debate on any amendment to an amendment, debatable motion, or appeal shall be limited to 30 minutes, to be equally divided between, and controlled by, the mover and the manager of the bill, except that in the event the manager of the bill is in favor of any such amendment, motion, or appeal, the time in opposition thereto shall be controlled by the minority leader or such leader's designee.

(iii) Final disposition. After 10 hours of consideration, the Senate shall proceed, without any further debate on any question, to vote on the final disposition thereof to the exclusion of all motions not then pending before the Senate at that time or necessary to resolve the differences between the Houses and to the exclusion of all other motions, except a motion to table, or to reconsider and one quorum call on demand to establish the presence of a quorum (and motions required to establish a quorum) immediately before the final vote begins.

(iv) Limitation. Clauses (i) through (iii) shall only apply to a conference report, message or the amendments thereto if the conference report, message, or an amendment thereto—

(I) is related only to the program under this title; and

(II) satisfies the requirements of subparagraphs (A)(i) and (C) of subsection (c)(2).

(F) Veto. If the President vetoes the bill debate on a veto message in the Senate under this subsection shall be 1 hour equally divided between the majority and minority leaders or their designees.

(5) Rules of the Senate and House of Representatives. This subsection and subsection (f)(2) are enacted by Congress—

(A) as an exercise of the rulemaking power of the Senate and the House of Representatives, respectively, and is deemed to be part of the rules of each House, respectively, but applicable only with respect to the procedure to be followed in that House in the case of bill under this section, and it supersedes other rules only to the extent that it is inconsistent with such rules; and

(B) with full recognition of the constitutional right of either House to change the rules (so far as they relate to the procedure of that House) at any time, in the same manner, and to the same extent as in the case of any other rule of that House.

(e) Implementation of proposal. (1) In general. Notwithstanding any other provision of law, the Secretary shall, except as provided in paragraph (3), implement the recommendations contained in a proposal submitted by the Board or the President to Congress pursuant to this section on August 15 of the year in which the proposal is so submitted.

(2) Application. (A) In general. A recommendation described in paragraph (1) shall apply as follows:

(i) In the case of a recommendation that is a change in the payment rate for an item or service under Medicare in which payment rates change on a fiscal year basis (or a cost reporting period basis that relates to a fiscal year), on a calendar year basis (or a cost reporting period basis that relates to a calendar year), or on a rate year basis (or a cost reporting period basis that relates to a rate year), such recommendation shall apply to items and services furnished on the first day of the first fiscal year, calendar year, or rate year (as the case may be) that begins after such August 15.

(ii) In the case of a recommendation relating to payments to plans under parts C and D [42 USCS §§ 1395w-21 et seq. and 1395w-101 et seq.], such recommendation shall apply to plan years beginning on the first day of the first calendar year that begins after such August 15.

(iii) In the case of any other recommendation, such recommendation shall be addressed in the regular regulatory process timeframe and shall apply as soon as practicable.

(B) Interim final rulemaking. The Secretary may use interim final rulemaking to implement any recommendation described in paragraph (1).

(3) Exceptions. (A) In general. The Secretary shall not implement the recommendations contained in a proposal submitted in a proposal year by the Board or the President to Congress pursuant to this section if—

(i) prior to August 15 of the proposal year, Federal legislation is enacted that includes the following provision: "This Act supercedes the recommendations of the Board contained in the proposal submitted, in the year which includes the date of enactment of this Act, to Congress under section 1899A of the Social Security Act."; and

(ii) in the case of implementation year 2020 and subsequent implementation years, a joint resolution described in subsection (f)(1) is enacted not later than August 15, 2017.

(B) Limited additional exception. (i) In general. Subject to clause (ii), the Secretary shall not implement the recommendations contained in a proposal submitted by the Board or the President to Congress pursuant to this section in a proposal year (beginning with proposal year 2019) if—

(I) the Board was required to submit a proposal to Congress under this section in the year preceding the proposal year; and

(II) the Chief Actuary of the Centers for Medicare & Medicaid Services makes a determination in the determination year that the growth rate described in subsection (c)(8) exceeds the growth rate described in subsection (c)(6)(A)(i).

(ii) Limited additional exception may not be applied in two consecutive years. This subparagraph shall not apply if the recommendations contained in a proposal submitted by the Board or the President to Congress pursuant to this section in the year preceding the proposal year were not required to be implemented by reason of this subparagraph.

(iii) No affect on requirement to submit proposals or for congressional consideration of proposals. Clause (i) and (ii) shall not affect—

(I) the requirement of the Board or the President to submit a proposal to Congress in a proposal year in accordance with the provisions of this section; or

(II) Congressional consideration of a legislative proposal (described in subsection (c)(3)(B)(iv)) contained such a proposal in accordance with subsection (d).

(4) No affect [effect] on authority to implement certain provisions. Nothing in paragraph (3) shall be construed to affect the authority of the Secretary to implement any recommendation contained in a proposal or advisory report under this section to the extent that the Secretary otherwise has the authority to implement such recommendation administratively.

(5) Limitation on review. There shall be no administrative or judicial review under section 1869 [42 USCS § 1395ff], section 1878 [42 USCS § 1395oo], or otherwise of the implementation by the Secretary under this subsection of the recommendations contained in a proposal.

(f) Joint resolution required to discontinue the Board. (1) In general. For purposes of subsection (e)(3)(B), a joint resolution described in this paragraph means only a joint resolution—

(A) that is introduced in 2017 by not later than February 1 of such year;

(B) which does not have a preamble;

(C) the title of which is as follows: "Joint resolution approving the discontinuation of the process for consideration and automatic implementation of the annual proposal of the Independent Medicare Advisory Board [Independent Payment Advisory Board] under section 1899A of the Social Security Act"; and

(D) the matter after the resolving clause of which is as follows: "That Congress approves the discontinuation of the process for consideration and automatic implementation of the annual proposal of the Independent Medicare Advisory Board [Independent Payment Advisory Board] under section 1899A of the Social Security Act.".

(2) Procedure. (A) Referral. A joint resolution described in paragraph (1) shall be referred to the Committee on Ways and Means and the Committee on Energy and Commerce of the House of Representatives and the Committee on Finance of the Senate.

(B) Discharge. In the Senate, if the committee to which is referred a joint resolution described in paragraph (1) has not reported such joint resolution (or an identical joint resolution) at the end of 20 days after the joint resolution described in paragraph (1) is introduced, such committee may be discharged from further consideration of such joint resolution upon a petition supported in writing by 30 Members of the Senate, and such joint resolution shall be placed on the calendar.

(C) Consideration. (i) In general. In the Senate, when the committee to which a joint resolution is referred has reported, or when a committee is discharged (under subparagraph (C)) from further consideration of a joint resolution described in paragraph (1), it is at any time thereafter in order (even though a previous motion to the same effect has been disagreed to) for a motion to proceed to the consideration of the joint resolution to be made, and all points of order against the joint resolution (and against consideration of the joint resolution) are waived, except for points of order under the Congressional Budget act of 1974 or under budget resolutions pursuant to that Act. The motion is not debatable. A motion to reconsider the vote by which the motion is agreed to or disagreed to shall not be in order. If a motion to proceed to the consideration of the joint resolution is agreed to, the joint resolution shall remain the unfinished business of the Senate until disposed of.

(ii) Debate limitation. In the Senate, consideration of the joint resolution, and on all debatable motions and appeals in connection therewith, shall be limited to not more than 10 hours, which shall be divided equally between the majority leader and the minority leader, or their designees. A motion further to limit debate is in order and not debatable. An amendment to, or a motion to postpone, or a motion to proceed to the consideration of other business, or a motion to recommit the joint resolution is not in order.

(iii) Passage. In the Senate, immediately following the conclusion of the debate on a joint resolution described in paragraph (1), and a single quorum call at the conclusion of the debate if requested in accordance with the rules of the Senate, the vote on passage of the joint resolution shall occur.

(iv) Appeals. Appeals from the decisions of the Chair relating to the application of the rules of the Senate to the procedure relating to a joint resolution described in paragraph (1) shall be decided without debate.

(D) Other House acts first. If, before the passage by 1 House of a joint resolution of that House described in paragraph (1), that House receives from the other House a joint resolution described in paragraph (1), then the following procedures shall apply:

(i) The joint resolution of the other House shall not be referred to a committee.

(ii) With respect to a joint resolution described in paragraph (1) of the House receiving the joint resolution—

(I) the procedure in that House shall be the same as if no joint resolution had been received from the other House; but

(II) the vote on final passage shall be on the joint resolution of the other House.

(E) Excluded days. For purposes of determining the period specified in subparagraph (B), there shall be excluded any days either House of Congress is adjourned for more than 3 days during a session of Congress.

(F) Majority required for adoption. A joint resolution considered under this subsection shall require an affirmative vote of three-fifths of the Members, duly chosen and sworn, for adoption.

(3) Termination. If a joint resolution described in paragraph (1) is enacted not later than August 15, 2017—

(A) the Chief Actuary of the Medicare & Medicaid Services shall not—

(i) make any determinations under subsection (c)(6) after May 1, 2017; or

(ii) provide any opinion pursuant to subsection (c)(3)(B)(iii) after January 16, 2018;

(B) the Board shall not submit any proposals, advisory reports, or advisory recommendations under this section or produce the public report under subsection (n) after January 16, 2018; and

(C) the Board and the consumer advisory council under subsection (k) shall terminate on August 16, 2018.

(g) Board membership; terms of office; Chairperson; removal. (1) Membership. (A) In general. The Board shall be composed of—

(i) 15 members appointed by the President, by and with the advice and consent of the Senate; and

(ii) the Secretary, the Administrator of the Center for Medicare & Medicaid Services, and the Administrator of the Health Resources and Services Administration, all of whom shall serve ex officio as nonvoting members of the Board.

(B) Qualifications. (i) In general. The appointed membership of the Board shall include individuals with national recognition for their expertise in health finance and economics, actuarial science, health facility management, health plans and integrated delivery systems, reimbursement of health facilities, allopathic and osteopathic physicians, and other providers of health services, and other related fields, who provide a mix of different professionals, broad geographic representation, and a balance between urban and rural representatives.

(ii) Inclusion. The appointed membership of the Board shall include (but not be limited to) physicians and other health professionals, experts in the area of pharmaco-economics or prescription drug benefit programs, employers, third-party payers, individuals skilled in the conduct and interpretation of biomedical, health services, and health economics research and expertise in outcomes and effectiveness research and technology assessment. Such membership shall also include representatives of consumers and the elderly.

(iii) Majority nonproviders. Individuals who are directly involved in the provision or management of the delivery of items and services covered under this title shall not constitute a majority of the appointed membership of the Board.

(C) Ethical disclosure. The President shall establish a system for public disclosure by appointed members of the Board of financial and other potential conflicts of interest relating to such members. Appointed members of the Board shall be treated as officers in the executive branch for purposes of applying title I of the Ethics in Government Act of 1978 (Public Law 95-521) [5 USCS Appx].

(D) Conflicts of interest. No individual may serve as an appointed member if that individual engages in any other business, vocation, or employment.

(E) Consultation with congress. In selecting individuals for nominations for appointments to the Board, the President shall consult with—

(i) the majority leader of the Senate concerning the appointment of 3 members;

(ii) the Speaker of the House of Representatives concerning the appointment of 3 members;

(iii) the minority leader of the Senate concerning the appointment of 3 members; and

(iv) the minority leader of the House of Representatives concerning the appointment of 3 members.

(2) Term of office. Each appointed member shall hold office for a term of 6 years except that—

(A) a member may not serve more than 2 full consecutive terms (but may be reappointed to 2 full consecutive terms after being appointed to fill a vacancy on the Board);

(B) a member appointed to fill a vacancy occurring prior to the expiration of the term for which that member's predecessor was appointed shall be appointed for the remainder of such term;

(C) a member may continue to serve after the expiration of the member's term until a successor has taken office; and

(D) of the members first appointed under this section, 5 shall be appointed for a term of 1 year, 5 shall be appointed for a term of 3 years, and 5 shall be appointed for a term of 6 years, the term of each to be designated by the President at the time of nomination.

(3) Chairperson. (A) In general. The Chairperson shall be appointed by the President, by and with the advice and consent of the Senate, from among the members of the Board.

(B) Duties. The Chairperson shall be the principal executive officer of the Board, and shall exercise all of the executive and administrative functions of the Board, including functions of the Board with respect to—

(i) the appointment and supervision of personnel employed by the Board;

(ii) the distribution of business among personnel appointed and supervised by the Chairperson and among administrative units of the Board; and

(iii) the use and expenditure of funds.

(C) Governance. In carrying out any of the functions under subparagraph (B), the Chairperson shall be governed by the general policies established by the Board and by the decisions, findings, and determinations the Board shall by law be authorized to make.

(D) Requests for appropriations. Requests or estimates for regular, supplemental, or deficiency appropriations on behalf of the Board may not be submitted by the Chairperson without the prior approval of a majority vote of the Board.

(4) Removal. Any appointed member may be removed by the President for neglect of duty or malfeasance in office, but for no other cause.

(h) Vacancies; quorum; seal; Vice Chairperson; voting on reports. (1) Vacancies. No vacancy on the Board shall impair the right of the remaining members to exercise all the powers of the Board.

(2) Quorum. A majority of the appointed members of the Board shall constitute a quorum for the transaction of business, but a lesser number of members may hold hearings.

(3) Seal. The Board shall have an official seal, of which judicial notice shall be taken.

(4) Vice chairperson. The Board shall annually elect a Vice Chairperson to act in the absence or disability of the Chairperson or in case of a vacancy in the office of the Chairperson.

(5) Voting on proposals. Any proposal of the Board must be approved by the majority of appointed members present.

(i) Powers of the Board. (1) Hearings. The Board may hold such hearings, sit and act at such times and places, take such testimony, and receive such evidence as the Board considers advisable to carry out this section.

(2) Authority to inform research priorities for data collection. The Board may advise the Secretary on priorities for health services research, particularly as such priorities pertain to necessary changes and issues regarding payment reforms under Medicare.

(3) Obtaining official data. The Board may secure directly from any department or agency of the United States information necessary to enable it to carry out this section. Upon request of the Chairperson, the head of that department or agency shall furnish that information to the Board on an agreed upon schedule.

(4) Postal services. The Board may use the United States mails in the same manner and under the same conditions as other departments and agencies of the Federal Government.

(5) Gifts. The Board may accept, use, and dispose of gifts or donations of services or property.

(6) Offices. The Board shall maintain a principal office and such field offices as it determines necessary, and may meet and exercise any of its powers at any other place.

(j) Personnel matters. (1) Compensation of members and Chairperson. Each appointed member, other than the Chairperson, shall be compensated at a rate equal to the annual rate of basic pay prescribed for level III of the

Executive Schedule under section 5315 of title 5, United States Code. The Chairperson shall be compensated at a rate equal to the daily equivalent of the annual rate of basic pay prescribed for level II of the Executive Schedule under section 5315 of title 5, United States Code.

(2) Travel expenses. The appointed members shall be allowed travel expenses, including per diem in lieu of subsistence, at rates authorized for employees of agencies under subchapter I of chapter 57 of title 5, United States Code [5 USCS §§ 5701 et seq.], while away from their homes or regular places of business in the performance of services for the Board.

(3) Staff. (A) In general. The Chairperson may, without regard to the civil service laws and regulations, appoint and terminate an executive director and such other additional personnel as may be necessary to enable the Board to perform its duties. The employment of an executive director shall be subject to confirmation by the Board.

(B) Compensation. The Chairperson may fix the compensation of the executive director and other personnel without regard to chapter 51 and subchapter III of chapter 53 of title 5, United States Code [5 USCS §§ 5101 et seq. and 5331 et seq.], relating to classification of positions and General Schedule pay rates, except that the rate of pay for the executive director and other personnel may not exceed the rate payable for level V of the Executive Schedule under section 5316 of such title [5 USCS § 5316].

(4) Detail of government employees. Any Federal Government employee may be detailed to the Board without reimbursement, and such detail shall be without interruption or loss of civil service status or privilege.

(5) Procurement of temporary and intermittent services. The Chairperson may procure temporary and intermittent services under section 3109(b) of title 5, United States Code, at rates for individuals which do not exceed the daily equivalent of the annual rate of basic pay prescribed for level V of the Executive Schedule under section 5316 of such title [5 USCS § 5316].

(k) Consumer advisory council. (1) In general. There is established a consumer advisory council to advise the Board on the impact of payment policies under this title on consumers.

(2) Membership. (A) Number and appointment. The consumer advisory council shall be composed of 10 consumer representatives appointed by the Comptroller General of the United States, 1 from among each of the 10 regions established by the Secretary as of the date of enactment of this section.

(B) Qualifications. The membership of the council shall represent the interests of consumers and particular communities.

(3) Duties. The consumer advisory council shall, subject to the call of the Board, meet not less frequently than 2 times each year in the District of Columbia.

(4) Open meetings. Meetings of the consumer advisory council shall be open to the public.

(5) Election of officers. Members of the consumer advisory council shall elect their own officers.

(6) Application of FACA. The Federal Advisory Committee Act (5 U.S.C. App.) shall apply to the consumer advisory council except that section 14 of such Act shall not apply.

(l) Definitions. In this section:

(1) Board; chairperson; member. The terms "Board", "Chairperson", and "Member" mean the Independent Medicare Advisory Board [Independent Payment Advisory Board] established under subsection (a) and the Chairperson and any Member thereof, respectively.

(2) Medicare. The term "Medicare" means the program established under this title, including parts A, B, C, and D [42 USCS §§ 1395c et seq., 1395j et seq., 1395w-21 et seq., 1395w-101 et seq.].

(3) Medicare beneficiary. The term "Medicare beneficiary" means an individual who is entitled to, or enrolled for, benefits under part A [42 USCS §§ 1395c et seq.] or enrolled for benefits under part B [42 USCS §§ 1395j et seq.].

(4) Medicare program spending. The term "Medicare program spending" means program spending under parts A, B, and D [42 USCS §§ 1395c et seq., 1395j et seq., and 1395w-101 et seq.] net of premiums.

(m) Funding. (1) In general. There are appropriated to the Board to carry out its duties and functions—

(A) for fiscal year 2012, $15,000,000; and

(B) for each subsequent fiscal year, the amount appropriated under this paragraph for the previous fiscal year increased by the annual percentage increase in the Consumer Price Index for All Urban Consumers (all items; United States city average) as of June of the previous fiscal year.

(2) From trust funds. Sixty percent of amounts appropriated under paragraph (1) shall be derived by transfer from the Federal Hospital Insurance Trust Fund under section

1817 and 40 percent of amounts appropriated under such paragraph shall be derived by transfer from the Federal Supplementary Medical Insurance Trust Fund under section 1841.

(n) Annual public report. (1) In general. Not later than July 1, 2014, and annually thereafter, the Board shall produce a public report containing standardized information on system-wide health care costs, patient access to care, utilization, and quality-of-care that allows for comparison by region, types of services, types of providers, and both private payers and the program under this title.

(2) Requirements. Each report produced pursuant to paragraph (1) shall include information with respect to the following areas:

(A) The quality and costs of care for the population at the most local level determined practical by the Board (with quality and costs compared to national benchmarks and reflecting rates of change, taking into account quality measures described in section 1890(b)(7)(B) [42 USCS § 1395aaa(b)(7)(B)]).

(B) Beneficiary and consumer access to care, patient and caregiver experience of care, and the cost-sharing or out-of-pocket burden on patients.

(C) Epidemiological shifts and demographic changes.

(D) The proliferation, effectiveness, and utilization of health care technologies, including variation in provider practice patterns and costs.

(E) Any other areas that the Board determines affect overall spending and quality of care in the private sector.

(o) Advisory recommendations for non-Federal health care programs. (1) In general. Not later than January 15, 2015, and at least once every two years thereafter, the Board shall submit to Congress and the President recommendations to slow the growth in national health expenditures (excluding expenditures under this title and in other Federal health care programs) while preserving or enhancing quality of care, such as recommendations—

(A) that the Secretary or other Federal agencies can implement administratively;

(B) that may require legislation to be enacted by Congress in order to be implemented;

(C) that may require legislation to be enacted by State or local governments in order to be implemented;

(D) that private sector entities can voluntarily implement; and

(E) with respect to other areas determined appropriate by the Board.

(2) Coordination. In making recommendations under paragraph (1), the Board shall coordinate such recommendations with recommendations contained in proposals and advisory reports produced by the Board under subsection (c).

(3) Available to public. The Board shall make recommendations submitted to Congress and the President under this subsection available to the public.

(Aug. 14, 1935, ch 531, Title XVIII, Part E, § 1899A, as added and amended March 23, 2010, P. L. 111-148, Title III, Subtitle E, § 3403(a)(1), Title X, Subtitle C, § 10320, 124 Stat. 489, 949.)

HISTORY; ANCILLARY LAWS AND DIRECTIVES

Other provisions:

References to "Independent Medicare Advisory Board". Act March 23, 2010, P. L. 111-148, Title X, Subtitle C, § 10320(b), 124 Stat. 952, provides: "Any reference in the provisions of, or amendments made by, section 3403 to the 'Independent Medicare Advisory Board' shall be deemed to be a reference to the 'Independent Payment Advisory Board'.".

Rule of construction. Act March 23, 2010, P. L. 111-148, Title X, Subtitle C, § 10320(c), 124 Stat. 952, provides: "Nothing in the amendments made by this section [amending this section] shall preclude the Independent Medicare Advisory Board, as established under section 1899A of the Social Security Act (as added by section 3403), from solely using data from public or private sources to carry out the amendments made by subsection (a)(4) [amending subsec. (f)(3)(B) of this section].".

§ 1395kkk-1. GAO study and report on determination and implementation of payment and coverage policies under the Medicare program.

(1) Initial study and report. (A) Study. The Comptroller General of the United States (in this section referred to as the "Comptroller General") shall conduct a study on changes to payment policies, methodologies, and rates and coverage policies and methodologies under the Medicare program under title XVIII of the Social Security Act [42 USCS §§ 1395 et seq.] as a result of the recommendations contained in the proposals made by the Independent Medicare Advisory Board [Independent Payment Advisory Board] under section 1899A of such Act [42 USCS § 1395kkk] (as added by subsection (a)), including an analysis of the effect of such recommendations on—

(i) Medicare beneficiary access to providers and items and services;

(ii) the affordability of Medicare premiums and cost-sharing (including deductibles, coinsurance, and copayments);

(iii) the potential impact of changes on other government or private-sector purchasers and payers of care; and

(iv) quality of patient care, including patient experience, outcomes, and other measures of care.

(B) Report. Not later than July 1, 2015, the Comptroller General shall submit to Congress a report containing the results of the study conducted under subparagraph (A), together with recommendations for such legislation and administrative action as the Comptroller General determines appropriate.

(2) Subsequent studies and reports. The Comptroller General shall periodically conduct such additional studies and submit reports to Congress on changes to Medicare payments policies, methodologies, and rates and coverage policies and methodologies as the Comptroller General determines appropriate, in consultation with the Committee on Ways and Means and the Committee on Energy and Commerce of the House of Representatives and the Committee on Finance of the Senate.

(March 23, 2010, P. L. 111-148, Title III, Subtitle E, § 3403(b), 124 Stat. 506.)

TITLE XIX. GRANTS TO STATES FOR MEDICAL ASSISTANCE PROGRAMS

§ 1396. Medicaid and CHIP Payment and Access Commission

(a) Establishment. There is hereby established the Medicaid and CHIP Payment and Access Commission (in this section referred to as "MACPAC").

(b) Duties. (1) Review of access policies for all States and annual reports. MACPAC shall—

(A) review policies of the Medicaid program established under this title [42 USCS §§ 1396 et seq.] (in this section referred to as "Medicaid") and the State Children's Health Insurance Program established under title XXI [42 USCS §§ 1397aa et seq.] (in this section referred to as "CHIP") affecting access to covered items and services, including topics described in paragraph (2);

(B) make recommendations to Congress, the Secretary, and States concerning such access policies;

(C) by not later than March 15 of each year (beginning with 2010), submit a report to Congress containing the results of such reviews and MACPAC's recommendations concerning such policies; and

(D) by not later than June 15 of each year (beginning with 2010), submit a report to Congress containing an examination of issues affecting Medicaid and CHIP, including the implications of changes in health care delivery in the United States and in the market for health care services on such programs.

(2) Specific topics to be reviewed. Specifically, MACPAC shall review and assess the following:

(A) Medicaid and CHIP payment policies. Payment policies under Medicaid and CHIP, including—

(i) the factors affecting expenditures for the efficient provision of items and services in different sectors, including the process for updating payments to medical, dental, and health professionals, hospitals, residential and long-term care providers, providers of home and community based services, Federally-qualified health centers and rural health clinics, managed care entities, and providers of other covered items and services;

(ii) payment methodologies; and

(iii) the relationship of such factors and methodologies to access and quality of care for Medicaid and CHIP beneficiaries (including how such factors and methodologies enable such beneficiaries to obtain the services for which they are eligible, affect provider supply, and affect providers that serve a disproportionate share of low-income and other vulnerable populations).

(B) Eligibility policies. Medicaid and CHIP eligibility policies, including a determination of the degree to which Federal and State policies provide health care coverage to needy populations.

(C) Enrollment and retention processes. Medicaid and CHIP enrollment and retention processes, including a determination of the degree to which Federal and State policies encourage the enrollment of individuals who are eligible for such programs and screen out individuals who are ineligible, while minimizing the share of program expenses devoted to such processes.

(D) Coverage policies. Medicaid and CHIP benefit and coverage policies, including a determination of the degree to which Federal and State policies provide access to the services enrollees require to improve and maintain their health and functional status.

(E) Quality of care. Medicaid and CHIP policies as they relate to the quality of care provided under those programs, including a determination of the degree to which Federal and State policies achieve their stated goals and interact with similar goals established by other purchasers of health care services.

(F) Interaction of Medicaid and CHIP payment policies with health care delivery generally. The effect of Medicaid and CHIP payment policies on access to items and services for children and other Medicaid and CHIP populations other than under this title or title XXI [42 USCS §§ 1396 et seq. or 1397aa et seq.] and the implications of changes in health care delivery in the United States and in the general market for health care items and services on Medicaid and CHIP.

(G) Interactions with Medicare and Medicaid. Consistent with paragraph (11), the interaction of policies under Medicaid and the Medicare program under title XVIII [42 USCS §§ 1395 et seq.], including with respect to how such interactions affect access to services, payments, and dual eligible individuals.

(H) Other access policies. The effect of other Medicaid and CHIP policies on access to covered items and services, including policies relating to transportation and language barriers and preventive, acute, and long-term services and supports.

(3) Recommendations and reports of State-specific data. MACPAC shall—

(A) review national and State-specific Medicaid and CHIP data; and

(B) submit reports and recommendations to Congress, the Secretary, and States based on such reviews.

(4) Creation of early-warning system. MACPAC shall create an early-warning system to identify provider shortage areas, as well as other factors that adversely affect, or have the potential to adversely affect, access to care by, or the health care status of, Medicaid and CHIP beneficiaries. MACPAC shall include in the annual report required under paragraph (1)(D) a description of all such areas or problems identified with respect to the period addressed in the report.

(5) Comments on certain secretarial reports and regulations.

(A) Certain secretarial reports. If the Secretary submits to Congress (or a committee of Congress) a report that is required by law and that relates to access policies, including with respect to payment policies, under Medicaid or CHIP, the Secretary shall transmit a copy of the report to MACPAC. MACPAC shall review the report and, not later than 6 months after the date of submittal of the Secretary's report to Congress, shall submit to the appropriate committees of Congress and the Secretary written comments on such report. Such comments may include such recommendations as MACPAC deems appropriate.

(B) Regulations. MACPAC shall review Medicaid and CHIP regulations and may comment through submission of a report to the appropriate committees of Congress and the Secretary, on any such regulations that affect access, quality, or efficiency of health care.

(6) Agenda and additional reviews. MACPAC shall consult periodically with the chairmen and ranking minority members of the appropriate committees of Congress regarding MACPAC's agenda and progress towards achieving the agenda. MACPAC may conduct additional reviews, and submit additional reports to the appropriate committees of Congress, from time to time on such topics relating to the program under this title or title XXI [42 USCS §§ 1396 et seq. or 1397aa et seq.] as may be requested by such chairmen and members and as MACPAC deems appropriate.

(7) Availability of reports. MACPAC shall transmit to the Secretary a copy of each report submitted under this subsection and shall make such reports available to the public.

(8) Appropriate committee of Congress. For purposes of this section, the term "appropriate committees of Congress" means the Committee on Energy and Commerce of the House of Representatives and the Committee on Finance of the Senate.

(9) Voting and reporting requirements. With respect to each recommendation contained in a report submitted under paragraph (1), each member of MACPAC shall vote on the recommendation, and MACPAC shall include, by member, the results of that vote in the report containing the recommendation.

(10) Examination of budget consequences. Before making any recommendations, MACPAC shall examine the budget consequences of such recommendations, directly or through consultation with appropriate expert entities, and shall submit with any recommendations, a report on the Federal and State-specific budget consequences of the recommendations.

(11) Consultation and coordination with MedPAC. (A) In general. MACPAC shall consult with the Medicare Payment Advisory Commission (in this paragraph referred to as "MedPAC") established under section 1805 [42 USCS § 1395b-6] in carrying out its duties under this section, as appropriate and particularly with respect to the issues specified in paragraph (2) as they relate to those Medicaid beneficiaries who are dually eligible for Medicaid and the Medicare program under title

XVIII [42 USCS §§ 1395 et seq.], adult Medicaid beneficiaries (who are not dually eligible for Medicare), and beneficiaries under Medicare. Responsibility for analysis of and recommendations to change Medicare policy regarding Medicare beneficiaries, including Medicare beneficiaries who are dually eligible for Medicare and Medicaid, shall rest with MedPAC.

(B) Information sharing. MACPAC and MedPAC shall have access to deliberations and records of the other such entity, respectively, upon the request of the other such entity.

(12) Consultation with States. MACPAC shall regularly consult with States in carrying out its duties under this section, including with respect to developing processes for carrying out such duties, and shall ensure that input from States is taken into account and represented in MACPAC's recommendations and reports.

(13) Coordinate and consult with the Federal Coordinated Health Care Office. MACPAC shall coordinate and consult with the Federal Coordinated Health Care Office established under section 2081 [2602] of the Patient Protection and Affordable Care Act [42 USCS § 1315b] before making any recommendations regarding dual eligible individuals.

(14) Programmatic oversight vested in the Secretary. MACPAC's authority to make recommendations in accordance with this section shall not affect, or be considered to duplicate, the Secretary's authority to carry out Federal responsibilities with respect to Medicaid and CHIP.

(c) Membership. (1) Number and appointment. MACPAC shall be composed of 17 members appointed by the Comptroller General of the United States.

(2) Qualifications. (A) In general. The membership of MACPAC shall include individuals who have had direct experience as enrollees or parents or caregivers of enrollees in Medicaid or CHIP and individuals with national recognition for their expertise in Federal safety net health programs, health finance and economics, actuarial science, health plans and integrated delivery systems, reimbursement for health care, health information technology, and other providers of health services, public health, and other related fields, who provide a mix of different professions, broad geographic representation, and a balance between urban and rural representation.

(B) Inclusion. The membership of MACPAC shall include (but not be limited to) physicians, dentists, and other health professionals, employers, third-party payers, and individuals with expertise in the delivery of health services. Such membership shall also include representatives of children, pregnant women, the elderly, individuals with disabilities, caregivers, and dual eligible individuals, current or former representatives of State agencies responsible for administering Medicaid, and current or former representatives of State agencies responsible for administering CHIP.

(C) Majority nonproviders. Individuals who are directly involved in the provision, or management of the delivery, of items and services covered under Medicaid or CHIP shall not constitute a majority of the membership of MACPAC.

(D) Ethical disclosure. The Comptroller General of the United States shall establish a system for public disclosure by members of MACPAC of financial and other potential conflicts of interest relating to such members. Members of MACPAC shall be treated as employees of Congress for purposes of applying title I of the Ethics in Government Act of 1978 [5 USCS Appx. §§ 101 et seq.] (Public Law 95-521).

(3) Terms. (A) In general. The terms of members of MACPAC shall be for 3 years except that the Comptroller General of the United States shall designate staggered terms for the members first appointed.

(B) Vacancies. Any member appointed to fill a vacancy occurring before the expiration of the term for which the member's predecessor was appointed shall be appointed only for the remainder of that term. A member may serve after the expiration of that member's term until a successor has taken office. A vacancy in MACPAC shall be filled in the manner in which the original appointment was made.

(4) Compensation. While serving on the business of MACPAC (including travel time), a member of MACPAC shall be entitled to compensation at the per diem equivalent of the rate provided for level IV of the Executive Schedule under section 5315 of title 5, United States Code; and while so serving away from home and the member's regular place of business, a member may be allowed travel expenses, as authorized by the Chairman of MACPAC. Physicians serving as personnel of MACPAC may be provided a physician comparability allowance by MACPAC in the same manner as Government physicians may be provided such an allowance by an agency under section 5948 of title 5, United States Code, and for such purpose subsection (i) of such section shall apply to MACPAC in the same manner as it applies to the Tennessee Valley Authority. For purposes of pay (other than pay of members of

MACPAC) and employment benefits, rights, and privileges, all personnel of MACPAC shall be treated as if they were employees of the United States Senate.

(5) Chairman; Vice Chairman. The Comptroller General of the United States shall designate a member of MACPAC, at the time of appointment of the member as Chairman and a member as Vice Chairman for that term of appointment, except that in the case of vacancy of the Chairmanship or Vice Chairmanship, the Comptroller General of the United States may designate another member for the remainder of that member's term.

(6) Meetings. MACPAC shall meet at the call of the Chairman.

(d) Director and staff; experts and consultants. Subject to such review as the Comptroller General of the United States deems necessary to assure the efficient administration of MACPAC, MACPAC may—

(1) employ and fix the compensation of an Executive Director (subject to the approval of the Comptroller General of the United States) and such other personnel as may be necessary to carry out its duties (without regard to the provisions of title 5, United States Code, governing appointments in the competitive service);

(2) seek such assistance and support as may be required in the performance of its duties from appropriate Federal and State departments and agencies;

(3) enter into contracts or make other arrangements, as may be necessary for the conduct of the work of MACPAC (without regard to section 3709 of the Revised Statutes (41 U.S.C. 5));

(4) make advance, progress, and other payments which relate to the work of MACPAC;

(5) provide transportation and subsistence for persons serving without compensation; and

(6) prescribe such rules and regulations as it deems necessary with respect to the internal organization and operation of MACPAC.

(e) Powers. (1) Obtaining official data. MACPAC may secure directly from any department or agency of the United States and, as a condition for receiving payments under sections 1903(a) and 2105(a) [42 USCS §§ 1396b(a) and 1397ee(a)], from any State agency responsible for administering Medicaid or CHIP, information necessary to enable it to carry out this section. Upon request of the Chairman, the head of that department or agency shall furnish that information to MACPAC on an agreed upon schedule.

(2) Data collection. In order to carry out its functions, MACPAC shall—

(A) utilize existing information, both published and unpublished, where possible, collected and assessed either by its own staff or under other arrangements made in accordance with this section;

(B) carry out, or award grants or contracts for, original research and experimentation, where existing information is inadequate; and

(C) adopt procedures allowing any interested party to submit information for MACPAC's use in making reports and recommendations.

(3) Access of GAO to information. The Comptroller General of the United States shall have unrestricted access to all deliberations, records, and nonproprietary data of MACPAC, immediately upon request.

(4) Periodic audit. MACPAC shall be subject to periodic audit by the Comptroller General of the United States.

(f) Funding. (1) Request for appropriations. MACPAC shall submit requests for appropriations (other than for fiscal year 2010) in the same manner as the Comptroller General of the United States submits requests for appropriations, but amounts appropriated for MACPAC shall be separate from amounts appropriated for the Comptroller General of the United States.

(2) Authorization. There are authorized to be appropriated such sums as may be necessary to carry out the provisions of this section.

(3) Funding for fiscal year 2010. (A) In general. Out of any funds in the Treasury not otherwise appropriated, there is appropriated to MACPAC to carry out the provisions of this section for fiscal year 2010, $9,000,000.

(B) Transfer of funds. Notwithstanding section 2104(a)(13) [42 USCS § 1397dd(a)(13)], from the amounts appropriated in such section for fiscal year 2010, $2,000,000 is hereby transferred and made available in such fiscal year to MACPAC to carry out the provisions of this section.

(4) Availability. Amounts made available under paragraphs (2) and (3) to MACPAC to carry out the provisions of this section shall remain available until expended.

(Aug. 14, 1935, ch 531, Title XIX, § 1900, as added Feb. 4, 2009, P. L. 111-3, Title V, § 506(a), 123 Stat. 91; March 23, 2010, P. L. 111-148, Title II, Subtitle J, § 2801(a), 124 Stat. 328.)

HISTORY; ANCILLARY LAWS AND DIRECTIVES

Other provisions:

No Federal funding for illegal aliens; disallowance for unauthorized expenditures. Act Feb. 4, 2009, P. L. 111-3, Title VI, Subtitle A, § 605, 123 Stat. 100 (effective on 4/1/2009, and applicable to child health assistance and medical assistance provided on or after that date, as provided by § 3(a) of such Act, which appears as a note to this section); March 23, 2010, P. L. 111-148, Title II, Subtitle B, § 2102(a)(2), 124 Stat. 288 (effective as if included in the enactment of Act Feb. 4, 2009, as provided by § 2102(a) of the 2010 Act), provides: "Nothing in this Act [for full classification, consult USCS Tables volumes] allows Federal payment for individuals who are not lawfully residing in the United States. Titles XI, XIX, and XXI of the Social Security Act [42 USCS §§ 1301 et seq., 1396 et seq., and 1397aa et seq.] provide for the disallowance of Federal financial participation for erroneous expenditures under Medicaid and under CHIP, respectively.".

§ 1396a. State plans for medical assistance [Caution: See prospective amendment note below.]

(a) Contents. A State plan for medical assistance must—

(1) provide that it shall be in effect in all political subdivisions of the State, and, if administered by them, be mandatory upon them;

(2) provide for financial participation by the State equal to not less than 40 per centum of the non-Federal share of the expenditures under the plan with respect to which payments under section 1903 [42 USCS § 1396b] are authorized by this title [42 USCS §§ 1396 et seq.]; and, effective July 1, 1969, provide for financial participation by the State equal to all of such non-Federal share or provide for distribution of funds from Federal or State sources, for carrying out the State plan, on an equalization or other basis which will assure that the lack of adequate funds from local sources will not result in lowering the amount, duration, scope, or quality of care and services available under the plan;

(3) provide for granting an opportunity for a fair hearing before the State agency to any individual whose claim for medical assistance under the plan is denied or is not acted upon with reasonable promptness;

(4) provide (A) such methods of administration (including methods relating to the establishment and maintenance of personnel standards on a merit basis, except that the Secretary shall exercise no authority with respect to the selection, tenure of office, and compensation of any individual employed in accordance with such methods, and including provision for utilization of professional medical personnel in the administration and, where administered locally, supervision of administration of the plan) as are found by the Secretary to be necessary for the proper and efficient operation of the plan, (B) for the training and effective use of paid subprofessional staff, with particular emphasis on the full-time or part-time employment of recipients and other persons of low income, as community service aides, in the administration of the plan and for the use of nonpaid or partially paid volunteers in a social service volunteer program in providing services to applicants and recipients and in assisting any advisory committees established by the State agency, (C) that each State or local officer, employee, or independent contractor who is responsible for the expenditure of substantial amounts of funds under the State plan, each individual who formerly was such an officer, employee, or contractor, and each partner of such an officer, employee, or contractor shall be prohibited from committing any act, in relation to any activity under the plan, the commission of which, in connection with any activity concerning the United States Government, by an officer or employee of the United States Government, an individual who was such an officer or employee, or a partner of such an officer or employee is prohibited by section 207 or 208 of title 18, United States Code, and (D) that each State or local officer, employee, or independent contractor who is responsible for selecting, awarding, or otherwise obtaining items and services under the State plan shall be subject to safeguards against conflicts of interest that are at least as stringent as the safeguards that apply under section 27 of the Office of Federal Procurement Policy Act (41 U.S.C. 423) to persons described in subsection (a)(2) of such section of that Act;

(5) either provide for the establishment or designation of a single State agency to administer or to supervise the administration of the plan; or provide for the establishment or designation of a single State agency to administer or to supervise the administration of the plan, except that the determination of eligibility for medical assistance under the plan shall be made by the State or local agency administering the State plan approved under title I or XVI [42 USCS §§ 301 et seq. or 1381 et seq.] (insofar as it relates to the aged) if the State is eligible to participate in the State plan program established under title XVI [42 USCS §§ 1381 et seq.], or by the agency or agencies administering the supplemental security income program established under title XVI [42 USCS §§ 1381 et seq.] or the State Plan approved under part A of title IV [42 USCS §§ 601 et seq.] if the State is not eligible to participate in the State plan program established under title XVI [42 USCS §§ 1381 et

seq.];

(6) provide that the State agency will make such reports, in such form and containing such information, as the Secretary may from time to time require, and comply with such provisions as the Secretary may from time to time find necessary to assure the correctness and verification of such reports;

(7) provide safeguards which restrict the use or disclosure of information concerning applicants and recipients to purposes directly connected with—

(A) the administration of the plan; and

(B) at State option, the exchange of information necessary to verify the certification of eligibility of children for free or reduced price breakfasts under the Child Nutrition Act of 1966 [42 USCS §§ 1771 et seq.] and free or reduced price lunches under the Richard B. Russell National School Lunch Act [42 USCS §§ 1751 et seq.], in accordance with section 9(b) of that Act [42 USCS § 1758(b)], using data standards and formats established by the State agency;

(8) provide that all individuals wishing to make application for medical assistance under the plan shall have opportunity to do so, and that such assistance shall be furnished with reasonable promptness to all eligible individuals;

(9) provide—

(A) that the State health agency, or other appropriate State medical agency (whichever is utilized by the Secretary for the purpose specified in the first sentence of section 1864(a) [42 USCS § 1395aa(a)]), shall be responsible for establishing and maintaining health standards for private or public institutions in which recipients of medical assistance under the plan may receive care or services,

(B) for the establishment or designation of a State authority or authorities which shall be responsible for establishing and maintaining standards, other than those relating to health, for such institutions,

(C) that any laboratory services paid for under such plan must be provided by a laboratory which meets the applicable requirements of section 1861(e)(9) [42 USCS § 1395x(e)(9)] or paragraphs (16) and (17) of section 1861(s) [42 USCS § 1395x(s)(16) and (17)], or, in the case of a laboratory which is in a rural health clinic, of section 1861(aa)(2)(G) [42 USCS § 1395x(aa)(2)(G)], and

(D) that the State maintain a consumer-oriented website providing useful information to consumers regarding all skilled nursing facilities and all nursing facilities in the State, including for each facility, Form 2567 State inspection reports (or a successor form), complaint investigation reports, the facility's plan of correction, and such other information that the State or the Secretary considers useful in assisting the public to assess the quality of long term care options and the quality of care provided by individual facilities;

(10) provide—

(A) for making medical assistance available, including at least the care and services listed in paragraphs (1) through (5), (17), (21), and (28) of section 1905(a) [42 USCS § 1396d(a)], to—

(i) all individuals—

(I) who are receiving aid or assistance under any plan of the State approved under title I, X, XIV, or XVI, or part A or part E of title IV [42 USCS §§ 301 et seq., 1201 et seq., 1351 et seq., or 1381 et seq., or 601 et seq. or 670 et seq.] (including individuals eligible under this title [42 USCS §§ 1396 et seq.] by reason of section 402(a)(37), 406(h), or 473(b) [42 USCS § 673(b)], or considered by the State to be receiving such aid as authorized under section 482(e)(6)),

(II) (aa) with respect to whom supplemental security income benefits are being paid under title XVI [42 USCS § 1381 et seq.] (or were being paid as of the date of the enactment of section 211(a) of the Personal Responsibility and Work Opportunity Reconciliation Act of 1996 (P.L. 104-193) [enacted Aug. 22, 1996] and would continue to be paid but for the enactment of that section), (bb) who are qualified severely impaired individuals (as defined in section 1905(q) [42 USCS § 1396d(q)]), or (cc) who are under 21 years of age and with respect to whom supplemental security income benefits would be paid under title XVI [42 USCS §§ 1381 et seq.] if subparagraphs (A) and (B) of section 1611(c)(7) [42 USCS § 1382(c)(7)] were applied without regard to the phrase "the first day of the month following",

(III) who are qualified pregnant women or children as defined in section 1905(n) [42 USCS § 1396d(n)],

(IV) who are described in subparagraph (A) or (B) of subsection (l)(1) and whose family income does not exceed the minimum income level the State is required to establish under subsection (l)(2)(A) for such a family; [,] or

(V) who are qualified family members as defined in section 1905(m)(1) [42 USCS § 1396d(m)(1)],

(VI) who are described in subparagraph (C) of subsection (l)(1) and whose family income does not exceed the income level the State is required to establish under subsection (l)(2)(B)

for such a family,

(VII) who are described in subparagraph (D) of subsection (l)(1) and whose family income does not exceed the income level the State is required to establish under subsection (l)(2)(C) for such a family;

(VIII) beginning January 1, 2014, who are under 65 years of age, not pregnant, not entitled to, or enrolled for, benefits under part A of title XVIII [42 USCS §§ 1395c et seq.], or enrolled for benefits under part B of title XVIII [42 USCS §§ 1395j et seq.], and are not described in a previous subclause of this clause, and whose income (as determined under subsection (e)(14)) does not exceed 133 percent of the poverty line (as defined in section 2110(c)(5) [42 USCS § 1397jj(c)(5)]) applicable to a family of the size involved, subject to subsection (k); or

(IX) **[Caution: This subclause takes effect on January 1, 2014, as provided by § 2004(d) of Act March 23, 2010, P. L. 111-148, which appears as a note to this section.]** who—

(aa) are under 26 years of age;

(bb) are not described in or enrolled under any of subclauses (I) through (VII) of this clause or are described in any of such subclauses but have income that exceeds the level of income applicable under the State plan for eligibility to enroll for medical assistance under such subclause;

(cc) were in foster care under the responsibility of the State on the date of attaining 18 years of age or such higher age as the State has elected under section 475(8)(B)(iii) [42 USCS § 675(8)(B)(iii)]; and

(dd) were enrolled in the State plan under this title or under a waiver of the plan while in such foster care;

(ii) at the option of the State, to any group or groups of individuals described in section 1905(a) [42 USCS § 1396d(a)] (or, in the case of individuals described in section 1905(a)(i) [42 USCS § 1396d(a)(i)], to any reasonable categories of such individuals) who are not individuals described in clause (i) of this subparagraph but—

(I) who meet the income and resources requirements of the appropriate State plan described in clause (i) or the supplemental security income program (as the case may be),

(II) who would meet the income and resources requirements of the appropriate State plan described in clause (i) if their work-related child care costs were paid from their earnings rather than by a State agency as a service expenditure,

(III) who would be eligible to receive aid under the appropriate State plan described in clause (i) if coverage under such plan was as broad as allowed under Federal law,

(IV) with respect to whom there is being paid, or who are eligible, or would be eligible if they were not in a medical institution, to have paid with respect to them, aid or assistance under the appropriate State plan described in clause (i), supplemental security income benefits under title XVI [42 USCS §§ 1381 et seq.], or a State supplementary payment; [,]

(V) who are in a medical institution for a period of not less than 30 consecutive days (with eligibility by reason of this subclause beginning on the first day of such period), who meet the resource requirements of the appropriate State plan described in clause (i) or the supplemental security income program, and whose income does not exceed a separate income standard established by the State which is consistent with the limit established under section 1903(f)(4)(C) [42 USCS § 1396b(f)(4)(C)],

(VI) who would be eligible under the State plan under this title [42 USCS §§ 1396 et seq.] if they were in a medical institution, with respect to whom there has been a determination that but for the provision of home or community-based services described in subsection (c), (d), or (e) of section 1915 [42 USCS § 1396n(c), (d), or (e)] they would require the level of care provided in a hospital, nursing facility or intermediate care facility for the mentally retarded the cost of which could be reimbursed under the State plan, and who will receive home or community-based services pursuant to a waiver granted by the Secretary under subsection (c), (d), or (e) of section 1915 [42 USCS § 1396n(c), (d), or (e)],

(VII) who would be eligible under the State plan under this title [42 USCS §§ 1396 et seq.] if they were in a medical institution, who are terminally ill, and who will receive hospice care pursuant to a voluntary election described in section 1905(o) [42 USCS § 1396d(o)]; [,]

(VIII) who is a child described in section 1905(a)(i) [42 USCS § 1396d(a)(i)]—

(aa) for whom there is in effect an adoption assistance agreement (other than an agreement under part E of title IV [42 USCS §§ 670 et seq.]) between the State and an adoptive parent or parents,

(bb) who the State agency responsible for adoption assistance has determined cannot be placed with adoptive parents without medical assistance because such child has special needs for medical or rehabilitative care, and

(cc) who was eligible for medical assistance

under the State plan prior to the adoption assistance agreement being entered into, or who would have been eligible for medical assistance at such time if the eligibility standards and methodologies of the State's foster care program under part E of title IV [42 USCS §§ 670 et seq.] were applied rather than the eligibility standards and methodologies of the State's aid to families with dependent children program under part A of title IV [42 USCS §§ 601 et seq.]; [,]

(IX) who are described in subsection (l)(1) and are not described in clause (i)(IV), clause (i)(VI), or clause (i)(VII); [,]

(X) who are described in subsection (m)(1); [,]

(XI) who receive only an optional State supplementary payment based on need and paid on a regular basis, equal to the difference between the individual's countable income and the income standard used to determine eligibility for such supplementary payment (with countable income being the income remaining after deductions as established by the State pursuant to standards that may be more restrictive than the standards for supplementary security income benefits under title XVI [42 USCS §§ 1381 et seq.]), which are available to all individuals in the State (but which may be based on different income standards by political subdivision according to cost of living differences), and which are paid by a State that does not have an agreement with the Commissioner of Social Security under section 1616 or 1634 [42 USCS § 1382e or 1383c];

(XII) who are described in subsection (z)(1) (relating to certain TB-infected individuals);

(XIII) who are in families whose income is less than 250 percent of the income official poverty line (as defined by the Office of Management and Budget, and revised annually in accordance with section 673(2) of the Omnibus Budget Reconciliation Act of 1981 [42 USCS § 9902(2)]) applicable to a family of the size involved, and who but for earnings in excess of the limit established under section 1905(q)(2)(B) [42 USCS § 1396d(q)(2)(B)], would be considered to be receiving supplemental security income (subject, notwithstanding section 1916 [42 USCS § 1396o], to payment of premiums or other cost-sharing charges (set on a sliding scale based on income) that the State may determine);

(XIV) who are optional targeted low-income children described in section 1905(u)(2)(B) [42 USCS § 1396d(u)(2)(B)];

(XV) who, but for earnings in excess of the limit established under section 1905(q)(2)(B) [42 USCS § 1396d(q)(2)(B)], would be considered to be receiving supplemental security income, who is at least 16, but less than 65, years of age, and whose assets, resources, and earned or unearned income (or both) do not exceed such limitations (if any) as the State may establish;

(XVI) who are employed individuals with a medically improved disability described in section 1905(v)(1) [42 USCS § 1396d(v)(1)] and whose assets, resources, and earned or unearned income (or both) do not exceed such limitations (if any) as the State may establish, but only if the State provides medical assistance to individuals described in subclause (XV);

(XVII) who are independent foster care adolescents (as defined in section 1905(w)(1) [42 USCS § 1396d(w)(1)]), or who are within any reasonable categories of such adolescents specified by the State;

(XVIII) who are described in subsection (aa) (relating to certain breast or cervical cancer patients);

(XIX) who are disabled children described in subsection (cc)(1);

(XX) beginning January 1, 2014, who are under 65 years of age and are not described in or enrolled under a previous subclause of this clause, and whose income (as determined under subsection (e)(14)) exceeds 133 percent of the poverty line (as defined in section 2110(c)(5) [42 USCS § 1397jj(c)(5)]) applicable to a family of the size involved but does not exceed the highest income eligibility level established under the State plan or under a waiver of the plan, subject to subsection (hh);

(XXI) who are described in subsection (ii) (relating to individuals who meet certain income standards); or

(XXII) who are eligible for home and community-based services under needs-based criteria established under paragraph (1)(A) of section 1915(i) [42 USCS § 1396n(i)], or who are eligible for home and community-based services under paragraph (6) of such section, and who will receive home and community-based services pursuant to a State plan amendment under such subsection;

(B) that the medical assistance made available to any individual described in subparagraph (A)—

(i) shall not be less in amount, duration, or scope than the medical assistance made available to any other such individual, and

(ii) shall not be less in amount, duration, or scope than the medical assistance made available to individuals not described in subparagraph (A);

(C) that if medical assistance is included for any group of individuals described in section 1905(a) [42 USCS § 1396d(a)] who are not described in subparagraph (A) or (E), then—

(i) the plan must include a description of (I) the criteria for determining eligibility of individuals in the group for such medical assistance, (II) the amount, duration, and scope of medical assistance made available to individuals in the group, and (III) the single standard to be employed in determining income and resource eligibility for all such groups, and the methodology to be employed in determining such eligibility, which shall be no more restrictive than the methodology which would be employed under the supplemental security income program in the case of groups consisting of aged, blind, or disabled individuals in a State in which such program is in effect, and which shall be no more restrictive than the methodology which would be employed under the appropriate State plan (described in subparagraph (A)(i)) to which such group is most closely categorically related in the case of other groups;

(ii) the plan must make available medical assistance—

(I) to individuals under the age of 18 who (but for income and resources) would be eligible for medical assistance as an individual described in subparagraph (A)(i), and

(II) to pregnant women, during the course of their pregnancy, who (but for income and resources) would be eligible for medical assistance as an individual described in subparagraph (A);

(iii) such medical assistance must include (I) with respect to children under 18 and individuals entitled to institutional services, ambulatory services, and (II) with respect to pregnant women, prenatal care and delivery services; and

(iv) if such medical assistance includes services in institutions for mental diseases or in an intermediate care facility for the mentally retarded (or both) for any such group, it also must include for all groups covered at least the care and services listed in paragraphs (1) through (5) and (17) of section 1905(a) [42 USCS § 1396d(a)(1)–(5) and (17)] or the care and services listed in any 7 of the paragraphs numbered (1) through (24) of such section;

(D) for the inclusion of home health services for any individual who, under the State plan, is entitled to nursing facility services; and

(E)(i) but, for making medical assistance available for medicare cost-sharing (as defined in section 1905(p)(3) [42 USCS § 1396d(p)(3)]) for qualified medicare beneficiaries described in section 1905(p)(1) [42 USCS § 1396d(p)(1)];

(ii) for making medical assistance available for payment of medicare cost-sharing described in section 1905(p)(3)(A)(i) [42 USCS § 1396d(p)(3)(A)(i)] for qualified disabled and working individuals described in section 1905(s) [42 USCS § 1396d(s)];

(iii) for making medical assistance available for medicare cost sharing described in section 1905(p)(3)(A)(ii) [42 USCS § 1396d(p)(3)(A)(ii)] subject to section 1905(p)(4) [42 USCS § 1396d(p)(4)], for individuals who would be qualified medicare beneficiaries described in section 1905(p)(1) [42 USCS § 1396d(p)(1)] but for the fact that their income exceeds the income level established by the State under section 1905(p)(2) [42 USCS § 1396d(p)(2)] but is less than 110 percent in 1993 and 1994, and 120 percent in 1995 and years thereafter of the official poverty line (referred to in such section) for a family of the size involved; and

(iv) subject to sections 1933 and 1905(p)(4) [42 USCS §§ 1396u-3, 1396d(p)(4)], for making medical assistance available (but only for premiums payable with respect to months during the period beginning with January 1998, and ending with December 2010) for medicare cost-sharing described in section 1905(p)(3)(A)(ii) [42 USCS § 1396d(p)(3)(A)(ii)] for individuals who would be qualified medicare beneficiaries described in section 1905(p)(1) [42 USCS § 1396d(p)(1)] but for the fact that their income exceeds the income level established by the State under section 1905(p)(2) [42 USCS § 1396d(p)(2)] and is at least 120 percent, but less than 135 percent, of the official poverty line (referred to in such section) for a family of the size involved and who are not otherwise eligible for medical assistance under the State plan;

(F) at the option of a State, for making medical assistance available for COBRA premiums (as defined in subsection (u)(2)) for qualified COBRA continuation beneficiaries described in section 1902(u)(1) [subsec. (u)(1) of this section]; and

(G) that, in applying eligibility criteria of the supplemental security income program under title XVI [42 USCS §§ 1381 et seq.] for purposes of determining eligibility for medical assistance under the State plan of an individual who is not receiving supplemental security income, the State will disregard the provisions of subsections (c) and (e) of section 1613 [42 USCS § 1382b];

except that (I) the making available of the services described in paragraph (4), (14), or (16) of section 1905(a) [42 USCS § 1396d(a)(4), (14) or (16)] to individuals meeting the age requirements prescribed therein shall not, by reason of this paragraph (10), require the making available of any such services, or the making available of such services of the same amount, duration, and scope, to individuals of any other ages, (II) the making available of supplementary medical insurance benefits under part B of title XVIII [42 USCS §§ 1395j et seq.] to individuals eligible therefor (either pursuant to an agreement entered into under section 1843 [42 USCS § 1395v] or by reason of the payment of premiums under such title [42 USCS §§ 1395 et seq.] by the State agency on behalf of such individuals), or provision for meeting part or all of the cost of deductibles, cost sharing, or similar charges under part B of title XVIII [42 USCS §§ 1395j et seq.] for individuals eligible for benefits under such part [42 USCS §§ 1395j et seq.], shall not, by reason of this paragraph (10), require the making available of any such benefits, or the making available of services of the same amount, duration, and scope, to any other individuals, (III) the making available of medical assistance equal in amount, duration, and scope to the medical assistance made available to individuals described in clause (A) to any classification of individuals approved by the Secretary with respect to whom there is being paid, or who are eligible, or would be eligible if they were not in a medical institution, to have paid with respect to them, a State supplementary payment shall not, by reason of this paragraph (10), require the making available of any such assistance, or the making available of such assistance of the same amount, duration, and scope, to any other individuals not described in clause (A), (IV) the imposition of a deductible, cost sharing, or similar charge for any item or service furnished to an individual not eligible for the exemption under section 1916(a)(2) or (b)(2) [42 USCS § 1396o(a)(2) or (b)(2)] shall not require the imposition of a deductible, cost sharing, or similar charge for the same item or service furnished to an individual who is eligible for such exemption, (V) the making available to pregnant women covered under the plan of services relating to pregnancy (including prenatal, delivery, and postpartum services) or to any other condition which may complicate pregnancy shall not, by reason of this paragraph (10), require the making available of such services, or the making available of such services of the same amount, duration, and scope, to any other individuals, provided such services are made available (in the same amount, duration, and scope) to all pregnant women covered under the State plan, (VI) with respect to the making available of medical assistance for hospice care to terminally ill individuals who have made a voluntary election described in section 1905(o) [42 USCS § 1396d(o)] to receive hospice care instead of medical assistance for certain other services, such assistance may not be made available in an amount, duration, or scope less than that provided under title XVIII [42 USCS §§ 1395 et seq.], and the making available of such assistance shall not, by reason of this paragraph (10), require the making available of medical assistance for hospice care to other individuals or the making available of medical assistance for services waived by such terminally ill individuals, (VII) the medical assistance made available to an individual described in subsection (l)(1)(A) who is eligible for medical assistance only because of subparagraph (A)(i)(IV) or (A)(ii)(IX) shall be limited to medical assistance for services related to pregnancy (including prenatal, delivery, postpartum, and family planning services) and to other conditions which may complicate pregnancy, (VIII) the medical assistance made available to a qualified medicare beneficiary described in section 1905(p)(1) [42 USCS § 1396d(p)(1)] who is only entitled to medical assistance because the individual is such a beneficiary shall be limited to medical assistance for medicare cost-sharing (described in section 1905(p)(3) [42 USCS § 1396d(p)(3)]), subject to the provisions of subsection (n) and section 1916(b) [42 USCS § 1396o(b)], (IX) the making available of respiratory care services in accordance with subsection (e)(9) shall not, by reason of this paragraph (10), require the making available of such services, or the making available of such services of the same amount, duration, and scope, to any individuals not included under subsection (e)(9)(A), provided such services are made available (in the same amount, duration, and scope) to all individuals described in such subsection, (X) if the plan provides for any fixed durational limit on medical assistance for inpatient hospital services (whether or not such a limit varies by medical condition or diagnosis), the plan must establish exceptions to such a limit for medically necessary inpatient hospital services furnished with respect to individuals under one year of age in a hospital defined under the State plan, pursuant to section 1923(a)(1)(A) [42 USCS § 1396r-4], as a disproportionate share hospital and subparagraph (B) (relating to comparability) shall not be construed as requiring such an exception for other individuals, services, or hospitals, (XI) the making available of medical assistance to cover the costs of premiums, deductibles, coinsurance, and other cost-sharing obligations for certain individuals for private health coverage as described in section 1906 [42 USCS § 1396e] shall not, by reason of paragraph (10), require the making available of any such benefits or the making available of services of the same amount, duration, and scope of such private coverage to any other individuals, (XII) the medical assistance made available to an individual described in subsection (u)(1) who is eligible for medical assistance only because of subparagraph (F) shall be limited to medical assistance for COBRA continuation premiums (as defined in subsection (u)(2)), (XIII) the medical assistance made available to an individual described in subsection (z)(1) who is eligible for medical assistance only because of subparagraph (A)(ii)(XII) shall be limited to medical assistance for TB-related services (described in subsection (z)(2)), (XIV) the medical assistance made available to an individual described in subsection (aa) who is eligible for medical assistance only because of subparagraph (A)(10)(ii)(XVIII) shall be limited to medical assistance provided during the period in which such an individual requires treatment for breast or cervical cancer[,] (XV) the medical assistance made available to an individual described in subparagraph (A)(i)(VIII) shall be limited to medical assistance described in subsection (k)(1), [and] (XVI) the medical assistance made available to an individual described in subsection (ii) shall be limited to family planning services and supplies described in section 1905(a)(4)(C) [42 USCS § 1396d(a)(4)(C)] including medical diagnosis and treatment services that are provided pursuant to a family planning service in a family planning setting[,] and (XVI) [XVII] if an individual is described in subclause (IX) of subparagraph (A)(i) and is also described in subclause (VIII) of that subparagraph, the medical assistance shall be made available to the individual through subclause (IX) instead of through subclause (VIII);

(11) (A) provide for entering into cooperative arrangements with the State agencies responsible for administering or supervising the administration of health services and vocational rehabilitation services in the State looking toward maximum utilization of such services in the provision of medical assistance under the plan, (B) provide, to the extent prescribed by the Secretary, for entering into agreements, with any agency, institution, or organization receiving payments under (or through an allotment under) title V [42 USCS §§ 701 et seq.], (i) providing for utilizing such agency, institution, or organization in furnishing care and services which are available under such title [42 USCS §§ 701 et seq.] or allotment and which are included in the State plan approved under this section[,](ii) making such provision as may be appropriate for reimbursing such agency, institution, or organization for the cost of any such care and services furnished any individual for which payment would otherwise be made to the State with respect to the individual under section 1903 [42 USCS § 1396b], and (iii) providing for coordination of information and education on pediatric vaccinations and delivery of immunization services, and (C) provide for coordination of the operations under this title [42 USCS §§ 1396 et seq.], including the provision of information and education on pediatric vaccinations and the delivery of immunization services, with the State's operations under the special supplemental nutrition program for women, infants, and children under section 17 of the Child Nutrition Act of 1966 [42 USCS § 1786];

(12) provide that, in determining whether an individual is blind, there shall be an examination by a physician skilled in the diseases of the eye or by an optometrist, whichever the individual may select;

(13) provide—

(A) for a public process for determination of rates of payment under the plan for hospital services, nursing facility services, and services of intermediate care facilities for the mentally retarded under which—

(i) proposed rates, the methodologies underlying the establishment of such rates, and justifications for the proposed rates are published,

(ii) providers, beneficiaries and their representatives, and other concerned State residents are given a reasonable opportunity for review and comment on the proposed rates, methodologies, and justifications,

(iii) final rates, the methodologies underlying the establishment of such rates, and justifications for such final rates are published, and

(iv) in the case of hospitals, such rates take into account (in a manner consistent with section 1923 [42 USCS § 1396r-4]) the situation of hospitals which serve a disproportionate number of low-income patients with special needs;

(B) for payment for hospice care in amounts no lower than the amounts, using the same methodology, used under part A of title XVIII [42 USCS §§ 1395c et seq.] and for payment of amounts under section 1905(o)(3) [42 USCS § 1396d(o)(3)]; except that in the case of hospice care which is furnished to an individual who is a resident of a nursing facility or intermediate care facility for the mentally retarded, and who would be eligible under the plan for nursing facility services or services in an intermediate care facility for the mentally retarded if he had not elected to receive hospice care, there shall be paid an additional amount, to take into account the room and board furnished by the facility, equal to at least 95 percent of the rate that would have been paid by the State under the plan for facility services in that facility for that individual; and

(C) payment for primary care services (as defined in subsection (jj)) furnished in 2013 and 2014 by a physician with a primary specialty designation of family medicine, general internal medicine, or pediatric medicine at a rate not less than 100 percent of the payment rate that applies to such services and physician under part B of title XVIII [42 USCS §§ 1395j et seq.] (or, if greater, the payment rate that would be applicable under such part if the conversion factor under section 1848(d) [42 USCS § 1395w-4(d)] for the year involved were the conversion factor under such section for 2009);

(14) provide that enrollment fees, premiums, or similar charges, and deductions, cost sharing, or similar charges, may be imposed only as provided in section 1916 [42 USCS § 1396o];

(15) provide for payment for services described in clause (B) or (C) of section 1905(a)(2) [42 USCS § 1396d(a)(2)] under the plan in accordance with subsection (bb);

(16) provide for inclusion, to the extent required by regulations prescribed by the Secretary, of provisions (conforming to such regulations) with respect to the furnishing of medical assistance under the plan to individuals who are residents of the State but are absent therefrom;

(17) except as provided in subsections (e)(14), (l)(3), (m)(3), and (m)(4), include reasonable standards (which shall be comparable for all groups and may, in accordance with standards prescribed by the Secretary, differ with respect to income levels, but only in the case of applicants or recipients of assistance under the plan who are not receiving aid or assistance under any plan of the State approved under title I, X, XIV, or XVI, or part A of title IV [42 USCS §§ 301 et seq., 1201 et seq., 1351 et seq., or 1381 et seq., or 601 et seq.], and with respect to whom supplemental security income benefits are not being paid under title XVI [42 USCS §§ 1381 et seq.], based on the variations between shelter costs in urban areas and in rural areas) for determining eligibility for and the extent of medical assistance under the plan which (A) are consistent with the objectives of this title [42 USCS §§ 1396 et seq.], (B) provide for taking into account only such income and resources as are, as determined in accordance with standards prescribed by the Secretary, available to the applicant or recipient and (in the case of any applicant or recipient who would, except for income and resources, be eligible for aid or assistance in the form of money payments under any plan of the State approved under title I, X, XIV, or XVI, or part A of title IV [42 USCS §§ 301 et seq., 1201 et seq., 1351 et seq., or 1381 et seq., or 601 et seq.], or to have paid with respect to him supplemental security income benefits under title XVI [42 USCS §§ 1381 et seq.]) as would not be disregarded (or set aside for future needs) in determining his eligibility for such aid, assistance, or benefits, (C) provide for reasonable evaluation of any such income or resources, and (D) do not take into account the financial responsibility of any individual for any applicant or recipient of assistance under the plan unless such applicant or recipient is such individual's spouse or such individual's child who is under 21 or (with respect to States eligible to participate in the State program established under title XVI [42 USCS §§ 1381 et seq.]), is blind or permanently and totally disabled, or is blind or disabled as defined in section 1614 [42 USCS § 1382c] (with respect to States which are not eligible to participate in such program); and provide for flexibility in the application of such standards with respect to income by taking into account, except to the extent prescribed by the Secretary, the costs (whether in the form of insurance premiums, payments made to the State under section 1903(f)(2)(B) [42 USCS § 1396b(f)(2)(B)], or otherwise and regardless of whether such costs are reimbursed under another public program of the State or political subdivision thereof) incurred for medical care or for any other type of remedial care recognized under State law;

(18) comply with the provisions of section 1917 [42 USCS § 1396p] with respect to liens, adjustments and recoveries of medical assistance correctly paid, [,] transfers of assets, and treatment of certain trusts;

(19) provide such safeguards as may be necessary to assure that eligibility for care and services under the plan will be determined, and such care and services will be provided, in a

manner consistent with simplicity of administration and the best interests of the recipients;

(20) if the State plan includes medical assistance in behalf of individuals 65 years of age or older who are patients in institutions for mental diseases—

(A) provide for having in effect such agreements or other arrangements with State authorities concerned with mental diseases, and, where appropriate, with such institutions, as may be necessary for carrying out the State plan, including arrangements for joint planning and for development of alternate methods of care, arrangements providing assurance of immediate readmittance to institutions where needed for individuals under alternate plans of care, and arrangements providing for access to patients and facilities, for furnishing information, and for making reports;

(B) provide for an individual plan for each such patient to assure that the institutional care provided to him is in his best interests, including, to that end, assurances that there will be initial and periodic review of his medical and other needs, that he will be given appropriate medical treatment within the institution, and that there will be a periodic determination of his need for continued treatment in the institution; and

(C) provide for the development of alternate plans of care, making maximum utilization of available resources, for recipients 65 years of age or older who would otherwise need care in such institutions, including appropriate medical treatment and other aid or assistance; for services referred to in section 3(a)(4)(A)(i) and (ii) [42 USCS § 303(a)(4)(A)(i) and (ii)] or section 1603(a)(4)(A)(i) and (ii) which are appropriate for such recipients and for such patients; and for methods of administration necessary to assure that the responsibilities of the State agency under the State plan with respect to such recipients and such patients will be effectively carried out;

(21) if the State plan includes medical assistance in behalf of individuals 65 years of age or older who are patients in public institutions for mental diseases, show that the State is making satisfactory progress toward developing and implementing a comprehensive mental health program, including provision for utilization of community mental health centers, nursing facilities, and other alternatives to care in public institutions for mental diseases;

(22) include descriptions of (A) the kinds and numbers of professional medical personnel and supporting staff that will be used in the administration of the plan and of the responsibilities they will have, (B) the standards, for private or public institutions in which recipients of medical assistance under the plan may receive care or services, that will be utilized by the State authority or authorities responsible for establishing and maintaining such standards, (C) the cooperative arrangements with State health agencies and State vocational rehabilitation agencies entered into with a view to maximum utilization of and coordination of the provision of medical assistance with the services administered or supervised by such agencies, and (D) other standards and methods that the State will use to assure that medical or remedial care and services provided to recipients of medical assistance are of high quality;

(23) except as provided in subsection (g), in section 1915 [42 USCS § 1396n], and in section 1932(a) [42 USCS § 1396u-2(a)] and except in the case of Puerto Rico, the Virgin Islands, and Guam, provide that (A) any individual eligible for medical assistance (including drugs) may obtain such assistance from any institution, agency, community pharmacy, or person, qualified to perform the service or services required (including an organization which provides such services, or arranges for their availability, on a prepayment basis), who undertakes to provide him such services, and (B) an enrollment of an individual eligible for medical assistance in a primary care case-management system (described in section 1915(b)(1) [42 USCS § 1396n(b)(1)]), a medicaid managed care organization, or a similar entity shall not restrict the choice of the qualified person from whom the individual may receive services under section 1905(a)(4)(C) [42 USCS § 1396d(a)(4)(C)], except as provided in subsection (g) and in section 1915 [42 USCS § 1396n], except that this paragraph shall not apply in the case of Puerto Rico, the Virgin Islands, and Guam, and except that nothing in this paragraph shall be construed as requiring a State to provide medical assistance for such services furnished by a person or entity convicted of a felony under Federal or State law for an offense which the State agency determines is inconsistent with the best interests of beneficiaries under the State plan or by a provider or supplier to which a moratorium under subsection (ii)(4) is applied during the period of such moratorium;

(24) effective July 1, 1969, provide for consultative services by health agencies and other appropriate agencies of the State to hospitals, nursing facilities, home health agencies, clinics, laboratories, and such other institutions as the Secretary may specify in order to assist them (A) to qualify for payments under this

Act, (B) to establish and maintain such fiscal records as may be necessary for the proper and efficient administration of this Act, and (C) to provide information needed to determine payments due under this Act on account of care and services furnished to individuals;

(25) provide—

(A) that the State or local agency administering such plan will take all reasonable measures to ascertain the legal liability of third parties (including health insurers, self-insured plans, group health plans (as defined in section 607(1) of the Employee Retirement Income Security Act of 1974 [29 USCS § 1167(1)]), service benefit plans, managed care organizations, pharmacy benefit managers, or other parties that are, by statute, contract, or agreement, legally responsible for payment of a claim for a health care item or service) to pay for care and services available under the plan, including—

(i) the collection of sufficient information (as specified by the Secretary in regulations) to enable the State to pursue claims against such third parties, with such information being collected at the time of any determination or redetermination of eligibility for medical assistance, and

(ii) the submission to the Secretary of a plan (subject to approval by the Secretary) for pursuing claims against such third parties, which plan shall be integrated with, and be monitored as a part of the Secretary's review of, the State's mechanized claims processing and information retrieval systems required under section 1903(r) [42 USCS § 1396b(r)];

(B) that in any case where such a legal liability is found to exist after medical assistance has been made available on behalf of the individual and where the amount of reimbursement the State can reasonably expect to recover exceeds the costs of such recovery, the State or local agency will seek reimbursement for such assistance to the extent of such legal liability;

(C) that in the case of an individual who is entitled to medical assistance under the State plan with respect to a service for which a third party is liable for payment, the person furnishing the service may not seek to collect from the individual (or any financially responsible relative or representative of that individual) payment of an amount for that service (i) if the total of the amount of the liabilities of third parties for that service is at least equal to the amount payable for that service under the plan (disregarding section 1916 [42 USCS § 1396o]), or (ii) in an amount which exceeds the lesser of (I) the amount which may be collected under section 1916 [42 USCS § 1396o], or (II) the amount by which the amount payable for that service under the plan (disregarding section 1916 [42 USCS § 1396o]) exceeds the total of the amount of the liabilities of third parties for that service;

(D) that a person who furnishes services and is participating under the plan may not refuse to furnish services to an individual (who is entitled to have payment made under the plan for the services the person furnishes) because of a third party's potential liability for payment for the service;

(E) that in the case of prenatal or preventive pediatric care (including early and periodic screening and diagnosis services under section 1905(a)(4)(B) [42 USCS § 1396d(a)(4)(B)]) covered under the State plan, the State shall—

(i) make payment for such service in accordance with the usual payment schedule under such plan for such services without regard to the liability of a third party for payment for such services; and

(ii) seek reimbursement from such third party in accordance with subparagraph (B);

(F) that in the case of any services covered under such plan which are provided to an individual on whose behalf child support enforcement is being carried out by the State agency under part D of title IV of this Act [42 USCS §§ 651 et seq.], the State shall—

(i) make payment for such service in accordance with the usual payment schedule under such plan for such services without regard to any third-party liability for payment for such services, if such third-party liability is derived (through insurance or otherwise) from the parent whose obligation to pay support is being enforced by such agency, if payment has not been made by such third party within 30 days after such services are furnished; and

(ii) seek reimbursement from such third party in accordance with subparagraph (B);

(G) that the State prohibits any health insurer (including a group health plan, as defined in section 607(1) of the Employee Retirement Income Security Act of 1974 [29 USCS § 1167(1)], a self-insured plan, a service benefit plan, a managed care organization, a pharmacy benefit manager, or other party that is, by statute, contract, or agreement, legally responsible for payment of a claim for a health care item or service), in enrolling an individual or in making any payments for benefits to the individual or on the individual's behalf, from taking into account that the individual is eligible for or is provided medical assistance under a plan under this title [42 USCS §§ 1396 et seq.] for such State, or any other State;

(H) that to the extent that payment has been made under the State plan for medical assistance in any case where a third party has a legal liability to make payment for such assistance, the State has in effect laws under which, to the extent that payment has been made under the State plan for medical assistance for health care items or services furnished to an individual, the State is considered to have acquired the rights of such individual to payment by any other party for such health care items or services; and

(I) that the State shall provide assurances satisfactory to the Secretary that the State has in effect laws requiring health insurers, including self-insured plans, group health plans (as defined in section 607(1) of the Employee Retirement Income Security Act of 1974 [29 USCS § 1167(1)]), service benefit plans, managed care organizations, pharmacy benefit managers, or other parties that are, by statute, contract, or agreement, legally responsible for payment of a claim for a health care item or service, as a condition of doing business in the State, to—

(i) provide, with respect to individuals who are eligible (and, at State option, individuals who apply or whose eligibility for medical assistance is being evaluated in accordance with section 1902(e)(13)(D) [42 USCS § 1396a(e)(13)(D)]) for, or are provided, medical assistance under the State plan under this title [42 USCS §§ 1396 et seq.] (and, at State option, child health assistance under title XXI [42 USCS §§ 1397aa et seq.]), upon the request of the State, information to determine during what period the individual or their spouses or their dependents may be (or may have been) covered by a health insurer and the nature of the coverage that is or was provided by the health insurer (including the name, address, and identifying number of the plan) in a manner prescribed by the Secretary;

(ii) accept the State's right of recovery and the assignment to the State of any right of an individual or other entity to payment from the party for an item or service for which payment has been made under the State plan;

(iii) respond to any inquiry by the State regarding a claim for payment for any health care item or service that is submitted not later than 3 years after the date of the provision of such health care item or service; and

(iv) agree not to deny a claim submitted by the State solely on the basis of the date of submission of the claim, the type or format of the claim form, or a failure to present proper documentation at the point-of-sale that is the basis of the claim, if—

(I) the claim is submitted by the State within the 3-year period beginning on the date on which the item or service was furnished; and

(II) any action by the State to enforce its rights with respect to such claim is commenced within 6 years of the State's submission of such claim;

(26) if the State plan includes medical assistance for inpatient mental hospital services, provide, with respect to each patient receiving such services, for a regular program of medical review (including medical evaluation) of his need for such services, and for a written plan of care;

(27) provide for agreements with every person or institution providing services under the State plan under which such person or institution agrees (A) to keep such records as are necessary fully to disclose the extent of the services provided to individuals receiving assistance under the State plan, and (B) to furnish the State agency or the Secretary with such information, regarding any payments claimed by such person or institution for providing services under the State plan, as the State agency or the Secretary may from time to time request;

(28) provide—

(A) that any nursing facility receiving payments under such plan must satisfy all the requirements of subsections (b) through (d) of section 1919 [42 USCS § 1396r(b)–(d)] as they apply to such facilities;

(B) for including in "nursing facility services" at least the items and services specified (or deemed to be specified) by the Secretary under section 1919(f)(7) [42 USCS § 1396r(f)(7)] and making available upon request a description of the items and services so included;

(C) for procedures to make available to the public the data and methodology used in establishing payment rates for nursing facilities under this title [42 USCS §§ 1396 et seq.]; and

(D) for compliance (by the date specified in the respective sections) with the requirements of—

(i) section 1919(e) [42 USCS § 1396r(e)];

(ii) section 1919(g) [42 USCS § 1396r(g)] (relating to responsibility for survey and certification of nursing facilities); and

(iii) sections 1919(h)(2)(B) and 1919(h)(2)(D) [42 USCS § 1396r(h)(2)(B) and (D)] (relating to establishment and application of remedies);

(29) **[Caution: For contingency relating**

to effective date of 1990 repeal of paragraph, see § 4801(e)(11)(A) of Act Nov. 5, 1990, P. L. 101-508, which appears as a note to this section.] include a State program which meets the requirements set forth in section 1908 [42 USCS § 1396g], for the licensing of administrators of nursing homes;

(30)(A) provide such methods and procedures relating to the utilization of, and the payment for, care and services available under the plan (including but not limited to utilization review plans as provided for in section 1903(i)(4) [42 USCS § 1396b(i)(4)]) as may be necessary to safeguard against unnecessary utilization of such care and services and to assure that payments are consistent with efficiency, economy, and quality of care and are sufficient to enlist enough providers so that care and services are available under the plan at least to the extent that such care and services are available to the general population in the geographic area; and

(B) provide, under the program described in subparagraph (A), that—

(i) each admission to a hospital, intermediate care facility for the mentally retarded, or hospital for mental diseases is reviewed or screened in accordance with criteria established by medical and other professional personnel who are not themselves directly responsible for the care of the patient involved, and who do not have a significant financial interest in any such institution and are not, except in the case of a hospital, employed by the institution providing the care involved, and

(ii) the information developed from such review or screening, along with the data obtained from prior reviews of the necessity for admission and continued stay of patients by such professional personnel, shall be used as the basis for establishing the size and composition of the sample of admissions to be subject to review and evaluation by such personnel, and any such sample may be of any size up to 100 percent of all admissions and must be of sufficient size to serve the purpose of (I) identifying the patterns of care being provided and the changes occurring over time in such patterns so that the need for modification may be ascertained, and (II) subjecting admissions to early or more extensive review where information indicates that such consideration is warranted to a hospital, intermediate care facility for the mentally retarded, or hospital for mental diseases;

(31) with respect to services in an intermediate care facility for the mentally retarded (where the State plan includes medical assistance for such services) provide, with respect to each patient receiving such services, for a written plan of care, prior to admission to or authorization of benefits in such facility, in accordance with regulations of the Secretary, and for a regular program of independent professional review (including medical evaluation) which shall periodically review his need for such services;

(32) provide that no payment under the plan for any care or service provided to an individual shall be made to anyone other than such individual or the person or institution providing such care or service, under an assignment or power of attorney or otherwise; except that—

(A) in the case of any care or service provided by a physician, dentist, or other individual practitioner, such payment may be made (i) to the employer of such physician, dentist, or other practitioner if such physician, dentist, or practitioner is required as a condition of his employment to turn over his fee for such care or service to his employer, or (ii) (where the care or service was provided in a hospital, clinic, or other facility) to the facility in which the care or service was provided if there is a contractual arrangement between such physician, dentist, or practitioner and such facility under which such facility submits the bill for such care or service;

(B) nothing in this paragraph shall be construed (i) to prevent the making of such a payment in accordance with an assignment from the person or institution providing the care or service involved if such assignment is made to a governmental agency or entity or is established by or pursuant to the order of a court of competent jurisdiction, or (ii) to preclude an agent of such person or institution from receiving any such payment if (but only if) such agent does so pursuant to an agency agreement under which the compensation to be paid to the agent for his services for or in connection with the billing or collection of payments due such person or institution under the plan is unrelated (directly or indirectly) to the amount of such payments or the billings therefor, and is not dependent upon the actual collection of any such payment;

(C) in the case of services furnished (during a period that does not exceed 14 continuous days in the case of an informal reciprocal arrangement or 90 continuous days (or such longer period as the Secretary may provide) in the case of an arrangement involving per diem or other fee-for-time compensation) by, or incident to the services of, one physician to the patients of another physician who submits the claim for such services, payment shall be made to the physician submitting the claim (as if the services were furnished by, or incident to, the physician's services), but only if the claim identifies (in a manner specified by the Secretary) the physician who furnished the services; and

(D) in the case of payment for a childhood vaccine administered before October 1, 1994, to individuals entitled to medical assistance under the State plan, the State plan may make payment directly to the manufacturer of the vaccine under a voluntary replacement program agreed to by the State pursuant to which the manufacturer (i) supplies doses of the vaccine to providers administering the vaccine, (ii) periodically replaces the supply of the vaccine, and (iii) charges the State the manufacturer's price to the Centers for Disease Control and Prevention for the vaccine so administered (which price includes a reasonable amount to cover shipping and the handling of returns);

(33) provide—

(A) that the State health agency, or other appropriate State medical agency, shall be responsible for establishing a plan, consistent with regulations prescribed by the Secretary, for the review by appropriate professional health personnel of the appropriateness and quality of care and services furnished to recipients of medical assistance under the plan in order to provide guidance with respect thereto in the administration of the plan to the State agency established or designated pursuant to paragraph (5) and, where applicable, to the State agency described in the second sentence of this subsection; and

(B) that, except as provided in section 1919(g) [42 USCS § 1396r(g)], the State or local agency utilized by the Secretary for the purpose specified in the first sentence of section 1864(a) [42 USCS § 1395aa(a)], or, if such agency is not the State agency which is responsible for licensing health institutions, the State agency responsible for such licensing, will perform for the State agency administering or supervising the administration of the plan approved under this title [42 USCS §§ 1396 et seq.] the function of determining whether institutions and agencies meet the requirements for participation in the program under such plan, except that, if the Secretary has cause to question the adequacy of such determinations, the Secretary is authorized to validate State determinations and, on that basis, make independent and binding determinations concerning the extent to which individual institutions and agencies meet the requirements for participation;

(34) provide that in the case of any individual who has been determined to be eligible for medical assistance under the plan, such assistance will be made available to him for care and services included under the plan and furnished in or after the third month before the month in which he made application (or application was made on his behalf in the case of a deceased individual) for such assistance if such individual was (or upon application would have been) eligible for such assistance at the time such care and services were furnished;

(35) provide that any disclosing entity (as defined in section 1124(a)(2) [42 USCS § 1320a-3(a)(2)]) receiving payments under such plan complies with the requirements of section 1124 [42 USCS § 1320a-3];

(36) provide that within 90 days following the completion of each survey of any health care facility, laboratory, agency, clinic, or organization, by the appropriate State agency described in paragraph (9), such agency shall (in accordance with regulations of the Secretary) make public in readily available form and place the pertinent findings of each such survey relating to the compliance of each such health care facility, laboratory, clinic, agency, or organization with (A) the statutory conditions of participation imposed under this title [42 USCS §§ 1396 et seq.], and (B) the major additional conditions which the Secretary finds necessary in the interest of health and safety of individuals who are furnished care or services by any such facility, laboratory, clinic, agency, or organization;

(37) provide for claims payment procedures which (A) ensure that 90 per centum of claims for payment (for which no further written information or substantiation is required in order to make payment) made for services covered under the plan and furnished by health care practitioners through individual or group practices or through shared health facilities are paid within 30 days of the date of receipt of such claims and that 99 per centum of such claims are paid within 90 days of the date of receipt of such claims, and (B) provide for procedures of prepayment and postpayment claims review, including review of appropriate data with respect to the recipient and provider of a service and the nature of the service for which payment is claimed, to ensure the proper and efficient payment of claims and management of the program;

(38) require that an entity (other than an individual practitioner or a group of practitioners) that furnishes, or arranges for the furnishing of, items or services under the plan,

shall supply (within such period as may be specified in regulations by the Secretary or by the single State agency which administers or supervises the administration of the plan) upon request specifically addressed to such entity by the Secretary or such State agency, the information described in section 1128(b)(9) [42 USCS § 1320a-7(b)(9)];

(39) provide that the State agency shall exclude any specified individual or entity from participation in the program under the State plan for the period specified by the Secretary, when required by him to do so pursuant to section 1128 or section 1128A [42 USCS § 1320a-7 or 1320a-7a], and provide that no payment may be made under the plan with respect to any item or service furnished by such individual or entity during such period;

(40) require each health services facility or organization which receives payments under the plan and of a type for which a uniform reporting system has been established under section 1121(a) [42 USCS § 1320a(a)] to make reports to the Secretary of information described in such section in accordance with the uniform reporting system (established under such section) for that type of facility or organization;

(41) provide that whenever a provider of services or any other person is terminated, suspended, or otherwise sanctioned or prohibited from participating under the State plan, the State agency shall promptly notify the Secretary and, in the case of a physician and notwithstanding paragraph (7), the State medical licensing board of such action;

(42) provide that—

(A) the records of any entity participating in the plan and providing services reimbursable on a cost-related basis will be audited as the Secretary determines to be necessary to insure that proper payments are made under the plan; and

(B) not later than December 31, 2010, the State shall—

(i) establish a program under which the State contracts (consistent with State law and in the same manner as the Secretary enters into contracts with recovery audit contractors under section 1893(h) [42 USCS § 1395ddd(h)], subject to such exceptions or requirements as the Secretary may require for purposes of this title or a particular State) with 1 or more recovery audit contractors for the purpose of identifying underpayments and overpayments and recouping overpayments under the State plan and under any waiver of the State plan with respect to all services for which payment is made to any entity under such plan or waiver; and

(ii) provide assurances satisfactory to the Secretary that—

(I) under such contracts, payment shall be made to such a contractor only from amounts recovered;

(II) from such amounts recovered, payment—

(aa) shall be made on a contingent basis for collecting overpayments; and

(bb) may be made in such amounts as the State may specify for identifying underpayments;

(III) the State has an adequate process for entities to appeal any adverse determination made by such contractors; and

(IV) such program is carried out in accordance with such requirements as the Secretary shall specify, including—

(aa) for purposes of section 1903(a)(7) [42 USCS § 1396b(a)(7)], that amounts expended by the State to carry out the program shall be considered amounts expended as necessary for the proper and efficient administration of the State plan or a waiver of the plan;

(bb) that section 1903(d) [42 USCS § 1396(d)] shall apply to amounts recovered under the program; and

(cc) that the State and any such contractors under contract with the State shall coordinate such recovery audit efforts with other contractors or entities performing audits of entities receiving payments under the State plan or waiver in the State, including efforts with Federal and State law enforcement with respect to the Department of Justice, including the Federal Bureau of Investigations, the Inspector General of the Department of Health and Human Services, and the State Medicaid fraud control unit; and

(43) provide for—

(A) informing all persons in the State who are under the age of 21 and who have been determined to be eligible for medical assistance including services described in section 1905(r) [42 USCS § 1396d(r)], of the availability of early and periodic screening, diagnostic, and treatment services as described in section 1905(r) [42 USCS § 1396d(r)] and the need for age-appropriate immunizations against vaccine-preventable diseases,

(B) providing or arranging for the provision of such screening services in all cases where they are requested,

(C) arranging for (directly or through referral to appropriate agencies, organizations, or individuals) corrective treatment the need for which is disclosed by such child health screening services, and

(D) reporting to the Secretary (in a uniform form and manner established by the Secretary, by age group and by basis of eligibility for medical assistance, and by not later than April 1 after the end of each fiscal year, beginning with fiscal year 1990) the following information relating to early and periodic screening, diagnostic, and treatment services provided under the plan during each fiscal year:

(i) the number of children provided child health screening services,

(ii) the number of children referred for corrective treatment (the need for which is disclosed by such child health screening services),

(iii) the number of children receiving dental services and other information relating to the provision of dental services to such children described in section 2108(e) [42 USCS § 1397hh(e)], and

(iv) the State's results in attaining the participation goals set for the State under section 1905(r) [42 USCS § 1396d(r)];

(44) **[Caution: For application of 1987 amendment of paragraph, see § 4218(b) of Act Dec. 22, 1987, P. L. 100-203, which appears as a note to this section.]** in each case for which payment for inpatient hospital services, services in an intermediate care facility for the mentally retarded, or inpatient mental hospital services is made under the State plan—

(A) a physician (or, in the case of skilled nursing facility services or intermediate care facility services, a physician, or a nurse practitioner or clinical nurse specialist who is not an employee of the facility but is working in collaboration with a physician) certifies at the time of admission, or, if later, the time the individual applies for medical assistance under the State plan (and a physician, a physician assistant under the supervision of a physician, or, in the case of skilled nursing facility services or intermediate care facility services, a physician, or a nurse practitioner or clinical nurse specialist who is not an employee of the facility but is working in collaboration with a physician, recertifies, where such services are furnished over a period of time, in such cases, at least as often as required under section 1903(g)(6) [42 USCS § 1396b(g)(6)] (or, in the case of services that are services provided in an intermediate care facility for the mentally retarded, every year), and accompanied by such supporting material, appropriate to the case involved, as may be provided in regulations of the Secretary), that such services are or were required to be given on an inpatient basis because the individual needs or needed such services, and

(B) such services were furnished under a plan established and periodically reviewed and evaluated by a physician, or, in the case of skilled nursing facility services or intermediate care facility services, a physician, or a nurse practitioner or clinical nurse specialist who is not an employee of the facility but is working in collaboration with a physician;

(45) provide for mandatory assignment of rights of payment for medical support and other medical care owed to recipients, in accordance with section 1912 [42 USCS § 1396k];

(46)(A) provide that information is requested and exchanged for purposes of income and eligibility verification in accordance with a State system which meets the requirements of section 1137 of this Act [42 USCS § 1320b-7]; and

(B) provide, with respect to an individual declaring to be a citizen or national of the United States for purposes of establishing eligibility under this title [42 USCS §§ 1396 et seq.], that the State shall satisfy the requirements of—

(i) section 1903(x) [42 USCS § 1396b(x)]; or

(ii) subsection (ee);

(47) provide—

(A) at the option of the State, provide for making ambulatory prenatal care available to pregnant women during a presumptive eligibility period in accordance with section 1920 [42 USCS § 1396r-1] and provide for making medical assistance for items and services described in subsection (a) of section 1920A [42 USCS § 1396r-1a] available to children during a presumptive eligibility period in accordance with such section [42 USCS § 1396r-1a] and provide for making medical assistance available to individuals described in subsection (a) of section 1920B [42 USCS § 1396r-1b] during a presumptive eligibility period in accordance with such section and provide for making medical assistance available to individuals described in subsection (a) of section 1920C [42 USCS § 1396r-1c] during a presumptive eligibility period in accordance with such section; and

(B) **[Caution: This subparagraph takes effect on January 1, 2014, and applies to services furnished on or after that date, as provided by § 2202(c) of Act March 23, 2010, P. L. 111-148, which appears as a note to this section.]** that any hospital that is a participating provider under the State plan may elect to be a qualified entity for purposes of determining, on the basis of preliminary information, whether any individual is eligible for medical assistance under the State plan or under a waiver of the plan for purposes of providing the individual with medical assistance during a presumptive eligibility period, in the same manner, and subject to the same requirements, as apply to the State options with respect to populations described in section 1920, 1920A, 1920B, or 1920C [42 USCS § 1396r-1, 1396r-1a, 1396r-1b, or 1396r-1c] (but without regard to whether the State has elected to provide for a presumptive eligibility period under any such sections), subject to such guidance as the Secretary shall establish;

(48) provide a method of making cards evidencing eligibility for medical assistance available to an eligible individual who does not reside in a permanent dwelling or does not have a fixed home or mailing address;

(49) provide that the State will provide information and access to certain information respecting sanctions taken against health care practitioners and providers by State licensing authorities in accordance with section 1921 [42 USCS § 1396r-2];

(50) provide, in accordance with subsection (q), for a monthly personal needs allowance for certain institutionalized individuals and couples;

(51) meet the requirements of section 1924 [42 USCS § 1396r-5] (relating to protection of community spouses);

(52) meet the requirements of section 1925 [42 USCS § 1396r-6] (relating to extension of eligibility for medical assistance);

(53) provide—

(A) for notifying in a timely manner all individuals in the State who are determined to be eligible for medical assistance and who are pregnant women, breastfeeding or postpartum women (as defined in section 17 of the Child Nutrition Act of 1966 [42 USCS § 1786]), or children below the age of 5, of the availability of benefits furnished by the special supplemental nutrition program under such section, and

(B) for referring any such individual to the State agency responsible for administering such program;

(54) in the case of a State plan that provides medical assistance for covered outpatient drugs (as defined in section 1927(k) [42 USCS § 1396r-8(k)]), comply with the applicable requirements of section 1927 [42 USCS § 1396r-8];

(55) provide for receipt and initial processing of applications of individuals for medical assistance under subsection (a)(10)(A)(i)(IV), (a)(10)(A)(i)(VI), (a)(10)(A)(i)(VII), or (a)(10)(A)(ii)(IX)—

(A) at locations which are other than those used for the receipt and processing of applications for aid under part A of title IV [42 USCS §§ 601 et seq.] and which include facilities defined as disproportionate share hospitals under section 1923(a)(1)(A) [42 USCS § 1396r-4(a)(1)(A)] and Federally-qualified health centers described in section 1905(l)(2)(B) [42 USCS § 1396d(l)(2)(B)], and

(B) using applications which are other than those used for applications for aid under such part;

(56) provide, in accordance with subsection (s), for adjusted payments for certain inpatient hospital services;

(57) provide that each hospital, nursing facility, provider of home health care or personal care services, hospice program, or medicaid managed care organization (as defined in section 1903(m)(1)(A) [42 USCS § 1396b(m)(1)(A)]) receiving funds under the plan shall comply with the requirements of subsection (w);

(58) provide that the State, acting through a State agency, association, or other private nonprofit entity, develop a written description of the law of the State (whether statutory or as recognized by the courts of the State) concerning advance directives that would be distributed by providers or organizations under the requirements of subsection (w);

(59) maintain a list (updated not less often than monthly, and containing each physician's unique identifier provided under the system established under subsection (x)) of all physicians who are certified to participate under the State plan;

(60) provide that the State agency shall provide assurances satisfactory to the Secretary that the State has in effect the laws relating to medical child support required under section 1908A [42 USCS § 1396g-1];

(61) provide that the State must demonstrate that it operates a medicaid fraud and abuse control unit described in section 1903(q) [42 USCS § 1396b(q)] that effectively carries out the functions and requirements described in such section, as determined in accordance with standards established by the Secretary, unless the State demonstrates to the satisfaction of the Secretary that the effective operation of such a unit in the State would not be cost-effective because minimal fraud exists in connection with the provision of covered services to eligible individuals under the State plan, and that beneficiaries under the plan will be protected from abuse and neglect in connec-

tion with the provision of medical assistance under the plan without the existence of such a unit;

(62) provide for a program for the distribution of pediatric vaccines to program-registered providers for the immunization of vaccine-eligible children in accordance with section 1928 [42 USCS § 1396s];

(63) provide for administration and determinations of eligibility with respect to individuals who are (or seek to be) eligible for medical assistance based on the application of section 1931 [42 USCS § 1396u-1];

(64) provide, not later than 1 year after the date of the enactment of this paragraph [enacted Aug. 5, 1997], a mechanism to receive reports from beneficiaries and others and compile data concerning alleged instances of waste, fraud, and abuse relating to the operation of this title [42 USCS §§ 1396 et seq.];

(65) provide that the State shall issue provider numbers for all suppliers of medical assistance consisting of durable medical equipment, as defined in section 1861(n) [42 USCS § 1395x(n)], and the State shall not issue or renew such a supplier number for any such supplier unless—

(A)(i) full and complete information as to the identity of each person with an ownership or control interest (as defined in section 1124(a)(3) [42 USCS § 1320a-3(a)(3)]) in the supplier or in any subcontractor (as defined by the Secretary in regulations) in which the supplier directly or indirectly has a 5 percent or more ownership interest; and

(ii) to the extent determined to be feasible under regulations of the Secretary, the name of any disclosing entity (as defined in section 1124(a)(2) [42 USCS § 1320a-3(a)(2)]) with respect to which a person with such an ownership or control interest in the supplier is a person with such an ownership or control interest in the disclosing entity; and

(B) a surety bond in a form specified by the Secretary under section 1834(a)(16)(B) [42 USCS § 1395m(a)(16)(B)] and in an amount that is not less than $50,000 or such comparable surety bond as the Secretary may permit under the second sentence of such section;

(66) provide for making eligibility determinations under section 1935(a) [42 USCS § 1396u-5(a)];

(67) provide, with respect to services covered under the State plan (but not under title XVIII [42 USCS § 1395 et seq.]) that are furnished to a PACE program eligible individual enrolled with a PACE provider by a provider participating under the State plan that does not have a contract or other agreement with the PACE provider that establishes payment amounts for such services, that such participating provider may not require the PACE provider to pay the participating provider an amount greater than the amount that would otherwise be payable for the service to the participating provider under the State plan for the State where the PACE provider is located (in accordance with regulations issued by the Secretary);

(68) provide that any entity that receives or makes annual payments under the State plan of at least $5,000,000, as a condition of receiving such payments, shall—

(A) establish written policies for all employees of the entity (including management), and of any contractor or agent of the entity, that provide detailed information about the False Claims Act established under sections 3729 through 3733 of title 31, United States Code [31 USCS §§ 3729–3733], administrative remedies for false claims and statements established under chapter 38 of title 31, United States Code [31 USCS §§ 3801 et seq.], any State laws pertaining to civil or criminal penalties for false claims and statements, and whistleblower protections under such laws, with respect to the role of such laws in preventing and detecting fraud, waste, and abuse in Federal health care programs (as defined in section 1128B(f) [42 USCS § 1320a-7b(f)]);

(B) include as part of such written policies, detailed provisions regarding the entity's policies and procedures for detecting and preventing fraud, waste, and abuse; and

(C) include in any employee handbook for the entity, a specific discussion of the laws described in subparagraph (A), the rights of employees to be protected as whistleblowers, and the entity's policies and procedures for detecting and preventing fraud, waste, and abuse;

(69) provide that the State must comply with any requirements determined by the Secretary to be necessary for carrying out the Medicaid Integrity Program established under section 1936 [42 USCS § 1396u-6];

(70) at the option of the State and notwithstanding paragraphs (1), (10)(B), and (23), provide for the establishment of a non-emergency medical transportation brokerage program in order to more cost-effectively provide transportation for individuals eligible for medical assistance under the State plan who need access to medical care or services and have no other means of transportation which—

(A) may include a wheelchair van, taxi, stretcher car, bus passes and tickets, secured transportation, and such other transportation as the Secretary determines appropriate; and

(B) may be conducted under contract with a broker who—

(i) is selected through a competitive bidding process based on the State's evaluation of the broker's experience, performance, references, resources, qualifications, and costs;

(ii) has oversight procedures to monitor beneficiary access and complaints and ensure that transport personnel are licensed, qualified, competent, and courteous;

(iii) is subject to regular auditing and oversight by the State in order to ensure the quality of the transportation services provided and the adequacy of beneficiary access to medical care and services; and

(iv) complies with such requirements related to prohibitions on referrals and conflict of interest as the Secretary shall establish (based on the prohibitions on physician referrals under section 1877 and such other prohibitions and requirements as the Secretary determines to be appropriate);

(71) provide that the State will implement an asset verification program as required under section 1940 [42 USCS § 1396w];

(72) provide that the State will not prevent a Federally-qualified health center from entering into contractual relationships with private practice dental providers in the provision of Federally-qualified health center services;

(73) in the case of any State in which 1 or more Indian Health Programs or Urban Indian Organizations furnishes health care services, provide for a process under which the State seeks advice on a regular, ongoing basis from designees of such Indian Health Programs and Urban Indian Organizations on matters relating to the application of this title that are likely to have a direct effect on such Indian Health Programs and Urban Indian Organizations and that—

(A) shall include solicitation of advice prior to submission of any plan amendments, waiver requests, and proposals for demonstration projects likely to have a direct effect on Indians, Indian Health Programs, or Urban Indian Organizations; and

(B) may include appointment of an advisory committee and of a designee of such Indian Health Programs and Urban Indian Organizations to the medical care advisory committee advising the State on its State plan under this title [42 USCS §§ 1396 et seq.];

(74) provide for maintenance of effort under the State plan or under any waiver of the plan in accordance with subsection (gg);

(75) provide that, beginning January 2015, and annually thereafter, the State shall submit a report to the Secretary that contains—

(A) the total number of enrolled and newly enrolled individuals in the State plan or under a waiver of the plan for the fiscal year ending on September 30 of the preceding calendar year, disaggregated by population, including children, parents, nonpregnant childless adults, disabled individuals, elderly individuals, and such other categories or sub-categories of individuals eligible for medical assistance under the State plan or under a waiver of the plan as the Secretary may require;

(B) a description, which may be specified by population, of the outreach and enrollment processes used by the State during such fiscal year; and

(C) any other data reporting determined necessary by the Secretary to monitor enrollment and retention of individuals eligible for medical assistance under the State plan or under a waiver of the plan;

(76) provide that any data collected under the State plan meets the requirements of section 3101 of the Public Health Service Act [42 USCS § 300kk];

(77) provide that the State shall comply with provider and supplier screening, oversight, and reporting requirements in accordance with subsection (ii);

(78) **[Caution: This paragraph takes effect on January 1, 2011, as provided by § 6508(a) of Act March 23, 2010, P. L. 111-148, which appears as a note to this section.]** provide that the State agency described in paragraph (9) exclude, with respect to a period, any individual or entity from participation in the program under the State plan if such individual or entity owns, controls, or manages an entity that (or if such entity is owned, controlled, or managed by an individual or entity that)—

(A) has unpaid overpayments (as defined by the Secretary) under this title during such period determined by the Secretary or the State agency to be delinquent;

(B) is suspended or excluded from participation under or whose participation is terminated under this title during such period; or

(C) is affiliated with an individual or entity that has been suspended or excluded from participation under this title or whose participation is terminated under this title during such period;

(79) **[Caution: This paragraph takes effect on January 1, 2011, as provided by § 6508(a) of Act March 23, 2010, P. L. 111-**

148, which appears as a note to this section.] provide that any agent, clearinghouse, or other alternate payee (as defined by the Secretary) that submits claims on behalf of a health care provider must register with the State and the Secretary in a form and manner specified by the Secretary;

(80) **[Caution: This paragraph takes effect on January 1, 2011, as provided by § 6508(a) of Act March 23, 2010, P. L. 111-148, which appears as a note to this section.]** provide that the State shall not provide any payments for items or services provided under the State plan or under a waiver to any financial institution or entity located outside of the United States;

(81) **[Caution: This paragraph takes effect on January 1, 2011, as provided by § 8002(e) of Act March 23, 2010, P. L. 111-148, which appears as 42 USCS § 300ll note.]** provide that the State will comply with such regulations regarding the application of primary and secondary payor rules with respect to individuals who are eligible for medical assistance under this title and are eligible beneficiaries under the CLASS program established under title XXXII of the Public Health Service Act [42 USCS §§ 300ll et seq.] as the Secretary shall establish;

(82) **[Caution: This paragraph takes effect on January 1, 2011, as provided by § 8002(e) of Act March 23, 2010, P. L. 111-148, which appears as 42 USCS § 300ll note.]** provide that, not later than 2 years after the date of enactment of the Community Living Assistance Services and Supports Act [enacted March 23, 2010], each State shall—

(A) assess the extent to which entities such as providers of home care, home health services, home and community service providers, public authorities created to provide personal care services to individuals eligible for medical assistance under the State plan, and nonprofit organizations, are serving or have the capacity to serve as fiscal agents for, employers of, and providers of employment-related benefits for, personal care attendant workers who provide personal care services to individuals receiving benefits under the CLASS program established under title XXXII of the Public Health Service Act [42 USCS §§ 300ll et seq.], including in rural and underserved areas;

(B) designate or create such entities to serve as fiscal agents for, employers of, and providers of employment-related benefits for, such workers to ensure an adequate supply of the workers for individuals receiving benefits under the CLASS program, including in rural and underserved areas; and

(C) ensure that the designation or creation of such entities will not negatively alter or impede existing programs, models, methods, or administration of service delivery that provide for consumer controlled or self-directed home and community services and further ensure that such entities will not impede the ability of individuals to direct and control their home and community services, including the ability to select, manage, dismiss, co-employ, or employ such workers or inhibit such individuals from relying on family members for the provision of personal care services; and

(83) provide for implementation of the payment models specified by the Secretary under section 1115A(c) [42 USCS § 1315a(c)] for implementation on a nationwide basis unless the State demonstrates to the satisfaction of the Secretary that implementation would not be administratively feasible or appropriate to the health care delivery system of the State.

Notwithstanding paragraph (5), if on January 1, 1965, and on the date on which a State submits its plan for approval under this title [42 USCS §§ 1396 et seq.], the State agency which administered or supervised the administration of the plan of such State approved under title X [42 USCS §§ 1201 et seq.] (or title XVI [42 USCS §§ 1381 et seq.], insofar as it relates to the blind) was different from the State agency which administered or supervised the administration of the State plan approved under title I [42 USCS §§ 301 et seq.] (or title XVI [42 USCS §§ 1381 et seq.], insofar as it relates to the aged), the State agency which administered or supervised the administration of such plan approved under title X [42 USCS §§ 1201 et seq.] (or title XVI [42 USCS §§ 1381 et seq.], insofar as it relates to the blind) may be designated to administer or supervise the administration of the portion of the State plan for medical assistance which relates to blind individuals and a different State agency may be established or designated to administer or supervise the administration of the rest of the State plan for medical assistance; and in such case the part of the plan which each such agency administers, or the administration of which each such agency supervises, shall be regarded as a separate plan for purposes of this title [42 USCS §§ 1396 et seq.] (except for purposes of paragraph (10)). The provisions of paragraphs (9)(A), (31), and (33) and of section 1903(i)(4) [42 USCS § 1396b(i)(4)] shall not apply to a religious nonmedical health care institution (as defined in section 1861(ss)(1) [42 USCS § 1395x(ss)(1)]).

For purposes of paragraph (10) any individual who, for the month of August 1972, was eligible for or receiving aid or assistance under a State plan approved under title I, X, XIV, or XVI, or part A of title IV [42 USCS §§ 301 et seq., 1201 et seq., 1351 et seq., or 1381 et seq., or 601 et seq.] and who for such month was entitled to monthly insurance benefits under title II [42 USCS §§ 401 et seq.] shall for purposes of this title [42 USCS §§ 1396 et seq.] only be deemed to be eligible for financial aid or assistance for any month thereafter if such individual would have been eligible for financial aid or assistance for such month had the increase in monthly insurance benefits under title II [42 USCS §§ 401 et seq.] resulting from enactment of Public Law 92-336 not been applicable to such individual.

The requirement of clause (A) of paragraph (37) with respect to a State plan may be waived by the Secretary if he finds that the State has exercised good faith in trying to meet such requirement. For purposes of this title [42 USCS §§ 1396 et seq.], any child who meets the requirements of paragraph (1) or (2) of section 473(b) [42 USCS § 673(b)(1) or (2)] shall be deemed to be a dependent child as defined in section 406 [42 USCS § 606] and shall be deemed to be a recipient of aid to families with dependent children under part A of title IV [42 USCS §§ 601 et seq.] in the State where such child resides. Notwithstanding paragraph (10)(B) or any other provision of this subsection, a State plan shall provide medical assistance with respect to an alien who is not lawfully admitted for permanent residence or otherwise permanently residing in the United States under color of law only in accordance with section 1903(v) [42 USCS § 1396b(v)].

(b) Approval by Secretary. The Secretary shall approve any plan which fulfills the conditions specified in subsection (a), except that he shall not approve any plan which imposes, as a condition of eligibility for medical assistance under the plan—

(1) an age requirement of more than 65 years; or

(2) any residence requirement which excludes any individual who resides in the State, regardless of whether or not the residence is maintained permanently or at a fixed address; or

(3) any citizenship requirement which excludes any citizen of the United States.

(c) Lower payment levels or applying for benefits as condition of applying for, or receiving, medical assistance. Notwithstanding subsection (b), the Secretary shall not approve any State plan for medical assistance if the State requires individuals described in subsection (l)(1) to apply for assistance under the State program funded under part A of title IV [42 USCS §§ 601 et seq.] as a condition of applying for or receiving medical assistance under this title [42 USCS §§ 1396 et seq.].

(d) Performance of medical or utilization review functions. If a State contracts with an entity which meets the requirements of section 1152 [42 USCS § 1320c-1], as determined by the Secretary, or a utilization and quality control peer review organization having a contract with the Secretary under part B of title XI [42 USCS §§ 1320c et seq.] for the performance of medical or utilization review functions required under this title [42 USCS §§ 1396 et seq.] of a State plan with respect to specific services or providers (or services or providers in a geographic area of the State), such requirements shall be deemed to be met for those services or providers (or services or providers in that area) by delegation to an entity or organization under the contract of the State's authority to conduct such review activities if the contract provides for the performance of activities not inconsistent with part B of title XI [42 USCS §§ 1320c et seq.] and provides for such assurances of satisfactory performance by such an entity or organization as the Secretary may prescribe.

(e) Continued eligibility of families determined ineligible because of income and resources or hours of work limitations of plan; individuals enrolled with health maintenance organizations; persons deemed recipients of supplemental security income or State supplemental payments; entitlement for certain newborns; postpartum eligibility for pregnant women. (1)(A) Notwithstanding any other provision of this title [42 USCS §§ 1396 et seq.], effective January 1, 1974, subject to subparagraph (B) each State plan approved under this title [42 USCS §§ 1396 et seq.] must provide that each family which was receiving aid pursuant to a plan of the State approved under part A of title IV [42 USCS §§ 601 et seq.] in at least 3 of the 6 months immediately preceding the month in which such family became ineligible for such aid because of increased hours of, or increased income from, employment, shall, while a member of such family is employed, remain eligible for assistance under the plan approved under this title [42 USCS §§ 1396 et seq.] (as though the family was receiving aid under the plan approved under part A of title IV [42 USCS

§§ 601 et seq.]) for 4 calendar months beginning with the month in which such family became ineligible for aid under the plan approved under part A of title IV [42 USCS §§ 601 et seq.] because of income and resources or hours of work limitations contained in such plan.

(B) Subparagraph (A) shall not apply with respect to families that cease to be eligible for aid under part A of title IV [42 USCS §§ 601 et seq.] during the period beginning on April 1, 1990, and ending on December 31, 2010. During such period, for provisions relating to extension of eligibility for medical assistance for certain families who have received aid pursuant to a State plan approved under part A of title IV [42 USCS §§ 601 et seq.] and have earned income, see section 1925 [42 USCS § 1396r-6].

(2)(A) In the case of an individual who is enrolled with a medicaid managed care organization (as defined in section 1903(m)(1)(A) [42 USCS § 1396b(m)(1)(A)]), with a primary care case manager (as defined in section 1905(t) [42 USCS § 1396d(t)]), or with an eligible organization with a contract under section 1876 [42 USCS § 1395mm] and who would (but for this paragraph) lose eligibility for benefits under this title [42 USCS §§ 1396 et seq.] before the end of the minimum enrollment period (defined in subparagraph (B)), the State plan may provide, notwithstanding any other provision of this title [42 USCS §§ 1396 et seq.], that the individual shall be deemed to continue to be eligible for such benefits until the end of such minimum period, but, except for benefits furnished under section 1905(a)(4)(C) [42 USCS § 1396d(a)(4)(C)], only with respect to such benefits provided to the individual as an enrollee of such organization or entity or by or through the case manager.

(B) For purposes of subparagraph (A), the term "minimum enrollment period" means, with respect to an individual's enrollment with an organization or entity under a State plan, a period, established by the State, of not more than six months beginning on the date the individual's enrollment with the organization or entity becomes effective.

(3) At the option of the State, any individual who—

(A) is 18 years of age or younger and qualifies as a disabled individual under section 1614(a) [42 USCS § 1382c(a)];

(B) with respect to whom there has been a determination by the State that—

(i) the individual requires a level of care provided in a hospital, nursing facility, or intermediate care facility for the mentally retarded,

(ii) it is appropriate to provide such care for the individual outside such an institution, and

(iii) the estimated amount which would be expended for medical assistance for the individual for such care outside an institution is not greater than the estimated amount which would otherwise be expended for medical assistance for the individual within an appropriate institution; and

(C) if the individual were in a medical institution, would be eligible for medical assistance under the State plan under this title [42 USCS §§ 1396 et seq.],

shall be deemed, for purposes of this title [42 USCS §§ 1396 et seq.] only, to be an individual with respect to whom a supplemental security income payment, or State supplemental payment, respectively, is being paid under title XVI [42 USCS §§ 1381 et seq.].

(4) A child born to a woman eligible for and receiving medical assistance under a State plan on the date of the child's birth shall be deemed to have applied for medical assistance and to have been found eligible for such assistance under such plan on the date of such birth and to remain eligible for such assistance for a period of one year. During the period in which a child is deemed under the preceding sentence to be eligible for medical assistance, the medical assistance eligibility identification number of the mother shall also serve as the identification number of the child, and all claims shall be submitted and paid under such number (unless the State issues a separate identification number for the child before such period expires). Notwithstanding the preceding sentence, in the case of a child who is born in the United States to an alien mother for whom medical assistance for the delivery of the child is made available pursuant to section 1903(v) [42 USCS § 1396b(v)], the State immediately shall issue a separate identification number for the child upon notification by the facility at which such delivery occurred of the child's birth.

(5) A woman who, while pregnant, is eligible for, has applied for, and has received medical assistance under the State plan, shall continue to be eligible under the plan, as though she were pregnant, for all pregnancy-related and postpartum medical assistance under the plan, through the end of the month in which the 60-day period (beginning on the last day of her pregnancy) ends.

(6) In the case of a pregnant woman described in subsection (a)(10) who, because of a change in income of the family of which she is a member, would not otherwise continue to be

described in such subsection, the woman shall be deemed to continue to be an individual described in subsection (a)(10)(A)(i)(IV) and subsection (l)(1)(A) without regard to such change of income through the end of the month in which the 60-day period (beginning on the last day of her pregnancy) ends. The preceding sentence shall not apply in the case of a woman who has been provided ambulatory prenatal care pursuant to section 1920 [42 USCS § 1396r-1] during a presumptive eligibility period and is then, in accordance with such section, determined to be ineligible for medical assistance under the State plan.

(7) In the case of an infant or child described in subparagraph (B), (C), or (D) of subsection (l)(1) or paragraph (2) of section 1905(n) [42 USCS § 1396d(n)(2)]—

(A) who is receiving inpatient services for which medical assistance is provided on the date the infant or child attains the maximum age with respect to which coverage is provided under the State plan for such individuals, and

(B) who, but for attaining such age, would remain eligible for medical assistance under such subsection,

the infant or child shall continue to be treated as an individual described in such respective provision until the end of the stay for which the inpatient services are furnished.

(8) If an individual is determined to be a qualified medicare beneficiary (as defined in section 1905(p)(1) [42 USCS § 1396d(p)(1)]), such determination shall apply to services furnished after the end of the month in which the determination first occurs. For purposes of payment to a State under section 1903(a) [42 USCS § 1396b(a)], such determination shall be considered to be valid for an individual for a period of 12 months, except that a State may provide for such determinations more frequently, but not more frequently than once every 6 months for an individual.

(9)(A) At the option of the State, the plan may include as medical assistance respiratory care services for any individual who—

(i) is medically dependent on a ventilator for life support at least six hours per day;

(ii) has been so dependent for at least 30 consecutive days (or the maximum number of days authorized under the State plan, whichever is less) as an inpatient;

(iii) but for the availability of respiratory care services, would require respiratory care as an inpatient in a hospital, nursing facility, or intermediate care facility for the mentally retarded and would be eligible to have payment made for such inpatient care under the State plan;

(iv) has adequate social support services to be cared for at home; and

(v) wishes to be cared for at home.

(B) The requirements of subparagraph (A)(ii) may be satisfied by a continuous stay in one or more hospitals, nursing facilities, or intermediate care facilities for the mentally retarded.

(C) For purposes of this paragraph, respiratory care services means services provided on a part-time basis in the home of the individual by a respiratory therapist or other health care professional trained in respiratory therapy (as determined by the State), payment for which is not otherwise included within other items and services furnished to such individual as medical assistance under the plan.

(10)(A) The fact that an individual, child, or pregnant woman may be denied aid under part A of title IV [42 USCS §§ 601 et seq.] pursuant to section 402(a)(43) [42 USCS § 602(a)(43)] shall not be construed as denying (or permitting a State to deny) medical assistance under this title [42 USCS §§ 1396 et seq.] to such individual, child, or woman who is eligible for assistance under this title [42 USCS §§ 1396 et seq.] on a basis other than the receipt of aid under such part [42 USCS §§ 601 et seq.].

(B) If an individual, child, or pregnant woman is receiving aid under part A of title IV [42 USCS §§ 601 et seq.] and such aid is terminated pursuant to section 402(a)(43) [42 USCS § 602(a)(43)], the State may not discontinue medical assistance under this title [42 USCS §§ 1396 et seq.] for the individual, child, or woman until the State has determined that the individual, child, or woman is not eligible for assistance under this title [42 USCS §§ 1396 et seq.] on a basis other than the receipt of aid under such part [42 USCS §§ 601 et seq.].

(11)(A) In the case of an individual who is enrolled with a group health plan under section 1906 [42 USCS § 1396e] and who would (but for this paragraph) lose eligibility for benefits under this title [42 USCS §§ 1396 et seq.] before the end of the minimum enrollment period (defined in subparagraph (B)), the State plan may provide, notwithstanding any other provision of this title [42 USCS §§ 1396 et seq.], that the individual shall be deemed to continue to be eligible for such benefits until the end of such minimum period, but only with respect to such benefits provided to the individual as an enrollee of such plan.

(B) For purposes of subparagraph (A), the term "minimum enrollment period" means, with respect to an individual's enrollment with a group health plan, a period established by the State, of not more than 6 months beginning on the date the individual's enrollment under the plan becomes effective.

(12) At the option of the State, the plan may provide that an individual who is under an age specified by the State (not to exceed 19 years of age) and who is determined to be eligible for benefits under a State plan approved under this title under subsection (a)(10)(A) shall remain eligible for those benefits until the earlier of—

(A) the end of a period (not to exceed 12 months) following the determination; or

(B) the time that the individual exceeds that age.

(13) Express Lane option. (A) In general. (i) Option to use a finding from an Express Lane agency. At the option of the State, the State plan may provide that in determining eligibility under this title [42 USCS §§ 1396 et seq.] for a child (as defined in subparagraph (G)), the State may rely on a finding made within a reasonable period (as determined by the State) from an Express Lane agency (as defined in subparagraph (F)) when it determines whether a child satisfies one or more components of eligibility for medical assistance under this title [42 USCS §§ 1396 et seq.]. The State may rely on a finding from an Express Lane agency notwithstanding sections 1902(a)(46)(B) and 1137(d) [42 USCS §§ 1396a(a)(46)(B) and 1320b-7(d)] or any differences in budget unit, disregard, deeming or other methodology, if the following requirements are met:

(I) Prohibition on determining children ineligible for coverage. If a finding from an Express Lane agency would result in a determination that a child does not satisfy an eligibility requirement for medical assistance under this title [42 USCS §§ 1396 et seq.] and for child health assistance under title XXI [42 USCS §§ 1397aa et seq.], the State shall determine eligibility for assistance using its regular procedures.

(II) Notice requirement. For any child who is found eligible for medical assistance under the State plan under this title [42 USCS §§ 1396 et seq.] or child health assistance under title XXI [42 USCS §§ 1397aa et seq.] and who is subject to premiums based on an Express Lane agency's finding of such child's income level, the State shall provide notice that the child may qualify for lower premium payments if evaluated by the State using its regular policies and of the procedures for requesting such an evaluation.

(III) Compliance with screen and enroll requirement. The State shall satisfy the requirements under subparagraphs (A) and (B) of section 2102(b)(3) [42 USCS § 1397bb(b)(3)] (relating to screen and enroll) before enrolling a child in child health assistance under title XXI [42 USCS §§ 1397aa et seq.]. At its option, the State may fulfill such requirements in accordance with either option provided under subparagraph (C) of this paragraph.

(IV) Verification of citizenship or nationality status. The State shall satisfy the requirements of section 1902(a)(46)(B) or 2105(c)(9) [42 USCS § 1396a(a)(46)(B) or 1397ee(c)(9)], as applicable for verifications of citizenship or nationality status.

(V) Coding. The State meets the requirements of subparagraph (E).

(ii) Option to apply to renewals and redeterminations. The State may apply the provisions of this paragraph when conducting initial determinations of eligibility, redeterminations of eligibility, or both, as described in the State plan.

(B) Rules of construction. Nothing in this paragraph shall be construed—

(i) to limit or prohibit a State from taking any actions otherwise permitted under this title [42 USCS §§ 1396 et seq.] or title XXI [42 USCS §§ 1397aa et seq.] in determining eligibility for or enrolling children into medical assistance under this title [42 USCS §§ 1396 et seq.] or child health assistance under title XXI [42 USCS §§ 1397aa et seq.]; or

(ii) to modify the limitations in section 1902(a)(5) [42 USCS § 1396a(a)(5)] concerning the agencies that may make a determination of eligibility for medical assistance under this title [42 USCS §§ 1396 et seq.].

(C) Options for satisfying the screen and enroll requirement. (i) In general. With respect to a child whose eligibility for medical assistance under this title [42 USCS §§ 1396 et seq.] or for child health assistance under title XXI [42 USCS §§ 1397aa et seq.] has been evaluated by a State agency using an income finding from an Express Lane agency, a State may carry out its duties under subparagraphs (A) and (B) of section 2102(b)(3) [42 USCS § 1397bb(b)(3)] (relating to screen and enroll) in accordance with either clause (ii) or clause (iii).

(ii) Establishing a screening threshold. (I) In general. Under this clause, the State establishes a screening threshold set as a percentage of the Federal poverty level that exceeds the highest income threshold applicable under this title [42 USCS §§ 1396 et seq.] to the child by a minimum of 30 percentage points or, at State option, a higher number of percentage points that reflects the value (as determined by the State and described in the State plan) of any differences between income methodologies used by the program administered by the Express Lane agency and the methodologies used by the State in determining eligibility for medical assistance under this title [42 USCS §§ 1396 et seq.].

(II) Children with income not above threshold. If the income of a child does not exceed the screening threshold, the child is deemed to satisfy the income eligibility criteria for medical assistance under this title [42 USCS §§ 1396 et seq.] regardless of whether such child would otherwise satisfy such criteria.

(III) Children with income above threshold. If the income of a child exceeds the screening threshold, the child shall be considered to have an income above the Medicaid applicable income level described in section 2110(b)(4) [42 USCS § 1397jj(b)(4)] and to satisfy the requirement under section 2110(b)(1)(C) [42 USCS § 1397jj(b)(1)(C)] (relating to the requirement that CHIP matching funds be used only for children not eligible for Medicaid). If such a child is enrolled in child health assistance under title XXI [42 USCS §§ 1397aa et seq.], the State shall provide the parent, guardian, or custodial relative with the following:

(aa) Notice that the child may be eligible to receive medical assistance under the State plan under this title [42 USCS §§ 1396 et seq.] if evaluated for such assistance under the State's regular procedures and notice of the process through which a parent, guardian, or custodial relative can request that the State evaluate the child's eligibility for medical assistance under this title [42 USCS §§ 1396 et seq.] using such regular procedures.

(bb) A description of differences between the medical assistance provided under this title [42 USCS §§ 1396 et seq.] and child health assistance under title XXI [42 USCS §§ 1397aa et seq.], including differences in cost-sharing requirements and covered benefits.

(iii) Temporary enrollment in CHIP pending screen and enroll. (I) In general. Under this clause, a State enrolls a child in child health assistance under title XXI [42 USCS §§ 1397aa et seq.] for a temporary period if the child appears eligible for such assistance based on an income finding by an Express Lane agency.

(II) Determination of eligibility. During such temporary enrollment period, the State shall determine the child's eligibility for child health assistance under title XXI [42 USCS §§ 1397aa et seq.] or for medical assistance under this title [42 USCS §§ 1396 et seq.] in accordance with this clause.

(III) Prompt follow up. In making such a determination, the State shall take prompt action to determine whether the child should be enrolled in medical assistance under this title [42 USCS §§ 1396 et seq.] or child health assistance under title XXI [42 USCS §§ 1397aa et seq.] pursuant to subparagraphs (A) and (B) of section 2102(b)(3) [42 USCS § 1397bb(b)(3)] (relating to screen and enroll).

(IV) Requirement for simplified determination. In making such a determination, the State shall use procedures that, to the maximum feasible extent, reduce the burden imposed on the individual of such determination. Such procedures may not require the child's parent, guardian, or custodial relative to provide or verify information that already has been provided to the State agency by an Express Lane agency or another source of information unless the State agency has reason to believe the information is erroneous.

(V) Availability of CHIP matching funds during temporary enrollment period. Medical assistance for items and services that are provided to a child enrolled in title XXI [42 USCS §§ 1397aa et seq.] during a temporary enrollment period under this clause shall be treated as child health assistance under such title [42 USCS §§ 1396 et seq.].

(D) Option for automatic enrollment. (i) In general. The State may initiate and determine eligibility for medical assistance under the State Medicaid plan or for child health assistance under the State CHIP plan without a program application from, or on behalf of, the child based on data obtained from sources other than the child (or the child's family), but a child can only be automatically enrolled in the State Medicaid plan or the State CHIP plan if the child or the family affirmatively consents to being enrolled through affirmation in writing, by telephone, orally, through electronic signature, or through any other means specified by the Secretary or by signature on an Express Lane agency application, if the requirement of clause (ii) is met.

(ii) Information requirement. The requirement of this clause is that the State informs the parent, guardian, or custodial relative of the child of the services that will be covered, appropriate methods for using such services, premium or other cost sharing charges (if any) that apply, medical support obligations (under section 1912(a) [42 USCS § 1396k(a)]) created by enrollment (if applicable), and the actions the parent, guardian, or relative must take to maintain enrollment and renew coverage.

(E) Coding; application to enrollment error rates. (i) In general. For purposes of subparagraph (A)(iv), the requirement of this subparagraph for a State is that the State agrees to—

(I) assign such codes as the Secretary shall require to the children who are enrolled in the State Medicaid plan or the State CHIP plan through reliance on a finding made by an Express Lane agency for the duration of the State's election under this paragraph;

(II) annually provide the Secretary with a statistically valid sample (that is approved by Secretary) of the children enrolled in such plans through reliance on such a finding by conducting a full Medicaid eligibility review of the children identified for such sample for purposes of determining an eligibility error rate (as described in clause (iv)) with respect to the enrollment of such children (and shall not include such children in any data or samples used for purposes of complying with a Medicaid Eligibility Quality Control (MEQC) review or a payment error rate measurement (PERM) requirement);

(III) submit the error rate determined under subclause (II) to the Secretary;

(IV) if such error rate exceeds 3 percent for either of the first 2 fiscal years in which the State elects to apply this paragraph, demonstrate to the satisfaction of the Secretary the specific corrective actions implemented by the State to improve upon such error rate; and

(V) if such error rate exceeds 3 percent for any fiscal year in which the State elects to apply this paragraph, a reduction in the amount otherwise payable to the State under section 1903(a) [42 USCS § 1396b(a)] for quarters for that fiscal year, equal to the total amount of erroneous excess payments determined for the fiscal year only with respect to the children included in the sample for the fiscal year that are in excess of a 3 percent error rate with respect to such children.

(ii) No punitive action based on error rate. The Secretary shall not apply the error rate derived from the sample under clause (i) to the entire population of children enrolled in the State Medicaid plan or the State CHIP plan through reliance on a finding made by an Express Lane agency, or to the population of children enrolled in such plans on the basis of the State's regular procedures for determining eligibility, or penalize the State on the basis of such error rate in any manner other than the reduction of payments provided for under clause (i)(V).

(iii) Rule of construction. Nothing in this paragraph shall be construed as relieving a State that elects to apply this paragraph from being subject to a penalty under section 1903(u) [42 USCS § 1396b(u)], for payments made under the State Medicaid plan with respect to ineligible individuals and families that are determined to exceed the error rate permitted under that section (as determined without regard to the error rate determined under clause (i)(II)).

(iv) Error rate defined. In this subparagraph, the term "error rate" means the rate of erroneous excess payments for medical assistance (as defined in section 1903(u)(1)(D) [42 USCS § 1396b(u)(1)(D)]) for the period involved, except that such payments shall be limited to individuals for which eligibility determinations are made under this paragraph and except that in applying this paragraph under title XXI [42 USCS §§ 1397aa et seq.], there shall be substituted for references to provisions of this title [42 USCS §§ 1396 et seq.] corresponding provisions within title XXI [42 USCS §§ 1397aa et seq.].

(F) Express Lane agency. (i) In general. In this paragraph, the term "Express Lane agency" means a public agency that—

(I) is determined by the State Medicaid agency or the State CHIP agency (as applicable) to be capable of making the determinations of one or more eligibility requirements described in subparagraph (A)(i);

(II) is identified in the State Medicaid plan or the State CHIP plan; and

(III) notifies the child's family—

(aa) of the information which shall be disclosed in accordance with this paragraph;

(bb) that the information disclosed will be used solely for purposes of determining eligibility for medical assistance under the State Medicaid plan or for child health assistance under the State CHIP plan; and

(cc) that the family may elect to not have the information disclosed for such purposes; and

(IV) enters into, or is subject to, an interagency agreement to limit the disclosure and use of the information disclosed.

(ii) Inclusion of specific public agencies and Indian Tribes and Tribal Organizations. Such term includes the following:

(I) A public agency that determines eligibility for assistance under any of the following:

(aa) The temporary assistance for needy families program funded under part A of title IV [42 USCS §§ 601 et seq.].

(bb) A State program funded under part D of

title IV [42 USCS §§ 651 et seq.].

(cc) The State Medicaid plan.

(dd) The State CHIP plan.

(ee) The Food and Nutrition Act of 2008 (7 U.S.C. 2011 et seq.).

(ff) The Head Start Act (42 U.S.C. 9801 et seq.).

(gg) The Richard B. Russell National School Lunch Act (42 U.S.C. 1751 et seq.).

(hh) The Child Nutrition Act of 1966 (42 U.S.C. 1771 et seq.).

(ii) The Child Care and Development Block Grant Act of 1990 (42 U.S.C. 9858 et seq.).

(jj) The Stewart B. McKinney Homeless Assistance Act (42 U.S.C. 11301 et seq.).

(kk) The United States Housing Act of 1937 (42 U.S.C. 1437 et seq.).

(ll) The Native American Housing Assistance and Self-Determination Act of 1996 (25 U.S.C. 4101 et seq.).

(II) A State-specified governmental agency that has fiscal liability or legal responsibility for the accuracy of the eligibility determination findings relied on by the State.

(III) A public agency that is subject to an interagency agreement limiting the disclosure and use of the information disclosed for purposes of determining eligibility under the State Medicaid plan or the State CHIP plan.

(IV) The Indian Health Service, an Indian Tribe, Tribal Organization, or Urban Indian Organization (as defined in section 1139(c) [42 USCS § 1329b-9(c)]).

(iii) Exclusions. Such term does not include an agency that determines eligibility for a program established under the Social Services Block Grant established under title XX [42 USCS §§ 1397 et seq.] or a private, for-profit organization.

(iv) Rules of construction. Nothing in this paragraph shall be construed as—

(I) exempting a State Medicaid agency from complying with the requirements of section 1902(a)(4) [42 USCS § 1396a(a)(4)] relating to merit-based personnel standards for employees of the State Medicaid agency and safeguards against conflicts of interest); or

(II) authorizing a State Medicaid agency that elects to use Express Lane agencies under this subparagraph to use the Express Lane option to avoid complying with such requirements for purposes of making eligibility determinations under the State Medicaid plan.

(v) Additional definitions. In this paragraph:

(I) State. The term "State" means 1 of the 50 States or the District of Columbia.

(II) State CHIP agency. The term "State CHIP agency" means the State agency responsible for administering the State CHIP plan.

(III) State CHIP plan. The term "State CHIP plan" means the State child health plan established under title XXI [42 USCS §§ 1397aa et seq.] and includes any waiver of such plan.

(IV) State Medicaid agency. The term "State Medicaid agency" means the State agency responsible for administering the State Medicaid plan.

(V) State Medicaid plan. The term "State Medicaid plan" means the State plan established under title XIX [42 USCS §§ 1396 et seq.] and includes any waiver of such plan.

(G) Child defined. For purposes of this paragraph, the term "child" means an individual under 19 years of age, or, at the option of a State, such higher age, not to exceed 21 years of age, as the State may elect.

(H) State option to rely on state income tax data or return. At the option of the State, a finding from an Express Lane agency may include gross income or adjusted gross income shown by State income tax records or returns.

(I) Application. This paragraph shall not apply with respect to eligibility determinations made after September 30, 2013.

(14) Income determined using modified adjusted gross income **[Caution: This paragraph takes effect on January 1, 2014, as provided by § 2002(c) of Act March 23, 2010, P. L. 111-148, which appears as a note to this section.]**. (A) In general. Notwithstanding subsection (r) or any other provision of this title [42 USCS §§ 1396 et seq.], except as provided in subparagraph (D), for purposes of determining income eligibility for medical assistance under the State plan or under any waiver of such plan and for any other purpose applicable under the plan or waiver for which a determination of income is required, including with respect to the imposition of premiums and cost-sharing, a State shall use the modified adjusted gross income of an individual and, in the case of an individual in a family greater than 1, the household income of such family. A State shall establish income eligibility thresholds for populations to be eligible for medical assistance under the State plan or a waiver of the plan using modified adjusted gross income and household income that are not less than the effective income eligibility levels that applied under the State plan or waiver on the date of enactment of the Patient Protection and Affordable Care Act [enacted March 23, 2010]. For purposes of complying with the maintenance of effort requirements under subsection (gg) during the transition to modified adjusted gross income and household income, a State

shall, working with the Secretary, establish an equivalent income test that ensures individuals eligible for medical assistance under the State plan or under a waiver of the plan on the date of enactment of the Patient Protection and Affordable Care Act [enacted March 23, 2010], do not lose coverage under the State plan or under a waiver of the plan. The Secretary may waive such provisions of this title and title XXI [42 USCS §§ 1396 et seq. and 1397aa et seq.] as are necessary to ensure that States establish income and eligibility determination systems that protect beneficiaries.

(B) No income or expense disregards. Subject to subparagraph (I), no type of expense, block, or other income disregard shall be applied by a State to determine income eligibility for medical assistance under the State plan or under any waiver of such plan or for any other purpose applicable under the plan or waiver for which a determination of income is required.

(C) No assets test. A State shall not apply any assets or resources test for purposes of determining eligibility for medical assistance under the State plan or under a waiver of the plan.

(D) Exceptions. (i) Individuals eligible because of other aid or assistance, elderly individuals, medically needy individuals, and individuals eligible for Medicare cost-sharing. Subparagraphs (A), (B), and (C) shall not apply to the determination of eligibility under the State plan or under a waiver for medical assistance for the following:

(I) Individuals who are eligible for medical assistance under the State plan or under a waiver of the plan on a basis that does not require a determination of income by the State agency administering the State plan or waiver, including as a result of eligibility for, or receipt of, other Federal or State aid or assistance, individuals who are eligible on the basis of receiving (or being treated as if receiving) supplemental security income benefits under title XVI [42 USCS §§ 1381 et seq.], and individuals who are eligible as a result of being or being deemed to be a child in foster care under the responsibility of the State.

(II) Individuals who have attained age 65.

(III) Individuals who qualify for medical assistance under the State plan or under any waiver of such plan on the basis of being blind or disabled (or being treated as being blind or disabled) without regard to whether the individual is eligible for supplemental security income benefits under title XVI [42 USCS §§ 1381 et seq.] on the basis of being blind or disabled and including an individual who is eligible for medical assistance on the basis of section 1902(e)(3) [subsec. (e)(3) of this section].

(IV) Individuals described in subsection (a)(10)(C).

(V) Individuals described in any clause of subsection (a)(10)(E).

(ii) Express lane agency findings. In the case of a State that elects the Express Lane option under paragraph (13), notwithstanding subparagraphs (A), (B), and (C), the State may rely on a finding made by an Express Lane agency in accordance with that paragraph relating to the income of an individual for purposes of determining the individual's eligibility for medical assistance under the State plan or under a waiver of the plan.

(iii) Medicare prescription drug subsidies determinations. Subparagraphs (A), (B), and (C) shall not apply to any determinations of eligibility for premium and cost-sharing subsidies under and in accordance with section 1860D-14 [42 USCS § 1395w-114] made by the State pursuant to section 1935(a)(2) [42 USCS § 1396u-5(a)(2)].

(iv) Long-term care. Subparagraphs (A), (B), and (C) shall not apply to any determinations of eligibility of individuals for purposes of medical assistance for nursing facility services, a level of care in any institution equivalent to that of nursing facility services, home or community-based services furnished under a waiver or State plan amendment under section 1915 [42 USCS § 1396n] or a waiver under section 1115 [42 USCS § 1315], and services described in section 1917(c)(1)(C)(ii) [42 USCS § 1396p(c)(1)(C)(ii)].

(v) Grandfather of current enrollees until date of next regular redetermination. An individual who, on January 1, 2014, is enrolled in the State plan or under a waiver of the plan and who would be determined ineligible for medical assistance solely because of the application of the modified adjusted gross income or household income standard described in subparagraph (A), shall remain eligible for medical assistance under the State plan or waiver (and subject to the same premiums and cost-sharing as applied to the individual on that date) through March 31, 2014, or the date on which the individual's next regularly scheduled redetermination of eligibility is to occur, whichever is later.

(E) Transition planning and oversight. Each State shall submit to the Secretary for the Secretary's approval the income eligibility thresholds proposed to be established using modified adjusted gross income and household income, the methodologies and procedures to be used to determine income eligibility using modified adjusted gross income and household income and, if applicable, a State plan amendment establishing an optional eligibility category under subsection (a)(10)(A)(ii)(XX). To the extent practicable, the State shall use the same methodologies and procedures for purposes of making such determinations as the State used on the date of enactment of the Patient Protection and Affordable Care Act [enacted March 23, 2010]. The Secretary shall ensure that the income eligibility thresholds proposed to be established using modified adjusted gross income and household income, including under the eligibility category established under subsection (a)(10)(A)(ii)(XX), and the methodologies and procedures proposed to be used to determine income eligibility, will not result in children who would have been eligible for medical assistance under the State plan or under a waiver of the plan on the date of enactment of the Patient Protection and Affordable Care Act [enacted March 23, 2010] no longer being eligible for such assistance.

(F) Limitation on secretarial authority. The Secretary shall not waive compliance with the requirements of this paragraph except to the extent necessary to permit a State to coordinate eligibility requirements for dual eligible individuals (as defined in section 1915(h)(2)(B) [42 USCS § 1396n(h)(2)(B)]) under the State plan or under a waiver of the plan and under title XVIII [42 USCS § 1395 et seq.] and individuals who require the level of care provided in a hospital, a nursing facility, or an intermediate care facility for the mentally retarded.

(G) Definitions of modified adjusted gross income and household income. In this paragraph, the terms "modified adjusted gross income" and "household income" have the meanings given such terms in section 36B(d)(2) of the Internal Revenue Code of 1986 [26 USCS § 36B(d)(2)].

(H) Continued application of Medicaid rules regarding point-in-time income and sources of income. The requirement under this paragraph for States to use modified adjusted gross income and household income to determine income eligibility for medical assistance under the State plan or under any waiver of such plan and for any other purpose applicable under the plan or waiver for which a determination of income is required shall not be construed as affecting or limiting the application of—

(i) the requirement under this title [42 USCS §§ 1396 et seq.] and under the State plan or a waiver of the plan to determine an individual's income as of the point in time at which an application for medical assistance under the State plan or a waiver of the plan is processed; or

(ii) any rules established under this title [42 USCS §§ 1396 et seq.] or under the State plan or a waiver of the plan regarding sources of countable income.

(I) Treatment of portion of modified adjusted gross income. For purposes of determining the income eligibility of an individual for medical assistance whose eligibility is determined based on the application of modified adjusted gross income under subparagraph (A), the State shall—

(i) determine the dollar equivalent of the difference between the upper income limit on eligibility for such an individual (expressed as a percentage of the poverty line) and such upper income limit increased by 5 percentage points; and

(ii) notwithstanding the requirement in subparagraph (A) with respect to use of modified adjusted gross income, utilize as the applicable income of such individual, in determining such income eligibility, an amount equal to the modified adjusted gross income applicable to such individual reduced by such dollar equivalent amount.

(f) Effective date of State plan as determinative of duty of State to provide medical assistance to aged, blind, or disabled individuals. Notwithstanding any other provision of this title [42 USCS §§ 1396 et seq.], except as provided in subsection (e) and section 1619(b)(3) and section 1924 [42 USCS § 1382h(b)(3) and § 1396r-5], except with respect to qualified disabled and working individuals (described in section 1905(s) [42 USCS § 1396d(s)]), and except with respect to qualified medicare beneficiaries, qualified severely impaired individuals, and individuals described in subsection (m)(1), no State not eligible to participate in the State plan program established under title XVI [42 USCS §§ 1381 et seq.] shall be required to provide medical assistance to any aged, blind, or disabled individual (within the meaning of title XVI [42 USCS §§ 1381 et seq.]) for any month unless such State would be (or would have been) required to provide medical assistance to such individual for such month had its plan for medical assistance approved under this title [42 USCS §§ 1396 et seq.] and in effect on January 1, 1972, been in effect in such month, except that for this purpose any such individual shall be deemed eligible for medical assistance under such State plan if (in addition to meeting such other requirements as are or may be imposed under the State plan) the income of any such individual as determined in accordance with section 1903(f) [42 USCS § 1396b(f)] (after deducting any supplemental security income payment and State supplementary payment made with respect to such individual, and incurred expenses for medical care as recognized under State law regardless of whether such expenses are reimbursed under another public program of the State or political subdivision thereof, is not in excess of the standard for medical assistance established under the State plan as in effect on January 1, 1972. In States which provide medical assistance to individuals pursuant to paragraph (10)(C) of subsection (a) of this section, an individual who is eligible for medical assistance by reason of the requirements of this section concerning the deduction of incurred medical expenses from income shall be considered an individual eligible for medical assistance under paragraph (10)(A) of that subsection if that individual is, or is eligible to be (1) an individual with respect to whom there is payable a State supplementary payment on the basis of which similarly situated individuals are eligible to receive medical assistance equal in amount, duration, and scope to that provided to individuals eligible under paragraph (10)(A), or (2) an eligible individual or eligible spouse, as defined in title XVI [42 USCS §§ 1381 et seq.], with respect to whom supplemental security income benefits are payable; otherwise that individual shall be considered to be an individual eligible for medical assistance under paragraph (10)(C) of that subsection. In States which do not provide medical assistance to individuals pursuant to paragraph (10)(C) of that subsection, an individual who is eligible for medical assistance by reason of the requirements of this section concerning the deduction of incurred medical expenses from income shall be considered an individual eligible for medical assistance under paragraph (10)(A) of that subsection.

(g) Reduction of aid or assistance to providers of services attempting to collect from beneficiary in violation of third-party provisions. In addition to any other sanction available to a State, a State may provide for a reduction of any payment amount otherwise due with respect to a person who furnishes services under the plan in an amount equal to up to three times the amount of any payment sought to be collected by that person in violation of subsection (a)(25)(C).

(h) Payments for hospitals serving disproportionate number of low-income patients and for home and community care. Nothing in this title [42 USCS §§ 1396 et seq.] (including subsections (a)(13) and (a)(30) of this section) shall be construed as authorizing the Secretary to limit the amount of payment that may be made under a plan under this title [42 USCS §§ 1396 et seq.] for home and community care.

(i) Termination of certification for participation of and suspension of State payments to intermediate care facilities for the mentally retarded. (1) In addition to any other authority under State law, where a State determines that a [an] intermediate care facility for the mentally retarded which is certified for participation under its plan no longer substantially meets the requirements for such a facility under this title [42 USCS §§ 1396 et seq.] and further determines that the facility's deficiencies—

(A) immediately jeopardize the health and safety of its patients, the State shall provide for the termination of the facility's certification for participation under the plan and may provide, or

(B) do not immediately jeopardize the health and safety of its patients, the State may, in lieu of providing for terminating the facility's certification for participation under the plan, establish alternative remedies if the State demonstrates to the Secretary's satisfaction that the alternative remedies are effective in deterring noncompliance and correcting deficiencies, and may provide

that no payment will be made under the State plan with respect to any individual admitted to such facility after a date specified by the State.

(2) The State shall not make such a decision with respect to a facility until the facility has had a reasonable opportunity, following the initial determination that it no longer substantially meets the requirements for such a facility under this title [42 USCS §§ 1396 et seq.], to correct its deficiencies, and, following this period, has been given reasonable notice and opportunity for a hearing.

(3) The State's decision to deny payment may be made effective only after such notice to the public and to the facility as may be provided for by the State, and its effectiveness shall terminate (A) when the State finds that the facility is in substantial compliance (or is making good faith efforts to achieve substantial compliance) with the requirements for such a facility under this title [42 USCS §§ 1396 et seq.], or (B) in the case described in paragraph (1)(B), with the end of the eleventh month

following the month such decision is made effective, whichever occurs first. If a facility to which clause (B) of the previous sentence applies still fails to substantially meet the provisions of the respective section on the date specified in such clause, the State shall terminate such facility's certification for participation under the plan effective with the first day of the first month following the month specified in such clause.

(j) Waiver or modification of 42 USCS §§ 1396 et seq. requirements with respect to medical assistance program in American Samoa. Notwithstanding any other requirement of this title [42 USCS §§ 1396 et seq.], the Secretary may waive or modify any requirement of this title [42 USCS §§ 1396 et seq.] with respect to the medical assistance program in American Samoa and the Northern Mariana Islands, other than a waiver of the Federal medical assistance percentage, the limitation in section 1108(f) [42 USCS § 1308(f)], or the requirement that payment may be made for medical assistance only with respect to amounts expended by American Samoa or the Northern Mariana Islands for care and services described in a numbered paragraph of section 1905(a) [42 USCS § 1396d(a)].

(k) Provision of at least minimum essential coverage. (1) The medical assistance provided to an individual described in subclause (VIII) of subsection (a)(10)(A)(i) shall consist of benchmark coverage described in section 1937(b)(1) [42 USCS § 1396u-7(b)(1)] or benchmark equivalent coverage described in section 1937(b)(2) [42 USCS § 1396u-7(b)(2)]. Such medical assistance shall be provided subject to the requirements of section 1937 [42 USCS § 1396u-7], without regard to whether a State otherwise has elected the option to provide medical assistance through coverage under that section, unless an individual described in subclause (VIII) of subsection (a)(10)(A)(i) is also an individual for whom, under subparagraph (B) of section 1937(a)(2) [42 USCS § 1396u-7(a)(2)], the State may not require enrollment in benchmark coverage described in subsection (b)(1) of section 1937 [42 USCS § 1396u-7] or benchmark equivalent coverage described in subsection (b)(2) of that section.

(2) Beginning with the first day of any fiscal year quarter that begins on or after April 1, 2010, and before January 1, 2014, a State may elect through a State plan amendment to provide medical assistance to individuals who would be described in subclause (VIII) of subsection (a)(10)(A)(i) if that subclause were effective before January 1, 2014. A State may elect to phase-in the extension of eligibility for medical assistance to such individuals based on income, so long as the State does not extend such eligibility to individuals described in such subclause with higher income before making individuals described in such subclause with lower income eligible for medical assistance.

(3) If an individual described in subclause (VIII) of subsection (a)(10)(A)(i) is the parent of a child who is under 19 years of age (or such higher age as the State may have elected) who is eligible for medical assistance under the State plan or under a waiver of such plan (under that subclause or under a State plan amendment under paragraph (2), the individual may not be enrolled under the State plan unless the individual's child is enrolled under the State plan or under a waiver of the plan or is enrolled in other health insurance coverage. For purposes of the preceding sentence, the term 'parent' includes an individual treated as a caretaker relative for purposes of carrying out section 1931 [42 USCS § 1396u-1].

(l) Description of group. (1) Individuals described in this paragraph are—

(A) women during pregnancy (and during the 60-day period beginning on the last day of the pregnancy),

(B) infants under one year of age,

(C) children who have attained one year of age but have not attained 6 years of age, and

(D) children born after September 30, 1983 (or, at the option of a State, after any earlier date), who have attained 6 years of age but have not attained 19 years of age,

who are not described in any of subclauses (I) through (III) of subsection (a)(10)(A)(i) and whose family income does not exceed the income level established by the State under paragraph (2) for a family size equal to the size of the family, including the woman, infant, or child.

(2)(A)(i) For purposes of paragraph (1) with respect to individuals described in subparagraph (A) or (B) of that paragraph, the State shall establish an income level which is a percentage (not less than the percentage provided under clause (ii) and not more than 185 percent) of the income official poverty line (as defined by the Office of Management and Budget, and revised annually in accordance with section 673(2) of the Omnibus Budget Reconciliation Act of 1981) [42 USCS § 9902(2)] applicable to a family of the size involved.

(ii) The percentage provided under this clause, with respect to eligibility for medical assistance on or after—

(I) July 1, 1989, is 75 percent, or, if greater,

the percentage provided under clause (iii), and

(II) April 1, 1990, 133 percent, or, if greater, the percentage provided under clause (iv).

(iii) In the case of a State which, as of the date of the enactment of this clause [Dec. 19, 1989], has elected to provide, and provides, medical assistance to individuals described in this subsection or has enacted legislation authorizing, or appropriating funds, to provide such assistance to such individuals before July 1, 1989, the percentage provided under clause (ii)(I) shall not be less than—

(I) the percentage specified by the State in an amendment to its State plan (whether approved or not) as of the date of the enactment of this clause [Dec. 19, 1989], or

(II) if no such percentage is specified as of the date of the enactment of this clause [Dec. 19, 1989], the percentage established under the State's authorizing legislation or provided for under the State's appropriations;

but in no case shall this clause require the percentage provided under clause (ii)(I) to exceed 100 percent.

(iv) In the case of a State which, as of the date of the enactment of this clause [Dec. 19, 1989], has established under clause (i), or has enacted legislation authorizing, or appropriating funds, to provide for, a percentage (of the income official poverty line) that is greater than 133 percent, the percentage provided under clause (ii) for medical assistance on or after April 1, 1990, shall not be less than—

(I) the percentage specified by the State in an amendment to its State plan (whether approved or not) as of the date of the enactment of this clause [Dec. 19, 1989], or

(II) if no such percentage is specified as of the date of the enactment of this clause [Dec. 19, 1989], the percentage established under the State's authorizing legislation or provided for under the State's appropriations.

(B) For purposes of paragraph (1) with respect to individuals described in subparagraph (C) of such paragraph, the State shall establish an income level which is equal to 133 percent of the income official poverty line described in subparagraph (A) applicable to a family of the size involved.

(C) For purposes of paragraph (1) with respect to individuals described in subparagraph (D) of that paragraph, the State shall establish an income level which is equal to 133 percent of the income official poverty line described in subparagraph (A) applicable to a family of the size involved.

(3) Notwithstanding subsection (a)(17), for individuals who are eligible for medical assistance because of subsection (a)(10)(A)(i)(IV), (a)(10)(A)(i)(VI), (a)(10)(A)(i)(VII), or (a)(10)(A)(ii)(IX)—

(A) application of a resource standard shall be at the option of the State;

(B) any resource standard or methodology that is applied with respect to an individual described in subparagraph (A) of paragraph (1) may not be more restrictive than the resource standard or methodology that is applied under title XVI [42 USCS §§ 1381 et seq.];

(C) any resource standard or methodology that is applied with respect to an individual described in subparagraph (B), (C), or (D) of paragraph (1) may not be more restrictive than the corresponding methodology that is applied under the State plan under part A of title IV [42 USCS §§ 601 et seq.];

(D) the income standard to be applied is the appropriate income standard established under paragraph (2); and

(E) family income shall be determined in accordance with the methodology employed under the State plan under part A or E of title IV [42 USCS §§ 601 et seq. or 670 et seq.] (except to the extent such methodology is inconsistent with clause (D) of subsection (a)(17)), and costs incurred for medical care or for any other type of remedial care shall not be taken into account.

Any different treatment provided under this paragraph for such individuals shall not, because of subsection (a)(17), require or permit such treatment for other individuals.

(4)(A) In the case of any State which is providing medical assistance to its residents under a waiver granted under section 1115 [42 USCS § 1315], the Secretary shall require the State to provide medical assistance for pregnant women and infants under age 1 described in subsection (a)(10)(A)(i)(IV), and for children described in subsection (a)(10)(A)(i)(VI) or subsection (a)(10)(A)(i)(VII) in the same manner as the State would be required to provide such assistance for such individuals if the State had in effect a plan approved under this title [42 USCS §§ 1396 et seq.].

(B) In the case of a State which is not one of the 50 States or the District of Columbia, the State need not meet the requirement of subsection (a)(10)(A)(i)(IV), (a)(10)(A)(i)(VI), or (a)(10)(A)(i)(VII) and, for purposes of paragraph (2)(A), the State may substitute for the percentage provided under clause (ii) of such paragraph any percentage.

(m) Description of individuals. (1) Individuals described in this paragraph are individuals—

(A) who are 65 years of age or older or are disabled individuals (as determined under section 1614(a)(3) [42 USCS § 1382c(a)(3)]),

(B) whose income (as determined under section 1612 [42 USCS § 1382a] for purposes of the supplemental security income program, except as provided in paragraph (2)(C)) does not exceed an income level established by the State consistent with paragraph (2)(A), and

(C) whose resources (as determined under section 1613 [42 USCS § 1382b] for purposes of the supplemental security income program) do not exceed (except as provided in paragraph (2)(B)) the maximum amount of resources that an individual may have and obtain benefits under that program.

(2)(A) The income level established under paragraph (1)(B) may not exceed a percentage (not more than 100 percent) of the official poverty line (as defined by the Office of Management and Budget, and revised annually in accordance with section 673(2) of the Omnibus Budget Reconciliation Act of 1981 [42 USCS § 9902(2)]) applicable to a family of the size involved.

(B) In the case of a State that provides medical assistance to individuals not described in subsection (a)(10)(A) and at the State's option, the State may use under paragraph (1)(C) such resource level (which is higher than the level described in that paragraph) as may be applicable with respect to individuals described in paragraph (1)(A) who are not described in subsection (a)(10)(A).

(C) The provisions of section 1905(p)(2)(D) [42 USCS § 1396d(p)(2)(D)] shall apply to determinations of income under this subsection in the same manner as they apply to determinations of income under section 1905(p) [42 USCS § 1396d(p)].

(3) Notwithstanding subsection (a)(17), for individuals described in paragraph (1) who are covered under the State plan by virtue of subsection (a)(10)(A)(ii)(X)—

(A) the income standard to be applied is the income standard described in paragraph (1)(B), and

(B) except as provided in section 1612(b)(4)(B)(ii) [42 USCS § 1382a(b)(4)(B)(ii)], costs incurred for medical care or for any other type of remedial care shall not be taken into account in determining income.

Any different treatment provided under this paragraph for such individuals shall not, because of subsection (a)(17), require or permit such treatment for other individuals.

(4) Notwithstanding subsection (a)(17), for qualified medicare beneficiaries described in section 1905(p)(1) [42 USCS § 1396d(p)(1)]—

(A) the income standard to be applied is the income standard described in section 1905(p)(1)(B) [42 USCS § 1396d(p)(1)(B)], and

(B) except as provided in section 1612(b)(4)(B)(ii) [42 USCS § 1382a(b)(4)(B)(ii)], costs incurred for medical care or for any other type of remedial care shall not be taken into account in determining income.

Any different treatment provided under this paragraph for such individuals shall not, because of subsection (a)(17), require or permit such treatment for other individuals.

(n) Payment amounts. (1) In the case of medical assistance furnished under this title [42 USCS §§ 1396 et seq.] for medicare cost-sharing respecting the furnishing of a service or item to a qualified medicare beneficiary, the State plan may provide payment in an amount with respect to the service or item that results in the sum of such payment amount and any amount of payment made under title XVIII [42 USCS §§ 1395 et seq.] with respect to the service or item exceeding the amount that is otherwise payable under the State plan for the item or service for eligible individuals who are not qualified medicare beneficiaries.

(2) In carrying out paragraph (1), a State is not required to provide any payment for any expenses incurred relating to payment for deductibles, coinsurance, or copayments for medicare cost-sharing to the extent that payment under title XVIII [42 USCS §§ 1395 et seq.] for the service would exceed the payment amount that otherwise would be made under the State plan under this title [42 USCS §§ 1396 et seq.] for such service if provided to an eligible recipient other than a medicare beneficiary.

(3) In the case in which a State's payment for medicare cost-sharing for a qualified medicare beneficiary with respect to an item or service is reduced or eliminated through the application of paragraph (2)—

(A) for purposes of applying any limitation under title XVIII [42 USCS §§ 1395 et seq.] on the amount that the beneficiary may be billed or charged for the service, the amount of payment made under title XVIII [42 USCS §§ 1395 et seq.] plus the amount of payment (if any) under the State plan shall be considered to be payment in full for the service;

(B) the beneficiary shall not have any legal liability to make payment to a provider or to an organization described in section 1903(m)(1)(A) [42 USCS § 1396b(m)(1)(A)] for the service;

and

(C) any lawful sanction that may be imposed upon a provider or such an organization for excess charges under this title or title XVIII [42 USCS §§ 1396 et seq. or 1395 et seq.] shall apply to the imposition of any charge imposed upon the individual in such case.

This paragraph shall not be construed as preventing payment of any medicare cost-sharing by a medicare supplemental policy or an employer retiree health plan on behalf of an individual.

(o) Certain benefits disregarded for purposes of determining post-eligibility contributions. Notwithstanding any provision of subsection (a) to the contrary, a State plan under this title [42 USCS §§ 1396 et seq.] shall provide that any supplemental security income benefits paid by reason of subparagraph (E) or (G) of section 1611(e)(1) [42 USCS § 1382(e)(1)(E) or (G)] to an individual who—

(1) is eligible for medical assistance under the plan, and

(2) is in a hospital, skilled nursing facility, or intermediate care facility at the time such benefits are paid,

will be disregarded for purposes of determining the amount of any post-eligibility contribution by the individual to the cost of the care and services provided by the hospital, skilled nursing facility, or intermediate care facility.

(p) Exclusion power of State; exclusion as prerequisite for medical assistance payments; "exclude" defined. (1) In addition to any other authority, a State may exclude any individual or entity for purposes of participating under the State plan under this title [42 USCS §§ 1396 et seq.] for any reason for which the Secretary could exclude the individual or entity from participation in a program under title XVIII [42 USCS §§ 1395 et seq.] under section 1128, 1128A, or 1866(b)(2) [42 USCS § 1320a-7, 1320a-7a, or 1395cc(b)(2)].

(2) In order for a State to receive payments for medical assistance under section 1903(a) [42 USCS § 1396b(a)], with respect to payments the State makes to a medicaid managed care organization (as defined in section 1903(m) [42 USCS § 1396b(m)]) or to an entity furnishing services under a waiver approved under section 1915(b)(1) [42 USCS § 1396n(b)(1)], the State must provide that it will exclude from participation, as such an organization or entity, any organization or entity that—

(A) could be excluded under section 1128(b)(8) [42 USCS § 1320a-7(b)(8)] (relating to owners and managing employees who have been convicted of certain crimes or received other sanctions),

(B) has, directly or indirectly, a substantial contractual relationship (as defined by the Secretary) with an individual or entity that is described in section 1128(b)(8)(B) [42 USCS § 1320a-7(b)(8)(B)], or

(C) employs or contracts with any individual or entity that is excluded from participation under this title [42 USCS §§ 1396 et seq.] under section 1128 or 1128A [42 USCS § 1320a-7 or 1320a-7a] for the provision of health care, utilization review, medical social work, or administrative services or employs or contracts with any entity for the provision (directly or indirectly) through such an excluded individual or entity of such services.

(3) As used in this subsection, the term "exclude" includes the refusal to enter into or renew a participation agreement or the termination of such an agreement.

(q) Minimum monthly personal needs allowance deduction; "institutionalized individual or couple" defined. (1)(A) In order to meet the requirement of subsection (a)(50), the State plan must provide that, in the case of an institutionalized individual or couple described in subparagraph (B), in determining the amount of the individual's or couple's income to be applied monthly to payment for the cost of care in an institution, there shall be deducted from the monthly income (in addition to other allowances otherwise provided under the State plan) a monthly personal needs allowance—

(i) which is reasonable in amount for clothing and other personal needs of the individual (or couple) while in an institution, and

(ii) which is not less (and may be greater) than the minimum monthly personal needs allowance described in paragraph (2).

(B) In this subsection, the term "institutionalized individual or couple" means an individual or married couple—

(i) who is an inpatient (or who are inpatients) in a medical institution or nursing facility for which payments are made under this title [42 USCS §§ 1396 et seq.] throughout a month, and

(ii) who is or are determined to be eligible for medical assistance under the State plan.

(2) The minimum monthly personal needs allowance described in this paragraph [subsection] is $30 for an institutionalized individual and $60 for an institutionalized couple (if both are aged, blind, or disabled, and their incomes are considered available to each other in determining eligibility).

(r) Disregarding payments for certain medical expenses by institutionalized individuals. (1)(A) For purposes of sections 1902(a)(17) and 1924(d)(1)(D) [42 USCS §§ 1396a(a)(17) and 1396r-5(d)(1)(D)] and for purposes of a waiver under section 1915 [42 USCS § 1396n], with respect to the post-eligibility treatment of income of individuals who are institutionalized or receiving home or community-based services under such a waiver, the treatment described in subparagraph (B) shall apply, there shall be disregarded reparation payments made by the Federal Republic of Germany, and there shall be taken into account amounts for incurred expenses for medical or remedial care that are not subject to payment by a third party, including—

(i) medicare and other health insurance premiums, deductibles, or coinsurance, and

(ii) necessary medical or remedial care recognized under State law but not covered under the State plan under this title [42 USCS §§ 1396 et seq.], subject to reasonable limits the State may establish on the amount of these expenses. (B)(i) In the case of a veteran who does not have a spouse or a child, if the veteran—

(I) receives, after the veteran has been determined to be eligible for medical assistance under the State plan under this title [42 USCS §§ 1396 et seq.], a veteran's pension in excess of $90 per month, and

(II) resides in a State veterans home with respect to which the Secretary of Veterans Affairs makes per diem payments for nursing home care pursuant to section 1741(a) of title 38, United States Code,

any such pension payment, including any payment made due to the need for aid and attendance, or for unreimbursed medical expenses, that is in excess of $90 per month shall be counted as income only for the purpose of applying such excess payment to the State veterans home's cost of providing nursing home care to the veteran.

(ii) The provisions of clause (i) shall apply with respect to a surviving spouse of a veteran who does not have a child in the same manner as they apply to a veteran described in such clause.

(2)(A) The methodology to be employed in determining income and resource eligibility for individuals under subsection (a)(10)(A)(i)(III), (a)(10)(A)(i)(IV), (a)(10)(A)(i)(VI), (a)(10)(A)(i)(VII), (a)(10)(A)(ii), (a)(10)(C)(i)(III), or (f) or under section 1905(p) [1396d(p)] may be less restrictive, and shall be no more restrictive, than the methodology—

(i) in the case of groups consisting of aged, blind, or disabled individuals, under the supplemental security income program under title XVI [42 USCS §§ 1381 et seq.], or

(ii) in the case of other groups, under the State plan most closely categorically related.

(B) For purposes of this subsection and subsection (a)(10), methodology is considered to be "no more restrictive" if, using the methodology, additional individuals may be eligible for medical assistance and no individuals who are otherwise eligible are made ineligible for such assistance.

(s) Adjustment in payment for hospital services furnished to low-income children under the age of 6 years. In order to meet the requirements of subsection (a)[(56)](55), the State plan must provide that payments to hospitals under the plan for inpatient hospital services furnished to infants who have not attained the age of 1 year, and to children who have not attained the age of 6 years and who receive such services in a disproportionate share hospital described in section 1923(b)(1) [42 USCS § 1396r-4(b)(1)], shall—

(1) if made on a prospective basis (whether per diem, per case, or otherwise) provide for an outlier adjustment in payment amounts for medically necessary inpatient hospital services involving exceptionally high costs or exceptionally long lengths of stay,

(2) not be limited by the imposition of day limits with respect to the delivery of such services to such individuals, and

(3) not be limited by the imposition of dollar limits (other than such limits resulting from prospective payments as adjusted pursuant to paragraph (1)) with respect to the delivery of such services to any such individual who has not attained their first birthday (or in the case of such an individual who is an inpatient on his first birthday until such individual is discharged).

(t) Limitation on payments to States for expenditures attributable to taxes. Nothing in this title [42 USCS §§ 1396 et seq.] (including sections 1903(a) and 1905(a) [42 USCS §§ 1936b(a) and 1396d(a)]) shall be construed as authorizing the Secretary to deny or limit payments to a State for expenditures, for medical assistance for items or services, attributable to taxes of general applicability imposed with respect to the provision of such items or services.

(u) Qualified COBRA continuation beneficiaries. (1) Individuals described in this paragraph are individuals—

(A) who are entitled to elect COBRA continuation coverage (as defined in paragraph (3)),

(B) whose income (as determined under section 1612 [42 USCS § 1382a] for purposes of the supplemental security income program) does not exceed 100 percent of the official poverty line (as defined by the Office of Management and Budget, and revised annually in accordance with section 673(2) of the Omnibus Budget Reconciliation Act of 1981 [42 USCS § 9902(2)]) applicable to a family of the size involved,

(C) whose resources (as determined under section 1613 [42 USCS § 1382b] for purposes of the supplemental security income program) do not exceed twice the maximum amount of resources that an individual may have and obtain benefits under that program, and

(D) with respect to whose enrollment for COBRA continuation coverage the State has determined that the savings in expenditures under this title [42 USCS §§ 1396 et seq.] resulting from such enrollment is likely to exceed the amount of payments for COBRA premiums made.

(2) For purposes of subsection (a)(10)(F) and this subsection, the term "COBRA premiums" means the applicable premium imposed with respect to COBRA continuation coverage.

(3) In this subsection, the term "COBRA continuation coverage" means coverage under a group health plan provided by an employer with 75 or more employees provided pursuant to title XXII of the Public Health Service Act [42 USCS §§ 300bb-1 et seq.], section 4980B of the Internal Revenue Code of 1986 [26 USCS § 4980B], or title VI of the Employee Retirement Income Security Act of 1974 [29 USCS §§ 1161 et seq.].

(4) Notwithstanding subsection (a)(17), for individuals described in paragraph (1) who are covered under the State plan by virtue of subsection (a)(10)(A)(ii)(XI)—

(A) the income standard to be applied is the income standard described in paragraph (1)(B), and

(B) except as provided in section 1612(b)(4)(B)(ii) [42 USCS § 1383(b)(4)(B)(ii)], costs incurred for medical care or for any other type of remedial care shall not be taken into account in determining income.

Any different treatment provided under this paragraph for such individuals shall not, because of subsection (a)(10)(B) or (a)(17), require or permit such treatment for other individuals.

(v) State agency disability and blindness determinations for medical assistance eligibility. A State plan may provide for the making of determinations of disability or blindness for the purpose of determining eligibility for medical assistance under the State plan by the single State agency or its designee, and make medical assistance available to individuals whom it finds to be blind or disabled and who are determined otherwise eligible for such assistance during the period of time prior to which a final determination of disability or blindness is made by the Social Security Administration with respect to such an individual. In making such determinations, the State must apply the definitions of disability and blindness found in section 1614(a) of the Social Security Act [42 USCS § 1382c(a)].

(w) Maintenance of written policies and procedures respecting advance directives. (1) For purposes of subsection (a)(57) and sections 1903(m)(1)(A) and 1919(c)(2)(E) [42 USCS §§ 1396b(m)(1)(A) and 1396r(c)(2)(E)], the requirement of this subsection is that a provider or organization (as the case may be) maintain written policies and procedures with respect to all adult individuals receiving medical care by or through the provider or organization—

(A) to provide written information to each such individual concerning—

(i) an individual's rights under State law (whether statutory or as recognized by the courts of the State) to make decisions concerning such medical care, including the right to accept or refuse medical or surgical treatment and the right to formulate advance directives (as defined in paragraph (3)), and

(ii) the provider's or organization's written policies respecting the implementation of such rights;

(B) to document in the individual's medical record whether or not the individual has executed an advance directive;

(C) not to condition the provision of care or otherwise discriminate against an individual based on whether or not the individual has executed an advance directive;

(D) to ensure compliance with requirements of State law (whether statutory or as recognized by the courts of the State) respecting advance directives; and

(E) to provide (individually or with others) for education for staff and the community on issues concerning advance directives.

Subparagraph (C) shall not be construed as requiring the provision of care which conflicts with an advance directive.

(2) The written information described in paragraph (1)(A) shall be provided to an adult individual—

(A) in the case of a hospital, at the time of the individual's admission as an inpatient,

(B) in the case of a nursing facility, at the time of the individual's admission as a resident,

(C) in the case of a provider of home health care or personal care services, in advance of the individual coming under the care of the provider,

(D) in the case of a hospice program, at the time of initial receipt of hospice care by the individual from the program, and

(E) in the case of a medicaid managed care organization, at the time of enrollment of the individual with the organization.

(3) Nothing in this section shall be construed to prohibit the application of a State law which allows for an objection on the basis of conscience for any health care provider or any agent of such provider which as a matter of conscience cannot implement an advance directive.

(4) In this subsection, the term "advance directive" means a written instruction, such as a living will or durable power of attorney for health care, recognized under State law (whether statutory or as recognized by the courts of the State) and relating to the provision of such care when the individual is incapacitated.

(5) For construction relating to this subsection, see section 7 of the Assisted Suicide Funding Restriction Act of 1997 [42 USCS § 14406] (relating to clarification respecting assisted suicide, euthanasia, and mercy killing).

(x) Physician identifier system; establishment. The Secretary shall establish a system, for implementation by not later than July 1, 1991, which provides for a unique identifier for each physician who furnishes services for which payment may be made under a State plan approved under this title [42 USCS §§ 1396 et seq.].

(y) Intermediate sanctions for psychiatric hospitals. (1) In addition to any other authority under State law, where a State determines that a psychiatric hospital which is certified for participation under its plan no longer meets the requirements for a psychiatric hospital (referred to in section 1905(h) [42 USCS § 1396d(h)]) and further finds that the hospital's deficiencies—

(A) immediately jeopardize the health and safety of its patients, the State shall terminate the hospital's participation under the State plan; or

(B) do not immediately jeopardize the health and safety of its patients, the State may terminate the hospital's participation under the State plan, or provide that no payment will be made under the State plan with respect to any individual admitted to such hospital after the effective date of the finding, or both.

(2) Except as provided in paragraph (3), if a psychiatric hospital described in paragraph (1)(B) has not complied with the requirements for a psychiatric hospital under this title [42 USCS §§ 1396 et seq.]—

(A) within 3 months after the date the hospital is found to be out of compliance with such requirements, the State shall provide that no payment will be made under the State plan with respect to any individual admitted to such hospital after the end of such 3-month period, or

(B) within 6 months after the date the hospital is found to be out of compliance with such requirements, no Federal financial participation shall be provided under section 1903(a) [42 USCS § 1396b(a)] with respect to further services provided in the hospital until the State finds that the hospital is in compliance with the requirements of this title [42 USCS §§ 1396 et seq.].

(3) The Secretary may continue payments, over a period of not longer than 6 months from the date the hospital is found to be out of compliance with such requirements, if—

(A) the State finds that it is more appropriate to take alternative action to assure compliance of the hospital with the requirements than to terminate the certification of the hospital,

(B) the State has submitted a plan and timetable for corrective action to the Secretary for approval and the Secretary approves the plan of corrective action, and

(C) the State agrees to repay to the Federal Government payments received under this paragraph if the corrective action is not taken in accordance with the approved plan and timetable.

(z) TB-infected individuals; TB-related services. (1) Individuals described in this paragraph are individuals not described in subsection (a)(10)(A)(i)—

(A) who are infected with tuberculosis;

(B) whose income (as determined under the State plan under this title [42 USCS §§ 1396 et seq.] with respect to disabled individuals) does not exceed the maximum amount of income a disabled individual described in subsection (a)(10)(A)(i) may have and obtain medical assistance under the plan; and

(C) whose resources (as determined under the State plan under this title [42 USCS

§§ 1396 et seq.] with respect to disabled individuals) do not exceed the maximum amount of resources a disabled individual described in subsection (a)(10)(A)(i) may have and obtain medical assistance under the plan.

(2) For purposes of subsection (a)(10), the term "TB-related services" means each of the following services relating to treatment of infection with tuberculosis:

(A) Prescribed drugs.

(B) Physicians' services and services described in section 1905(a)(2) [42 USCS § 1396d(a)(2)].

(C) Laboratory and X-ray services (including services to confirm the presence of infection).

(D) Clinic services and Federally-qualified health center services.

(E) Case management services (as defined in section 1915(g)(2) [42 USCS § 1396n(g)(2)]).

(F) Services (other than room and board) designed to encourage completion of regimens of prescribed drugs by outpatients, including services to observe directly the intake of prescribed drugs.

(aa) Certain individuals with breast or cervical cancer. Individuals described in this subsection are individuals who—

(1) are not described in subsection (a)(10)(A)(i);

(2) have not attained age 65;

(3) have been screened for breast and cervical cancer under the Centers for Disease Control and Prevention breast and cervical cancer early detection program established under title XV of the Public Health Service Act (42 U.S.C. 300k et seq.) in accordance with the requirements of section 1504 of that Act (42 U.S.C. 300n) and need treatment for breast or cervical cancer; and

(4) are not otherwise covered under creditable coverage, as defined in section 2701(c) of the Public Health Service Act (42 U.S.C. 300gg(c)), but applied without regard to paragraph (1)(F) of such section.

(bb) Payment for services provided by federally-qualified health centers and rural health clinics. (1) In general. Beginning with fiscal year 2001 with respect to services furnished on or after January 1, 2001, and each succeeding fiscal year, the State plan shall provide for payment for services described in section 1905(a)(2)(C) [42 USCS § 1396d(a)(2)(C)] furnished by a Federally-qualified health center and services described in section 1905(a)(2)(B) [42 USCS § 1396(a)(2)(B)] furnished by a rural health clinic in accordance with the provisions of this subsection.

(2) Fiscal year 2001. Subject to paragraph (4), for services furnished on and after January 1, 2001, during fiscal year 2001, the State plan shall provide for payment for such services in an amount (calculated on a per visit basis) that is equal to 100 percent of the average of the costs of the center or clinic of furnishing such services during fiscal years 1999 and 2000 which are reasonable and related to the cost of furnishing such services, or based on such other tests of reasonableness as the Secretary prescribes in regulations under section 1833(a)(3) [42 USCS § 1395l(a)(3)], or, in the case of services to which such regulations do not apply, the same methodology used under section 1833(a)(3) [42 USCS § 1395l(a)(3)], adjusted to take into account any increase or decrease in the scope of such services furnished by the center or clinic during fiscal year 2001.

(3) Fiscal year 2002 and succeeding fiscal years. Subject to paragraph (4), for services furnished during fiscal year 2002 or a succeeding fiscal year, the State plan shall provide for payment for such services in an amount (calculated on a per visit basis) that is equal to the amount calculated for such services under this subsection for the preceding fiscal year—

(A) increased by the percentage increase in the MEI (as defined in section 1842(i)(3) [42 USCS § 1395u(i)(3)]) applicable to primary care services (as defined in section 1842(i)(4) [42 USCS § 1395u(i)(4)]) for that fiscal year; and

(B) adjusted to take into account any increase or decrease in the scope of such services furnished by the center or clinic during that fiscal year.

(4) Establishment of initial year payment amount for new centers or clinics. In any case in which an entity first qualifies as a Federally-qualified health center or rural health clinic after fiscal year 2000, the State plan shall provide for payment for services described in section 1905(a)(2)(C) [42 USCS § 1396d(a)(2)(C)] furnished by the center or services described in section 1905(a)(2)(B) [42 USCS § 1396d(a)(2)(B)] furnished by the clinic in the first fiscal year in which the center or clinic so qualifies in an amount (calculated on a per visit basis) that is equal to 100 percent of the costs of furnishing such services during such fiscal year based on the rates established under this subsection for the fiscal year for other such centers or clinics located in the same or adjacent area with a similar case load or, in the absence of such a center or clinic, in accordance with the regulations and methodology referred to in paragraph (2) or based on such

other tests of reasonableness as the Secretary may specify. For each fiscal year following the fiscal year in which the entity first qualifies as a Federally-qualified health center or rural health clinic, the State plan shall provide for the payment amount to be calculated in accordance with paragraph (3).

(5) Administration in the case of managed care. (A) In general. In the case of services furnished by a Federally-qualified health center or rural health clinic pursuant to a contract between the center or clinic and a managed care entity (as defined in section 1932(a)(1)(B) [42 USCS § 1396u-2(a)(1)(B)]), the State plan shall provide for payment to the center or clinic by the State of a supplemental payment equal to the amount (if any) by which the amount determined under paragraphs (2), (3), and (4) of this subsection exceeds the amount of the payments provided under the contract.

(B) Payment schedule. The supplemental payment required under subparagraph (A) shall be made pursuant to a payment schedule agreed to by the State and the Federally-qualified health center or rural health clinic, but in no case less frequently than every 4 months.

(6) Alternative payment methodologies. Notwithstanding any other provision of this section, the State plan may provide for payment in any fiscal year to a Federally-qualified health center for services described in section 1905(a)(2)(C) [42 USCS § 1396d(a)(2)(C)] or to a rural health clinic for services described in section 1905(a)(2)(B) [42 USCS § 1396d(a)(2)(B)] in an amount which is determined under an alternative payment methodology that—

(A) is agreed to by the State and the center or clinic; and

(B) results in payment to the center or clinic of an amount which is at least equal to the amount otherwise required to be paid to the center or clinic under this section.

(cc) Disabled children eligible to receive medical assistance at option of State. (1) Individuals described in this paragraph are individuals—

(A) who are children who have not attained 19 years of age and are born—

(i) on or after January 1, 2001 (or, at the option of a State, on or after an earlier date), in the case of the second, third, and fourth quarters of fiscal year 2007;

(ii) on or after October 1, 1995 (or, at the option of a State, on or after an earlier date), in the case of each quarter of fiscal year 2008; and

(iii) after October 1, 1989, in the case of each quarter of fiscal year 2009 and each quarter of any fiscal year thereafter;

(B) who would be considered disabled under section 1614(a)(3)(C) [42 USCS § 1382c(a)(3)(C)] (as determined under title XVI [42 USCS §§ 1381 et seq.] for children but without regard to any income or asset eligibility requirements that apply under such title with respect to children); and

(C) whose family income does not exceed such income level as the State establishes and does not exceed—

(i) 300 percent of the poverty line (as defined in section 2110(c)(5) [42 USCS § 1397jj(c)(5)]) applicable to a family of the size involved; or

(ii) such higher percent of such poverty line as a State may establish, except that—

(I) any medical assistance provided to an individual whose family income exceeds 300 percent of such poverty line may only be provided with State funds; and

(II) no Federal financial participation shall be provided under section 1903(a) [42 USCS § 1396b(a)] for any medical assistance provided to such an individual.

(2)(A) If an employer of a parent of an individual described in paragraph (1) offers family coverage under a group health plan (as defined in section 2791(a) of the Public Health Service Act [42 USCS § 300gg-91(a)]), the State shall—

(i) notwithstanding section 1906 [42 USCS § 1396e], require such parent to apply for, enroll in, and pay premiums for such coverage as a condition of such parent's child being or remaining eligible for medical assistance under subsection (a)(10)(A)(ii)(XIX) if the parent is determined eligible for such coverage and the employer contributes at least 50 percent of the total cost of annual premiums for such coverage; and

(ii) if such coverage is obtained—

(I) subject to paragraph (2) of section 1916(h) [42 USCS § 1396o(h)], reduce the premium imposed by the State under that section in an amount that reasonably reflects the premium contribution made by the parent for private coverage on behalf of a child with a disability; and

(II) treat such coverage as a third party liability under subsection (a)(25).

(B) In the case of a parent to which subparagraph (A) applies, a State, notwithstanding section 1906 [42 USCS § 1396e] but subject to paragraph (1)(C)(ii), may provide for payment of any portion of the annual premium for such family coverage that the parent is required to pay. Any payments made by the State under this subparagraph shall be considered, for purposes of section 1903(a) [42 USCS § 1396b(a)], to be payments for medical assistance.

(dd) Electronic transmission of information. If the State agency determining eligibility for medical assistance under this title [42 USCS §§ 1396 et seq.] or child health assistance under title XXI [42 USCS §§ 1397aa et seq.] verifies an element of eligibility based on information from an Express Lane Agency (as defined in subsection (e)(13)(F)), or from another public agency, then the applicant's signature under penalty of perjury shall not be required as to such element. Any signature requirement for an application for medical assistance may be satisfied through an electronic signature, as defined in section 1710(1) of the Government Paperwork Elimination Act (44 U.S.C. 3504 note). The requirements of subparagraphs (A) and (B) of section 1137(d)(2) [42 USCS § 1320b-7(d)(2)] may be met through evidence in digital or electronic form.

(ee) Alternative to documentation requirement. [Caution: This subsection takes effect on January 1, 2010, as provided by § 211(d) of Act Feb. 4, 2009, P. L. 111-3, which appears as a note to this section.] (1) For purposes of subsection (a)(46)(B)(ii), the requirements of this subsection with respect to an individual declaring to be a citizen or national of the United States for purposes of establishing eligibility under this title [42 USCS §§ 1396 et seq.], are, in lieu of requiring the individual to present satisfactory documentary evidence of citizenship or nationality under section 1903(x) [42 USCS § 1396b(x)] (if the individual is not described in paragraph (2) of that section), as follows:

(A) The State submits the name and social security number of the individual to the Commissioner of Social Security as part of the program established under paragraph (2).

(B) If the State receives notice from the Commissioner of Social Security that the name or social security number, or the declaration of citizenship or nationality, of the individual is inconsistent with information in the records maintained by the Commissioner—

(i) the State makes a reasonable effort to identify and address the causes of such inconsistency, including through typographical or other clerical errors, by contacting the individual to confirm the accuracy of the name or social security number submitted or declaration of citizenship or nationality and by taking such additional actions as the Secretary, through regulation or other guidance, or the State may identify, and continues to provide the individual with medical assistance while making such effort; and

(ii) in the case such inconsistency is not resolved under clause (i), the State—

(I) notifies the individual of such fact;

(II) provides the individual with a period of 90 days from the date on which the notice required under subclause (I) is received by the individual to either present satisfactory documentary evidence of citizenship or nationality (as defined in section 1903(x)(3) [42 USCS § 1396b(x)(3)]) or resolve the inconsistency with the Commissioner of Social Security (and continues to provide the individual with medical assistance during such 90-day period); and

(III) disenrolls the individual from the State plan under this title [42 USCS §§ 1396 et seq.] within 30 days after the end of such 90-day period if no such documentary evidence is presented or if such inconsistency is not resolved.

(2)(A) Each State electing to satisfy the requirements of this subsection for purposes of section 1902(a)(46)(B) [42 USCS § 1396a(a)(46)(B)] shall establish a program under which the State submits at least monthly to the Commissioner of Social Security for comparison of the name and social security number, of each individual newly enrolled in the State plan under this title [42 USCS §§ 1396 et seq.] that month who is not described in section 1903(x)(2) [42 USCS § 1396b(x)(2)] and who declares to be a United States citizen or national, with information in records maintained by the Commissioner.

(B) In establishing the State program under this paragraph, the State may enter into an agreement with the Commissioner of Social Security—

(i) to provide, through an on-line system or otherwise, for the electronic submission of, and response to, the information submitted under subparagraph (A) for an individual enrolled in the State plan under this title [42 USCS §§ 1396 et seq.] who declares to be citizen or national on at least a monthly basis; or

(ii) to provide for a determination of the consistency of the information submitted with the information maintained in the records of the Commissioner through such other method as agreed to by the State and the Commissioner and approved by the Secretary, provided that such method is no more burdensome for individuals to comply with than any burdens that may apply under a method described in clause (i).

(C) The program established under this paragraph shall provide that, in the case of any individual who is required to submit a social security number to the State under subparagraph (A) and who is unable to provide the State with such number, shall be provided with at least the reasonable opportunity to present satisfactory documentary evidence of citizenship or nationality (as defined in section 1903(x)(3) [42 USCS § 1396b(x)(3)]) as is provided under clauses (i) and (ii) of section 1137(d)(4)(A) [42 USCS § 1320b-7(d)(4)(A)] to an individual for the submittal to the State of evidence indicating a satisfactory immigration status.

(3)(A) The State agency implementing the plan approved under this title [42 USCS §§ 1396 et seq.] shall, at such times and in such form as the Secretary may specify, provide information on the percentage each month that the inconsistent submissions bears to the total submissions made for comparison for such month. For purposes of this subparagraph, a name, social security number, or declaration of citizenship or nationality of an individual shall be treated as inconsistent and included in the determination of such percentage only if—

(i) the information submitted by the individual is not consistent with information in records maintained by the Commissioner of Social Security;

(ii) the inconsistency is not resolved by the State;

(iii) the individual was provided with a reasonable period of time to resolve the inconsistency with the Commissioner of Social Security or provide satisfactory documentation of citizenship status and did not successfully resolve such inconsistency; and

(iv) payment has been made for an item or service furnished to the individual under this title [42 USCS §§ 1396 et seq.].

(B) If, for any fiscal year, the average monthly percentage determined under subparagraph (A) is greater than 3 percent—

(i) the State shall develop and adopt a corrective plan to review its procedures for verifying the identities of individuals seeking to enroll in the State plan under this title [42 USCS §§ 1396 et seq.] and to identify and implement changes in such procedures to improve their accuracy; and

(ii) pay to the Secretary an amount equal to the amount which bears the same ratio to the total payments under the State plan for the fiscal year for providing medical assistance to individuals who provided inconsistent information as the number of individuals with inconsistent information in excess of 3 percent of such total submitted bears to the total number of individuals with inconsistent information.

(C) The Secretary may waive, in certain limited cases, all or part of the payment under subparagraph (B)(ii) if the State is unable to reach the allowable error rate despite a good faith effort by such State.

(D) Subparagraphs (A) and (B) shall not apply to a State for a fiscal year if there is an agreement described in paragraph (2)(B) in effect as of the close of the fiscal year that provides for the submission on a real-time basis of the information described in such paragraph.

(4) Nothing in this subsection shall affect the rights of any individual under this title [42 USCS §§ 1396 et seq.] to appeal any disenrollment from a State plan.

(ff) Treatment of certain property from resources for Medicaid and CHIP eligibility. Notwithstanding any other requirement of this title [42 USCS §§ 1396 et seq.] or any other provision of Federal or State law, a State shall disregard the following property from resources for purposes of determining the eligibility of an individual who is an Indian for medical assistance under this title [42 USCS §§ 1396 et seq.]:

(1) Property, including real property and improvements, that is held in trust, subject to Federal restrictions, or otherwise under the supervision of the Secretary of the Interior, located on a reservation, including any federally recognized Indian Tribe's reservation, pueblo, or colony, including former reservations in Oklahoma, Alaska Native regions established by the Alaska Native Claims Settlement Act, and Indian allotments on or near a reservation as designated and approved by the Bureau of Indian Affairs of the Department of the Interior.

(2) For any federally recognized Tribe not described in paragraph (1), property located within the most recent boundaries of a prior Federal reservation.

(3) Ownership interests in rents, leases, royalties, or usage rights related to natural resources (including extraction of natural resources or harvesting of timber, other plants and plant products, animals, fish, and shellfish) resulting from the exercise of federally protected rights.

(4) Ownership interests in or usage rights to items not covered by paragraphs (1) through (3) that have unique religious, spiritual, traditional, or cultural significance or rights that support subsistence or a traditional lifestyle according to applicable tribal law or custom.

(gg) Maintenance of effort. (1) General requirement to maintain eligibility standards until state exchange is fully operational. Subject to the succeeding paragraphs of this subsection, during the period that begins on the date of enactment of the Patient Protection and Affordable Care Act [enacted March 23, 2010] and ends on the date on which the Secretary determines that an Exchange established by the State under section 1311 of the Patient Protection and Affordable Care Act [42 USCS § 18031] is fully operational, as a condition for receiving any Federal payments under section 1903(a) [42 USCS § 1396b(a)] for calendar quarters occurring during such period, a State shall not have in effect eligibility standards, methodologies, or procedures under the State plan under this title or under any waiver of such plan that is in effect during that period, that are more restrictive than the eligibility standards, methodologies, or procedures, respectively, under the plan or waiver that are in effect on the date of enactment of the Patient Protection and Affordable Care Act [enacted March 23, 2010].

(2) Continuation of eligibility standards for children until October 1, 2019. The requirement under paragraph (1) shall continue to apply to a State through September 30, 2019, with respect to the eligibility standards, methodologies, and procedures under the State plan under this title or under any waiver of such plan that are applicable to determining the eligibility for medical assistance of any child who is under 19 years of age (or such higher age as the State may have elected).

(3) Nonapplication. During the period that begins on January 1, 2011, and ends on December 31, 2013, the requirement under paragraph (1) shall not apply to a State with respect to nonpregnant, nondisabled adults who are eligible for medical assistance under the State plan or under a waiver of the plan at the option of the State and whose income exceeds 133 percent of the poverty line (as defined in section 2110(c)(5) [42 USCS § 1397jj(c)(5)]) applicable to a family of the size involved if, on or after December 31, 2010, the State certifies to the Secretary that, with respect to the State fiscal year during which the certification is made, the State has a budget deficit, or with respect to the succeeding State fiscal year, the State is projected to have a budget deficit. Upon submission of such a certification to the Secretary, the requirement under paragraph (1) shall not apply to the State with respect to any remaining portion of the period described in the preceding sentence.

(4) Determination of compliance. (A) States shall apply modified adjusted gross income. A State's determination of income in accordance with subsection (e)(14) shall not be considered to be eligibility standards, methodologies, or procedures that are more restrictive than the standards, methodologies, or procedures in effect under the State plan or under a waiver of the plan on the date of enactment of the Patient Protection and Affordable Care Act [enacted March 23, 2010] for purposes of determining compliance with the requirements of paragraph (1), (2), or (3).

(B) States may expand eligibility or move waivered populations into coverage under the State plan. With respect to any period applicable under paragraph (1), (2), or (3), a State that applies eligibility standards, methodologies, or procedures under the State plan under this title or under any waiver of the plan that are less restrictive than the eligibility standards, methodologies, or procedures, applied under the State plan or under a waiver of the plan on the date of enactment of the Patient Protection and Affordable Care Act [enacted March 23, 2010], or that makes individuals who, on such date of enactment, are eligible for medical assistance under a waiver of the State plan, after such date of enactment eligible for medical assistance through a State plan amendment with an income eligibility level that is not less than the income eligibility level that applied under the waiver, or as a result of the application of subclause (VIII) of section 1902(a)(10)(A)(i) [subsec. (a)(10)(A)(i) of this section], shall not be considered to have in effect eligibility standards, methodologies, or procedures that are more restrictive than the standards, methodologies, or procedures in effect under the State plan or under a waiver of the plan on the date of enactment of the Patient Protection and Affordable Care Act [enacted March 23, 2010] for purposes of determining compliance with the requirements of paragraph (1), (2), or (3).

(hh) State option for coverage for individuals with income that exceeds 133 percent of the poverty line. (1) A State may elect to phase-in the extension of eligibility for medical assistance to individuals described in subclause (XX) of subsection (a)(10)(A)(ii) based on the categorical group (including nonpregnant childless adults) or income, so long as the State does not extend such eligibility to individuals described in such subclause with higher income before making individuals described in such subclause with lower income eligible for medical assistance.

(2) If an individual described in subclause (XX) of subsection (a)(10)(A)(ii) is the parent of a child who is under 19 years of age (or such

higher age as the State may have elected) who is eligible for medical assistance under the State plan or under a waiver of such plan, the individual may not be enrolled under the State plan unless the individual's child is enrolled under the State plan or under a waiver of the plan or is enrolled in other health insurance coverage. For purposes of the preceding sentence, the term "parent" includes an individual treated as a caretaker relative for purposes of carrying out section 1931 [42 USCS § 1396u-1].

(ii) Individuals eligible for optional family planning services. (1) Individuals described in this subsection are individuals—

(A) whose income does not exceed an income eligibility level established by the State that does not exceed the highest income eligibility level established under the State plan under this title (or under its State child health plan under title XXI [42 USCS §§ 1397aa et seq.]) for pregnant women; and

(B) who are not pregnant.

(2) At the option of a State, individuals described in this subsection may include individuals who, had individuals applied on or before January 1, 2007, would have been made eligible pursuant to the standards and processes imposed by that State for benefits described in clause (XV) of the matter following subparagraph (G) of section subsection (a)(10) pursuant to a waiver granted under section 1115 [42 USCS § 1315].

(3) At the option of a State, for purposes of subsection (a)(17)(B), in determining eligibility for services under this subsection, the State may consider only the income of the applicant or recipient.

[(jj)](ii) Provider and supplier screening, oversight, and reporting requirements. For purposes of subsection (a)(77), the requirements of this subsection are the following:

(1) Screening. The State complies with the process for screening providers and suppliers under this title, as established by the Secretary under section 1886(j)(2) [42 USCS § 1395ww(j)(2)].

(2) Provisional period of enhanced oversight for new providers and suppliers. The State complies with procedures to provide for a provisional period of enhanced oversight for new providers and suppliers under this title, as established by the Secretary under section 1886(j)(3) [42 USCS § 1395ww(j)(3)].

(3) Disclosure requirements. The State requires providers and suppliers under the State plan or under a waiver of the plan to comply with the disclosure requirements established by the Secretary under section 1886(j)(4) [42 USCS § 1395ww(j)(4)].

(4) Temporary moratorium on enrollment of new providers or suppliers. (A) Temporary moratorium imposed by the Secretary. (i) In general. Subject to clause (ii), the State complies with any temporary moratorium on the enrollment of new providers or suppliers imposed by the Secretary under section 1886(j)(6) [42 USCS § 1395ww(j)(6)].

(ii) Exception. A State shall not be required to comply with a temporary moratorium described in clause (i) if the State determines that the imposition of such temporary moratorium would adversely impact beneficiaries' access to medical assistance.

(B) Moratorium on enrollment of providers and suppliers. At the option of the State, the State imposes, for purposes of entering into participation agreements with providers or suppliers under the State plan or under a waiver of the plan, periods of enrollment moratoria, or numerical caps or other limits, for providers or suppliers identified by the Secretary as being at high-risk for fraud, waste, or abuse as necessary to combat fraud, waste, or abuse, but only if the State determines that the imposition of any such period, cap, or other limits would not adversely impact beneficiaries' access to medical assistance.

(5) Compliance programs. The State requires providers and suppliers under the State plan or under a waiver of the plan to establish, in accordance with the requirements of section 1866(j)(7) [42 USCS § 1395ww(j)(7)], a compliance program that contains the core elements established under subparagraph (B) of that section 1866(j)(7) [42 USCS § 1395ww(j)(7)] for providers or suppliers within a particular industry or category.

(6) Reporting of adverse provider actions. The State complies with the national system for reporting criminal and civil convictions, sanctions, negative licensure actions, and other adverse provider actions to the Secretary, through the Administrator of the Centers for Medicare & Medicaid Services, in accordance with regulations of the Secretary.

(7) Enrollment and NPI of ordering or referring providers. The State requires—

(A) all ordering or referring physicians or other professionals to be enrolled under the State plan or under a waiver of the plan as a participating provider; and

(B) the national provider identifier of any ordering or referring physician or other professional to be specified on any claim for payment that is based on an order or referral of the physician or other professional.

(8) Other State oversight. Nothing in this subsection shall be interpreted to preclude or limit the ability of a State to engage in provider and supplier screening or enhanced provider and supplier oversight activities beyond those required by the Secretary.

[(kk)](jj) Primary care services defined. For purposes of subsection (a)(13)(C), the term "primary care services" means—

(1) evaluation and management services that are procedure codes (for services covered under title XVIII [42 USCS §§ 1395 et seq.]) for services in the category designated Evaluation and Management in the Healthcare Common Procedure Coding System (established by the Secretary under section 1848(c)(5) [42 USCS § 1395w-4(c)(5)] as of December 31, 2009, and as subsequently modified); and

(2) services related to immunization administration for vaccines and toxoids for which CPT codes 90465, 90466, 90467, 90468, 90471, 90472, 90473, or 90474 (as subsequently modified) apply under such System.

(Aug. 14, 1935, ch 531, Title XIX, § 1902, as added July 30, 1965, P. L. 89-97, Title I, Part 2, § 121(a), 79 Stat. 344; Jan. 2, 1968, P. L. 90-248, Title II, Part 1, § 210(a)(6), Part 2, §§ 223(a), 224(a), (c)(1), 227(a), 228(a), 229(a), 231, 234(a), 235(a), 236(a), 237, 238, Part 3, § 241(f)(1)–(4), Title III, § 302(b), 81 Stat. 896, 901-906, 908, 911, 917, 929; Aug. 9, 1969, P. L. 91-56, § 2(c), (d), 83 Stat. 99; Dec. 28, 1971, P. L. 92-223, § 4(b), 85 Stat. 809; Oct. 30, 1972, P. L. 92-603, Title II, §§ 208(a), 209(a), (b)(1), 221(c)(5), 231, 232(a), 236(b), 237(a)(2), 239(a), (b), 240, 246(a), 249(a), 255(a), 268(a), 274(a), 278(a)(18)–(20), (b)(14), 298, 299A, 299D(b), 86 Stat. 1381, 1389, 1410, 1415, 1416-1418, 1424, 1426, 1446, 1450, 1452–1454, 1460, 1462; Dec. 31, 1973, P. L. 93-233, §§ 13(a)(2)–(10), 18(o)–(q), (x)(1)–(4), 87 Stat. 960–963, 971, 972; Aug. 7, 1974, P. L. 93-368, § 9(a), 88 Stat. 422; July 1, 1975, P. L. 94-48, 89 Stat. 247; Dec. 31, 1975, P. L. 94-182, Title I, § 111(a), 89 Stat. 1054; Oct. 18, 1976, P. L. 94-552, § 1, 90 Stat. 2540; Oct. 25, 1977, P. L. 95-142, §§ 2(a)(3), (b)(1), 3(c)(1), 7(b), (c), 9, 19(b)(2), 20(b), 91 Stat. 1176, 1178, 1193, 1195, 1204, 1207; Dec. 13, 1977, P. L. 95-210, § 2(c), 91 Stat. 1488; Nov. 1, 1978, P. L. 95-559, § 14(a)(1), 92 Stat. 2140; June 17, 1980, P. L. 96-272, Title III, § 308(c), 94 Stat. 531; Dec. 5, 1980, P. L. 96-499, Title IX, Part A, Subpart I, §§ 902(b), 903(b), 905(a), Subpart II, § 912(b), 913(c), (d), 914(b)(1), 916(b)(1), 918(b)(1), Part C, § 962(a), 965(b), 94 Stat. 2613, 2615, 2618-2621, 2624, 2626, 2650, 2652; Dec. 28, 1980, P. L. 96-611, § 5(b), 94 Stat. 3568; Aug. 13, 1981, P. L. 97-35, Title XXI, Subtitle A, Ch. 2, § 2105(c), Ch. 3, § 2113(m), Subtitle C, Ch. 1, § 2161(b), Ch. 2, §§ 2171(a), (b), 2172(a), 2173(a), (b)(1), (d), 2174(a), 2175(a), (d)(1), 2178(b), Ch. 3, §§ 2181(a)(2), 2182, Subtitle D, § 2193(c)(9), 95 Stat. 792, 795, 804, 807–809, 811, 814–816, 828; Sept. 3, 1982, P. L. 97-248, Title I, Subtitle B, §§ 131(a), (c) [(b)], 132(a), (c), 134(a), 136(d), 137(a)(1), (3), (b)(7)–(10), (e), Subtitle C, § 146(a), 96 Stat. 367, 369, 370, 373, 375–377, 381, 394; Jan. 12, 1983, P. L. 97-448, Title III, § 309(a)(8), 96 Stat. 2408; July 18, 1984, P. L. 98-369, Division B, Title III, Subtitle A, Part I, §§ 2303(g)(1), 2314(b), Part II, § 2335(e), Subtitle B, §§ 2361(a), 2362(a), 2363(a)(1), 2367(a), 2368(a), (b), 2373(b)(1)–(10), Title VI, Subtitle C, § 2651(c), 98 Stat. 1066, 1079, 1091, 1104, 1105, 1108, 1109, 1111, 1149; Aug. 16, 1984, P. L. 98-378, § 20(c), 98 Stat. 1322; Nov. 8, 1984, P. L. 98-617, § 3(a)(7), (b)(10), 98 Stat. 3295, 3296; April 7, 1986, P. L. 99-272, Title IX, Subtitle B, §§ 9501(b), (c), 9503(a), 9505(b), (c)(1), (d), 9506(a), 9509(a), 9510(a), 9517(b), 9520, 9529(a)(1), (b)(1), Title XII, Subtitle C, § 12305(b)(3), 100 Stat. 201, 202, 205, 206, 208, 209–212, 216, 217, 220, 293; Oct. 21, 1986, P. L. 99-509, Title IX, Subtitle D, Part 2, § 9320(h)(3), Subtitle E, Part 1, §§ 9401(a)–(e)(1), 9402(a), (b), 9403(a), (c), (e)–(g)(1), (4)(A), 9404(a), 9405, 9406(b), 9407(a), 9408(a), (b), (c)(2), (3), Part 4, §§ 9431(a), (b)(1), 9433(a), 9435(b)(1), 100 Stat. 2015, 2049–2057, 2059, 2060, 2065, 2067, 2068; Oct. 27, 1986, P. L. 99-570, Title XI, Subtitle C, § 11005(b), 100 Stat. 3207-169; Nov. 10, 1986, P. L. 99-643, §§ 3(b), 7(b), 100 Stat. 3575, 3579; Oct. 22, 1986, P. L. 99-514, Title XVIII, Subtitle C, Ch 1, § 1895(c)(1), (3)(B), (C), (7), 100 Stat. 2935, 2936; Aug. 18, 1987, P. L. 100-93, §§ 5(a), 7, 8(f), 101 Stat. 689, 691, 694; Dec. 22, 1987, P. L. 100-203, Title IV, Subtitle B, Part 1, §§ 4101(a)(1), (2), (b)(1), (2)(A), (B), (c)(2), (e)(1)–(5), 4102(b)(1), 4104, Part 2, §§ 4113(a)(2), (b)(1), (2), (c)(1), (2), (d)(2), 4116, 4118(c)(1), (h)(1), (m)(1)(B), (p)(1)–(4), (6)–(8), Subtitle C, Part 2, §§ 4211(b)(1)(e)(1), (h)(1)–(5), 4212(d)(2), (3), 4213(b)(1), 4218(a), Title IX, Subtitle B, Part 1, §§ 9115(b)(1), 9119(d), 101 Stat. 1330-140, 1330-141, 1330-142, 1330-146, 1330-147, 1330-151, 1330-152, 1330-154, 1330-155, 1330-156, 1330-157, 1330-159, 1330-203, 1330-205, 1330-213, 1330-219, 1330-220, 1330-219, 1330-305, 1330-309; July 1, 1988, P. L. 100-360, Title II, Subtitle A, § 204(d)(3), Title III, §§ 301(e)(2), 302(a), (b)(1), (c)(1), (2), (d), (e)(1)–(3), 303(d), (e), Title IV, Subtitle B, § 411(k)(5)(B), (7)(B), (C), (10)(G)(ii), (iv), (17)(B), (l), (3)(E), (H), (6)(C), (D), (8)(C), (n)(2), (4), 102 Stat. 729, 749–753, 762, 763, 792, 794, 796, 800, 803–805, 807; Oct. 13, 1988, P. L. 100-485, Title II, § 202(c)(4), Title III, § 303(a)(2), (d), Title IV, § 401(d)(1), Title VI, § 608(d)(14)(I), (15)(A), (B), (16)(C), (27)(F), (G), (28), 102 Stat. 2378, 2391, 2392, 2396, 2416, 2418, 2423, 2433; Nov. 10, 1988, P. L. 100-647, Title VIII, Subtitle E, Part IV, § 8434(b)(1), (2), 102 Stat. 3805; Dec. 13, 1989, P. L. 101-234, Title II, § 201(a)(1), 103 Stat. 1981; Dec. 19, 1989, P. L. 101-239, Title VI, Subtitle A, Part 2, Subpart A, § 6115(c), Subtitle B, Part 1, §§ 6401(a), 6402(a), (c)(2), 6403(b), (d)(1), 6404(c), 6405(b), 6406(a), 6408(c), (1), (d)(1), (4)(C), Part 2, § 6411(a)(1), (d)(3)(B), (e)(2), 103 Stat. 2219, 2258, 2260, 2261, 2263–2266, 2268–2270; Nov. 5, 1990, P. L. 101-508, Subtitle B, Part 1, §§ 4401(a)(2), 4402(a)(1), (c), (d)(1), Part 2, § 4501(b), (e)(2), Part 3, §§ 4601(a)(1), 4602(a), 4603(a), 4604(a)(b), Part 4, Subpart A, §§ 4701(b)(1), 4704(a), (e)(1), 4708(a), Subpart B, §§ 4711(c)(1), (d), 4713(a), 4715(a), 4723(b), 4724(a), Subpart C, §§ 4732(b)(1), Subpart E, §§ 4751(a), 4752(a)(1)(A), (c)(1), 4754(a), 4755(a)(2), (c)(1), Part 5, § 4801(e)(1); Dec. 12, 1991, P. L. 102-234, §§ 2(b), 3(a), 105 Stat. 1799; Aug. 10, 1993, P. L. 103-66, Title XIII, Ch 2, Subch A, Part V, § 13581(b)(2), Subch B, Part I, §§ 13601(b), 13602(c), 13603(a)–(c), Part II, § 13611(d)(1), Part III, §§ 13622(a)(1), (b), (c), 13623(a), 13625(a), Part IV, § 13631(a), (e)(1), (f)(1), 107 Stat. 611, 613, 619, 626, 632, 633, 636, 643, 644; Aug. 15, 1994, P. L. 103-296, Title I, § 108(d)(1), 108 Stat. 1486; Nov. 2, 1994, P. L. 103-448, Title II, § 204(w)(2)(E), 108 Stat. 4746; Aug. 22, 1996, P. L. 104-193, Title I, §§ 108(k), 114(b), (c), (d)(1), Title IX, § 913, 110 Stat. 2169, 2180, 2354; Oct. 2, 1996, P. L. 104-226, § 1(b)(2), 110 Stat. 3033; Oct. 9, 1996, P. L. 104-248, § 1(a)(1), 110 Stat. 3148; April 30, 1997, P. L. 105-12, § 9(b)(2), 111 Stat. 26; Aug. 5, 1997, P. L. 105-33, Title IV, Subtitle B, § 4106(c), Subtitle D, Ch 5, § 4454(b)(1), Subtitle H, Ch 1, § 4701(b)(2)(A)(i)–(iv), (d)(1), 4702(b)(2), 4709, Ch 2, §§ 4711(a), 4712(a), (b)(1), (2), (c), 4714(a)(1), 4715(a), Ch 3, §§ 4724(c)(1), (d), (f), (g)(1), Ch 4, §§ 4731(a), (b), 4732(a), 4733, Ch 5, § 4741(a), Ch. 6, §§ 4751(a), (b), 4752(a), 4753(b), Subtitle J, Ch 2, §§ 4911(b), 4912(b)(1), 4913(a), 111 Stat. 368, 431, 493, 495, 506, 507–510, 516, 517, 519, 520, 522–525, 571, 573; Nov. 29, 1999, P. L. 106-113, Div B, § 1000(a)(6), 113 Stat. 1536; Dec. 14, 1999, P. L. 106-169, Title I, Subtitle C, § 121(a)(1), (c)(4), Title II, Subtitle A, §§ 205(c), 206(b), 113 Stat. 1829, 1830, 1834, 1837; Dec. 17, 1999, P. L. 106-170, Title II, § 201(a)(1), (2)(A), 113 Stat. 1891; Oct. 24, 2000, P. L. 106-354, § 2(a)(1)–(3), (b)(2)(A), 114 Stat. 1381, 1383; Dec. 21, 2000, P. L. 106-554, § 1(a)(6), 114 Stat. 2763; Jan. 15, 2002, P. L. 107-121, § 2(a), (b)(1), (2), 115 Stat. 2384; June 30, 2003, P. L. 108-40, § 7(b), 117 Stat. 837; Oct. 1, 2003, P. l. 108-89, Title IV, § 401(a), 117 Stat. 1134; Dec. 8, 2003, P. L. 108-173, Title I, § 103(a)(1), (f)(1), Title II, Subtitle D, § 236(b)(1), 117 Stat. 2154, 2160, 2211; June 30, 2004, P. L. 108-265, Title I, § 105(b), 118 Stat. 744; Dec. 8, 2004, P. L. 108-448, § 1(a), 118 Stat. 3467; Oct. 20, 2005, P. L. 109-91, Title I, § 101(a), 119 Stat. 2091; Feb. 8, 2006, P. L. 109-171, Title VI, Subtitle A, Ch. 3, §§ 6032(a), 6034(b), 6035(a), (b), Ch. 6, Subch. A, §§ 6062(a), 6065(a), Subch. C, § 6083(a), 120 Stat. 73, 76, 78, 96, 101, 120; Dec. 20, 2006, P. L. 109-432, Div B, Title IV, § 405(c)(2)(A)(iv), 120 Stat. 3000; Sept. 29, 2007, P. L. 110-90, § 3(a), 121 Stat. 984; Dec. 29, 2007, P. L. 110-173, Title II, § 203(a), 121 Stat. 2513; June 30, 2008, P. L. 110-252, Title VII, § 7001(d)(2), 122 Stat. 2394; July 15, 2008, P. L. 110-275, Title I, Subtitle A, Part II, § 111(a), 122 Stat. 2503; Feb. 4, 2009, P. L. 111-3, Title I, Subtitle B, § 113(b)(1), Title II, Subtitle A, § 203(a)(1), (c), (d)(3), Subtitle B, § 211(a)(1)(A), (b)(3)(B), Title V, § 501(d)(1), (e)(1), 123 Stat. 34, 40, 47, 49, 54, 87; Feb. 17, 2009, P. L. 111-5, Div B, Title V, §§ 5004(a)(1), 5005(a), 5006(b)(1), (e)(2)(A), 123 Stat. 503, 505, 506, 510; March 23, 2010, P. L. 111-148, Title II, Subtitle A, §§ 2001(a)(1), (2)(A), (4)(A), (5)(A), (B), (b), (d)(1), (e)(1), 2002(a), (b), 2004(a), Subtitle C, § 2202(a), Subtitle D, §§ 2301(b), 2303(a)(1)–(3), (b)(2)(A), Subtitle E, § 2402(d)(1), Subtitle K, § 2901(c), Title III, Subtitle A, Part III, § 3021(b), Title IV, Subtitle D, § 4302(b)(1)(A), Title VI, Subtitle B, Part I, § 6103(d)(2), Subtitle E, §§ 6401(b)(1), (3), 6411(a)(1), Subtitle F, §§ 6501–6503, 6505, Title VIII, § 8002(a)(2), (b), Title X, Subtitle B, Part I, § 10201(a)(1), (2), (b), 124 Stat. 271, 274, 275, 277, 278, 279, 283, 291, 292, 293, 296, 303, 333, 394, 581, 710, 751, 753, 754, 774, 776, 777, 846, 917, 918; March 30, 2010, P. L. 111-152, Title I, Subtitle A, § 1004(b)(1), (e), Subtitle C, § 1202(a)(1), 124 Stat. 1034, 1036, 1052.)

HISTORY; ANCILLARY LAWS AND DIRECTIVES

Prospective amendments:

Amendment of subsec. (a)(39), effective January 1, 2011. Act March 23, 2010, P. L. 111-148, Title VI, Subtitle F, § 6501, 124 Stat. 776 (effective 1/1/

2011, as provided by § 6508(a) of such Act, which appears as a note to this section), provides: "Section 1902(a)(39) of the Social Security Act (42 U.S.C. 42 U.S.C. 1396a(a)) is amended by inserting after '1128A,' the following: 'terminate the participation of any individual or entity in such program if (subject to such exceptions as are permitted with respect to exclusion under sections 1128(c)(3)(B) and 1128(d)(3)(B)) participation of such individual or entity is terminated under title XVIII or any other State plan under this title,'.".

Other provisions:

Applicability of amendment made by § 4218 of Act Dec. 22, 1987. Act Dec. 22, 1987, P. L. 100-203, Title IV, Subtitle C, Part 2, § 4218(b), 101 Stat. 1330-221, provides: "The amendments made by subsection (a) [amending subsec. (a)(44) of this section] shall apply with respect to certifications or recertifications during the period beginning on July 1, 1988, and ending on October 1, 1990.".

Contingent repeal of subsec. (a)(29). Act Nov. 5, 1990, P. L. 101-508, Title IV, Subtitle B, Part 5, § 4801(e)(11)(A), 104 Stat. 1388-215, provides:

"(11) Removal of duplicative requirement for qualifications of nursing home administrators. Effective on the date on which the Secretary promulgates standards regarding the qualifications of nursing facility administrators under section 1919(f)(4) of the Social Security Act [42 USCS § 1396r(f)(4)]—

"(A) paragraph (29) of section 1902(a) of such Act (42 U.S.C. 1396a(a)) is repealed;".

Effective date of amendments made by § 211 of Act Feb. 4, 2009. Act Feb. 4, 2009, P. L. 111-3, Title II, Subtitle B, § 211(d), 123 Stat. 54, provides:

"(1) In general. (A) In general. Except as provided in subparagraph (B), the amendments made by this section [amending 42 USCS §§ 1396a, 1396b, and 1397ee] shall take effect on January 1, 2010.

"(B) Technical amendments. The amendments made by—

"(i) paragraphs (1), (2), and (3) of subsection (b) [amending 42 USCS §§ 1396a, 1396b] shall take effect as if included in the enactment of section 6036 of the Deficit Reduction Act of 2005 [§ 6036 of Act Feb. 8, 2006] (Public Law 109-171; 120 Stat. 80); and

"(ii) paragraph (4) of subsection (b) [amending 42 USCS § 1396b] shall take effect as if included in the enactment of section 405 of division B of the Tax Relief and Health Care Act of 2006 [enacted Oct. 16, 2008] (Public Law 109-432; 120 Stat. 2996).

"(2) Restoration of eligibility. In the case of an individual who, during the period that began on July 1, 2006, and ends on October 1, 2009, was determined to be ineligible for medical assistance under a State Medicaid plan, including any waiver of such plan, solely as a result of the application of subsections (i)(22) and (x) of section 1903 of the Social Security Act [42 USCS § 1396b] (as in effect during such period), but who would have been determined eligible for such assistance if such subsections, as amended by subsection (b), had applied to the individual, a State may deem the individual to be eligible for such assistance as of the date that the individual was determined to be ineligible for such medical assistance on such basis.

"(3) Special transition rule for Indians. During the period that begins on July 1, 2006, and ends on the effective date of final regulations issued under subclause (II) of section 1903(x)(3)(B)(v) of the Social Security Act (42 U.S.C. 1396b(x)(3)(B)(v)) (as added by subsection (b)(1)(B)), an individual who is a member of a federally-recognized Indian tribe described in subclause (II) of that section who presents a document described in subclause (I) of such section that is issued by such Indian tribe, shall be deemed to have presented satisfactory evidence of citizenship or nationality for purposes of satisfying the requirement of subsection (x) of section 1903 of such Act [42 USCS § 1396b].".

Money follows the person rebalancing demonstration. Act Feb. 8, 2006, P. L. 109-171, Title VI, Subtitle A, Ch. 6, Subch. B, § 6071, 120 Stat. 102; March 23, 2010, P. L. 111-148, Title II, Subtitle E, § 2403(a), (b)(1), 124 Stat. 304 (amendment by § 2403(b)(1) effective 30 days after enactment, as provided by § 2403(b)(2) of such Act), provides:

"(a) Program purpose and authority. The Secretary is authorized to award, on a competitive basis, grants to States in accordance with this section for demonstration projects (each in this section referred to as an 'MFP demonstration project') designed to achieve the following objectives with respect to institutional and home and community-based long-term care services under State Medicaid programs:

"(1) Rebalancing. Increase the use of home and community-based, rather than institutional, long-term care services.

"(2) Money follows the person. Eliminate barriers or mechanisms, whether in the State law, the State Medicaid plan, the State budget, or otherwise, that prevent or restrict the flexible use of Medicaid funds to enable Medicaid-eligible individuals to receive support for appropriate and necessary long-term services in the settings of their choice.

"(3) Continuity of service. Increase the ability of the State Medicaid program to assure continued provision of home and community-based long-term care services to eligible individuals who choose to transition from an institutional to a community setting.

"(4) Quality assurance and quality improvement. Ensure that procedures are in place (at least comparable to those required under the qualified HCB program) to provide quality assurance for eligible individuals receiving Medicaid home and community-based long-term care services and to provide for continuous quality improvement in such services.

"(b) Definitions. For purposes of this section:

"(1) Home and community-based long-term care services. The term 'home and community-based long-term care services' means, with respect to a State Medicaid program, home and community-based services (including home health and personal care services) that are provided under the State's qualified HCB program or that could be provided under such a program but are otherwise provided under the Medicaid program.

"(2) Eligible individual. The term 'eligible individual' means, with respect to an MFP demonstration project of a State, an individual in the State—

"(A) who, immediately before beginning participation in the MFP demonstration project—

"(i) resides (and has resided for a period of not less than 90 consecutive days) in an inpatient facility;

"(ii) is receiving Medicaid benefits for inpatient services furnished by such inpatient facility; and

"(iii) with respect to whom a determination has been made that, but for the provision of home and community-based long-term care services, the individual would continue to require the level of care provided in an inpatient facility and, in any case in which the State applies a more stringent level of care standard as a result of implementing the State plan option permitted under section 1915(i) of the Social

Security Act [42 USCS § 1396n(i)], the individual must continue to require at least the level of care which had resulted in admission to the institution; and

"(B) who resides in a qualified residence beginning on the initial date of participation in the demonstration project.

"Any days that an individual resides in an institution on the basis of having been admitted solely for purposes of receiving short-term rehabilitative services for a period for which payment for such services is limited under title XVIII [42 USCS §§ 1395 et seq.] shall not be taken into account for purposes of determining the 90-day period required under subparagraph (A)(i).

"(3) Inpatient facility. The term 'inpatient facility' means a hospital, nursing facility, or intermediate care facility for the mentally retarded. Such term includes an institution for mental diseases, but only, with respect to a State, to the extent medical assistance is available under the State Medicaid plan for services provided by such institution.

"(4) Medicaid. The term 'Medicaid' means, with respect to a State, the State program under title XIX of the Social Security Act [42 USCS §§ 1396 et seq.] (including any waiver or demonstration under such title or under section 1115 of such Act [42 USCS § 1315] relating to such title).

"(5) Qualified HCB program. The term 'qualified HCB program' means a program providing home and community-based long-term care services operating under Medicaid, whether or not operating under waiver authority.

"(6) Qualified residence. The term 'qualified residence' means, with respect to an eligible individual—

"(A) a home owned or leased by the individual or the individual's family member;

"(B) an apartment with an individual lease, with lockable access and egress, and which includes living, sleeping, bathing, and cooking areas over which the individual or the individual's family has domain and control; and

"(C) a residence, in a community-based residential setting, in which no more than 4 unrelated individuals reside.

"(7) Qualified expenditures. The term 'qualified expenditures' means expenditures by the State under its MFP demonstration project for home and community-based long-term care services for an eligible individual participating in the MFP demonstration project, but only with respect to services furnished during the 12-month period beginning on the date the individual is discharged from an inpatient facility referred to in paragraph (2)(A)(i).

"(8) Self-directed services. The term 'self-directed' means, with respect to home and community-based long-term care services for an eligible individual, such services for the individual which are planned and purchased under the direction and control of such individual or the individual's authorized representative (as defined by the Secretary), including the amount, duration, scope, provider, and location of such services, under the State Medicaid program consistent with the following requirements:

"(A) Assessment. There is an assessment of the needs, capabilities, and preferences of the individual with respect to such services.

"(B) Service plan. Based on such assessment, there is developed jointly with such individual or the individual's authorized representative a plan for such services for such individual that is approved by the State and that—

"(i) specifies those services, if any, which the individual or the individual's authorized representative would be responsible for directing;

"(ii) identifies the methods by which the individual or the individual's authorized representative or an agency designated by an individual or representative will select, manage, and dismiss providers of such services;

"(iii) specifies the role of family members and others whose participation is sought by the individual or the individual's authorized representative with respect to such services;

"(iv) is developed through a person-centered process that—

"(I) is directed by the individual or the individual's authorized representative;

"(II) builds upon the individual's capacity to engage in activities that promote community life and that respects the individual's preferences, choices, and abilities; and

"(III) involves families, friends, and professionals as desired or required by the individual or the individual's authorized representative;

"(v) includes appropriate risk management techniques that recognize the roles and sharing of responsibilities in obtaining services in a self-directed manner and assure the appropriateness of such plan based upon the resources and capabilities of the individual or the individual's authorized representative; and

"(vi) may include an individualized budget which identifies the dollar value of the services and supports under the control and direction of the individual or the individual's authorized representative.

"(C) Budget process. With respect to individualized budgets described in subparagraph (B)(vi), the State application under subsection (c)—

"(i) describes the method for calculating the dollar values in such budgets based on reliable costs and service utilization;

"(ii) defines a process for making adjustments in such dollar values to reflect changes in individual assessments and service plans; and

"(iii) provides a procedure to evaluate expenditures under such budgets.

"(9) State. The term 'State' has the meaning given such term for purposes of title XIX of the Social Security Act [42 USCS §§ 1396 et seq.].

"(c) State application. A State seeking approval of an MFP demonstration project shall submit to the Secretary, at such time and in such format as the Secretary requires, an application meeting the following requirements and containing such additional information, provisions, and assurances, as the Secretary may require:

"(1) Assurance of a public development process. The application contains an assurance that the State has engaged, and will continue to engage, in a public process for the design, development, and evaluation of the MFP demonstration project that allows for input from eligible individuals, the families of such individuals, authorized representatives of such individuals, providers, and other interested parties.

"(2) Operation in connection with qualified HCB program to assure continuity of services. The State will conduct the MFP demonstration project for eligible individuals in conjunction with the operation of a qualified HCB program that is in operation (or approved) in the State for such individuals in a manner that assures continuity of Medicaid coverage for such individuals so long as such individuals continue to be eligible for medical assistance.

"(3) Demonstration project period. The application shall specify the period of the MFP demonstration project, which shall include at least 2 consecutive fiscal years in the 5-fiscal-year period beginning with fiscal year 2007.

"(4) Service area. The application shall specify the service area or areas of the MFP demonstration project, which may be a statewide area or 1 or more geographic areas of the State.

"(5) Targeted groups and numbers of individuals served. The application shall specify—

"(A) the target groups of eligible individuals to be assisted to transition from an inpatient facility to a qualified residence during each fiscal year of the MFP demonstration project;

"(B) the projected numbers of eligible individuals in each targeted group of eligible individuals to be so assisted during each such year; and

"(C) the estimated total annual qualified expenditures for each fiscal year of the MFP demonstration project.

"(6) Individual choice, continuity of care. The application shall contain assurances that—

"(A) each eligible individual or the individual's authorized representative will be provided the opportunity to make an informed choice regarding whether to participate in the MFP demonstration project;

"(B) each eligible individual or the individual's authorized representative will choose the qualified residence in which the individual will reside and the setting in which the individual will receive home and community-based long-term care services;

"(C) the State will continue to make available, so long as the State operates its qualified HCB program consistent with applicable requirements, home and community-based long-term care services to each individual who completes participation in the MFP demonstration project for as long as the individual remains eligible for medical assistance for such services under such qualified HCB program (including meeting a requirement relating to requiring a level of care provided in an inpatient facility and continuing to require such services, and, if the State applies a more stringent level of care standard as a result of implementing the State plan option permitted under section 1915(i) of the Social Security Act [42 USCS § 1396n(i)], meeting the requirement for at least the level of care which had resulted in the individual's admission to the institution).

"(7) Rebalancing. The application shall—

"(A) provide such information as the Secretary may require concerning the dollar amounts of State Medicaid expenditures for the fiscal year, immediately preceding the first fiscal year of the State's MFP demonstration project, for long-term care services and the percentage of such expenditures that were for institutional long-term care services or were for home and community-based long-term care services;

"(B) (i) specify the methods to be used by the State to increase, for each fiscal year during the MFP demonstration project, the dollar amount of such total expenditures for home and community-based long-term care services and the percentage of such total expenditures for long-term care services that are for home and community-based long-term care services; and

"(ii) describe the extent to which the MFP demonstration project will contribute to accomplishment of objectives described in subsection (a).

"(8) Money follows the person. The application shall describe the methods to be used by the State to eliminate any legal, budgetary, or other barriers to flexibility in the availability of Medicaid funds to pay for long-term care services for eligible individuals participating in the project in the appropriate settings of their choice, including costs to transition from an institutional setting to a qualified residence.

"(9) Maintenance of effort and cost-effectiveness. The application shall contain or be accompanied by such information and assurances as may be required to satisfy the Secretary that—

"(A) total expenditures under the State Medicaid program for home and community-based long-term care services will not be less for any fiscal year during the MFP demonstration project than for the greater of such expenditures for—

"(i) fiscal year 2005; or

"(ii) any succeeding fiscal year before the first year of the MFP demonstration project; and

"(B) in the case of a qualified HCB program operating under a waiver under subsection (c) or (d) of section 1915 of the Social Security Act (42 U.S.C. 1396n), but for the amount awarded under a grant under this section, the State program would continue to meet the cost-effectiveness requirements of subsection (c)(2)(D) of such section or comparable requirements under subsection (d)(5) of such section, respectively.

"(10) Waiver requests. The application shall contain or be accompanied by requests for any modification or adjustment of waivers of Medicaid requirements described in subsection (d)(3), including adjustments to the maximum numbers of individuals included and package of benefits, including one-time transitional services, provided.

"(11) Quality assurance and quality improvement. The application shall include—

"(A) a plan satisfactory to the Secretary for quality assurance and quality improvement for home and community-based long-term care services under the State Medicaid program, including a plan to assure the health and welfare of individuals participating in the MFP demonstration project; and

"(B) an assurance that the State will cooperate in carrying out activities under subsection (f) to develop and implement continuous quality assurance and quality improvement systems for home and community-based long-term care services.

"(12) Optional program for self-directed services. If the State elects to provide for any home and community-based long-term care services as self-directed services (as defined in subsection (b)(8)) under the MFP demonstration project, the application shall provide the following:

"(A) Meeting requirements. A description of how the project will meet the applicable requirements of such subsection for the provision of self-directed services.

"(B) Voluntary election. A description of how eligible individuals will be provided with the opportunity to make an informed election to receive self-directed services under the project and after the end of the project.

"(C) State support in service plan development. Satisfactory assurances that the State will provide support to eligible individuals who self-direct in developing and implementing their service plans.

"(D) Oversight of receipt of services. Satisfactory assurances that the State will provide oversight of eligible individual's receipt of such self-directed services, including steps to assure the quality of services provided and that the provision of such services are consistent with the service plan under such subsection.

Nothing in this section shall be construed as requiring a State to make an election under the project to provide for home and community-based long-term care services as self-directed services, or as requiring an individual to elect to receive self-directed services under the project.

"(13) Reports and evaluation. The application shall provide that—

"(A) the State will furnish to the Secretary such reports concerning the MFP demonstration project, on such timetable, in such uniform format, and containing such information as the Secretary may require, as will allow for reliable comparisons of MFP demonstration projects across States; and

"(B) the State will participate in and cooperate with the evaluation of the MFP demonstration project.

"(d) Secretary's award of competitive grants. (1) In general. The Secretary shall award grants under this section on a competitive basis to States selected from among those with applications meeting the requirements of subsection (c), in accordance with the provisions of this subsection.

"(2) Selection and modification of State applications. In selecting State applications for the awarding of such a grant, the Secretary—

"(A) shall take into consideration the manner in which, and extent to which, the State proposes to achieve the objectives specified in subsection (a);

"(B) shall seek to achieve an appropriate national balance in the numbers of eligible individuals, within different target groups of eligible individuals, who are assisted to transition to qualified residences under MFP demonstration projects, and in the geographic distribution of States operating MFP demonstration projects;

"(C) shall give preference to State applications proposing—

"(i) to provide transition assistance to eligible individuals within multiple target groups; and

"(ii) to provide eligible individuals with the opportunity to receive home and community-based long-term care services as self-directed services, as defined in subsection (b)(8); and

"(D) shall take such objectives into consideration in setting the annual amounts of State grant awards under this section.

"(3) Waiver authority. The Secretary is authorized to waive the following provisions of title XIX of the Social Security Act [42 USCS §§ 1396 et seq.], to the extent necessary to enable a State initiative to meet the requirements and accomplish the purposes of this section:

"(A) Statewideness. Section 1902(a)(1) [subsec. (a)(1) of this section], in order to permit implementation of a State initiative in a selected area or areas of the State.

"(B) Comparability. Section 1902(a)(10)(B) [subsec. (a)(10)(B) of this section], in order to permit a State initiative to assist a selected category or categories of individuals described in subsection (b)(2)(A).

"(C) Income and resources eligibility. Section 1902(a)(10)(C)(i)(III), [subsec. (a)(10)(C)(i)(III) of this section] in order to permit a State to apply institutional eligibility rules to individuals transitioning to community-based care.

"(D) Provider agreements. Section 1902(a)(27) [subsec. (a)(27) of this section], in order to permit a State to implement self-directed services in a cost-effective manner.

"(4) Conditional approval of outyear grant. In awarding grants under this section, the Secretary shall condition the grant for the second and any subsequent fiscal years of the grant period on the following:

"(A) Numerical benchmarks. The State must demonstrate to the satisfaction of the Secretary that it is meeting numerical benchmarks specified in the grant agreement for—

"(i) increasing State Medicaid support for home and community-based long-term care services under subsection (c)(5); and

"(ii) numbers of eligible individuals assisted to transition to qualified residences.

"(B) Quality of care. The State must demonstrate to the satisfaction of the Secretary that it is meeting the requirements under subsection (c)(11) to assure the health and welfare of MFP demonstration project participants.

"(e) Payments to States; carryover of unused grant amounts. (1) Payments. For each calendar quarter in a fiscal year during the period a State is awarded a grant under subsection (d), the Secretary shall pay to the State from its grant award for such fiscal year an amount equal to the lesser of—

"(A) the MFP-enhanced FMAP (as defined in paragraph (5)) of the amount of qualified expenditures made during such quarter; or

"(B) the total amount remaining in such grant award for such fiscal year (taking into account the application of paragraph (2)).

"(2) Carryover of unused amounts. Any portion of a State grant award for a fiscal year under this section remaining at the end of such fiscal year shall remain available to the State for the next 4 fiscal years, subject to paragraph (3).

"(3) Reawarding of certain unused amounts. In the case of a State that the Secretary determines pursuant to subsection (d)(4) has failed to meet the conditions for continuation of a MFP demonstration project under this section in a succeeding year or years, the Secretary shall rescind the grant awards for such succeeding year or years, together with any unspent portion of an award for prior years, and shall add such amounts to the appropriation for the immediately succeeding fiscal year for grants under this section.

"(4) Preventing duplication of payment. The payment under a MFP demonstration project with respect to qualified expenditures shall be in lieu of any payment with respect to such expenditures that could otherwise be paid under Medicaid, including under section 1903(a) of the Social Security Act [42 USCS § 1396b(a)]. Nothing in the previous sentence shall be construed as preventing the payment under Medicaid for such expenditures in a grant year after amounts available to pay for such expenditures under the MFP demonstration project have been exhausted.

"(5) MFP-enhanced FMAP. For purposes of paragraph (1)(A), the 'MFP-enhanced FMAP', for a State for a fiscal year, is equal to the Federal medical assistance percentage (as defined in the first sentence of section 1905(b) [42 USCS § 1396d(b)]) for the State increased by a number of percentage points equal to 50 percent of the number of percentage points by which (A) such Federal medical assistance percentage for the State, is less than (B) 100 percent; but in no case shall the MFP-enhanced FMAP for a State exceed 90 percent.

"(f) Quality assurance and improvement; technical assistance; oversight. (1) In general. The Secretary, either directly or by grant or contract, shall provide for technical assistance to, and oversight of, States for purposes of upgrading quality assurance and quality improvement systems under Medicaid home and community-based waivers, including—

"(A) dissemination of information on promising practices;

"(B) guidance on system design elements addressing the unique needs of participating beneficiaries;

"(C) ongoing consultation on quality, including assistance in developing necessary tools, resources, and monitoring systems; and

"(D) guidance on remedying programmatic and systemic problems.

"(2) Funding. From the amounts appropriated under subsection (h)(1) for the portion of fiscal year 2007 that begins on January 1, 2007, and ends on September 30, 2007, and for fiscal year 2008, not more than $2,400,000 shall be available to the Secretary to carry out this subsection during the period that begins on January 1, 2007, and ends on September 30, 2011.

"(g) Research and evaluation. (1) In general. The Secretary, directly or through grant or contract, shall provide for research on, and a national evaluation of, the program under this section, including assistance to the Secretary in preparing the final report required under paragraph (2). The evaluation shall include an analysis of projected and actual savings related to the transition of individuals to qualified residences in each State conducting an MFP demonstration project.

"(2) Final report. The Secretary shall make a final report to the President and Congress, not later than September 30, 2016, reflecting the evaluation described in paragraph (1) and providing findings and conclusions on the conduct and effectiveness of MFP demonstration projects.

"(3) Funding. From the amounts appropriated under subsection (h)(1) for each of fiscal years 2008 through 2016, not more than $1,100,000 per year shall be available to the Secretary to carry out this subsection.

"(h) Appropriations. (1) In general. There are appropriated, from any funds in the Treasury not otherwise appropriated, for grants to carry out this section—

"(A) $250,000,000 for the portion of fiscal year 2007 beginning on January 1, 2007, and ending on September 30, 2007;

"(B) $300,000,000 for fiscal year 2008;

"(C) $350,000,000 for fiscal year 2009;

"(D) $400,000,000 for fiscal year 2010; and

"(E) $450,000,000 for each of fiscal years 2011 through 2016.

"(2) Availability. Amounts made available under paragraph (1) for a fiscal year shall remain available for the awarding of grants to States by not later than September 30, 2016.".

Reports to Congress. Act March 23, 2010, P. L. 111-148, Title II, Subtitle A, § 2001(d)(2), 124 Stat. 278, provides: "Beginning April 2015, and annually thereafter, the Secretary of Health and Human Services shall submit a report to the appropriate committees of Congress on the total enrollment and new enrollment in Medicaid for the fiscal year ending on September 30 of the preceding calendar year on a national and State-by-State basis, and shall include in each such report such recommendations for administrative or legislative changes to improve enrollment in the Medicaid program as the Secretary determines appropriate.".

Effective date of amendments made by § 2002 of Act March 23, 2010. Act March 23, 2010, P. L. 111-148, Title II, Subtitle A, § 2002(c), 124 Stat. 282, provides: "The amendments made by subsections (a) and (b) [amending subsec. (a)(17) and adding subsec. (e)(14) of this section] take effect on January 1, 2014.".

Effective date of amendments made by § 2004 of Act March 23, 2010. Act March 23, 2010, P. L. 111-148, Title II, Subtitle A, § 2004(d), Title X, Subtitle B, Part I, § 10201(a)(3), 124 Stat. 283, 918, provides: "The amendments made by this section [amending 42 USCS §§ 1396a, 1396b, 1396r-1, and 1396u-7] take effect on January 1, 2014.".

Effective date and applicability of amendments made by § 2202 of Act March 23, 2010. Act March 23, 2010, P. L. 111-148, Title II, Subtitle C, § 2202(c), 124 Stat. 292, provides: "The amendments made by this section [amending 42 USCS §§ 1396a(a)(47) and 1396b(u)(1)(D)(v)] take effect on January 1, 2014, and apply to services furnished on or after that date.".

Effective date and applicability of amendments made by § 2301 of Act March 23, 2010. Act March 23, 2010, P. L. 111-148, Title II, Subtitle D, § 2301(c), 124 Stat. 293, provides:

"(1) In general. Except as provided in paragraph (2), the amendments made by this section [amending 42 USCS §§ 1396a and 1396d] shall take effect on the date of the enactment of this Act and shall apply to services furnished on or after such date.

"(2) Exception if State legislation required. In the case of a State plan for medical assistance under title XIX of the Social Security Act [42 USCS §§ 1396 et seq.] which the Secretary of Health and Human Services determines requires State legislation (other than legislation appropriating funds) in order for the plan to meet the additional requirement imposed by the amendments made by this section, the State plan shall not be regarded as failing to comply with the requirements of such title solely on the basis of its failure to meet this additional requirement before the first day of the first calendar quarter beginning after the close of the first regular session of the State legislature that begins after the date of the enactment of this Act. For purposes of the previous sentence, in the case of a State that has a 2-year legislative session, each year of such session shall be deemed to be a separate regular session of the State legislature.".

Effective date and applicability of amendments made by § 2303 of Act March 23, 2010. Act March 23, 2010, P. L. 111-148, Title II, Subtitle D, § 2303(d), 124 Stat. 296, provides: "The amendments made by this section [adding 42 USCS § 1396r-1c and amending 42 USCS §§ 1396a, 1396b, 1396d, and 1396u-7] take effect on the date of the enactment of this Act and shall apply to items and services furnished on or after such date.".

Effective date of amendments made by § 2402 of Act March 23, 2010. Act March 23, 2010, P. L. 111-148, Title II, Subtitle E, § 2402(g), 124 Stat. 304, provides: "The amendments made by subsections (b) through (f) [amending 42 USCS §§ 1396a, 1396b, 1396d, and 1396n(i)] take effect on the first day of the first fiscal year quarter that begins after the date of enactment of this Act.".

Demonstration project to evaluate integrated care around a hospitalization. Act March 23, 2010, P. L. 111-148, Title II, Subtitle I, § 2704, 124 Stat. 323, provides:

"(a) Authority to conduct project. (1) In general. The Secretary of Health and Human Services (in this section referred to as the 'Secretary') shall establish a demonstration project under title XIX of the Social Security Act [42 USCS §§ 1396 et seq.] to evaluate the use of bundled payments for the provision of integrated care for a Medicaid beneficiary—

"(A) with respect to an episode of care that includes a hospitalization; and

"(B) for concurrent physicians services provided during a hospitalization.

"(2) Duration. The demonstration project shall begin on January 1, 2012, and shall end on December 31, 2016.

"(b) Requirements. The demonstration project shall be conducted in accordance with the following:

"(1) The demonstration project shall be conducted in up to 8 States, determined by the Secretary based on consideration of the potential to lower costs under the Medicaid program while improving care for Medicaid beneficiaries. A State selected to participate in the demonstration project may target the demonstration project to particular categories of beneficiaries, beneficiaries with particular diagnoses, or particular geographic regions of the State, but the Secretary shall insure that, as a whole, the demonstration project is, to the greatest extent possible, representative of the demographic and geographic composition of Medicaid beneficiaries nationally.

"(2) The demonstration project shall focus on conditions where there is evidence of an opportunity for providers of services and suppliers to improve the quality of care furnished to Medicaid beneficiaries while reducing total expenditures under the State Medicaid programs selected to participate, as determined by the Secretary.

"(3) A State selected to participate in the demonstration project shall specify the 1 or more episodes of care the State proposes to address in the project, the services to be included in the bundled payments, and the rationale for the selection of such episodes of care and services. The Secretary may modify the episodes of care as well as the services to be included in the bundled payments prior to or after approving the project. The Secretary may also vary such factors among the different States participating in the demonstration project.

"(4) The Secretary shall ensure that payments made under the demonstration project are adjusted for severity of illness and other characteristics of Medicaid beneficiaries within a category or having a diagnosis targeted as part of the demonstration project. States shall ensure that Medicaid beneficiaries are not liable for any additional cost sharing than if their care had not been subject to payment under the demonstration project.

"(5) Hospitals participating in the demonstration project shall have or establish robust discharge planning programs to ensure that Medicaid beneficiaries requiring post-acute care are appropriately placed in, or have ready access to, post-acute care settings.

"(6) The Secretary and each State selected to participate in the demonstration project shall ensure that the demonstration project does not result in the Medicaid beneficiaries whose care is subject to payment under the demonstration project being provided with less items and services for which medical assistance is provided under the State Medicaid program than the items and services for which medical assistance would have been provided to such beneficiaries under the State Medicaid program in the absence of the demonstration project.

"(c) Waiver of provisions. Notwithstanding section 1115(a) of the Social Security Act (42 U.S.C. 1315(a)), the Secretary may waive such provisions of titles XIX, XVIII, and XI of that Act [42 USCS §§ 1396 et seq., 1395 et seq., and 1301 et seq.] as may be necessary to accomplish the goals of the demonstration, ensure beneficiary access to acute and post-acute care, and maintain quality of care.

"(d) Evaluation and report. (1) Data. Each State selected to participate in the demonstration project under this section shall provide to the Secretary, in such form and manner as the Secretary shall specify, relevant data necessary to monitor outcomes, costs, and quality, and evaluate the rationales for selection of the episodes of care and services specified by States under subsection (b)(3).

"(2) Report. Not later than 1 year after the conclusion of the demonstration project, the Secretary shall submit a report to Congress on the results of the demonstration project.".

Pediatric accountable care organization demonstration project. Act March 23, 2010, P. L. 111-148, Title II, Subtitle I, § 2706, 124 Stat. 325, provides:

"(a) Authority to conduct demonstration. (1) In general. The Secretary of Health and Human Services (referred to in this section as the "Secretary") shall establish the Pediatric Accountable Care Organization Demonstration Project to authorize a participating State to allow pediatric medical providers that meet specified requirements to be recognized as an accountable care organization for purposes of receiving incentive payments (as described under subsection (d)), in the same manner as an accountable care organization is recognized and provided with incentive payments under section 1899 of the Social Security Act [42 USCS § 1395jjj] (as added by section 3022).

"(2) Duration. The demonstration project shall begin on January 1, 2012, and shall end on December 31, 2016.

"(b) Application. A State that desires to participate in the demonstration project under this section shall submit to the Secretary an application at such time, in such manner, and containing such information as the Secretary may require.

"(c) Requirements. (1) Performance guidelines. The Secretary, in consultation with the States and pediatric providers, shall establish guidelines to ensure that the quality of care delivered to individuals by a provider recognized as an accountable care organization under this section is not less than the quality of care that would have otherwise been provided to such individuals.

"(2) Savings requirement. A participating State, in consultation with the Secretary, shall establish an annual minimal level of savings in expenditures for items and services covered under the Medicaid program under title XIX of the Social Security Act [42 USCS §§ 1396 et seq.] and the CHIP program under title XXI of such Act [42 USCS §§ 1397aa et seq.] that must be reached by an accountable care organization in order for such organization to receive an incentive payment under subsection (d).

"(3) Minimum participation period. A provider desiring to be recognized as an accountable care organization under the demonstration project shall enter into an agreement with the State to participate in the project for not less than a 3-year period.

"(d) Incentive payment. An accountable care organization that meets the performance guidelines established by the Secretary under subsection (c)(1) and achieves savings greater than the annual minimal savings level established by the State under subsection (c)(2) shall receive an incentive payment for such year equal to a portion (as determined appropriate by the Secretary) of the amount of such excess savings. The Secretary may establish an annual cap on incentive payments for an accountable care organization.

"(e) Authorization of appropriations. There are authorized to be appropriated such sums as are necessary to carry out this section.".

Medicaid emergency psychiatric demonstration project. Act March 23, 2010, P. L. 111-148, Title II, Subtitle I, § 2707, 124 Stat. 326, provides:

"(a) Authority to conduct demonstration project. The Secretary of Health and Human Services (in this section referred to as the 'Secretary') shall establish a demonstration project under which an eligible State (as described in subsection (c)) shall provide payment under the State Medicaid plan under title XIX of the Social Security Act to an institution for mental diseases that is not publicly owned or operated and that is subject to the requirements of section 1867 of the Social Security Act (42 U.S.C. 1395dd) for the provision of medical assistance available under such plan to individuals who—

"(1) have attained age 21, but have not attained age 65;

"(2) are eligible for medical assistance under such plan; and

"(3) require such medical assistance to stabilize an emergency medical condition.

"(b) Stabilization review. A State shall specify in its application described in subsection (c)(1) establish a mechanism for how it will ensure that institutions participating in the demonstration will determine whether or not such individuals have been stabilized (as defined in subsection (h)(5)). This mechanism shall commence before the third day of the inpatient stay. States participating in the demonstration project may manage the provision of services for the stabilization of medical emergency conditions through utilization review, authorization, or management practices, or the application of medical necessity and appropriateness criteria applicable to behavioral health.

"(c) Eligible State defined. (1) In general. An eligible State is a State that has made an application and has been selected pursuant to paragraphs (2) and (3).

"(2) Application. A State seeking to participate in the demonstration project under this section shall submit to the Secretary, at such time and in such format as the Secretary requires, an application that includes such information, provisions, and assurances, as the Secretary may require.

"(3) Selection. A State shall be determined eligible for the demonstration by the Secretary on a competitive basis among States with applications meeting the requirements of paragraph (1). In selecting State applications for the demonstration project, the Secretary shall seek to achieve an appropriate national balance in the geographic distribution of such projects.

"(d) Length of demonstration project. The demonstration project established under this section shall be conducted for a period of 3 consecutive years.

"(e) Limitations on Federal funding. (1) Appropriation. (A) In general. Out of any funds in the Treasury not otherwise appropriated, there is appropriated to carry out this section, $75,000,000 for fiscal year 2011.

"(B) Budget authority. Subparagraph (A) constitutes budget authority in advance of appropriations Act and represents the obligation of the Federal Government to provide for the payment of the amounts appropriated under that subparagraph.

"(2) 5-year availability. Funds appropriated under paragraph (1) shall remain available for obligation through December 31, 2015.

"(3) Limitation on payments. In no case may—

"(A) the aggregate amount of payments made by the Secretary to eligible States under this section exceed $75,000,000; or

"(B) payments be provided by the Secretary under this section after December 31, 2015.

"(4) Funds allocated to States. Funds shall be allocated to eligible States on the basis of criteria, including a State's application and the availability of funds, as determined by the Secretary.

"(5) Payments to States. The Secretary shall pay to each eligible State, from its allocation under paragraph (4), an amount each quarter equal to the Federal medical assistance percentage of expenditures in the quarter for medical assistance described in subsection (a). As a condition of receiving payment, a State shall collect and report information, as determined necessary by the Secretary, for the purposes of providing Federal oversight and conducting an evaluation under subsection (f)(1).

"(f) Evaluation and report to Congress. (1) Evaluation. The Secretary shall conduct an evaluation of the demonstration project in order to determine the impact on the functioning of the health and mental health service system and on individuals enrolled in the Medicaid program and shall include the following:

"(A) An assessment of access to inpatient mental health services under the Medicaid program; average lengths of inpatient stays; and emergency room visits.

"(B) An assessment of discharge planning by participating hospitals.

"(C) An assessment of the impact of the demonstration project on the costs of the full range of mental health services (including inpatient, emergency and ambulatory care).

"(D) An analysis of the percentage of consumers with Medicaid coverage who are admitted to inpatient facilities as a result of the demonstration project as compared to those admitted to these same facilities through other means.

"(E) A recommendation regarding whether the demonstration project should be continued after December 31, 2013, and expanded on a national basis.

"(2) Report. Not later than December 31, 2013, the Secretary shall submit to Congress and make available to the public a report on the findings of the evaluation under paragraph (1).

"(g) Waiver authority. (1) In general. The Secretary shall waive the limitation of subdivision (B) following paragraph (28) of section 1905(a) of the Social Security Act (42 U.S.C. 1396d(a)) (relating to limitations on payments for care or services for individuals under 65 years of age who are patients in an institution for mental diseases) for purposes of carrying out the demonstration project under this section.

"(2) Limited other waiver authority. The Secretary may waive other requirements of titles XI and XIX of the Social Security Act [42 USCS §§ 1301 et seq. and 1396 et seq.] (including the requirements of sections 1902(a)(1) (relating to statewideness) and 1902(1)(10)(B) (relating to comparability)) only to extent necessary to carry out the demonstration project under this section.

"(h) Definitions. In this section:

"(1) Emergency medical condition. The term 'emergency medical condition' means, with respect to an individual, an individual who expresses suicidal or homicidal thoughts or gestures, if determined dangerous to self or others.

"(2) Federal medical assistance percentage. The term 'Federal medical assistance percentage' has the meaning given that term with respect to a State under section 1905(b) of the Social Security Act (42 U.S.C. 1396d(b)).

"(3) Institution for mental diseases. The term 'institution for mental diseases' has the meaning given to that term in section 1905(i) of the Social Security Act (42 U.S.C. 1396d(i)).

"(4) Medical assistance. The term 'medical assistance' has the meaning given that term in section 1905(a) of the Social Security Act (42 U.S.C. 1396d(a)).

"(5) Stabilized. The term 'stabilized' means, with respect to an individual, that the emergency medical condition no longer exists with respect to the individual and the individual is no longer dangerous to self or others.

"(6) State. The term 'State' has the meaning given that term for purposes of title XIX of the Social Security Act (42 U.S.C. 1396 et seq.).".

Incentives for prevention of chronic diseases in Medicaid. Act March 23, 2010, P. L. 111-148, Title IV, Subtitle B, § 4108, 124 Stat. 561, provides:

"(a) Initiatives. (1) Establishment. (A) In general. The Secretary shall award grants to States to carry out initiatives to provide incentives to Medicaid beneficiaries who—

"(i) successfully participate in a program described in paragraph (3); and

"(ii) upon completion of such participation, demonstrate changes in health risk and outcomes, including the adoption and maintenance of healthy behaviors by meeting specific targets (as described in subsection (c)(2)).

"(B) Purpose. The purpose of the initiatives under this section is to test approaches that may encourage behavior modification and determine scalable solutions.

"(2) Duration. (A) Initiation of program; resources. The Secretary shall awards grants to States beginning on January 1, 2011, or beginning on the date on which the Secretary develops program criteria, whichever is earlier. The Secretary shall develop program criteria for initiatives under this section using relevant evidence-based research and resources, including the Guide to Community Preventive Services, the Guide to Clinical Preventive Services, and the National Registry of Evidence-Based Programs and Practices.

"(B) Duration of program. A State awarded a grant to carry out initiatives under this section shall carry out such initiatives within the 5-year period beginning on January 1, 2011, or beginning on the date on which the Secretary develops program criteria, whichever is earlier. Initiatives under this section shall be carried out by a State for a period of not less than 3 years.

"(3) Program described. (A) In general. A program described in this paragraph is a comprehensive, evidence-based, widely available, and easily accessible program, proposed by the State and approved by the Secretary, that is designed and uniquely suited to address the needs of Medicaid beneficiaries and has demonstrated success in helping individuals achieve one or more of the following:

"(i) Ceasing use of tobacco products.

"(ii) Controlling or reducing their weight.

"(iii) Lowering their cholesterol.

"(iv) Lowering their blood pressure.

"(v) Avoiding the onset of diabetes or, in the case of a diabetic, improving the management of that condition.

"(B) Co-morbidities. A program under this section may also address co-morbidities (including depression) that are related to any of the conditions described in subparagraph (A).

"(C) Waiver authority. The Secretary may waive the requirements of section 1902(a)(1) (relating to statewideness) of the Social Security Act [42 USCS § 1396a(a)(1)] for a State awarded a grant to conduct an initiative under this section and shall ensure that a State makes any program described in subparagraph (A) available and accessible to Medicaid beneficiaries.

"(D) Flexibility in implementation. A State may enter into arrangements with providers participating in Medicaid, community-based organizations, faith-based organizations, public-private partnerships, Indian tribes, or similar entities or organizations to carry out programs described in subparagraph (A).

"(4) Application. Following the development of program criteria by the Secretary, a State may submit an application, in such manner and containing such information as the Secretary may require, that shall include a proposal for programs described in paragraph (3)(A) and a plan to make Medicaid beneficiaries and providers participating in Medicaid who reside in the State aware and informed about such programs.

"(b) Education and outreach campaign. (1) State awareness. The Secretary shall conduct an outreach and education campaign to make States aware of the grants under this section.

"(2) Provider and beneficiary education. A State awarded a grant to conduct an initiative under this section shall conduct an outreach and education campaign to make Medicaid beneficiaries and providers participating in Medicaid who reside in the State aware of the programs described in subsection (a)(3) that are to be carried out by the State under the grant.

"(c) Impact. A State awarded a grant to conduct an initiative under this section shall develop and implement a system to—

"(1) track Medicaid beneficiary participation in the program and validate changes in health risk and outcomes with clinical data, including the adoption and maintenance of health behaviors by such beneficiaries;

"(2) to the extent practicable, establish standards and health status targets for Medicaid beneficiaries participating in the program and measure the degree to which such standards and targets are met;

"(3) evaluate the effectiveness of the program and provide the Secretary with such evaluations;

"(4) report to the Secretary on processes that have been developed and lessons learned from the program; and

"(5) report on preventive services as part of reporting on quality measures for Medicaid managed care programs.

"(d) Evaluations and reports. (1) Independent assessment. The Secretary shall enter into a contract with an independent entity or organization to conduct an evaluation and assessment of the initiatives carried out by States under this section, for the purpose of determining—

"(A) the effect of such initiatives on the use of health care services by Medicaid beneficiaries participating in the program;

"(B) the extent to which special populations (including adults with disabilities, adults with chronic illnesses, and children with special health care needs) are able to participate in the program;

"(C) the level of satisfaction of Medicaid beneficiaries with respect to the accessibility and quality of health care services provided through the program; and

"(D) the administrative costs incurred by State agencies that are responsible for administration of the program.

"(2) State reporting. A State awarded a grant to carry out initiatives under this section shall submit reports to the Secretary, on a semi-annual basis, regarding the programs that are supported by the grant funds. Such report shall include information, as specified by the Secretary, regarding—

"(A) the specific uses of the grant funds;

"(B) an assessment of program implementation and lessons learned from the programs;

"(C) an assessment of quality improvements and clinical outcomes under such programs; and

"(D) estimates of cost savings resulting from such programs.

"(3) Initial report. Not later than January 1, 2014, the Secretary shall submit to Congress an initial report on such initiatives based on information provided by States through reports required under paragraph (2). The initial report shall include an interim evaluation of the effectiveness of the initiatives carried out with grants awarded under this section and a recommendation regarding whether funding for expanding or extending the initiatives should be extended beyond January 1, 2016.

"(4) Final report. Not later than July 1, 2016, the Secretary shall submit to Congress a final report on the program that includes the results of the independent assessment required under paragraph (1), together with recommendations for such legislation and administrative action as the Secretary determines appropriate.

"(e) No effect on eligibility for, or amount of, Medicaid or other benefits. Any incentives provided to a Medicaid beneficiary participating in a program described in subsection (a)(3) shall not be taken into account for purposes of determining the beneficiary's eligibility for, or amount of, benefits under the Medicaid program or any program funded in whole or in part with Federal funds.

"(f) Funding. Out of any funds in the Treasury not otherwise appropriated, there are appropriated for the 5-year period beginning on January 1, 2011, $100,000,000 to the Secretary to carry out this section. Amounts appropriated under this subsection shall remain available until expended.

"(g) Definitions. In this section:

"(1) Medicaid beneficiary. The term 'Medicaid beneficiary' means an individual who is eligible for medical assistance under a State plan or waiver under title XIX of the Social Security Act (42 U.S.C. 1396 et seq.) and is enrolled in such plan or waiver.

"(2) State. The term 'State' has the meaning given that term for purposes of title XIX of the Social Security Act (42 U.S.C. 1396 et seq.).".

Coordination; regulations. Act March 23, 2010, P. L. 111-148, Title VI, Subtitle E, § 6411(a)(2), 124 Stat. 775, provides:

"(A) In general. The Secretary of Health and Human Services, acting through the Administrator of the Centers for Medicare & Medicaid Services, shall coordinate the expansion of the Recovery Audit Contractor program to Medicaid with States, particularly with respect to each State that enters into a contract with a recovery audit contractor for purposes of the State's Medicaid program prior to December 31, 2010.

"(B) Regulations. The Secretary of Health and Human Services shall promulgate regulations to carry out this subsection and the amendments made by this subsection [amending subsec. (a)(42) of this section], including with respect to conditions of Federal financial participation, as specified by the Secretary.".

Annual report. Act March 23, 2010, P. L. 111-148, Title VI, Subtitle E, § 6411(c), 124 Stat. 775, provides: "The Secretary of Health and Human Services, acting through the Administrator of the Centers for Medicare & Medicaid Services, shall submit an annual report to Congress concerning the effectiveness of the Recovery Audit Contractor program under Medicaid and Medicare and shall include such reports recommendations for expanding or improving the program.".

Effective date of amendments made by Subtitle F of Title VI of Act March 23, 2010; delay if State legislation required. Act March 23, 2010, P. L. 111-148, Title VI, Subtitle F, § 6508, 124 Stat. 778, provides:

"(a) In general. Except as otherwise provided in this subtitle, this subtitle and the amendments made by this subtitle [amending 42 USCS §§ 1396a and 1396b and appearing in part as 42 USCS § 1396b notes] take effect on January 1, 2011, without regard to whether final regulations to carry out such amendments and subtitle have been promulgated by that date.

"(b) Delay if State legislation required. In the case of a State plan for medical assistance under title XIX of the Social Security Act [42 USCS §§ 1396 et seq.] or a child health plan under title XXI of such Act [42 USCS §§ 1397aa et seq.] which the Secretary of Health and Human Services determines requires State legislation (other than legislation appropriating funds) in order for the plan to meet the additional requirement imposed by the amendments made by this subtitle, the State plan or child health plan shall not be regarded as failing to comply with the requirements of such title solely on the basis of its failure to meet this additional requirement before the first day of the first calendar quarter beginning after the close of the first regular session of the State legislature that begins after the date of the enactment of this Act. For purposes of the previous sentence, in the case of a State that has a 2-year legislative session, each year of such session shall be deemed to be a separate regular session of the State legislature.".

§ 1396b. Payment to States

(a) Computation of amount. From the sums appropriated therefor, the Secretary (except as otherwise provided in this section) shall pay to each State which has a plan approved under this title [42 USCS §§ 1396 et seq.] for each quarter, beginning with the quarter commencing January 1, 1966—

(1) an amount equal to the Federal medical assistance percentage (as defined in section 1905(b) [42 USCS § 1396d(b)], subject to subsections (g) and (j) of this section and section 1923(f) [42 USCS § 1396r-4(f)]) of the total amount expended during such quarter as medical assistance under the State plan; plus

(2)(A) an amount equal to 75 per centum of so much of the sums expended during such quarter (as found necessary by the Secretary for the proper and efficient administration of the State plan) as are attributable to compensation or training of skilled professional medical personnel, and staff directly supporting such personnel, of the State agency or any other public agency; plus

(B) notwithstanding paragraph (1) or subparagraph (A), with respect to amounts expended for nursing aide training and competency evaluation programs, and competency evaluation programs, described in section 1919(e)(1) [42 USCS § 1396r(e)(1)] (including the costs for nurse aides to complete such competency evaluation programs), regardless of whether the programs are provided in or outside nursing facilities or of the skill of the personnel involved in such programs, an amount equal to 50 percent (or, for calendar quarters beginning on or after July 1, 1988, and before October 1, 1990, the lesser of 90 percent or the Federal medical assistance percentage plus 25 percentage points) of so much of the sums expended during such quarter (as found necessary by the Secretary for the proper and efficient administration of the State plan) as are attributable to such programs; plus

(C) an amount equal to 75 percent of so much of the sums expended during such quarter (as found necessary by the Secretary for the proper and efficient administration of the State plan) as are attributable to preadmission screening and resident review activities conducted by the State under section 1919(e)(7) [42 USCS § 1396r(e)(7)]; plus

(D) for each calendar quarter during—

(i) fiscal year 1991, an amount equal to 90 percent,

(ii) fiscal year 1992, an amount equal to 85 percent,

(iii) fiscal year 1993, an amount equal to 80 percent, and

(iv) fiscal year 1994 and thereafter, an amount equal to 75 percent,

of so much of the sums expended during such quarter (as found necessary by the Secretary for the proper and efficient administration of the State plan) as are attributable to State activities under section 1919(g) [42 USCS § 1396r(g)]; plus

(E) an amount equal to 75 percent of so much of the sums expended during such quarter (as found necessary by the Secretary for the proper and efficient administration of the State plan) as are attributable to translation or interpretation services in connection with the enrollment of, retention of, and use of services under this title [42 USCS §§ 1396 et seq.] by, children of families for whom English is not the primary language; plus

(3) an amount equal to—

(A)(i) 90 per centum of so much of the sums expended during such quarter as are attributable to the design, development, or installation of such mechanized claims processing and information retrieval systems as the Secretary determines are likely to provide more efficient, economical, and effective administration of the plan and to be compatible with the claims processing and information retrieval systems utilized in the administration of title XVIII [42 USCS §§ 1395 et seq.], including the State's share of the cost of installing such a system to be used jointly in the administration of such State's plan and the plan of any other State approved under this title [42 USCS §§ 1396 et seq.],

(ii) 90 per centum of so much of the sums expended during any such quarter in the fiscal year ending June 30, 1972, or the fiscal year ending June 30, 1973, as are attributable to the design, development, or installation of cost determination systems for State-owned general hospitals (except that the total amount paid to all States under this clause for either such fiscal year shall not exceed $150,000), and

(iii) an amount equal to the Federal medical assistance percentage (as defined in section 1905(b) [42 USCS § 1396d(b)]) of so much of the sums expended during such quarter (as found necessary by the Secretary for the proper and efficient administration of the State plan) as are attributable to such developments or modifications of systems of the type described in clause (i) as are necessary for the efficient collection and reporting on child health measures; and

(B) 75 per centum of so much of the sums expended during such quarter as are attributable to the operation of systems (whether such systems are operated directly by the State or by another person under a contract with the State) of the type described in subparagraph (A)(i) (whether or not designed, developed, or installed with assistance under such subparagraph) which are approved by the Secretary and which include provision for prompt written notice to each individual who is furnished services covered by the plan, or to each individual in a sample group of individuals who are furnished such services, of the specific services (other than confidential services) so covered, the name of the person or persons furnishing the services, the date or dates on which the services were furnished, and the amount of the payment or payments made under the plan on account of the services; and

(C)(i) 75 per centum of the sums expended with respect to costs incurred during such quarter (as found necessary by the Secretary for the proper and efficient administration of the State plan) as are attributable to the performance of medical and utilization review by a utilization and quality control peer review organization or by an entity which meets the requirements of section 1152 [42 USCS § 1320c-1], as determined by the Secretary, under a contract entered into under section 1902(d) [42 USCS § 1396a(d)]; and

(ii) 75 percent of the sums expended with respect to costs incurred during such quarter (as found necessary by the Secretary for the proper and efficient administration of the State plan) as are attributable to the performance of independent external reviews conducted under section 1932(c)(2) [42 USCS § 1396u-2(c)(2)]; and

(D) 75 percent of so much of the sums expended by the State plan during a quarter in 1991, 1992, or 1993, as the Secretary determines is attributable to the statewide adoption of a drug use review program which conforms to the requirements of section 1927(g) [42 USCS § 1396r-8(g)];

(E) 50 percent of the sums expended with respect to costs incurred during such quarter as are attributable to providing—

(i) services to identify and educate individuals who are likely to be eligible for medical assistance under this title and who have Sickle Cell Disease or who are carriers of the sickle cell gene, including education regarding how to identify such individuals; or

(ii) education regarding the risks of stroke and other complications, as well as the prevention of stroke and other complications, in individuals who are likely to be eligible for medical assistance under this title [42 USCS §§ 1396 et seq.] and who have Sickle Cell Disease; and

(F)(i) 100 percent of so much of the sums expended during such quarter as are attributable to payments to Medicaid providers described in subsection (t)(1) to encourage the adoption and use of certified EHR technology; and

(ii) 90 percent of so much of the sums expended during such quarter as are attributable to payments for reasonable administrative expenses related to the administration of payments described in clause (i) if the State meets the condition described in subsection (t)(9); plus

[(G)](H)(i) 90 percent of the sums expended during the quarter as are attributable to the design, development, or installation of such mechanized verification and information retrieval systems as the Secretary determines are necessary to implement section 1902(ee) [42 USCS § 1396a(ee)] (including a system described in paragraph (2)(B) thereof), and

(ii) 75 percent of the sums expended during the quarter as are attributable to the operation of systems to which clause (i) applies, plus

(4) an amount equal to 100 percent of the sums expended during the quarter which are attributable to the costs of the implementation and operation of the immigration status verification system described in section 1137(d) [42 USCS § 1320b-7(d)]; plus

(5) an amount equal to 90 per centum of the sums expended during such quarter which are attributable to the offering, arranging, and furnishing (directly or on a contract basis) of family planning services and supplies;

(6) subject to subsection (b)(3), an amount equal to—

(A) 90 per centum of the sums expended during such a quarter within the twelve-quarter period beginning with the first quarter in which a payment is made to the State pursuant to this paragraph, and

(B) 75 per centum of the sums expended during each succeeding calendar quarter,

with respect to costs incurred during such quarter (as found necessary by the Secretary for the elimination of fraud in the provision and administration of medical assistance provided under the State plan) which are attributable to the establishment and operation of (including the training of personnel employed by) a State medicaid fraud control unit (described in subsection (q)); plus

(7) subject to section 1919(g)(3)(B) [42 USCS § 1396r(g)(3)(B)], an amount equal to 50 per centum of the remainder of the amounts expended during such quarter as found necessary by the Secretary for the proper and efficient administration of the State plan.

(b) Quarterly expenditures beginning after December 31, 1969. (1) Notwithstanding the preceding provisions of this section, the amount determined under subsection (a)(1) for any State for any quarter beginning after December 31, 1969, shall not take into account any amounts expended as medical assistance with respect to individuals aged 65 or over and disabled individuals entitled to hospital insurance benefits under title XVIII [42 USCS §§ 1395 et seq.] which would not have been so expended if the individuals involved had been enrolled in the insurance program established by part B of title XVIII [42 USCS §§ 1395j et seq.], other than amounts expended under provisions of the plan of such State required by section 1902(a)(34) [42 USCS § 1396a(a)(34)].

(2) For limitation on Federal participation for capital expenditures which are out of conformity with a comprehensive plan of a State or areawide planning agency, see section 1122 [42 USCS § 1320a-1].

(3) The amount of funds which the Secretary is otherwise obligated to pay a State during a quarter under subsection (a)(6) may not exceed the higher of—

(A) $125,000, or

(B) one-quarter of 1 per centum of the sums expended by the Federal, State, and local governments during the previous quarter in carrying out the State's plan under this title [42 USCS §§ 1396 et seq.].

(4) Amounts expended by a State for the use of an enrollment broker in marketing medicaid managed care organizations and other managed care entities to eligible individuals under this title [42 USCS §§ 1396 et seq.] shall be considered, for purposes of subsection (a)(7), to be necessary for the proper and efficient administration of the State plan but only if the following conditions are met with respect to the broker:

(A) The broker is independent of any such entity and of any health care providers (whether or not any such provider participates in the State plan under this title [42 USCS §§ 1396 et seq.]) that provide coverage of services in the same State in which the broker is conducting enrollment activities.

(B) No person who is an owner, employee, consultant, or has a contract with the broker either has any direct or indirect financial interest with such an entity or health care provider or has been excluded from participation in the program under this title or title XVIII [42 USCS §§ 1396 et seq. or 1395 et seq.] or debarred by any Federal agency, or subject to a civil money penalty under this Act [42 USCS §§ 301 et seq.].

(5) Notwithstanding the preceding provisions of this section, the amount determined under subsection (a)(1) for any State shall be decreased in a quarter by the amount of any health care related taxes (described in section 1902 [1903] (w)(3)(A) [subsec. (w)(3)(A) of this section]) that are imposed on a hospital described in subsection (w)(3)(F) in that quarter.

(c) Treatment of educationally-related services. Nothing in this title [42 USCS §§ 1396 et seq.] shall be construed as prohibiting or restricting, or authorizing the Secretary to prohibit or restrict, payment under subsection (a) for medical assistance for covered services furnished to a child with a disability because such services are included in the child's individualized education program established pursuant to part B of the Individuals with Disabilities Education Act [20 USCS §§ 1411 et seq.] or furnished to an infant or toddler with a disability because such services are included in the child's individualized family service plan adopted pursuant to part C of such Act [20 USCS §§ 1431 et seq.].

(d) Estimates of State entitlement; installments; adjustments to reflect overpayments or underpayments; time for recovery or adjustment; uncollectable or discharged debts; obligated appropriations; disputed claims. (1) Prior to the beginning of each quarter, the Secretary shall estimate the amount to which a State will be entitled under subsections (a) and (b) for such quarter, such estimates to be based on (A) a report filed by the State containing its estimate of the total sum to be expended in such quarter in accordance with the provisions of such subsections, and stating the amount appropriated or made available by the State and its political subdivisions for such expenditures in such quarter, and if such amount is less than the State's proportionate share of the total sum of such estimated expenditures, the source or sources from which the difference is expected to be derived, and (B) such other investigation as the Secretary may find necessary.

(2)(A) The Secretary shall then pay to the State, in such installments as he may determine, the amount so estimated, reduced or increased to the extent of any overpayment or underpayment which the Secretary determines was made under this section to such State for any prior quarter and with respect to which adjustment has not already been made under this subsection.

(B) Expenditures for which payments were made to the State under subsection (a) shall be treated as an overpayment to the extent that the State or local agency administering such plan has been reimbursed for such expenditures by a third party pursuant to the provisions of its plan in compliance with section 1902(a)(25) [42 USCS § 1396a(a)(25)].

(C) For purposes of this subsection, when an overpayment is discovered, which was made by a State to a person or other entity, the State shall have a period of 1 year in which to recover or attempt to recover such overpayment before adjustment is made in the Federal payment to such State on account of such overpayment. Except as otherwise provided in subparagraph (D), the adjustment in the Federal payment shall be made at the end of the 1-year period, whether or not recovery was made.

(D)(i) In any case where the State is unable to recover a debt which represents an overpayment (or any portion thereof) made to a person or other entity on account of such debt having been discharged in bankruptcy or otherwise being uncollectable, no adjustment shall be made in the Federal payment to such State on account of such overpayment (or portion thereof).

(ii) In any case where the State is unable to recover a debt which represents an overpayment (or any portion thereof) made to a person or other entity due to fraud within 1 year of discovery because there is not a final determination of the amount of the overpayment under an administrative or judicial process (as applicable), including as a result of a judgment being under appeal, no adjustment shall be made in the Federal payment to such State on account of such overpayment (or portion thereof) before the date that is 30 days after the date on which a final judgment (including, if applicable, a final determination on an appeal) is made.

(3)(A) The pro rata share to which the United States is equitably entitled, as determined by the Secretary, of the net amount recovered during any quarter by the State or any political subdivision thereof with respect to medical assistance furnished under the State plan shall be considered an overpayment to be adjusted under this subsection.

(B)(i) Subparagraph (A) and paragraph (2)(B) shall not apply to any amount recovered or paid to a State as part of the comprehensive settlement of November 1998 between manufacturers of tobacco products, as defined in section 5702(d) of the Internal Revenue Code of 1986 [26 USCS § 5702(d)], and State Attorneys General, or as part of any individual State settlement or judgment reached in litigation initiated or pursued by a State against one or more such manufacturers.

(ii) Except as provided in subsection (i)(19), a State may use amounts recovered or paid to the State as part of a comprehensive or individual settlement, or a judgment, described in clause (i) for any expenditures determined appropriate by the State.

(4) Upon the making of any estimate by the Secretary under this subsection, any appropriations available for payments under this section shall be deemed obligated.

(5) In any case in which the Secretary estimates that there has been an overpayment under this section to a State on the basis of a claim by such State that has been disallowed by the Secretary under section 1116(d) [42 USCS § 1316(d)], and such State disputes such disallowance, the amount of the Federal payment in controversy shall, at the option of the State, be retained by such State or recovered by the Secretary pending a final determination with respect to such payment amount. If such final determination is to the effect that any amount was properly disallowed, and the State chose to retain payment of the amount in controversy, the Secretary shall offset, from any subsequent payments made to such State under this title [42 USCS §§ 1396 et seq.], an amount equal to the proper amount of the disallowance plus interest on such amount disallowed for the period beginning on the date such amount was disallowed and ending on the date of such final determination at a rate (determined by the Secretary) based on the average of the bond equivalent of the weekly 90-day treasury bill auction rates during such period.

(6)(A) Each State (as defined in subsection (w)(7)(D)) shall include, in the first report submitted under paragraph (1) after the end of each fiscal year, information related to—

(i) provider-related donations made to the State or units of local government during such fiscal year, and

(ii) health care related taxes collected by the State or such units during such fiscal year.

(B) Each State shall include, in the first report submitted under paragraph (1) after the end of each fiscal year, information related to the total amount of payment adjustments made, and the amount of payment adjustments made to individual providers (by provider), under section 1923(c) [42 USCS § 1396r-4(c)] during such fiscal year.

(e) Transition costs of closures or conversions permitted. State plan approved under this title [42 USCS §§ 1396 et seq.] may include, as a cost with respect to hospital services under the plan under this title [42 USCS §§ 1396 et seq.], periodic expenditures made to reflect transitional allowances established with respect to a hospital closure or conversion under section 1884 [42 USCS § 1395uu].

(f) Limitation on Federal participation in medical assistance. (1)(A) Except as provided in paragraph (4), payment under the preceding provisions of this section shall not be made with respect to any amount expended as medical assistance in a calendar quarter, in any State, for any member of a family the annual income of which exceeds the applicable income limitation determined under this paragraph.

(B)(i) Except as provided in clause (ii) of this subparagraph, the applicable income limitation with respect to any family is the amount determined, in accordance with standards prescribed by the Secretary, to be equivalent to 133⅓ percent of the highest amount which would ordinarily be paid to a family of the same size without any income or resources, in the form of money payments, under the plan of the State approved under part A of title IV of this Act [42 USCS §§ 601 et seq.]

(ii) If the Secretary finds that the operation of a uniform maximum limits payments to families of more than one size, he may adjust the amount otherwise determined under clause (i) to take account of families of different sizes.

(C) The total amount of any applicable income limitation determined under subparagraph (B) shall, if it is not a multiple of $100 or such other amount as the Secretary may prescribe, be rounded to the next higher multiple of $100 or such other amount, as the case may be.

(2) (A) In computing a family's income for purposes of paragraph (1), there shall be excluded any costs (whether in the form of insurance premiums or otherwise and regardless of whether such costs are reimbursed under another public program of the State or political subdivision thereof) incurred by such family for medical care or for any other type of remedial care recognized under State law or, (B) notwithstanding section 1916 [42 USCS § 1396o] at State option, an amount paid by such family, at the family's option, to the State, provided that the amount, when combined with costs incurred in prior months, is sufficient when excluded from the family's income to reduce such family's income below the applicable income limitation described in paragraph (1). The amount of State expenditures for which medical assistance is available under subsection (a)(1) will be reduced by amounts paid to the State pursuant to this subparagraph.

(3) For purposes of paragraph (1)(B), in the case of a family consisting of only one individual, the "highest amount which would ordinarily be paid" to such family under the State's plan approved under part A of title IV of this Act [42 USCS §§ 601 et seq.] shall be the amount determined by the State agency (on the basis of reasonable relationship to the amounts payable under such plan to families consisting of two or more persons) to be the amount of the aid which would ordinarily be payable under such plan to a family (without any income or resources) consisting of one person if such plan provided for aid to such a family.

(4) The limitations on payment imposed by the preceding provisions of this subsection shall not apply with respect to any amount expended by a State as medical assistance for any individual described in section 1902(a)(10)(A)(i)(III), 1902(a)(10)(A)(i)(IV), 1902(a)(10)(A)(i)(V), 1902(a)(10)(A)(i)(VI), 1902(a)(10)(A)(i)(VII), 1902(a)(10)(A)(i)(VIII), 1902(a)(10)(A)(i)(IX), 1902(a)(10)(A)(ii)(IX), 1902(a)(10)(A)(ii)(X), 1902(a)(10)(A)(ii)(XIII), 1902(a)(10)(A)(ii)(XIV), [or] 1902(a)(10)(A)(ii)(XV), 1902(a)(10)(A)(ii)(XVI), 1902(a)(10)(A)(ii)(XVII), 1902(a)(10)(A)(ii)(XVIII), 1902(a)(10)(A)(ii)(XIX), 1902(a)(10)(A)(ii)(XX), 1902(a)(10)(A)(ii)(XXI), 1902(a)(10)(A)(ii)(XXII), [or] 1905(p)(1) [42 USCS § 1396a(a)(10)(A)(i)(III), (IV), (V), (VI), (VII), (VIII), (IX), (ii)(IX), (X), (XIII), (XIV), (XV), (XVI), (XVII), (XVIII), (XIX), (XXI), (XXII), or 1396d(p)(1)] or for any individual—

(A) who is receiving aid or assistance under any plan of the State approved under title I, X, XIV or XVI, or part A of title IV [42 USCS §§ 301 et seq., 1201 et seq., 1351 et seq., or 1381 et seq., or 601 et seq.], or with respect to whom supplemental security income benefits are being paid under title XVI [42 USCS §§ 1381 et seq.], or

(B) who is not receiving such aid or assistance, and with respect to whom such benefits are not being paid, but (i) is eligible to receive such aid or assistance, or to have such benefits paid with respect to him, or (ii) would be eligible to receive such aid or assistance, or to have such benefits paid with respect to him if he were not in a medical institution, or

(C) with respect to whom there is being paid, or who is eligible, or would be eligible if he were not in a medical institution, to have paid with respect to him, a State supplementary payment and is eligible for medical assistance equal in amount, duration, and scope to the medical assistance made available to individuals described in section 1902(a)(10)(A) [42 USCS § 1396a(a)(10)(A)], or who is a PACE program eligible individual enrolled in a PACE program under section 1934 [42 USCS § 1396u-4], but only if the income of such individual (as determined under section 1612 [42 USCS § 1382a], but without regard to subsection (b) thereof) does not exceed 300 percent of the supplemental security income benefit rate established by section 1611(b)(1) [42 USCS § 1382(b)(1)],

at the time of the provision of the medical assistance giving rise to such expenditure.

(g) Decrease in Federal medical assistance percentage of amounts paid for services furnished under State plan after June 30, 1973. (1) Subject to paragraph (3), with respect to amounts paid for the following services furnished under the State plan after June 30, 1973 (other than services furnished pursuant to a contract with a health maintenance organization as defined in section 1876 [42 USCS § 1395mm] or which is a qualified health maintenance organization (as defined in section 1310(d) of the Public Health Service Act), the Federal medical assistance percentage shall be decreased as follows: After an individual has received inpatient hospital services or services in an intermediate care facility for the mentally retarded for 60 days or inpatient mental hospital services for 90 days (whether or not such days are consecutive), during any fiscal year, the Federal medical assistance percentage with respect to amounts paid for any such care furnished thereafter to such individual shall be decreased by a per centum thereof (determined under paragraph (5)) unless the State agency responsible for the administration of the plan makes a showing satisfactory to the Secretary that, with respect to each calendar quarter for which the State submits a request for payment at the full Federal medical assistance percentage for amounts paid for inpatient hospital services or services in an intermediate care facility for the mentally retarded furnished beyond 60 days (or inpatient mental hospital services furnished beyond 90 days), such State has an effective program of medical review of the care of patients in mental hospitals, and intermediate care facilities for the mentally retarded pursuant to paragraphs (26) and (31) of section 1902(a) [42 USCS § 1396a(a)(26) and (31))] whereby the professional management of each case is reviewed and evaluated at least annually by independent professional review teams. In determining the number of days on which an individual has received services described in this subsection, there shall not be counted any days with respect to which such individual is entitled to have payments made (in whole or in part) on his behalf under section 1812 [42 USCS § 1395d].

(2) The Secretary shall, as part of his validation procedures under this subsection, conduct timely sample onsite surveys of private and public institutions in which recipients of medical assistance may receive care and services under a State plan approved under this title [42 USCS §§ 1396 et seq.], and his findings with respect to such surveys (as well as the showings of the State agency required under this subsection) shall be made available for public inspection.

(3)(A) No reduction in the Federal medical assistance percentage of a State otherwise required to be imposed under this subsection shall take effect—

(i) if such reduction is due to the State's unsatisfactory or invalid showing made with respect to a calendar quarter beginning before January 1, 1977;

(ii) before January 1, 1978;

(iii) unless a notice of such reduction has been provided to the State at least 30 days before the date such reduction takes effect; or

(iv) due to the State's unsatisfactory or invalid showing made with respect to a calendar quarter beginning after September 30, 1977, unless notice of such reduction has been provided to the State no later than the first day of the fourth calendar quarter following the calendar quarter with respect to which such showing was made.

(B) The Secretary shall waive application of any reduction in the Federal medical assistance percentage of a State otherwise required to be imposed under paragraph (1) because a showing by the State, made under such paragraph with respect to a calendar quarter ending after January 1, 1977, and before January 1, 1978, is determined to be either unsatisfactory under such paragraph or invalid under paragraph (2), if the Secretary determines that the State's showing made under paragraph (1) with respect to any calendar quarter ending on or before December 31, 1978, is satisfactory under such paragraph and is valid under paragraph (2).

(4)(A) The Secretary may not find the showing of a State, with respect to a calendar quarter under paragraph (1), to be satisfactory if the showing is submitted to the Secretary later than the 30th day after the last day of the calendar quarter, unless the State demonstrates to the satisfaction of the Secretary good cause for not meeting such deadline.

(B) The Secretary shall find a showing of a State, with respect to a calendar quarter under paragraph (1), to be satisfactory under such paragraph with respect to the requirement that the State conduct annual onsite inspections in mental hospitals and intermediate care facilities for the mentally retarded under paragraphs (26) and (31) of section 1902(a) [42

USCS § 1396a(a)(26) and (31)], if the showing demonstrates that the State has conducted such an onsite inspection during the 12-month period ending on the last date of the calendar quarter—

(i) in each of not less than 98 per centum of the number of such hospitals and facilities requiring such inspection, and

(ii) in every such hospital or facility which has 200 or more beds,

and that, with respect to such hospitals and facilities not inspected within such period, the State has exercised good faith and due diligence in attempting to conduct such inspection, or if the State demonstrates to the satisfaction of the Secretary that it would have made such a showing but for failings of a technical nature only.

(5) In the case of a State's unsatisfactory or invalid showing made with respect to a type of facility or institutional services in a calendar quarter, the per centum amount of the reduction of the State's Federal medical assistance percentage for that type of services under paragraph (1) is equal to 33⅓ per centum multiplied by a fraction, the denominator of which is equal to the total number of patients receiving that type of services in that quarter under the State plan in facilities or institutions for which a showing was required to be made under this subsection, and the numerator of which is equal to the number of such patients receiving such type of services in that quarter in those facilities or institutions for which a satisfactory and valid showing was not made for that calendar quarter.

(6)(A) Recertifications required under section 1902(a)(44) [42 USCS § 1396a(a)(44)] shall be conducted at least every 60 days in the case of inpatient hospital services.

(B) Such recertifications in the case of services in an intermediate care facility for the mentally retarded shall be conducted at least—

(i) 60 days after the date of the initial certification,

(ii) 180 days after the date of the initial certification,

(iii) 12 months after the date of the initial certification,

(iv) 18 months after the date of the initial certification,

(v) 24 months after the date of the initial certification, and

(vi) every 12 months thereafter.

(C) For purposes of determining compliance with the schedule established by this paragraph, a recertification shall be considered to have been done on a timely basis if it was performed not later than 10 days after the date the recertification was otherwise required and the State establishes good cause why the physician or other person making such recertification did not meet such schedule.

(h) [Repealed]

(i) Payment for organ transplants; item or service furnished by excluded individual, entity, or physicians; other restrictions. Payment under the preceding provisions of this section shall not be made—

(1) for organ transplant procedures unless the State plan provides for written standards respecting the coverage of such procedures and unless such standards provide that—

(A) similarly situated individuals are treated alike; and

(B) any restriction, on the facilities or practitioners which may provide such procedures, is consistent with the accessibility of high quality care to individuals eligible for the procedures under the State plan; or

(2) with respect to any amount expended for an item or service (other than an emergency item or service, not including items or services furnished in an emergency room of a hospital) furnished—

(A) under the plan by any individual or entity during any period when the individual or entity is excluded from participation under Title V, XVIII, or XX [42 USCS §§ 701 et seq., 1395 et seq., or 1397 et seq.] or under this title [42 USCS §§ 1396 et seq.] pursuant to section 1128, 1128A, 1156, or 1842(j)(2) [42 USCS § 1320a-7, 1320a-7a, 1320c-5, or 1395u(j)(2)],

(B) at the medical direction or on the prescription of a physician, during the period when such physician is excluded from participation under title V, XVIII, or XX or under this title [42 USCS §§ 701 et seq., 1395 et seq., or 1397 et seq., or 1396 et seq.] pursuant to section 1128, 1128A, 1156, or 1842(j)(2) [42 USCS § 1320a-7, 1320a-7a, 1320c-5, or 1395u(j)(2)] and when the person furnishing such item or service knew or had reason to know of the exclusion (after a reasonable time period after reasonable notice has been furnished to the person); or

(C) by any individual or entity to whom the State has failed to suspend payments under the plan during any period when there is pending an investigation of a credible allegation of fraud against the individual or entity, as determined by the State in accordance with regulations promulgated by the Secretary for purposes of section 1862(o) [42 USCS § 1395y(o)] and this subparagraph, unless the State determines in accordance with such regulations there is good cause not to suspend such payments; or

(3) with respect to any amount expended for inpatient hospital services furnished under the plan (other than amounts attributable to the special situation of a hospital which serves a disproportionate number of low income patients with special needs) to the extent that such amount exceeds the hospital's customary charges with respect to such services or (if such services are furnished under the plan by a public institution free of charge or at nominal charges to the public) exceeds an amount determined on the basis of those items (specified in regulations prescribed by the Secretary) included in the determination of such payment which the Secretary finds will provide fair compensation to such institution for such services; or

(4) with respect to any amount expended for care or services furnished under the plan by a hospital unless such hospital or skilled nursing facility has in effect a utilization review plan which meets the requirements imposed by section 1861(k) [42 USCS § 1395x(k)] for purposes of title XVIII [42 USCS §§ 1395 et seq.]; and if such hospital has in effect such a utilization review plan for purposes of title XVIII [42 USCS §§ 1395 et seq.], such plan shall serve as the plan required by this subsection (with the same standards and procedures and the same review committee or group) as a condition of payment under this title [42 USCS §§ 1396 et seq.]; the Secretary is authorized to waive the requirements of this paragraph if the State agency demonstrates to his satisfaction that it has in operation utilization review procedures which are superior in their effectiveness to the procedures required under section 1861(k) [42 USCS § 1395x(k)]; or

(5) with respect to any amount expended for any drug product for which payment may not be made under part B of title XVIII [42 USCS §§ 1395j et seq.] because of section 1862(c) [42 USCS § 1395y(c)]; or

(6) with respect to any amount expended for inpatient hospital tests (other than in emergency situations) not specifically ordered by the attending physician or other responsible practitioner; or

(7) with respect to any amount expended for clinical diagnostic laboratory tests performed by a physician, independent laboratory, or hospital, to the extent such amount exceeds the amount that would be recognized under section 1833(h) [42 USCS § 1395l(h)] for such tests performed for an individual enrolled under part B of title XVIII [42 USCS §§ 1395j et seq.]; or

(8) with respect to any amount expended for medical assistance (A) for nursing facility services to reimburse (or otherwise compensate) a nursing facility for payment of a civil money penalty imposed under section 1919(h) [42 USCS § 1396r(h)] or (B) for home and community care to reimburse (or otherwise compensate) a provider of such care for payment of a civil money penalty imposed under this title or title XI [42 USCS §§ 1396 et seq. or §§ 1301 et seq.] or for legal expenses in defense of an exclusion or civil money penalty under this title or title XI [42 USCS §§ 1396 et seq. or §§ 1301 et seq.] if there is no reasonable legal ground for the provider's case; or

(9) [Deleted]

(10)(A) with respect to covered outpatient drugs unless there is a rebate agreement in effect under section 1927 [42 USCS § 1396r-8] with respect to such drugs or unless section 1927(a)(3) [42 USCS § 1396r-8(a)(3)] applies,

(B) with respect to any amount expended for an innovator multiple source drug (as defined in section 1927(k) [42 USCS § 1396r-8(k)]) dispensed on or after July 1, 1991, if, under applicable State law, a less expensive multiple source drug could have been dispensed, but only to the extent that such amount exceeds the upper payment limit for such multiple source drug;[,]

(C) with respect to covered outpatient drugs described in section 1927(a)(7) [42 USCS § 1396r-8(a)(7)], unless information respecting utilization data and coding on such drugs that is required to be submitted under such section is submitted in accordance with such section, and

(D) with respect to any amount expended for reimbursement to a pharmacy under this title [42 USCS §§ 1396 et seq.] for the ingredient cost of a covered outpatient drug for which the pharmacy has already received payment under this title [42 USCS §§ 1396 et seq.] (other than with respect to a reasonable restocking fee for such drug); or

(11) with respect to any amount expended for physicians' services furnished on or after the first day of the first quarter beginning more than 60 days after the date of establishment of the physician identifier system under section 1902(x) [42 USCS § 1396a(x)], unless the claim for the services includes the unique physician identifier provided under such system; or

(12) [Deleted]

(13) with respect to any amount expended to reimburse (or otherwise compensate) a nursing facility for payment of legal expenses associ-

ated with any action initiated by the facility that is dismissed on the basis that no reasonable legal ground existed for the institution of such action; or

(14) with respect to any amount expended on administrative costs to carry out the program under section 1928 [42 USCS § 1396s]; or

(15) with respect to any amount expended for a single-antigen vaccine and its administration in any case in which the administration of a combined-antigen vaccine was medically appropriate (as determined by the Secretary); or

(16) with respect to any amount expended for which funds may not be used under the Assisted Suicide Funding Restriction Act of 1997; or

(17) with respect to any amount expended for roads, bridges, stadiums, or any other item or service not covered under a State plan under this title [42 USCS §§ 1396 et seq.]; or

(18) with respect to any amount expended for home health care services provided by an agency or organization unless the agency or organization provides the State agency on a continuing basis a surety bond in a form specified by the Secretary under paragraph (7) of section 1861(o) [42 USCS § 1395x(o)] and in an amount that is not less than $50,000 or such comparable surety bond as the Secretary may permit under the last sentence of such section; or

(19) with respect to any amount expended on administrative costs to initiate or pursue litigation described in subsection (d)(3)(B);

(20) with respect to amounts expended for medical assistance provided to an individual described in subclause (XV) or (XVI) of section 1902(a)(10)(A)(ii) [42 USCS § 1396a(a)(10)(A)(ii)] for a fiscal year unless the State demonstrates to the satisfaction of the Secretary that the level of State funds expended for such fiscal year for programs to enable working individuals with disabilities to work (other than for such medical assistance) is not less than the level expended for such programs during the most recent State fiscal year ending before the date of the enactment of this paragraph [enacted Dec. 17, 1999];

(21) with respect to amounts expended for covered outpatient drugs described in section 1927(d)(2)(K) [42 USCS § 1396r-8(d)(2)(K)] (relating to drugs when used for treatment of sexual or erectile dysfunction);

(22) with respect to amounts expended for medical assistance for an individual who declares under section 1137(d)(1)(A) [42 USCS § 1320b-7(d)(1)(A)] to be a citizen or national of the United States for purposes of establishing eligibility for benefits under this title [42 USCS §§ 1396 et seq.], unless the requirement of section 1902(a)(46)(B) [42 USCS § 1396a(a)(46)(B)] is met;

(23) with respect to amounts expended for medical assistance for covered outpatient drugs (as defined in section 1927(k)(2) [42 USCS § 1396r-8(k)(2)]) for which the prescription was executed in written (and non-electronic) form unless the prescription was executed on a tamper-resistant pad;

(24) if a State is required to implement an asset verification program under section 1940 [42 USCS § 1396w] and fails to implement such program in accordance with such section, with respect to amounts expended by such State for medical assistance for individuals subject to asset verification under such section, unless—

(A) the State demonstrates to the Secretary's satisfaction that the State made a good faith effort to comply;

(B) not later than 60 days after the date of a finding that the State is in noncompliance, the State submits to the Secretary (and the Secretary approves) a corrective action plan to remedy such noncompliance; and

(C) not later than 12 months after the date of such submission (and approval), the State fulfills the terms of such corrective action plan;

(25) with respect to any amounts expended for medical assistance for individuals for whom the State does not report enrollee encounter data (as defined by the Secretary) to the Medicaid Statistical Information System (MSIS) in a timely manner (as determined by the Secretary); or

(26) with respect to any amounts expended for medical assistance for individuals described in subclause (VIII) of subsection (a)(10)(A)(i) other than medical assistance provided through benchmark coverage described in section 1937(b)(1) [42 USCS § 1396u-7(b)(1)] or benchmark equivalent coverage described in section 1937(b)(2) [42 USCS § 1396u-7(b)(1)].

Nothing in paragraph (1) shall be construed as permitting a State to provide services under its plan under this title [42 USCS §§ 1396 et seq.] that are not reasonable in amount, duration, and scope to achieve their purpose. Paragraphs (1), (2), (16), (17), and (18) shall apply with respect to items or services furnished and amounts expended by or through a managed care entity (as defined in section 1932(a)(1)(B) [42 USCS § 1396u-2(a)(1)(B)]) in the same manner as such paragraphs apply to items or services furnished and amounts expended directly by the State.

(j) Adjustment of amount. Notwithstanding the preceding provisions of this section, the amount determined under subsection (a)(1) for any State for any quarter shall be adjusted in accordance with section 1914 [42 USCS § 1396m].

(k) Technical assistance to States. The Secretary is authorized to provide at the request of any State (and without cost to such State) such technical and actuarial assistance as may be necessary to assist such State to contract with any medicaid managed care organization which meets the requirements of subsection (m) of this section for the purpose of providing medical care and services to individuals who are entitled to medical assistance under this title [42 USCS §§ 1396 et seq.].

(l) [Repealed]

(m) "Health maintenance organization" defined; duties and functions of Secretary; payments to States; provisional determination of status by State. (1)(A) The term "health maintenance organization" means a health maintenance organization, an eligible organization with a contract under section 1876 [42 USCS § 1395mm] or a Medicare+Choice organization with a contract under part C of title XVIII [42 USCS §§ 1395w-21 et seq.], a provider sponsored organization, or any other public or private organization, which meets the requirement of section 1902(w) [42 USCS § 1396a(w)] and—

(i) makes services it provides to individuals eligible for benefits under this title [42 USCS §§ 1396 et seq.] accessible to such individuals, within the area served by the organization, to the same extent as such services are made accessible to individuals (eligible for medical assistance under the State plan) not enrolled with the organization, and

(ii) has made adequate provision against the risk of insolvency, which provision is satisfactory to the State, meets the requirements of subparagraph (C)(i) (if applicable), and which assures that individuals eligible for benefits under this title [42 USCS §§ 1396 et seq.] are in no case held liable for debts of the organization in case of the organization's insolvency.

An organization that is a qualified health maintenance organization (as defined in section 1310(d) of the Public Health Service Act) is deemed to meet the requirements of clauses (i) and (ii).

(B) The duties and functions of the Secretary, insofar as they involve making determinations as to whether an organization is a medicaid managed care organization within the meaning of subparagraph (A), shall be integrated with the administration of section 1312(a) and (b) of the Public Health Service Act [42 USCS § 300e-11(a) and (b)].

(C) (i) Subject to clause (ii), a provision meets the requirements of this subparagraph for an organization if the organization meets solvency standards established by the State for private health maintenance organizations or is licensed or certified by the State as a risk-bearing entity.

(ii) Clause (i) shall not apply to an organization if—

(I) the organization is not responsible for the provision (directly or through arrangements with providers of services) of inpatient hospital services and physicians' services;

(II) the organization is a public entity;

(III) the solvency of the organization is guaranteed by the State; or

(IV) the organization is (or is controlled by) one or more Federally-qualified health centers and meets solvency standards established by the State for such an organization.

For purposes of subclause (IV), the term "control" means the possession, whether direct or indirect, of the power to direct or cause the direction of the management and policies of the organization through membership, board representation, or an ownership interest equal to or greater than 50.1 percent.

(2)(A) Except as provided in subparagraphs (B), (C), and (G) no payment shall be made under this title [42 USCS §§ 1396 et seq.] to a State with respect to expenditures incurred by it for payment (determined under a prepaid capitation basis or under any other risk basis) for services provided by any entity (including a health insuring organization) which is responsible for the provision (directly or through arrangements with providers of services) of inpatient hospital services and any other service described in paragraph (2), (3), (4), (5), or (7) of section 1905(a) [42 USCS § 1396d(a)(2)–(5), or (7)] or for the provision of any three or more of the services described in such paragraphs unless—

(i) the Secretary has determined that the entity is a medicaid managed care organization as defined in paragraph (1);

(ii) [Deleted]

(iii) such services are provided for the benefit of individuals eligible for benefits under this title [42 USCS §§ 1396 et seq.] in accordance with a contract between the State and the entity under which prepaid payments to the entity are made on an actuarially sound basis and under which the Secretary must provide prior approval for contracts providing for expenditures in excess of $1,000,000 for 1998 and, for a subsequent year, the amount established under this clause for the previous year increased by the percentage increase in the consumer price index for all urban consumers over the previous year;

(iv) such contract provides that the Secretary and the State (or any person or organization designated by either) shall have the right to audit and inspect any books and records of the entity (and of any subcontractor) that pertain (I) to the ability of the entity to bear the risk of potential financial losses, or (II) to services performed or determinations of amounts payable under the contract;

(v) such contract provides that in the entity's enrollment, reenrollment, or disenrollment of individuals who are eligible for benefits under this title [42 USCS §§ 1396 et seq.] and eligible to enroll, reenroll, or disenroll with the entity pursuant to the contract, the entity will not discriminate among such individuals on the basis of their health status or requirements for health care services;

(vi) such contract (I) permits individuals who have elected under the plan to enroll with the entity for provision of such benefits to terminate such enrollment in accordance with section 1932(a)(4) [42 USCS § 1396u-2(a)(4)] [;], and (II) provides for notification in accordance with such section of each such individual, at the time of the individual's enrollment, of such right to terminate such enrollment;

(vii) such contract provides that, in the case of medically necessary services which were provided (I) to an individual enrolled with the entity under the contract and entitled to benefits with respect to such services under the State's plan and (II) other than through the organization because the services were immediately required due to an unforeseen illness, injury, or condition, either the entity or the State provides for reimbursement with respect to those services, [;]

(viii) such contract provides for disclosure of information in accordance with section 1124 [42 USCS § 1320a-3] and paragraph (4) of this subsection;

(ix) such contract provides, in the case of an entity that has entered into a contract for the provision of services with a Federally-qualified health center or a rural health clinic, that the entity shall provide payment that is not less than the level and amount of payment which the entity would make for the services if the services were furnished by a provider which is not a Federally-qualified health center or a rural health clinic;

(x) any physician incentive plan that it operates meets the requirements described in section 1876(i)(8) [42 USCS § 1395mm(i)(8)];

(xi) such contract provides for maintenance of sufficient patient encounter data to identify the physician who delivers services to patients and for the provision of such data to the State at a frequency and level of detail to be specified by the Secretary; and

(xii) such contract, and the entity complies with the applicable requirements of section 1932 [42 USCS § 1396u-2]; and

(xiii) such contract provides that (I) covered outpatient drugs dispensed to individuals eligible for medical assistance who are enrolled with the entity shall be subject to the same rebate required by the agreement entered into under section 1927 [42 USCS § 1396r-8] as the State is subject to and that the State shall collect such rebates from manufacturers, (II) capitation rates paid to the entity shall be based on actual cost experience related to rebates and subject to the Federal regulations requiring actuarially sound rates, and (III) the entity shall report to the State, on such timely and periodic basis as specified by the Secretary in order to include in the information submitted by the State to a manufacturer and the Secretary under section 1927(b)(2)(A) [42 USCS § 1396r-8(b)(2)(A)], information on the total number of units of each dosage form and strength and package size by National Drug Code of each covered outpatient drug dispensed to individuals eligible for medical assistance who are enrolled with the entity and for which the entity is responsible for coverage of such drug under this subsection (other than covered outpatient drugs that under subsection (j)(1) of section 1927 [42 USCS § 1396r-8] are not subject to the requirements of that section) and such other data as the Secretary determines necessary to carry out this subsection.

(B) Subparagraph (A) [,] except with respect to clause (ix) of subparagraph (A), does not apply with respect to payments under this title [42 USCS §§ 1396 et seq.] to a State with respect to expenditures incurred by it for payment for services provided by an entity which—

(i)(I) received a grant of at least $100,000 in the fiscal year ending June 30, 1976, under section 329(d)(1)(A) or 330(d)(1) of the Public Health Service Act, and for the period beginning July 1, 1976, and ending on the expiration of the period for which payments are to be made under this title [42 USCS §§ 1396 et seq.] has been the recipient of a grant under either such section; and

(II) provides to its enrollees, on a prepaid capitation risk basis or on any other risk basis, all of the services and benefits described in paragraphs (1), (2), (3), (4)(C), and (5) of section 1905(a) [42 USCS § 1396d(a)(1), (2), (3), (4)(C), and (5)] and, to the extent required by section 1902(a)(10)(D) [42 USCS § 1396a(a)(10)(D)] to be provided under a State plan for medical assistance, the services and benefits described in paragraph (7) of section 1905(a) [42 USCS § 1396d(a)(7)]; or

(ii) is a nonprofit primary health care entity located in a rural area (as defined by the Appalachian Regional Commission)—

(I) which received in the fiscal year ending June 30, 1976, at least $100,000 (by grant, subgrant, or subcontract) under the Appalachian Regional Development Act of 1965 [40 USCS §§ 14101 et seq.], and

(II) for the period beginning July 1, 1976, and ending on the expiration of the period for which payments are to be made under this title [42 USCS §§ 1396 et seq.] either has been the recipient of a grant, subgrant, or subcontract under such Act or has provided services under a contract (initially entered into during a year in which the entity was the recipient of such a grant, subgrant, or subcontract) with a State agency under this title [42 USCS §§ 1396 et seq.] on a prepaid capitation risk basis or on any other risk basis; or

(iii) which has contracted with the single State agency for the provision of services (but not including inpatient hospital services) to persons eligible under this title [42 USCS §§ 1396 et seq.] on a prepaid risk basis prior to 1970.

(C)–(F) [Deleted]

(G) In the case of an entity which is receiving (and has received during the previous two years) a grant of at least $100,000 under section 329(d)(1)(A) or 330(d)(1) of the Public Health Service Act or is receiving (and has received during the previous two years) at least $100,000 (by grant, subgrant, or subcontract) under the Appalachian Regional Development Act of 1965, clause (i) of subparagraph (A) shall not apply.

(H) In the case of an individual who—

(i) in a month is eligible for benefits under this title [42 USCS §§ 1396 et seq.] and enrolled with a medicaid managed care organization with a contract under this paragraph or with a primary care case manager with a contract described in section 1905(t)(3) [42 USCS § 1396d(t)(3)],

(ii) in the next month (or in the next 2 months) is not eligible for such benefits, but

(iii) in the succeeding month is again eligible for such benefits,

the State plan, subject to subparagraph (A)(vi), may enroll the individual for that succeeding month with the organization described in clause (i) if the organization continues to have a contract under this paragraph with the State or with the manager described in such clause if the manager continues to have a contract described in section 1905(t)(3) [42 USCS § 1396d(t)(3)] with the State.

(3) [Repealed]

(4)(A) Each medicaid managed care organization which is not a qualified health maintenance organization (as defined in section 1310(d) of the Public Health Service Act) must report to the State and, upon request, to the Secretary, the Inspector General of the Department of Health and Human Services, and the Comptroller General a description of transactions between the organization and a party in interest (as defined in section 1318(b) of such Act [42 USCS § 300e-17(b)]), including the following transactions:

(i) Any sale or exchange, or leasing of any property between the organization and such a party.

(ii) Any furnishing for consideration of goods, services (including management services), or facilities between the organization and such a party, but not including salaries paid to employees for services provided in the normal course of their employment.

(iii) Any lending of money or other extension of credit between the organization and such a party.

The State or Secretary may require that information reported respecting an organization which controls, or is controlled by, or is under common control with, another entity be in the form of a consolidated financial statement for the organization and such entity.

(B) Each organization shall make the information reported pursuant to subparagraph (A) available to its enrollees upon reasonable request.

(5)(A) If the Secretary determines that an entity with a contract under this subsection—

(i) fails substantially to provide medically necessary items and services that are required (under law or under the contract) to be provided to an individual covered under the contract, if the failure has adversely affected (or has substantial likelihood of adversely affecting) the individual;

(ii) imposes premiums on individuals enrolled under this subsection in excess of the premiums permitted under this title [42 USCS

§§ 1396 et seq.];

(iii) acts to discriminate among individuals in violation of the provision of paragraph (2)(A)(v), including expulsion or refusal to re-enroll an individual or engaging in any practice that would reasonably be expected to have the effect of denying or discouraging enrollment (except as permitted by this subsection) by eligible individuals with the organization whose medical condition or history indicates a need for substantial future medical services;

(iv) misrepresents or falsifies information that is furnished—

(I) to the Secretary or the State under this subsection, or

(II) to an individual or to any other entity under this subsection, [;] or

(v) fails to comply with the requirements of section 1876(i)(8) [42 USCS § 1395mm(i)(8)],

the Secretary may provide, in addition to any other remedies available under law, for any of the remedies described in subparagraph (B).

(B) The remedies described in this subparagraph are—

(i) civil money penalties of not more than $25,000 for each determination under subparagraph (A), or, with respect to a determination under clause (iii) or (iv)(I) of such subparagraph, of not more than $100,000 for each such determination, plus, with respect to a determination under subparagraph (A)(ii), double the excess amount charged in violation of such subparagraph (and the excess amount charged shall be deducted from the penalty and returned to the individual concerned), and plus, with respect to a determination under subparagraph (A)(iii), $15,000 for each individual not enrolled as a result of a practice described in such subparagraph, or

(ii) denial of payment to the State for medical assistance furnished under the contract under this subsection for individuals enrolled after the date the Secretary notifies the organization of a determination under subparagraph (A) and until the Secretary is satisfied that the basis for such determination has been corrected and is not likely to recur.

The provisions of section 1128A [42 USCS § 1320a-7a] (other than subsections (a) and (b)) shall apply to a civil money penalty under clause (i) in the same manner as such provisions apply to a penalty or proceeding under section 1128A(a) [42 USCS § 1320a-7a(a)].

(6)(A) For purposes of this subsection and section 1902(e)(2)(A) [42 USCS § 1396a(e)(2)(A)], in the case of the State of New Jersey, the term "contract" shall be deemed to include an undertaking by the State agency, in the State plan under this title [42 USCS §§ 1396 et seq.], to operate a program meeting all requirements of this subsection.

(B) The undertaking described in subparagraph (A) must provide—

(i) for the establishment of a separate entity responsible for the operation of a program meeting the requirements of this subsection, which entity may be a subdivision of the State agency administering the State plan under this title [42 USCS §§ 1396 et seq.];

(ii) for separate accounting for the funds used to operate such program; and

(iii) for setting the capitation rates and any other payment rates for services provided in accordance with this subsection using a methodology satisfactory to the Secretary designed to ensure that total Federal matching payments under this title [42 USCS §§ 1396 et seq.] for such services will be lower than the matching payments that would be made for the same services, if provided under the State plan on a fee for service basis to an actuarially equivalent population.

(C) The undertaking described in subparagraph (A) shall be subject to approval (and annual re-approval) by the Secretary in the same manner as a contract under this subsection.

(D) The undertaking described in subparagraph (A) shall not be eligible for a waiver under section 1915(b) [42 USCS § 1396n(b)].

(n) [Repealed]

(o) Restrictions on authorized payments to States. Notwithstanding the preceding provisions of this section, no payment shall be made to a State under the preceding provisions of this section for expenditures for medical assistance provided for an individual under its State plan approved under this title [42 USCS §§ 1396 et seq.] to the extent that a private insurer (as defined by the Secretary by regulation and including a group health plan (as defined in section 607(1) of the Employee Retirement Income Security Act of 1974 [29 USCS § 1167(1)]), a service benefit plan, and a health maintenance organization) would have been obligated to provide such assistance but for a provision of its insurance contract which has the effect of limiting or excluding such obligation because the individual is eligible for or is provided medical assistance under the plan.

(p) Assignment of rights of payment; incentive payments for enforcement and collection. (1) When a political subdivision of a State makes, for the State of which it is a political subdivision, or one State makes, for another State, the enforcement and collection of rights of support or payment assigned under section 1912 [42 USCS § 1396k], pursuant to a cooperative arrangement under such section (either within or outside of such State), there shall be paid to such political subdivision or such other State from amounts which would otherwise represent the Federal share of payments for medical assistance provided to the eligible individuals on whose behalf such enforcement and collection was made, an amount equal to 15 percent of any amount collected which is attributable to such rights of support or payment.

(2) Where more than one jurisdiction is involved in such enforcement or collection, the amount of the incentive payment determined under paragraph (1) shall be allocated among the jurisdictions in a manner to be prescribed by the Secretary.

(q) "State medicaid fraud control unit" defined. For the purposes of this section, the term "State medicaid fraud control unit" means a single identifiable entity of the State government which the Secretary certifies (and annually recertifies) as meeting the following requirements:

(1) The entity (A) is a unit of the office of the State Attorney General or of another department of State government which possesses statewide authority to prosecute individuals for criminal violations, (B) is in a State the constitution of which does not provide for the criminal prosecution of individuals by a statewide authority and has formal procedures, approved by the Secretary, that (i) assure its referral of suspected criminal violations relating to the program under this title [42 USCS §§ 1396 et seq.] to the appropriate authority or authorities in the State for prosecution and (ii) assure its assistance of, and coordination with, such authority or authorities in such prosecutions, or (C) has a formal working relationship with the office of the State Attorney General and has formal procedures (including procedures for its referral of suspected criminal violations to such office) which are approved by the Secretary and which provide effective coordination of activities between the entity and such office with respect to the detection, investigation, and prosecution of suspected criminal violations relating to the program under this title [42 USCS §§ 1396 et seq.].

(2) The entity is separate and distinct from the single State agency that administers or supervises the administration of the State plan under this title [42 USCS §§ 1396 et seq.].

(3) The entity's function is conducting a statewide program for the investigation and prosecution of violations of all applicable State laws regarding any and all aspects of fraud in connection with (A) any aspect of the provision of medical assistance and the activities of providers of such assistance under the State plan under this title [42 USCS §§ 1396 et seq.]; and (B) upon the approval of the Inspector General of the relevant Federal agency, any aspect of the provision of health care services and activities of providers of such services under any Federal health care program (as defined in section 1128B(f)(1) [42 USCS § 1320a-7(f)(1)]), if the suspected fraud or violation of law in such case or investigation is primarily related to the State plan under this title [42 USCS §§ 1396 et seq.].

(4)(A) The entity has—

(i) procedures for reviewing complaints of abuse or neglect of patients in health care facilities which receive payments under the State plan under this title [42 USCS §§ 1396 et seq.];

(ii) at the option of the entity, procedures for reviewing complaints of abuse or neglect of patients residing in board and care facilities; and

(iii) procedures for acting upon such complaints under the criminal laws of the State or for referring such complaints to other State agencies for action.

(B) For purposes of this paragraph, the term "board and care facility" means a residential setting which receives payment (regardless of whether such payment is made under the State plan under this title) from or on behalf of two or more unrelated adults who reside in such facility, and for whom one or both of the following is provided:

(i) Nursing care services provided by, or under the supervision of, a registered nurse, licensed practical nurse, or licensed nursing assistant.

(ii) A substantial amount of personal care services that assist residents with the activities of daily living, including personal hygiene, dressing, bathing, eating, toileting, ambulation, transfer, positioning, self-medication, body care, travel to medical services, essential shopping, meal preparation, laundry, and housework.

(5) The entity provides for the collection, or referral for collection to a single State agency, of overpayments that are made under the State plan or under any Federal health care program (as so defined) to health care facilities and that are discovered by the entity in carrying out its activities. All funds collected in accordance

with this paragraph shall be credited exclusively to, and available for expenditure under, the Federal health care program (including the State plan under this title [42 USCS §§ 1396 et seq.]) that was subject to the activity that was the basis for the collection.

(6) The entity employs such auditors, attorneys, investigators, and other necessary personnel and is organized in such a manner as is necessary to promote the effective and efficient conduct of the entity's activities.

(7) The entity submits to the Secretary an application and annual reports containing such information as the Secretary determines, by regulation, to be necessary to determine whether the entity meets the other requirements of this subsection.

(r) Mechanized claims processing and information retrieval systems; operational, etc., requirements. (1) In order to receive payments under subsection (a) for use of automated data systems in administration of the State plan under this title [42 USCS §§ 1396 et seq.], a State must, in addition to meeting the requirements of paragraph (3), have in operation mechanized claims processing and information retrieval systems that meet the requirements of this subsection and that the Secretary has found—

(A) are adequate to provide efficient, economical, and effective administration of such State plan;

(B) are compatible with the claims processing and information retrieval systems used in the administration of title XVIII [42 USCS §§ 1395 et seq.], and for this purpose—

(i) have a uniform identification coding system for providers, other payees, and beneficiaries under this title or title XVIII [42 USCS §§ 1396 et seq. or 1395 et seq.];

(ii) provide liaison between States and carriers and intermediaries with agreements under title XVIII [42 USCS §§ 1395 et seq.] to facilitate timely exchange of appropriate data;

(iii) provide for exchange of data between the States and the Secretary with respect to persons sanctioned under this title or title XVIII [42 USCS §§ 1396 et seq. or 1395 et seq.]; and

(iv) effective for claims filed on or after October 1, 2010, incorporate compatible methodologies of the National Correct Coding Initiative administered by the Secretary (or any successor initiative to promote correct coding and to control improper coding leading to inappropriate payment) and such other methodologies of that Initiative (or such other national correct coding methodologies) as the Secretary identifies in accordance with paragraph (4);

(C) are capable of providing accurate and timely data;

(D) are complying with the applicable provisions of part C of title XI [42 USCS §§ 1320d et seq.];

(E) are designed to receive provider claims in standard formats to the extent specified by the Secretary; and

(F) effective for claims filed on or after January 1, 1999, provide for electronic transmission of claims data in the format specified by the Secretary and consistent with the Medicaid Statistical Information System (MSIS) (including detailed individual enrollee encounter data and other information that the Secretary may find necessary and including, for data submitted to the Secretary on or after January 1, 2010, data elements from the automated data system that the Secretary determines to be necessary for program integrity, program oversight, and administration, at such frequency as the Secretary shall determine).

(2) In order to meet the requirements of this paragraph, mechanized claims processing and information retrieval systems must meet the following requirements:

(A) The systems must be capable of developing provider, physician, and patient profiles which are sufficient to provide specific information as to the use of covered types of services and items, including prescribed drugs.

(B) The State must provide that information on probable fraud or abuse which is obtained from, or developed by, the systems, is made available to the State's medicaid fraud control unit (if any) certified under subsection (q) of this section.

(C) The systems must meet all performance standards and other requirements for initial approval developed by the Secretary.

(3) In order to meet the requirements of this paragraph, a State must have in operation an eligibility determination system which provides for data matching through the Public Assistance Reporting Information System (PARIS) facilitated by the Secretary (or any successor system), including matching with medical assistance programs operated by other States.

(4) For purposes of paragraph (1)(B)(iv), the Secretary shall do the following:

(A) Not later than September 1, 2010:

(i) Identify those methodologies of the National Correct Coding Initiative administered by the Secretary (or any successor initiative to promote correct coding and to control improper coding leading to inappropriate payment) which are compatible to claims filed under this title [42 USCS §§ 1396 et seq.].

(ii) Identify those methodologies of such Initiative (or such other national correct coding methodologies) that should be incorporated into claims filed under this title with respect to items or services for which States provide medical assistance under this title and no national correct coding methodologies have been established under such Initiative with respect to title XVIII [42 USCS §§ 1395 et seq.].

(iii) Notify States of—

(I) the methodologies identified under subparagraphs (A) and (B) (and of any other national correct coding methodologies identified under subparagraph (B)); and

(II) how States are to incorporate such methodologies into claims filed under this title [42 USCS §§ 1396 et seq.].

(B) Not later than March 1, 2011, submit a report to Congress that includes the notice to States under clause (iii) of subparagraph (A) and an analysis supporting the identification of the methodologies made under clauses (i) and (ii) of subparagraph (A).

(s) Limitations on certain physician referrals. Notwithstanding the preceding provisions of this section, no payment shall be made to a State under this section for expenditures for medical assistance under the State plan consisting of a designated health service (as defined in subsection (h)(6) of section 1877 [42 USCS § 1395nn]) furnished to an individual on the basis of a referral that would result in the denial of payment for the service under title XVIII [42 USCS §§ 1395 et seq.] if such title provided for coverage of such service to the same extent and under the same terms and conditions as under the State plan, and subsections (f) and (g)(5) of such section shall apply to a provider of such a designated health service for which payment may be made under this title [42 USCS §§ 1396 et seq.] in the same manner as such subsections apply to a provider of such a service for which payment may be made under such title.

(t)(1) For purposes of subsection (a)(3)(F), the payments described in this paragraph to encourage the adoption and use of certified EHR technology are payments made by the State in accordance with this subsection —

(A) to Medicaid providers described in paragraph (2)(A) not in excess of 85 percent of net average allowable costs (as defined in paragraph (3)(E)) for certified EHR technology (and support services including maintenance and training that is for, or is necessary for the adoption and operation of, such technology) with respect to such providers; and

(B) to Medicaid providers described in paragraph (2)(B) not in excess of the maximum amount permitted under paragraph (5) for the provider involved.

(2) In this subsection and subsection (a)(3)(F), the term "Medicaid provider" means—

(A) an eligible professional (as defined in paragraph (3)(B))—

(i) who is not hospital-based and has at least 30 percent of the professional's patient volume (as estimated in accordance with a methodology established by the Secretary) attributable to individuals who are receiving medical assistance under this title;

(ii) who is not described in clause (i), who is a pediatrician, who is not hospital-based, and who has at least 20 percent of the professional's patient volume (as estimated in accordance with a methodology established by the Secretary) attributable to individuals who are receiving medical assistance under this title; and

(iii) who practices predominantly in a Federally qualified health center or rural health clinic and has at least 30 percent of the professional's patient volume (as estimated in accordance with a methodology established by the Secretary) attributable to needy individuals (as defined in paragraph (3)(F)); and

(B)(i) a children's hospital, or

(ii) an acute-care hospital that is not described in clause (i) and that has at least 10 percent of the hospital's patient volume (as estimated in accordance with a methodology established by the Secretary) attributable to individuals who are receiving medical assistance under this title.

An eligible professional shall not qualify as a Medicaid provider under this subsection unless any right to payment under sections 1848(o) and 1853(l) [42 USCS §§ 1395w-4(o) and 1395w-23(l)] with respect to the eligible professional has been waived in a manner specified by the Secretary. For purposes of calculating patient volume under subparagraph (A)(iii), insofar as it is related to uncompensated care, the Secretary may require the adjustment of such uncompensated care data so that it would be an appropriate proxy for charity care, including a downward adjustment to eliminate bad debt data from uncompensated care. In applying subparagraphs (A) and (B)(ii), the methodology established by the Secretary for patient volume shall include individuals enrolled in a Medicaid managed care plan (under section 1903(m) [42 USCS § 1396b(m)] or section 1932 [42 USCS § 1396u-2]).

(3) In this subsection and subsection (a)(3)(F):

(A) The term "certified EHR technology" means a qualified electronic health record (as defined in 3000(13) of the Public Health Service Act [42 USCS § 300jj(13)]) that is certified pursuant to section 3001(c)(5) of such Act [42 USCS § 300jj-11(c)(5)] as meeting standards adopted under section 3004 of such Act [42 USCS § 300jj-14] that are applicable to the type of record involved (as determined by the Secretary, such as an ambulatory electronic health record for office-based physicians or an inpatient hospital electronic health record for hospitals).

(B) The term "eligible professional" means a—

(i) physician;

(ii) dentist;

(iii) certified nurse mid-wife;

(iv) nurse practitioner; and

(v) physician assistant insofar as the assistant is practicing in a rural health clinic that is led by a physician assistant or is practicing in a Federally qualified health center that is so led.

(C) The term "average allowable costs" means, with respect to certified EHR technology of Medicaid providers described in paragraph (2)(A) for—

(i) the first year of payment with respect to such a provider, the average costs for the purchase and initial implementation or upgrade of such technology (and support services including training that is for, or is necessary for the adoption and initial operation of, such technology) for such providers, as determined by the Secretary based upon studies conducted under paragraph (4)(C); and

(ii) a subsequent year of payment with respect to such a provider, the average costs not described in clause (i) relating to the operation, maintenance, and use of such technology for such providers, as determined by the Secretary based upon studies conducted under paragraph (4)(C).

(D) The term "hospital-based" means, with respect to an eligible professional, a professional (such as a pathologist, anesthesiologist, or emergency physician) who furnishes substantially all of the individual's professional services in a hospital inpatient or emergency room setting and through the use of the facilities and equipment, including qualified electronic health records, of the hospital. The determination of whether an eligible professional is a hospital-based eligible professional shall be made on the basis of the site of service (as defined by the Secretary) and without regard to any employment or billing arrangement between the eligible professional and any other provider.

(E) The term "net average allowable costs" means, with respect to a Medicaid provider described in paragraph (2)(A), average allowable costs reduced by any payment that is made to such Medicaid provider from any other source (other than under this subsection or by a State or local government) that is directly attributable to payment for certified EHR technology or support services described in subparagraph (C).

(F) The term "needy individual" means, with respect to a Medicaid provider, an individual—

(i) who is receiving assistance under this title;

(ii) who is receiving assistance under title XXI [42 USCS §§ 1397aa et seq.];

(iii) who is furnished uncompensated care by the provider; or

(iv) for whom charges are reduced by the provider on a sliding scale basis based on an individual's ability to pay.

(4)(A) With respect to a Medicaid provider described in paragraph (2)(A), subject to subparagraph (B), in no case shall—

(i) the net average allowable costs under this subsection for the first year of payment (which may not be later than 2016), which is intended to cover the costs described in paragraph (3)(C)(i), exceed $25,000 (or such lesser amount as the Secretary determines based on studies conducted under subparagraph (C));

(ii) the net average allowable costs under this subsection for a subsequent year of payment, which is intended to cover costs described in paragraph (3)(C)(ii), exceed $10,000; and

(iii) payments be made for costs described in clause (ii) after 2021 or over a period of longer than 5 years.

(B) In the case of Medicaid provider described in paragraph (2)(A)(ii), the dollar amounts specified in subparagraph (A) shall be ⅔ of the dollar amounts otherwise specified.

(C) For the purposes of determining average allowable costs under this subsection, the Secretary shall study the average costs to Medicaid providers described in paragraph (2)(A) of purchase and initial implementation and upgrade of certified EHR technology described in paragraph (3)(C)(i) and the average costs to such providers of operations, maintenance, and use of such technology described in paragraph (3)(C)(ii). In determining such costs for such providers, the Secretary may utilize studies of such amounts submitted by States.

(5)(A) In no case shall the payments described in paragraph (1)(B) with respect to a Medicaid provider described in paragraph (2)(B) exceed—

(i) in the aggregate the product of—

(I) the overall hospital EHR amount for the provider computed under subparagraph (B); and

(II) the Medicaid share for such provider computed under subparagraph (C);

(ii) in any year 50 percent of the product described in clause (i); and

(iii) in any 2-year period 90 percent of such product.

(B) For purposes of this paragraph, the overall hospital EHR amount, with respect to a Medicaid provider, is the sum of the applicable amounts specified in section 1886(n)(2)(A) [42 USCS § 1395ww(n)(2)(A)] for such provider for the first 4 payment years (as estimated by the Secretary) determined as if the Medicare share specified in clause (ii) of such section were 1. The Secretary shall establish, in consultation with the State, the overall hospital EHR amount for each such Medicaid provider eligible for payments under paragraph (1)(B). For purposes of this subparagraph in computing the amounts under section 1886(n)(2)(C) [42 USCS § 1395ww(n)(2)(C)] for payment years after the first payment year, the Secretary shall assume that in subsequent payment years discharges increase at the average annual rate of growth of the most recent 3 years for which discharge data are available per year.

(C) The Medicaid share computed under this subparagraph, for a Medicaid provider for a period specified by the Secretary, shall be calculated in the same manner as the Medicare share under section 1886(n)(2)(D) [42 USCS § 1395ww(n)(2)(D)] for such a hospital and period, except that there shall be substituted for the numerator under clause (i) of such section the amount that is equal to the number of inpatient-bed-days (as established by the Secretary) which are attributable to individuals who are receiving medical assistance under this title and who are not described in section 1886(n)(2)(D)(i) [42 USCS § 1395ww(n)(2)(D)(i)]. In computing inpatient-bed-days under the previous sentence, the Secretary shall take into account inpatient-bed-days attributable to inpatient-bed-days that are paid for individuals enrolled in a Medicaid managed care plan (under section 1903(m) [42 USCS § 1396b(m)] or section 1932 [42 USCS § 1396u-2]).

(D) In no case may the payments described in paragraph (1)(B) with respect to a Medicaid provider described in paragraph (2)(B) be paid—

(i) for any year beginning after 2016 unless the provider has been provided payment under paragraph (1)(B) for the previous year; and

(ii) over a period of more than 6 years of payment.

(6) Payments described in paragraph (1) are not in accordance with this subsection unless the following requirements are met:

(A)(i) The State provides assurances satisfactory to the Secretary that amounts received under subsection (a)(3)(F) with respect to payments to a Medicaid provider are paid, subject to clause (ii), directly to such provider (or to an employer or facility to which such provider has assigned payments) without any deduction or rebate.

(ii) Amounts described in clause (i) may also be paid to an entity promoting the adoption of certified EHR technology, as designated by the State, if participation in such a payment arrangement is voluntary for the eligible professional involved and if such entity does not retain more than 5 percent of such payments for costs not related to certified EHR technology (and support services including maintenance and training) that is for, or is necessary for the operation of, such technology.

(B) A Medicaid provider described in paragraph (2)(A) is responsible for payment of the remaining 15 percent of the net average allowable cost.

(C)(i) Subject to clause (ii), with respect to payments to a Medicaid provider—

(I) for the first year of payment to the Medicaid provider under this subsection, the Medicaid provider demonstrates that it is engaged in efforts to adopt, implement, or upgrade certified EHR technology; and

(II) for a year of payment, other than the first year of payment to the Medicaid provider under this subsection, the Medicaid provider demonstrates meaningful use of certified EHR technology through a means that is approved by the State and acceptable to the Secretary, and that may be based upon the methodologies applied under section 1848(o) or 1886(n) [42 USCS § 1395w-4(o) or 1395ww(n)].

(ii) In the case of a Medicaid provider who has completed adopting, implementing, or upgrading such technology prior to the first year of payment to the Medicaid provider under this subsection, clause (i)(I) shall not apply and clause (i)(II) shall apply to each year of payment to the Medicaid provider under this subsection, including the first year of payment.

(D) To the extent specified by the Secretary,

the certified EHR technology is compatible with State or Federal administrative management systems.For purposes of subparagraph (B), a Medicaid provider described in paragraph (2)(A) may accept payments for the costs described in such subparagraph from a State or local government.

For purposes of subparagraph (C), in establishing the means described in such subparagraph, which may include clinical quality reporting to the State, the State shall ensure that populations with unique needs, such as children, are appropriately addressed.

(7) With respect to Medicaid providers described in paragraph (2)(A), the Secretary shall ensure coordination of payment with respect to such providers under sections 1848(o) and 1853(l) [42 USCS §§ 1395w-4(o) and 1395w-23(l)] and under this subsection to assure no duplication of funding. Such coordination shall include, to the extent practicable, a data matching process between State Medicaid agencies and the Centers for Medicare & Medicaid Services using national provider identifiers. For such purposes, the Secretary may require the submission of such data relating to payments to such Medicaid providers as the Secretary may specify.

(8) In carrying out paragraph (6)(C), the State and Secretary shall seek, to the maximum extent practicable, to avoid duplicative requirements from Federal and State governments to demonstrate meaningful use of certified EHR technology under this title and title XVIII [42 USCS §§ 1396 et seq. and 1395 et seq.]. In doing so, the Secretary may deem satisfaction of requirements for such meaningful use for a payment year under title XVIII [42 USCS §§ 1395 et seq.] to be sufficient to qualify as meaningful use under this subsection. The Secretary may also specify the reporting periods under this subsection in order to carry out this paragraph.

(9) In order to be provided Federal financial participation under subsection (a)(3)(F)(ii), a State must demonstrate to the satisfaction of the Secretary, that the State—

(A) is using the funds provided for the purposes of administering payments under this subsection, including tracking of meaningful use by Medicaid providers;

(B) is conducting adequate oversight of the program under this subsection, including routine tracking of meaningful use attestations and reporting mechanisms; and

(C) is pursuing initiatives to encourage the adoption of certified EHR technology to promote health care quality and the exchange of health care information under this title, subject to applicable laws and regulations governing such exchange.

(10) The Secretary shall periodically submit reports to the Committee on Energy and Commerce of the House of Representatives and the Committee on Finance of the Senate on status, progress, and oversight of payments described in paragraph (1), including steps taken to carry out paragraph (7). Such reports shall also describe the extent of adoption of certified EHR technology among Medicaid providers resulting from the provisions of this subsection and any improvements in health outcomes, clinical quality, or efficiency resulting from such adoption.

(u) Limitation of Federal financial participation in erroneous medical assistance expenditures. (1)(A) Notwithstanding subsection (a)(1), if the ratio of a State's erroneous excess payments for medical assistance (as defined in subparagraph (D)) to its total expenditures for medical assistance under the State plan approved under this title [42 USCS §§ 1396 et seq.] exceeds 0.03, for the period consisting of the third and fourth quarters of fiscal year 1983, or for any full fiscal year thereafter, then the Secretary shall make no payment for such period or fiscal year with respect to so much of such erroneous excess payments as exceeds such allowable error rate of 0.03.

(B) The Secretary may waive, in certain limited cases, all or part of the reduction required under subparagraph (A) with respect to any State if such State is unable to reach the allowable error rate for a period or fiscal year despite a good faith effort by such State.

(C) In estimating the amount to be paid to a State under subsection (d), the Secretary shall take into consideration the limitation on Federal financial participation imposed by subparagraph (A) and shall reduce the estimate he makes under subsection (d)(1), for purposes of payment to the State under subsection (d)(3), in light of any expected erroneous excess payments for medical assistance (estimated in accordance with such criteria, including sampling procedures, as he may prescribe and subject to subsequent adjustment, if necessary, under subsection (d)(2)).

(D)(i) For purposes of this subsection, the term "erroneous excess payments for medical assistance" means the total of—

(I) payments under the State plan with respect to ineligible individuals and families, and

(II) overpayments on behalf of eligible individuals and families by reason of error in determining the amount of expenditures for medical care required of an individual or family as a condition of eligibility.

(ii) In determining the amount of erroneous excess payments for medical assistance to an ineligible individual or family under clause (i)(I), if such ineligibility is the result of an error in determining the amount of the resources of such individual or family, the amount of the erroneous excess payment shall be the smaller of (I) the amount of the payment with respect to such individual or family, or (II) the difference between the actual amount of such resources and the allowable resource level established under the State plan.

(iii) In determining the amount of erroneous excess payments for medical assistance to an individual or family under clause (i)(II), the amount of the erroneous excess payment shall be the smaller of (I) the amount of the payment on behalf of the individual or family, or (II) the difference between the actual amount incurred for medical care by the individual or family and the amount which should have been incurred in order to establish eligibility for medical assistance.

(iv) In determining the amount of erroneous excess payments, there shall not be included any error resulting from a failure of an individual to cooperate or give correct information with respect to third-party liability as required under section 1912(a)(1)(C) [42 USCS § 1396k(a)(1)(C)] or 402(a)(26)(C) or with respect to payments made in violation of section 1906 [42 USCS § 1396e].

(v) In determining the amount of erroneous excess payments, there shall not be included any erroneous payments made for ambulatory prenatal care provided during a presumptive eligibility period (as defined in section 1920(b)(1) [42 USCS § 1396r-1(b)(1)]) for items and services described in subsection (a) of section 1920A [42 USCS § 1396r-1a] provided to a child during a presumptive eligibility period under such section, for medical assistance provided to an individual described in subsection (a) of section 1920B [42 USCS § 1396r-1(b)] during a presumptive eligibility period under such section, [or] for medical assistance provided to an individual described in subsection (a) of section 1920C [42 USCS § 1396r-1c] during a presumptive eligibility period under such section, or for medical assistance provided to an individual during a presumptive eligibility period resulting from a determination of presumptive eligibility made by a hospital that elects under section 1902(a)(47)(B) [42 USCS § 1396a(a)(47)(B)] to be a qualified entity for such purpose.

(E) For purposes of subparagraph (D), there shall be excluded, in determining both erroneous excess payments for medical assistance and total expenditures for medical assistance—

(i) payments with respect to any individual whose eligibility therefor was determined exclusively by the Secretary under an agreement pursuant to section 1634 [42 USCS § 1383c] and such other classes of individuals as the Secretary may by regulation prescribe whose eligibility was determined in part under such an agreement; and

(ii) payments made as the result of a technical error.

(2) The State agency administering the plan approved under this title [42 USCS §§ 1396 et seq.] shall, at such times and in such form as the Secretary may specify, provide information on the rates of erroneous excess payments made (or expected, with respect to future periods specified by the Secretary) in connection with its administration of such plan, together with any other data he requests that are reasonably necessary for him to carry out the provisions of this subsection.

(3)(A) If a State fails to cooperate with the Secretary in providing information necessary to carry out this subsection, the Secretary, directly or through contractual or such other arrangements as he may find appropriate, shall establish the error rates for that State on the basis of the best data reasonably available to him and in accordance with such techniques for sampling and estimating as he finds appropriate.

(B) In any case in which it is necessary for the Secretary to exercise his authority under subparagraph (A) to determine a State's error rates for a fiscal year, the amount that would otherwise be payable to such State under this title [42 USCS §§ 1396 et seq.] for quarters in such year shall be reduced by the costs incurred by the Secretary in making (directly or otherwise) such determination.

(4) This subsection shall not apply with respect to Puerto Rico, Guam, the Virgin Islands, the Northern Mariana Islands, or American Samoa.

(v) Medical assistance to aliens not lawfully admitted for permanent residence. (1) Notwithstanding the preceding provisions of this section, except as provided in paragraphs (2) and (4), no payment may be made to a State under this section for medical assistance furnished to an alien who is not lawfully admitted for permanent residence or otherwise permanently residing in the United States under color of law.

(2) Payment shall be made under this section for care and services that are furnished to an alien described in paragraph (1) only if—

(A) such care and services are necessary for the treatment of an emergency medical condition of the alien,

(B) such alien otherwise meets the eligibility requirements for medical assistance under the State plan approved under this title [42 USCS §§ 1396 et seq.] (other than the requirement of the receipt of aid or assistance under title IV [42 USCS §§ 601 et seq.], supplemental security income benefits under title XVI [42 USCS §§ 1381 et seq.], or a State supplementary payment), and

(C) such care and services are not related to an organ transplant procedure.

(3) For purposes of this subsection, the term "emergency medical condition" means a medical condition (including emergency labor and delivery) manifesting itself by acute symptoms of sufficient severity (including severe pain) such that the absence of immediate medical attention could reasonably be expected to result in—

(A) placing the patient's health in serious jeopardy,

(B) serious impairment to bodily functions, or

(C) serious dysfunction of any bodily organ or part.

(4)(A) A State may elect (in a plan amendment under this title [42 USCS §§ 1396 et seq.]) to provide medical assistance under this title, notwithstanding sections 401(a), 402(b), 403, and 421 of the Personal Responsibility and Work Opportunity Reconciliation Act of 1996 [8 USCS §§ 1611(a), 1612(b), 1613, and 1631], to children and pregnant women who are lawfully residing in the United States (including battered individuals described in section 431(c) of such Act [8 USCS § 1641(c)]) and who are otherwise eligible for such assistance, within either or both of the following eligibility categories:

(i) Pregnant women. Women during pregnancy (and during the 60-day period beginning on the last day of the pregnancy).

(ii) Children. Individuals under 21 years of age, including optional targeted low-income children described in section 1905(u)(2)(B) [42 USCS § 1396d(u)(2)(B)].

(B) In the case of a State that has elected to provide medical assistance to a category of aliens under subparagraph (A), no debt shall accrue under an affidavit of support against any sponsor of such an alien on the basis of provision of assistance to such category and the cost of such assistance shall not be considered as an unreimbursed cost.

(C) As part of the State's ongoing eligibility redetermination requirements and procedures for an individual provided medical assistance as a result of an election by the State under subparagraph (A), a State shall verify that the individual continues to lawfully reside in the United States using the documentation presented to the State by the individual on initial enrollment. If the State cannot successfully verify that the individual is lawfully residing in the United States in this manner, it shall require that the individual provide the State with further documentation or other evidence to verify that the individual is lawfully residing in the United States.

(w) Prohibition on use of voluntary contributions, and limitation on the use of provider-specific taxes to obtain Federal financial participation under Medicaid. (1)(A) Notwithstanding the previous provisions of this section, for purposes of determining the amount to be paid to a State (as defined in paragraph (7)(D)) under subsection (a)(1) for quarters in any fiscal year, the total amount expended during such fiscal year as medical assistance under the State plan (as determined without regard to this subsection) shall be reduced by the sum of any revenues received by the State (or by a unit of local government in the State) during the fiscal year—

(i) from provider-related donations (as defined in paragraph (2)(A)), other than—

(I) bona fide provider-related donations (as defined in paragraph (2)(B)), and

(II) donations described in paragraph (2)(C);

(ii) from health care related taxes (as defined in paragraph (3)(A)), other than broad-based health care related taxes (as defined in paragraph (3)(B));

(iii) from a broad-based health care related tax, if there is in effect a hold harmless provision (described in paragraph (4)) with respect to the tax; or

(iv) only with respect to State fiscal years (or portions thereof) occurring on or after January 1, 1992, and before October 1, 1995, from broad-based health care related taxes to the extent the amount of such taxes collected exceeds the limit established under paragraph (5).

(B) Notwithstanding the previous provisions of this section, for purposes of determining the amount to be paid to a State under subsection (a)(7) for all quarters in a Federal fiscal year (beginning with fiscal year 1993), the total amount expended during the fiscal year for administrative expenditures under the State plan (as determined without regard to this subsection) shall be reduced by the sum of any revenues received by the State (or by a unit of local government in the State) during such quarters from donations described in paragraph (2)(C), to the extent the amount of such donations exceeds 10 percent of the amounts expended under the State plan under this title [42 USCS §§ 1396 et seq.] during the fiscal year for purposes described in paragraphs (2), (3), (4), (6), and (7) of subsection (a).

(C)(i) Except as otherwise provided in clause (ii), subparagraph (A)(i) shall apply to donations received on or after January 1, 1992.

(ii) Subject to the limits described in clause (iii) and subparagraph (E), subparagraph (A)(i) shall not apply to donations received before the effective date specified in subparagraph (F) if such donations are received under programs in effect or as described in State plan amendments or related documents submitted to the Secretary by September 30, 1991, and applicable to State fiscal year 1992, as demonstrated by State plan amendments, written agreements, State budget documentation, or other documentary evidence in existence on that date.

(iii) In applying clause (ii) in the case of donations received in State fiscal year 1993, the maximum amount of such donations to which such clause may be applied may not exceed the total amount of such donations received in the corresponding period in State fiscal year 1992 (or not later than 5 days after the last day of the corresponding period).

(D)(i) Except as otherwise provided in clause (ii), subparagraphs (A)(ii) and (A)(iii) shall apply to taxes received on or after January 1, 1992.

(ii) Subparagraphs (A)(ii) and (A)(iii) shall not apply to impermissible taxes (as defined in clause (iii)) received before the effective date specified in subparagraph (F) to the extent the taxes (including the tax rate or base) were in effect, or the legislation or regulations imposing such taxes were enacted or adopted, as of November 22, 1991.

(iii) In this subparagraph and subparagraph (E), the term "impermissible tax" means a health care related tax for which a reduction may be made under clause (ii) or (iii) of subparagraph (A).

(E)(i) In no case may the total amount of donations and taxes permitted under the exception provided in subparagraphs (C)(ii) and (D)(ii) for the portion of State fiscal year 1992 occurring during calendar year 1992 exceed the limit under paragraph (5) minus the total amount of broad-based health care related taxes received in the portion of that fiscal year.

(ii) In no case may the total amount of donations and taxes permitted under the exception provided in subparagraphs (C)(ii) and (D)(ii) for State fiscal year 1993 exceed the limit under paragraph (5) minus the total amount of broad-based health care related taxes received in that fiscal year.

(F) In this paragraph in the case of a State—

(i) except as provided in clause (iii), with a State fiscal year beginning on or before July 1, the effective date is October 1, 1992,

(ii) except as provided in clause (iii), with a State fiscal year that begins after July 1, the effective date is January 1, 1993, or

(iii) with a State legislature which is not scheduled to have a regular legislative session in 1992, with a State legislature which is not scheduled to have a regular legislative session in 1993, or with a provider-specific tax enacted on November 4, 1991, the effective date is July 1, 1993.

(2)(A) In this subsection (except as provided in paragraph (6)), the term "provider-related donation" means any donation or other voluntary payment (whether in cash or in kind) made (directly or indirectly) to a State or unit of local government by—

(i) a health care provider (as defined in paragraph (7)(B)),

(ii) an entity related to a health care provider (as defined in paragraph (7)(C)), or

(iii) an entity providing goods or services under the State plan for which payment is made to the State under paragraph (2), (3), (4), (6), or (7) of subsection (a).

(B) For purposes of paragraph (1)(A)(i)(I), the term "bona fide provider-related donation" means a provider-related donation that has no direct or indirect relationship (as determined by the Secretary) to payments made under this title [42 USCS §§ 1396 et seq.] to that provider, to providers furnishing the same class of items and services as that provider, or to any related entity, as established by the State to the satisfaction of the Secretary. The Secretary may by regulation specify types of provider-related donations described in the previous sentence that will be considered to be bona fide provider-related donations.

(C) For purposes of paragraph (1)(A)(i)(II), donations described in this subparagraph are funds expended by a hospital, clinic, or similar entity for the direct cost (including costs of training and of preparing and distributing outreach materials) of State or local agency personnel who are stationed at the hospital, clinic, or entity to determine the eligibility of individuals for medical assistance under this title [42 USCS §§ 1396 et seq.] and to provide outreach services to eligible or potentially eligible individuals.

(3)(A) In this subsection (except as provided in paragraph (6)), the term "health care related tax" means a tax (as defined in paragraph (7)(F)) that—

(i) is related to health care items or services, or to the provision of, the authority to provide, or payment for, such items or services, or

(ii) is not limited to such items or services but provides for treatment of individuals or entities that are providing or paying for such items or services that is different from the treatment provided to other individuals or entities.

In applying clause (i), a tax is considered to relate to health care items or services if at least 85 percent of the burden of such tax falls on health care providers.

(B) In this subsection, the term "broad-based health care related tax" means a health care related tax which is imposed with respect to a class of health care items or services (as described in paragraph (7)(A)) or with respect to providers of such items or services and which, except as provided in subparagraphs (D), (E), and (F)—

(i) is imposed at least with respect to all items or services in the class furnished by all non-Federal, nonpublic providers in the State (or, in the case of a tax imposed by a unit of local government, the area over which the unit has jurisdiction) or is imposed with respect to all non-Federal, nonpublic providers in the class; and

(ii) is imposed uniformly (in accordance with subparagraph (C)).

(C)(i) Subject to clause (ii), for purposes of subparagraph (B)(ii), a tax is considered to be imposed uniformly if—

(I) in the case of a tax consisting of a licensing fee or similar tax on a class of health care items or services (or providers of such items or services), the amount of the tax imposed is the same for every provider providing items or services within the class;

(II) in the case of a tax consisting of a licensing fee or similar tax imposed on a class of health care items or services (or providers of such services) on the basis of the number of beds (licensed or otherwise) of the provider, the amount of the tax is the same for each bed of each provider of such items or services in the class;

(III) in the case of a tax based on revenues or receipts with respect to a class of items or services (or providers of items or services) the tax is imposed at a uniform rate for all items and services (or providers of such items or services) in the class on all the gross revenues or receipts, or net operating revenues, relating to the provision of all such items or services (or all such providers) in the State (or, in the case of a tax imposed by a unit of local government within the State, in the area over which the unit has jurisdiction); or

(IV) in the case of any other tax, the State establishes to the satisfaction of the Secretary that the tax is imposed uniformly.

(ii) Subject to subparagraphs (D) and (E), a tax imposed with respect to a class of health care items and services is not considered to be imposed uniformly if the tax provides for any credits, exclusions, or deductions which have as their purpose or effect the return to providers of all or a portion of the tax paid in a manner that is inconsistent with subclauses (I) and (II) of subparagraph (E)(ii) or provides for a hold harmless provision described in paragraph (4).

(D) A tax imposed with respect to a class of health care items and services is considered to be imposed uniformly—

(i) notwithstanding that the tax is not imposed with respect to items or services (or the providers thereof) for which payment is made under a State plan under this title or title XVIII [42 USCS §§ 1396 et seq. or 1395 et seq.], or

(ii) in the case of a tax described in subparagraph (C)(i)(III), notwithstanding that the tax provides for exclusion (in whole or in part) of revenues or receipts from a State plan under this title or title XVIII [42 USCS §§ 1396 et seq. or 1395 et seq.].

(E)(i) A State may submit an application to the Secretary requesting that the Secretary treat a tax as a broad-based health care related tax, notwithstanding that the tax does not apply to all health care items or services in class (or all providers of such items and services), provides for a credit, deduction, or exclusion, is not applied uniformly, or otherwise does not meet the requirements of subparagraph (B) or (C). Permissible waivers may include exemptions for rural or sole-community providers.

(ii) The Secretary shall approve such an application if the State establishes to the satisfaction of the Secretary that—

(I) the net impact of the tax and associated expenditures under this title [42 USCS

§§ 1396 et seq.] as proposed by the State is generally redistributive in nature, and

(II) the amount of the tax is not directly correlated to payments under this title [42 USCS §§ 1396 et seq.] for items or services with respect to which the tax is imposed.

The Secretary shall by regulation specify types of credits, exclusions, and deductions that will be considered to meet the requirements of this subparagraph.

(F) In no case shall a tax not qualify as a broad-based health care related tax under this paragraph because it does not apply to a hospital that is described in section 501(c)(3) of the Internal Revenue Code of 1986 [26 USCS § 501(c)(3)] and exempt from taxation under section 501(a) of such Code [26 USCS § 501(a)] and that does not accept payment under the State plan under this title [42 USCS §§ 1396 et seq.] or under title XVIII [42 USCS §§ 1395 et seq.].

(4) For purposes of paragraph (1)(A)(iii), there is in effect a hold harmless provision with respect to a broad-based health care related tax imposed with respect to a class of items or services if the Secretary determines that any of the following applies:

(A) The State or other unit of government imposing the tax provides (directly or indirectly) for a payment (other than under this title [42 USCS §§ 1396 et seq.]) to taxpayers and the amount of such payment is positively correlated either to the amount of such tax or to the difference between the amount of the tax and the amount of payment under the State plan.

(B) All or any portion of the payment made under this title [42 USCS §§ 1396 et seq.] to the taxpayer varies based only upon the amount of the total tax paid.

(C)(i) The State or other unit of government imposing the tax provides (directly or indirectly) for any payment, offset, or waiver that guarantees to hold taxpayers harmless for any portion of the costs of the tax.

(ii) For purposes of clause (i), a determination of the existence of an indirect guarantee shall be made under paragraph (3)(i) of section 433.68(f) of title 42, Code of Federal Regulations, as in effect on November 1, 2006, except that for portions of fiscal years beginning on or after January 1, 2008, and before October 1, 2011, "5.5 percent" shall be substituted for "6 percent" each place it appears.

The provisions of this paragraph shall not prevent use of the tax to reimburse health care providers in a class for expenditures under this title [42 USCS §§ 1396 et seq.] nor preclude States from relying on such reimbursement to justify or explain the tax in the legislative process.

(5)(A) For purposes of this subsection, the limit under this subparagraph with respect to a State is an amount equal to 25 percent (or, if greater, the State base percentage, as defined in subparagraph (B)) of the non-Federal share of the total amount expended under the State plan during a State fiscal year (or portion thereof), as it would be determined pursuant to paragraph (1)(A) without regard to paragraph (1)(A)(iv).

(B)(i) In subparagraph (A), the term "State base percentage" means, with respect to a State, an amount (expressed as a percentage) equal to—

(I) the total of the amount of health care related taxes (whether or not broad-based) and the amount of provider-related donations (whether or not bona fide) projected to be collected (in accordance with clause (ii)) during State fiscal year 1992, divided by

(II) the non-Federal share of the total amount estimated to be expended under the State plan during such State fiscal year.

(ii) For purposes of clause (i)(I), in the case of a tax that is not in effect throughout State fiscal year 1992 or the rate (or base) of which is increased during such fiscal year, the Secretary shall project the amount to be collected during such fiscal year as if the tax (or increase) were in effect during the entire State fiscal year.

(C)(i) The total amount of health care related taxes under subparagraph (B)(i)(I) shall be determined by the Secretary based on only those taxes (including the tax rate or base) which were in effect, or for which legislation or regulations imposing such taxes were enacted or adopted, as of November 22, 1991.

(ii) The amount of provider-related donations under subparagraph (B)(i)(I) shall be determined by the Secretary based on programs in effect on September 30, 1991, and applicable to State fiscal year 1992, as demonstrated by State plan amendments, written agreements, State budget documentation, or other documentary evidence in existence on that date.

(iii) The amount of expenditures described in subparagraph (B)(i)(II) shall be determined by the Secretary based on the best data available as of the date of the enactment of this subsection.

(6)(A) Notwithstanding the provisions of this subsection, the Secretary may not restrict States' use of funds where such funds are derived from State or local taxes (or funds appropriated to State university teaching hospitals) transferred from or certified by units of government within a State as the non-Federal share of expenditures under this title [42 USCS §§ 1396 et seq.], regardless of whether the unit of government is also a health care provider, except as provided in section 1902(a)(2) [42 USCS § 1396a(a)(2)], unless the transferred funds are derived by the unit of government from donations or taxes that would not otherwise be recognized as the non-Federal share under this section.

(B) For purposes of this subsection, funds the use of which the Secretary may not restrict under subparagraph (A) shall not be considered to be a provider-related donation or a health care related tax.

(7) For purposes of this subsection:

(A) Each of the following shall be considered a separate class of health care items and services:

(i) Inpatient hospital services.

(ii) Outpatient hospital services.

(iii) Nursing facility services (other than services of intermediate care facilities for the mentally retarded).

(iv) Services of intermediate care facilities for the mentally retarded.

(v) Physicians' services.

(vi) Home health care services.

(vii) Outpatient prescription drugs.

(viii) Services of managed care organizations (including health maintenance organizations, preferred provider organizations, and such other similar organizations as the Secretary may specify by regulation).

(ix) Such other classification of health care items and services consistent with this subparagraph as the Secretary may establish by regulation.

(B) The term "health care provider" means an individual or person that receives payments for the provision of health care items or services.

(C) An entity is considered to be "related" to a health care provider if the entity—

(i) is an organization, association, corporation or partnership formed by or on behalf of health care providers;

(ii) is a person with an ownership or control interest (as defined in section 1124(a)(3) [42 USCS § 1320a-3(a)(3)]) in the provider;

(iii) is the employee, spouse, parent, child, or sibling of the provider (or of a person described in clause (ii)); or

(iv) has a similar, close relationship (as defined in regulations) to the provider.

(D) The term "State" means only the 50 States and the District of Columbia but does not include any State whose entire program under this title [42 USCS §§ 1396 et seq.] is operated under a waiver granted under section 1115 [42 USCS § 1315].

(E) The "State fiscal year" means, with respect to a specified year, a State fiscal year ending in that specified year.

(F) The term "tax" includes any licensing fee, assessment, or other mandatory payment, but does not include payment of a criminal or civil fine or penalty (other than a fine or penalty imposed in lieu of or instead of a fee, assessment, or other mandatory payment).

(G) The term "unit of local government" means, with respect to a State, a city, county, special purpose district, or other governmental unit in the State.

(x)(1) For purposes of section 1902(a)(46)(B)(i) [42 USCS § 1396a(a)(46)(B)(i)], the requirement of this subsection is, with respect to an individual declaring to be a citizen or national of the United States, that, subject to paragraph (2), there is presented satisfactory documentary evidence of citizenship or nationality (as defined in paragraph (3)) of the individual.

(2) The requirement of paragraph (1) shall not apply to an individual declaring to be a citizen or national of the United States who is eligible for medical assistance under this title [42 USCS §§ 1396 et seq.]—

(A) and is entitled to or enrolled for benefits under any part of title XVIII [42 USCS §§ 1395 et seq.];

(B) and is receiving—

(i) disability insurance benefits under section 223 [42 USCS § 423] or monthly insurance benefits under section 202 [42 USCS § 402] based on such individual's disability (as defined in section 223(d) [42 USCS § 423(d)]); or

(ii) supplemental security income benefits under title XVI [42 USCS §§ 1381 et seq.];

(C) and with respect to whom—

(i) child welfare services are made available under part B of title IV [42 USCS §§ 621 et seq.] on the basis of being a child in foster care; or

(ii) adoption or foster care assistance is made available under part E of title IV [42 USCS §§ 670 et seq.];

(D) pursuant to the application of section 1902(e)(4) [42 USCS § 1396a(e)(4)] (and, in the case of an individual who is eligible for medical assistance on such basis, the individual shall be deemed to have provided satisfactory documentary evidence of citizenship or nationality and shall not be required to provide further documentary evidence on any date that occurs during or after the period in which the individual is eligible for medical assistance on such basis); or

(E) on such basis as the Secretary may specify under which satisfactory documentary evidence of citizenship or nationality has been previously presented.

(3)(A) For purposes of this subsection, the term "satisfactory documentary evidence of citizenship or nationality" means—

(i) any document described in subparagraph (B); or

(ii) a document described in subparagraph (C) and a document described in subparagraph (D).

(B) The following are documents described in this subparagraph:

(i) A United States passport.

(ii) Form N-550 or N-570 (Certificate of Naturalization).

(iii) Form N-560 or N-561 (Certificate of United States Citizenship).

(iv) A valid State-issued driver's license or other identity document described in section 274A(b)(1)(D) of the Immigration and Nationality Act [8 USCS § 1324a(b)(1)(D)], but only if the State issuing the license or such document requires proof of United States citizenship before issuance of such license or document or obtains a social security number from the applicant and verifies before certification that such number is valid and assigned to the applicant who is a citizen.

(v)(I) Except as provided in subclause (II), a document issued by a federally recognized Indian tribe evidencing membership or enrollment in, or affiliation with, such tribe (such as a tribal enrollment card or certificate of degree of Indian blood).

(II) With respect to those federally recognized Indian tribes located within States having an international border whose membership includes individuals who are not citizens of the United States, the Secretary shall, after consulting with such tribes, issue regulations authorizing the presentation of such other forms of documentation (including tribal documentation, if appropriate) that the Secretary determines to be satisfactory documentary evidence of citizenship or nationality for purposes of satisfying the requirement of this subsection.

(vi) Such other document as the Secretary may specify, by regulation, that provides proof of United States citizenship or nationality and that provides a reliable means of documentation of personal identity.

(C) The following are documents described in this subparagraph:

(i) A certificate of birth in the United States.

(ii) Form FS-545 or Form DS-1350 (Certification of Birth Abroad).

(iii) Form I-197 (United States Citizen Identification Card).

(iv) Form FS-240 (Report of Birth Abroad of a Citizen of the United States).

(v) Such other document (not described in subparagraph (B)(iv)) as the Secretary may specify that provides proof of United States citizenship or nationality.

(D) The following are documents described in this subparagraph:

(i) Any identity document described in section 274A(b)(1)(D) of the Immigration and Nationality Act [8 USCS § 1324a(b)(1)(D)].

(ii) Any other documentation of personal identity of such other type as the Secretary finds, by regulation, provides a reliable means of identification.

(E) A reference in this paragraph to a form includes a reference to any successor form.

(4) In the case of an individual declaring to be a citizen or national of the United States with respect to whom a State requires the presentation of satisfactory documentary evidence of citizenship or nationality under section 1902(a)(46)(B)(i) [42 USCS § 1396a(a)(46)(B)(i)], the individual shall be provided at least the reasonable opportunity to present satisfactory documentary evidence of citizenship or nationality under this subsection as is provided under clauses (i) and (ii) of section 1137(d)(4)(A) [42 USCS § 1320b-7(d)(4)(A)] to an individual for the submittal to the State of evidence indicating a satisfactory immigration status.

(5) Nothing in subparagraph (A) or (B) of section 1902(a)(46) [42 USCS § 1396a(a)(46)], the preceding paragraphs of this subsection, or the Deficit Reduction Act of 2005, including section 6036 of such Act, shall be construed as changing the requirement of section 1902(e)(4) [42 USCS § 1396a(e)(4)] that a child born in the United States to an alien mother for whom medical assistance for the delivery of such child is available as treatment of an emergency medical condition pursuant to subsection (v) shall be deemed eligible for medical assistance during the first year of such child's life.

(y) Payments for establishment of alternate non-emergency services providers. (1) Payments. In addition to the payments otherwise provided under subsection (a), subject to paragraph (2), the Secretary shall provide for payments to States under such subsection for the establishment of alternate non-emergency service providers (as defined in section 1916A(e)(5)(B) [42 USCS § 1396o-1(e)(5)(B)]), or networks of such providers.

(2) Limitation. The total amount of payments under this subsection shall not exceed $50,000,000 during the 4-year period beginning with 2006. This subsection constitutes budget authority in advance of appropriations Acts and represents the obligation of the Secretary to provide for the payment of amounts provided under this subsection.

(3) Preference. In providing for payments to States under this subsection, the Secretary shall provide preference to States that establish, or provide for, alternate non-emergency services providers or networks of such providers that—

(A) serve rural or underserved areas where beneficiaries under this title [42 USCS §§ 1396 et seq.] may not have regular access to providers of primary care services; or

(B) are in partnership with local community hospitals.

(4) Form and manner of payment. Payment to a State under this subsection shall be made only upon the filing of such application in such form and in such manner as the Secretary shall specify. Payment to a State under this subsection shall be made in the same manner as other payments under section 1903(a) [42 USCS § 1396b(a)].

(z) Medicaid transformation payments. (1) In general. In addition to the payments provided under subsection (a), subject to paragraph (4), the Secretary shall provide for payments to States for the adoption of innovative methods to improve the effectiveness and efficiency in providing medical assistance under this title [42 USCS §§ 1396 et seq.].

(2) Permissible uses of funds. The following are examples of innovative methods for which funds provided under this subsection may be used:

(A) Methods for reducing patient error rates through the implementation and use of electronic health records, electronic clinical decision support tools, or e-prescribing programs.

(B) Methods for improving rates of collection from estates of amounts owed under this title [42 USCS §§ 1396 et seq.].

(C) Methods for reducing waste, fraud, and abuse under the program under this title [42 USCS §§ 1396 et seq.], such as reducing improper payment rates as measured by annual payment error rate measurement (PERM) project rates.

(D) Implementation of a medication risk management program as part of a drug use review program under section 1927(g) [42 USCS § 1396r-8(g)].

(E) Methods in reducing, in clinically appropriate ways, expenditures under this title [42 USCS §§ 1396 et seq.] for covered outpatient drugs, particularly in the categories of greatest drug utilization, by increasing the utilization of generic drugs through the use of education programs and other incentives to promote greater use of generic drugs.

(F) Methods for improving access to primary and specialty physician care for the uninsured using integrated university-based hospital and clinic systems.

(3) Application; terms and conditions. (A) In general. No payments shall be made to a State under this subsection unless the State applies to the Secretary for such payments in a form, manner, and time specified by the Secretary.

(B) Terms and conditions. Such payments are made under such terms and conditions consistent with this subsection as the Secretary prescribes.

(C) Annual report. Payment to a State under this subsection is conditioned on the State submitting to the Secretary an annual report on the programs supported by such payment. Such report shall include information on—

(i) the specific uses of such payment;

(ii) an assessment of quality improvements and clinical outcomes under such programs; and

(iii) estimates of cost savings resulting from such programs.

(4) Funding. (A) Limitation on funds. The total amount of payments under this subsection shall be equal to, and shall not exceed—

(i) $75,000,000 for fiscal year 2007; and

(ii) $75,000,000 for fiscal year 2008.

This subsection constitutes budget authority in advance of appropriations Acts and represents the obligation of the Secretary to provide for the payment of amounts provided under this subsection.

(B) Allocation of funds. The Secretary shall specify a method for allocating the funds made available under this subsection among States. Such method shall provide preference for States that design programs that target health providers that treat significant numbers of Medicaid beneficiaries. Such method shall provide that not less than 25 percent of such funds shall be allocated among States the population of which (as determined according to data collected by the United States Census Bureau) as of July 1, 2004, was more than 105 percent of the population of the respective State (as so determined) as of April 1, 2000.

(C) Form and manner of payment. Payment

to a State under this subsection shall be made in the same manner as other payments under section 1903(a) [subsec. (a) of this section]. There is no requirement for State matching funds to receive payments under this subsection.

(5) Medication risk management program. (A) In general. For purposes of this subsection, the term "medication risk management program" means a program for targeted beneficiaries that ensures that covered outpatient drugs are appropriately used to optimize therapeutic outcomes through improved medication use and to reduce the risk of adverse events.

(B) Elements. Such program may include the following elements:

(i) The use of established principles and standards for drug utilization review and best practices to analyze prescription drug claims of targeted beneficiaries and identify outlier physicians.

(ii) On an ongoing basis provide outlier physicians—

(I) a comprehensive pharmacy claims history for each targeted beneficiary under their care;

(II) information regarding the frequency and cost of relapses and hospitalizations of targeted beneficiaries under the physician's care; and

(III) applicable best practice guidelines and empirical references.

(iii) Monitor outlier physician's prescribing, such as failure to refill, dosage strengths, and provide incentives and information to encourage the adoption of best clinical practices.

(C) Targeted beneficiaries. For purposes of this paragraph, the term "targeted beneficiaries" means Medicaid eligible beneficiaries who are identified as having high prescription drug costs and medical costs, such as individuals with behavioral disorders or multiple chronic diseases who are taking multiple medications.

(Aug. 14, 1935, ch 531, Title XIX, § 1903, as added July 30, 1965, P. L. 89-97, Title I, Part 2, § 121(a), 79 Stat. 349; Jan. 2, 1968, P. L. 90-248, Title II, Part 2, §§ 220(a), 222(c), (d), 225(a), 229(c), Part 3, § 241(f)(5), 81 Stat. 898, 901, 902, 904, 917; June 28, 1968, P. L. 90-364, Title III, § 303(a)(1), 82 Stat. 274; Aug. 9, 1969, P. L. 91-56, § 2(a), 83 Stat. 99; Oct. 30, 1972, P. L. 92-603, Title II, §§ 207(a), 221(c)(6), 224(c), 225, 226(e), 229(c), 230, 233(c), 235(a), 237(a)(1), 249B, 278(b)(1), (5), (7), (16), 290, 295, 299E(a), 86 Stat. 1379, 1380, 1389, 1395, 1396, 1404, 1410, 1411, 1414, 1415, 1428, 1453, 1454, 1457, 1459, 1462; July 9, 1973, P. L. 93-66, Title II, Part D, § 234(a), 87 Stat. 160; Dec. 31, 1973, P. L. 93-233, §§ 13(a)(11), (12), 18(r)–(v), (x)(5), (6), (y)(1), 87 Stat. 963, 971–973; Dec. 31, 1975, P. L. 94-182, Title I, §§ 110(a), 111(b), 89 Stat. 1054; Oct. 8, 1976, P. L. 94-460, Title II, § 202(a), 90 Stat. 1957; Oct. 18, 1976, P. L. 94-552, § 1, 90 Stat. 2540; Aug. 1, 1977, P. L. 95-83, Title I, § 105(a)(1), (2), 91 Stat. 384; Oct. 25, 1977, P. L. 95-142, §§ 3(c)(2), 8(c), 10(a), 11(a), 17(a)–(c), 20(a), 91 Stat. 1179, 1195, 1196, 1201, 1205; Nov. 1, 1978, P. L. 95-559, § 14(c), 92 Stat. 2141; Nov. 10, 1978, P. L. 95-626, Title I, Part A, § 102(b)(3), 92 Stat. 3551; Oct. 4, 1979, P. L. 96-79, Title I, § 128, 93 Stat. 629; Oct. 7, 1980, P. L. 96-398, Title IX, § 901, 94 Stat. 1609; Dec. 5, 1980, P. L. 96-499, Title IX, Part A, Subpart I, § 905(b), (c), Part C, §§ 961(a), 963, 964, 94 Stat. 2618, 2650, 2651; Aug. 13, 1981, P. L. 97-35, Title XXI, Subtitle A, ch 1, §§ 2101(a)(2), 2103(b)(1), ch 2, § 2106(b)(3), ch 3, § 2113(n), Subtitle C, ch 1, §§ 2161(a), (b), 2163, 2164(a), ch 2, §§ 2174(b), 2178(a), ch 3, § 2183(a), 95 Stat. 786, 788, 792, 795, 803, 806, 809, 813, 816; Sept 3, 1982, P. L. 97-248, Title I, Subtitle B, §§ 133(a), 137(a)(1), (2), (b)(11)–(16), 27, (g), Subtitle C, § 146(b), 96 Stat. 373, 376, 378, 379, 381, 394; Jan. 12, 1983, P. L. 97-448, Title III, § 309(b)(16), 96 Stat. 2409; July 18, 1984, P. L. 98-369, Division B, Title III, Subtitle A, Part I, §§ 2303(g)(2), Subtitle B, §§ 2363(a)(2), (4), (b), 2364(1), (2), 2373(b)(11)–(14), 98 Stat. 1066, 1106, 1107, 1111, 1112; Nov. 8, 1984, P. L. 98-617, § 3(a)(6), 98 Stat. 3295; April 7, 1986, P. L. 99-272, Title IX, Subtitle B, §§ 9503(b), (f), 9507(a), 9512(a), 9517(a), (c)(1), 9518(a), 100 Stat. 206, 207, 210, 212, 215, 216; Oct. 21, 1986, P. L. 99-509, Title IX, Subtitle E, Part 1, §§ 9401(e)(2), 9403(g)(2), 9406(a), (b), 9407(c), Part 4, §§ 9431(b)(2), 9434(a)(1), (2), (b), 100 Stat. 2051, 2054, 2057, 2059, 2065, 2067, 2068; Oct. 22, 1986, P. L. 99-514, Title XVIII, Subtitle C, Ch. 1, § 1895(c)(2), 100 Stat. 2935; Nov. 6, 1986, P. L. 99-603, Title I, Part C, § 121(b)(2), 100 Stat. 3390; Aug. 18, 1987, P. L. 100-93, § 8(g), (h)(1), 101 Stat. 694; Dec. 22, 1987, P. L. 100-203, Title IV, Subtitle B, Part 1, §§ 4112(b), 4113(a)(1)(B), (b)(3), 4118(d)(1)(e)(11)(h), (l), (p)(5), Subtitle C, Part 2, §§ 4211(d)(1), (g), (i), 4212(c)(1), (2), (d)(1), (e)(2), 4213(b), 101 Stat. 1330-148, 1330-150, 1330-151, 1330-152, 1330-155, 1330-156, 1330-159, 1330-204, 1330-205, 1330-207, 1330-212, 1330-213, 1330-219; July 1, 1988, P. L. 100-360, Title II, Subtitle A, § 202(h)(2), Title III, §§ 301(f), 302(c)(3), (e)(4), Title IV, Subtitle B, § 411(a)(3)(B)(iii), (k)(6)(B)(x), (7)(A), (D), (10)(D), (12)(A), (13)(A), 102 Stat. 718, 750, 752, 753, 794, 796-798; Oct. 13, 1988, P. L. 100-485, Title VI, § 608(d)(26)(K)(ii), (f)(4), 102 Stat. 2422, 2424;

Dec. 13, 1989, P. L. 101-234, Title II, § 201(a)(1), 103 Stat. 1981; Dec. 19, 1989, P. L. 101-239, Title VI, Subtitle B, Part 1, § 6401(b), Part 2, § 6411(d)(2), Subtitle F, § 6901(b)(5)(A), 103 Stat. 2259, 2271, 2299; Nov. 5, 1990, P. L. 101-508, Title IV, Subtitle B, Part 1, §§ 4401(a)(1), (b)(1), 4402(b), (d)(3), Part 3, § 4601(a)(3)(A), Part 4, Subpart A, §§ 4701(b)(2), 4704(b)(1), (2), Subpart B, §§ 4711(c)(2), 4723(a), Subpart C, §§ 4731(a), (b)(2), 4732(a), (b)(2)–(d), Subpart E, §§ 4751(b)(1), 4752(a)(2), (b)(1), (e), Part 5, § 4801(a)(8), (e)(16)(A), 104 Stat. 1388-143, 1388-159, 1388-163, 1388-164, 1388-166, 1388-170, 1388-172, 1388-187, 1388-194, 1388-195, 1388-205, 1388-206, 1388-207, 1388-211, 1388-218; Oct. 7, 1991, P. L. 102-119, § 26(i)(1), 105 Stat. 607; Dec. 12, 1991, P. L. 102-234, §§ 2(a), (b)(2), 3(b)(2)(B), 4(a), 105 Stat. 1793, 1799, 1803, 1804; Aug. 10, 1993, P. L. 103-66, Title XIII, Ch. 2, Subch B, Part I, §§ 13602(b), 13604(a), Part III, §§ 13622(a)(2), 13624(a), Part IV, § 13631(c), (h)(1), 107 Stat. 619, 621, 632, 636, 643, 645; Aug. 22, 1996, P. L. 104-193, Title I, § 114(d)(2), 110 Stat. 2180; Oct. 9, 1996, P. L. 104-248, § 1(b)(1), 110 Stat. 3148; April 30, 1997, P. L. 105-12, § 9(b)(1), 111 Stat. 26; Aug. 5, 1997, P. L. 105-33, Title IV, Subtitle H, Ch. 1, §§ 4701(b)(1), (2)(A)(v)–(viii), (B), (C), (c), (d)(2), 4702(b)(1), 4703(a), (b)(1), 4705(b), 4706, 4707(b), 4708(a), (d), 4712(b)(2), (c)(2), Ch. 3, §§ 4722(a), (b), 4724(a), (b)(1), Ch. 5, § 4742(a), Ch. 6, § 4753(a), Subtitle I, § 4802(b)(2), Subtitle J, Ch. 2, § 4912(b)(2), 111 Stat. 492, 493, 495, 500, 501, 505, 506, 509, 514, 516, 523, 525, 549, 573; Nov. 19, 1997, P. L. 105-100, Title I, § 162(4), 111 Stat. 2189; May 21, 1999, P. L. 106-31, Title III, Ch. 11, § 3031(a), (b), 113 Stat. 103; Nov. 29, 1999, P. L. 106-113, Div B, § 1000(a)(6), 113 Stat. 1536; Dec. 17, 1999, P. L. 106-170, Title II, § 201(a)(4), (b), Title IV, § 407(a)–(c), 113 Stat. 1893, 1913; Oct. 24, 2000, P. L. 106-354, § 2(b)(2)(B), 114 Stat. 1383; Dec. 21, 2000, P. L. 106-554, § 1(a)(6), 114 Stat. 2763; Oct. 22, 2004, P. L. 108-357, Title VII, § 712(b), 118 Stat. 1559; Dec. 3, 2004, P. L. 108-446, Title III, § 305(j)(1), 118 Stat. 2806; Oct. 20, 2005, P. L. 109-91, Title I, § 104(b), 119 Stat. 2092; Feb. 8, 2006, P. L. 109-171, Title VI, Subtitle A, Ch. 1, § 6002(b), Ch. 3, §§ 6033(a), 6036(a), Ch. 4, § 6043(b), Ch. 5, § 6051(a), Ch. 6, Subch. A, § 6062(c)(1), Subch. C, § 6081, 120 Stat. 59, 74, 80, 88, 92, 98, 111; Dec. 20, 2006, P. L. 109-432, Div B, Title IV, §§ 403, 405(c)(1)(A), 120 Stat. 2994, 2998; May 25, 2007, P. L. 110-28, Title VII, § 7002(b)(1), 121 Stat. 187; June 30, 2008, P. L. 110-252, Title VII, § 7001(d)(3), 122 Stat. 2394; Oct. 8, 2008, P. L. 110-379, § 3(a), 122 Stat. 4075; Feb. 4, 2009, P. L. 111-3, Title II, Subtitle A, § 201(b)(2)(A), Subtitle B, §§ 211(a)(1)(B), (3), (b)(1)–(3)(A), (4), 214(a), Title IV, § 401(b), 123 Stat. 39, 52, 54, 56, 82; Feb. 17, 2009, P. L. 111-5, Div B, Title IV, Subtitle B, § 4201(a), 123 Stat. 489; March 23, 2010, P. L. 111-148, Title II, Subtitle A, §§ 2001(a)(2)(B), (5)(D), (e)(2)(B), 2004(c)(1), Subtitle B, § 2102(a)(8), Subtitle C, § 2202(b), Subtitle D, § 2303(a)(4)(B), (b)(2)(B), Subtitle E, 2402(d)(2)(A), Subtitle F, § 2501(c)(1), Title VI, Subtitle E, § 6402(c), (h)(2), Subtitle F, §§ 6504(a), (b)(1), 6506(a)(1), 6507, 124 Stat. 272, 275, 279, 283, 288, 291, 294, 296, 303, 308, 757, 760, 776, 777, 778; April 15, 2010, P. L. 111-157, § 5(a)(2), 124 Stat. 1117.)

HISTORY; ANCILLARY LAWS AND DIRECTIVES

Prospective amendments:

Effective date of amendments made by § 2102(a) of Act March 23, 2010. Act March 23, 2010, P. L. 111-148, Title II, Subtitle B, § 2102(a), 124 Stat. 288, provides that the amendments made by such section [for full classification, consult USCS Tables volumes] are effective as if included in the enactment of the Children's Health Insurance Program Reauthorization Act of 2009 (Public Law 111-3) (in this section referred to as "CHIPRA")

Application of amendment made by § 6504(b) of Act March 23, 2010. Act March 23, 2010, P. L. 111-148, Title VI, Subtitle F, § 6504(b)(2), 124 Stat. 777, provides: "The amendment made by paragraph (1) [amending subsec. (m)(2)(A)(xi) of this section] shall apply with respect to contract years beginning on or after January 1, 2010.".

Effective date and application of amendments made by § 6506(a) of Act March 23, 2010. Act March 23, 2010, P. L. 111-148, Title VI, Subtitle F, § 6506(a)(2), 124 Stat. 777, provides: "The amendments made by this subsection [amending subsec. (d)(2) of this section] take effect on the date of enactment of this Act and apply to overpayments discovered on or after that date.".

Regulations. Act March 23, 2010, P. L. 111-148, Title VI, Subtitle F, § 6506(b), 124 Stat. 777 (effective on 1/1/2011, as provided by § 6508 of such Act, which appears as 42 USCS § 1395a note), provides: "The Secretary shall promulgate regulations that require States to correct Federally identified claims overpayments, of an ongoing or recurring nature, with new Medicaid Management Information System (MMIS) edits, audits, or other appropriate corrective action.".

§ 1396b-1. Payment adjustment for health care-acquired conditions

(a) In general. The Secretary of Health and Human Services (in this subsection referred to as the "Secretary") shall identify current State practices that prohibit payment for health care-acquired conditions and shall incorporate the practices identified, or elements of such practices, which the Secretary determines appropriate for application to the Medicaid program in regulations. Such regulations shall be effective as of July 1, 2011, and shall prohibit payments to States under section 1903 of the Social Security Act [42 USCS § 1396b] for any amounts expended for providing medical assistance for health care-acquired conditions specified in the regulations. The regulations shall ensure that the prohibition on payment for health care-acquired conditions shall not result in a loss of access to care or services for Medicaid beneficiaries.

(b) Health care-acquired condition. In this section. the term "health care-acquired condition" means a medical condition for which an individual was diagnosed that could be identified by a secondary diagnostic code described in section 1886(d)(4)(D)(iv) of the Social Security Act (42 U.S.C. 1395ww(d)(4)(D)(iv)).

(c) Medicare provisions. In carrying out this section, the Secretary shall apply to State plans (or waivers) under title XIX of the Social Security Act [42 USCS §§ 1396 et seq.] the regulations promulgated pursuant to section 1886(d)(4)(D) of such Act (42 U.S.C. 1395ww(d)(4)(D)) relating to the prohibition of payments based on the presence of a secondary diagnosis code specified by the Secretary in such regulations, as appropriate for the Medicaid program. The Secretary may exclude certain conditions identified under title XVIII of the Social Security Act [42 USCS §§ 1395 et seq.] for non-payment under title XIX of such Act [42 USCS §§ 1396 et seq.] when the Secretary finds the inclusion of such conditions to be inapplicable to beneficiaries under title XIX [42 USCS §§ 1396 et seq.].

(March 23, 2010, P. L. 111-148, Title II, Subtitle I, § 2702, 124 Stat. 318.)

§ 1396d. Definitions [Caution: See prospective amendment notes below.]

For purposes of this title [42 USCS §§ 1396 et seq.]—

(a) Medical assistance. The term "medical assistance" means payment of part or all of the cost of the following care and services or the care and services themselves, or both (if provided in or after the third month before the month in which the recipient makes application for assistance or, in the case of medicare cost-sharing with respect to a qualified medicare beneficiary described in subsection (p)(1), if provided after the month in which the individual becomes such a beneficiary) for individuals, and, with respect to physicians' or dentists' services, at the option of the State, to individuals (other than individuals with respect to whom there is being paid, or who are eligible, or would be eligible if they were not in a medical institution, to have paid with respect to them a State supplementary payment and are eligible for medical assistance equal in amount, duration, and scope to the medical assistance made available to individuals described in section 1902(a)(10)(A) [42 USCS § 1396a(a)(10)(A)]) not receiving aid or assistance under any plan of the State approved under title I, X, XIV, or XVI, or part A of title IV [42 USCS §§ 301 et seq., 1201 et seq., 1351 et seq., or 1381 et seq., or 601 et seq.], and with respect to whom supplemental security income benefits are not being paid under title XVI [42 USCS §§ 1381 et seq.], who are—

(i) under the age of 21, or, at the option of the State, under the age of 20, 19, or 18 as the State may choose,

(ii) relatives specified in section 406(b)(1) with whom a child is living if such child is (or would, if needy, be) a dependent child under part A of title IV [42 USCS §§ 601 et seq.],

(iii) 65 years of age or older,

(iv) blind, with respect to States eligible to participate in the State plan program established under title XVI [42 USCS §§ 1381 et seq.],

(v) 18 years of age or older and permanently and totally disabled, with respect to States eligible to participate in the State plan program established under title XVI [42 USCS §§ 1381 et seq.],

(vi) persons essential (as described in the second sentence of this subsection) to individuals receiving aid or assistance under State plans approved under title I, X, XIV, or XVI [42 USCS §§ 301 et seq., 1201 et seq., 1351 et seq., or 1381 et seq.],

(vii) blind or disabled as defined in section 1614 [42 USCS § 1382c], with respect to States not eligible to participate in the State plan program established under title XVI [42 USCS §§ 1381 et seq.],

(viii) pregnant women,

(ix) individuals provided extended benefits under section 1925 [42 USCS § 1396r-6],

(x) individuals described in section 1902(u)(1) [42 USCS § 1396a(u)(1)],

(xi) individuals described in section 1902(z)(1) [42 USCS § 1396a(z)(1)],

(xii) employed individuals with a medically improved disability (as defined in subsection (v)),

(xiii) individuals described in section 1902(aa) [42 USCS § 1396a(aa)],

(xiv) individuals described in section 1902(a)(10)(A)(i)(VIII) or 1902(a)(10)(A)(i)(IX) [42 USCS § 1396a(a)(10)(A)(i)(VIII) or (IX)],

(xv) individuals described in section 1902(a)(10)(A)(ii)(XX) [42 USCS § 1396a(a)(10)(A)(ii)(XX)],

(xvi) individuals described in section 1902(ii) [42 USCS § 1396a(ii)], or

(xvii) individuals who are eligible for home and community-based services under needs-based criteria established under paragraph (1)(A) of section 1915(i) [42 USCS § 1396n(i)], or who are eligible for home and community-based services under paragraph (6) of such section, and who will receive home and community-based services pursuant to a State plan amendment under such subsection,

but whose income and resources are insufficient to meet all of such cost—

(1) inpatient hospital services (other than services in an institution for mental diseases);

(2)(A) outpatient hospital services, (B) consistent with State law permitting such services, rural health clinic services (as defined in subsection (l)(1)) and any other ambulatory services which are offered by a rural health clinic (as defined in subsection (l)(1)) and which are otherwise included in the plan, and (C) Federally-qualified health center services (as defined in subsection (l)(2)) and any other ambulatory services offered by a Federally-qualified health center and which are otherwise included in the plan;

(3) other laboratory and X-ray services;

(4) (A) nursing facility services (other than services in an institution for mental diseases) for individuals 21 years of age or older; (B) early and periodic screening, diagnostic, and treatment services (as defined in subsection (r)) for individuals who are eligible under the plan and are under the age of 21; and (C) family planning services and supplies furnished (directly or under arrangements with others) to individuals of childbearing age (including minors who can be considered to be sexually active) who are eligible under the State plan and who desire such services and supplies;

(5) (A) physicians' services furnished by a physician (as defined in section 1861(r)(1) [42 USCS § 1395x(r)(1)]), whether furnished in the office, the patient's home, a hospital, or a nursing facility, or elsewhere, and (B) medical and surgical services furnished by a dentist (described in section 1861(r)(2) [42 USCS § 1395x(r)(2)]) to the extent such services may be performed under State law either by a doctor of medicine or by a doctor of dental surgery or dental medicine and would be described in clause (A) if furnished by a physician (as defined in section 1861(r)(1) [42 USCS § 1395x(r)(1)]);

(6) medical care, or any other type of remedial care recognized under State law, furnished by licensed practitioners within the scope of their practice as defined by State law;

(7) home health care services;

(8) private duty nursing services;

(9) clinic services furnished by or under the direction of a physician, without regard to whether the clinic itself is administered by a physician, including such services furnished outside the clinic by clinic personnel to an eligible individual who does not reside in a permanent dwelling or does not have a fixed home or mailing address;

(10) dental services;

(11) physical therapy and related services;

(12) prescribed drugs, dentures, and prosthetic devices; and eyeglasses prescribed by a physician skilled in diseases of the eye or by an optometrist, whichever the individual may select;

(13) other diagnostic, screening, preventive, and rehabilitative services, including any medical or remedial services (provided in a facility, a home, or other setting) recommended by a physician or other licensed practitioner of the healing arts within the scope of their practice under State law, for the maximum reduction of physical or mental disability and restoration of an individual to the best possible functional level;

(14) inpatient hospital services and nursing facility services for individuals 65 years of age or over in an institution for mental diseases;

(15) services in an intermediate care facility for the mentally retarded (other than in an institution for mental diseases) for individuals who are determined, in accordance with section 1902(a)(31) [42 USCS § 1396a(a)(31)], to be in need of such care;

(16) effective January 1, 1973, inpatient psychiatric hospital services for individuals under age 21, as defined in subsection (h);

(17) services furnished by a nurse-midwife (as defined in section 1861(gg) [42 USCS § 1395x(gg)]) which the nurse-midwife is legally authorized to perform under State law (or the State regulatory mechanism provided by State law), whether or not the nurse-midwife is under the supervision of, or associated with, a physician or other health care provider, and without regard to whether or not the services are performed in the area of management of the care of mothers and babies throughout the maternity cycle;

(18) hospice care (as defined in subsection (o));

(19) case management services (as defined

in section 1915(g)(2) [42 USCS § 1396n(g)(2)]) and TB-related services described in section 1902(z)(2)(F) [42 USCS § 1396a(z)(2)(F)];

(20) respiratory care services (as defined in section 1902(e)(9)(C) [42 USCS § 1396a(e)(9)(C)]);

(21) services furnished by a certified pediatric nurse practitioner or certified family nurse practitioner (as defined by the Secretary) which the certified pediatric nurse practitioner or certified family nurse practitioner is legally authorized to perform under State law (or the State regulatory mechanism provided by State law), whether or not the certified pediatric nurse practitioner or certified family nurse practitioner is under the supervision of, or associated with, a physician or other health care provider;

(22) home and community care (to the extent allowed and as defined in section 1929 [42 USCS § 1396t]) for functionally disabled elderly individuals;

(23) community supported living arrangements services (to the extent allowed and as defined in section 1930;

(24) personal care services furnished to an individual who is not an inpatient or resident of a hospital, nursing facility, intermediate care facility for the mentally retarded, or institution for mental disease that are (A) authorized for the individual by a physician in accordance with a plan of treatment or (at the option of the State) otherwise authorized for the individual in accordance with a service plan approved by the State, (B) provided by an individual who is qualified to provide such services and who is not a member of the individual's family, and (C) furnished in a home or other location;

(25) primary care case management services (as defined in subsection (t));

(26) services furnished under a PACE program under section 1934 [42 USCS § 1396u-4] to PACE program eligible individuals enrolled under the program under such section;

(27) subject to subsection (x), primary and secondary medical strategies and treatment and services for individuals who have Sickle Cell Disease;

(28) freestanding birth center services (as defined in subsection (l)(3)(A)) and other ambulatory services that are offered by a freestanding birth center (as defined in subsection (l)(3)(B)) and that are otherwise included in the plan; and

(29) any other medical care, and any other type of remedial care recognized under State law, specified by the Secretary,

except as otherwise provided in paragraph (16), such term does not include—

(A) any such payments with respect to care or services for any individual who is an inmate of a public institution (except as a patient in a medical institution); or

(B) any such payments with respect to care or services for any individual who has not attained 65 years of age and who is a patient in an institution for mental diseases.

For purposes of clause (vi) of the preceding sentence, a person shall be considered essential to another individual if such person is the spouse of and is living with such individual, the needs of such person are taken into account in determining the amount of aid or assistance furnished to such individual (under a State Plan approved under title I, X, XIV, or XVI [42 USCS §§ 301 et seq., 1201 et seq., 1351 et seq., or 1381 et seq.]), and such person is determined, under such a State plan, to be essential to the well-being of such individual. The payment described in the first sentence may include expenditures for medicare cost-sharing and for premiums under part B of title XVIII [42 USCS §§ 1395j et seq.] for individuals who are eligible for medical assistance under the plan and (A) are receiving aid or assistance under any plan of the State approved under title I, X, XIV, or XVI, or part A of title IV [42 USCS §§ 301 et seq., 1201 et seq., 1351 et seq., or 1381 et seq., or 601 et seq.], or with respect to whom supplemental security income benefits are being paid under title XVI [42 USCS §§ 1381 et seq.], or (B) with respect to whom there is being paid a State supplementary payment and are eligible for medical assistance equal in amount, duration, and scope to the medical assistance made available to individuals described in section 1902(a)(10)(A) [42 USCS § 1396a(a)(10)(A)], and, except in the case of individuals 65 years of age or older and disabled individuals entitled to health insurance benefits under title XVIII [42 USCS §§ 1395 et seq.] who are not enrolled under part B of title XVIII [42 USCS §§ 1395j et seq.], other insurance premiums for medical or any other type of remedial care or the cost thereof. No service (including counseling) shall be excluded from the definition of "medical assistance" solely because it is provided as a treatment service for alcoholism or drug dependency.

(b) Federal medical assistance percentage; State percentage; Indian health care percentage. Subject to subsections (y), (z), and (aa) and section 1933(d) [42 USCS § 1396u-3(d)], the term "Federal medical assistance percentage" for any State shall be 100 per centum less the State percentage; and the State percentage shall be that percentage which bears the same ratio to 45 per centum as the square of the per capital income of such State bears to the square of the per capita income of the continental United States (including Alaska) and Hawaii; except that (1) the Federal medical assistance percentage shall in no case be less than 50 per centum or more than 83 per centum, (2) the Federal medical assistance percentage for Puerto Rico, the Virgin Islands, Guam, the Northern Mariana Islands, and American Samoa shall be 50 per centum, (3) for purposes of this title and title XXI [42 USCS §§ 1396 et seq. and 1397aa et seq.], the Federal medical assistance percentage for the District of Columbia shall be 70 percent, and (4) the Federal medical assistance percentage shall be equal to the enhanced FMAP described in section 2105(b) [42 USCS § 1397ee(b)] with respect to medical assistance provided to individuals who are eligible for such assistance only on the basis of section 1902(a)(10)(A)(ii)(XVIII) [42 USCS § 1396a(a)(10)(A)(ii)(XVIII)]. The Federal medical assistance percentage for any State shall be determined and promulgated in accordance with the provisions of section 1101(a)(8)(B) [42 USCS § 1301(a)(8)(B)]. Notwithstanding the first sentence of this section, the Federal medical assistance percentage shall be 100 per centum with respect to amounts expended as medical assistance for services which are received through an Indian Health Service facility whether operated by the Indian Health Service or by an Indian tribe or tribal organization (as defined in section 4 of the Indian Health Care Improvement Act [25 USCS § 1603]). Notwithstanding the first sentence of this subsection, in the case of a State plan that meets the condition described in subsection (u)(1), with respect to expenditures (other than expenditures under section 1923 [42 USCS § 1396r-4]) described in subsection (u)(2)(A) or subsection (u)(3) for the State for a fiscal year, and that do not exceed the amount of the State's available allotment under section 2104 [42 USCS § 1397dd], the Federal medical assistance percentage is equal to the enhanced FMAP described in section 2105(b) [42 USCS § 1397ee(b)].

(c) Nursing facility. For definition of the term "nursing facility", see section 1919(a) [42 USCS § 1396r(a)].

(d) Intermediate care facility for mentally retarded. The term "intermediate care facility for the mentally retarded" means an institution (or distinct part thereof) for the mentally retarded or persons with related conditions if—

(1) the primary purpose of such institution (or distinct part thereof) is to provide health or rehabilitative services for mentally retarded individuals and the institution meets such standards as may be prescribed by the Secretary;

(2) the mentally retarded individual with respect to whom a request for payment is made under a plan approved under this title [42 USCS §§ 1396 et seq.] is receiving active treatment under such a program; and

(3) in the case of a public institution, the State or political subdivision responsible for the operation of such institution has agreed that the non-Federal expenditures in any calendar quarter prior to January 1, 1975, with respect to services furnished to patients in such institution (or distinct part thereof) in the State will not, because of payments made under this title [42 USCS §§ 1396 et seq.], be reduced below the average amount expended for such services in such institution in the four quarters immediately preceding the quarter in which the State in which such institution is located elected to make such services available under its plan approved under this title [42 USCS §§ 1396 et seq.].

(e) Physician's services. In the case of any State the State plan of which (as approved under this title [42 USCS §§ 1396 et seq.])—

(1) does not provide for the payment of services (other than services covered under section 1902(a)(12) [42 USCS § 1396a(a)(12)]) provided by an optometrist; but

(2) at a prior period did provide for the payment of services referred to in paragraph (1);

the term "physicians' services" (as used in subsection (a)(5)) shall include services of the type which an optometrist is legally authorized to perform where the State plan specifically provides that the term "physicians' services", as employed in such plan, includes services of the type which an optometrist is legally authorized to perform, and shall be reimbursed whether furnished by a physician or an optometrist.

(f) Nursing facility services. For purposes of this title [42 USCS §§ 1396 et seq.], the term "nursing facility services" means services which are or were required to be given an individual who needs or needed on a daily basis nursing care (provided directly by or requiring the supervision of nursing personnel) or other skilled rehabilitation services which as a practical matter can only be provided in a nursing facility on an inpatient basis.

(g) Chiropractors' services. If the State plan includes provision of chiropractors' services, such services include only—

(1) services provided by a chiropractor (A) who is licensed as such by the State and (B) who meets uniform minimum standards promulgated by the Secretary under section 1861(r)(5) [42 USCS § 1395x(r)(5)]; and

(2) services which consist of treatment by means of manual manipulation of the spine which the chiropractor is legally authorized to perform by the State.

(h) Inpatient psychiatric hospital services for individuals under age 21. (1) For purposes of paragraph (16) of subsection (a), the term "inpatient psychiatric hospital services for individuals under age 21" includes only—

(A) inpatient services which are provided in an institution (or distinct part thereof) which is a psychiatric hospital as defined in section 1861(f) [42 USCS § 1395x(f)] or in another inpatient setting that the Secretary has specified in regulations;

(B) inpatient services which, in the case of any individual (i) involve active treatment which meets such standards as may be prescribed in regulations by the Secretary, and (ii) a team, consisting of physicians and other personnel qualified to make determinations with respect to mental health conditions and the treatment thereof, has determined are necessary on an inpatient basis and can reasonably be expected to improve the condition, by reason of which such services are necessary, to the extent that eventually such services will no longer be necessary; and

(C) inpatient services which, in the case of any individual, are provided prior to (i) the date such individual attains age 21, or (ii) in the case of an individual who was receiving such services in the period immediately preceding the date on which he attained age 21, (I) the date such individual no longer requires such services, or (II) if earlier, the date such individual attains age 22;

(2) Such term does not include services provided during any calendar quarter under the State plan of any State if the total amount of the funds expended, during such quarter, by the State (and the political subdivisions thereof) from non-Federal funds for inpatient services included under paragraph (1), and for active psychiatric care and treatment provided on an outpatient basis for eligible mentally ill children, is less than the average quarterly amount of the funds expended, during the 4-quarter period ending December 31, 1971, by the State (and the political subdivisions thereof) from non-Federal funds for such services.

(i) Institution for mental diseases. The term "institution for mental diseases" means a hospital, nursing facility, or other institution of more than 16 beds, that is primarily engaged in providing diagnosis, treatment, or care of persons with mental diseases, including medical attention, nursing care, and related services.

(j) State supplementary payment. The term "State supplementary payment" means any cash payment made by a State on a regular basis to an individual who is receiving supplemental security income benefits under title XVI [42 USCS §§ 1381 et seq.] or who would but for his income be eligible to receive such benefits, as assistance based on need in supplementation of such benefits (as determined by the Commissioner of Social Security), but only to the extent that such payments are made with respect to an individual with respect to whom supplemental security income benefits are payable under title XVI [42 USCS §§ 1381 et seq.], or would but for his income be payable under that title.

(k) Supplemental security income benefits. Increased supplemental security income benefits payable pursuant to section 211 of Public Law 93-66 [42 USCS § 1382 note] shall not be considered supplemental security income benefits payable under title XVI [42 USCS §§ 1381 et seq.].

(l) Rural health clinics. (1) The terms "rural health clinic services" and "rural health clinic" have the meanings given such terms in section 1861(aa) [42 USCS § 1395x(aa)], except that (A) clause (ii) of section 1861(aa)(2) [42 USCS § 1395x(aa)(2)(ii)] shall not apply to such terms, and (B) the physician arrangement required under section 1861(aa)(2)(B) [42 USCS § 1395x(aa)(2)(B)] shall only apply with respect to rural health clinic services and, with respect to other ambulatory care services, the physician arrangement required shall be only such as may be required under the State plan for those services.

(2)(A) The term "Federally-qualified health center services" means services of the type described in subparagraphs (A) through (C) of section 1861(aa)(1) [42 USCS § 1395x(aa)(1)] when furnished to an individual as an [a] patient of a Federally-qualified health center and, for this purpose, any reference to a rural health clinic or a physician described in section 1861(aa)(2)(B) [42 USCS § 1395x(aa)(2)(B)] is deemed a reference to a Federally-qualified health center or a physician at the center, respectively.

(B) The term "Federally-qualified health center" means an entity which—

(i) is receiving a grant under section 330 of the Public Health Service Act [42 USCS § 254b],

(ii)(I) is receiving funding from such a grant under a contract with the recipient of such a grant, and

(II) meets the requirements to receive a grant under section 330 of such Act [42 USCS § 254b],

(iii) based on the recommendation of the Health Resources and Services Administration within the Public Health Service, is determined by the Secretary to meet the requirements for receiving such a grant, including requirements of the Secretary that an entity may not be owned, controlled, or operated by another entity, or

(iv) was treated by the Secretary, for purposes of part B of title XVIII [42 USCS §§ 1395j et seq.], as a comprehensive Federally funded health center as of January 1, 1990;

and includes an outpatient health program or facility operated by a tribe or tribal organization under the Indian Self-Determination Act (Public Law 93-638) or by an urban Indian organization receiving funds under title V of the Indian Health Care Improvement Act [25 USCS §§ 1651 et seq.] for the provision of primary health services. In applying clause (ii) [(iii)], the Secretary may waive any requirement referred to in such clause for up to 2 years for good cause shown.

(3)(A) The term "freestanding birth center services" means services furnished to an individual at a freestanding birth center (as defined in subparagraph (B)) at such center.

(B) The term "freestanding birth center" means a health facility—

(i) that is not a hospital;

(ii) where childbirth is planned to occur away from the pregnant woman's residence;

(iii) that is licensed or otherwise approved by the State to provide prenatal labor and delivery or postpartum care and other ambulatory services that are included in the plan; and

(iv) that complies with such other requirements relating to the health and safety of individuals furnished services by the facility as the State shall establish.

(C) A State shall provide separate payments to providers administering prenatal labor and delivery or postpartum care in a freestanding birth center (as defined in subparagraph (B)), such as nurse midwives and other providers of services such as birth attendants recognized under State law, as determined appropriate by the Secretary. For purposes of the preceding sentence, the term "birth attendant" means an individual who is recognized or registered by the State involved to provide health care at childbirth and who provides such care within the scope of practice under which the individual is legally authorized to perform such care under State law (or the State regulatory mechanism provided by State law), regardless of whether the individual is under the supervision of, or associated with, a physician or other health care provider. Nothing in this subparagraph shall be construed as changing State law requirements applicable to a birth attendant.

(m) Qualified family member. (1) Subject to paragraph (2), the term "qualified family member" means an individual (other than a qualified pregnant woman or child, as defined in subsection (n)) who is a member of a family that would be receiving aid under the State plan under part A of title IV [42 USCS §§ 601 et seq.] pursuant to section 407 if the State had not exercised the option under section 407(b)(2)(B)(i).

(2) No individual shall be a qualified family member for any period after September 30, 1998.

(n) Qualified pregnant woman or child. The term "qualified pregnant woman or child" means—

(1) a pregnant woman who—

(A) would be eligible for aid to families with dependent children under part A of title IV [42 USCS §§ 601 et seq.] (or would be eligible for such aid if coverage under the State plan under part A of title IV [42 USCS §§ 601 et seq.] included aid to families with dependent children of unemployed parents pursuant to section 407 [42 USCS § 607]) if her child had been born and was living with her in the month such aid would be paid, and such pregnancy has been medically verified;

(B) is a member of a family which would be eligible for aid under the State plan under part A of title IV [42 USCS §§ 601 et seq.] pursuant to section 407 [42 USCS § 607] if the plan required the payment of aid pursuant to such section; or

(C) otherwise meets the income and resources requirements of a State plan under part A of title IV [42 USCS §§ 601 et seq.]; and

(2) a child who has not attained the age of 19, who was born after September 30, 1983 (or such earlier date as the State may designate), and who meets the income and resources requirements of the State plan under part A of title IV [42 USCS §§ 601 et seq.].

(o) Optional hospice benefits. (1)(A) Subject to subparagraphs (B) and (C), the term "hospice care" means the care described in section 1861(dd)(1) [42 USCS § 1395x(dd)(1)] furnished by a hospice program (as defined in section 1861(dd)(2) [42 USCS § 1395x(dd)(2)]) to a terminally ill individual who has voluntarily elected (in accordance with paragraph (2)) to have payment made for hospice care instead of having payment made for certain benefits described in section 1812(d)(2)(A) [42 USCS § 1395d(d)(2)(A)] and for which payment may otherwise be made under title XVIII [42 USCS §§ 1395 et seq.] and intermediate care facility services under the plan. For purposes of such election, hospice care may be provided to an individual while such individual is a resident of a skilled nursing facility or intermediate care facility, but the only payment made under the State plan shall be for the hospice care.

(B) For purposes of this title [42 USCS §§ 1396 et seq.], with respect to the definition of hospice program under section 1861(dd)(2) [42 USCS § 1395x(dd)(2)], the Secretary may allow an agency or organization to make the assurance under subparagraph (A)(iii) of such section without taking into account any individual who is afflicted with acquired immune deficiency syndrome (AIDS).

(C) A voluntary election to have payment made for hospice care for a child (as defined by the State) shall not constitute a waiver of any rights of the child to be provided with, or to have payment made under this title for, services that are related to the treatment of the child's condition for which a diagnosis of terminal illness has been made.

(2) An individual's voluntary election under this subsection—

(A) shall be made in accordance with procedures that are established by the State and that are consistent with the procedures established under section 1812(d)(2) [42 USCS § 1395d(d)(2)];

(B) shall be for such a period or periods (which need not be the same periods described in section 1812(d)(1) [42 USCS § 1395d(d)(1)]) as the State may establish; and

(C) may be revoked at any time without a showing of cause and may be modified so as to change the hospice program with respect to which a previous election was made.

(3) In the case of an individual—

(A) who is residing in a nursing facility or intermediate care facility for the mentally retarded and is receiving medical assistance for services in such facility under the plan,

(B) who is entitled to benefits under part A of title XVIII [42 USCS §§ 1395c et seq.] and has elected, under section 1812(d) [42 USCS § 1395d(d)], to receive hospice care under such part [42 USCS §§ 1395c et seq.], and

(C) with respect to whom the hospice program under such title and the nursing facility or intermediate care facility for the mentally retarded have entered into a written agreement under which the program takes full responsibility for the professional management of the individual's hospice care and the facility agrees to provide room and board to the individual,

instead of any payment otherwise made under the plan with respect to the facility's services, the State shall provide for payment to the hospice program of an amount equal to the additional amount determined in section 1902(a)(13)(B) [42 USCS § 1396a(a)(13)(B)] and, if the individual is an individual described in section 1902(a)(10)(A) [42 USCS § 1396a(a)(10)(A)], shall provide for payment of any coinsurance amounts imposed under section 1813(a)(4) [42 USCS § 1395e(a)(4)].

(p) Qualified medicare beneficiary; medicare cost-sharing. (1) The term "qualified medicare beneficiary" means an individual—

(A) who is entitled to hospital insurance benefits under part A of title XVIII [42 USCS §§ 1395c et seq.] (including an individual entitled to such benefits pursuant to an enrollment under section 1818 [42 USCS § 1395i-2], but not including an individual entitled to such benefits only pursuant to an enrollment under section 1818A [42 USCS § 1395i-2a]),

(B) whose income (as determined under section 1612 [42 USCS § 1382a] for purposes of the supplemental security income program, except as provided in paragraph (2)(D) does not exceed an income level established by the State consistent with paragraph (2), and

(C) whose resources (as determined under section 1613 [42 USCS § 1382b] for purposes of the supplemental security income program) do not exceed twice the maximum amount of resources that an individual may have and obtain benefits under that program or, effective beginning with January 1, 2010, whose resources (as so determined) do not exceed the maximum resource level applied for the year under subparagraph (D) of section 1860D-14(a)(3)[42 USCS § 1395w-114(a)(3)] (determined without regard to the life insurance policy exclusion provided under subparagraph (G) of such section) applicable to an individual or to the individual and the individual's spouse (as the case may be).

(2)(A) The income level established under paragraph (1)(B) shall be at least the percent provided under subparagraph (B) (but not more than 100 percent) of the official poverty line (as defined by the Office of Management and Budget, and revised annually in accordance with section 673(2) of the Omnibus Budget Reconciliation Act of 1981 [42 USCS § 9902(2)]) applicable to a family of the size involved.

(B) Except as provided in subparagraph (C), the percent provided under this clause, with respect to eligibility for medical assistance on or after—

(i) January 1, 1989, is 85 percent,

(ii) January 1, 1990, is 90 percent, and

(iii) January 1, 1991, is 100 per cent.

(C) In the case of a State which has elected treatment under section 1902(f) [42 USCS § 1396a(f)] and which, as of January 1, 1987, used an income standard for individuals age 65 or older which was more restrictive than the income standard established under the supplemental security income program under title XVI [42 USCS §§ 1381 et seq.], the percent provided under subparagraph (B), with respect to eligibility for medical assistance on or after—

(i) January 1, 1989, is 80 percent,

(ii) January 1, 1990, is 85 percent,

(iii) January 1, 1991, is 95 percent, and

(iv) January 1, 1992, is 100 percent.

(D)(i) In determining under this subsection the income of an individual who is entitled to monthly insurance benefits under title II [42 USCS §§ 401 et seq.] for a transition month (as defined in clause (ii)) in a year, such income shall not include any amounts attributable to an increase in the level of monthly insurance benefits payable under such title which have occurred pursuant to section 215(i) [42 USCS § 415(i)] for benefits payable for months beginning with December of the previous year.

(ii) For purposes of clause (i), the term "transition month" means each month in a year through the month following the month in which the annual revision of the official poverty line, referred to in subparagraph (A), is published.

(3) The term "medicare cost-sharing" means (subject to section 1902(n)(2) [42 USCS § 1396a(n)(2)]) the following costs incurred with respect to a qualified medicare beneficiary, without regard to whether the costs incurred were for items and services for which medical assistance is otherwise available under the plan:

(A)(i) premiums under section 1818 or 1818A [42 USCS § 1395i-2 or 1395i-2a], and

(ii) premiums under section 1839 [42 USCS § 1395r], [.]

(B) Coinsurance under title XVIII [42 USCS §§ 1395 et seq.] (including coinsurance described in section 1813 [42 USCS § 1395e]).

(C) Deductibles established under title XVIII [42 USCS §§ 1395 et seq.] (including those described in section 1813 and section 1833(b) [42 USCS §§ 1395e and 1395l(b)]).

(D) The difference between the amount that is paid under section 1833(a) [42 USCS § 1395l(a)] and the amount that would be paid under such section if any reference to "80 percent" therein were deemed a reference to "100 percent".

Such term also may include, at the option of a State, premiums for enrollment of a qualified medicare beneficiary with an eligible organization under section 1876 [42 USCS § 1395mm].

(4) Notwithstanding any other provision of this title [42 USCS §§ 1396 et seq.], in the case of a State (other than the 50 States and the District of Columbia)—

(A) the requirement stated in section 1902(a)(10)(E) [42 USCS § 1396a(a)(10)(E)] shall be optional, and

(B) for purposes of paragraph (2), the State may substitute for the percent provided under subparagraph (B) [of such paragraph] or [section] 1902(a)(10)(E)(iii) [42 USCS § 1396a(a)(10)(E)(iii)] [of such paragraph] any percent.

In the case of any State which is providing medical assistance to its residents under a waiver granted under section 1115 [42 USCS § 1315], the Secretary shall require the State to meet the requirement of section 1902(a)(10)(E) [42 USCS § 1396a(a)(10)(E)] in the same manner as the State would be required to meet such requirement if the State had in effect a plan approved under this title [42 USCS §§ 1396 et seq.].

(5)(A) The Secretary shall develop and distribute to States a simplified application form for use by individuals (including both qualified medicare beneficiaries and specified low-income medicare beneficiaries) in applying for medical assistance for medicare cost-sharing under this title in the States which elect to use such form. Such form shall be easily readable by applicants and uniform nationally. The Secretary shall provide for the translation of such application form into at least the 10 languages (other than English) that are most often used by individuals applying for hospital insurance benefits under section 226 or 226A [42 USCS § 426 or 426-1] and shall make the translated forms available to the States and to the Commissioner of Social Security.

(B) In developing such form, the Secretary shall consult with beneficiary groups and the States.

(6) For provisions relating to outreach efforts to increase awareness of the availability of medicare cost-sharing, see section 1144 [42 USCS § 1320b-14].

(q) Qualified severely impaired individual. The term "qualified severely impaired individual" means an individual under age 65—

(1) who for the month preceding the first month to which this subsection applies to such individual—

(A) received (i) a payment of supplemental security income benefits under section 1611(b) [42 USCS § 1382(b)] on the basis of blindness or disability, (ii) a supplementary payment under section 1616 of this Act [42 USCS § 1382e] or under section 212 of Public Law 93-66 [42 USCS § 1382 note] on such basis, (iii) a payment of monthly benefits under section 1619(a) [42 USCS § 1382h(a)], or (iv) a supplementary payment under section 1616(c)(3) [42 USCS § 1382e(c)(3)], and

(B) was eligible for medical assistance under the State plan approved under this title [42 USCS §§ 1396 et seq.]; and

(2) with respect to whom the Commissioner of Social Security determines that—

(A) the individual continues to be blind or continues to have the disabling physical or mental impairment on the basis of which he was found to be under a disability and, except for his earnings, continues to meet all nondisability-related requirements for eligibility for benefits under title XVI [42 USCS §§ 1381 et seq.],

(B) the income of such individual would not, except for his earnings, be equal to or in excess of the amount which would cause him to be ineligible for payments under section 1611(b) [42 USCS § 1382(b)] (if he were otherwise eligible for such payments),

(C) the lack of eligibility for benefits under this title [42 USCS §§ 1396 et seq.] would seriously inhibit his ability to continue or obtain employment, and

(D) the individual's earnings are not sufficient to allow him to provide for himself a reasonable equivalent of the benefits under title XVI [42 USCS §§ 1381 et seq.] (including any federally administered State supplementary payments), this title [42 USCS §§ 1396 et seq.], and publicly funded attendant care services (including personal care assistance) that would be available to him in the absence of such earnings.

In the case of an individual who is eligible for medical assistance pursuant to section 1619(b) [42 USCS § 1382h(b)] in June, 1987, the individual shall be a qualified severely impaired individual for so long as such individual meets the requirements of paragraph (2).

(r) Early and periodic screening, diagnostic, and treatment services. The term "early and periodic screening, diagnostic, and treatment services" means the following items and services:

(1) Screening services—

(A) which are provided—

(i) at intervals which meet reasonable standards of medical and dental practice, as determined by the State after consultation with recognized medical and dental organizations involved in child health care and, with respect to immunizations under subparagraph (B)(iii), in accordance with the schedule referred to in section 1928(c)(2)(B)(i) [42 USCS § 1396s(c)(2)(B)(i)] for pediatric vaccines, and

(ii) at such other intervals, indicated as medically necessary, to determine the existence of certain physical or mental illnesses or conditions; and

(B) which shall at a minimum include—

(i) a comprehensive health and developmental history (including assessment of both physical and mental health development),

(ii) a comprehensive unclothed physical exam,

(iii) appropriate immunizations (according to the schedule referred to in section 1928(c)(2)(B)(i) [42 USCS § 1396s(c)(2)(B)(i)] for pediatric vaccines) according to age and health history,

(iv) laboratory tests (including lead blood level assessment appropriate for age and risk factors), and

(v) health education (including anticipatory guidance).

(2) Vision services—

(A) which are provided—

(i) at intervals which meet reasonable standards of medical practice, as determined by the State after consultation with recognized medical organizations involved in child health care, and

(ii) at such other intervals, indicated as medically necessary, to determine the existence of a suspected illness or condition; and

(B) which shall at a minimum include diagnosis and treatment for defects in vision, including eyeglasses.

(3) Dental services—

(A) which are provided—

(i) at intervals which meet reasonable standards of dental practice, as determined by the State after consultation with recognized dental organizations involved in child health care, and

(ii) at such other intervals, indicated as medically necessary, to determine the existence of a suspected illness or condition; and

(B) which shall at a minimum include relief of pain and infections, restoration of teeth, and maintenance of dental health.

(4) Hearing services—

(A) which are provided—

(i) at intervals which meet reasonable standards of medical practice, as determined by the State after consultation with recognized medical organizations involved in child health care, and

(ii) at such other intervals, indicated as medically necessary, to determine the existence of a suspected illness or condition; and

(B) which shall at a minimum include diagnosis and treatment for defects in hearing, including hearing aids.

(5) Such other necessary health care, diagnostic services, treatment, and other measures described in section 1905(a) [subsec. (a) of this section] to correct or ameliorate defects and physical and mental illnesses and conditions discovered by the screening services, whether or not such services are covered under the State plan.

Nothing in this title [42 USCS §§ 1396 et seq.] shall be construed as limiting providers of early and periodic screening, diagnostic, and treatment services to providers who are qualified to provide all of the items and services described in the previous sentence or as preventing a provider that is qualified under the plan to furnish one or more (but not all) of such items or services from being qualified to provide such items and services as part of early and periodic screening, diagnostic, and treatment services. The Secretary shall, not later than July 1, 1990, and every 12 months thereafter, develop and set annual participation goals for each State for participation of individuals who are covered under the State plan under this title [42 USCS §§ 1396 et seq.] in early and periodic screening, diagnostic, and treatment services.

(s) Qualified disabled and working individual. The term "qualified disabled and working individual" means an individual—

(1) who is entitled to enroll for hospital insurance benefits under part A of title XVIII [42 USCS §§ 1395c et seq.] under section 1818A [42 USCS § 1395i-2a] (as added by 6012 of the Omnibus Budget Reconciliation Act of 1989);

(2) whose income (as determined under section 1612 [42 USCS § 1382a] for purposes of the supplemental security income program) does not exceed 200 percent of the official poverty line (as defined by the Office of Management and Budget and revised annually in accordance with section 673(2) of the Omnibus Budget Reconciliation Act of 1981 [42 USCS § 9902(2)]) applicable to a family of the size involved;

(3) whose resources (as determined under section 1613 [42 USCS § 1382b] for purposes of the supplemental security income program) do not exceed twice the maximum amount of resources that an individual or a couple (in the case of an individual with a spouse) may have and obtain benefits for supplemental security income benefits under title XVI [42 USCS §§ 1381 et seq.]; and

(4) who is not otherwise eligible for medical assistance under this title [42 USCS §§ 1396 et seq.].

(t) Primary care case management services; primary care case manager; primary care case management contract; primary care. (1) The term "primary care case management services" means case-management related services (including locating, coordinating, and monitoring of health care services) provided by a primary care case manager under a primary care case management contract.

(2) The term "primary care case manager" means any of the following that provides services of the type described in paragraph (1) under a contract referred to in such paragraph:

(A) A physician, a physician group practice, or an entity employing or having other arrangements with physicians to provide such services.

(B) At State option—

(i) a nurse practitioner (as described in section 1905(a)(21) [subsec. (a)(21) of this section]);

(ii) a certified nurse-midwife (as defined in section 1861(gg) [42 USCS § 1395x(gg)]); or

(iii) a physician assistant (as defined in section 1861(aa)(5) [42 USCS § 1395x(aa)(5)]).

(3) The term "primary care case management contract" means a contract between a primary care case manager and a State under which the manager undertakes to locate, coordinate, and monitor covered primary care (and such other covered services as may be specified under the contract) to all individuals enrolled with the manager, and which—

(A) provides for reasonable and adequate hours of operation, including 24-hour availability of information, referral, and treatment with respect to medical emergencies;

(B) restricts enrollment to individuals residing sufficiently near a service delivery site of the manager to be able to reach that site within a reasonable time using available and affordable modes of transportation;

(C) provides for arrangements with, or referrals to, sufficient numbers of physicians and other appropriate health care professionals to ensure that services under the contract can be furnished to enrollees promptly and without compromise to quality of care;

(D) prohibits discrimination on the basis of health status or requirements for health care services in enrollment, disenrollment, or reenrollment of individuals eligible for medical assistance under this title [42 USCS §§ 1396 et seq.];

(E) provides for a right for an enrollee to terminate enrollment in accordance with section 1932(a)(4) [42 USCS § 1396u-2(a)(4)]; and

(F) complies with the other applicable provisions of section 1932 [42 USCS § 1396u-2].

(4) For purposes of this subsection, the term "primary care" includes all health care services customarily provided in accordance with State licensure and certification laws and regulations, and all laboratory services customarily provided by or through, a general practitioner, family medicine physician, internal medicine physician, obstetrician/gynecologist, or pediatrician.

(u) Use of State child health assistance funds for enhanced medicaid match for expanded medicaid eligibility. (1) The conditions described in this paragraph for a State plan are as follows:

(A) The State is complying with the requirement of section 2105(d)(1) [42 USCS § 1397ee(d)(1)].

(B) The plan provides for such reporting of information about expenditures and payments attributable to the operation of this subsection as the Secretary deems necessary in order to carry out the fourth sentence of subsection (b).

(2)(A) For purposes of subsection (b), the expenditures described in this subparagraph are expenditures for medical assistance for optional targeted low-income children described in subparagraph (B).

(B) For purposes of this paragraph, the term "optional targeted low-income child" means a targeted low-income child as defined in section 2110(b)(1) [42 USCS § 1397jj(b)(1)] (determined without regard to that portion of subparagraph (C) of such section concerning eligibility for medical assistance under this title [42 USCS §§ 1396 et seq.]) who would not qualify for medical assistance under the State plan under this title [42 USCS §§ 1396 et seq.] as in effect on March 31, 1997 (but taking into account the expansion of age of eligibility effected through the operation of section 1902(l)(1)(D) [42 USCS § 1396a(l)(1)(D)]). Such term excludes any child eligible for medical assistance only by reason of section 1902(a)(10)(A)(ii)(XIX) [42 USCS § 1396b(a)(10)(A)(ii)(XIX)].

(3) For purposes of subsection (b), the expenditures described in this paragraph are expenditures for medical assistance for children who are born before October 1, 1983, and who would be described in section 1902(l)(1)(D) [42 USCS § 1396a(l)(1)(D)] if they had been born on or after such date, and who are not eligible for such assistance under the State plan under this title [42 USCS §§ 1397aa et seq.] based on such State plan as in effect as of March 31, 1997.

(4) The limitations on payment under subsections (f) and (g) of section 1108 [42 USCS § 1308(f) and (g)] shall not apply to Federal payments made under section 1903(a)(1) [42 USCS § 1396b(a)(1)] based on an enhanced FMAP described in section 2105(b) [42 USCS § 1397ee(b)].

(v) Employed individual with a medically improved disability. (1) The term "employed individual with a medically improved disability" means an individual who—

(A) is at least 16, but less than 65, years of age;

(B) is employed (as defined in paragraph (2));

(C) ceases to be eligible for medical assistance under section 1902(a)(10)(A)(ii)(XV) [42 USCS § 1396a(a)(10)(A)(ii)(XV)] because the individual, by reason of medical improvement, is determined at the time of a regularly scheduled continuing disability review to no longer be eligible for benefits under section 223(d) or 1614(a)(3) [42 USCS § 423(d) or 1382c(a)(3)]; and

(D) continues to have a severe medically determinable impairment, as determined under regulations of the Secretary.

(2) For purposes of paragraph (1), an individual is considered to be "employed" if the individual—

(A) is earning at least the applicable minimum wage requirement under section 6 of the Fair Labor Standards Act (29 U.S.C. 206) and working at least 40 hours per month; or

(B) is engaged in a work effort that meets substantial and reasonable threshold criteria for hours of work, wages, or other measures, as defined by the State and approved by the

Secretary.

(w) Independent foster care adolescent. (1) For purposes of this title [42 USCS §§ 1396 et seq.], the term "independent foster care adolescent" means an individual—

(A) who is under 21 years of age;

(B) who, on the individual's 18th birthday, was in foster care under the responsibility of a State; and

(C) whose assets, resources, and income do not exceed such levels (if any) as the State may establish consistent with paragraph (2).

(2) The levels established by a State under paragraph (1)(C) may not be less than the corresponding levels applied by the State under section 1931(b) [42 USCS § 1396u-1(b)].

(3) A State may limit the eligibility of independent foster care adolescents under section 1902(a)(10)(A)(ii)(XVII) [42 USCS § 1396a(a)(10)(A)(ii)(XVII)] to those individuals with respect to whom foster care maintenance payments or independent living services were furnished under a program funded under part E of title IV [42 USCS §§ 670 et seq.] before the date the individuals attained 18 years of age.

(x) For purposes of subsection (a)(27), the strategies, treatment, and services described in that subsection include the following:

(1) Chronic blood transfusion (with deferoxamine chelation) to prevent stroke in individuals with Sickle Cell Disease who have been identified as being at high risk for stroke.

(2) Genetic counseling and testing for individuals with Sickle Cell Disease or the sickle cell trait to allow health care professionals to treat such individuals and to prevent symptoms of Sickle Cell Disease.

(3) Other treatment and services to prevent individuals who have Sickle Cell Disease and who have had a stroke from having another stroke.

(y) Increased FMAP for medical assistance for newly eligible mandatory individuals. (1) Amount of increase. Notwithstanding subsection (b), the Federal medical assistance percentage for a State that is one of the 50 States or the District of Columbia, with respect to amounts expended by such State for medical assistance for newly eligible individuals described in subclause (VIII) of section 1902(a)(10)(A)(i), shall be equal to—

(A) 100 percent for calendar quarters in 2014, 2015, and 2016;

(B) 95 percent for calendar quarters in 2017;

(C) 94 percent for calendar quarters in 2018;

(D) 93 percent for calendar quarters in 2019; and

(E) 90 percent for calendar quarters in 2020 and each year thereafter.

(2) Definitions. In this subsection:

(A) Newly eligible. The term "newly eligible" means, with respect to an individual described in subclause (VIII) of section 1902(a)(10)(A)(i) [42 USCS § 1396a(a)(10)(A)(i)], an individual who is not under 19 years of age (or such higher age as the State may have elected) and who, as of December 1, 2009, is not eligible under the State plan or under a waiver of the plan for full benefits or for benchmark coverage described in subparagraph (A), (B), or (C) of section 1937(b)(1) [42 USCS § 1396u-7(b)(1)] or benchmark equivalent coverage described in section 1937(b)(2) [42 USCS § 1396u-7(b)(2)] that has an aggregate actuarial value that is at least actuarially equivalent to benchmark coverage described in subparagraph (A), (B), or (C) of section 1937(b)(1) [42 USCS § 1396u-7(b)(1)], or is eligible but not enrolled (or is on a waiting list) for such benefits or coverage through a waiver under the plan that has a capped or limited enrollment that is full.

(B) Full benefits. The term "full benefits" means, with respect to an individual, medical assistance for all services covered under the State plan under this title [42 USCS §§ 1396 et seq.] that is not less in amount, duration, or scope, or is determined by the Secretary to be substantially equivalent, to the medical assistance available for an individual described in section 1902(a)(10)(A)(i) [42 USCS § 1396a(a)(10)(A)(i)].

(z) Equitable support for certain States. (1)(A) During the period that begins on January 1, 2014, and ends on December 31, 2015, notwithstanding subsection (b), the Federal medical assistance percentage otherwise determined under subsection (b) with respect to a fiscal year occurring during that period shall be increased by 2.2 percentage points for any State described in subparagraph (B) for amounts expended for medical assistance for individuals who are not newly eligible (as defined in subsection (y)(2)) individuals described in subclause (VIII) of section 1902(a)(10)(A)(i) [42 USCS § 1396a(a)(10)(A)(i)].

(B) For purposes of subparagraph (A), a State described in this subparagraph is a State that—

(i) is an expansion State described in paragraph (3);

(ii) the Secretary determines will not receive any payments under this title on the basis of an increased Federal medical assistance percentage under subsection (y) for expenditures for medical assistance for newly eligible individuals (as so defined); and

(iii) has not been approved by the Secretary to divert a portion of the DSH allotment for a State to the costs of providing medical assistance or other health benefits coverage under a waiver that is in effect on July 2009.

(2)(A) For calendar quarters in 2014 and each year thereafter, the Federal medical assistance percentage otherwise determined under subsection (b) for an expansion State described in paragraph (3) with respect to medical assistance for individuals described in section 1902(a)(10)(A)(i)(VIII) [42 USCS § 1396a(a)(10)(A)(i)(VIII)] who are nonpregnant childless adults with respect to whom the State may require enrollment in benchmark coverage under section 1937 [42 USCS § 1396u-7] shall be equal to the percent specified in subparagraph (B)(i) for such year.

(B)(i) The percent specified in this subparagraph for a State for a year is equal to the Federal medical assistance percentage (as defined in the first sentence of subsection (b)) for the State increased by a number of percentage points equal to the transition percentage (specified in clause (ii) for the year) of the number of percentage points by which—

(I) such Federal medical assistance percentage for the State, is less than

(II) the percent specified in subsection (y)(1) for the year.

(ii) The transition percentage specified in this clause for—

(I) 2014 is 50 percent;

(II) 2015 is 60 percent;

(III) 2016 is 70 percent;

(IV) 2017 is 80 percent;

(V) 2018 is 90 percent; and

(VI) 2019 and each subsequent year is 100 percent.

(3) A State is an expansion State if, on the date of the enactment of the Patient Protection and Affordable Care Act, the State offers health benefits coverage statewide to parents and nonpregnant, childless adults whose income is at least 100 percent of the poverty line, that includes inpatient hospital services, is not dependent on access to employer coverage, employer contribution, or employment and is not limited to premium assistance, hospital-only benefits, a high deductible health plan, or alternative benefits under a demonstration program authorized under section 1938 [42 USCS § 1396u-8]. A State that offers health benefits coverage to only parents or only nonpregnant childless adults described in the preceding sentence shall not be considered to be an expansion State.

(aa) Special adjustment to FMAP determination for certain states recovering from a major disaster. (1) Notwithstanding subsection (b), beginning January 1, 2011, the Federal medical assistance percentage for a fiscal year for a disaster-recovery FMAP adjustment State shall be equal to the following:

(A) In the case of the first fiscal year (or part of a fiscal year) for which this subsection applies to the State, the Federal medical assistance percentage determined for the fiscal year without regard to this subsection, subsection (y), subsection (z), and section 10202 of the Patient Protection and Affordable Care Act [note to this section], increased by 50 percent of the number of percentage points by which the Federal medical assistance percentage determined for the State for the fiscal year without regard to this subsection, subsection (y), subsection (z), and section 10202 of the Patient Protection and Affordable Care Act [note to this section], is less than the Federal medical assistance percentage determined for the State for the preceding fiscal year after the application of only subsection (a) of section 5001 of Public Law 111-5 [note to this section] (if applicable to the preceding fiscal year) and without regard to this subsection, subsection (y), and subsections (b) and (c) of section 5001 of Public Law 111-5 [note to this section].

(B) In the case of the second or any succeeding fiscal year for which this subsection applies to the State, the Federal medical assistance percentage determined for the preceding fiscal year under this subsection for the State, increased by 25 percent of the number of percentage points by which the Federal medical assistance percentage determined for the State for the fiscal year without regard to this subsection and subsection (y), is less than the Federal medical assistance percentage determined for the State for the preceding fiscal year under this subsection.

(2) In this subsection, the term "disaster-recovery FMAP adjustment State" means a State that is one of the 50 States or the District of Columbia, for which, at any time during the preceding 7 fiscal years, the President has declared a major disaster under section 401 of the Robert T. Stafford Disaster Relief and Emergency Assistance Act [42 USCS § 5170] and determined as a result of such disaster that every county or parish in the State warrant individual and public assistance or public assistance from the Federal Government under such Act and for which—

(A) in the case of the first fiscal year (or part of a fiscal year) for which this subsection applies to the State, the Federal medical assistance percentage determined for the State for the fiscal year without regard to this subsection and subsection (y), is less than the Federal medical assistance percentage determined for the State for the preceding fiscal year after the application of only subsection (a) of section 5001 of Public Law 111-5 [note to this section] (if applicable to the preceding fiscal year) and without regard to this subsection, subsection (y), and subsections (b) and (c) of section 5001 of Public Law 111-5 [note to this section], by at least 3 percentage points; and

(B) in the case of the second or any succeeding fiscal year for which this subsection applies to the State, the Federal medical assistance percentage determined for the State for the fiscal year without regard to this subsection, subsection (y), subsection (z), and section 10202 of the Patient Protection and Affordable Care Act, is less than the Federal medical assistance percentage determined for the State for the preceding fiscal year under this subsection by at least 3 percentage points.

(3) The Federal medical assistance percentage determined for a disaster-recovery FMAP adjustment State under paragraph (1) shall apply for purposes of this title (other than with respect to disproportionate share hospital payments described in section 1923 [42 USCS § 1396r-4] and payments under this title that are based on the enhanced FMAP described in 2105(b) [42 USCS § 1397ee(b)]) and shall not apply with respect to payments under title IV [42 USCS §§ 601 et seq.] (other than under part E of title IV [42 USCS §§ 670 et seq.]) or payments under title XXI [42 USCS §§ 1397aa et seq.].

(bb) Requiring coverage of counseling and pharmacotherapy for cessation of tobacco use by pregnant women. [Caution: This subsection takes effect on October 1, 2010, as provided by § 4107(d) of Act March 23, 2010, P. L. 111-148, which appears as a note to this section.] (1) For purposes of this title [42 USCS §§ 1396 et seq.], the term "counseling and pharmacotherapy for cessation of tobacco use by pregnant women" means diagnostic, therapy, and counseling services and pharmacotherapy (including the coverage of prescription and nonprescription tobacco cessation agents approved by the Food and Drug Administration) for cessation of tobacco use by pregnant women who use tobacco products or who are being treated for tobacco use that is furnished—

(A) by or under the supervision of a physician; or

(B) by any other health care professional who—

(i) is legally authorized to furnish such services under State law (or the State regulatory mechanism provided by State law) of the State in which the services are furnished; and

(ii) is authorized to receive payment for other services under this title or is designated by the Secretary for this purpose.

(2) Subject to paragraph (3), such term is limited to—

(A) services recommended with respect to pregnant women in "Treating Tobacco Use and Dependence: 2008 Update: A Clinical Practice Guideline", published by the Public Health Service in May 2008, or any subsequent modification of such Guideline; and

(B) such other services that the Secretary recognizes to be effective for cessation of tobacco use by pregnant women.

(3) Such term shall not include coverage for drugs or biologicals that are not otherwise covered under this title [42 USCS §§ 1396 et seq.].

(cc) Requirement for certain States. Notwithstanding subsections (y), (z), and (aa), in the case of a State that requires political subdivisions within the State to contribute toward the non-Federal share of expenditures required under the State plan under section 1902(a)(2) [42 USCS § 1396a(a)(2)], the State shall not be eligible for an increase in its Federal medical assistance percentage under such subsections if it requires that political subdivisions pay a greater percentage of the non-Federal share of such expenditures, or a greater percentage of the non-Federal share of payments under section 1923, than the respective percentages that would have been required by the State under the State plan under this title, State law, or both, as in effect on December 31, 2009, and without regard to any such increase. Voluntary contributions by a political subdivision to the non-Federal share of expenditures under the State plan under this title or to the non-Federal share of payments under section 1923 [42 USCS § 1396r-4], shall not be considered to be required contributions for purposes of this subsection. The treatment of voluntary contributions, and the treatment of contributions required by a State under the State plan under this title, or State law, as provided by this subsection, shall also apply to the increases in the Federal medical assistance percentage under section 5001 of the American Recovery and Reinvestment Act of 2009 [note to this section].

(dd) Increased FMAP for additional ex-

penditures for primary care services. Notwithstanding subsection (b), with respect to the portion of the amounts expended for medical assistance for services described in section 1902(a)(13)(C) [42 USCS § 1396a(a)(13)(C)] furnished on or after January 1, 2013, and before January 1, 2015, that is attributable to the amount by which the minimum payment rate required under such section (or, by application, section 1932(f) [42 USCS § 1396u-2(f)]) exceeds the payment rate applicable to such services under the State plan as of July 1, 2009, the Federal medical assistance percentage for a State that is one of the 50 States or the District of Columbia shall be equal to 100 percent. The preceding sentence does not prohibit the payment of Federal financial participation based on the Federal medical assistance percentage for amounts in excess of those specified in such sentence.

(Aug. 14, 1935, ch 531, Title XIX, § 1905, as added July 30, 1965, P. L. 89-97, Title I, Part 2, § 121(a), 79 Stat. 351; Jan. 2, 1968, P. L. 90-248, Title II, Part 2, §§ 230, 233, Part 3, § 241(f)(6), Part 4, § 248(e), Title III, § 302(a), 81 Stat. 905, 917, 919, 929; Dec. 28, 1971, P. L. 92-223, § 4(a), 85 Stat. 809; Oct. 30, 1972, P. L. 92-603, Title II, §§ 212(a), 247(b), 275(a), 278(a)(21)–(23), 280, 297(a), 299, 299B, 299E(b), 299L, 86 Stat. 1384, 1425, 1452–1454, 1459–1462, 1464; Dec. 31, 1973, P. L. 93-233, §§ 13(a)(13)–(18), 18(w), (x)(7)–(10), (y)(2), 87 Stat. 963, 964, 972, 973; Sept. 30, 1976, P. L. 94-437, Title IV, § 402(e), 90 Stat. 1410; Dec. 13, 1977, P. L. 95-210, § 2(a), (b), 91 Stat. 1488; June 13, 1978, P. L. 95-292, § 8(a), (b), 92 Stat. 316; Oct. 19, 1980, P. L. 96-473, § 6(k), 94 Stat. 2266; Dec. 5, 1980, P. L. 96-499, Title IX, Part C, § 965(a), 94 Stat. 2651; Aug. 13, 1981, P. L. 97-35, Title XXI, Subtitle C, ch 1, § 2162(a)(2), ch 2, § 2172(b), 95 Stat. 806, 808; Sept. 3, 1982, P. L. 97-248, Title I, Subtitle B, §§ 136(c), 137(b)(17), (18), (f), 96 Stat. 376, 379, 381; July 18, 1984, P. L. 98-369, Division B, Title III, Subtitle A, Part II, §§ 2335(f), 2340(b), Subtitle B, §§ 2361(b), 2371(a), 2373(b)(15)–(20), 98 Stat. 1091, 1093, 1104, 1110, 1112; April 7, 1986, P. L. 99-272, Title IX, Subtitle E, §§ 9501(a), 9505(a), 9511(a), 100 Stat. 201, 208, 212; Oct. 21, 1986, P. L. 99-509, Title IX, Subtitle E, Part 1, §§ 9403(b)(d), (g)(3), 9404(b), 9408(c)(1), Part 4, § 9435(b)(2), 100 Stat. 2052, 2053, 2055, 2060, 2069; Oct. 22, 1986, P. L. 99-514, Title XVIII, Subtitle C, Ch 1, § 1895(c)(3)(A), 100 Stat. 2935; Dec. 22, 1987, P. L. 100-203, Title IV, Subtitle A, Part 3, Subpart C, § 4073(d), Subtitle B, Part 1, §§ 4101(c)(1), 4103(a), 4105(a), Part 2, §§ 4114, 4118(p)(8), Subtitle C, Part 2, § 4211(c), (f), (h)(6), 101 Stat. 1330-119, 1330-141, 1330-146, 1330-147, 1330-152, 1330-159, 1330-204–1330-206; July 1, 1988, P. L. 100-360, Title III, § 301(a)(2)–(d), (g)(2), Title IV, Subtitle B, § 411(h)(4)(E), (k)(4), (8), (14)(A), 102 Stat. 748–750, 787, 791, 794, 798; Oct. 13, 1988, P. L. 100-485, Title III, § 303(b)(2), Title IV, § 401(d)(2), Title VI, § 608(d)(14)(A)–(G), (J), (f)(3), 102 Stat. 2396, 2392, 2415, 2416, 2424; Nov. 10, 1988, P. L. 100-647, Title VIII, Subtitle E, Part IV, § 8434(a), (b)(3), (4), 102 Stat. 3805; Dec. 13, 1989, P. L. 101-234, Title II, § 201(b), 103 Stat. 1981; Dec. 19, 1989, P. L. 101-239, Title VI, Subtitle B, Part 1, §§ 6402(c)(1), 6403(a), (c), (d)(2), 6404(a), (b), 6405(a), 6408(d)(2), (4)(A), (B), 103 Stat. 2261–2265, 2268, 2269; Nov. 5, 1990, P. L. 101-508, Title IV, Subtitle B, Part 1, § 4402(d)(2), Part 2, § 4501(a), (c), (e)(1), Part 3, § 4601(a)(2), Part 4, Subpart A, §§ 4704(c)–(e)(1), 4705(a), Subpart B, §§ 4711(a), 4712(a), 4713(b), 4717, 4719(a), 4721(a), Subpart E, § 4755(a)(1)(A), 104 Stat. 1388-164, 1388-165, 1388-166, 1388-172, 1388-174, 1388-187, 1388-191, 1388-194, 1388-209; Aug. 10, 1993, P. L. 103-66, Title XIII, Ch 2, Subch B, Part I, §§ 13601(a), 13603(e), 13605(a), 13606(a), Part IV, § 13631(g)(1), 107 Stat. 612, 620, 621, 644, 645; Aug. 15, 1994, P. L. 103-296, Title I, § 108(d)(2), (3), 108 Stat. 1486; Oct. 11, 1996, P. L. 104-299, § 4(b)(2), 110 Stat. 3645; Aug. 5, 1997, P. L. 105-33, Title IV, Subtitle H, Ch 1, § 4702(a), Ch 2, § 4711(c)(1), 4712(d)(1), 4714(b)(2), Ch 3, § 4725(b)(1), Ch 4, § 4732(b), Subtitle I, § 4802(a)(1), Subtitle J, Ch 2, § 4911(a), 111 Stat. 494, 508–510, 518, 520, 538, 570; Nov. 19, 1997, P. L. 105-100, Title I, § 162(2), 111 Stat. 2188; Nov. 29, 1999, P. L. 106-113, Div B, § 1000(a)(6), 113 Stat. 1536; Dec. 14, 1999, P. L. 106-169, Title I, Subtitle C, § 121(a)(2), (c)(5), 113 Stat. 1829, 1830; Dec. 17, 1999, P. L. 106-170, Title II, § 201(a)(2)(B), (C), 113 Stat. 1892; Oct. 24, 2000, P. L. 106-354, § 2(a)(4), (c), 114 Stat. 1382, 1384; Dec. 21, 2000, P. L. 106-554, § 1(a)(6), 114 Stat. 2763; Oct. 22, 2004, P. L. 108-357, Title VII, § 712(a)(1), 118 Stat. 1558; Feb. 8, 2006, P. L. 109-171, Title VI, Subtitle A, Ch. 6, Subch. A, § 6062(c)(2), 120 Stat. 98; July 15, 2008, P. L. 110-275, Title I, Subtitle A, Part II, §§ 112, 118(a), 122 Stat. 2503, 2507; March 23, 2010, P. L. 111-148, Title II, Subtitle A, §§ 2001(a)(3), (5)(C), (e)(2)(A), 2005(c)(1), 2006, Subtitle D, §§ 2301(a), 2302(a), 2303(a)(4)(A), 2304, Subtitle E, § 2402(d)(2)(B), Title IV, Subtitle B, §§ 4106(a), (b), 4107(a), Title X, Subtitle B, Part I, § 10201(c), 124 Stat. 272, 275, 279, 284,

292, 293, 294, 296, 304, 559, 560, 918; March 30, 2010, P. L. 111-152, Title I, Subtitle C, §§ 1201, 1202(b), 124 Stat. 1051, 1053.)

HISTORY; ANCILLARY LAWS AND DIRECTIVES

Prospective amendments:

Amendment of subsec. (b), effective July 1, 2011. Act March 23, 2010, P. L. 111-148, Title II, Subtitle A, § 2005(c)(1), 124 Stat. 284 (effective on 7/1/2011, as provided by § 2005(c)(2) of such Act, as amended, which appears as a note to this section), provides: "The first sentence of section 1905(b) of the Social Security Act (42 U.S.C. 1396d(b)) is amended by striking 'shall be 50 per centum' and inserting 'shall be 55 percent'.".

Amendment of subsecs. (a)(13) and (b), effective January 1, 2013. Act March 23, 2010, P. L. 111-148, Title IV, Subtitle B, § 4106(a), (b), 124 Stat. 559 (effective on 1/1/2013, as provided by § 4106(c) of such Act, which appears as a note to this section), provides:

"(a) Clarification of inclusion of services. Section 1905(a)(13) of the Social Security Act (42 U.S.C. 1396d(a)(13)) is amended to read as follows:

" '(13) other diagnostic, screening, preventive, and rehabilitative services, including—

" '(A) any clinical preventive services that are assigned a grade of A or B by the United States Preventive Services Task Force;

" '(B) with respect to an adult individual, approved vaccines recommended by the Advisory Committee on Immunization Practices (an advisory committee established by the Secretary, acting through the Director of the Centers for Disease Control and Prevention) and their administration; and

" '(C) any medical or remedial services (provided in a facility, a home, or other setting) recommended by a physician or other licensed practitioner of the healing arts within the scope of their practice under State law, for the maximum reduction of physical or mental disability and restoration of an individual to the best possible functional level;'.

"(b) Increased FMAP. Section 1905(b) of the Social Security Act (42 U.S.C. 1396d(b)), as amended by sections 2001(a)(3)(A) and 2004(c)(1), is amended in the first sentence—

"(1) by striking ', and (4)' and inserting ', (4)'; and

"(2) by inserting before the period the following: ', and (5) in the case of a State that provides medical assistance for services and vaccines described in subparagraphs (A) and (B) of subsection (a)(13), and prohibits cost-sharing for such services and vaccines, the Federal medical assistance percentage, as determined under this subsection and subsection (y) (without regard to paragraph (1)(C) of such subsection), shall be increased by 1 percentage point with respect to medical assistance for such services and vaccines and for items and services described in subsection (a)(4)(D)'.".

Amendment of subsec. (a)(4), effective October 1, 2010. Act March 23, 2010, P. L. 111-148, Title IV, Subtitle B, § 4107(a)(1), 124 Stat. 560 (effective 10/1/2010, as provided by § 4107(d) of such Act, which appears as a note to this section), provides:

"Section 1905 of the Social Security Act (42 U.S.C. 1396d), as amended by sections 2001(a)(3)(B) and 2303, is further amended—

"(1) in subsection (a)(4)—

"(A) by striking 'and' before '(C)'; and

"(B) by inserting before the semicolon at the end the following new subparagraph: '; and (D) counseling and pharmacotherapy for cessation of tobacco use by pregnant women (as defined in subsection (bb))';".

Other provisions:

Effective date of amendment made by § 2005(c) of Act March 23, 2010. Act March 23, 2010, P. L. 111-148, Title II, Subtitle A, § 2005(c)(2), 124 Stat. 284; March 30, 2010, P. L. 111-152, Title I, Subtitle C, § 1204(b)(2)(B), 124 Stat. 1056, provides: "The amendment made by paragraph (1) [amending subsec. (b) of this section] takes effect on July 1, 2011.".

Effective date of amendments made by § 4106 of Act March 23, 2010. Act March 23, 2010, P. L. 111-148, Title IV, Subtitle B, § 4106(c), 124 Stat. 560, provides: "The amendments made under this section [amending subsecs. (a)(13) and (b) of this section] shall take effect on January 1, 2013.".

Effective date of amendments made by § 4107 of Act March 23, 2010. Act March 23, 2010, P. L. 111-148, Title IV, Subtitle B, § 4107(d), 124 Stat. 561, provides: "The amendments made by this section [amending 42 USCS §§ 1396d, 1396o, 1396o-1, and 1396r-8] shall take effect on October 1, 2010.".

Incentives for States to offer home and community-based services as a long-term care alternative to nursing homes. Act March 23, 2010, P. L. 111-148, Title X, Subtitle B, Part I, § 10202, 124 Stat. 923, provides:

"(a) State balancing incentive payments program. Notwithstanding section 1905(b) of the Social Security Act (42 U.S.C. 1396d(b)), in the case of a balancing incentive payment State, as defined in subsection (b), that meets the conditions described in subsection (c), during the balancing incentive period, the Federal medical assistance percentage determined for the State under section 1905(b) of such Act and, if applicable, increased under subsection (z) or (aa) shall be increased by the applicable percentage points determined under subsection (d) with respect to eligible medical assistance expenditures described in subsection (e).

"(b) Balancing incentive payment State. A balancing incentive payment State is a State—

"(1) in which less than 50 percent of the total expenditures for medical assistance under the State Medicaid program for a fiscal year for long-term services and supports (as defined by the Secretary under subsection (f))(1)) are for non-institutionally-based long-term services and supports described in subsection (f)(1)(B);

"(2) that submits an application and meets the conditions described in subsection (c); and

"(3) that is selected by the Secretary to participate in the State balancing incentive payment program established under this section.

"(c) Conditions. The conditions described in this subsection are the following:

"(1) Application. The State submits an application to the Secretary that includes, in addition to such other information as the Secretary shall require—

"(A) a proposed budget that details the State's plan to expand and diversify medical assistance for non-institutionally-based long-term services and supports described in subsection (f)(1)(B) under the State Medicaid program during the balancing incentive period and achieve the target spending percentage applicable to the State under paragraph (2), including through structural changes to how the State furnishes such assistance, such as through the establishment of a 'no wrong door single entry point system', optional presumptive eligibility, case management services, and the use of core standardized assessment instruments, and that includes a description of the new or expanded offerings of such services that the State will provide and the projected costs of such services; and

"(B) in the case of a State that proposes to expand the provision of home and community-based services under its State Medicaid program through a State plan amendment under section 1915(i) of the Social Security Act [42 USCS § 1396n(i)], at the option of the State, an election to increase the income eligibility for such services from 150 percent of the poverty line to such higher percentage as the State may establish for such purpose, not to exceed 300 percent of the supplemental security income benefit rate established by section 1611(b)(1) of the Social Security Act (42 U.S.C. 1382(b)(1)).

"(2) Target spending percentages. (A) In the case of a balancing incentive payment State in which less than 25 percent of the total expenditures for long-term services and supports under the State Medicaid program for fiscal year 2009 are for home and community-based services, the target spending percentage for the State to achieve by not later than October 1, 2015, is that 25 percent of the total expenditures for long-term services and supports under the State Medicaid program are for home and community-based services.

"(B) In the case of any other balancing incentive payment State, the target spending percentage for the State to achieve by not later than October 1, 2015, is that 50 percent of the total expenditures for long-term services and supports under the State Medicaid program are for home and community-based services.

"(3) Maintenance of eligibility requirements. The State does not apply eligibility standards, methodologies, or procedures for determining eligibility for medical assistance for non-institutionally-based long-term services and supports described in subsection (f)(1)(B) under the State Medicaid program that are more restrictive than the eligibility standards, methodologies, or procedures in effect for such purposes on December 31, 2010.

"(4) Use of additional funds. The State agrees to use the additional Federal funds paid to the State as a result of this section only for purposes of providing new or expanded offerings of non-institutionally-based long-term services and supports described in subsection (f)(1)(B) under the State Medicaid program.

"(5) Structural changes. The State agrees to make, not later than the end of the 6-month period that begins on the date the State submits an application under this section, the following changes:

"(A) 'No wrong door single entry point system'. Development of a statewide system to enable consumers to access all long-term services and supports through an agency, organization, coordinated network, or portal, in accordance with such standards as the State shall establish and that shall provide information regarding the availability of such services, how to apply for such services, referral services for services and supports otherwise available in the community, and determinations of financial and functional eligibility for such services and supports, or assistance with assessment processes for financial and functional eligibility.

"(B) Conflict-free case management services. Conflict-free case management services to develop a service plan, arrange for services and supports, support the beneficiary (and, if appropriate, the beneficiary's caregivers) in directing the provision of services and supports for the beneficiary, and conduct ongoing monitoring to assure that services and supports are delivered to meet the beneficiary's needs and achieve intended outcomes.

"(C) Core standardized assessment instruments. Development of core standardized assessment instruments for determining eligibility for non-institutionally-based long-term services and supports described in subsection (f)(1)(B), which shall be used in a uniform manner throughout the State, to determine a beneficiary's needs for training, support services, medical care, transportation, and other services, and develop an individual service plan to address such needs.

"(6) Data collection. The State agrees to collect from providers of services and through such other means as the State determines appropriate the following data:

"(A) Services data. Services data from providers of non-institutionally-based long-term services and supports described in subsection (f)(1)(B) on a per-beneficiary basis and in accordance with such standardized coding procedures as the State shall establish in consultation with the Secretary.

"(B) Quality data. Quality data on a selected set of core quality measures agreed upon by the Secretary and the State that are linked to population-specific outcomes measures and accessible to providers.

"(C) Outcomes measures. Outcomes measures data on a selected set of core population-specific outcomes measures agreed upon by the Secretary and the State that are accessible to providers and include—

"(i) measures of beneficiary and family caregiver experience with providers;

"(ii) measures of beneficiary and family caregiver satisfaction with services; and

"(iii) measures for achieving desired outcomes appropriate to a specific beneficiary, including employment, participation in community life, health stability, and prevention of loss in function.

"(d) Applicable percentage points increase in FMAP. The applicable percentage points increase is—

"(1) in the case of a balancing incentive payment State subject to the target spending percentage described in subsection (c)(2)(A), 5 percentage points; and

"(2) in the case of any other balancing incentive payment State, 2 percentage points.

"(e) Eligible medical assistance expenditures. (1) In general. Subject to paragraph (2), medical assistance described in this subsection is medical assistance for non-institutionally-based long-term services and supports described in subsection (f)(1)(B) that is provided by a balancing incentive payment State under its State Medicaid program during the balancing incentive payment period.

"(2) Limitation on payments. In no case may the aggregate amount of payments made by the Secretary to balancing incentive payment States under this section during the balancing incentive period exceed $3,000,000,000.

"(f) Definitions. In this section:

"(1) Long-term services and supports defined. The term 'long-term services and supports' has the meaning given that term by Secretary and may include any of the following (as defined for purposes of State Medicaid programs):

"(A) Institutionally-based long-term services and supports. Services provided in an institution, including the following:

"(i) Nursing facility services.

"(ii) Services in an intermediate care facility for the mentally retarded described in subsection (a)(15) of section 1905 of such Act [this section].

"(B) Non-institutionally-based long-term services and supports. Services not provided in an institution, including the following:

"(i) Home and community-based services provided under subsection (c), (d), or (i) of section 1915 of such Act [this section] or under a waiver under section 1115 of such Act [42 USCS § 1315].

"(ii) Home health care services.

"(iii) Personal care services.

"(iv) Services described in subsection (a)(26) of section 1905 of such Act [this section] (relating to PACE program services).

"(v) Self-directed personal assistance services described in section 1915(j) of such Act [42 USCS § 1396n(j)].

"(2) Balancing incentive period. The term 'balancing incentive period' means the period that begins on October 1, 2011, and ends on September 30, 2015.

"(3) Poverty line. The term 'poverty line' has the meaning given that term in section 2110(c)(5) of the Social Security Act (42 U.S.C. 1397jj(c)(5)).

"(4) State Medicaid program. The term 'State Medicaid program' means the State program for medical assistance provided under a State plan under title XIX of the Social Security Act [42 USCS §§ 1396 et seq.] and under any waiver approved with respect to such State plan.".

§ 1396e. Enrollment of individuals under group health plans

(a) Requirements of each State plan; guidelines. Each State plan—

(1) may implement guidelines established by the Secretary, consistent with subsection (b), to identify those cases in which enrollment of an individual otherwise entitled to medical assistance under this title [42 USCS §§ 1396 et seq.] in a group health plan (in which the individual is otherwise eligible to be enrolled) is cost-effective (as defined in subsection (e)(2));

(2) may require, in case of an individual so identified and as a condition of the individual being or remaining eligible for medical assistance under this title [42 USCS §§ 1396 et seq.] and subject to subsection (b)(2), notwithstanding any other provision of this title [42 USCS §§ 1396 et seq.], that the individual (or in the case of a child, the child's parent) apply for enrollment in the group health plan; and

(3) in the case of such enrollment (except as provided in subsection (c)(1)(B)), shall provide for payment of all enrollee premiums for such enrollment and all deductibles, coinsurance, and other cost-sharing obligations for items and services otherwise covered under the State plan under this title [42 USCS §§ 1396 et seq.] (exceeding the amount otherwise permitted under section 1916 [42 USCS § 1396o]), and shall treat coverage under the group health plan as a third party liability (under section 1902(a)(25) [42 USCS § 1396a(a)(25)]).

(b) Timing of enrollment; failure to enroll. (1) In establishing guidelines under subsection (a)(1), the Secretary shall take into account that an individual may only be eligible to enroll in group health plans at limited times and only if other individuals (not entitled to medical assistance under the plan) are also enrolled in the plan simultaneously.

(2) If a parent of a child fails to enroll the child in a group health plan in accordance with subsection (a)(2), such failure shall not affect the child's eligibility for benefits under this title [42 USCS §§ 1396 et seq.].

(c) Premiums considered payments for medical assistance; eligibility. (1)(A) In the case of payments of premiums, deductibles, coinsurance, and other cost-sharing obligations under this section shall be considered, for purposes of section 1903(a) [42 USCS § 1396b(a)], to be payments for medical assistance.

(B) If all members of a family are not eligible for medical assistance under this title [42 USCS §§ 1396 et seq.] and enrollment of the members so eligible in a group health plan is not possible without also enrolling members not so eligible—

(i) payment of premiums for enrollment of such other members shall be treated as payments for medical assistance for eligible individuals, if it would be cost-effective (taking into account payment of all such premiums), but

(ii) payment of deductibles, coinsurance, and other cost-sharing obligations for such other members shall not be treated as payments for medical assistance for eligible individuals.

(2) The fact that an individual is enrolled in a group health plan under this section shall not change the individual's eligibility for benefits under the State plan, except insofar as section 1902(a)(25) [42 USCS § 1396a(a)(25)] provides that payment for such benefits shall first be made by such plan.

(d) [Deleted]

(e) Definitions. In this section:

(1) The term "group health plan" has the meaning given such term in section 5000(b)(1) of the Internal Revenue Code of 1986 [26 USCS § 5000(b)(1)], and includes the provision of continuation coverage by such a plan pursuant to title XXII of the Public Health Service Act [42 USCS §§ 300bb-1 et seq.], section 4980B of the Internal Revenue Code of 1986 [26 USCS § 4980B], or title VI of the Employee Retirement Income Security Act of 1974.

(2) The term "cost-effective" has the meaning given that term in section 2105(c)(3)(A) [42 USCS § 1397ee(c)(3)(A)].

(Aug. 14, 1935, ch 531, Title XIX, § 1906, as added Nov. 5, 1990, P. L. 101-508, Title IV, Subtitle B, Part 1, § 4402(a)(2), 104 Stat. 1388-161; Aug. 5, 1997, P. L. 105-33, Title IV, Subtitle H, Ch 5, § 4741(b), 111 Stat. 523; March 23, 2010, P. L. 111-148, Title X, Subtitle B, Part I, § 10203(b)(1), 124 Stat. 927.)

HISTORY; ANCILLARY LAWS AND DIRECTIVES

Other provisions:

Effective date of amendments made by § 10203(b) of Act March 23, 2010. Act March 23, 2010, P. L. 111-148, Title X, Subtitle B, Part I, § 10203(b), 124 Stat. 927, provides that the amendments made by such section [for full classification, consult USCS Tables volumes] are effective as if included in the enactment of the Children's Health Insurance Program Reauthorization Act of 2009 (Public Law 111-3).

§ 1396e-1. Premium assistance option for children [Caution: See prospective amendment note below.]

(a) In general. A State may elect to offer a premium assistance subsidy (as defined in subsection (c)) for qualified employer-sponsored coverage (as defined in subsection (b)) to all individuals under age 19 who are entitled to medical assistance under this title [42 USCS §§ 1396 et seq.] (and to the parent of such an individual) who have access to such coverage if the State meets the requirements of this section and the offering of such a subsidy is cost-effective, as defined for purposes of section 2105(c)(3)(A) [42 USCS § 1397ee(c)(3)(A)].

(b) Qualified employer-sponsored coverage. (1) In general. Subject to paragraph (2)), in this paragraph, the term "qualified employer-sponsored coverage" means a group health plan or health insurance coverage offered through an employer—

(A) that qualifies as creditable coverage as a group health plan under section 2701(c)(1) of the Public Health Service Act [42 USCS § 300gg(c)(1)];

(B) for which the employer contribution toward any premium for such coverage is at least 40 percent; and

(C) that is offered to all individuals in a manner that would be considered a nondiscriminatory eligibility classification for purposes of paragraph (3)(A)(ii) of section 105(h) of the Internal Revenue Code of 1986 [26 USCS § 105(h)] (but determined without regard to clause (i) of subparagraph (B) of such paragraph).

(2) Exception. Such term does not include coverage consisting of—

(A) benefits provided under a health flexible spending arrangement (as defined in section 106(c)(2) of the Internal Revenue Code of 1986 [26 USCS § 106(c)(2)]); or

(B) a high deductible health plan (as defined in section 223(c)(2) of such Code [26 USCS § 223(c)(2)]), without regard to whether the plan is purchased in conjunction with a health savings account (as defined under section 223(d) of such Code [26 USCS § 223(d)]).

(3) Treatment as third party liability. The State shall treat the coverage provided under qualified employer-sponsored coverage as a third party liability under section 1902(a)(25) [42 USCS § 1396a(a)(25)].

(c) Premium assistance subsidy. In this section, the term "premium assistance subsidy" means the amount of the employee contribution for enrollment in the qualified employer-sponsored coverage by the individual under age 19 or by the individual's family. Premium assistance subsidies under this section shall be considered, for purposes of section 1903(a) [42 USCS § 1396b(a)], to be a payment for medical assistance.

(d) Voluntary participation. (1) Employers. Participation by an employer in a premium assistance subsidy offered by a State under this section shall be voluntary. An employer may notify a State that it elects to opt-out of being directly paid a premium assistance subsidy on behalf of an employee.

(2) Beneficiaries. No subsidy shall be provided to an individual under age 19 under this section unless the individual (or the individual's parent) voluntarily elects to receive such a subsidy. A State may not require such an election as a condition of receipt of medical assistance. State may not require, as a condition of an individual under age 19 (or the individual's parent) being or remaining eligible for medical assistance under this title, apply for enrollment in qualified employer-sponsored coverage under this section.

(3) Opt-out permitted for any month. A State shall establish a process for permitting the parent of an individual under age 19 receiving a premium assistance subsidy to disenroll the individual from the qualified employer-sponsored coverage.

(e) Requirement to pay premiums and cost-sharing and provide supplemental coverage. In the case of the participation of an individual under age 19 (or the individual's parent) in a premium assistance subsidy under this section for qualified employer-sponsored coverage, the State shall provide for payment of all enrollee premiums for enrollment in such coverage and all deductibles, coinsurance, and other cost-sharing obligations for items and services otherwise covered under the State plan under this title [42 USCS §§ 1396 et seq.] (exceeding the amount otherwise permitted under section 1916 [42 USCS § 1396o] or, if applicable, section 1916A [42 USCS § 1396o-1]). The fact that an individual under age 19 (or a parent) elects to enroll in qualified employer-sponsored coverage under this section shall not change the individual's (or parent's) eligibility for medical assistance under the State plan, except insofar as section 1902(a)(25) [42 USCS § 1396a(a)(25)] provides that payments for such assistance shall first be made under such coverage.

(Aug. 14, 1935, ch 531, Title XIX, § 1906A, as added Feb. 4, 2009, P. L. 111-3, Title III, Subtitle A, § 301(b), 123 Stat. 61; March 23, 2010, P. L. 111-148, Title II, Subtitle A, § 2003(a), (b), Title X, Subtitle B, Part I, § 10203(b)(2)(A), 124 Stat. 282, 927.)

HISTORY; ANCILLARY LAWS AND DIRECTIVES

Prospective amendments:

Amendment of section and heading, effective January 1, 2014. Act March 23, 2010, P. L. 111-148, Title II, Subtitle A, § 2003(a), (b), 124 Stat. 282 (effective 1/1/2014, as provided by § 2003(c) of such Act, which appears as a note to this section), provides:

"(a) In general. Section 1906A of such Act (42 U.S.C. 1396e-1) is amended—

"(1) in subsection (a)—

"(A) by striking 'may elect to' and inserting 'shall';

"(B) by striking 'under age 19'; and

"(C) by inserting ', in the case of an individual under age 19,' after '(and';

"(2) in subsection (c), in the first sentence, by striking 'under age 19'; and

"(3) in subsection (d)—

"(A) in paragraph (2)—

"(i) in the first sentence, by striking 'under age 19'; and

"(ii) by striking the third sentence and inserting 'A State may not require, as a condition of an individual (or the individual's parent) being or remaining eligible for medical assistance under this title, that the individual (or the individual's parent) apply for enrollment in qualified employer-sponsored coverage under this section.'; and

"(B) in paragraph (3), by striking 'the parent of an individual under age 19' and inserting 'an individual (or the parent of an individual)'; and

"(4) in subsection (e), by striking 'under age 19' each place it appears.

"(b) Conforming amendment. The heading for section 1906A of such Act (42 U.S.C. 1396e-1) is amended by striking 'option for children'.".

Other provisions:

Effective date of March 23, 2010 amendments. Act March 23, 2010, P. L. 111-148, Title II, Subtitle A, § 2003(c), 124 Stat. 283, provides: "The amendments made by this section [amending this section] take effect on January 1, 2014.".

Application of amendment by § 2003(a)(1)(A) of Act March 23, 2010. Act March 23, 2010, P. L. 111-148, Title X, Subtitle B, Part I, § 10203(b)(2)(B), 124 Stat. 927, provides: "This Act shall be applied without regard to subparagraph (A) of section 2003(a)(1) of this Act and that subparagraph and the amendment made by that subparagraph [substituting 'shall' for 'may elect to' in subsec. (a) of this section] are hereby deemed null, void, and of no effect.".

§ 1396n. Compliance with State plan and payment provisions

(a) Activities deemed as compliance. A State shall not be deemed to be out of compliance with the requirements of paragraphs (1), (10), or (23) of section 1902(a) [42 USCS § 1396a(1), (10), or (23)] solely by reason of the fact that the State (or any political subdivision thereof)—

(1) has entered into—

(A) a contract with an organization which has agreed to provide care and services in addition to those offered under the State plan to individuals eligible for medical assistance who reside in the geographic area served by such organization and who elect to obtain such care and services from such organization, or by reason of the fact that the plan provides for payment for rural health clinic services only if those services are provided by a rural health clinic; or

(B) arrangements through a competitive bidding process or otherwise for the purchase of laboratory services referred to in section 1905(a)(3) [42 USCS § 1396d(a)(3)] or medical devices if the Secretary has found that—

(i) adequate services or devices will be available under such arrangements, and

(ii) any such laboratory services will be provided only through laboratories—

(I) which meet the applicable requirements of section 1861(e)(9) [42 USCS § 1395x(e)(9)] or paragraphs (16) and (17) of section 1861(s) [42 USCS § 1395x(s)(16) and (17)], and such additional requirements as the Secretary may require, and

(II) no more than 75 percent of whose charges for such services are for services provided to individuals who are entitled to benefits under this title [42 USCS §§ 1396 et seq.] or under part A or part B of title XVIII [42 USCS §§ 1395c et seq. or 1395j et seq.]; or

(2) restricts for a reasonable period of time the provider or providers from which an individual (eligible for medical assistance for items or services under the State plan) can receive such items or services, if—

(A) the State has found, after notice and opportunity for a hearing (in accordance with procedures established by the State), that the individual has utilized such items or services at a frequency or amount not medically necessary (as determined in accordance with utilization guidelines established by the State), and

(B) under such restriction, individuals eligible for medical assistance for such services have reasonable access (taking into account geographic location and reasonable travel time) to such services of adequate quality.

(b) Waivers to promote cost-effectiveness and efficiency. The Secretary, to the extent he finds it to be cost-effective and efficient and not inconsistent with the purposes of this title [42 USCS §§ 1396 et seq.], may waive such requirements of section 1902 [42 USCS § 1396a] (other than subsection (s)) (other than sections 1902(a)(15), 1902(bb), and 1902(a)(10)(A) [42 USCS § 1396a(a)(15), (bb), and (a)(10)(A)] insofar as it requires provision of the care and services described in section 1905(a)(2)(C) [42 USCS § 1396d(a)(2)(C)]) as may be necessary for a State—

(1) to implement a primary care case-management system or a specialty physician services arrangement which restricts the provider from (or through) whom an individual (eligible for medical assistance under this title [42 USCS §§ 1396 et seq.]) can obtain medical care services (other than in emergency circumstances), if such restriction does not substantially impair access to such services of adequate quality where medically necessary,

(2) to allow a locality to act as a central broker in assisting individuals (eligible for medical assistance under this title [42 USCS §§ 1396 et seq.]) in selecting among competing health care plans, if such restriction does not substantially impair access to services of adequate quality where medically necessary,

(3) to share (through provision of additional services) with recipients of medical assistance under the State plan cost savings resulting from use by the recipient of more cost-effective medical care, and

(4) to restrict the provider from (or through) whom an individual (eligible for medical assistance under this title [42 USCS §§ 1396 et seq.]) can obtain services (other than in emergency circumstances) to providers or practitioners who undertake to provide such services and who meet, accept, and comply with the reimbursement, quality, and utilization standards under the State plan, which standards shall be consistent with the requirements of section 1923 [42 USCS § 1396r-4] and are consistent with access, quality, and efficient and economic provision of covered care and services, if such restriction does not discriminate among classes of providers on grounds unrelated to their demonstrated effectiveness and efficiency in providing those services and if providers under such restriction are paid on a timely basis in the same manner as health care practitioners must be paid under section 1902(a)(37)(A) [42 USCS § 1396a(a)(37)(A)].

No waiver under this subsection may restrict the choice of the individual in receiving services under section 1905(a)(4)(C) [42 USCS § 1396d(a)(4)(C)]. Subsection (h)(2) shall apply to a waiver under this subsection.

(c) Waiver respecting medical assistance requirement in State plan; scope, etc.; "habilitation services" defined; imposition of certain regulatory limits prohibited; computation of expenditures for certain disabled patients; coordinated services; substitution of participants. (1) The Secretary may by waiver provide that a State plan approved under this title [42 USCS §§ 1396 et seq.] may include as "medical assistance" under such plan payment for part or all of the cost of home or community-based services (other than room and board) approved by the Secretary which are provided pursuant to a written plan of care to individuals with respect to whom there has been a determination that but for the provision of such services the individuals would require the level of care provided in a hospital or a nursing facility or intermediate care facility for the mentally retarded the cost of which could be reimbursed under the State plan. For purposes of this subsection, the term "room and board" shall not include an amount established under a method determined by the State to reflect the portion of costs of rent and food attributable to an unrelated personal caregiver who is residing in the same household with an individual who, but for the assistance of such caregiver, would require admission to a hospital, nursing facility, or intermediate care facility for the mentally retarded.

(2) A waiver shall not be granted under this subsection unless the State provides assurances satisfactory to the Secretary that—

(A) necessary safeguards (including adequate standards for provider participation) have been taken to protect the health and welfare of individuals provided services under the waiver and to assure financial accountability for funds expended with respect to such services;

(B) the State will provide, with respect to individuals who—

(i) are entitled to medical assistance for inpatient hospital services, nursing facility services, or services in an intermediate care facility for the mentally retarded under the State plan,

(ii) may require such services, and

(iii) may be eligible for such home or community-based care under such waiver,

for an evaluation of the need for inpatient hospital services, nursing facility services, or services in an intermediate care facility for the mentally retarded;

(C) such individuals who are determined to be likely to require the level of care provided in a hospital, nursing facility, or intermediate care facility for the mentally retarded are informed of the feasible alternatives, if available under the waiver, at the choice of such individuals, to the provision of inpatient hospital services, nursing facility services, or services in an intermediate care facility for the mentally retarded;

(D) under such waiver the average per capita expenditure estimated by the State in any fiscal year for medical assistance provided with respect to such individuals does not exceed 100 percent of the average per capita expenditure that the State reasonably estimates would have been made in that fiscal year for expenditures under the State plan for such individuals if the waiver had not been granted; and

(E) the State will provide to the Secretary annually, consistent with a data collection plan designed by the Secretary, information on the impact of the waiver granted under this subsection on the type and amount of medical assistance provided under the State plan and on the health and welfare of recipients.

(3) A waiver granted under this subsection may include a waiver of the requirements of section 1902(a)(1) [42 USCS § 1396a(a)(1)] (relating to statewideness), section 1902(a)(10)(B) [42 USCS § 1396a(a)(10)(B)] (relating to comparability), and section 1902(a)(10)(C)(i)(III) [42 USCS § 1396a(a)(10)(C)(i)(III)] (relating to income and resource rules applicable in the community). A waiver under this subsection (other than a waiver described in subsection (h)(2)) shall be for an initial term of three years and, upon the request of a State, shall be extended for additional five-year periods unless the Secretary determines that for the previous waiver period the assurances provided under paragraph (2) have not been met. A waiver may provide, with respect to post-eligibility treatment of income of all individuals receiving services under that waiver, that the maximum amount of the individual's income which may be disregarded for any month for the maintenance needs of the individual may be an amount greater than the maximum allowed for that purpose under the regulations in effect on July 1, 1985.

(4) A waiver granted under this subsection may, consistent with paragraph (2)—

(A) limit the individuals provided benefits under such waiver to individuals with respect to whom the State has determined that there is a reasonable expectation that the amount of medical assistance provided with respect to the individual under such waiver will not exceed the amount of such medical assistance provided for such individual if the waiver did not apply, and

(B) provide medical assistance to individuals (to the extent consistent with written plans of care, which are subject to the approval of the State) for case management services, homemaker/home health aide services and personal care services, adult day health services, habilitation services, respite care, and such other services requested by the State as the Secretary may approve and for day treatment or other partial hospitalization services, psychosocial rehabilitation services, and clinic services (whether or not furnished in a facility) for individuals with chronic mental illness.

Except as provided under paragraph (2)(D), the Secretary may not restrict the number of hours or days of respite care in any period which a State may provide under a waiver under this subsection.

(5) For purposes of paragraph (4)(B), the term "habilitation services"—

(A) means services designed to assist individuals in acquiring, retaining, and improving the self-help, socialization, and adaptive skills necessary to reside successfully in home and community based settings; and

(B) includes (except as provided in subparagraph (C)) prevocational, educational, and supported employment services; but

(C) does not include—

(i) special education and related services (as such terms are defined in section 602 of the Individuals with Disabilities Education Act (20 U.S.C. 1401)) which otherwise are available to the individual through a local educational agency; and

(ii) vocational rehabilitation services which otherwise are available to the individual through a program funded under section 110 of the Rehabilitation Act of 1973 (29 U.S.C. 730).

(6) The Secretary may not require, as a condition of approval of a waiver under this section under paragraph (2)(D), that the actual total expenditures for home and community-based services under the waiver (and a claim

for Federal financial participation in expenditures for the services) cannot exceed the approved estimates for these services. The Secretary may not deny Federal financial payment with respect to services under such a waiver on the ground that, in order to comply with paragraph (2)(D), a State has failed to comply with such a requirement.

(7)(A) In making estimates under paragraph (2)(D) in the case of a waiver that applies only to individuals with a particular illness or condition who are inpatients in, or who would require the level of care provided in, hospitals,[,] nursing facilities, or intermediate care facilities for the mentally retarded, the State may determine the average per capita expenditure that would have been made in a fiscal year for those individuals under the State plan separately from the expenditures for other individuals who are inpatients in, or who would require the level of care provided in, those respective facilities.

(B) In making estimates under paragraph (2)(D) in the case of a waiver that applies only to individuals with developmental disabilities who are inpatients in a nursing facility and whom the State has determined, on the basis of an evaluation under paragraph (2)(B), to need the level of services provided by an intermediate care facility for the mentally retarded, the State may determine the average per capita expenditures that would have been made in a fiscal year for those individuals under the State plan on the basis of the average per capita expenditures under the State plan for services to individuals who are inpatients in an intermediate care facility for the mentally retarded, without regard to the availability of beds for such inpatients.

(C) In making estimates under paragraph (2)(D) in the case of a waiver to the extent that it applies to individuals with mental retardation or a related condition who are resident in an intermediate care facility for the mentally retarded the participation of which under the State plan is terminated, the State may determine the average per capita expenditures that would have been made in a fiscal year for those individuals without regard to any such termination.

(8) The State agency administering the plan under this title [42 USCS §§ 1396 et seq.] may, whenever appropriate, enter into cooperative arrangements with the State agency responsible for administering the program for children with special health care needs under title V [42 USCS §§ 701 et seq.] in order to assure improved access to coordinated services to meet the needs of such children.

(9) In the case of any waiver under this subsection which contains a limit on the number of individuals who shall receive home or community-based services, the State may substitute additional individuals to receive such services to replace any individuals who die or become ineligible for services under the State plan.

(10) The Secretary shall not limit to fewer than 200 the number of individuals in the State who may receive home and community-based services under a waiver under this subsection.

(d) Home and community-based services for elderly. (1) Subject to paragraph (2), the Secretary shall grant a waiver to provide that a State plan approved under this title [42 USCS §§ 1396 et seq.] shall include as "medical assistance" under such plan payment for part or all of the cost of home or community-based services (other than room and board) which are provided pursuant to a written plan of care to individuals 65 years of age or older with respect to whom there has been a determination that but for the provision of such services the individuals would be likely to require the level of care provided in a skilled nursing facility or intermediate care facility the cost of which could be reimbursed under the State plan. For purposes of this subsection, the term "room and board" shall not include an amount established under a method determined by the State to reflect the portion of costs of rent and food attributable to an unrelated personal caregiver who is residing in the same household with an individual who, but for the assistance of such caregiver, would require admission to a hospital, nursing facility, or intermediate care facility for the mentally retarded.

(2) A waiver shall not be granted under this subsection unless the State provides assurances satisfactory to the Secretary that—

(A) necessary safeguards (including adequate standards for provider participation) have been taken to protect the health and welfare of individuals provided services under the waiver and to assure financial accountability for funds expended with respect to such services;

(B) with respect to individuals 65 years of age or older who—

(i) are entitled to medical assistance for skilled nursing or intermediate care facility services under the State plan,

(ii) may require such services, and

(iii) may be eligible for such home or community-based services under such waiver, the State will provide for an evaluation of the need for such skilled nursing facility or intermediate care facility services; and

(C) such individuals who are determined to be likely to require the level of care provided in a skilled nursing facility or intermediate care facility are informed of the feasible alternatives to the provision of skilled nursing facility or intermediate care facility services, which such individuals may choose if available under the waiver.

Each State with a waiver under this subsection shall provide to the Secretary annually, consistent with a reasonable data collection plan designed by the Secretary, information on the impact of the waiver granted under this subsection on the type and amount of medical assistance provided under the State plan and on the health and welfare of recipients.

(3) A waiver granted under this subsection may include a waiver of the requirements of section 1902(a)(1) [42 USCS § 1396a(a)(1)] (relating to statewideness), section 1902(a)(10)(B) [42 USCS § 1396a(a)(10)(B)] (relating to comparability), and section 1902(a)(10)(C)(i)(III) [42 USCS § 1396a(a)(10)(C)(i)(III)] (relating to income and resource rules applicable in the community). Subject to a termination by the State (with notice to the Secretary) at any time, a waiver under this subsection (other than a waiver described in subsection (h)(2)) shall be for an initial term of 3 years and, upon the request of a State, shall be extended for additional 5-year periods unless the Secretary determines that for the previous waiver period the assurances provided under paragraph (2) have not been met. A waiver may provide, with respect to post-eligibility treatment of income of all individuals receiving services under the waiver, that the maximum amount of the individual's income which may be disregarded for any month is equal to the amount that may be allowed for that purpose under a waiver under subsection (c).

(4) A waiver under this subsection may, consistent with paragraph (2), provide medical assistance to individuals for case management services, homemaker/home health aide services and personal care services, adult day health services, respite care, and other medical and social services that can contribute to the health and well-being of individuals and their ability to reside in a community-based care setting.

(5)(A) In the case of a State having a waiver approved under this subsection, notwithstanding any other provision of section 1903 [42 USCS § 1396b] to the contrary, the total amount expended by the State for medical assistance with respect to skilled nursing facility services, intermediate care facility services, and home and community-based services under the State plan for individuals 65 years of age or older during a waiver year under this subsection may not exceed the projected amount determined under subparagraph (B).

(B) For purposes of subparagraph (A), the projected amount under this subparagraph is the sum of the following:

(i) The aggregate amount of the State's medical assistance under this title [42 USCS §§ 1396 et seq.] for skilled nursing facility services and intermediate care facility services furnished to individuals who have attained the age of 65 for the base year increased by a percentage which is equal to the lesser of 7 percent times the number of years (rounded to the nearest quarter of a year) beginning after the base year and ending at the end of the waiver year involved or the sum of—

(I) the percentage increase (based on an appropriate market-basket index representing the costs of elements of such services) between the beginning of the base year and the beginning of the waiver year involved, plus

(II) the percentage increase between the beginning of the base year and the beginning of waiver year involved in the number of residents in the State who have attained the age of 65, plus

(III) 2 percent for each year (rounded to the nearest quarter of a year) beginning after the base year and ending at the end of the waiver year.

(ii) The aggregate amount of the State's medical assistance under this title [42 USCS §§ 1396 et seq.] for home and community-based services for individuals who have attained the age of 65 for the base year increased by a percentage which is equal to the lesser of 7 percent times the number of years (rounded to the nearest quarter of a year) beginning after the base year and ending at the end of the waiver year involved or the sum of—

(I) the percentage increase (based on an appropriate market-basket index representing the costs of elements of such services) between the beginning of the base year and the beginning of the waiver year involved, plus

(II) the percentage increase between the beginning of the base year and the beginning of the waiver year involved in the number of residents in the State who have attained the age of 65, plus

(III) 2 percent for each year (rounded to the nearest quarter of a year) beginning after the base year and ending at the end of the waiver year.

(iii) The Secretary shall develop and promulgate by regulation (by not later than October 1, 1989)—

(I) a method, based on an index of appropriately weighted indicators of changes in the wages and prices of the mix of goods and services which comprise both skilled nursing facility services and intermediate care facility services (regardless of the source of payment for such services), for projecting the percentage increase for purposes of clause (i)(I);

(II) a method, based on an index of appropriately weighted indicators of changes in the wages and prices of the mix of goods and services which comprise home and community-based services (regardless of the source of payment for such services), for projecting the percentage increase for purposes of clause (ii)(I); and

(III) a method for projecting, on a State specific basis, the percentage increase in the number of residents in each State who are over 65 years of age for any period.

The Secretary shall develop (by not later than October 1, 1989) a method for projecting, on a State-specific basis, the percentage increase in the number of residents in each State who are over 65 years of age for any period. Effective on and after the date the Secretary promulgates the regulation under clause (iii), any reference in this subparagraph to the "lesser of 7 percent" shall be deemed to be a reference to the "greater of 7 percent".

(iv) If there is enacted after December 22, 1987, an Act which amends this title [42 USCS §§ 1396 et seq.] whose provisions become effective on or after such date and which results in an increase in the aggregate amount of medical assistance under this title [42 USCS §§ 1396 et seq.] for nursing facility services and home and community-based services for individuals who have attained the age of 65 years, the Secretary, at the request of a State with a waiver under this subsection for a waiver year or years and in close consultation with the State, shall adjust the projected amount computed under this subparagraph for the waiver year or years to take into account such increase.

(C) In this paragraph:

(i) The term "home and community-based services" includes services described in sections 1905(a)(7) and 1905(a)(8) [42 USCS § 1396d(a)(7) and (8)], services described in subsection (c)(4)(B), services described in paragraph (4), and personal care services.

(ii)(I) Subject to subclause (II), the term "base year" means the most recent year (ending before the date of the enactment of this subsection [enacted Dec. 22, 1986]) for which actual final expenditures under this title [42 USCS §§ 1396 et seq.] have been reported to, and accepted by, the Secretary.

(II) For purposes of subparagraph (C), in the case of a State that does not report expenditures on the basis of the age categories described in such subparagraph for a year ending before the date of the enactment of this subsection, the term "base year" means fiscal year 1989.

(iii) The term "intermediate care facility services" does not include services furnished in an institution certified in accordance with section 1905(d) [42 USCS § 1396d(d)].

(6)(A) A determination by the Secretary to deny a request for a waiver (or extension of waiver) under this subsection shall be subject to review to the extent provided under section 1116(b) [42 USCS § 1316(b)].

(B) Notwithstanding any other provision of this Act, if the Secretary denies a request of the State for an extension of a waiver under this subsection, any waiver under this subsection in effect on the date such request is made shall remain in effect for a period of not less than 90 days after the date on which the Secretary denies such request (or, if the State seeks review of such determination in accordance with subparagraph (A), the date on which a final determination is made with respect to such review).

(e) Waiver for children infected with AIDS or drug dependent at birth. (1)(A) Subject to paragraph (2), the Secretary shall grant a waiver to provide that a State plan approved under this title [42 USCS §§ 1396 et seq.] shall include as "medical assistance" under such plan payment for part or all of the cost of nursing care, respite care, physicians' services, prescribed drugs, medical devices and supplies, transportation services, and such other services requested by the State as the Secretary may approve which are provided pursuant to a written plan of care to a child described in subparagraph (B) with respect to whom there has been a determination that but for the provision of such services the infants would be likely to require the level of care provided in a hospital or nursing facility the cost of which could be reimbursed under the State plan.

(B) Children described in this subparagraph are individuals under 5 years of age who—

(i) at the time of birth were infected with (or tested positively for) the etiologic agent for acquired immune deficiency syndrome (AIDS),

(ii) have such syndrome, or

(iii) at the time of birth were dependent on heroin, cocaine, or phencyclidine,

and with respect to whom adoption or foster care assistance is (or will be) made available under part E of title IV [42 USCS §§ 670 et seq.].

(2) A waiver shall not be granted under this subsection unless the State provides assurances satisfactory to the Secretary that—

(A) necessary safeguards (including adequate standards for provider participation) have been taken to protect the health and welfare of individuals provided services under the waiver and to assure financial accountability for funds expended with respect to such services;

(B) under such waiver the average per capita expenditure estimated by the State in any fiscal year for medical assistance provided with respect to such individuals does not exceed 100 percent of the average per capita expenditure that the State reasonably estimates would have been made in that fiscal year for expenditures under the State plan for such individuals if the waiver had not been granted; and

(C) the State will provide to the Secretary annually, consistent with a data collection plan designed by the Secretary, information on the impact of the waiver granted under this subsection on the type and amount of medical assistance provided under the State plan and on the health and welfare of recipients.

(3) A waiver granted under this subsection may include a waiver of the requirements of section 1902(a)(1) [42 USCS § 1396a(a)(1)] (relating to statewideness) and section 1902(a)(10)(B) [42 USCS § 1396a(a)(10)(B)] (relating to comparability). A waiver under this subsection shall be for an initial term of 3 years and, upon the request of a State, shall be extended for additional five-year periods unless the Secretary determines that for the previous waiver period the assurances provided under paragraph (2) have not been met.

(4) The provisions of paragraph (6) of subsection (d) shall apply to this subsection in the same manner as it applies to subsection (d).

(f) Monitor of implementation of waivers; termination of waiver for noncompliance; time limitation for action on requests for plan approval, amendments, or waivers. (1) The Secretary shall monitor the implementation of waivers granted under this section to assure that the requirements for such waiver are being met and shall, after notice and opportunity for a hearing, terminate any such waiver where he finds noncompliance has occurred.

(2) A request to the Secretary from a State for approval of a proposed State plan or plan amendment or a waiver of a requirement of this title [42 USCS §§ 1396 et seq.] submitted by the State pursuant to a provision of this title [42 USCS §§ 1396 et seq.] shall be deemed granted unless the Secretary, within 90 days after the date of its submission to the Secretary, either denies such request in writing or informs the State agency in writing with respect to any additional information which is needed in order to make a final determination with respect to the request. After the date the Secretary receives such additional information, the request shall be deemed granted unless the Secretary, within 90 days of such date, denies such request.

(g) Optional targeted case management services. (1) A State may provide, as medical assistance, case management services under the plan without regard to the requirements of section 1902(a)(1) and section 1902(a)(10)(B) [42 USCS § 1396a(a)(1) and (a)(10)(B)]. The provision of case management services under this subsection shall not restrict the choice of the individual to receive medical assistance in violation of section 1902(a)(23) [42 USCS § 1396a(a)(23)]. A State may limit the provision of case management services under this subsection to individuals with acquired immune deficiency syndrome (AIDS), or with AIDS-related conditions, or with either, or to individuals described in section 1902(z)(1)(A) [42 USCS § 1396a(z)(1)(A)] and a State may limit the provision of case management services under this subsection to individuals with chronic mental illness. The State may limit the case managers available with respect to case management services for eligible individuals with developmental disabilities or with chronic mental illness in order to ensure that the case managers for such individuals are capable of ensuring that such individuals receive needed services.

(2) For purposes of this subsection:

(A)(i) The term "case management services" means services which will assist individuals eligible under the plan in gaining access to needed medical, social, educational, and other services.

(ii) Such term includes the following:

(I) Assessment of an eligible individual to determine service needs, including activities that focus on needs identification, to determine the need for any medical, educational, social, or other services. Such assessment activities include the following:

(aa) Taking client history.

(bb) Identifying the needs of the individual, and completing related documentation.

(cc) Gathering information from other sources such as family members, medical providers, social workers, and educators, if necessary, to form a complete assessment of the eligible individual.

(II) Development of a specific care plan based on the information collected through an assessment, that specifies the goals and actions to address the medical, social, educational, and other services needed by the eligible individual, including activities such as ensuring the active participation of the eligible individual and working with the individual (or the individual's authorized health care decision maker) and others to develop such goals and identify a course of action to respond to the assessed needs of the eligible individual.

(III) Referral and related activities to help an individual obtain needed services, including activities that help link eligible individuals with medical, social, educational providers or other programs and services that are capable of providing needed services, such as making referrals to providers for needed services and scheduling appointments for the individual.

(IV) Monitoring and followup activities, including activities and contacts that are necessary to ensure the care plan is effectively implemented and adequately addressing the needs of the eligible individual, and which may be with the individual, family members, providers, or other entities and conducted as frequently as necessary to help determine such matters as—

(aa) whether services are being furnished in accordance with an individual's care plan;

(bb) whether the services in the care plan are adequate; and

(cc) whether there are changes in the needs or status of the eligible individual, and if so, making necessary adjustments in the care plan and service arrangements with providers.

(iii) Such term does not include the direct delivery of an underlying medical, educational, social, or other service to which an eligible individual has been referred, including, with respect to the direct delivery of foster care services, services such as (but not limited to) the following:

(I) Research gathering and completion of documentation required by the foster care program.

(II) Assessing adoption placements.

(III) Recruiting or interviewing potential foster care parents.

(IV) Serving legal papers.

(V) Home investigations.

(VI) Providing transportation.

(VII) Administering foster care subsidies.

(VIII) Making placement arrangements.

(B) The term "targeted case management services" are case management services that are furnished without regard to the requirements of section 1902(a)(1) [42 USCS § 1396a(a)(1)] and section 1902(a)(10)(B) [42 USCS § 1396a(a)(10)(B)] to specific classes of individuals or to individuals who reside in specified areas.

(3) With respect to contacts with individuals who are not eligible for medical assistance under the State plan or, in the case of targeted case management services, individuals who are eligible for such assistance but are not part of the target population specified in the State plan, such contacts—

(A) are considered an allowable case management activity, when the purpose of the contact is directly related to the management of the eligible individual's care; and

(B) are not considered an allowable case management activity if such contacts relate directly to the identification and management of the noneligible or nontargeted individual's needs and care.

(4)(A) In accordance with section 1902(a)(25) [42 USCS § 1396a(a)(25)], Federal financial participation only is available under this title [42 USCS §§ 1396 et seq.] for case management services or targeted case management services if there are no other third parties liable to pay for such services, including as reimbursement under a medical, social, educational, or other program.

(B) A State shall allocate the costs of any part of such services which are reimbursable under another federally funded program in accordance with OMB Circular A-87 (or any related or successor guidance or regulations regarding allocation of costs among federally funded programs) under an approved cost allocation program.

(5) Nothing in this subsection shall be construed as affecting the application of rules with respect to third party liability under programs, or activities carried out under title XXVI of the Public Health Service Act [42 USCS §§ 300ff-11 et seq.] or by the Indian Health Service.

(h) Period of waivers; continuations. (1) No waiver under this section (other than a waiver under subsection (c), (d), or (e), or a waiver described in paragraph (2)) may extend over a period of longer than two years unless the State requests continuation of such waiver, and such request shall be deemed granted unless the Secretary, within 90 days after the date of its submission to the Secretary, either denies such request in writing or informs the State agency in writing with respect to any additional information which is needed in order to make a final determination with respect to the request. After the date the Secretary receives such additional information, the request shall be deemed granted unless the Secretary, within 90 days of such date, denies such request.

(2)(A) Notwithstanding subsections (c)(3) and (d) (3), any waiver under subsection (b), (c), or (d), or a waiver under section 1115 [42 USCS § 1315], that provides medical assistance for dual eligible individuals (including any such waivers under which non dual eligible individuals may be enrolled in addition to dual eligible individuals) may be conducted for a period of 5 years and, upon the request of the State, may be extended for additional 5-year periods unless the Secretary determines that for the previous waiver period the conditions for the waiver have not been met or it would no longer be cost-effective and efficient, or consistent with the purposes of this title, to extend the waiver.

(B) In this paragraph, the term "dual eligible individual" means an individual who is entitled to, or enrolled for, benefits under part A of title XVIII [42 USCS §§ 1395c et seq.], or enrolled for benefits under part B of title XVIII [42 USCS §§ 1395j et seq.], and is eligible for medical assistance under the State plan under this title or under a waiver of such plan.

(i) State plan amendment option to provide home and community-based services for elderly and disabled individuals. (1) In general. Subject to the succeeding provisions of this subsection, a State may provide through a State plan amendment for the provision of medical assistance for home and community-based services (within the scope of services described in paragraph (4)(B) of subsection (c) for which the Secretary has the authority to approve a waiver and not including room and board) for individuals eligible for medical assistance under the State plan whose income does not exceed 150 percent of the poverty line (as defined in section 2110(c)(5) [42 USCS § 1397jj(c)(5)]), without determining that but for the provision of such services the individuals would require the level of care provided in a hospital or a nursing facility or intermediate care facility for the mentally retarded, but only if the State meets the following requirements:

(A) Needs-based criteria for eligibility for, and receipt of, home and community-based services. The State establishes needs-based criteria for determining an individual's eligibility under the State plan for medical assistance for such home and community-based services, and if the individual is eligible for such services, the specific home and community-based services that the individual will receive.

(B) Establishment of more stringent needs-based eligibility criteria for institutionalized care. The State establishes needs-based criteria for determining whether an individual requires the level of care provided in a hospital, a nursing facility, or an intermediate care facility for the mentally retarded under the State plan or under any waiver of such plan that are more stringent than the needs-based criteria established under subparagraph (A) for determining eligibility for home and community-based services.

(C) Projection of number of individuals to be provided home and community-based services. The State submits to the Secretary, in such form and manner, and upon such frequency as the Secretary shall specify, the projected number of individuals to be provided home and community-based services.

(D) Criteria based on individual assessment. (i) In general. The criteria established by the State for purposes of subparagraphs (A) and (B) requires an assessment of an individual's support needs and capabilities, and may take into account the inability of the individual to perform 2 or more activities of daily living (as defined in section 7702B(c)(2)(B) of the Internal Revenue Code of 1986 [26 USCS § 7702B(c)(2)(B)]) or the need for significant assistance to perform such activities, and such other risk factors as the State determines to be appropriate.

(ii) Adjustment authority. The State plan amendment provides the State with the option to modify the criteria established under subparagraph (A) (without having to obtain prior approval from the Secretary) in the event that the enrollment of individuals eligible for home and community-based services exceeds the projected enrollment submitted for purposes of subparagraph (C), but only if—

(I) the State provides at least 60 days notice to the Secretary and the public of the proposed modification;

(II) the State deems an individual receiving home and community-based services on the basis of the most recent version of the criteria in effect prior to the effective date of the modification to continue to be eligible for such services after the effective date of the modification and until such time as the individual no longer meets the standard for receipt of such services under such pre-modified criteria; and

(III) after the effective date of such modification, the State, at a minimum, applies the criteria for determining whether an individual requires the level of care provided in a hospital, a nursing facility, or an intermediate care facility for the mentally retarded under the State plan or under any waiver of such plan which applied prior to the application of the more stringent criteria developed under subparagraph (B).

(E) Independent evaluation and assessment. (i) Eligibility determination. The State uses an independent evaluation for making the determinations described in subparagraphs (A) and (B).

(ii) Assessment. In the case of an individual who is determined to be eligible for home and community-based services, the State uses an independent assessment, based on the needs of the individual to—

(I) determine a necessary level of services and supports to be provided, consistent with an individual's physical and mental capacity;

(II) prevent the provision of unnecessary or inappropriate care; and

(III) establish an individualized care plan for the individual in accordance with subparagraph (G).

(F) Assessment. The independent assessment required under subparagraph (E)(ii) shall include the following:

(i) An objective evaluation of an individual's inability to perform 2 or more activities of daily living (as defined in section 7702B(c)(2)(B) of the Internal Revenue Code of 1986 [26 USCS § 7702B(c)(2)(B)]) or the need for significant assistance to perform such activities.

(ii) A face-to-face evaluation of the individual by an individual trained in the assessment and evaluation of individuals whose physical or mental conditions trigger a potential need for home and community-based services.

(iii) Where appropriate, consultation with the individual's family, spouse, guardian, or other responsible individual.

(iv) Consultation with appropriate treating and consulting health and support professionals caring for the individual.

(v) An examination of the individual's relevant history, medical records, and care and support needs, guided by best practices and research on effective strategies that result in improved health and quality of life outcomes.

(vi) If the State offers individuals the option to self-direct the purchase of, or control the receipt of, home and community-based service, an evaluation of the ability of the individual or the individual's representative to self-direct the purchase of, or control the receipt of, such services if the individual so elects.

(G) Individualized care plan. (i) In general. In the case of an individual who is determined to be eligible for home and community-based services, the State uses the independent assessment required under subparagraph (E)(ii) to establish a written individualized care plan for the individual.

(ii) Plan requirements. The State ensures that the individualized care plan for an individual—

(I) is developed—

(aa) in consultation with the individual, the individual's treating physician, health care or support professional, or other appropriate individuals, as defined by the State, and, where appropriate the individual's family, caregiver, or representative; and

(bb) taking into account the extent of, and need for, any family or other supports for the individual;

(II) identifies the necessary home and community-based services to be furnished to the individual (or, if the individual elects to self-direct the purchase of, or control the receipt of, such services, funded for the individual); and

(III) is reviewed at least annually and as needed when there is a significant change in the individual's circumstances.

(iii) State option to offer election for self-directed services. (I) Individual choice. At the option of the State, the State may allow an individual or the individual's representative to elect to receive self-directed home and community-based services in a manner which gives them the most control over such services consistent with the individual's abilities and the requirements of subclauses (II) and (III).

(II) Self-directed services. The term "self-directed" means, with respect to the home and community-based services offered under the State plan amendment, such services for the individual which are planned and purchased under the direction and control of such individual or the individual's authorized representative, including the amount, duration, scope, provider, and location of such services, under the State plan consistent with the following requirements:

(aa) Assessment. There is an assessment of the needs, capabilities, and preferences of the individual with respect to such services.

(bb) Service plan. Based on such assessment, there is developed jointly with such individual or the individual's authorized representative a plan for such services for such individual that is approved by the State and that satisfies the requirements of subclause (III).

(III) Plan requirements. For purposes of subclause (II)(bb), the requirements of this subclause are that the plan—

(aa) specifies those services which the individual or the individual's authorized representative would be responsible for directing;

(bb) identifies the methods by which the individual or the individual's authorized representative will select, manage, and dismiss providers of such services;

(cc) specifies the role of family members and others whose participation is sought by the individual or the individual's authorized representative with respect to such services;

(dd) is developed through a person-centered process that is directed by the individual or the individual's authorized representative, builds upon the individual's capacity to engage in activities that promote community life and that respects the individual's preferences, choices, and abilities, and involves families, friends, and professionals as desired or required by the individual or the individual's authorized representative;

(ee) includes appropriate risk management techniques that recognize the roles and sharing of responsibilities in obtaining services in a self-directed manner and assure the appropriateness of such plan based upon the resources and capabilities of the individual or the individual's authorized representative; and

(ff) may include an individualized budget which identifies the dollar value of the services and supports under the control and direction of the individual or the individual's authorized representative.

(IV) Budget process. With respect to individualized budgets described in subclause (III)(ff), the State plan amendment—

(aa) describes the method for calculating the dollar values in such budgets based on reliable costs and service utilization;

(bb) defines a process for making adjustments in such dollar values to reflect changes in individual assessments and service plans; and

(cc) provides a procedure to evaluate expenditures under such budgets.

(H) Quality assurance; conflict of interest standards. (i) Quality assurance. The State ensures that the provision of home and community-based services meets Federal and State guidelines for quality assurance.

(ii) Conflict of interest standards. The State establishes standards for the conduct of the independent evaluation and the independent assessment to safeguard against conflicts of interest.

(I) Redeterminations and appeals. The State allows for at least annual redeterminations of eligibility, and appeals in accordance with the frequency of, and manner in which, redeterminations and appeals of eligibility are made under the State plan.

(J) Presumptive eligibility for assessment. The State, at its option, elects to provide for a period of presumptive eligibility (not to exceed a period of 60 days) only for those individuals that the State has reason to believe may be eligible for home and community-based services. Such presumptive eligibility shall be limited to medical assistance for carrying out the independent evaluation and assessment under subparagraph (E) to determine an individual's eligibility for such services and if the individual is so eligible, the specific home and community-based services that the individual will receive.

(2) Definition of individual's representative. In this section, the term "individual's representative" means, with respect to an individual, a parent, a family member, or a guardian of the individual, an advocate for the individual, or any other individual who is authorized to represent the individual.

(3) Nonapplication. A State may elect in the State plan amendment approved under this section to not comply with the requirements of 1902(a)(10)(B) [42 USCS § 1396a(a)(10)(B)] (relating to comparability) and section 1902(a)(10)(C)(i)(III) [42 USCS § 1396a(a)(10)(C)(i)(III)] (relating to income and resource rules applicable in the community), but only for purposes of provided home and community-based services in accordance with such amendment. Any such election shall not be construed to apply to the provision of services to an individual receiving medical assistance in an institutionalized setting as a result of a determination that the individual requires the level of care provided in a hospital or a nursing facility or intermediate care facility for the mentally retarded.

(4) No effect on other waiver authority. Nothing in this subsection shall be construed as affecting the option of a State to offer home and community-based services under a waiver under subsections (c) or (d) of this section or under section 1115 [42 USCS § 1315].

(5) Continuation of Federal financial partic-

ipation for medical assistance provided to individuals as of effective date of State plan amendment. Notwithstanding paragraph (1)(B), Federal financial participation shall continue to be available for an individual who is receiving medical assistance in an institutionalized setting, or home and community-based services provided under a waiver under this section or section 1115 [42 USCS § 1315] that is in effect as of the effective date of the State plan amendment submitted under this subsection, as a result of a determination that the individual requires the level of care provided in a hospital or a nursing facility or intermediate care facility for the mentally retarded, without regard to whether such individuals satisfy the more stringent eligibility criteria established under that paragraph, until such time as the individual is discharged from the institution or waiver program or no longer requires such level of care.

(6) State option to provide home and community-based services to individuals eligible for services under a waiver. (A) In general. A State that provides home and community-based services in accordance with this subsection to individuals who satisfy the needs-based criteria for the receipt of such services established under paragraph (1)(A) may, in addition to continuing to provide such services to such individuals, elect to provide home and community-based services in accordance with the requirements of this paragraph to individuals who are eligible for home and community-based services under a waiver approved for the State under subsection (c), (d), or (e) or under section 1115 [42 USCS § 1315] to provide such services, but only for those individuals whose income does not exceed 300 percent of the supplemental security income benefit rate established by section 1611(b)(1) [42 USCS § 1382(b)(1)].

(B) Application of same requirements for individuals satisfying needs-based criteria. Subject to subparagraph (C), a State shall provide home and community-based services to individuals under this paragraph in the same manner and subject to the same requirements as apply under the other paragraphs of this subsection to the provision of home and community-based services to individuals who satisfy the needs-based criteria established under paragraph (1)(A).

(C) Authority to offer different type, amount, duration, or scope of home and community-based services. A State may offer home and community-based services to individuals under this paragraph that differ in type, amount, duration, or scope from the home and community-based services offered for individuals who satisfy the needs-based criteria established under paragraph (1)(A), so long as such services are within the scope of services described in paragraph (4)(B) of subsection (c) for which the Secretary has the authority to approve a waiver and do not include room or board.

(7) State option to offer home and community-based services to specific, targeted populations. (A) In general. A State may elect in a State plan amendment under this subsection to target the provision of home and community-based services under this subsection to specific populations and to differ the type, amount, duration, or scope of such services to such specific populations.

(B) 5-year term. (i) In general. An election by a State under this paragraph shall be for a period of 5 years.

(ii) Phase-in of services and eligibility permitted during initial 5-year period. A State making an election under this paragraph may, during the first 5-year period for which the election is made, phase-in the enrollment of eligible individuals, or the provision of services to such individuals, or both, so long as all eligible individuals in the State for such services are enrolled, and all such services are provided, before the end of the initial 5-year period.

(C) Renewal. An election by a State under this paragraph may be renewed for additional 5-year terms if the Secretary determines, prior to beginning of each such renewal period, that the State has—

(i) adhered to the requirements of this subsection and paragraph in providing services under such an election; and

(ii) met the State's objectives with respect to quality improvement and beneficiary outcomes.

(j)(1) A State may provide, as "medical assistance", payment for part or all of the cost of self-directed personal assistance services (other than room and board) under the plan which are provided pursuant to a written plan of care to individuals with respect to whom there has been a determination that, but for the provision of such services, the individuals would require and receive personal care services under the plan, or home and community-based services provided pursuant to a waiver under subsection (c). Self-directed personal assistance services may not be provided under this subsection to individuals who reside in a home or property that is owned, operated, or controlled by a provider of services, not related by blood or marriage.

(2) The Secretary shall not grant approval for a State self-directed personal assistance services program under this section unless the State provides assurances satisfactory to the Secretary of the following:

(A) Necessary safeguards have been taken to protect the health and welfare of individuals provided services under the program, and to assure financial accountability for funds expended with respect to such services.

(B) The State will provide, with respect to individuals who—

(i) are entitled to medical assistance for personal care services under the plan, or receive home and community-based services under a waiver granted under subsection (c);

(ii) may require self-directed personal assistance services; and

(iii) may be eligible for self-directed personal assistance services,

an evaluation of the need for personal care under the plan, or personal services under a waiver granted under subsection (c).

(C) Such individuals who are determined to be likely to require personal care under the plan, or home and community-based services under a waiver granted under subsection (c) are informed of the feasible alternatives, if available under the State's self-directed personal assistance services program, at the choice of such individuals, to the provision of personal care services under the plan, or personal assistance services under a waiver granted under subsection (c).

(D) The State will provide for a support system that ensures participants in the self-directed personal assistance services program are appropriately assessed and counseled prior to enrollment and are able to manage their budgets. Additional counseling and management support may be provided at the request of the participant.

(E) The State will provide to the Secretary an annual report on the number of individuals served and total expenditures on their behalf in the aggregate. The State shall also provide an evaluation of overall impact on the health and welfare of participating individuals compared to non-participants every three years.

(3) A State may provide self-directed personal assistance services under the State plan without regard to the requirements of section 1902(a)(1) [42 USCS § 1396a(a)(1)] and may limit the population eligible to receive these services and limit the number of persons served without regard to section 1902(a)(10)(B) [42 USCS § 1396a(a)(10)(B)].

(4)(A) For purposes of this subsection, the term "self-directed personal assistance services" means personal care and related services, or home and community-based services otherwise available under the plan under this title [42 USCS §§ 1396 et seq.] or subsection (c), that are provided to an eligible participant under a self-directed personal assistance services program under this section, under which individuals, within an approved self-directed services plan and budget, purchase personal assistance and related services, and permits participants to hire, fire, supervise, and manage the individuals providing such services.

(B) At the election of the State—

(i) a participant may choose to use any individual capable of providing the assigned tasks including legally liable relatives as paid providers of the services; and

(ii) the individual may use the individual's budget to acquire items that increase independence or substitute (such as a microwave oven or an accessibility ramp) for human assistance, to the extent that expenditures would otherwise be made for the human assistance.

(5) For purpose of this section, the term "approved self-directed services plan and budget" means, with respect to a participant, the establishment of a plan and budget for the provision of self-directed personal assistance services, consistent with the following requirements: (A) Self-direction. The participant (or in the case of a participant who is a minor child, the participant's parent or guardian, or in the case of an incapacitated adult, another individual recognized by State law to act on behalf of the participant) exercises choice and control over the budget, planning, and purchase of self-directed personal assistance services, including the amount, duration, scope, provider, and location of service provision.

(B) Assessment of needs. There is an assessment of the needs, strengths, and preferences of the participants for such services.

(C) Service plan. A plan for such services (and supports for such services) for the participant has been developed and approved by the State based on such assessment through a person-centered process that—

(i) builds upon the participant's capacity to engage in activities that promote community life and that respects the participant's preferences, choices, and abilities; and

(ii) involves families, friends, and professionals in the planning or delivery of services or supports as desired or required by the participant.

(D) Service budget. A budget for such services and supports for the participant has been developed and approved by the State based on such assessment and plan and on a methodology that uses valid, reliable cost data, is open to public inspection, and includes a calculation of the expected cost of such services if those services were not self-directed. The budget may not restrict access to other medically necessary care and services furnished under the plan and approved by the State but not included in the budget.

(E) Application of quality assurance and risk management. There are appropriate quality assurance and risk management techniques used in establishing and implementing such plan and budget that recognize the roles and responsibilities in obtaining services in a self-directed manner and assure the appropriateness of such plan and budget based upon the participant's resources and capabilities.

(6) A State may employ a financial management entity to make payments to providers, track costs, and make reports under the program. Payment for the activities of the financial management entity shall be at the administrative rate established in section 1903(a) [42 USCS § 1396b(a)].

(k) State plan option to provide home and community-based attendant services and supports. (1) In general. Subject to the succeeding provisions of this subsection, beginning October 1, 2011, a State may provide through a State plan amendment for the provision of medical assistance for home and community-based attendant services and supports for individuals who are eligible for medical assistance under the State plan whose income does not exceed 150 percent of the poverty line (as defined in section 2110(c)(5) [42 USCS § 1397jj(c)(5)]) or, if greater, the income level applicable for an individual who has been determined to require an institutional level of care to be eligible for nursing facility services under the State plan and with respect to whom there has been a determination that, but for the provision of such services, the individuals would require the level of care provided in a hospital, a nursing facility, an intermediate care facility for the mentally retarded, or an institution for mental diseases, the cost of which could be reimbursed under the State plan, but only if the individual chooses to receive such home and community-based attendant services and supports, and only if the State meets the following requirements:

(A) Availability. The State shall make available home and community-based attendant services and supports to eligible individuals, as needed, to assist in accomplishing activities of daily living, instrumental activities of daily living, and health-related tasks through hands-on assistance, supervision, or cueing—

(i) under a person-centered plan of services and supports that is based on an assessment of functional need and that is agreed to in writing by the individual or, as appropriate, the individual's representative;

(ii) in a home or community setting, which does not include a nursing facility, institution for mental diseases, or an intermediate care facility for the mentally retarded;

(iii) under an agency-provider model or other model (as defined in paragraph (6)(C)); and

(iv) the furnishing of which—

(I) is selected, managed, and dismissed by the individual, or, as appropriate, with assistance from the individual's representative;

(II) is controlled, to the maximum extent possible, by the individual or where appropriate, the individual's representative, regardless of who may act as the employer of record; and

(III) provided by an individual who is qualified to provide such services, including family members (as defined by the Secretary).

(B) Included services and supports. In addition to assistance in accomplishing activities of daily living, instrumental activities of daily living, and health related tasks, the home and community-based attendant services and supports made available include—

(i) the acquisition, maintenance, and enhancement of skills necessary for the individual to accomplish activities of daily living, instrumental activities of daily living, and health related tasks;

(ii) back-up systems or mechanisms (such as the use of beepers or other electronic devices) to ensure continuity of services and supports; and

(iii) voluntary training on how to select, manage, and dismiss attendants.

(C) Excluded services and supports. Subject to subparagraph (D), the home and community-based attendant services and supports made available do not include—

(i) room and board costs for the individual;

(ii) special education and related services provided under the Individuals with Disabilities Education Act [20 USCS §§ 1400 et seq.] and vocational rehabilitation services provided under the Rehabilitation Act of 1973 [29 USCS §§ 701 et seq.];

(iii) assistive technology devices and assistive technology services other than those under (1)(B)(ii);

(iv) medical supplies and equipment; or

(v) home modifications.

(D) Permissible services and supports. The home and community-based attendant services and supports may include—

(i) expenditures for transition costs such as rent and utility deposits, first month's rent and utilities, bedding, basic kitchen supplies, and other necessities required for an individual to make the transition from a nursing facility, institution for mental diseases, or intermediate care facility for the mentally retarded to a community-based home setting where the individual resides; and

(ii) expenditures relating to a need identified in an individual's person-centered plan of services that increase independence or substitute for human assistance, to the extent that expenditures would otherwise be made for the human assistance.

(2) Increased Federal financial participation. For purposes of payments to a State under section 1903(a)(1) [42 USCS § 1396b(a)(1)], with respect to amounts expended by the State to provide medical assistance under the State plan for home and community-based attendant services and supports to eligible individuals in accordance with this subsection during a fiscal year quarter occurring during the period described in paragraph (1), the Federal medical assistance percentage applicable to the State (as determined under section 1905(b) [42 USCS § 1396d(b)]) shall be increased by 6 percentage points.

(3) State requirements. In order for a State plan amendment to be approved under this subsection, the State shall—

(A) develop and implement such amendment in collaboration with a Development and Implementation Council established by the State that includes a majority of members with disabilities, elderly individuals, and their representatives and consults and collaborates with such individuals;

(B) provide consumer controlled home and community-based attendant services and supports to individuals on a statewide basis, in a manner that provides such services and supports in the most integrated setting appropriate to the individual's needs, and without regard to the individual's age, type or nature of disability, severity of disability, or the form of home and community-based attendant services and supports that the individual requires in order to lead an independent life;

(C) with respect to expenditures during the first full fiscal year in which the State plan amendment is implemented, maintain or exceed the level of State expenditures for medical assistance that is provided under section 1905(a) [42 USCS § 1396d(a)], section 1915 [42 USCS § 1396n], section 1115 [42 USCS § 1315], or otherwise to individuals with disabilities or elderly individuals attributable to the preceding fiscal year;

(D) establish and maintain a comprehensive, continuous quality assurance system with respect to community- based attendant services and supports that—

(i) includes standards for agency-based and other delivery models with respect to training, appeals for denials and reconsideration procedures of an individual plan, and other factors as determined by the Secretary;

(ii) incorporates feedback from consumers and their representatives, disability organizations, providers, families of disabled or elderly individuals, members of the community, and others and maximizes consumer independence and consumer control;

(iii) monitors the health and well-being of each individual who receives home and community-based attendant services and supports, including a process for the mandatory reporting, investigation, and resolution of allegations of neglect, abuse, or exploitation in connection with the provision of such services and supports; and

(iv) provides information about the provisions of the quality assurance required under clauses (i) through (iii) to each individual receiving such services; and

(E) collect and report information, as determined necessary by the Secretary, for the purposes of approving the State plan amendment, providing Federal oversight, and conducting an evaluation under paragraph (5)(A), including data regarding how the State provides home and community-based attendant services and supports and other home and community-based services, the cost of such services and supports, and how the State provides individuals with disabilities who otherwise qualify for institutional care under the State plan or under a waiver the choice to instead receive home and community-based services in lieu of institutional care.

(4) Compliance with certain laws. A State shall ensure that, regardless of whether the State uses an agency-provider model or other models to provide home and community-based attendant services and supports under a State plan amendment under this subsection, such services and supports are provided in accordance with the requirements of the Fair Labor Standards Act of 1938 [29 USCS §§ 201 et seq.] and applicable Federal and State laws

regarding—

(A) withholding and payment of Federal and State income and payroll taxes;

(B) the provision of unemployment and workers compensation insurance;

(C) maintenance of general liability insurance; and

(D) occupational health and safety.

(5) Evaluation, data collection, and report to Congress. (A) Evaluation. The Secretary shall conduct an evaluation of the provision of home and community-based attendant services and supports under this subsection in order to determine the effectiveness of the provision of such services and supports in allowing the individuals receiving such services and supports to lead an independent life to the maximum extent possible; the impact on the physical and emotional health of the individuals who receive such services; and an comparative analysis of the costs of services provided under the State plan amendment under this subsection and those provided under institutional care in a nursing facility, institution for mental diseases, or an intermediate care facility for the mentally retarded.

(B) Data collection. The State shall provide the Secretary with the following information regarding the provision of home and community-based attendant services and supports under this subsection for each fiscal year for which such services and supports are provided:

(i) The number of individuals who are estimated to receive home and community-based attendant services and supports under this subsection during the fiscal year.

(ii) The number of individuals that received such services and supports during the preceding fiscal year.

(iii) The specific number of individuals served by type of disability, age, gender, education level, and employment status.

(iv) Whether the specific individuals have been previously served under any other home and community based services program under the State plan or under a waiver.

(C) Reports. Not later than—

(i) December 31, 2013, the Secretary shall submit to Congress and make available to the public an interim report on the findings of the evaluation under subparagraph (A); and

(ii) December 31, 2015, the Secretary shall submit to Congress and make available to the public a final report on the findings of the evaluation under subparagraph (A).

(6) Definitions. In this subsection:

(A) Activities of daily living. The term "activities of daily living" includes tasks such as eating, toileting, grooming, dressing, bathing, and transferring.

(B) Consumer controlled. The term "consumer controlled" means a method of selecting and providing services and supports that allow the individual, or where appropriate, the individual's representative, maximum control of the home and community-based attendant services and supports, regardless of who acts as the employer of record.

(C) Delivery models. (i) Agency-provider model. The term "agency-provider model" means, with respect to the provision of home and community-based attendant services and supports for an individual, subject to paragraph (4), a method of providing consumer controlled services and supports under which entities contract for the provision of such services and supports.

(ii) Other models. The term "other models" means, subject to paragraph (4), methods, other than an agency-provider model, for the provision of consumer controlled services and supports. Such models may include the provision of vouchers, direct cash payments, or use of a fiscal agent to assist in obtaining services.

(D) Health-related tasks. The term "health-related tasks" means specific tasks related to the needs of an individual, which can be delegated or assigned by licensed health-care professionals under State law to be performed by an attendant.

(E) Individual's representative. The term "individual's representative" means a parent, family member, guardian, advocate, or other authorized representative of an individual

(F) Instrumental activities of daily living. The term "instrumental activities of daily living" includes (but is not limited to) meal planning and preparation, managing finances, shopping for food, clothing, and other essential items, performing essential household chores, communicating by phone or other media, and traveling around and participating in the community.

(Aug. 14, 1935, ch 531, Title XIX § 1915, as added Aug. 13, 1981, P. L. 97-35, Title XXI, Subtitle C, Ch. 2, § 2175(b), 95 Stat. 809; Aug. 13, 1981, P. L. 97-35, Title XXI, Subtitle C, Ch. 2, §§ 2176, 2177(a) 95 Stat. 812, 813; Sept. 3, 1982, P. L. 97-248, Title I, Subtitle B, § 137(b)(19)(A), (20)–(25), 96 Stat. 380; Jan. 12, 1983, P. L. 97-448, Title III, § 309(b)(17), 96 Stat. 2409; July 18, 1984, P. L. 98-369, Division B, Title III, Subtitle B, § 2373(b)(21), 98 Stat. 1112; April 7, 1986, P. L. 99-272, Title IX, Subtitle B, §§ 9502(a)–(e), (g)–(i), 9508(a), 100 Stat. 202-204, 210; Oct. 21, 1986, P. L. 99-509,

Title IX, Subtitle D, Part 2, § 9320(h)(3), Subtitle E, Part 2, § 9411(a)–(d), 100 Stat. 2015, 2060; Aug. 18, 1987, P. L. 100-93, § 8(h)(2), 101 Stat. 694; Dec. 22, 1987, P. L. 100-203, Title IV, Subtitle A, Part 3, Subpart C, § 4072(d), Subtitle B, Part 1, § 4102(a)(1), (b)(2), (c), Part 2, § 4118(a), (b), (i)(1), (k), (l)(1), (p)(10), Subtitle C, Part 2, § 4211(h)(10), 101 Stat. 1330-117, 1330-143, 1330-146, 1330-154, 1330-155, 1330-156, 1330-157, 1330-160, 1330-206; July 1, 1988, P. L. 100-360, Title II, Subtitle A, § 204(d)(3), Title IV, Subtitle B, § 411(k)(3)(A), (B), (10)(A), (H), (I), (17)(A), (l)(3)(G), 102 Stat. 729, 791, 794, 796, 799, 800, 803; Oct. 13, 1988, P. L. 100-485, Title VI, § 608(d)(26)(M), (f)(2) 102 Stat. 2422, 2424; Nov. 10, 1988, P. L. 100-647, Title VIII, Subtitle E, Part IV, §§ 8432(b), 8437(a), 102 Stat. 3804, 3806; Dec. 13, 1989, P. L. 101-234, Title II, § 201(a)(1), 103 Stat. 1981; Dec. 19, 1989, P. L. 101-239, Title VI, Subtitle A, Part 2, Subpart A, § 6115(c), Subtitle B, Part 2, § 6411(c)(2), 103 Stat. 2219, 2270; Nov. 5, 1990, P. L. 101-508, Title IV, Subtitle B, Part 3, § 4604(c), Part 4, Subpart A, § 4704(b)(3), 104 Stat. 1388-169, 1388-172, 1388-197, 1388-198; Oct. 7, 1991, P. L. 102-119, § 26(i)(2), 105 Stat. 607; Aug. 10, 1993, P. L. 103-66, Title XIII, Ch. 2, Subch B, Part I, § 13603(d), 107 Stat. 620; Aug. 5, 1997, P. L. 105-33, Title IV, Subtitle B, § 4106(c), Subtitle H, Ch 5, § 4743(a), 111 Stat. 368, 524; Nov. 29, 1999, P. L. 106-113, Div B, § 1000(a)(6), 113 Stat. 1536; Dec. 21, 2000, P. L. 106-554, § 1(a)(6), 114 Stat. 2763; Jan. 15, 2002, P. L. 107-121, § 2(b)(3), 115 Stat. 2384; Dec. 3, 2004, P. L. 108-446, Title III, § 305(j)(2), 118 Stat. 2806; Feb. 8, 2006, P. L. 109-171, Title VI, Subtitle A, Ch. 5, § 6052(a), Ch. 6, Subch. C, § 6086(a), 6087(a), 120 Stat. 93, 121, 127; March 23, 2010, P. L. 111-148, Title II, Subtitle E, §§ 2401, 2402(b), (c), (e), (f), Subtitle H, § 2601(a), (b)(1), 124 Stat. 297, 302, 304, 314; March 30, 2010, P. L. 111-152, Title I, Subtitle C, § 1205, 124 Stat. 1056.)

HISTORY; ANCILLARY LAWS AND DIRECTIVES

Other provisions:

Oversight and assessment of the administration of home and community-based services. Act March 23, 2010, P. L. 111-148, Title II, Subtitle E, § 2402(a), 124 Stat. 301, provides:

"The Secretary of Health and Human Services shall promulgate regulations to ensure that all States develop service systems that are designed to—

"(1) allocate resources for services in a manner that is responsive to the changing needs and choices of beneficiaries receiving non-institutionally-based long-term services and supports (including such services and supports that are provided under programs other the State Medicaid program), and that provides strategies for beneficiaries receiving such services to maximize their independence, including through the use of client-employed providers;

"(2) provide the support and coordination needed for a beneficiary in need of such services (and their family caregivers or representative, if applicable) to design an individualized, self-directed, community-supported life; and

"(3) improve coordination among, and the regulation of, all providers of such services under federally and State-funded programs in order to—

"(A) achieve a more consistent administration of policies and procedures across programs in relation to the provision of such services; and

"(B) oversee and monitor all service system functions to assure—

"(i) coordination of, and effectiveness of, eligibility determinations and individual assessments;

"(ii) development and service monitoring of a complaint system, a management system, a system to qualify and monitor providers, and systems for role-setting and individual budget determinations; and

"(iii) an adequate number of qualified direct care workers to provide self-directed personal assistance services.".

§ 1396o. Use of enrollment fees, premiums, deductions, cost sharing, and similar charges [Caution: See prospective amendment note below.]

(a) Imposition of certain charges under the plan in the case of individuals described in 42 USCS § 1396a(a)(10)(A). Subject to subsections (g), (i), and (j), the State plan shall provide that in the case of individuals described in subparagraph (A) or (E)(i) of section 1902(a)(10) [42 USCS § 1396a(a)(10)(A) or (E)(i)] who are eligible under the plan—

(1) no enrollment fee, premium, or similar charge will be imposed under the plan (except for a premium imposed under subsection (c));

(2) no deduction, cost sharing or similar charge will be imposed under the plan with respect to—

(A) services furnished to individuals under 18 years of age (and, at the option of the State, individuals under 21, 20, or 19 years of age, or any reasonable category of individuals 18 years of age or over),

(B) services furnished to pregnant women, if such services relate to the pregnancy or to any other medical condition which may complicate the pregnancy (or, at the option of the State, any services furnished to pregnant women),

(C) services furnished to any individual who is an inpatient in a hospital, nursing facility, intermediate care facility for the mentally retarded, or other medical institution, if such individual is required, as a condition of receiving services in such institution under the State plan, to spend for costs of medical care all but a minimal amount of his income required for personal needs,

(D) emergency services (as defined by the Secretary), family planning services and supplies described in section 1905(a)(4)(C) [42 USCS § 1396d(a)(4)(C)], or

(E) services furnished to an individual who is receiving hospice care (as defined in section 1905(o) [42 USCS § 1396d(o)]); and

(3) any deduction, cost sharing, or similar charge imposed under the plan with respect to other such individuals or other care and services will be nominal in amount (as determined by the Secretary in regulations which shall, if the definition of "nominal" under the regulations in effect on July 1, 1982 is changed, take into account the level of cash assistance provided in such State and such other criteria as the Secretary determines to be appropriate); except that a deduction, cost-sharing, or similar charge of up to twice the nominal amount established for outpatient services may be imposed by a State under a waiver granted by the Secretary for services received at a hospital emergency room if the services are not emergency services (referred to in paragraph (2)(D)) and the State has established to the satisfaction of the Secretary that individuals eligible for services under the plan have actually available and accessible to them alternative sources of nonemergency, outpatient services.

(b) Imposition of certain charges under the plan in the case of individuals other than those described in 42 USCS § 1396a(a)(10)(A) or (E). The State plan shall provide that in the case of individuals other than those described in subparagraph (A) or (E) of section 1902(a)(10) [42 USCS § 1396a(a)(10)(A) or (E)] who are eligible under the plan—

(1) there may be imposed an enrollment fee, premium, or similar charge, which (as determined in accordance with standards prescribed by the Secretary) is related to the individual's income,

(2) no deduction, cost sharing, or similar charge will be imposed under the plan with respect to—

(A) services furnished to individuals under 18 years of age (and, at the option of the State, individuals under 21, 20, or 19 years of age, or any reasonable category of individuals 18 years of age or over),

(B) services furnished to pregnant women, if such services relate to the pregnancy or to any other medical condition which may complicate the pregnancy (or, at the option of the State, any services furnished to pregnant women),

(C) services furnished to any individual who is an inpatient in a hospital, nursing facility, intermediate care facility for the mentally retarded, or other medical institution, if such individual is required, as a condition of receiving services in such institution under the State plan, to spend for costs of medical care all but a minimal amount of his income required for personal needs,

(D) emergency services (as defined by the Secretary), family planning services and supplies described in section 1905(a)(4)(C) [42 USCS § 1396d(a)(4)(C)], or

(E) services furnished to an individual who is receiving hospice care (as defined in section 1905(o) [42 USCS § 1396d(o)]); and

(3) any deduction, cost sharing, or similar charge imposed under the plan with respect to other such individuals or other care and services will be nominal in amount (as determined by the Secretary in regulations which shall, if the definition of "nominal" under the regulations in effect on July 1, 1982 is changed, take into account the level of cash assistance provided in such State and such other criteria as the Secretary determines to be appropriate); except that a deduction, cost-sharing, or similar charge of up to twice the nominal amount established for outpatient services may be imposed by a State under a waiver granted by the Secretary for services received at a hospital emergency room if the services are not emergency services (referred to in paragraph (2)(D)) and the State has established to the satisfaction of the Secretary that individuals eligible for services under the plan have actually available and accessible to them alternative sources of nonemergency, outpatient services.

(c) Imposition of monthly premium; persons affected; amount; prepayment; failure to pay; use of funds from other programs. (1) The State plan of a State may at the option of the State provide for imposing a monthly premium (in an amount that does not exceed the limit established under paragraph (2)) with respect to an individual described in subparagraph (A) or (B) of section 1902(l)(1) [42 USCS § 1396a(l)(1)] who is receiving medical assistance on the basis of section 1902(a)(10)(A)(ii)(IX) [42 USCS § 1396a(a)(10)(A)(ii)(IX)] and whose family income (as determined in accordance with the methodology specified in section 1902(l)(3)) [42 USCS § 1396a(l)(3)] equals or exceeds 150 percent of the income official poverty line (as defined by the Office of Management and Budget, and revised annually in accordance with section 673(2) of the Omnibus Budget Reconciliation Act of 1981 [42 USCS § 9902(2)]) applicable to a family of the size involved.

(2) In no case may the amount of any premium imposed under paragraph (1) exceed 10 percent of the amount by which the family income (less expenses for the care of a dependent child) of an individual exceeds 150 percent of the line described in paragraph (1).

(3) A State shall not require prepayment of a premium imposed pursuant to paragraph (1) and shall not terminate eligibility of an individual for medical assistance under this title [42 USCS §§ 1396 et seq.] on the basis of failure to pay any such premium until such failure continues for a period of not less than 60 days. The State may waive payment of any such premium in any case where the State determines that requiring such payment would create an undue hardship.

(4) A State may permit State or local funds available under other programs to be used for payment of a premium imposed under paragraph (1). Payment of a premium with such funds shall not be counted as income to the individual with respect to whom such payment is made.

(d) Premiums for qualified disabled and working individuals described in 42 USCS § 1396d(s). With respect to a qualified disabled and working individual described in section 1905(s) [42 USCS § 1396d(s)] whose income (as determined under paragraph (3) of that section) exceeds 150 percent of the official poverty line referred to in that paragraph, the State plan of a State may provide for the charging of a premium (expressed as a percentage of the medicare cost-sharing described in section 1905(p)(3)(A)(i) [42 USCS § 1396d(p)(3)(A)(i)] provided with respect to the individual) according to a sliding scale under which such percentage increases from 0 percent to 100 percent, in reasonable increments (as determined by the Secretary), as the individual's income increases from 150 percent of such poverty line to 200 percent of such poverty line.

(e) Prohibition of denial of services on basis of individuals' inability to pay certain charges. The State plan shall require that no provider participating under the State plan may deny care or services to an individual eligible for such care or services under the plan on account of such individual's inability to pay a deduction, cost sharing, or similar charge. The requirements of this subsection shall not extinguish the liability of the individual to whom the care or services were furnished for payment of the deduction, cost sharing, or similar charge.

(f) Charges imposed under waiver authority of Secretary. No deduction, cost sharing, or similar charge may be imposed under any waiver authority of the Secretary, except as provided in subsections (a)(3) and (b)(3) and section 1916A [42 USCS § 1396o-1], unless such waiver is for a demonstration project which the Secretary finds after public notice and opportunity for comment—

(1) will test a unique and previously untested use of copayments,

(2) is limited to a period of not more than two years,

(3) will provide benefits to recipients of medical assistance which can reasonably be expected to be equivalent to the risks to the recipients,

(4) is based on a reasonable hypothesis which the demonstration is designed to test in a methodologically sound manner, including the use of control groups of similar recipients of medical assistance in the area, and

(5) is voluntary, or makes provision for assumption of liability for preventable damage to the health of recipients of medical assistance resulting from involuntary participation.

(g) State authority to impose income-related premiums and cost-sharing. With respect to individuals provided medical assistance only under subclause (XV) or (XVI) of section 1902(a)(10)(A)(ii) [42 USCS § 1396a(a)(10)(A)(ii)]—

(1) a State may (in a uniform manner for individuals described in either such subclause)—

(A) require such individuals to pay premiums or other cost-sharing charges set on a sliding scale based on income that the State may determine; and

(B) require payment of 100 percent of such premiums for such year in the case of such an individual who has income for a year that exceeds 250 percent of the income official poverty line (referred to in subsection (c)(1)) applicable to a family of the size involved, except that in the case of such an individual who has income for a year that does not exceed 450 percent of such poverty line, such requirement may only apply to the extent such premiums do not exceed 7.5 percent of such income; and

(2) such State shall require payment of 100 percent of such premiums for a year by such an individual whose adjusted gross income (as defined in section 62 of the Internal Revenue Code of 1986 [26 USCS § 62]) for such year exceeds $75,000, except that a State may choose to subsidize such premiums by using State funds which may not be federally

matched under this title [42 USCS §§ 1396 et seq.].

In the case of any calendar year beginning after 2000, the dollar amount specified in paragraph (2) shall be increased in accordance with the provisions of section 215(i)(2)(A)(ii) [42 USCS § 415(i)(2)(A)(ii)].

(h) In applying this section and subsections (c) and (e) of section 1916A [42 USCS § 1396o-1], with respect to cost sharing that is "nominal" in amount, the Secretary shall increase such "nominal" amounts for each year (beginning with 2006) by the annual percentage increase in the medical care component of the consumer price index for all urban consumers (U.S. city average) as rounded up in an appropriate manner.

(i)(1) With respect to disabled children provided medical assistance under section 1902(a)(10)(A)(ii)(XIX) [42 USCS § 1396a(a)(10)(A)(ii)(XIX)], subject to paragraph (2), a State may (in a uniform manner for such children) require the families of such children to pay monthly premiums set on a sliding scale based on family income.

(2) A premium requirement imposed under paragraph (1) may only apply to the extent that—

(A) in the case of a disabled child described in that paragraph whose family income—

(i) does not exceed 200 percent of the poverty line, the aggregate amount of such premium and any premium that the parent is required to pay for family coverage under section 1902(cc)(2)(A)(i) [42 USCS § 1396a(cc)(2)(A)(i)] and other cost-sharing charges do not exceed 5 percent of the family's income; and

(ii) exceeds 200, but does not exceed 300, percent of the poverty line, the aggregate amount of such premium and any premium that the parent is required to pay for family coverage under section 1902(cc)(2)(A)(i) [42 USCS § 1396a(cc)(2)(A)(i)] and other cost-sharing charges do not exceed 7.5 percent of the family's income; and

(B) the requirement is imposed consistent with section 1902(cc)(2)(A)(ii)(I) [42 USCS § 1396a(cc)(2)(A)(ii)(I)].

(3) A State shall not require prepayment of a premium imposed pursuant to paragraph (1) and shall not terminate eligibility of a child under section 1902(a)(10)(A)(ii)(XIX) [42 USCS § 1396a(a)(10)(A)(ii)(XIX)] for medical assistance under this title [42 USCS §§ 1396 et seq.] on the basis of failure to pay any such premium until such failure continues for a period of at least 60 days from the date on which the premium became past due. The State may waive payment of any such premium in any case where the State determines that requiring such payment would create an undue hardship.

(j) No premiums or cost sharing for Indians furnished items or services directly by Indian health programs or through referral under contract health services. (1) No cost sharing for items or services furnished to Indians through Indian health programs. (A) In general. No enrollment fee, premium, or similar charge, and no deduction, copayment, cost sharing, or similar charge shall be imposed against an Indian who is furnished an item or service directly by the Indian Health Service, an Indian Tribe, Tribal Organization, or Urban Indian Organization or through referral under contract health services for which payment may be made under this title [42 USCS §§ 1396 et seq.].

(B) No reduction in amount of payment to Indian health providers. Payment due under this title to the Indian Health Service, an Indian Tribe, Tribal Organization, or Urban Indian Organization, or a health care provider through referral under contract health services for the furnishing of an item or service to an Indian who is eligible for assistance under such title, may not be reduced by the amount of any enrollment fee, premium, or similar charge, or any deduction, copayment, cost sharing, or similar charge that would be due from the Indian but for the operation of subparagraph (A).

(2) Rule of construction. Nothing in this subsection shall be construed as restricting the application of any other limitations on the imposition of premiums or cost sharing that may apply to an individual receiving medical assistance under this title [42 USCS §§ 1396 et seq.] who is an Indian.

(Aug. 14, 1935, ch 531, Title XIX, § 1916, as added Sept. 3, 1982, P. L. 97-248, Title I, Subtitle B, § 131(b), 96 Stat. 367; Jan. 12, 1983, P. L. 97-448, Title III, § 309(b)(18)–(20), 96 Stat. 2409, 2410; April 7, 1986, P. L. 99-272, Title IX, Subtitle B, § 9505(c)(2), 100 Stat. 209; Oct. 21, 1986, P. L. 99-509, Title IX, Subtitle E, Part 1, § 9403(g)(4)(B), 100 Stat. 2055; Dec. 22, 1987, P. L. 100-203, Title IV, Subtitle B, Part 1, § 4101(d)(1), Subtitle C, Part 2, § 4211(h)(11), 101 Stat. 1330-141, 1330-208; July 1, 1988, P. L. 100-360, Title IV, Subtitle B, § 411(k)(2), 102 Stat. 791; Dec. 19, 1989, P. L. 101-239, Title VI, Subtitle B, Part 1, § 6408(d)(3), 103 Stat. 2269; Aug. 5, 1997, P. L. 105-33, Title IV, Subtitle H, Ch 1, § 4708(b), 111 Stat. 506; Dec. 17, 1999, P. L. 106-170, Title II, § 201(a)(3), 113 Stat. 1893; Feb. 8, 2006, P. L. 109-171, Title VI, Subtitle A,

Ch. 4, § 6041(b), Ch. 6, Subch A, § 6062(b), 120 Stat. 84, 98; Feb. 17, 2009, P. L. 111-5, Div B, Title V, § 5006(a)(1), 123 Stat. 505; March 23, 2010, P. L. 111-148, Title IV, Subtitle B, § 4107(c)(1), 124 Stat. 561.)

HISTORY; ANCILLARY LAWS AND DIRECTIVES

Prospective amendments:

Amendment of subsecs. (a)(2)(B) and (b)(2)(B), effective October 1, 2010. Act March 23, 2010, P. L. 111-148, Title IV, Subtitle B, § 4107(c)(1), 124 Stat. 561 (effective on 10/1/2010, as provided by § 4107(d) of such Act, which appears as 42 USCS § 1396d note), provides: "Section 1916 of the Social Security Act (42 U.S.C. 1396o) is amended in each of subsections (a)(2)(B) and (b)(2)(B) by inserting ', and counseling and pharmacotherapy for cessation of tobacco use by pregnant women (as defined in section 1905(bb)) and covered outpatient drugs (as defined in subsection (k)(2) of section 1927 and including non-prescription drugs described in subsection (d)(2) of such section) that are prescribed for purposes of promoting, and when used to promote, tobacco cessation by pregnant women in accordance with the Guideline referred to in section 1905(bb)(2)(A)' after 'complicate the pregnancy'.".

§ 1396o-1. State option for alternative premiums and cost sharing [Caution: See prospective amendment note below.]

(a) State flexibility. (1) In general. Notwithstanding sections 1916 and 1902(a)(10)(B) [42 USCS §§ 1396o and 1396a(a)(10)(B)], but subject to paragraph (2), a State, at its option and through a State plan amendment, may impose premiums and cost sharing for any group of individuals (as specified by the State) and for any type of services (other than drugs for which cost sharing may be imposed under subsection (c) and non-emergency services furnished in a hospital emergency department for which cost sharing may be imposed under subsection (e)), and may vary such premiums and cost sharing among such groups or types, consistent with the limitations established under this section. Nothing in this section shall be construed as superseding (or preventing the application of) subsection (g), (i), or (j) of section 1916 [42 USCS § 1396o].

(2) Exemption for individuals with family income not exceeding 100 percent of the poverty line. (A) In general. Paragraph (1) and subsection (d) shall not apply, and sections 1916 and 1902(a)(10)(B) [42 USCS §§ 1396o and 1396a(a)(10)(B)] shall continue to apply, in the case of an individual whose family income does not exceed 100 percent of the poverty line applicable to a family of the size involved.

(B) Limit on aggregate cost sharing. To the extent cost sharing under subsections (c) and (e) or under section 1916 [42 USCS § 1396o] is imposed against individuals described in subparagraph (A), the limitation under subsection (b)(1)(B)(ii) on the total aggregate amount of cost sharing shall apply to such cost sharing for all individuals in a family described in subparagraph (A) in the same manner as such limitations apply to cost sharing and families described in subsection (b)(1)(B)(ii).

(3) Definitions. In this section:

(A) Premium. The term "premium" includes any enrollment fee or similar charge.

(B) Cost sharing. The term "cost sharing" includes any deduction, copayment, or similar charge.

(b) Limitations on exercise of authority. (1) Individuals with family income between 100 and 150 percent of the poverty line. In the case of an individual whose family income exceeds 100 percent, but does not exceed 150 percent, of the poverty line applicable to a family of the size involved—

(A) no premium may be imposed under the plan; and

(B) with respect to cost sharing—

(i) the cost sharing imposed under subsection (a) with respect to any item or service may not exceed 10 percent of the cost of such item or service; and

(ii) the total aggregate amount of cost sharing imposed under this section (including any cost sharing imposed under subsection (c) or (e)) for all individuals in the family may not exceed 5 percent of the family income of the family involved, as applied on a quarterly or monthly basis (as specified by the State).

(2) Individuals with family income above 150 percent of the poverty line. In the case of an individual whose family income exceeds 150 percent of the poverty line applicable to a family of the size involved—

(A) the total aggregate amount of premiums and cost sharing imposed under this section (including any cost sharing imposed under subsection (c) or (e)) for all individuals in the family may not exceed 5 percent of the family income of the family involved, as applied on a quarterly or monthly basis (as specified by the State); and

(B) with respect to cost sharing, the cost sharing imposed with respect to any item or service under subsection (a) may not exceed 20 percent of the cost of such item or service.

(3) Additional limitations. (A) Premiums. No premiums shall be imposed under this section with respect to the following:

(i) Individuals under 18 years of age that are required to be provided medical assistance under section 1902(a)(10)(A)(i) [42 USCS

§ 1396a(a)(10)(A)(i)], and including individuals with respect to whom child welfare services are made available under part B of title IV [42 USCS §§ 620 et seq.] on the basis of being a child in foster care and individuals with respect to whom adoption or foster care assistance is made available under part E of such title [42 USCS §§ 670 et seq.], without regard to age.

(ii) Pregnant women.

(iii) Any terminally ill individual who is receiving hospice care (as defined in section 1905(o) [42 USCS § 1396d(o)]).

(iv) Any individual who is an inpatient in a hospital, nursing facility, intermediate care facility for the mentally retarded, or other medical institution, if such individual is required, as a condition of receiving services in such institution under the State plan, to spend for costs of medical care all but a minimal amount of the individual's income required for personal needs.

(v) Women who are receiving medical assistance by virtue of the application of sections 1902(a)(10)(A)(ii)(XVIII) and 1902(aa) [42 USCS § 1396a(a)(10)(A)(ii)(XVIII) and (aa)].

(vi) Disabled children who are receiving medical assistance by virtue of the application of sections 1902(a)(10)(A)(ii)(XIX) and 1902(cc) [42 USCS § 1396a(a)(10)(A)(ii)(XIX) and (cc)].

(vii) An Indian who is furnished an item or service directly by the Indian Health Service, an Indian Tribe, Tribal Organization or Urban Indian Organization or through referral under contract health services.

(B) Cost sharing. Subject to the succeeding provisions of this section, no cost sharing shall be imposed under subsection (a) with respect to the following:

(i) Services furnished to individuals under 18 years of age that are required to be provided medical assistance under section 1902(a)(10)(A)(i) [42 USCS § 1396a(a)(10)(A)(i)], and including services furnished to individuals with respect to whom child welfare services are made available under part B of title IV [42 USCS §§ 620 et seq.] on the basis of being a child in foster care or [and] individuals with respect to whom adoption or foster care assistance is made available under part E of such title [42 USCS §§ 670 et seq.], without regard to age.

(ii) Preventive services (such as well baby and well child care and immunizations) provided to children under 18 years of age regardless of family income.

(iii) Services furnished to pregnant women, if such services relate to the pregnancy or to any other medical condition which may complicate the pregnancy.

(iv) Services furnished to a terminally ill individual who is receiving hospice care (as defined in section 1905(o) [42 USCS § 1396d(o)]).

(v) Services furnished to any individual who is an inpatient in a hospital, nursing facility, intermediate care facility for the mentally retarded, or other medical institution, if such individual is required, as a condition of receiving services in such institution under the State plan, to spend for costs of medical care all but a minimal amount of the individual's income required for personal needs.

(vi) Emergency services (as defined by the Secretary for purposes of section 1916(a)(2)(D) [42 USCS § 1396o(a)(2)(D)]).

(vii) Family planning services and supplies described in section 1905(a)(4)(C) [42 USCS § 1396d(a)(4)(C)].

(viii) Services furnished to women who are receiving medical assistance by virtue of the application of sections 1902(a)(10)(A)(ii)(XVIII) and 1902(aa) [42 USCS § 1396a(a)(10)(A)(ii)(XVIII) and (aa)].

(ix) Services furnished to disabled children who are receiving medical assistance by virtue of the application of sections 1902(a)(10)(A)(ii)(XIX) and 1902(cc) [42 USCS § 1396a(a)(10)(A)(ii)(XIX) and (cc)].

(x) Items and services furnished to an Indian directly by the Indian Health Service, an Indian Tribe, Tribal Organization or Urban Indian Organization or through referral under contract health services.

(C) Construction. Nothing in this paragraph shall be construed as preventing a State from exempting additional classes of individuals from premiums under this section or from exempting additional individuals or services from cost sharing under subsection (a).

(4) Determinations of family income. In applying this subsection, family income shall be determined in a manner specified by the State for purposes of this subsection, including the use of such disregards as the State may provide. Family income shall be determined for such period and at such periodicity as the State may provide under this title [42 USCS §§ 1396 et seq.].

(5) Poverty line defined. For purposes of this section, the term "poverty line" has the meaning given such term in section 673(2) of the Community Services Block Grant Act (42 U.S.C. 9902(2)), including any revision required by such section.

(6) Construction. Nothing in this section shall be construed—

(A) as preventing a State from further limiting the premiums and cost sharing imposed under this section beyond the limitations provided under this section;

(B) as affecting the authority of the Secretary through waiver to modify limitations on premiums and cost sharing under this section; or

(C) as affecting any such waiver of requirements in effect under this title [42 USCS §§ 1396 et seq.] before the date of the enactment of this section [enacted Feb. 8, 2006] with regard to the imposition of premiums and cost sharing.

(c) Special rules for cost sharing for prescription drugs. (1) In general. In order to encourage beneficiaries to use drugs (in this subsection referred to as "preferred drugs") identified by the State as the most (or more) cost effective prescription drugs within a class of drugs (as defined by the State), with respect to one or more groups of beneficiaries specified by the State, subject to paragraph (2), the State may—

(A) provide cost sharing (instead of the level of cost sharing otherwise permitted under section 1916 [42 USCS § 1396o], but subject to paragraphs (2) and (3)) with respect to drugs that are not preferred drugs within a class; and

(B) waive or reduce the cost sharing otherwise applicable for preferred drugs within such class and shall not apply any such cost sharing for such preferred drugs for individuals for whom cost sharing may not be imposed under subsection (a) due to the application of subsection (b)(3)(B).

(2) Limitations. (A) By income group. In no case may the cost sharing under paragraph (1)(A) with respect to a non-preferred drug exceed—

(i) in the case of an individual whose family income does not exceed 150 percent of the poverty line applicable to a family of the size involved, the amount of nominal cost sharing (as otherwise determined under section 1916 [42 USCS § 1396o]); or

(ii) in the case of an individual whose family income exceeds 150 percent of the poverty line applicable to a family of the size involved, 20 percent of the cost of the drug.

(B) Limitation to nominal for exempt populations. In the case of an individual who is not subject to cost sharing under subsection (a) due to the application of paragraph (1)(B), any cost sharing under paragraph (1)(A) with respect to a non-preferred drug may not exceed a nominal amount (as otherwise determined under section 1916 [42 USCS § 1396o]).

(C) Continued application of aggregate cap. In addition to the limitations imposed under subparagraphs (A) and (B), any cost sharing under paragraph (1)(A) continues to be subject to the aggregate cap on cost sharing applied under subsection (a)(2)(B) or under paragraph (1) or (2) of subsection (b), as the case may be.

(3) Waiver. In carrying out paragraph (1), a State shall provide for the application of cost sharing levels applicable to a preferred drug in the case of a drug that is not a preferred drug if the prescribing physician determines that the preferred drug for treatment of the same condition either would not be as effective for the individual or would have adverse effects for the individual or both.

(4) Exclusion authority. Nothing in this subsection shall be construed as preventing a State from excluding specified drugs or classes of drugs from the application of paragraph (1).

(d) Enforceability of premiums and other cost sharing. (1) Premiums. Notwithstanding section 1916(c)(3) [42 USCS § 1396o(c)(3)] and section 1902(a)(10)(B) [42 USCS § 1396a(a)(10)(B)], a State may, at its option, condition the provision of medical assistance for an individual upon prepayment of a premium authorized to be imposed under this section, or may terminate eligibility for such medical assistance on the basis of failure to pay such a premium but shall not terminate eligibility of an individual for medical assistance under this title [42 USCS §§ 1396 et seq.] on the basis of failure to pay any such premium until such failure continues for a period of not less than 60 days. A State may apply the previous sentence for some or all groups of beneficiaries as specified by the State and may waive payment of any such premium in any case where the State determines that requiring such payment would create an undue hardship.

(2) Cost sharing. Notwithstanding section 1916(e) [42 USCS § 1396o(e)] or any other provision of law, a State may permit a provider participating under the State plan to require, as a condition for the provision of care, items, or services to an individual entitled to medical assistance under this title for such care, items, or services, the payment of any cost sharing authorized to be imposed under this section with respect to such care, items, or services. Nothing in this paragraph shall be construed as preventing a provider from reducing or waiving the application of such cost sharing on a case-by-case basis.

(e) State option for permitting hospitals to impose cost sharing for non-emergency care furnished in an emergency depart-

ment. (1) In general. Notwithstanding section 1916 [42 USCS § 1396o] and section 1902(a)(1) [42 USCS § 1396a(a)(1)] or the previous provisions of this section, but subject to the limitations of paragraph (2), a State may, by amendment to its State plan under this title [42 USCS §§ 1396 et seq.], permit a hospital to impose cost sharing for non-emergency services furnished to an individual (within one or more groups of individuals specified by the State) in the hospital emergency department under this subsection if the following conditions are met:

(A) Access to non-emergency room provider. The individual has actually available and accessible (as such terms are applied by the Secretary under section 1916(b)(3) [42 USCS § 1396o(b)(3)]) an alternate non-emergency services provider with respect to such services.

(B) Notice. The hospital must inform the beneficiary after receiving an appropriate medical screening examination under section 1867 [42 USCS § 1395dd] and after a determination has been made that the individual does not have an emergency medical condition, but before providing the non-emergency services, of the following:

(i) The hospital may require the payment of the State specified cost sharing before the service can be provided.

(ii) The name and location of an alternate non-emergency services provider (described in subparagraph (A)) that is actually available and accessible (as described in such subparagraph).

(iii) The fact that such alternate provider can provide the services without the imposition of cost sharing described in clause (i).

(iv) The hospital provides a referral to coordinate scheduling of this treatment.

Nothing in this subsection shall be construed as preventing a State from applying (or waiving) cost sharing otherwise permissible under this section to services described in clause (iii).

(2) Limitations. (A) Individuals with family income between 100 and 150 percent of the poverty line. In the case of an individual described in subsection (b)(1) who is not described in subparagraph (B), the cost sharing imposed under this subsection may not exceed twice the amount determined to be nominal under section 1916 [42 USCS § 1396o], subject to the percent of income limitation otherwise applicable under subsection (b)(1)(B)(ii).

(B) Application to exempt populations. In the case of an individual described in subsection (a)(2)(A) or who is not subject to cost sharing under subsection (b)(3)(B) with respect to non-emergency services described in paragraph (1), a State may impose cost sharing under paragraph (1) for care in an amount that does not exceed a nominal amount (as otherwise determined under section 1916 [42 USCS § 1396o]) so long as no cost sharing is imposed to receive such care through an outpatient department or other alternative health care provider in the geographic area of the hospital emergency department involved.

(C) Continued application of aggregate cap; relation to other cost sharing. In addition to the limitations imposed under subparagraphs (A) and (B), any cost sharing under paragraph (1) is subject to the aggregate cap on cost sharing applied under subsection (a)(2)(B) or under paragraph (1) or (2) of subsection (b), as the case may be. Cost sharing imposed for services under this subsection shall be instead of any cost sharing that may be imposed for such services under subsection (a) or section 1916 [42 USCS § 1396o].

(3) Construction. Nothing in this section shall be construed—

(A) to limit a hospital's obligations with respect to screening and stabilizing treatment of an emergency medical condition under section 1867 [42 USCS § 1395dd]; or

(B) to modify any obligations under either State or Federal standards relating to the application of a prudent-layperson standard with respect to payment or coverage of emergency services by any managed care organization.

(4) Definitions. For purposes of this subsection:

(A) Non-emergency services. The term "non-emergency services" means any care or services furnished in an emergency department of a hospital that do not constitute an appropriate medical screening examination or stabilizing examination and treatment required to be provided by the hospital under section 1867 [42 USCS § 1395dd].

(B) Alternate non-emergency services provider. The term "alternative non-emergency services provider" means, with respect to non-emergency services for the diagnosis or treatment of a condition, a health care provider, such as a physician's office, health care clinic, community health center, hospital outpatient department, or similar health care provider, that can provide clinically appropriate services for the diagnosis or treatment of a condition contemporaneously with the provision of the non-emergency services that would be provided in an emergency department of a hospital for the diagnosis or treatment of a condition, and that is participating in the program under this title [42 USCS §§ 1396 et seq.].

(Aug. 14, 1935, ch 531, Title XIX, § 1916A, as added and amended Feb. 8, 2006, P. L. 109-171, Title VI, Subtitle A, Ch. 4, §§ 6041(a), 6042(a), 6043(a), 120 Stat. 81, 85, 86; Dec. 20, 2006, P. L. 109-432, Div B, Title IV, § 405(a)(1)–(5), 120 Stat. 2996; Feb. 17, 2009, P. L. 111-5, Div B, Title V, § 5006(a)(2), 123 Stat. 506; March 23, 2010, P. L. 111-148, Title II, Subtitle B, § 2102(b), Title IV, Subtitle B, § 4107(c)(2), 124 Stat. 289, 561.)

HISTORY; ANCILLARY LAWS AND DIRECTIVES

Prospective amendments:

Amendment of subsec. (b)(3)(B)(iii), effective October 1, 2010. Act March 23, 2010, P. L. 111-148, Title IV, Subtitle B, § 4107(c)(2), 124 Stat. 561 (effective on 10/1/2010, as provided by § 4107(d) of such Act, which appears as 42 USCS § 1396d note), provides: "Section 1916A(b)(3)(B)(iii) of such Act (42 U.S.C. 1396o-1(b)(3)(B)(iii)) is amended by inserting ', and counseling and pharmacotherapy for cessation of tobacco use by pregnant women (as defined in section 1905(bb))' after 'complicate the pregnancy'.".

Other provisions:

Effective date of March 23, 2010 amendment. Act March 23, 2010, P. L. 111-148, Title II, Subtitle B, § 2102(b), 124 Stat. 289, provides that the amendment by such section to subsec. (a)(1) of this section is effective as if included in the enactment of section 5006(a) of division B of the American Recovery and Reinvestment Act of 2009 (Public Law 111-5).

§ 1396p. Liens, adjustments and recoveries, and transfers of assets

(a) Imposition of lien against the property of an individual on account of medical assistance rendered to him under a State plan. (1) No lien may be imposed against the property of any individual prior to his death on account of medical assistance paid or to be paid on his behalf under the State plan, except—

(A) pursuant to the judgment of a court on account of benefits incorrectly paid on behalf of such individual, or

(B) in the case of the real property of an individual—

(i) who is an inpatient in a nursing facility, intermediate care facility for the mentally retarded, or other medical institution, if such individual is required, as a condition of receiving services in such institution under the State plan, to spend for costs of medical care all but a minimal amount of his income required for personal needs, and

(ii) with respect to whom the State determines, after notice and opportunity for a hearing (in accordance with procedures established by the State), that he cannot reasonably be expected to be discharged from the medical institution and to return home,

except as provided in paragraph (2).

(2) No lien may be imposed under paragraph (1)(B) on such individual's home if—

(A) the spouse of such individual,

(B) such individual's child who is under age 21, or (with respect to States eligible to participate in the State program established under title XVI [42 USCS §§ 1381 et seq.]) is blind or permanently and totally disabled, or (with respect to States which are not eligible to participate in such program) is blind or disabled as defined in section 1614 [42 USCS § 1382c], or

(C) a sibling of such individual (who has an equity interest in such home and who was residing in such individual's home for a period of at least one year immediately before the date of the individual's admission to the medical institution),

is lawfully residing in such home.

(3) Any lien imposed with respect to an individual pursuant to paragraph (1)(B) shall dissolve upon that individual's discharge from the medical institution and return home.

(b) Adjustment or recovery of medical assistance correctly paid under a State plan. (1) No adjustment or recovery of any medical assistance correctly paid on behalf of an individual under the State plan may be made, except that the State shall seek adjustment or recovery of any medical assistance correctly paid on behalf of an individual under the State plan in the case of the following individuals:

(A) In the case of an individual described in subsection (a)(1)(B), the State shall seek adjustment or recovery from the individual's estate or upon sale of the property subject to a lien imposed on account of medical assistance paid on behalf of the individual.

(B) In the case of an individual who was 55 years of age or older when the individual received such medical assistance, the State shall seek adjustment or recovery from the individual's estate, but only for medical assistance consisting of—

(i) nursing facility services, home and community-based services, and related hospital and prescription drug services, or

(ii) at the option of the State, any items or services under the State plan (but not including medical assistance for medicare cost-sharing or for benefits described in section 1902(a)(10)(E) [42 USCS § 1396a(a)(10)(E)]).

(C)(i) In the case of an individual who has received (or is entitled to receive) benefits under a long-term care insurance policy in connection with which assets or resources are disregarded in the manner described in clause (ii), except as provided in such clause, the State shall seek adjustment or recovery from the individual's estate on account of medical assistance paid on behalf of the individual for nursing facility and other long-term care services.

(ii) Clause (i) shall not apply in the case of an individual who received medical assistance under a State plan of a State which had a State plan amendment approved as of May 14, 1993, and which satisfies clause (iv), or which has a State plan amendment that provides for a qualified State long-term care insurance partnership (as defined in clause (iii)) which provided for the disregard of any assets or resources—

(I) to the extent that payments are made under a long-term care insurance policy; or

(II) because an individual has received (or is entitled to receive) benefits under a long-term care insurance policy.

(iii) For purposes of this paragraph, the term "qualified State long-term care insurance partnership" means an approved State plan amendment under this title [42 USCS §§ 1396 et seq.] that provides for the disregard of any assets or resources in an amount equal to the insurance benefit payments that are made to or on behalf of an individual who is a beneficiary under a long-term care insurance policy if the following requirements are met:

(I) The policy covers an insured who was a resident of such State when coverage first became effective under the policy.

(II) The policy is a qualified long-term care insurance policy (as defined in section 7702B(b) of the Internal Revenue Code of 1986 [26 USCS § 7702B(b)]) issued not earlier than the effective date of the State plan amendment.

(III) The policy meets the model regulations and the requirements of the model Act specified in paragraph (5).

(IV) If the policy is sold to an individual who—

(aa) has not attained age 61 as of the date of purchase, the policy provides compound annual inflation protection;

(bb) has attained age 61 but has not attained age 76 as of such date, the policy provides some level of inflation protection; and

(cc) has attained age 76 as of such date, the policy may (but is not required to) provide some level of inflation protection.

(V) The State Medicaid agency under section 1902(a)(5) [42 USCS § 1396a(a)(5)] provides information and technical assistance to the State insurance department on the insurance department's role of assuring that any individual who sells a long-term care insurance policy under the partnership receives training and demonstrates evidence of an understanding of such policies and how they relate to other public and private coverage of long-term care.

(VI) The issuer of the policy provides regular reports to the Secretary, in accordance with regulations of the Secretary, that include notification regarding when benefits provided under the policy have been paid and the amount of such benefits paid, notification regarding when the policy otherwise terminates, and such other information as the Secretary determines may be appropriate to the administration of such partnerships.

(VII) The State does not impose any requirement affecting the terms or benefits of such a policy unless the State imposes such requirement on long-term care insurance policies without regard to whether the policy is covered under the partnership or is offered in connection with such a partnership.

In the case of a long-term care insurance policy which is exchanged for another such policy, subclause (I) shall be applied based on the coverage of the first such policy that was exchanged. For purposes of this clause and paragraph (5), the term "long-term care insurance policy" includes a certificate issued under a group insurance contract.

(iv) With respect to a State which had a State plan amendment approved as of May 14, 1993, such a State satisfies this clause for purposes of clause (ii) if the Secretary determines that the State plan amendment provides for consumer protection standards which are no less stringent than the consumer protection standards which applied under such State plan amendment as of December 31, 2005.

(v) The regulations of the Secretary required under clause (iii)(VI) shall be promulgated after consultation with the National Association of Insurance Commissioners, issuers of long-term care insurance policies, States with experience with long-term care insurance partnership plans, other States, and representatives of consumers of long-term care insurance policies, and shall specify the type and format of the data and information to be reported and the frequency with which such reports are to be made. The Secretary, as appropriate, shall provide copies of the reports provided in accordance with that clause to the State involved.

(vi) The Secretary, in consultation with other appropriate Federal agencies, issuers of long-term care insurance, the National Association of Insurance Commissioners, State insurance commissioners, States with experience with long-term care insurance partnership plans, other States, and representatives of consumers of long-term care insurance policies, shall develop recommendations for Congress to authorize and fund a uniform minimum data set to be reported electronically by all issuers of long-term care insurance policies under qualified State long-term care insurance partnerships to a secure, centralized electronic query and report-generating mechanism that the State, the Secretary, and other Federal agencies can access.

(2) Any adjustment or recovery under paragraph (1) may be made only after the death of the individual's surviving spouse, if any, and only at a time—

(A) when he has no surviving child who is under age 21, or (with respect to States eligible to participate in the State program established under title XVI [42 USCS §§ 1381 et seq.]) is blind or permanently and totally disabled, or (with respect to States which are not eligible to participate in such program) is blind or disabled as defined in section 1614 [42 USCS § 1382c]; and

(B) in the case of a lien on an individual's home under subsection (a)(1)(B), when—

(i) no sibling of the individual (who was residing in the individual's home for a period of at least one year immediately before the date of the individual's admission to the medical institution), and

(ii) no son or daughter of the individual (who was residing in the individual's home for a period of at least two years immediately before the date of the individual's admission to the medical institution, and who establishes to the satisfaction of the State that he or she provided care to such individual which permitted such individual to reside at home rather than in an institution),

is lawfully residing in such home who has lawfully resided in such home on a continuous basis since the date of the individual's admission to the medical institution.

(3)(A) The State agency shall establish procedures (in accordance with standards specified by the Secretary) under which the agency shall waive the application of this subsection (other than paragraph (1)(C)) if such application would work an undue hardship as determined on the basis of criteria established by the Secretary.

(B) The standards specified by the Secretary under subparagraph (A) shall require that the procedures established by the State agency under subparagraph (A) exempt income, resources, and property that are exempt from the application of this subsection as of April 1, 2003, under manual instructions issued to carry out this subsection (as in effect on such date) because of the Federal responsibility for Indian Tribes and Alaska Native Villages. Nothing in this subparagraph shall be construed as preventing the Secretary from providing additional estate recovery exemptions under this title for Indians.

(4) For purposes of this subsection, the term "estate", with respect to a deceased individual—

(A) shall include all real and personal property and other assets included within the individual's estate, as defined for purposes of State probate law; and

(B) may include, at the option of the State (and shall include, in the case of an individual to whom paragraph (1)(C)(i) applies), any other real and personal property and other assets in which the individual had any legal title or interest at the time of death (to the extent of such interest), including such assets conveyed to a survivor, heir, or assign of the deceased individual through joint tenancy, tenancy in common, survivorship, life estate, living trust, or other arrangement.

(5)(A) For purposes of clause (iii)(III), the model regulations and the requirements of the model Act specified in this paragraph are:

(i) In the case of the model regulation, the following requirements:

(I) Section 6A (relating to guaranteed renewal or noncancellability), other than paragraph (5) thereof, and the requirements of section 6B of the model Act relating to such section 6A.

(II) Section 6B (relating to prohibitions on limitations and exclusions) other than paragraph (7) thereof.

(III) Section 6C (relating to extension of benefits).

(IV) Section 6D (relating to continuation or conversion of coverage).

(V) Section 6E (relating to discontinuance and replacement of policies).

(VI) Section 7 (relating to unintentional lapse).

(VII) Section 8 (relating to disclosure), other than sections 8F, 8G, 8H, and 8I thereof.

(VIII) Section 9 (relating to required disclosure of rating practices to consumer).

(IX) Section 11 (relating to prohibitions against post-claims underwriting).

(X) Section 12 (relating to minimum standards).

(XI) Section 14 (relating to application forms

and replacement coverage).

(XII) Section 15 (relating to reporting requirements).

(XIII) Section 22 (relating to filing requirements for marketing).

(XIV) Section 23 (relating to standards for marketing), including inaccurate completion of medical histories, other than paragraphs (1), (6), and (9) of section 23C.

(XV) Section 24 (relating to suitability).

(XVI) Section 25 (relating to prohibition against preexisting conditions and probationary periods in replacement policies or certificates).

(XVII) The provisions of section 26 relating to contingent nonforfeiture benefits, if the policyholder declines the offer of a nonforfeiture provision described in paragraph (4).

(XVIII) Section 29 (relating to standard format outline of coverage).

(XIX) Section 30 (relating to requirement to deliver shopper's guide).

(ii) In the case of the model Act, the following:

(I) Section 6C (relating to preexisting conditions).

(II) Section 6D (relating to prior hospitalization).

(III) The provisions of section 8 relating to contingent nonforfeiture benefits.

(IV) Section 6F (relating to right to return).

(V) Section 6G (relating to outline of coverage).

(VI) Section 6H (relating to requirements for certificates under group plans).

(VII) Section 6J (relating to policy summary).

(VIII) Section 6K (relating to monthly reports on accelerated death benefits).

(IX) Section 7 (relating to incontestability period).

(B) For purposes of this paragraph and paragraph (1)(C)—

(i) the terms "model regulation" and "model Act" mean the long-term care insurance model regulation, and the long-term care insurance model Act, respectively, promulgated by the National Association of Insurance Commissioners (as adopted as of October 2000);

(ii) any provision of the model regulation or model Act listed under subparagraph (A) shall be treated as including any other provision of such regulation or Act necessary to implement the provision; and

(iii) with respect to a long-term care insurance policy issued in a State, the policy shall be deemed to meet applicable requirements of the model regulation or the model Act if the State plan amendment under paragraph (1)(C)(iii) provides that the State insurance commissioner for the State certifies (in a manner satisfactory to the Secretary) that the policy meets such requirements.

(C) Not later than 12 months after the National Association of Insurance Commissioners issues a revision, update, or other modification of a model regulation or model Act provision specified in subparagraph (A), or of any provision of such regulation or Act that is substantively related to a provision specified in such subparagraph, the Secretary shall review the changes made to the provision, determine whether incorporating such changes into the corresponding provision specified in such subparagraph would improve qualified State long-term care insurance partnerships, and if so, shall incorporate the changes into such provision.

(c) Taking into account certain transfers of assets. (1)(A) In order to meet the requirements of this subsection for purposes of section 1902(a)(18) [42 USCS § 1396a(a)(18)], the State plan must provide that if an institutionalized individual or the spouse of such an individual (or, at the option of a State, a noninstitutionalized individual or the spouse of such an individual) disposes of assets for less than fair market value on or after the look-back date specified in subparagraph (B)(i), the individual is ineligible for medical assistance for services described in subparagraph (C)(i) (or, in the case of a noninstitutionalized individual, for the services described in subparagraph (C)(ii)) during the period beginning on the date specified in subparagraph (D) and equal to the number of months specified in subparagraph (E).

(B)(i) The look-back date specified in this subparagraph is a date that is 36 months (or, in the case of payments from a trust or portions of a trust that are treated as assets disposed of by the individual pursuant to paragraph (3)(A)(iii) or (3)(B)(ii) of subsection (d) or in the case of any other disposal of assets made on or after the date of the enactment of the Deficit Reduction Act of 2005 [enacted Feb. 8, 2006], 60 months) before the date specified in clause (ii).

(ii) The date specified in this clause, with respect to—

(I) an institutionalized individual is the first date as of which the individual both is an institutionalized individual and has applied for medical assistance under the State plan, or

(II) a noninstitutionalized individual is the date on which the individual applies for medical assistance under the State plan or, if later, the date on which the individual disposes of assets for less than fair market value.

(C)(i) The services described in this subparagraph with respect to an institutionalized individual are the following:

(I) Nursing facility services.

(II) A level of care in any institution equivalent to that of nursing facility services.

(III) Home or community-based services furnished under a waiver granted under subsection (c) or (d) of section 1915 [42 USCS § 1396n(c) or (d)].

(ii) The services described in this subparagraph with respect to a noninstitutionalized individual are services (not including any services described in clause (i)) that are described in paragraph (7), (22), or (24) of section 1905(a) [42 USCS § 1396d(a)(7), (22), or (24)], and, at the option of a State, other long-term care services for which medical assistance is otherwise available under the State plan to individuals requiring long-term care.

(D)(i) In the case of a transfer of asset made before the date of the enactment of the Deficit Reduction Act of 2005 [enacted Feb. 8, 2006], the date specified in this subparagraph is the first day of the first month during or after which assets have been transferred for less than fair market value and which does not occur in any other periods of ineligibility under this subsection.

(ii) In the case of a transfer of asset made on or after the date of the enactment of the Deficit Reduction Act of 2005 [enacted Feb. 8, 2006], the date specified in this subparagraph is the first day of a month during or after which assets have been transferred for less than fair market value, or the date on which the individual is eligible for medical assistance under the State plan and would otherwise be receiving institutional level care described in subparagraph (C) based on an approved application for such care but for the application of the penalty period, whichever is later, and which does not occur during any other period of ineligibility under this subsection.

(E)(i) With respect to an institutionalized individual, the number of months of ineligibility under this subparagraph for an individual shall be equal to—

(I) the total, cumulative uncompensated value of all assets transferred by the individual (or individual's spouse) on or after the look-back date specified in subparagraph (B)(i), divided by

(II) the average monthly cost to a private patient of nursing facility services in the State (or, at the option of the State, in the community in which the individual is institutionalized) at the time of application.

(ii) With respect to a noninstitutionalized individual, the number of months of ineligibility under this subparagraph for an individual shall not be greater than a number equal to—

(I) the total, cumulative uncompensated value of all assets transferred by the individual (or individual's spouse) on or after the look-back date specified in subparagraph (B)(i), divided by

(II) the average monthly cost to a private patient of nursing facility services in the State (or, at the option of the State, in the community in which the individual is institutionalized) at the time of application.

(iii) The number of months of ineligibility otherwise determined under clause (i) or (ii) with respect to the disposal of an asset shall be reduced—

(I) in the case of periods of ineligibility determined under clause (i), by the number of months of ineligibility applicable to the individual under clause (ii) as a result of such disposal, and

(II) in the case of periods of ineligibility determined under clause (ii), by the number of months of ineligibility applicable to the individual under clause (i) as a result of such disposal.

(iv) A State shall not round down, or otherwise disregard any fractional period of ineligibility determined under clause (i) or (ii) with respect to the disposal of assets.

(F) For purposes of this paragraph, the purchase of an annuity shall be treated as the disposal of an asset for less than fair market value unless—

(i) the State is named as the remainder beneficiary in the first position for at least the total amount of medical assistance paid on behalf of the institutionalized individual under this title [42 USCS §§ 1396 et seq.]; or

(ii) the State is named as such a beneficiary in the second position after the community spouse or minor or disabled child and is named in the first position if such spouse or a representative of such child disposes of any such remainder for less than fair market value.

(G) For purposes of this paragraph with respect to a transfer of assets, the term "assets" includes an annuity purchased by or on behalf of an annuitant who has applied for medical assistance with respect to nursing facility services or other long-term care services under this title [42 USCS §§ 1396 et seq.] unless—

(i) the annuity is—

(I) an annuity described in subsection (b) or (q) of section 408 of the Internal Revenue Code of 1986 [26 USCS § 408]; or

(II) purchased with proceeds from—

(aa) an account or trust described in subsection (a), (c), or (p) of section 408 of such Code [26 USCS § 408];

(bb) a simplified employee pension (within the meaning of section 408(k) of such Code [26 USCS § 408(k)]); or

(cc) a Roth IRA described in section 408A of such Code [26 USCS § 408A]; or

(ii) the annuity—

(I) is irrevocable and nonassignable;

(II) is actuarially sound (as determined in accordance with actuarial publications of the Office of the Chief Actuary of the Social Security Administration); and

(III) provides for payments in equal amounts during the term of the annuity, with no deferral and no balloon payments made.

(H) Notwithstanding the preceding provisions of this paragraph, in the case of an individual (or individual's spouse) who makes multiple fractional transfers of assets in more than 1 month for less than fair market value on or after the applicable look-back date specified in subparagraph (B), a State may determine the period of ineligibility applicable to such individual under this paragraph by—

(i) treating the total, cumulative uncompensated value of all assets transferred by the individual (or individual's spouse) during all months on or after the look-back date specified in subparagraph (B) as 1 transfer for purposes of clause (i) or (ii) (as the case may be) of subparagraph (E); and

(ii) beginning such period on the earliest date which would apply under subparagraph (D) to any of such transfers.

(I) For purposes of this paragraph with respect to a transfer of assets, the term "assets" includes funds used to purchase a promissory note, loan, or mortgage unless such note, loan, or mortgage—

(i) has a repayment term that is actuarially sound (as determined in accordance with actuarial publications of the Office of the Chief Actuary of the Social Security Administration);

(ii) provides for payments to be made in equal amounts during the term of the loan, with no deferral and no balloon payments made; and

(iii) prohibits the cancellation of the balance upon the death of the lender.

In the case of a promissory note, loan, or mortgage that does not satisfy the requirements of clauses (i) through (iii), the value of such note, loan, or mortgage shall be the outstanding balance due as of the date of the individual's application for medical assistance for services described in subparagraph (C).

(J) For purposes of this paragraph with respect to a transfer of assets, the term "assets" includes the purchase of a life estate interest in another individual's home unless the purchaser resides in the home for a period of at least 1 year after the date of the purchase.

(2) An individual shall not be ineligible for medical assistance by reason of paragraph (1) to the extent that—

(A) the assets transferred were a home and title to the home was transferred to—

(i) the spouse of such individual;

(ii) a child of such individual who (I) is under age 21, or (II) (with respect to States eligible to participate in the State program established under title XVI [42 USCS §§ 1381 et seq.]) is blind or permanently and totally disabled, or (with respect to States which are not eligible to participate in such program) is blind or disabled as defined in section 1614 [42 USCS § 1382c];

(iii) a sibling of such individual who has an equity interest in such home and who was residing in such individual's home for a period of at least one year immediately before the date the individual becomes an institutionalized individual; or

(iv) a son or daughter of such individual (other than a child described in clause (ii)) who was residing in such individual's home for a period of at least two years immediately before the date the individual becomes an institutionalized individual, and who (as determined by the State) provided care to such individual which permitted such individual to reside at home rather than in such an institution or facility;

(B) the assets—

(i) were transferred to the individual's spouse or to another for the sole benefit of the individual's spouse,

(ii) were transferred from the individual's spouse to another for the sole benefit of the individual's spouse,

(iii) were transferred to, or to a trust (including a trust described in subsection (d)(4)) established solely for the benefit of, the individual's child described in subparagraph (A)(ii)(II), or

(iv) were transferred to a trust (including a trust described in subsection (d)(4)) established solely for the benefit of an individual under 65 years of age who is disabled (as defined in section 1614(a)(3)) [42 USCS § 1382c(a)(3)];

(C) a satisfactory showing is made to the State (in accordance with regulations promulgated by the Secretary) that (i) the individual intended to dispose of the assets either at fair market value, or for other valuable consideration, (ii) the assets were transferred exclusively for a purpose other than to qualify for medical assistance, or (iii) all assets transferred for less than fair market value have been returned to the individual; or

(D) the State determines, under procedures established by the State (in accordance with standards specified by the Secretary), that the denial of eligibility would work an undue hardship as determined on the basis of criteria established by the Secretary.

The procedures established under subparagraph (D) shall permit the facility in which the institutionalized individual is residing to file an undue hardship waiver application on behalf of the individual with the consent of the individual or the personal representative of the individual. While an application for an undue hardship waiver is pending under subparagraph (D) in the case of an individual who is a resident of a nursing facility, if the application meets such criteria as the Secretary specifies, the State may provide for payments for nursing facility services in order to hold the bed for the individual at the facility, but not in excess of payments for 30 days.

(3) For purposes of this subsection, in the case of an asset held by an individual in common with another person or persons in a joint tenancy, tenancy in common, or similar arrangement, the asset (or the affected portion of such asset) shall be considered to be transferred by such individual when any action is taken, either by such individual or by any other person, that reduces or eliminates such individual's ownership or control of such asset.

(4) A State (including a State which has elected treatment under section 1902(f) [42 USCS § 1396a(f)]) may not provide for any period of ineligibility for an individual due to transfer of resources for less than fair market value except in accordance with this subsection. In the case of a transfer by the spouse of an individual which results in a period of ineligibility for medical assistance under a State plan for such individual, a State shall, using a reasonable methodology (as specified by the Secretary), apportion such period of ineligibility (or any portion of such period) among the individual and the individual's spouse if the spouse otherwise becomes eligible for medical assistance under the State plan.

(5) In this subsection, the term "resources" has the meaning given such term in section 1613 [42 USCS § 1382b], without regard to the exclusion described in subsection (a)(1) thereof.

(d) Treatment of trust amounts. (1) For purposes of determining an individual's eligibility for, or amount of, benefits under a State plan under this title [42 USCS §§ 1396 et seq.], subject to paragraph (4), the rules specified in paragraph (3) shall apply to a trust established by such individual.

(2)(A) For purposes of this subsection, an individual shall be considered to have established a trust if assets of the individual were used to form all or part of the corpus of the trust and if any of the following individuals established such trust other than by will:

(i) The individual.

(ii) The individual's spouse.

(iii) A person, including a court or administrative body, with legal authority to act in place of or on behalf of the individual or the individual's spouse.

(iv) A person, including any court or administrative body, acting at the direction or upon the request of the individual or the individual's spouse.

(B) In the case of a trust the corpus of which includes assets of an individual (as determined under subparagraph (A)) and assets of any other person or persons, the provisions of this subsection shall apply to the portion of the trust attributable to the assets of the individual.

(C) Subject to paragraph (4), this subsection shall apply without regard to—

(i) the purposes for which a trust is established,

(ii) whether the trustees have or exercise any discretion under the trust,

(iii) any restrictions on when or whether distributions may be made from the trust, or

(iv) any restrictions on the use of distributions from the trust.

(3)(A) In the case of a revocable trust—

(i) the corpus of the trust shall be considered resources available to the individual,

(ii) payments from the trust to or for the benefit of the individual shall be considered income of the individual, and

(iii) any other payments from the trust shall be considered assets disposed of by the individual for purposes of subsection (c).

(B) In the case of an irrevocable trust—

(i) if there are any circumstances under which payment from the trust could be made to or for the benefit of the individual, the portion of the corpus from which, or the income on the corpus from which, payment to the individual could be made shall be considered resources available to the individual, and payments from that portion of the corpus or income—

(I) to or for the benefit of the individual, shall be considered income of the individual, and

(II) for any other purpose, shall be considered a transfer of assets by the individual subject to subsection (c); and

(ii) any portion of the trust from which, or any income on the corpus from which, no payment could under any circumstances be made to the individual shall be considered, as of the date of establishment of the trust (or, if later, the date on which payment to the individual was foreclosed) to be assets disposed by the individual for purposes of subsection (c), and the value of the trust shall be determined for purposes of such subsection by including the amount of any payments made from such portion of the trust after such date.

(4) This subsection shall not apply to any of the following trusts:

(A) A trust containing the assets of an individual under age 65 who is disabled (as defined in section 1614(a)(3) [42 USCS § 1382c(a)(3)]) and which is established for the benefit of such individual by a parent, grandparent, legal guardian of the individual, or a court if the State will receive all amounts remaining in the trust upon the death of such individual up to an amount equal to the total medical assistance paid on behalf of the individual under a State plan under this title [42 USCS §§ 1396 et seq.].

(B) A trust established in a State for the benefit of an individual if—

(i) the trust is composed only of pension, Social Security, and other income to the individual (and accumulated income in the trust),

(ii) the State will receive all amounts remaining in the trust upon the death of such individual up to an amount equal to the total medical assistance paid on behalf of the individual under a State plan under this title [42 USCS §§ 1396 et seq.], and

(iii) the State makes medical assistance available to individuals described in section 1902(a)(10)(A)(ii)(V) [42 USCS § 1396a(a)(10)(A)(ii)(V)], but does not make such assistance available to individuals for nursing facility services under section 1902(a)(10)(C) [42 USCS § 1396a(a)(10)(C)].

(C) A trust containing the assets of an individual who is disabled (as defined in section 1614(a)(3)) [42 USCS § 1382c(a)(3)] that meets the following conditions:

(i) The trust is established and managed by a non-profit association.

(ii) A separate account is maintained for each beneficiary of the trust, but, for purposes of investment and management of funds, the trust pools these accounts.

(iii) Accounts in the trust are established solely for the benefit of individuals who are disabled (as defined in section 1614(a)(3)) [42 USCS § 1382c(a)(3)] by the parent, grandparent, or legal guardian of such individuals, by such individuals, or by a court.

(iv) To the extent that amounts remaining in the beneficiary's account upon the death of the beneficiary are not retained by the trust, the trust pays to the State from such remaining amounts in the account an amount equal to the total amount of medical assistance paid on behalf of the beneficiary under the State plan under this title [42 USCS §§ 1396 et seq.].

(5) The State agency shall establish procedures (in accordance with standards specified by the Secretary) under which the agency waives the application of this subsection with respect to an individual if the individual establishes that such application would work an undue hardship on the individual as determined on the basis of criteria established by the Secretary.

(6) The term "trust" includes any legal instrument or device that is similar to a trust but includes an annuity only to such extent and in such manner as the Secretary specifies.

(e)(1) In order to meet the requirements of this section for purposes of section 1902(a)(18) [42 USCS § 1396a(a)(18)], a State shall require, as a condition for the provision of medical assistance for services described in subsection (c)(1)(C)(i) (relating to long-term care services) for an individual, the application of the individual for such assistance (including any recertification of eligibility for such assistance) shall disclose a description of any interest the individual or community spouse has in an annuity (or similar financial instrument, as may be specified by the Secretary), regardless of whether the annuity is irrevocable or is treated as an asset. Such application or recertification form shall include a statement that under paragraph (2) the State becomes a remainder beneficiary under such an annuity or similar financial instrument by virtue of the provision of such medical assistance.

(2)(A) In the case of disclosure concerning an annuity under subsection (c)(1)(F), the State shall notify the issuer of the annuity of the right of the State under such subsection as a preferred remainder beneficiary in the annuity for medical assistance furnished to the individual. Nothing in this paragraph shall be construed as preventing such an issuer from notifying persons with any other remainder interest of the State's remainder interest under such subsection.

(B) In the case of such an issuer receiving notice under subparagraph (A), the State may require the issuer to notify the State when there is a change in the amount of income or principal being withdrawn from the amount that was being withdrawn at the time of the most recent disclosure described in paragraph (1). A State shall take such information into account in determining the amount of the State's obligations for medical assistance or in the individual's eligibility for such assistance.

(3) The Secretary may provide guidance to States on categories of transactions that may be treated as a transfer of asset for less than fair market value.

(4) Nothing in this subsection shall be construed as preventing a State from denying eligibility for medical assistance for an individual based on the income or resources derived from an annuity described in paragraph (1).

(f)(1)(A) Notwithstanding any other provision of this title [42 USCS §§ 1396 et seq.], subject to subparagraphs (B) and (C) of this paragraph and paragraph (2), in determining eligibility of an individual for medical assistance with respect to nursing facility services or other long-term care services, the individual shall not be eligible for such assistance if the individual's equity interest in the individual's home exceeds $500,000.

(B) A State may elect, without regard to the requirements of section 1902(a)(1) [42 USCS § 1396a(a)(1)] (relating to statewideness) and section 1902(a)(10)(B) [42 USCS § 1396a(a)(10)(B)] (relating to comparability), to apply subparagraph (A) by substituting for "$500,000", an amount that exceeds such amount, but does not exceed $750,000.

(C) The dollar amounts specified in this paragraph shall be increased, beginning with 2011, from year to year based on the percentage increase in the consumer price index for all urban consumers (all items; United States city average), rounded to the nearest $1,000.

(2) Paragraph (1) shall not apply with respect to an individual if—

(A) the spouse of such individual, or

(B) such individual's child who is under age 21, or (with respect to States eligible to participate in the State program established under title XVI [42 USCS §§ 1381 et seq.]) is blind or permanently and totally disabled, or (with respect to States which are not eligible to participate in such program) is blind or disabled as defined in section 1614 [42 USCS § 1382c],

is lawfully residing in the individual's home.

(3) Nothing in this subsection shall be construed as preventing an individual from using a reverse mortgage or home equity loan to reduce the individual's total equity interest in the home.

(4) The Secretary shall establish a process whereby paragraph (1) is waived in the case of a demonstrated hardship.

(g) Treatment of entrance fees of individuals residing in continuing care retirement communities. (1) In general. For purposes of determining an individual's eligibility for, or amount of, benefits under a State plan under this title [42 USCS §§ 1396 et seq.], the rules specified in paragraph (2) shall apply to individuals residing in continuing care retirement communities or life care communities that collect an entrance fee on admission from such individuals.

(2) Treatment of entrance fee. For purposes of this subsection, an individual's entrance fee in a continuing care retirement community or life care community shall be considered a resource available to the individual to the extent that—

(A) the individual has the ability to use the entrance fee, or the contract provides that the entrance fee may be used, to pay for care should other resources or income of the individual be insufficient to pay for such care;

(B) the individual is eligible for a refund of any remaining entrance fee when the individual dies or terminates the continuing care retirement community or life care community contract and leaves the community; and

(C) the entrance fee does not confer an ownership interest in the continuing care retirement community or life care community.

(h) Definitions. In this section, the following definitions shall apply:

(1) The term "assets", with respect to an individual, includes all income and resources of the individual and of the individual's spouse, including any income or resources which the individual or such individual's spouse is entitled to but does not receive because of action—

(A) by the individual or such individual's spouse,

(B) by a person, including a court or administrative body, with legal authority to act in place of or on behalf of the individual or such individual's spouse, or

(C) by any person, including any court or administrative body, acting at the direction or upon the request of the individual or such individual's spouse.

(2) The term "income" has the meaning given such term in section 1612 [42 USCS

§ 1382a].

(3) The term "institutionalized individual" means an individual who is an inpatient in a nursing facility, who is an inpatient in a medical institution and with respect to whom payment is made based on a level of care provided in a nursing facility, or who is described in section 1902(a)(10)(A)(ii)(VI) [42 USCS § 1396a(a)(10)(A)(ii)(VI)].

(4) The term "noninstitutionalized individual" means an individual receiving any of the services specified in subsection (c)(1)(C)(ii).

(5) The term "resources" has the meaning given such term in section 1613 [42 USCS § 1382b], without regard (in the case of an institutionalized individual) to the exclusion described in subsection (a)(1) of such section.

(Aug. 14, 1935, ch 531, Title XIX, § 1917, as added Sept. 3, 1982, P. L. 97-248, Title I, Subtitle B, § 132(b), 96 Stat. 370; Jan. 12, 1983, P. L. 97-448, Title III, § 309(b)(21), (22), 96 Stat. 2410; Dec. 22, 1987, P. L. 100-203, Title IV, Subtitle C, Part 2, § 4211(h)(12), 101 Stat. 1330-208; July 1, 1988, P. L. 100-360, Title III, § 303(b), Title IV, Subtitle B, § 411(l)(3)(1), 102 Stat. 760, 803; Oct. 13, 1988, P. L. 100-485, Title VI, § 608(d)(16)(B), 102 Stat. 2417; Dec. 19, 1989, P. L. 101-239, Title VI, Subtitle B, Part 2, § 6411(e)(1), 103 Stat. 2271; Aug. 10, 1993, P. L. 103-66, Title XIII, Ch. 2, Subch B, Part II, §§ 13611(a)–(c), 13612(a)–(c), 107 Stat. 622, 627; Feb. 8, 2006, P. L. 109-171, Title VI, Subtitle A, Ch. 2, Subch. A, §§ 6011(a), (b), (e), 6012(a)–(c), 6014(a), 6015(b), 6016(a)–(d), Subch. B, § 6021(a)(1), 120 Stat. 61, 62, 64, 65, 68; Dec. 20, 2006, P. L. 109-432, Div B, Title IV, § 405(b)(1), 120 Stat. 2998; July 15, 2008, P. L. 110-275, Title I, Subtitle A, Title I, Part II, § 115(a), 122 Stat. 2507; Feb. 17, 2009, P. L. 111-5, Div B, Title V, § 5006(c), 123 Stat. 507.)

HISTORY; ANCILLARY LAWS AND DIRECTIVES

Other provisions:

Expanded access to certain benefits. Act Feb. 8, 2006, P. L. 109-171, Title VI, Subtitle A, Ch. 2, Subch. B, § 6021, 120 Stat. 68, provides:

"(a) Expansion authority. (1) [Omitted—This paragraph amended subsec. (b)(1)(C) of this section.]

"(2) State reporting requirements. Nothing in clauses (iii)(VI) and (v) of section 1917(b)(1)(C) of the Social Security Act [subsec. (b)(1)(C) of this section] (as added by paragraph (1)) shall be construed as prohibiting a State from requiring an issuer of a long-term care insurance policy sold in the State (regardless of whether the policy is issued under a qualified State long-term care insurance partnership under section 1917(b)(1)(C)(iii) of such Act [subsec. (b)(1)(C)(iii) of this section]) to require the issuer to report information or data to the State that is in addition to the information or data required under such clauses.

"(3) Effective date. A State plan amendment that provides for a qualified State long-term care insurance partnership under the amendments made by paragraph (1) [amending subsec. (b)(1)(C) of this section] may provide that such amendment is effective for long-term care insurance policies issued on or after a date, specified in the amendment, that is not earlier than the first day of the first calendar quarter in which the plan amendment was submitted to the Secretary of Health and Human Services.

"(b) Standards for reciprocal recognition among partnership States. In order to permit portability in long-term care insurance policies purchased under State long-term care insurance partnerships, the Secretary of Health and Human Services shall develop, not later than January 1, 2007, and in consultation with the National Association of Insurance Commissioners, issuers of long-term care insurance policies, States with experience with long-term care insurance partnership plans, other States, and representatives of consumers of long-term care insurance policies, standards for uniform reciprocal recognition of such policies among States with qualified State long-term care insurance partnerships under which—

"(1) benefits paid under such policies will be treated the same by all such States; and

"(2) States with such partnerships shall be subject to such standards unless the State notifies the Secretary in writing of the State's election to be exempt from such standards.

"(c) Annual reports to Congress. (1) In general. The Secretary of Health and Human Services shall annually report to Congress on the long-term care insurance partnerships established in accordance with section 1917(b)(1)(C)(ii) of the Social Security Act (42 U.S.C. 1396p(b)(1)(C)(ii)) (as amended by subsection (a)(1)). Such reports shall include analyses of the extent to which such partnerships expand or limit access of individuals to long-term care and the impact of such partnerships on Federal and State expenditures under the Medicare and Medicaid programs. Nothing in this section shall be construed as requiring the Secretary to conduct an independent review of each long-term care insurance policy offered under or in connection with such a partnership.

"(2) Appropriation. Out of any funds in the Treasury not otherwise appropriated, there is appropriated to the Secretary of Health and Human Services, $1,000,000 for the period of fiscal years 2006 through 2010 to carry out paragraph (1).

"(d) National Clearinghouse for Long-Term Care Information. (1) Establishment. The Secretary of Health and Human Services shall establish a National Clearinghouse for Long-Term Care Information. The Clearinghouse may be established through a contract or interagency agreement.

"(2) Duties. (A) In general. The National Clearinghouse for Long-Term Care Information shall—

"(i) educate consumers with respect to the availability and limitations of coverage for long-term care under the Medicaid program and provide contact information for obtaining State-specific information on long-term care coverage, including eligibility and estate recovery requirements under State Medicaid programs;

"(ii) provide objective information to assist consumers with the decisionmaking process for determining whether to purchase long-term care insurance or to pursue other private market alternatives for purchasing long-term care and provide contact information for additional objective resources on planning for long-term care needs; and "(iii) maintain a list of States with State long-term care insurance partnerships under the Medicaid program that provide reciprocal recognition of long-term care insurance policies issued under such partnerships.

"(B) Requirement. In providing information to consumers on long-term care in accordance with this subsection, the National Clearinghouse for Long-Term Care Information shall not advocate in favor of a specific long-term care insurance provider or a specific long-term care insurance policy.

"(3) Appropriation. Out of any funds in the Treasury not otherwise appropriated, there is appropriated to carry out this subsection, $3,000,000 for each of fiscal years 2006 through 2010.".

Amendment of subsec. (d)(2), (3) of § 6021(d) of Act Feb. 8, 2006, P. L. 109-171 (note above), effective January 1, 2011. Act March 23, 2010, P. L. 111-148, Title VIII, § 8002(d), 124 Stat. 847 (effective on 1/1/2011, as provided by § 8002(e) of such Act, which appears as 42 USCS § 300ll note), as amended March 23, 2010, P. L. 111-148, Title X, Subtitle G, § 10801(c), 124 Stat. 1015, provides:

"Section 6021(d) of the Deficit Reduction Act of 2005 (42 U.S.C. 1396p note) is amended—

"(1) in paragraph (2)(A)—

"(A) in clause (ii), by striking 'and' at the end;

"(B) in clause (iii), by striking the period at the end and inserting '; and'; and

"(C) by adding at the end the following:

" '(iv) include information regarding the CLASS program established under title XXXII of the Public Health Service Act [42 USCS §§ 300ll et seq.] and information regarding how benefits provided under a CLASS Independence Benefit Plan differ from disability insurance benefits.'; and

"(2) in paragraph (3), by striking '2010' and inserting '2015'.".

§ 1396r. Requirements for nursing facilities [Caution: See prospective amendment notes below.]

(a) "Nursing facility" defined. In this title [42 USCS §§ 1396 et seq.], the term "nursing facility" means an institution (or a distinct part of an institution) which—

(1) is primarily engaged in providing to residents—

(A) skilled nursing care and related services for residents who require medical or nursing care,

(B) rehabilitation services for the rehabilitation of injured, disabled, or sick persons, or

(C) on a regular basis, health-related care and services to individuals who because of their mental or physical condition require care and services (above the level of room and board) which can be made available to them only through institutional facilities,

and is not primarily for the care and treatment of mental diseases;

(2) has in effect a transfer agreement (meeting the requirements of section 1861(l) [42 USCS § 1395x(l)) with one or more hospitals having agreements in effect under section 1866 [42 USCS § 1395cc]; and

(3) meets the requirements for a nursing facility described in subsections (b), (c), and (d) of this section.

Such term also includes any facility which is located in a State on an Indian reservation and is certified by the Secretary as meeting the requirements of paragraph (1) and subsections (b), (c), and (d).

(b) Requirements relating to provision of services. (1) Quality of life. (A) In general. A nursing facility must care for its residents in such a manner and in such an environment as will promote maintenance or enhancement of the quality of life of each resident.

(B) Quality assessment and assurance. A nursing facility must maintain a quality assessment and assurance committee, consisting of the director of nursing services, a physician designated by the facility, and at least 3 other members of the facility's staff, which (i) meets at least quarterly to identify issues with respect to which quality assessment and assurance activities are necessary and (ii) develops and implements appropriate plans of action to correct identified quality deficiencies. A State or the Secretary may not require disclosure of the records of such committee except insofar as such disclosure is related to the compliance of such committee with the requirements of this subparagraph.

(2) Scope of services and activities under plan of care. A nursing facility must provide services and activities to attain or maintain the highest practicable physical, mental, and psychosocial well-being of each resident in accordance with a written plan of care which—

(A) describes the medical, nursing, and psychosocial needs of the resident and how such needs will be met;

(B) is initially prepared, with the participation to the extent practicable of the resident or the resident's family or legal representative, by a team which includes the resident's attending physician and a registered professional nurse with responsibility for the resident; and

(C) is periodically reviewed and revised by such team after each assessment under paragraph (3).

(3) Residents' assessment. (A) Requirement. A nursing facility must conduct a comprehensive, accurate, standardized, reproducible assessment of each resident's functional capacity, which assessment—

(i) describes the resident's capability to perform daily life functions and significant impairments in functional capacity;

(ii) is based on a uniform minimum data set

specified by the Secretary under subsection (f)(6)(A);

(iii) uses an instrument which is specified by the State under subsection (e)(5); and

(iv) includes the identification of medical problems.

(B) Certification. (i) In general. Each such assessment must be conducted or coordinated (with the appropriate participation of health professionals) by a registered professional nurse who signs and certifies the completion of the assessment. Each individual who completes a portion of such an assessment shall sign and certify as to the accuracy of that portion of the assessment.

(ii) Penalty for falsification. (I) An individual who willfully and knowingly certifies under clause (i) a material and false statement in a resident assessment is subject to a civil money penalty of not more than $1,000 with respect to each assessment.

(II) An individual who willfully and knowingly causes another individual to certify under clause (i) a material and false statement in a resident assessment is subject to a civil money penalty of not more than $5,000 with respect to each assessment.

(III) The provisions of section 1128A [42 USCS § 1320a-7a] (other than subsections (a) and (b)) shall apply to a civil money penalty under this clause in the same manner as such provisions apply to a penalty or proceeding under section 1128A(a) [42 USCS § 1320a-7a(a)].

(iii) Use of independent assessors. If a State determines, under a survey under subsection (g) or otherwise, that there has been a knowing and willful certification of false assessments under this paragraph, the State may require (for a period specified by the State) that resident assessments under this paragraph be conducted and certified by individuals who are independent of the facility and who are approved by the State.

(C) Frequency. (i) In general. Such an assessment must be conducted—

(I) promptly upon (but no later than 14 days after the date of) admission for each individual admitted on or after October 1, 1990, and by not later than October 1, 1991, for each resident of the facility on that date;

(II) promptly after a significant change in the resident's physical or mental condition; and

(III) in no case less often than once every 12 months.

(ii) Resident review. The nursing facility must examine each resident no less frequently than once every 3 months and, as appropriate, revise the resident's assessment to assure the continuing accuracy of the assessment.

(D) Use. The results of such an assessment shall be used in developing, reviewing, and revising the resident's plan of care under paragraph (2).

(E) Coordination. Such assessments shall be coordinated with any State-required preadmission screening program to the maximum extent practicable in order to avoid duplicative testing and effort. In addition, a nursing facility shall notify the State mental health authority or State mental retardation or developmental disability authority, as applicable, promptly after a significant change in the physical or mental condition of a resident who is mentally ill or mentally retarded.

(F) Requirements relating to preadmission screening for mentally ill and mentally retarded individuals. Except as provided in clauses (ii) and (iii) of subsection (e)(7)(A), a nursing facility must not admit, on or after January 1, 1989, any new resident who—

(i) is mentally ill (as defined in subsection (e)(7)(G)(i)) unless the State mental health authority has determined (based on an independent physical and mental evaluation performed by a person or entity other than the State mental health authority) prior to admission that, because of the physical and mental condition of the individual, the individual requires the level of services provided by a nursing facility, and, if the individual requires such level of services, whether the individual requires specialized services for mental illness, or

(ii) is mentally retarded (as defined in subsection (e)(7)(G)(ii)) unless the State mental retardation or developmental disability authority has determined prior to admission that, because of the physical and mental condition of the individual, the individual requires the level of services provided by a nursing facility, and, if the individual requires such level of services, whether the individual requires specialized services for mental retardation.

A State mental health authority and a State mental retardation or developmental disability authority may not delegate (by subcontract or otherwise) their responsibilities under this subparagraph to a nursing facility (or to an entity that has a direct or indirect affiliation or relationship with such a facility).

(4) Provision of services and activities. (A) In general. To the extent needed to fulfill all plans of care described in paragraph (2), a nursing facility must provide (or arrange for the provision of)—

(i) nursing and related services and specialized rehabilitative services to attain or maintain the highest practicable physical, mental, and psychosocial well-being of each resident;

(ii) medically-related social services to attain or maintain the highest practicable physical, mental, and psychosocial well-being of each resident;

(iii) pharmaceutical services (including procedures that assure the accurate acquiring, receiving, dispensing, and administering of all drugs and biologicals) to meet the needs of each resident;

(iv) dietary services that assure that the meals meet the daily nutritional and special dietary needs of each resident;

(v) an on-going program, directed by a qualified professional, of activities designed to meet the interests and the physical, mental, and psychosocial well-being of each resident;

(vi) routine dental services (to the extent covered under the State plan) and emergency dental services to meet the needs of each resident; and

(vii) treatment and services required by mentally ill and mentally retarded residents not otherwise provided or arranged for (or required to be provided or arranged for) by the State.

The services provided or arranged by the facility must meet professional standards of quality.

(B) Qualified persons providing services. Services described in clauses (i), (ii), (iii), (iv), and (vi) of subparagraph (A) must be provided by qualified persons in accordance with each resident's written plan of care.

(C) Required nursing care; facility waivers. (i) General requirements. With respect to nursing facility services provided on or after October 1, 1990, a nursing facility—

(I) except as provided in clause (ii), must provide 24-hour licensed nursing services which are sufficient to meet the nursing needs of its residents, and

(II) except as provided in clause (ii), must use the services of a registered professional nurse for at least 8 consecutive hours a day, 7 days a week.

(ii) Waiver by State. To the extent that a facility is unable to meet the requirements of clause (i), a State may waive such requirements with respect to the facility if—

(I) the facility demonstrates to the satisfaction of the State that the facility has been unable, despite diligent efforts (including offering wages at the community prevailing rate for nursing facilities), to recruit appropriate personnel,

(II) the State determines that a waiver of the requirement will not endanger the health or safety of individuals staying in the facility,

(III) the State finds that, for any such periods in which licensed nursing services are not available, a registered nurse or a physician is obligated to respond immediately to telephone calls from the facility,

(IV) the State agency granting a waiver of such requirements provides notice of the waiver to the State long-term care ombudsman (established under section 307(a)(12) of the Older Americans Act of 1965 [42 USCS § 3027(a)(12)]) and the protection and advocacy system in the State for the mentally ill and the mentally retarded, and

(V) the nursing facility that is granted such a waiver by a State notifies residents of the facility (or, where appropriate, the guardians or legal representatives of such residents) and members of their immediate families of the waiver.

A waiver under this clause shall be subject to annual review and to the review of the Secretary and subject to clause (iii) shall be accepted by the Secretary for purposes of this title [42 USCS §§ 1396 et seq.] to the same extent as is the State's certification of the facility. In granting or renewing a waiver, a State may require the facility to employ other qualified, licensed personnel.

(iii) Assumption of waiver authority by Secretary. If the Secretary determines that a State has shown a clear pattern and practice of allowing waivers in the absence of diligent efforts by facilities to meet the staffing requirements, the Secretary shall assume and exercise the authority of the State to grant waivers.

(5) Required training of nurse aides. (A) In general. (i) Except as provided in clause (ii), a nursing facility must not use on a full-time basis any individual, as a nurse aide in the facility on or after October 1, 1990, for more than 4 months unless the individual—

(I) has completed a training and competency evaluation program, or a competency evaluation program, approved by the State under subsection (e)(1)(A), and

(II) is competent to provide nursing and nursing-related services.

(ii) A nursing facility must not use on a temporary, per diem, leased, or on any other basis other than as a permanent employee any individual as a nurse aide in the facility on or after January 1, 1991, unless the individual meets the requirements described in clause (i).

(B) Offering competency evaluation programs for current employees. A nursing facility must provide, for individuals used as a nurse aide by the facility as of January 1, 1990, for a competency evaluation program approved by the State under subsection (e)(1) and such preparation as may be necessary for the individual to complete such a program by October 1, 1990.

(C) Competency. The nursing facility must not permit an individual, other than in a training and competency evaluation program approved by the State, to serve as a nurse aide or provide services of a type for which the individual has not demonstrated competency and must not use such an individual as a nurse aide unless the facility has inquired of any State registry established under subsection (e)(2)(A) that the facility believes will include information concerning the individual.

(D) Re-training required. For purposes of subparagraph (A), if, since an individual's most recent completion of a training and competency evaluation program, there has been a continuous period of 24 consecutive months during none of which the individual performed nursing or nursing-related services for monetary compensation, such individual shall complete a new training and competency evaluation program, or a new competency evaluation program.

(E) Regular in-service education. The nursing facility must provide such regular performance review and regular in-service education as assures that individuals used as nurse aides are competent to perform services as nurse aides, including training for individuals providing nursing and nursing-related services to residents with cognitive impairments.

(F) Nurse aide defined. In this paragraph, the term "nurse aide" means any individual providing nursing or nursing-related services to residents in a nursing facility, but does not include an individual—

(i) who is a licensed health professional (as defined in subparagraph (G)) or a registered dietician, or

(ii) who volunteers to provide such services without monetary compensation.

(G) Licensed health professional defined. In this paragraph, the term "licensed health professional" means a physician, physician assistant, nurse practitioner, physical, speech, or occupational therapist, physical or occupational therapy assistant, registered professional nurse, licensed practical nurse, or licensed or certified social worker.

(6) Physician supervision and clinical records. A nursing facility must—

(A) require that the health care of every resident be provided under the supervision of a physician (or, at the option of a State, under the supervision of a nurse practitioner, clinical nurse specialist, or physician assistant who is not an employee of the facility but who is working in collaboration with a physician);

(B) provide for having a physician available to furnish necessary medical care in case of emergency; and

(C) maintain clinical records on all residents, which records include the plans of care (described in paragraph (2)) and the residents' assessments (described in paragraph (3)), as well as the results of any pre-admission screening conducted under subsection (e)(7).

(7) Required social services. In the case of a nursing facility with more than 120 beds, the facility must have at least one social worker (with at least a bachelor's degree in social work or similar professional qualifications) employed full-time to provide or assure the provision of social services.

(8) Information on nurse staffing. (A) In general. A nursing facility shall post daily for each shift the current number of licensed and unlicensed nursing staff directly responsible for resident care in the facility. The information shall be displayed in a uniform manner (as specified by the Secretary) and in a clearly visible place.

(B) Publication of data. A nursing facility shall, upon request, make available to the public the nursing staff data described in subparagraph (A).

(c) Requirements relating to residents' rights. (1) General rights. (A) Specified rights. A nursing facility must protect and promote the rights of each resident, including each of the following rights:

(i) Free choice. The right to choose a personal attending physician, to be fully informed in advance about care and treatment, to be fully informed in advance of any changes in care or treatment that may affect the resident's well-being, and (except with respect to a resident adjudged incompetent) to participate in planning care and treatment or changes in care and treatment.

(ii) Free from restraints. The right to be free from physical or mental abuse, corporal punishment, involuntary seclusion, and any physical or chemical restraints imposed for purposes of discipline or convenience and not required to treat the resident's medical symptoms. Restraints may only be imposed—

(I) to ensure the physical safety of the resident or other residents, and

(II) only upon the written order of a physician that specifies the duration and circumstances under which the restraints are to be used (except in emergency circumstances specified by the Secretary until such an order could reasonably be obtained).

(iii) Privacy. The right to privacy with regard to accommodations, medical treatment, written and telephonic communications, visits, and meetings of family and of resident groups.

(iv) Confidentiality. The right to confidentiality of personal and clinical records and to access to current clinical records of the resident upon request by the resident or the resident's legal representative, within 24 hours (excluding hours occurring during a weekend or holiday) after making such a request.

(v) Accommodation of needs. The right—

(I) to reside and receive services with reasonable accommodation of individual needs and preferences, except where the health or safety of the individual or other residents would be endangered, and

(II) to receive notice before the room or roommate of the resident in the facility is changed.

(vi) Grievances. The right to voice grievances with respect to treatment or care that is (or fails to be) furnished, without discrimination or reprisal for voicing the grievances and the right to prompt efforts by the facility to resolve grievances the resident may have, including those with respect to the behavior of other residents.

(vii) Participation in resident and family groups. The right of the resident to organize and participate in resident groups in the facility and the right of the resident's family to meet in the facility with the families of other residents in the facility.

(viii) Participation in other activities. The right of the resident to participate in social, religious, and community activities that do not interfere with the rights of other residents in the facility.

(ix) Examination of survey results. The right to examine, upon reasonable request, the results of the most recent survey of the facility conducted by the Secretary or a State with respect to the facility and any plan of correction in effect with respect to the facility.

(x) Refusal of certain transfers. The right to refuse a transfer to another room within the facility, if a purpose of the transfer is to relocate the resident from a portion of the facility that is not a skilled nursing facility (for purposes of title XVIII [42 USCS §§ 1395 et seq.]) to a portion of the facility that is such a skilled nursing facility.

(xi) Other rights. Any other right established by the Secretary.

Clause (iii) shall not be construed as requiring the provision of a private room. A resident's exercise of a right to refuse transfer under clause (x) shall not affect the resident's eligibility or entitlement to medical assistance under this title [42 USCS §§ 1396 et seq.] or a State's entitlement to Federal medical assistance under this title [42 USCS §§ 1396 et seq.] with respect to services furnished to such a resident.

(B) Notice of rights. A nursing facility must—

(i) inform each resident, orally and in writing at the time of admission to the facility, of the resident's legal rights during the stay at the facility and of the requirements and procedures for establishing eligibility for medical assistance under this title [42 USCS §§ 1396 et seq.], including the right to request an assessment under section 1924(c)(1)(B) [42 USCS § 1396r-5(c)(1)(B)];

(ii) make available to each resident, upon reasonable request, a written statement of such rights (which statement is updated upon changes in such rights) including the notice (if any) of the State developed under subsection (e)(6);

(iii) inform each resident who is entitled to medical assistance under this title [42 USCS §§ 1396 et seq.]—

(I) at the time of admission to the facility or, if later, at the time the resident becomes eligible for such assistance, of the items and services (including those specified under section 1902(a)(28)(B) [42 USCS § 1396a(a)(28)(B)]) that are included in nursing facility services under the State plan and for which the resident may not be charged (except as permitted in section 1916 [42 USCS § 1396o]), and of those other items and services that the facility offers and for which the resident may be charged and the amount of the charges for such items and services, and

(II) of changes in the items and services described in subclause (I) and of changes in the charges imposed for items and services described in that subclause; and

(iv) inform each other resident, in writing before or at the time of admission and periodically during the resident's stay, of services available in the facility and of related charges for such services, including any charges for services not covered under title XVIII [42 USCS §§ 1395 et seq.] or by the facility's basic per diem charge.

The written description of legal rights under this subparagraph shall include a description of the protection of personal funds under paragraph (6) and a statement that a resident may file a complaint with a State survey and certification agency respecting resident abuse and neglect and misappropriation of resident property in the facility.

(C) Rights of incompetent residents. In the case of a resident adjudged incompetent under the laws of a State, the rights of the resident under this title [42 USCS §§ 1396 et seq.] shall devolve upon, and, to the extent judged necessary by a court of competent jurisdiction, be exercised by, the person appointed under State law to act on the resident's behalf.

(D) Use of psychopharmacologic drugs. Psychopharmacologic drugs may be administered only on the orders of a physician and only as part of a plan (included in the written plan of care described in paragraph (2)) designed to eliminate or modify the symptoms for which the drugs are prescribed and only if, at least annually an independent, external consultant reviews the appropriateness of the drug plan of each resident receiving such drugs.

(2) Transfer and discharge rights. (A) In general. A nursing facility must permit each resident to remain in the facility and must not transfer or discharge the resident from the facility unless—

(i) the transfer or discharge is necessary to meet the resident's welfare and the resident's welfare cannot be met in the facility;

(ii) the transfer or discharge is appropriate because the resident's health has improved sufficiently so the resident no longer needs the services provided by the facility;

(iii) the safety of individuals in the facility is endangered;

(iv) the health of individuals in the facility would otherwise be endangered;

(v) the resident has failed, after reasonable and appropriate notice, to pay (or to have paid under this title [42 USCS §§ 1396 et seq.] or title XVIII [42 USCS §§ 1395 et seq.] on the resident's behalf) for a stay at the facility; or

(vi) the facility ceases to operate.

In each of the cases described in clauses (i) through (iv), the basis for the transfer or discharge must be documented in the resident's clinical record. In the cases described in clauses (i) and (ii), the documentation must be made by the resident's physician, and in the case described in clause (iv) the documentation must be made by a physician. For purposes of clause (v), in the case of a resident who becomes eligible for assistance under this title [42 USCS §§ 1396 et seq.] after admission to the facility, only charges which may be imposed under this title [42 USCS §§ 1396 et seq.] shall be considered to be allowable.

(B) Pre-transfer and pre-discharge notice. (i) In general. Before effecting a transfer or discharge of a resident, a nursing facility must—

(I) notify the resident (and, if known, an immediate family member of the resident or legal representative) of the transfer or discharge and the reasons therefor,

(II) record the reasons in the resident's clinical record (including any documentation required under subparagraph (A)), and

(III) include in the notice the items described in clause (iii).

(ii) Timing of notice. The notice under clause (i)(I) must be made at least 30 days in advance of the resident's transfer or discharge except—

(I) in a case described in clause (iii) or (iv) of subparagraph (A);

(II) in a case described in clause (ii) of subparagraph (A), where the resident's health improves sufficiently to allow a more immediate transfer or discharge;

(III) in a case described in clause (i) of subparagraph (A), where a more immediate transfer or discharge is necessitated by the resident's urgent medical needs; or

(IV) in a case where a resident has not resided in the facility for 30 days.

In the case of such exceptions, notice must be given as many days before the date of the transfer or discharge as is practicable.

(iii) Items included in notice. Each notice under clause (i) must include—

(I) for transfers or discharges effected on or after I) October 1, 1989, notice of the resident's right to appeal the transfer or discharge under the State process established under subsection (e)(3);

(II) the name, mailing address, and telephone number of the State long-term care ombudsman (established under title III or VII of the Older Americans Act of 1965 [42 USCS §§ 3021 et seq. or 3058 et seq.] in accordance with section 712 of the Act [42 USCS § 3058g]);

(III) in the case of residents with developmental disabilities, the mailing address and telephone number of the agency responsible for the protection and advocacy system for developmentally disabled individuals established under subtitle C [of title I] of the Developmental Disabilities Assistance and Bill of Rights Act [42 USCS §§ 15041 et seq.]; and

(IV) in the case of mentally ill residents (as defined in subsection (e)(7)(G)(i)), the mailing address and telephone number of the agency responsible for the protection and advocacy system for mentally ill individuals established under the Protection and Advocacy for Mentally Ill Individuals Act [42 USCS §§ 10801 et seq.].

(C) Orientation. A nursing facility must provide sufficient preparation and orientation to residents to ensure safe and orderly transfer or discharge from the facility.

(D) Notice on bed-hold policy and readmission. (i) Notice before transfer. Before a resident of a nursing facility is transferred for hospitalization or therapeutic leave, a nursing facility must provide written information to the resident and an immediate family member or legal representative concerning—

(I) the provisions of the State plan under this title [42 USCS §§ 1396 et seq.] regarding the period (if any) during which the resident will be permitted under the State plan to return and resume residence in the facility, and

(II) the policies of the facility regarding such a period, which policies must be consistent with clause (iii).

(ii) Notice upon transfer. At the time of transfer of a resident to a hospital or for therapeutic leave, a nursing facility must provide written notice to the resident and an immediate family member or legal representative of the duration of any period described in clause (i).

(iii) Permitting resident to return. A nursing facility must establish and follow a written policy under which a resident—

(I) who is eligible for medical assistance for nursing facility services under a State plan,

(II) who is transferred from the facility for hospitalization or therapeutic leave, and

(III) whose hospitalization or therapeutic leave exceeds a period paid for under the State plan for the holding of a bed in the facility for the resident,

will be permitted to be readmitted to the facility immediately upon the first availability of a bed in a semiprivate room in the facility if, at the time of readmission, the resident requires the services provided by the facility.

(E) Information respecting advance directives. A nursing facility must comply with the requirement of section 1902(w) [42 USCS § 1396a(w)] (relating to maintaining written policies and procedures respecting advance directives).

(F) Continuing rights in case of voluntary withdrawal from participation. (i) In general. In the case of a nursing facility that voluntarily withdraws from participation in a State plan under this title [42 USCS §§ 1396 et seq.] but continues to provide services of the type provided by nursing facilities—

(I) the facility's voluntary withdrawal from participation is not an acceptable basis for the transfer or discharge of residents of the facility who were residing in the facility on the day before the effective date of the withdrawal (including those residents who were not entitled to medical assistance as of such day);

(II) the provisions of this section continue to apply to such residents until the date of their discharge from the facility; and

(III) in the case of each individual who begins residence in the facility after the effective date of such withdrawal, the facility shall provide notice orally and in a prominent manner in writing on a separate page at the time the individual begins residence of the information described in clause (ii) and shall obtain from each such individual at such time an acknowledgment of receipt of such information that is in writing, signed by the individual, and separate from other documents signed by such individual.

Nothing in this subparagraph shall be construed as affecting any requirement of a participation agreement that a nursing facility provide advance notice to the State or the Secretary, or both, of its intention to terminate the agreement.

(ii) Information for new residents. The information described in this clause for a resident is the following:

(I) The facility is not participating in the program under this title with respect to that resident.

(II) The facility may transfer or discharge the resident from the facility at such time as the resident is unable to pay the charges of the facility, even though the resident may have become eligible for medical assistance for nursing facility services under this title.

(iii) Continuation of payments and oversight authority. Notwithstanding any other provision of this title [42 USCS §§ 1396 et seq.], with respect to the residents described in clause (i)(I), a participation agreement of a facility described in clause (i) is deemed to continue in effect under such plan after the effective date of the facility's voluntary withdrawal from participation under the State plan for purposes of—

(I) receiving payments under the State plan for nursing facility services provided to such residents;

(II) maintaining compliance with all applicable requirements of this title [42 USCS §§ 1396 et seq.]; and

(III) continuing to apply the survey, certification, and enforcement authority provided under subsections (g) and (h) (including involuntary termination of a participation agreement deemed continued under this clause).

(iv) No application to new residents. This paragraph (other than subclause (III) of clause (i)) shall not apply to an individual who begins residence in a facility on or after the effective date of the withdrawal from participation under this subparagraph.

(3) Access and visitation rights. A nursing facility must—

(A) permit immediate access to any resident by any representative of the Secretary, by any representative of the State, by an ombudsman or agency described in subclause (II), (III), or (IV) of paragraph (2)(B)(iii), or by the resident's individual physician;

(B) permit immediate access to a resident, subject to the resident's right to deny or withdraw consent at any time, by immediate family or other relatives of the resident;

(C) permit immediate access to a resident, subject to reasonable restrictions and the resident's right to deny or withdraw consent at any time, by others who are visiting with the consent of the resident;

(D) permit reasonable access to a resident by any entity or individual that provides health, social, legal, or other services to the resident, subject to the resident's right to deny or withdraw consent at any time; and

(E) permit representatives of the State ombudsman (described in paragraph (2)(B)(iii)(II)), with the permission of the resident (or the resident's legal representative) and consistent with State law, to examine a resident's clinical records.

(4) Equal access to quality care. (A) In general. A nursing facility must establish and maintain identical policies and practices regarding transfer, discharge, and the provision of services required under the State plan for all individuals regardless of source of payment.

(B) Construction. (i) Nothing prohibiting any charges for non-medicaid patients. Subparagraph (A) shall not be construed as prohibiting a nursing facility from charging any amount for services furnished, consistent with the notice in paragraph (1)(B) describing such charges.

(ii) No additional services required. Subparagraph (A) shall not be construed as requiring a State to offer additional services on behalf of a resident than are otherwise provided under the State plan.

(5) Admissions policy. (A) Admissions. With respect to admissions practices, a nursing facility must—

(i) (I) not require individuals applying to reside or residing in the facility to waive their rights to benefits under this title [42 USCS §§ 1396 et seq.] or title XVIII [42 USCS §§ 1395 et seq.], (II) subject to subparagraph (B)(v), not require oral or written assurance that such individuals are not eligible for, or will not apply for, benefits under this title [42 USCS §§ 1396 et seq.] or title XVIII [42 USCS §§ 1395 et seq.], and (III) prominently display in the facility written information, and provide to such individuals oral and written information, about how to apply for and use such benefits and how to receive refunds for previous payments covered by such benefits;

(ii) not require a third party guarantee of payment to the facility as a condition of admission (or expedited admission) to, or continued stay in, the facility; and

(iii) in the case of an individual who is entitled to medical assistance for nursing facility services, not charge, solicit, accept, or receive, in addition to any amount otherwise required to be paid under the State plan under this title [42 USCS §§ 1396 et seq.], any gift, money, donation, or other consideration as a precondition of admitting (or expediting the admission of) the individual to the facility or as a requirement for the individual's continued stay in the facility.

(B) Construction. (i) No preemption of stricter standards. Subparagraph (A) shall not be construed as preventing States or political subdivisions therein from prohibiting, under State or local law, the discrimination against individuals who are entitled to medical assistance under the State plan with respect to admissions practices of nursing facilities.

(ii) Contracts with legal representatives. Subparagraph (A)(ii) shall not be construed as preventing a facility from requiring an individual, who has legal access to a resident's income or resources available to pay for care in the facility, to sign a contract (without incurring personal financial liability) to provide payment from the resident's income or resources for such care.

(iii) Charges for additional services requested. Subparagraph (A)(iii) shall not be construed as preventing a facility from charging a resident, eligible for medical assistance under the State plan, for items or services the resident has requested and received and that are not specified in the State plan as included in the term "nursing facility services".

(iv) Bona fide contributions. Subparagraph (A)(iii) shall not be construed as prohibiting a nursing facility from soliciting, accepting, or receiving a charitable, religious, or philanthropic contribution from an organization or from a person unrelated to the resident (or potential resident), but only to the extent that such contribution is not a condition of admission, expediting admission, or continued stay in the facility.

(v) Treatment of continuing care retirement communities admission contracts. Notwithstanding subclause (II) of subparagraph (A)(i), subject to subsections (c) and (d) of section 1924 [42 USCS § 1396r-5], contracts for admission to a State licensed, registered, certified, or equivalent continuing care retirement community or life care community, including services in a nursing facility that is part of such community, may require residents to spend on their care resources declared for the purposes of admission before applying for medical assistance.

(6) Protection of resident funds. (A) In general. The nursing facility—

(i) may not require residents to deposit their personal funds with the facility, and

(ii) upon the written authorization of the resident, must hold, safeguard, and account for such personal funds under a system established and maintained by the facility in accordance with this paragraph.

(B) Management of personal funds. Upon a facility's acceptance of written authorization of a resident under subparagraph (A)(ii), the facility must manage and account for the personal funds of the resident deposited with the facility as follows:

(i) Deposit. The facility must deposit any amount of personal funds in excess of $50 with respect to a resident in an interest bearing account (or accounts) that is separate from any of the facility's operating accounts and credits all interest earned on such separate account to such account. With respect to any other personal funds, the facility must maintain such funds in a non-interest bearing account or petty cash fund.

(ii) Accounting and records. The facility must assure a full and complete separate accounting of each such resident's personal funds, maintain a written record of all financial transactions involving the personal funds of a resident deposited with the facility, and afford the resident (or a legal representative of the resident) reasonable access to such record.

(iii) Notice of certain balances. The facility must notify each resident receiving medical assistance under the State plan under title XIX [42 USCS §§ 1396 et seq.] when the amount in the resident's account reaches $200 less than the dollar amount determined under section 1611(a)(3)(B) [42 USCS § 1382(a)(3)(B)] and the fact that if the amount in the account (in addition to the value of the resident's other nonexempt resources) reaches the amount determined under such section the resident may lose eligibility for such medical assistance or for benefits under title XVI [42 USCS §§ 1381 et seq.].

(iv) Conveyance upon death. Upon the death of a resident with such an account, the facility must convey promptly the resident's personal funds (and a final accounting of such funds) to the individual administering the resident's estate.

(C) Assurance of financial security. The facility must purchase a surety bond, or otherwise provide assurance satisfactory to the Secretary, to assure the security of all personal funds of residents deposited with the facility.

(D) Limitation on charges to personal funds. The facility may not impose a charge against the personal funds of a resident for any item or service for which payment is made under this title [42 USCS §§ 1396 et seq.] or title XVIII [42 USCS §§ 1395 et seq.].

(7) Limitation on charges in case of Medicaid-eligible individuals. (A) In general. A nursing facility may not impose charges, for certain medicaid-eligible individuals for nursing facility services covered by the State under its plan under this title [42 USCS §§ 1396 et seq.], that exceed the payment amounts established by the State for such services under this title [42 USCS §§ 1396 et seq.].

(B) "Certain medicaid-eligible individuals" defined. In subparagraph (A), the term "certain medicaid-eligible individual" means an individual who is entitled to medical assistance for nursing facility services in the facility under this title [42 USCS §§ 1396 et seq.] but with respect to whom such benefits are not being paid because, in determining the amount of the individual's income to be applied monthly to payment for the costs of such services, the amount of such income exceeds the payment amounts established by the State for such services under this title [42 USCS §§ 1396 et seq.].

(8) Posting of survey results. A nursing facility must post in a place readily accessible to residents, and family members and legal representatives of residents, the results of the most recent survey of the facility conducted under subsection (g).

(d) Requirements relating to administration and other matters. (1) Administration. (A) In general. A nursing facility must be administered in a manner that enables it to use its resources effectively and efficiently to attain or maintain the highest practicable physical, mental, and psychosocial well-being of each resident (consistent with requirements established under subsection (f)(5)).

(B) Required notices. If a change occurs in—

(i) the persons with an ownership or control interest (as defined in section 1124(a)(3) [42 USCS § 1320a-3(a)(3)]) in the facility,

(ii) the persons who are officers, directors, agents, or managing employees (as defined in section 1126(b) [42 USCS § 1320a-5(b)]) of the facility,

(iii) the corporation, association, or other company responsible for the management of the facility, or

(iv) the individual who is the administrator or director of nursing of the facility,

the nursing facility must provide notice to the State agency responsible for the licensing of the facility, at the time of the change, of the change and of the identity of each new person, company, or individual described in the respective clause.

(C) Nursing facility administrator. The administrator of a nursing facility must meet standards established by the Secretary under subsection (f)(4).

(2) Licensing and Life Safety Code. (A) Licensing. A nursing facility must be licensed under applicable State and local law.

(B) Life Safety Code. A nursing facility must meet such provisions of such edition (as specified by the Secretary in regulation) of the Life Safety Code of the National Fire Protection Association as are applicable to nursing homes; except that—

(i) the Secretary may waive, for such periods as he deems appropriate, specific provisions of such Code which if rigidly applied would result in unreasonable hardship upon a facility, but only if such waiver would not adversely affect the health and safety of residents or personnel, and

(ii) the provisions of such Code shall not apply in any State if the Secretary finds that in such State there is in effect a fire and safety code, imposed by State law, which adequately protects residents of and personnel in nursing facilities.

(3) Sanitary and infection control and physical environment. A nursing facility must—

(A) establish and maintain an infection control program designed to provide a safe, sanitary, and comfortable environment in which residents reside and to help prevent the development and transmission of disease and infection, and

(B) be designed, constructed, equipped, and maintained in a manner to protect the health and safety of residents, personnel, and the general public.

(4) Miscellaneous. (A) Compliance with Federal, State, and local laws and professional standards. A nursing facility must operate and provide services in compliance with all applicable Federal, State, and local laws and regulations (including the requirements of section 1124 [42 USCS § 1320a-3]) and with accepted professional standards and principles which apply to professional providing services in such a facility.

(B) Other. A nursing facility must meet such other requirements relating to the health and safety of residents or relating to the physical facilities thereof as the Secretary may find necessary.

(e) State requirements relating to nursing facility requirements. As a condition of approval of its plan under this title [42 USCS §§ 1396 et seq.], a State must provide for the following:

(1) Specification and review of nurse aide training and competency evaluation programs and of nurse aide competency evaluation programs. The State must—

(A) by not later than January 1, 1989, specify those training and competency evaluation programs, and those competency evaluation programs, that the State approves for purposes of subsection (b)(5) and that meet the requirements established under subsection (f)(2), and

(B) by not later than January 1, 1990, provide for the review and reapproval of such programs, at a frequency and using a methodology consistent with the requirements established under subsection (f)(2)(A)(iii).

The failure of the Secretary to establish requirements under subsection (f)(2) shall not relieve any State of its responsibility under this paragraph.

(2) Nurse aide registry. (A) In general. By not later than January 1, 1989, the State shall establish and maintain a registry of all individuals who have satisfactorily completed a nurse aide training and competency evaluation program, or a nurse aide competency evaluation program, approved under paragraph (1) in the State, or any individual described in subsection (f)(2)(B)(ii) or in subparagraph (B), (C), or (D) of section 6901(b)(4) of the Omnibus Budget Reconciliation Act of 1989 [42 USCS § 1395i-3 note].

(B) Information in registry. The registry under subparagraph (A) shall provide (in accordance with regulations of the Secretary) for the inclusion of specific documented findings by a State under subsection (g)(1)(C) of resident neglect or abuse or misappropriation of resident property involving an individual listed in the registry, as well as any brief statement of the individual disputing the findings. In the case of inquiries to the registry concerning an individual listed in the registry, any information disclosed concerning such a finding shall also include disclosure of any such statement in the registry relating to the finding or a clear and accurate summary of such a statement.

(C) Prohibition against charges. A State may not impose any charges on a nurse aide relating to the registry established and maintained under subparagraph (A).

(3) State appeals process for transfers and discharges. The State, for transfers and discharges from nursing facilities effected on or after October 1, 1989, must provide for a fair mechanism, meeting the guidelines established under subsection (f)(3), for hearing appeals on transfers of residents of such facilities; but the failure of the Secretary to establish such guidelines under such subsection shall not relieve any State of its responsibility under this paragraph.

(4) Nursing facility administrator standards. By not later than July 1, 1989, the State must have implemented and enforced the nursing facility administrator standards developed under subsection (f)(4) respecting the qualification of administrators of nursing facilities.

(5) Specification of resident assessment instrument. Effective July 1, 1990, the State shall specify the instrument to be used by nursing facilities in the State in complying with the requirement of subsection (b)(3)(A)(iii). Such instrument shall be—

(A) one of the instruments designated under subsection (f)(6)(B), or

(B) an instrument which the Secretary has approved as being consistent with the minimum data set of core elements, common definitions, and utilization guidelines specified by the Secretary under subsection (f)(6)(A).

(6) Notice of medicaid rights. Each State, as a condition of approval of its plan under this title [42 USCS §§ 1396 et seq.], effective April 1, 1988, must develop (and periodically update) a written notice of the rights and obligations of residents of nursing facilities (and spouses of such residents) under this title [42 USCS §§ 1396 et seq.].

(7) State requirements for preadmission screening and resident review. (A) Preadmission screening. (i) In general. Effective January 1, 1989, the State must have in effect a preadmission screening program, for making determinations (using any criteria developed under subsection (f)(8)) described in subsection (b)(3)(F) for mentally ill and mentally retarded individuals (as defined in subparagraph (G)) who are admitted to nursing facilities on or after January 1, 1989. The failure of the Secretary to develop minimum criteria under subsection (f)(8) shall not relieve any State of its responsibility to have a preadmission screening program under this subparagraph or to perform resident reviews under subparagraph (B).

(ii) Clarification with respect to certain readmissions. The preadmission screening program under clause (i) need not provide for determinations in the case of the readmission to a nursing facility of an individual who, after being admitted to the nursing facility, was transferred for care in a hospital.

(iii) Exception for certain hospital discharges. The preadmission screening program under clause (i) shall not apply to the admission to a nursing facility of an individual—

(I) who is admitted to the facility directly from a hospital after receiving acute inpatient care at the hospital,

(II) who requires nursing facility services for the condition for which the individual received care in the hospital, and

(III) whose attending physician has certified, before admission to the facility, that the individual is likely to require less than 30 days of nursing facility services.

(B) State requirement for resident review. (i) For mentally ill residents. As of April 1, 1990, in the case of each resident of a nursing facility who is mentally ill, the State mental health authority must review and determine (using any criteria developed under subsection (f)(8) and based on an independent physical and mental evaluation performed by a person or entity other than the State mental health authority)—

(I) whether or not the resident, because of the resident's physical and mental condition, requires the level of services provided by a nursing facility or requires the level of services of an inpatient psychiatric hospital for individuals under age 21 (as described in section 1905(h) [42 USCS § 1396d(h)]) or of an institution for mental diseases providing medical assistance to individuals 65 years of age or older; and

(II) whether or not the resident requires specialized services for mental illness.

(ii) For mentally retarded residents. As of

April 1, 1990, in the case of each resident of a nursing facility who is mentally retarded, the State mental retardation or developmental disability authority must review and determine (using any criteria developed under subsection (f)(8))—

(I) whether or not the resident, because of the resident's physical and mental condition, requires the level of services provided by a nursing facility or requires the level of services of an intermediate care facility described under section 1905(d) [42 USCS § 1396d(d)]; and

(II) whether or not the resident requires specialized services for mental retardation.

(iii) Review required upon change in resident's condition. A review and determination under clause (i) or (ii) must be conducted promptly after a nursing facility has notified the State mental health authority or State mental retardation or developmental disability authority, as applicable, under subsection (b)(3)(E) with respect to a mentally ill or mentally retarded resident, that there has been a significant change in the resident's physical or mental condition.

(iv) Prohibition of delegation. A State mental health authority, a State mental retardation or developmental disability authority, and a State may not delegate (by subcontract or otherwise) their responsibilities under this subparagraph to a nursing facility (or to an entity that has a direct or indirect affiliation or relationship with such a facility).

(C) Response to preadmission screening and resident review. As of April 1, 1990, the State must meet the following requirements:

(i) Long-term residents not requiring nursing facility services, but requiring specialized services. In the case of a resident who is determined, under subparagraph (B), not to require the level of services provided by a nursing facility, but to require specialized services for mental illness or mental retardation, and who has continuously resided in a nursing facility for at least 30 months before the date of the determination, the State must, in consultation with the resident's family or legal representative and care-givers—

(I) inform the resident of the institutional and noninstitutional alternatives covered under the State plan for the resident,

(II) offer the resident the choice of remaining in the facility or of receiving covered services in an alternative appropriate institutional or noninstitutional setting,

(III) clarify the effect on eligibility for services under the State plan if the resident chooses to leave the facility (including its effect on readmission to the facility), and

(IV) regardless of the resident's choice, provide for (or arrange for the provision of) such specialized services for the mental illness or mental retardation.

A State shall not be denied payment under this title [42 USCS §§ 1396 et seq.] for nursing facility services for a resident described in this clause because the resident does not require the level of services provided by such a facility, if the resident chooses to remain in such a facility.

(ii) Other residents not requiring nursing facility services, but requiring specialized services. In the case of a resident who is determined, under subparagraph (B), not to require the level of services provided by a nursing facility, but to require specialized services for mental illness or mental retardation, and who has not continuously resided in a nursing facility for at least 30 months before the date of the determination, the State must, in consultation with the resident's family or legal representative and care-givers—

(I) arrange for the safe and orderly discharge of the resident from the facility, consistent with the requirements of subsection (c)(2),

(II) prepare and orient the resident for such discharge, and

(III) provide for (or arrange for the provision of) such specialized services treatment for the mental illness or mental retardation.

(iii) Residents not requiring nursing facility services and not requiring specialized services. In the case of a resident who is determined, under subparagraph (B), not to require the level of services provided by a nursing facility and not to require specialized services for mental illness or mental retardation, the State must—

(I) arrange for the safe and orderly discharge of the resident from the facility, consistent with the requirements of subsection (c)(2), and

(II) prepare and orient the resident for such discharge.

(iv) Annual report. Each State shall report to the Secretary annually concerning the number and disposition of residents described in each of clauses (ii) and (iii).

(D) Denial of payment. (i) For failure to conduct preadmission screening or review. No payment may be made under section 1903(a) [42 USCS § 1396b(a)] with respect to nursing facility services furnished to an individual for whom a determination is required under subsection (b)(3)(F) or subparagraph (B) but for whom the determination is not made.

(ii) For certain residents not requiring nursing facility level of services. No payment may be made under section 1903(a) [42 USCS § 1396b(a)] with respect to nursing facility services furnished to an individual (other than an individual described in subparagraph (C)(i)) who does not require the level of services provided by a nursing facility.

(E) Permitting alternative disposition plans. With respect to residents of a nursing facility who are mentally retarded or mentally ill and who are determined under subparagraph (B) not to require the level of services of such a facility, but who require specialized services for mental illness or mental retardation, a State and the nursing facility shall be considered to be in compliance with the requirements of subparagraphs (A) through (C) of this paragraph if, before April 1, 1989, the State and the Secretary have entered into an agreement relating to the disposition of such residents of the facility and the State is in compliance with such agreement. Such an agreement may provide for the disposition of the residents after the date specified in subparagraph (C). The State may revise such an agreement, subject to the approval of the Secretary, before October 1, 1991, but only if, under the revised agreement, all residents subject to the agreement who do not require the level of services of such a facility are discharged from the facility by not later than April 1, 1994.

(F) Appeals procedures. Each State, as a condition of approval of its plan under this title [42 USCS §§ 1396 et seq.], effective January 1, 1989, must have in effect an appeals process for individuals adversely affected by determinations under subparagraph (A) or (B).

(G) Definitions. In this paragraph and in subsection (b)(3)(F):

(i) An individual is considered to be "mentally ill" if the individual has a serious mental illness (as defined by the Secretary in consultation with the National Institute of Mental Health) and does not have a primary diagnosis of dementia (including Alzheimer's disease or a related disorder) or a diagnosis (other than a primary diagnosis) of dementia and a primary diagnosis that is not a serious mental illness.

(ii) An individual is considered to be "mentally retarded" if the individual is mentally retarded or a person with a related condition (as described in section 1905(d) [42 USCS § 1396d(d)]).

(iii) The term "specialized services" has the meaning given such term by the Secretary in regulations, but does not include, in the case of a resident of a nursing facility, services within the scope of services which the facility must provide or arrange for its residents under subsection (b)(4).

(f) Responsibilities of Secretary relating to nursing facility requirements. (1) General responsibility. It is the duty and responsibility of the Secretary to assure that requirements which govern the provision of care in nursing facilities under State plans approved under this title [42 USCS §§ 1396 et seq.], and the enforcement of such requirements, are adequate to protect the health, safety, welfare, and rights of residents and to promote the effective and efficient use of public moneys.

(2) Requirements for nurse aide training and competency evaluation programs and for nurse aide competency evaluation programs. (A) In general. For purposes of subsections (b)(5) and (e)(1)(A), the Secretary shall establish, by not later than September 1, 1988—

(i) requirements for the approval of nurse aide training and competency evaluation programs, including requirements relating to (I) the areas to be covered in such a program (including at least basic nursing skills, personal care skills, recognition of mental health and social service needs, care of cognitively impaired residents, basic restorative services, and residents' rights) and content of the curriculum, (II) minimum hours of initial and ongoing training and retraining (including not less than 75 hours in the case of initial training), (III) qualifications of instructors, and (IV) procedures for determination of competency;

(ii) requirements for the approval of nurse aide competency evaluation programs, including requirement relating to the areas to be covered in such a program, including at least basic nursing skills, personal care skills, recognition of mental health and social service needs, care of cognitively impaired residents, basic restorative services, and residents' rights, and procedures for determination of competency;

(iii) requirements respecting the minimum frequency and methodology to be used by a State in reviewing such programs compliance with the requirements for such programs; and

(iv) requirements, under both such programs, that—

(I) provide procedures for determining competency that permit a nurse aide, at the nurse aide's option, to establish competency through procedures or methods other than the passing of a written examination and to have the competency evaluation conducted at the nursing facility at which the aide is (or will be) employed (unless the facility is described in subparagraph (B)(iii)(I)),

(II) prohibit the imposition on a nurse aide who is employed by (or who has received an offer of employment from) a facility on the date on which the aide begins either such program of any charges (including any charges for textbooks and other required course materials and any charges for the competency evaluation) for either such program, and

(III) in the case of a nurse aide not described in subclause (II) who is employed by (or who has received an offer of employment from) a facility not later than 12 months after completing either such program, the State shall provide for the reimbursement of costs incurred in completing such program on a prorata basis during the period in which the nurse aide is so employed.

(B) Approval of certain programs. Such requirements—

(i) may permit approval of programs offered by or in facilities, as well as outside facilities (including employee organizations), and of programs in effect on the date of the enactment of this section [Dec. 22, 1987];

(ii) shall permit a State to find that an individual who has completed (before July 1, 1989) a nurse aide training and competency evaluation program shall be deemed to have completed such a program approved under subsection (b)(5) if the State determines that, at the time the program was offered, the program met the requirements for approval under such paragraph; and

(iii) subject to subparagraphs (C) and (D), shall prohibit approval of such a program—

(I) offered by or in a nursing facility which, within the previous 2 years—

(a) has operated under a waiver under subsection (b)(4)(C)(ii) that was granted on the basis of a demonstration that the facility is unable to provide the nursing care required under subsection (b)(4)(C)(i) for a period in excess of 48 hours during a week;

(b) has been subject to an extended (or partial extended) survey under section 1819(g)(2)(B)(i) [42 USCS § 1395i-3(g)(2)(B)(i)] or subsection (g)(2)(B)(i);or

(c) has been assessed a civil money penalty described in section 1819(h)(2)(B)(ii) [42 USCS § 1395i-3(h)(2)(B)(ii)] or subsection (h)(2)(A)(ii) of not less than $5,000, or has been subject to a remedy described in subsection (h)(1)(B)(i), clauses (i), (iii), or (iv) of subsection (h)(2)(A), clauses [clause] (i) or (iii) of section 1819(h)(2)(B), or section 1819(h)(4) [42 USCS § 1395i-3(h)(2)(B)(i) or (iii) or (h)(4)], or

(II) offered by or in a nursing facility unless the State makes the determination, upon an individual's completion of the program, that the individual is competent to provide nursing and nursing-related services in nursing facilities.

A State may not delegate (through subcontract or otherwise) its responsibility under clause (iii)(II) to the nursing facility.

(C) Waiver authorized. Clause (iii)(I) of subparagraph (B) shall not apply to a program offered in (but not by) a nursing facility (or skilled nursing facility for purposes of title XVIII [42 USCS §§ 1395 et seq.]) in a State if the State—

(i) determines that there is no other such program offered within a reasonable distance of the facility,

(ii) assures, through an oversight effort, that an adequate environment exists for operating the program in the facility, and

(iii) provides notice of such determination and assurances to the State long-term care ombudsman.

(D) Waiver of disapproval of nurse-aide training programs. Upon application of a nursing facility, the Secretary may waive the application of subparagraph (B)(iii)(I)(c) if the imposition of the civil monetary penalty was not related to the quality of care provided to residents of the facility. Nothing in this subparagraph shall be construed as eliminating any requirement upon a facility to pay a civil monetary penalty described in the preceding sentence.

(3) Federal guidelines for State appeals process for transfers and discharges. For purposes of subsections (c)(2)(B)(iii) and (e)(3), by not later than October 1, 1988, the Secretary shall establish guidelines for minimum standards which State appeals processes under subsection (e)(3) must meet to provide a fair mechanism for hearing appeals on transfers and discharges of residents from nursing facilities.

(4) Secretarial standards qualification of administrators. For purposes of subsections (d)(1)(C) and (e)(4), the Secretary shall develop, by not later than March 1, 1988, standards to be applied in assuring the qualifications of administrators of nursing facilities.

(5) Criteria for administration. The Secretary shall establish criteria for assessing a nursing facility's compliance with the requirement of subsection (d)(1) with respect to—

(A) its governing body and management,

(B) agreements with hospitals regarding transfers of residents to and from the hospitals and to and from other nursing facilities,

(C) disaster preparedness,

(D) direction of medical care by a physician,

(E) laboratory and radiological services,

(F) clinical records, and

(G) resident and advocate participation.

(6) Specification of resident assessment data set and instruments. The Secretary shall—

(A) not later than January 1, 1989, specify a minimum data set of core elements and common definitions for use by nursing facilities in conducting the assessments required under subsection (b)(3), and establish guidelines for utilization of the data set; and

(B) by not later than April 1, 1990, designate one or more instruments which are consistent with the specification made under subparagraph (A) and which a State may specify under subsection (e)(5)(A) for use by nursing facilities in complying with the requirements of subsection (b)(3)(A)(iii).

(7) List of items and services furnished in nursing facilities not chargeable to the personal funds of a resident. (A) Regulations required. Pursuant to the requirement of section 21(b) of the Medicare-Medicaid Anti-Fraud and Abuse Amendments of 1977 [42 USCS § 1395x note], the Secretary shall issue regulations, on or before the first day of the seventh month to begin after the date of enactment of this section [Dec. 22, 1987], that define those costs which may be charged to the personal funds of residents in nursing facilities who are individuals receiving medical assistance with respect to nursing facility services under this title [42 USCS §§ 1396 et seq.] and those costs which are to be included in the payment amount under this title [42 USCS §§ 1396 et seq.] for nursing facility services.

(B) Rule if failure to publish regulations. If the Secretary does not issue the regulations under subparagraph (A) on or before the date required in that subparagraph, in the case of a resident of a nursing facility who is eligible to receive benefits for nursing facility services under this title [42 USCS §§ 1396 et seq.], for purposes of section 1902(a)(28)(B) [42 USCS § 1396a(a)(28)(B)], the Secretary shall be deemed to have promulgated regulations under this paragraph which provide that the costs which may not be charged to the personal funds of such resident (and for which payment is considered to be made under this title [42 USCS §§ 1396 et seq.]) include, at a minimum, the costs for routine personal hygiene items and services furnished by the facility.

(8) Federal minimum criteria and monitoring for preadmission screening and resident review. (A) Minimum criteria. The Secretary shall develop, by not later than October 1, 1988, minimum criteria for States to use in making determinations under subsections (b)(3)(F) and (e)(7)(B) and in permitting individuals adversely affected to appeal such determinations, and shall notify the States of such criteria.

(B) Monitoring compliance. The Secretary shall review, in a sufficient number of cases to allow reasonable inferences, each State's compliance with the requirements of subsection (e)(7)(C)(ii) (relating to discharge and placement for active treatment of certain residents).

(9) Criteria for monitoring state waivers. The Secretary shall develop, by not later than October 1, 1988, criteria and procedures for monitoring State performances in granting waivers pursuant to subsection (b)(4)(C)(ii).

(10) Special focus facility program. (A) In general. The Secretary shall conduct a special focus facility program for enforcement of requirements for nursing facilities that the Secretary has identified as having substantially failed to meet applicable requirements of this Act [42 USCS §§ 301 et seq.].

(B) Periodic surveys. Under such program the Secretary shall conduct surveys of each facility in the program not less often than once every 6 months.

(g) Survey and certification process. (1) State and Federal responsibility. (A) In general. Under each State plan under this title [42 USCS §§ 1396 et seq.], the State shall be responsible for certifying, in accordance with surveys conducted under paragraph (2), the compliance of nursing facilities (other than facilities of the State) with the requirements of subsections (b), (c), and (d). The Secretary shall be responsible for certifying, in accordance with surveys conducted under paragraph (2), the compliance of State nursing facilities with the requirements of such subsections.

(B) Educational program. Each State shall conduct periodic educational programs for the staff and residents (and their representatives) of nursing facilities in order to present current regulations, procedures, and policies under this section.

(C) Investigation of allegations of resident neglect and abuse and misappropriation of resident property. The State shall provide, through the agency responsible for surveys and certification of nursing facilities under this subsection, for a process for the receipt and timely review, and investigation of allegations of neglect and abuse and misappropriation of resident property by a nurse aide of a resident in a nursing facility or by another individual used by the facility in providing services to such a resident. The State shall, after notice to the individual involved and a reasonable opportunity for a hearing for the individual to rebut allegations, make a finding as to the accuracy of the allegations. If the State finds that a nurse aide has neglected or abused a resident or misappropriated resident property in a facility, the State shall notify the nurse aide and the registry of such finding. If the State finds that any other individual used by the facility has neglected or abused a resident or misappropriated resident property in a facility, the State shall notify the appropriate licensure authority. A State shall not make a finding that an individual has neglected a resident if the individual demonstrates that such neglect was caused by factors beyond the control of the individual.

(D) Removal of name from nurse aide registry. (i) In general. In the case of a finding of neglect under subparagraph (C), the State shall establish a procedure to permit a nurse aide to petition the State to have his or her name removed from the registry upon a determination by the State that—

(I) the employment and personal history of the nurse aide does not reflect a pattern of abusive behavior or neglect; and

(II) the neglect involved in the original finding was a singular occurrence.

(ii) Timing of determination. In no case shall a determination on a petition submitted under clause (i) be made prior to the expiration of the 1-year period beginning on the date on which the name of the petitioner was added to the registry under subparagraph (C).

(E) Construction. The failure of the Secretary to issue regulations to carry out this subsection shall not relieve a State of its responsibility under this subsection.

(2) Surveys. (A) Annual standard survey. (i) In general. Each nursing facility shall be subject to a standard survey, to be conducted without any prior notice to the facility. Any individual who notifies (or causes to be notified) a nursing facility of the time or date on which such a survey is scheduled to be conducted is subject to a civil money penalty of not to exceed $2,000. The provisions of section 1128A [42 USCS § 1320a-7a] (other than subsections (a) and (b)) shall apply to a civil money penalty under the previous sentence in the same manner as such provisions apply to a penalty or proceeding under section 1128A(a) [42 USCS § 1320a-7a(a)]. The Secretary shall review each State's procedures for scheduling and conduct of standard surveys to assure that the State has taken all reasonable steps to avoid giving notice of such a survey through the scheduling procedures and the conduct of the surveys themselves.

(ii) Contents. Each standard survey shall include, for a case-mix stratified sample of residents—

(I) a survey of the quality of care furnished, as measured by indicators of medical, nursing, and rehabilitative care, dietary and nutrition services, activities and social participation, and sanitation, infection control, and the physical environment,

(II) written plans of care provided under subsection (b)(2) and an audit of the residents' assessments under subsection (b)(3) to determine the accuracy of such assessments and the adequacy of such plans of care, and

(III) a review of compliance with residents' rights under subsection (c).

(iii) Frequency. (I) In general. Each nursing facility shall be subject to a standard survey not later than 15 months after the date of the previous standard survey conducted under this subparagraph. The statewide average interval between standard surveys of a nursing facility shall not exceed 12 months.

(II) Special surveys. If not otherwise conducted under subclause (I), a standard survey (or an abbreviated standard survey) may be conducted within 2 months of any change of ownership, administration, management of a nursing facility, or director of nursing in order to determine whether the change has resulted in any decline in the quality of care furnished in the facility.

(B) Extended surveys. (i) In general. Each nursing facility which is found, under a standard survey, to have provided substandard quality of care shall be subject to an extended survey. Any other facility may, at the Secretary's or State's discretion, be subject to such an extended survey (or a partial extended survey).

(ii) Timing. The extended survey shall be conducted immediately after the standard survey (or, if not practicable, not later than 2 weeks after the date of completion of the standard survey).

(iii) Contents. In such an extended survey, the survey team shall review and identify the policies and procedures which produced such substandard quality of care and shall determine whether the facility has complied with all the requirements described in subsections (b), (c), and (d). Such review shall include an expansion of the size of the sample of residents' assessments reviewed and a review of the staffing, of in-service training, and, if appropriate, of contracts with consultants.

(iv) Construction. Nothing in this paragraph shall be construed as requiring an extended or partial extended survey as a prerequisite to imposing a sanction against a facility under subsection (h) on the basis of findings in a standard survey.

(C) Survey protocol. Standard and extended surveys shall be conducted—

(i) based upon a protocol which the Secretary has developed, tested, and validated by not later than January 1, 1990, and

(ii) by individuals, of a survey team, who meet such minimum qualifications as the Secretary establishes by not later than such date.

The failure of the Secretary to develop, test, or validate such protocols or to establish such minimum qualifications shall not relieve any State of its responsibility (or the Secretary of the Secretary's responsibility) to conduct surveys under this subsection.

(D) Consistency of surveys. Each State shall implement programs to measure and reduce inconsistency in the application of survey results among surveyors.

(E) Survey teams. (i) In general. Surveys under this subsection shall be conducted by a multidisciplinary team of professionals (including a registered professional nurse).

(ii) Prohibition of conflicts of interest. A State may not use as a member of a survey team under this subsection an individual who is serving (or has served within the previous 2 years) as a member of the staff of, or as a consultant to, the facility surveyed respecting compliance with the requirements of subsections (b), (c), and (d), or who has a personal or familial financial interest in the facility being surveyed.

(iii) Training. The Secretary shall provide for the comprehensive training of State and Federal surveyors in the conduct of standard and extended surveys under this subsection, including the auditing of resident assessments and plans of care. No individual shall serve as a member of a survey team unless the individual has successfully completed a training and testing program in survey and certification techniques that has been approved by the Secretary.

(3) Validation surveys. (A) In general. The Secretary shall conduct onsite surveys of a representative sample of nursing facilities in each State, within 2 months of the date of surveys conducted under paragraph (2) by the State, in a sufficient number to allow inferences about the adequacies of each State's surveys conducted under paragraph (2). In conducting such surveys, the Secretary shall use the same survey protocols as the State is required to use under paragraph (2). If the State has determined that an individual nursing facility meets the requirements of subsections (b), (c), and (d), but the Secretary determines that the facility does not meet such requirements, the Secretary's determination as to the facility's noncompliance with such requirements is binding and supersedes that of the State survey.

(B) Scope. With respect to each State, the Secretary shall conduct surveys under subparagraph (A) each year with respect to at least 5 percent of the number of nursing facilities surveyed by the State in the year, but in no case less than 5 nursing facilities in the State.

(C) Reduction in administrative costs for substandard performance. If the Secretary finds, on the basis of such surveys, that a State has failed to perform surveys as required under paragraph (2) or that a State's survey and certification performance otherwise is not adequate, the Secretary may provide for the training of survey teams in the State and shall provide for a reduction of the payment otherwise made to the State under section 1903(a)(2)(D) [42 USCS § 1396b(a)(2)(D)] with respect to a quarter equal to 33 percent multiplied by a fraction, the denominator of which is equal to the total number of residents in nursing facilities surveyed by the Secretary that quarter and the numerator of which is equal to the total number of residents in nursing facilities which were found pursuant to such surveys to be not in compliance with any of the requirements of subsections (b), (c), and (d). A State that is dissatisfied with the Secretary's findings under this subparagraph may obtain reconsideration and review of the findings under section 1116 [42 USCS § 1316] in the same manner as a State may seek reconsideration and review under that section of the Secretary's determination under section 1116(a)(1) [42 USCS § 1316(a)(1)].

(D) Special surveys of compliance. Where the Secretary has reason to question the compliance of a nursing facility with any of the requirements of subsections (b), (c), and (d), the Secretary may conduct a survey of the facility and, on the basis of that survey make independent and binding determinations concerning the extent to which the nursing facility meets such requirements.

(4) Investigation of complaints and monitoring nursing facility compliance. Each State shall maintain procedures and adequate staff

to—

(A) investigate complaints of violations of requirements by nursing facilities, and

(B) monitor, on-site, on a regular, as needed basis, a nursing facility's compliance with the requirements of subsections (b), (c), and (d), if—

(i) the facility has been found not to be in compliance with such requirements and is in the process of correcting deficiencies to achieve such compliance;

(ii) the facility was previously found not to be in compliance with such requirements, has corrected deficiencies to achieve such compliance, and verification of continued compliance is indicated; or

(iii) the State has reason to question the compliance of the facility with such requirements.

A State may maintain and utilize a specialized team (including an attorney, an auditor, and appropriate health care professionals) for the purpose of identifying, surveying, gathering and preserving evidence, and carrying out appropriate enforcement actions against substandard nursing facilities.

(5) Disclosure of results of inspections and activities. (A) Public information. Each State, and the Secretary, shall make available to the public—

(i) information respecting all surveys and certifications made respecting nursing facilities, including statements of deficiencies, within 14 calendar days after such information is made available to those facilities, and approved plans of correction,

(ii) copies of cost reports of such facilities filed under this title [42 USCS §§ 1396 et seq.] or under title XVIII [42 USCS §§ 1395 et seq.],

(iii) copies of statements of ownership under section 1124 [42 USCS § 1320a-3], and

(iv) information disclosed under section 1126 [42 USCS § 1320a-5].

(B) Notice to ombudsman. Each State shall notify the State long-term care ombudsman (established under title III or VII of the Older Americans Act of 1965 [42 USCS §§ 3021 et seq. or 3058 et seq.] in accordance with section 712 of the Act [42 USCS § 3058g]) of the State's findings of noncompliance with any of the requirements of subsections (b), (c), and (d), or of any adverse action taken against a nursing facility under paragraphs [paragraph] (1), (2), or (3) of subsection (h), with respect to a nursing facility in the State.

(C) Notice to physicians and nursing facility administrator licensing board. If a State finds that a nursing facility has provided substandard quality of care, the State shall notify—

(i) the attending physician of each resident with respect to which such finding is made, and

(ii) any State board responsible for the licensing of the nursing facility administrator of the facility.

(D) Access to fraud control units. Each State shall provide its State medicaid fraud and abuse control unit (established under section 1903(q) [42 USCS § 1396b(q)]) with access to all information of the State agency responsible for surveys and certifications under this subsection.

(E) **[Caution: This subparagraph takes effect on March 23, 2011, pursuant to § 6103(b)(2)(B) of Act March 23, 2010, PL. 111-148, which appears as a note to this section.]** Submission of survey and certification information to the Secretary. In order to improve the timeliness of information made available to the public under subparagraph (A) and provided on the Nursing Home Compare Medicare website under subsection (i), each State shall submit information respecting any survey or certification made respecting a nursing facility (including any enforcement actions taken by the State) to the Secretary not later than the date on which the State sends such information to the facility. The Secretary shall use the information submitted under the preceding sentence to update the information provided on the Nursing Home Compare Medicare website as expeditiously as practicable but not less frequently than quarterly.

(h) Enforcement process. (1) In general. If a State finds, on the basis of a standard, extended, or partial extended survey under subsection (g)(2) or otherwise, that a nursing facility no longer meets a requirement of subsection (b), (c), or (d), and further finds that the facility's deficiencies—

(A) immediately jeopardize the health or safety of its residents, the State shall take immediate action to remove the jeopardy and correct the deficiencies through the remedy specified in paragraph (2)(A)(iii), or terminate the facility's participation under the State plan and may provide, in addition, for one or more of the other remedies described in paragraph (2); or

(B) do not immediately jeopardize the health or safety of its residents, the State may—

(i) terminate the facility's participation under the State plan,

(ii) provide for one or more of the remedies described in paragraph (2), or

(iii) do both.

Nothing in this paragraph shall be construed as restricting the remedies available to a State to remedy a nursing facility's deficiencies. If a State finds that a nursing facility meets the requirements of subsections (b), (c), and (d), but, as of a previous period, did not meet such requirements, the State may provide for a civil money penalty under paragraph (2)(A)(ii) for the days in which it finds that the facility was not in compliance with such requirements.

(2) Specified remedies. (A) Listing. Except as provided in subparagraph (B)(ii), each State shall establish by law (whether statute or regulation) at least the following remedies:

(i) Denial of payment under the State plan with respect to any individual admitted to the nursing facility involved after such notice to the public and to the facility as may be provided for by the State.

(ii) A civil money penalty assessed and collected, with interest, for each day in which the facility is or was out of compliance with a requirement of subsection (b), (c), or (d). Funds collected by a State as a result of imposition of such a penalty (or as a result of the imposition by the State of a civil money penalty for activities described in subsections (b)(3)(B)(ii)(I), (b)(3)(B)(ii)(II), or (g)(2)(A)(i)) shall be applied to the protection of the health or property of residents of nursing facilities that the State or the Secretary finds deficient, including payment for the costs of relocation of residents to other facilities, maintenance of operation of a facility pending correction of deficiencies or closure, and reimbursement of residents for personal funds lost.

(iii) The appointment of temporary management to oversee the operation of the facility and to assure the health and safety of the facility's residents, where there is a need for temporary management while—

(I) there is an orderly closure of the facility, or

(II) improvements are made in order to bring the facility into compliance with all the requirements of subsections (b), (c), and (d).

The temporary management under this clause shall not be terminated under subclause (II) until the State has determined that the facility has the management capability to ensure continued compliance with all the requirements of subsections (b), (c), and (d).

(iv) The authority, in the case of an emergency, to close the facility, to transfer residents in that facility to other facilities, or both.

The State also shall specify criteria, as to when and how each of such remedies is to be applied, the amounts of any fines, and the severity of each of these remedies, to be used in the imposition of such remedies. Such criteria shall be designed so as to minimize the time between the identification of violations and final imposition of the remedies and shall provide for the imposition of incrementally more severe fines for repeated or uncorrected deficiencies. In addition, the State may provide for other specified remedies, such as directed plans of correction.

(B) Deadline and guidance. (i) Except as provided in clause (ii), as a condition for approval of a State plan for calendar quarters beginning on or after October 1, 1989, each State shall establish the remedies described in clauses (i) through (iv) of subparagraph (A) by not later than October 1, 1989. The Secretary shall provide, through regulations by not later than October 1, 1988, guidance to States in establishing such remedies; but the failure of the Secretary to provide such guidance shall not relieve a State of the responsibility for establishing such remedies.

(ii) A State may establish alternative remedies (other than termination of participation) other than those described in clauses (i) through (iv) of subparagraph (A), if the State demonstrates to the Secretary's satisfaction that the alternative remedies are as effective in deterring noncompliance and correcting deficiencies as those described in subparagraph (A).

(C) Assuring prompt compliance. If a nursing facility has not complied with any of the requirements of subsections (b), (c), and (d), within 3 months after the date the facility is found to be out of compliance with such requirements, the State shall impose the remedy described in subparagraph (A)(i) for all individuals who are admitted to the facility after such date.

(D) Repeated noncompliance. In the case of a nursing facility which, on 3 consecutive standard surveys conducted under subsection (g)(2), has been found to have provided substandard quality of care, the State shall (regardless of what other remedies are provided)—

(i) impose the remedy described in subparagraph (A)(i), and

(ii) monitor the facility under subsection (g)(4)(B),

until the facility has demonstrated, to the satisfaction of the State, that it is in compliance with the requirements of subsections (b), (c), and (d), and that it will remain in compliance with such requirements.

(E) Funding. The reasonable expenditures of

a State to provide for temporary management and other expenses associated with implementing the remedies described in clauses (iii) and (iv) of subparagraph (A) shall be considered, for purposes of section 1903(a)(7) [42 USCS § 1396b(a)(7)], to be necessary for the proper and efficient administration of the State plan.

(F) Incentives for high quality care. In addition to the remedies specified in this paragraph, a State may establish a program to reward, through public recognition, incentive payments, or both, nursing facilities that provide the highest quality care to residents who are entitled to medical assistance under this title [42 USCS §§ 1396 et seq.]. For purposes of section 1903(a)(7) [42 USCS § 1396b(a)(7)], proper expenses incurred by a State in carrying out such a program shall be considered to be expenses necessary for the proper and efficient administration of the State plan under this title [42 USCS §§ 1396 et seq.].

(3) Secretarial authority. (A) For State nursing facilities. With respect to a State nursing facility, the Secretary shall have the authority and duties of a State under this subsection, including the authority to impose remedies described in clauses (i), (ii), and (iii) of paragraph (2)(A).

(B) Other nursing facilities. With respect to any other nursing facility in a State, if the Secretary finds that a nursing facility no longer meets a requirement of subsection (b), (c), (d), or (e), and further finds that the facility's deficiencies—

(i) immediately jeopardize the health or safety of its residents, the Secretary shall take immediate action to remove the jeopardy and correct the deficiencies through the remedy specified in subparagraph (C)(iii), or terminate the facility's participation under the State plan and may provide, in addition, for one or more of the other remedies described in subparagraph (C); or

(ii) do not immediately jeopardize the health or safety of its residents, the Secretary may impose any of the remedies described in subparagraph (C).

Nothing in this subparagraph shall be construed as restricting the remedies available to the Secretary to remedy a nursing facility's deficiencies. If the Secretary finds that a nursing facility meets such requirements but, as of a previous period, did not meet such requirements, the Secretary may provide for a civil money penalty under subparagraph (C)(ii) for the days on which he finds that the facility was not in compliance with such requirements.

(C) Specified remedies. The Secretary may take the following actions with respect to a finding that a facility has not met an applicable requirement:

(i) Denial of payment. The Secretary may deny any further payments to the State for medical assistance furnished by the facility to all individuals in the facility or to individuals admitted to the facility after the effective date of the finding.

(ii) Authority with respect to civil money penalties.

(I) In general. Subject to subclause (II), the Secretary may impose a civil money penalty in an amount not to exceed $10,000 for each day of noncompliance. The provisions of section 1128A [42 USCS § 1320a-7a] (other than subsections (a) and (b)) shall apply to a civil money penalty under the previous sentence in the same manner as such provisions apply to a penalty or proceeding under section 1128A(a) [42 USCS § 1320a-7a(a)].

(II) **[Caution: This subclause takes effect 1 year after enactment of Act March 23, 2011, P. L. 111-148, as provided by § 6111(c) of such Act, which appears as a note to this section.]** Reduction of civil money penalties in certain circumstances. Subject to subclause (III), in the case where a facility self-reports and promptly corrects a deficiency for which a penalty was imposed under this clause not later than 10 calendar days after the date of such imposition, the Secretary may reduce the amount of the penalty imposed by not more than 50 percent.

(III) **[Caution: This subclause takes effect 1 year after enactment of Act March 23, 2011, P. L. 111-148, as provided by § 6111(c) of such Act, which appears as a note to this section.]** Prohibitions on reduction for certain deficiencies. (aa) Repeat deficiencies. The Secretary may not reduce the amount of a penalty under subclause (II) if the Secretary had reduced a penalty imposed on the facility in the preceding year under such subclause with respect to a repeat deficiency.

(bb) Certain other deficiencies. The Secretary may not reduce the amount of a penalty under subclause (II) if the penalty is imposed on the facility for a deficiency that is found to result in a pattern of harm or widespread harm, immediately jeopardizes the health or safety of a resident or residents of the facility, or results in the death of a resident of the facility.

(IV) **[Caution: This subclause takes effect 1 year after enactment of Act March 23, 2011, P. L. 111-148, as provided by § 6111(c) of such Act, which appears as a**

note to this section.] Collection of civil money penalties. In the case of a civil money penalty imposed under this clause, the Secretary shall issue regulations that—

(aa) subject to item (cc), not later than 30 days after the imposition of the penalty, provide for the facility to have the opportunity to participate in an independent informal dispute resolution process which generates a written record prior to the collection of such penalty;

(bb) in the case where the penalty is imposed for each day of noncompliance, provide that a penalty may not be imposed for any day during the period beginning on the initial day of the imposition of the penalty and ending on the day on which the informal dispute resolution process under item (aa) is completed;

(cc) may provide for the collection of such civil money penalty and the placement of such amounts collected in an escrow account under the direction of the Secretary on the earlier of the date on which the informal dispute resolution process under item (aa) is completed or the date that is 90 days after the date of the imposition of the penalty;

(dd) may provide that such amounts collected are kept in such account pending the resolution of any subsequent appeals;

(ee) in the case where the facility successfully appeals the penalty, may provide for the return of such amounts collected (plus interest) to the facility; and

(ff) in the case where all such appeals are unsuccessful, may provide that some portion of such amounts collected may be used to support activities that benefit residents, including assistance to support and protect residents of a facility that closes (voluntarily or involuntarily) or is decertified (including offsetting costs of relocating residents to home and community-based settings or another facility), projects that support resident and family councils and other consumer involvement in assuring quality care in facilities, and facility improvement initiatives approved by the Secretary (including joint training of facility staff and surveyors, technical assistance for facilities implementing quality assurance programs, the appointment of temporary management firms, and other activities approved by the Secretary).

(iii) Appointment of temporary management. In consultation with the State, the Secretary may appoint temporary management to oversee the operation of the facility and to assure the health and safety of the facility's residents, where there is a need for temporary management while—

(I) there is an orderly closure of the facility, or

(II) improvements are made in order to bring the facility into compliance with all the requirements of subsections (b), (c), and (d).

The temporary management under this clause shall not be terminated under subclause (II) until the Secretary has determined that the facility has the management capability to ensure continued compliance with all the requirements of subsections (b), (c), and (d).

The Secretary shall specify criteria, as to when and how each of such remedies is to be applied, the amounts of any fines, and the severity of each of these remedies, to be used in the imposition of such remedies. Such criteria shall be designed so as to minimize the time between the identification of violations and final imposition of the remedies and shall provide for the imposition of incrementally more severe fines for repeated or uncorrected deficiencies. In addition, the Secretary may provide for other specified remedies, such as directed plans of correction.

(D) Continuation of payments pending remediation. The Secretary may continue payments, over a period of not longer than 6 months after the effective date of the findings, under this title [42 USCS §§ 1396 et seq.] with respect to a nursing facility not in compliance with a requirement of subsection (b), (c), or (d), if—

(i) the State survey agency finds that it is more appropriate to take alternative action to assure compliance of the facility with the requirements than to terminate the certification of the facility, and

(ii) the State has submitted a plan and timetable for corrective action to the Secretary for approval and the Secretary approves the plan of corrective action.

The Secretary shall establish guidelines for approval of corrective actions requested by States under this subparagraph.

(4) Effective period of denial of payment. A finding to deny payment under this subsection shall terminate when the State or Secretary (or both, as the case may be) finds that the facility is in substantial compliance with all the requirements of subsections (b), (c), and (d).

(5) Immediate termination of participation for facility where State or Secretary finds noncompliance and immediate jeopardy. If either the State or the Secretary finds that a nursing facility has not met a requirement of subsection (b), (c), or (d), and finds that the failure immediately jeopardizes the health or safety of its residents, the State or the Secretary, respectively[,] shall notify the other of such finding,

and the State or the Secretary, respectively, shall take immediate action to remove the jeopardy and correct the deficiencies through the remedy specified in paragraph (2)(A)(iii) or (3)(C)(iii), or terminate the facility's participation under the State plan. If the facility's participation in the State plan is terminated by either the State or the Secretary, the State shall provide for the safe and orderly transfer of the residents eligible under the State plan consistent with the requirements of subsection (c)(2).

(6) Special rules where state and secretary do not agree on finding of noncompliance. (A) State finding of noncompliance and no secretarial finding of noncompliance. If the Secretary finds that a nursing facility has met all the requirements of subsections (b), (c), and (d), but a State finds that the facility has not met such requirements and the failure does not immediately jeopardize the health or safety of its residents, the State's findings shall control and the remedies imposed by the State shall be applied.

(B) Secretarial finding of noncompliance and no State finding of noncompliance. If the Secretary finds that a nursing facility has not met all the requirements of subsections (b), (c), and (d), and that the failure does not immediately jeopardize the health or safety of its residents, but the State has not made such a finding, the Secretary—

(i) may impose any remedies specified in paragraph (3)(C) with respect to the facility, and

(ii) shall (pending any termination by the Secretary) permit continuation of payments in accordance with paragraph (3)(D).

(7) Special rules for timing of termination of participation where remedies overlap. If both the Secretary and the State find that a nursing facility has not met all the requirements of subsections (b), (c), and (d), and neither finds that the failure immediately jeopardizes the health or safety of its residents—

(A)(i) if both find that the facility's participation under the State plan should be terminated, the State's timing of any termination shall control so long as the termination date does not occur later than 6 months after the date of the finding to terminate;

(ii) if the Secretary, but not the State, finds that the facility's participation under the State plan should be terminated, the Secretary shall (pending any termination by the Secretary) permit continuation of payments in accordance with paragraph (3)(D); or

(iii) if the State, but not the Secretary, finds that the facility's participation under the State plan should be terminated, the State's decision to terminate, and timing of such termination, shall control; and

(B)(i) if the Secretary or the State, but not both, establishes one or more remedies which are additional or alternative to the remedy of terminating the facility's participation under the State plan, such additional or alternative remedies shall also be applied, or

(ii) if both the Secretary and the State establish one or more remedies which are additional or alternative to the remedy of terminating the facility's participation under the State plan, only the additional or alternative remedies of the Secretary shall apply.

(8) Construction. The remedies provided under this subsection are in addition to those otherwise available under State or Federal law and shall not be construed as limiting such other remedies, including any remedy available to an individual at common law. The remedies described in clauses (i), (ii)(IV), (iii), and (iv) of paragraph (2)(A) may be imposed during the pendency of any hearing. The provisions of this subsection shall apply to a nursing facility (or portion thereof) notwithstanding that the facility (or portion thereof) also is a skilled nursing facility for purposes of title XVIII [42 USCS §§ 1395 et seq.].

(9) Sharing of information. Notwithstanding any other provision of law, all information concerning nursing facilities required by this section to be filed with the Secretary or a State agency shall be made available by such facilities to Federal or State employees for purposes consistent with the effective administration of programs established under this title [42 USCS §§ 1396 et seq.] and title XVIII [42 USCS §§ 1395 et seq.], including investigations by State medicaid fraud control units.

(i) Nursing Home Compare website. (1) Inclusion of additional information. (A) In general. The Secretary shall ensure that the Department of Health and Human Services includes, as part of the information provided for comparison of nursing homes on the official Internet website of the Federal Government for Medicare beneficiaries (commonly referred to as the "Nursing Home Compare" Medicare website) (or a successor website), the following information in a manner that is prominent, updated on a timely basis, easily accessible, readily understandable to consumers of long-term care services, and searchable:

(i) Staffing data for each facility (including resident census data and data on the hours of care provided per resident per day) based on data submitted under section 1128I(g) [42 USCS § 1320a-7j(g)], including information on staffing turnover and tenure, in a format that is clearly understandable to consumers of long-term care services and allows such consumers to compare differences in staffing between facilities and State and national averages for the facilities. Such format shall include—

(I) concise explanations of how to interpret the data (such as plain English explanation of data reflecting "nursing home staff hours per resident day");

(II) differences in types of staff (such as training associated with different categories of staff);

(III) the relationship between nurse staffing levels and quality of care; and

(IV) an explanation that appropriate staffing levels vary based on patient case mix.

(ii) Links to State Internet websites with information regarding State survey and certification programs, links to Form 2567 State inspection reports (or a successor form) on such websites, information to guide consumers in how to interpret and understand such reports, and the facility plan of correction or other response to such report. Any such links shall be posted on a timely basis.

(iii) The standardized complaint form developed under section 1128I(f) [42 USCS § 1320a-7j(f)], including explanatory material on what complaint forms are, how they are used, and how to file a complaint with the State survey and certification program and the State long-term care ombudsman program.

(iv) Summary information on the number, type, severity, and outcome of substantiated complaints.

(v) The number of adjudicated instances of criminal violations by a facility or the employees of a facility—

(I) that were committed inside of the facility; and

(II) with respect to such instances of violations or crimes committed outside of the facility, that were violations or crimes that resulted in the serious bodily injury of an elder.

(B) Deadline for provision of information. (i) In general. Except as provided in clause (ii), the Secretary shall ensure that the information described in subparagraph (A) is included on such website (or a successor website) not later than 1 year after the date of the enactment of this subsection [enacted March 23, 2010].

(ii) Exception. The Secretary shall ensure that the information described in subparagraph (A)(i) is included on such website (or a successor website) not later than the date on which the requirements under section 1128I(g) [42 USCS § 1320a-7j(g)] are implemented.

(2) Review and modification of website. (A) In general. The Secretary shall establish a process—

(i) to review the accuracy, clarity of presentation, timeliness, and comprehensiveness of information reported on such website as of the day before the date of the enactment of this subsection [enacted March 23, 2010]; and

(ii) not later than 1 year after the date of the enactment of this subsection [enacted March 23, 2010], to modify or revamp such website in accordance with the review conducted under clause (i).

(B) Consultation. In conducting the review under subparagraph (A)(i), the Secretary shall consult with—

(i) State long-term care ombudsman programs;

(ii) consumer advocacy groups;

(iii) provider stakeholder groups;

(iv) skilled nursing facility employees and their representatives; and

(v) any other representatives of programs or groups the Secretary determines appropriate.

(j) Construction. Where requirements or obligations under this section are identical to those provided under section 1819 of this Act [42 USCS § 1395i-3], the fulfillment of those requirements or obligations under section 1819 [42 USCS § 1395i-3] shall be considered to be the fulfillment of the corresponding requirements or obligations under this section.

(Aug. 14, 1935, ch 531, Title XIX, § 1919, as added Dec. 22, 1987, P. L. 100-203, Title IV, Subtitle C, Part 2, § 4211(a)(3), 101 Stat. 1330-182; Dec. 22, 1987, P. L. 100-203, Title IV, Subtitle C, Part 2, §§ 4211(c), 4212(a), (b), 4213(a), 4216, 101 Stat. 1330-182, 1330-196, 1330-204, 1330-208, 1330-212, 1330-213, 1330-220; July 1, 1988, P. L. 100-360, Title III, § 303(a)(2) Title IV, Subtitle B, § 411(l)(2)(A)–(D), (F)–(L), (3)(A), (C)(ii), (iii), (B), (D), (5)–(6)(B), (7)(A), (B), (8)(A)–(B)(iii), 102 Stat. 760, 801–805; Oct. 13, 1988, P. L. 100-485, Title VI, § 608(d)(27)(C)–(E), (I), 102 Stat. 2423; Dec. 19, 1989, P. L. 101-239, Title VI, Subtitle F, § 6901(b)(1), (3), (4)(A), (d)(1), (4), 103 Stat. 2298-2301; Nov. 5, 1990, P. L. 101-508, Title IV, Subtitle B, Part 4, Subpart E, §§ 4751(b)(2), Part 5, § 4801(a)(2)–(6)(A), (7), (b)(2)–(8), (d)(1), (e)(2)–(7)(A), (8)–(10), (12)–(15), (18), 104 Stat. 1388-205, 1388-211–1388-219; Sept. 30, 1992, P. L. 102-375, Title VII, § 708(a)(1)(B), 106 Stat. 1292; Oct. 19, 1996, P. L. 104-315, §§ 1(a), 2(a), (b), 3824; May 15, 1997, P. L. 105-15, § 1, 111 Stat. 34;

Aug. 5, 1997, P. L. 105-33, Title IV, Subtitle H, Ch 6, §§ 4754(a), 4755(b), 111 Stat. 526; March 25, 1999, P. L. 106-4, § 2(a), 113 Stat. 7; Nov. 29, 1999, P. L. 106-113, Div B, § 1000(a)(6), 113 Stat. 1536; Oct. 30, 2000, P. L. 106-402, Title IV, § 401(b)(6)(A), 114 Stat. 1738; Dec. 21, 2000, P. L. 106-554, § 1(a)(6), 114 Stat. 2763; Dec. 8, 2003, P. L. 108-173, Title IX, Subtitle D, § 932(c)(2), 117 Stat. 2401; Feb. 8, 2006, P. L. 109-171, Title VI, Subtitle A, Ch. 2, Subch. A, § 6015(a), 120 Stat. 65; Dec. 20, 2006, P. L. 109-432, Div B, Title IV, § 405(c)(2)(B), 120 Stat. 3000; March 23, 2010, P. L. 111-148, Title VI, Subtitle B, Part I, §§ 6101(c)(1)(B), 6103(b)(1), (2)(A), (3), (c)(2), Part II, § 6111(b), Part III, § 6121(b), 124 Stat. 702, 707, 709, 715, 721.)

HISTORY; ANCILLARY LAWS AND DIRECTIVES

Prospective amendments:

Amendment of subsec. (d)(1), effective on the date on which the Secretary makes public the information reported in accordance with final regulations promulgated. Act March 23, 2010, P. L. 111-148, Title VI, Subtitle B, Part I, § 6101(c)(1)(B), 124 Stat. 702 (effective on the date on which the Secretary makes public the information reported in accordance with final regulations promulgated, as provided by § 6101(c)(2) of such Act, which appears as 42 USCS § 1395i-3 note), provides: "Section 1919(d)(1) of the Social Security Act (42 U.S.C. 1396r(d)(1)) is amended by striking subparagraph (B) and redesignating subparagraph (C) as subparagraph (B).".

Amendment of subsec. (d)(1), effective March 23, 2011. Act March 23, 2010, P. L. 111-148, Title VI, Subtitle B, Part I, § 6103(c)(2), 124 Stat. 709 (effective 1 year after enactment, as provided by § 6103(c)(3) of such Act, which appears as 42 USCS § 1395i-3 note), provides:

"Section 1919(d)(1) of the Social Security Act (42 U.S.C. 1396r(d)(1)), as amended by section 6101, is amended by adding at the end the following new subparagraph:

" '(V) Availability of survey, certification, and complaint investigation reports. A nursing facility must—

" '(i) have reports with respect to any surveys, certifications, and complaint investigations made respecting the facility during the 3 preceding years available for any individual to review upon request; and

" '(iii) post notice of the availability of such reports in areas of the facility that are prominent and accessible to the public.

The facility shall not make available under clause (i) identifying information about complainants or residents.'.".

Amendment of subsecs. (b)(5)(F) and (f)(2)(A), effective March 23, 2011. Act March 23, 2010, P. L. 111-148, Title VI, Subtitle B, Part III, § 6121(b), 124 Stat. 721 (effective 1 year after enactment, as provided by § 6121(c) of such Act, which appears as 42 USCS § 1395i-3 note), provides:

"(1) In general. Section 1919(f)(2)(A)(i)(I) of the Social Security Act (42 U.S.C. 1396r(f)(2)(A)(i)(I)) is amended by inserting '(including, in the case of initial training and, if the Secretary determines appropriate, in the case of ongoing training, dementia management training, and patient abuse prevention training' before ', (II)'.

"(2) Clarification of definition of nurse aide. Section 1919(b)(5)(F) of the Social Security Act (42 U.S.C. 1396r(b)(5)(F)) is amended by adding at the end the following flush sentence:

" 'Such term includes an individual who provides such services through an agency or under a contract with the facility.'.".

Other provisions:

Effective date of amendments made by § 6103(b)(2) of Act March 23, 2010. Act March 23, 2010, P. L. 111-148, Title VI, Subtitle B, Part I, § 6103(b)(2)(B), 124 Stat. 709, provides: "The amendment made by this paragraph [adding subsec. (g)(5)(E) of this section] shall take effect 1 year after the date of the enactment of this Act.".

§ 1396r-1. Presumptive eligibility for pregnant women

(a) Ambulatory prenatal care. A State plan approved under section 1902 [42 USCS § 1396a] may provide for making ambulatory prenatal care available to a pregnant woman during a presumptive eligibility period.

(b) Definitions. For purposes of this section—

(1) the term "presumptive eligibility period" means, with respect to a pregnant woman, the period that—

(A) begins with the date on which a qualified provider determines, on the basis of preliminary information, that the family income of the woman does not exceed the applicable income level of eligibility under the State plan, and

(B) ends with (and includes) the earlier of—

(i) the day on which a determination is made with respect to the eligibility of the woman for medical assistance under the State plan, or

(ii) in the case of a woman who does not file an application by the last day of the month following the month during which the provider makes the determination referred to in subparagraph (A), such last day; and

(2) the term "qualified provider" means any provider that—

(A) is eligible for payments under a State plan approved under this title [42 USCS §§ 1396 et seq.],

(B) provides services of the type described in subparagraph (A) or (B) of section 1905(a)(2) or in section 1905(a)(9) [42 USCS § 1396d(a)(2) or (9)],

(C) is determined by the State agency to be capable of making determinations of the type described in paragraph (1)(A), and

(D)(i) receives funds under—

(I) section 330 or 330A of the Public Health

Service Act [42 USCS § 254b or 254c], or

(II) title V of this Act [42 USCS §§ 701 et seq.], or

(III) title V of the Indian Health Care Improvement Act;

(ii) participates in a program established under—

(I) section 17 of the Child Nutrition Act of 1966 [42 USCS § 1786], or

(II) section 4(a) of the Agriculture and Consumer Protection Act of 1973 [7 USCS § 612c note];

(iii) participates in a State perinatal program, or

(iv) is the Indian Health Service or is a health program or facility operated by a tribal organization under the Indian Self-Determination Act (Public Law 93-628).

The term "qualified provider" also includes a qualified entity, as defined in section 1920A(b)(3) [42 USCS § 1396r-1a(b)(3)].

(c) Duties of State agency, qualified providers, and presumptively eligible pregnant women. (1) The State agency shall provide qualified providers with—

(A) such forms as are necessary for a pregnant woman to make application for medical assistance under the State plan, and

(B) information on how to assist such women in completing and filing such forms.

(2) A qualified provider that determines under subsection (b)(1)(A) that a pregnant woman is presumptively eligible for medical assistance under a State plan shall—

(A) notify the State agency of the determination within 5 working days after the date on which determination is made, and

(B) inform the woman at the time the determination is made that she is required to make application for medical assistance under the State plan by not later than the last day of the month following the month during which the determination is made.

(3) A pregnant woman who is determined by a qualified provider to be presumptively eligible for medical assistance under a State plan shall make application for medical assistance under such plan by not later than the last day of the month following the month during which the determination is made, which application may be the application used for the receipt of medical assistance by individuals described in section 1902(l)(1)(A) [42 USCS § 1396a(l)(1)(A)].

(d) Ambulatory prenatal care as medical assistance. Notwithstanding any other provision of this title [42 USCS §§ 1396 et seq.], ambulatory prenatal care that—

(1) is furnished to a pregnant woman—

(A) during a presumptive eligibility period,

(B) by a provider that is eligible for payments under the State plan; and

(2) is included in the care and services covered by a State plan;

shall be treated as medical assistance provided by such plan for purposes of section 1903 [42 USCS § 1396b].

(e) Presumptive eligibility. If the State has elected the option to provide a presumptive eligibility period under this section or section 1920A [42 USCS § 1396r-1a], the State may elect to provide a presumptive eligibility period (as defined in subsection (b)(1)) for individuals who are eligible for medical assistance under clause (i)(VIII), clause (i)(IX), or clause (ii)(XX) of subsection (a)(10)(A) or section 1931 [42 USCS § 1396u-1] in the same manner as the State provides for such a period under this section or section 1920A [42 USCS § 1396r-1a], subject to such guidance as the Secretary shall establish.

(Aug. 14, 1935, ch 531, Title XIX, § 1920, as added Oct. 21, 1986, P. L. 99-509, Title IX, Subtitle E, Part 1, § 9407(b) in part, 100 Stat. 2057; July 1, 1988, P. L. 100-360, Title IV, Subtitle B, § 411(k)(16)(A), (B), 102 Stat. 799; Oct. 13, 1988, P. L. 100-485, Title VI, § 608(d)(26)(L), 102 Stat. 2422; Nov. 5, 1990, P. L. 101-508, Title IV, Subtitle B, Part 3, § 4605(a), (b), 104 Stat. 1388-169; Nov. 29, 1999, P. L. 106-113, Div B, § 1000(a)(6), 113 Stat. 1536; Feb. 4, 2009, P. L. 111-3, Title I, Subtitle B, § 113(b)(2), 123 Stat. 34; March 23, 2010, P. L. 111-148, Title II, Subtitle A, §§ 2001(a)(4)(B), (e)(2)(C), 2004(b), 124 Stat. 274, 279, 283.)

§ 1396r-1c. Presumptive eligibility for family planning services

(a) State option. State plan approved under section 1902 [42 USCS § 1396a] may provide for making medical assistance available to an individual described in section 1902(ii) [42 USCS § 1396a(ii)] (relating to individuals who meet certain income eligibility standard) during a presumptive eligibility period. In the case of an individual described in section 1902(ii) [42 USCS § 1396a(ii)], such medical assistance shall be limited to family planning services and supplies described in 1905(a)(4)(C) [42 USCS § 1396d(a)(4)(C)] and, at the State's option, medical diagnosis and treatment services that are provided in conjunction with a family planning service in a family planning setting.

(b) Definitions. For purposes of this section:

(1) Presumptive eligibility period. The term "presumptive eligibility period" means, with respect to an individual described in subsection (a), the period that—

(A) begins with the date on which a qualified entity determines, on the basis of preliminary information, that the individual is described in section 1902(ii) [42 USCS § 1396a(ii)]; and

(B) ends with (and includes) the earlier of—

(i) the day on which a determination is made with respect to the eligibility of such individual for services under the State plan; or

(ii) in the case of such an individual who does not file an application by the last day of the month following the month during which the entity makes the determination referred to in subparagraph (A), such last day.

(2) Qualified entity. (A) In general. Subject to subparagraph (B), the term "qualified entity" means any entity that—

(i) is eligible for payments under a State plan approved under this title; and

(ii) is determined by the State agency to be capable of making determinations of the type described in paragraph (1)(A).

(B) Rule of construction. Nothing in this paragraph shall be construed as preventing a State from limiting the classes of entities that may become qualified entities in order to prevent fraud and abuse.

(c) Administration. (1) In general. The State agency shall provide qualified entities with—

(A) such forms as are necessary for an application to be made by an individual described in subsection (a) for medical assistance under the State plan; and

(B) information on how to assist such individuals in completing and filing such forms.

(2) Notification requirements. A qualified entity that determines under subsection (b)(1)(A) that an individual described in subsection (a) is presumptively eligible for medical assistance under a State plan shall—

(A) notify the State agency of the determination within 5 working days after the date on which determination is made; and

(B) inform such individual at the time the determination is made that an application for medical assistance is required to be made by not later than the last day of the month following the month during which the determination is made.

(3) Application for medical assistance. In the case of an individual described in subsection (a) who is determined by a qualified entity to be presumptively eligible for medical assistance under a State plan, the individual shall apply for medical assistance by not later than the last day of the month following the month during which the determination is made.

(d) Payment. Notwithstanding any other provision of law, medical assistance that—

(1) is furnished to an individual described in subsection (a)—

(A) during a presumptive eligibility period; and

(B) by a entity that is eligible for payments under the State plan; and

(2) is included in the care and services covered by the State plan,

is included in the care and services covered by the State plan,shall be treated as medical assistance provided by such plan for purposes of clause (4) of the first sentence of section 1905(b) [42 USCS § 1396d(b)].

(Aug. 14, 1935, ch 531, Title XIX, § 1920C, as added March 23, 2010, P. L. 111-148, Title II, Subtitle D, § 2303(b)(1), 124 Stat. 294.)

§ 1396r-2. Information concerning sanctions taken by State licensing authorities against health care practitioners and providers [Caution: See prospective amendment note below.]

(a) Information reporting requirement; access to documents. The requirement referred to in section 1902(a)(49) [42 USCS § 1396a(a)(49)] is that the State must provide for the following:

(1) Information reporting system. The State must have in effect a system of reporting the following information with respect to formal proceedings (as defined by the Secretary in regulations) concluded against a health care practitioner or entity by any authority of the State (or of a political subdivision thereof) responsible for the licensing of health care practitioners (or any peer review organization or private accreditation entity reviewing the services provided by health care practitioners) or entities:

(A) Any adverse action taken by such licensing authority as a result of the proceeding, including any revocation or suspension of a license (and the length of any such suspension), reprimand, censure, or probation.

(B) Any dismissal or closure of the proceedings by reason of the practitioner or entity surrendering the license or leaving the State or jurisdiction.

(C) Any other loss of the license of the practitioner or entity, whether by operation of law, voluntary surrender, or otherwise.

(D) Any negative action or finding by such authority, organization, or entity regarding the practitioner or entity.

(2) Access to documents. The State must provide the Secretary (or an entity designated by the Secretary) with access to such documents of the authority described in paragraph (1) as may be necessary for the Secretary to determine the facts and circumstances concerning the actions and determinations described in such paragraph for the purpose of carrying out this Act.

(b) Form of information. The information described in subsection (a)(1) shall be provided to the Secretary (or to an appropriate private or public agency, under suitable arrangements made by the Secretary with respect to receipt, storage, protection of confidentiality, and dissemination of information) in such a form and manner as the Secretary determines to be appropriate in order to provide for activities of the Secretary under this Act and in order to provide, directly or through suitable arrangements made by the Secretary, information—

(1) to agencies administering Federal health care programs, including private entities administering such programs under contract,

(2) to licensing authorities described in subsection (a)(1),

(3) to State agencies administering or supervising the administration of State health care programs (as defined in section 1128(h) [42 USCS § 1320a-7(h)]),

(4) to utilization and quality control peer review organizations described in part B of title XI [42 USCS §§ 1320c et seq.] and to appropriate entities with contracts under section 1154(a)(4)(C) [42 USCS § 1320c-3(a)(4)(C)] with respect to eligible organizations reviewed under the contracts,

(5) to State medicaid fraud control units (as defined in section 1903(q) [42 USCS § 1396b(q)]),

(6) to hospitals and other health care entities (as defined in section 431 of the Health Care Quality Improvement Act of 1986 [42 USCS § 11151]), with respect to physicians or other licensed health care practitioners that have entered (or may be entering) into an employment or affiliation relationship with, or have applied for clinical privileges or appointments to the medical staff of, such hospitals or other health care entities (and such information shall be deemed to be disclosed pursuant to section 427 [42 USCS § 11137] of, and be subject to the provisions of, that Act [42 USCS §§ 11101 et seq.]),

(7) to the Attorney General and such other law enforcement officials as the Secretary deems appropriate, and

(8) upon request, to the Comptroller General,

in order for such authorities to determine the fitness of individuals to provide health care services, to protect the health and safety of individuals receiving health care through such programs, and to protect the fiscal integrity of such programs.

(c) Confidentiality of information provided. The Secretary shall provide for suitable safeguards for the confidentiality of the information furnished under subsection (a). Nothing in this subsection shall prevent the disclosure of such information by a party which is otherwise authorized, under applicable State law, to make such disclosure.

(d) Appropriate coordination. The Secretary shall provide for the maximum appropriate coordination in the implementation of subsection (a) of this section and section 422 of the Health Care Quality Improvement Act of 1986 [42 USCS § 11132].

(Aug. 14, 1935, ch 531, Title XIX, § 1921, as added Aug. 18, 1987, P. L. 100-93, § 5(b), 101 Stat. 690; Nov. 5, 1990, P. L. 101-508, Title IV, Subtitle B, Part 4, Subpart E, § 4752(f)(1), 104 Stat. 1388-208; March 23, 2010, P. L. 111-148, Title VI, Subtitle E, § 6403(b), 124 Stat. 764.)

HISTORY; ANCILLARY LAWS AND DIRECTIVES

Prospective amendments:

Amendment of section, effective on later of March 23, 2011, or effective date of regulations. Act March 23, 2010, P. L. 111-148, Title VI, Subtitle E, § 6403(b), 124 Stat. 764 (effective as provided by § 6403(d)(6) of such Act, which appears as 42 USCS § 1320a-7e note), provides:

"Section 1921 of the Social Security Act (42 U.S.C. 1396r-2) is amended—

"(1) in subsection (a)—

"(A) in paragraph (1)—

"(i) by striking 'system. The State' and all that follows through the semicolon and inserting "system. (A) Licensing or certification actions. The State must have in effect a system of reporting the following information with respect to formal proceedings (as defined by the Secretary in regulations) concluded against a health care practitioner or entity by a State licensing or certification agency:';

"(ii) by redesignating subparagraphs (A) through (D) as clauses (i) through (iv), respectively, and indenting appropriately;

"(iii) in subparagraph (A)(iii) (as so redesignated)—

"(I) by striking 'the license of' and inserting 'license or the right to apply for, or renew, a license by'; and

"(II) by inserting 'nonrenewability,' after 'voluntary surrender,'; and

"(iv) by adding at the end the following new subparagraph:

" '(B) Other final adverse actions. The State must have in effect a system of reporting information with respect to any final adverse action (not including settlements in which no findings of liability have been made) taken against a health care provider, supplier, or practitioner by a State law or fraud enforcement agency.'; and

"(B) in paragraph (2), by striking 'the authority described in paragraph (1)' and inserting 'a State licensing or certification agency or State law or fraud enforcement agency';

"(2) in subsection (b)—

"(A) by striking paragraph (2) and inserting the following:

" '(2) to State licensing or certification agencies and Federal agencies responsible for the licensing and certification of health care providers, suppliers, and licensed health care practitioners;';

"(B) in each of paragraphs (4) and (6), by inserting ', but only with respect to information provided pursuant to subsection (a)(1)(A)' before the comma at the end;

"(C) by striking paragraph (5) and inserting the following:

" '(5) to State law or fraud enforcement agencies,';

"(D) by redesignating paragraphs (7) and (8) as paragraphs (8) and (9), respectively; and

"(E) by inserting after paragraph (6) the following new paragraph:

" '(7) to health plans (as defined in section 1128C(c) [42 USCS § 1320a-7c(c)]);';

"(3) by redesignating subsection (d) as subsection (h), and by inserting after subsection (c) the following new subsections:

" '(d) Disclosure and correction of information. (1) Disclosure. With respect to information reported pursuant to subsection (a)(1), the Secretary shall—

" '(A) provide for disclosure of the information, upon request, to the health care practitioner who, or the entity that, is the subject of the information reported; and

" '(B) establish procedures for the case where the health care practitioner or entity disputes the accuracy of the information reported.

" '(2) Corrections. Each State licensing or certification agency and State law or fraud enforcement agency shall report corrections of information already reported about any formal proceeding or final adverse action described in subsection (a), in such form and manner as the Secretary prescribes by regulation.

" '(e) Fees for disclosure. The Secretary may establish or approve reasonable fees for the disclosure of information under this section. The amount of such a fee may not exceed the costs of processing the requests for disclosure and of providing such information. Such fees shall be available to the Secretary to cover such costs.

" '(f) Protection from liability for reporting. No person or entity, including any agency designated by the Secretary in subsection (b), shall be held liable in any civil action with respect to any reporting of information as required under this section, without knowledge of the falsity of the information contained in the report.

" '(g) References. For purposes of this section:

" '(1) State licensing or certification agency. The term "State licensing or certification agency" includes any authority of a State (or of a political subdivision thereof) responsible for the licensing of health care practitioners (or any peer review organization or private accreditation entity reviewing the services provided by health care practitioners) or entities.

" '(2) State law or fraud enforcement agency. The term "State law or fraud enforcement agency" includes—

" '(A) a State law enforcement agency; and

" '(B) a State Medicaid fraud control unit (as defined in section 1903(q) [42 USCS § 1396b(q)]).

" '(3) Final adverse action. (A) In general. Subject to subparagraph (B), the term "final adverse action" includes—

" '(i) civil judgments against a health care provider, supplier, or practitioner in State court related to the delivery of a health care item or service;

" '(ii) State criminal convictions related to the delivery of a health care item or service;

" '(iii) exclusion from participation in State health care programs (as defined in section 1128(h) [42 USCS § 1320a-7(h)]);

" '(iv) any licensing or certification action described in subsection (a)(1)(A) taken against a supplier by a State licensing or certification agency; and

" '(v) any other adjudicated actions or decisions that the Secretary shall establish by regulation.

" '(B) Exception. Such term does not include any action with respect to a malpractice claim.'; and

"(4) in subsection (h), as so redesignated, by striking 'The Secretary' and all that follows through the period at the end and inserting 'In implementing this section, the Secretary shall provide for the maximum appropriate coordination with part B of the Health Care Quality Improvement Act of 1986 (42 U.S.C. 11131 et seq.) and section 1128E [42 USCS § 1320a-7e].' ".

§ 1396r-4. Adjustment in payment for inpatient hospital services furnished by disproportionate share hospitals

(a) Implementation of requirement. (1) A State plan under this title [42 USCS §§ 1396 et seq.] shall not be considered to meet the requirement of section 1902(a)(13)(A)(iv) [42 USCS § 1396a(a)(13)(A)(iv)] (insofar as it requires payments to hospitals to take into account the situation of hospitals which serve a disproportionate number of low income patients with special needs), as of July 1, 1988, unless the State has submitted to the Secretary, by not later than such date, an amendment to such plan that—

(A) specifically defines the hospitals so described (and includes in such definition any disproportionate share hospital described in subsection (b)(1) which meets the requirements of subsection (d)), and

(B) provides, effective for inpatient hospital services provided not later than July 1, 1988, for an appropriate increase in the rate or amount of payment for such services provided by such hospitals, consistent with subsection (c).

(2)(A) In order to be considered to have met such requirement of section 1902(a)(13)(A) [42 USCS § 1396a(a)(13)(A)] as of July 1, 1989, the State must submit to the Secretary of Health and Human Services by not later than April 1, 1989, the State plan amendment described in paragraph (1), consistent with subsection (c), effective for inpatient hospital services provided on or after July 1, 1989.

(B) In order to be considered to have met such requirement of section 1902(a)(13)(A) [42 USCS § 1396a(a)(13)(A)] as of July 1, 1990, the State must submit to the Secretary of Health and Human Services by not later than April 1, 1990, the State plan amendment described in paragraph (1), consistent with subsections (c) and (f), effective for inpatient hospital services provided on or after July 1, 1990.

(C) If a State plan under this title [42 USCS §§ 1396 et seq.] provides for payments for inpatient hospital services on a prospective basis (whether per diem, per case, or otherwise), in order for the plan to be considered to have met such requirement of section 1902(a)(13)(A) [42 USCS § 1396a(a)(13)(A)] as of July 1, 1989, the State must submit to the Secretary by not later than April 1, 1989, a State plan amendment that provides, in the case of hospitals defined by the State as disproportionate share hospitals under paragraph (1)(A), for an outlier adjustment in payment amounts for medically necessary inpatient hospital services provided on or after July 1, 1989, involving exceptionally high costs or exceptionally long lengths of stay for individuals under one year of age.

(D) A State plan under this title [42 USCS §§ 1396 et seq.] shall not be considered to meet the requirements of section 1902(a)(13)(A)(iv) [42 USCS § 1396a(a)(13)(A)(iv)] (insofar as it requires payments to hospitals to take into account the situation of hospitals that serve a disproportionate number of low-income patients with special needs), as of October 1, 1998, unless the State has submitted to the Secretary by such date a description of the methodology used by the State to identify and to make payments to disproportionate share hospitals, including children's hospitals, on the basis of the proportion of low-income and medicaid patients (including such patients who receive benefits through a managed care entity) served by such hospitals. The State shall provide an annual report to the Secretary describing the disproportionate share payments to each such disproportionate share hospital.

(3) The Secretary shall, not later than 90 days after the date a State submits an amendment under this subsection, review each such amendment for compliance with such requirement and by such date shall approve or disapprove each such amendment. If the Secretary disapproves such an amendment, the State shall immediately submit a revised amendment which meets such requirement.

(4) The requirement of this subsection may not be waived under section 1915(b)(4) [42 USCS § 1396n(b)(4)].

(b) Hospitals deemed disproportionate share. (1) For purposes of subsection (a)(1), a hospital which meets the requirements of subsection (d) is deemed to be a disproportionate share hospital if—

(A) the hospital's medicaid inpatient utilization rate (as defined in paragraph (2)) is at least one standard deviation above the mean medicaid inpatient utilization rate for hospitals receiving medicaid payments in the State; or

(B) the hospital's low-income utilization rate (as defined in paragraph (3)) exceeds 25 percent.

(2) For purposes of paragraph (1)(A), the term "medicaid inpatient utilization rate" means, for a hospital, a fraction (expressed as a percentage), the numerator of which is the hospital's number of inpatient days attributable to patients who (for such days) were eligible for medical assistance under a State plan approved under this title [42 USCS §§ 1396 et seq.] in a period (regardless of whether such patients receive medical assistance on a fee-for-service basis or through a managed care entity), and the denominator of which is the total number of the hospital's inpatient days in that period. In this paragraph, the term "inpatient day" includes each day in which an individual (including a newborn) is an inpatient in the hospital, whether or not the individual is in a specialized ward and whether or not the individual remains in the hospital for lack of suitable placement elsewhere.

(3) For purposes of paragraph (1)(B), the term "low-income utilization rate" means, for a hospital, the sum of—

(A) the fraction (expressed as a percentage)—

(i) the numerator of which is the sum (for a period) of (I) the total revenues paid the hospital for patient services under a State plan under this title [42 USCS §§ 1396 et seq.] (regardless of whether the services were furnished on a fee-for-service basis or through a managed care entity) and (II) the amount of the cash subsidies for patient services received directly from State and local governments, and

(ii) the denominator of which is the total amount of revenues of the hospital for patient services (including the amount of such cash subsidies) in the period; and

(B) a fraction (expressed as a percentage)—

(i) the numerator of which is the total amount of the hospital's charges for inpatient hospital services which are attributable to charity care in a period, and less the portion of any cash subsidies described in clause (i)(II) of subparagraph (A) in the period reasonably attributable to inpatient hospital services, and

(ii) the denominator of which is the total amount of the hospital's charges for inpatient hospital services in the hospital in the period.

The numerator under subparagraph (B)(i) shall not include contractual allowances and discounts (other than for indigent patients not eligible for medical assistance under a State plan approved under this title [42 USCS §§ 1396 et seq.]).

(4) The Secretary may not restrict a State's authority to designate hospitals as disproportionate share hospitals under this section. The previous sentence shall not be construed to affect the authority of the Secretary to reduce payments pursuant to section 1903(w)(1)(A)(iii) [42 USCS § 1396b(w)(1)(A)(iii)] if the Secretary determines that, as a result of such designations, there is in effect a hold harmless provision described in section 1903(w)(4) [42 USCS § 1396b(w)(4)].

(c) Payment adjustment. Subject to subsections (f) and (g), in order to be consistent with this subsection, a payment adjustment for a disproportionate share hospital must either—

(1) be in an amount equal to at least the product of (A) the amount paid under the State plan to the hospital for operating costs for inpatient hospital services (of the kind described in section 1886(a)(4) [42 USCS § 1395ww(a)(4)]), and (B) the hospital's disproportionate share adjustment percentage (established under section 1886(d)(5)(F)(iv) [42 USCS § 1395ww(d)(5)(F)(iv)]);

(2) provide for a minimum specified additional payment amount (or increased percentage payment) and (without regard to whether the hospital is described in subparagraph (A) or (B) of subsection (b)(1)) for an increase in such a payment amount (or percentage payment) in proportion to the percentage by which the hospital's medicaid utilization rate (as defined in subsection (b)(2)) exceeds one standard deviation above the mean medicaid inpatient utilization rate for hospitals receiving medicaid payments in the State or the hospital's low-income utilization rate (as defined in paragraph [subsection] (b)(2)); or

(3) provide for a minimum specified additional payment amount (or increased percentage payment) that varies according to type of hospital under a methodology that—

(A) applies equally to all hospitals of each type; and

(B) results in an adjustment for each type of hospital that is reasonably related to the costs, volume, or proportion of services provided to patients eligible for medical assistance under a State plan approved under this title [42 USCS §§ 1396 et seq.] or to low-income patients,

except that, for purposes of paragraphs (1)(B) and (2)(A) of subsection (a), the payment adjustment for a disproportionate share hospital is consistent with this subsection if the appropriate increase in the rate or amount of payment is equal to at least one-third of the increase otherwise applicable under this subsection (in the case of such paragraph (1)(B)) and two-thirds of such increase (in the case of such paragraph (2)(A)). In the case of a hospital described in subsection (d)(2)(A)(i) (relating to children's hospitals), in computing the hospital's disproportionate share adjustment percentage for purposes of paragraph (1)(B) of this subsection, the disproportionate patient percentage (defined in section 1886(d)(5)(F)(vi) [42 USCS § 1395ww(d)(5)(F)(vi)]) shall be computed by substituting for the fraction described in subclause (I) of such section the fraction described in subclause (II) of that section. If a State elects in a State plan amendment under subsection (a) to provide the payment adjustment described in paragraph (2), the State must include in the amendment a detailed description of the specific methodology to be used in determining the specified additional payment amount (or increased percentage payment) to be made to each hospital qualifying for such a payment adjustment and must publish at least annually the name of each hospital qualifying for such a payment adjustment and the amount of such payment adjustment made for each such hospital.

(d) Requirements to qualify as disproportionate share hospital. (1) Except as provided in paragraph (2), no hospital may be defined or deemed as a disproportionate share hospital under a State plan or under subsection (b) of this section unless the hospital has at least 2 obstetricians who have staff privileges at the hospital and who have agreed to provide obstetric services to individuals who are entitled to medical assistance for such services under such State plan.

(2)(A) Paragraph (1) shall not apply to a hospital—

(i) the inpatients of which are predominantly individuals under 18 years of age; or

(ii) which does not offer nonemergency obstetric services to the general population as of the date of the enactment of this Act [Dec. 22, 1987].

(B) In the case of a hospital located in a rural

area (as defined for purposes of section 1886 [42 USCS § 1395ww]), in paragraph (1) the term "obstetrician" includes any physician with staff privileges at the hospital to perform nonemergency obstetric procedures.

(3) No hospital may be defined or deemed as a disproportionate share hospital under a State plan under this title [42 USCS §§ 1396 et seq.] or under subsection (b) or (e) of this section unless the hospital has a medicaid inpatient utilization rate (as defined in subsection (b)(2)) of not less than 1 percent.

(e) Special rule. (1) A State plan shall be considered to meet the requirement of section 1902(a)(13)(A)(iv) [42 USCS § 1396a(a)(13)(A)(iv)] (insofar as it requires payments to hospitals to take into account the situation of hospitals which serve a disproportionate number of low income patients with special needs) without regard to the requirement of subsection (a) if (A)(i) the plan provided for payment adjustments based on a pooling arrangement involving a majority of the hospitals participating under the plan for disproportionate share hospitals as of January 1, 1984, or (ii) the plan as of January 1, 1987, provided for payment adjustments based on a statewide pooling arrangement involving all acute care hospitals and the arrangement provides for reimbursement of the total amount of uncompensated care provided by each participating hospital, (B) the aggregate amount of the payment adjustments under the plan for such hospitals is not less than the aggregate amount of such adjustments otherwise required to be made under such subsection, and (C) the plan meets the requirement of subsection (d)(3) and such payment adjustments are made consistent with the last sentence of subsection (c).

(2) In the case of a State that used a health insuring organization before January 1, 1986, to administer a portion of its plan on a statewide basis, beginning on July 1, 1988—

(A) the requirements of subsections (b) and (c) (other than the last sentence of subsection (c)) shall not apply if the aggregate amount of the payment adjustments under the plan for disproportionate share hospitals (as defined under the State plan) is not less than the aggregate amount of payment adjustments otherwise required to be made if such subsections applied,

(B) subsection (d)(2)(B) shall apply to hospitals located in urban areas, as well as in rural areas,

(C) subsection (d)(3) shall apply, and

(D) subsection (g) shall apply.

(f) Limitation on Federal financial participation. (1) In general. Payment under section 1903(a) [42 USCS § 1396b(a)] shall not be made to a State with respect to any payment adjustment made under this section for hospitals in a State for quarters in a fiscal year in excess of the disproportionate share hospital (in this subsection referred to as "DSH") allotment for the State for the fiscal year, as specified in paragraphs (2), (3), and (7).

(2) State DSH allotments for fiscal years 1998 through 2002. Subject to paragraph (4), the DSH allotment for a State for each fiscal year during the period beginning with fiscal year 1998 and ending with fiscal year 2002 is determined in accordance with the following table:

State or District	DSH Allotment (in millions of dollars)				
	FY98	FY99	FY00	FY01	FY02
Alabama	293	269	248	246	246
Alaska	10	10	10	9	9
Arizona	81	81	81	81	81
Arkansas	2	2	2	2	2
California	1,085	1,068	986	931	877
Colorado	93	85	79	74	74
Connecticut	200	194	164	160	160
Delaware	4	4	4	4	4
District of Columbia	23	23	49	49	49
Florida	207	203	197	188	160
Georgia	253	248	241	228	215
Hawaii	0	0	0	0	0
Idaho	1	1	1	1	1
Illinois	203	199	193	182	172
Indiana	201	197	191	181	171
Iowa	8	8	8	8	8
Kansas	51	49	42	36	33
Kentucky	137	134	130	123	116
Louisiana	880	795	713	658	631
Maine	103	99	84	84	84
Maryland	72	70	68	64	61
Massachusetts	288	282	273	259	244
Michigan	249	244	237	224	212
Minnesota	16	16	33	33	33
Mississippi	143	141	136	129	122
Missouri	436	423	379	379	379
Montana	0.2	0.2	0.2	0.2	0.2
Nebraska	5	5	5	5	5
Nevada	37	37	37	37	37
New Hampshire	140	136	130	130	130
New Jersey	600	582	515	515	515
New Mexico	5	5	9	9	9
New York	1,512	1,482	1,436	1,361	1,285
North Carolina	278	272	264	250	236
North Dakota	1	1	1	1	1
Ohio	382	374	363	344	325
Oklahoma	16	16	16	16	16
Oregon	20	20	20	20	20
Pennsylvania	529	518	502	476	449
Rhode Island	62	60	58	55	52
South Carolina	313	303	262	262	262

State or District	DSH Allotment (in millions of dollars)				
	FY98	FY99	FY00	FY01	FY02
South Dakota	1	1	1	1	1
Tennessee	0	0	0	0	0
Texas	979	950	806	765	765
Utah	3	3	3	3	3
Vermont	18	18	18	18	18
Virginia	70	68	66	63	59
Washington	174	171	166	157	148
West Virginia	64	63	61	58	54
Wisconsin	7	7	7	7	7
Wyoming	0	0	0.1	0.1	0.1

(3) State DSH allotments for fiscal year 2003 and thereafter. (A) In general. Except as provided in paragraphs (6) and (7) and subparagraph (E), the DSH allotment for any State for fiscal year 2003 and each succeeding fiscal year is equal to the DSH allotment for the State for the preceding fiscal year under paragraph (2) or this paragraph, increased, subject to subparagraphs (B) and (C) and paragraph (5), by the percentage change in the consumer price index for all urban consumers (all items; U.S. city average), for the previous fiscal year.

(B) Limitation. The DSH allotment for a State shall not be increased under subparagraph (A) for a fiscal year to the extent that such an increase would result in the DSH allotment for the year exceeding the greater of—

(i) the DSH allotment for the previous year, or

(ii) 12 percent of the total amount of expenditures under the State plan for medical assistance during the fiscal year.

(C) Special, temporary increase in allotments on a one-time, non-cumulative basis. The DSH allotment for any State (other than a State with a DSH allotment determined under paragraph (5))—

(i) for fiscal year 2004 is equal to 116 percent of the DSH allotment for the State for fiscal year 2003 under this paragraph, notwithstanding subparagraph (B); and

(ii) for each succeeding fiscal year is equal to the DSH allotment for the State for fiscal year 2004 or, in the case of fiscal years beginning with the fiscal year specified in subparagraph (D) for that State, the DSH allotment for the State for the previous fiscal year increased by the percentage change in the consumer price index for all urban consumers (all items; U.S. city average), for the previous fiscal year.

(D) Fiscal year specified. For purposes of subparagraph (C)(ii), the fiscal year specified in this subparagraph for a State is the first fiscal year for which the Secretary estimates that the DSH allotment for that State will equal (or no longer exceed) the DSH allotment for that State under the law as in effect before the date of the enactment of this subparagraph [enacted Dec. 8, 2003].

(E) Temporary increase in allotments during recession. (i) In general. Subject to clause (ii), the DSH allotment for any State—

(I) for fiscal year 2009 is equal to 102.5 percent of the DSH allotment that would be determined under this paragraph for the State for fiscal year 2009 without application of this subparagraph, notwithstanding subparagraphs (B) and (C);

(II) for fiscal year 2010 is equal to 102.5 percent of the DSH allotment for the State for fiscal year 2009, as determined under subclause (I); and

(III) for each succeeding fiscal year is equal to the DSH allotment for the State under this paragraph determined without applying subclauses (I) and (II).

(ii) Application. Clause (i) shall not apply to a State for a year in the case that the DSH allotment for such State for such year under this paragraph determined without applying clause (i) would grow higher than the DSH allotment specified under clause (i) for the State for such year.

(4) Special rule for fiscal years 2001 and 2002. (A) In general. Notwithstanding paragraph (2), the DSH allotment for any State for—

(i) fiscal year 2001, shall be the DSH allotment determined under paragraph (2) for fiscal year 2000 increased, subject to subparagraph (B) and paragraph (5), by the percentage change in the consumer price index for all urban consumers (all items; U.S. city average) for fiscal year 2000; and

(ii) fiscal year 2002, shall be the DSH allotment determined under clause (i) increased, subject to subparagraph (B) and paragraph (5), by the percentage change in the consumer price index for all urban consumers (all items; U.S. city average) for fiscal year 2001.

(B) Limitation. Subparagraph (B) of paragraph (3) shall apply to subparagraph (A) of this paragraph in the same manner as that subparagraph (B) applies to paragraph (3)(A).

(C) No application to allotments after fiscal year 2002. The DSH allotment for any State for fiscal year 2003 or any succeeding fiscal year shall be determined under paragraph (3) without regard to the DSH allotments determined under subparagraph (A) of this paragraph.

(5) Special rule for low DSH States. (A) For fiscal years 2001 through 2003 for extremely low DSH States. In the case of a State in which

the total expenditures under the State plan (including Federal and State shares) for disproportionate share hospital adjustments under this section for fiscal year 1999, as reported to the Administrator of the Health Care Financing Administration as of August 31, 2000, is greater than 0 but less than 1 percent of the State's total amount of expenditures under the State plan for medical assistance during the fiscal year, the DSH allotment for fiscal year 2001 shall be increased to 1 percent of the State's total amount of expenditures under such plan for such assistance during such fiscal year. In subsequent fiscal years before fiscal year 2004, such increased allotment is subject to an increase for inflation as provided in paragraph (3)(A).

(B) For fiscal year 2004 and subsequent fiscal years. In the case of a State in which the total expenditures under the State plan (including Federal and State shares) for disproportionate share hospital adjustments under this section for fiscal year 2000, as reported to the Administrator of the Centers for Medicare & Medicaid Services as of August 31, 2003, is greater than 0 but less than 3 percent of the State's total amount of expenditures under the State plan for medical assistance during the fiscal year, the DSH allotment for the State with respect to—

(i) fiscal year 2004 shall be the DSH allotment for the State for fiscal year 2003 increased by 16 percent;

(ii) each succeeding fiscal year before fiscal year 2009 shall be the DSH allotment for the State for the previous fiscal year increased by 16 percent; and

(iii) fiscal year 2009 and any subsequent fiscal year, shall be the DSH allotment for the State for the previous year subject to an increase for inflation as provided in paragraph (3)(A).

(6) Allotment adjustments. (A) Tennessee. (i) In general. Only with respect to fiscal year 2007, the DSH allotment for Tennessee for such fiscal year, notwithstanding the table set forth in paragraph (2) or the terms of the TennCare Demonstration Project in effect for the State, shall be the greater of—

(I) the amount that the Secretary determines is equal to the Federal medical assistance percentage component attributable to disproportionate share hospital payment adjustments for the demonstration year ending in 2006 that is reflected in the budget neutrality provision of the TennCare Demonstration Project; and

(II) $280,000,000.

Only with respect to fiscal years 2008, 2009, 2010, and 2011, the DSH allotment for Tennessee for the fiscal year, notwithstanding such table or terms, shall be the amount specified in the previous sentence for fiscal year 2007. Only with respect to fiscal year 2012 for the period ending on December 31, 2011, the DSH allotment for Tennessee for such portion of the fiscal year, notwithstanding such table or terms, shall be ¼ of the amount specified in the first sentence for fiscal year 2007.

(ii) Limitation on amount of payment adjustments eligible for federal financial participation. Payment under section 1903(a) [42 USCS § 1396b(a)] shall not be made to Tennessee with respect to the aggregate amount of any payment adjustments made under this section for hospitals in the State for fiscal year 2007, 2008, 2009, 2010, 2011, or for [a] period in fiscal year 2012 described in clause (i) that is in excess of 30 percent of the DSH allotment for the State for such fiscal year or period determined pursuant to clause (i).

(iii) State plan amendment. The Secretary shall permit Tennessee to submit an amendment to its State plan under this title [42 USCS §§ 1396 et seq.] that describes the methodology to be used by the State to identify and make payments to disproportionate share hospitals, including children's hospitals and institutions for mental diseases or other mental health facilities. The Secretary may not approve such plan amendment unless the methodology described in the amendment is consistent with the requirements under this section for making payment adjustments to disproportionate share hospitals. For purposes of demonstrating budget neutrality under the TennCare Demonstration Project, payment adjustments made pursuant to a State plan amendment approved in accordance with this subparagraph shall be considered expenditures under such project.

(iv) Offset of Federal share of payment adjustments for fiscal years 2007 through 2011 and the first calendar quarter of fiscal year 2012 and the against essential access hospital supplemental pool payments under the TennCare demonstration project. (I) The total amount of Essential Access Hospital supplemental pool payments that may be made under the TennCare Demonstration Project for fiscal year 2007, 2008, 2009, 2010, 2011, or for a period in fiscal year 2012 described in clause (i) shall be reduced on a dollar for dollar basis by the amount of any payments made under section 1903(a) [42 USCS § 1396b(a)] to Tennessee with respect to payment adjustments made under this section for hospitals in the State for such fiscal year or period.

(II) The sum of the total amount of payments made under section 1903(a) [42 USCS § 1396b(a)] to Tennessee with respect to payment adjustments made under this section for hospitals in the State for fiscal year 2007, 2008, 2009, 2010, 2011, or for a period in fiscal year 2012 described in clause (i) and the total amount of Essential Access Hospital supplemental pool payments made under the TennCare Demonstration Project for such fiscal year or period shall not exceed the State's DSH allotment for such fiscal year or period established under clause (i).

(v) Allotment for 2d, 3rd, and 4th quarters of fiscal year 2012 and for fiscal year 2013. Notwithstanding the table set forth in paragraph (2):

(I) 2d, 3rd, and 4th quarters of fiscal year 2012. In the case of a State that has a DSH allotment of $0 for the 2d, 3rd, and 4th quarters of fiscal year 2012, the DSH allotment shall be $47,200,000 for such quarters.

(II) Fiscal year 2013. In the case of a State that has a DSH allotment of $0 for fiscal year 2013, the DSH allotment shall be $53,100,000 for such fiscal year.

(B) Hawaii. (i) In general. Only with respect to each of fiscal years 2007 through 2011, the DSH allotment for Hawaii for such fiscal year, notwithstanding the table set forth in paragraph (2), shall be $10,000,000. Only with respect to fiscal year 2012 for the period ending on December 31, 2011, the DSH allotment for Hawaii for such portion of the fiscal year, notwithstanding the table set forth in paragraph (2), shall be $2,500,000.

(ii) State plan amendment. The Secretary shall permit Hawaii to submit an amendment to its State plan under this title that describes the methodology to be used by the State to identify and make payments to disproportionate share hospitals, including children's hospitals and institutions for mental diseases or other mental health facilities. The Secretary may not approve such plan amendment unless the methodology described in the amendment is consistent with the requirements under this section for making payment adjustments to disproportionate share hospitals.

(iii) Allotment for 2d, 3rd, and 4th quarter of fiscal year 2012, fiscal year 2013, and succeeding fiscal years. Notwithstanding the table set forth in paragraph (2):

(I) 2d, 3rd, and 4th quarter of fiscal year 2012. The DSH allotment for Hawaii for the 2d, 3rd, and 4th quarters of fiscal year 2012 shall be $7,500,000.

(II) Treatment as a low-DSH state for fiscal year 2013 and succeeding fiscal years. With respect to fiscal year 2013, and each fiscal year thereafter, the DSH allotment for Hawaii shall be increased in the same manner as allotments for low DSH States are increased for such fiscal year under clause (iii) of paragraph (5)(B).

(III) Certain hospital payments. The Secretary may not impose a limitation on the total amount of payments made to hospitals under the QUEST section 1115 Demonstration Project except to the extent that such limitation is necessary to ensure that a hospital does not receive payments in excess of the amounts described in subsection (g), or as necessary to ensure that such payments under the waiver and such payments pursuant to the allotment provided in this clause do not, in the aggregate in any year, exceed the amount that the Secretary determines is equal to the Federal medical assistance percentage component attributable to disproportionate share hospital payment adjustments for such year that is reflected in the budget neutrality provision of the QUEST Demonstration Project.

(7) Medicaid DSH reductions. (A) Reductions. (i) In general. For each of fiscal years 2014 through 2020 the Secretary shall effect the following reductions:

(I) Reduction in DSH allotments. The Secretary shall reduce DSH allotments to States in the amount specified under the DSH health reform methodology under subparagraph (B) for the State for the fiscal year.

(II) Reductions in payments. The Secretary shall reduce payments to States under section 1903(a) [42 USCS § 1396b(a)] for each calendar quarter in the fiscal year, in the manner specified in clause (iii), in an amount equal to ¼ of the DSH allotment reduction under subclause (I) for the State for the fiscal year.

(ii) Aggregate reductions. The aggregate reductions in DSH allotments for all States under clause (i)(I) shall be equal to—

(I) $500,000,000 for fiscal year 2014;

(II) $600,000,000 for fiscal year 2015;

(III) $600,000,000 for fiscal year 2016;

(IV) $1,800,000,000 for fiscal year 2017;

(V) $5,000,000,000 for fiscal year 2018;

(VI) $5,600,000,000 for fiscal year 2019; and

(VII) $4,000,000,000 for fiscal year 2020. The Secretary shall distribute such aggregate reductions among States in accordance with subparagraph (B).

(iii) Manner of payment reduction. The amount of the payment reduction under clause (i)(II) for a State for a quarter shall be deemed an overpayment to the State under this title to be disallowed against the State's regular quarterly draw for all spending under section 1903(d)(2) [42 USCS § 1396b(d)(2)]. Such a disallowance is not subject to a reconsideration under subsections (d) and (e) of section 1116 [42 USCS § 1316].

(iv) Definition. In this paragraph, the term "State" means the 50 States and the District of Columbia.

(B) DSH health reform methodology. The Secretary shall carry out subparagraph (A) through use of a DSH Health Reform methodology that meets the following requirements:

(i) The methodology imposes the largest percentage reductions on the States that—

(I) have the lowest percentages of uninsured individuals (determined on the basis of data from the Bureau of the Census, audited hospital cost reports, and other information likely to yield accurate data) during the most recent year for which such data are available; or

(II) do not target their DSH payments on—

(aa) hospitals with high volumes of Medicaid inpatients (as defined in subsection (b)(1)(A)); and

(bb) hospitals that have high levels of uncompensated care (excluding bad debt).

(ii) The methodology imposes a smaller percentage reduction on low DSH States described in paragraph (5)(B).

(iii) The methodology takes into account the extent to which the DSH allotment for a State was included in the budget neutrality calculation for a coverage expansion approved under section 1115 [42 USCS § 1315] as of July 31, 2009.

(8) Definition of State. In this subsection, the term "State" means the 50 States and the District of Columbia.

(g) Limit on amount of payment to hospital. (1) Amount of adjustment subject to uncompensated costs. (A) In general. A payment adjustment during a fiscal year shall not be considered to be consistent with subsection (c) with respect to a hospital if the payment adjustment exceeds the costs incurred during the year of furnishing hospital services (as determined by the Secretary and net of payments under this title [42 USCS §§ 1396 et seq.], other than under this section, and by uninsured patients) by the hospital to individuals who either are eligible for medical assistance under the State plan or have no health insurance (or other source of third party coverage) for services provided during the year. For purposes of the preceding sentence, payments made to a hospital for services provided to indigent patients made by a State or a unit of local government within a State shall not be considered to be a source of third party payment.

(B) Limit to public hospitals during transition period. With respect to payment adjustments during a State fiscal year that begins before January 1, 1995, subparagraph (A) shall apply only to hospitals owned or operated by a State (or by an instrumentality or a unit of government within a State).

(C) Modifications for private hospitals. With respect to hospitals that are not owned or operated by a State (or by an instrumentality or a unit of government within a State), the Secretary may make such modifications to the manner in which the limitation on payment adjustments is applied to such hospitals as the Secretary considers appropriate.

(2) Additional amount during transition period for certain hospitals with high disproportionate share. (A) In general. In the case of a hospital with high disproportionate share (as defined in subparagraph (B)), a payment adjustment during a State fiscal year that begins before January 1, 1995, shall be considered consistent with subsection (c) if the payment adjustment does not exceed 200 percent of the costs of furnishing hospital services described in paragraph (1)(A) during the year, but only if the Governor of the State certifies to the satisfaction of the Secretary that the hospital's applicable minimum amount is used for health services during the year. In determining the amount that is used for such services during a year, there shall be excluded any amounts received under the Public Health Service Act [42 USCS §§ 201 et seq.], title V [42 USCS §§ 701 et seq.], title XVIII [42 USCS §§ 1395 et seq.], or from third party payors (not including the State plan under this title [42 USCS §§ 1396 et seq.]) that are used for providing such services during the year.

(B) Hospitals with high disproportionate share defined. In subparagraph (A), a hospital is a "hospital with high disproportionate share" if—

(i) the hospital is owned or operated by a State (or by an instrumentality or a unit of government within a State); and

(ii) the hospital—

(I) meets the requirement described in subsection (b)(1)(A), or

(II) has the largest number of inpatient days attributable to individuals entitled to benefits under the State plan of any hospital in such State for the previous State fiscal year.

(C) Applicable minimum amount defined. In subparagraph (A), the "applicable minimum amount" for a hospital for a fiscal year is equal to the difference between the amount of the hospital's payment adjustment for the fiscal year and the costs to the hospital of furnishing hospital services described in paragraph (1)(A) during the fiscal year.

(h) Limitation on certain State DSH expenditures. (1) In general. Payment under section 1903(a) [42 USCS § 1396b(a)] shall not be made to a State with respect to any payment adjustments made under this section for quarters in a fiscal year (beginning with fiscal year 1998) to institutions for mental diseases or other mental health facilities, to the extent the aggregate of such adjustments in the fiscal year exceeds the lesser of the following:

(A) 1995 IMD DSH payment adjustments. The total State DSH expenditures that are attributable to fiscal year 1995 for payments to institutions for mental diseases and other mental health facilities (based on reporting data specified by the State on HCFA Form 64 as mental health DSH, and as approved by the Secretary).

(B) Applicable percentage of 1995 total DSH payment allotment. The amount of such payment adjustments which are equal to the applicable percentage of the Federal share of payment adjustments made to hospitals in the State under subsection (c) that are attributable to the 1995 DSH allotment for the State for payments to institutions for mental diseases and other mental health facilities (based on reporting data specified by the State on HCFA Form 64 as mental health DSH, and as approved by the Secretary).

(2) Applicable percentage. (A) In general. For purposes of paragraph (1), the applicable percentage with respect to—

(i) each of fiscal years 1998, 1999, and 2000, is the percentage determined under subparagraph (B); or

(ii) a succeeding fiscal year is the lesser of the percentage determined under subparagraph (B) or the following percentage:

(I) For fiscal year 2001, 50 percent.

(II) For fiscal year 2002, 40 percent.

(III) For each succeeding fiscal year, 33 percent.

(B) 1995 percentage. The percentage determined under this subparagraph is the ratio (determined as a percentage) of—

(i) the Federal share of payment adjustments made to hospitals in the State under subsection (c) that are attributable to the 1995 DSH allotment for the State (as reported by the State not later than January 1, 1997, on HCFA Form 64, and as approved by the Secretary) for payments to institutions for mental diseases and other mental health facilities, to

(ii) the State 1995 DSH spending amount.

(C) State 1995 DSH spending amount. For purposes of subparagraph (B)(ii), the "State 1995 DSH spending amount", with respect to a State, is the Federal medical assistance percentage (for fiscal year 1995) of the payment adjustments made under subsection (c) under the State plan that are attributable to the fiscal year 1995 DSH allotment for the State (as reported by the State not later than January 1, 1997, on HCFA Form 64, and as approved by the Secretary).

(i) Requirement for direct payment. (1) In general. No payment may be made under section 1903(a)(1) [42 USCS § 1396b(a)(1)] with respect to a payment adjustment made under this section, for services furnished by a hospital on or after October 1, 1997, with respect to individuals eligible for medical assistance under the State plan who are enrolled with a managed care entity (as defined in section 1932(a)(1)(B) [42 USCS § 1396u-2(a)(1)(B)]) or under any other managed care arrangement unless a payment, equal to the amount of the payment adjustment—

(A) is made directly to the hospital by the State; and

(B) is not used to determine the amount of a prepaid capitation payment under the State plan to the entity or arrangement with respect to such individuals.

(2) Exception for current arrangements. Paragraph (1) shall not apply to a payment adjustment provided pursuant to a payment arrangement in effect on July 1, 1997.

(j) Annual reports and other requirements regarding payment adjustments. With respect to fiscal year 2004 and each fiscal year thereafter, the Secretary shall require a State, as a condition of receiving a payment under section 1903(a)(1) [42 USCS § 1396b(a)(1)] with respect to a payment adjustment made under this section, to do the following:

(1) Report. The State shall submit an annual report that includes the following:

(A) An identification of each disproportionate share hospital that received a payment adjustment under this section for the preceding fiscal year and the amount of the payment adjustment made to such hospital for the preceding fiscal year.

(B) Such other information as the Secretary determines necessary to ensure the appropriateness of the payment adjustments made under this section for the preceding fiscal year.

(2) Independent certified audit. The State shall annually submit to the Secretary an independent certified audit that verifies each of the following:

(A) The extent to which hospitals in the State have reduced their uncompensated care costs to reflect the total amount of claimed expenditures made under this section.

(B) Payments under this section to hospitals that comply with the requirements of subsection (g).

(C) Only the uncompensated care costs of providing inpatient hospital and outpatient hospital services to individuals described in paragraph (1)(A) of such subsection are included in the calculation of the hospital-specific limits under such subsection.

(D) The State included all payments under this title [42 USCS §§ 1396 et seq.], including supplemental payments, in the calculation of such hospital-specific limits.

(E) The State has separately documented and retained a record of all of its costs under this title [42 USCS §§ 1396 et seq.], claimed expenditures under this title [42 USCS §§ 1396 et seq.], uninsured costs in determining payment adjustments under this section, and any payments made on behalf of the uninsured from payment adjustments under this section.

(Aug. 14, 1935, ch 531, Title XIX, § 1923, as added Dec. 22, 1987, P. L. 100-203, Title IV, Subtitle B, Part 2, § 4112, 101 Stat. 1330-148; July 1, 1988, P. L. 100-360, Title III, Title IV, Subtitle B, § 411(k)(6)(A)–(B)(ix) 102 Stat. 752, 792; 21.2113, 1988, P. L. 100-485, Title VI, § 608(d)(15)(C), (26)(A)–(F), 102 Stat. 2417, 2421; Dec. 19, 1989, P. L. 101-239, Title VI, Subtitle B, Part 2, § 6411(c)(1), 103 Stat. 2270; Nov. 5, 1990, P. L. 101-508, Title IV, Subtitle B, Part 4, Subpart A, §§ 4702(a), 4703(a)–(c), 104 Stat. 1388-171; Dec. 12, 1991, P. L. 102-234, §§ 3(b)(1), (2)(A), (c), 105 Stat. 1799, 1803; Aug. 10, 1993, P. L. 103-66, Title XIII, Ch 2, Subch B, Part III, § 13621(a)(1), (b)(1), (2), 107 Stat. 629, 630; Aug. 5, 1997, P. L. 105-33, Title IV, Subtitle H, Ch 2, § 4711(c)(2), Ch 3, § 4721(a)(1), (b)–(d), 111 Stat. 508, 511, 513; Nov. 29, 1999, P. L. 106-113, Div B, § 1000(a)(6), 113 Stat. 1536; Dec. 21, 2000, P. L. 106-554, § 1(a)(6), 114 Stat. 2763; Dec. 8, 2003, P. L. 108-173, Title X, Subtitle A, § 1001(a)–(d), 117 Stat. 2428; Feb. 8, 2006, P. L. 109-171, Title VI, Subtitle A, Ch. 5, § 6054(a), 120 Stat. 96; Dec. 20, 2006, P. L. 109-432, Div B, Title IV, § 404, 120 Stat. 2995; Dec. 29, 2007, P. L. 110-173, Title II, § 204, 121 Stat. 2513; July 15, 2008, P. L. 110-275, Title II, § 202, 122 Stat. 2591; Feb. 4, 2009, P. L. 111-3, Title VI, Subtitle B, § 616, 123 Stat. 103; Feb. 17, 2009, P. L. 111-5, Div B, Title V, § 5002, 123 Stat. 502; March 23, 2010, P. L. 111-148, Title II, Subtitle G, § 2551(a), Title X, Subtitle B, Part I, § 10201(e), 124 Stat. 312, 920; March 30, 2010, P. L. 111-152, Title I, Subtitle C, § 1203, 124 Stat. 1053.)

HISTORY; ANCILLARY LAWS AND DIRECTIVES

Other provisions:

Repeal of provisions relating to effective date of March 23, 2010 amendments. Act March 23, 2010, P. L. 111-148, Title II, Subtitle G, § 2551(b), 124 Stat. 314, which provided that the amendment made by § 2551(a) of such Act to subsec. (f) of this section should take effect on 10/1/2011, was repealed by Act March 23, 2010, P. L. 111-148, Title X, Subtitle B, Part I, § 10201(f), 124 Stat. 922.

§ 1396r-5. Treatment of income and resources for certain institutionalized spouses

(a) Special treatment for institutionalized spouses. (1) Supersedes other provisions. In determining the eligibility for medical assistance of an institutionalized spouse (as defined in subsection (h)(1)), the provisions of this section supersede any other provision of this title (including sections 1902(a)(17) and 1902(f) [42 USCS § 1396a(a)(17) and (f)]) which is inconsistent with them.

(2) No comparable treatment required. Any different treatment provided under this section for institutionalized spouses shall not, by reason of paragraph (10) or (17) of section 1902(a) [42 USCS § 1396a(a)(10) or (17)], require such treatment for other individuals.

(3) Does not affect certain determinations. Except as this section specifically provides, this section does not apply to—

(A) the determination of what constitutes income or resources, or

(B) the methodology and standards for determining and evaluating income and resources.

(4) Application in certain States and territories. (A) Application in States operating under demonstration projects. In the case of any State which is providing medical assistance to its residents under a waiver granted under section 1115 [42 USCS § 1315], the Secretary shall require the State to meet the requirements of this section in the same manner as the State would be required to meet such requirement if the State had in effect a plan approved under this title [42 USCS §§ 1396 et seq.].

(B) No application in commonwealths and

territories. This section shall only apply to a State that is one of the 50 States or the District of Columbia.

(5) Application to individuals receiving services under PACE programs. This section applies to individuals receiving institutional or noninstitutional services under a PACE demonstration waiver program (as defined in section 1934(a)(7) [42 USCS § 1396u-4(a)(7)]) or under a PACE program under section 1934 or 1894 [42 USCS § 1396u-4 or 1395eee].

(b) Rules for treatment of income. (1) Separate treatment of income. During any month in which an institutionalized spouse is in the institution, except as provided in paragraph (2), no income of the community spouse shall be deemed available to the institutionalized spouse.

(2) Attribution of income. In determining the income of an institutionalized spouse or community spouse for purposes of the post-eligibility income determination described in subsection (d), except as otherwise provided in this section and regardless of any State laws relating to community property or the division of marital property, the following rules apply:

(A) Non-trust property. Subject to subparagraphs (C) and (D), in the case of income not from a trust, unless the instrument providing the income otherwise specifically provides—

(i) if payment of income is made solely in the name of the institutionalized spouse or the community spouse, the income shall be considered available only to that respective spouse;

(ii) if payment of income is made in the names of the institutionalized spouse and the community spouse, one-half of the income shall be considered available to each of them; and

(iii) if payment of income is made in the names of the institutionalized spouse or the community spouse, or both, and to another person or persons, the income shall be considered available to each spouse in proportion to the spouse's interest (or, if payment is made with respect to both spouses and no such interest is specified, one-half of the joint interest shall be considered available to each spouse).

(B) Trust property. In the case of a trust—

(i) except as provided in clause (ii), income shall be attributed in accordance with the provisions of this title [42 USCS §§ 1396 et seq.] (including sections 1902(a)(17) and 1917(d) [42 USCS §§ 1396a(a)(17) and 1396p(d)]), and

(ii) income shall be considered available to each spouse as provided in the trust, or, in the absence of a specific provision in the trust—

(I) if payment of income is made solely to the institutionalized spouse or the community spouse, the income shall be considered available only to that respective spouse;

(II) if payment of income is made to both the institutionalized spouse and the community spouse, one-half of the income shall be considered available to each of them; and

(III) if payment of income is made to the institutionalized spouse or the community spouse, or both, and to another person or persons, the income shall be considered available to each spouse in proportion to the spouse's interest (or, if payment is made with respect to both spouses and no such interest is specified, one-half of the joint interest shall be considered available to each spouse).

(C) Property with no instrument. In the case of income not from a trust in which there is no instrument establishing ownership, subject to subparagraph (D), one-half of the income shall be considered to be available to the institutionalized spouse and one-half to the community spouse.

(D) Rebutting ownership. The rules of subparagraphs (A) and (C) are superseded to the extent that an institutionalized spouse can establish, by a preponderance of the evidence, that the ownership interests in income are other than as provided under such subparagraphs.

(c) Rules for treatment of resources. (1) Computation of spousal share at time of institutionalization. (A) Total joint resources. There shall be computed (as of the beginning of the first continuous period of institutionalization (beginning on or after September 30, 1989) of the institutionalized spouse)—

(i) the total value of the resources to the extent either the institutionalized spouse or the community spouse has an ownership interest, and

(ii) a spousal share which is equal to ½ of such total value.

(B) Assessment. At the request of an institutionalized spouse or community spouse, at the beginning of the first continuous period of institutionalization (beginning on or after September 30, 1989) of the institutionalized spouse and upon the receipt of relevant documentation of resources, the State shall promptly assess and document the total value described in subparagraph (A)(i) and shall provide a copy of such assessment and documentation to each spouse and shall retain a copy of the assessment for use under this section. If the request is not part of an application for medical assistance under this title [42 USCS §§ 1396 et seq.], the State may, at its option as a condition of providing the assessment, require payment of a fee not exceeding the reasonable expenses of providing and documenting the assessment. At the time of providing the copy of the assessment, the State shall include a notice indicating that the spouse will have a right to a fair hearing under subsection (e)(2).

(2) Attribution of resources at time of initial eligibility determination. In determining the resources of an institutionalized spouse at the time of application for benefits under this title [42 USCS §§ 1396 et seq.], regardless of any State laws relating to community property or the division of marital property—

(A) except as provided in subparagraph (B), all the resources held by either the institutionalized spouse, community spouse, or both, shall be considered to be available to the institutionalized spouse, and

(B) resources shall be considered to be available to an institutionalized spouse, but only to the extent that the amount of such resources exceeds the amount computed under subsection (f)(2)(A) (as of the time of application for benefits).

(3) Assignment of support rights. The institutionalized spouse shall not be ineligible by reason of resources determined under paragraph (2) to be available for the cost of care where—

(A) the institutionalized spouse has assigned to the State any rights to support from the community spouse;

(B) the institutionalized spouse lacks the ability to execute an assignment due to physical or mental impairment but the State has the right to bring a support proceeding against a community spouse without such assignment; or

(C) the State determines that denial of eligibility would work an undue hardship.

(4) Separate treatment of resources after eligibility for benefits established. During the continuous period in which an institutionalized spouse is in an institution and after the month in which an institutionalized spouse is determined to be eligible for benefits under this title [42 USCS §§ 1396 et seq.], no resources of the community spouse shall be deemed available to the institutionalized spouse.

(5) Resources defined. In this section, the term "resources" does not include—

(A) resources excluded under subsection (a) or (d) of section 1613 [42 USCS § 1382b(a) or (d)], and

(B) resources that would be excluded under section 1613(a)(2)(A) [42 USCS § 1382b(a)(2)(A)] but for the limitation on total value described in such section.

(d) Protecting income for community spouse. (1) Allowances to be offset from income of institutionalized spouse. After an institutionalized spouse is determined or redetermined to be eligible for medical assistance, in determining the amount of the spouse's income that is to be applied monthly to payment for the costs of care in the institution, there shall be deducted from the spouse's monthly income the following amounts in the following order:

(A) A personal needs allowance (described in section 1902(q)(1) [42 USCS § 1396a(q)(1)]), in an amount not less than the amount specified in section 1902(q)(2) [42 USCS § 1396a(q)(2)].

(B) A community spouse monthly income allowance (as defined in paragraph (2)), but only to the extent income of the institutionalized spouse is made available to (or for the benefit of) the community spouse.

(C) A family allowance, for each family member, equal to at least ⅓ of the amount by which the amount described in paragraph (3)(A)(i) exceeds the amount of the monthly income of that family member.

(D) Amounts for incurred expenses for medical or remedial care for the institutionalized spouse (as provided under section 1902(r) [42 USCS § 1396a(r)]).

In subparagraph (C), the term "family member" only includes minor or dependent children, dependent parents, or dependent siblings of the institutionalized or community spouse who are residing with the community spouse.

(2) Community spouse monthly income allowance defined. In this section (except as provided in paragraph (5)), the "community spouse monthly income allowance" for a community spouse is an amount by which—

(A) except as provided in subsection (e), the minimum monthly maintenance needs allowance (established under and in accordance with paragraph (3)) for the spouse, exceeds

(B) the amount of monthly income otherwise available to the community spouse (determined without regard to such an allowance).

(3) Establishment of minimum monthly maintenance needs allowance. (A) In general. Each State shall establish a minimum monthly maintenance needs allowance for each community spouse which, subject to subparagraph (C), is equal to or exceeds—

(i) the applicable percent (described in subparagraph (B)) of 1/12 of the income official poverty line (defined by the Office of Management and Budget and revised annually in accordance with section 673(2) of the Omnibus Budget Reconciliation Act of 1981 [42 USCS § 9902(2)]) for a family unit of 2 members; plus

(ii) an excess shelter allowance (as defined in paragraph (4)).

A revision of the official poverty line referred to in clause (i) shall apply to medical assistance furnished during and after the second calendar quarter that begins after the date of publication of the revision.

(B) Applicable percent. For purposes of subparagraph (A)(i), the "applicable percent" described in this paragraph, effective as of—

(i) September 30, 1989, is 122 percent,

(ii) July 1, 1991, is 133 percent, and

(iii) July 1, 1992, is 150 percent.

(C) Cap on minimum monthly maintenance needs allowance. The minimum monthly maintenance needs allowance established under subparagraph (A) may not exceed $1,500 (subject to adjustment under subsections (e) and (g)).

(4) Excess shelter allowance defined. In paragraph (3)(A)(ii), the term "excess shelter allowance" means, for a community spouse, the amount by which the sum of—

(A) the spouse's expenses for rent or mortgage payment (including principal and interest), taxes and insurance and, in the case of a condominium or cooperative, required maintenance charge, for the community spouse's principal residence, and

(B) the standard utility allowance (used by the State under section 5(e) of the Food and Nutrition Act of 2008 [7 USCS § 2014(e)]) or, if the State does not use such an allowance, the spouse's actual utility expenses,

exceeds 30 percent of the amount described in paragraph (3)(A)(i), except that, in the case of a condominium or cooperative, for which a maintenance charge is included under subparagraph (A), any allowance under subparagraph (B) shall be reduced to the extent the maintenance charge includes utility expenses.

(5) Court ordered support. If a court has entered an order against an institutionalized spouse for monthly income for the support of the community spouse, the community spouse monthly income allowance for the spouse shall be not less than the amount of the monthly income so ordered.

(6) Application of "income first" rule to revision of community spouse resource allowance. For purposes of this subsection and subsections (c) and (e), a State must consider that all income of the institutionalized spouse that could be made available to a community spouse, in accordance with the calculation of the community spouse monthly income allowance under this subsection, has been made available before the State allocates to the community spouse an amount of resources adequate to provide the difference between the minimum monthly maintenance needs allowance and all income available to the community spouse.

(e) Notice and fair hearing. (1) Notice. Upon—

(A) a determination of eligibility for medical assistance of an institutionalized spouse, or

(B) a request by either the institutionalized spouse, or the community spouse, or a representative acting on behalf of either spouse,

each State shall notify both spouses (in the case described in subparagraph (A)) or the spouse making the request (in the case described in subparagraph (B)) of the amount of the community spouse monthly income allowance (described in subsection (d)(1)(B)), of the amount of any family allowances (described in subsection (d)(1)(C)), of the method for computing the amount of the community spouse resources allowance permitted under subsection (f), and of the spouse's right to a fair hearing under this subsection respecting ownership or availability of income or resources, and the determination of the community spouse monthly income or resource allowance.

(2) Fair hearing. (A) In general. If either the institutionalized spouse or the community spouse is dissatisfied with a determination of—

(i) the community spouse monthly income allowance;

(ii) the amount of monthly income otherwise available to the community spouse (as applied under subsection (d)(2)(B));

(iii) the computation of the spousal share of resources under subsection (c)(1);

(iv) the attribution of resources under subsection (c)(2); or

(v) the determination of the community spouse resource allowance (as defined in subsection (f)(2));

such spouse is entitled to a fair hearing described in section 1902(a)(3) [42 USCS § 1396a(a)(3)] with respect to such determination if an application for benefits under this title [42 USCS §§ 1396 et seq.] has been made on behalf of the institutionalized spouse. Any such hearing respecting the determination of the community spouse resource allowance shall be held within 30 days of the date of the request for the hearing.

(B) Revision of minimum monthly maintenance needs allowance. If either such spouse establishes that the community spouse needs income, above the level otherwise provided by the minimum monthly maintenance needs allowance, due to exceptional circumstances resulting in significant financial duress, there shall be substituted, for the minimum monthly maintenance needs allowance in subsection (d)(2)(A), an amount adequate to provide such additional income as is necessary.

(C) Revision of community spouse resource allowance. If either such spouse establishes that the community spouse resource allowance (in relation to the amount of income generated by such an allowance) is inadequate to raise the community spouse's income to the minimum monthly maintenance needs allowance, there shall be substituted, for the community spouse resource allowance under subsection (f)(2), an amount adequate to provide such a minimum monthly maintenance needs allowance.

(f) Permitting transfer of resources to community spouse. (1) In general. An institutionalized spouse may, without regard to section 1917(c)(1) [42 USCS § 1396p(c)(1)], transfer an amount equal to the community spouse resource allowance (as defined in paragraph (2)), but only to the extent the resources of the institutionalized spouse are transferred to (or for the sole benefit of) the community spouse. The transfer under the preceding sentence shall be made as soon as practicable after the date of the initial determination of eligibility, taking into account such time as may be necessary to obtain a court order under paragraph (3).

(2) Community spouse resource allowance defined. In paragraph (1), the "community spouse resource allowance" for a community spouse is an amount (if any) by which—

(A) the greatest of—

(i) $12,000 (subject to adjustment under subsection (g)), or, if greater (but not to exceed the amount specified in clause (ii)(II)) an amount specified under the State plan,

(ii) the lesser of (I) the spousal share computed under subsection (c)(1), or (II) $60,000 (subject to adjustment under subsection (g)),

(iii) the amount established under subsection (e)(2); or

(iv) the amount transferred under a court order under paragraph (3);

exceeds

(B) the amount of the resources otherwise available to the community spouse (determined without regard to such an allowance).

(3) Transfers under court orders. If a court has entered an order against an institutionalized spouse for the support of the community spouse, section 1917 [42 USCS § 1396p] shall not apply to amounts of resources transferred pursuant to such order for the support of the spouse or a family member (as defined in subsection (d)(1)).

(g) Indexing dollar amounts. For services furnished during a calendar year after 1989, the dollar amounts specified in subsections (d)(3)(C), (f)(2)(A)(i), and (f)(2)(A)(ii)(II) shall be increased by the same percentage as the percentage increase in the consumer price index for all urban consumers (all items; U.S. city average) between September 1988 and the September before the calendar year involved.

(h) Definitions. In this section:

(1) The term "institutionalized spouse" means an individual who—

(A) is in a medical institution or nursing facility or who (at the option of the State) is described in section 1902(a)(10)(A)(ii)(VI) [42 USCS § 1396a(a)(10)(A)(ii)(VI)], and

(B) is married to a spouse who is not in a medical institution or nursing facility;

but does not include any such individual who is not likely to meet the requirements of subparagraph (A) for at least 30 consecutive days.

(2) The term "community spouse" means the spouse of an institutionalized spouse.

(Aug. 14, 1935, ch 531, Title XIX, § 1924, as added July 1, 1988, P. L. 100-360, Title III, § 303(a)(1)(B), 102 Stat. 754; Oct. 13, 1988, P. L. 100-485, Title VI, § 608(d)(16)(A), 102 Stat. 2417; Dec. 19, 1989, P. L. 101-239, Title VI, Subtitle B, Part 2, § 6411(e)(3), 103 Stat. 2271; Nov. 5, 1990, P. L. 101-508, Title IV, Subtitle B, Part 4, Subpart B, § 4714(a)–(c), Subpart D, § 4744(b)(1), 104 Stat. 1388-191, 1388-198; Aug. 10, 1993, P. L. 103-66, Title XIII, Ch 2, Subch B, Part II, § 13611(d)(2), Part V, § 13643(c)(1), 107 Stat. 627, 647; May 18, 1994, P. L. 103-252, Title I, § 125(b), 108 Stat. 650; Aug. 5, 1997, P. L. 105-33, Title IV, Subtitle I, § 4802(b)(1), 111 Stat. 549; Feb. 8, 2006, P. L. 109-171, Title VI, Subtitle A, Ch. 2, Subch. A, § 6013(a), 120 Stat. 64; May 22, 2008, P. L. 110-234, Title IV, Subtitle A, Part I, § 4002(b)(1)(B), (2)(V), 122 Stat. 1096, 1097; June 18, 2008, P. L. 110-246, § 4(a), Title IV, Subtitle A, Part I, § 4002(b)(1)(B), (2)(V), 122 Stat. 1664, 1857, 1858.)

HISTORY; ANCILLARY LAWS AND DIRECTIVES

Other provisions:

Protection for recipients of home and community-based services against spousal impoverishment. Act March 23, 2010, P. L. 111-148, Title II, Subtitle E, § 2404, 124 Stat. 305, provides: "During the 5-year period that begins on January 1, 2014, section 1924(h)(1)(A) of the Social Security Act (42 U.S.C. 1396r-5(h)(1)(A)) shall be applied as though 'is eligible for medical assistance for home and community-based services provided under subsection (c), (d), or (i) of section 1915 [42 USCS § 1396n], under a waiver approved under section 1115 [42 USCS § 1315], or who is eligible for such medical assistance by reason of being determined eligible under section 1902(a)(10)(C) [42 USCS § 1396a(a)(10)(C)] or by reason of section 1902(f) [42 USCS § 1396a(f)] or otherwise on the basis of a reduction of income based on costs incurred for medical or other remedial care, or who is eligible for medical assistance for home and community-based attendant services and supports under section 1915(k) [42 USCS § 1396n(k)]' were substituted in such section for '(at the option of the State) is described in section 1902(a)(10)(A)(ii)(VI)'.".

§ 1396r-8. Payment for covered outpatient drugs [Caution: See prospective amendment note below.]

(a) Requirement for rebate agreement. (1) In general. In order for payment to be available under section 1903(a) [42 USCS § 1396b(a)] or under part B of title XVIII [42 USCS §§ 1395j et seq.] for covered outpatient drugs of a manufacturer, the manufacturer must have entered into and have in effect a rebate agreement described in subsection (b) with the Secretary, on behalf of States (except that, the Secretary may authorize a State to enter directly into agreements with a manufacturer), and must meet the requirements of paragraph (5) (with respect to drugs purchased by a covered entity on or after the first day of the first month that begins after the date of the enactment of title VI of the Veterans Health Care Act of 1992 [enacted Nov. 4, 1992]) and paragraph (6). Any agreement between a State and a manufacturer prior to April 1, 1991, shall be deemed to have been entered into on January 1, 1991, and payment to such manufacturer shall be retroactively calculated as if the agreement between the manufacturer and the State had been entered into on January 1, 1991. If a manufacturer has not entered into such an agreement before March 1, 1991, such an agreement, subsequently entered into, shall become effective as of the date on which the agreement is entered into or, at State option, on any date thereafter on or before the first day of the calendar quarter that begins more than 60 days after the date the agreement is entered into.

(2) Effective date. Paragraph (1) shall first apply to drugs dispensed under this title [42 USCS §§ 1396 et seq.] on or after January 1, 1991.

(3) Authorizing payment for drugs not covered under rebate agreements. Paragraph (1), and section 1903(i)(10)(A) [42 USCS § 1396b(i)(10)(A)], shall not apply to the dispensing of a single source drug or innovator multiple source drug if (A)(i) the State has made a determination that the availability of the drug is essential to the health of beneficiaries under the State plan for medical assistance; (ii) such drug has been given a rating of 1-A by the Food and Drug Administration; and (iii)(I) the physician has obtained approval for use of the drug in advance of its dispensing in accordance with a prior authorization program described in subsection (d), or (II) the Secretary has reviewed and approved the State's determination under subparagraph (A); or (B) the Secretary determines that in the first calendar quarter of 1991, there were extenuating circumstances.

(4) Effect on existing agreements. In the case of a rebate agreement in effect between a State and a manufacturer on the date of the enactment of this section [Nov. 5, 1990], such agreement, for the initial agreement period specified therein, shall be considered to be a rebate agreement in compliance with this section with respect to that State, if the State agrees to report to the Secretary any rebates paid pursuant to the agreement and such agreement provides for a minimum aggregate rebate of 10 percent of the State's total expenditures under the State plan for coverage of the manufacturer's drugs under this title [42 USCS §§ 1396 et seq.]. If, after the initial agreement period, the State establishes to the satisfaction of the Secretary that an agreement in effect on the date of the enactment of this section [enacted Nov. 5, 1990] provides for rebates that are at least as large as the rebates otherwise required under this section, and the State agrees to report any rebates under the agreement to the Secretary, the agreement shall be considered to be a rebate agreement in compliance with the section for the renewal periods of such agreement.

(5) Limitation on prices of drugs purchased by covered entities. (A) Agreement with Secretary. A manufacturer meets the requirements of this paragraph if the manufacturer has entered into an agreement with the Secretary that meets the requirements of section 340B of the Public Health Service Act [42 USCS § 256b] with respect to covered outpatient drugs purchased by a covered entity on or after the first day of the first month that begins after the date of the enactment of this paragraph.

(B) Covered entity defined. In this subsection, the term "covered entity" means an entity described in section 340B(a)(4) of the Public Health Service Act [42 USCS § 256b(a)(4)] and a children's hospital described in section 1886(d)(1)(B)(iii) [42 USCS § 1395ww(d)(1)(B)(iii)] which meets the requirements of clauses (i) and (iii) of section 340B(b)(4)(L) of the Public Health Service Act [42 USCS § 256b(b)(4)(L)] and which would meet the requirements of clause (ii) of such section if that clause were applied by taking into account the percentage of care provided by the hospital to patients eligible for medical assistance under a State plan under this title [42 USCS §§ 1396 et seq.].

(C) Establishment of alternative mechanism to ensure against duplicate discounts or rebates. If the Secretary does not establish a mechanism under section 340B(a)(5)(A) of the Public Health Service Act [42 USCS § 256b(a)(5)(A)] within 12 months of the date of the enactment of such section [enacted Nov. 4, 1992], the following requirements shall apply:

(i) Entities. Each covered entity shall inform the single State agency under section 1902(a)(5) [42 USCS § 1396a(a)(5)] when it is seeking reimbursement from the State plan for medical assistance described in section 1905(a)(12) [42 USCS § 1396d(a)(12)] with respect to a unit of any covered outpatient drug which is subject to an agreement under section 340B(a) of such Act [42 USCS § 256b(a)].

(ii) State agency. Each such single State agency shall provide a means by which a covered entity shall indicate on any drug reimbursement claims form (or format, where electronic claims management is used) that a unit of the drug that is the subject of the form is subject to an agreement under section 340B of such Act [42 USCS § 256b], and not submit to any manufacturer a claim for a rebate payment under subsection (b) with respect to such a drug.

(D) Effect of subsequent amendments. In determining whether an agreement under subparagraph (A) meets the requirements of section 340B of the Public Health Service Act [42 USCS § 256b], the Secretary shall not take into account any amendments to such section that are enacted after the enactment of title VI of the Veterans Health Care Act of 1992 [enacted Nov. 4, 1992].

(E) Determination of compliance. A manufacturer is deemed to meet the requirements of this paragraph if the manufacturer establishes to the satisfaction of the Secretary that the manufacturer would comply (and has offered to comply) with the provisions of section 340B of the Public Health Service Act [42 USCS § 256b] (as in effect immediately after the enactment of this paragraph [enacted Nov. 4, 1992]) and would have entered into an agreement under such section (as such section was in effect at such time), but for a legislative change in such section after the date of the enactment of this paragraph.

(6) Requirements relating to master agreements for drugs procured by department of veterans affairs and certain other Federal agencies. (A) In general. A manufacturer meets the requirements of this paragraph if the manufacturer complies with the provisions of section 8126 of title 38, United States Code, including the requirement of entering into a master agreement with the Secretary of Veterans Affairs under such section.

(B) Effect of subsequent amendments. In determining whether a master agreement described in subparagraph (A) meets the requirements of section 8126 of title 38, United States Code, the Secretary shall not take into account any amendments to such section that are enacted after the enactment of title VI of the Veterans Health Care Act of 1992 [enacted Nov. 4, 1992].

(C) Determination of compliance. A manufacturer is deemed to meet the requirements of this paragraph if the manufacturer establishes to the satisfaction of the Secretary that the manufacturer would comply (and has offered to comply) with the provisions of section 8126 of title 38, United States Code (as in effect immediately after the enactment of this paragraph) and would have entered into an agreement under such section (as such section was in effect at such time), but for a legislative change in such section after the date of the enactment of this paragraph.

(7) Requirement for submission of utilization data for certain physician administered drugs. (A) Single source drugs. In order for payment to be available under section 1903(a) [42 USCS § 1396b(a)] for a covered outpatient drug that is a single source drug that is physician administered under this title [42 USCS §§ 1396 et seq.] (as determined by the Secretary), and that is administered on or after January 1, 2006, the State shall provide for the collection and submission of such utilization data and coding (such as J-codes and National Drug Code numbers) for each such drug as the Secretary may specify as necessary to identify the manufacturer of the drug in order to secure rebates under this section for drugs administered for which payment is made under this title [42 USCS §§ 1396 et seq.].

(B) Multiple source drugs. (i) Identification of most frequently physician administered multiple source drugs. Not later than January 1, 2007, the Secretary shall publish a list of the 20 physician administered multiple source drugs that the Secretary determines have the highest dollar volume of physician administered drugs dispensed under this title [42 USCS §§ 1396 et seq.]. The Secretary may modify such list from year to year to reflect changes in such volume.

(ii) Requirement. In order for payment to be available under section 1903(a) [42 USCS § 1396b(a)] for a covered outpatient drug that is a multiple source drug that is physician administered (as determined by the Secretary), that is on the list published under clause (i), and that is administered on or after January 1, 2008, the State shall provide for the submission of such utilization data and coding (such as J-codes and National Drug Code numbers) for each such drug as the Secretary may specify as necessary to identify the manufacturer of the drug in order to secure rebates under this section.

(C) Use of NDC codes. Not later than January 1, 2007, the information shall be submitted under subparagraphs (A) and (B)(ii) using National Drug Code codes unless the Secretary specifies that an alternative coding system should be used.

(D) Hardship waiver. The Secretary may delay the application of subparagraph (A) or (B)(ii), or both, in the case of a State to prevent hardship to States which require additional time to implement the reporting system required under the respective subparagraph.

(b) Terms of rebate agreement. (1) Periodic rebates. (A) In general. A rebate agreement under this subsection shall require the manufacturer to provide, to each State plan approved under this title [42 USCS §§ 1396 et seq.], a rebate for a rebate period in an amount specified in subsection (c) for covered outpatient drugs of the manufacturer dispensed after December 31, 1990, for which payment was made under the State plan for such period, including such drugs dispensed to individuals enrolled with a Medicaid managed care organization if the organization is responsible for coverage of such drugs. Such rebate shall be paid by the manufacturer not later than 30 days after the date of receipt of the information described in paragraph (2) for the period involved.

(B) Offset against medical assistance. Amounts received by a State under this section (or under an agreement authorized by the Secretary under subsection (a)(1) or an agreement described in subsection (a)(4)) in any quarter shall be considered to be a reduction in the amount expended under the State plan in the quarter for medical assistance for purposes of section 1903(a)(1) [42 USCS § 1396b(a)(1)].

(C) Special rule for increased minimum rebate percentage. (i) In general. In addition to the amounts applied as a reduction under subparagraph (B), for rebate periods beginning on or after January 1, 2010, during a fiscal year, the Secretary shall reduce payments to a State under section 1903(a) [42 USCS § 1396b(a)] in the manner specified in clause (ii), in an amount equal to the product of—

(I) 100 percent minus the Federal medical assistance percentage applicable to the rebate period for the State; and

(II) the amounts received by the State under such subparagraph that are attributable (as estimated by the Secretary based on utilization and other data) to the increase in the minimum rebate percentage effected by the amendments made by subsections (a)(1), (b), and (d) of section 2501 of the Patient Protection and Affordable Care Act, taking into account the additional drugs included under the amendments made by subsection (c) of section 2501 of such Act. The Secretary shall adjust such payment reduction for a calendar quarter to the extent the Secretary determines, based upon subsequent utilization and other data, that the reduction for such quarter was greater or less than the amount of payment reduction that should have been made.

(ii) Manner of payment reduction. The amount of the payment reduction under clause (i) for a State for a quarter shall be deemed an overpayment to the State under this title to be disallowed against the State's regular quarterly draw for all Medicaid spending under section 1903(d)(2) [42 USCS § 1396b(d)(2)]. Such a disallowance is not subject to a reconsideration under section 1116(d) [42 USCS § 1316(d)].

(2) State provision of information. (A) State responsibility. Each State agency under this title [42 USCS §§ 1396 et seq.] shall report to each manufacturer not later than 60 days after the end of each rebate period and in a form consistent with a standard reporting format established by the Secretary, information on the total number of units of each dosage form and strength and package size of each covered outpatient drug dispensed after December 31, 1990, for which payment was made under the plan during the period, including such information reported by each Medicaid managed care organization, and shall promptly transmit a copy of such report to the Secretary.

(B) Audits. A manufacturer may audit the information provided (or required to be provided) under subparagraph (A). Adjustments to rebates shall be made to the extent that information indicates that utilization was greater or less than the amount previously specified.

(3) Manufacturer provision of price information. (A) In general. Each manufacturer with an agreement in effect under this section shall report to the Secretary—

(i) not later than 30 days after the last day of each rebate period under the agreement—

(I) on the average manufacturer price (as defined in subsection (k)(1)) for covered outpatient drugs for the rebate period under the agreement (including for all such drugs that are sold under a new drug application approved under section 505(c) of the Federal Food, Drug, and Cosmetic Act [21 USCS § 355(c)]); and

(II) for single source drugs and innovator multiple source drugs (including all such drugs that are sold under a new drug application approved under section 505(c) of the Federal Food, Drug, and Cosmetic Act [21 USCS § 355(c)]), on the manufacturer's best price (as defined in subsection (c)(1)(C)) for such drugs for the rebate period under the agreement;

(ii) not later than 30 days after the date of entering into an agreement under this section on the average manufacturer price (as defined in subsection (k)(1)) as of October 1, 1990[,] for each of the manufacturer's covered outpatient drugs (including for such drugs that are sold under a new drug application approved under section 505(c) of the Federal Food, Drug, and Cosmetic Act [21 USCS § 355(c)]); and

(iii) for calendar quarters beginning on or after January 1, 2004, in conjunction with reporting required under clause (i) and by National Drug Code (including package size)—

(I) the manufacturer's average sales price (as defined in section 1847A(c) [42 USCS § 1395w-3a(c)]) and the total number of units specified under section 1847A(b)(2)(A) [42 USCS § 1395w-3a(b)(2)(A)];

(II) if required to make payment under section 1847A [42 USCS § 1395w-3a], the manufacturer's wholesale acquisition cost, as defined in subsection (c)(6) of such section; and

(III) information on those sales that were made at a nominal price or otherwise described in section 1847A(c)(2)(B) [42 USCS § 1395w-3a(c)(2)(B)];

for a drug or biological described in subparagraph (C), (D), (E), or (G) of section 1842(o)(1) [42 USCS § 1395u(o)(1)] or section 1881(b)(13)(A)(ii) [42 USCS § 1395rr(b)(13)(A)(ii)], and, for calendar quarters beginning on or after January 1, 2007 and only with respect to the information described in subclause (III), for covered outpatient drugs.

Information reported under this subparagraph is subject to audit by the Inspector General of the Department of Health and Human Services. Beginning July 1, 2006, the Secretary shall provide on a monthly basis to States under subparagraph (D)(iv) the most recently reported average manufacturer prices for single source drugs and for multiple source drugs and shall, on at least a quarterly basis, update the information posted on the website under subparagraph (D)(v).

(B) Verification surveys of average manufacturer price and manufacturer's average sales price. The Secretary may survey wholesalers and manufacturers that directly distribute their covered outpatient drugs, when necessary, to verify manufacturer prices and manufacturer's average sales prices (including wholesale acquisition cost) if required to make payment reported under subparagraph (A). The Secretary may impose a civil monetary penalty in an amount not to exceed $100,000 on a wholesaler, manufacturer, or direct seller, if the wholesaler, manufacturer, or direct seller of a covered outpatient drug refuses a request for information about charges or prices by the Secretary in connection with a survey under this subparagraph or knowingly provides false information. The provisions of section 1128A [42 USCS § 1320a-7a] (other than subsections (a) (with respect to amounts of penalties or additional assessments) and (b)) shall apply to a civil money penalty under this subparagraph in the same manner as such provisions apply to a penalty or proceeding under section 1128A(a) [42 USCS § 1320a-7a(a)].

(C) Penalties. (i) Failure to provide timely information. In the case of a manufacturer with an agreement under this section that fails to provide information required under subparagraph (A) on a timely basis, the amount of the penalty shall be increased by $10,000 for each day in which such information has not been provided and such amount shall be paid to the Treasury, and, if such information is not reported within 90 days of the deadline imposed, the agreement shall be suspended for services furnished after the end of the 90-day period and until the date such information is reported (but in no case shall such suspension be for a period of less than 30 days).

(ii) False information. Any manufacturer with an agreement under this section that knowingly provides false information is subject to a civil money penalty in an amount not to exceed $100,000 for each item of false information. Such civil money penalties are in addition to other penalties as may be prescribed by law. The provisions of section 1128A [42 USCS

§ 1320a-7a] (other than subsections (a) and (b)) shall apply to a civil money penalty under this subparagraph in the same manner as such provisions apply to a penalty or proceeding under section 1128A(a) [42 USCS § 1320a-7a(a)].

(D) Confidentiality of information. Notwithstanding any other provision of law, information disclosed by manufacturers or wholesalers under this paragraph or under an agreement with the Secretary of Veterans Affairs described in subsection (a)(6)(A)(ii) (other than the wholesale acquisition cost for purposes of carrying out section 1847A [42 USCS § 1395w-3a]) is confidential and shall not be disclosed by the Secretary or the Secretary of Veterans Affairs or a State agency (or contractor therewith) in a form which discloses the identity of a specific manufacturer or wholesaler, prices charged for drugs by such manufacturer or wholesaler, except—

(i) as the Secretary determines to be necessary to carry out this section, to carry out section 1847A [42 USCS § 1395w-3a] (including the determination and implementation of the payment amount), or to carry out section 1847B [42 USCS § 1395w-3b],

(ii) to permit the Comptroller General to review the information provided,

(iii) to permit the Director of the Congressional Budget Office to review the information provided,

(iv) to States to carry out this title [42 USCS §§ 1396 et seq.], and

(v) to the Secretary to disclose (through a website accessible to the public) average manufacturer prices.

The previous sentence shall also apply to information disclosed under section 1860D-2(d)(2) or 1860D-4(c)(2)(E) [42 USCS § 1395w-102(d)(2) or 1395w-104(c)(2)(E)] and drug pricing data reported under the first sentence of section 1860D-31(i)(1) [42 USCS § 1395w-141(i)(1)].

(4) Length of agreement. (A) In general. A rebate agreement shall be effective for an initial period of not less than 1 year and shall be automatically renewed for a period of not less than one year unless terminated under subparagraph (B).

(B) Termination. (i) By the Secretary. The Secretary may provide for termination of a rebate agreement for violation of the requirements of the agreement or other good cause shown. Such termination shall not be effective earlier than 60 days after the date of notice of such termination. The Secretary shall provide, upon request, a manufacturer with a hearing concerning such a termination, but such hearing shall not delay the effective date of the termination.

(ii) By a manufacturer. A manufacturer may terminate a rebate agreement under this section for any reason. Any such termination shall not be effective until the calendar quarter beginning at least 60 days after the date the manufacturer provides notice to the Secretary.

(iii) Effectiveness of termination. Any termination under this subparagraph shall not affect rebates due under the agreement before the effective date of its termination.

(iv) Notice to States. In the case of a termination under this subparagraph, the Secretary shall provide notice of such termination to the States within not less than 30 days before the effective date of such termination.

(v) Application to terminations of other agreements. The provisions of this subparagraph shall apply to the terminations of agreements described in section 340B(a)(1) of the Public Health Service Act [42 USCS § 256b(a)(1)] and master agreements described in section 8126(a) of title 38, United States Code.

(C) Delay before reentry. In the case of any rebate agreement with a manufacturer under this section which is terminated, another such agreement with the manufacturer (or a successor manufacturer) may not be entered into until a period of 1 calendar quarter has elapsed since the date of the termination, unless the Secretary finds good cause for an earlier reinstatement of such an agreement.

(c) Determination of amount of rebate. (1) Basic rebate for single source drugs and innovator multiple source drugs. (A) In general. Except as provided in paragraph (2), the amount of the rebate specified in this subsection for a rebate period (as defined in subsection (k)(8)) with respect to each dosage form and strength of a single source drug or an innovator multiple source drug shall be equal to the product of—

(i) the total number of units of each dosage form and strength paid for under the State plan in the rebate period (as reported by the State); and

(ii) subject to subparagraph (B)(ii), the greater of—

(I) the difference between the average manufacturer price and the best price (as defined in subparagraph (C)) for the dosage form and strength of the drug, or

(II) the minimum rebate percentage (specified in subparagraph (B)(i)) of such average manufacturer price, for the rebate period.

(B) Range of rebates required. (i) Minimum rebate percentage. For purposes of subparagraph (A)(ii)(II), the "minimum rebate percentage" for rebate periods beginning—

(I) after December 31, 1990, and before October 1, 1992, is 12.5 percent;

(II) after September 30, 1992, and before January 1, 1994, is 15.7 percent;

(III) after December 31, 1993, and before January 1, 1995, is 15.4 percent;

(IV) after December 31, 1994, and before January 1, 1996, is 15.2 percent;

(V) after December 31, 1995 and before January 1, 2010, is 15.1 percent; and

(VI) except as provided in clause (iii), after December 31, 2009, 23.1 percent.

(ii) Temporary limitation on maximum rebate amount. In no case shall the amount applied under subparagraph (A)(ii) for a rebate period beginning—

(I) before January 1, 1992, exceed 25 percent of the average manufacturer price; or

(II) after December 31, 1991, and before January 1, 1993, exceed 50 percent of the average manufacturer price.

(iii) Minimum rebate percentage for certain drugs. (I) In general. In the case of a single source drug or an innovator multiple source drug described in subclause (II), the minimum rebate percentage for rebate periods specified in clause (i)(VI) is 17.1 percent.

(II) Drug described. For purposes of subclause (I), a single source drug or an innovator multiple source drug described in this subclause is any of the following drugs:

(aa) A clotting factor for which a separate furnishing payment is made under section 1842(o)(5) [42 USCS § 1395u(o)(5)] and which is included on a list of such factors specified and updated regularly by the Secretary.

(bb) A drug approved by the Food and Drug Administration exclusively for pediatric indications.

(C) Best price defined. For purposes of this section—

(i) In general. The term "best price" means, with respect to a single source drug or innovator multiple source drug of a manufacturer (including the lowest price available to any entity for any such drug of a manufacturer that is sold under a new drug application approved under section 505(c) of the Federal Food, Drug, and Cosmetic Act [21 USCS § 355(c)]), the lowest price available from the manufacturer during the rebate period to any wholesaler, retailer, provider, health maintenance organization, nonprofit entity, or governmental entity within the United States, excluding—

(I) any prices charged on or after October 1, 1992, to the Indian Health Service, the Department of Veterans Affairs, a State home receiving funds under section 1741 of title 38, United States Code, the Department of Defense, the Public Health Service, or a covered entity described in subsection (a)(5)(B) (including inpatient prices charged to hospitals described in section 340B(a)(4)(L) of the Public Health Service Act [42 USCS § 256b(a)(4)(L)]);

(II) any prices charged under the Federal Supply Schedule of the General Services Administration;

(III) any prices used under a State pharmaceutical assistance program;

(IV) any depot prices and single award contract prices, as defined by the Secretary, of any agency of the Federal Government;

(V) the prices negotiated from drug manufacturers for covered discount card drugs under an endorsed discount card program under section 1860D-31 [42 USCS § 1395w-141]; and

(VI) any prices charged which are negotiated by a prescription drug plan under part D of title XVIII [42 USCS §§ 1395w-101 et seq.], by an MA-PD plan under part C of such title [42 USCS §§ 1395w-21 et seq.] with respect to covered part D drugs or by a qualified retiree prescription drug plan (as defined in section 1860D-22(a)(2) [42 USCS § 1395w-132(a)(2)]) with respect to such drugs on behalf of individuals entitled to benefits under part A [42 USCS §§ 1395c et seq.] or enrolled under part B of such title [42 USCS §§ 1395j et seq.], or any discounts provided by manufacturers under the Medicare coverage gap discount program under section 1860D-14A [42 USCS § 1395w-114a].

(ii) Special rules. The term "best price"—

(I) shall be inclusive of cash discounts, free goods that are contingent on any purchase requirement, volume discounts, and rebates (other than rebates under this section);

(II) shall be determined without regard to special packaging, labeling, or identifiers on the dosage form or product or package;

(III) shall not take into account prices that are merely nominal in amount; and

(IV) in the case of a manufacturer that approves, allows, or otherwise permits any other drug of the manufacturer to be sold under a new drug application approved under section 505(c) of the Federal Food, Drug, and Cosmetic Act [21 USCS § 355(c)], shall be inclusive of the lowest price for such authorized drug available from the manufacturer during the rebate period to any manufacturer, wholesaler, retailer, provider, health maintenance organization, nonprofit entity, or governmental entity within the United States, excluding those prices described in subclauses (I) through (IV) of clause (i).

(iii) Application of auditing and recordkeeping requirements. With respect to a covered entity described in section 340B(a)(4)(L) of the Public Health Service Act [42 USCS § 256b(a)(4)(L)], any drug purchased for inpatient use shall be subject to the auditing and recordkeeping requirements described in section 340B(a)(5)(C) of the Public Health Service Act [42 USCS § 256b(a)(5)(C)].

(D) Limitation on sales at a nominal price. (i) In general. For purposes of subparagraph (C)(ii)(III) and subsection (b)(3)(A)(iii)(III), only sales by a manufacturer of covered outpatient drugs at nominal prices to the following shall be considered to be sales at a nominal price or merely nominal in amount:

(I) A covered entity described in section 340B(a)(4) of the Public Health Service Act [42 USCS § 256b(a)(4)].

(II) An intermediate care facility for the mentally retarded.

(III) A State-owned or operated nursing facility.

(IV) An entity that—

(aa) is described in section 501(c)(3) of the Internal Revenue Code of 1986 [26 USCS § 501(c)(3)] and exempt from tax under section 501(a) of such Act [26 USCS § 501(a)] or is State-owned or operated; and

(bb) would be a covered entity described in section 340(B)(a)(4) [340B(a)(4)] of the Public Health Service Act [42 USCS § 256b(a)(4)] insofar as the entity provides the same type of services to the same type of populations as a covered entity described in such section provides, but does not receive funding under a provision of law referred to in such section;

(V) A public or nonprofit entity, or an entity based at an institution of higher learning whose primary purpose is to provide health care services to students of that institution, that provides a service or services described under section 1001(a) of the Public Health Service Act, 42 U.S.C. 300.

(VI) Any other facility or entity that the Secretary determines is a safety net provider to which sales of such drugs at a nominal price would be appropriate based on the factors described in clause (ii).

(ii) Factors. The factors described in this clause with respect to a facility or entity are the following:

(I) The type of facility or entity.

(II) The services provided by the facility or entity.

(III) The patient population served by the facility or entity.

(IV) The number of other facilities or entities eligible to purchase at nominal prices in the same service area.

(iii) Nonapplication. Clause (i) shall not apply with respect to sales by a manufacturer at a nominal price of covered outpatient drugs pursuant to a master agreement under section 8126 of title 38, United States Code [38 USCS § 8126].

(iv) Rule of construction. Nothing in this subparagraph shall be construed to alter any existing statutory or regulatory prohibition on services with respect to an entity described in clause (i)(IV), including the prohibition set forth in section 1008 of the Public Health Service Act [42 USCS § 300a-6].

(2) Additional rebate for single source and innovator multiple source drugs. (A) In general. The amount of the rebate specified in this subsection for a rebate period, with respect to each dosage form and strength of a single source drug or an innovator multiple source drug, shall be increased by an amount equal to the product of—

(i) the total number of units of such dosage form and strength dispensed after December 31, 1990, for which payment was made under the State plan for the rebate period; and

(ii) the amount (if any) by which—

(I) the average manufacturer price for the dosage form and strength of the drug for the period, exceeds

(II) the average manufacturer price for such dosage form and strength for the calendar quarter beginning July 1, 1990 (without regard to whether or not the drug has been sold or transferred to an entity, including a division or subsidiary of the manufacturer, after the first day of such quarter), increased by the percentage by which the consumer price index for all urban consumers (United States city average) for the month before the month in which the rebate period begins exceeds such index for September 1990.

(B) Treatment of subsequently approved drugs. In the case of a covered outpatient drug approved by the Food and Drug Administration after October 1, 1990, clause (ii)(II) of subparagraph (A) shall be applied by substituting "the first full calendar quarter after the day on which the drug was first marketed" for "the calendar quarter beginning July 1, 1990" and "the month prior to the first month of the first full calendar quarter after the day on which the drug was first marketed" for "September 1990".

(C) Treatment of new formulations. In the case of a drug that is a line extension of a single source drug or an innovator multiple source drug that is an oral solid dosage form, the rebate obligation with respect to such drug under this section shall be the amount computed under this section for such new drug or, if greater, the product of—

(i) the average manufacturer price of the line extension of a single source drug or an innovator multiple source drug that is an oral solid dosage form;

(ii) the highest additional rebate (calculated as a percentage of average manufacturer price) under this section for any strength of the original single source drug or innovator multiple source drug; and

(iii) the total number of units of each dosage form and strength of the line extension product paid for under the State plan in the rebate period (as reported by the State).

In this subparagraph, the term "line extension" means, with respect to a drug, a new formulation of the drug, such as an extended release formulation.

(D) Maximum rebate amount. In no case shall the sum of the amounts applied under paragraph (1)(A)(ii) and this paragraph with respect to each dosage form and strength of a single source drug or an innovator multiple source drug for a rebate period beginning after December 31, 2009, exceed 100 percent of the average manufacturer price of the drug.

(3) Rebate for other drugs. (A) In general. The amount of the rebate paid to a State for a rebate period with respect to each dosage form and strength of covered outpatient drugs (other than single source drugs and innovator multiple source drugs) shall be equal to the product of—

(i) the applicable percentage (as described in subparagraph (B)) of the average manufacturer price for the dosage form and strength for the rebate period, and

(ii) the total number of units of such dosage form and strength dispensed after December 31, 1990, for which payment was made under the State plan for the rebate period.

(B) Applicable percentage defined. For purposes of subparagraph (A)(i), the "applicable percentage" for rebate periods beginning—

(i) before January 1, 1994, is 10 percent,

(ii) after December 31, 1993, and before January 1, 2010, is 11 percent; and

(iii) after December 31, 2009, is 13 percent.

(d) Limitations on coverage of drugs. (1) Permissible restrictions. (A) A State may subject to prior authorization any covered outpatient drug. Any such prior authorization program shall comply with the requirements of paragraph (5).

(B) A State may exclude or otherwise restrict coverage of a covered outpatient drug if—

(i) the prescribed use is not for a medically accepted indication (as defined in subsection (k)(6));

(ii) the drug is contained in the list referred to in paragraph (2);

(iii) the drug is subject to such restrictions pursuant to an agreement between a manufacturer and a State authorized by the Secretary under subsection (a)(1) or in effect pursuant to subsection (a)(4); or

(iv) the State has excluded coverage of the drug from its formulary established in accordance with paragraph (4).

(2) **[Caution: For provisions applicable before January 1, 2014, see 2010 amendment note below.]** List of drugs subject to restriction. The following drugs or classes of drugs, or their medical uses, may be excluded from coverage or otherwise restricted:

(A) Agents when used for anorexia, weight loss, or weight gain.

(B) Agents when used to promote fertility.

(C) Agents when used for cosmetic purposes or hair growth.

(D) Agents when used for the symptomatic relief of cough and colds.

(E) Prescription vitamins and mineral products, except prenatal vitamins and fluoride preparations.

(F) Nonprescription drugs.

(G) Covered outpatient drugs which the manufacturer seeks to require as a condition of sale that associated tests or monitoring services be purchased exclusively from the manufacturer or its designee.

(H) Agents when used for the treatment of sexual or erectile dysfunction, unless such agents are used to treat a condition, other than sexual or erectile dysfunction, for which the agents have been approved by the Food and Drug Administration.

(I)–(K) [Redesignated]

(3) Update of drug listings. The Secretary shall, by regulation, periodically update the list of drugs or classes of drugs described in paragraph (2) or their medical uses, which the Secretary has determined, based on data collected by surveillance and utilization review programs of State medical assistance programs, to be subject to clinical abuse or inappropriate use.

(4) Requirements for formularies. A State may establish a formulary if the formulary

meets the following requirements:

(A) The formulary is developed by a committee consisting of physicians, pharmacists, and other appropriate individuals appointed by the Governor of the State (or, at the option of the State, the State's drug use review board established under subsection (g)(3)).

(B) Except as provided in subparagraph (C), the formulary includes the covered outpatient drugs of any manufacturer which has entered into and complies with an agreement under subsection (a) (other than any drug excluded from coverage or otherwise restricted under paragraph (2)).

(C) A covered outpatient drug may be excluded with respect to the treatment of a specific disease or condition for an identified population (if any) only if, based on the drug's labeling (or, in the case of a drug the prescribed use of which is not approved under the Federal Food, Drug, and Cosmetic Act [21 USCS §§ 301 et seq.] but is a medically accepted indication, based on information from the appropriate compendia described in subsection (k)(6)), the excluded drug does not have a significant, clinically meaningful therapeutic advantage in terms of safety, effectiveness, or clinical outcome of such treatment for such population over other drugs included in the formulary and there is a written explanation (available to the public) of the basis for the exclusion.

(D) The State plan permits coverage of a drug excluded from the formulary (other than any drug excluded from coverage or otherwise restricted under paragraph (2)) pursuant to a prior authorization program that is consistent with paragraph (5).

(E) The formulary meets such other requirements as the Secretary may impose in order to achieve program savings consistent with protecting the health of program beneficiaries.

A prior authorization program established by a State under paragraph (5) is not a formulary subject to the requirements of this paragraph.

(5) Requirements of prior authorization programs. A State plan under this title [42 USCS §§ 1396 et seq.] may require, as a condition of coverage or payment for a covered outpatient drug for which Federal financial participation is available in accordance with this section, with respect to drugs dispensed on or after July 1, 1991, the approval of the drug before its dispensing for any medically accepted indication (as defined in subsection (k)(6)) only if the system providing for such approval—

(A) provides response by telephone or other telecommunication device within 24 hours of a request for prior authorization; and

(B) except with respect to the drugs on the list referred to in paragraph (2), provides for the dispensing of at least 72-hour supply of a covered outpatient prescription drug in an emergency situation (as defined by the Secretary).

(6) Other permissible restrictions. A State may impose limitations, with respect to all such drugs in a therapeutic class, on the minimum or maximum quantities per prescription or on the number of refills, if such limitations are necessary to discourage waste, and may address instances of fraud or abuse by individuals in any manner authorized under this Act [42 USCS §§ 301 et seq.].

(7) **[Caution: This paragraph applies to services furnished on or after January 1, 2014, as provided by § 2502(b) of Act March 23, 2010, P. L. 111-148, which appears as a note to this section.]** Non-excludable drugs. The following drugs or classes of drugs, or their medical uses, shall not be excluded from coverage:

(A) Agents when used to promote smoking cessation, including agents approved by the Food and Drug Administration under the over-the-counter monograph process for purposes of promoting, and when used to promote, tobacco cessation.

(B) Barbiturates.

(C) Benzodiazepines.

(e) Treatment of pharmacy reimbursement limits. (1) In general. During the period beginning on January 1, 1991, and ending on December 31, 1994—

(A) a State may not reduce the payment limits established by regulation under this title [42 USCS §§ 1396 et seq.] or any limitation described in paragraph (3) with respect to the ingredient cost of a covered outpatient drug or the dispensing fee for such a drug below the limits in effect as of January 1, 1991, and

(B) except as provided in paragraph (2), the Secretary may not modify by regulation the formula established under sections 447.331 through 447.334 of title 42, Code of Federal Regulations, in effect on November 5, 1990, to reduce the limits described in subparagraph (A).

(2) Special rule. If a State is not in compliance with the regulations described in paragraph (1)(B), paragraph (1)(A) shall not apply to such State until such State is in compliance with such regulations.

(3) Effect on State maximum allowable cost limitations. This section shall not supersede or affect provisions in effect prior to January 1,

1991, or after December 31, 1994, relating to any maximum allowable cost limitation established by a State for payment by the State for covered outpatient drugs, and rebates shall be made under this section without regard to whether or not payment by the State for such drugs is subject to such a limitation or the amount of such a limitation.

[(4)] Establishment of upper payment limits. Subject to paragraph (5), the Secretary shall establish a Federal upper reimbursement limit for each multiple source drug for which the FDA has rated three or more (or, effective January 1, 2007, two or more) products therapeutically and additional formulations are rated as such and shall use only such formulations when determining any such upper limit.

(5) Use of AMP in upper payment limits. Effective January 1, 2007, in applying the Federal upper reimbursement limit under paragraph (4) and section 447.332(b) of title 42 of the Code of Federal Regulations, the Secretary shall substitute 250 percent of the average manufacturer price (as computed without regard to customary prompt pay discounts extended to wholesalers) for 150 percent of the published price.

(f) Survey of retail prices; state payment and utilization rates; and performance rankings. (1) Survey of retail prices.

(A) Use of vendor. The Secretary may contract services for—

(i) the determination on a monthly basis of retail survey prices for covered outpatient drugs that represent a nationwide average of consumer purchase prices for such drugs, net of all discounts and rebates (to the extent any information with respect to such discounts and rebates is available); and

(ii) the notification of the Secretary when a drug product that is therapeutically and pharmaceutically equivalent and bioequivalent becomes generally available.

(B) Secretary response to notification of availability of multiple source products. If contractor notifies the Secretary under subparagraph (A)(ii) that a drug product described in such subparagraph has become generally available, the Secretary shall make a determination, within 7 days after receiving such notification, as to whether the product is now described in subsection (e)(4).

(C) Use of competitive bidding. In contracting for such services, the Secretary shall competitively bid for an outside vendor that has a demonstrated history in—

(i) surveying and determining, on a representative nationwide basis, retail prices for ingredient costs of prescription drugs;

(ii) working with retail pharmacies, commercial payers, and States in obtaining and disseminating such price information; and

(iii) collecting and reporting such price information on at least a monthly basis.

In contracting for such services, the Secretary may waive such provisions of the Federal Acquisition Regulation as are necessary for the efficient implementation of this subsection, other than provisions relating to confidentiality of information and such other provisions as the Secretary determines appropriate.

(D) Additional provisions. A contract with a vendor under this paragraph shall include such terms and conditions as the Secretary shall specify, including the following:

(i) The vendor must monitor the marketplace and report to the Secretary each time there is a new covered outpatient drug generally available.

(ii) The vendor must update the Secretary no less often than monthly on the retail survey prices for covered outpatient drugs.

(iii) The contract shall be effective for a term of 2 years.

(E) Availability of information to States. Information on retail survey prices obtained under this paragraph, including applicable information on single source drugs, shall be provided to States on at least a monthly basis. The Secretary shall devise and implement a means for providing access to each State agency designated under section 1902(a)(5) [42 USCS § 1396a(a)(5)] with responsibility for the administration or supervision of the administration of the State plan under this title [42 USCS §§ 1396 et seq.] of the retail survey price determined under this paragraph.

(2) Annual State report. Each State shall annually report to the Secretary information on—

(A) the payment rates under the State plan under this title [42 USCS §§ 1396 et seq.] for covered outpatient drugs;

(B) the dispensing fees paid under such plan for such drugs; and

(C) utilization rates for noninnovator multiple source drugs under such plan.

(3) Annual State performance rankings. (A) Comparative analysis. The Secretary annually shall compare, for the 50 most widely prescribed drugs identified by the Secretary, the national retail sales price data (collected under paragraph (1)) for such drugs with data on prices under this title [42 USCS §§ 1396 et seq.] for each such drug for each State.

(B) Availability of information. The Secretary shall submit to Congress and the States full information regarding the annual rankings made under subparagraph (A).

(4) Appropriation. Out of any funds in the Treasury not otherwise appropriated, there is appropriated to the Secretary of Health and Human Services $5,000,000 for each of fiscal years 2006 through 2010 to carry out this subsection.

(g) Drug use review. (1) In general. (A) In order to meet the requirement of section 1903(i)(10)(B) [42 USCS § 1396b(i)(10)(B)], a State shall provide, by not later than January 1, 1993, for a drug use review program described in paragraph (2) for covered outpatient drugs in order to assure that prescriptions (i) are appropriate, (ii) are medically necessary, and (iii) are not likely to result in adverse medical results. The program shall be designed to educate physicians and pharmacists to identify and reduce the frequency of patterns of fraud, abuse, gross overuse, or inappropriate or medically unnecessary care, among physicians, pharmacists, and patients, or associated with specific drugs or groups of drugs, as well as potential and actual severe adverse reactions to drugs including education on therapeutic appropriateness, overutilization and underutilization, appropriate use of generic products, therapeutic duplication, drug-disease contraindications, drug-drug interactions, incorrect drug dosage or duration of drug treatment, drug-allergy interactions, and clinical abuse/misuse.

(B) The program shall assess date on drug use against predetermined standards, consistent with the following:

(i) compendia which shall consist of the following:

(I) American Hospital Formulary Service Drug Information;

(II) United States Pharmacopeia-Drug Information (or its successor publications); and

(III) the DRUGDEX Information System; and

(IV) [Deleted]

(ii) the peer-reviewed medical literature.

(C) The Secretary, under the procedures established in section 1903 [42 USCS § 1396b], shall pay to each State an amount equal to 75 per centum of so much of the sums expended by the State plan during calendar years 1991 through 1993 as the Secretary determines is attributable to the statewide adoption of a drug use review program which conforms to the requirements of this subsection.

(D) States shall not be required to perform additional drug use reviews with respect to drugs dispensed to residents of nursing facilities which are in compliance with the drug regimen review procedures prescribed by the Secretary for such facilities in regulations implementing section 1919 [42 USCS § 1396r], currently at section 483.60 of title 42, Code of Federal Regulations.

(2) Description of program. Each drug use review program shall meet the following requirements for covered outpatient drugs:

(A) Prospective drug review. (i) The State plan shall provide for a review of drug therapy before each prescription is filled or delivered to an individual receiving benefits under this title [42 USCS §§ 1396 et seq.], typically at the point-of-sale or point of distribution. The review shall include screening for potential drug therapy problems due to therapeutic duplication, drug-disease contraindications, drug-drug interactions (including serious interactions with nonprescription or over-the-counter drugs), incorrect drug dosage or duration of drug treatment, drug-allergy interactions, and clinical abuse/misuse. Each State shall use the compendia and literature referred to in paragraph (1)(B) as its source of standards for such review.

(ii) As part of the State's prospective drug use review program under this subparagraph applicable State law shall establish standards for counseling of individuals receiving benefits under this title [42 USCS §§ 1396 et seq.] by pharmacists which includes at least the following:

(I) The pharmacist must offer to discuss with each individual receiving benefits under this title [42 USCS §§ 1396 et seq.] or caregiver of such individual (in person, whenever practicable, or through access to a telephone service which is toll-free for long-distance calls) who presents a prescription, matters which in the exercise of the pharmacist's professional judgment (consistent with State law respecting the provision of such information), the pharmacist deems significant including the following:

(aa) The name and description of the medication.

(bb) The route, dosage form, dosage, route of administration, and duration of drug therapy.

(cc) Special directions and precautions for preparation, administration and use by the patient.

(dd) Common severe side or adverse effects or interactions and therapeutic contraindications that may be encountered, including their avoidance, and the action required if they occur.

(ee) Techniques for self-monitoring drug therapy.

(ff) Proper storage.

(gg) Prescription refill information.

(hh) Action to be taken in the event of a missed dose.

(II) A reasonable effort must be made by the pharmacist to obtain, record, and maintain at least the following information regarding individuals receiving benefits under this title [42 USCS §§ 1396 et seq.]:

(aa) Name, address, telephone number, date of birth (or age) and gender.

(bb) Individual history where significant, including disease state or states, known allergies and drug reactions, and a comprehensive list of medications and relevant devices.

(cc) Pharmacist comments relevant to the individual's drug therapy.

Nothing in this clause shall be construed as requiring a pharmacist to provide consultation when an individual receiving benefits under this title [42 USCS §§ 1396 et seq.] or caregiver of such individual refuses such consultation, or to require verification of the offer to provide consultation or a refusal of such offer.

(B) Retrospective drug use review. The program shall provide, through its mechanized drug claims processing and information retrieval systems (approved by the Secretary under section 1903(r) [42 USCS § 1396b(r)]) or otherwise, for the ongoing periodic examination of claims data and other records in order to identify patterns of fraud, abuse, gross overuse, or inappropriate or medically unnecessary care, among physicians, pharmacists and individuals receiving benefits under this title [42 USCS §§ 1396 et seq.], or associated with specific drugs or groups of drugs.

(C) Application of standards. The program shall, on an ongoing basis, assess data on drug use against explicit predetermined standards (using the compendia and literature referred to in subsection [paragraph] (1)(B) as the source of standards for such assessment) including but not limited to monitoring for therapeutic appropriateness, overutilization and underutilization, appropriate use of generic products, therapeutic duplication, drug-disease contraindications, drug-drug interactions, incorrect drug dosage or duration of drug treatment, and clinical abuse/misuse and, as necessary, introduce remedial strategies, in order to improve the quality of care and to conserve program funds or personal expenditures.

(D) Educational program. The program shall, through its State drug use review board established under paragraph (3), either directly or through contracts with accredited health care educational institutions, State medical societies or State pharmacists associations/societies or other organizations as specified by the State, and using data provided by the State drug use review board on common drug therapy problems, provide for active and ongoing educational outreach programs (including the activities described in paragraph (3)(C)(iii) of this subsection) to educate practitioners on common drug therapy problems with the aim of improving prescribing or dispensing practices.

(3) State drug use review board. (A) Establishment. Each State shall provide for the establishment of a drug use review board (hereinafter referred to as the "DUR Board") either directly or through a contract with a private organization.

(B) Membership. The membership of the DUR Board shall include health care professionals who have recognized knowledge and expertise in one or more of the following:

(i) The clinically appropriate prescribing of covered outpatient drugs.

(ii) The clinically appropriate dispensing and monitoring of covered outpatient drugs.

(iii) Drug use review, evaluation, and intervention.

(iv) Medical quality assurance. The membership of the DUR Board shall be made up at least ⅓ but no more than 51 percent licensed and actively practicing physicians and at least ⅓ [* * *] licensed and actively practicing pharmacists.

(C) Activities. The activities of the DUR Board shall include but not be limited to the following:

(i) Retrospective DUR as defined in section [paragraph] (2)(B).

(ii) Application of standards as defined in section [paragraph] (2)(C).

(iii) Ongoing interventions for physicians and pharmacists, targeted toward therapy problems or individuals identified in the course of retrospective drug use reviews performed under this subsection. Intervention programs shall include, in appropriate instances, at least:

(I) information dissemination sufficient to ensure the ready availability to physicians and pharmacists in the State of information concerning its duties, powers, and basis for its standards;

(II) written, oral, or electronic reminders containing patient-specific or drug-specific (or both) information and suggested changes in prescribing or dispensing practices, communicated in a manner designed to ensure the privacy of patient-related information;

(III) use of face-to-face discussions between health care professionals who are experts in rational drug therapy and selected prescribers and pharmacists who have been targeted for educational intervention, including discussion of optimal prescribing, dispensing, or pharmacy care practices, and follow-up face-to-face discussions; and

(IV) intensified review or monitoring of selected prescribers or dispensers.

The Board shall re-evaluate interventions after an appropriate period of time to determine if the intervention improved the quality of drug therapy, to evaluate the success of the interventions and make modifications as necessary.

(D) Annual report. Each State shall require the DUR Board to prepare a report on an annual basis. The State shall submit a report on an annual basis to the Secretary which shall include a description of the activities of the Board, including the nature and scope of the prospective and retrospective drug use review programs, a summary of the interventions used, an assessment of the impact of these educational interventions on quality of care, and an estimate of the cost savings generated as a result of such program. The Secretary shall utilize such report in evaluating the effectiveness of each State's drug use review program.

(h) Electronic claims management. (1) In general. In accordance with chapter 35 of title 44, United States Code [44 USCS §§ 3501 et seq.] (relating to coordination of Federal information policy), the Secretary shall encourage each State agency to establish, as its principal means of processing claims for covered outpatient drugs under this title [42 USCS §§ 1396 et seq.], a point-of-sale electronic claims management system, for the purpose of performing on-line, real time eligibility verifications, claims data capture, adjudication of claims, and assisting pharmacists (and other authorized persons) in applying for and receiving payment.

(2) Encouragement. In order to carry out paragraph (1)—

(A) for calendar quarters during fiscal years 1991 and 1992, expenditures under the State plan attributable to development of a system described in paragraph (1) shall receive Federal financial participation under section 1903(a)(3)(A)(i) [42 USCS § 1396b(a)(3)(A)(i)] (at a matching rate of 90 percent) if the State acquires, through applicable competitive procurement process in the State, the most cost-effective telecommunications network and automatic data processing services and equipment; and

(B) the Secretary may permit, in the procurement described in subparagraph (A) in the application of part 433 of title 42, Code of Federal Regulations, and parts 95, 205, and 307 of title 45, Code of Federal Regulations, the substitution of the State's request for proposal in competitive procurement for advance planning and implementation documents otherwise required.

(i) Annual report. (1) In general. Not later than May 1 of each year the Secretary shall transmit to the Committee on Finance of the Senate, the Committee on Energy and Commerce of the House of Representatives, and the Committees on Aging of the Senate and the House of Representatives a report on the operation of this section in the preceding fiscal year.

(2) Details. Each report shall include information on—

(A) ingredient costs paid under this title [42 USCS §§ 1396 et seq.] for single source drugs, multiple source drugs, and nonprescription covered outpatient drugs;

(B) the total value of rebates received and number of manufacturers providing such rebates;

(C) how the size of such rebates compare with the size or [of] rebates offered to other purchasers of covered outpatient drugs;

(D) the effect of inflation on the value of rebates required under this section;

(E) trends in prices paid under this title [42 USCS §§ 1396 et seq.] for covered outpatient drugs; and

(F) Federal and State administrative costs associated with compliance with the provisions of this title [42 USCS §§ 1396 et seq.].

(j) Exemption of organized health care settings.

(1) Covered outpatient drugs are not subject to the requirements of this section if such drugs are—

(A) dispensed by health maintenance organizations, including Medicaid managed care organizations that contract under section 1903(m) [42 USCS § 1396b(m)]; and

(B) subject to discounts under section 340B of the Public Health Service Act [42 USCS § 256b].

(2) The State plan shall provide that a hospital (providing medical assistance under such plan) that dispenses covered outpatient drugs using drug formulary systems, and bills the plan no more than the hospital's purchasing

costs for covered outpatient drugs (as determined under the State plan) shall not be subject to the requirements of this section.

(3) Nothing in this subsection shall be construed as providing that amounts for covered outpatient drugs paid by the institutions described in this subsection should not be taken into account for purposes of determining the best price as described in subsection (c).

(k) Definitions. In this section—

(1) Average manufacturer price. (A) In general. Subject to paragraph (B), the term "average manufacturer price" means, with respect to a covered outpatient drug of a manufacturer for a rebate period, the average price paid to the manufacturer for the drug in the United States by wholesalers for drugs distributed to the retail pharmacy class of trade.

(B) Exclusion of customary prompt pay discounts extended to wholesalers. The average manufacturer price for a covered outpatient drug shall be determined without regard to customary prompt pay discounts extended to wholesalers.

(C) Inclusion of section 505(c) drugs. In the case of a manufacturer that approves, allows, or otherwise permits any drug of the manufacturer to be sold under a new drug application approved under section 505(c) of the Federal Food, Drug, and Cosmetic Act [21 USCS § 355(c)], such term shall be inclusive of the average price paid for such drug by wholesalers for drugs distributed to the retail pharmacy class of trade.

(2) Covered outpatient drug. Subject to the exceptions in paragraph (3), the term "covered outpatient drug" means—

(A) of those drugs which are treated as prescribed drugs for purposes of section 1905(a)(12) [42 USCS § 1396d(a)(12)], a drug which may be dispensed only upon prescription (except as provided in paragraph (5)), and—

(i) which is approved for safety and effectiveness as a prescription drug under section 505 or 507 of the Federal Food, Drug, and Cosmetic Act [21 USCS § 355 or former 357] or which is approved under section 505(j) of such Act [21 USCS § 355(j)];

(ii)(I) which was commercially used or sold in the United States before the date of the enactment of the Drug Amendments of 1962 [enacted Oct. 10, 1962] or which is identical, similar, or related (within the meaning of section 310.6(b)(1) of title 21 of the Code of Federal Regulations) to such a drug, and (II) which has not been the subject of a final determination by the Secretary that it is a "new drug" (within the meaning of section 201(p) of the Federal Food, Drug, and Cosmetic Act [21 USCS § 321(p)]) or an action brought by the Secretary under section 301, 302(a), or 304(a) of such Act [21 USCS § 331, 332(a), or 334(a)] to enforce section 502(f) or 505(a) of such Act [21 USCS § 352(f) or 355(a)]; or

(iii) (I) which is described in section 107(c)(3) of the Drug Amendments of 1962 [21 USCS § 321 note] and for which the Secretary has determined there is a compelling justification for its medical need, or is identical, similar, or related (within the meaning of section 310.6(b)(1) of title 21 of the Code of Federal Regulations) to such a drug, and (II) for which the Secretary has not issued a notice of an opportunity for a hearing under section 505(e) of the Federal Food, Drug, and Cosmetic Act [21 USCS § 355(e)] on a proposed order of the Secretary to withdraw approval of an application for such drug under such section because the Secretary has determined that the drug is less than effective for some or all conditions of use prescribed, recommended, or suggested in its labeling; and

(B) a biological product, other than a vaccine which—

(i) may only be dispensed upon prescription,

(ii) is licensed under section 351 of the Public Health Service Act [42 USCS § 262], and

(iii) is produced at an establishment licensed under such section to produce such product; and

(C) insulin certified under section 506 of the Federal Food, Drug, and Cosmetic Act [42 USCS § 356].

(3) Limiting definition. The term "covered outpatient drug" does not include any drug, biological product, or insulin provided as part of, or as incident to and in the same setting as, any of the following (and for which payment may be made under this title [42 USCS §§ 1396 et seq.] as part of payment for the following and not as direct reimbursement for the drug):

(A) Inpatient hospital services.

(B) Hospice services.

(C) Dental services, except that drugs for which the State plan authorizes direct reimbursement to the dispensing dentist are covered outpatient drugs.

(D) Physicians' services.

(E) Outpatient hospital services.

(F) Nursing facility services and services provided by an intermediate care facility for the mentally retarded.

(G) Other laboratory and x-ray services.

(H) Renal dialysis.

Such term also does not include any such

drug or product for which a National Drug Code number is not required by the Food and Drug Administration or a drug or biological [product] used for a medical indication which is not a medically accepted indication. Any drug, biological product, or insulin excluded from the definition of such term as a result of this paragraph shall be treated as a covered outpatient drug for purposes of determining the best price (as defined in subsection (c)(1)(C)) for such drug, biological product, or insulin.

(4) Nonprescription drugs. If a State plan for medical assistance under this title [42 USCS §§ 1396 et seq.] includes coverage of prescribed drugs as described in section 1905(a)(12) [42 USCS § 1396d(a)(12)] and permits coverage of drugs which may be sold without a prescription (commonly referred to as "over-the-counter" drugs), if they are prescribed by a physician (or other person authorized to prescribe under State law), such a drug shall be regarded as a covered outpatient drug.

(5) Manufacturer. The term "manufacturer" means any entity which is engaged in—

(A) the production, preparation, propagation, compounding, conversion, or processing of prescription drug products, either directly or indirectly by extraction from substances of natural origin, or independently by means of chemical synthesis, or by a combination of extraction and chemical synthesis, or

(B) in the packaging, repackaging, labeling, relabeling, or distribution of prescription drug products.

Such term does not include a wholesale distributor of drugs or a retail pharmacy licensed under State law.

(6) Medically accepted indication. The term "medically accepted indication" means any use for a covered outpatient drug which is approved under the Federal Food, Drug, and Cosmetic Act [21 USCS §§ 301 et seq.] or the use of which is supported by one or more citations included or approved for inclusion in any of the compendia described in subsection (g)(1)(B)(i).

(7) Multiple source drug; innovator multiple source drug; noninnovator multiple source drug; single source drug. (A) Defined. (i) Multiple source drug. The term "multiple source drug" means, with respect to a rebate period, a covered outpatient drug (not including any drug described in paragraph (5)) for which there [is] at least 1 other drug product which—

(I) is rated as therapeutically equivalent (under the Food and Drug Administration's most recent publication of "Approved Drug Products with Therapeutic Equivalence Evaluations"),

(II) except as provided in subparagraph (B), is pharmaceutically equivalent and bioequivalent, as defined in subparagraph (C) and as determined by the Food and Drug Administration, and

(III) is sold or marketed in the State during the period.

(ii) Innovator multiple source drug. The term "innovator multiple source drug" means a multiple source drug that was originally marketed under an original new drug application approved by the Food and Drug Administration.

(iii) Noninnovator multiple source drug. The term "noninnovator multiple source drug" means a multiple source drug that is not an innovator multiple source drug.

(iv) Single source drug. The term "single source drug" means a covered outpatient drug which is produced or distributed under an original new drug application approved by the Food and Drug Administration, including a drug product marketed by any cross-licensed producers or distributors operating under the new drug application.

(B) Exception. Subparagraph (A)(i)(II) shall not apply if the Food and Drug Administration changes by regulation the requirement that, for purposes of the publication described in subparagraph (A)(i)(I), in order for drug products to rated as therapeutically equivalent, they must be pharmaceutically equivalent and bioequivalent, as defined in subparagraph (C).

(C) Definitions. For purposes of this paragraph—

(i) drug products are pharmaceutically equivalent if the products contain identical amounts of the same active drug ingredient in the same dosage form and meet compendial or other applicable standards of strength, quality, purity, and identity;

(ii) drugs are bioequivalent if they do not present a known or potential bioequivalence problem, or, if they do present such a problem, they are shown to meet an appropriate standard of bioequivalence; and

(iii) a drug product is considered to be sold or marketed in a State if it appears in a published national listing of average wholesale prices selected by the Secretary, provided that the listed product is generally available to the public through retail pharmacies in that State.

(8) Rebate period. The term "rebate period" means, with respect to an agreement under subsection (a), a calendar quarter or other period specified by the Secretary with respect to the payment of rebates under such

agreement.

(9) State agency. The term "State agency" means the agency designated under section 1902(a)(5) [42 USCS § 1396a(a)(5)] to administer or supervise the administration of the State plan for medical assistance.

(Aug. 14, 1935, ch 531, Title XIX, § 1927, as added Nov. 5, 1990, P. L. 101-508, Title IV, Subtitle B, Part 1, § 4401(a)(3), 104 Stat. 1388-143; Nov. 4, 1992, P. L. 102-585, Title VI, § 601(a)–(c), 106 Stat. 4962; April 12, 1993, P. L. 103-18, § 2(a), 107 Stat. 54; Aug. 10, 1993, P. L. 103-66, Title XIII, Ch 2, Subch B, Part I, § 13602(a), 107 Stat. 613; Aug. 5, 1997, P. L. 105-33, Title IV, Subtitle H, Ch 1, § 4701(b)(2)(A)(x), Ch 6, § 4756, 111 Stat. 493, 527; Nov. 29, 1999, P. L. 106-113, Div B, § 1000(a)(6), 113 Stat. 1536; Dec. 8, 2003, P. L. 108-173, Title I, §§ 101(e)(4), (9), 103(e)(1), 105(b), Title III, § 303(i)(4), Title IX, § 900(e)(1)(K), (L), Title X, Subtitle A, § 1002, 117 Stat. 2151, 2152, 2159, 2166, 2254, 2372, 2431; Oct. 20, 2005, P. L. 109-91, Title I, § 104(a), 119 Stat. 2092; Feb. 8, 2006, P. L. 109-171, Title VI, Subtitle A, Ch. 1, §§ 6001(a)–(c)(2), (d)–(f)(2), 6002(a), 6003(a), (b), 6004(a), 120 Stat. 54, 56, 59, 60, 61; Dec. 20, 2006, P. L. 109-432, Div B, Title IV, § 405(c)(2)(A)(ii), 120 Stat. 3000; March 11, 2009, P. L. 111-8, Div F, Title II, § 221(a), 123 Stat. 783; March 23, 2010, P. L. 111-148, Title II, Subtitle F, §§ 2501(a), (b), (c)(2), (d)(1), (e), 2502(a), 2503(a)–(c), Title III, Subtitle D, § 3301(d)(2), Title IV, Subtitle B, § 4107(b), 124 Stat. 306, 308, 309, 310, 468, 560; March 30, 2010, P. L. 111-152, Title I, Subtitle B, § 1101(c), Subtitle C, § 1206(a), 124 Stat. 1039, 1056.)

HISTORY; ANCILLARY LAWS AND DIRECTIVES

References in text:

"Section 2501 of the Patient Protection and Affordable Health Care Act", referred to in subsec. (b)(1)(C), is § 2501 of Act March 23, 2010, P. L. 111-148. For full classification of such section, consult USCS Tables volumes.

With respect to the Committee on Energy and Commerce of the House of Representatives, referred to in this section, § 1(a)(4), (c)(1) of Act June 3, 1995, P. L. 104-14, which appears as a note preceding 2 USCS § 21, provides that any reference to such Committee in any provision of law enacted before January 4, 1995, shall be treated as referring to the Committee on Commerce of the House of Representatives, except that it shall be treated as referring to (A) the Committee on Agriculture of the House of Representatives, in the case of a provision of law relating to inspection of seafood or seafood products, (B) the Committee on Banking and Financial Services of the House of Representatives, in the case of a provision of law relating to bank capital markets activities generally or to depository institution securities activities generally, and (C) the Committee on Transportation and Infrastructure of the House of Representatives, in the case of a provision of law relating to railroads, railway labor, or railroad retirement and unemployment (except revenue measures related thereto).

Prospective amendments:

Amendment of subsecs. (b), (e), and (k), effective October 1, 2010. Act March 23, 2010, P. L. 111-148, Title II, Subtitle F, § 2503(a)–(c), 124 Stat. 310, provides:

"(a) Pharmacy reimbursement limits. (1) In general. Section 1927(e) of the Social Security Act (42 U.S.C. 1396r-8(e)) is amended—

"(A) in paragraph (4), by striking '(or, effective January 1, 2007, two or more)'; and

"(B) by striking paragraph (5) and inserting the following:

" '(5) Use of AMP in upper payment limits. The Secretary shall calculate the Federal upper reimbursement limit established under paragraph (4) as no less than 175 percent of the weighted average (determined on the basis of utilization) of the most recently reported monthly average manufacturer prices for pharmaceutically and therapeutically equivalent multiple source drug products that are available for purchase by retail community pharmacies on a nationwide basis. The Secretary shall implement a smoothing process for average manufacturer prices. Such process shall be similar to the smoothing process used in determining the average sales price of a drug or biological under section 1847A [42 USCS § 1395w-3a].'.

"(2) Definition of AMP. Section 1927(k)(1) of such Act (42 U.S.C. 1396r-8(k)(1)) is amended—

"(A) in subparagraph (A), by striking 'by' and all that follows through the period and inserting 'by—

" '(i) wholesalers for drugs distributed to retail community pharmacies; and

" '(ii) retail community pharmacies that purchase drugs directly from the manufacturer.'; and

"(B) by striking subparagraph (B) and inserting the following:

" '(B) Exclusion of customary prompt pay discounts and other payments.—

" '(i) In general. The average manufacturer price for a covered outpatient drug shall exclude—

" '(I) customary prompt pay discounts extended to wholesalers;

" '(II) bona fide service fees paid by manufacturers to wholesalers or retail community pharmacies, including (but not limited to) distribution service fees, inventory management fees, product stocking allowances, and fees associated with administrative services agreements and patient care programs (such as medication compliance programs and patient education programs);

" '(III) reimbursement by manufacturers for recalled, damaged, expired, or otherwise unsalable returned goods, including (but not limited to) reimbursement for the cost of the goods and any reimbursement of costs associated with return goods handling and processing, reverse logistics, and drug destruction;

" '(IV) payments received from, and rebates or discounts provided to, pharmacy benefit managers, managed care organizations, health maintenance organizations, insurers, hospitals, clinics, mail order pharmacies, long term care providers, manufacturers, or any other entity that does not conduct business as a wholesaler or a retail community pharmacy [; and]

" '(V) discounts provided by manufacturers under

section 1860D-14A [1395w-114a].

" '(ii) Inclusion of other discounts and payments. Notwithstanding clause (i), any other discounts, rebates, payments, or other financial transactions that are received by, paid by, or passed through to, retail community pharmacies shall be included in the average manufacturer price for a covered outpatient drug.'; and

"(C) in subparagraph (C), by striking 'the retail pharmacy class of trade' and inserting 'retail community pharmacies'.

"(3) Definition of multiple source drug. Section 1927(k)(7) of such Act (42 U.S.C. 1396r-8(k)(7)) is amended—

"(A) in subparagraph (A)(i)(III), by striking 'the State' and inserting 'the United States'; and

"(B) in subparagraph (C)—

"(1) in clause (i), by inserting 'and' after the semicolon;

"(ii) in clause (ii), by striking '; and' and inserting a period; and

"(iii) by striking clause (iii).

"(4) Definitions of retail community pharmacy; wholesaler. Section 1927(k) of such Act (42 U.S.C. 1396r-8(k)) is amended by adding at the end the following new paragraphs:

" '(10) Retail community pharmacy. The term 'retail community pharmacy' means an independent pharmacy, a chain pharmacy, a supermarket pharmacy, or a mass merchandiser pharmacy that is licensed as a pharmacy by the State and that dispenses medications to the general public at retail prices. Such term does not include a pharmacy that dispenses prescription medications to patients primarily through the mail, nursing home pharmacies, long-term care facility pharmacies, hospital pharmacies, clinics, charitable or not-for-profit pharmacies, government pharmacies, or pharmacy benefit managers.

" '(11) Wholesaler. The term 'wholesaler' means a drug wholesaler that is engaged in wholesale distribution of prescription drugs to retail community pharmacies, including (but not limited to) manufacturers, repackers, distributors, own-label distributors, private-label distributors, jobbers, brokers, warehouses (including manufacturer's and distributor's warehouses, chain drug warehouses, and wholesale drug warehouses) independent wholesale drug traders, and retail community pharmacies that conduct wholesale distributions.'.

"(b) Disclosure of Price Information to the Public. Section 1927(b)(3) of such Act (42 U.S.C. 1396r-8(b)(3)) is amended—

"(1) in subparagraph (A)—

"(A) in the first sentence, by inserting after clause (iii) the following:

" '(iv) not later than 30 days after the last day of each month of a rebate period under the agreement, on the manufacturer's total number of units that are used to calculate the monthly average manufacturer price for each covered outpatient drug;'; and

"(B) in the second sentence, by inserting '(relating to the weighted average of the most recently reported monthly average manufacturer prices)' after '(D)(v)'; and

"(2) in subparagraph (D)(v), by striking 'average manufacturer prices' and inserting 'the weighted average of the most recently reported monthly average manufacturer prices and the average retail survey price determined for each multiple source drug in accordance with subsection (f)'.

"(c) Clarification of application of survey of retail prices. Section 1927(f)(1) of such Act (42 U.S.C. 1396r-8(b)(1)) is amended—

"(1) in subparagraph (A)(i), by inserting 'with respect to a retail community pharmacy,' before 'the determination'; and

"(2) in subparagraph (C)(ii), by striking 'retail pharmacies' and inserting 'retail community pharmacies'.".

Amendment of subsec. (d)(2)(F), effective October 1, 2010. Act March 23, 2010, P. L. 111-148, Title IV, Subtitle B, § 4107(b), 124 Stat. 560 (effective 10/1/2010, as provided by § 4107(d) of such Act, which appears as 42 USCS § 1396d note), provides: "Section 1927(d)(2)(F) of the Social Security Act (42 U.S.C. 1396r-8(d)(2)(F)), as redesignated by section 2502(a), is amended by inserting before the period at the end the following: ', except, in the case of pregnant women when recommended in accordance with the Guideline referred to in section 1905(bb)(2)(A), agents approved by the Food and Drug Administration under the over-the-counter monograph process for purposes of promoting, and when used to promote, tobacco cessation'.".

Amendments:

2010. Act March 23, 2010, in subsec. (b), in para. (1), in subpara. (A), inserted ', including such drugs dispensed to individuals enrolled with a Medicaid managed care organization if the organization is responsible for coverage of such drugs", and added subpara. (C), and in para. (2)(A), inserted 'including such information reported by each Medicaid managed care organization,"; in subsec. (c), in para. (1)(B), in cl. (i), in subcl. (IV), deleted 'and" following the semicolon, in subcl. (V), inserted 'and before January 1, 2010" and substituted '; and" for a concluding period, and added subcl. (VI), and added cl. (iii), in para. (2), added subpara. (D), and in para. (3)(B), in cl. (i), deleted 'and" following the concluding comma, in cl. (ii), inserted 'and before January 1, 2010," and substituted '; and" for a concluding period, and added cl. (iii); and in subsec. (j), substituted para. (1) for one which read: '(1) Covered outpatient drugs dispensed by health maintenance organizations, including medicaid managed care organizations that contract under section 1903(m), are not subject to the requirements of this section.".

Such Act further (applicable to drugs that are paid for by a State after 12/31/2009, as provided by § 2501(d)(2) of such Act, which appears as a note to this section), in subsec. (c)(2), added subpara. (C).

Such Act further (applicable to services furnished on or after 1/1/2014, as provided by § 2502(b) of such Act, which appears as a note to this section), in subsec. (d), in para. (2), deleted subpara. (E), which read: '(E) Agents when used to promote smoking cessation.", redesignated subparas. (F)–(H) as subparas. (E)–(G), respectively, deleted subparas. (I) and (J), which read:

"(I) Barbiturates.

"(J) Benzodiazepines.",

and redesignated subpara. (K) as subpara. (H), and added para. (7).

Such Act further (applicable to drugs dispensed on or after 7/1/2010, as provided by § 3301(d)(3) of such Act, which appears as 42 USCS § 1320a-7b note), in subsec. (c)(1)(C)(i)(VI), inserted ', or any discounts provided by manufacturers under the Medicare coverage gap discount program under section 1860D-14A".

Act March 30, 2010, in subsec. (k)(1)(B)(i), in subcl. (III), deleted 'and" following the concluding semicolon, in subcl. (IV), deleted a concluding period, and added subcl. (V).

Such Act further (effective as if included in the enactment of Act March 23, 2010, as provided by § 1206(b) of Act March 30, 2010, which appears as a note to this section), in subsec. (c)(2), substituted subpara. (C) for one which read:
"(C) Treatment of new formulations. (i) In general. Except as provided in clause (ii), in the case of a drug that is a new formulation, such as an extended-release formulation, of a single source drug or an innovator multiple source drug, the rebate obligation with respect to the drug under this section shall be the amount computed under this section for the new formulation of the drug or, if greater, the product of—

"(I) the average manufacturer price for each dosage form and strength of the new formulation of the single source drug or innovator multiple source drug;

"(II) the highest additional rebate (calculated as a percentage of average manufacturer price) under this section for any strength of the original single source drug or innovator multiple source drug; and

"(III) the total number of units of each dosage form and strength of the new formulation paid for under the State plan in the rebate period (as reported by the State).

"(ii) No application to new formulations of orphan drugs. Clause (i) shall not apply to a new formulation of a covered outpatient drug that is or has been designated under section 526 of the Federal Food, Drug, and Cosmetic Act (21 U.S.C. 360bb) for a rare disease or condition, without regard to whether the period of market exclusivity for the drug under section 527 of such Act has expired or the specific indication for use of the drug.".

Other provisions:

Effective date of amendment made by § 2501(d) of Act March 23, 2010. Act March 23, 2010, P. L. 111-148, Title II, Subtitle F, § 2501(d)(2), 124 Stat. 309, provides: "The amendment made by paragraph (1) [adding subsec. (c)(2)(C) of this section] shall apply to drugs that are paid for by a State after December 31, 2009.".

Effective date of amendment made by § 2502 of Act March 23, 2010. Act March 23, 2010, P. L. 111-148, Title II, Subtitle F, § 2502(b), 124 Stat. 310, provides: "The amendments made by this section [amending subsec. (d) of this section] shall apply to services furnished on or after January 1, 2014.".

Effective date of amendment made by § 2503 of Act March 23, 2010. Act March 23, 2010, P. L. 111-148, Title II, Subtitle F, § 2503(d), 124 Stat. 312, provides: "The amendments made by this section [amending subsecs. (b), (e), and (k) of this section] shall take effect on the first day of the first calendar year quarter that begins at least 180 days after the date of enactment of this Act, without regard to whether or not final regulations to carry out such amendments have been promulgated by such date.".

Effective date of amendment made by § 1206 of Act March 30, 2010. Act March 30, 2010, P. L. 111-152, Title I, Subtitle C, § 1206(b), 124 Stat. 1057, provides: "The amendment made by subsection (a) [amending subsec. (c)(2) of this section] shall take effect as if included in the enactment of the Patient Protection and Affordable Care Act [Act March 23, 2010, P. L. 111-148].".

§ 1396u-6. Medicaid integrity program

(a) In general. There is hereby established the Medicaid Integrity Program (in this section referred to as the "Program") under which the Secretary shall promote the integrity of the program under this title [42 USCS §§ 1396 et seq.] by entering into contracts in accordance with this section with eligible entities to carry out the activities described in subsection (b).

(b) Activities described. Activities described in this subsection are as follows:

(1) Review of the actions of individuals or entities furnishing items or services (whether on a fee-for-service, risk, or other basis) for which payment may be made under a State plan approved under this title [42 USCS §§ 1396 et seq.] (or under any waiver of such plan approved under section 1115 [42 USCS § 1315]) to determine whether fraud, waste, or abuse has occurred, is likely to occur, or whether such actions have any potential for resulting in an expenditure of funds under this title [42 USCS §§ 1396 et seq.] in a manner which is not intended under the provisions of this title [42 USCS §§ 1396 et seq.].

(2) Audit of claims for payment for items or services furnished, or administrative services rendered, under a State plan under this title [42 USCS §§ 1396 et seq.], including—

(A) cost reports;

(B) consulting contracts; and

(C) risk contracts under section 1903(m) [42 USCS § 1396b(m)].

(3) Identification of overpayments to individuals or entities receiving Federal funds under this title [42 USCS §§ 1396 et seq.].

(4) Education or training, including at such national, State, or regional conferences as the Secretary may establish, of State or local officers, employees, or independent contractors responsible for the administration or the supervision of the administration of the State plan under this title [42 USCS §§ 1396 et seq.], providers of services, managed care entities, beneficiaries, and other individuals with respect to payment integrity and quality of care.

(c) Eligible entity and contracting requirements. (1) In general. An entity is eligible to enter into a contract under the Program to carry out any of the activities described in subsection (b) if the entity satisfies the requirements of paragraphs (2) and (3).

(2) Eligibility requirements. The requirements of this paragraph are the following:

(A) The entity has demonstrated capability to carry out the activities described in subsection (b).

(B) In carrying out such activities, the entity agrees to cooperate with the Inspector General of the Department of Health and Human Services, the Attorney General, and other law enforcement agencies, as appropriate, in the investigation and deterrence of fraud and abuse in relation to this title [42 USCS §§ 1396 et seq.] and in other cases arising out of such activities.

(C) The entity complies with such conflict of interest standards as are generally applicable to Federal acquisition and procurement.

(D) The entity agrees to provide the Secretary and the Inspector General of the Department of Health and Human Services with such performance statistics (including the number and amount of overpayments recovered, the number of fraud referrals, and the return on investment of such activities by the entity) as the Secretary or the Inspector General may request.

(E) The entity meets such other requirements as the Secretary may impose.

(3) Contracting requirements. The entity has contracted with the Secretary in accordance with such procedures as the Secretary shall by regulation establish, except that such procedures shall include the following:

(A) Procedures for identifying, evaluating, and resolving organizational conflicts of interest that are generally applicable to Federal acquisition and procurement.

(B) Competitive procedures to be used—

(i) when entering into new contracts under this section;

(ii) when entering into contracts that may result in the elimination of responsibilities under section 202(b) of the Health Insurance Portability and Accountability Act of 1996; and

(iii) at any other time considered appropriate by the Secretary.

(C) Procedures under which a contract under this section may be renewed without regard to any provision of law requiring competition if the contractor has met or exceeded the performance requirements established in the current contract.

The Secretary may enter into such contracts without regard to final rules having been promulgated.

(4) Limitation on contractor liability. The Secretary shall by regulation provide for the limitation of a contractor's liability for actions taken to carry out a contract under the Program, and such regulation shall, to the extent the Secretary finds appropriate, employ the same or comparable standards and other substantive and procedural provisions as are contained in section 1157 [42 USCS § 1320c-6].

(d) Comprehensive plan for program integrity. (1) 5-year plan. With respect to the 5-fiscal year period beginning with fiscal year 2006, and each such 5-fiscal year period that begins thereafter, the Secretary shall establish a comprehensive plan for ensuring the integrity of the program established under this title [42 USCS §§ 1396 et seq.] by combatting fraud, waste, and abuse.

(2) Consultation. Each 5-fiscal year plan established under paragraph (1) shall be developed by the Secretary in consultation with the Attorney General, the Director of the Federal Bureau of Investigation, the Comptroller General of the United States, the Inspector General of the Department of Health and Human Services, and State officials with responsibility for controlling provider fraud and abuse under State plans under this title [42 USCS §§ 1396 et seq.].

(e) Appropriation. (1) In general. Out of any money in the Treasury of the United States not otherwise appropriated, there are appropriated to carry out the Medicaid Integrity Program under this section, without further appropriation—

(A) for fiscal year 2006, $5,000,000;

(B) for each of fiscal years 2007 and 2008, $50,000,000;

(C) for each of fiscal years 2009 and 2010, $75,000,000; and

(D) for each fiscal year after fiscal year 2010, the amount appropriated under this paragraph for the previous fiscal year, increased by the percentage increase in the consumer price index for all urban consumers (all items; United States city average) over the previous year.

(2) Availability; authority for use of funds. (A) Availability. Amounts appropriated pursuant to paragraph (1) shall remain available until expended.

(B) Authority for use of funds for transportation and travel expenses for attendees at education, training, or consultative activities. (i) In general. The Secretary may use amounts appropriated pursuant to paragraph (1) to pay for transportation and the travel expenses, including per diem in lieu of subsistence, at rates authorized for employees of agencies under subchapter I of chapter 57 of title 5, United States Code [5 USCS §§ 5701 et seq.], while away from their homes or regular places of business, of individuals described in subsection (b)(4) who attend education, training, or consultative activities conducted under the authority of that subsection.

(ii) Public disclosure. The Secretary shall make available on a website of the Centers for Medicare & Medicaid Services that is accessible to the public—

(I) the total amount of funds expended for each conference conducted under the authority of subsection (b)(4); and

(II) the amount of funds expended for each such conference that were for transportation and for travel expenses.

(3) Increase in CMS staffing devoted to protecting Medicaid program integrity. From the amounts appropriated under paragraph (1), the Secretary shall increase by 100 the number of full-time equivalent employees whose duties consist solely of protecting the integrity of the Medicaid program established under this section by providing effective support and assistance to States to combat provider fraud and abuse.

(4) Evaluations. The Secretary shall conduct evaluations of eligible entities which the Secretary contracts with under the Program not less frequently than every 3 years.

(5) Annual report. Not later than 180 days after the end of each fiscal year (beginning with fiscal year 2006), the Secretary shall submit a report to Congress which identifies—

(A) the use of funds appropriated pursuant to paragraph (1); and

(B) the effectiveness of the use of such funds.

(Aug. 14, 1935, ch 531, Title XIX, § 1936, as added Feb. 8, 2006, P. L. 109-171, Title VI, Subtitle A, Ch. 3, § 6034(a)(2), 120 Stat. 74; Oct. 8, 2008, P. L. 110-379, § 5(a)(1), (b)(1), 122 Stat. 4078; March 23, 2010, P. L. 111-148, Title VI, Subtitle E, § 6402(j)(2), 124 Stat. 762; March 30, 2010, P. L. 111-152, Title I, Subtitle D, § 1303(b), 124 Stat. 1058.)

§ 1396u-7. State flexibility in benefit packages

(a) State option of providing benchmark benefits. (1) Authority. (A) In general. Notwithstanding section 1902(a)(1) [42 USCS § 1396(a)(1)] (relating to statewideness), section 1902(a)(10)(B) [42 USCS § 1396(a)(10)(B)] (relating to comparability) and any other provision of this title [42 USCS §§ 1396 et seq.] which would be directly contrary to the authority under this section and subject to subsection (E), a State, at its option as a State plan amendment, may provide for medical assistance under this title [42 USCS §§ 1396 et seq.] to individuals within one or more groups of individuals specified by the State through coverage that—

(i) provides benchmark coverage described in subsection (b)(1) or benchmark equivalent coverage described in subsection (b)(2); and

(ii) for any individual described in section 1905(a)(4)(B) [42 USCS § 1396d(a)(4)(B)] who is eligible under the State plan in accordance with paragraphs (10) and (17) of section 1902(a) [42 USCS § 1396(a)], consists of the items and services described in section 1905(a)(4)(B) [42 USCS § 1396d(a)(4)(B)](relating to early and periodic screening, diagnostic, and treatment services defined in section 1905(r) [42 USCS § 1396d(r)]) and provided in accordance with the requirements of section 1902(a)(43) [42 USCS § 1396(a)(43)].

(B) Limitation. The State may only exercise the option under subparagraph (A) for an individual eligible under subclause (VIII) of section 1902(a)(10)(A)(i) or under an eligibility category that had been established under the State plan on or before the date of the enactment of this section [enacted Feb. 8, 2006].

(C) Option of additional benefits. In the case of coverage described in subparagraph (A), a State, at its option, may provide such additional benefits as the State may specify.

(D) Treatment as medical assistance. Payment of premiums for such coverage under this subsection shall be treated as payment of other insurance premiums described in the third sentence of section 1905(a) [42 USCS § 1396d(a)].

(E) Rule of construction. Nothing in this paragraph shall be construed as—

(i) requiring a State to offer all or any of the items and services required by subparagraph (A)(ii) through an issuer of benchmark coverage described in subsection (b)(1) or benchmark equivalent coverage described in subsection (b)(2);

(ii) preventing a State from offering all or any of the items and services required by subparagraph (A)(ii) through an issuer of benchmark coverage described in subsection (b)(1) or benchmark equivalent coverage described in subsection (b)(2); or

(iii) affecting a child's entitlement to care and services described in subsections (a)(4)(B) and (r) of section 1905 [42 USCS § 1396d] and provided in accordance with section 1902(a)(43) [42 USCS § 1396a(a)(43)] whether provided through benchmark coverage, benchmark equivalent coverage, or otherwise.

(2) Application. (A) In general. Except as provided in subparagraph (B), a State may require that a full-benefit eligible individual (as defined in subparagraph (C)) within a group obtain benefits under this title [42 USCS §§ 1396 et seq.] through enrollment in coverage described in paragraph (1)(A). A State may apply the previous sentence to individuals within 1 or more groups of such individuals.

(B) Limitation on application. A State may not require under subparagraph (A) an individual to obtain benefits through enrollment described in paragraph (1)(A) if the individual is within one of the following categories of individuals:

(i) Mandatory pregnant women. The individual is a pregnant woman who is required to be covered under the State plan under section 1902(a)(10)(A)(i) [42 USCS § 1396a(a)(10)(A)(i)].

(ii) Blind or disabled individuals. The individual qualifies for medical assistance under the State plan on the basis of being blind or disabled (or being treated as being blind or disabled) without regard to whether the individual is eligible for supplemental security income benefits under title XVI [42 USCS §§ 1381 et seq.] on the basis of being blind or disabled and including an individual who is eligible for medical assistance on the basis of section 1902(e)(3) [42 USCS § 1396a(e)(3)].

(iii) Dual eligibles. The individual is entitled to benefits under any part of title XVIII [42 USCS §§ 1395 et seq.].

(iv) Terminally ill hospice patients. The individual is terminally ill and is receiving benefits for hospice care under this title [42 USCS §§ 1396 et seq.].

(v) Eligible on basis of institutionalization. The individual is an inpatient in a hospital, nursing facility, intermediate care facility for the mentally retarded, or other medical institution, and is required, as a condition of receiving services in such institution under the State plan, to spend for costs of medical care all but a minimal amount of the individual's income required for personal needs.

(vi) Medically frail and special medical needs individuals. The individual is medically frail or otherwise an individual with special medical needs (as identified in accordance with regulations of the Secretary).

(vii) Beneficiaries qualifying for long-term care services. The individual qualifies based on medical condition for medical assistance for long-term care services described in section 1917(c)(1)(C) [42 USCS § 1396p(c)(1)(C)].

(viii) Children in foster care receiving child welfare services and children receiving foster care or adoption assistance. The individual is an individual with respect to whom child welfare services are made available under part B of title IV [42 USCS §§ 620 et seq.] on the basis of being a child in foster care or with respect to whom adoption or foster care assistance is made available under part E of such title [42 USCS §§ 620 et seq.], without regard to age.

(ix) TANF and section 1931 parents. The individual qualifies for medical assistance on the basis of eligibility to receive assistance under a State plan funded under part A of title IV [42 USCS §§ 601 et seq.] (as in effect on or after the welfare reform effective date defined in section 1931(i) [42 USCS § 1396u-1(i)]).

(x) Women in the breast or cervical cancer program. The individual is a woman who is receiving medical assistance by virtue of the application of sections 1902(a)(10)(A)(ii)(XVIII) and 1902(aa) [42 USCS §§ 1396a(a)(10)(A)(ii)(XVIII) and (aa)].

(xi) Limited services beneficiaries. The individual—

(I) qualifies for medical assistance on the basis of section 1902(a)(10)(A)(ii)(XII) [42 USCS §§ 1396a(a)(10)(A)(ii)(XII)]; or

(II) is not a qualified alien (as defined in section 431 of the Personal Responsibility and Work Opportunity Reconciliation Act of 1996 [8 USCS § 1641]) and receives care and services necessary for the treatment of an emergency medical condition in accordance with section 1903(v) [42 USCS § 1396b(v)].

(C) Full-benefit eligible individuals. (i) In general. For purposes of this paragraph, subject to clause (ii), the term "full-benefit eligible individual" means for a State for a month an individual who is determined eligible by the State for medical assistance for all services defined in section 1905(a) [42 USCS § 1396d(a)] which are covered under the State plan under this title [42 USCS §§ 1396 et seq.] for such month under section 1902(a)(10)(A) [42 USCS § 1396a(a)(10)(A)] or under any other category of eligibility for medical assistance for all such services under this title [42 USCS §§ 1396 et seq.], as determined by the Secretary.

(ii) Exclusion of medically needy and spend-down populations. Such term shall not include an individual determined to be eligible by the State for medical assistance under section 1902(a)(10)(C) [42 USCS § 1396a(a)(10)(C)] or by reason of section 1902(f) [42 USCS § 1396a(f)] or otherwise eligible based on a reduction of income based on costs incurred for medical or other remedial care.

(b) Benchmark benefit packages. (1) In general. For purposes of subsection (a)(1), subject to paragraphs (5) and (6), each of the following coverages shall be considered to be benchmark coverage:

(A) FEHBP-equivalent health insurance coverage. The standard Blue Cross/ Blue Shield preferred provider option service benefit plan, described in and offered under section 8903(1) of title 5, United States Code [5 USCS § 8903(1)].

(B) State employee coverage. A health benefits coverage plan that is offered and generally available to State employees in the State involved.

(C) Coverage offered through HMO. The health insurance coverage plan that—

(i) is offered by a health maintenance organization (as defined in section 2791(b)(3) of the Public Health Service Act [42 USCS §§ 300gg-91(b)(3)]), and

(ii) has the largest insured commercial, non-medicaid enrollment of covered lives of such coverage plans offered by such a health maintenance organization in the State involved.

(D) Secretary-approved coverage. Any other health benefits coverage that the Secretary determines, upon application by a State, provides appropriate coverage for the population proposed to be provided such coverage.

(2) Benchmark-equivalent coverage. For purposes of subsection (a)(1), subject to paragraphs (5) and (6) coverage that meets the following requirement shall be considered to be benchmark-equivalent coverage:

(A) Inclusion of basic services. The coverage includes benefits for items and services within each of the following categories of basic services:

(i) Inpatient and outpatient hospital services.

(ii) Physicians' surgical and medical services.

(iii) Laboratory and x-ray services.

(iv) Coverage of prescription drugs.

(v) Mental health services.

(vi) Well-baby and well-child care, including age-appropriate immunizations.

(vii) Other appropriate preventive services, as designated by the Secretary.

(B) Aggregate actuarial value equivalent to benchmark package. The coverage has an aggregate actuarial value that is at least actuarially equivalent to one of the benchmark benefit packages described in paragraph (1).

(C) Substantial actuarial value for additional services included in benchmark package. With respect to each of the following categories of additional services for which coverage is provided under the benchmark benefit package used under subparagraph (B), the coverage has an actuarial value that is equal to at least 75 percent of the actuarial value of the coverage of that category of services in such package:

(i) Vision services.

(ii) Hearing services.

(iii), (iv) [Redesignated]

(3) Determination of actuarial value. The actuarial value of coverage of benchmark benefit packages shall be set forth in an actuarial opinion in an actuarial report that has been prepared—

(A) by an individual who is a member of the American Academy of Actuaries;

(B) using generally accepted actuarial principles and methodologies;

(C) using a standardized set of utilization and price factors;

(D) using a standardized population that is representative of the population involved;

(E) applying the same principles and factors in comparing the value of different coverage (or categories of services);

(F) without taking into account any differences in coverage based on the method of delivery or means of cost control or utilization used; and

(G) taking into account the ability of a State to reduce benefits by taking into account the increase in actuarial value of benefits coverage offered under this title [42 USCS §§ 1396 et seq.] that results from the limitations on cost sharing under such coverage.

The actuary preparing the opinion shall select and specify in the memorandum the standardized set and population to be used under subparagraphs (C) and (D).

(4) Coverage of rural health clinic and FQHC services. Notwithstanding the previous provisions of this section, a State may not provide for medical assistance through enrollment of an individual with benchmark coverage or benchmark equivalent coverage under this section unless—

(A) the individual has access, through such coverage or otherwise, to services described in subparagraphs (B) and (C) of section 1905(a)(2) [42 USCS § 1396d(a)(2)]; and

(B) payment for such services is made in accordance with the requirements of section 1902(bb) [42 USCS § 1396a(bb)].

(5) Minimum standards. Effective January 1, 2014, any benchmark benefit package under paragraph (1) or benchmark equivalent coverage under paragraph (2) must provide at least essential health benefits as described in section 1302(b) of the Patient Protection and Affordable Care Act [42 USCS § 18022(b)].

(6) Mental health services parity. (A) In general. In the case of any benchmark benefit package under paragraph (1) or benchmark equivalent coverage under paragraph (2) that is offered by an entity that is not a Medicaid managed care organization and that provides both medical and surgical benefits and mental health or substance use disorder benefits, the entity shall ensure that the financial require-

ments and treatment limitations applicable to such mental health or substance use disorder benefits comply with the requirements of section 2705(a) of the Public Health Service Act [42 USCS § 300gg-4(a)] in the same manner as such requirements apply to a group health plan.

(B) Deemed compliance. Coverage provided with respect to an individual described in section 1905(a)(4)(B) [42 USCS § 1396d(a)(4)(B)] and covered under the State plan under section 1902(a)(10)(A) [42 USCS § 1396a(a)(10)(A)] of the services described in section 1905(a)(4)(B) [42 USCS § 1396d(a)(4)(B)] (relating to early and periodic screening, diagnostic, and treatment services defined in section 1905(r) [42 USCS § 1396d(r)]) and provided in accordance with section 1902(a)(43) [42 USCS § 1396a(a)(43)], shall be deemed to satisfy the requirements of subparagraph (A).

(7) Coverage of family planning services and supplies. Notwithstanding the previous provisions of this section, a State may not provide for medical assistance through enrollment of an individual with benchmark coverage or benchmark-equivalent coverage under this section unless such coverage includes for any individual described in section 1905(a)(4)(C) [42 USCS § 1396d(a)(4)(C)], medical assistance for family planning services and supplies in accordance with such section.

(c) Publication of provisions affected. With respect to a State plan amendment to provide benchmark benefits in accordance with subsections (a) and (b) that is approved by the Secretary, the Secretary shall publish on the Internet website of the Centers for Medicare & Medicaid Services, a list of the provisions of this title [42 USCS §§ 1396 et seq.] that the Secretary has determined do not apply in order to enable the State to carry out the plan amendment and the reason for each such determination on the date such approval is made, and shall publish such list in the Federal Register and not later than 30 days after such date of approval.

(Aug. 14, 1935, ch 531, Title XIX, § 1937, as added Feb. 8, 2006, P. L. 109-171, Title VI, Subtitle A, Ch. 4, § 6044(a), 120 Stat. 88; Feb. 4, 2009, P. L. 111-3, Title VI, Subtitle B, § 611(a)–(c), 123 Stat. 100; March 23, 2010, P. L. 111-148, Title II, Subtitle A, §§ 2001(a)(5)(E), (c), 2004(c)(2), Subtitle D, § 2303(c), 124 Stat. 275, 276, 283, 296.)

§ 1396w-1. Medicaid Improvement Fund

(a) Establishment. The Secretary shall establish under this title [42 USCS §§ 1396 et seq.] a Medicaid Improvement Fund (in this section referred to as the "Fund") which shall be available to the Secretary to improve the management of the Medicaid program by the Centers for Medicare & Medicaid Services, including oversight of contracts and contractors and evaluation of demonstration projects. Payments made for activities under this subsection shall be in addition to payments that would otherwise be made for such activities.

(b) Funding. (1) In general. There shall be available to the Fund, for expenditures from the Fund—

(A) for fiscal year 2014, $0; and

(B) for each of fiscal years 2015 through 2018, $0.

(2) Funding limitation. Amounts in the Fund shall be available in advance of appropriations but only if the total amount obligated from the Fund does not exceed the amount available to the Fund under paragraph (1). The Secretary may obligate funds from the Fund only if the Secretary determines (and the Chief Actuary of the Centers for Medicare & Medicaid Services and the appropriate budget officer certify) that there are available in the Fund sufficient amounts to cover all such obligations incurred consistent with the previous sentence.

(Aug. 14, 1935, ch 531, Title XIX, § 1941, as added June 30, 2008, P. L. 110-252, Title VII, § 7002(b), 122 Stat. 2395; March 11, 2009, P. L. 111-8, Div F, Title II, § 226, 123 Stat. 784; Jan. 27, 2010, P. L. 111-127, § 4, 124 Stat. 5; March 23, 2010, P. L. 111-148, Title II, Subtitle A, § 2007(b), 124 Stat. 285.)

§ 1396w-3. Enrollment simplification and coordination with State health insurance exchanges

(a) Condition for participation in Medicaid. As a condition of the State plan under this title and receipt of any Federal financial assistance under section 1903(a) [42 USCS § 1396b(a)] for calendar quarters beginning after January 1, 2014, a State shall ensure that the requirements of subsection (b) is met.

(b) Enrollment simplification and coordination with State health insurance exchanges and CHIP. (1) In general. A State shall establish procedures for—

(A) enabling individuals, through an Internet website that meets the requirements of paragraph (4), to apply for medical assistance under the State plan or under a waiver of the plan, to be enrolled in the State plan or waiver, to renew their enrollment in the plan or waiver, and to consent to enrollment or reenrollment in the State plan through electronic signature;

(B) enrolling, without any further determination by the State and through such website, individuals who are identified by an Exchange established by the State under section 1311 of the Patient Protection and Affordable Care Act [42 USCS § 18031] as being eligible for—

(i) medical assistance under the State plan or under a waiver of the plan; or

(ii) child health assistance under the State child health plan under title XXI [42 USCS §§ 1397aa et seq.];

(C) ensuring that individuals who apply for but are determined to be ineligible for medical assistance under the State plan or a waiver or ineligible for child health assistance under the State child health plan under title XXI [42 USCS §§ 1397aa et seq.], are screened for eligibility for enrollment in qualified health plans offered through such an Exchange and, if applicable, premium assistance for the purchase of a qualified health plan under section 36B of the Internal Revenue Code of 1986 [26 USCS § 36B] (and, if applicable, advance payment of such assistance under section 1412 of the Patient Protection and Affordable Care Act [42 USCS § 18082]), and, if eligible, enrolled in such a plan without having to submit an additional or separate application, and that such individuals receive information regarding reduced cost-sharing for eligible individuals under section 1402 of the Patient Protection and Affordable Care Act [42 USCS § 18071], and any other assistance or subsidies available for coverage obtained through the Exchange;

(D) ensuring that the State agency responsible for administering the State plan under this title (in this section referred to as the "State Medicaid agency"), the State agency responsible for administering the State child health plan under title XXI [42 USCS §§ 1397aa et seq.] (in this section referred to as the "State CHIP agency") and an Exchange established by the State under section 1311 of the Patient Protection and Affordable Care Act [42 USCS § 18031] utilize a secure electronic interface sufficient to allow for a determination of an individual's eligibility for such medical assistance, child health assistance, or premium assistance, and enrollment in the State plan under this title, title XXI [42 USCS §§ 1397aa et seq.], or a qualified health plan, as appropriate;

(E) coordinating, for individuals who are enrolled in the State plan or under a waiver of the plan and who are also enrolled in a qualified health plan offered through such an Exchange, and for individuals who are enrolled in the State child health plan under title XXI [42 USCS §§ 1397aa et seq.] and who are also enrolled in a qualified health plan, the provision of medical assistance or child health assistance to such individuals with the coverage provided under the qualified health plan in which they are enrolled, including services described in section 1905(a)(4)(B) [42 USCS § 1396d(a)(4)(B)] (relating to early and periodic screening, diagnostic, and treatment services defined in section 1905(r) [42 USCS § 1396d(r)]) and provided in accordance with the requirements of section 1902(a)(43) [42 USCS § 1396a(a)(43)]; and

(F) conducting outreach to and enrolling vulnerable and underserved populations eligible for medical assistance under this title XIX [42 USCS §§ 1396 et seq.] or for child health assistance under title XXI [42 USCS §§ 1397aa et seq.], including children, unaccompanied homeless youth, children and youth with special health care needs, pregnant women, racial and ethnic minorities, rural populations, victims of abuse or trauma, individuals with mental health or substance-related disorders, and individuals with HIV/AIDS.

(2) Agreements with State health insurance exchanges. The State Medicaid agency and the State CHIP agency may enter into an agreement with an Exchange established by the State under section 1311 of the Patient Protection and Affordable Care Act [42 USCS § 18031] under which the State Medicaid agency or State CHIP agency may determine whether a State resident is eligible for premium assistance for the purchase of a qualified health plan under section 36B of the Internal Revenue Code of 1986 [26 USCS § 36B] (and, if applicable, advance payment of such assistance under section 1412 of the Patient Protection and Affordable Care Act [42 USCS § 18082]), so long as the agreement meets such conditions and requirements as the Secretary of the Treasury may prescribe to reduce administrative costs and the likelihood of eligibility errors and disruptions in coverage.

(3) Streamlined enrollment system. The State Medicaid agency and State CHIP agency shall participate in and comply with the requirements for the system established under section 1413 of the Patient Protection and Affordable Care Act [42 USCS § 18083] (relating to streamlined procedures for enrollment through an Exchange, Medicaid, and CHIP).

(4) Enrollment website requirements. The procedures established by State under paragraph (1) shall include establishing and having in operation, not later than January 1, 2014, an

Internet website that is linked to any website of an Exchange established by the State under section 1311 of the Patient Protection and Affordable Care Act [42 USCS § 18031] and to the State CHIP agency (if different from the State Medicaid agency) and allows an individual who is eligible for medical assistance under the State plan or under a waiver of the plan and who is eligible to receive premium credit assistance for the purchase of a qualified health plan under section 36B of the Internal Revenue Code of 1986 [26 USCS § 36B] to compare the benefits, premiums, and cost-sharing applicable to the individual under the State plan or waiver with the benefits, premiums, and cost-sharing available to the individual under a qualified health plan offered through such an Exchange, including, in the case of a child, the coverage that would be provided for the child through the State plan or waiver with the coverage that would be provided to the child through enrollment in family coverage under that plan and as supplemental coverage by the State under the State plan or waiver.

(5) Continued need for assessment for home and community-based services. Nothing in paragraph (1) shall limit or modify the requirement that the State assess an individual for purposes of providing home and community-based services under the State plan or under any waiver of such plan for individuals described in subsection (a)(10)(A)(ii)(VI).

(Aug. 14, 1935, ch 531, Title XIX, § 1943, as added March 23, 2010, P. L. 111-148, Title II, Subtitle C, § 2201, 124 Stat. 289.)

§ 1396w-4. State option to provide coordinated care through a health home for individuals with chronic conditions

(a) In general. Notwithstanding section 1902(a)(1) [42 USCS § 1396a(a)(1)] (relating to statewideness), section 1902(a)(10)(B) [42 USCS § 1396a(a)(10)(B)] (relating to comparability), and any other provision of this title for which the Secretary determines it is necessary to waive in order to implement this section, beginning January 1, 2011, a State, at its option as a State plan amendment, may provide for medical assistance under this title to eligible individuals with chronic conditions who select a designated provider (as described under subsection (h)(5)), a team of health care professionals (as described under subsection (h)(6)) operating with such a provider, or a health team (as described under subsection (h)(7)) as the individual's health home for purposes of providing the individual with health home services.

(b) Health home qualification standards. The Secretary shall establish standards for qualification as a designated provider for the purpose of being eligible to be a health home for purposes of this section.

(c) Payments. (1) In general. A State shall provide a designated provider, a team of health care professionals operating with such a provider, or a health team with payments for the provision of health home services to each eligible individual with chronic conditions that selects such provider, team of health care professionals, or health team as the individual's health home. Payments made to a designated provider, a team of health care professionals operating with such a provider, or a health team for such services shall be treated as medical assistance for purposes of section 1903(a) [42 USCS § 1396b(a)], except that, during the first 8 fiscal year quarters that the State plan amendment is in effect, the Federal medical assistance percentage applicable to such payments shall be equal to 90 percent.

(2) Methodology. (A) In general. The State shall specify in the State plan amendment the methodology the State will use for determining payment for the provision of health home services. Such methodology for determining payment—

(i) may be tiered to reflect, with respect to each eligible individual with chronic conditions provided such services by a designated provider, a team of health care professionals operating with such a provider, or a health team, as well as the severity or number of each such individual's chronic conditions or the specific capabilities of the provider, team of health care professionals, or health team; and

(ii) shall be established consistent with section 1902(a)(30)(A) [42 USCS § 1396a(a)(30)(A)].

(B) Alternate models of payment. The methodology for determining payment for provision of health home services under this section shall not be limited to a per-member per-month basis and may provide (as proposed by the State and subject to approval by the Secretary) for alternate models of payment.

(3) Planning grants. (A) In general. Beginning January 1, 2011, the Secretary may award planning grants to States for purposes of developing a State plan amendment under this section. A planning grant awarded to a State under this paragraph shall remain available until expended.

(B) State contribution. A State awarded a planning grant shall contribute an amount equal to the State percentage determined under section 1905(b) [42 USCS § 1396d(b)] (without regard to section 5001 of Public Law 111-5 [42 USCS § 1396d note]) for each fiscal year for which the grant is awarded.

(C) Limitation. The total amount of payments made to States under this paragraph shall not exceed $25,000,000.

(d) Hospital referrals. A State shall include in the State plan amendment a requirement for hospitals that are participating providers under the State plan or a waiver of such plan to establish procedures for referring any eligible individuals with chronic conditions who seek or need treatment in a hospital emergency department to designated providers.

(e) Coordination. A State shall consult and coordinate, as appropriate, with the Substance Abuse and Mental Health Services Administration in addressing issues regarding the prevention and treatment of mental illness and substance abuse among eligible individuals with chronic conditions.

(f) Monitoring. A State shall include in the State plan amendment—

(1) a methodology for tracking avoidable hospital readmissions and calculating savings that result from improved chronic care coordination and management under this section; and

(2) a proposal for use of health information technology in providing health home services under this section and improving service delivery and coordination across the care continuum (including the use of wireless patient technology to improve coordination and management of care and patient adherence to recommendations made by their provider).

(g) Report on quality measures. As a condition for receiving payment for health home services provided to an eligible individual with chronic conditions, a designated provider shall report to the State, in accordance with such requirements as the Secretary shall specify, on all applicable measures for determining the quality of such services. When appropriate and feasible, a designated provider shall use health information technology in providing the State with such information.

(h) Definitions. In this section:

(1) Eligible individual with chronic conditions. (A) In general. Subject to subparagraph (B), the term "eligible individual with chronic conditions" means an individual who—

(i) is eligible for medical assistance under the State plan or under a waiver of such plan; and

(ii) has at least—

(I) 2 chronic conditions;

(II) 1 chronic condition and is at risk of having a second chronic condition; or

(III) 1 serious and persistent mental health condition.

(B) Rule of construction. Nothing in this paragraph shall prevent the Secretary from establishing higher levels as to the number or severity of chronic or mental health conditions for purposes of determining eligibility for receipt of health home services under this section.

(2) Chronic condition. The term "chronic condition" has the meaning given that term by the Secretary and shall include, but is not limited to, the following:

(A) A mental health condition.

(B) Substance use disorder.

(C) Asthma.

(D) Diabetes.

(E) Heart disease.

(F) Being overweight, as evidenced by having a Body Mass Index (BMI) over 25.

(3) Health home. The term "health home" means a designated provider (including a provider that operates in coordination with a team of health care professionals) or a health team selected by an eligible individual with chronic conditions to provide health home services.

(4) Health home services. (A) In general. The term "health home services" means comprehensive and timely high-quality services described in subparagraph (B) that are provided by a designated provider, a team of health care professionals operating with such a provider, or a health team.

(B) Services described. The services described in this subparagraph are—

(i) comprehensive care management;

(ii) care coordination and health promotion;

(iii) comprehensive transitional care, including appropriate follow-up, from inpatient to other settings;

(iv) patient and family support (including authorized representatives);

(v) referral to community and social support services, if relevant; and

(vi) use of health information technology to link services, as feasible and appropriate.

(5) Designated provider. The term "designated provider" means a physician, clinical practice or clinical group practice, rural clinic, community health center, community mental health center, home health agency, or any other entity or provider (including pediatricians, gynecologists, and obstetricians) that is determined by the State and approved by the Secretary to be qualified to be a health home for eligible individuals with chronic conditions on

the basis of documentation evidencing that the physician, practice, or clinic—

(A) has the systems and infrastructure in place to provide health home services; and

(B) satisfies the qualification standards established by the Secretary under subsection (b).

(6) Team of health care professionals. The term "team of health care professionals" means a team of health professionals (as described in the State plan amendment) that may—

(A) include physicians and other professionals, such as a nurse care coordinator, nutritionist, social worker, behavioral health professional, or any professionals deemed appropriate by the State; and

(B) be free standing, virtual, or based at a hospital, community health center, community mental health center, rural clinic, clinical practice or clinical group practice, academic health center, or any entity deemed appropriate by the State and approved by the Secretary.

(7) Health team. The term "health team" has the meaning given such term for purposes of section 3502 of the Patient Protection and Affordable Care Act [42 USCS § 256a-1].

(Aug. 14, 1935, ch 531, Title XIX, § 1945, as added March 23, 2010, P. L. 111-148, Title II, Subtitle I, § 2703(a), 124 Stat. 319.)

HISTORY; ANCILLARY LAWS AND DIRECTIVES

Other provisions:

Survey and interim report. Act March 23, 2010, P. L. 111-148, Title II, Subtitle I, § 2703(b)(2), 124 Stat. 322, provides:

"(A) In general. Not later than January 1, 2014, the Secretary of Health and Human Services shall survey States that have elected the option under section 1945 of the Social Security Act [this section] (as added by subsection (a)) and report to Congress on the nature, extent, and use of such option, particularly as it pertains to—

"(i) hospital admission rates;

"(ii) chronic disease management;

"(iii) coordination of care for individuals with chronic conditions;

"(iv) assessment of program implementation;

"(v) processes and lessons learned (as described in subparagraph (B));

"(vi) assessment of quality improvements and clinical outcomes under such option; and

"(vii) estimates of cost savings.

"(B) Implementation reporting. A State that has elected the option under section 1945 of the Social Security Act [this section] (as added by subsection (a)) shall report to the Secretary, as necessary, on processes that have been developed and lessons learned regarding provision of coordinated care through a health home for Medicaid beneficiaries with chronic conditions under such option.".

§ 1396w-5. Addressing health care disparities

(a) Evaluating data collection approaches. The Secretary shall evaluate approaches for the collection of data under this title and title XXI [42 USCS §§ 1396 et seq. and 1397aa et seq.], to be performed in conjunction with existing quality reporting requirements and programs under this title and title XXI [42 USCS §§ 1396 et seq. and 1397aa et seq.], that allow for the ongoing, accurate, and timely collection and evaluation of data on disparities in health care services and performance on the basis of race, ethnicity, sex, primary language, and disability status. In conducting such evaluation, the Secretary shall consider the following objectives:

(1) Protecting patient privacy.

(2) Minimizing the administrative burdens of data collection and reporting on States, providers, and health plans participating under this title or title XXI [42 USCS §§ 1396 et seq. or 1397aa et seq.].

(3) Improving program data under this title and title XXI [42 USCS §§ 1396 et seq. and 1397aa et seq.] on race, ethnicity, sex, primary language, and disability status.

(b) Reports to Congress. (1) Report on evaluation. Not later than 18 months after the date of the enactment of this section [enacted March 23, 2010], the Secretary shall submit to Congress a report on the evaluation conducted under subsection (a). Such report shall, taking into consideration the results of such evaluation—

(A) identify approaches (including defining methodologies) for identifying and collecting and evaluating data on health care disparities on the basis of race, ethnicity, sex, primary language, and disability status for the programs under this title and title XXI [42 USCS §§ 1396 et seq. and 1397aa et seq.]; and

(B) include recommendations on the most effective strategies and approaches to reporting HEDIS quality measures as required under section 1852(e)(3) [42 USCS § 1395w-22(e)(3)] and other nationally recognized quality performance measures, as appropriate, on such bases.

(2) Reports on data analyses. Not later than 4 years after the date of the enactment of this section [enacted March 23, 2010], and 4 years thereafter, the Secretary shall submit to Congress a report that includes recommendations for improving the identification of health care disparities for beneficiaries under this title [42 USCS §§ 1396 et seq.] and under title XXI [42 USCS §§ 1397aa et seq.] based on analyses of the data collected under subsection (c).

(c) Implementing effective approaches. Not later than 24 months after the date of the enactment of this section [enacted March 23, 2010], the Secretary shall implement the approaches identified in the report submitted under subsection (b)(1) for the ongoing, accurate, and timely collection and evaluation of data on health care disparities on the basis of race, ethnicity, sex, primary language, and disability status.

(Aug. 14, 1935, ch 531, Title XIX, § 1946, as added March 23, 2010, P. L. 111-148, Title IV, Subtitle D, § 4302(b)(2), 124 Stat. 581.)

TITLE XX. BLOCK GRANTS TO STATES FOR SOCIAL SERVICES AND ELDER JUSTICE

SUBTITLE A. BLOCK GRANTS TO STATES FOR SOCIAL SERVICES

§ 1397. Purposes; authorization of appropriations

For the purposes of consolidating Federal assistance to States for social services into a single grant, increasing State flexibility in using social service grants, and encouraging each State, as far as practicable under the conditions in that State, to furnish services directed at the goals of—

(1) achieving or maintaining economic self-support to prevent, reduce, or eliminate dependency;

(2) achieving or maintaining self-sufficiency, including reduction or prevention of dependency;

(3) preventing or remedying neglect, abuse, or exploitation of children and adults unable to protect their own interests, or preserving, rehabilitating or reuniting families;

(4) preventing or reducing inappropriate institutional care by providing for community-based care, home-based care, or other forms of less intensive care; and

(5) securing referral or admission for institutional care when other forms of care are not appropriate, or providing services to individuals in institutions,

there are authorized to be appropriated for each fiscal year such sums as may be necessary to carry out the purposes of this subtitle [42 USCS §§ 1397 et seq.].

(Aug. 14, 1935, ch 531, Title XX, Subtitle A, § 2001, as added Aug. 13, 1981, P. L. 97-35, Title XXIII, Subtitle C, § 2352(a), 95 Stat. 867; March 23, 2010, P. L. 111-148, Title VI, Subtitle H, § 6703(a)(1)(B), (d)(1)(B), 124 Stat. 782, 803.)

§ 1397a. Payments to States

(a) Amount; covered services. (1) Each State shall be entitled to payment under this subtitle [42 USCS §§ 1397 et seq.] for each fiscal year in an amount equal to its allotment for such fiscal year, to be used by such State for services directed at the goals set forth in section 2001 [42 USCS § 1397], subject to the requirements of this subtitle [42 USCS §§ 1397 et seq.].

(2) For purposes of paragraph (1)—

(A) services which are directed at the goals set forth in section 2001 [42 USCS § 1397] include, but are not limited to, child care services, protective services for children and adults, services for children and adults in foster care, services related to the management and maintenance of the home, day care services for adults, transportation services, family planning services, training and related services, employment services, information, referral, and counseling services, the preparation and delivery of meals, health support services and appropriate combinations of services designed to meet the special needs of children, the aged, the mentally retarded, the blind, the emotionally disturbed, the physically handicapped, and alcoholics and drug addicts; and

(B) expenditures for such services may include expenditures for—

(i) administration (including planning and evaluation);

(ii) personnel training and retraining directly related to the provision of those services (including both short- and long-term training at educational institutions through grants to such institutions or by direct financial assistance to students enrolled in such institutions); and

(iii) conferences or workshops, and training or retraining through grants to nonprofit organizations within the meaning of section 501(c)(3) of the Internal Revenue Code of 1954 [1986] [26 USCS § 501(c)(3)] or to individuals with social services expertise, or through financial assistance to individuals participating in such conferences, workshops, and training or retraining (and this clause shall apply with respect to all persons involved in the delivery of such services).

(b) Funding requirements. The Secretary shall make payments in accordance with section 6503 of title 31, United States Code, to each State from its allotment for use under this subtitle [42 USCS §§ 1397 et seq.].

(c) Expenditure of funds. Payments to a State from its allotment for any fiscal year must be expended by the State in such fiscal year or in the succeeding fiscal year.

(d) Transfers of funds. A State may transfer up to 10 percent of its allotment under section 2003 [42 USCS § 1397b] for any fiscal year for its use for that year under other provisions of Federal law providing block grants for support of health services, health promotion and disease prevention activities, or low-income home energy assistance (or any combination of those activities). Amounts allotted to a State under any provisions of Federal law referred to in the preceding sentence and transferred by a State for use in carrying out the purposes of this subtitle [42 USCS §§ 1397 et seq.] shall be treated as if they were paid to the State under this subtitle [42 USCS §§ 1397 et seq.] but shall not affect the computation of the State's allotment under this subtitle [42 USCS §§ 1397 et seq.]. The State shall inform the Secretary of any such transfer of funds.

(e) Use of portion of funds. A State may use a portion of the amounts described in subsection (a) for the purpose of purchasing technical assistance from public or private entities if the State determines that such assistance is required in developing, implementing, or administering programs funded under this subtitle [42 USCS §§ 1397 et seq.].

(f) Authority to use vouchers. A State may use funds provided under this subtitle [42 USCS §§ 1397 et seq.] to provide vouchers, for services directed at the goals set forth in section 2001 [42 USCS § 1397], to families, including—

(1) families who have become ineligible for assistance under a State program funded under part A of title IV [42 USCS §§ 601 et seq.] by reason of a durational limit on the provision of such assistance; and

(2) families denied cash assistance under the State program funded under part A of title IV [42 USCS §§ 601 et seq.] for a child who is born to a member of the family who is—

(A) a recipient of assistance under the program; or

(B) a person who received such assistance at any time during the 10-month period ending with the birth of the child.

(Aug. 14, 1935, ch 531, Title XX, Subtitle A, § 2002, as added Aug. 13, 1981, P. L. 97-35, Title XXIII, Subtitle C, § 2352(a), 95 Stat. 867; July 18, 1984, P. L. 98-369, Division B, Title VI, Subtitle D, § 2663(h)(1), 98 Stat. 1169; Aug. 22, 1996, P. L. 104-193, Title IX, § 908(b), 110 Stat. 2351; March 23, 2010, P. L. 111-148, Title VI, Subtitle H, § 6703(a)(1)(B), (d)(1)(B), 124 Stat. 782, 803.)

§ 1397c. State reporting requirements

Prior to expenditure by a State of payments made to it under section 2002 [42 USCS § 1397a] for any fiscal year, the State shall report on the intended use of the payments the State is to receive under this subtitle [42 USCS §§ 1397 et seq.], including information on the types of activities to be supported and the categories or characteristics of individuals to be served. The report shall be transmitted to the Secretary and made public within the State in such manner as to facilitate comment by any person (including any Federal or other public agency) during development of the report and after its completion. The report shall be revised throughout the year as may be necessary to reflect substantial changes in the activities assisted under this subtitle [42 USCS §§ 1397 et seq.], and any revision shall be subject to the requirements of the previous sentence.

(Aug. 14, 1935, ch 531, Title XX, Subtitle A, § 2004, as added Aug. 13, 1981, P. L. 97-35, Title XXIII, Subtitle C, § 2352(a), 95 Stat. 869; March 23, 2010, P. L. 111-148, Title VI, Subtitle H, § 6703(a)(1)(B), (d)(1)(B), 124 Stat. 782, 803.)

§ 1397d. Limitations on use of grants; waiver

(a) Except as provided in subsection (b), grants made under this subtitle [42 USCS §§ 1397 et seq.] may not be used by the State, or by any other person with which the State makes arrangements to carry out the purposes of this subtitle [42 USCS §§ 1397 et seq.]—

(1) for the purchase or improvement of land, or the purchase, construction, or permanent improvement (other than minor remodeling) of any building or other facility;

(2) for the provision of cash payments for costs of subsistence or for the provision of room and board (other than costs of subsistence during rehabilitation, room and board provided for a short term as an integral but subordinate part of a social service, or temporary emergency shelter provided as a protective service);

(3) for payment of the wages of any individual as a social service (other than payment of the wages of welfare recipients employed in the provision of child day care services);

(4) for the provision of medical care (other than family planning services, rehabilitation services, or initial detoxification of an alcoholic or drug dependent individual) unless it is an integral but subordinate part of a social service for which grants may be used under this subtitle [42 USCS §§ 1397 et seq.];

(5) for social services (except services to an

alcoholic or drug dependent individual or rehabilitation services) provided in and by employees of any hospital, skilled nursing facility, intermediate care facility, or prison, to any individual living in such institution;

(6) for the provision of any educational service which the State makes generally available to its residents without cost and without regard to their income;

(7) for any child day care services unless such services meet applicable standards of State and local law;

(8) for the provisions of cash payments as a service (except as otherwise provided in this section);

(9) for payment for any item or service (other than an emergency item or service) furnished—

(A) by an individual or entity during the period when such individual or entity is excluded under this subtitle [42 USCS §§ 1397 et seq.] or title V, XVIII, or XIX [42 USCS §§ 701 et seq., 1395 et seq., or 1396 et seq.] pursuant to section 1128, 1128A, 1156, or 1842(j)(2) [42 USCS § 1320a-7, 1320a-7a, 1320c-5, or 1395u(j)(2)], or

(B) at the medical direction or on the prescription of a physician during the period when the physician is excluded under this subtitle [42 USCS §§ 1397 et seq.] or title V, XVIII, or XIX [42 USCS §§ 701 et seq., 1395 et seq., or 1396 et seq.] pursuant to section 1128, 1128A, 1156, or 1842(j)(2) [42 USCS § 1320a-7, 1320a-7a, 1320c-5, or 1395u(j)(2)] and when the person furnishing such item or service knew or had reason to know of the exclusion (after a reasonable time period after reasonable notice has been furnished to the person); or

(10) in a manner inconsistent with the Assisted Suicide Funding Restriction Act of 1997.

(b) The Secretary may waive the limitation contained in subsection (a)(1) and (4) upon the State's request for such a waiver if he finds that the request describes extraordinary circumstances to justify the waiver and that permitting the waiver will contribute to the State's ability to carry out the purposes of this subtitle [42 USCS §§ 1397 et seq.].

(Aug. 14, 1935, ch 531, Title XX, Subtitle A, § 2005, as added Aug. 13, 1981, P. L. 97-35, Title XXIII, Subtitle C, § 2352(a), 95 Stat. 869; Aug. 18, 1987, P. L. 100-93, § 8(i), 101 Stat. 695; Dec. 22, 1987, P. L. 100-203, Title IV, Subtitle B, Part 2, § 4118(e)(13), as added July 1, 1988, P. L. 100-360, Title IV, Subtitle B, § 411(k)(10)(D), 102 Stat. 796; Oct. 13, 1988, P. L. 100-485, Title VI, § 608(d)(26)(k)(ii), 102 Stat. 2422; April 30, 1997, P. L. 105-12, § 9(c), 111 Stat. 27; March 23, 2010, P. L. 111-148, Title VI, Subtitle H, § 6703(a)(1)(B), (d)(1)(B), 124 Stat. 782, 803.)

§ 1397e. Administrative and fiscal accountability

(a) Reporting requirements; form, contents, etc. Each State shall prepare reports on its activities carried out with funds made available (or transferred for use) under this subtitle [42 USCS §§ 1397 et seq.]. Reports shall be prepared annually covering the most recently completed fiscal year, and shall be in such form and contain such information (including but not limited to the information specified in subsection (c)) as the State finds necessary to provide an accurate description of such activities, to secure a complete record of the purposes for which funds were spent, and to determine the extent to which funds were spent in a manner consistent with the reports required by section 2004 [42 USCS § 1397c]. The State shall make copies of the reports required by this section available for public inspection within the State and shall transmit a copy to the Secretary. Copies shall also be provided, upon request, to any interested public agency, and each such agency may provide its views on these reports to the Congress.

(b) Audits; implementation, etc. Each State shall, not less often than every two years, audit its expenditures from amounts received (or transferred for use) under this subtitle [42 USCS §§ 1397 et seq.]. Such State audits shall be conducted by an entity independent of any agency administering activities funded under this subtitle [42 USCS §§ 1397 et seq.], in accordance with generally accepted auditing principles. Within 30 days following the completion of each audit, the State shall submit a copy of that audit to the legislature of the State and to the Secretary. Each State shall repay to the United States amounts ultimately found not to have been expended in accordance with this subtitle [42 USCS §§ 1397 et seq.], or the Secretary may offset such amounts against any other amount to which the State is or may become entitled under this subtitle [42 USCS §§ 1397 et seq.].

(c) State reports on expenditure and use of social services funds. Each report prepared and transmitted by a State under subsection (a) shall set forth (with respect to the fiscal year covered by the report)—

(1) the number of individuals who received services paid for in whole or in part with funds made available under this subtitle [42 USCS §§ 1397 et seq.], showing separately the number of children and the number of adults who

received such services, and broken down in each case to reflect the types of services and circumstances involved;

(2) the amount spent in providing each such type of service, showing separately for each type of service the amount spent per child recipient and the amount spent per adult recipient;

(3) the criteria applied in determining eligibility for services (such as income eligibility guidelines, sliding fee scales, the effect of public assistance benefits, and any requirements for enrollment in school or training programs); and

(4) the methods by which services were provided, showing separately the services provided by public agencies and those provided by private agencies, and broken down in each case to reflect the types of services and circumstances involved.

The Secretary shall establish uniform definitions of services for use by the States in preparing the information required by this subsection, and make such other provision as may be necessary or appropriate to assure that compliance with the requirements of this subsection will not be unduly burdensome on the States.

(d) Additional accounting requirements. For other provisions requiring States to account for Federal grants, see section 6503 of title 31, United States Code.

(Aug. 14, 1935, ch 531, Title XX, Subtitle A, § 2006, as added Aug. 13, 1981, P. L. 97-35, Title XXIII, Subtitle C, § 2352(a), 95 Stat. 870; July 18, 1984, P. L. 98-369, Division B, Title VI, Subtitle D, § 2663(h)(2), 98 Stat. 1169; Oct. 13, 1988, P. L. 100-485, Title VI, § 607, 102 Stat. 2410; March 23, 2010, P. L. 111-148, Title VI, Subtitle H, § 6703(a)(1)(B), (d)(1)(A), 124 Stat. 782, 803.)

§ 1397g. Demonstration projects to address health professions workforce needs

(a) Demonstration projects to provide low-income individuals with opportunities for education, training, and career advancement to address health professions workforce needs. (1) Authority to award grants. The Secretary, in consultation with the Secretary of Labor, shall award grants to eligible entities to conduct demonstration projects that are designed to provide eligible individuals with the opportunity to obtain education and training for occupations in the health care field that pay well and are expected to either experience labor shortages or be in high demand.

(2) Requirements. (A) Aid and supportive services. (i) In general. A demonstration project conducted by an eligible entity awarded a grant under this section shall, if appropriate, provide eligible individuals participating in the project with financial aid, child care, case management, and other supportive services.

(ii) Treatment. Any aid, services, or incentives provided to an eligible beneficiary participating in a demonstration project under this section shall not be considered income, and shall not be taken into account for purposes of determining the individual's eligibility for, or amount of, benefits under any means-tested program.

(B) Consultation and coordination. An eligible entity applying for a grant to carry out a demonstration project under this section shall demonstrate in the application that the entity has consulted with the State agency responsible for administering the State TANF program, the local workforce investment board in the area in which the project is to be conducted (unless the applicant is such board), the State workforce investment board established under section 111 of the Workforce Investment Act of 1998 [29 USCS § 2821], and the State Apprenticeship Agency recognized under the Act of August 16, 1937 (commonly known as the "National Apprenticeship Act" [29 USCS §§ 50 et seq.]) (or if no agency has been recognized in the State, the Office of Apprenticeship of the Department of Labor) and that the project will be carried out in coordination with such entities.

(C) Assurance of opportunities for Indian populations. The Secretary shall award at least 3 grants under this subsection to an eligible entity that is an Indian tribe, tribal organization, or Tribal College or University.

(3) Reports and evaluation. (A) Eligible entities. An eligible entity awarded a grant to conduct a demonstration project under this subsection shall submit interim reports to the Secretary on the activities carried out under the project and a final report on such activities upon the conclusion of the entities' participation in the project. Such reports shall include assessments of the effectiveness of such activities with respect to improving outcomes for the eligible individuals participating in the project and with respect to addressing health professions workforce needs in the areas in which the project is conducted.

(B) Evaluation. The Secretary shall, by grant, contract, or interagency agreement, evaluate the demonstration projects conducted under this subsection. Such evaluation shall include identification of successful activities for creating opportunities for developing and sustaining, particularly with respect to low-income individuals and other entry-level workers, a health professions workforce that has accessible entry points, that meets high standards for education, training, certification, and professional development, and that provides increased wages and affordable benefits, including health care coverage, that are responsive to the workforce's needs.

(C) Report to Congress. The Secretary shall submit interim reports and, based on the evaluation conducted under subparagraph (B), a final report to Congress on the demonstration projects conducted under this subsection.

(4) Definitions. In this subsection:

(A) Eligible entity. The term "eligible entity" means a State, an Indian tribe or tribal organization, an institution of higher education, a local workforce investment board established under section 117 of the Workforce Investment Act of 1998 [29 USCS § 2832], a sponsor of an apprenticeship program registered under the National Apprenticeship Act or a community-based organization.

(B) Eligible individual. (i) In general. The term "eligible individual" means a individual receiving assistance under the State TANF program.

(ii) Other low-income individuals. Such term may include other low-income individuals described by the eligible entity in its application for a grant under this section.

(C) Indian tribe; tribal organization. The terms "Indian tribe" and "tribal organization" have the meaning given such terms in section 4 of the Indian Self-Determination and Education Assistance Act (25 U.S.C. 450b).

(D) Institution of higher education. The term "institution of higher education" has the meaning given that term in section 101 of the Higher Education Act of 1965 (20 U.S.C. 1001).

(E) State. The term "State" means each of the 50 States, the District of Columbia, the Commonwealth of Puerto Rico, the United States Virgin Islands, Guam, and American Samoa.

(F) State TANF program. The term "State TANF program" means the temporary assistance for needy families program funded under part A of title IV [29 USCS §§ 601 et seq.].

(G) Tribal College or University. The term 'Tribal College or University' has the meaning given that term in section 316(b) of the Higher Education Act of 1965 (20 U.S.C. 1059c(b)).

(b) Demonstration project to develop training and certification programs for personal or home care aides. (1) Authority to award grants. Not later than 18 months after the date of enactment of this section [enacted March 23, 2010], the Secretary shall award grants to eligible entities that are States to conduct demonstration projects for purposes of developing core training competencies and certification programs for personal or home care aides. The Secretary shall—

(A) evaluate the efficacy of the core training competencies described in paragraph (3)(A) for newly hired personal or home care aides and the methods used by States to implement such core training competencies in accordance with the issues specified in paragraph (3)(B); and

(B) ensure that the number of hours of training provided by States under the demonstration project with respect to such core training competencies are not less than the number of hours of training required under any applicable State or Federal law or regulation.

(2) Duration. A demonstration project shall be conducted under this subsection for not less than 3 years.

(3) Core training competencies for personal or home care aides. (A) In general. The core training competencies for personal or home care aides described in this subparagraph include competencies with respect to the following areas:

(i) The role of the personal or home care aide (including differences between a personal or home care aide employed by an agency and a personal or home care aide employed directly by the health care consumer or an independent provider).

(ii) Consumer rights, ethics, and confidentiality (including the role of proxy decision-makers in the case where a health care consumer has impaired decision-making capacity).

(iii) Communication, cultural and linguistic competence and sensitivity, problem solving, behavior management, and relationship skills.

(iv) Personal care skills.

(v) Health care support.

(vi) Nutritional support.

(vii) Infection control.

(viii) Safety and emergency training.

(ix) Training specific to an individual consumer's needs (including older individuals, younger individuals with disabilities, individuals with developmental disabilities, individuals with dementia, and individuals with mental and behavioral health needs).

(x) Self-Care.

(B) Implementation. The implementation issues specified in this subparagraph include the following:

(i) The length of the training.

(ii) The appropriate trainer to student ratio.

(iii) The amount of instruction time spent in the classroom as compared to on-site in the home or a facility.

(iv) Trainer qualifications.

(v) Content for a "hands-on" and written certification exam.

(vi) Continuing education requirements.

(4) Application and selection criteria. (A) In general. (i) Number of States. The Secretary shall enter into agreements with not more than 6 States to conduct demonstration projects under this subsection.

(ii) Requirements for states. An agreement entered into under clause (i) shall require that a participating State—

(I) implement the core training competencies described in paragraph (3)(A); and

(II) develop written materials and protocols for such core training competencies, including the development of a certification test for personal or home care aides who have completed such training competencies.

(iii) Consultation and collaboration with community and vocational colleges. The Secretary shall encourage participating States to consult with community and vocational colleges regarding the development of curricula to implement the project with respect to activities, as applicable, which may include consideration of such colleges as partners in such implementation.

(B) Application and eligibility. A State seeking to participate in the project shall—

(i) submit an application to the Secretary containing such information and at such time as the Secretary may specify;

(ii) meet the selection criteria established under subparagraph (C); and

(iii) meet such additional criteria as the Secretary may specify.

(C) Selection criteria. In selecting States to participate in the program, the Secretary shall establish criteria to ensure (if applicable with respect to the activities involved)—

(i) geographic and demographic diversity;

(ii) that participating States offer medical assistance for personal care services under the State Medicaid plan;

(iii) that the existing training standards for personal or home care aides in each participating State—

(I) are different from such standards in the other participating States; and

(II) are different from the core training competencies described in paragraph (3)(A);

(iv) that participating States do not reduce the number of hours of training required under applicable State law or regulation after being selected to participate in the project; and

(v) that participating States recruit a minimum number of eligible health and long-term care providers to participate in the project.

(D) Technical assistance. The Secretary shall provide technical assistance to States in developing written materials and protocols for such core training competencies.

(5) Evaluation and report. (A) Evaluation. The Secretary shall develop an experimental or control group testing protocol in consultation with an independent evaluation contractor selected by the Secretary. Such contractor shall evaluate—

(i) the impact of core training competencies described in paragraph (3)(A), including curricula developed to implement such core training competencies, for personal or home care aides within each participating State on job satisfaction, mastery of job skills, beneficiary and family caregiver satisfaction with services, and additional measures determined by the Secretary in consultation with the expert panel;

(ii) the impact of providing such core training competencies on the existing training infrastructure and resources of States; and

(iii) whether a minimum number of hours of initial training should be required for personal or home care aides and, if so, what minimum number of hours should be required.

(B) Reports. (i) Report on initial implementation. Not later than 2 years after the date of enactment of this section [enacted March 23, 2010], the Secretary shall submit to Congress a report on the initial implementation of activities conducted under the demonstration project, including any available results of the evaluation conducted under subparagraph (A) with respect to such activities, together with such recommendations for legislation or administrative action as the Secretary determines appropriate.

(ii) Final report. Not later than 1 year after the completion of the demonstration project, the Secretary shall submit to Congress a report containing the results of the evaluation conducted under subparagraph (A), together with such recommendations for legislation or administrative action as the Secretary determines appropriate.

(6) Definitions. In this subsection:

(A) Eligible health and long-term care provider. The term "eligible health and long-term care provider" means a personal or home care agency (including personal or home care public authorities), a nursing home, a home health agency (as defined in section 1861(o) [42 USCS

§ 1395x(o)]), or any other health care provider the Secretary determines appropriate which—

(i) is licensed or authorized to provide services in a participating State; and

(ii) receives payment for services under title XIX [42 USCS §§ 1396 et seq.].

(B) Personal care services. The term "personal care services" has the meaning given such term for purposes of title XIX [42 USCS §§ 1396 et seq.].

(C) Personal or home care aide. The term "personal or home care aide" means an individual who helps individuals who are elderly, disabled, ill, or mentally disabled (including an individual with Alzheimer's disease or other dementia) to live in their own home or a residential care facility (such as a nursing home, assisted living facility, or any other facility the Secretary determines appropriate) by providing routine personal care services and other appropriate services to the individual.

(D) State. The term "State" has the meaning given that term for purposes of title XIX [42 USCS §§ 1396 et seq.].

(c) Funding. (1) In general. Subject to paragraph (2), out of any funds in the Treasury not otherwise appropriated, there are appropriated to the Secretary to carry out subsections (a) and (b), $85,000,000 for each of fiscal years 2010 through 2014.

(2) Training and certification programs for personal and home care aides. With respect to the demonstration projects under subsection (b), the Secretary shall use $5,000,000 of the amount appropriated under paragraph (1) for each of fiscal years 2010 through 2012 to carry out such projects. No funds appropriated under paragraph (1) shall be used to carry out demonstration projects under subsection (b) after fiscal year 2012.

(d) Nonapplication. (1) In general. Except as provided in paragraph (2), the preceding sections of this subtitle shall not apply to grant awarded under this section.

(2) Limitations on use of grants. Section 2005(a) [42 USCS § 1397d(a)] (other than paragraph (6)) shall apply to a grant awarded under this section to the same extent and in the same manner as such section applies to payments to States under this subtitle [42 USCS §§ 1397 et seq.].

(Aug. 14, 1935, ch 531, Title XX, Subtitle A, § 2008, as added March 23, 2010, P. L. 111-148, Title V, Subtitle F, § 5507(a), Title VI, Subtitle H, § 6703(a)(1)(B), (d)(1)(B), 124 Stat. 663, 782, 803.)

§ 1397h. Program for early detection of certain medical conditions related to environmental health hazards

(a) Program establishment. The Secretary shall establish a program in accordance with this section to make competitive grants to eligible entities specified in subsection (b) for the purpose of—

(1) screening at-risk individuals (as defined in subsection (c)(1)) for environmental health conditions (as defined in subsection (c)(3)); and

(2) developing and disseminating public information and education concerning—

(A) the availability of screening under the program under this section;

(B) the detection, prevention, and treatment of environmental health conditions; and

(C) the availability of Medicare benefits for certain individuals diagnosed with environmental health conditions under section 1881A [42 USCS § 1395rr-1].

(b) Eligible entities. (1) In general. For purposes of this section, an eligible entity is an entity described in paragraph (2) which submits an application to the Secretary in such form and manner, and containing such information and assurances, as the Secretary determines appropriate.

(2) Types of eligible entities. The entities described in this paragraph are the following:

(A) A hospital or community health center.

(B) A Federally qualified health center.

(C) A facility of the Indian Health Service.

(D) A National Cancer Institute-designated cancer center.

(E) An agency of any State or local government.

(F) A nonprofit organization.

(G) Any other entity the Secretary determines appropriate.

(c) Definitions. In this section:

(1) At-risk individual. The term "at-risk individual" means an individual who— (A)

(i) as demonstrated in such manner as the Secretary determines appropriate, has been present for an aggregate total of 6 months in the geographic area subject to an emergency declaration specified under paragraph (2), during a period ending—

(I) not less than 10 years prior to the date of such individual's application under subparagraph (B); and

(II) prior to the implementation of all the remedial and removal actions specified in the Record of Decision for Operating Unit 4 and the Record of Decision for Operating Unit 7; or

(ii) meets such other criteria as the Secretary determines appropriate considering the type of environmental health condition at issue; and

(B) has submitted an application (or has an application submitted on the individual's behalf), to an eligible entity receiving a grant under this section, for screening under the program under this section.

(2) Emergency declaration. The term "emergency declaration" means a declaration of a public health emergency under section 104(a) of the Comprehensive Environmental Response, Compensation, and Liability Act of 1980 [42 USCS § 9604(a)].

(3) Environmental health condition. The term "environmental health condition" means—

(A) asbestosis, pleural thickening, or pleural plaques, as established by—

(i) interpretation by a "B Reader" qualified physician of a plain chest x-ray or interpretation of a computed tomographic radiograph of the chest by a qualified physician, as determined by the Secretary; or

(ii) such other diagnostic standards as the Secretary specifies;

(B) mesothelioma, or malignancies of the lung, colon, rectum, larynx, stomach, esophagus, pharynx, or ovary, as established by—

(i) pathologic examination of biopsy tissue;

(ii) cytology from bronchioalveolar lavage; or

(iii) such other diagnostic standards as the Secretary specifies; and

(C) any other medical condition which the Secretary determines is caused by exposure to a hazardous substance or pollutant or contaminant at a Superfund site to which an emergency declaration applies, based on such criteria and as established by such diagnostic standards as the Secretary specifies.

(4) Hazardous substance; pollutant; contaminant. The terms "hazardous substance", "pollutant", and "contaminant" have the meanings given those terms in section 101 of the Comprehensive Environmental Response, Compensation, and Liability Act of 1980 (42 U.S.C. 9601).

(5) Superfund site. The term "Superfund site" means a site included on the National Priorities List developed by the President in accordance with section 105(a)(8)(B) of the Comprehensive Environmental Response, Compensation, and Liability Act of 1980 (42 U.S.C. 9605(a)(8)(B)).

(d) Health coverage unaffected. Nothing in this section shall be construed to affect any coverage obligation of a governmental or private health plan or program relating to an at-risk individual.

(e) Funding. (1) In general. Out of any funds in the Treasury not otherwise appropriated, there are appropriated to the Secretary, to carry out the program under this section—

(A) $23,000,000 for the period of fiscal years 2010 through 2014; and

(B) $20,000,000 for each 5-fiscal year period thereafter.

(2) Availability. Funds appropriated under paragraph (1) shall remain available until expended.

(f) Nonapplication. (1) In general. Except as provided in paragraph (2), the preceding sections of this title [42 USCS §§ 1397 et seq.] shall not apply to grants awarded under this section.

(2) Limitations on use of grants. Section 2005(a) [42 USCS § 1397d(a)] shall apply to a grant awarded under this section to the same extent and in the same manner as such section applies to payments to States under this title [42 USCS §§ 1397 et seq.], except that paragraph (4) of such section shall not be construed to prohibit grantees from conducting screening for environmental health conditions as authorized under this section.

(Aug. 14, 1935, ch 531, Title XX, § 2009, as added March 23, 2010, P. L. 111-148, Title X, Subtitle C, § 10323(b), 124 Stat. 957.)

SUBTITLE B. ELDER JUSTICE

§ 1397j. Definitions

In this subtitle [42 USCS §§ 1397j et seq.]:

(1) Abuse. The term "abuse" means the knowing infliction of physical or psychological harm or the knowing deprivation of goods or services that are necessary to meet essential needs or to avoid physical or psychological harm.

(2) Adult protective services. The term "adult protective services" means such services provided to adults as the Secretary may specify and includes services such as—

(A) receiving reports of adult abuse, neglect, or exploitation;

(B) investigating the reports described in subparagraph (A);

(C) case planning, monitoring, evaluation, and other case work and services; and

(D) providing, arranging for, or facilitating the provision of medical, social service, economic, legal, housing, law enforcement, or other protective, emergency, or support services.

(3) Caregiver. The term "caregiver" means an individual who has the responsibility for the care of an elder, either voluntarily, by contract, by receipt of payment for care, or as a result of the operation of law, and means a family mem-

ber or other individual who provides (on behalf of such individual or of a public or private agency, organization, or institution) compensated or uncompensated care to an elder who needs supportive services in any setting.

(4) Direct care. The term "direct care" means care by an employee or contractor who provides assistance or long-term care services to a recipient.

(5) Elder. The term "elder" means an individual age 60 or older.

(6) Elder justice. The term "elder justice" means—

(A) from a societal perspective, efforts to—

(i) prevent, detect, treat, intervene in, and prosecute elder abuse, neglect, and exploitation; and

(ii) protect elders with diminished capacity while maximizing their autonomy; and

(B) from an individual perspective, the recognition of an elder's rights, including the right to be free of abuse, neglect, and exploitation.

(7) Eligible entity. The term "eligible entity" means a State or local government agency, Indian tribe or tribal organization, or any other public or private entity that is engaged in and has expertise in issues relating to elder justice or in a field necessary to promote elder justice efforts.

(8) Exploitation. The term "exploitation" means the fraudulent or otherwise illegal, unauthorized, or improper act or process of an individual, including a caregiver or fiduciary, that uses the resources of an elder for monetary or personal benefit, profit, or gain, or that results in depriving an elder of rightful access to, or use of, benefits, resources, belongings, or assets.

(9) Fiduciary. The term "fiduciary"—

(A) means a person or entity with the legal responsibility—

(i) to make decisions on behalf of and for the benefit of another person; and

(ii) to act in good faith and with fairness; and

(B) includes a trustee, a guardian, a conservator, an executor, an agent under a financial power of attorney or health care power of attorney, or a representative payee.

(10) Grant. The term "grant" includes a contract, cooperative agreement, or other mechanism for providing financial assistance.

(11) Guardianship. The term "guardianship" means—

(A) the process by which a State court determines that an adult individual lacks capacity to make decisions about self-care or property, and appoints another individual or entity known as a guardian, as a conservator, or by a similar term, as a surrogate decisionmaker;

(B) the manner in which the court-appointed surrogate decisionmaker carries out duties to the individual and the court; or

(C) the manner in which the court exercises oversight of the surrogate decisionmaker.

(12) Indian tribe. (A) In general. The term "Indian tribe" has the meaning given such term in section 4 of the Indian Self-Determination and Education Assistance Act (25 U.S.C. 450b).

(B) Inclusion of Pueblo and Rancheria. The term "Indian tribe" includes any Pueblo or Rancheria.

(13) Law enforcement. The term "law enforcement" means the full range of potential responders to elder abuse, neglect, and exploitation including—

(A) police, sheriffs, detectives, public safety officers, and corrections personnel;

(B) prosecutors;

(C) medical examiners;

(D) investigators; and

(E) coroners.

(14) Long-term care. (A) In general. The term "long-term care" means supportive and health services specified by the Secretary for individuals who need assistance because the individuals have a loss of capacity for self-care due to illness, disability, or vulnerability.

(B) Loss of capacity for self-care. For purposes of subparagraph (A), the term "loss of capacity for self-care" means an inability to engage in 1 or more activities of daily living, including eating, dressing, bathing, management of one's financial affairs, and other activities the Secretary determines appropriate.

(15) Long-term care facility. The term "long-term care facility" means a residential care provider that arranges for, or directly provides, long-term care.

(16) Neglect. The term "neglect" means—

(A) the failure of a caregiver or fiduciary to provide the goods or services that are necessary to maintain the health or safety of an elder; or

(B) self-neglect.

(17) Nursing facility. (A) In general. The term "nursing facility" has the meaning given such term under section 1919(a) [42 USCS § 1396r(a)].

(B) Inclusion of skilled nursing facility. The term "nursing facility" includes a skilled nursing facility (as defined in section 1819(a) [42 USCS § 1395i-3(a)]).

(18) Self-neglect. The term "self-neglect" means an adult's inability, due to physical or mental impairment or diminished capacity, to perform essential self-care tasks including—

(A) obtaining essential food, clothing, shelter, and medical care;

(B) obtaining goods and services necessary to maintain physical health, mental health, or general safety; or

(C) managing one's own financial affairs.

(19) Serious bodily injury. (A) In general. The term "serious bodily injury" means an injury—

(i) involving extreme physical pain;

(ii) involving substantial risk of death;

(iii) involving protracted loss or impairment of the function of a bodily member, organ, or mental faculty; or

(iv) requiring medical intervention such as surgery, hospitalization, or physical rehabilitation.

(B) Criminal sexual abuse. Serious bodily injury shall be considered to have occurred if the conduct causing the injury is conduct described in section 2241 (relating to aggravated sexual abuse) or 2242 (relating to sexual abuse) of title 18, United States Code [18 USCS § 2241 or 2242], or any similar offense under State law.

(20) Social. The term "social", when used with respect to a service, includes adult protective services.

(21) State legal assistance developer. The term "State legal assistance developer" means an individual described in section 731 of the Older Americans Act of 1965 [42 USCS § 3058j].

(22) State long-term care ombudsman. The term "State Long-Term Care Ombudsman" means the State Long-Term Care Ombudsman described in section 712(a)(2) of the Older Americans Act of 1965 [42 USCS § 3058g(a)(2)].

(Aug. 14, 1935, ch 531, Title XX, Subtitle B, § 2011, as added March 23, 2010, P. L. 111-148, Title VI, Subtitle H, § 6703(a)(1)(C), 124 Stat. 782.)

§ 1397j-1. General provisions

(a) Protection of privacy. In pursuing activities under this subtitle [42 USCS §§ 1397j et seq.], the Secretary shall ensure the protection of individual health privacy consistent with the regulations promulgated under section 264(c) of the Health Insurance Portability and Accountability Act of 1996 [42 USCS § 1320d-2 note] and applicable State and local privacy regulations.

(b) Rule of construction. Nothing in this subtitle [42 USCS §§ 1397j et seq.] shall be construed to interfere with or abridge an elder's right to practice his or her religion through reliance on prayer alone for healing when this choice—

(1) is contemporaneously expressed, either orally or in writing, with respect to a specific illness or injury which the elder has at the time of the decision by an elder who is competent at the time of the decision;

(2) is previously set forth in a living will, health care proxy, or other advance directive document that is validly executed and applied under State law; or

(3) may be unambiguously deduced from the elder's life history.

(Aug. 14, 1935, ch 531, Title XX, Subtitle B, § 2012, as added March 23, 2010, P. L. 111-148, Title VI, Subtitle H, § 6703(a)(1)(C), 124 Stat. 785.)

PART I. NATIONAL COORDINATION OF ELDER JUSTICE ACTIVITIES AND RESEARCH

SUBPART A. ELDER JUSTICE COORDINATING COUNCIL AND ADVISORY BOARD ON ELDER ABUSE, NEGLECT, AND EXPLOITATION

§ 1397k. Elder Justice Coordinating Council

(a) Establishment. There is established within the Office of the Secretary an Elder Justice Coordinating Council (in this section referred to as the "Council").

(b) Membership. (1) In general. The Council shall be composed of the following members:

(A) The Secretary (or the Secretary's designee).

(B) The Attorney General (or the Attorney General's designee).

(C) The head of each Federal department or agency or other governmental entity identified by the Chair referred to in subsection (d) as having responsibilities, or administering programs, relating to elder abuse, neglect, and exploitation.

(2) Requirement. Each member of the Council shall be an officer or employee of the Federal Government.

(c) Vacancies. Any vacancy in the Council shall not affect its powers, but shall be filled in the same manner as the original appointment was made.

(d) Chair. The member described in subsection (b)(1)(A) shall be Chair of the Council.

(e) Meetings. The Council shall meet at least 2 times per year, as determined by the Chair.

(f) Duties. (1) In general. The Council shall make recommendations to the Secretary for the coordination of activities of the Department of Health and Human Services, the Department of Justice, and other relevant Federal, State, local, and private agencies and entities, relating to elder abuse, neglect, and exploitation and other crimes against elders.

(2) Report. Not later than the date that is 2 years after the date of enactment of the Elder Justice Act of 2009 [enacted March 23, 2010] and every 2 years thereafter, the Council shall submit to the Committee on Finance of the Senate and the Committee on Ways and Means and the Committee on Energy and Commerce of the House of Representatives a report that—

(A) describes the activities and accomplishments of, and challenges faced by—

(i) the Council; and

(ii) the entities represented on the Council; and

(B) makes such recommendations for legislation, model laws, or other action as the Council determines to be appropriate.

(g) Powers of the Council. (1) Information from federal agencies. Subject to the requirements of section 2012(a) [42 USCS § 1397j-1(a)], the Council may secure directly from any Federal department or agency such information as the Council considers necessary to carry out this section. Upon request of the Chair of the Council, the head of such department or agency shall furnish such information to the Council.

(2) Postal services. The Council may use the United States mails in the same manner and under the same conditions as other departments and agencies of the Federal Government.

(h) Travel expenses. The members of the Council shall not receive compensation for the performance of services for the Council. The members shall be allowed travel expenses, including per diem in lieu of subsistence, at rates authorized for employees of agencies under subchapter I of chapter 57 of title 5, United States Code [5 USCS §§ 5701 et seq.], while away from their homes or regular places of business in the performance of services for the Council. Notwithstanding section 1342 of title 31, United States Code, the Secretary may accept the voluntary and uncompensated services of the members of the Council.

(i) Detail of Government employees. Any Federal Government employee may be detailed to the Council without reimbursement, and such detail shall be without interruption or loss of civil service status or privilege.

(j) Status as permanent Council. Section 14 of the Federal Advisory Committee Act (5 U.S.C. App.) shall not apply to the Council.

(k) Authorization of appropriations. There are authorized to be appropriated such sums as are necessary to carry out this section.

(Aug. 14, 1935, ch 531, Title XX, Subtitle B, Part I, Subpart A, § 2021, as added March 23, 2010, P. L. 111-148, Title VI, Subtitle H, § 6703(a)(1)(C), 124 Stat. 786.)

§ 1397k-1. Advisory Board on Elder Abuse, Neglect, and Exploitation

(a) Establishment. There is established a board to be known as the "Advisory Board on Elder Abuse, Neglect, and Exploitation" (in this section referred to as the "Advisory Board") to create short- and long-term multidisciplinary strategic plans for the development of the field of elder justice and to make recommendations to the Elder Justice Coordinating Council established under section 2021 [42 USCS § 1397k].

(b) Composition. The Advisory Board shall be composed of 27 members appointed by the Secretary from among members of the general public who are individuals with experience and expertise in elder abuse, neglect, and exploitation prevention, detection, treatment, intervention, or prosecution.

(c) Solicitation of nominations. The Secretary shall publish a notice in the Federal Register soliciting nominations for the appointment of members of the Advisory Board under subsection (b).

(d) Terms. (1) In general. Each member of the Advisory Board shall be appointed for a term of 3 years, except that, of the members first appointed—

(A) 9 shall be appointed for a term of 3 years;

(B) 9 shall be appointed for a term of 2 years; and

(C) 9 shall be appointed for a term of 1 year.

(2) Vacancies. (A) In general. Any vacancy on the Advisory Board shall not affect its powers, but shall be filled in the same manner as the original appointment was made.

(B) Filling unexpired term. An individual chosen to fill a vacancy shall be appointed for the unexpired term of the member replaced.

(3) Expiration of terms. The term of any member shall not expire before the date on which the member's successor takes office.

(e) Election of officers. The Advisory Board shall elect a Chair and Vice Chair from among its members. The Advisory Board shall elect its initial Chair and Vice Chair at its initial meeting.

(f) Duties. (1) Enhance communication on promoting quality of, and preventing abuse, neglect, and exploitation in, long-term care. The Advisory Board shall develop collaborative and innovative approaches to improve the quality of, including preventing abuse, neglect, and exploitation in, long-term care.

(2) Collaborative efforts to develop consensus around the management of certain quality-related factors.

(A) In general. The Advisory Board shall establish multidisciplinary panels to address, and develop consensus on, subjects relating to improving the quality of long-term care. At least 1 such panel shall address, and develop consensus on, methods for managing resident-to-resident abuse in long-term care.

(B) Activities conducted. The multidisciplinary panels established under subparagraph (A) shall examine relevant research and data, identify best practices with respect to the subject of the panel, determine the best way to carry out those best practices in a practical and feasible manner, and determine an effective manner of distributing information on such subject.

(3) Report. Not later than the date that is 18 months after the date of enactment of the Elder Justice Act of 2009 [enacted March 23, 2010], and annually thereafter, the Advisory Board shall prepare and submit to the Elder Justice Coordinating Council, the Committee on Finance of the Senate, and the Committee on Ways and Means and the Committee on Energy and Commerce of the House of Representatives a report containing—

(A) information on the status of Federal, State, and local public and private elder justice activities;

(B) recommendations (including recommended priorities) regarding—

(i) elder justice programs, research, training, services, practice, enforcement, and coordination;

(ii) coordination between entities pursuing elder justice efforts and those involved in related areas that may inform or overlap with elder justice efforts, such as activities to combat violence against women and child abuse and neglect; and

(iii) activities relating to adult fiduciary systems, including guardianship and other fiduciary arrangements;

(C) recommendations for specific modifications needed in Federal and State laws (including regulations) or for programs, research, and training to enhance prevention, detection, and treatment (including diagnosis) of, intervention in (including investigation of), and prosecution of elder abuse, neglect, and exploitation;

(D) recommendations on methods for the most effective coordinated national data collection with respect to elder justice, and elder abuse, neglect, and exploitation; and

(E) recommendations for a multidisciplinary strategic plan to guide the effective and efficient development of the field of elder justice.

(g) Powers of the Advisory Board. (1) Information from Federal agencies. Subject to the requirements of section 2012(a) [42 USCS §§ 1397j-1(a)], the Advisory Board may secure directly from any Federal department or agency such information as the Advisory Board considers necessary to carry out this section. Upon request of the Chair of the Advisory Board, the head of such department or agency shall furnish such information to the Advisory Board.

(2) Sharing of data and reports. The Advisory Board may request from any entity pursuing elder justice activities under the Elder Justice Act of 2009 or an amendment made by that Act, any data, reports, or recommendations generated in connection with such activities.

(3) Postal services. The Advisory Board may use the United States mails in the same manner and under the same conditions as other departments and agencies of the Federal Government.

(h) Travel expenses. The members of the Advisory Board shall not receive compensation for the performance of services for the Advisory Board. The members shall be allowed travel expenses for up to 4 meetings per year, including per diem in lieu of subsistence, at rates authorized for employees of agencies under subchapter I of chapter 57 of title 5, United States Code [5 USCS §§ 5701 et seq.], while away from their homes or regular places of business in the performance of services for the Advisory Board. Notwithstanding section 1342 of title 31, United States Code, the Secretary may accept the voluntary and uncompensated services of the members of the Advisory Board.

(i) Detail of Government employees. Any Federal Government employee may be detailed to the Advisory Board without reimbursement, and such detail shall be without interruption or loss of civil service status or privilege.

(j) Status as permanent advisory committee. Section 14 of the Federal Advisory Committee Act (5 U.S.C. App.) shall not apply to the advisory board.

(k) Authorization of appropriations. There are authorized to be appropriated such sums as are necessary to carry out this section.

(Aug. 14, 1935, ch 531, Title XX, Subtitle B, Part I, Subpart A, § 2022, as added March 23, 2010, P. L. 111-148, Title VI, Subtitle H, § 6703(a)(1)(C), 124 Stat. 787.)

§ 1397k-2. Research protections

(a) Guidelines. The Secretary shall promulgate guidelines to assist researchers working in the area of elder abuse, neglect, and exploitation, with issues relating to human subject protections.

(b) Definition of legally authorized representative for application of regulations. For purposes of the application of subpart A of part 46 of title 45, Code of Federal Regulations, to research conducted under this subpart, the term "legally authorized representative" means, unless otherwise provided by law, the individual or judicial or other body authorized under the applicable law to consent to medical treatment on behalf of another person.

(Aug. 14, 1935, ch 531, Title XX, Subtitle B, Part I, Subpart A, § 2023, as added March 23, 2010, P. L. 111-148, Title VI, Subtitle H, § 6703(a)(1)(C), 124 Stat. 789.)

§ 1397k-3. Authorization of appropriations

There are authorized to be appropriated to carry out this subpart [42 USCS §§ 1397k et seq.]—

(1) for fiscal year 2011, $6,500,000; and

(2) for each of fiscal years 2012 through 2014, $7,000,000.

(Aug. 14, 1935, ch 531, Title XX, Subtitle B, Part I, Subpart A, § 2024, as added March 23, 2010, P. L. 111-148, Title VI, Subtitle H, § 6703(a)(1)(C), 124 Stat. 790.)

SUBPART B. ELDER ABUSE, NEGLECT, AND EXPLOITATION FORENSIC CENTERS

§ 1397l. Establishment and support of elder abuse, neglect, and exploitation forensic centers

(a) In general. The Secretary, in consultation with the Attorney General, shall make grants to eligible entities to establish and operate stationary and mobile forensic centers, to develop forensic expertise regarding, and provide services relating to, elder abuse, neglect, and exploitation.

(b) Stationary forensic centers. The Secretary shall make 4 of the grants described in subsection (a) to institutions of higher education with demonstrated expertise in forensics or commitment to preventing or treating elder abuse, neglect, or exploitation, to establish and operate stationary forensic centers.

(c) Mobile centers. The Secretary shall make 6 of the grants described in subsection (a) to appropriate entities to establish and operate mobile forensic centers.

(d) Authorized activities. (1) Development of forensic markers and methodologies. An eligible entity that receives a grant under this section shall use funds made available through the grant to assist in determining whether abuse, neglect, or exploitation occurred and whether a crime was committed and to conduct research to describe and disseminate information on—

(A) forensic markers that indicate a case in which elder abuse, neglect, or exploitation may have occurred; and

(B) methodologies for determining, in such a case, when and how health care, emergency service, social and protective services, and legal service providers should intervene and when the providers should report the case to law enforcement authorities.

(2) Development of forensic expertise. An eligible entity that receives a grant under this section shall use funds made available through the grant to develop forensic expertise regarding elder abuse, neglect, and exploitation in order to provide medical and forensic evaluation, therapeutic intervention, victim support and advocacy, case review, and case tracking.

(3) Collection of evidence. The Secretary, in coordination with the Attorney General, shall use data made available by grant recipients under this section to develop the capacity of geriatric health care professionals and law enforcement to collect forensic evidence, including collecting forensic evidence relating to a potential determination of elder abuse, neglect, or exploitation.

(e) Application. To be eligible to receive a grant under this section, an entity shall submit an application to the Secretary at such time, in such manner, and containing such information as the Secretary may require.

(f) Authorization of appropriations. There are authorized to be appropriated to carry out this section—

(1) for fiscal year 2011, $4,000,000;

(2) for fiscal year 2012, $6,000,000; and

(3) for each of fiscal years 2013 and 2014, $8,000,000.

(Aug. 14, 1935, ch 531, Title XX, Subtitle B, Part I, Subpart B, § 2031, as added March 23, 2010, P. L. 111-148, Title VI, Subtitle H, § 6703(a)(1)(C), 124 Stat. 790.)

PART II. PROGRAMS TO PROMOTE ELDER JUSTICE

§ 1397m. Enhancement of long-term care

(a) Grants and incentives for long-term care staffing. (1) In general. The Secretary shall carry out activities, including activities described in paragraphs (2) and (3), to provide incentives for individuals to train for, seek, and maintain employment providing direct care in long-term care.

(2) Specific programs to enhance training, recruitment, and retention of staff. (A) Coordination with secretary of labor to recruit and train long-term care staff. The Secretary shall coordinate activities under this subsection with the Secretary of Labor in order to provide incentives for individuals to train for and seek employment providing direct care in long-term care.

(B) Career ladders and wage or benefit increases to increase staffing in long-term care. (i) In general. The Secretary shall make grants to eligible entities to carry out programs through which the entities—

(I) offer, to employees who provide direct care to residents of an eligible entity or individuals receiving community-based long-term care from an eligible entity, continuing training and varying levels of certification, based on observed clinical care practices and the amount of time the employees spend providing direct care; and

(II) provide, or make arrangements to provide, bonuses or other increased compensation or benefits to employees who achieve certification under such a program.

(ii) Application. To be eligible to receive a grant under this subparagraph, an eligible entity shall submit an application to the Secretary at such time, in such manner, and containing such information as the Secretary may require (which may include evidence of consultation with the State in which the eligible entity is located with respect to carrying out activities funded under the grant).

(iii) Authority to limit number of applicants. Nothing in this subparagraph shall be construed as prohibiting the Secretary from limiting the number of applicants for a grant under this subparagraph.

(3) Specific programs to improve management practices. (A) In general. The Secretary shall make grants to eligible entities to enable the entities to provide training and technical assistance.

(B) Authorized activities. An eligible entity that receives a grant under subparagraph (A) shall use funds made available through the grant to provide training and technical assistance regarding management practices using methods that are demonstrated to promote retention of individuals who provide direct care, such as—

(i) the establishment of standard human resource policies that reward high performance, including policies that provide for improved wages and benefits on the basis of job reviews;

(ii) the establishment of motivational and thoughtful work organization practices;

(iii) the creation of a workplace culture that respects and values caregivers and their needs;

(iv) the promotion of a workplace culture that respects the rights of residents of an eligible entity or individuals receiving community-based long-term care from an eligible entity and results in improved care for the residents or the individuals; and

(v) the establishment of other programs that promote the provision of high quality care, such as a continuing education program that provides additional hours of training, including on-the-job training, for employees who are certified nurse aides.

(C) Application. To be eligible to receive a grant under this paragraph, an eligible entity shall submit an application to the Secretary at such time, in such manner, and containing such information as the Secretary may require (which may include evidence of consultation with the State in which the eligible entity is located with respect to carrying out activities funded under the grant).

(D) Authority to limit number of applicants. Nothing in this paragraph shall be construed as prohibiting the Secretary from limiting the number of applicants for a grant under this paragraph.

(4) Accountability measures. The Secretary shall develop accountability measures to ensure that the activities conducted using funds made available under this subsection benefit individuals who provide direct care and increase the stability of the long-term care workforce.

(5) Definitions. In this subsection:

(A) Community-based long-term care. The term "community-based long-term care" has the meaning given such term by the Secretary.

(B) Eligible entity. The term "eligible entity" means the following:

(i) A long-term care facility.

(ii) A community-based long-term care entity (as defined by the Secretary).

(b) Certified EHR technology grant program. (1) Grants authorized. The Secretary is authorized to make grants to long-term care facilities for the purpose of assisting such entities in offsetting the costs related to purchasing, leasing, developing, and implementing certified EHR technology (as defined in section 1848(o)(4) [42 USCS § 1395w-4(o)(4)]) designed to improve patient safety and reduce adverse events and health care complications resulting from medication errors.

(2) Use of grant funds. Funds provided under grants under this subsection may be used for any of the following:

(A) Purchasing, leasing, and installing computer software and hardware, including handheld computer technologies.

(B) Making improvements to existing computer software and hardware.

(C) Making upgrades and other improvements to existing computer software and hardware to enable e-prescribing.

(D) Providing education and training to eligible long-term care facility staff on the use of such technology to implement the electronic transmission of prescription and patient information.

(3) Application. (A) In general. To be eligible to receive a grant under this subsection, a long-term care facility shall submit an application to the Secretary at such time, in such manner, and containing such information as the Secretary may require (which may include evidence of consultation with the State in which the long-term care facility is located with respect to carrying out activities funded under the grant).

(B) Authority to limit number of applicants. Nothing in this subsection shall be construed as prohibiting the Secretary from limiting the number of applicants for a grant under this subsection.

(4) Participation in state health exchanges. A long-term care facility that receives a grant under this subsection shall, where available, participate in activities conducted by a State or a qualified State-designated entity (as defined in section 3013(f) of the Public Health Service Act [42 USCS § 300jj-33(f)]) under a grant under section 3013 of the Public Health Service Act [42 USCS § 300jj-33] to coordinate care and for other purposes determined appropriate by the Secretary.

(5) Accountability measures. The Secretary shall develop accountability measures to ensure that the activities conducted using funds made available under this subsection help improve patient safety and reduce adverse events and health care complications resulting from medication errors.

(c) Adoption of standards for transactions involving clinical data by long-term care facilities. (1) Standards and compatibility. The Secretary shall adopt electronic standards for the exchange of clinical data by long-term care facilities, including, where available, standards for messaging and nomenclature. Standards adopted by the Secretary under the preceding sentence shall be compatible with standards established under part C of title XI [42 USCS §§ 1320d et seq.], standards established under subsections (b)(2)(B)(i) and (e)(4) of section 1860D-4 [42 USCS § 1395w-104], standards adopted under section 3004 of the Public Health Service Act [42 USCS § 300jj-14], and general health information technology standards.

(2) Electronic submission of data to the Secretary. (A) In general. Not later than 10 years after the date of enactment of the Elder Justice Act of 2009 [enacted March 23, 2010], the Secretary shall have procedures in place to accept the optional electronic submission of clinical data by long-term care facilities pursuant to the standards adopted under paragraph (1).

(B) Rule of construction. Nothing in this subsection shall be construed to require a long-term care facility to submit clinical data electronically to the Secretary.

(3) Regulations. The Secretary shall promulgate regulations to carry out this subsection. Such regulations shall require a State, as a condition of the receipt of funds under this part, to conduct such data collection and reporting as the Secretary determines are necessary to satisfy the requirements of this subsection.

(d) Authorization of appropriations.

There are authorized to be appropriated to carry out this section—

(1) for fiscal year 2011, $20,000,000;

(2) for fiscal year 2012, $17,500,000; and

(3) for each of fiscal years 2013 and 2014, $15,000,000.

(Aug. 14, 1935, ch 531, Title XX, Subtitle B, Part II § 2041, as added March 23, 2010, P. L. 111-148, Title VI, Subtitle H, § 6703(a)(1)(C), 124 Stat. 791.)

§ 1397m-1. Adult protective services functions and grant programs

(a) Secretarial responsibilities. (1) In general. The Secretary shall ensure that the Department of Health and Human Services—

(A) provides funding authorized by this part to State and local adult protective services offices that investigate reports of the abuse, neglect, and exploitation of elders;

(B) collects and disseminates data annually relating to the abuse, exploitation, and neglect of elders in coordination with the Department of Justice;

(C) develops and disseminates information on best practices regarding, and provides training on, carrying out adult protective services;

(D) conducts research related to the provision of adult protective services; and

(E) provides technical assistance to States and other entities that provide or fund the provision of adult protective services, including through grants made under subsections (b) and (c).

(2) Authorization of appropriations. There are authorized to be appropriated to carry out this subsection, $3,000,000 for fiscal year 2011 and $4,000,000 for each of fiscal years 2012 through 2014.

(b) Grants to enhance the provision of adult protective services. (1) Establishment. There is established an adult protective services grant program under which the Secretary shall annually award grants to States in the amounts calculated under paragraph (2) for the purposes of enhancing adult protective services provided by States and local units of government.

(2) Amount of payment. (A) In general. Subject to the availability of appropriations and subparagraphs (B) and (C), the amount paid to a State for a fiscal year under the program under this subsection shall equal the amount appropriated for that year to carry out this subsection multiplied by the percentage of the total number of elders who reside in the United States who reside in that State.

(B) Guaranteed minimum payment amount. (i) 50 States. Subject to clause (ii), if the amount determined under subparagraph (A) for a State for a fiscal year is less than 0.75 percent of the amount appropriated for such year, the Secretary shall increase such determined amount so that the total amount paid under this subsection to the State for the year is equal to 0.75 percent of the amount so appropriated.

(ii) Territories. In the case of a State other than 1 of the 50 States, clause (i) shall be applied as if each reference to "0.75" were a reference to "0.1".

(C) Pro rata reductions. The Secretary shall make such pro rata reductions to the amounts described in subparagraph (A) as are necessary to comply with the requirements of subparagraph (B).

(3) Authorized activities. (A) Adult protective services. Funds made available pursuant to this subsection may only be used by States and local units of government to provide adult protective services and may not be used for any other purpose.

(B) Use by agency. Each State receiving funds pursuant to this subsection shall provide such funds to the agency or unit of State government having legal responsibility for providing adult protective services within the State.

(C) Supplement not supplant. Each State or local unit of government shall use funds made available pursuant to this subsection to supplement and not supplant other Federal, State, and local public funds expended to provide adult protective services in the State.

(4) State reports. Each State receiving funds under this subsection shall submit to the Secretary, at such time and in such manner as the Secretary may require, a report on the number of elders served by the grants awarded under this subsection.

(5) Authorization of appropriations. There are authorized to be appropriated to carry out this subsection, $100,000,000 for each of fiscal years 2011 through 2014.

(c) State demonstration programs. (1) Establishment. The Secretary shall award grants to States for the purposes of conducting demonstration programs in accordance with paragraph (2).

(2) Demonstration programs. Funds made available pursuant to this subsection may be used by States and local units of government to conduct demonstration programs that test—

(A) training modules developed for the purpose of detecting or preventing elder abuse;

(B) methods to detect or prevent financial

exploitation of elders;

(C) methods to detect elder abuse;

(D) whether training on elder abuse forensics enhances the detection of elder abuse by employees of the State or local unit of government; or

(E) other matters relating to the detection or prevention of elder abuse.

(3) Application. To be eligible to receive a grant under this subsection, a State shall submit an application to the Secretary at such time, in such manner, and containing such information as the Secretary may require.

(4) State reports. Each State that receives funds under this subsection shall submit to the Secretary a report at such time, in such manner, and containing such information as the Secretary may require on the results of the demonstration program conducted by the State using funds made available under this subsection.

(5) Authorization of appropriations. There are authorized to be appropriated to carry out this subsection, $25,000,000 for each of fiscal years 2011 through 2014.

(Aug. 14, 1935, ch 531, Title XX, Subtitle B, Part II § 2042, as added March 23, 2010, P. L. 111-148, Title VI, Subtitle H, § 6703(a)(1)(C), 124 Stat. 794.)

§ 1397m-2. Long-term care ombudsman program grants and training

(a) Grants to support the long-term care ombudsman program. (1) In general. The Secretary shall make grants to eligible entities with relevant expertise and experience in abuse and neglect in long-term care facilities or long-term care ombudsman programs and responsibilities, for the purpose of—

(A) improving the capacity of State long-term care ombudsman programs to respond to and resolve complaints about abuse and neglect;

(B) conducting pilot programs with State long-term care ombudsman offices or local ombudsman entities; and

(C) providing support for such State long-term care ombudsman programs and such pilot programs (such as through the establishment of a national long-term care ombudsman resource center).

(2) Authorization of appropriations. There are authorized to be appropriated to carry out this subsection—

(A) for fiscal year 2011, $5,000,000;

(B) for fiscal year 2012, $7,500,000; and

(C) for each of fiscal years 2013 and 2014, $10,000,000.

(b) Ombudsman training programs. (1) In general. The Secretary shall establish programs to provide and improve ombudsman training with respect to elder abuse, neglect, and exploitation for national organizations and State long-term care ombudsman programs.

(2) Authorization of appropriations. There are authorized to be appropriated to carry out this subsection, for each of fiscal years 2011 through 2014, $10,000,000.

(Aug. 14, 1935, ch 531, Title XX, Subtitle B, Part II § 2043, as added March 23, 2010, P. L. 111-148, Title VI, Subtitle H, § 6703(a)(1)(C), 124 Stat. 796.)

§ 1397m-3. Provision of information regarding, and evaluations of, elder justice programs

(a) Provision of information. To be eligible to receive a grant under this part, an applicant shall agree—

(1) except as provided in paragraph (2), to provide the eligible entity conducting an evaluation under subsection (b) of the activities funded through the grant with such information as the eligible entity may require in order to conduct such evaluation; or

(2) in the case of an applicant for a grant under section 2041(b) [42 USCS § 1397m(b)], to provide the Secretary with such information as the Secretary may require to conduct an evaluation or audit under subsection (c).

(b) Use of eligible entities to conduct evaluations. (1) Evaluations required. Except as provided in paragraph (2), the Secretary shall—

(A) reserve a portion (not less than 2 percent) of the funds appropriated with respect to each program carried out under this part; and

(B) use the funds reserved under subparagraph (A) to provide assistance to eligible entities to conduct evaluations of the activities funded under each program carried out under this part.

(2) Certified EHR technology grant program not included. The provisions of this subsection shall not apply to the certified EHR technology grant program under section 2041(b).

(3) Authorized activities. A recipient of assistance described in paragraph (1)(B) shall use the funds made available through the assistance to conduct a validated evaluation of the effectiveness of the activities funded under a program carried out under this part.

(4) Applications. To be eligible to receive assistance under paragraph (1)(B), an entity shall submit an application to the Secretary at such time, in such manner, and containing such

information as the Secretary may require, including a proposal for the evaluation.

(5) Reports. Not later than a date specified by the Secretary, an eligible entity receiving assistance under paragraph (1)(B) shall submit to the Secretary, the Committee on Ways and Means and the Committee on Energy and Commerce of the House of Representatives, and the Committee on Finance of the Senate a report containing the results of the evaluation conducted using such assistance together with such recommendations as the entity determines to be appropriate.

(c) Evaluations and audits of certified EHR technology grant program by the Secretary. (1) Evaluations. The Secretary shall conduct an evaluation of the activities funded under the certified EHR technology grant program under section 2041(b) [42 USCS § 1397m(b)]. Such evaluation shall include an evaluation of whether the funding provided under the grant is expended only for the purposes for which it is made.

(2) Audits. The Secretary shall conduct appropriate audits of grants made under section 2041(b) [42 USCS § 1397m(b)].

(Aug. 14, 1935, ch 531, Title XX, Subtitle B, Part II § 2044, as added March 23, 2010, P. L. 111-148, Title VI, Subtitle H, § 6703(a)(1)(C), 124 Stat. 796.)

§ 1397m-4. Report

Not later than October 1, 2014, the Secretary shall submit to the Elder Justice Coordinating Council established under section 2021 [42 USCS § 1397k], the Committee on Ways and Means and the Committee on Energy and Commerce of the House of Representatives, and the Committee on Finance of the Senate a report—

(1) compiling, summarizing, and analyzing the information contained in the State reports submitted under subsections (b)(4) and (c)(4) of section 2042 [42 USCS § 1397m-1]; and

(2) containing such recommendations for legislative or administrative action as the Secretary determines to be appropriate.

(Aug. 14, 1935, ch 531, Title XX, Subtitle B, Part II § 2045, as added March 23, 2010, P. L. 111-148, Title VI, Subtitle H, § 6703(a)(1)(C), 124 Stat. 797.)

§ 1397m-5. Rule of construction

Nothing in this subtitle [42 USCS §§ 1397j et seq.] shall be construed as—

(1) limiting any cause of action or other relief related to obligations under this subtitle [42 USCS §§ 1397j et seq.] that is available under the law of any State, or political subdivision thereof; or

(2) creating a private cause of action for a violation of this subtitle [42 USCS §§ 1397j et seq.].

(Aug. 14, 1935, ch 531, Title XX, Subtitle B, Part II § 2046, as added March 23, 2010, P. L. 111-148, Title VI, Subtitle H, § 6703(a)(1)(C), 124 Stat. 798.)

TITLE XXI. STATE CHILDREN'S HEALTH INSURANCE PROGRAM

§ 1397bb. General contents of State child health plan; eligibility; outreach

(a) General background and description. A State child health plan shall include a description, consistent with the requirements of this title [42 USCS §§ 1397aa et seq.], of—

(1) the extent to which, and manner in which, children in the State, including targeted low-income children and other classes of children classified by income and other relevant factors, currently have creditable health coverage (as defined in section 2110(c)(2) [42 USCS § 1397jj(c)(2)]);

(2) current State efforts to provide or obtain creditable health coverage for uncovered children, including the steps the State is taking to identify and enroll all uncovered children who are eligible to participate in public health insurance programs and health insurance programs that involve public-private partnerships;

(3) how the plan is designed to be coordinated with such efforts to increase coverage of children under creditable health coverage;

(4) the child health assistance provided under the plan for targeted low-income children, including the proposed methods of delivery, and utilization control systems;

(5) eligibility standards consistent with subsection (b);

(6) outreach activities consistent with subsection (c); and

(7) methods (including monitoring) used—

(A) to assure the quality and appropriateness of care, particularly with respect to well-baby care, well-child care, and immunizations provided under the plan, and

(B) to assure access to covered services, including emergency services and services described in section 2103(c)(5) [42 USCS § 1397cc(c)(5)].

(b) General description of eligibility standards and methodology. (1) Eligibility standards. (A) In general. The plan shall include a description of the standards used to determine the eligibility of targeted low-income children for child health assistance under the plan. Such standards may include (to the extent consistent with this title [42 USCS §§ 1397aa et seq.]) those relating to the geographic areas to be served by the plan, age, income and resources (including any standards relating to spenddowns and disposition of resources), residency, disability status (so long as any standard relating to such status does not restrict eligibility), access to or coverage under other health coverage, and duration of eligibility. Such standards may not discriminate on the basis of diagnosis.

(B) Limitations on eligibility standards. Such eligibility standards—

(i) shall, within any defined group of covered targeted low-income children, not cover such children with higher family income without covering children with a lower family income;

(ii) may not deny eligibility based on a child having a preexisting medical condition;

(iii) may not apply a waiting period (including a waiting period to carry out paragraph (3)(C)) in the case of a targeted low-income pregnant woman provided pregnancy-related assistance under section 2112 [42 USCS § 1397ll];

(iv) at State option, may not apply a waiting period in the case of a child provided dental-only supplemental coverage under section 2110(b)(5) [42 USCS § 1397jj(b)(5)]; and

(v) shall, beginning January 1, 2014, use modified adjusted gross income and household income (as defined in section 36B(d)(2) of the Internal Revenue Code of 1986 [26 USCS § 36B(d)(2)]) to determine eligibility for child health assistance under the State child health plan or under any waiver of such plan and for any other purpose applicable under the plan or waiver for which a determination of income is required, including with respect to the imposition of premiums and cost-sharing, consistent with section 1902(e)(14) [42 USCS § 1396a(e)(14)].

(2) Methodology. The plan shall include a description of methods of establishing and continuing eligibility and enrollment.

(3) Eligibility screening; coordination with other health coverage programs. The plan shall include a description of procedures to be used to ensure—

(A) through both intake and followup screening, that only targeted low-income children are furnished child health assistance under the State child health plan;

(B) that children found through the screening to be eligible for medical assistance under the State medicaid plan under title XIX [42 USCS §§ 1396 et seq.] are enrolled for such assistance under such plan;

(C) that the insurance provided under the State child health plan does not substitute for coverage under group health plans;

(D) the provision of child health assistance to targeted low-income children in the State who are Indians (as defined in section 4(c) of the Indian Health Care Improvement Act, 25 U.S.C. 1603(c)); and

(E) coordination with other public and private programs providing creditable coverage for low-income children.

(4) Reduction of administrative barriers to enrollment. (A) In general. Subject to subparagraph (B), the plan shall include a description of the procedures used to reduce administrative barriers to the enrollment of children and pregnant women who are eligible for medical assistance under title XIX [42 USCS §§ 1396a et seq.] or for child health assistance or health benefits coverage under this title [42 USCS §§ 1397aa et seq.]. Such procedures shall be established and revised as often as the State determines appropriate to take into account the most recent information available to the State identifying such barriers.

(B) Deemed compliance if joint application and renewal process that permits application other than in person. A State shall be deemed to comply with subparagraph (A) if the State's application and renewal forms and supplemental forms (if any) and information verification process is the same for purposes of establishing and renewing eligibility for children and pregnant women for medical assistance under title XIX [42 USCS §§ 1396a et seq.] and child health assistance under this title, and such process does not require an application to be made in person or a face-to-face interview.

(5) Nonentitlement. Nothing in this title [42 USCS §§ 1397aa et seq.] shall be construed as providing an individual with an entitlement to child health assistance under a State child health plan.

(c) Outreach and coordination. A State child health plan shall include a description of the procedures to be used by the State to accomplish the following:

(1) Outreach. Outreach (through community health workers and others) to families of children likely to be eligible for child health assistance under the plan or under other public or private health coverage programs to inform these families of the availability of, and to assist them in enrolling their children in, such a program.

(2) Coordination with other health insurance programs. Coordination of the administration of the State program under this title [42 USCS §§ 1397aa et seq.] with other public and private health insurance programs.

(3) Premium assistance subsidies. In the case of a State that provides for premium assistance subsidies under the State child health plan in accordance with paragraph (2)(B), (3), or (10) of section 2105(c) [42 USCS § 1397ee(c)], or a waiver approved under section 1115 [42 USCS § 1315], outreach, education, and enrollment assistance for families of children likely to be eligible for such subsidies, to inform such families of the availability of, and to assist them in enrolling their children in, such subsidies, and for employers likely to provide coverage that is eligible for such subsidies, including the specific, significant resources the State intends to apply to educate employers about the availability of premium assistance subsidies under the State child health plan.

(Aug. 14, 1935, ch 531, Title XXI, § 2102, as added Aug. 5, 1997, P. L. 105-33, Title IV, Subtitle J, Ch 1, § 4901(a), 111 Stat. 552; Feb. 4, 2009, P. L. 111-3, Title I, Subtitle B, § 111(b)(2), Title II, Subtitle A, § 201(b)(2)(B)(i), Subtitle B, § 212, Title III, Subtitle A, § 302(a), Title V, § 501(a)(2), (b)(2), 123 Stat. 28, 39, 55, 63, 85, 86; March 23, 2010, P. L. 111-148, Title II, Subtitle B, § 2101(d)(1), 124 Stat. 287; March 30, 2010, P. L. 111-152, Title I, Subtitle A, § 1004(b)(2)(A), 124 Stat. 1034.)

§ 1397dd. Allotments

(a) Appropriation; total allotment. For the purpose of providing allotments to States under this section, subject to subsection (d), there is appropriated, out of any money in the Treasury not otherwise appropriated—

(1) for fiscal year 1998, $4,295,000,000;
(2) for fiscal year 1999, $4,275,000,000;
(3) for fiscal year 2000, $4,275,000,000;
(4) for fiscal year 2001, $4,275,000,000;
(5) for fiscal year 2002, $3,150,000,000;
(6) for fiscal year 2003, $3,150,000,000;
(7) for fiscal year 2004, $3,150,000,000;
(8) for fiscal year 2005, $4,050,000,000;
(9) for fiscal year 2006, $4,050,000,000;
(10) for fiscal year 2007, $5,000,000,000;
(11) for fiscal year 2008, $5,000,000,000.
(12) for fiscal year 2009, $10,562,000,000;
(13) for fiscal year 2010, $12,520,000,000;
(14) for fiscal year 2011, $13,459,000,000;
(15) for fiscal year 2012, $14,982,000,000;
(16) for fiscal year 2013, $17,406,000,000;
(17) for fiscal year 2014, $19,147,000,000; and
(18) for fiscal year 2015, for purposes of making 2 semi-annual allotments—

(A) $2,850,000,000 for the period beginning on October 1, 2014, and ending on March 31, 2015, and

(B) $2,850,000,000 for the period beginning on April 1, 2015, and ending on September 30, 2015.

(b) Allotments to 50 States and District of Columbia. (1) In general. Subject to paragraph (4) and subsections (d) and (m), of the amount available for allotment under subsection (a) for a fiscal year, reduced by the amount of allotments made under subsection (c) (determined without regard to paragraph (4) thereof) for the fiscal year, the Secretary shall allot to each State (other than a State described in such subsection) with a State child health plan approved under this title [42 USCS §§ 1397aa et seq.] the same proportion as the ratio of—

(A) the product of (i) the number of children described in paragraph (2) for the State for the fiscal year and (ii) the State cost factor for that State (established under paragraph (3)); to

(B) the sum of the products computed under subparagraph (A).

(2) Number of children. (A) In general. The number of children described in this paragraph for a State for—

(i) each of fiscal years 1998 and 1999 is equal to the number of low-income children in the State with no health insurance coverage for the fiscal year;

(ii) fiscal year 2000 is equal to—

(I) 75 percent of the number of low-income children in the State for the fiscal year with no health insurance coverage, plus

(II) 25 percent of the number of low-income children in the State for the fiscal year; and

(iii) each succeeding fiscal year is equal to—

(I) 50 percent of the number of low-income children in the State for the fiscal year with no health insurance coverage, plus

(II) 50 percent of the number of low-income children in the State for the fiscal year.

(B) Determination of number of children. For purposes of subparagraph (A), a determination of the number of low-income children (and of such children who have no health insurance coverage) for a State for a fiscal year shall be made on the basis of the arithmetic average of the number of such children, as reported and defined in the 3 most recent March supplements to the Current Population Survey of the Bureau of the Census before the beginning of the calendar year in which such fiscal year year begins.

(3) Adjustment for geographic variations in health costs. (A) In general. For purposes of paragraph (1)(A)(ii), the "State cost factor" for a State for a fiscal year equal to the sum of—

(i) 0.15, and

(ii) 0.85 multiplied by the ratio of—

(I) the annual average wages per employee for the State for such year (as determined under subparagraph (B)), to

(II) the annual average wages per employee for the 50 States and the District of Columbia.

(B) Annual average wages per employee. For purposes of subparagraph (A), the "annual average wages per employee" for a State, or for all the States, for a fiscal year is equal to the average of the annual wages per employee for the State or for the 50 States and the District of Columbia for employees in the health services industry (SIC code 8000), as reported by the Bureau of Labor Statistics of the Department of Labor for each of the most recent 3 years before the beginning of the calendar year in which such fiscal year begins.

(4) Floors and ceilings in State allotments. (A) In general. The proportion of the allotment under this subsection for a subsection (b) State (as defined in subparagraph (D)) for fiscal year 2000 and each fiscal year thereafter shall be subject to the following floors and ceilings:

(i) Floor of $2,000,000. A floor equal to $2,000,000 divided by the total of the amount available under this subsection for all such allotments for the fiscal year.

(ii) Annual floor of 10 percent below preceding fiscal year's proportion. A floor of 90 percent of the proportion for the State for the preceding fiscal year.

(iii) Cumulative floor of 30 percent below the FY 1999 proportion. A floor of 70 percent of the proportion for the State for fiscal year 1999.

(iv) Cumulative ceiling of 45 percent above FY 1999 proportion. A ceiling of 145 percent of the proportion for the State for fiscal year 1999.

(B) Reconciliation. (i) Elimination of any deficit by establishing a percentage increase ceiling for States with highest annual percentage increases. To the extent that the application of subparagraph (A) would result in the sum of the proportions of the allotments for all subsection (b) States exceeding 1.0, the Secretary shall establish a maximum percentage increase in such proportions for all subsection (b) States for the fiscal year in a manner so that such sum equals 1.0.

(ii) Allocation of surplus through pro rata increase. To the extent that the application of subparagraph (A) would result in the sum of the proportions of the allotments for all subsection (b) States being less than 1.0, the proportions of such allotments (as computed before the application of floors under clauses (i), (ii), and (iii) of subparagraph (A)) for all subsection (b) States shall be increased in a pro rata manner (but not to exceed the ceiling established under subparagraph (A)(iv)) so that (after the application of such floors and ceiling) such sum equals 1.0.

(C) Construction. This paragraph shall not be construed as applying to (or taking into account) amounts of allotments redistributed under subsection (f).

(D) Definitions. In this paragraph:

(i) Proportion of allotment. The term "proportion" means, with respect to the allotment of a subsection (b) State for a fiscal year, the amount of the allotment of such State under this subsection for the fiscal year divided by the total of the amount available under this subsection for all such allotments for the fiscal year.

(ii) Subsection (b) State. The term "subsection (b) State" means one of the 50 States or the District of Columbia.

(c) Allotments to territories. (1) In general. Of the amount available for allotment under subsection (a) for a fiscal year, subject to subsections (d) and (m)(4), the Secretary shall allot 0.25 percent among each of the commonwealths and territories described in paragraph (3) in the same proportion as the percentage specified in paragraph (2) for such commonwealth or territory bears to the sum of such percentages for all such commonwealths or territories so described.

(2) Percentage. The percentage specified in this paragraph for—

(A) Puerto Rico is 91.6 percent,

(B) Guam is 3.5 percent,

(C) the Virgin Islands is 2.6 percent,

(D) American Samoa is 1.2 percent, and

(E) the Northern Mariana Islands is 1.1 percent.

(3) Commonwealths and territories. A commonwealth or territory described in this paragraph is any of the following if it has a State child health plan approved under this title [42 USCS §§ 1397aa et seq.]:

(A) Puerto Rico.

(B) Guam.

(C) The Virgin Islands.

(D) American Samoa.

(E) The Northern Mariana Islands.

(4) Additional allotment. (A) In general. In addition to the allotment under paragraph (1), the Secretary shall allot each commonwealth

and territory described in paragraph (3) the applicable percentage specified in paragraph (2) of the amount appropriated under subparagraph (B).

(B) Appropriations. For purposes of providing allotments pursuant to subparagraph (A), there is appropriated, out of any money in the Treasury not otherwise appropriated $32,000,000 for fiscal year 1999, $34,200,000 for each of fiscal years 2000 and 2001, $25,200,000 for each of fiscal years 2002 through 2004, $32,400,000 for each of fiscal years 2005 and 2006, and $40,000,000 for each of fiscal years 2007 through 2009.

(d) Additional allotments to eliminate funding shortfalls. (1) Appropriation; allotment authority. For the purpose of providing additional allotments to shortfall States described in paragraph (2), there is appropriated, out of any money in the Treasury not otherwise appropriated, $283,000,000 for fiscal year 2006.

(2) Shortfall States described. For purposes of paragraph (1), a shortfall State described in this paragraph is a State with a State child health plan approved under this title [42 USCS §§ 1397aa et seq.] for which the Secretary estimates, on the basis of the most recent data available to the Secretary as of December 16, 2005, that the projected expenditures under such plan for such State for fiscal year 2006 will exceed the sum of—

(A) the amount of the State's allotments for each of fiscal years 2004 and 2005 that will not be expended by the end of fiscal year 2005;

(B) the amount, if any, that is to be redistributed to the State during fiscal year 2006 in accordance with subsection (f); and

(C) the amount of the State's allotment for fiscal year 2006.

(3) Allotments. In addition to the allotments provided under subsections (b) and (c), subject to paragraph (4), of the amount available for the additional allotments under paragraph (1) for fiscal year 2006, the Secretary shall allot—

(A) to each shortfall State described in paragraph (2) such amount as the Secretary determines will eliminate the estimated shortfall described in such paragraph for the State; and

(B) to each commonwealth or territory described in subsection (c)(3), the same proportion as the proportion of the commonwealth's or territory's allotment under subsection (c) (determined without regard to subsection (f)) to 1.05 percent of the amount appropriated under paragraph (1).

(4) Use of additional allotment. Additional allotments provided under this subsection are only available for amounts expended under a State plan approved under this title [42 USCS §§ 1397aa et seq.] for child health assistance for targeted low-income children.

(5) 1-year availability; no redistribution of unexpended additional allotments. Notwithstanding subsections (e) and (f), amounts allotted to a State pursuant to this subsection for fiscal year 2006 shall only remain available for expenditure by the State through September 30, 2006. Any amounts of such allotments that remain unexpended as of such date shall not be subject to redistribution under subsection (f) and shall revert to the Treasury on October 1, 2006.

(e) Availability of amounts allotted. (1) In general. Except as provided in paragraph (2), amounts allotted to a State pursuant to this section—

(A) for each of fiscal years 1998 through 2008, shall remain available for expenditure by the State through the end of the second succeeding fiscal year; and

(B) for fiscal year 2009 and each fiscal year thereafter, shall remain available for expenditure by the State through the end of the succeeding fiscal year.

(2) Availability of amounts redistributed. Amounts redistributed to a State under subsection (f) shall be available for expenditure by the State through the end of the fiscal year in which they are redistributed.

(f) Procedure for redistribution of unused allotments. (1) In general. The Secretary shall determine an appropriate procedure for redistribution of allotments from States that were provided allotments under this section for a fiscal year but that do not expend all of the amount of such allotments during the period in which such allotments are available for expenditure under subsection (e), to States that the Secretary determines with respect to the fiscal year for which unused allotments are available for redistribution under this subsection, are shortfall States described in paragraph (2) for such fiscal year, but not to exceed the amount of the shortfall described in paragraph (2)(A) for each such State (as may be adjusted under paragraph (2)(C)).

(2) Shortfall States described. (A) In general. For purposes of paragraph (1), with respect to a fiscal year, a shortfall State described in this subparagraph is a State with a State child health plan approved under this title [42 USCS §§ 1397aa et seq.] for which the Secretary estimates on the basis of the most recent data available to the Secretary, that the projected expenditures under such plan for the

State for the fiscal year will exceed the sum of—

(i) the amount of the State's allotments for any preceding fiscal years that remains available for expenditure and that will not be expended by the end of the immediately preceding fiscal year;

(ii) the amount (if any) of the child enrollment contingency fund payment under subsection (n); and

(iii) the amount of the State's allotment for the fiscal year.

(B) Proration rule. If the amounts available for redistribution under paragraph (1) for a fiscal year are less than the total amounts of the estimated shortfalls determined for the year under subparagraph (A), the amount to be redistributed under such paragraph for each shortfall State shall be reduced proportionally.

(C) Retrospective adjustment. The Secretary may adjust the estimates and determinations made under paragraph (1) and this paragraph with respect to a fiscal year as necessary on the basis of the amounts reported by States not later than November 30 of the succeeding fiscal year, as approved by the Secretary.

(g) Rule for redistribution and extended availability of fiscal years 1998, 1999, 2000, and 2001 allotments. (1) Amount redistributed. (A) In general. In the case of a State that expends all of its allotment under subsection (b) or (c) for fiscal year 1998 by the end of fiscal year 2000, or for fiscal year 1999 by the end of fiscal year 2001, or for fiscal year 2000 by the end of fiscal year 2002, or for fiscal year 2001 by the end of fiscal year 2003, the Secretary shall redistribute to the State under subsection (f) (from the fiscal year 1998, 1999, 2000, or 2001 allotments of other States, respectively, as determined by the application of paragraphs (2) and (3) with respect to the respective fiscal year) the following amount:

(i) State. In the case of 1 of the 50 States or the District of Columbia, with respect to—

(I) the fiscal year 1998 allotment, the amount by which the State's expenditures under this title [42 USCS §§ 1397aa et seq.] in fiscal years 1998, 1999, and 2000 exceed the State's allotment for fiscal year 1998 under subsection (b);

(II) the fiscal year 1999 allotment, the amount by which the State's expenditures under this title [42 USCS §§ 1397aa et seq.] in fiscal years 1999, 2000, and 2001 exceed the State's allotment for fiscal year 1999 under subsection (b);

(III) the fiscal year 2000 allotment, the amount specified in subparagraph (C)(i) (less the total of the amounts under clause (ii) for such fiscal year), multiplied by the ratio of the amount specified in subparagraph (C)(ii) for the State to the amount specified in subparagraph (C)(iii); or

(IV) the fiscal year 2001 allotment, the amount specified in subparagraph (D)(i) (less the total of the amounts under clause (ii) for such fiscal year), multiplied by the ratio of the amount specified in subparagraph (D)(ii) for the State to the amount specified in subparagraph (D)(iii).

(ii) Territory. In the case of a commonwealth or territory described in subsection (c)(3), an amount that bears the same ratio to 1.05 percent of the total amount described in paragraph (2)(B)(i)(I) as the ratio of the commonwealth's or territory's fiscal year 1998, 1999, 2000, or 2001 allotment under subsection (c) (as the case may be) bears to the total of all such allotments for such fiscal year under such subsection.

(B) Expenditure rules. An amount redistributed to a State under this paragraph—

(i) shall not be included in the determination of the State's allotment for any fiscal year under this section;

(ii) notwithstanding subsection (e), with respect to fiscal year 1998, 1999, or 2000, shall remain available for expenditure by the State through the end of fiscal year 2004;

(iii) notwithstanding subsection (e), with respect to fiscal year 2001, shall remain available for expenditure by the State through the end of fiscal year 2005; and

(iv) shall be counted as being expended with respect to a fiscal year allotment in accordance with applicable regulations of the Secretary.

(C) Amounts used in computing redistributions for fiscal year 2000. For purposes of subparagraph (A)(i)(III)—

(i) the amount specified in this clause is the amount specified in paragraph (2)(B)(i)(I) for fiscal year 2000, less the total amount remaining available pursuant to paragraph (2)(A)(iii);

(ii) the amount specified in this clause for a State is the amount by which the State's expenditures under this title [42 USCS §§ 1397aa et seq.] in fiscal years 2000, 2001, and 2002 exceed the State's allotment for fiscal year 2000 under subsection (b); and

(iii) the amount specified in this clause is the sum, for all States entitled to a redistribution under subparagraph (A) from the allotments for fiscal year 2000, of the amounts specified in clause (ii).

(D) Amounts used in computing redistributions for fiscal year 2001. For purposes of subparagraph (A)(i)(IV)—

(i) the amount specified in this clause is the amount specified in paragraph (2)(B)(i)(I) for fiscal year 2001, less the total amount remaining available pursuant to paragraph (2)(A)(iv);

(ii) the amount specified in this clause for a State is the amount by which the State's expenditures under this title [42 USCS §§ 1397aa et seq.] in fiscal years 2001, 2002, and 2003 exceed the State's allotment for fiscal year 2001 under subsection (b); and

(iii) the amount specified in this clause is the sum, for all States entitled to a redistribution under subparagraph (A) from the allotments for fiscal year 2001, of the amounts specified in clause (ii).

(2) Extension of availability of portion of unexpended fiscal years 1998 through 2001 allotments. (A) In general. Notwithstanding subsection (e):

(i) Fiscal year 1998 allotment. Of the amounts allotted to a State pursuant to this section for fiscal year 1998 that were not expended by the State by the end of fiscal year 2000, the amount specified in subparagraph (B) for fiscal year 1998 for such State shall remain available for expenditure by the State through the end of fiscal year 2004.

(ii) Fiscal year 1999 allotment. Of the amounts allotted to a State pursuant to this subsection for fiscal year 1999 that were not expended by the State by the end of fiscal year 2001, the amount specified in subparagraph (B) for fiscal year 1999 for such State shall remain available for expenditure by the State through the end of fiscal year 2004.

(iii) Fiscal year 2000 allotment. Of the amounts allotted to a State pursuant to this section for fiscal year 2000 that were not expended by the State by the end of fiscal year 2002, 50 percent of that amount shall remain available for expenditure by the State through the end of fiscal year 2004.

(iv) Fiscal year 2001 allotment. Of the amounts allotted to a State pursuant to this section for fiscal year 2001 that were not expended by the State by the end of fiscal year 2003, 50 percent of that amount shall remain available for expenditure by the State through the end of fiscal year 2005.

(B) Amount remaining available for expenditure. The amount specified in this subparagraph for a State for a fiscal year is equal to—

(i) the amount by which (I) the total amount available for redistribution under subsection (f) from the allotments for that fiscal year, exceeds (II) the total amounts redistributed under paragraph (1) for that fiscal year; multiplied by

(ii) the ratio of the amount of such State's unexpended allotment for that fiscal year to the total amount described in clause (i)(I) for that fiscal year.

(C) Use of up to 10 percent of retained 1998 allotments for outreach activities. Notwithstanding section 2105(c)(2)(A) [42 USCS § 1397ee(c)(2)(A)], with respect to any State described in subparagraph (A)(i), the State may use up to 10 percent of the amount specified in subparagraph (B) for fiscal year 1998 for expenditures for outreach activities approved by the Secretary.

(3) Determination of amounts. For purposes of calculating the amounts described in paragraphs (1) and (2) relating to the allotment for fiscal year 1998, fiscal year 1999, fiscal year 2000, or fiscal year 2001, the Secretary shall use the amounts reported by the States not later than December 15, 2000, November 30, 2001, November 30, 2002, or November 2003, respectively, on HCFA Form 64 or HCFA Form 21, or CMS Form 64 of CMS Form 21, as the case may be, as approved by the Secretary.

(h) Special rules to address fiscal year 2007 shortfalls. (1) Redistribution of unused fiscal year 2004 allotments. (A) In general. Notwithstanding subsection (f) and subject to subparagraphs (C) and (D), with respect to months beginning during fiscal year 2007, the Secretary shall provide for a redistribution under such subsection from the allotments for fiscal year 2004 under subsection (b) that are not expended by the end of fiscal year 2006, to a shortfall State described in subparagraph (B), such amount as the Secretary determines will eliminate the estimated shortfall described in such subparagraph for such State for the month.

(B) Shortfall State described. For purposes of this paragraph, a shortfall State described in this subparagraph is a State with a State child health plan approved under this title [42 USCS §§ 1397aa et seq.] for which the Secretary estimates, on a monthly basis using the most recent data available to the Secretary as of such month, that the projected expenditures under such plan for such State for fiscal year 2007 will exceed the sum of—

(i) the amount of the State's allotments for each of fiscal years 2005 and 2006 that was not expended by the end of fiscal year 2006; and

(ii) the amount of the State's allotment for fiscal year 2007.

(C) Funds redistributed in the order in which states realize funding shortfalls. The Secretary shall redistribute the amounts available for redistribution under subparagraph (A) to shortfall States described in subparagraph (B) in the order in which such States realize monthly funding shortfalls under this title [42 USCS §§ 1397aa et seq.] for fiscal year 2007. The Secretary shall only make redistributions under this paragraph to the extent that there are unexpended fiscal year 2004 allotments under subsection (b) available for such redistributions.

(D) Proration rule. If the amounts available for redistribution under subparagraph (A) for a month are less than the total amounts of the estimated shortfalls determined for the month under that subparagraph, the amount computed under such subparagraph for each shortfall State shall be reduced proportionally.

(2) Funding part of shortfall for fiscal year 2007 through redistribution of certain unused fiscal year 2005 allotments. (A) In general. Subject to subparagraphs (C) and (D) and paragraph (5)(B), with respect to months beginning during fiscal year 2007 after March 31, 2007, the Secretary shall provide for a redistribution under subsection (f) from amounts made available for redistribution under paragraph (3) to each shortfall State described in subparagraph (B), such amount as the Secretary determines will eliminate the estimated shortfall described in such subparagraph for such State for the month.

(B) Shortfall State described. For purposes of this paragraph, a shortfall State described in this subparagraph is a State with a State child health plan approved under this title [42 USCS §§ 1397aa et seq.] for which the Secretary estimates, on a monthly basis using the most recent data available to the Secretary as of March 31, 2007, that the projected expenditures under such plan for such State for fiscal year 2007 will exceed the sum of—

(i) the amount of the State's allotments for each of fiscal years 2005 and 2006 that was not expended by the end of fiscal year 2006;

(ii) the amount, if any, that is to be redistributed to the State in accordance with paragraph (1); and

(iii) the amount of the State's allotment for fiscal year 2007.

(C) Funds redistributed in the order in which States realize funding shortfalls. The Secretary shall redistribute the amounts available for redistribution under subparagraph (A) to shortfall States described in subparagraph (B) in the order in which such States realize monthly funding shortfalls under this title [42 USCS §§ 1397aa et seq.] for fiscal year 2007. The Secretary shall only make redistributions under this paragraph to the extent that such amounts are available for such redistributions.

(D) Proration rule. If the amounts available for redistribution under paragraph (3) for a month are less than the total amounts of the estimated shortfalls determined for the month under subparagraph (A), the amount computed under such subparagraph for each shortfall State shall be reduced proportionally.

(3) Treatment of certain States with fiscal year 2005 allotments unexpended at the end of the first half of fiscal year 2007. (A) Identification of States. The Secretary, on the basis of the most recent data available to the Secretary as of March 31, 2007—

(i) shall identify those States that received an allotment for fiscal year 2005 under subsection (b) which have not expended all of such allotment by March 31, 2007; and

(ii) for each such State shall estimate—

(I) the portion of such allotment that was not so expended by such date; and

(II) whether the State is described in subparagraph (B).

(B) States with funds in excess of 200 percent of need. A State described in this subparagraph is a State for which the Secretary determines, on the basis of the most recent data available to the Secretary as of March 31, 2007, that the total of all available allotments under this title [42 USCS §§ 1397aa et seq.] to the State as of such date, is at least equal to 200 percent of the total projected expenditures under this title [42 USCS §§ 1397aa et seq.] for the State for fiscal year 2007.

(C) Redistribution and limitation on availability of portion of unused allotments for certain states. (i) In general. In the case of a State identified under subparagraph (A)(i) that is also described in subparagraph (B), notwithstanding subsection (e), the applicable amount described in clause (ii) shall not be available for expenditure by the State on or after April 1, 2007, and shall be redistributed in accordance with paragraph (2).

(ii) Applicable amount. For purposes of clause (i), the applicable amount described in this clause is the lesser of—

(I) 50 percent of the amount described in subparagraph (A)(ii)(I); or

(II) $20,000,000.

(4) Additional amounts to eliminate remainder of fiscal year 2007 funding shortfalls. (A) In general. From the amounts provided in advance in appropriations Acts, the Secretary shall allot to each remaining shortfall State described in subparagraph (B) such amount as the Secretary determines will eliminate the estimated shortfall described in such subpara-

graph for the State for fiscal year 2007.

(B) Remaining shortfall State described. For purposes of subparagraph (A), a remaining shortfall State is a State with a State child health plan approved under this title for which the Secretary estimates, on the basis of the most recent data available to the Secretary as of the date of the enactment of this paragraph, that the projected Federal expenditures under such plan for the State for fiscal year 2007 will exceed the sum of—

(i) the amount of the State's allotments for each of fiscal years 2005 and 2006 that will not be expended by the end of fiscal year 2006;

(ii) the amount of the State's allotment for fiscal year 2007; and

(iii) the amounts, if any, that are to be redistributed to the State during fiscal year 2007 in accordance with paragraphs (1) and (2).

(5) Retrospective adjustment. (A) In general. The Secretary may adjust the estimates and determinations made under paragraphs (1), (2), (3), and (4) as necessary on the basis of the amounts reported by States not later than November 30, 2007, on CMS Form 64 or CMS Form 21, as the case may be and as approved by the Secretary, but in no case may the applicable amount described in paragraph (3)(C)(ii) exceed the amount determined by the Secretary on the basis of the most recent data available to the Secretary as of March 31, 2007.

(B) Funding of any retrospective adjustments only from unexpended 2005 allotments. Notwithstanding subsections (e) and (f), to the extent the Secretary determines it necessary to adjust the estimates and determinations made for purposes of paragraphs (1), (2), and (3), the Secretary may use only the allotments for fiscal year 2005 under subsection (b) that remain unexpended through the end of fiscal year 2007 for providing any additional amounts to States described in paragraph (2)(B) (without regard to whether such unexpended allotments are from States described in paragraph (3)(B)).

(C) Rules of construction. Nothing in this subsection shall be construed as—

(i) authorizing the Secretary to use the allotments for fiscal year 2006 or 2007 under subsection (b) of States described in paragraph (3)(B) to provide additional amounts to States described in paragraph (2)(B) for purposes of eliminating the funding shortfall for such States for fiscal year 2007; or

(ii) limiting the authority of the Secretary to redistribute the allotments for fiscal year 2005 under subsection (b) that remain unexpended through the end of fiscal year 2007 and are available for redistribution under subsection (f) after the application of subparagraph (B).

(6) 1-year availability; no further redistribution. Notwithstanding subsections (e) and (f), amounts redistributed or allotted to a State pursuant to this subsection for fiscal year 2007 shall only remain available for expenditure by the State through September 30, 2007, and any amounts of such redistributions or allotments that remain unexpended as of such date, shall not be subject to redistribution under subsection (f). Nothing in the preceding sentence shall be construed as limiting the ability of the Secretary to adjust the determinations made under paragraphs (1), (2), (3), and (4) in accordance with paragraph (5).

(7) Definition of State. For purposes of this subsection, the term "State" means a State that receives an allotment for fiscal year 2007 under subsection (b).

(i) Redistribution of unused fiscal year 2005 allotments to States with estimated funding shortfalls for fiscal year 2008. (1) In general. Notwithstanding subsection (f) and subject to paragraphs (3) and (4), with respect to months beginning during fiscal year 2008, the Secretary shall provide for a redistribution under such subsection from the allotments for fiscal year 2005 under subsection (b) that are not expended by the end of fiscal year 2007, to a fiscal year 2008 shortfall State described in paragraph (2), such amount as the Secretary determines will eliminate the estimated shortfall described in such paragraph for such State for the month.

(2) Fiscal year 2008 shortfall State described. A fiscal year 2008 shortfall State described in this paragraph is a State with a State child health plan approved under this title for which the Secretary estimates, on a monthly basis using the most recent data available to the Secretary as of such month, that the projected expenditures under such plan for such State for fiscal year 2008 will exceed the sum of—

(A) the amount of the State's allotments for each of fiscal years 2006 and 2007 that was not expended by the end of fiscal year 2007; and

(B) the amount of the State's allotment for fiscal year 2008.

(3) Funds redistributed in the order in which States realize funding shortfalls. The Secretary shall redistribute the amounts available for redistribution under paragraph (1) to fiscal year 2008 shortfall States described in paragraph (2) in the order in which such States realize monthly funding shortfalls under this title for fiscal year 2008. The Secretary shall only make redistributions under this subsec-

tion to the extent that there are unexpended fiscal year 2005 allotments under subsection (b) available for such redistributions.

(4) Proration rule. If the amounts available for redistribution under paragraph (1) are less than the total amounts of the estimated shortfalls determined for the month under that paragraph, the amount computed under such paragraph for each fiscal year 2008 shortfall State for the month shall be reduced proportionally.

(5) Retrospective adjustment. The Secretary may adjust the estimates and determinations made to carry out this subsection as necessary on the basis of the amounts reported by States not later than November 30, 2007, on CMS Form 64 or CMS Form 21, as the case may be, and as approved by the Secretary.

(6) 1-Year availability; no further redistribution. Notwithstanding subsections (e) and (f), amounts redistributed to a State pursuant to this subsection for fiscal year 2008 shall only remain available for expenditure by the State through September 30, 2008, and any amounts of such redistributions that remain unexpended as of such date, shall not be subject to redistribution under subsection (f).

(j) Additional allotments to eliminate funding shortfalls for fiscal year 2008. (1) Appropriation; allotment authority. For the purpose of providing additional allotments described in subparagraphs (A) and (B) of paragraph (3), there is appropriated, out of any money in the Treasury not otherwise appropriated, such sums as may be necessary, not to exceed $1,600,000,000 for fiscal year 2008.

(2) Shortfall States described. For purposes of paragraph (3), a shortfall State described in this paragraph is a State with a State child health plan approved under this title for which the Secretary estimates, on the basis of the most recent data available to the Secretary as of November 30, 2007, that the Federal share amount of the projected expenditures under such plan for such State for fiscal year 2008 will exceed the sum of—

(A) the amount of the State's allotments for each of fiscal years 2006 and 2007 that will not be expended by the end of fiscal year 2007;

(B) the amount, if any, that is to be redistributed to the State during fiscal year 2008 in accordance with subsection (i); and

(C) the amount of the State's allotment for fiscal year 2008.

(3) Allotments. In addition to the allotments provided under subsections (b) and (c), subject to paragraph (4), of the amount available for the additional allotments under paragraph (1) for fiscal year 2008, the Secretary shall allot—

(A) to each shortfall State described in paragraph (2) not described in subparagraph (B), such amount as the Secretary determines will eliminate the estimated shortfall described in such paragraph for the State; and

(B) to each commonwealth or territory described in subsection (c)(3), an amount equal to the percentage specified in subsection (c)(2) for the commonwealth or territory multiplied by 1.05 percent of the sum of the amounts determined for each shortfall State under subparagraph (A).

(4) Proration rule. If the amounts available for additional allotments under paragraph (1) are less than the total of the amounts determined under subparagraphs (A) and (B) of paragraph (3), the amounts computed under such subparagraphs shall be reduced proportionally.

(5) Retrospective adjustment. The Secretary may adjust the estimates and determinations made to carry out this subsection as necessary on the basis of the amounts reported by States not later than November 30, 2008, on CMS Form 64 or CMS Form 21, as the case may be, and as approved by the Secretary.

(6) One-year availability; no redistribution of unexpended additional allotments. Notwithstanding subsections (e) and (f), amounts allotted to a State pursuant to this subsection for fiscal year 2008, subject to paragraph (5), shall only remain available for expenditure by the State through September 30, 2008. Any amounts of such allotments that remain unexpended as of such date shall not be subject to redistribution under subsection (f).

(k) Redistribution of unused fiscal year 2006 allotments to States with estimated funding shortfalls during fiscal year 2009. (1) In general. Notwithstanding subsection (f) and subject to paragraphs (3) and (4), with respect to months beginning during fiscal year 2009, the Secretary shall provide for a redistribution under such subsection from the allotments for fiscal year 2006 under subsection (b) that are not expended by the end of fiscal year 2008, to a fiscal year 2009 shortfall State described in paragraph (2), such amount as the Secretary determines will eliminate the estimated shortfall described in such paragraph for such State for the month.

(2) Fiscal year 2009 shortfall State described. A fiscal year 2009 shortfall State described in this paragraph is a State with a State child health plan approved under this title for which the Secretary estimates, on a monthly basis using the most recent data avail-

able to the Secretary as of such month, that the Federal share amount of the projected expenditures under such plan for such State for the first 2 quarters of fiscal year 2009 will exceed the sum of—

(A) the amount of the State's allotments for each of fiscal years 2007 and 2008 that was not expended by the end of fiscal year 2008; and

(B) the amount of the State's allotment for fiscal year 2009.

(3) Funds redistributed in the order in which States realize funding shortfalls. The Secretary shall redistribute the amounts available for redistribution under paragraph (1) to fiscal year 2009 shortfall States described in paragraph (2) in the order in which such States realize monthly funding shortfalls under this title for fiscal year 2009. The Secretary shall only make redistributions under this subsection to the extent that there are unexpended fiscal year 2006 allotments under subsection (b) available for such redistributions.

(4) Proration rule. If the amounts available for redistribution under paragraph (1) are less than the total amounts of the estimated shortfalls determined for the month under that paragraph, the amount computed under such paragraph for each fiscal year 2009 shortfall State for the month shall be reduced proportionally.

(5) Retrospective adjustment. The Secretary may adjust the estimates and determinations made to carry out this subsection as necessary on the basis of the amounts reported by States not later than May 31, 2009, on CMS Form 64 or CMS Form 21, as the case may be, and as approved by the Secretary.

(6) Availability; no further redistribution. Notwithstanding subsections (e) and (f), amounts redistributed to a State pursuant to this subsection for fiscal year 2009 shall only remain available for expenditure by the State through September 30, 2009, and any amounts of such redistributions that remain unexpended as of such date, shall not be subject to redistribution under subsection (f).

(l) Additional allotments to eliminate funding shortfalls for the first 2 quarters of fiscal year 2009. (1) Appropriation; allotment authority. For the purpose of providing additional allotments described in subparagraphs (A) and (B) of paragraph (3), there is appropriated, out of any money in the Treasury not otherwise appropriated, such sums as may be necessary, not to exceed $275,000,000 for the first 2 quarters of fiscal year 2009.

(2) Shortfall states described. For purposes of paragraph (3), a shortfall State described in this paragraph is a State with a State child health plan approved under this title for which the Secretary estimates, on the basis of the most recent data available to the Secretary, that the Federal share amount of the projected expenditures under such plan for such State for the first 2 quarters of fiscal year 2009 will exceed the sum of—

(A) the amount of the State's allotments for each of fiscal years 2007 and 2008 that will not be expended by the end of fiscal year 2008;

(B) the amount, if any, that is to be redistributed to the State during fiscal year 2009 in accordance with subsection (k); and

(C) the amount of the State's allotment for fiscal year 2009.

(3) Allotments. In addition to the allotments provided under subsections (b) and (c), subject to paragraph (4), of the amount available for the additional allotments under paragraph (1) for the first 2 quarters of fiscal year 2009, the Secretary shall allot—

(A) to each shortfall State described in paragraph (2) not described in subparagraph (B) such amount as the Secretary determines will eliminate the estimated shortfall described in such paragraph for the State; and

(B) to each commonwealth or territory described in subsection (c)(3), an amount equal to the percentage specified in subsection (c)(2) for the commonwealth or territory multiplied by 1.05 percent of the sum of the amounts determined for each shortfall State under subparagraph (A).

(4) Proration rule. If the amounts available for additional allotments under paragraph (1) are less than the total of the amounts determined under subparagraphs (A) and (B) of paragraph (3), the amounts computed under such subparagraphs shall be reduced proportionally.

(5) Retrospective adjustment. The Secretary may adjust the estimates and determinations made to carry out this subsection as necessary on the basis of the amounts reported by States not later than May 31, 2009, on CMS Form 64 or CMS Form 21, as the case may be, and as approved by the Secretary.

(6) Availability; no redistribution of unexpended additional allotments. Notwithstanding subsections (e) and (f), amounts allotted to a State pursuant to this subsection for fiscal year 2009, subject to paragraph (5), shall only remain available for expenditure by the State through March 31, 2009. Any amounts of such allotments that remain unexpended as of such date shall not be subject to redistribution under subsection (f).

(m) Allotments for fiscal years 2009 through 2015. (1) For fiscal year 2009. (A) For the 50 states and the District of Columbia. Subject to the succeeding provisions of this paragraph and paragraph (4), the Secretary shall allot for fiscal year 2009 from the amount made available under subsection (a)(12), to each of the 50 States and the District of Columbia 110 percent of the highest of the following amounts for such State or District:

(i) The total Federal payments to the State under this title [42 USCS §§ 1397aa et seq.] for fiscal year 2008, multiplied by the allotment increase factor determined under paragraph (5) for fiscal year 2009.

(ii) The amount allotted to the State for fiscal year 2008 under subsection (b), multiplied by the allotment increase factor determined under paragraph (5) for fiscal year 2009.

(iii) The projected total Federal payments to the State under this title [42 USCS §§ 1397aa et seq.] for fiscal year 2009, as determined on the basis of the February 2009 projections certified by the State to the Secretary by not later than March 31, 2009.

(B) For the commonwealths and territories. Subject to the succeeding provisions of this paragraph and paragraph (4), the Secretary shall allot for fiscal year 2009 from the amount made available under subsection (a)(12) to each of the commonwealths and territories described in subsection (c)(3) an amount equal to the highest amount of Federal payments to the commonwealth or territory under this title [42 USCS §§ 1397aa et seq.] for any fiscal year occurring during the period of fiscal years 1999 through 2008, multiplied by the allotment increase factor determined under paragraph (5) for fiscal year 2009, except that subparagraph (B) thereof shall be applied by substituting "the United States" for "the State".

(C) Adjustment for qualifying states. In the case of a qualifying State described in paragraph (2) of section 2105(g) [42 USCS § 1397ee(g)], the Secretary shall permit the State to submit a revised projection described in subparagraph (A)(iii) in order to take into account changes in such projections attributable to the application of paragraph (4) of such section.

(2) For fiscal years 2010 through 2014. (A) In general. Subject to paragraphs (4) and (6), from the amount made available under paragraphs (13) through (15) of subsection (a) for each of fiscal years 2010 through 2012, respectively, the Secretary shall compute a State allotment for each State (including the District of Columbia and each commonwealth and territory) for each such fiscal year as follows:

(i) Growth factor update for fiscal year 2010. For fiscal year 2010, the allotment of the State is equal to the sum of—

(I) the amount of the State allotment under paragraph (1) for fiscal year 2009; and

(II) the amount of any payments made to the State under subsection (k), (l), or (n) for fiscal year 2009, multiplied by the allotment increase factor under paragraph (5) for fiscal year 2010.

(ii) Rebasing in fiscal year 2011. For fiscal year 2011, the allotment of the State is equal to the Federal payments to the State that are attributable to (and countable towards) the total amount of allotments available under this section to the State in fiscal year 2010 (including payments made to the State under subsection (n) for fiscal year 2010 as well as amounts redistributed to the State in fiscal year 2010), multiplied by the allotment increase factor under paragraph (5) for fiscal year 2011.

(iii) Growth factor update for fiscal year 2012. For fiscal year 2012, the allotment of the State is equal to the sum of—

(I) the amount of the State allotment under clause (ii) for fiscal year 2011; and

(II) the amount of any payments made to the State under subsection (n) for fiscal year 2011, multiplied by the allotment increase factor under paragraph (5) for fiscal year 2012.

(B) Fiscal years 2013 and 2014. Subject to paragraphs (4) and (6), from the amount made available under paragraphs (16) and (17) of subsection (a) for fiscal years 2013 and 2014, respectively, the Secretary shall compute a State allotment for each State (including the District of Columbia and each commonwealth and territory) for each such fiscal year as follows:

(i) Rebasing in fiscal year 2013. For fiscal year 2013, the allotment of the State is equal to the Federal payments to the State that are attributable to (and countable towards) the total amount of allotments available under this section to the State in fiscal year 2012 (including payments made to the State under subsection (n) for fiscal year 2012 as well as amounts redistributed to the State in fiscal year 2012), multiplied by the allotment increase factor under paragraph (5) for fiscal year 2013.

(ii) Growth factor update for fiscal year 2014. For fiscal year 2014, the allotment of the State is equal to the sum of—

(I) the amount of the State allotment under clause (i) for fiscal year 2013; and

(II) the amount of any payments made to the State under subsection (n) for fiscal year 2013, multiplied by the allotment increase factor under paragraph (5) for fiscal year 2014.

(3) For fiscal year 2015. (A) First half. Subject to paragraphs (4) and (6), from the amount made available under subparagraph (A) of paragraph (18) of subsection (a) for the semi-annual period described in such paragraph, increased by the amount of the appropriation for such period under section 108 of the Children's Health Insurance Program Reauthorization Act of 2009 [unclassified], the Secretary shall compute a State allotment for each State (including the District of Columbia and each commonwealth and territory) for such semi-annual period in an amount equal to the first half ratio (described in subparagraph (D)) of the amount described in subparagraph (C).

(B) Second half. Subject to paragraphs (4) and (6), from the amount made available under subparagraph (B) of paragraph (18) of subsection (a) for the semi-annual period described in such paragraph, the Secretary shall compute a State allotment for each State (including the District of Columbia and each commonwealth and territory) for such semi-annual period in an amount equal to the amount made available under such subparagraph, multiplied by the ratio of—

(i) the amount of the allotment to such State under subparagraph (A); to

(ii) the total of the amount of all of the allotments made available under such subparagraph.

(C) Full year amount based on rebased amount. The amount described in this subparagraph for a State is equal to the Federal payments to the State that are attributable to (and countable towards) the total amount of allotments available under this section to the State in fiscal year 2014 (including payments made to the State under subsection (n) for fiscal year 2014 as well as amounts redistributed to the State in fiscal year 2014), multiplied by the allotment increase factor under paragraph (5) for fiscal year 2015.

(D) First half ratio. The first half ratio described in this subparagraph is the ratio of—

(i) the sum of—

(I) the amount made available under subsection (a)(18)(A); and

(II) the amount of the appropriation for such period under section 108 of the Children's Health Insurance Program Reauthorization Act of 2009 [unclassified]; to

(ii) the sum of the—

(I) amount described in clause (i); and

(II) the amount made available under subsection (a)(18)(B).

(4) Proration rule. If, after the application of this subsection without regard to this paragraph, the sum of the allotments determined under paragraph (1), (2), or (3) for a fiscal year (or, in the case of fiscal year 2015, for a semi-annual period in such fiscal year) exceeds the amount available under subsection (a) for such fiscal year or period, the Secretary shall reduce each allotment for any State under such paragraph for such fiscal year or period on a proportional basis.

(5) Allotment increase factor. The allotment increase factor under this paragraph for a fiscal year is equal to the product of the following:

(A) Per capita health care growth factor. 1 plus the percentage increase in the projected per capita amount of National Health Expenditures from the calendar year in which the previous fiscal year ends to the calendar year in which the fiscal year involved ends, as most recently published by the Secretary before the beginning of the fiscal year.

(B) Child population growth factor. 1 plus the percentage increase (if any) in the population of children in the State from July 1 in the previous fiscal year to July 1 in the fiscal year involved, as determined by the Secretary based on the most recent published estimates of the Bureau of the Census before the beginning of the fiscal year involved, plus 1 percentage point.

(6) Increase in allotment to account for approved program expansions. In the case of one of the 50 States or the District of Columbia that—

(A) has submitted to the Secretary, and has approved by the Secretary, a State plan amendment or waiver request relating to an expansion of eligibility for children or benefits under this title [42 USCS §§ 1397aa et seq.] that becomes effective for a fiscal year (beginning with fiscal year 2010 and ending with fiscal year 2015); and

(B) has submitted to the Secretary, before the August 31 preceding the beginning of the fiscal year, a request for an expansion allotment adjustment under this paragraph for such fiscal year that specifies—

(i) the additional expenditures that are attributable to the eligibility or benefit expansion provided under the amendment or waiver described in subparagraph (A), as certified by the State and submitted to the Secretary by not later than August 31 preceding the beginning of the fiscal year; and

(ii) the extent to which such additional expenditures are projected to exceed the allotment of the State or District for the year,

subject to paragraph (4), the amount of the

allotment of the State or District under this subsection for such fiscal year shall be increased by the excess amount described in subparagraph (B)(i). A State or District may only obtain an increase under this paragraph for an allotment for fiscal year 2010, fiscal year 2012, or fiscal year 2014.

(7) Adjustment of fiscal year 2010 allotments to account for changes in projected spending for certain previously approved expansion programs. For purposes of recalculating the fiscal year 2010 allotment, in the case of one of the 50 States or the District of Columbia that has an approved State plan amendment effective January 1, 2006, to provide child health assistance through the provision of benefits under the State plan under title XIX [42 USCS §§ 1396a et seq.] for children from birth through age 5 whose family income does not exceed 200 percent of the poverty line, the Secretary shall increase the allotment by an amount that would be equal to the Federal share of expenditures that would have been claimed at the enhanced FMAP rate rather than the Federal medical assistance percentage matching rate for such population.

(8) Availability of amounts for semi-annual periods in fiscal year 2015. Each semi-annual allotment made under paragraph (3) for a period in fiscal year 2015 shall remain available for expenditure under this title [42 USCS §§ 1397aa et seq.] for periods after the end of such fiscal year in the same manner as if the allotment had been made available for the entire fiscal year.

(n) Child Enrollment Contingency Fund. (1) Establishment. There is hereby established in the Treasury of the United States a fund which shall be known as the "Child Enrollment Contingency Fund" (in this subsection referred to as the "Fund"). Amounts in the Fund shall be available without further appropriations for payments under this subsection.

(2) Deposits into Fund. (A) Initial and subsequent appropriations. Subject to subparagraphs (B) and (D), out of any money in the Treasury of the United States not otherwise appropriated, there are appropriated to the Fund—

(i) for fiscal year 2009, an amount equal to 20 percent of the amount made available under paragraph (12) of subsection (a) for the fiscal year; and

(ii) for each of fiscal years 2010 through 2014 (and for each of the semi-annual allotment periods for fiscal year 2015), such sums as are necessary for making payments to eligible States for such fiscal year or period, but not in excess of the aggregate cap described in subparagraph (B).

(B) Aggregate cap. The total amount available for payment from the Fund for each of fiscal years 2010 through 2014 (and for each of the semi-annual allotment periods for fiscal year 2015), taking into account deposits made under subparagraph (C), shall not exceed 20 percent of the amount made available under subsection (a) for the fiscal year or period.

(C) Investment of Fund. The Secretary of the Treasury shall invest, in interest bearing securities of the United States, such currently available portions of the Fund as are not immediately required for payments from the Fund. The income derived from these investments constitutes a part of the Fund.

(D) Availability of excess funds for performance bonuses. Any amounts in excess of the aggregate cap described in subparagraph (B) for a fiscal year or period shall be made available for purposes of carrying out section 2105(a)(3) [42 USCS § 1397ee(a)(3)] for any succeeding fiscal year and the Secretary of the Treasury shall reduce the amount in the Fund by the amount so made available.

(3) Child Enrollment Contingency Fund payments. (A) In general. If a State's expenditures under this title [42 USCS §§ 1397aa et seq.] in fiscal year 2009, fiscal year 2010, fiscal year 2011, fiscal year 2012, fiscal year 2013, fiscal year 2014, or a semi-annual allotment period for fiscal year 2015, exceed the total amount of allotments available under this section to the State in the fiscal year or period (determined without regard to any redistribution it receives under subsection (f) that is available for expenditure during such fiscal year or period, but including any carryover from a previous fiscal year) and if the average monthly unduplicated number of children enrolled under the State plan under this title [42 USCS §§ 1397aa et seq.] (including children receiving health care coverage through funds under this title [42 USCS §§ 1397aa et seq.] pursuant to a waiver under section 1115 [42 USCS § 1315]) during such fiscal year or period exceeds its target average number of such enrollees (as determined under subparagraph (B)) for that fiscal year or period, subject to subparagraph (D), the Secretary shall pay to the State from the Fund an amount equal to the product of—

(i) the amount by which such average monthly caseload exceeds such target number of enrollees; and

(ii) the projected per capita expenditures under the State child health plan (as determined under subparagraph (C) for the fiscal year), multiplied by the enhanced FMAP (as defined in section 2105(b) [42 USCS § 1397ee(b)]) for the State and fiscal year involved (or in which the period occurs).

(B) Target average number of child enrollees. In this paragraph, the target average number of child enrollees for a State—

(i) for fiscal year 2009 is equal to the monthly average unduplicated number of children enrolled in the State child health plan under this title [42 USCS §§ 1397aa et seq.] (including such children receiving health care coverage through funds under this title [42 USCS §§ 1397aa et seq.] pursuant to a waiver under section 1115 [42 USCS § 1315]) during fiscal year 2008 increased by the population growth for children in that State for the year ending on June 30, 2007 (as estimated by the Bureau of the Census) plus 1 percentage point; or

(ii) for a subsequent fiscal year (or semi-annual period occurring in a fiscal year) is equal to the target average number of child enrollees for the State for the previous fiscal year increased by the child population growth factor described in subsection (m)(5)(B) for the State for the prior fiscal year.

(C) Projected per capita expenditures. For purposes of subparagraph (A)(ii), the projected per capita expenditures under a State child health plan—

(i) for fiscal year 2009 is equal to the average per capita expenditures (including both State and Federal financial participation) under such plan for the targeted low-income children counted in the average monthly caseload for purposes of this paragraph during fiscal year 2008, increased by the annual percentage increase in the projected per capita amount of National Health Expenditures (as estimated by the Secretary) for 2009; or

(ii) for a subsequent fiscal year (or semi-annual period occurring in a fiscal year) is equal to the projected per capita expenditures under such plan for the previous fiscal year (as determined under clause (i) or this clause) increased by the annual percentage increase in the projected per capita amount of National Health Expenditures (as estimated by the Secretary) for the year in which such subsequent fiscal year ends.

(D) Proration rule. If the amounts available for payment from the Fund for a fiscal year or period are less than the total amount of payments determined under subparagraph (A) for the fiscal year or period, the amount to be paid under such subparagraph to each eligible State shall be reduced proportionally.

(E) Timely payment; reconciliation. Payment under this paragraph for a fiscal year or period shall be made before the end of the fiscal year or period based upon the most recent data for expenditures and enrollment and the provisions of subsection (e) of section 2105 [42 USCS § 1397ee] shall apply to payments under this subsection in the same manner as they apply to payments under such section.

(F) Continued reporting. For purposes of this paragraph and subsection (f), the State shall submit to the Secretary the State's projected Federal expenditures, even if the amount of such expenditures exceeds the total amount of allotments available to the State in such fiscal year or period.

(G) Application to commonwealths and territories. No payment shall be made under this paragraph to a commonwealth or territory described in subsection (c)(3) until such time as the Secretary determines that there are in effect methods, satisfactory to the Secretary, for the collection and reporting of reliable data regarding the enrollment of children described in subparagraphs (A) and (B) in order to accurately determine the commonwealth's or territory's eligibility for, and amount of payment, under this paragraph.

(Aug. 14, 1935, ch 531, Title XXI, § 2104, as added Aug. 5, 1997, P. L. 105-33, Title IV, Subtitle J, Ch 1, § 4901(a), 111 Stat. 558; Nov. 19, 1997, P. L. 105-100, Title I, § 162(6), (8), 111 Stat. 2189, 2190; Oct. 21, 1998, P. L. 105-277, Div A, § 101(f) [Title VII, § 706], 112 Stat. 2681-389; Nov. 29, 1999, P. L. 106-113, Div B, § 1000(a)(6), 113 Stat. 1536; Dec. 21, 2000, P. L. 106-554, § 1(a)(6), 114 Stat. 2763; Aug. 15, 2003, P. L. 108-74, § 1(a)(1)–(3), 117 Stat. 892; Dec. 8, 2003, P. L. 108-173, Title IX, § 900(e)(1)(M), 117 Stat. 2372; Feb. 8, 2006, P. L. 109-171, Title VI, Subtitle B, § 6101(a), (b), 120 Stat. 130; Jan. 15, 2007, P. L. 109-482, Title II, § 201(a), 120 Stat. 3698; May 25, 2007, P. L. 110-28, Title VII, § 7001, 121 Stat. 186; Sept. 29, 2007, P. L. 110-92, § 136(c), 121 Stat. 994; Dec. 29, 2007, P. L. 110-173, Title II, § 201(a)(1), (c)(1), 121 Stat. 2509, 2510; Feb. 4, 2009, P. L. 111-3, Title I, Subtitle A, §§ 101–103, 105, 106(a)(1), (b), 123 Stat. 11, 23, 24; March 23, 2010, P. L. 111-148, Title II, Subtitle B, § 2102(a)(1), Title X, Subtitle B, Part I, § 10203(d)(1)–(2)(B), 124 Stat. 288, 928.)

§ 1397ee. Payments to States

(a) Payments. (1) In general. Subject to the succeeding provisions of this section, the

Secretary shall pay to each State with a plan approved under this title, from its allotment under section 2104 [42 USCS § 1397c], an amount for each quarter equal to the enhanced FMAP (or, in the case of expenditures described in subparagraph (D)(iv), the higher of 75 percent or the sum of the enhanced FMAP plus 5 percentage points) of expenditures in the quarter—

(A) for child health assistance under the plan for targeted low-income children in the form of providing medical assistance for which payment is made on the basis of an enhanced FMAP under the fourth sentence of section 1905(b) [42 USCS § 1396d(b)];

(B) [reserved]

(C) for child health assistance under the plan for targeted low-income children in the form of providing health benefits coverage that meets the requirements of section 2103 [42 USCS § 1397cc]; and

(D) only to the extent permitted consistent with subsection (c)—

(i) for payment for other child health assistance for targeted low-income children;

(ii) for expenditures for health services initiatives under the plan for improving the health of children (including targeted low-income children and other low-income children);

(iii) for expenditures for outreach activities as provided in section 2102(c)(1) [42 USCS § 1397bb(c)(1)] under the plan;

(iv) for translation or interpretation services in connection with the enrollment of, retention of, and use of services under this title [42 USCS §§ 1397aa et seq.] by, individuals for whom English is not their primary language (as found necessary by the Secretary for the proper and efficient administration of the State plan); and

(v) for other reasonable costs incurred by the State to administer the plan.

(2) Order of payments. Payments under paragraph (1) from a State's allotment shall be made in the following order:

(A) First, for expenditures for items described in paragraph (1)(A).

(B) Second, for expenditures for items described in paragraph (1)(B).

(C) Third, for expenditures for items described in paragraph (1)(C).

(D) Fourth, for expenditures for items described in paragraph (1)(D).

(3) Performance bonus payment to offset additional Medicaid and CHIP child enrollment costs resulting from enrollment and retention efforts. (A) In general. In addition to the payments made under paragraph (1), for each fiscal year (beginning with fiscal year 2009 and ending with fiscal year 2013), the Secretary shall pay from amounts made available under subparagraph (E), to each State that meets the condition under paragraph (4) for the fiscal year, an amount equal to the amount described in subparagraph (B) for the State and fiscal year. The payment under this paragraph shall be made, to a State for a fiscal year, as a single payment not later than the last day of the first calendar quarter of the following fiscal year.

(B) Amount for above baseline Medicaid child enrollment costs. Subject to subparagraph (E), the amount described in this subparagraph for a State for a fiscal year is equal to the sum of the following amounts:

(i) First tier above baseline Medicaid enrollees. An amount equal to the number of first tier above baseline child enrollees (as determined under subparagraph (C)(i)) under title XIX [42 USCS §§ 1396 et seq.] for the State and fiscal year, multiplied by 15 percent of the projected per capita State Medicaid expenditures (as determined under subparagraph (D)) for the State and fiscal year under title XIX [42 USCS §§ 1396 et seq.].

(ii) Second tier above baseline Medicaid enrollees. An amount equal to the number of second tier above baseline child enrollees (as determined under subparagraph (C)(ii)) under title XIX for the State [42 USCS §§ 1396 et seq.] and fiscal year, multiplied by 62.5 percent of the projected per capita State Medicaid expenditures (as determined under subparagraph (D)) for the State and fiscal year under title XIX [42 USCS §§ 1396 et seq.].

(C) Number of first and second tier above baseline child enrollees; baseline number of child enrollees. For purposes of this paragraph:

(i) First tier above baseline child enrollees. The number of first tier above baseline child enrollees for a State for a fiscal year under title XIX [42 USCS §§ 1396 et seq.] is equal to the number (if any, as determined by the Secretary) by which—

(I) the monthly average unduplicated number of qualifying children (as defined in subparagraph (F)) enrolled during the fiscal year under the State plan under title XIX [42 USCS §§ 1396 et seq.]; exceeds

(II) the baseline number of enrollees described in clause (iii) for the State and fiscal year under title XIX [42 USCS §§ 1396 et seq.];

but not to exceed 10 percent of the baseline number of enrollees described in subclause (II).

(ii) Second tier above baseline child enrollees. The number of second tier above baseline child enrollees for a State for a fiscal year under title XIX [42 USCS §§ 1396 et seq.] is equal to the number (if any, as determined by the Secretary) by which—

(I) the monthly average unduplicated number of qualifying children (as defined in subparagraph (F)) enrolled during the fiscal year under title XIX [42 USCS §§ 1396 et seq.] as described in clause (i)(I); exceeds

(II) the sum of the baseline number of child enrollees described in clause (iii) for the State and fiscal year under title XIX [42 USCS §§ 1396 et seq.], as described in clause (i)(II), and the maximum number of first tier above baseline child enrollees for the State and fiscal year under title XIX [42 USCS §§ 1396 et seq.], as determined under clause (i).

(iii) Baseline number of child enrollees. Subject to subparagraph (H), the baseline number of child enrollees for a State under title XIX [42 USCS §§ 1396 et seq.]—

(I) for fiscal year 2009 is equal to the monthly average unduplicated number of qualifying children enrolled in the State plan under title XIX [42 USCS §§ 1396 et seq.] during fiscal year 2007 increased by the population growth for children in that State from 2007 to 2008 (as estimated by the Bureau of the Census) plus 4 percentage points, and further increased by the population growth for children in that State from 2008 to 2009 (as estimated by the Bureau of the Census) plus 4 percentage points;

(II) for each of fiscal years 2010, 2011, and 2012, is equal to the baseline number of child enrollees for the State for the previous fiscal year under title XIX [42 USCS §§ 1396 et seq.], increased by the population growth for children in that State from the calendar year in which the respective fiscal year begins to the succeeding calendar year (as estimated by the Bureau of the Census) plus 3.5 percentage points;

(III) for each of fiscal years 2013, 2014, and 2015, is equal to the baseline number of child enrollees for the State for the previous fiscal year under title XIX [42 USCS §§ 1396 et seq.], increased by the population growth for children in that State from the calendar year in which the respective fiscal year begins to the succeeding calendar year (as estimated by the Bureau of the Census) plus 3 percentage points; and

(IV) for a subsequent fiscal year is equal to the baseline number of child enrollees for the State for the previous fiscal year under title XIX [42 USCS §§ 1396 et seq.], increased by the population growth for children in that State from the calendar year in which the fiscal year involved begins to the succeeding calendar year (as estimated by the Bureau of the Census) plus 2 percentage points.

(D) Projected per capita state Medicaid expenditures. For purposes of subparagraph (B), the projected per capita State Medicaid expenditures for a State and fiscal year under title XIX [42 USCS §§ 1396 et seq.] is equal to the average per capita expenditures (including both State and Federal financial participation) for children under the State plan under such title, including under waivers but not including such children eligible for assistance by virtue of the receipt of benefits under title XVI [42 USCS §§ 1381 et seq.], for the most recent fiscal year for which actual data are available (as determined by the Secretary), increased (for each subsequent fiscal year up to and including the fiscal year involved) by the annual percentage increase in per capita amount of National Health Expenditures (as estimated by the Secretary) for the calendar year in which the respective subsequent fiscal year ends and multiplied by a State matching percentage equal to 100 percent minus the Federal medical assistance percentage (as defined in section 1905(b) [42 USCS § 1396d(b)]) for the fiscal year involved.

(E) Amounts available for payments. (i) Initial appropriation. Out of any money in the Treasury not otherwise appropriated, there are appropriated $3,225,000,000 for fiscal year 2009 for making payments under this paragraph, to be available until expended.

(ii) Transfers. Notwithstanding any other provision of this title [42 USCS §§ 1397aa et seq.], the following amounts shall also be available, without fiscal year limitation, for making payments under this paragraph:

(I) Unobligated national allotment. (aa) Fiscal years 2009 through 2012. As of December 31 of fiscal year 2009, and as of December 31 of each succeeding fiscal year through fiscal year 2012, the portion, if any, of the amount appropriated under subsection (a) for such fiscal year that is unobligated for allotment to a State under subsection (m) for such fiscal year or set aside under subsection (a)(3) or (b)(2) of section 2111 for such fiscal year.

(bb) First half of fiscal year 2013. As of December 31 of fiscal year 2013, the portion, if any, of the sum of the amounts appropriated under subsection (a)(16)(A) and under section 108 of the Children's Health Insurance Reauthorization Act of 2009 [unclassified] for the period beginning on October 1, 2012, and ending on March 31, 2013, that is unobligated for allotment to a State under subsection (m) for such fiscal year or set aside under subsection (b)(2) of section 2111 for such fiscal year.

(cc) Second half of fiscal year 2013. As of

June 30 of fiscal year 2013, the portion, if any, of the amount appropriated under subsection (a)(16)(B) for the period beginning on April 1, 2013, and ending on September 30, 2013, that is unobligated for allotment to a State under subsection (m) for such fiscal year or set aside under subsection (b)(2) of section 2111 for such fiscal year.

(II) Unexpended allotments not used for redistribution. As of November 15 of each of fiscal years 2010 through 2013, the total amount of allotments made to States under section 2104 [42 USCS § 1397dd] for the second preceding fiscal year (third preceding fiscal year in the case of the fiscal year 2006, 2007, and 2008 allotments) that is not expended or redistributed under section 2104(f) [42 USCS § 1397dd(f)] during the period in which such allotments are available for obligation.

(III) Excess child enrollment contingency funds. As of October 1 of each of fiscal years 2010 through 2013, any amount in excess of the aggregate cap applicable to the Child Enrollment Contingency Fund for the fiscal year under section 2104(n) [42 USCS § 1397dd(n)].

(iii) Proportional reduction. If the sum of the amounts otherwise payable under this paragraph for a fiscal year exceeds the amount available for the fiscal year under this subparagraph, the amount to be paid under this paragraph to each State shall be reduced proportionally.

(F) Qualifying children defined. (i) In general. For purposes of this subsection, subject to clauses (ii) and (iii), the term "qualifying children" means children who meet the eligibility criteria (including income, categorical eligibility, age, and immigration status criteria) in effect as of July 1, 2008, for enrollment under title XIX [42 USCS §§ 1396 et seq.], taking into account criteria applied as of such date under title XIX [42 USCS §§ 1396 et seq.] pursuant to a waiver under section 1115 [42 USCS § 1315].

(ii) Limitation. A child described in clause (i) who is provided medical assistance during a presumptive eligibility period under section 1920A [42 USCS § 1396r-1a] shall be considered to be a "qualifying child" only if the child is determined to be eligible for medical assistance under title XIX [42 USCS §§ 1396 et seq.].

(iii) Exclusion. Such term does not include any children for whom the State has made an election to provide medical assistance under paragraph (4) of section 1903(v) [42 USCS § 1396b(v)] or any children enrolled on or after October 1, 2013.

(G) Application to commonwealths and territories. The provisions of subparagraph (G) of section 2104(n)(3) [42 USCS § 1397dd(n)(3)] shall apply with respect to payment under this paragraph in the same manner as such provisions apply to payment under such section.

(H) Application to States that implement a Medicaid expansion for children after fiscal year 2008. In the case of a State that provides coverage under section 115 of the Children's Health Insurance Program Reauthorization Act of 2009 [42 USCS § 1396d note] for any fiscal year after fiscal year 2008—

(i) any child enrolled in the State plan under title XIX [42 USCS §§ 1396 et seq.] through the application of such an election shall be disregarded from the determination for the State of the monthly average unduplicated number of qualifying children enrolled in such plan during the first 3 fiscal years in which such an election is in effect; and

(ii) in determining the baseline number of child enrollees for the State for any fiscal year subsequent to such first 3 fiscal years, the baseline number of child enrollees for the State under title XIX [42 USCS §§ 1396 et seq.] for the third of such fiscal years shall be the monthly average unduplicated number of qualifying children enrolled in the State plan under title XIX [42 USCS §§ 1396 et seq.] for such third fiscal year.

(4) Enrollment and retention provisions for children. For purposes of paragraph (3)(A), a State meets the condition of this paragraph for a fiscal year if it is implementing at least 5 of the following enrollment and retention provisions (treating each subparagraph as a separate enrollment and retention provision) throughout the entire fiscal year:

(A) Continuous eligibility. The State has elected the option of continuous eligibility for a full 12 months for all children described in section 1902(e)(12) [42 USCS § 1396a(e)(12)] under title XIX [42 USCS §§ 1396 et seq.] under 19 years of age, as well as applying such policy under its State child health plan under this title [42 USCS §§ 1397aa et seq.].

(B) Liberalization of asset requirements. The State meets the requirement specified in either of the following clauses:

(i) Elimination of asset test. The State does not apply any asset or resource test for eligibility for children under title XIX or this title [42 USCS §§ 1396 et seq. or 1397aa et seq.].

(ii) Administrative verification of assets. The State—

(I) permits a parent or caretaker relative who is applying on behalf of a child for medical assistance under title XIX [42 USCS §§ 1396 et seq.] or child health assistance under this title

[42 USCS §§ 1397aa et seq.] to declare and certify by signature under penalty of perjury information relating to family assets for purposes of determining and redetermining financial eligibility; and

(II) takes steps to verify assets through means other than by requiring documentation from parents and applicants except in individual cases of discrepancies or where otherwise justified.

(C) Elimination of in-person interview requirement. The State does not require an application of a child for medical assistance under title XIX [42 USCS §§ 1396 et seq.] (or for child health assistance under this title [42 USCS §§ 1397aa et seq.]), including an application for renewal of such assistance, to be made in person nor does the State require a face-to-face interview, unless there are discrepancies or individual circumstances justifying an in-person application or face-to-face interview.

(D) Use of joint application for Medicaid and CHIP. The application form and supplemental forms (if any) and information verification process is the same for purposes of establishing and renewing eligibility for children for medical assistance under title XIX [42 USCS §§ 1396 et seq.] and child health assistance under this title [42 USCS §§ 1397aa et seq.].

(E) Automatic renewal (use of administrative renewal). (i) In general. The State provides, in the case of renewal of a child's eligibility for medical assistance under title XIX [42 USCS §§ 1396 et seq.] or child health assistance under this title [42 USCS §§ 1397aa et seq.], a pre-printed form completed by the State based on the information available to the State and notice to the parent or caretaker relative of the child that eligibility of the child will be renewed and continued based on such information unless the State is provided other information. Nothing in this clause shall be construed as preventing a State from verifying, through electronic and other means, the information so provided.

(ii) Satisfaction through demonstrated use of ex parte process. A State shall be treated as satisfying the requirement of clause (i) if renewal of eligibility of children under title XIX [42 USCS §§ 1396 et seq.] or this title [42 USCS §§ 1397aa et seq.] is determined without any requirement for an in-person interview, unless sufficient information is not in the State's possession and cannot be acquired from other sources (including other State agencies) without the participation of the applicant or the applicant's parent or caretaker relative.

(F) Presumptive eligibility for children. The State is implementing section 1920A [42 USCS § 1396r-1a] under title XIX [42 USCS §§ 1396 et seq.] as well as, pursuant to section 2107(e)(1) [42 USCS § 1397gg(e)(1)], under this title [42 USCS §§ 1397aa et seq.].

(G) Express lane. The State is implementing the option described in section 1902(e)(13) [42 USCS § 1396a(e)(13)] under title XIX [42 USCS §§ 1396 et seq.] as well as, pursuant to section 2107(e)(1) [42 USCS § 1397gg(e)(1)], under this title [42 USCS §§ 1397aa et seq.].

(H) Premium assistance subsidies. The State is implementing the option of providing premium assistance subsidies under section 2105(c)(10) or section 1906A [42 USCS § 1397ee(c)(10) or 1396e-1].

(b) Enhanced FMAP. For purposes of subsection (a), the "enhanced FMAP", for a State for a fiscal year, is equal to the Federal medical assistance percentage (as defined in the first sentence of section 1905(b) [42 USCS § 1396d(b)]) for the State increased by a number of percentage points equal to 30 percent of the number of percentage points by which (1) such Federal medical assistance percentage for the State, is less than (2) 100 percent; but in no case shall the enhanced FMAP for a State exceed 85 percent. Notwithstanding the preceding sentence, during the period that begins on October 1, 2015, and ends on September 30, 2019, the enhanced FMAP determined for a State for a fiscal year (or for any portion of a fiscal year occurring during such period) shall be increased by 23 percentage points, but in no case shall exceed 100 percent. The increase in the enhanced FMAP under the preceding sentence shall not apply with respect to determining the payment to a State under subsection (a)(1) for expenditures described in subparagraph (D)(iv), paragraphs (8), (9), (11) of subsection (c), or clause (4) of the first sentence of section 1905(b) [42 USCS § 1396d(b)].

(c) Limitation on certain payments for certain expenditures. (1) General limitations. Funds provided to a State under this title [42 USCS §§ 1397aa et seq.] shall only be used to carry out the purposes of this title [42 USCS §§ 1397aa et seq.] (as described in section 2101 [42 USCS § 1397aa]) and may not include coverage of a nonpregnant childless adult, and any health insurance coverage provided with such funds may include coverage of abortion only if necessary to save the life of the mother or if the pregnancy is the result of an act of rape or incest. For purposes of the preceding sentence, a caretaker relative (as such term is defined for purposes of carrying out section 1931 [42 USCS § 1396u-1]) shall not be considered a childless adult.

(2) Limitation on expenditures not used for medicaid or health insurance assistance. (A) In general. Except as provided in this paragraph, the amount of payment that may be made under subsection (a) for a fiscal year for expenditures for items described in paragraph (1)(D) of such subsection shall not exceed 10 percent of the total amount of expenditures for which payment is made under subparagraphs (A), (C), and (D) of paragraph (1) of such subsection.

(B) Waiver authorized for cost-effective alternative. The limitation under subparagraph (A) on expenditures for items described in subsection (a)(1)(D) shall not apply to the extent that a State establishes to the satisfaction of the Secretary that—

(i) coverage provided to targeted low-income children through such expenditures meets the requirements of section 2103 [42 USCS § 1397cc];

(ii) the cost of such coverage is not greater, on an average per child basis, than the cost of coverage that would otherwise be provided under section 2103 [42 USCS § 1397cc]; and

(iii) such coverage is provided through the use of a community-based health delivery system, such as through contracts with health centers receiving funds under section 330 of the Public Health Service Act [42 USCS § 254c] or with hospitals such as those that receive disproportionate share payment adjustments under section 1886(d)(5)(F) or 1923 [42 USCS § 1395ww(d)(5)(F) or 1396r-4].

(C) Nonapplication to certain expenditures. The limitation under subparagraph (A) shall not apply with respect to the following expenditures:

(i) Expenditures to increase outreach to, and the enrollment of, Indian children under this title and title XIX. Expenditures for outreach activities to families of Indian children likely to be eligible for child health assistance under the plan or medical assistance under the State plan under title XIX [42 USCS §§ 1396 et seq.] (or under a waiver of such plan), to inform such families of the availability of, and to assist them in enrolling their children in, such plans, including such activities conducted under grants, contracts, or agreements entered into under section 1139(a) [42 USCS § 1320b-9(a)].

(ii) Expenditures to comply with citizenship or nationality verification requirements. Expenditures necessary for the State to comply with paragraph (9)(A).

(iii) Expenditures for outreach to increase the enrollment of children under this title and title XIX through premium assistance subsidies. Expenditures for outreach activities to families of children likely to be eligible for premium assistance subsidies in accordance with paragraph (2)(B), (3), or (10), or a waiver approved under section 1115 [42 USCS § 1315], to inform such families of the availability of, and to assist them in enrolling their children in, such subsidies, and to employers likely to provide qualified employer-sponsored coverage (as defined in subparagraph (B) of such paragraph), but not to exceed an amount equal to 1.25 percent of the maximum amount permitted to be expended under subparagraph (A) for items described in subsection (a)(1)(D).

(iv) Payment error rate measurement (perm) expenditures. Expenditures related to the administration of the payment error rate measurement (PERM) requirements applicable to the State child health plan in accordance with the Improper Payments Information Act of 2002 [31 USCS § 3321 note] and parts 431 and 457 of title 42, Code of Federal Regulations (or any related or successor guidance or regulations).

(3) Waiver for purchase of family coverage. Payment may be made to a State under subsection (a)(1) for the purchase of family coverage under a group health plan or health insurance coverage that includes coverage of targeted low-income children only if the State establishes to the satisfaction of the Secretary that—

(A) purchase of such coverage is cost-effective relative to—

(i) the amount of expenditures under the State child health plan, including administrative expenditures, that the State would have made to provide comparable coverage of the targeted low-income child involved or the family involved (as applicable); or

(ii) the aggregate amount of expenditures that the State would have made under the State child health plan, including administrative expenditures, for providing coverage under such plan for all such children or families; and

(B) such coverage shall not be provided if it would otherwise substitute for health insurance coverage that would be provided to such children but for the purchase of family coverage.

(4) Use of non-Federal funds for State matching requirement. Amounts provided by the Federal Government, or services assisted or subsidized to any significant extent by the Federal Government, may not be included in determining the amount of non-Federal contributions required under subsection (a).

(5) Offset of receipts attributable to premiums and other cost-sharing. For purposes of subsection (a), the amount of the expenditures under the plan shall be reduced by the amount of any premiums and other cost-sharing received by the State.

(6) Prevention of duplicative payments. (A) Other health plans. No payment shall be made to a State under this section for expenditures for child health assistance provided for a targeted low-income child under its plan to the extent that a private insurer (as defined by the Secretary by regulation and including a group health plan (as defined in section 607(1) of the Employee Retirement Income Security Act of 1974 [29 USCS § 1167(1)]), a service benefit plan, and a health maintenance organization) would have been obligated to provide such assistance but for a provision of its insurance contract which has the effect of limiting or excluding such obligation because the individual is eligible for or is provided child health assistance under the plan.

(B) Other Federal governmental programs. Except as provided in subparagraph (A) or (B) of subsection (a)(1) or any other provision of law, no payment shall be made to a State under this section for expenditures for child health assistance provided for a targeted low-income child under its plan to the extent that payment has been made or can reasonably be expected to be made promptly (as determined in accordance with regulations) under any other federally operated or financed health care insurance program, other than an insurance program operated or financed by the Indian Health Service, as identified by the Secretary. For purposes of this paragraph, rules similar to the rules for overpayments under section 1903(d)(2) [42 USCS § 1396b(d)(2)] shall apply.

(7) Limitation on payment for abortions. (A) In general. Payment shall not be made to a State under this section for any amount expended under the State plan to pay for any abortion or to assist in the purchase, in whole or in part, of health benefit coverage that includes coverage of abortion.

(B) Exception. Subparagraph (A) shall not apply to an abortion only if necessary to save the life of the mother or if the pregnancy is the result of an act of rape or incest.

(C) Rule of construction. Nothing in this section shall be construed as affecting the expenditure by a State, locality, or private person or entity of State, local, or private funds (other than funds expended under the State plan) for any abortion or for health benefits coverage that includes coverage of abortion.

(8) Limitation on matching rate for expenditures for child health assistance provided to children whose effective family income exceeds 300 percent of the poverty line. (A) FMAP applied to expenditures. Except as provided in subparagraph (B), for fiscal years beginning with fiscal year 2009, the Federal medical assistance percentage (as determined under section 1905(b) [42 USCS § 1396d(b)] without regard to clause (4) of such section) shall be substituted for the enhanced FMAP under subsection (a)(1) with respect to any expenditures for providing child health assistance or health benefits coverage for a targeted low-income child whose effective family income would exceed 300 percent of the poverty line but for the application of a general exclusion of a block of income that is not determined by type of expense or type of income.

(B) Exception. Subparagraph (A) shall not apply to any State that, on the date of enactment of the Children's Health Insurance Program Reauthorization Act of 2009 [enacted Feb. 4, 2009], has an approved State plan amendment or waiver to provide, or has enacted a State law to submit a State plan amendment to provide, expenditures described in such subparagraph under the State child health plan.

(9) Citizenship documentation requirements. (A) In general. No payment may be made under this section with respect to an individual who has, or is, declared to be a citizen or national of the United States for purposes of establishing eligibility under this title [42 USCS §§ 1397aa et seq.] unless the State meets the requirements of section 1902(a)(46)(B) [42 USCS § 1396a(a)(46)(B)] with respect to the individual.

(B) Enhanced payments. Notwithstanding subsection (b), the enhanced FMAP with respect to payments under subsection (a) for expenditures described in clause (i) or (ii) of section 1903(a)(3)(G) [42 USCS § 1396b(a)(3)(G)] necessary to comply with subparagraph (A) shall in no event be less than 90 percent and 75 percent, respectively.

(10) State option to offer premium assistance. (A) In general. A State may elect to offer a premium assistance subsidy (as defined in subparagraph (C)) for qualified employer-sponsored coverage (as defined in subparagraph (B)) to all targeted low-income children who are eligible for child health assistance under the plan and have access to such coverage in accordance with the requirements of this paragraph if the offering of such a subsidy is cost-effective, as defined for purposes of paragraph (3)(A). No

subsidy shall be provided to a targeted low-income child under this paragraph unless the child (or the child's parent) voluntarily elects to receive such a subsidy. A State may not require such an election as a condition of receipt of child health assistance.

(B) Qualified employer-sponsored coverage. (i) In general. Subject to clause (ii), in this paragraph, the term "qualified employer-sponsored coverage" means a group health plan or health insurance coverage offered through an employer—

(I) that qualifies as creditable coverage as a group health plan under section 2701(c)(1) of the Public Health Service Act [42 USCS § 300gg(c)(1)];

(II) for which the employer contribution toward any premium for such coverage is at least 40 percent; and

(III) that is offered to all individuals in a manner that would be considered a nondiscriminatory eligibility classification for purposes of paragraph (3)(A)(ii) of section 105(h) of the Internal Revenue Code of 1986 [26 USCS § 105(h)] (but determined without regard to clause (i) of subparagraph (B) of such paragraph).

(ii) Exception. Such term does not include coverage consisting of—

(I) benefits provided under a health flexible spending arrangement (as defined in section 106(c)(2) of the Internal Revenue Code of 1986 [26 USCS § 106(c)(2)]); or

(II) a high deductible health plan (as defined in section 223(c)(2) of such Code [26 USCS § 223(c)(2)]), without regard to whether the plan is purchased in conjunction with a health savings account (as defined under section 223(d) of such Code [26 USCS § 223(d)]).

(C) Premium assistance subsidy. (i) In general. In this paragraph, the term "premium assistance subsidy" means, with respect to a targeted low-income child, the amount equal to the difference between the employee contribution required for enrollment only of the employee under qualified employer-sponsored coverage and the employee contribution required for enrollment of the employee and the child in such coverage, less any applicable premium cost-sharing applied under the State child health plan (subject to the limitations imposed under section 2103(e) [42 USCS § 1397cc(e)], including the requirement to count the total amount of the employee contribution required for enrollment of the employee and the child in such coverage toward the annual aggregate cost-sharing limit applied under paragraph (3)(B) of such section).

(ii) State payment option. A State may provide a premium assistance subsidy either as reimbursement to an employee for out-of-pocket expenditures or, subject to clause (iii), directly to the employee's employer.

(iii) Employer opt-out. An employer may notify a State that it elects to opt-out of being directly paid a premium assistance subsidy on behalf of an employee. In the event of such a notification, an employer shall withhold the total amount of the employee contribution required for enrollment of the employee and the child in the qualified employer-sponsored coverage and the State shall pay the premium assistance subsidy directly to the employee.

(iv) Treatment as child health assistance. Expenditures for the provision of premium assistance subsidies shall be considered child health assistance described in paragraph (1)(C) of subsection (a) for purposes of making payments under that subsection.

(D) Application of secondary payor rules. The State shall be a secondary payor for any items or services provided under the qualified employer-sponsored coverage for which the State provides child health assistance under the State child health plan.

(E) Requirement to provide supplemental coverage for benefits and cost-sharing protection provided under the state child health plan. (i) In general. Notwithstanding section 2110(b)(1)(C) [42 USCS § 1397jj(b)(1)(C)], the State shall provide for each targeted low-income child enrolled in qualified employer-sponsored coverage, supplemental coverage consisting of—

(I) items or services that are not covered, or are only partially covered, under the qualified employer-sponsored coverage; and

(II) cost-sharing protection consistent with section 2103(e) [42 USCS § 1397ee(e)].

(ii) Record keeping requirements. For purposes of carrying out clause (i), a State may elect to directly pay out-of-pocket expenditures for cost-sharing imposed under the qualified employer-sponsored coverage and collect or not collect all or any portion of such expenditures from the parent of the child.

(F) Application of waiting period imposed under the State. Any waiting period imposed under the State child health plan prior to the provision of child health assistance to a targeted low-income child under the State plan shall apply to the same extent to the provision of a premium assistance subsidy for the child under this paragraph.

(G) Opt-out permitted for any month. A State shall establish a process for permitting the parent of a targeted low-income child receiving a premium assistance subsidy to disenroll the child from the qualified employer-sponsored coverage and enroll the child in, and receive child health assistance under, the State child health plan, effective on the first day of any month for which the child is eligible for such assistance and in a manner that ensures continuity of coverage for the child.

(H) Application to parents. If a State provides child health assistance or health benefits coverage to parents of a targeted low-income child in accordance with section 2111(b) [42 USCS § 1397kk(b)], the State may elect to offer a premium assistance subsidy to a parent of a targeted low-income child who is eligible for such a subsidy under this paragraph in the same manner as the State offers such a subsidy for the enrollment of the child in qualified employer-sponsored coverage, except that—

(i) the amount of the premium assistance subsidy shall be increased to take into account the cost of the enrollment of the parent in the qualified employer-sponsored coverage or, at the option of the State if the State determines it cost-effective, the cost of the enrollment of the child's family in such coverage; and

(ii) any reference in this paragraph to a child is deemed to include a reference to the parent or, if applicable under clause (i), the family of the child.

(I) Additional State option for providing premium assistance. (i) In general. A State may establish an employer-family premium assistance purchasing pool for employers with less than 250 employees who have at least 1 employee who is a pregnant woman eligible for assistance under the State child health plan (including through the application of an option described in section 2112(f) [42 USCS § 1397ll]) or a member of a family with at least 1 targeted low-income child and to provide a premium assistance subsidy under this paragraph for enrollment in coverage made available through such pool.

(ii) Access to choice of coverage. A State that elects the option under clause (i) shall identify and offer access to not less than 2 private health plans that are health benefits coverage that is equivalent to the benefits coverage in a benchmark benefit package described in section 2103(b) [42 USCS § 1397cc(b)] or benchmark-equivalent coverage that meets the requirements of section 2103(a)(2) [42 USCS § 1397cc(a)(2)] for employees described in clause (i).

(iii) Clarification of payment for administrative expenditures. Nothing in this subparagraph shall be construed as permitting payment under this section for administrative expenditures attributable to the establishment or operation of such pool, except to the extent that such payment would otherwise be permitted under this title [42 USCS §§ 1397aa et seq.].

(J) No effect on premium assistance waiver programs. Nothing in this paragraph shall be construed as limiting the authority of a State to offer premium assistance under section 1906 or 1906A [42 USCS § 1396e or 1396e-1], a waiver described in paragraph (2)(B) or (3), a waiver approved under section 1115 [42 USCS § 1315], or other authority in effect prior to the date of enactment of the Children's Health Insurance Program Reauthorization Act of 2009 [enacted Feb. 4, 2009].

(K) Notice of availability. If a State elects to provide premium assistance subsidies in accordance with this paragraph, the State shall—

(i) include on any application or enrollment form for child health assistance a notice of the availability of premium assistance subsidies for the enrollment of targeted low-income children in qualified employer-sponsored coverage;

(ii) provide, as part of the application and enrollment process under the State child health plan, information describing the availability of such subsidies and how to elect to obtain such a subsidy; and

(iii) establish such other procedures as the State determines necessary to ensure that parents are fully informed of the choices for receiving child health assistance under the State child health plan or through the receipt of premium assistance subsidies.

(L) Application to qualified employer-sponsored benchmark coverage. If a group health plan or health insurance coverage offered through an employer is certified by an actuary as health benefits coverage that is equivalent to the benefits coverage in a benchmark benefit package described in section 2103(b) [42 USCS § 1397cc(b)] or benchmark-equivalent coverage that meets the requirements of section 2103(a)(2) [42 USCS § 1397cc(a)(2)], the State may provide premium assistance subsidies for enrollment of targeted low-income children in such group health plan or health insurance coverage in the same manner as such subsidies are provided under this paragraph for enrollment in qualified employer-sponsored coverage, but without regard to the requirement to provide supplemental coverage for benefits and cost-sharing protection provided under the State child health plan under subparagraph (E).

(M) Coordination with Medicaid. In the case of a targeted low-income child who receives child health assistance through a State plan under title XIX [42 USCS §§ 1396 et seq.] and who voluntarily elects to receive a premium assistance subsidy under this section, the provisions of section 1906A [42 USCS § 1396e-1] shall apply and shall supersede any other provisions of this paragraph that are inconsistent with such section.

(11) Enhanced payments. Notwithstanding subsection (b), the enhanced FMAP with respect to payments under subsection (a) for expenditures related to the administration of the payment error rate measurement (PERM) requirements applicable to the State child health plan in accordance with the Improper Payments Information Act of 2002 [31 USCS § 3321 note] and parts 431 and 457 of title 42, Code of Federal Regulations (or any related or successor guidance or regulations) shall in no event be less than 90 percent.

(d) Maintenance of effort. (1) In medicaid eligibility standards. No payment may be made under subsection (a) with respect to child health assistance provided under a State child health plan if the State adopts income and resource standards and methodologies for purposes of determining a child's eligibility for medical assistance under the State plan under title XIX [42 USCS §§ 1396 et seq.] that are more restrictive than those applied as of June 1, 1997, except as required under section 1902(e)(14) [42 USCS § 1396a(e)(14)].

(2) In amounts of payment expended for certain State-funded health insurance programs for children. (A) In general. The amount of the allotment for a State in a fiscal year (beginning with fiscal year 1999) shall be reduced by the amount by which—

(i) the total of the State children's health insurance expenditures in the preceding fiscal year, is less than

(ii) the total of such expenditures in fiscal year 1996.

(B) State children's health insurance expenditures. The term "State children's health insurance expenditures" means the following:

(i) The State share of expenditures under this title [42 USCS §§ 1397aa et seq.].

(ii) The State share of expenditures under title XIX [42 USCS §§ 1396 et seq.] that are attributable to an enhanced FMAP under the fourth sentence of section 1905(b) [42 USCS § 1396d(b)].

(iii) State expenditures under health benefits coverage under an existing comprehensive State-based program, described in section 2103(d) [42 USCS § 1397cc(d)].

(3) Continuation of eligibility standards for children until October 1, 2019. (A) In general. During the period that begins on the date of enactment of the Patient Protection and Affordable Care Act [enacted March 23, 2010] and ends on September 30, 2019, as a condition of receiving payments under section 1903(a) [42 USCS § 1396b(a)], a State shall not have in effect eligibility standards, methodologies, or procedures under its State child health plan (including any waiver under such plan) for children (including children provided medical assistance for which payment is made under section 2105(a)(1)(A) [subsec. (a)(1)(A) of this section]) that are more restrictive than the eligibility standards, methodologies, or procedures, respectively, under such plan (or waiver) as in effect on the date of enactment of that Act [enacted March 23, 2010]. The preceding sentence shall not be construed as preventing a State during such period from—

(i) applying eligibility standards, methodologies, or procedures for children under the State child health plan or under any waiver of the plan that are less restrictive than the eligibility standards, methodologies, or procedures, respectively, for children under the plan or waiver that are in effect on the date of enactment of such Act [enacted March 23, 2010];

(ii) after September 30, 2015, enrolling children eligible to be targeted low-income children under the State child health plan in a qualified health plan that has been certified by the Secretary under subparagraph (C); or

(iii) imposing a limitation described in section 2112(b)(7) [42 USCS § 1397ll(b)(7)] for a fiscal year in order to limit expenditures under the State child health plan to those for which Federal financial participation is available under this section for the fiscal year.

(B) Assurance of exchange coverage for targeted low-income children unable to be provided child health assistance as a result of funding shortfalls. In the event that allotments provided under section 2104 [42 USCS § 1397dd] are insufficient to provide coverage to all children who are eligible to be targeted low-income children under the State child health plan under this title, a State shall establish procedures to ensure that such children are screened for eligibility for medical assistance under the State plan under title XIX [42 USCS §§ 1396 et seq.] or a waiver of that plan and, if found eligible, enrolled in such plan or a waiver. In the case of such children who, as a result of such screening, are determined to not be eligible for medical assistance under the State plan or a waiver under title XIX, the State shall establish procedures to ensure that the children are enrolled in a qualified health plan that has been certified by the Secretary under subparagraph (C) and is offered through an Exchange established by the State under section 1311 of the Patient Protection and Affordable Care Act [42 USCS § 18031]. For purposes of eligibility for premium assistance for the purchase of a qualified health plan under section 36B of the Internal Revenue Code of 1986 [26 USCS § 36B] and reduced cost-sharing under section 1402 of the Patient Protection and Affordable Care Act [42 USCS § 18071], children described in the preceding sentence shall be deemed to be ineligible for coverage under the State child health plan.

(C) Certification of comparability of pediatric coverage offered by qualified health plans. With respect to each State, the Secretary, not later than April 1, 2015, shall review the benefits offered for children and the cost-sharing imposed with respect to such benefits by qualified health plans offered through an Exchange established by the State under section 1311 of the Patient Protection and Affordable Care Act [42 USCS § 18031] and shall certify those plans that offer benefits for children and impose cost-sharing with respect to such benefits that the Secretary determines are at least comparable to the benefits offered and cost-sharing protections provided under the State child health plan.

(e) Advance payment; retrospective adjustment. The Secretary may make payments under this section for each quarter on the basis of advance estimates of expenditures submitted by the State and such other investigation as the Secretary may find necessary, and may reduce or increase the payments as necessary to adjust for any overpayment or underpayment for prior quarters.

(f) Flexibility in submittal of claims. Nothing in this section or subsections (e) and (f) of section 2104 [42 USCS § 1397dd(e) and (f)] shall be construed as preventing a State from claiming as expenditures in the quarter expenditures that were incurred in a previous quarter.

(g) Authority for qualifying States to use certain funds for Medicaid expenditures. (1) State option. (A) In general. Notwithstanding any other provision of law, subject to paragraph (4), a qualifying State (as defined in paragraph (2)) may elect to use not more than 20 percent of any allotment under section 2104 [42 USCS § 1397dd] for fiscal year 1998, 1999, 2000, 2001, 2004, 2005, 2006, 2007, or 2008 (insofar as it is available under subsections (e) and (g) of such section) for payments under title XIX [42 USCS §§ 1396 et seq.] in accordance with subparagraph (B), instead of for expenditures under this title [42 USCS §§ 1397aa et seq.].

(B) Payments to States. (i) In general. In the case of a qualifying State that has elected the option described in subparagraph (A), subject to the availability of funds under such subparagraph with respect to the State, the Secretary shall pay the State an amount each quarter equal to the additional amount that would have been paid to the State under title XIX [42 USCS §§ 1396 et seq.] with respect to expenditures described in clause (ii) if the enhanced FMAP (as determined under subsection (b)) had been substituted for the Federal medical assistance percentage (as defined in section 1905(b) [42 USCS § 1396d(b)]).

(ii) Expenditures described. For purposes of this subparagraph, the expenditures described in this clause are expenditures, made after the date of the enactment of this subsection [enacted Aug. 15, 2003] and during the period in which funds are available to the qualifying State for use under subparagraph (A), for medical assistance under title XIX [42 USCS §§ 1396 et seq.] to individuals who have not attained age 19 and whose family income exceeds 150 percent of the poverty line.

(iii) No impact on determination of budget neutrality for waivers. In the case of a qualifying State that uses amounts paid under this subsection for expenditures described in clause (ii) that are incurred under a waiver approved for the State, any budget neutrality determinations with respect to such waiver shall be determined without regard to such amounts paid.

(2) Qualifying State. In this subsection, the term "qualifying State" means a State that, on and after April 15, 1997, has an income eligibility standard that is at least 184 percent of the poverty line with respect to any 1 or more categories of children (other than infants) who are eligible for medical assistance under section 1902(a)(10)(A) [42 USCS § 1396a(a)(10)(A)] or, in the case of a State that has a statewide waiver in effect under section 1115 [42 USCS § 1315] with respect to title XIX [42 USCS §§ 1396 et seq.] that was first implemented on August 1, 1994, or July 1, 1995, has an income eligibility standard under such waiver for children that is at least 185 percent of the poverty line, or, in the case of a State that has a statewide waiver in effect

under section 1115 [42 USCS § 1315] with respect to title XIX [42 USCS §§ 1396 et seq.] that was first implemented on January 1, 1994, has an income eligibility standard under such waiver for children who lack health insurance that is at least 185 percent of the poverty line, or, in the case of a State that had a statewide waiver in effect under section 1115 [42 USCS § 1315] with respect to title XIX [42 USCS §§ 1396 et seq.] that was first implemented on October 1, 1993, had an income eligibility standard under such waiver for children that was at least 185 percent of the poverty line and on and after July 1, 1998, has an income eligibility standard for children under section 1902(a)(10)(A) [42 USCS § 1396a(a)(10)(A)] or a statewide waiver in effect under section 1115 [42 USCS § 1315] with respect to title XIX [42 USCS §§ 1396 et seq.] that is at least 185 percent of the poverty line.

(3) Construction. Nothing in paragraphs (1) and (2) shall be construed as modifying the requirements applicable to States implementing State child health plans under this title [42 USCS §§ 1397aa et seq.].

(4) Option for allotments for fiscal years 2009 through 2015. (A) Payment of enhanced portion of matching rate for certain expenditures. In the case of expenditures described in subparagraph (B), a qualifying State (as defined in paragraph (2)) may elect to be paid from the State's allotment made under section 2104 [42 USCS § 1397dd] for any of fiscal years 2009 through 2015 (insofar as the allotment is available to the State under subsections (e) and (m) of such section) an amount each quarter equal to the additional amount that would have been paid to the State under title XIX [42 USCS §§ 1396 et seq.] with respect to such expenditures if the enhanced FMAP (as determined under subsection (b)) had been substituted for the Federal medical assistance percentage (as defined in section 1905(b) [42 USCS § 1396d(b)]).

(B) Expenditures described. For purposes of subparagraph (A), the expenditures described in this subparagraph are expenditures made after the date of the enactment of this paragraph [enacted Feb. 4, 2009] and during the period in which funds are available to the qualifying State for use under subparagraph (A), for the provision of medical assistance to individuals residing in the State who are eligible for medical assistance under the State plan under title XIX [42 USCS §§ 1396 et seq.] or under a waiver of such plan and who have not attained age 19 (or, if a State has so elected under the State plan under title XIX [42 USCS §§ 1396 et seq.], age 20 or 21), and whose family income equals or exceeds 133 percent of the poverty line but does not exceed the Medicaid applicable income level.

(Aug. 14, 1935, ch 531, Title XXI, § 2105, as added Aug. 5, 1997, P. L. 105-33, Title IV, Subtitle J, Ch 1, § 4901(a), 111 Stat. 560; Nov. 19, 1997, P. L. 105-100, Title I, § 162(5), (7), 111 Stat. 2189, 2190; Nov. 29, 1999, P. L. 106-113, Div B, § 1000(a)(6), 113 Stat. 1536; Dec. 21, 2000, P. L. 106-554, § 1(a)(6), 114 Stat. 2763; Aug. 15, 2003, P. L. 108-74, § 1(b), 117 Stat. 895; Nov. 17, 2003, P. L. 108-127, § 1, 117 Stat. 1354; Feb. 8, 2006, P. L. 109-171, Title VI, Subtitle B, §§ 6102(b), 6103(a), 120 Stat. 131, 132; Jan. 15, 2007, P. L. 109-482, Title II, § 201(b), 120 Stat. 3701; Sept. 29, 2007, P. L. 110-92, § 136(d), 121 Stat. 995; Dec. 29, 2007, P. L. 110-173, Title II, § 201(b)(1), 121 Stat. 2510; Feb. 4, 2009, P. L. 111-3, Title I, Subtitle A, §§ 104, 107(a), Subtitle B, § 113(a), 114(a), Title II, Subtitle A, §§ 201(b)(1), 202(b), Subtitle B, § 211(c), Title III, Subtitle A, §§ 301(a)(1), (2)(A), 302(b), Title VI, Subtitle A, § 601(a), 123 Stat. 17, 24, 34, 39, 40, 54, 57, 63, 96; March 23, 2010, P. L. 111-148, Title II, Subtitle B, §§ 2101(a)–(c), 2102(a)(3)–(5), Title X, Subtitle B, Part I, §§ 10201(g), 10203(b)(3), (4), (c), (d)(2)(C), 124 Stat. 286, 288, 922, 927, 930.)

§ 1397gg. Strategic objectives and performance goals; plan administration

(a) Strategic objectives and performance goals. (1) Description. A State child health plan shall include a description of—

(A) the strategic objectives,

(B) the performance goals, and

(C) the performance measures,

the State has established for providing child health assistance to targeted low-income children under the plan and otherwise for maximizing health benefits coverage for other low-income children and children generally in the State.

(2) Strategic objectives. Such plan shall identify specific strategic objectives relating to increasing the extent of creditable health coverage among targeted low-income children and other low-income children.

(3) Performance goals. Such plan shall specify one or more performance goals for each such strategic objective so identified.

(4) Performance measures. Such plan shall describe how performance under the plan will be—

(A) measured through objective, independently verifiable means, and

(B) compared against performance goals, in order to determine the State's performance under this title [42 USCS §§ 1397aa et seq.].

(b) Records, reports, audits, and evaluation. (1) Data collection, records, and reports. A State child health plan shall include an assurance that the State will collect the data, maintain the records, and furnish the reports to the Secretary, at the times and in the standardized format the Secretary may require in order to enable the Secretary to monitor State program administration and compliance and to evaluate and compare the effectiveness of State plans under this title [42 USCS §§ 1397aa et seq.].

(2) State assessment and study. A State child health plan shall include a description of the State's plan for the annual assessments and reports under section 2108(a) [42 USCS § 1397hh(a)] and the evaluation required by section 2108(b) [42 USCS § 1397hh(b)].

(3) Audits. A State child health plan shall include an assurance that the State will afford the Secretary access to any records or information relating to the plan for the purposes of review or audit.

(c) Program development process. A State child health plan shall include a description of the process used to involve the public in the design and implementation of the plan and the method for ensuring ongoing public involvement.

(d) Program budget. A State child health plan shall include a description of the budget for the plan. The description shall be updated periodically as necessary and shall include details on the planned use of funds and the sources of the non-Federal share of plan expenditures, including any requirements for cost-sharing by beneficiaries.

(e) Application of certain general provisions. The following sections of this Act shall apply to States under this title [42 USCS §§ 1397aa et seq.] in the same manner as they apply to a State under title XIX [42 USCS §§ 1396 et seq.]:

(1) Title XIX provisions. (A) Section 1902(a)(4)(C) [42 USCS § 1396a(a)(4)(C)] (relating to conflict of interest standards).

(B) Section 1902(a)(72) [42 USCS § 1396a(a)(72)] (relating to limiting FQHC contracting for provision of dental services).

(C) Section 1902(a)(73) [42 USCS § 1396a(a)(73)] (relating to requiring certain States to seek advice from designees of Indian Health Programs and Urban Indian Organizations).

(D) Subsections (a)(77) and (ii) of section 1902 [42 USCS § 1396a] (relating to provider and supplier screening, oversight, and reporting requirements).

(E) Section 1902(e)(13) [42 USCS § 1396a(e)(13)] (relating to the State option to rely on findings from an Express Lane agency to help evaluate a child's eligibility for medical assistance).

(F) Section 1902(e)(14) [42 USCS § 1396a(e)(14)] (relating to income determined using modified adjusted gross income and household income).

(G) Section 1902(bb) [42 USCS § 1396a(bb)] (relating to payment for services provided by Federally-qualified health centers and rural health clinics).

(H) Section 1902(ff) [42 USCS § 1396a(ff)] (relating to disregard of certain property for purposes of making eligibility determinations).

(I) Paragraphs (2), (16), and (17) of section 1903(i) [42 USCS § 1396b(i)] (relating to limitations on payment).

(J) Paragraph (4) of section 1903(v) [42 USCS § 1396b(v)] (relating to optional coverage of categories of lawfully residing immigrant children or pregnant women), but only if the State has elected to apply such paragraph with respect to such category of children or pregnant women under title XIX [42 USCS §§ 1396 et seq.].

(K) Section 1903(w) [42 USCS § 1396b(w)] (relating to limitations on provider taxes and donations).

(L) Section 1920A [42 USCS § 1396r-1a] (relating to presumptive eligibility for children).

(M) Subsections (a)(2)(C) and (h) of section 1932 [42 USCS § 1396u-2].

(N) Section 1942 [42 USCS § 1396w-2] (relating to authorization to receive data directly relevant to eligibility determinations).

[(O)](N) Section 1943(b) [42 USCS § 1396w-3(b)] (relating to coordination with State Exchanges and the State Medicaid agency).

(2) Title XI provisions. (A) Section 1115 [42 USCS § 1315] (relating to waiver authority).

(B) Section 1116 [42 USCS § 1316] (relating to administrative and judicial review), but only insofar as consistent with this title [42 USCS §§ 1397aa et seq.].

(C) Section 1124 [42 USCS § 1320a-3] (relating to disclosure of ownership and related information).

(D) Section 1126 [42 USCS § 1320a-5] (relating to disclosure of information about certain convicted individuals).

(E) Section 1128A [42 USCS § 1320a-7a] (relating to civil monetary penalties).

(F) Section 1128B(d) [42 USCS § 1320a-

7b(d)] (relating to criminal penalties for certain additional charges).

(G) Section 1132 [42 USCS § 1320b-2] (relating to periods within which claims must be filed).

(f) Limitation of waiver authority. Notwithstanding subsection (e)(2)(A) and section 1115(a) [42 USCS § 1315(a)]:

(1) The Secretary may not approve a waiver, experimental, pilot, or demonstration project that would allow funds made available under this title to be used to provide child health assistance or other health benefits coverage to a nonpregnant childless adult or a parent (as defined in section 2111(c)(2)(A) [42 USCS § 1397kk(c)(2)(A)]), who is not pregnant, of a targeted low-income child.

(2) The Secretary may not approve, extend, renew, or amend a waiver, experimental, pilot, or demonstration project with respect to a State after the date of enactment of the Children's Health Insurance Program Reauthorization Act of 2009 [enacted Feb. 4, 2009] that would waive or modify the requirements of section 2111 [42 USCS § 1397kk].

(Aug. 14, 1935, ch 531, Title XXI, § 2107, as added Aug. 5, 1997, P. L. 105-33, Title IV, Subtitle J, Ch 1, § 4901(a), 111 Stat. 565; Dec. 21, 2000, P. L. 106-554, § 1(a)(6), 114 Stat. 2763; Feb. 8, 2006, P. L. 109-171, Title VI, Subtitle B, § 6102(a), 120 Stat. 131; Feb. 4, 2009, P. L. 111-3, Title I, Subtitle B, § 112(a)(2)(A), Title II, Subtitle A, §§ 203(a)(2), (d)(2), 214(b), Title V, §§ 501(d)(2), 503(a)(1), 123 Stat. 33, 46, 49, 57, 87, 89; Feb. 17, 2009, P. L. 111-5, Div B, Title V, § 5006(b)(2), (d)(2), (e)(2)(B), 123 Stat. 506, 510; March 23, 2010, P. L. 111-148, Title II, Subtitle B, § 2101(d)(2), (e), Title VI, Subtitle E, § 6401(c), 124 Stat. 287, 753; March 30, 2010, P. L. 111-152, Title I, Subtitle A, § 1004(b)(2)(B), 124 Stat. 1034.)

§ 1397hh. Annual reports; evaluations

(a) Annual report. Subject to subsection (e), the State shall—

(1) assess the operation of the State plan under this title [42 USCS §§ 1397aa et seq.] in each fiscal year, including the progress made in reducing the number of uncovered low-income children; and

(2) report to the Secretary, by January 1 following the end of the fiscal year, on the result of the assessment.

(b) State evaluations. (1) In general. By March 31, 2000, each State that has a State child health plan shall submit to the Secretary an evaluation that includes each of the following:

(A) An assessment of the effectiveness of the State plan in increasing the number of children with creditable health coverage.

(B) A description and analysis of the effectiveness of elements of the State plan, including—

(i) the characteristics of the children and families assisted under the State plan including age of the children, family income, and the assisted child's access to or coverage by other health insurance prior to the State plan and after eligibility for the State plan ends,

(ii) the quality of health coverage provided including the types of benefits provided,

(iii) the amount and level (including payment of part or all of any premium) of assistance provided by the State,

(iv) the service area of the State plan,

(v) the time limits for coverage of a child under the State plan,

(vi) the State's choice of health benefits coverage and other methods used for providing child health assistance, and

(vii) the sources of non-Federal funding used in the State plan.

(C) An assessment of the effectiveness of other public and private programs in the State in increasing the availability of affordable quality individual and family health insurance for children.

(D) A review and assessment of State activities to coordinate the plan under this title [42 USCS §§ 1397aa et seq.] with other public and private programs providing health care and health care financing, including medicaid and maternal and child health services.

(E) An analysis of changes and trends in the State that affect the provision of accessible, affordable, quality health insurance and health care to children.

(F) A description of any plans the State has for improving the availability of health insurance and health care for children.

(G) Recommendations for improving the program under this title [42 USCS §§ 1397aa et seq.].

(H) Any other matters the State and the Secretary consider appropriate.

(2) Report of the Secretary. The Secretary shall submit to Congress and make available to the public by December 31, 2001, a report based on the evaluations submitted by States under paragraph (1), containing any conclusions and recommendations the Secretary considers appropriate.

(c) Federal evaluation. (1) In general. The Secretary, directly or through contracts or interagency agreements, shall conduct an independent evaluation of 10 States with approved child health plans.

(2) Selection of States. In selecting States for the evaluation conducted under this subsection, the Secretary shall choose 10 States that utilize diverse approaches to providing child health assistance, represent various geographic areas (including a mix of rural and urban areas), and contain a significant portion of uncovered children.

(3) Matters included. In addition to the elements described in subsection (b)(1), the evaluation conducted under this subsection shall include each of the following:

(A) Surveys of the target population (enrollees, disenrollees, and individuals eligible for but not enrolled in the program under this title [42 USCS §§ 1397aa et seq.]).

(B) Evaluation of effective and ineffective outreach and enrollment practices with respect to children (for both the program under this title [42 USCS §§ 1397aa et seq.] and the medicaid program under title XIX [42 USCS §§ 1396 et seq.]), and identification of enrollment barriers and key elements of effective outreach and enrollment practices, including practices (such as through community health workers and others) that have successfully enrolled hard-to-reach populations such as children who are eligible for medical assistance under title XIX [42 USCS §§ 1396 et seq.] but have not been enrolled previously in the medicaid program under that title.

(C) Evaluation of the extent to which State medicaid eligibility practices and procedures under the medicaid program under title XIX [42 USCS §§ 1396 et seq.] are a barrier to the enrollment of children under that program, and the extent to which coordination (or lack of coordination) between that program and the program under this title [42 USCS §§ 1397aa et seq.] affects the enrollment of children under both programs.

(D) An assessment of the effect of cost-sharing on utilization, enrollment, and coverage retention.

(E) Evaluation of disenrollment or other retention issues, such as switching to private coverage, failure to pay premiums, or barriers in the recertification process.

(4) Submission to Congress. Not later than December 31, 2001, the Secretary shall submit to Congress the results of the evaluation conducted under this subsection.

(5) Subsequent evaluation using updated information. (A) In general. The Secretary, directly or through contracts or interagency agreements, shall conduct an independent subsequent evaluation of 10 States with approved child health plans.

(B) Selection of States and matters included. Paragraphs (2) and (3) shall apply to such subsequent evaluation in the same manner as such provisions apply to the evaluation conducted under paragraph (1).

(C) Submission to Congress. Not later than December 31, 2011, the Secretary shall submit to Congress the results of the evaluation conducted under this paragraph.

(D) Funding. Out of any money in the Treasury of the United States not otherwise appropriated, there are appropriated $10,000,000 for fiscal year 2010 for the purpose of conducting the evaluation authorized under this paragraph. Amounts appropriated under this subparagraph shall remain available for expenditure through fiscal year 2012.

(d) Access to records for IG and GAO audits and evaluations. For the purpose of evaluating and auditing the program established under this title [42 USCS §§ 1397aa et seq.], or title XIX [42 USCS §§ 1396 et seq.], the Secretary, the Office of Inspector General, and the Comptroller General shall have access to any books, accounts, records, correspondence, and other documents that are related to the expenditure of Federal funds under this title [42 USCS §§ 1397aa et seq.] and that are in the possession, custody, or control of States receiving Federal funds under this title [42 USCS §§ 1397aa et seq.] or political subdivisions thereof, or any grantee or contractor of such States or political subdivisions.

(e) Information required for inclusion in State annual report. The State shall include the following information in the annual report required under subsection (a):

(1) Eligibility criteria, enrollment, and retention data (including data with respect to continuity of coverage or duration of benefits).

(2) Data regarding the extent to which the State uses process measures with respect to determining the eligibility of children under the State child health plan, including measures such as 12-month continuous eligibility, self-declaration of income for applications or renewals, or presumptive eligibility.

(3) Data regarding denials of eligibility and redeterminations of eligibility.

(4) Data regarding access to primary and specialty services, access to networks of care, and care coordination provided under the State child health plan, using quality care and consumer satisfaction measures included in the Consumer Assessment of Healthcare Providers

and Systems (CAHPS) survey.

(5) If the State provides child health assistance in the form of premium assistance for the purchase of coverage under a group health plan, data regarding the provision of such assistance, including the extent to which employer-sponsored health insurance coverage is available for children eligible for child health assistance under the State child health plan, the range of the monthly amount of such assistance provided on behalf of a child or family, the number of children or families provided such assistance on a monthly basis, the income of the children or families provided such assistance, the benefits and cost-sharing protection provided under the State child health plan to supplement the coverage purchased with such premium assistance, the effective strategies the State engages in to reduce any administrative barriers to the provision of such assistance, and, the effects, if any, of the provision of such assistance on preventing the coverage provided under the State child health plan from substituting for coverage provided under employer-sponsored health insurance offered in the State.

(6) To the extent applicable, a description of any State activities that are designed to reduce the number of uncovered children in the State, including through a State health insurance connector program or support for innovative private health coverage initiatives.

(7) Data collected and reported in accordance with section 3101 of the Public Health Service Act [42 USCS § 300kk], with respect to individuals enrolled in the State child health plan (and, in the case of enrollees under 19 years of age, their parents or legal guardians), including data regarding the primary language of such individuals, parents, and legal guardians.

[(f)](e) Information on dental care for children. (1) In general. Each annual report under subsection (a) shall include the following information with respect to care and services described in section 1905(r)(3) [42 USCS § 1396d(r)(3)] provided to targeted low-income children enrolled in the State child health plan under this title [42 USCS § 1397aa et seq.] at any time during the year involved:

(A) The number of enrolled children by age grouping used for reporting purposes under section 1902(a)(43) [42 USCS § 1396a(a)(43)].

(B) For children within each such age grouping, information of the type contained in questions 12(a)–(c) of CMS Form 416 (that consists of the number of enrolled targeted low income children who receive any, preventive, or restorative dental care under the State plan).

(C) For the age grouping that includes children 8 years of age, the number of such children who have received a protective sealant on at least one permanent molar tooth.

(2) Inclusion of information on enrollees in managed care plans. The information under paragraph (1) shall include information on children who are enrolled in managed care plans and other private health plans and contracts with such plans under this title [42 USCS §§ 1397aa et seq.] shall provide for the reporting of such information by such plans to the State.

(Aug. 14, 1935, ch 531, Title XXI, § 2108, as added Aug. 5, 1997, P. L. 105-33, Title IV, Subtitle J, Ch 1, § 4901(a), 111 Stat. 566; Nov. 29, 1999, P. L. 106-113, Div B, § 1000(a)(6), 113 Stat. 1536; Feb. 4, 2009, P. L. 111-3, Title II, Subtitle A, § 201(b)(2)(B)(ii), Title IV, § 402(a), Title V, § 501(e)(2), Title VI, Subtitle A, §§ 603, 604, 123 Stat. 39, 82, 87, 99; March 11, 2009, P. L. 111-8, Div G, Title I, § 1301(e), 123 Stat. 829; March 23, 2010, P. L. 111-148, Title IV, Subtitle D, § 4302(b)(1)(B), 124 Stat. 581.)

§ 1397ii. Miscellaneous provisions

(a) Relation to other laws. (1) HIPAA. Health benefits coverage provided under section 2101(a)(1) [42 USCS § 1397aa(a)(1)] (and coverage provided under a waiver under section 2105(c)(2)(B) [42 USCS § 1397ee(c)(2)(B)]) shall be treated as creditable coverage for purposes of part 7 of subtitle B of title I of the Employee Retirement Income Security Act of 1974 [29 USCS §§ 1181 et seq.], title XXVII of the Public Health Service Act [42 USCS §§ 300gg et seq.], and subtitle K of the Internal Revenue Code of 1986 [26 USCS §§ 9801 et seq.].

(2) ERISA. Nothing in this title [42 USCS §§ 1397aa et seq.] shall be construed as affecting or modifying section 514 of the Employee Retirement Income Security Act of 1974 (29 U.S.C. 1144) with respect to a group health plan (as defined in section 2791(a)(1) of the Public Health Service Act (42 U.S.C. 300gg-91(a)(1))).

(b) Adjustment to current population survey to include State-by-State data relating to children without health insurance coverage. (1) In general. The Secretary of Commerce shall make appropriate adjustments to the annual Current Population Survey conducted by the Bureau of the Census in order to produce statistically reliable annual State data on the number of low-income children who do not have health insurance coverage, so that real changes in the uninsurance rates of children can reasonably be detected. The Current Population Survey should produce data under this subsection that categorizes such children by family income, age, and race or ethnicity. The adjustments made to produce such data shall include, where appropriate, expanding the sample size used in the State sampling units, expanding the number of sampling units in a State, and an appropriate verification element.

(2) Additional requirements. In addition to making the adjustments required to produce the data described in paragraph (1), with respect to data collection occurring for fiscal years beginning with fiscal year 2009, in appropriate consultation with the Secretary of Health and Human Services, the Secretary of Commerce shall do the following:

(A) Make appropriate adjustments to the Current Population Survey to develop more accurate State-specific estimates of the number of children enrolled in health coverage under title XIX or this title [42 USCS §§ 1396 et seq. or 1397aa et seq.].

(B) Make appropriate adjustments to the Current Population Survey to improve the survey estimates used to determine a high-performing State under section 2111(b)(3)(B) [42 USCS § 1397kk(b)(3)(B)] and any other data necessary for carrying out this title [42 USCS §§ 1397aa et seq.].

(C) Include health insurance survey information in the American Community Survey related to children.

(D) Assess whether American Community Survey estimates, once such survey data are first available, produce more reliable estimates than the Current Population Survey with respect to the purposes described in subparagraph (B).

(E) On the basis of the assessment required under subparagraph (D), recommend to the Secretary of Health and Human Services whether American Community Survey estimates should be used in lieu of, or in some combination with, Current Population Survey estimates for the purposes described in subparagraph (B).

(F) Continue making the adjustments described in the last sentence of paragraph (1) with respect to expansion of the sample size used in State sampling units, the number of sampling units in a State, and using an appropriate verification element.

(3) Authority for the Secretary of Health and Human Services to transition to the use of all, or some combination of, ACS estimates upon recommendation of the Secretary of Commerce. If, on the basis of the assessment required under paragraph (2)(D), the Secretary of Commerce recommends to the Secretary of Health and Human Services that American Community Survey estimates should be used in lieu of, or in some combination with, Current Population Survey estimates for the purposes described in paragraph (2)(B), the Secretary of Health and Human Services, in consultation with the States, may provide for a period during which the Secretary may transition from carrying out such purposes through the use of Current Population Survey estimates to the use of American Community Survey estimates (in lieu of, or in combination with the Current Population Survey estimates, as recommended), provided that any such transition is implemented in a manner that is designed to avoid adverse impacts upon States with approved State child health plans under this title [42 USCS §§ 1397aa et seq.].

(4) Appropriation. Out of any money in the Treasury of the United States not otherwise appropriated, there are appropriated $20,000,000 for fiscal year 2009 and each fiscal year thereafter for the purpose of carrying out this subsection (except that only with respect to fiscal year 2008, there are appropriated $20,000,000 for the purpose of carrying out this subsection, to remain available until expended).

(Aug. 14, 1935, ch 531, Title XXI, § 2109, as added Aug. 5, 1997, P. L. 105-33, Title IV, Subtitle J, Ch 1, § 4901(a), 111 Stat. 567; Nov. 29, 1999, P. L. 106-113, Div B, § 1000(a)(6), 113 Stat. 1536; Dec. 29, 2008, P. L. 110-173, Title II, § 205, 121 Stat. 2514; Feb. 4, 2009, P. L. 111-3, Title VI, Subtitle A, § 602, 123 Stat. 98; March 23, 2010, P. L. 111-148, Title II, Subtitle B, § 2102(a)(6), 124 Stat. 288.)

§ 1397jj. Definitions

(a) Child health assistance. For purposes of this title [42 USCS §§ 1397aa et seq.], the term "child health assistance" means payment for part or all of the cost of health benefits coverage for targeted low-income children that includes any of the following (and includes, in the case described in section 2105(a)(1)(D)(i) [42 USCS §§ 1397ee(a)(1)(D)(i)], payment for part or all of the cost of providing any of the following), as specified under the State plan:

(1) Inpatient hospital services.

(2) Outpatient hospital services.

(3) Physician services.

(4) Surgical services.

(5) Clinic services (including health center

services) and other ambulatory health care services.

(6) Prescription drugs and biologicals and the administration of such drugs and biologicals, only if such drugs and biologicals are not furnished for the purpose of causing, or assisting in causing, the death, suicide, euthanasia, or mercy killing of a person.

(7) Over-the-counter medications.

(8) Laboratory and radiological services.

(9) Prenatal care and prepregnancy family planning services and supplies.

(10) Inpatient mental health services, other than services described in paragraph (18) but including services furnished in a State-operated mental hospital and including residential or other 24-hour therapeutically planned structured services.

(11) Outpatient mental health services, other than services described in paragraph (19) but including services furnished in a State-operated mental hospital and including community-based services.

(12) Durable medical equipment and other medically-related or remedial devices (such as prosthetic devices, implants, eyeglasses, hearing aids, dental devices, and adaptive devices).

(13) Disposable medical supplies.

(14) Home and community-based health care services and related supportive services (such as home health nursing services, home health aide services, personal care, assistance with activities of daily living, chore services, day care services, respite care services, training for family members, and minor modifications to the home).

(15) Nursing care services (such as nurse practitioner services, nurse midwife services, advanced practice nurse services, private duty nursing care, pediatric nurse services, and respiratory care services) in a home, school, or other setting.

(16) Abortion only if necessary to save the life of the mother or if the pregnancy is the result of an act of rape or incest.

(17) Dental services.

(18) Inpatient substance abuse treatment services and residential substance abuse treatment services.

(19) Outpatient substance abuse treatment services.

(20) Case management services.

(21) Care coordination services.

(22) Physical therapy, occupational therapy, and services for individuals with speech, hearing, and language disorders.

(23) Hospice care (concurrent, in the case of an individual who is a child, with care related to the treatment of the child's condition with respect to which a diagnosis of terminal illness has been made[)].

(24) Any other medical, diagnostic, screening, preventive, restorative, remedial, therapeutic, or rehabilitative services (whether in a facility, home, school, or other setting) if recognized by State law and only if the service is—

(A) prescribed by or furnished by a physician or other licensed or registered practitioner within the scope of practice as defined by State law,

(B) performed under the general supervision or at the direction of a physician, or

(C) furnished by a health care facility that is operated by a State or local government or is licensed under State law and operating within the scope of the license.

(25) Premiums for private health care insurance coverage.

(26) Medical transportation.

(27) Enabling services (such as transportation, translation, and outreach services) only if designed to increase the accessibility of primary and preventive health care services for eligible low-income individuals.

(28) Any other health care services or items specified by the Secretary and not excluded under this section.

(b) Targeted low-income child defined. For purposes of this title [42 USCS §§ 1397aa et seq.]—

(1) In general. Subject to paragraph (2), the term "targeted low-income child" means a child—

(A) who has been determined eligible by the State for child health assistance under the State plan;

(B)(i) who is a low-income child, or

(ii) is a child—

(I) whose family income (as determined under the State child health plan) exceeds the medicaid applicable income level (as defined in paragraph (4)), but does not exceed 50 percentage points above the medicaid applicable income level;

(II) whose family income (as so determined) does not exceed the medicaid applicable income level (as defined in paragraph (4) but determined as if "June 1, 1997" were substituted for "March 31, 1997"); or

(III) who resides in a State that does not have a medicaid applicable income level (as defined in paragraph (4)); and

(C) who is not found to be eligible for medical assistance under title XIX [42 USCS §§ 1396 et seq.] or, subject to paragraph (5), covered under a group health plan or under health insurance coverage (as such terms are defined in section 2791 of the Public Health Service Act [42 USCS § 300gg-91]).

(2) Children excluded. Such term does not include—

(A) a child who is an inmate of a public institution or a patient in an institution for mental diseases; or

(B) except as provided in paragraph (6), a child who is a member of a family that is eligible for health benefits coverage under a State health benefits plan on the basis of a family member's employment with a public agency in the State.

(3) Special rule. A child shall not be considered to be described in paragraph (1)(C) notwithstanding that the child is covered under a health insurance coverage program that has been in operation since before July 1, 1997, and that is offered by a State which receives no Federal funds for the program's operation.

(4) Medicaid applicable income level. The term "medicaid applicable income level" means, with respect to a child, the effective income level (expressed as a percent of the poverty line) that has been specified under the State plan under title XIX [42 USCS §§ 1396 et seq.] (including under a waiver authorized by the Secretary or under section 1902(r)(2) [42 USCS § 1396a(r)(2)]), as of March 31, 1997, for the child to be eligible for medical assistance under section 1902(l)(2) or 1905(n)(2) [42 USCS § 1396a(l)(2) or 1396d(n)(2)] (as selected by a State) for the age of such child.

(5) Option for States with a separate CHIP program to provide dental-only supplemental coverage. (A) In general. Subject to subparagraphs (B) and (C), in the case of any child who is enrolled in a group health plan or health insurance coverage offered through an employer who would, but for the application of paragraph (1)(C), satisfy the requirements for being a targeted low-income child under a State child health plan that is implemented under this title [42 USCS §§ 1397aa et seq.], a State may waive the application of such paragraph to the child in order to provide—

(i) dental coverage consistent with the requirements of subsection (c)(5) of section 2103 [42 USCS § 1397cc]; or

(ii) cost-sharing protection for dental coverage consistent with such requirements and the requirements of subsection (e)(3)(B) of such section.

(B) Limitation. A State may limit the application of a waiver of paragraph (1)(C) to children whose family income does not exceed a level specified by the State, so long as the level so specified does not exceed the maximum income level otherwise established for other children under the State child health plan.

(C) Conditions. A State may not offer dental-only supplemental coverage under this paragraph unless the State satisfies the following conditions:

(i) Income eligibility. The State child health plan under this title [42 USCS §§ 1397aa et seq.]—

(I) has the highest income eligibility standard permitted under this title [42 USCS §§ 1397aa et seq.] (or a waiver) as of January 1, 2009;

(II) does not limit the acceptance of applications for children or impose any numerical limitation, waiting list, or similar limitation on the eligibility of such children for child health assistance under such State plan; and

(III) provides benefits to all children in the State who apply for and meet eligibility standards.

(ii) No more favorable treatment. The State child health plan may not provide more favorable dental coverage or cost-sharing protection for dental coverage to children provided dental-only supplemental coverage under this paragraph than the dental coverage and cost-sharing protection for dental coverage provided to targeted low-income children who are eligible for the full range of child health assistance provided under the State child health plan.

(6) Exceptions to exclusion of children of employees of a public agency in the State. (A) In general. A child shall not be considered to be described in paragraph (2)(B) if—

(i) the public agency that employs a member of the child's family to which such paragraph applies satisfies subparagraph (B); or

(ii) subparagraph (C) applies to such child.

(B) Maintenance of effort with respect to per person agency contribution for family coverage. For purposes of subparagraph (A)(i), a public agency satisfies this subparagraph if the amount of annual agency expenditures made on behalf of each employee enrolled in health coverage paid for by the agency that includes dependent coverage for the most recent State fiscal year is not less than the amount of such expenditures made by the agency for the 1997 State fiscal year, increased by the percentage increase in the medical care expenditure category of the Consumer Price Index for All-Urban Consumers (all items: U.S. City Average) for such preceding fiscal year.

(C) Hardship exception. For purposes of subparagraph (A)(ii), this subparagraph applies to a child if the State determines, on a case-by-case basis, that the annual aggregate amount of premiums and cost-sharing imposed for coverage of the family of the child would exceed 5 percent of such family's income for the year involved.

(c) Additional definitions. For purposes of this title [42 USCS §§ 1397aa et seq.]:

(1) Child. The term "child" means an individual under 19 years of age.

(2) Creditable health coverage. The term "creditable health coverage" has the meaning given the term "creditable coverage" under section 2701(c) of the Public Health Service Act (42 U.S.C. 300gg(c)) and includes coverage that meets the requirements of section 2103 [42 USCS § 1397cc] provided to a targeted low-income child under this title [42 USCS §§ 1397aa et seq.] or under a waiver approved under section 2105(c)(2)(B) [42 USCS § 1396d(c)(2)(B)] (relating to a direct service waiver).

(3) Group health plan; health insurance coverage; etc. The terms "group health plan", "group health insurance coverage", and "health insurance coverage" have the meanings given such terms in section 2791 of the Public Health Service Act [42 USCS § 300gg-91].

(4) Low-income. The term "low-income child" means a child whose family income is at or below 200 percent of the poverty line for a family of the size involved.

(5) Poverty line defined. The term "poverty line" has the meaning given such term in section 673(2) of the Community Services Block Grant Act (42 U.S.C. 9902(2)), including any revision required by such section.

(6) Preexisting condition exclusion. The term "preexisting condition exclusion" has the meaning given such term in section 2701(b)(1)(A) of the Public Health Service Act (42 U.S.C. 300gg(b)(1)(A)).

(7) State child health plan; plan. Unless the context otherwise requires, the terms "State child health plan" and "plan" mean a State child health plan approved under section 2106 [42 USCS § 1397ff].

(8) Uncovered child. The term "uncovered child" means a child that does not have creditable health coverage.

(9) School-based health center. (A) In general. The term "school-based health center" means a health clinic that—

(i) is located in or near a school facility of a school district or board or of an Indian tribe or tribal organization;

(ii) is organized through school, community, and health provider relationships;

(iii) is administered by a sponsoring facility;

(iv) provides through health professionals primary health services to children in accordance with State and local law, including laws relating to licensure and certification; and

(v) satisfies such other requirements as a State may establish for the operation of such a clinic.

(B) Sponsoring facility. For purposes of subparagraph (A)(iii), the term "sponsoring facility" includes any of the following:

(i) A hospital.

(ii) A public health department.

(iii) A community health center.

(iv) A nonprofit health care agency.

(v) A local educational agency (as defined under section 9101 of the Elementary and Secondary Education Act of 1965 [20 USCS § 7801] [])].

(vi) A program administered by the Indian Health Service or the Bureau of Indian Affairs or operated by an Indian tribe or a tribal organization.

(Aug. 14, 1935, ch 531, Title XXI, § 2110, as added Aug. 5, 1997, P. L. 105-33, Title IV, Subtitle J, Ch 1, § 4901(a), 111 Stat. 567; Nov. 19, 1997, P. L. 105-100, Title I, § 162(3), (9), 111 Stat. 2189, 2190; Dec. 21, 2000, P. L. 106-554, § 1(a)(6), 114 Stat. 2763; Feb. 4, 2009, P. L. 111-3, Title V, §§ 501(b)(1), 505(b), 123 Stat. 85, 90; March 23, 2010, P. L. 111-148, Title II, Subtitle B, § 2102(a)(7), Subtitle D, § 2302(b), Title X, Subtitle B, Part I, § 10203(d)(2)(D), 124 Stat. 288, 293, 930.)

HISTORY; ANCILLARY LAWS AND DIRECTIVES

Other provisions:

CHIP eligibility for children ineligible for Medicaid as a result of elimination of disregards. Act March 23, 2010, P. L. 111-148, Title II, Subtitle B, § 2101(f), 124 Stat. 287, provides: "Notwithstanding any other provision of law, a State shall treat any child who is determined to be ineligible for medical assistance under the State Medicaid plan or under a waiver of the plan as a result of the elimination of the application of an income disregard based on expense or type of income, as required under section 1902(e)(14) of the Social Security Act [42 USCS § 1396a(e)(14)] (as added by this Act), as a targeted low-income child under section 2110(b) [subsec. (b) of this section] (unless the child is excluded under paragraph (2) of that section) and shall provide child health assistance to the child under the State child health plan (whether implemented under title XIX or XXI, or both, of the Social Security Act [42 USCS §§ 1396 et seq. or 1397aa et seq.]).".

§ 1397mm. Grants to improve outreach and enrollment

(a) Outreach and enrollment grants; national campaign. (1) In general. From the amounts appropriated under subsection (g), subject to paragraph (2), the Secretary shall award grants to eligible entities during the period of fiscal years 2009 through 2015 to conduct outreach and enrollment efforts that are designed to increase the enrollment and participation of eligible children under this title [42 USCS §§ 1397aa et seq.] and title XIX [42 USCS §§ 1396 et seq.].

(2) Ten percent set aside for national enrollment campaign. An amount equal to 10 percent of such amounts shall be used by the Secretary for expenditures during such period to carry out a national enrollment campaign in accordance with subsection (h).

(b) Priority for award of grants. (1) In general. In awarding grants under subsection (a), the Secretary shall give priority to eligible entities that—

(A) propose to target geographic areas with high rates of—

(i) eligible but unenrolled children, including such children who reside in rural areas; or

(ii) racial and ethnic minorities and health disparity populations, including those proposals that address cultural and linguistic barriers to enrollment; and

(B) submit the most demonstrable evidence required under paragraphs (1) and (2) of subsection (c).

(2) Ten percent set aside for outreach to Indian children. An amount equal to 10 percent of the funds appropriated under subsection (g) shall be used by the Secretary to award grants to Indian Health Service providers and urban Indian organizations receiving funds under title V of the Indian Health Care Improvement Act (25 U.S.C. 1651 et seq.) for outreach to, and enrollment of, children who are Indians.

(c) Application. An eligible entity that desires to receive a grant under subsection (a) shall submit an application to the Secretary in such form and manner, and containing such information, as the Secretary may decide. Such application shall include—

(1) evidence demonstrating that the entity includes members who have access to, and credibility with, ethnic or low-income populations in the communities in which activities funded under the grant are to be conducted;

(2) evidence demonstrating that the entity has the ability to address barriers to enrollment, such as lack of awareness of eligibility, stigma concerns and punitive fears associated with receipt of benefits, and other cultural barriers to applying for and receiving child health assistance or medical assistance;

(3) specific quality or outcomes performance measures to evaluate the effectiveness of activities funded by a grant awarded under this section; and

(4) an assurance that the eligible entity shall—

(A) conduct an assessment of the effectiveness of such activities against the performance measures;

(B) cooperate with the collection and reporting of enrollment data and other information in order for the Secretary to conduct such assessments; and

(C) in the case of an eligible entity that is not the State, provide the State with enrollment data and other information as necessary for the State to make necessary projections of eligible children and pregnant women.

(d) Dissemination of enrollment data and information determined from effectiveness assessments; annual report. The Secretary shall—

(1) make publicly available the enrollment data and information collected and reported in accordance with subsection (c)(4)(B); and

(2) submit an annual report to Congress on the outreach and enrollment activities conducted with funds appropriated under this section.

(e) Maintenance of effort for States awarded grants; no match required for any eligible entity awarded a grant. (1) State maintenance of effort. In the case of a State that is awarded a grant under this section, the State share of funds expended for outreach and enrollment activities under the State child health plan shall not be less than the State share of such funds expended in the fiscal year preceding the first fiscal year for which the grant is awarded.

(2) No matching requirement. No eligible entity awarded a grant under subsection (a) shall be required to provide any matching funds as a condition for receiving the grant.

(f) Definitions. In this section:

(1) Eligible entity. The term "eligible entity" means any of the following:

(A) A State with an approved child health plan under this title [42 USCS §§ 1397aa et seq.].

(B) A local government.

(C) An Indian tribe or tribal consortium, a tribal organization, an urban Indian organization receiving funds under title V of the Indian Health Care Improvement Act (25 U.S.C. 1651 et seq.), or an Indian Health Service provider.

(D) A Federal health safety net organization.

(E) A national, State, local, or community-based public or nonprofit private organization, including organizations that use community health workers or community-based doula programs.

(F) A faith-based organization or consortia, to the extent that a grant awarded to such an entity is consistent with the requirements of section 1955 of the Public Health Service Act (42 U.S.C. 300x-65) relating to a grant award to nongovernmental entities.

(G) An elementary or secondary school.

(2) Federal health safety net organization. The term "Federal health safety net organization" means—

(A) a Federally-qualified health center (as defined in section 1905(l)(2)(B) [42 USCS § 1396d(l)(2)(B)]);

(B) a hospital defined as a disproportionate share hospital for purposes of section 1923 [42 USCS § 1396r-4];

(C) a covered entity described in section 340B(a)(4) of the Public Health Service Act (42 U.S.C. 256b(a)(4)); and

(D) any other entity or consortium that serves children under a federally funded program, including the special supplemental nutrition program for women, infants, and children (WIC) established under section 17 of the Child Nutrition Act of 1966 (42 U.S.C. 1786), the Head Start and Early Head Start programs under the Head Start Act (42 U.S.C. 9801 et seq.), the school lunch program established under the Richard B. Russell National School Lunch Act [42 USCS §§ 1751 et seq.], and an elementary or secondary school.

(3) Indians; Indian tribe; tribal organization; urban Indian organization. The terms "Indian", "Indian tribe", "tribal organization", and "urban Indian organization" have the meanings given such terms in section 4 of the Indian Health Care Improvement Act (25 U.S.C. 1603).

(4) Community health worker. The term 'community health worker' means an individual who promotes health or nutrition within the community in which the individual resides—

(A) by serving as a liaison between communities and health care agencies;

(B) by providing guidance and social assistance to community residents;

(C) by enhancing community residents' ability to effectively communicate with health care providers;

(D) by providing culturally and linguistically appropriate health or nutrition education;

(E) by advocating for individual and community health or nutrition needs; and

(F) by providing referral and followup services.

(g) Appropriation. There is appropriated, out of any money in the Treasury not otherwise appropriated, $140,000,000 for the period of fiscal years 2009 through 2015, for the purpose of awarding grants under this section. Amounts appropriated and paid under the authority of this section shall be in addition to amounts appropriated under section 2104 [42 USCS § 1397dd] and paid to States in accordance with section 2105 [42 USCS § 1397ee], including with respect to expenditures for outreach activities in accordance with subsections (a)(1)(D)(iii) and (c)(2)(C) of that section.

(h) National enrollment campaign. From the amounts made available under subsection (a)(2), the Secretary shall develop and implement a national enrollment campaign to improve the enrollment of underserved child populations in the programs established under this title [42 USCS §§ 1397aa et seq.] and title XIX [42 USCS §§ 1396 et seq.]. Such campaign may include—

(1) the establishment of partnerships with the Secretary of Education and the Secretary of Agriculture to develop national campaigns to link the eligibility and enrollment systems for the assistance programs each Secretary administers that often serve the same children;

(2) the integration of information about the programs established under this title [42 USCS §§ 1397aa et seq.] and title XIX [42 USCS §§ 1396 et seq.] in public health awareness campaigns administered by the Secretary;

(3) increased financial and technical support for enrollment hotlines maintained by the Secretary to ensure that all States participate in such hotlines;

(4) the establishment of joint public awareness outreach initiatives with the Secretary of Education and the Secretary of Labor regarding the importance of health insurance to building strong communities and the economy;

(5) the development of special outreach materials for Native Americans or for individuals with limited English proficiency; and

(6) such other outreach initiatives as the Secretary determines would increase public awareness of the programs under this title [42 USCS §§ 1397aa et seq.] and title XIX [42 USCS §§ 1396 et seq.].

(Aug. 14, 1935, ch 531, Title XXI, § 2113, as added Feb. 4, 2009, P. L. 111-3, Title II, Subtitle A, § 201(a), 123 Stat. 35; March 23, 2010, P. L. 111-148, Title X, Subtitle B, Part I, § 10203(d)(2)(E), 124 Stat. 931.)

CHAPTER 21. CIVIL RIGHTS

INSTITUTIONALIZED PERSONS

§ 1997a-1. Subpoena authority

(a) Authority. The Attorney General, or at the direction of the Attorney General, any officer or employee of the Department of Justice may require by subpoena access to any institution that is the subject of an investigation under this Act and to any document, record, material, file, report, memorandum, policy, procedure, investigation, video or audio recording, or quality assurance report relating to any institution that is the subject of an investigation under this Act [42 USCS §§ 1997 et seq.] to determine whether there are conditions which deprive persons residing in or confined to the institution of any rights, privileges, or immunities secured or protected by the Constitution or laws of the United States.

(b) Issuance and enforcement of subpoenas. (1) Issuance. Subpoenas issued under this section—

(A) shall bear the signature of the Attorney General or any officer or employee of the Department of Justice as designated by the Attorney General; and

(B) shall be served by any person or class of persons designated by the Attorney General or a designated officer or employee for that purpose.

(2) Enforcement. In the case of contumacy or failure to obey a subpoena issued under this section, the United States district court for the judicial district in which the institution is located may issue an order requiring compliance. Any failure to obey the order of the court may be punished by the court as a contempt that court.

(c) Protection of subpoenaed records and information. Any document, record, material, file, report, memorandum, policy, procedure, investigation, video or audio recording, or quality assurance report or other information obtained under a subpoena issued under this section—

(1) may not be used for any purpose other than to protect the rights, privileges, or immunities secured or protected by the Constitution or laws of the United States of persons who reside, have resided, or will reside in an institution;

(2) may not be transmitted by or within the Department of Justice for any purpose other than to protect the rights, privileges, or immunities secured or protected by the Constitution or laws of the United States of persons who reside, have resided, or will reside in an institution; and

(3) shall be redacted, obscured, or otherwise altered if used in any publicly available manner so as to prevent the disclosure of any personally identifiable information.

(May 23, 1980, P. L. 96-247, § 3A, as added March 23, 2010, P. L. 111-148, Title X, Subtitle F, § 10606(d)(2), 124 Stat. 1008.)

CHAPTER 122. NATIVE HAWAIIAN HEALTH CARE

§ 11705. Native Hawaiian health care systems

(a) Comprehensive health promotion, disease prevention, and primary health services. (1)(A) The Secretary, in consultation with Papa Ola Lokahi, may make grants to, or enter into contracts with, any qualified entity for the purpose of providing comprehensive health promotion and disease prevention services as well as primary health services to Native Hawaiians.

(B) In making grants and entering into contracts under this paragraph, the Secretary shall give preference to Native Hawaiian health care systems and Native Hawaiian organizations and, to the extent feasible, health promotion and disease prevention services shall be performed through Native Hawaiian health care systems.

(2) In addition to paragraph (1), the Secretary may make a grant to, or enter into a contract with, Papa Ola Lokahi for the purpose of planning Native Hawaiian health care systems to serve the health needs of Native Hawaiian communities on each of the islands of O'ahu, Moloka'i, Maui, Hawai'i, Lana'i, Kaua'i, and Ni'ihau in the State of Hawaii.

(b) Qualified entity. An entity is a qualified entity for purposes of subsection (a)(1) if the entity is a Native Hawaiian health care system.

(c) Services to be provided. (1) Each recipient of funds under subsection (a)(1) shall provide the following services:

(A) outreach services to inform Native Hawaiians of the availability of health services;

(B) education in health promotion and disease prevention of the Native Hawaiian population by, wherever possible, Native Hawaiian health care practitioners, community outreach workers, counselors, and cultural educators;

(C) services of physicians, physicians' assistants, nurse practitioners or other health professionals;

(D) immunizations;

(E) prevention and control of diabetes, high blood pressure, and otitis media;

(F) pregnancy and infant care; and

(G) improvement of nutrition.

(2) In addition to the mandatory services under paragraph (1), the following services may be provided pursuant to subsection (a)(1):

(A) identification, treatment, control, and reduction of the incidence of preventable illnesses and conditions endemic to Native Hawaiians;

(B) collection of data related to the prevention of diseases and illnesses among Native Hawaiians; and

(C) services within the meaning of the terms "health promotion", "disease prevention", and "primary health services", as such terms are defined in section 12 [42 USCS § 11711], which are not specifically referred to in paragraph (1) of this subsection.

(3) The health care services referred to in paragraphs (1) and (2) which are provided under grants or contracts under subsection (a)(1) may be provided by traditional Native Hawaiian healers.

(4) Health and education. In order to enable privately funded organizations to continue to supplement public efforts to provide educational programs designed to improve the health, capability, and well-being of Native Hawaiians and to continue to provide health services to Native Hawaiians, notwithstanding any other provision of Federal or State law, it shall be lawful for the private educational organization identified in section 7202(16) of the Elementary and Secondary Education Act of 1965 (20 U.S.C. 7512(16)) to continue to offer its educational programs and services to Native Hawaiians (as defined in section 7207 of that Act (20 U.S.C. 7517)) first and to others only after the need for such programs and services by Native Hawaiians has been met.

(d) Limitation of number of entities. During a fiscal year, the Secretary under this Act may make a grant to, or hold a contract with, not more than 5 Native Hawaiian health care systems.

(e) Matching funds. (1) The Secretary may not make a grant or provide funds pursuant to a contract under subsection (a)(1) of this section to a Native Hawaiian health care system—

(A) in an amount exceeding 83.3 percent of the costs of providing health services under the grant or contract; and

(B) unless the Native Hawaiian health care system agrees that the Native Hawaiian health care system or the State of Hawaii will make available, directly or through donations to the Native Hawaiian health care system, non-Federal contributions toward such costs in an amount equal to not less than $1 (in cash or in kind under paragraph (2)) for each $5 of Federal funds provided in such grant or contract.

(2) Non-Federal contributions required in paragraph (1) may be in cash or in kind, fairly evaluated, including plant, equipment, or services. Amounts provided by the Federal Government or services assisted or subsidized to any significant extent by the Federal Government may not be included in determining the amount of such non-Federal contributions.

(3) The Secretary may waive the requirement established in paragraph (1) if—

(A) the Native Hawaiian health care system involved is a nonprofit private entity described in subsection (b); and

(B) the Secretary, in consultation with Papa Ola Lokahi, determines that it is not feasible for the Native Hawaiian health care system to comply with such requirement.

(f) Restriction on use of grant and contract funds. The Secretary may not make a grant to, or enter into a contract with, any entity under subsection (a)(1) unless the entity agrees that, amounts received pursuant to such subsection will not, directly or through contract, be expended—

(1) for any purpose other than the purposes described in subsection (c) of this section;

(2) to provide inpatient services;

(3) to make cash payments to intended recipients of health services; or

(4) to purchase or improve real property (other than minor remodeling of existing improvements to real property) or to purchase major medical equipment.

(g) Limitation on charges for services. The Secretary may not make a grant, or enter into a contract with, any entity under subsection (a)(1) unless the entity agrees that, whether health services are provided directly or through contract—

(1) health services under the grant or contract will be provided without regard to ability to pay for the health services; and

(2) the entity will impose a charge for the delivery of health services, and such charge—

(A) will be made according to a schedule of charges that is made available to the public, and

(B) will be adjusted to reflect the income of the individual involved.

(h) Authorization of appropriations. (1) There are authorized to be appropriated such sums as may be necessary for fiscal years 1993 through 2019 to carry out subsection (a)(1).

(2) There are authorized to be appropriated such sums as may be necessary to carry out

subsection (a)(2).

(Oct. 31, 1988, P. L. 100-579, § 6, 102 Stat. 2919, and Nov. 18, 1988, P. L. 100-690, Title II, Subtitle D, § 2306, 102 Stat. 4226; Oct. 6, 1992, P. L. 102-396, Title IX, § 9168, 106 Stat. 1948; March 23, 2010, P. L. 111-148, Title X, Subtitle B, Part III, § 10221(a), 124 Stat. 935.)

HISTORY; ANCILLARY LAWS AND DIRECTIVES

Other provisions:

Effective date of subsec. (c)(4). Act March 23, 2010, P. L. 111-148, Title X, Subtitle B, Part III, § 10221(a), 124 Stat. 935 (enacting into law § 202(b)(2) of Title II of S. 1790, as reported in the Senate on Dec. 16, 2009), provides: "The amendment made by paragraph (1) [adding subsec. (c)(4) of this section] takes effect on December 5, 2006.".

§ 11706. Administrative grant for Papa Ola Lokahi

(a) In general. In addition to any other grant or contract under this Act, the Secretary may make grants to, or enter into contracts with, Papa Ola Lokahi for—

(1) coordination, implementation, and updating (as appropriate) of the comprehensive health care master plan developed pursuant to section 4 [42 USCS § 11703];

(2) training for the persons described in section 6(c)(1)(B) [42 USCS § 11705(c)(1)(B)];

(3) identification of and research into the diseases that are most prevalent among Native Hawaiians, including behavioral, biomedical, epidemiological, and health services;

(4) the development of an action plan outlining the contributions that each member organization of Papa Ola Lokahi will make in carrying out the policy of this Act;

(5) a clearinghouse function for—

(A) the collection and maintenance of data associated with the health status of Native Hawaiians;

(B) the identification and research into diseases affecting Native Hawaiians; and

(C) the availability of Native Hawaiian project funds, research projects and publications;

(6) the coordination of the health care programs and services provided to Native Hawaiians; and

(7) the administration of special project funds.

(b) Authorization of appropriations. There are authorized to be appropriated such sums as may be necessary for fiscal years 1993 through 2019 to carry out subsection (a).

(Oct. 31, 1988, P. L. 100-579, § 7, 102 Stat. 2921, and Nov. 18, 1988, P. L. 100-690, Title II, Subtitle D, § 2307, 102 Stat. 4227; Oct. 6, 1992, P. L. 102-396, Title IX, § 9168, 106 Stat. 1948; March 23, 2010, P. L. 111-148, Title X, Subtitle B, Part III, § 10221(a), 124 Stat. 935.)

§ 11709. Native Hawaiian health scholarships

(a) Eligibility. Subject to the availability of funds appropriated under the authority of subsection (c) of this section, the Secretary shall provide funds through a direct grant or a cooperative agreement to Papa Ola Lokahi for the purpose of providing scholarship assistance to students who—

(1) meet the requirements of paragraphs (1), (3), and (4) of section 338A(b) of the Public Health Service Act (42 U.S.C. 254l(b)), and

(2) are Native Hawaiians.

(b) Terms and conditions. (1) The scholarship assistance provided under subsection (a) of this section shall be provided under the same terms and subject to the same conditions, regulations, and rules that apply to scholarship assistance provided under section 338A of the Public Health Service Act (42 U.S.C. 254l), provided that—

(A) the provision of scholarships in each type of health care profession training shall correspond to the need for each type of health care professional identified in the Native Hawaiian comprehensive health care master plan implemented under section 4 [42 USCS § 11703] to serve the Native Hawaiian health care systems, as identified by Papa Ola Lokahi;

(B) the primary health services covered under the scholarship assistance program under this section shall be the services included under the definition of that term under section 12(8) [42 USCS § 11711(8)];

(C) to the maximum extent practicable, the Secretary shall select scholarship recipients from a list of eligible applicants submitted by the Papa Ola Lokahi;

(D) the obligated service requirement for each scholarship recipient shall be fulfilled through the full-time clinical or nonclinical practice of the health profession of the scholarship recipient, in an order of priority that would provide for practice—

(i) first, in any one of the five Native Hawaiian health care systems; and

(ii) second, in—

(I) a health professional shortage area or medically underserved area located in the State of Hawaii; or

(II) a geographic area or facility that is—

(aa) located in the State of Hawaii; and

(bb) has a designation that is similar to a

designation described in subclause (I) made by the Secretary, acting through the Public Health Service; and

(E) the provision of counseling, retention and other support services shall not be limited to scholarship recipients, but shall also include recipients of other scholarship and financial aid programs enrolled in appropriate health professions training programs, [;]

(F) the obligated service of a scholarship recipient shall not be performed by the recipient through membership in the National Health Service Corps; and

(G) the requirements of sections 331 through 338 of the Public Health Service Act (42 U.S.C. 254d through 254k), section 338C of that Act (42 U.S.C. 254m), other than subsection (b)(5) of that section, and section 338D of that Act (42 U.S.C. 254n) applicable to scholarship assistance provided under section 338A of that Act (42 U.S.C. 254l) shall not apply to the scholarship assistance provided under subsection (a) of this section.

(2) The Native Hawaiian Health Scholarship program shall not be administered by or through the Indian Health Service.

(c) Authorization of appropriations. There are authorized to be appropriated such sums as may be necessary for fiscal years 1993 through 2019 for the purpose of funding the scholarship assistance provided under subsection (a) of this section.

(Oct. 31, 1988, P. L. 100-579, § 10, as added Act Oct. 6, 1992, P. L. 102-396, Title IX, § 9168, 106 Stat. 1948; Oct. 14, 1998, P. L. 105-256, § 12, 112 Stat. 1899; Jan. 10, 2002, P. L. 107-116, Title V, § 514(a), 115 Stat. 2219; March 23, 2010, P. L. 111-148, Title X, Subtitle B, Part III, § 10221(a), 124 Stat. 935.)

§ 11711. Definitions

For purposes of this Act:

(1) Disease prevention. The term "disease prevention" includes—

(A) immunizations,

(B) control of high blood pressure,

(C) control of sexually transmittable diseases,

(D) prevention and control of diabetes,

(E) control of toxic agents,

(F) occupational safety and health,

(G) accident prevention,

(H) fluoridation of water,

(I) control of infectious agents, and

(J) provision of mental health care.

(2) Health promotion. The term "health promotion" includes—

(A) pregnancy and infant care, including prevention of fetal alcohol syndrome,

(B) cessation of tobacco smoking,

(C) reduction in the misuse of alcohol and drugs,

(D) improvement of nutrition,

(E) improvement in physical fitness,

(F) family planning,

(G) control of stress, and

(H) educational programs with the mission of improving the health, capability, and well-being of Native Hawaiians.

(3) Native Hawaiian. The term "Native Hawaiian" means any individual who is—

(A) a citizen of the United States, and

(B) a descendant of the aboriginal people, who prior to 1778, occupied and exercised sovereignty in the area that now constitutes the State of Hawaii, as evidenced by—

(i) genealogical records,

(ii) Kupuna (elders) or Kama'aina (long-term community residents) verification, or

(iii) birth records of the State of Hawaii.

(4) Native Hawaiian health center. The term "Native Hawaiian health center" means an entity—

(A) which is organized under the laws of the State of Hawaii,

(B) which provides or arranges for health care services through practitioners licensed by the State of Hawaii, where licensure requirements are applicable,

(C) which is a public or nonprofit private entity, and

(D) in which Native Hawaiian health practitioners significantly participate in the planning, management, monitoring, and evaluation of health services.

(5) Native Hawaiian organization. The term "Native Hawaiian organization" means any organization—

(A) which serves the interests of Native Hawaiians,

(B) which is—

(i) recognized by Papa Ola Lokahi for the purpose of planning, conducting, or administering programs (or portions of programs) authorized under this Act for the benefit of Native Hawaiians, and

(ii) certified by Papa Ola Lokahi as having the qualifications and capacity to provide the services, and meet the requirements, under the contract the organization enters into with, or grant the organization receives from, the Secretary under this Act,

(C) in which Native Hawaiian health practitioners significantly participate in the planning, management, monitoring, and evaluation of health services, and

(D) which is a public or nonprofit private entity.

(6) Native Hawaiian health care system. The term "Native Hawaiian health care system" means an entity—

(A) which is organized under the laws of the State of Hawaii,

(B) which provides or arranges for health care services through practitioners licensed by the State of Hawaii, where licensure requirements are applicable,

(C) which is a public or nonprofit private entity,

(D) in which Native Hawaiian health practitioners significantly participate in the planning, management, monitoring, and evaluation of health care services,

(E) which may be composed of as many Native Hawaiian health centers as necessary to meet the health care needs of each island's Native Hawaiians, and

(F) which is—

(i) recognized by Papa Ola Lokahi for the purpose of planning, conducting, or administering programs, or portions of programs, authorized by this Act for the benefit of Native Hawaiians, and

(ii) certified by Papa Ola Lokahi as having the qualifications and the capacity to provide the services and meet the requirements under the contract the Native Hawaiian health care system enters into with the Secretary or the grant the Native Hawaiian health care system receives from the Secretary pursuant to this Act.

(7) Papa Ola Lokahi. (A) The term "Papa Ola Lokahi" means an organization composed of—

(i) E Ola Mau;

(ii) the Office of Hawaiian Affairs of the State of Hawaii;

(iii) Alu Like Inc.;

(iv) the University of Hawaii;

(v) the Office of Hawaiian Health of the Hawaii State Department of Health;

(vi) Ho'ola Lahui Hawaii, or a health care system serving the islands of Kaua'i and Ni'ihau, and which may be composed of as many health care centers as are necessary to meet the health care needs of the Native Hawaiians of those islands;

(vii) Ke Ola Mamo, or a health care system serving the island of O'ahu, and which may be composed of as many health care centers as are necessary to meet the health care needs of the Native Hawaiians of that island;

(viii) Na Pu'uwai or a health care system serving the islands of Moloka'i and Lana'i, and which may be composed of as many health care centers as are necessary to meet the health care needs of the Native Hawaiians of those islands;

(ix) Hui No Ke Ola Pono, or a health care system serving the island of Maui, and which may be composed of as many health care centers as are necessary to meet the health care needs of the Native Hawaiians of that island;

(x) Hui Malama Ola Ha'Oiwi or a health care system serving the island of Hawaii, and which may be composed of as many health care centers as are necessary to meet the health care needs of the Native Hawaiians of that island; and

(xi) such other member organizations as the Board of Papa Ola Lokahi may admit from time to time, based upon satisfactory demonstration of a record of contribution to the health and well-being of Native Hawaiians, and upon satisfactory development of a mission statement in relation to this Act, including clearly defined goals and objectives, a 5-year action plan outlining the contributions that each organization will make in carrying out the policy of this Act, and an estimated budget.

(B) Such term does not include any such organization identified in subparagraph (A) if the Secretary determines that such organization has not developed a mission statement with clearly defined goals and objectives for the contributions the organization will make to the Native Hawaiian health care systems, and an action plan for carrying out those goals and objectives.

(8) Primary health services. The term "primary health services" means—

(A) services of physicians, physicians' assistants, nurse practitioners, and other health professionals;

(B) diagnostic laboratory and radiologic services;

(C) preventive health services (including children's eye and ear examinations to determine the need for vision and hearing correction, perinatal services, well child services, and family planning services);

(D) emergency medical services;

(E) transportation services as required for adequate patient care;

(F) preventive dental services; and

(G) pharmaceutical services, as may be appropriate for particular health centers.

(9) Secretary. The term "Secretary" means the Secretary of Health and Human Services.

(10) Traditional Native Hawaiian healer. The term "traditional Native Hawaiian healer" means a practitioner—

(A) who—

(i) is of Hawaiian ancestry, and

(ii) has the knowledge, skills, and experience in direct personal health care of individuals, and

(B) whose knowledge, skills, and experience are based on demonstrated learning of Native Hawaiian healing practices acquired by—

(i) direct practical association with Native Hawaiian elders, and

(ii) oral traditions transmitted from generation to generation.

(Oct. 31, 1988, P. L. 100-579, § 11, 102 Stat. 2923, and Nov. 18, 1988, P. L. 100-690, Title II, Subtitle D, § 2311, 102 Stat. 4230; Oct. 6, 1992, P. L. 102-396, Title IX, § 9168, 106 Stat. 1948; March 23, 2010, P. L. 111-148, Title X, Subtitle B, Part III, § 10221(a), 124 Stat. 935.)

CHAPTER 157. QUALITY AFFORDABLE HEALTH CARE FOR ALL AMERICANS

IMMEDIATE ACTIONS TO PRESERVE AND EXPAND COVERAGE

§ 18001. Immediate access to insurance for uninsured individuals with a preexisting condition

(a) In general. Not later than 90 days after the date of enactment of this Act [enacted March 23, 2010], the Secretary shall establish a temporary high risk health insurance pool program to provide health insurance coverage for eligible individuals during the period beginning on the date on which such program is established and ending on January 1, 2014.

(b) Administration. (1) In general. The Secretary may carry out the program under this section directly or through contracts to eligible entities.

(2) Eligible entities. To be eligible for a contract under paragraph (1), an entity shall—

(A) be a State or nonprofit private entity;

(B) submit to the Secretary an application at such time, in such manner, and containing such information as the Secretary may require; and

(C) agree to utilize contract funding to establish and administer a qualified high risk pool for eligible individuals.

(3) Maintenance of effort. To be eligible to enter into a contract with the Secretary under this subsection, a State shall agree not to reduce the annual amount the State expended for the operation of one or more State high risk pools during the year preceding the year in which such contract is entered into.

(c) Qualified high risk pool. (1) In general. Amounts made available under this section shall be used to establish a qualified high risk pool that meets the requirements of paragraph (2).

(2) Requirements. A qualified high risk pool meets the requirements of this paragraph if such pool—

(A) provides to all eligible individuals health insurance coverage that does not impose any preexisting condition exclusion with respect to such coverage;

(B) provides health insurance coverage—

(i) in which the issuer's share of the total allowed costs of benefits provided under such coverage is not less than 65 percent of such costs; and

(ii) that has an out of pocket limit not greater than the applicable amount described in section 223(c)(2) of the Internal Revenue Code of 1986 [26 USCS § 223(c)(2)] for the year involved, except that the Secretary may modify such limit if necessary to ensure the pool meets the actuarial value limit under clause (i);

(C) ensures that with respect to the premium rate charged for health insurance coverage offered to eligible individuals through the high risk pool, such rate shall—

(i) except as provided in clause (ii), vary only as provided for under section 2701 of the Public Health Service Act [42 USCS § 300gg] (as amended by this Act and notwithstanding the date on which such amendments take effect);

(ii) vary on the basis of age by a factor of not greater than 4 to 1; and

(iii) be established at a standard rate for a standard population; and

(D) meets any other requirements determined appropriate by the Secretary.

(d) Eligible individual. An individual shall be deemed to be an eligible individual for purposes of this section if such individual—

(1) is a citizen or national of the United States or is lawfully present in the United States (as determined in accordance with section 1411 [42 USCS § 18081]);

(2) has not been covered under creditable coverage (as defined in section 2701(c)(1) of the Public Health Service Act [42 USCS § 300gg(c)(1)] as in effect on the date of enactment of this Act [enacted March 23, 2010]) during the 6-month period prior to the date on which such individual is applying for coverage through the high risk pool; and

(3) has a pre-existing condition, as determined in a manner consistent with guidance issued by the Secretary.

(e) Protection against dumping risk by insurers. (1) In general. The Secretary shall establish criteria for determining whether health insurance issuers and employment-based health plans have discouraged an individual from remaining enrolled in prior coverage based on that individual's health status.

(2) Sanctions. An issuer or employment-based health plan shall be responsible for reimbursing the program under this section for the medical expenses incurred by the program for an individual who, based on criteria established by the Secretary, the Secretary finds was encouraged by the issuer to disenroll from health benefits coverage prior to enrolling in coverage through the program. The criteria shall include at least the following circumstances:

(A) In the case of prior coverage obtained through an employer, the provision by the employer, group health plan, or the issuer of money or other financial consideration for disenrolling from the coverage.

(B) In the case of prior coverage obtained directly from an issuer or under an employment-based health plan—

(i) the provision by the issuer or plan of money or other financial consideration for disenrolling from the coverage; or

(ii) in the case of an individual whose premium for the prior coverage exceeded the premium required by the program (adjusted based on the age factors applied to the prior coverage)—

(I) the prior coverage is a policy that is no longer being actively marketed (as defined by the Secretary) by the issuer; or

(II) the prior coverage is a policy for which duration of coverage form issue or health status are factors that can be considered in determining premiums at renewal.

(3) Construction. Nothing in this subsection shall be construed as constituting exclusive remedies for violations of criteria established under paragraph (1) or as preventing States from applying or enforcing such paragraph or other provisions under law with respect to health insurance issuers.

(f) Oversight. The Secretary shall establish—

(1) an appeals process to enable individuals to appeal a determination under this section; and

(2) procedures to protect against waste, fraud, and abuse.

(g) Funding; termination of authority. (1) In general. There is appropriated to the Secretary, out of any moneys in the Treasury not otherwise appropriated, $5,000,000,000 to pay claims against (and the administrative costs of) the high risk pool under this section that are in excess of the amount of premiums collected from eligible individuals enrolled in the high risk pool. Such funds shall be available without fiscal year limitation.

(2) Insufficient funds. If the Secretary estimates for any fiscal year that the aggregate amounts available for the payment of the expenses of the high risk pool will be less than the actual amount of such expenses, the Secretary shall make such adjustments as are necessary to eliminate such deficit.

(3) Termination of authority. (A) In general. Except as provided in subparagraph (B), coverage of eligible individuals under a high risk pool in a State shall terminate on January 1, 2014.

(B) Transition to exchange. The Secretary shall develop procedures to provide for the transition of eligible individuals enrolled in health insurance coverage offered through a high risk pool established under this section into qualified health plans offered through an Exchange. Such procedures shall ensure that there is no lapse in coverage with respect to the individual and may extend coverage after the termination of the risk pool involved, if the Secretary determines necessary to avoid such a lapse.

(4) Limitations. The Secretary has the authority to stop taking applications for participation in the program under this section to comply with the funding limitation provided for in paragraph (1).

(5) Relation to State laws. The standards established under this section shall supersede any State law or regulation (other than State licensing laws or State laws relating to plan solvency) with respect to qualified high risk pools which are established in accordance with this section.

(March 23, 2010, P. L. 111-148, Title I, Subtitle B, § 1101, 124 Stat. 141.)

HISTORY; ANCILLARY LAWS AND DIRECTIVES

Effective date of section:

This section took effect on enactment, as provided by § 1105 of Act March 23, 2010, P. L. 111-148, which appears as 42 USCS § 1320d note.

Short title:

Act March 23, 2010, P. L. 111-148, § 1(a), 124 Stat. 119, provides: "This Act may be cited as the 'Patient Protection and Affordable Care Act'.". For full classification of such Act, consult USCS Tables volumes.

§ 18002. Reinsurance for early retirees

(a) Administration. (1) In general. Not later than 90 days after the date of enactment of this Act [enacted March 23, 2010], the Secretary shall establish a temporary reinsurance program to provide reimbursement to participating employment-based plans for a portion of the cost of providing health insurance coverage to early retirees (and to the eligible spouses, surviving spouses, and dependents of such retirees) during the period beginning on the date on which such program is established and ending on January 1, 2014.

(2) Reference. In this section:

(A) Health benefits. The term "health benefits" means medical, surgical, hospital, prescription drug, and such other benefits as shall be determined by the Secretary, whether self-funded, or delivered through the purchase of insurance or otherwise.

(B) Employment-based plan. The term "employment-based plan" means a group benefits plan providing health benefits that—

(i) is—

(I) maintained by one or more current or former employers (including without limitation any State or local government or political subdivision thereof or any agency or instrumentality of any of the foregoing), employee organization, a voluntary employees' beneficiary association, or a committee or board of individuals appointed to administer such plan; or

(II) a multiemployer plan (as defined in section 3(37) of the Employee Retirement Income Security Act of 1974) [29 USCS § 1002(37)]; and

(ii) provides health benefits to early retirees.

(C) Early retirees. The term "early retirees" means individuals who are age 55 and older but are not eligible for coverage under title XVIII of the Social Security Act [42 USCS §§ 1395 et seq.], and who are not active employees of an employer maintaining, or currently contributing to, the employment-based plan or of any employer that has made substantial contributions to fund such plan.

(b) Participation. (1) Employment-based plan eligibility. A participating employment-based plan is an employment-based plan that—

(A) meets the requirements of paragraph (2) with respect to health benefits provided under the plan; and

(B) submits to the Secretary an application for participation in the program, at such time, in such manner, and containing such information as the Secretary shall require.

(2) Employment-based health benefits. An employment-based plan meets the requirements of this paragraph if the plan—

(A) implements programs and procedures to generate cost-savings with respect to participants with chronic and high-cost conditions;

(B) provides documentation of the actual cost of medical claims involved; and

(C) is certified by the Secretary.

(c) Payments. (1) Submission of claims. (A) In general. A participating employment-based plan shall submit claims for reimbursement to the Secretary which shall contain documentation of the actual costs of the items and services for which each claim is being submitted.

(B) Basis for claims. Claims submitted under subparagraph (A) shall be based on the actual amount expended by the participating employment-based plan involved within the plan year for the health benefits provided to an early retiree or the spouse, surviving spouse, or dependent of such retiree. In determining the amount of a claim for purposes of this subsection, the participating employment-based plan shall take into account any negotiated price concessions (such as discounts, direct or indirect subsidies, rebates, and direct or indirect remunerations) obtained by such plan with respect to such health benefit. For purposes of determining the amount of any such claim, the costs paid by the early retiree or the retiree's spouse, surviving spouse, or dependent in the form of deductibles, co-payments, or co-insurance shall be included in the amounts paid by the participating employment-based plan.

(2) Program payments. If the Secretary determines that a participating employment-based plan has submitted a valid claim under paragraph (1), the Secretary shall reimburse such plan for 80 percent of that portion of the costs attributable to such claim that exceed $15,000, subject to the limits contained in paragraph (3).

(3) Limit. To be eligible for reimbursement under the program, a claim submitted by a participating employment-based plan shall not be less than $15,000 nor greater than $90,000. Such amounts shall be adjusted each fiscal year based on the percentage increase in the Medical Care Component of the Consumer Price Index for all urban consumers (rounded to the nearest multiple of $1,000) for the year involved.

(4) Use of payments. Amounts paid to a participating employment-based plan under this subsection shall be used to lower costs for the plan. Such payments may be used to reduce premium costs for an entity described in subsection (a)(2)(B)(i) or to reduce premium contributions, co-payments, deductibles, co-insurance, or other out-of-pocket costs for plan participants. Such payments shall not be used

as general revenues for an entity described in subsection (a)(2)(B)(i). The Secretary shall develop a mechanism to monitor the appropriate use of such payments by such entities.

(5) Payments not treated as income. Payments received under this subsection shall not be included in determining the gross income of an entity described in subsection (a)(2)(B)(i) that is maintaining or currently contributing to a participating employment-based plan.

(6) Appeals. The Secretary shall establish—

(A) an appeals process to permit participating employment-based plans to appeal a determination of the Secretary with respect to claims submitted under this section; and

(B) procedures to protect against fraud, waste, and abuse under the program.

(d) Audits. The Secretary shall conduct annual audits of claims data submitted by participating employment-based plans under this section to ensure that such plans are in compliance with the requirements of this section.

(e) Funding. There is appropriated to the Secretary, out of any moneys in the Treasury not otherwise appropriated, $5,000,000,000 to carry out the program under this section. Such funds shall be available without fiscal year limitation.

(f) Limitation. The Secretary has the authority to stop taking applications for participation in the program based on the availability of funding under subsection (e).

(March 23, 2010, P. L. 111-148, Title I, Subtitle B, § 1102, Title X, § 10102(a), 124 Stat. 143, 892.)

§ 18003. Immediate information that allows consumers to identify affordable coverage options

(a) Internet portal to affordable coverage options. (1) Immediate establishment. Not later than July 1, 2010, the Secretary, in consultation with the States, shall establish a mechanism, including an Internet website, through which a resident of any, or small business in, State may identify affordable health insurance coverage options in that State.

(2) Connecting to affordable coverage. An Internet website established under paragraph (1) shall, to the extent practicable, provide ways for residents of, and small businesses in, any State to receive information on at least the following coverage options:

(A) Health insurance coverage offered by health insurance issuers, other than coverage that provides reimbursement only for the treatment or mitigation of—

(i) a single disease or condition; or

(ii) an unreasonably limited set of diseases or conditions (as determined by the Secretary).

(B) Medicaid coverage under title XIX of the Social Security Act [42 USCS §§ 1396 et seq.].

(C) Coverage under title XXI of the Social Security Act [42 USCS §§ 1397aa et seq.].

(D) A State health benefits high risk pool, to the extent that such high risk pool is offered in such State; and

(E) Coverage under a high risk pool under section 1101 [42 USCS § 18001].

(F) Coverage within the small group market for small businesses and their employees, including reinsurance for early retirees under section 1102 [42 USCS § 18002], tax credits available under section 45R of the Internal Revenue Code of 1986 [26 USCS § 45R] (as added by section 1421), and other information specifically for small businesses regarding affordable health care options.

(b) Enhancing comparative purchasing options. (1) In general. Not later than 60 days after the date of enactment of this Act [enacted March 23, 2010], the Secretary shall develop a standardized format to be used for the presentation of information relating to the coverage options described in subsection (a)(2). Such format shall, at a minimum, require the inclusion of information on the percentage of total premium revenue expended on nonclinical costs (as reported under section 2718(a) of the Public Health Service Act [42 USCS § 300gg-18(a)]), eligibility, availability, premium rates, and cost sharing with respect to such coverage options and be consistent with the standards adopted for the uniform explanation of coverage as provided for in section 2715 of the Public Health Service Act [42 USCS § 300gg-15].

(2) Use of format. The Secretary shall utilize the format developed under paragraph (1) in compiling information concerning coverage options on the Internet website established under subsection (a).

(c) Authority To contract. The Secretary may carry out this section through contracts entered into with qualified entities.

(March 23, 2010, P. L. 111-148, Title I, Subtitle B, § 1103, Title X, Subtitle A, § 10102(b), 124 Stat. 146, 892.)

OTHER PROVISIONS

§ 18011. Preservation of right to maintain existing coverage

(a) No changes to existing coverage. (1) In general. Nothing in this Act (or an amendment made by this Act) shall be construed to require that an individual terminate coverage under a group health plan or health insurance coverage in which such individual was enrolled on the date of enactment of this Act.

(2) Continuation of coverage. Except as provided in paragraph (3), with respect to a group health plan or health insurance coverage in which an individual was enrolled on the date of enactment of this Act [enacted March 23, 2010], this subtitle and subtitle A (and the amendments made by such subtitles) shall not apply to such plan or coverage, regardless of whether the individual renews such coverage after such date of enactment.

(3) Application of certain provisions. The provisions of sections 2715 and 2718 of the Public Health Service Act [42 USCS §§ 300gg-15 and 300gg-18] (as added by subtitle A) shall apply to grandfathered health plans for plan years beginning on or after the date of enactment of this Act [enacted March 23, 2010].

(4) Application of certain provisions. (A) In general. The following provisions of the Public Health Service Act (as added by this title) shall apply to grandfathered health plans for plan years beginning with the first plan year to which such provisions would otherwise apply:

(i) Section 2708 [42 USCS § 300gg-7] (relating to excessive waiting periods).

(ii) Those provisions of section 2711 [42 USCS § 300gg-11] relating to lifetime limits.

(iii) Section 2712 [42 USCS § 300gg-12] (relating to rescissions).

(iv) Section 2714 [42 USCS § 300gg-14] (relating to extension of dependent coverage).

(B) Provisions applicable only to group health plans. (i) Provisions described. Those provisions of section 2711 [42 USCS § 300gg-11] relating to annual limits and the provisions of section 2704 [42 USCS § 300gg-3] (relating to pre-existing condition exclusions) of the Public Health Service Act (as added by this subtitle) shall apply to grandfathered health plans that are group health plans for plan years beginning with the first plan year to which such provisions otherwise apply.

(ii) Adult child coverage. For plan years beginning before January 1, 2014, the provisions of section 2714 of the Public Health Service Act [42 USCS § 300gg-14] (as added by this subtitle) shall apply in the case of an adult child with respect to a grandfathered health plan that is a group health plan only if such adult child is not eligible to enroll in an eligible employer-sponsored health plan (as defined in section 5000A(f)(2) of the Internal Revenue Code of 1986 [26 USCS § 5000A(f)(2)]) other than such grandfathered health plan.

(b) Allowance for family members to join current coverage. With respect to a group health plan or health insurance coverage in which an individual was enrolled on the date of enactment of this Act [enacted March 23, 2010] and which is renewed after such date, family members of such individual shall be permitted to enroll in such plan or coverage if such enrollment is permitted under the terms of the plan in effect as of such date of enactment.

(c) Allowance for new employees to join current plan. A group health plan that provides coverage on the date of enactment of this Act [enacted March 23, 2010] may provide for the enrolling of new employees (and their families) in such plan, and this subtitle and subtitle A (and the amendments made by such subtitles) shall not apply with respect to such plan and such new employees (and their families).

(d) Effect on collective bargaining agreements. In the case of health insurance coverage maintained pursuant to one or more collective bargaining agreements between employee representatives and one or more employers that was ratified before the date of enactment of this Act [enacted March 23, 2010], the provisions of this subtitle and subtitle A (and the amendments made by such subtitles) shall not apply until the date on which the last of the collective bargaining agreements relating to the coverage terminates. Any coverage amendment made pursuant to a collective bargaining agreement relating to the coverage which amends the coverage solely to conform to any requirement added by this subtitle or subtitle A (or amendments) shall not be treated as a termination of such collective bargaining agreement.

(e) Definition. In this title, the term "grandfathered health plan" means any group health plan or health insurance coverage to which this section applies.

(March 23, 2010, P. L. 111-148, Title I, Subtitle C, Part II, § 1251, Title X, Subtitle A, § 10103(d), 124 Stat. 161, 895; March 30, 2010, P. L. 111-152, Title II, Subtitle B, § 2301(a), 124 Stat. 1081.)

§ 18012. Rating reforms must apply uniformly to all health insurance issuers and group health plans [Caution: This section is effective for plan years beginning on or after January 1, 2014, as provided by § 1255 of Act March 23, 2010, P. L. 111-148, which appears as 42 USCS § 300gg note.]

Any standard or requirement adopted by a

State pursuant to this title, or any amendment made by this title, shall be applied uniformly to all health plans in each insurance market to which the standard and requirements apply. The preceding sentence shall also apply to a State standard or requirement relating to the standard or requirement required by this title (or any such amendment) that is not the same as the standard or requirement but that is not preempted under section 1321(d) [42 USCS § 18041(d)].

(March 23, 2010, P. L. 111-148, Title I, Subtitle C, Part II, § 1252, 124 Stat. 162.)

§ 18013. Annual report on self-insured plans

Not later than 1 year after the date of enactment of this Act [enacted March 23, 2010], and annually thereafter, the Secretary of Labor shall prepare an aggregate annual report, using data collected from the Annual Return/Report of Employee Benefit Plan (Department of Labor Form 5500), that shall include general information on self-insured group health plans (including plan type, number of participants, benefits offered, funding arrangements, and benefit arrangements) as well as data from the financial filings of self-insured employers (including information on assets, liabilities, contributions, investments, and expenses). The Secretary shall submit such reports to the appropriate committees of Congress.

(March 23, 2010, P. L. 111-148, Title I, Subtitle C, Part II, § 1253, as added Title X, Subtitle A, § 10103(f)(2), 124 Stat. 895.)

AVAILABLE COVERAGE CHOICES FOR ALL AMERICANS

ESTABLISHMENT OF QUALIFIED HEALTH PLANS

§ 18021. Qualified health plan defined

(a) Qualified health plan. In this title:

(1) In general. The term "qualified health plan" means a health plan that—

(A) has in effect a certification (which may include a seal or other indication of approval) that such plan meets the criteria for certification described in section 1311(c) [42 USCS § 18031(c)] issued or recognized by each Exchange through which such plan is offered;

(B) provides the essential health benefits package described in section 1302(a) [42 USCS § 18022(a)]; and

(C) is offered by a health insurance issuer that—

(i) is licensed and in good standing to offer health insurance coverage in each State in which such issuer offers health insurance coverage under this title;

(ii) agrees to offer at least one qualified health plan in the silver level and at least one plan in the gold level in each such Exchange;

(iii) agrees to charge the same premium rate for each qualified health plan of the issuer without regard to whether the plan is offered through an Exchange or whether the plan is offered directly from the issuer or through an agent; and

(iv) complies with the regulations developed by the Secretary under section 1311(d) [42 USCS § 18031(d)] and such other requirements as an applicable Exchange may establish.

(2) Inclusion of CO-OP plans and multi-State qualified health plans. Any reference in this title to a qualified health plan shall be deemed to include a qualified health plan offered through the CO-OP program under section 1322 [42 USCS § 18042], and a multi-State plan under section 1334 [42 USCS § 18054], unless specifically provided for otherwise.

(3) Treatment of qualified direct primary care medical home plans. The Secretary of Health and Human Services shall permit a qualified health plan to provide coverage through a qualified direct primary care medical home plan that meets criteria established by the Secretary, so long as the qualified health plan meets all requirements that are otherwise applicable and the services covered by the medical home plan are coordinated with the entity offering the qualified health plan.

(4) Variation based on rating area. A qualified health plan, including a multi-State qualified health plan, may as appropriate vary premiums by rating area (as defined in section 2701(a)(2) of the Public Health Service Act [42 USCS § 300gg(a)(2)]).

(b) Terms relating to health plans. In this title:

(1) Health plan. (A) In general. The term "health plan" means health insurance coverage and a group health plan.

(B) Exception for self-insured plans and MEWAs. Except to the extent specifically provided by this title, the term "health plan" shall not include a group health plan or multiple employer welfare arrangement to the extent the plan or arrangement is not subject to State insurance regulation under section 514 of the Employee Retirement Income Security Act of 1974 [29 USCS § 1144].

(2) Health insurance coverage and issuer.

The terms "health insurance coverage" and "health insurance issuer" have the meanings given such terms by section 2791(b) of the Public Health Service Act [42 USCS § 300gg-91(b)].

(3) Group health plan. The term "group health plan" has the meaning given such term by section 2791(a) of the Public Health Service Act [42 USCS § 300gg-91(a)].

(March 23, 2010, P. L. 111-148, Title I, Subtitle D, Part I, § 1301, Title X, Subtitle A, § 10104(a), 124 Stat. 162, 896.)

§ 18022. Essential health benefits requirements

(a) Essential health benefits package. In this title, the term "essential health benefits package" means, with respect to any health plan, coverage that—

(1) provides for the essential health benefits defined by the Secretary under subsection (b);

(2) limits cost-sharing for such coverage in accordance with subsection (c); and

(3) subject to subsection (e), provides either the bronze, silver, gold, or platinum level of coverage described in subsection (d).

(b) Essential health benefits. (1) In general. Subject to paragraph (2), the Secretary shall define the essential health benefits, except that such benefits shall include at least the following general categories and the items and services covered within the categories:

(A) Ambulatory patient services.

(B) Emergency services.

(C) Hospitalization.

(D) Maternity and newborn care.

(E) Mental health and substance use disorder services, including behavioral health treatment.

(F) Prescription drugs.

(G) Rehabilitative and habilitative services and devices.

(H) Laboratory services.

(I) Preventive and wellness services and chronic disease management.

(J) Pediatric services, including oral and vision care.

(2) Limitation. (A) In general. The Secretary shall ensure that the scope of the essential health benefits under paragraph (1) is equal to the scope of benefits provided under a typical employer plan, as determined by the Secretary. To inform this determination, the Secretary of Labor shall conduct a survey of employer-sponsored coverage to determine the benefits typically covered by employers, including multiemployer plans, and provide a report on such survey to the Secretary.

(B) Certification. In defining the essential health benefits described in paragraph (1), and in revising the benefits under paragraph (4)(H), the Secretary shall submit a report to the appropriate committees of Congress containing a certification from the Chief Actuary of the Centers for Medicare & Medicaid Services that such essential health benefits meet the limitation described in paragraph (2).

(3) Notice and hearing. In defining the essential health benefits described in paragraph (1), and in revising the benefits under paragraph (4)(H), the Secretary shall provide notice and an opportunity for public comment.

(4) Required elements for consideration. In defining the essential health benefits under paragraph (1), the Secretary shall—

(A) ensure that such essential health benefits reflect an appropriate balance among the categories described in such subsection, so that benefits are not unduly weighted toward any category;

(B) not make coverage decisions, determine reimbursement rates, establish incentive programs, or design benefits in ways that discriminate against individuals because of their age, disability, or expected length of life;

(C) take into account the health care needs of diverse segments of the population, including women, children, persons with disabilities, and other groups;

(D) ensure that health benefits established as essential not be subject to denial to individuals against their wishes on the basis of the individuals' age or expected length of life or of the individuals' present or predicted disability, degree of medical dependency, or quality of life;

(E) provide that a qualified health plan shall not be treated as providing coverage for the essential health benefits described in paragraph (1) unless the plan provides that—

(i) coverage for emergency department services will be provided without imposing any requirement under the plan for prior authorization of services or any limitation on coverage where the provider of services does not have a contractual relationship with the plan for the providing of services that is more restrictive than the requirements or limitations that apply to emergency department services received from providers who do have such a contractual relationship with the plan; and

(ii) if such services are provided out-of-network, the cost-sharing requirement (expressed as a copayment amount or coinsurance rate) is the same requirement that would apply if such services were provided in-network;

(F) provide that if a plan described in section

1311(b)(2)(B)(ii) [42 USCS § 18031(b)(2)(B)(ii)] (relating to stand-alone dental benefits plans) is offered through an Exchange, another health plan offered through such Exchange shall not fail to be treated as a qualified health plan solely because the plan does not offer coverage of benefits offered through the stand-alone plan that are otherwise required under paragraph (1)(J); and

(G) periodically review the essential health benefits under paragraph (1), and provide a report to Congress and the public that contains—

(i) an assessment of whether enrollees are facing any difficulty accessing needed services for reasons of coverage or cost;

(ii) an assessment of whether the essential health benefits needs to be modified or updated to account for changes in medical evidence or scientific advancement;

(iii) information on how the essential health benefits will be modified to address any such gaps in access or changes in the evidence base;

(iv) an assessment of the potential of additional or expanded benefits to increase costs and the interactions between the addition or expansion of benefits and reductions in existing benefits to meet actuarial limitations described in paragraph (2); and

(H) periodically update the essential health benefits under paragraph (1) to address any gaps in access to coverage or changes in the evidence base the Secretary identifies in the review conducted under subparagraph (G).

(5) Rule of construction. Nothing in this title shall be construed to prohibit a health plan from providing benefits in excess of the essential health benefits described in this subsection.

(c) Requirements relating to cost-sharing. (1) Annual limitation on cost-sharing. (A) 2014. The cost-sharing incurred under a health plan with respect to self-only coverage or coverage other than self-only coverage for a plan year beginning in 2014 shall not exceed the dollar amounts in effect under section 223(c)(2)(A)(ii) of the Internal Revenue Code of 1986 [26 USCS § 223(c)(2)(A)(ii)] for self-only and family coverage, respectively, for taxable years beginning in 2014.

(B) 2015 and later. In the case of any plan year beginning in a calendar year after 2014, the limitation under this paragraph shall—

(i) in the case of self-only coverage, be equal to the dollar amount under subparagraph (A) for self-only coverage for plan years beginning in 2014, increased by an amount equal to the product of that amount and the premium adjustment percentage under paragraph (4) for the calendar year; and

(ii) in the case of other coverage, twice the amount in effect under clause (i).

If the amount of any increase under clause (i) is not a multiple of $50, such increase shall be rounded to the next lowest multiple of $50.

(2) Annual limitation on deductibles for employer-sponsored plans. (A) In general. In the case of a health plan offered in the small group market, the deductible under the plan shall not exceed—

(i) $2,000 in the case of a plan covering a single individual; and

(ii) $4,000 in the case of any other plan.

The amounts under clauses (i) and (ii) may be increased by the maximum amount of reimbursement which is reasonably available to a participant under a flexible spending arrangement described in section 106(c)(2) of the Internal Revenue Code of 1986 (determined without regard to any salary reduction arrangement).

(B) Indexing of limits. In the case of any plan year beginning in a calendar year after 2014—

(i) the dollar amount under subparagraph (A)(i) shall be increased by an amount equal to the product of that amount and the premium adjustment percentage under paragraph (4) for the calendar year; and

(ii) the dollar amount under subparagraph (A)(ii) shall be increased to an amount equal to twice the amount in effect under subparagraph (A)(i) for plan years beginning in the calendar year, determined after application of clause (i).

If the amount of any increase under clause (i) is not a multiple of $50, such increase shall be rounded to the next lowest multiple of $50.

(C) Actuarial value. The limitation under this paragraph shall be applied in such a manner so as to not affect the actuarial value of any health plan, including a plan in the bronze level.

(D) Coordination with preventive limits. Nothing in this paragraph shall be construed to allow a plan to have a deductible under the plan apply to benefits described in section 2713 of the Public Health Service Act [42 USCS § 300gg-13].

(3) Cost-sharing. In this title—

(A) In general. The term "cost-sharing" includes—

(i) deductibles, coinsurance, copayments, or similar charges; and

(ii) any other expenditure required of an insured individual which is a qualified medical expense (within the meaning of section 223(d)(2) of the Internal Revenue Code of 1986 [42 USCS § 223(d)(2)]) with respect to essential health benefits covered under the plan.

(B) Exceptions. Such term does not include premiums, balance billing amounts for non-network providers, or spending for non-covered services.

(4) Premium adjustment percentage. For purposes of paragraphs (1)(B)(i) and (2)(B)(i), the premium adjustment percentage for any calendar year is the percentage (if any) by which the average per capita premium for health insurance coverage in the United States for the preceding calendar year (as estimated by the Secretary no later than October 1 of such preceding calendar year) exceeds such average per capita premium for 2013 (as determined by the Secretary).

(d) Levels of coverage. (1) Levels of coverage defined. The levels of coverage described in this subsection are as follows:

(A) Bronze level. A plan in the bronze level shall provide a level of coverage that is designed to provide benefits that are actuarially equivalent to 60 percent of the full actuarial value of the benefits provided under the plan.

(B) Silver level. A plan in the silver level shall provide a level of coverage that is designed to provide benefits that are actuarially equivalent to 70 percent of the full actuarial value of the benefits provided under the plan.

(C) Gold level. A plan in the gold level shall provide a level of coverage that is designed to provide benefits that are actuarially equivalent to 80 percent of the full actuarial value of the benefits provided under the plan.

(D) Platinum level. A plan in the platinum level shall provide a level of coverage that is designed to provide benefits that are actuarially equivalent to 90 percent of the full actuarial value of the benefits provided under the plan.

(2) Actuarial value. (A) In general. Under regulations issued by the Secretary, the level of coverage of a plan shall be determined on the basis that the essential health benefits described in subsection (b) shall be provided to a standard population (and without regard to the population the plan may actually provide benefits to).

(B) Employer contributions. The Secretary shall issue regulations under which employer contributions to a health savings account (within the meaning of section 223 of the Internal Revenue Code of 1986 [26 USCS § 223]) may be taken into account in determining the level of coverage for a plan of the employer.

(C) Application. In determining under this title, the Public Health Service Act [42 USCS §§ 201 et seq.], or the Internal Revenue Code of 1986 [26 USCS §§ 1 et seq.] the percentage of the total allowed costs of benefits provided under a group health plan or health insurance coverage that are provided by such plan or coverage, the rules contained in the regulations under this paragraph shall apply.

(3) Allowable variance. The Secretary shall develop guidelines to provide for a de minimis variation in the actuarial valuations used in determining the level of coverage of a plan to account for differences in actuarial estimates.

(4) Plan reference. In this title, any reference to a bronze, silver, gold, or platinum plan shall be treated as a reference to a qualified health plan providing a bronze, silver, gold, or platinum level of coverage, as the case may be.

(e) Catastrophic plan. (1) In general. A health plan not providing a bronze, silver, gold, or platinum level of coverage shall be treated as meeting the requirements of subsection (d) with respect to any plan year if—

(A) the only individuals who are eligible to enroll in the plan are individuals described in paragraph (2); and

(B) the plan provides—

(i) except as provided in clause (ii), the essential health benefits determined under subsection (b), except that the plan provides no benefits for any plan year until the individual has incurred cost-sharing expenses in an amount equal to the annual limitation in effect under subsection (c)(1) for the plan year (except as provided for in section 2713 [42 USCS § 300gg-13]); and

(ii) coverage for at least three primary care visits.

(2) Individuals eligible for enrollment. An individual is described in this paragraph for any plan year if the individual—

(A) has not attained the age of 30 before the beginning of the plan year; or

(B) has a certification in effect for any plan year under this title that the individual is exempt from the requirement under section 5000A of the Internal Revenue Code of 1986 [26 USCS § 5000A] by reason of—

(i) section 5000A(e)(1) of such Code [26 USCS § 5000A(e)(1)] (relating to individuals without affordable coverage); or

(ii) section 5000A(e)(5) of such Code [26 USCS § 5000A(e)(5)] (relating to individuals with hardships).

(3) Restriction to individual market. If a health insurance issuer offers a health plan described in this subsection, the issuer may only offer the plan in the individual market.

(f) Child-only plans. If a qualified health plan is offered through the Exchange in any level of coverage specified under subsection (d), the issuer shall also offer that plan through the Exchange in that level as a plan in which the only enrollees are individuals who, as of the beginning of a plan year, have not attained the age of 21, and such plan shall be treated as a qualified health plan.

(g) Payments to Federally-qualified health centers. If any item or service covered by a qualified health plan is provided by a Federally-qualified health center (as defined in section 1905(l)(2)(B) of the Social Security Act (42 U.S.C. 1396d(l)(2)(B)) to an enrollee of the plan, the offeror of the plan shall pay to the center for the item or service an amount that is not less than the amount of payment that would have been paid to the center under section 1902(bb) of such Act (42 U.S.C. 1396a(bb)) for such item or service.

(March 23, 2010, P. L. 111-148, Title I, Subtitle D, Part I, § 1302, Title X, Subtitle A, § 10104(b), 124 Stat. 163, 896.)

§ 18023. Special rules

(a) State opt-out of abortion coverage. (1) In general. A State may elect to prohibit abortion coverage in qualified health plans offered through an Exchange in such State if such State enacts a law to provide for such prohibition.

(2) Termination of opt out. A State may repeal a law described in paragraph (1) and provide for the offering of such services through the Exchange.

(b) Special rules relating to coverage of abortion services. (1) Voluntary choice of coverage of abortion services. (A) In general. Notwithstanding any other provision of this title (or any amendment made by this title)—

(i) nothing in this title (or any amendment made by this title), shall be construed to require a qualified health plan to provide coverage of services described in subparagraph (B)(i) or (B)(ii) as part of its essential health benefits for any plan year; and

(ii) subject to subsection (a), the issuer of a qualified health plan shall determine whether or not the plan provides coverage of services described in subparagraph (B)(i) or (B)(ii) as part of such benefits for the plan year.

(B) Abortion services. (i) Abortions for which public funding is prohibited. The services described in this clause are abortions for which the expenditure of Federal funds appropriated for the Department of Health and Human Services is not permitted, based on the law as in effect as of the date that is 6 months before the beginning of the plan year involved.

(ii) Abortions for which public funding is allowed. The services described in this clause are abortions for which the expenditure of Federal funds appropriated for the Department of Health and Human Services is permitted, based on the law as in effect as of the date that is 6 months before the beginning of the plan year involved.

(2) Prohibition on the use of Federal funds. (A) In general. If a qualified health plan provides coverage of services described in paragraph (1)(B)(i), the issuer of the plan shall not use any amount attributable to any of the following for purposes of paying for such services:

(i) The credit under section 36B of the Internal Revenue Code of 1986 [26 USCS § 36B] (and the amount (if any) of the advance payment of the credit under section 1412 of the Patient Protection and Affordable Care Act [42 USCS § 18082]).

(ii) Any cost-sharing reduction under section 1402 of the Patient Protection and Affordable Care Act [42 USCS § 18071] (and the amount (if any) of the advance payment of the reduction under section 1412 of the Patient Protection and Affordable Care Act [42 USCS § 18082]).

(B) Establishment of allocation accounts. In the case of a plan to which subparagraph (A) applies, the issuer of the plan shall—

(i) collect from each enrollee in the plan (without regard to the enrollee's age, sex, or family status) a separate payment for each of the following:

(I) an amount equal to the portion of the premium to be paid directly by the enrollee for coverage under the plan of services other than services described in paragraph (1)(B)(i) (after reduction for credits and cost-sharing reductions described in subparagraph (A)); and

(II) an amount equal to the actuarial value of the coverage of services described in paragraph (1)(B)(i), and

(ii) shall deposit all such separate payments into separate allocation accounts as provided in subparagraph (C).

In the case of an enrollee whose premium for coverage under the plan is paid through employee payroll deposit, the separate payments required under this subparagraph shall each be paid by a separate deposit.

(C) Segregation of funds. (i) In general. The issuer of a plan to which subparagraph (A) applies shall establish allocation accounts described in clause (ii) for enrollees receiving amounts described in subparagraph (A).

(ii) Allocation accounts. The issuer of a plan to which subparagraph (A) applies shall deposit—

(I) all payments described in subparagraph (B)(i)(I) into a separate account that consists solely of such payments and that is used exclusively to pay for services other than services described in paragraph (1)(B)(i); and

(II) all payments described in subparagraph (B)(i)(II) into a separate account that consists solely of such payments and that is used exclusively to pay for services described in paragraph (1)(B)(i).

(D) Actuarial value. (i) In general. The issuer of a qualified health plan shall estimate the basic per enrollee, per month cost, determined on an average actuarial basis, for including coverage under the qualified health plan of the services described in paragraph (1)(B)(i).

(ii) Considerations. In making such estimate, the issuer—

(I) may take into account the impact on overall costs of the inclusion of such coverage, but may not take into account any cost reduction estimated to result from such services, including prenatal care, delivery, or postnatal care;

(II) shall estimate such costs as if such coverage were included for the entire population covered; and

(III) may not estimate such a cost at less than $1 per enrollee, per month.

(E) Ensuring compliance with segregation requirements. (i) In general. Subject to clause (ii), State health insurance commissioners shall ensure that health plans comply with the segregation requirements in this subsection through the segregation of plan funds in accordance with applicable provisions of generally accepted accounting requirements, circulars on funds management of the Office of Management and Budget, and guidance on accounting of the Government Accountability Office.

(ii) Clarification. Nothing in clause (i) shall prohibit the right of an individual or health plan to appeal such action in courts of competent jurisdiction.

(3) Rules relating to notice. (A) Notice. A qualified health plan that provides for coverage of the services described in paragraph (1)(B)(i) shall provide a notice to enrollees, only as part of the summary of benefits and coverage explanation, at the time of enrollment, of such coverage.

(B) Rules relating to payments. The notice described in subparagraph (A), any advertising used by the issuer with respect to the plan, any information provided by the Exchange, and any other information specified by the Secretary shall provide information only with respect to the total amount of the combined payments for services described in paragraph (1)(B)(i) and other services covered by the plan.

(4) No discrimination on basis of provision of abortion. No qualified health plan offered through an Exchange may discriminate against any individual health care provider or health care facility because of its unwillingness to provide, pay for, provide coverage of, or refer for abortions

(c) Application of State and Federal laws regarding abortion. (1) No preemption of State laws regarding abortion. Nothing in this Act shall be construed to preempt or otherwise have any effect on State laws regarding the prohibition of (or requirement of) coverage, funding, or procedural requirements on abortions, including parental notification or consent for the performance of an abortion on a minor.

(2) No effect on Federal laws regarding abortion. (A) In general. Nothing in this Act shall be construed to have any effect on Federal laws regarding—

(i) conscience protection;

(ii) willingness or refusal to provide abortion; and

(iii) discrimination on the basis of the willingness or refusal to provide, pay for, cover, or refer for abortion or to provide or participate in training to provide abortion.

(3) No effect on Federal civil rights law. Nothing in this subsection shall alter the rights and obligations of employees and employers under title VII of the Civil Rights Act of 1964 [42 USCS §§ 2000e et seq.].

(d) Application of emergency services laws. Nothing in this Act shall be construed to relieve any health care provider from providing emergency services as required by State or Federal law, including section 1867 of the Social Security Act [42 USCS § 1395dd] (popularly known as 'EMTALA').

(March 23, 2010, P. L. 111-148, Title I, Subtitle D, Part I, § 1303, Title X, Subtitle A, § 10104(c), 124 Stat. 168, 896.)

§ 18024. Related definitions

(a) Definitions relating to markets. In this title:

(1) Group market. The term "group market" means the health insurance market under which individuals obtain health insurance coverage (directly or through any arrangement) on behalf of themselves (and their dependents) through a group health plan maintained by an employer.

(2) Individual market. The term "individual market" means the market for health insur-

ance coverage offered to individuals other than in connection with a group health plan.

(3) Large and small group markets. The terms "large group market" and "small group market" mean the health insurance market under which individuals obtain health insurance coverage (directly or through any arrangement) on behalf of themselves (and their dependents) through a group health plan maintained by a large employer (as defined in subsection (b)(1)) or by a small employer (as defined in subsection (b)(2)), respectively.

(b) Employers. In this title:

(1) Large employer. The term "large employer" means, in connection with a group health plan with respect to a calendar year and a plan year, an employer who employed an average of at least 101 employees on business days during the preceding calendar year and who employs at least 1 employee on the first day of the plan year.

(2) Small employer. The term "small employer" means, in connection with a group health plan with respect to a calendar year and a plan year, an employer who employed an average of at least 1 but not more than 100 employees on business days during the preceding calendar year and who employs at least 1 employee on the first day of the plan year.

(3) State option to treat 50 employees as small. In the case of plan years beginning before January 1, 2016, a State may elect to apply this subsection by substituting "51 employees" for "101 employees" in paragraph (1) and by substituting "50 employees" for "100 employees" in paragraph (2).

(4) Rules for determining employer size. For purposes of this subsection—

(A) Application of aggregation rule for employers. All persons treated as a single employer under subsection (b), (c), (m), or (o) of section 414 of the Internal Revenue Code of 1986 [26 USCS § 414] shall be treated as 1 employer.

(B) Employers not in existence in preceding year. In the case of an employer which was not in existence throughout the preceding calendar year, the determination of whether such employer is a small or large employer shall be based on the average number of employees that it is reasonably expected such employer will employ on business days in the current calendar year.

(C) Predecessors. Any reference in this subsection to an employer shall include a reference to any predecessor of such employer.

(D) Continuation of participation for growing small employers. If—

(i) a qualified employer that is a small employer makes enrollment in qualified health plans offered in the small group market available to its employees through an Exchange; and

(ii) the employer ceases to be a small employer by reason of an increase in the number of employees of such employer;

the employer shall continue to be treated as a small employer for purposes of this subtitle for the period beginning with the increase and ending with the first day on which the employer does not make such enrollment available to its employees.

(c) Secretary. In this title, the term "Secretary" means the Secretary of Health and Human Services.

(d) State. In this title, the term "State" means each of the 50 States and the District of Columbia.

(e) Educated health care consumers. The term "educated health care consumer" means an individual who is knowledgeable about the health care system, and has background or experience in making informed decisions regarding health, medical, and scientific matters.

(March 23, 2010, P. L. 111-148, Title I, Subtitle D, Part I, § 1304, Title X, Subtitle A, § 10104(d), 124 Stat. 171, 900.)

CONSUMER CHOICES AND INSURANCE COMPETITION THROUGH HEALTH BENEFIT EXCHANGES

§ 18031. Affordable choices of health benefit plans

(a) Assistance to States to establish American Health Benefit Exchanges. (1) Planning and establishment grants. There shall be appropriated to the Secretary, out of any moneys in the Treasury not otherwise appropriated, an amount necessary to enable the Secretary to make awards, not later than 1 year after the date of enactment of this Act [enacted March 23, 2010], to States in the amount specified in paragraph (2) for the uses described in paragraph (3).

(2) Amount specified. For each fiscal year, the Secretary shall determine the total amount that the Secretary will make available to each State for grants under this subsection.

(3) Use of funds. A State shall use amounts awarded under this subsection for activities (including planning activities) related to establishing an American Health Benefit Exchange, as described in subsection (b).

(4) Renewability of grant. (A) In general.

Subject to subsection (d)(4), the Secretary may renew a grant awarded under paragraph (1) if the State recipient of such grant—

(i) is making progress, as determined by the Secretary, toward—

(I) establishing an Exchange; and

(II) implementing the reforms described in subtitles A and C (and the amendments made by such subtitles); and

(ii) is meeting such other benchmarks as the Secretary may establish.

(B) Limitation. No grant shall be awarded under this subsection after January 1, 2015.

(5) Technical assistance to facilitate participation in SHOP exchanges. The Secretary shall provide technical assistance to States to facilitate the participation of qualified small businesses in such States in SHOP Exchanges.

(b) American Health Benefit Exchanges. (1) In general. Each State shall, not later than January 1, 2014, establish an American Health Benefit Exchange (referred to in this title as an "Exchange") for the State that—

(A) facilitates the purchase of qualified health plans;

(B) provides for the establishment of a Small Business Health Options Program (in this title referred to as a "SHOP Exchange") that is designed to assist qualified employers in the State who are small employers in facilitating the enrollment of their employees in qualified health plans offered in the small group market in the State; and

(C) meets the requirements of subsection (d).

(2) Merger of individual and SHOP exchanges. A State may elect to provide only one Exchange in the State for providing both Exchange and SHOP Exchange services to both qualified individuals and qualified small employers, but only if the Exchange has adequate resources to assist such individuals and employers.

(c) Responsibilities of the Secretary. (1) In general. The Secretary shall, by regulation, establish criteria for the certification of health plans as qualified health plans. Such criteria shall require that, to be certified, a plan shall, at a minimum—

(A) meet marketing requirements, and not employ marketing practices or benefit designs that have the effect of discouraging the enrollment in such plan by individuals with significant health needs;

(B) ensure a sufficient choice of providers (in a manner consistent with applicable network adequacy provisions under section 2702(c) of the Public Health Service Act [42 USCS § 300gg-1(c)]), and provide information to enrollees and prospective enrollees on the availability of in-network and out-of-network providers;

(C) include within health insurance plan networks those essential community providers, where available, that serve predominately low-income, medically-underserved individuals, such as health care providers defined in section 340B(a)(4) of the Public Health Service Act [42 USCS § 256b(a)(4)] and providers described in section 1927(c)(1)(D)(i)(IV) of the Social Security Act [42 USCS § 1396r-8(c)(1)(D)(i)(IV)] as set forth by section 221 of Public Law 111-8, except that nothing in this subparagraph shall be construed to require any health plan to provide coverage for any specific medical procedure;

(D)(i) be accredited with respect to local performance on clinical quality measures such as the Healthcare Effectiveness Data and Information Set, patient experience ratings on a standardized Consumer Assessment of Healthcare Providers and Systems survey, as well as consumer access, utilization management, quality assurance, provider credentialing, complaints and appeals, network adequacy and access, and patient information programs by any entity recognized by the Secretary for the accreditation of health insurance issuers or plans (so long as any such entity has transparent and rigorous methodological and scoring criteria); or

(ii) receive such accreditation within a period established by an Exchange for such accreditation that is applicable to all qualified health plans;

(E) implement a quality improvement strategy described in subsection (g)(1);

(F) utilize a uniform enrollment form that qualified individuals and qualified employers may use (either electronically or on paper) in enrolling in qualified health plans offered through such Exchange, and that takes into account criteria that the National Association of Insurance Commissioners develops and submits to the Secretary;

(G) utilize the standard format established for presenting health benefits plan options;

(H) provide information to enrollees and prospective enrollees, and to each Exchange in which the plan is offered, on any quality measures for health plan performance endorsed under section 399JJ of the Public Health Service Act [42 USCS § 280j-3], as applicable; and

(I) report to the Secretary at least annually and in such manner as the Secretary shall require, pediatric quality reporting measures consistent with the pediatric quality reporting measures established under section 1139A of the Social Security Act [42 USCS § 1320b-9a].

(2) Rule of construction. Nothing in paragraph (1)(C) shall be construed to require a qualified health plan to contract with a provider described in such paragraph if such provider refuses to accept the generally applicable payment rates of such plan.

(3) Rating system. The Secretary shall develop a rating system that would rate qualified health plans offered through an Exchange in each benefits level on the basis of the relative quality and price. The Exchange shall include the quality rating in the information provided to individuals and employers through the Internet portal established under paragraph (4).

(4) Enrollee satisfaction system. The Secretary shall develop an enrollee satisfaction survey system that would evaluate the level of enrollee satisfaction with qualified health plans offered through an Exchange, for each such qualified health plan that had more than 500 enrollees in the previous year. The Exchange shall include enrollee satisfaction information in the information provided to individuals and employers through the Internet portal established under paragraph (5) in a manner that allows individuals to easily compare enrollee satisfaction levels between comparable plans.

(5) Internet portals. The Secretary shall—

(A) continue to operate, maintain, and update the Internet portal developed under section 1103(a) [42 USCS § 18003(a)] and to assist States in developing and maintaining their own such portal; and

(B) make available for use by Exchanges a model template for an Internet portal that may be used to direct qualified individuals and qualified employers to qualified health plans, to assist such individuals and employers in determining whether they are eligible to participate in an Exchange or eligible for a premium tax credit or cost-sharing reduction, and to present standardized information (including quality ratings) regarding qualified health plans offered through an Exchange to assist consumers in making easy health insurance choices.

Such template shall include, with respect to each qualified health plan offered through the Exchange in each rating area, access to the uniform outline of coverage the plan is required to provide under section 2716 of the Public Health Service Act [42 USCS § 300gg-16] and to a copy of the plan's written policy.

(6) Enrollment periods. The Secretary shall require an Exchange to provide for—

(A) an initial open enrollment, as determined by the Secretary (such determination to be made not later than July 1, 2012);

(B) annual open enrollment periods, as determined by the Secretary for calendar years after the initial enrollment period;

(C) special enrollment periods specified in section 9801 of the Internal Revenue Code of 1986 [26 USCS § 9801] and other special enrollment periods under circumstances similar to such periods under part D of title XVIII of the Social Security Act [42 USCS §§ 1395w-101 et seq.]; and

(D) special monthly enrollment periods for Indians (as defined in section 4 of the Indian Health Care Improvement Act [25 USCS § 1603]).

(d) Requirements. (1) In general. An Exchange shall be a governmental agency or nonprofit entity that is established by a State.

(2) Offering of coverage. (A) In general. An Exchange shall make available qualified health plans to qualified individuals and qualified employers.

(B) Limitation. (i) In general. An Exchange may not make available any health plan that is not a qualified health plan.

(ii) Offering of stand-alone dental benefits. Each Exchange within a State shall allow an issuer of a plan that only provides limited scope dental benefits meeting the requirements of section 9832(c)(2)(A) of the Internal Revenue Code of 1986 [42 USCS § 9832(c)(2)(A)] to offer the plan through the Exchange (either separately or in conjunction with a qualified health plan) if the plan provides pediatric dental benefits meeting the requirements of section 1302(b)(1)(J) [42 USCS § 18022(b)(1)(J)]).

(3) Rules relating to additional required benefits. (A) In general. Except as provided in subparagraph (B), an Exchange may make available a qualified health plan notwithstanding any provision of law that may require benefits other than the essential health benefits specified under section 1302(b) [42 USCS § 18022(b)].

(B) States may require additional benefits. (i) In general. Subject to the requirements of clause (ii), a State may require that a qualified health plan offered in such State offer benefits in addition to the essential health benefits specified under section 1302(b) [42 USCS § 18022(b)].

(ii) State must assume cost. A State shall make payments—

(I) to an individual enrolled in a qualified health plan offered in such State; or

(II) on behalf of an individual described in subclause (I) directly to the qualified health plan in which such individual is enrolled; to defray the cost of any additional benefits described in clause (i).

(4) Functions. An Exchange shall, at a minimum—

(A) implement procedures for the certification, recertification, and decertification, consistent with guidelines developed by the Secretary under subsection (c), of health plans as qualified health plans;

(B) provide for the operation of a toll-free telephone hotline to respond to requests for assistance;

(C) maintain an Internet website through which enrollees and prospective enrollees of qualified health plans may obtain standardized comparative information on such plans;

(D) assign a rating to each qualified health plan offered through such Exchange in accordance with the criteria developed by the Secretary under subsection (c)(3);

(E) utilize a standardized format for presenting health benefits plan options in the Exchange, including the use of the uniform outline of coverage established under section 2715 of the Public Health Service Act [42 USCS § 300gg-15];

(F) in accordance with section 1413 [42 USCS § 18083], inform individuals of eligibility requirements for the Medicaid program under title XIX of the Social Security Act [42 USCS §§ 1396 et seq.], the CHIP program under title XXI of such Act [42 USCS §§ 1397aa et seq.], or any applicable State or local public program and if through screening of the application by the Exchange, the Exchange determines that such individuals are eligible for any such program, enroll such individuals in such program;

(G) establish and make available by electronic means a calculator to determine the actual cost of coverage after the application of any premium tax credit under section 36B of the Internal Revenue Code of 1986 [26 USCS § 36B] and any cost-sharing reduction under section 1402 [42 USCS § 18071];

(H) subject to section 1411 [52 USCS § 18081], grant a certification attesting that, for purposes of the individual responsibility penalty under section 5000A of the Internal Revenue Code of 1986 [26 USCS § 5000A], an individual is exempt from the individual requirement or from the penalty imposed by such section because—

(i) there is no affordable qualified health plan available through the Exchange, or the individual's employer, covering the individual; or

(ii) the individual meets the requirements for any other such exemption from the individual responsibility requirement or penalty;

(I) transfer to the Secretary of the Treasury—

(i) a list of the individuals who are issued a certification under subparagraph (H), including the name and taxpayer identification number of each individual;

(ii) the name and taxpayer identification number of each individual who was an employee of an employer but who was determined to be eligible for the premium tax credit under section 36B of the Internal Revenue Code of 1986 [26 USCS § 36B] because—

(I) the employer did not provide minimum essential coverage; or

(II) the employer provided such minimum essential coverage but it was determined under section 36B(c)(2)(C) of such Code [26 USCS § 36B(c)(2)(C)] to either be unaffordable to the employee or not provide the required minimum actuarial value; and

(iii) the name and taxpayer identification number of each individual who notifies the Exchange under section 1411(b)(4) [42 USCS § 18081(b)(4)] that they have changed employers and of each individual who ceases coverage under a qualified health plan during a plan year (and the effective date of such cessation);

(J) provide to each employer the name of each employee of the employer described in subparagraph (I)(ii) who ceases coverage under a qualified health plan during a plan year (and the effective date of such cessation); and

(K) establish the Navigator program described in subsection (i).

(5) Funding limitations. (A) No Federal funds for continued operations. In establishing an Exchange under this section, the State shall ensure that such Exchange is self-sustaining beginning on January 1, 2015, including allowing the Exchange to charge assessments or user fees to participating health insurance issuers, or to otherwise generate funding, to support its operations.

(B) Prohibiting wasteful use of funds. In carrying out activities under this subsection, an Exchange shall not utilize any funds intended for the administrative and operational expenses of the Exchange for staff retreats, promotional giveaways, excessive executive compensation, or promotion of Federal or State legislative and regulatory modifications.

(6) Consultation. An Exchange shall consult with stakeholders relevant to carrying out the

activities under this section, including—

(A) educated health care consumers who are enrollees in qualified health plans;

(B) individuals and entities with experience in facilitating enrollment in qualified health plans;

(C) representatives of small businesses and self-employed individuals;

(D) State Medicaid offices; and

(E) advocates for enrolling hard to reach populations.

(7) Publication of costs. An Exchange shall publish the average costs of licensing, regulatory fees, and any other payments required by the Exchange, and the administrative costs of such Exchange, on an Internet website to educate consumers on such costs. Such information shall also include monies lost to waste, fraud, and abuse.

(e) Certification. (1) In general. An Exchange may certify a health plan as a qualified health plan if—

(A) such health plan meets the requirements for certification as promulgated by the Secretary under subsection (c)(1); and

(B) the Exchange determines that making available such health plan through such Exchange is in the interests of qualified individuals and qualified employers in the State or States in which such Exchange operates, except that the Exchange may not exclude a health plan—

(i) on the basis that such plan is a fee-for-service plan;

(ii) through the imposition of premium price controls; or

(iii) on the basis that the plan provides treatments necessary to prevent patients' deaths in circumstances the Exchange determines are inappropriate or too costly.

(2) Premium considerations. The Exchange shall require health plans seeking certification as qualified health plans to submit a justification for any premium increase prior to implementation of the increase. Such plans shall prominently post such information on their websites. The Exchange shall take this information, and the information and the recommendations provided to the Exchange by the State under section 2794(b)(1) of the Public Health Service Act [42 USCS § 300gg-94(b)(1)] (relating to patterns or practices of excessive or unjustified premium increases), into consideration when determining whether to make such health plan available through the Exchange. The Exchange shall take into account any excess of premium growth outside the Exchange as compared to the rate of such growth inside the Exchange, including information reported by the States.

(3) Transparency in coverage. (A) In general. The Exchange shall require health plans seeking certification as qualified health plans to submit to the Exchange, the Secretary, the State insurance commissioner, and make available to the public, accurate and timely disclosure of the following information:

(i) Claims payment policies and practices.

(ii) Periodic financial disclosures.

(iii) Data on enrollment.

(iv) Data on disenrollment.

(v) Data on the number of claims that are denied.

(vi) Data on rating practices.

(vii) Information on cost-sharing and payments with respect to any out-of-network coverage.

(viii) Information on enrollee and participant rights under this title.

(ix) Other information as determined appropriate by the Secretary.

(B) Use of plain language. The information required to be submitted under subparagraph (A) shall be provided in plain language. The term "plain language" means language that the intended audience, including individuals with limited English proficiency, can readily understand and use because that language is concise, well-organized, and follows other best practices of plain language writing. The Secretary and the Secretary of Labor shall jointly develop and issue guidance on best practices of plain language writing.

(C) Cost sharing transparency. The Exchange shall require health plans seeking certification as qualified health plans to permit individuals to learn the amount of cost-sharing (including deductibles, copayments, and coinsurance) under the individual's plan or coverage that the individual would be responsible for paying with respect to the furnishing of a specific item or service by a participating provider in a timely manner upon the request of the individual. At a minimum, such information shall be made available to such individual through an Internet website and such other means for individuals without access to the Internet.

(D) Group health plans. The Secretary of Labor shall update and harmonize the Secretary's rules concerning the accurate and timely disclosure to participants by group health plans of plan disclosure, plan terms and conditions, and periodic financial disclosure with the standards established by the Secretary under subparagraph (A).

(f) Flexibility. (1) Regional or other interstate exchanges. An Exchange may operate in more than one State if—

(A) each State in which such Exchange operates permits such operation; and

(B) the Secretary approves such regional or interstate Exchange.

(2) Subsidiary exchanges. A State may establish one or more subsidiary Exchanges if—

(A) each such Exchange serves a geographically distinct area; and

(B) the area served by each such Exchange is at least as large as a rating area described in section 2701(a) of the Public Health Service Act [42 USCS § 300gg(a)].

(3) Authority to contract. (A) In general. A State may elect to authorize an Exchange established by the State under this section to enter into an agreement with an eligible entity to carry out 1 or more responsibilities of the Exchange.

(B) Eligible entity. In this paragraph, the term "eligible entity" means—

(i) a person—

(I) incorporated under, and subject to the laws of, 1 or more States;

(II) that has demonstrated experience on a State or regional basis in the individual and small group health insurance markets and in benefits coverage; and

(III) that is not a health insurance issuer or that is treated under subsection (a) or (b) of section 52 of the Internal Revenue Code of 1986 [26 USCS § 52] as a member of the same controlled group of corporations (or under common control with) as a health insurance issuer; or

(ii) the State Medicaid agency under title XIX of the Social Security Act [42 USCS §§ 1396 et seq.].

(g) Rewarding quality through market-based incentives. (1) Strategy described. A strategy described in this paragraph is a payment structure that provides increased reimbursement or other incentives for—

(A) improving health outcomes through the implementation of activities that shall include quality reporting, effective case management, care coordination, chronic disease management, medication and care compliance initiatives, including through the use of the medical home model, for treatment or services under the plan or coverage;

(B) the implementation of activities to prevent hospital readmissions through a comprehensive program for hospital discharge that includes patient-centered education and counseling, comprehensive discharge planning, and post discharge reinforcement by an appropriate health care professional;

(C) the implementation of activities to improve patient safety and reduce medical errors through the appropriate use of best clinical practices, evidence based medicine, and health information technology under the plan or coverage;

(D) the implementation of wellness and health promotion activities; and

(E) the implementation of activities to reduce health and health care disparities, including through the use of language services, community outreach, and cultural competency trainings.

(2) Guidelines. The Secretary, in consultation with experts in health care quality and stakeholders, shall develop guidelines concerning the matters described in paragraph (1).

(3) Requirements. The guidelines developed under paragraph (2) shall require the periodic reporting to the applicable Exchange of the activities that a qualified health plan has conducted to implement a strategy described in paragraph (1).

(h) Quality improvement. (1) Enhancing patient safety. Beginning on January 1, 2015, a qualified health plan may contract with—

(A) a hospital with greater than 50 beds only if such hospital—

(i) utilizes a patient safety evaluation system as described in part C of title IX of the Public Health Service Act [42 USCS §§ 299b-21 et seq.]; and

(ii) implements a mechanism to ensure that each patient receives a comprehensive program for hospital discharge that includes patient-centered education and counseling, comprehensive discharge planning, and post discharge reinforcement by an appropriate health care professional; or

(B) a health care provider only if such provider implements such mechanisms to improve health care quality as the Secretary may by regulation require.

(2) Exceptions. The Secretary may establish reasonable exceptions to the requirements described in paragraph (1).

(3) Adjustment. The Secretary may by regulation adjust the number of beds described in paragraph (1)(A).

(i) Navigators. (1) In general. An Exchange shall establish a program under which it awards grants to entities described in paragraph (2) to carry out the duties described in paragraph (3).

(2) Eligibility. (A) In general. To be eligible to receive a grant under paragraph (1), an

entity shall demonstrate to the Exchange involved that the entity has existing relationships, or could readily establish relationships, with employers and employees, consumers (including uninsured and underinsured consumers), or self-employed individuals likely to be qualified to enroll in a qualified health plan.

(B) Types. Entities described in subparagraph (A) may include trade, industry, and professional associations, commercial fishing industry organizations, ranching and farming organizations, community and consumer-focused nonprofit groups, chambers of commerce, unions, resource partners of the Small Business Administration, other licensed insurance agents and brokers, and other entities that—

(i) are capable of carrying out the duties described in paragraph (3);

(ii) meet the standards described in paragraph (4); and

(iii) provide information consistent with the standards developed under paragraph (5).

(3) Duties. An entity that serves as a navigator under a grant under this subsection shall—

(A) conduct public education activities to raise awareness of the availability of qualified health plans;

(B) distribute fair and impartial information concerning enrollment in qualified health plans, and the availability of premium tax credits under section 36B of the Internal Revenue Code of 1986 [26 USCS § 36B] and cost-sharing reductions under section 1402 [42 USCS § 18071];

(C) facilitate enrollment in qualified health plans;

(D) provide referrals to any applicable office of health insurance consumer assistance or health insurance ombudsman established under section 2793 of the Public Health Service Act [42 USCS § 300gg-93], or any other appropriate State agency or agencies, for any enrollee with a grievance, complaint, or question regarding their health plan, coverage, or a determination under such plan or coverage; and

(E) provide information in a manner that is culturally and linguistically appropriate to the needs of the population being served by the Exchange or Exchanges.

(4) Standards. (A) In general. The Secretary shall establish standards for navigators under this subsection, including provisions to ensure that any private or public entity that is selected as a navigator is qualified, and licensed if appropriate, to engage in the navigator activities described in this subsection and to avoid conflicts of interest. Under such standards, a navigator shall not—

(i) be a health insurance issuer; or

(ii) receive any consideration directly or indirectly from any health insurance issuer in connection with the enrollment of any qualified individuals or employees of a qualified employer in a qualified health plan.

(5) Fair and impartial information and services. The Secretary, in collaboration with States, shall develop standards to ensure that information made available by navigators is fair, accurate, and impartial.

(6) Funding. Grants under this subsection shall be made from the operational funds of the Exchange and not Federal funds received by the State to establish the Exchange.

(j) Applicability of mental health parity. Section 2726 of the Public Health Service Act [42 USCS § 300gg-26] shall apply to qualified health plans in the same manner and to the same extent as such section applies to health insurance issuers and group health plans.

(k) Conflict. An Exchange may not establish rules that conflict with or prevent the application of regulations promulgated by the Secretary under this subtitle [42 USCS §§ 18021 et seq.].

(March 23, 2010, P. L. 111-148, Title I, Subtitle D, Part II, § 1311, Title X, Subtitle A, § 10104(e)–(h), Subtitle B, § 10203(a), 124 Stat. 173, 900, 927.)

§ 18032. Consumer choice

(a) Choice. (1) Qualified individuals. A qualified individual may enroll in any qualified health plan available to such individual and for which such individual is eligible.

(2) Qualified employers. (A) Employer may specify level. A qualified employer may provide support for coverage of employees under a qualified health plan by selecting any level of coverage under section 1302(d) [42 USCS § 18022(d)] to be made available to employees through an Exchange.

(B) Employee may choose plans within a level. Each employee of a qualified employer that elects a level of coverage under subparagraph (A) may choose to enroll in a qualified health plan that offers coverage at that level.

(b) Payment of premiums by qualified individuals. A qualified individual enrolled in any qualified health plan may pay any applicable premium owed by such individual to the health insurance issuer issuing such qualified health plan.

(c) Single risk pool. (1) Individual market. A health insurance issuer shall consider all enrollees in all health plans (other than grandfathered health plans) offered by such issuer in the individual market, including those enrollees who do not enroll in such plans through the Exchange, to be members of a single risk pool.

(2) Small group market. A health insurance issuer shall consider all enrollees in all health plans (other than grandfathered health plans) offered by such issuer in the small group market, including those enrollees who do not enroll in such plans through the Exchange, to be members of a single risk pool.

(3) Merger of markets. A State may require the individual and small group insurance markets within a State to be merged if the State determines appropriate.

(4) State law. A State law requiring grandfathered health plans to be included in a pool described in paragraph (1) or (2) shall not apply.

(d) Empowering consumer choice. (1) Continued operation of market outside exchanges. Nothing in this title shall be construed to prohibit—

(A) a health insurance issuer from offering outside of an Exchange a health plan to a qualified individual or qualified employer; and

(B) a qualified individual from enrolling in, or a qualified employer from selecting for its employees, a health plan offered outside of an Exchange.

(2) Continued operation of state benefit requirements. Nothing in this title shall be construed to terminate, abridge, or limit the operation of any requirement under State law with respect to any policy or plan that is offered outside of an Exchange to offer benefits.

(3) Voluntary nature of an exchange. (A) Choice to enroll or not to enroll. Nothing in this title shall be construed to restrict the choice of a qualified individual to enroll or not to enroll in a qualified health plan or to participate in an Exchange.

(B) Prohibition against compelled enrollment. Nothing in this title shall be construed to compel an individual to enroll in a qualified health plan or to participate in an Exchange.

(C) Individuals allowed to enroll in any plan. A qualified individual may enroll in any qualified health plan, except that in the case of a catastrophic plan described in section 1302(e) [42 USCS § 18022(e)], a qualified individual may enroll in the plan only if the individual is eligible to enroll in the plan under section 1302(e)(2) [42 USCS § 18022(e)(2)].

(D) Members of Congress in the Exchange. (i) Requirement. Notwithstanding any other provision of law, after the effective date of this subtitle [effective March 23, 2010], the only health plans that the Federal Government may make available to Members of Congress and congressional staff with respect to their service as a Member of Congress or congressional staff shall be health plans that are—

(I) created under this Act (or an amendment made by this Act); or

(II) offered through an Exchange established under this Act (or an amendment made by this Act).

(ii) Definitions. In this section:

(I) Member of Congress. The term "Member of Congress" means any member of the House of Representatives or the Senate.

(II) Congressional staff. The term "congressional staff" means all full-time and part-time employees employed by the official office of a Member of Congress, whether in Washington, DC or outside of Washington, DC.

(4) No penalty for transferring to minimum essential coverage outside exchange. An Exchange, or a qualified health plan offered through an Exchange, shall not impose any penalty or other fee on an individual who cancels enrollment in a plan because the individual becomes eligible for minimum essential coverage (as defined in section 5000A(f) of the Internal Revenue Code of 1986 [26 USCS § 5000A(f)] without regard to paragraph (1)(C) or (D) thereof) or such coverage becomes affordable (within the meaning of section 36B(c)(2)(C) of such Code [26 USCS § 36B(c)(2)(C)]).

(e) Enrollment through agents or brokers. The Secretary shall establish procedures under which a State may allow agents or brokers—

(1) to enroll individuals and employers in any qualified health plans in the individual or small group market as soon as the plan is offered through an Exchange in the State; and

(2) to assist individuals in applying for premium tax credits and cost-sharing reductions for plans sold through an Exchange.

(f) Qualified individuals and employers; access limited to citizens and lawful residents. (1) Qualified individuals. In this title:

(A) In general. The term "qualified individual" means, with respect to an Exchange, an individual who—

(i) is seeking to enroll in a qualified health plan in the individual market offered through the Exchange; and

(ii) resides in the State that established the Exchange.

(B) Incarcerated individuals excluded. An individual shall not be treated as a qualified individual if, at the time of enrollment, the individual is incarcerated, other than incarceration pending the disposition of charges.

(2) Qualified employer. In this title:

(A) In general. The term "qualified employer" means a small employer that elects to make all full-time employees of such employer eligible for 1 or more qualified health plans offered in the small group market through an Exchange that offers qualified health plans.

(B) Extension to large groups. (i) In general. Beginning in 2017, each State may allow issuers of health insurance coverage in the large group market in the State to offer qualified health plans in such market through an Exchange. Nothing in this subparagraph shall be construed as requiring the issuer to offer such plans through an Exchange.

(ii) Large employers eligible. If a State under clause (i) allows issuers to offer qualified health plans in the large group market through an Exchange, the term "qualified employer" shall include a large employer that elects to make all full-time employees of such employer eligible for 1 or more qualified health plans offered in the large group market through the Exchange.

(3) Access limited to lawful residents. If an individual is not, or is not reasonably expected to be for the entire period for which enrollment is sought, a citizen or national of the United States or an alien lawfully present in the United States, the individual shall not be treated as a qualified individual and may not be covered under a qualified health plan in the individual market that is offered through an Exchange.

(March 23, 2010, P. L. 111-148, Title I, Subtitle D, Part II, § 1312, Title X, Subtitle A, § 10104(i), 124 Stat. 182, 901.)

§ 18033. Financial integrity

(a) Accounting for expenditures. (1) In general. An Exchange shall keep an accurate accounting of all activities, receipts, and expenditures and shall annually submit to the Secretary a report concerning such accountings.

(2) Investigations. The Secretary, in coordination with the Inspector General of the Department of Health and Human Services, may investigate the affairs of an Exchange, may examine the properties and records of an Exchange, and may require periodic reports in relation to activities undertaken by an Exchange. An Exchange shall fully cooperate in any investigation conducted under this paragraph.

(3) Audits. An Exchange shall be subject to annual audits by the Secretary.

(4) Pattern of abuse. If the Secretary determines that an Exchange or a State has engaged in serious misconduct with respect to compliance with the requirements of, or carrying out of activities required under, this title, the Secretary may rescind from payments otherwise due to such State involved under this or any other Act administered by the Secretary an amount not to exceed 1 percent of such payments per year until corrective actions are taken by the State that are determined to be adequate by the Secretary.

(5) Protections against fraud and abuse. With respect to activities carried out under this title, the Secretary shall provide for the efficient and non-discriminatory administration of Exchange activities and implement any measure or procedure that—

(A) the Secretary determines is appropriate to reduce fraud and abuse in the administration of this title; and

(B) the Secretary has authority to implement under this title or any other Act.

(6) Application of the False Claims Act.

(A) In general. Payments made by, through, or in connection with an Exchange are subject to the False Claims Act (31 U.S.C. 3729 et seq.) if those payments include any Federal funds. Compliance with the requirements of this Act concerning eligibility for a health insurance issuer to participate in the Exchange shall be a material condition of an issuer's entitlement to receive payments, including payments of premium tax credits and cost-sharing reductions, through the Exchange.

(B) Damages. Notwithstanding paragraph (1) of section 3729(a) of title 31, United States Code, and subject to paragraph (2) of such section, the civil penalty assessed under the False Claims Act on any person found liable under such Act as described in subparagraph (A) shall be increased by not less than 3 times and not more than 6 times the amount of damages which the Government sustains because of the act of that person.

(b) GAO oversight. Not later than 5 years after the first date on which Exchanges are required to be operational under this title, the Comptroller General shall conduct an ongoing study of Exchange activities and the enrollees in qualified health plans offered through Exchanges. Such study shall review—

(1) the operations and administration of Exchanges, including surveys and reports of qualified health plans offered through Exchanges and on the experience of such plans (including data on enrollees in Exchanges and individuals

purchasing health insurance coverage outside of Exchanges), the expenses of Exchanges, claims statistics relating to qualified health plans, complaints data relating to such plans, and the manner in which Exchanges meet their goals;

(2) any significant observations regarding the utilization and adoption of Exchanges;

(3) where appropriate, recommendations for improvements in the operations or policies of Exchanges;

(4) a survey of the cost and affordability of health care insurance provided under the Exchanges for owners and employees of small business concerns (as defined under section 3 of the Small Business Act (15 U.S.C. 632)), including data on enrollees in Exchanges and individuals purchasing health insurance coverage outside of Exchanges; and

(5) how many physicians, by area and specialty, are not taking or accepting new patients enrolled in Federal Government health care programs, and the adequacy of provider networks of Federal Government health care programs.

(March 23, 2010, P. L. 111-148, Title I, Subtitle D, Part II, § 1313, Title X, Subtitle A, § 10104(k), 124 Stat. 184, 902.)

HISTORY; ANCILLARY LAWS AND DIRECTIVES

References in text:

"This title", referred to in this section, is Title I of Act March 23, 2010, P. L. 111-148, which appears generally as 42 USCS §§ 18001 et seq. For full classification of such Act, consult USCS Tables volumes.

Other provisions:

Subsec. (a)(6)(B) deemed null and void. Act March 23, 2010, P. L. 111-148, Title X, Subtitle A, § 10104(j)(1), 124 Stat. 901, provides: "Subparagraph (B) of section 1313(a)(6) of this Act [subsec. (a)(6)(B) of this section] is hereby deemed null, void, and of no effect.".

STATE FLEXIBILITY RELATING TO EXCHANGES

§ 18041. State flexibility in operation and enforcement of exchanges and related requirements

(a) Establishment of standards. (1) In general. The Secretary shall, as soon as practicable after the date of enactment of this Act, issue regulations setting standards for meeting the requirements under this title, and the amendments made by this title, with respect to—

(A) the establishment and operation of Exchanges (including SHOP Exchanges);

(B) the offering of qualified health plans through such Exchanges;

(C) the establishment of the reinsurance and risk adjustment programs under part V [42 USCS §§ 18061 et seq.]; and

(D) such other requirements as the Secretary determines appropriate.

The preceding sentence shall not apply to standards for requirements under subtitles A and C (and the amendments made by such subtitles) for which the Secretary issues regulations under the Public Health Service Act [42 USCS §§ 201 et seq.].

(2) Consultation. In issuing the regulations under paragraph (1), the Secretary shall consult with the National Association of Insurance Commissioners and its members and with health insurance issuers, consumer organizations, and such other individuals as the Secretary selects in a manner designed to ensure balanced representation among interested parties.

(b) State action. Each State that elects, at such time and in such manner as the Secretary may prescribe, to apply the requirements described in subsection (a) shall, not later than January 1, 2014, adopt and have in effect—

(1) the Federal standards established under subsection (a); or

(2) a State law or regulation that the Secretary determines implements the standards within the State.

(c) Failure to establish exchange or implement requirements. (1) In general. If—

(A) a State is not an electing State under subsection (b); or

(B) the Secretary determines, on or before January 1, 2013, that an electing State—

(i) will not have any required Exchange operational by January 1, 2014; or

(ii) has not taken the actions the Secretary determines necessary to implement—

(I) the other requirements set forth in the standards under subsection (a); or

(II) the requirements set forth in subtitles A and C and the amendments made by such subtitles;

the Secretary shall (directly or through agreement with a not-for-profit entity) establish and operate such Exchange within the State and the Secretary shall take such actions as are necessary to implement such other requirements.

(2) Enforcement authority. The provisions of section 2736(b) of the Public Health Services Act [42 USCS § 300gg-22(b)] shall apply to the enforcement under paragraph (1) of require-

ments of subsection (a)(1) (without regard to any limitation on the application of those provisions to group health plans).

(d) No interference with State regulatory authority. Nothing in this title shall be construed to preempt any State law that does not prevent the application of the provisions of this title.

(e) Presumption for certain state-operated exchanges. (1) In general. In the case of a State operating an Exchange before January 1, 2010, and which has insured a percentage of its population not less than the percentage of the population projected to be covered nationally after the implementation of this Act, that seeks to operate an Exchange under this section, the Secretary shall presume that such Exchange meets the standards under this section unless the Secretary determines, after completion of the process established under paragraph (2), that the Exchange does not comply with such standards.

(2) Process. The Secretary shall establish a process to work with a State described in paragraph (1) to provide assistance necessary to assist the State's Exchange in coming into compliance with the standards for approval under this section.

(March 23, 2010, P. L. 111-148, Title I, Subtitle D, Part III, § 1321, 124 Stat. 186.)

§ 18042. Federal program to assist establishment and operation of nonprofit, member-run health insurance issuers

(a) Establishment of program. (1) In general. The Secretary shall establish a program to carry out the purposes of this section to be known as the Consumer Operated and Oriented Plan (CO-OP) program.

(2) Purpose. It is the purpose of the CO-OP program to foster the creation of qualified nonprofit health insurance issuers to offer qualified health plans in the individual and small group markets in the States in which the issuers are licensed to offer such plans.

(b) Loans and grants under the CO-OP program. (1) In general. The Secretary shall provide through the CO-OP program for the awarding to persons applying to become qualified nonprofit health insurance issuers of—

(A) loans to provide assistance to such person in meeting its start-up costs; and

(B) grants to provide assistance to such person in meeting any solvency requirements of States in which the person seeks to be licensed to issue qualified health plans.

(2) Requirements for awarding loans and grants. (A) In general. In awarding loans and grants under the CO-OP program, the Secretary shall—

(i) take into account the recommendations of the advisory board established under paragraph (3);

(ii) give priority to applicants that will offer qualified health plans on a Statewide basis, will utilize integrated care models, and have significant private support; and

(iii) ensure that there is sufficient funding to establish at least 1 qualified nonprofit health insurance issuer in each State, except that nothing in this clause shall prohibit the Secretary from funding the establishment of multiple qualified nonprofit health insurance issuers in any State if the funding is sufficient to do so.

(B) States without issuers in program. If no health insurance issuer applies to be a qualified nonprofit health insurance issuer within a State, the Secretary may use amounts appropriated under this section for the awarding of grants to encourage the establishment of a qualified nonprofit health insurance issuer within the State or the expansion of a qualified nonprofit health insurance issuer from another State to the State.

(C) Agreement. (i) In general. The Secretary shall require any person receiving a loan or grant under the CO-OP program to enter into an agreement with the Secretary which requires such person to meet (and to continue to meet)—

(I) any requirement under this section for such person to be treated as a qualified nonprofit health insurance issuer; and

(II) any requirements contained in the agreement for such person to receive such loan or grant.

(ii) Restrictions on use of Federal funds. The agreement shall include a requirement that no portion of the funds made available by any loan or grant under this section may be used—

(I) for carrying on propaganda, or otherwise attempting, to influence legislation; or

(II) for marketing. Nothing in this clause shall be construed to allow a person to take any action prohibited by section 501(c)(29) of the Internal Revenue Code of 1986 [26 USCS § 501(c)(29)].

(iii) Failure to meet requirements. If the Secretary determines that a person has failed to meet any requirement described in clause (i) or (ii) and has failed to correct such failure within a reasonable period of time of when the person first knows (or reasonably should have known) of such failure, such person shall repay to the Secretary an amount equal to the sum of—

(I) 110 percent of the aggregate amount of loans and grants received under this section; plus

(II) interest on the aggregate amount of loans and grants received under this section for the period the loans or grants were outstanding. The Secretary shall notify the Secretary of the Treasury of any determination under this section of a failure that results in the termination of an issuer's tax-exempt status under section 501(c)(29) of such Code [26 USCS § 501(c)(29)].

(D) Time for awarding loans and grants. The Secretary shall not later than July 1, 2013, award the loans and grants under the CO-OP program and begin the distribution of amounts awarded under such loans and grants.

(3) Repayment of loans and grants. Not later than July 1, 2013, and prior to awarding loans and grants under the CO-OP program, the Secretary shall promulgate regulations with respect to the repayment of such loans and grants in a manner that is consistent with State solvency regulations and other similar State laws that may apply. In promulgating such regulations, the Secretary shall provide that such loans shall be repaid within 5 years and such grants shall be repaid within 15 years, taking into consideration any appropriate State reserve requirements, solvency regulations, and requisite surplus note arrangements that must be constructed in a State to provide for such repayment prior to awarding such loans and grants.

(4) Advisory board. (A) In general. The advisory board under this paragraph shall consist of 15 members appointed by the Comptroller General of the United States from among individuals with qualifications described in section 1805(c)(2) of the Social Security Act [42 USCS § 1395b-6(c)(2)].

(B) Rules relating to appointments. (i) Standards. Any individual appointed under subparagraph (A) shall meet ethics and conflict of interest standards protecting against insurance industry involvement and interference.

(ii) Original appointments. The original appointment of board members under subparagraph (A)(ii) shall be made no later than 3 months after the date of enactment of this Act [enacted March 23, 2010].

(C) Vacancy. Any vacancy on the advisory board shall be filled in the same manner as the original appointment.

(D) Pay and reimbursement. (i) No compensation for members of advisory board. Except as provided in clause (ii), a member of the advisory board may not receive pay, allowances, or benefits by reason of their service on the board.

(ii) Travel expenses. Each member shall receive travel expenses, including per diem in lieu of subsistence under subchapter I of chapter 57 of title 5, United States Code [5 USCS §§ 5701 et seq.].

(E) Application of FACA. The Federal Advisory Committee Act (5 U.S.C. App.) shall apply to the advisory board, except that section 14 of such Act shall not apply.

(F) Termination. The advisory board shall terminate on the earlier of the date that it completes its duties under this section or December 31, 2015.

(c) Qualified nonprofit health insurance issuer. For purposes of this section—

(1) In general. The term "qualified nonprofit health insurance issuer" means a health insurance issuer that is an organization—

(A) that is organized under State law as a nonprofit, member corporation;

(B) substantially all of the activities of which consist of the issuance of qualified health plans in the individual and small group markets in each State in which it is licensed to issue such plans; and

(C) that meets the other requirements of this subsection.

(2) Certain organizations prohibited. An organization shall not be treated as a qualified nonprofit health insurance issuer if—

(A) the organization or a related entity (or any predecessor of either) was a health insurance issuer on July 16, 2009; or

(B) the organization is sponsored by a State or local government, any political subdivision thereof, or any instrumentality of such government or political subdivision.

(3) Governance requirements. An organization shall not be treated as a qualified nonprofit health insurance issuer unless—

(A) the governance of the organization is subject to a majority vote of its members;

(B) its governing documents incorporate ethics and conflict of interest standards protecting against insurance industry involvement and interference; and

(C) as provided in regulations promulgated by the Secretary, the organization is required to operate with a strong consumer focus, including timeliness, responsiveness, and accountability to members.

(4) Profits inure to benefit of members. An organization shall not be treated as a qualified nonprofit health insurance issuer unless any profits made by the organization are required to be used to lower premiums, to improve

benefits, or for other programs intended to improve the quality of health care delivered to its members.

(5) Compliance with State insurance laws. An organization shall not be treated as a qualified nonprofit health insurance issuer unless the organization meets all the requirements that other issuers of qualified health plans are required to meet in any State where the issuer offers a qualified health plan, including solvency and licensure requirements, rules on payments to providers, and compliance with network adequacy rules, rate and form filing rules, any applicable State premium assessments and any other State law described in section 1324(b) [42 USCS § 18044(b)].

(6) Coordination with state insurance reforms. An organization shall not be treated as a qualified nonprofit health insurance issuer unless the organization does not offer a health plan in a State until that State has in effect (or the Secretary has implemented for the State) the market reforms required by part A of title XXVII of the Public Health Service Act [42 USCS §§ 300gg et seq.] (as amended by subtitles A and C of this Act).

(d) Establishment of private purchasing council. (1) In general. Qualified nonprofit health insurance issuers participating in the CO-OP program under this section may establish a private purchasing council to enter into collective purchasing arrangements for items and services that increase administrative and other cost efficiencies, including claims administration, administrative services, health information technology, and actuarial services.

(2) Council may not set payment rates. The private purchasing council established under paragraph (1) shall not set payment rates for health care facilities or providers participating in health insurance coverage provided by qualified nonprofit health insurance issuers.

(3) Continued application of antitrust laws. (A) In general. Nothing in this section shall be construed to limit the application of the antitrust laws to any private purchasing council (whether or not established under this subsection) or to any qualified nonprofit health insurance issuer participating in such a council.

(B) Antitrust laws. For purposes of this subparagraph, the term "antitrust laws" has the meaning given the term in subsection (a) of the first section of the Clayton Act (15 U.S.C. 12(a)). Such term also includes section 5 of the Federal Trade Commission Act (15 U.S.C. 45) to the extent that such section 5 applies to unfair methods of competition.

(e) Limitation on participation. No representative of any Federal, State, or local government (or of any political subdivision or instrumentality thereof), and no representative of a person described in subsection (c)(2)(A), may serve on the board of directors of a qualified nonprofit health insurance issuer or with a private purchasing council established under subsection (d).

(f) Limitations on Secretary. (1) In general. The Secretary shall not—

(A) participate in any negotiations between 1 or more qualified nonprofit health insurance issuers (or a private purchasing council established under subsection (d)) and any health care facilities or providers, including any drug manufacturer, pharmacy, or hospital; and

(B) establish or maintain a price structure for reimbursement of any health benefits covered by such issuers.

(2) Competition. Nothing in this section shall be construed as authorizing the Secretary to interfere with the competitive nature of providing health benefits through qualified nonprofit health insurance issuers.

(g) Appropriations. There are hereby appropriated, out of any funds in the Treasury not otherwise appropriated, $6,000,000,000 to carry out this section.

(h) [Omitted]

(i) GAO study and report. (1) Study. The Comptroller General of the General Accountability Office shall conduct an ongoing study on competition and market concentration in the health insurance market in the United States after the implementation of the reforms in such market under the provisions of, and the amendments made by, this Act. Such study shall include an analysis of new issuers of health insurance in such market.

(2) Report. The Comptroller General shall, not later than December 31 of each even-numbered year (beginning with 2014), report to the appropriate committees of the Congress the results of the study conducted under paragraph (1), including any recommendations for administrative or legislative changes the Comptroller General determines necessary or appropriate to increase competition in the health insurance market.

(March 23, 2010, P. L. 111-148, Title I, Subtitle D, Part III, § 1322, Title X, Subtitle A, § 10104(l), 124 Stat. 187, 902.)

§ 18043. Funding for the territories

(a) In general. A territory that—

(1) elects consistent with subsection (b) to establish an Exchange in accordance with part II of this subtitle [42 USCS §§ 18031 et seq.]

and establishes such an Exchange in accordance with such part shall be treated as a State for purposes of such part and shall be entitled to payment from the amount allocated to the territory under subsection (c); or

(2) does not make such election shall be entitled to an increase in the dollar limitation applicable to the territory under subsections (f) and (g) of section 1108 of the Social Security Act (42 U.S.C. 1308) for such period in such amount for such territory and such increase shall not be taken into account in computing any other amount under such subsections.

(b) Terms and conditions. An election under subsection (a)(1) shall—

(1) not be effective unless the election is consistent with section 1321 [42 USCS § 18041] and is received not later than October 1, 2013; and

(2) be contingent upon entering into an agreement between the territory and the Secretary that requires that—

(A) funds provided under the agreement shall be used only to provide premium and cost-sharing assistance to residents of the territory obtaining health insurance coverage through the Exchange; and

(B) the premium and cost-sharing assistance provided under such agreement shall be structured in such a manner so as to prevent any gap in assistance for individuals between the income level at which medical assistance is available through the territory's Medicaid plan under title XIX of the Social Security Act [42 USCS §§ 1396 et seq.] and the income level at which premium and cost-sharing assistance is available under the agreement.

(c) Appropriation and allocation. (1) Appropriation. Out of any funds in the Treasury not otherwise appropriated, there is appropriated for purposes of payment pursuant to subsection (a) $1,000,000,000, to be available during the period beginning with 2014 and ending with 2019.

(2) Allocation. The Secretary shall allocate the amount appropriated under paragraph (1) among the territories for purposes of carrying out this section as follows:

(A) For Puerto Rico, $925,000,000.

(B) For another territory, the portion of $75,000,000 specified by the Secretary.

(March 23, 2010, P. L. 111-148, Title I, Subtitle D, Part III, § 1323, as added March 30, 2010, P. L. 111-152, Title I, Subtitle C, § 1204(a), 124 Stat. 1055.)

HISTORY; ANCILLARY LAWS AND DIRECTIVES

Explanatory notes:

A prior § 18043 (Act March 23, 2010, P. L. 111-148, Title I, Subtitle D, Part III, § 1323, 124 Stat. 192) was repealed by Act March 23, 2010, P. L. 111-148, Title X, Subtitle A, § 10104(m), 124 Stat. 902. It provided for a community health insurance option.

§ 18044. Level playing field

(a) In general. Notwithstanding any other provision of law, any health insurance coverage offered by a private health insurance issuer shall not be subject to any Federal or State law described in subsection (b) if a qualified health plan offered under the Consumer Operated and Oriented Plan program under section 1322 [42 USCS § 18042], or a multi-State qualified health plan under section 1334 [42 USCS § 18054], is not subject to such law.

(b) Laws described. The Federal and State laws described in this subsection are those Federal and State laws relating to—

(1) guaranteed renewal;
(2) rating;
(3) preexisting conditions;
(4) non-discrimination;
(5) quality improvement and reporting;
(6) fraud and abuse;
(7) solvency and financial requirements;
(8) market conduct;
(9) prompt payment;
(10) appeals and grievances;
(11) privacy and confidentiality;
(12) licensure; and
(13) benefit plan material or information.

(March 23, 2010, P. L. 111-148, Title I, Subtitle D, Part III, § 1324, Title X, Subtitle A, § 10104(n), 124 Stat. 199, 902.)

STATE FLEXIBILITY TO ESTABLISH ALTERNATIVE PROGRAMS

§ 18051. State flexibility to establish basic health programs for low-income individuals not eligible for Medicaid

(a) Establishment of program. (1) In general. The Secretary shall establish a basic health program meeting the requirements of this section under which a State may enter into contracts to offer 1 or more standard health plans providing at least the essential health benefits described in section 1302(b) [42 USCS § 18022(b)] to eligible individuals in lieu of offering such individuals coverage through an Exchange.

(2) Certifications as to benefit coverage and costs. Such program shall provide that a State may not establish a basic health program under this section unless the State establishes to the satisfaction of the Secretary, and the Sec-

retary certifies, that—

(A) in the case of an eligible individual enrolled in a standard health plan offered through the program, the State provides—

(i) that the amount of the monthly premium an eligible individual is required to pay for coverage under the standard health plan for the individual and the individual's dependents does not exceed the amount of the monthly premium that the eligible individual would have been required to pay (in the rating area in which the individual resides) if the individual had enrolled in the applicable second lowest cost silver plan (as defined in section 36B(b)(3)(B) of the Internal Revenue Code of 1986 [26 USCS § 36B(b)(3)(B)]) offered to the individual through an Exchange; and

(ii) that the cost-sharing an eligible individual is required to pay under the standard health plan does not exceed—

(I) the cost-sharing required under a platinum plan in the case of an eligible individual with household income not in excess of 150 percent of the poverty line for the size of the family involved; and

(II) the cost-sharing required under a gold plan in the case of an eligible individual not described in subclause (I); and

(B) the benefits provided under the standard health plans offered through the program cover at least the essential health benefits described in section 1302(b) [42 USCS § 18022(b)].

For purposes of subparagraph (A)(i), the amount of the monthly premium an individual is required to pay under either the standard health plan or the applicable second lowest cost silver plan shall be determined after reduction for any premium tax credits and cost-sharing reductions allowable with respect to either plan.

(b) Standard health plan. In this section, the term "standard heath plan" means a health benefits plan that the State contracts with under this section—

(1) under which the only individuals eligible to enroll are eligible individuals;

(2) that provides at least the essential health benefits described in section 1302(b) [42 USCS § 18022(b)]; and

(3) in the case of a plan that provides health insurance coverage offered by a health insurance issuer, that has a medical loss ratio of at least 85 percent.

(c) Contracting process. (1) In general. A State basic health program shall establish a competitive process for entering into contracts with standard health plans under subsection (a), including negotiation of premiums and cost-sharing and negotiation of benefits in addition to the essential health benefits described in section 1302(b) [42 USCS § 18022(b)].

(2) Specific items to be considered. A State shall, as part of its competitive process under paragraph (1), include at least the following:

(A) Innovation. Negotiation with offerors of a standard health plan for the inclusion of innovative features in the plan, including—

(i) care coordination and care management for enrollees, especially for those with chronic health conditions;

(ii) incentives for use of preventive services; and

(iii) the establishment of relationships between providers and patients that maximize patient involvement in health care decision-making, including providing incentives for appropriate utilization under the plan.

(B) Health and resource differences. Consideration of, and the making of suitable allowances for, differences in health care needs of enrollees and differences in local availability of, and access to, health care providers. Nothing in this subparagraph shall be construed as allowing discrimination on the basis of pre-existing conditions or other health status-related factors.

(C) Managed care. Contracting with managed care systems, or with systems that offer as many of the attributes of managed care as are feasible in the local health care market.

(D) Performance measures. Establishing specific performance measures and standards for issuers of standard health plans that focus on quality of care and improved health outcomes, requiring such plans to report to the State with respect to the measures and standards, and making the performance and quality information available to enrollees in a useful form.

(3) Enhanced availability. (A) Multiple plans. A State shall, to the maximum extent feasible, seek to make multiple standard health plans available to eligible individuals within a State to ensure individuals have a choice of such plans.

(B) Regional compacts. A State may negotiate a regional compact with other States to include coverage of eligible individuals in all such States in agreements with issuers of standard health plans.

(4) Coordination with other state programs. A State shall seek to coordinate the administration of, and provision of benefits under, its program under this section with the State Medicaid program under title XIX of the Social Security Act [42 USCS §§ 1396 et seq.], the

State child health plan under title XXI of such Act [42 USCS §§ 1397aa et seq.], and other State-administered health programs to maximize the efficiency of such programs and to improve the continuity of care.

(d) Transfer of funds to States. (1) In general. If the Secretary determines that a State electing the application of this section meets the requirements of the program established under subsection (a), the Secretary shall transfer to the State for each fiscal year for which 1 or more standard health plans are operating within the State the amount determined under paragraph (3).

(2) Use of funds. A State shall establish a trust for the deposit of the amounts received under paragraph (1) and amounts in the trust fund shall only be used to reduce the premiums and cost-sharing of, or to provide additional benefits for, eligible individuals enrolled in standard health plans within the State. Amounts in the trust fund, and expenditures of such amounts, shall not be included in determining the amount of any non-Federal funds for purposes of meeting any matching or expenditure requirement of any federally-funded program.

(3) Amount of payment. (A) Secretarial determination. (i) In general. The amount determined under this paragraph for any fiscal year is the amount the Secretary determines is equal to 95 percent of the premium tax credits under section 36B of the Internal Revenue Code of 1986 [26 USCS § 36B], and the cost-sharing reductions under section 1402 [42 USCS § 18071], that would have been provided for the fiscal year to eligible individuals enrolled in standard health plans in the State if such eligible individuals were allowed to enroll in qualified health plans through an Exchange established under this subtitle.

(ii) Specific requirements. The Secretary shall make the determination under clause (i) on a per enrollee basis and shall take into account all relevant factors necessary to determine the value of the premium tax credits and cost-sharing reductions that would have been provided to eligible individuals described in clause (i), including the age and income of the enrollee, whether the enrollment is for self-only or family coverage, geographic differences in average spending for health care across rating areas, the health status of the enrollee for purposes of determining risk adjustment payments and reinsurance payments that would have been made if the enrollee had enrolled in a qualified health plan through an Exchange, and whether any reconciliation of the credit or cost-sharing reductions would have occurred if the enrollee had been so enrolled. This determination shall take into consideration the experience of other States with respect to participation in an Exchange and such credits and reductions provided to residents of the other States, with a special focus on enrollees with income below 200 percent of poverty.

(iii) Certification. The Chief Actuary of the Centers for Medicare & Medicaid Services, in consultation with the Office of Tax Analysis of the Department of the Treasury, shall certify whether the methodology used to make determinations under this subparagraph, and such determinations, meet the requirements of clause (ii). Such certifications shall be based on sufficient data from the State and from comparable States about their experience with programs created by this Act.

(B) Corrections. The Secretary shall adjust the payment for any fiscal year to reflect any error in the determinations under subparagraph (A) for any preceding fiscal year.

(4) Application of special rules. The provisions of section 1303 [42 USCS § 18023] shall apply to a State basic health program, and to standard health plans offered through such program, in the same manner as such rules apply to qualified health plans.

(e) Eligible individual. (1) In general. In this section, the term "eligible individual" means, with respect to any State, an individual—

(A) who a resident of the State who is not eligible to enroll in the State's Medicaid program under title XIX of the Social Security Act [42 USCS §§ 1396 et seq.] for benefits that at a minimum consist of the essential health benefits described in section 1302(b) [42 USCS § 18022(b)];

(B) whose household income exceeds 133 percent but does not exceed 200 percent of the poverty line for the size of the family involved, or, in the case of an alien lawfully present in the United States, whose income is not greater than 133 percent of the poverty line for the size of the family involved but who is not eligible for the Medicaid program under title XIX of the Social Security Act [42 USCS §§ 1396 et seq.] by reason of such alien status;

(C) who is not eligible for minimum essential coverage (as defined in section 5000A(f) of the Internal Revenue Code of 1986 [42 USCS § 5000A(f)]) or is eligible for an employer-sponsored plan that is not affordable coverage (as determined under section 5000A(e)(2) of such Code [42 USCS § 5000A(e)(2)]); and

(D) who has not attained age 65 as of the

beginning of the plan year.

Such term shall not include any individual who is not a qualified individual under section 1312 [42 USCS § 18032] who is eligible to be covered by a qualified health plan offered through an Exchange.

(2) Eligible individuals may not use exchange. An eligible individual shall not be treated as a qualified individual under section 1312 [42 USCS § 18032] eligible for enrollment in a qualified health plan offered through an Exchange established under section 1311 [42 USCS § 18031].

(f) Secretarial oversight. The Secretary shall each year conduct a review of each State program to ensure compliance with the requirements of this section, including ensuring that the State program meets—

(1) eligibility verification requirements for participation in the program;

(2) the requirements for use of Federal funds received by the program; and

(3) the quality and performance standards under this section.

(g) Standard health plan offerors. A State may provide that persons eligible to offer standard health plans under a basic health program established under this section may include a licensed health maintenance organization, a licensed health insurance insurer, or a network of health care providers established to offer services under the program.

(h) Definitions. Any term used in this section which is also used in section 36B of the Internal Revenue Code of 1986 [26 USCS § 36B] shall have the meaning given such term by such section.

(March 23, 2010, P. L. 111-148, Title I, Subtitle D, Part IV, § 1331, Title X, Subtitle A, § 10104(o), 124 Stat. 199, 902.)

§ 18052. Waiver for State innovation

(a) Application. (1) In general. A State may apply to the Secretary for the waiver of all or any requirements described in paragraph (2) with respect to health insurance coverage within that State for plan years beginning on or after January 1, 2017. Such application shall—

(A) be filed at such time and in such manner as the Secretary may require;

(B) contain such information as the Secretary may require, including—

(i) a comprehensive description of the State legislation and program to implement a plan meeting the requirements for a waiver under this section; and

(ii) a 10-year budget plan for such plan that is budget neutral for the Federal Government; and

(C) provide an assurance that the State has enacted the law described in subsection (b)(2).

(2) Requirements. The requirements described in this paragraph with respect to health insurance coverage within the State for plan years beginning on or after January 1, 2014, are as follows:

(A) Part I of subtitle D [42 USCS §§ 18021 et seq.].

(B) Part II of subtitle D [42 USCS §§ 18031 et seq.].

(C) Section 1402 [42 USCS § 18071].

(D) Sections 36B, 4980H, and 5000A of the Internal Revenue Code of 1986 [26 USCS §§ 36B, 4980H, and 5000A].

(3) Pass through of funding. With respect to a State waiver under paragraph (1), under which, due to the structure of the State plan, individuals and small employers in the State would not qualify for the premium tax credits, cost-sharing reductions, or small business credits under sections 36B of the Internal Revenue Code of 1986 [26 USCS § 36B] or under part I of subtitle E for which they would otherwise be eligible, the Secretary shall provide for an alternative means by which the aggregate amount of such credits or reductions that would have been paid on behalf of participants in the Exchanges established under this title had the State not received such waiver, shall be paid to the State for purposes of implementing the State plan under the waiver. Such amount shall be determined annually by the Secretary, taking into consideration the experience of other States with respect to participation in an Exchange and credits and reductions provided under such provisions to residents of the other States.

(4) Waiver consideration and transparency. (A) In general. An application for a waiver under this section shall be considered by the Secretary in accordance with the regulations described in subparagraph (B).

(B) Regulations. Not later than 180 days after the date of enactment of this Act [enacted March 23, 2010], the Secretary shall promulgate regulations relating to waivers under this section that provide—

(i) a process for public notice and comment at the State level, including public hearings, sufficient to ensure a meaningful level of public input;

(ii) a process for the submission of an application that ensures the disclosure of—

(I) the provisions of law that the State involved seeks to waive; and

(II) the specific plans of the State to ensure

that the waiver will be in compliance with subsection (b);

(iii) a process for providing public notice and comment after the application is received by the Secretary, that is sufficient to ensure a meaningful level of public input and that does not impose requirements that are in addition to, or duplicative of, requirements imposed under the Administrative Procedures Act, or requirements that are unreasonable or unnecessarily burdensome with respect to State compliance;

(iv) a process for the submission to the Secretary of periodic reports by the State concerning the implementation of the program under the waiver; and

(v) a process for the periodic evaluation by the Secretary of the program under the waiver.

(C) Report. The Secretary shall annually report to Congress concerning actions taken by the Secretary with respect to applications for waivers under this section.

(5) Coordinated waiver process. The Secretary shall develop a process for coordinating and consolidating the State waiver processes applicable under the provisions of this section, and the existing waiver processes applicable under titles XVIII, XIX, and XXI of the Social Security Act [42 USCS §§ 1395 et seq., 1396 et seq., and 1397aa et seq.], and any other Federal law relating to the provision of health care items or services. Such process shall permit a State to submit a single application for a waiver under any or all of such provisions.

(6) Definition. In this section, the term "Secretary" means—

(A) the Secretary of Health and Human Services with respect to waivers relating to the provisions described in subparagraph (A) through (C) of paragraph (2); and

(B) the Secretary of the Treasury with respect to waivers relating to the provisions described in paragraph (2)(D).

(b) Granting of waivers. (1) In general. The Secretary may grant a request for a waiver under subsection (a)(1) only if the Secretary determines that the State plan—

(A) will provide coverage that is at least as comprehensive as the coverage defined in section 1302(b) [42 USCS § 18022(b)] and offered through Exchanges established under this title as certified by Office of the Actuary of the Centers for Medicare & Medicaid Services based on sufficient data from the State and from comparable States about their experience with programs created by this Act and the provisions of this Act that would be waived;

(B) will provide coverage and cost sharing protections against excessive out-of-pocket spending that are at least as affordable as the provisions of this title would provide;

(C) will provide coverage to at least a comparable number of its residents as the provisions of this title would provide; and

(D) will not increase the Federal deficit.

(2) Requirement to enact a law. (A) In general. A law described in this paragraph is a State law that provides for State actions under a waiver under this section, including the implementation of the State plan under subsection (a)(1)(B).

(B) Termination of opt out. A State may repeal a law described in subparagraph (A) and terminate the authority provided under the waiver with respect to the State.

(c) Scope of waiver. (1) In general. The Secretary shall determine the scope of a waiver of a requirement described in subsection (a)(2) granted to a State under subsection (a)(1).

(2) Limitation. The Secretary may not waive under this section any Federal law or requirement that is not within the authority of the Secretary.

(d) Determinations by Secretary. (1) Time for determination. The Secretary shall make a determination under subsection (a)(1) not later than 180 days after the receipt of an application from a State under such subsection.

(2) Effect of determination. (A) Granting of waivers. If the Secretary determines to grant a waiver under subsection (a)(1), the Secretary shall notify the State involved of such determination and the terms and effectiveness of such waiver.

(B) Denial of waiver. If the Secretary determines a waiver should not be granted under subsection (a)(1), the Secretary shall notify the State involved, and the appropriate committees of Congress of such determination and the reasons therefore.

(e) Term of waiver. No waiver under this section may extend over a period of longer than 5 years unless the State requests continuation of such waiver, and such request shall be deemed granted unless the Secretary, within 90 days after the date of its submission to the Secretary, either denies such request in writing or informs the State in writing with respect to any additional information which is needed in order to make a final determination with respect to the request.

(March 23, 2010, P. L. 111-148, Title I, Subtitle D, Part IV, § 1332, 124 Stat. 203.)

§ 18053. Provisions relating to offering of plans in more than one State

(a) Health care choice compacts. (1) In general. Not later than July 1, 2013, the Secretary shall, in consultation with the National Association of Insurance Commissioners, issue regulations for the creation of health care choice compacts under which 2 or more States may enter into an agreement under which—

(A) 1 or more qualified health plans could be offered in the individual markets in all such States but, except as provided in subparagraph (B), only be subject to the laws and regulations of the State in which the plan was written or issued;

(B) the issuer of any qualified health plan to which the compact applies—

(i) would continue to be subject to market conduct, unfair trade practices, network adequacy, and consumer protection standards (including standards relating to rating), including addressing disputes as to the performance of the contract, of the State in which the purchaser resides;

(ii) would be required to be licensed in each State in which it offers the plan under the compact or to submit to the jurisdiction of each such State with regard to the standards described in clause (i) (including allowing access to records as if the insurer were licensed in the State); and

(iii) must clearly notify consumers that thc policy may not be subject to all the laws and regulations of the State in which the purchaser resides.

(2) State authority. A State may not enter into an agreement under this subsection unless the State enacts a law after the date of the enactment of this title that specifically authorizes the State to enter into such agreements.

(3) Approval of compacts. The Secretary may approve interstate health care choice compacts under paragraph (1) only if the Secretary determines that such health care choice compact—

(A) will provide coverage that is at least as comprehensive as the coverage defined in section 1302(b) and offered through Exchanges established under this title;

(B) will provide coverage and cost sharing protections against excessive out-of-pocket spending that are at least as affordable as the provisions of this title would provide;

(C) will provide coverage to at least a comparable number of its residents as the provisions of this title would provide;

(D) will not increase the Federal deficit; and

(E) will not weaken enforcement of laws and regulations described in paragraph (1)(B)(i) in any State that is included in such compact.

(4) Effective date. A health care choice compact described in paragraph (1) shall not take effect before January 1, 2016.

(b) [Deleted]

(March 23, 2010, P. L. 111-148, Title I, Subtitle D, Part IV, § 1333, Title X, Subtitle A, § 10104(p), 124 Stat. 206, 902.)

§ 18054. Multi-state plans

(a) Oversight by the Office of Personnel Management. (1) In general. The Director of the Office of Personnel Management (referred to in this section as the 'Director') shall enter into contracts with health insurance issuers (which may include a group of health insurance issuers affiliated either by common ownership and control or by the common use of a nationally licensed service mark), without regard to section 5 of title 41, United States Code, or other statutes requiring competitive bidding, to offer at least 2 multi-State qualified health plans through each Exchange in each State. Such plans shall provide individual, or in the case of small employers, group coverage.

(2) Terms. Each contract entered into under paragraph (1) shall be for a uniform term of at least 1 year, but may be made automatically renewable from term to term in the absence of notice of termination by either party. In entering into such contracts, the Director shall ensure that health benefits coverage is provided in accordance with the types of coverage provided for under section 2701(a)(1)(A)(i) of the Public Health Service Act [42 USCS § 300gg(a)(1)(A)(i)].

(3) Non-profit entities. In entering into contracts under paragraph (1), the Director shall ensure that at least one contract is entered into with a non-profit entity.

(4) Administration. The Director shall implement this subsection in a manner similar to the manner in which the Director implements the contracting provisions with respect to carriers under the Federal employees health benefit program under chapter 89 of title 5, United States Code [5 USCS §§ 8901 et seq.], including (through negotiating with each multi-state plan)—

(A) a medical loss ratio;

(B) a profit margin;

(C) the premiums to be charged; and

(D) such other terms and conditions of coverage as are in the interests of enrollees in such plans.

(5) Authority to protect consumers. The Director may prohibit the offering of any multi-State health plan that does not meet the terms and conditions defined by the Director with

respect to the elements described in subparagraphs (A) through (D) of paragraph (4).

(6) Assured availability of varied coverage. In entering into contracts under this subsection, the Director shall ensure that with respect to multi-State qualified health plans offered in an Exchange, there is at least one such plan that does not provide coverage of services described in section 1303(b)(1)(B)(i) [42 USCS § 18023(b)(1)(B)(i)].

(7) Withdrawal. Approval of a contract under this subsection may be withdrawn by the Director only after notice and opportunity for hearing to the issuer concerned without regard to subchapter II of chapter 5 and chapter 7 of title 5, United States Code [5 USCS §§ 551 et seq. and 701 et seq.].

(b) Eligibility. A health insurance issuer shall be eligible to enter into a contract under subsection (a)(1) if such issuer—

(1) agrees to offer a multi-State qualified health plan that meets the requirements of subsection (c) in each Exchange in each State;

(2) is licensed in each State and is subject to all requirements of State law not inconsistent with this section, including the standards and requirements that a State imposes that do not prevent the application of a requirement of part A of title XXVII of the Public Health Service Act [42 USCS §§ 300gg et seq.] or a requirement of this title;

(3) otherwise complies with the minimum standards prescribed for carriers offering health benefits plans under section 8902(e) of title 5, United States Code, to the extent that such standards do not conflict with a provision of this title; and

(4) meets such other requirements as determined appropriate by the Director, in consultation with the Secretary.

(c) Requirements for multi-State qualified health plan. (1) In general. A multi-State qualified health plan meets the requirements of this subsection if, in the determination of the Director—

(A) the plan offers a benefits package that is uniform in each State and consists of the essential benefits described in section 1302 [42 USCS § 18022];

(B) the plan meets all requirements of this title with respect to a qualified health plan, including requirements relating to the offering of the bronze, silver, and gold levels of coverage and catastrophic coverage in each State Exchange;

(C) except as provided in paragraph (5), the issuer provides for determinations of premiums for coverage under the plan on the basis of the rating requirements of part A of title XXVII of the Public Health Service Act [42 USCS §§ 300gg et seq.]; and

(D) the issuer offers the plan in all geographic regions, and in all States that have adopted adjusted community rating before the date of enactment of this Act [enacted March 23, 2010].

(2) States may offer additional benefits. Nothing in paragraph (1)(A) shall preclude a State from requiring that benefits in addition to the essential health benefits required under such paragraph be provided to enrollees of a multi-State qualified health plan offered in such State.

(3) Credits. (A) In general. An individual enrolled in a multi-State qualified health plan under this section shall be eligible for credits under section 36B of the Internal Revenue Code of 1986 [26 USCS § 36B] and cost sharing assistance under section 1402 [42 USCS § 18071] in the same manner as an individual who is enrolled in a qualified health plan.

(B) No additional federal cost. A requirement by a State under paragraph (2) that benefits in addition to the essential health benefits required under paragraph (1)(A) be provided to enrollees of a multi-State qualified health plan shall not affect the amount of a premium tax credit provided under section 36B of the Internal Revenue Code of 1986 [26 USCS § 36B] with respect to such plan.

(4) State must assume cost. A State shall make payments—

(A) to an individual enrolled in a multi-State qualified health plan offered in such State; or

(B) on behalf of an individual described in subparagraph (A) directly to the multi-State qualified health plan in which such individual is enrolled;

to defray the cost of any additional benefits described in paragraph (2).

(5) Application of certain state rating requirements. With respect to a multi-State qualified health plan that is offered in a State with age rating requirements that are lower than 3:1, the State may require that Exchanges operating in such State only permit the offering of such multi-State qualified health plans if such plans comply with the State's more protective age rating requirements.

(d) Plans deemed to be certified. A multi-State qualified health plan that is offered under a contract under subsection (a) shall be deemed to be certified by an Exchange for purposes of section 1311(d)(4)(A) [42 USCS § 18031(d)(4)(A)].

(e) Phase-in. Notwithstanding paragraphs

(1) and (2) of subsection (b), the Director shall enter into a contract with a health insurance issuer for the offering of a multi-State qualified health plan under subsection (a) if—

(1) with respect to the first year for which the issuer offers such plan, such issuer offers the plan in at least 60 percent of the States;

(2) with respect to the second such year, such issuer offers the plan in at least 70 percent of the States;

(3) with respect to the third such year, such issuer offers the plan in at least 85 percent of the States; and

(4) with respect to each subsequent year, such issuer offers the plan in all States.

(f) Applicability. The requirements under chapter 89 of title 5, United States Code [5 USCS §§ 8901 et seq.], applicable to health benefits plans under such chapter shall apply to multi-State qualified health plans provided for under this section to the extent that such requirements do not conflict with a provision of this title.

(g) Continued support for FEHBP. (1) Maintenance of effort. Nothing in this section shall be construed to permit the Director to allocate fewer financial or personnel resources to the functions of the Office of Personnel Management related to the administration of the Federal Employees Health Benefit Program under chapter 89 of title 5, United States Code [5 USCS §§ 8901 et seq.],.

(2) Separate risk pool. Enrollees in multi-State qualified health plans under this section shall be treated as a separate risk pool apart from enrollees in the Federal Employees Health Benefit Program under chapter 89 of title 5, United States Code [5 USCS §§ 8901 et seq.],.

(3) Authority to establish separate entities. The Director may establish such separate units or offices within the Office of Personnel Management as the Director determines to be appropriate to ensure that the administration of multi-State qualified health plans under this section does not interfere with the effective administration of the Federal Employees Health Benefit Program under chapter 89 of title 5, United States Code [5 USCS §§ 8901 et seq.],.

(4) Effective oversight. The Director may appoint such additional personnel as may be necessary to enable the Director to carry out activities under this section.

(5) Assurance of separate program. In carrying out this section, the Director shall ensure that the program under this section is separate from the Federal Employees Health Benefit Program under chapter 89 of title 5, United States Code [5 USCS §§ 8901 et seq.],. Premiums paid for coverage under a multi-State qualified health plan under this section shall not be considered to be Federal funds for any purposes.

(6) FEHBP plans not required to participate. Nothing in this section shall require that a carrier offering coverage under the Federal Employees Health Benefit Program under chapter 89 of title 5, United States Code [5 USCS §§ 8901 et seq.], also offer a multi-State qualified health plan under this section.

(h) Advisory board. The Director shall establish an advisory board to provide recommendations on the activities described in this section. A significant percentage of the members of such board shall be comprised of enrollees in a multi-State qualified health plan, or representatives of such enrollees.

(i) Authorization of appropriations. There is authorized to be appropriated, such sums as may be necessary to carry out this section.

(March 23, 2010, P. L. 111-148, Title I, Subtitle D, Part IV, § 1334, as added Title X, Subtitle A, § 10104(q), 124 Stat. 902.)

REINSURANCE AND RISK ADJUSTMENT

§ 18061. Transitional reinsurance program for individual market in each State

(a) In general. Each State shall, not later than January 1, 2014—

(1) include in the Federal standards or State law or regulation the State adopts and has in effect under section 1321(b) [42 USCS § 18041(b)] the provisions described in subsection (b); and

(2) establish (or enter into a contract with) 1 or more applicable reinsurance entities to carry out the reinsurance program under this section.

(b) Model regulation. (1) In general. In establishing the Federal standards under section 1321(a) [42 USCS § 18041(a)], the Secretary, in consultation with the National Association of Insurance Commissioners (the "NAIC"), shall include provisions that enable States to establish and maintain a program under which—

(A) health insurance issuers, and third party administrators on behalf of group health plans, are required to make payments to an applicable reinsurance entity for any plan year beginning in the 3-year period beginning January 1, 2014 (as specified in paragraph (3); and

(B) the applicable reinsurance entity collects

payments under subparagraph (A) and uses amounts so collected to make reinsurance payments to health insurance issuers described in subparagraph (A) that cover high risk individuals in the individual market (excluding grandfathered health plans) for any plan year beginning in such 3-year period.

(2) High-risk individual; payment amounts. The Secretary shall include the following in the provisions under paragraph (1):

(A) Determination of high-risk individuals. The method by which individuals will be identified as high risk individuals for purposes of the reinsurance program established under this section. Such method shall provide for identification of individuals as high-risk individuals on the basis of—

(i) a list of at least 50 but not more than 100 medical conditions that are identified as high-risk conditions and that may be based on the identification of diagnostic and procedure codes that are indicative of individuals with pre-existing, high-risk conditions; or

(ii) any other comparable objective method of identification recommended by the American Academy of Actuaries.

(B) Payment amount. The formula for determining the amount of payments that will be paid to health insurance issuers described in paragraph (1)(B) that insure high-risk individuals. Such formula shall provide for the equitable allocation of available funds through reconciliation and may be designed—

(i) to provide a schedule of payments that specifies the amount that will be paid for each of the conditions identified under subparagraph (A); or

(ii) to use any other comparable method for determining payment amounts that is recommended by the American Academy of Actuaries and that encourages the use of care coordination and care management programs for high risk conditions.

(3) Determination of required contributions. (A) In general. The Secretary shall include in the provisions under paragraph (1) the method for determining the amount each health insurance issuer and group health plan described in paragraph (1)(A) contributing to the reinsurance program under this section is required to contribute under such paragraph for each plan year beginning in the 36-month period beginning January 1, 2014. The contribution amount for any plan year may be based on the percentage of revenue of each issuer and the total costs of providing benefits to enrollees in self-insured plans or on a specified amount per enrollee and may be required to be paid in advance or periodically throughout the plan year.

(B) Specific requirements. The method under this paragraph shall be designed so that—

(i) the contribution amount for each issuer proportionally reflects each issuer's fully insured commercial book of business for all major medical products and the total value of all fees charged by the issuer and the costs of coverage administered by the issuer as a third party administrator;

(ii) the contribution amount can include an additional amount to fund the administrative expenses of the applicable reinsurance entity;

(iii) the aggregate contribution amounts for all States shall, based on the best estimates of the NAIC and without regard to amounts described in clause (ii), equal $10,000,000,000 for plan years beginning in 2014, $6,000,000,000 for plan years beginning 2015, and $4,000,000,000 for plan years beginning in 2016; and

(iv) in addition to the aggregate contribution amounts under clause (iii), each issuer's contribution amount for any calendar year under clause (iii) reflects its proportionate share of an additional $2,000,000,000 for 2014, an additional $2,000,000,000 for 2015, and an additional $1,000,000,000 for 2016.

Nothing in this subparagraph shall be construed to preclude a State from collecting additional amounts from issuers on a voluntary basis.

(4) Expenditure of funds. The provisions under paragraph (1) shall provide that—

(A) the contribution amounts collected for any calendar year may be allocated and used in any of the three calendar years for which amounts are collected based on the reinsurance needs of a particular period or to reflect experience in a prior period; and

(B) amounts remaining unexpended as of December, 2016, may be used to make payments under any reinsurance program of a State in the individual market in effect in the 2-year period beginning on January 1, 2017.

Notwithstanding the preceding sentence, any contribution amounts described in paragraph (3)(B)(iv) shall be deposited into the general fund of the Treasury of the United States and may not be used for the program established under this section.

(c) Applicable reinsurance entity. For purposes of this section—

(1) In general. The term "applicable reinsurance entity" means a not-for-profit organization—

(A) the purpose of which is to help stabilize premiums for coverage in the individual market in a State during the first 3 years of operation of an Exchange for such markets within the State when the risk of adverse selection related to new rating rules and market changes is greatest; and

(B) the duties of which shall be to carry out the reinsurance program under this section by coordinating the funding and operation of the risk-spreading mechanisms designed to implement the reinsurance program.

(2) State discretion. A State may have more than 1 applicable reinsurance entity to carry out the reinsurance program under this section within the State and 2 or more States may enter into agreements to provide for an applicable reinsurance entity to carry out such program in all such States.

(3) Entities are tax-exempt. An applicable reinsurance entity established under this section shall be exempt from taxation under chapter 1 of the Internal Revenue Code of 1986 [26 USCS §§ 1 et seq.]. The preceding sentence shall not apply to the tax imposed by section 511 such Code [26 USCS § 511] (relating to tax on unrelated business taxable income of an exempt organization).

(d) Coordination with State high-risk pools. The State shall eliminate or modify any State high-risk pool to the extent necessary to carry out the reinsurance program established under this section. The State may coordinate the State high-risk pool with such program to the extent not inconsistent with the provisions of this section.

(March 23, 2010, P. L. 111-148, Title I, Subtitle D, Part V, § 1341, Title X, Subtitle A, § 10104(r), 124 Stat. 208, 906.)

§ 18062. Establishment of risk corridors for plans in individual and small group markets

(a) In general. The Secretary shall establish and administer a program of risk corridors for calendar years 2014, 2015, and 2016 under which a qualified health plan offered in the individual or small group market shall participate in a payment adjustment system based on the ratio of the allowable costs of the plan to the plan's aggregate premiums. Such program shall be based on the program for regional participating provider organizations under part D of title XVIII of the Social Security Act [42 USCS §§ 1395w-101 et seq.].

(b) Payment methodology. (1) Payments out. The Secretary shall provide under the program established under subsection (a) that if—

(A) a participating plan's allowable costs for any plan year are more than 103 percent but not more than 108 percent of the target amount, the Secretary shall pay to the plan an amount equal to 50 percent of the target amount in excess of 103 percent of the target amount; and

(B) a participating plan's allowable costs for any plan year are more than 108 percent of the target amount, the Secretary shall pay to the plan an amount equal to the sum of 2.5 percent of the target amount plus 80 percent of allowable costs in excess of 108 percent of the target amount.

(2) Payments in. The Secretary shall provide under the program established under subsection (a) that if—

(A) a participating plan's allowable costs for any plan year are less than 97 percent but not less than 92 percent of the target amount, the plan shall pay to the Secretary an amount equal to 50 percent of the excess of 97 percent of the target amount over the allowable costs; and

(B) a participating plan's allowable costs for any plan year are less than 92 percent of the target amount, the plan shall pay to the Secretary an amount equal to the sum of 2.5 percent of the target amount plus 80 percent of the excess of 92 percent of the target amount over the allowable costs.

(c) Definitions. In this section:

(1) Allowable costs. (A) In general. The amount of allowable costs of a plan for any year is an amount equal to the total costs (other than administrative costs) of the plan in providing benefits covered by the plan.

(B) Reduction for risk adjustment and reinsurance payments. Allowable costs shall [be] reduced by any risk adjustment and reinsurance payments received under section 1341 and 1343 [42 USCS §§ 18061 and 18063].

(2) Target amount. The target amount of a plan for any year is an amount equal to the total premiums (including any premium subsidies under any governmental program), reduced by the administrative costs of the plan.

(March 23, 2010, P. L. 111-148, Title I, Subtitle D, Part V, § 1342, 124 Stat. 211.)

§ 18063. Risk adjustment

(a) In general. (1) Low actuarial risk plans. Using the criteria and methods developed under subsection (b), each State shall assess a charge on health plans and health insurance issuers (with respect to health insurance coverage) described in subsection (c) if the actuarial risk of the enrollees of such plans or coverage for a year is less than the average actuarial risk of all enrollees in all plans or coverage in such State for such year that are not self-insured group health plans (which are subject to the provisions of the Employee Retirement Income Security Act of 1974).

(2) High actuarial risk plans. Using the criteria and methods developed under subsection (b), each State shall provide a payment to health plans and health insurance issuers (with respect to health insurance coverage) described in subsection (c) if the actuarial risk of the enrollees of such plans or coverage for a year is greater than the average actuarial risk of all enrollees in all plans and coverage in such State for such year that are not self-insured group health plans (which are subject to the provisions of the Employee Retirement Income Security Act of 1974).

(b) Criteria and methods. The Secretary, in consultation with States, shall establish criteria and methods to be used in carrying out the risk adjustment activities under this section. The Secretary may utilize criteria and methods similar to the criteria and methods utilized under part C or D of title XVIII of the Social Security Act [42 USCS §§ 1395w-21 et seq. or 1395w-101 et seq.]. Such criteria and methods shall be included in the standards and requirements the Secretary prescribes under section 1321 [42 USCS § 18041].

(c) Scope. A health plan or a health insurance issuer is described in this subsection if such health plan or health insurance issuer provides coverage in the individual or small group market within the State. This subsection shall not apply to a grandfathered health plan or the issuer of a grandfathered health plan with respect to that plan.

(March 23, 2010, P. L. 111-148, Title I, Subtitle D, Part V, § 1343, 124 Stat. 212.)

AFFORDABLE COVERAGE CHOICES FOR ALL AMERICANS

COST-SHARING REDUCTIONS

§ 18071. Reduced cost-sharing for individuals enrolling in qualified health plans

(a) In general. In the case of an eligible insured enrolled in a qualified health plan—

(1) the Secretary shall notify the issuer of the plan of such eligibility; and

(2) the issuer shall reduce the cost-sharing under the plan at the level and in the manner specified in subsection (c).

(b) Eligible insured. In this section, the term "eligible insured" means an individual—

(1) who enrolls in a qualified health plan in the silver level of coverage in the individual market offered through an Exchange; and

(2) whose household income exceeds 100 percent but does not exceed 400 percent of the poverty line for a family of the size involved.In the case of an individual described in section 36B(c)(1)(B) of the Internal Revenue Code of 1986 [26 USCS § 36B(c)(1)(B)], the individual shall be treated as having household income equal to 100 percent for purposes of applying this section.

(c) Determination of reduction in cost-sharing. (1) Reduction in out-of-pocket limit. (A) In general. The reduction in cost-sharing under this subsection shall first be achieved by reducing the applicable out-of pocket limit under section 1302(c)(1) [42 USCS § 18022(c)(1)] in the case of—

(i) an eligible insured whose household income is more than 100 percent but not more than 200 percent of the poverty line for a family of the size involved, by two-thirds;

(ii) an eligible insured whose household income is more than 200 percent but not more than 300 percent of the poverty line for a family of the size involved, by one-half; and

(iii) an eligible insured whose household income is more than 300 percent but not more than 400 percent of the poverty line for a family of the size involved, by one-third.

(B) Coordination with actuarial value limits. (i) In general. The Secretary shall ensure the reduction under this paragraph shall not result in an increase in the plan's share of the total allowed costs of benefits provided under the plan above—

(I) 94 percent in the case of an eligible insured described in paragraph (2)(A);

(II) 87 percent in the case of an eligible insured described in paragraph (2)(B);

(III) 73 percent in the case of an eligible insured whose household income is more than 200 percent but not more than 250 percent of the poverty line for a family of the size involved; and

(IV) 70 percent in the case of an eligible insured whose household income is more than 250 percent but not more than 400 percent of the poverty line for a family of the size involved.

(ii) Adjustment. The Secretary shall adjust the out-of pocket limits under paragraph (1) if necessary to ensure that such limits do not cause the respective actuarial values to exceed the levels specified in clause (i).

(2) Additional reduction for lower income insureds. The Secretary shall establish proce-

dures under which the issuer of a qualified health plan to which this section applies shall further reduce cost-sharing under the plan in a manner sufficient to—

(A) in the case of an eligible insured whose household income is not less than 100 percent but not more than 150 percent of the poverty line for a family of the size involved, increase the plan's share of the total allowed costs of benefits provided under the plan to 94 percent of such costs;

(B) in the case of an eligible insured whose household income is more than 150 percent but not more than 200 percent of the poverty line for a family of the size involved, increase the plan's share of the total allowed costs of benefits provided under the plan to 87 percent of such costs; and

(C) in the case of an eligible insured whose household income is more than 200 percent but not more than 250 percent of the poverty line for a family of the size involved, increase the plan's share of the total allowed costs of benefits provided under the plan to 73 percent of such costs.

(3) Methods for reducing cost-sharing. (A) In general. An issuer of a qualified health plan making reductions under this subsection shall notify the Secretary of such reductions and the Secretary shall make periodic and timely payments to the issuer equal to the value of the reductions.

(B) Capitated payments. The Secretary may establish a capitated payment system to carry out the payment of cost-sharing reductions under this section. Any such system shall take into account the value of the reductions and make appropriate risk adjustments to such payments.

(4) Additional benefits. If a qualified health plan under section 1302(b)(5) [42 USCS § 18022(b)(5)] offers benefits in addition to the essential health benefits required to be provided by the plan, or a State requires a qualified health plan under section 1311(d)(3)(B) [42 USCS § 18031(d)(3)(B)] to cover benefits in addition to the essential health benefits required to be provided by the plan, the reductions in cost-sharing under this section shall not apply to such additional benefits.

(5) Special rule for pediatric dental plans. If an individual enrolls in both a qualified health plan and a plan described in section 1311(d)(2)(B)(ii)(I) [42 USCS § 18031(d)(2)(B)(ii)(I)] for any plan year, subsection (a) shall not apply to that portion of any reduction in cost-sharing under subsection (c) that (under regulations prescribed by the Secretary) is properly allocable to pediatric dental benefits which are included in the essential health benefits required to be provided by a qualified health plan under section 1302(b)(1)(J) [42 USCS § 18022(b)(1)(J)].

(d) Special rules for Indians. (1) Indians under 300 percent of poverty. If an individual enrolled in any qualified health plan in the individual market through an Exchange is an Indian (as defined in section 4(d) of the Indian Self-Determination and Education Assistance Act (25 U.S.C. 450b(d))) whose household income is not more than 300 percent of the poverty line for a family of the size involved, then, for purposes of this section—

(A) such individual shall be treated as an eligible insured; and

(B) the issuer of the plan shall eliminate any cost-sharing under the plan.

(2) Items or services furnished through Indian health providers. If an Indian (as so defined) enrolled in a qualified health plan is furnished an item or service directly by the Indian Health Service, an Indian Tribe, Tribal Organization, or Urban Indian Organization or through referral under contract health services—

(A) no cost-sharing under the plan shall be imposed under the plan for such item or service; and

(B) the issuer of the plan shall not reduce the payment to any such entity for such item or service by the amount of any cost-sharing that would be due from the Indian but for subparagraph (A).

(3) Payment. The Secretary shall pay to the issuer of a qualified health plan the amount necessary to reflect the increase in actuarial value of the plan required by reason of this subsection.

(e) Rules for individuals not lawfully present. (1) In general. If an individual who is an eligible insured is not lawfully present—

(A) no cost-sharing reduction under this section shall apply with respect to the individual; and

(B) for purposes of applying this section, the determination as to what percentage a taxpayer's household income bears to the poverty level for a family of the size involved shall be made under one of the following methods:

(i) A method under which—

(I) the taxpayer's family size is determined by not taking such individuals into account, and

(II) the taxpayer's household income is equal to the product of the taxpayer's household income (determined without regard to this subsection) and a fraction—

(aa) the numerator of which is the poverty line for the taxpayer's family size determined after application of subclause (I), and

(bb) the denominator of which is the poverty line for the taxpayer's family size determined without regard to subclause (I).

(ii) A comparable method reaching the same result as the method under clause (i).

(2) Lawfully present. For purposes of this section, an individual shall be treated as lawfully present only if the individual is, and is reasonably expected to be for the entire period of enrollment for which the cost-sharing reduction under this section is being claimed, a citizen or national of the United States or an alien lawfully present in the United States.

(3) Secretarial authority. The Secretary, in consultation with the Secretary of the Treasury, shall prescribe rules setting forth the methods by which calculations of family size and household income are made for purposes of this subsection. Such rules shall be designed to ensure that the least burden is placed on individuals enrolling in qualified health plans through an Exchange and taxpayers eligible for the credit allowable under this section.

(f) Definitions and special rules. In this section:

(1) In general. Any term used in this section which is also used in section 36B of the Internal Revenue Code of 1986 [26 USCS § 36B] shall have the meaning given such term by such section.

(2) Limitations on reduction. No cost-sharing reduction shall be allowed under this section with respect to coverage for any month unless the month is a coverage month with respect to which a credit is allowed to the insured (or an applicable taxpayer on behalf of the insured) under section 36B of such Code [26 USCS § 36B].

(3) Data used for eligibility. Any determination under this section shall be made on the basis of the taxable year for which the advance determination is made under section 1412 [42 USCS § 18082] and not the taxable year for which the credit under section 36B of such Code [26 USCS § 36B] is allowed.

(March 23, 2010, P. L. 111-148, Title I, Subtitle E, Part I, Subpart A, § 1402, 124 Stat. 220; March 30, 2010, P. L. 111-152, Title I, Subtitle A, § 1001(b), 124 Stat. 1031.)

ELIGIBILITY DETERMINATIONS

§ 18081. Procedures for determining eligibility for exchange participation, premium tax credits and reduced cost-sharing, and individual responsibility exemptions

(a) Establishment of program. The Secretary shall establish a program meeting the requirements of this section for determining—

(1) whether an individual who is to be covered in the individual market by a qualified health plan offered through an Exchange, or who is claiming a premium tax credit or reduced cost-sharing, meets the requirements of sections 1312(f)(3), 1402(e), and 1412(d) of this title [42 USCS §§ 18032(f)(3), 18071(e), and 18082(d)] and section 36B(e) of the Internal Revenue Code of 1986 [26 USCS § 36B(e)] that the individual be a citizen or national of the United States or an alien lawfully present in the United States;

(2) in the case of an individual claiming a premium tax credit or reduced cost-sharing under section 36B of such Code [26 USCS § 36B] or section 1402 [42 USCS § 18071]—

(A) whether the individual meets the income and coverage requirements of such sections; and

(B) the amount of the tax credit or reduced cost-sharing;

(3) whether an individual's coverage under an employer-sponsored health benefits plan is treated as unaffordable under sections 36B(c)(2)(C) and 5000A(e)(2) [26 USCS §§ 36B(c)(2)(C) and 5000A(e)(2)]; and

(4) whether to grant a certification under section 1311(d)(4)(H) [42 USCS § 18031(d)(4)(H)] attesting that, for purposes of the individual responsibility requirement under section 5000A of the Internal Revenue Code of 1986 [26 USCS § 5000A], an individual is entitled to an exemption from either the individual responsibility requirement or the penalty imposed by such section.

(b) Information required to be provided by applicants. (1) In general. An applicant for enrollment in a qualified health plan offered through an Exchange in the individual market shall provide—

(A) the name, address, and date of birth of each individual who is to be covered by the plan (in this subsection referred to as an "enrollee"); and

(B) the information required by any of the following paragraphs that is applicable to an enrollee.

(2) Citizenship or immigration status. The following information shall be provided with respect to every enrollee:

(A) In the case of an enrollee whose eligibility is based on an attestation of citizenship of the enrollee, the enrollee's social security number.

(B) In the case of an individual whose eligibility is based on an attestation of the enrollee's immigration status, the enrollee's social security number (if applicable) and such identifying information with respect to the enrollee's immigration status as the Secretary, after consultation with the Secretary of Homeland Security, determines appropriate.

(3) Eligibility and amount of tax credit or reduced cost-sharing. In the case of an enrollee with respect to whom a premium tax credit or reduced cost-sharing under section 36B of such Code [26 USCS § 36B] or section 1402 [42 USCS § 18071] is being claimed, the following information:

(A) Information regarding income and family size. The information described in section 6103(l)(21) [26 USCS § 6103(l)(21)] for the taxable year ending with or within the second calendar year preceding the calendar year in which the plan year begins.

(B) Changes in circumstances. The information described in section 1412(b)(2) [42 USCS § 18082(b)(2)], including information with respect to individuals who were not required to file an income tax return for the taxable year described in subparagraph (A) or individuals who experienced changes in marital status or family size or significant reductions in income.

(4) Employer-sponsored coverage. In the case of an enrollee with respect to whom eligibility for a premium tax credit under section 36B of such Code [26 USCS § 36B] or cost-sharing reduction under section 1402 [42 USCS § 18071] is being established on the basis that the enrollee's (or related individual's) employer is not treated under section 36B(c)(2)(C) of such Code [26 USCS § 36B(c)(2)(C)] as providing minimum essential coverage or affordable minimum essential coverage, the following information:

(A) The name, address, and employer identification number (if available) of the employer.

(B) Whether the enrollee or individual is a full-time employee and whether the employer provides such minimum essential coverage.

(C) If the employer provides such minimum essential coverage, the lowest cost option for the enrollee's or individual's enrollment status and the enrollee's or individual's required contribution (within the meaning of section 5000A(e)(1)(B) of such Code [26 USCS § 5000A(e)(1)(B)]) under the employer-sponsored plan.

(D) If an enrollee claims an employer's minimum essential coverage is unaffordable, the information described in paragraph (3).

If an enrollee changes employment or obtains additional employment while enrolled in a qualified health plan for which such credit or reduction is allowed, the enrollee shall notify the Exchange of such change or additional employment and provide the information described in this paragraph with respect to the new employer.

(5) Exemptions from individual responsibility requirements. In the case of an individual who is seeking an exemption certificate under section 1311(d)(4)(H) [42 USCS § 18031(d)(4)(H)] from any requirement or penalty imposed by section 5000A [26 USCS § 5000A], the following information:

(A) In the case of an individual seeking exemption based on the individual's status as a member of an exempt religious sect or division, as a member of a health care sharing ministry, as an Indian, or as an individual eligible for a hardship exemption, such information as the Secretary shall prescribe.

(B) In the case of an individual seeking exemption based on the lack of affordable coverage or the individual's status as a taxpayer with household income less than 100 percent of the poverty line, the information described in paragraphs (3) and (4), as applicable.

(c) Verification of information contained in records of specific Federal officials. (1) Information transferred to secretary. An Exchange shall submit the information provided by an applicant under subsection (b) to the Secretary for verification in accordance with the requirements of this subsection and subsection (d).

(2) Citizenship or immigration status. (A) Commissioner of Social Security. The Secretary shall submit to the Commissioner of Social Security the following information for a determination as to whether the information provided is consistent with the information in the records of the Commissioner:

(i) The name, date of birth, and social security number of each individual for whom such information was provided under subsection (b)(2).

(ii) The attestation of an individual that the individual is a citizen.

(B) Secretary of Homeland Security. (i) In general. In the case of an individual—

(I) who attests that the individual is an alien lawfully present in the United States; or

(II) who attests that the individual is a citizen but with respect to whom the Commissioner of Social Security has notified the Secretary under subsection (e)(3) that the attestation is inconsistent with information in the records maintained by the Commissioner;

the Secretary shall submit to the Secretary of Homeland Security the information described in clause (ii) for a determination as to whether the information provided is consistent with the information in the records of the Secretary of Homeland Security.

(ii) Information. The information described in clause (ii) is the following:

(I) The name, date of birth, and any identifying information with respect to the individual's immigration status provided under subsection (b)(2).

(II) The attestation that the individual is an alien lawfully present in the United States or in the case of an individual described in clause (i)(II), the attestation that the individual is a citizen.

(3) Eligibility for tax credit and cost-sharing reduction. The Secretary shall submit the information described in subsection (b)(3)(A) provided under paragraph (3), (4), or (5) of subsection (b) to the Secretary of the Treasury for verification of household income and family size for purposes of eligibility.

(4) Methods. (A) In general. The Secretary, in consultation with the Secretary of the Treasury, the Secretary of Homeland Security, and the Commissioner of Social Security, shall provide that verifications and determinations under this subsection shall be done—

(i) through use of an on-line system or otherwise for the electronic submission of, and response to, the information submitted under this subsection with respect to an applicant; or

(ii) by determining the consistency of the information submitted with the information maintained in the records of the Secretary of the Treasury, the Secretary of Homeland Security, or the Commissioner of Social Security through such other method as is approved by the Secretary.

(B) Flexibility. The Secretary may modify the methods used under the program established by this section for the Exchange and verification of information if the Secretary determines such modifications would reduce the administrative costs and burdens on the applicant, including allowing an applicant to request the Secretary of the Treasury to provide the information described in paragraph (3) directly to the Exchange or to the Secretary. The Secretary shall not make any such modification unless the Secretary determines that any applicable requirements under this section and section 6103 of the Internal Revenue Code of 1986 [26 USCS § 6103] with respect to the confidentiality, disclosure, maintenance, or use of information will be met.

(d) Verification by Secretary. In the case of information provided under subsection (b) that is not required under subsection (c) to be submitted to another person for verification, the Secretary shall verify the accuracy of such information in such manner as the Secretary determines appropriate, including delegating responsibility for verification to the Exchange.

(e) Actions relating to verification. (1) In general. Each person to whom the Secretary provided information under subsection (c) shall report to the Secretary under the method established under subsection (c)(4) the results of its verification and the Secretary shall notify the Exchange of such results. Each person to whom the Secretary provided information under subsection (d) shall report to the Secretary in such manner as the Secretary determines appropriate.

(2) Verification. (A) Eligibility for enrollment and premium tax credits and cost-sharing reductions. If information provided by an applicant under paragraphs (1), (2), (3), and (4) of subsection (b) is verified under subsections (c) and (d)—

(i) the individual's eligibility to enroll through the Exchange and to apply for premium tax credits and cost-sharing reductions shall be satisfied; and

(ii) the Secretary shall, if applicable, notify the Secretary of the Treasury under section 1412(c) [42 USCS § 18082(c)] of the amount of any advance payment to be made.

(B) Exemption from individual responsibility. If information provided by an applicant under subsection (b)(5) is verified under subsections (c) and (d), the Secretary shall issue the certification of exemption described in section 1311(d)(4)(H) [42 USCS § 18031(d)(4)(H)].

(3) Inconsistencies involving attestation of citizenship or lawful presence. If the information provided by any applicant under subsection (b)(2) is inconsistent with information in the records maintained by the Commissioner of Social Security or Secretary of Homeland Security, whichever is applicable, the applicant's eligibility will be determined in the same manner as an individual's eligibility under the Medicaid program is determined under section 1902(ee) of the Social Security Act [42 USCS § 1396a(ee)] (as in effect on January 1, 2010).

(4) Inconsistencies involving other information. (A) In general. If the information provided by an applicant under subsection (b) (other than subsection (b)(2)) is inconsistent with information in the records maintained by

persons under subsection (c) or is not verified under subsection (d), the Secretary shall notify the Exchange and the Exchange shall take the following actions:

(i) Reasonable effort. The Exchange shall make a reasonable effort to identify and address the causes of such inconsistency, including through typographical or other clerical errors, by contacting the applicant to confirm the accuracy of the information, and by taking such additional actions as the Secretary, through regulation or other guidance, may identify.

(ii) Notice and opportunity to correct. In the case the inconsistency or inability to verify is not resolved under subparagraph (A), the Exchange shall—

(I) notify the applicant of such fact;

(II) provide the applicant an opportunity to either present satisfactory documentary evidence or resolve the inconsistency with the person verifying the information under subsection (c) or (d) during the 90-day period beginning the date on which the notice required under subclause (I) is sent to the applicant.

The Secretary may extend the 90-day period under subclause (II) for enrollments occurring during 2014.

(B) Specific actions not involving citizenship or lawful presence. (i) In general. Except as provided in paragraph (3), the Exchange shall, during any period before the close of the period under subparagraph (A)(ii)(II), make any determination under paragraphs (2), (3), and (4) of subsection (a) on the basis of the information contained on the application.

(ii) Eligibility or amount of credit or reduction. If an inconsistency involving the eligibility for, or amount of, any premium tax credit or cost-sharing reduction is unresolved under this subsection as of the close of the period under subparagraph (A)(ii)(II), the Exchange shall notify the applicant of the amount (if any) of the credit or reduction that is determined on the basis of the records maintained by persons under subsection (c).

(iii) Employer affordability. If the Secretary notifies an Exchange that an enrollee is eligible for a premium tax credit under section 36B of such Code [26 USCS § 36B] or cost-sharing reduction under section 1402 [42 USCS § 18071] because the enrollee's (or related individual's) employer does not provide minimum essential coverage through an employer-sponsored plan or that the employer does provide that coverage but it is not affordable coverage, the Exchange shall notify the employer of such fact and that the employer may be liable for the payment assessed under section 4980H of such Code [26 USCS § 4980H].

(iv) Exemption. In any case where the inconsistency involving, or inability to verify, information provided under subsection (b)(5) is not resolved as of the close of the period under subparagraph (A)(ii)(II), the Exchange shall notify an applicant that no certification of exemption from any requirement or payment under section 5000A of such Code [26 USCS § 5000A] will be issued.

(C) Appeals process. The Exchange shall also notify each person receiving notice under this paragraph of the appeals processes established under subsection (f).

(f) Appeals and redeterminations. (1) In general. The Secretary, in consultation with the Secretary of the Treasury, the Secretary of Homeland Security, and the Commissioner of Social Security, shall establish procedures by which the Secretary or one of such other Federal officers—

(A) hears and makes decisions with respect to appeals of any determination under subsection (e); and

(B) redetermines eligibility on a periodic basis in appropriate circumstances.

(2) Employer liability. (A) In general. The Secretary shall establish a separate appeals process for employers who are notified under subsection (e)(4)(C) that the employer may be liable for a tax imposed by section 4980H of the Internal Revenue Code of 1986 [26 USCS § 4980H] with respect to an employee because of a determination that the employer does not provide minimum essential coverage through an employer-sponsored plan or that the employer does provide that coverage but it is not affordable coverage with respect to an employee. Such process shall provide an employer the opportunity to—

(i) present information to the Exchange for review of the determination either by the Exchange or the person making the determination, including evidence of the employer-sponsored plan and employer contributions to the plan; and

(ii) have access to the data used to make the determination to the extent allowable by law.

Such process shall be in addition to any rights of appeal the employer may have under subtitle F of such Code [26 USCS §§ 6001 et seq.].

(B) Confidentiality. Notwithstanding any provision of this title (or the amendments made by this title) or section 6103 of the Internal Revenue Code of 1986 [26 USCS § 6103], an employer shall not be entitled to any taxpayer return information with respect to an employee for purposes of determining whether the employer is subject to the penalty under section 4980H of such Code [26 USCS § 4980H] with respect to the employee, except that—

(i) the employer may be notified as to the name of an employee and whether or not the employee's income is above or below the threshold by which the affordability of an employer's health insurance coverage is measured; and

(ii) this subparagraph shall not apply to an employee who provides a waiver (at such time and in such manner as the Secretary may prescribe) authorizing an employer to have access to the employee's taxpayer return information.

(g) Confidentiality of applicant information. (1) In general. An applicant for insurance coverage or for a premium tax credit or cost-sharing reduction shall be required to provide only the information strictly necessary to authenticate identity, determine eligibility, and determine the amount of the credit or reduction.

(2) Receipt of information. Any person who receives information provided by an applicant under subsection (b) (whether directly or by another person at the request of the applicant), or receives information from a Federal agency under subsection (c), (d), or (e), shall—

(A) use the information only for the purposes of, and to the extent necessary in, ensuring the efficient operation of the Exchange, including verifying the eligibility of an individual to enroll through an Exchange or to claim a premium tax credit or cost-sharing reduction or the amount of the credit or reduction; and

(B) not disclose the information to any other person except as provided in this section.

(h) Penalties. (1) False or fraudulent information. (A) Civil penalty. (i) In general. If—

(I) any person fails to provides correct information under subsection (b); and

(II) such failure is attributable to negligence or disregard of any rules or regulations of the Secretary,

such person shall be subject, in addition to any other penalties that may be prescribed by law, to a civil penalty of not more than $25,000 with respect to any failures involving an application for a plan year. For purposes of this subparagraph, the terms "negligence" and "disregard" shall have the same meanings as when used in section 6662 of the Internal Revenue Code of 1986 [26 USCS § 6662].

(ii) Reasonable cause exception. No penalty shall be imposed under clause (i) if the Secretary determines that there was a reasonable cause for the failure and that the person acted in good faith.

(B) Knowing and willful violations. Any person who knowingly and willfully provides false or fraudulent information under subsection (b) shall be subject, in addition to any other penalties that may be prescribed by law, to a civil penalty of not more than $250,000.

(2) Improper use or disclosure of information. Any person who knowingly and willfully uses or discloses information in violation of subsection (g) shall be subject, in addition to any other penalties that may be prescribed by law, to a civil penalty of not more than $25,000.

(3) Limitations on liens and levies. The Secretary (or, if applicable, the Attorney General of the United States) shall not—

(A) file notice of lien with respect to any property of a person by reason of any failure to pay the penalty imposed by this subsection; or

(B) levy on any such property with respect to such failure.

(i) Study of administration of employer responsibility. (1) In general. The Secretary of Health and Human Services shall, in consultation with the Secretary of the Treasury, conduct a study of the procedures that are necessary to ensure that in the administration of this title and section 4980H of the Internal Revenue Code of 1986 [26 USCS § 4980H] (as added by section 1513) that the following rights are protected:

(A) The rights of employees to preserve their right to confidentiality of their taxpayer return information and their right to enroll in a qualified health plan through an Exchange if an employer does not provide affordable coverage.

(B) The rights of employers to adequate due process and access to information necessary to accurately determine any payment assessed on employers.

(2) Report. Not later than January 1, 2013, the Secretary of Health and Human Services shall report the results of the study conducted under paragraph (1), including any recommendations for legislative changes, to the Committees on Finance and Health, Education, Labor and Pensions of the Senate and the Committees of Education and Labor and Ways and Means of the House of Representatives.

(March 23, 2010, P. L. 111-148, Title I, Subtitle E, Part I, Subpart B, § 1411, 124 Stat. 224.)

§ 18082. Advance determination and payment of premium tax credits and cost-sharing reductions

(a) In general. The Secretary, in consultation with the Secretary of the Treasury, shall establish a program under which—

(1) upon request of an Exchange, advance determinations are made under section 1411 [42 USCS § 18081] with respect to the income eligibility of individuals enrolling in a qualified health plan in the individual market through the Exchange for the premium tax credit allowable under section 36B of the Internal Revenue Code of 1986 [26 USCS § 36B] and the cost-sharing reductions under section 1402 [42 USCS § 18071];

(2) the Secretary notifies—

(A) the Exchange and the Secretary of the Treasury of the advance determinations; and

(B) the Secretary of the Treasury of the name and employer identification number of each employer with respect to whom 1 or more employee of the employer were determined to be eligible for the premium tax credit under section 36B of the Internal Revenue Code of 1986 [26 USCS § 36B] and the cost-sharing reductions under section 1402 [42 USCS § 18071] because—

(i) the employer did not provide minimum essential coverage; or

(ii) the employer provided such minimum essential coverage but it was determined under section 36B(c)(2)(C) of such Code [26 USCS § 36B(c)(2)(C)] to either be unaffordable to the employee or not provide the required minimum actuarial value; and

(3) the Secretary of the Treasury makes advance payments of such credit or reductions to the issuers of the qualified health plans in order to reduce the premiums payable by individuals eligible for such credit.

(b) Advance determinations. (1) In general. The Secretary shall provide under the program established under subsection (a) that advance determination of eligibility with respect to any individual shall be made—

(A) during the annual open enrollment period applicable to the individual (or such other enrollment period as may be specified by the Secretary); and

(B) on the basis of the individual's household income for the most recent taxable year for which the Secretary, after consultation with the Secretary of the Treasury, determines information is available.

(2) Changes in circumstances. The Secretary shall provide procedures for making advance determinations on the basis of information other than that described in paragraph (1)(B) in cases where information included with an application form demonstrates substantial changes in income, changes in family size or other household circumstances, change in filing status, the filing of an application for unemployment benefits, or other significant changes affecting eligibility, including—

(A) allowing an individual claiming a decrease of 20 percent or more in income, or filing an application for unemployment benefits, to have eligibility for the credit determined on the basis of household income for a later period or on the basis of the individual's estimate of such income for the taxable year; and

(B) the determination of household income in cases where the taxpayer was not required to file a return of tax imposed by this chapter for the second preceding taxable year.

(c) Payment of premium tax credits and cost-sharing reductions. (1) In general. The Secretary shall notify the Secretary of the Treasury and the Exchange through which the individual is enrolling of the advance determination under section 1411 [42 USCS § 18081].

(2) Premium tax credit. (A) In general. The Secretary of the Treasury shall make the advance payment under this section of any premium tax credit allowed under section 36B of the Internal Revenue Code of 1986 [26 USCS § 36B] to the issuer of a qualified health plan on a monthly basis (or such other periodic basis as the Secretary may provide).

(B) Issuer responsibilities. An issuer of a qualified health plan receiving an advance payment with respect to an individual enrolled in the plan shall—

(i) reduce the premium charged the insured for any period by the amount of the advance payment for the period;

(ii) notify the Exchange and the Secretary of such reduction;

(iii) include with each billing statement the amount by which the premium for the plan has been reduced by reason of the advance payment; and

(iv) in the case of any nonpayment of premiums by the insured—

(I) notify the Secretary of such nonpayment; and

(II) allow a 3-month grace period for nonpayment of premiums before discontinuing coverage.

(3) Cost-sharing reductions. The Secretary shall also notify the Secretary of the Treasury and the Exchange under paragraph (1) if an advance payment of the cost-sharing reductions under section 1402 [42 USCS § 18071] is to be made to the issuer of any qualified health plan with respect to any individual enrolled in the plan. The Secretary of the Treasury shall make such advance payment at such time and in such amount as the Secretary specifies in the

notice.

(d) No Federal payments for individuals not lawfully present. Nothing in this subtitle or the amendments made by this subtitle allows Federal payments, credits, or cost-sharing reductions for individuals who are not lawfully present in the United States.

(e) State flexibility. Nothing in this subtitle or the amendments made by this subtitle shall be construed to prohibit a State from making payments to or on behalf of an individual for coverage under a qualified health plan offered through an Exchange that are in addition to any credits or cost-sharing reductions allowable to the individual under this subtitle and such amendments.

(March 23, 2010, P. L. 111-148, Title I, Subtitle E, Part I, Subpart B, § 1412, 124 Stat. 231.)

§ 18083. Streamlining of procedures for enrollment through an Exchange and State Medicaid, CHIP, and health subsidy programs

(a) In general. The Secretary shall establish a system meeting the requirements of this section under which residents of each State may apply for enrollment in, receive a determination of eligibility for participation in, and continue participation in, applicable State health subsidy programs. Such system shall ensure that if an individual applying to an Exchange is found through screening to be eligible for medical assistance under the State Medicaid plan under title XIX [42 USCS §§ 1396 et seq.], or eligible for enrollment under a State children's health insurance program (CHIP) under title XXI of such Act [42 USCS §§ 1397aa et seq.], the individual is enrolled for assistance under such plan or program.

(b) Requirements relating to forms and notice. (1) Requirements relating to forms. (A) In general. The Secretary shall develop and provide to each State a single, streamlined form that—

(i) may be used to apply for all applicable State health subsidy programs within the State;

(ii) may be filed online, in person, by mail, or by telephone;

(iii) may be filed with an Exchange or with State officials operating one of the other applicable State health subsidy programs; and

(iv) is structured to maximize an applicant's ability to complete the form satisfactorily, taking into account the characteristics of individuals who qualify for applicable State health subsidy programs.

(B) State authority to establish form. A State may develop and use its own single, streamlined form as an alternative to the form developed under subparagraph (A) if the alternative form is consistent with standards promulgated by the Secretary under this section.

(C) Supplemental eligibility forms. The Secretary may allow a State to use a supplemental or alternative form in the case of individuals who apply for eligibility that is not determined on the basis of the household income (as defined in section 36B of the Internal Revenue Code of 1986 [26 USCS § 36B]).

(2) Notice. The Secretary shall provide that an applicant filing a form under paragraph (1) shall receive notice of eligibility for an applicable State health subsidy program without any need to provide additional information or paperwork unless such information or paperwork is specifically required by law when information provided on the form is inconsistent with data used for the electronic verification under paragraph (3) or is otherwise insufficient to determine eligibility.

(c) Requirements relating to eligibility based on data exchanges. (1) Development of secure interfaces. Each State shall develop for all applicable State health subsidy programs a secure, electronic interface allowing an exchange of data (including information contained in the application forms described in subsection (b)) that allows a determination of eligibility for all such programs based on a single application. Such interface shall be compatible with the method established for data verification under section 1411(c)(4) [42 USCS § 18081(c)(4)].

(2) Data matching program. Each applicable State health subsidy program shall participate in a data matching arrangement for determining eligibility for participation in the program under paragraph (3) that—

(A) provides access to data described in paragraph (3);

(B) applies only to individuals who—

(i) receive assistance from an applicable State health subsidy program; or

(ii) apply for such assistance—

(I) by filing a form described in subsection (b); or

(II) by requesting a determination of eligibility and authorizing disclosure of the information described in paragraph (3) to applicable State health coverage subsidy programs for purposes of determining and establishing eligibility; and

(C) consistent with standards promulgated

by the Secretary, including the privacy and data security safeguards described in section 1942 of the Social Security Act [42 USCS § 1396w-2] or that are otherwise applicable to such programs.

(3) Determination of eligibility. (A) In general. Each applicable State health subsidy program shall, to the maximum extent practicable—

(i) establish, verify, and update eligibility for participation in the program using the data matching arrangement under paragraph (2); and

(ii) determine such eligibility on the basis of reliable, third party data, including information described in sections 1137, 453(i), and 1942(a) of the Social Security Act [42 USCS §§ 1320b-7, 653(i), and 1396w-2(a)], obtained through such arrangement.

(B) Exception. This paragraph shall not apply in circumstances with respect to which the Secretary determines that the administrative and other costs of use of the data matching arrangement under paragraph (2) outweigh its expected gains in accuracy, efficiency, and program participation.

(4) Secretarial standards. The Secretary shall, after consultation with persons in possession of the data to be matched and representatives of applicable State health subsidy programs, promulgate standards governing the timing, contents, and procedures for data matching described in this subsection. Such standards shall take into account administrative and other costs and the value of data matching to the establishment, verification, and updating of eligibility for applicable State health subsidy programs.

(d) Administrative authority. (1) Agreements. Subject to section 1411 [42 USCS § 18081] and section 6103(l)(21) of the Internal Revenue Code of 1986 [26 USCS § 6103(l)(21)] and any other requirement providing safeguards of privacy and data integrity, the Secretary may establish model agreements, and enter into agreements, for the sharing of data under this section.

(2) Authority of exchange to contract out. Nothing in this section shall be construed to—

(A) prohibit contractual arrangements through which a State Medicaid agency determines eligibility for all applicable State health subsidy programs, but only if such agency complies with the Secretary's requirements ensuring reduced administrative costs, eligibility errors, and disruptions in coverage; or

(B) change any requirement under title XIX [42 USCS §§ 1396 et seq.] that eligibility for participation in a State's Medicaid program must be determined by a public agency.

(e) Applicable State health subsidy program. In this section, the term "applicable State health subsidy program" means—

(1) the program under this title for the enrollment in qualified health plans offered through an Exchange, including the premium tax credits under section 36B of the Internal Revenue Code of 1986 [26 USCS § 36B] and cost-sharing reductions under section 1402 [42 USCS § 18071];

(2) a State Medicaid program under title XIX of the Social Security Act [42 USCS §§ 1396 et seq.];

(3) a State children's health insurance program (CHIP) under title XXI of such Act [42 USCS §§ 1397aa et seq.]; and

(4) a State program under section 1331 [42 USCS § 18051] establishing qualified basic health plans.

(March 23, 2010, P. L. 111-148, Title I, Subtitle E, Part I, Subpart B, § 1413, 124 Stat. 233.)

§ 18084. Premium tax credit and cost-sharing reduction payments disregarded for Federal and Federally-assisted programs

For purposes of determining the eligibility of any individual for benefits or assistance, or the amount or extent of benefits or assistance, under any Federal program or under any State or local program financed in whole or in part with Federal funds—

(1) any credit or refund allowed or made to any individual by reason of section 36B of the Internal Revenue Code of 1986 [26 USCS § 36B] (as added by section 1401) shall not be taken into account as income and shall not be taken into account as resources for the month of receipt and the following 2 months; and

(2) any cost-sharing reduction payment or advance payment of the credit allowed under such section 36B [26 USCS § 36B] that is made under section 1402 or 1412 [42 USCS § 18071 or 18082] shall be treated as made to the qualified health plan in which an individual is enrolled and not to that individual.

(March 23, 2010, P. L. 111-148, Title I, Subtitle E, Part I, Subpart B, § 1415, 124 Stat. 237.)

SHARED RESPONSIBILITY FOR HEALTH CARE

INDIVIDUAL RESPONSIBILITY

§ 18091. Requirement to maintain minimum essential coverage; congressional findings

Congress makes the following findings:

(1) In general. The individual responsibility requirement provided for in this section (in this subsection referred to as the "requirement") is commercial and economic in nature, and substantially affects interstate commerce, as a result of the effects described in paragraph (2).

(2) Effects on the national economy and interstate commerce. The effects described in this paragraph are the following:

(A) The requirement regulates activity that is commercial and economic in nature: economic and financial decisions about how and when health care is paid for, and when health insurance is purchased. In the absence of the requirement, some individuals would make an economic and financial decision to forego health insurance coverage and attempt to self-insure, which increases financial risks to households and medical providers.

(B) Health insurance and health care services are a significant part of the national economy. National health spending is projected to increase from $2,500,000,000,000, or 17.6 percent of the economy, in 2009 to $4,700,000,000,000 in 2019. Private health insurance spending is projected to be $854,000,000,000 in 2009, and pays for medical supplies, drugs, and equipment that are shipped in interstate commerce. Since most health insurance is sold by national or regional health insurance companies, health insurance is sold in interstate commerce and claims payments flow through interstate commerce.

(C) The requirement, together with the other provisions of this Act, will add millions of new consumers to the health insurance market, increasing the supply of, and demand for, health care services, and will increase the number and share of Americans who are insured.

(D) The requirement achieves near-universal coverage by building upon and strengthening the private employer-based health insurance system, which covers 176,000,000 Americans nationwide. In Massachusetts, a similar requirement has strengthened private employer-based coverage: despite the economic downturn, the number of workers offered employer-based coverage has actually increased.

(E) The economy loses up to $207,000,000,000 a year because of the poorer health and shorter lifespan of the uninsured. By significantly reducing the number of the uninsured, the requirement, together with the other provisions of this Act, will significantly reduce this economic cost.

(F) The cost of providing uncompensated care to the uninsured was $43,000,000,000 in 2008. To pay for this cost, health care providers pass on the cost to private insurers, which pass on the cost to families. This cost-shifting increases family premiums by on average over $1,000 a year. By significantly reducing the number of the uninsured, the requirement, together with the other provisions of this Act, will lower health insurance premiums.

(G) 62 percent of all personal bankruptcies are caused in part by medical expenses. By significantly increasing health insurance coverage, the requirement, together with the other provisions of this Act, will improve financial security for families.

(H) Under the Employee Retirement Income Security Act of 1974 (29 U.S.C. 1001 et seq.), the Public Health Service Act (42 U.S.C. 201 et seq.), and this Act, the Federal Government has a significant role in regulating health insurance. The requirement is an essential part of this larger regulation of economic activity, and the absence of the requirement would undercut Federal regulation of the health insurance market.

(I) Under sections 2704 and 2705 of the Public Health Service Act [42 USCS §§ 300gg-3 and 300gg-4] (as added by section 1201 of this Act), if there were no requirement, many individuals would wait to purchase health insurance until they needed care. By significantly increasing health insurance coverage, the requirement, together with the other provisions of this Act, will minimize this adverse selection and broaden the health insurance risk pool to include healthy individuals, which will lower health insurance premiums. The requirement is essential to creating effective health insurance markets in which improved health insurance products that are guaranteed issue and do not exclude coverage of pre-existing conditions can be sold.

(J) Administrative costs for private health insurance, which were $90,000,000,000 in 2006, are 26 to 30 percent of premiums in the current individual and small group markets. By significantly increasing health insurance coverage and the size of purchasing pools, which will increase economies of scale, the requirement, together with the other provisions of this Act, will significantly reduce administrative costs and lower health insurance premiums. The requirement is essential to creating effective health insurance markets that do not require underwriting and eliminate its associated administrative costs.

(3) Supreme court ruling. In United States v. South-Eastern Underwriters Association (322 U.S. 533 (1944)), the Supreme Court of the United States ruled that insurance is interstate commerce subject to Federal regulation.

(March 23, 2010, P. L. 111-148, Title I, Subtitle F, Part I, § 1501(a), Title X, Subtitle A, § 10106(a), 124 Stat. 242, 907.)

§ 18092. Notification of nonenrollment.

Not later than June 30 of each year, the Secretary of the Treasury, acting through the Internal Revenue Service and in consultation with the Secretary of Health and Human Services, shall send a notification to each individual who files an individual income tax return and who is not enrolled in minimum essential coverage (as defined in section 5000A of the Internal Revenue Code of 1986 [26 USCS § 5000A]). Such notification shall contain information on the services available through the Exchange operating in the State in which such individual resides.

(March 23, 2010, P. L. 111-148, Title I, Subtitle F, Part I, § 1502(c), 124 Stat. 251.)

EMPLOYER RESPONSIBIITIES

§ 18101. Free choice vouchers

(a) In general. An offering employer shall provide free choice vouchers to each qualified employee of such employer.

(b) Offering employer. For purposes of this section, the term "offering employer" means any employer who—

(1) offers minimum essential coverage to its employees consisting of coverage through an eligible employer-sponsored plan; and

(2) pays any portion of the costs of such plan.

(c) Qualified employee. For purposes of this section—

(1) In general. The term "qualified employee" means, with respect to any plan year of an offering employer, any employee—

(A) whose required contribution (as determined under section 5000A(e)(1)(B) [42 USCS § 5000A(e)(1)(B)]) for minimum essential coverage through an eligible employer-sponsored plan—

(i) exceeds 8 percent of such employee's household income for the taxable year described in section 1412(b)(1)(B) [42 USCS § 18082(b)(1)(B)] which ends with or within in the plan year; and

(ii) does not exceed 9.8 percent of such employee's household income for such taxable year;

(B) whose household income for such taxable year is not greater than 400 percent of the poverty line for a family of the size involved; and

(C) who does not participate in a health plan offered by the offering employer.

(2) Indexing. In the case of any calendar year beginning after 2014, the Secretary shall adjust the 8 percent under paragraph (1)(A)(i) and 9.8 percent under paragraph (1)(A)(ii) for the calendar year to reflect the rate of premium growth between the preceding calendar year and 2013 over the rate of income growth for such period.

(d) Free choice voucher. (1) Amount. (A) In general. The amount of any free choice voucher provided under subsection (a) shall be equal to the monthly portion of the cost of the eligible employer-sponsored plan which would have been paid by the employer if the employee were covered under the plan with respect to which the employer pays the largest portion of the cost of the plan. Such amount shall be equal to the amount the employer would pay for an employee with self-only coverage unless such employee elects family coverage (in which case such amount shall be the amount the employer would pay for family coverage).

(B) Determination of cost. The cost of any health plan shall be determined under the rules similar to the rules of section 2204 of the Public Health Service Act [42 USCS § 300bb-4], except that such amount shall be adjusted for age and category of enrollment in accordance with regulations established by the Secretary.

(2) Use of vouchers. An Exchange shall credit the amount of any free choice voucher provided under subsection (a) to the monthly premium of any qualified health plan in the Exchange in which the qualified employee is enrolled and the offering employer shall pay any amounts so credited to the Exchange.

(3) Payment of excess amounts. If the amount of the free choice voucher exceeds the amount of the premium of the qualified health plan in which the qualified employee is enrolled for such month, such excess shall be paid to the employee.

(e) Other definitions. Any term used in this section which is also used in section 5000A of the Internal Revenue Code of 1986 [26 USCS § 5000A] shall have the meaning given such term under such section 5000A [26 USCS § 5000A].

(March 23, 2010, P. L. 111-148, Title X, Subtitle A, § 10108(a)–(e), 124 Stat. 912.)

MISCELLANEOUS PROVISIONS

§ 18111. Definitions

Unless specifically provided for otherwise, the definitions contained in section 2791 of the Public Health Service Act (42 U.S.C. 300gg-91) shall apply with respect to this title.

(March 23, 2010, P. L. 111-148, Title I, Subtitle G, § 1551, 124 Stat. 258.)

§ 18112. Transparency in Government

Not later than 30 days after the date of enactment of this Act [enacted March 23, 2010], the Secretary of Health and Human Services shall publish on the Internet website of the Department of Health and Human Services, a list of all of the authorities provided to the Secretary under this Act (and the amendments made by this Act).

(March 23, 2010, P. L. 111-148, Title I, Subtitle G, § 1552, 124 Stat. 258.)

§ 18113. Prohibition against discrimination on assisted suicide

(a) In general. The Federal Government, and any State or local government or health care provider that receives Federal financial assistance under this Act (or under an amendment made by this Act) or any health plan created under this Act (or under an amendment made by this Act), may not subject an individual or institutional health care entity to discrimination on the basis that the entity does not provide any health care item or service furnished for the purpose of causing, or for the purpose of assisting in causing, the death of any individual, such as by assisted suicide, euthanasia, or mercy killing.

(b) Definition. In this section, the term "health care entity" includes an individual physician or other health care professional, a hospital, a provider-sponsored organization, a health maintenance organization, a health insurance plan, or any other kind of health care facility, organization, or plan.

(c) Construction and treatment of certain services. Nothing in subsection (a) shall be construed to apply to, or to affect, any limitation relating to—

(1) the withholding or withdrawing of medical treatment or medical care;

(2) the withholding or withdrawing of nutrition or hydration;

(3) abortion; or

(4) the use of an item, good, benefit, or service furnished for the purpose of alleviating pain or discomfort, even if such use may increase the risk of death, so long as such item, good, benefit, or service is not also furnished for the purpose of causing, or the purpose of assisting in causing, death, for any reason.

(d) Administration. The Office for Civil Rights of the Department of Health and Human Services is designated to receive complaints of discrimination based on this section.

(March 23, 2010, P. L. 111-148, Title I, Subtitle G, § 1553, 124 Stat. 259.)

§ 18114. Access to therapies

Notwithstanding any other provision of this Act, the Secretary of Health and Human Services shall not promulgate any regulation that—

(1) creates any unreasonable barriers to the ability of individuals to obtain appropriate medical care;

(2) impedes timely access to health care services;

(3) interferes with communications regarding a full range of treatment options between the patient and the provider;

(4) restricts the ability of health care providers to provide full disclosure of all relevant information to patients making health care decisions;

(5) violates the principles of informed consent and the ethical standards of health care professionals; or

(6) limits the availability of health care treatment for the full duration of a patient's medical needs.

(March 23, 2010, P. L. 111-148, Title I, Subtitle G, § 1554, 124 Stat. 259.)

§ 18115. Freedom not to participate in Federal health insurance programs

No individual, company, business, nonprofit entity, or health insurance issuer offering group or individual health insurance coverage shall be required to participate in any Federal health insurance program created under this Act (or any amendments made by this Act), or in any Federal health insurance program expanded by this Act (or any such amendments), and there shall be no penalty or fine imposed upon any such issuer for choosing not to participate in such programs.

(March 23, 2010, P. L. 111-148, Title I, Subtitle G, § 1555, 124 Stat. 260.)

§ 18116. Nondiscrimination

(a) In general. Except as otherwise provided for in this title (or an amendment made by this title), an individual shall not, on the ground prohibited under title VI of the Civil Rights Act of 1964 (42 U.S.C. 2000d et seq.), title IX of the Education Amendments of 1972 (20 U.S.C. 1681 et seq.), the Age Discrimination Act of 1975 (42 U.S.C. 6101 et seq.), or section 504 of the Rehabilitation Act of 1973 (29 U.S.C. 794), be excluded from participation in, be denied the benefits of, or be subjected to discrimination under, any health program or activity, any part of which is receiving Federal financial assistance, including credits, subsidies, or contracts of insurance, or under any program or activity that is administered by an Executive Agency or any entity established under this title (or amendments). The enforcement mechanisms provided for and available under such title VI, title IX, section 504, or such Age Discrimination Act shall apply for purposes of violations of this subsection.

(b) Continued application of laws. Nothing in this title (or an amendment made by this title) shall be construed to invalidate or limit the rights, remedies, procedures, or legal standards available to individuals aggrieved under title VI of the Civil Rights Act of 1964 (42 U.S.C. 2000d et seq.), title VII of the Civil Rights Act of 1964 (42 U.S.C. 2000e et seq.), title IX of the Education Amendments of 1972 (20 U.S.C. 1681 et seq.), section 504 of the Rehabilitation Act of 1973 (29 U.S.C. 794), or the Age Discrimination Act of 1975 (42 U.S.C. 611 et seq.), or to supersede State laws that provide additional protections against discrimination on any basis described in subsection (a).

(c) Regulations. The Secretary may promulgate regulations to implement this section.

(March 23, 2010, P. L. 111-148, Title I, Subtitle G, § 1557, 124 Stat. 260.)

§ 18117. Oversight

The Inspector General of the Department of Health and Human Services shall have oversight authority with respect to the administration and implementation of this title as it relates to such Department.

(March 23, 2010, P. L. 111-148, Title I, Subtitle G, § 1559, 124 Stat. 261.)

§ 18118. Rules of construction

(a) No effect on antitrust laws. Nothing in this title (or an amendment made by this title) shall be construed to modify, impair, or supersede the operation of any of the antitrust laws. For the purposes of this section, the term "antitrust laws" has the meaning given such term in subsection (a) of the first section of the Clayton Act [15 USCS § 12], except that such term includes section 5 of the Federal Trade Commission Act [15 USCS § 45] to the extent that such section 5 applies to unfair methods of competition.

(b) Rule of construction regarding Hawaii's Prepaid Health Care Act. Nothing in this title (or an amendment made by this title) shall be construed to modify or limit the application of the exemption for Hawaii's Prepaid Health Care Act (Haw. Rev. Stat. 393-1 et seq.) as provided for under section 514(b)(5) of the Employee Retirement Income Security Act of 1974 (29 U.S.C. 1144(b)(5)).

(c) Student health insurance plans. Nothing in this title (or an amendment made by this title) shall be construed to prohibit an institution of higher education (as such term is defined for purposes of the Higher Education Act of 1965) from offering a student health insurance plan, to the extent that such requirement is otherwise permitted under applicable Federal, State or local law.

(d) No effect on existing requirements. Nothing in this title (or an amendment made by this title, unless specified by direct statutory reference) shall be construed to modify any existing Federal requirement concerning the State agency responsible for determining eligibility for programs identified in section 1413 [42 USCS § 18083].

(March 23, 2010, P. L. 111-148, Title I, Subtitle G, § 1560, 124 Stat. 261.)

§ 18119. Small business procurement

Part 19 of the Federal Acquisition Regulation, section 15 of the Small Business Act (15 U.S.C. 644), and any other applicable laws or regulations establishing procurement requirements relating to small business concerns (as defined in section 3 of the Small Business Act (15 U.S.C. 632)) may not be waived with respect to any contract awarded under any program or other authority under this Act or an amendment made by this Act.

(March 23, 2010, P. L. 111-148, Title I, Subtitle G, § 1563, as added Title X, Subtitle A, § 10107(b)(2), 124 Stat. 912.)

§ 18120. Application

Notwithstanding any other provision of the Patient Protection and Affordable Care Act, nothing in such Act (or an amendment made by such Act) shall be construed to—

(1) prohibit (or authorize the Secretary of Health and Human Services to promulgate regulations that prohibit) a group health plan or health insurance issuer from carrying out utilization management techniques that are commonly used as of the date of enactment of

this Act [enacted March 23, 2010]; or

(2) restrict the application of the amendments made by this subtitle.

(March 23, 2010, P. L. 111-148, Title I, Subtitle G, § 1563(d) [1562(d)], Title X, Subtitle A, § 10107(b)(1), 124 Stat. 269, 911.)

CHAPTER 158. SUPPORT FOR PREGNANT AND PARENTING TEENS AND WOMEN

§ 18201. Definitions

In this part [42 USCS §§ 18201 et seq.]:

(1) Accompaniment. The term "accompaniment" means assisting, representing, and accompanying a woman in seeking judicial relief for child support, child custody, restraining orders, and restitution for harm to persons and property, and in filing criminal charges, and may include the payment of court costs and reasonable attorney and witness fees associated therewith.

(2) Eligible institution of higher education. The term "eligible institution of higher education" means an institution of higher education (as such term is defined in section 101 of the Higher Education Act of 1965 (20 U.S.C. 1001)) that has established and operates, or agrees to establish and operate upon the receipt of a grant under this part [42 USCS §§ 18201 et seq.], a pregnant and parenting student services office.

(3) Community service center. The term "community service center" means a non-profit organization that provides social services to residents of a specific geographical area via direct service or by contract with a local governmental agency.

(4) High school. The term "high school" means any public or private school that operates grades 10 through 12, inclusive, grades 9 through 12, inclusive or grades 7 through 12, inclusive.

(5) Intervention services. The term "intervention services" means, with respect to domestic violence, sexual violence, sexual assault, or stalking, 24-hour telephone hotline services for police protection and referral to shelters.

(6) Secretary. The term "Secretary" means the Secretary of Health and Human Services.

(7) State. The term "State" includes the District of Columbia, any commonwealth, possession, or other territory of the United States, and any Indian tribe or reservation.

(8) Supportive social services. The term "supportive social services" means transitional and permanent housing, vocational counseling, and individual and group counseling aimed at preventing domestic violence, sexual violence, sexual assault, or stalking.

(9) Violence. The term "violence" means actual violence and the risk or threat of violence.

(March 23, 2010, P. L. 111-148, Title X, Subtitle B, Part II, § 10211, 124 Stat. 931.)

§ 18202. Establishment of Pregnancy Assistance Fund

(a) In general. The Secretary, in collaboration and coordination with the Secretary of Education (as appropriate), shall establish a Pregnancy Assistance Fund to be administered by the Secretary, for the purpose of awarding competitive grants to States to assist pregnant and parenting teens and women.

(b) Use of Fund. A State may apply for a grant under subsection (a) to carry out any activities provided for in section 10213 [42 USCS § 18203].

(c) Applications. To be eligible to receive a grant under subsection (a), a State shall submit to the Secretary an application at such time, in such manner, and containing such information as the Secretary may require, including a description of the purposes for which the grant is being requested and the designation of a State agency for receipt and administration of funding received under this part [42 USCS §§ 18201 et seq.].

(March 23, 2010, P. L. 111-148, Title X, Subtitle B, Part II, § 10212, 124 Stat. 932.)

§ 18203. Permissible uses of Fund

(a) In general. A State shall use amounts received under a grant under section 10212 [42 USCS § 18202] for the purposes described in this section to assist pregnant and parenting teens and women.

(b) Institutions of higher education. (1) In general. A State may use amounts received under a grant under section 10212 [42 USCS § 18202] to make funding available to eligible institutions of higher education to enable the eligible institutions to establish, maintain, or operate pregnant and parenting student services. Such funding shall be used to supplement, not supplant, existing funding for such services.

(2) Application. An eligible institution of higher education that desires to receive funding under this subsection shall submit an application to the designated State agency at such time, in such manner, and containing such information as the State agency may require.

(3) Matching requirement. An eligible insti-

tution of higher education that receives funding under this subsection shall contribute to the conduct of the pregnant and parenting student services office supported by the funding an amount from non-Federal funds equal to 25 percent of the amount of the funding provided. The non-Federal share may be in cash or in-kind, fairly evaluated, including services, facilities, supplies, or equipment.

(4) Use of funds for assisting pregnant and parenting college students. An eligible institution of higher education that receives funding under this subsection shall use such funds to establish, maintain or operate pregnant and parenting student services and may use such funding for the following programs and activities:

(A) Conduct a needs assessment on campus and within the local community—

(i) to assess pregnancy and parenting resources, located on the campus or within the local community, that are available to meet the needs described in subparagraph (B); and

(ii) to set goals for—

(I) improving such resources for pregnant, parenting, and prospective parenting students; and

(II) improving access to such resources.

(B) Annually assess the performance of the eligible institution in meeting the following needs of students enrolled in the eligible institution who are pregnant or are parents:

(i) The inclusion of maternity coverage and the availability of riders for additional family members in student health care.

(ii) Family housing.

(iii) Child care.

(iv) Flexible or alternative academic scheduling, such as telecommuting programs, to enable pregnant or parenting students to continue their education or stay in school.

(v) Education to improve parenting skills for mothers and fathers and to strengthen marriages.

(vi) Maternity and baby clothing, baby food (including formula), baby furniture, and similar items to assist parents and prospective parents in meeting the material needs of their children.

(vii) Post-partum counseling.

(C) Identify public and private service providers, located on the campus of the eligible institution or within the local community, that are qualified to meet the needs described in subparagraph (B), and establishes programs with qualified providers to meet such needs.

(D) Assist pregnant and parenting students, fathers or spouses in locating and obtaining services that meet the needs described in subparagraph (B).

(E) If appropriate, provide referrals for prenatal care and delivery, infant or foster care, or adoption, to a student who requests such information. An office shall make such referrals only to service providers that serve the following types of individuals:

(i) Parents.

(ii) Prospective parents awaiting adoption.

(iii) Women who are pregnant and plan on parenting or placing the child for adoption.

(iv) Parenting or prospective parenting couples.

(5) Reporting. (A) Annual report by institutions. (i) In general. For each fiscal year that an eligible institution of higher education receives funds under this subsection, the eligible institution shall prepare and submit to the State, by the date determined by the State, a report that—

(I) itemizes the pregnant and parenting student services office's expenditures for the fiscal year;

(II) contains a review and evaluation of the performance of the office in fulfilling the requirements of this section, using the specific performance criteria or standards established under subparagraph (B)(i); and

(III) describes the achievement of the office in meeting the needs listed in paragraph (4)(B) of the students served by the eligible institution, and the frequency of use of the office by such students.

(ii) Performance criteria. Not later than 180 days before the date the annual report described in clause (i) is submitted, the State—

(I) shall identify the specific performance criteria or standards that shall be used to prepare the report; and

(II) may establish the form or format of the report.

(B) Report by state. The State shall annually prepare and submit a report on the findings under this subsection, including the number of eligible institutions of higher education that were awarded funds and the number of students served by each pregnant and parenting student services office receiving funds under this section, to the Secretary.

(c) Support for pregnant and parenting teens. A State may use amounts received under a grant under section 10212 [42 USCS § 18202] to make funding available to eligible high schools and community service centers to establish, maintain or operate pregnant and parenting services in the same general manner and in accordance with all conditions and requirements described in subsection (b), except that paragraph (3) of such subsection shall not apply for purposes of this subsection.

(d) Improving services for pregnant women who are victims of domestic violence, sexual violence, sexual assault, and stalking. (1) In general. A State may use amounts received under a grant under section 10212 [42 USCS § 18202] to make funding available tp [to] its State Attorney General to assist Statewide offices in providing—

(A) intervention services, accompaniment, and supportive social services for eligible pregnant women who are victims of domestic violence, sexual violence, sexual assault, or stalking.

(B) technical assistance and training (as described in subsection (c)) relating to violence against eligible pregnant women to be made available to the following:

(i) Federal, State, tribal, territorial, and local governments, law enforcement agencies, and courts.

(ii) Professionals working in legal, social service, and health care settings.

(iii) Nonprofit organizations.

(iv) Faith-based organizations.

(2) Eligibility. To be eligible for a grant under paragraph (1), a State Attorney General shall submit an application to the designated State agency at such time, in such manner, and containing such information, as specified by the State.

(3) Technical assistance and training described. For purposes of paragraph (1)(B), technical assistance and training is—

(A) the identification of eligible pregnant women experiencing domestic violence, sexual violence, sexual assault, or stalking;

(B) the assessment of the immediate and short-term safety of such a pregnant woman, the evaluation of the impact of the violence or stalking on the pregnant woman's health, and the assistance of the pregnant woman in developing a plan aimed at preventing further domestic violence, sexual violence, sexual assault, or stalking, as appropriate;

(C) the maintenance of complete medical or forensic records that include the documentation of any examination, treatment given, and referrals made, recording the location and nature of the pregnant woman's injuries, and the establishment of mechanisms to ensure the privacy and confidentiality of those medical records; and

(D) the identification and referral of the pregnant woman to appropriate public and private nonprofit entities that provide intervention services, accompaniment, and supportive social services.

(4) Eligible pregnant woman. In this subsection, the term "eligible pregnant woman" means any woman who is pregnant on the date on which such woman becomes a victim of domestic violence, sexual violence, sexual assault, or stalking or who was pregnant during the one-year period before such date.

(e) Public awareness and education. A State may use amounts received under a grant under section 10212 [42 USCS § 18202] to make funding available to increase public awareness and education concerning any services available to pregnant and parenting teens and women under this part [42 USCS §§ 18201 et seq.], or any other resources available to pregnant and parenting women in keeping with the intent and purposes of this part [42 USCS §§ 18201 et seq.]. The State shall be responsible for setting guidelines or limits as to how much of funding may be utilized for public awareness and education in any funding award.

(March 23, 2010, P. L. 111-148, Title X, Subtitle B, Part II, § 10213, 124 Stat. 932.)

§ 18204. Appropriations

There is authorized to be appropriated, and there are appropriated, $25,000,000 for each of fiscal years 2010 through 2019, to carry out this part [42 USCS §§ 18201 et seq.].

(March 23, 2010, P. L. 111-148, Title X, Subtitle B, Part II, § 10214, 124 Stat. 935.)

INDEX

[References are to sections.]

A

B

C

[References are to sections.]

D

[References are to sections.]

[References are to sections.]

F

[References are to sections.]

[References are to sections.]

[References are to sections.]

[References are to sections.]

[References are to sections.]

[References are to sections.]

[References are to sections.]

[References are to sections.]

[References are to sections.]

Q

[References are to sections.]

[References are to sections.]

[References are to sections.]

[References are to sections.]

U

V

W